WHO WAS WHO
A CUMULATED INDEX
1897–2000

WHO'S WHO

An annual biographical dictionary
first published in 1849

WHO WAS WHO

Ten volumes containing the biographies removed from
WHO'S WHO each year on account of death, with
final details and date of death added.

Volume I	1897–1915
Volume II	1916–1928
Volume III	1929–1940
Volume IV	1941–1950
Volume V	1951–1960
Volume VI	1961–1970
Volume VII	1971–1980
Volume VIII	1981–1990
Volume IX	1991–1995
Volume X	1996–2000

WHO'S WHO 1897–1998

One hundred and two years of biography on CD-ROM.
The complete text of
WHO WAS WHO up to 1997 and WHO'S WHO 1998.

WHO WAS WHO

A CUMULATED INDEX

INDEX

1897–2000

A & C BLACK
LONDON

FIRST PUBLISHED 2002
A & C BLACK PUBLISHERS LIMITED
37 SOHO SQUARE, LONDON W1D 3QZ

ISBN 0 7136 6125 9

PRINTED AND BOUND IN GREAT BRITAIN
BY WILLIAM CLOWES LTD, BECCLES AND LONDON

PREFACE

THIS INDEX has been prepared to give easy access to the ten volumes of *Who Was Who* for those who may come upon a name, in newspapers, journals, diaries or memoirs, which was obviously so familiar to the writer that he saw no need to explain it; for those who know that an entry should appear in one of the ten volumes, but do not know which volume—because the date of death is not to hand; for researchers in social and political history. The entries thus brought into one list are far from uniform; they range from very brief to expansive, from very personal to official in tone; but they are alike in that they were compiled, for the most part, by their subjects, published in their lifetimes, and sent for correction each year. They give at worst a clue, at best a full answer, to the enquirer seeking to turn a name into a person.

In the one hundred and four years of publication recorded there have been many changes, not so much of editorial policy as in the sort of person whose name and career attracted general public interest. *Who's Who* has reflected this interest faithfully; an invitation to have an entry has always signified the compilers' response thereto, rather than the capricious accolade sometimes supposed.

In the early days of *Who's Who* consistency seems, not surprisingly, to have been thought relatively unimportant. The result is a wide variety of forms of heading to entries, which required adaptation to fit into a single list. A form has been chosen for the Index which leaves no doubt as to which entry is referred to, but which is not necessarily exactly as printed in the book. Individuals preferred to appear under styles such as The MacDermot, or, in the case of titles, with forms or numberings not now regarded as correct. They spelt their names (for example) M'Taggart, Mactaggart or McTaggart. Where it is conceivable that a name might be hard to find a cross-reference is given, as it is to the part of a double surname under which an entry appears from the other part. There are also cross-references from pseudonyms, maiden names, married names, and other forms appearing in entries.

For hereditary peerages the Index gives the title only; where for any reason one holder of the title is missing from the sequence this is indicated. For life peerages, courtesy titles, and the titles of Lords of Session it gives the forenames and family name also; life peers have a cross-reference under their former names if these differ from their eventual title, and Lords of Session also have a cross-reference to their judicial titles from their family names and forenames. Baronets appear in alphabetical order among other entries; if there are two or more baronetcies of the same surname they are distinguished by the date of creation, and any missing from the sequences are noted.

In the case of names preceded by prefixes such as von or de, which may appear under the prefix or under the main part of the name in *Who Was Who*, the Index gives them as they appear in the book with no cross-reference to the other possible form.

It has always been necessary to include some entries in Addenda to the volumes of *Who Was Who*, because the compilers did not learn of the deaths in question until the main part of the volumes had been completed; such entries are transferred to the appropriate volume when a new edition is published, and in these cases both appearances of the entry are indexed. Where entries appear in the Addenda they are distinguished by (A) after the volume number. There were, however, occasions, particularly in the earlier years, when an entry was removed from *Who's Who* and included in *Who Was Who* by mistake; when the mistake was discovered the entry was returned to *Who's Who* but remained also, wrongly, in *Who Was Who*. In these cases the earlier, incorrect, appearance of the name has not been indexed. In the course of preparation of the Index a number of entries have been found without a date of death appended or with incomplete names. Where possible the dates and names have been discovered and included; they are added to the volumes of *Who Was Who* as new editions are published.

It is normal for entries once included in *Who's Who* to remain until death, but there has been one major exception to this. In 1943 the paper shortage was so acute that, even though the book was treated generously by the authorities, it became necessary to reduce the number of entries sharply. Very few of those entries then deleted were ever returned to *Who's Who*, and they do not appear in *Who Was Who*.

Since publication of the Index covering 1897–1990, the text of *Who Was Who* has been transferred to CD-ROM. The current version, *Who's Who 1897–1998*, includes all the entries of those who died between 1897 and 1997, and the biographies in *Who's Who 1998*.

April 2002

A

A. K. H. B; *see* Boyd, Very Rev. A. K. H.
Aalto, Alvar; *see* Aalto, H. A. H.
Aalto, (Hugo) Alvar (Henrik), 1898–1976, vol. VII
Aaltonen, Wäinö Valdemar, 1894–1966, vol. VI
Aaron, Richard Ithamar, 1901–1987, vol. VIII
Aarons, Sir Daniel Sidney, 1885–1983, vol. VIII
Aarvold, Sir Carl Douglas, 1907–1991, vol. IX
Abadie, Major Eustace Henry Egremont,
  1877–1914, vol. I
Abadie, Captain George Howard Fanshawe,
  1873–1904, vol. I
Abadie, Maj.-Gen. Henry Richard, 1841–1915,
  vol. I
Abady, Jacques, 1872–1964, vol. VI
Abayomi, Sir Kofo Adekunle, 1896–1979, vol. VII
Abbas, Kuli Khan (Nawab), 1864–1938, vol. III
Abbay, Col Bryan Norman, 1881–1947, vol. IV
Abbay, Rev. Richard, 1844–1924, vol. II
Abbe, Cleveland, 1838–1916, vol. II
Abbey, Edwin Austin, 1852–1911, vol. I
Abbey, Lt-Col Walter Bulmer Tate, 1872–1949,
  vol. IV
Abbey, William Henry, 1864–1943, vol. IV
Abbiss, Sir George, 1884–1966, vol. VI
Abbot, Charles Greeley, 1872–1973, vol. VII
Abbot, Dermot Charles Hyatt, 1908–1990, vol. VIII
Abbot, Dame Elsie Myrtle, 1907–1983, vol. VIII
Abbot, Lt-Col Frederick William, 1862–1942,
  vol. IV
Abbott, Albert, 1872–1950, vol. IV
Abbott, Albert Holden, 1871–1934, vol. III
Abbott, Alexander Crever, 1860–1935, vol. III
Abbott, Anthony Cecil, 1923–1992, vol. IX
Abbott, Arthur, 1879–1955, vol. V
Abbott, Arthur William, 1893–1986, vol. VIII
Abbott, Hon. Sir Charles (Arthur Hillas) Lempriere,
  1889–1960, vol. V
Abbott, Charles Lydiard Aubrey, 1886–1975,
  vol. VII
Abbott, Charles Theodore, *died* 1956, vol. V
Abbott, Claude Colleer, 1889–1971, vol. VII
Abbott, Hon. Douglas Charles, 1899–1987,
  vol. VIII
Abbott, Edwin, 1878–1947, vol. IV
Abbott, Rev. Edwin Abbott, 1838–1926, vol. II
Abbott, Rev. Eric Symes, 1906–1983, vol. VIII
Abbott, Evelyn Robins, 1873–1950, vol. IV
Abbott, Francis Charles, 1867–1938, vol. III
Abbott, Frank Frost, 1860–1924, vol. II
Abbott, Brig.-Gen. Henry Alexius, 1849–1924,
  vol. II
Abbott, Rt Rev. Henry Pryon Almon, 1881–1945,
  vol. IV

Abbott, Col Rev Preb. Herbert Alldridge,
  1881–1962, vol. VI
Abbott, Col Herbert Edward Stacy, 1855–1939,
  vol. III
Abbott, John Sutherland, 1900–1979, vol. VII
Abbott, Hon. Sir Joseph Palmer, 1842–1901, vol. I
Abbott, Brig.-Gen. Leonard Henry, 1875–1949,
  vol. IV
Abbott, Rev. Lyman, 1835–1922, vol. II
Abbott, Morris Percy, 1922–1998, vol. X
Abbott, Sir Myles John, 1906–1984, vol. VIII
Abbott, Percival William Henry, 1869–1954, vol. V
Abbott, Lt-Col Percy Phipps, 1869–1940, vol. III
Abbott, Brig. Reginald Stuart, 1882–1964, vol. VI
Abbott, Rt Rev. Robert Crowther, 1869–1927,
  vol. II
Abbott, Thomas Charles, *died* 1927, vol. II
Abbott, Rev. Thomas Kingsmill, *died* 1912, vol. I
Abbott, Rev. Thomas Kingsmill, 1829–1913, vol. I
Abbott, Trevor Michael, 1950–1997, vol. X
Abbott, William, 1891–1963, vol. VI
Abdela, Jack Samuel Ronald, 1913–1994, vol. IX
Abdool Raoof, Khan Bahadur Sir Muhammad, *died*
  1947, vol. IV
Abdoolcader, Sir Husein Hasanally, 1890–1974,
  vol. VII
Abdul, Sir Husain Sahib, Khan Bahadur Mirza,
  vol. III
Abdul Maliki, Alhaji, 1914–1969, vol. VI
Abdul Qaiyum, Nawab Sir Sahibzada, 1866–1937,
  vol. III
Abdul Rahman Putra, Tunku (Prince), 1903–1990,
  vol. VIII
Abdul Razak bin Hussein, Hon. Tun Haji,
  1922–1976, vol. VII
Abdulrahman Khan, Ameer of Afghanistan, *died*
  1901, vol. I
Abdussamad Khan, Sahibzada Sir, 1874–1943,
  vol. IV
Abdy, Sir Anthony Charles Sykes, 3rd Bt,
  1848–1921, vol. II
Abdy, Brig.-Gen. Anthony John, 1856–1924, vol. II
Abdy, Sir Henry Beadon, 4th Bt, 1854–1921, vol. II
Abdy, Richard Combe, *died* 1938, vol. III
Abdy, Sir Robert Henry Edward, 5th Bt,
  1896–1976, vol. VII
Abdy, Sir William Neville, 2nd Bt, 1844–1910,
  vol. I
à Beckett, Ada Mary; *see* à Beckett, Mrs T. A.
à Beckett, Sir Albert, 1840–1904, vol. I
A'Beckett, Arthur William, 1844–1909, vol. I
A'Beckett, Hon. Sir Thomas, 1837–1919, vol. II

à Beckett, Mrs Thomas Archibald, (Ada Mary à Beckett), 1872–1948, vol. IV
Abel, Arthur Lawrence, 1895–1978, vol. VII
Abel, Sir Frederick Augustus, 1st Bt, 1826–1902, vol. I
Abel, Henry George, 1875–1945, vol. IV
Abel Smith, Sir Alexander, 1904–1980, vol. VII
Abel-Smith, Brian, 1926–1996, vol. X
Abel Smith, Vice Adm. Sir Conolly; see Abel Smith, Sir E. M. C.
Abel Smith, Desmond, 1892–1974, vol. VII
Abel Smith, Vice Adm. Sir (Edward Michael) Conolly, 1899–1985, vol. VIII
Abel-Smith, Geoffrey Samuel, 1871–1926, vol. II
Abel Smith, Col Sir Henry, 1900–1993, vol. IX
Abel-Smith, Brig.-Gen. Lionel, 1870–1946, vol. IV
Abel Smith, Reginald Henry Macaulay, 1890–1964, vol. VI
Abeles, Sir (Emil Herbert) Peter, 1924–1999, vol. X
Abeles, Sir Peter; see Abeles, Sir E. H. P.
Abell, Sir Anthony Foster, 1906–1994, vol. IX
Abell, Charles, 1910–1992, vol. IX
Abell, Sir George Edmond Brackenbury, 1904–1989, vol. VIII
Abell, George Foster, 1875–1946, vol. IV
Abell, Lt-Col Robert Lloyd, 1889–1957, vol. V
Abell, Thomas Bertrand, 1880–1956, vol. V
Abell, Sir Westcott Stile, 1877–1961, vol. VI
Abend, Hallett, 1884–1955, vol. V
Abensur, Isaac Aaron, 1861–1937, vol. III
Abeokuta, The Alake of, (Ademola II), Sir Ladapo Ademola, 1873–1962, vol. VI
Aberconway, 1st Baron, 1850–1934, vol. III
Aberconway, 2nd Baron, 1879–1953, vol. V
Abercorn, 2nd Duke of, 1838–1913, vol. I
Abercorn, 3rd Duke of, 1869–1953, vol. V
Abercorn, 4th Duke of, 1904–1979, vol. VII
Abercorn, Dowager Duchess of; (Rosalind Cecilia Caroline), 1869–1958, vol. V
Abercrombie, Captain Alexander Ralph, 1896–1918, vol. II
Abercrombie, Col Charles Murray, 1874–1933, vol. III
Abercrombie, David, 1909–1992, vol. IX
Abercrombie, George Francis, 1896–1978, vol. VII
Abercrombie, Sir John Robertson, 1888–1960, vol. V
Abercrombie, Lascelles, 1881–1938, vol. III
Abercrombie, Sir (Leslie) Patrick, 1879–1957, vol. V
Abercrombie, Michael, 1912–1979, vol. VII
Abercrombie, Nigel James, 1908–1986, vol. VIII
Abercrombie, Sir Patrick; see Abercrombie, Sir L. P.
Abercrombie, Peter Henderson, 1867–1950, vol. IV
Abercrombie, Robert James, 1898–1992, vol. IX
Abercromby, 4th Baron, 1838–1917, vol. II
Abercromby, 5th Baron, 1841–1924, vol. II
Abercromby, Bt-Col Sir George William, 8th Bt, 1886–1964, vol. VI
Abercromby, Sir Robert Alexander, 9th Bt, 1895–1972, vol. VII
Aberdare, 2nd Baron, 1851–1929, vol. III
Aberdare, 3rd Baron, 1885–1957, vol. V
Aberdeen, David du Rieu, 1913–1987, vol. VIII

Aberdeen and Temair, 1st Marquess of, 1847–1934, vol. III
Aberdeen and Temair, 2nd Marquis of, 1879–1965, vol. VI
Aberdeen and Temair, 3rd Marquis of, 1883–1972, vol. VII
Aberdeen and Temair, 4th Marquess of, 1908–1974, vol. VII
Aberdeen and Temair, 5th Marquess of, 1913–1984, vol. VIII
Aberdeen and Temair, Marchioness of; (Ishbel Maria), 1857–1939, vol. III
Abergavenny, 1st Marquess of, 1826–1915, vol I
Abergavenny, 2nd Marquess of, 1853–1927, vol. II
Abergavenny, 3rd Marquess of, 1854–1938, vol. III
Abergavenny, 4th Marquess of, 1883–1954, vol. V
Abergavenny, 5th Marquess of, 1914–2000, vol. X
Aberhart, Hon. William, 1878–1943, vol. IV
Abernethy, James Smart, 1907–1976, vol. VII
Abertay, 1st Baron, 1875–1940, vol. III
Abinash Chandra Sen, Rai Bahadur, 1870–1922, vol. II
Abingdon, 7th Earl of, 1836–1928, vol. II
Abinger, 4th Baron, 1871–1903, vol. I
Abinger, 5th Baron, 1872–1917, vol. I
Abinger, 6th Baron, 1876–1927, vol. II
Abinger, 7th Baron, 1878–1943, vol. IV
Ableson, Frank; see Vaughan, Frankie.
Ablett, Thomas Robert, died 1945, vol. IV
Abney, Sir William de Wiveleslie, 1843–1921, vol. II
Abrahall, Rt Rev. Anthony Leigh Egerton H.; see Hoskyns-Abrahall.
Abrahall, Bennet H.; see Hoskyns-Abrahall.
Abrahall, Sir Theo Chandos H.; see Hoskyns-Abrahall.
Abraham, Ashley Perry, 1876–1951, vol. V
Abraham, Rt Rev. C. T., 1857–1945, vol. IV
Abraham, Rt Rev. Charles John, 1814–1903, vol. I
Abraham, Edgar Gaston Furtado, 1880–1955, vol. V
Abraham, Sir Edward Penley, 1913–1999, vol. X
Abraham, George Dixon, 1872–1965, vol. VI
Abraham, Gerald Ernest Heal, 1904–1988, vol. VIII
Abraham, James Johnston, 1876–1963, vol. VI
Abraham, Sir John Bradley, 1881–1945, vol. IV
Abraham, John Conrad, 1889–1939, vol. III
Abraham, Louis Arnold, 1893–1983, vol. VIII
Abraham, Rt Rev. Philip Selwyn, 1897–1955, vol. V
Abraham, Phineas Simon, died 1921, vol. II
Abraham, Robert John Elliot, 1927–1985, vol. VIII
Abraham, William, 1840–1915, vol. I
Abraham, Rt. Hon. William, 1842–1922, vol. II
Abraham, Maj.-Gen. Sir William Ernest Victor, 1897–1980, vol. VII
Abrahams, Sir Adolphe, 1883–1967, vol. VI
Abrahams, Allan Rose, 1908–1991, vol. IX
Abrahams, Major Sir Arthur Cecil, 1878–1944, vol. IV
Abrahams, Bertram, 1870–1908, vol. I
Abrahams, Sir Charles Myer, 1914–1985, vol. VIII
Abrahams, Doris Caroline; see Brahms, Caryl
Abrahams, Gerald, 1907–1980, vol. VII
Abrahams, Gerald Milton, 1917–1999, vol. X

Abrahams, Harold Maurice, 1899–1978, vol. VII
Abrahams, Israel, 1858–1925, vol. II
Abrahams, Sir Lionel, 1869–1919, vol. II
Abrahams, Louis Barnett, 1839–1918, vol. II
Abrahams, Rt Hon. Sir Sidney Solomon, 1885–1957, vol. V
Abrahamson, Sir Martin Arnold, 1870–1962, vol. VI
Abram, Sir George Stewart, 1866–1928, vol. II
Abram, John Hill, died 1933, vol. III
Abrams, Mark Alexander, 1906–1994, vol. IX
Abramson, Major Albert, 1876–1944, vol. IV
Abramson, Sidney, 1921–1994, vol. IX
Abruzzi, Duke of; Prince Luigi Amedeo Giuseppé Maria Ferdinando Francesco, 1873–1933, vol. III
Abu Bakar, Datuk Jamaluddin, 1929–1992, vol. IX
Abubakr, Seiyid Sir, bin Sheik al Kaf, 1885–1965, vol. VI
Achard, Marcel, 1899–1974, vol. VII
Acharya, Sir Vijaya Ragahava, 1875–1953, vol. V
Acheampong, Ignatius Kutu, 1931–1979, vol. VII
Acheson, Capt. Albert Edward, 1862–1945, vol. IV
Acheson, Andrew Basil, 1895–1959, vol. V
Acheson, Anne Crawford, died 1962, vol. VI
Acheson, Dean, 1893–1971, vol. VII
Acheson, Maj.-Gen. Hon. Edward Archibald Brabazon, 1844–1921, vol. II
Acheson, Edward Goodrich, 1856–1931, vol. III
Acheson, Sir James Glasgow, 1889–1973, vol. VII
Acheson, Hon. Patrick George Edward Cavendish-, 1883–1957, vol. V
Achurch, Janet, (Janet Achurch Sharp), died 1916, vol. II
Ackerley, Rev. Frederick George, 1871–1954, vol. V
Ackermann, Gerald, 1876–1960, vol. V (A), vol. VI
Ackerman, Myron, 1913–1985, vol. VIII
Ackers, Benjamin St John, 1839–1915, vol. I
Ackland, Robert Craig, died 1923, vol. II
Ackland, Rodney, 1908–1991, vol. IX
Ackland, William Alfred, 1875–1940, vol. III (A), vol. IV
Ackland, Major William Robert, 1863–1949, vol. IV
Acklom, Captain Cecil Ryther, 1872–1937, vol. III
Acklom, Maj. Spencer, died 1918, vol. II
Ackner, Brian Gerard Conrad, 1918–1966, vol. VI
Ackner, Conrad Adolf, 1880–1976, vol. VII
Ackroyd, Sir Cuthbert Lowell, 1st Bt, 1892–1973, vol. VII
Ackroyd, Dame (Dorothy) Elizabeth, 1910–1987, vol. VIII
Ackroyd, Sir Edward James, 1838–1904, vol. I
Ackroyd, Dame Elizabeth; see Ackroyd, Dame D. E.
Ackroyd, Sir John Robert Whyte, 2nd Bt, 1932–1995, vol. IX
Ackroyd, Thomas Raven, 1861–1946, vol. IV
Acland, Col Alfred Dyke, 1858–1937, vol. III
Acland, Sir Antony Guy, 5th Bt (cr 1890), 1916–1983, vol. VIII
Acland, Arthur Geoffrey Dyke, 1909–1964, vol. VI
Acland, Rt Hon. Sir Arthur Herbert Dyke, 13th Bt (cr 1644), 1847–1926, vol. II
Acland, Lt-Gen. Arthur Nugent F.; see Floyer-Acland.

Acland, Sir (Charles) Thomas Dyke, 12th Bt (cr 1644), 1842–1919, vol. II
Acland, Engr-Rear-Adm. Edward Leopold Dyke, 1878–1968, vol. VI
Acland, F. A., 1861–1950, vol. IV (A), vol. V
Acland, Rt Hon. Sir Francis Dyke, 14th Bt (cr 1644), 1874–1939, vol. III
Acland, Captain Frank Edward Dyke, 1857–1943, vol. IV
Acland, Henry Dyke, 1867–1942, vol. IV
Acland, Sir Henry Wentworth Dyke, 1st Bt (cr 1890), 1815–1900, vol. I
Acland, Captain Sir Hubert Guy Dyke, 4th Bt (cr 1890), 1890–1978, vol. VII
Acland, Sir (Hugh) John (Dyke), 1904–1981, vol. VIII
Acland, Col Sir Hugh Thomas Dyke, 1874–1956, vol. V
Acland, Sir John; see Acland, Sir H. J. D.
Acland, Brig. Peter Bevil Edward, 1902–1993, vol. IX
Acland, Sir Reginald Brodie Dyke, 1856–1924, vol. II
Acland, Rt Rev. Richard Dyke, 1881–1954, vol. V
Acland, Sir Richard Thomas Dyke, 15th Bt, 1906–1990, vol. VIII
Acland, Theodore Dyke, 1851–1931, vol. III
Acland, Rev. Theodore William Gull, 1890–1960, vol. V
Acland, Sir Thomas; see Acland, Sir C. T. D.
Acland, Rt Hon. Sir Thomas Dyke, 11th Bt (cr 1644), 1809–1898, vol. I
Acland, Adm. Sir William Alison Dyke, 2nd Bt (cr 1890), 1847–1924, vol. II
Acland, Sir William Henry Dyke, 3rd Bt (cr 1890), 1888–1970, vol. VI
Acland-Troyte, Lt-Col Sir Gilbert John, 1876–1964, vol. VI
Acomb, Henry Waldo, 1891–1962, vol. VI
A'Court-Repington, Lt-Col Charles; see Repington.
A'Court-Repington, Charles Henry Wyndham, 1819–1903, vol. I
Acton, 1st Baron, 1834–1902, vol. I
Acton, 2nd Baron, 1870–1924, vol. II
Acton, 3rd Baron, 1907–1989, vol. VIII
Acton, Antony; see Acton, W. A.
Acton, Hon. Sir Edward, 1865–1945, vol. IV
Acton, Dame (Ellen) Marian, 1887–1971, vol. VII
Acton, Fitzmaurice, 1874–1921, vol. II
Acton, Frederick, 1845–1933, vol. III
Acton, Sir Harold Mario Mitchell, 1904–1994, vol. IX
Acton, Harry Burrows, 1908–1974, vol. VII
Acton, Lt-Col Hugh William, 1883–1935, vol. III
Acton, John Adams, died 1910, vol. I
Acton, Dame Marian, see Acton, Dame E. M.
Acton, Murray A.; see Adams-Acton.
Acton, Maj.-Gen. Thomas Heward, 1917–1977, vol. VII
Acton, (William) Antony, 1904–1993, vol. IX
Acton, Lt-Col William Maxwell, 1878–1939, vol. III
Acutt, Sir Keith (Courtney), 1909–1986, vol. VIII
Acworth, Captain Bernard, 1885–1963, vol. VI
Acworth, Harry Arbuthnot, 1849–1933, vol. III

Acworth, Col Louis Raymond, 1872–1934, vol. III
Acworth, Sir William Mitchell, 1850–1925, vol. II
Adair, Maj.-Gen. Sir Allan Henry Shafto, 6th Bt, 1897–1988, vol. VIII
Adair, Arthur Robin, 1913–1981, vol. VIII
Adair, Cecil; *see* Everett-Green, Evelyn.
Adair, Adm. Charles Henry, 1851–1920, vol. II
Adair, Sir Charles William, 1822–1897, vol. I
Adair, Mrs Cornelia, *died* 1922, vol. II
Adair, Edward Robert, 1888–1967, vol. VI
Adair, Sir Frederick Edward Shafto, 4th Bt, 1860–1915, vol. I
Adair, Gilbert Smithson, 1896–1979, vol. VII
Adair, Sir Hugh Edward, 3rd Bt, 1815–1902, vol. I
Adair, Brig.-Gen. Hugh Robert, 1863–1946, vol. IV
Adair, Sir (Robert) Shafto, 5th Bt, 1862–1949, vol. IV
Adair, Sir Shafto; *see* Adair, Sir R. S.
Adair, Rear-Adm. Thomas Benjamin Stratton, *died* 1928, vol. II
Adair, Gen. Sir William Thompson, 1850–1931, vol. III
Adam, Hon. Lord; James Adam, 1824–1914, vol. I
Adam, Hon. Sir Alexander Duncan Grant, 1902–1986, vol. VIII
Adam, Sir Charles Elphinstone, 1st Bt (*cr* 1882), 1859–1922, vol. II
Adam, Charles Fox Frederick, 1852–1913, vol. I
Adam, Captain Charles Keith, 1891–1971, vol. VII
Adam, Colin Gurdon Forbes, 1889–1982, vol. VIII
Adam, Rev. David Stow, 1859–1925, vol. II
Adam, (David Stuart) Gordon, 1927–1995, vol. IX
Adam, Edwin, 1862–1931, vol. III
Adam, Eric Graham Forbes, 1888–1925, vol. II
Adam, Sir Frank Forbes, 1st Bt (*cr* 1917), 1846–1926, vol. II
Adam, Maj.-Gen. Frederick Archibald, 1860–1924, vol. II
Adam, Frederick Edward Fox, 1887–1969, vol. VI
Adam, Major Frederick Loch, 1864–1907, vol. I
Adam, Mrs George, (H. Pearl Adam), 1882–1957, vol. V
Adam, George Jefferys, 1883–1930, vol. III
Adam, Gordon; *see* Adam, D. S. G.
Adam, H. Pearl; *see* Adam, Mrs George.
Adam, Captain Herbert Algernon, 1872–1920, vol. II
Adam, J. Millen, 1853–1941, vol. IV
Adam, James, 1860–1907, vol. I
Adam, Sir James, 1870–1949, vol. IV
Adam, John Hunter, 1882–1958, vol. IV
Adam, Mme Juliette, 1836–1936, vol. III
Adam, Karl, 1876–1966, vol. VI
Adam, Kenneth, 1908–1978, vol. VII
Adam, Neil Kensington, 1891–1973, vol. VII
Adam, Patrick William, 1854–1929, vol. III
Adam, Randle R.; *see* Reid-Adam.
Adam, Robert Wilson, (Robin), 1923–1993, vol. IX
Adam, Robin; *see* Adam, R. W.
Adam, General Sir Ronald Forbes, 2nd Bt (*cr* 1917), 1885–1982, vol. VIII
Adam, Major William Augustus, 1865–1940, vol. III
Adam Smith, Janet Buchanan, (Mrs John Carleton), 1905–1999, vol. X

Adami, John George, 1862–1926, vol. II
Adami, Sir Leonard Christian, 1874–1952, vol. V
Adamic, Louis, 1899–1951, vol. V
Adams, 1st Baron, 1890–1960, vol. V
Adams, Rt Rev. (Albert) James, 1915–1999, vol. X
Adams, Alexander Annan, 1884–1955, vol. V
Adams, Air Vice-Marshal Alexander Annan, 1908–1990, vol. VIII
Adams, Hon. Alexander Samuel, 1861–1937, vol. III
Adams, Allen; *see* Adams, Allender S.
Adams, Allender Steele, (Allen), 1946–1990, vol. VIII
Adams, Rev. Arthur, 1852–1926, vol. II
Adams, Arthur Henry, 1872–1936, vol. III
Adams, Sir Arthur Robert, 1861–1937, vol. III
Adams, Beale, *died* 1939, vol. III
Adams, Bernard, *died* 1965, vol. VI
Adams, Brooks, 1848–1927, vol. II
Adams, Captain Bryan Fullerton, 1887–1971, vol. VII
Adams, (Charles) Christian Wilfred, 1939–1996, vol. X
Adams, Charles Edward, 1870–1945, vol. IV
Adams, Charles Francis, 1835–1915, vol. I
Adams, Charles Kingsley, 1899–1971, vol. VII
Adams, Christian Wilfred; *see* Adams, C. C. W.
Adams, Colin Wallace Maitland, 1928–1990, vol. VIII
Adams, Air Cdre Cyril Douglas, 1897–1988, vol. VIII
Adams, Dartrey; *see* Adams, H. D. C.
Adams, David, 1871–1943, vol. IV
Adams, David Morgan, 1875–1942, vol. IV
Adams, Miss E. Proby, *died* 1945, vol. IV
Adams, Ephraim Douglass, 1865–1930, vol. III
Adams, Sir Ernest Charles, 1886–1974, vol. VII
Adams, Col Francis, 1874–1945, vol. IV
Adams, Sir Francis Boyd, 1888–1974, vol. VII
Adams, Rev. Francis John, 1858–1929, vol. III
Adams, Frank; *see* Adams, J. F.
Adams, Frank Alexander, 1907–1998, vol. X
Adams, Frank Dawson, 1859–1942, vol. IV
Adams, Frederick James, 1885–1957, vol. V
Adams, George Burton, 1851–1925, vol. II
Adams, George Francis, 1870–1921, vol. II
Adams, Gerald Edward, 1930–1998, vol. X
Adams, Col Gofton Gee, 1861–1936, vol. III
Adams, Sir Grantley Herbert, 1898–1971, vol. VII
Adams, Major Sir Hamilton John G.; *see* Goold-Adams.
Adams, (Harold) Richard, 1912–1978, vol. VII
Adams, Harry William, 1868–1947, vol. IV
Adams, Henry, 1846–1935, vol. III
Adams, Henry Carter, 1851–1921, vol. II
Adams, Henry Charles, 1873–1952, vol. V
Adams, Col Sir Henry Edward Fane G.; *see* Goold-Adams.
Adams, Captain Henry George Homer, 1879–1960, vol. V
Adams, Ven. Henry Joseph, 1870–1946, vol. IV
Adams, Comdr Henry William Allen, 1884–1962, vol. VI
Adams, Herbert, 1858–1945, vol. IV
Adams, Herbert, 1874–1958, vol. V

4

Adams, Herbert Louis, 1910–1972, vol. VII
Adams, Hervey Cadwallader, 1903–1996, vol. X
Adams, (Howard) Dartrey (Charles), 1897–1958, vol. V
Adams, Rt Rev. James; see Adams, Rt Rev. A. J.
Adams, James Alexander, died 1930, vol. III
Adams, James Elwin Cokayne, 1876–1961, vol. VI
Adams, James Truslow, 1878–1949, vol. IV
Adams, James Whyte Leitch, 1909–1983, vol. VIII
Adams, Rev. James Williams, 1839–1903, vol. I
Adams, Comdr Sir Jameson Boyd, 1880–1962, vol. VI
Adams, Sir John, 1857–1934, vol. III
Adams, John, 1872–1950, vol. IV
Adams, Sir John Bertram, 1920–1984, vol. VIII
Adams, Sir John Coode-, 1859–1934, vol. III
Adams, J(ohn) Frank, 1930–1989, vol. VIII
Adams, Ven. John Michael G.; see Goold-Adams.
Adams, Rt Hon. John Michael Geoffrey Manningham, 1931–1985, vol. VIII
Adams, John Nicholas William B.; see Bridges-Adams.
Adams, John Roland, 1894–1961, vol. VI
Adams, (John) Roland, 1900–1983, vol. VIII
Adams, Captain Joseph Ebenezer, 1878–1926, vol. II
Adams, Joseph Robert George, 1859–1919, vol. II
Adams, Katharine; see Webb, Katharine.
Adams, Louis, 1853–1931, vol. III
Adams, Marcus Algernon, 1875–1959, vol. V
Adams, Mary Grace Agnes, 1898–1984, vol. VIII
Adams, Sir Maurice Edward, 1901–1982, vol. VIII
Adams, Surg. Rear-Adm. Maurice Henry, 1908–1992, vol. IX
Adams, Col Noel Percy, 1882–1954, vol. V
Adams, Paul, 1903–1972, vol. VII
Adams, Philip Edward Homer, 1879–1948, vol. IV
Adams, Rev. Reginald Arthur, 1864–1939, vol. III
Adams, Rev. Reginald Samuel, died 1928, vol. II
Adams, Richard; see Adams, H. R.
Adams, Richard, 1846–1908, vol. I
Adams, Richard John Moreton G.; see Goold-Adams.
Adams, Robert, 1917–1984, vol. VIII
Adams, Maj.-Gen. Sir Robert Bellew, 1856–1928, vol. II
Adams, Roland; see Adams, J. R.
Adams, Rev. Canon Samuel Trerice, died 1936, vol. III
Adams, Samuel Vyvyan Trerice, 1900–1951, vol. V
Adams, Sherman, 1899–1986, vol. VIII
Adams, Sidney Herbert; see Sidney, Herbert.
Adams, Stanley John, 1893–1965, vol. VI
Adams, Stephen; see Maybrick, Michael.
Adams, Sydney, 1905–1980, vol. VII
Adams, Sir Theodore Samuel, 1885–1961, vol. VI
Adams, Thomas, died 1929, vol. III
Adams, Thomas, 1871–1940, vol. III
Adams, Sir Walter, 1906–1975, vol. VII
Adams, Most Rev. Walter Robert, 1877–1957, vol. V
Adams, Walter Sydney, 1876–1956, vol. V
Adams, Wilfrid George, 1885–1936, vol. III
Adams, William B.; see Bridges-Adams.
Adams, William Dacres, 1864–1951, vol. V

Adams, William Davenport, 1851–1904, vol. I
Adams, William George Stewart, 1874–1966, vol. VI
Adams, William Grylls, 1836–1915, vol. I
Adams, William Henry, 1844–1928, vol. II, vol. III
Adams, Rev. Canon William John Telia Phythian P.; see Phythian-Adams.
Adams, Rear-Adm. William Leslie Graham, 1901–1963, vol. VI
Adams, William Thomas, 1884–1949, vol. IV
Adams-Acton, Gladstone Murray, 1886–1971, vol. VII
Adams-Beck, John Melliar, 1909–1979, vol. VII
Adams-Connor, Captain Harry George, 1859–1939, vol. III
Adams-Schneider, Rt Hon. Sir Lancelot Raymond, 1919–1995, vol. IX (AII)
Adamson, Very Rev. Alexander Campbell, 1921–1983, vol. VIII
Adamson, Sir Campbell; see Adamson, Sir W. O. C.
Adamson, Lt-Col Charles Henry Ellison, 1846–1930, vol. III
Adamson, Estelle Inez Ommanney, 1910–1990, vol. VIII
Adamson, Sir Harvey, 1854–1941, vol. IV
Adamson, Col Henry Mackenzie, 1861–1939, vol. III
Adamson, Horatio George, 1865–1955, vol. V
Adamson, Mrs Jennie Laurel, died 1962, vol. VI
Adamson, John, 1865–1918, vol. II
Adamson, John, 1886–1969, vol. VI
Adamson, Sir John Ernest, 1867–1950, vol. IV
Adamson, Hon. John Evans, 1884–1961, vol. VI
Adamson, Col John George, 1855–1932, vol. III
Adamson, John William, 1857–1947, vol. IV
Adamson, Joy-Friederike Victoria, 1910–1980, vol. VII
Adamson, Sir Kenneth Thomas, 1904–1976, vol. VII
Adamson, Lawrence Arthur, 1860–1932, vol. III
Adamson, Robert, 1852–1902, vol. I
Adamson, Lt-Col and Hon. Col Robert Hay, 1869–1936, vol. III
Adamson, Robert Stephen, 1885–1965, vol. VI
Adamson, Rt Rev. Mgr Canon Thomas, 1901–1991, vol. IX
Adamson, William, 1830–1910, vol. I
Adamson, Sir William, 1832–1917, vol. II
Adamson, Rt Hon. William, 1863–1936, vol. III
Adamson, William Murdoch, 1881–1945, vol. IV
Adamson, Sir (William Owen) Campbell, 1922–2000, vol. X
Adcock, (Arthur) St John, 1864–1930, vol. III
Adcock, Sir Frank Ezra, 1886–1968, vol. VI
Adcock, Sir Hugh, 1847–1920, vol. II
Adcock, St John; see Adcock, A. St J.
Adcock, Sir Robert Henry, 1899–1990, vol. VIII
Addams, Jane, 1860–1935, vol. III
Addams Williams, Christopher, 1877–1944, vol. IV
Adderley, Sir Augustus John, 1835–1905, vol. I
Adderley, Hubert John Broughton-, 1860–1931, vol. III
Adderley, Hon. and Rev. James Granville, 1861–1942, vol. IV

Adderley, Hon. Reginald Edmund, 1857–1934, vol. III
Addington, 2nd Baron, 1842–1915, vol. I
Addington, 3rd Baron, 1883–1966, vol. VI
Addington, 4th Baron, 1884–1971, vol. VII
Addington, 5th Baron, 1930–1982, vol. VIII
Addinsell, Richard Stewart, 1904–1977, vol. VII
Addis, Sir Charles Stewart, 1861–1945, vol. IV
Addis, Sir John Mansfield, 1914–1983, vol. VIII
Addis, Sir William, 1901–1978, vol. VII
Addis, Rev. William Edward, 1844–1917, vol. II
Addison, 1st Viscount, 1869–1951, vol. V
Addison, 2nd Viscount, 1904–1976, vol. VII
Addison, 3rd Viscount, 1914–1992, vol. IX
Addison, Adm. Sir (Albert) Percy, 1875–1952, vol. V
Addison, Cyril Clifford, 1913–1994, vol. IX
Addison, D'Arcy Wentworth, 1872–1955, vol. V
Addison, Air Vice-Marshal Edward Barker, 1898–1987, vol. VIII
Addison, Maj.-Gen. George Henry, 1876–1964, vol. VI
Addison, Sir James, 1879–1949, vol. IV
Addison, John Edmund Wentworth, 18380–1907, vol. I
Addison, Sir Joseph, 1879–1953, vol. V
Addison, Brig. Leonard Joseph Lancelot, 1902–1975, vol. VII
Addison, Margaret E. T., 1868–1940, vol. III (A), vol. IV
Addison, Oswald Lacy, 1874–1942, vol. IV
Addison, Adm. Sir Percy; see Addison, Adm. Sir A. P.
Addison, Philip Harold, 1909–1996, vol. X
Addison, Hon. William, 1890–1966, vol. VI
Addison, William Innes, 1857–1912, vol. I
Addison, Rev. William Robert Fountaine, *died* 1962, vol. VI
Addison, Sir William Wilkinson, 1905–1992, vol. IX
Addison-Smith, Chilton Lind, 1875–1955, vol. V
Addison-Smith, George Lind, 1870–1934, vol. III
Addleshaw, Very Rev. George William Outram, 1906–1982, vol. VIII
Addleshaw, John Lawrence, 1902–1989, vol. VIII
Addy, Sidney Oldall, 1848–1933, vol. III
Adeane, Baron (Life Peer); Michael Edward Adeane, 1910–1984, vol. VIII
Adeane, Charles Robert Whorwood, 1863–1943, vol. IV
Adeane, Col Sir Robert Philip Wyndham, 1905–1979, vol. VII
Adebo, Simeon Olaosebikan, Chief; The Okanlomo of Itoko and Egbaland, 1913–1994, vol. IX
Adeler, Max, (Charles Heber Clark), 1841–1915, vol. I
Adelstein, Abraham Manie, 1916–1992, vol. IX
Ademola, Rt Hon. Sir Adetokunbo Adegboyega, 1906–1993, vol. IX
Adenauer, Konrad, 1876–1967, vol. VI
Adeney, Bernard, *died* 1966, vol. VI
Adeney, Walter Frederick, 1849–1920, vol. II
Aderemi I; *see* Ife.
Adermann, Rt Hon. Sir Charles Frederick, 1896–1979, vol. VII

Adey, (Arthur) Victor, 1912–1990, vol. VIII
Adey, Victor; *see* Adey, A. V.
Adey, William James, 1874–1956, vol. V
Adie, Edward Percival, 1890–1977, vol. VII
Adie, Jack Jesson, 1913–1992, vol. IX
Adie, William John, 1886–1935, vol. III
Adie-Shepherd, Harold Richard Bowman, 1904–1979, vol. VII
Adjaye, Sir Edward; *see* Asafu-Adaye.
Adkin, Harry Kenrick K.; *see* Knight-Adkin.
Adkin, Rev. Walter Kenrick K.; *see* Knight-Adkin.
Adkins, Sir Ryland; *see* Adkins, Sir W. R. D.
Adkins, Sir (William) Ryland Dent, 1862–1925, vol. II
Adlam, George Henry Joseph, 1876–1946, vol. IV
Adlam, Lt-Col Tom Edwin, 1893–1975, vol. VII
Adler, Alfred, 1870–1937, vol. III
Adler, Cyrus, 1863–1940, vol. III
Adler, Elkan Nathan, 1861–1946, vol. IV
Adler, Felix, 1851–1933, vol. III
Adler, Very Rev. Hermann, 1839–1911, vol. I
Adler, Lawrence James, 1931–1988, vol. VIII
Adler, Rev. Michael, 1868–1944, vol. IV
Adler, Miss N., *died* 1950, vol. IV
Adler, Saul, 1895–1966, vol. VI
Adlercron, Brig.-Gen. Rodolph Ladeveze, 1873–1966, vol. VI
Adley, Robert James, 1935–1993, vol. IX
Adoo, Juius S.; *see* Sarkodee-Adoo.
Adorian, Paul, 1905–1983, vol. VIII
Adrian, 1st Baron, 1889–1977, vol. VII
Adrian, 2nd Baron, 1927–1995, vol. IX
Adrian, Alfred Douglas, 1845–1922, vol. II
Adrian, Frederick Obadiah, 1836–1909, vol. I
Adrian, Lady; (Hester Agnes), 1899–1966, vol. VI
Adrian, Max, 1903–1973, vol. VII
Adshead, Mary, 1904–1995, vol. IX
Adshead, Prof. Stanley Davenport, 1868–1946, vol. IV
Ady, Julia, (Mrs Henry Ady), *died* 1924, vol. II
Adye, Frederick James, 1874–1945, vol. IV
Adye, Maj.-Gen. Sir John, 1857–1930, vol. III
Adye, Gen. Sir John (Miller), 1819–1900, vol. I
Adye, Col Walter, 1858–1915, vol. I
Æ; *see* Russell, G. W.
Aehrenthal, Count Alois, 1854–1912, vol. I
Aelen, Most Rev. John, 1853–1929, vol. III
Aeron-Thomas, Gwilym Ewart, 1885–1958, vol. V
Affleck, Sir Frederick Danby James, 8th Bt, 1856–1939, vol. III
Affleck, Sir James Ormiston, *died* 1922, vol. II
Affleck, John Barr, 1878–1941, vol. IV
Affleck, Sir Robert, 7th Bt, 1852–1919, vol. II
Afghanistan, Ameer of; *see* Abdulrahman Khan.
Aflalo, Frederick George, 1870–1918, vol. II
Afsur-Ul-Mulk, Afsur-ud-Dowla, Afsur Jung, Mirza Mahomed Ali Beg, Khan Bahadur, Nawab, Maj.-Gen., *died* 1930, vol. III
Aga Khan (III), HH Rt Hon. Aga Sultan Sir Mohomed Shah, 1877–1957, vol. V
Agar, Sir Arthur Kirwan, 1877–1942, vol. IV
Agar, Captain Augustus Willington Shelton, 1890–1968, vol. VI
Agar, Charles Phipp, 1886–1963, vol. VI
Agar, Col Edward, 1859–1930, vol. III

Agar, Sir Francis, 1859–1934, vol. III
Agar, Hon. Francis William Arthur, 1873–1936, vol. III
Agar, Herbert Sebastian, 1897–1980, vol. VII
Agar, Lt-Col John Arnold Shelton, *died* 1951, vol. V
Agar, Wilfred Eade, 1882–1951, vol. V
Agar-Robartes, Hon. Thomas Charles Reginald, 1880–1915, vol. I
Agarwala, Sir Clifford Manmohan, 1890–1964, vol. VI
Agassiz, Alexander, 1835–1910, vol. I
Agate, James Evershed, 1877–1947, vol. IV
Ager, Rear-Adm. Kenneth Gordon, 1920–1998, vol. X
Aggey, Most Rev. John Kwao Amuzu, 1908–1972, vol. VII
Aghnides, Thanassis, 1889–1984, vol. VIII
Aglen, Anthony John, 1911–1984, vol. VIII
Aglen, Ven. Anthony Stocker, 1836–1908, vol. I
Aglen, Sir Francis Arthur, 1869–1932, vol. III
Aglen, John; *see* Aglen, A. J.
Aglionby, Col Arthur, 1832–1911, vol. I
Aglionby, Rev. Canon Francis Keyes, 1848–1937, vol. III
Aglionby, Rt Rev. John Orfeur, 1884–1963, vol. VI
Agnew, Alan Graeme, 1887–1962, vol. VI
Agnew, Sir Andrew, 1882–1955, vol. V
Agnew, Sir Andrew Noel, 9th Bt (*cr* 1629), 1850–1928, vol. II
Agnew, Sir Anthony; *see* Agnew, Sir J. A. S.
Agnew, (Sir) Fulque Melville Gerald Noel, 10th Bt (*cr* 1629), 1900–1975, vol. VII
Agnew, Maj. Sir (George) Keith, 5th Bt, 1918–1994, vol. IX
Agnew, Sir George William, 2nd Bt (*cr* 1895), 1852–1941, vol. IV
Agnew, Sir Geoffrey William Gerald, 1908–1986, vol. VIII
Agnew, Sir Godfrey; *see* Agnew, Sir W. G.
Agnew, Comdr Hugh Ladas, 1894–1975, vol. VII
Agnew, Hon. Sir James Wilson, 1815–1901, vol. I
Agnew, Sir (John) Anthony Stuart, 4th Bt, 1914–1993, vol. IX
Agnew, Hon. John Hume, 1863–1908, vol. I
Agnew, Sir John Stuart, 3rd Bt (*cr* 1895), 1879–1957, vol. V
Agnew, Sir Keith; *see* Agnew, Sir G. K.
Agnew, Sir Norris Montgomerie, 1895–1973, vol. VII
Agnew, Sir Patrick Dalreagle, 1868–1925, vol. II
Agnew, Comdr Sir Peter Garnett, 1st Bt, 1900–1990, vol. VIII
Agnew, Philip Leslie, 1863–1938, vol. III
Agnew, Col Quentin Graham Kinnaird, 1861–1937, vol. III
Agnew, Sir Robert David Garrick, 1930–1987, vol. VIII
Agnew, Spiro Theodore, 1918–1996, vol. X
Agnew, Sir Stair, 1831–1916, vol. II
Agnew, Sir William, 1st Bt (*cr* 1895), 1825–1910, vol. I
Agnew, Vice-Adm. Sir William Gladstone, 1898–1960, vol. V
Agnew, Sir (William) Godfrey, 1913–1995, vol. IX

Agnew, William Lockett, 1858–1918, vol. II
Agnew, Sir William Thomas Fischer, 1847–1903, vol. I
Agnon, Shmuel Yosef Halevi, 1888–1970, vol. VI
Agostini, L. E., 1858–1918, vol. II
Agron, Gershon, 1893–1959, vol. V
Agronsky, Gershon; *see* Agron, G.
Aguet, Gustave Charles, *died* 1927, vol. II
Ah-Chuen, Sir Moi Lin Jean Etienne, 1911–1992, vol. IX
Ahearne, Christopher Dominic, 1886–1964, vol. VI
Ahern, Maj.-Gen. Donal Maurice, 1911–1966, vol. VI
Ahern, Most Rev. John James, 1911–1997, vol. X
Ahern, Maj.-Gen. Timothy Michael Richard, 1908–1980, vol. VII
Aherne, Rev. David, 1871–1941, vol. IV
Ahlefeldt-Laurvig, Count Preben Ferdinand, 1872–1946, vol. IV
Ahlmann, Hans Wilhelmson, 1889–1974, vol. VII
Ahmad, Hon. Ahsanuddin, 1849–1918, vol. II
Admad, Maulvi Sir Nizam-ud-Din-Niwab Nizamat Jung Bahadur, 1871–1955, vol. V
Ahmad, Maulvi Sir Rafiuddin, 1865–1954, vol. V
Admad, Sir Zia-Uddin, 1879–1947, vol. IV
Admad Khan, Sardar Sahibzada Sir Sultan, 1864–1936, vol. III
Admed, Fakhruddin Ali, 1905–1977, vol. VII
Ahmed, Kabeerud-Din, 1888–1939, vol. III (A), vol. IV
Ahmed, Sir Syed Sultan, 1880–1963, vol. VI
Aicard, Jean, 1848–1921, vol. II
Aickin, Very Rev. George Ellis, *died* 1937, vol. III
Aickin, Hon. Sir Keith Arthur, 1916–1982, vol. VIII
Aickin, Thomas Reginald, 1886–1948, vol. IV (A)
Aidé, Charles Hamilton, 1826–1906, vol. I
Aiers, David Pascoe, 1922–1983, vol. VIII
Aiken, Conrad Potter, 1889–1973, vol. VII
Aiken, Frank, 1898–1983, vol. VIII
Aiken, John Elliott, 1909–1977, vol. VII
Aiken, John Macdonald, 1880–1961, vol. VI
Aikenhead, Brig. David Francis, 1895–1955, vol. V
Aikins, Hon. Sir James Albert Manning, 1851–1929, vol. III
Aikman, Sir Alexander, 1886–1968, vol. VI
Aikman, David Wann, 1863–1931, vol. III
Aikman, George, 1830–1905, vol. I
Aikman, Robert Gordon, 1905–1962, vol. VI
Aikman, Sir Robert Smith, 1844–1917, vol. II
Aikman, Col Thomas S. G. H. Robertson-, 1860–1948, vol. IV
Ailesbury, 5th Marquess of, 1842–1911, vol. I
Ailesbury, 6th Marquess of, 1873–1961, vol. VI
Ailesbury, 7th Marquess of, 1904–1974, vol. VII
Ailsa, 3rd Marquess of, 1847–1938, vol. III
Ailsa, 4th Marquess of, 1872–1943, vol. IV
Ailsa, 5th Marquess of, 1875–1956, vol. V
Ailsa, 6th Marquess of, 1882–1957, vol. V
Ailsa, 7th Marquess of, 1925–1994, vol. IX
Ailwyn, 1st Baron, 1855–1924, vol. II
Ailwyn, 2nd Baron, 1886–1936, vol. III
Ailwyn, 3rd Baron, 1887–1976, vol. VII
Ailwyn, 4th Baron, 1896–1988, vol. VIII
Ainger, Rev. Alfred, 1837–1904, vol. I
Ainger, Arthur Campbell, 1841–1919, vol. II

Ainley, Sir (Alfred) John, 1906–1992, vol. IX
Ainley, Eric Stephen, 1918–1986, vol. VIII
Ainley, Henry Hinchcliffe, 1879–1945, vol. IV
Ainley, Sir John; *see* Ainley, Sir A. J.
Ainley-Walker, Ernest William, 1871–1955, vol. V
Ainscough, Sir Thomas Martland, 1886–1976, vol. VII
Ainsley, John William, 1899–1976, vol. VII
Ainslie, Ainslie Douglas, 1838–1929, vol. III
Ainslie, Ven. Alexander Colvin, *died* 1903, vol. I
Ainslie, Lt-Col Charles Marshall, 1878–1940, vol. III
Ainslie, Charlotte, 1863–1960, vol. V
Ainslie, Grant Duff Douglas, 1865–1948, vol. IV
Ainslie, Lt-Col Henry Sandys, 1869–1948, vol. IV
Ainslie, James Percival, 1899–1973, vol. VII
Ainslie, Rev. Richard Montague, 1858–1924, vol. II
Ainsworth, Alfred Richard, 1879–1959, vol. V
Ainsworth, Bt Col Charles, 1874–1956, vol. V
Ainsworth, Sir David; *see* Ainsworth, Sir T. D.
Ainsworth, David, 1842–1906, vol. I
Ainsworth, Harry, 1888–1965, vol. VI
Ainsworth, John, 1864–1946, vol. IV
Ainsworth, Sir John Francis, 3rd Bt, 1912–1981, vol. VIII
Ainsworth, Sir John Stirling, 1st Bt, 1844–1923, vol. II
Ainsworth, Maj.-Gen. Sir Ralph Bignell, 1875–1952, vol. V
Ainsworth, Mrs Robert; *see* Brunskill, Muriel.
Ainsworth, Sir Thomas, 2nd Bt, 1886–1971, vol. VII
Ainsworth, Sir (Thomas) David, 4th Bt, 1926–1999, vol. X
Ainsworth, Lt-Col William John, 1873–1945, vol. IV
Ainsworth-Davis, James Richard, 1861–1934, vol. III
Ainsworth-Davis, John Creyghton, 1895–1976, vol. VII
Ainsworth Dickson, Thomas, 1881–1935, vol. III
Aird, Ian, 1905–1962, vol. VI
Aird, Sir John, 1st Bt, 1833–1911, vol. I
Aird, Sir John, 2nd Bt, 1861–1934, vol. III
Aird, Sir John, 1855–1938, vol. III
Aird, Col Sir John Renton, 3rd Bt, 1898–1973, vol. VII
Aird, Ronald, 1902–1986, vol. VIII
Airedale, 1st Baron, 1835–1911, vol. I
Airedale, 2nd Baron, 1863–1944, vol. IV
Airedale, 3rd Baron, 1882–1958, vol. V
Airedale, 4th Baron, 1915–1996, vol. X
Airey of Abingdon, Baroness (Life Peer); Diana Josceline Barbara Neave Airey, 1919–1992, vol. IX
Airey, Sir Edwin, 1878–1955, vol. V
Airey, Paymr Rear-Adm. Frederick W. I., 1861–1922, vol. II
Airey, Harold M.; *see* Morris-Airey.
Airey, Col Henry Parke, 1844–1911, vol. I
Airey, Sir James Talbot, 1812–1898, vol. I
Airey, John Robinson, *died* 1937, vol. III
Airey, Col Robert Berkeley, 1874–1933, vol. III
Airey, Lt-Gen. Sir Terence Sydney, 1900–1983, vol. VIII
Airlie, 8th Earl of, 1856–1900, vol. I

Airlie, 12th (*de facto* 9th) Earl of, 1893–1968, vol. VI
Airlie, Countess of; (Mabell Frances Elizabeth), 1866–1956, vol. V
Airy, Anna, 1882–1964, vol. VI
Airy, Rev. Basil Reginald, 1845–1924, vol. II
Airy, Osmund, 1845–1928, vol. II
Airy, Wilfrid, *died* 1925, vol. II
Aisher, Sir Owen Arthur, 1900–1993, vol. IX
Aitchison, Rt Hon. Lord; Craigie Mason Aitchison, 1882–1941, vol. IV
Aitchison, Gen. Charles Terrington, 1825–1919, vol. II
Aitchison, Craigie Mason; *see* Aitchison, Rt Hon. Lord.
Aitchison, Sir David, 1892–1975, vol. VII
Aitchison, George, 1825–1910, vol. I
Aitchison, George, 1877–1954, vol. V
Aitchison, James, 1899–1968, vol. VI
Aitchison, James Edward Tierney, 1835–1898, vol. I
Aitchison, Patrick Edward, 1881–1945, vol. IV
Aitchison, Sir Stephen, 1st Bt, 1863–1942, vol. IV
Aitchison, Sir Stephen Charles de Lancey, 3rd Bt, 1923–1958, vol. V
Aitchison, Sir Walter de Lancey, 2nd Bt, 1892–1953, vol. V
Aitken, Alexander Craig, 1895–1967, vol. VI
Aitken, Sir Arthur Percival Hay, (Sir Peter Aitken), 1905–1984, vol. VIII
Aitken, Rt Rev. Aubrey; *see* Aitken, Rt Rev. W. A.
Aitken, Cecil Edward, 1888–1959, vol. V
Aitken, Charles, 1869–1936, vol. III
Aitken, Edward Hamilton, 1851–1909, vol. I
Aitken, George Atherton, 1860–1917, vol. II
Aitken, George Benjamin Johnston, *died* 1942, vol. IV
Aitken, George Lewis, 1864–1940, vol. III
Aitken, Henry, 1851–1931, vol. III
Aitken, Ian Hugh, 1919–1986, vol. VIII
Aitken, Hon. J. G. W., *died* 1921, vol. II
Aitken, Sir James, 1880–1948, vol. IV
Aitken, James Hume, 1890–1955, vol. V
Aitken, Janet Kerr, 1886–1982, vol. VIII
Aitken, John, *died* 1919, vol. II
Aitken, John E., *died* 1957, vol. V
Aitken, John Hobson, 1851–1923, vol. II
Aitken, Col John James, 1878–1946, vol. IV
Aitken, John Thomas, 1913–1992, vol. IX
Aitken, Sir (John William) Max, 2nd Bt, 1910–1985, vol. VIII
Aitken, Sir Max; *see* Aitken, Sir J. W. M.
Aitken, Major Nigel Woodford, 1882–1963, vol. VI
Aitken, Sir Peter; *see* Aitken, Sir A. P. H.
Aitken, Sir Robert, 1863–1924, vol. II
Aitken, Rev. Canon Robert Aubrey, 1870–1941, vol. IV
Aitken, Robert Grant, 1864–1951, vol. V
Aitken, Air Vice-Marshal (Robert) Stanley, 1896–1982, vol. VIII
Aitken, Sir Robert Stevenson, 1901–1997, vol. X
Aitken, Air Vice-Marshal Stanley; *see* Aitken, Air Vice-Marshal R. S.
Aitken, Stephen Rowan, 1883–1943, vol. IV
Aitken, Col William, 1846–1917, vol. II

Aitken, Rt Rev. William Aubrey, 1911–1985, vol. VIII
Aitken, Rev. William Hay Macdowall Hunter, 1841–1927, vol. II
Aitken, Sir William Traven, 1905–1964, vol. VI
Aiton, Sir Arthur; see Aiton, Sir J. A.
Aiton, Sir (John) Arthur, 1864–1950, vol. IV
Aiyangar, Sir Venbakam B.; see Bashyam Aiyangar.
Aiyar, Sir Chetpat Pattabhirama R.; see Ramaswami Aiyar.
Aiyar, N. Chandrasekhara, 1888–1957, vol. V
Aiyar, Sir Theagaraja; see Sadasiva Aiyar.
Aiyer, Sir Pazhamarneri Sundaram Sivaswamy, 1864–1946, vol. IV
Ajasa, Sir Kitoyi, 1866–1937, vol. III
Akbar, Hon. M. T., 1880–1944, vol. IV (A)
Aked, Charles Frederic, 1864–1941, vol. IV
Akeley, Carl Ethan, 1864–1926, vol. II
Akenhead, David, 1894–1978, vol. VII
Akenhead, Rev. Edmund, died 1931, vol. III
Akerman, John Camille, died 1950, vol. IV
Akerman, Hon. Sir John William, 1825–1905, vol. I
Akerman, Air Vice-Marshal Walter Joseph Martin, 1901–1964, vol. VI
Akerman, Maj.-Gen. William Philip Jopp, 1888–1971, vol. VII
Akers, Sir Wallace Alan, 1888–1954, vol. V
Akhurst, Captain Algernon Frederic, 1893–1972, vol. VII
Akrill-Jones, Rev. Canon David, 1868–1945, vol. IV
Alabaster, Sir Chaloner, 1838–1898, vol. I
Alabaster, Sir Chaloner Grenville, 1880–1958, vol. V
Alagappa Chettiar, Sir Ramanatha, 1909–1957, vol. V
Alam, Hon. Anthony Alexander, 1898–1983, vol. VIII
Alanbrooke, 1st Viscount, 1883–1963, vol. VI
Alanbrooke, 2nd Viscount, 1920–1972, vol. VII
Alba, 17th Duque de, 1878–1953, vol. V
Alban, Sir Frederick John, 1882–1965, vol. VI
Alban Davies, Jenkin, 1901–1968, vol. VI
Albanesi, Mme, (Effe Henderson), 1859–1936, vol. III
Albani, Dame Emma, 1852–1930, vol. III
Albee, Ernest, 1865–1927, vol. II
Albemarle, 8th Earl of, 1858–1942, vol. IV
Albemarle, 9th Earl of, 1882–1979, vol. VII
Albert, Sir Alexis François, 1904–1997, vol. X
Albert, Carl Bert, 1908–2000, vol. X
Albert-Buisson, François, 1881–1961, vol. VI
Albertini, Luigi, 1871–1941, vol. IV
Alberts, Col Johannes Joachim, 1872–1947, vol. IV
Albery, Sir Bronson James, 1881–1971, vol. VII
Albery, Sir Donald Arthur Rolleston, 1914–1988, vol. VIII
Albery, Sir Irving James, 1879–1967, vol. VI
Albery, Michael James, 1910–1975, vol. VII
Albrecht, Ralph Gerhart, 1896–1985, vol. VIII
Albright, George Stacey, 1855–1945, vol. IV
Albright, William Foxwell, 1891–1971, vol. VII
Albrow, Desmond, 1925–1998, vol. X
Albu, Austen Harry, 1903–1994, vol. IX
Albu, Sir George, 1st Bt, 1857–1935, vol. III

Albu, Major Sir George Werner, 2nd Bt, 1905–1963, vol. VI
Albu, Leopold, died 1938, vol. III
Alcazar, Sir Henry Albert, 1860–1930, vol. III
Alchin, Gordon, died 1947, vol. IV
Alcock, Lt-Col Alfred William, 1859–1933, vol. III
Alcock, Charles William, 1842–1907, vol. I
Alcock, Henry, 1886–1948, vol. IV
Alcock, Rev. Preb. John Mark, died 1955, vol. V
Alcock, Captain Sir John William, 1892–1919, vol. II
Alcock, Nathaniel Henry, 1871–1913, vol. I
Alcock, Reginald, 1868–1944, vol. IV
Alcock, Sir Rutherford, 1809–1897, vol. I
Alcock, Sir Walter Galpin, 1861–1947, vol. IV
Alcorn, George Oscar, 1850–1930, vol. III
Aldam, Jeffery Heaton, 1922–1993, vol. IX
Aldam, Col William St Andrew W.; see Warde-Aldam.
Aldanov, Mark, 1889–1957, vol. V
Alden, Henry Mills, 1836–1919, vol. II
Alden, John Hewlett, 1900–1976, vol. VII
Alden, Sir Percy, 1865–1944, vol. IV
Aldenham, 1st Baron, 1819–1907, vol. I
Aldenham, 2nd Baron, 1846–1936, vol. III
Aldenham, 3rd Baron, 1879–1939, vol. III
Aldenham, 4th Baron, and Hunsdon of Hunsdon, 2nd Baron, 1888–1969, vol. VI
Aldenham, 5th Baron, 1922–1986, vol. VIII
Alder, Kurt, 1902–1958, vol. V
Alder, Wilfred, died 1962, vol. VI
Alderdice, Hon. Frederick Charles, 1872–1936, vol. III
Alderman, Edwin Anderson, 1861–1931, vol. III
Alderman, Harry Graham, 1895–1962, vol. VI
Alderman, Major Robert Edward, 1887–1934, vol. III
Alderman, Col Walter William, 1874–1935, vol. III
Aldersey, Captain Ralph, 1890–1971, vol. VII
Alderson, Rt Rev. Cecil William, 1900–1968, vol. VI
Alderson, Sir Charles Henry, 1831–1913, vol. I
Alderson, Sir Edward Hall, 1864–1951, vol. V
Alderson, Lt-Gen. Sir Edwin Alfred Hervey, 1859–1927, vol. II
Alderson, Rev. Frederick Cecil, 1836–1907, vol. I
Alderson, Sir George Beeton, 1844–1926, vol. II
Alderson, Sir Harold George, 1891–1978, vol. VII
Alderson, Michael Rowland, 1931–1988, vol. VIII
Alderson, Vice-Adm. William John Standly, died 1946, vol. IV
Alderton, George Edwin Lisle, 1888–1969, vol. VI (AII)
Aldham, Rev. Canon Vernon Harcourt, 1843–1929, vol. III
Aldin, Cecil Charles Windsor, 1870–1935, vol. III
Aldington, 1st Baron, 1914–2000, vol. X
Aldington, Charles, 1862–1922, vol. II
Aldington, Edward Godfree, 1892–1962, vol. VI
Aldington, Sir Geoffrey William, 1907–1992, vol. IX
Aldington, Hubert Edward, 1883–1967, vol. VI
Aldington, John Norman, 1905–1987, vol. VIII
Aldington, Richard; see Aldington, E. G.
Aldous, Alan Harold, 1923–1992, vol. IX

Aldous, Guy Travers, 1906–1981, vol. VIII
Aldred, Cyril, 1914–1991, vol. IX
Aldred-Brown, George Ronald Pym, 1896–1946, vol. IV
Aldren Turner, John William; see Turner.
Aldrich, Gertrude; see Lawrence, G.
Aldrich, Adm. Pelham, 1844–1930, vol. III
Aldrich, Thomas Bailey, 1836–1906, vol. I
Aldrich, Winthrop Williams, 1885–1974, vol. VII
Aldrich-Blake, Dame Louisa Brandreth, 1865–1925, vol. II
Aldridge, Lt-Col Arthur Russell, 1864–1947, vol. IV
Aldridge, Sir Frederick, 1891–1966, vol. VI
Aldridge, John Arthur Malcolm, 1905–1983, vol. VIII
Aldridge, Major John Barttelot, 1871–1909, vol. I
Aldridge, Very Rev. John Mullings, died 1920, vol. II
Aldridge, Leonard, 1892–1952, vol. V
Aldridge, Michael William ffolliott, 1920–1994, vol. IX
Aldworth, Lt-Col William, 1855–1900, vol. I
Alec-Smith, Col Rupert Alexander, 1913–1983, vol. VIII
Aleixandre, Vicente Pio Marcelino Cirilo, 1898–1984, vol. VIII
Alekhine, Alexander; see Alekhine, A. A.
Alekhine, (Aljechin) Alexander, 1892–1946, vol. IV
Alepoudelis, Odysseus; see Elytis, Odysseus.
Alers Hankey, Richard Lyons, 1906–1969, vol. VI
Alexander of Hillsborough, 1st Earl, 1885–1965, vol. VI
Alexander of Hillsborough, Countess; (Esther Ellen), 1877–1969, vol. VI
Alexander of Tunis, 1st Earl, 1891–1969, vol. VI
Alexander of Potterhill, Baron (Life Peer); William Picken Alexander, 1905–1993, vol. IX
Alexander, Mrs; see Hector, Annie Alexander.
Alexander, Alexander, 1849–1928, vol. II
Alexander, Sir Alexander Sandor, (Sir Alex), 1916–1994, vol. IX
Alexander, Anthony Victor, 1928–1999, vol. X
Alexander, Rev. Archibald, 1874–1942, vol. IV
Alexander, Rev. Archibald Browning Drysdale, 1855–1931, vol. III
Alexander, Arthur Harvey, 1843–1905, vol. I
Alexander, Col Aubrey de Vere, 1849–1923, vol. II
Alexander, Boyd, 1873–1910, vol. I
Alexander, Lt-Col Boyd Francis, 1834–1917, vol. II
Alexander, Charles, see Alexander, R. C.
Alexander, Brig.-Gen. Charles Henry, 1856–1946, vol. IV
Alexander, Charles McCallon, 1867–1920, vol. II
Alexander, Rear-Adm. Charles Otway, 1888–1970, vol. VI
Alexander, Maj.-Gen. Sir Claud, 1st Bt (cr 1886), 1831–1899, vol. I
Alexander, Sir Claud, 2nd Bt (cr 1886), 1867–1945, vol. IV
Alexander, Conel Hugh O'Donel, 1909–1974, vol. VII
Alexander, Conel W. O'D. L., 1879–1920, vol. II
Alexander, Cyril Wilson, 1879–1947, vol. IV
Alexander, Sir Darnley Arthur Raymond, 1920–1989, vol. VIII

Alexander, David, died 1944, vol. IV
Alexander, David, 1906–1972, vol. VII
Alexander, David Lindo, 1842–1922, vol. II
Alexander, Sir Desmond William Lionel C.; see Cable-Alexander.
Alexander, Sir Douglas, 1st Bt (cr 1921), 1864–1949, vol. IV
Alexander, Sir Douglas Hamilton, 2nd Bt, 1900–1983, vol. VIII
Alexander, Major Dudley Henry, 1863–1931, vol. III
Alexander, Duncan Hubert David, 1911–1985, vol. VIII
Alexander, Edward Bruce, 1872–1955, vol. V
Alexander, Maj.-Gen. Edward Currie, 1875–1964, vol. VI
Alexander, Edwin, 1870–1926, vol. II
Alexander, Eleanor Jane, died 1939, vol. III
Alexander, Ernest Edward, 1872–1946, vol. IV
Alexander, Maj.-Gen. Ernest Wright, 1870–1934, vol. III
Alexander, Lt-Col Francis David, 1878–1956, vol. V
Alexander, Sir Frank Samuel, 1st Bt (cr 1945), 1881–1959, vol. V
Alexander, Frederick Matthias, 1869–1955, vol. V
Alexander, Frederick William, 1859–1937, vol. III
Alexander, Sir George, 1858–1918, vol. II
Alexander, George Edward, 1865–1931, vol. III
Alexander, Gilchrist Gibb, 1871–1958, vol. V
Alexander, Harold Vincent, 1886–1950, vol. IV
Alexander, Col Harvey, 1859–1936, vol. III
Alexander, Lt-Col Heber Maitland, 1881–1942, vol. IV
Alexander, Henry, 1841–1914, vol. I
Alexander, Sir Henry, 1875–1940, vol. III
Alexander, Henry Clay, 1902–1969, vol. VI
Alexander, Henry Joachim, 1897–1988, vol. VIII
Alexander, Maj.-Gen. Henry Lethbridge, 1878–1944, vol. IV
Alexander, Maj.-Gen. Henry Templer, 1911–1977, vol. VII
Alexander, Herbert, 1874–1946, vol. IV
Alexander, Lt-Col Hon. Herbrand Charles, 1888–1965, vol. VI
Alexander, James Browning, 1888–1962, vol. VI
Alexander, Rt Hon. Sir James Ulick F. C.; see Alexander, Rt Hon. Sir Ulick.
Alexander, Very Rev. John, 1833–1908, vol. I
Alexander, Hon. John, 1876–1941, vol. IV
Alexander, Col John Donald, 1867–1922, vol. II
Alexander, Sir (John) Lindsay, 1920–2000, vol. X
Alexander, John W., 1856–1915, vol. I
Alexander, Joseph Gundry, 1848–1918, vol. II
Alexander, Sir Lindsay; see Alexander, Sir J. L.
Alexander, Sir Lionel Cecil William, 6th Bt (cr 1809), 1885–1956, vol. V
Alexander, Lt-Col Maurice, 1889–1945, vol. IV
Alexander, Nell Haigh, 1915–1986, vol. VIII
Alexander, Sir Norman Stanley, 1907–1997, vol. X
Alexander, Peter, 1893–1969, vol. VI
Alexander, Reginald Gervase, 1859–1916, vol. II
Alexander, (Richard) Charles, 1884–1968, vol. VI
Alexander, Robert, died 1923, vol. II
Alexander, Lt-Col Robert Donald Thain, 1878–1969, vol. VI

Alexander, Robert Edward, 1874–1946, vol. IV
Alexander, Rear-Adm. Robert Love, 1913–1993, vol. IX
Alexander, Maj.-Gen. Ronald Okeden, 1888–1949, vol. IV
Alexander, Samuel, 1859–1938, vol. III
Alexander, Rev. Sidney Arthur, 1866–1948, vol. IV
Alexander, Sir Sidney Robert, 1863–1929, vol. III
Alexander, Stanley Walker, 1895–1980, vol. VII
Alexander, Thomas, *died* 1933, vol. III
Alexander, Thomas Hood Wilson, 1878–1941, vol. IV
Alexander, Rt Hon. Sir Ulick, 1889–1973, vol. VII
Alexander, Walter, 1895–1964, vol. VI
Alexander, Most Rev. William, 1824–1911, vol. I
Alexander, William, *died* 1921, vol. II
Alexander, Brig.-Gen. Sir William, 1874–1954, vol. V
Alexander, William Cleverly, 1840–1916, vol. II
Alexander, Rev. William Menzies, *died* 1929, vol. III
Alexander, Lt-Col William Nathaniel Stuart, 1874–1956, vol. V
Alexander, Col Hon. William Sigismund Patrick, 1895–1972, vol. VII
Alexander-Sinclair, Adm. Sir Edwyn Sinclair, 1865–1945, vol. IV
Alexander-Sinclair, John Alexis Clifford Cerda, 1906–1988, vol. VIII
Alexandrowicz, Charles Henry, 1902–1975, vol. VII
Alfieri, Ernest, 1864–1913, vol. I
Alfieri, Maj.-Gen. Frederick John 1892–1961, vol. VI
Alford, Rt Rev. Charles Richard, 1816–1898, vol. I
Alford, Rev. Preb. Charles Symes Leslie, 1885–1963, vol. VI
Alford, Sir Edward Fleet, 1850–1905, vol. I
Alford, (Edward) John (Gregory), 1890–1960, vol. V (A)
Alford, Lt-Col Henry, *died* 1955, vol. V
Alford, Rev. Henry Powell, *died* 1921, vol. II
Alford, John; *see* Alford, E. J. G.
Alford, Ven. John Richard, 1919–1995, vol. IX
Alford, Rev. Josiah George, 1847–1924, vol. II
Alford, Sir Robert Edmund, 1904–1979, vol. VII
Alfvén, Hannes Olaf Gösta, 1908–1995, vol. IX
Algar, Claudius Randleson, 1900–1988, vol. VIII
Algeo, Sir Arthur, 1903–1967, vol. VI
Alger, John Goldworth, 1836–1907, vol. I
Algie, Sir Ronald Macmillan, 1888–1978, vol. VII
Ali, Abdullah Yusuf, 1872–1953, vol. V
Ali, Khan Bahadur Nawab Sir Chaudri Fazal, *died* 1942, vol. IV
Ali, (Chaudri) Mohamad, 1905–1980, vol. VII
Ali, Mir Aula, *died* 1898, vol. I
Ali, Mohamad; *see* Ali, C. M.
Ali, Mohammed, 1909–1963, vol. VI
Ali, Rt Hon. (Syed) A.; *see* Ameer-Ali.
Ali, Syed Waris A.; *see* Ameer Ali.
Ali, Sir Torick A.; *see* Ameer-Ali.
Ali Chowdhuri, Hon. Nawab Bahadur Syed Nawab, 1863–1929, vol. III
Ali-Rajpur, Raja of, 1881–1948, vol. IV (A), vol. V
Alice, HRH Princess; *see* Athlone, Countess of.
Alington, 1st Baron, 1825–1904, vol. I

Alington, 2nd Baron, 1859–1919, vol. II
Alington, 3rd Baron, 1896–1940, vol. III
Alington, Adrian Richard, 1895–1958, vol. V
Alington, Vice-Adm. Argentine Hugh, 1876–1945, vol. IV
Alington, Adm. Arthur Hildebrand, 1839–1925, vol. II
Alington, Very Rev. Cyril Argentine, 1872–1955, vol. V
Alington, Hon. Mrs Cyril, (Hester Margaret), 1874–1958, vol. V
Alington, Hon. Hester Margaret; *see* Alington, Hon. Mrs Cyril.
Alison, Sir Archibald, 2nd Bt, 1826–1907, vol. I
Alison, Sir Archibald, 3rd Bt, 1862–1921, vol. II
Alison, Comdr Sir Archibald, 4th Bt, 1888–1967, vol. VI
Alison, David, *died* 1955, vol. V
Alison, Sir Frederick Black, 5th Bt, 1893–1970, vol. VI
Alison, John, 1861–1952, vol. V
Alker, Thomas, 1904–1981, vol. VIII
Allan of Kilmahew, Baron (Life Peer); Robert Alexander Allan, 1914–1979, vol. VII
Allan, Albert, 1893–1948, vol. IV
Allan, Archibald Russell Watson, 1878–1959, vol. V
Allan, Arthur Percy, 1868–1927, vol. II
Allan, Charles Edward, 1861–1929, vol. III
Allan, Sir Colin Hamilton, 1921–1993, vol. IX
Allan, Donald James, 1907–1978, vol. VII
Allan, Douglas Alexander, 1896–1967, vol. VI
Allan, F. L., 1893–1964, vol. VI
Allan, Francis John, 1858–1932, vol. III
Allan, George William, 1860–1940, vol. III
Allan, Gordon Buchanan, 1914–1994, vol. IX
Allan, Sir Harold Egbert, 1894–1953, vol. V
Allan, Sir Henry Marshman H.; *see* Havelock-Allan.
Allan, Sir Henry Ralph Moreton H.; *see* Havelock-Allan.
Allan, Captain Henry Samuel, 1892–1979, vol. VII
Allan, Sir Henry Spencer Moreton H.; *see* Havelock-Allan.
Allan, Hugh A., 1857–1938, vol. III
Allan, Col Sir Hugh Montagu, 1860–1951, vol. V
Allan, Rev. J. B., 1873–1932, vol. III
Allan, Janet Laurie, 1892–1985, vol. VIII
Allan, Hon. John, 1866–1936, vol. III
Allan, John, *died* 1955, vol. V
Allan, John, 1927–1979, vol. VII
Allan, John Arthur Briscoe, 1911–1981, vol. VIII
Allan, John Clifford, 1920–1997, vol. X
Allan, John Gray, 1915–1994, vol. IX
Allan, Captain John Steele, 1889–1979, vol. VII (AII)
Allan, Maud, *died* 1956, vol. V
Allan, Philip Bertram Murray, 1884–1973, vol. VII
Allan, Sir Robert George, 1879–1972, vol. VII
Allan, Robert W., *died* 1942, vol. IV
Allan, Maj.-Gen. William, 1832–1918, vol. II
Allan, Sir William, 1837–1903, vol. I
Allan, Lt-Col William David, 1879–1961, vol. VI
Allan, William Nimmo, 1896–1984, vol. VIII
Allanby, Ven. Christopher Gibson, *died* 1917, vol. II
Allanson, Col Cecil John Lyons, 1877–1943, vol. IV

Allanson, Harry Llewelyn Lyons, 1876–1955, vol. V
Allard, Sir George Mason, 1866–1953, vol. V
Allard, Sir Gordon Laidlaw, 1909–1994, vol. IX
Allard, Gen. Jean Victor, 1913–1996, vol. X
Allard, Hon. Jules, 1859–1945, vol. IV
Allardyce, Elsie Elizabeth, (Lady Allardyce), died 1962, vol. VI
Allardyce, Brig. John Grahame Buchanan, 1878–1949, vol. IV
Allardyce, Robert Moir, 1882–1951, vol. V
Allardyce, Sir William Lamond, 1861–1930, vol. III
Allason, Maj.-Gen. Sir Richard B.; see Bannatine-Allason.
Allason, Brig.-Gen. Walter, 1875–1960, vol. V
Allberry, Albert Spenser, 1880–1949, vol. IV
Allbon, Charles F., 1856–1926, vol. II, vol. III
Allbutt, Rt Hon. Sir Clifford; see Allbutt, Rt Hon. Sir T. C.
Allbutt, Rt Hon. Sir (Thomas) Clifford, 1836–1925, vol. II
Allchin, Sir Geoffrey Cuthbert, 1895–1968, vol. VI
Allchin, Thomas, 1848–1936, vol. III
Allchin, Sir William Henry, 1846–1911, vol. I
Allcock, Rev. Arthur Edmund, 1851–1924, vol. II
Allcock, John Gladding Major, 1905–1986, vol. VIII
Allcott, Walter Herbert, 1880–1951, vol. V
Allcroft, Herbert John, 1865–1911, vol. I
Allcroft, Sir Philip M.; see Magnus-Allcroft.
Allden, John Eric, 1886–1949, vol. IV
Allderidge, Charles Donald, 1889–1958, vol. V
Alldis, Rev. Canon John, 1849–1930, vol. III
Alldridge, Thomas Joshua, 1847–1916, vol. II
Alldritt, Walter, 1918–1990, vol. VIII
Allegro, John Marco, 1923–1988, vol. VIII
Allen of Fallowfield, Baron (Life Peer); Alfred Walter Henry Allen, 1914–1985, vol. VIII
Allen of Hurtwood, 1st Baron, 1889–1939, vol. III
Allen of Hurtwood, Lady; (Marjory), 1897–1976, vol. VII
Allen, A. Stuart, 1890–1957, vol. V
Allen, Sir (Albert) George, 1888–1956, vol. V
Allen, Hon. Alfred Ernest, 1912–1987, vol. VIII
Allen, Brig.-Gen. Alfred James Whitacre, 1857–1939, vol. III
Allen, Arthur Acland, 1868–1939, vol. III
Allen, Arthur Cecil, 1887–1981, vol. VIII
Allen, Maj.-Gen. Arthur Samuel, 1894–1959, vol. V
Allen, Rev. Barten Wilcockson, died 1940, vol. III
Allen, Basil Copleston, 1870–1935, vol. III
Allen, Benjamin, 1845–1929, vol. III
Allen, Rear-Adm. Sir Bertram Cowles, 1875–1957, vol. V
Allen, Sir Carleton Kemp, 1887–1966, vol. VI
Allen, Lt-Col Carleton Woodford, 1878–1938, vol. III
Allen, Col Sir Charles, 1852–1920, vol. II
Allen, Air Vice-Marshal Charles Edward Hamilton, 1899–1975, vol. VII
Allen, Charles Francis Egerton, 1847–1927, vol. II
Allen, Major Rt Hon. Charles Peter, 1861–1930, vol. III
Allen, Charles Peter Selwyn, 1917–1977, vol. VII
Allen, Charles Turner, 1877–1958, vol. V
Allen, Clabon Walter, 1904–1987, vol. VIII
Allen, Clarence Edgar, 1871–1951, vol. V

Allen, Rear-Adm. Sir David, 1933–1995, vol. IX
Allen, Sir Denis; see Allen, Sir W. D.
Allen, Derek Fortrose, 1910–1975, vol. VII
Allen, Rev. Canon Derek William, 1925–1991, vol. IX
Allen, Sir Donald Richard, 1894–1983, vol. VIII
Allen, Edgar Johnson, 1866–1942, vol. IV
Allen, Edgar Malpas, 1883–1967, vol. VI
Allen, Lt-Col Edward, 1859–1933, vol. III
Allen, Edward H.; see Heron-Allen.
Allen, Col Edward Watts, 1883–1965, vol. VI
Allen, Edwin Hopkins, 1878–1967, vol. VI
Allen, Ernest Joshua, 1871–1955, vol. V
Allen, Sir Ernest King, 1864–1937, vol. III
Allen, F. M.; see Downey, Edmund.
Allen, Sir Francis Raymond, 2nd Bt, 1910–1939, vol. III
Allen, Frank, 1874–1965, vol. VI
Allen, Sir Frederick Charles, 1st Bt, 1864–1934, vol. III
Allen, Frederick Lewis, 1890–1954, vol. V
Allen, Frederick Martin Brice, 1898–1972, vol. VII
Allen, Rt Rev. Geoffrey Francis, 1902–1982, vol. VIII
Allen, Sir George; see Allen, Sir A. G.
Allen, Engr Rear-Adm. George Bennett, 1888–1948, vol. IV
Allen, George Berney, 1862–1917, vol. II
Allen, George Cyril, 1900–1982, vol. VIII
Allen, Rev. George Kendall, 1883–1975, vol. VII
Allen, Sir George Oswald Browning, 1902–1989, vol. VIII
Allen, George Thomas, 1852–1940, vol. III
Allen, Sir George Vance, 1894–1970, vol. VI
Allen, Rt Rev. Gerald Burton, 1885–1956, vol. V
Allen, Godfrey; see Allen, W. G.
Allen, Grant, 1848–1899, vol. I
Allen, Rear-Adm. Hamilton Colclough, 1883–1964, vol. VI
Allen, Harold Major, 1911–1977, vol. VII
Allen, (Harold) Norman (Gwynne), 1912–1995, vol. IX
Allen, Harold Tuckwell, 1879–1950, vol. IV
Allen, Sir Harry Brookes, 1854–1926, vol. II
Allen, Harry Cranbrook, 1917–1998, vol. X
Allen, Harry Epworth, 1894–1958, vol. V
Allen, Henry George, died 1908, vol. I
Allen, Brig. Henry Isherwood, 1887–1979, vol. VII
Allen, Henry Seymour, 1847–1928, vol. II
Allen, Maj.-Gen. Henry Tureman, 1859–1930, vol. III
Allen, Herbert Stanley, 1873–1954, vol. V
Allen, Herbert Warner, 1881–1968, vol. VI
Allen, Rev. Canon Herbert William, died 1944, vol. IV
Allen, Hervey, 1889–1949, vol. IV
Allen, Lt-Col Hugh Morris, 1867–1932, vol. III
Allen, Sir Hugh Percy, 1869–1946, vol. IV
Allen, Inglis, 1879–1943, vol. IV
Allen, Jack, 1905–1984, vol. VIII
Allen, Very Rev. James, 1802–1897, vol. I
Allen, Col Hon. Sir James, 1885–1942, vol. IV
Allen, James Godfrey Colquhoun, 1904–1982, vol. VIII
Allen, James Lane, 1849–1925, vol. II

Allen, Vice-Adm. John Derwent, 1875–1958, vol. V
Allen, John Edsall, 1861–1944, vol. IV
Allen, John Ernest, 1872–1962, vol. VI
Allen, John Hunter, *died* 1997, vol. X
Allen, John Romilly, 1847–1907, vol. I
Allen, Sir John Sandeman, 1865–1935, vol. III
Allen, Col John Sandeman, 1892–1949, vol. IV
Allen, Col John Woolley, 1865–1942, vol. IV
Allen, Joseph Stanley, 1898–1997, vol. X
Allen, Sir Kenneth; *see* Allen, Sir W. K. G.
Allen, Kenneth William, 1923–1997, vol. X
Allen, Leslie Holdsworth, 1879–1964, vol. VI
Allen, Comdt Mary Sophia, 1878–1964, vol. VI
Allen, Maurice; *see* Allen, W. M.
Allen, Sir Milton Pentonville, 1888–1981, vol. VIII
Allen, Col Newton Seymour, 1957–1934, vol. III
Allen, Norman; *see* Allen, H. N. G.
Allen, Norman Percy, 1903–1972, vol. VII
Allen, Sir Oswald Coleman, 1887–1959, vol. V
Allen, Percy Stafford, 1869–1933, vol. III
Allen, Sir Peter Christopher, 1905–1993, vol. IX
Allen, Maj.-Gen. Ralph Edward, 1846–1910, vol. I
Allen, Raymond Cecil, 1872–1937, vol. III
Allen, Raymond Seaforth Stirling, 1905–1974,
  vol. VII
Allen, Sir Richard Hugh Sedley, 1903–1996, vol. X
Allen, Rev. Richard Watson, 1833–1914, vol. I
Allen, Richard William, 1876–1921, vol. II
Allen, Sir Richard William, 1867–1955, vol. V
Allen, Captain Robert Calder, 1812–1903, vol. I
Allen, Lt-Col Robert Candlish, 1881–1942, vol. IV
Allen, Col Robert Franklin, 1860–1916, vol. II
Allen, Maj.-Gen. Robert Hall, 1886–1981, vol. VIII
Allen, Sir Roger, 1909–1972, vol. VII
Allen, Brig. Ronald Lewis, 1916–1986, vol. VIII
Allen, Sir Ronald Wilberforce, 1889–1936, vol. III
Allen, Rowland Lancelot, 1908–1992, vol. IX
Allen, Sir Roy George Douglas, 1906–1983,
  vol. VIII
Allen, Col Sir Stephen Shepherd, 1882–1964,
  vol. VI
Allen, Sydney Scholefield, 1898–1974, vol. VII
Allen, Rev. Thomas, 1837–1912, vol. I
Allen, Very Rev. Thomas, 1873–1927, vol. II
Allen, Sir Thomas, 1864–1943, vol. IV
Allen, Thomas Carleton, 1852–1927, vol. II
Allen, Thomas Palmer, 1899–1979, vol. VII
Allen, Walter Ernest, 1911–1995, vol. IX
Allen, W(alter) Godfrey, 1891–1986, vol. VIII
Allen, Walter John Gardener, 1916–1999, vol. X
Allen, Sir Walter Macarthur, 1870–1943, vol. IV
Allen, Wilfred Baugh, 1849–1922, vol. II
Allen, William, 1892–1941, vol. IV
Allen, William, 1870–1945, vol. IV
Allen, William Alexander, 1914–1998, vol. X
Allen, Major William Barnsley, 1892–1933, vol. III
Allen, Sir (William) Denis, 1910–1987, vol. VIII
Allen, William Edward David, 1901–1973, vol. VII
Allen, William Gilbert, 1892–1970, vol. VI
Allen, Sir William Guilford, 1898–1977, vol. VII
Allen, William Henry, 1844–1926, vol. II
Allen, Lt-Col Sir William James, 1866–1947,
  vol. IV
Allen, Sir (William) Kenneth (Gwynne),
  1907–2000, vol. X

Allen, Major William Lynn, 1871–1914, vol. I
Allen, (William) Maurice, 1908–1988, vol. VIII
Allen, William Philip, 1888–1958, vol. V
Allen, William Shepherd, 1831–1915, vol. I
Allen, Rev. Willoughby Charles, 1867–1953, vol. V
Allen-Jones, Air Vice-Marshal John Ernest,
  1909–1999, vol. X
Allen-Williams, Brig.-Gen. Sir Arthur John,
  1869–1949, vol. IV
Allenby, 1st Viscount, 1861–1936, vol. III
Allenby, 2nd Viscount, 1903–1984, vol. VIII
Allenby, Rt Rev. (David Howard) Nicholas,
  1909–1995, vol. IX
Allenby, Captain Frederick Claude Hynman,
  1864–1934, vol. III
Allenby, Rt Rev. Nicholas; *see* Allenby, Rt Rev.
  D. H. N.
Allenby, Adm. Reginald Arthur, 1861–1936, vol. III
Allendale, 1st Baron, 1829–1907, vol. I
Allendale, 1st Viscount, 1860–1923, vol. II
Allendale, 2nd Viscount, 1890–1956, vol. V
Allerton, 1st Baron, 1840–1917, vol. II
Allerton, 2nd Baron, 1867–1925, vol. II
Allerton, 3rd Baron, 1903–1991, vol. IX
Allerton, Air Cdre Ord Denny, 1902–1977, vol. VII
Allerton, Reginald John, 1898–1990, vol. VIII
Alletson, Major G. C., *died* 1928, vol. II
Alley, Ronald Edgar, 1926–1999, vol. X
Alleyne, Maj.-Gen. Sir James, *died* 1899, vol. I
Alleyne, Sir John Gay Newton, 3rd Bt, 1820–1912,
  vol. I
Alleyne, Captain Sir John Meynell, 4th Bt,
  1889–1983, vol. VIII
Allford, David, 1927–1997, vol. X
Allfrey, Lt-Gen. Sir Charles Walter, 1895–1964,
  vol. VI
Allfrey, Major Edward Mortimer, 1886–1957,
  vol. V
Allfrey, Captain Maurice Charles, 1916–1942,
  vol. IV
Allgeyer, Rt Rev. Emile Auguste, 1856–1924,
  vol. II
Allgood, Maj.-Gen. George, 1827–1907, vol. I
Allgood, Brig.-Gen. William Henry Loraine,
  1868–1957, vol. V
Allhusen, (Augustus) Henry (Eden), 1867–1925,
  vol. II
Allhusen, Beatrice May, *died* 1918, vol. II
Allhusen, Maj. Derek Swithin, 1914–2000, vol. X
Allhusen, Lt-Col. Frederick Henry, 1872–1957,
  vol. V
Allhusen, Henry; *see* Allhusen, A. H. E.
Allhusen, William Hutt, 1845–1923, vol. II
Allies, Mary H. A., 1852–1927, vol. II
Allighan, Garry, *born* 1900, vol. VII (AII)
Allin, Norman, 1884–1973, vol. VII
Allin, Samuel John Henry Wallis, 1871–1933,
  vol. III
Allingham, Helen, (Mrs William Allingham),
  1848–1926, vol. II
Allingham, Herbert William, *died* 1904, vol. I
Allingham, Margery Louise, 1904–1966, vol. VI
Allingham, Mrs William; *see* Allingham, H.
Allinson, Adrian Paul, 1890–1959, vol. V

Allinson, Air Vice-Marshal Norman Stuart, 1904–1984, vol. VIII
Allison, Charles Ralph, 1903–1991, vol. IX
Allison, Sir Charles William, 1886–1972, vol. VII
Allison, Rev. David, died 1940, vol. III
Allison, Rt Rev. Falkner; see Allison, Rt Rev. S. F.
Allison, James, 1865–1951, vol. V
Allison, James Anthony, 1915–1976, vol. VII
Allison, Sir John; see Allison, Sir W. J.
Allison, Captain John Hamilton, 1902–1968, vol. VI
Allison, John William, died 1934, vol. III
Allison, Rt Rev. Oliver Claude, 1908–1989, vol. VIII
Allison, Philip Rowland, 1907–1974, vol. VII
Allison, Ralph Victor, 1900–1987, vol. VIII
Allison, Sir Richard John, 1869–1958, vol. V
Allison, Richard Sydney, 1899–1978, vol. VII
Allison, Sir Robert Andrew, 1838–1926, vol. II
Allison, Rt Rev. Sherard Falkner, 1907–1993, vol. IX
Allison, William, 1851–1925, vol. II
Allison, Sir (William) John, 1903–1966, vol. VI
Alliston, Sir Frederick Prat, 1832–1912, vol. I
Allitsen, Frances, (Mary Frances Bumpus), 1849–1912, vol. I
Allitt, Sir (John) William, 1896–1972, vol. VII
Allitt, Sir William; see Allitt, Sir J. W.
Allix, Charles Peter, 1842–1920, vol. II
Allman, George James, 1812–1898, vol. I
Allman, George Johnston, 1824–1904, vol. I
Allman, Robert, 1854–1917, vol. II, vol. III
Allmand, Arthur John, 1885–1951, vol. V
Allnutt, Col Edward Bruce, 1885–1972, vol. VII
Allnutt, Rev. George Herbert, 1843–1919, vol. II
Allom, Sir Charles Carrick, 1865–1947, vol. IV
Allott, Eric Newmarch, 1899–1980, vol. VII
Allport, Alfred, 1867–1949, vol. IV
Allsebrook, George Clarence, 1877–1957, vol. V
Allsebrook, Peter Winder, 1917–1991, vol. IX
Allsop, Hon. Sir James Joseph Whittlesea, 1887–1963, vol. VI
Allsop, Kenneth, 1920–1973, vol. VII
Allsop, Lt-Col William Gillian, 1874–1951, vol. V
Allsopp, Hon. Alfred Percy, 1861–1929, vol. III
Allsopp, Bruce; see Allsopp, H. B.
Allsopp, Cecil Benjamin, 1904–1989, vol. VIII
Allsopp, Hon. Frederic Ernest, 1857–1928, vol. II
Allsopp, Hon. George Higginson, 1846–1907, vol. I
Allsopp, (Harold) Bruce, 1912–2000, vol. X
Allsopp, Captain Hon. Herbert Tongue, 1855–1920, vol. II
Allsopp, Samuel Ranulph, 1899–1975, vol. VII
Allsup, Major Edward Saunders, 1879–1928, vol. II
Allt, Wilfrid Greenhouse, 1889–1969, vol. VI
Allum, Frederick Warner, 1869–1963, vol. VI
Allum, Horace Benjamin, 1884–1966, vol. VI
Allum, Sir John Andrew Charles, 1889–1972, vol. VII
Allward, Walter Seymour, 1876–1955, vol. V
Allwood, James, died 1933, vol. III
Allwork, Rev. Robert Long, 1863–1919, vol. II
Allworthy, Rev. Thomas Bateson, 1879–1964, vol. VI
Alma-Tadema, Miss Anna, died 1943, vol. IV

Alma-Tadema, Laura Theresa, (Lady Alma-Tadema), died 1909, vol. I
Alma-Tadema, Miss Laurence, died 1940, vol. III
Alma-Tadema, Sir Lawrence, 1836–1912, vol. I
Almedingen, Edith Martha, 1898–1971, vol. VII
Almond, Hely Hutchinson, 1837–1903, vol. I
Almond, Sir James, 1891–1964, vol. VI
Almond, Hon. Col Ven. John Macpherson, 1872–1939, vol. III (A), vol. IV
Almond, W. Douglas, died 1916, vol. III
Alness, 1st Baron, 1868–1955, vol. V
Alpass, Joseph Herbert, 1873–1969, vol. VI
Alpe, Frank Theodore, died 1952, vol. V
Alphand, Hervé Jean-Charles, 1907–1994, vol. IX
Alport, Baron (Life Peer); Cuthbert James McCall Alport, 1912–1998, vol. X
Alsop, James Willcox, 1846–1921, vol. II
Alsop, Ralph, died 1950, vol. IV
Alstead, Robert, 1873–1946, vol. IV
Alstead, Stanley, 1905–1992, vol. IX
Alston, Alexander Rowland, 1863–1945, vol. IV
Alston, Rt Rev. Arthur Fawssett, 1872–1954, vol. V
Alston, (Arthur) Rex, 1901–1994, vol. IX
Alston, Rt Hon. Sir Beilby Francis, 1868–1929, vol. III
Alston, Sir Charles Ross, 1862–1937, vol. III
Alston, Sir Francis Beilby, 1820–1905, vol. I
Alston, Brig.-Gen. Francis George, 1878–1961, vol. VI
Alston, Hilda, (Lady Alston), died 1945, vol. IV
Alston, Captain Hubert George, 1866–1939, vol. III
Alston, Leonard, 1875–1953, vol. V
Alston, Brig. Llewllyn Arthur Augustus, 1890–1968, vol. VI
Alston, Rex; see Alston, A. R.
Alston, Rowland Crewe, 1852–1933, vol. III
Alston Roberts West, Gen. Sir Michael Montgomerie; see West.
Alt, Col William John, 1840–1908, vol. I
Altham, Captain Edward, 1882–1950, vol. IV
Altham, Lt-Gen. Sir Edward Altham, 1856–1943, vol. IV
Altham, Harry Surtees, 1888–1965, vol. VI
Althaus, Frederick Rudolph, 1895–1975, vol. VII
Althaus, Friedrich, 1829–1897, vol. I
Altman, Sir Albert Joseph, 1839–1912, vol. I
Alton, Ernest Henry, died 1952, vol. V
Alton, Sir Francis Cooke, 1856–1926, vol. II
Altrincham, 1st Baron, 1879–1955, vol. V
Alty, Thomas, 1899–1982, vol. VIII
Alun Roberts, Robert, 1894–1969, vol. VI
Aluwihare, Sir Richard, 1895–1976, vol. VII
Alvarez, Justin Charles William, 1859–1934, vol. III
Alvarez, Luis Walter, 1911–1988, vol. VIII
Alvarez de Rocafuarte, Marguerite; see D'Alvarez, Madame.
Alverstone, 1st Viscount, 1842–1915, vol. I
Alves, Duncan Elliott, 1870–1940, vol. III
Alves, Lt-Col Henry Malcolm Jerome, 1883–1940, vol. III
Alvin, Juliette Louise, died 1982, vol. VIII
Alvingham, 1st Baron, 1889–1955, vol. V
Alvord, Clarence Walworth, 1868–1928, vol. II
Alwar, HH Raj Rishi Shri Sewai Sir Jey Singhji

Veerendra Shiromani Dev, Bharat Dharam Prabhakar, Maharaj of, 1882–1937, vol. III
Alwyn, William, 1905–1985, vol. VIII
Aly Khan, Shah, 1911–1960, vol. V
Amaldi, Edoardo, 1908–1989, vol. VIII
Amand de Mendieta, Rev. Emmanuel Alexandre, 1907–1976, vol. VII
Amar Singh, Gen. Raja Sir, 1864–1909, vol. I
Amarjit Singh, Lt-Col Maharajkumar, 1893–1944, vol. IV
Ambartsumian, Victor, 1908–1996, vol. X
Ambedkar, Bhimrao Ramji, 1893–1956, vol. V
Ambler, Eric Clifford, 1909–1998, vol. X
Ambler, Air Vice-Marshal Geoffrey Hill, 1904–1978, vol. VII
Ambler, Harry, 1908–1988, vol. VIII
Ambrose, Edmund Jack, 1914–1996, vol. X
Ambrose, James Walter Davy, 1909–1993, vol. IX
Ambrose, Robert, 1855–1940, vol. III
Ambrose, Brig. Robert Denis, 1896–1974, vol. VII
Ambrose, William, 1832–1908, vol. I
Amcotts, Lt-Comdr John C.; *see* Cracroft-Amcotts.
Amcotts, Lt-Col Sir Weston C.; *see* Cracroft-Amcotts.
Ameer-Ali, Rt Hon. (Syed), 1849–1928, vol. II
Ameer Ali, (Syed) Waris, 1886–1975, vol. VII
Ameer Ali, Sir Torick, 1891–1975, vol. VII
Amers, Maj.-Gen. John Henry, 1904–1990, vol. VIII
Amery of Lustleigh, Baron (Life Peer); Julian Amery, 1919–1996, vol. X
Amery, Rt Hon. Leopold Stennett, 1873–1955, vol. V
Amery, William Bankes, 1883–1951, vol. V
Ames, Sir Cecil Geraint, 1897–1977, vol. VII
Ames, Frederick, 1836–1918, vol. II
Ames, Sir Herbert Brown, 1863–1954, vol. V
Ames, Jennifer; *see* Greig, Maysie.
Ames, John Richard Woodland, 1872–1947, vol. IV
Ames, Lt-Col Oswald Henry, 1862–1927, vol. II
Ames, Percy W., 1853–1919, vol. II
Ames, Rachel, (Sarah), (Mrs Kenneth Ames); *see* Gainham, S.
Amherst, 3rd Earl, 1836–1910, vol. I
Amherst, 4th Earl, 1856–1927, vol. II
Amherst, 5th Earl, 1896–1993, vol. IX
Amherst of Hackney, 1st Baron, 1835–1909, vol. I
Amherst of Hackney, Baroness (2nd in line), 1857–1919, vol. II
Amherst of Hackney, 3rd Baron, 1912–1980, vol. VII
Amherst, Rev. Hon. Percy Arthur, 1839–1910, vol. I
Amherst, Hon. Sybil Margaret, *died* 1926, vol. II
Ami, Henry M., 1858–1931, vol. III
Amies, Sir Arthur Barton Pilgrim, 1902–1976, vol. VII
Amigo, Most Rev. Peter E., 1864–1949, vol. IV
Amin, All Hajj Mohammud; *see* Keane, John Fryer Thomas.
Amis, Sir Kingsley, 1922–1995, vol. IX
Ammon, 1st Baron, 1873–1960, vol. V
Amod, Thakor of, Sardar Nawab Sir Naharsinhji Ishwarsinhji, *died* 1945, vol. IV
Amoore, Rt Rev. Frederick Andrew, 1913–1996, vol. X

Amor, Arthur Joseph, 1897–1966, vol. VI
Amoroso, Emmanuel Ciprian, 1901–1982, vol. VIII
Amory, 1st Viscount, 1899–1981, vol. VIII
Amory, Sir Ian Murray Heathcoat Heathcoat-, 2nd Bt, 1865–1931, vol. III
Amory, Major Sir John Heathcoat-, 3rd Bt, 1894–1972, vol. VII
Amory, Sir John Heathcoat H.; *see* Heathcoat-Amory.
Amory, Sir William H.; *see* Heathcoat Amory.
Amos, Major Herbert Gilbert Maclachlan, 1866–1924, vol. II
Amos, Sir Maurice Sheldon, 1872–1940, vol. III
Amphlett, Major Charles Grove, 1862–1921, vol. II
Amphlett, Richard Holmden, 1847–1925, vol. II
Ampthill, 2nd Baron, 1869–1935, vol. III
Ampthill, 3rd Baron, 1896–1973, vol. VII
Ampthill, Lady; (Margaret), 1874–1957, vol. V
Amritanand, Rt Rev. Joseph, 1917–1993, vol. IX
Amshewitz, J. H., 1882–1942, vol. IV
Amulree, 1st Baron, 1860–1942, vol. IV
Amulree, 2nd Baron, 1900–1983, vol. VIII
Amundsen, Captain Roald, 1872–1928, vol. II
Amwell, 1st Baron, 1876–1966, vol. VI
Amwell, 2nd Baron; Frederick Norman Montagne, 1912–1990, vol. VIII
Amyand, Arthur; *see* Haggard, Major E. A.
Amyot, Lt-Col Hon. George Elie, 1856–1940, vol. III
Amyot, Lt-Col John Andrew, 1867–1940, vol. III
Ancaster, 1st Earl of, 1830–1910, vol. I
Ancaster, 2nd Earl of, 1867–1951, vol. V
Ancaster, 3rd Earl of, 1907–1983, vol. VIII
Anda, Géza, 1921–1976, vol. VII
Anderson, Hon. Lord; Andrew Macbeth Anderson, 1862–1936, vol. III
Anderson, Dame Adelaide Mary, 1868–1936, vol. III
Anderson, Sir Alan Garrett, 1877–1952, vol. V
Anderson, Alan Orr, 1879–1958, vol. V
Anderson, Alexander, 1850–1904, vol. I
Anderson, Alexander, (Surfaceman), 1845–1909, vol. I
Anderson, Alexander, 1858–1936, vol. III
Anderson, Alexander, 1888–1954, vol. V
Anderson, Maj.-Gen. Alexander Dingwall, 1843–1916, vol. II
Anderson, Sir Alexander Greig, 1885–1961, vol. VI
Anderson, Sir Alexander James, 1879–1965, vol. VI
Anderson, Alexander Knox, 1892–1955, vol. V
Anderson, Alexander Richard, *died* 1933, vol. III
Anderson, Maj.-Gen. Alexander Vass, 1895–1963, vol. VI
Anderson, Maj.-Gen. Alfred, 1842–1909, vol. I
Anderson, Andrew Macbeth; *see* Anderson, Hon. Lord.
Anderson, Andrew Newton, 1880–1950, vol. IV
Anderson, Archibald Stirling Kennedy, 1887–1972, vol. VII
Anderson, Arthur Emilius David, 1886–1967, vol. VI
Anderson, Arthur Ingham, 1916–1976, vol. VII
Anderson, Arthur John Ritchie, (Iain), 1933–1996, vol. X
Anderson, Sir Arthur Robert, 1860–1924, vol. II

Anderson, Maj.-Gen. Arthur William Leslie, 1842–1929, vol. III
Anderson, Sir Athol Lancelot, 1875–1955, vol. V
Anderson, Sir Austin Innes, 1897–1973, vol. VII
Anderson, Brig.-Gen. Austin Thomas, *died* 1949, vol. IV
Anderson, Lt-Col Barton Edward, 1881–1927, vol. II
Anderson, C. Goldsborough, 1865–1936, vol. III
Anderson, Carl David, 1905–1991, vol. IX
Anderson, Charles, 1876–1944, vol. IV
Anderson, Major Charles, 1886–1954, vol. V
Anderson, Lt-Gen. Sir Charles Alexander, 1857–1940, vol. III
Anderson, Charles Buxton, 1879–1953, vol. V
Anderson, Lt-Col Charles Groves Wright, 1897–1988, vol. VIII
Anderson, Charles Martin, 1918–1961, vol. VI
Anderson, Rt Rev. Charles Palmerston, 1865–1930, vol. III
Anderson, Clinton Presba, 1895–1975, vol. VII
Anderson, Sir Colin Skelton, 1904–1980, vol. VII
Anderson, Daniel Elie, *died* 1928, vol. II
Anderson, Gen. David, 1821–1909, vol. I
Anderson, Sir David, 1880–1953, vol. V
Anderson, David; *see* Hon. Lord St Vigeans.
Anderson, David Colville, 1916–1995, vol. IX
Anderson, David Dick, 1889–1980, vol. VII
Anderson, David Fyfe, 1904–1988, vol. VIII
Anderson, David Martin, 1880–1955, vol. V
Anderson, Adm. Sir (David) Murray, 1874–1936, vol. III
Anderson, David Steel, 1902–1986, vol. VIII
Anderson, Sir David Stirling, 1895–1981, vol. VIII
Anderson, Brig. David William, 1929–1999, vol. X
Anderson, Lt-Gen. Sir Desmond Francis, 1885–1967, vol. VI
Anderson, Sir Donald Forsyth, 1906–1973, vol. VII
Anderson, Sir Donald George, 1917–1975, vol. VII
Anderson, Sir Duncan Law, 1901–1980, vol. VII
Anderson, Edith Muriel, (Lady Anderson), 1878–1958, vol. V
Anderson, Col Edmund Bullar, 1857–1935, vol. III
Anderson, Sir Edward Arthur, 1908–1979, vol. VII
Anderson, Rev. Edward Erskine, 1872–1950, vol. IV
Anderson, Lt-Col Edward Philip, 1883–1934, vol. III
Anderson, Edward William, 1901–1981, vol. VIII
Anderson, Elizabeth Garrett, 1836–1917, vol. II
Anderson, Emily, 1891–1962, vol. VI
Anderson, Col Eric Litchfield Brooke, 1889–1959, vol. V
Anderson, Eric Oswald, 1870–1935, vol. III
Anderson, Rt Rev. Ernest Augustus, 1859–1945, vol. IV
Anderson, Major Ernest Chester, 1863–1913, vol. I
Anderson, Dame Frances Margaret, 1898–1992, vol. IX
Anderson, Lt-Col Francis, 1888–1925, vol. II
Anderson, Sir Francis, 1858–1941, vol. IV
Anderson, Brig.-Gen. Sir Francis James, *died* 1920, vol. II
Anderson, Francis Sheed, 1897–1966, vol. VI
Anderson, Frank, 1889–1959, vol. V

Anderson, Sir Frederick, 1884–1961, vol. VI
Anderson, Rev. Frederick Ingall, 1874–1961, vol. VI
Anderson, Lt-Col Frederick Jasper, 1886–1957, vol. V
Anderson, Sir George, 1845–1923, vol. II
Anderson, Sir George, 1876–1943, vol. IV
Anderson, Dr George Cranston, 1879–1944, vol. IV
Anderson, George David, 1913–1983, vol. VIII
Anderson, Major George Denis, 1885–1971, vol. VII
Anderson, George Henry Garstin, 1896–1959, vol. V
Anderson, Hon. George James, 1860–1935, vol. III
Anderson, George Knox, 1854–1941, vol. IV
Anderson, Sir Gilmour M.; *see* Menzies Anderson.
Anderson, Lt-Col Guy Willoughby, 1885–1949, vol. IV
Anderson, Gen. Harry Cortlandt, 1826–1921, vol. II
Anderson, Lt-Gen. Sir Hasting; *see* Anderson, Lt-Gen. Sir W. H.
Anderson, Rev. Hector David, 1906–1989, vol. VIII
Anderson, Henry Aiken, 1851–1936, vol. III
Anderson, Major Henry Graeme, 1882–1925, vol. II
Anderson, Lt-Col Henry Stewart, 1872–1961, vol. VI
Anderson, Gen. Sir Horace Searle, 1833–1907, vol. I
Anderson, Hugh Alfred, 1867–1933, vol. III
Anderson, Hugh Fraser, 1910–1986, vol. VIII
Anderson, Sir Hugh Kerr, 1865–1928, vol. II
Anderson, Iain; *see* Anderson, A. J. R.
Anderson, Ian, 1891–1970, vol. VI
Anderson, J. Wemyss, 1868–1930, vol. III
Anderson, James, 1881–1915, vol. I
Anderson, James, 1857–1932, vol. III
Anderson, Col James, 1872–1955, vol. V
Anderson, James B., 1886–1938, vol. III
Anderson, Col James Dalgliesh, 1877–1947, vol. IV
Anderson, James Drummond, 1852–1920, vol. II
Anderson, Sir James Drummond, 1886–1968, vol. VI
Anderson, James Maitland, 1852–1927, vol. II
Anderson, Sir (James) Norman (Dalrymple), 1908–1994, vol. IX
Anderson, James Stirling, 1891–1976, vol. VII
Anderson, Hon. James Thomas Milton, 1878–1946, vol. IV
Anderson, James Wallace, *born* 1848, vol. II
Anderson, John, 1833–1900, vol. I
Anderson, John, 1840–1910, vol. I
Anderson, Sir John, 1858–1918, vol. II
Anderson, Sir John, 1852–1924, vol. II
Anderson, John, 1886–1935, vol. III
Anderson, Lt-Col John, 1852–1936, vol. III
Anderson, John, 1855–1938, vol. III
Anderson, Sir John, 1st Bt (*cr* 1920), 1878–1963, vol. VI
Anderson, Sir John, 1908–1965, vol. VI
Anderson, John, 1896–1984, vol. VIII
Anderson, John Allan Dalrymple, 1926–2000, vol. X
Anderson, Gen. Sir John D'Arcy, 1908–1988, vol. VIII

Anderson, Most Rev. John George, 1866–1943, vol. IV
Anderson, John George Clark, 1870–1952, vol. V
Anderson, John Gerard, 1836–1912, vol. I
Anderson, John Hubback, 1883–1950, vol. IV
Anderson, Rt Rev. John Ogle, 1912–1969, vol. VI
Anderson, John Stuart, 1908–1990, vol. VIII
Anderson, John William Stewart, 1874–1920, vol. II
Anderson, Joseph, 1832–1916, vol. II
Anderson, Major Joseph Ringland, 1894–1961, vol. VI
Anderson, Dame Judith; see Anderson, Dame, F. M.
Anderson, Rev. K. C., vol. II
Anderson, Sir Kenneth, 1906–1992, vol. IX
Anderson, Gen. Sir Kenneth Arthur Noel, 1891–1959, vol. V
Anderson, Hon. Sir Kenneth McColl, 1909–1985, vol. VIII
Anderson, Sir Kenneth Skelton, 1st Bt (cr 1919), 1866–1942, vol. IV
Anderson, Dame Kitty, 1903–1979, vol. VII
Anderson, Lindsay Gordon, 1923–1994, vol. IX
Anderson, Maj.-Gen. Louis Edward, 1861–1941, vol. IV
Anderson, Louisa Garrett, 1873–1943, vol. IV
Anderson, Marian, (Mrs Orpheus H. Fisher), 1897–1993, vol. IX
Anderson, Mark Louden, 1895–1961, vol. VI
Anderson, Martin Cynicus, 1854–1932, vol. III
Anderson, Mary Reid; see Macarthur, M. R.
Anderson, Sir Maurice Abbot, 1861–1938, vol. III
Anderson, Maxwell, 1888–1959, vol. V
Anderson, Captain Sir Maxwell Hendry Maxwell-, 1879–1951, vol. V
Anderson, Melville Best, 1851–1933, vol. III
Anderson, Adm. Sir Murray; see Anderson, Adm. Sir D. M.
Anderson, Maj.-Gen. Nelson Graham, 1875–1945, vol. IV
Anderson, Lt-Col Sir Neville, 1881–1963, vol. VI
Anderson, Ven. Nicol Keith, 1882–1953, vol. V
Anderson, Sir Norman; see Anderson, Sir J. N. D.
Anderson, Air Vice-Marshal Norman Russel, died 1948, vol. IV
Anderson, Col Patrick Campbell, 1894–1965, vol. VI
Anderson, Peter Corsar, 1871–1955, vol. V
Anderson, Peter John, died 1926, vol. II
Anderson, Richard John, 1848–1914, vol. I
Anderson, Lt-Gen. Sir Richard Neville, 1907–1979, vol. VII
Anderson, Sir Robert, 1841–1918, vol. II
Anderson, Sir Robert, 1st Bt (cr 1911), 1837–1921, vol. II
Anderson, Sir Robert Albert, 1866–1942, vol. IV
Anderson, Robert Bernerd, 1910–1989, vol. VIII
Anderson, Major Robert Grenville G.; see Gayer-Anderson.
Anderson, Brig. Robert Heath, 1882–1940, vol. III
Anderson, Brig.-Gen. Sir Robert Murray McCheyne, 1867–1940, vol. III (A), vol. IV
Anderson, Rt Hon. Sir Robert Newton, 1871–1948, vol. IV
Anderson, Sir Robert Rowand, 1834–1921, vol. II
Anderson, Roger Charles, 1883–1976, vol. VII

Anderson, Col Rowland James Percy, 1873–1950, vol. IV
Anderson, Major Roy Dunlop, 1878–1932, vol. III
Anderson, Rudolph Martin, 1876–1961, vol. VI
Anderson, Rupert Darnley, 1859–1944, vol. IV
Anderson, Samuel Boyd, 1878–1934, vol. III
Anderson, Sherwood, died 1941, vol. IV
Anderson, Stanley, 1884–1966, vol. VI
Anderson, Brig.-Gen. Stuart Milligan, 1879–1954, vol. V
Anderson, Tempest, 1846–1913, vol. I
Anderson, Theodore Farnworth, 1901–1979, vol. VII
Anderson, Thomas, 1844–1926, vol. II
Anderson, Thomas, 1904–1990, vol. VIII
Anderson, Thomas Alexander Harvie, died 1953, vol. V
Anderson, Thomas David, 1853–1932, vol. III
Anderson, Col Thomas Gayer G.; see Gayer-Anderson.
Anderson, Sir Thomas M'Call, 1836–1908, vol. I
Anderson, Thomas Scott, 1853–1919, vol. II
Anderson, Brig. Thomas Stephen James, 1909–1969, vol. VI
Anderson, Maj.-Gen. Thomas Victor, 1881–1972, vol. VII
Anderson, Walter Charles, 1910–1995, vol. IX
Anderson, Lt-Gen. Sir (Warren) Hastings, 1872–1930, vol. III
Anderson, Maj.-Gen. Warren Melville, 1894–1973, vol. VII
Anderson, Sir William, 1835–1898, vol. I
Anderson, William, 1842–1900, vol. I
Anderson, William, 1831–1913, vol. I
Anderson, Col William, 1886–1944, vol. IV
Anderson, William, 1889–1955, vol. V
Anderson, William Alexander, 1890–1971, vol. VII
Anderson, Maj.-Gen. William Beaumont, 1877–1959, vol. V
Anderson, William Blair, 1877–1959, vol. V
Anderson, Col William Campbell, 1868–1926, vol. II
Anderson, Brig.-Gen. William Christian, 1867–1942, vol. IV
Anderson, William Crawford, 1877–1919, vol. II
Anderson, William Galloway Macdonald, 1905–1978, vol. VII
Anderson, William Geddes, 1858–1932, vol. III
Anderson, Brig. William Henniker, 1880–1958, vol. V
Anderson, Sir William Hewson, 1897–1968, vol. VI
Anderson, Sir William John, 1846–1908, vol. I
Anderson, Rt Rev. William Louis, 1892–1972, vol. VII
Anderson, Lt-Col William Maurice, 1873–1946, vol. IV
Anderson, Lt-Col William Menzies, 1883–1940, vol. III
Anderson, Col William Patrick, 1851–1927, vol. II
Anderson, Col William Robert le Geyt, 1850–1908, vol. I
Anderson, William Thomas, 1872–1948, vol. IV
Anderson, Very Rev. W(illiam) White, 1888–1956, vol. V

Anderson-Morshead, Lt-Col Rupert Henry, *died* 1918, vol. II

Andersson, Lt-Col Sir (Charles) Llewellyn, 1861–1948, vol. IV

Andersson, Lt-Col Sir Llewellyn; *see* Andersson, Lt-Col Sir C. L.

Anderton, Sir Francis Robert Ince, 1859–1950, vol. IV

Anderton, Francis Swithin, 1868–1909, vol. I

Anderton, Col Geoffrey, 1902–1981, vol. VIII

Anderton, James, 1904–1994, vol. IX (AII)

Andoe, Vice-Adm. Sir Hilary Gustavus, 1841–1905, vol. I

Andrade, Edward Neville da Costa, 1887–1971, vol. VII

André, Brig. James Richard Glencoe, 1899–1981, vol. VIII

Andreades, Andrew, 1876–1935, vol. III

Andreae, Herman Anton, 1876–1965, vol. VI

Andrew, Rt Rev. Agnellus Matthew, 1908–1987, vol. VIII

Andrew, Alistair Hugh, 1908–1947, vol. IV

Andrew, George, 1873–1956, vol. V

Andrew, Engr-Capt. George Edward, 1869–1945, vol. IV

Andrew, Rev. Sir (George) Herbert, 1910–1985, vol. VIII

Andrew, Rev. Sir Herbert; *see* Andrew, Rev. Sir G. H.

Andrew, Ian Graham, 1893–1962, vol. VI

Andrew, Sir John, 1896–1968, vol. VI

Andrew, John Harold, 1887–1961, vol. VI

Andrew, Brig. Leslie Wilton, 1897–1969, vol. VI

Andrew, Col Richard Hynman, 1885–1964, vol. VI

Andrew, Samuel Ogden, 1868–1952, vol. V

Andrew, Walter Jonathan, *died* 1934, vol. III

Andrew, William Monro, 1895–1973, vol. VII

Andrew, Rev. Canon William Shaw, 1884–1963, vol. VI

Andrewes, Antony, 1910–1990, vol. VIII

Andrewes, Sir Christopher Howard, 1896–1988, vol. VIII

Andrewes, David; *see* Andrewes, E. D. E.

Andrewes, Edward David Eden, 1909–1990, vol. VIII

Andrewes, Major Francis Edward, 1878–1920, vol. II

Andrewes, Sir Frederick William, 1859–1932, vol. III

Andrewes, Rev. Canon Gerrard Thomas, 1855–1941, vol. IV

Andrewes, Rev. John Brereton, *died* 1920, vol. II

Andrewes, Adm. Sir William Gerrard, 1899–1974, vol. VII

Andrews, Albert Andrew, 1896–1976, vol. VII

Andrews, (Arthur) John (Francis), 1906–1984, vol. VIII

Andrews, Lt-Col Cecil Rollo Payton, 1870–1951, vol. V

Andrews, Charles Beresford Eaton B.; *see* Burt-Andrews.

Andrews, Rev. Charles Freer, 1871–1940, vol. III

Andrews, Charles M'Lean, 1863–1943, vol. IV

Andrews, Charles William, 1866–1924, vol. II

Andrews, Cyril Frank Wilton, 1892–1978, vol. VII

Andrews, Éamonn, 1922–1987, vol. VIII

Andrews, Edward Gordon, *died* 1915, vol. II

Andrews, Sir Edwin Arthur C.; *see* Chapman-Andrews.

Andrews, Hon. Elisha Benjamin, 1844–1917, vol. II

Andrews, Ernest Clayton, 1870–1948, vol. IV

Andrews, Sir Ernest Herbert, 1873–1961, vol. VI

Andrews, Captain Francis Arthur Lavington, 1869–1944, vol. IV

Andrews, Rev. George Whitefield, 1833–1931, vol. III

Andrews, Lt-Col Harold Marcus E.; *see* Ervine-Andrews.

Andrews, Harry Fleetwood, 1911–1989, vol. VIII

Andrews, Harry Thomson, 1897–1985, vol. VIII

Andrews, Henry Russell, 1871–1942, vol. IV

Andrews, Rev. Herbert T., 1864–1928, vol. II

Andrews, Hugh, *died* 1926, vol. II

Andrews, Rt Hon. Sir James, 1st Bt, 1877–1951, vol. V

Andrews, James Frank, 1848–1922, vol. II

Andrews, James Peter, 1902–1968, vol. VI

Andrews, John Alban, *died* 1964, vol. VI

Andrews, John; *see* Andrews, A. J. F.

Andrews, John Launcelot, 1893–1968, vol. VI

Andrews, Rt Hon. Sir John Lawson Ormrod, 1903–1986, vol. VIII

Andrews, Rt Hon. John Miller, 1871–1956, vol. V

Andrews, Air Vice-Marshal John Oliver, 1896–1989, vol. VIII

Andrews, Joseph Ormond, 1873–1909, vol. I

Andrews, Rev. Canon Leonard Martin, 1886–1989, vol. VIII

Andrews, Lewis Yelland, 1896–1937, vol. III

Andrews, Sir Linton; *see* Andrews, Sir W. L.

Andrews, Rev. Canon Martin; *see* Andrews, Rev. Canon L. M.

Andrews, Norman Roy F.; *see* Fox-Andrews.

Andrews, Surgeon Captain Octavius William, 1865–1936, vol. III

Andrews, Raymond Denzil Anthony, 1925–1999, vol. X

Andrews, Rear-Adm. Robert Walter Benjamin, 1876–1965, vol. VI

Andrews, Roland Stuart, 1897–1961, vol. VI

Andrews, Roy Chapman, 1884–1960, vol. V

Andrews, Stanley George B.; *see* Burt-Andrews.

Andrews, Thomas, 1847–1907, vol. I

Andrews, Rt Hon. Thomas, 1843–1916, vol. II

Andrews, Rt Rev. Walter, 1852–1932, vol. III

Andrews, Wilfrid, 1892–1975, vol. VII

Andrews, William, 1848–1908, vol. I

Andrews, Rt Hon. William Drennan, 1832–1924, vol. II

Andrews, William Horner, 1887–1953, vol. V

Andrews, Sir (William) Linton, 1886–1972, vol. VII

Andrews, Winifred Agnes, 1918–1983, vol. VIII

Andrews-Speed, James, 1876–1939, vol. III

Andric, Ivo, 1892–1975, vol. VII

Andrus, Brig.-Gen. Thomas Alchin, 1872–1959, vol. V

Anethan, Baroness Albert d', *died* 1935, vol. III

Aney, Madhao Shrihari, 1880–1968, vol. VI

Anfinsen, Christian Boehmer, 1916–1995, vol. IX

Angas, Sir (John) Keith, 1900–1977, vol. VII

Angas, Sir Keith; see Angas, Sir J. K.
Angas, Major Lawrence Lee Bazley, 1893–1973, vol. VII
Angel, John, 1881–1960, vol. V
Angell, Col Frederick John, 1861–1922, vol. II
Angell, James Burrill, 1829–1916, vol. II
Angell, James Rowland, 1869–1949, vol. IV
Angell, Sir Norman; see Angell, Sir R. N.
Angell, Sir (Ralph) Norman, 1872–1967, vol. VI
Angellier, Auguste Jean, 1848–1911, vol. I
Angers, Hon. Sir Auguste Réal, 1837–1919, vol. II
Angers, Hon. Eugène-Réal, 1883–1956, vol. V
Angier, Sir Theodore Vivian Samuel, 1843–1935, vol. III
Anglesey, 4th Marquess of, 1835–1898, vol. I
Anglesey, 5th Marquess of, 1875–1905, vol. I
Anglesey, 6th Marquess of, 1885–1947, vol. IV
Angless, Violet B.; see Brunton-Angless.
Anglin, Arthur H., 1850–1934, vol. III
Anglin, Arthur Whyte, 1867–1955, vol. V
Anglin, Eric Jack, 1923–1999, vol. X
Anglin, Rt Hon. Francis Alexander, 1865–1933, vol. III
Angliss, Dame Jacobena Victoria Alice, 1897–1980, vol. VII (AII)
Angliss, Hon. Sir William Charles, 1865–1957, vol. V
Angst, Sir Henry, 1847–1922, vol. II
Angus, Alfred Henry, 1873–1957, vol. V
Angus, Col Edmund Graham, 1889–1983, vol. VIII
Angus, Henry Brunton, 1867–1927, vol. II
Angus, J. Mortimer, 1850–1945, vol. IV
Angus, Richard Bladworth, 1831–1922, vol. II
Angus, Rev. Samuel, 1881–1943, vol. IV
Angus, Brig. Tom Hardy, 1899–1984, vol. VIII
Angus, Sir William, 1841–1912, vol. I
Angus, Col William Mathwin, 1851–1934, vol. III
Angwin, Col Sir (Arthur) Stanley, 1883–1959, vol. V
Angwin, Hugh Thomas Moffitt, 1888–1949, vol. IV
Angwin, Col Sir Stanley; see Angwin, Col Sir A. S.
Angwin, Hon. William Charles, 1863–1944, vol. IV
Anley, Brig.-Gen. Barnett Dyer Lempriere Gray, 1873–1954, vol. V
Anley, Brig.-Gen. Frederick Gore, 1864–1936, vol. III
Anley, Col Henry Augustus, 1864–1942, vol. IV
Anley, Major Philip Francis Ross, 1874–1956, vol. V
Ann, Sir Edwin Thomas, 1852–1913, vol. I
Annaly, 3rd Baron, 1857–1922, vol. II
Annaly, 4th Baron, 1885–1970, vol. VI
Annaly, 5th Baron, 1927–1990, vol. VIII
Annamunthodo, Sir Harry, 1920–1986, vol. VIII
Annan, Baron (Life Peer); Noël Gilroy Annan, 1916–2000, vol. X
Annan, Robert, 1885–1981, vol. VIII
Annan, William, 1872–1952, vol. V
Annand, James, 1843–1906, vol. I
Annandale, Charles, 1843–1915, vol. I
Annandale, Nelson; see Annandale, T. N.
Annandale, Thomas, 1838–1907, vol. I
Annandale, (Thomas) Nelson, 1876–1924, vol. II
Anne, Ernest Lambert Swinburne, 1852–1939, vol. III

Anne, George Charlton, 1886–1960, vol. V
Annesley, 5th Earl, 1831–1908, vol. I
Annesley, 6th Earl, 1884–1914, vol. I
Annesley, 7th Earl, 1861–1934, vol. III
Annesley, 8th Earl, 1894–1957, vol. V
Annesley, 9th Earl, 1900–1979, vol. VII
Annesley, Captain Hon. Arthur, 1880–1914, vol. I
Annesley, Lt-Gen. Sir Arthur Lyttelton L.; see Lyttelton-Annesley.
Annesley, Col Arthur Stephen Robert, 1869–1939, vol. III
Annesley, Lt-Col James Howard Adolphus, 1868–1919, vol. II
Annesley, Captain John Campbell, 1895–1964, vol. VI
Annesley, Lt-Col William Henry, 1876–1934, vol. III
Annesley, Major William Richard Norton, 1863–1914, vol. I
Annett, Engr-Captain George Lewis, 1887–1980, vol. VII
Annett, Henry Edward, 1871–1945, vol. IV (A), vol. V
Annigoni, Pietro, 1910–1988, vol. VIII
Anningson, Bushell, died 1916, vol. II
Annis, Philip Geoffrey Walter, 1936–1998, vol. X
Annois, Leonard Lloyd, 1906–1966, vol. VI
Anns, Bryan Herbert, 1929–1975, vol. VII
Anouilh, Jean, 1910–1987, vol. VIII
Anrep, Gleb V., 1891–1955, vol. V
Anscomb, Major Allen-Mellers, born 1849, vol. II
Ansell, Rev. Preb. George Frederick James, 1886–1951, vol. V
Ansell, James Lawrence Bunting, 1912–1978, vol. VII
Ansell, John, 1874–1948, vol. IV
Ansell, William Henry, 1872–1959, vol. V
Ansell, William James David, 1858–1920, vol. II
Ansell, Sir Michael Picton, 1905–1994, vol. IX
Ansermet, Ernest, 1883–1969, vol. VI
Ansett, Sir Reginald Myles, 1909–1981, vol. VIII
Anslow, 1st Baron, 1850–1933, vol. III
Anson, Viscount; Thomas William Arnold Anson, 1913–1958, vol. V
Anson, Rt Rev. and Hon. Adelbert John Robert, 1840–1909, vol. I
Anson, Captain Hon. Alfred, 1876–1944, vol. IV
Anson, Rear-Adm. Algernon Horatio, 1854–1913, vol. I
Anson, Maj.-Gen. Sir Archibald Edward Harbord, 1826–1925, vol. II
Anson, Adm. Charles Eustace, 1859–1940, vol. III
Anson, Hon. Claud, 1864–1947, vol. IV
Anson, Sir Denis George William, 4th Bt, 1888–1914, did not have an entry in Who's Who.
Anson, Sir Edward Reynell, 6th Bt, 1902–1951, vol. V
Anson, Hon. Frederic William, 1862–1917, vol. II
Anson, Lt-Col Hon. Sir George Augustus, 1857–1947, vol. IV
Anson, George H., died 1957, vol. V
Anson, Ven. George Henry Greville, died 1898, vol. I
Anson, Sir (George) Wilfrid, 1893–1974, vol. VII

Anson, Rev. Harold, 1867–1954, vol. V
Anson, Sir John Henry Algernon, 5th Bt,
1897–1918, vol. II
Anson, Malcolm Allinson, 1924–1992, vol. IX
Anson, Sir Wilfrid; see Anson, Sir G. W.
Anson, Rt Hon. Sir William Reynell, 3rd Bt,
1843–1914, vol. I
Ansorge, Sir Eric Cecil, 1887–1977, vol. VII
Ansorge, William John, 1850–1913, vol. I
Anstead, Rudolph David, 1876–1962, vol. VI
Anstey, Most Rev. Arthur Henry, died 1955, vol. V
Anstey, Brig. Edgar Carnegie, 1882–1958, vol. V
Anstey, Edgar Harold Macfarlane, 1907–1987,
vol. VIII
Anstey, F.; see Guthrie, T. A.
Anstey, Hon. Frank, 1865–1940, vol. III
Anstey, Gilbert Tomkins, 1889–1974, vol. VII
Anstey, Brig. Sir John, 1907–2000, vol. X
Anstey, Percy, 1876–1920, vol. II
Anstey, Sidney Herbert, 1910–1991, vol. IX
Anstey, Vera, 1889–1976, vol. VII
Anstey, Engr-Rear-Adm. William John, 1860–1936,
vol. III
Anstice, Hon. Col Sir Arthur, 1846–1929, vol. III
Anstice, Vice-Adm. Sir Edmund Walter,
1899–1979, vol. VII
Anstice, Lt-Col Sir Robert Henry, 1843–1922,
vol. II
Anstie, James, 1836–1924, vol. II
Anstruther, Brig. Alexander Meister, 1902–1969,
vol. VI
Anstruther, Arthur Wellesley, 1864–1938, vol. III
Anstruther, Col Charles Frederick St Clair,
1855–1925, vol. II
Anstruther, Hon. Dame Eva Isabella Henrietta,
1869–1935, vol. III
Anstruther, George Elliot, 1870–1940, vol. III
Anstruther, Henry Torrens, 1860–1926, vol. II
Anstruther, Col Philip Noel, 1891–1960, vol. V
Anstruther, Sir Ralph William, 6th Bt (cr 1694),
1858–1934, vol. III
Anstruther, Adm. Robert Hamilton, 1862–1938,
vol. III
Anstruther, Lt-Col Robert Hamilton Lloyd-,
1841–1914, vol. I
Anstruther, Sir Windham Charles James
Carmichael, 8th Bt (cr 1700 and 1798),
1824–1898, vol. I
Anstruther, Sir Windham Eric Francis Carmichael-,
11th Bt (cr 1700 and 1798), 1900–1980, vol. VII
Anstruther, Sir Windham Frederick Carmichael-,
10th Bt (cr 1700 and 1798), 1902–1928, vol. II
Anstruther, Sir Windham Robert Carmichael, 9th Bt
(cr 1700 and 1798), 1877–1903, vol. I
Anstruther-Gough-Calthorpe, Sir FitzRoy Hamilton,
1st Bt, 1872–1957, vol. V
Anstruther-Gough-Calthorpe, Brig. Sir Richard
Hamilton, 2nd Bt, 1908–1985, vol. VIII
Anstruther-Gray, Lt-Col William, 1859–1938,
vol. III
Anstruther-Gray, William John St Clair; see Baron
Kilmany.
Anstruther-Thomson, John, 1818–1904, vol. I
Antcliffe, Kenneth Arthur, 1923–1992, vol. IX
Antelme, Hon. Sir Celicourt, 1818–1899, vol. I

Anthonisz, James Oliver, 1860–1921, vol. II
Anthonisz, Peter Daniel, 1822–1903, vol. I
Anthony, C. L.; see Smith, Dodie.
Anthony, Henry Montesquieu, 1873–1949, vol. IV
Anthony, Herbert Douglas, 1892–1968, vol. VI
Anthony, Irvin, 1890–1971, vol. VII
Anthony, Sir John, died 1935, vol. III
Anthony, Sir Mobolaji B.; see Bank-Anthony.
Anthony, Philip Arnold, 1873–1949, vol. IV
Anthony, Maj.-Gen. Richard William, 1874–1940,
vol. III
Anthony, Maj.-Gen. William Samuel, 1874–1943,
vol. IV
Antill, Maj.-Gen. John Macquarie, 1866–1937,
vol. III
Antonio; see Ruiz Soler, Antonio.
Antony, Jonquil, 1912–1980, vol. VII
Antrim, 11th Earl of, 1851–1918, vol. II
Antrim, 12th Earl of, 1878–1932, vol. III
Antrim, 13th Earl of, 1911–1977, vol. VII
Antrobus, Sir Cosmo Gordon, 5th Bt, 1859–1939,
vol. III
Antrobus, Dame Edith Marion, 1862–1944, vol. IV
Antrobus, Sir Edmund, 3rd Bt, 1818–1899, vol. I
Antrobus, Sir Edmund, 4th Bt, 1848–1915, vol. I
Antrobus, Edward Gream, 1860–1940, vol. III
Antrobus, John Coutts, 1829–1916, vol. II
Antrobus, Maurice Edward, 1895–1985, vol. VIII
Antrobus, Sir Philip Coutts, 7th Bt, 1908–1995,
vol. IX
Antrobus, Captain Sir Philip Humphrey, 6th Bt,
1876–1968, vol. VI
Antrobus, Sir Reginald Laurence, 1853–1942,
vol. IV
Antrobus, Lt-Col Ronald Henry, 1891–1980,
vol. VII
Anwyl, Sir Edward, 1866–1914, vol. I
Anwyl, Rev. John Bodvan, 1875–1949, vol. IV (A),
vol. V
Anwyl-Davies, Thomas, 1891–1971, vol. VII
Anwyl-Passingham, Col Augustus Mervyn Owen,
1880–1955, vol. V
Anzon Caccamisi, Baronne; see Marchesi, Blanche
Aoki, Viscount, 1844–1914, vol. I
Apcar, Sir Apcar Alexander, 1851–1913, vol. I
Ap Ellis, Gp Captain Augustine, 1886–1969, vol. VI
Apley, Alan Graham, 1914–1996, vol. X
Aplin, Harold D'Auvergne, 1879–1958, vol. V
Aplin, Major John George Orlebar, died 1915, vol. I
Aplin, Col Philip John Hanham, 1858–1927, vol. II
Aplin, Col Stephen Lushington, 1863–1940, vol. III
Appelbe, Brig.-Gen. Edward Benjamin, 1855–1935,
vol. III
Apperley, (George Owen) Wynne, 1884–1960,
vol. V
Apperley, Newton Wynne, 1846–1925, vol. II
Apperley, Wynne; see Apperley, G. O. W.
Apperley, Sir Aldred, 1839–1913, vol. I
Apperly, Herbert, died 1932, vol. III
Apperson, George Latimer, 1857–1937, vol. III
Appleby, Sir Alfred, 1866–1952, vol. V
Appleby, Lt-Col Charles Bernard, 1905–1975,
vol. VII
Appleby, Maj.-Gen. David Stanley, 1918–1989,
vol. VIII

Appleby, Lt-Col John Pringle, 1891–1966, vol. VI
Appleby, Robert, 1913–1996, vol. X
Appleby, Sir Robert Rowland, 1887–1966, vol. VI
Applegarth, Robert, 1834–1924, vol. II
Appleton, Arthur Beeny, *died* 1950, vol. IV
Appleton, Sir Edward Victor, 1892–1965, vol. VI
Appleton, Rt Rev. George, 1902–1993, vol. IX
Appleton, George Webb, 1845–1909, vol. I
Appleton, Brig. Gilbert Leonard, 1894–1970, vol. VI
Appleton, Rev. Richard, 1849–1909, vol. I
Appleton, William, 1846–1906, vol. I
Appleton, Sir William, 1889–1958, vol. V
Appleton, William Archibald, 1859–1940, vol. III
Appleton, William Thomas, 1859–1930, vol. III
Appleyard, Maj.-Gen. Frederick Ernest, 1829–1911, vol. I
Appleyard, Col Kenelm Charles, 1894–1967, vol. VI
Appleyard, Rollo, 1867–1943, vol. IV
Applin, Captain Arthur, *died* 1949, vol. IV
Applin, Lt-Col Reginald Vincent Kempenfelt, 1869–1957, vol. V
Apponyi, Count Albert, 1846–1933, vol. III
Apps, Rear-Adm. Edgar Stephen, 1893–1958, vol. V
Apps, Engr-Captain William Richard, 1862–1947, vol. IV
ap Rees, Thomas, 1930–1996, vol. X
ap Rhys Pryce, Gen. Sir Henry Edward, 1874–1950, vol. IV
Apsey, Sir John, 1859–1930, vol. III
Apsley, Lord; Allen Algernon Bathurst, 1895–1942, vol. IV
Apsley, Lady; (Violet Emily Mildred), 1895–1966, vol. VI
Apthorp, Major Shirley East, 1882–1937, vol. III
Arabi, Sayed Ahmed Pasha, 1841–1911, vol. I
Aragon, Louis, 1897–1982, vol. VIII
Arbab Dost Muhammad Khan, Khan Bahadur Sir, *died* 1931, vol. III
Arber, Agnes, (Mrs E. A. Newell Arber), 1879–1960, vol. V
Arber, Mrs E. A. Newell; *see* Arber, Agnes.
Arber, Edward, 1836–1912, vol. I
Arber, Edward Alexander Newell, 1870–1918, vol. II
Arberry, Arthur John, 1905–1969, vol. VI
Arbuckle, Hon. Sir William, 1839–1915, vol. I
Arbuckle, Sir William Forbes, 1902–1966, vol. VI
Arbuthnot, Brig. Alexander George, 1873–1961, vol. VI
Arbuthnot, Sir Alexander John, 1822–1907, vol. I
Arbuthnot, Sir Charles George, 1824–1899, vol. I
Arbuthnot, Charles George, 1846–1928, vol. II
Arbuthnot, Vice-Adm. Charles Ramsay, 1850–1913, vol. I
Arbuthnot, Clifford William Ernest, 1885–1974, vol. VII
Arbuthnot, Brig.-Gen. Sir Dalrymple, 5th Bt, 1867–1941, vol. IV
Arbuthnot, Captain Ernest Kennaway, 1876–1945, vol. IV
Arbuthnot, Adm. Sir Geoffrey Schomberg, 1885–1957, vol. V

Arbuthnot, Ven. George, 1846–1922, vol. II
Arbuthnot, Sir George Gough, 1847–1929, vol. III
Arbuthnot, Gerald Archibald, 1872–1916, vol. II
Arbuthnot, Maj.-Gen. Henry Thomas, 1834–1919, vol. II
Arbuthnot, Sir Hugh Fitz-Gerald, 7th Bt, 1922–1983, vol. VIII
Arbuthnot, James Woodgate, 1848–1927, vol. II
Arbuthnot, Major John Bernard, 1875–1950, vol. IV
Arbuthnot, Sir John Sinclair-Wemyss, 1st Bt, 1912–1992, vol. IX
Arbuthnot, Major Sir Robert Dalrymple, 6th Bt, 1919–1944, vol. IV
Arbuthnot, Robert Edward Vaughan, 1871–1922, vol. II
Arbuthnot, Rear-Adm. Sir Robert Keith, 4th Bt, 1864–1916, vol. II
Arbuthnot, Robert Wemyss Muir, 1889–1962, vol. VI
Arbuthnot-Leslie of Warthill, William, 1878–1956, vol. V
Arbuthnott, 11th Viscount of, 1845–1914, vol. I
Arbuthnott, 12th Viscount of, 1849–1917, vol. II
Arbuthnott, 13th Viscount of, 1847–1920, vol. II
Arbuthnott, 14th Viscount of, 1882–1960, vol. V
Arbuthnott, 15th Viscount of, 1897–1966, vol. VI
Arbuthnott, Hon. David, 1820–1901, vol. I
Arbuthnott, John Campbell, 1858–1923, vol. II
Arbuthnott, Robert, 1900–1980, vol. VII
Arcedeckne-Butler, Maj.-Gen. St John Desmond, 1896–1959, vol. V
Arch, Joseph, 1826–1919, vol. II
Archambeault, Hon. Sir Horace, 1857–1918, vol. II
Archambeault, Rt Rev. Joseph Alfred, 1859–1913, vol. I
Archbold, William Arthur Jobson, 1865–1947, vol. IV
Archdale, Brig. Arthur Somerville, 1882–1948, vol. IV
Archdale, Rt Hon. Edward, 1850–1916, vol. II
Archdale, Rt Hon. Sir Edward Mervyn, 1st Bt, 1853–1943, vol. IV
Archdale, Rev. Canon Eyre William Preston, 1871–1955, vol. V
Archdale, Helen Alexander, 1876–1949, vol. IV
Archdale, Brig.-Gen. Hugh James, 1854–1921, vol. II
Archdale, Vice-Adm. Sir Nicholas Edward, 2nd Bt, 1881–1955, vol. V
Archdale, Major Theodore Montgomery, 1873–1918, vol. II
Archdale, Rev. Thomas Hewan, *died* 1924, vol. II
Archdall, Rev. Canon Henry Kingsley, 1886–1976, vol. VII
Archdall, Rt Rev. Mervyn, 1833–1913, vol. I
Archer, Allan; *see* Archer, H. A. F. B.
Archer, Sir Archibald, 1902–1983, vol. VIII
Archer, Gen. Sir (Arthur) John, 1924–1999, vol. X
Archer, Lt-Col Charles, 1861–1941, vol. IV
Archer, Sir Clyde Vernon Harcourt, 1904–1989, vol. IX (AI)
Archer, Adm. Sir Ernest Russell, 1891–1958, vol. V
Archer, Francis Kentdray, 1882–1962, vol. VI
Archer, Frank Joseph, 1912–1995, vol. IX
Archer, Sir Geoffrey Francis, 1882–1964, vol. VI

Archer, George, 1896–1960, vol. V
Archer, Sir Gilbert, 1882–1948, vol. IV
Archer, Maj.-Gen. Gilbert Thomas Lancelot, 1903–1986, vol. VIII
Archer, Major Henry, 1883–1917, vol. II
Archer, (Henry) Allan (Fairfax Best), 1887–1950, vol. IV
Archer, Captain Hugh Edward Murray, 1879–1930, vol. III
Archer, James, 1822–1904, vol. I
Archer, Col James Henry L.; see Lawrence-Archer.
Archer, Sir John; see Archer, Sir A. J.
Archer, Sir John, 1860–1949, vol. IV
Archer, John Beville, 1893–1949, vol. IV
Archer, John Mark, 1908–1965, vol. VI
Archer, Wing Comdr John Oliver, 1887–1968, vol. VI
Archer, Norman Ernest, 1892–1970, vol. VI
Archer, Richard Lawrence, 1874–1953, vol. V
Archer, Col Samuel Arthur, 1871–1943, vol. IV
Archer, Thomas, 1823–1905, vol. I
Archer, Walter E., 1855–1917, vol. II
Archer, William, 1856–1924, vol. II
Archer, William George, 1907–1979, vol. VII
Archer, William John, 1861–1934, vol. III
Archer-Hind, Richard Dacre, 1849–1910, vol. I
Archer Houblon, Mrs Doreen, 1899–1977, vol. VII
Archer-Houblon, Col George Bramston; see Houblon.
Archer-Jackson, Lt-Col Basil, 1884–1965, vol. VI
Archer-Shee, Lt-Col Sir Martin, 1873–1935, vol. III
Archey, Sir Gilbert Edward, 1890–1974, vol. VII
Archibald, 1st Baron, 1898–1975, vol. VII
Archibald, Barony of; see under Archibald, (George) Christopher.
Archibald, Christopher; see Archibald, G. C.
Archibald, (George) Christopher, 1926–1996, vol. X
Archibald, Col (temp. Brig.) Gordon King, died 1942, vol. IV
Archibald, (Harry) Munro, 1915–1996, vol. X
Archibald, James, 1863–1946, vol. IV
Archibald, James Montgomery, 1920–1983, vol. VIII
Archibald, Very Rev. John, died 1916, vol. II
Archibald, John Gordon, 1885–1970, vol. VI
Archibald, Hon. John Sprott, 1843–1932, vol. III
Archibald, Munro; see Archibald, H. M.
Archibald, Myles, 1898–1961, vol. VI
Archibald, Raymond Clare, 1875–1957, vol. V
Archibald, Sir Robert George, 1880–1953, vol. V
Archibald, Sir William Frederick Alphonse, 1846–1922, vol. II
Arcot, Prince of, 1882–1952, vol. V
Ardagh, Lt-Col George Hutchings, 1863–1930, vol. III
Ardagh, Maj.-Gen. Sir John Charles, 1840–1907, vol. I
Arden, Lt-Col John Henry Morris, 1875–1918, vol. II
Arden-Clarke, Sir Charles Noble, 1898–1962, vol. VI
Arden-Close, Col Sir Charles Frederick, 1865–1952, vol. V
Arden Wood, William Henry Heton, 1858–1932, vol. III
Ardilaun, 1st Baron, 1840–1915, vol. I

Ardill, Rev. John Roche, died 1947, vol. IV (A)
Arditi, Luigi, 1822–1903, vol. I
Ardizzone, Edward Jeffrey Irving, 1900–1979, vol. VII
Ardron, John, 1843–1919, vol. II
Ardwall, Hon. Lord; Andrew Jameson, 1845–1911, vol. I
Ardwick, Baron (Life Peer); John Cowburn Beavan, 1910–1994, vol. IX
Arenberg, Auguste Louis Alberic, Prince D', 1837–1924, vol. II
Arendzen, Rev. John, 1873–1954, vol. V
Arensky, Antony Stepanovich, 1861–1906, vol. I
Argenti, Philip Pandely, 1891–1974, vol. VII
Argles, Rev. Canon George Marsham, 1841–1920, vol. II
Argyle, Lt-Col Edward Percy, 1875–1935, vol. III
Argyle, Maj. Michael Victor, 1915–1998, vol. X
Argyle, Hon. Sir Stanley Seymour, 1867–1940, vol. III
Argyll, 8th Duke of, 1823–1900, vol. I
Argyll, 9th Duke of, 1845–1914, vol. I
Argyll, 10th Duke of, 1872–1949, vol. IV
Argyll, 11th Duke of, 1903–1973, vol. VII
Aria, Mrs, 1866–1931, vol. III
Arias, Dame Margot Fonteyn de, (Margot Fonteyn), 1919–1991, vol. IX
Arias, Roberto Emilio, 1918–1989, vol. VIII
Ariff, Sir Kamil Mohamed, 1893–1960, vol. V
Aris, Lt-Col Charles John, 1874–1931, vol. III
Aris, Ernest Alfred, 1882–1963, vol. VI
Aris, Major Herbert, 1868–1952, vol. V
Arisugawa, Prince Takehito, 1862–1913, vol. I
Arkell, Rev. Anthony John, 1898–1980, vol. VII
Arkell, John Heward, 1909–1999, vol. X
Arkell, Captain Sir Noël; see Arkell, Captain Sir T. N.
Arkell, Reginald, died 1959, vol. V
Arkell, Captain Sir (Thomas) Noël, 1893–1981, vol. VIII
Arkell, William Joscelyn, 1904–1958, vol. V
Arkfeld, Most Rev. Leo, 1912–1999, vol. X
Arkle, Harry, 1893–1973, vol. VII
Arkwright, Rev. Ernest Henry, 1868–1950, vol. IV
Arkwright, Esme Francis Wigsell, 1882–1934, vol. III
Arkwright, Francis, 1846–1915, vol. I
Arkwright, Frederic Charles, 1853–1923, vol. II
Arkwright, John Hungerford, 1833–1905, vol. I
Arkwright, John Peter, 1864–1931, vol. III
Arkwright, Sir John Stanhope, 1872–1954, vol. V
Arkwright, Sir Joseph Arthur, 1864–1944, vol. IV
Arkwright, Richard, 1835–1918, vol. II
Arkwright, Maj.-Gen. Robert Harry Bertram, 1903–1971, vol. VII
Arkwright, William, 1857–1925, vol. II
Arlen, Michael, 1895–1956, vol. V
Arlen, Stephen Walter, 1913–1972, vol. VII
Arliss, George, 1868–1946, vol. IV
Arliss, Vice-Adm. Stephen Harry Tolson, 1895–1954, vol. V
Arlott, John; see Arlott, L. T. J.
Arlott, (Leslie Thomas) John, 1914–1991, vol. IX
Armaghdale, 1st Baron, 1850–1924, vol. II
Armand, Louis, 1905–1971, vol. VII

Armbruster, Charles Hubert, 1874–1957, vol. V
Armer, Sir Frederick; see Armer, Sir I. F.
Armer, Sir (Isaac) Frederick, 1891–1982, vol. VIII
Armes, Col Reginald John, 1876–1948, vol. IV
Armfelt, Roger Noel, 1897–1955, vol. V
Armfield, Constance, (Mrs Maxwell Armfield); see Smedley, Constance.
Armfield, Maxwell Ashby, 1881–1972, vol. VII
Armitage, Captain Albert Borlase, 1864–1943, vol. IV
Armitage, Sir Arthur Llewellyn, 1916–1984, vol. VIII
Armitage, Bernard William, 1890–1976, vol. VII
Armitage, Sir Cecil; see Armitage, Sir S. C.
Armitage, Captain Sir Cecil Hamilton, 1869–1933, vol. III
Armitage, Cecil Henry, 1877–1955, vol. V
Armitage, Gen. Sir (Charles) Clement, 1881–1973, vol. VII
Armitage, Major Charles Leathley, 1871–1951, vol. V
Armitage, Gen. Sir Clement; see Armitage, Gen. Sir Charles C.
Armitage, Rev. Cyril Moxon, 1900–1966, vol. VI
Armitage, Brig.-Gen. Edward Hume, 1859–1949, vol. IV
Armitage, Elkanah, 1844–1929, vol. III
Armitage, Ella Sophia, 1841–1931, vol. III
Armitage, Francis Paul, 1875–1953, vol. V
Armitage, Frank, 1872–1955, vol. V
Armitage, Maj.-Gen. Geoffrey Thomas Alexander, 1917–1996, vol. X
Armitage, Rev. George, 1856–1948, vol. IV
Armitage, Hugh Traill, 1881–1963, vol. VI
Armitage, John, 1910–1980, vol. VII
Armitage, Robert, 1866–1944, vol. IV
Armitage, Rev. Robert, 1857–1954, vol. V
Armitage, Sir Robert Perceval, 1906–1990, vol. VIII
Armitage, Sir (Stephen) Cecil, 1889–1962, vol. VI
Armitage, Valentine Leathley, 1888–1964, vol. VI
Armitage, Ven. William James, 1860–1929, vol. III
Armitage-Smith, George, died 1923, vol. II
Armitage-Smith, Sir Sydney Armitage, 1876–1932, vol. III
Armitstead, 1st Baron, 1824–1915, vol. I
Armitstead, Ven. John Hornby, 1868–1941, vol. IV
Armitstead, Rev. John Richard, 1829–1918, vol. II
Armour, Donald John, died 1933, vol. III
Armour, Eric Norman, 1877–1934, vol. III
Armour, George Denholm, 1864–1949, vol. IV
Armour, Rev. James Brown, 1842–1928, vol. II
Armour, Hon. John Douglas, 1830–1903, vol. I
Armour, Jonathan Ogden, 1863–1927, vol. II
Armour, Margaret; see MacDougall, Margaret.
Armour, Rev. Samuel Crawford, 1839–1929, vol. III
Armour, Rt Rev. Thomas Makinson, 1890–1963, vol. VI
Armour, William, 1903–1979, vol. VII
Armour-Hannay, Samuel Beveridge, 1856–1919, vol. II
Arms, John Taylor, 1887–1953, vol. V
Armstead, Henry Hugh, 1828–1905, vol. I
Armstrong, 1st Baron cr 1887, 1810–1900, vol. I
(up to the 5th edition of vol. I this entry is

headed in error by the first three lines of the following entry: Armstrong, Sir Alexander)
Armstrong, 1st Baron cr 1903, 1863–1941, vol. IV
Armstrong, 2nd Baron cr 1903, 1892–1972, vol. VII
Armstrong, 3rd Baron cr 1903, 1919–1987, vol. VIII
Armstrong of Sanderstead, Baron (Life Peer); William Armstrong, 1915–1980, vol. VII
Armstrong, Sir Alexander, 1818–1899, vol. I
Armstrong, Sir Alfred Norman, 1899–1966, vol. VI
Armstrong, Sir Andrew Clarence Francis, 6th Bt, 1907–1997, vol. X
Armstrong, Sir Andrew Harvey, 3rd Bt, 1866–1922, vol. II
Armstrong, Sir Andrew St Clare, 5th Bt, 1912–1987, vol. VIII
Armstrong, Anthony (A. A.); see Willis, A. A.
Armstrong, Arthur Henry, 1893–1972, vol. VII
Armstrong, (Arthur) Hilary, 1909–1997, vol. X
Armstrong, Arthur Leopold, 1888–1973, vol. VII
Armstrong, Col Bertie Harold Olivier, 1873–1950, vol. IV
Armstrong, Brig. Charles Douglas, 1897–1985, vol. VIII
Armstrong, Sir Charles Herbert, 1862–1949, vol. IV
Armstrong, Brig.-Gen. Charles Johnstone, 1872–1934, vol. III
Armstrong, Christopher Wyborne, 1899–1986, vol. VIII
Armstrong, Rev. Canon Claude Blakeley, 1889–1982, vol. VIII
Armstrong, David, see Clewes, Winston.
Armstrong, Edmond Arrenton, 1899–1966, vol. VI
Armstrong, Edmund Clarence Richard, 1879–1923, vol. II
Armstrong, Rev. Sir Edmund Frederick, 2nd Bt, 1836–1899, vol. I
Armstrong, Edmund La Touche, 1864–1946, vol. IV
Armstrong, Edward, 1846–1928, vol. II
Armstrong, Lt-Col Edward, 1869–1951, vol. V
Armstrong, Maj.-Gen. Edward Francis Hunter, 1834–1917, vol. II
Armstrong, Edward Frankland, 1878–1945, vol. IV
Armstrong, Rt Hon. Ernest, 1915–1996, vol. X
Armstrong, Hon. Ernest Howard, vol. III
Armstrong, F. A. W. T., 1849–1920, vol. II
Armstrong, Francis Edwin, 1879–1921, vol. II
Armstrong, Sir Francis Philip, 3rd Bt, 1871–1944, vol. IV
Armstrong, Major Francis Savage Nesbitt S.; see Savage-Armstrong.
Armstrong, Francis William, 1919–1988, vol. VIII
Armstrong, Frederick Ernest, 1884–1962, vol. VI
Armstrong, Captain Sir George Carlyon Hughes, 1st Bt, 1836–1907, vol. I
Armstrong, George Eli, 1854–1933, vol. III
Armstrong, Sir George Elliot, 2nd Bt, 1866–1940, vol. III
Armstrong, George Francis S.; see Savage-Armstrong.
Armstrong, George Frederick, 1842–1900, vol. I
Armstrong, George Gilbert, 1870–1945, vol. IV
Armstrong, George James, 1901–1972, vol. VII
Armstrong, Col Gerald Denne, 1865–1931, vol. III
Armstrong, Sir Gloster; see Armstrong, Sir H. G.

Armstrong, Sir Godfrey, 1882–1964, vol. VI
Armstrong, Hamilton Fish, 1893–1973, vol. VII
Armstrong, Captain Harold Courtenay, 1892–1943, vol. IV
Armstrong, Sir (Harry) Gloster, 1861–1938, vol. III
Armstrong, Rt Hon. Henry Bruce, 1844–1943, vol. IV
Armstrong, Henry Edward, 1848–1937, vol. III
Armstrong, Hilary; see Armstrong, A. H.
Armstrong, Rev. James, died 1928, vol. II
Armstrong, James Shelley Phipps, 1899–1971, vol. VII
Armstrong, John, 1893–1973, vol. VII
Armstrong, Rt Rev. John, 1905–1992, vol. IX
Armstrong, Surg.-Dentist John Alexander, 1862–1928, vol. II
Armstrong, John Anderson, 1910–1990, vol. VIII
Armstrong, Brig. John Cardew, 1887–1953, vol. V
Armstrong, Col John Cecil, 1870–1961, vol. VI
Armstrong, Sir John Dunamace H.; see Heaton-Armstrong.
Armstrong, John Elliot, 1875–1962, vol. VI
Armstrong, Vice-Adm. John Garnet, 1870–1949, vol. IV
Armstrong, Hon. John Ignatius, 1908–1977, vol. VII
Armstrong, Most Rev. John Ward, 1915–1987, vol. VIII
Armstrong, John Warneford Scobell, 1877–1960, vol. V
Armstrong, Katharine Fairlie, 1892–1969, vol. VI
Armstrong, Louis Daniel, 1900–1971, vol. VII
Armstrong, Martin Donisthorpe, 1882–1974, vol. VII
Armstrong, Rt Rev. Mervyn, 1906–1984, vol. VIII
Armstrong, Dame Nellie; see Melba, Dame Nellie.
Armstrong, Sir Nesbitt William, 4th Bt, 1875–1953, vol. V
Armstrong, Col Oliver Carleton, 1859–1932, vol. III
Armstrong, Sir Richard Harold, 1874–1950, vol. IV
Armstrong, Gen. St George Bewes, 1871–1956, vol. V
Armstrong, Samuel, 1878–1959, vol. V
Armstrong, Rev. Simon Carter, 1856–1942, vol. IV
Armstrong, Terence Edward, 1920–1996, vol. X
Armstrong, Thomas, 1832–1911, vol. I
Armstrong, Thomas, 1899–1978, vol. VII
Armstrong, Thomas Graves Lowry Herbert, 1856–1940, vol. III
Armstrong, Rt Rev. Thomas Henry, 1857–1930, vol. III
Armstrong, Sir Thomas Henry Wait, 1898–1994, vol. IX
Armstrong, Thomas Mandeville Emerson, 1869–1922, vol. II
Armstrong, Wallace Edwin, 1896–1980, vol. VII
Armstrong, Sir Walter, 1850–1918, vol. II
Armstrong, Rev. Walter H., 1873–1949, vol. IV
Armstrong, William, 1882–1952, vol. V
Armstrong, William Charles H.; see Heaton-Armstrong.
Armstrong, Hon. William Drayton, 1861–1936, vol. III
Armstrong, William George, 1859–1941, vol. IV
Armstrong, Sir William Herbert Fletcher, 1892–1950, vol. IV

Armstrong Cowan, Sir Christopher; see Cowan, Sir C. G. A.
Armstrong-Jones, Sir Robert; see Jones.
Armstrong-Jones, Ronald Owen Lloyd, 1899–1966, vol. VI
Armytage, Rev. Canon Duncan, 1889–1954, vol. V
Armytage, Sir George, 5th Bt, 1819–1899, vol. I
Armytage, Brig.-Gen. Sir George Ayscough, 7th Bt, 1872–1953, vol. V
Armytage, Sir George John, 6th Bt, 1842–1918, vol. II
Armytage, Captain Sir John Lionel, 8th Bt, 1901–1983, vol. VIII
Armytage, Percy, 1853–1934, vol. III
Armytage, Rear-Adm. Reginald William, 1903–1984, vol. VIII
Armytage, Lt-Col Vivian Bartley G.; see Green-Armytage.
Armytage, Walter Harry Green, 1915–1998, vol. X
Arnason, Frú Barbara; see Moray Williams, B.
Arnaud, Emile, 1864–1921, vol. II
Arnaud, Yvonne, 1895–1958, vol. V
Arnavon, Jacques, 1877–1949, vol. IV
Arnell, Charles Christopher, 1881–1948, vol. IV
Arnett, Edward John, died 1940, vol. III
Arney, Frank Douglas, 1899–1983, vol. VIII
Arnheim, Edward Henry Silberstein Von, died 1925, vol. II
Arnison, William Christopher, 1837–1899, vol. I
Arno, Peter, 1906–1968, vol. VI
Arnold, 1st Baron, 1878–1945, vol. IV
Arnold, Sir Alfred, 1835–1908, vol. I
Arnold, Col Alfred James, 1866–1933, vol. III
Arnold, Maj.-Gen. Allan Cholmondeley, 1893–1962, vol. VI
Arnold, Sir Arthur, 1833–1902, vol. I
Arnold, Arthur, 1891–1961, vol. VI
Arnold, Bening Mourant, 1884–1955, vol. V
Arnold, Denis Midgley, 1926–1986, vol. VIII
Arnold, Edmund George, 1865–1939, vol. III
Arnold, Edward Augustus, 1857–1942, vol. IV
Arnold, Edward Carleton, died 1949, vol. IV
Arnold, Edward Vernon, 1857–1926, vol. II
Arnold, Sir Edwin, 1832–1904, vol. I
Arnold, Edwin Lester, died 1935, vol. III
Arnold, Sir Frederick Blackmore, 1906–1968, vol. VI
Arnold, Rt Rev. George Feversham, 1914–1998, vol. X
Arnold, George Frederick, died 1917, vol. II
Arnold, Henry Fraser James Coape-, 1846–1923, vol. II
Arnold, Gen. of the Army Henry H., 1886–1950, vol. IV
Arnold, Rev. Henry James Lawes, 1854–1928, vol. II
Arnold, Lt-Col Herbert Tollemache, 1867–1943, vol. IV
Arnold, Ivor Deiniol Osborn, 1895–1952, vol. V
Arnold, Major John Effingham, 1882–1939, vol. III
Arnold, John Oliver, 1858–1930, vol. III
Arnold, Ralph Crispian Marshall, 1906–1970, vol. VI
Arnold, Reginald Edward, 1853–1938, vol. III
Arnold, Ronald Nathan, 1908–1963, vol. VI

Arnold, Col Stanley, 1844–1906, vol. I
Arnold, Thomas, 1823–1900, vol. I
Arnold, Thomas George, 1866–1944, vol. IV
Arnold, Thomas James, 1879–1945, vol. IV
Arnold, Sir Thomas Walker, 1864–1930, vol. III
Arnold, Thurman Wesley, 1891–1969, vol. VI
Arnold, Tom, (Thomas Charles Arnold), died 1969,
vol. VI
Arnold, Vere Arbuthnot, 1902–1994, vol. IX
Arnold, Sir William Henry, 1903–1973, vol. VII
Arnold, William R., 1872–1929, vol. III
Arnold-Forster, Rear-Adm. Forster Delafield,
1876–1958, vol. V
Arnold-Forster, Major Francis Anson, 1890–1966,
vol. VI
Arnold-Forster, Comdr Hugh Christopher,
1890–1965, vol. VI
Arnold-Forster, Rt Hon. Hugh Oakeley, 1855–1909,
vol. I
Arnoldi, Frank, born 1848, vol. III
Arnoldi, Col Frank Fauquier, 1889–1953, vol. V
Arnott, Most Rev. Felix Raymond, 1911–1988,
vol. VIII
Arnott, Rev. Henry, died 1931, vol. III
Arnott, James Fullarton, 1914–1982, vol. VIII
Arnott, Sir John, 1st Bt, 1817–1898, vol. I
Arnott, John, 1871–1942, vol. IV
Arnott, Sir John Alexander, 2nd Bt, 1853–1940,
vol. III
Arnott, Col John Maclean, 1869–1945, vol. IV
Arnott, Sir John Robert Alexander, 5th Bt,
1927–1981, vol. VIII
Arnott, Sir Lauriston John, 3rd Bt, 1890–1958,
vol. V
Arnott, Leonard, 1887–1943, vol. IV
Arnott, Sir Melville; see Arnott, Sir W. M.
Arnott, Sir Robert John, 4th Bt, 1896–1966, vol. VI
Arnott, Maj.-Gen. Stanley, 1888–1972, vol. VII
Arnott, Brig.-Gen. William, 1860–1929, vol. III
Arnott, Sir (William) Melville, 1909–1999, vol. X
Arnould, Francis Graham, 1875–1941, vol. IV
Aron, Raymond Claude Ferdinand, 1905–1983,
vol. VIII
Aron, Robert, 1905–1975, vol. VII
Aronson, Geoffrey Fraser, 1914–1998, vol. X
Aronson, Victor Rees, 1880–1951, vol. V
Arp, Jean Hans, 1887–1966, vol. VI
Arran, 5th Earl of, 1839–1901, vol. I
Arran, 6th Earl of, 1868–1958, vol. V
Arran, 7th Earl of, 1903–1958, vol. II
Arran, 8th Earl of, 1910–1983, vol. VIII
Arran, Claudio, 1903–1991, vol. IX
Arrhenius, Svante August, 1859–1927, vol. II
Arrol, Sir William, 1839–1913, vol. I
Arrow, Gilbert John, 1873–1948, vol. IV
Arrowsmith, Sir Edwin Porter, 1909–1992, vol. IX
Arrowsmith, Hugh, 1888–1972, vol. VII
Arrowsmith, Rev. Preb. Walter Gordon, 1888–1964,
vol. VI
Arrowsmith-Brown, Lt-Col James Arnold,
1882–1937, vol. III
Arsenault, Hon. Aubin Edmond, 1870–1969, vol. VI
Artemus Jones, Sir Thomas; see Jones.
Arthington-Davy, Humphrey Augustine, 1920–1993,
vol. IX

Arthur, Sir Allan, 1857–1923, vol. II
Arthur, Allan James Vincent, 1915–1998, vol. X
Arthur, Hon. Sir Basil Malcolm, 5th Bt,
1928–1985, vol. VIII
Arthur, Col Sir Charles Gordon, 1884–1953, vol. V
Arthur, Major Christopher Geoffrey, 1882–1943,
vol. IV
Arthur, Donald Ramsay, 1917–1984, vol. VIII
Arthur, Sir Geoffrey George, 1920–1984, vol. VIII
Arthur, Sir George Compton Archibald, 3rd Bt,
1860–1946, vol. IV
Arthur, Sir George Malcolm, 4th Bt, 1908–1949,
vol. IV
Arthur, Col John Maurice, 1877–1954, vol. V
Arthur, Captain Leonard Robert Sunskersett,
1864–1903, vol. I
Arthur, Col Lionel Francis, 1876–1952, vol. V
Arthur, Sir (Oswald) Raynor, 1905–1973, vol. VII
Arthur, Peter Bernard, 1923–1998, vol. X
Arthur, Sir Raynor; see Arthur, Sir O. R.
Arthur, Hon. Richard, 1865–1932, vol. III
Arthur, Rt Rev. Robert Gordon, 1909–1992, vol. IX
Arthur, Humphrey George Edgar, 1906–1996,
vol. X
Arton, Maj. Anthony Temple B.; see Bourne-Arton,
A. T.
Artsibashev, Michel Petrovitch, 1878–1927, vol. II
Artus, Ronald Edward, 1931–1999, vol. X
Arunachalam, Sir Ponnambalam, 1853–1924, vol. II
Arundale, George Sydney, 1878–1945, vol. IV
Arundel and Surrey, Earl of; Philip Joseph Mary
Fitzalan-Howard, 1879–1902, vol. I
Arundel, Sir Arundel Tagg, 1843–1929, vol. III
Arundell of Wardour, 12th Baron, 1831–1906, vol. I
Arundell of Wardour, 13th Baron, 1834–1907, vol. I
Arundell of Wardour, 14th Baron, 1859–1921,
vol. II
Arundell of Wardour, 15th Baron, 1861–1939,
vol. III
Arundell of Wardour, 16th Baron, 1907–1944,
vol. IV
Arundell, Dennis Drew, 1898–1988, vol. VIII
Arundell, Brig. Sir Robert Duncan Harris,
1904–1989, vol. VIII
Arup, Sir Ove Nyquist, 1895–1988, vol. VIII
Arur Singh, Sir Sardar Bahadur Sardar, 1863–1926,
vol. II
Arwyn, Baron (Life Peer); Arwyn Randall Arwyn,
1897–1978, vol. VII
Asaad, Fikry Naguib M.; see Marcos-Asaad.
Asafu-Adjaye, Sir Edward Okyere, 1903–1976,
vol. VII
Asbury, William, 1889–1961, vol. VI
Asch, Sholem, 1880–1957, vol. V
Asche, Oscar, 1872–1936, vol. III
Ascoli, Frank David, 1883–1958, vol. V
Ascroft, Peter Byers, 1906–1965, vol. VI
Ascroft, Robert, 1847–1899, vol. I
Ascroft, Sir William, 1832–1916, vol. II
Ascroft, Sir William Fawell, 1876–1954, vol. V
Asfa Wossen Haile Sellassie, HIH Merd Azmatch,
1916–1997, vol. X
Ash, Audrey B., died 1958, vol. V
Ash, Edwin Lancelot Hopewell-, 1881–1964,
vol. VI

Ash, Rt Rev. Fortescue Leo, 1882–1956, vol. V
Ash, Graham Baron, 1889–1980, vol. VII
Ash, Rear-Adm. Walter William Hector, 1906–1998, vol. X
Ash, Major William Claudius Casson, 1870–1916, vol. II
Ashbee, C. R., 1863–1942, vol. IV
Ashbolt, Sir Alfred Henry, 1870–1930, vol. III
Ashbourne, 1st Baron, 1837–1913, vol. I
Ashbourne, 2nd Baron, 1868–1942, vol. IV
Ashbourne, 3rd Baron, 1901–1983, vol. VIII
Ashbridge, Sir Noel, 1889–1975, vol. VII
Ashbrook, 7th Viscount, 1830–1906, vol. I
Ashbrook, 8th Viscount, 1836–1919, vol. II
Ashbrook, 9th Viscount, 1870–1936, vol. III
Ashbrook, 10th Viscount, 1905–1995, vol. IX
Ashburner, Maj.-Gen. George Elliot, 1820–1907, vol. I
Ashburner, Lt-Col Lionel Forbes, 1874–1923, vol. II
Ashburner, Lionel Robert, 1827–1907, vol. I
Ashburner, Walter, 1864–1936, vol. III
Ashburnham, 5th Earl of, 1840–1913, vol. I
Ashburnham, 6th Earl of, 1855–1924, vol. II
Ashburnham, Sir Anchitel, 8th Bt, 1828–1899, vol. I
Ashburnham, Sir Anchitel Piers, 9th Bt; see Ashburnham-Clement.
Ashburnham, Sir Cromer, 1831–1917, vol. II
Ashburnham, Captain Sir Denny Reginald, 12th Bt, 1916–1999, vol. X
Ashburnham, Sir Fleetwood, 11th Bt, 1869–1953, vol. V
Ashburnham, Hon. John, 1845–1912, vol. I
Ashburnham, Sir Reginald, 10th Bt, 1865–1944, vol. IV
Ashburnham-Clement, Sir Anchitel Piers, 9th Bt, 1861–1935, vol. III
Ashburton, 5th Baron, 1866–1938, vol. III
Ashburton, 6th Baron, 1898–1991, vol. IX
Ashburton, Lady; (Louisa), died 1903, vol. I
Ashby, Baron (Life Peer); Eric Ashby, 1904–1992, vol. IX
Ashby, Arthur Wilfred, 1886–1953, vol. V
Ashby, Col George Ashby, 1856–1937, vol. III
Ashby, Hugh Tuke, 1880–1952, vol. V
Ashby, Sir James William Murray, 1822–1911, vol. I
Ashby, Dame Margery Irene C.; see Corbett Ashby.
Ashby, Very Rev. Paul Ogilvie, 1867–1937, vol. III
Ashby, Robert Claude, 1876–1963, vol. VI
Ashby, Thomas, 1874–1931, vol. III
Ashby-Sterry, Joseph, died 1917, vol. II
Ashcombe, 1st Baron, 1828–1917, vol. II
Ashcombe, 2nd Baron, 1867–1947, vol. IV
Ashcombe, 3rd Baron, 1899–1962, vol. VI
Ashcroft, Alex Hutchinson, 1887–1963, vol. VI
Ashcroft, (Charles) Neil, 1937–1984, vol. VIII
Ashcroft, D(udley) Walker, 1904–1963, vol. VI
Ashcroft, Dame Edith Margaret Emily, (Dame Peggy), 1907–1991, vol. IX
Ashcroft, James Geoffrey, 1928–2000, vol. X
Ashcroft, Ven. Lawrence, 1901–1996, vol. X
Ashcroft, Neil; see Ashcroft, C. N.
Ashcroft, Dame Peggy; see Ashcroft, Dame E. M. E.

Ashcroft, Thomas, 1890–1961, vol. VI
Ashdown, Baron (Life Peer); Arnold Silverstone, 1911–1977, vol. VII
Ashdown, Arthur Durham, 1872–1953, vol. V
Ashdown, Sir Curtis George, 1876–1933, vol. III
Ashdown, Sir George Henry, 1857–1924, vol. II
Ashdown, Rt Rev. Hugh Edward, 1904–1977, vol. VII
Ashe, Sir Derick Rosslyn, 1919–2000, vol. X
Ashe, Rear-Adm. Edward Percy, 1852–1914, vol. I
Ashe Lincoln, Fredman; see Lincoln, F. A.
Ashenheim, Sir Neville Noel, 1900–1984, vol. VIII
Asher, Alexander, 1835–1905, vol. I
Asher, Amy, (Mrs Peter Asher); see Shuard, A.
Asher, Sir Augustus Gordon Grant, 1861–1930, vol. III
Asher, Florence May, 1888–1977, vol. VII
Asher, Samuel Garcia, 1868–1938, vol. III
Asherson, Nehemiah, 1897–1989, vol. VIII
Ashfield, 1st Baron, 1874–1948, vol. IV
Ashfield, Percy John, 1870–1946, vol. IV
Ashford, (Albert) Reginald, 1914–1995, vol. IX
Ashford, Bailey K., died 1934, vol. III
Ashford, Sir Cyril Ernest, 1867–1951, vol. V
Ashford, George Francis, 1911–1998, vol. X
Ashford, Ven. Percival Leonard, 1927–1998, vol. X
Ashford, Reginald; see Ashford, A. R.
Ashford, Hon. William George, 1874–1925, vol. II
Ashkanasy, Maurice, 1901–1971, vol. VII
Ashley; see Harinden, A. E.
Ashley, Lord; Anthony Ashley-Cooper, 1900–1947, vol. IV
Ashley, Rt Hon. (Anthony) Evelyn Melbourne, 1836–1907, vol. I
Ashley, Hon. Cecil, 1849–1932, vol. III
Ashley, Rt Hon. Evelyn Melbourne; see Ashley, Rt Hon. A. E. M.
Ashley, Francis Noel, 1884–1976, vol. VII
Ashley, Francis Paul, 1942–2000, vol. X
Ashley, Lt-Col Frank, 1870–1923, vol. II
Ashley, Frederick Morewood, 1846–1933, vol. III
Ashley, Henry V., 1872–1945, vol. IV
Ashley, Maurice Percy, 1907–1994, vol. IX
Ashley, Sir Percy Walter Llewellyn, 1876–1945, vol. IV
Ashley, Walter, 1893–1937, vol. III
Ashley, Sir William James, 1860–1927, vol. II
Ashley-Brown, Ven. William, 1887–1970, vol. VI
Ashley-Scarlett, Lt-Col Henry, 1886–1976, vol. VII
Ashlin, George C., 1837–1922, vol. II
Ashmall, Rev. Francis James, 1856–1948, vol. IV
Ashman, Sir Frederick Herbert, 2nd Bt, 1875–1916, vol. II
Ashman, Sir Herbert, 1st Bt, 1854–1914, vol. I
Ashmead-Bartlett, Ellis, 1881–1931, vol. III
Ashmead-Bartlett, Sir Ellis; see Bartlett.
Ashmole, Bernard, 1894–1988, vol. VIII
Ashmore, Hon. Lord; John Wilson, 1857–1932, vol. III
Ashmore, Sir Alexander Murray, 1855–1906, vol. I
Ashmore, Maj.-Gen. Edward Bailey, 1872–1953, vol. V
Ashmore, Major Edwin James Caldwell, 1893–1959, vol. V

Ashmore, Vice-Adm. Leslie Haliburton, 1893–1974, vol. VII
Ashmore, William Caldwell, 1866–1931, vol. III
Ashton, 1st Baron, 1842–1930, vol. III
Ashton, Baroness; (Florence Maude), 1856–1944, vol. IV
Ashton of Hyde, 1st Baron, 1855–1933, vol. III
Ashton of Hyde, 2nd Baron, 1901–1983, vol. VIII
Ashton, Algernon Bennet Langton, 1859–1937, vol. III
Ashton, Arthur Jacob, 1855–1925, vol. II
Ashton, Sir (Arthur) Leigh (Bolland), 1897–1983, vol. VIII
Ashton, Lt-Col Edward Malcolm, 1895–1978, vol. VII
Ashton, Ellis, 1919–1985, vol. VIII
Ashton, Lt-Gen. Ernest Charles, 1873–1957, vol. V
Ashton, Sir Frederick William Mallandaine, 1904–1988, vol. VIII
Ashton, Gilbert, 1896–1981, vol. VIII
Ashton, Harry, 1882–1952, vol. V
Ashton, Helen, (Mrs Arthur Jordan), 1891–1958, vol. V
Ashton, Captain Henry Gordon Gooch, 1870–1951, vol. V
Ashton, Sir Hubert, 1898–1979, vol. VII
Ashton, Hon. James, 1864–1939, vol. III
Ashton, Engr Rear-Adm. James, 1883–1951, vol. V
Ashton, Rt Rev. John William, 1866–1964, vol. VI
Ashton, Julian Rossi, 1851–1942, vol. IV
Ashton, Sir Leigh; see Ashton, Sir A. L. B.
Ashton, Margaret, 1856–1937, vol. III
Ashton, Norman Henry, 1913–2000, vol. X
Ashton, Rev. Canon Patrick Thomas, 1916–1994, vol. IX
Ashton, Sir Ralph Percy, 1860–1921, vol. II
Ashton, Teddy; see Clarke, Charles Allen.
Ashton, Rt Hon. Thomas, 1844–1927, vol. II
Ashton, Thomas Southcliffe, 1889–1968, vol. VI
Ashton, Sir William, 1881–1963, vol. VI
Ashton, Winifred; see Dane, Clemence.
Ashton Hill, Norman, 1918–1991, vol. IX
Aston-Gwatkin, Frank Trelawny Arthur, 1889–1976, vol. VII
Ashton-Gwatkin, Rev. Walter Henry Trelawny; see Gwatkin.
Ashtown, 3rd Baron, 1868–1946, vol. IV
Ashtown, 4th Baron, 1897–1966, vol. VI
Ashtown, 5th Baron, 1901–1979, vol. VII
Ashtown, 6th Baron, 1931–1990, vol. VIII
Ashwanden, Col Sydney William Louis, 1878–1947, vol. IV
Ashwell, Maj. Arthur Lindley, 1886–1986, vol. VIII
Ashwell, Lena, died 1957, vol. V
Ashwin, Sir Bernard Carl, 1896–1975, vol. VII
Ashworth, Ernest Horatio, 1870–1934, vol. III
Ashworth, Harold Kenneth, 1903–1978, vol. VII
Ashworth, Sir Herbert, 1910–2000, vol. X
Ashworth, James Hartley, 1874–1936, vol. III
Ashworth, Brig. John Blackwood, 1910–1994, vol. IX
Ashworth, Sir John Percy, 1906–1975, vol. VII
Ashworth, Philip Arthur, 1853–1921, vol. II
Ashworth, Air Comdt Dame Veronica Margaret, 1910–1977, vol. VII

Ashworth, William, 1920–1991, vol. IX
Asimov, Isaac, 1920–1992, vol. IX
Aske, Sir Robert William, 1st Bt, 1872–1954, vol. V
Askew, Claude Arthur, died 1917, vol. II
Askew, Herbert Royston, 1891–1986, vol. VIII
Askew, John Marjoribanks Eskdale, 1908–1996, vol. X
Askew, William George, 1890–1968, vol. VI
Askew-Robertson, Watson, 1834–1907, vol. I
Askew Robertson, William Haggerston, 1868–1942, vol. IV
Askey, Arthur Bowden, 1900–1982, vol. VIII
Askin, Hon. Sir Robert William, 1909–1981, vol. VIII
Askuran, Sir Shantidas, 1882–1950, vol. IV (A), vol. V
Askwith, 1st Baron, 1861–1942, vol. IV
Askwith, Lady; (Ellen), died 1962, vol. VI
Askwith, Arthur Vivian, 1893–1971, vol. VII
Askwith, Hon. Betty Ellen, 1909–1995, vol. IX
Askwith, Rev. Edward Harrison, 1864–1946, vol. IV
Askwith, Col Henry Francis, 1865–1938, vol. III
Askwith, Rt Rev. Wilfred Marcus, 1890–1962, vol. VI
Askwith, Ven. William Henry, 1843–1911, vol. I
Aslett, Alfred, 1847–1928, vol. II
Aslin, Charles Herbert, 1893–1959, vol. V
Aslin, Elizabeth Mary, 1923–1989, vol. VIII
Asman, Rev. Harry Newbitt, 1877–1950, vol. IV
Aspden, Hartley, 1858–1940, vol. III
Aspell, Sir John, 1854–1938, vol. III
Aspinall, Sir Algernon Edward, 1871–1952, vol. V
Aspinall, Arthur, 1901–1972, vol. VII
Aspinall, Butler, 1861–1935, vol. III
Aspinall, Sir John Audley Frederick, 1851–1937, vol. III
Aspinall, John Bridge, 1877–1932, vol. III
Aspinall, Major John Ralph, 1878–1947, vol. IV
Aspinall, John Victor, 1926–2000, vol. X
Aspinall, Ven. Noël Lake, 1861–1934, vol. III
Aspinall, Lt-Col Robert Lowndes, 1869–1916, vol. II
Aspinall, Lt-Col Robert Stivala, 1895–1954, vol. V
Aspinall, William Briant Philip, 1912–1988, vol. VIII
Aspinall-Oglander, Brig.-Gen. Cecil Faber, 1878–1959, vol. V
Asprey, Algernon, 1912–1991, vol. IX
Asquith of Bishopstone, Baron (Life Peer); Cyril Asquith, 1890–1954, vol. V
Asquith of Yarnbury, Baroness (Life Peeress); Helen Violet Bonham Carter, 1887–1969, vol. VI
Asquith, Hon. Anthony, 1902–1968, vol. VI
Asquith, Hon. Arthur Melland, 1883–1939, vol. III
Asquith, Lady Cynthia, died 1960, vol. V
Asquith, Cyril Edward, 1902–1967, vol. VI
Asquith, Hon. Herbert, 1881–1947, vol. IV
Asquith, Raymond, 1878–1916, vol. II
Asser, Gen. Sir John; see Asser, Gen. Sir J. J.
Asser, Gen. Sir (Joseph) John, 1867–1949, vol. IV
Asser, Brig.-Gen. Verney, 1873–1944, vol. IV
Assheton, Ralph, 1830–1907, vol. I
Assheton, Sir Ralph Cockayne, 1st Bt, 1860–1955, vol. V

Assheton, Richard, 1863–1915, vol. I
Assheton-Smith, Sir Charles Garden, 1st Bt, 1851–1914, vol. I
Assheton-Smith, George William Duff, 1848–1904, vol. I
Astaire, Fred, 1899–1987, vol. VIII
Astbury, Arthur Ralph, 1880–1973, vol. VII
Astbury, Lt-Comdr Frederick Wolfe, 1872–1954, vol. V
Astbury, Rev. George, died 1926, vol. II
Astbury, Sir George, 1902–1985, vol. VIII
Astbury, Rev. Canon (Harold) Stanley, 1889–1962, vol. VI
Astbury, Herbert Arthur, 1870–1968, vol. VI
Astbury, Rt Hon. Sir John Meir, 1860–1939, vol. III
Astbury, Norman Frederick, 1908–1987, vol. VIII
Astbury, Rev. Canon Stanley; see Astbury, Rev. Canon H. S.
Astbury, William Thomas, 1898–1961, vol. VI
Astell, Maj.-Gen. Charles Edward, died 1901, vol. I
Astell, Richard John Vereker, 1890–1969, vol. VI
Astell, Captain Somerset Charles Godfrey Fairfax, 1866–1917, vol. II
Astell Hohler, Thomas Sidney, 1919–1989, vol. VIII
Asterley Jones, Philip; see Jones.
Astin, Alan Edgar, 1930–1991, vol. IX
Astley, Bertram Frankland Frankland-Russell-, 1857–1904, vol. I
Astley, Major Delaval Graham L'Estrange, 1868–1951, vol. V
Astley, Sir Francis Jacob Dugdale, 6th Bt, 1908–1994, vol. IX
Astley, Henry Jacob Delaval Frankland-Russell-, 1888–1912, vol. I
Astley, Hubert Delaval, 1860–1925, vol. II
Astley, Rev. Hugh John Dukinfield, 1856–1930, vol. III
Astley, Kathleen Mary; see Astley, Mrs Reginald.
Astley, Mrs Reginald, (Kathleen Mary Astley), 1880–1973, vol. VII
Astley, Reginald Basil, 1862–1942, vol. IV
Astley-Corbett, Sir Francis Edmund George, 4th Bt, 1859–1939, vol. III
Astley-Corbett, Sir (Francis) Henry (Rivers), 5th Bt, 1915–1943, vol. IV
Astley-Corbett, Sir Henry; see Astley-Corbett, Sir F. H. R.
Astley-Rushton, Vice-Adm. Edward Astley; see Rushton.
Aston, Alfred Withall, 1852–1929, vol. III
Aston, Arthur Vincent, 1896–1981, vol. VIII
Aston, Rev. Canon Basil, 1880–1957, vol. V
Aston, Bernard Cracroft, 1871–1951, vol. V
Aston, Sir Christopher Southcote, 1920–1982, vol. VIII
Aston, Francis William, 1877–1945, vol. IV
Aston, Maj.-Gen. Sir George Grey, 1861–1938, vol. III
Aston, Theodore, died 1910, vol. I
Aston, Thomas William, 1922–1981, vol. VIII
Aston, William George, 1841–1911, vol. I
Aston, Hon. Sir William John, 1916–1997, vol. X
Astor, 1st Viscount, 1848–1919, vol. II
Astor, 2nd Viscount, 1879–1952, vol. V
Astor, 3rd Viscount, 1907–1966, vol. VI

Astor, Nancy, Viscountess, 1879–1964, vol. VI
Astor of Hever, 1st Baron, 1886–1971, vol. VII
Astor of Hever, 2nd Baron, 1918–1984, vol. VIII
Astor, Hon. Hugh Waldorf, 1920–1999, vol. X
Astor, Hon. John, 1923–1987, vol. VIII
Astor, John Jacob, 1864–1912, vol. I
Astor, Major Hon. Sir John Jacob, 1918–2000, vol. X
Astor, Hon. Michael Langhorne, 1916–1980, vol. VII
Asturias, Miguel Angel, 1899–1974, vol. VII
Astwood, Lt-Col Sir Jeffrey Carlton, 1907–1996, vol. X
Atatürk, Kamâl, 1881–1938, vol. III
Atcherley, Air Vice-Marshal David Francis William, 1904–1952, vol. V
Atcherley, Col Sir Llewellyn William, 1871–1954, vol. V
Atcherley, Air Marshall Sir Richard Llewellyn Roger, 1904–1970, vol. VI
Atchison, Major Charles Ernest, 1875–1917, vol. II
Atchley, Chewton, 1850–1922, vol. II
Atchley, Shirley Clifford, 1871–1936, vol. III
Athaide, Most Rev. Dominic Romuald, 1909–1982, vol. VIII
Athawes, Edward James, died 1902, vol. I
Athelstan-Johnson, Wilfrid, 1876–1939, vol. III
Athenagoras, Archbishop, (Archbishop of Thyateira), died 1962, vol. VI
Athenagoras, Spyrou, 1886–1972, vol. VII
Athenagoras, Theodoritos, 1912–1979, vol. VII
Atherley, Major Evelyn George Hammond, 1852–1935, vol. III
Atherley-Jones, Llewellyn Archer, 1851–1929, vol. III
Atherton, Gertrude Franklin, died 1948, vol. IV
Atherton, Ray, 1885–1960, vol. V
Atherton, Col Thomas James, 1856–1920, vol. II
Athill, Charles Harold, died 1922, vol. II
Athill, Lt-Col Francis Remi Imbert, 1880–1958, vol. V
Athlone, 1st Earl of, 1874–1957, vol. V
Athlone, Countess of, (HRH Princess Alice), 1883–1981, vol. VIII
Athlumney, 6th Baron, 1865–1929, vol. III
Atholl, 7th Duke of, 1840–1917, vol. II
Atholl, 8th Duke of, 1871–1942, vol. IV
Atholl, 9th Duke of, 1879–1957, vol. V
Atholl, 10th Duke of, 1931–1996, vol. X
Atholl, Duchess of; (Katharine Marjory), died 1960, vol. V
Atholstan, 1st Baron, 1848–1938, vol. III
Atkey, Sir Albert (Reuben), 1867–1947, vol. IV
Atkey, Oliver Francis Haynes, died 1960, vol. V
Atkin, Baron (Life Peer); James Richard Atkin, 1867–1944, vol. IV
Atkin, Charles, died 1934, vol. III
Atkin, Peter Wilson, 1859–1931, vol. III
Atkins, family name of Baron Colnbrook.
Atkins, Maj.-Gen. Sir Alban Randell Crofton, 1870–1926, vol. II
Atkins, Alexander Robert; see Atkins, R.
Atkins, Charles Norman, 1885–1960, vol. V
Atkins, Col Ernest Clive, 1870–1953, vol. V
Atkins, Frederick Anthony, 1864–1929, vol. III

Atkins, Sir Hedley John Barnard, 1905–1983, vol. VIII
Atkins, Henry Gibson, 1871–1942, vol. IV
Atkins, Henry St J., 1896–1987, vol. IX (AI)
Atkins, Ian Robert, 1912–1979, vol. VII
Atkins, Sir Ivor Algernon, 1869–1953, vol. V
Atkins, Col Sir John, 1875–1963, vol. VI
Atkins, John Black, 1871–1954, vol. V
Atkins, John Spencer, 1905–1987, vol. VIII
Atkins, John William Hey, 1874–1951, vol. V
Atkins, Leonard Brian W.; see Walsh-Atkins.
Atkins, Malcolm Ramsay, 1881–1960, vol. V
Atkins, Robert, 1886–1972, vol. VII
Atkins, Thomas Frederick B.; see Burnaby-Atkins.
Atkins, William Ringrose Gelston, 1884–1959, vol. V
Atkins, Sir William Sydney Albert, 1902–1989, vol. VIII
Atkinson, Baron (Life Peer); John Atkinson, 1844–1932, vol. III
Atkinson, Major Sir Arthur Joseph, died 1959, vol. V
Atkinson, Brig.-Gen. Ben, 1872–1942, vol. IV
Atkinson, Brooks; see Atkinson, J. B.
Atkinson, Cecil Hewitt, 1894–1954, vol. V
Atkinson, Hon. Cecil Thomas, 1876–1919, vol. II
Atkinson, Ven. Charles Frederic, 1855–1942, vol. IV
Atkinson, Charles Milner, 1854–1920, vol. II
Atkinson, Colin Ronald Michael, 1931–1991, vol. IX
Atkinson, Hon. Sir Cyril, 1874–1967, vol. VI
Atkinson, Donald, 1886–1963, vol. VI
Atkinson, Rev. Edward, died 1915, vol. I
Atkinson, Ven. Edward Dupré, 1855–1937, vol. III
Atkinson, Sir Edward Hale Tindal, 1878–1957, vol. V
Atkinson, Surgeon-Captain Edward Leicester, 1882–1929, vol. III
Atkinson, Sir Edward Tindal, 1847–1930, vol. III
Atkinson, Major Edward William, 1873–1920, vol. II
Atkinson, Lt-Gen. Sir Edwin Henry de Vere, 1867–1947, vol. IV
Atkinson, Rt Hon. Sir Fenton, 1906–1980, vol. VII
Atkinson, Brig.-Gen. Francis Garnett, 1857–1941, vol. IV
Atkinson, Frank Buddle, 1866–1953, vol. V
Atkinson, Frank Stuart, 1899–1971, vol. VII
Atkinson, George, died 1941, vol. IV
Atkinson, Major George Prestage, 1885–1929, vol. III
Atkinson, Henry John Farmer-, 1828–1913, vol. I
Atkinson, Rev. Canon Henry Sadgrove, died 1927, vol. II
Atkinson, Henry Tindal, died 1918, vol. II
Atkinson, Rev. J. Augustus, died 1911, vol. I
Atkinson, Lt-Col John, died 1945, vol. IV
Atkinson, Sir (John) Kenneth, 1905–1989, vol. VIII
Atkinson, John Mitford, 1856–1917, vol. II
Atkinson, Sir John Nathaniel, 1857–1931, vol. III
Atkinson, Maj.-Gen. John Richard Breeks, 1844–1926, vol. II
Atkinson, (Justin) Brooks, 1894–1984, vol. VIII
Atkinson, Sir Kenneth; see Atkinson, Sir J. K.

Atkinson, Leonard Allan, 1906–1998, vol. X
Atkinson, Maj.-Gen. Sir Leonard Henry, 1910–1990, vol. VIII
Atkinson, Leslie, 1913–1994, vol. IX
Atkinson, Meredith, 1883–1929, vol. III
Atkinson, Richard John Copland, 1920–1994, vol. IX
Atkinson, Robert, 1883–1952, vol. V
Atkinson, Thomas Dinham, 1864–1948, vol. IV
Atkinson, Thomas John Day, 1882–1949, vol. IV
Atkinson, Vivian Buchanan, 1886–1960, vol. V
Atkinson, William Christopher, 1902–1992, vol. IX
Atkinson, Sir William Nicholas, 1850–1930, vol. III
Atkinson-Willes, Adm. Sir George Lambart, 1847–1921, vol. II
Atlay, James Beresford, 1860–1912, vol. I
Atlay, Rev. Marcus Ethelbert, died 1934, vol. III
Atlay, Sir Wilfrid, 1866–1929, vol. III
Atta, Nana Sir Ofori, 1881–1943, vol. IV
Attenborough, Charles Leete, 1853–1937, vol. III
Attenborough, Frederick L., 1887–1973, vol. VII
Attenborough, James, 1884–1984, vol. VIII
Attenborough, Walter Annis, 1850–1932, vol. III
Atterbury, Sir Frederick, 1853–1919, vol. II
Attewell, Humphry Cooper, 1894–1972, vol. VII
Attfield, John, 1835–1911, vol. I
Atthill, Major Anthony William Maunsell, 1861–1926, vol. II
Atthill, Lombe, 1827–1910, vol. I
Attlee, 1st Earl, 1883–1967, vol. VI
Attlee, 2nd Earl, 1927–1991, vol. IX
Attlee, Wilfrid Henry Waller, 1876–1962, vol. VI
Attwater, Harry Lawrence, 1885–1961, vol. VI
Attwell, Rt Rev. Arthur Henry, 1920–1991, vol. IX
Attwell, Mabel Lucie, (Mrs Harold Earnshaw), 1879–1964, vol. VI
Attwood, Harold Augustus F.; see Freeman-Attwood.
Attygalle, Sir Nicholas, 1894–1970, vol. VI (AII)
Atukorala, Nandasara Wijetilaka, 1915–1969, vol. VI
Atwater, Albert William, 1856–1929, vol. III
Atwell, Sir John William, 1911–1999, vol. X
Atwood, Clare, 1866–1962, vol. VI
Aubin, Charles Walter Duret, 1894–1972, vol. VII
Auboyneau, Adm. Philippe Marie Joseph Raymond, 1899–1961, vol. VI
Aubrey, Henry Miles W.; see Windsor-Aubrey.
Aubrey, Brig. Herbert Arthur Reginald, 1883–1954, vol. V
Aubrey, John Melbourn, 1921–1996, vol. X
Aubrey, Rev. Melbourn Evans, 1885–1957, vol. V
Aubrey, Sir Stanley James, 1883–1962, vol. VI
Aubrey, William Hickman Smith, 1858–1916, vol. II
Aubrey-Fletcher, Rt Hon. Sir Henry; see Fletcher.
Aubrey-Fletcher, Major Sir Henry Lancelot, 6th Bt, 1887–1969, vol. VI
Aubrey-Fletcher, Sir John Henry Lancelot, 7th Bt, 1912–1992, vol. IX
Aubrey-Fletcher, Sir Lancelot, 5th Bt, 1846–1937, vol. III
Auchinleck, Field-Marshal Sir Claude John Eyre, 1884–1981, vol. VIII
Auchinleck, William Douglas, 1848–1932, vol. III

Auchmuty, James Johnston, 1909–1981, vol. VIII
Auckland, 5th Baron, 1859–1917, vol. II
Auckland, 6th Baron, 1895–1941, vol. IV
Auckland, 7th Baron, 1891–1955, vol. V
Auckland, 8th Baron, 1892–1957, vol. V
Auckland, 9th Baron, 1926–1997, vol. X
Auden, George Augustus, 1872–1957, vol. V
Auden, Henry William, 1867–1940, vol. III
Auden, Rev. Thomas, 1836–1920, vol. II
Auden, Wystan Hugh, 1907–1973, vol. VII
Audette, Hon. Louis Arthur, 1856–1942, vol. IV
Audiffret-Pasquier, Duc d', (Edmé Armand Gaston), 1823–1905, vol. I
Audland, Brig. Edward Gordon, 1896–1976, vol. VII
Audley, Baroness (22nd in line), 1858–1942, vol. IV
Audley, 23rd Baron, 1913–1963, vol. VI
Audley, Baroness (24th in line), 1911–1973, vol. VII
Audley, 25th Baron, 1914–1997, vol. X
Audsley, Matthew Thomas, 1891–1975, vol. VII
Auer, Leopold, 1845–1930, vol. III
Auerbach, Charlotte, 1899–1994, vol. IX
Aufrecht, Theodor, 1821–1907, vol. I
Augagneur, Victor, 1855–1931, vol. III
Auger, Pierre Victor, 1899–1993, vol. IX
Augustine, Fennis Lincoln, 1932–1993, vol. IX
Aulard, Alphonse, 1849–1928, vol. II
Auld, Maj.-Gen. Robert, 1848–1911, vol. I
Auld, Lt-Col Samuel James Manson, 1884–1963, vol. VI
Ault, Norman, 1880–1950, vol. IV
Aumonier, Stacy, 1887–1928, vol. II
Aung, Maung Myat Tun, died 1920, vol. II
Auric, Georges, 1899–1983, vol. VIII
Auriol, Vincent, 1884–1966, vol. VI
Aurobindo, Sri, 1872–1950, vol. IV
Austen, Gen. Sir Alfred Reade G.; see Godwin-Austen.
Austen, Col Arthur Robert, 1860–1939, vol. III
Austen, Major Ernest Edward, 1867–1938, vol. III
Austen, Rev. George, 1839–1933, vol. III
Austen, Harold Cholmley Mansfield, 1878–1975, vol. VII
Austen, Harold William Colmer, 1868–1943, vol. IV
Austen, Henry Haversham G.; see Godwin-Austen.
Austen, Sir William Chandler R.; see Roberts-Austen.
Austen, Winifred Marie Louise, died 1964, vol. VI
Austen-Cartmell, James; see Cartmell.
Austen-Leigh, Rev. Augustus, 1840–1905, vol. I
Austen-Leigh, Charles Edward, 1833–1916, vol. II
Austen-Leigh, Richard Arthur, 1872–1961, vol. VI
Austerberry, Ven. Sidney Denham, 1908–1996, vol. X
Austick, David, 1920–1997, vol. X
Austin, 1st Baron, 1866–1941, vol. IV
Austin, Alfred, 1835–1913, vol. I
Austin, Maj.-Gen. Arthur Bramston, 1893–1967, vol. VI
Austin, Hon. Austin Albert, 1855–1925, vol. II
Austin, Vice-Adm. Sir Francis Murray, 1881–1953, vol. V
Austin, Frederic, 1872–1952, vol. V

Austin, Frederick Britten, 1885–1941, vol. IV
Austin, George Wesley, 1891–1975, vol. VII
Austin, Sir Harold Bruce Gardiner, 1877–1943, vol. IV
Austin, Sir Herbert, 1867–1929, vol. III
Austin, Brig.-Gen. Herbert Henry, 1868–1937, vol. III
Austin, James Valentine, 1850–1914, vol. I
Austin, Sir John, 1st Bt, 1824–1906, vol. I
Austin, Sir John Byron Fraser, 3rd Bt, 1897–1981, vol. VIII
Austin, Brig.-Gen. John Gardiner, died 1956, vol. V
Austin, John Langshaw, 1911–1960, vol. V
Austin, Sir John Worroker, died 1980, vol. VII (AII)
Austin, Lloyd James, 1915–1994, vol. IX
Austin, Mary Hunter, died 1934, vol. III
Austin, Dame (Mary) Valerie (Hall), 1900–1986, vol. VIII
Austin, Michael, 1855–1916, vol. II
Austin, Sir Michael Trescawen, 5th Bt, 1927–1995, vol. IX
Austin, Reginald McPherson, 1887–1950, vol. IV
Austin, Richard, 1903–1989, vol. VIII
Austin, Robert Sargent, 1895–1973, vol. VII
Austin, Roland, 1874–1954, vol. V
Austin, Roland Gregory, 1901–1974, vol. VII
Austin, Sumner Francis, 1888–1981, vol. VIII
Austin, Sir Thomas, 1887–1976, vol. VII
Austin, Thomas Aitken, 1895–1982, vol. VIII
Austin, Dame Valerie; see Austin, Dame M. V. H.
Austin, Warren Robinson, 1877–1962, vol. VI
Austin, Sir William Michael Byron, 2nd Bt, 1871–1940, vol. III
Austin, Sir William Ronald, 4th Bt, 1900–1989, vol. VIII
Austral, Florence, 1894–1968, vol. VI
Auswild, Sir James Frederick John, 1908–1985, vol. VIII
Auten, Captain Harold, died 1964, vol. VI
Auty, Richard Mossop, 1920–1996, vol. X
Auty, Robert, 1914–1978, vol. VII
Ava, Earl of; Archibald James Leofric Temple Blackwood, 1863–1900, vol. I
Avebury, 1st Baron, 1834–1913, vol. I
Avebury, 2nd Baron, 1858–1929, vol. III
Avebury, 3rd Baron, 1915–1971, vol. VII
Aveling, Alan John, 1928–1997, vol. X
Aveling, Arthur Francis, 1893–1954, vol. V
Aveling, Charles, 1873–1959, vol. V
Aveling, Claude, 1869–1943, vol. IV
Aveling, Francis Arthur Powell, 1875–1941, vol. IV
Avenol, Joseph Louis Anne, 1879–1952, vol. V
Averill, Most Rev. Alfred Walter, 1865–1957, vol. V
Averill, Leslie Cecil Lloyd, 1897–1981, vol. VIII
Avery, Charles Harold, 1867–1943, vol. IV
Avery, David Robert, 1921–1983, vol. VIII
Avery, Brig. Henry Esau, 1885–1961, vol. VI
Avery, Major Leonard, died 1953, vol. V
Avery, Percy Leonard, 1915–2000, vol. X
Avery, Thomas, 1862–1940, vol. III
Avery, Sir William Beilby, 1st Bt, 1854–1908, vol. I
Avery, Sir William Eric Thomas, 2nd Bt, 1890–1918, vol. II

Avery Jones, Sir Francis, 1910–1998, vol. X
Aves, Ernest, 1857–1917, vol. II
Aves, Dame Geraldine Maitland, 1898–1986, vol. VIII
Avezathe, Gerald Henry, 1889–1966, vol. VI
Avgherinos, George, 1906–1989, vol. VIII
Avis, John, 1851–1936, vol. III
Avon, 1st Earl of, 1897–1977, vol. VII
Avon, 2nd Earl of, 1930–1985, vol. VIII
Avonmore, 6th Viscount, 1866–1910, vol. I
Avonside, Rt Hon. Lord; Rt Hon. Ian Hamilton Shearer, 1914–1996, vol. X
Avory, Rt Hon. Sir Horace Edmund, 1851–1935, vol. III
Awbery, Stanley Stephen, 1888–1969, vol. VI
Awdry, Rev. Charles Hill, died 1910, vol. I
Awdry, Sir Richard Davis, 1843–1916, vol. II
Awdry, Rev. Wilbert Vere, 1911–1997, vol. X
Awdry, Rt Rev. William, 1842–1910, vol. I
Axford, Surg.-Rear-Adm. Walter Godfrey, 1861–1942, vol. IV
Axon, Sir Albert Edwin, 1898–1974, vol. VII
Axon, William Edward Armytage, 1846–1913, vol. I
Axworthy, Geoffrey John, 1923–1992, vol. IX
Ayala, Ramon Pérez de, 1880–1962, vol. VI
Aydelotte, Frank, 1880–1956, vol. V
Ayer, Sir Alfred Jules, 1910–1989, vol. VIII
Ayers, Charles William, 1880–1965, vol. VI
Ayers, Hon. Sir Henry, 1821–1897, vol. I
Ayers, Herbert Wilfred, 1889–1986, vol. VIII
Ayers, Engineer Captain Robert Bell, 1863–1940, vol. III
Ayerst, Rev. George Haughton, 1863–1931, vol. III
Ayerst, Rev. William, 1830–1904, vol. I
Aykroyd, Sir Aldred Hammond, 2nd Bt (cr 1920), 1894–1965, vol. VI
Aykroyd, Sir Cecil William, 2nd Bt, 1905–1993, vol. IX
Aykroyd, Sir Frederic Alfred, 1st Bt (cr 1929), 1873–1949, vol. IV
Aykroyd, Wallace Ruddell, 1899–1979, vol. VII
Aykroyd, Sir William Henry, 1st Bt (cr 1920), 1865–1947, vol. IV
Aylen, Rt Rev. Charles Arthur William, 1882–1972, vol. VII
Aylen, Helena Constance; see Romanne-James.
Ayles, Rev. Herbert Henry Baker, 1861–1940, vol. III
Ayles, Walter Henry, 1879–1953, vol. V
Aylesford, 8th Earl of, 1851–1924, vol. II
Aylesford, 9th Earl of, 1908–1940, vol. III (A), vol. IV
Aylesford, 10th Earl of, 1886–1958, vol. V
Aylestone, Baron (Life Peer); Herbert William Bowden, 1905–1994, vol. IX
Aylesworth, Hon. Sir Allen Bristol, 1854–1952, vol. V
Ayliff, Henry Kiell, died 1949, vol. IV
Ayling, Air Vice-Marshal Richard Cecil, 1916–1995, vol. IX

Ayling, Sir William Bock, 1867–1946, vol. IV
Aylmer, 7th Baron, 1814–1901, vol. I
Aylmer, 8th Baron, 1842–1923, vol. II
Aylmer, 9th Baron, 1880–1970, vol. VI (AII)
Aylmer, 10th Baron, 1883–1974, vol. VII
Aylmer, 11th Baron, 1886–1977, vol. VII
Aylmer, 12th Baron, 1907–1982, vol. VIII
Aylmer, Sir Arthur Percy Fitzgerald, 12th Bt (cr 1622), 1858–1928, vol. II
Aylmer, Col Edmund Kendal Grimston, 1859–1931, vol. III
Aylmer, Sir Felix, 1889–1979, vol. VII
Aylmer, Sir Fenton Gerald, 15th Bt, 1901–1987, vol. VIII
Aylmer, Lt-Gen. Sir Fenton John, 13th Bt (cr 1622), 1862–1935, vol. III
Aylmer, Sir Gerald (Arthur) Evans-Freke, 14th Bt (cr 1622), 1869–1939, vol. III
Aylmer, Gerald Edward, 1926–2000, vol. X
Aylmer, Gerald Percy Vivian, 1856–1936, vol. III
Aylmer, Rear-Adm. Henry Evans-Freke, 1878–1933, vol. III
Aylmer-Jones, Sir Felix E.; see Aylmer, Sir Felix.
Aylward, Florence, 1862–1950, vol. IV
Aylward, Francis, 1911–1978, vol. VII
Aylwen, Sir George, 1st Bt, 1880–1967, vol. VI
Aynsley, Vice-Adm. Charles Murray, 1821–1901, vol. I
Aynsley, Sir Charles Murray M.; see Murray-Aynsley.
Aynsley, George Ayton, 1896–1981, vol. VIII
Ayoub, John Edward Moussa, 1908–1999, vol. X
Ayre, Sir Amos Lowrey, 1885–1952, vol. V
Ayre, Captain Leslie Charles Edward, 1886–1979, vol. VII
Ayre, Sir Wilfrid, 1890–1971, vol. VII
Ayres, Sir Reginald John, 1900–1966, vol. VI
Ayres, Ruby Mildred, 1883–1955, vol. V
Ayrton, Hertha, died 1923, vol. II
Ayrton, Maxwell; see Ayrton, O.M.
Ayrton, Michael, 1921–1975, vol. VII
Ayrton, (Ormrod) Maxwell, died 1960, vol. V
Ayrton, William Edward, 1847–1908, vol. I
Ayscough, Florence, died 1942, vol. IV
Ayscough, John; see Bickerstaffe-Drew, Rt Rev. Mgr Count F. B. D.
Ayscough, Rev. Thomas Ayscough, 1830–1920, vol. II
Ayson, Hugh Fraser, 1884–1948, vol. IV
Aytoun, Col Andrew, 1860–1945, vol. IV
Ayub Khan, Field-Marshal Mohammad; see Khan, Field-Marshal M. A.
Azariah, Rt Rev. Vedanayakam Samuel, 1874–1945, vol. IV
Azcarate y Florez, Pablo de, 1890–1971, vol. VII
Azikiwe, Rt Hon. Nnamdi, 1904–1996, vol. X
Azizuddin Ahmad, Kazi Sir, 1861–1940, vol. III
Azizul Huque, Khan Bahadur Sir M., 1892–1947, vol. IV
Azopardi, James Frendo, 1866–1938, vol. III
Azopardi, Sir Vincent Frendo, 1865–1919, vol. II

B

Ba, Sir Maung, *died* 1937, vol. III
Baba, Hon. Sir Khem Singh Beda, 1830–1905, vol. I
Babb, S. Nicholson, 1874–1957, vol. V
Babbage, Maj.-Gen. Henry Prevost, 1824–1918, vol. II
Babbitt, Irving, 1865–1933, vol. III
Baber, Edward Cresswell, *died* 1910, vol. I
Baber, Ernest George, 1924–1994, vol. IX
Baber, Lt-Col John Barton, 1892–1967, vol. VI
Baber Shum Shere Jung Bahadur Rana, General, 1888–1960, vol. V
Babington, Rt Hon. Sir Anthony Brutus, 1877–1972, vol. VII
Babington, Col David Melville, 1863–1929, vol. III
Babington, Captain Gervase, 1890–1948, vol. IV
Babington, Lt-Gen. Sir James Melville, 1854–1936, vol. III
Babington, Air Marshal Sir John Tremayne; *see* Tremayne, Air Marshal Sir J. T.
Babington, Air Marshal Sir Philip, 1894–1965, vol. VI
Babington, Very Rev. Richard, 1869–1952, vol. V
Babington, Ven. Richard Hamilton, 1901–1984, vol. VIII
Babington, Col Stafford Charles, 1866–1951, vol. V
Babington, William, 1916–1998, vol. X
Babington Smith, Michael James, 1901–1984, vol. VIII
Babonau, Col Alexander Frederick, 1882–1949, vol. IV
Babtie, Lt-Gen. Sir William, 1859–1920, vol. II
Baby-Casgrain, Hon. Col Hon. Joseph Philippe; *see* Casgrain.
Bacchus, Captain Roy, 1883–1951, vol. V
Bach, Guido R., *died* 1905, vol. I
Bacharach, Alfred Louis, 1891–1966, vol. VI
Bachauer, Gina, (Mrs Alex Sherman), 1913–1976, vol. VII
Bache, Miss Constance, 1846–1903, vol. I
Bacheller, Irving, 1859–1950, vol. IV(A), vol. V
Bacher, William, 1850–1913, vol. I
Back, Ven. Hugh Cairns Alexander, 1863–1928, vol. II
Back, Ivor, *died* 1951, vol. V
Back, Kathleen, (Mrs J. H. Back); *see* Harrison, Kathleen.
Back, Ronald Eric George, 1926–1989, vol. VIII
Backhaus, Wilhelm, 1884–1969, vol. VI
Backhouse, Sir Edmund Trelawny, 2nd Bt, 1873–1944, vol. III
Backhouse, Col Edward Henry Walford, 1895–1973, vol. VII
Backhouse, Major Sir John Edmund, 3rd Bt, 1909–1944, vol. IV
Backhouse, Jonathan, 1907–1993, vol. IX
Backhouse, Sir Jonathan Edmund, 1st Bt, 1849–1918, vol. II
Backhouse, Lt-Col Julius Batt, 1854–1911, vol. I
Backhouse, Lt-Col Miles Roland Charles, 1878–1962, vol. VI

Backhouse, Adm. Oliver, 1876–1943, vol. IV
Backhouse, Adm. of the Fleet Sir Roger Roland Charles, 1878–1939, vol. III
Backhouse, Thomas Mercer, 1903–1955, vol. V
Bacon, Baroness (Life Peer); Alice Martha Bacon, 1909–1993, vol. IX
Bacon, Benjamin Wisner, 1860–1932, vol. III
Bacon, Sir Edmund Castell, 13th Bt, 1903–1982, vol. VIII
Bacon, Sir Edward Denny, 1860–1938, vol. III
Bacon, Edwin Munroe, 1844–1916, vol. II
Bacon, Francis, 1909–1992, vol. IX
Bacon, Francis Thomas, 1904–1992, vol. IX
Bacon, Frederic, 1880–1943, vol. IV
Bacon, Frederick Joseph, 1853–1929, vol. III
Bacon, Gertrude, (Mrs T. J. Foggitt), 1874–1949, vol. IV
Bacon, Sir Hickman Beckett, 11th Bt, 1855–1945, vol. IV
Bacon, Janet Ruth, 1891–1965, vol. VI
Bacon, John Henry Frederick, 1865–1914, vol. I
Bacon, John Mackenzie, 1846–1904, vol. I
Bacon, Sir Nicholas Henry, 12th Bt, 1857–1947, vol. IV
Bacon, Sir Ranulph Robert Maunsell, 1906–1988, vol. VIII
Bacon, Adm. Sir Reginald Hugh Spencer, 1863–1947, vol. IV
Bacon, Sir Roger Sewell, 1895–1962, vol. VI
Bacon, Comdr Sidney Kendrick, 1871–1950, vol. IV
Bacot, Arthur William, 1866–1922, vol. II
Badcock, Gen. Sir Alexander Robert, 1844–1907, vol. I
Badcock, Brig.-Gen. Francis Frederick, 1867–1926, vol. II
Badcock, Brig. Gerald Eliot, 1883–1966, vol. VI
Badcock, Isaac, 1842–1906, vol. I
Badcock, Jasper Capper, 1840–1924, vol. II
Badcock, Paymaster Captain Kenneth Edgar, 1886–1947, vol. IV
Baddeley, Angela; *see* Clinton-Baddeley, M. A.
Baddeley, Col Charles Edward, 1861–1923, vol. II
Baddeley, Sir Frank Morrish, 1874–1966, vol. VI
Baddeley, Hermione, 1908–1986, vol. VIII
Baddeley, Sir John Beresford, 3rd Bt, 1899–1979, vol. VII
Baddeley, John Halkett, 1920–1972, vol. VII
Baddeley, Sir John James, 1st Bt, 1842–1926, vol. II
Baddeley, Hon. John Marcus, 1881–1953, vol. V
Baddeley, Sir (John) William, 2nd Bt, 1869–1951, vol. V
Baddeley, Sir Vincent Wilberforce, 1874–1961, vol. VI
Baddeley, Sir William; *see* Baddeley, Sir J. W.
Baddeley, Very Rev. William Pye, 1914–1998, vol. X
Badè, William Frederic, 1871–1936, vol. III
Badel, Alan, 1923–1982, vol. VIII
Badeley, 1st Baron, 1874–1951, vol. V
Badeley, Rt Rev. Walter Hubert, 1894–1960, vol. V
Baden-Powell, 1st Baron, 1857–1941, vol. IV

Baden-Powell, 2nd Baron, 1913–1962, vol. VI
Baden-Powell, Lady; (Olave St Clair), 1889–1977, vol. VII
Baden-Powell, Agnes, 1858–1945, vol. IV
Baden-Powell, Major Baden Fletcher Smyth, 1860–1937, vol. III
Baden-Powell, Baden Henry, 1841–1901, vol. I
Baden-Powell, Frank Smyth, 1850–1933, vol. III
Baden-Powell, Sir George Smyth, 1847–1898, vol. I
Baden-Powell, (Henry) Warington (Smyth), 1847–1921, vol. II
Baden-Powell, Warington; see Baden-Powell, H. W. S.
Badenoch, Alec William, 1903–1991, vol. IX
Badenoch, Sir (Alexander) Cameron, 1889–1973, vol. VII
Badenoch, Sir Cameron; see Badenoch, Sir A. C.
Badenoch, Rev. George Roy, 1830–1912, vol. I
Badenoch, Sir John, 1920–1996, vol. X
Bader, Group Captain Sir Douglas Robert Steuart, 1910–1982, vol. VIII
Bader, Hubert Eugène, 1902–1936, vol. III
Badger, Rev. Canon George Edwin, 1868–1948, vol. IV
Badgerow, Sir George W., 1872–1937, vol. III
Badham, Edward Leslie, died 1944, vol. IV
Badham, Leonard, 1923–1992, vol. IX
Badham, Rev. Leslie Stephen Ronald, 1908–1975, vol. VII
Badham-Thornhill, Col George, 1876–1958, vol. V
Badley, John Haden, 1865–1967, vol. VI
Badmin, Stanley Roy, 1906–1989, vol. VIII
Badock, Sir Stanley Hugh, 1867–1945, vol. IV
Badock, Sir Walter, 1854–1931, vol. III
Baekeland, Leo Hendrik, 1863–1944, vol. IV
Baelz, Very Rev. Peter Richard, 1923–2000, vol. X
Baerlein, Edgar Max, 1879–1971, vol. VII
Baerlein, Henry, 1875–1960, vol. V, vol. VI
Baerlein, Richard Edgar, 1915–1995, vol. IX
Bagchi, Satischandra, 1882–1939, vol. III(A), vol. IV
Bagenal, Hope; see Bagenal, P. H. E.
Bagenal, (Philip) Hope (Edward), 1888–1979, vol. VII
Baggaley, Ernest James, 1900–1978, vol. VII
Baggallay, Claude, 1853–1906, vol. I
Baggallay, Ernest, 1850–1931, vol. III
Baggallay, Rev. Frederick, 1855–1928, vol. II
Baggallay, Lt-Col Richard Romer Claude, 1884–1975, vol. VII
Bagge, Sir Alfred Thomas, 3rd Bt, 1843–1916, vol. II
Bagge, Sir Alfred William Francis, 4th Bt, 1875–1939, vol. III
Bagge, Sir John Alfred Picton, 6th Bt, 1914–1990, vol. VIII
Bagge, Sir (John) Picton, 5th Bt, 1877–1967, vol. VI
Bagge, Sir Picton; see Bagge, Sir J. P.
Bagge, Major Sir Richard Ludwig, 1872–1933, vol. III
Bagge, Stephen Salisbury, 1859–1950, vol. IV
Baggley, Charles David Aubrey, 1923–1999, vol. X
Baggott, Ven. Louis John, 1891–1965, vol. VI
Baghot de la Bere, Stephen, 1877–1927, vol. II
Bagley, Desmond Simon, 1923–1983, vol. VIII

Bagley, Edward Albert Ashton, 1876–1961, vol. VI
Bagnall, Hon. Sir Arthur; see Bagnall, Hon. Sir W. A.
Bagnall, Colin; see Bagnall, F. C.
Bagnall, Frank Colin, 1909–1989, vol. VIII
Bagnall, Sir John, 1888–1954, vol. V
Bagnall, Richard Maurice, 1917–1997, vol. X
Bagnall, Rt Rev. Walter Edward, 1903–1984, vol. VIII
Bagnall, Hon. Sir (William) Arthur, 1917–1976, vol. VII
Bagnall-Wild, Ralph Bagnall, 1845–1925, vol. II
Bagnall-Wild, Brig.-Gen. Ralph Kirkby, 1873–1953, vol. V
Bagnold, Col Arthur Henry, 1854–1943, vol. IV
Bagnold, Enid, (Lady Jones), 1889–1981, vol. VIII
Bagnold, Brig. Ralph Alger, 1896–1990, vol. VIII
Bagot, 4th Baron, 1857–1932, vol. III
Bagot, 5th Baron, 1866–1946, vol. IV
Bagot, 6th Baron, 1877–1961, vol. VI
Bagot, 7th Baron, 1894–1973, vol. VII
Bagot, 8th Baron, 1897–1979, vol. VII
Bagot, Sir Alan Desmond, 1st Bt, 1896–1920, vol. II
Bagot, Col Charles Hervey, 1847–1911, vol. I
Bagot, Sir Charles Samuel, 1828–1906, vol. I
Bagot, (Sir) Josceline FitzRoy (1st Bt, but died before the passing under the Great Seal of the Patent of Baronetage), 1854–1913, vol. I
Bagot, Richard, 1860–1921, vol. II
Bagot, Theodosia, (Lady Bagot), 1865–1940, vol. III
Bagot, Major Hon. Walter Lewis, 1864–1927, vol. II
Bagot-Chester, Col Heneage Charles, 1836–1912, vol. I
Bagrit, Sir Leon, 1902–1979, vol. VII
Bagshawe, Arthur Clement, 1874–1937, vol. III
Bagshawe, Sir Arthur William Garrard, 1871–1950, vol. IV
Bagshawe, Most Rev. Edward Gilpin, 1829–1915, vol. I
Bagshawe, Edward Leonard, 1876–1955, vol. V
Bagshawe, Francis John Edward, 1877–1953, vol. V
Bagshawe, Col Frederick William, 1868–1945, vol. IV
Bagshawe, Lt-Col Herbert Vale, 1874–1962, vol. VI
Bagshawe, Thomas Wyatt, 1901–1976, vol. VII
Bagshawe, William Henry Gunning, 1825–1901, vol. I
Bagster, Robert, 1847–1924, vol. II
Baguley, Sir John Minty, 1880–1964, vol. VI
Bagwell, John, 1874–1946, vol. IV
Bagwell, Lt-Col John, 1884–1949, vol. IV
Bagwell, Richard, 1840–1918, vol. II
Bahadur Shamsher Jang Bahadur Rana, Commanding-General, 1892–1977, vol. VII
Bahauddin Khan, Resaldar Major, 1833–1901, vol. I
Bahawalpur, Ameer of, 1904–1966, vol. VI
Bahawalpur, Nawab of, 1883–1907, vol. I
Bahr, Sir Philip M; see Manson-Bahr.
Bahrain, Ruler of; HH Shaikh Sir Hamed bin Isa Al Khalifah, 1874–1942, vol. IV
Bahrain, Ruler of, HH Shaikh Sulman bin Hamad Al Khalifah, died 1961, vol. VI

Baig, Mirza Sir Abbas Ali, *died* 1932, vol. III
Baigent, Rt Rev. Mgr William Joseph, 1857–1930, vol. III
Baikie, Alfred, 1861–1947, vol. IV
Bailkie, Brig.-Gen. Sir Hugh Archie Dundas Simpson-, 1871–1924, vol. II
Baikie, Rev. James, 1866–1931, vol. III
Baildon, Henry Bellyse, *died* 1907, vol. I
Bailey, Sir Abe, 1st Bt, 1864–1940, vol. III
Bailey, Col Alfred John, 1867–1940, vol. III
Bailey, Arnold Savage, 1881–1935, vol. III
Bailey, Arthur, 1903–1979, vol. VII
Bailey, Arthur Charles John, 1886–1951, vol. V
Bailey, Captain Arthur Harold, 1873–1925, vol. II
Bailey, Charles Thomas Peach, 1882–1968, vol. VI
Bailey, Cyril, 1871–1957, vol. V
Bailey, Rev. (Derrick) Sherwin, 1910–1984, vol. VIII
Bailey, Desmond Patrick, 1907–1996, vol. X
Bailey, Sir Donald Coleman, 1901–1985, vol. VIII
Bailey, Lt-Col Edmund Wyndham-Grevis, 1858–1920, vol. II
Bailey, Sir Edward Battersby, 1881–1965, vol. VI
Bailey, Eric, 1913–1997, vol. X
Bailey, Ernest Edmond, 1907–1956, vol. V
Bailey, Fiona Mary; *see* Macpherson, F. M.
Bailey, Lt-Col Francis William, 1871–1932, vol. III
Bailey, Lt-Col Frederick George Glyn, 1880–1951, vol. V
Bailey, Frederick Manson, 1827–1915, vol. I
Bailey, Lt-Col Frederick Marshman, 1882–1967, vol. VI
Bailey, George Buchanan, 1898–1969, vol. VI
Bailey, Air Cdre George Cyril, 1890–1972, vol. VII
Bailey, Sir George Edwin, 1879–1965, vol. VI
Bailey, Sir George Leader, 1882–1953, vol. V
Bailey, George Leo, 1901–1979, vol. VII
Bailey, Gertrude Mary, 1870–1941, vol. IV
Bailey, Hamilton, 1894–1961, vol. VI
Bailey, Harold, 1914–1995, vol. IX
Bailey, Sir Harold Walter, 1899–1996, vol. X
Bailey, Rev. Henry, 1815–1906, vol. I
Bailey, Henry Christopher, 1878–1961, vol. VI
Bailey, Hon. Herbert Crawshay, *died* 1936, vol. III
Bailey, Horace Thomas, 1852–1945, vol. IV
Bailey, Miss (Irene) Temple, *died* 1953, vol. V
Bailey, Sir James, 1840–1910, vol. I
Bailey, James Vincent, 1908–1984, vol. VIII
Bailey, John, 1889–1957, vol. V
Bailey, Sir John, 1898–1969, vol. VI
Bailey, John Cann, 1864–1931, vol. III
Bailey, John E., 1897–1958, vol. V
Bailey, John Everett Creighton, 1905–2000, vol. X
Bailey, John Frederick, 1866–1938, vol. III
Bailey, Rev. J(ohn) H(enry) Shackleton, 1875–1956, vol. V
Bailey, Sir John Milner, 2nd Bt, 1900–1946, vol. IV
Bailey, John Walter, 1845–1930, vol. III
Bailey, Kenneth, 1909–1963, vol. VI
Bailey, Kenneth Claude, 1896–1951, vol. V
Bailey, Sir Kenneth Hamilton, 1898–1972, vol. VII
Bailey, Liberty Hyde, 1858–1954, vol. V
Bailey, Lionel Danyers, 1879–1967, vol. VI
Bailey, Philip James, 1816–1902, vol. I
Bailey, Reginald Bertram, 1916–1999, vol. X

Bailey, Sir Reginald Greenwood, 1894–1953, vol. V
Bailey, Richard William, 1885–1957, vol. V
Bailey, Sir Rowland, 1852–1930, vol. III
Bailey, Sidney Alfred, 1886–1972, vol. VII
Bailey, Rev. Sherwin; *see* Bailey, Rev. D. S.
Bailey, Adm. Sir Sidney Robert, 1882–1942, vol. IV
Bailey, Stanley John, 1901–1980, vol. VII
Bailey, Miss Temple; *see* Bailey, I. T.
Bailey, Victor Albert, 1895–1964, vol. VI
Bailey, Hon. Brig.-Gen. Vivian Telford, 1868–1938, vol. III
Bailey, Walter M.; *see* Milne-Bailey.
Bailey, Wilfrid, 1910–1993, vol. IX
Bailey, Wilfrid Norman, 1893–1961, vol. VI
Bailey, Rt Hon. William Frederick, 1857–1917, vol. II
Bailey, Sir William Henry, 1838–1913, vol. I
Bailey, William Henry, *born* 1855, vol. II
Bailey, Sir William Thomas, 1873–1949, vol. IV
Bailhache, Sir Clement Meacher, 1856–1924, vol. II
Bailie, Thomas, 1885–1957, vol. V
Bailie, Maj.-Gen. Thomas Maubourg, 1844–1918, vol. II
Baillet-Latour, Comte de; Henry, 1876–1942, vol. IV
Baillie, Sir Adrian William Maxwell, 6th Bt, 1898–1947, vol. IV
Baillie, Rev. Albert Victor, 1864–1955, vol. V
Baillie, Col Augustus Charles, 1861–1939, vol. III
Baillie, Rev. Donald Macpherson, 1887–1954, vol. V
Baillie, Sir Duncan Colvin, 1856–1919, vol. II
Baillie, Col Duncan Gus, 1872–1968, vol. VI
Baillie, Hon. Evan; *see* Baillie, Hon. G. E. M.
Baillie, Sir Frank, 1875–1921, vol. II
Baillie, Lt-Col Frederick David M.; *see* Murray Baillie.
Baillie, Sir Gawaine George Stuart, 5th Bt, 1893–1914, vol. I
Baillie, Hon. (George) Evan (Michael), 1894–1941, vol. IV
Baillie, George Henry, 1901–1970, vol. VI(AII)
Baillie, Col Hugh Frederick, 1879–1941, vol. IV
Baillie, Dame Isobel, 1895–1983, vol. VIII
Baillie, Sir James Black, 1872–1940, vol. III
Baillie, Gen. James Cadogan Parkison, 1835–1928, vol. II
Baillie, James Evan Bruce, 1859–1931, vol. III
Baillie, Very Rev. John, 1886–1960, vol. V
Baillie, John Gilroy, 1896–1960, vol. V
Baillie, John Strachan, 1896–1989, vol. VIII
Baillie, Lady Maud Louisa Emma, 1896–1975, vol. VII
Baillie, Sir Robert Alexander, 4th Bt, 1859–1907, vol. I
Baillie, Ronald Hugh, 1863–1948, vol. IV
Baillie-Gage, Thomas Robert; *see* Gage.
Baillie-Grohman, Vice-Adm. Harold Tom, 1888–1978, vol. VII
Baillie-Grohman, William A., 1851–1921, vol. II(A)
Baillie-Hamilton, Hon. Charles William, 1900–1939, vol. III
Baillie-Hamilton, Sir William Alexander, 1844–1920, vol. II
Baillie Reynolds, Paul Kenneth; *see* Reynolds.

34

Baillie-Saunders, Margaret, 1873–1949, vol. IV
Baillieu, 1st Baron, 1889–1967, vol. VI
Baillieu, 2nd Baron, 1915–1973, vol. VII
Baillon, Maj.-Gen. Joseph Aloysius, 1895–1951, vol. V
Baily, Francis Evans, *died* 1962, vol. VI
Baily, Francis Gibson, 1868–1945, vol. IV
Baily, J. T. Herbert, 1865–1914, vol. I
Baily, Rev. Johnson, 1835–1915, vol. I
Baily, Leslie, 1906–1976, vol. VII
Baily, Robert Edward Hartwell, 1885–1973, vol. VII
Bain, Sir (Albert) Ernest, 1875–1939, vol. III
Bain, Alexander, 1818–1903, vol. I
Bain, Cyril William Curtis, 1895–1987, vol. VIII
Bain, David, 1855–1933, vol. III
Bain, Donald Charles, 1913–1964, vol. VI
Bain, Sir Ernest; *see* Bain, Sir A. E.
Bain, Francis William, 1863–1940, vol. III
Bain, Sir Frederick, 1889–1950, vol. IV
Bain, Sir James, 1817–1898, vol. I
Bain, James Robert, 1851–1913, vol. I
Bain, Kenneth Bruce Findlater; *see* Findlater, Richard.
Bain, Robert Nisbet, 1854–1909, vol. I
Bain, William Alexander, 1905–1971, vol. VII
Bain-Marais, Colin, 1893–1942, vol. IV
Bainbridge, Col Sir Edmond, 1841–1911, vol. I
Bainbridge, Maj.-Gen. Sir (Edmund) Guy (Tulloch), 1867–1943, vol. IV
Bainbridge, Emerson, 1845–1911, vol. I
Bainbridge, Francis Arthur, 1874–1921, vol. II
Bainbridge, Maj.-Gen. Frederick Thomas, 1834–1915, vol. I
Bainbridge, Maj.-Gen. Sir Guy; *see* Bainbridge, Maj.-Gen. Sir E. G. T.
Bainbridge, Maj.-Gen. Henry, 1903–1993, vol. IX
Bainbridge, Herbert William, 1862–1940, vol. III
Bainbridge, Rev. Howard Gurney D.; *see* Daniell-Bainbridge.
Bainbridge, Rear-Adm. John Hugh, 1845–1901, vol. I
Bainbridge, Col Norman Bruce, 1869–1935, vol. III
Bainbridge, Brig.-Gen. Percy Agnew, 1864–1934, vol. III
Bainbridge, Brig.-Gen. William Frank, 1873–1953, vol. V
Bainbrigge, Rev. Philip Thomas, *died* 1919, vol. II
Baines, Ven. Albert, *died* 1951, vol. V
Baines, Anthony Cuthbert, 1912–1997, vol. X
Baines, Sir Frank, 1877–1933, vol. III
Baines, Frederick Ebenezer, 1832–1911, vol. I
Baines, Rt Rev. Frederick Samuel, *died* 1939, vol. III
Baines, Rt Rev. Henry Wolfe, 1905–1972, vol. VII
Baines, Hubert, 1874–1953, vol. V
Baines, Lt-Col J. C., 1876–1928, vol. II
Baines, Sir Jervoise Athelstane, 1847–1925, vol. II
Baines, Matthew Talbot, 1863–1925, vol. II
Baines, William, 1899–1922, vol. II
Baines, William Henry, 1879–1958, vol. V
Bainton, Edgar Leslie, 1880–1956, vol. V
Bairamian, Sir Vahé Robert, 1900–1984, vol. VIII
Baird, Sir Alexander, 1st Bt (*cr* 1897), 1849–1920, vol. II

Baird, Brig.-Gen. Alexander Walter Frederic, 1876–1931, vol. III
Baird, Rev. Andrew Cumming, 1883–1940, vol. III
Baird, Col Andrew Wilson, 1842–1908, vol. I
Baird, Sir David, 3rd Bt (*cr* 1809), 1832–1913, vol. I
Baird, Sir David, 4th Bt (*cr* 1809), 1865–1941, vol. IV
Baird, Sir David Charles, 5th Bt, 1912–2000, vol. X
Baird, Gen. Sir Douglas; *see* Baird, Gen. Sir H. B. D.
Baird, Douglas H., *died* 1940, vol. III
Baird, Sir Dugald, 1899–1986, vol. VIII
Baird, Edith Elina Helen, *died* 1924, vol. II
Baird, Brig.-Gen. Edward William David, 1864–1956, vol. V
Baird, Rear-Adm. Sir George Henry, 1871–1924, vol. II
Baird, Hon. George Thomas, 1847–1917, vol. II
Baird, Gen. Sir (Harry Beauchamp) Douglas, 1877–1963, vol. VI
Baird, James Craig, 1906–1973, vol. VII
Baird, Sir James Hozier Gardiner, 9th Bt (*cr* 1695), 1883–1966, vol. VI
Baird, Sir James Richard Gardiner, 10th Bt, 1913–1997, vol. X
Baird, John, 1906–1965, vol. VI
Baird, John George Alexander, 1854–1917, vol. II
Baird, Sir John Kennedy Erskine, 1832–1908, vol. I
Baird, John L., 1888–1946, vol. IV
Baird, May Deans, (Lady Baird), 1901–1983, vol. VIII
Baird, Percy Johnstone, 1877–1956, vol. V
Baird, Sir Robert Hugh Hanley, 1855–1934, vol. III
Baird, Ronald, 1930–1999, vol. X
Baird, Thomas Terence, 1916–1996, vol. X
Baird, William, 1848–1918, vol. II
Baird, Major Sir William, 1874–1956, vol. V
Baird, William Arthur, 1879–1933, vol. III
Baird, William George, 1889–1975, vol. VII
Baird, William James, 1893–1961, vol. VI
Baird, Sir William James Gardiner, 8th Bt (*cr* 1695), 1854–1921, vol. II
Baird, Sir William MacDonald, 1881–1946, vol. IV
Baird-Smith, David, *died* 1951, vol. V
Bairnsfather, Captain Bruce, 1888–1959, vol. V
Bairnsfather, Captain George Edward Beckwith, 1855–1945, vol. IV
Bairstow, Arthur William, 1855–1943, vol. IV
Bairstow, Sir Edward C., 1874–1946, vol. IV
Bairstow, Sir Leonard, 1880–1963, vol. VI
Bajpai, Sir Girja Shankar, 1891–1954, vol. V
Bajpai, Sir Seetla Prasad, Rai Bahadur, 1865–1947, vol. IV
Baker, Baron (Life Peer); John Fleetwood Baker, 1901–1985, vol. VIII
Baker, Rev. Albert Edward, 1884–1962, vol. VI
Baker, Alexander Shelley, 1915–1992, vol. IX
Baker, Alfred, *died* 1942, vol. IV
Baker, Sir Alfred, 1870–1943, vol. IV
Baker, Alfred Thomas, 1873–1936, vol. III
Baker, Alfreda Helen, 1897–1984, vol. VIII
Baker, Mrs Alice, *died* 1935, vol. III
Baker, Allan; *see* Baker, J. F. A.
Baker, Sir (Allan) Ivor, 1908–1994, vol. IX

Baker, Alma; *see* Baker, C. A.
Baker, Andrew Clement, 1842–1913, vol. I
Baker, Arthur, 1861–1939, vol. III
Baker, Major Arthur Brander, 1868–1918, vol. II
Baker, Arthur Harold, 1890–1962, vol. VI
Baker, Arthur Lemprière Lancey, 1905–1986, vol. VIII
Baker, Brig.-Gen. Arthur Slade, 1863–1943, vol. IV
Baker, Sir Augustine FitzGerald, 1851–1922, vol. II
Baker, Sir Benjamin, 1840–1907, vol. I
Baker, Lt-Col (Bernard) Granville, 1870–1957, vol. V
Baker, Bevan Braithwaite B.; *see* Bevan-Baker.
Baker, Bill; *see* Baker, W. H. K.
Baker, Air Marshal Sir Brian Edmund, 1896–1979, vol. VII
Baker, Bryant, 1881–1970, vol. VI
Baker, Vice-Adm. Casper Joseph, 1852–1918, vol. II
Baker, Col Cecil Norris, 1869–1934, vol. III
Baker, Charles, 1851–1934, vol. III
Baker, (Charles) Alma, 1857–1941, vol. IV
Baker, Charles Ernest S.; *see* Smalley-Baker.
Baker, Charles Gaffney, 1907–1969, vol. VI
Baker, Charles Henry Collins, 1880–1959, vol. V
Baker, Charles Maurice, 1872–1952, vol. V
Baker, Colin Lewis Gilbert, 1913–1982, vol. VIII
Baker, Lt-Col Sir Dodington George Richard S.; *see* Sherston-Baker.
Baker, Rt Rev. Donald, 1882–1968, vol. VI
Baker, Doris Manning, *died* 1971, vol. VII
Baker, Edmund Wilfrid, 1869–1953, vol. V
Baker, Edward Charles Stuart, 1864–1944, vol. IV
Baker, Lt-Col Edward Mervyn, 1875–1925, vol. II
Baker, Rev. Edward Morgan, 1874–1940, vol. III
Baker, Sir Edward Norman, 1857–1913, vol. I
Baker, Major Edwin Godfrey Phipps, 1885–1963, vol. VI
Baker, Rev. Eric Wilfred, 1899–1973, vol. VII
Baker, Ernest A., 1869–1941, vol. IV
Baker, Brig. Euston Edward Francis, 1895–1981, vol. VIII
Baker, Flora May, 1882–1949, vol. IV
Baker, Francis Douglas, 1884–1958, vol. V
Baker, Frederick Grenfell, *died* 1930, vol. III
Baker, Sir Frederick Spencer Arnold, 1885–1963, vol. VI
Baker, Field-Marshal Sir Geoffrey Harding, 1912–1980, vol. VII
Baker, Geoffrey Hunter, 1916–1999, vol. X
Baker, Col George, 1840–1910, vol. I
Baker, George Arthur, 1885–1976, vol. VII
Baker, Hon. George Barnard, 1834–1910, vol. I
Baker, Air Vice-Marshal George Brindley Aufrere, 1894–1968, vol. VI
Baker, George Edwin, 1876–1960, vol. V
Baker, George Fisher, 1840–1931, vol. III
Baker, Rt Hon. Sir George Gillespie, 1910–1984, vol. VIII
Baker, George Philip, 1879–1951, vol. V
Baker, Sir George Sherston, 4th Bt (*cr* 1796), 1846–1923, vol. II
Baker, George William, 1917–1996, vol. X
Baker, Lt-Col Granville; *see* Baker, Lt-Col B. G.
Baker, Granville Edwin Lloyd L.; *see* Lloyd-Baker.

Baker, Rt Hon. Harold Trevor, 1877–1960, vol. V
Baker, Henry, 1893–1975, vol. VII
Baker, Henry Frederick, *died* 1956, vol. V
Baker, Hon. Sir Henry Seymour, 1890–1968, vol. VI
Baker, Henry William Clinton-; *see* Clinton-Baker.
Baker, H(enry) Wright, 1893–1969, vol. VI
Baker, Sir Herbert, 1862–1946, vol. IV
Baker, Herbert Arthur, 1875–1946, vol. IV
Baker, Herbert Brereton, 1862–1935, vol. III
Baker, Sir Humphrey Dodington Benedict S.; *see* Sherston-Baker.
Baker, Sir Ivor; *see* Baker, Sir A. I.
Baker, J. Percy, 1859–1930, vol. III
Baker, Sir Jack Croft, 1894–1962, vol. VI
Baker, James, 1847–1920, vol. II
Baker, Adm. Sir Lewis C.; *see* Clinton-Baker.
Baker, James H., 1848–1925, vol. II
Baker, Lt-Gen. James Mitchell, 1878–1956, vol. V
Baker, Maj.-Gen. Jasper, 1877–1964, vol. VI
Baker, Joanna Constance, (Mrs Noel Baker); *see* Scott-Moncrieff, J. C.
Baker, Sir John, 1828–1909, vol. I
Baker, Sir John, 1861–1939, vol. III
Baker, John, 1867–1939, vol. III
Baker, John Alfred, 1882–1957, vol. V
Baker, John B.; *see* Brayne-Baker.
Baker, John Burkett, 1931–1997, vol. X
Baker, (John Frederic) Allan, 1903–1987, vol. VIII
Baker, John Gilbert, 1834–1920, vol. II
Baker, Rt Rev. John Gilbert Hindley, 1910–1986, vol. VIII
Baker, Ven. John Percy, 1871–1947, vol. IV
Baker, John Randal, 1900–1984, vol. VIII
Baker, Air Chief Marshal Sir John Wakeling, 1897–1978, vol. VII
Baker, Sir Joseph; *see* Baker, Sir S. J.
Baker, Joseph Allen, 1852–1918, vol. II
Baker, Julian Levett, 1873–1958, vol. V
Baker, Lawrence James, 1827–1921, vol. II
Baker, Adm. Sir Lewis C.; *see* Clinton-Baker.
Baker, Maurice Sidney, 1911–1998, vol. X
Baker, Newton Diehl, 1871–1937, vol. III
Baker, Sir Nicholas Brian, 1938–1997, vol. X
Baker, Olive Katherine Lloyd L.; *see* Lloyd-Baker.
Baker, Oliver, 1856–1939, vol. III
Baker, Percy M., 1872–1935, vol. III
Baker, Peter Frederick, 1939–1987, vol. VIII
Baker, Lt-Col Sir Randolf Littlehales, 4th Bt (*cr* 1802), 1879–1959, vol. V
Baker, Ray Stannard, 1870–1946, vol. IV
Baker, Reginald George Gillam, 1887–1971, vol. VII
Baker, Reginald Tustin, 1900–1966, vol. VI
Baker, Hon. Sir Richard Chaffey, 1842–1911, vol. I
Baker, Richard St Barbe, 1889–1982, vol. VIII
Baker, Richard Thomas, 1854–1941, vol. VI
Baker, Major Robert Joseph, 1857–1931, vol. III
Baker, Sir Rowland, 1908–1983, vol. VIII
Baker, Sir (Stanislaus) Joseph, 1898–1989, vol. VIII
Baker, Rev. Stanley, 1868–1950, vol. IV
Baker, Sir Stanley, 1928–1976, vol. VII
Baker, Stephen Leonard, 1888–1978, vol. VII
Baker, Rev. Sir Talbot Hastings Bendall, 3rd Bt (*cr* 1802), 1820–1900, vol. I

Baker, Sir Thomas, *died* 1926, vol. II
Baker, Verg Rev. Thomas George Adames, 1920–2000, vol. X
Baker, Col Thomas MacDonald, 1894–1976, vol. VII
Baker, Lt-Gen. Thomas Norris, 1833–1915, vol. I
Baker, Walter John, 1876–1930, vol. III
Baker, Walter Reginals, 1852–1929, vol. III
Baker, Will C., vol. III
Baker, Willfred Harold Kerton, (Bill), 1920–2000, vol. X
Baker, Rev. William, 1841–1910, vol. I
Baker, William, 1849–1920, vol. II
Baker, Ven. William Arthur, 1870–1950, vol. IV
Baker, Sir William Frederick, 1844–1929, vol. III
Baker, Ven. William George, *died* 1923, vol. II
Baker, Adm. William Henry Baker, 1862–1932, vol. III
Baker, Lt-Gen. Sir William Henry Goldney, 1888–1964, vol. VI
Baker, Rev. William James Furneaux Vashon, 1851–1932, vol. III
Baker, Rt Rev. William Scott, 1902–1990, vol. VIII
Baker, Sir William Thomas Webb, 1873–1948, vol. IV
Baker, Rev. William Wing Carew, 1860–1930, vol. III
Baker-Carr, Brig.-Gen. Christopher D'Arcy Bloomfield Saltern, 1878–1949, vol. IV
Baker-Carr, Air Marshal Sir John Darcy, 1906–1998, vol. X
Baker-Carr, Major Robert George Teesdale, 1867–1931, vol. III
Baker-Wilbraham, Sir George Barrington; *see* Wilbraham.
Baker-Wilbraham, Sir Philip Wilbraham; *see* Wilbraham.
Baker Wilbraham, Sir Randle John; *see* Wilbraham.
Bakewell, James Herbert, *died* 1931, vol. III
Bakewell, Robert Donald, 1899–1982, vol. VIII
Bakker, Cornelis Jan, 1904–1960, vol. V
Bakst, Léon, 1868–1924, vol. II
Balanchine, George Melitonovitch, 1904–1983, vol. VIII
Balasinor, Nawab of, 1894–1945, vol. IV
Balbo, Maresciallo dell'Aria Italo, 1896–1940, vol. III
Balch, Emily Greene, 1867–1961, vol. VI
Balchin, Brig. Nigel Marlin, 1908–1970, vol. VI
Balcombe, Rt Hon. Sir (Alfred) John, 1925–2000, vol. X
Balcombe, Frederick James, 1911–2000, vol. X
Balcombe, Rt Hon. Sir John; *see* Balcombe, Rt Hon. Sir A. J.
Balcon, Sir Michael, 1896–1977, vol. VII
Bald, Major Alfred Campbell, *died* 1905, vol. I
Bald, Lt-Col John Arthur, 1876–1960, vol. V
Bald, Robert Cecil, 1901–1965, vol. VI
Balderston, John Lloyd, 1889–1954 vol. V
Baldock, Maj.-Gen. Thomas Stanford, 1854–1937, vol. III
Baldock, William, 1850–1933, vol. III
Baldrey, Lt-Col Frank Shelson Headon, 1869–1935, vol. III
Baldry, Alfred Lys, 1858–1939, vol. III

Baldry, Harold Caparne, 1907–1991, vol. IX
Baldry, Walter Burton Burton-; *see* Burton-Baldry.
Baldwin of Bewdley, 1st Earl, 1867–1947, vol. IV
Baldwin of Bewdley, 2nd Earl, 1899–1958, vol. V
Baldwin of Bewdley, 3rd Earl, 1904–1976, vol. VII
Baldwin, Sir Archer Ernest, 1883–1966, vol. VI
Baldwin, Rev. Edward Curtis, 1844–1941, vol. IV
Baldwin, Ernest Hubert Francis, 1909–1969, vol. VI
Baldwin, Engr-Rear-Adm. George William, 1871–1955, vol. V
Baldwin, Brig.-Gen. Guy Melfort, 1865–1945, vol. IV
Baldwin, Sir Harry, 1862–1931, vol. III
Baldwin, James Arthur, 1924–1987, vol. VIII
Baldwin, James Mark, 1861–1934, vol. III
Baldwin, Air Marshal Sir John Eustace Arthur, 1892–1975, vol. VII
Baldwin, Lt-Col Sir John Grey, 1867–1939, vol. III
Baldwin, John Herbert Lacy, 1863–1945, vol. IV
Baldwin, Joseph Mason, 1878–1945, vol. IV
Baldwin, Nelson Mills, 1923–1980, vol. VII
Baldwin, Hon. Simeon Eben, 1840–1927, vol. II
Baldwin-Webb, Col James, *died* 1940, vol. III
Bale, Edwin, 1838–1923, vol. II
Bale, Hon. Sir Henry, 1854–1910, vol. I
Balerno, Baron (Life Peer); Alick Drummond Buchanan-Smith, 1898–1984, vol. VIII
Balewa, Alhaji Rt Hon. Sir Abubakar T.; *see* Tafawa Balewa.
Balfour, 1st Earl of, 1848–1930, vol. III
Balfour, 2nd Earl of, 1853–1945, vol. IV
Balfour, 3rd Earl of, 1902–1968, vol. VI
Balfour of Burleigh, 6th Lord, 1849–1921, vol. II
Balfour of Burleigh, 11th (*de facto* 7th) Lord, 1883–1967, vol. VI
Balfour of Inchrye, 1st Baron, 1897–1988, vol. VIII
Balfour, Alfred, 1885–1963, vol. VI
Balfour, Brig.-Gen. Sir Alfred Granville, 1858–1936, vol. III
Balfour, Alice Blanche, *died* 1936, vol. III
Balfour, Sir Andrew, 1873–1931, vol. III
Balfour, Ven. Andrew Jackson, 1845–1923, vol. II
Balfour, Col. Arthur Macintosh, 1862–1936, vol. III
Balfour, Charles Barrington, 1862–1921, vol. II
Balfour, Major Charles James, 1889–1939, vol. III
Balfour, Captain Christopher Egerton, 1872–1907, vol. I
Balfour, David, 1903–1989, vol. VIII
Balfour, Edward, 1849–1927, vol. II
Balfour, Brig. Edward William Sturgis, 1884–1955, vol. V
Balfour, Col Eustace James Anthony, *died* 1911, vol. I
Balfour, Lady Frances, 1858–1931, vol. III
Balfour, Lt-Col Francis Cecil Campbell, 1884–1965, vol. VI
Balfour, Rt Rev. Francis Richard Townley, 1846–1924, vol. II
Balfour, Lt-Col Frederick Robert Stephen, 1873–1945, vol. IV
Balfour, George, 1872–1941, vol. IV
Balfour, Rear-Adm. George Ian Mackintosh, 1912–1999, vol. X
Balfour, Sir Graham, 1858–1929, vol. III
Balfour, Henry, 1863–1939, vol. III

Balfour, Rear-Adm. Hugh Maxwell, 1933–1999, vol. X
Balfour, Sir Isaac Bayley, 1853–1922, vol. II
Balfour, Hon. James, 1830–1913, vol. I
Balfour, Hon. James Moncreiff, 1878–1960, vol. V
Balfour, James William, 1827–1907, vol. I
Balfour, Sir John, 1894–1983, vol. VIII
Balfour, Col John Edmond Heugh, 1863–1952, vol. V
Balfour, Lt-Col Kenneth Robert, 1863–1936, vol. III
Balfour, Margaret Ida, died 1945, vol. IV
Balfour, Hon. Mark Robin, 1927–1995, vol. IX
Balfour, Nancy, 1911–1997, vol. X
Balfour, Lt-Col Oswald Herbert Campbell, died 1953, vol. V
Balfour, Patrick; see Kinross, 3rd Baron.
Balfour, Lt-Gen. Sir Philip Maxwell, 1898–1977, vol. VIII
Balfour, Sir Robert, 1st Bt, 1844–1929, vol. III
Balfour, Sir Robert George Victor FitzGeorge; see FitzGeorge-Balfour.
Balfour, Rev. Robert Gordon, 1826–1905, vol. I
Balfour, Col William Edward Ligonier, 1855–1934, vol. III
Balfour-Browne, John Hutton; see Browne.
Balfour-Browne, Vincent Robert, 1880–1963, vol. VI
Balfour-Browne, William Alex Francis, 1874–1967, vol. VI
Balfour-Lynn, Stanley, 1922–1986, vol. VIII
Balfour-Melville, Leslie Melville, 1854–1937, vol. III
Baliol Scott, Edward, 1873–1963, vol. VI
Baliol Scott, Napier, 1903–1956, vol. V
Baline, Israel; see Berlin, Irving.
Ball, Alan Hugh, 1924–1987, vol. VIII
Ball, Sir Albert, 1862–1946, vol. IV
Ball, Sir Arthur; see Ball, Sir C. A. K.
Ball, Air Vice-Marshall Sir Benjamin, 1912–1977, vol. VII
Ball, Sir (Charles) Arthur (Kinahan), 2nd Bt, 1877–1945, vol. IV
Ball, Sir Charles Bent, 1st Bt, 1851–1916, vol. II
Ball, Charles Francis, 1869–1933, vol. III
Ball, Major Charles James Prior, 1893–1973, vol. VII
Ball, Rev. Charles Richard, died 1918, vol. II
Ball, E. Bruce, 1873–1944, vol. IV
Ball, Sir Edmund Lancaster, 1883–1971, vol. VII
Ball, Ernest, died 1927, vol. II
Ball, Eustace Alfred R.; see Reynolds-Ball.
Ball, Major George Joseph, 1880–1952, vol. V
Ball, Sir (George) Joseph, 1885–1961, vol. VI
Ball, Sir George Thomas T.; see Thalben-Ball.
Ball, Harry Standish, 1888–1941, vol. IV
Ball, James Barry, died 1926, vol. II
Ball, Sir James Benjamin, 1867–1920, vol. II
Ball, James Dyer, 1847–1919, vol. II
Ball, John, 1861–1940, vol. III
Ball, John, 1872–1941, vol. IV
Ball, Rt Hon. John Thomas, 1815–1898, vol. I
Ball, Sir Joseph; see Ball, Sir G. J.
Ball, Rev. Kenneth Vernon James, 1906–1986, vol. VIII
Ball, Michael George, 1937–1998, vol. X

Ball, Sir Nigel Gresley, 3rd Bt, 1892–1978, vol. VII
Ball, Robert Edward, 1911–1990, vol. VIII
Ball, Sir Robert Stawell, 1840–1913, vol. I
Ball, Thomas, 1846–1922, vol. II
Ball, Very Rev. Thomas Isaac, died 1916, vol. II
Ball, Walter William Rouse, 1850–1925, vol. II
Ball, Wilfrid, 1853–1917, vol. II
Ball, Willet, 1873–1962, vol. VI
Ball, William Antony, 1904–1973, vol. VII
Ball, Sir William Girling, died 1945, vol. IV
Ball, Sir William Valentine, 1874–1960, vol. V
Ballance, Sir Charles Alfred, 1856–1936, vol. III
Ballance, Rear-Adm. Frank Arthur, 1902–1978, vol. VII
Ballance, Sir Hamilton Ashley, 1867–1936, vol. III
Ballantine-Dykes, Col Frescheville Hubert; see Dykes.
Ballantrae, Baron (Life Peer); Bernard Edward Fergusson, 1911–1980, vol. VII
Ballantyne, Alexander Hanson, 1911–1983, vol. VIII
Ballantyne, Archibald Morton, 1908–1977, vol. VII
Ballantyne, Arthur James, 1876–1954, vol. V
Ballantyne, Colin Sandergrove, 1908–1988, vol. VIII(A)
Ballantyne, Air Vice-Marshal Gordon Arthur, 1900–1981, vol. VIII
Ballantyne, Sir Henry, 1855–1941, vol. IV
Ballantyne, Henry, 1912–1983, vol. VIII
Ballantyne, Horatio, 1871–1956, vol. V
Ballantyne, John Andrew, 1912–1960, vol. V
Ballantyne, John William, 1861–1923, vol. II
Ballard, Albert, 1888–1969, vol. VI
Ballard, Ven. Arthur Henry, 1912–1984, vol. VIII
Ballard, Lt-Col Basil W.; see Woods Ballard.
Ballard, Bristow Guy, 1902–1975, vol. VII
Ballard, Clifford Frederick, 1910–1997, vol. X
Ballard, Brig.-Gen. Colin Robert, 1868–1941, vol. IV
Ballard, Edward, 1820–1897, vol. I
Ballard, Rev. Frank, died 1931, vol. III
Ballard, Rev. Frank Hewett, died 1959, vol. V
Ballard, Adm. George Alexander, 1862–1948, vol. IV
Ballard, Geoffrey Horace, 1927–1990, vol. VIII
Ballard, Henry, 1840–1919, vol. II
Ballard, Brig. James Archibald William, 1905–1978, vol. VII
Ballard, Philip Boswood, 1865–1950, vol. IV
Ballentine, Maj.-Gen. John Steventon, 1897–1965, vol. VI
Ballin, Ada S., died 1906, vol. I
Ballingall, Lt-Col Henry Miller, 1878–1936, vol. III
Ballinger, Sir John, 1860–1933, vol. III
Ballou, Henry Arthur, 1872–1937, vol. III
Balls, William Lawrence, 1882–1960, vol. V
Bally, Maj.-Gen. John Ford, 1845–1912, vol. I
Balmain, Pierre Alexandre, 1914–1982, vol. VIII
Balme, Archibald Hamilton, died 1942, vol. IV
Balme, David Mowbray, 1912–1989, vol. VIII
Balme, Harold, died 1953, vol. V
Balmer, Sir Joseph Reginald, 1899–1993, vol. IX
Balmforth, Rev. Canon Henry, 1890–1977, vol. VII
Balogh, Baron (Life Peer); Thomas Balogh, 1905–1985, vol. VIII

Balrampur, Maharaja Bahadur of, 1879–1921, vol. II
Balsdon, John Percy Vyvian Dacre, 1901–1977, vol. VII
Balston, Thomas, 1883–1967, vol. VI
Baly, Edward Charles Cyril, 1871–1948, vol. IV
Balzani, Count Ugo, 1847–1916, vol. II
Bam, Lt-Col Pieter Canzius van Blommestein; see Stewart-Bam of Ards.
Bamber, Col Charles James, 1855–1941, vol. IV
Bamber, John, 1915–1976, vol. VII
Bamber, Captain Wyndham Lerrier, died 1924, vol. II
Bambridge, Sir George, 1883–1961, vol. VI
Bambridge, Henry James, 1881–1956, vol. V
Bambridge, Rev. Joseph John, died 1923, vol. II
Bambridge, Thomas, vol. III
Bamfield, Lt-Gen. Albert Henry, 1830–1908, vol. I
Bamfield, Maj.-Gen. Harold John Kinahan, died 1959, vol. V
Bamford, Clement Henry, 1912–1999, vol. X
Bamford, Major Edward, 1887–1928, vol. II
Bamford, Sir Eric St John, 1891–1957, vol. V
Bamford, Lt-Col Harry William Morrey, 1882–1968, vol. VI
Bamford, Percival Clifford, 1886–1960, vol. V
Bamford, Rt Rev. Thomas Ambrose, 1861–1945, vol. VI
Bamford-Slack, Sir John, 1857–1909, vol. I
Bammel, Caroline Penrose, 1940–1995, vol. IX
Bampton, Rev. Joseph M., 1854–1933, vol. III
Banarji, Hon. Sir Pramada Charan, died 1930, vol. III
Banatvala, Col Sir Hormasjee Eduljee, 1859–1932, vol. III
Banbury of Southam, 1st Baron, 1850–1936, vol. III
Banbury of Southam, 2nd Baron, 1915–1981, vol. VIII
Banbury, Brig.-Gen. Walter Edward, 1863–1927, vol. II
Bancroft, Baron (Life Peer); Ian Powell Bancroft, 1922–1996, vol. X
Bancroft, Claude Keith, 1885–1919, vol. II
Bancroft, Edgar Addison, 1857–1925, vol. II
Bancroft, Elias, died 1924, vol. II
Bancroft, George Pleydell, 1868–1956, vol. V
Bancroft, Hubert Howe, 1832–1918, vol. II
Bancroft, Marie Effie, (Lady Bancroft), 1839–1921, vol. II
Bancroft, Sir Oswald Lawrance, 1888–1964, vol. VI
Bancroft, Sir Squire Bancroft, 1841–1926, vol. II
Band, David, 1942–1996, vol. X
Banda, Hastings Kamuzu, (Ngwazi Dr H. Kamuzu Banda), 1905–1997, vol. X
Bandaranaike, Mrs Sirimavo Ratwatte Dias, 1916–2000, vol. X
Bandaranaike, Sir Solomon Dias, 1862–1946, vol. IV
Bandaranaike, Solomon West Ridgeway Dias, 1899–1959, vol. V
Bandon, 4th Earl of, 1850–1924, vol. II
Bandon, 5th Earl of, 1904–1979, vol. VII
Bandon, Countess of; (Georgina), 1853–1942, vol. IV
Banerjea, A. C., 1894–1979, vol. VII

Banerjea, Pramathanath, 1881–1960, vol. V(A)
Banerjea, Sir Surendranath, 1848–1925, vol. II
Banerjee, Sir Gooroo Dass, 1844–1919, vol. II
Banerjee, Rabindra Nath, 1895–1985, vol. VIII
Banerjee, Sarat Chandra, 1870–1932, vol. III
Banerji, Sir Albion Rajkumar, 1871–1950, vol. IV
Banerji, Amiya Charan, 1891–1968, vol. VI(AII)
Banes, George Edward, 1828–1907, vol. I
Banfield, John William, died 1945, vol. IV
Banfield, Col Rees John Francis, 1850–1926, vol. II
Banford, Leslie Jackson, died 1961, vol. VI
Bangor, 5th Viscount, 1828–1911, vol. I
Bangor, 6th Viscount, 1868–1950, vol. IV
Bangor, 7th Viscount, 1905–1993, vol. IX
Bangs, John Kendrick, 1862–1922, vol. II
Banham, Prof. (Peter) Reyner, 1922–1988, vol. VIII
Banham, Prof. Reyner; see Banham, Prof. P. R.
Banister, Col Fitzgerald Muirson, 1853–1928, vol. II
Banister, George Henry, died 1934, vol. III
Banister, John Bright, 1880–1938, vol. III
Banister, Rt Rev. William, 1855–1928, vol. II
Bank-Anthony, Sir Mobolaji, 1907–1991, vol. IX
Bankart, Sir Alfred Seymour, 1870–1933, vol. III
Bankart, Surg. Rear-Adm. Sir Arthur Reginald, 1868–1943, vol. IV
Bankart, Arthur Sydney Blundell, 1879–1951, vol. V
Bankart, Vice-Adm. Sir (George) Harold, 1893–1964, vol. VI
Bankart, Vice-Adm. Sir Harold; see Bankart, Vice-Adm. Sir G. H.
Bankes, Rev. Eldon Surtees, 1829–1915, vol. I
Bankes, Henry John Ralph, 1902–1981, vol. VIII
Bankes, Rt Hon. Sir John Eldon, 1854–1946, vol. IV
Bankes, Ralph George Scott, 1900–1948, vol. IV
Bankes, Ralph Vincent, 1867–1921, vol. II
Bankes, Robert Wynne, 1887–1975, vol. VII
Bankes, Walter Ralph, 1853–1904, vol. I
Bankes-Williams, Ivor Maredydd, 1896–1974, vol. VII
Bankole-Jones, Sir Samuel; see Jones.
Banks, Baron (Life Peer); Desmond Anderson Harvie Banks, 1918–1997, vol. X
Banks, Alan George, 1911–2000, vol. X
Banks, A(rthur) Leslie, 1904–1989, vol. VIII
Banks, Col Hon. Charles Arthur, 1885–1961, vol. VI
Banks, Col Cyril, 1901–1969, vol. VI
Banks, Sir Donald, 1891–1975, vol. VII
Banks, Edward Bernard, 1901–1968, vol. VI
Banks, Elizabeth, died 1938, vol. III
Banks, Air Cdre Francis Rodwell, 1898–1985, vol. VIII
Banks, Mrs George Linnaeus, 1821–1897, vol. I
Banks, Lt-Col Henry John Archibald, 1869–1939, vol. III
Banks, Isabella; see Banks, Mrs George Linnaeus
Banks, James Dallaway, 1917–1985, vol. VIII
Banks, Sir John Garnett, 1889–1974, vol. VII
Banks, Rev. John Shaw, 1835–1917, vol. II
Banks, Sir John Thomas, died 1908, vol. I
Banks, Leslie James, 1890–1952, vol. V

Banks, Sir Maurice Alfred Lister, 1901–1991, vol. IX
Banks, Sir Reginald Mitchell, 1880–1940, vol. III
Banks, Richard Alford, 1902–1997, vol. X
Banks, Rev. Samuel John Sherbrooke, 1861–1941, vol. IV
Banks, Sir Thomas Macdonald; see Banks, Sir Donald.
Banks, Captain William Eric, 1900–1986, vol. VIII
Banks, William Hartley, 1909–1998, vol. X
Banks, Sir William Mitchell, 1842–1904, vol. I
Banks-Davis, Henry John, 1867–1936, vol. III
Bannatine-Allason, Maj.-Gen. Sir Richard, 1855–1940, vol. III
Bannatyne, Rev. Colin A., 1849–1920, vol. II
Bannatyne, Maj.-Gen. Neil Charles, 1880–1970, vol. VI
Bannatyne, Sir Robert Reid, 1875–1956, vol. V
Banner, Sir George Knowles H.; see Harmood-Banner.
Banner, Major Sir Harmood H.-; see Harmood-Banner.
Banner, Hubert Stewart, 1891–1964, vol. VI
Banner, Sir John Sutherland H.; see Harmood-Banner.
Bannerman of Kildonan, Baron (Life Peer); John MacDonald Bannerman, 1901–1969, vol. VI
Bannerman, Sir Alexander, 11th Bt, 1871–1934, vol. III
Bannerman, Sir (Alexander) Patrick, 14th Bt, 1933–1989, vol. VIII
Bannerman, Lt-Col Sir Arthur D'Arcy Gordon, 12th Bt, 1866–1955, vol. V
Bannerman, Charles Edward Woolhouse, 1884–1943, vol. IV
Bannerman, David Armitage, 1886–1979, vol. VII
Bannerman, Lt-Col Sir Donald Arthur Gordon, 13th Bt, 1899–1989, vol. VIII
Bannerman, Sir George, 10th Bt, 1827–1901, vol. I
Bannerman, Rt Hon. Sir Henry C.; see Campbell-Bannerman.
Bannerman, Sir Patrick; see Bannerman, Sir A. P.
Bannerman, Gen. William, 1828–1914, vol. I
Bannerman, Maj.-Gen. William Burney, 1858–1924, vol. II
Banning, Lt-Col Stephen Thomas, 1859–1935, vol. III
Bannister, Rev. Arthur Thomas, 1862–1936, vol. III
Bannister, Charles Olden, 1876–1955, vol. V
Bannister, Frank Kenneth, 1909–1975, vol. VII
Bannister, Frederick Allan, 1901–1970, vol. VI
Bannister, Grace, died 1986, vol. VIII
Bannister, Rev. Henry Marriott, 1854–1919, vol. II
Banon, Brig.-Gen. Frederick Lionel, 1862–1950, vol. IV
Bansda, ex-Maharaja Saheb of, 1888–1951, vol. V
Banswara, Maharawal of, 1888–1944, vol. IV(A), vol. V
Banta, Arthur Mangun, 1877–1946, vol. IV(A), vol. V
Banting, Sir Frederick Grant, 1891–1941, vol. IV
Banting, Air Vice-Marshal George Gaywood, 1898–1973, vol. VII
Bantock, Geoffrey Herman, 1914–1997, vol. X
Bantock, George Granville, died 1913, vol. I

Bantock, Sir Granville, 1868–1946, vol. IV
Banton, George, 1856–1932, vol. III
Banwell, Sir (George) Harold, 1900–1982, vol. VIII
Banwell, Godwin Edward, 1897–1981, vol. VIII
Banwell, Sir Harold; see Banwell, Sir G. H.
Barbé, Louis A., 1845–1926, vol. II
Barbenson, Nicholas Peter Le Cocq, 1838–1928, vol. II
Barber, Alan Theodore, 1905–1985, vol. VIII
Barber, Arthur Vavasour, died 1957, vol. V
Barber, Rev. Benjamin Aquila, 1876–1946, vol. IV
Barber, Charles Alfred, 1860–1933, vol. III
Barber, Lt-Col Charles Harrison, 1877–1965, vol. VI
Barber, Lt-Gen. Sir Colin Muir, 1897–1964, vol. VI
Barber, Donald, 1905–1957, vol. V
Barber, Ven. Edward, 1841–1914, vol. I
Barber, Sir (Edward) Fairless, 1873–1958, vol. V
Barber, Hon. Sir (Edward Hamilton) Esler, 1905–1991, vol. IX
Barber, Elizabeth; see Barber, M. E.
Barber, Eric Arthur, 1888–1965, vol. VI
Barber, Hon. Sir Esler; see Barber, Hon. Sir E. H. E.
Barber, Sir Fairless; see Barber, Sir E. F.
Barber, Maj.-Gen. Frederick Charles, died 1908, vol. I
Barber, Maj.-Gen. George Walter, 1868–1951, vol. V
Barber, Sir George William, 1858–1945, vol. IV
Barber, Harold Wordsworth, 1886–1955, vol. V
Barber, Sir Henry; see Barber, Sir W. H.
Barber, Sir Herbert William, 1887–1978, vol. VII
Barber, Horace Newton, 1914–1971, vol. VII
Barber, Captain James William, 1884–1962, vol. VI
Barber, Rear-Adm. John L.; see Lee-Barber.
Barber, Leslie Claud Seton, 1894–1968, vol. VI
Barber, Mary, 1911–1965, vol. VI
Barber, (Mary) Elizabeth, 1911–1979, vol. VII
Barber, Michael, 1934–1991, vol. IX
Barber, Noël John Lysberg, 1909–1988, vol. VIII
Barber, Ohio C., 1841–1920, vol. II
Barber, Percival Ellison, died 1959, vol. V
Barber, Sir Philip; see Barber, Sir T. P.
Barber, Philip Stanley, 1895–1973, vol. VII
Barber, Samuel, 1910–1981, vol. VIII
Barber, Rev. Thomas Gerard, died 1952, vol. V
Barber, Sir (Thomas) Philip, 1st Bt (cr 1960), 1876–1961, vol. VI
Barber, William Charles, died 1921, vol. II
Barber, William David, died 1952, vol. V
Barber, W(illiam) Edmund, died 1958, vol. V
Barber, Col Sir William Francis, 1905–1995, vol. IX
Barber, Sir (William) Henry, 1st Bt (cr 1924), 1860–1927, vol. II
Barber, Rev. William Theodore Aquila, 1858–1945, vol. IV
Barber-Starkey, William Joseph Starkey, 1847–1924, vol. II
Barberton, Ivan Graham Mitford-, 1896–1976, vol. VII
Barbier, Paul, died 1921, vol. II
Barbier, Paul, 1873–1947, vol. IV

Barbieri, Bishop Guido Bastiani Pascucci, 1836–1910, vol. I
Barbirolli, Sir John Giovanni Battista, 1899–1970, vol. VI
Barbour, A. H. Freeland, 1856–1927, vol. II
Barbour, Sir David Miller, 1841–1928, vol. II
Barbour, George, 1841–1919, vol. II
Barbour, George Brown, 1890–1977, vol. VII(AII)
Barbour, George Freeland, 1882–1946, vol. IV
Barbour, Harold Adrian Milne, 1874–1938, vol. III
Barbour, Rt Hon. Sir John Milne, 1st Bt, 1868–1951, vol. V
Barbour, Major Robert, 1876–1928, vol. II
Barbour, Walworth, 1908–1982, vol. IX (AI)
Barbusse, Henri, 1873–1935, vol. III
Barchard, Col Charles Henry, 1828–1902, vol. I
Barclay, Alexander, 1896–1987, vol. VIII
Barclay, Alfred Ernest, 1876–1949, vol. IV
Barclay, Sir Cecil; see Barclay, Sir R. C. de B.
Barclay, Rt Hon. Sir Colville Adrian de Rune, 1869–1929, vol. III
Barclay, Brig. Cyril Nelson, 1896–1979, vol. VII
Barclay, Edward Exton, 1860–1948, vol. IV
Barclay, Florence Louisa, 1862–1920, vol. II
Barclay, Sir George Head, 1862–1921, vol. II
Barclay, Sir Harry John, 1861–1933, vol. III
Barclay, Col Henry Albert, 1858–1947, vol. IV
Barclay, Hugh Gurney, 1851–1936, vol. III
Barclay, Rev. Humphrey Gordon, died 1955, vol. V
Barclay, Rev. James, 1844–1920, vol. II
Barclay, John, 1845–1936, vol. III
Barclay, John Stephen, 1908–1968, vol. VI
Barclay, Major Maurice Edward, 1886–1962, vol. VI
Barclay, Sir Noton; see Barclay, Sir R. N.
Barclay, Col Reginald, 1861–1945, vol. IV
Barclay, Robert, 1837–1913, vol. I
Barclay, Robert Buchanan, 1843–1919, vol. II
Barclay, Sir (Robert) Cecil de Belzim, 13th Bt, 1862–1930, vol. III
Barclay, Robert Francis, 1867–1948, vol. IV
Barclay, Robert Leatham, 1869–1939, vol. III
Barclay, Sir (Robert) Noton, 1872–1957, vol. V
Barclay, Robert Wyvill, 1880–1951, vol. V
Barclay, Sir Roderick Edward, 1909–1996, vol. X
Barclay, Theodore David, 1906–1981, vol. VIII
Barclay, Sir Thomas, 1839–1921, vol. II
Barclay, Rev. Thomas, 1849–1935, vol. III
Barclay, Sir Thomas, 1853–1941, vol. IV
Barclay, William, 1907–1978, vol. VII
Barclay, William Singer, 1871–1947, vol. IV
Barclay-Harvey, Sir (Charles) Malcolm, 1890–1969, vol. VI
Barclay-Harvey, Sir Malcolm; see Barclay-Harvey, Sir C. M.
Barclay-Smith, Edward, died 1945, vol. IV
Barclay-Smith, (Ida) Phyllis, died 1980, vol. VII
Barclay-Smith, Phyllis; see Barclay-Smith, I. P.
Barcroft, Henry, 1904–1998, vol. X
Barcroft, John Coleraine Hanbury, 1908–1958, vol. V
Barcroft, Sir Joseph, 1872–1947, vol. IV
Barcŷnska, Countess Hélène Armiger Barclay, died 1930, vol. III
Bardeen, John, 1908–1991, vol. IX

Bardill, Ralph William, 1876–1935, vol. III
Bardoux, Jacques, 1874–1959, vol. V
Bardsley, Rt Rev. Cuthbert Killick Norman, 1907–1991, vol. IX
Bardsley, Rt Rev. Cyril Charles Bowman, 1870–1940, vol. III
Bardsley, Rev. Ernest John, 1868–1948, vol. IV
Bardsley, Rt Rev. John Wareing, 1835–1904, vol. I
Bardsley, Rev. Joseph Udell Norman, 1868–1928, vol. II
Bardsley, Robert Vickers, 1890–1952, vol. V
Bardswell, Charles William, 1832–1902, vol. I
Bardswell, Hugh Rosser, 1874–1962, vol. VI
Bardswell, Noel Dean, 1871–1938, vol. III
Bardwell, Thomas Newman Frederick, 1850–1931, vol. III
Bardwell, Captain William Scot, 1892–1968, vol. VI
Bare, Lt-Col Alfred Raymund, 1886–1967, vol. VI
Bare, Captain Arnold Edwin, 1880–1917, vol. II
Barea, Arturo, 1897–1957, vol. V
Barefoot, Lt-Col George Henry, 1864–1924, vol. II
Barfett, Ven. Thomas, 1916–2000, vol. X
Barff, Rev. Albert, died 1913, vol. I
Barff, Henry Ebenezer, 1857–1925, vol. II
Barff, Rev. Henry Tootai, 1834–1917, vol. II
Barff, Stafford Edward Douglas, 1909–1976, vol. VII
Barfoot, Most Rev. Walter Foster, 1893–1978, vol. VII
Barford, Edward, 1898–1980, vol. VII
Barford, Sir Leonard, 1908–1992, vol. IX
Barge, Lt-Col Kenneth, 1883–1971, vol. VII
Barger, George, 1878–1939, vol. III
Bargone, Frédéric Charles; see Farrère, Claude.
Barham, Col Arthur Saxby, 1869–1952, vol. V
Barham, Ven. Charles Mitchell, died 1935, vol. III
Barham, Rt Rev. E(dward) Lawrence, 1901–1973, vol. VII
Barham, Sir George, 1836–1913, vol. I
Barham, George Titus, 1860–1937, vol. III
Baria, Raja of, 1886–1949, vol. IV
Barillon, Rt Rev. Emile, 1860–1935, vol. III
Baring, Sir Charles Christian, 2nd Bt, 1898–1990, vol. VIII
Baring, Brig.-Gen. Hon. Everard, 1865–1932, vol. III
Baring, Hon. Francis Henry, 1850–1915, vol. I
Baring, Sir Godfrey, 1st Bt, 1871–1957, vol. V
Baring, Godfrey Nigel Everard, 1870–1934, vol. III
Baring, Major Hon. Guy Victor, 1873–1916, vol. II
Baring, Harold Herman John, 1869–1927, vol. II
Baring, Hon. Hugo, 1876–1949, vol. IV
Baring, Sir Mark, 1916–1988, vol. VIII
Baring, Wing Comdr Hon. Maurice, 1874–1945, vol. IV
Baring, Lady Rose Gwendolen Louisa, 1909–1993, vol. IX
Baring, Walter, 1844–1915, vol. I
Baring, Hon. Windham, 1880–1922, vol. II
Baring-Gould, Sabine, 1834–1924, vol. II
Bark, Evelyn Elizabeth Patricia, 1900–1993, vol. IX
Bark, Sir Peter, 1869–1937, vol. III
Barke, Allen; see Barke, J. A.
Barke, James Allen, 1903–1990, vol. VIII
Barker, Alan; see Barker, W. A.

Barker, Aldred Farrer, 1868–1964, vol. VI
Barker, Sir Alport; see Barker, Sir T. W. A.
Barker, Sir Alwyn Bowman, 1900–1998, vol. X
Barker, Anthony Raine, 1880–1963, vol. VI
Barker, Arthur Edward James, died 1916, vol. II
Barker, Lt-Col Arthur James, 1918–1981, vol. VIII
Barker, Augustine, 1887–1937, vol. III
Barker, Bertie Thomas Percival, 1877–1961, vol. VI
Barker, Cecil; see Barker, H. C. J.
Barker, Sir (Charles Frederic) James, 1914–1980, vol. VII
Barker, Col Charles William Panton, 1857–1926, vol. II
Barker, Air Vice-Marshal Clifford Cockcroft, 1909–1977, vol. VII
Barker, Captain Sir David W., 1858–1941, vol. IV
Barker, Denis William Knighton, 1908–1981, vol. VIII
Barker, Dennis Albert, 1926–1989, vol. VIII
Barker, Douglas William Ashley, 1905–1978, vol. VII
Barker, Edward, 1909–1999, vol. X
Barker, Edward Harrison, 1851–1919, vol. II
Barker, Eric Leslie, 1912–1990, vol. VIII
Barker, Sir Ernest, 1874–1960, vol. V
Barker, Col Ernest Francis William, 1877–1961, vol. VI
Barker, Gen. Sir Evelyn Hugh, 1894–1983, vol. VIII
Barker, Sir Francis Henry, 1865–1922, vol. II
Barker, Col Sir Francis William James, 1841–1924, vol. II
Barker, Lt-Col Frederic Allan, 1882–1959, vol. V
Barker, Hon. Sir Frederic Eustace, 1838–1916, vol. II
Barker, Lt-Col Frederick George, 1866–1951, vol. V
Barker, Maj.-Gen. Sir George, 1849–1930, vol. III
Barker, George, 1858–1936, vol. III(A), vol. IV
Barker, Gen. Sir George Digby, 1833–1914, vol. I
Barker, George Granville, 1913–1991, vol. IX
Barker, Rev. Canon Gilbert David, 1882–1958, vol. V
Barker, Harley Granville G.; see Granville-Barker.
Barker, (Harold) Cecil James, 1893–1974, vol. VII
Barker, Sir Harry Heaton, 1898–1994, vol. IX
Barker, Helen G.; see Granville-Barker.
Barker, Sir Henry Edward, 1872–1942, vol. IV
Barker, Henry James, 1852–1934, vol. III(A), vol. IV
Barker, Sir Herbert Atkinson, 1869–1950, vol. IV
Barker, Hugh Purslove, 1909–1984, vol. VIII
Barker, J. Ellis, 1870–1948, vol. IV
Barker, Sir James; see Barker, Sir C. F. J.
Barker, Sir John, 1st Bt, 1840–1914, vol. I
Barker, John, died 1970, vol. VI
Barker, John Edward, 1832–1912, vol. I
Barker, John Michael Adrian, 1932–1994, vol. IX
Barker, Lt-Col John Stafford, 1879–1959, vol. V
Barker, Maj.-Gen. John Stewart Scott, 1853–1918, vol. II
Barker, Very Rev. Joseph, 1834–1924, vol. II
Barker, Lancelot Elliot, 1908–1972, vol. VII
Barker, Lewellys F., 1867–1943, vol. IV

Barker, Brig. Lewis Ernest Stephen, 1895–1981, vol. VIII
Barker, Dame Lilian Charlotte, 1874–1955, vol. V
Barker, Louis William, 1879–1954, vol. V
Barker, Mary Ann, (Lady Barker); see Broome, M. A.
Barker, Lt-Gen. Michael George Henry, 1884–1960, vol. V
Barker, Rev. Peter, died 1937, vol. III
Barker, Lt-Col Randle Barnett-, 1870–1918, vol. II
Barker, Sir Rayner Childe, 1858–1945, vol. IV
Barker, Maj.-Gen. Richard Ernest, 1888–1962, vol. VI
Barker, Sir Robert Beacroft, 1890–1960, vol. V, vol. VI
Barker, Lt-Col Robert Hewitt, 1887–1961, vol. VI
Barker, Captain Roland Auriol, 1892–1954, vol. V
Barker, Ronald Ernest, 1920–1976, vol. VII
Barker, Sir Ross; see Barker, Sir W. R.
Barker, Rev. Rowland Vectis, 1846–1926, vol. II
Barker, Dame Sara Elizabeth, 1904–1973, vol. VII
Barker, Susan Vera; see Cooper, Susie.
Barker, Sydney George, 1887–1942, vol. IV
Barker, Thomas Vipond, 1881–1931, vol. III
Barker, Sir (Thomas William) Alport, died 1956, vol. V
Barker, Tom Battersby, died 1968, vol. VI
Barker, Sir (Wilberforce) Ross, 1874–1957, vol. V
Barker, Very Rev. William, 1838–1917, vol. II
Barker, Sir William, 1909–1992, vol. IX
Barker, (William) Alan, 1923–1988, vol. VIII
Barker, Lt-Col William Arthur John, 1879–1924, vol. II
Barker, Lt-Col William George, 1894–1930, vol. III
Barker, William Henry, 1882–1929, vol. III
Barker, Wright, died 1941, vol. IV
Barker-Benfield, Brig. Karl Vere, 1892–1969, vol. VI
Barker-Mill, William Claude Frederick V.; see Vaudrey-Barker-Mill.
Barkla, Charles Glover, 1877–1944, vol. IV
Barkley, Alben William, 1877–1956, vol. V
Barkley, Brenda Edith, (Mrs Harry Barkley); see Ryman, B. E.
Barkley, Rev. John Montieth, 1910–1997, vol. X
Barkley, Col Macdonald, 1871–1956, vol. V
Barkley, William Henry, 1869–1942, vol. IV
Barkly, Sir Henry, 1815–1898, vol. I
Barkway, Rt Rev. James Lumsden, 1878–1968, vol. VI
Barlas, Sir Richard Douglas, 1916–1982, vol. VIII
Barlee, Sir Kenneth William, died 1956, vol. V
Barley, Frederick, died 1915, vol. I
Barley, Lt-Col Leslie John, 1890–1979, vol. VII
Barley, Maurice Willmore, 1909–1991, vol. IX
Barling, Sir Gilbert; see Barling, Sir H. G.
Barling, Sir (Harry) Gilbert, 1st Bt, 1855–1940, vol. III
Barling, Joseph, born 1839, vol. III
Barling, Lt-Col Seymour Gilbert, died 1960, vol. V
Barlow, Sir Alan; see Barlow, Sir J. A. N.
Barlow, Rt Hon. Sir Anderson M.; see Montague-Barlow.
Barlow, Adm. Charles James, 1848–1921, vol. II

Barlow, Rt Rev. Christopher George, 1858–1915, vol. I
Barlow, Disney Charles, 1880–1965, vol. VI
Barlow, Donald Spiers Monteagle, 1905–1994, vol. IX
Barlow, Francis John, 1869–1940, vol. III
Barlow, Sir Frank Herbert, 1918–1979, vol. VII
Barlow, George Thomas, 1865–1919, vol. II
Barlow, Harold Everard Monteagle, 1899–1989, vol. VIII
Barlow, Rev. Henry Theodore Edward, 1863–1906, vol. I
Barlow, Sir Hilaro William Wellesley, 5th Bt (*cr* 1803), 1861 1941, vol. IV
Barlow, Horace M., 1884–1954, vol. V
Barlow, James, 1921–1973, vol. VII
Barlow, Sir (James) Alan (Noel), 2nd Bt (*cr* 1900), 1881–1968, vol. VI
Barlow, Rev. James William, 1826–1913, vol. I
Barlow, Jane, 1857–1917, vol. II
Barlow, Col John, *died* 1924, vol. II
Barlow, John, 1853–1943, vol. IV(A)
Barlow, Sir John Denman, 2nd Bt, 1898–1986, vol. VIII
Barlow, Sir John Emmott, 1st Bt (*cr* 1907), 1857–1932, vol. III
Barlow, Percy, 1867–1931, vol. III
Barlow, Ralph Mitford Marriott, 1904–1977, vol. VII
Barlow, Sir Richard Hugh, 6th Bt (*cr* 1803), 1904–1946, vol. IV
Barlow, Sir Richard Wellesley, 4th Bt (*cr* 1803), 1836–1904, vol. I
Barlow, Sir Robert, 1891–1976, vol. VII
Barlow, Thomas Bradwall, 1900–1988, vol. VIII
Barlow, Sir Thomas, 1st Bt (*cr* 1900), 1845–1945, vol. IV
Barlow, Sir Thomas Dalmahoy, 1883–1964, vol. VI
Barlow, Walter Sydney L.; *see* Lazarus-Barlow.
Barlow, William, 1834–1915, vol. I
Barlow, William, 1845–1934, vol. III
Barlow, William Henry, 1812–1902, vol. I
Barltrop, Ernest William, 1893–1957, vol. V
Barman, Christian August, 1898–1980, vol. VII
Barnaby, Sir Nathaniel, 1829–1915, vol. I
Barnard, 9th Baron, 1854–1918, vol. II
Barnard, 10th Baron, 1888–1964, vol. VI
Barnard, Andrew Bigoe, 1862–1928, vol. II
Barnard, Sir (Arthur) Thomas, 1893–1995, vol. IX
Barnard, Beverley Gayer, 1916–1973, vol. VII
Barnard, Sir Charles Loudon, 1823–1902, vol. I
Barnard, Rev. Charles William, *died* 1928, vol. II
Barnard, Brig.-Gen. Cyril Darcy Vivien C.; *see* Cary-Barnard.
Barnard, Sir Edmund Broughton, 1856–1930, vol. III
Barnard, Eric, 1891–1980, vol. VII
Barnard, Francis Pierrepont, 1854–1931, vol. III
Barnard, Hon. Sir Frank Stillman, 1856–1936, vol. III
Barnard, Vice-Adm. Sir Geoffrey, 1902–1974, vol. VII
Barnard, Captain Sir George Edward, 1907–1995, vol. IX
Barnard, George Grey, 1863–1938, vol. III

Barnard, George Henry, 1868–1948, vol. IV
Barnard, Sir Henry William, 1891–1981, vol. VIII
Barnard, Sir Herbert, 1831–1920, vol. II
Barnard, Howard Clive, 1884–1985, vol. VIII
Barnard, Brig.-Gen. John Henry, 1846–1901, vol. I
Barnard, Joseph Edwin, *died* 1949, vol. IV
Barnard, Joseph Terence Owen, 1872–1936, vol. III
Barnard,, Hon. Lance Herbert, 1919–1997, vol. X
Barnard, Leonard William, 1870–1951, vol. V
Barnard, Rev. Percy Mordaunt, 1868–1941, vol. IV
Barnard, Sir Thomas; *see* Barnard, Sir A. T.
Barnard, Thomas Theodore, 1898–1983, vol. VIII
Barnard, Hon. William Edward, 1886–1958, vol. V
Barnard, William George, 1892–1956, vol. V
Barnard, Maj.-Gen. William Osborne, 1838–1920, vol. II
Barnard, William Tyndall, 1855–1923, vol. II
Barnardiston, Col Nathaniel, 1832–1916, vol. II
Barnardiston, Maj.-Gen. Nathaniel Walter, 1858–1919, vol. II
Barnardiston, Lt-Col Samuel John Barrington, 1875–1924, vol. II
Barnardo, Fleming; *see* Barnardo, F. A. F.
Barnardo, (Frederick Adolphus) Fleming, 1874–1962, vol. VI
Barnardo, Thomas John, 1845–1905, vol. I
Barnato, Henry Isaac, *died* 1908, vol. I
Barnato, Woolf, 1895–1948, vol. IV
Barnby, 1st Baron, 1841–1929, vol. III
Barnby, 2nd Baron, 1884–1982, vol. VIII
Barne, Rt Rev. George Dunsford, 1879–1954, vol. V
Barne, Major Miles, 1874–1917, vol. II
Barne, Brig. William Bradley Gosset, 1880–1951, vol. V
Barneby, Lt-Col Henry Habington, 1909–1995, vol. IX
Barneby, William Theodore, 1873–1946, vol. IV
Barnell, Herbert Rex, 1907–1973, vol. VII
Barnes, Alexander, 1855–1924, vol. II
Barnes, Alfred Edward, 1881–1956, vol. V
Barnes, Rt Hon. Alfred John, 1887–1974, vol. VII
Barnes, Alfred Schwartz, 1868–1949, vol. IV
Barnes, Dame (Alice) Josephine (Mary Taylor), (Dame Josephine Warren), 1912–1999, vol. X
Barnes, Anthony Charles, 1891–1974, vol. VII
Barnes, Gen. Ardley Henry Falwasser, 1837–1910, vol. I
Barnes, Arthur Chapman, 1891–1985, vol. VIII
Barnes, Rev. Canon Arthur Hubert, *died* 1952, vol. V
Barnes, Arthur Kentish, 1872–1954, vol. V
Barnes, Rt Rev. Mgr Arthur Stapylton, 1861–1936, vol. III
Barnes, Barry K., (Nelson Barry Mackintosh Barnes), 1906–1965, vol. VI
Barnes, Bernard, 1890–1950, vol. IV
Barnes, Bertie Frank, 1888–1965, vol. VI
Barnes, Captain Charles Roper Gorell, 1896–1918, vol. II
Barnes, Daniel Sennett, 1924–1996, vol. X
Barnes, Sir Denis Charles, 1914–1992, vol. IX
Barnes, Edwin Clay, 1864–1941, vol. IV
Barnes, Eric Cecil, 1899–1987, vol. VIII
Barnes, Air Cdre Eric Delano, 1900–1957, vol. V

Barnes, Sir (Ernest) John (Ward), 1917–1992, vol. IX
Barnes, Rt Rev. Ernest William, 1874–1953, vol. V
Barnes, Fancourt, died 1908, vol. I
Barnes, Francis Walter Ibbetson, 1914–2000, vol. X
Barnes, Frank, died 1960, vol. V
Barnes, Col Frank Purcell, 1880–1956, vol. V
Barnes, Sir Frederic Gorell, 1856–1939, vol. III
Barnes, Frederick Dallas, 1843–1899, vol. I
Barnes, Rt Hon. George Nicoll, 1859–1940, vol. III
Barnes, Sir George Reginald, 1904–1960, vol. V
Barnes, Sir George Stapylton, 1858–1946, vol. IV
Barnes, Harold Charles Edward, 1871–1940, vol. III
Barnes, Harold William, 1912–1981, vol. VIII
Barnes, Major Harry, 1870–1935, vol. III
Barnes, Harry Cheetham, 1898–1961, vol. VI(AII)
Barnes, Harry Elmer, 1889–1968, vol. VI
Barnes, Sir Harry Jefferson, 1915–1982, vol. VIII
Barnes, Henry, 1842–1921, vol. II
Barnes, Howard Turner, 1873–1950, vol. IV(A)
Barnes, Sir Hugh Shakespear, 1853–1940, vol. III
Barnes, Major Humphry Aston, 1900–1940, vol. III
Barnes, Col James, 1866–1936, vol. III
Barnes, James Edwin, 1917–1991, vol. IX
Barnes, Sir James George, 1908–1995, vol. IX
Barnes, Sir James Horace, 1891–1969, vol. VI
Barnes, Sir (James) Sidney, 1881–1952, vol. V
Barnes, Sir John; see Barnes, Sir E. J. W.
Barnes, John Frederick Evelyn, 1851–1925, vol. II
Barnes, John Morrison, 1913–1975, vol. VII
Barnes, Dame Josephine; see Barnes, Dame A. J. M. T.
Barnes, Sir Kenneth Ralph, 1878–1957, vol. V
Barnes, Nelson Barry Mackintosh, see Barnes, Barry K.
Barnes, Col Osmond, 1834–1930, vol. III
Barnes, Rev. Peter, 1856–1921, vol. II
Barnes, Peter Robert, 1921–1996, vol. X
Barnes, Maj.-Gen. Sir Reginald Walter Ralph, 1871–1946, vol. IV
Barnes, Richard Cumberland, 1912–1970, vol. VI(AII)
Barnes, Roland, 1907–1998, vol. X
Barnes, Sir Sidney; see Barnes, Sir J. S.
Barnes, Stanley, 1875–1955, vol. V
Barnes, Sir Thomas James, 1888–1964, vol. VI
Barnes, Hon. Walter Henry, 1858–1933, vol. III
Barnes, Walter Mayhew, 1871–1950, vol. IV
Barnes, Air Vice-Marshal William Edward, 1897–1958, vol. V
Barnes, Rev. William Emery, 1859–1939, vol. III
Barnes, Sir William Lethbridge G.; see Gorell Barnes.
Barnes, Winston Herbert Frederick, 1909–1990, vol. VIII
Barnes-Lawrence, Rev. Arthur Evelyn, 1851–1931, vol. III
Barnes-Lawrence, Herbert Cecil, 1852–1921, vol. II
Barnetson, Baron (Life Peer); William Denholm Barnetson, 1917–1981, vol. VIII
Barnetson, Maj.-Gen. James Craw, 1907–1984, vol. VIII
Barnett, Lt-Col Alfred George, 1883–1955, vol. V
Barnett, Alfred John, 1857–1943, vol. IV
Barnett, Rev. Arthur Thomas, 1858–1941, vol. IV

Barnett, Sir Ben Lewis, 1894–1979, vol. VII
Barnett, Cecil Guy, 1881–1959, vol. V
Barnett, Charles Edward, 1848–1937, vol. III
Barnett, Cyril Harry, 1919–1970, vol. VI
Barnett, Air Chief Marshal Sir Denis Hensley Fulton, 1906–1992, vol. IX
Barnett, Rev. Ernest Judd, 1859–1955, vol. V
Barnett, Sir Geoffrey Morris, 1902–1970, vol. VI
Barnett, George Aldred, died 1903, vol. I
Barnett, Col George Henry, 1880–1942, vol. IV
Barnett, Sir George Percy, 1894–1965, vol. VI
Barnett, Guy; see Barnett, N. G.
Barnett, Harry Villiers, 1858–1928, vol. II
Barnett, Dame Henrietta; see Barnett, Dame M. H.
Barnett, Dame Henrietta Octavia, 1851–1936, vol. III
Barnett, Lt-Col Henry N.; see Norman Barnett.
Barnett, Rev. Herbert, 1851–1937, vol. III
Barnett, John Francis, 1837–1916, vol. II
Barnett, Lionel David, 1871–1960, vol. V
Barnett, Sir Louis Edward, 1865–1946, vol. IV
Barnett, Dame (Mary) Henrietta, 1905–1985, vol. VIII
Barnett, Rev. Maurice, 1917–1980, vol. VII
Barnett, (Nicolas) Guy, 1928–1986, vol. VIII
Barnett, Sir Oliver Charles, 1907–1995, vol. IX
Barnett, Percy Arthur, 1858–1941, vol. IV
Barnett, Richard David, 1909–1986, vol. VIII
Barnett, Major Sir Richard Whieldon, 1863–1930, vol. III
Barnett, Rev. Samuel Augustus, 1844–1913, vol. I
Barnett, Rev. T. Ratcliffe, 1868–1946, vol. IV
Barnett-Barker, Lt-Col Randle; see Barker.
Barnett-Clarke, Very Rev. Charles William, died 1916, vol. II
Barnewall, Sir John Robert, 11th Bt, 1850–1936, vol. III
Barnewall, Sir Reginald Aylmer John de Barneval, 10th Bt, 1838–1909, vol. I
Barnewall, Sir Reginald John, 12th Bt, 1888–1961, vol. VI
Barnewall, Hon. Reginald Nicholas Francis, 1897–1918, vol. II
Barnham, Henry Dudley, 1854–1936, vol. III
Barnhill, Alexander Perley, 1863–1935, vol. III
Barnicoat, John Wallis, 1814–1905, vol. I
Barnie, Marian, (Mrs Donald Barnie); see Veitch, Marian.
Barnish, Captain Geoffrey Howard, 1887–1941, vol. IV
Barns, Rev. John Wintour Baldwin, 1912–1974, vol. VII
Barns, Thomas Alexander, 1881–1930, vol. III
Barnsley, Alan Gabriel; see Fielding, Gabriel.
Barnsley, Brig.-Gen. Sir John, 1858–1926, vol. II
Barnsley, Maj.-Gen. Robert Eric, 1886–1968, vol. VI
Barnsley, Thomas Edward, 1919–1992, vol. IX
Barnsley, (William) Edward, 1900–1987, vol. VIII
Barnston, Sir Harry, 1st Bt, 1870–1929, vol. III
Barnwell, Col Ralph Ernest, 1895–1984, vol. VIII
Baroda, HH Maharaja Gaekwar Sir Sayaji Rao III, 1863–1939, vol. III
Baroda, Maharaja of, 1908–1968, vol. VI

Baroja Nessi, Pio, (Don Pio Baroja), 1872–1956, vol. V
Baron, Alexander; see Baron, J. A.
Baron, Sir Barclay Josiah, died 1919, vol. II
Baron, Bernhard, 1850–1929, vol. III
Baron, Sir Bernhard; see Baron, Sir L. B.
Baron, Colin, 1921–1987, vol. VIII
Baron, Cyril Faudel Joseph, 1903–1978, vol. VII
Baron, Sir Edward Samson, 1892–1962, vol. VI
Baron, (Joseph) Alexander, 1917–1999, vol. X
Baron, Sir (Louis) Bernhard, 1st Bt, 1876–1934, vol. III
Baron-Suckling, Rev. Charles William, 1862–1944, vol. IV
Barotseland, Litunga of, 1888–1968, vol. VI
Barr, A. W. Cleeve, 1910–2000, vol. X
Barr, Alexander Wallace, 1886–1949, vol. IV
Barr, Alfred Hamilton, jun., 1902–1981, vol. VIII
Barr, Amelia Edith, 1831–1919, vol. II
Barr, Archibald, 1855–1931, vol. III
Barr, Lt-Col Sir David William Keith, 1846–1916, vol. II
Barr, Sir George William, 1881–1956, vol. V
Barr, Ian, 1927–1995, vol. IX
Barr, Comdr James, 1855–1937, vol. III
Barr, Sir James, 1849–1938, vol. III
Barr, Rev. James, 1862–1949, vol. IV
Barr, Sir James, 1884–1952, vol. V
Barr, James Angus Evan Abbot, 1862–1923, vol. II
Barr, James Gordon, 1908–1963, vol. VI
Barr, John, 1859–1940, vol. III
Barr, Mark, 1871–1950, vol. IV
Barr, Murray Llewellyn, 1908–1995, vol. IX
Barr, Robert, died 1912, vol. I
Barr, Thomas, 1846–1916, vol. II
Barr, Venie, died 1947, vol. IV
Barr Smith, Sir Tom Elder, 1904–1968, vol. VI
Barraclough, Frank, 1901–1974, vol. VII
Barraclough, Geoffrey, 1908–1984, vol. VIII
Barraclough, Henry, 1894–1982, vol. VIII
Barraclough, Sir Henry; see Barraclough, Sir S. H. E.
Barraclough, Brig. Sir John Ashworth, died 1981, vol. VIII
Barraclough, Sir (Samuel) Henry (Egerton), 1874–1958, vol. V
Barran, Sir John, 1st Bt, 1821–1905, vol. I
Barran, Sir John Leighton, 3rd Bt, 1904–1974, vol. VII
Barran, Sir John Nicholson, 2nd Bt, 1872–1952, vol. V
Barran, Sir Rowland Hirst, 1858–1949, vol. IV
Barrand, Arthur Rhys, 1861–1941, vol. IV
Barratt, Sir Albert, 1860–1941, vol. IV
Barratt, Air Chief Marshal Sir Arthur Sheridan, 1891–1966, vol. VI
Barratt, Sir Charles, 1910–1971, vol. VII
Barratt, Captain Sir Francis Henry Godolphin L., 2nd Bt; see Layland-Barratt.
Barratt, Sir Francis Layland-, 1st Bt, 1860–1933, vol. III
Barratt, Herbert George Harold, 1905–1993, vol. IX
Barratt, Col Herbert James, 1858–1952, vol. V
Barratt, John Arthur, 1857–1944, vol. IV

Barratt, John Oglethorpe Wakelin, 1862–1956, vol. V
Barratt, Reginald, 1861–1917, vol. II
Barratt, Major Stanley George Reeves E.; see Elton-Barratt.
Barratt, Sir Sydney, 1898–1975, vol. VII
Barratt, Rev. Thomas H., 1870–1951, vol. V
Barratt, Maj.-Gen. William Cross, 1862–1940, vol. III
Barratt, William Donald, 1883–1955, vol. V
Barraud, Francis, died 1924, vol. II
Barrault, Jean-Louis, 1910–1994, vol. IX
Barrell, Francis Richard, 1860–1915, vol. I
Barrer, Richard Maling, 1910–1996, vol. X
Barrère, Jean-Bertrand Marie, 1914–1985, vol. VIII
Barres, Maurice, 1862–1923, vol. II
Barret, Rt Rev. John Patrick, 1878–1946, vol. IV
Barrett, Major Alexander Gould, 1866–1954, vol. V
Barrett, Anthony Arthur, 1930–1986, vol. VIII
Barrett, Field Marshal Sir Arthur Arnold, 1857–1926, vol. II
Barrett, Sir Arthur George, 1895–1984, vol. VIII
Barrett, (Arthur) Michael, 1932–1994, vol. IX
Barrett, Ashley William, died 1939, vol. III
Barrett, Lt-Col Cyril Charles Johnson, 1884–1933, vol. III
Barrett, Col Dacre Lennard, 1858–1941, vol. IV
Barrett, Rev. Daniel William, died 1925, vol. II
Barrett, Denis Everett, 1911–1991, vol. IX
Barrett, Sir Dennis Charles T.; see Titchener-Barrett.
Barrett, Edith Helen, died 1939, vol. III
Barrett, Brig.-Gen. Edward Alfred M.; see Moulton-Barrett.
Barrett, Edward Ivo Medhurst, 1879–1950, vol. IV
Barrett, Edwin Cyril Geddes, 1909–1986, vol. VIII
Barrett, Ernest, 1917–1998, vol. X
Barrett, Florence Elizabeth, (Lady Barrett), died 1945, vol. IV
Barrett, Francis E. H. Joyce, died 1925, vol. II
Barrett, Frank, 1848–1926, vol. II
Barrett, Frank Ashley, died 1954, vol. V
Barrett, Rev. George Slatyer, 1839–1916, vol. II
Barrett, Col Henry Walter, 1857–1949, vol. IV
Barrett, Herbert Roper, 1873–1943, vol. IV
Barrett, Rev. Hugh S.; see Scott-Barrett.
Barrett, Hugh T.; see Tufnell-Barrett.
Barrett, Jack Wheeler, 1912–1998, vol. X
Barrett, Lt-Col Sir James Williams, 1862–1945, vol. IV
Barrett, Col John Cridlan, 1897–1977, vol. VII
Barrett, Group Captain John Francis Tufnell, 1898–1941, vol. IV
Barrett, Michael; see Barrett, A. M.
Barrett, Norman Rupert, 1903–1979, vol. VII
Barrett, Robert John, 1861–1942, vol. IV
Barrett, Thomas J., 1841–1914, vol. I
Barrett, William, 1863–1931, vol. III
Barrett, Very Rev. William Edward Colvile, 1880–1956, vol. V
Barrett, Sir William Fletcher, 1844–1925, vol. II
Barrett, Sir William Scott, 1843–1921, vol. II
Barrett, Wilson, 1846–1904, vol. I
Barrett-Lennard, Sir Fiennes Cecil Arthur, 1880–1963, vol. VI

Barrett-Lennard, Lt-Col John, 1863–1935, vol. III
Barrett-Lennard, Sir Richard Fiennes; see Lennard.
Barrett-Lennard, Sir Thomas, 2nd Bt; see Lennard.
Barrett-Lennard, Sir Thomas, 3rd Bt; see Lennard.
Barrett-Lennard, Sir Thomas Richard F.; see
  Lennard.
Barrie, Alexander Baillie, 1906–1957, vol. V
Barrie, Sir Charles, 1840–1921, vol. II
Barrie, Derek Stiven Maxwelton, 1907–1989,
  vol. VIII
Barrie, Rt Hon. Hugh Thom, 1860–1922, vol. II
Barrie, James, 1862–1932, vol. III
Barrie, Sir James Matthew, 1st Bt, 1860–1937,
  vol. III
Barrie, Sir Walter, 1901–1988, vol. VIII
Barringer, Paul Brandon, 1857–1941, vol. IV
Barrington, 8th Viscount, 1825–1901, vol. I
Barrington, 9th Viscount, 1848–1933, vol. III
Barrington, 10th Viscount, 1873–1960, vol. V
Barrington, 11th Viscount, 1908–1990, vol. VIII
Barrington, Hon. Bernard; see Barrington, Hon.
  W. B. L.
Barrington, Hon. Sir (Bernard) Eric (Edward),
  1847–1918, vol. II
Barrington, Sir Charles Bacon, 6th Bt, 1902–1980,
  vol. VII(AII)
Barrington, Sir Charles Burton, 5th Bt, 1848–1943,
  vol. IV
Barrington, Charles George, 1827–1911, vol. I
Barrington, Claud, 1893–1960, vol. V
Barrington, E.; see Beck, L. A.
Barrington, Emilie Isabel, died 1933, vol. III
Barrington, Hon. Sir Eric; see Barrington, Hon. Sir
  B. E. E.
Barrington, Ernest James William, 1909–1985,
  vol. VIII
Barrington, John Harcourt, 1907–1973, vol. VII
Barrington, Sir Kenneth Charles Peto, 1911–1987,
  vol. VIII
Barrington, Hon. Rupert Edward Selborne,
  1877–1975, vol. VII
Barrington, Sir Vincent Hunter Barrington K.; see
  Kennett-Barrington.
Barrington, Hon. (Walter)Bernard (Louis),
  1876–1959, vol. V
Barrington, Hon. Sir William Augustus Curzon,
  1842–1922, vol. II
Barrington-Fleet, George Rutland, 1853–1922,
  vol. II
Barrington-Kennett, Lt-Col Brackley Herbert
  Barrington, 1846–1919, vol. II
Barrington-Ward, Frederick Temple, 1880–1938,
  vol. III
Barrington-Ward, John Grosvenor, 1894–1946,
  vol. IV
Barrington-Ward, Sir Lancelot Edward, 1884–1953,
  vol. V
Barrington-Ward, Rev. Mark James, died 1924,
  vol. II
Barrington-Ward, Sir Michael; see Barrington-Ward,
  Sir V. M.
Barrington-Ward, Robert M'Gowan, 1891–1948,
  vol. IV
Barrington-Ward, Sir (Victor) Michael, 1887–1972,
  vol. VII

Barrios, Benjamin, 1878–1929, vol. III
Barritt, Sir David Thurlow, 1903–1990, vol. VIII
Barron, Claud Alexander, 1871–1948, vol. IV
Barron, Donovan Allaway, 1907–1980, vol. VII
Barron, Douglas Shield, 1904–1991, vol. IX
Barron, Elwyn Alfred, died 1929, vol. III
Barron, Evan Macleod, 1879–1965, vol. VI
Barron, Maj.-Gen. Frederick Wilmot, 1880–1963,
  vol. VI
Barron, Gladys Caroline, died 1967, vol. VI
Barron, Maj.-Gen. Sir Harry, 1847–1921, vol. II
Barron, Sir Henry Page-Turner, 2nd Bt, 1824–1900,
  vol. I
Barron, James, 1847–1919, vol. II
Barron, Brig.-Gen. Netterville Guy, 1867–1945,
  vol. IV
Barron, Oswald, 1868–1939, vol. III
Barron, Rt Rev. Patrick Harold Falkiner,
  1911–1991, vol. IX
Barron, Wilfrid Philip S.; see Shepherd-Barron.
Barron, Col Willie Netterville, 1872–1930, vol. III
Barrow, Albert Boyce, died 1939, vol. III
Barrow, Sir Alfred, 1850–1928, vol. II
Barrow, Adm. Arthur, 1853–1914, vol. I
Barrow, Col Arthur Frederick, 1850–1903, vol. I
Barrow, Rear-Adm. Benjamin Wingate, 1878–1966,
  vol. VI
Barrow, Gen. Sir Edmund George, 1852–1934,
  vol. III
Barrow, Rt Hon. Errol Walton, 1920–1987,
  vol. VIII
Barrow, Sir Francis Laurence John, 4th Bt,
  1862–1950, vol. IV
Barrow, Gen. Sir George de Symons, 1864–1959,
  vol. V
Barrow, Maj.-Gen. Harold Percy Waller,
  1876–1957, vol. V
Barrow, John, 1808–1898, vol. I
Barrow, Sir John Croker, 3rd Bt, 1833–1900, vol. I
Barrow, Rev. Canon John Harrison, 1881–1981,
  vol. VIII
Barrow, Hon. Sir Malcolm Palliser, 1900–1973,
  vol. VII
Barrow, Dame Nita; see Barrow, Dame R. N.
Barrow, Oscar Theodore, 1854–1937, vol. III
Barrow, Sir Reuben Vincent, 1838–1918, vol. II
Barrow, Dame (Ruth) Nita, 1916–1995, vol. IX
Barrow, Sir Samuel, 1859–1935, vol. III
Barrow, Walter, 1867–1954, vol. V
Barrow, Sir Wilfrid John Wilson Croker, 5th Bt,
  1897–1960, vol. V
Barrowclough, Rt Hon. Sir Harold Eric, 1894–1972,
  vol. VII
Barrows, William Leonard, 1905–1976, vol. VII
Barrs, Alfred George, 1853–1934, vol. III
Barry, Rt Rev. Alfred, 1826–1910, vol. I
Barry, Brig. Arthur Gordon, 1885–1942, vol. IV
Barry, Lt-Col Arthur John, 1859–1944, vol. IV
Barry, Lt-Col Cecil Charles Stewart, 1867–1933,
  vol. III
Barry, Charles, 1887–1963, vol. VI
Barry, Charles David, died 1928, vol. II
Barry, Rt Hon. Charles Robert, 1825–1897, vol. I
Barry, Adm. Sir Claud Barrington, 1891–1951,
  vol. V

Barry, Sir (Claude) Francis, 3rd Bt, 1883–1970, vol. VI
Barry, David Thomas, 1870–1955, vol. V
Barry, (Donald Angus) Philip, 1920–1987, vol. VIII
Barry, E. L. M.; see Milner-Barry.
Barry, Edward, 1852–1927, vol. II(A), vol. III
Barry, Lt-Col Edward, 1896–1952, vol. V
Barry, Sir Edward Arthur, 2nd Bt, 1858–1949, vol. IV
Barry, Sir Francis; see Barry, Sir C. F.
Barry, Sir Francis Tress, 1st Bt, 1825–1907, vol. I
Barry, Rt Rev. (Frank) Russell, 1890–1976, vol. VII
Barry, Sir Gerald Reid, 1898–1968, vol. VI
Barry, Geraldine Mary, 1897–1978, vol. VII
Barry, Rear-Adm. Sir Henry Deacon, 1849–1908, vol. I
Barry, Rt Rev. Hugh Van Lynden O.; see Otter-Barry.
Barry, Iris, 1895–1969, vol. VI
Barry, Hon. Lt-Col James, died 1920, vol. II
Barry, Major James D., died 1941, vol. IV
Barry, Hon. Jeremiah Hayes, 1858–1946, vol. IV
Barry, Rt Rev. John, 1875–1938, vol. III
Barry, John Arthur, 1850–1911, vol. I
Barry, Sir John Edmond, 1828–1919, vol. II
Barry, Hon. Sir John Vincent William, 1903–1969, vol. VI
Barry, Sir John Wolfe Wolfe-, 1836–1918, vol. II
Barry, Michael, (James Barry Jackson), 1910–1988, vol. VIII
Barry, Norman, 1916–1984, vol. VIII
Barry, Sir Patrick Redmond, 1898–1972, vol. VII
Barry, Philip; see Barry, D. A. P.
Barry, Sir Philip Stuart M.; see Milner-Barry.
Barry, Ralph Brereton, 1856–1920, vol. II
Barry, Redmond, 1866–1913, vol. I
Barry, Richard Fitzwilliam, 1861–1916, vol. II(A), vol. III
Barry, Maj.-Gen. Richard Hugh, 1908–1999, vol. X
Barry, Sir Rupert Rodney Francis Tress, 4th Bt, 1910–1977, vol. VII
Barry, Rt Rev. Russell; see Barry, Rt Rev. F. R.
Barry, Col Stanley Leonard, 1873–1943, vol. IV
Barry, Col Thomas David Collis, died 1943, vol. IV
Barry, Rt Rev. Thomas Francis, 1841–1920, vol. II
Barry, Most Rev. William, 1872–1929, vol. III
Barry, Rt Rev. Mgr William Francis, 1849–1930, vol. III
Barry, William James, 1864–1952, vol. V
Barry, William Whitmore O.; see Otter-Barry.
Barry-Doyle, Rt Rev. Mgr Richard; see Doyle.
Barrymore, 1st Baron, 1843–1925, vol. II
Barrymore, Ethel, 1879–1959, vol. V
Barrymore, John, 1882–1942, vol. IV
Barrymore, Lionel, 1878–1954, vol. V
Barson, Derek Emmanuel, 1922–1980, vol. VII
Barstow, Maj.-Gen. Arthur Edward, 1888–1942, vol. IV
Barstow, Sir George Lewis, 1874–1966, vol. VI
Barstow, Maj.-Gen. Henry, 1876–1952, vol. V
Barstow, Major John Nelson, 1890–1936, vol. III
Barstow, Mrs Montague; see Baroness Orczy
Barstow, Percy Gott, 1883–1969, vol. VI
Bart, Lionel, 1930–1999, vol. X

Bartell, Lt-Col (Hon.) Kenneth George William, 1914–1993, vol. IX
Barter, Lt-Gen. Sir Charles St Leger, 1857–1931, vol. III
Barter, Captain Frederick, died 1953, vol. V
Barter, Geoffrey Herbert, 1901–1952, vol. V
Barter, Rev. Herbert Francis Treseder, 1869–1949, vol. IV
Barter, John Wilfred, 1917–1983, vol. VIII
Barter, Sir Percy, 1886–1975, vol. VII
Barter, Sir Richard, 1837–1916, vol. II
Barth, Lt-Col Sir Jacob William, 1871–1941, vol. IV
Barth, Karl, 1886–1968, vol. VI
Bartholomé, Albert, 1848–1928, vol. II
Bartholomew, Maj.-Gen. Arthur Wollaston, 1878–1945, vol. IV
Bartholomew, Sir Clarence Edward, 1879–1946, vol. IV
Bartholomew, Col Hugh John, 1871–1938, vol. III
Bartholomew, James Rankin, 1887–1951, vol. V(A)
Bartholomew, John, 1870–1937, vol. III
Bartholomew, John, 1890–1962, vol. VI
Bartholomew, John Eric, (Eric Morecambe), 1926–1984, vol. VIII
Bartholomew, John George, 1860–1920, vol. II
Bartholomew, Gen. Sir William Henry, 1877–1962, vol. VI
Barthorpe, Major Sir Frederick James, died 1942, vol. IV
Bartington, Dennis Walter, 1901–1985, vol. VIII
Bartle, Anita Jane Craven, died 1962, vol. VI
Bartleet, Rev. Edwin Berry, 1872–1946, vol. IV
Bartleet, Rev. Samuel Edwin, 1835–1924, vol. II
Bartleman, Maj.-Gen. Woodburn Francis, 1840–1924, vol. II
Bartlet, James Vernon, 1863–1940, vol. III
Bartlet, Rev. T. J., 1833–1915, vol. I
Bartlett, Lt-Col Alfred James Napier, 1884–1956, vol. V
Bartlett, Ven. Arthur Robert, 1851–1923, vol. II
Bartlett, Lt-Col Sir Basil Hardington, 2nd Bt, 1905–1985, vol. VIII
Bartlett, Cdre Charles Alfred, 1868–1945, vol. IV
Bartlett, Sir Charles John, 1889–1955, vol. V
Bartlett, Rev. Charles Oldfeld, 1858–1937, vol. III
Bartlett, (Charles) Vernon (Oldfeld), 1894–1983, vol. VIII
Bartlett, Sir David; see Bartlett, Sir H. D. H.
Bartlett, Rt Rev. David Daniel, 1900–1977, vol. VII
Bartlett, Rev. Canon Donald Mackenzie Maynard, 1873–1969, vol. VI
Bartlett, Ellis A.; see Ashmead-Bartlett.
Bartlett, Sir Ellis Ashmead-, 1849–1902, vol. I
Bartlett, Sir Frederic Charles, 1886–1969, vol. VI
Bartlett, George Bertram, 1880–1944, vol. IV
Bartlett, Sir (Henry) David (Hardington), 3rd Bt, 1912–1989, vol. VIII
Bartlett, Sir Herbert Henry, 1st Bt, 1842–1921, vol. II
Bartlett, Humphrey Edward Gibson, 1880–1951, vol. V
Bartlett, Sir John Hardington, 4th Bt, 1938–1998, vol. X
Bartlett, Joseph Leslie, 1889–1968, vol. VI

Bartlett, Paul Wayland, 1865–1925, vol. II
Bartlett, Peter Geoffrey, 1922–1986, vol. VIII
Bartlett, Vernon; see Bartlett, C. V. O.
Bartlett, W. H., 1858–1932, vol. III
Bartlett-Burdett-Coutts, Rt Hon. William Lehman Ashmead; see Burdett-Coutts.
Bartley, Lt-Col Bryan Cole, 1875–1968, vol. VI
Bartley, Sir Charles, 1882–1968, vol. VI
Bartley, Sir George Christopher Trout, 1842–1910, vol. I
Bartley, Sir John, 1886–1954, vol. V
Bartley, Patrick, 1909–1956, vol. V
Bartley, William, 1885–1961, vol. VI
Bartley-Denniss, Lt-Col Cyril Edmund Bartley, 1882–1955, vol. V
Bartley-Denniss, Sir Edmund Robert Bartley, 1854–1931, vol. III
Bartók, Béla, 1881–1945, vol. IV
Bartolo, Hon. Sir Augustus, 1883–1937, vol. III
Bartolomé, Adm. Sir Charles Martin de, 1871–1941, vol. IV
Barton, Arthur Edward Victor, 1892–1983, vol. VIII
Barton, Most Rev. Arthur William, 1881–1962, vol. VI
Barton, Arthur Willoughby, 1899–1976, vol. VII
Barton, Lt-Col Baptist Johnston, 1876–1944, vol. IV
Barton, Major Basil Kelsey, 1879–1958, vol. V
Barton, Cecil James Juxon Talbot, 1891–1980, vol. VII
Barton, Cecil Molyneux, 1883–1962, vol. VI
Barton, Major Charles Gerard, 1860–1919, vol. II
Barton, Sir Charles Newton, 1907–1987, vol. VIII
Barton, Lt-Col Charles Walter, 1876–1950, vol. IV
Barton, Clarence, 1892–1957, vol. V
Barton, Sir Derek Harold Richard, 1918–1998, vol. X
Barton, Rt Hon. Sir (Dunbar) Plunket, 1st Bt, 1853–1937, vol. III
Barton, Rt Hon. Sir Edmund, 1849–1920, vol. II
Barton, Edwin Alfred, 1863–1953, vol. V
Barton, Edwin Henry, 1858–1925, vol. II
Barton, Adm. Ernest Gillbe, 1861–1938, vol. III
Barton, Captain Francis Rickman, 1865–1947, vol. IV
Barton, Frederick Sherbrooke, 1895–1969, vol. VI
Barton, Maj.-Gen. Sir Geoffry, 1844–1922, vol. II
Barton, Rev. George Aaron, 1859–1942, vol. IV
Barton, George Alexander Heaton, 1865–1924, vol. II
Barton, George Samuel Horace, 1883–1962, vol. VI
Barton, Guy Trayton, 1908–1977, vol. VII
Barton, Sir Harold Montague, 1882–1962, vol. VI
Barton, Ven. Harry Douglas, 1898–1968, vol. VI
Barton, Lt-Col Sir Henry Baldwin, 1869–1952, vol. V
Barton, Sir John George, 1850–1937, vol. III
Barton, Rt Rev. Mgr John Mackintosh Tilney, 1898–1977, vol. VII
Barton, John Saxon, 1875–1961, vol. VI
Barton, Joseph Edwin, 1875–1959, vol. V
Barton, Lt-Col Leslie Eric, 1889–1952, vol. V
Barton, Margaret, born 1897, vol. IX
Barton, Col Maurice Charles, 1852–1939, vol. III

Barton, Rt Hon. Sir Plunket; see Barton, Rt Hon. Sir D. P.
Barton, Richard, 1850–1927, vol. II
Barton, Lt-Col Richard Lionel, 1875–1942, vol. IV
Barton, Robert Childers, 1881–1975, vol. VII
Barton, Rose, died 1929, vol. III
Barton, Samuel Saxon, died 1957, vol. V
Barton, Sir Sidney, 1876–1946, vol. IV
Barton, Sidney James, 1909–1986, vol. VIII
Barton, Rev. Walter John, died 1955, vol. V
Barton, Wilfred Alexander, 1880–1953, vol. V
Barton, Sir William, 1862–1957, vol. V
Barton, William Henry, 1869–1928, vol. II
Barton, Lt-Col William Hugh, 1874–1945, vol. IV
Barton, Sir William Pell, 1871–1956, vol. V
Bartram, Rev. Henry, 1849–1934, vol. III
Bartram, Sir Robert Appleby, 1835–1925, vol. II
Barttelot, Adm. Sir Brian Herbert Fairbairn, 1867–1942, vol. IV
Barttelot, Major Sir Walter Balfour, 3rd Bt, 1880–1918, vol. II
Barttelot, Lt-Col Sir Walter de Stopham, 4th Bt, 1904–1944, vol. IV
Barttelot, Sir Walter George, 2nd Bt, 1855–1900, vol. I
Barty, James Webster, 1841–1915, vol. I
Baruch, Bernard Mannes, 1870–1965, vol. VI
Barwell, Rev. Arthur Henry Sanxay, 1834–1913, vol. I
Barwell, Claud Foster, 1912–1971, vol. VII
Barwell, Harold Shuttleworth, 1875–1959, vol. V
Barwell, Hon. Sir Henry Newman, 1877–1959, vol. V
Barwick, Rt Hon. Sir Garfield Edward John, 1903–1997, vol. X
Barwick, George Frederick, 1853–1931, vol. III
Barwick, Sir John Storey, 1st Bt, 1840–1915, vol. I
Barwick, Sir John Storey, 2nd Bt, 1876–1953, vol. V
Barwick, Sir Richard Llewellyn, 3rd Bt, 1916–1979, vol. VII
Barzellotti, Giacomo, 1844–1917, vol. II
Basden, Rev. George Thomas, 1873–1944, vol. IV
Basedow, Herbert, 1881–1933, vol. III
Bashford, Ernest Francis, 1873–1923, vol. II
Bashford, Sir Henry Howarth, 1880–1961, vol. VI
Bashford, Rt Rev. James W., 1849–1919, vol. II
Bashford, John Laidlay, died 1908, vol. I
Bashford, Major Lindsay; see Bashford, Major R. J. L.
Bashford, Major (Radcliffe James) Lindsay, 1881–1921, vol. II
Bashyam Aiyangar, Sir Venbakam, died 1908, vol. I
Basing, 2nd Baron, 1860–1919, vol. II
Basing, 3rd Baron, 1890–1969, vol. VI
Basing, 4th Baron, 1903–1983, vol. VIII
Basinski, Zbigniew Stanislaw, 1928–1999, vol. X
Baskcomb-Harrison, Captain Henry Neville; see Harrison.
Baskerville, Beatrice; see Guichard, B. C.
Baskerville, Rev. Charles Gardiner, 1830–1921, vol. II
Baskerville, Lt-Col Charles Herbert Lethbridge, 1860–1946, vol. IV
Baskerville, Geoffrey, 1870–1944, vol. IV

Baskerville, Rev. Canon George Knyfton, 1867–1941, vol. IV
Baskerville, Ralph Hopton, 1883–1918, vol. II
Baskett, Charles H., 1872–1953, vol. V
Baskett, Sir Ronald Gilbert, 1901–1972, vol. VII
Basnett, Baron (Life Peer); David Basnett, 1924–1989, vol. VIII
Bason, Fred, (Frederick Thomas Bason), 1907–1973, vol. VII
Bass, Hamar Alfred, 1842–1898, vol. I
Bass, John Stuart, 1905–1954, vol. V
Bass, Col Philip de Salis, 1862–1936, vol. III
Bass, Sir William Arthur Hamar, 2nd Bt, 1879–1952, vol. V
Bassano, 3rd Duc de, 1844–1906, vol. I
Basser, Sir Adolph, 1887–1964, vol. VI
Basset, Alfred Barnard, 1854–1930, vol. III
Basset, Lady Elizabeth, 1908–2000, vol. X
Bassett, Arthur Francis, 1873–1950, vol. IV
Bassett, Maj.-Gen. Richard Augustin Marriott, 1891–1954, vol. V
Basset, Ronald Lambart, 1898–1972, vol. VII
Bassett, Arthur Tilney, 1869–1964, vol. VI
Bassett, George Arthur, 1884–1971, vol. VII
Bassett, Henry, 1881–1965, vol. VI
Bassett, Herbert Harry, 1874–1939, vol. III(A), vol. IV
Bassett, John Harold, died 1974, vol. VII
Bassett, John Spencer, 1867–1928, vol. II
Bassett, Ralph Henry, 1896–1962, vol. VI
Bassett, Sir Walter Eric, 1892–1978, vol. VII
Bassett Smith, Guy; see Bassett Smith, N. G.
Bassett Smith, (Newlands) Guy, 1910–1984, vol. VIII
Bassett-Smith, Surg.-Rear-Adm. Sir Percy William, 1861–1927, vol. II
Bastable, Charles F., 1855–1945, vol. IV
Bastard, Bt Col Reginald, 1880–1960, vol. V
Bastard, Rev. William Pollexfen, 1832–1915, vol. I
Basten, Sir Henry Bolton, 1903–1992, vol. IX
Bastian, Henry Charlton, 1837–1915, vol. I
Bastin, Brig. David Terence, 1904–1982, vol. VIII
Bastin, Maj.-Gen. George Edward Restalic, 1902–1960, vol. V
Bastyan, Lt-Gen. Sir Edric Montague, 1903–1980, vol. VII
Bastyan, Maj.-Gen. Kenneth Cecil Orville, 1906–1975, vol. VII
Basu, Bhupendra Nath, 1859–1924, vol. II
Basu, Hon. Bijay Kumar, 1885–1937, vol. III
Batchelor, Alfred Alexander Meston, 1901–1982, vol. VIII
Batchelor, Rev. Alfred Williams, 1864–1961, vol. VI
Batchelor, Denzil Stanley, 1906–1969, vol. VI
Batchelor, Hon. Egerton Lee, 1865–1911, vol. I
Batchelor, Ferdinand Campion, died 1916, vol. II
Batchelor, Francis Malcolm, 1865–1937, vol. III
Batchelor, George Frederick Grant, 1902–1984, vol. VIII
Batchelor, George Keith, 1920–2000, vol. X
Batchelor, Col Gordon Guthrie Malcolm, 1908–1976, vol. VII
Batchelor, John Stanley, 1905–1987, vol. VIII
Batchelor, Meston; see Batchelor, A. A. M.

Batchelor, Sir Stanley Lockhart, 1868–1938, vol. III
Batchelor, Lt-Col Vivian Allan, 1882–1960, vol. V
Bate, Ven. Alban F., 1893–1986, vol. VIII
Bate, Col Albert Louis Frederick, 1862–1924, vol. II
Bate, Maj.-Gen. (Alfred) Christopher, 1927–1980, vol. VII
Bate, Maj.-Gen. Christopher; see Bate, Maj.-Gen. A. C.
Bate, Captain Claude Lindsay, died 1957, vol. V
Bate, Edward Raoul, 1859–1948, vol. IV
Bate, Sir Edwin; see Bate, Sir W. E.
Bate, Francis, died 1950, vol. IV
Bate, Henry, see Bate, I. H.
Bate, Sir Henry Newel, 1828–1917, vol. II
Bate, Very Rev. Herbert Newell, 1871–1941, vol. IV
Bate, (Isaac) Henry, 1899–1986, vol. VIII
Bate, John Pawley, 1857–1921, vol. II
Bate, Percy, 1868–1913, vol. I
Bate, Col Thomas Elwood Lindsay, 1852–1937, vol. III
Bate, Brig.-Gen. Thomas Reginald Fraser, 1881–1964, vol. VI
Bate, Sir (Walter) Edwin, 1901–1999, vol. X
Bate, Walter Jackson, 1918–1999, vol. X
Bate, Dame Zara Kate, 1909–1989, vol. VIII
Bate-Smith, Edgar Charles, 1900–1989, vol. VIII
Bateman, 2nd Baron, 1826–1901, vol. I
Bateman, 3rd Baron, 1856–1931, vol. III
Bateman, Sir Alfred Edmund, 1844–1929, vol. III
Bateman, Alys, died 1924, vol. II
Bateman, Rev. Arthur Fitzroy D.; see Dobbie-Bateman.
Bateman, Arthur Leonard, 1879–1957, vol. V
Bateman, Brig.-Gen. Bernard Montague, 1865–1937, vol. III
Bateman, Sir Cecil Joseph, 1910–1997, vol. X
Bateman, Sir Charles Harold, 1892–1986, vol. VIII
Bateman, Maj.-Gen. Donald Roland Edwin Rowan, 1901–1969, vol. VI
Bateman, Edward Louis, 1834–1909, vol. I
Bateman, Francis John Harvey, died 1920, vol. II
Bateman, Sir Frederic, 1824–1904, vol. I
Bateman, Sir Geoffrey Hirst, 1906–1998, vol. X
Bateman, George Cecil, 1882–1963, vol. VI
Bateman, Lt-Col Harold Henry, 1888–1974, vol. VII
Bateman, Harry, 1882–1946, vol. IV
Bateman, Henry Mayo, 1887–1970, vol. VI
Bateman, James, died 1959, vol. V
Bateman, John, 1839–1910, vol. I
Bateman, Sir Ralph Melton, 1910–1996, vol. X
Bateman, Rev. William Fairbairn La Trobe-, 1845–1926, vol. II
Bateman, Rev. William Henry Fraser, 1855–1923, vol. II
Bateman-Champain, Brig.-Gen. Hugh Frederick, 1869–1933, vol. III
Bateman-Champain, Rt Rev. John Norman, 1880–1950, vol. IV
Bateman-Hanbury, Rev. Hon. Arthur Allen, 1829–1919, vol. II
Bateman-Hanbury, Captain Hon. Charles Stanhope Melville, 1877–1931, vol. III

Bateman-Hanbury, Major Edward Reginald, 1859–1907, vol. I
Bater, Rev. Alfred Brenchly, *died* 1933, vol. III
Bates, Sir Alfred, 1897–1979, vol. VII
Bates, Allan Frederick, 1911–1991, vol. IX
Bates, Arlo, 1850–1918, vol. II
Bates, Arthur Henry, *died* 1947, vol. IV
Bates, Lt-Col Austin Graves, 1891–1961, vol. VI
Bates, Major Cecil Robert, 1882–1935, vol. III
Bates, Brig.-Gen. Sir (Charles) Loftus, 1863–1951, vol. V
Bates, Sir Darrell; *see* Bates, Sir J. D.
Bates, Sir David Robert, 1916–1994, vol. IX
Bates, Sir Dawson; *see* Bates, Sir J. D.
Bates, Rt Hon. Sir Dawson; *see* Bates, Rt Hon. Sir R. D.
Bates, Sir Edward Bertram, 3rd Bt (*cr* 1880), 1877–1903, vol. I
Bates, Maj.-Gen. Sir (Edward) John (Hunter), 1911–1992, vol. IX
Bates, Sir Edward Percy, 2nd Bt (*cr* 1880), 1845–1899, vol. I
Bates, Eric, 1908–1999, vol. X
Bates, Air-Vice-Marshal Eric Cecil, 1906–1975, vol. VII
Bates, Brig.-Gen. Francis Stewart Montague, 1876–1954, vol. V
Bates, Frederic Alan, 1884–1957, vol. V
Bates, Harry, 1851–1899, vol. I
Bates, Harry Stuart, 1893–1985, vol. VIII
Bates, Henry Montague, 1849–1928, vol. II
Bates, Henry Thomas Roy, 1902–1958, vol. V
Bates, Herbert Ernest, 1905–1974, vol. VII
Bates, Maj.-Gen. Sir John; *see* Bates Maj.-Gen. Sir E. J. H.
Bates, Sir John David, 1904–1992, vol. IX
Bates, Sir (John) Dawson, 2nd Bt, 1921–1998, vol. X
Bates, Sir (Julian) Darrell, 1913–1989, vol. VIII
Bates, Leslie Fleetwood, 1897–1978, vol. VII
Bates, Air Vice-Marshal Sir Leslie John Vernon, 1896–1966, vol. VI
Bates, Brig.-Gen. Sir Loftus; *see* Bates, Brig.-Gen. Sir C. L.
Bates, Ven. Mansel Harry, 1912–1980, vol. VII
Bates, Oric, 1883–1918, vol. II
Bates, Sir Percy Elly, 4th Bt (*cr* 1880), 1879–1946, vol. IV
Bates, Ralph, 1899–2000, vol. X
Bates, Rt Hon. Sir (Richard) Dawson, 1st Bt (*cr* 1937), 1876–1949, vol. IV
Bates, Stewart Taverner, 1926–1999, vol. X
Bates, Rev. Canon T., 1842–1911, vol. I
Bates, Thorpe, 1883–1958, vol. V
Bates, William Stanley, 1920–1993, vol. IX
Bateson, Sir Alexander Dingwall, 1866–1935, vol. III
Bateson, Andrew James, 1929–1995, vol. IX
Bateson, Lt-Col David Mayhew, 1906–1975, vol. VII
Bateson, Sir Dingwall Latham, 1898–1967, vol. VI
Bateson, Frederick Wilse, 1901–1978, vol. VII
Bateson, Col John Holgate, 1880–1956, vol. V
Bateson, Rev. Joseph Harger, 1865–1935, vol. III
Bateson, Mary, 1865–1906, vol. I

Bateson, Air Vice-Marshal Robert Norman, 1912–1986, vol. VIII
Bateson, Rear-Adm. Stuart Latham, 1898–1980, vol. VII
Bateson, Williams, 1861–1926, vol. II
Batey, Charles Edward, 1893–1981, vol. VIII
Batey, Joseph, 1867–1949, vol. IV
Batey, Rowland William John S.; *see* Scott-Batey.
Bath, 5th Marquess of, 1862–1946, vol. IV
Bath, 6th Marquess of, 1905–1992, vol. IX
Bath, Engr-Rear-Adm. George Clark, 1862–1925, vol. II
Bath, Hon. Thomas Henry, 1875–1956, vol. V
Bather, Elizabeth Constance, 1904–1988, vol. VIII
Bather, Francis Arthur, 1863–1934, vol. III
Bather, Ven. Henry Francis, 1832–1905, vol. I
Bather, Rear-Adm. Rowland Henry, 1873–1961, vol. VI
Batho, Sir Charles Albert, 1st Bt, 1872–1938, vol. III
Batho, Cyril, 1885–1951, vol. V
Batho, Edith Clara, 1895–1986, vol. VIII
Batho, Sir Maurice Benjamin, 2nd Bt, 1910–1990, vol. VIII
Bathurst, 7th Earl, 1864–1943, vol. IV
Bathurst, Lt-Col Hon. (Allen) Benjamin, 1872–1947, vol. IV
Bathurst, Lt-Col Hon. Benjamin; *see* Bathurst, Lt-Col Hon. A. B.
Bathurst, Charles, 1836–1907, vol. I
Bathurst, Ven. Frederick, *died* 1910, vol. I
Bathurst, Major Sir Frederick Edward William Hervey-, 5th Bt, 1870–1956, vol. V
Bathurst, Sir Frederick Peter Methuen Hervey-, 6th, Bt, 1903–1995, vol. IX
Bathurst, Sir Frederick Thomas Arthur Hervey, 4th Bt, 1833–1900, vol. I
Bathurst, Joan Caroline, (Lady Bathurst); *see* Petrie, J. C.
Bathurst, Hon. William Ralph Seymour, 1903–1970, vol. VI
Batiffol, Pierre Henry, 1861–1929, vol. III
Batley, Mabel Terry; *see* Lewis, M. T.
Batsford, Sir Brian Caldwell Cook, 1910–1991, vol. IX
Batson, Col Herbert, 1853–1941, vol. IV
Batson, Reginald George, 1885–1974, vol. VII
Batt, Rear-Adm. Charles Ernest, 1874–1958, vol. V
Batt, Francis Raleigh, 1890–1961, vol. VI
Batt, Lt-Col Reginald Cossley, 1872–1952, vol. V
Batt, Reginald Joseph Alexander, 1920–1991, vol. IX
Batt, Lt-Col William Elliott, 1882–1971, vol. VII
Batt, William Loren, 1885–1965, vol. VI
Battcock, Col Grenville Arthur, 1882–1964, vol. VI
Batten, Adm.Alexander William Chisholm, 1851–1925, vol. II
Batten, Edith Mary, 1905–1985, vol. VIII
Batten, Frederick Eustace, 1865–1918, vol. II
Batten, (Harry) Mortimer, 1888–1958, vol. V
Batten, Col Herbert Cary George, 1849–1926, vol. II
Batten, Col Herbert Copeland Cary, 1884–1963, vol. VI
Batten, Herbert Ernest, 1877–1950, vol. IV

Batten, Jean Gardner, 1909–1982, vol. VIII
Batten, Sir John Kaye, 1865–1938, vol. III
Batten, Col John Mount, 1843–1916, vol. II
Batten, John Winterbotham, 1831–1901, vol. I
Batten, Lauriston Leonard, 1863–1934, vol. III
Batten, Mark Wilfrid, 1905–1993, vol. IX
Batten, Mortimer; see Batten, H. M.
Batten, Maj.-Gen. Richard Hutchison, 1908–1972, vol. VII
Batterbee, Sir Harry Fagg, 1880–1976, vol. VII
Battersby, Edmund James, 1911–1978, vol. VII
Battersby, Rev. Preb. Gerald William, 1911–1961, vol. VI
Battersby, Henry Francis Prevost, died 1949, vol. IV
Battersby, Maj.-Gen. John Prevost, 1826–1917, vol. II
Battersby, Maj.-Gen. Thomas Preston, died 1941, vol. IV
Battersby, Thomas Stephenson Francis, 1855–1933, vol. III
Battersea, 1st Baron, 1843–1907, vol. I
Battersea, Lady; (Constance), 1843–1931, vol. III
Battershill, Sir William Denis, 1896–1959, vol. V
Battey, Mrs E. J.; see White, E. E. McI.
Batthyany-Strattmann, HSH Edmund, 1826–1914, vol. I
Battine, Lt-Col Reginald St Clair, 1869–1942, vol. IV
Battiscombe, Rear-Adm. Albert Henry William, 1831–1918, vol. II
Battistini, Mattia, 1858–1928, vol. II
Battle, George Frederick Newsum, 1897–1966, vol. VI
Battle, Richard John Vulliamy, 1907–1982, vol. VIII
Battle, William Henry, died 1936, vol. III
Battley, John Rose, 1880–1952, vol. V
Batty, Archibald Douglas George Staunton, 1877–1961, vol. VI
Batty, Rt Rev. Basil Staunton, died 1952, vol. V
Batty, Christina Agnes Lillian, (Mrs Ronald Batty); see Foyle, C. A. L.
Batty, Rt Rev. Francis de Witt, 1879–1961, vol. VI
Batty, Herbert, 1849–1923, vol. II
Batty, James Henly, 1868–1946, vol. IV
Batty, Tom, 1906–1980, vol. VII
Batty-Smith, Henry, died 1927, vol. II
Battye, Maj.-Gen. Arthur, 1839–1909, vol. I
Battye, Aubyn Bernard Rochfort T.; see Trevor-Battye.
Battye, Col Basil Condon, 1882–1932, vol. III
Battye, Lt-Col Clinton Wynyard, 1874–1917, vol. II
Battye, Maj.-Gen. Henry Doveton, 1833–1915, vol. I
Battye, Brig. Ivan Urmston, 1875–1953, vol. V
Battye, James Sykes, 1871–1954, vol. V
Battye, Lt-Col Montague M'Pherson, 1836–1929, vol. III
Battye, Major Richmond Keith Molesworth, 1905–1958, vol. V
Battye, Maj.-Gen. Stuart Hedley Molesworth, 1907–1987, vol. VIII
Battye, Lt-Col Walter Rothney, 1874–1943, vol. IV
Baty, Charles Witcomb, 1900–1979, vol. VII
Baty, Thomas, 1869–1954, vol. V

Bauchop, Lt-Col Arthur, 1871–1915, vol. I
Baud, Rt Rev. Joseph A., 1890–1980, vol. VII(AII)
Baudains, Captain George La Croix, 1892–1942, vol. IV
Baudains, Captain Philip, 1836–1909, vol. I
Baudouin, Charles, 1893–1963, vol. VI
Baudoux, Most Rev. Maurice, 1902–1988, vol. VIII
Baudrillart, Cardinal Henri Marie Alfred, 1859–1942, vol. IV
Bauer, Louis Hopewell, 1888–1964, vol. VI(AII)
Baugh, Charles Herbert, 1881–1953, vol. V
Baugh, Captain George Johnstone, 1862–1924, vol. II
Baughan, Edward Algernon, 1865–1938, vol. III
Baughan, William Frederick, 1834–1908, vol. I
Baulkwill, Sir Pridham; see Baulkwill, Sir R. P.
Baulkwill, Sir (Reginald) Pridham, 1895–1974, vol. VII
Baulkwill, Rev. William Robert Kellaway, 1860–1915, vol. I
Baum, David; see Baum, J. D.
Baum, (John) David, 1940–1999, vol. X
Baum, Vicki, 1896–1960, vol. V
Baumann, Arthur Anthony, 1856–1936, vol. III
Baume, Eric; see Baume, F. E.
Baume, Frederick Ehrenfried, (Eric Baume), 1900–1967, vol. VI
Baumer, Lewis C. E., 1870–1963, vol. VI
Baverstock, Rev. Alban Henry, 1871–1950, vol. IV
Baverstock, Donald Leighton, 1924–1995, vol. IX
Bavin, John Thomas, died 1937, vol. III
Bavin, Hon. Sir Thomas Rainsford, 1874–1941, vol. IV
Bawden, Edward, 1903–1989, vol. VIII
Bawden, Sir Frederick Charles, 1908–1972, vol. VII
Bawden, Michael George, 1935–1999, vol. X
Bax, Sir Arnold Edward Trevor, 1883–1953, vol. V
Bax, Clifford, 1886–1962, vol. VI
Bax, Ernest Belfort, 1854–1926, vol. II
Bax, Adm. Robert Nesham, 1875—1969, vol. VI
Bax, Rodney Ian Shirley, 1920–1983, vol. VIII
Bax-Ironside, Sir Henry George Outram, 1859–1929, vol. III
Baxandall, David Kighley, 1905–1992, vol. IX
Baxendale, Col Joseph Francis Noel, 1877–1957, vol. V
Baxendale, Joseph William, 1848–1915, vol. I
Baxter, Alexander Duncan, 1908–1988, vol. VIII
Baxter, Sir (Arthur) Beverley, 1891–1964, vol. VI
Baxter, Cdre Sir Arthur James, 1890–1951, vol. V
Baxter, Sir Beverley; see Baxter, Sir A. B.
Baxter, Charles William, 1895–1969, vol. VI
Baxter, Frederick William, 1897–1980, vol. VII
Baxter, George Herbert, 1894–1962, vol. VI
Baxter, Sir George Washington, 1st Bt, 1853–1926, vol. II
Baxter, Herbert James, 1900–1974, vol. VII
Baxter, James, 1886–1964, vol. VI
Baxter, James Houson, 1894–1973, vol. VII
Baxter, James Sinclair, died 1933, vol. III
Baxter, James Thomson, 1925–1985, vol. VIII
Baxter, Jeremy Richard, 1929–1991, vol. IX
Baxter, John Babington Macaulay, 1868–1946, vol. IV
Baxter, Sir (John) Philip, 1905–1989, vol. VIII

51

Baxter, Rev. Michael Paget, 1834–1910, vol. I
Baxter, Sir Philip; see Baxter, Sir J. P.
Baxter, Sir Thomas, 1878–1951, vol. V
Baxter, Thomas Tennant, 1894–1947, vol. IV
Baxter, Walter, 1915–1994, vol. IX
Baxter, William, 1911–1979, vol. VII
Baxter, Sir William James, 1845–1918, vol. II
Baxter, Wynne Edwin, 1844–1920, vol. II
Bayard, Brig.-Gen. Reginald, 1860–1925, vol. II
Bayer, Sir Horace, 1878–1965, vol. VI
Bayes, Gilbert, 1872–1952, vol. V
Bayes, Walter, 1869–1956, vol. V
Bayfield, Rev. Matthew Albert, 1852–1922, vol. II
Bayford, 1st Baron, 1867–1940, vol. III
Bayford, Major Edmund Heseltine, 1873–1942, vol. IV
Bayford, Robert Augustus, 1838–1922, vol. II
Bayford, Robert Frederic, 1871–1951, vol. V
Baykov, Alexander M., 1899–1963, vol. VI
Baylay, Brig.-Gen. Sir Atwell Charles, 1879–1957, vol. V
Baylay, Brig.-Gen. Frederick, 1865–1956, vol. V
Bayles, Herbert Laurence, 1886–1940, vol. III
Bayley, Col Arthur George, 1878–1949, vol. IV
Bayley, Charles Butterworth, 1876–1926, vol. II
Bayley, Charles Clive, 1864–1923, vol. II
Bayley, Sir Charles Stuart, 1854–1935, vol. III
Bayley, Lt-Col Edward Charles, 1867–1924, vol. II
Bayley, Brig.-Gen. Gerald Edward, 1874–1955, vol. V
Bayley, Sir H. Dennis R.; see Readett-Bayley.
Bayley, Lt-Col Hadrian, died 1931, vol. II
Bayley, Dame Iris; see Murdoch, Dame J. I.
Bayley, Sir John, 1852–1952, vol. V
Bayley, Maj.-Gen. Kennett, 1903–1967, vol. VI
Bayley, Col Lionel Seton, 1875–1940, vol. III
Bayley, Sir Lyttelton Holyoake, 1827–1910, vol. I
Bayley, Sir Steuart Colvin, 1836–1925, vol. II
Bayley, Lt-Col Steuart Farquharson, 1863–1938, vol. III
Bayley, Thomas, 1846–1906, vol. I
Bayley, Vernon Thomas, 1908–1966, vol. VI
Bayley, Victor, 1880–1972, vol. VII
Bayliffe, Col Alfred Danvers, 1873–1942, vol. IV
Baylis, Clifford Henry, 1915–1998, vol. X
Baylis, Rev. Frederick, died 1935, vol. III
Baylis, Harry Arnold, 1889–1972, vol. VII
Baylis, Lilian Mary, 1874–1937, vol. III
Baylis, Thomas Henry, 1817–1908, vol. I
Bayliss, Edwin, 1894–1971, vol. VII
Bayliss, Col George Sheldon, 1900–1984, vol. VIII
Bayliss, Sir Noel Stanley, 1906–1996, vol. X
Bayliss, William, 1886–1963, vol. VI
Bayliss, Sir William Maddock, 1860–1924, vol. II
Bayliss, Sir Wyke, 1835–1906, vol. I
Bayly, Lt-Col Abingdon Robert, 1871–1952, vol. V
Bayly, Ada Ellen, 1857–1903, vol. I
Bayly, Maj.-Gen. Sir Alfred William Lambart, 1856–1928, vol. II
Bayly, Edward, 1865–1934, vol. III
Bayly, Major Edward Archibald Theodore, 1877–1959, vol. V
Bayly, Francis Albert, died 1911, vol. I
Bayly, Hugh Wansey, 1873–1946, vol. IV
Bayly, Gen. John, 1821–1905, vol. I

Bayly, Adm. Sir Lewis, 1857–1938, vol. III
Bayly, Vice-Adm. Sir Patrick Uniacke, 1914–1998, vol. X
Bayly, Col Richard Kerr, 1838–1903, vol. I
Bayly, William Reynolds, 1867–1937, vol. III
Bayne, Charles Gerwien, 1860–1947, vol. IV
Bayne, Charles S., 1876–1952, vol. V
Bayne, Charles Walter, 1872–1937, vol. III
Bayne, John, died 1994, vol. IX
Bayne, Ven. Percy Matheson, 1865–1942, vol. IV
Bayne, Rt Rev. Stephen Fielding, Jr, 1908–1974, vol. VII
Bayne, Thomas Wilson, 1845–1931, vol. III
Bayne, William, died 1922, vol. II
Bayne-Jardine, Brig. Christian West, 1888–1959, vol. V
Bayne-Powell, Robert Lane, 1910–1994, vol. IX
Baynes, Rt Rev. Arthur Hamilton, 1854–1942, vol. IV
Baynes, Sir Christopher William, 4th Bt, 1847–1936, vol. III
Baynes, Dorothy Julia C.; see Colston-Baynes.
Baynes, Edward Stuart Augustus, 1889–1972, vol. VII
Baynes, Edward William, 1880–1962, vol. VI
Baynes, Frederic William Wilberforce, 1889–1967, vol. VI
Baynes, Frederick, 1848–1917, vol. II
Baynes, Lt-Gen. George Edward, 1823–1906, vol. I
Baynes, Helton Godwin, 1882–1943, vol. IV
Baynes, Hon. Joseph, 1842–1925, vol. II
Baynes, Keith Stuart, 1887–1977, vol. VII
Baynes, Norman Hepburn, 1877–1961, vol. VI
Baynes, Robert Edward, 1849–1921, vol. II
Baynes, Sir Rory Malcolm Stuart, 6th Bt, 1886–1979, vol. VII
Baynes, Sir William Edward Colston, 5th Bt, 1876–1971, vol. VII
Baynes, Sir William John Walter, 3rd Bt, 1820–1897, vol. I
Baynham, Brig. Cuthbert Theodore, 1889–1966, vol. VI
Baynham, Tom, 1904–1985, vol. VIII
Baynham, Captain Sir Walter de Mouchet, 1876–1936, vol. III
Bazarrabusa, Byabasakuzi Timothy, 1912–1966, vol. VI
Bazeley, Rev. William, 1843–1925, vol. II
Bazell, Charles Ernest, 1909–1984, vol. VIII
Bazett, Henry Cuthbert, 1885–1950, vol. IV
Bazin, Germain René Michel, 1901–1990, vol. VIII
Bazin, René François Nicolas Marie, died 1932, vol. III
Bazire, Rev. Canon Reginald Victor, 1900–1990, vol. VIII
Bazley, Sir Thomas Sebastian, 2nd Bt, 1829–1919, vol. II
Bazley, Sir Thomas Stafford, 3rd Bt, 1907–1997, vol. X
Bazley-White, John, 1847–1927, vol. II
Bea, HE Cardinal Agostino, 1881–1968, vol. VI
Beach, Charles Fisk, 1854–1934, vol. III
Beach, Col Gerald, 1881–1955, vol. V
Beach, Rex, 1887–1949, vol. IV
Beach, Col Thomas Boswall, 1866–1941, vol. IV

Beach, Lady Victoria Alexandrina H.; *see* Hicks-Beach.
Beach, William Frederick H.; *see* Hicks Beach.
Beach, Maj.-Gen. William Henry, 1871–1952, vol. V
Beach, Surg. Rear-Adm. William Vincent, 1903–1995, vol. IX
Beach, Major William Whitehead H.; *see* Hicks Beach.
Beach, William Wither Bramston H.; *see* Hicks-Beach.
Beachcomber; *see* Morton, J. C. A. B. M.
Beachcroft, Sir Charles Porten, 1871–1927, vol. II
Beachcroft, Maurice; *see* Beachcroft, P. M.
Beachcroft, Sir Melvill; *see* Beachcroft, Sir R. M.
Beachcroft, (Philip) Maurice, 1879–1969, vol. VI
Beachcroft, Sir (Richard) Melvill, 1846–1926, vol. II
Beachcroft, Thomas Owen, 1902–1988, vol. VIII
Beadle, George Wells, 1903–1989, vol. VIII
Beadle, Sir Gerald Clayton, 1899–1976, vol. VII
Beadle, Rt Hon. Sir Hugh; *see* Beadle, Rt Hon. Sir T. H. W.
Beadle, James Prinsep Barnes, 1863–1947, vol. IV
Beadle, Rt Hon. Sir (Thomas) Hugh (William), 1905–1980, vol. VII
Beadnell, Surg. Rear-Adm. Charles Marsh, 1872–1947, vol. IV
Beadnell, Hugh John Llewellyn, 1874–1944, vol. IV
Beadon, Lt-Col Henry Cecil, 1869–1959, vol. V
Beadon, Bt Col Lancelot Richmond, 1875–1922, vol. II
Beadon, Col Roger Hammet, 1887–1945, vol. IV
Beaglehole, John Cawte, 1901–1971, vol. VII
Beak, Maj.-Gen. Daniel Marcus William, 1891–1967, vol. VI
Beak, George Bailey, 1872–1934, vol. III
Beal, Vice-Adm. Alister Francis, 1875–1962, vol. VI
Beal, Charles, 1841–1921, vol. II
Beal, Col Henry, 1843–1905, vol. I
Beal, Col Robert, *died* 1907, vol. I
Beal, Rev. T. Gilbert, 1865–1948, vol. IV
Beale, Charles Gabriel, *died* 1912, vol. I
Beale, Dame Doris Wiifred, 1889–1971, vol. VII
Beale, Dorothea, 1831–1906, vol. I
Beale, Edward; *see* Beale, T. E.
Beale, Evelyn Martin Lansdowne, 1928–1985, vol. VIII
Beale, George Galloway, 1868–1936, vol. III
Beale, Lt-Col Henry Yelverton, 1860–1930, vol. III
Beale, Hon. Sir Howard; *see* Beale, Hon. Sir O. H.
Beale, Sir John Field, 1874–1935, vol. III
Beale, Lionel Smith, 1828–1906, vol. I
Beale, Sir Louis Bernhardt George Stephen, 1879–1971, vol. VII
Beale, Hon. Sir (Oliver) Howard, 1898–1983, vol. VIII
Beale, Percival Spencer, 1906–1981, vol. VIII
Beale, Peter; *see* Beale, Percival S.
Beale, Peyton Todd Bowman, 1864–1957, vol. V
Beale, Sir Samuel Richard, 1881–1964, vol. VI
Beale, (Thomas) Edward, 1904–1998, vol. X
Beale, Sir William Francis, 1908–1992, vol. IX

Beale, Sir William Phipson, 1st Bt, 1839–1922, vol. II
Beale-Browne, Brig.-Gen. Desmond John Edward, 1870–1953, vol. V
Beales, Arthur Charles Frederick, 1905–1974, vol. VII
Beales, Hugh Lancelot, 1889–1988, vol. VIII
Beales, Lance; *see* Beales, H. L.
Beales, Reginald Edwin, 1909–1980, vol. VII
Beall, Lt-Col Edward Metcalfe, 1877–1950, vol. IV
Beall, Captain George, 1840–1918, vol. II
Beals, Carlyle Smith, 1899–1979, vol. VII
Beam, Jacob Dyneley, 1908–1993, vol. IX
Beaman, Bt Lt-Col Ardern Arthur Hulme, 1886–1950, vol. IV
Beaman, Ardern George Hulme, 1857–1929, vol. III
Beaman, Sir Frank Clement Offley, 1858–1928, vol. II
Beaman, Lt-Col Winfrid Kelsey, *died* 1929, vol. III
Beament, Brig. Arthur Warwick, 1898–1966, vol. VI
Beamish, Air Vice-Marshal Cecil Howard, 1915–1999, vol. X
Beamish, Wing-Comdr Francis Victor, 1903–1942, vol. IV
Beamish, Air Marshal Sir George Robert, 1905–1967, vol. VI
Beamish, Rear-Adm. Henry Hamilton, 1829–1901, vol. I
Beamish, Rear-Adm. Tufton Percy Hamilton, 1874–1951, vol. V
Beamish, Tufton Victor Hamilton; *see* Baron Chelwood.
Bean, Rev. Alexander Henry Stillingfleet, 1849–1929, vol. III
Bean, Ven. Arthur Selwyn, 1886–1981, vol. VIII
Bean, Charles Edwin Woodrow, 1879–1968, vol. VI
Bean, Sir Edgar Layton, 1893–1977, vol. VII
Bean, Sir George, 1855–1924, vol. II
Bean, Hon. Sir George Joseph, 1915–1973, vol. VII
Bean, John Harper, 1885–1963, vol. VI
Bean, Robert Ernest, 1935–1987, vol. VIII
Bean, Thomas Ernest, 1900–1983, vol. VIII
Bean, William Jackson, 1863–1947, vol. IV
Beane, Sir Francis Adams, 1872–1959, vol. V
Beaney, Alan, 1905–1985, vol. VIII
Beanland, Maj.-Gen. Douglas, 1893–1963, vol. VI
Beanlands, Rev. Arthur John, 1857–1917, vol. II
Bear, Leslie William, 1911–2000, vol. X
Bearblock, Engr Rear-Adm. Charles William John, 1865–1929, vol. III
Bearcroft, Col Edward Hugh, 1852–1932, vol. III
Bearcroft, Adm. John Edward, 1851–1931, vol. III
Beard, Charles A., 1874–1948, vol. IV
Beard, Charles Thomas, 1858–1918, vol. II
Beard, Derek, 1930–1999, vol. X
Beard, Maj.-Gen. Edmund Charles, 1894–1974, vol. VII
Beard, Lt-Col George John Allen, *died* 1922, vol. II
Beard, James Robert, 1885–1962, vol. VI
Beard, John, 1871–1950, vol. IV
Beard, John Stanley Coombe, 1890–1970, vol. VI
Beard, Sir Lewis, 1858–1933, vol. III
Beard, Paul, 1901–1989, vol. VIII
Beard, Paul Michael, 1930–1989, vol. VIII

Beard, Sidney Hartnoll, 1862–1938, vol. III
Beard, Wilfred Blackwell, 1892–1967, vol. VI
Beardmore, Rt Rev. Harold, 1898–1968, vol. VI
Beards, Paul Francis Richmond, 1916–1993, vol. IX
Beards, Samuel Arthur, *died* 1975, vol. VII
Beardsell, Sir William Arthur, 1865–1940, vol. III
Beardsley, Aubrey, 1874–1898, vol. I
Beardsworth, Air Vice-Marshal George Braithwaite, 1904–1959, vol. V
Beare, Daniel Robert O'S.; *see* O'Sullivan-Beare.
Beare, Ernest Edwin, 1877–1956, vol. V
Beare, John Isaac, *died* 1918, vol. II
Beare, Josias Crocker, 1881–1962, vol. VI
Beare, Sir Thomas Hudson, 1859–1940, vol. III
Beare, William, 1900–1963, vol. VI
Bearn, Edward Gordon, 1887–1945, vol. IV
Bearn, Col Frederic Arnot, 1890–1981, vol. VIII
Bearne, Catherine Mary, *died* 1923, vol. II
Bearne, Lt-Col Lewis Collinwood, 1878–1940, vol. III
Bearsted, 1st Viscount, 1853–1927, vol. II
Bearsted, 2nd Viscount, 1882–1948, vol. IV
Bearsted, 3rd Viscount, 1909–1986, vol. VIII
Bearsted, 4th Viscount, 1911–1996, vol. X
Beasley, Cyril George, 1901–1956, vol. V
Beasley, Sir (Horace) Owen (Compton), 1877–1960, vol. V
Beasley, Rt Hon. John Albert, 1895–1949, vol. IV
Beasley, John T.; *see* Telford Beasley.
Beasley, Sir Owen; *see* Beasley, Sir H. O. C.
Beasley-Murray, George Raymond, 1916–2000, vol. X
Beath, John Henry, 1835–1904, vol. I
Beaton, Lt-Col Angus John, 1858–1945, vol. IV
Beaton, Arthur Charles, 1904–1990, vol. VIII
Beaton, Sir Cecil Walter Hardy, 1904–1980, vol. VII
Beaton, Surg. Rear-Adm. Douglas Murdo, 1901–1990, vol. VIII
Beaton, John Angus, 1909–1987, vol. VIII
Beatson, Col Charles Henry, 1851–1938, vol. III
Beatson, Maj.-Gen. Finlay Cochrane, 1855–1933, vol. III
Beatson, Sir George Thomas, 1848–1933, vol. III
Beatson, Maj.-Gen. Sir Stuart Brownlow, 1854–1914, vol. I
Beatson-Bell, Col John, 1866–1929, vol. III
Beattie, Hon. Sir Alexander Craig, 1912–1999, vol. X
Beattie, Lt-Col Alexander Elder, 1888–1951, vol. V
Beattie, Rt Hon. Sir Andrew, *died* 1923, vol. II
Beattie, Arthur James, 1914–1996, vol. X
Beattie, Sir Carruthers; *see* Beattie, Sir J. C.
Beattie, Charles Innes, 1875–1952, vol. V
Beattie, Charles Noel, 1912–1998, vol. X
Beattie, Colin Panton, 1902–1987, vol. VIII
Beattie, Francis, 1885–1945, vol. IV
Beattie, Sir James, 1861–1933, vol. III
Beattie, James Martin, 1868–1955, vol. V
Beattie, John; *see* Beattie, W. J. H. M.
Beattie, John, *died* 1960, vol. V
Beattie, John, 1899–1976, vol. VII
Beattie, Sir (John) Carruthers, 1866–1946, vol. IV
Beattie, Brig. Joseph Hamilton, 1903–1985, vol. VIII

Beattie, Captain Kenneth Adair, 1883–1940, vol. III
Beattie, Rt Rev. Philip Rodger, 1912–1960, vol. V
Beattie, Robert, 1873–1940, vol. III
Beattie, Captain Stephen Halden, 1908–1975, vol. VII
Beattie, Thomas Brunton, 1924–2000, vol. X
Beattie, William, 1903–1986, vol. VIII
Beattie, Hon. Col Rev. William, 1873–1943, vol. IV
Beattie, (William) John (Hunt Montgomery), 1902–1993, vol. IX
Beattie-Brown, William, 1831–1909, vol. I
Beatty, 1st Earl, 1871–1936, vol. III
Beatty, 2nd Earl, 1905–1972, vol. VII
Beatty, Sir (Alfred) Chester, 1875–1968, vol. VI
Beatty, (Alfred) Chester, 1907–1983, vol. VIII
Beatty, Major Charles Harold Longfield, 1870–1917, vol. II
Beatty, Sir Chester; *see* Beatty, Sir A. C.
Beatty, Chester; *see* Beatty, A. C.
Beatty, Sir Edward Wentworth, 1877–1943, vol. IV
Beatty, Maj.-Gen. Sir Guy Archibald Hastings, 1870–1954, vol. V
Beatty, Haslitt Michael, *died* 1916, vol. II
Beatty, James, 1870–1947, vol. IV
Beatty, Sir Kenneth James, 1878–1966, vol. VI
Beatty, Brig.-Gen. Lionel Nicholson, 1867–1929, vol. III
Beatty, Pakenham Thomas, 1855–1930, vol. III
Beatty, Rose Mabel, 1879–1932, vol. III
Beatty, Wallace, 1853–1923, vol. III
Beatty, Wing-Comdr William Dawson, 1884–1941, vol. IV
Beaty-Pownall, Adm. Charles Pipon, 1872–1938, vol. III
Beaubien, Hon. Charles Philippe, 1870–1949, vol. IV
Beaubien, De Gaspé, 1881–1969, vol. VI(AII)
Beaubien, Justine Lacoste, (Mme L. De G. Beaubien), 1877–1967, vol. VI
Beauchamp, 7th Earl, 1872–1938, vol. III
Beauchamp, 8th Earl, 1903–1979, vol. VII
Beauchamp, Sir Brograve Campbell, 2nd Bt (*cr* 1911), 1897–1976, vol. VII
Beauchamp, Sir Douglas Clifford, (Sir Peter Beauchamp), 2nd Bt, 1903–1983, vol. VIII
Beauchamp, Sir Edward, 1st Bt (*cr* 1911), 1849–1925, vol. II
Beauchamp, Col Sir Frank, 1st Bt (*cr* 1918), 1866–1950, vol. IV
Beauchamp, Guy, 1902–1981, vol. VIII
Beauchamp, Sir Harold, 1858–1938, vol. III
Beauchamp, Rt Rev. Mgr Henry, 1884–1948, vol. IV
Beauchamp, Henry King, 1866–1907, vol. I
Beauchamp, Col Sir Horace George Proctor-, 6th Bt (*cr* 1744), 1856–1915, vol. I
Beauchamp, Rev. Sir Ivor Cuthbert Proctor-, 8th Bt (*cr* 1744), 1900–1971, vol. VII
Beauchamp, Rev. Sir Montagu Harry Proctor-, 7th Bt (*cr* 1744), 1860–1939, vol. III
Beauchamp, Sir Peter; *see* Beauchamp, Sir D. C.
Beauchamp, Sir Reginald William Proctor-, 5th Bt (*cr* 1744), 1853–1912, vol. I
Beauchamp, Sir Sydney, 1861–1921, vol. II
Beauchesne, Arthur, 1876–1959, vol. V

54

Beauclerk, Lord William de Vere, 1883–1954, vol. I
Beauclerk, William Nelthorpe, 1849–1908, vol. I
Beaufort, 8th Duke of, 1824–1899, vol. I
Beaufort, 9th Duke of, 1847–1924, vol. II
Beaufort, 10th Duke of, 1900–1984, vol. VIII
Beaufort, Sir Leicester Paul, 1853–1926, vol. II
Beaufoy, Henry Mark, 1887–1958, vol. V
Beaufoy, Mark Hanbury, 1854–1922, vol. II
Beaufoy, Samuel Leslie George, 1899–1961, vol. VI
Beauman, Brig.-Gen. Archibald Bentley, 1888–1977, vol. VII
Beauman, Wing Comdr Eric Bentley, 1891–1989, vol. VIII
Beaumarchais, Jacques Delarüe Caron de, 1913–1979, vol. VII
Beaumont, Baroness (11th in line), 1894–1971, vol. VII
Beaumont, Cyril William, 1891–1976, vol. VII
Beaumont, Rev. Francis Morton, 1838–1915, vol. I
Beaumont, Air Cdre Frank, 1896–1968, vol. VI
Beaumont, Sir George Arthur Hamilton, 11th Bt, 1881–1933, vol. III
Beaumont, George Ernest, 1888–1974, vol. VII
Beaumont, Sir George Howland William, 10th Bt, 1851–1914, vol. I
Beaumont, Henry Frederick, 1833–1913, vol. I
Beaumont, Sir Henry Hamond Dawson, 1867–1949, vol. IV
Beaumont, Hon. Hubert, 1864–1922, vol. II
Beaumont, Captain Hubert, died 1948, vol. IV
Beaumont, Hugh, 1908–1973, vol. VII
Beaumont, James Buchan, 1925–1973, vol. VII
Beaumont, Rt Hon. Sir John William Fisher, 1877–1974, vol. VII
Beaumont, Kenneth Macdonald, 1884–1965, vol. VI
Beaumont, Adm. Sir Lewis Anthony, 1847–1922, vol. II
Beaumont, Michael Wentworth, 1903–1958, vol. V
Beaumont, Hon. Ralph Edward Blackett, 1901–1977, vol. VII
Beaumont, Roberts, born 1862, vol. II
Beaumont, Somerset Archibald, 1836–1921, vol. II
Beaumont, W(illiam) Comyns, 1879–1955, vol. V
Beaumont, Sir William Henry, 1851–1930, vol. III
Beaumont, William Worby, 1848–1929, vol. III
Beaumont-Nesbitt, Maj.-Gen. Frederick George, 1893–1971, vol. VII
Beaumont-Thomas, Col Lionel, 1893–1942, vol. IV
Beaurepaire, Sir Frank, 1891–1956, vol. V
Beaurepaire, Ian Francis, 1922–1997, vol. X
Beauvoir, Simone Lucie Ernestine Marie Bertrand de, 1908–1986, vol. VIII
Beavan, family name of Baron Ardwick.
Beavan, Arthur Henry, 1844–1907, vol. I
Beavan, Margaret, died 1931, vol. III
Beavan, Rt Rev. Frederic Hicks, 1855–1941, vol. IV
Beaver, Sir Hugh Eyre Campbell, 1890–1967, vol. VI
Beaver, James Addams, 1837–1914, vol. I
Beaverbrook, 1st Baron, 1879–1964, vol. VI
Beavis, Arthur Beagley, 1867–1934, vol. III
Beavis, David, 1913–1987, vol. VIII
Beavis, Maj.-Gen. Leslie Ellis, 1895–1975, vol. VII
Beazeley, Lt-Col George Adam, 1870–1961, vol. VI
Beazley, Sir (Charles) Raymond, 1868–1955, vol. V

Beazley, Col Sir Geoffrey; see Beazley, Col Sir J. G. B.
Beazley, Sir Hugh Loveday, 1880–1964, vol. VI
Beazley, Col Sir (James) Geoffrey (Brydon), 1884–1962, vol. VI
Beazley, Sir John Davidson, 1885–1970, vol. VI
Beazley, John Godfrey, 1885–1948, vol. IV
Beazley, Patrick Langford, 1859–1923, vol. II
Beazley, Sir Raymond; see Beazley, Sir C. R.
Beazley, Lt-Col Walter Edwin, 1886–1969, vol. VI
Bebb, Rev. Llewellyn John Montfort, 1862–1915, vol. I
Bebbington, Bernard Nicolas, 1910–1980, vol. VII
Bebbington, Rev. John Henry, died 1936, vol. III
Bebel, Ferdinand August, 1840–1913, vol. I
Beberrua, 3rd Count of, born 1839, vol. III
Bech, Joseph, 1887–1975, vol. VII
Becher, Maj.-Gen. Andrew Cracroft, 1858–1929, vol. III
Becher, Dame Ethel Hope, 1867–1948, vol. IV
Becher, Sir Eustace William Windham Wrixon-, 4th Bt, 1859–1934, vol. III
Becher, Lt-Col Henry Wrixon-, 1866–1951, vol. V
Becher, Sir John Wrixon-, 3rd Bt, 1828–1914, vol. I
Becher, Rear-Adm. Otto Humphrey, 1908–1977, vol. VII
Becher, Gen. Septimus Harding, 1817–1908, vol. I
Becher, Major Sir William Fane Wrixon-, 5th Bt, 1915–2000, vol. X
Béchervaise, Albert Eric, 1884–1969, vol. VI
Beck, Col Hon. Sir Adam, 1857–1925, vol. II
Beck, Arnold Hugh William, 1916–1997, vol. X
Beck, Sir (Arthur) Cecil (Tyrrell), 1878–1932, vol. III
Beck, Arthur Clement, 1865–1949, vol. IV
Beck, Sir Cecil; see Beck, Sir A. C. T.
Beck, Lt-Col Charles Harrop, 1861–1910, vol. I
Beck, Conrad, died 1944, vol. IV
Beck, Diana Jean Kinloch, 1902–1956, vol. V
Beck, Sir Edgar Charles, 1911–2000, vol. X
Beck, Edward Anthony, 1848–1916, vol. II
Beck, Maj.-Gen. Edward Archibald, 1880–1974, vol. VII
Beck, Rev. Edward Josselyn, 1832–1924, vol. II
Beck, Egerton, 1858–1941, vol. IV
Beck, Rev. Frederick John, died 1922, vol. II
Beck, Most Rev. George Andrew, 1904–1978, vol. VII
Beck, Harvey Mortimer, 1868–1948, vol. IV
Beck, Hon. James Montgomery, 1861–1936, vol. III
Beck, Hon. Sir Johannes Henricus Meiring, 1855–1919, vol. II
Beck, John Melliar A.; see Adams-Beck.
Beck, Mrs L. Adams, died 1931, vol. III
Beck, Hon. Nicholas Du Bois Dominic, 1857–1928, vol. III
Beck, Captain Oliver Lawrence, died 1947, vol. IV
Beck, Sir Raymond, 1861–1953, vol. V
Beck, (Richard) Theodore, 1905–2000, vol. X
Beck, Rolf; see Beck, Rudolph R.
Beck, (Rudolph) Rolf, (Baron Rolf Beck), 1914–1991, vol. IX
Beck, Theodore; see Beck, R. T.
Beck, Very Rev. William Ernest, 1884–1957, vol. V
Beck, William Hopkins, 1892–1957, vol. V

Becke, George Louis, 1848–1913, vol. I
Becke, Major Sir Jack, 1878–1962, vol. VI
Becke, Brig.-Gen. John Harold Whitworth, 1879–1949, vol. IV
Becker, Sir Ellerton; see Becker, Sir J. E.
Becker, Sir Frederick Edward Robert, 1871–1936, vol. III
Becker, Harry Thomas Alfred, 1892–1980, vol. VII
Becker, Sir (Jack) Ellerton, 1904–1979, vol. VII
Becker, Neal Dow, 1883–1955, vol. V
Becker, Sir Walter Frederick, 1855–1927, vol. II
Beckett, Angus; see Beckett, J. A.
Beckett, Arthur, died 1943, vol. IV
Beckett, Brig.-Gen. Charles Edward, 1849–1925, vol. II
Beckett, Maj.-Gen. Clifford Thomason, 1891–1972, vol. VII
Beckett, Sir Eric; see Beckett, Sir W. E.
Beckett, Sir Eric Frederick, 1895–1971, vol. VII
Beckett, Geoffrey Bernard, 1903–1965, vol. VI
Beckett, Hon. Sir Gervase; see Beckett, Hon. Sir W. G.
Beckett, Harold, 1891–1952, vol. V
Beckett, James, 1891–1970, vol. VI
Beckett, James Camlin, 1912–1996, vol. X
Beckett, John Angus, 1909–1990, vol. VIII
Beckett, Lt-Col John Douglas Mortimer, 1881–1918, vol. II
Beckett, John Michael, 1929–1991, vol. IX
Beckett, John Warburton, 1894–1964, vol. VI(AII)
Beckett, Noel George Stanley, 1916–1990, vol. VIII
Beckett, Richard Henry, 1882–1981, vol. VIII
Beckett, Ronald Brymer, 1891–1970, vol. VI
Beckett, Hon. Rupert Evelyn, 1870–1955, vol. V
Beckett, Samuel Barclay, 1906–1989, vol. VIII
Beckett, Col Stephen, 1840–1921, vol. II
Beckett, Captain Walter Napier Thomason, 1893–1941, vol. IV
Beckett, Walter Ralph Durie, 1864–1917, vol. II
Beckett, Sir (William) Eric, 1896–1966, vol. VI
Beckett, Hon. Sir (William) Gervase, 1st Bt, 1866–1937, vol. III
Beckett, Brig.-Gen. William Thomas Clifford, 1862–1956, vol. V
Beckingham, Charles Fraser, 1914–1998, vol. X
Beckles, Rt Rev. Edward Hyndman, died 1902, vol. I
Beckles, Gordon, 1901–1954, vol. V
Beckwith, Brig.-Gen. Arthur Thackeray, 1875–1942, vol. IV
Beckwith, Edward George Ambrose, died 1935, vol. III
Beckwith, John Gordon, 1918–1991, vol. IX
Beckwith, Air Vice-Marshal William Flint, 1913–1971, vol. VII
Beckwith-Smith, Maj.-Gen. Merton, 1890–1942, vol. IV
Bective, Countess of; (Alice), died 1928, vol. II
Bedale, Rev. Frederick, died 1924, vol. II
Bedale, Rear-Adm. Sir John Leigh, 1891–1964, vol. VI
Bedale, Rev. Stephen Frederick Burstal, 1888–1961, vol. VI
Bedbrook, Sir George, 1921–1991, vol. IX
Beddall, Hugh Richard Muir, 1922–1999, vol. X

Beddall, Maj.-Gen. Walter Samuel, 1894–1973, vol. VII
Beddard, Arthur Philip, died 1939, vol. III
Beddard, Frank Evers, 1858–1926, vol. II
Beddard, Frederick Denys, 1917–1985, vol. VIII
Beddington, Brig. Sir Edward Henry Lionel, 1884–1966, vol. VI
Beddington, Frances Ethel, (Mrs Claude Beddington), died 1963, vol. VI
Beddington, Gerald Ernest, 1867–1958, vol. V
Beddington, Jack, 1893–1959, vol. V
Beddington, Nadine Dagmar, 1915–1990, vol. VIII
Beddington, Reginald, 1877–1962, vol. VI
Beddington, Maj.-Gen. William Richard, 1893–1975, vol. VII
Beddington-Behrens, Sir Edward, 1897–1968, vol. VI
Beddoe, Jack Eglinton, 1914–1990, vol. VIII
Beddoe, John, 1826–1911, vol. I
Beddoes, Air Vice-Marshal John Geoffrey Genior, 1925–1993, vol. IX
Beddome, Col Richard Henry, died 1910, vol. I
Beddow, Lt-Col Arnold Bellamy, 1883–1965, vol. VI
Beddy, James Patrick, 1900–1976, vol. VII
Beddy, Brig. Percy Langdon, died 1945, vol. IV
Bedell, Frederick, 1868–1958, vol. V(A)
Bedells, Charles Herbert, 1862–1943, vol. IV
Bedford, 11th Duke of, 1858–1940, vol. III
Bedford, 12th Duke of, 1888–1953, vol. V
Bedford, Duchess of; (Mary du Caurroy), 1865–1937, vol. III
Bedford, Alfred William, (Bill), 1920–1996, vol. X
Bedford, Vice-Adm. Arthur Edward Frederick, 1881–1949, vol. IV
Bedford, Bill; see Bedford, A. W.
Bedford, Lt-Col Sir Charles Henry, 1866–1931, vol. III
Bedford, Davis Evan, 1898–1978, vol. VII
Bedford, Adm. Sir Frederick George Denham, 1838–1913, vol. I
Bedford, Henry Hall, 1847–1930, vol. III
Bedford, Herbert, 1867–1945, vol. IV
Bedford, Mrs Herbert; see Lehmann, Liza.
Bedford, James Douglas Hardy, 1884–1960, vol. V
Bedford, John, 1903–1980, vol. VII
Bedford, Leslie Herbert, 1900–1989, vol. VIII
Bedford, Richard Perry, 1883–1967, vol. VI
Bedford, Maj.-Gen. Sir Walter George Augustus, 1858–1922, vol. II
Bedford, Rev. William Campbell Riland, 1852–1922, vol. II
Bedford, Rev. William Kirkpatrick Riland, 1826–1905, vol. I
Bedi, Raja Sir Baba Gurbukhsh Singh, died 1945, vol. IV
Bedier, Joseph, 1864–1938, vol. III
Bedingfeld, Sir Henry Edward P.; see Paston-Bedingfeld.
Bedingfeld, Sir Henry George P.; see Paston-Bedingfeld.
Bedingfield, Christopher Ohl Macredie, 1935–1995, vol. IX
Bednall, Maj.-Gen. Sir (Cecil Norbury) Peter, 1895–1982, vol. VIII

Bednall, Maj.-Gen. Sir Peter; *see* Bednall, Maj.-Gen. Sir C. N. P.
Bedson, Peter Phillips, 1853–1943, vol. IV
Bedson, Sir Samuel Phillips, 1886–1969, vol. VI
Bedwell, Cyril Edward Alfred, *died* 1950, vol. IV
Bedwell, Rev. Francis, *died* 1925, vol. II
Bedwell, Horace, 1868–1954, vol. V
Beebe, (Charles) William, 1877–1962, vol. VI
Beebe, William; *see* Beebe, C. W.
Beeby, Clarence Edward, 1902–1998, vol. X
Beeby, George Harry, 1902–1994, vol. IX
Beeby, Sir George Stephenson, 1869–1942, vol. IV
Beech, Francis William, 1885–1969, vol. VI
Beech, Lt-Col John Robert, 1860 1915, vol. I
Beech, Patrick Mervyn, 1912–1993, vol. IX
Beecham, Sir Adrian Welles, 3rd Bt, 1904–1982, vol. VIII
Beecham, Sir Joseph, 1st Bt, 1848–1916, vol. II
Beecham, Sir Thomas, 2nd Bt, 1879–1961, vol. VI
Beecher, Most Rev. Leonard James, 1906–1987, vol. VIII
Beecher, Rev. Patrick A., 1870–1940, vol. III
Beecher, Willis Judson, 1838–1912, vol. I
Beechey, Rev. St Vincent, 1841–1905, vol. I
Beeching, Baron (Life Peer); Richard Beeching, 1913–1985, vol. VIII
Beeching, Maj.-Gen. Frank, 1839–1916, vol. II
Beeching, Very Rev. Henry Charles, 1859–1919, vol. II
Beechman, Captain Alec; *see* Beechman, Captain N. A.
Beechman, Captain Nevil Alexander, (Captain Alec Beechman), *died* 1965, vol. VI
Beeding, Francis; *see* Saunders, H. A. St G.
Beeck, Sir Marcus Truby, 1923–1986, vol. VIII
Beeman, Christina May, *died* 1935, vol. III
Beeman, Engr Rear-Adm.Sir Robert, *died* 1963, vol. VI
Beeman, Brig. William Gilbert, 1884–1953, vol. V
Beer, Sir Frederick Tidbury T.; *see* Tidbury-Beer.
Beer, Harry, 1896–1970, vol. VI
Beer, Ven. Henry, 1844–1937, vol. III
Beer, Col James Henry Elias, 1848–1925, vol. II
Beer, Mrs Nellie, 1900–1988, vol. VIII
Beer, Patricia, (Mrs J. D. Parsons), 1919–1999, vol. X
Beer Bikram Singh, Rajkumar, *died* 1923, vol. II
Beerbohm, Sir Max, 1872–1956, vol. V
Beere, Mrs Bernard, (Fanny Mary), 1856–1915, vol. I
Beernaert, Auguste Marie François, 1829–1912, vol. I
Beery, Wallace, 1885–1949, vol. IV
Beesley, Dodie, (Mrs A. M. Beesley); *see* Smith, D.
Beesley, Michael Edwin, 1924–1999, vol. X
Beesly, Edward Spenser, 1831–1915, vol. I
Beesly, Lewis Rowland, 1912–1978, vol. VII
Beeson, Cyril Frederick Cherrington, 1889–1975, vol. VII
Beeston, Alfred Felix Landon, 1911–1995, vol. IX
Beeston, Col Joseph Livesley, 1859–1921, vol. II
Beet, Rev. Joseph Agar, 1840–1924, vol. II
Beetham, Sir Edward Betham, 1905–1979, vol. VII
Beeton, Alan, 1880–1942, vol. IV
Beeton, Sir Mayson, *died* 1947, vol. IV

Beeton, William Hugh, 1903–1976, vol. VII
Beets, Nicolaas, 1814–1903, vol. I
Beevor, Charles Edward, 1854–1908, vol. I
Beevor, Sir Hugh Reeve, 5th Bt, 1858–1939, vol. III
Beevor, Rt Rev. Humphry, 1903–1965, vol. VI
Beevor, John Grosvenor, 1905–1987, vol. VIII
Beevor, Miles, 1900–1994, vol. IX
Beevor, Comdr Sir Thomas Lubbock, 6th Bt, 1897–1943, vol. IV
Beevor, Lt-Col Walter Calverley, 1858–1927, vol. II
Begas, Reinhold, 1831–1911, vol. I
Begbie, Maj.-Gen. Elphinstone Waters, 1842–1915, vol. I
Begble, Col Francis Warburton, 1864–1922, vol. II
Begbie, Major George Edward, 1868–1907, vol. I
Begbie, Harold, 1871–1929, vol. III
Begbie, Rt Rev. Herbert Gordon Smirnoff, 1905–1973, vol. VII
Begbie, Ven. Herbert Smirnoff, 1871–1951, vol. V
Begbie, Sir James, 1859–1934, vol. III
Begg, Col Charles Mackie, *died* 1919, vol. II
Begg, Ferdinand Faithfull, 1847–1926, vol. II
Begg, Rt Rev. Ian Forbes, 1910–1989, vol. VIII
Begg, Jean, 1887–1971, vol. VII
Begg, John Henderson, 1844–1911, vol. I
Begg, Sir Neil Colquhoun, 1915–1995, vol. IX
Begg, Col Robert B.; *see* Burns-Begg.
Begg, Adm. of the Fleet Sir Varyl Cargill, 1908–1995, vol. IX
Begg, Rev William H.; *see* Henderson-Begg.
Beggs, Engr-Captain James, *died* 1949, vol. IV
Beggs, Hon. Theodore, 1859–1940, vol. III
Begin, His Eminence Cardinal Louis Nazaire, 1840–1925, vol. II
Begin, Menachem, 1913–1992, vol. IX
Behan, Brendan, 1923–1964, vol. VI
Behan, Sir Harold Garfield, 1901–1979, vol. VII(AII)
Behan, Sir John Clifford Valentine, 1881–1957, vol. V
Beharrell, Sir Edward; *see* Beharrell, Sir G. E.
Beharrel, Sir George; *see* Beharrell, Sir J. G.
Beharrel, Sir (George) Edward, 1899–1972, vol. VII
Beharrell, Sir (John) George, 1873–1959, vol. V
Behne, Edmond Rowlands, 1906–1994, vol. X (AI)
Behr, Fritz Bernhard, 1842–1927, vol. II
Behram, Sir Jehangir Bomonji B.; *see* Bomon-Behram.
Behrend, George L., 1868–1950, vol. IV
Behrens, Sir Charles, 1848–1925, vol. II
Behrens, Major Clive, 1871–1935, vol. III
Behrens, Edgar Charles, 1885–1975, vol. VII
Behrens, Sir Edward B.; *see* Beddington-Behrens.
Behrens, Gustav, 1846–1936, vol. III
Behrens, Sir Leonard Frederick, 1890–1978, vol. VII
Behrens, Walter, 1856–1922, vol. II
Behrman, Samuel Nathaniel, 1893–1973, vol. VII
Behrman, Simon, 1902–1988, vol. VIII
Beibitz, Rev. Joseph Hugh, 1868–1936, vol. III
Beilby, Sir George Thomas, 1850–1924, vol. II
Beinart, Ben Zion, 1914–1979, vol. VII
Beique, Hon. Frederic Liguori, 1845–1933, vol. III
Beirne, Hon. Thomas Charles, 1860–1949, vol. IV
Beit, Alfred, 1853–1906, vol. I

Beit, Sir Alfred Lane, 2nd Bt, 1903–1994, vol. IX
Beit, Sir Otto John, 1st Bt, 1865–1930, vol. III
Beith, Sir John Greville Stanley, 1914–2000, vol. X
Beith, Maj.-Gen. John Hay, 1876–1952, vol. V
Beith, John William, 1909–2000, vol. X
Beith, Hon. Robert, 1843–1922, vol. II
Béjot, Eugène, *died* 1931, vol. III
Békésy, Dr Georg von, 1899–1972, vol. VII
Belam, Noël Stephen, 1920–1991, vol. IX
Beland, Hon. Henri, 1869–1935, vol. III
Belasco, David, 1859–1931, vol. III
Belch, Alexander, 1890–1967, vol. VI
Belch, Sir (Alexander) Ross, 1920–1999, vol. X
Belch, Sir Ross; *see* Belch, Sir A. R.
Belchem, David; *see* Belchem, Maj.-Gen. R. F. K.
Belchem, Maj.-Gen. Ronald Frederick King, (David), 1911–1981, vol. VIII
Belcher, Rev. Arthur Hayes, 1876–1947, vol. IV
Belcher, Sir Charles Frederic, 1876–1970, vol. VI
Belcher, Captain Douglas Walter, 1889–1953, vol. V
Belcher, Major Ernest Albert, 1871–1949, vol. IV
Belcher, George Frederick Arthur, 1875–1947, vol. IV
Belcher, Lt-Col Harold Thomas, 1875–1917, vol. II
Belcher, John, 1841–1913, vol. I
Belcher, John William, 1905–1964, vol. VI
Belcher, Major Robert, 1849–1919, vol. II
Belcher, Rev. Thomas Waugh, 1831–1910, vol. I
Belcher, Rt Rev. Wilfrid Bernard, 1891–1963, vol. VI
Belcourt, Hon Napoleon Antoine, 1860–1932, vol. III
Belden, Rev. Albert David, 1883–1964, vol. VI
Belfield, Sir Henry Conway, 1855–1923, vol. II
Belfield, Lt-Gen. Sir Herbert Eversley, 1857–1934, vol. III
Belfield, Lt-Col Sydney, 1862–1946, vol. IV
Belfield, Major William Seymour, *died* 1924, vol. II(A), vol. III
Belfrage, Leif Axel Lorentz, 1910–1990, vol. VIII
Belfrage, Sydney Henning, 1871–1950, vol. IV
Belgion, (Harold) Montgomery, 1892–1973, vol. VII
Belgion, Montgomery; *see* Belgion, H. M.
Belgrave, Sir Charles Dalrymple, 1894–1969, vol. VI
Belhaven and Stenton, 10th Lord, 1840–1920, vol. II
Belhaven and Stenton, 11th Lord, 1871–1950, vol. IV
Belhaven and Stenton, 12th Lord, 1903–1961, vol. VI
Belhaven, Master of; Hon. Ralph Gerard Alexander Hamilton, 1883–1918, vol. II
Belilios, Emanuel Raphael, 1837–1905, vol. I
Belisario, John Colquhoun, 1900–1976, vol. VII
Béliveau, Most Rev. Arthur, 1870–1955, vol. V
Beljame, Alexandre, *died* 1906, vol. I
Belk, John Thomas, 1837–1901, vol. I
Belk, Lt-Col William, 1869–1952, vol. V
Bell, Adam Carr, 1847–1912, vol. I
Bell, Captain Adolphus Edmund, 1850–1927, vol. II
Bell, Adrian Hanbury, 1901–1980, vol. VII
Bell, Alexander Foulis, 1876–1940, vol. III
Bell, Alexander Graham, 1847–1922, vol. II
Bell, Andrew Beatson, 1831–1913, vol. I

Bell, Andrew James, 1856–1932, vol. III
Bell, Lt-Comdr Archibald Colquhoun, *died* 1958, vol. V
Bell, Archibald Græme, 1868–1948, vol. IV
Bell, Rev. Archibald William, 1870–1938, vol. III
Bell, Sir Arthur Capel Herbert, 1904–1977, vol. VII
Bell, (Arthur) Clive (Heward), 1881–1964, vol. VI
Bell, Arthur Doyne Courtenay, 1900–1970, vol. VI
Bell, Arthur George, *died* 1916, vol. II
Bell, Maj.-Gen. Arthur Henry, 1871–1956, vol. V
Bell, Col Arthur Hugh, 1878–1968, vol. VI
Bell, Maj.-Gen. Sir Arthur Lynden L.; *see* Lynden-Bell.
Bell, Arthur William, 1868–1935, vol. III
Bell, Aubrey FitzGerald, 1881–1950, vol. IV
Bell, Rev. Benjamin, 1845–1930, vol. III
Bell, Sir (Bernard) Humphrey, *died* 1959, vol. V
Bell, Bertram Charles, 1893–1941, vol. IV
Bell, Sir Charles Alfred, 1870–1945, vol. IV
Bell, Rev. Canon Charles Carlyle, 1868–1954, vol. V
Bell, Rev. Charles Dent, 1818–1898, vol. I
Bell, Charles Francis, 1871–1966, vol. VI
Bell, Charles Frederick Moberly, 1847–1911, vol. I
Bell, Captain Charles Leigh de Hauteville, 1903–1972, vol. VII
Bell, Sir Charles Reginald Francis M.; *see* Morrison-Bell.
Bell, Sir Charles William, 1907–1988, vol. VIII
Bell, Sir Charles William M.; *see* Morrison-Bell.
Bell, Claude Waylen, 1891–1964, vol. VI
Bell, Sir Claude William Hedley M.; *see* Morrison-Bell.
Bell, Clive; *see* Bell, A. C. H.
Bell, Sir Clive M.; *see* Morrison-Bell.
Bell, Cyril Francis, 1883–1957, vol. V
Bell, Douglas; *see* Bell, G. D. H.
Bell, Sir Douglas James, 1904–1974, vol. VII
Bell, Douglas Maurice, 1914–1993, vol. IX
Bell, Sir Eastman, 2nd Bt (*cr* 1909), 1884–1955, vol. V
Bell, Edward, 1844–1926, vol. II
Bell, Col Edward, 1866–1937, vol. III
Bell, Edward Allen, 1884–1959, vol. V
Bell, Col Edward Horace Lynden L.; *see* Lynden-Bell.
Bell, (Edward) Percy, 1902–1987, vol. VIII
Bell, Sir (Edward) Peter (Stubbs), 1902–1957, vol. V
Bell, Edward Price, 1869–1943, vol. IV
Bell, Enid Moberly, 1881–1967, vol. VI
Bell, Eric Temple, 1883–1960, vol. V
Bell, Ernest, 1851–1933, vol. III
Bell, Sir Ernest Albert Seymour, *died* 1955, vol. V
Bell, Lt-Col Ernest FitzRoy M.; *see* Morrison-Bell.
Bell, Lt-Col Eustace Widdrington M.; *see* Morrison-Bell.
Bell, Eva Mary, *died* 1959, vol. V
Bell, Hon. Sir Francis Dillon, *died* 1898, vol. I
Bell, Sir Francis Gordon, 1887–1970, vol. VI
Bell, Rt Hon. Sir Francis Henry Dillon, 1851–1936, vol. III
Bell, Francis Jeffrey, *died* 1924, vol. II
Bell, Frank, 1878–1961, vol. VI
Bell, Frank, 1904–1992, vol. IX

Bell, Sir Frederick Archibald, 1891–1972, vol. VII
Bell, Col Frederick Charles, 1883–1971, vol. VII
Bell, Captain Frederick Secker, 1897–1973, vol. VII
Bell, Lt-Col Frederick William, *died* 1954, vol. V
Bell, Sir Gawain Westray, 1909–1995, vol. IX
Bell, Geoffrey Foxall, 1896–1984, vol. VIII
Bell, Geoffrey Y.; *see* Yates-Bell, J. G.
Bell, Hon. George Alexander, 1856–1927, vol. II
Bell, Rev. George Charles, *died* 1913, vol. I
Bell, George Douglas Hutton, 1905–1993, vol. IX
Bell, Rev. Canon George Fancourt, 1874–1952, vol. V
Bell, George Howard, 1905–1986, vol. VIII
Bell, Col George James Hamilton, 1861–1930, vol. VII
Bell, Col Hon. Sir George John, 1872–1944, vol. IV
Bell, Rt Rev. George Kennedy Allen, 1883–1958, vol. V
Bell, Rev. Preb. George Milner, 1872–1947, vol. IV
Bell, George Trafford, 1913–1984, vol. VIII
Bell, Gertrude Margaret Lowthian, 1868–1926, vol. II
Bell, Grace Effingham Laughton, (Mrs Harry Graham Bell), *died* 1875, vol. VII
Bell, Major Graham Airdrie, 1874–1929, vol. III
Bell, Harold Arthur, 1918–1978, vol. VII
Bell, Sir (Harold) Idris, 1879–1967, vol. VI
Bell, Lt-Col Sir Harold W.; *see* Wilberforce-Bell.
Bell, Harry, 1899–1984, vol. VIII
Bell, Harry Charles Purvis, 1851–1937, vol. III
Bell, Mrs Harry Graham; *see* Bell, G. E. L.
Bell, Rev. Henry, 1838–1919, vol. II
Bell, Sir Henry, 1st Bt (*cr* 1909), 1848–1931, vol. III
Bell, Henry, *died* 1935, vol. III
Bell, Henry McGrady, 1880–1958, vol. V
Bell, Lt-Col Henry Stanley, 1874–1949, vol. IV
Bell, (Henry Thomas) Mackenzie, 1856–1930, vol. III
Bell, Henry Thurburn Montague, 1873–1949, vol. IV
Bell, Herbert Clifford Francis, 1881–1966, vol. VI
Bell, Herbert Wright, 1857–1936, vol. III
Bell, Sir Hesketh, 1864–1952, vol. V
Bell, Sir Hugh, 2nd Bt (*cr* 1885), 1844–1931, vol. III
Bell, Sir Hugh Francis, 4th Bt (*cr* 1885), 1923–1970, vol. VI
Bell, Sir Humphrey; *see* Bell, Sir B. H.
Bell, Ian Wright, 1913–1998, vol. X
Bell, Sir Idris; *see* Bell, Sir H. I.
Bell, Isaac, 1879–1964, vol. VI
Bell, Sir (Isaac) Lowthian, 1st Bt (*cr* 1885), 1816–1904, vol. I
Bell, James, 1825–1908, vol. I
Bell, Rev. James, *died* 1918, vol. II
Bell, Sir James, 1st Bt (*cr* 1895), 1850–1929, vol. III
Bell, Sir James, 1866–1937, vol. III
Bell, Sir James, 1878–1948, vol. IV
Bell, James, 1872–1955, vol. V
Bell, James Alan, 1894–1968, vol. VI
Bell, Maj.-Gen. Sir James Alexander, 1856–1926, vol. II
Bell, Rev. James Allen, *died* 1934, vol. III

Bell, James Mackintosh, 1877–1934, vol. III
Bell, James Young, 1877–1966, vol. VI
Bell, Sir John, 2nd Bt (*cr* 1895), 1876–1943, vol. IV
Bell, John, 1890–1958, vol. V
Bell, Very Rev. John, 1898–1983, vol. VIII
Bell, Col John B.; *see* Beatson-Bell.
Bell, Sir John Charles, 1st Bt (*cr* 1908), 1844–1924, vol. II
Bell, John Elliott, 1886–1985, vol. VIII
Bell, Sir John Ferguson, 1856–1937, vol. III
Bell, John Geoffrey Y.; *see* Yates-Bell.
Bell, John Joy, 1871–1934, vol. III
Bell, John Keble, 1875–1928, vol. II
Bell, John Stewart, 1928–1990, vol. VIII
Bell, Ven. John White, *died* 1928, vol. II(A), vol. III
Bell, Lt-Col John William, 1844–1928, vol. II
Bell, Sir John William Anderson, 1873–1938, vol. III
Bell, Joseph, 1837–1911, vol. I
Bell, Joseph, 1899–1989, vol. VIII
Bell, Joseph Denis Milburn, 1920–1997, vol. X
Bell, Hon. Joshua Thomas, 1863–1911, vol. I
Bell, Julia, 1879–1979, vol. VII
Bell, Rev. Kenneth Norman, 1884–1951, vol. V
Bell, Laird, 1883–1965, vol. VI
Bell, Lilian, *died* 1929, vol. III
Bell, Louis, 1864–1923, vol. II
Bell, Sir Lowthian; *see* Bell, Sir I. L.
Bell, Mackenzie; *see* Bell, H. T. M.
Bell, Col Mark Sever, 1843–1906, vol. I
Bell, Mrs Mary Taylor Watson, *died* 1943, vol. IV
Bell, Lt-Col Matthew Gerald Edward, 1871–1926, vol. II
Bell, Col Sir Maurice Hugh Lowthian, 3rd Bt (*cr* 1885), 1871–1944, vol. IV
Bell, Nancy R. E., *died* 1933, vol. III
Bell, Rev. Sir Nicholas Dodd Beatson, 1867–1936, vol. III
Bell, Norris Garrett, 1860–1937, vol. III
Bell, Oliver, 1898–1952, vol. V
Bell, Percy; *see* Bell, E. P.
Bell, Sir Peter; *see* Bell, Sir E. P. S.
Bell, Maj.-Gen. Peter Harvey, 1886–1963, vol. VI
Bell, P(hilip) Ingress, 1900–1986, vol. VIII
Bell, Quentin Claudian Stephen, 1910–1996, vol. X
Bell, Richard, 1859–1930, vol. III
Bell, Robert, 1841–1917, vol. II
Bell, Robert, 1845–1926, vol. II
Bell, Robert, 1863–1937, vol. III
Bell, Robert Anning, 1863–1933, vol. III
Bell, Sir Robert Duncan, 1878–1953, vol. V
Bell, Robert Edward, 1918–1992, vol. IX
Bell, Robert Stanley Warren, 1871–1921, vol. II
Bell, Ronald Percy, 1907–1996, vol. X
Bell, Sir Ronald McMillan, 1914–1982, vol. VIII
Bell, Sir Stanley, 1899–1972, vol. VII
Bell, Stewart Edward, 1919–1992, vol. IX
Bell, Very Rev. Thomas, 1820–1917, vol. II
Bell, Sir Thomas, 1865–1952, vol. V
Bell, Sir Thomas Hugh; *see* Bell, Sir Hugh.
Bell, Thomas Reid Davys, *died* 1948, vol. IV
Bell, Hon. Valentine Græme, 1839–1908, vol. I
Bell, Rev. Vicars Walker, 1904–1988, vol. VIII
Bell, Walter George, *died* 1942, vol. IV

Bell, Col William, 1829–1913, vol. I
Bell, Rev. William, *died* 1918, vol. II
Bell, William, 1860–1946, vol. IV
Bell, William Abraham, 1841–1920, vol. II
Bell, William B.; *see* Blair-Bell.
Bell, Lt-Col William Cory Heward, 1875–1961, vol. VI
Bell, Rev. Canon William Godfrey, 1880–1953, vol. V
Bell, Sir William James, 1859–1913, vol. I
Bell, William Rupert Graham, 1920–1996, vol. X
Bell-Irving, Lt-Col Andrew, 1855–1929, vol. III
Bell-Irving, James Jardine, 1859–1936, vol. III
Bell-Irving, John, 1846–1925, vol. II
Bell-Smith, Frederic Marlett, 1846–1923, vol. II
Bell-Smyth, Brig.-Gen. John Ambard, 1868–1922, vol. II
Bellairs, Angus d'Albini, 1918–1990, vol. VIII
Bellairs, Comdr Carlyon, 1871–1955, vol. V
Bellairs, Hamon D'Albini, *died* 1932, vol. III
Bellairs, Rear-Adm. Roger Mowbray, 1884–1959, vol. V
Bellairs, Lt-Gen. Sir William, 1828–1913, vol. I
Bellamy, Albert, *died* 1931, vol. III
Bellamy, Albert Alexander, (Alec), 1914–1981, vol. VIII
Bellamy, Alec; *see* Bellamy, Albert A.
Bellamy, Alexander William, 1909–1999, vol. X (AII)
Bellamy, Basil Edmund, 1914–1989, vol. VIII
Bellamy, Charles Vincent, 1867–1938, vol. III
Bellamy, Dennis, 1894–1964, vol. VI
Bellamy, Edward, 1850–1898, vol. I
Bellamy, Rev. James, 1819–1909, vol. I
Bellamy, Sir Joseph Arthur, 1845–1918, vol. II
Bellamy, Lionel John, 1916–1982, vol. VIII
Bellamy, Lt-Col Robert, 1871–1927, vol. II
Bellamy, Brig. Robert Hugh, 1910–1972, vol. VII
Bellars, Rear-Adm. Edward Gerald Hyslop, 1894–1955, vol. V
Bellasis, Edward, 1852–1922, vol. II
Bellasis, Captain Richard O.; *see* Oliver-Bellasis.
Bellenger, Captain Rt Hon. Frederick John, 1894–1968, vol. VI
Bellerby, Rev. Alfred Courthope Benson, 1888–1979, vol. VII
Bellerby, Major John Rotherford, 1896–1977, vol. VII
Belleroche, Albert de, 1864–1944, vol. IV
Bellessort, André, 1861–1942, vol. IV
Bellew, 3rd Baron, 1855–1911, vol. I
Bellew, 4th Baron, 1857–1935, vol. III
Bellew, 5th Baron, 1889–1975, vol. VII
Bellew, 6th Baron, 1890–1981, vol. VIII
Bellew, Sir Arthur John G.; *see* Grattan-Bellew.
Bellew, Lt-Col Sir Charles Christopher G.; *see* Grattan-Bellew.
Bellew, Captain Edward Donald, 1882–1961, vol. VI
Bellew, Hon. Sir George Rothe, 1899–1993, vol. IX
Bellew, Sir Henry Christopher G.; *see* Grattan-Bellew.
Bellew, Hon. Richard Eustace, 1858–1933, vol. III
Belley, Hon. L. G., 1863–1930, vol. III
Bellhouse, Sir Gerald, 1867–1946, vol. IV

Bellingham, Sir (Alan) Henry, 4th Bt, 1846–1921, vol. II
Bellingham, Brig.-Gen. Sir Edward Henry Charles Patrick, 5th Bt, 1879–1956, vol. V
Bellingham, Sir Henry; *see* Bellingham, Sir A. H.
Bellingham, Sir Noel Peter Roger, 7th Bt, 1943–1999, vol. X
Bellingham, Sir Roger Carroll Patrick Stephen, 6th Bt, 1911–1973, vol. VII
Bellis, John Herbert, 1930–2000, vol. X
Bellman, Sir Harold, 1886–1963, vol. VI
Bello, Alhaji Sir Ahmadu, 1909–1966, vol. VI
Belloc, Hilaire; *see* Belloc, J. H. P.
Belloc, (Joseph) Hilaire (Pierre), 1870–1953, vol. V
Belloc, Marie Adelaide, (Mrs Belloc Lowndes), 1868–1947, vol. IV
Bellot, Hugh Hale, 1890–1969, vol. VI
Bellot, Hugh Hale Leigh, 1860–1928, vol. II
Bellville, Captain George Ernest, 1879–1967, vol. VI
Belmont, August, 1853–1924, vol. II
Belmont, Perry, 1851–1947, vol. IV
Belmore, 4th Earl of, 1835–1913, vol. I
Belmore, 5th Earl of, 1870–1948, vol. IV
Belmore, 6th Earl of, 1873–1949, vol. IV
Belmore, 7th Earl of, 1913–1960, vol. V
Beloe, Vice-Adm. Sir (Isaac) William (Trant), 1909–1966, vol. VI
Beloe, Robert, 1905–1984, vol. VIII
Beloe, Rev. Robert Douglas, 1868–1931, vol. III
Beloe, Vice-Adm. Sir William; *see* Beloe, Vice-Adm. Sir I. W. T.
Beloff, Baron (Life Peer); Max Beloff, 1913–1999, vol. X
Beloff, Nora, 1919–1997, vol. X
Belper, 2nd Baron, 1840–1914, vol. I
Belper, 3rd Baron, 1883–1956, vol. V
Belper, 4th Baron, 1912–1999, vol. X
Belsey, Sir Francis Flint, 1837–1914, vol. I
Belshaw, Edward, *died* 1916, vol. II
Belsky, Franta, 1921–2000, vol. X
Belstead, 1st Baron, 1882–1958, vol. V
Belt, Comdr Francis Walter, 1862–1938, vol. III
Belton, Rev. Francis George, *died* 1962, vol. VI
Belton, Leslie James, 1897–1949, vol. IV
Bemelmans, Ludwig, 1898–1962, vol. VI
Bemont, Charles, 1848–1939, vol. III(A), vol. IV
Bemrose, Sir Henry Howe, 1827–1911, vol. I
Bemrose, Sir John Maxwell; *see* Bemrose, Sir Max.
Bemrose, Sir Max, (John Maxwell), 1904–1986, vol. VIII
Ben-Gurion, David, 1886–1973, vol. VII
Benares, Maharajah Bahadur of, 1855–1931, vol. III
Benares, Maharaja of, 1874–1939, vol. III
Benas, Bertram Benjamin Baron, 1880–1968, vol. VI
Benavente, Jacinto, 1866–1954, vol. V
Benbow, Sir Henry, 1838–1916, vol. II
Bence, Cyril Raymond, 1902–1992, vol. IX
Bence-Jones, Col Philip Reginald, 1897–1972, vol. VII
Bence-Lambert, Col Guy Lenox, 1856–1930, vol. III
Benckendorff, Count de, Alexandre, 1849–1917, vol. II
Bencraft, Sir Henry William Russell, 1858–1943, vol. IV

Benda, Wladyslaw Theodor, 1873–1948, vol. IV, vol. V

Bendall, Cecil, 1856–1906, vol. I

Bendall, Ernest Alfred, 1846–1924, vol. II

Bendall, Col Frederic William Duffield, 1882–1953, vol. V

Bender, Rev. A. P., 1863–1937, vol. III

Bender, Arnold Eric, 1918–1999, vol. X

Bender, William Edward Gustave, 1885–1961, vol. VI

Bendern, Count; Arnold Maurice, 1879–1968, vol. VI

Bendit, Gladys; see Presland, John.

Benecke, Paul V. M., 1868–1944, vol. IV

Benedict, Ruth Fulton, 1887–1948, vol. IV

Benedite, Leonce, died 1925, vol. II

Benes, Dr Eduard, 1884–1948, vol. IV

Benét, Stephen Vincent,. 1898–1943, vol. IV

Benét, William Rose, 1886–1950, vol. IV

Benett, Lt-Col Henry Cleeve, 1877–1941, vol. IV

Beney, Frederick William, 1884–1986, vol. VIII

Benfield, Brig. Karl Vere B.; see Barker-Benfield.

Benger, Berenger, 1868–1935, vol. III

Bengough, Guy Dunstan, 1876–1945, vol. IV

Bengough, Maj.-Gen. Sir Harcourt Mortimer, 1837–1922, vol. II

Benham, Frederic Charles Courtenay, 1900–1962, vol. VI

Benham, Sir Gurney; see Benham, Sir W. G.

Benham, Rev. William, 1831–1910, vol. I

Benham, Sir William Blaxland, 1860–1950, vol. IV

Benham, Sir (William)Gurney, 1859–1944, vol. IV

Benians, Ernest Alfred, 1880–1952, vol. V

Benin, Oba of; Akenzua II; Godfrey Okoro, 1899–1978, vol. VII

Beningfield, Gordon George, 1936–1998, vol. X

Benjamin, Arthur, 1893–1960, vol. V

Benjamin, Sir Benjamin, 1834–1905, vol. I

Benjamin, Brooke; see Benjamin, T. B.

Benjamin, Lewis S., 1874–1932, vol. III

Benjamin, Louis, 1922–1994, vol. IX

Benjamin, Louis Edmund, 1865–1935, vol. III

Benjamin, Pauline, (Mrs Joseph Benjamin); see Crabbe, Pauline.

Benjamin, (Thomas) Brooke, 1929–1995, vol. IX

Benjamin-Constant, Jean Joseph, 1845–1902, vol. I

Benka-Coker, Sir Salako Ambrosius, 1900–1965, vol. VI

Benn, Alfred William, 1843–1916, vol. II

Benn, Edward Glanvill, 1905–2000, vol. X

Benn, Engr Rear-Adm. Edward Piercy St John, 1872–1947, vol. IV

Benn, Sir Ernest John Pickstone, 2nd Bt (cr 1914), 1875–1954, vol. V

Benn, Ion Bridges Hamilton, 1887–1956, vol. V

Benn, Captain Sir Ion Hamilton, 1st Bt (cr 1920), 1863–1961, vol. VI

Benn, Sir John Andrews, 3rd Bt, 1904–1984, vol. VIII

Benn, John Meriton, 1908–1992, vol. IX

Benn, Sir John Williams, 1st Bt (cr 1914), 1850–1922, vol. II

Benn, Captain Sir Patrick Ian Hamilton, 2nd Bt, 1922–1992, vol. IX

Benn, Lt-Col Robert Arthur Edward, 1867–1940, vol. III

Bennet, Sir Edward, 1880–1958, vol. V

Bennet, Edward Armstrong, died 1977, vol. VII

Bennet, Maj.-Gen. John, 1893–1976, vol. VII

Bennet-Clark, Thomas Archibald, 1903–1975, vol. VII

Bennett, 1st Viscount, 1870–1947, vol. IV

Bennett of Edgbaston, 1st Baron, 1880–1957, vol. V

Bennett, Sir Albert Edward, 1900–1972, vol. VII

Bennett, Sir Albert James, 1st Bt, 1872–1945, vol. IV

Bennett, Albert Joseph, 1913–1996, vol. X

Bennett, Alexander; see Bennett, F. O. A. G.

Bennett, Alexander John Munro, 1868–1943, vol. IV

Bennett, Lt-Col Alfred Charles, died 1915, vol. I

Bennett, Alfred Gordon, 1901–1962, vol. VI

Bennett, Col Alfred Joshua, 1865–1946, vol. IV

Bennett, Alfred Rosling, 1850–1928, vol. II

Bennett, Alfred William, 1833–1902, vol. I

Bennett, Andrew Percy, 1866–1943, vol. IV

Bennett, Arnold; see Bennett, E. A.

Bennett, Sir Arnold Lucas, 1908–1983, vol. VIII

Bennett, Arthur, 1862–1931, vol. III

Bennett, Cecil Harry Andrew, 1898–1967, vol. VI

Bennett, Engr-Rear-Adm. Cecil Reginald Percival, 1896–1976, vol. VII

Bennett, Sir Charles Alan, 1877–1943, vol. IV

Bennett, Lt-Col Charles Hugh, 1867–1932, vol. III

Bennett, (Charles John) Michael, 1906—1999, vol. X

Bennett, Sir Charles Moihi, 1913–1998, vol. X

Bennett, Lt-Col Sir C(harles) Wilfrid, 2nd Bt, 1898–1952, vol. V

Bennett, Sir Courtenay Walter, 1855–1937, vol. III

Bennett, Cyril, 1928–1976, vol. VII

Bennett, Daniel, 1900–1985, vol. VIII

Bennett, Air Vice-Marshal Donald Clifford Tyndall, 1910–1986, vol. VIII

Bennett, Edward Hallaran, 1837–1907, vol. I

Bennett, (Enoch) Arnold, 1867–1931, vol. III

Bennett, Sir Ernest Nathaniel, died 1947, vol. IV

Bennett, Captain (Eugene) Paul, 1892–1970, vol. VI

Bennett, Sir Francis Sowerby, 1863–1950, vol. VI

Bennett, Very Rev. Frank Selwyn Macaulay, 1866–1947, vol. III

Bennett, Rt Rev. Frederick Augustus, 1872–1950, vol. IV

Bennett, Rev. Frederick George, died 1937, vol. III

Bennett, Frederick Henry C.; see Curtis-Bennett.

Bennett, (Frederick Onslow) Alexander (Godwyn), 1913–1993, vol. IX

Bennett, Captain Geoffrey Martin, 1909–1983, vol. VIII

Bennett, Geoffrey Thomas, died 1943, vol. IV

Bennett, Rev. George, 1855–1930, vol. III

Bennett, Rt Rev. George Henry, 1875–1946, vol. IV

Bennett, George John, 1863–1930, vol. III

Bennett, George Lovett, 1846–1916, vol. II

Bennett, George Macdonald, 1892–1959, vol. VI

Bennett, George Wheatley, 1845–1921, vol. II

Bennett, Lt-Gen. Gordon; see Bennett, Lt-Gen. H. G.

Bennett, Henry Currie L.; see Leigh-Bennett.

Bennett, Sir Henry Curtis, 1846–1913, vol. I
Bennett, Lt-Gen. (Henry) Gordon, 1887–1962, vol. VI
Bennett, Sir Henry Honywood C.; see Curtis-Bennett.
Bennett, Rev. Henry Leigh, 1833–1912, vol. I
Bennett, Henry Stanley, 1889–1972, vol. VII
Bennett, Sir Hubert, 1909–2000, vol. X
Bennett, Jack Arthur Walter, 1911–1981, vol. VIII
Bennett, James, 1912–1984, vol. VIII
Bennett, James Allan Jamieson, 1903–1973, vol. VII
Bennett, James Gordon, 1841–1918, vol. II
Bennett, Engr Rear-Adm. James Martin Cameron, died 1922, vol. II
Bennett, Jill, 1929–1990, vol. VIII
Bennett, Joan, 1896–1986, vol. VIII
Bennett, Joan Geraldine, 1910–1990, vol. VIII
Bennett, Sir John, 1814–1897, vol. I
Bennett, Sir John, 1876–1948, vol. IV
Bennett, John, 1909–1975, vol. VII
Bennett, Sir John (Cecil) Sterndale, 1895–1969, vol. VI
Bennett, John Colburn, 1897–1969, vol. VI
Bennett, Sir John Mokonuiarangi, 1912–1997, vol. X
Bennett, Hon. Sir John R., 1866–1941, vol. IV
Bennett, John Reginald William, 1888–1971, vol. VII
Bennett, John Sloman, 1914–1990, vol. VIII
Bennett, John Still, 1911–1970, vol. VI
Bennett, Sir John Thorne Masey, 1894–1949, vol. IV
Bennett, John Wheeler W.; see Wheeler-Bennett.
Bennett, Sir John Wheeler W.; see Wheeler-Bennett.
Bennett, Kenneth Geoffrey, 1911–1974, vol. VII
Bennett, Michael; see Bennett, C. J. M.
Bennett, Sir Noel C.; see Curtis-Bennett.
Bennett, Sir Norman Godfrey, 1870–1947, vol. IV
Bennett, Captain Paul; see Bennett, Captain E. P.
Bennett, Percy Raymond L.; see Leigh-Bennett.
Bennett, Peter Ward, 1917–1996, vol. X
Bennett, Sir Reginald, died 1944, vol. IV
Bennett, Sir Reginald Frederick Brittain, 1911–2000, vol. X
Bennett, Reginald Robert, 1879–1966, vol. VI
Bennett, Rex George, 1885–1972, vol. VII
Bennett, Robert Augustus, 1855–1929, vol. III
Bennett, Maj.-Gen. Roland Anthony, 1899–1974, vol. VII
Bennett, Ronald Alistair, 1922–1996, vol. X
Bennett, Rev. Canon Ronald Du Pré G.; see Grange-Bennett.
Bennett, Roy Grissell, 1917–1996, vol. X
Bennett, Seymour John, 1848–1930, vol. III
Bennett, T. C. S.; see Sterndale-Bennett.
Bennett, T. Izod, 1887–1946, vol. IV
Bennett, Thomas Henry, died 1900, vol. I
Bennett, Sir Thomas Jewell, 1852–1925, vol. II
Bennett, Sir Thomas Penberthy, 1887–1980, vol. VII
Bennett, Comdr Thomas William, 1872–1939, vol. III
Bennett, Thomas William Westropp, 1867–1962, vol. VI

Bennett, Hon. Walter, 1864–1934, vol. III
Bennett, Lt-Col Sir Wilfrid; see Bennett, Lt-Col Sir C. W.
Bennett, Col William, 1835–1912, vol. I
Bennett, William, 1854–1935, vol. III
Bennett, William, 1873–1937, vol. III
Bennett, William Exall Tempest, 1858–1937, vol. III
Bennett, Sir William Gordon, died 1982, vol. VIII
Bennett, William H., 1859–1925, vol. II
Bennett, William Hart, 1861–1918, vol. II
Bennett, Sir William Henry, 1852–1931, vol. III
Bennett, Sir William James, 1896–1971, vol. VII
Bennett, William John, 1911–1991, vol. IX
Bennett-Edwards, Mrs; see Edwards, Mrs B.
Bennett-Goldney, Francis, 1865–1918, vol. II
Benney, Ernest Alfred Sallis, 1894–1966, vol. VI
Benning, Captain Charles Stuart, 1884–1924, vol. II
Bennion, Claud, 1886–1976, vol. VII
Bennison, John; see Bennison, R. J.
Bennison, (Robert) John, 1928–1989, vol. VIII
Bennitt, Mortimer Wilmot, 1910–1995, vol. IX
Benoit, Pierre, 1886–1962, vol. VI
Benoy, Brig. James Francis, 1896–1972, vol. VII
Benoy, Maj.-Gen. John Meredith, 1896–1977, vol. VII
Benskin, Gladys Sheffield, (Mrs Joseph Benskin), 1888–1978, vol. VII
Benskin, Col Joseph, 1883–1953, vol. V
Bensley, Benjamin Arthur, 1875–1934, vol. III
Bensley, Col Clement Henry, 1870–1940, vol. III
Bensley, Edward von Blomberg, 1863–1939, vol. III
Bensly, Rev. William James, 1874–1943, vol. IV
Benson, Baron (Life Peer); Henry Alexander Benson, 1909–1995, vol. IX
Benson, Arthur Christopher, 1862–1925, vol. II
Benson, Sir Arthur Edward Trevor, 1907–1987, vol. VIII
Benson, Arthur Henry, 1852–1912, vol. I
Benson, Rev. Sir (Clarence) Irving, 1897–1980, vol. VII(AII)
Benson, Air Cdre Constantine Evelyn, died 1960, vol. V
Benson, Rear-Adm. Cyril Herbert Gordon, 1884–1974, vol. VII
Benson, Edward Frederic, 1867–1940, vol. III
Benson, Maj.-Gen. Edward Riou, 1903–1985, vol. VIII
Benson, Hon. (Eleanor) Theodora Roby, 1906–1968, vol. VI
Benson, Sir Frank, 1878–1952, vol. V
Benson, Sir Frank Robert, 1858–1939, vol. III
Benson, Frank Weston, 1862–1951, vol. V
Benson, Maj.-Gen. Sir Frederick William, 1849–1916, vol. II
Benson, Sir George, 1889–1973, vol. VII
Benson, Guy Holford, 1888–1975, vol. VII
Benson, Hon. Lt-Col Henry Wightman, 1855–1935, vol. III
Benson, Horace Burford, 1904–1995, vol. X (AI)
Benson, Rev. Sir Irving; see Benson, Rev. Sir C. I.
Benson, Sir J. Hawtrey, 1843–1931, vol. III
Benson, James Bourne, 1848–1930, vol. III
Benson, Sir Jeffrey; see Benson, Sir W. J.
Benson, Jeremy Henry, 1925–1999, vol. X

Benson, Rev. John Peter, *died* 1944, vol. IV
Benson, Margaret J., *died* 1936, vol. III
Benson, Rev. Niale Shane Trevor, 1911–1980, vol. VII
Benson, Percy George Reginald, 1872–1961, vol. VI
Benson, Surg.-Gen. Percy Hugh, 1852–1933, vol. III
Benson, Philip de Gylpyn, 1883–1931, vol. III
Benson, Preston, 1896–1975, vol. VII
Benson, Col Ralph Hawtrey Rohde, 1880–1943, vol. IV
Benson, Sir Ralph Sillery, 1851–1920, vol. II
Benson, Lt-Col Sir Rex Lindsay, 1889–1968, vol. IV
Benson, Rev. Richard Meux, 1824–1915, vol. I
Benson, Brig.-Gen. Riou Philip, 1863–1939, vol. III
Benson, Brig. Robert, 1881–1952, vol. V
Benson, Vice-Adm. Robert Edmund Ross, *died* 1927, vol. II
Benson, Robert Henry, 1850–1929, vol. III
Benson, Very Rev. Mgr Robert Hugh, 1871–1914, vol. I
Benson, Col Starling Meux, 1846–1933, vol. III
Benson, Stella, 1892–1933, vol. III
Benson, Stephen Riou, *died* 1961, vol. VI
Benson, Hon. Theodora; *see* Benson, Hon. E. T. R.
Benson, Ven. Thomas M., *died* 1921, vol. II
Benson, Col Wallace, *died* 1951, vol. V
Benson, William Arthur Smith, 1854–1924, vol. II
Benson, William Denman, 1848–1919, vol. II
Benson, Col William George Sackville, 1861–1954, vol. V
Benson, Sir (William) Jeffrey, 1922–1994, vol. IX
Benson, William John, *died* 1941, vol. IV
Benson, William Noël, 1885–1957, vol. V
Benstead, Sir John, 1897–1979, vol. VII
Bensusan, Samuel Levy, 1872–1958, vol. V
Bent, Col Arthur Milton, 1870–1940, vol. III
Bent, Col Charles Edward, 1880–1955, vol. V
Bent, Rear-Adm. Eric Ritchie, 1888–1949, vol. IV
Bent, James Theodore, 1852–1897, vol. I
Bent, Mabel Virginia Anna, (Mrs Theodore Bent), *died* 1929, vol. III
Bent, Mrs Theodore; *see* Bent, M. V. A.
Bent, Hon. Sir Thomas, 1838–1909, vol. I
Bentall, Gerald Chalmers, 1903–1971, vol. VII
Bentall, (Leonard Edward) Rowan, 1911–1993, vol. IX
Bentall, Rowan; *see* Bentall, L. E. R.
Benthall, Sir (Arthur) Paul, 1902–1992, vol. IX
Benthall, Sir Edward Charles, 1893–1961, vol. VI
Benthall, Major John Lawrence, 1868–1947, vol. IV
Benthall, Michael Pickersgill, 1919–1974, vol. VII
Benthall, Sir Paul; *see* Benthall, Sir A. P.
Bentham, Ethel, *died* 1931, vol. III
Bentham, George Jackson, 1863–1929, vol. III
Bentham, Percy George, 1883–1936, vol. III
Bentinck, Baron Adolph Willem Carel, 1905–1970, vol. VI
Bentinck, Arthur Harold Walter, 1875–1964, vol. VI
Bentinck, Lt-Col Lord Charles C.; *see* Cavendish-Bentinck.
Bentinck, Rev. Charles D., 1866–1940, vol. III
Bentinck, Rev. Sir Charles Henry, 1879–1955, vol. V
Bentinck, Frederick Cavendish-, 1856–1948, vol. IV

Bentinck, Lord Henry Cavendish, 1863–1931, vol. III
Bentinck, Lady Norah, *died* 1939, vol. III
Bentinck, Adm. Sir Rudolph Walter, 1869–1947, vol. IV
Bentinck, Baron Walter Guy, 1864–1957, vol. V
Bentinck, Lord William Augustus Cavendish-, 1865–1903, vol. I
Bentinck, Count William Charles Philip Otho, 1848–1912, vol. I
Bentine, Michael, 1922–1996, vol. X
Bentley, Alfred, *died* 1923, vol. II
Bentley, Arthur Owen, 1898–1943, vol. IV
Bentley, Bertram Henry, 1873–1946, vol. IV
Bentley, Charles Albert, 1873–1949, vol. IV
Bentley, Rt Rev. David Williams Bentley, 1882–1970, vol. VI
Bentley, Edmund Clerihew, 1875–1956, vol. V
Bentley, Col Francis I., 1868–1938, vol. III
Bentley, Frederic Herbert, 1905–1980, vol. VII
Bentley, Rev. Canon Geoffrey Brian, 1909–1996, vol. X
Bentley, Nicolas Clerihew, 1907–1978, vol. VII
Bentley, Phyllis Eleanor, 1894–1977, vol. VII
Bentley, Richard, 1854–1936, vol. III
Bentley, Walter Owen, 1888–1971, vol. III
Bentley, Sir William, 1927–1998, vol. X
Bentley-Buckle, Lt-Col Arthur William; *see* Buckle.
Bentliff, Hubert David, 1891–1953, vol. V
Bentliff, Walter David, 1859–1940, vol. III
Benton, Gordon William, 1893–1983, vol. VIII
Benton, Sir John, 1850–1927, vol. II
Benton, Kenneth Carter, 1909–1999, vol. X
Benton, William, 1900–1973, vol. VII
Bentwich, Helen Caroline, (Mrs Norman Bentwich), 1892–1972, vol. VII
Bentwich, Herbert, 1856–1932, vol. III
Bentwich, Norman de Mathos, 1883–1971, vol. VII
Benuarrat, 7th Baron of, 1870–1935, vol. III
Benyon, Sir Henry Arthur, 1st Bt, 1884–1959, vol. V
Benyon, James Herbert, 1849–1935, vol. III
Benyon, Vice-Adm. Richard, 1892–1968, vol. VI
Benziger, August, 1867–1955, vol. V
Benzinger, Immanuel G. A., *born* 1865, vol. III
Beoku-Betts, Sir Ernest Samuel, 1895–1957, vol. V
Beovich, Most Rev. Matthew, 1896–1981, vol. VIII
Berar, State of; Gen. HH the Prince of, 1907–1970, vol. VI (AII)
Berard, Victor, 1864–1931, vol. III
Bercovici, Konrad, *died* 1961, vol. VI
Bere, Rennie Montague, 1907–1991, vol. IX
Bérégovoy, Pierre Eugène, 1925–1993, vol. IX
Berendsen, Sir Carl August, 1890–1973, vol. VII
Berens, Alexander Augustus, 1842–1926, vol. II
Berens, Herbert Cecil Benyon, 1908–1981, vol. VIII
Berenson, Bernhard, 1865–1959, vol. V
Beresford, 1st Baron, 1846–1919, vol. II
Beresford, Ven. Alfred Richard Angland, *died* 1936, vol. III
Beresford, Cecil Hugh W., *died* 1912, vol. I
Beresford, Col Charles Edward de la Poer, 1850–1921, vol. II
Beresford, Rev. Charles John, 1868–1936, vol. III
Beresford, Denis R. P.; *see* Pack-Beresford.

Beresford, Eric George Harold, 1901–1983, vol. VIII
Beresford, George de la Poer, 1831–1906, vol. I
Beresford, Maj.-Gen. Sir George de la Poer, 1885–1964, vol. VI
Beresford, Jack, 1899–1977, vol. VII
Beresford, Rev. John, 1839–1918, vol. II
Beresford, John Baldwyn, 1888–1940, vol. III
Beresford, Maj.-Gen. John Beresford, *born* 1828, vol. II
Beresford, John Davys, 1873–1947, vol. IV
Beresford, John George M.; *see* Massy-Beresford.
Beresford, John Stuart, 1845–1926, vol. II
Beresford, Lord Marcus de la Poer, 1848–1922, vol. II
Beresford, Marcus Henry de la Poer, 1857–1934, vol. III
Beresford, Lt-Gen. Mostyn de la Poer, 1835–1911, vol. I
Beresford, Hon. Seton Robert de la Poer Horsley, 1868–1928, vol. II
Beresford, Tristram de la Poer, 1887–1962, vol. VI
Beresford, Lady William, *died* 1909, vol. I
Beresford, Lord William Leslie de la Poer, 1847–1900, vol. I
Beresford-Peirse, Major Sir Henry Bernard de la Poer, 4th Bt, 1875–1949, vol. IV
Beresford-Peirse, Sir Henry Campbell de la Poer, 5th Bt, 1905–1972, vol. VII
Beresford-Peirse, Sir Henry Monson de la Poer, 3rd Bt, 1850–1926, vol. II
Beresford-Peirse, Lt-Gen. Sir Noel Monson de la Poer, 1887–1953, vol. V
Beresford-Peirse, Rev. Richard Windham de la Poer, 1876–1952, vol. V
Beresford-Peirse, Rev. Canon Windham de la Poer, 1858–1940, vol. III
Berg, Alban, 1885–1935, vol. III
Bergel, Franz, 1900–1987, vol. VIII
Berger, Francesco, 1834–1933, vol. III
Berget, Baron Alphonse, 1860–1933, vol. III
Bergh, Rt Rev. Frederick Thomas, 1840–1924, vol. II
Bergholt, Ernest George Binckes, 1856–1925, vol. II
Bergin, John Alexander, 1920–1986, vol. VIII
Bergin, Kenneth Glenny, 1911–1981, vol. VIII
Bergin, Osborn Joseph, *died* 1950, vol. IV
Bergin, William, 1864–1942, vol. IV
Bergius, Friedrich Karl Rudolph, 1884–1949, vol. IV
Bergman, Ingrid, 1915–1982, vol. VIII
Bergne, Sir John Henry Gibbs, 1842–1908, vol. I
Bergner, Elisabeth, 1900–1986, vol. VIII
Bergson, Henri Louis, 1859–1941, vol. IV
Beringer, Oscar, 1844–1922, vol. II
Beringer, Mrs Oscar, 1856–1936, vol. III
Beriozova, Svetlana, 1932–1998, vol. X
Berkeley, 8th Earl, 1865–1942, vol. IV
Berkeley, Baroness (15th in line), 1840–1899, vol. I
Berkeley, Baroness (16th in line), 1875–1964, vol. VI
Berkeley, Baroness (17th in line), 1905–1992, vol. IX
Berkeley, Rt Rev. Alfred Pakenham, 1862–1938, vol. III

Berkeley, Lt-Col Arthur Mowbray, 1870–1937, vol. III
Berkeley, (Augustus Fitzhardinge) Maurice, 1903–1991, vol. IX
Berkeley, Lt-Col Christopher Robert, 1877–1959, vol. V
Berkeley, Sir Comyns, 1865–1946, vol. IV
Berkeley, Sir Ernest James Lennox, 1857–1932, vol. III
Berkeley, Essex Digby, 1843–1936, vol. III
Berkeley, Frederic George, 1919–1999, vol. X
Berkeley, Maj.-Gen. Frederick George, 1841–1906, vol. I
Berkeley, Sir George, 1819–1905, vol. I
Berkeley, Sir Henry Spencer, 1851–1918, vol. II
Berkeley, Humphrey John, 1926–1994, vol. IX
Berkeley, Maj.-Gen. James Cavan, 1839–1926, vol. II
Berkeley, Sir Lennox Randal Francis, 1903–1989, vol. VIII
Berkeley, Maurice; *see* Berkeley, A. F. M.
Berkeley, Sir Maurice Julian, *died* 1931, vol. III
Berkeley, Captain Reginald Cheyne, 1890–1935, vol. III
Berkeley, Robert Valentine, 1853–1940, vol. III
Berkeley, Stanley, *died* 1909, vol. I
Berkhouwer, Cornelis, 1919–1992, vol. IX
Berkin, John Phillip, 1905–1979, vol. VII
Berle, Adolf Augustus, 1895–1971, vol. VII
Berlin, Irving, 1888–1989, vol. VIII
Berlin, Sir Isiah, 1909–1997, vol. X
Berliner, Emile, 1851–1929, vol. III
Berlyn, Alfred, *died* 1936, vol. III
Berlyn, Mrs Alfred, *died* 1943, vol. IV
Berlyn, Bernard Henry Alfred Forbes, 1886–1936, vol. III
Bermant, Chaim Icyk, 1929–1998, vol. X
Bermingham, Engr-Rear-Adm. Cecil Henry Alec, 1870–1938, vol. III
Bernacchi, Louis Charles, 1876–1942, vol. IV
Bernacchi, Michael Louis, 1911–1983, vol. VIII
Bernadotte, Count Folke, 1895–1948, vol. IV
Bernal, Frederic, 1828–1924, vol. II
Bernal, Lt-Col Greville Hugh Woodlee, *died* 1922, vol. II
Bernal, John Desmond, 1901–1971, vol. VII
Bernal, Ralph, 1867–1938, vol. III
Bernard, Albert Victor, 1885–1955, vol. V
Bernard, Andrew Milroy F.; *see* Fleming-Bernard.
Bernard, Anthony, 1891–1963, vol. VI
Bernard, Hon. Charles Brodrick Amyas, 1904–1977, vol. VII
Bernard, Sir Charles Edward, 1837–1901, vol. I
Bernard, Sir Dallas Gerald Mercer, 1st Bt, 1888–1975, vol. VII
Bernard, Lt-Gen. Sir Denis Kirwan, 1882–1956, vol. V
Bernard, Col Sir Edgar Edwin, 1866–1931, vol. III
Bernard, Rev. Edward Russell, 1842–1921, vol. II
Bernard, Rt Rev. Eustace Anthony M.; *see* Morrogh Bernard.
Bernard, Francis Georgius, 1908–1978, vol. VII
Bernard, Lt-Col Francis Tyringham H.; *see* Higgins Bernard.
Bernard, Jean-Jacques, 1888–1972, vol. VII

Bernard, Jeffrey Joseph, 1932–1997, vol. X
Bernard, Most Rev. and Rt Hon. John Henry, 1860–1927, vol. II
Bernard, Col Joseph Francis, 1871–1953, vol. V
Bernard, Oliver Percy, 1881–1939, vol. III
Bernard, Percy Brodrick, 1844–1912, vol. I
Bernard, Lt-Col Ronald Percy Hamilton, 1875–1921, vol. II
Bernard, Col Ronald Playfair St Vincent, 1888–1943, vol. IV
Bernard, Rev. Thomas Dehany, 1815–1904, vol. I
Bernard, Adm. Vivian Henry Gerald, 1868–1934, vol. III
Bernard, Lt-Col William Kingsmill, 1872–1933, vol. III
Bernays, Charles Arrowsmith, 1862–1940, vol. III
Bernays, Comdr Leopold Arthur, died 1917, vol. II
Bernays, Lewis Adolphus, 1831–1908, vol. I
Bernays, Lewis Edward, 1886–1972, vol. VII
Bernays, Robert Hamilton, 1902–1945, vol. IV
Berners, Baroness (7th in line), 1835–1917, vol. II
Berners, 8th Baron, 1855–1918, vol. II
Berners, 14th (de facto 9th) Baron, 1883–1950, vol. IV
Berners, Baroness (15th in line), 1901–1992, vol. IX
Berners, John Anstruther, died 1934, vol. III
Berners, Brig.-Gen. Ralph Abercrombie, 1871–1949, vol. IV
Berney, Sir Henry, 1862–1953, vol. V
Berney, Sir Henry Hanson, 9th Bt, 1843–1907, vol. I
Berney, Captain Sir Thomas Reedham, 10th Bt, 1893–1975, vol. VII
Berney-Ficklin, Maj.-Gen. Horatio Pettus Mackintosh, 1892–1961, vol. VI
Bernhardt, Sarah, 1845–1923, vol. II
Bernier, Captain Joseph Elzear, 1852–1934, vol. III
Bernier, Hon. Michel Esdras, 1841–1921, vol. II
Bernier, Hon. Thomas Alfred, 1844–1909, vol. I
Bernstein, Baron (Life Peer); Sidney Lewis Bernstein, 1899–1993, vol. IX
Bernstein, Basil Bernard, 1924–2000, vol. X
Bernstein, Cecil George, 1904–1981, vol. VIII
Bernstein, Henri, 1876–1953, vol. V
Bernstein, Leonard, 1918–1990, vol. VIII
Bernstorff, Count John, 1862–1939, vol. III
Berrangé, Major Christian Anthony Lawson, 1864–1922, vol. II
Berridge, Harold, 1872–1949, vol. IV
Berridge, Sir Thomas Henry Devereux, 1857–1924, vol. II
Berrie, John Archibald Alexander, 1887–1962, vol. VI
Berrill, Norman John, 1903–1996, vol. X
Berrow, William Lewis, 1862–1928, vol. II
Berry, Alan Percival, 1926–1983, vol. VIII
Berry, Lt-Col Alfred Eugene, 1869–1932, vol. III
Berry, Hon. Sir Anthony George, 1925–1984, vol. VIII
Berry, Arthur, 1862–1929, vol. III
Berry, Rev. Charles Albert, 1852–1899, vol. I
Berry, Rev. Edward Arthur, 1871–1949, vol. IV
Berry, (Frances) May Dickinson, 1857–1934, vol. III
Berry, Sir George Andreas, 1853–1940, vol. III

Berry, Hon. Sir Graham, 1822–1904, vol. I
Berry, Harry, 1890–1982, vol. VIII
Berry, Henry, 1883–1956, vol. V
Berry, Henry Fitz-Patrick, born 1847, vol. II
Berry, Sir (Henry) Vaughan, 1891–1979, vol. VII
Berry, Very Rev. Hugh Frederick, died 1961, vol. VI (AII)
Berry, Prof. Jack, 1918–1980, vol. VII (AII)
Berry, Sir James, 1860–1946, vol. IV
Berry, John Stanley, 1915–1975, vol. VII
Berry, John William Edward, 1901–1971, vol. VII
Berry, Col Hon. Julian, 1920–1988, vol. VIII
Berry, Martha McChesney, 1866–1942, vol. IV
Berry, May Dickinson; see Berry, F. M. D.
Berry, Michael Francis, 1906–1988, vol. VIII
Berry, Lady Pamela Margaret Elizabeth; see Hartwell, Lady.
Berry, Richard James Arthur, 1867–1962, vol. VI
Berry, Robert, 1825–1903, vol. I
Berry, Air Cdre Ronald, 1917–2000, vol. X
Berry, Rev. Sidney Malcolm, 1881–1961, vol. VI
Berry, Rt Rev. Thomas Sterling, 1854–1931, vol. III
Berry, Trevor T.; see Thornton-Berry.
Berry, Sir Vaughan; see Berry, Sir H. V.
Berry, Sir Walter Wheeler, 1857–1933, vol. III
Berry, Sir William John, 1865–1937, vol. III
Berry, Hon. Sir William Bisset-, 1839–1922, vol. II
Berry, William Grinton, 1873–1926, vol. II
Berryman, Lt-Gen. Sir Frank Horton, 1894–1981, vol. VIII
Berryman, Sir Frederick Henry, 1869–1952, vol. V
Berryman, John, 1914–1972, vol. VII
Berryman, Montague Levander, 1899–1974, vol. VII
Berteau, Francis Cyrus, 1856–1945, vol. IV
Berteaux, Henry Maurice, 1852–1911, vol. I
Bertenshaw, Eric Strickland, 1888–1957, vol. V
Berthon, Rear-Adm. Charles Pierre, 1893–1965, vol. VI
Berthon, Rev. Edward Lyon, 1813–1899, vol. I
Berthon, Henry Edward, 1862–1948, vol. IV
Berthoud, Edward Henry, 1876–1955, vol. VI
Berthoud, Sir Eric Alfred, 1900–1989, vol. VIII
Berthoulat, Georges, 1859–1930, vol. III
Bertie of Thame, 1st Viscount, 1844–1919, vol. II
Bertie of Thame, 2nd Viscount, 1878–1954, vol. V
Bertie, Rev. Hon. Alberic Edward, 1846–1928, vol. II
Berties, Major Hon. Arthur Michael, 1886–1957, vol. V
Berties, Lt-Col Hon. George Aubrey Vere, 1850–1926, vol. II
Bertie, Col Hon. Reginal Henry, 1856–1950, vol. IV
Bertillon, Alponse, 1853–1914, vol. I
Bertouch, Baroness de, Beatrice, died 1931, vol. III
Bertram, Brig.-Gen. Sir Alexander, 1853–1926, vol. II
Bertram, Anthony, 1897–1978, vol. VII
Bertram, Sir Anton, 1869–1937, vol. III
Bertram, (Cicely) Kate, 1912–1999, vol. X
Bertram, Douglas Somerville, 1913–1988, vol. VIII
Bertram, Edith, (Lady Bertram), died 1959, vol. V

Bertram, Francis George Lawder, 1875–1938, vol. III
Bertram, Sir George Clement, 1841–1915, vol. I
Bertram, Julius, 1866–1944, vol. IV
Bertram, Kate; see Bertram, C. K.
Bertram, Louis John, 1859–1940, vol. III
Bertram, Neville Rennie, 1909–1974, vol. VII
Bertram, Lt-Col William Robert, 1888–1970, vol. VI
Bertrand, Cavalier Léon, 1897–1980, vol. VII
Bertrand, Louis Marie Emile, 1866–1941, vol. IV
Beruete y Moret, Aureliano de, 1878–1922, vol. II (A), vol. III
Berwick, 7th Baron, 1847–1897, vol. I
Berwick, 8th Baron, 1877–1947, vol. IV
Berwick, 9th Baron, 1897–1953, vol. V
Berwick, T., 1826–1915, vol. I
Berwick, William Edward Hodgson, 1888–1944, vol. IV
Besant, Annie, 1847–1933, vol. III
Besant, Arthur Digby, 1869–1960, vol. V
Besant, Sir Walter, 1836–1901, vol. I
Besant, William Henry, 1828–1917, vol. II
Besicovitch, Abram Samoilovitch, 1891–1970, vol. VI
Besier, Rudolf, 1878–1942, vol. IV
Besley, Edward Thomas Edmonds, 1826–1901, vol. I
Besley, Rev. Walter Philip, 1870–1934, vol. III
Besly, Ernest Francis Withers, 1891–1965, vol. VI
Besly, Maurice, 1888–1945, vol. IV
Besnard, Paul Albert, 1849–1934, vol. III
Bessborough, 7th Earl of, 1821–1906, vol. I
Bessborough, 8th Earl of, 1851–1920, vol. II
Bessborough, 9th Earl of, 1880–1956, vol. V
Bessborough, 10th Earl of, 1913–1993, vol. IX
Bessell, Peter Joseph, 1921–1985, vol. VIII
Bessell-Browne, Brig.-Gen. Alfred Joseph; see Browne.
Bessemer, Sir Henry, 1813–1898, vol. I
Best, Alfred Charles, 1904–1993, vol. IX
Best, Charles Herbert, 1899–1978, vol. VII
Best, Edna, 1900–1974, vol. VII
Best, Edward Wallace, 1917–1993, vol. IX
Best, Elsdon, 1856–1931, vol. III
Best, George Percival, 1872–1953, vol. V
Best, Giles Bernard, 1925–1997, vol. X
Best, Captain Humphrey Willie, 1884–1959, vol. V
Best, Hon. James William, 1882–1960, vol. V
Best, Rev. John Dugdale, 1856–1933, vol. III
Best, Sir John Victor Hall, 1894–1972, vol. VII
Best, Ven. Joseph, 1880–1965, vol. VI
Best, Hon. Margaret, 1872–1941, vol. IV
Best, Adm. Hon. Sir Matthew Robert, 1878–1940, vol. III
Best, Rt Hon. Richard, died 1939, vol. III
Best, Richard Irvine, 1872–1959, vol. V
Best, Hon. Robert Rainy, 1834–1903, vol. I
Best, Hon. Sir Robert Wallace, 1856–1946, vol. IV
Best, Sir Thomas Alexander Vans, 1870–1941, vol. IV
Best, Rear-Adm. Thomas William, 1915–1984, vol. VIII
Best-Shaw, Sir John James Kenward, 9th Bt, 1895–1984, vol. VIII

Beste, Captain Sir Henry Aloysius Bruno D.; see Digby-Beste.
Besterman, Theodore Deodatus Nathaniel, 1904–1976, vol. VII
Bestor, Arthur Eugene, 1908–1994, vol. IX
Beswick, Baron (Life Peer); Frank Beswick, 1912–1987, vol. VIII
Beswick, John Reginald, 1919–1994, vol. IX
Betham, Lt-Col Sir Geoffrey Lawrence, 1889–1963, vol. VI
Betham, Brig.-Gen. Robert Mitchell, 1864–1939, vol. III
Betham-Edwards, Matilda; see Edwards.
Bethel, Albert, born 1874, vol. III
Bethell, 1st Baron, 1861–1945, vol. IV
Bethell, 2nd Baron, 1902–1965, vol. VI
Bethell, 3rd Baron, 1928–1967, vol. VI
Bethell, Captain Adrian, 1890–1941, vol. IV
Bethell, Hon. (Albert) Victor, 1864–1927, vol. II
Bethell, Adm. Hon. Sir Alexander Edward, 1855–1932, vol. III
Bethell, Col Alfred Bryan, 1875–1956, vol. V
Bethell, Maj.-Gen. Donald Andrew Douglas Jardine, (Drew), 1921–1988, vol. VIII
Bethell, Maj.-Gen. Drew; see Bethell, Maj.-Gen. Donald A. D. J.
Bethell, Col Edward Hugh, 1854–1940, vol. III
Bethell, George Richard, 1849–1919, vol. II
Bethell, Brig.-Gen. Henry Arthur, 1861–1939, vol. III
Bethell, Maj.-Gen. Sir (Hugh) Keppel, 1882–1947, vol. IV
Bethell, Maj.-Gen. Sir Keppel; see Bethell, Maj.-Gen. Sir H. K.
Bethell, Hon. Richard, 1883–1929, vol. III
Bethell, Richard Anthony, 1922–1996, vol. X
Bethell, Sir Thomas Robert, died 1957, vol. V
Bethell, Hon. Victor; see Bethell, Hon. A.V.
Bethell, William, 1847–1926, vol. II
Bethune, Sir Alexander Maitland Sharp, 10th Bt, 1909–1997, vol. X
Bethune, Rev. Charles James Stewart, 1838–1932, vol. III
Bethune, Lt.-Gen. Sir Edward Cecil, 1855–1930, vol. III
Bethune, Francis John, 1860–1954, vol. V
Bethune, Lt-Col Henry Alexander, 1866–1946, vol. IV
Bethune, Henry Leonard, 1858–1939, vol. III
Bethune, Rev. John Walter, 1882–1960, vol. V
Bethune, Strachan, 1821–1910, vol. I
Bethune-Baker, Rev. James Franklin, 1861–1951, vol. V
Betjeman, Sir John, 1906–1984, vol. VIII
Betjemann, Gilbert H., 1840–1921, vol. II
Bett, Rev. Henry, 1876–1953, vol. V
Bett, Surg. Rear-Adm. William, 1863–1946, vol. IV
Bettany, Frederick George, 1868–1942, vol. IV
Betteridge, Don; see Newman, Bernard.
Bettington, Gp Captain (Arthur) Vere, 1881–1950, vol. IV
Bettington, Gp Captain Vere; see Bettington, Gp Captain A. V.
Bettley, Francis Ray, 1909–1993, vol. IX
Bettley, Ray; see Bettley, F. R.

Bettmann, Siegfried, 1863–1951, vol. V
Betts, Mrs E. M.; *see* Hayes, Gertrude.
Betts, Edward William, 1881–1980, vol. VII
Betts, Captain Ernest Edward Alexander,
   1877–1951, vol. V
Betts, Sir Ernest Samuel B.; *see* Beoku-Betts.
Betts, Frederick Pimlott, 1853–1930, vol. III
Betts, James Anthony, 1897–1980, vol. VII
Betts, Reginald Robert, 1903–1961, vol. VI
Betts, William Andrew, 1866–1945, vol. IV
Betty, Vice-Adm. Arthur K.; *see* Kemmis Betty.
Betty, Lt-Col Paget K.; *see* Kemmis Betty.
Betuel, Herbert William Norman, 1908–1980,
   vol. VII
Beuttler, Brig. V. O., 1886–1948, vol. IV
Bevan, Sir Alfred Henry, 1837–1900, vol. I
Bevan, (Andrew) David Gilroy, 1928–1996, vol. X
Bevan, Rt Hon. Aneurin, 1897–1960, vol. V
Bevan, Anthony Ashley, 1859–1933, vol. III
Bevan, Bill; *see* Bevan, C. W. L.
Bevan, Cecil Wilfrid Luscombe, (Bill), 1920–1989,
   vol. VIII
Bevan, Cosmo, 1863–1935, vol. III
Bevan, David Gilroy; *see* Bevan, A. D. G.
Bevan, Sir David Martyn E.; *see* Evans Bevan.
Bevan, Rt Rev. Edward Latham, 1861–1934, vol. III
Bevan, Edwyn Robert, 1870–1943, vol. IV
Bevan, Francis Augustus, 1840–1919, vol. II
Bevan, Frederick Charles, *born* 1856, vol. III
Bevan, Captain George Parker, 1878–1920, vol. II
Bevan, Ven. Henry Edward James, 1854–1935,
   vol. III
Bevan, Ven. Hugh Henry Molesworth, 1884–1970,
   vol. VI
Bevan, Janet; *see* Baroness Lee of Asheridge.
Bevan, John Henry, 1894–1978, vol. VII
Bevan, John Sage, 1900–1978, vol. VII
Bevan, Rt Rev. Kenneth Graham, 1898–1993,
   vol. IX
Bevan, Lawrence Emlyn Douglas, 1903–1972,
   vol. VII
Bevan, Leonard, 1926–1990, vol. VIII
Bevan, Major Rev. Llewelyn David, 1842–1918,
   vol. II
Bevan, Hon. Dame Maud Elizabeth, 1856–1944,
   vol. IV
Bevan, Michael Guy Molesworth, 1926–1992,
   vol. IX
Bevan, Percy Archibald Thomas, 1909–1981,
   vol. VIII
Bevan, Rear-Adm. Sir Richard Hugh Loraine,
   1885–1976, vol. VII
Bevan, Richard Thomas, 1914–1997, vol. X
Bevan, Robert Alexander Polhill, 1901–1974,
   vol. VII
Bevan, Stuart James, *died* 1935, vol. III
Bevan, Wilfred, 1866–1940, vol. III
Bevan, Ven. William Latham, 1821–1908, vol. I
Bevan-Baker, Bevan Braithwaite, 1890–1963,
   vol. VI
Bevan-Lewis, William, 1847–1929, vol. III
Bevenot, Clovis, *died* 1925, vol. II
Beveridge, 1st Baron, 1879–1963, vol. VI
Beveridge, Lady; (Janet), 1876–1959, vol. V

Beveridge, Alexander William Morton, *died* 1959,
   vol. V
Beveridge, Maj.-Gen. Arthur Joseph, 1893–1959,
   vol. V
Beveridge, Erskine, 1851–1920, vol. II
Beveridge, Sir Gordon Smith Grieve, 1933–1999,
   vol. X
Beveridge, Rev. John, 1857–1943, vol. IV
Beveridge, Maj.-Gen. Sir Wildred William Ogilvy,
   1864–1962, vol. VI
Beverley, Rt Rev. Alton Ray, 1884–1956, vol. V
Beverley, Frank, 1880–1972, vol. VII
Beverley, Vice-Adm. Sir (William) York (La
   Roche), 1895–1982, vol. VIII
Beverley, Vice-Adm. Sir York; *see* Beverley,
   Vice-Adm. Sir W. Y. La R.
Bevers, Edmund Cecil, 1876–1961, vol. VI
Beverton, Raymond John Heaphy, 1922–1995,
   vol. IX
Beves, Donald Howard, 1896–1961, vol. VI
Beves, Brig.-Gen. Percival Scott, 1868–1924, vol. II
Beville, Lt-Col Charles Hamilton, 1865–1934,
   vol. III
Beville, Lt-Col Francis Granville, 1867–1923, vol. II
Beville, Gen. Sir George Francis, 1837–1913, vol. I
Bevin, Rt Hon. Ernest, 1881–1951, vol. V
Bevin, Dame Florence Anne, 1882–1968, vol. VI
Bevins, Rt Hon. John Reginald, 1908–1996, vol. X
Bevir, Sir Anthony, 1895–1977, vol. VII
Bevir, Vice-Adm. Oliver, 1891–1967, vol. VI
Bewerunge, Rev. Henry, *born* 1862, vol. II
Bewes, Lt-Col Arthur Edward, 1871–1922, vol. II
Bewes, Wyndham Austis, 1857–1942, vol. IV
Bewick, Herbert, 1911–1995, vol. X (AI)
Bewick, Ralph Martin, 1861–1934, vol. III
Bewick-Copley, Brig.-Gen. Sir Robert Calverley
   Alington Bewicke, 1855–1923, vol. II
Bewley, Col Alfred William, 1866–1939, vol. III
Bewley, Sir Edmund Thomas, 1837–1908, vol. I
Bewley, Henry, 1860–1945, vol. IV
Bewley, Thomas Kenneth, 1890–1943, vol. IV
Bewley, William Fleming, 1891–1976, vol. VII
Bewoor, Sir Gurunath Venkatesh, *died* 1950, vol. IV
Bews, John William, 1884–1938, vol. III
Bewsher, Brig. Frederick William, 1886–1950,
   vol. IV
Bewsher, Paul, 1894–1966, vol. VI
Bewsher, Lt-Col William Dent, 1868–1942, vol. IV
Bex, Charles James, *died* 1940, vol. III
Beyen, Johan Willem, 1897–1976, vol. VII
Beyers, Brig.-Gen. Hon. Christian Frederick,
   1869–1914, vol. I
Beyers, Hon. Fredrik William, 1867–1938, vol. III
Beyfus, Gilbert Hugh, 1885–1960, vol. V
Beynon, Albert Gwyn, 1908–1978, vol. VII
Beynon, Major Godfrey Evan Schaw P.; *see*
   Protheroe-Beynon.
Beynon, Sir Granville; *see* Beynon, Sir W. J. G.
Beynon, Brig.-Gen. Henry Lawrence Norman,
   1868–1950, vol. IV
Beynon, Ven. James Royston, 1907–1991, vol. IX
Beynon, Sir John Wyndham, 1st Bt, 1864–1944,
   vol. IV
Beynon, Maj.-Gen. Sir William George Lawrence,
   1866–1955, vol. V

Beynon, Sir (William John) Granville, 1914–1996, vol. X

Beytagh, Rev. Canon Gonville Aubie ff; see ffrench-Beytagh.

Bezzant, Rev. Canon James Stanley, 1897–1967, vol. VI

Bhabha, H. J., 1852–1941, vol. IV

Bhabha, Homi Jehangir, 1909–1966, vol. VI

Bhagat, Lt-Gen. Premindra Singh, 1918–1975, vol. VII

Bhalja, Govardhan Shankerlal, 1895–1948, vol. IV (A), vol. V

Bhan, Suraj, 1904–1980, vol. VII (AII)

Bhandari, Rai Bahadur Sir Gopal Das, 1860–1927, vol. II

Bhandarkar, Devadatta Ramkrishna, 1875–1950, vol. IV (A), vol. V

Bhandarkar, Sir Ramkrishna Gopal, 1837–1925, vol. II

Bhanot, Harnam Dass, 1897–1948, vol. IV

Bharatpur, Maharaja of, 1899–1929, vol. III

Bhatawadekar, Sir Bhalchandra Krishna, born 1852, vol. III

Bhatnagar, Sir Shanti Swarupa, 1895–1955, vol. V

Bhatt, Ramchandra Madhavram, 1874–1936, vol. III

Bhavnagar, HH Maharaja of, 1875–1919, vol. II

Bhopal, HH Nawab Shah Jahan Begum, 1838–1901, vol. I

Bhopal, HH Nawab Sultan Jehan Begum, 1858–1930, vol. III

Bhopal, Ruler of, 1894–1960, vol. V

Bhore, Sir Joseph William, 1878–1960, vol. V

Bhownagree, Sir Mancherjee Merwanjee, 1851–1933, vol. III

Bhutan, Maharajah of, 1861–1926, vol. II

Bhutto, Zulfikar Ali, 1928–1979, vol. VII

Biagi, Guido, 1855–1925, vol. II

Biancardi, Lt Col Nicola G.; see Grech-Biancardi.

Bibby, Major Sir (Arthur) Harold, 1st Bt, 1889–1986, vol. VIII

Bibby, Arthur Wilson, 1846–1935, vol. III

Bibby, Major Brian; see Bibby, Major F. B. F.

Bibby, Cyril, 1914–1987, vol. VIII

Bibby, Frank, 1857–1923, vol. II

Bibby, Major (Frank) Brian (Frederic), 1893–1929, vol. III

Bibby, Major Sir Harold; see Bibby, Major Sir A. H.

Bibby, John Hartley, 1864–1938, vol. III

Bibby, Joseph, 1851–1940, vol. III

Bibby, Samuel Leslie, 1897–1985, vol. VIII

Bibesco, Prince Antoine, 1878–1951, vol. V

Bice, Hon. Sir John George, 1853–1923, vol. II

Bicester, 1st Baron, 1867–1956, vol. V

Bicester, 2nd Baron, 1898–1968, vol. VI

Bickerdyke, John, (Charles Henry Cook), 1858–1933, vol. III

Bickerstaffe, Sir John, 1848–1930, vol. III

Bickerstaffe-Drew, Rt Rev. Mgr Count Francis Browning Drew, 1858–1928, vol. II

Bickersteth, Rt Rev. Edward, 1850–1897, vol. I

Bickersteth, Rt Rev. Edward Henry, 1825–1906, vol. I

Bickersteth, Rev. Canon Edward Monier, 1882–1976, vol. VII

Bickersteth, Geoffrey Langdale, 1884–1974, vol. VII

Bickersteth, John Burgon, 1888–1979, vol. VII

Bickersteth, John Joseph, 1850–1932, vol. III

Bickersteth, John Richard, 1897–1967, vol. VI

Bickersteth, Rev. Kenneth Julian Faithfull, 1885–1962, vol. VI

Bickersteth, Rev. Montagu Cyril, 1858–1936, vol. III

Bickersteth, Robert Alexander, 1862–1924, vol. II

Bickersteth, Rev. Samuel, 1857–1937, vol. III

Bickerton, Alexander William, 1842–1929, vol. III

Bickerton, John Myles, 1894–1977, vol. VII

Bickerton, Reginald Ernest, 1870–1949, vol. IV

Bicket, Sir Alexander, 1853–1931, vol. III

Bicket, Brig.-Gen. William Neilson, 1883–1978, vol. VII

Bickford, Adm. Andrew Kennedy, 1844–1927, vol. II

Bickford, Major Arthur Louis, 1870–1916, vol. II

Bickford, Brig.-Gen. Edward, 1861–1949, vol. IV

Bickford, Rt Rev. Mgr Francis P., 1889–1968, vol. VI

Bickford, Captain William George Hastings, died 1932, vol. III

Bickford, Rev. William Pennington, 1874–1941, vol. IV

Bickford, Col William Wilfrid, 1871–1951, vol. V

Bickford Smith, John Roger, 1915–1998, vol. X

Bickley, Francis Lawrance, 1885–1976, vol. VII

Bickley, William Gee, 1893–1969, vol. VI

Bicknell, Mrs Christine Betty, 1919–1999, vol. X

Bicknell, Rev. Edward John, died 1934, vol. III

Bicknell, Lt-Col Henry Percy Frank, 1879–1940, vol. III

Bidault, Georges, 1899–1983, vol. VIII

Bidder, George Parker, 1863–1953, vol. V

Bidder, Maurice McClean, 1879–1934, vol. III

Biddle, A. J. Drexel, 1874–1948, vol. IV

Biddle, Maj.-Gen. Anthony J. Drexel, 1896–1961, vol. VI

Biddle, Francis, 1886–1968, vol. VI

Biddle, Major Fred Leslie, 1885–1917, vol. II

Biddle, Maj.-Gen. John, 1859–1936, vol. III

Biddle, Sir Reginald Poulton, 1888–1970, vol. VI

Biddlecombe, Rev. Stuart Holman, 1879–1944, vol. IV

Biddulph, 1st Baron, 1834–1923, vol. II

Biddulph, 2nd Baron, 1869–1949, vol. IV

Biddulph, 3rd Baron, 1898–1972, vol. VII

Biddulph, 4th Baron, 1931–1988, vol. VIII

Biddulph, Assheton, 1850–1916, vol. II

Biddulph, Sir Francis Henry, 9th Bt, 1882–1980, vol. VII

Biddulph, Brig.-Gen. Harry, 1872–1952, vol. V

Biddulph, Lt-Col Hope, 1866–1940, vol. III

Biddulph, Gen. Sir Michael Anthony Shrapnel, 1823–1904, vol. I

Biddulph, Gen. Sir Robert, 1835–1918, vol. II

Biddulph, Sir Stuart Royden, 10th Bt, 1908–1986, vol. VIII

Biddulph, Sir Theophilus George, 8th Bt, 1874–1948, vol. IV

Biddulph, Thomas Henry Stillingfleet, 1846–1919, vol. II
Bidie, Surg.-Gen. George, 1830–1913, vol. I
Bidlake, Rev. Walter, 1865–1938, vol. III
Bidwell, Rt Rev. Edward John, 1866–1941, vol. IV
Bidwell, Hayward John, 1849–1931, vol. III
Bidwell, Leonard Arthur, 1865–1912, vol. I
Bidwell, Rt Rev. Mgr Manuel John, died 1930, vol. III
Bidwell, Rear-Adm. Roger Edward Shelford, 1899–1968, vol. VI
Bidwell, Shelford, 1848–1909, vol. I
Bidwell, Sydney James, 1917–1997, vol. X
Bierbach, Martin, 1926–1984, vol. VIII
Bierer, Joshua, 1901–1984, vol. VIII
Biermans, Rt Rev. John Henry Mary, 1871–1941, vol. IV
Biernacki, Roderick Korneli, died 1943, vol. IV
Biffen, Sir Rowland, 1874–1949, vol. IV
Bigelow, John, 1817–1911, vol. I
Bigelow, Melville Madison, 1846–1921, vol. II
Bigelow, Poultney, 1855–1954, vol. V
Bigg, Rev. Charles, 1840–1908, vol. I
Bigg, Henry Robert Heather, 1853–1911, vol. I
Bigg, Wilfred Joseph, 1897–1983, vol. VIII
Biggam, Maj.-Gen. Sir Alexander Gordon, 1888–1963, vol. VI
Biggar, Maj.-Gen. James Lyons, 1856–1922, vol. II
Biggar, Oliver Mowat, 1876–1948, vol. IV
Biggart, Sir John Henry, 1905–1979, vol. VII
Biggart, Sir Thomas, died 1949, vol. IV
Bigge, Sir Amherst S.; see Selby-Bigge, Sir L. A.
Bigge, Sir John Amherst S.; see Selby-Bigge.
Bigge, Col Thomas Arthur Hastings, 1866–1955, vol. V
Bigge, Maj.-Gen. Thomas Scovell, 1837–1914, vol. I
Bigge, Sir William Egelric, died 1916, vol. II
Bigger, Sir Edward Coey, 1861–1942, vol. IV
Bigger, Joseph Warwick, 1891–1951, vol. V
Biggs, Baroness, (Felicity Jane Ewart-Biggs); see Ewart-Biggs.
Biggs, Sir (Albert) Ashley, died 1938, vol. III
Biggs, Sir Arthur Worthington, 1846–1928, vol. II
Biggs, Sir Ashley; see Biggs, Sir A. A.
Biggs, Christopher Thomas Ewart E.; see Ewart-Biggs.
Biggs, George Nixon, 1881–1922, vol. II
Biggs, Col Henry Vero, 1860–1925, vol. II
Biggs, Hermann M., 1859–1923, vol. II
Biggs, Vice-Adm. Sir Hilary Worthington, 1905–1976, vol. VII
Biggs, Rt Rev. Huyshe Wolcott Y.; see Yeatman-Biggs.
Biggs, Leonard Vivian, 1873–1944, vol. IV
Biggs, Sir Lionel William, 1906–1985, vol. VIII
Biggs-Davison, Sir John Alec, 1918–1988, vol. VIII
Bigham, Hon. Sir (Frank) Trevor R., 1876–1954, vol. V
Bigham, Hon. Sir Trevor; see Bigham, Hon. Sir F. T. R.
Bigland, Alfred, 1855–1936, vol. III
Bigland, Eileen Anne Carstairs, (Mrs E. W. Bigland), 1898–1970, vol. VI
Bigland, Ernest Frank, 1913–1985, vol. VIII

Bigland, Rt Rev. Mgr John, 1871–1945, vol. IV
Bigland, Percy, died 1926, vol. II
Bignall, John Reginald, 1913–2000, vol. X
Bignold, Sir Arthur, 1839–1915, vol. I
Bignold, Sir (Charles) Robert, 1892–1970, vol. VI
Bignold, Sir Robert; see Bignold, Sir C. R.
Bigsby, Sydney Herbert, 1885–1946, vol. IV
Bigsworth, Air Cdre Arthur Wellesley, 1885–1961, vol. VI
Bigwood, Sir Cecil, 1863–1947, vol. IV
Bigwood, James, 1839–1919, vol. II
Bijawar State, HH Bharat Dharm-indu Maharajah Sawai Sir Sawant Singh Bahadur, 1877–1940, vol. III (A), vol. IV
Bikaner, Maharajah of; General HH Maharajadhiraj Sri Ganga Singbji Bahadur, 1880–1943, vol. IV
Bikaner, Maharajah of; Lt-Gen. HH Maharajadhiraj Raj Rajeshwar Narendra Shiromani (Sri Sadul Singhji Bahadur), 1902–1950, vol. IV
Bikaner, Maharaja of; Karni Singhji Bahadur, 1924–1988, vol. VIII
Bilainkin, George, 1903–1981, vol. VIII
Bilaspur (Kehlur) State, Chief HH Raja Bije Chand, 1873–1931, vol. III
Bilbrough, Rt Rev. Harold Ernest, 1867–1950, vol. IV
Biles, Sir John Harvard, 1854–1933, vol. III
Bilgrami, Syed Akeel, Nawab Sir Akeel Jung Bahadur, 1874–1945, vol. IV
Bilgrami, Sayyid Ali, Shamsul Ulama, 1853–1911, vol. I
Bilgrami, Syed Hossain, 1842–1926, vol. II
Bilgrami, Sayyid Sir Mehdi Husain, Nawab Mahdi Yar Jang Bahadur, died 1948, vol. IV
Biliotti, Sir Alfred, 1833–1915, vol. II
Bilkey, Paul Ernest, 1878–1962, vol. VI
Bill, Charles, 1843–1915, vol. I
Bill, Comdr Robert, 1910–1987, vol. VIII
Bill, Rt Rev. Sydney Alfred, 1884–1964, vol. VI
Billam, John Bertram Hardy, 1920–1986, vol. VIII
Bille, Frank Ernest, 1832–1918, vol. II
Billen, Rev. Albert Victor, died 1961, vol. VI
Billett, Rev. Canon Frederick, died 1941, vol. IV
Billimoria, Sir Shapoorjee, 1877–1958, vol. V
Billing, Rt Rev. Claudius, died 1898, vol. I
Billing, Melvin George, 1906–1992, vol. IX
Billing, N. Pemberton, 1880–1948, vol. IV
Billingham, Col John Alfred Lawrence, 1868–1955, vol. V
Billinghurst, Alfred John, 1880–1963, vol. VI
Billings, Rear-Adm. Frederick Stewart, 1900–1980, vol. VII
Billington, Mary Frances, died 1925, vol. II
Billington, Ray Allen, 1903–1981, vol. VIII
Billington, William, died 1932, vol. III
Billington, Lt-Col Lawson, 1882–1954, vol. V
Billmeir, Jack Albert, 1900–1963, vol. VI
Billson, Alfred, 1839–1907, vol. I
Billson, Hon. Alfred Arthur, 1858–1930, vol. III
Billson, Herbert George, 1871–1938, vol. III
Bilney, Air Vice-Marshal Christopher Neil Hope, 1898–1988, vol. VIII
Bilsborrow, Most Rev. James Romanus, 1862–1931, vol. III
Bilsborrow, Rt Rev. John, 1837–1903, vol. I

Bilsland, 1st Baron, 1892–1970, vol. VI
Bilsland, Sir William, 1st Bt, 1847–1921, vol. II
Bilton, Lt-Col Lewis Leonard, died 1954, vol. V
Bilton, Percy, 1896–1983, vol. VIII
Binney, H(arry) A(ugustus) Roy, 1907–1999, vol. X
Binchy, Daniel A., 1900–1989, vol. VIII
Binder, Sir Bernhard Heymann, 1876–1966, vol. VI
Bindley, Rev. Thomas Herbert, 1861–1931, vol. III
Bindloss, Harold, 1866–1945, vol. IV
Bindoff, Stanley Thomas, 1908–1980, vol. VII
Bing, Geoffrey Henry Cecil, 1909–1977, vol. VII
Bing, Gertrud, 1892–1964, vol. VI
Bing, Sir Rudolf Franz Joseph, 1902–1997, vol. X
Bingen, Sir Eric Albert, 1898–1972, vol. VII
Bingham, Col Sir Albert Edward, 2nd Bt,
    1868–1945, vol. IV
Bingham, Hon. Albert Yelverton, 1840–1907, vol. I
Bingham, Captain Alexander Gordon, 1873–1933,
    vol. III
Bingham, Rear-Adm. Hon. Barry; see Bingham,
    Rear-Adm. Hon. E. B. S.
Bingham, Caroline Margery Conyers, 1938–1998,
    vol. X
Bingham, Maj.-Gen. Hon. Sir Cecil Edward,
    1861–1934, vol. III
Bingham, Col Charles Henry Marion, 1873–1957,
    vol. V
Bingham, Lt-Col Hon. Denis; see Bingham, Lt-Col
    Hon. J. D. Y.
Bingham, Rear-Adm. Hon. (Edward) Barry
    (Stewart), 1881–1939, vol. III
Bingham, Maj.-Gen. Hon. Sir Francis Richard,
    1863–1935, vol. III
Bingham, James, 1916–1990, vol. VIII
Bingham, Lt-Col Hon. (John) Denis (Yelverton),
    died 1940, vol. III
Bingham, Sir John Edward, 1st Bt, 1839–1915,
    vol. I
Bingham, Lionel John, 1878–1919, vol. II
Bingham, Brig.-Gen. Oswald Buckley Bingham
    Smith-, 1868–1949, vol. IV
Bingham, Lt-Col Ralph Charles, 1885–1977,
    vol. VII
Bingham, Rear-Adm. Hon. Richard, 1847–1924,
    vol. II
Bingham, Richard Martin, 1915–1992, vol. IX
Bingham, Robert Porter, 1903–1982, vol. VIII
Bingham, Robert Worth, 1871–1937, vol. III
Bingham, Lt-Col Samuel, died 1941, vol. IV
Bingley, 1st Baron, 1870–1947, vol. IV
Bingley, Adm. Sir Alexander Noel Campbell,
    1905–1972, vol. VII
Bingley, Lt-Gen. Sir Alfred Horsford, 1865–1944,
    vol. IV
Bingley, Henry Campbell Alchorne, died 1939,
    vol. III
Bingley, Col Robert Albert Glanville, 1902–1976,
    vol. VII
Binnall, Rev. Canon Peter Blannin Gibbons,
    1907–1980, vol. VII
Binney, Anthony Lockhart, 1890–1973, vol. VII
Binney, Lt-Col Edward Victor, 1885–1942, vol. IV
Binney, Sir Frederick George; see Binney, Sir G.
Binney, Sir George, 1900–1972, vol. VII
Binney, Adm. Sir Hugh; see Binney, Adm. Sir T. H.

Binney, James, 1868–1935, vol. III
Binney, Captain Ralph Douglas, 1888–1944, vol. IV
Binney, Adm. Sir (Thomas) Hugh, 1883–1953,
    vol. V
Binney, Rev. William Hibbert, 1857–1916, vol. II
Binnie, Sir Alexander Richardson, 1839–1917,
    vol. II
Binnie, Rev. Alfred Jonathan, died 1926, vol. II
Binnie, Alfred Maurice, 1901–1986, vol. VIII
Binnie, Geoffrey Morse, 1908–1989, vol. VIII
Binnie, James, 1842–1930, vol. III
Binnie, Thomas Inglis, 1874–1954, vol. V
Binnie, William James Eames, 1867–1949, vol. IV
Binning, Col Lord; George Baillie-Hamilton,
    1856–1917, vol. II
Binning, Sir Arthur William, 1861–1931, vol. III
Binning, Lt-Col Joseph, 1845–1913, vol. I
Binns, Arthur, 1861–1952, vol. V
Binns, Sir Arthur Lennon, 1891–1971, vol. VII
Binns, Asa, 1873–1946, vol. IV
Binns, Sir Bernard Ottwell, 1898–1953, vol. V
Binns, Edward Ussher Elliott E.; see Elliott-Binns.
Binns, Sir Frank, 1898–1954, vol. V
Binns, Geoffrey John, 1930–2000, vol. X
Binns, Surg. Rear-Adm. George Augustus,
    1918–1990, vol. VIII
Binns, Howard Reed, 1909–1987, vol. VIII
Binns, John, 1914–1986, vol. VIII
Binns, Joseph, 1900–1975, vol. VII
Binns, Kenneth, 1882–1969, vol. VI
Binns, Kenneth Johnstone, 1912–1987, vol. VIII
Binns, Rev. Leonard Elliott Elliott-, 1885–1963,
    vol. VI
Binns, Percy, died 1920, vol. II
Binns, St John, 1914–1993, vol. IX
Binny, Graham, died 1929, vol. III
Binny, John Anthony Francis, 1911–1996, vol. X
Binny, Major Steuart Scott, 1871–1916, vol. II
Binstead, Arthur Morris, 1861–1914, vol. I
Binstead, Herbert Ernest, 1869–1937, vol. III
Binstead, Mary, died 1928, vol. II
Binyon, Basil, 1885–1977, vol. VII
Binyon, Laurence; see Binyon, R. L.
Binyon, (Robert) Laurence, 1869–1943, vol. IV
Bion, Frederick Fleetwood, 1870–1949, vol. IV
Birch, Sir Alan; see Birch, Sir J. A.
Birch, Albert Edward Henry, 1868–1954, vol. V
Birch, Alexander Hope, 1913–1995, vol. IX
Birch, Sir Arthur, 1837–1914, vol. I
Birch, Arthur John, 1915–1995, vol. IX
Birch, Claude Churchill, 1846–1940, vol. III
Birch, David; see Birch, W. H. D.
Birch, De Burgh, 1852–1937, vol. III
Birch, Col Edward Massy, 1875–1964, vol. VI
Birch, Sir Ernest Woodford, 1857–1929, vol. III
Birch, (Evelyn) Nigel (Chetwode); see Baron Rhyl.
Birch, Francis Lyall, 1889–1956, vol. V
Birch, George Henry, 1842–1904, vol. I
Birch, Henry William, 1854–1927, vol. II
Birch, Gen. Sir (James Frederick) Noel, 1865–1939,
    vol. III
Birch, Major James Richard Kemmis, 1859–1907,
    vol. I
Birch, Sir (John) Alan, 1909–1961, vol. VI
Birch, Rev. John George, born 1839, vol. II

Birch, John Henry Stopford, *died* 1949, vol. IV
Birch, Nigel; *see* Baron Rhyl.
Birch, Gen. Sir Noel; *see* Birch, Gen. Sir J. F. N.
Birch, Lt-Col Percy Yates, 1884–1939, vol. III
Birch, Reginald, 1914–1994, vol. IX
Birch, S. J. Lamorna, 1869–1955, vol. V
Birch, Walter de Gray, 1842–1924, vol. II
Birch, (William Henry) David, 1894–1968, vol. VI
Birch, Wyndham Lindsay, 1879–1950, vol. IV
Birch-Reynardson, Col Charles; *see* Reynardson.
Birch-Reynardson, Lt-Col Henry T.; *see* Reynardson.
Birchall, Derek; *see* Birchall, J. D.
Birchall, (James) Derek, 1930–1995, vol. IX
Birchall, Sir John Dearman, 1875–1941, vol. IV
Birchall, Sir Raymond; *see* Birchall, Sir W. R.
Birchall, Sir (Walter) Raymond, 1888–1968, vol. VI
Bircham, Sir Bernard Edward H.; *see* Halsey-Bircham.
Bircham, Sir Bertram Okeden, 1877–1961, vol. VI
Bircham, Major Humphry Francis William, 1875–1916, vol. II
Birchenough, Charles, 1882–1973, vol. VII
Birchenough, Very Rev. Godwin, 1880–1953, vol. V
Birchenough, Sir Henry, 1st Bt, 1853–1937, vol. III
Birchenough, Mabel, (Lady Birchenough), *died* 1936, vol. III
Bird, Sir Alfred Frederick, 1849–1922, vol. II
Bird, Archibald John, 1872–1939, vol. III
Bird, Col Arthur James Glover, 1883–1962, vol. VI
Bird, Hon. Bolton Stafford, 1840–1924, vol. II
Bird, Sir Charles Hayward, 1862–1944, vol. IV
Bird, Christopher John, 1855–1922, vol. II
Bird, Lt-Gen. Sir Clarence August, 1885–1986, vol. VIII
Bird, Cuthbert Hilton G.; *see* Golding-Bird.
Bird, Sir C(yril) Handley, 1896–1969, vol. VI
Bird, Rt Rev. Cyril Henry G.; *see* Golding-Bird.
Bird, (Cyril) Kenneth, 1887–1965, vol. VI
Bird, Sir Cyril Pangbourne, 1906–1984, vol. VIII
Bird, Sir Donald Geoffrey, 3rd Bt, 1906–1963, vol. VI
Bird, Elliott Beverley S.; *see* Steeds-Bird.
Bird, Eric Leslie, 1894–1965, vol. VI
Bird, Sir Ernest Edward, 1877–1945, vol. IV
Bird, Ernest Roy, 1883–1933, vol. III
Bird, Sir F. Hugh W. S.; *see* Stonehewer Bird.
Bird, Air Vice-Marshal Frank Ronald, 1918–1983, vol. VIII
Bird, Col Frederic Dougan, 1858–1929, vol. III
Bird, Captain Frederic Godfrey, 1868–1919, vol. II
Bird, Gen. Sir George Corrie, 1838–1907, vol. I
Bird, (George William) Terence, 1914–1985, vol. IV
Bird, Harington; *see* Bird, J. A. H.
Bird, Sir Harry, 1862–1944, vol. IV
Bird, Sir Henry Busby, 1856–1929, vol. III
Bird, Henry Edward, 1830–1908, vol. I
Bird, Isabella Lucy; *see* Bishop, Mrs I. L.
Bird, Sir James, 1863–1925, vol. II
Bird, Squadron Comdr Sir James, 1883–1946, vol. IV
Bird, Rev. James Grant, *died* 1920, vol. II
Bird, James Gurth, 1909–1999, vol. X
Bird, James William Fairbridge, 1858–1938, vol. III

Bird, (John Alexander) Harington, *died* 1936, vol. III
Bird, John Alfred William, 1924–1997, vol. X
Bird, John Louis Warner, 1929–1983, vol. VIII
Bird, Rev. John Turnbull, 1862–1930, vol. III
Bird, Lt-Col John Wilfred, 1872–1938, vol. III
Bird, Kenneth; *see* Bird, C. K.
Bird, Michael Gwynne, 1921–1991, vol. IX
Bird, Captain Oliver, 1880–1963, vol. VI
Bird, Sir Richard Dawnay M.; *see* Martin-Bird.
Bird, Lt-Col Robert, 1866–1918, vol. II
Bird, Sir Robert Bland, 2nd Bt, 1876–1960, vol. V
Bird, Rev. Samuel William Elderfield, *died* 1926, vol. II
Bird, Col Spencer Godfrey, 1854–1926, vol. II
Bird, Col Stanley, 1864–1938, vol. III
Bird, Col Stanley George, 1837–1905, vol. I
Bird, Terence; *see* Bird, G. W. T.
Bird, Terence Frederick, 1906–1979, vol. VII
Bird, Tom, *died* 1932, vol. III
Bird, Rt Hon. Vere Cornwall, 1910–1999, vol. X
Bird, Veronica, 1932–1986, vol. VIII
Bird, Maj.-Gen. Sir Wilkinson Dent, 1869–1943, vol. IV
Bird, Sir William Barrott Montfort, 1855–1950, vol. IV
Bird, William Seymour, 1846–1919, vol. II
Bird-Wilson, Air Vice-Marshal Harold Arthur Cooper, 1919–2000, vol. X
Birdwood, 1st Baron, 1865–1951, vol. V
Birdwood, 2nd Baron, 1899–1962, vol. VI
Birdwood, Lt-Col George Christopher McDowall, 1863–1944, vol. IV
Birdwood, Sir George Christopher Molesworth, 1832–1917, vol. II
Birdwood, Herbert Mills, 1837–1907, vol. I
Birgi, Muharrem Nuri, 1908–1986, vol. VIII
Birk, Baroness (Life Peer); Alma Birk, 1917–1996, vol. X
Birkbeck, Sir Edward, 1st Bt, 1838–1907, vol. I
Birkbeck, Geoffrey, 1875–1954, vol. V
Birkbeck, Harold Edward, 1902–1977, vol. VII
Birkbeck, Henry, 1853–1930, vol. III
Birkbeck, Major Henry Anthony, 1885–1956, vol. V
Birkbeck, Col Oliver, 1893–1952, vol. V
Birkbeck, Maj.-Gen. Theodore Henry, 1911–1976, vol. VII
Birkbeck, Maj.-Gen. Sir William Henry, 1863–1929, vol. III
Birkbeck, William John, 1859–1916, vol. II
Birkenhead, 1st Earl of, 1872–1930, vol. III
Birkenhead, 2nd Earl of, 1907–1975, vol. VII
Birkenhead, 3rd Earl of, 1936–1985, vol. VIII
Birkenruth, Adolphus, 1861–1940, vol. III
Birkett, 1st Baron, 1883–1962, vol. VI
Birkett, George William Alfred, 1908–1988, vol. VIII
Birkett, Brig.-Gen. Herbert Stanley, 1864–1942, vol. IV
Birkett, Brig. Richard Maule, 1882–1942, vol. IV
Birkett, Sir Thomas William, 1871–1957, vol. V
Birkin, Sir Alexander Russell, 4th Bt, 1861–1942, vol. IV
Birkin, Sir Charles Lloyd, 5th Bt, 1907–1985, vol. VIII

Birkin, Lt-Col Charles Wilfrid, 1865–1932, vol. III
Birkin, Sir Henry Ralph Stanley, 3rd Bt, 1896–1933, vol. III
Birkin, Air Cdre James Michael, 1912–1985, vol. VIII
Birkin, Lt-Col Richard Leslie, 1863–1936, vol. III
Birkin, Sir Stanley; see Birkin, Sir T. S.
Birkin, Sir Thomas Isaac, 1st Bt, 1831–1922, vol. II
Birkin, Sir (Thomas) Stanley, 2nd Bt, 1857–1931, vol. III
Birkinshaw, Air Cdre George William, 1896–1977, vol. VII
Birkinshaw, John Howard, 1894–1995, vol. IX
Birkmyre, Sir Archibald, 1st Bt, 1875–1935, vol. III
Birkmyre, Sir Henry, 2nd Bt, 1898–1992, vol. IX
Birks, Falconer Moffat, 1885–1960, vol. V
Birks, Maj.-Gen. Horace Leslie, 1897–1985, vol. VIII
Birley, Lt-Col Bevil Langton, 1884–1943, vol. IV
Birley, Eric, 1906–1995, vol. IX
Birley, Sir Frank, 1883–1940, vol. III
Birley, James Leatham, 1884–1934, vol. III
Birley, Leonard, 1875–1951, vol. V
Birley, Norman Pellew, 1891–1980, vol. VII
Birley, Captain Sir Oswald Hornby Joseph, 1880–1952, vol. V
Birley, Mrs Percy Langton, 1875–1956, vol. V
Birley, Col Richard Kennedy, 1845–1914, vol. I
Birley, Sir Robert, 1903–1982, vol. VIII
Birley, Rt Rev. Thomas Howard, 1864–1949, vol. IV
Birmingham, George A.; see Hannay, Rev. James O.
Birnage, Arthur, 1874–1953, vol. V
Birnam, Hon. Lord; (Thomas) David King Murray, 1884–1955, vol. V
Birnie, Col Eugene St John, 1900–1976, vol. VII
Birnie, Captain Harry Charles, 1882–1943, vol. IV
Biron, Sir Chartres, 1863–1940, vol. III
Biron, Sir (Moshe Chaim Efraim) Philip, 1909–1981, vol. VIII
Biron, Sir Philip; see Biron, Sir M. C. E. P.
Birrell, Rt Hon. Augustine, 1850–1933, vol. III
Birrell, Col Edwin Thomas Fairweather, 1874–1944, vol. IV
Birrell, Hon. Frederick William, died 1939, vol. III
Birrell, John, 1836–1902, vol. I
Birrell-Gray, Major William; see Gray, Major W. B.
Birsay, Hon. Lord; Harald Robert Leslie, 1905–1982, vol. VIII
Birt, Francis Bradley B.; see Bradley-Birt.
Birt, Guy Capper, 1884–1972, vol. VII
Birt, Rev. Canon Roderick Harold Capper, 1882–1975, vol. VII
Birt, Sir William, 1834–1911, vol. I
Birtchnell, Sir Cyril Augustine, 1887–1967, vol. VI
Birtles, Frank; see Langdon, Michael.
Birtwistle, Brig.-Gen. Arthur, 1877–1937, vol. III
Birtwistle, George, 1877–1929, vol. III
Birtwistle, Ivor Treharne, 1892–1976, vol. VII
Bisat, William S., 1886–1973, vol. VII
Bischoff, Thomas Hume, 1886–1951, vol. V
Bischoffesheim, Henry Louis, 1829–1908, vol. I
Biscoe, Rear Adm. Alec Julian T.; see Tyndale-Biscoe.
Biscoe, Rev. Cecil Earle T.; see Tyndale-Biscoe.

Biscoe, Lt-Col Sir Hugh Vincent, 1881–1932, vol. III
Biscoe, Brig.-Gen. Julian Dallas Tyndale T.; see Tyndale-Biscoe.
Biscoe, Walter Treweeke, 1892–1969, vol. VI
Biscoe, Lt-Gen. William Walters, 1841–1920, vol. II
Bisdee, Lt-Col John Hutton, 1869–1930, vol. III
Bisgood, Joseph John, 1861–1927, vol. II
Bishop, Alan; see Bishop, T. A. M.
Bishop, Maj.-Gen. Sir Alec; see Bishop, Maj.-Gen. Sir W. H. A.
Bishop, Ann, 1899–1990, vol. VIII
Bishop, Arthur Henry Burdick, 1898–1969, vol. VI
Bishop, Rt Rev. Clifford Leofric Purdy, 1908–1994, vol. IX
Bishop, Edward Stanley; see Baron Bishopston.
Bishop, Lt-Comdr Francis Charles, 1905–1965, vol. VI
Bishop, Sir (Frank) Patrick, 1900–1972, vol. VII
Bishop, Frederic Sillery, died 1913, vol. I
Bishop, Captain Frederick Edward, 1872–1931, vol. III
Bishop, Sir George Sidney, 1913–1999, vol. X
Bishop, George Walter, 1886–1965, vol. VI
Bishop, Sir Harold, 1900–1983, vol. VIII
Bishop, Henry, died 1939, vol. III
Bishop, Rev. Hugh William Fletcher, 1907–1989, vol. VIII
Bishop, Mrs Isabella Luey, 1832–1904, vol. I
Bishop, John, 1828–1913, vol. I
Bishop, Joseph Bucklin, 1847–1928, vol. II
Bishop, Dame Joyce; see Bishop, Dame M. J.
Bishop, Julius, 1855–1932, vol. III
Bishop, Laurence Arthur, 1895–1954, vol. V
Bishop, Dame (Margaret) Joyce, 1896–1993, vol. IX
Bishop, Matilda Ellen, 1844–1913, vol. I
Bishop, Sir Patrick; see Bishop, Sir F. P.
Bishop, Peter Maxwell Farrow, 1904–1979, vol. VII
Bishop, Richard Evelyn Donohue, 1925–1989, vol. VIII
Bishop, Hon. Robert Kirby, 1853–1930, vol. III
Bishop, Ronald Eric, 1903–1989, vol. VIII
Bishop, Terence Alan Martyn, 1907–1994, vol. IX
Bishop, Theodore Bendysh Watson, 1886–1967, vol. VI
Bishop, W. Follen, 1856–1936, vol. III
Bishop, Walter Frederick, 1879–1955, vol. V
Bishop, Rev. William; see Bishop, Rev. H. W. F.
Bishop, Rear-Adm. Sir William Alfred, 1899–1991, vol. IX
Bishop, Air Marshal William Avery, 1894–1956, vol. V
Bishop, Maj.-Gen. Sir (William Henry) Alexander, (Alec), 1897–1984, vol. VIII
Bishop, Sir William Poole, 1894–1977, vol. VII
Bishop, William Thomas, 1901–1982, vol. VIII
Bishopston, Baron (Life Peer); Edward Stanley Bishop, 1920–1984, vol. VIII
Bismarck, Prince Herbert von, 1849–1904, vol. I
Bispham, David, 1857–1921, vol. II
Bispham, James Webb, died 1956, vol. V
Biss, Godfrey Charles D'Arcy, 1909–1989, vol. VIII
Bisschop, Willem Roosegaarde, 1866–1944, vol. IV
Bisseker, Rev. Harry, 1878–1965, vol. VI

Bisset, Vice-Adm. Arthur William La Touche, 1892–1956, vol. V

Bisset, Captain Sir James Gordon Partridge, 1883–1967, vol. VI

Bisset, Sir Murray, 1876–1931, vol. III

Bisset, Col Sir William Sinclair Smith, 1843–1916, vol. II

Bisset-Berry, Hon. Sir William; see Berry.

Bisset-Smith, George Tulloch, 1863–1922, vol. II

Bissett, Maj.-Gen. Frederic William Lyon, 1888–1961, vol. VI

Bisson, Laurence Adophus, 1897–1965, vol. VI

Biswambhar Ray, Rai Bahadur (Vidyabenode), 1855–1930, vol. III

Biswas, Rt Rev. Nirod Kumar, 1905–1948, vol. IV

Bithell, Jethro, 1878–1962, vol. VI

Bizet, George; see Bisset-Smith, George Tulloch.

Bjoerling, Jussi, 1911–1960, vol. V

Björnson, Björnstjerne, 1832–1910, vol. I

Björnsson, Henrik Sveinsson, 1914–1985, vol. VIII

Blache, Jules Adolphe Lucien, 1893–1970, vol. VI

Blache-Fraser, Louis Nathaniel, 1904–1987, vol. VIII

Blachford, Lady; (Georgiana Mary), died 1900, vol. I

Black, Baron (Life Peer); William Rushton Black, 1893–1984, vol. VIII

Black, Sir Alec, 1st Bt (cr 1918), 1872–1942, vol. IV

Black, Alexander William, 1859–1906, vol. I

Black, Andrew, 1850–1916, vol. II

Black, Sir Archibald Campbell, 1877–1962, vol. VI

Black, Rt Hon. Arthur, 1888–1968, vol. VI

Black, Arthur John, 1855–1936, vol. III

Black, Sir Arthur William, 1863–1947, vol. IV

Black, Charles Crofton, 1880–1937, vol. III

Black, Lt-Col Claud Hamilton Griffith, died 1946, vol. IV

Black, Colin Mackenzie, 1877–1943, vol. IV

Black, Sir Cyril Wilson, 1902–1991, vol. IX

Black, Davidson, 1884–1934, vol. III

Black, Donald Harrison, 1899–1978, vol. VII

Black, Duncan, 1908–1991, vol. IX

Black, Ebenezer Charlton, 1861–1927, vol. II

Black, Eugene Robert, 1898–1992, vol. IX

Black, Francis, died 1939, vol. III

Black, Sir Frederick William, 1863–1930, vol. III

Black, Hon. George, 1873–1965, vol. VI

Black, Major George Cumine Strahan, 1882–1951, vol. V

Black, George Joseph, 1918–1984, vol. VIII

Black, George Norman, 1907–1955, vol. V

Black, Rev. Canon Gibson James Hunter Monahan, 1867–1950, vol. IV

Black, Gordon, 1923–1990, vol. VIII

Black, Sir Harold, 1914–1981, vol. VIII

Black, Henry, 1875–1960, vol. V, vol. VI

Black, Sir Hermann David, 1905–1990, vol. VIII

Black, Hervey Stuart; see Black, I. H. S.

Black, Rev. Hugh, 1868–1953, vol. V

Black, Hugo LaFayette, 1886–1971, vol. VII

Black, Iain James, died 2000, vol. X

Black, (Ian) Hervey Stuart, 1908–1986, vol. VIII

Black, Rt Rev. James, 1894–1968, vol. VI

Black, Very Rev. James Macdougall, 1879–1949, vol. IV

Black, James Watt, 1840–1918, vol. II

Black, John Bennett, 1883–1964, vol. VI

Black, Col John Campbell Lamont, 1869–1950, vol. IV

Black, Sir John Paul, 1895–1965, vol. VI

Black, John Stewart, 1865–1930, vol. III

Black, John Sutherland, 1846–1923, vol. II

Black, John Wycliffe, 1862–1951, vol. V

Black, Joseph, 1921–2000, vol. X

Black, Kenneth, 1879–1959, vol. V

Black, Kenneth Oscar, 1910–1987, vol. VIII

Black, Ladbroke Lionel Day, 1877–1940, vol. III

Black, Margaret McLeod, 1912–1993, vol. IX

Black, Rev. Matthew, 1908–1994, vol. IX

Black, Sir Misha, 1910–1977, vol. VII

Black, Peter Blair, 1917–1997, vol. X

Black, Robert Alastair Lucien, 1921–1967, vol. VI

Black, Sir Robert Andrew Stransham, 2nd Bt, 1902–1979, vol. VII

Black, Sir Robert Brown, (Sir Robin), 1906–1999, vol. X

Black, Sir Robert James, 1st Bt (cr 1922), 1860–1925, vol. II

Black, Sir Robin; see Black, Sir Robert B.

Black, Sir Samuel, 1830–1910, vol. I

Black, Sydney, 1908–1968, vol. VI

Black, Thomas Porteous, 1878–1915, vol. I

Black, Maj.-Gen. Walter Clarence, 1867–1930, vol. III

Black, William, 1841–1898, vol. I

Black, Hon. William Anderson, 1847–1934, vol. III

Black, Maj.-Gen. William Campbell, 1846–1931, vol. III

Black, William Charles, 1890–1959, vol. V (A)

Black, William George, 1857–1932, vol. III

Black, William John, 1872–1941, vol. IV

Black, Maj.-Gen. Sir Wilsone, 1837–1909, vol. I

Black-Hawkins, (Clive) David, 1915–1983, vol. VIII

Black-Hawkins, David; see Black-Hawkins, C. D.

Blackadder, William, 1877–1940, vol. III

Blackader, Alexander Dougall, 1847–1932, vol. III

Blackader, Maj.-Gen. Charles Guinand, 1869–1921, vol. II

Blackall, Sir Henry William Butler, 1889–1981, vol. VIII

Blackbourne, Rev. Jacob, 1862–1936, vol. III

Blackburn, Hon. Lord; Robert Francis Leslie Blackburn, 1864–1944, vol. IV

Blackburn, (Albert) Raymond, 1915–1991, vol. IX

Blackburn, Sir Arthur Dickinson, 1887–1970, vol. VI

Blackburn, Brig. Arthur Seaforth, 1892–1960, vol. V

Blackburn, Barbara; see Blackburn, E. B.

Blackburn, Lt-Col Sir Charles Bickerton, 1874–1972, vol. VII

Blackburn, Lt-Col Charles Cautley, 1867–1938, vol. III

Blackburn, (Evelyn) Barbara, 1898–1981, vol. VIII

Blackburn, Fred, 1902–1990, vol. VIII

Blackburn, Guy, 1911–1994, vol. IX

Blackburn, Henry, 1830–1897, vol. I

Blackburn, Col John Edward, 1851–1927, vol. II

Blackburn, John Graham, 1933–1994, vol. IX
Blackburn, Maurice McCrae, 1880–1944, vol. IV
Blackburn, Michael Scott, 1936–2000, vol. X
Blackburn, Raymond; see Blackburn, A. R.
Blackburn, Hon. Sir Richard Arthur, 1918–1987, vol. VIII
Blackburn, Robert Francis Leslie; see Blackburn, Hon. Lord.
Blackburn, Ronald Henry Albert, 1924–1993, vol. IX
Blackburn, Sir Thomas, died 1974, vol. VII
Blackburn, Vernon, died 1907, vol. I
Blackburn, William Ernest, 1873–1951, vol. V
Blackburne, Lt-Col Charles Harold, 1876–1918, vol. II
Blackburne, Rev. Foster Grey, died 1909, vol. I
Blackburne, Gertrude Mary Ireland, 1861–1951, vol. V
Blackburne, Very Rev. Harry William, 1878–1963, vol. VI
Blackburne, Rt Rev. Hugh Charles, 1912–1995, vol. IX
Blackburne, Joseph Henry, 1841–1924, vol. II
Blackburne, Sir Kenneth William, 1907–1980, vol. VII
Blackburne, Very Rev. Lionel Edward, 1874–1951, vol. V
Blackburne, Col Robert Ireland, 1850–1930, vol. III
Blackden, Col Leonard Shadwell, 1863–1937, vol. III
Blacker, Carlos Paton, 1895–1975, vol. VII
Blacker, Edward Carew, 1863–1932, vol. III
Blacker, Col Frederick St John, 1881–1942, vol. IV
Blacker, Sir George, 1865–1948, vol. IV
Blacker, Maj.-Gen. George Patrick Demaine, 1906–1974, vol. VII
Blacker, Harold Alfred Cecil, 1889–1944, vol. IV
Blacker, L(atham) V(alentine) Stewart, 1887–1964, vol. VI
Blacker, Lt-Col Stewart William Ward, 1865–1935, vol. III
Blacket, Wilfred, 1859–1937, vol. III
Blackett, Baron (Life Peer); Patrick Maynard Stuart Blackett, 1897–1974, vol. VII
Blackett, Sir Basil Phillott, 1882–1935, vol. III
Blackett, Sir Charles Douglas, 9th Bt, 1904–1968, vol. VI
Blackett, Sir Edward William, 7th Bt, 1831–1909, vol. I
Blackett, Maj. Sir Francis Hugh, 11th Bt, 1907–1995, vol. IX
Blackett, Sir George William, 10th Bt, 1906–1994, vol. IX
Blackett, Adm. Henry, 1867–1952, vol. V
Blackett, Sir Hugh Douglas, 8th Bt, 1873–1960, vol. V
Blackett, Rev. Selwyn, 1854–1935, vol. III
Blackett, Col William Cuthbert, 1859–1935, vol. III
Blackett Ord, Ven. Charles Edward, 1858–1931, vol. III
Blackford, 1st Baron, 1862–1947, vol. IV
Blackford, 2nd Baron, 1887–1972, vol. VII
Blackford, 3rd Baron, 1923–1977, vol. VII
Blackford, 4th Baron, 1962–1988, vol. VIII

Blackham, Maj.-Gen. Robert James, died 1951, vol. V
Blackie, Rt Rev. Ernest Morell, 1867–1943, vol. IV
Blackie, John Ernest Haldane, 1904–1985, vol. VIII
Blackie, Margery Grace, 1898–1981, vol. VIII
Blackie, Walter Wilfrid, 1860–1953, vol. V
Blacking, Randoll; see Blacking, W. H. R.
Blacking, (William Henry) Randoll, 1889–1958, vol. V
Blackledge, Geoffrey Glynn, 1894–1964, vol. VI
Blackledge, Rev. Canon George Robert, 1868–1935, vol. III
Blackley, Travers Robert, 1899–1982, vol. VIII
Blackley, Rev. William Lewery, 1830–1902, vol. I
Blacklock, Maj.-Gen. Cyril Aubrey, 1870–1936, vol. III
Blacklock, Donald Breadalbane, 1879–1955, vol. V
Blacklock, John William Stewart, died 1973, vol. VII
Blacklock, Captain Ronald William, 1889–1987, vol. VIII
Blackman, Aylward Manley, 1883–1956, vol. V
Blackman, Rear-Adm. Charles Maurice, 1890–1981, vol. VIII
Blackman, Frederick Frost, 1866–1947, vol. IV
Blackman, Geoffrey Emett, 1903–1980, vol. VII
Blackman, Moses, 1908–1983, vol. VIII
Blackman, Raymond Victor Bernard, 1910–1989, vol. VIII
Blackman, Vernon Herbert, 1872–1967, vol. VI
Blackman, Winifred Susan, died 1950, vol. IV
Blackmore, Sir Charles Henry, 1880–1967, vol. VI
Blackmore, Col Lindsay William Saul, 1896–1973, vol. VII
Blackmore, Richard Doddridge, 1825–1900, vol. I
Blackmun, Hon. Harry Andrew, 1908–1999, vol. X
Blackmur, Richard Palmer, 1904–1965, vol. VI
Blackshaw, J. F., 1875–1943, vol. IV
Blackshaw, James William, 1895–1983, vol. VIII
Blackshaw, Maurice Bantock, 1903–1975, vol. VII
Blackshaw, Rev. William, 1866–1953, vol. V
Blackton, James Stuart, 1875–1941, vol. IV
Blackwell, Sir Basil Henry, 1889–1984, vol. VIII
Blackwell, Sir (Cecil) Patrick, 1881–1944, vol. IV
Blackwell, Elizabeth, 1821–1910, vol. I
Blackwell, Sir Ernley Robertson Hay, 1868–1941, vol. IV
Blackwell, Francis Samuel, 1869–1951, vol. V
Blackwell, Major Francis Victor, died 1928, vol. II
Blackwell, John Humphrey, 1895–1979, vol. VII
Blackwell, John Kenneth, 1914–1986, vol. VIII
Blackwell, Sir Patrick; see Blackwell, Sir C. P.
Blackwell, Richard, 1918–1980, vol. VII
Blackwell, Thomas Francis, 1838–1907, vol. I
Blackwell, Thomas Francis, 1912–1983, vol. VIII
Blackwell, Thomas Geoffrey, 1884–1943, vol. IV
Blackwell, Maj.-Gen. William Richard, 1877–1946, vol. IV
Blackwood, Lt-Col Albemarle Price, 1881–1921, vol. II
Blackwood, Algernon Henry, 1869–1951, vol. V
Blackwood, Lord Basil; see Blackwood, Lord I.B.G.T.
Blackwood, Rt Rev. Donald Burns, 1884–1967, vol. VI (AII)

Blackwood, Sir Francis, 4th Bt, 1838–1924, vol. II
Blackwood, Sir Francis Elliot Temple, 6th Bt, 1901–1979, vol. VII
Blackwood, Captain Frederick Herbert, 1885–1926, vol. II
Blackwood, Wing Comdr George Douglas, 1909–1997, vol. X
Blackwood, George William, 1876–1942, vol. IV
Blackwood, Sir Henry Palmer Temple, 5th Bt, 1896–1948, vol. IV
Blackwood, Lord (Ian) Basil (Gawaine Temple), 1870–1917, vol. II
Blackwood, James H., 1878–1951, vol. V
Blackwood, Dame Margaret, 1909–1986, vol. VIII
Blackwood, Captain Maurice Baldwin Raymond, 1882–1941, vol. IV
Blackwood, Sir Robert Rutherford, 1906–1982, vol. VIII
Blackwood, William, 1836–1912, vol. I
Blackwood, William, 1878–1958, vol. V
Blackwood, William, 1911–1990, vol. VIII
Blackwood-Price, Rev. Canon Edward Hyde, 1875–1940, vol. III
Blades, Hon. Lord; Daniel Patterson Blades, 1888–1959, vol. V
Blades, Daniel Patterson; see Blades, Hon. Lord.
Blades, Major Walter William, 1863–1943, vol. IV
Bladin, Air Vice-Marshal Francis Masson, 1898–1978, vol. VII
Bladon, Air Cdre Graham Clarke, 1899–1967, vol. VI
Blagden, Charles Otto, 1864–1949, vol. IV
Blagden, Rt Rev. Claude Martin, 1874–1952, vol. V
Blagden, Rev. Henry, 1832–1922, vol. II
Blagden, John Basil, 1901–1964, vol. VI
Blagden, Sir John Ramsay, 1908–1985, vol. VIII
Blagrove, Col Henry John, 1854–1925, vol. II
Blaikie, Leonard, 1873–1951, vol. V
Blaikie, Walter Biggar, 1847–1928, vol. II
Blaikie, Rev. William Garden, 1820–1899, vol. I
Blaikley, John Barnard, 1906–1975, vol. VII
Blaiklock, George, 1856–1943, vol. IV
Blain, Hon. Sir Eric Herbert, 1904–1969, vol. VI
Blain, Sir Herbert Edwin, 1870–1942, vol. IV
Blain, William, died 1908, vol. I
Blain, Sir William Arbuthnot, 1833–1911, vol. I
Blaine, Sir Charles Frederick, died 1915, vol. I
Blaine, Brig. Charles Herbert, 1883–1958, vol. V
Blaine, Sir Robert Stickney, died 1897, vol. I
Blair; see Blair-Fish, W. W.
Blair, Sir Alastair Campbell, 1908–1999, vol. X
Blair, Alexander, 1864–1944, vol. IV
Blair, Lt-Col Alexander Stevenson, 1865–1936, vol. III
Blair, Hon. Andrew George, 1844–1907, vol. I
Blair, Rev. Andrew Hamish, 1901–1981, vol. VIII
Blair, Andrew James Fraser, (Hamish Blair), 1872–1935, vol. III
Blair, Hon. Sir Archibald William, 1875–1952, vol. V
Blair, Brig.-Gen. Arthur, 1869–1947, vol. IV
Blair, Charles Neil Molesworth, 1910–1988, vol. VIII
Blair, Gen. Charles Renny, 1837–1912, vol. I
Blair, Charles Samuel, 1859–1939, vol. III

Blair, David, 1932–1976, vol. VII
Blair, David Arthur, 1917–1985, vol. VIII
Blair, Rt Rev. Sir David H.; see Hunter-Blair.
Blair, Douglas MacColl, 1940–1990, vol. VIII
Blair, Duncan MacCallum, 1896–1944, vol. IV
Blair, Captain Sir Edward H.; see Hunter-Blair.
Blair, Dame Emily Mathieson, 1894–1963, vol. VI
Blair, Eric Arthur; see Orwell, George.
Blair, Brig.-Gen. Everard Macleod, 1866–1939, vol. III
Blair, Col Frederick Gordon, 1852–1943, vol. IV
Blair, George William S.; see Scott Blair.
Blair, Hamish; see Blair, A. J. F.
Blair, Rev. Canon Harold Arthur, 1902–1985, vol. VIII
Blair, Gen. James, 1828–1905, vol. I
Blair, Rt. Rev. James Douglas, 1906–1991, vol. IX
Blair, Sir James H.; see Hunter Blair.
Blair, Col James Molesworth, 1880–1925, vol. II
Blair, James Richard, 1890–1958, vol. V
Blair, Hon. Sir James William, 1871–1944, vol. IV
Blair, Kenneth Gloyne, 1882–1952, vol. V
Blair, Rt Rev. Laurence Frederick Devaynes, died 1925, vol. II
Blair, Oliver Robin, 1925–1975, vol. VII
Blair, Patrick James, 1865–1932, vol. III
Blair, Col Sir Patrick James, 1892–1972, vol. VII
Blair, Peter H.; see Hunter Blair.
Blair, Sir Reginald, 1st Bt, 1881–1962, vol. VI
Blair, Sir Robert, 1859–1935, vol. III
Blair, Robert Kerr, 1876–1942, vol. IV
Blair, Maj.-Gen. Walter Charles H.; see Hunter-Blair.
Blair, Very Rev. William, 1830–1916, vol. II
Blair-Bell, William, 1871–1936, vol. III
Blair-Cunynghame, Sir James Ogilvy, 1913–1990, vol. VIII
Blair-Fish, Wallace Wilfrid, 1889–1968, vol. VI
Blair-Kerr, Sir Alastair; see Blair-Kerr, Sir W. A.
Blair-Kerr, Sir William Alexander, (Sir Alastair), 1911–1992, vol. IX
Blais, Rt Rev. Andrew Albert, 1842–1919, vol. II
Blaize, Rt Hon. Herbert Augustus, 1918–1989, vol. VIII
Blake, Captain Sir Acton; see Blake, Captain Sir H. A.
Blake, Sir Arthur Ernest, 1869–1935, vol. III
Blake, Arthur John J.; see Jex-Blake.
Blake, Col Arthur Maurice, born 1852, vol. II
Blake, Lt-Col Arthur O'Brien ffrench, 1879–1973, vol. VII
Blake, Charles Henry, 1912–1994, vol. IX
Blake, Comdr Sir Cuthbert Patrick, 6th Bt (cr 1772), 1885–1975, vol. VII
Blake, Hon. Edward, 1833–1912, vol. I
Blake, Sir Edward; see Blake, Sir F. E. C.
Blake, Edwin Holmes, 1873–1956, vol. V
Blake, Sir Ernest Edward, 1845–1920, vol. II
Blake, Eugene Carson, 1906–1985, vol. VIII
Blake, Sir Francis Douglas, 1st Bt (cr 1907), 1856–1940, vol. III
Blake, Sir (Francis) Edward (Colquhoun), 2nd Bt (cr 1907), 1893–1950, vol. IV
Blake, Francis Gilman, 1887–1952, vol. V
Blake, Vice-Adm. Sir Geoffrey, 1882–1968, vol. VI

Blake, George, 1893–1961, vol. VI
Blake, Lt-Col Sir (George) Reginald, 1882–1949, vol. IV
Blake, Maj.-Gen. Gilbert Alan, 1887–1971, vol. VII
Blake, Henrietta J.; see Jex-Blake.
Blake, Sir Henry Arthur, 1840–1918, vol. II
Blake, Henry E.; see Elliott-Blake.
Blake, (Henry) Vincent, 1912–1998, vol. X
Blake, Gen. Henry William, 1815–1908, vol. I
Blake, Henry Wollaston, 1815–1899, vol. I
Blake, Captain Sir (Herbert) Acton, 1857–1926, vol. II
Blake, Herbert Frederick, 1866–1946, vol. IV
Blake, Jack Percy, died 1950, vol. IV
Blake, Rev. James Edward Huxley, 1863–1933, vol. III
Blake, Rev. James Martindale, 1863–1934, vol. III
Blake, John Clifford, 1901–1993, vol. IX
Blake, Rev. John Frederick, 1839–1906, vol. I
Blake, Sir John Lucian, 1898–1954, vol. V
Blake, John William, 1911–1987, vol. VIII
Blake, Katharine J.; see Jex-Blake.
Blake, Louisa Brandreth A.; see Aldrich-Blake.
Blake, Col Maurice Charles Joseph, 1837–1917, vol. II
Blake, Major Napoleon Joseph Rodolph, 1853–1926, vol. II
Blake, Nicholas; see Day-Lewis, Cecil.
Blake, Sir Patrick James Graham, 5th Bt (cr 1772), 1861–1930, vol. III
Blake, Lt-Col Sir Reginald; see Blake, Lt-Col Sir G. R.
Blake, Sophia J.; see Jex-Blake.
Blake, Lt-Col Terence Joseph Edward, 1886–1921, vol. II
Blake, Sir Thomas Patrick Ulick John Harvey, 15th Bt (cr 1622), 1870–1925, vol. II
Blake, Very Rev. Thomas William J.; see Jex-Blake.
Blake, Sir Ulick Temple, 16th Bt (cr 1622), 1904–1963, vol. VI
Blake, Vernon, 1875–1930, vol. III
Blake, Vincent; see Blake, H. V.
Blake, Brig.-Gen. William Alan, 1878–1959, vol. V
Blake-Daly, John Archer; see Daly.
Blake-Humfrey, Rev. John, 1847–1930, vol. III
Blake-Reed, Sir John Seymour, 1882–1966, vol. VI
Blakelock, Denys Martin, 1901–1970, vol. VI
Blakely, Hon. Arthur, 1886–1972, vol. VII
Blakely, Colin George Edward, 1930–1987, vol. VIII
Blakeman, Joan, (Mrs L. T. Blakeman); see Woodward, Joan.
Blakeman, John, 1881–1942, vol. IV
Blakeman, Leslie Thompson, 1904–1975, vol. VII
Blakemore, Alan, 1919–1989, vol. VIII
Blakemore, Frederick, 1906–1955, vol. V
Blakeney, Edward Henry, died 1955, vol. V
Blakeney, Frederick Joseph, 1913–1990, vol. VIII
Blakeney, Col Herbert Norwood, 1871–1946, vol. IV
Blakeney, Rev. Richard, 1857–1946, vol. IV
Blakeney, Rev. Robert Bibby, 1865–1948, vol. IV
Blakeney, Brig.-Gen. Robert Byron Drury, 1872–1952, vol. V

Blakeney, Col William Edward Albemarle, died 1942, vol. IV
Blakenham, 1st Viscount, 1911–1982, vol. VIII
Blaker, Cedric, 1889–1965, vol. VI
Blaker, Harry Rowsell, 1872–1953, vol. V
Blaker, Sir John George, 1st Bt, 1854–1926, vol. II
Blaker, Nathaniel Robert, 1921–1990, vol. VIII
Blaker, Sir Reginald, 2nd Bt, 1900–1975, vol. VII
Blaker, Richard, 1893–1940, vol. III
Blaker, Richard Henry, 1866–1940, vol. III
Blaker, Col William Frederick, 1877–1933, vol. III
Blakesley, Major Henry J., died 1931, vol. III
Blakesley, Thomas H., 1847–1929, vol. III
Blakeway, Ven. Charles Edward, 1868–1922, vol. II
Blakeway, Lt-Col Sir Denys Brooke, 1870–1933, vol. III
Blakeway, John Denys, 1918–1986, vol. VIII
Blakeway, Brig.-Gen. John Prestwich, 1867–1936, vol. III
Blakey, James, 1851–1929, vol. III
Blakiston, Sir Arthur Frederick, 7th Bt, 1892–1974, vol. VII
Blakiston, Sir (Arthur) Norman (Hunter), 8th Bt, 1899–1977, vol. VII
Blakiston, Sir Charles Edward, 6th Bt, 1862–1941, vol. IV
Blakiston, Cuthbert Harold, 1879–1949, vol. IV
Blakiston, Rev. Cyril Ralph Noel, 1880–1941, vol. IV
Blakiston, Rev. Herbert Edward Douglas, 1862–1942, vol. IV
Blakiston, Sir Horace Nevile, 5th Bt, 1861–1936, vol. III
Blakiston, John Frnacis, 1882–1965, vol. IV
Blakiston, Sir Norman; see Blakiston, Sir A. N. H.
Blakiston, Wilfrid Robert Louis, 1876–1955, vol. V
Blakiston-Houston, Major Charles, 1868–1935, vol. III
Blakiston-Houston, John, 1829–1920, vol. II
Blakiston-Houston, Maj.-Gen. John, 1881–1959, vol. V
Blamey, Col Edwin Herbert, 1877–1936, vol. III
Blamey, Norman Charles, 1914–2000, vol. X
Blamey, Field Marshal Sir Thomas Albert, 1884–1951, vol. V
Blampied, Edmund, 1886–1966, vol. VI
Blanc, Edmond, 1861–1920, vol. II
Blanc, Sir Henry Jules, 1831–1911, vol. I
Blanc, Hippolyte Jean, 1844–1917, vol. II
Blanch, Baron (Life Peer); Rt Rev. and Rt Hon. Stuart Yarworth Blanch, 1918–1994, vol. IX
Blanche, Rt Rev. Gustave, 1848–1916, vol. II
Blanche, Jaques Emile, 1862–1942, vol. IV
Blanco, Alfredo Ernesto, 1877–1945, vol. IV
Blanco White, Amber, 1887–1981, vol. VIII
Blanco White, George Rivers; see White.
Bland, Charles Heber, 1886–1966, vol. VI
Bland, E.; see Nesbit, E.
Bland, E. Beatrice, 1868–1951, vol. V
Bland, Brig.-Gen. Edward Humphry, 1866–1945, vol. IV
Bland, Edward Maltby, 1878–1946, vol. IV
Bland, Rev. Edward Michael, 1851–1936, vol. III
Bland, Francis Armand, 1882–1967, vol. VI
Bland, Francis Lawrence, 1873–1941, vol. IV

Bland, Sir (George) Nevile Maltby, 1886–1972, vol. VII
Bland, Sir Henry Armand, 1909–1997, vol. X
Bland, Lt-Col John Edward Michael, 1899–1976, vol. VII
Bland, John Otway Percy, 1863–1945, vol. IV
Bland, Sir Nevile; *see* Bland, Sir G. N. M.
Bland, Robert Norman, 1859–1948, vol. IV
Bland, Sir Thomas Maltby, 1906–1968, vol. VI
Bland, William Archdale, 1862–1934, vol. III
Bland, Col William St Colum, 1868–1950, vol. IV
Bland-Sutton, Sir John, 1st Bt, 1855–1936, vol. III
Blandford, Marchioness of; (Albertha Frances Anne), 1847–1932, vol. III
Blandford, George Fielding, 1829–1911, vol. I
Blandford, Heinz Hermann, 1908–1996, vol. X
Blandford, Laurence James, 1876–1944, vol. IV
Blandford, Hon. Sydney Dara, 1868–1929, vol. III
Blandy, Beatrice Charlotte, *died* 1950, vol. IV
Blandy, Sir Edmond Nicolas, *died* 1942, vol. IV
Blandy, Air Cdre Lyster Fettiplace, 1874–1964, vol. VI
Blandy, Richard Denis, 1891–1964, vol. VI
Blane, Brig.-Gen. Charles Forbes, 1859–1930, vol. III
Blane, Comdr Sir Charles Rodney, 4th Bt, 1879–1916, vol. II
Blane, Gilbert Gordon, 1851–1928, vol. II
Blane, Lt-Gen. Sir Seymour John, 3rd Bt, 1833–1911, vol. I
Blane, Thomas Andrew, 1881–1940, vol. III
Blane, William, 1864–1936, vol. III
Blanesborough, Baron (Life Peer); Robert Younger, 1861–1946, vol. IV
Blaney, Thomas, 1823–1903, vol. I
Blanford, William Thomas, 1832–1905, vol. I
Blank, Abraham Lewis, 1891–1967, vol. VI
Blankenberg, Sir Reginald Andrew, 1876–1960, vol. V (A)
Blankenhorn, Herbert, 1904–1991, vol. IX
Blanks, Howard John, 1932–1998, vol. X
Blantyre, 12th Baron, 1818–1900, vol. I
Blaschko, Hermann Karl Felix, (Hugh), 1900–1993, vol. IX
Blaschko, Hugh; *see* Blaschko, Hermann K. F.
Blaserna, Pietro, *died* 1918, vol. II
Blatch, Sir William Bernard, 1887–1965, vol. VI
Blatchford, Robert, 1851–1943, vol. IV
Blatherwick, Col Sir Thomas, 1887–1950, vol. IV
Blathwayt, Raymond, 1855–1935, vol. III
Blathwayt, Robert Wynter, 1850–1936, vol. III
Blaxland, Maj.-Gen. Alan Bruce, 1892–1963, vol. VI
Blaxland, Rev. George Cuthbert, 1852–1930, vol. III
Blaxland, Vice-Adm. John Edric, 1847–1935, vol. III
Blaxter, Sir Kenneth Lyon, 1919–1991, vol. IX
Blaxter, Kenneth William, 1895–1964, vol. VI
Blaydes, Frederick Henry Marvell, 1818–1908, vol. I
Blaylock, Col Harry Woodburn, 1878–1928, vol. II
Bleackley, Horace William, 1868–1931, vol. III
Bleackley, Engr Rear-Adm. Hubert, 1886–1950, vol. IV
Blease, W. Lyon, 1884–1963, vol. VI

Bleasdale, Raymond John, 1924–1982, vol. VIII
Blech, Harry, 1910–1999, vol. X
Bleck, Edward Charles, 1861–1919, vol. II
Bledisloe, 1st Viscount, 1867–1958, vol. V
Bledisloe, 2nd Viscount, 1899–1979, vol. VII
Blee, David, 1899–1979, vol. VII
Blegen, Carl William, 1887–1971, vol. VII
Blelloch, Ian William, 1901–1982, vol. VIII
Blencowe, Rev. Alfred James, *died* 1928, vol. II
Blenkin, Very Rev. George Wilfrid, 1861–1924, vol. II
Blenkinsop, Maj.-Gen. Sir Alfred Percy, 1865–1936, vol. III
Blenkinsop, Arthur, 1911–1979, vol. VII
Blenkinsop, Edward Robert Kaye, 1871–1954, vol. V
Blenkinsop, Maj.-Gen. Sir Layton John, 1862–1942, vol. IV
Blennerhassett, Sir Arthur Charles Francis Bernard, 5th Bt, 1871–1915, vol. I
Blennerhassett, Col Blennerhassett Montgomerie, 1849–1926, vol. II
Blennerhassett, Francis Alfred, 1916–1993, vol. IX
Blennerhassett, Sir Marmaduke Charles Henry Joseph, 6th Bt, 1902–1940, vol. III
Blennerhassett, Rt Hon. Sir Rowland, 4th Bt, 1839–1909, vol. I
Blennerhassett, Rowland Ponsonby, 1850–1913, vol. I
Blennerhassett, William Lewis Rowland Paul Sebastian, 1882–1958, vol. V
Bleriot, Louis, 1872–1936, vol. III
Blewett, Francis Richard, *born* 1869, vol. II
Blewett, Maj.-Gen. Robert Sidney, 1931–1987, vol. VIII
Blewitt, Maj.-Gen. William Edward, 1854–1939, vol. III
Bligh, Sir Edward Clare, 1887–1976, vol. VII
Bligh, John Murray, *died* 1968, vol. VI
Bligh, Sir Timothy James, 1918–1969, vol. VI
Blight, Francis James, 1858–1935, vol. III
Blind, Karl, 1826–1907, vol. I
Blind, Rudolf, 1850–1916, vol. II
Blindell, Sir James, 1884–1937, vol. III
Blishen, Edward, 1920–1996, vol. X
Bliss, 4th Baron, 1869–1926, vol. II
Bliss, Sir Arthur Edward Drummond, 1891–1975, vol. VII
Bliss, Major Charles, 1871–1914, vol. I
Bliss, Cuthbert Vivian, 1878–1963, vol. VI
Bliss, Col Ernest William, 1869–1934, vol. III
Bliss, Sir Henry William, 1840–1919, vol. II
Bliss, Rev. Howard S., 1860–1920, vol. II
Bliss, John Cordeux, 1914–1999, vol. X
Bliss, Rev. John Worthington, 1832–1917, vol. II
Bliss, Joseph, 1853–1939, vol. III
Bliss, Kathleen Mary, (Mrs Rupert Bliss), 1908–1989, vol. VIII
Bliss, Brig. Philip Wheeler, 1887–1966, vol. VI
Bliss, Gen. Tasker Howard, 1853–1930, vol. III
Bliss, Col Thomas Gordon, 1869–1949, vol. IV
Bliss, Rev. William Henry, 1834–1919, vol. II
Blissett, Alfreda Rose; *see* Hodgson, A. R.
Bliven, Bruce, 1889–1977, vol. VII
Blixen Finecke, Karen; *see* Dinesen, Isak.

Bloch, Ernest, 1880–1959, vol. V
Bloch, Felix, 1905–1983, vol. VIII
Bloch, Jean de, *died* 1902, vol. I
Bloch, Konrad Emil, 1912–2000, vol. X
Bloch, Sir Maurice, *died* 1964, vol. VI
Bloch, Olaf F., *died* 1944, vol. IV
Block, Maj.-Gen. Adam Johnstone Cheyne, 1908–1994, vol. IX
Block, Sir Adam Samuel James, 1856–1941, vol. IV
Block, Brig. Allen Prichard, 1899–1973, vol. VII
Block, Comdr Leslie Kenneth Allen, 1906–1980, vol. VII
Blockey, Air Vice-Marshal Paul Sandland, 1905–1963, vol. VI
Blodget, Cornelia Otis, (Mrs A. S. Blodget); *see* Skinner, C. O.
Blofeld, Rev. Stuart, 1872–1950, vol. IV
Blofeld, Thomas Calthorpe, 1836–1908, vol. I
Blofield, Edgar Glanville, 1899–1981, vol. VIII
Blois, Captain Sir Gervase Ralph Edmund, 10th Bt, 1901–1968, vol. VI
Blois, Sir Ralph Barrett Macnaghten, 9th Bt, 1866–1950, vol. IV
Blois-Johnson, Lt-Col Thomas Gordon; *see* Johnson.
Blom, Eric Walter, 1888–1959, vol. V
Blomefield, Edward Hugh, 1852–1938, vol. III
Blomefield, Peregrine Maitland, 1917–1988, vol. VIII
Blomefield, Sir Thomas Edward Peregrine, 5th Bt, 1907–1984, vol. VIII
Blomefield, Sir Thomas Wilmot Peregrine, 4th Bt, 1848–1928, vol. II
Blomfield, Arthur Conran, 1863–1935, vol. III
Blomfield, Sir Arthur William, 1829–1899, vol. I
Blomfield, Maj.-Gen. Charles James, 1855–1928, vol. II
Blomfield, Charles James, *died* 1932, vol. III
Blomfield, Douglas John, 1885–1979, vol. VII
Blomfield, Brig. John Reginald, 1916–1992, vol. IX
Blomfield, Joseph, 1870–1948, vol. IV
Blomfield, Sir Reginald, 1856–1942, vol. IV
Blomfield, Wing Comdr Richard Graham, 1890–1940, vol. III
Blomfield, Rear-Adm. Sir Richard Massie, 1835–1921, vol. II
Blomfield, Maj.-Gen. Valentine, 1898–1980, vol. VII
Blomfield, Rev. William Ernest, 1862–1934, vol. III
Blommers, Johannes Bernardus, 1845–1914, vol. I
Blond, Neville, 1896–1970, vol. VI
Blondin, Lt-Col Hon. Pierre Edouard, 1874–1943, vol. IV
Blood, Alexander, *died* 1933, vol. III
Blood, Gen. Sir Bindon, 1842–1940, vol. III
Blood, Sir Hilary Rudolph Robert, 1893–1967, vol. VI
Blood, Lancelot Ivan Neptune Lloyd-, 1896–1951, vol. V
Blood, Brig. William Edmund Robarts, 1897–1976, vol. VII
Blood, Brig. William Holcroft, 1887–1976, vol. VII
Blood-Smyth, Rev. William A., 1853–1940, vol. IV
Bloom, Cromarty; *see* Bloom, G. C.
Bloom, G(eorge) Cromarty, 1910–1992, vol. IX
Bloom, Ronald, 1926–1993, vol. IX

Bloom, Ursula Harvey, (Mrs Gower Robinson), 1892–1984, vol. VIII
Bloomer, Rt Rev. Thomas, 1894–1984, vol. VIII
Bloomfield, Lady; (Georgiana), 1822–1905, vol. I
Bloomfield, Sir John Stoughton, 1901–1989, vol. VIII
Bloomfield, Maurice, 1855–1928, vol. II (A), vol. III
Blore, Rev. George John, 1835–1916, vol. II
Blore, Lt-Col Herbert Richard, 1871–1955, vol. V
Blosse, Sir David Edward L.; *see* Lynch-Blosse.
Blosse, Sir Henry L.; *see* Lynch-Blosse.
Blosse, Sir Robert Cyril Lynch-, 13th Bt, 1887–1951, vol. V
Blosse, Sir Robert Geoffrey Lynch-, 14th Bt, 1915–1963, vol. VI
Blosse, Sir Robert Lynch, 12th Bt, 1861–1942, vol. IV
Blouet, Léon Paul; *see* O'Rell, Max
Blough, Roger Miles, 1904–1985, vol. VIII
Bloundelle-Burton, John Edward, *died* 1917, vol. II
Blount, Austin Ernest, 1870–1954, vol. V
Blount, Bertie Kennedy, 1907–1999, vol. X
Blount, Air Vice-Marshal Charles Hubert Boulby, 1893–1940, vol. III
Blount, Col Edward Augustine, *died* 1936, vol. III
Blount, Sir Edward Charles, 1809–1905, vol. I
Blount, Edward Francis Riddell-, 1865–1943, vol. IV
Blount, Sir Edward Robert, 11th Bt, 1884–1978, vol. VII
Blount, Vice-Adm. George Ronald, 1877–1964, vol. VI
Blount, Lt-Gen. Harold, 1881–1967, vol. VI
Blount, Sir Walter Aston, 10th Bt, 1876–1958, vol. V
Blount, Sir Walter de Sodington, 9th Bt, 1833–1915, vol. I
Blow, Detmar, 1867–1939, vol. III
Blow, Horatio John Hooper, 1855–1933, vol. III
Blow, Very Rev. Norman John, 1915–1950, vol. IV (A), vol. V
Blow, Sydney, *died* 1961, vol. VI
Blowers, Arthur R., 1868–1954, vol. V
Blowitz, Henri Georges Stephane Adolphe Opper de, 1832–1903, vol. I
Bloxam, John Astley, *died* 1926, vol. II
Bloy, Rt Rev. Francis Eric Irving, 1904–1993, vol. IX
Blucher von Wahlstatt, Prince; *see* Wahlstatt.
Blucke, Air Vice-Marshal Robert Stewart, 1897–1988, vol. VIII
Bluett, Maj.-Gen. Douglas, 1897–1981, vol. VIII
Blum, Léon, 1872–1950, vol. IV
Blumberg, Gen. Sir Herbert Edward, 1869–1934, vol. III
Blumenfeld, Ralph David, 1864–1948, vol. IV
Blumenthal, George, 1858–1941, vol. IV
Blumenthal, Jacques, 1829–1908, vol. I
Blumfield, Clifford William, 1922–1996, vol. X
Blumhardt, J. F., *died* 1922, vol. II
Blundell, Lt-Col Bryan Seymour Moss-, 1878–1932, vol. III
Blundell, Charles Joseph W.; *see* Weld-Blundell.
Blundell, Sir Denis; *see* Blundell, Sir E. D.
Blundell, Rev. Canon E. K., 1886–1961, vol. VI

Blundell, Edward, 1842–1932, vol. III
Blundell, Sir (Edward) Denis, 1907–1984, vol. VIII
Blundell, Mrs Francis, *died* 1930, vol. III
Blundell, Francis Nicholas, 1880–1936, vol. III
Blundell, Col Frederick Blundell Moss, 1873–1964, vol. VI
Blundell, Henry B. H.; *see* Blundell-Hollinshead-Blundell.
Blundell, Henry Seymour Moss-, 1871–1947, vol. IV
Blundell, Col John Eyles, 1843–1931, vol. III
Blundell, Lionel Alleyne, 1910–1975, vol. VII
Blundell, Sir Michael, 1907–1993, vol. IX
Blundell, Maj.-Gen. Richard H. B.; *see* Blundell-Hollinshead-Blundell.
Blundell, Sir Robert Henderson, 1901–1967, vol. IV
Blundell-Hollinshead-Blundell, Henry, 1831–1906, vol. I
Blundell-Hollinshead-Blundell, Maj.-Gen. Richard, 1835–1912, vol. I
Blunden, Edmund Charles, 1896–1974, vol. VII
Blunden, Sir John, 5th Bt, 1880–1923, vol. II
Blunden, Sir William, 4th Bt, 1840–1923, vol. II
Blunden, Sir William, 6th Bt, 1919–1985, vol. VIII
Blundstone, Ferdinand V., 1882–1951, vol. V
Blunt, Rev. Alexander Colvin, *died* 1920, vol. II
Blunt, Rt Rev. Alfred Walter Frank, 1879–1957, vol. V
Blunt, Lt-Col Allan St John, 1880–1931, vol. III
Blunt, Anthony Frederick, 1907–1983, vol. VIII
Blunt, Arthur Powlett, 1883–1946, vol. IV
Blunt, Col Charles Jasper, *died* 1933, vol. III
Blunt, Christopher Evelyn, 1904–1987, vol. VIII
Blunt, Col Conrad Edward Grant, 1868–1948, vol. IV
Blunt, Davenport Fabian Cartwright, 1888–1965, vol. VI
Blunt, Denzil Layton, 1891–1968, vol. VI
Blunt, Sir Edward Arthur Henry, 1877–1941, vol. IV
Blunt, Col Ernest, 1851–1932, vol. III
Blunt, Brig. Gerald Charles Gordon, 1883–1967, vol. VI
Blunt, Sir John Elijah, 1832–1916, vol. II
Blunt, Captain Sir John Harvey, 8th Bt, 1839–1922, vol. II
Blunt, Sir John Harvey, 9th Bt, 1872–1938, vol. III
Blunt, Sir John Lionel Reginald, 10th Bt, 1908–1969, vol. VI
Blunt, John Silvester, 1874–1943, vol. IV
Blunt, Reginald, 1857–1944, vol. IV
Blunt, Sir Richard David Harvey, 11th Bt, 1912–1975, vol. VII
Blunt, Rt Rev. Richard Lefevre, 1833–1910, vol. I
Blunt, Wilfrid Jasper Walter, 1901–1987, vol. VIII
Blunt, Wilfrid Scawen, 1840–1922, vol. II
Blunt, Sir William, 7th Bt, 1826–1902, vol. I
Blunt, Rear-Adm. William Frederick, 1870–1928, vol. II
Blyde, Sir Henry Ernest, 1896–1984, vol. VIII
Blyth, 1st Baron, 1841–1925, vol. II
Blyth, 2nd Baron, 1868–1943, vol. IV
Blyth, 3rd Baron, 1905–1977, vol. VII
Blyth, Alexander Wynter, *died* 1921, vol. II
Blyth, Alfred Carleton, 1865–1936, vol. III

Blyth, Benjamin Hall, 1849–1917, vol. II
Blyth, Lt-Col Charles Frederick Tolmé, 1868–1950, vol. IV
Blyth, Charles Henry, 1916–1986, vol. VIII
Blyth, Rt Rev. George Francis Popham, *died* 1914, vol. I
Blyth, Lt-Col James, 1869–1925, vol. II
Blyth, James, 1864–1933, vol. III
Blyth, James Pattison C.; *see* Currie-Blyth.
Blyth, Ormond Alfred, 1879–1947, vol. IV
Blyth, Robert Henderson, 1919–1970, vol. VI
Blyth, Rev. Thomas Allen, 1844–1913, vol. I
Blythe, Ernest, 1889–1975, vol. VII
Blythe, Wilfred Lawson, 1896–1975, vol. VII
Blythswood, 1st Baron, 1837–1908, vol. I
Blythswood, 2nd Baron, 1839–1916, vol. II
Blythswood, 3rd Baron, 1845–1918, vol. II
Blythswood, 4th Baron, 1870–1929, vol. III
Blythswood, 5th Baron, 1877–1937, vol. III
Blythswood, 6th Baron, 1881–1940, vol. III
Blythswood, 7th Baron, 1919–1940, vol. III
Blyton, Baron (Life Peer); William Reid Blyton, 1899–1987, vol. VIII
Blyton, Enid Mary, 1897–1968, vol. VI
Boag, Sir George Townsend, 1884–1969, vol. VI
Board, Air Cdre Andrew George, 1878–1973, vol. VII
Board, Sir (Archibald) Vyvyan, 1884–1973, vol. VII
Board, Ernest, 1877–1934, vol. III
Board, Peter, 1858–1945, vol. IV
Board, Sir Vyvyan; *see* Board, Sir A. V.
Board, Sir William John, 1869–1946, vol. IV
Boardman, Adm. Frederick Ross, 1843–1927, vol. II
Boardman, Harold, 1907–1994, vol. IX
Boardman, Paymaster Captain John Cogswell, *died* 1942, vol. IV
Boardman, Sir Kenneth Ormrod, 1914–1995, vol. IX
Boas, Franz, 1858–1942, vol. IV
Boas, Frederick S., 1862–1957, vol. V
Boas, Guy, 1896–1966, vol. VI
Boas, Leslie, 1912–1988, vol. VIII
Boase, Alan Martin, 1902–1982, vol. VIII
Boase, Lt-Gen. Allan Joseph, 1894–1964, vol. VI
Boase, Arthur Joseph, 1901–1986, vol. VIII
Boase, Col George Orlebar, 1881–1966, vol. VI
Boase, Thomas Sherrer Ross, 1898–1974, vol. VII
Boase, William Norman, 1870–1938, vol. III
Boateng, Ernest Amano, 1920–1997, vol. X
Bockett, Herbert Leslie, 1905–1977, vol. VII (AII)
Bocquet, Guy Sutton, 1882–1961, vol. VI
Bocquet, (Roland) Roscoe (Charles), 1839–1920, vol. II
Boddam, Maj.-Gen. Welby Wraughton, 1832–1906, vol. I
Boddam-Whetham, Rear-Adm. Edye Kington, 1887–1944, vol. IV
Boddam-Whetham, Major Sydney A., 1885–1925, vol. II
Boddie, Donald Raikes, 1917–1984, vol. VIII
Boddie, George Frederick, 1900–1985, vol. VIII
Boddie, Rear-Adm. Ronald Charles, 1886–1967, vol. VI

Boddington, Rev. Edward Henry, *died* 1920, vol. II
Boddington, Lewis, 1907–1994, vol. IX
Boddis, Alfred Charles, 1895–1958, vol. V
Bode, Major Louis William, 1860–1936, vol. III
Boden, Rev. Charles John, 1853–1937, vol. III
Boden, Edward Arthur, 1911–1990, vol. IX (AI)
Boden, Leonard, 1911–1999, vol. X
Boden, Thomas Bennion, 1915–1995, vol. IX
Bodenham-Lubienski, Count Louis, 1852–1909, vol. I
Bodenstein, Helgard Dewald Johannes, 1881–1943, vol. IV
Bodet, Jaime T.; *see* Torres Bodet.
Bodilly, Sir Jocelyn, 1913–1997, vol. X
Bodington, Rev. Charles, 1836–1918, vol. II
Bodington, Ven. Eric James, 1862–1929, vol. III
Bodington, Sir Nathan, 1848–1911, vol. I
Bodinnar, Sir John Francis, *died* 1958, vol. V
Bodkin, Sir Archibald Henry, 1862–1957, vol. V
Bodkin, Gilbert Edwin, 1886–1955, vol. V
Bodkin, Matthias M'Donnell, 1850–1933, vol. III
Bodkin, Thomas Patrick, 1887–1961, vol. VI
Bodkin, Fr William, 1867–1930, vol. III
Bodkin, Hon. Sir William Alexander, 1883–1964, vol. VI
Bodle, Brig.-Gen. William, 1855–1924, vol. II
Bodley, George Frederick, 1827–1907, vol. I
Bodley, John Edward Courtenay, 1853–1925, vol. II
Bodley Scott, Sir Ronald, 1906–1982, vol. VIII
Body, Rev. George, 1840–1911, vol. I
Body, Maj.-Gen. Kenneth Marten, 1883–1973, vol. VII
Boegner, Marc, 1881–1970, vol. VI
Boehm Boteler, Sir Edgar Collins; *see* Boteler.
Boerma, Addeke Hendrik, 1912–1992, vol. IX
Boevey, Sir Francis Hyde Crawley-, 6th Bt, 1868–1928, vol. II
Boevey, Sir Lance (Launcelot Valentine Hyde) C.; 7th Bt; *see* Crawley-Boevey.
Boevey, Sir Thomas Hyde Crawley, 5th Bt, 1837–1912, vol. I
Boffa, Sir Paul, 1890–1962, vol. VI
Bogard, Humphrey de Forest, 1899–1957, vol. V
Bogarde, Sir Dirk; *see* Van den Bogaerde, Sir D. N.
Boger, Lt-Col Dudley Coryndon, *died* 1935, vol. III
Boger, Major R. W., 1868–1910, vol. I
Bogert, Clarence Atkinson, 1864–1949, vol. IV
Bogert, Ven. James John, 1835–1920, vol. II
Boggis-Rolfe, Douglass Horace, 1874–1966, vol. VI
Boggon, Roland Hodgson, 1903–1983, vol. VIII
Bogie, David Wilson, 1946–1999, vol. X
Bogle, Very Rev. Andrew Nisbet, *died* 1957, vol. V
Bogle, David Blyth, 1903–2000, vol. X
Bogle, Lt-Col John Savile, 1872–1940, vol. III
Bogle, Lockhart, *died* 1900, vol. I
Bogle-Smith, Col Steuart, 1859–1921, vol. II
Bohane, (Albert) Edward, 1873–1940, vol. III
Bohane, Edward; *see* Bohane, A. E.
Boheman, Erik, 1895–1979, vol. VII (AII)
Bohlen, Charles Eustis, 1904–1974, vol. VII
Bohm, David Joseph, 1917–1992, vol. IX
Bohr, Niels Henrik David, 1885–1962, vol. VI
Boileau, Sir Edmond Charles, 7th Bt, 1903–1980, vol. VII

Boileau, Col Etienne Ronald Partridge, 1870–1947, vol. IV
Boileau, Sir Francis George Manningham, 2nd Bt, 1830–1900, vol. I
Boileau, Sir Francis James, 5th Bt, 1871–1945, vol. IV
Boileau, Col Francis William, 1835–1915, vol. I
Boileau, Col Frank Ridley Farrer, 1867–1914, vol. I
Boileau, Sir Gilbert George Benson, 6th Bt, 1898–1978, vol. VII
Boileau, Brig.-Gen. Guy Hamilton, 1870–1962, vol. VI
Boileau, Hugh Evan Ridley, 1906–1952, vol. V
Boileau, Sir Maurice Colborne, 3rd Bt, 1865–1937, vol. III
Boileau, Sir Raymond Frederic, 4th Bt, 1868–1942, vol. IV
Boillot, Félix, 1880–1961, vol. VI
Bois, Col John, 1881–1941, vol. IV
Bois, Sir Stanley, 1864–1938, vol. III
Boisragon, Col Guy Hudleston, 1864–1931, vol. III
Boissier, Arthur Paul, 1882–1953, vol. V
Boissier, Rev. George John, 1857–1929, vol. III
Boissier, Léopold, 1893–1968, vol. VI
Boissier, Marie Louis Gaston, 1823–1908, vol. I
Boito, Arrigo, 1842–1918, vol. II
Bojaxhiu, Agnes Gonxha; *see* Teresa, Mother.
Bojer, Johan, 1872–1959, vol. V
Bok, Edward William, 1863–1930, vol. III
Bolam, Rev. Cecil Edward, 1875–1960, vol. V
Bolam, Sir Robert, *died* 1939, vol. III
Boland, Bridget, 1913–1988, vol. VIII
Boland, Sir (Edward) Rowan, 1898–1972, vol. VII
Boland, Frederick Henry, 1904–1985, vol. VIII
Boland, Harry, *died* 1922, vol. II
Boland, John Pius, 1870–1958, vol. V
Boland, Sir Rowan; *see* Boland, Sir E. R.
Bolden, John Leonard, 1841–1929, vol. III
Boldero, Sir Harold Esmond Arnison, 1889–1960, vol. VI
Boldrewood, Rolf, (Thomas Alexander Browne), 1826–1915, vol. I
Bole, Hon. W. Norman, 1846–1923, vol. II
Boles, Lt-Col Dennis Coleridge, 1885–1958, vol. V
Boles, Lt-Col Sir Dennis Fortescue, 1st Bt, 1861–1935, vol. III
Boles, Sir Gerald Fortescue, 2nd Bt, 1900–1945, vol. IV
Boles, Rev. Richard Henry, 1855–1929, vol. III
Bolingbroke, 5th Viscount, **and St John,** 6th Viscount, 1820–1899, vol. I
Bolingbroke, 6th Viscount, **and St John,** 7th Viscount, 1896–1974, vol. VII
Bolingbroke, Leonard George, 1859–1927, vol. II
Bolitho, Lt-Col Sir Edward Hoblyn Warren, *died* 1969, vol. VI
Bolitho, Hector; *see* Bolitho, Henry H.
Bolitho, (Henry) Hector, 1897–1974, vol. VII
Bolitho, Captain Richard John Bruce, 1889–1965, vol. VI
Bolitho, Maj. Simon Edward, 1916–1991, vol. IX
Bolitho, Thomas Bedford, 1835–1915, vol. I
Bolitho, Thomas Robins, 1840–1925, vol. II
Bolitho, Lt-Col William Edward Thomas, 1862–1919, vol. II

Böll, Heinrich Theodor, 1917–1985, vol. VIII
Bolland, John, 1920–1993, vol. IX
Bolland, Robert William, 1915–1974, vol. VII
Bollard, Hon. R. F., *died* 1927, vol. II
Bolling, Cunliffe Lawrance, 1898–1938, vol. III
Bols, Hon. Maj.-Gen. Eric Louis, 1904–1985, vol. VIII
Bols, Major Louis Jean, 1867–1909, vol. I
Bols, Lt-Gen. Sir Louis Jean, 1867–1930, vol. III
Bolsover, George Henry, 1910–1990, vol. VIII
Bolst, Captain Clifford Charles Alan Lawrence E.; *see* Erskine-Bolst.
Bolster, Francis, *died* 1941, vol. IV
Bolster, Rev. Robert Crofts, *died* 1918, vol. II
Bolster, Captain Thomas Charles Carpenter, *died* 1955, vol. V
Bolt, Rear-Adm. Arthur Seymour, 1907–1994, vol. IX
Bolt, Rev. G. H., 1863–1947, vol. IV
Bolt, George Thomas, 1900–1971, vol. VII
Bolt, Robert Oxton, 1924–1995, vol. IX
Bolte, Dame Edith Lilian, (Lady Bolte), *died* 1986, vol. VIII
Bolte, Hon. Sir Henry Edward, 1908–1990, vol. VIII
Bolter, Albert Ernest, 1856–1933, vol. III
Bolton, 4th Baron, 1845–1922, vol. II
Bolton, 5th Baron, 1869–1944, vol. IV
Bolton, 6th Baron, 1900–1963, vol. VI
Bolton, Arthur Thomas, 1864–1945, vol. IV
Bolton, Charles, *died* 1947, vol. IV
Bolton, Brig. Charles Arthur, 1882–1964, vol. VI
Bolton, Rev. Charles Nelson, 1844–1918, vol. II
Bolton, Charles walter, 1850–1919, vol. II
Bolton, Lt-Col Edward Frederick, 1897–1977, vol. VII
Bolton, Edward Richards, 1878–1939, vol. III
Bolton, Sir Edwin, 1st Bt, 1858–1931, vol. III
Bolton, Elizabeth, 1878–1961, vol. VI
Bolton, Sir Frederic, 1851–1920, vol. II
Bolton, Gambier, *died* 1928, vol. II
Bolton, Col Geoffrey George Hargreaves, 1894–1983, vol. VIII
Bolton, Sir George Lewis French, 1900–1982, vol. VIII
Bolton, Guy, 1884–1979, vol. VII
Bolton, Herbert, *died* 1936, vol. III
Bolton, Sir (Horatio) Norman, 1875–1965, vol. VI
Bolton, Captain Sir Ian Frederick Cheney, 2nd Bt, 1889–1982, vol. VIII
Bolton, John, 1925–1986, vol. VIII
Bolton, Sir John Brown, 1902–1980, vol. VII (AII)
Bolton, Joseph Cheney, 1819–1901, vol. I
Bolton, Joseph Shaw, 1867–1946, vol. IV
Bolton, Louis Hamilton, 1884–1953, vol. V
Bolton, Sir Norman; *see* Bolton, Sir H. N.
Bolton, Percy, 1889–1981, vol. VIII
Bolton, Thomas Dolling, 1841–1906, vol. I
Bolton, Thomas Henry, 1841–1916, vol. II
Bolton, Brig.-Gen. William Kinsey, 1861–1941, vol. IV
Bomanji, Sir Dhunjibhoy, *died* 1937, vol. III
Bomford, Surg.-Gen. Sir Gerald, 1851–1915, vol. I
Bomford, Sir Hugh, 1882–1939, vol. III
Bomford, Richard Raymond, 1907–1981, vol. VIII

Bomon-Behram, Sir Jehangir Bomonji, 1868–1949, vol. IV
Bompas, Cecil Henry, 1868–1956, vol. V
Bompas, Henry Mason, 1836–1909, vol. I
Bompas, Rt Rev. William Carpenter, 1834–1906, vol. I
Bon, Christoph Rudolf, 1921–1999, vol. X
Bonallack, Sir Richard Frank, 1904–1996, vol. X
Bonaparte, Hon. Charles Joseph, 1851–1921, vol. II
Bonaparte, HIH Prince Roland, 1858–1924, vol. II
Bonaparte-Wyse, Andrew Nicholas, 1870–1940, vol. III
Bonar, Henry Alfred Constant, 1861–1935, vol. III
Bonar, Sir Herbert Vernon, 1907–1993, vol. IX
Bonar, James, 1852–1941, vol. IV
Bonavia, Hon. Edgar, 1868–1927, vol. II
Boncour, Joseph P.; *see* Paul-Boncour.
Bond, Arthur, 1907–1989, vol. VIII
Bond, Carrie Jacobs-, 1862–1946, vol. IV
Bond, Brig.-Gen. Charles Earbery, 1877–1953, vol. V
Bond, Charles John, *died* 1939, vol. III
Bond, Rev. Charles Watson, 1839–1922, vol. II
Bond, Lt-Col Chetwynd Rokeby Alfred, 1863–1944, vol. IV
Bond, Engr Captain Edmund Edward, 1865–1943, vol. IV
Bond, Edward, 1844–1920, vol. II
Bond, Sir Edward Augustus, 1815–1898, vol. I
Bond, Francis, *died* 1918, vol. II
Bond, Maj.-Gen. Sir Francis George, 1856–1930, vol. III
Bond, Frederick Bligh, 1864–1945, vol. IV
Bond, George, 1906–1988, vol. VIII
Bond, Maj.-Gen. George Alexander, 1901–1987, vol. VIII
Bond, Godfrey William, 1925–1997, vol. X
Bond, Henry, 1853–1938, vol. III
Bond, Henry Coulson, 1864–1937, vol. III
Bond, Sir Hubert, 1870–1945, vol. IV
Bond, Col James Henry Robinson, 1871–1943, vol. IV
Bond, Ven. John, 1841–1912, vol. I
Bond, Maj.-Gen. John Arthur Mallock, 1891–1959, vol. V
Bond, John Wentworth Garneys, 1865–1948, vol. IV
Bond, Joshua Walter MacGeough, 1831–1905, vol. I
Bond, Lt-Gen. Sir Lionel Vivian, 1884–1961, vol. VI
Bond, Maurice Francis, 1916–1983, vol. VIII
Bond, Ralph Norman, 1900–1984, vol. VIII
Bond, Sir Ralph Stuart, 1871–1968, vol. VI
Bond, Lt-Col Reginald Copleston, 1866–1936, vol. III
Bond, Surg. Vice-Adm. Sir Reginald St George Smallridge, 1872–1955, vol. V
Bond, Maj.-Gen. Richard Lawrence, 1890–1979, vol. VII
Bond, Richard Warwick, 1857–1943, vol. IV
Bond, Rt Hon. Sir Robert, 1857–1927, vol. II
Bond, Rev. Robert, *died* 1952, vol. V
Bond, Stanley Shaw, 1877–1943, vol. IV
Bond, Sir Walter Adrian M.; *see* Macgeough Bond.
Bond, Walter Fitzgerald; *see* Fitzgerald, Walter.

Bond, Most Rev. William Bennett, 1815–1906, vol. I
Bond, Maj.-Gen. William Dunn, 1836–1919, vol. II
Bond, William Langley, 1873–1947, vol. IV
Bond, William Linskill, 1892–1950, vol. IV
Bond, William Ralph Garneys, 1880–1952, vol. V
Bondfield, Rt Hon. Margaret Grace, 1873–1953, vol. V
Bone, Sir David William, 1874–1959, vol. V
Bone, Rev. Frederic James, 1844–1917, vol. II
Bone, Gertrude Helena, (Lady Bone), 1876–1962, vol. VI
Bone, Engr-Rear-Adm. Howard, 1869–1955, vol. V
Bone, Captain Howard Francis, 1908–1981, vol. VIII
Bone, James, 1872–1962, vol. VI
Bone, John Wardle, 1869–1949, vol. IV
Bone, Mary; see Adshead, Mary.
Bone, Sir Muirhead, 1876–1953, vol. V
Bone, Phyllis Mary, 1894–1972, vol. VII
Bone, Group Captain Reginald John, 1888–1972, vol. VII
Bone, Stephen, 1904–1958, vol. V
Bone, William Arthur, 1871–1938, vol. III
Bonet Maury, Amy-Gaston, 1842–1919, vol. II
Bonfield, John Martin, 1915–1976, vol. VII
Bonham, Lt-Col Charles Barnard, 1871–1943, vol. IV
Bonham, Major Sir Eric Henry, 3rd Bt, 1875–1937, vol. III
Bonham, Sir George Francis, 2nd Bt, 1847–1927, vol. II
Bonham, Col John, 1834–1928, vol. II
Bonham, Major Walter Floyd, 1869–1905, vol. I
Bonham-Carter, Baron (Life Peer); Mark Raymond Bonham Carter, 1922–1994, vol. IX
Bonham-Carter, Alfred, died 1910, vol. I
Bonham-Carter, Sir (Arthur) Desmond, 1908–1985, vol. VIII
Bonham-Carter, Arthur Thomas, 1869–1916, vol. II
Bonham-Carter, Gen. Sir Charles, 1876–1955, vol. V
Bonham Carter, Rear-Adm. Sir Christopher Douglas, 1907–1975, vol. VII
Bonham-Carter, Air Cdre David William Frederick, 1901–1974, vol. VII
Bonham-Carter, Sir Desmond; see Bonham-Carter, Sir A. D.
Bonham-Carter, Sir Edgar, 1870–1956, vol. V
Bonham Carter, Helen Violet; see Baroness Asquith of Yarnbury.
Bonham-Carter, Ian Malcolm 1882–1953, vol. V
Bonham-Carter, John Arkwright, 1915–1998, vol. X
Bonham Carter, Sir Maurice, 1880–1960, vol. V
Bonham-Carter, Richard Erskine, 1910–1994, vol. IX
Bonham-Carter, Adm. Sir Stuart Sumner, 1889–1972, vol. VII
Bonheur, Rosa, (Marie Rosalie Bonheur), 1822–1899, vol. I
Bonhote, Rev. Edward Frederic, 1888–1972, vol. VII
Boni, Giacomo, 1859–1925, vol. II
Boniwell, Martin Charles, 1883–1967, vol. VI
Bonn, Leo, 1850–1929, vol. III

Bonn, Sir Max J., 1877–1943, vol. IV
Bonnar, John Calderwood, 1888–1956, vol. V
Bonnat, Leon, died 1922, vol. II
Bonner, Rev. Carey, 1859–1938, vol. III
Bonner, Charles George, 1884–1951, vol. V
Bonner, Frederick Ernest, 1923–2000, vol. X
Bonner, Sir George Albert, 1862–1952, vol. V
Bonner, Hypatia Bradlaugh, 1858–1935, vol. III
Bonner, Captain Singleton, 1879–1917, vol. II
Bonner-Smith, David; see Smith.
Bonnet, Christian M.; see Melchior-Bonnet.
Bonnet, Georges, 1889–1973, vol. VII
Bonnetard, Sir France; see Bonnetard, Sir N. P. F.
Bonnetard, Sir (Nicholas Patrick) France, 1907–1969, vol. VI
Bonney, Rev. Edwin, 1873–1946, vol. IV
Bonney, Rev. Thomas George, 1833–1923, vol. II
Bonney, Victor, died 1953, vol. V
Bonsal, Stephen, 1865–1951, vol. V
Bonsall, Arthur Charles, 1859–1924, vol. II (A), vol. III
Bonsall, Major Hugh Edward, 1863–1928, vol. II
Bonser, Rev. Henry, 1884–1966, vol. VI
Bonser, Rt Hon. Sir John Winfield, 1847–1914, vol. I
Bonser, Air Vice-Marshal Stanley Haslam, 1916–1997, vol. X
Bonser, Wilfrid, 1887–1971, vol. VII
Bonsey, Henry Dawes, died 1919, vol. II
Bonsey, Mary, (Mrs Lionel Bonsey); see Norton, M.
Bonsey, Rev. William, 1845–1909, vol. I
Bonsor, Sir Bryan Cosmo, 3rd Bt, 1916–1977, vol. VII
Bonsor, Sir Cosmo; see Bonsor, Sir H. C. O.
Bonsor, Sir (Henry) Cosmo (Orme), 1st Bt, 1848–1929, vol. III
Bonsor, Major Sir Reginald, 2nd Bt, 1879–1959, vol. V
Bonus, Maj.-Gen. Joseph, 1836–1926, vol. II
Bonus, Col William John, 1862–1943, vol. IV
Bonvalot, Pierre Gabriel, 1853–1933, vol. III
Bonwick, Alfred James, 1883–1949, vol. IV
Bony, Jean V., 1908–1995, vol. IX
Bonython, Hon. Sir (John) Langdon, 1848–1939, vol. III
Bonython, Sir (John) Lavington, 1875–1960, vol. V
Bonython, Sir Lavington; see Bonython, Sir J. L.
Booker, Lt-Col George Edward Nussey, died 1938, vol. III
Booker, Sir William Lane, 1824–1905, vol. I
Bookey, Col John Trench Brownrigg, 1847–1921, vol. II
Boome, Brig.-Gen. Edward Herbert, 1865–1945, vol. IV
Boon, Sir Geoffrey Pearl, 1888–1970, vol. VI
Boon, Quartermaster George, 1846–1927, vol. II
Boon, George Counsell, 1927–1994, vol. IX
Boon, John, 1859–1928, vol. II
Boon, John Trevor, 1916–1996, vol. X
Boon, Sir Peter Coleman, 1916–1997, vol. X
Boon, William Robert, 1911–1994, vol. IX
Boord, Sir Arthur; see Boord, Sir W. A.
Boord, Sir Richard William, 3rd Bt, 1907–1975, vol. VII

Boord, Sir (Thomas) William, 1st Bt, 1838–1912, vol. I

Boord, Sir William; see Boord, Sir T. W.

Boord, Sir (William) Arthur, 2nd Bt, 1862–1928, vol. II

Boorman, Henry Roy Pratt, 1900–1992, vol. IX

Boos, Sir Werner James, 1911–1974, vol. VII

Boose, Major James Rufus, 1859–1936, vol. III

Boosey, Leslie Arthur, 1887–1979, vol. VII

Boot, Rev. Alfred, 1854–1937, vol. III

Boot, Henry Albert Howard, 1917–1983, vol. VIII

Boot, Sir Horace, 1873–1943, vol. IV

Boot, William Henry James, died 1918, vol. II

Boote, Col Charles Geoffrey Michael, 1909–1999, vol. X

Booth, Alfred, 1893–1965, vol. VI

Booth, Sir Alfred Allen, 1st Bt (cr 1916), 1872–1948, vol. IV

Booth, Sir Angus Josslyn G.; see Gore-Booth.

Booth, Sir Arthur; see Booth, Sir G. A. W.

Booth, Bramwell; see Booth, W. B.

Booth, Mrs Bramwell, (Florence Eleanor), 1861–1957, vol. V

Booth, Catherine B.; see Bramwell-Booth.

Booth, Rt Hon. Charles, 1840–1916, vol. II

Booth, Charles, 1868–1938, vol. III

Booth, Sir Charles H., 1853–1939, vol. III

Booth, Charles Leonard, 1925–1997, vol. X

Booth, Hon. Charles Lutley S.; see Sclater-Booth.

Booth, Sir Charles Sylvester, 1897–1970, vol. VI

Booth, Rev. Canon David Herbert, (Peter), 1907–1993, vol. IX

Booth, Edgar Harold, 1893–1963, vol. VI

Booth, Dame Edith; see Evans, Dame Edith.

Booth, Eva G.; see Gore-Booth.

Booth, Evangeline Cory, died 1950, vol. IV

Booth, Florence Eleanor; see Booth, Mrs Bramwell.

Booth, Rear-Adm. Sir Francis Fitzgerald H.; see Haworth-Booth.

Booth, Frederick Handel, 1867–1947, vol. IV

Booth, Sir (George) Arthur (Warrington), 1879–1972, vol. VII

Booth, George Macaulay, 1877–1971, vol. VII

Booth, Sir Henry William Gore-, 5th Bt (cr 1760), 1843–1900, vol. I

Booth, James, 1914–2000, vol. X

Booth, James William, died 1953, vol. V

Booth, John Bennion, 1880–1961, vol. VI

Booth, John Reginald Trevor, 1883–1963, vol. VI

Booth, John Wells, 1903–1994, vol. IX

Booth, Most Rev. Joseph John, 1886–1965, vol. VI

Booth, Sir Josslyn (Augustus Richard) Gore-, 6th Bt (cr 1760), 1869–1944, vol. IV

Booth, Very Rev. Lancelot Parker, died 1925, vol. II

Booth, Leonard William, 1856–1923, vol. II

Booth, Mary Booth, 1885–1969, vol. VI

Booth, Sir Michael Savile G.; see Gore-Booth.

Booth, Major Sir Paul, 1884–1963, vol. VI

Booth, Rev. Canon Peter; see Booth, Rev. Canon D. H.

Booth, Sir Philip, 2nd Bt (cr 1916), 1907–1960, vol. V

Booth, Sir Robert Camm, 1916–1996, vol. X

Booth, S. Lawson, died 1928, vol. II

Booth, W. S., 1896–1972, vol. VII

Booth, Col Hon. Walter Dashwood S.; see Sclater-Booth.

Booth, Walter Reynolds, 1891–1963, vol. VI

Booth, Rev. William, 1829–1912, vol. I

Booth, (William) Bramwell, 1856–1929, vol. III

Booth-Clibborn, Rt Rev. Stanley Eric Francis, 1924–1996, vol. X

Booth-Gravely, Sir Walter, 1882–1971, vol. VII

Booth Tucker, Frederick St George de Lautour, 1853–1929, vol. III

Boothby, Baron, (Life Peer); Robert John Graham Boothby, 1900–1986, vol. VIII

Boothby, Basil; see Boothby, E. B.

Boothby, Sir Brooke, 11th Bt, 1856–1913, vol. I

Boothby, Sir Charles Francis, 12th Bt, 1858–1926, vol. II

Boothby, (Evelyn) Basil, 1910–1990, vol. VIII

Boothby, Captain Evelyn Leonard Beridge, 1876–1937, vol. III

Boothby, Captain Frederick Lewis Maitland, 1881–1940, vol. III

Boothby, Guy Newell, 1867–1905, vol. I

Boothby, Rev. Sir Herbert Cecil, 13th Bt, 1863–1935, vol. III

Boothby, Comdr Hubert Basil, 1863–1941, vol. IV

Boothby, Sir Hugo Robert Brooke, 15th Bt, 1907–1986, vol. VIII

Boothby, Josiah, 1837–1916, vol. II

Boothby, Sir Robert Tuite, 1871–1941, vol. IV

Boothby, Sir Seymour William Brooke, 14th Bt, 1866–1951, vol. V

Boothby, Cdre William Osbert, 1866–1913, vol. I

Boothe, Clare; see Luce, Mrs Henry R.

Boothman, Air Chief Marshal Sir John Nelson, 1901–1957, vol. V

Boothroyd, (Edith) Hester, (Mrs Francis Boothroyd), 1915–1983, vol. VIII

Boothroyd, Hester, (Mrs Francis Boothroyd); see Boothroyd, E. H.

Boothroyd, (John) Basil, 1910–1988, vol. VIII

Booty, Arthur Ernest, 1875–1932, vol. III

Booty, Vice-Adm. Edward Leonard, 1871–1949, vol. IV

Boppe, Lucien, 1834–1909, vol. I

Bor, Gen. James Henry, 1857–1914, vol. I

Bor, Max; see Adrian, Max.

Bor, Norman Loftus, 1893–1972, vol. VII

Bor, Walter George, 1916–1999, vol. X

Borah, William Edgar, 1865–1940, vol. III

Boraston, Sir John, 1851–1920, vol. II

Boraston, Lt-Col John Herbert, 1885–1969, vol. VI

Borchgrevink, Carsten E., 1864–1934, vol. III

Bordeaux, Henry, 1870–1963, vol. VI

Borden, Rev. Byron Crane, 1850–1929, vol. III

Borden, Hon. Sir Frederick William, 1847–1917, vol. II

Borden, Henry, 1901–1989, vol. VIII

Borden, Mary, (Lady Spears), died 1968, vol. VI

Borden, Rt Hon. Sir Robert Laird, 1854–1937, vol. III

Border, Hugh William, 1890–1981, vol. VIII

Bordes, Charles, 1865–1909, vol. I

Bordet, Jules Jean Baptiste Vincent, 1870–1961, vol. VI

Bordonaro, Antonio Chiaramonte, 1877–1932, vol. III
Boreel, Sir Alfred, 12th Bt, 1883–1964, vol. VI
Boreel, Sir Francis William Robert, 11th Bt, 1882–1941, vol. IV
Boreel, Sir Jacob Willem Gustaaf, 10th Bt, 1852–1937, vol. III
Boreham, Sir (Arthur) John, 1925–1994, vol. IX
Boreham, Sir John; see Boreham, Sir A. J.
Boreham, Ven. Frederick, 1888–1966, vol. VI
Borenius, Tancred, 1885–1948, vol. IV
Borg, Sir George, 1887–1954, vol. V
Borg, Raphael, 1840–1903, vol. I
Borg Olivier, George, 1911–1980, vol. VII
Borgeaud, Charles, 1861–1940, vol. III
Borges, Jorge Luis, 1899–1986, vol. VIII
Borges, Thomas William Alfred, 1923–2000, vol. X
Boring, Edwin Garrigues, 1886–1968, vol. VI
Borland, David Morton, 1911–1996, vol. X
Borland, John Ernest, died 1937, vol. III
Borland, Captain John MacInnes, 1869–1946, vol. IV
Borland, Kenneth Alexander, died 1948, vol. IV
Borland, Rev. William, 1867–1945, vol. IV
Born, Max, 1882–1970, vol. VI
Borneman, Roy Ernest, 1904–1983, vol. VIII
Borodin, George; see Sava, George.
Borradaile, Col George William, 1838–1927, vol. II
Borradaile, Brig.-Gen. Harry Benn, 1860–1948, vol. IV
Borradaile, Maj.-Gen. Hugh Alastair, 1907–1993, vol. IX
Borradaile, Lancelot Alexander, 1872–1945, vol. IV
Borradaile, Rev. Robert Hudson, died 1914, vol. I
Borrajo, Edward Marto, 1853–1909, vol. I
Borrett, Ven. Charles Walter, 1916–2000, vol. X
Borrett, Adm. George Holmes, died 1952, vol. V
Borrett, Maj.-Gen. Herbert Charles, 1841–1919, vol. II
Borrett, Lt-Gen. Sir Oswald Cuthbert, 1878–1950, vol. IV
Borrie, Peter Forbes, 1918–1984, vol. VIII
Borrowes, Sir Erasmus Dixon, 9th Bt, 1831–1898, vol. I
Borrowes, Sir Eustace Dixon, 11th Bt, 1866–1939, vol. III
Borrowes, Lt-Col Sir Kildare Dixon, 10th Bt, 1852–1924, vol. II
Borschette, Albert, 1920–1976, vol. VII
Borthwick, 17th Baron, 1867–1910, vol. I
Borthwick, 23rd Lord, 1905–1996, vol. X
Borthwick, Albert William, died 1937, vol. III
Borthwick, Lt-Col Alexander, 1839–1914, vol. I
Borthwick, Captain Alfred Edward, 1871–1955, vol. V
Borthwick, Algernon Malcolm, 1907–1975, vol. VII
Borthwick, Brig.-Gen. Francis Henry, 1883–1977, vol. VII
Borthwick, Henry, 1868–1937, vol. III
Borthwick, Jason; see Borthwick, W. J. M.
Borthwick, Sir Thomas, 1st Bt, 1835–1912, vol. I
Borthwick, Sir Thomas Banks, 2nd Bt; see Whitburgh.
Borthwick, William Henry, 1832–1928, vol. II

Borthwick, (William) Jason (Maxwell), 1910–1998, vol. X
Borton, Air Vice-Marshal Amyas Eden, 1886–1969, vol. VI
Borton, Lt-Col Arthur Drummond, 1883–1933, vol. III
Borton, Col Charles Edward, 1857–1924, vol. II
Borton, Neville Travers, 1870–1938, vol. III
Borwick, 1st Baron, 1845–1936, vol. III
Borwick, 2nd Baron, 1880–1941, vol. IV
Borwick, 3rd Baron, 1886–1961, vol. VI
Borwick, Lt-Col George Oldroyd, 1879–1964, vol. VI
Borwick, Leonard, 1868–1925, vol. II
Borwick, Lt-Col Malcolm, 1882–1957, vol. V
Borwick, Lt-Col Michael George, 1916–1986, vol. VIII
Borwick, Lt-Col Sir Thomas Faulkner, 1890–1981, vol. VIII
Bosanquet, Sir Albert; see Bosanquet, Sir F. A.
Bosanquet, Bernard, 1848–1923, vol. II
Bosanquet, Bernard James Tindal, 1877–1936, vol. III
Bosanquet, Charles Ian Carr, 1903–1986, vol. VIII
Bosanquet, Adm. Sir Day Hort, 1843–1923, vol. II
Bosanquet, Sir (Frederick) Albert, 1837–1923, vol. II
Bosanquet, Major George Richard Bosanquet S.; see Smith-Bosanquet.
Bosanquet, Adm. George Stanley, 1835–1914, vol. I
Bosanquet, Helen, 1860–1925, vol. II
Bosanquet, Captain Henry Theodore Augustus, 1870–1959, vol. V
Bosanquet, Sir Oswald Vivian, 1866–1933, vol. III
Bosanquet, Robert Carr, 1871–1935, vol. III
Bosanquet, Robert Holford Macdowall, died 1912, vol. I
Bosanquet, Sir Ronald Courthope; see Bosanquet, Sir S. R. C.
Bosanquet, Sir (Samuel) Ronald Courthope, 1868–1952, vol. V
Bosanquet, Theodora, 1880–1961, vol. VI
Bosanquet, Vivian Henry Courthope, 1872–1943, vol. IV
Bosanquet, William Cecil, died 1941, vol. IV
Boscawen, Rt Hon. Sir Arthur Sackville Trevor G.; see Griffith-Boscawen.
Boscawen, Major Hon. George Edward, 1888–1918, vol. II
Boscawen, Hon. Hugh le Despencer, 1844–1908, vol. I
Boscawen, Hon. John Richard De Clare, 1860–1915, vol. I
Bosch, Carl, 1874–1940, vol. III
Bosch, Baron Jean van den, 1910–1985, vol. VIII
Bose, Sir Bipin Krishna, 1851–1933, vol. III
Bose, Rai Bahadur C.; see Chunilal Bose.
Bose, Sir Jagadis Chunder, 1858–1937, vol. III
Bose, Sir Kailas Chandra, Rai Bahadur, died 1927, vol. II
Bose, (L. M.) Vivian, 1891–1983, vol. VIII
Bose, Satyendranath, 1894–1974, vol. VII
Bose, Vivian; see Bose, L. M. V.
Bossom, Baron (Life Peer); Alfred Charles Bossom, 1881–1965, vol. VI

Bostock, Rev. Charles, 1869–1943, vol. IV
Bostock, Geoffrey, 1880–1961, vol. VI
Bostock, Henry, *died* 1923, vol. II
Bostock, Henry John, 1870–1956, vol. V
Bostock, Hon. Hewitt, 1864–1930, vol. III
Bostock, John, 1916–1977, vol. VII
Bostock, Col John Southey, 1875–1930, vol. III
Bostock, Rev. Canon Peter Geoffrey, 1911–1999, vol. X
Bostock, Samuel, *died* 1938, vol. III
Bostock, Air Vice-Marshal William Dowling, 1892–1968, vol. VI
Boston, 6th Baron, 1860–1941, vol. IV
Boston, 7th Baron, 1889 1958, vol. V
Boston, 8th Baron, 1897–1972, vol. VII
Boston, 9th Baron, 1897–1978, vol. VII
Boston, Sir Henry (Josiah) Lightfoot, 1898–1969, vol. VI
Boston, Lucy Maria, 1892–1990, vol. VIII
Boswall, Sir George Lauderdale H.; *see* Houstoun-Boswall.
Boswall, Sir George Reginald H.; *see* Houstoun-Boswall.
Boswall, Major Sir Gordon H.; *see* Houstoun-Boswall.
Boswall, Sir Thomas H.; *see* Houstoun-Boswall.
Boswall, Sir (Thomas) Randolph H.; *see* Houstoun-Boswall.
Boswall, Sir William Evelyn H.; *see* Houstoun-Boswall.
Boswell, Alexander Bruce, 1884–1962, vol. VI
Boswell, Arthur Radcliffe, *born* 1838, vol. II
Boswell, Maj.-Gen. John James, 1835–1908, vol. I
Boswell, Captain Lennox Albert Knox, 1898–1975, vol. VII
Boswell, Percy George Hamnall, 1886–1960, vol. V
Bosworth, George Herbert, 1896–1979, vol. VII
Bosworth, George Simms, 1916–1986, vol. VIII
Bosworth, Col William John, 1858–1923, vol. II
Bosworth-Smith, Nevil Digby, 1886–1964, vol. VI
Bosworth Smith, Reginald Montagu, 1872–1944, vol. IV
Boteler, Sir Edgar Collins Boehm, 2nd Bt, 1869–1928, vol. II
Botha, Colin Graham, 1883–1973, vol. VII
Botha, Rt Hon. Louis, 1863–1919, vol. II
Botham, Arthur William, 1874–1963, vol. VI
Bothamley, Rev. Hilton, *died* 1919, vol. II
Bothamley, Rev. Canon Westley, 1861–1933, vol. III
Bothe, Walther Wilhelm Georg Franz, 1891–1957, vol. V
Bott, Alan John, *died* 1952, vol. V
Bott, Lt-Col Robert Henry, 1882–1938, vol. III
Botteley, James, *born* 1839, vol. III
Botterell, Percy Dumville, 1880–1952, vol. V
Bottini, Reginald Norman, 1916–1999, vol. X
Bottome, Phyllis, (Mrs A. E. Forbes Dennis), 1884–1963, vol. VI
Bottomley, Baron (Life Peer); Arthur George Bottomley, 1907–1995, vol. IX
Bottomley, Lady; Bessie Ellen Bottomley, 1906–1998, vol. X
Bottomley, Albert Ernest, 1873–1950, vol. IV
Bottomley, Sir Cecil; *see* Bottomley, Sir W. C.

Bottomley, Edwin, *died* 1929, vol. III
Bottomley, Gordon, 1874–1948, vol. IV
Bottomley, Col Herbert, 1866–1926, vol. II (A), vol. III
Bottomley, James H., 1857–1934, vol. III
Bottomley, James Thomson, 1845–1926, vol. II
Bottomley, John Mellor, 1888–1960, vol. V (A)
Bottomley, Air Chief Marshal Sir Norman Howard, 1891–1970, vol. VI
Bottomley, William Beecroft, 1863–1922, vol. II
Bottomley, Sir (William) Cecil, 1878–1954, vol. V
Bottrall, (Francis James) Ronald, 1906–1989, vol. VIII
Bottrall, Ronald; *see* Bottrall, F. J. R.
Botvinnik, Mikhail Moisseyevich, 1911–1995, vol. IX
Boucaut, Hon. Sir James Penn, 1831–1916, vol. II
Bouch, Thomas, 1882–1963, vol. VI
Bouchard, Hon. Telesphore Damien, 1881–1962, vol. VI
Bouche-Leclercq, Auguste, 1842–1923, vol. II
Boucher, Lt-Col Benjamin Hamilton, 1864–1928, vol. II
Boucher, Rev. Charles Estcourt, 1856–1940, vol. III
Boucher, Maj.-Gen. Sir Charles Hamilton, 1898–1951, vol. V
Boucher, Rear-Adm. Maitland Walter Sabine, 1888–1963, vol. VI
Boucher, Maj.-Gen. Valentine, 1904–1961, vol. VI
Boucherett, Emilia Jessie, 1825–1905, vol. I
Bouchier, Air Vice-Marshal Sir Cecil Arthur, 1895–1979, vol. VII
Boucicault, Dion, 1859–1929, vol. III
Boughey, Rev. Anchitel Harry Fletcher, 1849–1936, vol. III
Boughey, Charles Lovell Fletcher, 1887–1934, vol. III
Boughey, Sir Francis, 8th Bt, 1848–1927, vol. II
Boughey, Rev. Sir George, 5th Bt, 1837–1910, vol. I
Boughey, Col George Fletcher Ottley, 1844–1918, vol. II
Boughey, Sir George Menteth, 9th Bt, 1879–1959, vol. V
Boughey, Maj.-Gen. John, 1845–1932, vol. III
Boughey, John Fenton C.; *see* Coplestone-Boughey.
Boughey, Sir Richard James, 10th Bt, 1925–1978, vol. VII
Boughey, Rev. Sir Robert, 7th Bt, 1843–1921, vol. II
Boughey, Sir Thomas Fletcher, 4th Bt, 1836–1906, vol. I
Boughey, Sir William Fletcher, 6th Bt, 1840–1912, vol. I
Boughton, Rev. Canon Charles Henry Knowler, 1883–1943, vol. IV
Boughton, Sir Charles Henry Rouse-, 11th Bt, 1825–1906, vol. I
Boughton, Sir Edward Hotham Rouse-, 13th Bt, 1893–1963, vol. VI
Boughton, George Henry, 1833–1905, vol. I
Boughton, Michael Linnell Gerald, 1925–1990, vol. VIII
Boughton, Rutland, 1878–1960, vol. V
Boughton, Sir William St Andrew Rouse-, 12th Bt, 1853–1937, vol. III

Boughton-Knight, Charles Andrew R.; *see* Rouse-Boughton-Knight.
Bougle, C., *died* 1940, vol. III
Bouguereau, Adolphe William, 1825–1905, vol. I
Boulanger, Nadia Juliette, 1887–1979, vol. VII
Bould, John, 1855–1938, vol. III
Boulden, Rev. Alfred William, 1849–1920, vol. II
Boulenger, Charles L., 1885–1940, vol. III
Boulenger, Edward George, 1888–1946, vol. IV
Boulenger, George Albert, *died* 1937, vol. III
Boulet, Gilles, 1926–1997, vol. X
Boulger, Demetrius Charles, 1853–1928, vol. II
Boulger, Dorothy Henrietta, 1847–1923, vol. II
Boulger, George Simonds, 1853–1922, vol. II
Boulnois, Charles, 1832–1912, vol. I
Boulnois, Edmund, 1838–1911, vol. I
Boult, Sir Adrian Cedric, 1889–1983, vol. VIII
Boulter, Eric Thomas, 1917–1989, vol. VIII
Boulter, Rev. Canon John Sidney, 1890–1969, vol. VI
Boulter, Robert, 1885–1973, vol. VII
Boulter, Stanley Carr, 1852–1917, vol. II
Boulter, Rev. Walter Easton, 1874–1936, vol. III
Boulting, John Edward, 1913–1985, vol. VIII
Boulting, Sydney Arthur; *see* Cotes, Peter.
Boulton, A. C. Forster, 1862–1949, vol. IV
Boulton, Lt-Col Aubrey Holmes, 1882–1932, vol. III
Boulton, Major Charles Percy, 1867–1916, vol. II
Boulton, Sir Christian; *see* Boulton, Sir H. H. C.
Boulton, Sir (Denis Duncan) Harold (Owen), 3rd Bt (*cr* 1905), 1892–1968, vol. VI
Boulton, Edward Henry Brooke, 1897–1982, vol. VIII
Boulton, Major Sir Edward John, 2nd Bt (*cr* 1944), 1907–1982, vol. VIII
Boulton, Maj.-Gen. Harold, 1872–1955, vol. V
Boulton, Sir Harold; *see* Boulton, Sir D. D. H. O.
Boulton, Sir Harold Edwin, 2nd Bt (*cr* 1905), 1859–1935, vol. III
Boulton, Sir (Harold Hugh) Christopher, (Sir Christian), 1918–1996, vol. X
Boulton, Norman Savage, 1899–1984, vol. VIII
Boulton, Percy, 1840–1909, vol. I
Boulton, Rev. Canon Peter Henry, 1925–1998, vol. X
Boulton, Sir Samuel Bagster, 1st Bt (*cr* 1905), 1830–1918, vol. II
Boulton, Sidney, 1855–1932, vol. III
Boulton, Very Rev. Walter, 1901–1984, vol. VIII
Boulton, William Savage, 1867–1954, vol. V
Boulton, Sir William Whytehead, 1st Bt (*cr* 1944), 1873–1949, vol. IV
Boumphrey, Geoffrey Maxwell, 1894–1969, vol. VI
Bouquet, Rev. Alan Coates, 1884–1976, vol. VII
Bourassa, Robert, 1933–1996, vol. X
Bourcard, Gustave Amaury René, 1846–1925, vol. II (A), vol. III
Bourcart, Charles Daniel, 1860–1940, vol. III
Bourchier, Arthur, 1864–1927, vol. II
Bourchier, Rev. Basil Graham, 1881–1934, vol. III
Bourchier, Lt-Gen. Eustace Fane, 1822–1902, vol. I
Bourchier, Sir George, 1821–1898, vol. I
Bourchier, James David, 1850–1920, vol. II

Bourchier, Col Hon. Murray William James, 1881–1937, vol. III
Bourchier, Violet, (Mrs Arthur Bourchier); *see* Vanbrugh, Violet.
Bourchier, Very Rev. William Chadwick, *died* 1924, vol. II
Bourdelle, Antoine; *see* Bourdelle, E. A.
Bourdelle, (Emile) Antoine, 1861–1929, vol. III
Bourdillon, Sir Bernard Henry, 1883–1948, vol. IV
Bourdillon, Francis Bernard, 1883–1970, vol. VI
Bourdillon, Francis William, 1852–1921, vol. II
Bourdillon, Henry Townsend, 1913–1991, vol. IX
Bourdillon, Sir James Austin, 1848–1913, vol. I
Bourdillon, Lancelot Gerard, 1888–1950, vol. IV
Bourdillon, Robert Benedict, 1889–1971, vol. VII
Bourgeois, Emile, 1857–1934, vol. III
Bourgeois, Jeanne; *see* Mistinguett.
Bourgeois, Léon Victor Auguste, 1851–1925, vol. II
Bourget, Paul, 1852–1935, vol. III
Bourinot, Sir John George, 1837–1903, vol. I
Bourke, Hon. Algernon Henry, 1854–1922, vol. II
Bourke, Ven. Cecil Frederick Joseph, *died* 1910, vol. I
Bourke, Edmund, 1857–1939, vol. III
Bourke, Maj.-Gen. Sir George Deane, 1852–1936, vol. III
Bourke, Rev. Hon. George Wingfield, 1829–1903, vol. I
Bourke, Major Sir Harry L.; *see* Legge-Bourke.
Bourke, Lt-Col Henry Beresford, 1855–1921, vol. II
Bourke, John Francis, 1889–1967, vol. VI
Bourke, Lt-Col John Joseph, 1865–1933, vol. III
Bourke, Matthew J., *died* 1936, vol. III
Bourke, Hon. Maurice Archibald, 1853–1900, vol. I
Bourke, Sir Paget John, 1906–1983, vol. VIII
Bourke, Paul Francis, 1938–1999, vol. X
Bourke, Lt-Comdr Roland, 1885–1958, vol. V
Bourke, Hon. Terence Theobald, 1865–1923, vol. II
Bourke, Gp Captain Ulick John Deane, 1884–1948, vol. IV
Bourke-White, Margaret, 1906–1971, vol. VII
Bourne, Baron (Life Peer); Geoffrey Kemp Bourne, 1902–1982, vol. VIII
Bourne, Gen. Sir Alan George Barwys, 1882–1967, vol. VI
Bourne, Aleck William, 1886–1974, vol. VII
Bourne, Sir Alfred Gibbs, 1859–1940, vol. III
Bourne, Rev. Charles William, 1846–1927, vol. II
Bourne, Edward John, 1922–1974, vol. VII
Bourne, His Eminence Cardinal Francis, 1861–1935, vol. III
Bourne, Sir Frederick Chalmers, 1891–1977, vol. VII
Bourne, Sir Frederick Samuel Augustus, 1854–1940, vol. III
Bourne, Geoffrey, 1893–1970, vol. VI
Bourne, Lt Col Geoffrey Howard, 1909–1988, vol. VIII
Bourne, George; *see* Sturt, G.
Bourne, Rev. George Hugh, *died* 1925, vol. II
Bourne, Gilbert Charles, 1861–1933, vol. III
Bourne, Sir (Henry) Roland (Murray), 1874–1931, vol. III
Bourne, Hugh Clarence, *died* 1909, vol. I
Bourne, James Gerald, 1906–1995, vol. IX

Bourne, Sir (John) Wilfred, 1922–1999, vol. X
Bourne, Kenneth, 1930–1992, vol. IX
Bourne, Kenneth Morison, 1893–1968, vol. VI
Bourne, Captain Rt Hon. Robert Croft, 1888–1938, vol. III
Bourne, Sir Roland; see Bourne, Sir H. R. M.
Bourne, Stafford, 1900–1986, vol. VIII
Bourne, Thomas Johnstone, 1864–1947, vol. IV
Bourne, Sir Wilfred; see Bourne, Sir J. W.
Bourne, Rev. William St Hill, 1846–1929, vol. III
Bourne-Arton, Maj. Anthony Temple, 1913–1996, vol. X
Bourns, Newcome Whitelaw, died 1927, vol. II
Bourton, Cyril Leonard, 1916–1995, vol. IX
Bousfield, Edward George Paul, 1880–1957, vol. V
Bousfield, Guy William John, 1893–1974, vol. VII
Bousfield, Rt Rev. Henry Brougham, 1832–1902, vol. I
Bousfield, Lt-Col Henry Richings, 1863–1930, vol. III
Bousfield, Col Hugh Delabere, 1872–1951, vol. V
Bousfield, Sir William, 1842–1910, vol. I
Bousfield, William Robert, 1854–1943, vol. IV
Boussac, Marcel, 1889–1980, vol. VII
Boustead, Rev. Canon Harry Wilson, 1858–1942, vol. IV
Boustead, Col Sir Hugh; see Boustead, Col Sir J. E. H.
Boustead, Col Sir (John Edmund) Hugh, 1895–1980, vol. VII
Boutens, Dr Peter Cornelis, 1870–1943, vol. IV
Boutflour, Robert, 1890–1961, vol. VI
Boutflower, Rt Rev. Cecil Henry, 1863–1942, vol. IV
Boutflower, Rev. Douglas Samuel, died 1940, vol. III
Boutroux, Emile, 1845–1921, vol. II
Boutwood, Rear-Adm. Laurence Arthur, 1898–1982, vol. VIII
Bouveret, Pascal Adolph Jean D.; see Dagnan-Bouveret.
Bouverie, Rev. Hon. Bertrand P.; see Pleydell-Bouverie.
Bouverie, Hon. Duncombe P.; see Pleydell-Bouverie.
Bouverie, Col Hon. Stuart P.; see Pleydell-Bouverie.
Bouverie-Pusey, Philip Francis, died 1933, vol. III
Bovell, Sir (Conrad Swire) Kerr, 1913–1973, vol. VII
Bovell, Sir Henry Alleyne, 1854–1938, vol. III
Bovell, Vice-Adm. Henry Cecil, 1893–1963, vol. VI
Bovell, John Redman, 1855–1928, vol. II (A), vol. III
Bovell, Sir Kerr; see Bovell, Sir C. S. K.
Bovell, Hon. Sir Stewart; see Bovell, Hon. Sir W. S.
Bovell, Hon. Sir (William) Stewart, 1906–1999, vol. IX
Bovell-Jones, Thomas Boughton, 1906–1967, vol. VI
Bovenschen, Sir Frederick Carl, 1884–1977, vol. VII
Bovet, David, 1907–1992, vol. IX
Bovey, Henry Taylor, died 1912, vol. I
Bovill, Major Anthony Charles Stevens, 1888–1943, vol. IV
Bovill, Charles Harry, 1878–1918, vol. II

Bovill, Edward William, 1892–1966, vol. VI
Boville, Thomas Cooper, 1860–1948, vol. IV
Bowater, Sir Dudley; see Bowater, Sir T. D. B.
Bowater, Sir Eric Vansittart, 1895–1962, vol. VI
Bowater, Major Sir Frank Henry, 1st Bt (cr 1939), 1866–1947, vol. IV
Bowater, Sir Frederick William, 1867–1924, vol. II
Bowater, Sir Ian Frank, 1904–1982, vol. VIII
Bowater, Sir Noël Vansittart, 2nd Bt (cr 1939) 1892–1984, vol. VIII
Bowater, Sir Rainald Vansittart, 2nd Bt (cr 1914), 1888–1945, vol. IV
Bowater, Sir (Thomas) Dudley Blennerhassett, 3rd Bt (cr 1914), 1889–1972, vol. VII
Bowater, Sir (Thomas) Vansittart, 1st Bt (cr 1914), 1862–1938, vol. III
Bowater, Sir Vansittart; see Bowater, Sir T. V.
Bowater, Sir William Henry, 1855–1932, vol. III
Bowcher, Frank, died 1938, vol. III
Bowdell, Wilfred, 1913–1989, vol. VIII
Bowden, family name of Baron Aylestone.
Bowden, Baron (Life Peer); Bertram Vivian Bowden, 1910–1989, vol. VIII
Bowden, Maj. Aubrey Henry, 1895–1987, vol. VIII
Bowden, Sir Frank, 1st Bt, 1848–1921, vol. II
Bowden, Captain Frank Lake, 1863–1906, vol. I
Bowden, Frank Philip, 1903–1968, vol. VI
Bowden, Major George Robert Harland, 1873–1927, vol. II
Bowden, Rev. Canon Guy Arthur George, 1909–1974, vol. VII
Bowden, Sir Harold, 2nd Bt, 1880–1960, vol. V
Bowden, Col James Hubert Thomas C.; see Cornish-Bowden.
Bowden, Lt-Col John, died 1948, vol. IV
Bowden, Kenneth Frank, 1916–1989, vol. VIII
Bowden, Norman Henry Martin, 1879–1968, vol. VI
Bowden, Richard Charles, 1887–1988, vol. VIII
Bowden, Vivian Gordon, 1884–1942, vol. IV
Bowden, Walter, 1859–1919, vol. II
Bowden, William Douglas, 1875–1944, vol. IV
Bowden-Smith, Adm. Sir Nathaniel, 1838–1921, vol. II
Bowden Smith, Vice-Adm. William, 1874–1962, vol. VI
Bowdler, Audley; see Bowdler, W. A.
Bowdler, Lt-Col Basil Wilfred Bowdler, 1873–1960, vol. V
Bowdler, Col Cyril William Bowdler, 1839–1918, vol. II
Bowdler, (William) Audley, 1884–1969, vol. VI
Bowdler-Henry, Cyril; see Henry.
Bowdon, John Erdeswick B.; see Butler-Bowdon.
Bowell, Hon. Sir Mackenzie, 1823–1917, vol. II
Bowen, Sir Albert, 1st Bt, 1858–1924, vol. II
Bowen, Lt-Col Alfred John Hamilton, 1885–1917, vol. II
Bowen, Arthur Charles M.; see Mainwaring-Bowen.
Bowen, Col Arthur Winniett Nunn, 1873–1964, vol. VI
Bowen, Catherine Drinker, died 1973, vol. VII
Bowen, Hon. Sir Charles Christopher, 1830–1917, vol. II
Bowen, Major Charles Otway Cole, 1867–1910, vol. I

Bowen, Rev. David, *died* 1928, vol. II (A), vol. III
Bowen, David, 1885–1950, vol. IV
Bowen, Edmund John, 1898–1980, vol. VII
Bowen, Major Sir Edward Crowther, 2nd Bt, 1885–1937, vol. III
Bowen, Edward Ernest, 1836–1901, vol. I
Bowen, Edward George, 1911–1991, vol. IX
Bowen, Elizabeth Dorothea Cole, 1899–1973, vol. VII
Bowen, Rear-Adm. Frank, 1930–1995, vol. IX
Bowen, Sir George Bevan, 1858–1940, vol. III
Bowen, Rt Hon. Sir George Ferguson, 1821–1899, vol. I
Bowen, Gordon, 1910–1991, vol. IX
Bowen, Col Herbert Walter, 1870–1944, vol. IV
Bowen, Col Hildred Edward W.; *see* Webb-Bowen.
Bowen, Horace George, *died* 1902, vol. I
Bowen, Ian; *see* Bowen, Ivor I.
Bowen, Ira Sprague, 1898–1973, vol. VII
Bowen, Ivor, *died* 1934, vol. III
Bowen, Ivor, 1902–1984, vol. VIII
Bowen, (Ivor) Ian, 1908–1984, vol. VIII
Bowen, James Bevan, 1828–1905, vol. I
Bowen, Air Cdre James Bevan, 1883–1969, vol. VI
Bowen, Sir John Cuthbert Grenside, 1860–1932, vol. III
Bowen, Sir John Edward Mortimer, 3rd Bt, 1918–1939, vol. III
Bowen, Sir John Poland, *died* 1955, vol. V
Bowen, Sir (John) William, 1876–1965, vol. VI
Bowen, Very Rev. Lawrence, 1914–1994, vol. IX
Bowen, Majorie; *see* Long, M. G.
Bowen, Hon. Sir Nigel Hubert, 1911–1994, vol. IX
Bowen, Norman Levi, 1887–1956, vol. V
Bowen, Owen, 1873–1967, vol. VI
Bowen, Stanley, 1910–1995, vol. IX
Bowen, Sir Thomas Frederic Charles, 4th Bt, 1921–1989, vol. VIII
Bowen, Air Vice-Marshal Sir Tom Ince W.; *see* Webb-Bowen.
Bowen, Trevor Alfred, *died* 1964, vol. VI
Bowen, Sir William; *see* Bowen, Sir J. W.
Bowen, Lt-Col William Allan, 1879–1937, vol. III
Bowen, Hon. and Rev. William Edward, 1862–1938, vol. III
Bowen, William Henry, *died* 1963, vol. VI
Bowen, William Herbert, 1843–1937, vol. III
Bowen, Maj.-Gen. William Oswald, 1898–1961, vol. VI
Bowen, York, 1884–1961, vol. VI
Bowen-Buscarlet, Air Vice-Marshal Sir Willett Amalric Bowen, 1898–1967, vol. VI
Bowen-Davies, Alan, 1907–1974, vol. VII
Bowen-Jones, Sir John Bowen; *see* Jones.
Bowen-Rowlands, Ernest Brown, 1866–1951, vol. V
Bower, Sir Alfred Louis, 1st Bt, 1858–1948, vol. IV
Bower, Sir Edmund Ernest N.; *see* Nott-Bower.
Bower, Sir Frank, 1894–1982, vol. VIII
Bower, Frederick Orpen, 1855–1948, vol. IV
Bower, Lt-Col George Haddon, 1871–1950, vol. IV (A)
Bower, George Spencer, 1854–1928, vol. II
Bower, Sir Graham John, 1848–1933, vol. III
Bower, Maj.-Gen. Sir Hamilton, 1858–1940, vol. III
Bower, Sir John D.; *see* Dykes Bower.

Bower, Comdr John Graham, 1886–1940, vol. III
Bower, Sir John Reginald Hornby N.; *see* Nott-Bower.
Bower, Air Marshal Sir Leslie William Clement, 1909–1991, vol. IX
Bower, Norman, 1907–1990, vol. VIII
Bower, Sir Percival, 1880–1948, vol. IV
Bower, Rev. Richard, 1845–1911, vol. I
Bower, Major Sir Robert Lister, 1860–1929, vol. III
Bower, Comdr Robert Tatton, 1894–1975, vol. VII
Bower, Lt-Gen. Sir Roger Herbert, 1903–1990, vol. VIII
Bower, Stephen Ernest D.; *see* Dykes Bower.
Bower, Sir (William) Guy N.; *see* Nott-Bower.
Bower, Captain Sir William N.; *see* Nott-Bower.
Bowerbank, Sir Fred Thompson, 1880–1960, vol. V
Bowering, John, 1894–1973, vol. VII
Bowerley, Amelia M., *died* 1916, vol. II
Bowerley, Walter, 1876–1952, vol. V
Bowerman, Rt Hon. Charles William, 1851–1947, vol. IV
Bowerman, David Alexander, 1903–1998, vol. X
Bowerman, Brig. John Francis, 1893–1983, vol. VIII
Bowers, Sir Edward Hardman, 1854–1914, vol. I
Bowers, Frederick Gatus, 1882–1937, vol. III
Bowers, Fredson Thayer, 1905–1991, vol. IX
Bowers, Rt Rev. John Phillips Allcot, 1854–1926, vol. II
Bowers, Ven. Percy Harris, 1856–1922, vol. II
Bowers, Col Percy Lloyd, 1879–1943, vol. IV
Bowes, Frederick, 1867–1958, vol. V
Bowes, Sir (Harold) Leslie, 1893–1988, vol. VIII
Bowes, Col Hugh, *died* 1952, vol. V
Bowes, Sir Leslie; *see* Bowes, Sir H. L.
Bowes, Robert Kenneth, 1904–1958, vol. V
Bowes, Brig.-Gen. William Hely, 1858–1932, vol. III
Bowes-Lyon, Hon. Sir David, 1902–1961, vol. VI
Bowes-Lyon, Hon. Francis, 1856–1948, vol. IV
Bowes-Lyon, Maj.-Gen. Sir (Francis) James (Cecil), 1917–1977, vol. VII
Bowes-Lyon, Captain Geoffrey Francis, 1886–1951, vol. V
Bowes-Lyon, Maj.-Gen. Sir James; *see* Bowes-Lyon, Maj.-Gen. Sir F. J. C.
Bowes-Lyon, Hon. John, 1886–1930, vol. III
Bowes-Lyon, Hon. Michael Claude Hamilton, 1893–1953, vol. V
Bowes-Lyon, Captain Ronald George, 1893–1960, vol. V
Bowhill, Air Chief Marshal Sir Frederick William, 1880–1960, vol. V
Bowick, David Marshall, 1923–1995, vol. IX
Bowie, James Alexander, 1888–1949, vol. IV
Bowie, John, *died* 1941, vol. IV
Bowie, Robert Forbes, 1860–1940, vol. III
Bowie, Sir William Tait, 1876–1949, vol. IV
Bowker, Alfred Johnstone, (John), 1922–1993, vol. IX
Bowker, Sir James; *see* Bowker, Sir R. J.
Bowker, John; *see* Bowker, A. J.
Bowker, Sir Leslie Cecil Blackmore, 1887–1965, vol. VI
Bowker, Sir (Reginald) James, 1901–1983, vol. VIII

Bowker, Lt-Col William James, 1869–1931, vol. III
Bowlby, Sir Anthony Alfred, 1st Bt, 1855–1929, vol. III
Bowlby, Sir Anthony Hugh Mostyn, 2nd Bt, 1906–1993, vol. IX
Bowlby, Arthur Salvin, 1872–1932, vol. III
Bowlby, Captain Cuthbert Francis Bond, 1895–1969, vol. VI
Bowlby, (Edward) John (Mostyn), 1907–1990, vol. VIII
Bowlby, Hon. Mrs Geoffrey, (Lettice), 1885–1988, vol. VIII
Bowlby, Rev. Henry Thomas, 1864–1940, vol. III
Bowlby, John; see Bowlby, E. J. M.
Bowlby, Hon. Lettice; see Bowlby, Hon. Mrs Geoffrey.
Bowle, Horace Edgar, 1886–1978, vol. VII
Bowle, John Edward, 1905–1985, vol. VIII
Bowle-Evans, Maj.-Gen. Charles Harford, 1867–1942, vol. IV
Bowler, Air Vice-Marshal Thomas Geoffrey, 1895–1974, vol. VII
Bowles, Baron (Life Peer); Francis George Bowles, 1902–1970, vol. VI
Bowles, Dame Ann P.; see Parker-Bowles.
Bowles, Chester, 1901–1986, vol. VIII
Bowles, Rt Rev. Cyril William Johnston, 1916–1999, vol. X
Bowles, Maj.-Gen. Frederick Augustus, 1851–1931, vol. III
Bowles, Maj.-Gen. Frederick Gilbert, died 1947, vol. IV
Bowles, George Frederic Stewart, 1877–1955, vol. V
Bowles, Hon. Brig.-Gen. Henry, 1854–1932, vol. III
Bowles, Sir Henry Ferryman, 1st Bt, 1858–1943, vol. IV
Bowles, Thomas Gibson, 1844–1922, vol. II
Bowley, Sir Arthur Lyon, 1869–1957, vol. V
Bowling, Paymaster-in-Chief Thomas Henry Lovelace, 1839–1922, vol. II
Bowling, Air Vice-Marshal Victor Swanton, 1908–1971, vol. VII
Bowly, Rev. Charles Henry, 1845–1913, vol. I
Bowly, Col William Arthur Travell, 1880–1957, vol. V
Bowman, Alexander, died 1941, vol. IV
Bowman, Archibald Allan, 1883–1936, vol. III
Bowman, Sir George, 2nd Bt, 1923–1990, vol. IX (AI)
Bowman, Herbert Lister, 1874–1942, vol. IV
Bowman, Humphrey Ernest, 1879–1965, vol. VI
Bowman, Isaiah, 1878–1950, vol. IV
Bowman, Sir James, 1st Bt, 1898–1978, vol. VII
Bowman, Maj.-Gen. John Francis, 1927–1997, vol. X
Bowman, Sir John Paget, 4th Bt, 1904–1994, vol. IX
Bowman, Laurence George, 1866–1950, vol. IV
Bowman, Rev. Sir Paget Mervyn, 3rd Bt, 1873–1955, vol. V
Bowman, Patrick; see Bowman, T. P.
Bowman, Robert Ritchie, 1883–1970, vol. VI (AII)
Bowman, Thomas, died 1945, vol. IV
Bowman, (Thomas) Patrick, 1915–1987, vol. VIII

Bowman, Sir William Paget, 2nd Bt, 1845–1917, vol. II
Bowman, William Powell, 1932–1998, vol. X
Bowman-Manifold, Maj.-Gen. Sir (Michael) Graham Egerton; see Manifold.
Bowmar, Sir (Charles) Erskine, 1913–1996, vol. X
Bowmar, Sir Erskine; see Bowmar, Sir C. E.
Bown, Rev. George Herbert, 1871–1918, vol. II
Bowra, Cecil Arthur Verner, 1869–1947, vol. IV
Bowra, Sir (Cecil) Maurice, 1898–1971, vol. VII
Bowra, Sir Maurice; see Bowra, Sir C. M.
Bowran, Rev. John George, 1869–1946, vol. IV
Bowring, Sir Charles Calvert, 1872–1945, vol. IV
Bowring, Sir (Charles) Clement, 1844–1907, vol. I
Bowring, Sir Clement; see Bowring, Sir C. C.
Bowring, Edgar Alfred, 1826–1911, vol. I
Bowring, Rev. Edgar Francis, 1854–1931, vol. III
Bowring, Hon. Sir Edgar Rennie, 1858–1943, vol. IV
Bowring, Edgar Rennie, 1899–1982, vol. VIII
Bowring, Sir Frederick Charles, 1857–1936, vol. III
Bowring, Col Frederick Thomas Nelson Spratt, 1847–1934, vol. III
Bowring, Adm. Humphrey Wykeham, 1874–1952, vol. V
Bowring, Maj.-Gen. John Humphrey Stephen, 1913–1998, vol. X
Bowring, Lewin Bentham, 1824–1910, vol. I
Bowring, Theodore Louis, 1901–1967, vol. VI
Bowring, Sir Thomas Benjamin, 1847–1915, vol. I
Bowring, Walter Andrew, 1875–1950, vol. IV
Bowring, Walter Armiger, 1874–1931, vol. III
Bowring, Sir William Benjamin, 1st Bt, 1837–1916, vol. II
Bowron, Sir Edward, 1857–1923, vol. II
Bowser, Ernest William, 1887–1969, vol. VI (AII)
Bowser, Hon. Sir John, 1856–1936, vol. III
Bowser, Rev. Sidney W., 1853–1928, vol. II
Bowser, William John, 1867–1933, vol. III
Bowstead, Rev. Canon Christopher J. K., 1844–1924, vol. II
Bowstead, John, 1897–1969, vol. VI
Bowyear, Vice-Adm. George le Geyt, 1817–1903, vol. I
Bowyear, Henry William Thomas, 1852–1936, vol. III
Bowyer, Sir Eric Blacklock, 1902–1964, vol. VI
Bowyer, Sir George Henry, 9th and 5th Bt, 1870–1950, vol. IV
Bowyer, John Francis, 1893–1974, vol. VII
Bowyer-Smijth, Sir William; see Smijth.
Bowyer-Smyth, Sir Alfred John; see Smyth.
Bowyer-Smyth, Captain Sir Philip Weyland; see Smyth.
Box, Betty Evelyn, 1915–1999, vol. X
Box, Charles Richard, died 1951, vol. V
Box, Donald Stewart, 1917–1993, vol. IX
Box, Rev. George Herbert, 1869–1933, vol. III
Box, Sydney, 1907–1983, vol. VIII
Boxall, Sir Alleyne Alfred, 1st Bt, 1855–1927, vol. II
Boxall, Col Sir Alleyne Percival, 2nd Bt, 1882–1945, vol. IV
Boxall, Bernard, 1906–1994, vol. IX
Boxall, Col Sir Charles Gervaise, 1852–1914, vol. I

Boxall, William Percival Gratwicke, 1848–1931, vol. III
Boxer, Air Vice-Marshal Sir Alan Hunter Cachemaille, 1916–1998, vol. X
Boxer, (Charles) Mark (Edward), 1931–1988, vol. VIII
Boxer, Charles Ralph, 1904–2000, vol. X
Boxer, Maj.-Gen. Edward M., *died* 1898, vol. I
Boxer, Rear-Adm. Henry Percy, 1885–1961, vol. VI
Boxer, Captain Herbert Martyn, 1882–1962, vol. VI
Boxer, Mark; *see* Boxer, C. M. E.
Boxshall, Col Henry Edwin, 1863–1936, vol. III
Boxwell, Lt-Col Ambrose, 1876–1959, vol. V
Boyagian, Henry Samuel Rogers, 1875–1947, vol. IV
Boyce, Arthur Cyril, 1867–1942, vol. IV
Boyce, Austin Alexander Rodney, 1870–1948, vol. IV (A)
Boyce, Col Charles Edward, 1882–1963, vol. VI
Boyce, Air Vice-Marshal Clayton Descou Clement, 1907–1987, vol. VIII
Boyce, Ven. Francis Bertie, 1884–1931, vol. III
Boyce, Francis Stewart, 1872–1940, vol. III
Boyce, Air Cdre George Harold, 1894–1975, vol. VII
Boyce, Gilbert L.; *see* Leighton-Boyce, Guy G.
Boyce, Guy Gilbert L.; *see* Leighton-Boyce.
Boyce, Sir (Harold) Leslie, 1st Bt, 1895–1955, vol. V
Boyce, Brig.-Gen. Harry Augustus, 1870–1954, vol. V
Boyce, James, 1947–1994, vol. IX
Boyce, Sir Leslie; *see* Boyce, Sir H. L.
Boyce, Sir Richard Leslie, 2nd Bt, 1929–1968, vol. VI
Boyce, Robert Henry, 1834–1909, vol. I
Boyce, Sir Rubert William, 1863–1911, vol. I
Boyce, Sarah, 1863–1939, vol. III
Boyce, Rev. Walter, 1853–1936, vol. III
Boyce, Maj.-Gen. Sir William George Bertram, 1868–1937, vol. III
Boycott, Arthur Edwin, 1877–1938, vol. III
Boycott, Brian Blundell, 1924–2000, vol. X
Boycott, Rev. Desmond M.; *see* Morse-Boycott.
Boycott, Lt-Col T. A. W.; *see* Wight-Boycott.
Boyd of Merton, 1st Viscount, 1904–1983, vol. VIII
Boyd, Alexander Michael, 1905–1973, vol. VII
Boyd, Alexander Stuart, 1854–1930, vol. III
Boyd, Sir Alexander William K.; *see* Keown-Boyd.
Boyd, Alfred Ernest, *died* 1949, vol. IV
Boyd, Very Rev. Andrew Kennedy Hutchison, 1825–1899, vol. I
Boyd, Sir Archibald John, 1888–1959, vol. V
Boyd, Arthur Merric Bloomfield, 1920–1999, vol. X
Boyd, Ven. Charles, 1842–1914, vol. I
Boyd, Col Charles Augustus R.; *see* Rochfort-Boyd.
Boyd, Charles Walter, 1869–1919, vol. II
Boyd, David Runciman, 1872–1955, vol. V
Boyd, Adm. Sir Denis William, 1891–1965, vol. VI
Boyd, Sir Donald James, 1877–1953, vol. V
Boyd, Douglas Thornley, 1896–1964, vol. VI
Boyd, Edmund Blaikie, 1894–1946, vol. IV
Boyd, Edward Charles Percy, 1871–1949, vol. IV
Boyd, Ernest, 1887–1946, vol. IV
Boyd, Sir Francis; *see* Boyd, Sir J. F.

Boyd, Francis Darby, 1866–1922, vol. II
Boyd, Rev. Francis Leith, 1856–1927, vol. II
Boyd, Frank M., 1863–1950, vol. IV
Boyd, Gavin, 1928–1993, vol. IX
Boyd, Maj.-Gen. Sir Gerald Farrell, 1877–1930, vol. III
Boyd, Rev. Halbert Johnstone, 1872–1957, vol. V
Boyd, Sir Harry Robert, 1876–1940, vol. III
Boyd, Henry, 1831–1922, vol. II
Boyd, Henry, *died* 1942, vol. IV
Boyd, Lt-Col Henry Alexander, 1877–1943, vol. IV
Boyd, Lt-Col Henry Charles R.; *see* Rochfort-Boyd.
Boyd, Rev. Herbert Buchanan, *died* 1941, vol. IV
Boyd, Maj.-Gen. Ian Herbert Fitzgerald, 1907–1978, vol. VII
Boyd, James, 1888–1944, vol. IV
Boyd, James, 1888–1963, vol. VI
Boyd, James, 1891–1970, vol. VI
Boyd, James Dixon, 1907–1968, vol. VI
Boyd, James Fleming, 1920–2000, vol. X
Boyd, Sir John, 1887–1967, vol. VI
Boyd, Hon. Sir John Alexander, 1837–1916, vol. II
Boyd, Col John Alexander, 1857–1931, vol. III
Boyd, Sir (John) Francis, 1910–1995, vol. IX
Boyd, Sir John McFarlane, 1917–1989, vol. VIII
Boyd, (John) Morton, 1925–1998, vol. X
Boyd, Sir John Smith, 1886–1963, vol. VI
Boyd, Brig. Sir John Smith Knox, 1891–1981, vol. VIII
Boyd, Maj.-Gen. Julius Middleton, 1837–1919, vol. II
Boyd, Lachlan Macpherson, 1904–1980, vol. VII
Boyd, Leslie Balfour, 1914–1998, vol. X
Boyd, Martin à Beckett, 1893–1972, vol. VII
Boyd, Mary Stuart, *died* 1937, vol. III
Boyd, Maurice James, 1911–1979, vol. VII
Boyd, Morton; *see* Boyd, J. M.
Boyd, Col Mossom Archibald, 1860–1943, vol. IV
Boyd, Air Vice-Marshal Owen Tudor, 1889–1944, vol. IV
Boyd, Robert, 1890–1959, vol. V
Boyd, Rt Rev. Robert McNeil, 1890–1958, vol. V
Boyd, Ven. Robert Wallace, *died* 1921, vol. II
Boyd, Sidney Arthur, 1880–1966, vol. VI
Boyd, Ven. Sydney Adolphus, 1857–1947, vol. IV
Boyd, Col Thomas Crawford, 1886–1967, vol. VI
Boyd, Thomas Herbert, 1890–1941, vol. IV
Boyd, Thomas J. L. Stirling, 1886–1973, vol. VII
Boyd, Sir Thomas Jamieson, 1818–1902, vol. I
Boyd, Rt Hon. Sir Walter, 1st Bt, 1833–1918, vol. II
Boyd, Sir Walter Herbert, 2nd Bt, 1867–1948, vol. IV
Boyd, William, 1867–1961, vol. VI (AII)
Boyd, William, 1874–1962, vol. VI
Boyd, William, 1885–1984, vol. VIII
Boyd, Rev. William Grenville, 1867–1941, vol. IV
Boyd-Carpenter, Baron (Life Peer); John Archibald Boyd-Carpenter, 1908–1998, vol. X
Boyd Carpenter, Major Sir Archibald Boyd, 1873–1937, vol. III
Boyd-Carpenter, Henry John, 1865–1923, vol. II
Boyd-Carpenter, Captain John Peers, 1871–1936, vol. III

Boyd Carpenter, Rt Rev. William, 1841–1918, vol. II
Boyd-Moss, Brig.-Gen. Lionel Boyd, 1875–1940, vol. III
Boyd Neel, Louis; see Neel.
Boyd Orr, 1st Baron, 1880–1971, vol. VII
Boyd-Rochfort, Sir Cecil Charles, 1887–1983, vol. VIII
Boyd-Rochfort, Captain George Arthur, 1880–1940, vol. III
Boyd-Wilson, Edwin John, 1886–1973, vol. VII
Boyden, Rev. A. H., died 1940, vol. III (A), vol. IV
Boyden, (Harold) James, 1910–1993, vol. IX
Boyden, James; see Boyden H. J.
Boyer, Hon. Arthur, 1851–1922, vol. II
Boyer, Rear-Adm. (S) George Christopher Aubin, 1862–1949, vol. IV
Boyer, Sir Richard James Fildes, 1891–1961, vol. VI
Boyes, Charles Edward, 1866–1920, vol. II
Boyes, Sir George Thomas Henry, died 1910, vol. I
Boyes, Rear-Adm. Hector, 1881–1960, vol. V
Boyes, John, 1912–1985, vol. VIII
Boyes, Maj.-Gen. John Edward, 1843–1915, vol. I
Boyes, John Henry, 1886–1958, vol. V
Boyle of Handsworth, Baron (Life Peer); Edward Charles Gurney Boyle, 1923–1981, vol. VIII
Boyle, Sir Alexander George, 1872–1943, vol. IV
Boyle, Adm. Hon. Sir Algernon Douglas Edward Harry, 1871–1949, vol. IV
Boyle, Andrew Philip More, 1919–1991, vol. IX
Boyle, Archibald Cabbourn, 1918–1998, vol. X
Boyle, Air Cdre Archibald Robert, 1887–1949, vol. IV
Boyle, (Arthur) Brian, 1913–1965, vol. VI
Boyle, Brian; see Boyle, A. B.
Boyle, Sir Cavendish, 1849–1916, vol. II
Boyle, Col Cecil Alexander, 1888–1941, vol. IV
Boyle, Sir Courtenay, 1845–1901, vol. I
Boyle, Daniel, 1859–1925, vol. II
Boyle, Marshal of the Royal Air Force Sir Dermot Alexander, 1904–1993, vol. IX
Boyle, Rev. Desmond; see Boyle, Rev. J. D.
Boyle, Sir Edward, 1st Bt, 1849–1909, vol. I
Boyle, Sir Edward, 2nd Bt, 1878–1945, vol. IV
Boyle, Rear-Adm. Edward Courtney, 1883–1967, vol. VI
Boyle, Comdr Edward Louis Dalrymple, 1864–1923, vol. II
Boyle, Very Rev. George David, 1828–1901, vol. I
Boyle, Harry, 1863–1937, vol. III
Boyle, Captain Harry Lumsden, died 1955, vol. V
Boyle, Henry Edmund Gaskin, 1875–1941, vol. IV
Boyle, Captain James, 1850–1931, vol. III
Boyle, James, 1863–1936, vol. III
Boyle, John Andrew, 1916–1978, vol. VII
Boyle, Air Cdre Hon. John David, 1884–1974, vol. VII
Boyle, Rev. (John) Desmond, 1897–1982, vol. VIII
Boyle, John R., 1870–1936, vol. III
Boyle, John Sebastian, 1933–1991, vol. IX
Boyle, Kay, (Baroness Joseph von Franckenstein), 1902–1992, vol. IX
Boyle, Sir Lawrence, 1920–1989, vol. VIII

Boyle, Col Lionel Richard Cavendish, 1851–1920, vol. II
Boyle, Sir Richard Gurney, 4th Bt, 1930–1983, vol. VIII
Boyle, Richard Vicars, 1822–1908, vol. I
Boyle, Maj.-Gen. Robert, 1823–1899, vol. I
Boyle, Robert Colquhoun, 1877–1934, vol. III
Boyle, Vice-Adm. Hon. Robert Francis, 1863–1922, vol. II
Boyle, Robert William, 1883–1955, vol. V
Boyle, Brig.-Gen. Roger Courtenay, 1863–1944, vol. IV
Boyle, Vincent, 1891–1956, vol. V
Boyle, Hon. Walter John Harry, 1869–1939, vol. III
Boyle, Lt-Col Hon. William George, 1830–1908, vol. I
Boyle, William Lewis, 1859–1918, vol. II
Boyle, Rev. William Skinner, 1844–1915, vol. I
Boyne, 8th Viscount, 1830–1907, vol. I
Boyne, 9th Viscount, 1864–1942, vol. IV
Boyne, 10th Viscount, 1931–1995, vol. IX
Boyne, Sir Harry; see Boyne, Sir H. B.
Boyne, Sir Henry Brian, (Sir Harry), 1910–1997, vol. X
Boyne, Robert John, died 1938, vol. III
Boynton, Sir Griffith Henry, 12th Bt, 1894–1937, vol. III
Boynton, Sir Griffith Wilfrid Norman, 13th Bt, 1889–1966, vol. VI
Boynton, Sir Henry Somerville, 11th Bt, 1844–1899, vol. I
Boynton, Captain Thomas Lamplugh W.; see Wickham-Boynton.
Boys, Sir Charles Vernon, 1855–1944, vol. IV
Boys, Sir Francis Theodore, 1870–1952, vol. V
Boys, Geoffrey Vernon, 1893–1945, vol. IV
Boys, Guy Ponsonby, 1871–1950, vol. IV
Boys, Henry Ward, 1874–1955, vol. V
Boys, Rt Rev. John, 1900–1972, vol. VII
Boys, Brig.-Gen. Reginald Harvey Henderson, 1867–1945, vol. IV
Boys-Smith, Captain Humphry Gilbert, 1904–1999, vol. X
Boys Smith, Rev. John Sandwith, 1901–1991, vol. IX
Boys-Smith, Winifred L., died 1939, vol. III
Boyson, Sir John Alexander, 1846–1926, vol. II
Boyton, Sir James, 1855–1926, vol. II
Bozman, Geoffrey Stephen, 1896–1973, vol. VII
Bozzoli, Guerino Renzo, 1911–1998, vol. X
Braadland, Erik, 1910–1988, vol. VIII
Brabant, Maj.-Gen. Sir Edward Yewd, 1839–1914, vol. I
Brabant, Rev. Frank Herbert, 1892–1972, vol. VII
Brabazon of Tara, 1st Baron, 1884–1964, vol. VI
Brabazon of Tara, 2nd Baron, 1910–1974, vol. VII
Brabazon, Maj.-Gen. Sir John Palmer, 1843–1922, vol. II
Brabin, Sir Daniel James, 1913–1975, vol. VII
Brabner, Rupert Arnold, 1911–1945, vol. IV
Brabourne, 2nd Baron, 1857–1909, vol. I
Brabourne, 3rd Baron, 1885–1915, vol. I
Brabourne, 4th Baron, 1863–1933, vol. III
Brabourne, 5th Baron, 1895–1939, vol. III
Brabourne, 6th Baron, 1922–1943, vol. IV

Brabrook, Sir Edward William, 1839–1930, vol. III
Braby, Frederick Cyrus, 1897–1983, vol. VIII
Brace, Col Henry Fergusson, 1888–1948, vol. IV
Brace, Sir Ivor Llewellyn, 1898–1952, vol. V
Brace, Rt Hon. William, 1865–1947, vol. IV
Bracegirdle, Rear-Adm. Sir Leighton Seymour, 1881–1970, vol. VI (AII)
Bracewell, Rev. Canon William, 1872–1954, vol. V
Bracewell-Smith, Sir George, (Sir Guy); see Smith.
Bracewell-Smith, Sir Guy; see Smith.
Bracewell-Smith, Sir Guy, 3rd Bt, 1952–1983, vol. VIII
Bracken, 1st Viscount, 1901–1958, vol. V
Bracken, Clio Hinton, died 1925, vol. II
Bracken, Sir Geoffrey Thomas Hirst, 1879–1951, vol. V
Brackenbury, Arthur Jocelyn, 1876–1935, vol. III
Brackenbury, Rev. Basil V. F., 1889–1965, vol. VI
Brackenbury, Sir Cecil Fabian, 1881–1958, vol. V
Brackenbury, Rt Hon. Gen. Sir Henry, 1837–1914, vol. I
Brackenbury, Sir Henry Britten, 1866–1942, vol. IV
Brackenbury, Col Henry Langton, 1868–1920, vol. II
Brackenbury, Hereward Irenius, died 1938, vol. III
Brackenbury, Adm. John William, 1842–1918, vol. II
Brackenbury, Laura, 1868–1937, vol. III
Brackenbury, Col Maule Campbell, 1844–1915, vol. I
Brackenridge, Sir Alexander, 1893–1964, vol. VI
Brackett, Oliver, 1875–1941, vol. IV
Brackley, Air Cdre Herbert George, 1894–1948, vol. IV
Bradbeer, Sir Albert Frederick, 1890–1963, vol. VI
Bradbrook, Muriel Clara, 1909–1993, vol. IX
Bradbury, 1st Baron, 1872–1950, vol. IV
Bradbury, 2nd Baron, 1914–1994, vol. IX
Bradbury, (Elizabeth) Joyce, 1918–1989, vol. VIII
Bradbury, John Buckley, 1841–1930, vol. III
Bradbury, Joyce; see Bradbury, E. J.
Bradbury, Sir Malcolm Stanley, 1932–2000, vol. X
Bradbury, Surg. Rear-Adm. William, 1884–1966, vol. VI
Bradby, Edward Lawrence, 1907–1996, vol. X
Bradby, Godfrey Fox, 1863–1947, vol. IV
Braddell, Darcy; see Braddell, T. A. D.
Braddell, Dorothy Adelaide, 1889–1981, vol. VIII
Braddell, Octavius Henry, 1843–1921, vol. II
Braddell, Sir Roland St John, 1880–1966, vol. VI
Braddell, (Thomas Arthur) Darcy, 1884–1970, vol. VI
Braddell, Sir Thomas de Multon Lee, 1856–1927, vol. II
Braddock, Mrs Elizabeth Margaret, 1899–1970, vol. VI
Braddock, Geoffrey Frank, 1881–1966, vol. VI
Braddock, Thomas, 1887–1976, vol. VII
Braddon, Rt Hon. Sir Edward Nicholas Coventry, 1829–1904, vol. I
Braddon, Hon. Sir Henry Yule, 1863–1955, vol. V
Braddon, Mary Elizabeth, (Mrs John Maxwell), 1837–1915, vol. I
Braddon, Russell Reading, 1921–1995, vol. IX
Brade, Sir Reginald Herbert, 1864–1933, vol. III

Braden, Bernard, 1916–1993, vol. IX
Bradfield, Lt-Gen. Sir Ernest William Charles, 1880–1963, vol. VI
Bradfield, Rt Rev. Harold William, 1898–1960, vol. V
Bradfield, John Job Crew, 1867–1943, vol. IV
Bradfield, William Walter, 1879–1925, vol. II
Bradford, 3rd Earl of, 1819–1898, vol. I
Bradford, 4th Earl of, 1845–1915, vol. I
Bradford, 5th Earl of, 1873–1957, vol. V
Bradford, 6th Earl of, 1911–1981, vol. VIII
Bradford, Rev. E. E., 1860–1944, vol. IV
Bradford, Adm. Sir Edward Eden, 1858–1935, vol. III
Bradford, Major Sir Edward Montagu Andrew, 3rd Bt (cr 1902), 1910–1952, vol. V
Bradford, Col Sir Edward Ridley Colborne, 1st Bt (cr 1902), 1836–1911, vol. I
Bradford, Ernle, 1922–1986, vol. VIII
Bradford, Lt-Col Sir Evelyn Ridley, 2nd Bt (cr 1902), 1869–1914, vol. I
Bradford, Sir James, 1841–1930, vol. III
Bradford, Sir John Ridley Evelyn, 4th Bt (cr 1902), 1941–1954, vol. V
Bradford, Sir John Rose, 1st Bt (cr 1931), 1863–1935, vol. III
Bradford, Ven. Richard Bleaden, 1913–1980, vol. VII
Bradford, Rev. Robert John, 1941–1981, vol. VIII
Bradford, Lt-Col Roland Boys, 1892–1917, vol. II
Bradford, Rt Hon. Roy Hamilton, 1921–1998, vol. X
Bradford, Samuel Clement, 1878–1948, vol. IV
Bradford, Sir Thomas Andrews, 1886–1966, vol. VI
Bradford, Wat; see Woodgate, W. B.
Bradford, William Vincent, 1883–1974, vol. VII
Bradford, Lt-Gen. Wilmot Henry, 1815–1914, vol. I
Brading, Keith, 1917–1996, vol. X
Brading, Brig. Norman Baldwin, 1896–1990, vol. VIII
Bradlaw, Sir Robert (Vivian), 1905–1992, vol. IX
Bradley, Miss; see Field, Michael.
Bradley, Albert James, 1899–1972, vol. VII
Bradley, Andrew Cecil, 1851–1935, vol. III
Bradley, Arthur Granville, 1850–1943, vol. IV
Bradley, Col Sir (Augustus) Montague, 1865–1953, vol. V
Bradley, Sir Burton Gyrth, B.; see Burton-Bradley.
Bradley, Brig.-Gen. Charles Edward, 1852–1931, vol. III
Bradley, Rev. Charles Lister, 1880–1957, vol. V
Bradley, Col Edward de Winton Herbert, 1889–1964, vol. VI
Bradley, Francis Ernest, died 1933, vol. III
Bradley, Francis Herbert, 1846–1924, vol. II
Bradley, Rear-Adm. Frederic Cyril, 1888–1957, vol. V
Bradley, Lt-Col Frederick Gardner, 1860–1935, vol. III
Bradley, Gladys Lilian, died 1978, vol. VII
Bradley, Harry, 1897–1982, vol. VIII
Bradley, Henry, 1845–1923, vol. II
Bradley, Herbert, 1856–1923, vol. II
Bradley, Herbert Dennis, 1878–1934, vol. III

Bradley, Air Marshal Sir John Stanley Travers, 1888–1982, vol. VIII
Bradley, Sir Kenneth Granville, 1904–1977, vol. VII
Bradley, Leslie Ripley, 1892–1968, vol. VI
Bradley, Col Sir Montague; see Bradley, Col Sir A. M.
Bradley, General of the Army Omar Nelson, 1893–1981, vol. VIII
Bradley, Orlando Charnock, 1871–1937, vol. III
Bradley, Peter Colley S.; see Sylvester-Bradley.
Bradley, Reginald Livingstone, 1894–1977, vol. VII
Bradley, Lt-Col Robert Anstruther, 1879–1965, vol. VI
Bradley, Thomas John, 1857–1936, vol. III
Bradley, Thomas Losco, 1869–1930, vol. III
Bradley, William, 1903–1972, vol. VII
Bradley-Birt, Francis Bradley, 1874–1963, vol. VI
Bradley-Williams, Col William Picton, 1890–1981, vol. VIII
Bradly, Henry George, 1876–1938, vol. III
Bradnack, Brian Oswald, 1898–1973, vol. VII
Bradney, George Preston, 1877–1959, vol. V
Bradney, Col Sir Joseph Alfred, 1859–1933, vol. III
Bradshaw, Mrs Albert S., died 1938, vol. III
Bradshaw, Surg.-Maj.-Gen. Sir (Alexander) Frederick, 1834–1923, vol. II
Bradshaw, Brig.-Gen. Charles Richard, 1873–1940, vol. III
Bradshaw, Constance H., died 1961, vol. VI
Bradshaw, Eric, 1909–1961, vol. VI
Bradshaw, Evelyn, 1862–1952, vol. V
Bradshaw, Surg.-Maj.-Gen. Sir Frederick; see Bradshaw, Surg.-Maj.-Gen. A. F.
Bradshaw, George Fagan, 1887–1960, vol. V
Bradshaw, Brig. George Rowley, 1898–1976, vol. VII
Bradshaw, Harold Chalton, 1893–1943, vol. IV
Bradshaw, Maj.-Gen. Laurence Julius Elliott, 1857–1929, vol. III
Bradshaw, Maurice Bernard, 1903–1991, vol. IX
Bradshaw, Octavius, 1845–1928, vol. II
Bradshaw, Lt-Gen. Sir Richard Phillip, 1920–1999, vol. X
Bradshaw, Thomas R., 1857–1927, vol. II
Bradshaw, Thornton Frederick, 1917–1988, vol. VIII
Bradshaw, William, 1844–1927, vol. II
Bradshaw, Sir William, 1876–1955, vol. V
Bradshaw, William Graham, 1861–1941, vol. IV
Bradshaw, Maj.-Gen. William Pat Arthur, 1897–1966, vol. VI
Bradshaw-Isherwood, Christopher William; see Isherwood.
Bradshaw-Isherwood, John Henry; see Isherwood.
Bradstock, Major George, died 1966, vol. VI
Bradstreet, Sir Edmond Simon, 6th Bt, 1820–1905, vol. I
Bradstreet, Sir Edward Simon Victor, 7th Bt, 1856–1924, vol. II
Bradwell, Baron (Life Peer); Thomas Edward Neil Driberg, 1905–1976, vol. VII
Brady, Sir Andrew N.; see Newton-Brady.
Brady, Sir Francis William, 2nd Bt, 1824–1909, vol. I

Brady, George Stewardson, 1832–1921, vol. II
Brady, Major Gerald Charles Jervis, died 1941, vol. IV
Brady, Rev. Canon Henry Westby, 1884–1934, vol. III
Brady, Patrick Joseph, 1868–1943, vol. IV
Brady, Sir Robert Maziere, 3rd Bt, 1854–1909, vol. I
Brady, Sir Thomas Francis, 1824–1904, vol. I
Brady, Thomas John Bellingham, 1841–1910, vol. I
Brady, Major Sir William Longfield, 4th Bt, 1864–1927, vol. II
Brækstad, H. L., 1845–1915, vol. I
Bragg, Sir Lawrence; see Bragg, Sir W. L.
Bragg, Sir William Henry, 1862–1942, vol. IV
Bragg, Sir (William) Lawrence, 1890–1971, vol. VII
Bragge, Rev. Charles Albert, died 1923, vol. II
Braggins, Maj.-Gen. Derek Henry, 1931–1999, vol. X
Braham, Dudley Disraeli, 1875–1951, vol. V
Braham, Harold, 1907–1995, vol. IX
Braham, Harry Vincent, 1886–1938, vol. III
Brahms, Caryl, (Doris Caroline Abrahams), 1901–1982, vol. VIII
Braidwood, Harold Lithgow, 1872–1949, vol. IV
Brailey, William A., died 1915, vol. I
Brailsford, Frederick, 1903–1985, vol. VIII
Brailsford, Henry Noel, 1873–1958, vol. V
Brailsford, John William, 1918–1988, vol. VIII
Brain, 1st Baron, 1895–1966, vol. VI
Brain, Dennis, 1921–1957, vol. V
Brain, Sir Francis William Thomas, 1855–1921, vol. II
Brain, Sir Hugh Gerner, 1890–1976, vol. VII
Brain, Lawrence L.; see Lewton-Brain.
Brain, Reginald T., 1894–1971, vol. VII
Brain, Ronald, 1914–1989, vol. VIII
Braine of Wheatley, Baron (Life Peer); Bernard Richard Braine, 1914–2000, vol. X
Braine, Brig. Herbert Edmund Reginald Rubens, 1876–1942, vol. IV
Braine, John Gerard, 1922–1986, vol. VIII
Braine, Rear-Adm. Richard Allix, 1900–1998, vol. X
Braintree, 1st Baron, 1884–1961, vol. VI
Brais, (François) Philippe, 1894–1972, vol. VII
Brais, Philippe; see Brais, F. P.
Braithwaite, Major Sir Albert Newby, 1893–1959, vol. V
Braithwaite, Charles, died 1941, vol. IV
Braithwaite, Air Vice-Marshal Francis Joseph St George, 1907–1956, vol. V
Braithwaite, Col Francis Powell, 1875–1952, vol. V
Braithwaite, Major John, 1871–1940, vol. III
Braithwaite, Sir John Bevan, 1884–1973, vol. VII
Braithwaite, Sir Joseph Gurney, 1st Bt, 1895–1958, vol. V
Braithwaite, Vice-Adm. Lawrence Walter, 1878–1961, vol. VI
Braithwaite, Dame Lilian, 1873–1948, vol. IV
Braithwaite, Rev. Philip Richard Pipon, 1849–1933, vol. III
Braithwaite, Richard Bevan, 1900–1990, vol. VIII
Braithwaite, Robert, 1824–1917, vol. II

Braithwaite, Gen. Sir Walter Pipon, 1865–1945, vol. IV
Braithwaite, Warwick, 1896–1971, vol. VII
Braithwaite, William Charles, 1862–192, vol. II
Braithwaite, Brig.-Gen. William Garnett, 1870–1937, vol. III
Braithwaite, William John, 1875–1938, vol. III
Brake, Sir Francis, 1889–1960, vol. V
Brake, Brig.-Gen. Herbert Edward John, 1866–1936, vol. III
Brakenridge, Col Francis John, 1871–1955, vol. V
Brakspear, Sir Harold, 1870–1934, vol. III
Braley, Rev. Evelyn Foley, 1884–1963, vol. VI
Bramah, David, 1875–1947, vol. IV
Bramah, Ernest, *died* 1942, vol. IV
Bramall, Sir Ashley; *see* Bramall, Sir E. A.
Bramall, Sir (Ernest) Ashley, 1916–1999, vol. X
Brambell, Francis William Rogers, 1901–1970, vol. VI
Bramble, Courtenay Parker, 1900–1987, vol. VIII
Bramble, Paymaster Rear-Adm. James, 1850–1930, vol. III
Brame, John Samuel Strafford, 1871–1952, vol. V
Brameld, Rev. William Arthur, *died* 1922, vol. II
Bramley, Frank, 1857–1915, vol. I
Bramley, Fred, 1874–1925, vol. II
Bramley, Rev. Henry Ramsden, 1833–1917, vol. II
Bramley-Moore, Rev. William, 1831–1918, vol. II
Brammer, Leonard Griffith, 1906–1994, vol. IX
Brampton, 1st Baron, 1817–1907, vol. I
Bramsdon, Sir Thomas Arthur, 1857–1935, vol. III
Bramston, Sir John, 1832–1921, vol. II
Bramston, Rev. John Trant, *died* 1931, vol. III
Bramwell, Sir Byrom, 1847–1931, vol. III
Bramwell, Edward George, 1865–1944, vol. IV
Bramwell, Edwin, 1873–1952, vol. V
Bramwell, Sir Frederick Joseph, 1st Bt, 1818–1903, vol. I
Bramwell, John Crighton, 1889–1976, vol. VII
Bramwell, John Milne, 1852–1925, vol. II
Bramwell-Booth, Catherine, 1883–1987, vol. VIII
Bramwell Davis, Maj.-Gen. Ronald Albert, 1905–1974, vol. VII
Branch, Sir (Charles Ernest) St John, *died* 1939, vol. III
Branch, James, 1845–1918, vol. II
Branch, Sir St John; *see* Branch, Sir C. E. St J.
Branch, Ven. Samuel Edmund, 1861–1932, vol. III
Branch, Sir William Allan Patrick, 1915–1993, vol. IX
Brancker, Sir (John Eustace) Theodore, 1909–1996, vol. X
Brancker, Air Vice-Marshal Sir Sefton; *see* Brancker, Air Vice-Marshal Sir W. S.
Brancker, Sir Theodore; *see* Brancker, Sir J. E. T.
Brancker, Air Vice-Marshal Sir (William) Sefton, 1877–1930, vol. III
Brand, 1st Baron, 1878–1963, vol. VI
Brand, Hon. Lord; David William Robert Brand, 1923–1996, vol. X
Brand, Sir Alfred; *see* Brand, Sir W. A.
Brand, Hon. Arthur George, 1853–1917, vol. II
Brand, Hon. Charles, 1855–1912, vol. I
Brand, Maj.-Gen. Charles Henry, 1873–1961, vol. VI

Brand, (Charles) Neville, 1895–1951, vol. V
Brand, Air Vice-Marshal Sir (Christopher Joseph) Quintin, 1893–1968, vol. VI
Brand, Sir David, 1837–1908, vol. I
Brand, Hon. Sir David, 1912–1979, vol. VII
Brand, Col David Ernest, 1884–1948, vol. IV
Brand, David William Robert; *see* Brand, Hon. Lord.
Brand, Ferdinand, 1846–1922, vol. II
Brand, Sir Harry F., 1873–1951, vol. V
Brand, Adm. Hon. Sir Hubert George, 1870–1955, vol. V
Brand, James, 1843–1907, vol. I
Brand, Engr-Captain James John Cantley, 1880–1952, vol. V
Brand, Lt-Col John Charles, 1885–1929, vol. III
Brand, Neville; *see* Brand, C. N.
Brand, Air Vice-Marshal Sir Quintin; *see* Brand, Air Vice-Marshal Sir C. J. Q.
Brand, Hon. Roger, 1880–1945, vol. IV
Brand, Rear-Adm. Hon. Thomas Seymour, 1847–1916, vol. II
Brand, Sir (William) Alfred, 1888–1979, vol. VII (AII)
Brandeis, Louis Dembitz, 1856–1941, vol. IV
Brander, George Maconachie, 1906–1977, vol. VII
Brander, Col Herbert Ralph, 1861–1933, vol. III
Brander, Maj.-Gen. Maxwell Spieker, 1884–1972, vol. VII
Brander, William Browne, 1880–1951, vol. V
Brandes, George, 1842–1927, vol. II
Brandin, Louis M., 1874–1940, vol. III
Brandis, Sir Dietrich, 1824–1907, vol. I
Brandon of Oakbrook, Baron (Life Peer); Henry Vivian Brandon, 1920–1999, vol. X
Brandon, Henry; *see* Brandon, Oscar H.
Brandon, Very Rev. Lowther E., *died* 1933, vol. III
Brandon, Col Oscar Gilbert, 1876–1968, vol. VI
Brandon, (Oscar) Henry, 1916–1993, vol. IX
Brandon, Percy Samuel, (Peter), 1916–1991, vol. IX
Brandon, Peter; *see* Brandon, Percy S.
Brandon, Rev. Samuel George Frederick, 1907–1971, vol. VII
Brandon, Captain Vivian R., 1882–1944, vol. IV
Brandram, Rosina, *died* 1907, vol. I
Brandt, William, (Bill Brandt), 1904–1983, vol. VIII
Brandt, Willy, 1913–1992, vol. IX
Branfill Harrison, Col Cholmeley Edward Carl; *see* Harrison.
Branfoot, Surg.-Gen. Sir Arthur Mudge, 1848–1914, vol. I
Brangwyn, Sir Frank, 1867–1956, vol. V
Branigan, Sir Patrick Francis, 1906–2000, vol. X
Branly, Edouard, 1844–1940, vol. III
Brannan, Charles Franklin, 1903–1992, vol. IX
Branner, John Casper, 1850–1922, vol. II
Brannigan, Owen, 1908–1973, vol. VII
Branson, Col Sir Douglas Stephenson, 1893–1981, vol. VIII
Branson, Rt Hon. Sir George Arthur Harwin, 1871–1951, vol. V
Branson, William Philip Sutcliffe, 1874–1950, vol. IV
Branson, William Rainforth, 1905–1997, vol. X

Brant, Richard William, 1852–1934, vol. III
Branthwaite, Robert Welsh, 1859–1929, vol. III
Braque, Georges, 1882–1963, vol. VI
Brash, James Couper, 1886–1958, vol. V
Brash, William Bardsley, 1877–1952, vol. V
Brasher, William Kenneth, 1897–1972, vol. VII
Braslau, Sophie, died 1935, vol. III
Brasnett, Rev. Bertrand Rippington, 1893–1988, vol. VIII
Brass, John, 1908–1999, vol. X
Brass, Sir Leslie Stuart, 1891–1958, vol. V
Brass, William, 1921–1999, vol. X
Brassey, 1st Earl, 1836–1918, vol. II
Brassey, 2nd Earl, 1863–1919, vol. II
Brassey of Apethorpe, 1st Baron, 1870–1958, vol. V
Brassey of Apethorpe, 2nd Baron, 1905–1967, vol. VI
Brassey, Albert, 1844–1918, vol. II
Brassey, Lt-Col Edgar Hugh, 1878–1946, vol. IV
Brassey, Captain Harold Ernest, 1877–1916, vol. II
Brassey, Col Sir Hugh Trefusis, 1915–1990, vol. VIII
Brassey, Lt-Col Hon. Peter Esmé, 1907–1995, vol. IX
Brassey, Captain Robert Bingham, 1875–1946, vol. IV
Brassington, William Salt, 1859–1939, vol. III
Bratby, John Randall, 1928–1992, vol. IX
Brattain, Walter Houser, 1902–1987, vol. VIII
Bratton, Rt Rev. Theodore Du Bose, 1862–1944, vol. IV
Braude, Ernest Alexander Rudolph, 1922–1956, vol. V
Braudel, Fernand, 1902–1985, vol. VIII
Braun, Adolphe Armand, 1869–1938, vol. III
Braund, Sir Henry Benedict Linthwaite, 1893–1969, vol. VI
Braunholtz, Eugen Gustav Wilhelm, 1859–1941, vol. IV
Braunholtz, Gustav Ernst Karl, 1887–1967, vol. VI
Braunholtz, Hermann Justus, 1888–1963, vol. VI
Bray, Maj.-Gen. Sir Claude Arthur, 1858–1934, vol. III
Bray, Sir Denys de Saumarez, 1875–1951, vol. V
Bray, Sir Edward, 1849–1926, vol. II
Bray, Sir Edward Hugh, 1874–1950, vol. IV
Bray, Francis Edmond, 1882–1950, vol. IV
Bray, Frederick, 1895–1977, vol. VII
Bray, Col George Arthur Theodore, 1864–1933, vol. III
Bray, Col Hubert Alaric, 1867–1935, vol. III
Bray, Captain Sir Jocelyn, 1880–1964, vol. VI
Bray, Hon. John Jefferson, 1912–1995, vol. IX
Bray, Rt Rev. Patrick Albert, 1883–1953, vol. V
Bray, Sir Reginald More, 1842–1923, vol. II
Bray, Brig.-Gen. Robert Napier, 1872–1921, vol. II
Bray, Gen. Sir Robert Napier Hubert Campbell, 1908–1983, vol. VIII
Bray, Ronald William Thomas, 1922–1984, vol. VIII
Bray, Sir Theodor Charles, 1905–2000, vol. X
Braybrooke, 5th Baron, 1823–1902, vol. I
Braybrooke, 6th Baron, 1827–1904, vol. I
Braybrooke, 7th Baron, 1855–1941, vol. IV
Braybrooke, 8th Baron, 1918–1943, vol. IV

Braybrooke, 9th Baron, 1897–1990, vol. VIII
Brayden, William Henry, 1865–1933, vol. III
Braye, 5th Baron, 1849–1928, vol. II
Braye, 6th Baron, 1874–1952, vol. V
Braye, 7th Baron, 1902–1985, vol. VIII
Braye, Philip George, 1894–1956, vol. V
Brayley, Baron (Life Peer); (John) Desmond Brayley. 1917–1977, vol. VII
Brayn, Sir Richard, 1850–1912, vol. I
Brayne, Albert Frederic Lucas, 1884–1970, vol. VI
Brayne, Charles Valentine, 1877–1964, vol. VI
Brayne, Frank Lugard, 1882–1952, vol. V
Brayne-Baker, John, 1905–1996, vol. X
Brayne-Nicholls, Brian; see Brayne-Nicholls, F. B. P.
Brayne-Nicholls, Rear-Adm. (Francis) Brian (Price), 1914–1998, vol. X
Braynen, Sir Alvin Rudolph, 1904–1992, vol. IX
Brayshaw, (Alfred) Joseph, 1912–1994, vol. IX
Brayshaw, Joseph; see Brayshaw, A. J.
Brayshay, Sir Maurice William, 1883–1959, vol. V
Brazel, Claude Hamilton, 1894–1959, vol. V
Brazendale, George William, 1909–1990, vol. VIII
Brazier-Creagh, Col George Washington, 1858–1942, vol. IV
Brazil, Angela, 1868–1947, vol. IV
Braza, Pierre Paul François Camille de, Count de Savorgnan, 1852–1905, vol. I
Brazier, Rt Rev. Percy James, 1903–1989, vol. VIII
Breadalbane, 1st Marquis of, 1851–1922, vol. II
Breadalbane, 8th Earl of, 1885–1923, vol. II
Breadalbane and Holland, 9th Earl of, 1889–1959, vol. V
Breadalbane and Holland, 10th Earl of, 1919–1995, vol. X (AI)
Breading, Lt-Col George Remington, 1877–1942, vol. IV
Breadner, Air Chief Marshall Lloyd Samuel, 1894–1952, vol. V
Breadner, Robert Walker, 1865–1935, vol. III
Breakey, Air Vice-Marshal John Denis, 1899–1965, vol. VI
Breaks, Rear-Adm. James, 1895–1968, vol. VI
Breakspear, W. A., died 1914, vol. I
Brealey, William Ramsden, 1889–1949, vol. IV
Breare, William Robert Ackrill, 1916–1993, vol. IX
Brearley, Sir Norman, 1890–1989, vol. VIII
Breasted, James Henry, 1865–1935, vol. III
Brebner, Sir Alexander, 1883–1979, vol. VII
Brebner, Arthur, 1870–1922, vol. II
Brebner, John Bartlet, 1895–1957, vol. V
Brebner, Percy James, 1864–1922, vol. II
Brechin, Sir Herbert Archbold, 1903–1979, vol. VII
Brecknock, Marjorie Countess of, (Marjorie Minna), 1900–1989, vol. VIII
Brecon, 1st Baron, 1905–1976, vol. VII
Bredin, George Richard Frederick, 1899–1983, vol. VIII
Bredin, James John, 1924–1998, vol. X
Bredius, Abraham, 1855–1946, vol. IV
Bredon, Sir Robert Edward, 1846–1918, vol. II
Bree, Rt Rev. Herbert, 1828–1899, vol. I
Bree, Ven. William, 1822–1917, vol. II
Breech, Ernest Robert, 1897–1978, vol. VII
Breeks, Brig.-Gen. Richard William, 1863–1920, vol. II

Breen, Air Marshal John Joseph, 1896–1964, vol. VI
Breen, Dame Marie Freda, 1902–1993, vol. IX
Breen, Timothy Florence, 1885–1966, vol. VI
Breene, Very Rev. Richard Simmons, 1886–1974, vol. VII
Breese, Air-Cdre Charles Dempster, 1889–1941, vol. IV
Breese, Major Charles Edward, 1867–1932, vol. III
Breithaupt, Hon. Louis Orville, 1890–1960, vol. V
Brema, Marie, 1856–1925, vol. II
Bremer, Walther Erich Emanuel Friedrich, 1887–1926, vol. II
Bremner, Alexander, 1890–1944, vol. IV
Bremner, Brig.-Gen. Arthur Grant, 1867–1950, vol. IV (A)
Bremner, Lt-Col Claude E. U., 1891–1965, vol. VI
Bremner, Captain Donald, 1864–1935, vol. III
Bremond, L'Abbé Henri, 1865–1933, vol. III
Bremridge, Sir John Henry, 1925–1994, vol. IX
Brenan, Byron, 1847–1927, vol. II
Brenan, (Edward Fitz-) Gerald, 1894–1987, vol. VIII
Brenan, Gerald; see Brenan, E. F.
Brenan, James, 1837–1907, vol. I
Brenan, Sir John Fitzgerald, 1883–1953, vol. V
Brenan, John Patrick Micklethwait, 1917–1985, vol. VIII
Brenan, Terence Vincent, 1887–1974, vol. VII
Brenchley, Winifred Elsie, 1883–1953, vol. V
Brend, William A., 1873–1944, vol. IV
Brennan, Brian John, 1918–1998, vol. X
Brennan, Charles John, 1876–1972, vol. VII
Brennan, Hon. Frank, died 1950, vol. IV
Brennan, Joseph, 1887–1976, vol. VII
Brennan, Louis, 1852–1932, vol. III
Brennan, Lt-Gen. Michael, died 1986, vol. VIII
Brennan, Very Rev. Nicholas J., 1854–1928, vol. II
Brennan, Maj.-Gen. William Brian Francis, 1907–1977, vol. VII
Brennan, Hon. William Joseph, Jr, 1906–1997, vol. X
Brent, Rt Rev. Charles Henry, 1862–1929, vol. III
Brentano, Heinrich von, 1904–1964, vol. VI
Brentford, 1st Viscount, 1865–1932, vol. III
Brentford, 2nd Viscount, 1896–1958, vol. V
Brentford, 3rd Viscount, 1902–1983, vol. VIII
Brereton, Alfred, 1849–1926, vol. II
Brereton, Austin, 1862–1922, vol. II
Brereton, Cloudesley, 1863–1937, vol. III
Brereton, Brig.-Gen. Edward Fitzgerald, died 1937, vol. III
Brereton, Very Rev. Eric Hugh, 1889–1962, vol. VI
Brereton, Bt Lt-Col Frederick Sadleir, 1872–1957, vol. V
Brereton, John Le Gay, 1871–1933, vol. III
Brereton, Maud Adeline Cloudesley-, died 1946, vol. IV
Brereton, Reginald Hugh, 1861–1944, vol. IV
Brereton, William Westropp, 1845–1924, vol. II
Bressey, Sir Charles Herbert, 1874–1951, vol. V
Bresson, Robert, 1901–1999, vol. X
Breteuil, Marquis de; Henri Charles Joseph, 1848–1916, vol. II
Bretherton, Frederick S.; see Stapleton-Bretherton.

Bretherton, Major George Howard, 1860–1904, vol. I
Bretherton, Russell Frederick, 1906–1991, vol. IX
Breton, Jules, 1827–1906, vol. I
Breton, Virginie Demont, 1859–1935, vol. III
Bretscher, Egon, 1901–1973, vol. VII
Brett, Arthur Cyril Adair, 1882–1936, vol. III
Brett, Sir Cecil Michael Wilford, 1852–1938, vol. III
Brett, Major Charles Arthur Hugh, 1865–1914, vol. I
Brett, Sir Charles Henry, 1839–1926, vol. II
Brett, Cyril Templeton, 1885–1960, vol. V
Brett, Francis William, 1885–1936, vol. III
Brett, Lt-Gen. George Howard, 1886–1963, vol. VI
Brett, George Platt, 1858–1936, vol. III
Brett, George Platt, jun., 1893–1984, vol. VIII
Brett, George Sidney, 1879–1944, vol. IV
Brett, Sir Henry, 1843–1927, vol. II
Brett, Henry James, 1878–1963, vol. VI
Brett, Very Rev. Henry Robert, 1868–1932, vol. III
Brett, James; see Brett, L. J.
Brett, Jeremy, (Peter Jeremy William Huggins), 1935–1995, vol. IX
Brett, John, 1831–1902, vol. I
Brett, John Alfred, 1915–1996, vol. X
Brett, Lt-Col John Aloysius, 1879–1955, vol. V
Brett, Sir Lionel, 1911–1990, vol. VIII
Brett, (Louis) James, 1910–1975, vol. VII
Brett, Lt-Col Hon. Maurice Vyner Baliol, 1882–1934, vol. III
Brett, Raymond Laurence, 1917–1996, vol. X
Brett, Hon. Robert George, 1851–1929, vol. III
Brett, Brig. Rupert John, 1890–1963, vol. VI
Brett, Sir Wilford, 1824–1901, vol. I
Brett, William Bailie, 1889–1947, vol. IV
Brett-James, Antony; see Brett-James, E. A.
Brett-James, (Eliot) Antony, 1920–1984, vol. VIII
Brett Young, Francis; see Young, F. B.
Brettell, Frederick Gilbert, 1884–1965, vol. VI
Bretton, Very Rev. William Frederick, 1909–1971, vol. VII
Breuil, Abbé Henri Édouard Prosper, 1877–1961, vol. VI
Breul, Karl Herman, 1860–1932, vol. III
Breun, J. E., 1862–1921, vol. II
Brevitt, Sir Horatio, 1843–1933, vol. III
Brew, Robert John, 1838–1911, vol. I
Brewer, Sir (Alfred) Herbert, 1865–1928, vol. II
Brewer, David J., died 1910, vol. I
Brewer, Rev. Ebenezer Cobham, 1810–1897, vol. I
Brewer, Rev. Edward, died 1922, vol. II
Brewer, Frank, 1915–1987, vol. VIII
Brewer, Rear-Adm. George Maxted Kenneth, 1930–1998, vol. X
Brewer, Sir Henry Campbell, 1885–1963, vol. VI
Brewer, Sir Herbert; see Brewer, Sir A. H.
Brewer, Rt Rev. John, 1929–2000, vol. X
Brewer, Rt Rev. Leigh Richmond, 1839–1916, vol. II
Brewerton, Elmore, 1867–1962, vol. VI
Brewill, Lt-Col Arthur William, 1861–1923, vol. II
Brewin, Arthur Winbolt, 1867–1946, vol. IV
Brewin, Elizabeth Maud, (Mrs P. K. Brewin); see Pepperell, E. M.

Brewis, Captain Charles Richard Wynn, 1874–1953, vol. V

Brewis, (Henry) John, 1920–1989, vol. VIII

Brewis, John; see Brewis, H. J.

Brewis, John Fenwick, 1910–1986, vol. VIII

Brewis, Rev. John Salusbury, 1902–1972, vol. VII

Brewis, Nathaniel Thomas, died 1924, vol. II

Brewitt, Rev. James C., 1843–1905, vol. I

Brews, Alan; see Brews, R. A.

Brews, (Richard) Alan, 1902–1965, vol. VI

Brewster, Adolph Brewster, 1854–1937, vol. III

Brewster, Rt Rev. Benjamin, 1860–1941, vol. IV

Brewster, Rt Rev. Chauncey Bunce, 1848–1941, vol. IV

Brewster, Edward John, died 1931, vol. III

Brewster, George, 1899–1991, vol. IX

Brewster, Kingman, 1919–1988, vol. VIII

Brewster, Willoughby Staples, 1860–1932, vol. III

Brewtnall, Edward Frederick, 1846–1902, vol. I

Breymann, Dr Hermann Wilhelm, died 1910, vol. I

Brezhnev, Leonid Ilyich, 1906–1982, vol. VIII

Brian, Percy Wragg, 1910–1979, vol. VII

Briance, John Albert, 1915–1989, vol. VIII

Briand, Aristide, 1862–1932, vol. III

Briant, Bernard Christian, 1917–1993, vol. IX

Briant, Bruce Edgar Dutton, 1895–1959, vol. V

Briant, Frank, 1865–1934, vol. III

Briault, Eric William Henry, 1911–1996, vol. X

Brice, Arthur John Hallam Montefiore, died 1927, vol. II

Brice, Rev. Edward Henry, died 1952, vol. V

Brice, Geoffrey James Barrington Groves, 1938–1999, vol. X

Brice, Seward, 1846–1914, vol. I

Brickdale, Sir Charles F.; see Fortescue-Brickdale.

Brickdale, Eleanor F.; see Fortescue-Brickdale.

Brickdale, John Matthew F.; see Fortescue-Brickdale.

Brickell, Daniel Francis Horseman, 1893–1967, vol. VI

Bricker, John William, 1893–1986, vol. VIII

Brickhill, Paul Chester Jerome, 1916–1991, vol. IX

Brickman, Brig. Ivan Pringle, 1891–1980, vol. VII

Brickwell, Alfred James, 1870–1937, vol. III

Brickwood, Sir John, 1st Bt, 1852–1932, vol. III

Brickwood, Sir Rupert Redvers, 2nd Bt, 1900–1974, vol. VII

Bridge, Ann, (Lady O'Malley), 1891–1974, vol. VII

Bridge, Adm. Sir (Arthur) Robin (Moore), 1894–1971, vol. VII

Bridge, Brig. Charles Edward Dunscomb, 1886–1961, vol. VI

Bridge, Brig.-Gen. Sir Charles Henry, 1852–1926, vol. II

Bridge, Adm. Sir Cyprian Arthur George, 1839–1924, vol. II

Bridge, Frank, 1879–1941, vol. IV

Bridge, Sir Frederick, 1844–1924, vol. II

Bridge, George Wilfred, 1894–1971, vol. VII

Bridge, Sir John, 1824–1900, vol. I

Bridge, John Crosthwaite, 1877–1947, vol. IV

Bridge, Joseph Cox, 1853–1929, vol. III

Bridge, Joseph James Rabnett, 1875–1959, vol. V

Bridge, Peter Gonzalez, 1885–1942, vol. IV

Bridge, Adm. Sir Robin; see Bridge, Adm. Sir A. R. M.

Bridge, Roy Arthur Odell, 1911–1978, vol. VII

Bridge, Maj.-Gen. Thomas Field Dunscomb, 1847–1934, vol. III

Bridge, Thomas William, 1848–1909, vol. I

Bridgeford, Lt-Gen. Sir William, 1894–1971, vol. VII

Bridgeman, 1st Viscount, 1864–1935, vol. III

Bridgeman, 2nd Viscount, 1896–1982, vol. VIII

Bridgeman, Viscountess; (Caroline Beatrix), died 1961, vol. VI

Bridgeman, Brig.-Gen. Hon. Francis Charles, 1846–1917, vol. II

Bridgeman, Adm. Sir Francis Charles Bridgeman-, 1848–1929, vol. III

Bridgeman, Hon. Geoffrey John Orlando, 1898–1974, vol. VII

Bridgeman, Col Hon. Henry George Orlando, 1882–1972, vol. VII

Bridgeman, John Wilfred, 1895–1992, vol. IX

Bridgeman, Hon. Sir Maurice Richard, 1904–1980, vol. VII

Bridgeman, Reginald Francis Orlando, 1884–1968, vol. VI

Bridgeman-Bridgeman, Adm. Sir Francis Charles; see Bridgeman.

Bridger, Rev. John, died 1911, vol. I

Bridger, Pearl, 1912–2000, vol. X

Bridges, 1st Baron, 1892–1969, vol. VI

Bridges, Col Arthur Holroyd, 1871–1953, vol. V

Bridges, Daisy Caroline, 1894–1972, vol. VII

Bridges, Sir Ernest Arthur, 1880–1953, vol. V

Bridges, Col Francis Doveton, 1871–1954, vol. V

Bridges, Col George, 1876–1962, vol. VI

Bridges, Rev. Sir George Talbot, 1818–1899, vol. I

Bridges, Lt-Gen. Sir (George) Tom (Molesworth), 1871–1939, vol. III

Bridges, Rear-Adm. Henry Dalrymple, 1881–1955, vol. V

Bridges, Col James Whiteside, 1863–1930, vol. III

Bridges, John Gourlay, 1901–1985, vol. VIII

Bridges, John Henry, 1832–1906, vol. I

Bridges, John Henry, 1852–1925, vol. II

Bridges, Lt-Col Lionel Forbes, 1871–1937, vol. III

Bridges, Robert, 1844–1930, vol. III

Bridges, Robert, 1858–1941, vol. IV

Bridges, Roy, 1885–1952, vol. V

Bridges, Lt-Gen. Sir Tom; see Bridges, Lt-Gen. Sir G. T. M.

Bridges, Rear-Adm. Walter Bogue, 1843–1917, vol. II

Bridges, Brig.-Gen. William Throsby, 1861–1915, vol. I

Bridges-Adams, John Nicholas William, 1930–1998, vol. X

Bridges-Adams, William, 1889–1965, vol. VI

Bridgewater, Bentley Powell Conyers, 1911–1996, vol. X

Bridgewater, Francis Matthew, 1851–1915, vol. I

Bridgford, Col Sir Robert, 1836–1905, vol. I

Bridgford, Brig.-Gen. Robert James, 1869–1954, vol. V

Bridgland, Albert Stanford, died 1944, vol. IV

Bridgland, Sir Aynsley Vernon, 1893–1966, vol. VI

Bridgman, Leonard Logoz, 1895–1980, vol. VII
Bridgman, Percy Williams, 1882–1961, vol. VI
Bridie, James, (O. H. Mavor), 1888–1951, vol. V
Bridport, 1st Viscount, 1814–1904, vol. I
Bridport, 2nd Viscount, 1839–1924, vol. II
Bridport, 3rd Viscount, 1911–1969, vol. VI
Briercliffe, Sir Rupert, 1889–1975, vol. VII
Brierley, Col Sir Charles Isherwood, 1879–1940, vol. III
Brierley, Edgar, 1858–1927, vol. II
Brierley, Col Geoffrey Teale, 1873–1961, vol. VI
Brierley, Captain Henry, 1897–1981, vol. VIII
Brierley, J., 1843–1914, vol. I
Brierley, Rev. Canon John, 1886–1964, vol. VI
Brierley, William Broadhurst, 1889–1963, vol. VI
Brierley, Sir Zachry, 1920–1993, vol. IX
Brierly, James Leslie, 1881–1955, vol. V
Brieux, Eugene, 1858–1932, vol. III
Briffa, Col Alfred, 1868–1952, vol. V
Briffault, Robert Stephen, 1876–1948, vol. IV
Brigden, James Bristock, 1887–1950, vol. IV (A)
Brigg, Sir John, 1834–1911, vol. I
Briggs, Albert William, 1900–1971, vol. VII
Briggs, Sir (Alfred) George (Ernest), 1900–1976, vol. VII
Briggs, Arthur Beecham, 1883–1937, vol. III
Briggs, Prof. Charles Augustus, 1841–1913, vol. I
Briggs, Lt-Gen. Sir Charles James, 1865–1941, vol. IV
Briggs, Adm. Sir Charles John, 1858–1951, vol. V
Briggs, D. H. Currer, 1893–1974, vol. VII
Briggs, Lt-Col Ernest, 1881–1947, vol. IV
Briggs, Ernest Edward, 1866–1913, vol. I
Briggs, Sir Francis Arthur, 1902–1983, vol. VIII
Briggs, Sir Geoffrey Gould, 1914–1993, vol. IX
Briggs, Sir George; see Briggs, Sir A. G. E.
Briggs, George Edward, 1893–1985, vol. VIII
Briggs, Rev. Canon George Wallace, 1875–1959, vol. V
Briggs, Harold; see Briggs, W. J. H.
Briggs, Captain Harold Douglas, 1877–1944, vol. IV
Briggs, Lt-Gen. Sir Harold Rawdon, 1894–1952, vol. V
Briggs, Hon. Sir Henry, born 1844, vol. II
Briggs, Henry, 1883–1935, vol. III
Briggs, Henry, died 1944, vol. IV
Briggs, James, 1855–1933, vol. III
Briggs, Sir John Henry, 1808–1897, vol. I
Briggs, Martin Shaw, 1882–1977, vol. VII
Briggs, Col Norman, 1891–1960, vol. V
Briggs, Percy, 1903–1980, vol. VII
Briggs, Rev. Rawdon, 1853–1936, vol. III
Briggs, Brig. Rawdon, 1892–1960, vol. V
Briggs, Maj.-Gen. Raymond, 1895–1985, vol. VIII
Briggs, Thomas, 1847–1934, vol. III
Briggs, Rear-Admiral Thomas Vallack, 1906–1999, vol. X
Briggs, (W. J.) Harold, 1870–1945, vol. IV
Briggs, Waldo Raven, 1883–1956, vol. V
Briggs, William, 1861–1932, vol. III
Briggs, Col William Hilton, 1871–1951, vol. V
Brighouse, Harold, 1882–1958, vol. V
Brighouse, Sir Samuel, died 1940, vol. III
Bright, Alfred Ernest, 1869–1938, vol. III
Bright, Allan Heywood, 1862–1941, vol. IV

Bright, Sir Charles, 1863–1937, vol. III
Bright, Charles Edward, 1829–1915, vol. I
Bright, Sir Charles Hart, 1912–1983, vol. VIII
Bright, Ernest Henry, 1864–1937, vol. III
Bright, Mrs Golding; see Egerton, George.
Bright, Ven. Hugh, 1867–1935, vol. III
Bright, Rt Rev. Humphrey Penderell, 1903–1964, vol. VI
Bright, Rt Hon. Jacob, 1821–1899, vol. I
Bright, James Franck, 1832–1920, vol. II
Bright, John Albert, 1848–1924, vol. II
Bright, Sir Joseph, 1849–1918, vol. II
Bright, Mary Chavelita; see Egerton, George.
Bright, Brig-Gen. Reginald Arthur, 1870–1942, vol. IV
Bright, Major Richard George Tyndall, 1872–1944, vol. IV
Bright, Rev. William, 1824–1901, vol. I
Bright, William Robert, 1857–1908, vol. I
Brighten, Lt-Col Edgar William, 1880–1966, vol. VI
Brightman, Rev. Frank Edward, 1856–1932, vol. III
Brightmore, A. W., 1864–1927, vol. II
Briginshaw, Baron (Life Peer); Richard William Briginshaw, 1908–1992, vol. IX
Brigstocke, Charles Reginald, 1876–1951, vol. V
Brigstocke, Geoffrey Reginald William, 1917–1974, vol. VII
Brigstocke, George Edward, died 1971, vol. VII
Brill, Abraham Arden, 1874–1948, vol. IV
Brillant, Jules-André, 1888–1973, vol. VII
Billiant, Fredda, (Mrs Herbert Marshall), 1904–1999, vol. X
Brimacombe, Richard William, 1867–1930, vol. III
Brimble, Lionel John Farnham, 1904–1965, vol. VI
Brimelow, Baron (Life Peer); Thomas Brimelow, 1915–1995, vol. IX
Brims, Charles William, 1877–1944, vol. IV
Brinckman, Col Sir Roderick Napoleon, 5th Bt, 1902–1985, vol. VIII
Brinckman, Major Sir Theodore Ernest Warren, 4th Bt, 1898–1954, vol. V
Brinckman, Col Sir Theodore Francis, 3rd Bt, 1862–1937, vol. III
Brinckman, Sir Theodore Henry, 2nd Bt, 1830–1905, vol. I
Brind, Adm. Sir (Eric James) Patrick, 1892–1963, vol. VI
Brind, George Walter Richard, 1911–1988, vol. VIII
Brind, Gen. Sir John Edward Spencer, 1878–1954, vol. V
Brind, Adm. Sir Patrick; see Brind, Adm. Sir E. J. P.
Brind, Maj.-Gen. Peter Holmes Walter, 1912–1999, vol. X
Brindle, Harry, died 1976, vol. VII
Brindle, Rt Rev. Robert, 1837–1916, vol. II
Brindley, Harold Hulme, 1865–1944, vol. IV
Brine, Edgar, 1856–1932, vol. III
Brink, Charles Oscar, 1907–1994, vol. IX
Brink, Lt-Gen. George Edwin, 1889–1971, vol. VII
Brinkley, Captain Frank, 1841–1912, vol. I
Brinkley, Captain John Turner, 1855–1928, vol. II
Brinkworth, George Harold, 1906–1989, vol. VIII
Brinson, Derek Neilson, 1921–1974, vol. VII

Brinson, J. Paul, *died* 1927, vol. II
Brinton, Denis Hubert, 1902–1986, vol. VIII
Brinton, Maj. Sir (Esme) Tatton (Cecil), 1916–1985, vol. VIII
Brinton, Lt-Col John Chaytor, 1867–1956, vol. V
Brinton, Selwyn, *died* 1940, vol. III
Brinton, Major Sir Tatton; *see* Brinton, Major Sir E. T. C.
Brisbane, Arthur, 1864–1936, vol. III
Brisbane, Sir (Hugh) Lancelot, 1893–1966, vol. VI
Brisbane, Sir Lancelot; *see* Brisbane, Sir H. L.
Brisco, Sir Aubrey Hylton, 6th Bt, 1873–1957, vol. V
Brisco, Sir Donald Gilfrid, 8th Bt, 1920–1995, vol. IX
Brisco, Sir Hylton Musgrave Campbell, 7th Bt, 1886–1968, vol. VI
Brisco, Sir Hylton Ralph, 5th Bt, 1871–1922, vol. II
Brisco, Sir Musgrave Horton, 4th Bt, 1833–1909, vol. I
Briscoe, Sir Alfred Leigh, 2nd Bt, 1870–1921, vol. II
Briscoe, Arthur John Trevor, 1873–1943, vol. IV
Briscoe, Sir Charlton; *see* Briscoe, Sir J. C.
Briscoe, Major Edward William, 1857–1928, vol. II
Briscoe, Captain Henry Villiers, 1896–1983, vol. VIII
Briscoe, Henry Vincent Aird, 1888–1961, vol. VI
Briscoe, Hugh Kynaston, 1879–1956, vol. V
Briscoe, Sir James; *see* Briscoe, Sir John J.
Briscoe, Sir (John) Charlton, 3rd Bt, 1874–1960, vol. V
Briscoe, Sir John James, 1st Bt, 1836–1919, vol. II
Briscoe, Sir (John) James, 5th Bt, 1951–1994, vol. IX
Briscoe, Sir John Leigh Charlton, 4th Bt, 1911–1993, vol. IX
Briscoe, John Potter, 1848–1926, vol. II
Briscoe, Percy Charles, *died* 1951, vol. V
Briscoe, Captain Richard George, 1893–1957, vol. V
Briscoe, William Richard Brunskill, 1855–1930, vol. III
Brise, Archibald Weyland R.; *see* Ruggles-Brise.
Brise, Col Sir Edward Archibald R.; *see* Ruggles-Brise.
Brise, Sir Evelyn John R.; *see* Ruggles-Brise.
Brise, Captain Guy Edward R.; *see* Ruggles-Brise.
Brise, Maj.-Gen. Sir Harold Goodeve R.; *see* Ruggles-Brise.
Brise, Col Sir Samuel Ruggles, 1825–1899, vol. I
Brisson, Adolphe, *died* 1925, vol. II
Brisson, Henri, 1835–1912, vol. I
Brisson, Rosalind, (Mrs F. Brisson); *see* Russell, R.
Bristol, 3rd Marquis of, 1834–1907, vol. I
Bristol, 4th Marquis of, 1863–1951, vol. V
Bristol, 5th Marquess of, 1870–1960, vol. V
Bristol, 6th Marquess of, 1915–1985, vol. VIII
Bristol, 7th Marquess of, 1954–1999, vol. X
Bristol, Hon. Edmund, 1861–1927, vol. II
Bristol, Major Everett, 1888–1976, vol. VII
Bristow, Sir Charles Holditch, 1887–1967, vol. VI
Bristow, Ernest, 1873–1968, vol. VI
Bristow, Frederick George, *died* 1945, vol. IV
Bristow, Very Rev. John, *died* 1909, vol. I

Bristow, Rev. Richard Rhodes, *died* 1914, vol. I
Bristow, Sir Robert Charles, 1880–1966, vol. VI
Bristow, Walter Rowley, 1882–1947, vol. IV
Bristowe, Ethel Susan Graham, 1866–1952, vol. V
Bristowe, Samuel Botelen, *died* 1897, vol. I
Bristowe, William Syer, 1901–1979, vol. VII
Brittain, Alida Luisa, (Lady Brittain), *died* 1943, vol. IV
Brittain, Rev. Canon Arthur Henry Barrett, 1854–1911, vol. I
Brittain, Frederick, *died* 1969, vol. VI
Brittain, Sir Harry Ernest, 1873–1974, vol. VII
Brittain, Sir Herbert, 1894–1961, vol. VI
Brittain, John, 1849–1913, vol. I
Brittain, Vera, 1893–1970, vol. VI
Brittain, Rear-Adm. Wilfred Geoffrey, 1903–1979, vol. VII
Brittain, William Henry, 1835–1922, vol. II
Brittain, William James, 1905–1977, vol. VII
Brittan, Maj.-Gen. Charles Gisborne, 1860–1939, vol. III
Britten, Baron (Life Peer); (Edward) Benjamin Britten, 1913–1976, vol. VII
Britten, Benjamin; *see* Baron Britten.
Britten, Brig. Charles Richard, 1894–1984, vol. VIII
Britten, Comdr Sir Edgar Theophilus, 1874–1936, vol. III
Britten, Forester Richard John, 1928–1977, vol. VII
Britten, Brig. George Vallette, 1909–1997, vol. X
Britten, James, 1846–1924, vol. II
Britten, Rae Gordon, 1920–1997, vol. X
Britten, Rear-Adm. Richard Frederick, 1843–1910, vol. I
Britten, Maj.-Gen. Robert Wallace Tudor, 1922–1995, vol. IX
Brittlebank, Lt-Col Joseph William Forster, 1876–1944, vol. IV
Britton, Major Arthur Henry Daniel, 1875–1934, vol. III
Britton, Hon. Byron Moffat, 1833–1921, vol. II
Britton, Brig. Edwin John James, 1880–1955, vol. V
Britton, George Bryant, 1863–1929, vol. III
Britton, Hubert Thomas Stanley, 1892–1960, vol. V
Britton, Rev. Canon John, 1881–1948, vol. IV
Britton, Karl William, 1909–1983, vol. VIII
Britton, Major Philip William Poole C.; *see* Carlyon-Britton.
Brittorous, Brig. Francis Gerard Russell, 1896–1974, vol. VII
Broackes, Sir Nigel, 1934–1999, vol. X
Broad, Lt-Gen. Sir Charles Noel Frank, 1882–1976, vol. VII
Broad, Charlie Dunbar, 1887–1971, vol. VII
Broad, Francis Alfred, 1874–1956, vol. V
Broad, George Alexander, 1844–1915, vol. I
Broad, Philip, 1903–1966, vol. VI
Broad, William Henry, 1875–1948, vol. IV
Broadbent, A., *died* 1919, vol. II(A), vol. III
Broadbent, Albert, 1867–1912, vol. I
Broadbent, Benjamin, 1850–1925, vol. II
Broadbent, Donald Eric, 1926–93, vol. IX
Broadbent, Maj.-Gen. Sir Edward Nicholson, 1875–1944, vol. IV
Broadbent, Sir Ewen, 1924–1993, vol. IX

Broadbent, Sqdn Leader Sir George, 4th Bt, 1935–1992, vol. IX
Broadbent, Captain Harvey William, 1864–1942, vol. IV
Broadbent, Henry, 1852–1935, vol. III
Broadbent, Col John, 1872–1938, vol. III
Broadbent, Sir John, 2nd Bt, 1865–1946, vol. IV
Broadbent, Col John Edward, 1845–1931, vol. III
Broadbent, Joseph Edward, 1883–1948, vol. IV
Broadbent, Walter, died 1951, vol. V
Broadbent, Sir William Francis, 3rd Bt, 1904–1987, vol. VIII
Broadbent, Sir William Henry, 1st Bt, 1835–1907, vol. I
Broadbridge, 1st Baron, 1869–1952, vol. V
Broadbridge, 2nd Baron, 1895–1972, vol. VII
Broadbridge, 3rd Baron, 1938–2000, vol. X
Broadbridge, Stanley Robertson, 1828–1978, vol. VII
Broadfoot, Col Archibald, 1843–1926, vol. II
Broadfoot, Hon. Sir Walter James, 1881–1965, vol. VI
Broadfoot, Major William, 1841–1922, vol. II
Broadhead, Rt Rev. Mgr Joseph, 1860–1929, vol. III
Broadhurst, Sir Edward Tootal, 1st Bt, 1858–1922, vol. II
Broadhurst, George H., 1866–1952, vol. V
Broadhurst, Air Chief Marshal Sir Harry, 1905–1995, vol. IX
Broadhurst, Henry, 1840–1911, vol. I
Broadhurst, Mary Aadelaide, died 1928, vol. II
Broadley, Alexander Meyrick, 1847–1916, vol. II
Broadley, Henry Broadley Harrison-, 1853–1914, vol. I
Broadley, Sir Herbert, 1892–1983, vol. VIII
Broadmead, Sir Philip Mainwaring, 1893–1977, vol. VII
Broadrick, Edward George, 1864–1929, vol. III
Broadus, Edmund Kemper, 1876–1936, vol. III
Broadway, Sir Alan Brice, 1873–1948, vol. IV
Broadway, Leonard Marsham, 1903–1974, vol. VII
Broadwood, Brig.-Gen. Arthur, 1849–1928, vol. II
Broadwood, Bertha Marion, 1846–1935, vol. III
Broadwood, Captain Evelyn Henry Tschudi, 1889–1975, vol. VII
Broadwood, Lt-Gen. Robert George, 1862–1917, vol. II
Broatch, Surg. Rear-Adm. George Thomas, 1862–1945, vol. IV
Broatch, James, 1900–1986, vol. VIII
Brock, Baron (Life Peer); Russell Claude Brock, 1903–1980, vol. VII
Brock, Alan Francis C.; see Clutton-Brock.
Brock, Lt-Col Alec Walter Saumarez, 1878–1949, vol. IV
Brock, Arthur C.; see Clutton-Brock.
Brock, (Arthur) Guy C.; see Clutton-Brock.
Brock, Charles Edmund, 1870–1938, vol. III
Brock, Captain Donald Carey, 1891–1970, vol. VI
Brock, Dame Dorothy; see Brock, Dame M. D.
Brock, Adm. Sir Frederic Edward Errington, 1854–1929, vol. III
Brock, Brig.-Gen. Henry Jenkins, 1870–1933, vol. III

Brock, Air Cdre Henry Le Marchant, 1889–1946, vol. VI
Brock, Henry Matthew, 1875–1960, vol. V
Brock, Sir Laurence George 1879–1949, vol. IV
Brock, Dame (Madeline) Dorothy, 1886–1969, vol. VI
Brock, Adm. of the Fleet Sir Osmond de Beauvoir, 1869–1947, vol. IV
Brock, Rear-Adm. Patrick Willet, 1902–1988, vol. VIII
Brock, Reginald Walter, 1874–1935, vol. III
Brock, Sir Thomas, 1847–1922, vol. II
Brockbank, A. E., 1862–1958, vol. V
Brockbank, (James) Tyrrell, 1920–1995, vol. IX
Brockbank, (John) Philip, 1922–1989, vol. VIII
Brockbank, Philip; see Brockbank, J. P.
Brockbank, Russell Partridge, 1913–1979, vol. VII
Brockbank, Tyrrell; see Brockbank, J. T.
Brockbank, William, 1900–1984, vol. VIII
Brocket, 1st Baron, 1866–1934, vol. III
Brocket, 2nd Baron, 1904–1967, vol. VI
Brockhoff, Sir Jack Stuart, 1908–1984, vol. IX (AI)
Brockholes, John William F.; see Fitzherbert-Brockholes.
Brockholes, Michael John F.; see Fitzherbert-Brockholes.
Brockholes, William Joseph F.; see Fitzherbert-Brockholes.
Brockhurst, Gerald Leslie, 1890–1978, vol. VII
Brockie, Thomas, 1906–1976, vol. VII
Brockington, Rev. Alfred Allen, 1872–1938, vol. III
Brockington, Leonard Walter, 1888–1966, vol. VI
Brockington, Sir William Allport, 1871–1959, vol. V
Brocklebank, Sir Aubrey, 3rd Bt, 1873–1929, vol. III
Brocklebank, Sir (Clement) Edmund (Royds), 1882–1949, vol. IV
Brocklebank, Sir Edmund; see Brocklebank, Sir C. E. R.
Brocklebank, Captain Henry Cyril Royds, 1874–1957, vol. V
Brocklebank, Major John Jasper, 1875–1942, vol. IV
Brocklebank, Sir John Montague, 5th Bt, 1915–1974, vol. VII
Brocklebank, Mary Petrena; see Brocklebank, Mrs Thomas.
Brocklebank, Sir Thomas, 1st Bt, 1814–1906, vol. I
Brocklebank, Sir Thomas, 2nd Bt, 1848–1911, vol. I
Brocklebank, Thomas, 1841–1919, vol. II
Brocklebank, Mrs Thomas, (Mary Petrena Brocklebank), 1849–1937, vol. III
Brocklebank, Sir Thomas Aubrey Lawies, 4th Bt, 1899–1953, vol. V
Brocklehurst, Maj.-Gen. Arthur Evers, 1905–1998, vol. X
Brocklehurst, Charles Douglas Fergusson P.; see Phillips Brocklehurst.
Brocklehurst, Rev. Canon George, 1868–1946, vol. IV
Brocklehurst, Captain Henry Dent, 1855–1932, vol. III
Brocklehurst, Major John Henry Dent-, 1882–1949, vol. IV

Brocklehurst, Sir John Ogilvy, 3rd Bt, 1926–1981, vol. VIII
Brocklehurst, Mary D.; see Dent-Brocklehurst.
Brocklehurst, Sir Philip Lancaster, 1st Bt, 1827–1904, vol. I
Brocklehurst, Sir Philip Lee, 2nd Bt, 1887–1975, vol. VII
Brocklehurst, Robert James, 1899–1995, vol. IX
Brocklehurst, Robert Walter Douglas Phillips, 1861–1948, vol. IV
Brocklehurst, William Brocklehurst, 1851–1929, vol. III
Brockman, Brig.-Gen. David Henry D.; see Drake-Brockman.
Brockman, Sir Digby Livingstone D.; see Drake-Brockman.
Brockman, Maj.-Gen. Edmund Alfred D.; see Drake-Brockman.
Brockman, Sir Edward Lewis, 1865–1943, vol. IV
Brockman, Edward Phillimore, died 1977, vol. VII
Brockman, Engr Rear-Adm. Henry Stafford, 1884–1958, vol. V
Brockman, Sir Henry Vernon D.; see Drake-Brockman.
Brockman, Lt-Col Ralph Evelyn D.; see Drake-Brockman.
Brockman, Ralph St Leger, 1889–1975, vol. VII
Brockman, Vice-Adm. Sir Ronald, 1909–1999, vol. X
Brockman, Hon. Sir Thomas Charles D.; see Drake-Brockman.
Brockway, Baron (Life Peer); (Archibald) Fenner Brockway, 1888–1988, vol. VIII
Brockwell, Esca Powys Butler, died 1934, vol. III
Brockwell, Rev. Canon John Cornthwaite, 1843–1927, vol. II
Brockwell, Maurice Walter, 1869–1958, vol. V
Broderick, Sir John Joyce, 1882–1933, vol. III
Broderick, Brig. Ralph Aalexander, 1888–1971, vol. VII
Brodetsky, Selig, 1888–1954, vol. V
Brodeur, Hon. Louis Philippe, 1862–1924, vol. II
Brodeur, Rear-Adm. Victor Gabriel, 1892–1976, vol. VII
Brodhurst, Henry William Frederick Cottingham, 1856–1943, vol. IV
Brodhurst, James George Joseph P.; see Penderel-Brodhurst.
Brodie, Captain Sir Benjamin Collins, 4th Bt, 1888–1971, vol VII
Brodie, Sir Benjamin Vincent Sellon, 3rd Bt, 1862–1938, vol. III
Brodie, Colin Alexander, 1929–1999, vol. X
Brodie, Captain Ewen James, 1878–1914, vol. I
Brodie, George Bernard, 1839–1919, vol. II
Brodie, Harry Cunningham, 1875–1956, vol. V
Brodie of Brodie, Ian, 1868–1943, vol. IV
Brodie, Rabbi Sir Israel, 1895–1979, vol. VII
Brodie, John A., 1858–1934, vol. III
Brodie, Rt Rev. Matthew Joseph, 1864–1943, vol. IV
Brodie, Neil, 1900–1968, vol. VI
Brodie, Peter Ewen, 1914–1989, vol. VIII
Brodie, Very Rev. Peter Philip, 1916–1990, vol. VIII

Brodie, Maj.-Gen. Thomas, 1903–1993, vol. IX
Brodie, Thomas Gregor, 1866–1916, vol. II
Brodie, Thomas Vernor Alexander, 1907–1975, vol. VII
Brodie, Bt Major Walter Lorrain, 1884–1918, vol. II
Brodrick, Rev. Hon. Alan, 1840–1909, vol. I
Brodrick, Alan Houghton, died 1973, vol. VII
Brodrick, Hon. Arthur Grenville, 1868–1934, vol. III
Brodrick, Elizabeth Ann, 1942–1996, vol. X
Brodrick, Hon. George Charles, 1831–1903, vol. I
Brodrick, Norman John Lee, 1912–1992, vol. IX
Brodrick, Sir Thomas, 1856–1925, vol. II
Brodrick, William John Henry, 1874–1964, vol. VI
Brodrick, Brig. William Le Couteur, 1888–1973, vol. VII
Brodsky, Adolph, 1851–1929, vol. III
Brodsky, Joseph Alexandrovich, 1940–1996, vol. X
Brogan, Colm, 1902–1977, vol. VII
Brogan, Sir Denis William, 1900–1974, vol. VII
Brogan, Lt-Gen. Sir Mervyn Francis, 1915–1994, vol. IX
Broglie, Duc de, Maurice, 1875–1960, vol. V
Broke-Smith, Brig. Philip William Lilian, 1882–1963, vol. VI
Bromage, Lt-Col John Aldhelm Raikes, 1891–1955, vol. V
Bromby, Rt Rev. Charles Henry, 1814–1907, vol. I
Bromet, Air Vice-Marshal Sir Geoffrey Rhodes, 1891–1983, vol. VIII
Bromet, Air Comdt Dame Jean (Lena Annette), (Lady Bromet); see Conan Doyle, Air Comdt Dame J. L. A.
Bromet, Mary (Mrs Alfred Bromet); see Pownall, Mary.
Bromfield, Rev. George Henry Worth, 1842–1920, vol. II
Bromfield, Major Harry Hickman, 1869–1916, vol. II
Bromfield, Louis, 1896–1956, vol. V
Bromfield, William, 1868–1950, vol IV
Bromhead, Lt-Col Alfred Claude, 1876–1963, vol. VI
Bromhead, Sir Benjamin Denis Gonville, 5th Bt, 1900–1981, vol. VIII
Bromhead, Col Sir Benjamin Parnell, 4th Bt, 1838–1935, vol. III
Bromhead, Col Charles James, 1840–1922, vol. II
Bromilow, Maj.-Gen (David) George, 1884–1959, vol. V
Bromilow, Maj.-Gen. George; see Bromilow, Maj.-Gen. D. G.
Bromilow, Brig.-Gen. Walter, 1863–1939, vol. III
Bromilow, Rev. William E., 1857–1929, vol. III
Bromley, Rear-Adm. Sir Arthur, 8th Bt, 1876–1961, vol. VI
Bromley, Rear-Adm. Arthur Charles Burgoyne, died 1909, vol. I
Bromley, Sir Henry, 5th Bt, 1849–1905, vol. I
Bromley, Sir John, 1849–1915, vol. I
Bromley, John, 1876–1945, vol. IV
Bromley, Lancelot, 1885–1949, vol. IV
Bromley, Leonard John, 1929–1999, vol. X
Bromley, Sir Maurice, 7th Bt; see Bromley-Wilson.
Bromley, Sir Robert, 6th Bt, 1874–1906, vol. I

Bromley, Sir Rupert Howe, 9th Bt, 1910–1966, vol. VI

Bromley, Sir Thomas Eardley, 1911–1987, vol. VIII

Bromley-Davenport, Dame Lilian Emily Isabel Jane, 1878–1972, vol. VII

Bromley-Davenport, Mrs Muriel Coomber, 1879–1956, vol. V

Bromley-Davenport, Lt-Col Sir Walter Henry, 1903–1989, vol. VIII

Bromley-Davenport, Brig.-Gen. Sir William, 1862–1949, vol. IV

Bromley-Derry, Henry, 1885–1954, vol. V

Bromley-Martin, Granville Edward, *died* 1941, vol. IV

Bromley-Wilson, Sir Maurice, 7th Bt, 1875–1957, vol. V

Brommage, Joseph Charles, 1897–1972, vol. VII

Brommelle, Norman Spencer, 1915–1989, vol. VIII

Bromwich, Engr Rear-Adm. George Herbert, 1871–1965, vol. VI

Bromwich, T. J. I'anson, *died* 1929, vol. III

Bronk, Detlev Wulf, 1897–1975, vol. VII

Bronowski, Jacob, 1908–1974, vol. VII

Bronson, Howard Logan, 1878–1968, vol. VI

Broodbank, Sir Joseph Guinness, 1857–1944, vol. IV

Brook, Rev. Canon Alfred Eyre-, *died* 1949, vol. IV

Brook, Barnaby; *see* Brooks, W. C.

Brook, Caspar, 1920–1983, vol. VIII

Brook, Charles, 1866–1930, vol. III

Brook, Clive, 1887–1974, vol. II

Brook, Rev. David, 1854–1933, vol. III

Brook, Donald Charles, 1894–1976, vol. VII

Brook, Sir Dryden, 1884–1971, vol. VII

Brook, Maj.-Gen. Edmund Smith, 1845–1910, vol. I

Brook, Edward Jonas, 1865–1924, vol. II

Brook, Captain Edward William, 1895–1963, vol. VI

Brook, Lt-Col Sir Frank, 1883–1960, vol. V

Brook, George Leslie, 1910–1987, vol. VIII

Brook, Helen Grace Mary, (Lady Brook), 1907–1997, vol. X

Brook, Herbert Arthur, 1855–1925, vol. II

Brook, Cdre James Kenneth, 1889–1976, vol. VII

Brook, John Herbert, 1912–1963, vol. VI

Brook, Sir Ralph Ellis; *see* Brook, Sir Robin.

Brook, Bt Col Reginald James, 1885–1965, vol. VI

Brook, Rt Rev. Richard, 1880–1969, vol. VI

Brook, Sir Robin, 1908–1998, vol. X

Brook, Rev. Victor John Knight, 1887–1974, vol. VII

Brook, Air Vice-Marshal William Arthur Darville, 1901–1953, vol. V

Brook, William Edward, 1922–1993, vol. IX

Brook-Jackson, Rev. Canon Edwin, 1877–1936, vol. III

Brooke of Cumnor, Baron (Life Peer); Henry Brooke, 1903–1984, vol. VIII

Brooke of Oakley, 1st Baron, 1869–1944, vol. IV

Brooke of Ystradfellte, Baroness (Life Peer); Barbara Brooke, 1908–2000, vol. X

Brooke, Rev. Alan England, 1863–1939, vol. III

Brooke, Sir (Arthur) Douglas, 4th Bt (*cr* 1822), 1865–1907, vol. I

Brooke, Captain Basil Richard, 1882–1929, vol. III

Brooke, Vice-Adm. Basil Charles Barrington, 1895–1983, vol. VIII

Brooke, Sir Basil Stanlake, 5th Bt (*cr* 1822); *see* Brookeborough, 1st Viscount.

Brooke, Rear-Adm. Sir Basil Vernon, 1876–1945, vol. IV

Brooke, (Bernard) Jocelyn, 1908–1966, vol. VI

Brooke, Lt-Gen. Sir Bertram Norman Sergison-, 1880–1967, vol. VI

Brooke, Bryan Nicholas, 1915–1998, vol. X

Brooke, Sir Charles Anthony Johnson; *see* Sarawak, Rajah of.

Brooke, Col. Louis, 1868–1938, vol. III

Brooke, Sir Charles Vyner, 1874–1963, vol. VI

Brooke, Brig.-Gen. Christopher Robert Ingham, 1869–1948, vol. IV

Brooke, Sir Douglas; *see* Brooke, Sir A. D.

Brooke, Sir Edward Geoffrey de C.; *see* de Capell Brooke.

Brooke, Lt-Col Edward William Saurin, 1873–1954, vol. V

Brooke, Emma Frances, *died* 1926, vol. II

Brooke, Sir Francis Hugh, 2nd Bt (*cr* 1903), 1882–1954, vol. V

Brooke, Rt Rev. Francis Key, 1852–1918, vol. II

Brooke, Rt Hon. Frank, 1851–1920, vol. II

Brooke, Maj.-Gen. Frank Hastings, 1909–1982, vol. V

Brooke, Maj-Gen. Geoffrey Francis Heremon, 1884–1966, vol. VI

Brooke, Sir George Cecil Francis, 3rd Bt (*cr* 1903), 1916–1982, vol. VIII

Brooke, George Cyril, 1884–1934, vol. III

Brooke, Lt-Col George Frank, *born* 1878, vol. II

Brooke, Sir George Frederick, 1st Bt (*cr* 1903), 1849–1926, vol. II

Brooke, Gilbert Edward, 1873–1936, vol. III

Brooke, Col Harry Morris Mitchelson, 1868–1934, vol. III

Brooke, Captain Sir Harry Vesey, 1845–1921, vol. II

Brooke, Brig.-Gen. Hugh Fenwick, 1871–1948, vol. IV

Brooke, Humphrey; *see* Brooke, T. H.

Brooke, Rev. James Mark Saurin, 1842–1918, vol. II

Brooke, Jocelyn; *see* Brooke, B. J.

Brooke, John, 1912–1987, vol. VIII

Brooke, Sir John Arthur, 1st Bt (*cr* 1919), 1844–1920, vol. II

Brooke, John Henry, *died* 1902, vol. I

Brooke, John Kendall, 1856–1939, vol. III

Brooke, Sir John Reeve, 1880–1937, vol. III

Brooke, Major Sir John Weston, 3rd Bt (*cr* 1919), 1911–1983, vol. VIII

Brooke, Ven. Joshua Ingham, 1836–1906, vol. I

Brooke, Gp-Captain Kennedy Gerard, 1882–1959, vol. V

Brooke, Leonard Leslie, 1862–1940, vol. III

Brooke, Brig.-Gen. Lionel Godolphin, 1849–1931, vol. III

Brooke, Margaret, (Lady Brooke); *see* Sarawak, Ranee of.

Brooke, Nevile John, 1891–1968, vol. VI

Brooke, Sir (Norman) Richard (Rowley), 1910–1989, vol. VIII
Brooke, Lt-Col Ralph, 1900–1982, vol. VIII
Brooke, Sir Richard; see Brooke, Sir N. R. R.
Brooke, Ven. Richard, died 1926, vol. II
Brooke, Sir Richard Christopher, 9th Bt (cr 1662), 1888–1981, vol. VIII
Brooke, Col Richard Edward Frederic H.; see Howard-Brooke.
Brooke, Sir Richard Marcus, 8th Bt (cr 1662), 1850–1920, vol. II
Brooke, Sir Richard Neville, 10th Bt, 1915–1997, vol. X
Brooke, Major Sir Robert Weston, 2nd Bt (cr 1919), 1885–1942, vol. IV
Brooke, Col Ronald George, 1866–1930, vol. III
Brooke, Rev. Stopford Augustus, 1832–1916, vol. II
Brooke, Stopford W. W., 1859–1938, vol. III
Brooke, Sir Thomas, 1st Bt (cr 1899), 1830–1908, vol. I
Brooke, (Thomas) Humphrey, 1914–1988, vol. VIII
Brooke, Major Victor Reginald, 1873–1914, vol. I
Brooke, Brig. Walter Headfort, 1887–1975, vol. VII
Brooke, Sir William Robert, 1842–1924, vol. II
Brooke, Willie, 1896–1939, vol. III
Brooke, Zachary Nugent, 1883–1946, vol. IV
Brooke-Hitching, Sir Thomas Henry, 1858–1926, vol. II
Brooke-Hunt, Violet, died 1910, vol. I
Brooke-Pechell, Sir Alexander; see Brooke-Pechell, Sir A. A.
Brooke-Pechell, Sir (Augustus) Alexander, 7th Bt, 1857–1937, vol. III
Brooke-Pechell, Sir George Samuel; see Pechell.
Brooke-Pechell, Sir Samuel George; see Pechell.
Brooke-Popham, Air Chief Marshal Sir Robert; see Popham.
Brookeborough, 1st Viscount, 1888–1973, vol. VII
Brookeborough, 2nd Viscount, 1922–1987, vol. VIII
Brooker, Brig.-Gen. Edward Part, 1866–1946, vol. IV
Brooker, William, 1918–1983, vol. VIII
Brookes, Hon. and Rev. Edgar Harry, 1897–1979, vol. VII
Brookes, Captain Sir Ernest Geoffrey, 1889–1969, vol. VI
Brookes, Ernest Roy, 1904–1972, vol. VII
Brookes, Air Vice-Marshal Hugh Hamilton, 1904–1988, vol. VIII
Brookes, Mabel Balcombe, (Lady Brookes), died 1975, vol. VII
Brookes, Sir Norman Everard, 1877–1968, vol. VI
Brookes, Warwick, died 1935, vol. III
Brookes, Sir Wilfred Deakin, 1906–1997, vol. X
Brookfield, Col Arthur Montagu, 1853–1940, vol. III
Brookfield, Charles Hallam Elton, 1857–1913, vol. I
Brookfield, G. Piers, 1894–1975, vol. VII
Brooking, Allan John, 1934–1980, vol. VII
Brooking, Maj.-Gen. Sir Harry Triscott, 1864–1944, vol. IV
Brooking, Adm. Patrick William Beresford, 1896–1964, vol. VI
Brookman, Sir George, 1853–1927, vol. II
Brooks, Sir (Arthur) David, 1864–1930, vol. III

Brooks, Captain Arthur William, 1887–1941, vol. IV
Brooks, Cleanth, 1906–1994, vol. IX
Brooks, Collin; see Brooks, W. C.
Brooks, Gen. Sir Dallas; see Brooks, Gen. Sir R. A. D.
Brooks, Sir David; see Brooks, Sir A. D.
Brooks, Eric Arthur Swatton, 1907–1997, vol. X
Brooks, Eric St John; see Brooks, W. E. St J.
Brooks, Ernest Walter, 1863–1955, vol. V
Brooks, Hon. Mrs Florence, died 1934, vol. III
Brooks, Francis, 1861–1936, vol. III
Brooks, Ven. Frederick Richard, died 1912, vol. I
Brooks, Frederick Tom, 1882–1952, vol. V
Brooks, Rt Rev. Gerald Henry, 1905–1974, vol. VII
Brooks, Herbert, 1842–1918, vol. II
Brooks, Iris Mary, died 1971, vol. VII
Brooks, James, 1825–1901, vol. I
Brooks, Sir James Henry, 1863–1941, vol. IV
Brooks, John Birtwhistle Tyrrell, 1889–1962, vol. VI
Brooks, Hon. Marshall Jones, 1855–1944, vol. IV
Brooks, Oliver, 1920–1985, vol. VIII
Brooks, Ralph Terence St J.; see St John-Brooks.
Brooks, Gen. Sir (Reginald Alexander) Dallas, 1896–1966, vol. VI
Brooks, Ronald Clifton, 1899–1980, vol. VII
Brooks, Sydney, 1872–1937, vol. III
Brooks, Thomas Judson, 1880–1958, vol. V
Brooks, Lt-Col T(homas) Marshall, 1893–1967, vol. VI
Brooks, Van Wyck, 1886–1963, vol. VI
Brooks, Hon. William, 1858–1937, vol. III
Brooks, (William) Collin, 1893–1959, vol. V
Brooks, Sir William Cunliffe, 1st Bt, 1819–1900, vol. I
Brooks, William Donald Wykeham, 1905–1993, vol. IX
Brooks, (William) Eric St John, 1883–1955, vol. V
Brooksbank, Sir Edward Clitherow, 1st Bt, 1858–1943, vol. IV
Brooksbank, Col Sir (Edward) William, 2nd Bt, 1915–1983, vol. VIII
Brooksbank, Kenneth, 1915–1990, vol. VIII
Brooksbank, Col Sir William; see Brooksbank, Col Sir E. W.
Brooksby; see Elmhirst, Capt. E. P.
Brooksby, John Burns, 1914–1998, vol. X
Broom, Cyril George Mitchell, 1889–1968, vol. VI
Broom, Sir James Thomson, 1866–1931, vol. III
Broom, Robert, 1866–1951, vol. V
Brooman-White, Major Charles James, 1883–1954, vol. V
Brooman-White, Richard Charles, 1912–1964, vol. VI
Broome, Viscount; Henry Franklin Chevallier Kitchener, 1878–1928, vol. II
Broome, Francis Napier, 1891–1980, vol. VII(AII)
Broome, Harold Holkar, 1875–1958, vol. V
Broome, Mary Ann, (Lady Broome), died 1911, vol. I
Broome, Maj.-Gen. Ralph Champneys, 1860–1915, vol. I
Broome, Hon. William, 1852–1930, vol. III

Broomfield, Sir Robert Stonehouse, 1882–1957, vol. V

Broomhall, Maj.-Gen. William Maurice, 1897–1995, vol. IX

Brophy, Brigid Antonia, (Lady Levey), 1929–1995, vol. IX

Brophy, John, 1899–1965, vol. VI

Bros, James Reader White, 1841–1923, vol. II

Brosio, Manlio, 1897–1980, vol. VII

Broster, Dorothy Kathleen, *died* 1950, vol. IV

Broster, Lennox Ross, *died* 1965, vol. VI

Brotchie, James Rayner, 1909–1956, vol. V

Brotherhood, Stanley, 1876–1938, vol. III

Brotherston, Sir John Howie Flint, 1915–1985, vol. VIII

Brotherton, 1st Baron, 1856–1930, vol. III

Brotherton, Charles Frederick Ratcliffe, 1882–1949, vol. IV

Brotherton, Harry George, 1890–1980, vol. VII(AII)

Brotherton, John, 1867–1941, vol. IV

Brough, Maj.-Gen. Alan, 1876–1956, vol. V

Brough, Bennett Hooper, 1860–1908, vol. I

Brough, Bertram C., *died* 1938, vol. III

Brough, Charles Allan La Touche, *died* 1925, vol. II

Brough, Major John, *died* 1917, vol. II

Brough, John, 1917–1984, vol. VIII

Brough, Joseph, 1852–1925, vol. II

Brough, Lionel, 1836–1909, vol. I

Brough, Mary Bessie, 1863–1937, vol. III

Brough, Robert, 1872–1905, vol. I

Broughall, Rt Rev. Lewis Wilmot Bovell, 1876–1958, vol. V

Brougham and Vaux, 3rd Baron, 1836–1927, vol. II

Brougham and Vaux, 4th Baron, 1909–1967, vol. VI

Brougham, Harold de Vaux, 1858–1930, vol. III

Brougham, Very Rev. Henry, 1827–1913, vol. I

Brougham, Captain Hon. Henry, 1883–1927, vol. II

Brougham, James Rigg, 1826–1919, vol. II

Broughshane, 1st Baron, 1872–1953, vol. V

Broughshane, 2nd Baron, 1903–1995, vol. IX

Broughton, Sir Alfred Davies Devonsher, 1902–1979, vol. VII

Broughton, Air Marshal Sir Charles, 1911–1998, vol. X

Broughton, Major Sir Delves; *see* Broughton, Major Sir H. J. D.

Broughton, Sir Delves Louis, 10th Bt, 1857–1914, vol. I

Broughton, Maj. Sir Evelyn, 12th Bt, 1915–1993, vol. IX

Broughton, Sir Henry Delves, 9th Bt, 1808–1899, vol. I

Broughton, Rev. Henry Ellis, *died* 1924, vol. II

Broughton, Major Sir (Henry John) Delves, 11th Bt, 1888–1942, vol. IV

Broughton, Leonard, 1924–2000, vol. X (AII)

Broughton, Leonard Gaston, 1864–1936, vol. III

Broughton, Miss Rhoda, 1840–1920, vol. II

Broughton, Urban Hanlon, 1857–1929, vol. III

Broughton-Adderley, Hubert John; *see* Adderley.

Broughton-Head, Leslie Charles, *died* 1961, vol. VI

Broumas, Nikolaas, *born* 1916, vol. IX (AI)

Broun, Sir (James) Lionel, 11th Bt, 1875–1962, vol. VI

Broun, John Alexander, 1856–1935, vol. III

Broun, Sir Lionel; *see* Broun, Sir J. L.

Broun, Sir Lionel John Law, 12th Bt, 1927–1995, vol. IX (AII)

Broun, Sir William, 10th Bt, 1848–1918, vol. II

Broun Lindsay, Major Sir (George) Humphrey (Maurice), 1888–1964, vol. VI

Broun Lindsay, Major Sir Humphrey; *see* Broun Lindsay, Major Sir G. H. M.

Brounger, Captain Kenneth, 1881–1942, vol. IV

Brounger, Richard Ernest, 1849–1922, vol. II

Brousson, Louis Maurice, *died* 1920, vol. II

Brouwer, Luitzen Egbertus Jan, 1881–1966, vol. VI

Browder, Earl Russell, 1891–1973, vol. VII

Browell, Col William Basil, 1870–1935, vol. III

Browett, Sir Leonard, 1884–1959, vol. V

Brown, Baron (Life Peer); Wilfred Banks Duncan Brown, 1908–1985, vol. VIII

Brown, A. Curtis, 1866–1945, vol. IV

Brown, Rev. A. Douglas, 1874–1940, vol. III

Brown, Adrian John, 1852–1919, vol. II

Brown, Alan Brock, 1911–1980, vol. VII

Brown, Alan Grahame, 1913–1972, vol. VII

Brown, Brig. Alan Ward, 1909–1971, vol. VII

Brown, Albert Joseph, 1861–1938, vol. III

Brown, (Albert) Peter (Graeme), 1913–1993, vol. IX

Brown, Hon. Alexander, 1851–1926, vol. II

Brown, Alexander Cosens Lindsay, 1920–1999, vol. X

Brown, Alexander Crum, 1838–1922, vol. II

Brown, Col Alexander Denis B.; *see* Burnett-Brown.

Brown, Sir Alexander Hargreaves, 1st Bt, 1844–1922, vol. II

Brown, Alexander Kellock, 1849–1922, vol. II

Brown, Alfred Barratt, 1887–1947, vol. IV

Brown, Rt Hon. (Alfred) Ernest, 1881–1962, vol. VI

Brown, Alfred Reginald R.; *see* Radcliffe-Brown.

Brown, Sir Alfred W., 1883–1955, vol. V

Brown, Sir Algernon; *see* Brown, Sir T. A.

Brown, Allan, 1884–1969, vol. VI

Brown, Sir Allen Stanley, 1911–1999, vol. X

Brown, Anthony Geoffrey Hopwood G.; *see* Gardner-Brown.

Brown, Anthony George C.; *see* Clifton-Brown.

Brown, Rev. Archibald Geikie, 1844–1922, vol. II

Brown, Armitage Noel B.; *see* Bryan-Brown.

Brown, Sir Arnesby; *see* Brown, Sir J. A. A.

Brown, Arthur, 1884–1939, vol. III

Brown, Arthur, 1921–1979, vol. VII

Brown, Rev. Arthur Ernest, 1882–1952, vol. V

Brown, Arthur Godfrey Kilner, 1915–1995, vol. IX

Brown, Wing Comdr Arthur James, 1884–1949, vol. IV

Brown, Sir (Arthur James) Stephen, 1906–1998, vol. X

Brown, Lt-Col Arthur Miles W,; *see* Weber-Brown.

Brown, Sir Arthur W.; *see* Whitten-Brown.

Brown, Ashley Geikie, *died* 1957, vol. V

Brown, Brig. Athol Earle McDonald, 1905–1987, vol. IX (AI)

Brown, Dame Beryl P.; *see* Paston Brown.

Brown, Major Cecil, *born* 1867, vol. II

Brown, Cecil Jermyn, 1886–1945, vol. IV

Brown, Air Vice-Marshal Cecil Leonard Morley, 1895–1955, vol. V
Brown, Cedric C.; see Clifton Brown.
Brown, Charles, 1849–1929, vol. III
Brown, Charles, 1884–1940, vol. III
Brown, Rev. Charles, 1855–1947, vol. IV
Brown, Lt-Col Sir Charles Frederick Richmond, 4th Bt, 1902–1995, vol. IX (AII)
Brown, Sir Charles Gage, 1826–1908, vol. I
Brown, Charles Herbert, 1868–1942, vol. IV
Brown, Sir (Charles) James Officer, 1897–1984, vol. VIII
Brown, Lt-Col Charles John, died 1939, vol. III
Brown, Adm. Charles Randall, 1899–1983, vol. VIII
Brown, Col Charles Turner, 1875–1939, vol. III(A), vol. IV
Brown, Christopher Wilson, 1891–1949, vol. IV
Brown, Col Claude R.; see Russell-Brown.
Brown, Captain Claude Wreford W.; see Wreford-Brown.
Brown, Air Vice-Marshal Colin Peter, 1898–1965, vol. VI
Brown, Rev. Cyril James, 1904–1997, vol. X
Brown, Sir David, 1904–1993, vol. IX
Brown, David, died 1935, vol. III
Brown, Rt Rev. David Alan, 1922–1982, vol. VIII
Brown, David Hownam, 1879–1961, vol. VI
Brown, Denise Jeanne Marie Lebreton, 1911–1998, vol. X
Brown, Denys Downing, 1918–1997, vol. X
Brown, Derek Ernest D.; see Denny-Brown.
Brown, Douglas James, 1925–1989, vol. VIII
Brown, Eden Tatton, 1877–1961, vol. VI
Brown, Dame Edith Mary, 1864–1956, vol. V
Brown, Sir Edward, 1851–1939, vol. III
Brown, Edward Clifton C.; see Clifton-Brown.
Brown, Sir Edward Joseph, 1913–1991, vol. IX
Brown, Edward Percy, 1911–1972, vol. VII
Brown, Edward Thomas, 1879–1943, vol. IV
Brown, Edwin Percy, 1917–1990, vol. VIII
Brown, Eric, died 1939, vol. III
Brown, Maj.-Gen. Eric Gilmour, 1900–1967, vol. VI
Brown, Ernest, 1878–1949, vol. IV
Brown, Rt Hon. Ernest; see Brown, Rt Hon. A. E.
Brown, Lt-Col Ernest C.; see Craig-Brown.
Brown, Rev. Ernest Faulkner, 1854–1933, vol. III
Brown, Sir (Ernest) Henry Phelps, 1906–1994, vol. IX
Brown, Ernest William, 1866–1938, vol. III
Brown, (Everard) Kenneth, 1879–1958, vol. V
Brown, F. Gregory, 1887–1941, vol. IV
Brown, Rev. Francis, 1849–1916, vol. II
Brown, Vice-Adm. Francis Clifton, 1874–1963, vol. VI
Brown, Francis David Wynyard, 1915–1967, vol. VI
Brown, Francis Y.; see Yeats-Brown.
Brown, Sir Frank, 1857–1931, vol. III
Brown, Sir Frank Herbert, 1868–1959, vol. V
Brown, Frank James, 1865–1958, vol. V
Brown, Frank Leslie, 1896–1977, vol. VII
Brown, Frank Percival, 1877–1958, vol. V
Brown, Frederick, 1851–1941, vol. IV

Brown, Adm. Frederick Dundas G.; see Gilpin-Brown.
Brown, Sir (Frederick Herbert) Stanley, 1910–1997, vol. X
Brown, Col Frederick John, 1857–1941, vol. IV
Brown, Lt-Col Geoffrey Benedict C.; see Clifton-Brown.
Brown, Hon. Geoffrey E.; see Ellman-Brown.
Brown, George, born 1844, vol. II
Brown, George, 1847–1934, vol. III
Brown, George, 1872–1946, vol. IV
Brown, George Alfred; see Baron George-Brown.
Brown, Hon. George Arthur, 1922–1993, vol. X (AI)
Brown, George Clifford, 1879–1944, vol. IV
Brown, George Edward, 1872–1934, vol. III
Brown, Rt Rev. George Francis G.; see Graham Brown.
Brown, George Frederick William, 1908–1991, vol. IX
Brown, Rear-Adm. George Herbert Hempson, 1893–1977, vol. VII
Brown, Rev. George James C.; see Cowley-Brown.
Brown, Sir (George) Lindor, 1903–1971, vol. VII
Brown, George Mackay, 1921–1996, vol. X
Brown, George Mackenzie, 1869–1946, vol. IV
Brown, Col Sir George McLaren, 1865–1939, vol. III
Brown, Sir (George) Malcolm, 1925–1997, vol. X
Brown, George Ronald Pym A.; see Aldred-Brown
Brown, Sir George Thomas, 1827–1906, vol. I
Brown, Hon. George William, 1860–1919, vol. II
Brown, Gerard Baldwin, 1849–1932, vol. III
Brown, Gilbert Alexander M.; see Murray-Brown.
Brown, Dame Gillian Gerda, 1923–1999, vol. X
Brown, Gordon, 1921–1985, vol. VIII
Brown, H. Harris, 1864–1948, vol. IV
Brown, Major Harold, died 1918, vol. II
Brown, Harold, 1895–1969, vol. VI
Brown, Harold Arrowsmith, died 1968, vol. VI
Brown, Engr Vice-Adm. Sir Harold Arthur, 1878–1968, vol. VI
Brown, Harold George, 1876–1949, vol. IV
Brown, Harold John, 1899–1975, vol. VII
Brown, Sir Harry Percy, 1878–1967, vol. VI
Brown, Haydn, died 1936, vol. III
Brown, Helen Gilman, 1869–1942, vol. IV
Brown, Henry Billings, 1836–1913, vol. I
Brown, Major Henry Coddington, 1876–1958, vol. V
Brown, Sir Henry Isaac Close, 1874–1962, vol. VI
Brown, Sir Henry Phelps; see Brown, Sir E. H. P.
Brown, Sir Herbert, 1869–1946, vol. IV
Brown, Herbert Charles, 1874–1940, vol. III (A), vol. IV
Brown, Herbert Macauley Sandes, 1897–1987, vol. VIII
Brown, Horace T., 1848–1925, vol. II
Brown, Horatio Robert Forbes, 1854–1926, vol. II
Brown, Brig.-Gen. Howard Clifton, 1868–1946, vol. IV
Brown, Howard Mayer, 1930–1993, vol. IX
Brown, Hubert Sydney, 1898–1949, vol. IV
Brown, Ivor John Carnegie, 1891–1974, vol. VII
Brown, J. H.; see Hullah-Brown.

Brown, Jack, 1929–1991, vol. IX
Brown, Rt Hon. James, 1862–1939, vol. III
Brown, James, *died* 1941, vol. IV
Brown, Maj.-Gen. James, 1928–2000, vol X
Brown, James Alan Calvert, 1922–1984, vol. VIII
Brown, James Alexander, 1914–1999, vol. X
Brown, Lt-Col James Arnold A.; *see* Arrowsmith-Brown.
Brown, James Arthur Kinnear, 1902–1971, vol. VII
Brown, Sir James Birch, 1888–1968, vol. VI
Brown, Lt-Col James C.; *see* Cross Brown
Brown, James Campbell, *died* 1910, vol. I
Brown, James Clifton, 1841–1917, vol. II
Brown, Hon. James Drysdale, 1850–1922, vol. II
Brown, James Duff, 1862–1914, vol. I
Brown, Sir James Officer; *see* Brown, Sir C. J. O.
Brown, Major James Pearson, 1868–1942, vol. IV
Brown, Sir James Raitt, 1892–1979, vol. VII
Brown, Brig. James Sutherland, 1881–1951, vol. V
Brown, Rev. (James) Wilson (Davy), 1839–1922, vol. II
Brown, Jethro; *see* Brown, W. J.
Brown, John, 1844–1905, vol. I
Brown, Very Rev. John, 1850–1919, vol. II
Brown, John, 1830–1922, vol. II
Brown, Sir John, *died* 1928, vol. II
Brown, Lt-Gen. Sir John, 1880–1958, vol. V
Brown, John, 1890–1977, vol. VII
Brown, Sir John, 1901–2000, vol. X
Brown, John A. H.; *see* Harvie-Brown.
Brown, Sir (John Alfred) Arnesby, 1866–1955, vol. V
Brown, John Cecil, 1911–1983, vol. VIII
Brown, Sir John Douglas Keith, 1913–2000, vol. X
Brown, Paymaster-Commander John Edwin Ambrose, 1879–1931, vol. III
Brown, John Francis Seccombe, 1917–1989, vol. VIII
Brown, John Frank, 1856–1941, vol. IV
Brown, Captain Sir John Hargreaves P.; *see* Pigott-Brown.
Brown, John James Graham, *died* 1925, vol. II
Brown, John Macdonald, *died* 1935, vol. III
Brown, Sir John McLeavy, 1842–1926, vol. II
Brown, John Macmillan, 1846–1935, vol. III
Brown, John Mason, 1900–1969, vol. VI
Brown, Very Rev. John Pierce, 1843–1925, vol. II
Brown, Sir John Rankine, *died* 1946, vol. IV
Brown, John T. T.; *died* 1933, vol. III
Brown, Rev. John Thomas, 1860–1929, vol. III
Brown, John Wesley, 1873–1944, vol. IV
Brown, Rev. Johnston Carnegie, 1862–1930, vol. III
Brown, Joseph, 1809–1902, vol. I
Brown, Sir Joseph, *died* 1919, vol. II
Brown, Joseph Pearce, 1850–1936, vol. III
Brown, Kenneth; *see* Brown, E. K.
Brown, Sir Kenneth Alfred Leader, 1906–1978, vol. VII
Brown, Rt Rev. Laurence Ambrose, 1907–1994, vol. IX
Brown, Laurence Morton, 1854–1910, vol. I
Brown, Leonard Graham, 1888–1950, vol. IV
Brown, Leslie, 1902–1998, vol. X
Brown, Leslie F.; *see* Farrer-Brown.

Brown, Air Vice-Marshal Sir Leslie Oswald, 1893–1978, vol. VII
Brown, Rt Rev. Leslie Wilfrid, 1912–1999, vol. X
Brown, Lilian Kate Rowland-, 1863–1959, vol. V
Brown, Lilian Mabel Alice, (Lady Richmond Brown), *died* 1946, vol. IV
Brown, Sir Lindor; *see* Brown, Sir G. L.
Brown, Maj.-Gen. Llewellyn; *see* Brown, Maj.-Gen. R. L.
Brown, Sir Malcolm; *see* Brown, Sir G. M.
Brown, Mary M. Annesley, 1856–1932, vol. III
Brown, Maud Frances F.; *see* Forrester-Brown.
Brown, Sir Melville Richmond, 3rd Bt, 1866–1944, vol. IV
Brown, Meredith Jemima, *died* 1908, vol. I
Brown, Maj.-Gen. Michael, 1931–1993, vol. IX
Brown, Michael George Harold, 1907–1969, vol. VI
Brown, Montagu Y.; *see* Yeats-Brown.
Brown, Nicol Paton, 1853–1934, vol. III
Brown, Rev. Nigel Mackenzie M.; *see* Morgan-Brown.
Brown, Lt-Col Sir Norman Seddon S.; *see* Seddon-Brown.
Brown, Ormond John, 1922–1989, vol. VIII
Brown, Lt-Col Oscar, 1864–1932, vol. III
Brown, Rev. Canon Oscar Henry, 1896–1982, vol. VIII
Brown, Pamela Mary, 1917–1975, vol. VII
Brown, Sir Percival, 1901–1962, vol. VI
Brown, Percy, 1872–1955, vol. V
Brown, Captain Percy George, 1874–1954, vol. V
Brown, Brig.-Gen. Percy Wilson, 1876–1954, vol. V
Brown, Peter; *see* Brown, A. P. G.
Brown, Sir Peter Boswell, 1866–1948, vol. IV
Brown, Peter Hume, 1850–1918, vol. II
Brown, Sir Raymond Frederick, 1920–1991, vol. IX
Brown, Raymond Gordon, 1912–1962, vol. VI
Brown, Reginald, *died* 1936, vol. III
Brown, Reginald Francis, 1910–1985, vol. VIII
Brown, Maj.-Gen. (Reginald) Llewellyn, 1895–1983, vol. VIII
Brown, Richard, 1844–1910, vol. I
Brown, Richard King, 1864–1942, vol. IV
Brown, Robert, 1908–1999, vol. X
Brown, Sir Robert Charles, 1836–1925, vol. II
Brown, Robert Crofton, 1921–1996, vol. X
Brown, Robert Cunyngham, 1867–1945, vol. IV
Brown, Major Sir Robert Hanbury, 1849–1926, vol. II
Brown, Robert J.; *see* Jardine-Brown.
Brown, Robert Neal R.; *see* Rudmose-Brown.
Brown, Robert Sidney, 1889–1959, vol. IV
Brown, Lt-Col Robert Tilbury, 1873–1928, vol. II
Brown, Robson Christie, 1898–1971, vol. VII
Brown, Ronald David S.; *see* Stewart-Brown.
Brown, Ronald S.; *see* Stewart-Brown.
Brown, Rear-Adm. Roy Stephenson F.; *see* Foster-Brown.
Brown, Rt Rev. Russel Featherstone, 1900–1988, vol. VIII
Brown, Samuel Edward, 1868–1929, vol. III
Brown, Sir Samuel Harold, 1903–1965, vol. VI
Brown, Samuel Lombard, *died* 1939, vol. III
Brown, Sidney George, 1873–1948, vol. IV

Brown, Spencer C.; *see* Curtis Brown.
Brown, Sir Stanley; *see* Brown, Sir F. H. S.
Brown, Sir Stephen; *see* Brown, Sir A. J. S.
Brown, Sir Stuart Kelson, 1885–1952, vol. V
Brown, Rear-Adm. Sydney, 1899–1970, vol. VI
Brown, Rev. Sydney Lawrence, 1880–1947, vol. IV
Brown, T. Austen, *died* 1924, vol. II
Brown, Sir (Thomas) Algernon, 1900–1960, vol. V
Brown, Thomas Brown R.; *see* Rudmose-Brown.
Brown, Thomas C.; *see* Craig-Brown.
Brown, Thomas Edwin Burton, 1833–1911, vol. I
Brown, Thomas G.; *see* Graham Brown.
Brown, Thomas James; *see* Brown, Tom.
Brown, Thomas Julian, 1923–1987, vol. VIII
Brown, Thomas Walter Falconer, 1901–1995,
   vol. IX
Brown, Rt Hon. Thomas Watters, 1879–1944,
   vol. IV
Brown, Tom, (Thomas James Brown), 1886–1970,
   vol. VI
Brown, Air Cdre Sir Vernon, 1889–1986, vol. VIII
Brown, Hon. Villiers, 1843–1915, vol. I
Brown, Vincent, *died* 1933, vol. III
Brown, Walter, 1886–1957, vol. V
Brown, Walter Graham S.; *see* Scott-Brown.
Brown, Lt-Col Walter Henry, 1867–1928, vol. II
Brown, Walter Hugh, *died* 1950, vol. IV
Brown, Sir Walter L.; *see* Langdon-Brown.
Brown, Walter Russell, 1879–1966, vol. VI
Brown, William, 1850–1929, vol. III
Brown, William, 1856–1945, vol. IV
Brown, William, 1881–1952, vol. V
Brown, William, 1888–1975, vol. VII
Brown, Sir William, 1929–1996, vol. X
Brown, Ven. William A.; *see* Ashley-Brown.
Brown, William Adams, 1865–1943, vol. IV
Brown, William Eden T.; *see* Tatton Brown.
Brown, William B.; *see* Beattie-Brown.
Brown, Brig.-Gen. William Baker, 1864–1947,
   vol. IV
Brown, Sir William Barrowclough, 1893–1947,
   vol. IV
Brown, Maj.-Gen. William Douglas Elmes,
   1913–1984, vol. VIII
Brown, Rt Rev. William F., 1862–1951, vol. V
Brown, William Glanville, 1907–1995, vol. IX
Brown, Very Rev. William Henry, *died* 1924, vol. II
Brown, William Henry, 1845–1918, vol. II
Brown, Rt Rev. Mgr William Henry, 1852–1934,
   vol. III
Brown, William Herbert, *died* 1927, vol. II
Brown, Col Sir William James, 1832–1918, vol. II
Brown, Very Rev. William James, 1889–1970,
   vol. VI
Brown, (William) Jethro, 1868–1930, vol. III
Brown, William John, 1894–1960, vol. V
Brown, William John, 1911–1977, vol. VII
Brown, William Lowe L.; *see* Lowe-Brown.
Brown, William Marshall, 1868–1936, vol. III
Brown, Rt Rev. William Montgomery, 1855–1937,
   vol. III
Brown, Sir William Nicholson, 1865–1939, vol. III
Brown, Sir William R.; *see* Robson Brown.
Brown, Sir William Richmond, 2nd Bt, 1840–1906,
   vol. I

Brown, Sir William Roger, 1831–1902, vol. I
Brown, Sir William Scott, 1890–1968, vol. VI
Brown, Sir William Slater, 1845–1917, vol. II
Brown, Rev. William Tom, 1865–1939, vol. III
Brown, Rev. Wilson; *see* Brown, Rev. J. W. D.
Browne, family name of Baron Craigton.
Browne, Col Abraham Walker, 1854–1939, vol. III
Browne, Hon. Sir Albert, 1860–1923, vol. II
Browne, Captain Alexander Crawford, *died* 1942,
   vol. IV
Browne, Maj. Alexander Simon Cadogan,
   1895–1987, vol. VIII
Browne, Alfred John J.; *see* Jukes-Browne.
Browne, Brig.-Gen. Alfred Joseph Bessell-,
   1877–1947, vol. IV
Browne, Lt-Col Alfred Percy, 1868–1930, vol. III
Browne, Maj.-Gen. Andrew Smythe Montague,
   1836–1916, vol. II
Browne, Lt-Gen. Sir Arthur George Frederic,
   1851–1935, vol. III
Browne, Rt Rev. Arthur Heber, 1864–1951, vol. V
Browne, Rt Rev. Arthur Henry Howe, *died* 1961,
   vol. VI
Browne, Arthur Scott, 1866–1946, vol. IV
Browne, Rev. Barrington Gore, *died* 1914, vol. I
Browne, Sir Benjamin Chapman, 1839–1917, vol. II
Browne, Maj.-Gen. Beverley Wood, *died* 1948,
   vol. IV
Browne, Rev. Bevil; *see* Browne, Rev. W. B.
Browne, Sir Buckston; *see* Browne, Sir G. B.
Browne, Charles Edward, *born* 1861, vol. III
Browne, Sir Charles Ernest Christopher, 1871–1953,
   vol. V
Browne, Charles Macaulay, 1846–1911, vol. I
Browne, Col Charles Michael, 1878–1929, vol. III
Browne, Coral Edith, (Mrs Vincent Price),
   1913–1991, vol. IX
Browne, Lt-Col Cuthbert Garrard, 1883–1951,
   vol. V
Browne, Daniel F., *died* 1913, vol. I
Browne, Denis, 1903–1965, vol. VI
Browne, Sir Denis John Wolko, 1892–1967, vol. VI
Browne, Brig.-Gen. Desmond John Edward B.; *see*
   Beale-Browne.
Browne, Brig. Dominick Andrew Sidney,
   1904–1982, vol. VIII
Browne, Edith A., *died* 1963, vol. VI
Browne, Sir Edmond, 1857–1928, vol. II
Browne, Maj.-Gen. Edward George, 1863–1952,
   vol. V
Browne, Edward Granville, 1862–1926, vol. II
Browne, Sir (Edward) Humphrey, 1911–1987,
   vol. VIII
Browne, (Edward) Michael (Andrew), 1910–1992,
   vol. IX
Browne, Edward Raban C.; *see* Cave-Browne.
Browne, E(lliott) Martin, 1900–1980, vol. VII
Browne, Col Sir Eric G.; *see* Gore-Browne.
Browne, Sir Francis G.; *see* Gore-Browne.
Browne, Francis James, 1879–1963, vol. VI
Browne, Major Frederick Macdonnell, 1873–1915,
   vol. I
Browne, George, *died* 1919, vol. II
Browne, Sir (George) Buckston, 1850–1945, vol. IV

Browne, Maj.-Gen. George Fitzherbert, 1851–1935, vol. III
Browne, Rt Rev. George Forrest, 1833–1930, vol. III
Browne, Col George Herbert Stewart, 1866–1944, vol. IV
Browne, Rev. George Rickards, 1854–1921, vol. II
Browne, George Sinclair, 1880–1946, vol. IV
Browne, George Stephenson, 1890–1970, vol. VI
Browne, Sir George Washington, 1853–1939, vol. III
Browne, Comdr Godfrey G.; see Gore-Browne.
Browne, Gordon Frederick, 1858–1932, vol. III
Browne, Sir Granville St John O.; see Orde Browne.
Browne, Hablot Robert Edgar, 1905–1984, vol. VIII
Browne, Hamilton Edward, 1860–1933, vol. III
Browne, Harold Carlyon Gore, 1844–1919, vol. II
Browne, Col Harold William Alexander Francis C.; see Crichton-Browne.
Browne, Henry Doughty, died 1907, vol. I
Browne, Henry George G.; see Gore-Browne.
Browne, Rev. Henry J., 1853–1941, vol. IV
Browne, Gen. Henry Ralph, 1828–1917, vol. II
Browne, Henry William Langley, 1848–1928, vol. II
Browne, Maj.-Gen. Herbert Jose Pierson, 1872–1953, vol. V
Browne, Gen. Horace Albert, 1832–1914, vol. I
Browne, Sir Humphrey; see Browne, Sir E. H.
Browne, Jack Nixon; see Craigton, Baron.
Browne, Maj.-Gen. James, 1840–1917, vol. II
Browne, Brig. James Clendinning, 1878–1953, vol. V
Browne, Sir James C.; see Crichton-Browne.
Browne, Gen. Sir James Frankfort Manners, 1823–1911, vol. I
Browne, John Campbell McClure, 1912–1978, vol. VII
Browne, John Edward Stevenson, 1910–1976, vol. VII
Browne, Brig.-Gen. John Gilbert, 1878–1968, vol. VI
Browne, John Hutton Balfour-, 1845–1921, vol. II
Browne, Sir John Walton, 1845–1923, vol. II
Browne, Major John William, 1857–1938, vol. III
Browne, Julius Basil, 1892–1947, vol. IV
Browne, Kathleen A., died 1943, vol. IV
Browne, Rev. Laurence Edward, 1887–1986, vol. VIII
Browne, Leonard Foster, 1887–1960, vol. V
Browne, Maurice, 1881–1955, vol. V
Browne, Col Maurice, 1884–1961, vol. VI
Browne, Michael; see Browne, E. M. A.
Browne, Most Rev. Michael, died 1980, vol. VII
Browne, His Eminence Cardinal Michael David, 1887–1971, vol. VII
Browne, Nassau Blair, died 1940, vol. III(A), vol. IV
Browne, Rt Hon. Sir Patrick Reginald Evelyn, 1907–1996, vol. X
Browne, Philip Austin, 1898–1961, vol. VI
Browne, Sir Philip Henry, 1877–1950, vol. IV
Browne, Maj.-Gen. Reginald Spencer, 1856–1943, vol. IV
Browne, Richard Charles, 1911–1980, vol. VII
Browne, Rt Rev. Robert, 1844–1935, vol. III

Browne, Col Samuel Haslett, 1850–1933, vol. III
Browne, Gen. Sir Samuel James, 1824–1901, vol. I
Browne, Col Sherwood Dighton, 1862–1947, vol. IV
Browne, Dame Sidney Jane, 1850–1941, vol. IV
Browne, Stanley George, 1907–1986, vol. VIII
Browne, Lt-Col Sir Stewart G.; see Gore-Browne.
Browne, Maj.-Gen. Swinton John, 1837–1914, vol. I
Browne, Thomas Alexander; see Boldrewood, R.
Browne, Sir Thomas Anthony G.; see Gore Browne.
Browne, Air Marshal Sir Thomas Arthur W.; see Warne-Browne.
Browne, Thomas George, 1888–1963, vol. VI
Browne, Ven. Thomas Robert, 1889–1978, vol. VII
Browne, Tom, 1872–1910, vol. I
Browne, Vincent R. B.; see Balfour-Browne.
Browne, Major Walter Hamilton, 1875–1933, vol. III
Browne, Ven. Walter Marshall, 1885–1959, vol. V
Browne, Rt Rev. Wilfred G.; see Gore-Browne.
Browne, William, 1838–1924, vol. II
Browne, William Alex Francis B.; see Balfour-Browne.
Browne, Rev. (William) Bevil, 1845–1928, vol. II
Browne, Maj.-Gen. William C.; see Cave-Browne.
Browne, Lt-Col William Percy, 1893–1972, vol. VII
Browne, Surg.-Gen. William Richard, 1850–1924, vol. II
Browne, Wynyard Barry, 1911–1964, vol. VI
Browne-Cave, Sir Clement Charles C.; see Cave-Browne-Cave.
Browne-Cave, Rev. Sir Genille C.; see Cave-Browne-Cave.
Browne-Cave, Air Vice-Marshal Henry Meyrick C.; see Cave-Browne-Cave.
Browne-Cave, Sir Mylles C.; see Cave.
Browne-Cave, Captain Sir Reginald Ambrose C.; see Cave-Browne-Cave.
Browne-Cave, Sir Rowland Henry C.; see Cave-Browne-Cave.
Browne-Cave, Sir Thomas C.; see Cave-Browne-Cave.
Browne-Cave, Wing Comdr Thomas Reginald C.; see Cave-Browne-Cave.
Browne Clayton, Hon. Brig.-Gen. Robert Clayton, 1870–1939, vol. III
Browne-Mason, Col Hubert Oliver Browne, 1872–1930, vol. III
Browne-Synge-Hutchinson, Col Edward Douglas, 1861–1940, vol. III
Browne-Wilkinson, Rev. Arthur Rupert, 1889–1961, vol. VI
Brownell, Franklin; see Brownell, P. F.
Brownell, (Peleg) Franklin, 1857–1946, vol. IV
Brownell, Reginald Samuel, 1893–1961, vol. VI
Brownell, William Crary, 1851–1928, vol. II
Brownfield, Vice-Adm. Leslie Newton, 1901–1968, vol. VI
Brownfield, Surg. Rear-Adm. Owen Deane, 1891–1955, vol. V
Browning, Mrs Adeline Elizabeth, 1869–1950, vol. IV
Browning, Amy Katherine, 1881–1978, vol. VII
Browning, Andrew, 1889–1972, vol. VII
Browning, Carl Hamilton, 1881–1972, vol. VII

Browning, Rev. Charles William, 1855–1930, vol. III

Browning, Colin Arrott Robertson, 1833–1908, vol. I

Browning, Dame Daphne, (Lady Browning); *see* du Maurier, Dame Daphne.

Browning, Lt-Gen. Sir Frederick Arthur Montague, 1896–1965, vol. VI

Browning, Lt-Col Frederick Henry, *died* 1929, vol. III

Browning, Col George Dansey-, 1870–1941, vol. IV

Browning, Col George William, 1901–1981, vol. VIII

Browning, Lt-Col Herbert Arrott, 1861–1951, vol. V

Browning, Sir Jeffrey, 1862–1933, vol. III

Browning, Maj.-Gen. Langley, 1891–1974, vol. VII

Browning, Col Montague Charles 1837–1905, vol. I

Browning, Adm. Sir Montague Edward, 1863–1947, vol. IV

Browning, Oscar, 1837–1923, vol. II

Browning, Robert, 1902–1974, vol. VII

Browning, Robert, 1914–1997, vol. X

Browning, Sidney, *died* 1928, vol. II

Browning, Lt-Col Winthrop Benjamin, 1855–1934, vol. III

Brownjohn, Gen. Sir Nevil Charles Dowell, 1897–1973, vol. VII

Brownlee, John Donald Mackenzie, 1901–1969, vol. VI

Brownlee, John Edward, 1884–1961, vol. VI

Brownlees, Sir Anthony Culling, 1817–1897, vol. I

Brownlie, James Thomas, 1865–1938, vol. III

Brownlow, 3rd Earl, 1844–1921, vol. II

Brownlow, 5th Baron, 1867–1927, vol. II

Brownlow, 6th Baron, 1899–1978, vol. VII

Brownlow, Lt-Col Celadon Charles, 1843–1925, vol. II

Brownlow, Field-Marshal Sir Charles Henry, 1831–1916, vol. II

Brownlow, Col Charles William, 1862–1924, vol. II

Brownlow, Brig.-Gen. d'Arcy Charles, 1869–1938, vol. III

Brownlow, Lt-Gen. Henry Alexander, 1831–1914, vol. I

Brownlow, Rt Rev. William Robert, 1830–1901, vol. I

Brownlow, Col William Stephen, 1921–1998, vol. X

Brownlow, Maj.-Gen. William Vesey, 1841–1926, vol. II

Brownrigg, Rt Rev. Abraham, 1836–1928, vol. II

Brownrigg, Charles Edward, 1865–1942, vol. IV

Brownrigg, Vice-Adm. Sir Douglas Egremont Robert, 4th Bt, 1867–1939, vol. III

Brownrigg, Adm. Sir (Henry John) Studholme, 1882–1943, vol. IV

Brownrigg, Sir Henry Moore, 3rd Bt, 1819–1900, vol. I

Brownrigg, Very Rev. John Studholme, 1841–1930, vol. III

Brownrigg, Col Metcalfe Studholme, 1845–1924, vol. II

Brownrigg, Philip Henry Akerman, 1911–1998, vol. X

Brownrigg, Adm. Sir Studholme; *see* Brownrigg, Adm. Sir H. J. S.

Brownrigg, Captain Thomas Marcus, 1902–1967, vol. IV

Brownrigg, Lt-Gen. Sir W. Douglas S., 1886–1946, vol. IV

Broxbourne, Baron (Life Peer); Derek Colclough Walker-Smith, 1910–1992, vol. IX

Bruce of Melbourne, 1st Viscount, 1883–1967, vol. VI

Bruce, Vice-Adm. Alan Cameron, 1873–1947, vol. IV

Bruce, Alastair Henry, 1900–1988, vol. VIII

Bruce, Alexander, 1854–1911, vol. I

Bruce, Alexander, 1836–1920, vol. II

Bruce, Rev. Alexander Balmain, 1831–1899, vol. I

Bruce, Sir Alexander Carmichael, 1850–1926, vol. II

Bruce, Alexander Robson, 1907–1991, vol. IX

Bruce, Hon. Alice Moore, 1867–1951, vol. V

Bruce, Col Andrew Macrae, 1842–1920, vol. II

Bruce, Sir Arthur Atkinson, 1895–1992, vol. IX

Bruce, Sir Charles, 1836–1920, vol. II

Bruce, Lt-Col Charles Edward, 1876–1950, vol. IV

Bruce, Brig.-Gen. Hon. Charles Granville, 1866–1939, vol. III

Bruce, Charles Mathewes, 1875–1939, vol. III

Bruce, Very Rev. Charles Saul, *died* 1913, vol. I

Bruce, Brig.-Gen. Clarence Dalrymple, 1862–1934, vol. III

Bruce, Rev. David, *died* 1911, vol. I

Bruce, Maj.-Gen. Sir David, 1855–1931, vol. III

Bruce, Col Hon. David, 1888–1964, vol. VI

Bruce, David Kirkpatrick Este, 1898–1977, vol. VII

Bruce, Rev. Douglas William, 1885–1953, vol. V

Bruce, Col Edward, 1850–1911, vol. I

Bruce, Eric Henry Stuart, 1855–1935, vol. III

Bruce, Rev. Francis Rosslyn Courtenay, 1871–1956, vol. V

Bruce, Frederick Fyvie, 1910–1990, vol. VIII

Bruce, Rt Hon. Sir Gainsford, 1834–1912, vol. I

Bruce, George Gordon, 1891–1976, vol. VII

Bruce, Col Sir Gerald Trevor, 1872–1953, vol. V

Bruce, Adm. Sir Henry Harvey, 1862–1948, vol. IV

Bruce, Rt Hon. Sir Henry Hervey, 3rd Bt (*cr* 1804), 1820–1907, vol. I

Bruce, Henry James, 1880–1951, vol. V

Bruce, Lt-Gen. Sir Henry Le Geyt, 1824–1899, vol. I

Bruce, Hon. Henry Lyndhurst, 1881–1915, vol. I

Bruce, Herbert, 1877–1935, vol. III

Bruce, Col Hon. Herbert Alexander, *died* 1963, vol. VI

Bruce, Captain Sir Hervey John William, 6th Bt (*cr* 1804), 1919–1971, vol. VII

Bruce, Sir Hervey Juckes Lloyd, 4th Bt (*cr* 1804), 1843–1919, vol. II

Bruce, Sir Hervey Ronald, 5th Bt (*cr* 1804), 1872–1924, vol. II

Bruce, Howard, 1879–1961, vol. VI

Bruce, Adm. Sir James Andrew Thomas, 1846–1921, vol. II

Bruce, Rt Hon. Sir James Roualeyn Hovell-Thurlow-C.; *see* Cumming-Bruce.

Bruce, John, 1837–1907, vol. I

Bruce, Sir John, 1905–1975, vol. VII
Bruce, Maj.-Gen. John Geoffrey, 1896–1972, vol. VII
Bruce, Hon. John Hamilton, 1889–1964, vol. VI
Bruce, John Mitchell, 1846–1929, vol. III
Bruce, Joseph Percy, 1861–1934, vol. III
Bruce, Marcus James Henry, 1890–1956, vol. V
Bruce, Sir Michael William Selby, 11th Bt (cr 1629), 1894–1957, vol. V
Bruce, Mildred Mary; see Bruce, Hon. Mrs V.
Bruce, Hon. Randolph; see Bruce, Hon. Robert R.
Bruce, Richard Isaac, 1840–1924, vol. II
Bruce, Col Robert, 1825–1899, vol. I
Bruce, Rev. Robert, 1829–1908, vol. I
Bruce, Rev. Robert, died 1915, vol. I
Bruce, Sir Robert, 1855–1931, vol. III
Bruce, Robert, died 1949, vol. IV
Bruce, Sir Robert, 1871–1955, vol. V
Bruce, Major Hon. Robert, 1882–1959, vol. V
Bruce, Robert Elton Spencer, 1936–1971, vol. VII
Bruce of Sumburgh, Robert Hunter Wingate, 1907–1983, vol. VIII
Bruce, Robert Nigel Beresford Dalrymple, 1907–1997, vol. X
Bruce, Hon. (Robert) Randolph, 1863–1942, vol. IV
Bruce, Rev. Rosslyn; see Bruce, Rev. F. R. C.
Bruce, Tamara, (Mrs H. J. Bruce); see Karsavina, T.
Bruce, Brig.-Gen. Thomas, died 1966, vol. VI
Bruce, Thomas Dundas Hope, 1885–1940, vol. III
Bruce, Hon. Mrs Victor, (Mildred Mary), 1895–1990, vol. VIII
Bruce, Hon. Victoria Alexandrina Katherine, 1898–1951, vol. V
Bruce, Sir Wallace, 1878–1944, vol. IV
Bruce, Captain Wilfrid Montagu, 1874–1953, vol. V
Bruce, Ven. William Conybeare, died 1919, vol. II
Bruce, Sir William Cuningham, 9th Bt (cr 1629), 1825–1906, vol. I
Bruce, William Ironside, died 1921, vol. II
Bruce, William Napier, 1858–1936, vol. III
Bruce, William Speirs, 1867–1921, vol. II
Bruce, Rev. William Straton, 1846–1933, vol. III
Bruce, Sir William Waller, 10th Bt (cr 1629), 1856–1912, vol. I
Bruce-Chwatt, Leonard Jan, 1907–1989, vol. VIII
Bruce-Gardner, Sir Charles, 1st Bt, 1887–1960, vol. V
Bruce-Gardner, Sir Douglas Bruce, 2nd Bt, 1917–1997, vol. X
Bruce-Gardyne, Baron (Life Peer); John, (Jock), Bruce-Gardyne, 1930–1990, vol. VIII
Bruce-Joy, Albert, died 1924, vol. II
Bruce Lockhart, John Macgregor, 1914–1995, vol. IX
Bruce Lockhart, Rab Brougham, 1916–1990, vol. VIII
Bruce Lockhart, Sir Robert Hamilton, 1887–1970, vol. VI
Bruce-Mitford, Rupert Leo Scott, 1914–1994, vol. IX
Bruce Mitford, Terence; see Mitford.
Bruce-Porter, Sir (Harry Edwin) Bruce, 1869–1948, vol. IV
Bruce-Williams, Maj.-Gen. Sir Hugh Bruce; see Williams.

Bruche, Maj.-Gen. Sir Julius Henry, 1873–1961, vol. VI
Bruchesi, Most Rev. Paul, 1855–1939, vol. III
Brück, Hermann Alexander, 1905–2000, vol. X
Brudenell, George Lionel Thomas, 1880–1962, vol. VI
Bru-de-Wold, Col Hilmar Theodore, 1842–1913, vol. I
Bruen, Adm. Edward Francis, 1866–1952, vol. V
Bruen, Rt Hon. Henry, 1828–1912, vol. I
Bruford, Robert, 1868–1939, vol. III
Bruford, Walter Horace, 1894–1988, vol. VIII
Brugha, Cathal; see Burgess, Charles.
Bruhl, L. Burleigh, 1861–1942, vol. IV
Brühl, Paul, born 1855, vol. III
Bruhn, Erik Belton Evers, 1928–1986, vol. VIII
Bruller, Jean Marcel; see Vercors.
Brummer, Rev. Nicolaas Johannes, 1866–1947, vol. IV
Brumwell, George Murray, 1872–1963, vol. VI
Brumwell, Rev. Percy Middleton, 1881–1963, vol. VI
Brun, Constantin, 1860–1945, vol. IV
Brunault, Rt Rev. Joseph Simon-Hermann, 1857–1937, vol. III
Brundage, Avery, 1887–1975, vol. VII
Brundle, Frank Walter, 1890–1963, vol. VI
Brundrett, Sir Frederick, 1894–1974, vol. VII
Brundrit, Reginald Grange, 1883–1960, vol. V
Brune, Charles Glynn P.; see Prideaux-Brune.
Brune, Col Charles Robert P.; see Prideaux-Brune.
Brune, Sir Humphrey Ingelram P.; see Prideaux-Brune.
Bruneau, Hon. Arthur Aimé, 1864–1940, vol. III(A), vol. IV
Bruneau, Louis Charles Bonaventure Alfred, 1857–1934, vol. III
Brunel, Adrian Hope, 1892–1958, vol. V
Brunetiere, Ferdinand, 1849–1906, vol. I
Brunger, Captain Robert, 1893–1918, vol. II
Brüning, Heinrich, 1885–1970, vol. VI
Brunker, Brig.-Gen. Capel Molyneux, 1858–1936, vol. III
Brunker, Edward George, 1871–1951, vol. V
Brunker, Maj.-Gen. Sir James Milford Sutherland, 1854–1942, vol. IV
Brunner, Emil, 1889–1966, vol. VI
Brunner, Ernst August, died 1920, vol. II
Brunner, Sir Felix John Morgan, 3rd Bt, 1897–1982, vol. VIII
Brunner, Rt Rev. George, 1889–1969, vol. VI
Brunner, Guido, 1930–1997, vol. X
Brunner, Sir John Fowler, 2nd Bt, 1865–1929, vol. III
Brunner, Rt Hon. Sir John Tomlinson, 1st Bt, 1842–1919, vol. II
Brunner, Roscoe, 1871–1926, vol. II
Brunot, Ferdinand, died 1938, vol. III
Brunskill, Catherine Lavinia Bennett, 1891–1981, vol. VIII
Brunskill, Brig. George Stephen, 1891–1982, vol. VIII
Brunskill, Maj.-Gen. Gerald, 1897–1964, vol. VI
Brunskill, Gerald FitzGibbon, 1866–1918, vol. II
Brunskill, Hubert Fawcett, 1873–1951, vol. V

Brunskill, Lt-Col John Handfield, 1875–1940, vol. III
Brunskill, Muriel, 1899–1980, vol. VII
Brunskill, Ven. Thomas Redmond, 1870–1936, vol. III
Brunt, Sir David, 1886–1965, vol. VI
Brunt, Robert Nigel Bright, 1902–1982, vol. VIII
Bruntisfield, 1st Baron, 1899–1993, vol. IX
Bruntnell, Albert, 1866–1929, vol. III
Brunton, Frederick William, 1879–1953, vol. V
Brunton, Sir (James) Stopford (Lauder), 2nd Bt, 1884–1943, vol. IV
Brunton, John Stirling, 1903–1977, vol. VII
Brunton, Sir Lauder; see Brunton, Sir T. L.
Brunton, Sir Stopford; see Brunton, Sir J. S. L.
Brunton, Sir (Thomas) Lauder, 1st Bt, 1844–1916, vol. II
Brunton, Sir William, 1867–1938, vol. III
Brunton-Angless, Violet, 1878–1951, vol. V
Brunwin-Hales, Rev. Canon G. T., 1859–1932, vol. III
Brunyate, Sir James Bennett, 1871–1951, vol. V
Brunyate, Sir William Edwin, 1867–1943, vol. IV
Brush, Lt-Col Edward James Augustus Howard, (Peter), 1901–1984, vol. VIII
Brush, Lt-Col Peter; see Brush, Lt-Col E. J. A. H.
Bruton, Charles Lamb, 1890–1969, vol. VI
Bruton, Rear-Adm. Charles William, 1875–1952, vol. V
Bruton, Sir James, 1848–1933, vol. III
Brutton, Charles Phipps, 1899–1964, vol. VI
Bruxner, Lt-Col Sir Michael Frederick, 1882–1970, vol. VI(AII).
Bruyne, Pieter Louis de, 1845–1917, vol. II
Bryan, Sir Andrew Meikle, 1893–1988, vol. VIII
Bryan, Charles Walter Gordon, 1883–1954, vol. V
Bryan, Denzil Arnold, 1909–1987, vol. VIII
Bryan, George Hartley, 1864–1928, vol. II
Bryan, Col Sir Herbert, 1865–1950, vol. IV
Bryan, Rev. J. Ingram, 1868–1953, vol. V
Bryan, Walter Burr-, died 1940, vol. III
Bryan, Col William Booth, died 1914, vol. I
Bryan, William Jennings, 1860–1925, vol. II
Bryan, Willoughby Guy, 1911–1987, vol. VIII
Bryan-Brown, Armitage Noel, 1900–1968, vol. VI
Bryans, Rev. John Lonsdale, 1853–1945, vol. IV
Bryant, Sir Arthur, 1899–1985, vol. VIII
Bryant, Rear-Adm. Benjamin, 1905–1994, vol. IX
Bryant, Charles David Jones, 1883–1937, vol. III
Bryant, Charles William, died 1935, vol. III
Bryant, Sir Francis Morgan, 1859–1938, vol. III
Bryant, Frederick, 1878–1942, vol. IV
Bryant, Frederick Beadon, 1858–1922, vol. II
Bryant, Col Frederick Carkeet, 1879–1956, vol. V
Bryant, Lt-Col George Herbert, 1883–1952, vol. V
Bryant, Captain Henry Grenville, 1872–1915, vol. I
Bryant, J. H., 1867–1906, vol. I
Bryant, Marguerite, (Mrs Munn), 1870–1962, vol. VI
Bryant, Sophie, 1850–1922, vol. II
Bryant, Thomas, 1828–1914, vol. I
Bryce, 1st Viscount, 1838–1922, vol. II
Bryce, Viscountess; (Elizabeth Marion), died 1939, vol. III
Bryce, Alexander Joshua Caleb, 1868–1940, vol. III

Bryce, Lt-Col Edward Daniel, 1879–1936, vol. III
Bryce, Rev. George, 1844–1931, vol. III
Bryce, Dame Isabel G.; see Graham-Bryce.
Bryce, James McKie, died 1946, vol. IV
Bryce, John Annan, 1844–1923, vol. II
Bryce, Thomas Hastie, 1862–1946, vol. IV
Bryce, William Kirk, 1867–1954, vol. V
Bryceson, Sir Arthur Benjamin, 1861–1943, vol. IV
Bryden, Henry Anderson, 1854–1937, vol. III
Bryden, Robert, 1865–1939, vol. III
Bryden, Sir William James, 1909–1986, vol. VIII
Brydon, James Herbert, 1881–1960, vol. V
Bryher, (Annie) Winifred, 1894–1983, vol. VIII
Bryher, Winifred; see Bryher, A. W.
Brymer, Ven. Frederick Augustus, died 1917, vol. II
Brymer, William Ernest, 1840–1909, vol. I
Brymner, William, born 1855, vol. III
Bryson, Charles; see Barry, Charles.
Bryson, George Murray, 1904–1970, vol. VI
Buber, Martin, 1878–1965, vol. VI
Buccleuch, 6th Duke of, and Queensberry, 8th Duke of, 1831–1914, vol. I
Buccleuch, 7th Duke of, and Queensberry, 9th Duke of, 1864–1935, vol. III
Buccleuch, 8th Duke of, and Queensberry, 10th Duke of, 1894–1973, vol. VII
Buchan, 13th Earl of, 1815–1899, vol. I
Buchan, 14th Earl of, 1850–1934, vol. III
Buchan, 15th Earl of, 1878–1960, vol. V
Buchan, 16th Earl of, 1899–1984, vol. VIII
Buchan, Hon. Alastair Francis, 1918–1976, vol. VII
Buchan, Alexander, 1829–1907, vol. I
Buchan, Anna, died 1948, vol. IV
Buchan, Lt-Col Charles Forbes, 1869–1954, vol. V
Buchan, Brig. David Adye, 1890–1950, vol. IV
Buchan, Captain James Ivory, 1885–1958, vol. V
Buchan, John; see Tweedsmuir, 1st Baron.
Buchan, Sir John; see Buchan, Sir T. J.
Buchan, Brig.-Gen. Lawrence, 1847–1909, vol. I
Buchan, Norman Findlay, 1922–1990, vol. VIII
Buchan, Priscilla Jean Fortescue; see Baroness Tweedsmuir of Belhelvie.
Buchan, Stevenson, 1907–1996, vol. X
Buchan, Sir Thomas Johnston, (Sir John), 1912–1998, vol. X
Buchan-Hepburn, Sir Archibald, 4th Bt, 1852–1929, vol. III
Buchan-Hepburn, Sir John Karslake Thomas, 5th Bt, 1894–1961, vol. VI
Buchan-Hepburn, Sir Ninian Buchan Archibald John, 6th Bt, 1922–1992, vol. IX
Buchanan, Most Rev. Alan Alexander, 1907–1984, vol. VIII
Buchanan, Sir Alexander Wellesley George Thomas L.; see Leith-Buchanan.
Buchanan, Captain Angus, 1886–1954, vol. V
Buchanan, Lt-Col Arthur Louis Hamilton, 1866–1925, vol. II
Buchanan, Arthur William Patrick, 1870–1939, vol. III
Buchanan, Major Sir Charles James, 4th Bt, 1899–1984, vol. VIII
Buchanan, Sir David Carrick Robert C.; see Carrick-Buchanan.

Buchanan, David William Ramsay C.; *see* Carrick-Buchanan.
Buchanan, Hon. Sir (Ebenezer) John, 1844–1930, vol. III
Buchanan, Brig. Edgar James Bernard, 1892–1979, vol. VII
Buchanan, Sir Eric Alexander, 3rd Bt, 1848–1928, vol. II
Buchanan, George, 1827–1906, vol. I
Buchanan, Rt Hon. George, 1890–1955, vol. V
Buchanan, Sir George Cunningham, 1865–1940, vol. III
Buchanan, Sir George Hector L.; *see* Leith-Buchanan.
Buchanan, Sir George Hector Macdonald L.; *see* Leith-Buchanan.
Buchanan, George Henry Perrott, 1904–1989, vol. VIII
Buchanan, Sir George Seaton, 1869–1936, vol. III
Buchanan, Rt Hon. Sir George William, 1854–1924, vol. II
Buchanan, Lt-Gen. Henry James, 1830–1903, vol. I
Buchanan, Rear-Adm. Herbert James, 1902–1965, vol. VI
Buchanan, J. Courtney, 1877–1949, vol. IV
Buchanan, Jack, (Walter John), 1890–1957, vol. V
Buchanan, Sir James, 2nd Bt, 1840–1901, vol. I
Buchanan, Rev. John, *died* 1945, vol. IV
Buchanan, Hon. Sir John; *see* Buchanan, Hon. Sir E. J.
Buchanan, Sir John Cecil Rankin, 1896–1976, vol. VII
Buchanan, John Lee, 1831–1922, vol. II
Buchanan, John Nevile, 1887–1969, vol. VI
Buchanan, Sir John Scoular, 1883–1966, vol. VI
Buchanan, John Young, 1844–1925, vol. II
Buchanan, Joseph Andrew William, *died* 1929, vol. III
Buchanan, Maj.-Gen. Sir Kenneth Gray, 1880–1973, vol. VII
Buchanan, Brig.-Gen. Kenneth James, 1863–1933, vol. III
Buchanan, Leslie, 1868–1943, vol. IV
Buchanan, Lewis Mansergh, 1836–1908, vol. I
Buchanan, Rev. Louis George, 1871–1952, vol. V
Buchanan, Milton Alexander, 1878–1952, vol. V
Buchanan, Major Sir Reginald Narcissus M.; *see* Macdonald-Buchanan.
Buchanan, Robert, 1841–1901, vol. I
Buchanan, Robert J. M., *died* 1925, vol. II
Buchanan, Rev. Robert M., 1871–1945, vol. IV
Buchanan, Robert Ogilvie, 1894–1980, vol. VII
Buchanan, Ven. Thomas Boughton, 1833–1924, vol. II
Buchanan, Rt Hon. Thomas Ryburn, 1846–1911, vol. I
Buchanan, Hon. Sir Walter Clarke, 1838–1924, vol. II
Buchanan, Sir Walter James, 1861–1924, vol. II
Buchanan, Walter John; *see* Buchanan, Jack.
Buchanan, Hon. William A., 1876–1954, vol. V
Buchanan-Dunlop, Col Henry Donald, 1878–1950, vol. IV
Buchanan-Dunlop, Captain David Kennedy, 1911–1985, vol. VIII

Buchanan-Jardine, Captain Sir John William; *see* Jardine.
Buchanan-Riddell, Sir John Walter; *see* Riddell.
Buchanan-Riddell, Sir Walter Robert; *see* Riddell.
Buchanan-Smith, Alick Drummond; *see* Baron Balerno.
Buchanan-Smith, Alick Laidlaw, 1932–1991, vol. IX
Buchanan-Smith, Sir Walter, 1879–1944, vol. IV
Buchanan-Wollaston, Vice-Adm. Herbert Arthur; *see* Wollaston.
Bucher, Gen. Sir Francis Robert Roy; *see* Bucher, Gen. Sir R.
Bucher, Fredrick Newell, *died* 1964, vol. VI
Bucher, Gen. Sir Roy, 1895–1980, vol. VII
Buchheim, Charles Adolphus, 1828–1900, vol. I
Büchler, Adolph, 1867–1939, vol. III
Buchman, Frank N. D., 1878–1961, vol. VI
Buchthal, Hugo, 1909–1996, vol. X
Buck, Albert Charles, 1910–1992, vol. IX
Buck, Sir Edward Charles, 1838–1916, vol. II
Buck, Edward Clarke, 1873–1950, vol. IV(A)
Buck, Sir Edward John, *died* 1948, vol. IV
Buck, George Stucley; *see* Stucley, Sir G. S.
Buck, Leslie William, 1915–1984, vol. VIII
Buck, Pearl Sydenstricker, 1892–1973, vol. VII
Buck, Sir Percy Carter, 1871–1947, vol. IV
Buck, Sir Peter Henry, *died* 1951, vol. V
Buckee, Henry Thomas, 1913–1989, vol. VIII
Buckell, Sir Robert, 1841–1925, vol. II
Buckeridge, Surg. Rear-Adm. Guy Leslie, 1877–1944, vol. IV
Buckham, Bernard, 1882–1963, vol. VI
Buckham, Sir George Thomas, 1863–1928, vol. II
Buckhurst, John William, 1853–1943, vol. IV
Buckingham and Chandos, Duchess of; (Alice Anne), *died* 1931, vol. III
Buckingham, Rev. Frederick Finney, *died* 1934, vol. III
Buckingham, George Somerset, 1903–1989, vol. VIII
Buckingham, Sir Henry Cecil, 1867–1931, vol. III
Buckingham, Col Sir James, 1843–1912, vol. I
Buckingham, John, 1894–1982, vol. VIII
Buckingham, Richard Arthur, 1911–1994, vol. IX
Buckinghamshire, 7th Earl of, 1860–1930, vol. III
Buckinghamshire, 8th Earl of, 1906–1963, vol. VI
Buckinghamshire, 9th Earl of, 1901–1983, vol. VIII
Buckland, 1st Baron, 1877–1928, vol. II
Buckland, Captain Arthur Edgar, 1890–1969, vol. VI
Buckland, Charles Edward, 1847–1941, vol. IV
Buckland, Geoffrey Ronald Aubert, 1889–1968, vol. VI
Buckland, Brig. Gerald Charles Balfour, 1884–1967, vol. VI
Buckland, Sir Henry, 1870–1957, vol. V
Buckland, Sir Philip Lindsay, 1874–1952, vol. V
Buckland, Maj.-Gen. Sir Reginald Ulick Henry, 1864–1933, vol. III
Buckland, Sir Thomas, 1848–1947, vol. IV
Buckland, William Warwick, 1859–1946, vol. IV
Buckle, Comdr Archibald Walter, *died* 1927, vol. II
Buckle, Lt-Col Arthur William Bentley-, 1860–1923, vol. II

Buckle, Maj.-Gen. Charles Randolph, 1835–1920, vol. II
Buckle, Maj.-Gen. Christopher Reginald, 1862–1952, vol. V
Buckle, Adm. Claude Edward, 1839–1930, vol. III
Buckle, Col Cuthbert, 1885–1971, vol. VII
Buckle, Maj.-Gen. Denys Herbert Vintcent, 1902–1994, vol. IX
Buckle, Rt. Rev. Edward Gilbert, 1926–1993, vol. IX
Buckle, George Earle, 1854–1935, vol. III
Buckle, John, 1867–1925, vol. II
Buckle, Rev. Martin Brereton, 1853–1915, vol. I
Buckle, Major Matthew Perceval, 1869–1914, vol. I
Buckler, Georgina Grenfell, (Mrs William Buckler), died 1953, vol. V
Buckler, William Hepburn, 1867–1952, vol. V
Buckleton, Sir Henry, 1864–1934, vol. III
Buckley, Abel, 1835–1908, vol. I
Buckley, Lt-Col Albert, 1877–1965, vol. VI
Buckley, Anthony James Henthorne, 1934–2000, vol. X
Buckley, Col Arthur Dashwood Bulkeley, 1860–1915, vol. I
Buckley, Brig.-Gen. Basil Thorold, 1874–1954, vol. V
Buckley, Charles William, 1874–1955, vol. V
Buckley, Rt Hon. Sir Denys Burton, 1906–1998, vol. X
Buckley, Sir Edmund, 1st Bt, 1834–1910, vol. I
Buckley, Sir Edmund, 2nd Bt, 1861–1919, vol. II
Buckley, Edward Dunscombe Henry, 1860–1931, vol. III
Buckley, Ven. Eric Rede, 1868–1948, vol. IV
Buckley, Rev. Felix J., 1834–1911, vol. I
Buckley, Rear-Adm. Frederic Arthur, 1887–1952, vol. V
Buckley, Lt-Col George Alexander Maclean, 1866–1937, vol. III
Buckley, George James, 1935–1991, vol. IX
Buckley, Howard; see Buckley, W. H.
Buckley, Maj.-Gen. Sir Hugh Clive, 1880–1962, vol. VI
Buckley, Rev. James Monroe, 1836–1920, vol. II
Buckley, Ven. James Rice, 1849–1924, vol. II
Buckley, John J., 1863–1939, vol. III
Buckley, John Joseph Cronin, 1904–1972, vol. VII
Buckley, Sir John William, 1913–2000, vol. X
Buckley, Rev. Jonathan Charles, died 1927, vol. II
Buckley, Llewellyn Eddison, 1866–1944, vol. IV
Buckley, Rear-Adm. Sir Kenneth Robertson, 1904–1992, vol. IX
Buckley, Lt-Col Neville, 1867–1953, vol. V
Buckley, Rear-Adm. Peter Noel, 1909–1988, vol. VIII
Buckley, Robert Burton, 1847–1927, vol. II
Buckley, Hon. Dame Ruth Burton, 1898–1986, vol. VIII
Buckley, Ven. Thomas Richard, 1859–1936, vol. III
Buckley, Trevor, 1938–1993, vol. IX
Buckley, Wilfred, 1873–1933, vol. III
Buckley, William, 1859–1937, vol. III
Buckley, (William) Howard, 1909–1974, vol. VII
Buckley, Lt-Col William Howell, 1896–1981, vol. VIII

Buckley, Maj. William Kemmis, 1921–2000, vol. X
Buckley, Brig. William Percy, 1887–1968, vol. VI
Buckman, Edwin, 1841–1930, vol. III
Buckman, Rosina, died 1948, vol. IV
Buckmaster, 1st Viscount, 1861–1934, vol. III
Buckmaster, 2nd Viscount, 1890–1974, vol. VII
Buckmaster, Charles A., 1854–1949, vol. IV
Buckmaster, Rev. Cuthbert Harold Septimus, 1903–1994, vol. IX
Buckmaster, Engr Rear-Adm. Frederick Henry, 1883–1947, vol. IV
Buckmaster, George Alfred, 1859–1937, vol. III
Buckmaster, Martin A., 1862–1960, vol. V
Buckmaster, Col Maurice James, 1902–1992, vol. IX
Bucknall, Lt-Gen. Gerard Corfield, 1894–1980, vol. VII
Bucknill, Rt Hon. Sir Alfred Townsend, 1880–1963, vol. VI
Bucknill, Sir John Alexander-Strachey, 1873–1926, vol. II
Bucknill, Sir John Charles, 1817–1897, vol. I
Bucknill, Peter Thomas, 1910–1987, vol. VIII
Bucknill, Rt Hon. Sir Thomas Townsend, 1845–1915, vol. I
Buckrose, J. E., died 1931, vol. III
Bucks, Ven. Michael William, 1940–1997, vol. X
Buckston, George Moreton, 1881–1942, vol. IV
Buckston, Rev. Henry, 1834–1916, vol. II
Buckton, Baron (Life Peer); Samuel Storey, 1896–1978, vol. VII
Buckton, Ernest James, 1883–1973, vol. VII
Buckton, Raymond William, 1922–1995, vol. IX
Buckton, Ven. Thomas Frederick, 1858–1933, vol. III
Buckworth-Herne-Soame, Sir Charles; see Soame.
Buckworth-Herne-Soame, Sir Charles Burnett; see Soame.
Buday, George, 1907–1990, vol. VIII
Budd, Alfred, died 1927, vol. II
Budd, Sir Cecil Lindsay, 1865–1945, vol. IV
Budd, Hon. Sir Harry Vincent, 1900–1979, vol. VII
Budd, Herbert Ashwin, 1881–1950, vol. IV
Budd, John Wreford, 1838–1922, vol. II
Budd, Stanley Alec, 1931–1989, vol. VIII
Budden, Rev. Charles William, 1878–1952, vol. V
Budden, Lt-Col F. H., 1887–1953, vol. V
Budden, Henry Ebenezer, 1871–1944, vol. IV
Budden, Lionel, 1891–1966, vol. VI
Budden, Lionel Bailey, 1887–1956, vol. V
Buddo, Hon. David, 1856–1937, vol. III
Budge, Sir Ernest A. Wallis, 1857–1934, vol. III
Budge, Sir Henry Sinclair Campbell, 1874–1946, vol. IV
Budge, Rev. Ronald Henderson Gunn, 1909–1976, vol. VII
Budgen, Rear-Adm. Douglas Adams, died 1947, vol. IV
Budgen, Nicholas William, 1937–1998, vol. X
Budgett, Hubert Maitland, 1882–1951, vol. V
Budworth, Maj.-Gen. Charles Edward Dutton, 1869–1921, vol. II
Budworth, Rev. Richard Dutton, 1867–1937, vol. III
Buell, Lt-Col William Senkler, 1868–1941, vol. IV
Buer, Mabel Craven, 1881–1942, vol. IV

Buesst, Captain Aylmer, 1883–1970, vol. VI
Buffet, Bernard, 1928–1999, vol. X
Buffey, Brig. William, 1899–1984, vol. VIII
Bufton, Air Vice-Marshal Sydney Osborne, 1908–1993, vol. IX
Buganda, Kabaka (King) of, 1896–1939, vol. III
Buganda, HH The Kabaka of, 1924–1969, vol. VI
Bugotu, Francis, 1937–1992, vol. IX
Buhl, Frants Peter William, 1850–1932, vol. III
Buhler, Robert, 1916–1989, vol. VIII
Buick, Thomas Lindsay, died 1938, vol. III
Buisson, Ferdinand Édouard, 1841–1932, vol. III
Buisson, François A.; see Albert-Buisson.
Buist, Comdr Colin, 1896–1981, vol. VIII
Buist, Maj.-Gen. David Simson, 1829–1908, vol. I
Buist, Col Herbert John Martin, 1868–1956, vol. V
Buist, H(ugo) Massac, 1878–1966, vol. VI
Buist, Robert Cochrane, 1860–1939, vol. III
Bülbring, Edith, 1903–1990, vol. VIII
Bulfin, Gen. Sir Edward Stanislaus, 1862–1939, vol. III
Bulganin, Marshal Nikolai Alexandrovich, 1895–1975, vol. VII
Bulger, Anthony Clare, 1912–1996, vol. X
Bulkeley, Lt-Col C. Rivers, 1840–1934, vol. III
Bulkeley, Lt-Col Henry Charles, 1860–1938, vol. III
Bulkeley, John Pierson, died 1958, vol. V
Bulkeley, Sir Richard Harry David W.; see Williams-Bulkeley.
Bulkeley, Sir Richard Henry Williams-, 12th Bt, 1862–1942, vol. IV
Bulkeley, Captain Thomas Henry Rivers, 1876–1914, vol. I
Bulkeley-Evans, William, 1870–1952, vol. V
Bulkeley-Owen, Rev. Thomas M. Bulkeley, died 1910, vol. I
Bull, A. J., 1875–1950, vol. IV
Bull, Amy Frances, 1902–1982, vol. VIII
Bull, Archibald William Major, 1888–1970, vol. VI
Bull, Bartle, 1902–1950, vol. IV
Bull, George, 1864–1929, vol. III
Bull, Sir George, 3rd Bt, 1906–1986, vol. VIII
Bull, George Lucien, 1876–1972, vol. VII
Bull, Sir Graham MacGregor, 1918–1987, vol. VIII
Bull, Hedley Norman, 1932–1985, vol. VIII
Bull, Henry Cecil Herbert, 1892–1964, vol. VI
Bull, James William Douglas, 1911–1987, vol. VIII
Bull, Megan Patricia, (Lady Bull), 1922–1995, vol. IX
Bull, Rev. Paul Bertie, 1864–1942, vol. IV
Bull, René, died 1942, vol. IV
Bull, Sir Stephen John, 2nd Bt, 1904–1942, vol. IV
Bull, Sir Walter Edward Avenon, 1902–1995, vol. IX
Bull, Rt Hon. Sir William, 1st Bt, 1863–1931, vol. III
Bull, William Charles, 1858–1933, vol. III
Bull, William Perkins, 1870–1948, vol. IV
Bullard, Maj.-Gen. Colin, 1900–1981, vol. VIII
Bullard, Denys Gradwell, 1912–1994, vol. IX
Bullard, Sir Edward Crisp, 1907–1980, vol. VII
Bullard, Sir Giles Lionel, 1926–1992, vol. IX
Bullard, Sir Harry, 1841–1903, vol. I
Bullard, John Eric, 1903–1961, vol. VI
Bullard, Rev. John Vincent, 1869–1941, vol. IV

Bullard, Sir Reader William, 1885–1976, vol. VII
Bullard, Lt-Gen. Robert Lee, 1861–1947, vol. IV
Bulleid, C. H., 1883–1956, vol. V
Bulleid, G. Lawrence, 1858–1933, vol. III
Bulleid, Oliver Vaughan Snell, 1882–1970, vol. VI
Bullen, Arthur Henry, 1857–1920, vol. II
Bullen, Frank Thomas, 1857–1915, vol. I
Bullen, Rt Rev. Herbert Guy, 1896–1937, vol. III
Bullen, Keith Edward, 1906–1976, vol. VII
Bullen, Percy Sutherland, 1867–1958, vol. V
Bullen, William Alexander, died 1992, vol. IX
Bullen-Smith, Col George Moultrie, 1870–1934, vol. III
Buller, Sir Alexander, 1834–1903, vol. I
Buller, Arthur Henry Reginald, 1874–1944, vol. IV
Buller, Arthur Tremayne, 1850–1917, vol. II
Buller, Dame (Audrey Charlotte) Georgiana, 1883–1953, vol. V
Buller, Charles William Dunbar-, 1847–1924, vol. II
Buller, Rear-Adm. Francis Alexander Waddilove, 1879–1943, vol. IV
Buller, Dame Georgiana; see Buller, Dame A. C. G.
Buller, Adm. Sir Henry Tritton, 1873–1960, vol. V
Buller, Brig.-Gen. Hon. Sir Henry Y.; see Yarde-Buller.
Buller, Major Herbert Cecil, 1882–1916, vol. II
Buller, Lt-Col John Dashwood, 1878–1961, vol. VI
Buller, Lt-Col Sir Mervyn Edward M.; see Manningham-Buller.
Buller, Sir Morton Edward Manningham-, 2nd Bt, 1825–1910, vol. I
Buller, Ralph Buller H.; see Hughes-Buller.
Buller, Gen. Rt Hon. Sir Redvers Henry, 1839–1908, vol. I
Buller, Sir Walter Lawry, 1838–1906, vol. I
Buller, Lt-Col Walter Thomas More, 1886–1938, vol. III
Buller, Hon. Walter Y.; see Yarde-Buller.
Bullerwell, William, 1916–1977, vol. VII
Bullett, Gerald William, 1893–1958, vol. V
Bulley, Rt Rev. Cyril; see Bulley, Rt Rev. S. C.
Bulley, Rt Rev. Sydney Cyril, 1907–1989, vol. VIII
Bullin, Major Sir Reginald, 1879–1969, vol. VI
Bullinger, Ethelbert William, 1837–1913, vol. I
Bullitt, William Christian, 1891–1967, vol. VI
Bulloch, Rev. James Boyd Prentice, 1915–1981, vol. VIII
Bulloch, John Malcolm, 1867–1938, vol. III
Bulloch, William, 1868–1941, vol. IV
Bullock, Rev. Charles, 1829–1911, vol. I
Bullock, Charles, died 1952, vol. V
Bullock, Sir Christopher Llewellyn, 1891–1972, vol. VII
Bullock, Lt-Col Edward George T.; see Troyte-Bullock.
Bullock, Sir Ernest, 1890–1979, vol. VII
Bullock, Ernest Henry, 1911–1957, vol. V
Bullock, Fred, 1878–1946, vol. IV
Bullock, Frederick Shore, 1847–1914, vol. I
Bullock, Lt-Gen. Sir George Mackworth, 1851–1926, vol. II
Bullock, Guy Henry, 1887–1956, vol. V
Bullock, Captain Sir (Harold) Malcolm, 1st Bt, 1890–1966, vol. VI
Bullock, Hugh, 1898–1996, vol. X

Bullock, Brig. Humphry, 1899–1959, vol. V
Bullock, Kenneth, 1901–1985, vol. VIII
Bullock, Captain Sir Malcolm; see Bullock, Captain Sir H. M.
Bullock, Ralph, 1868–1946, vol. IV
Bullock, Rev. Richard, 1839–1918, vol. II
Bullock, Richard Henry Watson, 1920–1998, vol. X
Bullock, Samuel, 1844–1922, vol. II
Bullock, Shan F., 1865–1935, vol. III
Bullock, Thomas Lowndes, 1845–1915, vol. I
Bullock, Walter L1., 1890–1944, vol. IV
Bullock, Ven. William, 1885–1944, vol. IV
Bullock, Willoughby, 1882–1950, vol. IV
Bullock-Marsham, Brig. Francis William; see Marsham.
Bullock-Marsham, Robert H.; see Marsham.
Bullock-Webster, Rev. George Russell, 1858–1934, vol. III
Bullough, Geoffrey, 1901–1982, vol. VIII
Bullough, Sir George, 1st Bt, 1870–1939, vol. III
Bullough, Major Ian, died 1936, vol. III
Bulman, Henry Herbert, 1871–1928, vol. II
Bulman, Oliver Meredith Boone, 1902–1974, vol. VII
Bulman, Paul Ward Spencer, 1896–1963, vol. VI
Bulmer, Edward Frederick, 1865–1941, vol. IV
Bulmer, James Alfred, died 1914, vol. I
Bulmer, Sir James William, 1881–1936, vol. III
Bulmer-Thomas, Ivor, 1905–1993, vol. IX
Bulstrode, Herbert Timbrell, died 1911, vol. I
Bulteel, Christopher Harris, 1921–1999, vol. X
Bulteel, Major Sir John Crocker, 1890–1956, vol. V
Bulwer, Gen. Sir Edward Earle Gascoyne, 1829–1910, vol. I
Bulwer, Sir Henry Ernest Gascoyne, 1836–1914, vol. I
Bulwer, James Redfoord, 1820–1899, vol. I
Bulwer, William Dering Earle, 1856–1915, vol. I
Bulwer, Brig.-Gen. William Earle Gascoyne Lytton, 1829–1910, vol. I
Bulyea, George Hedley Vicars, 1859–1928, vol. II
Bumpus, Mary Frances; see Allitsen, Frances.
Bumstead, Kenneth, 1908–1987, vol. VIII
Bun Behari Kapur, Raja Bahadur, 1853–1924, vol. II
Bunbury, Cecil Edward Francis, 1864–1932, vol. III
Bunbury, Sir Charles Henry Napier, 11th Bt (cr 1681), 1886–1963, vol. VI
Bunbury, Evelyn James, 1888–1965, vol. VI
Bunbury, Brig. Francis Ramsay St Pierre, 1910–1990, vol. VIII
Bunbury, Sir Henry Charles John, 10th Bt (cr 1681), 1855–1930, vol. VII
Bunbury, Sir Henry Noel, 1876–1968, vol. VI
Bunbury, Maj.-Gen. Sir Herbert Napier, 1851–1922, vol. II
Bunbury, Sir (John) William Napier, 12th Bt, 1915–1985, vol. VIII
Bunbury, Rev. Sir John Richardson, 3rd Bt (cr 1787), 1813–1909, vol. I
Bunbury, Sir Mervyn William Richardson-, 4th Bt (cr 1787), 1874–1952, vol. V
Bunbury, Brig. Noël Louis St Pierre, 1890–1971, vol. VII
Bunbury, Rt Rev. Thomas, died 1907, vol. I

Bunbury, Brig.-Gen. Vesey Thomas, 1859–1934, vol. III
Bunbury, Sir William; see Bunbury, Sir J. W. N.
Bunbury, Maj.-Gen. William Edwin, 1858–1925, vol. II
Bunce, John Thackray, 1828–1899, vol. I
Bunch, John L., died 1941, vol. IV
Bunche, Ralph Johnson, 1904–1971, vol. VII
Bund, John William W.; see Willis-Bund.
Bundey, Hon. Sir Henry; see Bundey, Hon. Sir W. H.
Bundey, Hon. Sir (William) Henry, 1838–1909, vol. I
Bundi, HH Maharao Raja, 1869–1927, vol. II
Bundi, HH Maharao Raja of, 1893–1945, vol. IV
Bundy, Edgar, died 1922, vol. II
Bundy, McGeorge, 1919–1996, vol. X
Bune, John, died 1925, vol. II
Bunford, John Farrant, 1901–1992, vol. IX
Bunin, Ivan Alexseyevich, 1870–1953, vol. V
Bunker, Albert Rowland, 1913–1998, vol. X
Bunker, Lt-Col Sidney Waterfield, 1889–1968, vol. VI
Bunn, Charles William, 1905–1990, vol. VIII
Bunning, Arthur John Farrant, 1895–1968, vol. VI
Bunning, Herbert, 1863–1937, vol. III
Bunny, Rupert Charles Wolston, 1864–1947, vol. IV
Bunoz, Rt Rev. Emile Marie, 1864–1945, vol. IV
Bunt, Rev. Frederick Darrell, 1902–1977, vol. VII
Buntine, James Robertson, 1841–1920, vol. II
Bunting, Basil, 1900–1985, vol. VIII
Bunting, D. G.; see George, Daniel.
Bunting, Sir (Edward) John, 1918–1995, vol. IX
Bunting, Sir John; see Bunting, Sir E. J.
Bunting, Sir Percy William, 1836–1911, vol. I
Bunton, George Louis, 1920–1997, vol. X
Buñuel, Luis, 1900–1983, vol. VIII
Burbank, Luther, 1849–1926, vol. II
Burbidge, Rev. Frederick William, 1840–1915, vol. I
Burbidge, Frederick William Thomas, 1847–1905, vol. I
Burbidge, Hon. George W., died 1908, vol. I
Burbidge, Sir John Richard Woodman, 4th Bt, 1930–1974, vol. VII
Burbidge, Percy William, 1891–1984, vol. VIII
Burbidge, Sir Richard, 1st Bt, 1847–1917, vol. II
Burbidge, Sir Richard Grant Woodman, 3rd Bt, 1897–1966, vol. VI
Burbidge, Sir (Richard) Woodman, 2nd Bt, 1872–1945, vol. IV
Burbidge, Sir Woodman; see Burbidge, Sir R. W.
Burbury, Samuel Hawksley, 1831–1911, vol. I
Burbury, Hon. Sir Stanley Charles, 1909–1995, vol. IX
Burch, Cecil Reginald, 1901–1983, vol. VIII
Burch, Maj.-Gen. Frederick Whitmore, 1893–1977, vol. VII
Burch, Maj.-Gen. Geoffrey, 1923–1990, vol. VIII
Burch, George James, 1852–1914, vol. I
Burch, Lt-Col William Edward Scarth, died 1940, vol. III
Burchardt, Frank A., 1902–1958, vol. V
Burchmore, Air Cdre Eric, 1920–1994, vol. IX

Burchnall, Joseph Langley, 1892–1975, vol. VII
Burckhardt, Charles James, 1891–1974, vol. VII
Burd, Rev. Frederick, 1826–1915, vol. I
Burd, Rev. Prebendary John, 1828–1918, vol. II
Burd, Rt Rev. Walter, 1888–1939, vol. III
Burden, 1st Baron, 1885–1970, vol. VI
Burden, 2nd Baron, 1916–1995, vol. IX
Burden, Sqn Ldr Sir Frederick Frank Arthur, 1905–1987, vol. VIII
Burden, Frederick Parker, 1874–1971, vol. VII
Burden, Major Geoffrey Noel, 1898–1990, vol. VIII
Burden, Col Henry, 1867–1953, vol. V
Burder, Brig.-Gen. Ernest Sumner, 1866–1946, vol. IV
Burder, Sir John Henry, 1900–1988, vol. VIII
Burdett, Sir Charles Coventry, 9th Bt (cr 1665), 1902–1940, vol. III
Burdett, Sir Francis, 8th Bt (cr 1618), 1869–1951, vol. V
Burdett, Sir Henry, 1847–1920, vol. II
Burdett, Sir Henry Aylmer, 10th Bt (cr 1665), 1881–1943, vol. IV
Burdett, Osbert, 1885–1936, vol. III
Burdett, Scott Langshaw, 1897–1961, vol. VI
Burdett-Coutts, Baroness (1st in line), 1814–1906, vol. I
Burdett-Coutts, Rt Hon. William Lehman Ashmead Bartlett-, 1851–1921, vol. II
Burditt, George Frederick, 1862–1933, vol. III
Burdon, Sir Ernest, 1881–1957, vol. V
Burdon, Major Sir John Alder, 1866–1933, vol. III
Burdon, Rt Rev. John Shaw, 1826–1907, vol. I
Burdon, Rowland, 1857–1944, vol. III
Burdon-Sanderson, Sir John Scott, 1st Bt, 1828–1905, vol. I(A)
Burdwan, Maharajadhiraja Bahadur of, 1881–1941, vol. IV
Bureau, Jacques, 1860–1933, vol. III
Buret, Captain Theobald John Claud P.; see Purcell-Buret.
Burford, Eleanor; see Hibbert, Eleanor.
Burford, George Henry, 1856–1937, vol. III
Burge, Sir Charles Henry, 1846–1921, vol. II
Burge, Rt Rev. Hubert Murray, 1862–1925, vol. II
Burge, James Charles George, 1906–1990, vol. VIII
Burge, Milward Rodon Kennedy, 1894–1968, vol. VI
Burger, Schalk William, died 1918, vol. II
Burger, Warren Earl, 1907–1995, vol. IX
Burges, Betty; see Burges, M. B. P.
Burges, Lt-Col Dan, 1873–1946, vol. IV
Burges, Ven. Ernest Travers, 1851–1921, vol. II
Burges, (Margaret) Betty (Pierpoint), died 1999, vol. X
Burges, Col Ynyr Henry, 1834–1908, vol. I
Burgess, Anthony, 1917–1993, vol. IX
Burgess, Arthur Henry, 1874–1948, vol. IV
Burgess, Arthur James Wetherall, 1879–1957, vol. V
Burgess, Charles, (Cathal Brugha), 1874–1922, vol. II
Burgess, Lt-Col Charles Roscoe, 1874–1966, vol. VI(AII)
Burgess, Clarkson Leo, 1902–1975, vol. VII
Burgess, Claude Bramall, 1910–1998, vol. X

Burgess, Duncan, 1850–1917, vol. II
Burgess, Rev. Francis, 1879–1948, vol. IV
Burgess, (Frank) Gelett, 1866–1951, vol. V
Burgess, Rt Rev. Frederick, 1853–1925, vol. II
Burgess, Frederick George, died 1951, vol. V
Burgess, Frederick William, 1855–1945, vol. IV
Burgess, Gelett; see Burgess, F. G.
Burgess, Geoffrey, 1906–1972, vol. VII
Burgess, Rt Hon. Henry Givens, 1859–1937, vol. III
Burgess, Herbert Edward, 1863–1948, vol. IV
Burgess, James, 1832–1916, vol. II
Burgess, James John Haldane, 1862–1927, vol. II
Burgess, John Bagnold, 1830–1897, vol. I
Burgess, Sir John Lawie, 1912–1987, vol. VIII
Burgess, Norman Francis Clifford, 1902–1940, vol. III
Burgess, Robert Arthur, 1946–1999, vol. X
Burgess, Robert Nelson, 1867–1945, vol. IV
Burgess, Russell Brian, 1931–1979, vol. VII
Burgess, Sir Thomas Arthur Collier, 1906–1977, vol. VII
Burgess, Thomas Joseph Workman, 1849–1926, vol. II
Burgess, Hon. William Henry, 1847–1917, vol. II
Burgess, William Leslie, 1886–1954, vol. V
Burgess, Maj.-Gen. Sir William Livingstone Hatchwell S,; see Sinclair-Burgess.
Burgett, Rt Rev. Arthur Edward, 1869–1942, vol. IV
Burgh, 5th Baron, 1866–1926, vol. II
Burgh, 8th (otherwise 6th) Baron, 1906–1959, vol. V
Burghard, Frédéric François, 1864–1947, vol. IV
Burghard, Rear-Adm. Geoffrey Frederic, 1900–1981, vol. VIII
Burghclere, 1st Baron, 1846–1921, vol. II
Burghclere, Lady; (Winifred Henrietta Christina), 1864–1933, vol. III
Burgin, Rt Hon. Edward Leslie, 1887–1945, vol. IV
Burgin, George B., 1856–1944, vol. IV
Burgis, Sir Edwin Cooper, 1878–1966, vol. VI
Burgis, Lawrence Franklin, 1892–1972, vol. VII
Burgmann, Rt Rev. Ernest Henry, 1885–1967, vol. VI
Burgoyne, Lt-Col Sir Alan Hughes, 1880–1929, vol. III
Burgoyne, Major Gerald Achilles, 1874–1936, vol. III
Burgoyne, Sir John, 1875–1969, vol. VI
Burgoyne, Col Sir John Montagu, 10th Bt, 1832–1921, vol. II
Burhop, Eric Henry Stoneley, 1911–1980, vol. VII
Burke, Rt Rev. Mgr Alfred Edward, 1862–1927, vol. II
Burke, Adm. Arleigh Albert, 1901–1996, vol. X
Burke, Sir Aubrey Francis, 1904–1989, vol. VIII
Burke, Col Bernard Bruce, 1876–1938, vol. III
Burke, Major Charles James, 1882–1917, vol. II
Burke, Desmond Peter Meredyth, 1912–1987, vol. VIII
Burke, Edmund Haviland, died 1914, vol. I
Burke, Edmund Tytler, 1888–1941, vol. IV
Burke, Rt Rev. Geoffrey, 1913–1999, vol. X
Burke, Captain Sir Gerald Howe, 7th Bt (cr 1797), 1893–1954, vol. V

Burke, Lt-Col Gerald Tyler, 1882–1952, vol. V
Burke, Harold Arthur, 1852–1942, vol. IV
Burke, Sir Henry Farnham, 1859–1930, vol. III
Burke, Sir Henry George, 5th Bt (*cr* 1797), 1859–1910, vol. I
Burke, Henry Lardner, 1850–1927, vol. II
Burke, Col Herbert Francis Lardner, 1883–1950, vol. IV
Burke, Captain James Henry Thomas, 1853–1902, vol. I
Burke, Sir John, *died* 1922, vol. II
Burke, John Barclay, 1924–1983, vol. VIII
Burke, John Benjamin Butler, 1871–1946, vol. IV
Burke, Sir Joseph Terence Anthony, 1913–1992, vol. IX
Burke, Kathleen, 1887–1958, vol. V
Burke, Rt Rev. Maurice Francis, 1845–1923, vol. II
Burke, Lt-Col Sir Richard John Charles, 1878–1960, vol. V
Burke, Sir Ronald; *see* Burke, Sir U. R.
Burke, Sir Theobald Hubert, 13th Bt (*cr* 1628), 1833–1909, vol. I
Burke, Thomas, 1886–1945, vol. IV
Burke, Sir Thomas Mallachy, 6th Bt (*cr* 1797), 1864–1913, vol. I
Burke, Thomas Michael, 1870–1949, vol. IV
Burke, Sir Thomas Stanley, 8th Bt, 1916–1989, vol. VIII
Burke, Sir (Ulick) Roland, 1872–1958, vol. V
Burke, Wilfrid Andrew, *died* 1968, vol. VI
Burke-Gaffney, Maj.-Gen. Edward Sebastian, 1900–1981, vol. VIII
Burkett, Sir William Robert, 1840–1908, vol. I
Burkhardt, Col Valentine Rodolphe, 1884–1967, vol. IV
Burkhart, Harvey J., 1864–1946, vol. IV
Burkill, Charles; *see* Burkill, J. C.
Burkill, Isaac Henry, 1870–1965, vol. VI
Burkill, John Charles, 1900–1993, vol. IX
Burkitt, Col Bernard Maynard H.; *see* Humble-Burkitt.
Burkitt, Denis Parsons, 1911–1993, vol. IX
Burkitt, Francis Crawford, 1864–1935, vol. III
Burkitt, Francis Holy, 1880–1952, vol. V
Burkitt, Miles Crawford, 1890–1971, vol. VII
Burkitt, Ven. Robert Scott Bradshaw, 1857–1940, vol. III(A), vol. IV
Burkitt, Robert William, 1908–1976, vol. VII
Burland, Col Jeffrey Hale, 1861–1914, vol. I
Burland, John Burland H.; *see* Harris-Burland.
Burland, Col William Watt, 1877–1935, vol. III
Burleigh, Bennet, *died* 1914, vol. I
Burleigh, Captain Cecil Wills, 1870–1940, vol. III
Burleigh, George Hall, 1928–1991, vol. IX
Burleigh, Very Rev. John H. S., 1894–1985, vol. VIII
Burleigh, Thomas Haydon, 1911–1999, vol. X
Burleson, Rt Rev. Hugh Latimer, 1865–1933, vol. III
Burlingame, Edward Livermore, 1848–1922, vol. II
Burls, Sir Edwin Grant, 1844–1926, vol. II
Burlton, Lt-Col Philip Sykes Murphy, 1865–1950, vol. IV
Burman, Sir Charles; *see* Burman, Sir J. C.
Burman, Sir John Bedford, 1867–1941, vol. IV

Burman, Sir (John) Charles, 1908–1999, vol. X
Burman, Sir Stephen France, 1904–1992, vol. IX
Burmester, Adm. Sir Rudolf Miles, 1875–1956, vol. V
Burn, Col Alexander Henderson, 1885–1949, vol. IV
Burn, Very Rev. Andrew Ewbank, 1864–1927, vol. II
Burn, Andrew Robert, (Robin), 1902–1991, vol. IX
Burn, Lt-Col Charles Pelham Maitland, 1880–1925, vol. II
Burn, Sir Clive; *see* Burn, Sir R. C. W.
Burn, Dugald Stuart, 1877–1951, vol. V
Burn, Duncan Lyall, 1902–1988, vol. VIII
Burn, Sir George, 1847–1932, vol. III
Burn, Col Harold Septimus, *died* 1970, vol. VI
Burn, Sir Harry Harrison, 1888–1961, vol. VI
Burn, Brig.-Gen. Henry Pelham, 1882–1958, vol. V
Burn, Rev. John Henry, 1858–1937, vol. III
Burn, Sir Joseph, 1871–1950, vol. IV
Burn, Joshua Harold, 1892–1981, vol. VIII
Burn, Sir Richard, 1871–1947, vol. IV
Burn, Rev. Robert, 1829–1904, vol. I
Burn, Robin; *see* Burn, A. R.
Burn, Rodney Joseph, 1899–1984, vol. VIII
Burn, Sir (Roland) Clive (Wallace), 1882–1955, vol. V
Burn, Sir Sidney, 1881–1963, vol. VI
Burn, William Laurence, 1904–1966, vol. VI
Burn-Murdoch, Hector, 1881–1958, vol. V
Burn-Murdoch, Rev. Canon James McGibbon, 1828–1904, vol. I
Burn-Murdoch, Maj.-Gen. Sir John Francis, 1859–1931, vol. III
Burn-Murdoch, W. G., 1862–1939, vol. III
Burnaby, Major Algernon Edwyn, 1868–1938, vol. III
Burnaby, Davy; *see* Burnaby, G. D.
Burnaby, Lt-Col Eustace Beaumont, 1842–1916, vol. II
Burnaby, (George) Davy, 1881–1949, vol. IV
Burnaby, Lt-Col Hugo Beaumont, 1874–1916, vol. II
Burnaby, Rev. John, 1891–1978, vol. VII
Burnaby-Atkins, Thomas Frederick, 1836–1918, vol. II
Burnage, Col Granville John, 1858–1945, vol. IV
Burnand, Sir Francis Cowley, 1836–1917, vol. II
Burnand, Sir Frank; *see* Burnand, Sir R. F.
Burnand, Sir (Richard) Frank, 1887–1969, vol. VI
Burnand, Victor Wyatt, 1868–1940, vol. III
Burnard, Major Charles Francis, 1876–1931, vol. III
Burne, Lt-Col Alfred Higgins, 1886–1959, vol. V
Burne, Gen. Henry Knightley, 1825–1901, vol. I
Burne, Sir Lewis Charles, 1898–1978, vol. VII
Burne, Lt-Col Lindsay Eliott Lumley, 1877–1944, vol. IV
Burne, Col Newdigate Halford Marriot, 1872–1950, vol. IV(A), vol. V
Burne, Maj.-Gen. Sir Owen Tudor, 1837–1909, vol. I
Burne, Brig.-Gen. Rainald Owen, 1871–1923, vol. II
Burne, Richard Higgins, 1868–1953, vol. V

Burne, Ven. Richard Vernon Higgins, 1882–1970, vol. VI
Burne-Jones, Sir Edward Coley, 1st Bt, 1833–1898, vol. I
Burne-Jones, Sir Philip, 2nd Bt, 1861–1926, vol. II
Burnell, Lt-Col Charles Desborough, 1876–1969, vol. VI
Burnell-Nugent, Brig.-Gen. Frank, 1880–1942, vol. IV
Burnes, Sheila; see Bloom, Ursula.
Burnet, Rev. Amos, 1857–1926, vol. II
Burnet, Sir (Frank) Macfarlane, 1899–1985, vol. VIII
Burnet, John, 1863–1928, vol. II
Burnet, Sir John James, 1857–1938, vol. III
Burnet, John Rudolph Wardlaw, 1886–1941, vol. IV
Burnet, Pauline Ruth, 1920–1991, vol. IX
Burnet, Sir Robert William, 1851–1931, vol. III
Burnett of Leys, Major Sir Alexander Edwin, 14th Bt (cr 1626), 1881–1959, vol. V
Burnett, Col Allan Harrington, 1884–1966, vol. VI
Burnett, Most Rev. Bill Bendyshe, 1917–1994, vol. IX
Burnett, Cecil Ross, 1872–1933, vol. III
Burnett, Gen. Sir Charles John, 1843–1915, vol. I
Burnett, Brig.-Gen. Charles Kenyon, 1868–1950, vol. IV
Burnett, Air Chief Marshal Sir Charles Stuart, 1882–1945, vol. IV
Burnett, Sir David, 1st Bt (cr 1913), 1851–1930, vol. III
Burnett, Sir Digby Vere, died 1958, vol. V
Burnett, Maj.-Gen. Edward John Sidney, 1921–1978, vol. VII
Burnett, Sir (Edward) Napier, 1872–1923, vol. II
Burnett, Mrs Frances (Eliza) Hodgson, 1849–1924, vol. II
Burnett, George Murray, 1921–1980, vol. VII
Burnett, Dame Ivy C.; see Compton-Burnett.
Burnett of Leys, Maj.-Gen. Sir James Lauderdale Gilbert, 13th Bt (cr 1626), 1880–1953, vol. V
Burnett, Major John Chaplyn, 1863–1943, vol. IV
Burnett, Brig. John Curteis, 1882–1968, vol. VI
Burnett, John George, 1876–1962, vol. VI
Burnett, Col Sir Leslie Trew, 2nd Bt (cr 1913), 1884–1955, vol. V
Burnett, Dame Maud, 1863–1950, vol. IV
Burnett, Lt-Col Maurice John Brownless, 1904–1988, vol. VIII
Burnett, Sir Napier; see Burnett, Sir E. N.
Burnett, Rev. Canon (Philip) Stephen, 1914–1991, vol. IX
Burnett, Rear-Adm. Philip Whitworth, 1908–1996, vol. X
Burnett, Adm. Sir Robert Lindsay, 1887–1959, vol. V
Burnett, Lt-Col Robert Richardson, 1897–1975, vol. VII
Burnett, Rev. Canon Stephen; see Burnett, Rev. Canon P. S.
Burnett of Leys, Sir Thomas, 12th Bt (cr 1626), 1840–1926, vol. II
Burnett, William Freshfield, 1865–1935, vol. III

Burnett, William George Esterbrooke, 1886–1978, vol. VII
Burnett-Brown, Col Alexander Denis, 1894–1966, vol. VI
Burnett-Hitchcock, Lt-Gen. Sir Basil Ferguson; see Hitchcock.
Burnett-Stuart, George Eustace, 1876–1938, vol. III
Burnett-Stuart, Gen. Sir John Theodosius, 1875–1958, vol. V
Burney, Sir Anthony George Bernard, 1909–1989, vol. VIII
Burney, Lt-Col Arthur Edward Cave, 1883–1931, vol. III
Burney, Admiral of the Fleet Sir Cecil, 1st Bt, 1858–1929, vol. III
Burney, Ven. Charles, died 1907, vol. I
Burney, Charles, 1840–1912, vol. I
Burney, Comdr Sir (Charles) Dennistoun, 2nd Bt, 1888–1968, vol. VI
Burney, Rev. Charles Fox, 1868–1925, vol. II
Burney, Comdr Sir Dennistoun; see Burney, Comdr Sir C. D.
Burney, Brig.-Gen. Herbert Henry, 1858–1932, vol. III
Burney, Brig.-Gen. Percy de Sausmarez, 1863–1934, vol. III
Burney, Sydney Bernard, died 1951, vol. V
Burnham, 1st Baron, 1833–1916, vol. II
Burnham, 1st Viscount (and 2nd Baron), 1862–1933, vol. III
Burnham, 3rd Baron, 1864–1943, vol. IV
Burnham, 4th Baron, 1890–1963, vol. VI
Burnham, 5th Baron, 1920–1993, vol. IX
Burnham, Lady; (Marie Enid), died 1979, vol. VII
Burnham, Cecil, 1887–1965, vol. VI
Burnham, Forbes; see Burnham, L. F. S.
Burnham, James, 1905–1987, vol. VIII
Burnham, John Charles, 1866–1943, vol. IV
Burnham, (Linden) Forbes (Sampson), 1923–1985, vol. VIII
Burnie, James, 1882–1975, vol. VII
Burniston, George Garrett, 1914–1992, vol. IX
Burniston, Surg. Rear-Adm. Hugh Somerville, 1870–1962, vol. VI
Burnley, James, died 1919, vol. II
Burns, Sir Alan Cuthbert, 1887–1980, vol. VII
Burns, Arthur F., 1904–1987, vol. VIII
Burns, Bryan Hartop, 1896–1984, vol. VIII
Burns, Cecil Delisle, 1879–1942, vol. IV
Burns, Cecil Laurence, 1863–1929, vol. III
Burns, Sir Charles Ritchie, 1898–1985, vol. VIII
Burns, David, 1884–1969, vol. VI
Burns, Lt-Gen. Eedson Louis Millard, 1897–1985, vol. VIII
Burns, George, 1903–1970, vol. VI
Burns, Maj.-Gen. Sir George; see Burns, Maj.-Gen. Sir W. A. G.
Burns, Henry Stuart Mackenzie, 1900–1971, vol. VII
Burns, Col Hon. Sir James, 1846–1923, vol. II
Burns, James, 1859–1929, vol. III
Burns, Rev. James, 1865–1948, vol. IV
Burns, James, 1902–1994, vol. IX
Burns, Rt Hon. John, 1858–1943, vol. IV
Burns, Sir John Crawford, 1903–1991, vol. IX

Burns, John George, 1880–1950, vol. IV
Burns, Brig. Lionel Bryan Douglas, 1895–1966, vol. VI
Burns, Sir Malcolm McRae, 1910–1986, vol. VIII
Burns, Very Rev. Michael John, 1863–1949, vol. IV
Burns, Philip Leonard, 1896–1968, vol. VI
Burns, Robert, 1869–1941, vol. IV
Burns, Robert, 1859–1951, vol. V
Burns, Robert, 1912–1971, vol. VII
Burns, Rev. Thomas, 1853–1938, vol. III
Burns, Thomas Ferrier, 1906–1995, vol. IX
Burns, Maj.-Gen. Sir (Walter Arthur) George, 1911–1997, vol. X
Burns, Sir Wilfred, 1923–1984, vol. VIII
Burns, William, 1884–1970, vol. VI
Burns, William Alexander, 1921–1972, vol. VII
Burns-Begg, Col Robert, 1872–1918, vol. II
Burns-Lindow, Lt-Col Isaac William, 1868–1946, vol. IV
Burnside, Dame Edith, died 1992, vol. IX
Burnside, Rev. Frederick, died 1904, vol. I
Burnside, Helen Marion, 1844–1923, vol. II
Burnside, Robert Bruce, 1862–1929, vol. III
Burnside, Rev. Walter Fletcher, 1874–1949, vol. IV
Burnside, William, 1852–1927, vol. II
Burnside, William Snow, died 1920, vol. II
Burntwood, Baron (Life Peer); Julian Ward Snow, 1910–1982, vol. VIII
Burnyeat, William John Dalzell, 1874–1916, vol. II
Burpee, Lawrence Johnston, 1873–1946, vol. IV
Burr, Alfred, 1855–1952, vol. V
Burr, Rear-Adm. John Leslie, 1847–1917, vol. II
Burr, Malcolm, 1878–1954, vol. V
Burr-Bryan, Walter; see Bryan, W. B.
Burra, Edward, 1905–1976, vol. VII
Burrage, Alfred McLelland, 1889–1956, vol. V
Burrard, Major Sir Gerald, 8th Bt, 1888–1965, vol. VI
Burrard, Col Harry George, 1871–1963, vol. VI
Burrard, Sir Harry Paul, 6th Bt, 1846–1933, vol. III
Burrard, Col Sir Sidney Gerald, 7th Bt, 1860–1943, vol. IV
Burrard, Col William Dutton, 1861–1938, vol. III
Burrell, Sir Charles Raymond, 6th Bt, 1848–1899, vol. I
Burrell, Derek William, 1925–1999, vol. X
Burrell, Harry James, 1873–1945, vol. IV
Burrell, Vice-Adm. Sir Henry MacKay, 1904–1988, vol. VIII
Burrell, John; see Burrell, R. J.
Burrell, John Glyn, 1912–1984, vol. VIII
Burrell, John Percy, 1910–1972, vol. VII
Burrell, Joseph Frederick, 1909–1983, vol. VIII
Burrell, Lancelot S. T., 1883–1938, vol. III
Burrell, Hon. Martin, 1858–1938, vol. III
Burrell, Sir Merrik Raymond, 7th Bt, 1877–1957, vol. V
Burrell, Percy Saville, 1871–1958, vol. V
Burrell, Peter Eustace, 1905–1999, vol. X
Burrell, Robert Eric, 1890–1968, vol. VI
Burrell, (Robert) John, 1923–1985, vol. VIII
Burrell, Sir Walter Raymond, 8th Bt, 1903–1985, vol. VIII
Burrell, Sir William, 1861–1958, vol. V

Burrenchobay, Sir Dayendranath, 1919–1999, vol. X
Burridge, Frederick Vango, 1869–1945, vol. IV
Burridge, Captain Robert Archibald Morison, died 1957, vol. V
Burrington, Arthur, died 1924, vol. II
Burrough, Adm. Sir Harold Martin, 1888–1977, vol. VII
Burrough, John Outhit Harold, 1916–1996, vol. X
Burroughes, Dorothy Mary Burroughes-, died 1963, vol. VI
Burroughs, Edgar Rice, 1875–1950, vol. IV
Burroughs, Rt Rev. Edward Arthur, 1882–1934, vol. III
Burroughs, Lt-Gen. Sir Frederick William Traill, 1831–1905, vol. I
Burroughs, John, 1837–1921, vol. II
Burroughs, Ronald Arthur, 1917–1980, vol. VII
Burroughs, Rev. William Edward, 1845–1931, vol. III
Burroughs-Fowler, Walter, died 1930, vol. III
Burrow, Edward John, 1869–1935, vol. III
Burrow, Harold, 1903–1987, vol. VIII
Burrow, Joseph le Fleming, 1888–1967, vol. VI
Burrow, Thomas, 1909–1986, vol. VIII
Burrowes, Lt-Col Algernon St Leger, 1847–1925, vol. II
Burrowes, Rt Rev. Arnold Brian, 1896–1963, vol. VI
Burrowes, Brig.-Gen. Arnold Robinson, 1867–1949, vol. IV
Burrowes, Herbert Alleyne Nathanael, 1870–1933, vol. III
Burrowes, Thomas Cosby, 1856–1925, vol. II(A), vol. III
Burrowes, Thomas Fraser, died 1947, vol. IV
Burrowes, William Henry Aglionby, died 1922, vol. II
Burrows, Albert, 1919–1972, vol. VII
Burrows, Alfred John, died 1957, vol. V
Burrows, Christine Mary Elizabeth, 1872–1959, vol. V
Burrows, Col Edmund Augustine, 1855–1927, vol. II
Burrows, Sir Ernest Pennington, 3rd Bt, 1851–1917, vol. II
Burrows, Rev. Francis Henry, 1857–1928, vol. II
Burrows, Sir Frederick Abernethy, 2nd Bt, 1845–1904, vol. I
Burrows, Sir Frederick John, 1887–1973, vol. VII
Burrows, Gen. George Reynolds Scott, 1827–1917, vol. II
Burrows, George Thomas, 1876–1949, vol. IV
Burrows, Harold, 1875–1955, vol. V
Burrows, Harold Jackson, 1902–1981, vol. VIII
Burrows, Very Rev. Hedley Robert, 1887–1983, vol. VIII
Burrows, Comdr Henry Montagu, 1899–1979, vol. VII
Burrows, Brig. Hollis Martin, 1884–1952, vol. V
Burrows, Sir John; see Burrows, Sir R. J. F.
Burrows, Rt Rev. Leonard Hedley, 1857–1940, vol. III
Burrows, Lionel Burton, 1883–1970, vol. VI
Burrows, Rev. Millar, 1889–1980, vol. VII
Burrows, Captain Montagu, 1819–1905, vol. I

Burrows, Lt-Gen. Montagu Brocas, 1894–1967, vol. VI

Burrows, Sir Robert Abraham, 1884–1964, vol. VI

Burrows, Sir (Robert) John (Formby), 1901–1987, vol. VIII

Burrows, Sir Roland, 1882–1952, vol. V

Burrows, Ronald Montagu, 1867–1920, vol. II

Burrows, Sir Stephen Montagu, 1856–1935, vol. III

Burrows, Theodore Arthur, 1857–1929, vol. III

Burrows, Rt Rev. Winfrid Oldfield, 1858–1929, vol. III

Burry, Bessie P.; see Pullen-Burry.

Burstall, Aubrey Frederic, 1902–1984, vol. VIII

Burstall, Frederick William, 1865–1934, vol. III

Burstall, Lt-Gen. Sir Henry Edward, 1870–1945, vol. IV

Burstall, Sara Annie, 1859–1939, vol. III

Burston, Maj.-Gen. Sir Samuel Roy, 1888–1960, vol. V

Burt, Brig.-Gen. Alfred, 1875–1949, vol. IV

Burt, Alfred LeRoy, 1888–1971, vol. VII

Burt, Sir Bryce Chudleigh, 1881–1943, vol. IV

Burt, Sir Charles, 1832–1913, vol. I

Burt, Charles Kingley J.; see Johnstone-Burt.

Burt, Clive Stuart Saxon, 1900–1981, vol. VIII

Burt, Sir Cyril Lodowic, 1883–1971, vol. VII

Burt, Sir George Mowlem, 1884–1964, vol. VI

Burt, Rear-Adm. Gerald George Percy, 1888–1965, vol. VI

Burt, Henry, 1844–1940, vol. III

Burt, Rev. Henry Chadwick, 1871–1959, vol. V(A)

Burt, Sir Henry Parsall, 1857–1936, vol. III

Burt, Hugh Armitage, 1911–1976, vol. VII

Burt, Col John Marshall, 1860–1931, vol. III

Burt, Sir John Mowlem, 1845–1918, vol. II

Burt, Joseph Barnes, died 1953, vol. V

Burt, Leonard James, 1892–1983, vol. VIII

Burt, Octavius, 1849–1940, vol. III

Burt, Hon. Septimus, 1847–1919, vol. II

Burt, Rt Hon. Thomas, 1837–1922, vol. II

Burt-Andrews, Air Cdre Charles Beresford Eaton, 1913–1995, vol. IX

Burt-Andrews, Stanley George, 1908–1990, vol. VIII

Burtchaell, Lt-Gen. Sir Charles Henry, 1866–1932, vol. III

Burtchaell, George Dames, 1853–1921, vol. II

Burton, 1st Baron, 1837–1909, vol. I

Burton, Baroness (2nd in line), 1873–1962, vol. VI

Burton of Coventry, Baroness (Life Peer); Elaine Frances Burton, 1904–1991, vol. IX

Burton, Alan Chadburn, 1904–1979, vol. VII

Burton, Rev. Arthur Daniel, 1852–1933, vol. III

Burton, Arthur Davis, 1887–1962, vol. VI

Burton, Maj.-Gen. Benjamin, 1855–1921, vol. II(A), vol. III

Burton, Sir Bunnell Henry, 1858–1943, vol. IV

Burton, Sir Charles William Cuffe, 5th Bt, 1823–1902, vol. I

Burton, Claud Peter Primrose, 1916–1957, vol. V

Burton, Brig. Colin, 1883–1945, vol. IV

Burton, Donald, 1892–1966, vol. VI

Burton, Brig.-Gen. Edmund Boteler, 1861–1942, vol. IV

Burton, Rev. Canon Edwin Hubert, 1870–1925, vol. II

Burton, Eli Franklin, 1879–1948, vol. IV

Burton, Rev. Ernest De Witt, 1856–1925, vol. II

Burton, Gen. Sir Fowler, 1822–1904, vol. I

Burton, Sir Francis Charles Edward D.; see Denys-Burton.

Burton, Frank Ernest, 1865–1948, vol. IV

Burton, Sir Frederick William, 1816–1900, vol. I

Burton, Captain Sir Geoffrey Duke, 1893–1954, vol. V

Burton, Sir Geoffrey Pownall, 1884–1972, vol. VII

Burton, Rt Rev. George Ambrose, 1852–1931, vol. III

Burton, Major Sir Gerald Arthur Fowler, 1869–1930, vol. III

Burton, Captain Gerard William, 1879–1915, vol. I

Burton, Harold, 1901–1966, vol. VI

Burton, Harold Hitz, 1888–1964, vol. VI

Burton, Air Marshal Sir Harry, 1919–1993, vol. IX

Burton, Rt Hon. Henry, 1866–1935, vol. III

Burton, Henry, 1907–1952, vol. V

Burton, Rev. Henry Darwin, 1858–1943, vol. IV

Burton, Col Henry Walter, 1876–1947, vol. IV

Burton, Rev. Canon Humphrey Philipps Walcot, 1888–1957, vol. V

Burton, John Adam Gib, 1888–1962, vol. VI

Burton, John Edward B.; see Bloundelle-Burton.

Burton, John Frederick, 1870–1937, vol. III

Burton, Rev. John Harold Stanley, 1913–1993, vol. IX

Burton, Rev. John James, 1849–1927, vol. II

Burton, Rev. John Richard, 1847–1939, vol. III

Burton, Rt Rev. Lewis William, 1852–1940, vol. III(A), vol. IV

Burton, Maurice, 1898–1992, vol. IX

Burton, Sir Montague, 1885–1952, vol. V

Burton, Neil Edward David, 1930–1990, vol. VIII

Burton, Sir Pomeroy, 1869–1947, vol. IV

Burton, Brig.-Gen. Reginald George, 1864–1951, vol. V

Burton, Richard, 1925–1984, vol. VIII

Burton, Brig.-Gen. St George Edward William, died 1943, vol. IV

Burton, Rt Rev. Spence, 1881–1966, vol. VI

Burton, William, died 1954, vol. V

Burton, Sir William James Miller, 1862–1946, vol. IV

Burton, Sir William Parker, 1864–1942, vol. IV

Burton-Baldry, Walter Burton, 1888–1940, vol. III

Burton-Bradley, Sir Burton Gyrth, 1914–1994, vol. X (AI)

Burton-Chadwick, Sir Peter; see Burton-Chadwick, Sir R.

Burton-Chadwick, Sir Robert, 1st Bt, 1869–1951, vol. V

Burton-Chadwick, Sir Robert, (Sir Peter Burton-Chadwick), 2nd Bt, 1911–1983, vol. VIII

Burton-Fanning, Frederick William, 1863–1937, vol. III

Burton-Taylor, Sir Alvin, 1912–1991, vol. IX

Burtt Davy, Joseph, 1870–1940, vol. III

Burwash, Lachlin Taylor, 1874–1940, vol. III

Burwash, Rev. Nathanael, 1839–1918, vol. II

Bury, Viscount; Derek William Charles Keppel, 1911–1968, vol. VI
Bury, Lt-Col Charles Kenneth Howard, 1883–1963, vol. VI
Bury, Francis George, *died* 1926, vol. II
Bury, Sir George, 1866–1958, vol. V
Bury, George Wyman, 1874–1920, vol. II
Bury, Rt Rev. Herbert, *died* 1933, vol. III
Bury, John, 1925–2000, vol. X
Bury, John Bagnell, 1861–1927, vol. II
Bury, Judson Sykes, *died* 1944, vol. IV
Bury, Hon. Leslie Harry Ernest, 1913–1986, vol. VIII
Bury, Lindsay Edward, 1882–1952, vol. V
Bury, Oliver R. H., *died* 1946, vol. IV
Bury, Ralph Frederic, 1876–1954, vol. V
Bury, Shirley Joan, 1925–1999, vol. X
Bury, Rev. William, 1839–1920, vol. II
Busby, Sir Matthew, 1909–1994, vol. IX
Buscarlet, Air Vice-Marshal Sir Willett Amalric Bowen B.; *see* Bowen-Buscarlet.
Busch, Adolf, 1891–1952, vol. V
Busch, Fritz, 1890–1951, vol. V
Bush, Alan Dudley, 1900–1995, vol. IX
Bush, Hon. Sir Brian Drex, 1925–1989, vol. VIII
Bush, Douglas; *see* Bush, J. N. D.
Bush, Captain Eric Wheler, 1899–1985, vol. VIII
Bush, Frank Whittaker, 1825–1903, vol. I
Bush, Harry, 1883–1957, vol. V
Bush, Col Harry Stebbing, 1871–1942, vol. IV
Bush, Ian Elcock, 1928–1986, vol. VIII
Bush, Irving T., 1869–1948, vol. IV
Bush, Col (James) Paul, 1857–1930, vol. III
Bush, Rear-Adm. James Tobin, 1874–1949, vol. IV
Bush, (John Nash) Douglas, 1896–1983, vol. VIII
Bush, Brig.-Gen. John Ernest, 1858–1943, vol. IV
Bush, Col Paul; *see* Bush, Col J. P.
Bush, Adm. Sir Paul Warner, 1855–1930, vol. III
Bush, Raymond G. W., 1885–1972, vol. VII
Bush, Reginald Edgar James, 1869–1956, vol. V
Bush, Robert Edwin, 1855–1939, vol. III
Bush, Ronald Paul, 1902–1986, vol. VIII
Bush, Rev. Thomas Cromwell, *died* 1919, vol. II
Bush, Vannevar, 1890–1974, vol. VII
Bushby, Sir Edmund Fleming, 1879–1943, vol. IV
Bushby, Geoffrey Henry, 1899–1935, vol. III
Bushby, Henry Jeffreys, 1820–1903, vol. I
Bushby, Thomas, *died* 1916, vol. II
Bushby, Walter Edwin, 1889–1963, vol. VI
Bushe, Sir Grattan; *see* Bushe, Sir H. G.
Bushe, Sir (Henry) Grattan, 1886–1961, vol. VI
Bushe, Robert Gervase, 1851–1927, vol. II
Bushe, Seymour Coghill Hort, 1853–1922, vol. II
Bushe, Brig.-Gen. Thomas Francis, 1858–1951, vol. V
Bushe-Fox, Joscelyn Plunket, 1880–1954, vol. V
Bushe-Fox, Loftus Henry Kendal, 1863–1916, vol. II
Bushe-Fox, Patrick Loftus, 1907–1982, vol. VIII
Bushell, John Christopher Wyndowe, 1919–1995, vol. IX
Bushell, Stephen Wootton, 1844–1908, vol. I
Bushell, W. F., 1885–1974, vol. VII
Bushell, Rev. William Done, 1838–1917, vol. II

Bushman, Maj.-Gen. Sir Henry Augustus, 1841–1930, vol. III
Bushnell, Frank George, 1868–1941, vol. IV
Bushnell, Geoffrey Hext Sutherland, 1903–1978, vol. VII
Bushnell, George Herbert, 1896–1973, vol. VII
Busia, Kofi Abrefa, 1913–1978, vol. VII
Busk, Air Cdre Clifford Westly, 1898–1970, vol. VI
Busk, Sir Douglas Laird, 1906–1990, vol. VIII
Busk, Sir Edward Henry, 1844–1926, vol. II
Busk, Henrietta, 1845–1936, vol. III
Busk, Mrs Mary, 1854–1935, vol. III
Busoni, Ferruccio Benvenuto, 1866–1924, vol. II
Bussau, Hon. Sir (Albert) Louis, 1884–1947, vol. IV
Bussau, Hon. Sir Louis; *see* Bussau, Hon. Sir A. L.
Bussé, John, 1903–1956, vol. V
Bussell, Rev. Frederick William, 1862–1944, vol. IV
Bussell, Ven. William, *died* 1936, vol. III
Bussey, Ernest William, 1891–1958, vol. V
Bussey, Harry Youngman, 1858–1951, vol. V
Bussy, (George Francis) Philip, 1871–1933, vol. III
Bussy, Philip; *see* Bussy, G. F. P.
Bustamante, Rt Hon. and Exc. Sir Alexander; *see* Bustamante, Rt Hon. and Exc. Sir W. A.
Bustamante, Rt Hon. and Exc. Sir (William) Alexander, 1884–1977, vol. VII
Busteed, Bde-Surgeon Henry Elmsley, 1833–1912, vol. I
Buston, Brig.-Gen. Philip Thomas, 1853–1938, vol. III
Buswell, Col Ferberd Richard, *died* 1937, vol. III
Buswell, Ven. Henry Dison, 1839–1940, vol. III
Buszard, Marston Clarke, 1837–1921, vol. II
Butchart, Bt Lt-Col Henry Jackson, 1882–1971, vol. VII
Butcher, Arthur Douglas Deane, 1884–1944, vol. IV
Butcher, Very Rev. Charles Henry, 1833–1907, vol. I
Butcher, Maj.-Gen. Sir George James, 1860–1939, vol. III
Butcher, Sir Herbert Walter, 1st Bt, 1901–1966, vol. VI
Butcher, Paymaster Captain Reginald, 1880–1935, vol. III
Butcher, Rt Rev. Reginald Albert Claver, 1905–1975, vol. VII
Butcher, Samuel Henry, 1850–1910, vol. I
Butcher, William Deane, 1846–1919, vol. II
Bute, 3rd Marquess of, 1847–1900, vol. I
Bute, 4th Marquess of, 1881–1947, vol. IV
Bute, 5th Marquess of, 1907–1956, vol. V
Bute, 6th Marquess of, 1933–1993, vol. IX
Butement, William Alan Stewart, 1904–1990, vol. VIII
Butenandt, Adolf Friedrich Johann, 1903–1995, vol. IX
Butland, Sir Jack Richard, *died* 1982, vol. VIII
Butler of Saffron Walden, Baron (Life Peer); Richard Austen Butler, 1902–1982, vol. VIII
Butler, Rev. Alexander Douglas, *died* 1926, vol. II
Butler, Alfred J., 1850–1936, vol. III
Butler, Alfred Trego, 1880–1946, vol. IV
Butler, Col Arnold Charles Paul, 1890–1973, vol. VII

Butler, Arthur Gardiner, 1844–1925, vol. II
Butler, Col Arthur Graham, 1872–1949, vol. IV
Butler, Rev. Arthur Gray, 1831–1909, vol. I
Butler, Rt Rev. Arthur Hamilton, 1912–1991, vol. IX
Butler, (Arthur) Hugh (Montagu), 1873–1943, vol. IV
Butler, Arthur John, 1844–1910, vol. I
Butler, Arthur Stanley, 1854–1923, vol. II
Butler, Arthur Stanley George, 1888–1965, vol. VI
Butler, Lt-Col Arthur Townley, 1867–1948, vol. IV
Butler, Rt Rev. (Basil) Christopher, 1902–1986, vol. VIII
Butler, Lt-Col Charles Henry, 1881–1941, vol. IV
Butler, Sir (Charles) Owen, 1896–1968, vol. VI
Butler, Rt Rev. Christopher; see Butler, Rt Rev. B. C.
Butler, Sir Clifford Charles, 1922–1999, vol. X
Butler, Rt Rev. Cuthbert; see Butler, Rt Rev. E. C.
Butler, Sir Cyril Kendall, 1864–1936, vol. III
Butler, Rev. Dugald, 1862–1926, vol. II
Butler, Edward Clive Barber, 1904–1999, vol. X
Butler, Rt Rev. (Edward) Cuthbert, 1858–1934, vol. III
Butler, Sir Edwin John, 1874–1943, vol. IV
Butler, Eliza Marian, 1885–1959, vol. V
Butler, Elizabeth, (Lady Butler), 1846–1933, vol. III
Butler, Air Vice-Marshal Eric Scott, 1907–1996, vol. X
Butler, Maj.-Gen. Ernest Reuben Charles, 1864–1959, vol. V
Butler, Esmond Unwin, 1922–1989, vol. VIII
Butler, Captain Hon. Francis Almeric, 1872–1925, vol. II
Butler, Frank Chatterton, 1907–1984, vol. VIII
Butler, Frank Hedges, 1855–1928, vol. II
Butler, Sir Frederick George Augustus, 1873–1961, vol. VI
Butler, Sir Geoffrey, 1887–1929, vol. III
Butler, Maj.-Gen. Geoffrey Ernest, 1905–1981, vol. VIII
Butler, George, 1904–1999, vol. X
Butler, Sir George Beresford, 1857–1924, vol. II
Butler, George Grey, 1852–1935, vol. III
Butler, Sir Gerald Snowden, 1885–1969, vol. VI
Butler, Sir Harcourt; see Butler, Sir S. H.
Butler, Sir Harold Beresford, 1883–1951, vol. V
Butler, Harold Edgeworth, 1878–1951, vol. V
Butler, Harold Edwin, 1893–1973, vol. VII
Butler, Maj.-Gen. Henry, died 1907, vol. I
Butler, Rev. Henry Montagu, 1833–1918, vol. II
Butler, Herbert William, 1897–1971, vol. VII
Butler, Rev. Hercules Scott, 1850–1928, vol. II
Butler, Hon. (Horace) Somerset Edmond, 1903–1962, vol. VI
Butler, Hugh; see Butler, A. H. M.
Butler, Hugh Montagu, 1890–1972, vol. VII
Butler, Hugh Myddleton, 1857–1943, vol. IV
Butler, Lt-Col Humphrey, 1894–1953, vol. V
Butler, James Bayley, died 1964, vol. VI
Butler, Sir James Ramsay Montagu, 1889–1975, vol. VII
Butler, Rev. Lord (James) Theobald Bagot John, 1852–1929, vol. III
Butler, John Alfred Valentine, 1899–1977, vol. VII

Butler, Captain John Fitzhardinge Paul, 1888–1916, vol. II
Butler, Josephine Elizabeth, 1828–1906, vol. I
Butler, Mrs Joyce Shore, 1910–1992, vol. IX
Butler, Kathleen Teresa Blake, 1883–1950, vol. IV
Butler, Brig.-Gen. Hon. Lesley James Probyn, 1876–1955, vol. V
Butler, Lionel Harry, 1923–1981, vol. VIII
Butler, Maria, 1868–1901, vol. I
Butler, Matthew Joseph, 1856–1933, vol. III
Butler, Gen. Sir Mervyn Andrew Haldane, 1913–1976, vol. VII
Butler, Mildred, died 1941, vol. IV
Butler, Hon. Sir Milo Broughton, 1906–1979, vol. VII
Butler, Sir Montagu Sherard Dawes, 1873–1952, vol. V
Butler, Sir Nevile Montagu, 1893–1973, vol. VII
Butler, Nicholas Murray, 1862–1947, vol. IV
Butler, Sir Owen; see Butler, Sir C. O.
Butler, Lt-Col Patrick Richard, 1880–1967, vol. VI
Butler, Sir Paul Dalrymple, 1886–1955, vol. V
Butler, Pierce Essex O'B.; see O'Brien-Butler.
Butler, Reg, (Reginald Cotterell Butler), 1913–1981, vol. VIII
Butler, Sir Reginald; see Butler, Sir R. R. F.
Butler, Comdr Sir (Reginald) Thomas, 2nd Bt (cr 1922), 1901–1959, vol. VII
Butler, Hon. Sir Richard, 1850–1925, vol. II
Butler, Col Richard Barry, died 1957, vol. V
Butler, Lt-Col Richard F.; see Fowler-Butler.
Butler, Lt-Gen. Sir Richard Harte Keatinge, 1870–1935, vol. III
Butler, Richard Jago, 1884–1931, vol. III
Butler, Hon. Sir Richard Layton, 1885–1966, vol. IV
Butler, Sir Richard Pierce, 11th Bt (cr 1628), 1872–1955, vol. V
Butler, Richard William, 1844–1928, vol. II
Butler, Maj.-Gen. Robert Henry F.; see Fowler-Butler.
Butler, Sir (Robert) Reginald Frederick, 1st Bt (cr 1922), 1866–1933, vol. III
Butler, Major Hon. Robert Thomas Rowley Probyn, 1882–1938, vol. III
Butler, Rohan D'Olier, 1917–1996, vol. X
Butler, Rudolph Maximilian, 1872–1943, vol. IV
Butler, Maj.-Gen. St John Desmond A.; see Arcedeckne-Butler.
Butler, Samuel, 1835–1902, vol. I
Butler, Slade, died 1923, vol. II
Butler, Hon. Somerset; see Butler, Hon. H. S. E.
Butler, Sir (Spencer) Harcourt, 1869–1938, vol. III
Butler, Spencer Perceval, 1828–1915, vol. I
Butler, Maj.-Gen. Stephen Seymour, 1880–1964, vol. VI
Butler, Col Sydney George, 1874–1940, vol. III
Butler, Rev. Lord Theobold; see Butler, Rev. Lord J. T. B. J.
Butler, Maj.-Gen. Hon. Theobald Patrick Probyn, 1884–1970, vol. VI
Butler, Theobald Richard Fitzwalter, 1894–1976, vol. VII
Butler, Thomas, died 1937, vol. III

Butler, Comdr Sir Thomas; *see* Butler, Comdr Sir R. T.
Butler, Major Thomas Adair, 1836–1901, vol. I
Butler, Captain Sir Thomas Dacres, 1845–1937, vol. III
Butler, Thomas Harrison, 1871–1945, vol. IV
Butler, Sir Thomas Pierce, 10th Bt (*cr* 1628), 1836–1909, vol. I
Butler, Col Sir Thomas Pierce, 12th Bt (*cr* 1628), 1910–1994, vol. IX
Butler, Rear-Adm. Vernon Saumarez, 1885–1954, vol. V
Butler, Victor Spencer, 1900–1969, vol. VI
Butler, William F. I., *died* 1930, vol. III
Butler, Rt Hon. Sir William Francis, 1838–1910, vol. I
Butler, Brig-Gen. William John Chesshyre, 1864–1946, vol. IV
Butler, Sir William Waters, 1st Bt (*cr* 1926), 1866–1939, vol. III
Butler-Bowdon, John Erdeswick, 1850–1929, vol. III
Butler Brockwell, Esca Powys; *see* Brockwell, E. P. B.
Butler-Henderson, Hon. Eric Brand, 1884–1953, vol. V
Butler-Smythe, Albert Charles, 1852–1936, vol. III
Butlin, Sir Henry Guy Trentham, 2nd Bt, 1893–1916, vol. II
Butlin, Sir Henry Tretham, 1st Bt, 1845–1912, vol. I
Butlin, Sir William, 1851–1923, vol. II
Butlin, Sir William Edmund, 1899–1980, vol. VII
Butt, Sir Alfred, 1st Bt, 1878–1962, vol. VI
Butt, Sir (Alfred) Kenneth (Dudley), 2nd Bt, 1908–1999, vol. X
Butt, Charles Sinclair, 1900–1973, vol. VII
Butt, Dame Clara Ellen, 1873–1936, vol. III
Butt, John Everett, 1906–1965, vol. VI
Butt, Most Rev. Joseph, 1869–1944, vol. IV
Butt, Sir Kenneth; *see* Butt, Sir A. K. D.
Buttenshaw, Hon. Ernest Albert, 1876–1950, vol. IV, vol. V
Butter, Archibald Edward, 1874–1928, vol. II
Butter, Peter Herbert, 1921–1999, vol. X
Butterfield, Baron (Life Peer); William John Hughes Butterfield, 1920–2000, vol. X
Butterfield, Fred, *died* 1935, vol. III
Butterfield, Sir Frederick William Louis d'Hilliers Roosevelt Theodore, *died* 1943, vol. IV
Butterfield, Sir Harry Durham, 1898–1976, vol. VII
Butterfield, Sir Herbert, 1900–1979, vol. VII
Butterfield, Robert William Fitzmaurice, 1889–1967, vol. VI
Butterfield, William, 1814–1900, vol. I
Butters, Sir John Henry, 1885–1969, vol. VI
Butterworth, Alan, 1864–1937, vol. III
Butterworth, Sir Alexander-Kaye, 1854–1946, vol. IV
Butterworth, Arthur Reginald, 1850–1924, vol. II
Butterworth, George Esmond, 1946–2000, vol. X
Butterworth, Sir (George) Neville, 1911–1995, vol. IX
Butterworth, Comdr Henry, 1866–1926, vol. II
Butterworth, Henry, 1926–1996, vol. X
Butterworth, Sir Neville; *see* Butterworth, Sir G. N.
Butterworth, Reginald, 1879–1951, vol. V

Butterworth, Col Reginald Francis Amherst, 1876–1960, vol. V
Butterworth, Hon. W. Walton, 1903–1975, vol. VII
Butti, Rt Rev. Mgr Peter L., *died* 1932, vol. III
Buttigieg, Anton, 1912–1983, vol. VIII
Buttle, Gladwin Albert Hurst, 1899–1983, vol. VIII
Button, Air Vice-Marshal Arthur Daniel, 1916–1991, vol. IX
Button, Frederick Stephen, 1873–1948, vol. IV
Button, Howard, 1875–1965, vol. VI
Button, Sir Howard Stransom, 1873–1943, vol. IV
Buttrose, Murray, 1903–1987, vol. VIII
Butts, S., *died* 1906, vol. I
Buxton, 1st Earl, 1853–1934, vol. III
Buxton, Countess; (Mildred Anne), *died* 1955, vol. V
Buxton, Alfred Fowell, 1854–1952, vol. V
Buxton, Alfred St Clair, 1854–1920, vol. II
Buxton, Major Anthony, 1881–1970, vol. VI
Buxton, Comdr Bernard, 1882–1923, vol. II
Buxton, Charles Roden, 1875–1942, vol. IV
Buxton, Denis Alfred Jex, 1895–1964, vol. VI
Buxton, Maj. Desmond Gurney, 1898–1987, vol. VIII
Buxton, Dudley Wilmot, *died* 1931, vol. III
Buxton, Edward Gurney, 1865–1929, vol. III
Buxton, Edward North, 1840–1924, vol. II
Buxton, Francis William, 1847–1911, vol. I
Buxton, Geoffrey Powell, 1852–1929, vol. III
Buxton, Gladys, 1891–1971, vol. VII
Buxton, Rt Rev. Harold Jocelyn, 1880–1976, vol. VII
Buxton, Henry Fowell, 1876–1949, vol. IV
Buxton, James Basil, *died* 1954, vol. V
Buxton, John Henry, 1849–1934, vol. III
Buxton, Col John Lawrence, 1877–1951, vol. V
Buxton, Leonard Halford Dudley, 1889–1939, vol. III
Buxton, Lionel Gurney, 1876–1962, vol. VI
Buxton, Patrick Alfred, 1892–1955, vol. V
Buxton, Richard; *see* Shanks, Edward.
Buxton, Captain Richard Gurney, 1887–1972, vol. VII
Buxton, Dame Rita Mary, 1900–1982, vol. VIII
Buxton, Robert Vere, 1883–1953, vol. V
Buxton, Captain Roden Henry Victor, 1890–1970, vol. VI
Buxton, St John Dudley, 1891–1981, vol. VIII
Buxton, Sir Thomas Fowell, 3rd Bt, 1837–1915, vol. I
Buxton, Sir Thomas Fowell, 5th Bt, 1889–1945, vol. IV
Buxton, Sir (Thomas Fowell) Victor, 4th Bt, 1865–1919, vol. II
Buxton, Sir Thomas Fowell Victor, 6th Bt, 1925–1996, vol. X
Buxton, Sir Victor; *see* Buxton, Sir T. F. V.
Buxton, William Leonard, 1894–1964, vol. VI
Buzacott, Charles Hardie, 1835–1918, vol. II
Buzacott, William James, 1866–1937, vol. III
Buzzard, Rear-Adm. Sir Anthony Wass, 2nd Bt, 1902–1972, vol. VII
Buzzard, Lt-Col Charles Norman, 1873–1861, vol. VI

123

Buzzard, Sir (Edward) Farquhar, 1st Bt, 1871–1945, vol. IV
Buzzard, Brig.-Gen. Frank Anstie, 1875–1950, vol. IV
Buzzard, John Huxley, 1912–1984, vol. VIII
Buzzard, Thomas, 1831–1919, vol. II
Byam, Maj.-Gen. William, 1841–1906, vol. I
Byam, William, 1882–1963, vol. VI
Byam Shaw, Glencairn Alexander, 1904–1986, vol. VIII
Byam Shaw, James; *see* Byam Shaw, John J.
Byam Shaw, (John) James, 1903–1992, vol. IX
Byass, Bt Col Sir Geoffrey Robert Sidney, 2nd Bt, 1895–1976, vol. VII
Byass, Col Harry Nicholl, 1863–1956, vol. V
Byass, Sir Sidney Hutchinson, 1st Bt, 1862–1929, vol. III
Byatt, Edwin, 1888–1948, vol. IV
Byatt, Sir Horace Archer, 1875–1933, vol. III
Byers, Baron (Life Peer); Charles Frank Byers, 1915–1984, vol. VIII
Byers, Sir John William, *died* 1920, vol. II
Byers, Joseph Austen, 1895–1977, vol. VII
Byers, Mrs Margaret, *died* 1912, vol. I
Byers, Sir Maurice Hearne, 1917–1999, vol. X
Byford, Donald, 1898–1981, vol. VIII
Byford, Sir John, 1860–1931, vol. III
Byles, William Hounsom, 1872–1928, vol. II
Byles, Sir William Pollard, 1839–1917, vol. II
Byng, 1st Viscount, 1862–1935, vol. III
Byng, Lt-Col Hon. Antony Schomberg, 1876–1934, vol. III
Byng, Col Hon. Charles Cavendish George, 1849–1918, vol. II
Byng, Hon. Ivo Francis, 1874–1949, vol. IV
Byng, L. C.; *see* Crammer-Byng.
Byng, Major Hon. Lionel Francis George, 1858–1915, vol. I
Byng, Lady Mary Elizabeth Agnes; *see* Mauny-Talvande, Countess of.
Byng, Hon. Sydney, 1844–1920, vol. II
Bynner, Witter, 1881–1968, vol. VI
Byrd, Rear-Adm. Richard E., 1888–1957, vol. V
Byrde, Ven. Louis, *died* 1917, vol. II
Byrne, Alfred, 1882–1956, vol. V
Byrne, Brian Oswald D., *see* Byrne, Donn.
Byrne, Sir Clarence Askew, 1903–1987, vol. IX (AI)

Byrne, Donn, 1889–1928, vol. II
Byrne, Sir Edmund Widdrington, 1844–1904, vol. I
Byrne, Most Rev. Edward J., 1872–1940, vol. III
Byrne, Rt Rev. Mgr Frederick, *born* 1834, vol. II
Byrne, Col Frederick Joseph, 1873–1929, vol. III
Byrne, Col Henry, 1840–1915, vol. I
Byrne, Rt Rev. Herbert Kevin, 1884–1978, vol. VII
Byrne, Rt Rev. James, 1870–1938, vol. III
Byrne, James Patrick, 1854–1935, vol. III
Byrne, Lt-Col John Dillon, 1875–1925, vol. II
Byrne, Brig-Gen. Sir Joseph Aloysius, 1874–1942, vol. IV
Byrne, Hon. Sir Laurence Austin, 1896–1965, vol. VI
Byrne, Louis Campbell, *died* 1923. vol. II
Byrne, Muriel St Clare, 1895–1983, vol. VIII
Byrne, Patrick Sarsfield, 1913–1980, vol. VII
Byrne, Rev. Peter, *born* 1840, vol. II
Byrne, Air Cdre Reginald, 1888–1965, vol. VI
Byrne, Richard, *died* 1942, vol. IV
Byrne, Rt Hon. Sir William Patrick, 1859–1935, vol. III
Byrnes, James Francis, 1879–1972, vol. VII
Byrnes, Hon. Sir Percy Thomas, 1893–1973, vol. VII
Byrnes, Hon. Thomas Joseph, 1860–1898, vol. I
Byrom, Charles Reginald, 1878–1952, vol. V
Byrom, Thomas Emmett, 1871–1956, vol. V
Byron, 9th Baron, 1855–1917, vol. II
Byron, 10th Baron, 1861–1949, vol. IV
Byron, 11th Baron, 1903–1983, vol. VIII
Byron, 12th Baron, 1899–1989, vol. VIII
Byron, Captain Augustus William, 1856–1939, vol. III
Byron, Paymaster Rear-Adm. Charles Edgar, *died* 1940, vol. III
Byron, Edmund, 1843–1921, vol. II
Byron, Brig.-Gen. John, 1872–1944, vol. IV
Byron, Brig.-Gen. Hon. John Joseph, *died* 1935, vol. III
Byron, Col Richard, 1870–1939, vol. III
Byron, Robert, 1905–1941, vol. IV
Byrt, Albert Henry, 1881–1966, vol. VI
Bythesea, Rear-Adm. John, 1827–1906, vol. I
Bywater, Hector Charles, 1884–1940, vol. III
Bywater, Ingram, 1840–1914, vol. I
Bywater, Thomas Lloyd, 1905–1979, vol. VII
Bywaters, Hubert William, 1881–1966, vol. VI

C

Cabell, James Branch, 1879–1958, vol. V
Cable, 1st Baron, 1859–1927, vol. II
Cable, Boyd, *died* 1943, vol. IV
Cable, Eric Grant, 1887–1970, vol. VI
Cable, George Washington, 1844–1925, vol. II
Cable-Alexander, Sir Desmond William Lionel, 7th Bt, 1910–1988, vol. VIII
Caborne, Captain Warren Frederick, 1849–1924, vol. II
Cabot, Sir Daniel Alfred Edmond, 1888–1974, vol. VII

Cabot, Lt-Col Hugh, 1872–1945, vol. IV
Cabrol, Rt Rev. Fernand, 1855–1937, vol. III
Caccamisi, Baronne Anzon; *see* Marchesi, Blanche
Caccia, Baron (Life Peer); Harold Anthony Caccia, 1905–1990, vol. VIII
Caccia, Anthony Mario Felix, 1869–1962, vol. VI
Caclamanos, Demetrius, 1872–1949, vol. VI
Cacoyannis, Hon. Sir Panayotis Loizou, 1893–1980, vol. VII
Cadbury, Barrow, 1862–1958, vol. V
Cadbury, Edward, 1873–1948, vol. IV

Cadbury, Sir Egbert, 1893–1967, vol. IV
Cadbury, Dame Elizabeth Mary, (Mrs George Cadbury), 1858–1951, vol. V
Cadbury, George, 1839–1922, vol. II
Cadbury, George Woodall, 1907–1995, vol. IX
Cadbury, Henry Joel, 1883–1974, vol. VII
Cadbury, Henry Tylor, 1882–1952, vol. V
Cadbury, Jocelyn Benedict Laurence, 1946–1982, vol. VIII
Cadbury, Kenneth Hotham, 1919–1991, vol. IX
Cadbury, Laurence John, 1889–1982, vol. VIII
Cadbury, Paul Strangman, 1895–1984, vol. VIII
Caddell, Col Henry Mortimer, 1875–1944, vol. IV
Caddy, Adrian, 1879–1966, vol. VI
Caddy, Col Hector Osman, 1882–1935, vol. III
Cade, Sir Stanford, 1895–1973, vol. VII
Cadell, Alan, 1841–1921, vol. II
Cadell, Lt-Gen. Charles Alexander Elliott, 1888–1951, vol. V
Cadell, Colin Simson, 1905–1996, vol. X
Cadell, Francis Campbell Boileau, 1883–1937, vol. III
Cadell, Lt-Col Harry Ernest, 1867–1939, vol. III
Cadell, Henry Moubray, 1860–1934, vol. III
Cadell of Grange, Col Henry Moubray, 1892–1967, vol. VI
Cadell, Vice-Adm. Sir John Frederick, 1929–1998, vol. X
Cadell, Sir Patrick Robert, 1871–1961, vol. VI
Cadell, Sir Robert, 1825–1897, vol. I
Cadell, Simon John, 1950–1996, vol. X
Cadell, Col Thomas, 1835–1919, vol. III
Cadenhead, James, 1858–1927, vol. II
Cadge, William, died 1903, vol. I
Cadic, Edouard, 1858–1914, vol. I
Cadman, 1st Baron, 1877–1941, vol. IV
Cadman, 2nd Baron, 1909–1966, vol. VI
Cadman, Hon. Sir Alfred Jerome, died 1905, vol. I
Cadman, James, 1878–1947, vol. IV
Cadman, John Heaton, 1839–1906, vol. I
Cadman, Rev. Samuel Parkes, 1864–1936, vol. III
Cadman, Rev. William Healey, 1891–1965, vol. VI
Cadogan, 5th Earl, 1840–1915, vol. I
Cadogan, 6th Earl, 1869–1933, vol. III
Cadogan, 7th Earl, 1914–1997, vol. X
Cadogan, Rt Hon. Sir Alexander George Montagu, 1884–1968, vol. VI
Cadogan, Hon. Sir Edward Cecil George, 1880–1962, vol. VI
Cadogan, Hon. Frederick William, 1821–1904, vol. I
Cadogan, Hon. William George Sydney, 1879–1914, vol. I
Cadoux, Cecil John, 1883–1947, vol. IV
Cadwallader, Air Vice-Marshal Howard George, 1919–1998, vol. X
Cadwallader, Sir John, 1902–1991, vol. IX
Cadzow, Sir Norman James Kerr, 1912–1981, vol. VIII
Caesar, Irving, 1895–1996, vol. X
Cafe, T. Watt, 1856–1925, vol. II
Cafe, Gen. William Martin, 1826–1906, vol. I
Caffery, Jefferson, 1886–1974, vol. VII
Caffieri, H., died 1932, vol. III
Caffin, Albert Edward, 1902–1992, vol. IX

Caffin, Arthur Crawford, 1910–2000, vol. X
Caffyn, Brig. Sir Edward Roy, 1904–1990, vol. VIII
Caffyn, Kathleen Mannington, died 1926, vol. II
Caffyn, Sir Sydney Morris, 1901–1976, vol. VII
Cage, Edward Edwin Henry, 1912–1984, vol. VIII
Cahal, Dennis Abraham, 1921–1983, vol. VIII
Cahan, Hon. Charles Hazlitt, 1861–1944, vol. IV
Cahan, J(ohn) Flint, 1912–1961, vol. VI
Cahill, Rt Rev. John Baptist, 1841–1910, vol. I
Cahill, John Conway, 1930–1995, vol. IX
Cahill, Sir (Joseph) Robert, 1879–1953, vol. V
Cahill, Michael Leo, 1928–1999, vol. X
Cahill, Patrick Richard, 1912–1990, vol. VIII
Cahill, Sir Robert; see Cahill, Sir J. R.
Cahill, Most Rev. Thomas Vincent, 1913–1978, vol. VII
Cahill, Lt-Col William Geoffrey, 1854–1931, vol. III
Cahn, Charles Montague, 1900–1985, vol. VIII
Cahn, Sir Julien, 1st Bt, died 1994, vol. IV
Cahn, Sammy, 1913–1993, vol. IX
Cahusac, Col William Fremantle, 1857–1930, vol. III
Caie, John Morrison, 1878–1949, vol. IV
Caillard, Alfred, 1841–1900, vol. I
Caillard, Sir Vincent Henry Penalver, 1856–1930, vol. III
Caillaux, Joseph, died 1944, vol. IV
Cain, Sir Edward Thomas, 1916–1996, vol. X
Cain, Sir Ernest, 2nd Bt, 1891–1969, vol. VI
Cain, Maj.-Gen. George Robert T.; see Turner Cain.
Cain, Georges, died 1919, vol. II
Cain, John Cannell, 1871–1921, vol. II
Cain, Sir Jonathan Robert, 1869–1938, vol. III
Cain, Major Robert Henry, 1909–1974, vol. VII
Cain, Sir William, 1st Bt, 1864–1924, vol. II
Caine, Sir Derwent Hall, 1st Bt, 1891–1971, vol. VII
Caine, Gordon Ralph H.; see Hall Caine.
Caine, Sir Hall, 1853–1931, vol. III
Caine, Sir Michael Harris, 1927–1999, vol. X
Caine, Sir Sydney, 1902–1991, vol. IX
Caine, William, 1873–1925, vol. II
Caird, William Douglas Sime, 1917–1999, vol. X
Caine, William Ralph Hall, 1856–1939, vol. III
Caine, William Sproston, 1842–1903, vol. I
Caines, Clement Guy, 1882–1952, vol. V
Caird, Sir Andrew, 1870–1956, vol. V
Caird, David, 1863–1934, vol. III
Caird, Edward, 1835–1908, vol. I
Caird, Francis M., died 1926, vol. II
Caird, Rev. George Bradford, 1917–1984, vol. VIII
Caird, Sir James, 1st Bt (cr 1928), 1864–1954, vol. V
Caird, Sir James Key, 1st Bt (cr 1913), 1837–1916, vol. II
Caird, Very Rev. John, 1820–1898, vol. I
Caird, Mrs Mona, died 1932, vol. III
Cairncross, Sir Alec; see Cairncross, Sir A. K.
Cairncross, Sir Alexander Kirkland, (Sir Alec), 1911–1998, vol. X
Cairncross, Maj.-Gen. John, 1835–1914, vol. I
Cairnes, Captain William Elliot, 1862–1902, vol. I
Cairnes, William Plunket, 1857–1925, vol. II
Cairney, John, 1898–1966, vol. VI

Cairns, 3rd Earl, 1863–1905, vol. I
Cairns, 4th Earl, 1865–1946, vol. IV
Cairns, 5th Earl, 1909–1989, vol. VIII
Cairns, Rt Hon. Sir David Arnold Scott,
   1902–1987, vol. VIII
Cairns, Very Rev. David Smith, 1862–1946, vol. IV
Cairns, Sir Hugh William Bell, 1896–1952, vol. V
Cairns, James, 1885–1939, vol. III
Cairns, James George Hamilton Dickson,
   1920–1995, vol. IX
Cairns, John, 1859–1923, vol. II
Cairns, John Arthur Robert, died 1933, vol. III
Cairns, Sir Joseph Foster, 1920–1981, vol. VIII
Cairns, Julia, (Mrs Paul Davidson), 1893–1985,
   vol. VIII
Cairns, T., died 1908, vol. I
Cairns, William Murray, 1866–1949, vol. IV
Caithness, 17th Earl of, 1857–1914, vol. I
Caithness, 18th Earl of, 1862–1947, vol. IV
Caithness, 19th Earl of, 1906–1965, vol. VI
Cakobau, Ratu Sir Etuate Tui-Vanuavou Tugi,
   1908–1973, vol. VII
Cakobau, Ratu Sir George Kadavulevu, 1911–1989,
   vol. VIII
Caldecot, Ivone K.; see Kirkpatrick-Caldecot.
Caldecote, 1st Viscount, 1876–1947, vol. IV
Caldecote, 2nd Viscount, 1917–1999, vol. X
Caldecott, Rev. Alfred, 1850–1936, vol. III
Caldecott, Andrew; see Caldecott, J. A.
Caldecott, Sir Andrew, 1884–1951, vol. V
Caldecott, Lt-Col Ernest Lawrence, 1874–1927,
   vol. II
Caldecott, Maj.-Gen. Francis James, 1842–1926,
   vol. II
Caldecott, (John) Andrew, 1924–1990, vol. VIII
Calder, Alexander, 1898–1976, vol. VII
Calder, George, 1894–1968, vol. VI
Calder, George Alexander, 1859–1945, vol. IV
Calder, James, 1869–1940, vol. III
Calder, Col (Hon.) James, 1898–1968, vol. VI
Calder, Hon. James Alexander, 1868–1956, vol. V
Calder, Sir James Charles, 1869–1962, vol. VI
Calder, James William, 1914–1975, vol. VII
Calder, Sir John Alexander, 1889–1974, vol. VII
Calder, Air Vice-Marshal Malcolm Frederick,
   1907–1978, vol. VII (AII)
Calder, (Peter) Ritchie; see Baron Ritchie-Calder.
Calder, Ritchie; see Baron Ritchie-Calder.
Calder, Robert, 1838–1912, vol. I
Calder, Ven. William, 1848–1923, vol. II
Calder, Sir William Moir, 1881–1960, vol. V
Calder-Marshall, Arthur, 1908–1992, vol. IX
Calder-Marshall, Sir Robert, 1877–1955, vol. V
Calderbank, Philip Hugh, 1919–1988, vol. VIII
Calderon, George, 1868–1915, vol. I
Calderon, Philip Hermogenes, 1833–1898, vol. I
Calderon, W. Frank, 1865–1943, vol. IV
Calderwood, Henry, 1830–1897, vol. I
Calderwood, W. L., 1865–1950, vol. IV
Caldicott, Hon. Sir John Moore, 1900–1986,
   vol. VIII
Caldwell, Alexander Francis Somerville,
   1873–1940, vol. III
Caldwell, Surg. Vice-Adm. Sir Dick; see Caldwell,
   Surg. Vice-Adm. Sir E. D.

Caldwell, Surg. Vice-Adm. Sir (Eric) Dick,
   1907–2000, vol. X
Caldwell, Erskine, 1903–1987, vol. VIII
Caldwell, Francis, 1860–1934, vol. III
Caldwell, Maj.-Gen. Frederick Crofton H.; see
   Heath-Caldwell.
Caldwell, Godfrey David, 1920–1985, vol. VIII
Caldwell, Rt Hon. James, 1839–1925, vol. II
Caldwell, John, 1903–1974, vol. VII
Caldwell, John Foster, 1892–1981, vol. VIII
Caldwell, Peter Christopher, 1927–1979, vol. VII
Caldwell, Robert Nixon, 1888–1967, vol. VI
Caldwell, Col Robert Townley, 1843–1914, vol. I
Caldwell, Taylor, 1900–1985, vol. VIII
Caldwell, Thomas Fisher, 1866–1940, vol. III
Caldwell, William, 1863–1942, vol. IV
Caledon, 4th Earl of, 1846–1898, vol. I
Caledon, 5th Earl of, 1885–1968, vol. VI
Caledon, 6th Earl of, 1920–1980, vol. VII
Calhoun, Eleanor; see Lazarovich-Hrebelianovich.
Calkin, Lance, 1859–1936, vol. III
Call, Frank Oliver, 1878–1956, vol. V
Callaghan, Sir Alfred John, 1865–1940, vol. III
Callaghan, Sir Allan Robert, 1903–1993, vol. IX
Callaghan, Sir Bede Bertrand, 1912–1993, vol. IX
Callaghan, Maj.-Gen. Cecil Arthur, 1890–1967,
   vol. VI
Callaghan, Rear-Adm. Desmond Noble, 1915–2000,
   vol. X
Callaghan, Admiral of the Fleet Sir George Astley,
   1852–1920, vol. II
Callaghan, Morley Edward, 1903–1990, vol. VIII
Callahan, James Morton, 1864–1956, vol. V
Callan, Harold Garnet, 1917–1993, vol. IX
Callan, John Bartholomew, 1882–1951, vol. V
Callander, Lt-Gen. Sir Colin Bishop, 1897–1979,
   vol. VII
Callander, George Frederick William, 1848–1916,
   vol. II
Callander, Sir James, 1877–1952, vol. V
Callander, John Graham, 1873–1938, vol. III
Callander, Thomas, 1877–1959, vol. V
Callander, Major William Henry Burn, 1890–1967,
   vol. VI
Callard, Sir Eric John, (Sir Jack), 1913–1998,
   vol. X
Callard, Sir Jack; see Callard, Sir E. J.
Callas, Maria, 1923–1977, vol. VII
Callaway, Charles, 1838–1915, vol. I
Callaway, Air Vice-Marshal William Bertram,
   1889–1974, vol. VII
Callcott, F. T., died 1923, vol. II
Callender, Hugh Longbourne, 1863–1930, vol. III
Callender, Lt-Col David Aubrey, 1868–1953, vol. V
Callender, Eustace Maud, 1864–1952, vol. V
Callender, Sir Geoffrey Arthur Romaine,
   1875–1946, vol. IV
Callender, Sir Thomas Octavius, 1855–1938, vol. III
Calley, Sir Henry Algernon, 1914–1997, vol. X
Calley, Hon. Maj.-Gen. Thomas Charles Pleydell,
   1856–1932, vol. III
Callinan, Sir Bernard James, 1913–1995, vol. IX
Callow, Charles Thomas Cheslyn, 1852–1933,
   vol. III
Callow, Graham, 1894–1960, vol. V

Callow, Robert Kenneth, 1901–1983, vol. VIII
Callow, William, 1812–1908, vol. I
Callwell, Maj.-Gen. Sir Charles Edward, 1859–1923, vol. II
Calman, William Thomas, 1871–1952, vol. V
Calman, Mel, 1931–1994, vol. IX
Calmette, Leon Charles Albert, 1863–1933, vol. III
Calnan, Denis, died 1939, vol. III
Calovski, Mitko, 1930–1994, vol. IX
Calry, 6th Count de, 1854–1950, vol. IV (A), vol. V
Calthorpe, 6th Baron, 1829–1910, vol. I
Calthorpe, 7th Baron, 1831–1912, vol. I
Calthorpe, 8th Baron, 1862–1940, vol. III
Calthorpe, 9th Baron, 1924–1945, vol. IV
Calthorpe, 10th Baron, 1927–1997, vol. X
Calthorpe, Sir FitzRoy Hamilton A. G.; see Anstruther-Gough-Calthorpe.
Calthorpe, Hon. Frederick Somerset Gough-, 1892–1935, vol. III
Calthorpe, Brig. Sir Richard Hamilton A. G.; see Anstruther-Gough-Calthorpe.
Calthorpe, Admiral of the Fleet Hon. Sir Somerset Arthur Gough-, 1864–1937, vol. III
Calthrop, Sir Cathrop Guy Spencer, 1st Bt, 1870–1919, vol. II
Calthrop, Col Christopher William C.; see Carr-Calthrop.
Calthrop, Dion Clayton, 1878–1937, vol. III
Calve, Emma, 1866–1942, vol. IV
Calver, Sir Robert Henry Sherwood, died 1963, vol. VI
Calverley, 1st Baron, 1877–1955, vol. V
Calverley, 2nd Baron, 1914–1971, vol. VII
Calverley, Joseph Ernest Goodfellow, 1872–1953, vol. V
Calvert, Albert Frederick, 1872–1946, vol. IV
Calvert, Albert Spencer, 1897–1953, vol. V
Calvert, Archibald Motteux, 1827–1906, vol. I
Calvert, Mrs Charles, 1836–1921, vol. II
Calvert, Edwin George Bleakley, died 1976, vol. VII
Calvert, Rt Rev. George Reginald, 1900–1976, vol. VII
Calvert, Henry Reginald, 1904–1992, vol. IX
Calvert, Hubert, 1875–1961, vol. VI
Calvert, James, died 1932, vol. III
Calvert, Lt-Col John Telfer, died 1944, vol. IV
Calvert, Sir Joseph, 1853–1931, vol. III
Calvert, Rear-Adm. Thomas Frederick Parker, 1883–1938, vol. III
Calvert, William Archibald, 1868–1943, vol. IV
Calvert, William Robinson, 1882–1949, vol. IV
Calvert-Jones, Maj.-Gen. Percy George, 1894–1977, vol. VII
Calvin, Melvin, 1911–1997, vol. X
Calvino, Italo, 1923–1985, vol. VIII
Calwell, Rt Hon. Arthur Augustus, 1896–1973, vol. VII
Cam, Helen Maud, 1885–1968, vol. VI
Camacho, Sir Maurice Vivian, 1885–1941, vol. IV
Cambage, Richard Hind, 1859–1928, vol. II
Cambell, Rear-Adm. Dennis Royle Farquharson, 1907–2000, vol. X
Camber-Williams, Rev. Robert, 1860–1924, vol. II
Cambon, Paul, 1843–1924, vol. II

Cambon, Roger Paul Jules, 1881–1970, vol. VI
Cambridge, 2nd Duke of, 1819–1904, vol. I
Cambridge, 1st Marquess of, 1868–1927, vol. II
Cambridge, 2nd Marquess of, 1895–1981, vol. VIII
Cambridge, Ada, 1844–1926, vol. II
Cambridge, Sir Arthur Wallace P.; see Pickard-Cambridge.
Cambridge, Elizabeth; see Hodges, Barbara K.
Cambridge, Rev. Octavius P.; see Pickard-Cambridge.
Cambridge, William Adair P.; see Pickard-Cambridge.
Camden, 4th Marquess of, 1872–1943, vol. IV
Camden, 5th Marquess, 1899–1983, vol. VIII
Camden, John, 1925–1996, vol. X
Came, William Gerald, 1889–1984, vol. VIII
Cameron of Balhousie, Baron (Life Peer); Marshal of the Royal Air Force Neil Cameron, 1920–1985, vol. VIII
Cameron, Hon. Lord; John Cameron, 1900–1996, vol. X
Cameron, Rev. A. D., died 1946, vol. IV
Cameron, Alexander Gordon, 1886–1944, vol. IV
Cameron, Lt-Gen. Sir Alexander Maurice, 1898–1986, vol. VIII
Cameron, Alexander T., 1882–1947, vol. IV
Cameron, Rev. Allan Thomas, 1870–1932, vol. III
Cameron, Archibald, 1902–1964, vol. VI
Cameron, Gen. Sir Archibald Rice, 1870–1944, vol. IV
Cameron, Rev. Archibald Stuart, died 1936, vol. III
Cameron, Col Aylmer, 1833–1909, vol. I
Cameron, Basil; see Cameron, G. B.
Cameron, (Caroline) Emily, (Mrs Lovett Cameron), died 1921, vol. II
Cameron, Major Cecil Aylmer, 1883–1924, vol. II
Cameron, Sir Charles, 1st Bt, 1841–1924, vol. II
Cameron, Charles, 1886–1968, vol. VI
Cameron, Sir Charles Alexander, 1830–1921, vol. II
Cameron, Rev. Charles Leslie L.; see Lovett-Cameron.
Cameron, Charlotte, died 1946, vol. IV
Cameron, Clive Bremner, 1921–1996, vol. X
Cameron, Sir Cornelius, 1896–1975, vol. VII
Cameron, Col Hon. Cyril St Clair, 1857–1941, vol. IV
Cameron, Vice-Adm. Cyril St Clair, 1879–1973, vol. VII
Cameron, Sir David Young, 1865–1945, vol. IV
Cameron of Lochiel, Donald, 1835–1905, vol. I
Cameron, Donald Andreas, 1856–1936, vol. III
Cameron, Sir Donald Charles, 1872–1948, vol. IV
Cameron, Lt-Col Sir Donald Charles, 1879–1960, vol. V (A), vol. VI
Cameron, Sir Donald Charles, 1877–1962, vol. VI
Cameron, Lt-Col Donald Hay, 1867–1932, vol. III
Cameron, Hon. Donald Norman, died 1931, vol. III
Cameron, Maj.-Gen. Donald Roderick, 1834–1921, vol. II
Cameron of Lochiel, Col Sir Donald Walter, 1876–1951, vol. V
Cameron, Hon. Sir Douglas Colin, 1854–1921, vol. II
Cameron, Sir Edward John, 1858–1947, vol. IV
Cameron, Edward Robert, 1857–1931, vol. III

Cameron, Elizabeth Dorothea Cole, (Mrs Alan Charles Cameron); see Bowen, E. D. C.
Cameron, Emily; see Cameron, C. E.
Cameron, Sir (Eustace) John, 1913–1998, vol. X
Cameron, Lt-Col Ewan Cornwallis, 1865–1932, vol. III
Cameron, Sir Ewen, 1841–1908, vol. I
Cameron of Lundavra, Col Ewen Allan, 1877–1958, vol. V
Cameron, Hon. Sir Ewen Paul, 1892–1964, vol. VI
Cameron, Finlay James, 1880–1954, vol. V
Cameron, (George) Basil, 1884–1975, vol. VII
Cameron, Lt-Col George Cecil Minett Sorell-, 1871–1947, vol. IV
Cameron, George Edmund, 1911–1997, vol. X
Cameron, Ven. George Henry, 1861–1940, vol. III
Cameron, Gordon Campbell, 1937–1990, vol. VIII
Cameron, Gordon Stewart, 1916–1994, vol. IX
Cameron, Hector Charles, 1878–1958, vol. V
Cameron, Sir Hector Clare, 1843–1928, vol. II
Cameron, Hugh, 1835–1918, vol. II
Cameron, Col Hugh Alan, 1871–1929, vol. III
Cameron, Irving Heward, 1855–1933, vol. III
Cameron, Isabella Douglas, died 1945, vol. IV
Cameron, James; see Cameron, M. J. W.
Cameron, Col James Black, 1882–1946, vol. IV
Cameron, Sir James Clark, 1905–1991, vol. IX
Cameron, Sir James Davidson Stuart, 1900–1969, vol. VI
Cameron, James Munro, 1910–1995, vol. IX
Cameron, James Nield, 1884–1960, vol. V
Cameron, James Spottiswoode, died 1918, vol. II
Cameron, Sir John; see Cameron, Sir E. J.
Cameron, John, 1873–1960, vol. V
Cameron, Sir John, 2nd Bt, 1903–1968, vol. VI
Cameron, John Donald, 1858–1923, vol. II
Cameron, Adm. John Ewen, 1874–1939, vol. III
Cameron, John Forbes, 1873–1952, vol. V
Cameron, John Gordon Patrick, 1885–1970, vol. VI
Cameron, Rev. John Kennedy, 1860–1944, vol. IV
Cameron, Col John Philip, 1879–1950, vol. IV
Cameron, John Robson, 1845–1907, vol. I
Cameron, Brig. John S.; see Sorel Cameron.
Cameron, Sir John Watson, 1901–1997, vol. X
Cameron, Col Kenneth, 1863–1939, vol. III (A), vol. IV
Cameron, Mrs Lovett; see Cameron, C. E.
Cameron, Captain Ludovick Charles Richard Duncombe-Jewell, 1866–1947, vol. IV
Cameron, Malcolm Graeme, 1857–1925, vol. II
Cameron, (Mark) James (Walter), 1911–1985, vol. VIII
Cameron, Matthew Brown, 1867–1952, vol. V
Cameron, Major Sir Maurice Alexander, 1855–1936, vol. III
Cameron, Murdoch, died 1930, vol. III
Cameron, Maj.-Gen. Neville John Gordon, 1873–1955, vol. V
Cameron, Brig. Orford Somerville, 1878–1958, vol. V
Cameron, Robert, 1825–1913, vol. I
Cameron, Maj.-Gen. Roderic Duncan, 1893–1975, vol. VII
Cameron, Sir Roderick William, 1825–1900, vol. I
Cameron, Sir Roy, 1899–1966, vol. VI

Cameron, Samuel J., 1878–1959, vol. V
Cameron, Thomas Wright Moir, 1894–1980, vol. VII (AII)
Cameron, William, died 1954, vol. V
Cameron, Gen. Sir William Gordon, 1827–1913, vol. I
Cameron, William Lochiel Sapte Lovett, 1854–1938, vol. III
Cameron, Rt Rev. William Mouat, 1854–1915, vol. I
Cameron-Head, Francis Somerville Cameron, 1896–1957, vol. V
Cameron-Head, James, 1851–1922, vol. II
Cameron-Ramsay-Fairfax-Lucy, Major Sir Brian Fulke; see Fairfax-Lucy.
Cameron-Ramsay-Fairfax-Lucy, Sir Henry William; see Fairfax-Lucy.
Cameron-Swan, Captain Donald, 1863–1951, vol. V
Camidge, Rt Rev. Charles Edward, 1838–1911, vol. I
Camilleri, Emanuel, 1887–1968, vol. VI (AII)
Camilleri, Rt Rev. Giovanni M., born 1843, vol. II
Camilleri, Sir Luigi A., 1892–1989, vol. VIII
Camm, Dom Bede, 1864–1942, vol. IV
Camm, John Sutcliffe, 1925–1985, vol. VIII
Camm, Sir Sydney, 1893–1966, vol. VI
Cammaerts, Emile, died 1953, vol. V
Cammell, Major Gerald Arthur, 1889–1933, vol. III
Cammidge, Percy John, 1872–1956, vol. V (A)
Camoys, 4th Baron, 1856–1897, vol. I
Camoys, 5th Baron, 1884–1968, vol. VI
Camoys, 6th Baron, 1913–1976, vol. VII
Camp, Harold Robert, 1893–1968, vol. VI
Camp, Instr Captain J., 1877–1962, vol. VI
Camp, Samuel James, 1876–1936, vol. III
Campagnac, E. T., died 1952, vol. V
Campbell of Eskan, Baron (Life Peer); John (Jock) Middleton Campbell, 1912–1994, vol. IX
Campbell, Alan Johnston, 1895–1982, vol. VIII
Campbell, Captain Alexander, 1839–1914, vol. I
Campbell, Sir Alexander, 6th Bt (cr 1667), 1841–1914, vol. I
Campbell, Lt-Col Alexander, 1881–1941, vol. IV
Campbell, Alexander, died 1961, vol. VI
Campbell, Sir Alexander, 1892–1963, vol. VI
Campbell, (Alexander) Colin (Patton), 1908–1996, vol. X
Campbell, Brig. Alexander Donald Powys, 1894–1974, vol. VII
Campbell, Maj.-Gen. Sir (Alexander) Douglas, 1899–1980, vol. VII
Campbell, Lt-Col Alexander George, 1889–1936, vol. III
Campbell, Maj.-Gen. Alexander Henry Edward, 1835–1929, vol. III
Campbell, Alexander McCulloch, 1879–1955, vol. V
Campbell, Sir Alexander Thomas Cockburn-, 5th Bt (cr 1821), 1872–1935, vol. III
Campbell, Adm. Alexander Victor, 1874–1957, vol. V
Campbell, Lt-Col Sir Alexander William Dennistoun, 4th Bt (cr 1831), 1848–1931, vol. III
Campbell, Maj.-Gen. Alfred Edward, 1901–1973, vol. VII

Campbell, Alistair, 1907–1974, vol. VII
Campbell, Very Rev. Andrew James, 1875–1950, vol. IV
Campbell, Hon. Angus Dudley, 1895–1967, vol. VI
Campbell, Lord Archibald, 1846–1913, vol. I
Campbell, Lady Archibald; (Janey Sevilla), *died* 1923, vol. II
Campbell, Hon. Archibald, 1846–1913, vol. I
Campbell, Archibald, 1877–1963, vol. VI
Campbell, Archibald, 1914–1994, vol. IX
Campbell, Sir Archibald Augustus Ava, 4th Bt (*cr* 1831), 1879–1916, vol. II
Campbell, Sir Archibald Ava, 3rd Bt (*cr* 1831), 1844–1913, vol. I
Campbell, Archibald Duncan, 1919–1975, vol. VII
Campbell, Rt Rev. Archibald Ean, 1856–1921, vol. II
Campbell, Maj.-Gen. Archibald Edwards, 1834–1921, vol. II
Campbell, Sir Archibald Henry, 1870–1948, vol. IV
Campbell, Archibald Hunter, 1902–1989, vol. VIII
Campbell, Major Archibald James Hamilton Douglas, 1884–1936, vol. III
Campbell of Achalader, Brig. Archibald Pennant, 1896–1983, vol. VIII
Campbell, Rt Rev. Archibald Rollo G.; *see* Graham-Campbell.
Campbell, Sir Archibald Spencer Lindsey, 5th Bt (*cr* 1808), 1852–1941, vol. IV
Campbell, Archibald Y., 1885–1958, vol. V
Campbell, Sir Archibald Young Gipps, 1872–1957, vol. V
Campbell, Arnold Everitt, 1906–1980, vol. VII (AII)
Campbell, Lt-Col Aylmer MacIver, 1837–1915, vol. I
Campbell, Beatrice Stella; *see* Campbell, Mrs Patrick.
Campbell, Brig. Sir Bruce Atta, 1888–1954, vol. V
Campbell, Lt-Col Hon. Sir Cecil James Henry, 1891–1952, vol. V
Campbell, Vice-Adm. Sir Charles, 1847–1911, vol. I
Campbell, Charles Arthur, 1897–1974, vol. VII
Campbell, Charles Douglas, 1905–1975, vol. VII
Campbell, Sir (Charles) Duncan Macnair, 2nd Bt (*cr* 1939), 1906–1954, vol. V
Campbell, Lt-Col Charles Ferguson, *died* 1925, vol. II
Campbell, Charles Graham, 1880–1971, vol. VII
Campbell, Lt-Col Charles Lionel Kirwan, 1873–1918, vol. II
Campbell, Sir Charles Ralph, 11th Bt (*cr* 1628), 1850–1919, vol. II
Campbell, Sir Charles Ralph, 12th Bt (*cr* 1628), 1881–1948, vol. IV
Campbell, Hon. Sir Charles Rudolph, 1885–1969, vol. VI
Campbell, Charles Sandwith, 1858–1923, vol. II
Campbell, Charles Stewart, 1875–1942, vol. IV
Campbell, Charles William, 1861–1927, vol. II
Campbell, Captain Claude Henry, 1878–1916, vol. II
Campbell, Sir Clifford Clarence, 1892–1991, vol. IX
Campbell, Colin; *see* Campbell, A. C. P.
Campbell, Lady Colin, *died* 1911, vol. I
Campbell, Rev. Colin, 1848–1931, vol. III

Campbell, Colin, 1851–1933, vol. III
Campbell, Sir Colin, 1891–1979, vol. VII
Campbell, Colin Algernon, 1874–1957, vol. V
Campbell, Ven. Colin Arthur Fitzgerald, 1863–1916, vol. II
Campbell, Col Colin Charles, 1842–1929, vol. III
Campbell, Colin George, 1852–1911, vol. I
Campbell, Colin George Pelham, 1872–1955, vol. V
Campbell, Sir Colin Moffat, 8th Bt, 1925–1997, vol. X
Campbell, Sir David, 1889–1978, vol. VII
Campbell, Rt Hon. Sir David Callender, 1891–1963, vol. VI
Campbell, Gen. Sir David Graham Muschet, 1869–1936, vol. III
Campbell, David John G.; *see* Graham-Campbell.
Campbell, Col David Wilkinson, 1832–1903, vol. I
Campbell, Most Rev. Donald Alphonsus, 1894–1963, vol. VI
Campbell, Ven. Donald F., 1886–1933, vol. III
Campbell, Donald Malcolm, 1921–1967, vol. VI
Campbell, Dorothy, (Mrs Alan Campbell); *see* Parker, D.
Campbell, Maj.-Gen. Sir Douglas; *see* Campbell, Maj.-Gen. Sir A. D.
Campbell, Douglas Colin, 1891–1957, vol. V
Campbell, Douglas Graham, 1867–1918, vol. II
Campbell, Douglas Mason, 1905–1978, vol. VII
Campbell, Lt-Col Duncan, 1880–1954, vol. V
Campbell, Sir Duncan Alexander Dundas, 3rd Bt (*cr* 1831), 1856–1926, vol. II
Campbell, Major Duncan Elidor, *died* 1930, vol. III
Campbell, Captain Duncan Lorn, 1881–1923, vol. II
Campbell, Sir Duncan John Alfred, 5th Bt (*cr* 1831), 1854–1932, vol. III
Campbell, Captain Duncan Lorn, 1881–1923, vol. II
Campbell, Sir Duncan Macnair; *see* Campbell, Sir C. D. M.
Campbell, Col Edmund George, 1893–1972, vol. VII
Campbell, Rev. Edward Fitzhardinge, 1880–1957, vol. V
Campbell, Sir Edward Taswell, 1st Bt (*cr* 1939), 1879–1945, vol. IV
Campbell, Captain Sir Eric Francis Dennistoun, 6th Bt (*cr* 1831), 1892–1963, vol. VI
Campbell, Major Hon. Eric Octavius, 1885–1918, vol. II
Campbell, Esther Helen, (Mrs Mungo Campbell); *see* McCracken, E. H.
Campbell, Evan Roy, 1908–1980, vol. VII
Campbell, Ewen, 1897–1975, vol. VII
Campbell, Fergus William, 1924–1993, vol. IX
Campbell, Sir Francis Alexander, 1852–1911, vol. I
Campbell, Sir Francis Joseph, 1832–1914, vol. I
Campbell, Freda K., (Mrs Ian McIvor); *see* Corbet, F. K.
Campbell, Col Frederick, 1843–1926, vol. II
Campbell, Gen. Sir Frederick, 1860–1943, vol. IV
Campbell, Maj.-Gen. Frederick Lorn, 1850–1931, vol. III
Campbell, George Archibald, 1875–1964, vol. VI
Campbell, Engr Captain George Douglas, 1884–1972, vol. VII

Campbell, Col George Frederick Colin, 1858–1937, vol. III

Campbell, Lord George Granville, 1850–1915, vol. I

Campbell, Sir George Ilay, 6th Bt (*cr* 1808), 1894–1967, vol. VI

Campbell, George James, 1842–1931, vol. III

Campbell, Brig.-Gen. George Polding, 1864–1928, vol. II

Campbell, Sir George Riddoch, 1887–1965, vol. VI

Campbell, Col George Tupper Campbell C.; *see* Carter-Campbell.

Campbell, Vice-Adm. George William McOran, 1877–1948, vol. IV

Campbell, Sir George William Robert, 1835–1905, vol. I

Campbell, Sir Gerald, 1879–1964, vol. VI

Campbell, Gerald FitzGerald, 1862–1933, vol. III

Campbell, Gertrude Elizabeth; *see* Campbell, Lady Colin.

Campbell, Vice-Adm. Gordon, 1886–1953, vol. V

Campbell, Sir Gordon Huntly, 1864–1953, vol. V

Campbell, Grace Margaret; *see* Wilson, G. M.

Campbell, Gen. Gunning Morehead, *died* 1920, vol. II

Campbell, Major Sir Guy Colin, 4th Bt (*cr* 1815), 1885–1960, vol. V

Campbell, Lt-Col Sir Guy Theophilus, 3rd Bt (*cr* 1815), 1854–1931, vol. III

Campbell, Sir Guy Theophilus Halswell, 5th Bt (*cr* 1815), 1910–1993, vol. IX

Campbell, H. Donald, 1879–1969, vol. VI

Campbell, Maj.-Gen. Rev. Sir Hamish Manus, 1905–1993, vol. IX

Campbell, Sir Harold Alfred Maurice, 1892–1959, vol. V

Campbell, Harold Ernest, 1902–1980, vol. VII

Campbell, Captain Sir Harold George, 1888–1969, vol. VI

Campbell, Harry, *died* 1938, vol. III

Campbell, Lt-Col Harry La Trobe, *born* 1881, vol. II

Campbell, Brig. Hector, 1877–1972, vol. VII

Campbell, Sir Henry, 1856–1924, vol. II

Campbell, Henry Alexander, 1851–1907, vol. I

Campbell, Rt Rev. and Rt Hon. Henry Colville M.; *see* Montgomery Campbell.

Campbell, Adm. Sir Henry Hervey, 1865–1933, vol. III

Campbell, Rear-Adm. Henry John Fletcher, 1837–1914, vol. I

Campbell, Henry Johnstone, 1859–1935, vol. III

Campbell, Lt-Col Hon. Henry Walter, 1835–1910, vol. I

Campbell, Ven. Herbert Ernest, *died* 1930, vol. III

Campbell, Brig.-Gen. Herbert M.; *see* Montgomery-Campbell.

Campbell, Hugh, 1916–1998, vol. X

Campbell, Ian George Hallyburton, 1909–1986, vol. VIII

Campbell, Ian Macdonald, 1922–1994, vol. IX

Campbell, Ian McIntyre, 1915–1982, vol. VIII

Campbell, Col Hon. Ian Malcolm, 1883–1962, vol. VI

Campbell of Airds, Bt Col Ian Maxwell, 1870–1954, vol. V

Campbell, Vice-Adm. Sir Ian Murray Robertson, 1898–1980, vol. VII

Campbell, Maj.-Gen. Ian Ross, 1900–1997, vol. X

Campbell, Sir Ian Vincent Hamilton, 7th Bt (*cr* 1831), 1895–1978, vol. VII

Campbell, Ignatius Roy Dunnachie, 1901–1957, vol. V

Campbell, Captain Hon. Ivan, 1859–1917, vol. II

Campbell, Sir James, 5th Bt (*cr* 1667), 1818–1903, vol. I

Campbell, Sir James, 1842–1925, vol. II

Campbell, James, 1895–1957, vol. V

Campbell, Rt Hon. James Alexander, 1825–1908, vol. I

Campbell, Maj.-Gen. James Alexander, 1886–1964, vol. VI

Campbell, James Argyll, 1884–1944, vol. IV

Campbell, Sir James Clark, 1882–1964, vol. VI

Campbell, Rear-Adm. James Douglas, 1882–1954, vol. V

Campbell, James Duncan, 1833–1907, vol. I

Campbell, James Grant, 1914–1989, vol. VIII

Campbell, James Hugh, 1889–1934, vol. III

Campbell, Sir (James) Keith, 1928–1983, vol. VIII

Campbell, James Lang, 1858–1936, vol. III

Campbell, Sir James Macnabb, 1846–1903, vol. I

Campbell, Very Rev. James Montgomery, 1859–1937, vol. III

Campbell, James Reid, 1930–1985, vol. VIII

Campbell, Dame Janet Mary, *died* 1954, vol. V

Campbell, Surg.-Maj. John, 1817–1904, vol. I

Campbell, Lt-Col John, 1872–1928, vol. II

Campbell, Sir John, 1862–1929, vol. III

Campbell, Maj.-Gen. John, 1871–1941, vol. IV

Campbell, Sir John, 1874–1944, vol. IV

Campbell, Mrs John; *see* Campbell, May Eudora.

Campbell, Sir John Alexander Coldstream, 7th Bt (*cr* 1667), 1877–1960, vol. V

Campbell, Captain Hon. John Beresford, 1866–1915, vol. I

Campbell, Lt-Col Sir John Bruce Stuart, 2nd Bt (*cr* 1913), 1877–1943, vol. IV

Campbell, John Dermot, 1898–1945, vol. IV

Campbell, John Edward, 1862–1924, vol. II

Campbell, Lt-Col John Edward Robert, 1855–1936, vol. III

Campbell, John Gordon Drummond, 1864–1935, vol. III

Campbell, Brig.-Gen. John Hasluck, *died* 1921, vol. II

Campbell, Lt-Col John Hay, 1871–1946, vol. IV

Campbell, Sir John Home-Purves Hume-, 1879–1960, vol. V

Campbell, Sir John Johnston, 1897–1983, vol. VIII

Campbell, John L., 1906–1996, vol. X

Campbell, Sir John Logan, 1817–1912, vol. I

Campbell, Rev. John McLeod, *died* 1961, vol. VI

Campbell, John Macmaster, 1859–1939, vol. III

Campbell, (John) Maurice (Hardman), 1891–1973, vol. VII

Campbell, J(ohn) Menzies, 1887–1974, vol. VII

Campbell, John Ross, 1894–1969, vol. VI

Campbell, Sir John Stratheden, 1863–1928, vol. II

Campbell, Brig.-Gen. John Vaughan, 1876–1944, vol. IV

Campbell, Maj.-Gen. Sir John William, 1st Bt (*cr* 1913) (styled 8th, of Ardnamurchan), 1836–1915, vol. I

Campbell, Rev. Joseph William Robert, 1853–1935, vol. III

Campbell, Dame Kate Isabel, 1899–1986, vol. VIII

Campbell, Sir Keith; *see* Campbell, Sir J. K.

Campbell, Kenneth, *died* 1943, vol. IV

Campbell of Strachur, Lt-Col Kenneth John, 1878–1965, vol. VI

Campbell, Lt-Col Kenneth Rankin, 1863–1931, vol. III

Campbell, Lawson; *see* Campbell, W. L.

Campbell, Leila, 1911–1993, vol. IX

Campbell, Brig.-Gen. Leslie Warner Yule, 1867–1946, vol. IV

Campbell, Captain Leveson Granville Byron Alexander, 1881–1951, vol. V

Campbell, Rev. Lewis, 1830–1908, vol. I

Campbell, Lloyd, *died* 1950, vol. IV

Campbell, Maj.-Gen. Lorn Robert Henry Dick, 1846–1913, vol. I

Campbell, Sir Louis Hamilton, 14th Bt (*cr* 1628), 1885–1970, vol. VI

Campbell, Sir Malcolm, 1848–1935, vol. III

Campbell, Major Sir Malcolm, 1885–1948, vol. IV

Campbell, Col Rev. Malcolm Sydenham Clarke, 1863–1949, vol. IV

Campbell, Hon. Sir Marshall, 1849–1918, vol. II

Campbell, Sir Matthew, 1907–1998, vol. X

Campbell, Maurice; *see* Campbell, J. M. H.

Campbell, May Eudora, (Mrs John Campbell), *died* 1975, vol. VII

Campbell, Lt-Col Montagu Douglas, 1852–1916, vol. II

Campbell, Mungo, 1900–1983, vol. VIII

Campbell, Sir Nigel Leslie, *died* 1948, vol. IV

Campbell, Sir Norman Dugald Ferrier, 13th Bt (*cr* 1628), 1883–1968, vol. VI

Campbell, Sir Norman Montgomery Abercromby, 10th Bt (*cr* 1628), 1846–1901, vol. I

Campbell, Norman Robert, 1880–1949, vol. IV

Campbell, Lt-Col Norman St Clair, 1877–1949, vol. IV

Campbell, Mrs Patrick, 1865–1940, vol. III

Campbell, Patrick; *see* Glenavy, 3rd Baron.

Campbell, Percy Gerald Cadogan, 1878–1960, vol. V(A), vol. VI (AI)

Campbell, Peter, 1856–1951, vol. V

Campbell, Sir Ralph Abercromby, 1906–1989, vol. VIII

Campbell, Lt-Col Hon. Ralph Alexander, 1877–1945, vol. IV

Campbell, Rev. Reginald John, 1867–1956, vol. V

Campbell, (Renton) Stuart, 1908–1966, vol. VI

Campbell, Richard Hamilton, *died* 1923, vol. II

Campbell, Richard Mitchelson, 1897–1974, vol. VII

Campbell, Very Rev. Richard Stewart Dobbs, *died* 1913, vol. I

Campbell, Richard Vary, 1840–1901, vol. I

Campbell, Maj.-Gen. Robert Dallas, 1832–1916, vol. II

Campbell, Robert Garrett, 1858–1931, vol. III

Campbell, Brig. Robert Morris, 1883–1949, vol. IV

Campbell, Col Sir Robert Neil, 1854–1928, vol. II

Campbell, Robert Peel William, 1853–1929, vol. III

Campbell, Robert Richmond, 1901–1972, vol. VII

Campbell, Lt-Col Robert Wemyss, *died* 1939, vol. III

Campbell, Robin Francis, 1912–1985, vol. VIII

Campbell, Maj.-Gen. Robin Hasluck, 1894–1964, vol. VI

Campbell, Sir Rollo Frederick G.; *see* Graham-Campbell.

Campbell, Col Ronald Bruce, 1878–1963, vol. VI

Campbell, Ronald Francis Boyd, 1912–1996, vol. X

Campbell, Rt Hon. Sir Ronald Hugh, 1883–1953, vol. V

Campbell, Rt Hon. Sir Ronald Ian, 1890–1983, vol. VIII

Campbell, Ross, 1916–1996, vol. X

Campbell, Major Roy Neil Boyd, 1884–1950, vol. IV

Campbell, Samuel George, 1861–1926, vol. II

Campbell, Sidney George, 1875–1956, vol. V

Campbell, Sidney Scholfield, 1909–1974, vol. VII

Campbell, Lt-Col Spurgeon, 1870–1935, vol. III

Campbell, Rev Canon Stephen, *died* 1918, vol. II

Campbell, Stuart; *see* Campbell, R. S.

Campbell, Sybil, 1889–1977, vol. VII

Campbell, Hon. Thane A., 1895–1978, vol. VII

Campbell, Sir Thomas C.; *see* Cockburn-Campbell.

Campbell, Thomas Joseph, *died* 1946, vol. IV

Campbell, Ven. Thomas Robert Curwen, 1843–1911, vol. I

Campbell, Maj.-Gen. Victor David Graham, 1905–1990, vol. VIII

Campbell, Lt-Gen. Sir Walter, 1864–1936, vol. III

Campbell, Captain Sir Walter Douglas Somerset, 1853–1919, vol. II

Campbell, Lt-Col Sir Walter Fendall, 1894–1973, vol. VII

Campbell, Walter Stanley, 1887–1957, vol. V

Campbell, Gen. Sir William, 1847–1918, vol. II

Campbell, Rev. William, 1841–1921, vol. II

Campbell, William, 1889–1953, vol. V

Campbell, William, 1895–1976, vol. VII

Campbell, William; *see* Skerrington, Hon. Lord.

Campbell, Sir William Andrewes Ava, 5th Bt (*cr* 1831), 1880–1949, vol. IV

Campbell, Major William Charles, *died* 1958, vol. V

Campbell, William Gordon, 1891–1974, vol. VII

Campbell, Maj.-Gen. William Henry McNeile V.; *see* Verschoyle-Campbell.

Campbell, Col William Kentigern Hamilton, 1865–1917, vol. II

Campbell, Major William Lachlan, *died* 1937, vol. III

Campbell, (William) Lawson, 1890–1970, vol. VI

Campbell, Brig.-Gen. William MacLaren, 1864–1924, vol. II

Campbell, William Middleton, 1849–1919, vol. II

Campbell, Brig.-Gen. William Nevile, 1863–1933, vol. III

Campbell, Lt-Gen. Sir William Pitcairn, 1856–1933, vol. III

Campbell, Major William Robinson, 1879–1915, vol. I

Campbell, Maj.-Gen. William Tait, 1912–1999, vol. X

Campbell of Airds, Brig. Lorne Maclaine, 1902–1991, vol. IX
Campbell-Bannerman, Rt Hon. Sir Henry, 1836–1908, vol. I
Campbell-Colquhoun, William Erskine, 1866–1922, vol. II
Campbell Golding, Frederick; *see* Golding.
Campbell-Johnson, Alan, 1913–1998, vol. X
Campbell-Johnston, Malcolm, 1871–1931, vol. III
Campbell Orde, Alan Colin, 1898–1992, vol. IX
Campbell-Orde, Sir John William Powlett; *see* Orde.
Campbell-Orde, Major Sir Simon Arthur; *see* Orde.
Campbell-Preston, Hon. Mrs Angela, 1910–1981, vol. VIII
Campbell-Preston of Ardchattan, Robert Modan Thorne, 1909–1996, vol. X
Campbell-Purdie, Cora Gwendolyn Jean, (Wendy), 1925–1985, vol. VIII
Campbell-Purdie, Wendy; *see* Campbell-Purdie, C. G. J.
Campbell-Smith, Walter; *see* Smith.
Campbell Swinton, Brig. Alan Henry; *see* Swinton.
Campbell-Walter, Rear-Adm. Keith McNeil, 1904–1976, vol. VII
Camperdown, 3rd Earl of, 1841–1918, vol. II
Camperdown, 4th Earl of, 1845–1933, vol. III
Campinchi, César, 1882–1941, vol. IV
Campion, 1st Baron, 1882–1958, vol. V
Campion, Bernard, *died* 1952, vol. V
Campion, Cecil; *see* Campion, J. C.
Campion, Col Douglas John Montriou, 1883–1963, vol. VI
Campion, George, 1846–1926, vol. II
Campion, George Goring, 1862–1946, vol. IV
Campion, Sir Harry, 1905–1996, vol. X
Campion, Rev. Canon Herbert Roper, 1868–1941, vol. IV
Campion, Rear-Adm. Hubert, 1825–1900, vol. I
Campion, (John) Cecil, 1907–1971, vol. VII
Campion, Sidney Ronald, 1891–1978, vol. VII
Campion, Col William Henry, 1836–1923, vol. II
Campion, William Magan, *died* 1898, vol. I
Campion, Col Sir William Robert, 1870–1951, vol. V
Campling, Rev. Canon William Charles, 1888–1973, vol. VII
Campney, Hon. Ralph Osborne, 1894–1967, vol. VI
Campoli, Alfredo, 1906–1991, vol. IX
Camps, Francis Edward, 1905–1972, vol. VII
Camps, William Anthony, 1910–1997, vol. X
Camrose, 1st Viscount, 1879–1954, vol. V
Camrose, 2nd Viscount, 1909–1995, vol. IX
Camsell, Charles, 1876–1958, vol. V
Camus, Albert, 1913–1960, vol. V
Cana, Frank Richardson, 1865–1935, vol. III
Canaway, Arthur Pitcairn, 1857–1949, vol. IV
Canby, Henry Seidel, 1878–1961, vol. VI
Cancellor, Henry Lannoy, 1862–1929, vol. III
Candau, Marcolino Gomes, 1911–1983, vol. VIII
Candela Outeriño, Felix, 1910–1997, vol. X
Candler, Edmund, 1874–1926, vol. II
Candlish, Joseph John, 1855–1913, vol. I
Candy, Rear-Adm. Algernon Henry Chester, 1877–1959, vol. V

Candy, Air Vice-Marshal Charles Douglas, 1912–1985, vol. VIII
Candy, Sir Edward Townshend, 1854–1913, vol. I
Candy, George, 1841–1899, vol. I
Candy, Major Henry Augustus, 1842–1911, vol. I
Candy, Hugh Charles Herbert, *died* 1935, vol. III
Candy, Maj.-Gen. Ronald Herbert, *died* 1972, vol. VII
Cane, Arthur Beresford, 1864–1939, vol. III
Cane, Sir Cyril Hubert, 1891–1959, vol. V
Cane, Lucy Mary, (Mrs Arthur Beresford Cane), *died* 1926, vol. II
Cane, Robert Alexander Gordon, 1893–1975, vol. VII
Canet, Maj.-Gen. Lawrence George, 1910–1996, vol. X
Canetti, Elias, 1905–1994, vol. IX
Canfield, Cass, 1897–1986, vol. VIII
Canfield, Dorothy, (Dorothea Frances Canfield Fisher), 1879–1958, vol. V
Canfield, James Hulme, 1847–1909, vol. I
Canham, Brian John, 1930–1990, vol. VIII
Canham, Bryan Frederick, (Peter), 1920–1993, vol. IX
Canham, Erwin Dain, 1904–1982, vol. VIII
Canham, Peter; *see* Canham, B. F.
Canham, Ven. Thomas Henry, *died* 1947, vol. IV
Cann, Hon. John Henry, 1860–1940, vol. III
Cann, Percy Walter, 1884–1973, vol. VII
Cann, Robert John, 1901–1983, vol. VIII
Cann, Sir William Moore, 1856–1947, vol. IV
Cannan, Charles, 1858–1919, vol. II
Cannan, Rt. Rev. Edward Alexander Capparis, 1920–1992, vol. IX
Cannan, Edwin, 1861–1935, vol. III
Cannan, Gilbert, 1884–1955, vol. V
Cannan, Maj.-Gen. James Harold, 1882–1976, vol. VII
Cannan, Joanna, (Mrs H. J. Pullein-Thompson), 1898–1961, vol. VI
Cannell, John, vol. III
Canney, Maurice Arthur, 1872–1942, vol. IV
Canning, Col Albert, 1861–1960, vol. V
Canning, Hon. Albert Stratford George, 1832–1916, vol. II
Canning, Rev. Clifford Brooke, 1882–1957, vol. V
Canning, Hon. Conway Stratford George, 1854–1926, vol. II
Canning, Sir Ernest R., 1876–1966, vol. VI
Canning, Frederick, 1882–1968, vol. VI
Canning, Hugh, *died* 1927, vol. II
Canning, Sir Samuel, 1823–1908, vol. I
Canning, Victor, 1911–1986, vol. VIII
Cannon, Annie Jump, 1863–1941, vol. IV
Cannon, George Harry Franklyn, 1885–1966, vol. VI
Cannon, Henry White, 1850–1934, vol. III
Cannon, Herbert Graham, 1897–1963, vol. VI
Cannon, James, 1864–1944, vol. IV
Cannon, Hon. Lawrence Arthur Dumoulin, 1877–1939, vol. III
Cannon, Lawrence John, 1852–1921, vol. II
Cannon, Sir Leslie, 1920–1970, vol. VI
Cannon, Air Vice-Marshal Leslie William, 1904–1986, vol. VIII

Carden, Sir Lionel Edward Gresley, 1851–1915, vol. I
Carden, Col Louis Peile, 1860–1942, vol. IV
Carden, Adm. Sir Sackville Hamilton, 1857–1930, vol. III
Carden, Stephen; *see* Carden, G. S. P.
Carden Roe, Brig. William, 1894–1977, vol. VII
Cardew, Sir Alexander Gordon, 1861–1937, vol. III
Cardew, Claud Ambrose, 1870–1959, vol. V
Cardew, Evelyn Roberta, (Lady Cardew), *died* 1953, vol. V
Cardew, Col Sir Frederic, 1839–1921, vol. II
Cardew, Rev. Prebendary Frederic Anstruther, 1866–1942, vol. IV
Cardew, Lt-Col George Ambrose, *died* 1941, vol. IV
Cardew, Col George Hereward, 1861–1949, vol. IV
Cardew, Michael Ambrose, 1901–1983, vol. VIII
Cardiff, Brig. Ereld Boteler Wingfield, 1909–1988, vol. VIII
Cardigan and Lancastre, Countess of; (Adeline Louise Maria), 1825–1915, vol. I
Cardin, James Joseph, 1839–1917, vol. II
Cardinale, Most Rev. Hyginus Eugene, 1916–1983, vol. VIII
Cardinall, Sir Allan Wolsey, 1887–1956, vol. V
Cardon, Philip Vincent, 1889–1965, vol. VI
Cardot, Rt Rev. Alexander, 1857–1925, vol. II
Cardozo, Benjamin N., 1870–1938, vol. III
Cardozo, Henry O'Connell, 1839–1905, vol. I
Carducci, Giosue, 1835–1907, vol. I
Cardus, Sir Neville, 1889–1975, vol. VII
Cardwell, Sir David, 1920–1982, vol. VIII
Cardwell, George, 1882–1962, vol. VI
Cardwell, Rev. John Henry, 1842–1921, vol. II
Care, Henry Clifford, 1892–1979, vol. VII
Carew, 3rd Baron, 1860–1923, vol. II
Carew, 4th Baron, 1863–1926, vol. II
Carew, 5th Baron, 1860–1927, vol. II
Carew, 6th Baron, 1905–1994, vol. IX
Carew, Charles Robert Sydenham, 1853–1939, vol. III
Carew, Major George Albert Lade, 1862–1937, vol. III
Carew, Sir Henry Palk, 9th Bt, 1870–1934, vol. III
Carew, Mrs James; *see* Terry, Dame Ellen.
Carew, James Laurence, *died* 1903, vol. I
Carew, Lt-Gen. Sir Reginald Pole, 1849–1924, vol. II
Carew, Major Robert John Henry, 1888–1982, vol. VIII
Carew, Sir Thomas Palk, 10th Bt, 1890–1976, vol. VII
Carew, William Desmond, 1899–1981, vol. VIII
Carew, William James, 1890–1990, vol. VIII
Carew-Gibson, Harry Frederick, 1869–1953, vol. V
Carew Hunt, Rear-Adm. Geoffrey Harry, 1917–1979, vol. VII
Carew Hunt, Captain Roland Cecil, 1880–1959, vol. V
Carew-Hunt, Lt-Col Thomas Edward, 1874–1950, vol. IV
Carew Pole, Col Sir John Gawen, 12th Bt, 1902–1993, vol. IX
Carey, Rev. Albert Darell T.; *see* Tupper-Carey.

Carey, Brig.-Gen. Arthur Basil, 1872–1961, vol. VI
Carey, Sir Bernard Sausmarez, 1864–1919, vol. II
Carey, Maj.-Gen. Carteret Walter, 1853–1932, vol. III
Carey, Cecil William Victor, 1887–1976, vol. VII
Carey, Chapple G.; *see* Gill-Carey.
Carey, Charles William, 1862–1943, vol. IV
Carey, Clive; *see* Carey, F. C. S.
Carey, Maj.-Gen. Constantine Phipps, 1835–1906, vol. I
Carey, David Macbeth Moir, 1917–2000, vol. X
Carey, Denis, 1909–1986, vol. VIII
Carey, (Francis) Clive (Savill), 1883–1968, vol. VI
Carey, Frank Stanton, 1860–1928, vol. II
Carey, Maj.-Gen. George Glas Sandeman, 1867–1948, vol. IV
Carey, Gordon Vero, 1886–1969, vol. VI
Carey, Brig.-Gen. Harold Eustace, 1874–1944, vol. IV
Carey, Col Herbert Clement, 1865–1948, vol. IV
Carey, Herbert Simon, 1856–1947, vol. IV
Carey, Rt Rev. Kenneth Moir, 1908–1979, vol. VII
Carey, Maj.-Gen. Laurence Francis de Vic, 1904–1972, vol. VII
Carey, Lionel Mohun, 1911–1988, vol. VIII
Carey, Very Rev. Michael Sausmarez, 1913–1985, vol. VIII
Carey, Brig.-Gen. Octavius William, 1865–1938, vol. III
Carey, Rosa Nouchette, 1840–1909, vol. I
Carey, Sir Thomas Godfrey, 1832–1906, vol. I
Carey, Sir Victor Gosselin, 1871–1957, vol. V
Carey, Captain Walter, *died* 1932, vol. III
Carey, Rt Rev. Walter Julius, 1875–1955, vol. V
Carey, Brig. Walter Louis John, 1872–1953, vol. V
Carey, Lt-Col Wilfrid Leathes de Mussenden, 1881–1937, vol. III
Carey, Col William, 1833–1905, vol. I
Carey, Sir Willoughby Langer, 1875–1933, vol. III
Carey Evans, Lady Olwen Elizabeth, 1892–1990, vol. VIII
Carey-Foster, George Arthur, 1907–1994, vol. IX
Carey Jones, Norman Stewart, 1911–1997, vol. X
Carey Taylor, Alan; *see* Taylor.
Cargill, Featherston, 1870–1959, vol. V
Cargill, Air Comdt Dame Helen Wilson, 1896–1969, vol. VI
Cargill, Sir (Ian) Peter (Macgillivray), 1915–1981, vol. VIII
Cargill, Sir John Traill, 1st Bt, 1867–1954, vol. V
Cargill, Lionel Vernon, *died* 1955, vol. V
Cargill, Sir Peter; *see* Cargill, Sir I. P. M.
Cargill Thompson, William David James, 1930–1978, vol. VII
Carill-Worsley, Philip Ernest T.; *see* Tindal-Carill-Worsley.
Carington, Herbert Hanbury Smith-, 1851–1917, vol. II
Carington, Neville Woodford S.; *see* Smith-Carington.
Carington, Lt-Col Rt Hon. Sir William Henry Peregrine, 1845–1914, vol. I
Carisbrooke, 1st Marquess of, 1886–1960, vol. V
Carkeek, Sir Arthur, 1861–1933, vol. III
Carlaw, John, *died* 1934, vol. III

Carlebach, Col Sir Philip, 1873–1949, vol. IV
Carles, William Richard, 1848–1929, vol. III
Carless, Albert, *died* 1936, vol. III
Carleston, Hadden Hamilton, 1904–1986, vol. VIII
Carleton, Hon. Brig.-Gen. Frank Robert Crofton, 1856–1924, vol. II
Carleton, Brig.-Gen. Frederick Montgomerie, 1867–1922, vol. II
Carleton, Ven. George Dundas, 1877–1961, vol. VI
Carleton, Major Guy Audouin, 1859–1941, vol. IV
Carleton, Gen. Henry Alexander, 1814–1900, vol. I
Carleton, Rev. James George, 1848–1918, vol. II
Carleton, Janet Buchanan, (Mrs John Carleton); *see* Adam Smith, J. B.
Carleton, John Dudley, 1908–1974, vol. VII
Carleton, Brig.-Gen. Lancelot Richard, 1861–1937, vol. III
Carleton, Brig.-Gen. Mongtomery Launcelot, 1861–1942, vol. IV
Carleton, Maj.-Gen. Richard Langford L.; *see* Leir-Carleton.
Carlier, Edmond William Wace, 1861–1940, vol. III
Carlile, Sir Edward, 1845–1917, vol. II
Carlile, Sir (Edward) Hildred, 1st Bt (*cr* 1917), 1852–1942, vol. IV
Carlile, Rev. Edward Wilson, 1915–1996, vol. X
Carlile, Sir Hildred; *see* Carlile, Sir E. H.
Carlile, Rev. John Charles, *died* 1941, vol. IV
Carlile, Sir Walter; *see* Carlile, Sir W. W.
Carlile, Sir (William) Walter, 1st Bt (*cr* 1928), 1862–1950, vol. IV
Carlile, Rev. Wilson, 1847–1942, vol. IV
Carlill, Harold Flamank, 1875–1959, vol. V
Carlill, Hildred, *died* 1942, vol. IV
Carlill, Vice-Adm. Sir Stephen Hope, 1902–1996, vol. X
Carlin, Gaston, *died* 1922, vol. II
Carline, George, 1855–1920, vol. II
Carline, Sydney W., 1888–1929, vol. III
Carling, Sir Ernest Rock, 1877–1960, vol. V
Carling, Rt Hon. Sir John, 1828–1911, vol. I
Carlingford, 1st Baron, 1823–1898, vol. I
Carlisle, 9th Earl of, 1843–1911, vol. I
Carlisle, 10th Earl of, 1867–1912, vol. I
Carlisle, 11th Earl of, 1895–1963, vol. VI
Carlisle, 12th Earl of, 1923–1994, vol. IX
Carlisle, Rt Hon. Alexander Montgomery, 1854–1926, vol. II
Carlisle, Rt Rev. Arthur, 1881–1943, vol. IV
Carlisle, Lt-Col Denton; *see* Carlisle, Lt-Col J. C. D.
Carlisle, Engr Rear-Adm. Frank Scott, 1882–1941, vol IV
Carlisle, Lt-Col (John Charles) Denton, 1888–1972, vol. VII
Carlisle, Kenneth Ralph Malcolm, 1908–1983, vol. VIII
Carlisle, R. H., 1865–1941, vol. IV
Carlos, Don; Duke of Madrid, 1848–1909, vol. I
Carlow, Viscount; George Lionel Seymour, 1907–1944, vol. IV
Carlow, Charles Augustus, *died* 1954, vol. V
Carlton, Sir Arthur, *died* 1931, vol. III
Carlton, C. Hope, 1889–1951, vol. V
Carlyle, Rev. Alexander James, 1861–1943, vol. IV
Carlyle, Edward Irving, 1871–1952, vol. V

Carlyle, Sir Robert Warrand, 1859–1934, vol. III
Carlyon, Sir Alexander Keith, 1848–1936, vol. III
Carlyon, Thomas Symington, 1902–1982, vol. VIII
Carlyon-Britton, Major Philip William Poole, 1863–1938, vol. III
Carman, Bliss, 1861–1929, vol. III
Carmichael, 1st Baron, 1859–1926, vol. II
Carmichael, Alexander, *died* 1912, vol. I
Carmichael, Captain Hon. Ambrose Campbell, 1872–1953, vol. V
Carmichael, Claude Dundas James, 1862–1915, vol. I
Carmichael, Sir Duncan, 1866–1923, vol. II
Carmichael, Sir Eardley Charles William G. C.; *see* Gibson-Craig-Carmichael.
Carmichael, Edward Arnold, 1896–1978, vol. VII
Carmichael, Rev. Frederic Falkiner, 1831–1919, vol. II
Carmichael, Sir George, 1866–1936, vol. III
Carmichael, George Chapman, 1924–1970, vol. VI
Carmichael, Captain Sir Henry Thomas G. C.; *see* Gibson-Craig-Carmichael.
Carmichael, James, 1846–1927, vol. II
Carmichael, Sir James, 1858–1934, vol. III
Carmichael, James, 1894–1966, vol. VI
Carmichael, James, *died* 1972, vol. VII
Carmichael, James Armstrong Gordon, 1913–1990, vol. VIII
Carmichael, Lt-Col Sir James Forrest Halkett, 1868–1934, vol. III
Carmichael, Sir James Morse, 3rd Bt, 1844–1902, vol. I
Carmichael, Sir John, 1910–1996, vol. X
Carmichael, John Murray G.; *see* Gibson-Carmichael.
Carmichael, Leonard, 1898–1973, vol. VII
Carmichael, Mary, *died* 1935, vol. III
Carmichael, Mary Gertrude, (Lady Carmichael), *died* 1941, vol. IV
Carmichael, Montgomery, 1857–1936, vol. III
Carmichael, Norman Scott, 1883–1951, vol. V
Carmichael, Peter, 1933–1999, vol. X
Carmichael, Sir William G. C.; *see* Gibson-Craig-Carmichael, Sir A. H. W.
Carmichael Anstruther, Sir Windham Charles James; *see* Anstruther.
Carmichael-Anstruther, Sir Windham Eric Francis; *see* Anstruther.
Carmichael-Anstruther, Sir Windham Frederick; *see* Anstruther.
Carmichael-Anstruther, Sir Windham Robert; *see* Anstruther.
Carmichael-Ferrall, John, 1855–1923, vol. II
Carmody, Sir Alan Thomas, 1920–1978, vol. VII (AII)
Carmody, Very Rev. William P., *died* 1938, vol. III
Carmont, Hon. Lord; John Francis Carmont, 1880–1965, vol. VI
Carmont, John Francis; *see* Carmont, Hon. Lord.
Carnac, Charles James R.; *see* Rivett-Carnac.
Carnac, Sir Claud James R.; *see* Rivett-Carnac.
Carnac, Rev. Sir George R.; *see* Rivett-Carnac.
Carnac, Sir Henry George Crabbe R.; *see* Rivett-Carnac.

Carnac, Vice-Adm. James William R.; *see* Rivett-Carnac.
Carnac, Col John Henry R.; *see* Rivett-Carnac.
Carnac, Col Percy Temple R.; *see* Rivett-Carnac.
Carnac, Sir William Percival R.; *see* Rivett-Carnac.
Carnarvon, 5th Earl of, 1866–1923, vol. II
Carnarvon, 6th Earl of, 1898–1987, vol. VIII
Carncross, Hon. Sir Walter Charles Frederick, 1855–1940, vol. III
Carnduff, Sir Herbert William Cameron, 1862–1915, vol. I
Carne, Col James Power, 1906–1986, vol. VIII
Carnegie, Andrew, 1835–1919, vol. II
Carnegie, Hon. Charles, 1883–1906, vol. I
Carnegie, Col David, 1868–1949, vol. IV
Carnegie, Air Vice-Marshal David Vaughan, 1897–1964, vol. VI
Carnegie, Hon. David Wynford, 1871–1900, vol. I
Carnegie, Lt-Col Hon. Douglas George, 1870–1937, vol. III
Carnegie, Sir Francis, 1874–1946, vol. IV
Carnegie, Lady Helena Mariota, 1865–1943, vol. IV
Carnegie, Rt Hon. Sir Lancelot Douglas, 1861–1933, vol. III
Carnegie, Louise, (Mrs Andrew Carnegie), 1857–1946, vol. IV
Carnegie, Rev. William Hartley, 1860–1936, vol. III
Carnegy, Gen. Alexander, 1829–1900, vol. I
Carnegy, Col Charles Gilbert, 1864–1928, vol. II
Carnegy of Lour, Lt-Col Elliott; *see* Carnegy of Lour, Lt-Col U. E. C.
Carnegy, Rev. Canon Patrick Charles Alexander, 1893–1969, vol. VI
Carnegy, Maj.-Gen. Sir Philip Mainwaring, 1858–1927, vol. II
Carnegy of Lour, Lt-Col (Ughtred) Elliott (Carnegy), 1886–1973, vol. VII
Carner, Mosco, 1904–1985, vol. VIII
Carney, Most Rev. James F., 1915–1990, vol. VIII
Carney, Adm. Robert Bostwick, 1895–1990, vol. VIII
Carnochan, John Golder, 1910–1981, vol. VIII
Carnock, 1st Baron, 1849–1928, vol. II
Carnock, 2nd Baron, 1883–1952, vol. V
Carnock, 3rd Baron, 1884–1982, vol. VIII
Carnwath, 12th Earl of, 1847–1910, vol. I
Carnwath, 15th (de facto 13th) Earl of, 1883–1931, vol. III
Carnwath, 16th (de facto 14th) Earl of, 1851–1941, vol. IV
Carnwath, Sir Andrew Hunter, 1909–1995, vol. IX
Carnwath, Thomas, 1878–1954, vol. V
Caröe, Sir Athelstan; *see* Caröe, Sir E. A. G.
Caröe, Sir (Einar) Athelstan (Gordon), 1903–1988, vol. VIII
Caroe, Martin Bragg, 1933–1999, vol. X
Caroe, Sir Olaf Kirkpatrick, 1892–1981, vol. VIII
Caroe, William Douglas, 1857–1938, vol. III
Carolus-Duran, Emile Auguste, 1838–1917, vol. II
Caron, Hon. Joseph Edouard, 1866–1930, vol. III
Caron, Hon. Sir Joseph Philippe Rene Adolphe, 1842–1908, vol. I
Carozzi, Joseph L., 1866–1933, vol. III
Carpendale, Vice-Adm. Sir Charles Douglas, 1874–1968, vol. VI

Carpendale, Major Frederic Maxwell-, 1887–1958, vol. V
Carpenter, Captain Alfred, 1847–1925, vol. II
Carpenter, Vice-Adm. Alfred Francis Blakeney, 1881–1955, vol. V
Carpenter, Major Sir Archibald Boyd B.; *see* Boyd Carpenter.
Carpenter, Charles Claude, 1858–1938, vol. III
Carpenter, Brig.-Gen. Charles Murray, 1870–1942, vol. IV
Carpenter, David, 1866–1935, vol. III
Carpenter, Edward, 1844–1929, vol. III
Carpenter, Rev. Edward Frederick, 1910–1998, vol. X
Carpenter, Sir Eric Ashton, 1896–1973, vol. VII
Carpenter, Geoffrey Douglas Hale, 1882–1953, vol. V
Carpenter, George, 1859–1910, vol. I
Carpenter, Lt-Gen. George, 1877–1952, vol. V
Carpenter, George Frederick, 1917–1992, vol. IX
Carpenter, Rev. George Herbert, 1865–1939, vol. III
Carpenter, George Lyndon, 1872–1948, vol. IV
Carpenter, Sir H. C. Harold, 1875–1940; vol. III
Carpenter, Rt. Rev. Harry James, 1901–1993, vol. IX
Carpenter, Ven. Harry William, 1854–1936, vol. III
Carpenter, Henry John B.; *see* Boyd-Carpenter.
Carpenter, Ven. Horace John, 1887–1965, vol. VI
Carpenter, Rev. J. Estlin, 1844–1927, vol. II
Carpenter, Rev. James Nelson, *died* 1949, vol. IV (A), vol. V
Carpenter, John MacGregor Kendall K.; *see* Kendall-Carpenter.
Carpenter, Maj.-Gen. John Owen, 1894–1967, vol. VI
Carpenter, Captain John Peers B.; *see* Boyd-Carpenter.
Carpenter, Percy Frederick, 1901–1964, vol. VI
Carpenter, Percy Henry, 1879–1962, vol. VI
Carpenter, Rhys, 1889–1980, vol. VII
Carpenter, Rev. Spencer Cecil, 1877–1959, vol. V
Carpenter, Trevor Charles, 1917–1986, vol. VIII
Carpenter, Adm. Hon. Walter Cecil, 1834–1904, vol. I
Carpenter, Sir Walter Randolph, 1877–1954, vol. V
Carpenter, Rt Rev. William B.; *see* Boyd Carpenter.
Carpenter-Garnier, John, 1839–1926, vol. II
Carpenter-Garnier, Rt Rev. Mark Rodolph, 1881–1969, vol. VI
Carpentier, Général d'Armée Marcel Maurice, 1895–1977, vol. VII
Carpmael, Kenneth S., 1885–1975, vol. VII
Carpmael, Raymond, 1875–1950, vol. IV
Carr, Alwyn C. E., *died* 1940, vol. III
Carr, Sir Arthur Strettell C.; *see* Comyns Carr.
Carr, Sir Bernard; *see* Carr, Sir F. B.
Carr, Sir Cecil Thomas, 1878–1966, vol. VI
Carr, Rt Rev. Charles Lisle, 1871–1942, vol. IV
Carr, Air Marshal Sir (Charles) Roderick, 1891–1971, vol. VII
Carr, Charles Telford, 1905–1976, vol. VII
Carr, Brig.-Gen. Christopher D'Arcy Bloomfield Saltern B.; *see* Baker-Carr.
Carr, Cyril Eric, 1926–1981, vol. VIII

Carr, David, 1847–1920, vol. II
Carr, Denis Edward Bernard, 1920–1981, vol. VIII
Carr, Rev. Edmund, 1826–1916, vol. II
Carr, Edward Arthur, 1903–1966, vol. VI
Carr, Col Edward Elliott, 1854–1926, vol. II
Carr, Edward Hallett, 1892–1982, vol. VIII
Carr, Sir Emsley, 1867–1941, vol. IV
Carr, Francis Howard, 1874–1969, vol. VI
Carr, Frank Arnold, 1873–1942, vol. IV
Carr, Frank George Griffith, 1903–1991, vol. IX
Carr, Sir (Frederick) Bernard, 1893–1981, vol. VIII
Carr, Rev. Frederick Robert, 1869–1952, vol. V
Carr, George Shadwell Quartano, 1866–1905, vol. I
Carr, Gilbert Harry, 1884–1954, vol. V
Carr, Harry Lascelles, 1907–1943, vol. IV
Carr, Lt-Col Henry Arbuthnot, 1872–1951, vol. V
Carr, Adm. Henry John, 1839–1914, vol. I
Carr, Henry Lambton, 1899–1988, vol. VIII
Carr, Henry Lascelles, 1841–1902, vol. I
Carr, Henry Marvell, 1894–1970, vol. VI
Carr, Herbert Reginald Culling, 1896–1986, vol. VIII
Carr, Herbert Wildon, 1857–1931, vol. III
Carr, Maj.-Gen. Howard, 1863–1944, vol. IV
Carr, Howard, 1880–1960, vol. V
Carr, Sir Hubert Winch, 1877–1955, vol. V
Carr, J. W. Comyns, 1849–1916, vol. II
Carr, Rev. James Haslewood, 1831–1915, vol. I
Carr, Sir James Henry Brownlow, 1913–1984, vol. VIII
Carr, James Lloyd, 1912–1994, vol. IX
Carr, Hon. John, 1819–1913, vol. I
Carr, Air Marshal Sir John Darcy B.; see Baker-Carr.
Carr, John Dickson, died 1977, vol. VII
Carr, John Walter, 1862–1942, vol. IV
Carr, John Wesley, 1862–1939, vol. III
Carr, Lt-Gen. Laurence, 1886–1954, vol. V
Carr, Rear-Adm. Lawrence George, 1920–1990, vol. IX (AI)
Carr, Michael, 1947–1990, vol. VIII
Carr, Norman Alexander, 1899–1970, vol. VI
Carr, Rev. Owen Charles, died 1929, vol. III
Carr, Philippa; see Hibbert, Eleanor.
Carr, Major Robert George Teesdale B.; see Baker-Carr.
Carr, Air Marshal Sir Roderick; see Carr, Air Marshal Sir C. R.
Carr, Rupert Ellis, 1910–1974, vol. VII
Carr, Theodore; see Carr, W. T.
Carr, Thomas Ernest Ashdown, 1915–1999, vol. X
Carr, Most Rev. Thomas Joseph, 1839–1917, vol. II
Carr, Rev. Walter Raleigh, 1843–1907, vol. I
Carr, Sir William, 1872–1949, vol. IV
Carr, Sir William Emsley, 1912–1977, vol. VII
Carr, Brig. William Greenwood, 1901–1982, vol. VIII
Carr, Rev. William Henry, 1857–1932, vol. III
Carr, Surg. Rear-Adm. William James, 1883–1966, vol. VI
Carr, Col William Moncrieff, 1886–1956, vol. V
Carr, Sir William St John, 1848–1928, vol. II
Carr, (William) Theodore, 1866–1931, vol. III

Carr-Calthrop, Col Christopher William, 1844–1934, vol. III
Carr-Gomm, Francis Culling, 1834–1919, vol. II
Carr-Gomm, Hubert William Culling, 1877–1939, vol. III
Carr-Hall, Col Ralph Ellis; see Hall.
Carr-Saunders, Sir Alexander Morris, 1886–1966, vol. VI
Carr-White, Maj.-Gen. Percy, 1856–1934, vol. III
Carrara, Arthur Charles, died 1949, vol. IV
Carre, Major Ralph G. Riddell, 1868–1941, vol. IV
Carrel, Alexis, 1873–1944, vol. IV
Carrel, Philip, 1915–2000, vol. X
Carreras, Sir James, 1909–1990, vol. VIII
Carrick, 5th Earl of, 1835–1901, vol. I
Carrick, 6th Earl of, 1851–1909, vol. I
Carrick, 7th Earl of, 1873–1931, vol. III
Carrick, 8th Earl of, 1903–1957, vol. V
Carrick, 9th Earl of, 1931–1992, vol. IX
Carrick, Alexander, died 1966, vol. VI
Carrick, Edward; see Craig, E. A.
Carrick, Maj.-Gen. Thomas Welsh, 1914–2000, vol. X
Carrick-Buchanan, Sir David Carrick Robert, 1825–1904, vol. I
Carrick-Buchanan, David William Ramsay, 1834–1925, vol. II
Carrier, Philippe Leslie Caro, 1893–1975, vol. VII
Carrigan, William, died 1951, vol. V
Carrington, 4th Baron, 1852–1929, vol. III
Carrington, 5th Baron, 1891–1938, vol. III
Carrington, Charles Edmund, 1897–1990, vol. VIII
Carrington, Brig. Charles Ronald Brownlow, 1880–1948, vol. IV
Carrington, Very Rev. Charles Walter, 1859–1941, vol. IV
Carrington, Maj.-Gen. Sir Frederick, 1844–1913, vol. I
Carrington, Lt-Gen. Sir Harold; see Carrington, Lt-Gen. Sir R. H.
Carrington, Very Rev. Henry, 1814–1906, vol. I
Carrington, Vice-Adm. John Walsh, 1879–1964, vol. VI
Carrington, Sir John Worrell, 1847–1913, vol. I
Carrington, Most Rev. Philip, 1892–1975, vol. VII
Carrington, Richard, 1921–1971, vol. VII
Carrington, Lt-Gen. Sir (Robert) Harold, 1882–1964, vol. VI
Carrington, Roger Clifford, 1905–1971, vol. VII
Carrington, Sir William Speight, 1904–1975, vol. VII
Carritt, David; see Carritt, H. D. G.
Carritt, Edgar Frederick, 1876–1964, vol. VI
Carritt, (Hugh) David (Graham), 1927–1982, vol. VIII
Carroll, Sir Alfred Thomas, (Sir Turi Carroll), 1890–1975, vol. VII
Carroll, Maj.-Gen. Derek Raymond, 1919–1996, vol. X
Carroll, Rt Rev. Francis P., 1890–1967, vol. VI
Carroll, Francis Patrick, 1887–1955, vol. VI
Carroll, Col Frederick Fitzgerald, died 1932, vol. III
Carroll, Hon. Henry George, 1865–1939, vol. III
Carroll, Sir James, died 1905, vol. I
Carroll, Hon. Sir James, 1857–1926, vol. II

Carroll, Sir John Anthony, 1899–1974, vol. VII
Carroll, Most Rev. John J., 1865–1949, vol. IV
Carroll, Brig.-Gen. John William Vincent, 1869–1927, vol. II
Carroll, Lewis, (Rev. Charles L. Dodgson), 1832–1898, vol. I
Carroll, Madeleine, 1906–1987, vol. VIII
Carroll, Paul Vincent, 1900–1968, vol. VI
Carroll, Sydney Wentworth, 1877–1958, vol. V
Carroll, Sir Turi; see Carroll, Sir Alfred Thomas.
Carroll, Rev. William Alexander, 1863–1935, vol. III
Carron, Baron (Life Peer); William John Carron, 1902–1969, vol. VI
Carrow, Comdr John Hinton, 1890–1973, vol. VII
Carruthers, Adam, 1857–1937, vol. III
Carruthers, Agnes Lucy Mary, 1872–1961, vol. VI
Carruthers, (Alexander) Douglas (Mitchell), *died* 1962, vol. VI
Carruthers, Engr-Rear-Adm. David John, 1867–1940, vol. III
Carruthers, Douglas; see Carruthers, A. D. M.
Carruthers, Lt-Col Francis John, 1868–1945, vol. IV
Carruthers, George, 1917–1992, vol. IX
Carruthers, Ian Douglas, 1938–1996, vol. X
Carruthers, Lt-Col James, 1876–1936, vol. III
Carruthers, Rev. James E., 1848–1932, vol. III
Carruthers, John Bennett, 1869–1910, vol. I
Carruthers, Hon. Sir Joseph Hector M'Neil, 1857–1932, vol. III
Carruthers, Brig.-Gen. Robert Alexander, 1862–1945, vol. IV
Carruthers, Violet Rosa; see Markham, V. R.
Carruthers, William, 1830–1922, vol. II
Carruthers, Sir William, 1858–1936, vol. III
Carse, William Mitchell, 1899–1987, vol. VIII
Carslaw, Horatio Scott, 1870–1954, vol. V
Carson, Baron (Life Peer); Rt Hon. Sir Edward Henry Carson, 1854–1935, vol. III
Carson, Col Charles John Lloyd, 1866–1953, vol. V
Carson, Sir Charles William Charteris, 1874–1945, vol. IV
Carson, Hon. Edward, 1920–1987, vol. VIII
Carson, Brig. Sir Frederick, 1886–1960, vol. V
Carson, Herbert William, 1870–1930, vol. III
Carson, Howard Adams, 1842–1931, vol. III
Carson, Maj.-Gen. Sir John Wallace, 1864–1922, vol. II
Carson, Rev. Joseph, *died* 1898, vol. I
Carson, Lionel, 1873–1937, vol. III
Carson, Murray, 1865–1917, vol. II
Carson, Sir Norman John, 1877–1964, vol. VI
Carson, Rachel Louise, 1907–1964, vol. VI
Carson, Air Cdre Robert John, 1924–1991, vol. IX
Carson, Thomas Henry, 1843–1917, vol. II
Carson, Captain Hon. Walter Seymour, 1890–1946, vol. IV
Carstairs, Charles Young, 1910–1993, vol. IX
Carstairs, George Morrison, 1916–1991, vol. IX
Carsten, Francis Ludwig, 1911–1998, vol. X
Carstens, Karl, 1914–1992, vol. IX
Carswell, Catherine Roxburgh, 1879–1946, vol. IV
Carswell, Donald, 1882–1940, vol. III
Carswell, John Patrick, 1918–1997, vol. X

Cart de Lafontaine, Lt-Col Henry Philip L., 1884–1963, vol. VI
Cartan, Elie Joseph, 1869–1951, vol. V
Carte, D'Oyly; see Carte, R. D.
Carte, (Richard) D'Oyly, 1844–1901, vol. I
Carte, Rupert D'Oyly; see D'Oyly Carte.
Carte, Col Thomas Elliott, 1861–1945, vol. IV
Carter, Albert Charles Robinson, 1864–1957, vol. V
Carter, Albert Thomas, 1861–1946, vol. IV
Carter, Alexander Scott, 1879–1969, vol. VI (AII)
Carter, Alfred B.; see Bonham-Carter.
Carter, Alfred Henry, 1849–1918, vol. II
Carter, Col Alfred Henry, 1856–1934, vol. III
Carter, Angela, 1940–1992, vol. IX
Carter, Ven. Anthony Basil, 1881–1942, vol. IV
Carter, Sir Archibald; see Carter, Sir R. H. A.
Carter, Sir (Arthur) Desmond B.; see Bonham-Carter.
Carter, Arthur Herbert, 1890–1979, vol. VII
Carter, Hon. Arthur John, 1847–1917, vol. II
Carter, Arthur Thomas B.; see Bonham-Carter.
Carter, Major Aubrey John, 1872–1914, vol. I
Carter, Barry Robin Octavius, 1928–1981, vol. VIII
Carter, Maj.-Gen. Beresford Cecil Molyneux, 1872–1923, vol. II
Carter, Captain (S) Bernard, 1885–1954, vol. V
Carter, Bruce; see Hough, R. A.
Carter, Gen. Sir Charles B.; see Bonham-Carter.
Carter, Brig.-Gen. Charles Herbert Philip, 1864–1943, vol. IV
Carter, Rev. Charles Sydney, 1876–1963, vol. VI
Carter, Sir Christopher Douglas B.; see Bonham Carter.
Carter, Rev. Cyril Robert, 1863–1930, vol. III
Carter, Air Cdre David William Frederick B.; see Bonham Carter.
Carter, Sir Derrick Hunton, 1906–1997, vol. X
Carter, Desmond, *died* 1939, vol. III
Carter, Dorothy Ethel Fleming, (Jane), 1928–1995, vol. IX
Carter, Douglas, 1911–1998, vol. X
Carter, Hon. Sir Douglas Julian, 1908–1988, vol. VIII
Carter, Col Duncan Campbell, 1856–1942, vol. IV
Carter, Sir Edgar B.; see Bonham-Carter.
Carter, Edward Henry, 1876–1953, vol. V
Carter, Edward Julian, 1902–1982, vol. VIII
Carter, Edward Robert Erskine, 1923–1982, vol. VIII
Carter, Eric Bairstow, 1912–1997, vol. X
Carter, Col Ernest Augustus Frederick, 1858–1934, vol. III
Carter, Ernestine Marie, 1906–1983, vol. VIII
Carter, Maj.-Gen. Sir Evan Eyare, 1866–1933, vol. III
Carter, Brig.-Gen. Francis Charles, 1858–1931, vol. III
Carter, Rev. Francis Edward, 1851–1935, vol. III
Carter, Francis Edward, 1886–1977, vol. VII
Carter, Francis Jackson, 1899–1999, vol. X
Carter, Frank Ernest Lovell, 1909–1995, vol. IX
Carter, Frank W., 1870–1933, vol. III
Carter, Sir Frank Willington, 1865–1945, vol. IV
Carter, Franklin, 1837–1919, vol. II

Carter, Frederick, *died* 1967, vol. VI
Carter, Sir Frederick Bowker Terrington, 1819–1900, vol. I
Carter, Frederick William, 1870–1952, vol. V
Carter, Geoffrey William, 1909–1989, vol. VIII
Carter, Sir George John, 1860–1922, vol. II
Carter, George Stuart, 1893–1969, vol. VI
Carter, Sir Gerald Francis, 1881–1959, vol. V
Carter, Sir Gilbert Thomas G.; *see* Gilbert-Carter.
Carter, Lt-Col Godfrey Lambert, 1868–1932, vol. III
Carter, Lt-Col Sir Gordon, 1853–1941, vol. IV
Carter, Harry Graham, 1901–1982, vol. VIII
Carter, Col Harry Molyneux, 1850–1914, vol. I
Carter, Rev. Henry, 1874–1951, vol. V
Carter, Rev. Henry Child, 1875–1954, vol. V
Carter, Captain Herbert Augustine, 1874–1916, vol. II
Carter, Herbert James, 1858–1940, vol. III (A), vol. IV
Carter, Hester Marion, 1867–1944, vol. IV
Carter, Howard, 1873–1939, vol. III
Carter, Hugh Hoyles, *died* 1919, vol. II
Carter, Humphrey G.; *see* Gilbert-Carter.
Carter, Huntly, *died* 1942, vol. IV
Carter, Ian Malcolm B.; *see* Bonham-Carter.
Carter, Jane; *see* Carter, D. E. F.
Carter, Maj.-Gen. James Norman, 1906–1994, vol. IX
Carter, Rev. John, 1861–1944, vol. IV
Carter, John Arkwright B.; *see* Bonham-Carter.
Carter, John Corrie, 1839–1927, vol. II
Carter, Lt-Col John Fillis Carré, 1882–1944, vol. IV
Carter, John Hilton, *died* 1926, vol. II
Carter, John Ridgely, 1865–1944, vol. IV
Carter, John Somers, 1901–1989, vol. VIII
Carter, Maj. Gen. Sir John Thomas, 1855–1939, vol. III
Carter, John Waynflete, 1905–1975, vol. VII
Carter, Malcolm Ogilvy, 1898–1982, vol. VIII
Carter, Sir Maurice B.; *see* Bonham-Carter.
Carter, Sir Morris; *see* Carter, Sir W. M.
Carter, Norman St Clair, 1875–1963, vol. VI
Carter, Air Cdre North, 1902–1984, vol. VIII
Carter, Octavius Cyril, 1893–1964, vol. VI
Carter, Peter Anthony, 1914–1983, vol. VIII
Carter, Reginald, 1868–1936, vol. III
Carter, Rei Alfred Deakin, 1856–1938, vol. III
Carter, Richard Erskine B.; *see* Bonham-Carter.
Carter, Sir (Richard Henry) Archibald, 1887–1958, vol. V
Carter, Robert Brudenell, 1828–1918, vol. II
Carter, Lt-Col Robert Markham, 1875–1961, vol. VI
Carter, Adm. Sir Stuart Sumner B.; *see* Bonham-Carter.
Carter, Hon. Thomas Fortescue, 1855–1945, vol. IV
Carter, Vivian, 1878–1956, vol. V
Carter, W. Horsfall, 1900–1976, vol. VII
Carter, Walter, 1883–1964, vol. VI
Carter, Walter, 1873–1975, vol. VII
Carter, Sir Walker Kelly, 1899–1985, vol. VIII
Carter, Air Vice-Marshal Wilfred, 1912–1999, vol. X

Carter, Wilfred George, *died* 1969, vol. VI
Carter, William, 1836–1913, vol. I
Carter, Sir William, 1848–1932, vol. III
Carter, William, *died* 1932, vol. III
Carter, William, 1867–1940, vol. III
Carter, William Edward, 1885–1965, vol. VI
Carter, Col William Graydon, 1857–1938, vol. III
Carter, William Henry, 1868–1944, vol. IV
Carter, Most Rev. William Marlborough, 1850–1941, vol. IV
Carter, Sir (William) Morris, 1873–1960, vol. V
Carter, Sir William Oscar, 1905–2000, vol. X
Carter, William Stovold, 1915–1985, vol. VIII
Carter-Campbell, Col George Tupper Campbell, 1869–1921, vol. II
Carter-Cotton, Francis, 1847–1919, vol. II
Carteret, Captain Charles Edward M. de; *see* Malet de Carteret.
Carteret, Lt-Col E. C. M. de; *see* Malet de Carteret.
Carteret, Reginald M. de; *see* Malet de Carteret.
Carthew, Lt-Col Thomas Walter Colby, 1880–1955, vol. V
Carthew-Yorstoun, Brig.-Gen. Archibald Morden, 1855–1925, vol. III
Cartier De Marchienne, Baron de, 1871–1946, vol. IV
Cartier, Rudolph, 1904–1994, vol. IX
Cartland, Dame Barbara; *see* Cartland, Dame B. H.
Cartland, Dame Barbara Hamilton, 1901–2000, vol. X
Cartland, J. Ronald H., 1907–1940, vol. III
Cartland, Major John Howard, 1849–1940, vol. III
Cartledge, Jack Pickering, 1900–1966, vol. VI
Cartmel, Lt-Col Alfred Edward, 1893–1974, vol. VII
Cartmel-Robinson, Sir Harold Francis, 1889–1957, vol. V
Cartmell, Sir Harry, *died* 1923, vol. II
Cartmell, James Austen-, 1862–1921, vol. II
Carton, Richard Claude, 1856–1928, vol. II
Carton, Richard Paul, 1836–1907, vol. I
Carton, Ronald Lewis, 1888–1960, vol. V
Carton de Wiart, Lt-Gen. Sir Adrian, 1880–1963, vol. VI
Carton de Wiart, Count Edmund, 1876–1959, vol. V (A), vol. VI (AI)
Carton de Wiart, Comte Henry, 1869–1951, vol. V
Carton de Wiart, Léon Constant Ghislain, 1854–1915, vol. I
Carton de Wiart, Rt Rev. Mgr Maurice E., 1872–1935, vol. III
Cartwright, Albert, 1868–1956, vol. V
Cartwright, (Aubrey) Ralph Thomas, 1880–1936, vol. III
Cartwright, Beatrice, *died* 1947, vol. IV
Cartwright, Charles Frederic, 1846–1929, vol. III
Cartwright, Sir Charles Henry, 1865–1959, vol. V
Cartwright, Col Charles Marling, 1862–1946, vol. IV
Cartwright, Sir Chauncy, 1853–1933, vol. III
Cartwright, Rt Rev. David; *see* Cartwright, Rt Rev. E. D.
Cartwright, Rt Rev. (Edward) David, 1920–1997, vol. X

Cartwright, Rt Hon. Sir Fairfax Leighton, 1857–1928, vol. II
Cartwright, Lt-Col Francis Lennox, 1874–1957, vol. V
Cartwright, Frederick; see Cartwright, W. F.
Cartwright, Brig.-Gen. Garnier Norton, 1868–1924, vol. II
Cartwright, Brig.-Gen. George Strachan, 1866–1959, vol. V
Cartwright, Col Henry Antrobus, 1887–1957, col. V
Cartwright, Lt-Col Henry Aubrey, 1858–1945, vol. IV
Cartwright, Sir Henry Edmund, 1821–1899, vol. I
Cartwright, J. R., died 1919, vol. II
Cartwright, Rev. Canon James Lawrence, 1889–1978, vol. VII
Cartwright, Rt Hon. John Robert, 1895–1979, vol. VII (AII)
Cartwright, Lt-Col John Rogers, 1882–1942, vol. IV
Cartwright, Julia; see Ady, J.
Cartwright, Dame Mary Lucy, 1900–1998, vol. X
Cartwright, Ralph Thomas; see Cartwright, A. R. T.
Cartwright, Rt Hon. Sir Richard John, 1835–1912, vol. I
Cartwright, Lt-Col Robert, 1860–1942, vol. IV
Cartwright, Thomas Robert Brook Leslie-Melville, 1830–1921, vol. II
Cartwright, Sir William Bramwell, 1876–1958, vol. V
Cartwright, William Cornwallis, 1826–1915, vol. I
Cartwright, (William) Frederick, 1906–1998, vol. X
Cartwright Sharp, John Michael; see Sharp.
Cartwright-Taylor, Gen. Sir Malcolm Cartwright, 1911–1969, vol. VI
Caruana, Col Alfred Joseph, 1865–1953, vol. V
Caruana, Most Rev. Maurus, 1867–1943, vol. IV
Carus, Dr Paul, 1852–1919, vol. II
Carus-Wilson, Mrs C. Ashley, (Mary Louisa Georgina), died 1935, vol. III
Carus-Wilson, Charles Ashley, 1860–1942, vol. IV
Carus-Wilson, Eleanora Mary, 1897–1977, vol. VII
Caruso, Enrico, 1873–1921, vol. II
Carvell, John Eric Maclean, 1894–1978, vol. VII
Carver, Rev. Alfred James, 1826–1909, vol. I
Carver, David Dove, 1903–1974, vol. VII
Carver, Captain Edmund Clifton, 1873–1942, vol. IV
Carver, Rev. George Albert, 1862–1930, vol. III
Carver, Sir Stanley Roy, 1897–1967, vol. VI
Carver, Sydney Ralph Pitts, died 1940, vol. III
Carver, Thomas Gilbert, 1848–1906, vol. I
Carver, Col William Henton, 1868–1961, vol. VI
Carvill, Patrick George Hamilton, 1839–1924, vol. II
Carwardine, Thomas, died 1947, vol. IV
Cary, (Arthur) Joyce (Lunel), 1888–1957, vol. V
Cary, Sir (Arthur Lucius) Michael, 1914–1976, vol. VII
Cary, Joyce; see Cary, A. J. L.
Cary, Max, 1881–1958, vol. V
Cary, Sir Michael; see Cary, Sir A. L. M.
Cary, Hon. Philip Plantagenet, 1895–1968, vol. VI
Cary, Sir Robert Archibald, 1st Bt, 1898–1979, vol. VII

Cary, Maj.-Gen. Rupert Tristram Oliver, 1896–1980, vol. VII
Cary-Barnard, Brig.-Gen. Cyril Darcy Vivien, 1876–1933, vol. III
Cary-Elwes, Rt Rev. Dudley Charles, 1868–1932, vol. III
Cary-Elwes, Gervase Henry; see Elwes.
Cary-Elwes, Valentine Dudley Henry; see Elwes.
Caryll, Ivan, died 1921, vol. II
Carysfort, 5th Earl of, 1836–1909, vol. I
Casadesus, Robert, 1899–1972, vol. VII
Casalis, Jeanne de, 1898–1966, vol. VI
Casalone, Carlo D.; see Dionisotti-Casalone.
Casals, Pablo, 1876–1973, vol. VII
Casartelli, Rt Rev. Louis Charles, 1852–1925, vol. II
Casault, Hon. Sir Louis Edelmar Napoleon, 1822–1908, vol. I
Case, Air Vice-Marshal Albert Avion, 1916–1990, vol. VIII
Case, Air Vice-Marshal Avion; see Case, Air Vice-Marshal Albert A.
Case, Col Horace Akroyd, 1879–1968, vol. VI
Case, Captain Richard Vere Essex, 1904–1991, vol. IX
Case, Robert Hope, 1857–1944, vol. IV
Case, Thomas, 1844–1925, vol. II
Casella, Alfredo, 1883–1947, vol. IV
Casement, Maj.-Gen. Francis, 1881–1967, vol. VI
Casement, Adm. John Moore, 1877–1952, vol. V
Casey, Baron (Life Peer); Richard Gardiner Casey, 1890–1976, vol. VII
Casey, Captain Denis Arthur, 1889–1968, vol. VI
Casey, Hon. James Joseph, 1831–1913, vol. I
Casey, Rt Rev. Patrick, 1873–1940, vol. III
Casey, Rt Rev. Patrick Joseph, 1913–1999, vol. X
Casey, Dame Stella Katherine, 1924–2000, vol. X
Casey, Terence Anthony, 1920–1987, vol. VIII
Casey, Thomas Worrall, 1869–1949, vol. IV
Casey, Most Rev. Timothy, 1862–1931, vol. III
Casey, William Francis, 1884–1957, vol. V
Casgrain, Alexandre Chase-, 1879–1941, vol. IV
Casgrain, Hon. Col Hon. Joseph Philippe Baby-, born 1856, vol. III
Casgrain, Rev. Philippe Henri Duperron, 1864–1942, vol. IV
Casgrain, Rt Hon. Thomas Chase, 1852–1916, vol. II
Cash, J. Theodore, 1854–1936, vol. III
Cash, Col Sir Reginald John, 1892–1959, vol. V
Cash, Sir Thomas James, 1888–1978, vol. VII
Cash, Sir William, 1891–1964, vol. VI
Cash, Rt Rev. William Wilson, 1880–1955, vol. V
Cash-Reed, Bellamy Alexander, 1888–1965, vol. VI
Cashin, Hon. Sir Michael Patrick, 1864–1926, vol. II
Cashman, Rt Rev. David John, 1912–1971, vol. VII
Cashmore, Herbert Maurice, 1882–1972, vol. VII
Cashmore, Rt Rev. Thomas Herbert, 1892–1984, vol. VIII
Casimir-Perier, Jean Paul Pierre, 1847–1907, vol. I
Caslon, Vice-Adm. Clifford, 1896–1973, vol. VII
Caspersz, Charles P., 1855–1951, vol. V
Cass, Major Charles Herbert Davis, 1858–1929, vol. III

140

Cass, Brig. Edward Earnshaw Eden, 1898–1968, vol. VI
Cass, Rev. Gilbert Henning, 1873–1931, vol. III
Cass, Sir John, 1832–1898, vol. I
Cass, Sir John Patrick, 1909–1995, vol. IX (AII)
Cass, Col Walter Edmund Hutchinson, 1876–1931, vol. III
Cassal, Col Charles Edward, 1858–1921, vol. II
Cassar De Sain, 9th Marquess, 1880–1927, vol. II
Cassar De Sain, 10th Marquess, 1907–1958, vol. V
Cassatt, Alexander Johnston, 1839–1906, vol. I
Cassel, Rt Hon. Sir Ernest Joseph, 1852–1921, vol. II
Cassel, Rt Hon. Sir Felix, 1st Bt, 1869–1953, vol. V
Cassel, Sir Francis Edward, 2nd Bt, 1912–1969, vol. VI
Cassel, Gustav, 1866–1945, vol. IV
Cassells, Alexander, 1883–1967, vol. VI
Cassells, Hugh Hutchison, 1886–1950, vol. IV
Cassells, Thomas, 1902–1944, vol. IV
Cassels, Field-Marshal Sir (Archibald) James (Halkett), 1907–1996, vol. X
Cassels, Francis Henry, 1910–1987, vol. VIII
Cassels, Brig. George Hamilton, 1882–1944, vol. IV
Cassels, Brig.-Gen. Gilbert Robert, 1870–1951, vol. V
Cassels, Field-Marshal Sir James; see Cassels, A. J. H.
Cassels, Sir James Dale, 1877–1972, vol. VII
Cassels, James Macdonald, 1924–1994, vol. IX
Cassels, Gen. Sir Robert Archibald, 1876–1959, vol. V
Cassels, Hon. Sir Walter, 1845–1923, vol. II
Cassels, Walter Richard, 1826–1907, vol. I
Cassels, Walter Seton, 1873–1932, vol. III
Cassels, Rt Rev. William Wharton, 1858–1925, vol. II
Casserly, Col Gordon, died 1947, vol. IV
Cassia, Francis Joseph Nicholas Paul S.; see Sant-Cassia.
Cassidy, David Mackay, 1846–1936, vol. III
Cassidy, Sir Jack Evelyn, 1894–1975, vol. VII
Cassidy, John, 1860–1939, vol. III
Cassidy, Sir Maurice Alan, 1880–1949, vol. IV
Cassie, Arnold Blatchford David, 1905–1982, vol. VIII
Cassie, W(illiam) Fisher, 1905–1985, vol. VIII
Cassie, William Riach, 1861–1908, vol. I
Cassilly, Richard, 1927–1998, vol. X
Cassin, René, 1887–1976, vol. VII
Casson, Elizabeth, 1881–1954, vol. V
Casson, Herbert Alexander, 1867–1952, vol. V
Casson, Brig.-Gen. Hugh Gilbert, 1866–1951, vol. VI
Casson, Sir Hugh Maxwell, 1910–1999, vol. X
Casson, Rev. Canon John, 1869–1955, vol. V
Casson, Sir Lewis, 1875–1969, vol. VI
Casson, Margaret MacDonald, (Lady Casson), 1913–1999, vol. X
Casson, Stanley, 1889–1944, vol. IV
Casson, Dame Sybil; see Thorndike, Dame Sybil.
Casswell, Joshua David, died 1963, vol. VI
Castaing, Jacques C. de; see Chastenet de Castaing.
Catcheside, David Guthrie, 1907–1994, vol. IX
Castéja, Marie Emmanuel Alvar de

Biaudos-Scarisbrick, the Marquis de, 1849–1911, vol. I
Castellani, Marchese Count Aldo, 1877–1971, vol. VII
Castenskiold, H. Grevenkop, 1862–1921, vol. II
Casteret, Norbert, 1897–1987, vol. VIII
Castillejo, José, 1877–1945, vol. IV
Castle, Baron (Life Peer); Edward Cyril Castle, 1907–1979, vol. VII
Castle, Agnes, died 1922, vol. II
Castle, Edgar Bradshaw, 1897–1973, vol. VII
Castle, Egerton, 1858–1920, vol. II
Castle, Frances; see Blackburn, E. B.
Castle, Marcellus Purnell, 1849–1917, vol. II
Castle, Norman Henry, 1913–1988, vol. VIII
Castle, Lt-Col Reginald Wingfield, 1874–1952, vol. V
Castle, Walter Frances Raphael, 1892–1926, vol. II
Castle, William, 1833–1911, vol. I
Castle-Miller, Rudolph Valdemar Thor, 1905–1987, vol. VIII
Castle Stewart (styled Castlestewart), 5th Earl, 1837–1914, vol. I
Castle Stewart (styled Castlestewart), 6th Earl, 1841–1921, vol. II
Castle Stewart, 7th Earl, 1889–1961, vol. VI
Castlemaine, 5th Baron, 1863–1937, vol. III
Castlemaine, 6th Baron, 1864–1954, vol. V
Castlemaine, 7th Baron, 1904–1973, vol. VII
Castleman-Smith, Col Edward Castleman, died 1943, vol. IV
Castletown, 2nd Baron, 1849–1937, vol. III
Catarinich, John, 1882–1974, vol. VII
Catchpool, Egerton St John Pettifor, 1890–1971, vol. VII
Cater, Sir (Alexander) Norman (Ley), 1880–1957, vol. V
Cater, Douglass, 1923–1995, vol. IX (AII)
Cater, Sir John James, 1885–1962, vol. VI
Cater, Sir John Robert, (Sir Robin), 1919–1997, vol. X
Cater, Sir Robin; see Cater, Sir J. R.
Cater, Sir Norman; see Cater, Sir A. N. L.
Cates, Arthur, 1829–1901, vol. I
Cathcart, 3rd Earl, 1828–1905, vol. I
Cathcart, 4th Earl, 1856–1911, vol. I
Cathcart, 5th Earl, 1862–1927, vol. II
Cathcart, 6th Earl, 1919–1999, vol. X
Cathcart, Col Hon. Augustus Murray, 1830–1914, vol. I
Cathcart, Charles Walker, 1853–1932, vol. III
Cathcart, Edward Provan, 1877–1954, vol. V
Cathcart, George Clark, died 1951, vol. V
Cathcart, Sir Reginald Archibald Edward, 6th Bt, 1838–1916, vol. II
Cathcart, Robert, died 1907, vol. I
Cathcart, William Taylor, 1859–1940, vol. III
Cathels, Rt Rev. David, 1853–1925, vol. II
Cather, Willa Sibert, 1876–1947, vol. IV
Cathery, Edmund, 1852–1925, vol. III
Cathie, Ian Aysgarth Bewley, 1908–1989, vol. VIII
Catledge, Turner, 1901–1983, vol. VIII
Catlin, Sir George Edward Gordon, 1896–1979, vol. VII
Catling, Thomas, 1838–1920, vol. II

141

Catlow, Sir John William, *died* 1947, vol. IV
Catnach, Agnes, 1891–1979, vol. VII
Cato, Sir Arnott Samuel, 1912–1998, vol. X
Cato, Rt Hon. Robert Milton, 1915–1997, vol. X
Caton, Richard, *died* 1926, vol. II
Caton-Jones, Col Frederick William, 1860–1944, vol. IV
Caton-Thompson, Gertrude, 1888–1985, vol. VIII
Cator, Maj.-Gen. Albemarle Bertie Edward, 1877–1932, vol. III
Cator, Sir Geoffrey Edmund, 1884–1973, vol. VII
Cator, Lt-Col Henry John, 1897–1965, vol. VI
Cator, John, 1862–1944, vol. IV
Cator, Lt-Col Philip James, 1901–1944, vol. IV
Cator, Sir Ralph Bertie Peter, 1861–1945, vol. IV
Cator, Rev. William Lumley Bertie, *died* 1918, vol. II
Catroux, Gén. Georges Albert Julian, 1877–1969, vol. VI
Cattanach, Brig. Helen, 1920–1994, vol. IX
Cattanach, William, 1863–1932, vol. III
Cattell, George Harold Bernard, 1920–1996, vol. X
Catterall, Arthur, 1884–1943, vol. IV
Catterall, Sir Robert, 1880–1962, vol. VI
Cattermole, Lancelot Harry Mosse, 1898–1992, vol. IX
Catterns, Basil Gage, 1886–1969, vol. VI
Catterson-Smith, John Keats, 1882–1945, vol. IV
Cattley, M. H., *died* 1958, vol. V
Catto, 1st Baron, 1879–1959, vol. V
Catton, Bruce, 1899–1978, vol. VII
Catty, Col Thomas Claude, 1879–1967, vol. VI
Caughey, Sir Harcourt; *see* Caughey, Sir T. H. S.
Caughey, Sir (Thomas) Harcourt (Clarke), 1911–1993, vol. IX
Caulcutt, Sir John, 1876–1943, vol. IV
Caulfeild, Major Algernon Montgomerie, 1858–1915, vol. I
Caulfeild, Algernon Thomas St George, 1869–1933, vol. III
Caulfeild, Brig.-Gen. Charles Trevor, 1863–1947, vol. IV
Caulfeild, Francis St George, 1852–1933, vol. III
Caulfeild, Vice-Adm. Francis Wade, 1872–1947, vol. IV
Caulfeild, Brig.-Gen. Francis William John, 1859–1938, vol. III
Caulfeild, Col Gordon Napier, 1862–1922, vol. II
Caulfeild, Brig.-Gen. James Edward Wilmot Smyth, 1850–1925, vol. II
Caulfeild, Captain James Montgomerie, 1855–1946, vol. IV
Caulfield, Sir Bernard, 1914–1994, vol. IX
Caulfield, Sidney Burgoyne Kitchener, *died* 1964, vol. VI
Caullery, Maurice, 1868–1958, vol. V
Caulton, Rt Rev. Sidney Gething, 1895–1976, vol. VII
Caumont, Rt Rev. Mgr Fortunatus Henry, 1871–1930, vol. III
Caunt, Ven. Frederic, *died* 1933, vol. III
Caunter, Brig. Alan; *see* Caunter, Brig. J. A. L.
Caunter, Brig.-Gen. James Eales, 1859–1937, vol. III

Caunter, Brig. John Alan Lyde, 1889–1981, vol. VIII
Causer, William Sidney, *died* 1958, vol. V
Causey, Gilbert, 1907–1996, vol. X
Causton, Rev. Francis Jervoise, *died* 1932, vol. III
Cauthery, Harold William, 1914–1987, vol. VIII
Cautley, 1st Baron, 1863–1946, vol. IV
Cautley, Edmund, *died* 1944, vol. IV
Cauty, Sir Arthur Belcher, 1870–1954, vol. V
Cavalcanti, Alberto de Almeida, 1897–1982, vol. VIII
Cavalieri, Lina, 1874–1944, vol. IV
Cavallera, Rt Rev. Charles, 1909–1990, vol. X (AI)
Cavan, 9th Earl of, 1839–1900, vol. I
Cavan, 10th Earl of, 1865–1946, vol. IV
Cavan, 11th Earl of, 1878–1950, vol. IV
Cavan, 12th Earl of, 1911–1988, vol. VIII
Cavanagh, Captain John Duncan Macaulay, 1881–1957, vol. V
Cavaye, Maj.-Gen. William Frederick, *died* 1926, vol. II
Cave, 1st Viscount, 1856–1928, vol. II
Cave of Richmond, Countless; (1st in line), *died* 1938, vol. III
Cave, Rev. Alfred, 1847–1900, vol. I
Cave, Arthur Wilson, *died* 1930, vol. III
Cave, Sir Basil Shillito, 1865–1931, vol. III
Cave, Sir Charles Daniel, 1st Bt (*cr* 1896), 1832–1922, vol. II
Cave, Sir Charles Edward Coleridge, 4th Bt, 1927–1997, vol. X
Cave, Sir Charles Henry, 2nd Bt (*cr* 1896), 1861–1932, vol. III
Cave, Charles John Philip, 1871–1950, vol. IV
Cave, Sir (Charles) Philip H.; *see* Haddon-Cave.
Cave, Edmund, 1859–1946, vol. IV
Cave, Sir Edward Charles, 3rd Bt (*cr* 1896), 1893–1946, vol. IV
Cave, Edward Watkins, *died* 1948, vol. IV
Cave, Captain George Ellis, 1867–1938, vol. III
Cave, Air Vice-Marshal Henry Meyrick C.-B.; *see* Cave-Browne-Cave.
Cave, John Arthur, 1915–1998, vol. X
Cave, Adm. John Halliday, 1827–1913, vol. I
Cave, Hon. Sir Lewis William, 1832–1897, vol. I
Cave, Sir Mylles Cave-Browne-, 11th Bt (*cr* 1641), 1822–1907, vol. I
Cave, Sir Philip; *see* Haddon-Cave.
Cave, Sir Richard Guy, 1920–1986, vol. VIII
Cave, Sir Richard Philip, 1912–1988, vol. VIII
Cave, Rev. Sydney, 1883–1953, vol. V
Cave, Sir Thomas C.-B.; *see* Cave-Browne-Cave.
Cave, Wing Comdr Thomas Reginald C.-B.; *see* Cave-Browne-Cave.
Cave, Sir Thomas Sturmy, 1846–1936, vol. III
Cave, Walter F., *died* 1939, vol. III
Cave-Browne, Edward Raban, 1835–1907, vol. I
Cave-Browne, Maj.-Gen. William, 1884–1967, vol. VI
Cave-Browne-Cave, Sir Clement Charles, 15th Bt (*cr* 1641), 1896–1945, vol. IV
Cave-Browne-Cave, Rev. Sir Genille, 12th Bt (*cr* 1641), 1869–1929, vol. III
Cave-Browne-Cave, Air Vice-Marshal Henry Meyrick, 1887–1965, vol. VI

Cave-Browne-Cave, Sir Mylles; *see* Cave.
Cave-Browne-Cave, Captain Sir Reginald Ambrose, 13th Bt (*cr* 1641), 1860–1930, vol. III
Cave-Browne-Cave, Sir Rowland Henry, 14th Bt (*cr* 1641), 1865–1943, vol. IV
Cave-Browne-Cave, Sir Thomas, 1835–1924, vol. II
Cave-Browne-Cave, Wing Comdr Thomas Reginald, 1885–1969, vol. VI
Caven, Rev. Principal, 1830–1904, vol. I
Caven, Robert Martin, 1870–1934, vol. III
Cavenagh, Prof. Francis Alexander, 1884–1946, vol. IV
Cavendish; *see* Jones, Henry.
Cavendish, Brig.-Gen Alfred Edward John, 1859–1943, vol. IV
Cavendish, Lord Charles A. F., 1905–1944, vol. IV
Cavendish, Major Frederick George, 1891–1936, vol. III
Cavendish, Brig.-Gen. Frederick William Lawrence Sheppard Hart, 1878–1931, vol. III
Cavendish, Captain Lord John Spencer, 1875–1914, vol. I
Cavendish, Col Ralph Henry Voltelin, 1887–1968, vol. VI
Cavendish, Richard Charles Alexander, 1885–1941, vol. IV
Cavendish, Rt Hon. Lord Richard Frederick, 1871–1946, vol. IV
Cavendish, Brig.-Gen. Hon. William Edwin, 1862–1931, vol. III
Cavendish-Acheson, Hon. Patrick George Edward; *see* Acheson.
Cavendish-Bentinck, Lt-Col Lord Charles, 1868–1956, vol. V
Cavendish-Bentinck, Frederick; *see* Bentinck.
Cavendish-Bentinck, Lord William Augustus; *see* Bentinck.
Caverhill, William Melville; *see* Melville, Alan.
Cavill, William Victor, *died* 1959, vol. V
Caw, Sir James Lewis, 1864–1950, vol. IV
Cawadias, Alexander Pocnagioti, *died* 1971, vol. VII
Cawdor, 2nd Earl, 1817–1898, vol. I
Cawdor, 3rd Earl, 1847–1911, vol. I
Cawdor, 4th Earl, 1870–1914, vol. I
Cawdor, 5th Earl, 1900–1970, vol. VI
Cawdor, 6th Earl, 1932–1993, vol. IX
Cawley, 1st Baron, 1850–1937, vol. III
Cawley, 2nd Baron, 1877–1954, vol. V
Cawley, Sir Charles Mills, 1907–2000, vol. X
Cawley, Rev. Frederick, 1884–1978, vol. VII
Cawley, George, 1848–1927, vol. II
Cawley, Harold Thomas, 1878–1915, vol. I
Cawley, Hon. Oswald, 1882–1918, vol. II
Cawley, Robert Hugh, 1924–1999, vol. X
Cawood, Herbert Harry, 1890–1957, vol. V
Cawood, Sir Walter, 1907–1967, vol. VI
Caws, Genevra Fiona Penelope Victoria, (Mrs J. W. O Curtis), 1948–1997, vol. X
Caws, Richard Byron, 1927–1997, vol. X
Cawston, (Edwin) Richard, 1923–1986, vol. VIII
Cawston, Sir John Westerman, 1859–1927, vol. II
Cawston, Richard; *see* Cawston, E. R.
Cawthorn, Maj.-Gen. Sir Walter Joseph, 1896–1970, vol. VI (AII)

Cawthorne, Sir Terence Edward, 1902–1970, vol. VI
Cawthra-Elliot, Maj.-Gen. Harry Macintire, 1867–1949, vol. IV
Cay, Armistead, 1872–1957, vol. V
Cayford, Dame Florence Evelyn, 1897–1987, vol. X (AI)
Cayley, Hon. Maj.-Gen. Douglas Edward, 1870–1951, vol. V
Cayley, Adm. George Cuthbert, 1866–1944, vol. IV
Cayley, Sir George Everard Arthur, 9th Bt, 1861–1917, vol. II
Cayley, Captain Harry Francis, 1873–1954, vol. V
Cayley, Dep. Surg.-Gen. Henry, 1834–1904, vol. I
Cayley, Henry Douglas, 1904–1991, vol. IX
Cayley, Sir Kenelm Henry Ernest, 10th Bt, 1896–1967, vol. VI
Cayley, Sir Richard, 1833–1908, vol. I
Cayley, Maj.-Gen. Sir Walter de Sausmarez, 1863–1952, vol. V
Cayley, William, 1836–1916, vol. II
Cayley-Robinson, Frederic; *see* Robinson.
Cayzer, Baron (Life Peer); William Nicholas Cayzer, Bt, 1910–1999, vol. X
Cayzer, Hon. Anthony; *see* Cayzer, Hon. M. A. R.
Cayzer, Sir August Bernard Tellefsen, 1st Bt (*cr* 1921), 1876–1943, vol. IV
Cayzer, Sir Charles, 1st Bt (*cr* 1904), 1843–1916, vol. II
Cayzer, Sir Charles William, 2nd Bt (*cr* 1904), 1869–1917, vol. II
Cayzer, Sir Charles William, 3rd Bt (*cr* 1904), 1896–1940, vol. III
Cayzer, Major Harold Stanley, 1882–1948, vol. IV
Cayzer, Major John Sanders, 1871–1908, vol. I
Cayzer, Hon. (Michael) Anthony (Rathborne), 1920–1990, vol. VIII
Cayzer, Sir Nigel John, 4th Bt (*cr* 1904), 1920–1943, vol. IV
Cazalet, Edward Alexander, *died* 1923, vol. II
Cazalet, Vice-Adm. Sir Peter Grenville Lyon, 1899–1982, vol. VIII
Cazalet, Peter Victor Ferdinand, 1907–1973, vol. VII
Cazalet, Lt-Col Victor Alexander, 1896–1943, vol. IV
Cazalet, William Marshall, 1865–1932, vol. III
Cazalet-Keir, Thelma, 1899–1989, vol. VIII
Cazamian, Louis, 1877–1965, vol. VI
Cazenove, Brig. Arnold de Lerisson, *died* 1969, vol. VI
Cazenove, Philip Henry de Lerisson, 1901–1978, vol. VII
Cecil of Chelwood, 1st Viscount, 1864–1958, vol. V
Cecil, Algernon, 1879–1953, vol. V
Cecil, Lord Arthur, 1851–1913, vol. I
Cecil, Lord David; *see* Cecil, Lord E. C. D. G.
Cecil, Ean Francis, 1880–1942, vol. IV
Cecil, Lord (Edward Christian) David (Gascoyne), 1902–1986, vol. VIII
Cecil, Col Lord Edward Herbert, 1867–1918, vol. II
Cecil, Lord Eustace Brownlow Henry, 1834–1921, vol. II
Cecil, Henry; *see* Leon, H. C.

143

Cecil, Lord John Pakenham Joicey-, 1867–1942, vol. IV
Cecil, Rev. Philip Henry, 1918–1977, vol. VII
Cecil, Robert, 1913–1994, vol. IX
Cecil, Victor Alexander G.; see Gascoyne-Cecil.
Cecil, Lord William, 1854–1943, vol. IV
Cecil, Hon. William Amherst, 1886–1914, vol. I
Cecil, Rt Rev. Lord William Gascoyne-, 1863–1936, vol. III
Cecil-Williams, Sir John Lias Cecil, 1892–1964, vol. VI
Cecil-Wright, Air Cdre John Allan Cecil, 1886–1982, vol. VIII
Cederström, Baron Rolf, died 1947, vol. IV
Cederström, Baroness Rolf, see Patti, Mme Adelina.
Céitinn, Seán; see Keating, John.
Celibidache, Sergiu, 1912–1996, vol. X
Cellier, Jacobus Stephanus, born 1878, vol. III
Cemlyn-Jones, Sir E. Wynne, 1888–1966, vol. VI
Cenez, Rt Rev. Jules Joseph, 1865–1944, vol. IV
Centlivres, Hon. Albert van de Sandt, 1887–1966, vol. VI
Ceram, C. W.; see Marek, K. W.
Cerf, Bennett, 1898–1971, vol. VII
Cerny, Jaroslav, 1898–1970, vol. VI
Cerretti, His Eminence Cardinal Bonaventura, 1872–1933, vol. III
Cerutty, Charles John, 1870–1941, vol. IV
Cervera, Adm. Pascual Cervera y Topete, 1839–1909, vol. I
Chaban-Delmas, Jacques Pierre Michel, 1915–2000, vol. X
Chacksfield, Air Vice-Marshal Sir Bernard, 1913–1999, vol. X
Chadburn, George Haworthe, 1870–1950, vol. IV
Chadburn, Maud Mary, died 1957, vol. V
Chaddock, Dennis Hilliar, 1908–1992, vol. IX
Chads, Adm. Sir Henry, 1819–1906, vol. I
Chads, Maj.-Gen. William John, 1830–1915, vol. I
Chadwell, Rt Rev. Arthur Ernest, 1892–1967, vol. VI
Chadwick, Sir Albert Edward, 1897–1983, vol. VIII
Chadwick, Brig. Cecil Arthur Harrop, 1901–1970, vol. VI
Chadwick, Rev. Charles Egerton, 1880–1958, vol. V
Chadwick, Sir David Thomas, 1876–1954, vol. V
Chadwick, Edward Marion, 1840–1921, vol. II
Chadwick, Rt Rev. George Alexander, 1840–1923, vol. II
Chadwick, Hector Munro, 1870–1947, vol. IV
Chadwick, Helen, 1953–1996, vol. X
Chadwick, Sir James, 1891–1974, vol. VII
Chadwick, John, 1920–1998, vol. X
Chadwick, John Courtenay Chasman, 1846–1932, vol. III
Chadwick, Sir John Edward, 1911–1987, vol. VIII
Chadwick, Nora Kershaw, 1891–1972, vol. VII
Chadwick, Osbert, 1844–1913, vol. I
Chadwick, Sir Peter B.; see Burton-Chadwick, Sir R.
Chadwick, Rev. Canon Robert, died 1927, vol. II
Chadwick, Sir Robert B.; see Burton-Chadwick.
Chadwick, Robert Everard, 1916–2000, vol. X
Chadwick, Roy, 1893–1947, vol. IV
Chadwick, Rev. Samuel, 1860–1932, vol. III

Chadwick, Sir Thomas, 1888–1969, vol. VI
Chadwick, Rev. William Edward, died 1934, vol. III
Chadwick, Rt Rev. William Frank Percival, 1905–1991, vol. IX
Chadwyck-Healey, Sir Charles Arthur, 4th Bt, 1910–1986, vol. VIII
Chadwyck-Healey, Sir Charles Edward Heley, 1st Bt, 1845–1919, vol. II
Chadwyck-Healey, Sir Edward Randal, 3rd Bt, 1898–1979, vol. VII
Chadwyck-Healey, Sir Gerald Edward, 2nd Bt, 1873–1955, vol. V
Chadwyck-Healey, Oliver Nowell, 1886–1960, vol. V
Chaffey, Hon. Frank A., 1888–1940, vol. III
Chaffey, Col Ralph Anderson, 1856–1925, vol. II
Chagall, Marc, 1887–1985, vol. VIII
Chagla, Shri Mohomedali Currim, 1900–1981, vol. VIII
Chain, Sir Ernst Boris, 1906–1979, vol. VII
Chaine, Lt-Col William, 1838–1916, vol. II
Chaldecott, John Anthony, 1916–1998, vol. X
Chaliapin, Fedor Ivanovitch, 1873–1938, vol. III
Chalk, Hon. Sir Gordon William Wesley, 1913–1991, vol. IX
Chalkley, Alfred Philip, 1886–1959, vol. V
Chalkley, Sir (Harry) Owen, 1882–1958, vol. V
Chalkley, Sir Owen; see Chalkley, Sir H. O.
Challacombe, Rev. William Allen, died 1951, vol. V
Challans, Mary; see Renault, M.
Challe, Général d'Armée Aérienne Maurice, 1905–1979, vol. VII
Challen, Charles, 1894–1960, vol. V
Challenger, Frederick, 1887–1983, vol. VIII
Challenor, Brig.-Gen. Edward Lacy, 1873–1935, vol. III
Challinor, William Francis, 1882–1967, vol. VI
Challis, Anthony Arthur Leonard, 1921–1996, vol. X
Challis, John Humphrey Thornton, 1896–1958, vol. V
Challis, Margaret Joan, 1917–1994, vol. IX
Chalmer, Col Francis George, 1884–1951, vol. V
Chalmer, Col Reginald, 1844–1911, vol. I
Chalmers, 1st Baron, 1858–1938, vol. III
Chalmers, Albert John, 1870–1920, vol. II
Chalmers, Sir Alfred John George, 1845–1937, vol. III
Chalmers, Archibald Kerr, 1856–1942, vol. IV
Chalmers, Archibald MacDonald, 1883–1977, vol. VII
Chalmers, Arthur Morison, 1862–1949, vol. IV
Chalmers, Sir Charles, 1861–1924, vol. II
Chalmers, Sir David Patrick, died 1899, vol. I
Chalmers, Lt-Col Frederick Roydon, 1881–1943, vol. IV
Chalmers, George Buchanan, 1929–1989, vol. VIII
Chalmers, John, 1915–1983, vol. VIII
Chalmers, Sir Mackenzie Dalzell, 1847–1927, vol. II
Chalmers, P. MacGregor, 1859–1922, vol. II
Chalmers, Patrick Reginald, died 1942, vol. IV
Chalmers, Rev. Reginald, 1893–1974, vol. VII
Chalmers, Thomas Andrew, died 1944, vol. IV
Chalmers, Thomas Wightman, 1913–1995, vol. IX

Chalmers, William John, 1914–1986, vol. VIII

Chalmers, Rear-Adm. William Scott, 1888–1971, vol. VII

Chamba, Raja of, 1869–1919, vol. II

Chamberlain, Arthur, *died* 1913, vol. I

Chamberlain, Rt Hon. (Arthur) Neville, 1869–1940, vol. III

Chamberlain, Rt Hon. Sir Austen; *see* Chamberlain, Rt Hon. Sir J. A.

Chamberlain, Basil Hall, 1850–1935, vol. III

Chamberlain, Gen. Sir Crawford Trotter, 1821–1902, vol. I

Chamberlain, Digby, 1896–1962, vol. VI

Chamberlain, Rev. Elsie Dorothea; *see* Chamberlain-Garrington, Rev. E. D.

Chamberlain, Fernley John, 1879–1958, vol. V

Chamberlain, Francis Walter, 1892–1970, vol. VI

Chamberlain, Rt Rev. (Frank) Noel, 1900–1975, vol. VII

Chamberlain, George Digby, 1898–1994, vol. IX

Chamberlain, Air Vice-Marshal George Philip, 1905–1995, vol. IX

Chamberlain, Sir Henry Hamilton Erroll, 4th Bt, 1857–1936, vol. III

Chamberlain, Henry Richardson, 1859–1911, vol. I

Chamberlain, Sir Henry Wilmot, 5th Bt, 1899–1980, vol. VII (AII)

Chamberlain, Houston Stewart, 1855–1927, vol. II

Chamberlain, Ivy Muriel, (Lady Chamberlain), *died* 1941, vol. IV

Chamberlain, Rt Hon. Joseph, 1836–1914, vol. I

Chamberlain, Rt Hon. Sir (Joseph) Austen, 1863–1937, vol. III

Chamberlain, Rt Hon. Neville; *see* Chamberlain, Rt Hon. A. N.

Chamberlain, Field Marshal Sir Nevile Bowles, 1820–1902, vol. I

Chamberlain, Col Sir Neville Francis Fitzgerald, 1856–1944, vol. IV

Chamberlain, Rt Rev. Noel; *see* Chamberlain, Rt Rev. F. N.

Chamberlain, Hon. Sir (Reginald) Roderic (St Clair), 1901–1990, vol. IX

Chamberlain, Hon. Sir Roderic; *see* Chamberlain, Hon. Sir (Reginald) R.

Chamberlain, Ronald, 1901–1987, vol. VIII

Chamberlain, Ven. Thomas, *born* 1854, vol. II

Chamberlain, Sir William, 1877–1944, vol. IV

Chamberlain-Garrington, Rev. Elsie Dorothea, 1910–1991, vol. IX

Chamberlayne, Air Cdre Paul Richard Tankerville James Michael Isidore Camille, 1898–1972, vol. VII

Chamberlayne, Tankerville, 1843–1924, vol. II

Chamberlayne, Gen. William John, 1821–1910, vol. I

Chamberlin, Arthur George, *died* 1925, vol. II

Chamberlin, Edson J., *died* 1924, vol. II

Chamberlin, Frederick, 1870–1943, vol. IV

Chamberlin, Sir George, 1846–1928, vol. II

Chamberlin, Sir Michael, 1891–1972, vol. VII

Chamberlin, Peter Hugh Girard, 1919–1978, vol. VII

Chambers, Rev. Arthur, *died* 1918, vol. II

Chambers, Adm. Bertram Mordaunt, 1866–1945, vol. IV

Chambers, Maj.-Gen. Brooke Rynd, 1834–1915, vol. I

Chambers, Charles Edward Stuart, 1859–1936, vol. III

Chambers, Charles Haddon, 1860–1921, vol. II

Chambers, Sir Cornelius, 1862–1941, vol. IV

Chambers, Sir Edmund Kerchever, 1866–1954, vol. V

Chambers, Rev. Frederick Charles, 1860–1933, vol. III

Chambers, Rt Rev. George Alexander, *died* 1963, vol. VI

Chambers, George Frederick, 1841–1915, vol. I

Chambers, Sir George Henry, 1816–1903, vol. I

Chambers, George Lawson, 1852–1934, vol. III

Chambers, George Michael, 1928–1997, vol. X

Chambers, Helen, *died* 1935, vol. III

Chambers, James, 1863–1917, vol. II

Chambers, John Ferguson, 1894–1941, vol. IV

Chambers, Major John Reginald, 1882–1953, vol. V

Chambers, Jonathan David, 1898–1970, vol. VI

Chambers, Surg. Vice-Adm. Sir Joseph, 1864–1935, vol. III

Chambers, Lt-Col Joseph Charles, 1857–1940, vol. III (A), vol. IV

Chambers, Julius, 1850–1920, vol. II

Chambers, Lloyd Eld, 1863–1930, vol. III

Chambers, Sir Newman Pitts-, *died* 1922, vol. II

Chambers, Sir Paul; *see* Chambers, Sir S. P.

Chambers, Raymond Wilson, 1874–1942, vol. IV

Chambers, Rev. Robert Halley, 1853–1934, vol. III

Chambers, Maj.-Gen. Robert Macdonald, 1833–1924, vol. II

Chambers, Robert Sharp Borgnis H.; *see* Hammond-Chambers.

Chambers, Robert William, 1865–1933, vol. III

Chambers, Sir (Stanley) Paul, 1904–1981, vol. VIII

Chambers, Sir Theodore Gervase, 1871–1957, vol. V

Chambers, William Walker, 1913–1985, vol. VIII

Chamier, Sir Edward Maynard Des Champs, 1866–1945, vol. IV

Chamier, Maj.-Gen. Francis Edward Archibald, 1833–1923, vol. II

Chamier, Brig.-Gen. George Daniel, 1860–1920, vol. II

Chamier, Air Cdre Sir John Adrian, 1883–1974, vol. VII

Chamier, Lt-Col Richard Outram, 1888–1980, vol. VII

Chamier, Lt-Gen. Stephen, 1834–1910, vol. I

Chaminade, Cécile, *died* 1944, vol. IV

Chamney, Lt-Col Henry, 1861–1947, vol. IV

Champain, Brig.-Gen. Hugh Frederick B.; *see* Bateman-Champain.

Champain, Rt Rev. John Norman B.; *see* Bateman-Champain.

Champernowne, David Gawen, 1912–2000, vol. X

Champion, Baron (Life Peer); Arthur Joseph Champion, 1897–1985, vol. VIII

Champion, Arthur Mortimer, 1885–1950, vol. IV

Champion, Frank Clive, 1907–1976, vol. VII

Champion, Sir Harry George, 1891–1979, vol. VII

145

Champion, Henry Hyde, 1859–1928, vol. II
Champion, Captain John Pelham, 1883–1955, vol. V
Champion, John Stuart, 1921–1994, vol. IX
Champion, Pierre, 1880–1942, vol. IV
Champion, Rev. Sir Reginald Stuart, 1895–1982, vol. VIII
Champion de Crespigny, Captain Claude, 1873–1910, vol. I
Champion de Crespigny, Sir Claude, 4th Bt, 1847–1935, vol. III
Champion de Crespigny, Brig.-Gen. Sir Claude Raul, 5th Bt, 1878–1941, vol. IV
Champion-de Crespigny, Col Sir (Constantine) Trent, 1882–1952, vol. V
Champion de Crespigny, Comdr Sir Frederick Philip, 7th Bt, 1884–1947, vol. IV
Champion de Crespigny, Lt-Col George Harrison, 1863–1945, vol. IV
Champion de Crespigny, Sir Henry, 6th Bt, 1882–1946, vol. IV
Champion de Crespigny, Air Vice-Marshal Hugh Vivian, 1897–1969, vol. VI
Champion de Crespigny, Rose, (Mrs Philip Champion de Crespigny), died 1935, vol. III
Champion-de Crespigny, Col Sir Trent; see Champion-de Crespigny, Col Sir C. T.
Champion de Crespigny, Sir Vivian Tyrell, 8th Bt, 1907–1952, vol. V
Champness, Captain Charles Henry, 1889–1963, vol. VI
Champness, Henry Robert, 1852–1923, vol. II
Champness, Major Sir William Henry, 1873–1956, vol. V
Champneys, Basil, 1842–1935, vol. III
Champneys, Sir Francis Henry, 1848–1930, vol. III
Champneys, Rev. Francis Weldon, died 1929, vol. III
Champneys, Captain Sir Weldon D.; see Dalrymple-Champneys.
Champtaloup, Sydney Taylor, 1880–1921, vol. II
Chamson, André, 1900–1983, vol. VIII
Chan, Chun Hung Jerome, 1951–1997, vol. X
Chance, Sir Arthur, 1859–1928, vol. II
Chance, Frederick Selby, 1886–1946, vol. IV
Chance, Sir Frederick William, 1852–1932, vol. III
Chance, Maj. Geoffrey Henry Barrington, 1893–1987, vol. VIII
Chance, George Ferguson, 1854–1933, vol. III
Chance, Sir Hugh; see Chance, Sir W. H. S.
Chance, Ivan Oswald, 1910–1984, vol. VIII
Chance, James Frederick, 1856–1938, vol. III
Chance, Sir James Timmins, 1st Bt, 1814–1902, vol. I
Chance, Kenneth Macomb, 1879–1966, vol. VI
Chance, Kenneth Miles, 1893–1980, vol. VII
Chance, Miles; see Chance, K. M.
Chance, Brig.-Gen. Oswald Kesteven, 1880–1935, vol. III
Chance, Percival Vincent, 1888–1970, vol. VI
Chance, Sir Robert Christopher, 1883–1960, vol. V
Chance, Sir Roger James Ferguson, 3rd Bt, 1893–1987, vol. VIII
Chance, Thomas Williams, 1872–1954, vol. V
Chance, Walter Lucas, 1880–1963, vol. VI

Chance, Sir William, 2nd Bt, 1853–1935, vol. III
Chance, Sir (William) Hugh (Stobart), 1896–1981, vol. VIII
Chancellor, Alexander Richard, 1869–1959, vol. V
Chancellor, Sir Christopher John, 1904–1989, vol. VIII
Chancellor, Edwin Beresford, 1868–1937, vol. III
Chancellor, Henry George, 1863–1945, vol. IV
Chancellor, Lt-Col Sir John Robert, 1870–1952, vol. V
Chand, Masheerud-dowal Rai Bahadur N.; see Nanak Chand.
Chandavarkar, Sir Narayen Ganesh, 1855–1923, vol. II
Chandavarkar, Sir Vithal Narayan, 1887–1959, vol. V
Chandler, Alfred, 1853–1923, vol. II
Chandler, Rt Rev. Arthur, 1860–1939, vol. III
Chandler, Edwin George, 1914–1991, vol. IX
Chandler, Frederick George, died 1942, vol. IV
Chandler, George, 1915–1992, vol. IX
Chandler, Hon. Sir Gilbert Lawrence, 1903–1974, vol. VII
Chandler, Sir John Beals, 1887–1962, vol. VI
Chandler, Sir John DeLisle, 1889–1967, vol. VI
Chandler, Louise; see Moulton, Mrs.
Chandler, Pretor Whitty, 1858–1941, vol. IV
Chandler, Raymond Thornton, 1888–1959, vol. V
Chandler, Sir William Kellman, 1857–1940, vol. III
Chandley, Peter Warren, 1934–1996, vol. X
Chandos, 1st Viscount, 1893–1972, vol. VII
Chandos, 2nd Viscount, 1920–1980, vol. VII
Chandos-Pole, Brig.-Gen. Harry Anthony, died 1934, vol. III
Chandos-Pole, Lt-Col John, 1909–1993, vol. IX
Chandos-Pole, Maj. John Walkelyne, 1913–1994, vol. IX
Chandrasekhar, Subrahmanyan, 1910–1995, vol. IX
Chandy, Ven. Jacob, born 1852, vol. III
Chaney, Henry James, 1842–1906, vol. I
Chaney, Maj.-Gen. James E., 1885–1967, vol. VI
Channell, Rt Hon. Sir Arthur Moseley, 1838–1928, vol. II
Channer, Col Bernard, 1846–1916, vol. II
Channer, Frederick Francis Ralph, 1875–1950, vol. IV
Channer, Gen. George Nicholas, 1843–1905, vol. I
Channer, Maj.-Gen. George Osborne De Renzy, 1890–1969, vol. VI
Channing of Wellingborough, 1st Baron, 1841–1926, vol. II
Channing, Edward, 1856–1931, vol. III
Channing Williams, Maj.-Gen. John William, 1908–1990, vol. VIII
Channon, Harold John, 1897–1979, vol. VII
Channon, Sir Henry, 1897–1958, vol. V
Chant, Clarence Augustus, 1865–1956, vol. V
Chant, Mrs Laura Ormiston, 1848–1923, vol. II
Chanter, Hon. John Moore, 1845–1931, vol. III
Chantler, Philip, 1911–1988, vol. VIII
Chapais, Hon. Sir Thomas, 1858–1946, vol. IV
Chapel, Sir William, 1870–1950, vol. IV (A)
Chapin, Harold, 1886–1915, vol. I
Chapin, Captain Sidney H., 1875–1918, vol. II

Chapleau, Hon. Sir Joseph Adolphe, 1840–1898, vol. I

Chapleau, Samuel Edmour St Onge, 1839–1921, vol. II

Chaplin, 1st Viscount, 1840–1923, vol. II (A)

Chaplin, 2nd Viscount, 1877–1949, vol. IV

Chaplin, 3rd Viscount, 1906–1981, vol. VIII

Chaplin, Alan Geoffrey Tunstal, 1908–1967, vol. VI

Chaplin, Arnold; see Chaplin, T. H. A.

Chaplin, Arthur Hugh, 1905–1996, vol. X

Chaplin, Sir Charles Spencer, 1889–1977, vol. VII

Chaplin, Sir Drummond Percy; see Chaplin, Sir F. D. P.

Chaplin, Sir (Francis) Drummond Percy, 1866–1933, vol. III

Chaplin, Frederick Leslie, 1905–1977, vol. VII

Chaplin, Sir George Frederick, 1900–1975, vol. VII

Chaplin, Brig.-Gen. James Graham, 1873–1956, vol. V

Chaplin, Col John Worthy, 1840–1920, vol. II

Chaplin, Judith; see Chaplin, S. J.

Chaplin, (Sybil) Judith, 1939–1993, vol. IX

Chaplin, (T. H.) Arnold, 1864–1944, vol. IV

Chaplin, Rev. W. Knight, 1863–1951, vol. V

Chaplin, William Robert, 1888–1974, vol. VII

Chapling, Norman Charles, 1903–1986, vol. VIII

Chapman, Abel, 1851–1929, vol. III

Chapman, Captain Alexander Colin, 1897–1970, vol. VI

Chapman, Alfred Chaston, 1869–1932, vol. III

Chapman, Allan, 1897–1966, vol. VI

Chapman, (Anthony) Colin (Bruce), 1928–1982, vol. VIII

Chapman, Brig.-Gen. Archibald John, 1862–1950, vol. IV

Chapman, Sir Arthur, 1851–1918, vol. II

Chapman, Sir Arthur Wakefield, 1849–1926, vol. II

Chapman, Hon. Sir Austin, 1864–1926, vol. II

Chapman, Sir Benjamin Rupert, 6th Bt, 1865–1914, vol. I

Chapman, Brian, 1923–1981, vol. VIII

Chapman, Rev. C., 1828–1922, vol. II

Chapman, Cecil Maurice, 1852–1938, vol. III

Chapman, Charles Williams, 1843–1941, vol. IV

Chapman, Very Rev. Clifford Thomas, 1913–1982, vol. VIII

Chapman, Colin; see Chapman, A. C. B.

Chapman, Rear-Adm. Cuthbert Godfrey, 1862–1931, vol. III

Chapman, David Leonard, 1869–1958, vol. V

Chapman, Col David Phelips, 1855–1939, vol. III

Chapman, Dennis, 1927–1999, vol. X

Chapman, Dorothy, 1878–1967, vol. VI

Chapman, Edmund Pelly, 1867–1923, vol. II

Chapman, Edward, died 1906, vol. I

Chapman, Gen. Sir Edward Francis, 1840–1926, vol. II

Chapman, Edward Henry, 1874–1933, vol. III

Chapman, Rev. Edward William, 1841–1919, vol. II

Chapman, Captain Ernest John Collis, 1876–1958, vol. V

Chapman, Fitzroy Tozer, 1880–1976, vol. VII

Chapman, Frank M., 1864–1945, vol. IV

Chapman, Ven. Frank Robert, died 1924, vol. II

Chapman, Col Frederic Hamilton, 1863–1925, vol. II

Chapman, Frederick, 1864–1943, vol. IV

Chapman, Sir Frederick Revans, 1849–1936, vol. III

Chapman, Lt-Col Frederick S.; see Spencer Chapman.

Chapman, Guy Patterson, 1889–1972, vol. VII

Chapman, Maj.-Gen. Hamilton, 1835–1926, vol. II

Chapman, Harold Thomas, 1896–1985, vol. VIII

Chapman, Henry, died 1908, vol. I

Chapman, Sir Henry, died 1947, vol. IV

Chapman, Henry George, 1879–1934, vol. III

Chapman, Rt Rev. Henry Palmer, 1865–1933, vol. III

Chapman, Col Herbert Alexander, 1858–1939, vol. III

Chapman, Mrs Hester Wolferstan, (Mrs R. L. Griffin), 1899–1976, vol. VII

Chapman, Air Vice-Marshal Hubert Huntlea, 1910–1972, vol. VII

Chapman, Rev. Hugh Boswell, died 1933, vol. III

Chapman, Rev. James, 1849–1913, vol. I

Chapman, James Ernest, died 1941, vol. IV

Chapman, Rt Rev. John; see Chapman, Rt Rev. H. P.

Chapman, Maj.-Gen. John Austin, 1896–1963, vol. VI

Chapman, John Henry Benjamin, 1899–1997, vol. X

Chapman, Kathleen Violet, 1903–1996, vol. X

Chapman, Kenneth Herbert, 1908–1989, vol. VIII

Chapman, Brig.-Gen. Lawrence Joseph, 1867–1930, vol. III

Chapman, Lewis, 1890–1963, vol. VI

Chapman, Martin, 1846–1924, vol. II

Chapman, Sir Montagu Richard, 5th Bt (cr 1782), 1853–1907, vol. I

Chapman, Mrs Murray, (Olive Chapman), died 1977, vol. VII

Chapman, Olive; see Chapman, Mrs Murray.

Chapman, Oscar Littleton, 1896–1978, vol. VII

Chapman, Rev. Percy Hugh, 1866–1953, vol. V

Chapman, Col Philip Francis, 1870–1956, vol. V

Chapman, Col Sir Robert, 1st Bt (cr 1958), 1880–1963, vol. VI

Chapman, Robert Barclay, 1829–1909, vol. I

Chapman, Robert Hall, 1890–1953, vol. V

Chapman, Sir Robert William, 1866–1942, vol. IV

Chapman, Robert William, 1881–1960, vol. V

Chapman, Sir Robin (Robert Macgowan), 2nd Bt, 1911–1987, vol. VIII

Chapman, Air Chief Marshal Sir Ronald I.; see Ivelaw-Chapman.

Chapman, Sir Samuel, 1859–1947, vol. IV

Chapman, Hon. Sir Stephen, 1907–1991, vol. IX

Chapman, Sydney, 1888–1970, vol. VI

Chapman, Sir Sydney John, 1871–1951, vol. V

Chapman, Rt Rev. Thomas Alfred, 1867–1949, vol. IV

Chapman, Thomas Algernon, 1842–1921, vol. II

Chapman, Sir Thomas Robert Tighe, 7th Bt (cr 1782), 1846–1919, vol. II

Chapman, William Arthur, 1849–1917, vol. II

Chapman, Major William P.; see Percy-Chapman.

Chapman-Andrews, Sir Edwin Arthur, 1903–1980, vol. VII
Chapman-Huston, Major Desmond Wellesley William Desmond Mountjoy, *died* 1952, vol. V
Chapman-Mortimer, William Charles, 1907–1988, vol. VIII
Chappel, Rev. William Haighton, 1860–1922, vol. II
Chappell, (Edwin) Philip, 1929–1993, vol. IX
Chappell, Sir Ernest, 1864–1943, vol. IV
Chappell, Philip; *see* Chappell, E. P.
Chappell, Robert Kingsley, 1884–1937, vol. III
Chappell, T. Stanley, *died* 1933, vol. III
Chappell, William, 1908–1994, vol. IX
Chapple, Charles Roberts, 1874–1965, vol. VI
Chapple, Frederic, 1845–1924, vol. II
Chapple, Harold, 1881–1945, vol. IV
Chapple, Paymaster Rear-Adm. Sir John Henry George, 1859–1925, vol. II
Chapple, Stanley, 1900–1987, vol. VIII
Chapple, William Allan, 1864–1936, vol. III
Chapuis, Mgr Marie Auguste, 1869–1930, vol. III
Chaput de Saintonge, Rev. Rolland Alfred Aimé, 1912–1989, vol. VIII
Charbonneau, Most Rev. Joseph, *died* 1959, vol. V
Charbonneau, Napoleon, 1853–1916, vol. II
Charcot, Dr Jean Baptiste Etienne Auguste, 1867–1936, vol. III
Chari, P. N., vol. III
Charkhari, HH Maharaja Dhiraj Sipah-Darul-Mulk Sir Malkhan Sinh Ju Dev Bahadur, 1872–1908, vol. I
Charkhari State, HH Maharaja-Dhiraja Sipahdar-ul-Mulk Arimardan Singh Ju Deo Bahadur, 1903–1941, vol. IV
Charlemont, 7th Viscount, 1830–1913, vol. I
Charlemont, 8th Viscount, 1880–1949, vol. IV
Charlemont, 9th Viscount, 1887–1964, vol. VI
Charlemont, 10th Viscount, 1881–1967, vol. VI
Charlemont, 11th Viscount, 1884–1971, vol. VII
Charlemont, 12th Viscount, 1887–1979, vol. VII
Charlemont, 13th Viscount (Ireland), 1899–1985, vol. VIII
Charles, Captain Sir Allen Aitchison Havelock, 2nd Bt, 1887–1936, vol. III
Charles, Anthony Harold, 1908–1990, vol. VIII
Charles, Rt Hon. Sir Arthur, 1839–1921, vol. II
Charles, Sir Arthur Eber Sydney, 1910–1965, vol. VI
Charles, Enid, 1894–1972, vol. VII
Charles, Brig. Eric Montagu Seton, 1878–1964, vol. VI
Charles, Sir Ernest Bruce, 1871–1950, vol. IV
Charles, Rev. George B., 1862–1936, vol. III
Charles, Rt Rev. Harold John, 1914–1987, vol. VIII
Charles, Rev. James Hamilton, 1854–1939, vol. III
Charles, Lt-Gen. Sir (James) Ronald (Edmondston), 1875–1955, vol. V
Charles, Cdre Sir James Thomas Walter, 1865–1928, vol. II
Charles, Sir John Alexander, *died* 1971, vol. VII
Charles, John James, 1845–1912, vol. I
Charles, Sir John Pendrill, 1914–1984, vol. VIII
Charles, John Roger, 1872–1962, vol. VI
Charles, Sir Joseph Quentin, 1908–1993, vol. IX

Charles, Leslie Stanley Francis, 1917–2000, vol. X
Charles, Sir Noel Hughes Havelock, 3rd Bt, 1891–1975, vol. VII
Charles, Maj.-Gen. Sir Richard Havelock, 1st Bt, 1858–1934, vol. III
Charles, Ven. Robert Henry, 1855–1931, vol. III
Charles, Robert Henry, 1882–1951, vol. V
Charles, Robert Lonsdale, 1916–1977, vol. VII
Charles, Lt-Gen. Sir Ronald; *see* Charles, Lt-Gen. Sir J. R. E.
Charles, Rev. Canon Sebastian, 1932–1989, vol. VIII
Charles, Captain Ulick de Burgh, 1884–1947, vol. IV
Charles, William Travers, 1908–1990, vol. VIII
Charles-Edwards, Rt Rev. Lewis Mervyn, 1902–1983, vol. VIII
Charles-Roux, François, 1879–1961, vol. VI
Charleson, Ian, 1949–1990, vol. VIII
Charleston, Robert Jesse, 1916–1994, vol. IX
Charlesworth, Albany Hawke, 1854–1914, vol. I
Charlesworth, Col Henry, 1851–1926, vol. II
Charlesworth, John, 1893–1957, vol. V
Charlesworth, John Kaye, 1889–1972, vol. VII
Charlesworth, Lilian E., *died* 1970, vol. VI
Charlesworth, Rev. Martin Percival, 1895–1950, vol. IV
Charlesworth, Stanley, 1920–1992, vol. IX
Charleton, Henry Charles, 1870–1959, vol. V
Charley, Col Harold Richard, 1875–1956, vol. V
Charley, Sir Philip Belmont, 1893–1976, vol. VII
Charley, Sir William Thomas, 1833–1904, vol. I
Charlish, Dennis Norman, 1918–1999, vol. X
Charlot, André Eugene Maurice, 1882–1956, vol. V
Charlton, Archibald Campbell, 1877–1952, vol. V
Charlton, Brig.-Gen. Claud Edward Charles Graham, *died* 1961, vol. VI
Charlton, Adm. Sir Edward Francis Benedict, 1865–1937, vol. III
Charlton, Ferrier Harvey; *see* Charlton, F. F. H.
Charlton, (Foster) Ferrier Harvey, 1923–1999, vol. X
Charlton, (Frederick) Noel, 1906–2000, vol. X
Charlton, George, 1899–1979, vol. VII
Charlton, Henry Buckley, 1890–1961, vol. VI
Charlton, Hon. John, 1829–1910, vol. I
Charlton, John, *died* 1917, vol. II
Charlton, Air Cdre Lionel Evelyn Oswald, 1879–1958, vol. V
Charlton, Matthew, 1866–1948, vol. IV
Charlton, Noël; *see* Charlton, F. N.
Charlton, Thomas Malcolm, 1923–1997, vol. X
Charlton, Sir William Arthur, 1893–1983, vol. VIII
Charlton, Captain William Henry, 1876–1950, vol. IV
Charlton-Meyrick, Col Sir Thomas, 1st Bt, 1837–1921, vol. II
Charmes, Francis, 1848–1916, vol. II
Charnley, Sir John, 1911–1982, vol. VIII
Charnock, George Frederick, 1860–1929, vol. III
Charnock, Henry, 1920–1997, vol. X
Charnwood, 1st Baron, 1864–1945, vol. IV
Charnwood, 2nd Baron, 1901–1955, vol. V
Charoux, Siegfried Joseph, 1896–1967, vol. VI
Charpentier, Gustave, 1860–1956, vol. V

Charques, Mrs Dorothy, (Mrs S. A. G. Emms), 1899–1976, vol. VII
Charrington, Captain Eric, 1872–1927, vol. II
Charrington, Lt-Col Francis, 1858–1921, vol. II
Charrington, Frederick Nicholas, 1850–1936, vol. III
Charrington, John, 1856–1939, vol. III
Charrington, Sir John, 1886–1977, vol. VII
Charrington, John Arthur Pepys, 1905–1979, vol. VII
Charrington, Spencer, 1818–1904, vol. I
Charrington, Lt-Col Sydney Herbert, 1878–1954, vol. V
Charry, Sir Vembakkam C. D.; see Desika-Charry.
Chart, Edwin, 1848–1926, vol. II
Charteris of Amisfield, Baron (Life Peer); Martin Michael Charles Charteris, 1913–1999, vol. X
Charteris, Very Rev. Archibald Hamilton, 1835–1908, vol. I
Charteris, Archibald Hamilton, 1874–1940, vol. III
Charteris, Hon. Sir Evan, 1864–1940, vol. III
Charteris, Francis James, 1875–1964, vol. VI
Charteris, Hon. Guy Lawrence, 1886–1967, vol. VI
Charteris, Hugo Francis Guy, 1922–1970, vol. VI
Charteris, Brig.-Gen. John, 1877–1946, vol. IV
Charteris, Leslie, 1907–1993, vol. IX
Charteris, Col Nigel Keppel, 1878–1967, vol. VI
Charters, Col Alexander Burnet, 1876–1948, vol. IV
Chase, Anya Seton; see Seton, A.
Chase, Beatrice; see Parr, Olive Katharine.
Chase, Rev. Drummond Percy, 1820–1902, vol. I
Chase, Rt Rev. Frederic Henry, 1853–1925, vol. II
Chase, Rt Rev. George Armitage, 1886–1971, vol. VII
Chase, Lewis, 1873–1937, vol. III (A), vol. IV
Chase, Marian Emma, 1844–1905, vol. I
Chase, Mary Ellen, 1887–1973, vol. VII
Chase, Stuart, 1888–1985, vol. VIII
Chase, William Henry, 1880–1965, vol. VI
Chase, Col William St Lucian, 1856–1908, vol. I
Chase-Casgrain, Alexandre; see Casgrain.
Chastel De Boinville, Rev. Basil William, died 1943, vol. IV
Chastenet de Castaing, Jacques, 1893–1978, vol. VII
Chasteney, Howard Everson, 1888–1947, vol. IV
Chatelain, Henri Louis, 1877–1915, vol. I
Chater, Maj.-Gen. Arthur Reginald, 1896–1979, vol. VII
Chater, Sir Catchick Paul, 1846–1926, vol. II
Chater, Daniel, 1870–1959, vol. V
Chater, Nancy, 1915–2000, vol. X
Chater, Col Vernor, 1842–1923, vol. II
Chatfeild-Clarke, Sir Edgar, 1863–1925, vol. II
Chatfield, 1st Baron, 1873–1967, vol. VI
Chatfield, Adm. Alfred John, 1831–1910, vol. I
Chatfield, George Ernle, 1875–1930, vol. III
Chatfield-Taylor, Hobart Chatfield, 1865–1945, vol. IV
Chatham, William, 1859–1940, vol. III
Chatt, Joseph, 1914–1994, vol. IX
Chattaway, Edward, 1873–1956, vol. V
Chattaway, Frederick Daniel, died 1944, vol. IV
Chatterjee, Sir Atul Chandra, 1874–1955, vol. V
Chatterjee, Gopal Chunder, 1873–1953, vol. V

Chatterji, Sir Nalini Ranjan, died 1942, vol. IV
Chatterji, Sir Protul Chandra, 1848–1917, vol. II
Chatterton, Sir Alfred, 1866–1958, vol. V
Chatterton, Edward Keble, 1878–1944, vol. IV
Chatterton, Rt Rev. Eyre, 1863–1950, vol. IV
Chatterton, Col Frank Beauchamp Macaulay, 1873–1934, vol. III
Chatterton, Col Frank William, 1839–1924, vol. II
Chatterton, Frederick, died 1934, vol. III
Chatterton, Rev. Sir Percy, 1898–1984, vol. VIII
Chattisham, 1st Baron, 1886–1945, vol. IV
Chattock, Arthur Prince, 1860–1934, vol. III
Chatwin, Bruce; see Chatwin, C. B.
Chatwin, (Charles) Bruce, 1940–1989, vol. VIII
Chau, Hon. Sir Sik-Nin, born 1903, vol. VIII
Chau Tsun-Nin, Sir, 1893–1971, vol. VII
Chaubal, Sir Mahadev Bhaskar, 1857–1933, vol. III
Chaudhuri, Asutosh, 1860–1924, vol. II
Chaudhuri, Nirad Chandra, 1897–1999, vol. X
Chaumeix, André, 1874–1955, vol. V
Chauncy, Col Charles Henry Kemble, died 1945, vol. IV
Chauncy, Maj. Frederick Charles Leslie, 1904–1986, vol. VIII
Chauvel, Gen. Sir Henry George, 1865–1945, vol. IV
Chauvel, Jean Michel Henri, 1897–1979, vol. VII
Chauvel, Ven. John Henry Allan, 1895–1946, vol. IV
Chavan, Yeshwantrao Balvantrao, 1913–1984, vol. VIII
Chavasse, Rt Rev. Christopher Maude, 1884–1962, vol. VI
Chavasse, Rt Rev. Francis James, 1846–1928, vol. II
Chavasse, Michael Louis Maude, 1923–1983, vol. VIII
Chavasse, Sir Thomas Frederick, 1854–1913, vol. I
Chave, Captain Sir Benjamin, 1870–1954, vol. V
Chave, Elmer Hargreaves, 1891–1957, vol. VI
Chawner, William, 1848–1911, vol. I
Chaworth-Musters, Col John Nevile, 1890–1970, vol. VI
Chaytor, Alfred Henry, 1869–1931, vol. III
Chaytor, Lt-Col Clervaux Alexander, died 1941, vol. IV
Chaytor, Col D'Arcy, 1873–1960, vol. V
Chaytor, Sir Edmund Hugh, 6th Bt, 1876–1935, vol. III
Chaytor, Maj.-Gen. Sir Edward Walter Clervaux, 1868–1939, vol. III
Chaytor, Rev. Henry John, 1871–1954, vol. V
Chaytor, Lt-Col John Clervaux, 1888–1964, vol. VI
Chaytor, Sir Walter Clervaux, 5th Bt, 1874–1913, vol. I
Chaytor, Sir William Henry Clervaux, 7th Bt, 1914–1976, vol. VII
Chaytor, Sir William Henry Edward, 4th Bt, 1867–1908, vol. I
Cheadle, Sir Eric Wallers, 1908–1992, vol. IX
Cheadle, Walter Butler, 1835–1910, vol. I
Cheape, Brig.-Gen. (George) Ronald (Hamilton), 1881–1957, vol. V
Cheape, Lt-Col Hugh Annesley Gray-, 1878–1918, vol. II

Cheape, James, 1853–1943, vol. IV
Cheape, Brig.-Gen. Ronald; see Cheape, Brig.-Gen. G. R. H.
Cheatle, Arthur Henry, 1866–1929, vol. III
Cheatle, Sir (George) Lenthal, 1865–1951, vol. V
Cheatle, Sir Lenthal; see Cheatle, Sir G. L.
Checkland, Sydney George, 1916–1986, vol. VIII
Checkley, Frank S., died 1918, vol. II
Cheeseman, A. K. A.; see Wymark, Patrick Carl.
Cheeseman, Eric Arthur, 1912–1987, vol. VIII
Cheeseman, Harold Ambrose Robinson, 1889–1961, vol. VI
Cheeseman, Lt-Col William Joseph Robert, 1894–1938, vol. III
Cheesewright, William Frederick, died 1934, vol. III
Cheesman, Rev. Alfred Hunter, 1864–1941, vol. IV
Cheesman, Evelyn; see Cheesman, L. E.
Cheesman, (Lucy) Evelyn, 1881–1969, vol. VI
Cheesman, Col Robert Ernest, 1878–1962, vol. VI
Cheetham, Rev. Canon Frederic Philip, 1890–1970, vol. VI
Cheetham, Maj.-Gen. Geoffrey, 1891–1962, vol. VI
Cheetham, Rt Rev. Henry, 1827–1899, vol. I
Cheetham, Rt Hon. John Frederick, 1835–1916, vol. II
Cheetham, John Frederick Thomas, 1919–1999, vol. X
Cheetham, Sir Milne, 1869–1938, vol. III
Cheetham, Ven. Samuel, 1827–1908, vol. I
Cheever, John, 1912–1982, vol. VIII
Chegwidden, Sir Thomas Sidney, 1895–1986, vol. VIII
Cheiro; see Hamon, Count Louis
Cheke, Dudley John, 1912–1993, vol. IX
Cheke, Sir Marcus John, 1906–1960, vol. V
Chelmer, Baron (Life Peer); Eric Cyril Boyd Edwards, 1914–1997, vol. X
Chelmick, William George Hamar, 1882–1969, vol. VI
Chelmsford, 1st Viscount, 1868–1933, vol. III
Chelmsford, 2nd Viscount, 1903–1970, vol. VI
Chelmsford, 3rd Viscount, 1931–1999, vol. X
Chelmsford, Viscountess; (Frances Charlotte), 1869–1957, vol. V
Chelmsford, 2nd Baron, 1827–1905, vol. I
Chelsea, Viscount; Edward George Humphry John Cadogan, 1903–1910, vol. I
Chelsea, Viscount; Henry Arthur Cadogan, 1868–1908, vol. I
Chelwood, Baron (Life Peer); Tufton Victor Hamilton Beamish, 1917–1989, vol. VIII
Chenevix-Trench, Anthony, 1919–1979, vol. VII
Chenevix-Trench, Col Arthur Henry, 1884–1968, vol. VI
Chenevix-Trench, Charles Godfrey, 1877–1964, vol. VI
Chenevix-Trench, Lt-Col George Frederick, 1859–1937, vol. III
Chenevix-Trench, Col Lawrence, 1883–1958, vol. V
Chenevix-Trench, Brig. Ralph, 1885–1974, vol. VII
Chenevix-Trench, Lt-Col Sir Richard Henry, 1876–1954, vol. V
Cheney, Christopher Robert, 1906–1987, vol. VIII
Cheney, E. John, 1862–1921, vol. II
Cheng, F. T.; see Cheng, Tien-Hsi.

Cheng, Tien-Hsi, (F. T. Cheng), 1884–1970, vol. VI
Cherenkov, Pavel Alexeevich, 1904–1990, vol. IX (AI)
Chéret, Jules, 1836–1932, vol. III
Cherkassky, Shura, 1911–1995, vol. IX
Chermayeff, Serge, 1900–1996, vol. X
Chermont, Jayme Sloan, 1903–1983, vol. IX (AI)
Chermside, Lt-Gen. Sir Herbert Charles, 1850–1929, vol. III
Cherniavsky, Mischel, 1893–1982, vol. VIII
Cherrington, Rt Rev. Cecil Arthur, died 1950, vol. IV
Cherry, Sir Benjamin Lennard, 1869–1932, vol. III
Cherry, Colin; see Cherry, E. C.
Cherry, (Edward) Colin, 1914–1979, vol. VII
Cherry, Gordon Emanuel, 1931–1996, vol. X
Cherry, Sir John Arnold, 1879–1950, vol. IV
Cherry, Rt Hon. Richard Robert, 1859–1923, vol. II
Cherry, Sir Thomas MacFarland, 1898–1966, vol. VI
Cherry-Garrard, Maj.-Gen. Apsley, 1832–1907, vol. I
Cherry-Garrard, Apsley George Benet, 1886–1959, vol. V
Cherwell, 1st Viscount, 1886–1957, vol. V
Chesebrough, Robert Augustus, 1837–1933, vol. III
Chesham, 3rd Baron, 1850–1907, vol. I
Chesham, 4th Baron, 1894–1952, vol. V
Chesham, 5th Baron, 1916–1989, vol. VIII
Cheshire, Baron (Life Peer); Geoffrey Leonard Cheshire, 1917–1992, vol. IX
Cheshire, Frederic John, 1860–1939, vol. III
Cheshire, Geoffrey Chevalier, 1886–1978, vol. VII
Cheshire, Rt Rev. Joseph Blount, 1850–1932, vol. III
Cheshire, Comdt Dame Mary Kathleen, 1902–1972, vol. VII
Cheshire, Air Chief Marshal Sir Walter Graemes, 1907–1978, vol. VII
Chesney, Col Alexander George, 1858–1939, vol. III
Chesney, Lt-Col Clement Hope Rawdon, 1883–1962, vol. VI
Chesney, Col Harold Frank, 1859–1920, vol. II
Chesney, Kathleen, 1899–1976, vol. VII
Chesser, Elizabeth Sloan, died 1940, vol. III
Chesser, Eustace, 1902–1973, vol. VII
Chesshire, Rev. Reginald Stanley Pargeter, 1869–1940, vol. III
Chesson, Nora; see Hopper, N.
Chester, Cecil Harry, 1900–1964, vol. VI
Chester, Sir (Daniel) Norman, 1907–1986, vol. VIII
Chester, Sir George, 1886–1949, vol. IV
Chester, Col Heneage Charles B.; see Bagot-Chester.
Chester, Sir Norman; see Chester, Sir D. N.
Chester, Theodore Edward, 1908–1991, vol. IX
Chester Jones, Ian, 1916–1996, vol. X
Chester-Master, Rev. Harold, 1889–1948, vol. IV
Chester-Master, Lt-Col Richard, 1870–1917, vol. II
Chester-Master, Thomas William Chester, 1841–1914, vol. I
Chester-Master, Col William Alfred, 1903–1963, vol. VI
Chesterfield, 10th Earl of, 1854–1933, vol. III

Chesterfield, 11th Earl of, 1855–1935, vol. III
Chesterfield, 12th Earl of, 1889–1952, vol. V
Chesterfield, Arthur Desborough, 1905–1991, vol. IX
Chesterman, Sir Clement Clapton, 1894–1983, vol. VIII
Chesterman, Sir Ross, 1909–1999, vol. X
Chesters, Charles Geddes Coull, 1904–1993, vol. IX
Chesters, John Hugh, 1906–1994, vol. IX
Chesterton, Ada Elizabeth, (Mrs Cecil Chesterton), died 1962, vol. VI
Chesterton, Cecil Edward, 1879–1918, vol. II
Chesterton, Gilbert Keith, 1874–1936, vol. III
Cheston, Charles Sidney, died 1960, vol. V
Cheston, Evelyn, died 1929, vol. III
Chesworth, Donald Piers, 1923–1991, vol. IX
Chetham-Strode, Edward David, 1871–1958, vol. V
Chetham-Strode, Warren, 1896–1974, vol. VII
Chettiar, Rajah Sir Annamalai Chettiar of Chettinad, 1881–1948, vol. IV
Chettiar, Sir M. C. T. M.; see Muthiah Chettiar.
Chettiar, Sir Ramanatha A.; see Alagappa Chettiar.
Chettle, Major Henry Francis, 1882–1958, vol. V
Chettur, Govinda Krishna, 1898–1936, vol. III (A)
Chetty, Amatyasiromani Sir Bernard T. T.; see Thumboo Chetty.
Chetty, Sir Krishnarajapur Palligondé P.; see Puttanna Chetty.
Chetty, Sir Shanmukham, 1892–1953, vol. V
Chetwode, 1st Baron, 1869–1950, vol. IV
Chetwode, Adm. Sir George Knightley, 1877–1957, vol. V
Chetwynd, 7th Viscount, 1823–1911, vol. I
Chetwynd, 8th Viscount, 1863–1936, vol. III
Chetwynd, 9th Viscount, 1904–1965, vol. VI
Chetwynd, Sir (Arthur Henry) Talbot, 7th Bt, 1887–1972, vol. VII
Chetwynd, Lady Florence Cecilia; see Hastings, Marchioness of
Chetwynd, Sir George, 4th Bt, 1849–1917, vol. II
Chetwynd, Sir (George) Guy, 5th Bt, 1874–1935, vol. III
Chetwynd, Sir George Roland, 1916–1982, vol. VIII
Chetwynd, Sir Guy; see Chetwynd, Sir George G.
Chetwynd, Henry Goulburn Willoughby, 1858–1909, vol. I
Chetwynd, Hon. Richard Walter, 1859–1908, vol. I
Chetwynd, Sir Talbot; see Chetwynd, Sir A. H. T.
Chetwynd, Sir Victor James Guy, 6th Bt, 1902–1938, vol. III
Chetwynd-Stapylton, Col Bryan Henry, died 1958, vol. V
Chetwynd-Stapylton, Granville Brian, 1887–1964, vol. VI
Chetwynd-Stapylton, Lt-Gen. Granville George, 1823–1915, vol. I
Chetwynd-Stapylton, Rev. William, 1825–1919, vol. II
Chetwynd-Talbot, Richard Michael Arthur; see Talbot.
Chevalier, Albert, 1861–1923, vol. II
Chevalier, Maurice, 1888–1972, vol. VII
Chevallier, Captain Barrington Henry, 1851–1930, vol. III

Chevassût, Rev. Frederick George, died 1932, vol. III
Chevassût, Rev. Canon Frederick George, 1889–1974, vol. VII
Cheveley, Stephen William, 1900–1991, vol. IX
Chevis, Sir William, 1864–1939, vol. III
Chevrier, Hon. Lionel, 1903–1987, vol. VIII
Chevrillon, André, 1864–1957, vol. V
Chew, Frederic Robert Gansel, 1907–1970, vol. VI
Cheylesmore, 2nd Baron, 1843–1902, vol. I
Cheylesmore, 3rd Baron, 1848–1925, vol. II
Cheylesmore, 4th Baron, 1893–1974, vol. VII
Cheyne, Brig. Douglas Gordon, 1889–1966, vol. VI
Cheyne, James, 1894–1973, vol. VII
Cheyne, Sir John, 1841–1907, vol. I
Cheyne, Col Sir Joseph Lister, 2nd Bt, 1888–1957, vol. V
Cheyne, Rev. Thomas Kelly, 1841–1915, vol. I
Cheyne, Sir Watson; see Cheyne, Sir William W.
Cheyne, Sir (William) Watson, 1st Bt, 1852–1932, vol. III
Cheyney, Peter, (Major Reginald Evelyn Peter Southouse-Cheyney), 1896–1951, vol. V
Cheyney, Major Reginald Evelyn Peter Southouse-; see Cheyney, Peter.
Chhajju Ram Chowdhry, Sir, born 1865, vol. V
Chhatarpur, Sir Maharaja of, 1866–1932, vol. III
Chhotu Ram, Rao Bahadur Chaudhri Sir, died 1945, vol. IV
Chhota Udepur, Maharawal Shri Natwarsinhji Fatehsinhji, Raja of, 1906–1946, vol. IV
Chiang, Yee, 1903–1977, vol. VII
Chiang Kai-Shek, Generalissimo, 1887–1975, vol. VII
Chiasson, Rt Rev. Patrice Alexandre, 1867–1942, vol. IV
Chiazzari, Comdr Nicholas William, 1868–1929, vol. III
Chibnall, Albert Charles, 1894–1988, vol. VIII
Chichele-Plowden, Sir Trevor John Chichele, 1846–1905, vol. I
Chichester, 4th Earl of, 1838–1902, vol. I
Chichester, 5th Earl of, 1844–1905, vol. I
Chichester, 6th Earl of, 1871–1926, vol. II
Chichester, 7th Earl of, 1905–1926, vol. II
Chichester, 8th Earl of, 1912–1944, vol. IV
Chichester, Lt-Col Alan, died 1947, vol. IV
Chichester, Maj.-Gen. Sir Arlington Augustus, 1863–1948, vol. IV
Chichester, Sir Arthur, 8th Bt, 1822–1898, vol. I
Chichester, Lt-Col Arthur O'Neill Cubitt, 1889–1972, vol. VII
Chichester, Most Rev. Aston, 1879–1962, vol. VI
Chichester, Rear-Adm. Sir Edward, 9th Bt, 1849–1906, vol. I
Chichester, Rev. Edward Arthur, 1849–1925, vol. II
Chichester, Sir Edward George, 10th Bt, 1888–1940, vol. III
Chichester, Sir Francis, 1901–1972, vol. VII
Chichester, Hon. Sir Gerald Henry Crofton, 1886–1939, vol. III
Chichester, Lord Henry Fitzwarine, 1834–1928, vol. II
Chichester, Maj.-Gen. Robert Bruce, 1825–1902, vol. I

Chichester, Col Robert Peel Dawson Spencer, 1873–1921, vol. II
Chichester-Clark, Captain James Lenox, 1884–1933, vol. III
Chichester-Constable, Brig. Raleigh Charles Joseph, 1890–1963, vol. VI
Chichester-Constable, Walter George Raleigh, 1863–1942, vol. IV
Chichester Smith, Charles Henry, 1897–1966, vol. VI
Chick, Sir (Alfred) Louis, 1904–1972, vol. VII
Chick, Dame Harriette, 1875–1977, vol. VII
Chick, Herbert George, 1882–1951, vol. V
Chick, Sir Louis; see Chick, Sir A. L.
Chiene, George Lyall, 1873–1951, vol. V
Chiene, John, 1843–1923, vol. II
Chiesman, Sir Walter Eric, 1900–1973, vol. VII
Chifley, Rt Hon. Joseph Benedict, 1885–1951, vol. V
Chignell, Rev. Hugh Scott, died 1950, vol. IV
Chilcott, Rear-Adm. Ronald Evered, 1876–1935, vol. III
Chilcott, Lt-Comdr Sir Warden Stanley, 1871–1942, vol. IV
Chilcott, William Winsland, 1848–1915, vol. I
Child, Arthur, 1852–1902, vol. I
Child, Clifton James, 1912–1994, vol. IX
Child, Sir Coles, 1st Bt (cr 1919), 1862–1929, vol. III
Child, Major Sir (Coles) John, 2nd Bt (cr 1919), 1906–1971, vol. VII
Child, Harold Hannyngton, 1869–1945, vol. IV
Child, Lieut Herbert Alexander, died 1914, vol. I
Child, Brig.-Gen. Sir Hill; see Child, Brig.-Gen. Sir S. H.
Child, Major Sir John; see Child, Major Sir C. J.
Child, Ven. Kenneth, 1916–1983, vol. VIII
Child, Rev. Robert Leonard, 1891–1971, vol. VII
Child, Brig.-Gen. Sir (Smith) Hill, 2nd Bt (cr 1868), 1880–1958, vol. V
Childe, Rev. Christopher Venn, died 1937, vol. III
Childe, Col Ralph Bromfield Willington F.; see Fisher-Childe.
Childe, V. Gordon, 1892–1957, vol. V
Childe, Wilfred Rowland Mary, 1890–1952, vol. V
Childe-Pemberton, William Shakespear, 1859–1924, vol. II
Childers, Charles Edward Eardley, 1851–1931, vol. III
Childers, Col Edmund Spencer Eardley, 1854–1919, vol. II
Childers, Lt-Comdr Erskine; see Childers, Lt-Comdr R. E.
Childers, Erskine Hamilton, 1905–1974, vol. VII
Childers, Lt-Col Hugh Francis Eardley, 1886–1941, vol. IV
Childers, Lt-Comdr (Robert) Erskine, 1870–1922, vol. II
Childs, Maj.-Gen. Sir (Borlase Elward) Wyndham, 1876–1946, vol. IV
Childs, Most Rev. Derrick Greenslade, 1918–1987, vol. VIII
Childs, Hubert, 1905–1983, vol. VIII
Childs, Leonard, 1897–1982, vol. VIII
Childs, William Macbride, 1869–1939, vol. III

Childs, Maj.-Gen. Sir Wyndham; see Childs, Maj.-Gen. Sir B. E. W.
Childs-Clarke, Col Charles, 1861–1934, vol. III
Childs-Clarke, Rev. Septimus John, 1876–1964, vol. VI
Chilston, 1st Viscount, 1851–1926, vol. II
Chilston, 2nd Viscount, 1876–1947, vol. IV
Chilston, 3rd Viscount, 1910–1982, vol. VIII
Chilton, Rev. Arthur, 1864–1947, vol. IV
Chilton, Charles, 1860–1926, vol. III
Chilton, Air Marshal Sir (Charles) Edward, 1906–1992, vol. IX
Chilton, Donovan, 1909–1978, vol. VII
Chilton, Air Marshal Sir Edward; see Chilton, Air Marshal Sir C. E.
Chilton, Vice-Adm. Francis George Gillilan, 1879–1964, vol. VI
Chilton, Sir Henry Getty, 1877–1954, vol. V
Chilton, Lt-Gen. Sir Maurice Somerville, 1898–1956, vol. V
Chilver, Guy Edward Farquhar, 1910–1982, vol. VIII
Chilver, Richard Clementson, 1912–1985, vol. VIII
Chilvers, Rev. H. Tydeman, 1872–1963, vol. VI
Chimay, Lt-Col Prince Alphonse de, 1899–1973, vol. VII
China, William Edward, 1895–1979, vol. VII
Chinda, Count Sutemi, 1856–1929, vol. III
Chinn, Wilfred Henry, 1901–1970, vol. VI
Chinnery, E. W. Pearson, 1887–1972, vol. VII
Chinnery-Haldane, James Brodrick, 1868–1941, vol. IV
Chinnery-Haldane, Rt Rev. James Robert Alexander, 1842–1906, vol. I
Chinoy, Hon. Fazulbhoy Meherally, died 1915, vol. I
Chinoy, Sir Rahimtoola Meherally, 1882–1957, vol. V
Chinoy, Sir Sultan Meherally, 1885–1968, vol. VI
Chintamani, Sir Chirravoori Yajneswara, 1880–1941, vol. IV
Chipman, Warwick Fielding, 1880–1967, vol. VI
Chippindall, Lt-Gen. Edward, 1827–1902, vol. I
Chippindall, Sir Giles Tatlock, 1893–1969, vol. VI
Chirgwin, Rev. Arthur Mitchell, 1885–1966, vol. VI
Chirico, Giorgio de, 1888–1978, vol. VII
Chirnside, Captain John Percy, 1856–1944, vol. IV
Chirol, Sir Valentine, 1852–1929, vol. III
Chisholm, Rt Rev. Aeneas, 1836–1918, vol. II
Chisholm, Sir (Albert) Roderick, 1897–1967, vol. VI
Chisholm, Ven. Alexander, 1887–1975, vol. VII
Chisholm, Alexander Hugh, 1890–1977, vol. VII
Chisholm, Dame Alice, 1856–1954, vol. V
Chisholm, Archibald Hugh Tennent, 1902–1992, vol. IX
Chisholm, Brock; see Chisholm, G. B.
Chisholm, Catherine, 1878–1952, vol. V
Chisholm, Hon. Christopher P., 1854–1934, vol. III
Chisholm, Geoffrey Duncan, 1931–1994, vol. IX
Chisholm, (George) Brock, 1896–1971, vol. VII
Chisholm, George Goudie, 1850–1930, vol. III
Chisholm, Sir Henry, 1900–1981, vol. VIII
Chisholm, Hugh, 1866–1924, vol. II
Chisholm, Col Hugh Alexander, 1883–1940, vol. III (A), vol. IV

Chisholm, John, 1857–1929, vol. III
Chisholm, Most Rev. John Wallace, 1922–1975, vol. VII
Chisholm, Hon. Sir Joseph Andrew, 1863–1950, vol. IV
Chisholm, Dr Murdoch, *died* 1929, vol. III
Chisholm, Sir Roderick; *see* Chisholm, Sir A. R.
Chisholm, Roderick Æneas, 1911–1994, vol. IX
Chisholm, Roderick William, 1925–1979, vol. VII
Chisholm, Ronald George, 1910–1972, vol. VII
Chisholm, Sir Samuel, 1st Bt, 1836–1923, vol. II
Chisholm, William Wilson, 1854–1935, vol. III
Chitham, Sir Charles Carter, 1886–1972, vol. VII
Chitnavis, Sir Gangadhar Madhav, 1863–1929, vol. III
Chitnavis, Sir Shankar Madhavi, 1863–1931, vol. III
Chitral, Major HH Muhammad Sir Nasir-ul-Mulk, Mehtar of, 1898–1943, vol. IV
Chittenden, Frederick James, 1873–1950, vol. IV
Chittenden, Russell Henry, 1856–1943, vol. IV
Chitty, Anthony Merlott, 1907–1976, vol. VII
Chitty, Sir Arthur, 1864–1948, vol. IV
Chitty, Arthur Whatley, 1824–1905, vol. I
Chitty, Sir Charles William, 1859–1932, vol. III
Chitty, Sir Henry Willes; *see* Chitty, Sir T. H. W.
Chitty, Sir Joseph Henry Pollock, 1861–1942, vol. IV
Chitty, Rt Hon. Sir Joseph William, 1828–1899, vol. I
Chitty, Letitia, 1897–1982, vol. VIII
Chitty, Sir (Thomas) Henry Willes, 2nd Bt, 1891–1955, vol. V
Chitty, Sir Thomas Willes, 1st Bt, 1855–1930, vol. III
Chitty, Rev. Walter Henry, 1867–1940, vol. III
Chitty, Col Walter Willis, 1866–1933, vol. III
Chivers, Edgar Warren, 1906–1979, vol. VII
Chivers, Stephen Oswald, 1899–1975, vol. VII
Chlapowska, Helena M.; *see* Modjeska-Chlapowska.
Chloros, Alexander George, 1926–1982, vol. VIII
Choate, Joseph Hodges, 1832–1917, vol. II
Chodat, Robert, 1865–1934, vol. III
Choksy, Khan Bahadur Sir Nasarvanji Hormasji, 1861–1939, vol. III
Cholmeley, Francis William Alfred F.; *see* Fairfax-Cholmeley.
Cholmeley, Sir Hugh Arthur Henry, 3rd Bt (*cr* 1806), 1839–1904, vol. I
Cholmeley, Major Sir Hugh John Francis Sibthorp, 5th Bt (*cr* 1806), 1906–1964, vol. VI
Cholmeley, John Adye, 1902–1995, vol. IX
Cholmeley, Sir Montague Aubrey Rowley, 4th Bt (*cr* 1806), 1876–1914, vol. I
Cholmeley, Sir Montague John, 6th Bt (*cr* 1806), 1935–1998, vol. X
Cholmeley, Norman Goodford, 1863–1947, vol. IV
Cholmeley, Robert Francis, 1862–1947, vol. IV
Cholmondeley, 4th Marquess of, 1858–1923, vol. II
Cholmondeley, 5th Marquess of, 1883–1968, vol. VI
Cholmondeley, 6th Marquess of, 1919–1990, vol. VIII
Cholmondeley, Lord George Hugo, 1887–1958, vol. V
Cholmondeley, Rev. Hon. Henry Pitt, 1820–1905, vol. I

Cholmondeley, Brig.-Gen. Hugh Cecil, 1852–1941, vol. IV
Cholmondeley, Mary, 1859–1925, vol. II
Cholmondeley-Pennell, Henry; *see* Pennell.
Chomley, Arthur Wolfe, 1837–1914, vol. I
Chomley, Charles Henry, 1868–1942, vol. IV
Chope, Brig. Arthur John Herbert, 1884–1942, vol. IV
Chope, Robert Charles, 1913–1988, vol. VIII
Chopping, Col Arthur, 1871–1951, vol. V
Chopra, Iqbal Chand, 1896–1976, vol. VII
Choquette, Rt Rev. Mgr Charles Philippe, *died* 1947, vol. IV
Choquette, Hon. Philippe Auguste, *born* 1854, vol. III
Chorley, 1st Baron, 1895–1978, vol. VII
Chorley, (Charles) Harold, 1912–1990, vol. VIII
Chorley, Francis Kenneth, 1926–1993, vol. IX
Chorley, Harold; *see* Chorley, C. H.
Chorlton, Alan Ernest Leofric, 1874–1946, vol. IV
Chorlton, Rev. Samuel, *died* 1911, vol. I
Chotzner, Alfred James, 1873–1958, vol. V
Chou En-Lai, 1898–1976, vol. VII
Chouinard, Honore Julien Jean Baptiste, 1850–1928, vol. II
Chow, Sir Shou-Son, 1861–1959, vol. V
Chowdhury, Abu Sayeed, 1921–1987, vol. VIII
Chowdhury, Maharaja Sir Manmatha Nath Ray, *died* 1939, vol. III
Chown, Maj.-Gen. Ernest Edward, 1864–1922, vol. II
Chown, John, *died* 1922, vol. II
Choyce, Charles Coley, 1875–1937, vol. III
Chree, Charles, 1860–1928, vol. II
Chree, Sir William, 1858–1936, vol. III
Chrimes, Sir Bertram; *see* Chrimes, Sir W. B.
Chrimes, Henry Bertram, 1915–1997, vol. X
Chrimes, Stanley Bertram, 1907–1984, vol. VIII
Chrimes, Sir (William) Bertram, 1883–1972, vol. VII
Chris, A. Lauri; *see* Christensen, A. L.
Christ, George Elgie, 1904–1972, vol. VII
Christelow, Allan, 1911–1975, vol. VII
Christensen, Arent Lauri, (A. Lauri Chris), 1893–1982, vol. VIII
Christensen, Christian Neils, 1901–1982, vol. VIII
Christensen, Elsa, (Mrs Adolph Christensen); *see* Stralia, E.
Christensen, Eric Herbert, 1923–1990, vol. IX (AI)
Christian, Adm. Arthur Henry, 1863–1926, vol. II
Christian, Bertram, *died* 1953, vol. V
Christian, Rear-Adm. Charles Arbuthnot, 1862–1937, vol. III
Christian, Clifford Stuart, 1907–1996, vol. X
Christian, Edmund Brown Viney, 1864–1938, vol. III
Christian, Brig.-Gen. Gerard, 1867–1930, vol. III
Christian, Adm. Henry, 1828–1916, vol. II
Christian, Henry A., 1876–1951, vol. V
Christian, Brig.-Gen. Sydney Ernest, 1867–1931, vol. III
Christian, Lt-Col William Francis, 1879–1954, vol. V
Christiansen, Arthur, 1904–1963, vol. VI
Christiansen, Michael Robin, 1927–1984, vol. VIII

Christie, Dame Agatha Mary Clarissa, 1890–1976, vol. VII
Christie, Alexander Wishart, 1871–1955, vol. V
Christie, Col Archibald, 1889–1962, vol. VI
Christie, Augustus Langham, 1857–1930, vol. III
Christie, Maj.-Gen. Campbell Manning, 1893–1963, vol. VI
Christie, Charles Henry, 1924–1992, vol. IX
Christie, Daniel Hall, 1881–1965, vol. VI
Christie, Dugald, 1855–1936, vol. III
Christie, Harold Alfred Hunter, 1884–1960, vol. V
Christie, Hon. Sir Harold George, 1896–1973, vol. VII
Christie, Henry; see Christie, C. H.
Christie, Herbert Bertram, 1863–1916, vol. II
Christie, Brig.-Gen. Herbert Willie Andrew, 1868–1946, vol. IV
Christie, Ian Ralph, 1919–1998, vol. X
Christie, James, died 1960, vol. V (A)
Christie, James Archibald, 1873–1958, vol. V
Christie, James Roberton, 1866–1932, vol. III
Christie, John, 1882–1962, vol. VI
Christie, John Arthur Kingsley, 1915–1994, vol. IX
Christie, John Denham, died 1950, vol. IV
Christie, John Traill, 1899–1980, vol. VII
Christie, Joseph MacNaughtan, 1871–1936, vol. III
Christie, Gp-Captain Malcolm Grahame, 1881–1971, vol. VII
Christie, Richard Copley, 1830–1901, vol. I
Christie, Ronald Victor, 1902–1986, vol. VIII
Christie, Hon. Sir Vernon Howard Colville, 1909–1994, vol. IX
Christie, Walter Henry John, 1905–1983, vol. VIII
Christie, Sir William, 1896–1983, vol. VIII
Christie, Sir William Henry Mahoney, 1845–1922, vol. II
Christie, William Langham, 1830–1913, vol. I
Christie, Very Rev. William Leslie, 1858–1931, vol. III
Christie, William Lorenzo, 1858–1962, vol. VI
Christie-Miller, Col. Sir Geoffry, 1881–1969, vol. VI
Christie-Miller, Samuel Vandeleur, 1911–1968, vol. VI
Christie-Miller, Sydney Richardson, 1874–1931, vol. III
Christison, Sir Alexander, 2nd Bt, 1828–1918, vol. II
Christison, Gen. Sir (Alexander Frank) Philip, 4th Bt, 1893–1993, vol. IX
Christison, Gen. Sir Philip; see Christison, Gen. Sir A. F. P.
Christison, Sir Robert Alexander, 3rd Bt, 1870–1945, vol. IV
Christmas, Arthur Napier, 1913–1993, vol. IX
Christmas, E. W., died 1918, vol. II
Christofas, Sir Kenneth Cavendish, 1917–1992, vol. IX
Christoff, Boris, 1914–1993, vol. IX
Christoffelsz, Arthur Eric, born 1890, vol. VII
Christoffelsz, William Sperling, 1846–1937, vol. III
Christopher, Rev. Alfred Millard William, 1820–1913, vol. I
Christopher, Col Charles de Lona, 1885–1942, vol. IV
Christopher, Eleanor Caroline, 1873–1959, vol. V

Christopher, Sir George Perrin, 1890–1977, vol. VII
Christopher, Maj.-Gen. Leonard William, 1848–1927, vol. II
Christophers, Bt Col Sir Richard; see Christophers, Bt Col Sir S. R.
Christophers, Bt Col Sir (Samuel) Rickard, 1873–1978, vol. VII
Christopherson, Sir Derman Guy, 1915–2000, vol. X
Christopherson, Douglas, 1869–1944, vol. IV
Christopherson, John Brian, 1868–1955, vol. V
Christopherson, Very Rev. Noel Charles, died 1968, vol. VI
Christopherson, Stanley, died 1949, vol. IV
Christy, Cuthbert, 1863–1932, vol. III
Christy, Ronald Kington, 1905–1987, vol. VIII
Christy, Stephen Henry, 1879–1914, vol. I
Chrystal, George, 1851–1911, vol. I
Chrystal, Sir George William, 1880–1944, vol. IV
Chrystall, Brig. John Inglis, 1887–1960, vol. V
Chubb, Sir Cecil Herbert Edward, 1st Bt, 1876–1934, vol. III
Chubb, Hon. Charles Edward, 1845–1930, vol. III
Chubb, Gilbert Charles, died 1966, vol. VI
Chubb, Harry Emory, 1880–1960, vol. V
Chubb, Sir John Corbin, 2nd Bt, 1904–1957, vol. V
Chubb, John Oliver, 1920–1996, vol. X
Chubb, Sir Lawrence Wensley, 1873–1948, vol. IV
Chudoba, Franti¢ek, 1878–1941, vol. IV
Chula-Chakrabongse of Thailand, HRH Prince, 1908–1963, vol. VI
Chulaparambil, Rt Rev. Alexander, 1877–1951, vol. V
Chunilal Bose, Rai Bahadur, 1861–1930, vol. III
Church, Rev. Alfred John, 1829–1912, vol. I
Church, Major Archibald George, 1886–1954, vol. V
Church, Arthur Frederick, 1868–1939, vol. III
Church, Arthur Harry, died 1937, vol. III
Church, Sir Arthur Herbert, 1834–1915, vol. I
Church, Col Arthur John Bromley, 1869–1954, vol. V
Church, Rev. Charles Marcus, died 1915, vol. I
Church, Eric Edmund Raitt, 1907–1972, vol. VII
Church, Brig. Sir Geoffrey Selby, 2nd Bt, 1887–1979, vol. VII
Church, Col George Earl, 1835–1910, vol. I
Church, Col George Ross Marryat, 1868–1940, vol. III
Church, Rev. Leslie Frederic, 1886–1961, vol. VI
Church, Richard Thomas, 1893–1972, vol. VII
Church, Robert William, 1882–1923, vol. II
Church, Ronald James H.; see Harrison-Church.
Church, Samuel Harden, 1858–1943, vol. IV
Church, Maj.-Gen. Thomas Ross, 1831–1926, vol. II
Church, Vice-Adm. William Drummond, died 1937, vol. III
Church, Sir William Selby, 1st Bt, 1837–1928, vol. II
Churcher, Col Sir Arthur, 1871–1951, vol. V
Churcher, Maj.-Gen. John Bryan, 1905–1997, vol. X
Churchill, 1st Viscount, 1864–1934, vol. III
Churchill, 2nd Viscount, 1890–1973, vol. VII

Churchill, Surg.-Gen. Alexander Ferrier, 1839–1928, vol. II
Churchill, Col Arthur Gillespie, 1860–1940, vol. III
Churchill, Clementine Ogilvy S.; *see* Baroness Spencer-Churchill.
Churchill, Diana Josephine, 1913–1994, vol. IX
Churchill, Captain Edward George Spencer-, 1876–1964, vol. VI
Churchill, Lord Edward Spencer-, 1853–1911, vol. I
Churchill, George Percy, 1877–1973, vol. VII
Churchill, Hon. Gordon, 1898–1985, vol. VIII
Churchill, Harry Lionel, 1860–1924, vol. II
Churchill, Lord Ivor Charles Spencer, 1898–1956, vol. V
Churchill, Jennie Spencer; *see* Churchill, Lady Randolph Spencer.
Churchill, Brig. John Atherton, 1887–1965, vol. VI
Churchill, John George Spencer, 1909–1992, vol. IX
Churchill, Very Rev. John Howard, 1920–1990, vol. VIII
Churchill, John Strange Spencer, 1880–1947, vol. IV
Churchill, Peter Morland, 1909–1972, vol. VII
Churchill, Hon. Randolph Frederick Edward Spencer, 1911–1968, vol. VI
Churchill, Lady Randolph Spencer, 1854–1921, vol. II
Churchill, Rev. Robert Reginald, 1890–1970, vol. VI
Churchill, Lt-Col Seton, *died* 1933, vol. III
Churchill, Sidney John Alexander, 1862–1921, vol. II
Churchill, Stella, *died* 1954, vol. V
Churchill, Maj.-Gen. Thomas Bell Lindsay, 1907–1990, vol. VIII
Churchill, William, 1859–1920, vol. II (A), vol. III
Churchill, William Foster Norton, 1898–1963, vol. VI
Churchill, Winston, 1871–1947, vol. IV
Churchill, Rt Hon. Sir Winston Leonard Spencer, 1874–1965, vol. VI
Churchman, Air Cdre Allan Robert, 1896–1970, vol. VI
Churchman, Sir William Alfred, 1st Bt, 1863–1947, vol. IV
Churchward, Captain Alaric Watts, 1845–1929, vol. III
Churchward, George Jackson, *died* 1933, vol. III
Churchward, Rev. Marcus Wellesley, 1860–1940, vol. III
Churchward, Col Paul Rycaut Stanbury, 1858–1935, vol. III
Churchward, Percy Albert, 1862–1924, vol. II
Churchward, William Brown, 1844–1920, vol. II
Churston, 2nd Baron, 1846–1910, vol. I
Churston, 3rd Baron, 1873–1930, vol. III
Churston, 4th Baron, 1910–1991, vol. IX
Churton, Rt Rev. Edward Townson, 1841–1912, vol. I
Churton, Rt Rev. Henry Norris, 1843–1904, vol. I
Churton, Ven. Theodore Townson, 1853–1915, vol. I
Churton, Lt-Col William Arthur Vere, 1876–1949, vol. IV

Chute, Ven. Anthony William, 1884–1958, vol. V
Chute, Sir Charles Lennard, 1st Bt, 1879–1956, vol. V
Chute, Ven. John Chaloner, 1881–1961, vol. VI
Chute, Marchette Gaylord, 1909–1994, vol. IX
Chuter-Ede, Baron (Life-Peer); James Chuter Chuter-Ede, 1882–1965, vol. VI
Chwatt, Prof. Leonard Jan B.; *see* Bruce-Chwatt.
Ciano, Conte Cortellazzo, Galeazzo, 1903–1944, vol. IV
Cilcennin, 1st Viscount, 1903–1960, vol. V
Cilea, Francesco, 1866–1950, vol. IV
Cilento, Sir Raphael West, 1893–1985, vol. VIII
Cippico, Count Antonio, 1877–1935, vol. III
Citrine, 1st Baron, 1887–1983, vol. VIII
Citrine, 2nd Baron, 1914–1997, vol. X
Civil, Alan, 1928–1989, vol. VIII
Clague, Ven. Arthur Ashford, 1915–1983, vol. VIII
Clague, Col Sir Douglas; *see* Clague, Col Sir J. D.
Clague, Sir John, 1882–1958, vol. V
Clague, Col Sir (John) Douglas, 1917–1981, vol. VIII
Clair, René, 1898–1981, vol. VIII
Clamageran, Alice Germaine Suzanne, 1906–1998, vol. X
Clampett, Ven. Albert Wyndham, 1860–1953, vol. V
Clancarty, 5th Earl of, 1868–1929, vol. III
Clancarty, 6th Earl of, 1891–1971, vol. VII
Clancarty, 7th Earl of, 1902–1975, vol. VII
Clancarty, 8th Earl of, 1911–1995, vol. IX
Clancey, John Charles, 1854–1932, vol. III
Clancy, Rt Rev. John, 1856–1912, vol. I
Clancy, John Joseph, 1847–1928, vol. II
Clancy, Sir John Sydney James, 1895–1970, vol. VI (AII)
Clanmorris, 5th Baron, 1852–1916, vol. II
Clanmorris, 6th Baron, 1879–1960, vol. V
Clanmorris, 7th Baron, 1908–1988, vol. VIII
Clanricarde, 2nd Marquis of, 1832–1916, vol. II
Clanwilliam, 4th Earl of, 1832–1907, vol. I
Clanwilliam, 5th Earl of, 1873–1953, vol. V
Clanwilliam, 6th Earl of; John Charles Edmund Carson Meade, 1914–1989, vol. VIII
Clapham, Sir Alfred William, 1883–1950, vol. IV
Clapham, Arthur Roy, 1904–1990, vol. VIII
Clapham, Brian Ralph, 1913–1998, vol. X
Clapham, Edward William, *died* 1943, vol. IV
Clapham, Sir John Harold, 1873–1946, vol. IV
Clapin, Adolphus Philip, 1828–1914, vol. I
Clapp, Sir Harold Winthrop, 1875–1952, vol. V
Clappen, Air Cdre Donald William, 1895–1978, vol. VII
Clapperton, Alan Ernest, *died* 1931, vol. III
Clapperton, T. J., 1879–1962, vol. VI
Clarabut, Maj.-Gen. Reginald Blaxland, 1893–1977, vol. VII
Clare, Captain Chapman James, 1853–1940, vol. III
Clare, Ernest E. S.; *see* Sabben-Clare.
Clare, Sir Harcourt Everard, 1854–1922, vol. II
Clare, Henry Lewis, 1858–1920, vol. II
Clare, Mary, (Mrs L. Mawhood), 1892–1970, vol. VI
Clare, Octavius Leigh, 1841–1912, vol. I
Clare, Lt-Col Oliver Cecil, 1881–1933, vol. III

Clark, John Willis, 1833–1910, vol. I
Clark, Joseph, 1834–1926, vol. II
Clark, Col Joseph Arthur Myles Ariel, 1872–1935, vol. III
Clark, (Josiah) Latimer, 1822–1898, vol. I
Clark, Kenneth MacKenzie, 1868–1932, vol. III
Clark, Latimer; see Clark, J. L.
Clark, Leo; see Clark, F. L.
Clark, Leonard, 1905–1981, vol. VIII
Clark, Leslie Joseph, 1914–1992, vol. IX
Clark, Sir Lindesay; see Clark, Sir G. C. L.
Clark, Sir Marcus; see Clark, Sir R. M.
Clark, Mrs Margaret; see Storm, Lesley.
Clark, Marjorie, (Georgia Rivers), died 1989, vol. VIII
Clark, Gen. Mark Wayne, 1896–1984, vol. VIII
Clark, Michael Lindsey, 1918–1990, vol. VIII
Clark, Rt Rev. Patrick; see Clark, Rt Rev. F. P.
Clark, Percy, 1917–1985, vol. VIII
Clark, Col Percy William, 1888–1943, vol. IV
Clark, Philip Lindsey, 1889–1977, vol. VII
Clark, Reginald, 1895–1981, vol. VIII
Clark, Sir (Reginald) Marcus, 1883–1953, vol. V
Clark, Col Robert, 1859–1940, vol. III (A), vol. IV
Clark, Rev. Canon Robert James Vodden 1907–1998, vol. X
Clark, Lt-Gen. (Samuel) Findlay, 1909–1998, vol. X
Clark, Ven. Sidney H.; see Harvie-Clark.
Clark, Sir Stewart S.; see Stewart-Clark.
Clark, Stuart Ellis, born 1899, vol. VIII
Clark, Rev. Canon Stuart Harrington, 1869–1947, vol. IV
Clark, Sir Thomas, 1st Bt (cr 1886), 1823–1900, vol. I
Clark, Sir Thomas, 3rd Bt (cr 1886), 1886–1977, vol. VII
Clark, Thomas Archibald B.; see Bennet-Clark.
Clark, Thomas Campbell, (Tom C. Clark), 1899–1977, vol. VII
Clark, Sir (Thomas) Fife, 1907–1985, vol. VIII
Clark, Sir Wilfrid Edward Le Gros, 1895–1971, vol. VII
Clark, William Andrews, 1839–1925, vol. II
Clark, Sir (William) Arthur (Weir), 1908–1967, vol. VI
Clark, William Clifford, 1889–1952, vol. V
Clark, William Donaldson, 1916–1985, vol. VIII
Clark, Brig. William Ellis, 1877–1969, vol. VI
Clark, Hon. William George, 1865–1948, vol. IV
Clark, Rev. William Gilchrist; see Clark-Maxwell.
Clark, Sir William Henry, 1876–1952, vol. V
Clark, Sir William Mortimer, 1836–1917, vol. II
Clark, Sir William Ovens, 1849–1937, vol. III
Clark, Rt Rev. William Reid, died 1925, vol. II
Clark, Rev. William Robinson, died 1912, vol. I
Clark-Eddington, Paul; see Eddington.
Clark-Hall, Air Marshal Sir Robert Hamilton, 1883–1964, vol. VI
Clark Hutchison, Alan Michael; see Hutchison.
Clark-Kennedy, Archibald Edmund, 1893–1985, vol. VIII
Clark-Kennedy, John William James; see Kennedy.
Clark-Kennedy of Knockgray, Lt-Col William Hew; see Kennedy of Knockgray.

Clark-Maxwell, Rev. William Gilchrist, 1865–1935, vol. III
Clarke, Lt-Col Albert Edward Stanley, 1879–1926, vol. II
Clarke, Col Alexander Ross, 1828–1914, vol. I
Clarke, Alfred Henry, 1860–1942, vol. IV
Clarke, Hon. Sir Andrew, 1824–1902, vol. I
Clarke, Andrew B., died 1940, vol. III
Clarke, Vice-Adm. Arthur Calvert, 1848–1926, vol. II
Clarke, Brig. Arthur Christopher Lancelot S.; see Stanley-Clarke.
Clarke, Rev. Arthur Frederic, 1848–1932, vol. III
Clarke, Arthur Grenfell, 1906–1993, vol. IX
Clarke, Col Arthur Lionel Crisp, 1874–1935, vol. III
Clarke, Captain Sir Arthur Wellesley, 1857–1932, vol. III
Clarke, Captain Arthur Wellesley, 1898–1985, vol. VIII
Clarke, Sir Ashley; see Clarke, Sir H. A.
Clarke, Astley Vavasour, 1870–1945, vol. IV
Clarke, Austin, 1896–1974, vol. VII
Clarke, Sir Basil, 1879–1947, vol. IV
Clarke, Rev. Basil Fulford Lowther, 1903–1978, vol. VII
Clarke, Brig. Bowcher Campbell Senhouse, 1882–1969, vol. VI
Clarke, Sir Campbell, 1835–1902, vol. I
Clarke, Maj.-Gen. Sir Campbell; see Clarke, Maj.-Gen. Sir E. M. C.
Clarke, Sir Caspar Purdon, 1846–1911, vol. I
Clarke, Rev. Sir Charles, 2nd Bt (cr 1831), 1812–1899, vol. I
Clarke, Charles Agacy, 1872–1939, vol. III
Clarke, Charles Allen, 1863–1935, vol. III
Clarke, Charles Baron, 1832–1906, vol. I
Clarke, Col Charles C.; see Childs-Clarke.
Clarke, Charles Cyril, 1882–1968, vol. VI
Clarke, Charles Edward, 1912–1981, vol. VIII
Clarke, Charles Goddard, 1849–1908, vol. I
Clarke, Bt-Col (Charles Henry Geoffrey) Mansfield, 1873–1919, vol. II
Clarke, Charles Kirk, 1857–1924, vol. II
Clarke, Gen. Sir Charles Mansfield, 3rd Bt (cr 1831), 1839–1932, vol. III
Clarke, Sir Charles Noble A.; see Arden-Clark.
Clarke, Rear-Adm. Sir (Charles) Philip, 1898–1966, vol. VI
Clarke, Ven. Charles Philip Stewart, 1871–1947, vol. IV
Clarke, Hon. Sir Charles Pitcher, 1857–1926, vol. II
Clarke, Very Rev. Charles William B.; see Barnett-Clarke.
Clarke, Comdr Courtney; see Clarke, Comdr H. C. C.
Clarke, Sir Cyril Astley, 1907–2000, vol. X
Clarke, Dennis Robert, 1902–1967, vol. VI
Clarke, Denzil Robert Noble, 1908–1985, vol. VIII
Clarke, Maj.-Gen. Desmond Alexander Bruce, 1912–1986, vol. VIII
Clarke, Sir Douglas, 1901–1969, vol. VI
Clarke, Brig. Dudley Wrangel, 1899–1974, vol. VII
Clarke, Sir Edgar C.; see Chatfeild-Clarke.
Clarke, Edith, 1844–1926, vol. II

Clarke, Edward, 1908–1989, vol. VIII
Clarke, Edward Ashley Walrond, 1860–1913, vol. I
Clarke, Edward de Courcy, 1880–1958, vol. V
Clarke, Captain Edward Denman, 1898–1966, vol. VI
Clarke, Rt Hon. Sir Edward George, 1841–1931, vol. III
Clarke, Lt-Col Sir Edward Henry St Lawrence, 4th Bt (cr 1804), 1857–1926, vol. II
Clarke, Edward Henry Scamander, 1856–1947, vol. IV
Clarke, Major Edward John Arundell, 1868–1932, vol. III
Clarke, Edward Lionel Alexander, 1837–1917, vol. II
Clarke, Maj.-Gen. Sir (Edward Montagu) Campbell, 1885–1971, vol. VII
Clarke, Edwin Sisterson, 1919–1996, vol. X
Clarke, Elizabeth Bleckly, 1915–1993, vol. IX
Clarke, Sir Ernest, 1856–1923, vol. II
Clarke, Ernest, died 1932, vol. III
Clarke, (Ernest) Meredyth H.; see Hyde-Clarke.
Clarke, Sir Ernest Michael, 1868–1956, vol. V
Clarke, Hon. Sir Fielding, 1851–1928, vol. II
Clarke, Hon. Sir Francis Grenville, 1879–1955, vol. V
Clarke, Frank Edward, 1886–1938, vol. III
Clarke, Frank Wigglesworth, 1847–1931, vol. III
Clarke, Sir Fred, 1880–1952, vol. V
Clarke, Brig. Frederick Arthur Stanley, 1892–1972, vol. VII
Clarke, Ven. Frederick James, 1858–1937, vol. III
Clarke, Hon. Sir Frederick James, 1859–1944, vol. IV
Clarke, Sir Frederick Joseph, 1912–1980, vol. VII (AII)
Clarke, Frederick Seymour, 1855–1932, vol. III
Clarke, Sir Frederick William Alfred, 1857–1927, vol. II
Clarke, Sir Geoffrey, died 1950, vol. IV
Clarke, George, 1878–1944, vol. IV
Clarke, Gen. George Calvert, 1814–1900, vol. I
Clarke, George Johnson, died 1917, vol. II
Clarke, Gerald Bryan, 1909–1981, vol. VIII
Clarke, Brig.-Gen. Goland Vanhalt, 1875–1944, vol. IV
Clarke, Very Rev. Harold George Michael, 1898–1978, vol. VII
Clarke, Henry, 1854–1936, vol. III
Clarke, Sir (Henry) Ashley, 1903–1994, vol. IX
Clarke, Brig.-Gen. Henry Calvert Stanley, 1872–1943, vol. IV
Clarke, Comdr H(enry) C(ecil) Courtney, 1890–1968, vol. VI
Clarke, Adm. Henry James Langford, 1866–1944, vol. IV
Clarke, Most Rev. Henry Lowther, 1850–1926, vol. II
Clarke, Sir Henry O.; see Osmond-Clarke.
Clarke, Herbert, 1863–1925, vol. II
Clarke, Ven. Herbert Lovell, 1881–1962, vol. VI
Clarke, Hilton Swift, 1909–1995, vol. IX
Clarke, Sir Horace William, 1883–1963, vol. VI
Clarke, Sir Humphrey Orme, 5th Bt (cr 1831), 1906–1973, vol. VII

Clarke, Isabel Constance, died 1951, vol. V
Clarke, Col J. de W. L.; see Lardner-Clarke.
Clarke, J. Jackson, died 1940, vol. III (A), vol. IV
Clarke, James Greville, 1854–1901, vol. I
Clarke, Rev. John, died 1923, vol. II
Clarke, John, died 1939, vol. III
Clarke, John Courtenay, 1880–1939, vol. III
Clarke, Rev. John Erskine, 1827–1920, vol. II
Clarke, John Henry, 1852–1931, vol. III
Clarke, John Joseph, 1879–1969, vol. VI
Clarke, Brig.-Gen. John Louis Justice, 1870–1944, vol. IV
Clarke, John Mason, 1857–1925, vol. II
Clarke, John Smith, 1885–1959, vol. V
Clarke, Col John Thomas, 1870–1947, vol. IV (A)
Clarke, Joseph Percival, 1862–1930, vol. III
Clarke, Col Lancelot Fox, 1858–1925, vol. II
Clarke, Captain Lionel Altham G.; see Graham-Clarke.
Clarke, Hon. Lionel H., 1859–1922, vol. II
Clarke, Loftus Otway, 1871–1954, vol. V
Clarke, Louis Colville Gray, 1881–1960, vol. V, vol. VI
Clarke, Bt-Col Mansfield; see Clarke, Bt-Col C. H. G. M.
Clarke, Lt-Col Sir Marshal James, 1841–1909, vol. I
Clarke, Adm. Sir Marshal Llewelyn, 1887–1959, vol. V
Clarke, Mary Gavin, 1881–1976, vol. VII
Clarke, Mrs Mary Victoria Cowden, 1809–1898, vol. I
Clarke, Lt-Col Matthew John, 1895–1954, vol. V
Clarke, Maude Violet, 1892–1935, vol. III
Clarke, Meredyth H.; see Hyde-Clarke, E. M.
Clarke, Rear-Adm. Noel Edward Harwood, 1904–1980, vol. VII
Clarke, Norman Eley, 1930–1993, vol. IX
Clarke, Rt Rev. Norman Harry, 1892–1974, vol. VII
Clarke, Sir Orme Bigland, 4th Bt (cr 1831), 1880–1949, vol. IV
Clarke, Paul Henry Francis, 1921–1989, vol. VIII
Clarke, Sir Percival, 1872–1936, vol. III
Clarke, Rear-Adm. Sir Philip; see Clarke, Rear-Adm. Sir C. P.
Clarke, Sir Philip Haughton, 11th Bt (cr 1617), 1819–1898, vol. I
Clarke, Col Sir Ralph Stephenson, 1892–1970, vol. VI
Clarke, Sir Reginald, 1876–1956, vol. V
Clarke, Reginald Arnold, 1921–1989, vol. VIII
Clarke, Col Reginald Graham, 1879–1959, vol. V
Clarke, Sir Richard William Barnes, 1910–1975, vol. VII
Clarke, Robert Coningsby, 1879–1934, vol. III
Clarke, Col Robert Ffoulke Noel, 1853–1904, vol. I
Clarke, Lt-Col Robert Joyce, 1874–1949, vol. IV
Clarke, Roger Simon Woodchurch, 1903–1988, vol. VIII
Clarke, Sir Rupert Turner Havelock, 2nd Bt (cr 1882), 1865–1926, vol. II
Clarke, Samuel Harrison, 1903–1994, vol. IX
Clarke, Sir Selwyn S.; see Selwyn-Clarke.
Clarke, Rev. Septimus John C.; see Childs-Clarke.
Clarke, Rev. Sidney Lampard, 1871–1945, vol. IV

Clarke, Somers, 1841–1926, vol. II
Clarke, Lt-Gen. Somerset Molyneux W.; *see* Wiseman-Clarke.
Clarke, Maj.-Gen. Sir Stanley de Astel Calvert, 1837–1911, vol. I
Clarke, Stephenson Robert, 1862–1948, vol. IV
Clarke, Rev. Sydney Herbert, 1894–1974, vol. VII
Clarke, Brig. Terence Hugh, 1904–1992, vol. IX
Clarke, Ven. Thomas, 1907–1965, vol. VI
Clarke, Col Thomas Cecil Arthur, 1898–1979, vol. VII
Clarke, Thomas Ernest Bennett, 1907–1989, vol. VIII
Clarke, Col Thomas Henry Matthews, 1869–1941, vol. IV
Clarke, Tom, 1884–1957, vol. V
Clarke, Tom, 1918–1993, vol. IX
Clarke, Lt-Gen. Sir Travers Edwards, 1871–1962, vol. VI
Clarke, William, 1842–1918, vol. II
Clarke, William Bruce, *died* 1914, vol. I
Clarke, William Eagle, 1853–1938, vol. III
Clarke, Sir William Henry, *died* 1930, vol. III
Clarke, Sir William Henry, 1847–1930, vol. III
Clarke, Sir William John, 1st Bt (*cr* 1882), 1831–1897, vol. I
Clarke, William John, 1857–1951, vol. V
Clarke, Rev. William Kemp Lowther, 1879–1968, vol. VI
Clarke, Hon. William Lionel Russell, 1876–1954, vol. V
Clarke, Brig. William Stanhope, 1899–1973, vol. VII
Clarke, Maj.-Gen. Willoughby Charles Stanley, 1833–1909, vol. I
Clarke Hall, Edna (Lady Clarke Hall), 1879–1979, vol. VII
Clarke-Jervoise, Sir Arthur Henry; *see* Jervoise.
Clarke-Jervoise, Sir Dudley Alan Lestock; *see* Jervoise.
Clarke Taylor, Air Vice-Marshal James; *see* Taylor.
Clarke-Thornhill, Thomas Bryan, 1857–1934, vol. III
Clarke-Travers, Sir Guy Francis Travers; *see* Travers.
Clarkson, Anthony; *see* Clarkson, G. W. A.
Clarkson, Lt-Col Bertie St John, 1868–1954, vol. V
Clarkson, (George Wensley) Anthony, 1912–1977, vol. VII
Clarkson, Rt Rev. George William, 1897–1977, vol. VII
Clarkson, Mabel, *died* 1950, vol. IV
Clarkson, Patrick Wensley, 1911–1969, vol. VI
Clarkson, Rev. Peter, 1871–1936, vol. III
Clarkson, Randolph Norman Macgregor, 1889–1967, vol. VI
Clarkson, Engr-Vice-Adm. Sir William, 1859–1934, vol. III
Clarry, Sir Reginald, 1882–1945, vol. IV
Clasen, Andrew Joseph, 1906–1984, vol. VIII
Claude, Albert, 1898–1983, vol. VIII
Claudel, Paul, 1868–1955, vol. V
Claughton, Sir Gilbert Henry, 1st Bt, 1856–1921, vol. II
Claughton, Sir Harold, 1882–1969, vol. VI

Claus, Emile, 1849–1924, vol. II
Clause, William Lionel, 1887–1946, vol. IV
Clausen, Sir George, 1852–1944, vol. IV
Clausen, Raymond John, *died* 1966, vol. VI
Clauson, 1st Baron, 1870–1946, vol. IV
Clauson, Sir Gerard Leslie Makins, 1891–1974, vol. VII
Clauson, Major Sir John Eugene, 1866–1918, vol. II
Clavell, James, 1924–1994, vol. IX
Clavering, Sir Albert, 1887–1972, vol. VII
Clavering, Col Charles Warren N.; *see* Napier-Clavering.
Clavering, Maj.-Gen. Noel Warren N.; *see* Napier-Clavering.
Claxton, Hon. Brooke, 1898–1960, vol. V
Claxton, Rt Rev. Charles Robert, 1903–1992, vol. IX
Claxton, John Francis, 1911–1991, vol. IX
Claxton, Maj.-Gen. Patrick Fisher, 1915–2000, vol. X
Claxton, Thomas Folkes, 1874–1952, vol. V
Clay, Sir Arthur Temple Felix, 4th Bt, 1842–1928, vol. II
Clay, Brig.-Gen. Bertie Gordon, 1874–1937, vol. III
Clay, Charles Felix, 1861–1947, vol. IV
Clay, Charles John Jervis, 1910–1988, vol. VIII
Clay, Sir Charles Travis, 1885–1978, vol. VII
Clay, Lt-Col Ernest Charles, 1872–1955, vol. V
Clay, Sir Felix, 5th Bt, 1871–1941, vol. IV
Clay, Sir Geoffrey Fletcher, 1895–1969, vol. VI
Clay, Col Henry, 1872–1945, vol. IV
Clay, Sir Henry, 1883–1954, vol. V
Clay, Sir Henry Felix, 6th Bt, 1909–1985, vol. VIII
Clay, Lt-Col Rt Hon. Herbert Henry S.; *see* Spender-Clay.
Clay, Col John, *died* 1962, vol. VI
Clay, Rev. John Harden, *died* 1923, vol. II
Clay, Sir Joseph Miles, 1881–1949, vol. IV
Clay, Gen. Lucius DuBignon, 1897–1978, vol. VII
Clay, Reginald S., *died* 1954, vol. V
Clay, Trevor Reginald, 1936–1994, vol. IX
Clay, William Henry, 1841–1921, vol. II
Clay, Rev. William Leslie, 1863–1928, vol. II
Clayden, Arthur William, 1855–1944, vol. IV
Clayden, Rt Hon. Sir (Henry) John, 1904–1986, vol. VIII
Clayden, Rt Hon. Sir John; *see* Clayden, Rt Hon. Sir H. J.
Clayden, Peter William, 1827–1902, vol. I
Claydon, Rev. Canon Ernest Henry Beales, 1863–1930, vol. III
Claye, Sir Andrew Moynihan, 1896–1977, vol. VII
Claye, Rev. Canon Arthur Needham, 1863–1956, vol. V
Clayhills, George, 1877–1914, vol. I
Clayson, Sir Eric Maurice, 1908–1989, vol. VIII
Clayson, Rev. Canon Jesse Alec Maynard, 1905–1971, vol. VII
Clayton, Rev. Albert, *died* 1907, vol. I
Clayton, Sir Arthur Harold, 11th Bt, 1903–1985, vol. VIII
Clayton, Arthur Ross, 1876–1963, vol. VI
Clayton, Sir Christopher; *see* Clayton, Sir G. C.
Clayton, Colin, 1895–1975, vol. VII
Clayton, Edward, 1856–1938, vol. III

Clayton, Edward Chapman, 1837–1935, vol. III
Clayton, Major Edward Francis, 1864–1922, vol. II
Clayton, Major Sir Edward Gilbert, 1841–1917, vol. II
Clayton, Maj.-Gen. Edward Hadrill, 1899–1962, vol. VI
Clayton, Col Edward Robert, 1877–1957, vol. V
Clayton, Edwin, 1887–1973, vol. VII
Clayton, Col Sir Fitz-Roy Augustus Talbot, 1834–1913, vol. I
Clayton, Col Forrester, 1878–1942, vol. IV
Clayton, Sir Francis Hare, 1869–1956, vol. V
Clayton, Frederick, 1872–1932, vol. III
Clayton, Lt-Gen. Sir Frederick Thomas, 1855–1933, vol. III
Clayton, Frederick William, 1913–1999, vol. X
Clayton, Air Marshal Sir Gareth Thomas Butler, 1914–1992, vol. IX
Clayton, Most Rev. Geoffrey Hare, 1884–1957, vol. V
Clayton, Sir (George) Christopher, 1869–1945, vol. IV
Clayton, Brig.-Gen. Sir Gilbert Falkingham, 1875–1929, vol. III
Clayton, Harold, 1874–1963, vol. VI
Clayton, Sir Harold Dudley, 10th Bt (cr 1732), 1877–1951, vol. V
Clayton, Col Hon. Sir Hector Joseph Richard, 1885–1975, vol. VII
Clayton, Rev. Horace Evelyn, 1853–1916, vol. II
Clayton, Sir Hugh Byard, 1877–1947, vol. IV
Clayton, Brig. Sir Iltyd Nicholl, 1886–1955, vol. V
Clayton, Jack, 1921–1995, vol. IX
Clayton, Rev. John Francis, 1883–1947, vol. IV
Clayton, Rear-Adm. John Wittewronge, 1888–1952, vol. V
Clayton, Joseph, 1868–1943, vol. IV
Clayton, Rt Rev. Lewis, 1838–1917, vol. II
Clayton, Lucie; see Kark, Evelyn F.
Clayton, Michael Thomas Emilius, 1917–1995, vol. IX
Clayton, Lt-Col Muirhead Collins, 1892–1957, vol. V
Clayton, Col Patrick Andrew, 1896–1962, vol. VI
Clayton, Rev. Philip Thomas Byard, 1885–1972, vol. VII
Clayton, Reginald John Byard, 1875–1962, vol. VI
Clayton, Richard Henry Michael, (William Haggard), 1907–1993, vol. IX
Clayton, Adm. Sir Richard Pilkington, 1925–1984, vol. VIII
Clayton, Hon. Brig.-Gen. Robert Clayton B.; see Browne Clayton.
Clayton, Sir Robert James, 1915–1998, vol. X
Clayton, Sir Stanley George, 1911–1986, vol. VIII
Clayton, Lt-Col William Kitson, died 1937, vol. III
Clayton, William Lockhart, 1880–1966, vol. VI
Clayton, Sir William Robert, 6th Bt (cr 1732), 1842–1914, vol. I
Clayton-East, Sir George Frederick Lancelot, 8th Bt and 4th Bt; see East.
Clayton East, Sir Gilbert Augustus Clayton, 7th Bt and 3rd Bt; see East.
Clayton East Clayton, Sir Robert Alan, 9th Bt (cr 1732), and 5th Bt (cr 1838), 1908–1932, vol. III

Clayton-Greene, William Henry, died 1926, vol. II
Cleall, Ven. Aubrey Victor George, 1898–1982, vol. VIII
Cleary, Denis Mackrow, 1907–1997, vol. X
Cleary, Frederick Ernest, 1905–1984, vol. VIII
Cleary, Rt Rev. Henry William, 1859–1929, vol. III
Cleary, Rt. Rev. Joseph Francis, 1912–1991, vol. IX
Cleary, Sir Joseph Jackson, 1902–1993, vol. IX
Cleary, Ven. Robert, died 1919, vol. II
Cleary, Hon. Sir Timothy Patrick, 1900–1962, vol. VI
Cleary, Sir William Castle, 1886–1971, vol. VII
Cleather, Edward Gordon, 1872–1967, vol. VI
Cleaton, John Davies, died 1901, vol. I
Cleave, John, 1837–1928, vol. II
Cleave, John Kyrie Frederick, 1861–1947, vol. IV
Cleaver, Sir Frederick, 1875–1936, vol. III
Cleaver, Col Frederick Holden, 1875–1944, vol. IV
Cleaver, Leonard Harry, 1909–1993, vol. IX
Cleaver, Air Vice-Marshal Peter Charles, 1919–1999, vol. X
Cleaver, Reginald; see Cleaver, T. R.
Cleaver, (Thomas) Reginald, died 1954, vol. V
Clee, Sir Charles Beaupré Bell, 1893–1980, vol. VII
Cleeve, Brig. Francis Charles Frederick, 1896–1975, vol. VII
Cleeve, Lt-Col Herbert, 1870–1948, vol. IV
Cleeve, Lucas, (Mrs Howard Kingscote), died 1908, vol. I
Cleeve, Col Stewart Dalrymple, 1856–1939, vol. III
Cleeve, Sir Thomas Henry, 1844–1908, vol. I
Cleeve, Maj.-Gen. William Frederick, 1853–1922, vol. II
Clegg, Sir Alec, (Alexander Bradshaw Clegg), 1909–1986, vol. VIII
Clegg, Sir (Alfred) Rowland, 1872–1957, vol. V
Clegg, Sir Cuthbert Barwick, 1904–1986, vol. VIII
Clegg, Hugh Anthony, 1900–1983, vol. VIII
Clegg, Hugh Armstrong, 1920–1995, vol. IX
Clegg, Sir James Travis T.; see Travis-Clegg.
Clegg, Rev. James Whitehead, died 1930, vol. III
Clegg, Sir John Charles, 1850–1937, vol. III
Clegg, Rear-Adm. John Harry Kay, 1884–1962, vol. VI
Clegg, Sir Robert Bailey, 1865–1929, vol. III
Clegg, Ronald Anthony, (Tony), 1937–1995, vol. IX
Clegg, Sir Rowland; see Clegg, Sir A. R.
Clegg, Tony; see Clegg, Ronald Anthony.
Clegg, Sir Walter, 1920–1994, vol. IX
Clegg, Sir William Edwin, 1852–1932, vol. III
Clegg, William Henry, died 1945, vol. IV
Cleghorn, Isabel, died 1922, vol. II
Cleghorn, Surg.-Gen. James, 1841–1920, vol. II
Cleland, Sir Charles, 1867–1941, vol. IV
Cleland, Brig. Sir Donald Mackinnon, 1901–1975, vol. VII
Cleland, Edward Erskine, 1869–1943, vol. IV (A)
Cleland, James William, 1874–1914, vol. I
Cleland, John, 1835–1924, vol. II
Cleland, Sir John Burton, 1878–1971, vol. VII
Clemenceau, Georges, 1841–1929, vol. III
Clemens, Benjamin, died 1957, vol. V
Clemens, Samuel Langhorne; see Twain, Mark.
Clemens, Sir William James, 1873–1941, vol. IV

Clement, Sir Anchitel Piers A.; *see* Ashburnham-Clement.
Clement, Ernest Wilson, 1860–1941, vol. IV
Clément, René, 1913–1996, vol. X
Clement, Sir Thomas, *died* 1956, vol. V
Clementi, Sir Cecil, 1875–1947, vol. IV
Clementi, Air Vice-Marshal Cresswell Montagu, 1918–1981, vol. VIII
Clements, Arthur; *see* Baker, Andrew Clement.
Clements, Arthur Frederick, 1877–1968, vol. VI
Clements, Bernard; *see* Clements, W. D. B.
Clements, Clyde Edwin, 1897–1983, vol. VIII
Clements, Rev. Jacob, 1820–1898, vol. I
Clements, Sir John Selby, 1910–1988, vol. VIII
Clements, Kay, (Dorothy Katharine), (Lady Clements); *see* Hammond, Kay.
Clements, Rt Rev. Kenneth John, 1905–1992, vol. IX
Clements, Maj.-Gen. Ralph Arthur Penrhyn, 1855–1909, vol. I
Clements, Col Robert William, *died* 1941, vol. IV
Clements, (William Dudley) Bernard, 1880–1942, vol. IV
Clemesha, Lt-Col William Wesley, 1871–1958, vol. V
Cleminson, Frederick John, 1878–1943, vol. IV
Cleminson, Henry Millican, 1885–1970, vol. VI
Clemitson, Rear-Adm. Francis Edward, 1899–1981, vol. VIII
Clemitson, Ivor Malcolm, 1931–1997, vol. X
Clemmey, Sir William Henry, 1846–1933, vol. III
Clemo, George Roger, 1889–1983, vol. VIII
Clemoes, Peter Alan Martin, 1920–1996, vol. X
Clemow, Frank Gerard, *died* 1939, vol. III
Clemson, Brig.-Gen. William Fletcher, 1866–1946, vol. IV
Clerici, Charles John Emil, *died* 1938, vol. III
Clerk, Sir Dugald, 1854–1932, vol. III
Clerk, Sir George Douglas, 8th Bt, 1852–1911, vol. I
Clerk, Sir George James Robert, 9th Bt, 1876–1943, vol. IV
Clerk, Rt Hon. Sir George Russell, 1874–1951, vol. V
Clerk, Gen. Sir Godfrey, 1835–1908, vol. I
Clerk, Maj.-Gen. Henry, 1821–1913, vol. I
Clerk, Hugh Edward, 1859–1942, vol. IV
Clerk, Col John, *died* 1919, vol. II
Clerk-Rattray, Lt-Gen. Sir James, 1832–1910, vol. I
Clerke, Agnes Mary, 1842–1907, vol. I
Clerke, Major Augustus Basil Holt, 1871–1949, vol. IV
Clerke, Ellen Mary, 1840–1906, vol. I
Clerke, Sir William Francis, 11th Bt, 1856–1930, vol. III
Clermont-Ganneau, Charles Simon, *born* 1846, vol. II
Clery, Arthur Edward, *died* 1932, vol. III
Clery, Maj.-Gen. Carleton Buckley Laming, 1869–1937, vol. III
Clery, Lt-Gen. Sir Francis, 1838–1926, vol. II
Clery, Surg.-Gen. James Albert, 1846–1920, vol. II
Cleugh, Eric Arthur, 1894–1964, vol. VI
Cleveland, Duchess of; (Catherine Lucy Wilhelmina), 1819–1901, vol. I

Cleveland, Sir Charles Raitt, 1866–1929, vol. III
Cleveland, Grover, 1837–1908, vol. I
Cleveland, Adm. Henry Forster, 1834–1924, vol. II
Cleveland, Col Henry Francis, 1863–1938, vol. III
Cleveland, Sydney Dyson, 1898–1975, vol. VII
Cleveland-Stevens, William, 1881–1957, vol. V
Cleverdon, Douglas; *see* Cleverdon, T. D. J.
Cleverdon, (Thomas) Douglas (James), 1903–1987, vol. VIII
Cleverley Ford, Rev. Preb. Douglas William, 1914–1996, vol. X
Cleverly, Charles F. M., *died* 1921, vol. II
Cleverly, Sir Osmund Somers, 1891–1966, vol. VI
Clewer, Maj.-Gen. Donald, 1892–1945, vol. IV
Clewes, Howard Charles Vivian, 1912–1988, vol. VIII
Clewes, Winston, 1906–1957, vol. V
Cleworth, Ralph, 1896–1975, vol. VII
Cleworth, Rev. Thomas Ebenezer, 1854–1909, vol. I
Clibborn, Donovan Harold, 1917–1996, vol. X
Clibborn, Col John, 1847–1938, vol. III
Clibborn, Rt Rev. Stanley Eric Francis B.; *see* Booth-Clibborn.
Clifden, 5th Viscount, 1829–1899, vol. I
Clifden, 6th Viscount, 1844–1930, vol. III
Clifden, 7th Viscount, 1883–1966, vol. VI
Clifden, 8th Viscount, 1887–1974, vol. VII
Cliff, Eric Francis, 1884–1969, vol. VI
Cliffe, Anthony Loftus, 1861–1922, vol. II
Cliffe, Michael, 1904–1964, vol. VI
Clifford of Chudleigh, 9th Baron, 1851–1916, vol. II
Clifford of Chudleigh, 10th Baron, 1858–1943, vol. IV
Clifford of Chudleigh, 11th Baron, 1887–1962, vol. VI
Clifford of Chudleigh, 12th Baron, 1889–1964, vol. VI
Clifford of Chudleigh, 13th Baron, 1916–1988, vol. VIII
Clifford, Rt Rev. Alfred, 1849–1931, vol. III
Clifford, Captain Hon. Sir Bede Edmund Hugh, 1890–1969, vol. VI
Clifford, Sir Charles, *died* 1936, vol. III
Clifford, Sir Charles Lewis, 3rd Bt, 1885–1938, vol. III
Clifford, Clark McAdams, 1906–1998, vol. X
Clifford, Edward C., *died* 1910, vol. I
Clifford, Elizabeth Lydia Rosabelle, (Lady Clifford), (Mrs Henry de la Pasture), *died* 1945, vol. IV
Clifford, Vice-Adm. Sir Eric George Anderson, 1900–1964, vol. VI
Clifford, Col Esmond Humphrey Miller, 1895–1970, vol. VI
Clifford, Ethel, *died* 1959, vol. V
Clifford, Frederick, 1828–1904, vol. I
Clifford, Sir (Geoffrey) Miles, 1897–1986, vol. VIII
Clifford, Sir George Hugh Charles, 2nd Bt, 1847–1930, vol. III
Clifford, Graham Douglas, 1913–1989, vol. VIII
Clifford, Henry Charles, 1861–1947, vol. IV
Clifford, Brig.-Gen. Henry Frederick Hugh, 1867–1916, vol. II
Clifford, Sir Hugh, 1866–1941, vol. IV
Clifford, James Lowry, 1901–1978, vol. VII
Clifford, Rev. John, 1836–1923, vol. II

Clifford, Julian, 1877–1921, vol. II
Clifford, Rev. Sir Lewis Arthur Joseph, 5th Bt, 1896–1970, vol. VI
Clifford, Sir Miles; see Clifford, Sir G. M.
Clifford, Maj.-Gen. Richard Melville, 1841–1915, vol. I
Clifford, Lt-Gen. Robert Cecil Richard, 1839–1930, vol. III
Clifford, Rev. Robert Rowntree, 1867–1943, vol. IV
Clifford, Sir Roger Charles Joseph Gerrard, 6th Bt, 1910–1982, vol. VIII
Clifford, Sir Walter Lovelace, 4th Bt, 1852–1944, vol. IV
Clifford, Brig.-Gen. Walter Rees, 1866–1947, vol. IV
Clifford, Major Wigram, 1876–1917, vol. II
Clifford, William Henry Morton, 1909–1996, vol. X
Clifford, Mrs William Kingdom, (Lucy Clifford), died 1929, vol. III
Clifford-Turner, Raymond, 1906–1995, vol. IX
Clift, Hon. James Augustus, 1857–1923, vol. II
Clift, Col Sir Sidney William, 1885–1951, vol. V
Clifton, Baroness (17th in line), 1900–1937, vol. III
Clifton, Augustus Wykeham, 1829–1915, vol. I
Clifton, John Talbot, 1868–1928, vol. II
Clifton, Leon James Thomas, 1912–1978, vol. VII
Clifton, Lt-Col Percy Robert, 1872–1944, vol. IV
Clifton, Peter Thomas, 1911–1996, vol. X
Clifton, Robert Bellamy, 1836–1921, vol. II
Clifton, Robert Cecil, 1854–1931, vol. III
Clifton, Violet Mary, (Mrs Talbot Clifton), 1883–1961, vol. VI
Clifton-Brown, Anthony George, 1903–1984, vol. VIII
Clifton Brown, Cedric, 1887–1968, vol. VI
Clifton-Brown, Edward Clifton, 1870–1944, vol. IV
Clifton-Brown, Lt-Col Geoffrey Benedict, 1899–1983, vol. VIII
Clifton-Taylor, Alec, 1907–1985, vol. VIII
Climie, Robert, 1868–1929, vol. III
Climo, Lt-Gen. Sir Skipton Hill, 1868–1937, vol. III
Clinch, George, 1860–1921, vol. II
Clinton, 20th Baron, 1834–1904, vol. I
Clinton, 21st Baron, 1863–1957, vol. V
Clinton, David Osbert F.; see Fynes-Clinton.
Clinton, Lord Edward William Pelham-, 1836–1907, vol. I
Clinton, (Francis) Gordon, 1912–1988, vol. VIII
Clinton, Gordon; see Clinton, F. G.
Clinton, Rev. Henry Joy F.; see Fynes-Clinton.
Clinton, Michael Denys Arthur, 1918–1976, vol. VII
Clinton, Osbert Henry F.; see Fynes-Clinton.
Clinton, Ven. Thomas William, died 1926, vol. II
Clinton-Baddeley, Madeline Angela, (Angela Baddeley), 1904–1976, vol. VII
Clinton-Baker, Henry William, 1865–1935, vol. III
Clinton-Baker, Adm. Sir Lewis, 1866–1939, vol. III
Clinton-Thomas, Robert Antony, 1913–1981, vol. VIII
Clipperton, Sir Charles Bell Child, 1864–1927, vol. II
Clissitt, William Cyrus, 1898–1977, vol. VII
Clissold, Major Harry, died 1917, vol. II
Clitheroe, 1st Baron, 1901–1984, vol. VIII

Clitherow, Lt-Col John Bourchier S.; see Stracey-Clitherow.
Clitherow, Richard, 1902–1947, vol. IV
Clitherow, Rt Rev. Richard George, 1909–1984, vol. VIII
Clive, Viscount; Mervyn Horatio Herbert, 1904–1943, vol. IV
Clive, Viscount; Percy Robert Herbert, 1892–1916, vol. II
Clive, Gen. Edward Henry, 1837–1916, vol. II
Clive, Lt-Col Hon. George Herbert Windsor W.; see Windsor-Clive.
Clive, Lt-Gen. Sir (George) Sidney, 1874–1959, vol. V
Clive, Lt-Col George W.; se Windsor-Clive.
Clive, Col Harry, 1880–1963, vol. VI
Clive, Captain Percy Archer, 1873–1918, vol. II
Clive, Rt Hon. Sir Robert Henry, 1877–1948, vol. IV
Clive, Lt-Gen. Sir Sidney; see Clive, Lt-Gen. Sir G. S.
Cloake, Philip Cyril, 1890–1969, vol. VI
Clodd, Edward, 1840–1930, vol. III
Clode, Dame (Emma) Frances (Heather), 1903–1994, vol. IX
Clode, Dame Frances; see Clode, Dame E. F. H.
Clode, Sir Walter Baker, 1856–1937, vol. III
Cloete, (Edward Fairly) Stuart (Graham), 1897–1976, vol. VII
Cloete, Col Evelyn, 1863–1943, vol. IV
Cloete, Hendrik, 1851–1920, vol. II
Cloete, Lt-Gen. Josias Gordon, 1840–1907, vol. I
Cloete, Stuart; see Cloete, E. F. S. G.
Cloete, William Broderick, 1851–1915, vol. I
Clogg, Rev. Bertram; see Clogg, Rev. F. B.
Clogg, Rev. (Frank) Bertram, 1884–1955, vol. V
Clogg, Herbert Sherwell, died 1932, vol. III
Clogstoun, Herbert Cunningham, 1857–1936, vol. III
Clonbrock, 4th Baron, 1834–1917, vol. II
Clonbrock, 5th Baron, 1869–1926, vol. II
Cloncurry, 4th Baron, 1840–1928, vol. II
Cloncurry, 5th Baron, 1847–1929, vol. III
Clonmell, 6th Earl of, 1847–1898, vol. I
Clonmell, 7th Earl of, 1877–1928, vol. II
Clonmell, 8th Earl of, 1853–1935, vol. III
Cloran, Hon. Henry Joseph, 1855–1928, vol. II
Clore, Sir Charles, 1904–1979, vol. VII
Close, Col Sir Charles Frederick A.; see Arden-Close.
Close, Etta, died 1945, vol. IV
Close, Adm. Francis Arden, 1829–1918, vol. II
Close, Brig.-Gen. Geoffrey Dominic, 1866–1942, vol. IV
Close, Harold Arden, 1863–1932, vol. III
Close, Col Lewis Henry, 1869–1924, vol. II
Close, Major Maxwell Archibald, 1853–1935, vol. III
Close, Ralph William, 1867–1945, vol. IV
Close, Richard Charles, 1949–2000, vol. X
Close, S. P., vol. II
Close-Smith, Charles Nugent, 1911–1988, vol. VIII
Closs, August, 1898–1990, vol. VIII
Clothier, Henry Williamson, 1878–1958, vol. V
Clothier, Wilfrid, 1887–1967, vol. VI
Clotworthy, Stanley Edward, 1902–1983, vol. VIII

162

Cloudesley-Brereton, Maud Adeline; *see* Brereton.

Clough, Lt-Col Alfred Herrick Butler, 1856–1935, vol. III

Clough, (Arthur) Gordon, 1934–1996, vol. X

Clough, Arthur Harold, 1897–1967, vol. VI

Clough, Blanche Athena, 1861–1960, vol. V

Clough, (Ernest Marshall) Owen, 1873–1964, vol. VI

Clough, Frederic Horton, 1878–1957, vol. V

Clough, Gordon; *see* Clough, A. G.

Clough, Howard James Butler, 1890–1967, vol. VI

Clough, Sir John, 1836–1922, vol. II

Clough, Owen; *see* Clough, E. M. O.

Clough, Prunella, 1919–1999, vol. X

Clough, Sir Robert, 1873–1965, vol. VI

Clough, Tom, 1867–1943, vol. IV

Clough, Walter Owen, 1846–1922, vol. II

Clough, William, 1862–1937, vol. III

Clouston, Air Cdre Arthur Edmond, 1908–1984, vol. VIII

Clouston, David, 1872–1948, vol. IV

Clouston, Sir Edward Seaborne, 1st Bt, 1849–1912, vol. I

Clouston, J. Storer, 1870–1944, vol. IV

Clouston, Sir Thomas Smith, 1840–1915, vol. I

Cloutier, Rt Rev. Francis Xavier, 1848–1933, vol. III

Cloutman, Sir Brett Mackay, 1891–1971, vol. VII

Cloutman, Air Vice-Marshal Geoffrey William, 1920–2000, vol. X

Clover, Maj.-Gen. Frederick Sherwood, 1894–1962, vol. VI

Clover, Gordon; *see* Clover, R. G.

Clover, (Robert) Gordon, 1911–1993, vol. IX

Clow, Sir Andrew Gourlay, 1890–1957, vol. V

Clow, Paymaster Rear-Adm. George James, *died* 1932, vol. III

Clow, Lt-Col William, 1863–1934, vol. III

Clow, William McCallum, 1853–1930, vol. III

Clowes, Lt-Gen. Cyril Albert, 1892–1968, vol. VI

Clowes, Frank, 1848–1923, vol. II

Clowes, Geoffrey Swinford Laird, 1883–1937, vol. III

Clowes, Col George Charles Knight, 1882–1941, vol. IV

Clowes, Sir Harold, 1903–1968, vol. VI

Clowes, Hon. Sir Henry Nelson, 1911–1993, vol. IX

Clowes, Maj.-Gen. Norman, 1893–1980, vol. VII

Clowes, Lt-Col Peter Legh, 1853–1925, vol. II

Clowes, Samuel, 1864–1928, vol. II

Clowes, William Archibald, 1866–1937, vol. III

Clowes, Sir William Laird, 1856–1905, vol. I

Clubb, Hon. William Reid, 1884–1962, vol. VI

Clubbe, Sir Charles Percy Barlee, *died* 1932, vol. III

Clucas, Sir Frederick; *see* Clucas, Sir G. F.

Clucas, Sir (George) Frederick, 1870–1937, vol. III

Cluer, Albert Rowland, 1852–1942, vol. IV

Clune, Most Rev. Patrick Joseph, 1864–1935, vol. III

Clunes, Alec Sheriff de Moro, 1912–1970, vol. VI

Clunie, James, 1889–1974, vol. VII

Clunies-Ross, Sir Ian, 1899–1959, vol. V

Cluny Macpherson; *see* Macpherson, A. C.

Cluny Macpherson; *see* Macpherson, Brig. A. D.

Cluny Macpherson, *see* Macpherson, Brig.-Gen. E. H. D.

Cluse, William Sampson, 1875–1955, vol. V

Cluskey, Frank, 1930–1989, vol. IX (AI)

Clute, Hon. Roger Conger, 1848–1921, vol. II

Clutsam, George H., 1866–1951, vol. V

Clutterbuck, Sir Alexander; *see* Clutterbuck, Sir P. A.

Clutterbuck, Edmund Harry Michael, 1920–1991, vol. IX

Clutterbuck, Sir (Peter) Alexander, 1897–1975, vol. VII

Clutterbuck, Sir Peter Henry, 1868–1951, vol. V

Clutterbuck, Maj.-Gen. Richard Lewis, 1917–1998, vol. X

Clutterbuck, Maj.-Gen. Walter Edmond, 1894–1987, vol. VIII

Clutton, Sir George Lisle, 1909–1970, vol. VI

Clutton, Henry Hugh, 1850–1909, vol. I

Clutton-Brock, Alan Francis, *died* 1976, vol. VII

Clutton-Brock, Arthur, 1868–1924, vol. II

Clutton-Brock, (Arthur) Guy, 1906–1995, vol. IX

Clutton-Brock, Guy; *see* Clutton-Brock, A. G.

Cluver, Eustace Henry, 1894–1982, vol. VIII

Clwyd, 1st Baron, 1863–1955, vol. V

Clwyd, 2nd Baron, 1900–1987, vol. VIII

Clyde, Rt Hon. Lord; Rt Hon. James Avon Clyde, 1863–1944, vol. IV

Clyde, Rt Hon. Lord; Rt Hon. James Latham McDiarmid Clyde, 1898–1975, vol. VII

Clyde, Col Sir David, 1894–1966, vol. VI

Clyde, Rt Hon. James Avon; *see* Clyde, Rt Hon. Lord.

Clyde, Rt Hon. James Latham McDiarmid; *see* Clyde, Rt Hon. Lord.

Clyde, William McCallum, 1901–1972, vol. VII

Clydesmuir, 1st Baron, 1894–1954, vol. V

Clydesmuir, 2nd Baron, 1917–1996, vol. X

Clyne, Hon. Sir Thomas Stuart, 1887–1967, vol. VI

Clynes, Rt Hon. John Robert, 1869–1949, vol. IV

Coad, Maj.-Gen. Aubrey; *see* Coad, Maj.-Gen. B. A.

Coad, Maj.-Gen. Basil Aubrey, 1906–1980, vol. VII

Coad, Rev. Canon William Samuel, 1882–1965, vol. VI

Coade, Thorold Francis, 1896–1963, vol. VI

Coaker, Maj.-Gen. Ronald Edward, 1917–1983, vol. VIII

Coaker, Hon. Sir William Ford, 1871–1938, vol. III

Coakes, Ven. E. Lloyd, 1853–1930, vol. III

Coales, John Flavell, 1907–1999, vol. X

Coape-Arnold, Henry Fraser James; *see* Arnold.

Coape-Smith, Maj.-Gen. Henry, 1829–1921, vol. II

Coast, James Percy Chatterton, 1880–1962, vol. VI

Coatalen, Louis Hervé, 1879–1962, vol. VI

Coate, Rev. Harry, *died* 1939, vol. III

Coate, Maj.-Gen. Sir Raymond Douglas, 1908–1983, vol. VIII

Coaten, Arthur Wells, 1879–1939, vol. III (A), vol. IV

Coates, Abraham George, 1861–1928, vol. II

Coates, Albert, 1882–1953, vol. V

Coates, Sir Albert Ernest, 1895–1977, vol. VII

Coates, Captain Sir Clive Milnes-, 2nd Bt (*cr* 1911), 1879–1971, vol. VII

Coates, David Wilson, 1886–1968, vol. VI
Coates, Dora; see Meeson, D.
Coates, Edith, 1908–1983, vol. VIII
Coates, Major Sir Edward Feetham, 1st Bt (cr 1911), 1853–1921, vol. II
Coates, Eric, 1886–1957, vol. V
Coates, Sir Eric Thomas, 1897–1968, vol. VI
Coates, Sir Ernest William, 1916–1994, vol. IX
Coates, Florence Earle, died 1927, vol. II
Coates, Brig. Sir Frederick Gregory Lindsay, 1916–1994, vol. IX
Coates, George James, 1869–1930, vol. III
Coates, Henry, 1880–1963, vol. VI
Coates, Sir James Hugh Buchanan, 1851–1935, vol. III
Coates, John, 1865–1941, vol. IV
Coates, Rev. John Rider, 1879–1956, vol. V
Coates, Joseph Edward, 1883–1973, vol. VII
Coates, Rt Hon. Joseph Gordon, 1878–1943, vol. IV
Coates, Kenneth Howard, 1933–1998, vol. X
Coates, Sir Leonard James, 1883–1944, vol. IV
Coates, Patrick Devereux, 1916–1990, vol. VIII
Coates, Rev. Percy, 1855–1925, vol. II
Coates, Brig.-Gen. Reginald Carlyon, 1869–1958, vol. V
Coates, Sir Robert Edward James Clive M.; see Milnes Coates.
Coates, Maj.-Gen. Thomas Seymour, 1879–1954, vol. V
Coates, Wells Wintemute, 1895–1958, vol. V
Coates, Col Sir William, 1860–1962, vol. VI
Coates, Sir William Frederick, 1st Bt (cr 1921), 1866–1932, vol. III
Coates, Sir William Henry, 1882–1963, vol. VI
Coath, Howell Lang L.; see Lang-Coath.
Coatman, John, 1889–1963, vol. VI
Coats, Major Andrew, 1862–1930, vol. III
Coats, George, 1876–1915, vol. I
Coats, Col George Henry Brook, 1852–1919, vol. II
Coats, Sir James, 1st Bt (cr 1905), 1834–1913, vol. I
Coats, Sir James Stuart, 3rd Bt (cr 1905), 1894–1966, vol. VI
Coats, Rev. Jervis, 1844–1921, vol. II
Coats, Joseph, 1846–1899, vol. I
Coats, Robert Hamilton, 1874–1960, vol. V
Coats, Rev. Robert Hay, 1873–1956, vol. V
Coats, Air Cdre Rowland, 1904–1974, vol. VII
Coats, Sir Stuart Auchincloss, 2nd Bt (cr 1905), 1868–1959, vol. V
Coats, Sir Thomas Coats Glen Glen-, 2nd Bt (cr 1894), 1878–1954, vol. V
Coats, Sir Thomas Glen G., 1st Bt; see Glen-Coats.
Coats, Rev. Walter William, 1856–1941, vol. IV
Coats, William Hodge, 1866–1928, vol. II
Coatsworth, Emerson, 1854–1943, vol. IV
Cobb, Lt-Col Charles, 1884–1947, vol. IV
Cobb, Sir Cyril Stephen, 1861–1938, vol. III
Cobb, Captain Edward Charles, 1891–1957, vol. V
Cobb, Maj.-Gen. Edwyn Harland Wolstenholme, 1902–1955, vol. V
Cobb, Frederick Arthur, 1901–1950, vol. IV
Cobb, Geoffry Edward Wheatly, 1858–1931, vol. III
Cobb, Gerard Francis, 1838–1904, vol. I

Cobb, Col Henry Frederick, 1881–1939, vol. III
Cobb, Henry Venn, 1864–1949, vol. IV
Cobb, Ivo Geikie-, 1887–1953, vol. V
Cobb, Sir John Francis Scott, 1922–1977, vol. VII
Cobb, John Leslie, 1923–1977, vol. VII
Cobb, John Rhodes, 1899–1952, vol. V
Cobb, John William, 1873–1950, vol. IV
Cobb, Richard Charles, 1917–1996, vol. X
Cobb, Rear-Adm. Robert Harborne, 1900–1978, vol. VII
Cobb, Thomas, 1854–1932, vol. III
Cobb, Rev. William Frederick G.; see Geikie-Cobb.
Cobban, Alfred, 1901–1968, vol. VI
Cobban, Sir James Macdonald, 1910–1999, vol. X
Cobban, James MacLaren, 1849–1903, vol. I
Cobbe, Gen. Sir Alexander Stanhope, 1870–1931, vol. III
Cobbe, Frances Power, 1822–1904, vol. I
Cobbe, Col Henry Hercules, 1869–1939, vol. III
Cobbe, Hon. John George, died 1944, vol. IV
Cobbett, Louis, 1862–1947, vol. IV
Cobbett, Pitt, died 1919, vol. II
Cobbett, Sir Walter Palmer, 1871–1955, vol. V
Cobbett, Walter Willson, 1847–1937, vol. III
Cobbett, Sir William, 1846–1926, vol. II
Cobbold, 1st Baron, 1904–1987, vol. VIII
Cobbold, David; see Cobbold, M. D. N.
Cobbold, Lt-Col Ernest Cazenove, 1866–1932, vol. III
Cobbold, Lady Evelyn, died 1963, vol. VI
Cobbold, Felix Thornley, 1841–1909, vol. I
Cobbold, Herbert St George, died 1944, vol. IV
Cobbold, John Dupuis, 1861–1929, vol. III
Cobbold, Lt-Col John Murray, 1897–1944, vol. IV
Cobbold, (Michael) David (Nevill), 1919–1994, vol. IX
Cobbold, Patrick Mark, 1934–1994, vol. IX
Cobden, Lt-Col George Gough, 1878–1949, vol. IV
Cobden-Ramsay, Louis Eveleigh Bawtree, 1873–1962, vol. VI
Cobham, 8th Viscount, 1842–1922, vol. II
Cobham, 9th Viscount, 1881–1949, vol. IV
Cobham, 10th Viscount, 1909–1977, vol. VII
Cobham, 15th Baron, 1880–1933, vol. III
Cobham, 16th Baron, 1885–1951, vol. V
Cobham, Sir Alan John, 1894–1973, vol. VII
Cobham, Claude Delaval, 1842–1915, vol. I
Cobham, Brig.-Gen. Horace Walter, died 1958, vol. V
Cobham, Ven. John Lawrence, 1873–1960, vol. V, vol. VI
Cobham, Ven. John Oldcastle, 1899–1987, vol. VIII
Cobley, Walter Henry, 1850–1938, vol. III
Coborn, Charles, (Colin Whitton McCallum), 1852–1945, vol. IV
Coburn, Kathleen, 1905–1991, vol. IX
Coburn, Sir (Marmaduke) Robert, 1885–1966, vol. VI
Coburn, Sir Robert; see Coburn, Sir M. R.
Cochin, Rajah of, died 1932, vol. III
Cochin, Maharaja of, 1861–1941, vol. IV
Cochin, Maharaja of, died 1943, vol. IV
Cochin, Henry Denys Benoit Marie, 1854–1922, vol. II
Cochran, Alexander, died 1961, vol. VI

Cochran, Sir Charles Blake, 1872–1951, vol. V
Cochran, Vice-Adm. Charles Home, 1850–1930, vol. III
Cochran-Patrick, Major Charles Kennedy; *see* Patrick.
Cochran-Patrick, Sir Neil James Kennedy, 1866–1958, vol. V
Cochrane of Cults, 1st Baron, 1857–1951, vol. V
Cochrane of Cults, 2nd Baron, 1883–1968, vol. VI
Cochrane of Cults, 3rd Baron, 1922–1990, vol. VIII
Cochrane, Alfred, 1865–1948, vol. IV
Cochrane, Dame Anne Annette Minnie, *died* 1943, vol. IV
Cochrane, Rear-Adm. Archibald, 1874–1952, vol. V
Cochrane, Captain Hon. Sir Archibald Douglas, 1885–1958, vol. V
Cochrane, Hon. Sir Arthur Auckland Leopold Pedro, 1824–1905, vol. I
Cochrane, Sir Arthur William Steuart, 1872–1954, vol. V
Cochrane, Vice-Adm. Basil Edward, 1841–1922, vol. II
Cochrane, Sir Cecil Algernon, 1869–1960, vol. V
Cochrane, Mrs Catherine, 1849–1934, vol. III
Cochrane, Charles Walter Hamilton, 1876–1932, vol. III
Cochrane, Sir Desmond Oriel Alastair George Weston, 3rd Bt (*cr* 1903), 1918–1979, vol. VII
Cochrane, Rev. Canon Edmund Lewis, 1876–1955, vol. V
Cochrane, Rear-Adm. Sir Edward Owen, 1881–1972, vol. VII
Cochrane, Captain Sir Ernest Cecil, 2nd Bt (*cr* 1903), 1873–1952, vol. V
Cochrane, Captain Hon. Ernest Grey Lambton, 1834–1911, vol. I
Cochrane, Hon. Francis, 1852–1919, vol. II
Cochrane, Helen Lavinia, *died* 1946, vol. IV
Cochrane, Sir Henry, 1st Bt (*cr* 1903), *died* 1904, vol. I
Cochrane, Brig.-Gen. James Kilvington, 1873–1948, vol. IV
Cochrane, Maj.-Gen. James Rupert, 1904–1978, vol. VII
Cochrane, Col John Ernest Charles James, 1870–1938, vol. III
Cochrane, Julia Dorothy, (Hon. Lady Cochrane), 1888–1971, vol. VII
Cochrane, Lt-Col R. C., 1871–1925, vol. III
Cochrane, Air Chief Marshal Hon. Sir Ralph Alexander, 1895–1977, vol. VII
Cochrane, Robert Greenhill, 1899–1985, vol. VIII
Cochrane, Sir Stanley Herbert, 1st Bt (*cr* 1915), 1877–1949, vol. IV
Cochrane, Col Thomas Henry, 1867–1950, vol. IV
Cochrane, Col William Francis Dundonald, 1847–1928, vol. II
Cock, Rev. Albert A., 1883–1953, vol. V
Cock, F. William, 1858–1943, vol. IV
Cock, Gerald, 1887–1973, vol. VII
Cock, Henry, 1842–1922, vol. II
Cock, Julia, *died* 1914, vol. I
Cockayne, Edward Alfred, 1880–1956, vol. V
Cockayne, Dame Elizabeth, 1894–1988, vol. VIII
Cockayne, Leonard, 1855–1934, vol. III

Cockbill, Ven. Charles Shipley, 1888–1965, vol. VI
Cockburn, Archibald William, 1887–1969, vol. VI
Cockburn, Col Charles Douglas L.; *see* Learoyd-Cockburn.
Cockburn, Claud, 1904–1981, vol. VIII
Cockburn, Sir Edward Cludde, 8th Bt, 1834–1903, vol. I
Cockburn, Major Ernest Radcliffe, 1875–1955, vol. V
Cockburn, Col George, 1856–1925, vol. II
Cockburn, Sir George Jack, 1848–1927, vol. II
Cockburn, Major H. Z. C., *died* 1913, vol. I
Cockburn, Henry, 1859–1927, vol. II
Cockburn, Gen. Henry Alexander, 1831–1922, vol. II
Cockburn, Very Rev. James Hutchinson, 1882–1973, vol. VII
Cockburn, Sir James Stanhope, 10th Bt, 1867–1947, vol. IV
Cockburn, Hon. Sir John Alexander, 1850–1929, vol. III
Cockburn, Lt-Col Sir John Brydges, 11th Bt, 1870–1949, vol. IV
Cockburn, Nathaniel Clayton, 1866–1924, vol. II
Cockburn, Sir Robert, 9th Bt, 1861–1938, vol. III
Cockburn, Sir Robert, 1909–1994, vol. IX
Cockburn, Captain William, 1893–1970, vol. VI
Cockburn, Sir William Robert Marshall, 1891–1957, vol. V
Cockburn-Campbell, Sir Alexander Thomas; *see* Campbell.
Cockburn-Campbell, Sir Thomas, 6th Bt, 1918–1999, vol. X
Cockcraft, Lt-Col Louis William la Trobe, 1880–1963, vol. VI
Cockcroft, Janet Rosemary, 1916—2000, vol. X
Cockcroft, Sir John Douglas, 1897–1967, vol. VI
Cockcroft, Sir Wilfred Halliday, 1923–1999, vol. X
Cocke, Sir Hugh, *died* 1958, vol. V
Cockell, Seton F.; *see* Forbes-Cockell.
Cocker, Ralph, 1908–1986, vol. VIII
Cocker, William Hollis, 1896–1962, vol. VI
Cocker, Sir William Wiggins, 1896–1982, vol. VIII
Cockeram, William Henry, 1857–1946, vol. IV
Cockerell, Sir Christopher Sydney, 1910–1999, vol. X
Cockerell, Douglas Bennett, 1870–1945, vol. IV
Cockerell, Horace Abel, 1832–1908, vol. I
Cockerell, Sir Sydney Carlyle, 1867–1962, vol. VI
Cockerell, Sydney Morris, 1906–1987, vol. VIII
Cockerill, Brig.-Gen. Sir George Kynaston, 1867–1957, vol. V
Cockerline, Sir Walter Herbert, 1856–1941, vol. IV
Cockey, Air Cdre Leonard Herbert, 1893–1978, vol. VII
Cockin, Rt Rev. Frederic Arthur, 1888–1969, vol. VI
Cockin, Rt Rev. George Eyles Irwin, 1908–1996, vol. X
Cockin, Ven John Irwin Browne, 1850–1924, vol. II
Cocking, John Martin, 1914–1986, vol. VIII
Cocking, William Trusting, 1862–1912, vol. I
Cockram, Ben, 1903–1981, vol. VIII
Cockram, George, 1861–1950, vol. IV
Cockram, Sir John, 1908–1999, vol. X

Cockran, William Bourke, 1854–1923, vol. II
Cocks, Hon. Sir Arthur Alfred Clement, 1862–1943, vol. IV
Cocks, Sir Barnett; see Cocks, Sir T. G. B.
Cocks, Charles Sebastian Somers, 1870–1951, vol. V
Cocks, Rt Rev. Francis William, 1913–1998, vol. X
Cocks, Frederick Seymour, 1882–1953, vol. V
Cocks, George Arthur, died 1933, vol. III
Cocks, Rev. Henry Lawrence S.; see Somers-Cocks.
Cocks, John Sebastian S.; see Somers Cocks.
Cocks, John Somers-; see Somers, 8th Baron.
Cocks, Philip Alphonso Somers, 1862–1940, vol. III
Cocks, Sir (Thomas George) Barnett, 1907–1989, vol. VIII
Cockshutt, Col Hon. Henry, 1868–1944, vol. IV
Cocoto, Spiridon Gerge, 1843–1916, vol. II
Cocteau, Jean, 1889–1963, vol. VI
Codd, Rt Rev. William, 1864–1938, vol. III
Coddington, Fitzherbert John Osbourne, 1881–1956, vol. V
Coddington, Col Herbert Adolphe, 1864–1939, vol. III
Coddington, Sir William, 1st Bt, 1830–1918, vol. II
Code, Rev. Canon George Brereton, 1886–1946, vol. IV
Code Holland, Robert Henry; see Holland.
Coderre, Louis, 1865–1935, vol. III
Codling, Sir William Richard, 1879–1947, vol. IV
Codner, Maurice Frederick, 1888–1958, vol. V
Codrington, Lt-Gen. Sir Alfred Edward, 1854–1945, vol. IV
Codrington, Sir Christopher William Gerald Henry, 2nd Bt (cr 1876), 1894–1979, vol. VII
Codrington, Engr-Comdr Claude Alexander, 1877–1955, vol. V
Codrington, Col Sir Geoffrey Ronald, 1888–1973, vol. VII
Codrington, Sir Gerald William Henry, 1st Bt (cr 1876), 1850–1929, vol. III
Codrington, Brig.-Gen. Hubert Walter, 1864–1940, vol. III
Codrington, Kenneth de Burgh, 1899–1986, vol. VIII
Codrington, Robert Edward, 1869–1908, vol. I
Codrington, Rev. Robert Henry, 1830–1922, vol. II
Codrington, Sir William Mary Joseph, 5th Bt (cr 1721), 1829–1904, vol. I
Codrington, William Melville, 1892–1963, vol. VI
Codrington, Sir William Richard, 7th Bt (cr 1721), 1904–1961, vol. VI
Codrington, Lt-Col Sir William Robert, 6th Bt (cr 1721), 1867–1932, vol. III
Cody, Rev. Henry John, 1868–1951, vol. V
Coe, Captain; see Mitchell, Edward Card.
Coe, Peter Leonard, 1929–1987, vol. VIII
Coen, Sir Terence Bernard C.; see Creagh Coen.
Coffer, David Edwin, 1913–1998, vol. X
Coffey, Christopher, 1902–1976, vol. VII
Coffey, Denis Joseph, died 1945, vol. IV
Coffey, George, 1857–1916, vol. II
Coffey, Rt Rev. John, died 1904, vol. I
Coffey, John Nimmo, 1929–1981, vol. VIII
Coffey, Rev. Peter, 1876–1943, vol. IV
Coffey, Hon. Thomas, 1843–1914, vol. I

Coffey, Thomas Malo, 1894–1968, vol. VI
Coffin, Col Campbell, 1867–1952, vol. V
Coffin, Charles Hayden, 1862–1935, vol. III
Coffin, Maj.-Gen. Clifford, 1870–1959, vol. V
Coffin, Rev. Henry Sloane, 1877–1954, vol. V
Coffin, Major John Edward P.; see Pine-Coffin.
Coffin, Gen. Roger P.; see Pine-Coffin.
Coffin, Walter Harris, 1853–1916, vol. II
Cofman-Nicoresti, Carol Adolph, 1881–1938, vol. III (A), vol. IV
Cogan, Rev. Horace Barbut, died 1933, vol. III
Coggan, Baron (Life Peer); Rt Rev. and Rt Hon. Frederick Donald Coggan, 1909–2000, vol. X
Coghill, Col Charles Edward, 1861–1948, vol. IV
Coghill, Douglas Harry, 1855–1928, vol. II
Coghill, Sir Egerton Bushe, 5th Bt, 1853–1921, vol. II
Coghill, Sir Egerton James Nevill Tobias, (Sir Toby), 8th Bt, 1930–2000, vol. X
Coghill, Rev. Canon Ernest Arthur, 1859–1941, vol. IV
Coghill, Sir John Joscelyn, 4th Bt, 1826–1905, vol. I
Coghill, John Percival, 1902–1984, vol. VIII
Coghill, Sir Joscelyn Ambrose Cramer, 7th Bt, 1902–1983, vol. VIII
Coghill, Col Kendal Josiah William, 1832–1919, vol. II
Coghill, Sir (Marmaduke Nevill) Patrick (Somerville), 6th Bt, 1896–1981, vol. VIII
Coghill, Nevill Henry Kendal Aylmer, 1899–1980, vol. VII
Coghill, Sir Patrick; see Coghill, Sir M. N. P. S.
Coghill, Sir Toby; see Coghill, Sir E. J. N. T.
Coghlan, Col Charles, 1852–1921, vol. II
Coghlan, Hon. Sir Charles Patrick John, 1863–1927, vol. II
Coghlan, Rt Rev. Mgr John, 1887–1963, vol. VI
Coghlan, Hon. Sir Timothy Augustine, 1857–1926, vol. II
Cogswell, Mark James, died 1934, vol. III
Cogswell, Rev. Canon William, 1845–1917, vol. II
Cohalan, Most Rev. Daniel, 1858–1952, vol. V
Cohalan, Most Rev. Daniel, 1884–1965, vol. VI
Cohan, George Michael, 1878–1942, vol. IV
Cohen, Baron (Life Peer); Lionel Leonard Cohen, 1888–1973, vol. VII
Cohen of Birkenhead, 1st Baron, 1900–1977, vol. VII
Cohen of Brighton, Baron (Life Peer); Lewis Coleman Cohen, 1897–1966, vol. VI
Cohen, Sir Andrew Benjamin, 1909–1968, vol. VI
Cohen, Arthur; see Cohen, N. A. J.
Cohen, Rt Hon. Arthur, 1830–1914, vol. I
Cohen, Arthur S.; see Sefton-Cohen.
Cohen, Augustus, died 1903, vol. I
Cohen, Sir Benjamin Arthur, 1862–1942, vol. IV
Cohen, Sir Benjamin Louis, 1st Bt, 1844–1909, vol. I
Cohen, Sir Bernard Nathaniel W.; see Waley-Cohen.
Cohen, Major Sir Brunel; see Cohen, Major Sir J. B. B.
Cohen, Lt-Col Charles Waley, 1879–1963, vol. VI
Cohen, Clifford Theodore, 1906–1972, vol. VII
Cohen, Sir Edgar Abraham, 1908–1973, vol. VII

Cohen, Rabbi Francis Lyon, 1862–1934, vol. III
Cohen, George Cormack, 1909–1999, vol. X
Cohen, Hannah F., *died* 1946, vol. IV
Cohen, Brig. Hon. Harold Edward, 1881–1946, vol. IV
Cohen, Harriet, 1895–1967, vol. VI
Cohen, Harry F.; *see* Freeman-Cohen.
Cohen, Hon. Henry Emanuel, 1840–1912, vol. I
Cohen, Hon. Henry Isaac, 1872–1942, vol. IV
Cohen, Sir Herbert Benjamin, 2nd Bt, 1874–1968, vol. VI
Cohen, Isaac Michael, 1884–1951, vol. V
Cohen, Israel, 1879–1961, vol. VI
Cohen, Sir Jack, 1896–1982, vol. VIII
Cohen, Major Sir (Jack Benn) Brunel, 1886–1965, vol. VI
Cohen, Col Jacob Waley, 1874–1948, vol. IV
Cohen, Sir John Edward, 1898–1979, vol. VII
Cohen, John, 1911–1985, vol. VIII
Cohen, John Michael, 1903–1989, vol. VIII
Cohen, Joseph L., *died* 1940, vol. III
Cohen, Julius Berend, 1859–1935, vol. III
Cohen, Sir Karl Cyril, *died* 1973, vol. VII
Cohen, Comdr Kenneth H. S., 1900–1984, vol. VIII
Cohen, Sir Leonard Lionel, 1858–1938, vol. III
Cohen, Sir Lewis, 1849–1933, vol. III
Cohen, Louis, 1925–1997, vol. X
Cohen, Marcel, 1884–1974, vol. VII
Cohen, Mary Gwendolen, (Mrs Arthur M. Cohen), 1893–1962, vol. VI
Cohen, Nat, 1905–1988, vol. VIII
Cohen, Lt-Col Nathan Leslie, 1908–2000, vol. X
Cohen, (Nathaniel) Arthur Jim, 1898–1995, vol. IX
Cohen, Mrs Nathaniel Louis, *died* 1917, vol. II
Cohen, Percy, 1891–1987, vol. VIII
Cohen, Reuben, 1880–1958, vol. V
Cohen, Reuben K.; *see* Kelf-Cohen.
Cohen, Sir Rex Arthur Louis, 1906–1988, vol. VIII
Cohen, Richard Henry Lionel, 1907–1998, vol. X
Cohen, Sir Robert Waley, 1877–1952, vol. V
Cohen, Ruth Louisa, 1906–1991, vol. IX
Cohen, Samuel; *see* Cahn, Sammy.
Cohen, Sir Samuel Sydney, 1869–1948, vol. IV
Cohen, Jefferson Davis, 1881–1951, vol. V
Coia, Jack Antonio, 1898–1981, vol. VIII
Coiley, John Arthur, 1932–1998, vol. X
Coit, Stanton, 1857–1944, vol. IV
Cokayne, George Edward, 1825–1911, vol. I
Coke, Adm. Sir Charles Henry, 1854–1945, vol. IV
Coke, Charlotte, (Mrs Talbot Coke), 1843–1922, vol. II
Coke, Captain Desmond, 1879–1931, vol. III
Coke, Dorothy Josephine, 1897–1979, vol. VII (AII)
Coke, Brig.-Gen. Edward Beresford, 1850–1924, vol. II
Coke, Brig.-Gen. Edward Sacheverell D'Ewes, 1872–1941, vol. IV
Coke, Gerald Edward, 1907–1990, vol. VIII
Coke, Hon. Henry John, 1827–1916, vol. II
Coke, Col Jacynth d'Ewes FitzErcald, 1879–1963, vol. VI
Coke, Sir John, 1807–1897, vol. I
Coke, Captain John Gilbert de Odingsells, 1874–1937, vol. III

Coke, Major Hon. Sir John Spencer, 1880–1957, vol. V
Coke, Maj.-Gen. John Talbot, 1841–1912, vol. I
Coke, Captain Hon. Reginald, 1883–1969, vol. VI
Coke, Major Hon. Richard, 1876–1964, vol. VI
Coke, Comdr Hon. Roger, 1886–1960, vol. V
Coke, Mrs Talbot; *see* Coke, Charlotte.
Coke, Lt-Col Wenman Clarence Walpole, 1828–1907, vol. I
Coke Wallis, Leonard George, 1900–1974, vol. VII
Coker, Col Edmund Rogers, 1844–1914, vol. I
Coker, Dame Elizabeth, 1915–1988, vol. VIII
Coker, Ernest George, 1869–1946, vol. IV
Coker, Sir Salako Ambrosius B.; *see* Benka-Coker.
Colahan, Nicholas Whistler, *died* 1930, vol. III
Colahan, Air Vice-Marshal William Edward, 1923–1991, vol. IX
Colam, Sir Harold Nugent, 1882–1956, vol. V
Colam, Robert Frederick, *died* 1942, vol. IV
Colban, Erik Andreas, 1876–1956, vol. V
Colbeck, Edmund Henry, 1865–1942, vol. IV
Colbeck-Welch, Air Vice-Marshal Edward Lawrence, 1914–1994, vol. IX
Colbert, Claudette, 1903–1996, vol. X
Colbert, John Patrick, 1898–1975, vol. VII
Colborne, Col Hon. Francis Lionel Lydstone, 1855–1924, vol. II
Colborne, Surg. Rear-Adm. William John, 1865–1945, vol. IV
Colborne, Surg. Rear-Adm. William John, *died* 1971, vol. VII
Colburn, Oscar Henry, 1925–1990, vol. VIII
Colby, Col Cecil John Herbert S.; *see* Spence-Colby.
Colby, Charles W., 1867–1955, vol. V
Colby, Sir Geoffrey Francis Taylor, 1901–1958, vol. V
Colchester, 3rd Baron, 1842–1919, vol. II
Colchester, Rev. Halsey Sparrowe, 1918–1995, vol. IX
Colchester, Nicholas Benedict Sparrowe, 1946–1996, vol. X
Colchester-Wemyss, Sir Francis, 1872–1954, vol. V
Colchester-Wemyss, Maynard Willoughby, 1846–1930, vol. III
Colclough, Rear-Adm. (S) Beauchamp Urquhart, 1867–1949, vol. IV
Coldrick, Albert Percival, (Percy), 1913–1999, vol. X
Coldrick, Percy; *see* Coldrick, A. P.
Coldrick, William, 1896–1975, vol. VII
Coldridge, Ward, 1864–1926, vol. II
Coldstream, Sir John, 1877–1954, vol. V
Coldstream, John Phillips, 1842–1909, vol. I
Coldstream, Col William Menzies, 1869–1943, vol. IV
Coldstream, Sir William Menzies, 1908–1987, vol. VIII
Coldwell, Hon. George Robson, 1858–1924, vol. II
Coldwell-Smith, Lt-Col Frederick Lawrence, 1895–1967, vol. VI (AII)
Cole, Viscount; Michael Galbraith Lowry Cole, 1921–1956, vol. V
Cole, Baron (Life Peer); George James Cole, 1906–1979, vol. VII

Cole, Air Vice-Marshal Adrian Trevor, 1895–1966, vol. VI
Cole, Alan Summerly, 1846–1934, vol. III
Cole, Alfred Clayton, 1854–1920, vol. II
Cole, Vice-Adm. Sir Antony Bartholomew, 1909–1967, vol. VI
Cole, Brig.-Gen. Arthur Willoughby George Lowry, 1860–1915, vol. I
Cole, Major Aubrey du Plat Thorold, 1877–1939, vol. III
Cole, Madame Belle, died 1904, vol. I
Cole, Boris Norman, 1924–1999, vol. X
Cole, Charles Woolsey, 1906–1978, vol. VII
Cole, Sir David Lee, 1920–1997, vol. X
Cole, Col Sir Edward Hearle, 1863–1949, vol. IV
Cole, Edward Nicholas, 1909–1977, vol. VII
Cole, Rev. Edward Pattinson, died 1926, vol. II
Cole, Eric Kirkham, 1901–1966, vol. VI
Cole, Maj.-Gen. Eric Stuart, 1906–1992, vol. IX
Cole, Francis Joseph, 1872–1959, vol. V
Cole, George, died 1913, vol. I
Cole, George Douglas Howard, 1889–1959, vol. V
Cole, Lt-Gen. Sir George Sinclair, 1911–1973, vol. VII
Cole, Maj.-Gen. George Wynne, 1836–1908, vol. I
Cole, Grenville Arthur James, 1859–1924, vol. II
Cole, Harold William, 1884–1959, vol. V
Cole, Lt-Col Henry W.; see Wells-Cole.
Cole, Lt-Col Sir Henry Walter George, died 1932, vol. III
Cole, Herbert Aubrey, 1911–1984, vol. VIII
Cole, Maj.-Gen. Sir Herbert Covington, died 1959, vol. V
Cole, James S.; see Stuart-Cole.
Cole, John, 1903–1975, vol. VII
Cole, Rev. John Francis, died 1921, vol. II
Cole, John Sydney Richard, 1907–1989, vol. VIII
Cole, Leslie Barrett, 1898–1983, vol. VIII
Cole, Dame Margaret Isabel, 1893–1980, vol. VII
Cole, Monica Mary, 1922–1994, vol. IX
Cole, Sir Noel, 1892–1975, vol. VII
Cole, Norman John, 1909–1979, vol. VII
Cole, Percival Pasley, died 1948, vol. IV
Cole, Percy Frederick, 1882–1968, vol. VI
Cole, Reginald John Vicat; see Cole, John.
Cole, Rex Vicat, 1870–1940, vol. III
Cole, Gp Captain Robert Arthur Alexander, 1901–1949, vol. IV
Cole, Rev. Robert Eden George, died 1921, vol. II
Cole, Robert Henry, 1866–1926, vol. II
Cole, Ven. Robert Henry, died 1934, vol. III
Cole, Robert Langton, 1858–1928, vol. II
Cole, Robin John, 1935–1988, vol. VIII
Cole, Ven. Ronald Berkeley, 1913–1996, vol. X
Cole, Sophie, 1862–1947, vol. IV
Cole, Lt-Col Stanley James, 1884–1949, vol. IV
Cole, Rev. Theodore Edward Fortescue, died 1944, vol. IV
Cole, Thomas Loftus, died 1961, vol. VI
Cole, Walton Adamson, 1912–1963, vol. VI
Cole, William Charles, 1909–1997, vol. X
Cole, Rev. William John, died 1933, vol. III
Cole, Maj.-Gen. William Scott, 1902–1992, vol. IX
Cole-Deacon, Gerald John, 1890–1968, vol. VI
Cole-Hamilton, Lt-Col Claud George; see Hamilton.

Cole-Hamilton, John, 1899–1991, vol. IX
Cole-Hamilton, Air Vice-Marshal John Beresford, 1894–1945, vol. IV
Colebatch, Hon. Sir Hal Pateshall, 1872–1953, vol. V
Colebrook, Edward Hilder, 1898–1977, vol. VII
Colebrook, Leonard, 1883–1967, vol. VI
Colebrooke, 1st Baron, 1861–1939, vol. III
Colefax, Sir Arthur, died 1936, vol. III
Colegate, Sir Arthur, died 1956, vol. V
Coleman, Arthur Percy, 1922–2001, vol. X
Coleman, Arthur Philemon, 1852–1939, vol. III
Coleman, Lt-Gen. Sir Charles; see Coleman, Lt-Gen. Sir C. F. C.
Coleman, Charles James, died 1908, vol. I
Coleman, Lt-Gen. Sir (Cyril Frederick) Charles, died 1974, vol. VII
Coleman, D'Alton Corry, 1879–1956, vol. V
Coleman, Donald Cuthbert, 1920–1995, vol. IX
Coleman, Donald Richard, 1925–1991, vol. IX
Coleman, Ephraim Herbert, 1890–1961, vol. VI
Coleman, Frank, 1876–1962, vol. VI
Coleman, Lt-Col George Burdett, died 1923, vol. II
Coleman, Herbert Cecil, 1893–1965, vol. VI
Coleman, Rev. James, 1831–1913, vol. I
Coleman, Rt Rev. John Aloysius, 1887–1947, vol. IV, vol. V
Coleman, Laurence Vail, 1893–1982, vol. VIII
Coleman, Leslie Charles, died 1954, vol. V
Coleman, Rt Rev. Michael Edward, 1902–1969, vol. VI
Coleman, Rev. Canon Noel Dolben, 1891–1948, vol. IV
Coleman, Rt Rev. William Robert, 1917–1992, vol. IX
Colenbrander, Col Johann William, 1859–1918, vol. II
Coleraine, 1st Baron, 1901–1980, vol. VII
Coleridge, 2nd Baron, 1851–1927, vol. II
Coleridge, 3rd Baron, 1877–1955, vol. V
Coleridge, 4th Baron, 1905–1984, vol. VIII
Coleridge, Christabel Rose, 1843–1921, vol. II
Coleridge, Ernest Hartley, 1846–1920, vol. II
Coleridge, Hon. Gilbert James Duke, 1859–1953, vol. V
Coleridge, Lt-Col Hugh Fortescue, 1859–1928, vol. II
Coleridge, Gen. Sir John Francis Stanhope Duke, 1878–1951, vol. V
Coleridge, Miss Mary Elizabeth, 1861–1907, vol. I
Coleridge, Hon. Stephen, 1854–1936, vol. III
Coleridge, Wilfrid Duke, 1889–1956, vol. V
Coleridge-Taylor, Samuel, 1875–1912, vol. I
Coles, Captain Arthur Edward, 1902–1982, vol. VIII
Coles, Col Arthur Horsman, 1856–1931, vol. III
Coles, Sir Arthur William, 1892–1982, vol. VIII
Coles, Bryan Randell, 1926–1997, vol. X
Coles, Charles, 1853–1926, vol. II
Coles, Charles, 1878–1947, vol. IV
Coles, Sir Edgar Barton, 1899–1981, vol. VIII
Coles, Edward Horsman, 1865–1948, vol. IV
Coles, Sir George James, 1885–1977, vol. VII
Coles, Gordon Robert, 1913–1975, vol. VII
Coles, Hon. Sir Jenkin, 1842–1911, vol. I
Coles, John, died 1919, vol. II

Coles, Sir Kenneth Frank, 1896–1985, vol. VIII
Coles, Dame Mabel Irene, *died* 1993, vol. IX
Coles, Col Morton Calverley, 1863–1943, vol. IV
Coles, Norman, 1914–1999, vol. X
Coles, Sir Norman Cameron, 1907–1989, vol. VIII
Coles, Sir Richard James, 1862–1935, vol. III
Coles, Sherard Osborn C.; *see* Cowper-Coles.
Coles, Rev. Vincent Stuckey Stratton, 1845–1929, vol. III
Coles, Air Marshal Sir William Edward, 1913–1979, vol. VII
Coles, Major William Hewett, 1882–1955, vol. V
Colette, 1873–1954, vol. V
Coley, Frederic Collins, *died* 1928, vol. II
Coley, (Howard William) Maitland, 1910–1981, vol. VIII
Coley, Maitland; *see* Coley, H. W. M.
Colfox, Lt-Col Sir Philip; *see* Colfox, Lt-Col Sir W. P.
Colfox, Lt-Col Sir (William) Philip, 1st Bt, 1888–1966, vol. VI
Colgan, Most Rev. Joseph, 1824–1911, vol. I
Colgate, Dennis Harvey, 1922–1990, vol. VIII
Colgrain, 1st Baron, 1866–1954, vol. V
Colgrain, 2nd Baron, 1891–1973, vol. VII
Colijn, Hendrikus, 1869–1944, vol. IV
Colin, Rt Rev. Gerald Fitzmaurice, 1913–1995, vol. IX
Colivet, Michael Patrick, 1884–1955, vol. V
Coll, Sir Anthony Michael, 1861–1931, vol. III
Collar, (Arthur) Roderick, 1908–1986, vol. VIII
Collar, Roderick; *see* Collar, A. R.
Collard, Maj.-Gen. Albert Sydney, 1876–1938, vol. III (A), vol. IV
Collard, Col Alexander Arthur Lysons, 1871–1947, vol. IV
Collard, Major Alfred Stephen, 1865–1941, vol. IV
Collard, Allan Ovenden, 1861–1928, vol. II
Collard, Vice-Adm. Bernard St G., 1876–1962, vol. VI
Collard, Lt-Col Charles Edwin, *died* 1942, vol. IV
Collard, Sir George, 1840–1921, vol. II
Collard, Patrick John, 1920–1989, vol. VIII
Collard, Gp Captain Richard Charles Marler, 1911–1962, vol. VI
Collcutt, Thomas Edward, 1840–1924, vol. II
Colledge, Lionel, 1883–1948, vol. IV
Collen, Lt-Col Edwin Henry Ethelbert, 1875–1943, vol. IV
Collen, Lt-Gen. Sir Edwin Henry Hayter, 1843–1911, vol. I
Collens, John Antony, 1930–1988, vol. VIII
Coller, Frank Herbert, 1866–1938, vol. III
Colles, Comdr Sir Dudley; *see* Colles, Comdr Sir E. D. G.
Colles, Comdr Sir (Ernest) Dudley (Gordon), 1889–1976, vol. VII
Colles, Henry Cope, 1879–1943, vol. IV
Colles, Ramsay, 1862–1919, vol. II
Colles, William Morris, *died* 1926, vol. II
Collet, Clara E., 1860–1948, vol. IV
Collet, Sir Mark Edlmann, 2nd Bt, 1864–1944, vol. IV
Collet, Sir Mark Wilks, 1st Bt, 1816–1905, vol. I
Collet, Sir Wilfred, 1856–1929, vol. III

Colleton, Sir Robert Augustus William, 9th Bt, 1854–1938, vol. III
Collett, Charles Benjamin, 1871–1952, vol. V
Collett, Sir Charles Henry, 1st Bt, 1864–1938, vol. III
Collett, Rear-Adm. George Kempthorne, 1907–1982, vol. VIII
Collett, Sir Henry, 1836–1901, vol. I
Collett, Sir Henry Seymour, 2nd Bt, 1893–1971, vol. VII
Collett, Col Hon. Herbert Brayley, 1877–1947, vol. IV
Collett, Col John Henry, 1876–1942, vol. IV
Collett, Sir Kingsley; *see* Collett, Sir T. K.
Collett, Rt Rev. Dom Martin, 1879–1948, vol. IV
Collett, Sir (Thomas) Kingsley, 1906–1987, vol. VIII
Collette, Charles, 1842–1924, vol. II
Colley, David Isherwood, 1916–1975, vol. VII
Colley, Richard, 1893–1964, vol. VI
Colley, Robert D.; *see* Davies-Colley.
Colley, Thomas, 1894–1983, vol. VIII
Collick, Percy Henry, 1899–1984, vol. VIII
Collie, Alexander Conn, 1913–1999, vol. X
Collie, J. Norman, 1859–1942, vol. IV
Collie, Sir John, 1860–1935, vol. III
Collie, Ruth, *died* 1936, vol. III
Collier, Air Vice-Marshal Sir (Alfred) Conrad, 1895–1986, vol. VIII
Collier, Maj.-Gen. Angus Lyell, 1893–1971, vol. VII
Collier, Charles Saint John, 1880–1944, vol. IV
Collier, Air Vice-Marshal Sir Conrad; *see* Collier, Air Vice-Marshal, Sir A. C.
Collier, Constance, 1880–1955, vol. V
Collier, Dorothy Josephine, 1894–1972, vol. VII
Collier, Lt-Col Ernest Victor, 1878–1964, vol. VI
Collier, Frank Simon, 1900–1964, vol. VI
Collier, Frederick William, 1851–1925, vol. II
Collier, Sir George Herman, 1856–1941, vol. IV
Collier, Gerald; *see* Collier, K. G.
Collier, Horace Stansfield, *died* 1930, vol. III
Collier, James, 1846–1925, vol. II (A), vol. III
Collier, James, 1870–1935, vol. III
Collier, Hon. John, 1850–1934, vol. III
Collier, John Francis, 1829–1913, vol. I
Collier, John Gordon, 1935–1995, vol. IX
Collier, Joseph, *died* 1967, vol. VI
Collier, Air Cdre Kenneth Dowsett Gould, 1892–1971, vol. VII
Collier, (Kenneth) Gerald, 1910–1998, vol. X
Collier, Sir Laurence, 1890–1976, vol. VII
Collier, Hon. Margaret Isabella; *see* Galletti di Cadilhac, Countess.
Collier, Marie Elizabeth, 1927–1971, vol. VII
Collier, Mayo, 1857–1931, vol. III
Collier, Most Rev. Patrick, 1880–1964, vol. VI
Collier, Peter Fenelon, 1849–1909, vol. I
Collier, Hon. Philip, 1874–1948, vol. IV
Collier, Rev. Samuel Francis, 1855–1921, vol. II
Collier, Rev. Thomas Grey, 1844–1933, vol. III
Collier, William, 1856–1935, vol. III
Collier, William Adrian Larry, 1913–1984, vol. VIII
Collier, William Douglas, 1894–1953, vol. V
Colligan, John Clifford, 1906–1999, vol. X

Collin, Annie Rosalie, 1852–1957, vol. V
Collindridge, Frank, *died* 1951, vol. V
Colling, Rev. James, *died* 1929, vol. III
Collinge, Walter E., *died* 1947, vol. IV
Collingridge, George Rooke, 1867–1944, vol. IV
Collingridge, William, 1854–1927, vol. II
Collings, Albert Henry, *died* 1947, vol. IV
Collings, Col Alfred Henry, 1847–1933, vol. III
Collings, Col Godfrey Disney, 1855–1941, vol. IV
Collings, Rt Hon. Jesse, 1831–1920, vol. II
Collings, Maj.-Gen. Wilfred d'Auvergne,
  1893–1984, vol. VIII
Collingwood, Adrian Redman, 1910–1987, vol. VIII
Collingwood, Arthur, 1879–1952, vol. V
Collingwood, Bertram James, *died* 1934, vol. III
Collingwood, Sir Charles Arthur, 1887–1964, vol. VI
Collingwood, Brig.-Gen. Clennell William,
  1873–1960, vol. V
Collingwood, Cuthbert, 1826–1908, vol. I
Collingwood, Rt Rev. Mgr Canon Cuthbert,
  1908–1980, vol. VII
Collingwood, Col Cuthbert George, 1848–1933,
  vol. III
Collingwood, Sir Edward Foyle, 1900–1970, vol. VI
Collingwood, Lt-Gen. Sir George; *see* Collingwood,
  Lt-Gen. Sir R. G.
Collingwood, Rear-Adm. George Trevor,
  1863–1922, vol. II
Collingwood, Harry; *see* Lancaster, W. J. C.
Collingwood, Lawrance Arthur, 1887–1982,
  vol. VIII
Collingwood, Lt-Gen. Sir (Richard) George,
  1903–1986, vol. VIII
Collingwood, Robin George, 1889–1943, vol. IV
Collingwood, Brig. Sydney, 1892–1986, vol. VIII
Collingwood, Sir William, 1855–1928, vol. II
Collingwood, William Gershom, 1854–1932, vol. III
Collins, Baron (Life Peer); Richard Henn Collins,
  1842–1911, vol. I
Collins, Alfred Tenison, 1852–1945, vol. IV
Collins, Sir Archibald John, 1890–1955, vol. V
Collins, Lt-Col Arthur, 1845–1911, vol. I
Collins, Arthur, 1880–1952, vol. V
Collins, Arthur Ernest, 1871–1926, vol. II
Collins, Brig. Arthur Francis St Clair, 1892–1980,
  vol. VII
Collins, Sir Arthur James Robert, 1911–2000, vol. X
Collins, Arthur Jefferies, 1893–1976, vol. VII
Collins, Sir Arthur John Hammond, 1834–1915,
  vol. I
Collins, Arthur Pelham, 1863–1932, vol. III
Collins, Bernard Abdy, 1880–1951, vol. V
Collins, Bernard John, 1909–1989, vol. VIII
Collins, Charles, *died* 1921, vol. II
Collins, Maj.-Gen. Charles Edward E.; *see*
  Edward-Collins.
Collins, Sir Charles Henry, 1887–1983, vol. VIII
Collins, Cyril George, 1880–1947, vol. IV
Collins, Dale, 1897–1956, vol. V
Collins, Sir D(aniel) George, 1869–1959, vol. V
Collins, Sir David Charles, 1908–1983, vol. VIII
Collins, Maj.-Gen. Dennis Joseph, *died* 1939,
  vol. III
Collins, Douglas, 1912–1972, vol. VII
Collins, Douglas Henry, 1907–1964, vol. VI

Collins, Maj.-Gen. Sir Dudley Stuart, 1881–1959,
  vol. V
Collins, Edward Treacher, 1862–1932, vol. III
Collins, Adm. Sir Frederick (Basset) E.; *see*
  Edward-Collins.
Collins, Sir Geoffrey Abdy, 1888–1986, vol. VIII
Collins, Sir George, *see* Collins, Sir D. G.
Collins, George Edward, 1880–1968, vol. VI
Collins, Adm. Sir (George) Frederick (Basset) E.;
  see Edward-Collins.
Collins, Hon. George Thomas, 1839–1926, vol. II
Collins, Brig. Gerald E.; *see* Edward-Collins.
Collins, Sir Godfrey Ferdinando Stratford,
  1888–1952, vol. V
Collins, Rt Hon. Sir Godfrey P., 1875–1936, vol. III
Collins, Herbert Frederick, 1890–1967, vol. VI
Collins, Herbert Jeffery, 1907–1968, vol. VI
Collins, Horatio John, 1894–1963, vol. VI
Collins, Sir James Patrick, 1891–1964, vol. VI
Collins, James Richard, 1869–1934, vol. III
Collins, Rev. Canon John; *see* Collins, Rev. Canon
  L. J.
Collins, Vice-Adm. Sir John Augustine, 1899–1989,
  vol. VIII
Collins, John Churton, 1848–1908, vol. I
Collins, John Henry, 1880–1952, vol. V
Collins, Rt Rev. John J., 1857–1934, vol. III
Collins, John Philip, *died* 1954, vol. V
Collins, John Rupert, *died* 1965, vol. VI
Collins, Maj.-Gen. John Stratford, 1851–1908, vol. I
Collins, Maj.-Gen. Joseph Clinton, 1895–1991,
  vol. IX
Collins, Gen. J(oseph) Lawton, 1896–1987,
  vol. VIII
Collins, Joseph Thomas, 1863–1938, vol. III
Collins, Rear-Adm. Kenneth St Barbe, 1904–1982,
  vol. VIII
Collins, Rev. Canon Lewis John, 1905–1982,
  vol. VIII
Collins, Brig. Lionel Peter, 1878–1957, vol. V
Collins, Mabel; *see* Cook, Mrs M.
Collins, Mark, vol. III
Collins, Michael, 1890–1922, vol. II
Collins, Norman Richard, 1907–1982, vol. VIII
Collins, Patrick, 1859–1943, vol. IV
Collins, Rev. Percy Herbert, *died* 1941, vol. IV
Collins, Rear-Adm. Ralph, 1877–1957, vol. V
Collins, Rev. Reginald Francis, 1851–1933, vol. III
Collins, Rt Rev. Richard, 1857–1924, vol. II
Collins, Lt-Col Hon. Richard Henn, 1873–1952,
  vol. V
Collins, Sir Robert Hawthorn, 1841–1908, vol. I
Collins, Maj.-Gen. Robert John, 1880–1950, vol. IV
Collins, Col Robert Joseph, 1848–1924, vol. II
Collins, Sir Robert Muirhead, 1852–1927, vol. II
Collins, Seymour John, 1906–1970, vol. VI
Collins, Sir Stephen, 1847–1925, vol. II
Collins, Hon. Sir Stephen Ogle H.; *see*
  Henn-Collins.
Collins, Stuart Verdun, 1916–1997, vol. X
Collins, Sir Thomas, 1860–1944, vol. IV
Collins, Brig. Thomas Frederick James, 1905–1999,
  vol. X
Collins, Most Rev. Thomas Gibson George,
  1873–1927, vol. II

Collins, Victor John; see Baron Stonham.
Collins, Rt Rev. W. E., 1867–1911, vol. I
Collins, Lt-Col William Alexander, 1873–1945, vol. IV
Collins, Sir William Alexander Roy, 1900–1976, vol. VII
Collins, Col Hon. William Edward, 1853–1934, vol. III
Collins, Sir William Henry, died 1947, vol. IV
Collins, Sir William Job, 1859–1946, vol. IV
Collins, Col Comdt Hon. William Richard, 1876–1944, vol. IV
Collins, William Wiehe, 1862–1951, vol. V
Collinson, Alfred Howe, 1866–1927, vol. II
Collinson, Col Harold, 1876–1945, vol. IV
Collinson, Lt-Col John, 1859–1901, vol. I
Collinson, Joseph, 1871–1952, vol. V
Collinson, Richard Jeffreys Hampton, 1924–1983, vol. VIII
Collinson, Thomas Henry, 1858–1928, vol. II
Collinson, William Edward, 1889–1969, vol. VI
Collip, James Bertram, 1892–1965, vol. VI
Collis, Edgar Leigh, 1870–1957, vol. V
Collis, Maj.-Gen. Francis William, 1839–1905, vol. I
Collis, Maj.-Gen. Sir James Norman C.; see Cooke-Collis.
Collis, John Stewart, 1900–1984, vol. VIII
Collis, Maurice, 1889–1973, vol. VII
Collis, Very Rev. Maurice Henry Fitzgerald, 1859–1947, vol. IV
Collis, Lt-Col Robert Henry, 1874–1930, vol. III
Collis, Col William C.; see Cooke-Collis.
Collis, William Robert FitzGerald, 1900–1975, vol. VII
Collishaw, Air Vice-Marshal Raymond, 1893–1976, vol. VII
Collison, Baron (Life Peer); Harold Francis Collison, 1909–1995, vol. IX
Collison, Bt Col Charles Sydney, 1871–1935, vol. III
Collison, Levi, 1875–1965, vol. VI (AII)
Collison, Lewis Herbert, 1908–1988, vol. VIII
Collison, Ven. William Henry, 1847–1922, vol. II
Collisson, Rev. William Alexander Houston, 1865–1920, vol. II
Collister, Sir Harold James, 1885–1950, vol. IV
Colls, John Howard, died 1910, vol. I
Collyer, Ven. Daniel, 1848–1924, vol. II
Collyer, Maj.-Gen. John Johnston, 1870–1941, vol. IV
Collyer, Robert, 1823–1912, vol. I
Collyer, William Robert, 1842–1928, vol. II
Collymore, Sir Allan; see Collymore, Sir E. A.
Collymore, Sir (Ernest) Allan, 1893–1962, vol. VI
Colman, Alec; see Colman, E. A.
Colman, Cecil, 1878–1954, vol. V
Colman, David Stacy, 1906–1993, vol. IX
Colman, (Elijah) Alec, 1903–1991, vol. IX
Colman, Lt-Col Frederick Gordon Dalziel, died 1969, vol. VI
Colman, Sir (George) Stanley, died 1966, vol. VI
Colman, Grace Mary, 1892–1971, vol. VII
Colman, Sir Jeremiah, 1st Bt (cr 1907), 1859–1942, vol. IV

Colman, Sir Jeremiah, 2nd Bt (cr 1907), 1886–1961, vol. VI
Colman, Sir Nigel Claudian Dalziel, 1st Bt (cr 1952), died 1966, vol. VI
Colman, Col Percy Edward, 1875–1951, vol. V
Colman, Ronald, 1891–1958, vol. V
Colman, Russell James, 1861–1946, vol. IV
Colman, Stacy; see Colman, D. S.
Colman, Sir Stanley; see Colman, Sir G. S.
Colmer, Joseph Grose, 1856–1937, vol. III
Colmore, G.; see Weaver, Mrs Baillie.
Colmore, Wing-Comdr Reginald Blayney Bulteel, 1888–1930, vol. III
Colmore, Thomas Milnes, 1845–1916, vol. II
Colnaghi, Sir Dominic Ellis, 1834–1908, vol. I
Colnbrook, Baron (Life Peer); Humphrey Edward Gregory Atkins, 1922–1996, vol. X
Colomb, Brig.-Gen. George Henry Cooper, 1862–1934, vol. III
Colomb, Vice-Adm. Philip Howard, 1831–1899, vol. I
Colomb, Adm. Philip Howard, 1867–1958, vol. V
Colomb, Rupert Palmer, 1869–1955, vol. V
Colombos, C(onstantine) John, died 1968, vol. VI
Colonne, Edouard, 1838–1910, vol. I
Colquhoun, Col Sir Alan John, 6th Bt cr 1786 (styled 13th Bt, cr 1625), 1838–1910, vol. I
Colquhoun, Archibald Ross, 1848–1914, vol. I
Colquhoun, Brian; see Colquhoun, C. B. H.
Colquhoun, (Cecil) Brian (Hugh), 1902–1977, vol. VII
Colquhoun, Maj.-Gen. Sir Cyril Harry, 1903–1996, vol. X
Colquhoun, Ethel M., (Mrs Tawse Jollie), died 1950, vol. IV (A), vol. V
Colquhoun, Rev. Canon Frank, 1909–1997, vol. X
Colquhoun, Sir Iain, 7th Bt (cr 1786), 1887–1948, vol. IV
Colquhoun, Sir James, 5th Bt cr 1786 (styled 12th Bt, cr 1625), 1844–1907, vol. I
Colquhoun, Major Julian Campbell, 1870–1937, vol. III
Colquhoun, Col Malcolm Alexander, 1870–1950, vol. IV
Colquhoun, Robert, 1914–1962, vol. VI
Colquhoun, Ven. William, died 1920, vol. II
Colquhoun, William Erskine C.; see Campbell-Colquhoun.
Colquhoun, Comdr William Jarvie, 1859–1908, vol. I
Colson, Charles, 1839–1915, vol. I
Colson, Charles Henry, 1864–1939, vol. III
Colson, Francis Henry, 1857–1943, vol. III
Colson, Rev. Francis Tovey, 1858–1929, vol. III
Colson, Surg. Vice-Adm. Sir Henry St Clair, 1887–1968, vol. VI
Colson, Lionel Hewitt, 1887–1943, vol. IV
Colson, Percy, 1873–1952, vol. V
Colson, Phyllis Constance, 1904–1972, vol. VII
Colston, Sir Charles Blampied, 1891–1969, vol. VI
Colston-Baynes, Dorothy Julia, died 1973, vol. VII
Colt, Rev. Sir Edward Harry Dutton, 8th Bt, 1850–1931, vol. III
Colt, George Frederick Russell, 1837–1909, vol. I
Colt, Sir Henry Archer, 9th Bt, 1882–1951, vol. V

Coltart, Captain Cyril George Bucknill, 1889–1964, vol. VI
Coltart, James Milne, 1903–1986, vol. VIII
Colthurst, Sir George Oliver, 7th Bt, 1882–1951, vol. V
Colthurst, Sir George St John, 6th Bt, 1850–1925, vol. II
Colthurst, Captain Sir Richard St John Jefferyes, 8th Bt, 1887–1955, vol. V
Colthurst-Vesey, Captain Charles Nicholas, 1860–1915, vol. I
Coltman-Rogers, Muriel Augusta Gillian, *died* 1952, vol. V
Colton, Cyril Hadlow, 1902–1988, vol. VIII
Colton, Gladys, 1909–1986, vol. VIII
Colton, Hon. Sir John, 1823–1902, vol. I
Colton, William Robert, 1867–1921, vol. II
Colum, Padraic, 1881–1972, vol. VII
Colvile, Ernest Frederick, 1879–1967, vol. VI
Colvile, Lt-Gen. Sir Fiennes Middleton, 1832–1917, vol. II
Colvile, Brig.-Gen. George Northcote, 1867–1940, vol. III
Colvile, Lancelot Edward, 1876–1947, vol. IV
Colvile, Comdr Mansel Brabazon Fiennes, 1887–1942, vol. IV
Colvill, Lt-Col David Chaigneau, 1898–1979, vol. VII
Colvill, Robert Frederick Stewart, 1860–1936, vol. III
Colville of Culross, 1st Viscount, 1818–1903, vol. I
Colville of Culross, 2nd Viscount, 1854–1928, vol. II
Colville of Culross, 3rd Viscount, 1888–1945, vol. IV
Colville, Brig.-Gen. Arthur Edward William, 1857–1942, vol. IV
Colville, Sir Cecil; *see* Colville, Sir H. C.
Colville, Lady Cynthia; *see* Colville, Lady H. C.
Colville, Maj.-Gen. Edward Charles, 1905–1982, vol. VIII
Colville, Hon. George Charles, 1867–1943, vol. IV
Colville, Lady (Helen) Cynthia, 1884–1968, vol. VI
Colville, Sir (Henry) Cecil, 1891–1984, vol. VIII
Colville, Maj.-Gen. Sir Henry Edward, 1852–1907, vol. I
Colville, Rev. James, *died* 1953, vol. V
Colville, John, 1852–1901, vol. I
Colville, Lt-Col John Ross, 1878–1935, vol. III
Colville, Sir John Rupert, 1915–1987, vol. VIII
Colville, Norman Robert, 1893–1974, vol. VII
Colville, Comdr Sir Richard, 1907–1975, vol. VII
Colville, Adm. Hon. Sir Stanley Cecil James, 1861–1939, vol. III
Colville, Col Hon. Sir William James, 1827–1903, vol. I
Colvin, Arthur Edmund, 1884–1966, vol. VI (AII)
Colvin, Sir Auckland, 1838–1908, vol. I
Colvin, Sir C. Preston, 1879–1950, vol. IV
Colvin, Col Cecil Hodgson, 1858–1938, vol. III
Colvin, Sir Elliot Graham, 1861–1940, vol. III
Colvin, Lt-Col Elliot James Dowell, 1885–1950, vol. IV
Colvin, Lt-Col Forrester Farnell, 1860–1936, vol. III
Colvin, Sir George Lethbridge, 1878–1962, vol. VI
Colvin, Major Hugh, 1887–1962, vol. VI

Colvin, Ian Duncan, 1877–1938, vol. III
Colvin, Col J. M. C., 1870–1945, vol. IV
Colvin, Brig. Dame Mary Katherine Rosamond, 1907–1988, vol. VIII
Colvin, Michael Keith Beale, 1932–2000, vol. X
Colvin, Sir Preston; *see* Colvin, Sir C. P.
Colvin, Adm. Sir Ragnar Musgrave, 1882–1954, vol. V
Colvin, Brig.-Gen. Sir Richard Beale, 1856–1936, vol. III
Colvin, Sir Sidney, 1845–1927, vol. II
Colvin, Thomas, 1863–1940, vol. III (A), vol. IV
Colvin, Sir Walter Mytton, 1847–1908, vol. I
Colvin, Very Rev. William Evans, *died* 1949, vol. IV
Colvin-Smith, Surg.-Gen. Sir Colvin, 1829–1913, vol. I
Colwell, Gen. George Harrie Thorn, 1841–1913, vol. I
Colwell, Hector Alfred, 1875–1946, vol. IV
Colwell, Rev. James, 1860–1930, vol. III
Colwyn, 1st Baron, 1859–1946, vol. IV
Colwyn, 2nd Baron, 1914–1966, vol. VI
Colyer, Air Marshal Douglas, 1893–1978, vol. VII
Colyer, Sir Frank, 1866–1954, vol. V
Colyer-Fergusson, Sir Thomas Colyer, 3rd Bt, 1865–1951, vol. V
Colyton, 1st Baron, 1902–1996, vol. X
Comay, Michael, 1908–1987, vol. VIII
Combe, Maj.-Gen. Boyce Albert, 1841–1920, vol. II
Combe, Charles, 1836–1920, vol. II
Combe, Charles Harvey, 1863–1935, vol. III
Combe, Captain Christian, 1858–1940, vol. III
Combe, George Alexander, 1877–1933, vol. III
Combe, Air Vice-Marshal Gerard, 1902–1979, vol. VII
Combe, Harvey Trewythen Brabazon, 1852–1923, vol. II
Combe, Lt-Col Herbert, 1878–1931, vol. III
Combe, Maj.-Gen. John Frederick Boyce, 1895–1967, vol. VI
Combe, Brig.-Gen. Lionel, 1861–1950, vol. IV
Combe, Sir Ralph Molyneux, 1872–1946, vol. IV
Combe, Richard Henry, 1829–1900, vol. I
Combe, Simon Harvey, 1903–1965, vol. VI
Comben, Robert Stone, 1868–1957, vol. V
Comber, Henry Gordon, 1869–1935, vol. III
Comber, Norman Mederson, 1888–1953, vol. V
Combermere, 4th Viscount, 1887–1969, vol. VI
Combermere, 5th Viscount, 1929–2000, vol. X
Combes, Emile, 1839–1921, vol. II
Combridge, Annie, 1862–1949, vol. IV
Combs, Sir Willis Ide, 1916–1994, vol. IX
Comerford, Lt-Col Augustine Ambrose, 1886–1944, vol. IV
Comfort, Alexander, 1920–2000, vol. X
Comfort, Mrs Bessie; *see* Marchant, Bessie.
Comfort, Charles Fraser, 1900–1994, vol. IX
Comino, Demetrius, 1902–1988, vol. VIII
Comins, Ven. Richard Blundell, *died* 1919, vol. II
Commager, Henry Steele, 1902–1998, vol. X
Commerell, Sir John Edmund, 1829–1901, vol. I
Commings, Maj.-Gen. Percy Ryan Conway, 1880–1958, vol. V
Commins, Andrew, 1829–1916, vol. II

Common, Sir Andrew; *see* Common, Sir L. A.
Common, Andrew Ainslie, 1841–1903, vol. I
Common, Frank Breadon, 1891–1969, vol. VI
Common, Sir (Lawrence) Andrew, 1889–1953, vol. V
Commons, John Rogers, 1862–1945, vol. IV
Commy, Rt Rev. John, 1843–1911, vol. I
Comparetti, Domenico, 1835–1927, vol. II
Comper, Sir (John) Ninian, 1864–1960, vol. V, vol. VI
Comper, Sir Ninian; *see* Comper, Sir J. N.
Compston, Rev. Herbert Fuller Bright, 1866–1931, vol. III
Compston, John Albert, *died* 1930, vol. III
Compston, Nigel Dean, 1918–1986, vol. VIII
Compston, Vice-Adm. Sir Peter Maxwell, 1915–2000, vol. X
Compton, Rt Rev. Lord Alwyne, 1825–1906, vol. I
Compton, Lord Alwyne Frederick, 1855–1911, vol. I
Compton, Arthur Holly, 1892–1962, vol. VI
Compton, Brig.-Gen. Charles William, 1869–1933, vol. III
Compton, Denis Charles Scott, 1918–1997, vol. X
Compton, Col. Lord Douglas James Cecil, 1865–1944, vol. IV
Compton, Sir Edmund Gerald, 1906–1994, vol. IX
Compton, Edward Robert Francis, 1891–1977, vol. VII
Compton, Eric Henry, 1902–1982, vol. VIII
Compton, Fay, 1894–1978, vol. VII
Compton, Henry Francis, 1872–1943, vol. IV
Compton, Herbert Eastwick, 1853–1906, vol. I
Compton, Joseph, 1881–1937, vol. III
Compton, Joseph, 1891–1964, vol. VI
Compton, Karl Taylor, 1887–1954, vol. V
Compton, Maurice, 1908–1974, vol. VII
Compton, Robert Herbert K.; *see* Keppel-Compton.
Compton, Captain Walter Burge, *died* 1932, vol. III
Compton, Rev. William Cookworthy, 1854–1936, vol. III
Compton, Air Vice-Marshal William Vernon C.; *see* Crawford-Compton.
Compton-Burnett, Dame Ivy, 1884–1969, vol. VI
Compton Mackenzie, Faith; *see* Mackenzie, Lady.
Compton Miller, Sir John Francis, 1900–1992, vol. IX
Compton-Rickett, Arthur, 1869–1937, vol. III
Compton-Rickett, Rt Hon. Sir Joseph, 1847–1919, vol. II
Compton-Thornhill, Sir Anthony John; *see* Thornhill.
Comrie, John Dixon, 1875–1939, vol. III
Comrie, Leslie John, 1893–1950, vol. IV
Comyn, Lt-Col Edward Walter, 1868–1949, vol. IV
Comyn, Henry Ernest Fitzwilliam, 1854–1941, vol. IV
Comyn, Hon. Sir James, 1921–1997, vol. X
Comyn, Col Lewis James, 1878–1961, vol. VI
Comyn, Michael, 1877–1952, vol. V
Comyn-Platt, Sir Thomas Walter; *see* Platt.
Comyns, Henry Joseph, 1868–1943, vol. IV
Comyns, Louis, *died* 1962, vol. VI
Comyns Carr, Sir Arthur Strettell, 1882–1965, vol. VI

Conacher, Hamilton, 1881–1939, vol. III
Conacher, Mungo, 1901–1977, vol. VII
Conan Doyle, Adrian Malcolm, 1910–1970, vol. VI
Conan Doyle, Air Comdt Dame Jean Lena Annette, (Lady Bromet), 1912–1997, vol. X
Conant, James Bryant, 1893–1978, vol. VII
Conant, Sir Roger John Edward, 1st Bt, 1899–1973, vol. VII
Concanon, Col Henry, 1861–1926, vol. II
Concannon, Terence Patrick, 1932–1990, vol. VIII
Conde, Harold Graydon, *died* 1959, vol. V
Conder, Charles, 1868–1909, vol. I
Conder, Claude Reignier, 1848–1910, vol. I
Conder, Rev. Canon Edward Baines, 1872–1936, vol. III
Condliffe, John Bell, 1891–1981, vol. VIII
Condon, Edward Uhler, 1902–1974, vol. VII
Conerney, Very Rev. John Pirrie, *died* 1940, vol. III (A), vol. IV
Conesford, 1st Baron, 1892–1974, vol. VII
Coney, Rev. Canon Harold Robert Harvey, 1889–1982, vol. VIII
Coneybeer, Hon. Frederick William, 1859–1950, vol. IV
Congdon, Col Arthur Edward Osmond, *died* 1924, vol. II
Conger, Edwin H., 1843–1907, vol. I
Congleton, 4th Baron, 1839–1906, vol. I
Congleton, 5th Baron, 1890–1914, vol. I
Congleton, 6th Baron, 1892–1932, vol. III
Congleton, 7th Baron, 1925–1967, vol. VI
Congreve, Cecil Ralph Townshend, 1876–1952, vol. V
Congreve, Comdr Sir Geoffrey, 1st Bt, *died* 1941, vol. IV
Congreve, John, 1872–1957, vol. V
Congreve, Gen. Sir Walter Norris, 1862–1927, vol. II
Coni, Peter Richard Carstairs, 1935–1993, vol. IX
Coningham, Air Marshal Sir Arthur, 1895–1948, vol. IV
Coningham, Maj.-Gen. Frank Evelyn, 1870–1934, vol. III
Coningham, Captain Herbert John, 1867–1936, vol. III
Coningsby, Eric Alfred, 1909–1955, vol. V
Conklin, Edwin Grant, 1863–1952, vol. V
Conlay, William Lance, 1869–1927, vol. II
Conn, John Farquhar Christie, 1903–1993, vol. IX
Connal, Benjamin Michael, 1861–1944, vol. IV
Connal, Col Kenneth Hugh Munro, 1870–1949, vol. IV
Connally, John Bowden, 1917–1993, vol. IX
Connally, Thomas Terry; *see* Connally, Tom.
Connally, Tom, (Thomas Terry Connally), 1877–1963, vol. VI
Connard, Philip, 1875–1958, vol. V
Connaught, Prince Arthur of, 1883–1938, vol. III
Connaught, HRH Princess Arthur of; *see* Fife, Duchess of.
Connaught and Strathearn, 2nd Duke of, 1914–1943, vol. IV
Connel, John Arthur, 1903–1961, vol. VI
Connell, Rev. Alexander, 1866–1920, vol. II
Connell, Sir Charles, 1900–1972, vol. VII

Connell, Sir Charles Gibson, 1899–1985, vol. VIII
Connell, Major Hugh John, 1884–1934, vol. III
Connell, Sir Isaac, 1858–1935, vol. III
Connell, James MacLuckie, 1867–1947, vol. IV
Connell, Jim, *died* 1929, vol. III
Connell, John, (John Henry Robertson), 1909–1965, vol. VI
Connell, John Morris, 1911–1999, vol. X
Connell, Philip Henry, 1921–1998, vol. X
Connell, Rev. Robert, 1852–1936, vol. III
Connell, Sir Robert Lowden, 1867–1936, vol. III
Connell, Walter Thomas, 1873–1964, vol. VI
Connellan, Joseph, *died* 1967, vol. VI (AII)
Connelly, Sir Francis Raymond, 1895–1949, vol. IV
Connelly, Marc, 1890–1980, vol. VII
Connelly, Thomas John, 1925–1991, vol. IX
Connely, Willard, 1888–1967, vol. VI
Connemara, 1st Baron, 1827–1901, vol. I
Conner, Cyril, 1900–1981, vol. VIII
Conner, Henry Daniel, 1859–1925, vol. II
Conner, Lewis Atterbury, 1867–1950, vol. IV (A), vol. V
Conner, Rearden; *see* Connor, Patrick Reardon.
Connibere, Sir Charles Wellington, *died* 1941, vol. IV
Connolly, Col Benjamin Bloomfield, 1845–1924, vol. II
Connolly, Cyril Vernon, 1903–1974, vol. VII
Connolly, Air Cdre Hugh Patrick, 1915–1968, vol. VI
Connolly, Hon. Sir James Daniel, 1869–1962, vol. VI
Connolly, Martin, 1874–1945, vol. IV
Connolly, Richard Joseph, 1873–1948, vol. IV
Connolly, Thomas James D.; *see* Doull-Connolly.
Connolly, William Patrick Joseph, *died* 1935, vol. III
Connolly, Sir Willis Henry, 1901–1981, vol. VIII
Connor, Dame (Annie) Jean, 1899–1968, vol. VI
Connor, Comdr Edward Richard, *died* 1903, vol. I
Connor, Francis Richard, 1870–1956, vol. V
Connor, Maj.-Gen. Sir Frank Powell, *died* 1954, vol. V
Connor, Captain Harry George A.; *see* Adams-Connor.
Connor, Dame Jean; *see* Connor, Dame A. J.
Connor, Col John Colpoys, 1867–1936, vol. III
Connor, Rev. Muirhead Mitchell, *died* 1930, vol. III
Connor, Patrick Reardon, (Rearden Conner), 1907–1991, vol. IX
Connor, Ralph, (Rev. Charles W. Gordon), 1860–1937, vol. III
Connor, Sir William Neil, 1909–1967, vol. VI
Conolly, Major Edward Michael, 1874–1956, vol. V
Conolly, Brig. John James Pollock, 1896–1950, vol. IV
Conor, William, 1881–1968, vol. VI
Conrad, Joseph, 1857–1924, vol. II
Conran, (George) Loraine, 1912–1986, vol. VIII
Conran, Loraine; *see* Conran, G. L.
Conran-Smith, Sir Eric Conran, 1890–1960, vol. V
Conroy, Charles O'Neill, 1871–1946, vol. IV
Conroy, Sir Diarmaid William, 1913–1978, vol. VII
Conroy, J. G., *died* 1915, vol. I
Conroy, Sir John, 3rd Bt, 1845–1900, vol. I

Conry, Major James Lionel Joyce, 1873–1914, vol. I
Conry, Brig. John de Lisle, 1882–1971, vol. VII
Consett, Rear-Adm. Montagu William Warcop Peter, 1871–1945, vol. IV
Considine, Sir Heffernan James Fritz, 1846–1912, vol. I
Constable, Hon. Lord; Andrew Henderson Briggs Constable, 1865–1928, vol. II
Constable, Andrew Henderson Briggs; *see* Constable, Hon. Lord.
Constable, Frank Challice, 1846–1937, vol. III
Constable, Sir Henry Marmaduke S.; *see* Strickland-Constable.
Constable, Brig. Raleigh Charles Joseph C.; *see* Chichester-Constable.
Constable, Sir Robert Frederick S.; *see* Strickland-Constable.
Constable, Walter George Raleigh C.; *see* Chichester-Constable.
Constable, William George, 1887–1976, vol. VII
Constable-Maxwell-Scott, Mary Monica; *see* Scott, Hon. Mrs Maxwell.
Constanduros, Mabel, *died* 1957, vol. V
Constant, Antony, 1916–1996, vol. X
Constant, Hayne, 1904–1968, vol. VI
Constant, Jean Joseph B.; *see* Benjamin-Constant.
Constantine, Baron (Life Peer); Learie Nicholas Constantine, 1901–1971, vol. VII
Constantine, Maj.-Gen. Charles Francis, *died* 1953, vol. V
Constantine, Sir George Baxandall, 1902–1969, vol. VI
Constantine, Air Chief Marshal Sir Hugh Alex, 1908–1992, vol. IX
Constantine, Tom, 1926–1981, vol. VIII
Constantinides, Most Rev. Michael, 1892–1958, vol. V
Constandin, Fernand Joseph Désiré; *see* Fernandel.
Conti, Italia, *died* 1946, vol. IV
Converse, Frederick Shepherd, 1871–1940, vol. III (A), vol. IV
Conway of Allington, 1st Baron, 1856–1937, vol. III
Conway, Brig. Albert Edward, 1891–1974, vol. VII
Conway, Arthur William, 1875–1950, vol. IV (A)
Conway, Conway Joseph, *died* 1953, vol. V
Conway, Most Rev. Dominic Joseph, 1918–1996, vol. X
Conway, Edward Joseph, 1894–1968, vol. VI
Conway, Essie Ruth, *died* 1934, vol. III
Conway, Hugh Graham, 1914–1989, vol. VIII
Conway, James, 1915–1974, vol. VII
Conway, Lt-Col John Marcus Hobson, *died* 1940, vol. III
Conway, Marmaduke Percy, 1885–1961, vol. VI
Conway, Moncure Daniel, 1832–1907, vol. I
Conway, Robert Russ, 1863–1950, vol. IV
Conway, Prof. Robert Seymour, 1864–1933, vol. III
Conway, His Eminence Cardinal William, 1913–1977, vol. VII
Conway-Gordon, Col Esme Cosmo William, 1875–1962, vol. VI
Conway-Gordon, Col Gwynnedd, 1868–1936, vol. III
Conway-Gordon, Lt-Gen. Lewis, 1863–1933, vol. III

Conwy, Rear-Adm. Rafe Grenville Rowley-, 1875–1951, vol. V
Conybeare, Alfred Edward, 1875–1952, vol. V
Conybeare, Charles Augustus Vansittart, 1853–1919, vol. II
Conybeare, Charles Frederick Pringle, 1860–1927, vol. II
Conybeare, Rear-Adm. Crawford James Markland, 1854–1937, vol. III
Conybeare, Frederick Cornwallis, 1856–1924, vol. II
Conybeare, Sir John Josias, 1888–1967, vol. VI
Conybeare, John William Edward, 1843–1931, vol. III
Conybeare, Very Rev. William James, 1871–1955, vol. V
Conyers, Dorothea, 1873–1949, vol. IV
Conyers, Evelyn Augusta, died 1944, vol. IV
Conyers, Sir James Reginald, 1879–1948, vol. IV
Conyngham, 4th Marquess, 1857–1897, vol. I
Conyngham, 5th Marquess, 1883–1906, vol. I
Conyngham, 6th Marquess, 1890–1974, vol. VII
Conyngham, Col Sir Gerald Ponsonby L.; see Lenox-Conyngham.
Conyngham, Sir William Fitzwilliam L.; see Lenox-Conyngham.
Cooch, Col Charles, 1829–1917, vol. II
Cooch Behar, Col Maharajah Sir Nripendra Narayan Bhup Bahadur of, 1862–1911, vol. I
Cooch Behar, Maharaja of, died 1913, vol. I
Cooch Behar, Maharaja Bhup Bahadur of, 1886–1922, vol. II
Coode, Sir Bernard Henry, 1887–1962, vol. VI
Coode, Rear-Adm. Charles Penrose Rushton, 1870–1939, vol. III
Coode, Captain Percival, died 1902, vol. I
Coode-Adams, Sir John; see Adams.
Coo-ee; see Walker, William Sylvester.
Cook, Air Vice-Marshal Albert Frederick, 1901–1980, vol. VII
Cook, Sir Albert Ruskin, 1870–1951, vol. V
Cook, Albert Stanburrough, 1853–1927, vol. II
Cook, Alexander Edward, 1906–1984, vol. VIII
Cook, (Alfred) Melville, 1912–1993, vol. IX
Cook, Arthur Bernard, 1868–1952, vol. V
Cook, Arthur Herbert, 1911–1988, vol. VIII
Cook, Arthur James, 1885–1931, vol. III
Cook, Arthur Kemball, 1851–1928, vol. II
Cook, Rev. Canon Arthur Malcolm, 1883–1964, vol. VI
Cook, Maj.-Gen. Arthur Thompson, 1923–2000, vol. X
Cook, Arthur Willsteed, died 1930, vol. III
Cook, Sir Basil (Alfred) Kemball-, 1876–1949, vol. IV
Cook, Bernard Christopher Allen, 1906–1985, vol. VIII
Cook, Brian Caldwell; see Batsford, Sir B. C. C.
Cook, Sir Charles Archer, 1849–1934, vol. III
Cook, Col Charles Chesney, 1866–1937, vol. III
Cook, Charles Henry; see Bickerdyke, John.
Cook, Edgar T., 1880–1953, vol. II
Cook, Sir Edmund Ralph, died 1942, vol. IV
Cook, Sir Edward Mitchener, 1881–1955, vol. V
Cook, Sir Edward Tyas, 1857–1919, vol. II

Cook, Ven. Edwin Arthur, 1888–1972, vol. VII
Cook, Lt-Col Edwin Berkeley, 1869–1914, vol. I
Cook, Elsie, (Mrs E. Thornton Cook), died 1960, vol. V
Cook, Air Vice-Marshal Eric, 1920–1985, vol. VIII
Cook, Eric William, 1920–1998, vol. X
Cook, Vice-Adm. Eric William L.; see Longley-Cook.
Cook, Ernest Benjamin, 1879–1952, vol. V
Cook, Sir Ernest Henry, 1855–1945, vol. IV
Cook, Sir Francis, 1st Bt, 1817–1901, vol. I
Cook, Sir Francis Ferdinand Maurice, 4th Bt, 1907–1978, vol. VII
Cook, Francis John Granville, 1913–1997, vol. X
Cook, Frank, 1888–1972, vol. VII
Cook, Frank Allan Grafton, 1902–1973, vol. VII
Cook, Sir Frederick Charles, 1875–1947, vol. IV
Cook, Sir Frederick Lucas, 2nd Bt, 1844–1920, vol. II
Cook, George Steveni L.; see Littlejohn Cook.
Cook, Lt-Col George Trevor-Roper, 1877–1918, vol. II
Cook, Gilbert, 1885–1951, vol. V
Cook, Sir Halford; see Cook, Sir P. H.
Cook, Harold James, 1926–1997, vol. X
Cook, Sir Henry, 1848–1928, vol. II
Cook, Henry Caldwell, 1886–1939, vol. III
Cook, Rt Rev. Henry George, 1906–1995, vol. X (AI)
Cook, Ven. Henry Lucas, died 1928, vol. II
Cook, Brig.-Gen. Henry Rex, 1863–1950, vol. IV
Cook, Sir Herbert Frederick, 3rd Bt, 1868–1939, vol. III
Cook, Herbert George Graham, 1864–1939, vol. III
Cook, Maj.-Gen. James, 1844–1928, vol. II
Cook, James Allan, 1858–1933, vol. III
Cook, Hon. James H.; see Hume-Cook.
Cook, Sir James Wilfred, 1900–1975, vol. VII
Cook, John Edward E.; see Evan-Cook.
Cook, John Gilbert, 1911–1979, vol. VII
Cook, John Irvine, 1892–1952, vol. V
Cook, John Manuel, 1910–1994, vol. IX
Cook, Rt Hon. Sir Joseph, 1860–1947, vol. IV
Cook, Mrs Keningale, (Mabel Collins), 1851–1927, vol. II
Cook, Melville; see Cook, A. M.
Cook, Norman Charles, 1906–1994, vol. IX
Cook, Norman Edgar, 1920–1995, vol. IX
Cook, Percival Robert, 1867–1939, vol. III
Cook, Peter Edward, 1937–1995, vol. IX
Cook, Sir (Philip) Halford, 1912–1990, vol. VIII
Cook, Reginald, 1918–1997, vol. X
Cook, Maj.-Gen. Robert Francis Leonard, 1939–1997, vol. X
Cook, Robert Manuel, 1909–2000, vol. X
Cook, Stanley Arthur, 1873–1949, vol. IV
Cook, Stanley Smith, 1875–1952, vol. V
Cook, Hon. Sir Tasker Keech, 1867–1937, vol. III
Cook, Sir Theodore Andrea, 1867–1928, vol. II
Cook, Thomas Fotheringham, 1908–1952, vol. V
Cook, Thomas Reginald Hague, 1866–1925, vol. II
Cook, Lt-Col Thomas Russell Albert Mason, 1902–1970, vol. VI
Cook, Rt Rev. Thomas William, 1866–1928, vol. II
Cook, Sir William, 1834–1908, vol. I

Cook, Sir William Richard Joseph, 1905–1987, vol. VIII
Cooke, Alexander Macdougall, 1899–1999, vol. X
Cooke, Col Alfred Fothergill, 1871–1946, vol. IV
Cooke, Rev. Alfred Hands, *died* 1937, vol. III
Cooke, Amos John, 1885–1961, vol. VI
Cooke, Lt-Gen. Anthony Charles, 1826–1905, vol. I
Cooke, Arthur Hafford, 1912–1987, vol. VIII
Cooke, Lt-Col Aubrey St John, 1872–1935, vol. III
Cooke, Brig.-Gen. Bertram Hewett Hunter, 1874–1946, vol. IV
Cooke, Brian K.; *see* Kennedy-Cooke.
Cooke, Cecil; *see* Cooke, R. C.
Cooke, Sir Charles Arthur John, 11th Bt, 1905–1978, vol. VII
Cooke, Rev. Canon Charles Edward, 1860–1939, vol. III
Cooke, Charles John Bowen, 1859–1920, vol. II
Cooke, Charles Wallwyn Radcliffe-, *died* 1911, vol. I
Cooke, Christopher Herbert, 1899–1979, vol. VII
Cooke, Sir Clement K.; *see* Kinloch-Cooke.
Cooke, Conrad William, 1843–1926, vol. II
Cooke, Air Marshal Sir Cyril Bertram, 1895–1972, vol. VII
Cooke, Deryck Victor, 1919–1976, vol. VII
Cooke, Sir Douglas; *see* Cooke, Sir J. D.
Cooke, Sir (Edward) Marriott, 1852–1931, vol. III
Cooke, Rev. George Albert, 1865–1939, vol. III
Cooke, George William, 1916–1992, vol. IX
Cooke, Rev. Canon Greville Vaughan Turner, 1894–1989, vol. VIII
Cooke, Henry Arthur, 1862–1946, vol. IV
Cooke, Sir Henry Frank, 1900–1973, vol. VII
Cooke, Sir Henry P.; *see* Paget-Cooke.
Cooke, Lt-Gen. Sir Herbert Fothergill, 1871–1936, vol. III
Cooke, Isaac, 1846–1922, vol. II
Cooke, Sir (James) Douglas, *died* 1949, vol. IV
Cooke, Rear-Adm. John Ernest, 1899–1980, vol. VII
Cooke, Sir John F.; *see* Fletcher-Cooke.
Cooke, John Fitzpatrick, *died* 1930, vol. III
Cooke, Rear-Adm. John Gervaise Beresford, 1911–1976, vol. VII
Cooke, John Hunt, 1828–1908, vol. I
Cooke, John Sholto Fitzpatrick, 1906–1975, vol. VII
Cooke, Kenneth; *see* Cooke, R. K.
Cooke, Sir Leonard, 1901–1976, vol. VII
Cooke, Rev. Leslie Edward, 1908–1967, vol. VI
Cooke, Lewis Henry, *died* 1929, vol. III
Cooke, Sir Marriott; *see* Cooke, Sir E. M.
Cooke, Michael Joseph, 1881–1960, vol. V
Cooke, Mordecai Cubitt, 1825–1913, vol. I
Cooke, Oliver Dayrell Paget P.; *see* Paget-Cooke.
Cooke, Peter Maurice, 1927–1995, vol. IX
Cooke, Col Philip Ralph D.; *see* Davies-Cooke.
Cooke, Philip Tatton Davies-, 1863–1946, vol. IV
Cooke, (Richard) Kenneth, 1917–2000, vol. X
Cooke, Sir Robert Gordon, 1930–1987, vol. VIII
Cooke, Rev. Canon Robert Herbert Michael, 1864–1939, vol. III
Cooke, Brig. Robert Thomas, 1897–1984, vol. VIII
Cooke, Robert Victor, 1902–1978, vol. VII
Cooke, Roger Gresham, 1907–1970, vol. VI

Cooke, (Roland) Cecil, 1899–1991, vol. IX
Cooke, Maj.-Gen. Ronald Basil Bowen Bancroft, 1899–1971, vol. VII
Cooke, Rupert C.; *see* Croft-Cooke.
Cooke, Hon. Sir Samuel Burgess Ridgway, 1912–1978, vol. VII
Cooke, Maj.-Gen. Sidney Arthur, 1903–1977, vol. VII
Cooke, Sir Stenson, 1874–1942, vol. IV
Cooke, Temple, 1851–1925, vol. II
Cooke, Theodore, 1836–1910, vol. I
Cooke, Thomas Fitzpatrick, 1911–1994, vol. IX
Cooke, Tom Harry, 1923–1987, vol. VIII
Cooke, William Charles Cyril, 1881–1966, vol. VI
Cooke, William Cubitt, 1866–1951, vol. V
Cooke, William Ernest, 1863–1947, vol. IV
Cooke, William Henry, 1843–1921, vol. II
Cooke, Sir William Henry Charles Wemyss, 10th Bt, 1872–1964, vol. VI
Cooke-Collis, Maj.-Gen. Sir James; *see* Cooke-Collis, Maj.-Gen. Sir W. J. N.
Cooke-Collis, Col William, 1847–1933, vol. III
Cooke-Collis, Maj.-Gen. Sir (William) James Norman, 1876–1941, vol. IV
Cooke-Hurle, Col Edward Forbes; *see* Hurle.
Cooke-Hurle, John A.; *see* Hurle.
Cooke-Taylor, Richard Whately, 1842–1918, vol. II
Cooke-Yarborough, George Eustace, 1876–1938, vol. III
Cooke-Yarborough, Rev. John James; *see* Yarborough.
Cookman, Anthony Victor, 1894–1962, vol. VI
Cooksley, Clarence Harrington, 1915–1991, vol. IX
Cookson, Dame Catherine Ann, 1906–1998, vol. X
Cookson, Sir Charles Alfred, 1829–1906, vol. I
Cookson, Charles Lisle Stirling, 1855–1919, vol. II
Cookson, Christopher, *died* 1948, vol. IV
Cookson, Captain Claude Edward, 1879–1963, vol. VI
Cookson, Clive, 1879–1971, vol. VII
Cookson, Maj.-Gen. George Arthur, 1860–1929, vol. III
Cookson, Henry Anstey, 1886–1949, vol. IV
Cookson, John Blencowe, 1843–1910, vol. I
Cookson, Lt-Col John Cookson F.; *see* Fife-Cookson.
Cookson, Col Philip Blencowe, 1871–1928, vol. II
Cookson, Roland Antony, 1908–1991, vol. IX
Cookson, Sydney Spencer S.; *see* Sawrey-Cookson.
Cooley, Sir Alan Sydenham, 1920–1997, vol. X
Coolidge, Archibald Cary, 1866–1928, vol. II
Coolidge, Calvin, 1872–1933, vol. III
Coolidge, William Augustus Brevoort, 1850–1926, vol. II
Coolidge, William David, 1873–1975, vol. VII
Cools-Lartigue, Alexander Raphael, 1899–1973, vol. VII
Cools-Lartigue, Sir Louis, 1905–1993, vol. IX
Coomaraswamy, Ananda K., 1877–1947, vol. IV
Coomaraswamy, Sir Velupillai, 1892–1972, vol. VII
Coombe, Sir Thomas Melrose, 1877–1959, vol. V
Coomber, John Edward, 1901–1963, vol. VI
Coombes, Very Rev. George Frederick, 1856–1922, vol. II
Coombs, Carey Franklin, 1879–1932, vol. III

Coombs, Herbert Cole, 1906–1997, vol. X
Coombs, Captain Thomas Edward, 1884–1953, vol. V
Coombs, William Harry, 1893–1969, vol. VI
Coombs, William Heron, 1851–1931, vol. III
Coombs, Rev. Canon William Joseph Mundy, 1871–1966, vol. VI
Coop, Hubert, 1872–1953, vol. V
Coop, Rev. James Ogden, 1869–1928, vol. II
Coop, Sir Maurice Fletcher, 1907–1996, vol. X
Coope, Edward Jesser, 1849–1918, vol. II
Cooper of Culross, 1st Baron, 1892–1955, vol. V
Cooper of Stockton Heath, Baron (Life Peer); John Cooper, 1908–1988, vol. VIII
Cooper, Very Rev. Alan; see Cooper, Very Rev. W. H. A.
Cooper, Sqdn Ldr Albert Edward, 1910–1986, vol. VIII
Cooper, Rev. Albert Samuel, 1905–1998, vol. X
Cooper, Sir Alfred, 1838–1908, vol. I
Cooper, Sir Alfred, 1846–1916, vol. II
Cooper, Alfred B., 1863–1936, vol. III
Cooper, Rt Rev. Alfred Cecil, died 1964, vol. VI
Cooper, Alfred Heaton, died 1929, vol. III
Cooper, Rev. Alfred William Francis, died 1920, vol. II
Cooper, Alice J., died 1917, vol. II
Cooper, Captain Archibald Frederick, 1885–1975, vol. VII
Cooper, Archibald Samuel, 1871–1942, vol. IV
Cooper, Col Arthur; see Aglionby, Col A.
Cooper, Rev. Arthur Nevile, 1850–1943, vol. IV
Cooper, (Arthur William) Douglas, 1911–1984, vol. VIII
Cooper, Sir Astley Paston P.; see Paston-Cooper.
Cooper, Austin Edwin, 1869–1954, vol. V
Cooper, Bryan Ricco, 1884–1930, vol. III
Cooper, Very Rev. Cecil Henry Hamilton, 1871–1942, vol. IV
Cooper, Charles Alfred, 1829–1916, vol. II
Cooper, Maj.-Gen. Charles Duncan, 1849–1929, vol. III
Cooper, Sir Charles Eric Daniel, 5th Bt (cr 1863), 1906–1984, vol. VIII
Cooper, Col Charles James, died 1931, vol. III
Cooper, Sir Charles Naunton Paston P., 4th Bt (cr 1821); see Paston-Cooper.
Cooper, Sir Clive F.; see Forster-Cooper.
Cooper, Major Colin, 1892–1938, vol. III
Cooper, Sir Daniel, 1st Bt (cr 1863), 1821–1902, vol. I
Cooper, Sir Daniel, 2nd Bt (cr 1863), 1848–1909, vol. I
Cooper, Sir Daniel; see Cooper, Sir W. G. D.
Cooper, David, 1855–1940, vol. III
Cooper, Sir Dhanjishah Bomanjee, died 1947, vol. IV
Cooper, Lady Diana, (Diana, Viscountess Norwich), 1892–1986, vol. VIII
Cooper, Douglas; see Cooper, A. W. D.
Cooper, Sir Edward Ernest, 1st Bt (cr 1920), 1848–1922, vol. II
Cooper, Rt Hon. Edward Henry, 1827–1902, vol. I
Cooper, Edward Herbert, 1867–1910, vol. I

Cooper, Maj.-Gen. Edward Joshua, 1858–1945, vol. IV
Cooper, Sir Edwin, 1874–1942, vol. IV
Cooper, Sir Ernest Herbert, 1877–1962, vol. VI
Cooper, Francis Alfred, 1860–1933, vol. III
Cooper, Sir Francis Ashmole, (Sir Frank), 4th Bt, 1905–1987, vol. VIII
Cooper, Sir Francis D'Arcy, 1st Bt (cr 1941), 1882–1941, vol. IV
Cooper, Hon. Frank Arthur, 1872–1949, vol. IV
Cooper, Col Frank Sandiford, 1873–1936, vol. III
Cooper, Frank Shewell, 1864–1949, vol. IV
Cooper, Frank Towers, 1863–1915, vol. I
Cooper, Rev. Frederic Wilson, 1860–1941, vol. IV
Cooper, Gary Frank James, 1901–1961, vol. VI
Cooper, Wing Comdr Geoffrey, 1907–1995, vol. X (AI)
Cooper, Sir George Alexander, 1st Bt (cr 1905, of Hursley), 1856–1940, vol. III
Cooper, Captain Sir George James Robertson, 2nd Bt (cr 1905, of Hursley), 1890–1961, vol. VI
Cooper, George Joseph, died 1909, vol. I
Cooper, Gerald Melbourne, 1892–1947, vol. IV
Cooper, Sir Gilbert Alexander, 1903–1989, vol. VIII
Cooper, Giles Stannus, 1918–1966, vol. VI
Cooper, Dame Gladys Constance, 1888–1971, vol. VII
Cooper, Sir Guy; see Cooper, Sir H. G.
Cooper, Harold H.; see Hinton-Cooper.
Cooper, Sir (Harold) Stanford, 1889–1976, vol. VII
Cooper, Col Harry, 1847–1928, vol. III
Cooper, Sir Henry, 1873–1962, vol. VI
Cooper, Sir Henry; see Cooper, Sir W. H.
Cooper, Henry, 1877–1947, vol. IV
Cooper, Rt Rev. Henry Edward, 1845–1916, vol. II
Cooper, Sir (Henry) Guy, 1890–1975, vol. VII
Cooper, Sir Henry Lovick, 5th Bt (cr 1821), 1875–1959, vol. V
Cooper, Henry St John, 1869–1926, vol. II
Cooper, Very Rev. James, 1846–1922, vol. II
Cooper, James, 1882–1949, vol. IV
Cooper, Sir James Alexander, died 1936, vol. III
Cooper, Rev. James Hughes, died 1909, vol. I
Cooper, James Lees, 1907–1980, vol. VII
Cooper, Rev. Canon James Sidmouth, 1869–1961, vol. VI
Cooper, Joan Davies, 1914–1999, vol. X
Cooper, John Newton, 1923–2000, vol. X
Cooper, John Paul, died 1933, vol. III
Cooper, Joshua Edward Synge, 1901–1981, vol. VIII
Cooper, Maj.-Gen. Kenneth Christie, 1905–1981, vol. VIII
Cooper, Kenneth Ernest, 1903–1993, vol. IX
Cooper, Lance Harries, 1890–1972, vol. VII
Cooper, Leslie Hugh Norman, 1905–1985, vol. VIII
Cooper, Col Lyall Newcomen, died 1929, vol. III
Cooper, Malcolm Edward, 1907–1977, vol. VII
Cooper, Prof. Malcolm McGregor, 1910–1989, vol. VIII
Cooper, Margaret, died 1922, vol. II
Cooper, Martin Du Pré, 1910–1986, vol. VIII
Cooper, Sir Patrick Ashley, 1887–1961, vol. VI
Cooper, Percival Martin, 1887–1951, vol. V

Cooper, Peter James, 1947–2000, vol. X
Cooper, Hon. Sir Pope Alexander, 1848–1923, vol. II
Cooper, Sir Richard Ashmole, 2nd Bt (*cr* 1905, of Shenstone Court), 1874–1946, vol. IV
Cooper, Brig.-Gen. Richard Joshua, 1860–1938, vol. III
Cooper, Sir Richard Powell, 1st Bt (*cr* 1905, of Shenstone Court), 1847–1913, vol. I
Cooper, Sir Robert Elliott-, 1845–1942, vol. IV
Cooper, Robert Higham, 1878–1944, vol. IV
Cooper, Robert William, 1877–1970, vol. VI
Cooper, Rear-Adm. Sidney G.; *see* Grattan-Cooper.
Cooper, Susie, (Mrs Susan Vera Barker), 1902–1995, vol. IX
Cooper, Sir Stanford; *see* Cooper, Sir H. S.
Cooper, Rev. Canon Sydney, 1862–1942, vol. IV
Cooper, Hon. Sir Theo, 1850–1925, vol. II
Cooper, Thomas Edwin; *see* Utley, T. E.
Cooper, Rev. Thomas John, 1837–1911, vol. I
Cooper, Thomas Sidney, 1803–1902, vol. I
Cooper, Rev. Vincent King, 1849–1922, vol. II
Cooper, Hon. Sir Walter Jackson, 1892–1973, vol. VII
Cooper, Dame Whina, 1895–1994, vol. IX
Cooper, Wilbraham Villiers, 1876–1955, vol. V
Cooper, Wilfred Edward S.; *see* Shewell-Cooper.
Cooper, Sir William Charles, 3rd Bt (*cr* 1863), 1851–1925, vol. II
Cooper, William Edward Deck, 1877–1962, vol. VI
Cooper, Lt-Col Sir William Earnshaw, 1843–1924, vol. II
Cooper, Sir (William George) Daniel, 4th Bt (*cr* 1863), 1877–1954, vol. V
Cooper, Sir (William) Henry, 1909–1990, vol. VIII
Cooper, Sir William Herbert, 3rd Bt (*cr* 1905, of Shenstone Court), 1901–1970, vol. VI
Cooper, Very Rev. (William Hugh) Alan, 1909–1999, vol. X
Cooper, Sir William M.; *see* Mansfield Cooper.
Cooper, William Ranson, 1868–1926, vol. II
Cooper, Lt-Col William Weldon H.; *see* Herring-Cooper.
Cooper-Key, Major Sir Aston, 1861–1930, vol. III
Cooper-Key, Captain Edmund Moore Cooper, 1862–1933, vol. III
Cooper-Key, Sir Neill, 1907–1981, vol. VIII
Coopland, George William, 1875–1975, vol. VII
Cooray, Edmund Joseph, 1907–1979, vol. VII
Cooray, His Eminence Thomas Benjamin, Cardinal, 1901–1988, vol. VIII
Coote, Rev. Sir Algernon, 11th Bt, 1817–1899, vol. I
Coote, Sir Algernon Charles Plumptre, 12th Bt, 1847–1920, vol. II
Coote, Captain Sir Colin Reith, 1893–1979, vol. VII
Coote, Sir Eyre, 1857–1925, vol. II
Coote, Rt Rev. Mgr Canon George, 1881–1961, vol. VI
Coote, Howard, 1865–1943, vol. IV
Coote, John Oldham, 1921–1993, vol. IX
Coote, Rear-Adm. Sir John Ralph, 14th Bt, 1905–1978, vol. VII
Coote, Sir Ralph Algernon, 13th Bt, 1874–1941, vol. IV

Coote, Rt Rev. Roderic Norman, 1915–2000, vol. X
Coote, William, 1863–1924, vol. II
Coote, William Alexander, 1842–1919, vol. II
Copas, Most Rev. Virgil, 1915–1993, vol. IX
Cope, 1st Baron, 1870–1946, vol. IV
Cope, Sir Alfred, *died* 1954, vol. V
Cope, Sir Anthony, 13th Bt (*cr* 1611), 1842–1932, vol. III
Cope, Sir Anthony Mohun Leckonby, 15th Bt (*cr* 1611), 1927–1966, vol. VI
Cope, Sir Arthur Stockdale, 1857–1940, vol. III
Cope, Charles Elvey, *died* 1943, vol. IV
Cope, Captain Sir Denzil, 14th Bt (*cr* 1611), 1873–1940, vol. III
Cope, Frederick Wolverson, 1909–2000, vol. X
Cope, John Hautenville, *died* 1942, vol. IV
Cope, John Wigley, 1907–1987, vol. VIII
Cope, Maclachlan Alan Carl S.; *see* Silverwood-Cope.
Cope, Sir Mordaunt Leckonby, 16th Bt (*cr* 1611), 1878–1972, vol. VII
Cope, Sir Ralph, 1862–1949, vol. IV
Cope, Sir Thomas, 1st Bt (*cr* 1918), 1840–1924, vol. II
Cope, Brig.-Gen. Sir Thomas George, 2nd Bt (*cr* 1918), 1884–1966, vol. VI
Cope, Sir (Vincent) Zachary, 1881–1974, vol. VII
Cope, Sir Zachary; *see* Cope, Sir V. Z.
Copeau, Jacques, 1879–1949, vol. IV
Copeland, Edwin Bingham, 1873–1964, vol. VI
Copeland, Hon. Henry, 1839–1904, vol. I
Copeland, Ida, (Mrs Ronald Copeland), *died* 1964, vol. VI
Copeland, Ralph, 1837–1905, vol. I
Copeland, (Richard) Ronald (John), *died* 1958, vol. V
Copeland, Ronald; *see* Copeland, Richard R. J.
Copeland, Theodore Benfey, 1878–1952, vol. V
Copeman, Col Charles Edward Fraser, *died* 1949, vol. IV
Copeman, Constance Gertrude, 1864–1953, vol. V (A), vol. VI
Copeman, Lt-Col Hugh Charles, 1862–1955, vol. V
Copeman, Vice-Adm. Sir Nicholas Alfred, 1906–1969, vol. VI
Copeman, Sydney A. Monckton, 1862–1947, vol. IV
Copeman, William Sydney Charles, 1900–1970, vol. VI
Copestake, Barry; *see* Copestake, T. B.
Copestake, Thomas Barry, 1930–1989, vol. VIII
Copinger, Walter Arthur, 1847–1910, vol. I
Copland, Aaron, 1900–1990, vol. VIII
Copland, Col Alexander, 1833–1908, vol. I
Copland, Sir Douglas Berry, 1894–1971, vol. VII
Copland, Harold W.; *see* Wallace-Copland.
Copland, Sir William Robertson, 1838–1907, vol. I
Copland, William Wallace, 1853–1922, vol. II
Copland-Griffiths, Brig. Felix Alexander Vincent, 1894–1967, vol. VI
Copland Simmons, Rev. Frederic Pearson; *see* Simmons.
Copland-Sparkes, Rear-Adm. Robert, 1851–1924, vol. II
Coplans, Major Myer, *died* 1961, vol. VI

Copleston, Rt Rev. Ernest Arthur, *died* 1933, vol. III
Copleston, Ernest Reginald, 1909–1993, vol. X (AI)
Copleston, Rev. Frederick Charles, 1907–1994, vol. IX
Copleston, Frederick Selwyn, 1850–1935, vol. III
Copleston, Most Rev. Reginald Stephen, 1845–1925, vol. II
Copleston, Waters Edward, *died* 1949, vol. IV
Coplestone, Frederick, 1850–1932, vol. III
Coplestone-Boughey, John Fenton, 1912–2000, vol. X
Copley, Ethel Leontine; *see* Gabain, E. L.
Copley, John, 1875–1950, vol. IV
Copley, Mrs John; *see* Gabain, Ethel Leontine.
Copley, Very Rev. John Robert, *died* 1923, vol. II
Copley, Brig.-Gen. Sir Robert Calverley Alington Bewicke B.; *see* Bewicke-Copley.
Copley, Samuel William, 1859–1937, vol. III
Copnall, Bainbridge; *see* Copnall, E. B.
Copnall, (Edward) Bainbridge, 1903–1973, vol. VII
Copp, (Douglas) Harold, 1915–1998, vol. X
Copp, Harold; *see* Copp, D. H.
Coppard, Alfred Edgar, 1878–1957, vol. V
Coppee, François Edouard Joachim, 1842–1908, vol. I
Coppel, Elias Godfrey, 1896–1978, vol. VII
Coppel, Rt Rev. Francis Stephen, 1867–1933, vol. III
Coppin, Hon. George, 1820–1906, vol. I
Copping, Arthur E., 1865–1941, vol. IV
Copping, Harold, *died* 1932, vol. III
Coppinger, Rear-Adm. Robert Henry, 1877–1967, vol. VI
Coppinger, Maj.-Gen. Walter Valentine, 1875–1957, vol. V
Coppleson, Sir Lionel Wolfe, 1901–1980, vol. VII (AII)
Coppleson, Sir Victor Marcus, 1893–1965, vol. VI
Copplestone, Bennet; *see* Kitchin, F. H.
Copplestone, Frank Henry, 1925–1996, vol. X
Coppock, John Terence, (Terry), 1921–2000, vol. X
Coppock, Sir Richard, 1885–1971, vol. VII
Coppock, Terry; *see* Coppock, J. T.
Copson, Edward Thomas, 1901–1980, vol. VII
Copus, George Frederick, 1868–1949, vol. IV
Coquelin, Benoit Constant, (Coquelin aîné), 1841–1909, vol. I
Coquelin, Ernest Alexandre Honoré, (Coquelin cadet), 1848–1909, vol. I
Corah, Sir John Harold, 1884–1978, vol. VII
Corbally, Elias, 1868–1933, vol. III
Corban, Maj.-Gen. William Watts, 1829–1916, vol. II
Corbet, Maj.-Gen. Arthur Domville, 1847–1918, vol. II
Corbet, Eustace Kynaston, 1854–1920, vol. II
Corbet, Freda Kunzlen, 1900–1993, vol. IX
Corbet, Hon. Frederick Hugh Mackenzie, 1862–1916, vol. II
Corbet, Sir Gerald Vincent, 6th Bt, 1868–1955, vol. V
Corbet, Lieut-Col Sir John Vincent, 7th Bt, 1911–1996, vol. X
Corbet, Hon. Mrs (Katherine), 1861–1950, vol. IV

Corbet, Air Vice-Marshal Lancelot Miller, 1898–1990, vol. VIII
Corbet, Reginald, 1857–1945, vol. IV
Corbet, Sir Roland James, 5th Bt, 1892–1915, vol. I
Corbet, Sir Walter Orlando, 4th Bt, 1856–1910, vol. I
Corbet, William Joseph, 1824–1909, vol. I
Corbett, Adm. Charles Frederick, 1867–1955, vol. V
Corbett, Charles Henry Joseph, 1853–1935, vol. III
Corbett, Edward, 1843–1918, vol. II
Corbett, (Edward) James, (Jim Corbett), 1875–1955, vol. V
Corbett, Sir Francis Edmund George A.; *see* Astley-Corbett.
Corbett, Sir (Francis) Henry (Rivers) A.; *see* Astley-Corbett.
Corbett, Rev. Frederick St John, 1862–1919, vol. II
Corbett, Sir Geoffrey Latham, 1881–1937, vol. III
Corbett, Captain Godfrey Edwin, 1871–1929, vol. III
Corbett, Harvey Wiley, 1873–1954, vol. V
Corbett, J. Soden, 1871–1935, vol. III
Corbett, James; *see* Corbett, E. J.
Corbett, Rt Rev. James Francis, 1840–1912, vol. I
Corbett, Jim; *see* Corbett, E. J.
Corbett, John, 1817–1901, vol. I
Corbett, John Patrick, 1916–1999, vol. X
Corbett, Rev. John Reginald, 1844–1920, vol. II
Corbett, Sir Julian Stafford, 1854–1922, vol. II
Corbett, Peter Edgar, 1920–1992, vol. IX
Corbett, Col Robert de la Cour, 1844–1904, vol. I
Corbett, Captain Roland, 1881–1938, vol. III
Corbett, Rupert Shelton, 1893–1985, vol. VIII
Corbett, Thomas Lorimer, 1854–1910, vol. I
Corbett, Lt-Gen. Thomas William, 1888–1981, vol. VIII
Corbett, Captain Sir Vincent Edwin Henry, 1861–1936, vol. III
Corbett, William John, *died* 1941, vol. IV
Corbett Ashby, Dame Margery Irene, 1882–1981, vol. VIII
Corbett-Smith, Arthur, 1879–1945, vol. IV
Corbett-Winder, Col John Lyon, 1911–1990, vol. VIII
Corbett-Winder, Major William John, 1875–1950, vol. IV
Corbin, (André) Charles, 1881–1970, vol. VI
Corbin, Charles; *see* Corbin, A. C.
Corbin, John, 1870–1959, vol. V
Corbishley, Rev. Thomas, 1903–1976, vol. VII
Corby, Henry, *died* 1917, vol. II
Corbyn, Ernest Nugent, 1881–1961, vol. VI
Corcoran, Sir John A., 1862–1932, vol. III
Corcoran, Percy John, 1920–1984, vol. VIII
Corcoran, Rev. Timothy, 1872–1943, vol. IV
Cordeaux, Captain Edward Cawdron, 1894–1963, vol. VI
Cordeaux, Col Edward Kyme, 1866–1946, vol. IV
Cordeaux, Major Sir Harry Edward Spiller, 1870–1943, vol. IV
Cordeaux, Lt-Col John Kyme, 1902–1982, vol. VIII
Cordeiro, His Eminence Cardinal Joseph, 1918–1994, vol. IX
Cordellis, Mrs M.; *see* Groom, Gladys Laurence.

Corder, Lt-Col Arthur Annerley, *died* 1923, vol. II
Corder, Frederick, 1852–1932, vol. III
Corder, Paul Walford, 1879–1942, vol. IV
Corder, Philip, 1891–1961, vol. VI
Cordes, Thomas, 1826–1901, vol. I
Cordier, Andrew Wellington, 1901–1975, vol. VII
Cordiner, George Ritchie Mather, *died* 1957, vol. V
Cordiner, Thomas Smith, 1902–1965, vol. VI
Cordingley, Charles, 1862–1914, vol. I
Cordingley, Air Vice-Marshal Sir John Walter, 1890–1977, vol. VII
Cordingley, Reginald Annandale, 1896–1962, vol. VI
Cordingly, Rt Rev. Eric William Bradley, 1911–1976, vol. VII
Cordon, Cecil Gilbert William, *died* 1952, vol. V
Core, Thomas Hamilton, 1836–1910, vol. I
Corea, Sir Claude; *see* Corea, Sir G. C. S.
Corea, Sir (George) Claude (Stanley), 1894–1962, vol. VI
Corelli, Marie, 1855–1924, vol. II
Corfe, Rt Rev. Charles John, 1843–1921, vol. II
Corfiato, Hector Othon, *died* 1963, vol. VI
Corfield, Rt Rev. Bernard Conyngham, 1890–1965, vol. VI
Corfield, Rev. Claud Evelyn Lacey, *died* 1926, vol. II
Corfield, Sir Conrad Laurence, 1893–1980, vol. VII
Corfield, Col Frederick Alleyne, 1884–1939, vol. III
Corfield, Gerald Frederick Conyngham, 1886–1961, vol. VI
Corfield, William Henry, 1843–1903, vol. I
Cori, Carl Ferdinand, 1896–1984, vol. VIII
Cori, Gerty Theresa, 1896–1957, vol. V
Corish, Brendan, 1918–1990, vol. VIII
Cork and Orrery, 9th Earl of, 1829–1904, vol. I
Cork and Orrery, 10th Earl of, 1861–1925, vol. II
Cork and Orrery, 11th Earl of, 1864–1934, vol. III
Cork and Orrery, 12th Earl of, 1873–1967, vol. VI
Cork and Orrery, 13th Earl of, 1910–1995, vol. IX
Cork, Sir Kenneth Russell, 1913–1991, vol. IX
Cork, Philip Clark, 1854–1936, vol. III (A), vol. IV
Corke, Sir John Henry, *died* 1927, vol. II
Corker, Maj.-Gen. Thomas Martin, 1856–1937, vol. III
Corkery, Daniel, 1878–1964, vol. VI
Corkey, Very Rev. Rt Hon. Robert, 1881–1966, vol. VI
Corkhill, Percy Fullerton, *died* 1959, vol. V
Corkill, Norman Lace, 1898–1966, vol. VI
Corkill, Thomas Frederick, 1893–1965, vol. VI
Corkran, Alice, *died* 1916, vol. II
Corkran, Maj.-Gen. Sir Charles Edward, 1872–1939, vol. III
Corkran, Sir Victor Seymour, 1873–1934, vol. III
Corless, Richard, 1884–1967, vol. VI
Corlett, John, 1841–1915, vol. I
Corlette, Major Hubert Christian, 1869–1956, vol. V
Corlette, Brig. James Montagu Christian, 1880–1969, vol. VI (AII)
Corley, Michael Early Ferrand, 1909–1998, vol. X
Corley Smith, Gerard Thomas, 1909–1997, vol. X
Cormack, Allan MacLeod, 1924–1998, vol. X
Cormack, Benjamin George, 1866–1936, vol. III

Cormack, James Maxwell Ross, 1909–1975, vol. VII
Cormack, John Dewar, 1870–1935, vol. III
Cormack, Sir Magnus Cameron, 1906–1994, vol. IX
Cormie, David; *see* Cormie, J. D.
Cormie, (John) David, 1930–1983, vol. VIII
Cornaby, Rev. William Arthur, 1860–1921, vol. II
Cornelius, Percival, 1874–1960, vol. V
Cornell, Katharine, 1898–1974, vol. VII
Cornell, Ward MacLaurin, 1924–2000, vol. X
Corner, Edred John Henry, 1906–1996, vol. X
Corner, Edred Moss, 1873–1950, vol. IV
Corner, George, 1869–1947, vol. IV
Corner, George Washington, 1889–1981, vol. VIII
Corner, Engr Rear-Adm. John Thomas, 1849–1912, vol. I
Cornewall, Sir Geoffrey, 6th Bt, 1869–1951, vol. V
Cornewall, Rev. Sir George Henry, 5th Bt, 1833–1908, vol. I
Cornewall, Sir William Francis, 7th Bt, 1871–1962, vol. VI
Corney, Bolton Glanvill, 1851–1924, vol. II
Corney, Leonard George, 1886–1955, vol. V
Cornford, Sir Clifford; *see* Cornford, Sir E. C.
Cornford, Sir (Edward) Clifford, 1918–1999, vol. X
Cornford, Frances Crofts, 1886–1960, vol. V
Cornford, Francis Macdonald, 1874–1943, vol. IV
Cornford, Leslie Cope, *died* 1927, vol. II
Cornil, Georges, 1863–1944, vol. IV
Cornish, Rt Rev. Charles Edward, 1842–1936, vol. III
Cornish, Charles John, 1859–1906, vol. I
Cornish, Rev. Ebenezer Darrel, 1849–1922, vol. II
Cornish, Francis Warre, 1839–1916, vol. II
Cornish, George Augustus, 1874–1960, vol. V
Cornish, Rt Rev. George Kestell K.; *see* Kestell-Cornish.
Cornish, Henry Dauncey, 1877–1948, vol. IV
Cornish, Herbert, 1862–1945, vol. IV
Cornish, Hubert Warre, 1872–1934, vol. III
Cornish, Rt Rev. John Rundle, 1837–1918, vol. II
Cornish, Rt Rev. (John) Vernon (Kestell), 1931–1982, vol. VIII
Cornish, Josiah Easton, 1841–1912, vol. I
Cornish, Rt Rev. Robert Kestell K.; *see* Kestell-Cornish.
Cornish, Ronald James, 1898–1986, vol. VIII
Cornish, Vaughan, 1862–1948, vol. IV
Cornish, Rt Rev. Vernon; *see* Cornish, Rt Rev. J. V. K.
Cornish, William Herbert, 1906–1995, vol. IX
Cornish-Bowden, Col James Hubert Thomas, 1870–1938, vol. III
Cornwall, Ven. Alan Whitmore, 1858–1932, vol. III
Cornwall, Rt Hon. Sir Edwin, 1st Bt, 1863–1953, vol. V
Cornwall, Ernest, 1875–1966, vol. VI
Cornwall, Ian Wolfran, 1909–1994, vol. IX
Cornwall, Gen. Sir James Handyside M.; *see* Marshall-Cornwall.
Cornwall, Lt-Col John Wolfran, 1870–1947, vol. IV
Cornwall, Rt Rev. Nigel Edmund, 1903–1984, vol. VIII
Cornwall, Sir Reginald Edwin, 2nd Bt, 1887–1962, vol. VI

Cornwall, Maj.-Gen. Richard Frank, 1902–1967, vol. VI
Cornwall-Jones, Brig. Arthur Thomas, 1900–1980, vol. VII
Cornwallis, 1st Baron, 1864–1935, vol. III
Cornwallis, 2nd Baron, 1892–1982, vol. VIII
Cornwallis, Sir Kinahan, 1883–1959, vol. V
Cornwallis-West, Major George F. M., 1874–1951, vol. V
Cornwallis-West, William Cornwallis; see West.
Cornwell, Ven. Leonard Cyril, 1893–1971, vol. VII
Corrance, Frederick Snowden, died 1906, vol. I
Corrie, Major Alfred Wynne, 1856–1919, vol. II
Corrie, Sir Owen Cecil Kirkpatrick, 1882–1965, vol. VI
Corrie, Rodney; see Corrie, W. R.
Corrie, W(allace) Rodney, 1919–1997, vol. X
Corrie, Maj.-Gen. William Taylor, 1838–1931, vol. III
Corrigan, Most Rev. Michael Augustine, 1839–1902, vol. I
Corrigan, Rev. Terence Edward, 1915–1975, vol. VII
Corrin, John Bowes, 1922–1994, vol. IX
Corry, Adm. Hon. Armar L.; see Lowry-Corry.
Corry, Lt-Col Sir Henry Charles L.; see Lowry-Corry.
Corry, Col Hon. Henry William L.; see Lowry-Corry.
Corry, Sir James Perowne Ivo Myles, 3rd Bt, 1892–1987, vol. VIII
Corry, Major John Beaumont, 1874–1914, vol. I
Corry, Brig.-Gen. Noel Armar L.; see Lowry-Corry.
Corry, Sir William, 2nd Bt, 1859–1926, vol. II
Corry, Lt-Comdr Sir William James, 4th Bt, 1924–2000, vol. X
Corsan, Brig. Reginald Arthur, 1893–1942, vol. IV
Corser, Captain Charles Huskisson, 1886–1962, vol. VI
Corser, Haden, 1845–1906, vol. I
Corson, Rear-Adm. Eric Reid, 1887–1972, vol. VII
Corstorphine, George Steuart, 1868–1919, vol. II
Cortelyou, George Bruce, 1862–1940, vol. III
Cortie, Rev. Father Aloysius Laurence, 1859–1925, vol. II
Cortis-Stanford, Gp Captain C. E., 1874–1933, vol. III
Cortissoz, Royal, 1869–1948, vol. IV
Cortlandt, Lyn, 1926–1979, vol. VII
Cortot, Alfred, 1877–1962, vol. VI
Corwin, Edward Samuel, 1878–1963, vol. VI
Cory, Ven. Alexander, 1890–1973, vol. VII
Cory, Ven. Charles Page, 1859–1942, vol. IV
Cory, Sir Clifford John, 1st Bt (cr 1907), 1859–1941, vol. IV
Cory, Sir Clinton James Donald, 4th Bt, 1909–1991, vol. IX
Cory, Elizabeth Cansh, (Lady Cory), died 1956, vol. V
Cory, Lt-Col Evan James Trevor, 1863–1957, vol. V
Cory, Sir George Edward, 1862–1935, vol. III
Cory, Lt-Gen. Sir George Norton, 1874–1968, vol. VI
Cory, Sir Herbert; see Cory, Sir J. H.

Cory, Sir Herbert George Donald, 2nd Bt (cr 1919), 1879–1935, vol. III
Cory, Sir (James) Herbert, 1st Bt (cr 1919), 1857–1933, vol. III
Cory, John, 1828–1910, vol. I
Cory, John Herbert, 1889–1939, vol. III
Cory, Percy Albert, 1870–1936, vol. III
Cory, Richard, 1830–1914, vol. I
Cory, Surg. Rear-Adm. Robert Francis Preston, 1885–1961, vol. VI
Cory, Mrs Theodore; see Graham, W.
Cory, Sir Vyvyan Donald, 3rd Bt (cr 1919), 1906–1941, vol. IV
Cory, William Wallace, 1865–1943, vol. IV
Cory, Winifred; see Graham, W.
Cory-Wright, Sir Arthur Cory, 2nd Bt, 1869–1951, vol. V
Cory-Wright, Sir Cory Francis, 1st Bt, 1839–1909, vol. I
Cory-Wright, Sir Geoffrey, 3rd Bt, 1892–1969, vol. VI
Coryndon, Sir Robert Thorne, 1870–1925, vol. II
Coryton, Air Chief Marshal Sir Alec; see Coryton, Air Chief Marshal Sir W. A.
Coryton, Frederick, 1850–1924, vol. II
Coryton, William, 1847–1919, vol. II
Coryton, Air Chief Marshal Sir (William) Alec, 1895–1981, vol. VIII
Cosby, Dudley Sydney Ashworth, 1862–1923, vol. II
Cosby, Brig. Noel Robert Charles, 1890–1981, vol. VIII
Cosby, Col Robert Ashworth Godolphin, 1837–1920, vol. II
Cosgrave, Rev. Francis Herbert, 1880–1971, vol. VII
Cosgrave, Col L. Moore, 1890–1971, vol. VII
Cosgrave, MacDowel, died 1925, vol. II
Cosgrave, Mary Josephine, died 1941, vol. IV
Cosgrave, Sir William Alexander, 1879–1952, vol. V
Cosgrave, Rev. William Frederick, 1857–1936, vol. III
Cosgrave, William Thomas, 1880–1965, vol. VI
Cosgrove, Dame Gertrude Ann, 1882–1962, vol. VI
Cosgrove, Hon. Sir Robert, 1884–1969, vol. VI
Coslett, Air Marshal Sir Norman; see Air Marshal Sir T. N.
Coslett, Air Marshal Sir (Thomas) Norman, 1909–1987, vol. VIII
Cossar, George Carter, 1880–1942, vol. IV
Cossimbazar, Maharaja Srischandra Nandy, 1897–1952, vol. V
Cosslett, Ellis; see Cosslett, V. E.
Cosslett, (Vernon) Ellis, 1908–1990, vol. VIII
Costain, Sir Albert Percy, 1910–1987, vol. VIII
Costain, Rev. Alfred James, 1881–1963, vol. VI
Costain, Sir Richard Rylandes, 1902–1966, vol. VI
Costain, Thomas Bertram, 1885–1965, vol. VI
Costaki, Anthopoulos Pasha, 1838–1902, vol. I
Costar, Sir Norman Edgar, 1909–1995, vol. IX
Coste, John Henry, 1871–1949, vol. IV
Costeker, Captain John Henry Dives, 1879–1915, vol. I
Costello, Desmond Patrick, 1912–1964, vol. VI

Costello, Brig.-Gen. Edmund W., 1873–1949, vol. IV
Costello, John Aloysius, 1891–1976, vol. VII
Costello, Sir Leonard Wilfred James, 1881–1972, vol. VII
Coster, Howard, (Howard Sydney Musgrave Coster), died 1959, vol. V
Costigan, Captain Charles Telford, died 1917, vol. II
Costigan, Hon. John, 1835–1916, vol. II
Costigan, Rev. John, 1916–1978, vol. VII
Costin, Maj.-Gen. Eric Boyd, 1889–1971, vol. VII
Costin, William Conrad, 1893–1970, vol. VI
Costley-White, Cyril Grove, 1913–1979, vol. VII
Costley-White, Very Rev. Harold, 1878–1966, vol. VI
Cot, Pierre Donatien Alphonse, 1911–1993, vol. IX
Cotes, Lt-Col Charles James, 1847–1913, vol. I
Cotes, Mrs Everard; see Cotes, S. J.
Cotes, Everard, 1862–1944, vol. IV
Cotes, Sara Jeanette, (Mrs Everard Cotes), 1861–1922, vol. II
Cotes, Sir Merton Russell, 1835–1921, vol. II
Cotes, Peter, (Sydney Arthur Boulting), 1912–1998, vol. X
Cotes-Preedy, Digby, 1875–1942, vol. IV
Cotman, Frederic George, 1850–1920, vol. II
Cotsworth, Moses B., 1859–1943, vol. IV
Cott, Hugh Bamford, 1900–1987, vol. VIII
Cottam, Rev. Maj.-Gen. Algernon Edward, 1893–1964, vol. VI
Cottell, Col Reginald James Cope, 1858–1924, vol. II
Cottenham, 4th Earl of, 1874–1919, vol. II
Cottenham, 5th Earl of, 1901–1922, vol. II
Cottenham, 6th Earl of, 1903–1943, vol. IV
Cottenham, 7th Earl of, 1907–1968, vol. VI
Cottenham, 8th Earl of, 1948–2000, vol. X
Cotter, Col Edward, 1892–1961, vol. VI
Cotter, Maj.-Gen. Francis Gibson, 1857–1928, vol. II
Cotter, Lt-Col Harry John, 1871–1921, vol. II
Cotter, Sir James Laurence, 5th Bt, 1887–1924, vol. II
Cotter, Most Rev. William Timothy, 1866–1940, vol. III
Cotterell, Cecil Bernard, 1875–1957, vol. V
Cotterell, Sir Geers Henry, 3rd Bt, 1834–1900, vol. I
Cotterell, Gilbert Thorp, 1891–1963, vol. VI
Cotterell, Sir John Richard Geers, 4th Bt, 1866–1937, vol. III
Cotterell, Mabel, died 1968, vol. VI
Cotterell, Lt-Col Sir Richard Charles Geers, 5th Bt, 1907–1978, vol. VII
Cotterill, James Henry, 1836–1922, vol. II
Cotterill, Sir (Joseph) Montagu, 1851–1933, vol. III
Cotterill, Sir Montagu; see Cotterill, Sir J. M.
Cottesloe, 2nd Baron, 1830–1918, vol. II
Cottesloe, 3rd Baron, 1862–1956, vol. V
Cottesloe, 4th Baron, 1900–1994, vol. IX
Cottet, Charles, died 1925, vol. II
Cottier, Sir Charles Edward, 1869–1928, vol. II
Cottingham, Lt-Col Edward Roden, 1866–1930, vol. III

Cottingham, Dame Margaret; see Teyte, Dame Maggie.
Cottington-Taylor, Dorothy Daisy, died 1944, vol. IV
Cottle, Adela, 1861–1940, vol. III
Cotton, Lt-Col Arthur Egerton, 1876–1922, vol. II
Cotton, Brig.-Gen. Arthur Stedman, 1873–1952, vol. V
Cotton, Sir Arthur Thomas, 1803–1899, vol. I
Cotton, Baron Francis C.; see Carter-Cotton.
Cotton, Charles, 1856–1939, vol. III
Cotton, Sir Charles Andrew, 1885–1970, vol. VI (AII)
Cotton, Charles William Egerton, died 1931, vol. III
Cotton, Sir Evan; see Cotton, Sir H. E. A.
Cotton, Maj.-Gen. Frederic Conyers, 1807–1901, vol. I
Cotton, Sir George, 1842–1905, vol. I
Cotton, Sir George Frederick, 1877–1943, vol. IV
Cotton, Harry, 1889–1985, vol. VIII
Cotton, Sir (Harry) Evan Auguste, 1868–1939, vol. III
Cotton, Henry; see Cotton, T. H.
Cotton, Rev. Henry Aldrich, 1835–1927, vol. II
Cotton, Henry Egerton, 1929–1993, vol. IX
Cotton, Sir Henry John Stedman, 1845–1915, vol. I
Cotton, Jack, 1903–1964, vol. VI
Cotton, Rev. (James) Stapleton, 1849–1932, vol. III
Cotton, James Sutherland, 1847–1918, vol. II
Cotton, Sir James Temple, 1879–1965, vol. VI
Cotton, Leo Arthur, 1883–1963, vol. VI
Cotton, Leonard Thomas, 1922–1992, vol. IX
Cotton, Michael James, 1920–1981, vol. VIII
Cotton, Montagu Arthur Finch, 1885–1915, vol. I
Cotton, Percy Horace Gordon P.; see Powell-Cotton.
Cotton, Adm. Richard Greville Arthur Wellington S.; see Stapleton-Cotton.
Cotton, Col Hon. Richard Southwell George S.; see Stapleton-Cotton.
Cotton, Lt-Col Ronald Egerton, 1876–1932, vol. III
Cotton, Rev. Stapleton; see Cotton, Rev. J. S.
Cotton, Captain Stapleton Charles, 1831–1908, vol. I
Cotton, Thomas Forrest, died 1965, vol. VI
Cotton, (Thomas) Henry, 1907–1987, vol. VIII
Cotton, Lt-Col Vere Egerton, 1888–1970, vol. VI
Cotton, William Francis, 1847–1917, vol. II
Cotton, Sir William James Richmond, 1822–1902, vol. I
Cotton-Jodrell, Col Sir Edward Thomas Davenant, 1847–1917, vol. II
Cottrell, Brig. Arthur Foulkes Baglietto, 1891–1962, vol. VI
Cottrell, Sir Edward Baglietto, 1896–1976, vol. VII
Cottrell, Leonard, 1913–1974, vol. VII
Cottrell, Lt-Col Reginald Foulkes, 1885–1924, vol. II
Cottrell, Tom Leadbetter, 1923–1973, vol. VII
Cottrell, William Henry, 1863–1926, vol. II
Cottrell-Dormer, Charles Walter, 1860–1945, vol. IV
Cottrell-Hill, Maj.-Gen. Robert Charles, 1903–1965, vol. VI

Cotts, Sir Campbell Mitchell; *see* Cotts, Sir W. C. M.
Cotts, Sir Crichton; *see* Cotts, Sir R. C. M.
Cotts, Sir (Robert) Crichton Mitchell, 3rd Bt, 1903–1995, vol. IX
Cotts, Sir (William) Campbell Mitchell-, 2nd Bt, 1902–1964, vol. VI
Cotts, Sir William Dingwall Mitchell, 1st Bt, 1871–1932, vol. III
Coty, René, 1882–1962, vol. VI
Coubertin, Pierre de Fredi, Baron de, 1863–1937, vol. III
Coubrough, Anthony Cathcart, 1877–1963, vol. VI
Couch, Sir Arthur Thomas Q.; *see* Quiller-Couch.
Couch, Rt Hon. Sir Richard, 1817–1905, vol. I
Couch, William Charles Milford, 1894–1975, vol. VII
Couchman, Dame Elizabeth May Ramsay, 1878–1982, vol. VIII
Couchman, Sir Francis Dundas, 1864–1948, vol. IV
Couchman, Col George Henry Holbeche, 1859–1936, vol. III
Couchman, Brig. Sir Harold John, 1882–1956, vol. V
Couchman, Malcolm Edward, 1869–1938, vol. III
Couchman, Rev. Reginald Henry, 1874–1948, vol. IV
Couchman, Adm. Sir Walter Thomas, 1905–1981, vol. VIII
Coudenhove-Kalergi, Richard N., 1894–1972, vol. VII
Coudert, Most Rev. Antony, 1861–1929, vol. III
Coudurier de Chassaigne, Joseph, 1878–1961, vol. VI
Coué, Emile, *died* 1926, vol. II
Coughlan, Cornelius, 1828–1915, vol. I
Coughtrie, Thomas, 1895–1985, vol. VIII
Coulcher, Mary Caroline, 1852–1925, vol. II
Couldrey, Robert Charles, 1890–1974, vol. VII
Couling, Samuel, 1859–1922, vol. II
Coull, Hon. William, 1857–1918, vol. II
Coulshaw, Rev. Leonard, 1896–1988, vol. VIII
Coulshed, Dame Frances; *see* Coulshed, Dame M. F.
Coulshed, Dame (Mary) Frances, 1904–1998, vol. X
Coulson, Charles Alfred, 1910–1974, vol. VII
Coulson, Lt-Col Frank Morris, 1880–1953, vol. V
Coulson, Frederick Raymond, 1864–1922, vol. II
Coulson, Lt-Col John, 1873–1929, vol. III
Coulson, Sir John Eltringham, 1909–1997, vol. X
Coulson, John Metcalfe, 1910–1990, vol. VIII
Coulson, Noel James, 1928–1986, vol. VIII
Coulson, Maj.-Gen. Samuel M.; *see* Moore-Coulson.
Coulson, William Lisle B., 1840–1911, vol. I
Coultas, Frederick George, 1888–1961, vol. VI
Coultas, William Whitham, 1890–1973, vol. VII
Coulter, Very Rev. Isaac, 1851–1934, vol. III
Coulter, Ven. J. W., 1867–1956, vol. V
Coulter, Robert, 1914–1987, vol. VIII
Coulter, Robert Millar, 1857–1927, vol. II
Coulthard, Rev. Canon Hugh Robert, 1860–1939, vol. III
Coulthard, Alan George Weall, 1924–1988, vol. VIII
Coulthard, William Henderson, 1913–1993, vol. IX
Coulton, George Gordon, 1858–1947, vol. IV

Counsell, John William, 1905–1987, vol. VIII
Counsell, Paul Hayward, 1926–1993, vol. IX
Couper, Sir George Ebenezer Wilson, 2nd Bt, 1824–1908, vol. I
Couper, Major Sir George Robert Cecil, 5th Bt, 1898–1975, vol. VII
Couper, Sir Guy, 4th Bt, 1889–1973, vol. VII
Couper, James Brown, *died* 1946, vol. IV
Couper, John, *died* 1918, vol. II
Couper, Sir John C., 1867–1937, vol. III
Couper, John Duncan Campbell, 1876–1962, vol. VI
Couper, Leslie, 1871–1929, vol. III
Couper, Sir Ramsay George Henry, 3rd Bt, 1855–1949, vol. IV
Couper, Sir Thomas, 1878–1954, vol. V
Couper, Maj.-Gen. Sir Victor Arthur, 1859–1938, vol. III
Couperus, Louis, 1863–1923, vol. II
Coupland, Sir Reginald, 1884–1952, vol. V
Coupland, Sidney, 1849–1930, vol. III
Coupland, William Chatterton, 1838–1915, vol. I
Courage, Brig.-Gen. Anthony, 1875–1944, vol. IV
Courage, Edward Raymond, 1906–1982, vol. VIII
Courage, James Francis, 1903–1963, vol. VI
Courage, Lt-Col John Hubert, 1891–1967, vol. VI
Courage, John Michell, 1868–1931, vol. III
Courage, Comdr Rafe Edward, 1902–1960, vol. V
Courage, Richard Hubert, 1915–1994, vol. IX
Couratin, Rev. Canon Arthur Hubert, 1902–1988, vol. VIII
Courcel, Baron de; (Geoffroy Louis Chodron de Courcel), 1912–1992, vol. IX
Courchesne, Most Rev. Georges, 1880–1950, vol IV (A), vol. V
Courlander, Alphonse, 1881–1914, vol. I
Cournand, André Frédéric, 1895–1988, vol. VIII
Cournos, John, 1881–1966, vol. VI
Courroux, George Augustus, 1852–1923, vol. II
Court, Donald; *see* Court, S. D. M.
Court, Emily, *died* 1957, vol. V
Court, Sir Josiah, 1841–1938, vol. III
Court, (Seymour) Donald (Mayneord), 1912–1994, vol. IX
Court, William Henry Bassano, 1904–1971, vol. VII
Courtauld, Augustine, 1904–1959, vol. V
Courtauld, Major John Sewell, 1880–1942, vol. IV
Courtauld, Samuel, 1876–1947, vol. IV
Courtauld, Samuel Augustine, 1865–1953, vol. V
Courtauld, Sir Stephen Lewis, 1883–1967, vol. VI
Courtauld, Sir William Julien, 1st Bt, 1870–1940, vol. III
Courtauld Thomson, 1st Baron, 1865–1954, vol. V
Courtenay, Lord; Henry Reginald Courtenay, 1836–1898, vol. I
Courtenay, Col Arthur Henry, 1852–1927, vol. II
Courtenay, Brig.-Gen. Edward Reginald, 1853–1919, vol. II
Courtenay, Hon. Sir Harrison; *see* Courtenay, Hon. Sir W. H.
Courtenay, Henry, *died* 1921, vol. II
Courtenay, Sir Irving; *see* Courtenay, Sir J. I.
Courtenay, Sir (John) Irving, 1837–1912, vol. I
Courtenay, Rt Rev. Reginald, 1813–1906, vol. I

Courtenay, Hon. Sir (Woldrich) Harrison, 1904–1982, vol. VIII
Courthope, 1st Baron, 1877–1955, vol. V
Courthope, William John, 1842–1917, vol. II
Courthope-Munroe, Sir Harry, 1860–1951, vol. V
Courtice, Col James George, died 1939, vol. III
Courtis, Sir John Wesley, 1859–1939, vol. III
Courtneidge, Dame Cicely; see Courtneidge, Dame E. C.
Courtneidge, Dame (Esmerelda) Cicely, 1893–1980, vol. VII
Courtney of Penwith, 1st Baron, 1832–1918, vol. II
Courtney, Comdr Anthony Tosswill, 1908–1988, vol. VIII
Courtney, Air Chief Marshal Sir Christopher Lloyd, 1890–1976, vol. VII
Courtney, Col Edward Arthur Waldegrave, 1868–1926, vol. II
Courtney, Maj.-Gen. Edward Henry, 1836–1913, vol. I
Courtney, Rt Rev. Frederick, 1837–1918, vol. II
Courtney, Lt-Col Frederick Harold, 1875–1937, vol. III
Courtney, Gp Captain Ivon Terence, 1885–1978, vol. VII
Courtney, Janet Elizabeth, 1865–1954, vol. V
Courtney, John Mortimer, 1838–1920, vol. II
Courtney, Dame Kathleen D'Olier, 1878–1974, vol. VII
Courtney, Col Richard Edmond, 1870–1919, vol. II
Courtney, Victor Desmond, 1894–1970, vol. VI (AII)
Courtney, William Leonard, 1850–1928, vol. II
Courtney, William Prideaux, 1845–1913, vol. I
Courtown, 5th Earl of, 1823–1914, vol. I
Courtown, 6th Earl of, 1853–1933, vol. III
Courtown, 7th Earl of, 1877–1957, vol. V
Courtown, 8th Earl of, 1908–1975, vol. VII
Coury, Captain Gabriel George, 1896–1956, vol. V
Cousens, Col Robert Baxter, 1880–1943, vol. IV
Cousin, David Ross, 1904–1984, vol. VIII
Cousins, Arthur George, 1882–1949, vol. IV
Cousins, Clarence W., died 1954, vol. V
Cousins, Donald, 1900–1964, vol. VI
Cousins, Edmund Richard John Ratcliffe, 1888–1955, vol. V
Cousins, Rt Hon. Frank, 1904–1986, vol. VIII
Cousins, Sir Harry, 1852–1935, vol. III
Cousins, Herbert H., 1869–1949, vol. IV
Cousins, John Ratcliffe, 1863–1928, vol. II
Cousins, Norman, 1915–1990, vol. VIII
Cousins, William Henry, 1833–1917, vol. II
Coussey, Sir James Henley, 1891–1958, vol. V
Coussirat, Rev. Daniel, 1841–1907, vol. I
Coussmaker, Col Lannoy John, 1883–1937, vol. III
Cousteau, Jacques-Yves, 1910–1997, vol. X
Coutanche, Baron (Life Peer); Alexander Moncrieff Coutanche, 1892–1973, vol. VII
Coutts, Charles Ronald Vawdrey, 1876–1938, vol. III
Coutts, Francis James Henderson, 1865–1949, vol. IV
Coutts, Gen. Frederick, 1899–1986, vol. VIII
Coutts, James, 1852–1913, vol. I
Coutts, Sir Walter Fleming, 1912–1988, vol. VIII

Coutts, Rt Hon. William Lehman Ashmead Bartlett-B.; see Burdett-Coutts.
Coutts, William Strachan, 1873–1963, vol. VI
Coutts Donald, William, 1906–1974, vol. VII
Couve de Murville, Maurice, 1907–1999, vol. X
Covacevich, Sir (Anthony) Thomas, 1915–1999, vol. X
Covacevich, Sir Thomas; see Covacevich, Sir A. T.
Covell, Maj.-Gen. Sir Gordon, 1887–1975, vol. VII
Coventry, Rev. John Seton, 1915–1998, vol. X
Coverdale, Ralph, 1918–1975, vol. VII
Couvreur, Mme Jessie, died 1897, vol. I
Couzens, Sir George Edwin, 1851–1925, vol. II
Couzens, Sir Henry Herbert, died 1944, vol. IV
Cove, Captain George Edward, 1889–1967, vol. VI
Cove, William George, 1888–1963, vol. VI
Coventry, 9th Earl of, 1838–1930, vol. III
Coventry, 10th Earl of, 1900–1940, vol. III
Coventry, Bernard, 1859–1929, vol. III
Coventry, Col Hon. Charles John, 1867–1929, vol. III
Coventry, Henry Arthur, 1852–1925, vol. II
Coventry, Henry Robert Beauclerk, 1871–1953, vol. V
Coventry, Hon. Henry Thomas, 1868–1934, vol. III
Coventry, Rev. Henry William, died 1920, vol. II
Coventry, Millis, 1838–1930, vol. III
Coventry, R. M. G., died 1914, vol. I
Coventry, Hon. Sir Reginald, 1869–1940, vol. III
Covernton, Alfred Laurence, 1872–1961, vol. VI
Covernton, James Gargrave, 1868–1957, vol. V
Covington, Stenton, 1857–1935, vol. III
Covington, Walter George, died 1939, vol. III
Covington, Rev. William, died 1908, vol. I
Cowan, Brig. Alan; see Cowan, Brig. J. A. C.
Cowan, Sir Christopher (George) Armstrong, 1889–1979, vol. VII
Cowan, Sir Darcy Rivers Warren, 1885–1958, vol. V
Cowan, Rev. David Galloway, died 1921, vol. II
Cowan, Maj.-Gen. David Tennant, 1896–1983, vol. VIII
Cowan, Dugald M'Coig, 1865–1933, vol. III
Cowan, Rev. Henry, 1844–1932, vol. III
Cowan, Sir Henry, 1862–1932, vol. III
Cowan, Sir (Henry) Kenneth, 1900–1971, vol. VII
Cowan, Col Henry Vivian, 1854–1918, vol. II
Cowan, Ian Borthwick, 1932–1990, vol. VIII
Cowan, James, 1870–1943, vol. IV
Cowan, Brig. (James) Alan (Comrie), 1923–1999, vol. X
Cowan, Col James Henry, 1856–1943, vol. IV
Cowan, James Macfarlane, 1912–1967, vol. VI
Cowan, Captain James William Alston, 1868–1899, vol. I
Cowan, Sir John, 1st Bt (cr 1894), 1814–1900, vol. I
Cowan, John, 1849–1926, vol. II
Cowan, Hon. John, 1847–1927, vol. II
Cowan, Sir John, 1844–1929, vol. III
Cowan, John, 1869–1935, vol. III
Cowan, John, 1870–1947, vol. IV
Cowan, Hon. Sir John, 1866–1953, vol. V
Cowan, Sir Kenneth; see Cowan, Sir H. K.
Cowan, Lt-Col Percy John, died 1954, vol. V

Cowan, Sir Robert, 1932–1993, vol. IX
Cowan, Samuel, 1835–1914, vol. I
Cowan, Thomas William, 1840–1926, vol. II
Cowan, Adm. Sir Walter Henry, 1st Bt (*cr* 1921), 1871–1956, vol. V
Cowan, William Christie, 1878–1950, vol. IV (A)
Cowan, William Graham, 1919–1997, vol. X
Cowan-Douglas, Hugh, 1895–1960, vol. V
Cowans, Harry Lowes, 1932–1985, vol. VIII
Cowans, Gen. Sir John Steven, 1862–1921, vol. II
Coward, Sir Cecil Allen, 1845–1938, vol. III
Coward, Sir Henry, 1849–1944, vol. IV
Coward, Sir (John Charles) Lewis, 1852–1930, vol. III
Coward, Sir Noel, 1899–1973, vol. VII
Coward, Thomas Alfred, 1867–1933, vol. III
Cowderoy, Most Rev. Mgr Cyril Conrad, 1905–1976, vol. VII
Cowdray, 1st Viscount, 1856–1927, vol. II
Cowdray, 2nd Viscount, 1882–1933, vol. III
Cowdray, 3rd Viscount, 1910–1995, vol. IX
Cowdrey of Tonbridge, Baron (Life Peer); Michael Colin Cowdrey, 1932–2000, vol. X
Cowdroy, Joan Alice, *died* 1946, vol. IV
Cowdry, Rt Rev. Roy Walter Frederick, 1915–1984, vol. VIII
Cowe, Collin; *see* Cowe, R. G. C.
Cowe, (Robert George) Collin, 1917–1999, vol. X
Cowell, Maj.-Gen. Sir Ernest Marshall, 1886–1971, vol. VII
Cowell, Frank Richard, 1897–1978, vol. VII
Cowell, George, 1836–1927, vol. II
Cowell, Very Rev. George Young, 1838–1930, vol. III
Cowell, Hubert Russell, *died* 1967, vol. VI
Cowell, John Richard, 1933–1998, vol. X
Cowell, Rev. Maurice Byles, *died* 1919, vol. II
Cowell, Philip Herbert, *died* 1949, vol. IV
Cowell, Sibert Forrest, 1863–1949, vol. IV
Cowell, Stuart Jasper, 1891–1971, vol. VII
Cowell-Stepney, Sir Emile Algernon Arthur Keppel, 2nd Bt, 1834–1909, vol. I
Cowen, Alan Biddulph, 1896–1989, vol. VIII
Cowen, Sir Frederic Hyman, 1852–1935, vol. III
Cowen, John David, 1904–1981, vol. VIII
Cowen, John Edward, 1873–1938, vol. III
Cowen, Joseph, 1831–1899, vol. I
Cowen, Richard John, 1871–1928, vol. II
Cowern, Raymond Teague, 1913–1986, vol. VIII
Cowey, Brig. Bernard Turing Vionnée, 1911–1997, vol. X
Cowgill, John Vincent, 1888–1959, vol. V
Cowgill, Rt Rev. Joseph Robert, 1860–1936, vol. III
Cowham, Hilda, *died* 1964, vol. VI
Cowie, Brig.-Gen. Alexander Hugh, 1860–1933, vol. III
Cowie, Very Rev. Benjamin Morgan, *died* 1900, vol. I
Cowie, Maj.-Gen. Charles Henry, 1861–1941, vol. IV
Cowie, Col Henry Edward Colvin, 1872–1963, vol. VI
Cowie, Major Hugh Norman Ramsay, 1872–1915, vol. I

Cowie, Rev. James Ratchford de Wolfe, 1855–1935, vol. III
Cowie, Mervyn Hugh, 1909–1996, vol. X
Cowie, Rt Rev. William Garden, 1831–1902, vol. I
Cowie, William Patrick, *died* 1924, vol. II
Cowland, Rear-Adm. Geoffrey; *see* Cowland, Rear-Adm. W. G.
Cowland, Bt Lt-Col Walter Storey, 1888–1942, vol. IV
Cowland, Rear-Adm. (William) Geoffrey, 1895–1966, vol. VI
Cowles, Virginia, 1910–1983, vol. VIII
Cowles-Voysey, Charles, 1889–1981, vol. VIII
Cowley, 3rd Earl, 1866–1919, vol. II
Cowley, 4th Earl, 1890–1962, vol. VI
Cowley, 5th Earl, 1921–1968, vol. VI
Cowley, 6th Earl, 1946–1975, vol. VII
Cowley, Hon. Sir Alfred Sandlings Cowley, 1848–1926, vol. II
Cowley, Sir Arthur Ernest, 1861–1931, vol. III
Cowley, Air Vice-Marshal Arthur Thomas Noel, 1888–1960, vol. V
Cowley, Rev. Canon Colin Patrick, 1902–1993, vol. IX
Cowley, Denis Martin, 1919–1985, vol. VIII
Cowley, Herbert, 1885–1967, vol. VI
Cowley, John Duncan, 1897–1944, vol. IV
Cowley, Lt-Gen. Sir John Guise, 1905–1993, vol. IX
Cowley, Kenneth Martin, 1912–1998, vol. X
Cowley, Sir Percy; *see* Cowley, Sir W. P.
Cowley, Sir (William) Percy, 1886–1958, vol. V
Cowley-Brown, Rev. George James, 1832–1924, vol. II
Cowlin, Sir Francis Nicholas, 1868–1945, vol. IV
Cowling, Donald George, 1904–1975, vol. VII
Cowling, George H., 1881–1946, vol. IV
Cowling, Richard John, 1911–1987, vol. VIII
Cowling, Thomas George, 1906–1990, vol. VIII
Cowper, 7th Earl, 1834–1905, vol. I
Cowper, Brig. Anthony William, 1913–1983, vol. VIII
Cowper, Cecil, 1856–1916, vol. II
Cowper, Frank, 1849–1930, vol. III
Cowper, Frank Cadogan, 1877–1958, vol. V
Cowper, Henry Swainson, 1865–1941, vol. IV
Cowper, Maj.-Gen. Maitland, 1859–1932, vol. III
Cowper, Lt-Col Malcolm Gordon, 1877–1931, vol. III
Cowper, Sir Norman Lethbridge, 1896–1987, vol. VIII
Cowper, Sydney, 1854–1922, vol. II
Cowper-Coles, Sherard Osborn, *died* 1936, vol. III
Cowtan, Air Vice-Marshal Frank Cuninghame, 1888–1950, vol. IV
Cox; *see* Roxbee Cox, family name of Baron Kings Norton.
Cox, A. W., 1857–1919, vol. II
Cox, Adelaide, 1860–1945, vol. IV
Cox, Col Alexander Temple, 1836–1907, vol. I
Cox, Albert Edward, 1916–1992, vol. IX
Cox, Alfred, 1866–1954, vol. V
Cox, Alfred Innes, 1894–1970, vol. VI
Cox, Rev. Alfred Peachey, 1862–1930, vol. III
Cox, Sir Anthony Wakefield, 1915–1993, vol. IX
Cox, Arthur Frederick, 1849–1925, vol. II

Cox, Arthur Henry, 1888–1971, vol. VII
Cox, Arthur Hubert, 1884–1961, vol. VI
Cox, Arthur Sambell, 1876–1951, vol. V
Cox, Captain Bernard Thomas, 1884–1935, vol. III
Cox, Rt Rev. Charles, 1848–1936, vol. III
Cox, Maj.-Gen. Charles Frederick, 1863–1947, vol. IV
Cox, Lt-Col Sir (Charles) Henry (Fortnom), 1880–1953, vol. V
Cox, Charles Leslie, 1880–1963, vol. VI
Cox, Sir Charles Thomas, 1858–1933, vol. III
Cox, Maj.-Gen. Charles Vyvyan, 1819–1903, vol. I
Cox, Sir Christopher William Machell, 1899–1982, vol. VIII
Cox, Cuthbert Eustace Connop, 1885–1958, vol. V
Cox, Cuthbert Machell, 1881–1962, vol. VI
Cox, E. Albert, 1876–1955, vol. V
Cox, Col Edgar William, 1882–1918, vol. II
Cox, Edmund Charles, 1856–1935, vol. III
Cox, Bt-Col Sir (Edward) Geoffrey Hippisley, 1884–1954, vol. V
Cox, Lt-Col Edward Henry, 1863–1925, vol. II
Cox, Hon. Sir (Edward) Owen, 1866–1932, vol. III
Cox, Lt-Col Edwin Charles, 1868–1958, vol. V
Cox, Sir (Ernest) Gordon, 1906–1996, vol. X
Cox, Euan Hillhouse Methven, 1893–1977, vol. VII
Cox, Major Eustace R.; see Richardson-Cox.
Cox, Francis Albert, 1862–1920, vol. II
Cox, Bt-Col Sir Geoffrey Hippisley; see Cox, Bt Col Sir E. G. H.
Cox, Maj.-Gen. George, 1838–1909, vol. I
Cox, Hon. George Albertus, 1840–1914, vol. I
Cox, Rt Rev. George Bede, 1854–1938, vol. III
Cox, George Henry, 1848–1935, vol. III
Cox, George Lissant, 1879–1967, vol. VI
Cox, Sir (George) Trenchard, 1905–1995, vol. IX
Cox, Rev. Sir George William, 14th Bt (cr 1706), 1827–1902, vol. I
Cox, Sir Gordon; see Cox, Sir E. G.
Cox, Gen. Sir H. Vaughan, 1860–1923, vol. II
Cox, Major Harding, died 1944, vol. IV
Cox, Harold, 1859–1936, vol. III
Cox, Harry Bernard, 1906–1989, vol. VIII
Cox, Lt-Col Sir Henry; see Cox, Lt-Col Sir C. H. F.
Cox, Rev. Heraclitus Matthew, 1816–1938, vol. III
Cox, Sir Herbert Charles Fahie, 1893–1973, vol. VII
Cox, Hugh Bertram, 1861–1930, vol. III
Cox, Ian Herbert, 1910–1990, vol. VIII
Cox, Irwin Edward Bainbridge, 1838–1922, vol. II
Cox, Sir Ivor Richard, 1891–1964, vol. VI
Cox, Surg. Rear-Adm. James, 1928–1991, vol. IX
Cox, Rev. James Taylor, 1865–1948, vol. IV
Cox, John Charles, 1843–1919, vol. II
Cox, John Hugh, 1870–1922, vol. II
Cox, John S.; see Snead-Cox.
Cox, Sir John William, 1821–1901, vol. I
Cox, Sir John William, 1900–1990, vol. VIII
Cox, Air Vice-Marshal Joseph, 1904–1986, vol. VIII
Cox, Keith Gordon, 1933–1998, vol. X
Cox, Leonard Bell, 1894–1976, vol. VII (AII)
Cox, Leslie Reginald, 1897–1965, vol. VI
Cox, Sir Lionel; see Cox, Sir W. H. L.
Cox, Rev. Lionel; Edgar, 1868–1945, vol. IV

Cox, Maj.-Gen. Lionel Howard, 1893–1949, vol. IV
Cox, Louisa Belle, (Lady Cox), died 1956, vol. V
Cox, Dame Marjorie Sophie, 1893–1979, vol. VII
Cox, Brig. Sir Matthew Henry, 1892–1966, vol. VI
Cox, Maj.-Gen. Maurice L.; see Lea-Cox.
Cox, Sir Mencea Ethereal, 1906–1994, vol. IX
Cox, Rt Hon. Michael Francis, 1852–1926, vol. II
Cox, Sir Montagu Hounsel, 1873–1936, vol. III
Cox, Hon. Sir Owen; see Cox, Hon. Sir E. O.
Cox, Palmer, 1840–1924, vol. II
Cox, Percy Stuart, 1868–1929, vol. III
Cox, Maj.-Gen. Sir Percy Zachariah, 1864–1937, vol. III
Cox, Sir Reginald Henry, 1st Bt (cr 1921), died 1922, vol. II
Cox, Sir Reginald Kennedy K.; see Kennedy-Cox.
Cox, Robert, 1845–1899, vol. I
Cox, Sir Robert; see Cox, Sir W. R.
Cox, Ronald, 1916–1991, vol. IX
Cox, S. Herbert, died 1920, vol. II
Cox, Lt-Col St John Augustus, 1869–1936, vol. III
Cox, Stephen, 1870–1943, vol. IV
Cox, Thomas, 1865–1947, vol. IV
Cox, Thomas Richard Fisher, 1907–1986, vol. VIII
Cox, Sir Thomas S.; see Skewes-Cox.
Cox, Sir Trenchard; see Cox, Sir G. T.
Cox, William Edward, 1880–1960, vol. V
Cox, Sir (William Henry) Lionel, 1864–1921, vol. II
Cox, Ven. William Lang Paige, 1855–1934, vol. III
Cox, Maj.-Gen. William Reginald, 1905–1988, vol. VIII
Cox, Sir (William) Robert, 1922–1981, vol. VIII
Cox, Lt-Col Sir William Thomas, 1881–1939, vol. III
Cox-Davies, Rachael Annie, 1863–1944, vol. IV
Cox-Edwards, Rev. John Cox, died 1926, vol. II
Cox-Taylor, Col Herbert James; see Taylor.
Coxe, Henry Reynell Holled, 1863–1938, vol. III
Coxe, Rev. Seymour Richard, 1842–1922, vol. II
Coxen, Maj.-Gen. Walter Adams, 1870–1949, vol. IV
Coxen, Sir William George, 1st Bt, 1867–1946, vol. IV
Coxhead, Brig.-Gen. James Alfred, 1851–1929, vol. III
Coxhead, Lt-Col Thomas Langhorne, 1864–1939, vol. III
Coxwell, Charles Blake, 1889–1967, vol. VI
Coxwell-Rogers, Maj.-Gen. Norman Annesley, 1896–1985, vol. VIII
Coyajee, Sir Jahangir Cooverjee, 1875–1943, vol. IV (A), vol. V
Coyle, James Vincent, 1864–1948, vol. IV
Coyle, William Thomas, died 1951, vol. V
Cozens, Brig. Dame Barbara; see Cozens, Brig. Dame F. B.
Cozens, Brig. Dame (Florence) Barbara, 1906–1995, vol. IX
Cozens, Air Cdre Henry Iliffe, 1904–1995, vol. IX
Cozens-Hardy, 1st Baron, 1838–1920, vol. III
Cozens-Hardy, 2nd Baron, 1868–1924, vol. II
Cozens-Hardy, 3rd Baron, 1873–1956, vol. V
Cozens-Hardy, 4th Baron, 1907–1975, vol. VII
Cozens-Hardy, Archibald, 1869–1957, vol. V

Cozens-Hardy, Edgar Wrigly, 1872–1945, vol. IV
Cozzens, James Gould, 1903–1978, vol. VII
Crabb, Edward, 1853–1914, vol. I
Crabbe, Sir Cecil Brooksby, 1898–1971, vol. VII
Crabbe, Brig.-Gen. Eyre Macdonnell Stewart, 1852–1905, vol. I
Crabbe, Herbert Ernest, 1867–1940, vol. III
Crabbe, Col Sir John Gordon, 1892–1961, vol. VI
Crabbe, Vice-Adm. Lewis Gonne Eyre, 1882–1951, vol. V
Crabbe, Mrs Pauline, (Mrs Joseph Benjamin), 1914–1998, vol. X
Crabbe, Reginald James Williams, 1909–1996, vol. X
Crabbe, Rt Rev. Reginald Percy, 1883–1964, vol. VI
Crabbie, (Margaret) Veronica, 1910–1998, vol. X
Crabbie, Veronica; see Crabbie, M. V.
Crabtree, Harold, 1884–1956, vol. V
Crace, Adm. Sir John Gregory, 1887–1968, vol. VI
Crackanthorpe, Dayrell Montague, died 1950, vol. IV
Crackanthorpe, Montague Hughes, 1832–1913, vol. I
Cracknall, Walter Borthwick, 1850–1902, vol. I
Cracroft-Amcotts, Lt-Comdr John, died 1956, vol. V
Cracroft-Amcotts, Lt-Col Sir Weston, 1888–1975, vol. VII
Craddock, Col Alexander Bainbridge, 1893–1962, vol. VI
Craddock, Sir Beresford; see Craddock, Sir G. B.
Craddock, Charles Egbert; see Murfree, Mary Noailles.
Craddock, George, 1897–1974, vol. VII
Craddock, Sir (George) Beresford, 1898–1976, vol. VII
Craddock, Sir Reginald Henry, 1864–1937, vol. III
Craddock, Lt-Gen. Sir Richard Walter, 1910–1977, vol. VII
Craddock, Sir Walter Merry, 1883–1972, vol. VII
Cradock, Rear-Adm. Sir Christopher George Francis Maurice, 1862–1914, vol. I
Cradock, Lt-Col Montagu, 1859–1929, vol. III
Cradock, Major Sheldon William Keith, 1858–1922, vol. II
Cradock-Hartopp, Sir Charles Edward; see Hartopp.
Cradock-Hartopp, Sir Charles (William Everard); see Hartopp.
Cradock-Hartopp, Sir Frederick; see Hartopp.
Cradock-Hartopp, Sir George Francis Fleetwood; see Hartopp.
Cradock-Hartopp, Sir John Edmund; see Hartopp.
Cradock-Hartopp, Lt-Comdr Kenneth Alston, 10th Bt, 1918–2000, vol. X
Cradock-Watson, Henry, 1864–1951, vol. V
Crafer, Rev. Thomas Wilfrid, 1870–1949, vol. IV
Craft, Percy Robert, died 1934, vol. III
Crafts, Wilbur Fisk, 1850–1922, vol. II
Cragg, Ven. Herbert Wallace, 1910–1980, vol. VII
Cragg, James Birkett, 1910–1996, vol. X
Cragg, Major William Gilliat, 1883–1956, vol. V
Craggs, John Drummond, 1915–1999, vol. X
Craggs, Sir John George, 1856–1928, vol. II
Craib, William Grant, 1882–1933, vol. III
Craies, William Feilden, 1854–1911, vol. I

Craig, Alexander, died 1935, vol. III
Craig, Major Sir Algernon Tudor T.; see Tudor-Craig.
Craig, Sir Archibald, died 1927, vol. II
Craig, Sir Archibald Charles G.; see Gibson-Craig.
Craig, Very Rev. Archibald Campbell, 1888–1985, vol. VIII
Craig, Maj.-Gen. Archibald Maxwell, 1895–1953, vol. V
Craig, Sir Arthur John Edward, 1886–1972, vol. VII
Craig, Barry; see Craig, F. B.
Craig, Captain Rt Hon. Charles Curtis, 1869–1960, vol. V
Craig, Charles James, 1919–1997, vol. X
Craig, Clifford, 1896–1986, vol. VIII
Craig, Edward Anthony, 1905–1998, vol. X
Craig, Edward Gordon, 1872–1966, vol. VI
Craig, Edward Hubert Cunningham, 1874–1946, vol. IV
Craig, Edwin Stewart, 1865–1939, vol. III
Craig, Elizabeth Josephine, 1883–1980, vol. VII
Craig, Sir Ernest, 1st Bt, 1859–1933, vol. III
Craig, Sir (Ernest) Gordon, 1891–1966, vol. VI
Craig, Frank, 1874–1918, vol. II
Craig, Frank Barrington, (Barry Craig), 1902–1951, vol. V
Craig, George, 1873–1947, vol. IV
Craig, Sir Gilfrid Gordon, 1871–1953, vol. V
Craig, Sir Gordon; see Craig, Sir E. G.
Craig, Very Rev. Graham, died 1904, vol. I
Craig, Hamish M.; see Millar-Craig.
Craig, Herbert James, 1869–1934, vol. III
Craig, J. Humbert, died 1944, vol. IV
Craig, James, 1851–1931, vol. III
Craig, Lt-Col James, 1864–1931, vol. III
Craig, Sir James, 1861–1933, vol. III
Craig, James A., died 1958, vol. V
Craig, James Alfred, 1858–1942, vol. IV
Craig, James Douglas, 1882–1950, vol. IV
Craig, Sir James Henry G.; see Gibson-Craig.
Craig, James Ireland, 1868–1952, vol. V
Craig, Sir John, 1874–1957, vol. V
Craig, John, 1898–1977, vol. VII
Craig, John Douglas, 1887–1968, vol. VI
Craig, Col John Francis, 1856–1927, vol. II
Craig, Sir John Herbert McCutcheon, 1885–1977, vol. VII
Craig, John Manson, 1896–1970, vol. VI
Craig, Sir (John) Walker, 1847–1926, vol. II
Craig, Sir Marshall Millar, 1880–1957, vol. V
Craig, Sir Maurice, 1866–1935, vol. III
Craig, Col Noel Newman Lombard, died 1968, vol. VI
Craig, Lt-Comdr Norman Carlyle, 1868–1919, vol. II
Craig, Rev. Oswald, 1867–1935, vol. III
Craig, R. Hunter, 1839–1913, vol. I
Craig, Very Rev. Robert, 1917–1995, vol. IX
Craig, Col Robert Annesley, 1869–1932, vol. III
Craig, Stuart E., died 1904, vol. I
Craig, Thomas Joseph Alexander, 1881–1970, vol. IV
Craig, Thomas Rae, 1906–1994, vol. IX
Craig, Sir Walker; see Craig, Sir J. W.

Craig, Dep. Surg.-Gen. William Maxwell, 1859–1914, vol. I
Craig, William Stuart McRae, 1903–1975, vol. VII
Craig-Brown, Lt-Col Ernest, 1871–1966, vol. VI
Craig-Brown, Thomas, 1844–1922, vol. II
Craigavon, 1st Viscount, 1871–1940, vol. III
Craigavon, 2nd Viscount, 1906–1974, vol. VII
Craigavon, Viscountess; (Cecil Mary Nowell Dering), died 1960, vol. V
Craighead, Edwin Boone, 1861–1920, vol. II (A), vol. III
Craigie, Rev. Charles Edward, died 1922, vol. II
Craigie, Hugh Brechin, 1908–1993, vol. IX
Craigie, James, 1899–1978, vol. VII
Craigie, John, 1857–1919, vol. II
Craigie, John Hubert, 1887–1989, vol. IX (AI)
Craigie, Major Patrick George, 1843–1930, vol. III
Craigie, Pearl Mary Teresa; see Hobbes, John Oliver.
Craigie, Rt Hon. Sir Robert Leslie, 1883–1959, vol. V
Craigie, Adm. Robert William, 1849–1911, vol. I
Craigie, Sir William A., 1867–1957, vol. V
Craigmyle, 1st Baron, 1850–1937, vol. III
Craigmyle, 2nd Baron, 1883–1944, vol. IV
Craigmyle, 3rd Baron, 1923–1998, vol. X
Craigton, Baron (Life Peer); Jack Nixon Browne, 1904–1993, vol. IX
Craik, Duncan Robert Steele, 1916–1999, vol. X
Craik, Sir George Lillie, 2nd Bt, 1874–1929, vol. III
Craik, Rt Hon. Sir Henry, 1st Bt, 1846–1927, vol. II
Craik, Sir Henry Duffield, 3rd Bt, 1876–1955, vol. V
Craik, Lt-Col James, 1871–1942, vol. IV
Craik, Robert, 1829–1906, vol. I
Cram, Alastair Lorimer, 1909–1994, vol. IX
Cram, Ralph Adams, 1863–1942, vol. IV
Cramb, Alexander Charles, 1874–1956, vol. V
Cramb, J. A., 1862–1913, vol. I
Cramer, Hon. Sir John Oscar, 1896–1994, vol. IX
Cramer, Dame Mary Theresa, died 1984, vol. VIII
Cramer, William, 1878–1945, vol. IV
Cramer-Roberts, Major Marmaduke Torin; see Roberts.
Cramp, Charles Henry, 1828–1913, vol. I
Cramp, Concemore Thomas, 1876–1933, vol. III
Cramp, Karl Reginald, 1878–1956, vol. V
Cramp, William, 1876–1939, vol. III
Cramp, Sir William Dawkins, 1840–1927, vol. II
Crampton, (Arthur Edward) Seán, 1918–1999, vol. X
Crampton, Vice-Adm. Denis Burke, 1873–1936, vol. III
Crampton, Brig.-Gen. Fiennes Henry, 1862–1938, vol. III
Crampton, Harold Percy, 1878–1969, vol. VI
Crampton, Col Philip John Ribton, 1860–1932, vol. III
Crampton, Seán; see Crampton, A. E. S.
Cran, Marion, 1875–1942, vol. IV
Cranage, Very Rev. David Herbert Somerset, 1866–1957, vol. V
Cranbrook, 1st Earl of, 1814–1906, vol. I

Cranbrook, 2nd Earl of, 1839–1911, vol. I
Cranbrook, 3rd Earl of, 1870–1915, vol. I
Cranbrook, 4th Earl of, 1900–1978, vol. VII
Crane, Sir Alfred Victor, 1892–1955, vol. V
Crane, Lt-Col Charles Paston, died 1939, vol. III
Crane, Sir Edmund Frank, 1886–1957, vol. V
Crane, Geoffrey David, 1934–1995, vol. IX
Crane, Sir Harry Walter Victor, 1903–1986, vol. VIII
Crane, Sir James William Donald, 1921–1994, vol. X (AI)
Crane, Morley Benjamin, 1890–1983, vol. VIII
Crane, Robert Newton, 1848–1927, vol. II
Crane, Walter, 1845–1915, vol. I
Crane, Sir William, 1874–1959, vol. V
Crane, William Alfred James, 1925–1982, vol. VIII
Cranfield, Arthur Leslie, 1892–1957, vol. V
Cranko, John, 1927–1973, vol. VII
Crankshaw, Edward, 1909–1984, vol. VIII
Crankshaw, Lt-Col Sir Eric Norman Spencer, 1885–1966, vol. VI
Cranmer-Byng, L., 1872–1945, vol. IV
Cranston, Maurice William, 1920–1993, vol. IX
Cranston, Robert, died 1906, vol. I
Cranston, Brig.-Gen. Sir Robert, 1843–1923, vol. II
Cranston, William Patrick, 1913–1967, vol. VI
Cranstone, Bryan Allan Lefevre, 1918–1989, vol. VIII
Cranstoun, Lady; (Elizabeth), died 1899, vol. I
Cranstoun, Charles Joseph Edmondstoune-, 1877–1950, vol. IV
Cranstoun, James, died 1931, vol. III
Cranswick, Rt Rev. Geoffrey Franceys, 1894–1978, vol. VII
Cranswick, Rt Rev. George Harvard, 1882–1954, vol. V
Cranworth, 1st Baron, 1829–1902, vol. I
Cranworth, 2nd Baron, 1877–1964, vol. VI
Craske, A(rthur) H(ugh) Glenn, 1904–1967, vol. VI
Craske, Rt Rev. Frederick William Thomas, 1901–1971, vol. VII
Craske, Glenn; see Craske, A. H. G.
Craske, Lt-Col John, 1869–1936, vol. III
Craster, Sir Edmund; see Craster, Sir H. H. E.
Cra'ster, Lt-Col Edmund Henry Bertram, 1869–1942, vol. IV
Craster, Col George, 1878–1958, vol. V
Craster, Maj.-Gen. George Ayton, 1830–1912, vol. I
Craster, Sir (Herbert Henry) Edmund, 1879–1959, vol. V
Craster, Sir John Montagu, 1901–1975, vol. VII
Cra'ster, Col Shafto Longfield, 1862–1943, vol. IV
Craster, Thomas William, 1860–1938, vol. III
Crathorne, 1st Baron, 1897–1977, vol. VII
Craufurd, Rev. Alexander Henry, 1843–1917, vol. II
Craufurd, Sir Alexander John Fortescue, 7th Bt, 1876–1966, vol. VI
Craufurd, Sir Charles William Frederick, 4th Bt, 1847–1939, vol. III
Craufurd, Mrs Eleanor Louisa Houison, died 1950, vol. IV
Craufurd, Brig.-Gen. Sir (George) Standish (Gage), 5th Bt, 1872–1957, vol. V

Craufurd, Sir James Gregan, 8th Bt, 1886–1970, vol. VI
Craufurd, Brig.-Gen. John Archibald Houison, 1862–1933, vol. III
Craufurd, Sir Quentin Charles Alexander, 6th Bt, 1875–1957, vol. V
Craufurd, Col Robert Quentin, 1880–1943, vol. IV
Craufurd, Brig.-Gen. Sir Standish; see Craufurd, Brig.-Gen. Sir G. S. G.
Craufurd-Stuart, Lt-Col Charles Kennedy; see Stuart.
Cravath, Paul Drennan, 1861–1940, vol. III
Craven, 4th Earl of, 1868–1921, vol. II
Craven, 5th Earl of, 1897–1932, vol. III
Craven, 6th Earl of, 1917–1965, vol. VI
Craven, 7th Earl of, 1957–1983, vol. VIII
Craven, 8th Earl of, 1961–1990, vol. VIII
Craven, Brig.-Gen. Arthur Julius, 1867–1933, vol. III
Craven, Arthur Scott, (Captain Arthur Keedwell Harvey James), 1875–1917, vol. II
Craven, Avery O., 1886–1980, vol. VII
Craven, Comdr Sir Charles Worthington, 1st Bt, 1884–1944, vol. IV
Craven, Sir Derek Worthington Clunes, 2nd Bt, 1910–1946, vol. IV
Craven, Rt Rev. George L., 1884–1967, vol. VI
Craven, Ven. James Brown, 1850–1924, vol. II
Craven, Majorie Eadon, 1895–1983, vol. VIII
Craven, Hon. Osbert William, 1848–1923, vol. II
Craven, Sir Robert Martin, 1824–1903, vol. I
Craven, Major Hon. Rupert Cecil, 1870–1959, vol. V
Craven, Lt-Col Waldemar Sigismund Dacre, 1880–1928, vol. II
Craven, William George, 1835–1906, vol. I
Craven-Ellis, William, died 1959, vol. V
Craw, Sir Henry Hewat, 1882–1964, vol. VI
Crawford, 26th Earl of, and Balcarres, 9th Earl of, 1847–1913, vol. I
Crawford, 27th Earl of, and Balcarres, 10th Earl of, 1871–1940, vol. III
Crawford, 28th Earl of, and Balcarres, 11th Earl of, 1900–1975, vol. VII
Crawford, Brig. Alastair Wardrop Euing, 1896–1978, vol. VII
Crawford, Alexander W., 1866–1933, vol. III
Crawford, Andrew, 1871–1936, vol. III
Crawford, Archibald, 1882–1960, vol. V
Crawford, Sir (Archibald James) Dirom, 1899–1983, vol. VIII
Crawford, Arthur Muir, 1882–1962, vol. VI
Crawford, Arthur Travers, 1835–1911, vol. I
Crawford, Captain Charles Wispington Glover, died 1934, vol. III
Crawford, Colin Grant, 1890–1959, vol. V
Crawford, David Gordon, 1928–1981, vol. VIII
Crawford, Sir Dirom; see Crawford, Sir A. J. D.
Crawford, Donald, 1837–1919, vol. II
Crawford, Brig. Sir Douglas Inglis, 1904–1981, vol. VIII
Crawford, Very Rev. Edward Patrick, 1846–1912, vol. I
Crawford, Col Edward William, 1879–1961, vol. VI
Crawford, Mrs Emily, died 1915, vol. I

Crawford, Sir Ferguson; see Crawford, Sir W. F.
Crawford, Sir Francis Collum, 1862–1934, vol. III
Crawford, Francis Marion, 1854–1909, vol. I
Crawford, Sir Frederick, 1906–1978, vol. VII
Crawford, Lt-Col Frederick Hugh, 1861–1952, vol. V
Crawford, Hon. Sir George Hunter, 1911–1923, vol. IX
Crawford, Maj.-Gen. George Oswald, 1902–1994, vol. IX
Crawford, Col George Rainier, 1862–1915, vol. I
Crawford, Lt-Col Gilbert Stewart, 1868–1953, vol. V
Crawford, Henry Leighton, 1855–1931, vol. III
Crawford, Sir Homewood, 1850–1936, vol. III
Crawford, Hugh Adam, 1898–1982, vol. VIII
Crawford, James, 1896–1982, vol. VIII
Crawford, James Archibald, 1905–1953, vol. V
Crawford, Joan, died 1977, vol. VII
Crawford, Very Rev. John, died 1924, vol. II
Crawford, John Balfour, 1887–1962, vol. VI
Crawford, John Dawson, 1861–1946, vol. IV
Crawford, Sir John Grenfell, 1910–1984, vol. VIII
Crawford, Lt-Col John Halket, 1868–1936, vol. III
Crawford, Maj.-Gen. John Scott, 1889–1978, vol. VII
Crawford, Captain John Stuart, 1900–1985, vol. VIII
Crawford, Gen. Sir Kenneth Noel, 1895–1961, vol. VI
Crawford, Lawrence, 1867–1951, vol. V
Crawford, Captain Lawrence Hugh, died 1918, vol. II
Crawford, Norman; see Crawford, R. N.
Crawford, Osbert Guy Stanhope, 1886–1957, vol. V
Crawford, Col Raymund, 1858–1927, vol. II
Crawford, Sir Richard Frederick, 1863–1919, vol. II
Crawford, Col Richmond Irvine, 1839–1910, vol. I
Crawford, Robert, died 1946, vol. IV
Crawford, Col Robert Duncan, died 1936, vol. III
Crawford, Col Rt Hon. Robert Gordon S.; see Sharman-Crawford.
Crawford, (Robert) Norman, 1923–1998, vol. X
Crawford, Susan Fletcher, died 1919, vol. II
Crawford, Sir Theodore, (Sir Theo), 1911–1993, vol. IX
Crawford, Rev. Thomas, 1860–1937, vol. III
Crawford, Thomas Clark, 1886–1955, vol. V
Crawford, Col Vincent James, 1877–1932, vol. III
Crawford, Sir (Walter) Ferguson, 1894–1978, vol. VII
Crawford, Sir William, 1840–1922, vol. II
Crawford, Lt-Col William Loftus, 1868–1951, vol. V
Crawford, William Neil Kennedy Mellon, 1910–1978, vol. VII
Crawford, Sir William S., 1878–1950, vol. IV
Crawford-Compton, Air Vice-Marshal William Vernon, 1915–1988, vol. VIII
Crawfurd, Major Horace Evelyn, 1882–1958, vol. V
Crawfurd, Rt Rev. Lionel Payne, 1864–1934, vol. III
Crawfurd, Oswald John Frederick, 1834–1909, vol. I

Crawfurd, Sir Raymond Henry Payne, 1865–1938, vol. III
Crawfurd-Price, Walter Harrington, 1881–1967, vol. VI
Crawfurd-Stirling-Stuart, William, 1854–1938, vol. III
Crawhall, Joseph, died 1913, vol. I
Crawhall, Rev. Thomas Emerson, 1866–1934, vol. III
Crawley, Aidan Merivale, 1908–1993, vol. IX
Crawley, Alfred Ernest, 1869–1924, vol. II
Crawley, Rev. Canon Arthur Stafford, 1876–1948, vol. IV
Crawley, Cecil, 1862–1931, vol. III
Crawley, Charles William, 1899–1992, vol. IX
Crawley, Desmond John Chetwode, 1917–1993, vol. IX
Crawley, Francis, 1853–1914, vol. I
Crawley, Frank C., 1871–1935, vol. III
Crawley, Major Sir Philip Arthur Sambrooke, 1869–1933, vol. III
Crawley, Col Richard Parry, 1876–1933, vol. III
Crawley, Virginia, (Mrs Aidan Crawley); see Cowles, V.
Crawley, William John Chetwode, 1844–1916, vol. II
Crawley-Boevey, Sir Francis Hyde; see Boevey.
Crawley-Boevey, Sir Lance, (Launcelot Valentine Hyde), 7th Bt, 1900–1968, vol. VI
Crawshaw, 1st Baron, 1825–1908, vol. I
Crawshaw, 2nd Baron, 1853–1929, vol. III
Crawshaw, 3rd Baron, 1884–1946, vol. IV
Crawshaw, 4th Baron, 1933–1997, vol. X
Crawshaw of Aintree, Baron (Life Peer); Lt-Col Richard Crawshaw, 1917–1986, vol. VIII
Crawshaw, Sir Daniel; see Crawshaw, Sir E. D. W.
Crawshaw, Sir (Edward) Daniel (Weston), 1903–1991, vol. IX
Crawshaw, Lionel Townsend, died 1949, vol. IV
Crawshaw, Philip, 1912–1984, vol. VIII
Crawshay, Lt-Col Codrington Howard Rees, 1882–1937, vol. III
Crawshay, Captain Geoffrey Cartland Hugh, 1892–1954, vol. V
Crawshay, Col Sir William Robert, 1920–1997, vol. X
Crawshay-Williams, Lt-Col Eliot, 1879–1962, vol. VI
Craxton, Antony, 1918–1999, vol. X
Craxton, Harold, 1885–1971, vol. VII
Cray, Rev. Canon Frank Maynard, 1898–1967, vol. VI
Creagh, Maj.-Gen. Arthur Gethin, 1855–1941, vol. IV
Creagh, Col Arthur Henry Dopping, 1866–1941, vol. IV
Creagh, Charles Vandeleur, 1842–1917, vol. II
Creagh, Maj.-Gen. Edward Philip Nagle, 1896–1981, vol. VIII
Creagh, Col George Washington B.; see Brazier-Creagh.
Creagh, Rear-Adm. James Vandeleur, 1883–1956, vol. V
Creagh, Maj.-Gen. Sir Michael O'Moore, 1892–1970, vol. VI
Creagh, Gen. Sir O'Moore, 1848–1923, vol. II
Creagh, Lt-Col Peter H., 1882–1933, vol. III
Creagh Coen, Sir Terence Bernard, 1903–1970, vol. VI
Creagh-Osborne, Captain F.; see Osborne.
Creak, Captain Ettrick William, 1835–1920, vol. II
Crealock, Major John Mansfield, died 1959, vol. V
Creamer, Amos Albert, 1917–1978, vol. VII
Crean, Sir Bernard Arthur, 1881–1956, vol. V
Crean, Eugene, 1856–1939, vol. III
Crean, Major Thomas Joseph, 1873–1923, vol. II
Crease, Hon. Sir Henry Pering Pellew, 1823–1905, vol. I
Crease, Maj.-Gen. Sir John Frederick, died 1907, vol. I
Crease, Captain Thomas Evans, 1875–1942, vol. IV
Creasey, Gordon Leonard, 1873–1943, vol. IV
Creasey, John, 1908–1973, vol. VII
Creasey, Gen. Sir Timothy May, 1923–1986, vol. VIII
Creasy, Adm. of the Fleet Sir George Elvey, 1895–1972, vol. VII
Creasy, Sir Gerald Hallen, 1897–1983, vol. VIII
Creasy, Harold Thomas, 1873–1950, vol. IV
Creasy, Leonard, 1854–1922, vol. II
Cree, Maj.-Gen. Gerald, 1862–1932, vol. III
Cree, Brig. Gerald Hilary, 1905–1998, vol. X
Cree, Kate; see Rorke, K.
Creed, Albert Lowry, 1909–1987, vol. VIII
Creed, Clarence James, 1894–1955, vol. V
Creed, Edward ffolliott, 1893–1947, vol. IV
Creed, Rev. John Martin, 1889–1940, vol. III
Creed, Hon. John Mildred, 1842–1930, vol. III
Creed, Richard Stephen, 1898–1964, vol. VI
Creed, Sir Thomas Percival, 1897–1969, vol. VI
Creedy, Sir Herbert James, 1878–1973, vol. VII
Creeggan, Rt Rev. Jack Burnett, 1902–1994, vol. IX
Creelman, James, 1859–1915, vol. I
Creelman, Col John Jennings, 1882–1949, vol. IV
Crees, James Harold Edward, 1882–1941, vol. IV
Cregan, Rev. James, 1857–1935, vol. III
Creightmore, Peter Beauchamp, 1928–1997, vol. X
Creighton, Charles, 1847–1927, vol. II
Creighton, Rev. Cuthbert, 1876–1963, vol. VI
Creighton, Donald Grant, 1902–1979, vol. VII
Creighton, James George Aylwin, 1850–1930, vol. III
Creighton, Rear-Adm. Sir Kenelm Everard Lane, 1883–1963, vol. VI
Creighton, Mrs Louise, 1850–1936, vol. III
Creighton, Rt Hon. and Rt Rev. Mandell, 1843–1901, vol. I
Cremer, Herbert William, 1893–1970, vol. VI
Cremer, Robert Wyndham K.; see Ketton-Cremer.
Cremer, Sir William Randal, 1838–1908, vol. I
Cremieu-Javal, Paul, 1857–1927, vol. II
Cremin, Cornelius Christopher, 1908–1987, vol. VIII
Crerar, Gen. Henry Duncan Graham, 1888–1965, vol. VI
Crerar, Sir James, 1877–1960, vol. V
Crerar, Hon. Thomas Alexander, 1876–1975, vol. VII
Crespi, Caesar James, 1928–1992, vol. IX
Crespi, James; see Crespi, C. J.

Cresswell, Rev. Cyril Leonard, 1890–1974, vol. VII
Cresswell, Col George Francis Addison, 1852–1926, vol. II
Cresswell, Herbert Osborn, 1860–1919, vol. II
Creswell, Jack Norman, 1913–1999, vol. X
Cresswell, Col Pearson Robert, 1834–1905, vol. I
Cresswell, Stuart Cornwallis, died 1959, vol. V
Cresswell, William Foy, 1895–1981, vol. VIII
Cressy-Marcks, Violet Olivia, (Mrs Francis Fisher), died 1970, vol. VI
Creston, Dormer; see Colston-Baynes, D. J.
Creswell, Sir Archibald; see Creswell, Sir K. A. C.
Creswell, Col Edmund Fraser, 1876–1941, vol. IV
Creswell, Lt-Col Hon. Frederic Hugh Page, 1866–1948, vol. IV
Creswell, Rear-Adm. George Hector, 1889–1967, vol. VI
Creswell, Harry Bulkeley, 1869–1960, vol. V
Creswell, John Edwards, 1864–1928, vol. II
Creswell, Sir (Keppel) Archibald (Cameron), 1879–1974, vol. VII
Creswell, Margaret Susan, died 1936, vol. III
Creswell, Sir Michael Justin, 1909–1986, vol. VIII
Creswell, Vice-Adm. Sir William Rooke, 1852–1933, vol. III
Creswell, William Thomas, 1872–1946, vol. IV
Creswick, Sir Alexander Reid, (Sir Alec Creswick), 1912–1983, vol. VIII
Creswick, Harry Richardson, 1902–1988, vol. VIII
Creswick, Col Sir Nathaniel, 1831–1917, vol. II
Creswick, Paul, 1866–1947, vol. IV
Cretney, Sir Godfrey; see Cretney, Sir W. G.
Cretney, Sir (William) Godfrey, 1912–1971, vol. VII
Crew, Albert, died 1942, vol. IV
Crew, Francis Albert Eley, 1886–1973, vol. VII
Crewdson, Bernard Francis, 1887–1966, vol. VI
Crewdson, Rev. George, 1840–1920, vol. II
Crewdson, Bt-Col William Dillworth, 1897–1972, vol. VII
Crewdson, Wilson, 1856–1918, vol. II
Crewe, 1st Marquess of, 1858–1945, vol. IV
Crewe, Marchioness of; (Margaret Etrenne Hannah), died 1967, vol. VI
Crewe, Bertie Gibson, 1884–1971, vol. VII
Crewe, Brig.-Gen. Hon. Sir Charles Preston, 1858–1936, vol. III
Crewe, Major James Hugh Hamilton D.; see Dodds Crewe.
Crewe, Quentin Hugh, 1926–1998, vol. X
Crewe, Sir Vauncey Harpur, 10th Bt, 1846–1924, vol. II
Crewe-Read, Col Randulph Offley, died 1932, vol. III
Creyke, Ralph, 1849–1908, vol. I
Cribbett, Sir George; see Cribbett, Sir W. C. G.
Cribbett, Sir (Wilfrid Charles) George, 1897–1964, vol. VI
Crichton, Sir Andrew Maitland-Makgill-, 1910–1995, vol. IX
Crichton, Hon. Arthur Owen, 1876–1970, vol. VI
Crichton, Charles Ainslie, 1910–1999, vol. X
Crichton, Lt-Col Hon. Charles Frederick, 1841–1918, vol. II
Crichton, David George, 1914–1997, vol. X

Crichton, Lady Emma, died 1936, vol. III
Crichton, Col Hon. Sir George Arthur Charles, 1874–1952, vol. V
Crichton, Lt-Col Gerald Charles Lawrence, 1900–1969, vol. VI
Crichton, Brig. Henry Coventry Maitland-Makgill-, 1880–1953, vol. V
Crichton, Col Hon. Sir Henry George Louis, 1844–1922, vol. II
Crichton, Air Cdre Henry Lumsden, 1890–1952, vol. V
Crichton, Captain Hon. James Archibald, 1877–1956, vol. V
Crichton, Sir (John) Robertson (Dunn), 1912–1985, vol. VIII
Crichton, Engr Captain Peter Thomson, 1863–1935, vol. III
Crichton, Lt-Col Richmond Trevor, 1865–1934, vol. III
Crichton, Sir Robert, 1881–1950, vol. IV
Crichton, Sir Robertson; see Crichton, Sir J. R. D.
Crichton, Col Walter Hugh, 1896–1984, vol. VIII
Crichton-Browne, Col Harold William Alexander Francis, 1866–1937, vol. III
Crichton-Browne, Sir James, 1840–1938, vol. III
Crichton-Maitland, Maj.-Gen. David M.; see Makgill-Crichton-Maitland.
Crichton-Miller, Donald, 1906–1997, vol. X
Crichton-Miller, Hugh, 1877–1959, vol. V
Crichton-Stuart, Lord Colum Edmund, 1886–1957, vol. V
Crichton-Stuart, Lord Ninian Edward, 1883–1915, vol. I
Crick, Alan John Pitts, 1913–1995, vol. IX
Crick, Rt Rev. Douglas Henry, died 1973, vol. VII
Crick, Rt Rev. Philip Charles Thurlow, 1882–1937, vol. III
Crick, Very Rev. Thomas, 1885–1970, vol. VI
Crick, Hon. William P., died 1908, vol. I
Crickmay, John Rackstrow, 1914–1997, vol. X
Cridland, Charles Elliot Tapscott, 1900–1983, vol. VIII
Cridland, Frank, 1873–1954, vol. V
Crighton, David George, 1942–2000, vol. X
Crilly, Daniel, 1857–1923, vol. II
Crimmin, Col John, 1859–1945, vol. IV
Cripps, Anthony Leonard; see Cripps, M. A. L.
Cripps, Col Arthur William, 1862–1945, vol. IV
Cripps, Sir (Cyril) Humphrey, 1915–2000, vol. X
Cripps, Sir Cyril Thomas, 1892–1979, vol. VII
Cripps, Sir Edward Stewart, 1885–1955, vol. V
Cripps, Major Sir Frederick William Beresford, 1873–1959, vol. V
Cripps, Henry William, died 1899, vol. I
Cripps, Sir Humphrey; see Cripps, Sir C. H.
Cripps, Dame Isobel, 1891–1979, vol. VII
Cripps, Sir John Stafford, 1912–1993, vol. IX
Cripps, Major Hon. Leonard Harrison, died 1959, vol. V
Cripps, Hon. Lionel, 1863–1950, vol. IV
Cripps, (Matthew) Anthony Leonard, 1913–1997, vol. X
Cripps, Rt Hon. Sir (Richard) Stafford, 1889–1952, vol. V

Cripps, Rt Hon. Sir Stafford; *see* Cripps, Rt Hon. Sir R. S.
Cripps, W. Harrison, *died* 1923, vol. II
Cripps, William Parry, 1903–1972, vol. VII
Crisham, Air Vice-Marshal William Joseph, 1906–1987, vol. VIII
Crisp, Col Rev. Alan Percy, 1889–1972, vol. VII
Crisp, Sir Frank, 1st Bt, 1843–1919, vol. II
Crisp, Sir Frank Morris, 2nd Bt, 1872–1938, vol. III
Crisp, Frederick Arthur, 1851–1922, vol. II
Crisp, Sir Harold, 1874–1942, vol. IV
Crisp, Dennis John, 1916–1990, vol. VIII
Crisp, Sir John Wilson, 3rd Bt, 1873–1950, vol. IV
Crisp, Leslie Finlay, 1917–1984, vol. VIII
Crisp, Sir (Malcolm) Peter, 1912–1984, vol. VIII
Crisp, Sir Peter; *see* Crisp, Sir M. P.
Crispe, Thomas Edward, *died* 1911, vol. I
Crispi, Francesco, 1819–1901, vol. I
Crispin, Edward Smyth, 1874–1958, vol. V
Crispin, Geoffrey Hollis, 1905–1976, vol. VII
Critchell, James Troubridge, 1850–1917, vol. II
Critchett, Sir George Anderson, 1st Bt, *died* 1925, vol. II
Critchett, Sir (George) Montague, 2nd Bt, 1884–1941, vol. IV
Critchett, Sir Montague; *see* Critchett, Sir G. M.
Critchley, Alexander, 1893–1974, vol. VII
Critchley, Brig.-Gen. Alfred Cecil, 1890–1963, vol. VI
Critchley, Sir Julian Michael Gordon, 1930–2000, vol. X
Critchley, Macdonald, 1900–1997, vol. X
Critchley, Thomas Alan, 1919–1991, vol. IX
Critchley-Waring, Captain Arthur Cunliffe Bernard, 1886–1930, vol. III
Crittall, Francis Henry, *died* 1935, vol. III
Croal, John P., 1852–1932, vol. III
Croce, Benedetto, 1866–1952, vol. V
Crockatt, Lieut Comdr Allan; *see* Crockatt, D. A.
Crockatt, Lieut Comdr (Douglas) Allan, 1923–1996, vol. X
Crockatt, James Laird, 1876–1936, vol. III
Crockatt, Brig. Norman Richard, 1894–1956, vol. V
Crocker, George, 1846–1923, vol. II
Crocker, Antony James Gulliford, 1918–1988, vol. VIII
Crocker, Brig.-Gen. George Delamain, *died* 1938, vol. III
Crocker, Henry Radcliffe, 1845–1909, vol. I
Crocker, Lt-Col Herbert Edmund, 1877–1962, vol. VI
Crocker, Gen. Sir John Tredinnick, 1896–1963, vol. VI
Crocker, Brig.-Gen. Sydney Francis, 1864–1952, vol. V
Crocker, Sir William Charles, 1886–1973, vol. VII
Crocker, Rear-Adm. (S) William Ernest, *died* 1951, vol. V
Crocket, Henry Edgar, *died* 1926, vol. II
Crocket, James, 1878–1944, vol. IV
Crocket, Oswald Smith, 1868–1945, vol. IV
Crockett, Sir James Henry Clifden, 1848–1931, vol. III
Crockett, Samuel Rutherford, 1860–1914, vol. I

Crockett, Rev. William Shillinglaw, 1866–1945, vol. IV
Crockford, Brig. Allen Lepard, 1897–1992, vol. IX
Crocombe, Leonard Cecil, 1890–1968, vol. VI
Croft, 1st Baron, 1881–1947, vol. IV
Croft, 2nd Baron, 1916–1997, vol. X
Croft, Sir Alfred Woodley, 1841–1925, vol. II
Croft, Andrew; *see* Croft, N. A.C.
Croft, Sir Arthur, 1886–1961, vol. VI
Croft, Sir Bernard Hugh Denman, 13th Bt (*cr* 1671), 1903–1984, vol. VIII
Croft, Sir Frederick Leigh, 3rd Bt (*cr* 1818), 1860–1930, vol. III
Croft, Henry Herbert Stephen, 1842–1923, vol. II
Croft, Sir Herbert Archer, 10th Bt (*cr* 1671), 1868–1915, vol. I
Croft, Sir Herbert George Denman, 9th Bt (*cr* 1671), 1838=n1902, vol. I
Croft, Sir Hugh Matthew Fiennes, 12th Bt (*cr* 1671), 1874–1954, vol. V
Croft, Sir James Herbert, 11th Bt (*cr* 1671), 1907–1941, vol. IV
Croft, Major Sir John Archibald Radcliffe, 5th Bt, 1910–1990, vol. VIII
Croft, Sir John Frederick, 2nd Bt (*cr* 1818), 1828–1904, vol. I
Croft, (John) Michael, 1922–1986, vol. VIII
Croft, Sir John William Graham, 4th Bt (*cr* 1818), 1910–1979, vol. VII
Croft, Michael; *see* Croft, J. M.
Croft, Col (Noel) Andrew (Cotton), 1906–1998, vol. X
Croft, Major Owen George Scudamore, 1880–1956, vol. V
Croft, Richard Benyon, 1843–1912, vol. I
Croft, Sir William Dawson, 1892–1964, vol. VI
Croft, Brig.-Gen. William Denman, 1879–1968, vol. VI
Croft-Cooke, Rupert, 1903–1979, vol. VII
Croft-Murray, Edward, 1907–1980, vol. VII
Crofton, 3rd Baron, 1834–1911, vol. I
Crofton, 4th Baron, 1866–1942, vol. IV
Crofton, 5th Baron, 1926–1974, vol. VII
Crofton, 6th Baron, 1949–1989, vol. VIII
Crofton, Brig.-Gen. Cyril Randell, 1867–1941, vol. IV
Crofton, Denis Hayes, 1908–1995, vol. IX
Crofton, Vice-Adm. Edward George L.; *see* Lowther-Crofton.
Crofton, Major Sir Henry; *see* Crofton, Major Sir M. R. H.
Crofton, Sir Hugh Denis, 5th Bt (*cr* 1801), 1878–1902, vol. I
Crofton, Lt-Gen. James, 1826–1908, vol. I
Crofton, Sir Malby, 3rd Bt (*cr* 1838), 1857–1926, vol. II
Crofton, Major Sir (Malby Richard) Henry, 4th Bt (*cr* 1838), 1881–1962, vol. VI
Crofton, Col Morgan, 1850–1916, vol. II
Crofton, Sir Morgan George, 4th Bt (*cr* 1801), 1850–1900, vol. I
Crofton, Sir Morgan George, 6th Bt (*cr* 1801), 1879–1958, vol. V
Crofton, Morgan William, 1826–1915, vol. I

Crofton, Sir Patrick Simon, 7th Bt, 1936–1987, vol. VIII
Crofton, Sir Richard Marsh, 1891–1955, vol. V
Crofton, Brig. Roger, 1888–1972, vol. VII
Crofton, Rt Hon. Sir Walter Frederic, 1815–1897, vol. I
Crofts, Surg.-Gen. Aylmer Martin, 1854–1915, vol. I
Crofts, Ernest, 1847–1911, vol. I
Crofts, Freeman Wills, 1879–1957, vol. V
Crofts, John Ernest Victor, 1887–1972, vol. VII
Crofts, Lt-Col Leonard Markham, 1867–1942, vol. IV
Crofts, Major Richard, 1859–1916, vol. II
Crofts, Thomas Robert Norman, 1874–1949, vol. IV
Crofts, Rev. William John H.; see Humble-Crofts.
Croiset, Alfred, 1845–1923, vol. II
Croisset, Francis de, 1885–1937, vol. III
Croke, Air Cdre Lewis George Le Blount, 1894–1971, vol. VII
Croke, Most Rev. Thomas W., 1824–1902, vol. I
Croker, Bithia Mary, died 1920, vol. II
Croker, Edgar Alfred, 1924–1992, vol. IX
Croker, Engr Rear-Adm. Edward James O'Brien, 1881–1960, vol. V
Croker, Maj.-Gen. Sir Henry Leycester, 1864–1938, vol. III
Croker, Richard, 1841–1922, vol. II
Croker, Ted; see Croker, E. A.
Croker, Captain Thomas Joseph, 1876–1956, vol. V
Crole, Charles Stewart, died 1916, vol. II
Crole, Gerard Lake, 1855–1927, vol. II
Croll, Hon. David Arnold, 1900–1991, vol. IX
Croll, David Gifford, 1885–1948, vol. IV
Croly, Very Rev. Daniel George Hayes, died 1916, vol. II
Croly, Brig. Henry Gray, 1910–1998, vol. X
Cromartie, Countess of (3rd in line), 1878–1962, vol. VI
Cromartie, 4th Earl of, 1904–1989, vol. VIII
Cromartie, Ian; see Cromartie, R. I. T.
Cromartie, (Ronald) Ian (Talbot), 1929–1987, vol. VIII
Cromb, David Lyall, 1875–1961, vol. VI
Crombie, Alan Douglas, 1894–1958, vol. V
Crombie, Bde-Surg. Lt-Col Alexander, 1845–1906, vol. I
Crombie, Alistair Cameron, 1915–1996, vol. X
Crombie, Col David Campbell, 1877–1952, vol. V
Crombie, George Edmond, 1908–1972, vol. VII
Crombie, Sir James Ian Cormack, 1902–1969, vol. VI
Crombie, Rear-Adm. John Harvey Forbes, 1900–1972, vol. VII
Crombie, John William, 1858–1908, vol. I
Crombie, Leslie, 1923–1999, vol. X
Cromer, 1st Earl of, 1841–1917, vol. II
Cromer, 2nd Earl of, 1877–1953, vol. V
Cromer, 3rd Earl of, 1918–1991, vol. IX
Cromie, Captain Charles Francis, 1858–1907, vol. I
Cromie, Comdr Francis Newton Allen, 1882–1918, vol. II
Cromie, Robert, 1856–1907, vol. I
Cromie, Rev. William Patrick, died 1927, vol. II

Crommelin, Andrew Claude de la Cherois, 1865–1939, vol. III
Crommelin, May de la Cherois, died 1930, vol. III
Crompton, James Shaw, 1853–1916, vol. II
Crompton, John Gilbert Frederic, 1869–1919, vol. II
Crompton, Richmal; see Lamburn, R. C.
Crompton, Robert, 1869–1958, vol. V
Crompton, Col Rookes Evelyn Bell, 1845–1940, vol. III
Crompton, Air Cdre Roy Hartley, 1921–1992, vol. IX
Crompton-Inglefield, Col Sir John Frederick, 1904–1988, vol. VIII
Crompton-Roberts, Lt-Col Henry Roger; see Roberts.
Cromwell, 5th Baron, 1893–1966, vol. VI
Cromwell, 6th Baron, 1929–1982, vol. VIII
Crone, Anne, 1915–1972, vol. VII
Crone, Col Desmond Roe, 1900–1974, vol. VII
Crone, John Smyth, 1858–1945, vol. IV
Cronin, Archibald Joseph, 1896–1981, vol. VIII
Cronin, Rt Rev. Mgr Francis, 1879–1939, vol. III
Cronin, Henry Francis, 1894–1977, vol. VII
Cronin, John Desmond, 1916–1986, vol. VIII
Cronin, John Walton, 1915–1990, vol. VIII
Cronin, Rt Rev. Mgr Michael, 1871–1943, vol. IV
Cronje, Gen. Piet A., 1835–1911, vol. I
Cronne, Henry Alfred, 1904–1990, vol. VIII
Cronshaw, Cecil John Turrell, 1889–1961, vol. VI
Cronshaw, Rev. Christopher, died 1921, vol. II
Cronshaw, Rev. George Bernard, died 1928, vol. II
Cronshaw, Rev. Herbert Priestley, 1863–1930, vol. III
Cronwright, Samuel Cron, 1863–1936, vol. III (A), vol. IV
Cronwright Schreiner, Mrs S. C.; see Schreiner, Olive.
Cronyn, Captain St John, 1901–1973, vol. VII
Crook, 1st Baron, 1901–1989, vol. VIII
Crook, Charles W., 1862–1926, vol. II
Crook, Eric Ashley, 1894–1984, vol. VIII
Crook, Thomas Mewburn, 1869–1949, vol. IV
Crook, William Montgomery, 1860–1945, vol. IV
Crooke, Lt-Col Charles Douglas Parry, 1870–1948, vol. IV
Crooke, Adm. Sir (Henry) Ralph, 1875–1952, vol. V
Crooke, Sir (John) Smedley, died 1951, vol. V
Crooke, Adm. Sir Ralph; see Crooke, Adm. Sir H. R.
Crooke, Sir Smedley; see Crooke, Sir J. S.
Crooke, William, 1848–1923, vol. II
Crooke-Lawless, Surg. Lt-Col Sir Warren Roland; see Lawless.
Crookenden, Col Arthur, 1877–1962, vol. VI
Crookenden, Harry Mitten, 1862–1947, vol. IV
Crookes, Sir William, 1832–1919, vol. II
Crookham, Rev. William Thomas Rupert, died 1945, vol. IV
Crooks, Sir James, 1858–1940, vol. III
Crooks, James, 1901–1980, vol. VII
Crooks, Rev. John Robert Megaw, 1914–1995, vol. IX
Crooks, Air Vice-Marshal Lewis M.; see Mackenzie Crooks.

Crooks, Captain Robert Crawford, 1894–1951, vol. V
Crooks, Very Rev. Samuel Bennett, 1920–1986, vol. VIII
Crooks, Rt Hon. William, 1852–1921, vol. II
Crookshank, 1st Viscount, 1893–1961, vol. VI
Crookshank, Col Chichester de Windt, *died* 1958, vol. V
Crookshank, Francis Graham, 1873–1933, vol. III
Crookshank, Harry Maule, 1849–1914, vol. I
Crookshank, Henry, 1893–1972, vol. VII
Crookshank, Maj.-Gen. Sir Sydney D'Aguilar, 1870–1941, vol. IV
Croom, Sir Halliday; *see* Croom, Sir J. H.
Croom, Sir (J.) Halliday, 1847–1923, vol. II
Croom, Sir John Halliday, 1909–1986, vol. VIII
Croom-Johnson, Rt Hon. Sir David Powell, 1914–2000, vol. X
Croom-Johnson, Henry Powell, 1910–1994, vol. IX
Croom-Johnson, Hon. Sir Reginald Powell, *died* 1957, vol. V
Croome, Honor Renée Minturn, 1908–1960, vol. V
Croome, William Iveson, 1891–1967, vol. VI
Croot, Sir (Horace) John, 1907–1981, vol. VIII
Croot, Sir John; *see* Croot, Sir H. J.
Cropper, Anthony Charles, 1912–1967, vol. VI
Cropper, Charles James, 1852–1924, vol. II
Cropper, Rev. James, *died* 1938, vol. III
Cropper, James Winstanley, 1879–1956, vol. V
Crosbie, Lt-Gen. Adolphus Brett, *died* 1916, vol. II
Crosbie, George, 1864–1934, vol. III
Crosbie, Henry, 1852–1928, vol. II
Crosbie, Brig.-Gen. James Dayrolles, 1865–1947, vol. IV
Crosbie, Hon. Sir John Chalker, 1876–1932, vol. III
Crosbie, Robert Edward Harold, 1886–1950, vol. IV
Crosbie, William, 1915–1999, vol. X
Crosbie, Sir William Edward Douglas, 8th Bt, 1855–1936, vol. III
Crosby, Bing; *see* Crosby, H. L.
Crosby, Very Rev. Ernest Henry L.; *see* Lewis-Crosby.
Crosby, Fanny, 1820–1915, vol. I
Crosby, Harry Lillis, (Bing Crosby), 1904–1977, vol. VII
Crosby, John Michael, 1940–1988, vol. VIII
Crosby, Sir Josiah, 1880–1958, vol. V
Crosby, Theo, 1925–1994, vol. IX
Crosby, Sir Thomas Boor, 1830–1916, vol. II
Crosby, William, 1832–1910, vol. I
Crosfield, Sir Arthur Henry, 1st Bt, 1865–1938, vol. III
Crosfield, Bertram Fothergill, 1882–1951, vol. V
Crosfield, Domini, (Lady Crosfield), *died* 1963, vol. VI
Crosfield, Lt-Col George Rowlandson, 1877–1962, vol. VI
Crosland, Rt Hon. Anthony; *see* Crosland, Rt Hon. C. A. R.
Crosland, Rt Hon. (Charles) Anthony (Raven), 1918–1977, vol. VII
Crosland, Brig. Harold Powell, 1893–1973, vol. VII
Crosland, Sir Joseph, 1826–1904, vol. I
Crosland, Joseph Beardsell, 1874–1935, vol. III
Crosland, T. W. H., 1868–1924, vol. II

Crosland, Brig. Walter Hugh, 1894–1960, vol. V
Cross, 1st Viscount, 1823–1914, vol. I
Cross, 2nd Viscount, 1882–1932, vol. III
Cross of Chelsea, Baron (Life Peer); (Arthur) Geoffrey (Neale) Cross, 1904–1989, vol. VIII
Cross, Ada, (Mrs George Frederick Cross); *see* Cambridge, A.
Cross, (Alan) Beverley, 1931–1998, vol. X
Cross, Sir Alexander, 1st Bt (*cr* 1912), 1847–1914, vol. I
Cross, Sir Alexander, 3rd Bt (*cr* 1912), 1880–1963, vol. VI
Cross, Alexander Galbraith, 1908–1996, vol. X
Cross, Alexander George, 1858–1919, vol. II
Cross, Alexander Urquhart, 1906–1992, vol. IX
Cross, Sir (Alfred) Rupert (Neale), 1912–1980, vol. VII
Cross, Alfred William Stephens, 1860–1932, vol. III
Cross, Arthur Lyon, 1873–1940, vol. III (A), vol. IV
Cross, Sir Barry Albert, 1925–1994, vol. IX
Cross, Beverley; *see* Cross, A. B.
Cross, Sir Cecil Lancelot Stewart, (Sir Lance), 1912–1989, vol. VIII
Cross, Rev. Hon. Charles Francis, 1860–1937, vol. III
Cross, Charles Frederick, 1855–1935, vol. III
Cross, Adm. Charles Henry, *died* 1915, vol. I
Cross, Charles Wilson, *died* 1928, vol. II
Cross, Rt Rev. (David) Stewart, 1928–1989, vol. VIII
Cross, Sir Eugene, 1896–1981, vol. VIII
Cross, Francis John Kynaston, 1865–1950, vol. IV
Cross, Francis Richardson, *died* 1931, vol. III
Cross, Rev. Frank Leslie, 1900–1968, vol. VI
Cross, Frederick Victor, 1907–1981, vol. VIII
Cross, Herbert S.; *see* Shepherd-Cross.
Cross, Col James Albert, 1876–1952, vol. V
Cross, Joan, 1900–1993, vol. IX
Cross, Hon. John Edward, 1858–1921, vol. II
Cross, Kenneth Mervyn Baskerville, 1890–1968, vol. VI
Cross, Kenneth William, 1916–1990, vol. VIII
Cross, Sir Lance; *see* Cross, Sir C. L. S.
Cross, Rev. Leslie Basil, 1895–1974, vol. VII
Cross, Brig. Lionel Lesley, 1899–1984, vol. VIII
Cross, Mark; *see* Pechey, Archibald T.
Cross, Richard Basil, 1881–1952, vol. V
Cross, Robert Craigie, 1911–2000, vol. X
Cross, Rev. Robert Nicol, 1883–1970, vol. VI
Cross, Rt Hon. Sir Ronald Hibbert, 1st Bt (*cr* 1941), 1896–1968, vol. VI
Cross, Sir Rupert; *see* Cross, Sir A. R. N.
Cross, Rt Rev. Stewart; *see* Cross, Rt Rev. D. S.
Cross, Rev. Thomas George, *died* 1932, vol. III
Cross, Sir William Coats, 2nd Bt (*cr* 1912), 1877–1947, vol. IV
Cross Brown, Lt-Col James, 1884–1969, vol. VI
Crosse, Ven. Arthur B., 1830–1909, vol. I
Crosse, Rev. Arthur John William, 1857–1948, vol. IV
Crosse, Lt-Col Charles Robert, 1851–1921, vol. II
Crosse, Ven. Edmond Francis, 1858–1941, vol. IV
Crosse, Rev. Canon Ernest Courtenay, 1887–1955, vol. V

Crosse, Rev. Frank Parker, 1897–1979, vol. VII
Crosse, Herbert D. H., 1863–1908, vol. I
Crossfield, Robert Sands, 1904–1978, vol. VII
Crossing, William, 1847–1928, vol. II
Crossland, Sir Leonard, 1914–1999, vol. X
Crossley, Madame Ada, died 1929, vol. III
Crossley, Anthony Crommelin, 1903–1939, vol. III
Crossley, Arthur William, 1869–1927, vol. II
Crossley, Sir Christopher John, 3rd Bt, 1931–1989, vol. VIII
Crossley, Edward; see Crossley, J. E.
Crossley, Eric Lomax, 1903–1982, vol. VIII
Crossley, Harry, 1918–1997, vol. X
Crossley, Lt-Col Henry Joseph, 1874–1936, vol. III
Crossley, (Joseph) Edward, 1908–1969, vol. VI
Crossley, Sir Julian Stanley, 1899–1971, vol. VII
Crossley, Sir Kenneth Irwin, 2nd Bt, 1877–1957, vol. V
Crossley, Wing-Comdr Michael Nicholson, 1912–1987, vol. VIII
Crossley, St Nicholas John, 4th Bt, 1962–2000, vol. X
Crossley, Rt Rev. Owen Thomas Lloyd, 1860–1926, vol. II
Crossley, Thomas Hastings Henry, 1846–1926, vol. II
Crossley, Sir William John, 1st Bt, 1844–1911, vol. I
Crossley-Holland, Frank William, 1878–1956, vol. V
Crossman, Hon. Sir (Charles) Stafford, 1870–1941, vol. IV
Crossman, Sir (Douglas) Peter, 1908–1989, vol. VIII
Crossman, Maj.-Gen. Francis Lindisfarne Morley, 1888–1947, vol. IV
Crossman, Col George Lytton, 1877–1947, vol. IV
Crossman, Percy, 1872–1929, vol. III
Crossman, Sir Peter; see Crossman, Sir D. P.
Crossman, Rt Hon. Richard Howard Stafford, 1907–1974, vol. VII
Crossman, Hon. Sir Stafford; see Crossman, Hon. Sir C. S.
Crossman, Sir William, 1830–1901, vol. I
Crossman, Sir William Smith, 1854–1929, vol. III
Crosswell, Noel Alfred, 1909–1964, vol. VI
Crosthwait, Col Herbert Leland, 1867–1940, vol. III
Crosthwaite, Arthur Tinley, 1880–1951, vol. V
Crosthwaite, Sir Bertram Maitland, 1880–1974, vol. VII
Crosthwaite, Cecil, 1909–1978, vol. VII
Crosthwaite, Lt-Col Charles Gilbert, 1878–1940, vol. III
Crosthwaite, Sir Charles Haukes Todd, 1835–1915, vol. I
Crosthwaite, Lt-Col Henry Robert, 1876–1956, vol. V
Crosthwaite, Sir Hugh Stuart, 1879–1952, vol. V
Crosthwaite, Sir Moore; see Crosthwaite, Sir P. M.
Crosthwaite, Sir (Ponsonby) Moore, 1907–1989, vol. VIII
Crosthwaite, Robert, 1868–1953, vol. V
Crosthwaite, Rt Rev. Robert Jarratt, 1837–1925, vol. II
Crosthwaite, Sir Robert Joseph, 1841–1917, vol. II
Crosthwaite, W. M., died 1956, vol. V

Crosthwaite, Sir William Henry, 1880–1968, vol. VI
Crosthwaite-Eyre, Sir Oliver Eyre, 1913–1978, vol. VII
Crotch, William Walter, 1874–1947, vol. IV
Crothers, Thomas Wilson, 1850–1921, vol. II
Crotty, Rt Rev. Horace, 1886–1952, vol. V
Crouch, Sir David Lance, 1919–1998, vol. X
Crouch, Lt-Col Ernest George, 1875–1935, vol. III
Crouch, Henry Arthur, 1870–1955, vol. V
Crouch, Col Hon. Richard Armstrong, 1869–1949, vol. IV, vol. V
Crouch, Robert Fisher, 1904–1957, vol. V
Croudace, Rev. William Darnell, 1848–1942, vol. IV
Crousaz, Engr Rear-Adm. Augustus George, 1884–1977, vol. VII
Crouse, Russel, 1893–1966, vol. VI
Crout, Dame Mabel, 1890–1984, vol. VIII
Crow, Sir Alwyn Douglas, 1894–1965, vol. VI
Crow, Douglas Arthur, 1889–1945, vol. IV
Crow, Francis Edward, 1863–1939, vol. III
Crowden, Rev. Charles, 1836–1936, vol. III
Crowden, Guy Pascoe, 1894–1966, vol. VI
Crowder, F(rederick) Petre, 1919–1999, vol. X
Crowder, Sir John Ellenborough, 1890–1961, vol. VI
Crowder, Michael, 1934–1988, vol. VIII
Crowdy, Edith Frances, died 1947, vol. IV
Crowdy, James Fuidge, 1876–1934, vol. III
Crowdy, Mary, died 1961, vol. VI
Crowdy, Dame Rachel Eleanor, (Dame Rachel Thornhill), 1884–1964, vol. VI
Crowe, Sir Colin Tradescant, 1913–1989, vol. VIII
Crowe, Sir Edward Thomas Frederick, 1877–1960, vol. V
Crowe, Eric Eyre, 1905–1952, vol. V
Crowe, Eyre, 1824–1910, vol. I
Crowe, Sir Eyre, 1864–1925, vol. II
Crowe, F. J. W., 1864–1931, vol. III
Crowe, Captain Fritz Hauch Eden, 1849–1904, vol. I
Crowe, Brig.-Gen. John Henry Verinder, 1862–1948, vol. IV
Crowe, Col Mordaunt Abingdon Carlisle, 1867–1939, vol. III
Crowe, Percy Robert, 1904–1979, vol. VII
Crowe, Philip Kingsland, 1908–1976, vol. VII
Crowe, Ralph Vernon, 1915–1990, vol. VIII
Crowe, Dame Sylvia, 1901–1997, vol. X
Crowe, Maj.-Gen. Thomas Carlisle, 1830–1917, vol. II
Crowe, William Henry, 1844–1925, vol. II
Crowest, Frederick J., 1860–1927, vol. II
Crowfoot, Rev. John Henchman, 1841–1926, vol. II
Crowfoot, John Winter, 1873–1959, vol. V
Crowley, Sir Brian Hurtle, 1896–1982, vol. VIII
Crowley, Rear Adm. George Clement, 1916–1999, vol. X
Crowley, James, died 1946, vol. IV
Crowley, John, died 1934, vol. III
Crowley, Niall, 1926–1998, vol. X
Crowley, Ralph Henry, 1869–1953, vol. V
Crowley, Rt Rev. Timothy, 1880–1946, vol. IV
Crowley, Dep. Insp.-Gen. Timothy Joseph, died 1912, vol. I

Crowley, Thomas Michael, 1917–1988, vol. VIII
Crowley-Milling, Air Marshal Sir Denis, 1919–1996, vol. X
Crowly, Joseph Patrick, 1859–1917, vol. II
Crown, Jennifer Brigit, (Mrs Leon Crown); see Vyvyan, J. B.
Crowther, Baron (Life Peer); Geoffrey Crowther, 1907–1972, vol. VII
Crowther, Charles, 1876–1964, vol. VI
Crowther, Edward, 1897–1979, vol. VII
Crowther, Francis Harold, 1914–1984, vol. VIII
Crowther, Henry, 1848–1937, vol. III
Crowther, James Arnold, 1883–1950, vol. IV
Crowther, Sir William Edward Lodewyk Hamilton, 1887–1981, vol. VIII
Crowther-Hunt, Baron (Life Peer); Norman Crowther Crowther-Hunt, 1920–1987, vol. VIII
Crowther-Smith, Vivian Francis, 1875–1961, vol. VI
Croxton, Arthur, died 1956, vol. V
Croxton-Smith, Claude, 1901–1996, vol. X
Croysdale, Sir James, 1886–1971, vol. VII
Croysdill, Clifford William, 1874–1935, vol. III
Crozier, Maj.-Gen. Baptist Barton, 1878–1957, vol. V
Crozier, Douglas James Smyth, 1908–1976, vol. VII
Crozier, Rev. Edward Travers, died 1940, vol. III
Crozier, Eric John, 1914–1994, vol. IX
Crozier, Brig.-Gen. Frank Percy, 1879–1937, vol. III
Crozier, George, died 1914, vol. I
Crozier, Most Rev. John Baptist, 1853–1920, vol. II
Crozier, John Beattie, 1849–1921, vol. II
Crozier, Rt Rev. John Winthrop, 1879–1966, vol. VI
Crozier, Major Sir Thomas Henry, died 1948, vol. IV
Crozier, William Percival, 1879–1944, vol. IV
Cru, Robert L., 1884–1944, vol. IV
Cruddas, Bt Col Bernard, 1882–1959, vol. V
Cruddas, Col Hamilton Maxwell, 1874–1955, vol. V
Cruddas, Lt-Col Hugh Wilson, 1868–1916, vol. II
Cruddas, Maj.-Gen. Ralph Cyril, 1900–1979, vol. VII
Cruddas, Rear-Adm. Thomas Rennison, 1921–2000, vol. X
Cruddas, William Donaldson, 1831–1912, vol. I
Cruickshank, Alexander Walmsley, 1851–1925, vol. II
Cruickshank, Rev. Alfred Hamilton, 1862–1927, vol. II
Cruickshank, Andrew John Maxton, 1907–1988, vol. VIII
Cruickshank, Charles Grieg, 1914–1989, vol. VIII
Cruickshank, Ernest William Henderson, 1888–1964, vol. VI
Cruickshank, Herbert James, 1912–1995, vol. IX
Cruickshank, Dame Joanna Margaret, died 1958, vol. V
Cruickshank, John, 1884–1966, vol. VI
Cruickshank, John, 1924–1995, vol. IX
Cruickshank, John Cecil, 1899–1956, vol. V
Cruickshank, Col Martin Melvin, 1888–1964, vol. VI
Cruickshank, Robert, 1899–1974, vol. VII

Cruickshank, Robert James, 1898–1956, vol. V
Cruickshank, Sir William Dickson, 1845–1929, vol. III
Cruickshank, John Merrill, 1901–1984, vol. VIII
Cruise, Sir Francis Richard, 1834–1912, vol. I
Cruise, Sir Richard Robert, died 1946, vol. IV
Crum, Rev. John Macleod Campbell, 1872–1958, vol. V
Crum, Maj.-Gen. Vernon Forbes E.; see Erskine Crum.
Crum, Sir Walter Erskine, 1874–1923, vol. II
Crum, Walter Ewing, 1865–1944, vol. IV
Crumly, Patrick, vol. II
Crump, Basil Woodward, 1866–1945, vol. IV
Crump, Charles George, 1862–1935, vol. III
Crump, Edwin Samuel, 1882–1961, vol. VI
Crump, Frederick Octavius, 1840–1900, vol. I
Crump, Sir Henry Ashbrooke, 1863–1941, vol. IV
Crump, Rev. John Herbert, 1849–1924, vol. II
Crump, Leslie Maurice, 1875–1929, vol. III
Crump, Sir Louis Charles, 1869–1960, vol. V
Crump, Maurice; see Crump, W. M. E.
Crump, Norman Easedale, 1896–1964, vol. VI
Crump, Sir William John, 1850–1923, vol. II
Crump, (William) Maurice (Esplen), 1908–1996, vol. X
Crundall, Sir William Henry, 1847–1934, vol. III
Cruse, Rt Rev. John Howard, 1908–1979, vol. VII
Crutchley, Arthur Felton, 1883–1966, vol. VI
Crutchley, Maj.-Gen. Sir Charles, 1856–1920, vol. II
Crutchley, Ernest Tristram, 1878–1940, vol. III
Crutchley, Percy Edward, 1855–1940, vol. III
Crutchley, Adm. Sir Victor Alexander Charles, 1893–1986, vol. VIII
Crutchley, William Caius, 1848–1923, vol. II
Crute, Robert, 1907–1967, vol. VI (AII)
Cruttwell, Charles Robert Mowbray Fraser, 1887–1941, vol. IV
Cruttwell, Rev. Charles Thomas, 1847–1911, vol. I
Cruz, Joao Carlos Lopes Cardoso de F.; see de Freitas-Cruz.
Cryer, (George) Robert, 1934–1994, vol. IX
Cryer, Robert; see Cryer, G. R.
Crymble, Percival Templeton, 1880–1970, vol. VI
Cubbon, Maj.-Gen. John Hamilton, 1911–1997, vol. X
Cubbon, William, 1865–1955, vol. V
Cubitt, Sir Bertram Blakiston, 1862–1942, vol. IV
Cubitt, Hon. (Charles) Guy, 1903–1979, vol. VII
Cubitt, Edward George, 1860–1933, vol. III
Cubitt, Hon. Guy; see Cubitt, Hon. C. G.
Cubitt, James William Archibald, 1914–1983, vol. VIII
Cubitt, Thomas, 1870–1947, vol. IV
Cubitt, Gen. Sir Thomas Astley, 1871–1939, vol. III
Cubitt, Col William George, 1835–1903, vol. I
Cuckney, Air Vice-Marshall Ernest John, 1896–1965, vol. VI
Cudlip, Mrs Pender; see Thomas, Annie.
Cudlipp, Baron (Life Peer); Hugh Cudlipp, 1913–1998, vol. X
Cudlipp, Percy, 1905–1962, vol. VI
Cudmore, Sir Arthur Murray, 1870–1951, vol. V

Cudmore, Hon. Sir Collier Robert, 1885–1971, vol. VII

Cudmore, Derek George, 1923–1981, vol. VIII

Cuff, Maj.-Gen. Brian, 1889–1970, vol. VI

Cuffe, Sir Charles Frederick Denny Wheeler-, 2nd Bt, 1832–1915, vol. I

Cuffe, Surg.-Gen. Sir Charles M'Donough, 1842–1915, vol. I

Cuffe, Sir George Eustace, 1892–1962, vol. VI

Cuffe, Col James Aloysius Francis, 1876–1957, vol. V

Cuffe, Sir Otway Fortescue Luke Wheeler-, 3rd Bt, 1866–1934, vol. III

Cuffe, Hon. Otway Frederick Seymour, 1853–1912, vol. I

Cuke, Sir Hampden Archibald, 1892–1968, vol. VI

Culbertson, Ely, 1891–1955, vol. V

Culhane, Rosalind, (Lady Padmore), died 1995, vol. IX

Cull, Vice-Adm. Sir Malcolm Giffard Stebbing, 1891–1962, vol. VI

Cullen, Hon. Lord; William James Cullen, 1859–1941, vol. IV

Cullen of Ashbourne, 1st Baron, 1864–1932, vol. III

Cullen of Ashbourne, 2nd Baron, 1912–2000, vol. X

Cullen, Mrs Alice, (Mrs William Reynolds), died 1969, vol. VI

Cullen, Rt Rev. Archibald Howard, 1887–1968, vol. VI

Cullen, Brian; see Cullen, J. B.

Cullen, Brig.-Gen. Ernest Henry Scott, 1869–1951, vol. V

Cullen, Gordon; see Cullen, T. G.

Cullen, (James) Brian, 1905–1972, vol. VII

Cullen, James Reynolds, 1900–1995, vol. IX

Cullen, Rev. John, 1836–1914, vol. I

Cullen, Kenneth Douglas, 1889–1956, vol. V

Cullen, Rt Rev. Matthew, 1864–1936, vol. III

Cullen, Comdr Percy, 1861–1918, vol. II

Cullen, (Thomas) Gordon, 1914–1994, vol. IX

Cullen, William, 1867–1948, vol. IV

Cullen, William James; see Cullen, Hon. Lord.

Cullen, Hon. Sir William Portus, 1855–1935, vol. III

Culley, Rev. Arnold Duncan, 1867–1947, vol. IV

Culley, Gp Captain Stuart Douglas, 1895–1975, vol. VII

Cullinan, Edward Revill, 1901–1965, vol. VI

Cullinan, Sir Frederick Fitzjames, 1845–1913, vol. I

Cullinan, Sir Thomas Major, 1862–1936, vol. III

Cullinan, Paymaster-Rear-Adm. William Frederick, 1876–1937, vol. III

Culling, James William Henry, 1870–1949, vol. IV

Culling, Maj.-Gen. John Chislett, 1858–1938, vol. III

Cullingford, Rev. Cecil Howard Dunstan, 1904–1990, vol. VIII

Cullingworth, Charles James, 1841–1908, vol. I

Cullis, Charles Edgar, 1899–1964, vol. VI

Cullis, Carles Gilbert, 1871–1941, vol. IV

Cullis, Winifred Clara, 1875–1956, vol. V

Culliton, Hon. Edward Milton, 1906–1991, vol. IX

Cullum, George Gery Milner-Gibson, 1857–1921, vol. II

Cullum, Ridgwell, 1867–1943, vol. IV

Cullwick, Ernest Geoffrey, 1903–1981, vol. VIII

Culme-Seymour, Sir Michael; see Seymour.

Culme-Seymour, Vice-Adm. Sir Michael; see Seymour.

Culpin, Ewart Gladstone, 1877–1946, vol. IV

Culpin, Millais, 1874–1952, vol. V

Culshaw, John Royds, 1924–1980, vol. VII

Culver, Roland Joseph, 1900–1984, vol. VIII

Culverwell, Cyril Tom, 1895–1963, vol. VI

Culverwell, Edward Parnall, 1855–1931, vol. III

Cumber, Sir John Alfred, 1920–1991, vol. IX

Cumber, William John, 1878–1974, vol. VII

Cumberbatch, Arthur Noel, 1895–1982, vol. VIII

Cumberbatch, Elkin Percy, 1880–1939, vol. III

Cumberbatch, Henry Alfred, 1858–1918, vol. II

Cumberbatch, Sir Hugh Douglas, 1897–1951, vol. V

Cumberbatch, Isaac William, 1888–1971, vol. VII

Cumberland, Maj.-Gen. Charles Edward, 1830–1920, vol. II

Cumberland, Major Charles Sperling, 1847–1922, vol. II

Cumberland, Gerald, 1879–1926, vol. II

Cumberlege, Geoffrey Fenwick Jocelyn, 1891–1979, vol. VII

Cumbrae-Stewart, Francis William Sutton, 1865–1938, vol. III

Cumine, Alexander, died 1909, vol. I

Cuming, Sir Arthur Herbert, died 1941, vol. IV

Cuming, Edward William Dirom, 1862–1941, vol. IV

Cuming, Col Helier Brohier, 1867–1950, vol. IV (A)

Cuming, Mariannus Adrian, 1901–1988, vol. VIII

Cuming, Adm. Robert Stevenson Dalton, 1852–1940, vol. III

Cumings, Sir Charles Cecil George, 1904–1981, vol. VIII

Cumings, John Nathaniel, 1905–1974, vol. VII

Cumming, Alan; see Cumming, J. A.

Cumming, Alexander Neilson, died 1913, vol. I

Cumming, Major Sir Alexander Penrose G.; see Gordon-Cumming.

Cumming, Brig. Arthur Edward, 1896–1971, vol. VII

Cumming, Col Charles Chevin, 1875–1947, vol. IV

Cumming, Miss Constance Frederica G.; see Gordon-Cumming.

Cumming, Sir Duncan Cameron, 1903–1979, vol. VII

Cumming, Rev. James, died 1946, vol. IV

Cumming, (John) Alan, 1932–1993, vol. IX

Cumming, Sir John Ghest, 1868–1958, vol. V

Cumming, Sir Kenneth William, 7th Bt, 1837–1915, vol. I

Cumming, Lt-Col Malcolm Edward Durant, 1907–1985, vol. VIII

Cumming, Captain Sir Mansfield, 1859–1923, vol. II

Cumming, Lt-Col Sir Ronald Stuart, 1900–1982, vol. VIII

Cumming, Ronald William, 1920–1986, vol. VIII

Cumming, Roualeyn Charles Rossiter, 1891–1981, vol. VIII

Cumming, Col William Gordon, 1842–1908, vol. I

Cumming, Sir William Gordon G.; *see* Gordon-Cumming.

Cumming, William Richard, 1911–1984, vol. VIII

Cumming-Bruce, Rt Hon. Sir (James) Roualeyn Hovell-Thurlow-, 1912–2000, vol. X

Cumming-Bruce, Rt Hon. Sir Roualeyn; *see* Cumming-Bruce, Rt Hon. Sir J. R. H. T.

Cummings, Arthur John, *died* 1957, vol. V

Cummings, David Charles, 1861–1942, vol. IV

Cummings, Edward Estlin, 1894–1962, vol. VI

Cummings, William Hayman, 1831–1915, vol. I

Cummins, Ashley; *see* Cummins, W. E. A.

Cummins, Geraldine Dorothy, 1890–1969, vol. VI

Cummins, Maj.-Gen. Harry Ashley Vane, 1870–1953, vol. V

Cummins, Major Henry Alfred, 1864–1938, vol. III

Cummins, Henry Ashley Travers, 1847–1926, vol. II

Cummins, Herbert Ashley Cunard, 1871–1943, vol. IV

Cummins, Maj.-Gen. James Turner, 1843–1912, vol. I

Cummins, Rt Rev. John Ildefonsus, 1850–1938, vol. III

Cummins, Col Stevenson Lyle, 1873–1949, vol. IV

Cummins, Walter Herbert, 1881–1953, vol. V

Cummins, (William Edward) Ashley, *died* 1923, vol. II

Cumont, Franz Valery Marie, 1868–1947, vol. IV

Cumpston, John Howard Lidgett, 1880–1954, vol. V

Cunard, Sir Bache, 3rd Bt, 1851–1925, vol. II

Cunard, Sir Edward, 5th Bt, 1891–1962, vol. VI

Cunard, Ernest Haliburton, 1862–1926, vol. II

Cunard, Sir Gordon, 4th Bt, 1857–1933, vol. III

Cunard, Major Sir Guy Alick, 7th Bt, 1911–1989, vol. VIII

Cunard, Sir Henry Palmes, 6th Bt, 1909–1973, vol. VII

Cundall, Charles, 1890–1971, vol. VII

Cundall, Frank, 1858–1937, vol. III

Cundall, Herbert Minton, 1848–1940, vol. III

Cundall, Joseph Leslie, 1906–1964, vol. VI

Cundell, Edric, 1893–1961, vol. VI

Cundiff, Major Frederick William, 1895–1982, vol. VIII

Cundiff, Sir William, 1861–1935, vol. III

Cuneo, Cyrus Cincinatto, *died* 1916, vol. II

Cuneo, Terence Tenison, 1907–1996, vol. X

Cuningham, Maj.-Gen. Charles Alexander, 1842–1925, vol. II

Cuningham, Granville Carlyle, 1847–1927, vol. II

Cuningham, Surg.-Gen. James Macnabb, 1829–1905, vol. I

Cuningham, Sir William John, 1848–1929, vol. III

Cuninghame, Sir Alfred Edward F., 12th Bt (*cr* 1630); *see* Fairlie-Cuninghame.

Cuninghame, Sir Charles Arthur F., 11th Bt (*cr* 1630); *see* Fairlie-Cuninghame.

Cuninghame, Lt-Col Edward William Montgomery, 1878–1935, vol. III

Cuninghame, Sir Hussey Burgh Fairlie-, 14th Bt (*cr* 1630), 1890–1939, vol. III

Cuninghame, Col John Anstruther Smith, 1852–1921, vol. II

Cuninghame, John Charles, 1851–1917, vol. II

Cuninghame, Sir Thomas Andrew Alexander Montgomery-, 10th Bt (*cr* 1672), 1877–1945, vol. IV

Cuninghame, Sir William Alan F.; *see* Fairlie-Cuninghame.

Cuninghame, Sir (William) Andrew Malcolm Martin Oliphant Montgomery-, 11th Bt (*cr* 1672), 1929–1959, vol. V

Cuninghame, Sir William Edward Fairlie-, 13th Bt (*cr* 1630), 1856–1929, vol. III

Cuninghame, Sir William Henry F.; *see* Fairlie-Cuninghame.

Cuninghame, Sir William James Montgomery-, 9th Bt (*cr* 1672), 1834–1897, vol. I

Cuninghame, Lt-Col William Wallace Smith, 1889–1959, vol. V

Cunliffe, 1st Baron, 1855–1920, vol. II

Cunliffe, 2nd Baron, 1899–1963, vol. VI

Cunliffe, Christopher Joseph, 1916–1995, vol. IX

Cunliffe, Sir Cyril Henley, 8th Bt, 1901–1969, vol. VI

Cunliffe, Sir Ellis; *see* Cunliffe, Sir R. E.

Cunliffe, Sir Foster Hugh Egerton, 6th Bt, 1875–1916, vol. II

Cunliffe, Brig.-Gen. Frederick Hugh Gordon, 1861–1955, vol. V

Cunliffe, Hon. Geoffrey, 1903–1978, vol. VII

Cunliffe, Sir Herbert; *see* Cunliffe, Sir J. H.

Cunliffe, Sir John Robert Ellis, 1886–1967, vol. VI

Cunliffe, John William, 1865–1946, vol. IV

Cunliffe, Sir (Joseph) Herbert, 1867–1963, vol. VI

Cunliffe, Marcus Falkner, 1922–1990, vol. VIII

Cunliffe, Sir Robert Alfred, 5th Bt, 1839–1905, vol. I

Cunliffe, Sir (Robert) Ellis, 1858–1927, vol. II

Cunliffe, Capt. Robert Lionel Brooke, 1895–1990, vol. VIII

Cunliffe, Sir Robert Neville Henry, 7th Bt, 1884–1949, vol. IV

Cunliffe, Thomas, 1895–1966, vol. VI

Cunliffe, Thomas Alfred, 1905–1993, vol. IX

Cunliffe-Jones, Rev. Hubert, 1905–1991, vol. IX

Cunliffe-Owen, Brig.-Gen. Charles, 1863–1932, vol. III

Cunliffe-Owen, Sir Dudley Herbert, 2nd Bt, 1923–1983, vol. VIII

Cunliffe-Owen, Lt-Col F., *died* 1946, vol. IV

Cunliffe-Owen, Sir Hugo, 1st Bt, 1870–1947, vol. IV

Cunning, Joseph, 1872–1948, vol. IV

Cunningham of Hyndhope, 1st Viscount, 1883–1963, vol. VI

Cunningham, Gen. Sir Alan Gordon, 1887–1983, vol. VIII

Cunningham, Air Cdre Alexander Duncan, 1888–1981, vol. VIII

Cunningham, Sir (Alexander) Frederick (Douglas), 1852–1935, vol. III

Cunningham, Alfred, 1870–1918, vol. II

Cunningham, Alfred G., 1870–1951, vol. V

Cunningham, Lt-Col Aylmer Basil, 1879–1940, vol. III (A), vol. IV

Cunningham, Rev. Bertram Keir, 1871–1944, vol. IV

Cunningham, Brysson, 1868–1950, vol. IV

Cunningham, Sir Charles Banks, 1884–1967, vol. VI

Cunningham, Sir Charles Craik, 1906–1998, vol. X

Cunningham, Daniel John, 1850–1909, vol. I

Cunningham, David, 1924–1995, vol. IX

Cunningham, Col David Douglas, 1843–1914, vol. I

Cunningham, E. Margaret, 1872–1940, vol. III

Cunningham, Ebenezer, 1881–1977, vol. VII

Cunningham, Edward Charles, 1872–1929, vol. III

Cunningham, Sir Edward Sheldon, 1859–1957, vol. V

Cunningham, Sir Frederick; see Cunningham, Sir A, F, D,

Cunningham, Sir George, 1888–1964, vol. VI

Cunningham, George Charles, 1883–1950, vol. IV

Cunningham, Brig.-Gen. George Glencairn, 1862–1943, vol. IV

Cunningham, George John, 1906–1994, vol. IX

Cunningham, Sir George M.; see Miller-Cunningham.

Cunningham, Gordon Herriot, 1892–1962, vol. VI

Cunningham, Sir Graham, 1892–1978, vol. VII

Cunningham, Sir Henry Stewart, 1832–1920, vol. II

Cunningham, Rt Rev. Jack, 1926–1978, vol. VII

Cunningham, Rt Rev. James, 1910–1974, vol. VII

Cunningham, Lt-Col John, died 1968, vol. VI

Cunningham, Engr-Rear-Adm. John Edward Greig, 1878–1954, vol. V

Cunningham, Rt Rev. John F., 1842–1919, vol. II (A), vol. III

Cunningham, John Francis, died 1932, vol. III

Cunningham, Adm. of the Fleet Sir John Henry Dacres, 1885–1962, vol. VI

Cunningham, John Jeffrey, 1907–1959, vol. V

Cunningham, Rev. Canon John Manstead, 1879–1947, vol. III

Cunningham, John Richard, 1876–1942, vol. IV

Cunningham, Lt-Col John Sydney, 1876–1943, vol. IV

Cunningham, Joseph Thomas, 1859–1935, vol. III

Cunningham, Sir Josias, 1934–2000, vol. X

Cunningham, Sir Knox; see Cunningham, Sir S. K.

Cunningham, Lallie S. C., died 1937, vol. III

Cunningham, Marta, died 1937, vol. III

Cunningham, Mary Elizabeth, died 1939, vol. III

Cunningham, Patrick, died 1960, vol. V

Cunningham, Robert Kerr, 1923–2000, vol. X

Cunningham, Rt Hon. Samuel, 1862–1946, vol. IV

Cunningham, Sir (Samuel) Knox, 1st Bt, 1909–1976, vol. VII

Cunningham, Wilfred Bertram, 1882–1960, vol. V

Cunningham, Ven. William, 1849–1919, vol. II

Cunningham, William Allison, died 1939, vol. III

Cunningham, Maj.-Gen. Sir William Henry, 1883–1959, vol. V

Cunningham, William Ross, 1890–1953, vol. V

Cunningham Craig, Edward Hubert; see Craig.

Cunningham-Reid, Captain Alec Stratford, died 1977, vol. VII

Cunninghame, Sir James Fraser, 1870–1952, vol. V

Cunninghame Graham of Gartmore, Adm. Sir Angus Edward Malise Bontine, 1893–1981, vol. VIII

Cunninghame Graham, Comdr Charles Elphinstone Fleeming, 1854–1917, vol. II

Cunninghame Graham, Robert Bontine, 1852–1936, vol. III

Cunnington, Cecil Willett, 1878–1961, vol. VI

Cunnington, Maud Edith, 1869–1951, vol. V

Cunnison, Sir Alexander, 1879–1959, vol. V

Cunnison, David Keith, 1881–1972, vol. VII

Cunyngham, Major Sir Colin Keith Dick-, 11th Bt, 1908–1941, vol. IV

Cunyngham, Maj.-Gen. James Keith D.; see Dick-Cunyngham.

Cunyngham of Lamburghtoun, Sir Robert Keith Alexander Dick-, 9th Bt, 1836–1897, vol. I

Cunyngham, Lt-Col William Henry Dick-, died 1900, vol. I

Cunyngham, Sir William Stewart-Dick-, 10th Bt, 1871–1922, vol. II

Cunynghame, Sir David; see Cunynghame, Sir H. D. St L. B. S.

Cunynghame, Sir Francis George Thurlow, 9th Bt, 1835–1900, vol. I

Cunynghame, Sir (Henry) David St Leger Brooke Selwyn, 11th Bt, 1905–1978, vol. VII

Cunynghame, Sir Henry Hardinge, 1848–1935, vol. III

Cunynghame, Sir James Ogilvy B.; see Blair-Cunynghame.

Cunynghame, Hon. Pamela Margaret, (Hon. Lady Cunynghame); see Stanley.

Cunynghame, Sir Percy, 10th Bt, 1867–1941, vol. IV

Curci, Amelita G.; see Galli-Curci.

Cure, Sir Edward Capel, 1866–1923, vol. II

Cure, Col Herbert Capel, 1859–1909, vol. I

Curgenven, Sir Arthur Joseph, 1876–1965, vol. VI

Curie, Jean F. J.; see Joliot-Curie.

Curie, Madame Marie, 1867–1934, vol. III

Curie, Pierre, 1859–1906, vol. I

Curle, Alexander Ormiston, 1866–1955, vol. V

Curle, James, 1862–1944, vol. IV

Curle, Sir John Noel Ormiston, 1915–1997, vol. X

Curle, Richard Henry Parnell, 1883–1968, vol. VI

Curlewis, Sir Adrian Herbert, 1901–1985, vol. VIII

Curlewis, Ethel; see Turner, E.

Curlewis, Rt Hon. John Stephen, 1863–1940, vol. III

Curling, Brig.-Gen. Bryan James, 1877–1955, vol. V

Curling, Rev. Joseph James, 1844–1906, vol. I

Curling, Rev. Canon Thomas Higham, 1872–1944, vol. IV

Curnick, Captain Alfred James, 1865–1936, vol. III

Curnock, Rev. Nehemiah, 1840–1915, vol. I

Curnow, John, 1846–1902, vol. I

Curphey, Col Sir Aldington George, 1880–1958, vol. V

Curran, Charles, 1903–1972, vol. VII

Curran, Sir Charles John, 1921–1980, vol. VII

Curran, Desmond, 1903–1985, vol. VIII

Curran, Harry Gibson, 1901–1986, vol. VIII

Curran, John Adye, 1837–1919, vol. II

Curran, Rt Hon. Sir Lancelot Ernest, 1899–1984, vol. VIII

Curran, Pete, 1860–1910, vol. I

Curran, Sir Samuel Crowe, 1912–1998, vol. X

Curran, Thomas, died 1913, vol. I

Curran, Thomas Bartholomew, 1870–1929, vol. III
Curre, Augusta, (Lady Curre), died 1956, vol. V
Curre, John Mathew, 1859–1919, vol. II
Curre, Sir William Edward Carne, 1855–1930, vol. III
Currer Briggs, D. H.; see Briggs.
Currey, Adm. Bernard, died 1936, vol. III
Currey, Rear-Adm. Edmund Neville Vincent, 1906–1998, vol. X
Currey, Harry Lloyd Fairbridge, 1925–1998, vol. X
Currey, Rear-Adm. Harry Philip, 1902–1979, vol. VII
Currey, Henry Latham, 1863–1945, vol. IV
Currey, Brig. Henry Percivall, 1886–1969, vol. VI
Currey, Rear-Adm. Hugh Schomberg, 1876–1955, vol. V
Currey, Ronald Fairbridge, 1894–1983, vol. VIII
Currie, 1st Baron, 1834–1906, vol. I
Currie, Agnes Jean, 1899–1968, vol. VI
Currie, Major Hon. Sir Alan; see Currie, Major Hon. Sir H. A.
Currie, Sir Alastair Robert, 1921–1994, vol. IX
Currie, Sir Alick Bradley, 6th Bt, 1904–1987, vol. VIII
Currie, Brig.-Gen. Arthur Cecil, died 1942, vol. IV
Currie, Gen. Sir Arthur William, 1875–1933, vol. III
Currie, Captain Bertram Francis George, 1899–1959, vol. V
Currie, David, 1870–1933, vol. III
Currie, Sir Donald, 1825–1909, vol. I
Currie, Brig. Douglas Hendrie, 1892–1966, vol. VI
Currie, Sir Edmund Hay, 1834–1913, vol. I
Currie, Very Rev. Edward Reid, 1844–1921, vol. II
Currie, Maj.-Gen. Fendall, 1841–1920, vol. II
Currie, Rev. Sir Frederick Larkins, 2nd Bt, 1823–1900, vol. I
Currie, Sir Frederick Reeve, 3rd Bt, 1851–1930, vol. III
Currie, Sir George Alexander, 1896–1984, vol. VIII
Currie, George Boyle Hanna, 1905–1978, vol. VII
Currie, Lt-Col George Selkirk, 1889–1975, vol. VII
Currie, George Welsh, 1870–1950, vol. IV
Currie, Harry Augustus Frederick, 1866–1912, vol. I
Currie, Major Hon. Sir (Henry) Alan, 1868–1942, vol. IV
Currie, Rev. Hugh Penton, 1854–1903, vol. I
Currie, Lt-Col Ivor Bertram Fendall, 1872–1924, vol. II
Currie, Sir James, 1868–1937, vol. III
Currie, Sir James, 1907–1983, vol. VIII
Currie, Sir James Thomson, 1868–1943, vol. IV
Currie, John Ronald, died 1949, vol. IV
Currie, Laurence, 1867–1934, vol. III
Currie, Mark Mainwaring Lee, 1882–1951, vol. V
Currie, Mary Montgomerie, (Lady Currie), 1843–1905, vol. I
Currie, Sir Neil Smith, 1926–1999, vol. X
Currie, Patrick, 1883–1949, vol. IV
Currie, Rev. Piers William Edward, 1913–1999, vol. X
Currie, Rear-Adm. Robert Alexander, 1905–1995, vol. IX
Currie, Ronald Ian, 1928–1996, vol. X

Currie, Col Ryves Alexander Mark, 1875–1920, vol. II
Currie, Col Thomas, 1851–1931, vol. III
Currie, Sir Walter Louis Rackham, 4th Bt, 1856–1941, vol. IV
Currie, Sir Walter Mordaunt Cyril, 5th Bt, 1894–1978, vol. VII
Currie, Sir William Crawford, 1884–1961, vol. VI
Currie, Major William Leopold, 1856–1929, vol. III
Currie-Blyth, James Pattison, 1824–1908, vol. I
Currin, Richard William, 1872–1942, vol. IV
Curry, Aaron Charlton, 1887–1957, vol. V
Curry, Comdr Hugh Fortescue, 1890–1932, vol. III
Curry, John Anthony, 1949–1994, vol. IX
Curry, Brig.-Gen. Montagu Crichton, died 1931, vol. III
Cursetjee, Maj.-Gen. Sir Heerajee Jehangir Manockjee, 1885–1964, vol. VI
Cursiter, Stanley, 1887–1976, vol. VII
Cursley, Norman Sharpe, 1898–1972, vol. VII
Curson, Bernard Robert, 1913–1988, vol. VIII
Curteis, Adm. Sir Alban Thomas Buckley, 1887–1961, vol. VI
Curteis, Col Cyril Samuel Sackville, 1874–1943, vol. IV
Curteis, Brig.-Gen. Francis Algernon, 1856–1928, vol. II
Curteis, Captain Sir Gerald, 1892–1972, vol. VII
Curteis, Maj.-Gen. Reginald Lawrence Herbert, 1843–1919, vol. II
Curthoys, Alfred, died 1969, vol. VI
Curthoys, Roy Lancaster, 1892–1971, vol. VII
Curtice, Harlow H., 1893–1962, vol. VI
Curtin, Rt Rev. Mgr Canon Jeremiah John, 1907–1988, vol. VIII
Curtin, Rt Hon. John, 1885–1945, vol. IV
Curtis, Maj.-Gen. Alfred Cyril, 1894–1971, vol. VII
Curtis, Amy, 1894–1970, vol. VI
Curtis, Sir Arthur Colin, 3rd Bt (cr 1794), 1858–1898, vol. I
Curtis, Sqdn Ldr Sir Arthur Randolph Wormeley, 1889–1966, vol. VI
Curtis, Vice-Adm. Berwick, 1876–1965, vol. VI
Curtis, Charles, 1860–1936, vol. III
Curtis, Cyrus Hermann Kotzschmar, 1850–1933, vol. III
Curtis, Sir (Edgar) Francis (Egerton), 5th Bt (cr 1802), 1875–1943, vol. IV
Curtis, Edmund, 1881–1943, vol. IV
Curtis, Edward Beaumont Cotton, 1863–1939, vol. III
Curtis, Col Edward George, 1868–1923, vol. II
Curtis, Edward Herbert, 1867–1937, vol. III
Curtis, Most Rev. Ernest Edwin, 1906–1999, vol. X
Curtis, Sir Francis; see Curtis, Sir E. F. E.
Curtis, Brig. Francis Cockburn, 1898–1986, vol. VIII
Curtis, Col Francis George Savage, 1836–1906, vol. I
Curtis, Genevra Fiona Penelope Victoria, (Mrs J. W. O. Curtis); see Caws, G. F. P. V.
Curtis, Very Rev. Canon George, 1861–1948, vol. IV
Curtis, George Byron, 1843–1907, vol. I
Curtis, Sir George Harold, 1902–1972, vol. VII

Curtis, Col George Reginald, 1892–1958, vol. V
Curtis, Sir George Seymour, 1867–1931, vol. III
Curtis, Henry, *died* 1944, vol. IV
Curtis, Maj.-Gen. Henry Osborne, 1888–1964, vol. VI
Curtis, Sir James, 1868–1942, vol. IV
Curtis, Rt Rev. John, 1880–1962, vol. VI
Curtis, John S.; *see* Sutton Curtis.
Curtis, Lionel George, 1872–1955, vol. V
Curtis, Dame Myra, 1886–1971, vol. VII
Curtis, Percy John, 1900–1985, vol. VIII
Curtis, Sir Peter, 6th Bt (*cr* 1802), 1907–1976, vol. VII
Curtis, Philip, 1908–1998, vol. X
Curtis, Maj.-Gen. Sir Reginald Salmond, 1863–1922, vol. II
Curtis, Richard James Seymour, 1900–1985, vol. VIII
Curtis, Sir Roger Colin Molyneux, 4th Bt (*cr* 1794), 1886–1954, vol. V
Curtis, Air Vice-Marshal Walter John Brice, 1888–1973, vol. VII
Curtis, Air Marshal Wilfred Austin, 1893–1977, vol. VII
Curtis, Wilfred Harry, 1897–1988, vol. VIII
Curtis, Rev. William Alexander, 1876–1961, vol. VI
Curtis, William Edward, 1889–1969, vol. VI
Curtis, Sir William Michael, 4th Bt (*cr* 1802), 1859–1916, vol. II
Curtis-Bennett, Derek; *see* Curtis-Bennett, F. H.
Curtis-Bennett, Sir (Francis) Noel, 1882–1950, vol. IV
Curtis-Bennett, Frederick Henry, (Derek), 1904–1956, vol. V
Curtis-Bennett, Sir Henry Honywood, 1879–1936, vol. III
Curtis-Bennett, Sir Noel; *see* Curtis-Bennett, Sir F. N.
Curtis Brown, Spencer, 1906–1980, vol. VII
Curtis-Raleigh, Nigel Hugh, 1914–1986, vol. VIII
Curtis-Willson, William Thomas, 1888–1957, vol. V
Curtoys, Maj.-Gen. Charles Ernest Edward, 1863–1940, vol. III
Curwen, Alan de Lancy, 1869–1930, vol. III
Curwen, Dame (Anne) May, 1889–1973, vol. VII
Curwen, Annie J., 1845–1932, vol. III
Curwen, Rev. Edward Hasell, 1847–1929, vol. III
Curwen, Eldred Vincent Morris, 1842–1927, vol. II
Curwen, Harold Spedding, 1885–1949, vol. IV
Curwen, Henry, 1879–1946, vol. IV
Curwen, John Spencer, 1847–1916, vol. II
Curwen, Dame May; *see* Curwen, Dame A. M.
Curwood, James Oliver, 1879–1927, vol. II
Curzon of Kedleston, 1st Marquess, 1859–1925, vol. II
Curzon of Kedleston, Marchioness; (Grace Elvina), *died* 1958, vol. V
Curzon, Hon. Alfred Nathaniel, 1860–1920, vol. II
Curzon, Rt Rev. Charles Edward, *died* 1954, vol. V
Curzon, Sir Clifford Michael, 1907–1982, vol. VIII
Curzon, Mrs Edith Basset Penn, 1861–1943, vol. IV
Curzon, Hon. Francis Nathaniel, 1865–1941, vol. IV
Curzon, Frank, 1868–1927, vol. II
Curzon, Col George Augustus, 1836–1912, vol. I

Curzon, Harry Edward James, 1880–1935, vol. III
Curzon, Hon. Henry Dugdale, 1824–1910, vol. I
Curzon, Col Hon. Montagu, 1846–1907, vol. I
Curzon-Howe, Adm. Hon. Sir Assheton Gore, 1850–1911, vol. I
Curzon-Howe, Captain Leicester Charles Assheton St John, 1894–1941, vol. IV
Curzon-Siggers, Ven. William, 1860–1947, vol. IV
Cusack, Henry Vernon, 1895–1996, vol. X
Cusack, John, 1867–1940, vol. III
Cusack, John Winder, 1907–1968, vol. VI
Cusack, Sir Ralph Smith, 1822–1910, vol. I
Cusack, Hon. Sir Ralph Vincent, 1916–1978, vol. VII
Cusack-Smith, Sir Berry, 5th Bt, 1859–1929, vol. III
Cusack-Smith, Sir Dermot; *see* Cusack-Smith, Sir W. R. D. J.
Cusack-Smith, Sir William, 4th Bt, 1822–1919, vol. II
Cusack-Smith, Sir (William Robert) Dermot (Joshua), 6th Bt, 1907–1970, vol. VI
Cuscaden, Maj.-Gen. Sir George, 1857–1933, vol. III
Cuscaden, William Andrew, 1853–1936, vol. III
Cusden, Victor Vincent, 1893–1980, vol. VII
Cushendun, 1st Baron, 1861–1936, vol. III
Cushing, Harvey Williams, 1869–1939, vol. III
Cushion, Air Vice-Marshal Sir William Boston, 1891–1978, vol. VII
Cushny, Arthur Robertson, 1866–1926, vol. II
Cusins, Col Albert George Teeling, 1871–1936, vol. III
Cussen, Edward James Patrick, 1904–1973, vol. VII
Cussen, Hon. Sir Leo Finn Bernard, 1859–1933, vol. III
Cust, Aleen Isabel, *died* 1937, vol. III
Cust, Col Sir Archer; *see* Cust, Col Sir L. G. A.
Cust, Very Rev. Arthur Perceval Purey-, 1828–1916, vol. II
Cust, Sir Charles Leopold, 3rd Bt, 1864–1931, vol. III
Cust, Mrs Henry, (Emmeline Mary Elizabeth), (Nina), *died* 1955, vol. V
Cust, Henry John Cockayne, 1861–1917, vol. II
Cust, Adm. Sir Herbert Edward Purey-, 1857–1938, vol. III
Cust, Col Sir (Lionel George) Archer, 1896–1962, vol. VI
Cust, Sir Lionel Henry, 1859–1929, vol. III
Cust, Nina; *see* Cust, Mrs Henry.
Cust, Sir Reginald John, 1828–1912, vol. I
Cust, Brig. Richard Brownlow P.; *see* Purey-Cust.
Cust, Robert Henry Hobart, 1861–1940, vol. III
Cust, Robert Needham, 1821–1909, vol. I
Cust, Rev. Canon William Arthur Purey, 1855–1938, vol. III
Custance, Col Frederic Hambleton, 1844–1925, vol. II
Custance, Michael Magnus Vere, 1916–1999, vol. X
Custance, Adm. Sir Reginald Neville, 1847–1935, vol. III
Custance, Rear-Adm. Wilfred Neville, 1884–1939, vol. III
Custard, Reginald G.; *see* Goss-Custard.
Custard, Walter Henry Goss, 1871–1964, vol. VI

Cutbill, Col Reginald Heaton Locke, 1878–1956, vol. V
Cutforth, Sir Arthur Edwin, 1881–1958, vol. V
Cutforth, Maj.-Gen. Sir Lancelot Eric, 1899–1980, vol. VII
Cuthbert, Very Rev. Father, 1866–1939, vol. III
Cuthbert, David, 1866–1953, vol. V
Cuthbert, Maj.-Gen. Gerald James, 1861–1931, vol. III
Cuthbert, Harold David, 1909–1959, vol. V
Cuthbert, Hon. Sir Henry, 1829–1907, vol. I
Cuthbert, Captain James Harold, 1876–1915, vol. I
Cuthbert, Vice-Adm. Sir John Wilson, 1902–1987, vol. VIII
Cuthbert, Lt-Col Thomas Wilkinson, *died* 1936, vol. III
Cuthbert, William Moncrieff, 1936–1989, vol. VIII
Cuthbert, William Nicolson, *died* 1960, vol. V
Cuthbertson, Clive, 1863–1943, vol. IV
Cuthbertson, David, 1856–1935, vol. III
Cuthbertson, Sir David Paton, 1900–1989, vol. VIII
Cuthbertson, Brig.-Gen. Edward Boustead, 1880–1942, vol. IV
Cuthbertson, Sir Harold Alexander, 1911–1994, vol. IX
Cuthbertson, Henry, 1859–1903, vol. I
Cuthbertson, Sir John Neilson, 1829–1905, vol. I
Cuthbertson, Joseph William, 1901–1984, vol. VIII
Cutlack, Col William Philip, 1881–1965, vol. VI
Cutler, Edward, 1831–1916, vol. II
Cutler, Elliott Carr, 1888–1947, vol. IV
Cutler, Sir Horace Walter, 1912–1997, vol. X
Cutler, John, 1839–1924, vol. II
Cutner, Solomon; *see* Solomon.
Cuttell, Rev. Canon Colin, 1908–1992, vol. IX
Cuttle, William Linsdell, 1896–1958, vol. V
Cutts, Rt Rev. Richard Stanley, 1919–1997, vol. X
Cuyler, Sir Charles, 4th Bt, 1867–1919, vol. II
Cuyler, Sir George Hallifax, 5th Bt, 1876–1947, vol. IV
Cuyler, Rev. Theodore Ledyard, *died* 1909, vol. I
Cynan; *see* Evans-Jones, Rev. Sir Albert.
Cyriax, James Henry, 1904–1985, vol. VIII
Czaplicka, Marie Antoinette, *died* 1921, vol. II
Cziffra, György, 1921–1994, vol. IX

D

Dabbs, George Henry Roque, 1846–1913, vol. I
D'Abernon, 1st Viscount, 1857–1941, vol. IV
Dabholkar, Sir Vasantrao Anandrao, 1881–1933, vol. III
Dabney, Hon. Charles William, 1855–1945, vol. IV
d'Abo, Gerard Louis, 1884–1962, vol. VI
d'Abreu, Alphonso Liguori, 1906–1976, vol. VII
d'Abreu, Francis Arthur, 1904–1995, vol. IX
Dacca, Nawab Bahadur, Sir Khwaya Salimulla, *died* 1915, vol. I
D'Ache, Caran, (Emmanuel Poire), *died* 1909, vol. I
D'Costa, Sir Alfred Horace, 1873–1967, vol. VI
Da Costa, Brig.-Gen. Evan Campbell, 1871–1949, vol. IV
Da Costa, John, 1867–1931, vol. III
Dacre, Air Cdre George Bentley, 1891–1962, vol. VI
Dadabhoy, Sir Maneckji Byramji, 1865–1953, vol. V
Dadd, Frank, 1851–1929, vol. III
Dadzie, Kenneth Kweku Sinaman, 1930–1995, vol. IX
Daeniker, Armin, 1898–1983, vol. VIII
D'Aeth, Rear-Adm. Arthur Cloudesley Shovel H.; *see* Hughes D'Aeth.
D'Aeth, John, 1853–1922, vol. II
D'Aeth, Air Vice-Marshal Narborough Hughes, 1901–1986, vol. VIII
Da Fano, Corrado Donato, 1879–1927, vol. II
Da Fano, Dorothea, (Mrs C. D. Da Fano); *see* Landau, D.
Dafoe, Allan Roy, 1883–1943, vol. IV
Dafoe, John Wesley, 1866–1944, vol. IV
Daga, Sir Dewan Bahadur Kasturchand, 1855–1917, vol. II
Daga, Raja Rai Bahadur Sir Seth Bisesardass, 1877–1941, vol. IV (A), vol. V
Daggar, George, *died* 1950, vol. IV
Daggett, William Ingledew, 1900–1980, vol. VII
Daglish, Eric Fitch, 1892–1966, vol. VI
Daglish, Hon. Henry, 1866–1920, vol. II
Dagnan-Bouveret, Pascal Adolph Jean, 1852–1929, vol. III
Dagonet; *see* Sims, George Robert.
D'Aguilar, Sir Charles Lawrence, 1821–1912, vol. I
Dahl, Knut, 1871–1953, vol. V
Dahl, Murdoch Edgcumbe, 1914–1991, vol. IX
Dahl, Roald, 1916–1990, vol. VIII
Dahl, Robert Henry, 1910–1999, vol. X
Dahlgaard, Tyge, 1921–1985, vol. VIII
Daiches, Lionel Henry, 1911–1999, vol. X
Dain, Charles Kenneth, 1879–1950, vol. IV (A)
Dain, George Rutherford, 1884–1954, vol. V
Dain, Sir Guy; *see* Dain, Sir H. G.
Dain, Sir (Harry) Guy, 1870–1966, vol. VI
Dain, Sir John Rutherford, 1883–1957, vol. V
Daines, Percy, *died* 1957, vol. V
Dainton, Baron (Life Peer); Frederick Sydney Dainton, 1914–1997, vol. X
Daintree, Captain John Dodson, 1864–1952, vol. V
Dakers, A. W., 1868–1947, vol. IV
Dakers, Jane, (Mrs Andrew Dakers); *see* Lane, J.
Dakin, Henry Drysdale, 1880–1952, vol. V
Dakin, William John, 1883–1950, vol. IV
Dakin, William Radford, 1860–1935, vol. III
Dakyns, George Doherty, 1856–1939, vol. III (A), vol. IV
Dakyns, Winifred, 1875–1960, vol. V
Daladier, Edouard, 1884–1970, vol. VI
Dalais, Sir (Adrien) Pierre, 1929–1991, vol. IX
Dalais, Sir Pierre; *see* Dalais, Sir A. P.

Dalal, Sir Ardeshir Rustomji, 1884–1949, vol. IV
Dalal, Sirdar Sir Bamanjee Ardeshire, 1854–1932, vol. III
Dalal, Sir Barjor Jamshedji, 1871–1936, vol. III
Dalal, Sir Dadiba Merwanjee, 1870–1941, vol. IV
Dalal, Sir Ratanji Dinshaw, 1868–1957, vol. V
d'Albe, Edmund Edward F.; see Fournier d'Albe.
D'Albert, Eugen, 1864–1932, vol. III
D'Albiac, Air Marshal Sir John Henry, 1894–1963, vol. VI
Dalbiac, Philip Hugh, 1855–1927, vol. II
d'Albuquerque, Nino Pedroso, 1894–1969, vol. VI
Dalby, Rev. Francis Higgs, 1853–1933, vol. III
Dalby, Maj.-Gen. Thomas Gerald, 1880–1963, vol. VI
Dalby, W. Ernest, died 1936, vol. III
Dalby, Sir William Bartlett, 1840–1918, vol. II
Dalcroze, Emile J.; see Jaques-Dalcroze.
Daldry, Sir Leonard Charles, 1908–1988, vol. VIII
Daldy, Ven. Alfred Edward, 1865–1935, vol. III
Daldy, Frederick Francis, 1857–1928, vol. II
Dale, Adm. Alfred Taylor, 1840–1925, vol. II
Dale, Sir Alfred William Winterslow, 1855–1921, vol. II
Dale, Rt Rev. Basil Montague, 1903–1976, vol. VII
Dale, Benjamin James, 1885–1943, vol. IV
Dale, Charles Ernest, 1867–1956, vol. V
Dale, Major Claude Henry, 1882–1946, vol. IV
Dale, Darley; see Steele, F. M.
Dale, Sir Edgar Thorniley, 1886–1966, vol. VI
Dale, Francis Richard, 1883–1976, vol. VII
Dale, Frank Harry, 1871–1918, vol. II
Dale, Brig.-Gen. George Arthur, 1866–1940, vol. III
Dale, Harold Edward, 1875–1954, vol. V
Dale, Rev. Harold Montague, 1873–1951, vol. V
Dale, Henry Angley L.; see Lewis-Dale.
Dale, Sir Henry Hallett, 1875–1968, vol. VI
Dale, Henry Sheppard, 1852–1921, vol. II
Dale, James A., 1874–1951, vol. V
Dale, Sir James Backhouse, 2nd Bt, 1855–1932, vol. III
Dale, John Ainsworth, 1887–1938, vol. III
Dale, John Gilbert, 1869–1926, vol. II
Dale, Louise Mary, (Lady Mulleneux-Grayson), died 1954, vol. V
Dale, Ven. Canon Percy John, 1876–1957, vol. V
Dale, Rev. Thomas F., died 1923, vol. II
Dale, Rev. William, 1841–1924, vol. II
Dale, Sir William Leonard, 1906–2000, vol. X
Dalen, Nils Gustaf, 1869–1937, vol. III
Daley, Sir Allen; see Daley, Sir W. A.
Daley, Sir Denis Leo, 1888–1965, vol. VI
Daley, Sir (William) Allen, 1887–1969, vol. VI
Dalgetty, James Simpson, 1907–1981, vol. VIII
Dalgety, Arthur William Hugh, 1899–1972, vol. VII
Dalgety, Col Edmund Henry, 1847–1914, vol. I
Dalgety, Major Frederick John, 1866–1926, vol. II
Dalgleish, Wing Comdr James William O.; see Ogilvy-Dalgleish.
Dalgleish, Oakley Hedley, 1910–1963, vol. VI
Dalgleish, Walter Scott, 1834–1897, vol. I
Dalgleish, Sir William Ogilvy, 1st Bt, 1832–1913, vol. I
Dalgliesh, Richard, 1844–1922, vol. II
Dalgliesh, Theodore Irving, died 1941, vol. IV

Dalglish, Capt. James Stephen, 1913–1995, vol. IX
Dalglish, Rear-Adm. Robin Campsie, 1880–1934, vol. III
Dalhoff, Most Rev. T., died 1906, vol. I
Dalhousie, 14th Earl of, 1878–1928, vol. II
Dalhousie, 15th Earl of, 1904–1950, vol. IV
Dalhousie, 16th Earl of, 1914–1999, vol. X
Dali, Salvador Felipe Jacinto, 1904–1989, vol. VIII
Dalison, Maj.-Gen. John Bernard, 1898–1964, vol. VI
Dalison, Rev. Canon Roger William H., 1860–1939, vol. III
Dallapiccola, Luigi, 1904–1975, vol. VII
Dallard, Berkeley Lionel Scudamore, 1889–1983, vol. VIII
Dallas, Lt-Col Alexander Egerton, 1869–1949, vol. IV
Dallas, Surg.-Gen. Alexander Morison, 1830–1912, vol. I
Dallas, Maj.-Gen. Alister Grant, 1866–1931, vol. III
Dallas, Lt-Col Charles Mowbray, 1861–1936, vol. III
Dallas, Hon. Francis Henry, 1865–1920, vol. II
Dallas, George, 1878–1961, vol. VI
Dallas, Sir George Edward, 3rd Bt, 1842–1918, vol. II
Dalley, Christopher Mervyn, 1913–1999, vol. X
Dallin, Cyrus Edwin, 1861–1944, vol. IV
Dalling, Sir Thomas, 1892–1982, vol. VIII
Dallinger, Rev. William Henry, 1842–1909, vol. I
Dally, John Frederick Halls, died 1944, vol. IV
Dalmahoy, Maj.-Gen. Patrick Carfrae, 1840–1926, vol. II
Dalmahoy, Patrick Carfrae, 1872–1928, vol. II
Dalmahoy, Patrick James Edward, 1896–1963, vol. VI
Dalmeny, Lord; Archibald Ronald Primrose, 1910–1931, vol. III
Dalrymple, Rt Hon. Sir Charles, 1st Bt (cr 1887), 1839–1916, vol. II
Dalrymple, Sir (Charles) Mark, 3rd Bt (cr 1887), 1915–1971, vol. VII
Dalrymple, Sir David Charles Herbert, 2nd Bt (cr 1887), 1879–1932, vol. III
Dalrymple, Hon. David Hay, 1840–1912, vol. II
Dalrymple, Sir Edward Arthur E.; see Elphinstone-Dalrymple.
Dalrymple, Col Sir Francis Napier E.; see Elphinstone-Dalrymple.
Dalrymple, Sir Hew (Clifford) Hamilton-, 9th Bt (cr 1697), 1888–1959, vol. V
Dalrymple, Hon. Sir Hew Hamilton, 1857–1945, vol. IV
Dalrymple, Ian Murray, 1903–1989, vol. VIII
Dalrymple, James, 1859–1934, vol. III
Dalrymple, Joseph, 1869–1949, vol. IV
Dalrymple, Sir Mark; see Dalrymple, Sir C. M.
Dalrymple, Sir Robert Graeme E.; see Elphinstone-Dalrymple.
Dalrymple, Sir Walter Hamilton-, 8th Bt (cr 1697), 1854–1920, vol. II
Dalrymple, Col Sir William, 1864–1941, vol. IV
Dalrymple, Maj.-Gen. William Liston, 1845–1938, vol. III

Dalrymple-Champneys, Captain Sir Weldon, 2nd Bt, 1892–1980, vol. VII

Dalrymple-Hamilton, Adm. Sir Frederick Hew George, 1890–1974, vol. VII

Dalrymple-Hamilton, Col Hon. North de Coigny, 1853–1906, vol. I

Dalrymple-Hamilton, Col Sir North Victor Cecil, 1883–1953, vol. V

Dalrymple Hay, Sir Charles John, 5th Bt, 1865–1952, vol. V

Dalrymple-Hay, Sir Harley Hugh, 1861–1940, vol. III

Dalrymple-Horn-Elphinstone, Sir Græme Hepburn; *see* Elphinstone.

Dalrymple-Smith, Captain Hugh, 1901–1987, vol. VIII

Dalrymple-White, Lt-Col Sir Godfrey Dalrymple, 1st Bt, 1866–1954, vol. V

Dalton, Baron (Life Peer); Edward Hugh John Neale Dalton, 1887–1962, vol. VI

Dalton, Rev. Prebendary Arthur Edison, 1853–1938, vol. III

Dalton, Charles, 1850–1913, vol. I

Dalton, Hon. Charles, 1850–1933, vol. III

Dalton, Captain Charles G.; *see* Grant-Dalton.

Dalton, Maj.-Gen. Sir Charles James George, 1902–1989, vol. VIII

Dalton, Sir Cornelius Neale, 1842–1920, vol. II

Dalton, Lt-Col Duncan G.; *see* Grant-Dalton.

D'Alton, Rt Rev. Edward A., 1860–1941, vol. IV

Dalton, Emilie Hilda; *see* Dalton, Mrs John E.

Dalton, Surg.-Rear-Adm. Frederick James Abercrombie, 1868–1940, vol. III

Dalton, Frederick Thomas, 1855–1927, vol. II

Dalton, Sir Henry, 1891–1966, vol. VI

Dalton, Rev. Herbert Andrew, 1852–1928, vol. II

Dalton, Adm. Hubert G.; *see* Grant-Dalton.

Dalton, Maj.-Gen. James Cecil, 1848–1931, vol. III

D'Alton, His Eminence Cardinal John, *died* 1963, vol. VI

Dalton, Maj.-Gen. John Cecil D'Arcy, 1907–1981, vol. VIII

Dalton, Sir John Cornelius, *died* 1959, vol. V

Dalton, Mrs John E., (Emilie Hilda Dalton), 1886–1950, vol. IV

Dalton, Rev. John Neale, 1839–1931, vol. III

Dalton, John Patrick, 1886–1965, vol. VI

Dalton, Comdr (E) Lionel Sydney, 1902–1941, vol. IV

Dalton, Sir Llewelyn Chisholm, 1879–1945, vol. IV

Dalton, Norman, *died* 1923, vol. II

Dalton, Vice-Adm. Sir Norman Eric, 1904–1992, vol. IX

Dalton, Ormonde Maddock, 1866–1945, vol. IV

Dalton, Philip Neale, 1909–1989, vol. VIII

Dalton, Sir Robert William, 1882–1961, vol. VI

Dalton, Seymour Berkeley P.; *see* Portman-Dalton.

Dalton, Thomas Wilson Fox, 1886–1977, vol. VII

Dalton, William Bower, 1868–1965, vol. VI

Dalton-Morris, Air Marshal Sir Leslie, 1906–1976, vol. VII

D'Alvarez, Marguerite, 1886–1953, vol. V

D'Alviella, Count Goblet, 1846–1925, vol. II

Dalwood, Hubert, 1924–1976, vol. VII

Dalwood, Lt-Col John H.; *see* Hall-Dalwood.

Daly, Maj.-Gen. Arthur Crawford, 1871–1936, vol. III

Daly, Ashley Skeffington, 1882–1977, vol. VII

Daly, Augustin, 1838–1899, vol. I

Daly, Lt-Col Sir Clive Kirkpatrick, 1888–1966, vol. VI

Daly, Major Denis St George, 1862–1942, vol. IV

Daly, Lt-Col Francis Augustus Bonner, 1855–1946, vol. IV

Daly, Francis Charles, 1868–1945, vol. IV

Daly, Harry John, 1893–1980, vol. VII (AII)

Daly, Very Rev. Henry Edward, *died* 1949, vol. IV

Daly, Ven. Henry Varian, 1838–1925, vol. II

Daly, Lt-Col Sir Hugh, 1860–1939, vol. III

Daly, Ivan de Burgh, 1893–1974, vol. VII

Daly, John Archer Blake-, 1835–1917, vol. II (A), vol. III

Daly, Rt Rev. John Charles Sydney, 1903–1993, vol. IX

Daly, Col Louis Dominic, 1885–1967, vol. VI

Daly, Lt-Col Ludger Jules Olivier G.; *see* Gingras-Daly.

Daly, Hon. Sir Malachy Bowes, 1836–1920, vol. II

Daly, Dame Mary Dora, *died* 1983, vol. VIII

Daly, Sir Oscar Bedford, 1880–1953, vol. V

Daly, Col Patrick Joseph, 1872–1931, vol. III

Daly, Col Thomas, *died* 1917, vol. II

Daly, Thomas Denis, 1890–1956, vol. V

Daly Lewis, Edward; *see* Lewis.

Dalyell of the Binns, Lt-Col Gordon, 1887–1953, vol. V

Dalyell, Major Sir James Bruce Wilkie-, 9th Bt, 1867–1935, vol. III

Dalyell, Lt-Gen. John Thomas, 1827–1919, vol. II

Dalyell, Ralph, 1834–1915, vol. I

Dalzell, Lord; Robert Hippisley Dalzell, 1877–1904, vol. I

Dalzell, Lt-Col John Norton, 1897–1957, vol. V

Dalzell, Reginald Alexander, 1865–1928, vol. II

Dalziel of Kirkcaldy, 1st Baron, 1868–1935, vol. III

Dalziel of Wooler, 1st Baron, 1854–1928, vol. II

Dalziel, Edward, 1817–1905, vol. I

Dalziel, George, 1815–1902, vol. I

Dalziel, Gilbert, 1853–1930, vol. III

Dalziel, Keith, 1921–1994, vol. IX

Dalziel, Sir Kennedy, 1861–1924, vol. II

Dalziel, Walter Watson, 1900–1967, vol. VI

Dam, (Carl Peter) Henrik, 1895–1976, vol. VII

Dam, Henrik; *see* Dam, C. P. H.

D'Amade, Albert, 1856–1941, vol. IV

Damant, Lt-Col Frederick Hugh, 1864–1926, vol. II

Damant, Captain Guybon Chesney Castell, *died* 1963, vol. VI

d'Ambrumenil, Sir Philip, 1886–1974, vol. VII

Damiano, Most Rev. Celestine Joseph, *died* 1967, vol. VI

D'Amico Inguanez, Baroness Mary Frances Carmen Maria Teresa Sceberras Trigona, 1865–1947, vol. IV

Damle, Keshav Govind, 1868–1930, vol. III

Dampier, Adm. Cecil Frederick, 1868–1950, vol. IV

Dampier, Henry Lucius, 1828–1913, vol. I

Dampier, Sir William Cecil Dampier, 1867–1952, vol. V

Damrosch, Walter, 1862–1950, vol. IV

Dana, Charles L., 1852–1935, vol. III
Dana, John Cotton, 1856–1929, vol. III
Dana, Paul, 1852–1930, vol. III
Dana, Robert Washington, 1868–1956, vol. V
Danby, Vice-Adm. Sir Clinton Francis Samuel, 1882–1945, vol. IV
Danby, Frank, 1864–1916, vol. II
Danby, Rev. Herbert, 1889–1953, vol. V
Dance, Sir George, died 1932, vol. III
Dance, James, 1907–1971, vol. VII
Dancer, Sir Thomas Johnston, 7th Bt, 1852–1933, vol. III
Danckwerts, Rt Hon. Sir Harold Otto, 1888–1978, vol. VII
Danckwerts, Peter Victor, 1916–1984, vol. VIII
Danckwerts, Rear-Adm. Victor Hilary, died 1944, vol. IV
Danckwerts, William Otto Adolph Julius, 1853–1914, vol. I
Dandie, James Naughton, 1894–1976, vol. VII
Dando, Kenneth Walter, 1921–1980, vol. VII
Dandridge, Cecil Gerald Graham, 1890–1960, vol. V
Dandurand, Rt Hon. Raoul, 1861–1942, vol. IV
Dandy, Rev. Henry Edward, died 1930, vol. III
Dandy, James Edgar, 1903–1976, vol. VII
Dane, Clemence, (Winifred Ashton), 1888–1965, vol. VI
Dane, Hal; see Macfall, Haldane.
Dane, Lt-Col James Auchinleck, 1883–1927, vol. II
Dane, Sir Louis William, 1856–1946, vol. IV
Dane, Richard Martin, 1852–1903, vol. I
Dane, Sir Richard Morris, 1854–1940, vol. III
Dane, William Surrey, 1892–1978, vol. VII
Danesfort, 1st Baron, 1853–1935, vol. III
Dangar, Rev. James George, 1841–1917, vol. II
Danger, Frank Charles, 1873–1943, vol. IV
Dangerfield, Roland Edmund, 1897–1964, vol. VI
Dangin, François T.; see Thureau-Dangin.
Dangin, Paul Marie Pierre T.; see Thureau-Dangin.
Danglow, Rabbi Jacob, 1880–1962, vol. VI
Daniel, Sir Augustus Moore, 1866–1950, vol. IV
Daniel, Rev. Charles Henry Olive, 1836–1919, vol. II
Daniel, Lt-Col Charles James, 1861–1949, vol. IV
Daniel, Adm. Sir Charles Saumarez, 1894–1981, vol. VIII
Daniel, Lt-Col Edward Yorke, 1865–1941, vol. IV
Daniel, Rev. Canon Evan, 1837–1904, vol. I
Daniel, Glyn Edmund, 1914–1986, vol. VIII
Daniel, Henry Cave, 1896–1980, vol. VII
Daniel, Brig. James Alfred, 1893–1959, vol. V
Daniel, Sir John, 1870–1938, vol. III
Daniel, (John) Stuart, 1912–1977, vol. VII
Daniel, Hon. John Waterhouse, 1845–1933, vol. III
Daniel, Norman Alexander, 1919–1992, vol. IX
Daniel, Peter Maxwell, 1910–1998, vol. X
Daniel, Stuart; see Daniel, J. S.
Daniel, Thomas Ernest, 1898–1968, vol. VI
Daniel, Rev. Wilson Eustace, 1841–1924, vol. II
Daniel-Rops, Henry, 1901–1965, vol. VI
Daniell, Major Edward Henry Edwin, 1868–1914, vol. I
Daniell, Very Rev. Edward M., 1864–1952, vol. V

Daniell, Emily Hilda, (Mrs J. A. H. Daniell); see Young, E. H.
Daniell, Major Francis Edward Lloyd, 1874–1916, vol. II
Daniell, Brig.-Gen. Frederick Francis Williamson, 1866–1937, vol. III
Daniell, Rev. George William, 1853–1931, vol. III
Daniell, John, 1878–1963, vol. VI
Daniell, Maj.-Gen. Sir John Frederic, 1859–1943, vol. IV
Daniell, Percy John, 1889–1946, vol. IV
Daniell, Roy Lorentz, died 1992, vol. IX
Daniell, Lt-Col William Augustus Bampfylde, 1875–1956, vol. V
Daniell-Bainbridge, Rev. Howard Gurney, died 1950, vol. IV
Danielli, James Frederic, 1911–1984, vol. VIII
Daniels, Charles Wilberforce, died 1927, vol. II
Daniels, David Kingsley, 1905–1986, vol. VIII
Daniels, George William, 1878–1937, vol. III
Daniels, Harold Griffith, 1874–1952, vol. V
Daniels, Lt-Col Harry, 1884–1953, vol. V
Daniels, Henry Ellis, 1912–2000, vol. X
Daniels, Jeffery, 1932–1986, vol. VIII
Daniels, Laurence John, 1916–1994, vol. IX
Daniels, Sir Percy, 1875–1951, vol. V
Daniels, Robert George Reginald, 1916–1993, vol. IX
Daniels, Sidney Reginald, 1873–1937, vol. III
Danielsen, Col Frederick Gustavus, 1874–1951, vol. V
Danilova, Alexandra, 1903–1997, vol. X
Danks, Sir Aaron Turner, 1861–1928, vol. II
Danks, Sir Alan John, 1914–1993, vol. X
Danks, Ven. William, 1845–1916, vol. II
Dann, Alfred Clarence, 1893–1953, vol. V
Dann, Howard Ernest, 1914–1986, vol. VIII
Dann, Brig.-Gen. William Rowland Harris, 1876–1957, vol. V
Dannatt, Sir Cecil, 1896–1981, vol. VIII
Dannay, Frederic, 1905–1982, vol. VIII
Dannreuther, Edward, 1844–1905, vol. I
Dannreuther, Rear-Adm. Hubert Edward, 1880–1977, vol. VII
Dannreuther, Sir Sigmund, 1873–1965, vol. VI
D'Annunzio, Gabriele, 1864–1938, vol. III
Dansey, Lt-Col Sir Claude Edward Marjoribanks, 1876–1947, vol. IV
Dansey, Col Francis Henry, 1878–1953, vol. V
Dansey-Browning, Col George; see Browning.
Danson, Rt Rev. Ernest Denny Logie, 1880–1946, vol. IV
Danson, Sir Francis Chatillon, 1855–1926, vol. II
Danter, Harold Walter Phillips, 1886–1976, vol. VII
Danvers, Frederick Charles, 1833–1906, vol. I
Danvers, Sir Juland, 1826–1902, vol. I
d'Aranyi, Jelly, died 1966, vol. VI
Darbhanga, Maharajadhiraja of, 1907–1962, vol. VI
Darbishire, Charles William, 1875–1925, vol. II
Darbishire, David Harold, 1914–1986, vol. VIII
Darbishire, Helen, 1881–1961, vol. VI
Darbishire, Otto Vernon, 1870–1934, vol. III
Darbourne, John William Charles, 1935–1991, vol. IX
Darboux, Jean Gaston, 1842–1917, vol. II

Darby, Sir Clifford; *see* Darby, Sir H. C.
Darby, Francis John, 1920–1996, vol. X
Darby, Rt. Rev. Harold Richard, 1919–1993, vol. IX
Darby, Sir (Henry) Clifford, 1909–1992, vol. IX
Darby, Very Rev. John Lionel, 1831–1919, vol. II
Darby, William Evans, 1844–1922, vol. II
Darbyshire, Most Rev. John Russell, 1880–1948, vol. IV
Darbyshire, Ruth Eveline, *died* 1946, vol. IV
Darbyshire, Taylor, 1875–1943, vol. IV
D'Arcy, Most Rev. Charles Frederick, 1859–1938, vol. III
D'Arcy, Dame Constance Elizabeth, *died* 1950, vol. IV
D'Arcy, Rev. George James Audomar, 1861–1941, vol. IV
D'Arcy, Lt-Gen. John Conyers, 1894–1966, vol. VI
D'Arcy, Very Rev. Martin Cyril, 1888–1976, vol. VII
D'Arcy, Surgeon Rear-Adm. Thomas Norman, 1896–1987, vol. VIII
D'Arcy, William Knox, 1849–1917, vol. II
Darcy de Knayth, Baroness (16th in line), 1865–1929, vol. III
Darcy de Knayth, 17th Baron; *see* Clive, Viscount, vol. IV
D'Arcy-Irvine, Rt Rev. Gerard Addington, 1862–1932, vol. III
D'Arcy-Irvine, Adm. Sir St George Caufield; *see* Irvine.
Dare, Adm. Sir Charles Holcombe, 1854–1924, vol. II
Dare, Edith Graham, 1883–1969, vol. VI
Dare, Robert Westley H.; *see* Hall-Dare.
Darell, Lt-Col Harry Francis, 1872–1934, vol. III
Darell, Sir Lionel Edward, 5th Bt, 1845–1919, vol. II
Darell, Sir Lionel Edward Hamilton Marmaduke, 6th Bt, 1876–1954, vol. V
Darell, Sir Oswald; *see* Darell, Sir W. O.
Darell, Brig.-Gen. William Harry Verelst, 1878–1954, vol. V
Darell, Sir (William) Oswald, 7th Bt, 1910–1959, vol. V
Daresbury, 1st Baron, 1867–1938, vol. III
Daresbury, 2nd Baron, 1902–1990, vol. VIII
Daresbury, 3rd Baron, 1928–1996, vol. X
Darewski, Herman, *died* 1947, vol. IV
Dargan, William J., *died* 1944, vol. IV
Dark, Sidney, 1874–1947, vol. IV
Darke, Harold Edwin, 1888–1976, vol. VII
Darke, Rear-Adm. Reginald Burnard, 1885–1962, vol. VI
Darkin, Maj.-Gen. Roy Bertram, 1916–1987, vol. VIII
Darlan, Admiral de la Flotte Jean François, 1881–1942, vol. IV
Darley, Sir Bernard D'Olier, 1880–1953, vol. V
Darley, Cecil West, 1842–1928, vol. II
Darley, Air Cdre Charles Curtis, 1890–1962, vol. VI
Darley, Rt Hon. Sir Frederick Matthew, 1830–1910, vol. I
Darley, Major Henry Read, 1865–1931, vol. III

Darley, J. F., *died* 1932, vol. III
Darley, Lt-Col James Russell, 1868–1951, vol. V
Darling, 1st Baron, 1849–1936, vol. III
Darling of Hillsborough, Baron (Life Peer); George Darling, 1905–1985, vol. VIII
Darling, Arthur Ivan, 1916–1987, vol. VIII
Darling, Rev. Charles Brian Auchinleck, 1905–1978, vol. VII
Darling, Col Charles Henry, 1852–1931, vol. III
Darling, Charles Robert, 1870–1942, vol. IV
Darling, Maj.-Gen. Douglas Lyall, 1914–1978, vol. VII
Darling, Rev. Canon Edward M.; *see* Moore Darling.
Darling, Frank, 1850–1923, vol. II
Darling, Sir Frank F.; *see* Fraser Darling.
Darling, Frederick, 1884–1953, vol. V
Darling, George Kenneth, 1879–1964, vol. VI
Darling, Gerald Ralph Auchinleck, 1921–1996, vol. X
Darling, Henry Shillington, 1914–1995, vol. IX
Darling, Sir James Carlisle S.; *see* Stormonth Darling.
Darling, Ven. James George Reginald, 1868–1938, vol. III
Darling, Sir James Ralph, 1899–1995, vol. IX
Darling, Major Hon. John Clive, 1887–1933, vol. III
Darling, Major John Collier S.; *see* Stormonth-Darling.
Darling, John Ford, 1864–1938, vol. III
Darling, Major John May, 1878–1942, vol. IV
Darling, Hon. Joseph, 1870–1946, vol. IV
Darling, Gen. Sir Kenneth Thomas, 1909–1998, vol X
Darling, Sir Malcolm Lyall, 1880–1969, vol. VI
Darling, Moir Tod Stormonth; *see* Hon. Lord Stormonth-Darling.
Darling, Sir William Young, 1885–1962, vol. VI
Darlington, Rear Adm. Sir Charles Roy, 1910–1998, vol. X
Darlington, Cyril Dean, 1903–1981, vol. VIII
Darlington, Edwin, 1839–1928, vol. II
Darlington, Col Sir Henry Clayton, 1877–1959, vol. V
Darlington, Rt Rev. James Henry, 1856–1930, vol. III
Darlington, Rev. John, 1868–1947, vol. IV
Darlington, Rev. Joseph, 1850–1939, vol. III
Darlington, Reginald Ralph, 1903–1977, vol. VII
Darlington, William Aubrey, 1890–1979, vol. VII
Darlow, Rev. Thomas Herbert, 1858–1927, vol. II
Darnley, 7th Earl of, 1851–1900, vol. I
Darnley, 8th Earl of, 1859–1927, vol. II
Darnley, 9th Earl of, 1886–1955, vol. V
Darnley, 10th Earl of, 1915–1980, vol. VII
Darracott, Sir William, 1860–1947, vol. IV
Darrah, Henry Zouch, 1854–1909, vol. I
Darrell, Hon. Richard Darrell, 1827–1904, vol. I
Darroch, Alexander, 1862–1924, vol. II
Darrow, Clarence, ?1854?–1938, vol. III
Dart, Rt Rev. John, 1837–1910, vol. I
Dart, Rev. John Lovering Campbell, 1882–1961, vol. VI
Dart, Raymond Arthur, 1893–1988, vol. VIII
Dart, Thurston, 1921–1971, vol. VII

Dartmouth, 6th Earl of, 1851–1936, vol. III
Dartmouth, 7th Earl of, 1881–1958, vol. V
Dartmouth, 8th Earl of, 1888–1962, vol. VI
Dartmouth, 9th Earl of, 1924–1997, vol. X
Dartnell, Maj.-Gen. Sir John George, 1838–1913, vol. I
Dartrey, 1st Earl of, 1817–1897, vol. I
Dartrey, 2nd Earl of, 1842–1920, vol. II
Dartrey, 3rd Earl of, 1855–1933, vol. III
Darvall, Frank Ongley, 1906–1987, vol. VIII
Darvall, Air Marshal Sir Lawrence, 1898–1968, vol. VI
Darvil-Smith, Major Percy George, 1880–1962, vol. VI
Darvill, Harold Edgar, 1908–1972, vol. VII
Darwall, Lt-Gen. Robert Henry, 1879–1956, vol. V
Darwen, 1st Baron, 1885–1950, vol. IV
Darwen, 2nd Baron, 1915–1988, vol. VIII
Darwin, Bernard, 1876–1961, vol. VI
Darwin, Sir Charles Galton, 1887–1962, vol. VI
Darwin, Squadron Leader Charles John Wharton, 1894–1941, vol. IV
Darwin, Col Charles Waring, 1855–1928, vol. II
Darwin, Sir Francis, 1848–1925, vol. II
Darwin, Sir George Howard, 1845–1912, vol. I
Darwin, Henry Galton, 1929–1992, vol. IX
Darwin, Sir Horace, 1851–1928, vol. II
Darwin, John Henry, 1884–1962, vol. VI
Darwin, Major Leonard, 1850–1943, vol. IV
Darwin, Robert Vere; see Darwin, Sir Robin.
Darwin, Sir Robin, 1910–1974, vol. VII
Darwin, Ruth, died 1972, vol. VII
Darwood, Sir John William, 1873–1951, vol. V
Daryngton, 1st Baron, 1867–1949, vol. IV
Daryngton, 2nd Baron, 1908–1994, vol. IX
Das, Sir Kedarnath; see Kedarnath Das.
Das, Hon. M. S., 1848–1934, vol. III
Das, Hon. Satish Ranjan, 1872–1928, vol. II
Das, Sudhi Ranjan, 1894–1977, vol. VII
Dasent, Arthur Irwin, died 1939, vol. III
Dasent, Sir John Roche, 1847–1914, vol. I
Dasgupta, Surendra Nath, 1887–1952, vol. V
Dash, Sir Arthur Jules, 1887–1974, vol. VII
Dash, Sir Roydon Englefield Ashford, 1888–1984, vol. VIII
Dashwood, Arthur George Frederick, 1860–1922, vol. II
Dashwood, Charles James, 1843–1919, vol. II
Dashwood, Col Edmund William, 1858–1946, vol. IV
Dashwood, Elizabeth Monica, 1890–1943, vol. IV
Dashwood, Sir Francis John Vernon Hereward, 11th Bt (cr 1707), 1925–2000, vol. X
Dashwood, Sir George John Egerton, 6th Bt (cr 1684), 1851–1933, vol. III
Dashwood, Sir Henry George Massy, 8th Bt (cr 1684), 1908–1972, vol. VII
Dashwood, Sir Henry Thomas Alexander, 1878–1959, vol. V
Dashwood, Sir John Lindsay, 10th Bt (cr 1707), 1896–1966, vol. VII
Dashwood, Maj.-Gen. Richard Lewes, 1837–1905, vol. I
Dashwood, Major Sir Robert Henry Seymour, 7th Bt (cr 1684), 1876–1947, vol. IV

Dashwood, Sir Robert John, 9th Bt (cr 1707), 1859–1908, vol. I
Datar Singh, Sardar Bahadur Sir, died 1973, vol. VII
Datia, HH Maharajah Sir Govind Singh Bahadur, 1886–1951, vol. V
Datia, HH Maharajah Sir Lockindar Bhawani Singh Bahadur, 1846–1907, vol. I
Datta, Surendra Kumar, 1878–1942, vol. IV
Daube, David, 1909–1999, vol. X
Daubeney, Brig.-Gen. Edward Kaye, 1858–1932, vol. III
Daubeney, Gen. Sir Henry Charles Barnston, 1810–1903, vol. I
Daubeny, Sir Peter Lauderdale, 1921–1975, vol. VII
Daubeny, Col Reginald Ernest, 1877–1935, vol. III
Dauber, J. H., died 1915, vol. I
Daubney, Robert, 1891–1977, vol. VII
Daudet, Alphonse, 1840–1897, vol. I
Daudet, Léon, 1867–1942, vol. IV
Dauglish, Captain Edward Heath, 1882–1950, vol. IV
Dauglish, Rt Rev. John, 1879–1952, vol. V
Daukes, Lt-Col Sir Clendon Turberville, 1879–1947, vol. IV
Daukes, Rt Rev. Francis Whitfield, 1877–1954, vol. V
Daukes, Frederick Clendon, 1848–1915, vol. I
Daukes, Sidney Herbert, 1879–1947, vol. IV
Daultana, Mumtaz Mohammad Khan, 1916–1996, vol. X (AI)
Daunt, Maj.-Gen. Brian, 1900–1996, vol. X
Daunt, Very Rev. Ernest George, 1909–1966, vol. VI
Daunt, Lt-Col Richard Algernon Craigie, 1872–1928, vol. II
Daunt, Maj.-Gen. William, 1831–1899, vol. I
Daunt, Ven. William, 1841–1919, vol. II
Dauntesey, Lt-Col William Bathurst, 1864–1937, vol. III
Davar, Sir Dinsha Dhurjibhai, 1856–1916, vol. II
Daven-Thomas, Rev. Canon Dennis; see Thomas.
Davenport, Brian John, 1936–2000, vol. X
Davenport, Charles Benedict, 1866–1944, vol. IV
Davenport, Major Cyril James H., 1848–1941, vol. IV
Davenport, Rear-Adm. Dudley Leslie, 1919–1990, vol. VIII
Davenport, Frederic Richard, 1872–1952, vol. V
Davenport, Hon. Sir George Arthur, 1893–1970, vol. VI
Davenport, Harold, 1907–1969, vol. VI
Davenport, Sir Henry Edward, 1866–1941, vol. IV
Davenport, Major John Lewes, 1910–1964, vol. VI
Davenport, Dame Lilian Emily Isabel Jane B.; see Bromley-Davenport.
Davenport, Muriel Coomber B.; see Bromley-Davenport.
Davenport, Robert Cecil, 1893–1961, vol. VI
Davenport, Vice-Adm. Robert Clutterbuck, 1882–1965, vol. VI
Davenport, Sir Samuel, 1818–1906, vol. I
Davenport, Lt-Col Sir Walter Henry B.; see Bromley-Davenport.
Davenport, Brig.-Gen. Sir William B.; see Bromley-Davenport.

Daventry, 1st Viscountess, 1869–1962, vol. VI
Daventry, 2nd Viscount, 1893–1986, vol. VIII
Daventry, 3rd Viscount, 1921–2000, vol. X
Daverin, John, 1851–1922, vol. II
Davey, Baron (Life Peer); Horace Davey, 1833–1907, vol. I
Davey, Maj.-Gen. Basil Charles, 1897–1959, vol. V
Davey, Comdr Charles Henry, 1879–1940, vol. III
Davey, David Garnet, 1912–1997, vol. X
Davey, George, 1911–1959, vol. V
Davey, Henry, 1843–1928, vol. II
Davey, Herbert, 1871–1931, vol. III
Davey, Lt-Col Hon. Horace Scott, 1865–1935, vol. III
Davey, Idris Wyn, 1917–1996, vol. X
Davey, Lt-Col James Edgar, 1873–1969, vol. VI
Davey, Rev. J(ames) Ernest, 1890–1960, vol. V, vol. VI
Davey, Rev. James Penry, 1878–1939, vol. III
Davey, John Trevor, 1923–1996, vol. X
Davey, Rev. Thomas Arthur Edwards, died 1944, vol. IV
Davey, Thomas Herbert, 1899–1978, vol. VII
Davey, Very Rev. William Harrison, 1825–1917, vol. II
Davey, William Kendall, 1887–1968, vol. VI
David, Rt Rev. Albert Augustus, 1867–1950, vol. IV
David, Alexander Jones, 1851–1929, vol. III
David, Ven. Arthur Evan, 1861–1913, vol. I
David, Brian Guvney, 1926–1990, vol. VIII
David, Lt-Col Sir Edgeworth; see David, Lt-Col Sir T. W. E.
David, Sir Edgeworth Beresford, 1908–1965, vol. VI
David, Elizabeth, 1913–1992, vol. IX
David, Herman Francis, 1905–1974, vol. VII
David, Hon. Laurent Olivier, 1840–1926, vol. II
David, Sir Percival Victor, 2nd Bt, 1892–1964, vol. VI
David, Rev. Richard, died 1947, vol. IV (A)
David, Richard William, 1912–1993, vol. IX
David, Sir Sassoon, 1st Bt, 1849–1926, vol. II
David, Lt-Col Sir (Tannatt William) Edgeworth, 1858–1934, vol. III
David, Bt-Col Thomas Jenkins, 1881–1926, vol. II
David, Tudor, 1921–2000, vol. X
David, W. T., died 1948, vol. IV
David-Weill, David, 1871–1952, vol. V
Davidge, Cecil William, 1863–1936, vol. III
Davidge, William Robert, died 1961, vol. VI
Davids, Caroline A. F. Rhys, died 1942, vol. IV
Davids, Thomas William Rhys, 1843–1922, vol. II
Davidson, 1st Viscount, 1889–1970, vol. VI
Davidson, Dowager Viscountess; Frances Joan Davidson; Baroness Northchurch (Life Peer), 1894–1985, vol. VIII
Davidson, 1st Baron, 1848–1930, vol. III
Davidson, Rev. Alan Munro, 1894–1959, vol. V
Davidson, Albert, 1869–1932, vol. III
Davidson, Maj.-Gen. Alexander Elliott, 1880–1962, vol. VI
Davidson, Air Vice-Marshal Sir Alexander Paul, 1894–1971, vol. VII

Davidson, Vice-Adm. Alexander Percy, 1868–1930, vol. III
Davidson, Sir Alfred Charles, 1882–1952, vol. V
Davidson, Allan Douglas, 1873–1932, vol. III
Davidson, Sir Andrew, 1892–1962, vol. VI
Davidson, Rev. Andrew Bruce, 1840–1902, vol. I
Davidson, Andrew Hope, 1895–1967, vol. VI
Davidson, Very Rev. (Andrew) Nevile, 1899–1976, vol. VII
Davidson, Col Sir Arthur, 1856–1922, vol. II
Davidson, Brian, 1909–1995, vol. IX
Davidson, Sir Charles, 1878–1927, vol. II
Davidson, Charles Findlay, 1911–1967, vol. VI
Davidson, Lt-Col Charles George Francis, 1884–1956, vol. V
Davidson, Col Charles John Lloyd, 1858–1941, vol. IV
Davidson, Sir Charles Peers, 1841–1929, vol. III
Davidson, Charles Rundle, 1875–1970, vol. VI
Davidson, Brig.-Gen. Charles Steer, 1866–1942, vol. IV
Davidson, Hon. Sir Charles William, 1897–1985, vol. VIII
Davidson, Sir Colin George Watt, 1878–1954, vol. V
Davidson, Sir Colin John, 1878–1930, vol. III
Davidson, Lt-Col Colin Keppel, 1895–1943, vol. IV
Davidson, Col Sir David, 1811–1900, vol. I
Davidson, Brig. Douglas Stewart, 1892–1958, vol. V
Davidson, Duncan, 1865–1917, vol. II
Davidson, Brig. Edmund, 1875–1945, vol. IV
Davidson, Sir Edward; see Davidson, Sir W. E.
Davidson, Lt-Col Edward Humphrey, 1886–1962, vol. VI
Davidson, Rt Rev. Edwin John, 1899–1958, vol. V
Davidson, Ethel Sarah, 1877–1939, vol. III
Davidson, Francis, 1905–1999, vol. X
Davidson, Maj.-Gen. Francis Henry Norman, 1892–1973, vol. VII
Davidson, Frederick Lewis Maitland, died 1936, vol. III
Davidson, George, died 1928, vol. II
Davidson, Major George Harry, 1866–1927, vol. II
Davidson, Ven. Gilbert Farquhar, 1871–1930, vol. III
Davidson, Howard William, 1911–1995, vol. IX
Davidson, Ian Douglas, 1901–1989, vol. VIII
Davidson, Col James, 1853–1932, vol. III
Davidson, Ven. James, died 1933, vol. III
Davidson, Lt-Col James, 1865–1933, vol. III
Davidson, James, 1885–1945, vol. IV
Davidson, James, 1875–1959, vol. V
Davidson, James, 1896–1985, vol. VIII
Davidson, Sir James Inglis, 1852–1934, vol. III
Davidson, James Leigh S.; see Strachan-Davidson.
Davidson, Sir James Mackenzie, 1856–1919, vol. II
Davidson, (James) Norman, 1911–1972, vol. VII
Davidson, James Walker, 1872–1939, vol. III
Davidson, James Wightman, 1915–1973, vol. VII
Davidson, Jo, 1883–1952, vol. V
Davidson, John, 1869–1905, vol. I
Davidson, John, 1857–1909, vol. I
Davidson, Col John, 1845–1917, vol. II
Davidson, John, 1878–1957, vol. V
Davidson, John, 1882–1960, vol. V

Davidson, Maj.-Gen. Sir John Humphrey, 1876–1954, vol. V

Davidson, John Wallace Ord, 1888–1973, vol. VII

Davidson, Col Sir Jonathan Roberts, 1874–1961, vol. VI

Davidson, Maj.-Gen. Kenneth Chisholm, 1897–1985, vol. VIII

Davidson, Major Leslie Evan Outram, 1882–1925, vol. II

Davidson, Sir Leybourne Francis Watson, 1859–1934, vol. III

Davidson, Sir (Leybourne) Stanley (Patrick), 1894–1981, vol. VIII

Davidson, Lindsay Gordon, 1893–1965, vol. VI

Davidson, Sir Lionel, 1868–1944, vol. IV

Davidson, Dame Margaret Agnes, 1871–1964, vol. VI

Davidson, Mark George, 1859–1933, vol. III

Davidson, Maurice, 1883–1967, vol. VI

Davidson, Very Rev. Nevile; *see* Davidson, Very Rev. A. N.

Davidson, Sir Nigel George, 1873–1961, vol. VI

Davidson, Norman; *see* Davidson, J. N.

Davidson, Lt-Col Peers, 1870–1920, vol. II

Davidson, Lt-Col Percival, 1874–1930, vol. III

Davidson, Randall George, 1874–1963, vol. VI

Davidson, Rev. Richard, 1876–1944, vol. IV

Davidson, Robert, 1831–1913, vol. I

Davidson, Robert, 1888–1952, vol. V

Davidson, Roger Alastair McLaren, 1900–1983, vol. VIII

Davidson, Sir Samuel C., *died* 1921, vol. II

Davidson, Maj.-Gen. Sisley Richard, 1869–1952, vol. V

Davidson, Col Stuart, 1859–1941, vol. IV

Davidson, Sir Stanley; *see* Davidson, Sir L. S. P.

Davidson, Thomas, 1856–1923, vol. II

Davidson, Sir Walter Edward, 1859–1923, vol. II

Davidson, William Bird, 1912–1990, vol. VIII

Davidson, Sir (William) Edward, 1853–1923, vol. II

Davidson, Col William Leslie, 1850–1915, vol. I

Davidson, William Leslie, 1848–1929, vol. III

Davidson, William Tennent Gairdner, 1889–1949, vol. IV

Davidson-Houston, Maj. Aubrey Claud, 1906–1995, vol. IX

Davidson-Houston, Major Charles Elrington Duncan, 1873–1915, vol. I

Davidson-Houston, Lt-Col Wilfred Bennett, 1870–1960, vol. V

Davidson-Smith, Maj.-Gen. E.; *see* Smith.

Davie, Sir Antony Francis F.; *see* Ferguson Davie.

Davie, Major Arthur Francis Ferguson-, 1867–1916, vol. II

Davie, Rev. Sir Arthur Patrick F.; *see* Ferguson Davie.

Davie, Cedric Thorpe, 1913–1983, vol. VIII

Davie, Rt Rev. Charles James F.; *see* Ferguson-Davie.

Davie, Donald Alfred, 1922–1995, vol. IX

Davie, Sir Henry Augustus Ferguson-, 1865–1946, vol. IV

Davie, Sir John Davie Ferguson-, 2nd Bt, 1830–1907, vol. I

Davie, Sir John F.; *see* Ferguson Davie.

Davie, Sir Paul Christopher, 1901–1990, vol. VIII

Davie, Thomas Benjamin, 1895–1955, vol. V

Davie, Sir William Augustus Ferguson-, 3rd Bt, 1833–1915, vol. I

Davie, Major Sir William John F., 4th Bt; *see* Ferguson-Davie.

Davies, 1st Baron, 1880–1944, vol. IV

Davies, 2nd Baron, 1915–1944, vol. IV

Davies of Leek, Baron (Life Peer); Harold Davies, 1904–1985, vol. VIII

Davies of Penrhys, Baron (Life Peer); Gwilym Elfed Davies, 1913–1992, vol. IX

Davies, Aaron, 1830–1915, vol. I

Davies, Air Cdre Adolphus Dan, 1902–1984, vol. VIII

Davies, Alan B.; *see* Bowen-Davies.

Davies, Air Marshal Sir Alan Cyril, 1924–1998, vol. X

Davies, Sir Alan Meredyth H.; *see* Hudson-Davies.

Davies, Albert Edward, 1900–1953, vol. V

Davies, Albert Emil, 1875–1950, vol. IV

Davies, Albert John, 1919–1999, vol. X

Davies, Alfred, 1848–1907, vol. I

Davies, Sir Alfred Thomas, 1881–1941, vol. IV

Davies, Sir Alfred Thomas, 1861–1949, vol. IV

Davies, Alice Hollingdrake, 1878–1968, vol. VI

Davies, Alun Bennett O.; *see* Oldfield-Davies.

Davies, Sir Alun Talfan, 1913–2000, vol. X

Davies, Rt Hon. Sir Arthian; *see* Davies, Rt Hon. Sir W. A.

Davies, Sir Arthur; *see* Davies, Sir D. A.

Davies, Arthur, 1906–1998, vol. X

Davies, Arthur Cecil, 1889–1947, vol. IV

Davies, Arthur Charles F.; *see* Fox-Davies.

Davies, (Arthur Edward) Miles, 1903–1977, vol. VII

Davies, Adm. Sir Arthur John, *died* 1954, vol. V

Davies, Rev. Arthur Llywelyn, *died* 1957, vol. V

Davies, Lt-Gen. Arthur Matcham, 1832–1908, vol. I

Davies, Arthur Templer, 1858–1929, vol. III

Davies, Arthur Vernon, *died* 1942, vol. IV

Davies, Very Rev. Arthur Whitcliffe, *died* 1966, vol. VI

Davies, Arthur William 1878–1969, vol. VI

Davies, Ashton, 1874–1958, vol. V

Davies, Ben, 1858–1943, vol. IV

Davies, Rev. Canon Benjamin, 1880–1941, vol. IV

Davies, Bernard Nöel L.; *see* Langdon-Davies.

Davies, Brian H.; *see* Humphreys-Davies.

Davies, Carlton Griffith, 1895–1981, vol. VIII

Davies, Ven. Carlyle W.; *see* Witton-Davies.

Davies, Cecil Bertrand, 1876–1960, vol. VI

Davies, Sir Charles; *see* Davies, Sir R. C.

Davies, Rev. Charles Douglas Percy, *died* 1931, vol. III

Davies, Hon. Charles Ellis, 1848–1921, vol. II

Davies, Brig.-Gen. Charles Henry, 1867–1954, vol. V

Davies, Charles Llewelyn, 1860–1927, vol. II

Davies, Brig. Charles Stafford P.; *see* Price-Davies.

Davies, Lt-Col Charles Stewart, 1880–1946, vol. IV

Davies, Clara Novello, 1861–1943, vol. IV

Davies, Rt Hon. Clement, 1884–1962, vol. VI

Davies, Sir Colin R.; *see* Rees-Davies.

Davies, Cuthbert Collin, 1896–1974, vol. VII

Davies, Rt Rev. Daniel, 1863–1928, vol. II

Davies, Daniel James, 1880–1946, vol. IV
Davies, Sir Daniel Thomas, 1899–1966, vol. VI
Davies, Ven. David, 1858–1930, vol. III
Davies, David, 1862–1932, vol. III
Davies, Sir David, 1870–1958, vol. V
Davies, Sir David, 1889–1964, vol. VI
Davies, David, 1877–1966, vol. VI
Davies, David Alban, 1873–1951, vol. V
Davies, Sir (David) Arthur, 1913–1990, vol. VIII
Davies, Rt Rev. David E.; see Edwardes-Davies.
Davies, David F.; see Ffrangcon-Davies.
Davies, Sir David Henry, 1909–1998, vol. X
Davies, Rt Rev. David Henry S.; see
  Saunders-Davies.
Davies, Ven David John, 1879–1935, vol. III
Davies, Sir David Joseph, 1896–1991, vol. IX
Davies, David Lewis, died 1937, vol. III
Davies, David Lewis, 1911–1982, vol. VIII
Davies, David Percy, 1891–1946, vol. IV
Davies, David Richard Seaborne, 1904–1984,
  vol. VIII
Davies, David Ronald, 1910–1994, vol. IX
Davies, David Samuel, died 1933, vol. III
Davies, Sir David Sanders, 1852–1934, vol. III
Davies, David Vaughan, 1911–1969, vol. VI
Davies, Derek George G.; see Gill-Davies.
Davies, Donald Watts, 1924–2000, vol. X
Davies, Duncan Sheppey, 1921–1987, vol. VIII
Davies, Edward, died 1920, vol. II
Davies, Col Edward Campbell, died 1919, vol. II
Davies, Edward Gwynfryn, 1904–1980, vol. VII
  (AII)
Davies, Edward Harold, 1867–1947, vol. IV
Davies, Sir (Edward) John, 1898–1969, vol. VI
Davies, Elidir Leslie Wish, 1907–1993, vol. IX
Davies, Ellis William, 1871–1939, vol. III
Davies, Elwyn, 1908–1986, vol. VIII
Davies, Emily; see Davies, S. E.
Davies, Emlyn Glyndwr, 1916–1993, vol. IX
Davies, Eric John W.; see Warlow-Davies.
Davies, Ernest, 1873–1946, vol. IV
Davies, Ernest Albert John, 1902–1991, vol. IX
Davies, Ernest Herbert, died 1934, vol. III
Davies, Ernest James, 1875–1935, vol. III
Davies, Ernest S.; see Salter Davies.
Davies, Rev. Ernest William, 1901–1978, vol. VII
Davies, Eryl Oliver, 1922–1982, vol. VIII
Davies, Rev. Evan Thomas, died 1927, vol. II
Davies, Evan Thomas, 1878–1969, vol. VI
Davies, Evan Tom, 1904–1973, vol. VII
Davies, Fanny, 1861–1934, vol. III
Davies, Francis, 1897–1965, vol. VI
Davies, Gen. Sir Francis John, 1864–1948, vol. IV
Davies, Rev. (Francis Maurice) Russell, 1871–1956,
  vol. V
Davies, Rev. Francis Parry W.; see Watkin-Davies.
Davies, Rev. Frederick Charles, died 1929, vol. III
Davies, Frederick William Samuel, died 1919,
  vol. II
Davies, Rev. Canon George Colliss Boardman,
  1912–1982, vol. VIII
Davies, Sir George Edmund, 1857–1932, vol. III
Davies, George Francis, 1911–1987, vol. VIII (A)
Davies, Major Sir George Frederick, 1875–1950,
  vol. IV

Davies, Maj.-Gen. George Freshfield, 1872–1936,
  vol. III
Davies, George Maitland Lloyd, 1880–1949, vol. IV
Davies, Ven. George Middlecott, 1858–1937,
  vol. III
Davies, Rev. Gerald Stanley, 1845–1927, vol. II
Davies, Rev. Gilbert Austin, 1868–1948, vol. IV
Davies, Glyn; see Davies, T. G.
Davies, Dame Gwen F.; see Ffrangcon-Davies.
Davies, Gwendoline Elizabeth, died 1951, vol. V
Davies, Rev. Gwynne Henton, 1906–1998, vol. X
Davies, Harold Haydn, 1897–1982, vol. VIII
Davies, Harold Whitridge, died 1946, vol. IV
Davies, Harry, 1915–1993, vol. X (AI)
Davies, Haydn, 1905–1976, vol. VII
Davies, Hector Leighton, 1894–1980, vol. VII
Davies, Lt-Col Henry, 1867–1923, vol. II
Davies, Sir Henry, 1856–1936, vol. III
Davies, Lt-Gen. Henry Fanshawe, 1837–1914, vol. I
Davies, Henry J.; see Jones-Davies.
Davies, Maj.-Gen. Henry Lowrie, 1898–1975,
  vol. VII
Davies, Henry Meirion, 1875–1950, vol. IV (A),
  vol. V
Davies, Maj.-Gen. Henry Rodolph, 1865–1950,
  vol. IV
Davies, Sir (Henry) Walford, 1869–1941, vol. IV
Davies, Col Sir Horatio David, 1842–1912, vol. I
Davies, Sir Howell; see Davies, Sir H. W.
Davies, Hubert Henry, died 1917, vol. II
Davies, Hugh Morriston, 1879–1965, vol. VI
Davies, Rev. Canon Hywel Islwyn, 1909–1981,
  vol. VIII
Davies, Ifor, 1910–1982, vol. VIII
Davies, Iforwyn Glyndwr, 1901–1984, vol. VIII
Davies, Ven. Ivor Gordon, 1917–1992, vol. IX
Davies, Jack Gale Wilmot, 1911–1992, vol. IX
Davies, James Henry W.; see Wootton-Davies.
Davies, Jenkin A.; see Alban Davies.
Davies, Dame Jean; see Lancaster, Dame J.
Davies, Sir John; see Davies, Sir E. J.
Davies, John Alun Emlyn, 1909–1997, vol. X
Davies, John Bowen, 1876–1943, vol. IV
Davies, Sir John Cecil, 1864–1927, vol. II
Davies, John Cledwyn, died 1952, vol. V
Davies, John David Griffith, 1899–1953, vol. V
Davies, John Edward Henry, died 1939, vol. III
Davies, Rt Hon. John Emerson Harding,
  1916–1979, vol. VII
Davies, Hon. Sir John George, 1846–1913, vol. I
Davies, Rev. John Gordon, 1919–1990, vol. VIII
Davies, John Henry Vaughan, 1921–1994, vol. IX
Davies, John Howard Gay, 1923–2000, vol. X
Davies, John Humphreys, died 1926, vol. II
Davies, Rev. John J., 1863–1938, vol. III
Davies, John L.; see Langdon-Davies.
Davies, Rev. John Llewelyn, 1826–1916, vol. II
Davies, John Llewelyn, 1888–1959, vol. V
Davies, Hon. Sir John Mark, died 1919, vol. II
Davies, J(ohn) Prysor, 1900–1959, vol. V
Davies, John Robert, 1856–1934, vol. III
Davies, J(ohn) R(obert) L.; see Lloyd Davies.
Davies, John Tasman, 1924–1987, vol. VIII
Davies, Sir John Thomas, 1881–1938, vol. III

Davies, Very Rev. John Thomas, 1881–1966, vol. VI
Davies, Rev. John Timothy, *died* 1931, vol. III
Davies, Rev. (John) Trevor, 1907–1974, vol. VII
Davies, Sir Joseph, 1866–1954, vol. V
Davies, Joseph Edward, 1876–1958, vol. V
Davies, Very Rev. Joseph Gwyn, 1890–1952, vol. V
Davies, Joshua David, 1889–1966, vol. VI
Davies, Kenneth; *see* Davies, S. K.
Davies, Kenneth Arthur, 1897–1991, vol. IX
Davies, Sir Leonard Twiston, 1894–1953, vol. V
Davies, Lewis, 1886–1971, vol. VII
Davies, Maj.-Gen. Llewelyn Alberic Emilius P.; *see* Price-Davies.
Davies, Rt Hon. Sir Louis Henry, 1845–1924, vol. II
Davies, Col Lucy Myfanwy, 1913–1995, vol. IX
Davies, Margaret, (Lady Davies); *see* Kennedy, Margaret.
Davies, Sir Martin, 1908–1975, vol. VII
Davies, Mrs Mary, 1855–1930, vol. III
Davies, Hon. Sir Matthew Henry, 1850–1912, vol. I
Davies, Michael John, 1918–1984, vol. VIII
Davies, Miles; *see* Davies, A. E. M.
Davies, N. P.; *see* Prescott-Davies.
Davies, Neil; *see* Davies, W. M. N.
Davies, Sir Oswald, 1920–1996, vol. X
Davies, Oswald Vaughan L.; *see* Lloyd-Davies.
Davies, Owen Picton, 1872–1940, vol. III
Davies, Bt-Col Owen Stanley, *died* 1926, vol. II
Davies, Col Percy George, *died* 1947, vol. IV
Davies, Peter; *see* Davies, R. P. H.
Davies, Peter George, 1927–1994, vol. IX
Davies, Peter H.; *see* Humphreys-Davies.
Davies, Rev. Philip Latimer, 1864–1928, vol. II
Davies, Rev. R. W. F. S.; *see* Singers-Davies.
Davies, Rachael Annie C.; *see* Cox-Davies.
Davies, Randall Robert Henry, 1866–1946, vol. IV
Davies, Reginald, 1887–1971, vol. VII
Davies, Sir (Reginald) Charles, 1886–1958, vol. V
Davies, Rhisiart Morgan, 1903–1958, vol. V
Davies, Rhys, 1903–1978, vol. VII
Davies, Rhys John, 1877–1954, vol. V
Davies, Sir Richard, 1853–1939, vol. III
Davies, Vice-Adm. Richard Bell, *died* 1966, vol. VI
Davies, Sir Richard Harries, 1916–1995, vol. IX
Davies, Richard Humphrey, 1872–1970, vol. VI
Davies, Col Richard Hutton, *died* 1918, vol. II
Davies, Robert Ernest, 1919–1993, vol. IX
Davies, Robert Gwyneddon, 1870–1928, vol. II
Davies, Sir Robert Henry, 1824–1902, vol. I
Davies, Sir Robert John, 1900–1967, vol. VI
Davies, Robert Malcolm Deryck, 1918–1967, vol. VI
Davies, Rev. Robert Owen, 1857–1929, vol. III
Davies, (Roger) Peter (Havard), 1919–1993, vol. IX
Davies, Roy Dicker Salter, 1906–1984, vol. VIII
Davies, Rev. Rupert Eric, 1909–1994, vol. IX
Davies, Rev. Russell; *see* Davies, Rev. F. M. R.
Davies, Ven. Samuel Morris, 1879–1963, vol. VI
Davies, (Sarah) Emily, 1830–1921, vol. II
Davies, Rev. Sidney Edmund, *died* 1918, vol. II
Davies, (Stanley) Kenneth, 1899–1987, vol. VIII
Davies, Rt Rev. Stephen Harris, 1883–1961, vol. VI
Davies, Stephen Owen, 1886–1972, vol. VII
Davies, Stuart Duncan, 1906–1995, vol. IX

Davies, Sydney John, 1891–1967, vol. VI
Davies, T. Witton, 1851–1923, vol. II
Davies, Sir Thomas, 1858–1939, vol. III
Davies, Thomas A.; *see* Anwyl-Davies.
Davies, Col Thomas Arthur Harkness, 1857–1942, vol. IV
Davies, (Thomas) Glyn, 1905–1997, vol. X
Davies, Thomas H.; *see* Hart-Davies.
Davies, Thomas Walton, 1907–1948, vol. IV
Davies, Timothy, 1857–1951, vol. V
Davies, Rev. Trevor; *see* Davies, Rev. J. T.
Davies, Trevor Arthur L.; *see* Lloyd Davies.
Davies, Tudor, *died* 1958, vol. V
Davies, Sir Victor Caddy, *died* 1977, vol. VII (AII)
Davies, Sir Walford; *see* Davies, Sir H. W.
Davies, Walter, 1865–1939, vol. III
Davies, Hon. Brig.-Gen. Walter Percy Lionel, 1871–1952, vol. V
Davies, Col Warburton Edward, 1879–1956, vol. V
Davies, Rev. Canon Watkin, 1869–1943, vol. IV
Davies, Sir William, 1863–1935, vol. III
Davies, William, 1899–1968, vol. VI
Davies, Rt Hon. Sir (William) Arthian, 1901–1979, vol. VII
Davies, William Frank de Rolante, *died* 1942, vol. IV
Davies, Sir William George, 1828–1898, vol. I
Davies, William Henry, 1871–1940, vol. III
Davies, Sir (William) Howell, 1851–1932, vol. III
Davies, William John, 1848–1934, vol. IV
Davies, William John, 1891–1975, vol. VII
Davies, William John Abbott, 1890–1967, vol. VI
Davies, Sir William Llewelyn, 1887–1952, vol. V
Davies, (William Michael) Neil, 1931–1995, vol. IX (AII)
Davies, Sir William Rees-, 1863–1939, vol. III
Davies, William Robert, 1870–1949, vol. IV
Davies, William Rupert R.; *see* Rees-Davies.
Davies, William Thomas Frederick, 1860–1947, vol. IV
Davies, William Tudor, *died* 1978, vol. VII
Davies, William Watkin, 1895–1973, vol. VII
Davies, Wyndham Matabele, 1893–1972, vol. VII
Davies, Wyndham Roy, 1926–1984, vol. VIII
Davies, Zelma Ince, 1930–1994, vol. IX
Davies-Colley, Robert, *died* 1955, vol. V
Davies-Cooke, Col Philip Ralph, 1896–1974, vol. VII
Davies-Cooke, Philip Tatton; *see* Cooke.
Davies-Evans, Herbert, 1842–1928, vol. II
Davies-Gilbert, Mrs Grace Catherine Rose, *died* 1951, vol. V
d'Avigdor-Goldsmid, Major Sir Henry Joseph, 2nd Bt, 1909–1976, vol. VII
d'Avigdor-Goldsmid, Maj.-Gen. Sir James Arthur, 3rd Bt, 1912–1987, vol. VIII
d'Avigdor-Goldsmid, Sir Osmond Elim, 1st Bt, 1877–1940, vol. III
Davin, Daniel Marcus, (Dan Davin), 1913–1990, vol. VIII
Davin, Nicholas Flood, 1843–1901, vol. I
Daviot, Gordon, 1896–1952, vol. V
Davis, Alexander, 1861–1945, vol. IV
Davis, Sir Alfred George Fletcher H.; *see* Hall-Davis.

Davis, Sir Allan; *see* Davis, Sir W. A.
Davis, Anthony Tilton, 1931–1978, vol. VII
Davis, Archibald William, 1900–1979, vol. VII
Davis, Arthur Henry, 1886–1931, vol. III
Davis, Arthur J., 1878–1951, vol. V
Davis, Bette Ruth Elizabeth, 1908–1989, vol. VIII
Davis, Brian; *see* ffolkes, Michael.
Davis, Rt Rev. Brian Newton, 1934–1998, vol. X
Davis, Sir Charles, 1st Bt, 1878–1950, vol. IV
Davis, Ven. Charles Henderson, *died* 1915, vol. I
Davis, Sir Charles Henry, 1847–1938, vol. III
Davis, Charles Henry H.; *see* Hart-Davis.
Davis, Col Charles Herbert, 1872–1922, vol. II
Davis, Sir Charles Sigmund, 1909–1999, vol. X
Davis, Sir Charles Thomas, 1873–1938, vol. III
Davis, Mrs Chloë Marion, 1909–2000, vol. X
Davis, Brig. Cyril Elliott, 1892–1986, vol. VIII
Davis, David; *see* Davis, W. E.
Davis, David, 1877–1930, vol. III
Davis, Sir David, 1859–1938, vol. III
Davis, Ven. David Grimaldi, *died* 1936, vol. III
Davis, Derek Russell, 1914–1993, vol. IX
Davis, Hon. Sir (Dermot) Renn, 1928–1997, vol. X
Davis, Dwight Filley, 1879–1945, vol. IV
Davis, Sir Edmund, *died* 1939, vol. III
Davis, Edward David Darelan, 1880–1976, vol. VII
Davis, Air Vice-Marshal Edward Derek, 1895–1955, vol. V
Davis, Adm. Edward Henry Meggs, 1846–1929, vol. III
Davis, Eliza Jeffries, 1875–1943, vol. IV
Davis, Elmer Holmes, 1890–1958, vol. V
Davis, Sir Ernest, 1872–1962, vol. VI
Davis, Very Rev. Evans, 1848–1918, vol. II
Davis, Col Evans Greenwood, 1885–1951, vol. V
Davis, F. W., *died* 1919, vol. II
Davis, Francis John, 1900–1980, vol. VII
Davis, Francis Robert Edward, 1887–1960, vol. V
Davis, Hon. Frank Roy, 1888–1948, vol. IV
Davis, Sir George Francis, 1883–1947, vol. IV
Davis, Col George M'Bride, 1846–1909, vol. I
Davis, Sir Gilbert, 2nd Bt, 1901–1973, vol. VII
Davis, Sir Godfrey, 1890–1968, vol. VI
Davis, Godfrey Rupert Carless, 1917–1997, vol. X
Davis, Lt-Col Gronow John, 1869–1919, vol. II
Davis, H. Haldin; *see* Haldin-Davis.
Davis, Lt-Col Harold James Norman, 1882–1960, vol. V
Davis, Harold Sydney, 1908–1988, vol. VIII
Davis, Henry John B.; *see* Banks-Davis.
Davis, Henry William Banks, 1833–1914, vol. I
Davis, Henry William Carless, 1874–1928, vol. II
Davis, Sir Herbert, 1891–1972, vol. VII
Davis, Herbert John, 1893–1967, vol. VI
Davis, Captain Herbert Ludlow, 1887–1951, vol. V
Davis, James; *see* Hall, Owen.
Davis, James Corbett, 1870–1957, vol. V
Davis, James Richard A.; *see* Ainsworth-Davis.
Davis, Col John, 1834–1902, vol. I
Davis, John Creyghton A.; *see* Ainsworth-Davis.
Davis, Air Chief Marshal Sir John Gilbert, 1911–1989, vol. VIII
Davis, Sir John Henry Harris, 1906–1993, vol. IX
Davis, John King, 1884–1967, vol. VI
Davis, John Merle, 1875–1960, vol. V

Davis, John Samuel Champion, 1859–1926, vol. II
Davis, John William, 1873–1955, vol. V
Davis, Leslie John, 1899–1980, vol. VII
Davis, Lucien, 1860–1941, vol. IV
Davis, Dame Margaret; *see* Rutherford, Dame M.
Davis, Hon. Sir Maurice, 1912–1988, vol. IX (AI)
Davis, Morris Cael, 1907–1987, vol. VIII
Davis, Sir Mortimer Barnett, 1866–1928, vol. II
Davis, Lt-Col Nathaniel N.; *see* Newnham-Davis.
Davis, Rt Rev. Nathaniel William Newnham, 1903–1966, vol. VI
Davis, Nicholas Darnell, 1846–1915, vol. I
Davis, Norman, 1913–1989, vol. VIII
Davis, Hon. Norman H., *died* 1944, vol. IV
Davis, R. Bramwell, 1849–1932, vol. II
Davis, Ralph, 1915–1978, vol. VII
Davis, Ralph Henry Carless, 1918–1991, vol. IX
Davis, Hon. Sir Renn; *see* Davis Hon. Sir D. R.
Davis, Richard Harding, 1864–1916, vol. II
Davis, Sir Robert Henry, 1870–1965, vol. VI
Davis, Maj.-Gen. Ronald Albert B.; *see* Bramwell Davis.
Davis, Sir Rupert Charles H.; *see* Hart-Davis.
Davis, Rushworth Kennard, 1883–1969, vol. VI
Davis, Sir Spencer; *see* Davis, Sir S. S.
Davis, Sir (Steuart) Spencer, 1875–1950, vol. IV
Davis, Hon. Thomas C., 1889–1960, vol. V
Davis, Thomas Frederick, 1891–1974, vol. VII
Davis, Rev. Canon Thomas Henry, 1867–1947, vol. IV
Davis, Val, 1854–1930, vol. III
Davis, Vernon Mansfield, 1855–1931, vol. III
Davis, Sir (William) Allan, 1921–1994, vol. IX
Davis, William Eric, (David), 1908–1996, vol. X
Davis, Major William Hathaway, 1881–1928, vol. II (A), vol. III
Davis, William Morris, 1850–1934, vol. III
Davis, Most Rev. William Wallace, 1908–1987, vol. VIII
Davis, Adm. Sir William Wellclose, 1901–1987, vol. VIII
Davis-Goff, Sir Ernest William; *see* Goff.
Davis-Goff, Sir Herbert William; *see* Goff.
Davis-Goff, Sir William Goff; *see* Goff.
Davison Alan Nelson, 1925–1993, vol. IX
Davison, Archibald Thompson, 1883–1961, vol. VI
Davison, Arthur Clifford Percival, 1918–1992, vol. IX
Davison, Charles, 1858–1940, vol. III
Davison, Charles Stewart, 1855–1942, vol. IV (A), vol. V
Davison, Major Douglas Stewart, 1888–1929, vol. III
Davison, Frederick Charles, 1851–1935, vol. III
Davison, Rev. Gilderoy, 1892–1954, vol. V
Davison, Mrs J. W.; *see* Goddard, Arabella.
Davison, Sir John Alec B.; *see* Biggs-Davison.
Davison, John Armstrong, 1906–1966, vol. VI
Davison, John Clarke, 1875–1946, vol. IV
Davison, John Emanuel, 1870–1927, vol. II
Davison, Rt Hon. Sir Joseph, 1868–1948, vol. IV
Davison, Maj.-Gen. Kenneth Stewart, 1856–1934, vol. III
Davison, Rev. Leslie, 1906–1972, vol. VII
Davison, Ralph, 1914–1977, vol. VII

Davison, Sir Ronald Conway, 1884–1958, vol. V
Davison, T. Raffles, 1853–1937, vol. III
Davison, Rev. Canon William Holmes, 1884–1955, vol. V
Davison, William Norris, 1919–1986, vol. VIII
Davison, William Theophilus, 1846–1935, vol. III
Davisson, Clinton Joseph, 1881–1958, vol. V
Davitt, Cahir, 1894–1986, vol. VIII
Davitt, Michael, 1846–1906, vol. I
Davray, Henry D., 1873–1944, vol. IV
Davson, Sir Charles Simon, 1857–1933, vol. III
Davson, Sir Edward, 1st Bt, *died* 1937, vol. III
Davson, Sir Geoffrey Leo Simon, 2nd Bt; *see* Glyn, Sir Anthony, 2nd Bt.
Davson, Lt-Col Harry Miller, 1872–1961, vol. VI
Davson, Sir Henry Katz, 1830–1909, vol. I
Davson, Lt-Col Sir Ivan Buchanan, 1884–1947, vol. IV
Davy, Col Cecil William, 1868–1957, vol. V
Davy, Francis Herbert Mountjoy Nelson H.; *see* Humphrey-Davy.
Davy, Brig. George Mark Oswald, 1898–1983, vol. VIII
Davy, Georges Ambroise, 1883–1976, vol. VII
Davy, Sir Henry, 1855–1922, vol. II
Davy, Humphrey Augustine A.; *see* Arthington-Davy.
Davy, Sir James Stewart, 1848–1915, vol. I
Davy, Joseph B.; *see* Burtt Davy.
Davy, Lila, 1873–1949, vol. IV
Davy, Maurice John Bernard, 1892–1950, vol. IV
Davy, Lt-Col Philip Claude Tresilian, 1877–1951, vol. V
Davy, Richard, 1838–1920, vol. II
Davy, Sir William, 1863–1939, vol. III
Davys, Rev. Owen William, *died* 1914, vol. I
Daw, Sir John Edward, 1866–1959, vol. V
Daw, Sydney Ernest Henry, 1897–1963, vol. VI
Daw, Sir William Herbert, 1859–1941, vol. IV
Dawbarn, Charles, 1871–1925, vol. II
Dawbarn, Graham Richards, 1893–1976, vol. VII
Dawber, Sir Guy, 1861–1938, vol. III
Dawe, Sir Arthur James, 1891–1950, vol. IV
Dawe, Carlton, *died* 1935, vol. III
Dawe, Donovan Arthur, 1915–1996, vol. X
Dawes, Sir (Albert) Cecil, 1890–1959, vol. V
Dawes, Sir Cecil; *see* Dawes, Sir A. C.
Dawes, Charles Ambrose William, 1919–1982, vol. VIII
Dawes, Brig.-Gen. Charles Gates, 1865–1951, vol. V
Dawes, Edgar Rowland, 1902–1973, vol. VII
Dawes, Sir Edwyn Sandys, 1838–1903, vol. I
Dawes, Geoffrey Sharman, 1918–1996, vol. X
Dawes, Lt-Col George William Patrick, 1880–1960, vol. V
Dawes, Brig. Hugh Frank, 1884–1965, vol. VI
Dawes, James Arthur, 1866–1921, vol. II
Dawes, Rt Rev. Nathaniel, 1843–1910, vol. I
Dawes, William Charles, 1865–1920, vol. II
Dawkins, Lady Bertha Mabel, 1866–1943, vol. IV
Dawkins, Charles John Massey, 1905–1975, vol. VII
Dawkins, Maj.-Gen. Sir Charles Tyrwhitt, 1858–1919, vol. II
Dawkins, Charles William, 1870–1948, vol. IV

Dawkins, Sir Clinton Edward, 1859–1905, vol. I
Dawkins, Brig.-Gen. Henry Stopford, 1856–1933, vol. III
Dawkins, Sir Horace Christian, 1867–1944, vol. IV
Dawkins, Col John Wyndham George, 1861–1913, vol. I
Dawkins, Richard MacGillivray, 1871–1955, vol. V
Dawkins, Sir William Boyd, 1837–1929, vol. III
Dawnay, Col Alan Geoffrey Charles, 1888–1938, vol. III
Dawnay, Sir Archibald Davis, *died* 1919, vol. II
Dawnay, Lt-Col Christopher Payan, 1909–1989, vol. VIII
Dawnay, Lt-Col Cuthbert Henry, 1891–1964, vol. VI
Dawnay, Maj.-Gen. Sir David, 1903–1971, vol. VII
Dawnay, Hon. Eustace Henry, 1850–1928, vol. II (A), vol. III
Dawnay, Hon. George William ffolkes, 1909–1990, vol. VIII
Dawnay, Maj.-Gen. Guy Payan, 1878–1952, vol. V
Dawnay, Major Hon. Hugh, 1875–1914, vol. I
Dawnay, Lt-Col Hon. Lewis Payn, 1846–1910, vol. I
Dawnay, Captain Oliver Payan, 1920–1988, vol. VIII
Dawnay, Vice-Adm. Sir Peter, 1904–1989, vol. VIII
Dawnay, Hon. William Frederick, 1851–1904, vol. I
Dawood, Khan Sahib Sir Adamjee Hajee, *died* 1948, vol. IV
Dawson of Penn, 1st Viscount, 1864–1945, vol. IV
Dawson, A. J., 1872–1951, vol. V
Dawson, Very Rev. Abraham Dawson, 1826–1905, vol. I
Dawson, Aimée Evelyn, (Lady Dawson), *died* 1946, vol. IV
Dawson, Albert, 1866–1930, vol. III
Dawson, Col Algernon Cecil, 1849–1934, vol. III
Dawson, Alistair Benedict, 1922–1978, vol. VII
Dawson, Sir Anthony Michael, 1928–1997, vol. X
Dawson, Sir Arthur James, 1859–1943, vol. IV
Dawson, Maj.-Gen. Arthur Peel, 1888–1958, vol. V
Dawson, Sir (Arthur) Trevor, 1st Bt (*cr* 1920), 1866–1931, vol. III
Dawson, Sir Benajmin, 1st Bt (*cr* 1929), 1878–1966, vol. VI
Dawson, Sir Bernard; *see* Dawson, Sir J. B.
Dawson, Christopher, 1889–1970, vol. VI
Dawson, Christopher William, 1896–1983, vol. VIII
Dawson, Coningsby, 1883–1959, vol. V
Dawson, Brig.-Gen. Sir Douglas Frederick Rawdon, 1854–1933, vol. III
Dawson, Hon. Edward Stanley, 1843–1919, vol. II
Dawson, Rev. Edwin Collas, *died* 1925, vol. II
Dawson, Gen. Francis, 1827–1911, vol. I
Dawson, Captain Francis Evelyn M.; *see* Massy-Dawson.
Dawson, Frank Harold, 1896–1972, vol. VII
Dawson, Lt-Col Frederick Stewart, *died* 1920, vol. II
Dawson, Geoffrey, 1874–1944, vol. IV
Dawson, George Mercer, 1849–1901, vol. I
Dawson, George W., 1868–1959, vol. V
Dawson, Air Vice-Marshal Grahame George, *died* 1944, vol. IV
Dawson, Col Harry Leonard, 1854–1920, vol. II

Deakin, Rt Rev. Thomas Carlyle Joseph Robert Hamish, 1917–1985, vol. VIII
Dealtry, Lawrence Percival, 1896–1963, vol. VI
Dealy, Jane M.; *see* Lewis, Jane.
Dealy, Brig.-Gen. John Anderson, 1865–1935, vol. III
De Amicis, Edmondo, 1846–1908, vol. I
Dean of Beswick, Baron (Life Peer); Joseph Jabez Dean, 1922–1999, vol. X
Dean, Arthur, 1903–1968, vol. VI
Dean, Hon. Sir Arthur, 1893–1970, vol. VI
Dean, Arthur Edis, 1883–1961, vol. VI
Dean, Arthur Wellesley, 1857–1929, vol. III
Dean, Sir Arthur William Henry, 1892–1976, vol. VII
Dean, Barbara Florence, 1924–1989, vol. VIII
Dean, Bashford, 1867–1928, vol. II
Dean, Basil, 1888–1978, vol. VII
Dean, Comdr Brian, 1895–1976, vol. VII
Dean, David Edis, 1922–1994, vol. IX
Dean, Col Donald John, 1897–1985, vol. VIII
Dean, Eric Walter, 1906–1993, vol. IX
Dean, Engr Rear-Adm. Francis Edward, 1881–1965, vol. VI
Dean, Frederic William Charles, 1867–1942, vol. IV
Dean, (Frederick) Harold, 1908–1994, vol. IX
Dean, Frederick William, 1884–1959, vol. V
Dean, George, 1863–1914, vol. I
Dean, Brig.-Gen. George Henry, 1859–1953, vol. V
Dean, Gertrude Mary, 1878–1962, vol. VI
Dean, Gordon Evans, 1905–1958, vol. V
Dean, Harold; *see* Dean, F. H.
Dean, Henry Edwin, 1881–1973, vol. VII
Dean, Henry Percy, *died* 1931, vol. III
Dean, Henry Roy, 1879–1961, vol. VI
Dean, Herbert Samuel, 1870–1942, vol. IV
Dean, Sir John Norman, 1899–1988, vol. VIII
Dean, Sir Maurice Joseph, 1906–1978, vol. VII
Dean, Sir Patrick Henry, 1909–1994, vol IX
Dean, Lt-Comdr Percy Thompson, 1877–1939, vol. III
Dean, Rt Rev. Ralph Stanley, 1913–1987, vol. VIII
Dean, William John Lyon, 1911–1990, vol. VIII
Dean, William Reginald, 1896–1973, vol. VII
Dean-Leslie, John, 1860–1946, vol. IV
Deane, Rev. Anthony Charles, 1870–1946, vol. IV
Deane, Rev. Canon Arthur Mackreth, 1837–1926, vol. III
Deane, Augustus Henry, 1851–1928, vol. II
Deane, Maj.-Gen. Sir Dennis, 1874–1953, vol. V
Deane, Major Donald Victor, 1902–1978, vol. VII
Deane, Edgar Ernest, 1860–1933, vol. III
Deane, Rt Rev. Frederic Llewellyn, 1868–1952, vol. V
Deane, Sir George Campbell, 1873–1948, vol. IV (A), vol. V
Deane, Col George Williams, 1850–1931, vol. III
Deane, Lt-Col Sir Harold Arthur, 1854–1908, vol. I
Deane, Sir Henry Bargrave, 1846–1919, vol. II
Deane, Hermann Frederick Williams, 1858–1921, vol. II
Deane, Major James, 1863–1942, vol. IV
Deane, Rt Hon. Sir James Parker, 1812–1902, vol. I
Deane, Nora Bryan, 1902–1973, vol. VII
Deane, Percy Edgar, 1890–1946, vol. IV

Deane, Captain Richard Burton, 1848–1930, vol. III
Deane, Col Richard Woodforde, 1859–1940, vol. III
Deane, Lt-Col Robert, 1879–1969, vol. VI
Deane, Col Thomas, 1841–1907, vol. I
Deane, Sir Thomas Manly, 1851–1933, vol. III
Deane, Sir Thomas Newenham, 1830–1899, vol. I
Deane, Walter Meredith, 1840–1906, vol. I
Deane, William, 1894–1972, vol. VII
Deanesly, Margaret, 1885–1977, vol. VII
Deans, Harris, 1886–1961, vol. VI
Deans, Richard Storry, *died* 1938, vol. III
Deans, Rodger William, 1917–1995, vol. IX
Deans, Engr-Rear-Adm. William Jordan, *died* 1947, vol. IV
Dear, Hon. Sir John Stanley Bruce, 1925–1997, vol. X
Dearbergh, Geoffrey Frederick, 1924–1979, vol. VII
Dearden, Harold, 1883–1962, vol. VI
Deare, Maj.-Gen. Benjamin Hobbs, 1867–1940, vol. III
Deare, Ronald Frank Robert, 1927–1989, vol. VIII
Dearing, George Edmund, 1911–1968, vol. VI
Dearlove, Rev. William John, 1869–1935, vol. III
Dearmer, Mabel, 1872–1915, vol. I
Dearmer, Rev. Percy, 1867–1936, vol. III
Dearnley, Christopher Hugh, 1930–2000, vol. X
Dearnley, Gertrude, 1884–1982, vol. VIII
Deas, J. A. Charlton, 1874–1951, vol. V
Deas, (James) Stewart, 1903–1985, vol. VIII
Deas, Stewart; *see* Deas, J. S.
Dease, Edmund Gerald, 1829–1904, vol. I
Dease, Major Edmund J., 1861–1945, vol. IV
Dease, Col Sir Gerald Richard, 1831–1903, vol. I
Deasy, Major Henry Hugh Peter, 1866–1947, vol. IV
De'Ath, Lt-Col Ian Dudley, 1918–1960, vol. V
Deavin, Stanley Gwynne, 1905–1991, vol. IX
De Azcarate, Pablo; *see* Azcarate.
De Bathe, Sir Christopher Albert, 6th Bt, 1905–1941, vol. IV
De Bathe, Gen. Sir Henry Perceval, 4th Bt, 1823–1907, vol. I
De Bathe, Sir Hugo Gerald, 5th Bt, 1871–1940, vol. III
De Bathe, Patrick Wynne, 1876–1930, vol. III
de Bazus, Baroness; *see* Leslie, Mrs Frank.
de Beauvoir, Simone Lucie Ernestine Marie Bertrand; *see* Beauvoir.
de Beer, Esmond Samuel, 1895–1990, vol. VIII
de Beer, Sir Gavin Rylands, 1899–1972, vol. VII
de Belabre, Louis Fradin, Baron, 1862–1945, vol. IV
Debenham, Sir Ernest Ridley, 1st Bt, 1865–1952, vol. V
Debenham, Frank, 1883–1965, vol. VI
Debenham, Sir Piers Kenrick, 2nd Bt, 1904–1964, vol. VI
De Bernochi, Francesco, 1887–1962, vol. VI
de Berry, Brig.-Gen. Philip Patrick Evelyn, 1872–1938, vol. III
De Bildt, Baron, 1850–1931, vol. III
de Blank, Most Rev. Joost, 1908–1968, vol. VI
de Blaquiere, 6th Baron, 1856–1920, vol. II
de Blogue, Rev. Oswald William Charles, 1874–1959, vol. V

de Boer, Anthony Peter, 1918–1999, vol. X
de Boer, Henry Speldewinde, 1889–1957, vol. V
De Boinville, Rev. Basil William C.; *see* Chastel De Boinville.
Debono, Massimiliano, 1852–1932, vol. III
de Botton, Gilbert, 1935–2000, vol. X
De Boucherville, Hon. Sir Charles Eugene Boucher, 1822–1915, vol. I
de Brath, Lt-Gen. Sir Ernest, 1858–1933, vol. III
Debré, Michel Jean-Pierre, 1912–1996, vol. X
de Brett, Hon. Brig.-Gen. Harry Simonds, 1870–1965, vol. VI
De Brigard, Camilo, 1906–1972, vol. VII
de Broglie, 7th Duc, 1892–1987, vol. VIII
de Bruyne, Dirk, 1920–1993, vol. IX
de Bruyne, Norman Adrian, 1904–1997, vol. X
de Bruyne, Pieter Louis; *see* Bruyne.
De Bucy, 11th Marquess, 1864–1929, vol. III
de Bunsen, Sir Bernard, 1907–1990, vol. VIII
de Bunsen, Rt Hon. Sir Maurice William Ernest, 1st Bt, 1852–1932, vol. III
de Burgh, Captain Charles, 1886–1973, vol. VII
de Burgh, Gen. Sir Eric, 1881–1973, vol. VII
de Burgh, Lt-Col Thomas John, 1851–1931, vol. III
de Burgh, Col Ulick George Campbell, 1855–1922, vol. II
de Burgh, William George, 1866–1943, vol. IV
Debus, Heinrich, 1824–1915, vol. I
Debussy, Claude Achille, 1862–1918, vol. II
De Butts, Brig. Frederick Cromie, 1888–1977, vol. VII
Debye, Peter Joseph William, 1884–1966, vol. VI
de Candole, Eric Armar Vully, 1901–1989, vol. VIII
de Candole, Rt Rev. Henry Handley Vully, 1895–1971, vol. VII
de Candole, Very Rev. Henry Lawe Corry Vully, 1868–1933, vol. III
de Candolle, Maj.-Gen. Raymond, *died* 1935, vol. III
de Capell Brooke, Sir Edward Geoffrey, 6th Bt, 1880–1968, vol. VI
Decarie, Hon. Jeremie L., 1870–1927, vol. II
de Carteret, Rt Rev. George Frederick Cecil, 1886–1932, vol. III
de Carteret, Samuel Laurence, 1885–1956, vol. V
De Celles, Alfred Duclos, 1844–1925, vol. II
de Chair, Adm. Sir Dudley Rawson Stratford, 1864–1958, vol. V
de Chair, Rev. Frederick Blackett, 1888–1932, vol. III
de Chair, Somerset Struben, 1911–1995, vol. IX
Dechamps, Jules, 1888–1968, vol. VI
de Chazal, Hon. Pierre Edmond, 1837–1914, vol. I
Dechene, Hon. F. G. M., *died* 1902, vol. I
Decie, Brig.-Gen. Cyril Prescott-, 1865–1953, vol. V
Decies, 4th Baron, 1865–1910, vol. I
Decies, 5th Baron, 1866–1944, vol. IV
Decies, 6th Baron, 1915–1992, vol. IX
de Clifford, 25th Baron, 1884–1909, vol. I
de Clifford, 26th Baron, 1907–1982, vol. VIII
de Colyar, Henry Anselm, *died* 1925, vol. II
de Comarmond, Sir Joseph Henri Maxime, 1899–1957, vol. V
Decoppet, Camille, 1862–1925, vol. II
de Cordova, Rudolph, *died* 1941, vol. IV

de Courcel, Geoffrey Chodron; *see* Courcel, Baron de.
de Courcy, Kenneth Hugh, 1909–1999, vol. X
de Courcy-Ireland, Lt-Col Gerald Blakeney, 1895–1986, vol. VIII
de Courcy-Perry, Sir Gerald Raoul, 1836–1903, vol. I
De Courville, Albert Pierre, (Albert Peter Hugh), 1887–1960, vol. V
de Crespigny, Captain Claude C.; *see* Champion de Crespigny.
de Crespigny, Sir Claude C.; *see* Champion de Crespigny.
de Crespigny, Brig.-Gen. Sir Claude Raul C.; *see* Champion de Crespigny.
de Crespigny, Col Sir (Constantine) Trent C.; *see* Champion-de Crespigny.
de Crespigny, Comdr Sir Frederick Philip C.; *see* Champion de Crespigny.
de Crespigny, Lt-Col George Harrison C.; *see* Champion de Crespigny.
de Crespigny, Sir Henry C.; *see* Champion de Crespigny.
de Crespigny, Air Vice-Marshal Hugh Vivian C.; *see* Champion de Crespigny.
de Crespigny, Rose C.; *see* Champion de Crespigny.
de Crespigny, Col Sir Trent C.; *see* Champion-de Crespigny.
de Crespigny, Sir Vivian Tyrell C.; *see* Champion de Crespigny.
De Curel, Viscomte François, 1854–1928, vol. II
Dedijer, Vladimir, 1914–1990, vol. VIII
Dee, Philip Ivor, 1904–1983, vol. VIII
Deed, Basil Lingard, 1909–1991, vol. IX
Deed, Rev. Canon John George, 1842–1923, vol. II
Deedes, Rev. Arthur Gordon, 1861–1916, vol. II
Deedes, Ven. Brook, 1847–1922, vol. II
Deedes, Rev. Cecil, 1843–1920, vol. II
Deedes, Gen. Sir Charles Parker, 1879–1969, vol. VI
Deedes, John Gordon, 1892–1962, vol. VI
Deedes, Percy Gordon, 1899–1973, vol. VII
Deedes, Lt-Gen. Sir Ralph Bouverie, 1890–1954, vol. V
Deedes, Maj.-Gen. William Henry, 1839–1915, vol. I
Deedes, Brig.-Gen. Sir Wyndham Henry, 1883–1956, vol. V
Deegan, Joseph William, 1899–1992, vol. IX
Deeley, Sir Anthony Meyrick M.; *see* Mallaby-Deeley.
Deeley, Sir Guy Meyrick Mallaby M.; *see* Mallaby-Deeley.
Deeley, Sir Harry Mallaby M.; *see* Mallaby-Deeley.
Deeping, (George) Warwick, *died* 1950, vol. IV
Deeping, Warwick; *see* Deeping, G. W.
Deer, Sir Arthur Frederick, 1910–1995, vol. IX
Deer, Sir Frederick; *see* Deer, Sir A. F.
Deer, George, 1890–1974, vol. VII
Deer, Mrs Olive Gertrude, 1897–1983, vol. VIII
Deerhurst, Viscount; George William Coventry, 1865–1928, vol. II
Deerhurst, Viscount; Edward George William Omar Coventry, 1957–1997, vol. X
Deering, William Henry, 1848–1925, vol. II

Deeves, Thomas William, 1893–1977, vol. VII
De Falbe, Brig. Gen. Vigant William, 1867–1940, vol. III
De Falla, Manuel, 1876–1946, vol. IV
de Ferranti, Basil Reginald Vincent Ziani, 1930–1988, vol. VIII
de Ferranti, Sebastian Ziani, 1864–1930, vol. III
de Ferranti, Sir Vincent Ziani, 1893–1980, vol. VII
De Ferrieres, 3rd Baron, 1823–1908, vol. I
Defferre, Gaston, 1910–1986, vol. VIII
De Filippi, Cav. Filippo, 1869–1938, vol. III
de Fischer-Reichenbach, Henry-Béat, 1901–1984, vol. VIII
de Fonblanque, Maj.-Gen. Edward Barrington, 1895–1981, vol. VIII
de Fonblanque, Maj.-Gen. Philip, 1885–1940, vol. III
De Fonseka, Sir (Deepal) Susanta, 1900–1963, vol. VI
De Fonseka, Sir Susanta; see De Fonseka, Sir D. S.
De Foville, Alfred, 1842–1913, vol. I
de Frece, Lady; see Tilley, Vesta.
de Frece, Sir Walter, 1870–1935, vol. III
De Freitas, Sir Anthony, 1869–1940, vol. III
de Freitas, Rt Hon. Sir Geoffrey Stanley, 1913–1982, vol. VIII
de Freitas-Cruz, Jono Carlos Lopes Cardoso, born 1925, vol. VIII
De Freycinet, C. L., 1828–1923, vol. II
De Freyne, 4th Baron, 1855–1913, vol. I
De Freyne, 5th Baron, 1879–1915, vol. I
De Freyne, 6th Baron, 1884–1935, vol. III
Degacher, Maj.-Gen. Henry James, 1835–1902, vol. I
de Gale, Hugh Otway, 1891–1966, vol. VI
de Gale, Sir Leo Victor, 1921–1986, vol. VIII
De Garston, Edward Mervyn, 1869–1939, vol. III
Degas, Hilaire Germain Edgard, 1834–1917, vol. II
De Gasperi, Alcide, 1881–1954, vol. V
de Gaulle, Gén. Charles André Joseph Marie, 1890–1970, vol. VI
De Geer, Baron Gerard, 1858–1943, vol. IV
De Gerlache De Gomery, Baron, 1866–1934, vol. III
de Gex, Col Francis John, 1861–1917, vol. II
de Gex, Maj.-Gen. George Francis, 1911–1986, vol. VIII
De Giberne, Agnes; see Giberne, Agnes.
De Glanville, Sir Oscar James Lardner, died 1942, vol. IV (A), vol. V
De Glehn, Wilfrid Gabriel, 1870–1951, vol. V
De Greef, Arthur, 1862–1940, vol. III (A), vol. IV
de Grey, Nigel, 1886–1951, vol. V
de Grey, Sir Roger, 1918–1995, vol. IX
de Grunwald, Anatole, 1910–1967, vol. VI
De Gruyther, Leslie, died 1937, vol. III
de Guiche, Lillian; see Gish, L.
de Guingand, Maj.-Gen. Sir Francis Wilfred, 1900–1979, vol. VII
de Guiringaud, Louis; see Guiringaud.
d'Egville, Major Alan Hervey, 1891–1951, vol. V
d'Egville, Sir Howard, died 1965, vol. IV
de Gylpyn, Very Rev. Edwin, 1821–1906, vol. I
de Haan, Edward Peter Nayler, 1919–1977, vol. VII
de Haas, Wander Johannes, 1878–1960, vol. V
Dehan, Richard; see Graves, Clotilde I. M.

de Havilland, Captain Sir Geoffrey, 1882–1965, vol. VI
de Havilland, Maj.-Gen. Peter Hugh, 1904–1989, vol. VIII
de Havilland, Col Thomas Lyttleton, 1872–1939, vol. III
Dehlavi, Sir Ali Mahomed Khan, 1871–1952, vol. V
Dehlavi, Samiulla Khan, 1913–1976, vol. VII
Dehn, Adolf Arthur, 1895–1968, vol. VI
Dehn, Paul Edward, 1912–1976, vol. VII
de Hochepied, 10th Baron, 1900–1945, vol. IV
de Hochepied Larpent, Maj.-Gen. Lionel Henry Planta, 1834–1907, vol. I
de Hoghton, Sir Anthony; see de Hoghton, Sir H. P. A. M.
de Hoghton, Sir Cuthbert, 12th Bt, 1880–1958, vol. V
de Hoghton, Sir (Henry Philip) Anthony (Mary), 13th Bt, 1919–1978, vol. VII
de Hoghton, Sir James, 11th Bt, 1851–1938, vol. III
de Horsey, Adm. Sir Algernon Frederick Rous, 1827–1922, vol. II
de Horsey, Adm. Spencer, 1863–1937, vol. III
De Horsey, Lt-Gen. William Henry Beaumont, 1826–1915, vol. I
Deichmann, Baron Adolph Wilhelm, 1831–1907, vol. I
Deighton, Frederick, 1854–1924, vol. II
de Jersey, Rear-Adm. Gilbert Carey, 1905–1974, vol. VII
de Jersey, Rt Rev. Norman Stewart, 1866–1934, vol. III
De Jersey, Col William Grant, 1853–1935, vol. III
de Joux, Lt-Col John Sedley Newton, 1876–1949, vol. IV
De Kalb, Courtenay, 1861–1931, vol. III
de Kantzow, Comdr Arthur Henry, died 1928, vol. II
de Kerillis, Henri, 1889–1958, vol. V
De Keyser, Sir Polydore, 1832–1897, vol. I
Dekobra, Maurice, 1885–1973, vol. VII
de la Bedoyere, Count Michael, 1900–1973, vol. VII
De la Bere, Henry D., 1861–1937, vol. III
De La Bere, Brig. Sir Ivan, 1893–1970, vol. VI
de la Bere, Captain Richard Norman, 1869–1922, vol. II
De la Bère, Sir Rupert, 1st Bt, 1893–1978, vol. VII
de la Bere, Stephen B.; see Baghot de la Bere.
de Labilliere, Rt Rev. Paul Fulcrand Delacour, 1879–1946, vol. IV
Delacombe, Lt-Col Addis, 1865–1941, vol. IV
Delacombe, Maj.-Gen. Sir Rohan, 1906–1991, vol. IX
Delacourt-Smith, Baron (Life Peer); Charles George Percy Smith, 1917–1972, vol. VII
de Lacretelle, Jacques, 1888–1985, vol. VIII
Delafaye, Sir Louis Victor, 1842–1920, vol. II
de la Ferte, Air Chief Marshal Sir Philip Bennet J.; see Joubert de la Ferte.
Delafield, E. M.; see Dashwood, Elizabeth M.
Delafield, Max Everard, 1886–1974, vol. VII
de Lafontaine, Lt-Col Henry Philip L. C.; see Cart de Lafontaine.
Delaforce, Brig.-Gen. Edwin Francis, 1870–1954, vol. V
de La Fosse, Sir Claude Fraser, 1868–1950, vol. IV

de La Fosse, Maj.-Gen. Henry George, 1835–1905, vol. I
Delage, Hon. Cyrille Fraser, 1869–1957, vol. V
Delage, Yves, 1854–1920, vol. II
De la Gorce, Pierre, 1846–1934, vol. III
Delahaye, Col James Viner, 1890–1948, vol. IV
de la Hey, Rev. Richard Willis, 1872–1942, vol. IV
Delalle, Rt Rev. Henry, 1869–1949, vol. IV
Delamain, Lt-Gen. Sir Walter Sinclair, 1862–1932, vol. III
de la Mare, Sir Arthur James, 1914–1994, vol. IX
de la Mare, Peter Bernard David, 1920–1989, vol. VIII
de la Mare, Richard Herbert Ingpen, 1901–1986, vol. VIII
De La Mare, Walter, 1873–1956, vol. V
Delamere, 3rd Baron, 1870–1931, vol. III
Delamere, 4th Baron, 1900–1979, vol. VII
Delamere, Sir Monita Eru, 1921–1993, vol. IX
De La Mothe, Sir Joseph Terence, 1876–1953, vol. V
Delamothe, Hon. Sir Peter Roylance, 1906–1973, vol. VII
De Lancey Forth, Lt-Col Nowell Barnard, 1879–1933, vol. III
Deland, Margaret, 1857–1945, vol. IV
Delaney, Colin John, 1897–1969, vol. VI (AII)
De Laney, Brig.-Gen. Matthew A., 1874–1936, vol. III
de Lange, Daniel, 1841–1918, vol. II
Delano, William Adams, 1874–1960, vol. V
Delano-Osborne, Maj.-Gen. Osborne Herbert, 1879–1958, vol. V
Delany, Mgr Patrick, 1853–1926, vol. II
Delany, Rev. William, 1835–1924, vol. II
Delany, William P., 1855–1916, vol. II
Delap, Rev. Alexander, died 1906, vol. I
Delap, Col George Goslett, 1873–1945, vol. IV
de la Pasture, Elizabeth Lydia Rosabelle, (Mrs Henry de la Pasture); see Clifford, E. L. R.
de la Poer, Edmond, 1841–1915, vol. I
de la Poer, John William Rivallon de Poher, 1882–1939, vol. III
De la Pryme, Ven. Alexander George, 1870–1935, vol. III
de Lara, Adelina, (Lottie Adelina de Lara Shipwright), 1872–1961, vol. VI
De Lara, Isidore, 1858–1935, vol. III
de la Ramée, Marie Louise; see Ouida.
Delarey, Gen. Hon. Jacobus Hendrik, 1848–1914, vol. I
Delargey, His Eminence Cardinal Reginald John, 1914–1979, vol. VII
de Largie, Hon. Hugh, 1859–1947, vol. IV
Delargy, Captain Hugh James, 1908–1976, vol. VII
de la Roche, Mazo, 1885–1961, vol. VI
de la Rue, Sir Eric Vincent, 3rd Bt, 1906–1989, vol. VIII
de la Rue, Sir Ernest, 1852–1929, vol. III
de la Rue, Sir Evelyn Andros, 2nd Bt, 1879–1950, vol. IV
de la Rue, Stuart Andros, 1883–1927, vol. II
de la Rue, Sir Thomas Andros, 1st Bt, 1849–1911, vol. I
de la Rue, Warren William, 1847–1921, vol. II

de Lastic, Most Rev. Alen Basil, 1929–2000, vol. X
de Laszlo, Patrick David, 1909–1980, vol. VII
de Laszowska, (Jane) Emily; see Gerard, J. E.
de Lattre de Tassigny, Général d'Armée Jean Joseph Marie Gabriel, 1889–1952, vol. V
de Lavis-Trafford, Marcus Antonius Johnston, 1880–1960, vol. V
De la Voye, Brig.-Gen. Alexander Edwin, 1871–1940, vol. III
Delavoye, Col Alexander Marin, 1845–1917, vol. II
De La Warr, 8th Earl, 1869–1915, vol. I
De La Warr, 9th Earl, 1900–1976, vol. VII
De La Warr, 10th Earl, 1921–1988, vol. VIII
De La Warr, Sylvia Countess, died 1992, vol. IX
Delay, Jean, 1907–1987, vol. VIII
Delbridge, Rt Rev. Graham Richard, 1917–1980, vol. VII
Delbrück, Max, 1906–1981, vol. VIII
Delcasse, Théephile, 1852–1923, vol. II
Delderfield, Ronald Frederick, 1912–1972, vol. VII
Deledda, Grazia, 1875–1936, vol. III
De Lemos, Charles Herman, 1855–1928, vol. II (A), vol. III
Delepine, Sheridan, 1855–1921, vol. II
Delevingne, Sir Malcolm, 1868–1950, vol. IV
Delfont, Baron (Life Peer); Bernard Delfont, 1909–1994, vol. IX
De L'Hôpital, René le Brun (Count), 1877–1929, vol. III
De L'Isle, 1st Viscount, 1909–1991, vol. IX
De L'Isle and Dudley, 2nd Baron, 1828–1898, vol. I
De L'Isle and Dudley, 3rd Baron, 1853–1922, vol. III
De L'Isle and Dudley, 4th Baron, 1854–1945, vol. IV
De L'Isle and Dudley, 5th Baron, 1859–1945, vol. IV
de Lisle, Gen. Sir Beauvoir, 1864–1955, vol. V
de Lisle, Edwin Joseph Lisle March Phillipps, 1852–1920, vol. II
de Lisle, Everard March Phillipps, died 1947, vol. IV
De Lisle, Brig.-Gen. George de Saumarez, 1862–1954, vol. V
De Lisle, Leopold Victor, 1826–1910, vol. I
de Lisser, Herbert George, 1878–1944, vol. IV
Delius, Frederick, 1862–1934, vol. III
Dell, Draycot Montagu, 1888–1940, vol. III
Dell, Rt Hon. Edmund, 1921–1999, vol. X
Dell, Ethel Mary, 1881–1939, vol. III
Della Taflia, Marchioness, died 1953, vol. V
Della Torre Alta, Il Marchese Albert Félix Schmitt, 1873–1954, vol. V
Deller, Alfred, 1912–1979, vol. VII
Deller, Sir Edwin, 1883–1936, vol. III
Deller, Captain Harold Arthur, 1897–1976, vol. VII
Del Mar, Norman Rene, 1919–1994, vol. IX
Delmas, Jacques Pierre Michel C.; see Chaban-Delmas.
Delme-Radcliffe, Brig.-Gen. Sir Charles, 1864–1937, vol. III
Delme-Radcliffe, Sir Ralph Hubert John, 1877–1963, vol. VI
Delmege, Alfred Gideon, 1846–1923, vol. II
Delmer, (Denis) Sefton, 1904–1979, vol. VII
Delmer, Sefton; see Delmer, D. S.
de Longueuil, 8th Baron, 1856–1931, vol. III
de Longueuil, 9th Baron, 1861–1938, vol. III

De Lotbinière, Maj.-Gen. Alain Chartier Joly; *see* Joly De Lotbinière.
de Lotbinière, Lt-Col Sir Edmond; *see* Joly de Lotbinière.
de Lotbinière, Brig.-Gen. Henri Gustave J.; *see* Joly de Lotbinière.
de Lotbinière, Hon. Sir Henry Gustave J.; *see* Joly de Lotbinière.
de Lotbinière, Seymour Joly, 1905–1984, vol. VIII
de Lotbiniere-Harwood, Charles Auguste; *see* Harwood.
de Loynes, John Barraclough, 1909–1969, vol. VI
Delpech, Reginald George Marius, 1881–1935, vol. III
Delprat, Guillaume Daniel, 1856–1937, vol. III
del Re, Cavaliere Arundel, 1892–1974, vol. VII
del Riego, Teresa, 1876–1968, vol. VI
del Tufo, Sir (Moroböe) Vincent, 1901–1961, vol. VI
Delury, Justin Sarsfield, 1884–1968, vol. VI
Delve, Sir William Frederick, 1902–1995, vol. IX
Delves, Robert Harvey Addington, 1873–1952, vol. V
Delves Broughton, Major Sir Evelyn; *see* Broughton.
Delysia, Alice, 1889–1979, vol. VII
de Manio, Jack, 1914–1988, vol. VIII
de Majo, William Maks, 1917–1993, vol. IX
Demant, Rev. Vigo Auguste, 1893–1983, vol. VIII
de Marees-Van Swinderen, Jonkheer Rene; *see* Van Swinderen.
de Margerie, Emmanuel, 1862–1953, vol. V
de Margerie, Emmanuel Jacquin, 1924–1991, vol. IX
de Margerie, Pierre, 1861–1942, vol. IV
de Margerie, Roland Jacquin, 1899–1990, vol. VIII
de Mauley, 3rd Baron, 1843–1918, vol. II
de Mauley, 4th Baron, 1846–1945, vol. IV
de Mauley, 5th Baron, 1878–1962, vol. VI
de Mayo, Paul, 1924–1994, vol. IX
De Mel, Sir Henry Lawson, 1877–1936, vol. III
De Mel, Most Rev. (Hiyanirindu) Lakdasa Jacob, 1902–1976, vol. VII
De Mel, Most Rev. Lakdasa Jacob; *see* De Mel, Most Rev. H. L. J.
de Mendieta, Rev. Emmanuel Alexandre A.; *see* Amand de Mendieta.
de Meric, Rear-Adm. Martin John Coucher, 1887–1943, vol. IV
Demers, Marie Joseph, 1871–1940, vol. III (A), vol. IV
Demetriadi, Sir Stephen, 1880–1952, vol. V
de Mille, Agnes George, 1905–1993, vol. IX
deMille, Cecil Blount, 1881–1959, vol. V
de Miranda, Comtesse; *see* Nilsson, Mme Christine.
De Mole, Lancelot Eldin, 1880–1950, vol. IV
de Moleyns, Thomas, 1807–1900, vol. I
de Moleyns, Maj.-Gen. Townsend Aremberg, 1838–1926, vol. II
de Montalt, 1st Earl, 1817–1905, vol. I
de Monte, Frank Thomas, 1879–1950, vol. IV
de Montherlant, Henry; *see* Montherlant.
de Montmorency, Sir Angus; *see* de Montmorency, Sir H. A.
de Montmorency, Hon. Francis Raymond, 1835–1910, vol. I

de Montmorency, Sir Geoffrey Fitzhervey, 1876–1955, vol. V
de Montmorency, Sir (Hervey) Angus, 16th Bt, 1888–1959, vol. V
de Montmorency, Major Hervey Guy Francis Edward, 1868–1942, vol. IV
de Montmorency, James Edward Geoffrey, 1866–1934, vol. III
De Montmorency, Captain John Pratt, 1873–1960, vol. V
de Montmorency, Sir Miles Fletcher, 17th Bt, 1893–1963, vol. VI
de Montmorency, Hon. Raymond Hervey, 1867–1900, vol. I
de Montmorency, Sir Reginald D'Alton Lodge, 18th Bt, 1899–1979, vol. VII
de Montmorency, Reymond Hervey, 1871–1938, vol. III
de Montmorency, Ven. Waller, 1841–1924, vol. II
De Morgan, William Frend, 1839–1917, vol. II
de Morley, 21st Baron, 1844–1918, vol. II
de Mourgues, Odette Marie Hélène Louise, 1914–1988, vol. VIII
Dempsey, Sir Alexander, 1852–1920, vol. II
Dempsey, James, 1917–1982, vol. VIII
Dempsey, Gen. Sir Miles Christopher, 1896–1969, vol. VI
Dempster, Francis Erskine, 1858–1941, vol. IV
Dempster, Col Reginald Hawkins H.; *see* Hall-Dempster.
Denbigh, 9th Earl of, **and Desmond,** 8th Earl of, 1859–1939, vol. III
Denbigh, 10th Earl of, **and Desmond,** 9th Earl of, 1912–1966, vol. VI
Denbigh, 11th Earl of, **and Desmond,** 10th Earl of, 1943–1995, vol. IX
Denby, Elizabeth Marian, *died* 1965, vol. VI
Denby, Sir Ellis, 1856–1939, vol. III
Denby, Sir Richard Kenneth, 1915–1986, vol. VIII
Dence, Ernest Martin, 1873–1937, vol. III
Dench, William George, 1888–1963, vol. VI
Dendy, Arthur, 1865–1925, vol. II
Dendy, Edward Evershed, 1861–1929, vol. III
Dendy, Mary, 1855–1933, vol. III
Dendy, Brig. Murray Heathfield, 1885–1951, vol. V
Dene, Col Arthur Pollard, *died* 1945, vol. IV
Deneke, Margaret Clara Adèle, 1882–1969, vol. VI
de Neuflize, Baron Jean, 1850–1928, vol. II
Deneys, Comdr James Godfrey Wood, 1897–1962, vol. VI
Denham, 1st Baron, 1886–1948, vol. IV
Denham, Algernon, *died* 1961, vol. VI
Denham, Hon. Digby Frank, 1859–1944, vol. IV
Denham, Sir Edward Brandis, 1876–1938, vol. III
Denham, Godfrey Charles, 1883–1956, vol. V
Denham, Harold Arthur, 1878–1921, vol. II
Denham, Henry George, 1880–1943, vol. IV
Denham, Captain Henry Mangles, 1897–1993, vol. IX
Denham, Humphrey John, 1893–1970, vol. VI
Denham, Sir James, *died* 1927, vol. II
Denham, William Smith, 1878–1964, vol. VI
Denham-White, Lt-Col Arthur; *see* White.
Denholm, John, 1853–1937, vol. III

Denholm, Sir John Carmichael, 1893–1981, vol. VIII

Denholm, Col Sir William Lang, 1901–1986, vol. VIII

Deniker, Joseph, 1852–1918, vol. II

Dening, Sir Esler; see Dening, Sir M. E.

Dening, Lt-Gen. Sir Lewis, 1848–1911, vol. I

Dening, Sir (Maberly) Esler, 1897–1977, vol. VII

Dening, Maj.-Gen. Roland, 1888–1978, vol. VII

Denington, Baroness (Life Peer); Evelyn Joyce Denington, 1907–1998, vol. X

Denis de Vitré, Col Percy Theodosius, 1870–1940, vol. III

Denison, Rear-Adm. Hon. Albert Denison Somerville, 1835–1903, vol. I

Denison, Captain Edward C., 1888–1960, vol. V

Denison, Col George Taylor, 1839–1925, vol. II

Denison, Hon. Harold Albert, 1856–1948, vol. IV

Denison, Captain Hon. Henry, 1849–1936, vol. III

Denison, Brig.-Gen. Henry, 1847–1938, vol. III

Denison, Rev. Henry Phipps, 1848–1940, vol. III

Denison, Sir Hugh Robert, 1865–1940, vol. III

Denison, Adm. John, 1853–1939, vol. III

Denison, (John) Michael (Terence Wellesley), 1915–1998, vol. X

Denison, Michael; see Denison, J. M. T. W.

Denison, Robert Beckett, 1879–1951, vol. V

Denison, Maj.-Gen. Septimus Julius Augustus, 1859–1937, vol. III

Denison, William Evelyn, 1843–1916, vol. II

Denison-Pender, Sir John Denison; see Pender.

de Niverville, Air Vice-Marshal Joseph Lionel Elphege Albert, 1897–1968, vol. VI (AII)

Denman, 3rd Baron, 1874–1954, vol. V

Denman, 4th Baron, 1905–1971, vol. VII

Denman, Lady; (Gertrude Mary), 1884–1954, vol. V

Denman, Sir Arthur, 1857–1931, vol. III

Denman, Donald Robert, 1911–1999, vol. X

Denman, George Lewis, 1854–1929, vol. III

Denman, John Leopold, 1882–1975, vol. VII

Denman, Hon. Sir Richard Douglas, 1st Bt, 1876–1957, vol. V

Denne, Major William Henry, 1876–1917, vol. II

Dennehy, Sir Harold George, 1890–1956, vol. V

Dennehy, Maj.-Gen. Sir Thomas, 1829–1915, vol. I

Dennehy, William Francis, died 1918, vol. II (A), vol. III

Dennell, Ralph, 1907–1989, vol. VIII

Dennett, Richard Edward, 1857–1921, vol. II

Denney, Rev. James, 1856–1917, vol. II

Denning, Baron (Life Peer); Alfred Thompson Denning, 1899–1999, vol. X

Denning, Sir Howard, 1885–1943, vol. IV

Denning, Vice-Adm. Sir Norman Egbert, 1904–1979, vol. VII

Denning, Lt-Gen. Sir Reginald Francis Stewart, 1894–1990, vol. VIII

Denning, William Frederick, 1848–1931, vol. III

Dennis, Mrs A. E. Forbes; see Bottome, Phyllis.

Dennis, Sir Alfred Hull, 1858–1947, vol. IV

Dennis, Geoffrey Pomeroy, 1892–1963, vol. VI

Dennis, Sir (Herbert) Raymond, 1878–1939, vol. III

Dennis, Rev. Canon Herbert Wesley, died 1938, vol. III

Dennis, Rev. James Shepard, 1842–1914, vol. I

Dennis, Surg.-Rear-Adm. John Jeffreys, 1858–1958, vol. V

Dennis, Col John Stoughton, 1856–1938, vol. III

Dennis, John William, 1865–1949, vol. IV

Dennis, Maxwell Lewis, 1909–1999, vol. X

Dennis, Maj.-Gen. Meade Edward, 1893–1965, vol. VI

Dennis, Col Meade James Crosbie, 1865–1945, vol. IV

Dennis, Nigel Forbes, 1912–1989, vol. VIII

Dennis, Sir Raymond; see Dennis, Sir H. R.

Dennis, Ven. Thomas John, 1869–1917, vol. II

Dennis, Trevor, 1882–1950, vol. IV

Dennis, Will; see Townesend, Stephen.

Dennis, William, 1856–1920, vol. II

Dennis Smith, Edgar; see Smith.

Dennison, Major Charles George, born 1844, vol. III

Dennison, Major Gilbert, 1883–1957, vol. III

Dennison, Brig. Malcolm Gray, 1924–1996, vol. X

Dennison, Mervyn William, 1914–1993, vol. IX

Dennison, Robert, 1879–1951, vol. V

Dennison, Adm. Robert Lee, 1901–1980, vol. VII

Dennison, Stanley Raymond, 1912–1992, vol. IX

Dennison, Thomas Andrews, 1906–1972, vol. VII

Denniss, Charles Sherwood, 1860–1917, vol. II

Denniss, Lt-Col Cyril Edmund Bartley B.; see Bartley-Denniss.

Denniss, Sir Edmund Robert Bartley B.; see Bartley-Denniss.

Denniss, George Hamson, 1854–1940, vol. III (A), vol. IV

Denniston, Alexander Guthrie Alistair, 1881–1961, vol. VI

Denniston, John Dewar, 1887–1949, vol. IV

Denniston, Hon. Sir John Edward, 1845–1919, vol. II

Denniston, Sir Robert, 1890–1946, vol. IV

Dennistoun, Lt-Col Ian Onslow, 1879–1938, vol. III

Dennistoun, Lt-Col James George, 1871–1939, vol. II

Dennistoun, Hon. Robert Maxwell, 1864–1952, vol. V

Denny, Sir Alistair Maurice Archibald, 3rd Bt, 1922–1995, vol. IX

Denny, Sir Archibald, 1st Bt (cr 1913), 1860–1936, vol. III

Denny, Barbara Mary, (Mrs Edward Denny), 1880–1965, vol. VI

Denny, Captain Sir Cecil Edward, 6th Bt (cr 1782), 1850–1928, vol. II

Denny, Major Ernest Wriothesley, 1872–1949, vol. IV

Denny, Frederick Anthony, 1860–1941, vol. IV

Denny, Col Henry Cuthbert, 1858–1934, vol. III

Denny, Rev. Sir Henry Lyttelton Lyster, 7th Bt (cr 1782), 1878–1953, vol. V

Denny, Henry Samuel, died 1938, vol. III

Denny, Comdr Herbert Maynard, 1876–1957, vol. V

Denny, Surg. Rear-Adm. Herbert Reginald Harry, 1876–1943, vol. IV

Denny, James Runciman, 1908–1978, vol. VII

Denny, John M'Ausland, 1858–1922, vol. II

Denny, Sir J(onathan) Lionel P(ercy), 1897–1985, vol. VIII

Denny, Sir Lionel; see Denny, Sir J. L. P.

Denny, Margaret Bertha Alice, (Mrs E. L. Denny), 1907–1999, vol. X
Denny, Sir Maurice Edward, 2nd Bt (cr 1913), 1886–1955, vol. V
Denny, Adm. Sir Michael Maynard, 1896–1972, vol. VII
Denny, Sir Robert Arthur, 5th Bt (cr 1782), 1838–1921, vol. II
Denny, Rev. William Henry, died 1907, vol. I
Denny, Hon. William Joseph, died 1946, vol. IV
Denny-Brown, Derek Ernest, 1901–1981, vol. VIII
Dennys, Cyril George, 1897–1991, vol. IX
Dennys, Col George William Patrick, 1857–1924, vol. II
Dennys, Lt-Col Sir Hector Travers, 1864–1922, vol. II
Dennys, Gen. Julius Bentall, 1822–1907, vol. I
Dennys, Rodney Onslow, 1911–1993, vol. IX
de Normann, Sir Eric, 1893–1982, vol. VIII
Densham, Sir Harry Percival, 1866–1933, vol. III
Densmore, Emmet, 1837–1912, vol. I
Denson, John Boyd, 1926–1992, vol. IX
Dent, Alan Holmes, 1905–1978, vol. VII
Dent, Sir Alfred, 1844–1927, vol. II
Dent, Brig.-Gen. Bertie Coore, 1872–1960, vol. V
Dent, Charles Enrique, 1911–1976, vol. VI
Dent, Clinton Thomas, 1850–1912, vol. I
Dent, Adm. Douglas Lionel, 1869–1959, vol. V
Dent, Edward Joseph, 1876–1957, vol. V
Dent, Sir Francis Henry, 1866–1955, vol. V
Dent, Frederick James, 1905–1973, vol. VII
Dent, George Irving, 1918–1976, vol. VII
Dent, Harold Collett, 1894–1995, vol. IX
Dent, Lt-Col Henry Francis, 1839–1916, vol. II
Dent, Rear-Adm. John, 1899–1973, vol. VII
Dent, John James, 1856–1936, vol. III
Dent, Lt-Col John Ralph Congreve, 1884–1969, vol. VI
Dent, Major John William, 1857–1943, vol. IV
Dent, Rev. Joseph Jonathan Dent, 1829–1907, vol. I
Dent, Major Joseph Leslie, 1889–1917, vol. II
Dent, Joseph Mallaby, 1849–1926, vol. II
Dent, Major Leonard Maurice Edward, 1888–1987, vol. VIII
Dent, Sir Robert Annesley Wilkinson, 1895–1983, vol. VIII
Dent, (Robert) Stanley (Gorrell), 1909–1991, vol. IX
Dent, Sir Robin John, 1929–1999, vol. X
Dent, Ronald Henry, 1913–1993, vol. X
Dent, Stanley; see Dent, R. S. G.
Dent, Maj.-Gen. Wilkinson, 1883–1934, vol. III
Dent-Brocklehurst, Major John Henry; see Brocklehurst.
Dent-Brocklehurst, Mary, 1902–1988, vol. VIII
Denton, Sir George Chardin, 1851–1928, vol. II
Denton, Mrs H. S., died 1953, vol. V
Denton, William, 1844–1915, vol. I
Denton-Thompson, Merrick Arnold Bardsley, 1888–1969, vol. VI
d'Entrèves, Alexander Passerin, 1902–1985, vol. VIII
Denville, Alfred, 1876–1955, vol. V
Denyer, Charles Leonard, 1887–1969, vol. VI
Denyer, Stanley Edward, 1869–1931, vol. III

Denys, Sir (Charles) Peter, 4th Bt (cr 1813), 1899–1960, vol. V
Denys, Sir Peter; see Denys, Sir C. P.
Denys-Burton, Sir Francis Charles Edward, 3rd Bt (cr 1913), 1849–1922, vol. II
Denza, Luigi, 1846–1922, vol. II
Deol, Malkiat Singh, 1928–1999, vol. X
de Paravicini, Percy J., 1862–1921, vol. II
de Pass, Sir Eliot Arthur, 1851–1937, vol. III
de Pass, Col Guy Eliot, 1898–1985, vol. VIII
de Pauley, Rt Rev. William Cecil, 1893–1968, vol. VI
De Pencier, Most Rev. Adam Urias, 1866–1949, vol. IV
Depew, Chauncey Mitchell, 1834–1928, vol. II
de Peyer, Charles Hubert, 1905–1983, vol. VIII
d'Epinay, Charles Adrien Prosper; see Epinay.
de Polnay, Peter, 1906–1984, vol. VIII
de Pourtalès, Count Guy, 1881–1941, vol. IV
De Pree, Maj.-Gen. Hugo Douglas, 1870–1943, vol. IV
de Pury, David, 1943–2000, vol. X
de Putron, Air Cdre Owen Washington, 1893–1980, vol. VII
Deramore, 3rd Baron, 1865–1936, vol. III
Deramore, 4th Baron, 1870–1943, vol. IV
Deramore, 5th Baron, 1903–1964, vol. VI
De Ramsey, 2nd Baron, 1848–1925, vol. II
De Ramsey, 3rd Baron, 1910–1993, vol. IX
Derby, 16th Earl of, 1841–1908, vol. I
Derby, 17th Earl of, 1865–1948, vol. IV
Derby, 18th Earl of, 1918–1994, vol. IX
Derbyshire, Sir Harold, 1886–1972, vol. VII
Derbyshire, Job Nightingale, 1866–1954, vol. V
De Renzy, Sir Annesley Charles Castriot, 1829–1914, vol. I
De Renzy-Martin, Lt-Col Edward Cuthbert, 1883–1974, vol. VII
Derham, Sir David Plumley, 1920–1985, vol. VIII
Derham, Maj.-Gen. Frank Plumley, 1885–1957, vol. IV
Derham, Brig.-Gen. Frank Seymour, 1858–1941, vol. IV
Derham, Hon. Frederick Thomas, 1844–1922, vol. II
de Rhé-Philipe, Maj.-Gen. Arthur Terence, 1905–1971, vol. VII
Dering, Sir Anthony Myles Cholmeley, 11th Bt, 1901–1958, vol. V
Dering, Comdr Claud Lacy Yea, 1885–1943, vol. IV
Dering, Sir Henry Edward, 10th Bt, 1866–1931, vol. III
Dering, Sir Henry Nevill, 9th Bt, 1839–1906, vol. I
Dering, Sir Herbert Guy, 1867–1933, vol. III
Dering, Lt-Col Rupert Anthony Yea, 12th Bt, 1915–1975, vol. VII
d'Erlanger, Baron Emile Beaumont, 1866–1939, vol. III
d'Erlanger, Baron Frederic A., 1868–1943, vol. IV
d'Erlanger, Sir Gerard John Regis Leo, 1906–1962, vol. V
d'Erlanger, Leo Frederic Alfred, 1898–1978, vol. VII
de Robeck, 4th Baron, 1823–1904, vol. I

de Robeck, 5th Baron, 1859–1929, vol. III
de Robeck, 6th Baron, 1895–1965, vol. VI
de Robeck, Adm. of the Fleet Sir John Michael, 1st Bt, 1862–1928, vol. II
de Ros, 24th Baron, 1827–1907, vol. I
de Ros, Baroness (25th in line), 1854–1939, vol. III
de Ros, Baroness (26th in line), 1879–1956, vol. V
de Rothschild, Anthony Gustav; see Rothschild.
de Rougemont, Brig.-Gen. Cecil Henry, 1865–1951, vol. V
de Rougemont, Charles Irving, 1864–1939, vol. III
Deroulède, Paul, 1846–1914, vol. I
Derrick, Col George Alexander, 1860–1945, vol. IV
Derrick, Thomas, died 1954, vol. V
Derrig, Thomas; see O'Deirg, Tomás.
Derriman, Captain G. L., died 1915, vol. I
Derry, Cyril, 1895–1964, vol. VI
Derry, Henry B.; see Bromley-Derry.
Derry, Henry Forster H.; see Handley-Derry.
Derry, John, 1854–1937, vol. III
Derry, Ven. Percy A., 1859–1928, vol. II
Derry, Warren, 1899–1986, vol. VIII
de Ros, Baroness (27th in line), 1933–1983, vol. VIII
de Rutzen, Baron, John Frederick Foley, 1909–1944, vol. IV
de Rutzen, Sir Albert, 1831–1913, vol. I
Derviche-Jones, Lt-Col Arthur Daniel, 1873–1940, vol. III
Derville, Major Max T.; see Teichman-Derville.
Derwent, 1st Baron, 1829–1916, vol. II
Derwent, 2nd Baron, 1851–1929, vol. III
Derwent, 3rd Baron, 1899–1949, vol. IV
Derwent, 4th Baron, 1901–1986, vol. VIII
Derwent, William Raymond, 1883–1960, vol. V
de Sabata, Victor, 1892–1967, vol. VI
Desai, Shri Morarji Ranchhodji, 1896–1995, vol. IX
De St Jorre, Danielle Marie-Madelaine J.; see Jorre De St Jorre.
de Ste Croix, Geoffrey Ernest Maurice, 1910–2000, vol. X
de Sales La Terrière, Col. Fenwick Bulmer, 1856–1925, vol. II
De Salis, Sir Cecil Fane, 1857–1948, vol. IV
De Salis, Rt Rev. Charles Fane, 1860–1942, vol. IV
De Salis, Lt-Col Edward Augustus Alfred, 1874–1943, vol. IV
De Salis, Rev. Henry Jerome, 1828–1915, vol. I
de Salis, Lt-Col John Eugene, 8th Count De Salis, 1891–1949, vol. IV
de Salis, John Francis Charles, Count de Salis, 1864–1939, vol. III
De Salis, Rodolph Fane, 1854–1931, vol. III
De Salis, Adm. Sir William Fane, 1858–1939, vol. III
de Saram, John Henricus, 1844–1920, vol. II
Desart, 4th Earl of, 1845–1898, vol. I
Desart, 5th Earl of, 1848–1934, vol. III
Desart, Ellen Odette, 1857–1933, vol. III
de Satgé, Lt-Col Sir Henry Valentine Bache, 1874–1964, vol. VI
De Saumarez, 4th Baron, 1843–1937, vol. III
De Saumarez, 5th Baron, 1889–1969, vol. VI
de Saumarez, 6th Baron, 1924–1991, vol. IX

de Sausmarez, Annie Elizabeth, (Lady de Sausmarez), died 1947, vol. IV
De Sausmarez, Brig.-Gen. Cecil, 1870–1966, vol. VI
de Sausmarez, Sir Havilland Walter de; see Sausmarez.
de Sausmarez, (Lionel) Maurice, 1915–1969, vol. VI
de Sausmarez, Maurice; see de Sausmarez, L. M.
Desbarats, George Joseph, 1861–1944, vol. IV
Desborough, 1st Baron, 1855–1945, vol. IV
Desborough, Arthur Peregrine Henry, 1868–1949, vol. IV
Desborough, Maj.-Gen. John, 1824–1918, vol. II
Desborough, Vincent Robin d'Arba, 1914–1978, vol. VII
Descamps, Baron, died 1933, vol. III
Desch, Cecil Henry, 1874–1958, vol. V
Desch, Stephen Conway, 1939–1996, vol. X
Deschanel, Paul Eugène Louis, 1856–1922, vol. II
de Segonzac, A. D.; see Dunoyer de Segonzac.
de Selincourt, Anne Douglas, (Mrs Basil de Selincourt); see Sedgwick, A. D.
de Selincourt, Aubrey, 1894–1962, vol. VI
de Selincourt, Martin, 1864–1950, vol. IV
des Forges, Sir Charles Lee, 1879–1972, vol. VII
des Graz, Charles Geoffrey Maurice, 1893–1953, vol. V
Des Graz, Sir Charles Louis, 1860–1940, vol. III
Deshmukh, Sir Chintaman Dwarkanath, 1896–1982, vol. VIII
Deshon, Col Charles John, 1840–1929, vol. III
Deshon, Edward, 1836–1924, vol. II
Deshon, Lt-Gen. Frederick George Thomas, 1818–1913, vol. I
Deshon, H. F., 1858–1924, vol. II
Deshumbert, Marius, 1856–1943, vol. IV
De Sica, Vittorio, 1901–1974, vol. VII
Desika-Charry, Sir Vembakkam C., born 1861, vol. II
Desikachari, Diwan Bahadur Sir Tirumalai, 1868–1940, vol. III(A), vol. IV
de Silva, Sir Albert Ernest, 1887–1957, vol. V(A), vol. VI(AI)
de Silva, Sir Arthur Marcellus, 1879–1957, vol. V
de Silva, Rt Hon. Lucien Macull Dominic, 1893–1962, vol. VI
Desjardins, Hon. Alphonse, 1841–1912, vol. I
Deslandes, Sir Charles Frederick, 1884–1957, vol. V
Deslandes, Baronne M., vol. III
de Smidt, Lt-Col Errol Mervyn, 1877–1931, vol. III
de Smidt, Henry, 1845–1919, vol. II
de Smith, Stanley Alexander, 1922–1974, vol. VII
Desmond, Astra, (Lady Neame), 1893–1973, vol. VII
Desmond, John, died 1938, vol. III
Desmond, Shaw, 1877–1960, vol. V, vol. VI
de Soissons, Louis, 1890–1962, vol. VI
de Sola, Rev. Meldola, 1853–1918, vol. II
De Soveral, Marquess (Sir), died 1922, vol. II
de Soyres, Rev. John, 1849–1905, vol. I
de Soysa, Rt Rev. Charles Harold Wilfred, died 1971, vol. VII
de Soysa, Sir (Lambert) Wilfred (Alexander), 1884–1968, vol. VI
de Soysa, Sir Wilfred; see de Soysa, Sir L. W. A.
de Soyza, Gunasena, 1902–1961, vol. VI

Despard, Captain Herbert John, 1860–1937, vol. III
Despencer-Robertson, Lt-Col James Archibald St
George Fitzwarenne, 1893–1942, vol. IV
d'Esperey, Franchet, 1856–1942, vol. IV
Dessaulles, Hon. George Casimir, 1827–1930,
vol. III
de Stein, Sir Edward, 1887–1965, vol. VI
de Stacpoole, 4th Duke, 1860–1929, vol. III
de Stacpoole, 5th Duke, 1886–1965, vol. VI
d'Esterre, Elsa, died 1935, vol. III
Destinn, Emmy, 1878–1930, vol. III
D'Estournelles de Constant, Baron, 1852–1924,
vol. II
Desty, Denis Henry, 1923–1994, vol. IX
Des Vœux, Sir Charles Champagné, 6th Bt,
1827–1914, vol. I
Des Vœux, Lt-Gen. Sir Charles Hamilton,
1853–1911, vol. I
Des Vœux, Sir Edward Alfred, 8th Bt, 1864–1941,
vol. IV
Des Vœux, Sir Frederick, 7th Bt, 1857–1937, vol. III
Des Vœux, Sir George William, 1834–1909, vol. I
Des Vœux, Lt-Col Henry Bertram, 1868–1930,
vol. III
Des Vœux, Lt-Col Henry J., 1876–1940, vol. III
Des Vœux, Lt-Col Herbert, 1864–1945, vol. IV
Des Vœux, Lt-Col Sir Richard de Bacquencourt; see
Des Vœux, Lt-Col Sir W. R. de B.
Des Vœux, Sir William; see Des Vœux, Sir G. W.
Des Vœux, Lt-Col Sir (William) Richard de
Bacquencourt, 9th Bt, 1911–1944, vol. IV
De Tabley, Lady; (Elizabeth), died 1915, vol. I
Detaille, Edouard, died 1912, vol. I
de Teissier, Baron Henry de Teissier, 1862–1931,
vol. III
Deterding, Sir Henri Wilhelm August, 1866–1939,
vol. III
de Thier, Baron Jacques, 1900–1996, vol. X
de Thieusies, Vicomte Alain O.; see Obert de
Thieusies.
Dethridge, George James, 1864–1938, vol. III
Dethridge, Hon. George Leo, 1903–1978, vol. VII
Detmold, Edward J., 1883–1957, vol. V
Detmold, Maurice, 1883–1908, vol. I
de Torrenté, Henry, 1893–1962, vol. VI
De Trafford, Lt Augustus Francis, 1879–1904, vol. I
De Trafford, (Charles) Edmund, 1864–1951, vol. V
De Trafford, Edmund; see De Trafford, C. E.
de Trafford, Captain Sir Humphrey Edmund, 4th Bt,
1891–1971, vol. VII
de Trafford, Sir Humphrey Francis, 3rd Bt,
1862–1929, vol. III
de Trafford, Sir Rudolph Edgar Francis, 5th Bt,
1894–1983, vol. VIII
de Trafford, Sigismund Cathcart, 1853–1936,
vol. III
Dettmann, Herbert Stanley, 1875–1940, vol. III
Deuchar, William, 1849–1923, vol. II
Deutsch, André, 1917–2000, vol. X
Deutsch, John James, 1911–1976, vol. VII
Deutsch, Otto Erich, 1883–1967, vol. VI
Deutscher, Isaac, 1907–1967, vol. VI
Devadhar, Gopal Krishna, 1871–1935, vol. III
Devadoss, Sir David Muthiah, 1868–1955, vol. V
De Valera, Eamon, 1882–1975, vol. VII

Devals, Rt Rev. Adrian, 1882–1945, vol. IV
Devas, Anthony, 1911–1958, vol. V
Devas, Charles Stanton, 1848–1906, vol. I
Devas, Rev. Francis Charles, 1877–1951, vol. V
Devaux, J. Louis, 1884–1943, vol. IV
de Vaux, Father Roland, 1903–1971, vol. VII
de Veber, Hon. Leverett George, 1849–1925, vol. II
Devenish, Rev. Robert Cecil Silvester, 1888–1973,
vol. VII
Devenish, Very Rev. Robert Jones Sylvester, died
1916, vol. II
Devenish-Meares, Maj.-Gen. William Lewis,
1832–1907, vol. I
Devenport, Martyn Herbert, 1931–1991, vol. IX
Dever, Hon. James, 1825–1904, vol. I
de Vere, Aubrey Thomas, 1814–1902, vol. I
de Vere, Robert Stephen Vere, 1872–1936, vol. III
de Vere, Sir Stephen Edward, 4th Bt, 1812–1904,
vol. I
Deverell, Sir Colville Montgomery, 1907–1995,
vol. IX
Deverell, Field Marshal Sir Cyril John, 1874–1947,
vol. IV
Devereux, Rev. Edward Robert Price, died 1941,
vol. IV
Devereux, Sir Joseph, 1816–1903, vol. I
Devereux, Wallace Charles, 1893–1952, vol. V
de Vere White, Terence; see White.
Devers, Gen. Jacob Loucks, 1887–1979, vol. VII
de Versan, Raoul Couturier, 1848–1936, vol. III
De Vesci, 5th Viscount, 1881–1958, vol. V
de Vesci, 6th Viscount, 1919–1983, vol. VIII
de Veulle, Henry Marett, 1847–1930, vol. III
de Villiers, 1st Baron, 1842–1914, vol. I
de Villiers, 2nd Baron, 1871–1934, vol. III
de Villiers, Hon. Sir Etienne; see de Villiers, Hon.
Sir J. E. R.
de Villiers, Sir (H.) Nicolas, 1902–1958, vol. V
de Villiers, Maj.-Gen. Isaac Pierre, 1891–1967,
vol. VI
de Villiers, Jacob, 1868–1932, vol. III
de Villiers, Hon. Sir (Jean) Etienne (Reenen),
1875–1947, vol. IV
de Villiers, Sir John Abraham Jacob, 1863–1931,
vol. III
Devine, Alexander, 1865–1930, vol. III
Devine, George Alexander Cassady, 1910–1966,
vol. VI
Devine, Henry, 1879–1940, vol. III
Devine, Sir Hugh Berchmans, died 1959, vol. V
Devine, Major James Arthur, 1869–1939, vol. III
Devine, Rev. Minos, 1871–1937, vol. III
De Vinne, Theodore Low, 1828–1914, vol. I
De Vito, Gioconda, 1907–1994, vol. IX
Devitt, Sir Philip Henry, 1st Bt (cr 1931),
1876–1947, vol. IV
Devitt, Lt-Col Sir Thomas Gordon, 1902–1995,
vol. IX
Devitt, Sir Thomas Lane, 1st Bt (cr 1916),
1839–1923, vol. II
de Vivenot, Baroness; see Vivenot, Baroness de.
Devlin, Baron (Life Peer); Patrick Arthur Devlin,
1905–1992, vol. IX
Devlin, Hon. Charles Ramsay, 1858–1914, vol. I
Devlin, Emmanuel, 1872–1921, vol. II

Devlin, Joseph, 1872–1934, vol. III
Devlin, William, 1911–1987, vol. VIII
de Voil, Very Rev. Walter Harry, 1893–1964, vol. VI
Devon, 13th Earl of, 1811–1904, vol. I
Devon, 14th Earl of, 1870–1927, vol. II
Devon, 15th Earl of, 1872–1935, vol. III
Devon, 16th Earl of, 1875–1935, vol. III
Devon, 17th Earl of, 1916–1998, vol. X
Devon, James, 1866–1939, vol. III
Devonport, 1st Viscount, 1856–1934, vol. III
Devonport, 2nd Viscount, 1890–1973, vol. VII
Devons, Ely, 1913–1967, vol. VI
Devonshire, 9th Duke of, 1868–1938, vol. III
Devonshire, 10th Duke of, 1895–1950, vol. IV
Devonshire, Dowager Duchess of, (Mary Alice), 1895–1988, vol. VIII
Devonshire, Sir James Lyne, 1863–1946, vol. IV
DeVoto, Bernard Augustine, 1897–1955, vol. V
de Vries, Hugo, 1848–1935, vol. III
De Vries, Peter, 1910–1993, vol. IX
Dew, Col Sir Armine Brereton, 1867–1941, vol. IV
Dew, Armine Roderick, 1906–1945, vol. IV
Dew, Sir Harold Robert, 1891–1962, vol. VI
Dew, Leslie Robert, 1914–1996, vol. X
De Waal, Hon. Daniel, 1873–1938, vol. III
De Waal, Brig. Pieter, 1899–1977, vol. VII
Dewar, 1st Baron, 1864–1930, vol. III
Dewar, Hon. Lord; Arthur Dewar, died 1917, vol. II
Dewar, Rev. Alexander, 1864–1943, vol. IV
Dewar, Arthur; see Dewar, Hon. Lord.
Dewar, Rt Hon. Donald Campbell, 1937–2000, vol. X
Dewar, Douglas, 1875–1957, vol. V
Dewar, George A. B., 1862–1934, vol. III
Dewar, George Duncan Hamilton, 1916–1998, vol. X
Dewar, Sir James, 1842–1923, vol. II
Dewar, John, 1883–1964, vol. VI
Dewar, John Arthur, 1891–1954, vol. V
Dewar, Vice-Adm. Kenneth Gilbert Balmain, 1879–1964, vol. VI
Dewar, Rev. Canon Lindsay, 1891–1976, vol. VII
Dewar, Michael Bruce Urquhart, 1886–1950, vol. IV
Dewar, Michael James Steuart, 1918–1997, vol. X
Dewar, Brig. Michael Preston Douglas, 1906–1984, vol. VIII
Dewar, Robert, 1882–1956, vol. V
Dewar, Vice-Adm. Robert Gordon Douglas, died 1948, vol. IV
Dewar, Thomas Finlayson, 1866–1929, vol. III
Dewar, William McLachlan, 1905–1979, vol. VII
Dewas State, Maharaja Tukoji Rao Puar, 1888–1937, vol. III
de Watteville, Lt-Col Herman Gaston, 1875–1963, vol. VI
de Watteville, John Edward, 1892–1976, vol. VII
Dewdney, Rt Rev. Alfred Daniel Alexander, 1863–1945, vol. IV
Dewdney, Ven. Arthur John Bible, died 1946, vol. IV
Dewdney, Duncan Alexander Cox, 1911–1999, vol. X
de Wend-Fenton, West Fenton, 1881–1920, vol. II

Dewes, Sir Herbert John Salisbury, 1897–1988, vol. VIII
de Wesselow, Owen Lambert Vaughan, 1883–1959, vol. V
De Wet, Gen. Hon. Christian Rudolf, 1854–1922, vol. II
De Wet, Sir Jacobus Albertus, 1840–1911, vol. I
De Wet, Sir Jacobus Petrus, 1838–1900, vol. I
De Wet, Rt Hon. Nicolas Jacobus, 1873–1960, vol. V
de Wet, Captain Thomas Oloff, 1869–1940, vol. III
Dewey, (Alexander) Gordon, 1890–1953, vol. V
Dewey, Cyril Marston, 1907–1973, vol. VII
Dewey, Rt Rev. Mgr Edward, 1884–1965, vol. VI
Dewey, George, 1837–1917, vol. II
Dewey, Gordon; see Dewey, A. G.
Dewey, John, 1859–1952, vol. V
Dewey, Kenneth Thomas, 1902–1961, vol. VI
Dewey, Rev. Sir Stanley Daws, 2nd Bt, 1867–1948, vol. IV
Dewey, Sir Thomas Charles, 1st Bt, 1840–1926, vol. II
Dewey, Thomas Edmund, 1902–1971, vol. VII
Dewhurst, Captain Gerard Powys, 1872–1956, vol. V
Dewhurst, Lt-Comdr Harry, 1866–1931, vol. III
Dewhurst, Keith Ward, 1924–1984, vol. VIII
Dewhurst, Comdr Ronald Hugh, 1905–1990, vol. VIII
Dewhurst, Timothy Littleton, 1920–1993, vol. IX
Dewhurst, Wynford, died 1941, vol. IV
Dewick, Rev. E. C., 1884–1958, vol. V
De Windt, Harry, 1856–1933, vol. III
Dewing, Maj.-Gen. Maurice Nelson, 1896–1976, vol. VII
Dewing, Maj.-Gen. Richard Henry, 1891–1981, vol. VIII
de Winton, Brig.-Gen. Charles, 1860–1943, vol. IV
de Winton, Charles Henry, 1856–1936, vol. III
de Winton, Sir Francis Walter, 1835–1901, vol. I
de Winton, Ven. Frederic Henry, 1852–1932, vol. III
de Winton, Walter Bernard, 1850–1944, vol. IV
de Winton, Wilfred Seymour, 1856–1929, vol. III
DeWitt, Norman Wentworth, 1876–1958, vol. V
De Wolf, Vice-Adm. Harry George, 1903–2000, vol. X
Dewolfe, Rev. Henry Todd, 1867–1947, vol. IV
de Wolff, Brig. Charles Esmond, 1893–1986, vol. VIII
Dewrance, Sir John, 1858–1937, vol. III
Dews, Peter, 1929–1997, vol. X
Dewsnup, Ernest Ritson, 1874–1950, vol. IV
Dexter, Harold, 1920–2000, vol. X
Dexter, John, 1925–1990, vol. VIII
Dexter, Keith, 1928–1989, vol. VIII
Dexter, Walter, 1877–1944, vol. IV
Dexter, Walter, 1876–1958, vol. V
Dextraze, Gen. Jacques Alfred, 1919–1993, vol. IX
Dey, George Goodair, 1876–1955, vol. V
Dey, Helen, 1888–1968, vol. VI
Deym, Count; Franz de Paula, 1838–1903, vol. I
d'Eyncourt, Edmund Charles T.; see Tennyson-d'Eyncourt.

d'Eyncourt, Adm. Edwin Clayton Tennyson, *died* 1903, vol. I
d'Eyncourt, Sir Eustace Henry William T.; *see* Tennyson-d'Eyncourt.
d'Eyncourt, Sir Gervais T.; *see* Tennyson d'Eyncourt, Sir E. G.
d'Eyncourt, Sir Giles Gervais T.; *see* Tennyson-d'Eyncourt.
d'Eyncourt, Sir Jeremy T.; *see* Tennyson-d'Eyncourt, Sir John J. E.
d'Eyncourt, Sir (John) Jeremy (Eustace) T.; *see* Tennyson-d'Eyncourt.
de Young, Michel Harry, 1849–1925, vol. II
de Zouche, Dorothy Eva, 1886–1969, vol. VI
De Zoysa, Sir Cyril, 1897–1978, vol. VII
de Zulueta, Sir Philip Francis; *see* Zulueta.
Dhar, Lt-Col HH Maharaja Sir Udaji Rao Puar Major, Bahadur, 1886–1926, vol. II
Dharampur, Maharana of, 1863–1921, vol. II
D'Harcourt, Robert, 1881–1965, vol. VI(AII)
d'Hardelot, Guy; *see* Rhodes, Mrs Helen.
d'Hautpoul, Marquis, 1859–1934, vol. III
D'Herelle, Felix H., 1873–1949, vol. IV
Dhingra, Sir Behari Lal, 1873–1936, vol. III
Dholpur, Maharaj Rana of, 1893–1954, vol. V
Dholpur, Captain HH, 1883–1911, vol. I
Dhondup, Rai Bahadur Norbhu, *died* 1943, vol. IV
Dhrangadhra, Maharaja Raj Saheb of, 1889–1942, vol. IV
Diack, Sir Alexander Henderson, 1862–1929, vol. III
Diaghileff, Serge de, 1872–1929, vol. III
Diamand, Peter, 1913–1998, vol. X
Diamand, Arthur Sigismund, 1897–1978, vol. VII
Diamond, Charles, 1858–1934, vol. III
Diamond, George Clifford, 1902–1985, vol. VIII
Diamond, George le Boutillier, 1893–1964, vol. VI
Diamond, Jack, 1912–1990, vol. VIII
Diamond, Sir William Henry, 1865–1941, vol. IV
Diaz, Maresciallo d'Italia Armando, 1861–1928, vol. II
Diaz, Sir Porfirio, 1830–1915, vol. I
Dibben, Major Cecil Reginald, 1885–1965, vol. VI
Dibblee, George Binney, 1868–1952, vol. V
Dibbs, Alexander; *see* Dibbs, A. H. A.
Dibbs, (Arthur Henry) Alexander, 1918–1985, vol. VIII
Dibbs, Hon. Sir George Richard, 1834–1904, vol. I
Dibbs, Sir Thomas Allwright, 1832–1923, vol. II
Dibden, Edgar, 1888–1971, vol. VII
Dibdin, Aubrey, 1892–1958, vol. V
Dibdin, Charles, 1849–1910, vol. I
Dibdin, Edward Rimbault, 1853–1941, vol. IV
Dibdin, Sir Lewis Tonna, 1852–1938, vol. III
Dibdin, Sir Robert William, 1848–1933, vol. III
Dibdin, William Joseph, 1850–1925, vol. II
Dible, James Henry, *died* 1971, vol. VII
Dible, James Kenneth Victor, 1890–1976, vol. VII
Dible, William Cuthbert, 1886–1971, vol. VII
Dibley, Rear-Adm. Albert Kingsley, 1890–1958, vol. V
Dicconson, Hon. Robert Joseph Gerard-, 1857–1918, vol. II
Dicey, Albert Venn, 1835–1922, vol. II
Dicey, Edward, 1832–1911, vol. I

Dick, Air Vice-Marshal (Alan) David, 1924–1999, vol. X
Dick, Bt Col Alan Macdonald, 1884–1970, vol. VI
Dick, Alick Sydney, 1916–1986, vol. VIII
Dick, Brig.-Gen. Archibald Campbell Douglas, 1847–1927, vol. II
Dick, Col Sir Arthur Robert, 1860–1943, vol. IV
Dick, Charles George Cotsford, 1846–1911, vol. I
Dick, Clare L.; *see* Lawson Dick.
Dick, Air Vice-Marshal David; *see* Dick, Air Vice-Marshal A. D.
Dick, Lt-Col Dighton Hay Abercromby, 1869–1941, vol. IV
Dick, George Paris, 1866–1941, vol. IV
Dick, George Williamson Auchinvole, 1914–1997, vol. X
Dick, Gladys; *see* Ripley, G.
Dick, Henry Charles, 1872–1946, vol. IV
Dick, Col James Adam, 1866–1942, vol. IV
Dick, Sir James Nicholas, 1832–1920, vol. II
Dick, John, 1902–1970, vol. VI
Dick, Sir John Alexander, 1920–1994, vol. IX
Dick, John Kenneth, 1913–1997, vol. X
Dick, John Lawson, 1870–1944, vol. IV
Dick, Cdre John Mathew, 1899–1981, vol. VIII
Dick, Captain Quintin, 1847–1923, vol. II
Dick, Brig.-Gen. Robert Nicholas, 1879–1967, vol. VI
Dick, Rear-Adm. Roger Mylius, 1897–1991, vol. IX
Dick, Sir W(illiam) R.; *see* Reid Dick.
Dick-Cunyngham, Major Sir Colin Keith; *see* Cunyngham.
Dick-Cunyngham, Maj.-Gen. James Keith, 1877–1935, vol. III
Dick-Cunyngham of Lamburghtoun, Sir Robert Keith Alexander; *see* Cunyngham.
Dick-Cunyngham, Lt-Col William Henry; *see* Cunyngham.
Dick-Lauder, Sir George Andrew; *see* Lauder.
Dick-Lauder, Sir George William Dalrymple; *see* Lauder.
Dick-Lauder, Lt-Col Sir John North Dalrymple; *see* Lauder.
Dick-Lauder, Sir Thomas North; *see* Lauder.
Dick-Read, Grantly; *see* Read.
Dicken, Adm. Charles Gauntlett, 1854–1937, vol. III
Dicken, Charles Shortt, 1841–1902, vol. I
Dicken, Charles Vernon, 1881–1955, vol. V
Dicken, Rear-Adm. Edward Bernard Cornish, 1888–1964, vol. VI
Dicken, Col William Popham, 1834–1912, vol. I
Dickens, Craven Hildesley, 1822–1900, vol. I
Dickens, Frank, 1899–1986, vol. VIII
Dickens, Geoffrey Kenneth, 1931–1995, vol. IX
Dickens, Adm. Sir Gerald Charles, 1879–1962, vol. VI
Dickens, Sir Henry Fielding, 1849–1933, vol. III
Dickens, Sir Louis Walter, 1903–1988, vol. VIII
Dickens, Mary Angela, *died* 1948, vol. IV
Dickens, Monica Enid, (Mrs R. O. Stratton), 1915–1992, vol. IX
Dickens, Air Cdre Thomas Charles, 1906–1972, vol. VII
Dickenson, Lt-Col Edward Stanley Newton, *died* 1910, vol. I

Dickenson, Rev. Lenthall Greville T.; *see* Trotman-Dickenson.
Dickeson, Sir Richard, 1823–1900, vol. I
Dickey, Rev. Charles A., *died* 1910, vol. I
Dickey, Edward Montgomery O'Rorke, 1894–1977, vol. VII
Dickey, Robert H. F., 1856–1915, vol. I
Dickie, Archibald Campbell, 1868–1941, vol. IV
Dickie, Captain David, 1880–1930, vol. III
Dickie, Rev. Edgar Primrose, 1897–1991, vol. IX
Dickie, Rev. James F., 1845–1933, vol. III
Dickie, Very Rev. John, 1875–1942, vol. IV
Dickie, Maj.-Gen. John Elford, 1856–1939, vol. III
Dickie, William, 1856–1919, vol. II
Dickin, Maria Elisabeth, 1870–1951, vol. V
Dickins, Aileen Marian, 1917–1987, vol. VIII
Dickins, Basil Gordon, 1908–1996, vol. X
Dickins, Bruce, 1889–1978, vol. VII
Dickins, Brig. Frederick, 1879–1975, vol. VII
Dickins, Frederick Victor, 1838–1915, vol. I
Dickins, Rev. Henry Compton, 1838–1920, vol. II
Dickins, Col Spencer William Scrase-, 1862–1919, vol. II
Dickins, Rev. Thomas Bourne, 1832–1919, vol. II
Dickins, Col Vernon William Frank, 1867–1942, vol. IV
Dickins, Ven. William Arthur, *died* 1921, vol. II
Dickins, Maj.-Gen. William Drummond S.; *see* Scrase-Dickins.
Dickinson, 1st Baron, 1859–1943, vol. IV
Dickinson, Sir Alwin Robinson, 1873–1944, vol. IV
Dickinson, Anne Hepple, 1877–1959, vol. V
Dickinson, Arthur Harold, 1892–1978, vol. VII
Dickinson, Sir Arthur Lowes, 1859–1935, vol. III
Dickinson, Ven. Charles Henry, 1871–1930, vol. III
Dickinson, Croft; *see* Dickinson, W. C.
Dickinson, Maj.-Gen. Douglas Povah, 1886–1949, vol. IV
Dickinson, Frederic William, 1856–1922, vol. II
Dickinson, Gladys, 1895–1964, vol. VI
Dickinson, Goldsworthy Lowes, 1862–1932, vol. III
Dickinson, Henry Douglas, 1899–1969, vol. VI
Dickinson, Very Rev. Hercules Henry, 1827–1905, vol. I
Dickinson, James, *died* 1933, vol. III
Dickinson, Sir John, 1848–1933, vol. III
Dickinson, John Alfred Ernst, 1859–1933, vol. III
Dickinson, Rt Rev. John Hubert, 1901–1993, vol. IX
Dickinson, Major Neville Hope Campbell, 1862–1935, vol. III
Dickinson, Rear-Adm. Norman Vincent, 1901–1981, vol. VIII
Dickinson, Patric Thomas, 1914–1994, vol. IX
Dickinson, Reginald Percy, 1914–1987, vol. VIII
Dickinson, Hon. Richard Sebastian Willoughby, 1897–1935, vol. III
Dickinson, Robert Edmund, 1862–1947, vol. IV
Dickinson, Robert Eric, 1905–1981, vol. VIII
Dickinson, Ronald Arthur, 1910–1986, vol. VIII
Dickinson, Ronald Sigismund Shepherd, 1906–1984, vol. VIII
Dickinson, Thomas Vincent, 1858–1941, vol. IV
Dickinson, Thorold Barron, 1903–1984, vol. VIII
Dickinson, Lt-Col William, 1831–1917, vol. II
Dickinson, W(illiam) Croft, 1897–1963, vol. VI

Dickinson, William Howship, 1832–1913, vol. I
Dickinson, Col William Vicris, 1856–1917, vol. II
Dicks, Captain Henry Leage, 1870–1942, vol. IV
Dicksee, Sir Francis Bernard, (Frank), 1853–1928, vol. II
Dicksee, Frank; *see* Dicksee, Sir F. B.
Dicksee, Herbert, 1862–1942, vol. IV
Dicksee, Lawrence Robert, 1864–1932, vol. III
Dickson, Rt Hon. Lord; Scott Dickson, 1850–1922, vol. II
Dickson, Alec; *see* Dickson, Alexander G.
Dickson, Alexander Graeme, (Alec), 1914–1994, vol. IX
Dickson, Bertram Thomas, 1886–1982, vol. VIII
Dickson, Bonner William Arthur, 1887–1976, vol. VII
Dickson, Rt Hon. Brian, 1916–1998, vol. X
Dickson, Charles Gordon, 1884–1963, vol. VI
Dickson, Gen. Sir Collingwood, 1817–1904, vol. I
Dickson, Rev. Canon Daniel Eccles Lucas, *died* 1924, vol. II
Dickson, David, 1908–1982, vol. VIII
Dickson, Air Vice-Marshal Edward Dalziel, 1895–1979, vol. VII
Dickson, Maj.-Gen. Edward Thompson, 1850–1938, vol. III
Dickson, Eileen Wadham, 1908–1997, vol. X
Dickson, Frank, 1862–1936, vol. III
Dickson, Lt-Col George Arthur Hamilton, 1863–1918, vol. II
Dickson, Lt-Col Harold Richard Patrick, 1881–1959, vol. V
Dickson, Rev. Henry Granville, 1844–1929, vol. III
Dickson, Henry Newton, 1866–1922, vol. II
Dickson, (Horatio Henry) Lovat, 1902–1987, vol. VIII
Dickson, Ian Anderson, 1905–1982, vol. VIII
Dickson, James, 1859–1941, vol. IV
Dickson, James Douglas Hamilton, 1849–1931, vol. III
Dickson, James Hill, 1863–1938, vol. III
Dickson, Hon. Sir James Robert, 1832–1901, vol. I
Dickson, Maj.-Gen. John Baillie Ballantyne, 1842–1925, vol. II
Dickson, John Abernethy, 1915–1994, vol. IX
Dickson, John Harold, 1898–1967, vol. VI
Dickson, Col John Herbert, 1867–1938, vol. III
Dickson, John Robert, 1884–1937, vol. III
Dickson, Lovat; *see* Dickson, H. H. L.
Dickson, Lt-Col Maurice Rhynd, 1882–1940, vol. III
Dickson, Murray Graeme, 1911–1997, vol. X
Dickson, Norman Bonnington, 1868–1944, vol. IV
Dickson, Rear-Adm. Robert Kirk, 1898–1952, vol. V
Dickson, Scott; *see* Dickson, Rt Hon. Lord.
Dickson, Spencer Stuart, 1873–1951, vol. V
Dickson, Rt Hon. Thomas Alexander, 1833–1909, vol. I
Dickson, Rev. Thomas Knox Whitaker, *died* 1931, vol. III
Dickson, Thomas S., 1885–1935, vol. III
Dickson, Dame Violet Penelope, 1896–1991, vol. IX

Dickson, Brig.-Gen. William Edmund Ritchie, 1871–1957, vol. V
Dickson, Rev. William Edward, 1823–1910, vol. I
Dickson, William Elliot Carnegie, 1878–1954, vol. V
Dickson, William Everard, died 1945, vol. IV
Dickson, Marshal of the Royal Air Force Sir William Forster, 1898–1987, vol. VIII
Dickson, William Kirk, 1860–1949, vol. IV
Dickson, Rev. William Purdle, 1823–1901, vol. I
Dickson, Lt-Gen. William Thomas, 1830–1909, vol. I
Dickson Wright, Arthur; see Wright.
Diddams, Harry John Charles, 1864–1929, vol. III
Didon, Very Rev. Fr Henri, 1840–1900, vol. I
Didsbury, Brian, 1926–1970, vol. VI
Dieckhoff, Hans Heinrich, 1884–1952, vol. V
Diederichs, Hon. Nicolaas, 1903–1978, vol. VII
Diefenbaker, Rt Hon. John George, 1895–1979, vol. VII
Diehl, Alice Mangold, died 1912, vol. I
Diels, Otto Paul Hermann, 1876–1954, vol. V
Diesel, Rudolf, 1858–1913, vol. I
Dietrich, Maria Magdalena; see Dietrich, Marlene.
Dietrich, Marlene, 1901–1992, vol. IX
Digan, Lt-Col Augustine J., 1878–1926, vol. II
Digby, 10th Baron, 1846–1920, vol. II
Digby, 11th Baron, 1894–1964, vol. VI
Digby, Comdr Edward Aylmer, 1883–1935, vol. III
Digby, Col Hon. Everard Charles, 1852–1914, vol. I
Digby, Col Frederick James Bosworth Digby Wingfield, 1885–1952, vol. V
Digby, George F. Wingfield, 1911–1989, vol. VIII
Digby, Hon. Gerald Fitzmaurice, 1858–1942, vol. IV
Digby, John Kenelm Digby Wingfield, 1859–1904, vol. I
Digby, Sir Kenelm Edward, 1836–1916, vol. II
Digby, Kenelm George, 1890–1944, vol. IV
Digby, Kenelm Hutchinson, 1884–1954, vol. V
Digby, Hon. Robert Henry, 1903–1959, vol. V
Digby, Samuel, died 1925, vol. II
Digby, Simon Wingfield, 1910–1998, vol. X
Digby, Ven. Stephen Basil W.; see Wingfield-Digby.
Digby, Rev. Stephen Harold Wingfield, 1872–1942, vol. IV
Digby, William, 1849–1904, vol. I
Digby-Beste, Captain Sir Henry Aloysius Bruno 1883–1964, vol. VI
Diggines, Christopher Ewart, 1920–1990, vol. VIII
Diggines, Sir William Ewart, 1881–1952, vol. V
Diggle, F. Holt, 1886–1942, vol. IV
Diggle, Rt Rev. John William, 1847–1920, vol. II
Diggle, Joseph Robert, 1849–1917, vol. II
Diggle, Captain Neston William, 1880–1963, vol. VI
Diggle, Rev. Reginald Fraser, 1889–1975, vol. VII
Diggle, Wadham Neston, 1848–1934, vol. III
Dignan, Most Rev. John, died 1953, vol. V
Dike, Kenneth Onwuka, 1917–1983, vol. VIII
Dilhorne, 1st Viscount, 1905–1980, vol. VII
Dilke, Beaumont Albany F.; see Fetherstone-Dilke.
Dilke, Rt Hon. Sir Charles Wentworth, 2nd Bt, 1843–1911, vol. I

Dilke, Sir Charles Wentworth, 3rd Bt, 1874–1918, vol. II
Dilke, Emilia Francis, (Lady Dilke), 1840–1904, vol. I
Dilke, Sir Fisher Wentworth, 4th Bt, 1877–1944, vol. IV
Dilke, Sir John Fisher Wentworth, 5th Bt, 1906–1998, vol. X
Dill, Sir Bayard,; see Dill, Sir. N. B.
Dill, Field-Marshal Sir John Greer, 1881–1944, vol. IV
Dill, Sir (Nicholas) Bayard, 1905–1993, vol. IX
Dill, Very Rev. S. Marcus, 1843–1924, vol. II
Dill, Sir Samuel, 1844–1924, vol. II
Dill-Russell, Patrick Wimberley, 1910–1977, vol. VII
Dilley, Sir Arthur George, 1854–1938, vol. III
Dilling, Walter James, 1886–1950, vol. IV
Dillingham, Cyril Claud, 1886–1943, vol. IV
Dillistone, Rev. Canon Frederick William, 1903–1993, vol. IX
Dillon, 17th Viscount, 1844–1932, vol. III
Dillon, 18th Viscount, 1875–1934, vol. III
Dillon, 19th Viscount, 1881–1946, vol. IV
Dillon, 20th Viscount, 1911–1979, vol. VII
Dillon, 21st Viscount, 1945–1982, vol. VIII
Dillon, Hon. Conrad Adderly, 1845–1901, vol. I
Dillon, Captain Constantine Theobold Francis, 1873–1920, vol. II
Dillon, Emile Joseph, 1854–1933, vol. III
Dillon, Frank, 1823–1909, vol. I
Dillon, Frederick, 1887–1965, vol. VI
Dillon, Lt-Col George Frederick Horace, 1859–1906, vol. I
Dillon, Hon. Harry Lee Stanton; L., see Lee-Dillon.
Dillon, Major Henry Mountford, 1881–1918, vol. II
Dillon, John, 1851–1927, vol. II
Dillon, Sir John Fox, 7th Bt, 1843–1925, vol. II
Dillon, Sir John Vincent, 1908–1992, vol. IX
Dillon, Malcolm, 1859–1945, vol. IV
Dillon, Gen. Sir Martin Andrew, 1826–1913, vol. I
Dillon, Sir Max, 1913–1995, vol. IX (AII)
Dillon, Sir Robert William Charlier, 8th Bt, 1914–1982, vol. VIII
Dillon, Comdr Stafford Harry, 1887–1935, vol. III
Dillon, Thomas, 1884–1971, vol. VII
Dillwyn-Llewelyn, Sir John Talbot; see Llewelyn.
Dillwyn-Venables-Llewelyn, Sir Charles Leyshon; see Venables-Llewelyn.
Dillwyn-Venables-Llewelyn, Brig. Sir Michael; see Venables-Llewelyn, Brig. Sir C. M. D.
Dilnot, Frank, 1875–1946, vol. IV
Dilworth, W. J., 1863–1922, vol. II
Dilworth-Harrison, Ven. Talbot, 1886–1975, vol. VII
Di Maria, Most Rev. Pietro, 1865–1937, vol. III
Dimbleby, Richard, 1913–1965, vol. VI
Dimmer, Lt-Col John Henry Stephen, 1884–1918, vol. II
Dimmitt, Hon. James Albert, 1888–1957, vol. V
Dimnet, Very Rev. Abbè Ernest, 1866–1954, vol. V
Dimoline, Hon. Brig. Harry Kenneth, 1903–1972, vol. VI
Dimoline, Maj.-Gen. William Alfred, 1897–1965, vol. VI

Dimond, Maj.-Gen. William Elliot Randal, 1893–1960, vol. V
Dimont, Rev. Canon Charles Tunnacliff, 1872–1953, vol. V
Dimsdale, 6th Baron of the Russian Empire, 1828–1898, vol. I
Dimsdale, 7th Baron of the Russian Empire, 1856–1928, vol. II
Dimsdale, Mrs Helen Easdale, 1907–1977, vol. VII
Dimsdale, Sir John Holdsworth, 2nd Bt, 1874–1923, vol. II
Dimsdale, Sir John Holdsworth, 3rd Bt, 1901–1978, vol. VII
Dimsdale, Rt Hon. Sir Joseph Cockfield, 1st Bt, 1849–1912, vol. I
Dimsey, Surg. Rear-Adm. Edgar Ralph, 1861–1930, vol. III
Dimson, Gladys Felicia, (Mrs S. B. Dimson), 1917–1999, vol. X
Dinajpur, Bahadur of, 1860–1919, vol. II
D'Indy, (Paul Marie Théodore) Vincent, 1851–1931, vol. III
D'Indy, Vincent; *see* D'Indy, P. M. T. V.
Dineen, Rev. Canon Frederick George K.; *see* Kerr-Dineen.
Dines, Henry George, 1891–1964, vol. VI
Dines, William Henry, 1855–1927, vol. II
Dinesen, Isak, (Karen Blixen Finecke), 1885–1962, vol. VI
Dinesen, Thomas, 1892–1979, vol. VII
Dingle, Aylward Edward, *died* 1947, vol. IV
Dingle, Herbert, 1890–1978, vol. VII
Dingle, Percival Alfred, 1881–1963, vol. VI
Dingle, Sir Philip Burrington, 1906–1978, vol. VII
Dingley, Allen Roy, 1892–1978, vol. VII
Dingli, Sir Adriano, 1817–1900, vol. I
Dingwall, Baroness; *see* Lucas of Crudwell and Dingwall.
Dingwall, Eric John, 1890–1986, vol. VIII
Dingwall, John James, 1907–1996, vol. X
Dingwall, Walter Spender, 1900–1990, vol. VIII
Dingwall-Fordyce, Alexander, 1875–1940, vol. III
Dinkel, Ernest Michael, 1894–1983, vol. VIII
Dinkel, Michael; *see* Dinkel, E. M.
Dinneen, Rev. Patrick Stephen, *died* 1934, vol. III
Dinsdale, Richard Lewis, 1907–1995, vol. IX
Dinshaw, Sir Hormusjee Cowasjee, 1857–1939, vol. III
Dinwiddie, Melville, 1892–1975, vol. VII
Dinwiddy, Thomas Lutwyche, 1905–1992, vol. IX
Dinwoody, Very Rev. Loefric Matthews H.; *see* Hay-Dinwoody.
Diogenes; *see* Brown, W. J.
Dionisotti-Casalone, Carlo, 1908–1998, vol. X
Dionne, Narcisse-Eutrope, 1848–1917, vol. II
Dior, Christian Ernest, 1905–1957, vol. V
Diósy, Arthur, 1856–1923, vol. II
Diplock, Baron (Life Peer); (William John) Kenneth Diplock, 1907–1985, vol. VIII
Diplock, Anthony Tytherleigh, 1935–2000, vol. X
Dippie, Herbert, 1885–1945, vol. IV
Dirac, Paul Adrien Maurice, 1902–1984, vol. VIII
Dircks, Rudolf, *died* 1936, vol. III
Dirksen, Herbert von, 1882–1955, vol. V

Disbrowe-Wise, Lt-Col Henry Edward Disbrowe; *see* Wise.
Disher, Maurice Willson, 1893–1969, vol. VI
Disney, Harold Vernon, 1907–1998, vol. X
Disney, Lt-Col Henry Anthony Patrick, 1893–1974, vol. VII
Disney, Henry William, 1858–1925, vol. II
Disney, Hon. Sir James, 1896–1952, vol. V
Disney, Walter E., 1901–1966, vol. VI
Disraeli, Coningsby Ralph, 1867–1936, vol. III
Distant, William Lucas, 1845–1922, vol. II
Disturnal, William Josiah, *died* 1923, vol. II
Ditchburn, Robert William, 1903–1987, vol. VIII
Ditchfield, Rt Rev. John Edwin.; *see* Watts-Ditchfield.
Ditchfield, Rev. Peter Hampson, 1854–1930, vol. III
Ditmars, Raymond Lee, 1876–1942, vol. IV
Ditmas, Lt-Col Francis Ivan Leslie, 1876–1969, vol. VI
Ditzen, Rudolf, 1893–1947, vol. IV
Dive, Lt-Col Gilbert Henry, 1882–1939, vol. III
Diver, Captain Cyril Roper Pollock, 1892–1969, vol. VI
Diver, (Katherine Helen) Maud, *died* 1945, vol. IV
Diver, Hon. Sir Leslie Charles, 1899–1996, vol. IX (AII)
Diver, Maud; *see* Diver, K. H. M.
Diverres, Armel Hugh, 1914–1998, vol. X
Divers, Edward, 1837–1912, vol. I
Divers, Brig. Sydney Thomas, 1896–1979, vol. VII
Divine, Arthur Durham (David Divine), 1904–1987, vol. VIII
Divine, David; *see* Divine, A. D.
Dix, Bernard Hubert, 1925–1995, vol. IX
Dix, Comdr Charles Cabry, 1881–1951, vol. V
Dix, Dorothy Knight; *see* Waddy, D. K.
Dix, G. E. A., *see* Dix, Rev. Dom Gregory.
Dix, Rev. G. H., *died* 1932, vol. III
Dix, Rev. Dom Gregory, (G. E. A. Dix), 1901–1952, vol. V
Dix, Victor Wilkinson, *died* 1992, vol. IX
Dixey, Arthur Carlyne Niven, 1889–1954, vol. V
Dixey, Charles Neville Douglas, 1881–1947, vol. IV
Dixey, Sir Frank, 1892–1982, vol. VIII
Dixey, Frederick Augustus, 1855–1935, vol. III
Dixey, Sir Harry Edward, 1853–1927, vol. II
Dixey, Marmaduke; *see* Howard, Geoffrey.
Dixey, Paul Arthur Groser, 1915–1998, vol. X
Dixie, Sir (Alexander Archibald Douglas) Wolstan, 13th Bt, 1910–1975, vol. VII
Dixie, Sir Alexander Beaumont Churchill, 11th Bt, 1851–1924, vol. II
Dixie, Sir Douglas; *see* Dixie, Sir G. D.
Dixie, Llady Florence, 1857–1905, vol. I
Dixie, Sir (George) Douglas, 12th Bt, 1876–1948, vol. IV
Dixie, Sir Wolstan; *see* Dixie, Sir A. A. D. W.
Dixon, Alfred Cardew, 1865–1936, vol. III
Dixon, Sir Alfred Herbert, 1st Bt (cr 1918), 1857–1920, vol. II
Dixon, Amzi Clarence, 1854–1925, vol. II
Dixon, Andrew Francis, *died* 1936, vol. III
Dixon, Arthur Frederic William, 1892–1948, vol. IV
Dixon, Arthur Lee, 1867–1955, vol. V
Dixon, Sir Arthur Lewis, 1881–1969, vol. VI

Dixon, Augustus Edward, 1860–1946, vol. IV
Dixon, Bernard, 1906–1983, vol. VIII
Dixon, Maj.-Gen. Bernard Edward Cooke, 1896–1973, vol. VII
Dixon, Campbell; see Dixon, G. C.
Dixon, Cecil Edith Mary, 1891–1979, vol. VII
Dixon, Charles, 1858–1926, vol. II
Dixon, Charles, 1872–1934, vol. III
Dixon, Charles Harvey, 1862–1923, vol. II
Dixon, Sir Charles William, 1888–1976, vol. VII
Dixon, Rt Hon. Sir Daniel, 1st Bt (cr 1903), 1844–1907, vol. I
Dixon, Maj.-Gen. Edward George, 1837–1918, vol. II
Dixon, Ella Nora Hepworth, died 1932, vol. III
Dixon, Sir Francis Netherwood, 1879–1968, vol. VI
Dixon, Air Vice-Marshal Sir (Francis Wilfred) Peter, 1907–1988, vol. VIII
Dixon, Lt-Col Frederick Alfred, 1880–1925, vol. II
Dixon, George, 1820–1898, vol. I
Dixon, Col Sir George, 1st Bt (cr 1919), 1842–1924, vol. II
Dixon, (George) Campbell, 1895–1960, vol. V
Dixon, Gertrude Caroline, 1886–1966, vol. VI
Dixon, Col Graham Patrick, 1873–1947, vol. IV
Dixon, Guy Holford, 1902–1993, vol. IX
Dixon, Harold Baily, 1852–1930, vol. III
Dixon, Harry, 1861–1941, vol. IV
Dixon, Brig.-Gen. Sir Henry Grey, 1850–1933, vol. III
Dixon, Henry Horatio, 1869–1953, vol. V
Dixon, Henry Sydenham, 1848–1931, vol. III
Dixon, Ven. Henry Thomas, 1874–1939, vol. III
Dixon, Rt Rev. Horace Henry, 1869–1964, vol. VI
Dixon, Hubert John, 1895–1971, vol. VII
Dixon, Jack Shawcross, 1918–1997, vol. X
Dixon, Sir John, 2nd Bt (cr 1919), 1886–1976, vol. VII
Dixon, John Edwin F.; see Fowler-Dixon.
Dixon, Sir John George, 3rd Bt (cr 1919), 1911–1990, vol. VIII
Dixon, Most Rev. John Harkness, 1888–1972, vol. VII
Dixon, John Reginald, 1886–1972, vol. VII
Dixon, Kendal Cartwright, 1911–1990, vol. VIII
Dixon, Captain Kennet, died 1927, vol. II
Dixon, Kevin, 1902–1959, vol. V
Dixon, Leslie Charles G.; see Graham-Dixon.
Dixon, Malcolm, 1899–1985, vol. VIII
Dixon, Margaret Rumer Haynes; see Godden, Rumer.
Dixon, Maj.-Gen. Matthew Charles, 1821–1905, vol. I
Dixon, Michael George, 1920–1990, vol. VIII
Dixon, Lt-Col Oscar, 1883–1966, vol. VI
Dixon, Rt Hon. Sir Owen, 1886–1972, vol. VII
Dixon, Air Vice-Marshal Sir Peter; see Dixon, Air Vice-Marshal Sir F. W. P.
Dixon, Sir Pierson John, 1904–1965, vol. VI
Dixon, Sir Raylton, 1838–1901, vol. I
Dixon, Engr-Vice-Adm. Sir Robert Bland, 1867–1939, vol. III
Dixon, Sir Samuel G.; see Gurney-Dixon.
Dixon, Stanley, 1900–2000, vol. X
Dixon, Stephen Mitchell, died 1940, vol. III

Dixon, Rev. Thomas Harold, died 1963, vol. VI
Dixon, Rt Hon. Sir Thomas James, 2nd Bt (cr 1903), 1868–1950, vol. IV
Dixon, Walter Ernest, 1870–1931, vol. III
Dixon, Lt-Col William, 1868–1958, vol. V
Dixon, William Gray, 1854–1928, vol. II
Dixon, William Macneile, 1866–1946, vol. IV
Dixon, Gp Captain William Michael, 1920–1999, vol. X
Dixon, Sir William Vibart, 1850–1930, vol. III
Dixon-Hartland, Sir Frederick Dixon, 1st Bt, 1832–1909, vol. I
Dixon-Nuttall, Major William Francis, 1885–1981, vol. VIII
Dixon-Spain, John Edward, died 1955, vol. V
Dixon-Wright, Rev. Henry Dixon, 1870–1916, vol. II
Dixson, Sir Hugh, 1841–1926, vol. II
Dixson, Sir William, 1870–1952, vol. V
Dixwell-Oxenden, Sir Percy Dixwell Nowell; see Oxenden.
Doak, Sir James, 1904–1975, vol. VII
Doane, Rt Rev. W. Crosswell, 1832–1913, vol. I
Dobb, Erlam Stanley, 1910–1996, vol. X
Dobb, Harry, 1867–1928, vol. II
Dobb, Maurice Herbert, 1900–1976, vol. VII
Dobbie, Edward David, 1857–1915, vol. I
Dobbie, Sir James Johnston, 1852–1924, vol. II
Dobbie, Sir Joseph, 1862–1943, vol. IV
Dobbie, Mitchell Macdonald, 1901–1982, vol. VIII
Dobbie, William, 1878–1950, vol. IV
Dobbie, Lt-Gen. Sir William George Sheddon, 1879–1964, vol. VI
Dobbie, William Herbert, 1851–1941, vol. IV
Dobbie, Brig.-Gen. William Hugh, 1859–1922, vol. II
Dobbie-Bateman, Rev. Arthur Fitzroy, 1897–1974, vol. VII
Dobbin, Sir Alfred Graham, 1853–1942, vol. IV
Dobbin, Gertrude; see Page, G.
Dobbin, Brig.-Gen. Herbert Thomas, 1878–1946, vol. IV
Dobbin, Lt-Col Leonard George William, 1871–1936, vol. III
Dobbin, Lt-Col William James Knowles, 1856–1926, vol. II
Dobbing, John, 1922–1999, vol. X
Dobbs, Cecil Moore, 1882–1969, vol. VI
Dobbs, Col Charles Fairlie, 1872–1936, vol. III
Dobbs, Sir Henry Robert Conway, 1871–1934, vol. III
Dobbs, Lt-Col Richard Conway, 1878–1957, vol. V
Dobbs, Richard Heyworth, 1905–1980, vol. VII
Dobell, Lt-Gen. Sir Charles Macpherson, 1869–1954, vol. V
Dobell, Clifford, 1886–1949, vol. IV
Dobell, Air Cdre Frederic Osborne Storey, 1912–1965, vol. VI
Dobell, Rev. Joseph, 1844–1908, vol. I
Dobell, Hon. Richard Reid, 1837–1902, vol. I
Dobell, Sir William, 1899–1970, vol. VI
Dobereiner, Peter Arthur Bertram, 1925–1996, vol. X
Dobie, Very Rev. George Nelson, died 1933, vol. III
Dobie, Marryat Ross, 1888–1973, vol. VII

Dobie, William Jardine, 1892–1956, vol. V
Dobinson, Charles Henry, 1903–1980, vol. VII
Dobie, Rev. Gilbert Hunter, 1880–1945, vol. IV
Dobree, Alfred, 1864–1937, vol. III
Dobrée, Lt-Col Bonamy, 1891–1974, vol. VII
Dobree, Claude Hatherley, died 1960, vol. V, vol. VI
Dobree, George, 1873–1907, vol. I
Dobree, John Hatherley, 1914–1999, vol. X
Dobree, Rev. Osmond, 1832–1929, vol. III
Dobson, Alban Tabor Austin, 1885–1962, vol. VI
Dobson, Hon. Alfred, 1848–1908, vol. I
Dobson, Maj.-Gen. Anthony Henry George, 1911–1987, vol. VIII
Dobson, Sir Arthur Dudley, 1841–1934, vol. III
Dobson, Sir Benjamin Alfred, 1847–1898, vol. I
Dobson, Bernard Henry, 1881–1945, vol. IV
Dobson, Rear-Adm. Claude Congreve, 1885–1940, vol. III
Dobson, Cowan, died 1980, vol. VII
Dobson, Sir Denis William, 1908–1995, vol. IX
Dobson, Eric John, 1913–1984, vol. VIII
Dobson, Lt-Col Francis George, 1879–1941, vol. IV
Dobson, Frank, 1888–1963, vol. VI
Dobson, George, died 1938, vol. III
Dobson, Gordon Miller Bourne, 1889–1976, vol. VII
Dobson, Henry Austin, 1840–1921, vol. II
Dobson, Henry John, 1858–1928, vol. II
Dobson, John Frederic, 1875–1947, vol. IV
Dobson, Cdre John Petter, 1901–1985, vol. VIII
Dobson, Lt-Col Joseph Henry, 1878–1954, vol. V
Dobson, Mildred Eaton, died 1952, vol. V
Dobson, Raymond Francis Harvey, 1925–1980, vol. VII
Dobson, Sir Richard Portway, 1914–1993, vol. IX
Dobson, Richard Rhimes, 1877–1960, vol. V
Dobson, Sir Roy Hardy, 1891–1968, vol. VI
Dobson, Sydney George, 1883–1969, vol. VI
Dobson, Thomas William, 1853–1935, vol. III
Dobson, William Charles Thomas, 1817–1898, vol. I
Dobson, Sir William Lambert, 1833–1898, vol. I
Dobson, Col Sir William Warrington, 1861–1941, vol. IV
Docker, Sir Bernard Dudley Frank, 1896–1978, vol. VII
Docker, Frank Dudley, 1862–1944, vol. IV
Docker, Ludford Charles, 1860–1940, vol. III
Docker, Rev. Wilfrid Brougham, 1882–1956, vol. V
Dockrell, Benjamin Morgan, 1860–1920, vol. II
Dockrell, Sir Maurice Edward, 1850–1929, vol. III
Dockrill, Col Walter R., 1877–1942, vol. IV
Dod, Brig.-Gen. Owen Cadogan W.; see Wolley-Dod.
Dodd, Brig. Arthur Harvey Russell, 1883–1955, vol. V
Dodd, Catherine I., died 1932, vol. III
Dodd, Charles Edward Shuter, 1891–1974, vol. VII
Dodd, Rev. Charles Harold, 1884–1973, vol. VII
Dodd, Cyril, died 1913, vol. I
Dodd, Sir Edward James, 1909–1966, vol. VI
Dodd, Sir Edwin, died 1933, vol. III
Dodd, Francis, 1874–1949, vol. IV
Dodd, Air Vice-Marshal Frank Leslie, 1919–1993, vol. IX

Dodd, Frederick Henry, 1890–1950, vol. IV
Dodd, Major George, 1872–1914, vol. I
Dodd, Rev. Harold, 1899–1987, vol. VIII
Dodd, Henry Work, died 1921, vol. II
Dodd, James Munro, 1915–1986, vol. VIII
Dodd, Col John Richard, 1858–1930, vol. III
Dodd, Sir John Samuel, 1904–1973, vol. VII
Dodd, Norris Edward, 1879–1968, vol. VI
Dodd, Sir Robert John Sherwood, 1878–1950, vol. IV
Dodd, Stanley, died 1946, vol. IV
Dodd, Col Wilfrid T., died 1942, vol. IV
Dodd, Rev. William Harold Alfred; see Dodd, Rev. Harold.
Dodd, Rt Hon. William Huston, 1844–1930, vol. III
Dodds, Sir Charles; see Dodds, Sir E. C.
Dodds, Sir (Edward) Charles, 1st Bt, 1899–1973, vol. VII
Dodds, Eric Robertson, 1893–1979, vol. VII
Dodds, George Christopher Buchanan, 1916–1995, vol. IX
Dodds, George Elliott, 1889–1977, vol. VII
Dodds, Gladys Helen, 1898–1982, vol. VIII
Dodds, Harold Willis, 1889–1980, vol. VII
Dodds, Jackson, 1881–1961, vol. VI
Dodds, Sir James Leishman, 1891–1972, vol. VII
Dodds, Sir James Miller, 1861–1935, vol. III
Dodds, James Pickering, 1913–1996, vol. X
Dodds, Hon. Sir John Stokell, 1848–1914, vol. I
Dodds, Rev. Canon Matthew Archbold, 1864–1928, vol. II
Dodds, Norman Noel, 1903–1965, vol. VI
Dodds, Stephen Roxby, 1881–1943, vol. IV
Dodds, Maj.-Gen. Thomas Henry, 1873–1943, vol. IV
Dodds, Brig.-Gen. William Okell Holden, 1867–1934, vol. III
Dodds Crewe, Major James Hugh Hamilton, 1880–1956, vol. V
Dodge, Bayard, 1888–1972, vol. VII
Dodge, Grenville Mellen, 1831–1916, vol. II
Dodge, John Bigelow, 1894–1960, vol. V
Dodge, John Vilas, 1909–1991, vol. IX
Dodgson, Campbell, 1867–1948, vol. IV
Dodgson, Rev. Charles L.; see Carroll, Lewis.
Dodgson, Brig.-Gen. Golquhoun Scott, 1867–1947, vol. IV
Dodgson, Sir David Scott, 1821–1898, vol. I
Dodgson, Major Heathfield Butler, 1863–1937, vol. III
Dodgson, John Arthur, 1890–1969, vol. VI
Dodington, Brig.-Gen. Wilfred Marriott-, 1871–1931, vol. III
Dods, Alexander Waddell, died 1952, vol. V
Dods, Lt-Col Joseph Espie, 1874–1930, vol. III
Dods, Sir Lorimer Fenton, 1900–1981, vol. VIII
Dods, Marcus, 1834–1909, vol. I
Dods, Marcus, died 1935, vol. III
Dods-Withers, Isobelle, 1876–1939, vol. III
Dodson, Sir Gerald, 1884–1966, vol. VI
Dodson, John Michael, 1919–1977, vol. VII
Dodson, Rev. Canon Thomas Hatheway, 1862–1931, vol. III
Dodsworth, Sir Claude Matthew S., 7th Bt; see Smith-Dodsworth.

Dodsworth, Sir (Leonard) Lumley (Savage), 1890–1968, vol. VI
Dodsworth, Sir Lumley; see Dodsworth, Sir Leonard L. S.
Dodsworth, Sir Matthew Blayney Smith, 6th Bt, 1856–1931, vol. III
Dodwell, Charles Reginald, 1922–1994, vol. IX
Dodwell, David William, 1898–1980, vol. VII
Dodwell, Henry Herbert, 1879–1946, vol. IV
Doel, James, 1804–1902, vol. I
Doggart, Arthur Robert, 1866–1932, vol. III
Doggart, James Hamilton, 1900–1989, vol. VIII
Doggett, Frank John, 1910–1988, vol. VIII
Doherty, Rt Hon. Charles Joseph, 1855–1931, vol. III
Doherty, F. C., died 1959, vol. V
Doherty, William David, 1893–1966, vol. VI
Doherty-Holwell, Captain Raymond Vernon; see Holwell.
Dohnányi Ernest, 1877–1960, vol. V
Doidge, Sir Frederick Widdowson, 1884–1954, vol. V
Doig, Very Rev. Andrew Beveridge, 1914–1997, vol. X
Doig, Henry Stuart, 1874–1931, vol. III
Doig, Sir James Nimmo Crawford, 1913–1984, vol. VIII
Doig, Peter, 1882–1952, vol. V
Doig, Peter Muir, 1911–1996, vol. X
d'Oisly, (Emile) Maurice, 1882–1949, vol. IV
d'Oisly, Maurice; see d'Oisly, E. M.
Doisy, Edward A., 1893–1986, vol. VIII
Doke, Clement Martyn, 1893–1980, vol. VII
Dolamore, William Henry, died 1938, vol. III
Doland, Lt-Col George Frederick, 1872–1946, vol. IV
Dolbey, Robert Valentine, 1878–1937, vol. III
Dolby, Major Sir George Alexander, 1854–1939, vol. III
Dolci, Danilo, 1924–1997, vol. X
Dolgorouki, Prince Alexis, 1846–1915, vol. I
Dolgorouki, Princess Alexis, (Frances), died 1919, vol. II
Dolin, Sir Anton, 1904–1983, vol. VIII
Doll, William Alfred Millner, 1885–1977, vol. VII
Dollan, Sir Patrick Joseph, died 1963, vol. VI
Dollar, Jean Marguerite, 1900–1982, vol. VIII
Dolley, Michael, 1925–1983, vol. VIII
Dollfuss, Engelbert, 1892–1934, vol. III
Dolling, Francis Robert, 1923–1994, vol. IX
Dollman, John Charles, 1851–1934, vol. III
Dolman, Eric Charles, 1903–1969, vol. VI
Dolman, Frederick, born 1867, vol. II
Dolmetsch, Arnold, 1858–1940, vol. III
Dolmetsch, Carl Frederick, 1911–1997, vol. X
Dolphin, Albert Edward, 1895–1972, vol. VII
Dolphin, Lt-Comdr Edgar H., died 1930, vol. III
Dolphin, Rear-Adm. George Verner Motley, 1902–1979, vol. VII
Dolphin, John Robert Vernon, 1905–1973, vol. VII
Dolton, David, died 1932, vol. III
Domagk, Gerhard, 1895–1964, vol. VI
Domenichetti, Richard, died 1901, vol. I
Domett, Rear-Adm. Douglas Brian, 1932–1994, vol. IX

Dominguez, Florencio L., died 1910, vol. I
Dominguez, Don Vicente J., died 1916, vol. II
Dominy, Reginald Hugh, died 1953, vol. V
Domvile, Adm. Sir Barry Edward, 1878–1971, vol. VII
Domvile, Sir Compton Edward, 1842–1924, vol. II
Domvile, Sir Compton Meade, 4th Bt, 1857–1935, vol. III
Domvile, Sir Hugo Compton Domvile P.; see Pöe Domvile.
Domville, Rear-Adm. Sir Cecil; see Domville, Rear-Adm. Sir W. C. H.
Domville, Captain Sir Cecil Lionel, 6th Bt, 1892–1930, vol. III
Domville, Sir Gerald Guy, 7th Bt, 1896–1981, vol. VIII
Domville, Lt-Col Hon. James, 1842–1921, vol. II
Domville, Sir James Henry, 5th Bt, 1889–1919, vol. II
Domville, Rear-Adm. Sir (William) Cecil H., 4th Bt, 1849–1904, vol. I
Domville-Fife, Charles William, 1887–1960, vol. V
(A)
Don, Rev. Alan Campbell, 1885–1966, vol. VI
Don, Charles Davidson, 1874–1959, vol. V
Don, Air Vice-Marshal Francis Percival, 1886–1964, vol. VI
Don, Kaye Ernest, 1891–1981, vol. VIII
Don, Sir William, 1861–1926, vol. II
Don, Surg.-Gen. William Gerard, 1836–1920, vol. II
Don-Wauchope, Sir John Douglas; see Wauchope.
Don-Wauchope, Sir Patrick George; see Wauchope.
Donachy, Frank, 1899–1970, vol. VI
Donald, Alexander Douglas, died 1948, vol. IV
Donald, Archibald, 1860–1937, vol. III
Donald, Charles, 1896–1955, vol. V
Donald, Maj.-Gen. Colin George, 1854–1939, vol. III
Donald, David William Alexander, 1915–1986, vol. VIII
Donald, Douglas, 1865–1953, vol. V
Donald, Douglas Alexander, died 1975, vol. VII
Donald, Air Marshal Sir Grahame, 1891–1976, vol. VII
Donald, Ian, 1910–1987, vol. VIII
Donald, Sir James, 1873–1957, vol. V
Donald, Sir James Bell, 1879–1971, vol. VII
Donald, Sir John Stewart, 1861–1948, vol. IV
Donald, Kenneth William, 1911–1994, vol. IX
Donald, Mary Jane; see Longstaff, M. J.
Donald, Maxwell Bruce, 1897–1978, vol. VII
Donald, Sir Robert, 1861–1933, vol. III
Donald, William C.; see Coutts Donald.
Donaldson of Kingsbridge, Baron (Life Peer); John George Stuart Donaldson, 1907–1998, vol. X
Donaldson of Kingsbridge, Lady; see Donaldson, Frances Annesley.
Donaldson, Rev. Canon Alexander Edward, 1878–1960, vol. V
Donaldson, Rev. Augustus Blair, 1841–1903, vol. I
Donaldson, Comdr Charles Edward McArthur, 1903–1964, vol. VI
Donaldson, David Abercrombie, 1916–1996, vol. X
Donaldson, Sir Dawson, 1903–1990, vol. VIII

Donaldson, Air Cdre Edward Mortlock, 1912–1992, vol. IX
Donaldson, Eion Pelly, 1896–1963, vol. VI
Donaldson, Frances Annesley, (Lady Donaldson of Kingsbridge), 1907–1994, vol. IX
Donaldson, Rev. Frederic Lewis, 1860–1953, vol. V
Donaldson, Sir George, 1845–1925, vol. II
Donaldson, Gordon, 1913–1993, vol. IX
Donaldson, Sir Hey Frederick, 1856–1916, vol. II
Donaldson, Sir James, 1831–1915, vol. I
Donaldson, John Coote, 1895–1980, vol. VII
Donaldson, Adm. Leonard Andrew Boyd, 1875–1956, vol. V
Donaldson, Malcolm, 1884–1973, vol. VII
Donaldson, Mary Ethel Muir, 1876–1958, vol. V
Donaldson, Norman Patrick, 1878–1955, vol. V
Donaldson, Robert, died 1933, vol. III
Donaldson, Rt Rev. St Clair George, 1863–1935, vol. III
Donaldson, Rear-Adm. Vernon D'Arcy, 1906–1992, vol. IX
Donaldson, William, 1838–1924, vol. II
Donaldson-Hudson, Lt-Col Ralph Charles, 1874–1941, vol. IV
Donat, (Frederick) Robert, 1905–1958, vol. V
Donat, Robert; see Donat, F. R.
Doncaster, John Priestman, 1907–1981, vol. VIII
Doncaster, Leonard, 1877–1920, vol. II
Doncaster, Sir Robert, 1872–1955, vol. V
Done, Brig.-Gen. Herbert Richard, 1876–1950, vol. IV
Done, William Edward Pears, 1883–1976, vol. VII
Donegall, 5th Marquess of, 1822–1904, vol. I
Donegall, 6th Marquis of, 1903–1975, vol. VII
Donegan, Rt Rev. Horace William Baden, 1900–1991, vol. IX
Donegan, Lt-Col James Francis, 1863–1934, vol. III
Donelan, Captain Anthony J., 1846–1924, vol. II
Donelan, James, died 1922, vol. II
Doneraile, 6th Viscount, 1866–1941, vol. IV
Doneraile, 7th Viscount, 1869–1956, vol. V
Doneraile, 8th Viscount, 1878–1957, vol. V
Doneraile, 9th Viscount, 1923–1983, vol. VIII
Dönges, Theophilus Ebenhaézer, 1898–1968, vol. VI
Donington, 3rd Baron, 1859–1927, vol. II
Donkin, Sir Bryan; see Donkin, Sir H. B.
Donkin, Bryan, 1835–1902, vol. I
Donkin, Sir (Horatio) Bryan, 1845–1927, vol. II
Donkin, Air Cdre Peter Langloh, 1913–2000, vol. X
Donkin, Richard Sims, 1836–1919, vol. II
Donkin, Sydney Bryan, 1871–1952, vol. V
Donn-Byrne, Brian Oswald; see Byrne, Donn.
Donnan, Frederick George, 1870–1956, vol. V
Donnan, James, 1837–1915, vol. I
Donnay, Maurice, 1859–1945, vol. IV
Donne, Col Benjamin Donisthorpe Alsop, 1856–1907, vol. I
Donne, Col Henry Richard Beadon, 1860–1949, vol. IV
Donne, Thomas Edward, 1859–1945, vol. IV
Donne, Ven. William, 1845–1914, vol. I
Donnelly, Alex. E., died 1958, vol. V
Donnelly, Sir Arthur Telford, 1890–1954, vol. V
Donnelly, Desmond Louis, 1920–1974, vol. VII
Donnelly, Harry Hill, 1909–1969, vol. VI

Donnelly, Sir John Fretcheville Dykes, 1834–1902, vol. I
Donnelly, Rt Rev. Nicholas, 1837–1920, vol. II
Donnelly, Patrick, died 1947, vol. IV
Donner, Anna Maria, (Lady Donner), died 1935, vol. III
Donner, Sir Edward, 1st Bt, 1840–1934, vol. III
Donner, Frederic Garrett, 1902–1987, vol. VIII
Donner, Ossian, 1866–1957, vol. V
Donner, Sir Patrick William, 1904–1988, vol. VIII
Donnet of Balgay, Baron (Life Peer); Alexander Mitchell Donnet, 1916–1985, vol. VIII
Donnet, Sir James John Louis, 1816–1905, vol. I
Donnison, (Frank Siegfried) Vernon, 1898–1993, vol. IX
Donnison, Vernon; see Donnison F. S. V.
Donnithorne, Rev. Vyvyan Henry, 1886–1968, vol. VI
Donoghue, Stephen, (Steve), 1884–1945, vol. IV
Donohoe, Martin Henry, 1869–1927, vol. II
Donohue, Col William Edward, 1861–1945, vol. IV
Donoughmore, 5th Earl of, 1848–1900, vol. I
Donoughmore, 6th Earl of, 1875–1948, vol. IV
Donoughmore, 7th Earl of, 1902–1981, vol. VIII
Donovan, Baron (Life Peer); Terence Norbert Donovan, 1898–1971, vol. VII
Donovan, Dame Florence May; see Hancock, Dame F. M.
Donovan, Francis Desmond, 1894–1948, vol. IV
Donovan, Hedley Williams, 1914–1990, vol. VIII
Donovan, John, 1891–1971, vol. VII
Donovan, John Thomas, 1878–1922, vol. II
Donovan, John Thomas, 1885–1973, vol. VII
Donovan, Robert, 1862–1934, vol. III
Donovan, Terence Daniel, 1936–1996, vol. X
Donovan, Maj.-Gen. Sir William, 1850–1934, vol. III
Donovan, Maj.-Gen. William Joseph, 1883–1959, vol. V
Dontenwill, Most Rev. Augustin, 1857–1931, vol. III
Doodson, Arthur Thomas, 1890–1968, vol. VI
Doogan, P. C., died 1906, vol. I
Doolette, Sir George Philip, 1840–1924, vol. II
Doolin, William, 1887–1962, vol. VI
Doolittle, Gen. James H., 1896–1993, vol. IX
Dooner, Lt-Col William Dundas, 1876–1927, vol. II
Dooner, Col William Toke, died 1926, vol. II
Doorly, Sir Charles William, 1875–1942, vol. IV
Doorly, Most Rev. Edward, 1870–1950, vol. IV
Doorly, Rev. Canon Wiltshire Stokely, died 1932, vol. III
Dopping-Hepenstal, Major Lambert John, 1859–1928, vol. II
Dopping-Hepenstal, Col Maxwell Edward, 1872–1965, vol. VI
Doran, Alban Henry Griffiths, 1849–1927, vol. II
Doran, Maj.-Gen. Beauchamp John Colclough, 1860–1943, vol. IV
Doran, Edward, 1892–1945, vol. IV
Doran, Edward Anthony, died 1922, vol. II
Doran, Sir Henry Francis, 1856–1928, vol. II
Doran, Gen. Sir John, 1824–1903, vol. I
Doran, Brig. John Crampton Morton, 1880–1957, vol. V
Doran, John Frederick, 1916–1995, vol. IX

Doran, Brig.-Gen. Walter Robert Butler, 1861–1945, vol. IV

Doráti, Antal, 1906–1988, vol. VIII

Dorchester, 4th Baron, 1822–1897, vol. I

Dorchester, Baroness (5th in line), 1846–1925, vol. II

Dorchester, 6th Baron, 1876–1963, vol. VI

Dore, Gp Captain Alan Sydney Whitehorn, 1882–1953, vol. V

Dore, Ernest, died 1950, vol. IV

Doré, Victor, 1880–1954, vol V

Dorey, Edgar Aleck, 1886–1976, vol. VII

Dorey, Stanley Fabes, 1891–1972, vol. VII

Dorez, Léon Louis Marie, 1864–1922, vol. II (A), vol. III

Dorington, Hubert, 1878–1935, vol. III

Dorington, Rt Hon. Sir John Edward, 1st Bt, 1832–1911, vol. I

Doris, William, 1860–1926, vol. II

Dorland, Arthur Garratt, 1887–1980, vol. VII

Dorling, Captain Henry Taprell, 1883–1968, vol. VI

Dorling, Vice-Adm. James Wilfred Sussex, 1889–1966, vol. VI

Dorling, Col Lionel, 1860–1925, vol. II

Dorman, Sir Arthur John, 1st Bt, 1848–1931, vol. III

Dorman, Sir Bedford Lockwood, 2nd Bt, died 1956, vol. V

Dorman, Lt-Col Sir Charles Geoffrey, 3rd Bt, 1920–1996, vol. X

Dorman, Brig. Edward Mungo, 1885–1967, vol. VI

Dorman, Surg.-Gen. John Cotter, 1852–1944, vol. IV

Dorman, Sir Maurice Henry, 1912–1993, vol. IX

Dorman-Smith, Col Rt Hon. Sir Reginald Hugh, 1899–1977, vol. VII

Dormer, 12th Baron, 1830–1900, vol. I

Dormer, 13th Baron, 1862–1920, vol. II

Dormer, 14th Baron, 1864–1922, vol. II

Dormer, 15th Baron, 1903–1975, vol. VII

Dormer, 16th Baron, 1914–1995, vol. IX

Dormer, Sir Cecil Francis Joseph, 1883–1979, vol. VII

Dormer, Charles Walter C.; see Cottrell-Dormer.

D'Ormesson, Count Wladimir Olivier Marie François de Paule Le Fèvre, 1888–1973, vol. VII

Dornhorst, Frederick, 1849–1927, vol. II

Dorrell, Bt Lt-Col George Thomas, died 1971, vol. VII

Dorrien, Gen. Sir Horace Lockwood S.; see Smith-Dorrien.

Dorrien, Lady (Olive Crofton) S.; see Smith-Dorrien.

Dorrien, Rev. Walter Montgomery S.; see Smith-Dorrien.

Dorrien-Smith, Major Edward Pendarves, 1879–1937, vol. III

Dorrien-Smith, Thomas Algernon, 1846–1918, vol. II

Dorrity, Rev. David, died 1926, vol. II

Dorté, Philip Hoghton, 1904–1970, vol. VI

Dorward, Alan James, 1889–1956, vol. V

Dorward, Maj.-Gen. Sir Arthur Robert Ford, 1848–1934, vol. III

Dorward, Ivor Gardiner Menzies Gordon, 1927–1983, vol. VIII

Dos Passos, John, 1896–1970, vol. VI

Dos Santos, Sir Errol Lionel, 1890–1992, vol. IX

Dossor, Rear-Adm. Frederick, 1913–1990, vol. VIII

Dott, Norman McOmish, 1897–1973, vol. VII

Dottin, Henri Georges, 1863–1928, vol. II (A), vol. III

Dottridge, Edwin Thomas, 1876–1947, vol. IV

Doubleday, Rt Rev. Arthur, 1865–1951, vol. V

Doubleday, Frederic Nicklin, 1885–1971, vol. VII

Doubleday, John Gordon, 1920–1982, vol. VIII

Doubleday, Sir Leslie, 1887–1975, vol. VII

Doudney, Sarah, 1843–1926, vol. II

Dougal, Daniel, 1884–1948, vol. IV

Dougall, Lily, 1858–1923, vol. II

Dougan, James Lockhart, 1874–1941, vol. IV

Dougan, Thomas Wilson, died 1907, vol. I

Dougherty, His Eminence Cardinal Denis J., died 1951, vol. V

Dougherty, Maj.-Gen. Sir Ivan Noel, 1907–1998, vol. X

Dougherty, Rt Hon. Sir James Brown, 1844–1934, vol. III

Doughty, Dame Adelaide Baillieu, 1908–1986, vol. VIII

Doughty, Sir Arthur, died 1936, vol. III

Doughty, Sir Charles, 1878–1956, vol. V

Doughty, Charles John Addison, 1902–1973, vol. VII

Doughty, Charles Montagu, 1843–1926, vol. II

Doughty, Sir George, 1854–1914, vol. I

Doughty, George Henry, 1911–1998, vol. X

Doughty, Rear-Adm. Henry Montagu, 1870–1921, vol. II

Doughty-Tichborne, Sir Anthony Joseph Henry Doughty; see Tichborne.

Doughty-Tichborne, Sir Henry Alfred Joseph; see Tichborne.

Doughty-Tichborne, Sir Joseph Henry Bernard; see Tichborne.

Doughty-Wylie, Major Charles Hotham Montagu; see Wylie.

Douglas of Barloch, 1st Baron, 1889–1980, vol. VII

Douglas of Kirtleside, 1st Baron, 1893–1969, vol. VI

Douglas, Hon. Sir Adyl, 1815–1906, vol. I

Douglas, Alexander Edgar, 1916–1981, vol. VIII

Douglas, Alexander Stuart, 1921–1998, vol. X

Douglas, Lord Alfred Bruce, 1870–1945, vol. IV

Douglas, Andrew, died 1935, vol. III

Douglas, Very Rev. Canon Lord Archibald, 1850–1938, vol. III

Douglas, Archibald Campbell, 1872–1943, vol. IV

Douglas, Adm. Sir Archibald Lucius, 1842–1913, vol. I

Douglas, Col Archibald Philip, 1867–1953, vol. V

Douglas, Lt-Col Archibald Vivian Campbell, 1902–1977, vol. VII

Douglas, Arthur, 1850–1920, vol. II

Douglas, Rt Rev. Hon. Arthur Gascoigne, 1827–1905, vol. I

Douglas, Arthur Henry Johnstone-, 1846–1923, vol. II

Douglas, Arthur John Alexander, 1920–1995, vol. IX

Douglas, Sir Arthur Percy, 5th Bt (*cr* 1777), 1845–1913, vol. I
Douglas, Campbell Mellis, *died* 1909, vol. I
Douglas, Carstairs Cumming, 1866–1940, vol. III
Douglas, Lord Cecil Charles, 1898–1981, vol. VIII
Douglas, Cecil George, 1854–1919, vol. II
Douglas, Lt-Col Charles Edward, 1855–1943, vol. IV
Douglas, Charles Mackinnon, 1865–1924, vol. II
Douglas, Gen. Sir Charles Whittingham Horsley, 1850–1914, vol. I
Douglas, Claude, 1852–1945, vol. IV
Douglas, Claude Gordon, 1882–1963, vol. VI
Douglas, Clifford Hugh, 1879–1952, vol. V
Douglas, David, 1823–1916, vol. II
Douglas, David Charles, 1898–1982, vol. VIII
Douglas, Sir Donald Macleod, 1911–1993, vol. IX
Douglas, Donald Wills, 1892–1981, vol. VIII
Douglas, Brig.-Gen. Douglas Campbell, 1964–1927, vol. II
Douglas, Rt Rev. Edward, 1901–1967, vol. VI
Douglas, Hon. Edward Archibald, 1877–1947, vol. IV
Douglas, Sir (Edward) Sholto, 1909–1997, vol. X
Douglas, Rev. Evelyn Keith, 1959–1920, vol. II
Douglas, Francis John, 1858–1934, vol. III
Douglas, Sir George Brisbane, 5th Bt (*cr* 1786), 1856–1935, vol. III
Douglas, Rev. George Cunninghame Monteath, 1826–1904, vol. I
Douglas, Adm. Hon. George Henry, 1821–1905, vol. I
Douglas, Very Rev. George James Cosmo, *died* 1973, vol. VII
Douglas, (George) Keith, 1903–1949, vol. IV
Douglas, Lt-Col George Stuart, 1879–1947, vol IV
Douglas, Rt Rev. Gerald Wybergh, 1875–1934, vol. III
Douglas, Rev. Hon. Henry, 1822–1907, vol I
Douglas, Maj.-Gen. Henry Edward Manning, 1875–1939, vol. III
Douglas, Vice-Adm. Sir (Henry) Percy, 1876–1939, vol. III
Douglas, Horace James, 1866–1962, vol. VI
Douglas, Hugh C; *see* Cowan-Douglas
Douglas, Very Rev. Hugh Osborne, 1911–1986, vol. VIII
Douglas, Irvine; *see* Douglas, R. I.
Douglas, James, 1826–1904, vol. I
Douglas, James, 1837–1910, vol. I
Douglas, James, 1837–1918, vol. II
Douglas, James, 1867–1940, vol. III
Douglas, James Albert Sholto, 1913–1981, vol. VIII
Douglas, Maj.-Gen. James Archibald, 1862–1932, vol. III
Douglas, James Archibald, 1884–1978, vol. VII
Douglas, Sir James Boyd, 1893–1964, vol. VI
Douglas, James G., 1887–1954, vol. V
Douglas, Sir James Louis Fitzroy Scott, 6th Bt *cr* 1786), 1930–1969, vol. VI
Douglas, Hon. James Moffat, 1839–1921, vol. II
Douglas, James Sholto Cameron, 1879–1931, vol. III
Douglas, Major Sir James Stewart, 6th Bt (*cr* 1777), 1859–1940, vol. III

Douglas, Major James Wightman, 1873–1937, vol. III
Douglas, Hon. John, 1828–1904, vol. I
Douglas, Rev. Canon John Albert, *died* 1956, vol. V
Douglas, Maj.-Gen. John Primrose, 1908–1975, vol. VII
Douglas, Katharine Greenhill, 1908–1979, vol. VII
Douglas, Keith; *see* Douglas, G. K.
Douglas, Sir Kenneth, 4th Bt (*cr* 1831), 1868–1954, vol. V
Douglas, Lewis Williams, 1894–1974, vol. VII
Douglas, Lloyd C., 1877–1951, vol. V
Douglas, Lt-Col Montagu William, 1863–1957, vol. V
Douglas, Norman, 1868–1952, vol. V
Douglas, Col Norman, 1887–1968, vol. VI
Douglas, O.; *see* Buchan, Anna.
Douglas, Vice-Adm. Sir Percy; *see* Douglas, Vice-Adm. Sir H. P.
Douglas, Reginald Stair, 1877–1933, vol. III
Douglas, Lt-Col Robert Jeffray, 1869–1916, vol. II
Douglas, Sir Robert Kennaway, 1838–1913, vol. I
Douglas, Captain Robert Langton, 1864–1951, vol. V
Douglas, Sir Robert McCallum, 1899–1996, vol. X
Douglas, Rev. Robert Noel, 1868–1957, vol. V
Douglas, Major Robert Vaughan, 1881–1922, vol. II
Douglas, Col Roderick, 1898–1965, vol. VI
Douglas, Ronald Albert Neale, 1922–1993, vol. IX
Douglas, (Ronald) Irvine, 1899–1973, vol. VII
Douglas, Ronald Walter, 1910–2000, vol. X
Douglas, Sir Sholto; *see* Douglas, Sir E. S.
Douglas, Adm. Sholto, 1833–1913, vol. I
Douglas, Sir Sholto (Courtenay Mackenzie), 5th Bt, 1890–1986, vol. VIII
Douglas, Captain Sholto Grant, 1867–1956, vol. V
Douglas, Major Sholto William, 1870–1959, vol. V
Douglas, Captain Stewart Ranken, 1871–1936, vol. III
Douglas, Maj.-Gen. Sir William, 1858–1920, vol. II
Douglas, Brig.-Gen. William Charles, 1862–1938, vol. III
Douglas, William Douglas Robinson-, 1851–1921, vol. II
Douglas, William Orville, 1898–1980, vol. VII
Douglas, Comdr William Ramsay Binny, *died* 1919, vol. II
Douglas, Sir William Scott, 1890–1953, vol. V
Douglas, William Wilton, 1922–1998, vol. X
Douglas-Hamilton, Rev. Hamilton Anne, 1853–1929, vol. III
Douglas-Hamilton, Lord Malcolm Avendale, 1909–1964, vol. VI
Douglas-Hamilton, Percy Seymour, 1875–1940, vol. III
Douglas-Henry, Major James, 1881–1943, vol. IV
Douglas-Home, family name of Baron Home of the Hirsel.
Douglas-Home, Charles Cospatrick, 1937–1985, vol. VIII
Douglas-Home, Hon. William; *see* Home.
Douglas-Jones, Sir Crawford Douglas, 1874–1956, vol. V
Douglas-Mann, Bruce Leslie Home, 1927–2000, vol. X

Douglas-Mann, Keith John Sholto, 1931–1992, vol. IX
Douglas-Pennant, Hon. Alan George Sholto, 1890–1915, vol. I
Douglas-Pennant, Hon. Charles, 1877–1914, vol. I
Douglas-Pennant, Adm. Hon. Sir Cyril Eustace, 1894–1961, vol. VI
Douglas-Pennant, Captain Hon. George Henry, 1876–1915, vol. I
Douglas-Pennant, Hon. Violet Blanche, *died* 1945, vol. IV
Douglas-Scott, Lord Charles Thomas Montagu; *see* Scott
Douglas-Scott-Montagu, Hon. Robert Henry, 1867–1916, vol. II
Douglas-Withers, Maj.-Gen. John Keppel Ingold, 1919–1997, vol. X
Douglass of Cleveland, Baron (Life Peer); Harry Douglass, 1902–1978, vol. VII
Douglass, Sir James Nicholas, 1826–1898, vol. I
Douglass, Walter John, 1863–1945, vol. IV
Douglass, William Tregarthen, *died* 1913, vol. I
Douie, Charles Oswald Gaskell, 1896–1953, vol. V
Douie, Col Francis McCrone, 1886–1935, vol. III
Douie, Sir James McCrone, 1854–1935, vol. III
Doull, Rt Rev. Alexander John, 1870–1937, vol. III
Doull, John, 1878–1969, vol. VI (AII)
Doull-Connolly, Thomas James, 1878–1949, vol. IV (A)
Doulton, Alfred John Farre, 1911–1996, vol. X
Doulton, Sir Henry, 1820–1897, vol. I
Doulton, Henry Lewis, 1853–1930, vol. III
Doumer, Paul, 1857–1932, vol. III
Doumergue, Emile, 1844–1937, vol. III
Doumergue, Gaston, 1863–1937, vol. III
Doumic, Rene, *died* 1937, vol. III
Douthwaite, Arthur Henry, 1896–1974, vol. VII
Douthwaite, James Lungley, 1877–1960, vol. V
Douty, Edward Henry, 1861–1911, vol. I
Dove, Maj.-Gen. Arthur Julian Hadfield, 1902–1985, vol. VIII
Dove, Sir Clifford Alfred, 1904–1988, vol. VIII
Dove, Dame Frances, 1847–1942, vol. IV
Dove-Edwin, George Frederick, 1896–1973, vol. VII
Dove-Wilson, Sir John Carnegie; *see* Wilson
Dovener, John Montague, 1923–1981, vol. VIII
Dover, Rev. Thomas Birkett, 1846–1926, vol. II
Dovercourt, 1st Baron, 1878–1961, vol. VI
Doverdale, 1st Baron, 1836–1925, vol. II
Doverdale, 2nd Baron, 1872–1935, vol. III
Doverdale, 3rd Baron, 1904–1949, vol. IV
Doveton, Frederick Bazett, 1841–1911, vol. I
Dow, Alexander Warren, 1873–1948, vol. IV
Dow, Christopher; *see* Dow, J. C. R.
Dow, David Rutherford, 1887–1979, vol. VII
Dow, Sir Hugh, 1886–1978, vol. VII
Dow, James Findlay, 1911–1983, vol. VIII
Dow, (John) Christopher (Roderick), 1916–1998, vol. X
Dow, R(onald) Graham, 1909–1983, vol. VIII
Dow, Samuel, 1908–1976, vol. VII
Dow, Thomas Millie, *died* 1919, vol. II
Dowbiggin, Sir Herbert Layard, 1880–1966, vol. VI
Dowd, (Eric) Ronald; *see* Dowd, R.
Dowd, Ronald, 1914–1990, vol. VIII

Dowdall, Hon. Mary Frances Harriet, 1876–1939, vol. III
Dowdall, Harold Chaloner, 1868–1955, vol. V
Dowdall, Sir Laurence Charles Edward Downing, 1851–1936, vol. III
Dowdalls, Edward Joseph, 1926–1994, vol. IX
Dowden, Major Charles Henry, 1880–1937, vol. III
Dowden, Edward, 1843–1913, vol. I
Dowden, Rt Rev. John, 1840–1910, vol. I
Dowden, John Wheeler, 1866–1936, vol. III
Dowding, 1st Baron, 1882–1970, vol. VI
Dowding, 2nd Baron, 1919–1992, vol. IX
Dowding, Vice-Adm. Sir Arthur Ninian, 1886–1966, vol. VI
Dowding, Cdre John Charles Keith, 1891–1965, vol. VI
Dowding, Michael Frederick, 1918–1991, vol. IX
Dowding, Gen. Townley Ward, 1847–1927, vol. II
Dowell, Brig.-Gen. Arthur John William, 1861–1943, vol. IV
Dowell, Col George Cecil, 1862–1949, vol. IV
Dowell, Bt Lt-Col George William, 1860–1940, vol. III
Dowell, Sir William Montagu, 1825–1912, vol. I
Dower, Col Alan Vincent Gandar, 1898–1980, vol. VII
Dower, Eric Leslie G.; *see* Gandar Dower.
Dowker, Gen. Howard Codrington, 1829–1912, vol. I
Dowler, Lt-Gen. Sir Arthur Arnhold Bullick, 1895–1963, vol. VI
Dowley, Francis Michael, 1885–1948, vol. IV
Dowling, Geoffrey Barrow, 1891–1976, vol. VII
Dowling, Sir Hallam Walter, 1909–1983, vol. VIII
Dowling, Most Rev. John Pius, 1860–1940, vol. III
Dowling, Vice-Adm. Sir Roy Russell, 1901–1969, vol. VI
Dowling, Rev. Theodore Edward, 1937–1921, vol. II
Dowling, Rt Rev. Thomas Joseph, 1840–1924, vol. II
Down, Barbara Langdon; *see* Littlewood, Barbara, (Lady Littlewood).
Down, Lt-Comdr Sir Charles Edward, 1857–1927, vol. II
Down, Lt-Gen. Sir Ernest Edward, 1902–1980, vol. VII
Down, Air Cdre Harold Hunter, 1895–1974, vol. VII
Down, Norman Cecil Sommers, 1893–1984, vol. VIII
Down, Captain Richard Thornton, 1882–1944, vol. IV
Downe, 8th Viscount, 1844–1924, vol. II
Downe, 9th Viscount, 1872–1931, vol. III
Downe, 10th Viscount, 1903–1965, vol. VI
Downer, Hon. Sir Alexander Russell, 1910–1981, vol. VIII
Downer, Ven. George William, *died* 1912, vol. I
Downer, Sir Harold George, 1871–1935, vol. III
Downer, Hon. Sir John William, 1844–1915, vol. I
Downer, William James, 1851–1939, vol. III
Downes, Sir Arthur Henry, 1851–1938, vol. III
Downes, Commissary-Gen. Arthur William, 1827–1905, vol. I

235

Downes, Very Rev. Edmund Audley, 1877–1950, vol. IV
Downes, Sir Joseph, 1848–1925, vol. II
Downes, Maj.-Gen. Major Francis, 1834–1923 vol. II
Downes, Mollie Patricia P.; *see* Panter-Downes.
Downes, Ralph William, 1904–1993, vol. IX
Downes, Rev. Robert Percival, 1842–1924, vol. II
Downes, Ronald Geoffrey, 1916–1985, vol. VIII
Downes, Maj.-Gen. Rupert Major, 1885–1945, vol. IV
Downes, Col William Knox, 1855–1911, vol. I
Downes-Shaw, Sir (Archibald) Havergal, 1884–1961, vol. VI
Downes-Shaw, Sir Havergal; *see* Downes-Shaw, Sir A. H.
Downey, Edmund, *died* 1937, vol. III
Downey, Most Rev. Richard, 1881–1953, vol V
Downham, 1st Baron, 1853–1920, vol. II
Downham, Rev. Isaac, *died* 1923, vol. II
Downe, Major Fairbairn, 1880–1949, vol. IV
Downie, Allan Watt, 1901–1988, vol. VIII
Downie, Sir Harold Frederick, 1889–1966, vol. VI
Downie, Captain John, *died* 1921, vol. II
Downie, John P., *died* 1945, vol. IV
Downie, Hon. John Wallace, 1876–1940, vol. III
Downie, Walker, *died* 1921, vol. II
Downing, Arthur Matthew Weld, 1850–1917, vol. II
Downing, Col Cameron Macartney Harwood, 1845–1926, vol. II
Downing, Rev. Edward Andrew, *died* 1931, vol. III
Downing, George Henry, 1878–1940, vol. III (A), vol. IV
Downing, Henry Julian, 1919–1998, vol. X
Downing, Henry Philip Burke, 1865–1947, vol. IV
Downing, Richard Ivan, 1915–1975, vol. VII
Downing, Sir Stanford Edwin, 1870–1933, vol. III
Downing, Rev. Thomas William, 1864–1932, vol. III
Downman, Charles Beaumont Benoy, 1916–1982, vol. VIII
Downs, Brian Westerdale, 1893–1984, vol. VIII
Downs, Edgar, *died* 1963, vol. VI
Downs, James, 1856–1941, vol. IV
Downs, Leslie Hall, 1900–1992, vol. IX
Downshire, 6th Marquess of, 1871–1918, vol.II
Downshire, 7th Marquess of, 1894–1989, vol. VIII
Dowse, Rt Rev. Charles Benjamin, *died* 1934, vol. III
Dowse, Maj.-Gen. John Cecil Alexander, 1891–1964, vol. VI
Dowse, Rev. John Clarence, *died* 1930, vol. III
Dowse, Maj.-Gen. Sir Maurice Brian, 1899–1986, vol. VIII
Dowse, Very Rev. William, 1856–1939, vol.III
Dowsett, Charles James Frank, 1924–1998, vol. X
Dowsett, Col Ernest Blair, *died* 1951, vol. V
Dowson, Maj.-Gen. Arthur Henley, 1908–1989, vol. VIII
Dowson, Sir Ernest MacLeod, 1876–1950, vol. IV
Dowson, Sir Hubert Arthur, 1866–1946, vol. IV
Dowson, Joseph Emerson, 1844–1940, vol. III
Dowson, Sir Oscar Follett, 1879–1961, vol. VI
Dowty, Sir George Herbert, 1901–1975, vol. VII
Doxat, Major Alexis Charles, 1867–1942, vol. IV

Doxford, Sir William Theodore, 1841–1916, vol. II
Doxiadis, Constantinos Apostolos, 1913–1975, vol. VII
Doyen, E., 1859–1916, vol. II
Doyle, Adrian Malcolm C.; *see* Conan Doyle.
Doyle, Rear-Adm. Alec Broughton, 1888–1984, vol. VIII
Doyle, Sir Arthur Conan, 1859–1930, vol. III
Doyle, Col Sir Arthur Havelock James, 4th Bt, 1858–1948, vol. IV
Doyle, Charles Francis, 1866–1928, vol. II
Doyle, Edward, 1892–1965, vol. VI
Doyle, Lt-Col Eric Edward, 1886–1937, vol. III
Doyle, Sir Everard Hastings, 3rd Bt, 1852–1933, vol. III
Doyle, Hon. Henry Martin, *died* 1929, vol. III
Doyle, Major Ignatius Purcell, 1863–1923, vol. II
Doyle, Air Comdt Dame Jean (Lena Annette) C.; *see* Conan Doyle.
Doyle, John Andrew, 1844–1907, vol. I
Doyle, Lt-Col John Francis Innes Hay, 1873–1919, vol. II
Doyle, Sir John Francis Reginald William Hastings, 5th Bt, 1912–1987, vol. VIII
Doyle, Joseph, 1891–1974, vol. VII
Doyle, Lynn, (Leslie Alexander Montgomery), 1873–1961, vol. VI
Doyle, Sir Nicholas G.; *see* Grattan-Doyle.
Doyle, Rt Rev. Mgr Richard Barry-, 1878–1933, vol. III
Doyle, Brig. Richard Stanislaus, 1911–1982, vol. VIII
Doyle, Very Rev. Thomas, 1853–1926, vol. II
Doyle, William Patrick, 1927–1983, vol. VIII
Doyle-Jones, F. W., *died* 1938, vol. III
D'Oyly, Sir Charles Hastings, 12th Bt, 1898–1962, vol. VI
D'Oyly, Sir Charles Walters, 9th Bt, 1822–1900, vol. I
D'Oyly, Sir Hadley; *see* D'Oyly, Sir. H. H.
D'Oyly, Sir (Hastings) Hadley, 11th Bt, 1864–1948, vol. IV
D'Oyly, Sir John Rochfort, 13th Bt, 1900–1986, vol. VIII
D'Oyly, Sir Nigel Hadley Miller, 14th Bt, 1914–2000, vol. X
D'Oyly, Sir Warren Hastings, 10th Bt, 1838–1921, vol. II
D'Oyly Carte, Dame Bridget, 1908–1985, vol. VIII
D'Oyly Carte, Rupert, 1876–1948, vol. IV
D'Oyly-Hughes, Captain Guy, 1891–1940, vol. III
Doyne, Charles Mervyn, 1839–1924, vol.II
Doyne, Dermot Henry, 1871–1942, vol. IV
Doyne, Philip Geoffry, 1886–1959, vol. V
Doyne, Robert Walter, 1857–1916, vol. II
Drabble, John Frederick, 1906–1982, vol. VIII
Drachmann, Holger, 1846–1908, vol. I
Drage, Sir Benjamin, *died* 1952, vol. V
Drage, Geoffrey, 1860–1955, vol. V
Drage, Lt-Col William Henry, 1855–1915, vol. I
Drago, Luis Maria, 1859–1921, vol. II
Drain, Geoffrey Ayrton, 1918–1993, vol. IX
Drake, Antony Elliot, 1907–1990, vol. VIII
Drake, Sir (Arthur) Eric (Courtney), 1910–1996, vol. X

Drake, Brig.-Gen. Bernard Francis, 1862–1954, vol. V
Drake, Bernard Harpur, 1876–1941, vol. IV
Drake, Donald Henry Charles, 1887–1974, vol. VII
Drake, Sir Eric; see Drake, Sir. A. E. C.
Drake, Sir Eugen John Henry Vanderstegen M.; see Millington-Drake.
Drake, Rev. F. W., died 1930, vol. III
Drake, Sir Francis George Augustus Fuller-Eliott-, 2nd Bt, 1837–1916, vol. II
Drake, Lt-Col Francis Richard, 1862–1935, vol. III
Drake, Sir Garrard Tyrwhitt-; see Drake, Sir H, G, T,
Drake, Harold William, 1889–1973, vol. VII
Drake, Col Henry Dowrish, 1859–1931, vol. III
Drake, Sir (Hugh) Garrard Tyrwhitt-, 1881–1964, vol. VI
Drake, Sir James, 1907–1989, vol. VIII
Drake, Hon. James George, 1850–1941, vol. IV
Drake, James Mackay Henry M.; see Millington-Drake.
Drake, Brig. Dame Jean Elizabeth R.; see Rivett-Drake.
Drake, John Alexander, 1878–1952, vol. V
Drake, John Collard Bernard, 1884–1975, vol. VII
Drake, John Edmund Bernard, 1917–1991, vol. IX
Drake, Maurice, 1875–1923, vol. II
Drake, Hon. Montague W. Tyrwhitt-, died 1908, vol. I
Drake, Lt-Col Reginald John, died 1948, vol. IV
Drake, Robert James, died 1916, vol. II
Drake, Samuel Bingham, died 1935, vol. III
Drake, Captain Thomas Oakley, 1863–1928, vol. II
Drake, Col William Hacche, 1873–1956, vol. V
Drake, William James, 1872–1919, vol. II
Drake, William Wyckham Tyrwhitt, 1851–1919, vol. II
Drake-Brockman, Brig.-Gen. David Henry, 1868–1960, vol. V
Drake-Brockman, Sir Digby Livingstone, 1877–1959, vol. V
Drake-Brockman, Maj.-Gen. Edmund Alfred, 1884–1949, vol. IV
Drake-Brockman, Sir Henry Vernon, 1865–1933, vol. III
Drake-Brockman, Lt-Col Ralph Evelyn, 1875–1952, vol. V
Drake-Brockman, Hon. Sir Thomas Charles, 1919–1992, vol. IX
Drakeley, Thomas James, 1890–1981, vol. VIII
Drakoules, Platon Soterios, 1858–1942, vol. IV
Draper, Bernard Montagu, 1875–1950, vol. IV
Draper, Charles; see Draper, R. C.
Draper, Charles, 1869–1952, vol. V
Draper, Brig.-Gen. Denis Colbarn, 1873–1951, vol. V
Draper, Col Gerald Irving Anthony Dare, 1914–1989, vol. VIII
Draper, Herbert James, died 1920, vol. II
Draper, (Reginald) Charles, 1932–1983, vol. VIII
Draper, Ruth, 1884–1956, vol. V
Draper, Hon. Thomas Percy, 1864–1946, vol. IV
Draper, William Franklin, 1842–1910, vol. I
Draper, William H., Jr, 1894–1974, vol. VII
Draper, Rev. William Henry, 1855–1933, vol. III

Drawbell, James Wedgwood, 1899–1979, vol. VII
Drawbridge, Rev. Cyprian Leycester, 1868–1937, vol. III
Drax, Adm. Hon. Sir Reginald Aylmer Ranfurly P. E. E.; see Plunkett-Ernle-Erle-Drax.
Draycott, Douglas Patrick, 1918–1997, vol. X
Drayson, Rear-Adm. Edwin Howard, 1889–1977, vol. VII
Drayson, Brig. Fitz-Alan George, 1888–1964, vol. VI
Drayson, George Burnaby, 1913–1983, vol. VIII
Drayton, Edward Rawle, 1859–1927, vol. II
Drayton, Miss Gertrude Drayton Grimké, 1880–1941, vol. IV
Drayton, Harley; see Drayton, Harold Charles.
Drayton, Harold Charles, (Harley Drayton), died 1966, vol. VI
Drayton, Sir Henry Lumley, 1869–1950, vol. IV
Drayton, Sir Robert Harry, 1892–1963, vol. VI
Dreaper, Surg. Rear-Adm. George Albert, 1863–1927, vol. II
Dreaper, William Porter, 1868–1938, vol. III
Dredge, James, 1840–1906, vol. I
Dreiser, Theodore, 1871–1945, vol. IV
Drennan, Alexander Murray, 1884–1984, vol. VIII
Drennan, Basil St George, 1903–1976, vol. VII
Drennan, (C.) Max, 1870–1935, vol. III
Drennan, John Cherry, 1899–1982, vol. VIII
Drennan, Max; see Drennan, C. M.
Dreschfeld, Julius, 1846–1907, vol. I
Dreschfield, Ralph Leonard Emmanuel, 1911–1991, vol. IX
Dresdel, Sonia, 1909–1976, vol. VII
Dressel, Dettmar, 1878–1961, vol. VI
Dressel, Otto, 1880–1941, vol. IV
Dresser, Henry Eeles, 1838–1915, vol I
Dresser, Horatio Willis, 1866–1954, vol. V
Drever, James, 1873–1950, vol. IV (A)
Drever, James, 1910–1991, vol. IX
Drew, Brig.-Gen. Arthur Blanshard Hawley, 1865–1947, vol. IV
Drew, Sir Arthur Charles Walter, 1912–1993, vol. IX
Drew, Air Cdre Bertie Clephane Hawley, 1880–1969, vol. VI
Drew, Brig. Cecil Francis, 1890–1987, vol. VIII
Drew, Charles Edwin, 1916–1987, vol. VIII
Drew, Clifford Luxmoore, died 1919, vol. II
Drew, Douglas, 1867–1931, vol. III
Drew, Sir Ferdinand Caire, 1895–1986, vol. VIII
Drew, Maj.-Gen. Francis Barry, 1825–1905, vol. I
Drew, Rt Rev. Mgr Count Francis Browning Drew B.; see Bickerstaffe-Drew.
Drew, Brig. Francis Greville, 1892–1962, vol. VI
Drew, Lt-Col Hon. George Alexander, 1894–1973, vol. VII
Drew, Lt-Col George Barry, 1868–1930, vol. III
Drew, George Charles, 1911–1997, vol. X
Drew, Rev. Harry, died 1910, vol. I
Drew, Harry Edward, 1909–1988, vol. VIII
Drew, Gen. Henry Rawlins, 1822–1906, vol. I
Drew, Lt-Col Horace Robert Hawley, 1871–1936, vol. III
Drew, Maj.-Gen. Sir James Syme, 1883–1955, vol. V

Drew, Dame Jane Beverly, 1911–1996, vol. X
Drew, John Alexander, 1907–1995, vol. IX
Drew, Hon. John Michael, 1865–1947, vol. IV
Drew, Mary, 1847–1927, vol. II
Drew, Lt-Gen. Sir Robert; see Drew, Lt-Gen. Sir W. R. M.
Drew, Sir Thomas, 1838–1910, vol. I
Drew, Vice-Adm. Thomas Bernard, died 1960, vol. V
Drew, Lt-Gen. Sir (William) Robert (Macfarlane), 1907–1991, vol. IX
Drew, William Wilson, died 1923, vol. II
Drew-Wilkinson, Clennell Frank Massy, 1877–1956, vol. V
Drewe, Basil, 1894–1974, vol. VII
Drewe, Sir Cedric, 1896–1971, vol. VII
Drewe, Rev. Ernest, died 1935, vol. III
Drewe, Geoffrey Grabham, 1904–1986, vol. VIII
Drewitt, Frederic George Dawtrey, 1848–1942, vol. IV
Drewry, Arthur, 1891–1961, vol. VI
Drewry, Lt George Leslie, 1894–1918, vol. II
Dreyer, Adm. Sir Fredric Charles, 1878–1956, vol. V
Dreyer, Georges, 1873–1934, vol. III
Dreyer, John Louis Emil, 1852–1926, vol. II
Dreyer, Maj.-Gen. John Tuthill, 1876–1959, vol. V
Dreyfus, Henry, 1882–1944, vol. IV
Dreyfus, Pierre, 1907–1994, vol. IX
Driberg, Thomas Edward Neil; see Baron Bradwell.
Driesch, Hans, 1867–1941, vol. IV
Dring, Lt-Col Sir (Arthur) John, 1902–1991, vol. IX
Dring, (Dennis) William, 1904–1990, vol. VIII
Dring, Lt-Col Sir John; see Dring, Lt-Col Sir A. J.
Dring, William; see Dring, D. W.
Dring Sir William Arthur, 1859–1912, vol. I
Drinkwater, Daisy; see Kennedy, D.
Drinkwater, George, 1852–1930, vol. III
Drinkwater, George Carr, 1880–1941, vol. IV
Drinkwater, John, 1882–1937, vol. III
Drinkwater, Sir William Leece, 1812–1909, vol. I
Driscoll, Lt-Col Daniel Patrick, 1862–1934, vol. III
Driscoll, Very Rev. James, 1870–1927, vol. II
Driver, Sir Arthur John, 1900–1990, vol. VIII
Driver, Major Arthur Robert, 1909–1981, vol. VIII
Driver, Christopher Prout, 1932–1997, vol. X
Driver, Sir Godfrey Rolles, 1892–1975, vol. VII
Driver, John Edmund, 1900–1965, vol. VI
Driver, Rev. Samuel Rolles, 1846–1914, vol. I
Driver, Thomas, 1912–1988, vol. VIII
Droch; see Bridges, Robert.
Drogheda, 9th Earl of, 1846–1908, vol. I
Drogheda, 10th Earl of, 1884–1957, vol. V
Drogheda, 11th Earl of, 1910–1989, vol. VIII
Dromgoole, Charles, died 1927, vol. II
Dron, Robert Wilson, 1869–1932, vol. III
Dronfield, John, 1898–1983, vol. VIII
Droop, John Percival, 1882–1963, vol. VI
Drought, Rev. Charles Edward, 1847–1917, vol. II
Drought, Charles W.; see Worster-Drought.
Drower, Sir Edwin Mortimer, 1880–1951, vol. V
Drower, Ethel May Stefana, (Lady Drower), 1879–1972, vol. VII
Drower, John Edmund, 1853–1945, vol. IV

Drowley, Air Vice-Marshal Thomas Edward, 1894–1985; vol. VIII
Drown, Thomas Messinger, 1842–1904, vol. I
Druce, George Claridge, 1850–1932, vol. III
Drucker, Adolphus, 1868–1903, vol. I
Drucquer, Sir Leonard, 1902–1975, vol. VII
Drucquer, Maurice Nathaniel, 1876–1970, vol. VI
Drughorn, Sir John Frederick, 1st Bt, 1862–1943, vol. IV
Druitt, Rt. Rev. Cecil Henry, 1874–1921, vol. II
Druitt, Sir Harvey; see Druitt, Sir W. A. H.
Druitt, Sir (William Arthur) Harvey, 1910–1973, vol. VII
Drum, Col Lorne, 1871–1933, vol. III
Drumalbyn, 1st Baron, 1908–1987, vol. VIII
Drummond, Lt-Gen. Sir Alexander; see Drummond, Lt-Gen. Sir W. A. D.
Drummond, Allan Harvey, 1845–1913, vol. I
Drummond, Andrew Cecil, 1865–1913, vol. I
Drummond, Arthur, 1871–1951, vol. V
Drummond, Rev. Arthur Hislop, 1843–1925, vol. II
Drummond, Arthur William Henry H; see Hay-Drummond.
Drummond, Col Hon. Charles Rowley H.; see Hay-Drummond.
Drummond, Cyril Augustus, 1873–1945, vol. IV
Drummond, Sir David, 1852–1932, vol. III
Drummond, Lady Edith, 1854–1937, vol. III
Drummond, Dame (Edith) Margaret, 1917–1987, vol. VIII
Drummond, Adm. Edmund Charles, 1841–1911, vol. I
Drummond, Vice-Adm. Hon. Edmund Rupert, 1884–1965, vol. VI
Drummond, Sir Francis Dudley Williams, 1863–1935, vol. III
Drummond, Maj.-Gen. Sir Francis Henry Rutherford, 1857–1919, vol. II
Drummond, Lt-Comdr Geoffrey Heneage, 1886–1941, vol. III
Drummond, Hon. Sir George Alexander, 1829–1910, vol. I
Drummond, George Henry, 1883–1963, vol. VI
Drummond, Captain George Robinson Bridge, 1845–1917, vol. II
Drummond, Hon. Mrs Geraldine Margaret, died 1956, vol. V
Drummond, Hamilton, died 1935, vol. III
Drummond, Henry, 1851–1897, vol. I
Drummond, Lt-Col Henry Edward S. H.; see Stirling Home Drummond.
Drummond, Brig.-Gen. Sir Hugh Henry John, 1st Bt, 1859–1924, vol. II
Drummond, Isabella Martha, died 1949, vol. IV
Drummond, Sir Jack Cecil, 1891–1952, vol. V
Drummond, Rev. James, 1835–1918, vol. II
Drummond, James, 1869–1940, vol. III
Drummond, Sir James Hamlyn Williams-, 4th Bt, 1857–1913, vol. I
Drummond, Sir James Hamlyn Williams Williams-, 5th Bt, 1891–1970, vol. VI
Drummond, James Montagu Frank, 1881–1965, vol. VI
Drummond, Maj.-Gen. Laurence George, 1861–1946, vol. IV

Drummond, Lister Maurice, 1856–1916, vol. II
Drummond, Malcolm, 1856–1924, vol. II
Drummond, Captain Maldwin, 1872–1929, vol. III
Drummond, Dame Margaret; see Drummond, Dame E. M.
Drummond, Col Hon. Sir Maurice Charles Andrew, 1877–1957, vol. V
Drummond, Michael, 1850–1921, vol. II (A), vol. III
Drummond, Air Marshal Sir Peter Roy Maxwell, 1894–1945, vol. IV
Drummond, Rev. Robert J., 1858–1951, vol. V
Drummond, Rev. Robert Skiell, 1828–1911, vol. I
Drummond, Sir Victor Arthur Wellington, 1833–1907, vol. I
Drummond, Sir Walter James, 1891–1965, vol. VI
Drummond, Col William, 1880–1960, vol. V
Drummond, Lt-Gen. Sir (William) Alexander (Duncan), 1901–1988, vol. VIII
Drummond, Rev. William Hamilton, 1863–1945, vol. IV
Drummond, William Henry, 1854–1907, vol. I
Drummond, Sir William Hugh Dudley Williams-, 6th Bt, 1901–1976, vol. VII
Drummond, William Norman, 1927–1993, vol. IX
Drummond-Hay, Francis Edward; see Hay.
Drummond-Hay, Sir Francis Ringler; see Hay.
Drummond-Willoughby, Brig.-Gen. Hon. Charles Strathavon Heathcote; see Willoughby.
Drummond-Wolff, Henry, 1899–1982, vol. VIII
Drury, Sir Alan Nigel, 1889–1980, vol. VII
Drury, Alfred, 1856–1944, vol. IV
Drury, (Alfred) Paul (Dalou), 1903–1987, vol. VIII
Drury, Allen Stuart, 1918–1998, vol. X
Drury, Amy Gertrude (Lady Drury), died 1953, vol. V
Drury, Adm. Sir Charles Carter, 1846–1914, vol. I
Drury, Hon. Charles Mills, 1912–1991, vol. IX
Drury, Maj.-Gen. Charles William, 1856–1913, vol. I
Drury, George Thorn-, 1860–1931, vol. III
Drury, Henry Cooke, 1860–1944, vol. IV
Drury, Henry George, 1839–1941, vol. IV
Drury, Rev. John Frederick William, 1858–1923, vol. II
Drury, Paul; see Drury, A. P. D.
Drury, Lt-Col Richard Frederick, 1866–1956, vol. V
Drury, Rev. Thomas William Ernest, died 1960, vol. V
Drury, Rt. Rev. Thomas Wortley, 1847–1926, vol. II
Drury, William D., 1857–1928, vol. II
Drury, Lt-Col William Price, 1861–1949, vol. IV
Drury-Lowe, Sir Drury Curzon, 1830–1908, vol. I
Drury-Lowe, Vice-Adm. Sidney Robert, 1871–1945, vol. IV
Druso; see Lumley, Lyulph.
Dryburgh, Edward Gelderd, 1909–1965, vol. VI
Dryden, Sir Alfred Erasmus, 5th and 8th Bt, 1821–1912, vol. I
Dryden, Sir Arthur, 6th and 9th Bt, 1852–1938, vol. III
Dryden, Sir Henry Edward Leigh, 4th and 7th Bt, 1818–1899, vol. I

Dryden, Hon. John, 1840–1909, vol. I
Dryden, Sir Noel Percy Hugh, 7th and 10th Bt, 1910–1970, vol. VI
Dryerre, Henry, 1881–1959, vol. V
Dryfoos, Orvil E., 1912–1963, vol. VI
Dryhurst, Frederick John, died 1931, vol. III
Dryland, Alfred, 1865–1946, vol. IV
Drysdale, Rev. A. H., 1837–1924, vol. II
Drysdale, Arthur, 1857–1922, vol. II
Drysdale, Charles Vickery, 1874–1961, vol. VI
Drysdale, Sir (George) Russell, 1912–1981, vol. VIII
Drysdale, Learmont, 1866–1909, vol. I
Drysdale, Sir Matthew Watt, 1892–1962, vol. VI
Drysdale, Sir Russell; see Drysdale, Sir G. R.
Drysdale, Sir William, 1819–1900, vol. I
Drysdale, Lt-Col William, 1876–1916, vol. II
D'Silva, John Leonard, 1910–1973, vol. VII
D'Souza, Most Rev. Albert V., 1904–1977, vol. VII
D'Souza, Frank, 1883–1960, vol. V
Dube, Bhugwandin, 1876–1938, vol. III
Dubilier, William, 1888–1969, vol. VI
Dubois, Paul, 1829–1905, vol. I
Dubois, Théodore, 1837–1924, vol. II
Du Bois, William Edward Burghardt, 1868–1963, vol. VI
Du Boisrouvray, Rt Rev. Bernard Jacquelot, 1877–1970, vol. VI (AII)
Dubose, William Porcher, 1836–1918, vol. II
Dubost, Antonin, 1844–1921, vol. II
Du Boulay, George Cornibert, 1883–1951, vol. V
Du Boulay, Ven. Henry Houssemayne, 1840–1925, vol. II
Du Boulay, Sir James Houssemayne, 1868–1945, vol. IV
DuBridge, Lee Alvin, 1901–1994, vol. IX
Dubs, Homer H., 1892–1969, vol. VI
Dubuc, Arthur Edouard, 1880–1944, vol. IV
Dubuc, Sir Joseph, 1840–1914, vol. I
Dubuffet, Jean, 1901–1985, vol. VIII
Du Buisson, Very Rev. John Clement, 1871–1938, vol. III
Du Cane, Sir Edmund Frederick, 1830–1903, vol. I
Du Cane, Col Hubert John, 1859–1916, vol. II
Ducane, Gen. Sir John Philip, 1865–1947, vol. IV
Du Cane, Comdr Peter, 1901–1984, vol. VIII
du Cann, Richard Dillon Lott, 1929–1994, vol. IX
Ducat, Col Charles Merewether, 1860–1934, vol. III
Ducat, David, 1904–1989, vol. VIII
Ducat, Ven. William Methven Gordon, died 1922, vol. II
Du Chaillu, Paul Belloni, 1835–1903, vol. I
Duchemin, Rt Rev. Mgr Charles L. H., 1886–1965, vol. VI
Duchemin, Henry Pope, died 1950, vol. IV
Duchesne, Jacques; see Saint-Denis, M. J.
Duchesne, Mgr Louis Marie Olivier, 1843–1922, vol. II
Duchesne, Brig. (Peter) Robin, 1936–2000, vol. X
Duchesne, Brig. Robin; see Duchesne, Brig. P. R.
Ducie, 3rd Earl of, 1827–1921, vol. II
Ducie, 4th Earl of, 1834–1924, vol. II
Ducie, 5th Earl of, 1875–1952, vol. V
Ducie, 6th Earl of, 1917–1991, vol. IX
Duck, Vet. Col Sir Francis, 1845–1934, vol. III

Duck, Leslie, 1935–1989, vol. VIII
Ducker, Herbert Charles, 1900–1993, vol. IX
Duckett, Sir George Floyd, 3rd Bt, 1811–1902, vol. I
Duckett, Lt-Col John Steuart, 1876–1952, vol. V
Duckham, Alec Narraway, 1903–1988, vol. VIII
Duckham, Sir Arthur McDougall, 1879–1932, vol. III
Duckmanton, Sir Talbot Sydney, 1921–1995, vol. IX
Duckworth, Arthur; see Duckworth, G. A. V.
Duckworth, Sir Dyce, 1st Bt, 1840–1928, vol. II
Duckworth, Sir Edward Dyce, 2nd Bt, 1875–1945, vol. IV
Duckworth, Francis R. G., 1881–1964, vol. VI
Duckworth, Frederick Victor, 1901–1974, vol. VII
Duckworth, (George) Arthur (Victor), 1901–1986, vol. VIII
Duckworth, Sir George Herbert, 1868–1934, vol. III
Duckworth, Sir James, 1840–1915, vol. I
Duckworth, James, 1869–1937, vol. III
Duckworth, John, 1863–1946, vol. IV
Duckworth, Captain Ralph Campbell Musbury, 1907–1983, vol. VIII
Duckworth, Sir Richard Dyce, 3rd Bt, 1918–1997, vol. X
Duckworth, Rev. Robinson, 1834–1911, vol. I
Duckworth, Rev. William Arthur, 1829–1917, vol. II
Duckworth, William Rostron, 1879–1952, vol. V
Duckworth, Wynfrid Laurence Henry, 1870–1956, vol. V
Duckworth-King, Col Sir Dudley Gordon Alan, 5th Bt, 1851–1909, vol. I
Duckworth-King, Sir George Henry James, 6th Bt, 1891–1952, vol. V
Duckworth-King, Sir John Richard, 7th Bt, 1899–1972, vol. VII
Duclos, Arnold Willard, 1874–1947, vol. IV
Duclos, Hon. Joseph Adolphe, 1873–1933, vol. III
Du Cros, Alfred, 1868–1946, vol. IV
Du Cros, Sir Arthur Philip, 1st Bt, 1871–1955, vol. V
Du Cros, Sir (Harvey) Philip, 2nd Bt, 1898–1975, vol. VII
Du Cros, Sir Philip; see Du Cros, Sir H. P.
du Cros, William Harvey, 1846–1918, vol. II
Dudbridge, Bryan James, 1912–1996, vol. X
Duddell, W., 1872–1917, vol. II
Dudden, Rev. Frederick Homes, 1874–1955, vol. V
Dudding, Rear-Adm. Horatio Nelson, 1849–1917, vol. II
Dudding, Surg. Rear-Adm. John Scarbrough, 1877–1951, vol. V
Dudding, Sir John Scarbrough, 1915–1986, vol. VIII
Dudeney, Mrs Henry, died 1945, vol. IV
Dudeney, Henry Ernest, 1857–1930, vol. III
Dudgeon, Alastair; see Dudgeon, J. A.
Dudgeon, Major Cecil Randolph, 1885–1970, vol. VI
Dudgeon, Sir Charles John, 1855–1928, vol. II
Dudgeon, Maj.-Gen. Frederick Annesley, 1866–1943, vol. IV
Dudgeon, Gerald Cecil, 1867–1930, vol. III
Dudgeon, Henry Alexander, 1924–1984, vol. VIII
Dudgeon, (John) Alastair, 1916–1989, vol. VIII

Dudgeon, Leonard Stanley, 1876–1938, vol. III
Dudgeon, Lt-Col Robert Francis, 1851–1932, vol. III
Dudgeon, Brig.-Gen. Robert Maxwell, 1881–1962, vol. VI
Dudley, 2nd Earl of, 1867–1932, vol. III
Dudley, 3rd Earl of, 1894–1969, vol. VI
Dudley, 12th Baron, 1872–1936, vol. III
Dudley, 13th Baron, 1910–1972, vol. VII
Dudley, Sir Alan Alves, 1907–1971, vol. VII
Dudley, Donald Reynolds, 1910–1972, vol. VII
Dudley, Col George de Someri, 1874–1941, vol. IV
Dudley, Harold Ward, 1887–1935, vol. III
Dudley, Rev. Owen Francis, 1882–1952, vol. V
Dudley, Roland, 1879–1964, vol. VI
Dudley, Surg. Vice-Adm. Sir Sheldon Francis, 1884–1956, vol. V
Dudley, Sir Willem Edward, died 1938, vol. III
Dudley-Williams, Sir Rolf Dudley, 1st Bt, 1908–1987, vol. VIII
Dudman, George Edward, 1916–1984, vol. VIII
Dudman, Ven. Robert William, 1925–1984, vol. VIII
Dudok, Willem Marinus, 1884–1974, vol. VII
Duerden, J. E., died 1937, vol. III
Duesbury, Rt Rev. Charles Leonard T.; see Thornton-Duesbury.
Duesbery, Rev. Canon Julian Percy T.; see Thornton-Duesbery.
Duff, Major Adrian G.; see Grant-Duff.
Duff, Maj.-Gen. Alan Colquhoun, 1896–1973, vol. VII
Duff, Adm. Sir Alexander Ludovic, 1862–1933, vol. III
Duff, Rt Hon. Sir Antony; see Duff, Rt Hon. Sir Arthur A.
Duff, Archibald, 1845–1934, vol. III
Duff, Bt Lt-Col Arthur Abercromby S.; see Scott-Duff.
Duff, Adm. Sir Arthur Allan Morison, 1874–1952, vol. V
Duff, Rt Hon. Sir (Arthur) Antony, 1920–2000, vol. X
Duff, Sir Arthur Cuninghame G.; see Grant-Duff.
Duff, Gen. Sir Beauchamp, 1855–1918, vol. II
Duff, Lt-Col Benjamin Michael, 1840–1926, vol. II
Duff, Col Charles de Vertus, 1870–1950, vol. IV
Duff, Col Charles Edward, 1858–1936, vol. III
Duff, Sir (Charles) Michael (Robert Vivian), 3rd Bt, 1907–1980, vol. VII
Duff, Sir (Charles) Patrick, 1889–1972, vol. VII
Duff, Charles St Lawrence, 1894–1966, vol. VI
Duff, David, 1883–1959, vol. V
Duff, Edith Florence G.; see Grant-Duff.
Duff, Edward Gordon, 1863–1924, vol. II
Duff, Sir Evelyn G.; see Grant-Duff.
Duff, Francis Bluett, 1875–1947, vol. IV
Duff, Garden Alexander, 1853–1933, vol. III
Duff, Lt-Col Sir Garden Beauchamp, 1st Bt, 1879–1952, vol. V
Duff, Col George Mowat, 1862–1935, vol. III
Duff, Sir Hector Livingston, 1872–1954, vol. V
Duff, James Augustine, 1872–1943, vol. IV
Duff, Sir James Fitzjames, 1898–1970, vol. VI
Duff, Hon. James Stoddart, 1856–1916, vol. II
Duff, John, 1850–1921, vol. II

Duff, John Robert Keitley, 1862–1938, vol. III
Duff, John Wharton Wharton-, 1845–1935, vol. III
Duff, John Wight, 1866–1944, vol. IV
Duff, Rt. Hon. Sir Lyman Poore, 1865–1955, vol. V
Duff, Sir Michael; see Duff, Sir C. M. R. V.
Duff, Rt. Hon. Sir Mountstuart Elphinstone Grant, 1829–1906, vol. I
Duff, Sir Patrick; see Duff, Sir C. P.
Duff, Patrick Craigmile, 1922–2000, vol. X
Duff, Patrick William, 1901–1991, vol. IX
Duff, Sir Robert George Vivian, (Sir Robin), 2nd Bt, 1876–1914, vol. I
Duff, Sir Robin; see Duff, Sir R. G. V.
Duff, Stanley Lewis, 1881–1943, vol. IV
Duff, Thomas Duff Gordon, 1848–1923, vol. II
Duff, Col Thomas Robert G.; see Gordon-Duff.
Duff-Dunbar, Lt-Comdr Kenneth James; see Dunbar.
Duff Gordon, Sir Cosmo Edmund, 5th Bt; see Gordon.
Duff-Gordon, Sir Douglas Frederick, 7th Bt, 1892–1964, vol. VI
Duff-Gordon, Sir Henry William, 6th Bt, 1866–1953, vol. V
Duff-Sutherland-Dunbar, Sir George, 6th Bt; see Dunbar.
Duff-Sutherland-Dunbar, Sir George Cospatrick, 7th Bt, 1906–1963, vol. VI
Dufferin and Ava, 1st Marquess of, 1826–1902, vol. I
Dufferin and Ava, 2nd Marquess of, 1866–1918, vol. II
Dufferin and Ava, 3rd Marquess of, 1875–1930, vol. III
Dufferin and Ava, 4th Marquess of, 1909–1945, vol. IV
Dufferin and Ava, 5th Marquess of, 1938–1988, vol. VIII
Dufferin and Ava, Marchioness of; (Hariot), died 1936, vol. III
Dufferin and Clandeboye, 10th Baron, 1916–1991, vol. IX
Duffes, Arthur Paterson, 1880–1968, vol. VI
Duffey, Sir George Frederick, 1843–1903, vol. I
Duffield, Anne, died 1976, vol. VII
Duffield, Mary Elizabeth, 1819–1914, vol. I
Duffield, William Bartleet, died 1918, vol. II
Duffus, Brig.-Gen. Edward John, 1866–1937, vol. III
Duffus, Col Francis Ferguson, 1870–1953, vol. V
Duffus, Sir William Algernon Holwell, 1911–1981, vol. VIII
Duffy, Hon. Sir Charles Gavan, 1816–1903, vol. I
Duffy, Charles Gavan, 1855–1932, vol. III
Duffy, Hon. Sir Charles Leonard G.; see Gavan-Duffy.
Duffy, Rt. Hon. Sir Frank Gavan, 1852–1936, vol. III
Duffy, George Gavan, 1882–1951, vol. V
Duffy, Hon. H. Thomas, died 1903, vol. I
Duffy, Hugh Herbert White, 1917–1983, vol. VIII
Duffy, Peter Joseph Francis, 1954–1999, vol. X
Duffy, Terence, 1922–1985, vol. VIII
Duffy, Thomas G.; see Gavan-Duffy.
Dufty, (Arthur) Richard, 1911–1993, vol. IX

Dufty, Richard; see Dufty, A. R.
Dufy, Raoul, 1877–1953, vol. V
Dugan of Victoria, 1st Baron, 1877–1951, vol. V
Dugard, Arthur Charles, 1904–1996, vol. X
Dugas, Calixter Aimé, 1845–1918, vol. II
Dugas, François Octave, 1857–1918, vol. II (A), vol. III
Dugdale, Amy Katherine; see Browning, A. K.
Dugdale, Col Arthur, 1869–1941, vol. IV
Dugdale, Blanche Elizabeth Campbell; see Dugdale, Mrs Edgar Trevelyan Stratford.
Dugdale, Mrs Edgar Trevelyan Stratford, (Blanche Elizabeth Campbell Dugdale), died 1948, vol. IV
Dugdale, Col Frank, 1857–1925, vol. II
Dugdale, Frederick Brooks, died 1902, vol. I
Dugdale, James Broughton, 1855–1927, vol. II
Dugdale, Rt. Hon. John, 1905–1963, vol. VI
Dugdale, Sir John Robert Stratford, 1923–1994, vol. IX
Dugdale, John Stratford, 1835–1920, vol. II
Dugdale, Norman, 1921–1995, vol. IX
Dugdale, Peter Robin, 1928–1998, vol. X
Dugdale, Rev. Sydney, died 1942, vol. IV
Dugdale, Thomas Cantrell, 1880–1952, vol. V
Dugdale, Sir William Francis Stratford, 1st Bt, 1872–1965, vol. VI
Dugdale, Major William Marshall, 1881–1952, vol. V
Duggan, Alfred Leo, 1903–1964, vol. VI
Duggan, Edmund John, died 1936, vol. III
Duggan, Rear-Adm. Eyre Sturdy, 1891–1956, vol. V
Duggan, George Chester, died 1969, vol. VI
Duggan, Gordon Aldridge, 1937–1998, vol. X
Duggan, Major Harold Joseph, 1896–1942, vol. IV
Duggan, Hubert John, 1904–1943, vol. IV
Duggan, Col Sir Jamshedji, 1884–1957, vol. V
Duggan, Rt Rev. John Coote, 1918–2000, vol. X
Dugmore, Arthur Radclyffe, 1870–1955, vol. V
Dugmore, Rev. Clifford William, 1909–1990, vol. VIII
Dugmore, Rev. Ernest Edward, 1843–1925, vol. II
Dugmore Lt-Col William Francis Brougham Radclyffe, 1868–1917, vol. II
Duguid, Charles, 1864–1923, vol. II
Duguid, Maj.-Gen. David Robertson, 1888–1973, vol. VII
Duguid, John Bright, 1895–1980, vol. VII
Duguid-McCombie, Col William McCombie, 1874–1970, vol. VI
Duhamel, Georges, 1884–1966, vol. VI
du Heaume, Sir (Francis) Herbert, 1897–1988, vol. VIII
du Heaume, Sir Herbert; see du Heaume, Sir F. H.
Duhig, Sir James, 1871–1965, vol. VI
Duhm, Bernhard Laward, 1847–1928, vol. II
Duigan, Maj.-Gen. Sir John Evelyn, 1882–1950, vol. IV
Dukas, Paul, 1865–1935, vol. III
Duke, Lt-Col Augustus Cecil Hare, died 1943, vol. IV
Duke, Brig. Cecil Leonard Basil, 1896–1963, vol. IV
Duke, Sir Charles Beresford, 1905–1978, vol. VII
Duke, Hon. Edgar Mortimer, 1895–1965, vol. VI
Duke, Rev. Edward St Arnaud, 1854–1939, vol. III

Duke, Sir (Frederick) William, 1863–1924, vol. II
Duke, Maj.-Gen. Sir Gerald William, 1910–1992, vol. IX
Duke, Herbert Lyndhurst, 1883–1966, vol. VI
Duke, Sr James, 2nd Bt, 1865–1935, vol. III
Duke, James Buchanan, 1857–1925, vol. II
Duke, Brig. Jesse Pevensey, 1890–1980, vol. VII
Duke, Sir Norman; see Duke, Sir R. N.
Duke, Reginald Franklyn Hare, 1887–1929, vol. III
Duke, Sir (Robert) Norman, 1893–1969, vol. VI
Duke, Robin Antony Hare, 1916–1984, vol. VIII
Duke, Sir William; see Duke, Sir F. W.
Duke, Most Rev. William Mark, 1879–1971, vol. VII
Duke, Winifred, died 1962, vol. VI
Duke-Elder, Sir Stewart; see Duke-Elder, Sir W. S.
Duke-Elder, Sir (William) Stewart, 1898–1978, vol. VII
Dukes, Ashley, 1885–1959, vol. V
Dukes, Cuthbert Esquire, 1890–1977, vol. VII
Dukes, Dame Cyvia Myriam; see Rambert, Dame Marie.
Dukes, Dame Marie; see Rambert.
Dukes, Sir Paul, 1889–1967, vol. VI
Dukeston, 1st Baron, 1881–1948, vol. IV
Dulac, Edmund, 1882–1953, vol. V
Dulanty, John Whelan, died 1955, vol. V
Duleep Singh, Prince Frederick, 1868–1926, vol. II
Duleep Singh, Prince Victor Albert Jay, 1866–1918, vol. II
Dulles, Allen Welsh, 1893–1969, vol. VI
Dulles, John Foster, 1888–1959, vol. V
Dulverton, 1st Baron, 1880–1956, vol. V
Dulverton, 2nd Baron, 1915–1992, vol. IX
Duly, Surg. Rear-Adm. (D) Philip Reginald John, 1925–1989, vol. VIII
Duly, Sidney John, 1891–1991, vol. IX
Dumarchey, Pierre; see MacOrlan, Pierre.
Dumaresq, Rear-Adm. John Saumarez, 1873–1922, vol. II
Dumas, Hugh Charles Sowerby, 1865–1940, vol. III
Dumas, Sir Lloyd, 1891–1973, vol. VII
Dumas, Adm. Philip Wylie, 1868–1948, vol. IV
Dumas, Sir Russell John, 1887–1975, vol. VII
du Maurier, Dame Daphne, (Lady Browning), 1907–1989, vol. VIII
du Maurier, Sir Gerald, 1873–1934, vol. III
du Maurier, Lt-Col Guy Louis Busson, 1865–1915, vol. I
Dumayne, Sir Fredrick George, 1852–1930, vol. III
Dumbell, Sir Alured, 1835–1900, vol. I
Dumbell, Lt-Col Charles Harold, 1878–1935, vol. III
Dumbleton, Gen. Charles, 1824–1916, vol. II
Dumbutshena, Hon. Enoch, 1920–2000, vol. X
Duminy, Jacobus Petrus, 1897–1980, vol. VII
Dummett, Robert Bryan, 1912–1977, vol. VII
Dummett, Sir Robert Ernest, 1872–1941, vol. IV
Du Moulin, Rt Rev. John Philip, 1834–1911, vol. I
Dumpleton, Cyril Walter, 1897–1966, vol. VI
Dumraon, Zamindar of, died 1933, vol. III
Dun, Robert Hay, 1870–1940, vol. IV
Dun, William Gibb, died 1927, vol. II
Dunalley, 4th Baron, 1851–1927, vol. II
Dunalley, 5th Baron, 1877–1948, vol. IV

Dunalley, 6th Baron, 1912–1992, vol. IX
Dunbabin, Robert Leslie, 1869–1949, vol. IV
Dunbabin, Thomas, 1883–1973, vol. VII
Dunbabin, Thomas James, 1911–1955, vol. V
Dunbar of Mochrum, Sir Adrian Ivor, 12th Bt (cr 1694), 1893–1977, vol. VII
Dunbar, Sir Alexander, 1888–1955, vol. V
Dunbar, Sir Alexander James, 4th Bt (cr 1814), 1870–1900, vol. I
Dunbar, Alexander Robert, 1904–1980, vol. VII
Dunbar, Sir Archibald, 6th Bt (cr 1700), 1803–1898, vol. I
Dunbar, Sir (Archibald) Edward, 9th Bt (cr 1700), 1889–1969, vol. VI
Dunbar, Sir Archibald Hamilton, 7th Bt (cr 1700), 1828–1910, vol. I
Dunbar, Sir Basil Douglas H.; see Hope-Dunbar.
Dunbar, Charles, 1907–1997, vol. X
Dunbar, Paymaster Rear-Adm. Charles Augustus Royer Flood, 1849–1939, vol. III
Dunbar, Sir Charles Dunbar H.; see Hope-Dunbar.
Dunbar, Rev. Sir Charles Gordon-Cumming, 8th Bt (cr 1700), 1844–1916, vol. II
Dunbar, Maj.-Gen. Charles Whish, 1919–1981, vol. VIII
Dunbar, Maj.-Gen. Claude Ian Hurley, 1909–1971, vol. VII
Dunbar of Durn, Sir Drummond Cospatrick Ninian, 9th Bt, 1917–2000, vol. X
Dunbar, Sir Drummond Miles, 7th Bt (cr 1697), 1845–1903, vol. I
Dunbar, Sir Edward; see Dunbar, Sir A. E.
Dunbar, Evelyn Mary, died 1960, vol. V
Dunbar, Sir Frederick George, 5th Bt (cr 1814), 1875–1937, vol. III
Dunbar, Sir George Alexander Drummond, 8th Bt (cr 1697), 1879–1949, vol. IV
Dunbar, Sir George Cospatrick D. S., 7th Bt; see Duff-Sutherland-Dunbar.
Dunbar, Sir George Duff-Sutherland, 6th Bt, 1878–1962, vol. VI
Dunbar, Sir James George Hawker Rowland, 10th Bt (cr 1694), 1862–1953, vol. V
Dunbar of Mochrum, Sir Jean Ivor, 13th Bt (cr 1694), 1918–1993, vol. IX
Dunbar, Sir John Greig, 1906–1978, vol. VII
Dunbar, Major John Telfer, died 1957, vol. V
Dunbar, Lt-Comdr Kenneth James Duff-, 1886–1916, vol. II
Dunbar, Sir Loraine Geddes, 1865–1943, vol. IV
Dunbar of Hempriggs, Dame Maureen Daisy Helen, (Lady Dunbar of Hempriggs), Btss (8th in line), 1906–1997, vol. X
Dunbar, Sir Richard Fredrick Roberts, 1900–1965, vol. VI
Dunbar, Sir Richard Sutherland, 11th Bt (cr 1694), 1873–1953, vol. V
Dunbar, Robert, 1895–1970, vol. VI
Dunbar, Robert Haig, died 1919, vol. II
Dunbar, Sir Uthred James Hay, 8th Bt (cr 1694), 1843–1904, vol. I
Dunbar, Sir William Cospatrick, 9th Bt (cr 1694), 1844–1931, vol. III
Dunbar-Buller, Charles William; see Buller.

Dunbar Kilburn, Bertram Edward, 1872–1948, vol. IV
Dunbar-Nasmith, Rear-Adm. David Arthur, 1921–1997, vol. X
Dunbar-Nasmith, Adm. Sir Martin Eric; *see* Nasmith.
Dunboyne, 24th Baron, 1839–1899, vol. I
Dunboyne, 25th Baron, 1844–1913, vol. I
Dunboyne, 26th Baron, 1874–1945, vol. IV
Duncalfe, Sir Roger, 1884–1961, vol. VI
Duncan, Col Sir Alan Gomme Gomme-, 1893–1963, vol. VI
Duncan, Alexander, *died* 1943, vol. IV
Duncan, Alexander Mitchell, 1888–1965, vol. VI
Duncan, Alexander Robert, 1844–1927, vol. II
Duncan, Alfred Charles, 1886–1979, vol. VII
Duncan, Andrew, *died* 1912, vol. I
Duncan, Rt. Hon. Sir Andrew Rae, 1884–1952, vol. V
Duncan, Archibald Sutherland, 1914–1992, vol. IX
Duncan, Sir Arthur Bryce, 1909–1984, vol. VIII
Duncan, Brian Arthur Cullum, 1908–1997, vol. X
Duncan, Charles, 1865–1933, vol. III
Duncan, Sir (Charles Edgar) Oliver, 3rd Bt (*cr* 1905), 1892–1964, vol. VI
Duncan, Claude Woodruff, *died* 1945, vol. IV
Duncan, Colin; *see* Duncan, P. C.
Duncan, Sir David, *died* 1923, vol. II
Duncan, David, 1839–1923, vol. II
Duncan, Surg. Rear-Adm. David, 1900–1974, vol. VII
Duncan, Douglas John Stewart, 1945–2000, vol. X
Duncan, Edmondstoune, 1866–1920, vol. II
Duncan, Ellen, vol. III
Duncan, Maj.-Gen. Francis John, *died* 1960, vol. V
Duncan, Sir Frederick William, 2nd Bt (*cr* 1905), 1859–1929, vol. III
Duncan, Captain George, 1863–1937, vol. III
Duncan, Rev. George, *died* 1932, vol. III
Duncan, George, *died* 1949, vol. IV
Duncan, George B., 1869–1941, vol. IV
Duncan, Very Rev. George Simpson, 1884–1965, vol. VI
Duncan, Sir Harold Handasyde, 1885–1962, vol. VI
Duncan, Sir Hastings; *see* Duncan, Sir J. H.
Duncan, Maj.-Gen. Henry Clare, 1876–1961, vol. VI
Duncan, Sir James, *died* 1926, vol. II
Duncan, Sir James Alexander Lawson, 1st Bt (*cr* 1957), 1899–1974, vol. VII
Duncan, James Archibald, 1858–1911, vol. I
Duncan, Lt-Col James Fergus, *died* 1941, vol. IV
Duncan, Sir (James) Hastings, 1855–1928, vol. II
Duncan, James Lindsay, 1905–1954, vol. V
Duncan, James Stuart, 1893–1986, vol. VIII
Duncan, Jane, 1910–1976, vol. VII
Duncan, Sir John, 1846–1914, vol. I
Duncan, John, *died* 1945, vol. IV
Duncan, Maj.-Gen. Sir John, 1872–1948, vol. IV
Duncan, Comdr John Alexander, 1878–1943, vol. IV
Duncan, John Douglas Grace, 1899–1969, vol. VI
Duncan, John Hudson E.; *see* Elder-Duncan.
Duncan, Hon. Sir John James, 1845–1913, vol. I
Duncan, John Murray, *died* 1922, vol. II

Duncan, Sir John Norman Valette; *see* Duncan, Sir Val.
Duncan, John Shiels, 1886–1949, vol. IV
Duncan, Rev. Joseph, 1843–1915, vol. I
Duncan, Joseph Forbes, 1879–1964, vol. VI
Duncan, Kenneth Playfair, 1924–1999, vol. X
Duncan, Leland Lewis, 1862–1923, vol. II
Duncan, Col Macbeth Moir, 1866–1942, vol. IV
Duncan, Malcolm McGregor, 1922–1996, vol. X
Duncan, Michael John Freeman, 1926–1991, vol. IX
Duncan, Maj.-Gen. Nigel William, 1899–1987, vol. VIII
Duncan, Norman, 1871–1916, vol. II
Duncan, Sir Oliver; *see* Duncan, Sir C. E. O.
Duncan, Rt. Hon. Sir Patrick, 1870–1943, vol. IV
Duncan, (Peter) Colin, 1895–1979, vol. VII
Duncan, Lt-Col Ronald Cardew, 1886–1963, vol. VI
Duncan, Ronald Frederick Henry, 1914–1982, vol. VIII
Duncan, Sir Surr William, 1st Bt (*cr* 1905), 1834–1908, vol. I
Duncan, Sir Thomas Andrew, 1873–1960, vol. V
Duncan, Hon. Thomas Young, 1836–1914, vol. I
Duncan, Sir Val, (John Norman Valette), 1913–1975, vol. VII
Duncan, Hon. Sir Walter Gordon, 1885–1963, vol. VI
Duncan, Sir William Barr McKinnon, 1922–1984, vol. VIII
Duncan, Brig. William Edmonstone, 1890–1969, vol. VI
Duncan, William Jolly, 1894–1960, vol. V
Duncan-Hughes, Captain John Grant; *see* Hughes.
Duncan-Jones, Very Rev. Arthur Stuart, 1879–1955, vol. V
Duncan-Jones, Austin Ernest, 1908–1967, vol. VI
Duncan Millar, Ian Alastair, 1914–1997, vol. X
Duncan-Sandys, Baron (Life Peer); Duncan Edwin Duncan-Sandys, 1908–1987, vol. VIII
Duncanson, Sir John McLean, 1897–1963, vol. VI
Duncombe, Alfred Charles, 1843–1925, vol. II
Duncombe, Col (Charles) William (Ernest), 1862–1945, vol. IV
Duncombe, Maj.-Gen. Charles Wilmer, 1838–1911, vol. I
Duncombe, Sir Everard (Philip Digby) Pauncefort-, 3rd Bt (*cr* 1859), 1885–1971, vol. VII
Duncombe, Col Sir George Augustus, 1st Bt (*cr* 1919), 1848–1933, vol. III
Duncombe, Hon. Hubert Ernest Valentine, 1862–1918, vol. II
Duncombe, Walter Henry Octavius, 1846–1917, vol. II
Duncombe, Col William; *see* Duncombe, Col C. W. E.
Duncombe, Rev. William Duncombe Van der Horst, *died* 1925, vol. II
Dundas, Hon. Lord; David Dundas, 1854–1922, vol. II
Dundas of Dundas, Adam Duncan, 1903–1951, vol. V
Dundas, Sir Ambrose Dundas Flux, 1899–1973, vol. VII

Dundas of Dundas, Adm. Sir Charles, 1859–1924, vol. II
Dundas, Hon. Sir Charles Cecil Farquharson, 1884–1956, vol. V
Dundas, Sir Charles Henry, 4th Bt (*cr* 1821), 1851–1908, vol. I
Dundas, Rev. Charles Leslie, 1847–1932, vol. III
Dundas, David; *see* Dundas, Hon. Lord.
Dundas, Lt-Col Frederick Charles, 1868–1941, vol. IV
Dundas, Lord George Heneage Lawrence, 1882–1968, vol. VI
Dundas, George Smythe, 1842–1909, vol. I
Dundas, Sir George Whyte Melville, 5th Bt (*cr* 1821), 1856–1934, vol. III
Dundas, Sir Henry Herbert Philip, 3rd Bt (*cr* 1898), 1866–1930, vol. III
Dundas, Sir Henry Matthew, 5th Bt (*cr* 1898), 1937–1963, vol. VI
Dundas, Sir Hugh Spencer Lisle, 1920–1995, vol. IX
Dundas, Lt-Col James Colin, 1883–1966, vol. VI
Dundas, Sir James Durham, 6th Bt (*cr* 1898), 1905–1967, vol. VI
Dundas, Vice-Adm. John George Lawrence, 1893–1952, vol. V
Dundas, Hon. Kenneth Robert, 1882–1915, vol. I
Dundas, Major Laurance Charles, 1857–1908, vol. I
Dundas, Captain Lawrence Leopold, *died* 1939, vol. III
Dundas, Col Sir Lorenzo George, 1837–1917, vol. II
Dundas, Brig. Patrick Henry, 1871–1936, vol. III
Dundas, Sir Philip, 4th Bt (*cr* 1898), 1899–1952, vol. V
Dundas, Sir Robert, 1st Bt (*cr* 1898) 1823–1909, vol. I
Dundas, Lt-Col Sir Robert, 2nd Bt (*cr* 1898), 1857–1910, vol. I
Dundas, Robert Giffen, 1909–1984, vol. VIII
Dundas, Robert Hamilton, 1884–1960, vol. V
Dundas, Rev. Robert J., 1832–1904, vol. I
Dundas, Robert Thomas, *died* 1948, vol. IV
Dundas, Sir Robert Whyte-Melville, 6th Bt (*cr* 1821), 1881–1981, vol. VIII
Dundas, Sir Sidney James, 3rd Bt (*cr* 1821), 1849–1904, vol. I
Dundas, Sir Thomas Calderwood, 7th Bt (*cr* 1898), 1906–1970, vol. VI
Dundas, William Charles Michael, 1873–1933, vol. III
Dundas, William John, 1848–1921, vol. II
Dundas-Grant, Sir James; *see* Grant.
Dundee, 11th Earl of, 1902–1983, vol. VIII
Dundee, Col William John Daniell, 1862–1940, vol. III
Dunderdale, Comdr Wilfred Albert, 1899–1990, vol. VIII
Dundon, John, *died* 1952, vol. V
Dundonald, 12th Earl of, 1852–1935, vol. III
Dundonald, 13th Earl of, 1886–1958, vol. V
Dundonald, 14th Earl of, 1918–1986, vol. VIII
Dunedin, 1st Viscount, 1849–1942, vol. IV
Dunedin, Viscountess; (Jean Elmslie), *died* 1944, vol. IV
Dunfee, Col Vickers, 1861–1927, vol. II

Dunfield, Sir Brian Edward Spencer, 1888–1968, vol. VI
Dunham, Cyril John, 1908–1986, vol. VIII
Dunham, E. K. 1860–1923, vol. II
Dunhill, Alfred, 1872–1959, vol. V
Dunhill, Thomas Frederick, 1877–1946, vol. IV
Dunhill, Sir Thomas Peel, 1876–1957, vol. V
Dunican, Peter Thomas, 1918–1989, vol. VIII
Dunk, Susan S.; *see* Spain-Dunk.
Dunk, Sir William Ernest, 1897–1984, vol. VIII
Dunkerley, George William, 1919–1994, vol. IX
Dunkerley, Harvey John, 1902–1985, vol. VIII
Dunkerley, Ven. William Herbert Cecil, *died* 1922, vol. II
Dunkerly, John Samuel, 1881–1931, vol. III
Dunkin, Edwin, 1821–1898, vol. I
Dunkin, Major George William, 1886–1942, vol. IV
Dunkley, Rev. Charles, 1847–1936, vol. III
Dunkley, Sir Herbert Francis, 1886–1963, vol. VI (AII)
Dunkley, Captain James Lewis, 1908–1994, vol. IX
Dunkley, Philip Parker, 1922–1985, vol. VIII
Dunleath, 2nd Baron, 1854–1931, vol. III
Dunleath, 3rd Baron, 1886–1956, vol. V
Dunleath, 4th Baron, 1933–1993, vol. IX
Dunleath, 5th Baron, 1915–1997, vol. X
Dunleavy, Philip, 1915–1996, vol. X
Dunlop, Agnes Mary Robertson; *see* Kyle, Elisabeth.
Dunlop, Alexander Johnstone, 1848–1921, vol. II
Dunlop, Mrs Annie Isabella, 1897–1973, vol. VII
Dunlop, Charles Robertson, 1876–1932, vol. III
Dunlop, Major Colin Napier Buchanan, 1877–1915, vol. I
Dunlop, Rt Rev. David Colin, 1897–1968, vol. VI
Dunlop, Captain David Kennedy B.; *see* Buchanan-Dunlop.
Dunlop, Maj.-Gen. Dermott, 1898–1980, vol. VII
Dunlop, Sir Derrick Melville, 1902–1980, vol. VII
Dunlop, Douglas Morton, 1909–1987, vol. VIII
Dunlop, Sir Edward; *see* Dunlop, Sir E. E.
Dunlop, Sir (Ernest) Edward, 1907–1993, vol. IX
Dunlop, Ernest McMurchie, 1893–1969, vol. VI
Dunlop, Rev. Francis Wallace, 1875–1932, vol. III
Dunlop, Col Frank Passy, 1877–1940, vol. III
Dunlop, Gordon; *see* Dunlop, N. G. E.
Dunlop, Col Henry Donald B.; *see* Buchanan-Dunlop.
Dunlop, Hugh Alexander, 1903–1954, vol. V
Dunlop, James Crauford, *died* 1944, vol. IV
Dunlop, James Marcus Muntz, *died* 1938, vol. III
Dunlop, James Matthew, 1867–1949, vol. IV
Dunlop, Col James William, 1854–1923, vol. II
Dunlop, Hon. John, 1837–1916, vol. II
Dunlop, John, 1910–1996, vol. X
Dunlop, Sir John Kinninmont, 1892–1974, vol. VII
Dunlop, Sir John Wallace, 1910–1983, vol. VIII
Dunlop, Louis Vandalle, 1878–1954, vol. V
Dunlop, Ven. Maxwell Tulloch, 1898–1964, vol. VI
Dunlop, Sir Nathaniel, 1830–1919, vol. II
Dunlop, (Norman) Gordon (Edward), 1928–1995, vol. IX
Dunlop, Robert, *died* 1935, vol. III
Dunlop, Sir Robert William Layard, 1869–1962, vol. VI

Dunlop, Ronald Offory, 1894–1973, vol. VII
Dunlop, Roy Leslie, 1899–1981, vol. VIII
Dunlop, Col Samuel, 1838–1917, vol. II
Dunlop, Engr Rear-Adm. Samuel Harrison, 1884–1950, vol. IV
Dunlop, Sir Thomas, 1st Bt, 1855–1938, vol. III
Dunlop, Sir Thomas, 2nd Bt, 1881–1963, vol. VI
Dunlop, Sir Thomas, 3rd Bt, 1912–1999, vol. X
Dunlop, Bt Col Sir Thomas Charles, 1878–1960, vol. V
Dunlop, Sir Thomas Dacre, 1883–1963, vol. VI
Dunlop, Col William Bruce, 1877–1933, vol. III
Dunlop, Major William Hugh, 1857–1924, vol. II
Dunlop, William Louis Martial, 1882–1948, vol. IV
Dunlop, Sir William Norman Gough, 1914–1998, vol. X
Dunlop, William Wallace, 1846–1930, vol. III
Dunmore, 7th Earl of, 1841–1907, vol. I
Dunmore, 8th Earl of, 1871–1962, vol. VI
Dunmore, 9th Earl of, 1939–1980, vol. VII
Dunmore, 10th Earl of, 1911–1981, vol. VIII
Dunmore, 11th Earl of, 1913–1995, vol. IX
Dunn, Albert Edward, 1864–1937, vol. III
Dunn, Rt Rev. Andrew Hunter, 1839–1914, vol. I
Dunn, Captain Arthur Edward, 1876–1927, vol. II
Dunn, Charles William, 1877–1966, vol. VI
Dunn, Lt-Col Cuthbert Lindsay, 1875–1956, vol. V
Dunn, Edward, 1880–1945, vol. IV
Dunn, Most Rev. Edward Arthur, 1870–1955, vol. V
Dunn, Lt-Col Sir (Francis) Vivian, 1908–1995, vol. IX
Dunn, Col George Willoughby, 1914–1994, vol. IX
Dunn, Col Henry Nason, 1864–1952, vol. V
Dunn, Hugh Percy, 1854–1931, vol. III
Dunn, James Anthony, 1926–1985, vol. VIII
Dunn, James B., 1861–1930, vol. III
Dunn, Sir James Hamet, 1st Bt (cr 1921), 1875–1956, vol. V
Dunn, James Nicol, 1856–1919, vol. II
Dunn, James Stormont, 1879–1965, vol. VI
Dunn, John Freeman, 1874–1954, vol. V
Dunn, Sir John Henry, 2nd Bt (cr 1917), 1890–1971, vol. VII
Dunn, John Messenger, 1838–1904, vol. I
Dunn, John Shaw, 1883–1944, vol. IV
Dunn, Brig. Keith Frederick William, 1891–1985, vol. VIII
Dunn, John Thomas, 1858–1939, vol. III
Dunn, Louis Albert, 1858–1918, vol. II
Dunn, Naughton, 1884–1939, vol. III
Dunn, Patrick Smith, 1848–1932, vol. III
Dunn, Peter Douglas Hay, 1892–1965, vol. VI
Dunn, Sir Philip Gordon, 2nd Bt (cr 1921), 1905–1976, vol. VII
Dunn, Piers Duncan Williams, 1896–1957, vol. V
Dunn, Richard Johann, 1943–1998, vol. X
Dunn, Stanley Gerald, 1879–1964, vol. VI
Dunn, Rt Rev. Thomas, 1870–1931, vol. III
Dunn, Thomas Alexander, 1923–1988, vol. VIII
Dunn, Rev. Thomas Shelton, 1875–1949, vol. IV
Dunn, Thomas Smith, 1836–1916, vol. II
Dunn, Sir Vivian; see Dunn, Sir F. V.
Dunn, Sir William, 1st Bt (cr 1895), 1833–1912, vol. I

Dunn, William, 1876–1949, vol. IV
Dunn, Sir William Henry, 1st Bt (cr 1917), 1856–1926, vol. II
Dunn, William Norman, 1873–1961, vol. VI
Dunnachie, James Francis, (Jimmy), 1930–1997, vol. X
Dunne, Arthur Mountjoy, 1859–1947, vol. IV
Dunne, Lt-Col Edward Marten, 1864–1944, vol. IV
Dunne, Finley Peter, 1867–1936, vol. III
Dunne, Major Francis Plunkett Neville, 1872–1931, vol. III
Dunne, Irene Marie, 1898–1990, vol. VIII
Dunne, Rt Rev. Mgr James J, 1859–1934, vol. III
Dunne, Lt-Col James Stuart, 1877–1955, vol. V
Dunne, Sir John, 1825–1906, vol. I
Dunne, Rt Rev. John, 1846–1917, vol. II
Dunne, Gen. Sir John Hart, 1835–1924, vol. II
Dunne, Captain John J., 1837–1910, vol. I
Dunne, Rt Rev. John Mary, 1843–1919, vol. II
Dunne, John William died 1949, vol. IV
Dunne, Sir Laurence Rivers, 1893–1970, vol. VI
Dunne, Most Rev. Patrick, 1891–1988, vol. VIII
Dunne, Philip Russell Rendel, 1904–1965, vol. VI
Dunne, Col William, 1855–1932, vol. III
Dunnell, Sir Francis; see Dunnell, Sir R. F.
Dunnell, Sir (Robert) Francis, 1st Bt, 1868–1960, vol. V
Dunnet, George Mackenzie, 1928–1995, vol. IX
Dunnett, Sir Alastair MacTavish, 1908–1998, vol. X
Dunnett, Sir George Sangster, 1907–1984, vol. VIII
Dunnett, George Sinclair, 1906–1964, vol. VI
Dunnett, Sir James; see Dunnett, Sir L. J.
Dunnett, Sir James Macdonald, 1877–1953, vol. V
Dunnett, Sir (Ludovic) James, 1914–1997, vol. X
Dunnicliff, Rev. Canon Edward Frederick Holwell, 1901–1963, vol. VI
Dunnicliff, Horace Barratt, died 1958, vol. V
Dunnico, Rev. Sir Herbert, 1876–1953, vol. V
Dunnill, W. F., died 1936, vol. III
Dunning, Albert Elijah, 1844–1923, vol. II
Dunning, Hon. Charles Avery, 1885–1958, vol. V
Dunning, Sir Edwin Harris, 1858–1923, vol. III
Dunning, J. Thomson, 1851–1931, vol. III
Dunning, James, 1873–1931, vol. III
Dunning, John Ernest Patrick, 1912–1992, vol. IX
Dunning, John Ray, 1907–1975, vol. VII
Dunning, Sir Leonard, 1st Bt, 1860–1941, vol. IV
Dunning, Rev. Thomas George, 1885–1975, vol. VII
Dunning, William Archibald, died 1922, vol. II
Dunning, Sir William Leonard, 2nd Bt, 1903–1961, vol. VI
Dunnington-Jefferson, Lt-Col Sir John Alexander, 1st Bt, 1884–1979, vol. VII
Dunoyer de Segonzac, André, 1884–1974, vol. VII
Dunpark, Hon. Lord; Alastair McPherson Johnston, 1915–1991, vol. IX
Dunphie, Sir Alfred Edwin, died 1938, vol. III
Dunphie, Maj.-Gen. Sir Charles Anderson Lane, 1902–1999, vol. X
Dunphy, Rev. Thomas Patrick Joseph, 1913–1989, vol. VIII
Dunraven and Mount-Earl, 4th Earl of, 1841–1926, vol. II
Dunraven and Mount-Earl, 5th Earl of, 1857–1952, vol. V

245

Dunraven and Mount-Earl, 6th Earl of, 1887–1965, vol. VI

Dunrossil, 1st Viscount, 1893–1961, vol. VI

Dunrossil, 2nd Viscount, 1926–2000, vol. X

Duns, John, 1820–1909, vol. I

Dunsandle and Clan-Conal, 4th Baron, 1849–1911, vol. I

Dunsany, 17th Baron, 1853–1899, vol. I

Dunsany, 18th Baron, 1878–1957, vol. V

Dunsany, 19th Baron, 1906–1999, vol. X

Dunsford, Brig.-Gen. Francis Pearson Shaw, 1866–1931, vol. III

Dunsheath, Percy, 1886–1979, vol. VII

Dunsmuir, Hon. James, 1851–1921, vol. II

Dunstaffnage, The Captain of, 1888–1958, vol. V

Dunstan, Hon. Sir Albert Arthur, died 1950, vol. IV

Dunstan, Albert Ernest, 1878–1964, vol. VI

Dunstan, Hon. Donald Allan, 1926–1999, vol. X

Dunstan, Edgar Grieve, 1890–1963, vol. VI

Dunstan, Ven. Ephraim, died 1915, vol. I

Dunstan, Malcolm James Rowley, 1863–1938, vol. III

Dunstan, Victor Joseph, 1899–1970, vol. VI

Dunstan, William, 1895–1957, vol. V

Dunstan, Sir Wyndham Rowland, 1861–1949, vol. IV

Dunsterville, Col Arthur Bruce, 1859–1943, vol. IV

Dunsterville, Brig. Knightley Fletcher, 1883–1958, vol. V

Dunsterville, Col Knightley Stalker, 1857–1935, vol. III

Dunsterville, Maj.-Gen. Lionel Charles, 1865–1946, vol. IV

Dunsterville, Lt-Gen. Lionel D'Arcy, 1830–1912, vol. I

Dunton, Walter Theodore W.; see Watts-Dunton.

Duntze, Sir Daniel Evans, 8th Bt, 1926–1997, vol. X

Duntze, Sir George Alexander, 4th Bt, 1839–1922, vol. II

Duntze, Sir George Edwin Douglas, 6th Bt, 1913–1985, vol. VIII

Duntze, Sir George Puxley, 5th Bt, 1873–1947, vol. IV

Duntze, Sir John Alexander, 7th Bt, 1909–1987, vol. VIII

Dunville, Lt-Col John, 1866–1929, vol. III

Dunville, Robert Grimshaw, 1838–1910, vol. I

Dunwoodie, Lallah Bessie, died 1950, vol. IV

Dunwoody, Robert Browne, 1879–1966, vol. VI

Duparc, Marie Eugene Henri, 1848–1933, vol. III

du Parcq, Baron (Life Peer); Herbert du Parcq, 1880–1949, vol. IV

Duperier, Maj.-Gen. Henry William, 1851–1940, vol. III

Du-Plat-Taylor, Francis Maurice Gustavus, 1878–1954, vol. V

du Plat-Taylor, Lt-Col St John Louis Hyde; see Taylor.

du Pont, Lammot, 1880–1952, vol. V

Dupont-Sommer, André, 1900–1983, vol. VIII

Du Port, Lt-Col Osmond Charteris, 1875–1929, vol. III

Duppa-Miller, John Bryan Peter; see Miller, J. B. P.D.

Dupplin, Viscount; Edmund Alfred Rollo George Hay, 1879–1903, vol. I

Duppuy, Rt Rev. Charles Ridley, died 1944, vol. IV

Dupré, August, 1835–1907, vol. I

du Pré, Jacqueline Mary, 1945–1987, vol. VIII

Dupré, Hon. Maurice, 1888–1941, vol. IV

Du Pre, William Baring, 1875–1946, vol. IV

Dupree, Sir Vernon, 3rd Bt, 1884–1971, vol. VII

Dupree, Sir Victor, 4th Bt, 1887–1976, vol. VII

Dupree, Col Sir William, 2nd Bt, 1882–1953, vol. V

Dupree, Col Sir William Thomas, 1st Bt, 1856–1933, vol. III

Dupuch, Sir (Alfred) Etienne (Jerome), 1899–1991, vol. IX

Dupuch, Sir Etienne; see Dupuch, Sir A. E. J.

Dupuis, Charles George, 1886–1940, vol. III

Dupuis, Raymond, 1907–1970, vol. VI (AII)

Dupuis, Rev. Theodore Crane, 1830–1914, vol. I

Dupuy, Charles Alexander, 1851–1923, vol. II

Dupuy, Jean, died 1919, vol. II

Dupuy, Paul, died 1927, vol. II

Dupuy, Pierre, 1896–1969, vol. VI

Durack, Dame Mary, (Mrs Horrie Miller), 1913–1994, vol. IX

Duran, Emile Auguste C.; see Carolus-Duran.

Durand, Brig. Sir Alan Algernon Marion, 3rd Bt, 1893–1971, vol. VII

Durand, Col Algernon George Arnold, 1854–1923, vol. II

Durand, Rev. Sir Dickon; see Durand, Rev. Sir H. M. D. M. St G.

Durand, Sir Edward Law, 1st Bt, 1845–1920, vol. II

Durand, Major Sir Edward Percy Marion, 2nd Bt, 1884–1955, vol. V

Durand, Rt Hon. Sir (Henry) Mortimer, 1850–1924, vol. II

Durand, Rev. Sir (Henry Mortimer) Dickon (Marion St George), 4th Bt, 1934–1992, vol. IX

Durand, Rt Hon. Sir Mortimer; see Durand, Rt Hon. Sir H. M.

Durand, Victor Albert Charles, 1907–1994, vol. IX

Duranleau, Alfred, 1871–1951, vol. V

Durant, Rear-Adm. Bryan Cecil, 1910–1983, vol. VIII

Durant, Rt Rev. Henry Bickersteth, died 1932, vol. III

Durant, William James, 1885–1981, vol. VIII

Duranty, Walter, died 1957, vol. V

Duras, Marguerite, 1914–1996, vol. X

Durbhunga, Maharajadhiraj of, 1860–1929, vol. III

Durbin, Evan Frank Mottram, 1906–1948, vol. IV

Durbridge, Francis Henry, 1912–1998, vol. X

Durden, James, died 1964, vol. VI

Duret, Rt Rev. Augustin, 1846–1920, vol. II

Durga Gati, Banerji, died 1903, vol. I

Durham, 3rd Earl of, 1855–1928, vol. II

Durham, 4th Earl of, 1855–1929, vol. III

Durham, 5th Earl of, 1884–1970, vol. VI

Durham, Frances Hermia, 1873–1948, vol. IV

Durham, Lt-Col Frank Rogers, died 1947, vol. IV

Durham, Herbert Edward, 1866–1945, vol. IV

Durham, Mary Edith, 1863–1944, vol. IV

Durham, Rev. Thomas Charles, 1825–1904, vol. I

Durham, Rev. William Edward, 1857–1921, vol. II

246

Durlacher, Sir Esmond Otho, 1901–1982, vol. VIII
Durlacher, Adm. Sir Laurence George, 1904–1986, vol. VIII
Durley, Richard John, 1868–1948, vol. IV
Durnford, Lt-Gen. Cyril Maton Periam, 1891–1965, vol. VI
Durnford, Hugh George Edmund, 1886–1965, vol. VI
Durnford, Adm. Sir John, 1849–1914, vol. I
Durnford, Vice-Adm. John Walter, 1891–1967, vol. VI
Durnford, Richard, 1843–1934, vol. III
Durnford, Robert Chichester, 1895–1918, vol. II
Durnford, Sir Walter, 1847–1926, vol. II
Durnford-Slater, Adm. Sir Robin Leonard Francis, 1902–1984, vol. VIII
Durning-Lawrence, Sir Edwin, 1st Bt, 1837–1914, vol. I
Durrant, Albert Arthur Molteno, 1898–1984, vol. VIII
Durrant, Sir Arthur Isaac, 1864–1939, vol. III
Durrant, Frederick Chester W.; see Wells-Durrant.
Durrant, Maj.-Gen. James Murdoch Archer, 1885–1963, vol. VI
Durrant, Maj.-Gen. James Thom, 1913–1990, vol. VIII
Durrant, Sir William Henry Estridge, 6th Bt, 1872–1953, vol. V
Durrant, Sir William Henry Estridge, 7th Bt, 1901–1994, vol. IX
Durrant, Sir William Robert Estridge, 5th Bt, 1840–1912, vol. I
Durrant, William Scott, 1860–1932, vol. III
Durell, Col Arthur James Vavasor, 1871–1945, vol. IV
Durrell, Gerald Malcolm, 1925–1995, vol. IX
Durell, Henry E. Le Vavasseur dit, died 1921, vol. II
Durell, Rev. John Carlyon Vavasour, 1870–1946, vol. IV
Durrell, Lawrence George, 1912–1990, vol. VIII
Dürrenmatt, Friedrich, 1921–1990, vol. VIII
Durst, Alan Lydiat, 1883–1970, vol. VI
Durst, Rev. William, 1838–1922, vol. II
Durston, Air Marshal Sir Albert, 1894–1959, vol. V
Durston, Sir Albert John, 1846–1917, vol. II
Durward, Archibald, 1902–1964, vol. VI
Durward, James, 1892–1971, vol. VII
Dury, Theodore Seton, 1854–1932, vol. III
du Sautoy, Peter Francis, 1912–1995, vol. IX
Duse, Signora Eleonora, 1861–1924, vol. II
Duthie, George Ian, 1915–1967, vol. VI
Duthie, Sir John, 1858–1922, vol. II
Duthie, Sir William Smith, 1892–1980, vol. VII
du Toit, Alexander Logie, died 1948, vol. IV
du Toit, F. J., 1897–1961, vol. VI
du Toit, Very Rev. Lionel Meiring Spafford, 1903–1979, vol. VII
du Toit, P. J., 1888–1967, vol. VI
Dutoit, Rev. S. J., 1849–1911, vol. I
Dutt, Palme; see Dutt, R. P.
Dutt, (Rajani) Palme, 1896–1974, vol. VII
Dutt, Romesh Chunder, 1848–1909, vol. I
Dutt, William Alfred, 1870–1939, vol. III
Dutton, Alan Hart, 1913–1974, vol. VII

Dutton, Vice-Adm. Hon. Arthur Brandreth Scott, 1876–1932, vol. III
Dutton, Col Hon. Charles, 1842–1909, vol. I
Dutton, Eric Aldhelm Torlogh, 1895–1973, vol. VII
Dutton, Sir Ernest R.; see Rowe-Dutton.
Dutton, Sir Frederick, 1855–1930, vol. III
Dutton, Lt-Col Hugh Reginald, 1875–1950, vol. IV
Duval, Sir (Charles) Gaetan, 1930–1996, vol. X
Duval, Sir Francis John, 1909–1981, vol. VIII
Duval, Sir Gaetan; see Duval, Sir. C. G.
Duval, Herbert Philip, died 1929, vol. III
Duveen, 1st Baron, 1869–1939, vol. III
Duveen, Claude Henry, 1903–1976, vol. VII
Duveen, Edward Joseph, died 1944, vol. IV
Duveen, Sir Geoffrey, 1883–1975, vol. VII
Duveen, Sir Joseph Joel, 1843–1908, vol. I
Du Vernet, Most Rev. Frederick Herbert, 1860–1924, vol. II
du Vigneaud, Vincent, 1901–1978, vol. VII
Duxbury, Air Marshal Sir Barry; see Duxbury, Air Marshal J. B.
Duxbury, Air Marshal Sir (John) Barry, 1934–1997, vol. X
Dvorak, Pan Antonin, 1841–1904, vol. I
Dwelly, Very Rev. Frederick William, 1881–1957, vol. V
Dwight, Rev. Timothy, 1828–1916, vol. II
Dwyer, Edward, 1897–1916, vol. II
Dwyer, Lt-Col Ernest, 1880–1957, vol. V
Dwyer, Sir F. Conway, 1860–1935, vol. III
Dwyer, Most Rev. George Patrick, 1908–1987, vol. VIII
Dwyer, Sir John Patrick, 1880–1966, vol. VI
Dwyer, Rt Rev. Joseph Wilfred, 1869–1939, vol. III
Dwyer, Air Vice-Marshal Michael Harington, 1912–1989, vol. VIII
Dwyer, Rt Rev. Patrick Vincent, 1858–1931, vol. III
Dwyer, Hon. Sir Walter, 1875–1950, vol. IV, vol. V
Dwyer-Hampton, Lt-Col Bertie Cunynghame, 1872–1967, vol. VI
Dyall, Clarence George, 1858–1941, vol. IV
Dyall, Franklin, 1870–1950, vol. IV
Dyall, Valentine, 1908–1985, vol. VIII
Dyas, Col James Ridgeway, 1862–1933, vol. III
Dyball, Maj.-Gen. Antony John, 1919–1985, vol. VIII
Dyce, Col George Hugh Coles, 1846–1921, vol. II
Dyde, Samuel Walters, 1862–1947, vol. IV
Dye, Sidney, 1900–1958, vol. V
Dye, William David, 1887–1932, vol. III
Dyer, Sir Alfred, 1865–1947, vol. IV
Dyer, Ven. Alfred Saunders, 1853–1906, vol. I
Dyer, Arthur Reginald, 1877–1951, vol. V
Dyer, Bernard, 1856–1948, vol. IV
Dyer, Charles Edward, died 1937, vol. III
Dyer, Edward Jerome, died 1943, vol. IV
Dyer, Col George Nowers, died 1955, vol. V
Dyer, Maj.-Gen. Godfrey Maxwell, 1898–1979, vol. VII
Dyer, Henry, 1848–1918, vol. II
Dyer, Hugh Marshall, 1860–1938, vol. III
Dyer, James Ferguson, 1880–1940, vol. III
Dyer, Sir John Lodovick Swinnerton, 13th Bt, 1914–1940, vol. III

Dyer, Captain Sir John Swinnerton, 12th Bt, 1891–1917, vol. II
Dyer, Ven. Joseph Perry, 1855–1926, vol. II
Dyer, Sir Leonard Schroeder Swinnerton, 15th Bt, 1898–1975, vol. VII
Dyer, Sir Leonard Whitworth Swinnerton, 14th Bt, 1875–1947, vol. IV
Dyer, Brig.-Gen. Reginald Edward Harry, 1864–1927, vol. II
Dyer, Robert Morton, 1878–1936, vol. III
Dyer, Sidney Reginald, *died* 1934, vol. III
Dyer, Simon, 1939–1996, vol. X
Dyer, Major Stewart Barton Bythesea, 1875–1917, vol. II
Dyer, Sir Thomas Swinnerton, 11th Bt, 1859–1907, vol. I
Dyer, Sir William Turner T.; *see* Thiselton-Dyer.
Dyer-Smith, Rear-Adm. John Edward, 1918–1999, vol. X
Dyett, Sir Gilbert Joseph Cullen, 1891–1964, vol. VI
Dyke, Sir Arthur James, 1872–1933, vol. III
Dyke, Sir Derek William H.; *see* Hart Dyke.
Dyke, Rev. Edwin Francis, 1842–1919, vol. II
Dyke, Lt-Col John Samuel, 1859–1927, vol. II
Dyke, Sir Oliver Hamilton Augustus Hart, 8th Bt, 1885–1969, vol. VI
Dyke, Sidney Campbell, 1886–1975, vol. VII
Dyke, Rt Hon. Sir William Hart, 7th Bt, 1837–1931, vol. III
Dykes, David Oswald, 1876–1942, vol. IV
Dykes, Frederick James, 1880–1957, vol. V
Dykes, Col Frescheville Hubert Ballantine-, 1881–1949, vol. IV
Dykes, Rev. James Oswald, 1835–1912, vol. I

Dykes, Brig. Vivian, 1898–1943, vol. IV
Dykes, William Rickatson, 1877–1926, vol. II
Dykes Bower, Sir John, 1905–1981, vol. VIII
Dykes Bower, Stephen Ernest, 1903–1994, vol. IX
Dykstra, John, 1898–1972, vol. VII
Dyment, Clifford Henry, 1914–1971, vol. VII
Dymoke, Frank Scaman, 1862–1946, vol. IV
Dymond, Charles Edward, 1916–1985, vol. IX (AI)
Dymott, Rev. Sidney Edward, *died* 1924, vol. II
Dynes, Brig. Ernest, 1903–1968, vol. VI
Dynevor, 6th Baron, 1836–1911, vol. I
Dynevor, 7th Baron, 1873–1956, vol. V
Dynevor, 8th Baron, 1899–1962, vol. VI
Dynham, Edward, 1843–1914, vol. I
Dysart, 9th Earl of, 1859–1935, vol. III
Dysart, Countess of (10th in line), 1889–1975, vol. VII
Dyson, Rev. Anthony Oakley, 1935–1998, vol. X
Dyson, Sir (Charles) Frederick, 1854–1934, vol. III
Dyson, Sir Cyril Douglas, 1895–1976, vol. VII
Dyson, Edith Mary Beatrice, 1900–1986, vol. VIII
Dyson, Edward Trevor, 1886–1969, vol. VI
Dyson, Sir Frank Watson, 1868–1939, vol. III
Dyson, Fred, 1916–1987, vol. VIII
Dyson, Sir Frederick; *see* Dyson, Sir C. F.
Dyson, Sir George, 1883–1964, vol. VI
Dyson, Lt-Col Harry Hugo Bernard, 1869–1939, vol. III
Dyson, Herbert Kempton, 1880–1944, vol. IV
Dyson, James, 1914–1990, vol. VIII
Dyson, Richard George, 1909–1987, vol. VIII
Dyson, William, 1849–1928, vol. II
Dyson, William, 1871–1947, vol. IV
Dyson, William Henry, 1883–1938, vol. III

E

Eacott, Rev. Canon Henry James Theodore, 1882–1943, vol. IV
Eade, Charles Stanley, 1903–1964, vol. VI
Eade, Sir Peter, 1825–1915, vol. I
Eaden, Maurice Bryan, 1923–1993, vol. IX
Eades, Sir Thomas, 1888–1971, vol. VII
Eadie, Dennis, 1875–1928, vol. II
Eadie, Douglas, George Arnott, 1931–2000, vol. X
Eadie, William Ewing, 1896–1976, vol. VII
Eady, Sir (Crawfurd) Wilfrid Griffin, 1890–1962, vol. VI
Eady, George Hathaway, *died* 1941, vol. IV
Eady, Sir Wilfrid; *see* Eady, Sir C. W. G.
Eagar, Waldo McGillycuddy, 1884–1966, vol. VI
Eager, Sir Clifden Henry Andrews, 1882–1969, vol. VI
Eagers, Derek, 1924–1998, vol. X
Eagger, Brig. Arthur Austin, 1898–1993, vol. IX
Eagles, Rev. Charles Frederick, 1851–1931, vol. III
Eagles, Gen. Henry Cecil, 1855–1927, vol. II
Eaglesham, Eric John Ross, 1905–1988, vol. VIII
Eaglesome, Sir John, 1868–1950, vol. IV
Eagleston, Arthur John, 1870–1944, vol. IV
Eagleton, Guy Tryon, 1894–1988, vol. VIII

Eaker, Gen. Ira Clarence, 1896–1987, vol. VIII
Eakin, Rev. Thomas, 1871–1958, vol. V
Eales, Herbert, 1857–1927, vol. II
Eales, John Frederick, 1881–1936, vol. III
Eales, Shirley, 1883–1963, vol. VI
Eames, Alfred Edward, *died* 1924, vol. II
Eames, James Bromley, 1872–1916, vol. II
Eames, Sir William, 1821–1910, vol. I
Eames, Maj.-Gen. William L'Estrange, 1863–1956, vol. V
Eardley, Joan Kathleen Harding, 1921–1963, vol. VI
Eardley-Russell, Lt-Col Edmund Stuart Eardley Wilmot, 1869–1918, vol. II
Eardley-Wilmot, Col Arthur, 1856–1940, vol. III
Eardley-Wilmot, Captain Cecil F., 1855–1916, vol. II
Eardley-Wilmot, Rev. Ernest Augustus, 1848–1932, vol. III
Eardley-Wilmot, Hugh Eden, 1850–1926, vol. II
Eardley-Wilmot, Sir John, 4th Bt, 1882–1970, vol. VI
Eardley-Wilmot, Sir John Assheton, 5th Bt, 1917–1995, vol. IX

Eardley-Wilmot, May, 1883–1970, vol. VI
Eardley-Wilmot, Maj.-Gen. Revell, 1842–1922, vol. II
Eardley-Wilmot, Sir Sainthill, 1852–1929, vol. III
Eardley-Wilmot, Rear-Adm. Sir Sydney Marow, 1847–1929, vol. III
Earengey, William George, *died* 1961, vol. VI
Earl, Sir Austin, 1888–1958, vol. V
Earl, Frederick, 1857–1945, vol. IV
Earle, Rt Rev. Alfred, 1827–1918, vol. II
Earle, Air Chief Marshal Sir Alfred, 1907–1990, vol. VIII
Earle, Lt-Col Sir Algernon; *see* Earle, Lt Col Sir T. A.
Earle, Sir Archdale, 1861–1934, vol. III
Earle, Arthur, 1838–1919, vol. II
Earle, Mrs C. W., (Maria Theresa Villiers), 1836–1925, vol. II
Earle, Lt-Col Charles, 1913–1989, vol. VIII
Earle, Charles Westwood, 1871–1950, vol. IV
Earle, Ven. Edward Ernest Maples, 1900–1994, vol. IX
Earle, Edward Mead, 1894–1954, vol. V
Earle, Brig. Eric Greville, 1893–1965, vol. VI
Earle, Sir George Foster, 1890–1965, vol. VI
Earle, Gerald Frederick, 1864–1944, vol. II
Earle, Sir Hardman Alexander Mort, 5th Bt, 1902–1979, vol. VII
Earle, Lt-Col Sir Henry, 3rd Bt (*cr* 1869), 1854–1939, vol. III
Earle, Herbert Gastineau, 1882–1946, vol. IV
Earle, Rev. John, 1824–1903, vol. I
Earle, Hon. John, 1865–1932, vol. III
Earle, Gen. John March, 1825–1914, vol. I
Earle, Sir Lionel, 1866–1948, vol. IV
Earle, Col Maxwell, 1871–1953, vol. V
Earle, Rev. Canon Richard Cobden, 1867–1942, vol. IV
Earle, Col Robert Gilmour, 1874–1957, vol. V
Earle, Sir Thomas, 2nd Bt (*cr* 1869), 1820–1900, vol. I
Earle, Lt-Col Sir (Thomas) Algernon, 4th Bt (*cr* 1869), 1860–1945, vol. IV
Earle, Rev. Sir William, 11th Bt (*cr* 1629), *died* 1910, vol. I
Early, Stephen T., 1889–1951, vol. V
Earnshaw, Albert, 1865–1920, vol. II
Earnshaw, Mabel Lucie, (Mrs Harold Earnshaw); *see* Attwell, M. L.
Earp, Charles Anthony, 1871–1933, vol. III
Earp, Frank Russell, 1871–1955, vol. V
Earp, Hon. George Frederick, *died* 1933, vol. III
Earp, Thomas Wade, 1892–1958, vol. V
Eason, Sir Herbert Lightfoot, 1874–1949, vol. IV
Eason, John, 1874–1964, vol. VI
Eason, Robert Kinley, 1908–1991, vol. IX
Eassie, Brig.-Gen. Fitzpatrick, 1864–1943, vol. IV
Eassie, Maj.-Gen. William James Fitzpatrick, 1899–1974, vol. VII
Easson, Rt Rev. Edward Frederick, 1905–1988, vol. VIII
Easson, Eric Craig, 1915–1983, vol. VIII
East, Sir Alfred, 1849–1913, vol. I
East, Gen. Sir Cecil James, 1837–1908, vol. I
East, Col Charles Conran, 1866–1942, vol. IV

East, Charles Frederick Terence, 1894–1967, vol. VI
East, Frederick Henry, 1919–1996, vol. X
East, Sir George Frederick Lancelot Clayton-, 8th Bt (*cr* 1732), and 4th Bt (*cr* 1838), 1872–1926, vol. II
East, Gerald Reginald Ricketts, 1917–1991, vol. IX
East, Sir Gilbert Augustus Clayton, 7th Bt (*cr* 1732), and 3rd Bt (*cr* 1838), 1846–1925, vol. II
East, Grahame Richard, 1908–1993, vol. IX
East, Hubert Frazer, 1893–1959, vol. V
East, Sir (Lewis) Ronald, 1899–1994, vol. X (AI)
East, Col Lionel William Pellew, 1866–1918, vol. II
East, Sir Norwood; *see* East, Sir W. N.
East, Sir Ronald; *see* East, Sir L. R.
East, William Gordon, 1902–1998, vol. X
East, Sir (William) Norwood, 1872–1953, vol. V
Eastaugh, Rt Rev. Cyril, 1897–1988, vol. VIII
Eastaugh, Rt Rev. John Richard Gordon, 1920–1990, vol. VIII
Easten, Sir Stephen, *died* 1936, vol. III
Easter, Rev. Canon Arthur John Talbot, 1893–1969, vol. VI
Easter, Bertie Harry, 1893–1976, vol. VII (AII)
Easterbrook, James, 1851–1923, vol. II
Easterbrook, John Thomas, *died* 1934, vol. III
Easterbrook, William Thomas James, 1907–1985, vol. VIII
Easterfield, Sir Thomas Hill, 1866–1949, vol. IV
Eastes, Arthur Ernest, 1877–1948, vol. IV
Eastham, Leonard Ernest Sydney, 1893–1977, vol. VII
Eastham, Hon. Sir Michael; *see* Eastham, Hon. Sir T. M.
Eastham, Hon. Sir (Thomas) Michael, 1920–1993, vol. IX
Eastham, Sir Tom, *died* 1967, vol. VI
Eastick, Brig. Sir Thomas Charles, 1900–1988, vol. VIII
Eastlake, Charles Locke, 1836–1906, vol.I
Eastman, Ven. Derek Ian Tennent, 1919–1991, vol. IX
Eastman, George, 1854–1932, vol. III
Eastman, Gen. William Inglefield, 1856–1941, vol. IV
Easton, Brig.-Gen. Frederick Arthur, 1871–1949, vol. IV
Easton, Col George, 1868–1946, vol. IV
Easton, Hugh, *died* 1965, vol. VI
Easton, Admiral Sir Ian, 1917–1989, vol. VIII
Easton, Air Cdre Sir James (Alfred), 1908–1990, vol. VIII
Easton, John Francis, 1928–1994, vol. IX
Easton, John Murray, 1889–1975, vol. VII
Easton, Lt-Col Philip George, 1878–1960, vol. V
Eastwood, Benjamin, 1863–1943, vol. IV
Eastwood, Charles, 1868–1940, vol. III
Eastwood, Christopher Gilbert, 1905–1983, vol. VIII
Eastwood, Sir Eric, 1910–1981, vol. VIII
Eastwood, Frank Sandford, 1895–1971, vol. VII
Eastwood, Major Sir Geoffrey Hugh, 1895–1983, vol. VIII
Eastwood, (George) Granville, 1906–1989, vol. IX (AI)

Eastwood, Granville; *see* Eastwood, George G.
Eastwood, Harold, 1880–1941, vol. IV
Eastwood, Harold Edmund, 1889–1960, vol. V
Eastwood, Col Hugh de Crespigny, 1863–1934, vol. III
Eastwood, Sir John Bealby, 1909–1995, vol. IX
Eastwood, Col John Charles Basil, 1862–1934, vol. III
Eastwood, John Francis, 1887–1952, vol. V
Eastwood, Reginald Allen, 1893–1964, vol. VI
Eastwood, Lt-Gen. Sir T. Ralph, 1890–1959, vol. V
Eather, Maj.-Gen. Kenneth William, 1901–1993, vol. IX
Eaton, Rev. Arthur Wentworth Hamilton, 1849–1937, vol. III
Eaton, Air Vice-Marshal Brian Alexander, 1916–1992, vol. IX
Eaton, Cecil; *see* Eaton, W. C.
Eaton, Cyrus Stephen, 1883–1979, vol. VII
Eaton, Sir Frederick Alexis, 1838–1913, vol. I
Eaton, Hon. Herbert Edward, 1895–1962, vol. VI
Eaton, Sir John Craig, 1876–1922, vol. II
Eaton, Vice-Adm. Sir John Willson Musgrave, 1902–1981, vol. VIII
Eaton, Peter, 1914–1993, vol. IX
Eaton, Col Sir Richard William, 1876–1942, vol. IV
Eaton, (Walter) Cecil, 1875–1958, vol. V
Eayrs, Rev. George, 1864–1926, vol. II
Ebbels, Brig. Wilfred Austin, 1898–1976, vol. VII
Ebbisham, 1st Baron, 1868–1953, vol. V
Ebbisham, 2nd Baron, 1912–1991, vol. IX
Ebblewhite, Ernest Arthur, 1867–1947, vol. IV
Ebbs, William Alexander, 1890–1960, vol. V
Ebbutt, Norman, 1894–1968, vol. VI
Ebden, Mrs Agnes, *died* 1930, vol. III
Eberle, George Strachan John Fuller, 1881–1968, vol. VI
Ebers, Georg Maurice, 1837–1898, vol. I
Ebert, Carl Anton Charles, 1887–1980, vol. VII
Eberts, Hon. David MacEwen, 1850–1924, vol. II
Eberts, Edmond Melchior, 1873–1945, vol. IV
Eboo Pirbhai, Diwan Sir, 1905–1990, vol. VIII
Eborall, Sir Arthur; *see* Eborall, Sir E. A.
Eborall, Sir (Ernest) Arthur, 1878–1967, vol. VI
Ebrahim, Sir Currimbhoy; *see* Ebrahim, Sir H. C.
Ebrahim, Sir Currimbhoy, 1st Bt, 1840–1924, vol. II
Ebrahim, Sir Fazulbhoy Currimbhoy, 1873–1970, vol. VI (AII)
Ebrahim, Sir (Huseinali) Currimbhoy, 3rd Bt, 1903–1952, vol. V
Ebrahim, Sir Mahomedbhoy Currimbhoy, 2nd Bt, 1867–1928, vol. II
Ebrington, Viscount; Hugh Peter Fortescue, 1920–1942, vol. IV
Ebsworth, Brig. Wilfrid Algernon, 1897–1978, vol. VII
Eburne, Sir Sidney Alfred William, 1918–1994, vol. IX
Ebury, 2nd Baron, 1834–1918, vol. II
Ebury, 3rd Baron, 1868–1921, vol.II
Ebury, 4th Baron, 1883–1932, vol. III
Ebury, 5th Baron, 1914–1957, vol. V
Eccles, 1st Viscount, 1904–1999, vol. X

Eccles, Lt-Col Cuthbert John, 1870–1922, vol. II
Eccles, James Ronald, 1874–1956, vol. V
Eccles, Adm. Sir John Arthur Symons, 1898–1966, vol. VI
Eccles, Sir John Carew, 1903–1997, vol. X
Eccles, Rev. Canon John Charles, *born* 1845, vol. II
Eccles, Sir Josiah, 1897–1967, vol. VI
Eccles, Launcelot William Gregory, 1890–1955, vol. V
Eccles, Miss O'C.; *see* O'Conor-Eccles, Miss.
Eccles, Maj.-Gen. Ronald Whalley, 1912–1975, vol. VII
Eccles, William Henry, 1875–1966, vol. VI
Eccles, William McAdam, *died* 1946, vol. IV
Eccleshare, Colin Forster, 1916–1989, vol. VIII
Echegaray, José, 1832–1916, vol. II
Echlin, Sir Henry Frederick, 8th Bt, 1846–1923, vol. II
Echlin, Sir John Frederick, 9th Bt, 1890–1932, vol. III
Echlin, Sir Thomas, 7th Bt, 1844–1906, vol. I
Eck, Rev. Herbert Vincent Shortgrave, *died* 1934, vol. III
Eckener, Hugo, 1868–1954, vol. V
Eckersley, Eva Mary, 1871–1944, vol. IV
Eckersley, Peter Pendleton, 1892–1963, vol. VI
Eckersley, Peter Thorp, 1904–1940, vol. III
Eckersley, Roger Huxley, 1885–1955, vol. V
Eckersley, Thomas, 1914–1997, vol. X
Eckersley, Thomas Lydwell, 1886–1959, vol. V
Eckhoff, Nils Lovold Bjarne Victor, 1902–1969, vol. VI
Eckman, Samuel, Jr, *died* 1976, vol. VII
Eckstein, Captain Sir Bernard, 2nd Bt, 1894–1948, vol. IV
Eckstein, Sir Frederick, 1st Bt, 1857–1930, vol. III
Ecroyd, William Farrer, 1827–1915, vol. I
Edden, Alan John, 1912–1991, vol. IX
Edden, Vice-Adm. Sir Kaye; *see* Edden, Vice-Adm. Sir W. K.
Edden, Vice-Adm. Sir (William) Kaye, 1905–1990, vol. VIII
Eddie, Sir George Brand, 1893–1981, vol. VIII
Eddington, Sir Arthur Stanley, 1882–1944, vol. IV
Eddington, Paul Clark-, 1927–1995, vol. IX
Eddis, Sir Basil Eden Garth, *died* 1971, vol. VII
Eddis, Brig. Bruce Lindsay, 1883–1966, vol. VI
Eddison, Eric Rucker, 1882–1945, vol. IV
Eddison, John Edwin, 1842–1929, vol. III
Eddison, Rear-Adm. Talbot Leadam, 1908–1983, vol. VIII
Eddleman, Gen. Clyde Davis, 1902–1992, vol. X (AI)
Eddowes, Alfred, *died* 1946, vol. IV
Eddowes, Rev. Canon Edmund Edward, 1871–1963, vol. VI
Eddowes, Rev. John, 1826–1905, vol. I
Eddy, Sir (Edward) George, 1878–1967, vol. VI
Eddy, Sir George; *see* Eddy, Sir E. G.
Eddy, Sir (John) Montague, 1881–1949, vol. IV
Eddy, John Percy, 1881–1975, vol. VII
Eddy, Mary Baker Glover, 1821–1910, vol. VI
Eddy, Sir Montague; *see* Eddy, Sir J. M.
Ede, Comdr Lionel James Spencer, 1903–1956, vol. V

Ede, Very Rev. William Moore, *died* 1935, vol. III
Edel, (Joseph) Leon, 1907–1997, vol. X
Edel, Leon; *see* Edel, J. L.
Edelman, Maurice, 1911–1975, vol. VII
Edelsten, Col John Arthur, 1863–1931, vol. III
Edelsten, Adm. Sir John Hereward, 1891–1966, vol. VI
Edelston, Sir Thomas Dugald, 1878–1955, vol. V
Eden, Brig.-Gen. Archibald James Fergusson, 1872–1956, vol. V
Eden, Charles William Guy, 1874–1947, vol. IV
Eden, Conrad William, 1905–1994, vol. IX
Eden, Denis, 1878–1949, vol. IV
Eden, Edward Norman, 1921–1990, vol. VIII
Eden, Rev. Frederick Nugent, 1857–1926, vol. II
Eden, Hon. George, 1861–1924, vol. II
Eden, Rt Rev. George Rodney, 1853–1940, vol. III
Eden, Guy E. Morton, *died* 1954, vol. V
Eden, Helen Parry, 1885–1960, vol. V
Eden, Rev. Robert Allan, 1839–1912, vol. I
Eden, Robert H. H., *died* 1932, vol. III
Eden, Col Schomberg Henley, 1873–1934, vol. III
Eden, Thomas Watts, 1863–1946, vol. IV
Eden, Sir Timothy Calvert, 8th Bt, 1893–1963, vol. VI
Eden, Sir William, 7th and 5th Bt, 1849–1915, vol. I
Eden, Brig.-Gen. William Rushbrooke, 1873–1920, vol. II
Edenborough, Eric John Horatio, 1893–1965, vol. VI
Eder, Montagu David, *died* 1936, vol. III
Edgar, Clifford Blackburn, 1857–1931, vol. III
Edgar, Sir Edward Mackay, 1st Bt, 1876–1934, vol. III
Edgar, Frederick Percy, 1884–1972, vol. VII
Edgar, George, 1877–1918, vol. II
Edgar, Gilbert Harold Samuel, 1898–1978, vol. VII
Edgar, Lt-Gen. Hector Geoffrey, 1903–1978, vol. VII
Edgar, Hon. Sir James David, 1841–1899, vol. I
Edgar, John, *died* 1922, vol. II
Edgar, Sir John Ware, 1839–1902, vol. I
Edgar, Pelham, 1871–1948, vol. IV
Edgar, William C., 1856–1932, vol. III
Edgar, Surg. Rear-Adm. William Harold, 1885–1959, vol. V
Edgcumbe, Aubrey Pearce; *see* Edgcumbe, J. A. P.
Edgcumbe, Sir (Edward) Robert Pearce, 1851–1929, vol. III
Edgcumbe, (John) Aubrey Pearce, 1886–1974, vol. VI
Edgcumbe, Maj.-Gen. Oliver Pearce, 1892–1956, vol. V
Edgcumbe, Richard John Frederick, 1843–1937, vol. III
Edgcumbe, Sir Robert Pearce; *see* Edgcumbe, Sir E. R. P.
Edge, Frederick, 1863–1937, vol. III
Edge, James Broughton, *died* 1926, vol. II
Edge, Rt Hon. Sir John, 1841–1926, vol. II
Edge, Maj.-Gen. John Dallas, 1848–1937, vol. III
Edge, John Henry, 1841–1916, vol. II
Edge, Sir Knowles, 1853–1931, vol. III
Edge, Sir Knowles, 2nd Bt, 1905–1984, vol. VIII

Edge, Maj.-Gen. Raymond Cyril Alexander, 1912–1999, vol. X
Edge, Samuel Rathbone, 1848–1936, vol. III
Edge, Selwyn Francis, 1868–1940, vol. III
Edge, Captain Sir William, 1st Bt, 1880–1948, vol. IV
Edge-Partington, Rev. Canon Ellis Foster, 1885–1957, vol. V
Edgedale, Samuel Richards, 1897–1966, vol. VI
Edgell, Beatrice, 1871–1948, vol. IV
Edgell, George Harold, 1887–1954, vol. V
Edgell, Vice-Adm. Sir John Augustine, 1880–1962, vol. VI
Edgerley, Catherine Mabel, *died* 1946, vol. IV
Edgerley, Sir Steyning William, 1857–1935, vol. III
Edgeworth, Francis H., 1864–1943, vol. IV
Edgeworth, Francis Ysidro, 1845–1926, vol. II
Edgeworth, Lt-Col Kenneth Essex, 1880–1972, vol. VII
Edgeworth-Johnstone, Maj.-Gen. Ralph, 1893–1990, vol. VIII
Edgeworth Johnstone, Robert; *see* Johnstone, R. E.
Edgeworth-Johnstone, Lt-Col Sir Walter, *died* 1936, vol. III
Edghill, Rev. John Cox, *died* 1917, vol. II
Edginton May, *died* 1957, vol. V
Edgley, Sir Norman George Armstrong, 1888–1960, vol. V
Edie, Arthur George, 1872–1937, vol. III
Edie, Rev. William, 1865–1936, vol.III
Edington, Alexander Robert, 1895–1964, vol. VI
Edington, George Henry, 1870–1943, vol. IV
Edington, James William, *died* 1939, vol. III
Edington, William Gerald, 1895–1968, vol. VI
Edis, Sir Robert William, 1839–1927, vol. II
Edison, Thomas Alva, 1847–1931, vol. III
Edkins, John Sydney, 1863–1940, vol. III
Edlin, Sir Peter Henry, 1819–1903, vol. I
Edlmann, Major Ernest Elliot, 1868–1915, vol. I
Edlmann, Col Francis Joseph Frederick, 1885–1950, vol. IV
Edman, Irwin, 1896–1954, vol. V
Edman, Pehr Victor, 1916–1977, vol. VII
Edmeades, Major Henry, 1875–1952, vol. V
Edmeades, Lt-Col James Frederick, 1843–1917, vol. II
Edmeades, Lt-Col William Allaire, 1880–1942, vol. IV
Edmensen, Sir Walter Alexander, 1892–1992, vol. IX
Edmond, Colin Alexander, 1888–1956, vol. V
Edmond, James, 1859–1933, vol. III
Edmond, John Philip, 1850–1906, vol. I
Edmondes, Ven. Frederic William, 1840–1918, vol. II
Edmonds, Cecil John, 1889–1979, vol. VII
Edmonds, Air Vice-Marshal Charles Humphrey Kingsman, 1891–1954, vol. V
Edmonds, Edward Alfred Jubal, 1907–1974, vol. VII
Edmonds, Edward Reginald, 1901–1979, vol. VII
Edmonds, Garnham, 1866–1946, vol. IV
Edmonds, Brig.-Gen. Sir James Edward, 1861–1956, vol. V
Edmonds, Rev. Walter John, 1834–1914, vol.I

Edmonds, William Stanley, 1882–1969, vol. VI
Edmondson, George D'Arcy, 1904–1976, vol. VII
Edmondstoune-Cranstoun, Charles Joseph; see Cranstoun.
Edmonstone, Sir Archibald, 5th Bt, 1867–1954, vol. V
Edmonstone, Sir (Archibald) Charles, 6th Bt, 1898–1954, vol. V
Edmonstone, Sir Charles; see Edmonstone, Sir A. C.
Edmund-Davies, Baron (Life Peer); Herbert Edmund Edmund-Davies, 1906–1992, vol. IX
Edmunds, Arthur, 1874–1945, vol. IV
Edmunds, Christopher Montague, 1899–1990, vol. VIII
Edmunds, Rev. Horace Vaughan, 1886–1958, vol. V
Edmunds, Humfrey Henry, 1890–1962, vol. VI
Edmunds, Lewis Humfrey, 1860–1941, vol. IV
Edmunds, Nellie M. Hepburn, died 1953, vol. V
Edmunds, Sir Percy James, 1890–1959, vol. V
Edmunds, Walter, died 1930, vol. III
Edmundson, Rev. George, 1848–1930, vol. III
Edridge, Col Frederick Lockwood, 1831–1913, vol. I
Edridge, Sir Frederick Thomas, 1843–1921, vol. II
Edridge-Green, Frederick William, 1864–1953, vol. V
Edsall, Rt Rev. Samuel Cook, 1860–1917, vol. II
Edsberg, John Christian, 1938–1999, vol. X
Edser, Edwin, died 1932, vol. III
Edvina, Madame Marie Louise, died 1948, vol. IV
Edward, A. S., 1852–1915, vol. I
Edward-Collins, Maj.-Gen. Charles Edward, 1881–1967, vol. VI
Edward-Collins, Adm. Sir Frederick; see Edward-Collins, Adm. Sir G. F. B.
Edward-Collins, Adm. Sir (George) Frederick (Basset), 1883–1958, vol. V
Edward-Collins, Brig. Gerald 1885–1968, vol. VI
Edwardes, Lt-Col Alexander Coburn, 1873–1948, vol. IV
Edwardes, Arthur Henry Francis, 1885–1951, vol. V
Edwardes, Lt-Col Hon. Cuthbert Ellison, 1838–1911, vol. I
Edwardes, George, 1852–1915, vol. I
Edwardes, Sir Henry Hope, 10th Bt, 1829–1900, vol. I
Edwardes, Gen. Sir Stanley de Burgh, 1840–1918, vol. II
Edwardes, Col Stanley Malcolm, 1863–1937, vol. III
Edwardes, Stephen Meredyth, 1873–1927, vol. II
Edwardes, Tickner, 1865–1944, vol. IV
Edwardes-Davies, Rt Rev. David, 1897–1950, vol. IV
Edwardes Jones, Air Marshal Sir Humphrey; see Edwardes Jones, Sir J. H.
Edwardes Jones, Air Marshal Sir (John) Humphrey, 1905–1987, vol. VIII
Edwardes-Ker, Lt-Col Douglas Rous, 1886–1979, vol. VII
Edwards, family name of Baron Chelmer
Edwards, Agustin, 1878–1941, vol. IV
Edwards, Alfred, 1888–1958, vol. V

Edwards, Most Rev. Alfred George, 1848–1937, vol. III
Edwards, Maj.-Gen. Sir Alfred Hamilton Mackenzie, 1862–1944, vol. IV
Edwards, Rev. Canon Allen, 1844–1917, vol. II
Edwards, (Allen) Clement, 1869–1938, vol. III
Edwards, Brig. Arthur Bertie Duncan, 1898–1990, vol. VIII
Edwards, Arthur James Howie, 1884–1944, vol. IV
Edwards, Arthur John Charles, 1883–1963, vol. VI
Edwards, (Arthur) Trystan, 1884–1973, vol. VII
Edwards, Arthur Tudor, died 1946, vol. IV
Edwards, Lt-Col Sir Bartle Mordaunt Marsham, 1891–1977, vol. VII
Edwards, Hon. Sir Bassett; see Edwards, Hon. Sir W. B.
Edwards, Mrs Bennett-, 1844–1936, vol. III
Edwards, Ven. Bickerton Cross, 1874–1949, vol. IV
Edwards, Brig. Brian Bingay, 1895–1947, vol. IV
Edwards, Carl Johannes, 1914–1985, vol. VIII
Edwards, Rt Hon. Sir Charles, 1867–1954, vol. V
Edwards, Charles Alfred, 1882–1960, vol. V
Edwards, Charles Harold, 1913–1996, vol. X
Edwards, Charles Lewis, 1865–1928, vol. II
Edwards, Lt-Comdr Charles Peter, 1885–1960, vol. V
Edwards, Brig.-Gen. Christopher Vaughan, 1875–1955, vol. V
Edwards, Clement; see Edwards, A. C.
Edwards, Sir Clive; see Edwards, Sir J. C. L.
Edwards, Corwin D., 1901–1979, vol. VII
Edwards, Lt-Col Cosmo Grant Niven, 1896–1964, vol. VI
Edwards, D., 1858–1916, vol. II
Edwards, Sir David, 1892–1966, vol. VI
Edwards, Derek, 1931—1993, vol. IX
Edwards, Donald Isaac, 1904–1991, vol. IX
Edwards, Rev. Father Douglas Allen, 1893–1953, vol. V
Edwards, Ebby, 1884–1961, vol. VI
Edwards, Rev. Canon Edgar Thomas, 1880–1935, vol. III
Edwards, Edward, 1865–1933, vol. III
Edwards, Edward George, 1914–1996, vol. X
Edwards, Edward John Rogers, 1891–1965, vol. VI
Edwards, Rev. Ellis, 1844–1915, vol. I
Edwards, Enoch, 1852–1912, vol. I
Edwards, Evangeline Dora, 1888–1957, vol. V
Edwards, Brig.-Gen. Fitz-James Maine, 1861–1929, vol. III
Edwards, Lt-Col Rt Hon. Sir Fleetwood Isham, 1842–1910, vol. I
Edwards, Sir Francis, 1st Bt (cr 1907), 1852–1927, vol. II
Edwards, Lt-Gen. Frederick Charles, 1870–1947, vol. IV
Edwards, Frederick Laurence, 1903–1962, vol. VI
Edwards, Frederick Swinford, 1853–1939, vol. III
Edwards, Frederick Wallace, 1888–1940, vol. III
Edwards, G. Spencer, died 1916, vol. II
Edwards, Geoffrey, 1917–1990, vol. VIII
Edwards, Geoffrey Frances, 1917–1996, vol. X
Edwards, Geoffrey Richard, 1891–1961, vol. VI
Edwards, Sir George, 1850–1933, vol. III
Edwards, George, 1854–1946, vol. IV

Edwards, George, 1901–1989, vol. VIII
Edwards, Sir (George) Tristram, 1882–1960, vol. V
Edwards, Sir George William, 1818–1902, vol. I
Edwards, Gordon, 1899–1976, vol. VII
Edwards, Sir Goronwy; *see* Edwards, Sir J. G.
Edwards, Brig.-Gen. Graham Thomas George, 1864–1943, vol. IV
Edwards, Col Guy Janion, 1881–1962, vol. VI
Edwards, Gwilym Arthur, 1881–1963, vol. VI
Edwards, (H. C.) Ralph, 1894–1977, vol. VII
Edwards, Lt-Comdr Harington Douty, *died* 1916, vol. II
Edwards, Air Marshal Harold, 1892–1952, vol. V
Edwards, Harold Clifford, 1899–1989, vol. VIII
Edwards, Lt-Col Harold Walter, 1887–1973, vol. VII
Edwards, Sir Henry, 1820–1897, vol. I
Edwards, Sir Henry Charles Serrell Priestley, 4th Bt (*cr* 1866), 1893–1963, vol. VI
Edwards, Sir Henry Coster Lea, 2nd Bt (*cr* 1866), 1840–1896, vol. I
Edwards, Henry John, 1869–1923, vol. II
Edwards, Col Herbert Ivor Powell, 1884–1946, vol. IV
Edwards, Captain Hugh, 1873–1916, vol. II
Edwards, Air Cdre Sir Hughie Idwal, 1914–1982, vol. VIII
Edwards, Sir Ifan ab Owen, 1895–1970, vol. VI
Edwards, Iorweth Eiddon Stephen, 1909–1996, vol. X
Edwards, Very Rev. Irven David, 1907–1973, vol. VII
Edwards, Lt-Col Ivo Arthyr Exley, 1881–1947, vol. IV (A)
Edwards, Lt-Gen. Sir James Bevan, 1834–1922, vol. II
Edwards, James Keith O'Neill, 1920–1988, vol. VIII
Edwards, Jane Elizabeth; *see* Hayward, J. E.
Edwards, Rt Hon. John; *see* Edwards, Rt Hon. L. J.
Edwards, John, *died* 1954, vol. V
Edwards, John, 1882–1960, vol. V
Edwards, John, 1932–1989, vol. VIII
Edwards, Sir John Arthur, 1901–1983, vol. VIII
Edwards, John Basil, 1909–1996, vol. X
Edwards, John Braham Scott, 1928–1987, vol. VIII
Edwards, Sir John Bryn, 1st Bt (*cr* 1921), 1889–1922, vol. II
Edwards, Brig.-Gen. John Burnard, 1857–1937, vol. III
Edwards, Sir (John) Clive (Leighton), 2nd Bt (*cr* 1921), 1916–1999, vol. X
Edwards, Rev. John Cox C.; *see* Cox-Edwards.
Edwards, Vice-Adm. John Douglas, 1871–1952, vol. V
Edwards, John Francis H.; *see* Hall-Edwards.
Edwards, Sir (John) Goronwy, 1891–1976, vol. VII
Edwards, Sir John Henry Priestley Churchill, 3rd Bt (*cr* 1866), 1889–1942, vol. IV
Edwards, John Hugh, *died* 1945, vol. IV
Edwards, John Lionel, 1915–1999, vol. X
Edwards, John Passmore, 1823–1911, vol. I
Edwards, Rev. John Rosindale W.; *see* Wynne-Edwards.
Edwards, Joseph, 1854–1931, vol. III

Edwards, Joseph Robert, 1908–1997, vol. X
Edwards, Joshua Price, 1898–1966, vol. VI
Edwards, Kenneth Charles, 1904–1982, vol. VIII
Edwards, Laura Selina, (Lady Edwards), *died* 1919, vol. II
Edwards, Sir Lawrence, 1896–1968, vol. VI
Edwards, Rt Hon. (Lewis) John, 1904–1959, vol. V
Edwards, Rt Rev. Lewis Mervyn C.; *see* Charles-Edwards.
Edwards, Lionel D. R., 1878–1966, vol. VI
Edwards, Engr Rear-Adm. Macleod Gamul Arthur, 1884–1957, vol. V
Edwards, Rev. Maldwyn Lloyd, 1903–1974, vol. VII
Edwards, Sir Martin Llewellyn, 1909–1987, vol. VIII
Edwards, Matilda Betham-, *died* 1919, vol. II
Edwards, Rev. Maurice Henry, 1886–1961, vol. VI
Edwards, Rt Hon. Ness, 1897–1968, vol. VI
Edwards, Osman, 1864–1936, vol. III
Edwards, Sir Owen Morgan, 1858–1920, vol. II
Edwards, Ralph; *see* Edwards, H. C. R.
Edwards, Adm. Sir Ralph Alan Bevan, 1901–1963, vol. VI
Edwards, Brig.-Gen. Richard Fielding, 1866–1942, vol. IV
Edwards, Richard Lionel, 1907–1984, vol. VIII
Edwards, Robert, 1905–1990, vol. VIII
Edwards, Robert Hamilton, *born* 1872, vol. III
Edwards, Sir Robert Meredydd W.; *see* Wynne-Edwards.
Edwards, Captain Roderick Latimer Mackenzie 1900–1975, vol. VII
Edwards, Lt-Col Roderick Mackenzie, *died* 1940, vol. III
Edwards, Roger Snowden, 1904–1997, vol. X
Edwards, Sir Ronald Stanley, 1910–1976, vol. VII
Edwards, Rev. Canon Rowland Alexander, 1890–1973, vol. VII
Edwards, Rev. Thomas, vol. II
Edwards, Rev. Thomas Charles, 1837–1900, vol. I
Edwards, Sir Tristram; *see* Edwards, Sir G. T.
Edwards, Trystan; *see* Edwards, A. T.
Edwards, Vero Copner W.; *see* Wynne-Edwards.
Edwards, Walter James, 1900–1964, vol. VI
Edwards, Lt-Col Walter Manoel, 1885–1971, vol. VII
Edwards, Wilbraham Tollemache Arthur, 1836–1929, vol. III
Edwards, Wilfred Norman, 1890–1956, vol. V
Edwards, William, 1851–1940, vol. III
Edwards, William, 1874–1969, vol. VI
Edwards, Lt-Col William Bickerton, 1870–1933, vol. III
Edwards, Hon. William Cameron, 1844–1921, vol. II
Edwards, Col William Egerton, 1875–1921, vol. II
Edwards, Brig.-Gen. William Frederick Savery, 1872–1941, vol. IV
Edwards, Rev. Canon William George, 1858–1942, vol. IV
Edwards, Rev. William Gilbert, 1846–1936, vol. III
Edwards, Major William Mordaunt Marsh, 1855–1912, vol. I

Edwards, William Philip Neville, 1904–1995, vol. IX
Edwards, William Powell, 1854–1935, vol. III
Edwards, Hon. Maj.-Gen. Sir William Rice, 1862–1923, vol. II
Edwards, William Stuart, 1880–1944, vol. IV
Edwards, Hon. Sir (Worley) Bassett, 1850–1927, vol. II
Edwards-Heathcote, Justinian Heathcote; see Heathcote.
Edwards-Jones, Ian, 1923–1995, vol. IX
Edwards-Moss, Sir John Edwards, 2nd Bt, 1850–1935, vol. III
Edwards-Moss, Sir John Herbert Theodore, 4th Bt, 1913–1988, vol. VIII
Edwards-Moss, Sir Thomas, 3rd Bt, 1874–1960, vol. V
Edwin, George Frederick D.; see Dove-Edwin.
Edye, Sir Benjamin Thomas, 1884–1962, vol. VI
Eeles, Francis Carolus, 1876–1954, vol. V
Eeles, Air Cdre Henry, 1910–1992, vol. IX
Eestermans, Fabian Anthony, 1858–1931, vol. III
Effingham, 3rd Earl of, 1837–1898, vol. I
Effingham, 4th Earl of, 1866–1927, vol. II
Effingham, 5th Earl of, 1873–1946, vol. IV
Effingham, 6th Earl of, 1905–1996, vol. X
Egan, Harold, 1922–1984, vol. VIII
Egan, Sir Henry Kelly, 1848–1925, vol. II
Egan, Hon. Maurice Francis, 1852–1924, vol. II
Egan, Col Michael Henry, 1865–1940, vol. III
Egan, Rt Rev. T. Erkenwald, 1856–1939, vol. III
Egan, Major William, 1881–1929, vol. III
Egan, William Henry, 1869–1943, vol. IV
Egeland, Leif, 1903–1996, vol. X
Egbert, Hon. William, 1857–1936, vol. III
Egerton, 1st Earl, 1832–1909, vol. I
Egerton of Tatton, 3rd Baron, 1845–1920, vol. II
Egerton of Tatton, 4th Baron, 1874–1958, vol. V
Egerton, Sir Alfred Charles Glyn, 1886–1959, vol. V
Egerton, Col Sir Alfred Mordaunt, 1843–1908, vol. I
Egerton, Lady Alice, 1923–1977, vol. VII
Egerton, Lt-Col Arthur Frederick, 1866–1942, vol. IV
Egerton, Sir Brian, 1857–1940, vol. III
Egerton, Rev. Sir Brooke de Malpas Grey-, 13th Bt, 1845–1945, vol. IV
Egerton, Charles Augustus, died 1912, vol. I
Egerton, Field-Marshal Sir Charles Comyn, 1848–1921, vol. II
Egerton, Charles William, 1862–1939, vol. III
Egerton, Rt Hon. Edwin Henry, 1841–1916, vol. II
Egerton, Rear-Adm. Frederick Wilbraham, 1838–1909, vol. I
Egerton, George, (Mrs Golding Bright), (Mary Chavelita), 1859–1945, vol. IV
Egerton, Adm. Sir George le Clerc, 1852–1940, vol. III
Egerton, Major George M. L., 1837–1898, vol. I
Egerton, Maj.-Gen. Granville George Algernon, 1859–1951, vol. V
Egerton, Vice-Adm. (Henry) Jack, 1892–1972, vol. VII
Egerton, Hugh Edward, 1855–1927, vol. II

Egerton, Comdr Hugh Sydney, 1890–1969, vol. VI
Egerton, Jack; see Egerton, Sir J. A. R.
Egerton, Vice-Adm. Jack; see Egerton, Vice-Adm. H. J.
Egerton, Sir John Alfred Roy, (Sir Jack), 1918–1998, vol. X
Egerton, Lady Mabelle, 1865–1927, vol. II
Egerton, Sir Philip Henry Brian Grey-, 12th Bt, 1864–1937, vol. III
Egerton, Sir Philip Reginald le Belward G.; see Grey Egerton.
Egerton, Lt-Gen. Sir Raleigh Gilbert, 1860–1931, vol. III
Egerton, Sir Reginald Arthur, 1850–1930, vol. III
Egerton, Sir Robert Eyles, 1857–1912, vol. I
Egerton, Sir Seymour John Louis, 1915–1998, vol. X
Egerton, Hon. Thomas Henry Frederick, 1876–1953, vol. V
Egerton, Sir Walter, 1858–1947, vol. IV
Egerton, Rear-Adm. Wilfrid Allan, 1881–1931, vol. III
Egerton, William Francis, 1868–1949, vol. IV
Egerton, Rev. William Henry, 1811–1910, vol. I
Egerton, Vice-Adm. Wion De Malpas, 1879–1943, vol. IV
Egerton-Warburton, Geoffrey, 1888–1961, vol. VI
Egerton-Warburton, John, 1883–1915, vol. I
Egerton-Warburton, Piers, 1839–1914, vol. I
Eggar, Sir Arthur, 1877–1958, vol. V
Eggar, Sir Henry Cooper, 1851–1941, vol. IV
Eggar, James, 1880–1962, vol. VI
Eggeling, H. Julius, 1842–1918, vol. II
Eggers, Henry Howard, 1903–1980, vol. VII
Egginton, Wycliffe, 1875–1951, vol. V
Eggleston, Edward, 1837–1902, vol. I
Eggleston, Sir Frederic William, 1875–1954, vol. V
Eggleston, Harold Gordon, 1921–1999, vol. X
Eggleston, Hon. Sir Richard Moulton, 1909–1991, vol. IX
Eglington, Rev. Canon Arthur, 1871–1925, vol. II
Eglington, William, 1858–1933, vol. III
Eglinton and Winton, 15th Earl of, 1848–1919, vol. II
Eglinton and Winton, 16th Earl of, 1880–1945, vol. IV
Eglinton and Winton, 17th Earl of, 1914–1966, vol. VI
Egmont, 7th Earl of, 1845–1897, vol. I
Egmont, 8th Earl of, 1856–1910, vol. I
Egmont, 9th Earl of, 1858–1929, vol. III
Egmont, 10th Earl of, 1873–1932, vol. III
Egmont, Countess of; (Lucy), died 1932, vol. III
Egremont, 1st Baron, and Leconfield, 6th Baron, 1920–1972, vol. VII
Eha; see Aitken, E. H.
Ehrenberg, Victor Leopold, 1891–1976, vol. VII
Ehrenburg, Ilya, 1891–1967, vol. VI
Ehrhardt, Albert, 1862–1929, vol. III
Ehrlich, Georg, 1897–1966, vol. VI
Ehrlich, Paul, 1854–1915, vol. I
Eichholz, Alfred, 1869–1933, vol. III
Eiffel, Alexandre Gustave, 1832–1923, vol. II
Einaudi, Luigi, 1874–1961, vol. VI
Einstein, Albert, 1879–1955, vol. V

Einstein, Alfred, 1880–1952, vol. V
Einthoven, Willem, 1860–1927, vol. II
Einzig, Paul, 1897–1973, vol. VII
Eisdell, Hubert Mortimer, 1882–1948, vol. IV
Eisenberg, Maurice, 1902–1972, vol. VII
Eisenhower, Gen. Dwight David, 1890–1969, vol. VI
Eisenhower, Milton Stover, 1899–1985, vol. VIII
Eisenschitz, Robert Karl, 1898–1968, vol. VI
Ekin, Maj.-Gen. Roger Gillies, 1895–1990, vol. VIII
Eking, Maj.-Gen. Harold Cecil William, 1903–1978, vol. VII
Ekins, Emily Helen, 1879–1964, vol. VI
Ekwall, Bror Oscar Eilert, 1877–1964, vol. VI
Elam, Henry, 1903–1993, vol. IX
Eland, John Shenton, 1872–1933, vol. III
Elatu, Eliahu, 1903–1990, vol. VIII
Elborne, Sydney Lipscomb, 1890–1986, vol. VIII
Elcho, Lord; Iain David Charteris, 1945–1954, vol. V
Elcock, William Dennis, 1910–1960, vol. V
Elder, David Renwick, 1920–1996, vol. X
Elder, Hugh, 1905–1986, vol. VIII
Elder, Sir James Alexander MacKenzie, 1869–1946, vol. IV
Elder, John Munro, 1860–1922, vol. II
Elder, John Rawson, 1880–1962, vol. VI
Elder, Sir Stewart D.; see Duke-Elder
Elder, William, 1864–1931, vol. III
Elder, William Alexander, 1881–1946, vol. IV(A)
Elder, Rear-Adm. William Leslie, 1874–1961, vol. VI
Elder, Sir (William) Stewart D.; see Duke-Elder.
Elder-Duncan, John Hudson, 1877–1938, vol. III
Elder-Jones, Thomas, 1904–1988, vol. VIII
Elderton, Ethel Mary, 1878–1954, vol. V
Elderton, Captain Ferdinand Halford, 1865–1942, vol. IV
Elderton, Sir Thomas Howard, 1886–1970, vol. VI
Elderton, Sir William Palin, 1877–1962, vol. VI
Eldin-Taylor, Kenneth Roy, 1902–1990, vol. VIII
Eldon, 3rd Earl of, 1845–1926, vol. II
Eldon, 4th Earl of, 1899–1976, vol. VII
Eldred, Paymaster-Captain Edward Henry, 1864–1929, vol. III
Eldridge, Eric William, 1906–1991, vol. IX
Eldridge, Captain George Bernard, died 1944, vol. IV
Eldridge, Lt-Gen. Sir John; see Eldridge, Lt-Gen. Sir W. J.
Eldridge, John Barron, 1919–1998, vol. X
Eldridge, Lt-Col William James, 1917–1987, vol. VIII
Eldridge, Lt-Gen. Sir (William) John, 1898–1985, vol. VIII
Elek, Stephen Dyonis, 1914–1992, vol. IX
Eley, Col Edward Henry, 1874–1949, vol. IV
Eley, Sir Frederick, 1st Bt, 1866–1951, vol. V
Eley, Sir Geoffrey Cecil Ryves, 1904–1990, vol. VIII
Eley, John L.; see Lloyd-Eley.
Eley, Rt Rev. Stanley Albert Hallam, 1899–1970, vol. VI
Elford, William Joseph, 1900–1952, vol. V

Elgar, Sir Edward, 1st Bt, 1857–1934, vol. III
Elgar, Francis, 1845–1909, vol. I
Elgee, Captain Cyril Hammond, 1871–1917, vol. II
Elgee, Frank, 1880–1944, vol. IV
Elger, Major Edward Gwyn, 1864–1929, vol. III
Elgin, 9th Earl of, and Kincardine, 13th Earl of, 1849–1917, vol. II
Elgin, 10th Earl of, and Kincardine, 14th Earl of, 1881–1968, vol. VI
Elgood, Sir Frank Minshull, 1865–1948, vol. IV
Elgood, George S., 1851–1943, vol. IV
Elgood, Captain Leonard Alsager, 1892–1987, vol VIII
Elgood, Lt-Col Percival George, 1863–1941, vol. IV
Elhorst, Hendrik Jan, born 1861, vol. II
Elias, David Henry, 1882–1953, vol. V
Elias, Taslim Olawale, 1914–1991, vol. IX
Eliash, Mordecai, 1892–1950, vol. IV
Elibank, 1st Viscount, 1840–1927, vol. II
Elibank, 2nd Viscount, 1877–1951, vol. V
Elibank, 3rd Viscount, 1879–1962, vol. VI
Elibank, 13th Lord, 1902–1973, vol. VII
Elion, Gertrude Belle, 1918–1999, vol. X
Eliot, Lord; Edward Henry John Cornwallis Elliot, 1885–1909, vol. I
Eliot, Hon. Arthur Ernest Henry, 1874–1936, vol. III
Eliot, Rt Hon. Sir Charles Norton Edgcumbe, 1862–1931, vol. III
Eliot, Charles William, 1834–1926, vol. II
Eliot, Edward Carlyon, died 1940, vol. III
Eliot, Ven. Edward Francis Whately, 1864–1943, vol. IV
Eliot, Sir John, 1839–1908, vol. I
Eliot, Laurence Stirling, 1845–1922, vol. II
Eliot, Lt-Col Nevill, 1880–1957, vol. V
Eliot, Ven. Canon Peter Charles, 1910–1995, vol. IX
Eliot, Very Rev. Philip Frank, 1835–1917, vol. II
Eliot, Rt Rev. Philip Herbert, 1862–1946, vol. IV
Eliot, Vice-Adm. Ralph, 1881–1958, vol. V
Eliot, Hon. Reginald Huyshe H.; see Huyshe-Eliot.
Eliot, Rev. Samuel Atkins, 1862–1950, vol. IV (A), vol. V
Eliot, Thomas Stearns, 1888–1965, vol. VI
Eliot, Rev. W., 1832–1910, vol. I
Eliot, Sir Whately, 1841–1927, vol. II
Eliott of Stobs, Sir Arthur Boswell, 9th Bt, 1856–1926, vol. II
Eliott, Lt-Col Francis Augustus Heathfield, 1867–1937, vol. III
Eliott, Lt-Col Francis Hardinge, 1862–1928, vol. II
Eliott of Stobs, Sir Arthur Francis Augustus Boswell, 11th Bt, 1915–1989, vol. VIII
Eliott of Stobs, Sir Gilbert Alexander Boswell, 10th Bt, 1885–1958, vol. V
Eliott of Stobs, Sir William Francis Augustus, 8th Bt, 1827–1910, vol. I
Eliott Lockhart, Sir Allan Robert, 1905–1977, vol. VII
Eliott-Lockhart, Lt-Col Percy Clare, 1867–1915, vol. I
Elkan, Benno, 1877–1960, vol. V
Elkan, Lt-Col Clarence John, 1877–1940, vol. III
Elkan, John, 1849–1927, vol. II

El'Kanemi, Alhaji Sir Umar Ibn Muhammed El'Amin, 1873–1967, vol. VI
Elkin, Adolphus Peter, 1891–1979, vol. VII (AII)
Elkington, Frederick Pellatt, 1874–1940, vol. III (A), vol. IV
Elkington,, Geoffrey; see Elkington, R. G.
Elkington, John St Clair, died 1963, vol. VI
Elkington, John Simeon, born 1841, vol. II
Elkington, (Reginald) Geoffrey, 1907–1993, vol. IX
Elkington, Reginald Lawrence, 1898–1975, vol. VII
Elkington, Col Robert James Goodall, 1867–1939, vol. III
Elkins, Sir Anthony Joseph, 1904–1978, vol. VII
Elkins, Vice-Adm. Sir Robert Francis, 1903–1985, vol. VIII
Elkins, Stephen Benton, 1841–1911, vol. I
Elkins, Maj.-Gen. William Henry Pferinger, 1883–1964, vol. VI
Elkins, William Lukens, 1832–1903, vol. I
Elland, Percy, 1908–1960, vol. V
Ellenberger, Lt-Col Jules, 1871–1973, vol. VII
Ellenborough, 4th Baron, 1856–1902, vol. I
Ellenborough, 5th Baron, 1841–1915, vol. I
Ellenborough, 6th Baron, 1849–1931, vol. III
Ellenborough, 7th Baron, 1889–1945, vol. IV
Ellerman, Sir John Reeves, 1st Bt, 1862–1933, vol. III
Ellerman, Sir John Reeves, 2nd Bt, 1909–1973, vol. VII
Ellershaw, Brig.-Gen. Arthur, 1869–1929, vol. III
Ellershaw, Rev. Henry, 1863–1932, vol. III
Ellerton, Air Cdre Alban Spenser, 1894–1978, vol. VII
Ellerton, Rev. Arthur John Bicknell, 1865–1928, vol. II
Ellerton, Sir Cecil; see Ellerton, Sir F. C.
Ellerton, Sir (Frederick) Cecil, 1892–1962, vol. VI
Ellerton, Adm. Walter Maurice, 1870–1948, vol. IV
Ellery, Lt-Col Robert Lewis John, 1827–1908, vol. I
Elles, Lt-Gen. Sir Edmond Roche, 1848–1934, vol. III
Elles, Gen. Sir Hugh Jamieson, 1880–1945, vol. IV
Elles, Robin Jamieson, 1907–1987, vol. VIII
Ellesmere, 3rd Earl of, 1847–1914, vol. I
Ellesmere, 4th Earl of, 1872–1944, vol. IV
Ellice, Major Edward Charles, 1858–1934, vol. III
Ellicot, Rt Rev. Charles John, 1819–1905, vol. I
Ellicott, Arthur Becher, 1849–1931, vol. III
Ellicott, Langford Pannell, 1903–1972, vol. VII
Ellicott, Rosalind, died 1924, vol. II
Ellinger, Barnard, died 1947, vol. IV
Ellingford, Herbert Frederick, 1876–1966, vol. VI
Ellington,, Duke; see Ellington, Hon. E. K.
Ellington, Hon. Edward Kennedy, (Duke), 1899–1974, vol. VII
Ellington, Marshal of the Royal Air Force Sir Edward Leonard, 1877–1967, vol. VI
Elliot of Harwood, Baroness (Life Peer); Katharine Elliot, 1903–1994, vol. IX
Elliot, Maj.-Gen. Sir Alexander James Hardy, 1825–1909, vol. I
Elliot, Alison, 1891–1939, vol. III
Elliot, Hon. Arthur Ralph Douglas, 1846–1923, vol. II
Elliot, Sir Charles, 4th Bt, 1873–1911, vol. I

Elliot, Sir Duncan; see Elliot, Sir J. D.
Elliot, Major Sir Edmund Halbert, 1854–1926, vol. II
Elliot, Lt-Gen. Sir Edward Locke, 1850–1938, vol. III
Elliot, Sir Francis Edmund Hugh, 1851–1940, vol. III
Elliot, Frederick Augustus Hugh, 1847–1910, vol. I
Elliot, Frederick Barnard, 1877–1950, vol. IV
Elliot, Rev. Frederick Roberts, 1840–1918, vol. II
Elliot, Sir George, 1812–1901, vol. I
Elliot, Sir George, 3rd Bt, 1867–1904, vol. I
Elliot, Sir George, 1869–1956, vol. V
Elliot, Rev. Canon George Edward, 1851–1916, vol. II
Elliot, Maj.-Gen. Gilbert Minto, 1897–1969, vol. VI
Elliot, Brig.-Gen. Gilbert Sutherland McDowell, 1863–1937, vol. III
Elliot, Maj.-Gen. Harry Macintire C.; see Cawthra-Elliot.
Elliot, Rt Hon. Sir Henry George, 1817–1907, vol. I
Elliot, Sir Henry George, 1826–1912, vol. I
Elliot, Lt-Col Henry Hawes, 1891–1972, vol. VII
Elliot, Maj.-Gen. Henry Riversdale, 1836–1921, vol. II
Elliot, Hubert William Arthur, 1891–1967, vol. VI
Elliot, Hugh, 1881–1930, vol. III
Elliot, Hon. Hugh Frederick Hislop, 1848–1932, vol. III
Elliot, Sir (James) Duncan, 1862–1956, vol. V
Elliot, James Robert McDowell, 1896–1980, vol. VII
Elliot, Maj.-Gen. James S.; see Scott Elliot.
Elliot, Sir John, 1898–1988, vol. VIII
Elliot, Margaret, died 1901, vol. I
Elliot, Captain Mark F.; see Fogg Elliot.
Elliot, Maj.-Gen. Minto, 1833–1909, vol. I
Elliot, Robert H., 1837–1914, vol. I
Elliot, Lt-Col Robert Henry, died 1936, vol. III
Elliot, Captain Walter, 1910–1988, vol. VIII
Elliot, Rt Hon. Walter Elliot, 1888–1959, vol. V
Elliot, Walter Travers S.; see Scott-Elliot.
Elliot, Col William, 1861–1936, vol. III
Elliot, Air Chief Marshal Sir William, 1896–1971, vol. VII
Elliot, Col William Henry Wilson, 1864–1934, vol. III
Elliot, Lt-Col William Scott, 1873–1943, vol. IV
Elliot-Smith, Alan Guy, 1904–1997, vol. X
Elliott, Adshead, 1869–1922, vol. II
Elliott, Albert George, 1889–1975, vol. VII
Elliott, Lt-Col Alfred Charles, 1870–1952, vol. V
Elliott, Rt Rev. Alfred George, 1828–1915, vol. I
Elliott, Algernon, 1848–1934, vol. III
Elliott, Anthony; see Elliott, T. A. K.
Elliott, Rt Rev. Anthony Blacker, 1887–1970, vol. VI (AII)
Elliott, Archibald Campbell, 1861–1913, vol. I
Elliott, Sir Bignell George, 1857–1933, vol. III
Elliott, Bruce John, 1927–1993, vol. IX
Elliott, Sir Charles Alfred, 1835–1911, vol. I
Elliott, Sir Charles Bletterman, 1841–1911, vol. I
Elliott, Col Charles Hazell, 1882–1956, vol. V
Elliott, Charles Hugh Babington, 1852–1943, vol. IV

Elliott, Charles Kennedy, 1919–1992, vol. IX
Elliott, Rev. Canon Charles Lister Boileau, 1864–1940, vol. III
Elliott, Christopher, 1849–1933, vol. III
Elliott, Clarence, 1881–1969, vol. VI
Elliott, Sir Claude Aurelius, 1888–1973, vol. VII
Elliott, (Colin) Fraser, 1888–1969, vol. VI
Elliott, David Lee L.; see Lee-Elliott.
Elliott, Denholm Mitchell, 1922–1992, vol. IX
Elliott, Edward Cassleton, 1881–1967, vol. VI
Elliott, Maj.-Gen. Edward Draper, 1838–1918, vol. II
Elliott, Edwin Bailey, 1851–1937, vol. III
Elliott, Ven. Francis William Thomas, died 1930, vol. III
Elliott, Frank Herbert, 1878–1966, vol. VI
Elliott, Frank Louis Dumbell, 1874–1939, vol. III
Elliott, Fraser; see Elliott, C. F.
Elliott, George, 1860–1916, vol. II
Elliott, Sir George Samuel, died 1925, vol. II
Elliott, Col Gilbert Charles Edward, 1872–1934, vol. III
Elliott, Maj.-Gen. Harold Edward, 1878–1931, vol. III
Elliott, Harold William, 1905–1991, vol. IX
Elliott, Sir Hugh Francis Ivo, 3rd Bt, 1913–1989, vol. VIII
Elliott, Sir Ivo D'Oyly, 2nd Bt, 1882–1961, vol. VI
Elliott, Maj.-Gen. James Gordon, 1898–1990, vol. VIII
Elliott, Sir James Sands, 1880–1959, vol. V
Elliott, Mrs John; see Elliott, M. H.
Elliott, Col John, 1824–1911, vol. I
Elliott, Hon. John Campbell, 1872–1941, vol. IV
Elliott, Rev. John Robert Underwood, 1843–1936, vol. III
Elliott, John Wilson, 1886–1957, vol. V
Elliott, Maud Howe, (Mrs John Elliott), 1854–1948, vol. IV
Elliott, Vice-Adm. Sir Maurice Herbert, 1897–1972, vol. VII
Elliott, Michael Paul, 1931–1984, vol. VIII
Elliott, Sir Norman Randall, 1903–1992, vol. IX
Elliott, Ralph Edward, 1908–1981, vol. VIII
Elliott, Robert Charles Dunlop, 1886–1950, vol. IV
Elliott, Rt Rev. Robert Cyril Hamilton, 1890–1977, vol. VII
Elliott, Air Vice-Marshal Robert D.; see Deacon Elliott.
Elliott, Rowley, 1877–1944, vol. IV
Elliott, Rev. Canon Spencer Hayward, 1883–1967, vol. VI
Elliott, Sydney Robert, 1902–1987, vol. VIII
Elliott, (Thomas) Anthony (Keith), 1921–1976, vol. VI
Elliott, Sir Thomas Henry, 1st Bt, 1854–1926, vol. II
Elliott, Thomas Renton, 1877–1961, vol. VI
Elliott, Rev. Canon Wallace Harold, died 1957, vol. V
Elliott, Col William, 1879–1947, vol. IV
Elliott, William John, 1890–1940, vol. III
Elliott, William Rowcliffe, 1910–1996, vol. X
Elliott, Rev. William Thompson, 1880–1940, vol. III

Elliott-Binns, Edward Ussher Elliott, 1918–1990, vol. VIII
Elliott-Binns, Rev. Leonard Elliott; see Binns.
Elliott-Blake, Henry, 1902–1983, vol. VIII
Elliott-Cooper, Sir Robert; see Cooper.
Ellis, Sir Alan Edward, 1890–1960, vol. V
Ellis, Sir Albert Fuller, 1869–1951, vol. V
Ellis, Col Alfred Charles Samuel Burdon, 1876–1955, vol. V
Ellis, Annabel W.; see Williams-Ellis, M. A. N.
Ellis, Anthony Louis, died 1944, vol. IV
Ellis, Arthur, 1856–1918, vol. II
Ellis, Maj.-Gen. Sir Arthur Edward Augustus, 1837–1907, vol. I
Ellis, Arthur Isaac, 1883–1963, vol. VI
Ellis, Arthur Thomas, 1892–1964, vol. VI
Ellis, Sir Arthur William Mickle, died 1966, vol. VI
Ellis, Lt-Comdr Bernard Henry, 1885–1918, vol. II
Ellis, Sir (Bertram) Clough W.; see Williams-Ellis.
Ellis, Col Charles Conyngham, 1852–1921, vol. II
Ellis, Sir Charles Drummond, 1895–1980, vol. VII
Ellis, Sir Charles Edward, 1852–1937, vol. III
Ellis, Lt-Col Sir Charles Henry Brabazon H.; see Heaton-Ellis.
Ellis, Charles Howard, 1895–1975, vol. VII
Ellis, Col Clarence Isidore, 1871–1961, vol. VI
Ellis, Rear-Adm. (E.) Clement, died 1953, vol. V
Ellis, Colin Dare Bernard, 1895–1969, vol. VI
Ellis, Lt-Col Conyngham Richard Cecil, 1863–1938, vol. III
Ellis, David, 1874–1937, vol. III
Ellis, Rt Rev. Edward, 1899–1979, vol. VII
Ellis, Vice-Adm. Sir Edward Henry Fitzhardinge H.; see Heaton-Ellis.
Ellis, Engr Rear-Adm. Ernest Frank, 1855–1944, vol. IV
Ellis, Ernest Tetley, 1893–1953, vol. V
Ellis, Sir Evelyn Campbell, 1865–1920, vol. II
Ellis, Francis Newman, 1855–1934, vol. III
Ellis, Francis Robert, 1849–1915, vol. I
Ellis, Captain Frederick, 1826–1906, vol. I
Ellis, Sir Geoffrey; see Ellis, Sir R. G.
Ellis, Gerald Edward Harold, 1878–1967, vol. VI
Ellis, Harold Owen, 1906–1981, vol. VIII
Ellis, Rev. Canon Henry, 1909–1972, vol. VII
Ellis, Henry Arthur Augustus, died 1934, vol. III
Ellis, Henry Havelock, 1859–1939, vol. III
Ellis, Lt-Col Henry L.; see Leslie-Ellis.
Ellis, Col Herbert Charles, 1874–1952, vol. V
Ellis, Sir Herbert Mackay, 1851–1912, vol. I
Ellis, Sir Howard; see Ellis, Sir S. H.
Ellis, Humphrey Francis, 1907–2000, vol. X
Ellis, Rt Hon. John Edward, 1841–1910, vol. I
Ellis, J(ohn) Hugh, 1909–1959, vol. V
Ellis, Sir John Rogers, 1916–1998, vol. X
Ellis, Sir (John) Whittaker, 1st Bt (cr 1882), 1829–1912, vol. I
Ellis, Sir Joseph Baxter, died 1918, vol. II
Ellis, Joseph Stanley, 1907–1993, vol. IX
Ellis, Hon. Sir Kevin, 1908–1975, vol. VII
Ellis, Major Lionel Frederic, 1885–1970, vol. VI
Ellis, Lyle Fullam, 1887–1951, vol. V
Ellis, Malcolm Henry, 1890–1969, vol. VI (AII)
Ellis, Mary Annabel Nassau W.; see Williams-Ellis.
Ellis, Mary Baxter, 1892–1968, vol. VI

Ellis, Mary Jenny Lake, 1921–1983, vol. VIII
Ellis, Maxwell Philip, 1906–1996, vol. X
Ellis, Maj.-Gen. Philip George Saxon G.; *see* Gregson-Ellis.
Ellis, Raymond Joseph, 1923–1994, vol. IX
Ellis, Brig. Richard Stanley, 1884–1962, vol. VI
Ellis, Richard White Bernard, 1902–1966, vol. VI
Ellis, Sir (Robert) Geoffrey, 1st Bt (*cr* 1932), 1874–1956, vol. V
Ellis, Robert Powley, 1845–1918, vol. II
Ellis, Robinson, 1834–1913, vol. I
Ellis, Roger Henry, 1910–1998, vol. X
Ellis, Rt Rev. Rowland, 1841–1911, vol. I
Ellis, Sir (Samuel) Howard, 1889–1949, vol. IV
Ellis, Lt-Col Sherman Gordon Venn, 1880–1937, vol. III
Ellis, Stewart Marsh, *died* 1933, vol. III
Ellis, T. Mullett, 1850–1919, vol. II
Ellis, Thomas Edward, 1859–1899, vol. I
Ellis, Sir Thomas Hobart, 1894–1981, vol. VIII
Ellis, Thomas Iorwerth, 1899–1970, vol. VI
Ellis, Sir Thomas Ratcliffe R.; *see* Ratcliffe-Ellis.
Ellis, Tristram, 1844–1922, vol. II
Ellis, Valentine Herbert, *died* 1953, vol. V
Ellis, Vivian, 1904–1996, vol. X
Ellis, Very Rev. Vorley Spencer, 1882–1977, vol. VII
Ellis, Walter Devonshire, 1871–1957, vol. V
Ellis, Sir Whittaker; *see* Ellis, Sir J. W.
Ellis, Wilfred Desmond, 1914–1990, vol. VIII
Ellis, William, 1828–1916, vol. II
Ellis, William, 1868–1947, vol. IV
Ellis, William Barker, *died* 1934, vol. III
Ellis, William C.; *see* Craven-Ellis.
Ellis, Rev. Hon. William Charles, 1835–1923, vol. II
Ellis, Lt-Col W(illiam) Francis, 1878–1953, vol. V
Ellis, Sir William Henry, 1860–1945, vol. IV
Ellis, William Hodgson, 1845–1921, vol. II
Ellis, Col William Montague, 1862–1952, vol. V
Ellis-Fermor, Una Mary, 1894–1958, vol. V
Ellis-Griffith, Sir Elis Arundell; *see* Griffith, Sir E. A. E.
Ellis-Griffith, Rt Hon. Sir Ellis Jones; *see* Griffith.
Ellis-Rees, Sir Hugh, 1900–1974, vol. VII
Ellison, Rear-Adm. Alfred Astley, 1874–1932, vol. III
Ellison, Arthur James, 1920–2000, vol. X
Ellison, Ven. Charles Ottley, 1898–1978, vol. VII
Ellison, Rt Rev. and Rt Hon. Gerald Alexander, 1910–1992, vol. IX
Ellison, Lt-Gen. Sir Gerald Francis, 1861–1947, vol. IV
Ellison, Grace Mary, *died* 1935, vol. III
Ellison, John Harold, 1916–2000, vol. X
Ellison, Rev. John Henry Joshua, 1855–1944, vol. IV
Ellison, Randall Erskine, 1904–1984, vol. VIII
Ellison, Captain Richard Todd, *died* 1932, vol. III
Ellison, William, 1911–1978, vol. VII
Ellison, William Augustine, 1855–1917, vol. II
Ellison, Rev. Canon William Frederick Archdall, 1864–1936, vol. III
Ellison-Macartney, John William; *see* Macartney.

Ellison-Macartney, Rt Hon. Sir William Grey; *see* Macartney.
Ellissen, Lt-Col Sir Herbert, 1876–1952, vol. V
Elliston, Col George Sampson, 1844–1921, vol. II
Elliston, Sir George Sampson, 1875–1954, vol. V
Elliston, Guy, 1872–1918, vol. II
Elliston, Julian Clement Peter, 1911–1970, vol. VI
Elliston, William Alfred, 1840–1908, vol. I
Elliston, William Rowley, 1869–1954, vol. V
Ellman-Brown, Hon. Geoffrey, 1910–1994, vol. IX
Ellmann, Richard, 1918–1987, vol. VIII
Ellson, George, 1875–1949, vol. IV
Ellsworth, Lincoln, 1880–1951, vol. V
Ellwood, Bt Col Arthur Addison, 1886–1943, vol. IV
Ellwood, Air Marshal Sir Aubrey Beauclerk, 1897–1992, vol. IX
Ellwood, George Montague, 1875–1955, vol. V
Ellwood, Captain Michael Oliver Dundas, 1894–1984, vol. VIII
Elman, Mischa, 1891–1967, vol. VI
Elmhirst, Dorothy Whitney, 1887–1968, vol. VI
Elmhirst, Captain Edward Pennell, 1845–1916, vol. II
Elmhirst, Leonard Knight, *died* 1974, vol. VII
Elmhirst, Air Marshal Sir Thomas Walker, 1895–1982, vol. VIII
Elmitt, Lt-Col T. F., 1871–1938, vol. III
Elmsley, Maj.-Gen. James Harold, 1878–1954, vol. V
Elmslie, Christiana Deanes, 1869–1961, vol. VI
Elmslie, Brig.-Gen. Frederick Baumgardt, 1855–1936, vol. III
Elmslie, Noel, 1876–1956, vol. V
Elmslie, Reginald Cheyne, 1878–1940, vol. III
Elmslie, Rev. William Alexander Leslie, 1885–1965, vol. VI
Elnor, Rev. William George, *died* 1956, vol. V
Elphick, Ronald, 1918–1977, vol. VII
Elphinstone, 16th Lord, 1869–1955, vol. V
Elphinstone, 17th Lord, 1914–1975, vol. VII
Elphinstone, 18th Lord, 1953–1994, vol. IX
Elphinstone of Glack, Sir Alexander Logie, 10th Bt (*cr* 1701), 1880–1970, vol. VI
Elphinstone, Archibald Howard L., 1865–1936, vol. III
Elphinstone, Sir Arthur Percy Archibald, 11th Bt (*cr* 1628), *born* 1863 (this entry was not transferred to Who was Who).
Elphinstone, Sir Douglas; *see* Elphinstone, Sir M. D. W.
Elphinstone, Sir (George) Keith (Buller), 1865–1941, vol. IV
Elphinstone, Sir Græme Hepburn Dalrymple-Horn-, 4th Bt (*cr* 1828), 1841–1900, vol. I
Elphinstone, Sir Howard Graham, 4th Bt (*cr* 1816), 1898–1975, vol. VII
Elphinstone, Sir Howard Warburton, 3rd Bt (*cr* 1816), 1830–1917, vol. II
Elphinstone, Sir Keith; *see* Elphinstone, Sir G. K. B.
Elphinstone, Rev. Kenneth John Tristram, 1911–1980, vol. VII
Elphinstone, Kenneth Vaughan, 1878–1963, vol. VI
Elphinstone, Sir Lancelot Henry, 1879–1965, vol. VI

Elphinstone, Rev. Maurice Curteis, 1874–1969, vol. VI
Elphinstone, Sir (Maurice) Douglas (Warburton), 5th Bt, 1909–1995, vol. IX
Elphinstone, Hon. Mountstuart William, 1871–1957, vol. V
Elphinstone, Sir Nicholas, 10th Bt (*cr* 1628), 1825–1907, vol. I
Elphinstone-Dalrymple, Sir Edward Arthur, 6th Bt, 1877–1913, vol. I
Elphinstone-Dalrymple, Col Sir Francis Napier, 7th Bt, 1882–1956, vol. V
Elphinstone-Dalrymple, Sir Robert Graeme, 5th Bt, 1844–1908, vol. I
Elrington, Rev. Charles Andrew, 1856–1936, vol. III
Elrington, Gen. Frederick Robert, 1819–1904, vol. I
El-Sadat, Mohamed Anwar, 1918–1981, vol. VIII
Elsden, John Pascoe, 1887–1950, vol. IV
Else, John, 1911–1996, vol. X (AII)
Else, Joseph, 1874–1955, vol. V
Elsee, Rev. Charles, *died* 1960, vol. V
Elsee, Rev. Henry John, *died* 1936, vol. III
Elsey, Rt Rev. William Edward, 1880–1966, vol. VI
Elsley, Rev. William James, 1870–1942, vol. IV
Elsmie, Maj.-Gen. Alexander Montagu Spears, 1869–1958, vol. V
Elsmie, George Robert, 1838–1909, vol. I
Elsmore, Geoffrey William, 1925–1985, vol. VIII
Elsner, Col Otto William Alexander, 1871–1953, vol. V
Elstob, Rev. John George, *died* 1926, vol. II
Elstob, Lt-Col Wilfrith, *died* 1918, vol. II
Elstub, Sir St John de Holt, 1915–1989, vol. VIII
Eltisley, 1st Baron, 1879–1942, vol. IV
Elton, 1st Baron, 1892–1973, vol. VII
Elton, Sir Ambrose, 9th Bt, 1869–1951, vol. V
Elton, Sir Arthur Hallam Rice, 10th Bt, 1906–1973, vol. VII
Elton, Charles Isaac, 1839–1900, vol. I
Elton, Charles Sutherland, 1900–1991, vol. IX
Elton, Sir Edmund Harry, 8th Bt, 1846–1920, vol. II
Elton, Col Frederick Coulthurst, 1836–1920, vol. II
Elton, Sir Geoffrey Rudolph, 1921–1994, vol. IX
Elton, Maj.-Gen. Henry Strachan, 1841–1934, vol. III
Elton, John Bullen, 1916–1983, vol. VIII
Elton, Air Vice-Marshal John Goodenough, 1905–1954, vol. IX
Elton, Oliver, 1861–1945, vol. IV
Elton, Lt-Col William M.; *see* Marwood-Elton.
Elton-Barratt, Major Stanley George Reeves, 1900–1973, vol. VII
Eltringham, Harry, 1873–1941, vol. IV
Elveden, Viscount; Arthur Onslow Edward Guinness, 1912–1945, vol. IV
Elverston, Sir Harold, 1866–1941, vol. IV
Elvey, Lewis Edgar, 1908–1974, vol. VII
Elvey, Maurice, 1887–1967, vol. VI
Elvin, Sir Arthur J., 1899–1957, vol. V
Elvin, Herbert Henry, 1874–1949, vol. IV
Elvin, Ven. John Elijah, 1900–1964, vol. VI
Elwell, Col Francis Edwin, 1858–1922, vol. II, vol. III

Elwell, Frederick William, 1870–1958, vol. V
Elwes, Arthur Henry Stuart, 1858–1908, vol. I
Elwes, Rt Rev. Dudley Charles Cary-; *see* Cary-Elwes.
Elwes, Ven. Edward Leighton, 1848–1930, vol. III
Elwes, Lt-Col Frederick Fenn, 1875–1962, vol. VI
Elwes, Gervase Henry Carey-, 1866–1921, vol. II
Elwes, Henry John, 1846–1922, vol. II
Elwes, Captain Jeremy Gervase Geoffrey Philip, 1921–1999, vol. X
Elwes, Sir Richard Everard Augustine, 1901–1968, vol. VI
Elwes, Simon, 1902–1975, vol. VII
Elwes, Valentine Dudley Henry Cary-, 1832–1909, vol. I
Elwes, Ven. William Weston, *died* 1901, vol. I
Elwin, Rt Rev. Edmund Henry, 1871–1909, vol. I
Elwin, Verrier, 1902–1964, vol. VI
Elwood, Hon. Edward Lindsey, *born* 1868, vol. II
Elworthy, Baron (Life Peer); Marshal of the Royal Air Force Samuel Charles Elworthy, 1911–1993, vol. IX
Elworthy-Jarman, Air Cdre Lance Michael, 1907–1986, vol. VIII
Elwyn-Jones, Baron (Life Peer); Frederick Elwyn-Jones, 1909–1989, vol. VIII
Ely, 5th Marquess of, 1851–1925, vol. II
Ely, 6th Marquess of, 1854–1935, vol. III
Ely, 7th Marquess of, 1903–1969, vol. VI
Ely, Paul, 1897–1975, vol. VII
Elytis, Odysseus, 1911–1996, vol. X
Emanuel, Frank Lewis, 1865–1948, vol. IV
Emanuel, Joseph George, 1871–1958, vol. V
Emanuel, Samuel Henry, *died* 1925, vol. II
Emanuel, Walter, 1869–1915, vol. I
Emard, Most Rev. Mgr Joseph Medard, 1853–1927, vol. II
Emberton, John James, 1893–1976, vol. VII
Emberton, Lt-Col Sir (John) Wesley, 1896–1967, vol. VI
Emberton, Joseph, 1889–1956, vol. V
Emberton, Lt-Col Sir Wesley; *see* Emberton, Lt-Col Sir J. W.
Embleton, Dennis, 1881–1944, vol. IV
Embling, Air Vice-Marshal John Robert André, 1913–1959, vol. V
Embry, Air Chief Marshal Sir Basil Edward, 1902–1977, vol. VII
Embury, Brig.-Gen. Hon. John Fletcher Leopold, 1875–1943, vol. IV
Embury, Lt-Col P. Robinson, 1865–1952, vol. V
Emden, Alfred, 1849–1911, vol. I
Emden, Alfred Brotherston, 1888–1979, vol. VII
Emden, Walter, 1847–1913, vol. I
Emdin, Engr Rear-Adm. Archie Russell, 1865–1950, vol. IV
Emeleus, Harry Julius, 1903–1993, vol. IX
Emeleus, Karl George, 1901–1989, vol. VIII
Emerson, Hon. Charles H., 1864–1919, vol. II
Emerson, Hon. Sir Edward; *see* Emerson, Hon. Sir L. E.
Emerson, Ven. Edward Robert, 1838–1926, vol. II
Emerson, Edward Waldo, 1844–1930, vol. III
Emerson, Hon. George Henry, 1853–1916, vol. II

Emerson, Maj.-Gen. Henry Horace Andrews, 1881–1957, vol. V
Emerson, Sir Herbert William, 1881–1962, vol. VI
Emerson, Hon. Sir (Lewis) Edward, 1890–1949, vol. IV
Emerson, Very Rev. Norman David, 1900–1966, vol. VI
Emerson, Major Norman Zeal, 1872–1928, vol. II
Emerson, Sir Ralf Billing, 1897–1965, vol. VI
Emerson, Robert Jackson, *died* 1944, vol. IV
Emerson, Thomas, 1870–1956, vol. V
Emerson, Sir William, 1843–1924, vol. II
Emery, Rt Rev. Anthony Joseph, 1918–1988, vol. VIII
Emery, Douglas, 1915–1974, vol. VII
Emery, Sir Frederick; *see* Emery, Sir J. F.
Emery, George Edwin, 1859–1937, vol. III
Emery, Henry Crosby, 1872–1924, vol. II
Emery, Sir (James) Frederick, 1886–1983, vol. VIII
Emery, Walter Bryan, 1903–1971, vol. VII
Emery, Walter d'Este, *died* 1923, vol. II
Emery, Ven. William, 1825–1910, vol. I
Emery, Brig.-Gen. William Basil, 1871–1945, vol. IV
Emery, Winifred, (Isabel Winifred Maud Emery Maude), *died* 1924, vol. II
Emett, (Frederick) Rowland, 1906–1990, vol. VIII
Emett, Frederick William, 1865–1935, vol. III
Emett, Rowland; *see* Emett, F. R.
Emley, Herbert Barnes, 1891–1948, vol. IV
Emley, 2nd Baron, 1858–1932, vol. III
Emlyn-Jones, Hugh, 1902–1970, vol. VI
Emlyn-Jones, John Emlyn, 1889–1952, vol. V
Emlyn Williams, Arthur; *see* Williams.
Emmerson, Sir Harold Corti, 1896–1984, vol. VIII
Emmerson, Hon. Henry Robert, 1853–1914, vol. I
Emmerson, Thomas, 1909–1981, vol. VIII
Emmet of Amberley, Baroness (Life Peer); Evelyn Violet Elizabeth Emmet, 1899–1980, vol. VII
Emmet, Rev. Cyril William, 1875–1923, vol. II
Emmet, Dorothy Mary, 1904–2000, vol. X
Emmett, Harold Leslie, 1919–1991, vol. IX
Emminger, Otmar, 1911–1986, vol. VIII
Emmony, Harry Oliver, 1897–1956, vol. V
Emmott, 1st Baron, 1858–1926, vol. II
Emmott, Charles Ernest George Campbell, 1898–1953, vol. V
Emmott, George Henry, 1855–1916, vol. II
Emms, Mrs Dorothy, (Mrs S. A. G. Emms); *see* Charques, Mrs D.
Emms, John Frederick George, 1920–1990, vol. VIII
Empson, Sir Charles, 1898–1983, vol. VIII
Empson, Sir Derek; *see* Empson, Sir L. D.
Enpson, Adm. Sir (Leslie) Derek, 1918–1997, vol. X
Empson, Sir William, 1906–1984, vol. VIII
Emrys-Evans, John; *see* Evans.
Emrys-Evans, Paul Vychan, 1894–1967, vol. VI
Emrys-Roberts, Edward, 1878–1924, vol. II
Emslie, John William, 1901–1973, vol. VII
Emslie, Rosalie, 1891–1977, vol. VII
Emson, Air Marshal Sir Reginald Herbert Embleton, 1912–1995, vol. IX

Emtage, William Thomas Allder, 1862–1942, vol. IV
Encombe, Viscount; John Scott, 1870–1900, vol. I
Enderby, Kenneth Albert, 1920–2000, vol. X
Enderby, Col Samuel, 1907–1996, vol. X
Enderl, Kurt H., 1913–1985, vol. VIII
Enders, John Franklin, 1897–1985, vol. VIII
Endicott, Very Rev. James, 1865–1954, vol. V
Endicott, William, 1865–1941, vol. IV
Energlyn, Baron (Life Peer); William David Evans, 1912–1985, vol. VIII
Enever, Sir Francis Alfred, 1893–1966, vol. VI
Enfield, Sir Ralph Roscoe, 1885–1973, vol. VII
Engelbach, Alfred H. H., 1850–1928, vol. II
Engelbach, Archibald Frank, 1881–1961, vol. VI
Engelbach, Mrs Florence, *died* 1951, vol. V
Engelbach, Lewis William, 1837–1908, vol. I
Engelbach, Reginald, 1888–1946, vol. IV
Engelhard, Charles William, 1917–1971, vol. VII
Engelmann, Franklin, 1908–1972, vol. VII
Engels, Johan Peter, 1908–1981, vol. VIII
Engholm, Sir Basil Charles, 1912–1990, vol. VIII
England, Col Abraham, 1867–1949, vol. IV
England, Rev. Arthur Creyke, 1872–1946, vol. IV
England, Maj.-Gen. Edward Lutwyche, 1839–1910, vol. I
England, Edwin Bourdieu, 1847–1936, vol. III
England, Edwin Thirlwall, *died* 1945, vol. IV
England, E(ric) C. Gordon, 1891–1976, vol. VII
England, Frank Raymond Wilton, 1911–1995, vol. IX
England, Henry Barren, 1855–1942, vol. IV
England, Rear-Adm. Hugh Turnour, 1884–1978, vol. VII
England, Lt-Col Norman Ayrton, 1886–1939, vol. III
England, Peter Tiarks Ede, 1925–1978, vol. VII
England, Philip Remington, 1879–1959, vol. V
England, Sir Russell, *died* 1970, vol. VI
Engledow, Charles John, 1860–1933, vol. III (A), vol. IV
Engledow, Sir Frank Leonard, 1890–1985, vol. VIII
Engleheart, Lt-Col Evelyn Linzee, 1862–1943, vol. IV
Engleheart, Sir John Gardner Dillman, 1823–1923, vol. II
English, Alexander Emanuel, 1871–1962, vol. VI
English, Sir Crisp, *died* 1949, vol. IV
English, Sir Cyril Rupert, 1913–1997, vol. X
English, Sir David, 1931–1998, vol. X
English, Rev. Donald, 1930–1998, vol. X
English, Douglas, 1870–1939, vol. III
English, Lt-Col Ernest Robert Maling, 1874–1941, vol. IV
English, Col Frederick Paul, 1859–1946, vol. IV
English, Sir John; *see* English, Sir W. J.
English, Joseph Sandys, 1890–1971, vol. VII
English, Comdr Reginald Wastell, 1894–1980, vol. VII
English, Lt-Col William John, 1882–1941, vol. IV
English, Sir (William) John, 1903–1973, vol. VII
Ennals, Baron (Life Peer); David Hedley Ennals, 1922–1995, vol. IX
Ennals, John Arthur Ford, 1918–1988, vol. VIII

Ennals, Kenneth Frederick John, 1932–1995, vol. IX
Ennals, Martin, 1927–1991, vol. IX
Ennes Ulrich, Ruy, 1883–1966, vol. VI
Ennever, William Joseph, 1869–1947, vol. IV
Ennis, George Francis Macdaniel, 1868–1933, vol. III
Ennis, John Matthew, vol. II
Ennis, Lawrence, 1871–1938, vol. III
Ennisdale, 1st Baron, 1878–1963, vol. VI
Enniskillen, 4th Earl of, 1845–1924, vol. II
Enniskillen, 5th Earl of, 1876–1963, vol. VI
Enniskillen, 6th Earl of, 1918–1989, vol. VIII
Ennor, Sir Arnold Hughes, (Sir Hugh Ennor), 1912–1977, vol. VII
Ennor, Sir Hugh; see Ennor, Sir A. H.
Enock, Charles Reginald, 1868–1970, vol. VI
Enraght, Rev. Canon Hawtrey James, 1871–1938, vol. III
Enrici, Most Rev. Domenico, 1909–1997, vol. X
Enright, Derek Anthony, 1935–1995, vol. IX
Enright, Adm. Sir Philip King, 1894–1960, vol. V
Enslin, Brig.-Gen. Barend Gotfried Leopold, 1879–1955, vol. V
Ensor, Alick Charles Davidson, (David), 1906–1987, vol. VIII
Ensor, Arthur Hinton, 1891–1977, vol. VII
Ensor, David; see Ensor, A. C. D.
Ensor, Maj.-Gen. Howard, 1874–1942, vol. IV
Ensor, Sir Robert Charles Kirkwood, 1877–1958, vol. V
Ensor Walters, P. H. B.; see Walters.
Enters, Angna, 1907–1989, vol. VIII
Enthoven, Mrs (Augusta) Gabrielle (Eden), 1868–1950, vol. IV
Enthoven, Mrs Gabrielle; see Enthoven, Mrs A. G. E.
Enthoven, Reginald Edward, 1869–1952, vol. V
Enthoven, Roderick Eustace, 1900–1985, vol. VIII
Entrican, Lt-Col James, 1864–1935, vol. III
Entwisle, John Bertie Norreys, 1856–1945, vol. IV
Entwistle, Major Sir Cyril Fullard, 1887–1974, vol. VII
Entwistle, Sir (John Nuttall) Maxwell, 1910–1994, vol. IX
Entwistle, Sir Maxwell; see Entwistle, Sir J. N. M.
Entwistle, William James, died 1952, vol. V
Ephraim, Lee, died 1953, vol. V
Epinay, Charles Adrien Prosper d', 1836–1914, vol. I
Epps, Sir George Selby Washington, 1885–1951, vol. V
Eppstein, Rev. William Charles, 1864–1928, vol. II
Epstein, Sir Jacob, 1880–1959, vol. V
Epstein, Mortimer, died 1946, vol. IV
Erasmus, Hon. François Christiaan, 1896–1967, vol. VI
Ereaut, Sir Frank; see Ereaut, Sir H. F. C.
Ereaut, Sir (Herbert) Frank Cobbold, 1919–1998, vol. X
Erdelyi, Arthur, 1908–1977, vol. VII
Erhard, Ludwig, 1897–1977, vol. VII
Eri, Sir Serei; see Eri, Sir V. S.
Eri, Sir (Vincent) Serei, 1936–1993, vol. IX
Eriks, Sierd Sint, died 1966, vol. VI

Erith, Rev. Canon Lionel Edward Patrick, 1885–1939, vol. III
Erith, Raymond Charles, 1904–1973, vol. VII
Erkin, Feridun Cemal, 1899–1980, vol. IX (AI)
Erlanger, E. Joseph, 1874–1965, vol. VI
Erle, Twynihoe William, 1828–1908, vol. I
Erne, 4th Earl of, 1839–1914, vol. I
Erne, 5th Earl of, 1907–1940, vol. III
Ernest, Maurice, 1872–1955, vol. V
Ernle, 1st Baron, 1851–1937, vol. III
Ernst, Harold Clarence, died 1922, vol. II
Ernst, Max, 1891–1976, vol. VII
Ernst, Morris Leopold, 1888–1976, vol. VII
Ernst, Noel Edward, 1891–1965, vol. VI
Ernst, Oswald Herbert, 1842–1926, vol. II
Ernst, William Gordon, 1897–1939, vol. III
Errington, Sir Eric, 1st Bt (cr 1963), 1900–1973, vol. VII
Errington, Lt-Col Francis Henry Launcelot, 1857–1942, vol. IV
Errington, Sir George, 1st Bt (cr 1885), 1839–1920, vol. II
Errington, Richard Percy, 1904–1995, vol. IX
Errington, Col Roger, 1887–1960, vol. V
Errock, Michael Warden, 1921–1970, vol. VI
Erroll, 20th Earl of, 1852–1927, vol. II
Erroll, 21st Earl of, 1876–1928, vol. II
Erroll, 22nd Earl of, 1901–1941, vol. IV
Erroll, Countess of (23rd in line), 1926–1978, vol. VII
Erroll of Hale, 1st Baron, 1914–2000, vol. X
Erskine, 5th Baron, 1841–1913, vol. I
Erskine, 6th Baron, 1865–1957, vol. V
Erskine of Rerrick, 1st Baron, 1893–1980, vol. VII
Erskine of Rerrick, 2nd Baron, 1926–1995, vol. IX
Erskine, Lord; John Francis Ashley Erskine, 1895–1953, vol. V
Erskine, Col Sir Arthur Edward, 1881–1963, vol. VI
Erskine, David, died 1922, vol. II
Erskine, Sir Derek Quicke, 1905–1977, vol. VII
Erskine, Major Esmé Nourse, 1885–1962, vol. VI
Erskine, Sir ffolliott Williams, 3rd Bt, 1850–1912, vol. I
Erskine, Hon. Francis Walter, 1899–1972, vol. VII
Erskine, Sir George; see Erskine, Sir R. G.
Erskine, Maj.-Gen. George Elphinstone, 1841–1912, vol. I
Erskine, George Oswald Harry Erskine Biber, 1857–1931, vol. III
Erskine, Gen. Sir George Watkin Eben James, 1899–1965, vol. VI
Erskine, Col Henry Adeane, 1857–1953, vol. V
Erskine, Sir Henry David, 1838–1921, vol. II
Erskine, Maj.-Gen. (Hon.) Ian David, 1898–1973, vol. VII
Erskine, James; see Rosslyn, 5th Earl of.
Erskine, Adm. of the Fleet Sir James Elphinstone, 1838–1911, vol. I
Erskine, Brig.-Gen. James Francis, 1862–1936, vol. III
Erskine, Sir James Malcolm Monteith, 1863–1944, vol. IV
Erskine, John, 1879–1951, vol. V
Erskine, Lt-Col Keith David, 1863–1914, vol. I
Erskine, Keith David, 1907–1974, vol. VII

Erskine, Robert, 1874–1933, vol. III
Erskine, Sir (Robert) George, 1896–1984, vol. VIII
Erskine, Hon. Ruaraidh, 1869–1960, vol. V
Erskine, Adm. Seymour Elphinstone, 1863–1945, vol. IV
Erskine, Mrs Steuart, *died* 1948, vol. IV
Erskine, Sir Thomas, 2nd Bt, 1824–1902, vol. I
Erskine, Col Thomas Harry, 1860–1924, vol. II
Erskine, Sir Thomas Wilfred Hargreaves John, 4th Bt, 1880–1944, vol. IV
Erskine, Walter Hugh, 1870–1948, vol. IV
Erskine, Rt Hon. Sir William Augustus Forbes, 1871–1952, vol. V
Erskine-Bolst, Captain Clifford Charles Alan Lawrence, 1878–1946, vol. IV
Erskine Crum, Maj.-Gen. Vernon Forbes, 1918–1971, vol. VII
Erskine-Hill, Sir Alexander Galloway, 1st Bt, 1894–1947, vol. IV
Erskine-Hill, Sir Robert, 2nd Bt, 1917–1989, vol. VIII
Erskine-Lindop, Audrey Beatrice Noël, 1920–1986, vol. VIII
Erskine-Murray, Lt-Col Arthur, 1877–1948, vol. IV
Erskine-Wyse, Marjorie Anne, (Mrs Michael Erskine-Wyse), 1914–1976, vol. VII
Ertz, Edward, 1862–1954, vol. V
Ertz, Susan, (Mrs J. R. McCrindle), 1887–1985, vol. VIII
Ervine, St John Greer, 1883–1971, vol. VII
Ervine-Andrews, Lt-Col Harold Marcus, 1911–1995, vol. IX
Escombe, Captain Harold, *died* 1933, vol. III
Escombe, Rt Hon. Harry, 1838–1899, vol. I
Escombe, Captain William Malcolm Lingard, 1891–1973, vol. VII
Escott, Sir (Ernest) Bichkam S.; *see* Sweet-Escott.
Escott, Thomas Hay Sweet, *died* 1924, vol. II
Escreet, Ven. Charles Ernest, 1852–1919, vol. II
Escritt, (Charles) Ewart, 1905–1990, vol. VIII
Escritt, Ewart; *see* Escritt, C. E.
Escritt, Maj.-Gen. Frederick Knowles, 1893–1993, vol. IX
Escritt, Leonard Bushby, 1902–1973, vol. VII
Esdaile, Arundell James Kennedy, 1880–1956, vol. V
Esdaile, Katharine Ada, 1881–1950, vol. IV
Esdaile, Philippa Chichele, 1888–1989, vol. VIII
Eshelby, John Douglas, 1916–1981, vol. VIII
Esher, 1st Viscount, 1815–1899, vol. I
Esher, 2nd Viscount, 1852–1930, vol. III
Esher, 3rd Viscount, 1881–1963, vol. VI
Esler, Erminda Rentoul, *died* 1924, vol. II
Esmarch, Johannes Friedrich August von, 1823–1908, vol. I
Esmond, Eva; *see* Moore, E.
Esmond, Henry V., *died* 1922, vol. II
Esmonde, Sir Anthony Charles, 15th Bt, 1899–1981, vol. VIII
Esmonde, John, 1862–1915, vol. I
Esmonde, Sir John Henry Grattan, 16th Bt, 1928–1987, vol. VIII
Esmonde, Captain Sir John Lymbrick, 14th Bt, 1893–1958, vol. V

Esmonde, Lt-Col Sir Laurence Grattan, 13th Bt, 1863–1943, vol. IV
Esmonde, Sir Osmond Thomas Grattan, 12th Bt, 1896–1936, vol. III
Esmonde, Sir Thomas Henry Grattan, 11th Bt, 1862–1935, vol. III
Espin, Rev. John, 1836–1905, vol. I
Espin, Rev. Thomas Espinell, *died* 1912, vol. I
Espin, Rev. Thomas Henry Espinell Compton, 1858–1934, vol. III
Espinas, Alfred, 1844–1922, vol. II
'Espinasse, Paul Gilbert, 1900–1975, vol. VII
Espinosa, Augusto, 1919–1989, vol. IX (AI)
Espitalier-Noel, Andre; *see* Noel.
Esplen, Sir John, 1st Bt, 1863–1930, vol. III
Esplen, Sir William Graham, 2nd Bt, 1899–1989, vol. VIII
Espley, Arthur James, *died* 1971, vol. VII
Esposito, Michele, 1855–1929, vol. III
Essame, Enid Mary, 1906–1999, vol. X
Essame, Maj.-Gen. Hubert, 1896–1976, vol. VII
Essell, Col Frederick Knight, 1864–1951, vol. V
Essen, Louis, 1908–1997, vol. X
Essendon, 1st Baron, 1870–1944, vol. IV
Essendon, 2nd Baron, 1903–1978, vol. VII
Essenhigh, Reginald Clare, 1890–1955, vol. V
Essery, William Joseph, 1860–1955, vol. V
Essex, 7th Earl of, 1857–1916, vol. II
Essex, 8th Earl of, 1884–1966, vol. VI
Essex, 9th Earl of, 1906–1981, vol. VIII
Essex, Air Vice-Marshal Bertram Edward, 1897–1959, vol. V
Essex, Francis William, 1916–1995, vol. IX
Essex, Mary; *see* Bloom, Ursula.
Essex, Sir (Richard) Walter, 1857–1941, vol. IV
Essex, Rosamund Sibyl, 1900–1985, vol. VIII
Essex, Sir Walter; *see* Essex, Sir R. W.
Esslemont, George Birnie, 1860–1917, vol. II
Esslemont, Mary, 1891–1984, vol. VIII
Esson, Col James Jacob, 1869–1940, vol. III
Esson, William, 1838–1916, vol. II
Estall, Thomas, 1848–1920, vol. II
Estaunie, Édouard, 1862–1942, vol. IV
Estcourt, 1st Baron, 1839–1915, vol. I
Estcourt, Rev. Edmund Walter S.; *see* Sotheron-Estcourt.
Estcourt, Maj.-Gen. Edward Noel Keith, 1905–1982, vol. VIII
Estcourt, Captain Thomas Edmund S.; *see* Sotheron-Estcourt.
Estell, Hon. John, 1861–1928, vol. II
Estes, Elliott M(arantette), 1916–1988, vol. VIII
Estey, James Wilfred, 1889–1956, vol. V
Etchells, Ernest Fiander, 1876–1927, vol. II
Etchells, Frederick, *died* 1973, vol. VII
Etches, Major Charles Edward, 1872–1944, vol. IV
Eteson, Surg.-Gen. Alfred, *died* 1910, vol. I
Eteson, Col Harold Carleton Wetherall, 1863–1947, vol. IV
Ethe, C. Hermann, 184–1917, vol. II
Etheridge, Col Cecil de Courcy, 1860–1940, vol. III
Etheridge, Rt Rev. Edward Harold, 1872–1954, vol. V
Etheridge, Robert, 1819–1903, vol. I
Etherington, Col Frederick, 1878–1955, vol. V

Etherington-Smith, John Henry, 1841–1923, vol. II
Etherton, Sir George Hammond, 1876–1949, vol. IV
Etherton, Col P. T., 1879–1963, vol. VI
Etherton, Ralph Humphrey, 1904–1987, vol. VIII
Eton, Robert; see Meynell, L. W.
Ettles, William James M'Culloch, 1869–1918, vol. II
Ettlinger, Leopold David, 1913–1989, vol. VIII
Etzdorf, Hasso von, 1900–1989, vol. VIII
Etzel, Franz, 1902–1970, vol. VI (AII)
Euan-Smith, Col Sir Charles Bean; see Smith.
Eucken, Rudolf Christoph, 1846–1926, vol. II
Eugenie, Empress, 1826–1920, vol. II
Eugster, Gen. Sir Basil Oscar Paul, 1914–1984, vol. VIII
Eugster, Lt-Col Oscar Lewis, 1880–1930, vol. III
Eumorfopoulos, George, 1863–1939, vol. III
Eurich, Frederick William, 1867–1945, vol. IV
Eurich, Richard Ernst, 1903–1992, vol. IX
Eustace, Maj.-Gen. Alexander Henry, 1863–1939, vol. III
Eustace, Major Charles Legge Eustace R.; see Robertson-Eustace.
Eustace, Edward Arthur Rawlins, 1899–1972, vol. VII
Eustace, Maj.-Gen. Sir Francis John William, 1849–1925, vol. II
Eustace, Lt-Col Henry Montague, 1863–1926, vol. II
Eustace, Adm. John Bridges, 1861–1947, vol. IV
Eustace, John Curtis Wernher, 1906–1972, vol. VII
Eustace, Sir (Joseph) Lambert, 1908–1996, vol. X
Eustace, Sir Lambert; see Eustace, Sir J. L.
Eustace, Mrs Marjory Edith R.; see Robertson-Eustace.
Eustace, Robert William Barrington R.; see Robertson-Eustace.
Eustace-Jameson, Lt-Col John; see Jameson.
Eustice, John, 1864–1943, vol. IV
Euston, Earl of; Henry James Fitzroy, 1848–1912, vol. I
Euwe, Machgielis, 1901–1981, vol. VIII
Evan-Cook, John Edward, 1902–1991, vol. IX
Evan-Jones, Cecil Artimus, 1912–1978, vol. VII
Evan-Jones, Rev. Canon Richard, 1849–1925, vol. II
Evan-Thomas, Adm. Sir Hugh, 1862–1928, vol. II
Evan-Thomas, Llewelyn, 1859–1947, vol. IV
Evang, Karl, 1902–1981, vol. VIII
Evans, 1st Baron, 1903–1963, vol. VI
Evans of Claughton, Baron (Life Peer); David Thomas Gruffydd Evans, 1928–1992, vol. IX
Evans of Hungershall, Baron (Life Peer); Benjamin Ifor Evans, 1899–1982, vol. VIII
Evans, Alan Frederick Reginald, 1891–1960, vol. V
Evans, Albert, 1903–1988, vol. VIII
Evans, Ven. Albert Owen, 1864–1937, vol. III
Evans, Vice-Adm. Sir Alfred Englefield, 1884–1944, vol. IV
Evans, Sir Alfred Henry, 1847–1938, vol. III
Evans, Alfred Thomas, (Fred Evans), 1914–1987, vol. VIII
Evans, Annie Lloyd-, died 1938, vol. III
Evans, Arthur; see Evans, H. A.
Evans, Sir Arthur, 1851–1941, vol. IV

Evans, Col Sir Arthur, 1898–1958, vol. V
Evans, Rev. Canon Arthur Fitz-Gerald, 1854–1933, vol. III
Evans, Arthur Henry, died 1950, vol. IV
Evans, Rev. Arthur Norman, 1900–1975, vol. VII
Evans, Rev. Arthur Robertson, died 1923, vol. II
Evans, Sir Arthur Trevor, 1895–1983, vol. VIII
Evans, Rev. Arthur Wade W.; see Wade-Evans.
Evans, Sir Athol Donald, 1904–1988, vol. VIII
Evans, Sir Bernard, 1905–1981, vol. VIII
Evans, Bernard Walter, 1843–1922, vol. II
Evans, Captain Bertram Sutton, 1872–1919, vol. II
Evans, Brig. Brian P.; see Pennefather-Evans.
Evans, Rt Rev. Bruce Read, 1929–1993, vol. IX
Evans, Caradoc, died 1945, vol. IV
Evans, Cecil Herbert, 1898–1957, vol. V
Evans, Charles; see Evans, W. C.
Evans, Sir Charles; see Evans, Sir R. C.
Evans, Sir Charles Arthur Lovatt, died 1968, vol. VI
Evans, Charles Barnard, died 1920, vol. II
Evans, Charles Glyn, 1883–1961, vol. VI
Evans, Maj.-Gen. Charles Harford B.; see Bowle-Evans.
Evans, Vice-Adm. Sir Charles Leo Glandore, 1908–1981, vol. VIII
Evans, Col Charles Robert, 1873–1956, vol. V
Evans, Charles Seddon, 1883–1944, vol. IV
Evans, Charles Tunstall, 1903–1980, vol. VII
Evans, Col Charles William Henry, 1851–1909, vol. I
Evans, Collis William, 1895–1984, vol. VIII
Evans, Brig.-Gen. Cuthbert, 1871–1934, vol. III
Evans, Rt Rev. Daniel Ivor, 1900–1962, vol. VI
Evans, Rev. Daniel Silvan, 1818–1903, vol. I
Evans, Sir David, 1849–1907, vol. I
Evans, Ven. David, died 1910, vol. I
Evans, David, 1874–1948, vol. IV
Evans, David Carey Rees Jones, 1899–1982, vol. VIII
Evans, David Charles Exton, 1878–1938, vol. III
Evans, Ven. David Eifion, 1911–1997, vol. X
Evans, David Eifion Puleston, 1902–1984, vol. VIII
Evans, Sir (David) Emrys, 1891–1966, vol. VI
Evans, Sir David Gwynne, 1909–1984, vol. VIII
Evans, Sir David Lewis, 1893–1987, vol. VIII
Evans, David M.; see Monle-Evans.
Evans, (David) Meurig, 1906–1983, vol. VIII
Evans, David Morgan, 1892–1977, vol. VII
Evans, David Owen, 1876–1945, vol. IV
Evans, David Philip, 1908–1995, vol. IX (AII)
Evans, Sir (David) Rowland, died 1953, vol. V
Evans, Maj.-Gen. David Sydney Carlyon, 1893–1955, vol. V
Evans, Sir David William, 1866–1926, vol. II
Evans, Dennis Frederick, 1928–1990, vol. VIII
Evans, Air Chief Marshal Sir Donald Randell, 1912–1975, vol. VII
Evans, Rev. E. Gwyn, 1898–1958, vol. V
Evans, Sir E. Vincent, died 1934, vol. III
Evans, Dame Edith, (Dame Edith Mary Booth), 1888–1976, vol. VII
Evans, Sir Edward, 1846–1917, vol. II
Evans, Maj.-Gen. Sir Edward, 1872–1949, vol. IV
Evans, Edward, 1883–1960, vol. V
Evans, Edward Francis Herbert, 1873–1958, vol. V

Evans, Rt Rev. Edward Lewis, 1904–1996, vol. X
Evans, Col Edward Stokes, 1855–1926, vol. II
Evans, Edward Victor, 1882–1964, vol. VI
Evans, Edward Walter, 1890–1985, vol. VIII
Evans, Sir Edwin, *died* 1928, vol. II
Evans, Edwin, 1874–1945, vol. IV
Evans, Einion, 1896–1969, vol. VI
Evans, Ellen, 1891–1953, vol. V
Evans, Emily, *died* 1958, vol. V
Evans, Emlyn Hugh Garner, 1911–1963, vol. VI
Evans, Sir Emrys; *see* Evans, Sir D. E.
Evans, (Emyr) Estyn, 1905–1989, vol. VIII
Evans, Very Rev. Eric; *see* Evans, Very Rev. T. E.
Evans, Ven. Eric Herbert, 1902–1977, vol. VII
Evans, Ernest, 1885–1965, vol. VI
Evans, Estyn; *see* Evans, Emyr E.
Evans, Sir Evan Gwynne G.; *see* Gwynne-Evans.
Evans, Evan Jenkin, 1882–1944, vol. IV
Evans, Evan Laming, 1871–1945, vol. IV
Evans, Evan Stanley, 1904–1982, vol. VIII
Evans, Evan William, 1860–1925, vol. II
Evans, Sir Evelyn Ward, 3rd Bt (*cr* 1902), 1883–1970, vol. VI
Evans, Major Fisher Henry Freke, 1868–1961, vol. VI
Evans, Sir Francis Edward, 1897–1983, vol. VIII
Evans, Sir Francis Henry, 1st Bt (*cr* 1902), 1840–1907, vol. I
Evans, Sir Francis Loring G.; *see* Gwynne-Evans.
Evans, Frank Dudley, 1883–1941, vol. IV
Evans, Frankis Tilney, 1900–1974, vol. VII
Evans, Fred; *see* Evans, Alfred T.
Evans, Captain Frederic James, 1867–1945, vol. IV
Evans, Rev. Canon Frederic James, *died* 1946, vol. IV
Evans, Rev. Frederic Rawlins, 1842–1927, vol. II
Evans, Sir Frederick, 1849–1939, vol. III
Evans, Frederick Anthony, 1907–1999, vol. X
Evans, Frederick Buisson, 1874–1952, vol. V
Evans, Sir Geoffrey, 1883–1963, vol. VI
Evans, Geoffrey A., 1886–1951, vol. V
Evans, Lt-Gen. Sir Geoffrey Charles, 1901–1987, vol. VIII
Evans, George Ewart, 1909–1988, vol. VIII
Evans, Rear-Adm. George Hammond, 1917–1980, vol. VII
Evans, Col George Henry, 1863–1948, vol. IV
Evans, Rev. George Simon T.; *see* Tudor-Evans.
Evans, Rev. George William, 1867–1938, vol. III
Evans, Sir Geraint Llewellyn, 1922–1992, vol. IX
Evans, Godfrey; *see* Evans, T. G.
Evans, Lt-Col Granville P.; *see* Pennefather-Evans.
Evans, Griffith, 1835–1935, vol. III
Evans, Griffith Conrad, 1887–1973, vol. VII
Evans, Sir Griffith Humphrey Pugh, 1840–1902, vol. I
Evans, Griffith Ivor, 1889–1966, vol. VI
Evans, Sir Guildhaume M.; *see* Myrddin-Evans.
Evans, Sir Harold, 1st Bt, 1911–1983, vol. VIII
Evans, Harold Muir, 1866–1947, vol. IV
Evans, Lt-Col Harrie Smalley, 1887–1971, vol. VII
Evans, (Harry) Lindley, 1895–1982, vol. VIII
Evans, Rev. Henry, *died* 1924, vol. II
Evans, (Henry) Arthur, 1903–1965, vol. VI
Evans, Henry Farrington, 1845–1931, vol. III

Evans, Maj.-Gen. Henry Holland, 1914–1987, vol. VIII
Evans, Rt Rev. Henry St John Tomlinson, 1905–1956, vol. V
Evans, Major Herbert, 1868–1931, vol. III
Evans, Herbert D.; *see* Davies-Evans.
Evans, Herbert Edgar, 1884–1970, vol. VI (AII)
Evans, Herbert McLean, 1882–1971, vol. VII
Evans, Herbert Walter Lloyd, 1877–1956, vol. V
Evans, Gen. Sir Horace Moule, 1841–1923, vol. II
Evans, Brig.-Gen. Horatio James, 1850–1932, vol. III
Evans, Howard, 1839–1915, vol. I
Evans, Hubert John Filmer, 1904–1989, vol. VIII
Evans, Hywel Eifion, 1910–1997, vol. X
Evans, Sir Hywel Wynn, 1920–1988, vol. VIII
Evans, Sir Ian William G.; *see* Gwynne-Evans.
Evans, Ifor Leslie, 1897–1952, vol. V
Evans, Illtyd Buller P.; *see* Pole-Evans.
Evans, Ioan Lyonel, 1927–1984, vol. VIII
Evans, Rev. J. T., 1878–1950, vol. IV
Evans, James Donald, 1926–1997, vol. X
Evans, Col J(ames) Ellis, 1910–1998, vol. X
Evans, Major James John Pugh, 1885–1974, vol. VII
Evans, Dame Joan, *died* 1977, vol. VII
Evans, Sir John, 1823–1908, vol. I
Evans, Lt-Col John, *died* 1930, vol. III
Evans, Col John, 1868–1942, vol. IV
Evans, John, 1875–1961, vol. VI
Evans, John Cayo, 1879–1958, vol. V
Evans, Rev. John David, *died* 1912, vol. I
Evans, John Emrys-, 1853–1931, vol. III
Evans, John Gwenogvryn, 1852–1930, vol. III
Evans, Sir John Harold, 1904–1973, vol. VII
Evans, John Howell, 1870–1962, vol. VI
Evans, John Isaac Glyn, 1919–1991, vol. IX
Evans, John Jameson, 1871–1941, vol. IV
Evans, Rev. Canon John Mascal, 1915–1996, vol. X
Evans, John Owain, 1875–1943, vol. IV
Evans, Rev. John Thomas, 1869–1940, vol. III
Evans, John William, *died* 1930, vol. III
Evans, Hon. Sir John William, 1855–1943, vol. IV
Evans, Rev. John Young, 1865–1941, vol. IV
Evans, Rev. Joseph David Samuel P.; *see* Parry-Evans.
Evans, Rt Rev. Kenneth Charles, 1903–1970, vol. VI
Evans, Rt Hon. Sir Laming W.; *see* Worthington-Evans.
Evans, Laurence James, 1917–1991, vol. IX
Evans, L(eonard) G(lyde) Lavington, 1888–1976, vol. VII
Evans, Rev. Leonard Hugh, 1863–1939, vol. III
Evans, Maj.-Gen. Leopold Exxel, 1837–1916, vol. II
Evans, Lewis, 1853–1930, vol. III
Evans, Rev. Lewis Herbert, 1870–1942, vol. IV
Evans, Lewis Noel Vincent, 1886–1967, vol. VI
Evans, Brig.-Gen. Lewis Pugh, 1881–1962, vol. VI
Evans, Sir Lincoln, 1889–1970, vol. VI
Evans, Lindley; *see* Evans, H. L.
Evans, Mgr Canon Lionel Ella, 1882–1942, vol. IV
Evans, Lt-Col Llewelyn, *died* 1963, vol. VI
Evans, Luther Harris, 1902–1981, vol. VIII
Evans, Maurice Hubert, 1901–1989, vol. VIII

Evans, Maurice Smethurst, 1854–1920, vol. II, vol. III
Evans, Meredith Gwynne, 1904–1952, vol. V
Evans, Merlyn Oliver, 1910–1973, vol. VII
Evans, Meurig; see Evans, D. M.
Evans, Rev. Sir Murland de Grasse, 2nd Bt (cr 1902), 1874–1946, vol. IV
Evans, Nevil Norton, 1865–1948, vol. IV
Evans, Lady Olwen Elizabeth C.; see Carey Evans.
Evans, Ven. Owen, died 1914, vol. I
Evans, Patrick Fleming, 1851–1902, vol. I
Evans, Paul Vychan E.; see Emrys-Evans.
Evans, Col Percy, 1868–1945, vol. IV
Evans, Percy William, 1882–1951, vol. V
Evans, Peter MacIntyre, 1859–1944, vol. IV
Evans, Philip Rainsford, 1910–1990, vol. VIII
Evans, Phyllis Mary Carlyon, 1913–1990, vol. VIII
Evans, Very Rev. Raymond Ellis, 1908–1983, vol. VIII
Evans, Raymond John Morda, 1917–1992, vol. IX
Evans, Dame Regina Margaret, 1885–1969, vol. VI
Evans, Rhydwyn Harding, 1900–1993, vol. IX
Evans, (Richard) Stanley, 1883–1949, vol. IV
Evans, Richard Thomas, 1890–1946, vol. IV
Evans, Richardson, 1846–1928, vol. II
Evans, Sir Robert Charles, 1878–1961, vol. VI
Evans, Sir (Robert) Charles, 1918–1995, vol. IX
Evans, Maj.-Gen. Roger, 1886–1968, vol. VI
Evans, Sir Rowland; see Evans, Sir D. R.
Evans, Samuel T. G., 1829–1904, vol. I
Evans, Rt Hon. Sir Samuel Thomas, 1859–1918, vol. II
Evans, Very Rev. Seiriol John Arthur, 1894–1984, vol. VIII
Evans, Sir Shirley W.; see Worthington-Evans, Sir W. S. W.
Evans, Sir (Sidney) Harold; see Evans, Sir Harold.
Evans, Simon John, 1937–1999, vol. X
Evans, Stanley; see Evans, E. S.
Evans, Stanley; see Evans, R. S.
Evans, Rev. Canon Stanley George, 1912–1965, vol. VI
Evans, Stanley Norman, 1898–1970, vol. VI
Evans, Very Rev. Sydney Hall, 1915–1988, vol. VIII
Evans, T. Hopkin, 1879–1940, vol. III
Evans, Thomas, died 1943, vol. IV
Evans, Col Thomas Dixon Byron, 1860–1908, vol. I
Evans, Very Rev. (Thomas) Eric, 1928–1996, vol. X
Evans, Very Rev. Thomas Frye Lewis, 1845–1920, vol. II
Evans, (Thomas) Godfrey, 1920–1999, vol. X
Evans, Thomas Henry, 1907–1992, vol. IX
Evans, Major Sir Thomas John Carey, 1884–1947, vol. IV
Evans, Rev. Thomas Jones, 1856–1921, vol. II
Evans, Maj.-Gen. Thomas Julian Penrhys, 1854–1921, vol. II
Evans, Timothy, 1875–1945, vol. IV
Evans, Trefor Ellis, 1913–1974, vol. VII
Evans, Sir Trevor Maldwyn, 1902–1981, vol. VIII
Evans, Ulick Richardson, 1889–1980, vol. VII
Evans, Brig.-Gen. Usher Williamson, 1864–1946, vol. IV

Evans, Sir Walter, 1855–1935, vol. III
Evans, Sir Walter Harry, 1st Bt (cr 1920), 1872–1954, vol. V
Evans, Walter Jenkin, 1856–1927, vol. II
Evans, Walter John, 1864–1939, vol. III
Evans, Webster; see Evans, W. E. W.
Evans, Brig.-Gen. Wilfrid Keith, 1878–1934, vol. III
Evans, William, 1847–1918, vol. II
Evans, William, 1841–1919, vol. II
Evans, William, died 1936, vol. III
Evans, Brig.-Gen. William, 1871–1944, vol. IV
Evans, William, 1895–1988, vol. VIII
Evans, William B.; see Bulkeley-Evans.
Evans, William Campbell, 1916–1990, vol. VIII
Evans, (William) Charles, 1911–1988, vol. VIII
Evans, William David; see Baron Energlyn.
Evans, William Edis Webster, 1908–1982, vol. VIII
Evans, William Ewart, 1899–1990, vol. VIII
Evans, Sir William G.; see Gwynne-Evans.
Evans, William H., 1873–1934, vol. III
Evans, Brig. William Harry, 1876–1956, vol. V
Evans, William James, 1861–1944, vol. IV
Evans, William John, 1899–1983, vol. VIII
Evans, William Percival, 1864–1959, vol. V
Evans, Sir (William) Shirley (Worthington) W.; see Worthington-Evans.
Evans, Willmott Henderson, died 1938, vol. III
Evans Bevan, Sir David Martyn, 1st Bt, 1902–1973, vol. VII
Evans-Freke, Hon. Ralfe, 1897–1969, vol. VI
Evans-Gordon, Col Kenmure Alick Garth, 1885–1960, vol. V
Evans-Gwynne, Brig. Alfred Howel, 1882–1949, vol. IV
Evans-Jones, Rev. Sir Albert, 1895–1970, vol. VI
Evans-Lombe, Vice-Adm. Sir Edward Malcolm, 1901–1974, vol. VII
Evans-Pritchard, Sir Edward Evan, 1902–1973, vol. VII
Evanson, Maj.-Gen. Arthur Charles Tarver, 1895–1957, vol. V
Evatt, Maj.-Gen. Sir George Joseph Hamilton, 1843–1921, vol. II
Evatt, Rt Hon. Herbert Vere, 1894–1965, vol. VI
Evatt, Brig.-Gen. John Thorold, 1861–1949, vol. IV
Eve, Arthur Stewart, 1862–1948, vol. IV
Eve, Frank Cecil, died 1952, vol. V
Eve, Sir Frederic Samuel, died 1916, vol. II
Eve, George W., died 1914, vol. I
Eve, Rt Hon. Sir Harry Trelawney, 1856–1940, vol. III
Eve, Sir Herbert Trustram, 1865–1936, vol. III
Evelegh, Maj.-Gen. Vyvyan, 1898–1958, vol. V
Eveling, Walter Raphael Taylor, 1908–1987, vol. VIII
Evelyn, John Harcourt Chichester, 1876–1922, vol. II
Evelyn, (John) Michael, 1916–1992, vol. IX
Evelyn, Michael; see Evelyn, J. M.
Evelyn, William John, 1822–1908, vol. I
Even, Col George Eusebe, 1855–1924, vol. II
Evennett, Henry Outram, 1901–1964, vol. VI
Everall, John Harold, 1908–1984, vol. VIII

Everard, Captain Andrew Robert Guy, 1830–1925, vol. II, vol. III
Everard, Bernard, 1879–1963, vol. VI
Everard, Maj.-Gen. Sir Christopher Earle W.; see Welby-Everard.
Everard, Edward Everard Earle W.; see Welby-Everard.
Everard, Sir Lindsay; see Everard, Sir W. L.
Everard, Lt-Col Sir Nugent Henry, 3rd Bt, 1905–1984, vol. VIII
Everard, Col Sir Nugent Talbot, 1st Bt, 1849–1929, vol. III
Everard, Major Sir Richard William, 2nd Bt, 1874–1929, vol. III
Everard, Sir (William) Lindsay, died 1949, vol. IV
Everest, Arthur Ernest, 1888–1983, vol. VIII
Everest, David Anthony, 1926–1998, vol. X
Everett, Adm. Sir Allan Frederic, 1868–1938, vol. III
Everett, Rev. Bernard Charles Spencer, 1874–1943, vol. IV
Everett, Dorothy, 1894–1953, vol. V
Everett, Rear-Adm. Douglas Henry, 1900–1986, vol. VIII
Everett, Col Edward, 1837–1920, vol. II
Everett, Harry Poore, 1862–1955, vol. V
Everett, Maj.-Gen. Sir Henry Joseph, 1866–1951, vol. V
Everett, Joseph David, 1831–1904, vol. I
Everett, Sir Percy Winn, 1870–1952, vol. V
Everett, Richard Marven Hale, 1909–1978, vol. VII
Everett, Robert Lacey, 1833–1916, vol. II
Everett, Col Sir William, 1844–1908, vol. I
Everett-Green, Evelyn, 1856–1932, vol. III
Everidge, John, died 1955, vol. V
Everingham, Ven. William, 1856–1919, vol. II
Everington, Geoffrey Devas, 1915–1982, vol. VIII
Everitt, Sir Clement, 1873–1934, vol. III
Everitt, Major Sydney George, 1860–1932, vol. III
Evers, Claude Ronald, 1908–1988, vol. VIII
Evers, H(enry) Harvey, 1893–1979, vol. VII
Evershed, 1st Baron, 1899–1966, vol. VI
Evershed, Arthur, 1836–1919, vol. II
Evershed, John, 1864–1956, vol. V
Evershed, Sydney, 1825–1903, vol. I
Evershed, Sir Sydney Herbert, 1861–1937, vol. III
Evershed, Rear-Adm. Walter, 1907–1969, vol. VI
Eversley, 1st Baron, 1831–1928, vol. II
Eversley, David Edward Charles, 1921–1995, vol. IX
Eversley, William Pinder, 1850–1918, vol. II
Every, Rt Rev. Edward Francis, 1862–1941, vol. IV
Every, Sir Edward Oswald, 11th Bt, 1886–1959, vol. V
Every, Sir John Simon, 12th Bt, 1914–1988, vol. VIII
Eves, Sir Charles, 1864–1936, vol. III
Eves, Charles Washington, 1838–1899, vol. I
Eves, Sir Hubert Heath, 1883–1961, vol. VI
Eves, Reginald Grenville, 1876–1941, vol. IV
Evetts, Sir George, 1882–1958, vol. V
Evetts, Lt-Gen. Sir John Fullerton, 1891–1988, vol. VIII
Evill, Lt-Col Charles Ariel, 1874–1954, vol. V

Evill, Air Chief Marshal Sir Douglas Claude Strathern, 1892–1971, vol. VII
Evington, Rt Rev. Henry, 1848–1912, vol. I
Evoe; see Knox, E. G. V.
Ewald, Paul P., 1888–1985, vol. VIII
Ewan, Col Thomas George, 1856–1937, vol. III
Ewart, Alfred James, 1872–1937, vol. III
Ewart, Adm. Arthur Wartensleben, 1862–1922, vol. II
Ewart, Lt-Gen. Charles Brisbane, 1827–1903, vol. I
Ewart, David, 1841–1921, vol. II
Ewart, David Shanks, 1901–1965, vol. VI
Ewart, Lt-Col Ernest Andrew; see Cable, Boyd.
Ewart, Captain Frank Rowland, 1874–1906, vol. I
Ewart, Gavin Buchanan, 1916–1995, vol. IX
Ewart, George Arthur, 1886–1942, vol. IV
Ewart, Maj.-Gen. Sir Henry Peter, 1st Bt, 1838–1928, vol. II
Ewart, Sir Ivan; see Ewart, Sir W. I. C.
Ewart, James Cossar, 1851–1933, vol. III
Ewart, Gen. Sir John Alexander, 1821–1904, vol. I
Ewart, Sir John Murray, 1884–1939, vol. III
Ewart, John S., 1849–1933, vol. III
Ewart, Lt-Gen. Sir John Spencer, 1861–1930, vol. III
Ewart, Sir Joseph, 1831–1906, vol. I
Ewart, Sir Lavens Mathewson Algernon, 4th Bt, 1885–1939, did not have an entry in Who's Who.
Ewart, Richard, 1904–1953, vol. V
Ewart, Maj.-Gen. Sir Richard Henry, 1864–1928, vol. II
Ewart, Sir Robert Heard, 3rd Bt, 1879–1939, vol. III
Ewart, Sir Talbot, 5th Bt, 1878–1959, vol. V
Ewart, William, 1848–1929, vol. III
Ewart, William Herbert Lee, 1881–1953, vol. V
Ewart, Sir (William) Ivan (Cecil), 6th Bt, 1919–1995, vol. IX
Ewart, Sir William Quartus, 2nd Bt, 1844–1919, vol. II
Ewart-Biggs, Baroness (Life Peer); Felicity Jane Ewart-Biggs, 1929–1992, vol. IX
Ewart-Biggs, Christopher Thomas Ewart, 1921–1976, vol. VII
Ewart James, William Henry, 1910–1988, vol. VIII
Ewbank, Sir Robert Benson, 1883–1967, vol. VI
Ewbank, Maj.-Gen. Sir Robert Withers, 1907–1981, vol. VIII
Ewbank, Brig.-Gen. William, 1865–1930, vol. III
Ewen, Sir David Alexander, 1884–1957, vol. V
Ewen, Hon. Guy Seymour, 1871–1936, vol. III
Ewen, Peter, 1903–1993, vol. IX
Ewens, John Qualtrough, 1907–1992, vol. IX
Ewer, Col George Guy, 1883–1965, vol. VI
Ewer, Tom Keightley, 1911–1997, vol. X
Ewert, Alfred, 1891–1969, vol. VI
Ewing, Vice-Adm. Sir Alastair; see Ewing, Vice-Adm. Sir R. A.
Ewing, Sir Alexander William Gordon, 1896–1980, vol. VII
Ewing, Sir Alfred; see Ewing, Sir J. A.
Ewing, Alfred Cyril, 1899–1973, vol. VII
Ewing, Sir Archibald Ernest O.; see Orr-Ewing.
Ewing, Charles Lindsay O.; see Orr-Ewing.

Ewing, Sir Ian Leslie O.; *see* Orr Ewing.
Ewing, James, 1884–1975, vol. VII
Ewing, Major James Alexander O.; *see* Orr-Ewing.
Ewing, Sir (James) Alfred, 1855–1935, vol. III
Ewing, Rev. James Carruthers Rhea, 1854–1925, vol. II
Ewing, Rev. John William, 1864–1951, vol. V
Ewing, Brig.-Gen. Sir Norman Archibald O.; *see* Orr Ewing.
Ewing, Hon. Norman Kirkwood, 1870–1928, vol. II
Ewing, Peter Dewar, *died* 1932, vol. III
Ewing, Rev. Robert, 1847–1908, vol. I
Ewing, Robert, 1871–1957, vol. V
Ewing, Vice-Adm. Sir (Robert) Alastair, 1909–1997, vol. X
Ewing, Hon. Sir Thomas Thomson, 1856–1920, vol. II
Ewing, Air Vice-Marshal Vyvyan Stewart, 1898–1981, vol. VIII
Ewing, Rev. William, 1857–1932, vol. III
Ewing, Sir William O.; *see* Orr-Ewing.
Ewins, Arthur James, 1882–1957, vol. V
Exeter, 4th Marquess of, 1849–1898, vol. I
Exeter, 5th Marquess of, 1876–1956, vol. V
Exeter, 6th Marquess of, 1905–1981, vol. VIII
Exeter, 7th Marquess of, 1909–1988, vol. VIII
Exham, Lt-Col Harold, 1884–1950, vol. IV
Exham, Maj.-Gen. Kenneth Godfrey, 1903–1974, vol. VII
Exham, Col Richard, 1848–1915, vol. I
Exham, Maj.-Gen. Robert Kenah, 1907–1985, vol. VIII
Exham, Col Simeon Hardy,. 1850–1926, vol. II
Exley, J. R. Granville, 1878–1967, vol. VI
Exmouth, 4th Viscount, 1861–1899, vol. I
Exmouth, 5th Viscount, 1890–1922, vol. II
Exmouth, 6th Viscount, 1828–1923, vol. II
Exmouth, 7th Viscount, 1863–1945, vol. IV
Exmouth, 8th Viscount, 1868–1951, vol. V
Exmouth, 9th Viscount, 1908–1970, vol. VI
Exon, Charles, 1862–1962, vol. VI
Exton, Rodney Noel, 1927–1999, vol. X
Exton-Smith, Arthur Norman, 1920–1990, vol. VIII
Eyles, Sir Alfred, 1856–1945, vol. IV
Eyles, Sir George Lancelot, 1849–1919, vol. II

Eyles, Leonora; *see* Eyles, M. L.
Eyles, (Margaret) Leonora, 1889–1960, vol. V
Eyre, Rev. Alfred Collet, 1851–1929, vol. III
Eyre, Most Rev. Charles, 1817–1902, vol. I
Eyre, Ven. Christopher Benson, 1849–1928, vol. II
Eyre, Col. Edmund Henry, 1838–1919, vol. II
Eyre, Edward John, 1815–1901, vol. I
Eyre, Rev. Edward Vincent, 1851–1925, vol. II
Eyre, Sir Graham Newman, 1931–1999, vol. X
Eyre, Col Henry, 1834–1904, vol. I
Eyre, Col Henry Robert, 1842–1904, vol. I
Eyre, John, *died* 1927, vol. II
Eyre, Ven. John Rashdall, *died* 1912, vol. I
Eyre, John William Henry, 1869–1944, vol. IV
Eyre, Sir Oliver Eyre C.; *see* Crosthwaite-Eyre.
Eyre, Ronald, 1929–1992, vol. IX
Eyre-Brook, Rev. Canon Alfred; *see* Brook.
Eyre-Matcham, Col William Eyre, 1865–1938, vol. III
Eyre-Todd, George, 1862–1937, vol. III
Eyres, Adm. Cresswell John, 1862–1949, vol. IV
Eyres, Sir Harry Charles Augustus, 1856–1944, vol. IV
Eyres, Harry Maurice, 1898–1962, vol. VI
Eysenck, Hans Jürgen, 1916–1997, vol. X
Eyston, Charles Turbervile, 1868–1938, vol. III
Eyston, Captain George Edward Thomas, 1897–1979, vol. VII
Eyston, John Joseph, 1867–1916, vol. II
Eyston, Thomas More, 1902–1940, vol. III
Eyton, Alan John F. W.; *see* Fairbairn-Wynne-Eyton.
Eyton, Lt-Col Charles Reginald M.; *see* Morris-Eyton.
Eyton, Mrs Frances W.; *see* Wynne-Eyton, Mrs. S. F.
Eyton, Frank, 1894–1962, vol. VI
Eyton, Lt-Col Robert Charles Gilfrid M.; *see* Morris-Eyton.
Eyton, Mrs Selena Frances W.; *see* Wynne-Eyton.
Ezard, Bernard John Bycroft, 1900–1976, vol. VII
Ezard, Clarence Norbury, 1896–1986, vol. VIII
Ezechiel, Sir Percy Hubert, 1875–1950, vol. IV
Ezra, Sir Alwyn, 1900–1974, vol. VII
Ezra, Sir David, 1871–1947, vol. IV

F

Faber, 1st Baron, 1847–1920, vol. II
Faber, Sir Geoffrey Cust, 1889–1961, vol. VI
Faber, George Henry, 1839–1910, vol. I
Faber, Knud, 1862–1956, vol. V
Faber, Oscar, 1886–1956, vol. V
Faber, Lt-Col Walter Vavasour, 1857–1928, vol. II
Fabre, Hon. Hector, 1834–1910, vol. I
Fabre, Jean Henri, 1823–1915, vol. I
Fachiri, Adila Adrienne Adalbertina Marina, *died* 1962, vol. VI
Fadden, Rt Hon. Sir Arthur William, 1895–1973, vol. VII
Faed, John, 1819–1902, vol. I
Faed, Thomas, 1826–1900, vol. I

Fagan, Lt-Col Bernard Joseph, 1874–1939, vol. III
Fagan, Betty Maud Christian, *died* 1932, vol. III
Fagan, Brian Walter, 1893–1971, vol. VII
Fagan, Charles Edward, 1855–1921, vol. II
Fagan, Lt-Col Christopher George Forbes, 1856–1943, vol. IV
Fagan, Maj.-Gen. Sir Edward Arthur, 1871–1955, vol. V
Fagan, Hon. Henry Allan, 1889–1963, vol. VI
Fagan, James Bernard, 1873–1933, vol. III
Fagan, Maj.-Gen. James Lawtie, 1843–1919, vol. II
Fagan, Sir John, 1843–1930, vol. III
Fagan, Hon. Mark, 1873–1947, vol. IV
Fagan, Sir Patrick James, 1865–1942, vol. IV

Fagan, William Bateman, *died* 1948, vol. IV
Fagg, Bernard Evelyn Buller, 1915–1987, vol. VIII
Fagg, William Buller, 1914–1992, vol. IX
Fage, Arthur, 1890–1977, vol. VII
Fagge, Charles Herbert, 1873–1939, vol. III
Fagge, Sir John Charles, 9th Bt, 1866–1930, vol. III
Fagge, Sir John Harry Lee, 10th Bt, 1868–1940, vol. III
Fagge, Sir John William Charles, 8th Bt, 1830–1909, vol. I
Faguet, Emile, 1847–1916, vol. II
Fahey, Edward Henry, *died* 1907, vol. I
Fahey, Rt Rev. Mgr Jerome, 1843–1920, vol. II
Fahie, Sen. Comdr Pauline Mary de Peauly, *died* 1947, vol. IV
Fahy, Francis Patrick, 1880–1953, vol. V
Faichnie, Col Douglas Charles, *died* 1938, vol. III
Fair, Hon. Sir Arthur, 1885–1970, vol. VI (AII)
Fair, Lt-Col Frederick Kendall, 1868–1953, vol. V
Fair, Lt-Col James George, 1864–1946, vol. IV
Fairbairn, Sir Andrew, 1828–1901, vol. I
Fairbairn, Andrew Martin, 1838–1912, vol. I
Fairbairn, Sir Arthur Henderson, 3rd Bt, 1852–1915, vol. I
Fairbairn, Vice-Adm. Bernard William Murray, 1880–1960, vol. V
Fairbairn, David, 1924–1993, vol. IX
Fairbairn, Hon. Sir David Eric, 1917–1994, vol. IX (AII)
Fairbairn, Douglas Chisholm, 1904–1987, vol. VIII
Fairbairn, Douglas Foakes, 1919–1994, vol. IX
Fairbairn, Sir George, 1855–1943, vol. IV
Fairbairn, James, *died* 1950, vol. IV
Fairbairn, Hon. James Valentine, 1897–1940, vol. III
Fairbairn, John Shields, 1868–1944, vol. IV
Fairbairn, Sir Nicholas Hardwick, 1933–1995, vol. IX
Fairbairn, Richard Robert, 1867–1941, vol. IV
Fairbairn, Sir Robert Duncan, 1910–1988, vol. VIII
Fairbairn, Stephen, (Steve), 1862–1938, vol. III
Fairbairn, Thomas Charles, 1874–1978, vol. VII
Fairbairn, Sir Thomas Gordon, 4th Bt, 1854–1931, vol. III
Fairbairn, Sir William Albert, 5th Bt, 1902–1972, vol. VII
Fairbairn, William Ronald Dodds, 1889–1964, vol. VI
Fairbairn-Wynne-Eyton, Alan John, *died* 1960, vol. V
Fairbank, Alfred John, 1895–1982, vol. VIII
Fairbank, Sir (Harold Arthur) Thomas, 1876–1961, vol. VI
Fairbank, Sir Thomas; *see* Fairbank, Sir H. A. T.
Fairbank, Sir William, 1850–1929, vol. III
Fairbanks, Maj.-Gen. Cecil Benfield, 1903–1982, vol. VIII
Fairbanks, Charles Warren, 1852–1918, vol. II
Fairbanks, Douglas, 1883–1939, vol. III
Fairbanks, Douglas Elton, Jr, 1909–2000, vol. X
Fairbrother, Ven. Rupert, *died* 1947, vol. IV
Fairbrother, William Henry, 1859–1927, vol. II
Fairbrother, Col William Tomes, 1856–1924, vol. II
Fairburn, Charles Edward, 1887–1945, vol. IV
Fairburn, Harold, 1884–1973, vol. VII

Fairchild, Rev. John, *died* 1942, vol. IV
Fairclough, Col Brereton, 1870–1945, vol. IV
Fairclough, Henry Rushton, 1862–1938, vol. III
Fairclough, Wilfred, 1907–1996, vol. X
Faire, Sir Arthur William, 1854–1933, vol. III
Faire, Sir Samuel, 1849–1931, vol. III
Fairey, Sir (Charles) Richard, 1887–1956, vol. V
Fairey, Sir Richard; *see* Fairey, Sir C. R.
Fairfax, 11th Lord, 1830–1900, vol. I
Fairfax of Cameron, 12th Lord, 1870–1939, vol. III
Fairfax of Cameron, 13th Lord, 1923–1964, vol. VI
Fairfax, Col Bryan Charles, 1873–1950, vol. IV
Fairfax, Hon. Charles Edmund, 1876–1939, vol. III (A), vol. IV
Fairfax, Guy Thomas, 1870–1934, vol. III
Fairfax, James Griffyth, 1886–1976, vol. VII
Fairfax, Sir James Oswald, 1863–1928, vol. II
Fairfax, Sir James Reading, 1834–1919, vol. II
Fairfax, Sir Vincent Charles, 1909–1993, vol. IX
Fairfax, Sir Warwick Oswald, 1901–1987, vol. VIII
Fairfax, Comdr William George Astell R.; *see* Ramsay-Fairfax.
Fairfax, Sir William George Herbert Taylor Ramsay-, 2nd Bt, 1831–1902, vol. I
Fairfax-Cholmeley, Francis William Alfred, 1904–1983, vol. VIII
Fairfax-Lucy, Major Sir Brian Fulke Cameron-Ramsay-, 5th Bt, 1898–1974, vol. VII
Fairfax-Lucy, Captain Sir (Henry) Montgomerie (Ramsay), 4th Bt, 1896–1965, vol. VI
Fairfax-Lucy, Sir Henry William Cameron-Ramsay-, 3rd Bt, 1870–1944, vol. IV
Fairfax-Lucy, Captain Sir Montgomerie; *see* Fairfax-Lucy, Captain Sir H. M. R.
Fairfield, 1st Baron, 1863–1945, vol. IV
Fairfield, (Josephine) Letitia Denny, 1885–1978, vol. VII
Fairfield, Letitia; *see* Fairfield, J. L. D.
Fairfield, Sir Ronald McLeod, 1911–1978, vol. VII
Fairgrieve, James, 1870–1953, vol. V
Fairgrieve, Sir Russell; *see* Fairgrieve, Sir T. R.
Fairgrieve, Sir (Thomas) Russell, 1924–1999, vol. X
Fairhaven, 1st Baron, 1896–1966, vol. VI
Fairhaven, 2nd Baron, 1900–1973, vol. VII
Fairholme, Edward George, *died* 1956, vol. V
Fairholme, George Frederick, 1858–1940, vol. III
Fairholme, Brig.-Gen. William Ernest, 1860–1920, vol. II
Fairhurst, Frank, 1892–1953, vol. V
Fairhurst, James Ashton, 1867–1944, vol. IV
Fairhurst, William Albert, 1903–1982, vol. VIII
Fairless, Benjamin F., 1890–1962, vol. VI
Fairless, Margaret, *died* 1968, vol. VI
Fairley, Alan Brand, *died* 1987, vol. VIII
Fairley, Sir Andrew Walker, *died* 1965, vol. VI
Fairley, Barker, 1887–1986, vol. VIII
Fairley, Sir Neil Hamilton, 1891–1966, vol. VI
Fairlie, Alison Anna Bowie, 1917–1993, vol. IX
Fairlie, Hugh, 1919–1993, vol. IX
Fairlie, James Ogilvy Reginald, 1848–1916, vol. II
Fairlie, Margaret, *died* 1963, vol. VI
Fairlie, Reginald Francis Joseph, 1883–1952, vol. V
Fairlie-Cuninghame, Sir Alfred Edward, 12th Bt, 1852–1901, vol. I

Fairlie-Cuninghame, Sir Charles Arthur, 11th Bt, 1846–1897, vol. I
Fairlie-Cuninghame, Sir Hussey Burgh; *see* Cuninghame.
Fairlie-Cuninghame, Sir William Alan, 15th Bt, 1893–1981, vol. VIII
Fairlie-Cuninghame, Sir William Edward; *see* Cuninghame.
Fairlie-Cuninghame, Sir William Henry, 16th Bt, 1930–1999, vol. X
Fairman, Herbert Walter, 1907–1982, vol. VIII
Fairn, Duncan; *see* Fairn, R. D.
Fairn, (Richard) Duncan, 1906–1980, vol. VIII
Fairtlough, Major Edward Charles D'Heillemer, 1869–1925, vol. II
Fairtlough, Maj.-Gen. Eric Victor Howard, 1887–1944, vol. IV
Fairtlough, Col Frederick Howard, 1860–1915, vol. I
Fairway, Sidney; *see* Daukes, S. H.
Fairweather, Sir Charles Edward Stuart, 1889–1963, vol. VI
Fairweather, Lt-Col James McIntyre, 1876–1917, vol. II
Fairweather, Sir Wallace, 1853–1939, vol. III
Faisal, King; *see* Saudi Arabia, HM the King of.
Faisandier, Rt Rev. Augustin, 1853–1935, vol. III
Faithfull, Baroness (Life Peer); Lucy Faithfull, 1910–1996, vol. X
Faithfull, Lilian Mary, 1865–1952, vol. V
Faiyaz Ali Khan, Nawab, Sir Mumtazud-Dowlah, 1851–1922, vol. II
Falb, Rudolph, 1838–1903, vol. I
Falcon, Michael, 1888–1976, vol. VII
Falcon, Norman Leslie, 1904–1996, vol. X
Falcon, Thomas Adolphus, 1872–1944, vol. IV
Falconbridge, Hon. Sir Glenholme, 1846–1920, vol. II
Falconbridge, John Delatre, 1875–1968, vol. VI
Falconer, Alexander Frederick, *died* 1987, vol. VIII
Falconer, Lt-Col Alexander Robertson, 1874–1955, vol. V
Falconer, Arthur Wellesley, *died* 1954, vol. V
Falconer, Lt-Col Sir George Arthur, 1894–1981, vol. VIII
Falconer, James, 1856–1931, vol. III
Falconer, John B., *died* 1924, vol. II
Falconer, John Downie, 1876–1947, vol. IV
Falconer, Sir John Ireland, 1879–1954, vol. V
Falconer, Lanoe; *see* Hawker, M. E.
Falconer, Murray Alexander, 1910–1977, vol. VII
Falconer, Sir Robert Alexander, 1867–1943, vol. IV
Falconer Jameson, Mrs; *see* Buckrose, J. E.
Falconio, HE Cardinal Diomed, 1842–1917, vol. II
Falk, Bernard, 1882–1960, vol. V
Falk, Oswald Toynbee, 1879–1972, vol. VII
Falk, Sir Roger Salis, 1910–1997, vol. X
Falke, Otto von, 1862–1943, vol. IV
Falkiner, Sir Edmond Charles, 9th Bt, 1938–1997, vol. X
Falkiner, Rt Hon. Sir Frederick Richard, 1831–1908, vol. I (A)
Falkiner, Sir Leslie Edmond Percy Riggs, 7th Bt, 1866–1917, vol. II

Falkiner, Lt-Col Sir Terence Edmond Patrick, 8th Bt, 1903–1987, vol. VIII
Falkland, 12th Viscount, 1845–1922, vol. II
Falkland, 13th Viscount, 1880–1961, vol. VI
Falkland, 14th Viscount, 1905–1984, vol. VIII
Falkner, Sir (Donald) Keith, 1900–1994, vol. IX
Falkner, Brig. Eric Felton, 1880–1956, vol. V
Falkner, John Meade, 1858–1932, vol. III
Falkner, Sir Keith; *see* Falkner, Sir D. K.
Falkner, Rev. Thomas Felton, 1847–1924, vol. II
Falkus, Hugh Edward Lance, 1917–1996, vol. X
Fall, Captain Ernest Matson, 1883–1955, vol. V
Falla, Norris Stephen, 1883–1945, vol. IV
Falla, Sir Robert Alexander, 1901–1979, vol. VII
Fallada, Hans; *see* Ditzen, Rudolf.
Fallas, Carl, 1885–1962, vol. VI
Falle, Lt-Col Philip Vernon Le Geyt, 1885–1936, vol. III
Falle, Very Rev. Samuel, 1854–1937, vol. III
Fallieres, Armand, 1841–1931, vol. III
Fallis, Lt-Col Rev. George Oliver, 1885–1952, vol. V
Fallon, Rt Rev. Michael Francis, 1867–1931, vol. III
Falloon, C. H., 1875–1959, vol. V
Fallows, Rt Rev. Gordon; *see* Fallows, Rt Rev. W. G.
Fallows, Rt Rev. (William) Gordon, 1913–1979, vol. VII
Falls, Major Sir Charles Fausset, 1860–1936, vol. III
Falls, Captain Cyril Bentham, 1888–1971, vol. VII
Falls, Lt-Col Horace Edward, 1874–1937, vol. III
Fallside, Frank, 1932–1993, vol. IX
Falmouth, 7th Viscount, 1847–1918, vol. II
Falmouth, 8th Viscount, 1887–1962, vol. VI
Falshaw, Sir Donald James, 1905–1984, vol. VIII
Falvey, Sir John Neil, 1918–1990, vol. VIII
Falwasser, Arthur Thomas, 1873–1959, vol. V
Fancourt, Col St John Fancourt Michell, 1847–1917, vol. II
Fancourt, Ven. Thomas, 1840–1919, vol. II
Fane, Lady Augusta, *died* 1950, vol. IV
Fane, Col Cecil, 1875–1960, vol. V
Fane, Cecil Francis William, 1856–1914, vol. I
Fane, Adm. Sir Charles George, 1837–1909, vol. I
Fane, Sir Edmund Douglas Veitch, 1837–1900, vol. I
Fane, Frederick William, 1857–1933, vol. III
Fane, Harry Frank Brien, 1915–1993, vol. IX
Fane, Lenox; *see* Clifton, Baroness.
Fane, Major Hon. Mountjoy John Charles, Wedderburn, 1900–1963, vol. VI
Fane, Captain Octavius Edward, 1886–1918, vol. II
Fane, Rt Hon. Sir Spencer Cecil Brabazon P.; *see* Ponsonby-Fane.
Fane, Sydney Algernon, 1867–1929, vol. III
Fane, Maj.-Gen. Sir Vere Bonamy, 1863–1924, vol. II
Fane, Violet; *see* Currie, Mary Montgomerie, Lady.
Fane De Salis, Sir Cecil; *see* De Salis.
Fane De Salis, Rt Rev. Charles; *see* De Salis.
Fane De Salis, Rodolph; *see* De Salis.
Fane De Salis, Adm. Sir William; *see* De Salis.
Faning, Joseph Eaton, 1850–1927, vol. II
Fanner, John Lewis, 1921–1975, vol. VII

Fanning, Frederick William B.; *see* Burton-Fanning.
Fanning, Sir Roland Francis Nichol, 1829–1919, vol. II
Fanshawe, Sir Arthur Dalrymple, 1847–1936, vol. III
Fanshawe, Sir Arthur Upton, 1848–1931, vol. III
Fanshawe, Vice-Adm. Basil Hew, 1868–1929, vol. III
Fanshawe, Lt-Gen. Sir Edward Arthur, 1859–1952, vol. V
Fanshawe, Sir Edward Gennys, 1814–1906, vol. I
Fanshawe, Maj.-Gen. Sir Evelyn Dalrymple, 1895–1979, vol. VII
Fanshawe, Maj.-Gen. George Drew, 1901–1991, vol. IX
Fanshawe, Rev. Gerald Charles, 1870–1924, vol. II
Fanshawe, Captain Guy Dalrymple, *died* 1962, vol. VI
Fanshawe, Herbert Charles, 1852–1923, vol. II
Fanshawe, Lt-Gen. Sir Hew Dalrymple, 1860–1957, vol. V
Fanshawe, Brig. Lionel Arthur, 1874–1962, vol. VI
Fanshawe, Col Reginald Winnington, 1871–1932, vol. III
Fanshawe, Maj.-Gen. Sir Robert, 1863–1946, vol. IV
Fanshawe, Captain Thomas Evelyn, 1918–2000, vol. X
Fantham, Annie; *see* Porter, A.
Fantham, Harold Benjamin, *died* 1937, vol. III
Faraday, Wilfred Barnard, 1874–1953, vol. V
Fardell, Sir George; *see* Fardell, Sir T. G.
Fardell, Sir (Thomas) George, 1833–1917, vol. II
Fareed, Sir Razik, 1895–1984, vol. VIII
Farewell, Captain Michael Warren, 1868–1953, vol. V
Farey-Jones, Frederick William, 1904–1974, vol. VII
Farfan, Brig. Arthur Joseph Thomas, 1882–1953, vol. V
Fargher, John Adrian, 1901–1977, vol. VII
Fargus, Brig.-Gen. Harold, 1873–1962, vol. VI
Fargus, Lt-Col Nigel Harry Skinner, 1881–1962, vol. VI
Faridkot, Ruler of, 1915–1989, vol. VIII
Faridoonji Jamshedji, Nawab Sir Faridoon Jung, 1849–1928, vol. II
Farie, Rear-Adm. James Uchtred, *died* 1957, vol. V
Faringdon, 1st Baron, 1850–1934, vol. III
Faringdon, 2nd Baron, 1902–1977, vol. VII
Faris, Desmond William George, 1901–1957, vol. V
Farjeon, Benjamin Leopold, 1838–1903, vol. I
Farjeon, Eleanor, 1881–1965, vol. VI
Farjeon, Herbert, 1887–1945, vol. IV
Farjeon, Joseph Jefferson, 1883–1955, vol. V
Farleigh, John, 1900–1965, vol. VI
Farley, Albert Henry, 1887–1954, vol. V
Farley, Brig. Edward Lionel, 1889–1968, vol. VI
Farley, Sir Edwin Wood Thorp, 1864–1939, vol. III
Farley, HE Cardinal John, 1842–1918, vol. II
Farlow, Sir Sydney Nettleton K.; *see* King-Farlow.
Farman, Air Vice-Marshal Edward Crisp, 1897–1966, vol. VI
Farman, Henry, 1874–1958, vol. V

Farmar, Maj.-Gen. George Jasper, 1872–1958, vol. V
Farmar, Col Harold Mynors, 1878–1961, vol. VI
Farmar, Hugh William, 1908–1987, vol. VIII
Farmer, Charles Edward, 1847–1935, vol. III
Farmer, Edward Desmond, 1917–1999, vol. X
Farmer, Emily, 1826–1905, vol. I
Farmer, Ernest Harold, *died* 1952, vol. V
Farmer, Sir Francis Mark, *died* 1922, vol. II
Farmer, Sir George; *see* Farmer, Sir L. G. T.
Farmer, Col George Devey, 1866–1928, vol. II
Farmer, Henry George, 1882–1965, vol. VI
Farmer, Rev. Herbert Henry, 1892–1981, vol. VIII
Farmer, John, 1835–1901, vol. I
Farmer, Sir John Bretland, 1865–1944, vol. IV
Farmer, John Cotton, 1886–1952, vol. V
Farmer, Sir (Lovedin) George (Thomas), 1908–1996, vol. X
Farmer, Norman William, 1901–1971, vol. VII
Farmer, Sir William, 1831–1908, vol. I
Farmer-Atkinson, Henry John; *see* Atkinson.
Farmiloe, Ven. William Thomas, 1863–1946, vol. VII
Farnall, Edmund Waterton, 1855–1918, vol. II
Farnall, Harry de la Rosa Burrard, 1852–1929, vol. III
Farnan, R. P., *died* 1962, vol. VI
Farnborough, Louisa Johanna, (Lady Farnborough), *died* 1901, vol. I
Farncomb, Rear-Adm. Harold Bruce, 1899–1971, vol. VII
Farndale, Joseph, 1865–1954, vol. V
Farndale, Gen. Sir Martin Baker, 1929–2000, vol. X
Farndale, Rev. William Edward, 1881–1966, vol. VI
Farnell, Lewis Richard, 1856–1934, vol. III
Farnham, 10th Baron, 1849–1900, vol. I
Farnham, 11th Baron, 1879–1957, vol. V
Farnhill, Rear-Adm. Kenneth Haydn, 1913–1983, vol. VIII
Farnol, Jeffery; *see* Farnol, John J.
Farnol, (John) Jeffery, 1878–1952, vol. V
Farnsworth, John Windsor, 1912–1987, vol. VIII
Farnsworth, William Charles, 1892–1964, vol. VI
Farquhar, 1st Earl, 1844–1923, vol. II
Farquhar, Alfred, 1852–1928, vol. II
Farquhar, Sir Arthur, 1815–1908, vol. I
Farquhar, Adm. Sir Arthur Murray, 1855–1937, vol. III
Farquhar, Major Francis Douglas, 1874–1915, vol. I
Farquhar, George Neil, 1896–1948, vol. IV
Farquhar, Very Rev. George Taylor Shillito, *died* 1927, vol. II
Farquhar, Gilbert, 1850–1920, vol. II
Farquhar, Sir Harold Lister, 1894–1953, vol. V
Farquhar, Sir Henry Thomas, 4th Bt, 1838–1916, vol. II
Farquhar, John Nicol, 1861–1929, vol. III
Farquhar, Joseph, 1854–1929, vol. III
Farquhar, Lt-Col Sir Peter Walter, 6th Bt, 1904–1986, vol. VIII
Farquhar, Adm. Richard Bowles, 1859–1948, vol. IV
Farquhar, Sir Robert Townsend-, 6th Bt, 1841–1924, vol. II

Farquhar, Sir Walter Randolph Fitzroy, 5th Bt, 1878–1918, vol. II
Farquhar, Sir Walter Rockcliffe, 3rd Bt, 1810–1900, vol. I
Farquharson, Alexander Charles, 1864–1951, vol. V
Farquharson, Alexander Haldane, 1867–1936, vol. III
Farquharson, Bt Lt-Col Arthur Spenser Loat, *died* 1942, vol. IV
Farquharson, Sir Arthur Wildman, *died* 1947, vol. IV
Farquharson, Lt-Col David Lorraine Wilson-, 1862–1938, vol. III
Farquharson, Eric Leslie, 1905–1970, vol. VI
Farquharson, Lt-Gen. Henry Douglas, 1868–1947, vol. IV
Farquharson, James Miller, 1825–1906, vol. I
Farquharson, Col Sir John, 1839–1905, vol. I
Farquharson, John Malcolm, 1864–1936, vol. III
Farquharson, Joseph, 1846–1935, vol. III
Farquharson, Mrs Ogilvie-, *died* 1912, vol. I
Farquharson, Rt Hon. Robert, 1836–1918, vol. II
Farquharson-Lang, William Marshall, 1908–1988, vol. VIII
Farr, Clinton Coleridge, 1866–1943, vol. IV
Farr, Captain John, 1882–1951, vol. V
Farr, Sir John Arnold, 1922–1997, vol. X
Farr, William Edward, 1872–1923, vol. II
Farran, Sir Charles Frederick, 1840–1898, vol. I
Farran, Major George Lambert, *died* 1925, vol. II
Farrand, Livingston, 1867–1939, vol. III
Farrands, John Law, 1921–1996, vol. X
Farrant, Sir Geoffrey Upcott, 1881–1964, vol. VI
Farrant, Henry Gatchell, 1864–1946, vol. IV
Farrant, Maj.-Gen. Ralph Henry, 1909–1988, vol. VIII
Farrant, Reginald Douglas, 1877–1952, vol. V
Farrant, Sir Richard, 1835–1906, vol. I
Farrar, Rev. Adam Story, 1826–1905, vol. I
Farrar, Rev. Charles Frederick, *died* 1931, vol. III
Farrar, Hon. Ernest Henry, 1879–1952, vol. V
Farrar, Very Rev. Frederic William, 1831–1903, vol. I
Farrar, Sir George Herbert, 1st Bt, 1859–1915, vol. I
Farrar, Geraldine, 1882–1967, vol. VI
Farrar, Captain John Percy, 1857–1929, vol. III
Farrar, Rev. Piercy Austin, 1873–1947, vol. IV
Farrar, Rt Rev. Walter, 1865–1916, vol. II
Farrell, Arthur Acheson, 1898–1983, vol. VIII
Farrell, Arthur Denis, 1906–1990, vol. VIII
Farrell, Hon. Edward Matthew, 1854–1931, vol. III
Farrell, Frank James, 1877–1937, vol. III
Farrell, James, *died* 1985, vol. IX (AI)
Farrell, James A., 1863–1943, vol. IV
Farrell, James Gordon, 1935–1979, vol. VII
Farrell, James Patrick, 1865–1921, vol. II
Farrell, James T., 1904–1979, vol. VII
Farrell, Jerome; *see* Farrell, W. J.
Farrell, Joseph Jessop, 1866–1949, vol. IV
Farrell, M. J.; *see* Keane, M. N.
Farrell, Michael James, 1926–1975, vol. VII
Farrell, Robert Hamilton, 1895–1959, vol. V
Farrell, Sir Thomas, 1828–1900, vol. I
Farrell, (Wilfrid) Jerome, 1882–1960, vol. V

Farren, Most Rev. Neil, 1893–1980, vol. VII (AII)
Farren, Sir Richard Thomas, 1817–1909, vol. I
Farren, William, 1853–1937, vol. III
Farren, Sir William Scott, 1892–1970, vol. VI
Farrer, 1st Baron, 1819–1899, vol. I
Farrer, 2nd Baron, 1859–1940, vol. III
Farrer, 3rd Baron, 1893–1948, vol. IV
Farrer, 4th Baron, 1904–1954, vol. V
Farrer, 5th Baron, 1910–1964, vol. VI
Farrer, Augustine John Daniel, 1872–1954, vol. V
Farrer, Rev. Austin Marsden, 1904–1968, vol. VI
Farrer, Bryan, 1858–1944, vol. IV
Farrer, Claude St Aubyn, *died* 1940, vol. III
Farrer, Edmund Hugh, 1876–1955, vol. V
Farrer, Hon. Dame Frances Margaret, 1895–1977, vol. VII
Farrer, Harold Marson, 1882–1943, vol. IV
Farrer, Rev. Canon Henry Richard William, 1859–1933, vol. III
Farrer, Sir Leslie; *see* Farrer, Sir W. L.
Farrer, Margaret Irene, 1914–1997, vol. X
Farrer, Hon. Noel Maitland, 1867–1929, vol. III
Farrer, Philip Tonstall, 1877–1966, vol. VI
Farrer, Reginald, 1880–1920, vol. II
Farrer, Roland John, 1873–1956, vol. V
Farrer, Ven. Walter, 1862–1934, vol. III
Farrer, Sir (Walter) Leslie, 1900–1984, vol. VIII
Farrer, Sir William James, 1822–1911, vol. I
Farrer-Brown, Leslie, 1904–1994, vol. IX
Farrère, Claude, (Frédéric Charles Bargone), 1876–1957, vol. V
Farrington, Vice-Adm. Alexander, 1869–1933, vol. III
Farrington, Benjamin, 1891–1974, vol. VII
Farrington, Sir Henry Anthony, 6th Bt, 1871–1944, vol. IV
Farrington, Col Malcolm Charles, 1835–1925, vol. II
Farrington, Sir William Hicks, 5th Bt, 1838–1901, vol. I
Farris, Hon. John Lauchlan, 1911–1986, vol. VIII
Farris, Hon. John Wallace de Beque, 1878–1970, vol. VI
Farrow, G. Martin, 1896–1969, vol. VI(AII)
Farrow, Leslie William, 1888–1978, vol. VII
Farson, Negley, 1890–1960, vol. V
Farthing, Rt Rev. John Cragg, 1861–1947, vol. IV
Farthing, Walter John, 1889–1954, vol. V
Farwell, Sir Christopher John Wickens, 1877–1943, vol. IV
Farwell, Eveline Louisa Michell; *see* Forbes, Hon. Mrs Walter.
Farwell, Rt Hon. Sir George, 1845–1915, vol. I
Farwell, Rt Rev. Gerard Victor, 1913–1988, vol. VIII
Fasella, Paolo Maria, 1930–1999, vol. X
Fasken, Maj.-Gen. Charles Grant Mansell, 1855–1928, vol. II
Fasken, Brig.-Gen. William Henry, 1863–1943, vol. IV
Fass, Sir Ernest; *see* Fass, Sir H. E.
Fass, Sir (Herbert) Ernest, *died* 1969, vol. VI
Fassbinder, Rainer Werner, 1946–1982, vol. VIII
Fasson, Brig.-Gen. Disney John Menzies, 1864–1931, vol. III

Fatchett, Rt Hon. Derek John, 1945–1999, vol. X
Fateh Ali Khan, Hon. Sir Hajee, Nawab Kizilbash, 1862–1923, vol. II
Fathers, Henry, 1860–1937, vol. III
Faucit, Helen, (Lady Martin), 1820–1898, vol. I
Fauconberg and Conyers, Baroness (13th in line), (Countess of Yarborough), 1863–1926, vol. II
Faudel-Phillips, Sir Benjamin Samuel, 2nd Bt, 1871–1927, vol. II
Faudel-Phillips, Sir George Faudel, 1st Bt, 1840–1922, vol. II
Faudel-Phillips, Sir Lionel Lawson Faudel, 3rd Bt, 1877–1941, vol. IV
Faught, Surg.-Maj.-Gen. John George, 1832–1910, vol. I
Faulds, Archibald Galbraith, 1860–1940, vol. III
Faulds, Andrew Matthew William, 1923–2000, vol. X
Faulkner, Sir Alfred Edward, 1882–1963, vol. VI
Faulkner, Rt Hon. (Arthur) Brian (Deane), 1921–1977, vol. VII
Faulkner, Hon. Arthur James, 1921–1985, vol. VIII
Faulkner, Rt Hon. Brian; see Faulkner, Rt Hon. A. B. D.
Faulkner, Sir Eric Odin, 1914–1994, vol. IX
Faulkner, Major George Aubrey, died 1930, vol. III
Faulkner, Hon. George Everett, 1855–1931, vol. III
Faulkner, Captain George Haines, 1893–1983, vol. VIII
Faulkner, Harry, 1892–1971, vol. VII
Faulkner, Hugh Branston, 1916–1997, vol. X
Faulkner, Hugh Charles, 1912–1994, vol. IX
Faulkner, Rear-Adm. Hugh Webb, 1900–1969, vol. VI
Faulkner, Hon. James Albert, 1877–1944, vol. IV
Faulkner, John, 1871–1958, vol. V
Faulkner, Odin T., 1890–1958, vol. V
Faulkner, Sir Percy, 1907–1990, vol. VIII
Faulkner, Vincent Clements, 1888–1975, vol. VII
Faulkner, William Harrison, 1897–1962, vol. VI
Faulks, Hon. Sir Neville Major Ginner, 1908–1985, vol. VIII
Faulks, Peter Ronald, 1917–1998, vol. X
Faull, Joseph Horace, 1870–1961, vol. VI
Faunce, Brig. Bonham, 1872–1961, vol. VI
Faunce, William Herbert Perry, 1859–1930, vol. III
Faunthorpe, Lt-Col John Champion, 1872–1929, vol. III
Faunthorpe, Rev. John Pincher, 1839–1924, vol. II
Faure, Edgar Jean, 1908–1988, vol. VIII
Fauré, Gabriel, 1845–1924, vol. II
Faure, Hon. Sir Pieter Hendrik, 1848–1914, vol. I
Fausset, Rev. Andrew Robert, 1821–1910, vol. I
Fausset, Hugh I'Anson, 1895–1965, vol. VI
Fausset, Rev. William Yorke, died 1914, vol. I
Faussett, Captain Sir Bryan Godfrey G.; see Godfrey-Faussett.
Faussett, Brig. Bryan Trevor G.; see Godfrey-Faussett.
Faussett, Brig.-Gen. Edmund Godfrey G.; see Godfrey-Faussett.
Faussett, Lt-Col Owen Godfrey G.; see Godfrey Faussett.
Fauteux, Rt Hon. Gérald; see Fauteux, Rt Hon. J. H. G.

Fauteux, Rt Hon. (Joseph Honoré) Gérald, 1900–1980, vol. VII (AII)
Faux, Col Edward, 1857–1937, vol. III
Favell, Richard, died 1918, vol. II
Faviell, Captain Douglas, 1884–1947, vol. IV
Faviell, Lt-Col William Frederick Oliver, 1882–1950, vol. IV
Faville, Air Vice-Marshal Roy, 1908–1980, vol. VII
Fawcett, Charles Bungay, 1883–1952, vol. V
Fawcett, Sir Charles Gordon Hill, 1869–1952, vol. V
Fawcett, Colin, 1923–1996, vol. X
Fawcett, Douglas; see Fawcett, E. D.
Fawcett, Edgar, 1847–1904, vol. I
Fawcett, Edmund Alderson Sandford, 1868–1938, vol. III
Fawcett, Edward, 1867–1942, vol. IV
Fawcett, (Edward) Douglas, 1866–1960, vol. V
Fawcett, Edward Pinder, 1874–1954, vol. V
Fawcett, Sir Henry; see Fawcett, Sir J. H.
Fawcett, Henry Heath, 1863–1925, vol. II
Fawcett, Sir James Edmund Sandford, 1913–1991, vol. IX
Fawcett, John, 1866–1944, vol. IV
Fawcett, Sir (John) Henry, 1831–1898, vol. I
Fawcett, Sir Luke, 1881–1960, vol. V
Fawcett, Dame Millicent, 1847–1929, vol. III
Fawcett, Lt-Col Percy Harrison, 1867–1925, vol. II, vol. III
Fawcett, Philippa Garrett, died 1948, vol. IV
Fawcett, William, died 1941, vol. IV
Fawcett, Sir William Claude, 1868–1935, vol. III
Fawcett, Maj.-Gen. William James, 1848–1943, vol. IV
Fawcett, William Milner, 1832–1908, vol. I
Fawcus, Lt-Col Arthur, 1886–1936, vol. III
Fawcus, George Ernest, 1885–1958, vol. V
Fawcus, Lt-Gen. Sir Harold Ben, 1876–1947, vol. IV
Fawcus, Louis Reginald, 1887–1971, vol. VII
Fawdry, Reginald Charles, 1873–1965, vol. VI
Fawdry, Air Cdre Thomas, 1891–1968, vol. VI
Fawke, Sir Ernest John, died 1928, vol. II
Fawkes, Archibald Walter, 1855–1941, vol. IV
Fawkes, Frederick Hawksworth, 1870–1936, vol. III
Fawkes, Rear-Adm. George Barney Hamley, 1903–1967, vol. VI
Fawkes, Rowland Beattie, 1894–1965, vol. VI
Fawkes, Rupert Edward Francis, 1879–1967, vol. VI
Fawkes, Adm. Sir Wilmot Hawksworth, 1846–1926, vol. II
Fawsitt, Charles Edward, 1878–1960, vol. V(A)
Fay, Charles Ernest, 1846–1931, vol. III
Fay, Charles Ryle, 1884–1961, vol. VI
Fay, Rt Rev. Cyril Damian, 1903–1975, vol. VII
Fay, John David, 1919–1991, vol. IX
Fay, Sir Sam, 1856–1953, vol. V
Fay, Sidney Bradshaw, 1876–1967, vol. VI
Fayle, Lindley Robert Edmundson, 1903–1972, vol. VII
Fayolle, Emile, 1852–1928, vol. II
Fayrer, Sir Joseph, 1st Bt, 1824–1907, vol. I
Fayrer, Sir Joseph, 2nd Bt, 1859–1937, vol. III
Fayrer, Sir Joseph Herbert Spens, 3rd Bt, 1899–1976, vol. VII

Fazan, Sidney Herbert, 1888–1979, vol. VII
Fea, Allan, 1860–1956, vol. V
Fea, William Wallace, 1907–1993, vol. IX
Fearfield, Joseph, 1883–1941, vol. IV
Fearnley, John Thorn, 1921–1986, vol. VIII
Fearnley, Thomas, 1880–1961, vol. VI
Fearnley Scarr, J. G.; see Scarr.
Fearnley-Whittingstall, Francis Herbert, 1894–1945, vol. IV
Fearnley-Whittingstall, William Arthur, 1903–1959, vol. V
Fearnsides, Edwin Greaves, 1883–1919, vol. II
Fearnsides, William George, 1879–1968, vol. VI
Fearon, Daniel Robert, 1835–1919, vol. II
Fearon, John Francis, 1867–1940, vol. III
Fearon, Percy Hutton (Poy), 1874–1948, vol. IV
Fearon, Rev. William Andrewes, 1841–1924, vol. II
Fearon, William Robert, 1892–1959, vol. V
Feather, Baron (Life Peer); Victor Grayson Hardie Feather, 1908–1976, vol. VII
Feather, Norman, 1904–1978, vol. VII
Featherstone, Eric Kellett, 1896–1965, vol. VI
Featherstone, Henry Walter, 1894–1967, vol. VI
Featherstone, Col Patrick Davies; see Featherstone, Col W. P. D.
Featherstone, Col (William) Patrick Davies, 1919–1983, vol. VIII
Feavearyear, Sir Albert Edgar, 1896–1953, vol. V
Feaver, Rt Rev. Douglas Russell, 1914–1997, vol. X
Fechteler, Adm. William Morrow, 1896–1967, vol. VI
Fedden, Sir (Alfred Hubert) Roy, 1885–1973, vol. VII
Fedden, (Henry) Robin Romilly, 1908–1977, vol. VII
Fedden, Katharine Waldo Douglas, died 1939, vol. III
Fedden, Robin Romilly; see Fedden, H. R. R.
Fedden, Romilly, died 1939, vol. III
Fedden, Sir Roy; see Fedden, Sir A. H. R.
Fedden, Walter Fedde, died 1952, vol. V
Fedrick, Geoffrey Courtis, 1937–1994, vol. IX
Feeny, Max Howard, 1928–1995, vol. IX
Feetham, Brig.-Gen. Edward, 1863–1918, vol. II
Feetham, Rt Rev. John Oliver, 1873–1947, vol. IV
Feetham, Hon. Richard, 1874–1965, vol. VI
Fegen, Rear-Adm. Frederick Fogarty, 1855–1911, vol. I
Fegen, Col Magrath Fogarty, 1858–1935, vol. III
Fehily, Rt Rev. Mgr Canon Thomas Francis, 1917–1987, vol. VIII
Fehr, Basil Henry Frank, 1912–1999, vol. X
Fehr, Frank Emil, 1874–1948, vol. IV
Fehr, Henry Charles, died 1940, vol. III
Fehrenbacher, Rt Rev. Bruno, 1895–1965, vol. VI
Feibusch, Hans, 1898–1998, vol. X
Feilden, Cecil William Montague, 1863–1902, vol. I
Feilden, Major Granville Cholmondeley, 1863–1939, vol. III
Feilden, Major Guy; see Fielden, Major P. H. G.
Feilden, Maj.-Gen. Sir Henry Broome, 1834–1926, vol. II
Feilden, Col Henry Wemyss, 1838–1921, vol. II

Feilden, Major (Percy Henry) Guy, 1870–1944, vol. IV
Feilden, Maj.-Gen. Sir Randle Guy, 1904–1981, vol. VIII
Feilden, Lt-Col Randle Montague, 1871–1965, vol. VI
Feilden, Theodore John Valentine, 1863–1955, vol. V
Feilden, Col Wemyss Gawne Cunningham, 1870–1943, vol. IV
Feilden, Sir William Henry, 4th Bt, 1866–1946, vol. IV
Feilden, Rev. William Leyland, died 1907, vol. I
Feilden, Sir William Leyland, 3rd Bt, 1835–1912, vol. I
Feilden, Sir William Morton Buller, 5th Bt, 1893–1976, vol. VII
Feilding, Viscount; Lt-Col Rudolph Edmund Aloysius Feilding, 1885–1937, vol. III
Feilding, Maj.-Gen. Sir Geoffrey Percy Thynne, 1866–1932, vol. III
Feilding, Hon. Sir Percy Robert Basil, 1827–1904, vol. I
Feilding, Lt-Col Rowland Charles, died 1945, vol. IV
Feiling, Anthony, 1885–1975, vol. VII
Feiling, Sir Keith Grahame, 1884–1977, vol. VII
Feisal, King, died 1933, vol. III
Felberman, Louis, 1861–1927, vol. II
Feldberg, Wilhelm Siegmund, 1900–1993, vol. IX
Feldman, Rev. Dayan Asher, 1873–1950, vol. IV
Feldman, William Moses, died 1939, vol. III
Felgate, Air Vice-Marshal Frank Westerman, 1901–1974, vol. VII
Felix, Arthur, 1887–1956, vol. V
Felkin, Mrs A. L.; see Fowler, Hon. Ellen Thorneycroft.
Felkin, Alfred Laurence, 1856–1942, vol. IV
Fell, Sir Anthony, 1914–1998, vol. X
Fell, Sir Arthur, 1850–1934, vol. III
Fell, Aubrey Llewellyn Coventry, 1869–1948, vol. IV
Fell, Sir Bryan Hugh, 1869–1955, vol. V
Fell, Charles Percival, 1894–1989, vol. VIII
Fell, Eleanor, died 1946, vol. IV
Fell, Sir Godfrey Butler Hunter, 1872–1955, vol. V
Fell, Herbert Granville, 1872–1951, vol. V
Fell, Dame Honor Bridget, 1900–1986, vol. VIII
Fell, John Robert Massey, 1890–1969, vol. VI
Fell, Lt-Gen. Sir Matthew Henry Gregson, 1872–1959, vol. V
Fell, Vice-Adm. Sir Michael Frampton, 1918–1976, vol. VII
Fell, Brig.-Gen. Robert Black, 1859–1934, vol. III
Fell, Sheila Mary, 1931–1979, vol. VII
Fell, Thomas Edward, 1873–1926, vol. II
Fell, Captain William Richmond, 1897–1981, vol. VIII
Fell-Smith, Charlotte, died 1937, vol. III
Felling, Sir Christian Ludolph Neethling, 1880–1928, vol. II
Fellini, Federico, 1920–1993, vol. IX
Fellowes, Hon. Coulson Churchill, 1883–1915, vol. I
Fellowes, Daisy, (Hon. Mrs Reginald Fellowes), died 1962, vol. VI

Fellowes, Rev. Edmund Horace, 1870–1951, vol. V
Fellowes, Sir Edward Abdy, 1895–1970, vol. VI
Fellowes, Maj.-Gen. Halford David, 1906–1985, vol. VIII
Fellowes, Vice-Adm. Sir John, 1843–1912, vol. I
Fellowes, Air Cdre Peregrine Forbes Morant, 1883–1955, vol. V
Fellowes, Brig. Reginald William Lyon, 1895–1982, vol. VIII
Fellowes, Rear-Adm. Sir Thomas Hounsom Butler, 1827–1923, vol. II
Fellowes, Sir William Albemarle, 1899–1986, vol. VIII
Fellows, Brig.-Gen. Bertram Charles, 1877–1956, vol. V
Fellows, Col Bruce; see Fellows, Col R. B.
Fellows, Col (Robert) Bruce, 1830–1922, vol. II
Fells, John Manger, 1858–1925, vol. II
Fels, Willi, 1858–1946, vol. IV(A)
Feltham, John Alric Percy, 1862–1929, vol. III
Feltin, HE Cardinal Maurice, 1883–1975, vol. VII
Felton, Sir John Robinson, 1880–1962, vol. VI
Felton, Mrs Monica, 1906–1970, vol. VI
Felton, Samuel Morse, 1853–1930, vol. III
Fenby, Charles, 1905–1974, vol. VII
Fenby, Eric William, 1906–1997, vol. X
Fenby, Thomas Davis, 1875–1956, vol. V
Fendall, Brig.-Gen. Charles Pears, 1860–1933, vol. III
Fendall, Percy Paul Wentworth, 1879–1910, vol. I
Fender, Percy George Herbert, 1892–1985, vol. VIII
Fendick, Rev. George Harold, 1883–1962, vol. VI
Fenn, Col Ernest Harrold, 1850–1916, vol. II
Fenn, Frederick, 1868–1924, vol. II
Fenn, George Manville, 1831–1909, vol. I
Fenn, Harold Robert Backwell, 1894–1974, vol. VII
Fenn, John Cyril Douglas, 1879–1927, vol. II
Fenn, William Wallace, 1862–1932, vol. III
Fennell, John Lister Illingworth, 1918–1992, vol. IX
Fennelly, Sir Daniel; see Fennelly, Sir R. D.
Fennelly, Sir (Reginald) Daniel, 1890–1969, vol. VI
Fennelly, Most Rev. Thomas, 1845–1927, vol. II
Fenner, Tan Sri Sir Claude Harry, 1916–1978, vol. VII
Fenning, Captain Edward George, 1878–1932, vol. III
Fenning, Frederick William, 1919–1988, vol. VIII
Fenton, Brig.-Gen. Alexander Bulstrode, 1856–1942, vol. IV
Fenton, Charles; see Fenton, T. C.
Fenton, Ferrar, 1832–1911, vol. I
Fenton, Air Cdre Harold Arthur, 1909–1995, vol. IX
Fenton, Henry John Horstman, 1854–1929, vol. III
Fenton, James, 1884–1962, vol. VI
Fenton, Hon. James Edward, 1864–1950, vol. IV
Fenton, James Stevenson, 1891–1975, vol. VII
Fenton, Sir John Charles, 1880–1951, vol. V
Fenton, Sir Michael William, 1862–1941, vol. IV
Fenton, Sir Myles, 1830–1918, vol. II
Fenton, Rt Rev. Patrick, 1837–1918, vol. II
Fenton, Richard, 1899–1959, vol. V
Fenton, Roy Pentelow, 1918–1979, vol. VII
Fenton, (Thomas) Charles, died 1927, vol. II
Fenton, West Fenton de W.; see de Wend-Fenton.

Fenton, Wilfrid David Drysdale, 1908–1985, vol. VIII
Fenton, Col Sir William Charles, 1891–1976, vol. VII
Fenton, William Hugh, 1854–1928, vol. II
Fenton, William James, 1868–1957, vol. V
Fenwick, Bedford, 1855–1939, vol. III
Fenwick, Mrs Bedford; see Fenwick, Ethel Gordon.
Fenwick, Rt Hon. Charles, 1850–1918, vol. II
Fenwick, Maj.-Gen. Charles Philip, 1891–1954, vol. V
Fenwick, Christian Bedford, 1888–1969, vol. VI
Fenwick, E. Hurry, 1856–1944, vol. IV
Fenwick, Edward Nicholas Fenwick-, 1847–1908, vol. I
Fenwick, Major Ernest Guy, 1867–1937, vol. III
Fenwick, Ethel Gordon, (Mrs Bedford Fenwick), 1857–1947, vol. IV
Fenwick, Sir George, 1847–1929, vol. III
Fenwick, Hon. Sir (George) Townsend, 1846–1927, vol. II
Fenwick, Lt-Col Gerard, 1868–1935, vol. III
Fenwick, Col Henry Thomas, 1863–1939, vol. III
Fenwick, Col Percival Clennell, 1870–1958, vol. V
Fenwick, Robert George, 1913–1987, vol. VIII
Fenwick, Thomas FitzRoy Phillipps, 1856–1938, vol. III
Fenwick, Hon. Sir Townsend; see Fenwick, Hon. Sir G. T.
Fenwick-Fenwick, Edward Nicholas; see Fenwick.
Fenwick-Palmer, Lt-Col Roderick George, 1892–1968, vol. VI
Fenwicke, William Soltau, died 1944, vol. IV
Ferard, Arthur George, 1858–1943, vol. IV
Ferard, Henry Cecil, 1864–1936, vol. III
Ferard, John Edward, 1869–1944, vol. IV
Ferard, Reginald Herbert, 1866–1934, vol. III
Ferber, Edna, 1885–1968, vol. VI
Ferens, Rt Hon. Thomas Robinson, 1847–1930, vol. III
Ferens, Sir Thomas Robinson, 1903–1992, vol. IX
Ferens, Rev. Canon William, 1859–1935, vol. III
Fergus, Andrew Freeland, 1858–1932, vol. III
Fergus, Most Rev. James, 1895–1989, vol. VIII
Fergus, John F., 1865–1943, vol. IV
Fergus, Hon. Thomas, 1851–1914, vol. I
Ferguson, Alexander Stewart, 1883–1958, vol. V
Ferguson, Brig.-Gen. Algernon Francis Holford, 1867–1943, vol. IV
Ferguson, Allan, 1880–1951, vol. V
Ferguson, Lt-Col Sir Arthur George, 1862–1935, vol. III
Ferguson, Maj.-Gen. Augustus Klingner, 1898–1965, vol. VI
Ferguson, Charles Edward Hamilton, died 1958, vol. V
Ferguson, Hon. Sir David Gilbert, 1861–1941, vol. IV
Ferguson, Sir David Gordon, 1895–1969, vol. VI
Ferguson, Hon. Donald, 1839–1909, vol. I
Ferguson, Sir Edward Alexander James J.; see Johnson-Ferguson.
Ferguson, Sir Edward Brown, 1892–1967, vol. VI
Ferguson, Erne Cecil, 1911–1968, vol. VI
Ferguson, Fergus James, 1878–1948, vol. IV

Ferguson, Frederic Sutherland, 1878–1967, vol. VI
Ferguson, Col George Andrew, 1872–1933, vol. III
Ferguson, Lt-Col George Arthur, 1835–1924, vol. II
Ferguson, Hon. (George) Howard, 1870–1946, vol. IV
Ferguson, Sir Gordon; see Ferguson, Sir D. G.
Ferguson, Harry George, 1884–1960, vol. V
Ferguson, Sir (Henry) Lindo, 1858–1948, vol. IV
Ferguson, Herbert, 1874–1953, vol. V
Ferguson, Hon. Howard; see Ferguson, Hon. G. H.
Ferguson, Sir (Jabez) Edward J.; see Johnson-Ferguson.
Ferguson of Kinmundy, James, 1857–1917, vol. II
Ferguson, James, 1879–1949, vol. IV
Ferguson, James Brown Provan, 1935–1994, vol. IX
Ferguson, James Haig, 1862–1934, vol. III
Ferguson, Very Rev. John, died 1902, vol. I
Ferguson, John, 1842–1913, vol. I
Ferguson, John, 1854–1916, vol. II
Ferguson, Sir John, 1870–1932, vol. III
Ferguson, John, 1854–1939, vol. III
Ferguson, John, 1921–1989, vol. VIII
Ferguson, Hon. Sir John Alexander, 1882–1969, vol. VI
Ferguson, John Calvin, 1866–1945, vol. IV
Ferguson, Col John David, 1866–1961, vol. VI
Ferguson, Major Sir John Frederick, 1891–1975, vol. VII
Ferguson, John Macrae, 1849–1919, vol. II
Ferguson, Joshua, 1870–1951, vol. V
Ferguson, Sir Lindo; see Ferguson, Sir H. L.
Ferguson, Sir Neil Edward J.; see Johnson-Ferguson.
Ferguson, Col Nicholas Charles, 1862–1930, vol. III
Ferguson, Rachel, 1893–1957, vol. V
Ferguson, Richard Saul, 1837–1900, vol. I
Ferguson, Samuel Fergus, 1897–1971, vol. VII
Ferguson, Engr Rear-Adm. Samuel Pringle, 1871–1938, vol. III
Ferguson, Thomas, 1900–1977, vol. VII
Ferguson, William Alexander, 1902–1973, vol. VII
Ferguson, William Bates, 1853–1937, vol. III
Ferguson, Rev. Canon William Harold, 1874–1950, vol. IV
Ferguson, William Nassau, 1869–1928, vol. II, vol. III
Ferguson Davie, Sir Antony Francis, 6th Bt, 1952–1997, vol. X
Ferguson-Davie, Major Arthur Francis, see Davie.
Ferguson Davie, Rev. Sir Arthur Patrick, 5th Bt, 1909–1988, vol. VIII
Ferguson-Davie, Rt Rev. Charles James, 1872–1963, vol. VI
Ferguson-Davie, Sir Henry Augustus; see Davie.
Ferguson Davie, Sir John, 7th Bt, 1906–2000, vol. X
Ferguson-Davie, Sir John Davie; see Davie.
Ferguson-Davie, Sir William Augustus; see Davie.
Ferguson-Davie, Major Sir William John, 4th Bt, 1863–1947, vol. IV
Ferguson Jones, Hugh; see Jones.
Fergusson, Col Arthur Charles, 1871–1958, vol. V
Fergusson, Bernard Edward; see Baron Ballantrae.
Fergusson, Gen. Sir Charles, 7th Bt (cr 1703), 1865–1951, vol. V
Fergusson, Sir Donald; see Fergusson, Sir J. D. B.

Fergusson, Sir Ewen MacGregor Field, 1897–1974, vol. VII
Fergusson, Lt-Col Herbert Chaworth, 1865–1939, vol. III
Fergusson, Ian Victor Lyon, 1901–1990, vol. VIII
Fergusson, Rt Hon. Sir James, 6th Bt (cr 1703), 1832–1907, vol. I
Fergusson of Kilkerran, Sir James, 8th Bt (cr 1703), 1904–1973, vol. VII
Fergusson, Adm. Sir James Andrew, 1871–1942, vol. IV
Fergusson, James David, 1923–1991, vol. IX
Fergusson, Surg. Rear-Adm. James Herbert, 1874–1948, vol. IV
Fergusson, Sir James Ranken, 2nd Bt (cr 1866), 1835–1924, vol. II
Fergusson, John, 1835–1912, vol. I
Fergusson, Sir (John) Donald (Balfour), 1891–1963, vol. VI
Fergusson, John Douglas, 1909–1979, vol. VII
Fergusson, Rev. John Moore, 1863–1944, vol. IV
Fergusson, Sir Louis Forbes, 1878–1962, vol. VI
Fergusson, Sir Thomas Colyer C., 3rd Bt (cr 1866); see Colyer-Fergusson.
Fergusson, Lt-Col Vivian Moffatt, 1878–1926, vol. II
Fergusson, Col William James Smyth, 1864–1934, vol. III
Fergusson Hannay, Doris, (Lady Fergusson Hannay); see Leslie, D.
Fermi, Enrico, 1901–1954, vol. V
Fermor, Sir Lewis Leigh, 1880–1954, vol. V
Fermor, Una Mary E.; see Ellis-Fermor.
Fermor-Hesketh, Sir Thomas George; see Hesketh.
Fermoy, 2nd Baron, 1850–1920, vol. II
Fermoy, 3rd Baron, 1852–1920, vol. II
Fermoy, 4th Baron, 1885–1955, vol. V
Fermoy, 5th Baron, 1939–1984, vol. VIII
Fermoy, Ruth Lady; Ruth Sylvia Roche, 1908–1993, vol. IX
Fernald, Chester Bailey, 1869–1938, vol. III
Fernald, John Bailey, 1905–1985, vol. VIII
Fernandel, (Fernand Joseph Désiré Contandin), 1903–1971, vol. VII
Fernandes, Most Rev. Angelo, 1913–2000, vol. X
Fernando, Sir Ernest Peter Arnold, 1904–1956, vol. V
Fernando, Sir Hilarion Marcus, 1864–1935, vol. III
Fernando, Hugh Norman Gregory, 1910–1976, vol. VII
Fernow, Bernhard Eduard, born 1851, vol. II
Ferns, Henry Stanley, 1913–1992, vol. IX
Fernyhough, Ven. Bernard, 1932–2000, vol. X
Fernyhough, Rt Hon. Ernest, 1908–1993, vol. IX
Fernyhough, Col Hugh Clifford, 1872–1947, vol. IV
Fernyhough, Brig. Hugh Edward, 1904–1982, vol. VIII
Ferraby, H. C., 1884–1942, vol. IV
Ferrall, John C.; see Carmichael-Ferrall.
Ferrall, Sir Raymond Alfred, 1906–2000, vol. X
Ferrand, Major James Brian Patrick, 1895–1934, vol. III
Ferranti, Sir Vincent Ziani de; see de Ferranti.
Ferrar, Lt-Col Henry Minchin 1863–1949, vol. IV
Ferrar, Lt-Col Michael Lloyd, 1876–1971, vol. VII

Ferrar, William Leonard, 1893–1990, vol. VIII
Ferrari, Enzo, 1898–1988, vol. VIII
Ferrari, Ermanno W.; see Wolf-Ferrari.
Ferraro, Rev. Preb. Francis William, 1888–1963, vol. VI
Ferraro, Vincenzo Consolato Antonino, 1907–1974, vol. VII
Ferrer, José Vicente, 1912–1992, vol. IX
Ferrero, Gen. Annibale, 1839–1902, vol. I
Ferrero, Baron Augusto, vol. II
Ferrero, Guglielmo, 1871–1942, vol. IV
Ferrers, 10th Earl, 1847–1912, vol. I
Ferrers, 11th Earl, 1864–1937, vol. III
Ferrers, 12th Earl, 1894–1954, vol. V
Ferrers, Rev. Norman Macleod, 1829–1903, vol. I
Ferri, Enrico, 1856–1929, vol. III
Ferrie, Maj.-Gen. Alexander Martin, 1923–1995, vol. IX
Ferrier, Baron (Life Peer); Victor Ferrier Noel-Paton, 1900–1992, vol. IX
Ferrier, Sir David, 1843–1928, vol. II
Ferrier, Sir Grant; see Ferrier, Sir H. G.
Ferrier, Sir (Harold) Grant, 1905–1976, vol. VII
Ferrier, Maj.-Gen. James Archibald, 1854–1934, vol. III
Ferrier, Kathleen, 1912–1953, vol. V
Ferrier, Thomas Archibald, 1877–1968, vol. VI
Ferris, Hon. Rt Rev. Mgr Francis, 1860–1931, vol. III
Ferris, Rev. Thomas Boys Barraclough, 1845–1931, vol. III
Ferris, Rev. William Bridger, died 1931, vol. III
Ferry, Alexander, 1931–1994, vol. IX
Ferryman, Lt-Col Augustus Ferryman M.; see Mockler-Ferryman.
Ferryman, Col Eric Edward M.; see Mockler-Ferryman.
Fessenden, Clementina, died 1918, vol. II
Festetics de Tolna, Prince, 1850–1933, vol. III
Festing, Major Arthur Hoskyns-, 1870–1915, vol. I
Festing, Maj.-Gen. Edward Robert, 1839–1912, vol. I
Festing, Brig.-Gen. Francis Leycester, 1877–1948, vol. IV
Festing, Field Marshal Sir Francis Wogan, 1902–1976, vol. VII
Festing, Gabrielle, died 1924, vol. II
Festing, Major Harold England, 1886–1923, vol. II
Festing, Rt Rev. John Wogan, 1837–1902, vol. I
Fethers, Hon. Col Wilfrid Kent, 1885–1976, vol. VII
Fetherston, Rev. Sir George Ralph, 6th Bt, 1852–1923, vol. II
Fetherston-Dilke, Beaumont Albany, 1875–1968, vol. VI
Fetherston-Godley, Brig. Sir Francis William Crewe, 1893–1976, vol. VII
Fetherstonhaugh, Lt-Col Edward Phillips, 1879–1959, vol. V
Fetherstonhaugh, Frederick Barnard, 1864–1945, vol. IV
Fetherstonhaugh, Godfrey, 1858–1928, vol. II
Fetherstonhaugh, Captain Herbert Howard, died 1937, vol. III

Fetherstonhaugh, Adm. Hon. Sir Herbert M.; see Meade-Fetherstonhaugh.
Fetherstonhaugh, Hon. Keith Turnour-, 1848–1930, vol. III
Fetherstonhaugh, Lt-Col Timothy, 1869–1945, vol. IV
Fetherstonhaugh, Lt-Col Sir Timothy, 1899–1969, vol. VI
Fetherstonhaugh, Brig. William Albany, 1876–1947, vol. IV
Fetherstonhaugh-Whitney, Henry Ernest William, 1847–1921, vol. II
Fetterolf, Adam H., 1841–1912, vol. I
Feuchtwanger, Lion, 1884–1958, vol. V
Feuillère, Edwige, 1910–1998, vol. X
Feversham, 1st Earl of, 1829–1915, vol. I
Feversham, 2nd Earl of, 1879–1916, vol. II
Feversham, 3rd Earl of, 1906–1963, vol. VI
Few, Bt Col Robert Jebb, 1876–1965, vol. VI
Fewtrell, Maj.-Gen. Albert Cecil, 1885–1950, vol. IV
Feynman, Richard Phillips, 1918–1988, vol. VIII
ffarington, Henry Nowell, 1868–1947, vol. IV
ffennell, Raymond William, 1871–1944, vol. IV
Ffinch, Benjamin Traill, 1840–1910, vol. I
Ffinch, Captain Matthew Benjamin Dipnall, died 1951, vol. V .
Ffinch, Rev. Matthew Mortimer, 1838–1920, vol. II
ffolkes, Captain Sir (Edward John) Patrick (Boschetti), 6th Bt, 1899–1960, vol. V
Ffolkes, Sir Everard; see Ffolkes, Sir W. E. B.
Ffolkes, Rev. Sir Francis Arthur Stanley, 5th Bt, 1863–1938, vol. III
ffolkes, Michael, (Brian Davis), 1925–1988, vol. VIII
ffolkes, Captain Sir Patrick; see ffolkes, Captain Sir E. J. P. B.
Ffolkes, Sir (William) Everard Browne, 4th Bt, 1861–1930, vol. III
Ffolkes, Sir William Hovell Browne, 3rd Bt, 1847–1912, vol. I
fforde, Sir Arthur Frederic Brownlow, 1900–1985, vol. VIII
Fforde, Sir Cecil Robert, died 1951, vol. V
Fforde, John Standish, 1921–2000, vol. X
ffoulkes, Charles John, 1868–1947, vol. IV
ffoulkes, Captain Edmund Andrew, 1867–1949, vol. IV
Ffoulkes, William Wynne, died 1903, vol. I
Ffrangcon-Davies, David, 1850–1918, vol. II
Ffrangcon-Davies, Dame Gwen, 1891–1992, vol. IX
ffrench, 6th Baron, 1868–1955, vol. V
ffrench, 7th Baron, 1926–1986, vol. VIII
ffrench, Rev. James Frederick Metge, died 1914, vol. I
ffrench, Hon. John Martin Valentine, 1872–1946, vol. IV
Ffrench, Peter, 1844–1929, vol. III
ffrench-Beytagh, Rev. Canon Gonville Aubie, 1912–1991, vol. IX
Ffrench-Blake, Lt-Col Arthur O'Brien; see Blake.
Ffrench-Mullen, Lt-Col John Lawrence William, 1868–1951, vol. V
Fiaschi, Col Thomas Henry, 1853–1927, vol. II

Ficklin, Maj.-Gen. Horatio Pettus Mackintosh B.; *see* Berney-Ficklin.

Fiddament, Air Vice-Marshal Arthur Leonard, 1896–1976, vol. VII

Fiddes, Edward, 1864–1942, vol. IV

Fiddes, Sir George Vandeleur, 1858–1936, vol. III

Fiddes, Sir James Raffan, 1883–1961, vol. VI

Fiddes, James Raffan, 1919–1997, vol. X

Fidge, Sir (Harold) Roy, 1904–1981, vol. VIII

Fidge, Sir Roy; *see* Fidge, Sir H. R.

Fidler, Alwyn Gwilym S.; *see* Sheppard Fidler.

Fidler, Henry, *died* 1912, vol. I

Fidler, Michael M., 1916–1989, vol. VIII

Fiedler, Hermann George, 1862–1945, vol. IV

Field, 1st Baron, 1813–1907, vol. I

Field, Allan Bertram, 1875–1962, vol. VI

Field, Adm. Sir (Arthur) Mostyn, 1855–1950, vol. IV

Field, Bradda, *died* 1957, vol. V

Field, Lt-Col Sir Donald Moyle, 1881–1956, vol. V

Field, Adm. Edward, 1828–1912, vol. I

Field, Edward, 1898–1978, vol. VII

Field, Sir Ernest Wensley Lapthorn, 1889–1974, vol. VII

Field, Frank Meade, 1863–1943, vol. IV

Field, Adm. of the Fleet Sir Frederick Laurence, 1871–1945, vol. IV

Field, Frederick William, 1884–1960, vol. V

Field, George David, 1887–1975, vol. VII

Field, Guy Cromwell, 1887–1955, vol. V

Field, Henry St John, 1883–1949, vol. IV

Field, Gen. Sir John, 1821–1899, vol. I

Field, John, 1921–1991, vol. IX

Field, Sir John Osbaldiston, 1913–1985, vol. VIII

Field, John William, 1899–1981, vol. VIII

Field, Major Kenneth Douglas, *born* 1880, vol. II

Field, Brig. Leonard Frank, 1898–1978, vol. VII

Field, Marshall, 1893–1956, vol. V

Field, Mary, (Mrs Agnes Mary Hankin), 1896–1968, vol. VI

Field, Michael, *died* 1914, vol. I

Field, Adm. Sir Mostyn; *see* Field, Adm. Sir A. M.

Field, Gp Captain Roger Martin, 1890–1974, vol. VII

Field, Roland Alfred Reginald, *died* 1969, vol. VI

Field, Sid, (Sidney Arthur Field), 1904–1950, vol. IV

Field, Stanley Alfred, 1913–1986, vol. VIII

Field, Rev. Thomas, 1855–1936, vol. III

Field, Walter, *died* 1902, vol. I

Field, William, 1848–1935, vol. III

Field, Hon. Winston Joseph, 1904–1969, vol. VI

Fielden, Lt-Col Edward Anthony, 1886–1972, vol. VII

Fielden, Edward Brocklehurst, *died* 1942, vol. IV

Fielden, Air Vice-Marshal Sir Edward Hedley, 1903–1976, vol. VII

Fielden, Captain Harold, 1868–1937, vol. III

Fielden, Lionel, 1896–1974, vol. VII

Fielden, Thomas, 1854–1897, vol. I

Fielden, Thomas Perceval, *died* 1974, vol. VII

Fielden, Victor George Leopold, 1867–1946, vol. IV

Fieldgate, Alan Frederic Edmond, *born* 1889, vol. VIII

Fieldhouse, Baron (Life Peer); Adm. of the Fleet

John David Elliott Fieldhouse, 1928–1992, vol. IX

Fieldhouse, Arnold; *see* Fieldhouse, R. A.

Fieldhouse, Sir Harold, 1892–1991, vol. IX

Fieldhouse, (Richard) Arnold, 1916–1990, vol. VIII

Fieldhouse, William, 1932–1988, vol. VIII

Fieldhouse, William John, 1858–1928, vol. II

Fielding, Sir Charles William, 1863–1941, vol. IV

Fielding, Frank Stanley, 1918–1990, vol. VIII

Fielding, Gabriel, (Alan Gabriel Barnsley), 1916–1986, vol. VIII

Fielding, Ven. Harold Ormandy, 1912–1987, vol. VIII

Fielding, Marjorie, 1892–1956, vol. V

Fielding, Col Thomas Evelyn, 1873–1937, vol. III

Fielding, Rt Hon. William Stevens, 1848–1929, vol. III

Fielding-Hall, Harold, 1859–1917, vol. II

Fielding-Ould, Robert, 1872–1951, vol. V

Fields, Dame Gracie, 1898–1979, vol. VII

Fields, John Charles, 1863–1932, vol. III

Fienburgh, Wilfred, 1919–1958, vol. V

Fiennes, Hon. Sir Eustace Edward, 1st Bt, 1864–1943, vol. IV

Fiennes, Gerard Francis Gisborne T. W.; *see* Twisleton-Wykeham-Fiennes.

Fiennes, Gerard Yorke Twisleton-Wykeham, 1864–1926, vol. II

Fiennes, Sir John Saye Wingfield T. W.; *see* Twisleton-Wykeham-Fiennes.

Fiennes, Sir Maurice Alberic Twisleton-Wykeham-, 1907–1994, vol. IX

Fiennes, Lt-Col Sir Ranulph Twisleton-Wykeham-, 2nd Bt, 1902–1943, vol. II

Fife, Duchess of (2nd in line), 1891–1959, vol. V

Fife, Col Sir Aubone, 1846–1920, vol. II

Fife, Charles Morrison, 1903–1982, vol. VIII

Fife, Charles William D.; *see* Domville-Fife.

Fife, Herbert Legard, *died* 1941, vol. IV

Fife, Ian Braham, 1911–1990, vol. VIII

Fife, Lt-Col Ronald D'Arcy, 1868–1946, vol. IV

Fife-Cookson, Lt-Col John Cookson, 1844–1911, vol. I

Fifoot, Cecil Herbert Stuart, 1899–1975, vol. VII

Fifoot, (Erik) Richard (Sidney), 1925–1992, vol. IX

Fifoot, Richard; *see* Fifoot, E. R. S.

Figg, Sir Clifford, 1890–1947, vol. IV

Figg, Captain Donald Whitly, 1886–1917, vol. II

Figgess, Sir John George, 1909–1997, vol. X

Figgins, James Hugh Blair, 1893–1956, vol. V

Figgis, Rev. J. B., *died* 1916, vol. II

Figgis, Rev. John Neville, 1866–1919, vol. II

Figgures, Sir Frank Edward, 1910–1990, vol. VIII

Fihelly, Hon. John Arthur, 1883–1945, vol. IV

Fildes, Sir Henry, 1870–1948, vol. IV

Fildes, Sir Luke; *see* Fildes, Sir S. L.

Fildes, Sir Paul, 1882–1971, vol. VII

Fildes, Sir (Samuel) Luke, 1843–1927, vol. II

Filene, Edward A., *died* 1937, vol. III

Filer, Albert Jack, 1898–1989, vol. VIII

Filgate, John Victor Opynschae M.; *see* Macartney-Filgate.

Filgate, Captain Richard Alexander Baillie, 1877–1967, vol. VI

Filgate, Lt-Col Townley Richard, 1854–1931, vol. III
Filgate, William de Salis, 1834–1916, vol. II
Filliter, Douglas Freeland Shute, 1884–1968, vol. VI
Filliter, Freeland, 1814–1902, vol. I
Filmer, Sir Robert Marcus, 10th Bt, 1878–1916, vol. II
Filomena; see Miller, Florence Fenwick.
Filon, Louis Napoleon George, 1875–1937, vol. III
Filon, Sidney Philip Lawrence, 1905–1996, vol. X
Filose, Lt-Col Clement, 1853–1938, vol. III
Filose, Lt-Col Sir Michael, 1836–1925, vol. II
Filson, Alexander Warnock Andrew, 1913–1986, vol. VIII
Finberg, Alexander Joseph, 1866–1939, vol. III
Finberg, Herbert Patrick Reginald, 1900–1974, vol. VII
Finburgh, Samuel, 1867–1935, vol. III
Fincastle, Viscount; Edward David Murray, 1908–1940, vol. III
Finch, Charles Hugh, 1866–1954, vol. V
Finch, Sir Ernest Frederick, 1884–1960, vol. V, vol. VI
Finch, Surg. Rear-Adm. Ernest James, 1868–1934, vol. III
Finch, Ven. Geoffrey Grenville, 1923–1984, vol. VIII
Finch, Rt Hon. George Henry, 1835–1907, vol. I
Finch, George Ingle, 1888–1970, vol. VI
Finch, Lt-Col Hamilton Walter Edward, 1868–1935, vol. III
Finch, Sir Harold Josiah, 1898–1979, vol. VII (AII)
Finch, Col John Charles W.; see Wynne Finch.
Finch, Major John Philip Gordon, 1898–1965, vol. VI
Finch, Maj.-Gen. Lionel Hugh Knightley, 1888–1982, vol. VIII
Finch, Peter, (Peter Ingle-Finch), 1916–1977, vol. VII
Finch, Wilfred Henry Montgomery, 1883–1939, vol. III
Finch, Col Sir William Heneage W.; see Wynne Finch.
Finch, Rev. William Robert W.; see Wykes-Finch.
Finch Hatton, Brig.-Gen. Edward Heneage, 1868–1940, vol. III
Finch-Hatton, Hon. Harold Heneage, 1856–1904, vol. I
Finck, Henry T., 1854–1926, vol. II
Finck, Herman, 1872–1939, vol. III
Findlater, Alexander, died 1931, vol. III
Findlater, Jane Helen, died 1946, vol. IV
Findlater, Mary, 1865–1963, vol. VI
Findlater, Richard, (Kenneth Bruce Findlater Bain), 1921–1985, vol. VIII
Findlater, Sir William Huffington, 1824–1906, vol. I
Findlay, Adam Fyfe, 1869–1962, vol. VI
Findlay, Alexander, 1874–1921, vol. II
Findlay, Alexander, 1874–1966, vol. VI
Findlay, Alexander, 1926–1990, vol. VIII
Findlay, Alexander John, 1886–1976, vol. VII
Findlay, Sir Charles Stewart, 1874–1951, vol. V
Findlay, Sir Edmund; see Findlay, Sir J. E. R.

Findlay, Col George de Cardonnel Elmsall, 1889–1967, vol. VI
Findlay, Rev. George Gillanders, 1849–1919, vol. II
Findlay, George Hugo, 1888–1966, vol. VI
Findlay, George William Marshall, 1893–1952, vol. V
Findlay, Col Harold, 1875–1939, vol. III
Findlay, Harriet, (Lady Findlay), died 1954, vol. V
Findlay, Comdr James Buchanan, 1895–1983, vol. VIII
Findlay, James Thomas, 1875–1927, vol. II
Findlay, Surg.-Maj. John, 1851–1920, vol. II
Findlay, Col John, 1869–1946, vol. IV
Findlay, Sir (John) Edmund (Ritchie), 2nd Bt, 1902–1962, vol. VI
Findlay, Hon. Sir John George, 1862–1929, vol. III
Findlay, John Niemeyer, 1903–1987, vol. VIII
Findlay, John Ritchie, 1824–1898, vol. I
Findlay, Sir John Ritchie, 1st Bt, 1866–1930, vol. III
Findlay, Joseph John, 1860–1940, vol. III
Findlay, Leonard, 1878–1947, vol. IV
Findlay, Sir Mansfeldt de Cardonnel, 1861–1932, vol. III
Findlay, Brig.-Gen. Neil Douglas, 1859–1914, vol. I
Findlay, Lt-Col Sir Ronald Lewis, 3rd Bt, 1903–1979, vol. VII
Findlay, William, 1880–1953, vol. V
Findlay, Lt-Col William Henri de la Tour d'Auvergne, 1864–1941, vol. IV
Findlay-Hamilton, George Douglas, 1861–1941, vol. IV
Findon, Benjamin William, 1859–1943, vol. IV
Finegan, Most Rev. Patrick, 1858–1937, vol. III
Finer, Herman, 1898–1969, vol. VI
Finer, Sir Morris, 1917–1974, vol. VII
Finer, Samuel Edward, 1915–1993, vol. IX
Fingall, 11th Earl of, 1859–1929, vol. III
Fingall, 12th Earl of, 1896–1984, vol. VIII
Fingerhut, John Hyman, 1910–1996, vol. X
Fink, Hon. Theodore, 1855–1942, vol. IV
Finlaison, Alexander John, 1840–1900, vol. I
Finlaison, Brig. Alexander Montagu, 1904–1989, vol. VIII
Finlaison, Maj.-Gen. John Bruce, 1870–1950, vol. IV
Finlay, 1st Viscount, 1842–1929, vol. III
Finlay, 2nd Viscount, 1875–1945, vol. IV
Finlay, Bernard, 1913–1980, vol. VII(AII)
Finlay, Sir (Campbell) Kirkman, 1875–1937, vol. III
Finlay, Maj.-Gen. Charles Hector, 1910–1993, vol. IX
Finlay, David White, died 1923, vol. II
Finlay, Sir George Panton, 1886–1970, vol. VI (AII)
Finlay, Sir Graeme Bell, 1st Bt, 1917–1987, vol. VIII
Finlay, Ian; see Finlay, W. I. R.
Finlay, Ian Archibald, 1878–1925, vol. II
Finlay, James Fairbairn, died, 1930, vol. III
Finlay, Jane Little (Sheena), 1917–1985, vol. VIII
Finlay, Major John, 1833–1912, vol. I
Finlay, Very Rev. John, 1842–1921, vol. II
Finlay, John Alexander Robertson, 1917–1989, vol. VIII

Finlay, John Euston Bell, 1908–1982, vol. VIII
Finlay, Sir Kirkman, *see* Finlay, Sir C. K.
Finlay, Rev. Peter, 1851–1929, vol. III
Finlay, Sheena; *see* Finlay, J. L.
Finlay, Rev. Thomas A., 1848–1940, vol. III
Finlay, Thomas Victor William, 1899–1980, vol. VII
Finlay, (William) Ian (Robertson), 1906–1995, vol. IX
Finlay-Freundlich, Erwin, 1885–1964, vol. VI
Finlayson, Maj.-Gen. Forbes; *see* Finlayson, Maj.-Gen. W. F.
Finlayson, George Daniel, 1882–1955, vol. V
Finlayson, Surg. Captain Henry William, 1864–1944, vol. IV
Finlayson, Horace Courtenay Forbes, 1885–1969, vol. VI
Finlayson, Air Vice-Marshal James Richmond G.; *see* Gordon-Finlayson.
Finlayson, John Rankine, *died* 1935, vol. III
Finlayson, Lt-Col Robert Alexander, 1857–1940, vol. III
Finlayson, General Sir Robert G.; *see* Gordon-Finlayson.
Finlayson, Lt-Col Walter Taylor, 1877–1928, vol. II
Finlayson, Maj.-Gen. (William) Forbes, 1911–1989, vol. VIII
Finletter, Hon. Thomas Knight, 1893–1980, vol. VII
Finley, David Edward, 1890–1977, vol. VII
Finley, Frederick Gault, 1861–1940, vol. III
Finley, John Huston, 1863–1940, vol. III
Finley, Sir Moses, 1912–1986, vol. VIII
Finley, Sir Peter Hamilton, 1919–1994, vol. IX
Finlow, Robert Steel, 1877–1953, vol. V
Finn, Alexander, 1847–1919, vol. II
Finn, Donovan Bartley, 1900–1982, vol. VIII
Finn, Frank, 1868–1932, vol. III
Finn, Brig.-Gen. Harry, 1852–1924, vol. II
Finnegan, Thomas, 1901–1964, vol. VI
Finnemore, Sir Donald Leslie, 1889–1974, vol. VII
Finnemore, Joseph, 1860–1939, vol. III
Finnemore, Robert Isaac, 1842–1906, vol. I
Finney, Jarlath John, 1930–1999, vol. X
Finney, Samuel, 1857–1935, vol. III
Finney, Sir Stephen, 1852–1924, vol. II
Finney, Victor Harold, *died* 1970, vol. VI
Finnigan, Surg. Rear-Adm. Charles Joseph, 1901–1967, vol. VI
Finnis, Adm. Frank, 1851–1918, vol. II
Finnis, Col Frank Alexander, 1880–1941, vol. IV
Finnis, Col Henry, 1853–1929, vol. III
Finnis, Gen. Sir Henry, 1890–1945, vol. IV
Finnis, Rev. Herbert Robert, 1854–1936, vol. III
Finnis, Sidney Alexander, 1908–1969, vol. VI
Finniston, Sir (Harold) Montague, (Sir Monty), 1912–1991, vol. IX
Finniston, Sir Monty; *see* Finniston, Sir H. M.
Finny, Maj.-Gen. Charles Morgan, 1886–1955, vol. V
Finny, John Magee, 1841–1922, vol. II
Finot, Jean, 1856–1922, vol. II
Finsberg, Baron (Life Peer); Geoffrey Finsberg, 1926–1996, vol. X
Finsen, Niels Ryberg, 1860–1904, vol. I
Finucane, John, 1843–1902, vol. I

Finucane, Rt Hon. Michael, *died* 1911, vol. I
Finzi, Gerald, 1901–1956, vol. V
Finzi, Neville Samuel, 1881–1968, vol. VI
Firbank, (Arthur Annesley) Ronald, 1886–1926, vol. II
Firbank, Maj.-Gen. Cecil Llewellyn, 1903–1985, vol. VIII
Firbank, Sir Joseph Thomas, 1850–1910, vol. I
Firbank, Ronald; *see* Firbank, A. A. R.
Firebrace, Comdr Sir Aylmer Newton George, 1886–1972, vol. VII
Firman, Lt-Col Robert Bertram, 1859–1936, vol. III
Firminger, Ven. Walter K., 1870–1940, vol. III
Firth, Sir Algernon Freeman, 2nd Bt, 1856–1936, vol. III
Firth, Arthur Charles Douglas, *died* 1948, vol. IV
Firth, Arthur Percival, 1928–1987, vol. VIII
Firth, Maj.-Gen. Charles Edward Anson, 1902–1991, vol. IX
Firth, Sir Charles Harding, 1857–1936, vol. III
Firth, Col Sir Charles Henry, 1836–1910, vol. I
Firth, Rev. Edward Harding, 1863–1936, vol. III
Firth, Edward Michael Tyndall, 1903–1991, vol. IX
Firth, Sir Harriss, 1876–1950, vol. IV
Firth, James Brierley, 1888–1966, vol. VI
Firth, John B., 1868–1943, vol. IV
Firth, Rev. Canon John D'Ewes Evelyn, 1900–1957, vol. V
Firth, Joseph, *died* 1931, vol. III
Firth, Michael; *see* Firth, E. M. T.
Firth, Col Sir Robert Hammill, 1858–1931, vol. III
Firth, Sir Thomas Freeman, 1st Bt, 1825–1909, vol. I
Firth, Sir William John, 1881–1957, vol. V
Fischer, Rt Hon. Abraham, 1850–1913, vol. I
Fischer, Annie, 1914–1995, vol. IX
Fischer, Edwin, 1886–1960, vol. V
Fischer, Elsa; *see* Stralia, E.
Fischer, Ernst Kuno Berthold, 1824–1907, vol. I
Fischer, Hans, 1881–1945, vol. IV
Fischer, Harry Robert, 1903–1977, vol. VII
Fischer, John, 1910–1978, vol. VII
Fischer, Louis, 1896–1970, vol. VI
Fischer, Percy Ulrich, 1878–1957, vol. V
Fischer, Thomas Halhed, 1830–1914, vol. I
Fiset, Maj.-Gen. Hon. Sir Eugene Marie Joseph, 1874–1951, vol. V
Fiset, Jean Baptiste Romuald, 1843–1917, vol. II, vol. III
Fish, Anne Harriet, (Mrs Walter Sefton), *died* 1964, vol. VI
Fish, Anthony, 1937–1991, vol. IX
Fish, Elizabeth, *died* 1944, vol. IV
Fish, Sir (Eric) Wilfred, 1894–1974, vol. VII
Fish, Sir Hugh, 1923–1999, vol. X
Fish, Ven. Lancelot John, 1861–1924, vol. II
Fish, Stuyvesant, 1851–1923, vol. II
Fish, Wallace Wilfrid B.; *see* Blair-Fish.
Fish, Walter George, 1874–1947, vol. IV
Fish, Sir Wilfred; *see* Fish, Sir E. W.
Fishenden, Margaret White, *died* 1977, vol. VII
Fishenden, Richard Bertie, 1880–1956, vol. V
Fisher, 1st Baron, 1841–1920, vol. II
Fisher, 2nd Baron, 1868–1955, vol. V

Fisher of Camden, Baron (Life Peer); Samuel Fisher, 1905–1979, vol. VII
Fisher of Lambeth, Baron (Life Peer); Most Rev. and Rt Hon. Geoffrey Francis Fisher, 1887–1972, vol. VII
Fisher, A. Hugh, 1867–1945, vol. IV
Fisher, Mrs A. O.; see Peterson, Margaret.
Fisher, Alan Wainwright, 1922–1988, vol. VIII
Fisher, Alfred George Timbrell, died 1967, vol. VI
Fisher, Allan George Barnard, 1895–1976, vol. VII
Fisher, Rt Hon. Andrew, 1862–1928, vol. II
Fisher, Anne; see Fisher, P. A.
Fisher, Mrs Arabella B., 1840–1929, vol. III
Fisher, Arthur Bedford K., see Knapp-Fisher.
Fisher, Brig. Arthur Francis, 1899–1972, vol. VII
Fisher, Ben, died 1939, vol. III
Fisher, Rev. Canon Bernard Horatio Parry, 1875–1953, vol. V
Fisher, Lt-Gen. Sir Bertie Drew, 1878–1972, vol. VII
Fisher, Rev. Cecil Edward, 1838–1925, vol. II
Fisher, Col Cecil James, 1890–1961, vol. VI
Fisher, Brig. Charles Alexander, 1872–1934, vol. III
Fisher, Charles Alfred, 1916–1982, vol. VIII
Fisher, Charles Browning, died 1929, vol. III
Fisher, Hon. Charles Douglas, 1921–1978, vol. VII
Fisher, Major (Hon.) Charles Howard Kerridge, 1895–1987, vol. VIII
Fisher, Maj.-Gen. Donald Rutherford Dacre, 1890–1962, vol. VI
Fisher, Doris Gwenllian, 1907–1998, vol. X
Fisher, Dorothea Frances Canfield; see Canfield, Dorothy.
Fisher, Adm. Sir Douglas Blake, 1890–1963, vol. VI
Fisher, Sir Edward Francis K.; see Knapp-Fisher.
Fisher, Lt-Gen. Edward Henry, 1822–1910, vol. I
Fisher, Edwin, 1883–1947, vol. IV
Fisher, Hon. Francis Forman, 1919–1986, vol. VIII
Fisher, Francis George Robson, 1921–2000, vol. X
Fisher, Francis Marion Bates, 1877–1960, vol. V
Fisher, Col Francis Torriano, 1863–1938, vol. III
Fisher, Frank Lindsay, died 1947, vol. IV
Fisher, Frederic Henry, 1849–1926, vol. II
Fisher, Rev. Frederic Horatio, 1837–1915, vol. I
Fisher, Adm. Sir Frederic William, 1851–1943, vol. IV
Fisher, Vice-Adm. Frederick Charles, 1877–1958, vol. V
Fisher, Frederick Jack, 1908–1988, vol. VIII
Fisher, Frederick Victor, 1870–1954, vol. V
Fisher, Fredy; see Fisher, M. H.
Fisher, Rt Rev. George Carnac, 1844–1921, vol. II
Fisher, George Park, 1827–1909, vol. I
Fisher, Brig. Sir Gerald Thomas, 1887–1965, vol. VI
Fisher, Sir Godfrey Arthur, 1885–1969, vol. VI
Fisher, Captain Harold, 1877–1914, vol. I
Fisher, Harold Wallace, 1904–2000, vol. X (AII)
Fisher, Rt Hon. Herbert Albert Laurens, 1865–1940, vol. III
Fisher, Irving, 1867–1947, vol. IV
Fisher, James Maxwell McConnell, 1912–1970, vol. VI
Fisher, James Neil, 1917–1997, vol. X

Fisher, Inspector-Gen. James W., died 1919, vol. II
Fisher, Rev. John, 1862–1930, vol. III
Fisher, Brig.-Gen. John, 1862–1942, vol. IV
Fisher, Sir John, 1892–1983, vol. VIII
Fisher, John Campbell, 1880–1943, vol. IV
Fisher, John Cartwright Braddon, 1911–1968, vol. VI
Fisher, Maj.-Gen. John Frederick Lane, 1832–1917, vol. II
Fisher, John Henry, 1856–1937, vol. III
Fisher, John Herbert, 1867–1933, vol. III
Fisher, John Lenox, 1899–1976, vol. VII
Fisher, Brig. John Malcolm, 1890–1943, vol. IV
Fisher, Rev. John Martyn, 1873–1939, vol. III
Fisher, John Mortimer, 1915–1999, vol. X
Fisher, Joseph R., 1855–1939, vol. III
Fisher, Lt-Col Julian Lawrence, 1877–1953, vol. V
Fisher, Kenneth, 1882–1945, vol. IV
Fisher, Rt Rev. Leonard Noel, 1881–1963, vol. VI
Fisher, Ven. Leslie Gravatt, 1906–1988, vol. VIII
Fisher, Margery Lilian Edith, 1913–1992, vol. IX
Fisher, Mark, 1841–1923, vol. II
Fisher, Matthew George, 1888–1965, vol. VI
Fisher, Max Henry, (Fredy), 1922–1993, vol. IX
Fisher, Sir Nigel Thomas Loveridge, 1913–1996, vol. X
Fisher, Sir (Norman Fenwick) Warren, 1879–1948, vol. IV
Fisher, Norman George, 1910–1972, vol. VII
Fisher, Mrs. O. H.; see Anderson, Marian.
Fisher, Patricia, (Lady Fisher), 1921–1995, vol. IX
Fisher, Rev. Philip John, 1883–1961, vol. VI
Fisher, (Phyllis) Anne, 1913–1994, vol. IX
Fisher, Rear-Adm. Ralph Lindsay, 1903–1988, vol. VIII
Fisher, Reginald Brettauer, 1907–1986, vol. VIII
Fisher, Richard Colomb, 1923–1992, vol. IX
Fisher, Rev. Robert, 1848–1933, vol. III
Fisher, Rev. Robert, 1855–1938, vol. III
Fisher, Rev. Robert Howie, 1861–1934, vol. III
Fisher, Sir Ronald Aylmer, 1890–1962, vol. VI
Fisher, S. Melton, 1860–1939, vol. III
Fisher, Sophie Florence Lothrop; see Wavertree, Lady.
Fisher, Sir Stanley, 1867–1949, vol. IV
Fisher, Col Stanley Howe, 1891–1967, vol. VI
Fisher, Hon. Sydney Arthur, 1850–1921, vol. II
Fisher, Sydney Humbert, 1887–1980, vol. VII
Fisher, Sylvia Gwendoline Victoria, 1910–1996, vol. X
Fisher, Theodore, 1863–1949, vol. IV
Fisher, Comdr Sir Thomas, 1883–1925, vol. II
Fisher, Rt Rev. Thomas Cathrew, 1871–1929, vol. III
Fisher, Vardis, 1895–1968, vol. VI(AII)
Fisher, Violet Olivia; see Cressy-Marcks, V. O.
Fisher, W. R., 1846–1910, vol. I
Fisher, Rev. Walter Henry, died 1931, vol. III
Fisher, Sir Walter Newton, 1844–1932, vol. III
Fisher, Sir Warren; see Fisher, Sir N. F. W.
Fisher, William Bayne, 1916–1984, vol. VIII
Fisher, Adm. William Blake, 1853–1926, vol. II
Fisher, William James, died 1924, vol. II
Fisher, Adm. Sir William Wordsworth, 1875–1937, vol. III

Fisher, Sir Woolf, 1912–1975, vol. VII
Fisher-Childe, Col Ralph Bromfield Willington, 1854–1936, vol. III
Fisher Prout, Margaret, *died* 1963, vol. VI
Fisher-Rowe, Edward Rowe, 1832–1909, vol. I
Fisher-Rowe, Col Herbert Mayow, 1870–1938, vol. III
Fisher-Smith, Sir George Henry, 1846–1931, vol. III
Fishwick, Lt-Col Henry, 1835–1914, vol. I
Fisk, Sir Ernest Thomas, 1886–1965, vol. VI
Fisk, James Brown, 1910–1981, vol. VIII
Fiske, Baron (Life Peer); William Geoffrey Fiske, 1905–1975, vol. VII
Fiske, Rear-Adm. Bradley Allen, 1854–1942, vol. IV
Fiske, Rt Rev. Charles, 1868–1942, vol. IV
Fiske, Dudley Astley, 1929–1991, vol. IX
Fiske, John, 1842–1901, vol. I
Fisken, Archibald Clyde Wanliss, 1897–1970, vol. VI(AII)
Fison, Alfred Henry, 1857–1923, vol. II
Fison, Sir Clavering; *see* Fison, Sir F. G. C.
Fison, Captain Sir (Francis) Geoffrey, 2nd Bt, 1873–1948, vol. IV
Fison, Sir (Frank Guy) Clavering, 1892–1985, vol. VIII
Fison, Sir Frederick William, 1st Bt, 1847–1927, vol. II
Fison, Captain Sir Geoffrey; *see* Fison, Captain Sir F. G.
Fison, Sir Guy; *see* Fison, Sir W. G.
Fison, Rt Rev. Joseph Edward, 1906–1972, vol. VII
Fison, Sir (William) Guy, 3rd Bt, 1890–1964, vol. VI
Fistoulari, Anatole, 1907–1995, vol. IX
Fitch, Alan; *see* Fitch, E. A.
Fitch, Sir Cecil Edwin, 1870–1940, vol. III
Fitch, Charles Francis, 1860–1947, vol. IV
Fitch, Clyde, 1865–1909, vol. I
Fitch, Ven. Edward Arnold, *died* 1965, vol. VI
Fitch, (Ernest) Alan, 1915–1985, vol. VIII
Fitch, Sir Joshua Girling, 1824–1903, vol. I
Fitch, Marc; *see* Fitch, Marcus F. B.
Fitch, Marcus Felix Brudenell, (Marc), 1908–1994, vol. IX
Fitch, Adm. Sir Richard George Alison, 1929–1994, vol. IX
Fitchett, Very Rev. Alfred Robertson, *died* 1929, vol. III
Fitchett, Frederick, 1851–1930, vol. III
Fitchett, Rt Rev. William Alfred Robertson, 1872–1952, vol. V
Fitchett, Rev. William Henry, *died* 1928, vol. II
Fithian, Sir Edward William, 1845–1936, vol. III
Fitt, Mary; *see* Freeman, Kathleen.
Fitt, Robert Louis, 1905–1994, vol. IX
Fitton, Col Sir Charles Vernon, 1894–1967, vol. VI
Fitton, Col Guy William, 1862–1939, vol. III
Fitton, Hedley, 1857–1929, vol. III
Fitton, Col Hugh Gregory, 1863–1916, vol. II
Fitton, James, 1864–1952, vol. V
Fitton, James, 1899–1982, vol. VIII
Fitts, Sir Clive Hamilton, 1900–1984, vol. VIII
FitzAlan of Derwent, 1st Viscount, 1855–1947, vol. IV

FitzAlan of Derwent, 2nd Viscount, 1883–1962, vol. VI
FitzClarence, Lt-Col Charles, 1865–1914, vol. I
FitzClarence, Hon. Harold Edward, 1870–1926, vol. II
Fitze, Sir Kenneth Samuel, 1887–1960, vol. V
Fitzer, Clyde; *see* Fitzer, H. C.
Fitzer, Herbert Clyde, 1910–1994, vol. IX
FitzGeorge, Rear-Adm. Sir Adolphus Augustus Frederick, 1846–1922, vol. II
Fitzgeorge, Col Sir Augustus Charles Frederick, 1847–1933, vol. III
FitzGeorge-Balfour, Gen. Sir (Robert George) Victor, 1913–1994, vol. IX
FitzGeorge-Balfour, Sir Victor; *see* FitzGeorge-Balfour, Sir R. G. V.
Fitzgerald, Sir (Adolf) Alexander, 1890–1969, vol. VI(AII)
Fitzgerald, Sir Alexander; *see* Fitzgerald, Sir A. A.
FitzGerald, Sir Arthur Henry Brinsley, 4th Bt (*cr* 1880), 1885–1967, vol. VI
Fitzgerald, Brian Percy Seymour V.; *see* Vesey-Fitzgerald.
Fitzgerald, Lt-Col Brinsley, 1859–1931, vol. III
Fitzgerald, Adm. Charles Cooper Penrose, 1841–1921, vol. II
FitzGerald, Charles Edward, 1843–1916, vol. II
FitzGerald, Col Sir Charles John Oswald, 1840–1912, vol. I
Fitzgerald, Charles Patrick, 1902–1992, vol. IX
FitzGerald, Hon. David, 1847–1920, vol. II
Fitzgerald, Denis P., 1871–1947, vol. IV
FitzGerald, Captain Lord Desmond, 1888–1916, vol. II
Fitzgerald, Desmond, *died* 1947, vol. IV
Fitzgerald, Desmond Fitzjohn Lloyd, 1862–1936, vol. III
Fitz-Gerald, Desmond Windham Otho, 1901–1949, vol. IV
Fitzgerald, Sir Edward, 1st Bt (*cr* 1903), 1846–1927, vol. II
Fitzgerald, Edward, 1874–1969, vol. VI(AII)
Fitzgerald, Major Edward Arthur, 1871–1931, vol. III
Fitzgerald, Rev. (Sir) Edward Thomas, 3rd Bt, 1912–1988, vol. VIII
Fitz-Gerald, Hon. Evelyn Charles Joseph, *died* 1946, vol. IV
Fitzgerald, Maj.-Gen. Fitzgerald Gabbett, *died* 1954, vol. V
Fitzgerald, Francis John, 1864–1939, vol. III
FitzGerald, Lt-Col Lord Frederick, 1857–1924, vol. II
Fitzgerald, Garrett Ernest, 1894–1970, vol. VI
FitzGerald, Col George Alfred, 1868–1959, vol. V
Fitzgerald, Sir George Cumming, 5th Bt (*cr* 1822), 1823–1908, vol. I
Fitzgerald, George Francis, 1851–1901, vol. I
FitzGerald, Hon. George Parker, 1843–1917, vol. II
Fitzgerald, Sir Gerald; *see* Fitzgerald, Sir W. G. S. V.
Fitzgerald, Hon. Gerald, 1849–1925, vol. II
FitzGerald, Gerald A. R., 1844–1925, vol. II
Fitzgerald, Lt-Col Gerald James, 1869–1944, vol. IV

Fitzgerald, Brig. Gerald Loftus, 1907–1999, vol. X
FitzGerald, Maj.-Gen. Gerald Michael, 1889–1957, vol. V
Fitzgerald, Sir Gerald Seymour Vesey; *see* Fitz-gerald, Sir W. G. S. V.
FitzGerald, Brig.-Gen. Herbert Swayne, 1856–1924, vol. II
Fitzgerald, James, *died* 1909, vol. I
Fitzgerald, James Foster-Vesey-, 1846–1907, vol. I
Fitzgerald, Sir John, 1857–1930, vol. III
FitzGerald, Hon. John Donohoe, 1848–1918, vol. II
FitzGerald, John Foster V.; *see* Vesey-FitzGerald.
Fitzgerald, John Gerald, 1882–1940, vol. III(A), vol. IV
Fitzgerald, Sir John Joseph, 2nd Bt (*cr* 1903), 1876–1957, vol. V(A)
Fitzgerald, Sir John Peter Gerald Maurice, 3rd Bt (*cr* 1880), 1884–1957, vol. V
Fitzgerald, Rear-Adm. John Uniacke Penrose, 1888–1940, vol. III
FitzGerald, John Vesey V.; *see* Vesey-FitzGerald.
FitzGerald, Marion; *see* FitzGerald, Mrs Robert.
FitzGerald, Lord Maurice, 1852–1901, vol. I
FitzGerald, Sir Maurice, 2nd Bt (*cr* 1880), 1844–1916, vol. II
FitzGerald, Maurice F., *died* 1927, vol. II
Fitzgerald, Rev. Canon Maurice Henry, 1877–1963, vol. VI
Fitzgerald, Maurice Pembroke, *died* 1952, vol. V
Fitzgerald, Michael, 1851–1918, vol. II
Fitzgerald, Lt-Col Oswald Arthur Gerald, 1875–1916, vol. II
Fitz-Gerald, Sir Patrick Herbert, 1899–1978, vol. VII
Fitzgerald, Penelope Mary, (Mrs Desmond Fitzgerald), 1916–2000, vol. X
Fitzgerald, Brig.-Gen. Percy Desmond, 1875–1933, vol. III
FitzGerald, Percy Seymour Vesey, *died* 1924, vol. II
Fitzgerald, Sir Raymond; *see* Fitzgerald, Sir W. R.
FitzGerald, Richard Charles, 1905–1959, vol. V
Fitzgerald, Rt Rev. Richard Joseph, 1881–1956, vol. V
FitzGerald, Mrs Robert, (Marion), 1860–1928, vol. II
Fitzgerald, Sir Robert Uniacke-Penrose-, 1st Bt (*cr* 1896), 1839–1919, vol. II
FitzGerald, Hon. Rowan Robert, *born* 1847, vol. II
Fitzgerald, Seymour Gonne V.; *see* Vesey-Fitzgerald.
Fitz-Gerald, Shafto Justin Adair, 1859–1925, vol. II
FitzGerald, Terence, 1919–1985, vol. VIII
Fitzgerald, Thomas, 1879–1959, vol. V
Fitzgerald, Sir Thomas Naghten, 1838–1908, vol. I
FitzGerald, Lord Walter, 1858–1923, vol. II
Fitzgerald, Walter, 1898–1949, vol. IV
Fitzgerald, Walter, (Walter Fitzgerald Bond), 1896–1976, vol. VII
Fitzgerald, Sir (William) Gerald Seymour Vesey, 1841–1910, vol. I
FitzGerald, Sir William James, 1894–1989, vol. VIII
Fitzgerald, William Knight, 1909–1991, vol. IX
Fitzgerald, Most Rev. William Michael, 1906–1971, vol. VII

Fitzgerald, Sir (William) Raymond, 1890–1964, vol. VI
Fitzgerald, William Walter Augustine, *died* 1936, vol. III
Fitzgerald-Kenney, James C., 1878–1956, vol. V
FitzGibbon, Constantine; *see* FitzGibbon, R. L. C. L-D.
Fitzgibbon, Edmond Gerald, 1825–1905, vol. I
FitzGibbon, Brig. Francis, 1883–1964, vol. VI
Fitzgibbon, Rt Hon. Gerald, 1837–1909, vol. I
FitzGibbon, Gerald, *died* 1942, vol. IV
FitzGibbon, Gibbon, 1877–1952, vol. V
Fitzgibbon, Henry, 1824–1909, vol. I
Fitzgibbon, Henry Macaulay, 1855–1942, vol. IV
FitzGibbon, John, 1849–1919, vol. II
FitzGibbon, (Robert Louis) Constantine (Lee-Dillon), 1919–1983, vol. VIII
Fitz-Hardinge, 2nd Baron, 1826–1896, vol. I
Fitzhardinge, 3rd Baron, 1830–1916, vol. II
Fitzherbert, Basil Thomas, 1836–1919, vol. II
Fitzherbert, Cuthbert, 1899–1986, vol. VIII
Fitzherbert, Maj.-Gen. Edward Herbert, 1885–1979, vol. VII
FitzHerbert, Ven. Henry Edward, 1882–1958, vol. V
Fitzherbert, Adm. Sir Herbert, 1885–1958, vol. V
Fitzherbert, Sir Hugo Meynell, 6th Bt, 1872–1934, vol. III
FitzHerbert, Sir John Richard Frederick, 8th Bt, 1913–1989, vol. VIII
Fitz Herbert, Lt-Col Norman, 1858–1943, vol. IV
Fitzherbert, Rev. Sir Richard, 5th Bt, 1846–1906, vol. I
Fitzherbert, Sir William, 7th Bt, 1874–1963, vol. VI
Fitzherbert-Brockholes, John William, 1889–1963, vol. VI
Fitzherbert-Brockholes, Michael John, 1920–1998, vol. X
Fitzherbert-Brockholes, William Joseph, 1851–1924, vol. II
Fitzhugh, Maj.-Gen. Alfred, 1837–1929, vol. III
FitzHugh, James, 1917–1989, vol. VIII
Fitzhugh, Captain Terrick Charles, 1876–1939, vol. III
Fitzmaurice, 1st Baron, 1846–1935, vol. III
Fitzmaurice, Lt-Col Sir Desmond FitzJohn, 1893–1991, vol. IX
Fitzmaurice, Sir Gerald Gray, 1901–1982, vol. VIII
Fitzmaurice, Gerald Henry, 1865–1939, vol. III
Fitzmaurice, Rev. Sir Henry, 1886–1952, vol. V
Fitzmaurice, Sir Maurice, 1861–1924, vol. II
Fitz Maurice, Vice-Adm. Sir Maurice Swynfen, 1870–1927, vol. II
Fitzmaurice, Nicholas, 1887–1960, vol. V
Fitzmaurice, Vice-Adm. Sir Raymond, 1878–1943, vol. IV
Fitzmaurice, Brig.-Gen. Robert, 1866–1952, vol. V
Fitzpatrick, Rt Rev. Mgr Bartholomew, 1847–1925, vol. II
Fitzpatrick, Rt Hon. Sir Charles, 1851–1942, vol. IV
FitzPatrick, Air Cdre David Beatty, 1920–1997, vol. X
Fitzpatrick, Sir Dennis, 1837–1920, vol. II
Fitzpatrick, Brig.-Gen. Sir (Ernest) Richard, 1878–1949, vol. IV

FitzPatrick, Lt-Col Geoffrey Henry Julian, 1873–1939, vol. III
Fitz Patrick, Herbert Lindsay, 1868–1949, vol. IV
Fitz-Patrick, Horace James, 1894–1967, vol. VI
Fitzpatrick, Sir James Alexander Ossory, 1879–1937, vol. III
Fitzpatrick, Sir (James) Percy, 1862–1931, vol. III
Fitzpatrick, Brig. Noel Trew, 1888–1938, vol. III
Fitzpatrick, Sir Percy; see Fitzpatrick, Sir J. P.
Fitzpatrick, Brig.-Gen. Sir Richard; see Fitzpatrick, Brig.-Gen. Sir E. R.
Fitzpatrick, Rev. Thomas Cecil, 1861–1931, vol. III
Fitzpatrick, Thomas William, died 1965, vol. VI
Fitzpatrick, William Francis Joseph, 1854–1940, vol. III
Fitzroy, Sir Almeric William, 1851–1935, vol. III
FitzRoy, Charles, 1904–1989, vol. VIII
Fitzroy, Rev. Lord Charles Edward, 1857–1911, vol. I
FitzRoy, Sir Charles Edward, 1876–1954, vol. V
Fitzroy, Captain Rt Hon. Edward Algernon, 1869–1943, vol. IV
FitzRoy, Lord Frederick John, 1823–1919, vol. II
Fitzsimmons, William J., 1845–1913, vol. I
Fitzsimmons, Rt Hon. William Kennedy, 1909–1992, vol. IX
Fitzsimons, Frederick William, 1875–1951, vol. V
Fitzsimons, Robert Allen, 1892–1978, vol. VII
Fitzwalter, 20th Baron, 1860–1932, vol. III
Fitzwilliam, 6th Earl, 1815–1902, vol. I
Fitzwilliam, 7th Earl, 1872–1943, vol. IV
Fitzwilliam, 8th Earl, 1910–1948, vol. IV
Fitzwilliam, 9th Earl, 1883–1952, vol. V
Fitzwilliam, 10th Earl, 1904–1979, vol. VII
Fitzwilliam, Captain Hon. Sir Charles Wentworth-; see Fitzwilliam, Captain Hon. Sir W. C. W.
Fitzwilliam, George Charles Wentworth-, died 1935, vol. III
Fitzwilliam, Captain Hon. Sir (William) Charles (Wentworth-, 1848–1925, vol. II
Fitzwilliam, Hon. William Henry Wentworth-, 1840–1920, vol. II
Fitzwilliams, Duncan Campbell Lloyd, 1878–1954, vol. V
Fitzwilliams, Col Edward Crawford Lloyd, 1872–1936, vol. III
Fitzwygram, Sir Frederick Loftus Francis, 5th Bt, 1884–1920, vol. II
Fitzwygram, Sir Frederick Wellington John, 4th Bt, 1823–1904, vol. I
Flack, Harvey, 1912–1966, vol. VI
Flack, Martin, 1882–1931, vol. III
Fladgate, Maj.-Gen. Courtenay William, 1890–1958, vol. V
Fladgate, Sir Francis; see Fladgate, Sir W. F.
Fladgate, Sir (William) Francis, 1853–1937, vol. III
Flagstad, Kirsten, 1895–1962, vol. VI
Flaherty, Robert Joseph, 1884–1951, vol. V
Flahiff, His Eminence Cardinal George Bernard, 1905–1989, vol. VIII
Flammarion, Camille, 1842–1925, vol. II
Flanagan, Lt-Col Edward Martyn Woulfe, 1870–1954, vol. V
Flanagan, Rev. J., 1851–1918, vol. II
Flanagan, William Henry, 1871–1944, vol. IV

Flanders, Allan David, 1910–1973, vol. VII
Flanders, Dennis, 1915–1994, vol. IX
Flanders, Michael Henry, 1922–1975, vol. VII
Flandin, Pierre Etienne, 1889–1958, vol. V
Flannery, Sir Harold Fortescue, 2nd Bt, 1883–1959, vol. V
Flannery, Sir James F.; see Fortescue-Flannery.
Flather, James Henry, 1853–1928, vol. II
Flatley, Derek Comedy, 1920–1991, vol. IX
Flatt, Leslie Neeve, 1889–1957, vol. V
Flavell, Geoffrey, 1913–1994, vol. IX
Flavelle, Sir David; see Flavelle, Sir J. D. E
Flavelle, Sir Ellsworth; see Flavelle, Sir J. E.
Flavelle, Sir (Joseph) David (Ellsworth), 3rd Bt, 1921–1985, vol. IX (AI)
Flavelle, Sir (Joseph) Ellsworth, 2nd Bt, 1892–1977, vol. VII
Flavelle, Sir Joseph Wesley, 1st Bt, 1858–1939, vol. III
Flavin, Michael Joseph, 1861–1944, vol. IV
Flaxman, Brig. Sir Hubert James Marlowe, 1893–1976, vol. VII
Fleck, 1st Baron, 1889–1968, vol. VI
Flecker, H. L. O., 1896–1958, vol. V
Flecker, Rev. William Herman, 1859–1941, vol. IV
Fleet, Rear-Adm. Ernest James, 1850–1935, vol. III
Fleet, George Rutland B., see Barrington-Fleet.
Fleet, Vice-Adm. Henry Louis, 1850–1923, vol. II
Fleet, John Faithfull, 1847–1917, vol. II
Fleet, Kenneth George, 1929–2000, vol. X
Fleetwood, Susan Maureen, 1944–1995, vol. IX
Fleetwood-Hesketh, Charles Hesketh; see Hesketh.
Fleetwood-Hesketh, Peter; see Hesketh.
Fleetwood-Walker, Bernard, 1893–1965, vol. VI
Fleischmann, Louis, 1868–1954, vol. V
Fleming, Hon. Lord; David Pinkerton Fleming, 1877–1944, vol. IV
Fleming, Sir Alexander, 1881–1955, vol. V
Fleming, Sir Ambrose; see Fleming, Sir J. A.
Fleming, Amy Margaret, died 1981, vol. VIII
Fleming, Sir Andrew Fleming Hudleston le, 8th Bt, 1855–1925, vol. II
Fleming, Rev. Archibald, 1863–1941, vol. IV
Fleming, Rt Rev. Archibald Lang, 1883–1953, vol. V
Fleming, Col Archibald Nicol, 1870–1948, vol. IV
Fleming, Sir Arthur Percy Morris, 1881–1960, vol. V
Fleming, Dame Celia; see Johnson.
Fleming, Sir Charles Alexander, 1916–1987, vol. VIII
Fleming, Major Charles Christie, 1864–1917, vol. II
Fleming, Charles James, 1839–1904, vol. I
Fleming, Charles Mann, 1904–1985, vol. VIII
Fleming, Rev. David, died 1920, vol. II
Fleming, David Hay, 1849–1931, vol. III
Fleming, David Pinkerton; see Fleming, Hon. Lord.
Fleming, Hon. Donald Methuen, 1905–1986, vol. VIII
Fleming, Dorothy Leigh; see Sayers, D. L.
Fleming, Edward G.; see Gibson Fleming.
Fleming, Edward Lascelles, died 1950, vol. IV
Fleming, Edward Vandermere, 1869–1947, vol. IV
Fleming, Sir Francis, 1842–1922, vol. II
Fleming, Col Frank, 1876–1964, vol. VI

Fleming, Frederick, vol. II
Fleming, Geoffrey Balmanno, 1882–1952, vol. V
Fleming, George; see Fletcher, Constance.
Fleming, George, 1833–1901, vol. I
Fleming, Maj.-Gen. George, 1879–1957, vol. V
Fleming, Rev. Herbert James, 1873–1926, vol. II
Fleming, Horace, 1872–1941, vol. IV
Fleming, Very Rev. Horace Townsend, *died* 1909, vol. I
Fleming, Ian, 1906–1994, vol. IX
Fleming, Ian Lancaster, 1908–1964, vol. VI
Fleming, Rev. James, *died* 1908, vol. I
Fleming, James, 1841–1922, vol. II
Fleming, James Alexander, 1855–1926, vol. II
Fleming, Rev. James George Grant, 1895–1978, vol. VII
Fleming, Sir John, 1847–1925, vol. II
Fleming, Rear-Adm. Sir John, 1904–1994, vol. IX
Fleming, Sir (John) Ambrose, 1849–1945, vol. IV
Fleming, Rev. John Dick, *died* 1938, vol. III
Fleming, Col John Gibson, 1880–1936, vol. III
Fleming, Lt-Col John Kenneth Sprot, 1874–1944, vol. IV
Fleming, John Marcus, 1911–1976, vol. VII
Fleming, Rev. John Robert, 1858–1937, vol. III
Fleming, Rt Rev. Launcelot; see Fleming, Rt Rev. W. L. S.
Fleming, Marston Greig, 1913–1982, vol. VIII
Fleming, Maxwell, 1871–1935, vol. III
Fleming, Patrick D., *died* 1928, vol. II
Fleming, Patrick Lyons, 1905–1985, vol. VIII
Fleming, Peter; see Fleming, R. P.
Fleming, Major Philip, 1889–1971, vol. VII
Fleming, Richard Evelyn, 1911–1977, vol. VII
Fleming, Robert, 1845–1933, vol. III
Fleming, Robert Alexander, 1862–1947, vol. IV
Fleming, (Robert) Peter, 1907–1971, vol. VII
Fleming, Lt-Col Samuel, 1865–1925, vol. II
Fleming, Sir Sandford, 1827–1915, vol. I
Fleming, Sir Thomas Henry, 1863–1933, vol. III
Fleming, Valentine, 1882–1917, vol. II
Fleming, Wilfrid Louis Remi, 1869–1944, vol. IV
Fleming, William Arnot, 1879–1970, vol. VI
Fleming, Rt Rev. (William) Launcelot (Scott), 1906–1990, vol. VIII
Fleming-Bernard, Andrew Milroy, 1871–1953, vol. V
Fleming-Sandes, Alfred James Terence, 1894–1961, vol. VI
Flemington, Roger, 1932–1994, vol. IX
Flemington, Rev. William Frederick, 1901–1991, vol. IX
Flemming, Cecil Wood, 1902–1981, vol. VIII
Flemming, Sir Gilbert Nicolson, 1897–1981, vol. VIII
Flemming, Hon. James Kidd, 1868–1927, vol. II
Flemming, Percy, *died* 1941, vol. IV
Flemwell, George Jackson, 1865–1928, vol. II
Flenley, Ralph, 1886–1969, vol. VI
Flers, Marquis de, (Robert de Flers), 1872–1927, vol. II
Fletcher, Baron (Life Peer); Eric George Molyneux Fletcher, 1903–1990, vol. VIII
Fletcher, Hon. Sir Alan Roy, 1907–1991, vol. IX
Fletcher, Air Cdre Albert, *died* 1956, vol. V

Fletcher, Sir Alexander MacPherson, (Sir Alex Fletcher), 1929–1989, vol. VIII
Fletcher, Alfred Ewen, 1841–1915, vol. I
Fletcher, Sir Angus Somerville, 1883–1960, vol. V
Fletcher, Col Archibald Ian, 1924–1995, vol. IX
Fletcher, Sir (Arthur George) Murchison, 1878–1954, vol. V
Fletcher, Banister, 1833–1899, vol. I
Fletcher, Sir Banister Flight, *died* 1953, vol. V
Fletcher, Basil Alais, 1900–1983, vol. VIII
Fletcher, Benton; see Fletcher, G. H. B.
Fletcher, Sir Carteret Ernest, 1868–1934, vol. III
Fletcher, Charles Brunsdon, 1859–1946, vol. IV
Fletcher, Charles John, 1843–1914, vol. I
Fletcher, Charles Montague, 1911–1995, vol. IX
Fletcher, Charles Robert Leslie, 1857–1934, vol. III
Fletcher, Clarence George Eugene, 1875–1929, vol. III
Fletcher, Constance, 1858–1938, vol. III
Fletcher, Rev. Canon Denis, 1881–1942, vol. IV
Fletcher, Hon. Edward Ernest, vol. II
Fletcher, Surg. Rear-Adm. Edward Ernest, 1886–1968, vol. VI
Fletcher, Edward Joseph, 1911–1983, vol. VIII
Fletcher, Sir (Edward) Lionel, 1876–1968, vol. VI
Fletcher, Lt-Col Edward Walter, 1899–1958, vol. V
Fletcher, Sir Ernest Edward, 1869–1940, vol. III
Fletcher, Ernest Tertius Decimus, 1891–1961, vol. VI
Fletcher, Sir Frank, 1870–1954, vol. V
Fletcher, Frank, 1867–1956, vol. V
Fletcher, Frank Morley, 1866–1949, vol. IV
Fletcher, Frank Thomas Herbert, 1898–1977, vol. VII
Fletcher, Geoffrey Bernard Abbott, 1903–1995, vol. IX
Fletcher, George Hamilton, 1860–1930, vol. III
Fletcher, (George Henry) Benton, *died* 1944, vol. IV
Fletcher, Hanslip, 1874–1955, vol. V
Fletcher, Harold Roy, 1907–1978, vol. VII
Fletcher, Lt-Col Sir Henry Arthur, 1843–1925, vol. II
Fletcher, Rt Hon. Sir Henry Aubrey-, 4th Bt, 1835–1910, vol. I
Fletcher, Major Sir Henry Lancelot A.; see Aubrey-Fletcher.
Fletcher, Henry Prather, 1873–1959, vol. V
Fletcher, Herbert Morley, *died* 1950, vol. IV
Fletcher, Herbert Phillips, 1872–1917, vol. II
Fletcher, J. K.; see Kebty-Fletcher.
Fletcher, J. S., 1863–1935, vol. III
Fletcher, Sir James, 1886–1974, vol. VII
Fletcher, James Douglas, 1857–1927, vol. II
Fletcher, Rev. James Michael John, 1852–1940, vol. III
Fletcher, James Thomas, 1898–1990, vol. VIII
Fletcher, Lt-Col John, 1815–1902, vol. I
Fletcher, John, 1827–1903, vol. I
Fletcher, Rev. John Charles Ballett, *died* 1926, vol. II
Fletcher, John Gould, 1886–1950, vol. IV(A), vol. V
Fletcher, Sir John Henry Lancelot Aubrey; see Aubrey-Fletcher.

Fletcher, Sir John Samuel, 1st Bt, 1841–1924, vol. II
Fletcher, Sir Lancelot A.; *see* Aubrey-Fletcher.
Fletcher, Sir Lazarus, 1854–1921, vol. II
Fletcher, Leonard Ralph, 1917–1974, vol. VII
Fletcher, (Leopold) Raymond, 1921–1991, vol. IX
Fletcher, Leslie, 1906–1998, vol. X
Fletcher, Sir Lionel; *see* Fletcher, Sir E. L.
Fletcher, Michael Scott, 1868–1947, vol. IV
Fletcher, Sir Murchison; *see* Fletcher, Sir A. G. M.
Fletcher, Sir Norman Seymour, 1905–1986, vol. VIII
Fletcher, Hon. Sir Patrick Bisset, 1901–1981, vol. VIII
Fletcher, Paul Thomas, 1912–1998, vol. X
Fletcher, Air Chief Marshal Sir Peter Carteret, 1916–1999, vol. X
Fletcher, Rev. Philip, 1848–1928, vol. II
Fletcher, Raymond; *see* Fletcher, L. R.
Fletcher, Rev. Reginald James, 1865–1932, vol. III
Fletcher, Richard Cawthorne, 1916–1986, vol. VIII
Fletcher, Rev. Robert, *died* 1921, vol. II
Fletcher, Ven. Robert Crompton, 1850–1917, vol. II
Fletcher, Sir Walter, 1892–1956, vol. V
Fletcher, Sir Walter Morley, 1873–1933, vol. III
Fletcher, Surg.-Maj. William, 1863–1933, vol. III
Fletcher, Major William Alfred Littledale, 1869–1919, vol. II
Fletcher, William Charles, 1865–1959, vol. V
Fletcher, Rev. Canon William Dudley Saul, 1863–1948, vol. IV
Fletcher, Ven. William Henry, *died* 1926, vol. II
Fletcher, William Younger, 1830–1913, vol. I
Fletcher-Cooke, Sir John, 1911–1989, vol. VIII
Fletcher-Twemlow, George Fletcher; *see* Twemlow.
Fletcher-Watson, P., 1842–1907, vol. I
Flett, Sir John Smith, 1869–1947, vol. IV
Flett, Sir Martin Teall, 1911–1982, vol. VIII
Fleure, Herbert John, 1877–1969, vol. VI
Fleuriau, Aimé Joseph de, 1870–1938, vol. III
Flew, John Douglas Score, 1902–1972, vol. VII
Flew, Rev. Robert Newton, 1886–1962, vol. VI
Flewett, Rt Rev. William Edward, 1861–1938, vol. III
Flexner, Abraham, 1866–1959, vol. V
Flexner, Simon, 1863–1946, vol. IV
Flick, Brig.-Gen. Ccharles Leonard, 1869–1948, vol. IV
Flight, Claude, 1881–1955, vol. V
Flinn, D. Edgar, 1850–1926, vol. II
Flinn, Major William Henry, 1895–1973, vol. VII
Flint, Abraham John, 1903–1971, vol. VII
Flint, Alexander, 1877–1932, vol. III
Flint, Austin, 1836–1915, vol. I
Flint, Charles Ranlett, 1850–1934, vol. III
Flint, Ethelbert Rest, 1880–1956, vol. V
Flint, Henry Thomas, 1890–1971, vol. VII
Flint, Joseph, 1855–1925, vol. II
Flint, Percy Sydney George, (Pip), 1921–1990, vol. VIII
Flint, Pip; *see* Flint, Percy S. G.
Flint, Rev. Robert, 1838–1910, vol. I
Flint, Robert Purves, 1883–1947, vol. IV
Flint, Ven. Stamford R. R.; *see* Raffles-Flint.
Flint, Thomas Barnard, 1847–1919, vol. II

Flint, Sir William Russell, 1880–1969, vol. VI
Flintoff, Lt-Col Thomas, 1851–1907, vol. I
Flitcroft, Sir Thomas Evans, 1861–1938, vol. III
Floersheim, Cecil L. F., 1871–1936, vol. III
Flood, Maj.-Gen. Arthur S.; *see* Solly-Flood.
Flood, Maj.-Gen. Sir Frederick Richard S.; *see* Solly-Flood.
Flood, John Ernest William, 1886–1940, vol. III
Flood, Brig.-Gen. Richard Elles S.; *see* Solly-Flood.
Flood, Chevalier William Henry Grattan, 1859–1928, vol. II
Florence, Lt-Col Henry Louis, 1843–1916, vol. II
Florence, Mary S.; *see* Sargant-Florence.
Florence, Philip Sargant, 1890–1982, vol. VIII
Florey, Baron (Life Peer); Howard Walter Florey, 1898–1968, vol. VI
Flory, Paul John, 1910–1985, vol. VIII
Floud, Bernard Francis Castle, 1915–1967, vol. VI
Floud, Sir Francis Lewis Castle, 1875–1965, vol. VI
Floud, Peter Castle, 1911–1960, vol. V
Flower, Sir Archibald Dennis, *died* 1950, vol. IV
Flower, Group Capt. Arthur Hyde, 1892–1987, vol. VIII
Flower, Benjamin Orange, 1858–1918, vol. II
Flower, Sir Cyril Thomas, 1879–1961, vol. VI
Flower, Desmond John Newman, 1907–1997, vol. X
Flower, Sir Ernest Francis Swan, 1865–1926, vol. II
Flower, Lt-Col Sir Fordham, 1904–1966, vol. VI
Flower, Major Horace John, 1883–1919, vol. II
Flower, Sir Newman; *see* Flower, Sir W. N.
Flower, Robin Ernest William, 1881–1946, vol. IV
Flower, Major Victor Augustine, 1875–1917, vol. II
Flower, Rev. Walker, *died* 1910, vol. I
Flower, Sir (Walter) Newman, 1879–1964, vol. VI
Flower, Sir William Henry, 1831–1899, vol. I
Flowerdew, Herbert, 1866–1917, vol. II
Flowerdew, Richard Edward, 1886–1971, vol. VII
Flowerdew, Spencer Pelham, 1881–1959, vol. V
Flowers, Hon. Frederick, 1864–1928, vol. II
Floyd, Alfred Ernest, 1877–1974, vol. VII
Floyd, Charles Murray, 1905–1971, vol. VII
Floyd, Brig. Sir Henry Robert Kincaid, 5th Bt, 1899–1968, vol. VI
Floyd, Captain Sir Henry Robert Peel, 4th Bt, 1855–1915, vol. I
Floyd, Major Sir John, 3rd Bt, 1823–1909, vol. I
Floyd, John Anthony, 1923–1998, vol. X
Floyd, Sir John Duckett, 6th Bt, 1903–1975, vol. VII
Floyer, Michael Antony, 1920–2000, vol. X
Floyer-Acland, Lt-Gen. Arthur Nugent, 1885–1980, vol. VII
Fludyer, Sir Arthur John, 5th Bt, 1844–1922, vol. II
Fludyer, Col Henry, 1847–1920, vol. II
Flugel, John Carl, 1884–1955, vol. V
Flute, Peter Thomas, 1928–1999, vol. X
Flux, Sir Alfred William, 1867–1942, vol. IV
Flynn, Alfred Axen Leonard, *died* 1943, vol. IV
Flynn, Sir Charles Joseph, 1884–1938, vol. III
Flynn, Hon. Edmund James, 1847–1927, vol. II
Flynn, Sir J. Albert; *see* Flynn, Sir J(oshua) Albert.
Flynn, James Christopher, 1852–1922, vol. II
Flynn, Sir J(oshua) Albert, 1863–1933, vol. III
Flynn, Theodore Thomson, *died* 1968, vol. VI

Flynn, Rt Rev. Thomas Edward, 1880–1961, vol. VI

Foad, Roland Walter, 1908–1978, vol. VII

Foakes-Jackson, Rev. Frederick John, 1855–1941, vol. IV

Foch, Field-Marshal Ferdinand, 1851–1929, vol. III

Foden, Air Vice-Marshal Arthur, 1914–1990, vol. VIII

Foden, William Bertram, 1892–1981, vol. VIII

Foden-Pattinson, Peter Lawrence, 1925–1992, vol. IX

Fogarty, Air Chief Marshal Sir Francis, 1899–1973, vol. VII

Fogarty, Most Rev. Michael, 1859–1955, vol. V

Fogarty, Rt Rev. Nelson Wellesley, 1871–1933, vol. III

Fogarty, Sir Reginald Francis Graham, 1892–1967, vol. VI

Fogarty, Susan Winthrop, 1930–1983, vol. VIII

Fogazzaro, Antonio, 1842–1911, vol. I

Fogerty, Elsie, *died* 1945, vol. IV

Fogg, Albert, 1909–1989, vol. VIII

Fogg, Charles William Eric, 1903–1939, vol. III

Fogg, Ven. Peter Parry, 1832–1920, vol. II

Fogg Elliot, Captain Mark, 1898–1950, vol. IV

Foggie, David, 1878–1948, vol. IV

Foggin, Lancelot Middleton, 1876–1968, vol. VI

Foggin, Myers; *see* Foggin, W. M.

Foggin, (Wilhelm) Myers, 1908–1986, vol. VIII

Foggitt, Mrs T. J.; *see* Bacon, Gertrude.

Fogh, Torkel W.; *see* Weis-Fogh.

Fokker, A. H. G., 1890–1939, vol. III

Foldes, Andor, 1913–1992, vol. IX

Foletta, George Gotardo, 1892–1973, vol. VII

Foley, 5th Baron, 1850–1905, vol. I

Foley, 6th Baron, 1852–1918, vol. II

Foley, 7th Baron, 1898–1927, vol. II

Foley, Blanchard, 1869–1950, vol. IV

Foley, Rt Rev. Brian Charles, 1910–1999, vol. X

Foley, Most Rev. Daniel, 1865–1941, vol. IV

Foley, Sir (Ernest) Julian, 1881–1966, vol. VI

Foley, Major Francis Edward, 1884–1958, vol. V

Foley, Rear-Adm. Francis John, 1855–1911, vol. I

Foley, Col Frank Wigram, 1865–1949, vol. IV

Foley, Guy Francis, 1896–1970, vol. VI

Foley, Rt Rev. Mgr John, *died* 1937, vol. III

Foley, Sir Julian; *see* Foley, Sir E. J.

Foley, Rt Rev. Patrick, 1858–1926, vol. II

Foley, Paul Henry, 1857–1928, vol. II

Foley, Hon. Sir St George Gerald, 1814–1897, vol. I

Foley, Most Rev. William J., 1931–1991, vol. IX

Foley-Phillipps, Sir Richard Foley, 4th Bt, 1920–1962, vol. VI

Folger, Henry C., 1857–1930, vol. III

Folger, Col Karl Creighton, *died* 1941, vol. IV

Foligno, Cesare, 1878–1863, vol. VI

Foljambe, Rt Hon. Francis John Savile, 1830–1917, vol. II

Foljambe, George Savile, 1856–1920, vol. II

Folkard, Charles James, 1878–1963, vol. VI

Folkard, Henry Coleman, *died* 1914, vol. I

Folker, Horace S.; *see* Shepherd-Folker.

Foll, Hon. Hattil Spencer, 1890–1977, vol. VII

Follett, Cathleen; *see* Mann, C.

Follett, Sir Charles John, 1838–1921, vol. II

Follett, Sir David Henry, 1907–1982, vol. VIII

Follett, Lt-Col Gilbert Burrell Spencer, 1878–1918, vol. II

Follett, Lt-Col Henry Spencer, 1866–1940, vol. III

Follett, Lt-Col Robert Spencer, 1882–1941, vol. IV

Follett, Col Robert William Webb, 1844–1921, vol. II

Follett, Samuel Frank, 1904–1988, vol. VIII

Folley, Sydney John, 1906–1970, vol. VI

Follick, Mont, 1887–1958, vol. V

Follows, Sir (Charles) Geoffry (Shield), 1896–1983, vol. VIII

Follows, Sir Denis, 1908–1983, vol. VIII

Follows, Sir Geoffry; *see* Follows, Sir C. G. S.

Follows, Lt-Col John Henry, 1869–1938, vol. III

Fonda, Henry, 1905–1982, vol. VIII

Fontanne, Lynn, 1887–1983, vol. VIII

Fonteyn, Margot; *see* Arias, Dame M. F. de.

Fooks, Sir Raymond Hatherell, 1888–1978, vol. VII

Foord, Francis Layton, 1874–1942, vol. IV

Foord, Rev. James, *died* 1932, vol. III

Foord-Kelcey, Air Vice-Marshal Alick, 1913–1973, vol. VII

Foot, Baron (Life Peer); John Mackintosh Foot, 1909–1999, vol. X

Foot, Arthur Edward, 1901–1968, vol. VI

Foot, Adm. Cunningham Robert de Clare, 1864–1940, vol. III

Foot, Rt Hon. Sir Dingle Mackintosh, 1905–1978, vol. VII

Foot, Hugh Mackintosh; *see* Baron Caradon.

Foot, Rt Hon. Isaac, 1880–1960, vol. V

Foot, Brig.-Gen. Richard Mildmay, 1865–1933, vol. III

Foot, Robert William, 1889–1973, vol. VII

Foot, Stephen Henry, 1887–1966, vol. VI

Foot, Maj.-Gen. William, 1889–1971, vol. VII

Foote, Col F. Onslow Barrington, 1850–1911, vol. I

Foote, Maj.-Gen. Henry Robert Bowreman, 1904–1993, vol. IX

Foote, John Alderson, 1848–1922, vol. II

Foote, Rev. John Weir, 1904–1988, vol. VIII

Foote, Adm. Sir Randolph Frank Olive, 1853–1931, vol. III

Footman, Charles Worthington Fowden, 1905–1996, vol. X

Footman, David John, 1895–1983, vol. VIII

Footner, Col Foster Lake, 1881–1953, vol. V

Foott, Col Cecil Henry, 1876–1942, vol. IV

Foottet, Frederick Francis, *died* 1935, vol. III

Forain, Jean Louis, 1852–1931, vol. III

Forber, Sir Edward Rodolph, 1878–1960, vol. V

Forber, Janet Elizabeth, (Lady Forber), 1877–1967, vol. VI

Forbes, 19th Lord, 1829–1914, vol. I

Forbes, 20th (styled 21st) Lord, 1841–1916, vol. II

Forbes, 21st (styled 22nd) Lord, 1882–1953, vol. V

Forbes, Alexander, 1860–1942, vol. IV

Forbes, Archibald, 1838–1900, vol. I

Forbes, Sir Archibald Finlayson, 1903–1989, vol. VIII

Forbes, Archibald Jones, 1873–1901, vol. I

Forbes, Arthur, 1843–1919, vol. II

Forbes, Maj.-Gen. Arthur, 1869–1930, vol. III

Forbes, Arthur C., 1866–1950, vol. IV

Forbes, Arthur Harold, 1885–1967, vol. VI
Forbes, Hon. Brig.-Gen. Sir Arthur William, 1858–1935, vol. III
Forbes, Athol; see Phillips, Rev. Forbes Alexander.
Forbes, Lt-Col Atholl Murray Hay, 1870–1942, vol. IV
Forbes, Lt-Col Hon. Bertram Aloysius, 1882–1960, vol. V
Forbes of Pitsligo, Sir Charles Edward Stuart-, 12th Bt, 1903–1985, vol. VIII
Forbes, Charles Harington Gordon, 1896–1982, vol. VIII
Forbes of Pitsligo, Sir Charles Hay Hepburn Stuart-, 10th Bt (cr 1626), 1871–1927, vol. II
Forbes, Admiral of the Fleet Sir Charles Morton, 1880–1960, vol. V
Forbes, Sir Charles Stewart, 5th Bt (cr 1823), 1867–1927, vol. II
Forbes of Callendar, Charles William, 1871–1948, vol. IV
Forbes, Sir Courtenay; see Forbes, Sir V. C. W.
Forbes, Daniel, born 1853, vol. II
Forbes, Bt Col Hon. Donald Alexander, 1880–1938, vol. III
Forbes, Sir Douglas Stuart, 1890–1973, vol. VII
Forbes, Rev. Edward Archibald, 1869–1929, vol. III
Forbes, Elizabeth Adela, 1859–1912, vol. I
Forbes, Esther, died 1967, vol. VI
Forbes of Craigievar, Hon. Sir Ewan, 11th Bt, 1912–1991, vol. IX
Forbes, Lt-Col Frederick William Dempster, 1883–1957, vol. V
Forbes, George, 1849–1936, vol. III
Forbes, Sir George Arthur D. Ogilvie-, 1891–1954, vol. V
Forbes, Sir George Stuart, 1849–1940, vol. III
Forbes, Lt-Gen. George Wentworth, 1820–1907, vol. I
Forbes, Rt Hon. George William, 1869–1947, vol. IV
Forbes, Gilbert, 1908–1986, vol. VIII
Forbes, Gordon Stewart Drummond, 1868–1915, vol. I
Forbes, Most Rev. Mgr Guillaume, 1865–1940, vol. III
Forbes, Harry, 1866–1937, vol. III
Forbes, Lady Helen Emily, 1874–1926, vol. II
Forbes, Henry Ogg, 1851–1932, vol. III
Forbes, Hon. Sir Hugh Harry Valentine, 1917–1985, vol. VIII
Forbes of Pitsligo, Sir Hugh Stuart-, 11th Bt (cr 1626), 1896–1937, vol. III
Forbes, Ian, 1914–1996, vol. X
Forbes, Ian Alexander, 1915–1986, vol. VIII
Forbes, Col Ian Rose-Innes Joseph, 1875–1957, vol. V
Forbes, James, 1862–1919, vol. II
Forbes, James Graham, 1873–1941, vol. IV
Forbes, James Wright, 1866–1947, vol. IV
Forbes, (Joan) Rosita, (Mrs Arthur T. McGrath), died 1967, vol. VI
Forbes, John, 1838–1904, vol. I
Forbes, Gen. Sir John, 1817–1906, vol. I
Forbes, John Colin, 1846–1925, vol. II
Forbes, Lt-Col John Foster, 1835–1914, vol. I

Forbes, Col John Greenlaw, 1837–1910, vol. I
Forbes, Lt-Comdr John Hay, 1906–1940, vol. III(A), vol. IV
Forbes, John Houblon, 1852–1935, vol. III
Forbes, Col Sir John Stewart, 6th Bt, 1901–1984, vol. VIII
Forbes, Rev. John T., 1857–1936, vol. III
Forbes, Air Chief Comdt Dame Katherine Jane Trefusis; see Watson-Watt, Air Chief Comdt Dame K. J. T.
Forbes, Mansfield Duval, 1889–1936, vol. III
Forbes, Mrs Muriel Rose, 1894–1991, vol. IX
Forbes, Nevil, 1883–1929, vol. III
Forbes, Captain Hon. Reginald George Benedict, 1877–1908, vol. I
Forbes, Robert Brown, 1912–1989, vol. VIII
Forbes, Robert Jaffrey, 1878–1958, vol. V
Forbes, Col Ronald Foster, 1881–1936, vol. III
Forbes, Rosita; see Forbes, J. R.
Forbes, Stanhope Alexander, 1857–1947, vol. IV
Forbes, Sir (Victor) Courtenay (Walter), 1889–1958, vol. V
Forbes, Hon. Mrs Walter (Eveline Louisa Michell), 1866–1924, vol. II
Forbes, William, 1833–1914, vol. I
Forbes, Sir William, 1856–1936, vol. III
Forbes, William Alfred Beaumont, 1927–1981, vol. VIII
Forbes of Pitsligo, Sir William Stuart, 9th Bt (cr 1626), 1835–1906, vol. I
Forbes, Brig.-Gen. Willoughby Edward Gordon, 1851–1926, vol. II
Forbes-Cockell, Seton, 1927–1971, vol. VII
Forbes-Leith of Fyvie, Sir Andrew George, 3rd Bt, 1929–2000, vol. X
Forbes-Leith of Fyvie, Col Sir Charles Rosdew, 1st Bt, 1859–1930, vol. III
Forbes-Leith of Fyvie, Sir Ian; see Forbes-Leith of Fyvie, Sir R. I. A.
Forbes-Leith of Fyvie, Sir (Robert) Ian (Algernon), 2nd Bt, 1902–1973, vol. VII
Forbes-Robertson, Col James, 1884–1955, vol. V
Forbes-Robertson, Jean, 1905–1962, vol. VI
Forbes-Robertson, John, 1822–1903, vol. I
Forbes-Robertson, Sir Johnston, 1853–1937, vol. III
Forbes-Sempill, Major Hon. Douglas, 1865–1908, vol. I
Forbes-Trefusis, Hon. Henry Walter Hepburn-Stuart-; see Trefusis.
Forbes-Trefusis, Major Hon. John Frederick Hepburn-Stuart-; see Trefusis.
Ford, Ven. A. Lockett, 1853–1945, vol. IV
Ford, Col Arthur, 1834–1913, vol. I
Ford, Arthur Clow, died 1952, vol. V
Ford, Captain Sir Aubrey St C.; see St Clair-Ford.
Ford, Maj.-Gen. Barnett, died 1907, vol. I
Ford, Col Sir Bertram, 1869–1955, vol. V
Ford, Boris, 1917–1998, vol. X
Ford, Sir Brinsley; see Ford, Sir R. B.
Ford, Charles, 1844–1927, vol. II
Ford, Charles Edmund, 1912–1999, vol. X
Ford, Lt-Col Charles Hopewell, 1864–1950, vol. IV
Ford, Cdre Charles Musgrave, 1887–1974, vol. VII
Ford, Rt Hon. Sir Clare; see Ford, Rt Hon. Sir F. C.

Ford, Vice-Adm. Sir Denys Chester, 1890–1967, vol. VI
Ford, Rev. Preb. Douglas William C.; see Cleverley Ford.
Ford, Edmund Brisco, 1901–1988, vol. VIII
Ford, Sir Edward, 1902–1986, vol. VIII
Ford, Edward Onslow, 1852–1901, vol. I
Ford, Elbur; see Hibbert, Eleanor.
Ford, Ernest A. C., 1858–1919, vol. II
Ford, Rev. Ernest Robert, 1863–1942, vol. IV
Ford, Ford Madox, 1873–1939, vol. III
Ford, Sir (Francis Charles) Rupert, 5th Bt, 1877–1948, vol. IV
Ford, Rt Hon. Sir (Francis) Clare, 1830–1899, vol. I
Ford, Hon. Frank, 1873–1965, vol. VI
Ford, Ven. Frank Edward, 1902–1976, vol. VII
Ford, Col Frederick Samuel Lampson, 1869–1944, vol. IV
Ford, Rev. Gabriel Estwick, vol. II
Ford, Brig. Geoffrey Noel, 1883–1964, vol. VI
Ford, Ven. George Adam, died 1930, vol. III
Ford, Rev. George Paget, 1883–1950, vol. IV
Ford, Harold Frank, 1915–1994, vol. IX
Ford, Henry, 1863–1947, vol. IV
Ford, Henry, II, 1917–1987, vol. VIII
Ford, Henry Justice, 1860–1941, vol. IV
Ford, Sir Henry Russell, 2nd Bt, 1911–1989, vol. VIII
Ford, Air Vice-Marshal Howard, 1905–1986, vol. VIII
Ford, Hugh Alexander, 1885–1966, vol. VI
Ford, Isaac N., 1848–1912, vol. I
Ford, Sir James, 1863–1943, vol. IV
Ford, Jeremiah Denis Matthias, 1873–1958, vol. V
Ford, John, died 1917, vol. II
Ford, John, (Sean O'Feeney), 1895–1973, vol. VII
Ford, Maj.-Gen. John Randle Minshull-, 1881–1948, vol. IV
Ford, Joseph Francis, 1912–1993, vol. IX
Ford, Sir Leslie Ewart, 1897–1981, vol. VIII
Ford, Very Rev. Lionel George Bridges Justice, 1865–1932, vol. III
Ford, Sir Patrick Johnstone, 1st Bt, 1880–1945, vol. IV
Ford, Paul Leicester, 1865–1902, vol. I
Ford, Percy, 1894–1983, vol. VIII
Ford, Maj.-Gen. Sir Peter St C.; see St Clair-Ford.
Ford, Raymond Eustace, 1898–1994, vol. IX
Ford, Maj.-Gen. Sir Reginald, 1868–1951, vol. V
Ford, Sir (Richard) Brinsley, 1908–1999, vol. X
Ford, Gen. Sir Richard Vernon Tredinnick, 1878–1949, vol. IV
Ford, Surg.-Gen. Sir Richard William, 1857–1925, vol. II
Ford, Sir Rupert; see Ford, Sir F. C. R.
Ford, Sir Sidney William George, 1909–1983, vol. VIII
Ford, Sir Theodore Thomas, 1829–1920, vol. II
Ford, Brig. Vincent Tennyson Randle, 1885–1957, vol. V
Ford, Walter Armitage Justice, 1861–1938, vol. III
Ford, Adm. Sir Wilbraham Tennyson Randle, 1880–1964, vol. VI
Ford, Rev. Wilfred Franklin, 1920–1999, vol. X
Ford, William, 1821–1905, vol. I

Ford, William Justice, 1853–1904, vol. I
Ford, Worthington Chauncey, 1858–1941, vol. IV
Ford-Hutchinson, Lt-Col George Higginson, 1863–1933, vol. III
Ford-Robertson, Francis Calder, 1901–1993, vol. IX
Forde, Lt-Col Bernard, 1865–1939, vol. III
Forde, Daryll, 1902–1973, vol. VII
Forde, Rt Hon. Francis Michael, 1890–1983, vol. VIII
Forde, Sir Henry J., 1863–1929, vol. III
Forde, Rev. Hugh, died 1929, vol. III
Forde, Col Lionel, 1860–1926, vol. II
Forde, Rt Hon. William Brownlow, 1823–1902, vol. I
Forder, Rev. Frank George, 1883–1930, vol. III
Forder, Henry George, 1889–1981, vol. VIII
Fordham, Sir (Alfred) Stanley, 1907–1981, vol. VIII
Fordham, Edward Snow, 1858–1919, vol. II
Fordham, Sir George; see Fordham, Sir H. G.
Fordham, Sir (Herbert) George, 1854–1929, vol. III
Fordham, Montague Edward, 1864–1948, vol. IV
Fordham, Lt-Col Reginald Sydney Walter, 1897–1976, vol. VII
Fordham, Sir Stanley; see Fordham, Sir A. S.
Fordham, Wilfrid Gurney, 1902–1988, vol. VIII
Fordham, Brig. William Marshall, 1875–1959, vol. V
Fordyce, Alexander D.; see Dingwall-Fordyce.
Fordyce, Catherine Mary, 1898–1983, vol. VIII
Fordyce, Christian James, 1901–1974, vol. VII
Forecast, Kenneth George, 1925–1988, vol. VIII
Foreman, Carl, 1914–1984, vol. VIII
Foreman, Sir Henry, 1852–1924, vol. II
Foreman, James Kenneth, 1928–1980, vol. VII
Forest Smith, John, died 1973, vol. VII
Forester, 5th Baron, 1842–1917, vol. II
Forester, 6th Baron, 1867–1932, vol. III
Forester, 7th Baron, 1899–1977, vol. VII
Forester, Cecil Scott, 1899–1966, vol. VI
Forester, Hon. Charles Cecil Orlando Weld-, 1869–1937, vol. III
Forester, Major Hon. Edric Alfred Cecil Weld-, 1880–1963, vol. VI
Forester, Francis William, 1860–1942, vol. IV
Forester, Lt-Comdr Wolstan Beaumont Charles W.; see Weld-Forester.
Forestier, Amédée, died 1930, vol. III
Forestier-Walker, Sir (Charles) Leolin, 1st Bt, 1866–1934, vol. III
Forestier-Walker, Lt-Col Claude Edward; see Walker.
Forestier-Walker, Sir Clive Radzivill; see Walker.
Forestier-Walker, Gen. Sir Frederick William Edward Forestier; see Walker.
Forestier-Walker, Sir George Ferdinand; see Walker.
Forestier-Walker, Major Sir George Ferdinand; see Walker.
Forestier-Walker, Maj.-Gen. Sir George Townshend; see Walker.
Forestier-Walker, Sir Leolin; see Forestier-Walker, Sir C. L.
Forestier-Walker, Bt-Col Roland Stuart; see Walker.
Forgan, Very Rev. James Rae, 1876–1966, vol. VI
Forgan, Robert, 1891–1976, vol. VII
Forget, Sir Guy Joseph, 1902–1972, vol. VII

Forget, Sir (Joseph David) Rodolphe, 1861–1919, vol. II
Forget, Sir Rodolphe; see Forget, Sir J. D. R.
Forman, Rev. Adam, 1876–1977, vol. VII
Forman, Brig.-Gen. Arthur Baron, 1873–1951, vol. V
Forman, Lt-Col Douglas Evans, 1872–1949, vol. IV
Forman, E. Baxter, died 1925, vol. II
Forman, Harry Buxton, 1842–1917, vol. II
Forman, Brig. James Francis Robert, 1899–1969, vol. VI
Forman, John Calder, 1884–1975, vol. VII
Forman, Justus Miles, 1875–1915, vol. I
Forman, Louis, 1901–1988, vol. VIII
Forman, Rev. Thomas Pears Gordon, 1885–1965, vol. VI
Forman Hardy, Col Thomas Eben, 1919–1989, vol. VIII
Formby, George, 1904–1961, vol. VI
Formby, Myles Landseer, 1901–1994, vol. IX
Formilli, Cesare T. G., died 1942, vol. IV
Formosa, Mgr Canon John, 1869–1941, vol. IV
Formston, Clifford, 1907–1993, vol. IX
Forneret, Ven. George Augustus, died 1927, vol. II, vol. III
Forrer, Ludwig, 1845–1921, vol. II
Forres, 1st Baron, 1860–1931, vol. III
Forres, 2nd Baron, 1888–1954, vol. V
Forres, 3rd Baron, 1922–1978, vol. VII
Forrest, 1st Baron, 1847–1918, vol. II
Forrest, Andrew Bryson, 1884–1951, vol. V
Forrest, Archibald Stevenson, 1869–1963, vol. VI
Forrest, Sir Charles, 5th Bt, 1857–1928, vol. II
Forrest, Major Charles Evelyn, 1876–1915, vol. I
Forrest, Rev. David William, died 1918, vol. II
Forrest, Geoffrey, 1909–1997, vol. X
Forrest, Cdre Geoffrey Cornish, 1898–1996, vol. X
Forrest, George; see Forrest, W. G. G.
Forrest, George, 1922–1968, vol. VI
Forrest, Col George Atherley William, 1846–1904, vol. I
Forrest, George Topham, died 1945, vol. IV
Forrest, Sir George William, 1846–1926, vol. II
Forrest, Gilbert Alexander, 1912–1977, vol. VII
Forrest, Sir James, 4th Bt, 1853–1899, vol. I
Forrest, Lt-Col James, 1859–1939, vol. III
Forrest, Sir James Alexander, 1905–1990, vol. IX (AI)
Forrest, John Samuel, 1907–1992, vol. IX
Forrest, Col John Vincent, 1873–1953, vol. V
Forrest, Sir John William, 1867–1951, vol. V
Forrest, Richard Haddow, 1908–1977, vol. VII
Forrest, Robert Edward Treston, died 1914, vol. I
Forrest, Very Rev. Robert William, died 1908, vol. I
Forrest, Sir Walter, 1869–1939, vol. III
Forrest, Lt-Col William, 1868–1921, vol. II
Forrest, Rev. William, 1867–1936, vol. III
Forrest, Gen. William Charles, 1819–1902, vol. I
Forrest, Sir William Croft, died 1928, vol. II
Forrest, William George Grieve, 1925–1997, vol. X
Forrestal, James, 1892–1949, vol. IV
Forrester, Charles, 1895–1980, vol. VII
Forrester, Rev. Canon John Charles, 1874–1933, vol. III

Forrester, Joseph, 1871–1967, vol. VI
Forrester, Peter, 1864–1941, vol. IV
Forrester, Rev. William Roxburgh, 1892–1984, vol. VIII
Forrester-Brown, Maud Frances, died 1970, vol. VI
Forrow, Air Cdre Henry Edward, died 1959, vol. V
Forsberg, (Charles) Gerald, 1912–2000, vol. X
Forsberg, Gerald; see Forsberg, C. G.
Forsdyke, Sir (Edgar) John, 1883–1979, vol. VII
Forsdyke, Sir John; see Forsdyke, Sir E. J.
Forsey, Charles Benjamin, 1819–1908, vol. I
Forsey, George Frank, 1889–1974, vol. VII
Forsey, Sir John, 1856–1915, vol. I
Forshaw, John Henry, 1895–1973, vol. VII
Forshaw, Thomas, 1888–1976, vol. VII
Forson, A. J., 1872–1950, vol. IV(A)
Forssmann, Werner Theodor Otto, 1904–1979, vol. VII
Forster, 1st Baron, 1866–1936, vol. III
Forster, Lady; (Rachel Cecily), 1868–1962, vol. VI
Forster of Harraby, 1st Baron, 1888–1972, vol. VII
Forster, Lt-Gen. Alfred Leonard, died 1963, vol. VI
Forster, Arnold John, 1885–1968, vol. VI
Forster, Very Rev. Arthur Newburgh H.; see Haire-Forster.
Forster, Lt-Gen. Bowes Lennox, 1837–1919, vol. II
Forster, Sir Charles, 2nd Bt (cr 1874), 1841–1914, vol. I
Forster, Brig. David, 1878–1959, vol. V
Forster, Donald Murray, 1929–2000, vol. X
Forster, Edward Morgan, 1879–1970, vol. VI
Forster, Edward Seymour, 1879–1950, vol. IV
Forster, Brig. Eric Brown, 1917–1997, vol. X
Forster, Rear-Adm. Forster Delafield A.; see Arnold-Forster.
Forster, Major Francis Anson A.; see Arnold-Forster.
Forster, Sir (Francis) Villiers, 3rd Bt (cr 1874), 1850–1930, vol. III
Forster, Lt-Col George Norman Bowes, 1872–1918, vol. II
Forster, Rear-Adm. Herbert Acheson, died 1975, vol. VII
Forster, Comdr Hugh Christopher A.; see Arnold-Forster.
Forster, Rt Hon. Hugh Oakeley A.; see Arnold-Forster.
Forster, Maj.-Gen. John Burton, 1855–1938, vol. III
Forster, John Wycliffe Lowes, died 1938, vol. III
Forster, Lancelot, 1882–1968, vol. VI
Forster, Leonard Wilson, 1913–1997, vol. X
Forster, Sir Martin Onslow, 1872–1945, vol. IV
Forster, Lady Mary Louise Elizabeth; see Hamilton and Brandon, Duchess of.
Förster, Max Theodor Wilhelm, 1869–1954, vol. V
Forster, Norvela Felicia, 1931–1993, vol. IX
Forster, Sir Oliver Grantham, 1925–1999, vol. X
Forster, Sir Ralph Collingwood, 1st Bt (cr 1912), 1850–1930, vol. III
Forster, Ralph George Elliott, 1865–1931, vol. III
Forster, Sir Robert, 4th Bt (cr 1794), 1827–1904, vol. I
Forster, Robert Henry, 1867–1923, vol. II
Forster, Sir Sadler; see Forster, Sir S. A. S.

289

Forster, Sir (Samuel Alexander) Sadler, 1900–1973, vol. VII
Forster, Sir Samuel John, 1873–1940, vol. III
Forster, Sir Thomas Edwards, 1859–1939, vol. III
Forster, Sir Villiers; see Forster, Sir F. V.
Forster, Walter Leslie, 1903–1985, vol. VIII
Forster, Maj.-Gen. William Charles Hughan, 1874–1939, vol. III
Forster, Sir William Edward Stanley, 1921–1997, vol. X
Forster, Rev. William Thomlinson, died 1929, vol. III
Forster-Cooper, Sir Clive, 1880–1947, vol. IV
Forsyth, Andrew Russell, 1858–1942, vol. IV
Forsyth, Ven. David, 1845–1933, vol. III
Forsyth, David, 1877–1941, vol. IV
Forsyth, Lt-Col Frederick Richard Gerrard, 1882–1962, vol. VI
Forsyth, Gordon M., 1879–1952, vol. V
Forsyth, Ian McMillan, 1892–1969, vol. VI
Forsyth, James Alexander, 1921–1968, vol. VI
Forsyth, Lt-Col James Archibald Charteris, 1877–1922, vol. II
Forsyth, John Andrew Cairns, 1876–1935, vol. III
Forsyth, Maj.-Gen. John Keatly, 1867–1928, vol. II
Forsyth, Neil, 1866–1915, vol. I
Forsyth, Rev. Peter Taylor, 1848–1921, vol. II
Forsyth, Robert Sutherland, 1880–1942, vol. IV
Forsyth, Thomas Miller, 1871–1958, vol. V
Forsyth, William, 1812–1899, vol. I
Forsyth, William Douglass, 1909–1993, vol. IX
Forsyth, Major William Henry, 1882–1929, vol. III
Forsyth-Thompson, Aubrey Denzil, 1897–1982, vol. VIII
Forsythe, Clifford, 1929–2000, vol. X
Fort, George Seymour, 1858–1951, vol. V
Fort, Sir Hugh, 1862–1919, vol. II
Fort, Richard, 1856–1918, vol. II
Fort, Richard, 1907–1959, vol. V
Forte, Major Herbert Augustus Nourse, 1868–1938, vol. III
Forter, Alexis Kougoulsky, 1925–1983, vol. VIII
Fortes, Meyer, 1906–1983, vol. VIII
Fortescue, 3rd Earl, 1818–1905, vol. I
Fortescue, 4th Earl, 1854–1932, vol. III
Fortescue, 5th Earl, 1888–1958, vol. V
Fortescue, 6th Earl, 1893–1977, vol. VII
Fortescue, 7th Earl, 1922–1993, vol. IX
Fortescue, Rev. Adrian, 1874–1923, vol. II
Fortescue, Col Archer I.; see Irvine-Fortescue.
Fortescue, Cecil Lewis, 1881–1949, vol. IV
Fortescue, Brig.-Gen. Hon. Charles Granville, 1861–1951, vol. V
Fortescue, Hon. Dudley Francis, 1820–1909, vol. I
Fortescue, Brig.-Gen. Francis Alexander, 1858–1942, vol. IV
Fortescue, George Knottesford, 1847–1912, vol. I
Fortescue, John Bevill, 1850–1938, vol. III
Fortescue, Hon. Sir John William, 1859–1933, vol. III
Fortescue, Laurence Knottesford-, 1845–1924, vol. II
Fortescue, Captain Hon. Sir Seymour John, 1856–1942, vol. IV
Fortescue, Rev. Vincent, 1849–1932, vol. III

Fortescue, Hon. Lady; (Winifred), 1888–1951, vol. V
Fortescue-Brickdale, Sir Charles, 1857–1944, vol. IV
Fortescue-Brickdale, Eleanor, died 1945, vol. IV
Fortescue-Brickdale, John Matthew, died 1921, vol. II
Fortescue-Flannery, Sir James, 1st Bt, 1851–1943, vol. IV
Forteviot, 1st Baron, 1856–1929, vol. III
Forteviot, 2nd Baron, 1885–1947, vol. IV
Forteviot, 3rd Baron, 1906–1993, vol. IX
Forth, Francis Charles, died 1919, vol. II
Forth, Lt-Col Nowell Barnard De Lancey; see De Lancey Forth.
Fortin, Ven. Octave, 1842–1927, vol. II
Fortington, Harold Augustus, 1890–1944, vol. IV
Fortnum, Charles Drury Edward, 1820–1899, vol. I
Fortune, Allan Stewart, 1895–1975, vol. VII
Fortune, Maj.-Gen. Sir Victor Morven, 1883–1949, vol. IV
Forty, Francis John, 1900–1990, vol. VIII
Forward, Ernest Alfred, 1877–1959, vol. V
Forwood, Rt Hon. Sir Arthur Bower, 1st Bt, 1836–1898, vol. I
Forwood, Sir Dudley Baines, 2nd Bt, 1875–1961, vol. VI
Forwood, Sir William Bower, 1840–1928, vol. II
Fosbery, Hon. Edmund Walcott, 1834–1919, vol. II
Fosbery, Lt-Col George Vincent, died 1907, vol. I
Fosbery, Major Widenham Francis Widenham, 1869–1935, vol. III
Fosbrooke, Ven. Henry Leonard, died 1950, vol. IV
Fosdick, Rev. Harry Emerson, 1878–1969, vol. VI
Fosdick, Raymond Blaine, 1883–1969, vol. VI
Foskett, Rt Rev. Reginald, 1909–1973, vol. VII
Foss, Brig. Charles Calveley, 1885–1953, vol. V
Foss, Hubert James, 1899–1953, vol. V
Foss, Rt Rev. Hugh James, 1848–1932, vol. III
Foster, Sir (Albert) Ridgeby, 1907–1973, vol. VII
Foster, Alfred Edye Manning, died 1939, vol. III
Foster, Col Alfred James, 1864–1959, vol. V
Foster, Captain Alwyn, 1874–1953, vol. V
Foster, Rev. Arthur Austin, 1869–1942, vol. IV
Foster, Lt-Col Arthur Wellesley, 1855–1929, vol. III
Foster, Sir Augustus Vere, 4th Bt (cr 1831), 1873–1947, vol. IV
Foster, Sir Berkeley; see Foster, Sir H. W. B.
Foster, Birket, 1825–1899, vol. I
Foster, Rev. Canon Charles, 1907–1972, vol. VII
Foster, Rev. Charles Wilmer, 1866–1935, vol. III
Foster, Sir Clement Le Neve, 1841–1904, vol. I
Foster, Captain Sir Edward, 1881–1958, vol. V
Foster, Edward William Perceval, 1850–1932, vol. III
Foster, Ernest, died 1919, vol. II
Foster, Very Rev. Ernest, 1867–1925, vol. II
Foster, E(rnest) Marshall, 1907–1970, vol. VI
Foster, F(ermian) Le Neve, 1888–1972, vol. VII
Foster, Francis; see Foster, Major R. F.
Foster, Sir Frank Savin, 1879–1964, vol. VI
Foster, Geoffrey Norman, 1884–1971, vol. VII
Foster, George Arthur C.; see Carey-Foster.
Foster, George Carey, 1835–1919, vol. II

Foster, Rt Hon. Sir George Eulas, 1847–1931, vol. III
Foster, Hon. George G., 1860–1931, vol. III
Foster, George Ralph Cunliffe, 1869–1936, vol. III
Foster, Gilbert, 1855–1906, vol. I
Foster, Maj.-Gen. Gilbert Lafayette, 1874–1940, vol. III
Foster, Gordon Bentley, 1885–1963, vol. VI
Foster, Sir Gregory; see Foster, Sir T. G.
Foster, Lt-Col Harold William Alexander, died 1960, vol. V
Foster, Rt Hon. Sir Harry Braustyn Hylton H.; see Hylton-Foster
Foster, Sir Harry Seymour, 1855–1938, vol. III
Foster, Maj.-Gen. Henry Nedham, 1878–1951, vol. V
Foster, Sir (Henry William) Berkeley, 4th Bt (cr 1838), 1892–1960, vol. V
Foster, Herbert Anderton, 1853–1930, vol. III
Foster, Rev. Herbert Charles, died 1926, vol. II
Foster, Rev. Canon Herbert Henry, 1864–1927, vol. II
Foster, Sir Hugh Matheson, 1886–1955, vol. V
Foster, Sir Idris Llewelyn, 1911–1984, vol. VIII
Foster, Ivor, 1870–1959, vol. V
Foster, Rev. James, died 1926, vol. II
Foster, John, 1832–1910, vol. I
Foster, Rev. John, 1898–1973, vol. VII
Foster, John Frederick, 1903–1975, vol. VII
Foster, Sir John Galway, 1904–1982, vol. VIII
Foster, Maj.-Gen. John Hulbert, 1925–1980, vol. VII
Foster, (John) Kenneth, died 1930, vol. III
Foster, John Robert, 1916–1999, vol. X
Foster, John Stuart, 1890–1964, vol. VI
Foster, John Watson, 1836–1917, vol. II
Foster, Rev. Canon John William, 1921–2000, vol. X
Foster, Joseph, 1844–1905, vol. I
Foster, Joshua James, died 1923, vol. II
Foster, Kenneth; see Foster, J. K.
Foster, Leslie Thomas, 1905–1979, vol. VII
Foster, Sir Michael, 1836–1907, vol. I
Foster, Michael George, 1864–1934, vol. III
Foster, Major Montagu Amos, 1861–1940, vol. III
Foster, Sir Montagu Richard William, died 1935, vol. III
Foster, Muriel, died 1937, vol. III
Foster, Maj.-Gen. Norman Leslie, 1909–1995, vol. IX
Foster, Sir Norris Tildasley, 1855–1925, vol. II
Foster, Major Percy John, 1873–1969, vol. VI
Foster, Sir Peter Harry Batson Woodroffe, 1912–1985, vol. VIII
Foster, Philip Stanley, 1885–1965, vol. VI
Foster, Philip Staveley, 1865–1933, vol. III
Foster, Major Reginald Francis, 1896–1975, vol. VII
Foster, Gen. Sir Richard Foster Carter, 1879–1965, vol. VI
Foster, Hon. Richard Witty, 1856–1932, vol. III
Foster, Sir Ridgeby; see Foster, Sir A. R.
Foster, Robert, 1898–1989, vol. VIII
Foster, Robert Frederick, 1853–1945, vol. IV
Foster, Robert John, 1850–1925, vol. II

Foster, Air Chief Marshal Sir Robert Mordaunt, 1898–1973, vol. VII
Foster, Robert Spence, 1891–1947, vol. IV
Foster, Sidney, 1885–1958, vol. V
Foster, Brig. Thomas Francis Vere, 1885–1967, vol. VI
Foster, Sir (Thomas) Gregory, 1st Bt (cr 1930), died 1931, vol. III
Foster, Thomas Henry, 1888–1970, vol. VI
Foster, Sir Thomas Saxby Gregory, 2nd Bt (cr 1930), 1899–1957, vol. V
Foster, Sir Tom Scott, 1845–1918, vol. II
Foster, Brig.-Gen. Turville Douglas, 1865–1915, vol. I
Foster, Vere Henry Lewis, 1819–1900, vol. I
Foster, Major Wilfrid Lionel, 1874–1958, vol. V
Foster, Sir William, 2nd Bt (cr 1838), 1825–1911, vol. I
Foster, William, 1887–1947, vol. IV
Foster, Sir William, 1863–1951, vol. V
Foster, Sir William Edward, 1846–1921, vol. II
Foster, Air Vice-Marshal William Foster Mac-Neece, 1889–1978, vol. VII
Foster, Col William Henry, 1848–1908, vol. I
Foster, William Henry, 1846–1924, vol. II
Foster, Bt-Col William James, 1881–1927, vol. II
Foster, Maj.-Gen. William Wasbrough, died 1954, vol. V
Foster, Sir William Yorke, 3rd Bt (cr 1838), 1860–1948, vol. IV
Foster-Brown, Rear-Adm. Roy Stephenson, 1904–1999, vol. X
Foster Pegg, Rev. Canon Henry, 1857–1940, vol. III
Foster-Skeffington, Hon. Oriel John Clotworthy Whyte-Melville; see Skeffington.
Foster-Sutton, Sir Stafford William Powell, 1897–1991, vol. IX
Foster-Vesey-Fitzgerald, James; see Fitzgerald.
Fothergill, (Arthur) Brian, 1921–1990, vol. VIII
Fothergill, Brian; see Fothergill, A. B.
Fothergill, (Charles) Philip, 1906–1959, vol. V
Fothergill, John Rowland, 1876–1957, vol. V
Fothergill, Philip; see Fothergill, C. P.
Fothergill, William Edward, 1865–1926, vol. II
Fotheringham, Rev. David Ross, 1872–1939, vol. III
Fotheringham, John Knight, 1874–1936, vol. III
Fotheringham, John Taylor, 1860–1940, vol. III(A), vol. IV
Fothringham, Walter Thomas James S.; see Scrymsoure-Steuart-Fothringham.
Fottrell, Sir George, 1849–1925, vol. II
Fouché, Jacobus Johannes, 1898–1980, vol. VII
Fouché, Leo, 1880–1949, vol. IV
Fougasse; see Bird, C. K.
Fouhy, David Emmet, 1891–1967, vol. VI
Foulds, John H., died 1939, vol. III
Foulds, Linton Harry, 1897–1952, vol. V
Foulerton, Alexander Grant Russell, 1863–1931, vol. III
Foulger, Robert Edward, 1899–1969, vol. VI
Foulis, Sir Archibald Charles Liston, 12th Bt, 1903–1961, vol. VI
Foulis, Sir Charles Liston, 11th Bt, 1873–1936, vol. III
Foulis, Douglas Ainslie, 1885–1969, vol. VI

Foulis, Sir William Liston-, 10th Bt, 1869–1918, vol. II
Foulkes, Gen. Charles, 1903–1969, vol. VI
Foulkes, Maj.-Gen. Charles Howard, 1875–1969, vol. VI
Foulkes, Hedworth; see Foulkes, P. H.
Foulkes, P. Hedworth, 1871–1965, vol. VI
Foulkes, Maj.-Gen. Thomas Herbert Fisher, 1908–1986, vol. VIII
Foulsham, Sir Charles Sidney, 1892–1955, vol. V
Fountain, Sir Henry, 1870–1957, vol. V
Fountaine, Vice-Adm. Charles Andrew, 1879–1946, vol. IV
Fournier, Pierre, 1906–1986, vol. VIII
Fournier d'Albe, Edmund Edward, 1868–1933, vol. III
Foweraker, A. Moulton, 1873–1942, vol. IV
Fowke, Frank Rede, 1847–1927, vol. II, vol. III
Fowke, Sir Frederick Ferrers Conant, 3rd Bt, 1879–1948, vol. IV
Fowke, Sir Frederick Thomas, 2nd Bt, 1816–1897, vol. I
Fowke, Sir Frederick Woollaston Rawdon, 4th Bt, 1910–1987, vol. VIII
Fowke, Lt-Gen. Sir George Henry, 1864–1936, vol. III
Fowke, Villiers Loftus Philip, 1887–1940, vol. III
Fowkes, Maj.-Gen. Charles Christopher, 1894–1966, vol. VI
Fowlds, Hon. Sir George, 1860–1934, vol. III
Fowle, Brig. Francis Ernlé, 1893–1969, vol. VI
Fowle, Col Frederick Trenchard Thomas, 1853–1914, vol. I
Fowle, Col Sir (Henry) Walter Hamilton, 1871–1954, vol. V
Fowle, Col John, 1862–1923, vol. II
Fowle, Brig. John Le Clerc, 1893–1978, vol. VII
Fowle, Col Thomas Ernlé, 1862–1932, vol. III
Fowle, Sir Trenchard Craven William, 1884–1940, vol. III
Fowle, Col Sir Walter Hamilton; see Fowle, Col Sir H. W. H.
Fowler, Alfred, 1868–1940, vol. III
Fowler, Maj.-Gen. Charles Astley, 1865–1940, vol. III
Fowler, Lt Charles Wilson, 1859–1907, vol. I
Fowler, Adm. Cole Cortlandt, died 1936, vol. III
Fowler, Lt-Col Edward Gardiner, 1879–1953, vol. V
Fowler, Hon. Ellen Thorneycroft, died 1929, vol. III
Fowler, Maj.-Gen. Francis John, 1864–1939, vol. III
Fowler, Frank James, 1911–1981, vol. VIII
Fowler, George Herbert, 1861–1940, vol. III
Fowler, Sir George Jefford, 1858–1937, vol. III
Fowler, George Merrick, 1852–1935, vol. III
Fowler, Gerald Teasdale, 1935–1993, vol. IX
Fowler, Harold North, 1859–1955, vol. V
Fowler, Sir Henry, 1870–1938, vol. III
Fowler, Henry Hamill, 1908–2000, vol. X
Fowler, Henry Watson, 1858–1933, vol. III
Fowler, Sir James Kingston, 1852–1934, vol. III
Fowler, James Stewart, 1870–1925, vol. II
Fowler, Sir John, 1st Bt (cr 1890), 1817–1898, vol. I
Fowler, Sir John Arthur, 2nd Bt (cr 1890), 1854–1899, vol. I

Fowler, Sir John Edward, 3rd Bt (cr 1890), 1885–1915, vol. I
Fowler, Lt-Gen. Sir John Sharman, 1864–1939, vol. III
Fowler, Rev. Joseph Thomas, 1833–1924, vol. II
Fowler, Matthew, 1845–1898, vol. I
Fowler, Rev. Sir Montague, 4th Bt (cr 1890), 1858–1933, vol. III
Fowler, Peter Howard, 1923–1996, vol. X
Fowler, Sir Ralph Howard, 1889–1944, vol. IV
Fowler, Rees John, 1894–1974, vol. VII
Fowler, Robert, died 1926, vol. II
Fowler, Robert MacLaren, 1906–1980, vol. VII
Fowler, Sir Robert William Doughty, 1914–1985, vol. VIII
Fowler, Ronald Frederick, 1910–1997, vol. X
Fowler, Sir Thomas, 2nd Bt (cr 1885), 1868–1902, vol. I
Fowler, Rev. Thomas, 1832–1904, vol. I
Fowler, Walter B.; see Burroughs-Fowler.
Fowler, William, 1828–1905, vol. I
Fowler, William Alfred, 1911–1995, vol. IX
Fowler, William Hope, 1876–1933, vol. III
Fowler, William Warde, 1847–1921, vol. II
Fowler, Rev. William Weekes, 1849–1923, vol. II
Fowler-Butler, Lt-Col Richard, 1865–1931, vol. III
Fowler-Butler, Maj.-Gen. Robert Henry, 1838–1919, vol. II
Fowler-Dixon, John Edwin, 1850–1943, vol. IV
Fowweather, Frank Scott, 1892–1980, vol. VII
Fox, Rev. Canon Adam, 1883–1977, vol. VII
Fox, Lt-Col Arthur Claude, 1868–1917, vol. II
Fox, Arthur Wilson, 1861–1909, vol. I
Fox, Ven. (Benjamin) George (Burton), 1913–1978, vol. VII
Fox, Bernard Joshua, 1885–1977, vol. VII
Fox, Major Brabazon Hubert Maine, 1868–1940, vol. III
Fox, Rear-Adm. Cecil Henry, 1873–1963, vol. VI
Fox, Captain Charles, 1890–1977, vol. VII
Fox, Sir (Charles) Douglas, 1840–1921, vol. II
Fox, Sir Charles Edmund, 1854–1918, vol. II
Fox, Lt-Col Charles J., 1857–1930, vol. III
Fox, Major Charles Vincent, 1877–1928, vol. II
Fox, Sir Cyril Fred, 1882–1967, vol. VI
Fox, Sir Cyril Sankey, 1886–1951, vol. V
Fox, Sir David S.; see Scott Fox, Sir R. D. J.
Fox, Sir Douglas; see Fox, Sir C. D.
Fox, Douglas Gerard Arthur, 1893–1978, vol. VII
Fox, Hon. Mrs Eleanor Birch W.; see Wilson-Fox.
Fox, Dame Evelyn Emily Marion, 1874–1955, vol. V
Fox, Felicity L.; see Lane-Fox.
Fox, Sir Francis, 1844–1927, vol. II
Fox, Col Francis Gordon Ward L.; see Lane Fox.
Fox, Sir Frank, 1874–1960, vol. V
Fox, Ven. George; see Fox, Ven. B. G. B.
Fox, Rev. George, died 1911, vol. I
Fox, Sir Gifford Wheaton Grey, 2nd Bt, 1903–1959, vol. V
Fox, Sir Gilbert Wheaton, 1st Bt, 1863–1925, vol. II
Fox, H. B. Earle, died 1920, vol. II
Fox, Harold Munro, 1889–1967, vol. VI
Fox, Sir Harry Halton, 1872–1936, vol. III
Fox, Henry Benedict, 1875–1944, vol. IV

Fox, Rev. Henry Elliott, 1841–1926, vol. II
Fox, Sir (Henry) Murray, 1912–1999, vol. X
Fox, Henry Wilson-, 1863–1921, vol. II
Fox, Sir John, 1882–1970, vol. VI
Fox, Sir John Charles, 1855–1943, vol. IV
Fox, Major John Charles Ker, 1851–1929, vol. III
Fox, John Howard, 1864–1951, vol. V
Fox, Sir John Jacob, 1874–1944, vol. IV
Fox, John Junior, 1863–1919, vol. II
Fox, Major Sir John St Vigor, 1879–1968, vol. VI
Fox, John Scott, 1852–1918, vol. II
Fox, John Shirley S.; see Shirley-Fox.
Fox, Joscelyn Plunket B.; see Bushe-Fox.
Fox, Rt Rev. Langton Douglas, 1917–1997, vol. X
Fox, Leslie, 1918–1992, vol. IX
Fox, Sir Lionel Wray, 1895–1961, vol. VI
Fox, Loftus Henry Kendal B.; see Bushe-Fox.
Fox, Col Sir Malcolm, 1843–1918, vol. II
Fox, Sir Murray; see Fox, Sir H. M.
Fox, Patrick Loftus B.; see Bushe-Fox.
Fox, R. Fortescue, died 1940, vol. III
Fox, Richard Hodding, 1876–1966, vol. VI
Fox, Robert Barclay, 1873–1934, vol. III
Fox, Sir (Robert) David (John) S.; see Scott Fox.
Fox, Sir Robert Eyes, 1861–1924, vol. II
Fox, Brig.-Gen. Robert Fanshawe, 1862–1939,
    vol. III
Fox, Sir Sidney Joseph, died 1962, vol. VI
Fox, Terence Robert Corelli, 1912–1962, vol. VI
Fox, Sir Theodore Fortescue, 1899–1989, vol. VIII
Fox, Thomas Colcott, 1849–1916, vol. II
Fox, Rt Rev. Thomas Martin, 1893–1967,
    vol. VI(AII)
Fox, Surg.-Gen. Thomas William, 1830–1908, vol. I
Fox, Uffa, 1898–1972, vol. VII
Fox, Wilfrid S., died 1962, vol. VI
Fox, William, 1928–1991, vol. IX
Fox, William Sherwood, 1878–1967, vol. VI
Fox-Andrews, Norman Roy, 1894–1971, vol. VII
Fox-Davies, Arthur Charles, 1871–1928, vol. II
Fox-Pitt, Douglas, died 1922, vol. II
Fox-Pitt, Maj.-Gen. William Augustus Fitzgerald
    Lane, 1896–1988, vol. VIII
Fox-Pitt-Rivers, Augustus Henry Lane, 1820–1900,
    vol. I
Fox-Strangways, Maurice Walter, 1862–1938,
    vol. III
Fox-Symons, Sir Robert, 1870–1932, vol. III
Fox-Williams, Jack, 1893–1970, vol. VI
Foxcroft, Captain Charles Talbot, died 1929, vol. III
Foxcroft, Frederick Walter, 1858–1916, vol. II
Foxcroft, Miss H. C., died 1950, vol. IV
Foxell, Rev. Maurice Frederic, 1888–1981, vol. VIII
Foxell, Rev. William James, 1857–1933, vol. III
Foxlee, Richard William, 1885–1961, vol. VI
Foxley, Barbara, died 1958, vol. V
Foxon, George Eric Howard, 1908–1982, vol. VIII
Foxton, Maj.-Gen. Edwin Frederick, 1914–1996,
    vol. X
Foxton, Col Hon. Justin Fox Greenlaw, 1849–1916,
    vol. I, vol. II
Foxwell, Arthur, 1853–1909, vol. I
Foxwell, Herbert Somerton, 1849–1936, vol. III
Foy, Ernest Rudolph, died 1951, vol. V
Foy, Hon. James Joseph, 1847–1916, vol. II

Foy, Sir Thomas Arthur Wyness, 1895–1971,
    vol. VII
Foylan, Rt Rev. Michael, 1907–1976, vol. VII
Foyle, Christina Agnes Lilian, (Mrs Ronald Batty),
    1911–1999, vol. X
Foyle, Gilbert Samuel, 1886–1971, vol. VII
Foyle, William Alfred, 1885–1963, vol. VI
Fozard, John William, 1928–1996, vol. X
Fraenkel, Eduard, 1888–1970, vol. VI
Fraenkel, Heinrich, 1897–1986, vol. VIII
Frahm, Herbert Ernst Karl; see Brandt, Willy.
Frame, Sir Alistair Gilchrist, 1929–1993, vol. IX
Frames, Col Percival R.; see Ross-Frames.
Frampton, Algernon de Kewer, 1904–1974, vol. VII
Frampton, E. Reginald, died 1923, vol. II
Frampton, Sir George James, 1860–1928, vol. II
Frampton, Henry James, 1897–1980, vol. VII
Frampton, Meredith, 1894–1984, vol. VIII
Frampton, Rev. Samuel, 1862–1943, vol. IV
Frampton, Walter, 1871–1939, vol. III
Frampton, Walter Bennett, 1903–1981, vol. VIII
France, Anatole, (Jacques Anatole François
    Thibault), 1844–1924, vol. II
France, Sir Arnold William, 1911–1998, vol. X
France, Captain George Frederick Hayhurst H.; see
    Hayhurst-France.
France, Gerald Ashburner, 1870–1935, vol. III
France, Sir Joseph Nathaniel, 1907–1997, vol. X
France, Rev. Canon Walter Frederick, 1887–1963,
    vol. VI
France-Hayhurst, William Hosken; see Hayhurst.
Francia, Col. John Lewis, 1864–1934, vol. III
Francillon, Robert Edward, 1841–1919, vol. II
Francis, (Alan) David, 1900–1987, vol. VIII
Francis, Alfred Edwin, 1909–1985, vol. VIII
Francis, Arthur Gordon, 1880–1958, vol. V
Francis, Augustus Lawrence, 1848–1925, vol. II
Francis, Sir Brooke; see Francis, Sir C. G. B.
Francis, Lt-Col Charles John Henry Watson,
    1879–1959, vol. V
Francis, Charles King, 1851–1925, vol. II
Francis, Sir (Cyril Gerard) Brooke, 1883–1971,
    vol. VII
Francis, David; see Francis, A. D.
Francis, Francis, died 1941, vol. IV
Francis, Sir Frank Chalton, 1901–1988, vol. VIII
Francis, Grant Richardson, 1868–1940, vol. III(A),
    vol. IV
Francis, Very Rev. Henry, died 1924, vol. II
Francis, Herbert William Sidney, 1880–1968,
    vol. VI
Francis, Hugh Elvet, 1907–1986, vol. VIII
Francis, James Schreiber, 1843–1915, vol. I
Francis, Sir John, 1864–1937, vol. III
Francis, Major John, 1879–1960, vol. V
Francis, Lt-Col John Clement Wolstan, 1888–1978,
    vol. VII
Francis, John Collins, 1838–1916, vol. II
Francis, John Gordon Loveband, 1907–1976,
    vol. VII
Francis, Rt Rev. Joseph Marshall, 1862–1939,
    vol. III
Francis, Hon. Sir Josiah, 1890–1964, vol. VI
Francis, Sir Laurie Justice, 1918–1994, vol. X (AI)
Francis, M. E.; see Blundell, Mrs F.

Francis, Major Norton, 1871–1939, vol. III
Francis, Richard Henry, 1897–1961, vol. VI
Francis, Sir Richard Trevor Langford, 1934–1992, vol. IX
Francis, Brig.-Gen. Sidney Goodall, 1874–1955, vol. V
Francis, William Lancelot, 1906–1996, vol. X
Francis-Williams, Baron (Life Peer); Edward Francis Williams, 1903–1970, vol. VI
Francis-Williams, William St John, 1871–1930, vol. III
Franck, Harry Alverson, 1881–1962, vol. VI
Franck, James, 1882–1964, vol. VI
Franck, Sir Louis, 1868–1937, vol. III
Francke, Paul Mortimer, 1866–1929, vol. III
Franckenstein, Baroness Joseph von; see Boyle, Kay.
Franckenstein, Sir George, 1878–1953, vol. V
Francklin, John Liell, 1844–1915, vol. I
Francklin, Comdr (Mavourn Baldwin) Philip, 1913–1999, vol. X
Francklin, Philip; see Francklin, M. B. P.
Francklin, Captain Philip, 1874–1914, vol. I
Franco Bahamonde, General Don Francisco, 1892–1975, vol. VII
François-Poncet, André, 1887–1978, vol. VII
Franey, John Sharman, 1864–1947, vol. IV
Frangulis, A. F., 1888–1975, vol. VII
Frank, Bruno, 1887–1945, vol. IV
Frank, Sir Charles; see Frank, Sir F. C.
Frank, Sir (Frederick) Charles, 1911–1998, vol. X
Frank, Glenn, 1887–1940, vol. III
Frank, Sir Howard, 1st Bt, 1871–1932, vol. III
Frank, Sir Howard Frederick, 2nd Bt, 1923–1944, vol. IV
Frank, Ilya Mikhailovich, 1908–1990, vol. VIII
Frank, Leonhard, 1882–1961, vol. VI
Frank, Sir Peirson; see Frank, Sir T. P.
Frank, Phyllis Margaret Duncan, (Mrs Alan Frank); see Tate, P. M. D.
Frank, Sir Robert John, 3rd Bt, 1925–1987, vol. VIII
Frank, Tenney, 1876–1939, vol. III
Frank, Sir (Thomas) Peirson, 1881–1951, vol. V
Frankau, Sir Claude Howard Stanley, 1883–1967, vol. VI
Frankau, Captain Gilbert, 1884–1952, vol. V
Frankau, Mrs Julia; see Danby, Frank.
Frankau, Pamela, 1908–1967, vol. VI
Frankel, Benjamin, 1906–1973, vol. VII
Frankel, Dan, 1900–1988, vol. IX
Frankel, Herbert; see Frankel, S. H.
Frankel, Joseph, 1913–1989, vol. VIII
Frankel, Sir Otto Herzberg, 1900–1998, vol. X
Frankel, Paul Herzberg, 1903–1992, vol. IX
Frankel, (Sally) Herbert, 1903–1996, vol. X
Franken, Rose Dorothy, 1895–1988, vol. VIII
Frankenburg, John Beeching, 1921–1981, vol. VIII
Frankfort de Montmorency, 3rd Viscount, 1835–1902, vol. I
Frankfort de Montmorency, 4th Viscount, 1868–1917, vol. II
Frankfort, Henri, 1897–1954, vol. V
Frankfurter, Felix, 1882–1965, vol. VI

Frankham, Very Rev. Harold Edward, 1911–1996, vol. X
Frankland, Cecil J., 1884–1942, vol. IV
Frankland, Sir Edward, 1825–1899, vol. I
Frankland, Edward Percy, 1884–1958, vol. V
Frankland, Sir Frederick William Francis George, 10th Bt, 1868–1937, vol. III
Frankland, Grace C., (Mrs Percy Frankland), 1858–1946, vol. IV
Frankland, Percy Faraday, 1858–1946, vol. IV
Frankland, Major Hon. Sir Thomas William Assheton, 11th Bt, 1902–1944, vol. IV
Frankland-Payne-Gallwey, Sir John; see Gallwey.
Frankland-Russell-Astley, Bertram Frankland; see Astley.
Frankland-Russell-Astley, Henry Jacob Delaval; see Astley.
Franklen, Sir Thomas Mansel, 1840–1928, vol. II
Franklin, Alfred White, 1905–1984, vol. VIII
Franklin, Arthur Ellis, 1857–1938, vol. III
Franklin, Surg.-Gen. Sir Benjamin, 1844–1917, vol. II
Franklin, David, 1908–1973, vol. VII
Franklin, Sir Eric Alexander, 1910–1996, vol. X
Franklin, Ernest Louis, 1859–1950, vol. IV
Franklin, Fabian, died 1939, vol. III
Franklin, Sir George, 1853–1916, vol. II
Franklin, George Cooper, 1846–1919, vol. II
Franklin, Bt-Col George Dennne, 1877–1946, vol. IV
Franklin, George Frederic, 1897–1987, vol. VIII
Franklin, Brig.-Gen. Harold Scott Erskine, 1878–1948, vol. IV
Franklin, Hon. Mrs Henrietta, 1866–1964, vol. VI
Franklin, Henry William Fernehough, 1901–1985, vol. VIII
Franklin, Hon. James Thomas, 1854–1940, vol. III
Franklin, John Lewis, 1904–1972, vol. VII
Franklin, Kenneth James, 1897–1966, vol. VI
Franklin, Sir Leonard, 1862–1944, vol. IV
Franklin, Norman Laurence, 1924–1986, vol. VIII
Franklin, Olga Heather, 1895–1987, vol. VIII
Franklin, Philip, died 1951, vol. V
Franklin, Sir Reginald Hector, 1893–1957, vol. V
Franklin, Richard Harrington, 1906–1991, vol. IX
Franklin, Richard Penrose, 1884–1942, vol. IV
Franklin, Col Will Hodgson, 1871–1941, vol. IV
Franklin, Rt Rev. William Alfred, 1916–1998, vol. X
Frankling, Herbert George, 1876–1962, vol. VI
Franklyn, Charles Aubrey Hamilton, 1896–1982, vol. VIII
Franklyn, Brig. Geoffrey Ernest Warren, 1889–1967, vol. VI
Franklyn, Gen. Harold Edmund, 1885–1963, vol. VI
Franklyn, Lt-Gen. Sir William Edmund, 1856–1914, vol. I
Franks, Baron (Life Peer); Oliver Shewell Franks, 1905–1992, vol. IX
Franks, Sir Augustus Wollaston, 1826–1897, vol. I
Franks, Lt-Col George Despard, died 1918, vol. II
Franks, Maj.-Gen. Sir George McKenzie, 1868–1958, vol. V
Franks, Air Vice-Marshal John Gerald, 1905–1995, vol. X (AI)

Franks, Sir John Hamilton, 1848–1915, vol. I
Franks, Sir Kendal, 1851–1920, vol. II
Franks, Col Kendal Fergusson, 1886–1944, vol. IV
Franks, Captain Norman, 1843–1923, vol. II
Franks, Rev. Robert Sleightholme, 1871–1964, vol. VI
Franks, Maj.-Gen. William Astell, 1838–1929, vol. III
Franks, William Temple, 1863–1926, vol. II
Franqueville, Amable Charles Franquet, Comte de, 1840–1919, vol. II
Franzella, Albert, died 1935, vol. III
Franzos, Carl Emile, 1848–1904, vol. I
Fraser of Allander, 1st Baron, 1903–1966, vol. VI
Fraser of Kilmorack, Baron (Life Peer); Richard Michael Fraser, 1915–1996, vol. X
Fraser of Lonsdale, Baron (Life Peer); William Jocelyn Ian Fraser, 1897–1974, vol. VII
Fraser of North Cape, 1st Baron, 1888–1981, vol. VIII
Fraser of Tullybelton, Baron (Life Peer); Walter Ian Reid Fraser, 1911–1989, vol. VIII
Fraser, Agnes Frances MacNab, 1859–1944, vol. IV
Fraser, Major Hon. Alastair Thomas Joseph, 1877–1949, vol. IV
Fraser, Alexander Brodie, 1871–1936, vol. III
Fraser, Alexander Campbell, 1819–1914, vol. I
Fraser, Maj.-Gen. Alexander Donald, 1884–1960, vol. V
Fraser, Rev. Alexander Garden, 1873–1962, vol. VI
Fraser, Alexander Macdonald, 1921–1987, vol. IX (AI)
Fraser, Sir Andrew Henderson Leith, 1848–1919, vol. II
Fraser, Mrs Angela Zelia, (Alice Spinner), died 1925, vol. II
Fraser, Sir Angus, 1909–1963, vol. VI
Fraser, Major Arthur Ion, 1879–1917, vol. II
Fraser, Sir (Arthur) Ronald, 1888–1974, vol. VII
Fraser, Sir Basil Malcolm, 2nd Bt, 1920–1992, vol. IX
Fraser, Sir Bruce Donald, 1910–1993, vol. IX
Fraser, Lt-Col Cecil, 1885–1951, vol. V
Fraser, Sir Charles Frederick, 1850–1925, vol. II
Fraser, Charles Ian, 1903–1963, vol. VI
Fraser, Sir Colin, 1875–1944, vol. IV
Fraser, Colin Neil, 1905–1979, vol. VII
Fraser, Hon. Sir David MacDowall, 1825–1906, vol. I
Fraser, Lt-Col Sir Denholm de Montalt Stuart, 1889–1956, vol. V
Fraser, Very Rev. Donald, 1870–1933, vol. III
Fraser, Donald Blake, 1910–1998, vol. X
Fraser, Sir Douglas Were, 1899–1988, vol. VIII (A)
Fraser, Sir Drummond Drummond, 1867–1929, vol. III
Fraser, Rev. Duncan, 1814–1912, vol. I
Fraser, Duncan, 1880–1966, vol. VI
Fraser, Very Rev. Duncan, 1903–1977, vol. VII
Fraser, Surg.-Maj.-Gen. Duncan Alexander Campbell, 1831–1912, vol. I
Fraser, Sir Edward Cleather, 1853–1927, vol. II
Fraser, Sir Edward Henry, 1851–1921, vol. II
Fraser, Eric Malcolm, 1896–1960, vol. V, vol. VI

Fraser, Sir Everard Duncan Home, 1859–1922, vol. II
Fraser, Francis Charles, 1903–1978, vol. VII
Fraser, Sir Francis Richard, 1885–1964, vol. VI
Fraser, Frederick William, 1870–1936, vol. III
Fraser, Galloway, died 1925, vol. II
Fraser, Rear-Adm. Hon. George, 1887–1970, vol. VI
Fraser, Col George Ireland, 1876–1929, vol. III
Fraser, George M., 1862–1938, vol. III
Fraser, Gilbert, born 1848, vol. II
Fraser, Sir Gordon, 1873–1934, vol. III
Fraser, Captain Gordon Colquhoun, 1866–1952, vol. V
Fraser, Hanson Werry, 1850–1929, vol. III
Fraser, Col Henry Francis, 1872–1949, vol. IV
Fraser, Henry Lumsden Forbes, 1877–1951, vol. V
Fraser, Henry Ralph, 1896–1963, vol. VI
Fraser, Col Herbert Cecil, died 1943, vol. IV
Fraser, Col Howard Alan Denholm, 1867–1948, vol. IV
Fraser, Hon. Sir Hugh, died 1927, vol. II
Fraser, Mrs Hugh, (Mary), 1815–1922, vol. II, vol. III
Fraser, Sir Hugh, 2nd Bt, 1936–1987, vol. VIII
Fraser, Rt Hon. Sir Hugh Charles Patrick Joseph, 1918–1984, vol. VIII
Fraser, Air Vice-Marshal Hugh Henry Macleod, 1895–1962, vol. VI
Fraser, Sir Hugh Stein, 1863–1944, vol. IV
Fraser, Col Hugh Vincent, 1908–1993, vol. IX
Fraser, Sir Ian, 1901–1999, vol. X
Fraser, Ian George Inglis, 1923–1980, vol. VII
Fraser, Captain Ian Mackenzie, 1854–1922, vol. II
Fraser, Ian Montagu, 1916–1987, vol. VIII
Fraser, Very Rev. Ian Watson, 1907–1996, vol. X
Fraser, Rev. James, 1842–1913, vol. I
Fraser, James, 1861–1936, vol. III
Fraser, Rev. James, 1883–1966, vol. VI
Fraser, James Alexander L.; see Lovat-Fraser.
Fraser, Sir James David, 2nd Bt, 1924–1996, vol. X
Fraser, Col James Douglas, 1914–1981, vol. VIII
Fraser, James Duncan, 1915–1965, vol. VI
Fraser, Lt-Col James Johnson, 1876–1939, vol. III
Fraser, Lt-Col James Wilson, 1862–1943, vol. IV
Fraser, John, 1820–1911, vol. I
Fraser, John, born 1852, vol. II
Fraser, John, died 1925, vol. II
Fraser, John, 1882–1945, vol. IV
Fraser, Sir John, 1st Bt (cr 1943), 1885–1947, vol. IV
Fraser, Very Rev. John Annand, 1894–1985, vol. VIII
Fraser, Lt-Col John Edward, 1877–1934, vol. III
Fraser, Sir John Foster, 1868–1936, vol. III
Fraser, Sir John George, 1840–1927, vol. II
Fraser, Sir John George, 1864–1941, vol. IV
Fraser, John Henry Pearson, 1874–1949, vol. IV
Fraser, Sir John Hugh Ronald, 1878–1943, vol. IV
Fraser, Sir (John) Malcolm, 1st Bt (cr 1921), 1878–1949, vol. IV
Fraser, Rear-Adm. John Stewart Gordon, 1883–1973, vol. VII
Fraser, Kate, 1877–1957, vol. V

295

Fraser, Major Sir Keith Alexander, 5th Bt (cr 1806), 1867–1935, vol. III
Fraser, Sir Keith Charles Adolphus, 6th Bt (cr 1806), 1911–1979, vol. VII
Fraser, Kenneth, 1874–1941, vol. IV
Fraser, Sir Kenneth Barron, 1897–1969, vol. VI
Fraser, Kenneth Wharton, 1905–1981, vol. VIII
Fraser, Leon, 1889–1945, vol. IV
Fraser, Lindley Macnaghten, 1904–1963, vol. VI
Fraser, Louis Nathaniel B.; see Blache-Fraser.
Fraser, Lovat, 1871–1926, vol. II
Fraser, Brig.-Gen. Lyons David, 1868–1926, vol. II
Fraser, Sir Malcolm; see Fraser, Sir J. M.
Fraser, Hon. Sir Malcolm, 1834–1900, vol. I
Fraser, Malcolm, 1873–1949, vol. IV
Fraser, Marjory Kennedy, died 1930, vol. III
Fraser, Mary; see Fraser, Mrs Hugh
Fraser, Mary, died 1940, vol. III
Fraser, Sir Matthew Pollock, died 1937, vol. III
Fraser, Captain Norman, 1879–1914, vol. I
Fraser, Rt Hon. Peter, 1884–1950, vol. IV
Fraser, Rt Rev. Robert, 1858–1914, vol. I
Fraser, Sir Robert; see Fraser, Sir W. R.
Fraser, Sir Robert Brown, 1904–1985, vol. VIII
Fraser, Ronald; see Fraser, Sir A. R.
Fraser, Ronald Petrie, 1917–1998, vol. X
Fraser, Russell; see Fraser, T. R. C.
Fraser, Hon. Sir Simon, 1832–1919, vol. II
Fraser, Sir Stuart Mitford, 1864–1963, vol. VI
Fraser, Maj.-Gen. Sir Theodore, 1865–1953, vol. V
Fraser, Maj.-Gen. Sir Thomas, 1840–1922, vol. II
Fraser, Col Thomas, 1872–1951, vol. V
Fraser, Rt Hon. Thomas, 1911–1988, vol. VIII
Fraser, Thomas Cameron, 1909–1982, vol. VIII
Fraser, Sir Thomas Richard, 1841–1920, vol. II
Fraser, (Thomas) Russell (Cumming), 1908–1994, vol. IX
Fraser, Sir William, 1816–1898, vol. I
Fraser, Rev. William, 1851–1919, vol. II
Fraser, Hon. Sir William, 1840–1923, vol. II
Fraser, Brig. Hon. William, 1890–1964, vol. VI
Fraser, William, 1911–1990, vol. VIII
Fraser, William Alexander, died 1933, vol. III
Fraser, Maj.-Gen. William Archibald Kenneth, 1886–1969, vol. VI
Fraser, Sir William Augustus, 4th Bt (cr 1806), 1826–1898, vol. I
Fraser, William Donald, 1890–1941, vol. IV
Fraser, William Henry, 1853–1916, vol. II
Fraser, William Henry, died 1966, vol. VI
Fraser, W(illiam) Lionel, died 1965, vol. VI
Fraser, Sir (William) Robert, 1891–1985, vol. VIII
Fraser, William Stuart, 1876–1954, vol. V
Fraser Darling, Sir Frank, 1903–1979, vol. VII
Fraser-Harris, David Fraser, 1867–1937, vol. III
Fraser Roberts, John Alexander; see Roberts.
Fraser-Simson, Harold, 1878–1944, vol. IV
Fraser-Tytler, Christian Helen, 1897–1995, vol. IX
Fraser-Tytler, Edward Grant, 1856–1918, vol. II
Fraser-Tytler, Gen. Sir James Macleod Bannatyne, 1821–1914, vol. I
Fraser-Tytler, Bt Col Neil, 1889–1937, vol. III
Fraser-Tytler, Lt-Col Sir William Kerr, 1886–1963, vol. VI
Frayling, Frederick George, born 1846, vol. II

Frazer, Alastair Campbell, 1909–1969, vol. VI
Frazer, Hon. Charles Edward, 1880–1913, vol. I
Frazer, Hon. Sir Francis Vernon, 1880–1948, vol. IV
Frazer, Col George Stanley, 1865–1950, vol. IV(A), vol. V
Frazer, Sir James George, 1854–1941, vol. IV
Frazer, John Ernest Sullivan, 1870–1946, vol. IV
Frazer, Robert, 1878–1947, vol. IV
Frazer, Robert Alexander, 1891–1959, vol. V
Frazer, Robert Watson, 1854–1921, vol. II
Frazer, Sir Thomas, 1884–1969, vol. VI
Frazer, William Miller, 1864–1961, vol. VI
Frazer, William Mowll, 1888–1958, vol. V
Freake, Sir Charles Arland Maitland, 4th Bt, 1904–1951, vol. V
Freake, Sir Frederick Charles Maitland, 3rd Bt, 1876–1950, vol. IV
Freake, Sir Thomas George, 2nd Bt, 1848–1920, vol. II
Fream, William, died 1906, vol. I
Frears, John Newton, 1906–1981, vol. VIII
Fréchette, Achille, 1847–1927, vol. II
Fréchette, Louis, 1839–1908, vol. I
Frecheville, William, 1854–1940, vol. III
Frederic, Harold, 1856–1898, vol. I
Frederick, Lt-Col Sir Charles Arthur Andrew, 1861–1913, vol. I
Frederick, Sir Charles Edward, 7th Bt (cr 1723), 1843–1913, vol. I
Frederick, Sir Charles Edward St John, 8th Bt, 1876–1938, vol. III
Frederick, Lt-Col Sir Edward Boscawen, 9th Bt, 1880–1956, vol. V
Frederick, Captain George Charles, 1855–1951, vol. V
Freebody, Air Vice-Marshal Wilfred Leslie, 1906–1991, vol. IX
Freedman, Barnett, 1901–1958, vol. V
Freedman, Louis, 1917–1998, vol. X
Freedman, Maurice, 1920–1975, vol. VII
Freedman, Hon. Samuel, 1908–1993, vol. IX
Freeland, Maj.-Gen. Sir Henry Francis Edward, 1870–1946, vol. IV
Freeland, Lt-Gen. Sir Ian Henry, 1912–1979, vol. VII
Freeland, Col John Cavendish, 1877–1944, vol. IV
Freeling, Sir Charles Edward Luard, 9th Bt, 1858–1941, vol. IV
Freeling, Sir Clayton Pennington, 8th Bt, 1857–1927, vol. II
Freeling, Sir Harry, 6th Bt, 1852–1914, vol. I
Freeling, Rev. Sir James Robert, 7th Bt, 1825–1916, vol. II
Freeman, Anthony Mallows; see Freeman, P. A. M.
Freeman, Sir Bernard; see Freeman, Sir N. B.
Freeman, (Edgar) James (Albert), 1917–1992, vol. IX
Freeman, Edward Bothamley, 1838–1921, vol. II
Freeman, Col Ernest Carrick, 1860–1932, vol. III
Freeman, Comdr Frederick Arthur Peere W.; see Williams-Freeman.
Freeman, George Mallows, 1850–1934, vol. III
Freeman, George Robert, 1875–1972, vol. VII
Freeman, George Sydney, 1879–1938, vol. III

Freeman, Harold Webber, 1899–1994, vol. IX
Freeman, Harry, 1888–1959, vol. V
Freeman, Rev. Herbert Bentley, 1855–1950, vol. IV
Freeman, Ifan Charles Harold, 1910–1990, vol. VIII
Freeman, James; see Freeman, E. J. A.
Freeman, His Eminence Cardinal Sir James Darcy, 1907–1991, vol. IX
Freeman, James E., 1871–1929, vol. III
Freeman, Rt Rev. James Edward, 1866–1943, vol. IV
Freeman, John, 1880–1929, vol. III
Freeman, John, 1877–1962, vol. VI
Freeman, John Joseph, 1851–1937, vol. III
Freeman, Sir (John) Keith (Noel), 2nd Bt, 1923–1981, vol. VIII
Freeman, Kathleen, 1897–1959, vol. V
Freeman, Sir Keith; see Freeman, Sir J. K. N.
Freeman, Sir (Nathaniel) Bernard, 1896–1982, vol. VIII
Freeman, Nicholas Hall, 1939–1989, vol. VIII
Freeman, Patrick, 1919–1978, vol. VII
Freeman, Percy Tom, 1891–1956, vol. V
Freeman, Peter, 1888–1956, vol. V
Freeman, (Philip) Anthony Mallows, 1892–1971, vol. VII
Freeman, Sir Philip Horace, 1878–1933, vol. III
Freeman, Sir Ralph, 1880–1950, vol. IV
Freeman, Sir Ralph, 1911–1998, vol. X
Freeman, Richard Austin, 1862–1943, vol. IV
Freeman, Richard Gavin, 1910–1997, vol. X
Freeman, Captain Spencer, 1892–1982, vol. VIII
Freeman, Sterry Baines, 1875–1953, vol. V
Freeman, Air Chief Marshal Sir Wilfrid Rhodes, 1st Bt, 1888–1953, vol. V
Freeman, William Marshall, 1868–1953, vol. V
Freeman-Attwood, Harold Augustus, 1897–1963, vol. VI
Freeman-Cohen, Harry, died 1904, vol. I
Freeman-Mitford, Hon. Clement Bertram Ogilvy, 1876–1915, vol. I
Freeman-Mitford, Major Hon. Thomas David F.; see Mitford.
Freer, A. M. G.; see Goodrich-Freer.
Freer, Charles Edward Jesse, 1901–1998, vol. X
Freer, Charles L., 1854–1919, vol. II
Freer, Ven. T. Henry, 1833–1904, vol. I
Freer Smith, Sir Hamilton Pym, 1845–1929, vol. III
Freese-Pennefather, Harold Wilfrid Armine, 1907–1967, vol. VI
Freeston, Sir Brian; see Freeston, Sir L. B.
Freeston, Charles Lincoln, 1865–1942, vol. IV
Freeston, Sir (Leslie) Brian, 1892–1958, vol. V
Freestun, Col William Humphrey May, 1878–1964, vol. VI
Freeth, Sir Evelyn, 1846–1911, vol. I
Freeth, Francis Arthur, 1884–1970, vol. VI
Freeth, Maj.-Gen. George Henry Basil, 1872–1949, vol. IV
Freeth, H. Andrew, 1912–1986, vol. VIII
Freeth, Rt Rev. Robert Evelyn, 1886–1979, vol. VII
Freke, Cecil George, 1887–1974, vol. VII
Freke, Hon. Ralfe E.; see Evans-Freke.
Fremantle, Gen. Sir Arthur James Lyon, 1835–1901, vol. I
Fremantle, Charles Albert, 1878–1952, vol. V

Fremantle, Hon. Sir Charles William, 1834–1914, vol. I
Fremantle, Adm. Hon. Sir Edmund Robert, 1836–1929, vol. III
Fremantle, Francis David Eardley, 1906–1968, vol. VI
Fremantle, Sir Francis Edward, 1872–1943, vol. IV
Fremantle, Henry Eardley Stephen, 1874–1931, vol. III
Fremantle, John Morton, 1876–1936, vol. III
Fremantle, Sir Selwyn Howe, 1869–1942, vol. IV
Fremantle, Adm. Sir Sydney Robert, 1867–1958, vol. V
Fremantle, Very Rev. Hon. William Henry, 1831–1916, vol. II
Frémiet, Emmanuel, 1824–1910, vol. I
French, Alice Octave Thanet, 1850–1934, vol. III
French, Gen. Arthur, 1840–1928, vol. II
French, Major Arthur Cecil, 1896–1974, vol. VII
French, Col Arthur Harwood, 1876–1939, vol. III
French, Hon. Charles, 1851–1925, vol. II
French, Brig. Charles Newenham, 1875–1959, vol. V
French, Daniel Chester, 1850–1931, vol. III
French, Daniel O'Connell, 1843–1902, vol. I
French, Lt-Col Hon. (Edward) Gerald, 1883–1970, vol. VI
French, Edward Henry, 1850–1935, vol. III
French, Sir Edward Lee, 1857–1916, vol. II
French, Francis Coope, 1868–1940, vol. III
French, Rev. Francis Laurence, 1868–1936, vol. III
French, Captain Sir Frederick Edward, 1882–1947, vol. IV
French, Frederick George, 1889–1963, vol. VI
French, Maj.-Gen. Sir George Arthur, 1841–1921, vol. II
French, Col George Arthur, 1865–1950, vol. IV
French, Lt-Col Hon. Gerald; see French, Lt-Col Hon. E. G.
French, Sir Henry Leon, 1883–1966, vol. VI
French, Herbert Stanley, 1875–1951, vol. V
French, Captain Sir Houston, 1853–1932, vol. III
French, Sir James Weir, 1876–1953, vol. V
French, Maj.-Gen. John, 1906–1978, vol. VII
French, John Gay, died 1951, vol. V
French, Brig. John Linnaeus, 1896–1953, vol. V
French, Sir John Russell, 1847–1921, vol. II
French, Leslie Richard, 1904–1999, vol. X
French, Lewis, 1873–1945, vol. IV
French, Neville Arthur Irwin, 1920–1996, vol. X
French, Percy, 1854–1920, vol. II
French, Rev. Reginald, 1883–1961, vol. VI
French, Reginald Thomas George, 1881–1965, vol. VI
French, Sir Somerset Richard, 1848–1929, vol. III
French, Adm. Sir Wilfred Frankland, 1880–1958, vol. V
French, William Innes, 1910–1971, vol. VII
Frend, Charles Herbert, 1909–1977, vol. VII
Frend, Col George, 1857–1923, vol. II
Frere, Alexander Stewart, 1892–1984, vol. VIII
Frere, Sir Bartle Compton Arthur, 1854–1933, vol. III
Frere, Sir Bartle Henry Temple, 1862–1953, vol. V
Frere, Rev. Hugh Corrie, 1857–1938, vol. III

Frere, James Arnold, 1920–1994, vol. IX
Frere, Brig. Jasper Gray, 1894–1974, vol. VII
Frere, John Tudor, 1843–1918, vol. II
Frere, Noel Gray, 1885–1955, vol. V
Frere, Rt Rev. Walter Howard, 1863–1938, vol. III
Frere, William Edward, 1840–1900, vol. I
Freshfield, Douglas William, 1845–1934, vol. III
Freshwater, Douglas Hope, *died* 1945, vol. IV
Fresnay, Pierre, (Pierre Laudenbach), 1897–1975, vol. VII
Fressanges, Air Marshal Sir Francis J., 1902–1975, vol. VII
Fretwell, Sir George Herbert, 1900–1991, vol. IX
Freud, Anna, 1895–1982, vol. VIII
Freud, Sigmund, 1856–1939, vol. III
Freund, Sir Otto K.; *see* Kahn-Freund.
Freundlich, Erwin F.; *see* Finlay-Freundlich.
Freundlich, Herbert Max Finlay, 1880–1941, vol. IV
Frew, Rev. Dr, 1813–1910, vol. I
Frew, Sir John Lewtas, 1912–1985, vol. VIII
Frew, Air Vice-Marshal Sir Matthew Brown, 1895–1974, vol. VII
Frew, Engr Rear-Adm. Sir Sidney Oswell, *died* 1972, vol. VII
Frewen, Col Edward, 1850–1919, vol. II
Frewen, Adm. Sir John Byng, 1911–1975, vol. VII
Frewen, Moreton, 1853–1924, vol. II
Frewen-Laton, Col Stephen, 1857–1933, vol. III
Frewer, Rev. George Ernest, 1852–1935, vol. III
Frewer, Rt Rev. John, 1883–1974, vol. VII
Freyberg, 1st Baron, 1889–1963, vol. VI
Freyberg, 2nd Baron, 1923–1993, vol. IX
Freyberg, Lady; (Barbara), *died* 1973, vol. VII
Freyberg, Captain Geoffrey Herbert, 1881–1966, vol. VI
Freyer, Sir Peter J., *died* 1921, vol. II
Freyer, Lt-Col Samuel Forster, 1858–1947, vol. IV
Frick, Henry Clay, 1849–1919, vol. II
Frick, Winifred; *see* Austen, W. M. L.
Fricker, Edward T., *died* 1917, vol. II
Fricker, Peter Racine, 1920–1990, vol. VIII
Friederichs, Hulda, *died* 1927, vol. II
Friedlander, Max J., 1867–1958, vol. V
Friedlander, Michael, *died* 1910, vol. I
Friedman, Ignaz, 1882–1948, vol. IV
Friend, (Archibald) Gordon, 1912–1997, vol. X
Friend, Maj.-Gen. Arthur Leslie Irvine, 1886–1961, vol. VI
Friend, Bernard Ernest, 1924–1993, vol. IX
Friend, Gordon; *see* Friend, A. G.
Friend, John Albert Newton, 1881–1966, vol. VI
Friend, Maj.-Gen. Rt Hon. Sir Lovick Bransby, 1856–1944, vol. IV
Frigon, Augustin, 1888–1952, vol. V
Friml, Rudolf, 1879–1972, vol. VII
Frink, Dame Elisabeth Jean, 1930–1993, vol. IX
Fripp, Sir Alfred Downing, 1865–1930, vol. III
Fripp, Alfred Ernest, 1866–1938, vol. III
Fripp, Alfred Thomas, 1899–1995, vol. IX
Fripp, Charles E., 1854–1906, vol. I
Frisby, Major Cyril Hubert, 1885–1961, vol. VI
Frisby, Lt-Col Lionel Claud, 1889–1936, vol. III
Frisby, Maj.-Gen. Richard George Fellowes, 1911–1982, vol. VIII
Frisch, Otto Robert, 1904–1979, vol. VII

Frisch, Ragnar Anton Kittil, 1895–1973, vol. VII
Friswell, Sir Charles Hain, 1871–1926, vol. II
Frith, Col Cyril Halsted, 1877–1946, vol. IV
Frith, Donald Alfred, 1918–2000, vol. X
Frith, Brig. Sir Eric Herbert Cokayne, 1897–1984, vol. VIII
Frith, Brig.-Gen. Gilbert Robertson, 1873–1958, vol. V
Frith, Col Herbert Cokayne, 1861–1942, vol. IV
Frith, W. S., *died* 1924, vol. II
Frith, Walter, *died* 1941, vol. IV
Frith, William Powell, 1819–1909, vol. I
Fritsch, Felix Eugen, 1879–1954, vol. V
Frizell, Rev. Charles William, *died* 1920, vol. II
Frizell, Brig.-Gen. Charles William, 1888–1951, vol. V
Frizelle, Sir Joseph, 1841–1921, vol. II
Frizzell, Edward, 1918–1987, vol. VIII
Frodsham, Rt Rev. George Horsfall, 1863–1937, vol. III
Frohawk, Frederick William, 1861–1946, vol. IV
Fröhlich, Herbert, 1905–1991, vol. IX
Frohman, Charles, 1860–1915, vol. I
Frome, Sir Norman Frederick, 1899–1982, vol. VIII
Frood, Hester, 1882–1971, vol. VII
Froom, Sir Arthur Henry, 1873–1964, vol. VI
Frossard, Rev. Canon Edward Louis, 1887–1968, vol. VI
Frost, Edward Granville Gordon, 1886–1971, vol. VII
Frost, Edward Purkis, 1842–1922, vol. II
Frost, Brig.-Gen. Frank Dutton, *died* 1968, vol. VI
Frost, Hon. Sir John, 1828–1918, vol. II
Frost, Maj.-Gen. John Dutton, 1912–1993, vol. IX
Frost, Lt-Col John Meadows, 1885–1923, vol. II
Frost, Sir John Meadows, 1856–1935, vol. III
Frost, Mark Edwin Pescott, 1859–1953, vol. V
Frost, Captain Meadows, 1875–1954, vol. V
Frost, Norman, 1899–1985, vol. VIII
Frost, Percival, 1817–1898, vol. I
Frost, Robert, 1874–1963, vol. VI
Frost, Hon. Sir Sydney; *see* Frost, Hon. Sir T. S.
Frost, Sir Thomas Gibbons, 1820–1904, vol. I
Frost, Hon. Sir (Thomas) Sydney, 1916–1997, vol. X
Frostick, James Arthur, 1857–1931, vol. III
Froude, Ashley Anthony, 1863–1949, vol. IV
Froude, Robert Edmund, 1846–1924, vol. II
Frowde, Henry, 1841–1927, vol. II
Frowen, Brig. John Harold, 1898–1980, vol. VII
Frumkin, Gad, 1887–1960, vol. VI
Fry, (Anna) Ruth, 1878–1962, vol. VI
Fry, Col Arthur Brownfield, 1873–1954, vol. V
Fry, Augustine Sargood, 1890–1962, vol. VI
Fry, Cecil Roderick, 1890–1952, vol. V
Fry, Charles Burgess, 1872–1956, vol. V
Fry, Rev. Canon Charles Edward Middleton, 1882–1950, vol. IV
Fry, Maj.-Gen. Charles Irwin, 1858–1931, vol. III
Fry, Dennis Butler, 1907–1983, vol. VIII
Fry, Donald William, 1910–1992, vol. IX
Fry, Rt Hon. Sir Edward, 1827–1918, vol. II
Fry, E(dwin) Maxwell, 1899–1987, vol. VIII
Fry, Francis Gibson, 1864–1914, vol. I
Fry, Francis James, 1835–1918, vol. II

Fry, Sir (Francis) Wilfrid, 5th Bt, 1904–1987, vol. VIII
Fry, Sir Frederick Morris, 1851–1943, vol. IV
Fry, Sir Geoffrey Storrs, 1st Bt (*cr* 1929), 1888–1960, vol. V
Fry, George Samuel, 1853–1938, vol. III
Fry, Sir Henry James Wakely, 1849–1920, vol. II
Fry, Henry Kenneth, 1886–1959, vol. V(A), vol. VI(AI)
Fry, John, 1922–1994, vol. IX
Fry, Sir John Nicholas Pease, 4th Bt, 1897–1985, vol. VIII
Fry, Sir John Pease, 2nd Bt (*cr* 1894), 1864–1957, vol. V
Fry, Major Sir Leslie Alfred Charles, 1908–1976, vol. VII
Fry, Rt Hon. Lewis, 1832–1921, vol. II
Fry, Lewis G., 1860–1933, vol. III
Fry, Margery; *see* Fry, S. M.
Fry, Matthew Wyatt Joseph, *died* 1943, vol. IV
Fry, Oliver Armstrong, 1855–1931, vol. III
Fry, Sir Penrose; *see* Fry, Sir T. P.
Fry, Peter George, 1875–1925, vol. II
Fry, Peter George Robin Plantagenet S.; *see* Somerset Fry.
Fry, Roger E., 1866–1934, vol. III
Fry, Ruth; *see* Fry, A. R.
Fry, (Sara) Margery, 1874–1958, vol. V
Fry, Sir Theodore, 1st Bt (*cr* 1894), 1836–1912, vol. I
Fry, Sir (Theodore) Penrose, 3rd Bt (*cr* 1894), 1892–1971, vol. VII
Fry, Theodore Wilfrid, 1868–1947, vol. IV
Fry, Thomas, 1889–1958, vol. V
Fry, Very Rev. Thomas Charles, 1846–1930, vol. III
Fry, Sir Wilfrid; *see* Fry, Sir F. W.
Fry, Maj.-Gen. Sir William, 1858–1934, vol. III
Fry, Sir William, 1853–1939, vol. III
Fry, Hon. Sir William Gordon, 1909–2000, vol. X
Fry, Sir William Kelsey, 1889–1963, vol. VI
Fry, Windsor, *died* 1947, vol. IV
Fryar, Samuel, 1863–1938, vol. III
Fryars, Sir Robert Furness, 1887–1978, vol. VII(AII)
Fryberg, Sir Abraham, 1901–1993, vol. IX (AII)
Frye, Frederick Robert, 1851–1942, vol. IV
Frye, Jack, 1914–1975, vol. VII
Fryer, Sir Charles Edward, 1850–1920, vol. II
Fryer, David Richard, 1936–1996, vol. X
Fryer, Edward Harpur, 1879–1948, vol. IV
Fryer, Sir Frederic William Richards, 1845–1922, vol. II
Fryer, Herbert, 1877–1957, vol. V
Fryer, James, 1930–1981, vol. VIII
Fryer, Lt-Gen. Sir John, 1838–1917, vol. II
Fryer, Sir John Claud Fortescue, 1886–1948, vol. IV
Fryer, Walter John, 1871–1933, vol. III
Fryer, Maj.-Gen. Wilfred George, 1900–1993, vol. IX
Fuad, Mustafa Ziai, Bey, 1888–1968, vol. VI
Fuchs, Carl, 1865–1951, vol. V
Fuchs, Emile, 1866–1929, vol. III
Fuchs, Sir Vivian Ernest, 1908–1999, vol. X

Fudge, Edward George, 1888–1961, vol. VI
Fukui, Dr Kenichi, 1918–1998, vol. X
Fukushima, Gen. Baron, 1853–1919, vol. II
Fulbright, J(ames) William, 1905–1995, vol. IX
Fulcher, Derick Harold, 1917–1999, vol. X
Fulford, Dame Catherine, 1881–1960, vol. V
Fulford, Francis, 1861–1926, vol. II
Fulford, Rev. Frederick John, 1860–1927, vol. II
Fulford, Henry English, 1859–1929, vol. III
Fulford, Sir Roger Thomas Baldwin, 1902–1983, vol. VIII
Fullagar, Sir Wilfred Kelsham, 1892–1961, vol. VI
Fullard, George, 1923–1973, vol. VII
Fullbrook-Leggatt, Maj.-Gen. Charles St Quentin Outen; *see* Leggatt.
Fuller, Lt-Col Albert George Hubert, *died* 1969, vol. VI
Fuller, Maj.-Gen. Algernon Clement, 1885–1970, vol. VI
Fuller, Rev. Arthur Rose, 1874–1959, vol. V
Fuller, Sir Bampfylde; *see* Fuller, Sir J. B.
Fuller, Sir Benjamin John, 1875–1952, vol. V
Fuller, Maj.-Gen. Cuthbert Graham, 1874–1960, vol. V
Fuller, Adm. Sir Cyril Thomas Moulden, 1874–1942, vol. IV
Fuller, Sir Francis Charles, 1866–1944, vol. IV
Fuller, Brig.-Gen. Francis George, 1869–1961, vol. VI
Fuller, Francis Matthew, 1899–1963, vol. VI
Fuller, George Pargiter, 1833–1927, vol. II
Fuller, Hon. Sir George Warburton, 1861–1940, vol. III
Fuller, Major Sir Gerard; *see* Fuller, Major Sir J. G. H. F.
Fuller, Henry Roxburgh, *died* 1929, vol. III
Fuller, Air Cdre Herbert Francis, 1893–1967, vol. VI
Fuller, James Franklin, 1835–1924, vol. II
Fuller, Gen. John Augustus, 1828–1902, vol. I
Fuller, Maj.-Gen. John Frederick Charles, 1878–1966, vol. VI
Fuller, Major Sir (John) Gerard (Henry Fleetwood), 2nd Bt, 1906–1981, vol. VIII
Fuller, Rt Rev. John Latimer, 1870–1950, vol. IV
Fuller, Sir John Michael Fleetwood, 1st Bt, 1864–1915, vol. I
Fuller, Major Sir John William Fleetwood, 3rd Bt, 1936–1998, vol. X
Fuller, Sir (Joseph) Bampfylde, 1854–1935, vol. III
Fuller, Leonard J., 1891–1973, vol. VII
Fuller, Melville Weston, 1833–1910, vol. I
Fuller, Richard Buckminster, 1895–1983, vol. VIII
Fuller, Brig.-Gen. Richard Woodfield, 1861–1938, vol. III
Fuller, Roy Broadbent, 1912–1991, vol. IX
Fuller, Sir Thomas Ekins, 1831–1910, vol. I
Fuller, Walter Everard, 1879–1942, vol. IV
Fuller, William Fleetwood, 1865–1947, vol. IV
Fuller-Acland-Hood, Sir (Alexander) William; *see* Hood, Sir William Acland.
Fuller-Eliott-Drake, Sir Francis George Augustus; *see* Drake.
Fuller-Good, Air Vice-Marshal James Laurence Fuller, 1903–1983, vol. VIII

299

Fuller-Maitland, J. A., 1856–1936, vol. III
Fuller-Maitland, William, 1844–1932, vol. III
Fullerton, Andrew, *died* 1934, vol. III
Fullerton, Adm. Sir Eric John Arthur, *died* 1962, vol. VI
Fullerton, Harold Williams, 1905–1970, vol. VI
Fullerton, Hugh, 1851–1922, vol. II
Fullerton, Brig. John Parke, 1894–1977, vol. VII
Fullerton, Adm. Sir John Reginald Thomas, 1840–1918, vol. II
Fullerton, John Skipwith Herbert, 1865–1940, vol. III
Fullerton, Rev. William Young, 1857–1932, vol. III
Fulleylove, John, 1847–1908, vol. I
Fullwood, John, *died* 1931, vol. III
Fülop-Miller, René, 1891–1963, vol. VI
Fulthorpe, Henry Joseph, 1916–1999, vol. X
Fulton, Baron (Life Peer); John Scott Fulton, 1902–1986, vol. VIII
Fulton, Alexander Strathern, 1888–1976, vol. VII
Fulton, Sir Edmund McGilldowny Hope, 1848–1913, vol. I
Fulton, Eustace Cecil, 1880–1954, vol. V
Fulton, Sir Forrest, 1846–1925, vol. II
Fulton, Forrest, 1913–1971, vol. VII
Fulton, Frederick John, 1862–1936, vol. III
Fulton, Lt-Col Harry Townsend, 1869–1918, vol. II
Fulton, Lt-Col J. D. B., 1876–1915, vol. I
Fulton, John Farquhar, 1899–1960, vol. V
Fulton, Robert Burwell, 1849–1918, vol. II
Fulton, Sir Robert Fulton, 1844–1927, vol. II
Fulton, Thomas Alexander Wemyss, 1855–1929, vol. III
Fulton, Rev. William, 1876–1952, vol. V
Funch, Christian Holger, 1865–1915, vol. I
Funk, Isaac Kaufman, 1839–1912, vol. I
Funsten, Rt Rev. James Bowen, *died* 1918, vol. II
Funston, Brig.-Gen. Frederick, 1865–1917, vol. II
Funston, G(eorge) Keith, 1910–1992, vol. IX
Furber, Lt-Col Cecil Tidswell, 1883–1943, vol. IV
Furber, Douglas, 1885–1961, vol. VI
Furber, Edward Price, 1864–1940, vol. III
Fürer-Haimendorf, Christoph von, 1909–1995, vol. IX
Furkert, Frederick William, 1876–1949, vol. IV
Furley, Sir John, 1836–1919, vol. II
Furley, John Talfourd, 1878–1956, vol. V
Furlong, Hon. L. O'Brien, 1856–1908, vol. I
Furlong, Robert O'Brien, 1842–1917, vol. II
Furlong, Hon. Robert Stafford, 1904–1996, vol. X
Furlonge, Sir Geoffrey Warren, 1903–1984, vol. VIII
Furneaux, Rev. Henry, 1829–1900, vol. I
Furneaux, Rev. William Mordaunt, 1848–1928, vol. II
Furness, 1st Baron, 1852–1912, vol. I
Furness, 1st Viscount, 1883–1940, vol. III
Furness, 2nd Viscount, 1929–1995, vol. IX
Furness, Sir Christopher, 2nd Bt, 1900–1974, vol. VII
Furness, George James, 1868–1936, vol. III
Furness, George James Barnard, 1900–1962, vol. VI
Furness, Horace Howard, 1833–1912, vol. I
Furness, Reginald Albert, *died* 1951, vol. V

Furness, Sir Robert Allason, 1883–1954, vol. V
Furness, Sir Robert Howard, 1880–1959, vol. V
Furness, Stephen Noel, 1902–1974, vol. VII
Furness, Sir Stephen Wilson, 1st Bt, 1872–1914, vol. I
Furness-Smith, Sir Cecil, 1890–1971, vol. VII
Furney, Brig. John Leared, 1872–1936, vol. III
Furniss, Harry, 1854–1925, vol. II
Furniss, John Mawdsley, 1877–1956, vol. V
Furnival Jones, Sir (Edward) Martin, 1912–1997, vol. X
Furnival-Jones, Sir Martin; *see* Furnival-Jones, Sir E. M.
Furnivall, Baroness (19th in line), 1900–1968, vol. VI
Furnivall, Lt-Col Charles Hilton, 1873–1946, vol. IV
Furnivall, Frederick James, 1825–1910, vol. I
Furnivall, Maj.-Gen. Lewis Trevor, 1907–1986, vol. VIII
Furnivall, Percy, 1868–1938, vol. III
Furse, Ven. Charles Wellington, 1821–1900, vol. I
Furse, Charles Wellington, 1868–1904, vol. I
Furse, Rear-Adm. (John) Paul (Wellington), 1904–1978, vol. VII
Furse, Dame Katharine, 1875–1952, vol. V
Furse, Rt Rev. Michael Bolton, 1870–1955, vol. V
Furse, Rear-Adm. Paul; *see* Furse, Rear-Adm. J. P. W.
Furse, Major Ralph Dolignon, 1887–1973, vol. VII
Furse, Roger Kemble, 1903–1972, vol. VII
Furse, Lt-Gen. Sir William T., 1865–1953, vol. V
Furst, Herbert Ernest Augustus, 1874–1945, vol. IV
Furtado, Robert Audley, 1912–1992, vol. IX
Furtwängler, Wilhelm, 1886–1954, vol. V
Fussell, Edward Coldham, 1901–1978, vol. VII
Fussey, David Eric, 1943–2000, vol. X
Fust, Herbert J.; *see* Jenner-Fust.
Fyers, FitzRoy Hubert, 1899–1981, vol. VIII
Fyers, Major Hubert Alcock Nepean, 1862–1951, vol. V
Fyfe, Sir Cleveland, 1888–1959, vol. V
Fyfe, David Theodore, 1875–1945, vol. IV
Fyfe, H. Hamilton, 1869–1951, vol. V
Fyfe, Thomas Alexander, 1852–1928, vol. II
Fyfe, Sir William Hamilton, 1878–1965, vol. VI
Fyffe, Rev. David, 1866–1929, vol. III
Fyffe, Lt-Gen. Sir Richard Alan, 1912–1972, vol. VII
Fyffe, Rt Rev. Rollestone Sterritt, 1868–1964, vol. VI
Fyleman, Rose, *died* 1957, vol. V
Fyler, Maj.-Gen. Arthur Roderic, 1911–1980, vol. VII
Fyler, Adm. Herbert Arthur Stevenson, 1864–1934, vol. III
Fynes-Clinton, David Osbert, 1909–1978, vol. VII
Fynes-Clinton, Rev. Henry Joy, 1875–1959, vol. V
Fynes-Clinton, Osbert Henry, *died* 1941, vol. IV
Fynn, Sir Basil Mortimer L.; *see* Lindsay-Fynn.
Fynn, Hon. Sir Percival Donald Leslie, 1872–1940, vol. III
Fynne, Robert John, *died* 1953, vol. V
Fysh, Sir Hudson; *see* Fysh, Sir W. H.
Fysh, Hon. Sir Philip Oakley, 1835–1919, vol. II

Fysh, Sir (Wilmot) Hudson, 1895–1974, vol. VII
Fyson, Rt Rev. Philip Kemball, 1846–1928, vol. II

Fyvie, Isabella; *see* Mayo, Isabella, (Mrs John R. Mayo).

G

Gabain, Ethel Leontine, (Mrs John Copley), *died* 1950, vol. IV
Gabb, Harry; *see* Gabb, W. H.
Gabb, (William) Harry, 1909–1995, vol. IX
Gabbatt, John Percy, 1880–1956, vol. V
Gabin, Jean, (Alexis Jean Montgorge), 1904–1976, vol. VII
Gable, Christopher Michael, 1940–1998, vol. X
Gable, Clark, 1901–1960, vol. V
Gabor, Dennis, 1900–1979, vol. VII
Gabriel, Lt-Col Cecil Hamilton, 1879–1947, vol. IV
Gabriel, Col Sir (Edmund) Vivian, 1875–1950, vol. IV
Gabriel, Col Sir Vivian; *see* Gabriel, Col Sir E. V.
Gabriel, William Bashall, *died* 1975, vol. VII
Gadd, Maj.-Gen. Alfred Lockwood, (David), 1912–1986, vol. VIII
Gadd, Cyril John, 1893–1969, vol. VI
Gadd, Maj.-Gen. David; *see* Gadd, Maj.-Gen. A. L.
Gadd, John, 1925–1994, vol. IX
Gaddum, Arthur Graham, 1874–1948, vol. IV
Gaddum, Sir John Henry, 1900–1965, vol. VI
Gaddum, Captain Walter Frederick, 1888–1956, vol. V
Gadie, Lt-Col Sir Anthony, *died* 1948, vol. IV
Gadow, Hans Friedrich, 1855–1928, vol. II
Gadsby, Henry, 1842–1907, vol. I
Gadsby, John, 1884–1970, vol. VI
Gadsby, W. H., *died* 1924, vol. II
Gadsden, Cecil Holroyd, 1887–1957, vol. V
Gadsden, Edward Holroyd, 1859–1920, vol. II
Gadsdon, Sir Laurence Percival, 1897–1967, vol. VI(AII)
Gaekwad, Lt-Col Fatesinghrao P., 1930–1988, vol. VIII
Gaffney, Maj.-Gen. Edward Sebastian B.; *see* Burke-Gaffney.
Gaffney, Thomas Burke, 1839–1927, vol. II
Gagarin, Col Yuri Alexeyevich, 1934–1968, vol. VI
Gage, 5th Viscount, 1854–1912, vol. I
Gage, 6th Viscount, 1895–1982, vol. VIII
Gage, 7th Viscount, 1932–1993, vol. IX
Gage, Col Aella Molyneux Berkeley, 1863–1937, vol. III
Gage, Andrew Thomas, 1871–1945, vol. IV
Gage, Sir Berkeley Everard Foley, 1904–1994, vol. IX
Gage, Conolly Hugh, 1905–1984, vol. VIII
Gage, Hon. Lyman Judson, 1836–1927, vol. II
Gage, Brig.-Gen. Moreton Foley, 1873–1953, vol. V
Gage, Thomas Robert Baillie-, 1842–1914, vol. I
Gage, Sir William James, 1849–1921, vol. II
Gaggero, Sir George, 1897–1978, vol. VII
Gagnon, Rt Rev. Mgr Cyrille, *died* 1945, vol. IV
Gahan, Charles Joseph, 1862–1939, vol. III
Gahan, Frank, 1890–1971, vol. VII

Gaiger, Sydney Herbert, 1884–1934, vol. III
Gailey, James Hamilton, 1869–1938, vol. III
Gailey, Thomas William Hamilton, 1906–1986, vol. VIII
Gailor, Rt Rev. Thomas Frank, 1856–1935, vol. III
Gaimes, John Austin, 1886–1921, vol. II
Gainer, Sir Donald St Clair, 1891–1966, vol. VI
Gainer, Rev. Canon Harry, 1858–1920, vol. II
Gainford, 1st Baron, 1860–1943, vol. IV
Gainford, 2nd Baron, 1889–1971, vol. VII
Gainham, Sarah, (Rachel Ames), 1922–1999, vol. X
Gainsborough, 3rd Earl of, 1850–1926, vol. II
Gainsborough, 4th Earl of, 1884–1927, vol. II
Gainsborough, Hugh, 1893–1980, vol. VII
Gair, Col Sinclair, 1856–1939, vol. III
Gair, Walter Burgh, 1854–1951, vol. V
Gairdner, Arthur Charles Dalrymple, 1872–1950, vol. IV
Gairdner, Gen. Sir Charles Henry, 1898–1983, vol. VIII
Gairdner, Eric Dalrymple, 1878–1933, vol. III
Gairdner, James, 1828–1912, vol. I
Gairdner, Rev. Canon W. H. Temple, 1873–1928, vol. II
Gairdner, Sir William Tennant, 1824–1907, vol. I
Gairns, James Mather, 1880–1935, vol. III
Gairy, Rt Hon. Sir Eric Matthew, 1922–1997, vol. X
Gaisford, Hugh William, 1874–1954, vol. V
Gaisford, Lt-Col Sir Philip, 1891–1973, vol. VII
Gaisford, Brig.-Gen. Richard Boileau, 1854–1924, vol. II
Gaisford, Wilfrid Fletcher, 1902–1988, vol. VIII
Gaisford-St Lawrence, Julian Charles, 1862–1932, vol. III
Gait, Sir Edward Albert, 1863–1950, vol. IV
Gaither, H. Rowan, Jr, 1909–1961, vol. VI
Gaitskell, Baroness (Life Peer); Anna Dora Gaitskell, 1901–1989, vol. VIII
Gaitskell, Sir Arthur, 1900–1985, vol. VIII
Gaitskell, Maj.-Gen. Frederick, 1806–1901, vol. I
Gaitskell, Rt Hon. Hugh Todd Naylor, 1906–1963, vol. VI
Gaje Ghale, 1922–2000, vol. X
Gajjumal, Rai Sahib Lala, *born* 1857, vol. II
Galabin, Alfred Lewis, 1843–1913, vol. I
Galbraith, Angus, 1846–1915, vol. I
Galbraith, Very Rev. George, 1829–1911, vol. I
Galbraith, James Francis Wallace, 1872–1945, vol. IV
Galbraith, Lt-Col James Ponsonby, 1881–1950, vol. IV
Galbraith, Samuel, 1853–1936, vol. III
Galbraith, Hon. Sir Thomas Galloway Dunlop, 1917–1982, vol. VIII
Galbraith, Vivian Hunter, 1889–1976, vol. VII
Galbraith, Walter, 1839–1906, vol. I

Galbraith, Maj.-Gen. Sir William, 1837–1906, vol. I
Galbraith, Col William Campbell, 1870–1946, vol. IV
Galdos, Benito Perez, 1845–1920, vol. II
Gale, Anthony Eugene Myddelton, 1901–1959, vol. V
Gale, Arthur James Victor, 1895–1978, vol. VII
Gale, Rev. Canon Courtenay James Randolph, 1857–1937, vol. III
Gale, Hon. George Alexander, 1906–1997, vol. X
Gale, George Stafford, 1927–1990, vol. VIII
Gale, Brig. Henry John Gordon, 1883–1944, vol. IV
Gale, Brig.-Gen. Henry Richmond, 1866–1930, vol. III
Gale, Lt-Gen. Sir Humfrey Myddelton, 1890–1971, vol. VII
Gale, Rev. Isaac Sadler, died 1915, vol. I
Gale, James, 1833–1907, vol. I
Gale, Kenneth Frederick, 1914–1969, vol. VI
Gale, Sir Laurence George, 1905–1969, vol. VI
Gale, Malcolm Ruthven, 1909–1990, vol. VIII
Gale, Norman, died 1942, vol. IV
Gale, Gen. Sir Richard Nelson, 1896–1982, vol. VIII
Gale, Lt-Col Robert, 1887–1937, vol. III
Gale, Walter Frederick, 1865–1945, vol. IV
Gale, Zona, 1874–1939, vol. III
Galea, Robert V., 1882–1962, vol. VI (AII)
Galer, Sir Bertram; see Galer, Sir F. B.
Galer, Sir (Frederic) Bertram, 1873–1968, vol. VI
Galer, John Maxcey, 1839–1919, vol. II
Gales, Sir Robert Richard, 1864–1948, vol. IV
Gales, Wilfred Appleby, 1860–1937, vol. III
Galipeault, Hon. Antonin, 1879–1971, vol. VII
Gall, William James, 1867–1938, vol. III
Gallacher, William, 1876–1951, vol. V
Gallacher, William, 1881–1965, vol. VI
Gallagher, Lt-Col Albert Ernest, 1872–1940, vol. III
Gallagher, Sir James Michael, 1860–1926, vol. II
Gallagher, Rt Rev. John, 1846–1923, vol. II
Gallagher, John Andrew, 1919–1980, vol. VII
Gallagher, Patrick Joseph, 1921–1993, vol. IX
Gallagher, Sir William, 1851–1933, vol. III
Gallaher, Major Alexander, died 1938, vol. III
Gallaher, Patrick Edmund, 1917–1988, vol. VIII
Gallaher, Thomas, 1840–1927, vol. II
Gallannaugh, Bertram William Leonard, 1900–1957, vol. V
Gallarati Scotti, Tommaso, 1878–1966, vol. VI
Gallardo, Angel, 1867–1934, vol. III
Galleghan, Brig. Sir Frederick Gallagher, 1897–1971, vol. VII
Galletti di Cadilhac, Countess, (Hon. Margaret Isabella Collier), 1846–1928, vol. II
Galli-Curci, Amelita, 1882–1963, vol. VI
Gallichan, Walter M., died 1946, vol. IV
Gallico, Paul William, 1897–1976, vol. VII
Gallie, Bryce; see Gallie, W. B.
Gallie, Maj.-Gen. James Stuart, 1870–1943, vol. IV
Gallie, (Walter) Bryce, 1912–1998, vol. X
Gallieni, Joseph, 1849–1916, vol. II
Gallienne, Wilfred Hansford, 1897–1956, vol. V
Gallier, William Henry, 1855–1946, vol. IV
Galliers-Pratt, Anthony Malcolm, 1926–1998, vol. X

Galliffet, Marquis de; Gaston Alexandre Auguste, 1830–1909, vol. I
Galliher, Hon. William Alfred, 1860–1934, vol. III
Gallon, Tom, 1866–1914, vol. I
Gallon, William Anthony, 1898–1962, vol. VI
Gallop, Constantine, died 1967, vol. VI
Gallop, Rev. Edward Jordan, 1850–1928, vol. II
Gallop, Rodney Alexander, 1901–1948, vol. IV
Galloway, 10th Earl of, 1835–1901, vol. I
Galloway, 11th Earl of, 1836–1920, vol. II
Galloway, 12th Earl of, 1892–1978, vol. VII
Galloway, Countess of; (Mary Arabella Arthur Cecil), died 1903, vol. I
Galloway, Alexander, 1901–1965, vol. VI
Galloway, Lt-Gen. Sir Alexander, 1895–1977, vol. VII
Galloway, Lt-Col Arnold Crawshaw, 1901–1988, vol. VIII
Galloway, Adm. Arthur Archibald Campbell, 1855–1918, vol. II
Galloway, Sir David, 1858–1943, vol. IV
Galloway, Col Frank Lennox, 1869–1949, vol. IV
Galloway, George, died 1933, vol. III
Galloway, Sir James, 1862–1922, vol. II
Galloway, Maj.-Gen. John Mawby Clossey, 1840–1916, vol. II
Galloway, Maj.-Gen. Rudolf William, 1891–1976, vol. VII
Galloway, Sir William, 1840–1927, vol. II
Galloway, William Johnson, 1866–1931, vol. III
Gallwey, Col Edmond Joseph, 1850–1927, vol. II
Gallwey, Sir John Frankland-Payne-, 4th Bt, 1889–1955, vol. V
Gallwey, Hon. Sir Michael Henry, 1826–1912, vol. I
Gallwey, Sir Ralph William Frankland Payne-, 3rd Bt, 1843–1916, vol. II
Gallwey, Sir Reginald Frankland Payne-, 5th Bt, 1889–1964, vol. VI
Gallwey, Maj.-Gen. Sir Thomas Joseph, 1852–1933, vol. III
Gallwey, Sir Thomas Lionel, 1821–1906, vol. I
Gallwey, Captain William Thomas Frankland Payne-, 1881–1914, vol. I (A), vol. II
Galpern, Baron (Life Peer); Myer Galpern, 1903–1993, vol. IX
Galpin, Sir Albert James, 1903–1984, vol. VIII
Galpin, Rev. Arthur John, 1861–1926, vol. II
Galpin, Rev. Francis William, 1858–1945, vol. IV
Galsworthy, Sir Arthur Norman, 1916–1986, vol. VIII
Galsworthy, Sir Edwin Henry, 1831–1920, vol. II
Galsworthy, John, 1867–1933, vol. III
Galsworthy, Sir John Edgar, 1919–1992, vol. IX
Galt, Alexander, 1854–1938, vol. III
Galt, Alexander Casimir, 1853–1936, vol. III
Galt, Sir Thomas, 1815–1901, vol. I
Galton, Rt Rev. Compton Theodore, 1855–1931, vol. III
Galton, Sir Douglas, 1822–1899, vol. I
Galton, Sir Francis, 1822–1911, vol. I
Galton, Frank Wallis, 1867–1952, vol. V
Galtrey, Albert Sidney, died 1935, vol. III
Galway, 7th Viscount, 1844–1931, vol. III
Galway, 8th Viscount, 1882–1943, vol. IV
Galway, 9th Viscount, 1929–1971, vol. VII

Galway, 10th Viscount, 1894–1977, vol. VII
Galway, 11th Viscount, 1900–1980, vol. VII
Galway, Lt-Col Sir Henry Lionel, 1859–1949, vol. IV
Gamage, Albert Walter, 1855–1930, vol. III
Gamage, Sir Leslie, 1887–1972, vol. VII
Gambier, Kenyon; see Lathrop, L. A.
Gambier-Parry, Major Ernest, 1853–1936, vol. III
Gambier-Parry, Maj.-Gen. Michael Denman, 1891–1976, vol. VII
Gambier-Parry, Brig. Sir Richard, 1894–1965, vol. VI
Gambier-Parry, Thomas Robert, 1883–1935, vol. III
Gamble, Rev. Arthur Mellor, 1899–1975, vol. VII
Gamble, Sir David, 1st Bt, 1823–1907, vol. I
Gamble, Sir David, 3rd Bt, 1876–1943, vol. IV
Gamble, Sir David, 5th Bt, 1933–1984, vol. VIII
Gamble, Sir David Arthur Josias, 4th Bt, 1907–1982, vol. VIII
Gamble, Adm. Sir Douglas Austin, 1856–1934, vol. III
Gamble, Adm. Edward Harpur, 1849–1925, vol. II
Gamble, Sir (Frederick) Herbert, 1907–1983, vol. VIII
Gamble, Frederick William, 1869–1926, vol. II
Gamble, Brig. Geoffrey Massey, 1896–1970, vol. VI
Gamble, Very Rev. Henry Reginald, died 1931, vol. III
Gamble, Sir Herbert; see Gamble, Sir F. H.
Gamble, James Sykes, 1847–1925, vol. II
Gamble, Rev. John, 1859–1929, vol. III
Gamble, Sir Josias Christopher, 2nd Bt, 1848–1908, vol. I
Gamble, Sir Reginald Arthur, 1862–1930, vol. III
Gamble, Brig.-Gen. Richard Narrien, 1860–1937, vol. III
Gamble, Robert Edward, 1922–1975, vol. VII
Gamble, Victor Felix, 1886–1952, vol. V
Gamblin, Sir George Henry, 1870–1930, vol. III
Game, Henry Clement, died 1966, vol. VI
Game, Air Vice-Marshal Sir Philip Woolcott, 1876–1961, vol. VI
Gamelin, Général Maurice Gustave, 1872–1958, vol. V
Games, Abram, 1914–1996, vol. X
Games, Ven. Joshua H.; see Hughes-Games.
Gamgee, Arthur, 1841–1909, vol. I
Gaminara, Albert William, 1913–1993, vol. IX
Gamlen, John Charles Blagdon, 1885–1952, vol. V
Gamley, Henry Snell, 1865–1928, vol. II
Gamlin, Lionel James, 1903–1967, vol. VI
Gammans, Ann Muriel, (Lady Gammans), 1898–1989, vol. VIII
Gammans, Sir David; see Gammans, Sir L. D.
Gammans, Sir (Leonard) David, 1st Bt, 1895–1957, vol. V
Gammell, Lt-Gen. Sir James Andrew Harcourt, 1892–1975, vol. VII
Gammell, James Gilbert Sydney, 1920–1999, vol. X
Gammell, Sir Sydney James, 1867–1946, vol. IV
Gammie, John, 1896–1968, vol. VI
Gammon, John Charles, 1887–1973, vol. VII
Gamon, Hugh Reece Percival, 1880–1953, vol. V
Gamow, George, 1904–1968, vol. VI

Gandar, Hon. Leslie Walter, 1919–1994, vol. X (AI)
Gandar Dower, Eric Leslie, 1894–1987, vol. VIII
Gandee, John Stephen, 1909–1994, vol. IX
Gandell, Sir Alan Thomas, 1904–1988, vol. VIII
Gandell, Captain Wilfred Pearse, 1886–1986, vol. VIII
Gander, L(eonard) Marsland, 1902–1986, vol. VIII
Gandhi, Mrs Indira (Nehru), 1917–1984, vol. VIII
Gandhi, Mohandas Karamchand, 1869–1948, vol. IV
Gandhi, Nagardas P., 1886–1960, vol. V (A), vol. VI (AI)
Gandhi, Rajiv, 1944–1991, vol. IX
Gandier, Rev. Alfred, 1861–1932, vol. III
Gandolfi, Duke, 1846–1906, vol. I
Gandolfi, Duke, 1899–1937, vol. III
Gandy, Eric Worsley, 1879–1958, vol. V
Gandy, Henry Garnett, 1860–1939, vol. III
Gane, Sir Irving Blanchard, 1892–1972, vol. VII
Gane, Richard Howard, 1912–1988, vol. VIII
Ganesh Datta Shastri, born 1861, vol. III
Ganga Ram, Rai Bahadur Sir Lala, 1851–1927, vol. II
Gange, Edwin Stanley, 1871–1944, vol. IV
Gangulee, Nagendra Nath, 1889–1954, vol. V
Ganguly, Most Rev. Theotonius A., 1920–1977, vol. VII
Ganilan, Ratu Sir Penaia Kanatabatu, 1918–1993, vol. IX
Ganley, Mrs Caroline Selina, 1879–1966, vol. VI
Gann, Thomas William Francis, died 1938, vol. III
Ganneau, Charles Simon C.; see Clermont-Ganneau.
Gannon, Brig. Jack Rose Compton, 1882–1980, vol. VII
Gannon, Hon. James Conley, 1860–1924, vol. II
Gannon, Rev. Patrick Joseph, 1879–1953, vol. V
Gant, Hon. Tetley, 1856–1928, vol. II
Ganz, Wilhelm, 1833–1914, vol. I
Gaon, Soloman, 1912–1994, vol. IX
Garbe, Louis Richard, died 1957, vol. V
Garbett, Sir Colin Campbell, 1881–1972, vol. VII
Garbett, Most Rev. and Rt Hon. Cyril Forster, 1875–1955, vol. III
Garbett, Lt-Col Hubert Champion, 1873–1939, vol. III
Garbett, Captain Leonard Gillilan, 1879–1974, vol. VII
Garbo, Greta, (Greta Lovisa Gustafsson), 1905–1990, vol. VIII
Garcia, Manuel, 1805–1906, vol. I
García Robles, Alfonso, 1911–1991, vol. IX
Garcke, Emile, 1856–1930, vol. III
Garcke, Sidney, 1885–1948, vol. IV
Garçon, Maurice, 1889–1967, vol. VI
Gard, William Henry, 1854–1936, vol. III
Garde, Engr Captain Robert Boles, 1863–1921, vol. II
Garden, Mary, 1874–1967, vol. VI
Gardener, Sir (Alfred) John, 1897–1985, vol. VIII
Gardener, Sir John; see Gardener, Sir A. J.
Gardham, Arthur John, 1899–1983, vol. VIII
Gardham, Air Vice-Marshal Marcus Maxwell, (Max), 1916–1991, vol. IX

Gardham, Air Vice-Marshal Max; *see* Gardham, Air Vice-Marshal Marcus M.

Gardiner, Baron (Life Peer); Gerald Austin Gardiner, 1900–1990, vol. VIII

Gardiner, Sir Alan Henderson, 1879–1963, vol. VI

Gardiner, Alfred G., 1865–1946, vol. IV

Gardiner, Col Bernard Calwoodley, 1879–1932, vol. III

Gardiner, Sir Chittampalam Abraham, 1899–1960, vol. V

Gardiner, Lt-Col Christopher John, 1907–1986, vol. VIII

Gardiner, Edward Rawson, 1859–1929, vol. III

Gardiner, Ernest David, 1909–1988, vol. VIII

Gardiner, Rev. Frederic Evelyn, *died* 1928, vol. II

Gardiner, Sir Frederick Crombie, 1855–1937, vol. III

Gardiner, Hon. Frederick George, 1874–1935, vol. III

Gardiner, Frederick Keith, 1904–1989, vol. VIII

Gardiner, Frederick William, 1849–1918, vol. II

Gardiner, Gp Captain George Cecil, 1892–1940, vol. III

Gardiner, Col Henry Lawrence, 1860–1946, vol. IV

Gardiner, Gen. Sir (Henry) Lynedoch, 1820–1897, vol. I

Gardiner, Henry Rolf, 1902–1971, vol. VII

Gardiner, James, 1860–1924, vol. II

Gardiner, Rt Hon. James Garfield, 1883–1962, vol. VI

Gardiner, John, 1852–1932, vol. III

Gardiner, John Stanley, 1872–1946, vol. IV

Gardiner, Keith; *see* Gardiner, F. K.

Gardiner, Linda, *died* 1941, vol. IV

Gardiner, Gen. Sir Lynedoch; *see* Gardiner, Gen. Sir H. L.

Gardiner, Patrick Lancaster, 1922–1997, vol. X

Gardiner, Brig. Richard, 1874–1957, vol. V

Gardiner, Brig. Richard, 1900–1989, vol. VIII

Gardiner, Robert Kweku Atta, 1914–1993, vol. X (AI)

Gardiner, Sir Robert Septimus, 1856–1939, vol. III

Gardiner, Robert Strachan, 1874–1950, vol. IV

Gardiner, Samuel Rawson, 1829–1902, vol. I

Gardiner, Sir Thomas Robert, 1883–1964, vol. VI

Gardiner, Rev. Thory Gage, 1857–1941, vol. IV

Gardiner, Walter, 1859–1941, vol. IV

Gardiner, Rev. Canon William, 1848–1925, vol. II

Gardiner, William Dundas, 1830–1900, vol. I

Gardiner-Hill, Harold, 1891–1982, vol. VIII

Gardiner-Scott, Rev. William, 1906–1998, vol. X

Gardini, Raul, 1933–1993, vol. IX

Gardner, Hon. Mrs Alan, (Nora Beatrice), *died* 1944, vol. IV

Gardner, Col Alan Coulstoun, 1846–1907, vol. I

Gardner, Alice, 1854–1927, vol. II

Gardner, Arthur Duncan, 1884–1978, vol. VII

Gardner, Benjamin, 1896–1956, vol. V

Gardner, Benjamin Walter, 1865–1948, vol. IV

Gardner, Sir Charles B.; *see* Bruce-Gardner.

Gardner, Lt-Col Charles James Hookham, 1875–1962, vol. VI

Gardner, Christopher Thomas, 1842–1914, vol. I

Gardner, Sir Douglas Bruce B.; *see* Bruce-Gardner.

Gardner, Edmund, 1874–1960, vol. V

Gardner, Edmund Garratt, 1869–1935, vol. III

Gardner, Eric Stanley, 1889–1970, vol. VI

Gardner, Sir Ernest, 1846–1925, vol. II

Gardner, Ernest Arthur, 1862–1939, vol. III

Gardner, Major Fitzroy, 1856–1936, vol. III

Gardner, Dame Frances Violet, 1913–1989, vol. VIII

Gardner, Francis William, 1891–1976, vol. VII

Gardner, Frank Matthias, 1908–1980, vol. VII (AII)

Gardner, Ven. George Lawrence Harter, *died* 1925, vol. II

Gardner, Sir George William Hoggan, 1903–1975, vol. VII

Gardner, Dame Helen Louise, 1908–1986, vol. VIII

Gardner, Henry Willoughby, 1861–1948, vol. IV

Gardner, Hugh, 1910–1986, vol. VIII

Gardner, J. Starkie, 1844–1930, vol. III

Gardner, James; *see* Gardner, L. J.

Gardner, James Clark Molesworth, 1894–1970, vol. VI

Gardner, James Patrick, 1883–1937, vol. III

Gardner, Rt Hon. Sir James Tynte Agg, 1846–1928, vol. II

Gardner, John Addyman, 1867–1946, vol. IV

Gardner, John Dunn, 1811–1903, vol. I

Gardner, Kenneth Burslam, 1924–1995, vol. IX

Gardner, (Leslie) James, 1907–1995, vol. IX

Gardner, Hon. Mrs Nora Beatrice; *see* Gardner, Hon. Mrs Alan.

Gardner, Percy, 1846–1937, vol. III

Gardner, Ralph Bennett, 1919–1997, vol. X

Gardner, Sir Robert, 1838–1920, vol. II

Gardner, Robert Cotton Bruce, 1889–1964, vol. VI

Gardner, Robert Dickson Robertson, 1924–1998, vol. X

Gardner, W(alter) Frank, 1900–1983, vol. VIII

Gardner, Walter Myers, 1861–1939, vol. III

Gardner, William, 1845–1926, vol. II

Gardner, William Henry, 1895–1977, vol. VII

Gardner, William Maving, 1914–2000, vol. X

Gardner, Air Commodore William Steven, 1909–1983, vol. VIII

Gardner-Brown, Anthony Geoffrey Hopwood, 1913–1978, vol. VII

Gardner-Medwin, Robert Joseph, 1907–1995, vol. IX

Gardner-Thorpe, Col Sir Ronald Laurence, 1917–1991, vol. IX

Gardyne, Lt-Col Charles G.; *see* Greenhill-Gardyne.

Gardyne, John, (Jock), B.; *see* Baron Bruce-Gardyne.

Garfield, Leon, 1921–1996, vol. X

Garfit, William, 1840–1920, vol. II

Garforth, Rear-Adm. Edmund St John, 1836–1920, vol. II

Garforth, Captain Francis Edmund Musgrave, 1874–1953, vol. V

Garforth, Sir William Edward, 1845–1921, vol. II

Garforth, William Henry, 1856–1931, vol. III

Garioch, Lord, (Master of Mar); David Charles of Mar, 1944–1967, vol. VI

Garlake, Maj.-Gen. Storr, 1904–1983, vol. VIII

Garland, Ailsa Mary, (Mrs John Rollit Mason), *died* 1982, vol. VIII

Garland, Sir Archibald, 1867–1937, vol. III

Garland, Charles Alexander Spencer, 1861–1914, vol. I

Garland, Charles Samuel, 1887–1960, vol. V

Garland, Charles Tuller, *died* 1921, vol. II

Garland, Rev. David John, 1864–1939, vol. III

Garland, Col Ernest Alfred Crowder, 1857–1938, vol. III

Garland, (Frederick) Peter (Collison), 1912–2000, vol. X

Garland, Hamlin, 1860–1940, vol. III

Garland, Henry Burnard, 1907–1981, vol. VIII

Garland, Hon. John, 1863–1921, vol. II

Garland, Lester, V. L.; *see* Lester-Garland.

Garland, Patrick Joseph, 1867–1929, vol. III

Garland, Peter; *see* Garland, F. P. C.

Garlick, George Frederick John, 1919–1997, vol. X

Garlick, Rev. Canon Wilfred, 1910–1982, vol. VIII

Garmonsway, George Norman, 1898–1967, vol. VI

Garmoyle, Viscount; Hugh Wilfrid John Cairns, 1907–1942, vol. IV

Garnar, Sir James Wilson, 1871–1957, vol. V

Garneau, Sir George; *see* Garneau, Sir J. G.

Garneau, Sir (John) George, 1864–1944, vol. IV

Garneau, Hon. Némèse, 1847–1937, vol. III

Garner, Baron (Life Peer); (Joseph John) Saville Garner, 1908–1983, vol. IV

Garner, Col Cathcart, 1861–1928, vol. II

Garner, Frank Harold, 1904–1990, vol. VIII

Garner, Frederic Francis, 1910–1993, vol. IX

Garner, Frederic Horace, 1893–1964, vol. VI

Garner, Sir Harry Mason, 1891–1977, vol. VII

Garner, John Nance, 1868–1967, vol. VI

Garner, Robert Livingston, 1894–1975, vol. VII

Garner, Ronald Arthur, 1920–1994, vol. IX

Garner, Walter Wesley, 1864–1938, vol. III

Garner, William, 1870–1953, vol. V

Garner, William Edward, 1889–1960, vol. V

Garnett, Bernard John, 1913–1977, vol. VII

Garnett, David, 1892–1981, vol. VIII

Garnett, Edward, 1868–1937, vol. III

Garnett, Frank Walls, 1867–1922, vol. II

Garnett, Sir George, 1871–1955, vol. V

Garnett, Rear-Adm. Herbert Neville, 1875–1960, vol. V

Garnett, (James Clerk) Maxwell, 1880–1958, vol. V

Garnett, John; *see* Garnett, W. J. P. M.

Garnett, Lucy M. J., *died* 1934, vol. III

Garnett, Martha, 1869–1946, vol. IV

Garnett, Maxwell; *see* Garnett, J. C. M.

Garnett, Col Reginald, 1844–1910, vol. I

Garnett, Richard, 1835–1906, vol. I

Garnett, Robert Singleton, *died* 1932, vol. III

Garnett, Walter James, 1889–1958, vol. V

Garnett, William, 1850–1932, vol. III

Garnett, Lt-Col William Brooksbank, 1875–1946, vol. IV

Garnett, William James, 1878–1965, vol. VI

Garnett, (William) John Poulton Maxwell, 1921–1997, vol. X

Garnett-Orme, Ion Hunter Touchet, 1910–1991, vol. IX

Garnham, Percy Cyril Claude, 1901–1994, vol. IX

Garnier, Col Alan Parry, 1886–1963, vol. VI

Garnier, Rev. Edward Southwell, 1850–1938, vol. III

Garnier, John C.; *see* Carpenter-Garnier.

Garnier, Rt Rev. Mark Rodolph C.; *see* Carpenter-Garnier.

Garnier, Lt-Col Walter Keppel, 1882–1969, vol. VI

Garnons Williams, Basil Hugh, 1906–1992, vol. IX

Garnons Williams, Captain Nevill Glennie, 1899–1983, vol. VIII

Garnsey, Rt Rev. David Arthur, 1909–1996, vol. X

Garnsey, Sir Gilbert Francis, 1883–1932, vol. III

Garnsworthy, Baron (Life Peer); Charles James Garnsworthy, 1906–1974, vol. VIII

Garnsworthy, Most Rev. Lewis Samuel, 1922–1990, vol. VIII

Garofalo, Baron Raffaele, 1851–1934, vol. III

Garran, Hon. Andrew, 1825–1901, vol. I

Garran, Sir (Isham) Peter, 1910–1991, vol. IX

Garran, Sir Peter; *see* Garran, Sir I. P.

Garran, Sir Robert Randolph, 1867–1957, vol. V

Garrard, Maj.-Gen. Apsley C.; *see* Cherry-Garrard.

Garrard, Apsley George Benet C.; *see* Cherry-Garrard.

Garrard, Henry John, 1912–1990, vol. VIII

Garrard, Hon. Jacob, 1846–1931, vol. III

Garrard, Rev. Lancelot Austin, 1904–1993, vol. IX

Garratt, Brig.-Gen. Sir Francis Sudlow, 1859–1928, vol. II

Garratt, Geoffrey Theodore, 1888–1942, vol. IV

Garratt, Gerald Reginald Mansel, 1906–1989, vol. VIII

Garratt, Lt-Col John Arthur Thomas, 1842–1919, vol. II

Garratt, Rev. Samuel, 1817–1906, vol. I

Garraway, Sir Edward Charles Frederick, 1865–1932, vol. III

Garrett, Alexander Adnett, 1886–1986, vol. VIII

Garrett, Lt-Gen. Sir (Alwyn) Ragnar, 1900–1977, vol. VII

Garrett, Col Arthur Newson Bruff, 1868–1942, vol. IV

Garrett, Sir (Arthur) Wilfrid, 1880–1967, vol. VI

Garrett, Rev. Charles, 1823–1900, vol. I

Garrett, Sir Douglas Thornbury, 1883–1949, vol. IV

Garrett, Col Edmund, 1840–1914, vol. I

Garrett, Edmund William, 1850–1936, vol. III

Garrett, Edward; *see* Mayo, Isabella

Garrett, F. Edmund, 1865–1907, vol. I

Garrett, Lt-Col Sir Frank, 1869–1952, vol. V

Garrett, Rev. George Henry St Patrick, 1855–1937, vol. III

Garrett, George Mursell, 1834–1897, vol. I

Garrett, Herbert Leonard Offley, 1881–1941, vol. IV

Garrett, Sir Hugh; *see* Garrett, Sir J. H.

Garrett, John Walter Percy, 1902–1966, vol. VI

Garrett, Sir (Joseph) Hugh, 1880–1978, vol. VII

Garrett, Captain Peter Bruff, 1866–1950, vol. IV

Garrett, Philip Leslie, 1888–1978, vol. VII

Garrett, R. W., 1853–1925, vol. II

Garrett, Lt-Gen. Sir Ragnar; *see* Garrett, Lt-Gen. Sir A. R.

Garrett, Hon. Sir Raymond William, 1900–1994, vol. IX

Garrett, Sir Ronald Thornbury, 1888–1972, vol. VII

Garrett, Samuel, 1850–1923, vol. II

Garrett, Stephen Denis, 1906–1989, vol. VIII
Garrett, Sir Wilfrid; see Garrett, Sir A. W.
Garrett, William, 1890–1967, vol. VI
Garrett, William Edward, 1920–1993, vol. IX
Garrett, Sir William Herbert, 1900–1977, vol. VII
Garrick, Hon. Sir James Francis, 1836–1907, vol. I
Garrick, Rev. James Percy, died 1919, vol. II
Garrington, Rev. Elsie Dorothea C.; see
  Chamberlain-Garrington.
Garrison, Lindley Miller, 1864–1932, vol. III
Garrod, Sir Alfred Baring, 1819–1907, vol. I
Garrod, Air Chief Marshal Sir (Alfred) Guy
  (Roland), 1891–1965, vol. VI
Garrod, Sir Archibald Edward, 1856–1936, vol. III
Garrod, Dorothy Annie Elizabeth, 1892–1968,
  vol. VI
Garrod, Geoffrey, 1886–1974, vol. VII
Garrod, Rev. Canon George Watts, 1857–1936,
  vol. III
Garrod, Air Chief Marshal Sir Guy; see Garrod, Air
  Chief Marshal Sir A. G. R.
Garrod, Heathcote William, 1878–1960, vol. V
Garrod, Lawrence Paul, 1895–1979, vol. VII
Garrod, William Henry Edward, 1892–1967,
  vol. VI
Garrow, Alexander, 1923–1966, vol. VI
Garrow, Hon. James Thompson, 1843–1916, vol. II
Garrow, Sir Nicholas, 1895–1982, vol. VIII
Garrow, Col Robert G., 1876–1932, vol. III
Garry, Robert Campbell, 1900–1993, vol. IX
Garsia, Lt-Col Herbert George Anderson,
  1871–1965, vol. VI
Garsia, Lt-Col Michael Clare, 1838–1903, vol. I
Garsia, Lt-Col Willoughby Clive, 1881–1961,
  vol. VI
Garside, Captain Frederick Rodney, 1897–1940,
  vol. III
Garside, Kenneth, 1913–1983, vol. VIII
Garside, Air Vice-Marshal Kenneth Vernon,
  1913–1986, vol. VIII
Garside, Oswald, 1869–1942, vol. IV
Garson, Alexander Denis, 1904–1968, vol. VI
Garson, Greer, 1908–1996, vol. X
Garstang, Cecil, 1904–1979, vol. VII
Garstang, John, 1876–1956, vol. V
Garstang, Tim; see Garstang, W. L.
Garstang, Walter, 1868–1949, vol. IV
Garstang, Walter Lucian, (Tim), 1908–1991, vol. IX
Garsten, John Henry, 1838–1903, vol. I
Garstin, Brig.-Gen. Alfred Allan, 1850–1937,
  vol. III
Garstin, Charles Fortescue, 1880–1969, vol. VI
Garstin, Crosbie Alfred Norman, 1887–1930,
  vol. III
Garstin, John Ribton, 1836–1917, vol. II, vol. III
Garstin, Lt-Col William Arthur MacDonell,
  1882–1975, vol. VII
Garstin, Sir William Edmund, 1849–1925, vol. II
Garth, Rt Hon. Sir Richard, 1820–1903, vol. I
Garth, Thomas Colleton, 1822–1907, vol. I
Garth, Sir William, 1854–1923, vol. II
Garthwaite, Brig. Clive Charlton, 1909–1979,
  vol. VII
Garthwaite, Sir William, 1st Bt, 1874–1956, vol. V

Garthwaite, Sir William, 2nd Bt, 1906–1993,
  vol. IX
Gartlan, Maj.-Gen. Gerald Ion, 1889–1975, vol. VII
Garton, Lt-Col James Archibald, 1891–1969,
  vol. VI
Garton, John William 1895–1971, vol. VII
Garton, Sir Richard Charles, 1857–1934, vol. III
Gartrell, Rt Rev. Frederick Roy, 1914–1987,
  vol. VIII
Gartside-Tipping, Col Robert Francis, 1852–1926,
  vol. II
Garvagh, 3rd Baron, 1852–1915, vol. I
Garvagh, 4th Baron, 1878–1956, vol. V
Garvan, Sir John Joseph, 1873–1927, vol. II
Garvey, Sir Ronald Herbert, 1903–1991, vol. IX
Garvey, Sir Terence Willcocks, 1915–1986,
  vol. VIII
Garvice, Charles, died 1920, vol. II
Garvice, Major Chudleigh, 1875–1921, vol. II
Garvie, Rev. Alfred Ernest, 1861–1945, vol. IV
Garvin, James Louis, died 1947, vol. IV
Garvin, Thomas, 1843–1922, vol. II
Garvin, Sir Thomas Forrest, 1881–1940, vol. III
Garwood, Edmund Johnston, 1864–1949, vol. IV
Garwood, Lt-Col Henry Percy, 1882–1956, vol. V
Garwood, Engr-Rear-Adm. Hugh Sydney,
  1872–1948, vol. IV
Garwood, Lt-Col John Reginald, 1873–1948,
  vol. IV
Gary, Elbert Henry, died 1927, vol. II
Gary, Romain, 1914–1980, vol. VII
Gascoigne, Sir Alvary Douglas Frederick,
  1893–1970, vol. VI
Gascoigne, Lt-Col Cecil Claud Hugh Orby,
  1877–1929, vol. III
Gascoigne, Brig.-Gen. Sir (Ernest) Frederick (Orby),
  1873–1944, vol. IV
Gascoigne, Col Frederic Richard Thomas Trench,
  1851–1937, vol. III
Gascoigne, Brig.-Gen. Sir Frederick; see Gascoigne,
  Brig.-Gen. Sir E. F. O.
Gascoigne, Hubert Claude Victor, died 1959, vol. V
Gascoigne, John Henry, 1856–1928, vol. II
Gascoigne, Maj.-Gen. Sir Julian Alvery, 1903–1990,
  vol. VIII
Gascoigne, Laura Gwendolen, died 1949, vol. IV
Gascoigne, Maj.-Gen. Sir William Julius Gascoigne,
  1844–1926, vol. II
Gascoyne-Cecil, Victor Alexander, 1891–1977,
  vol. VII
Gascoyne-Cecil, Rt Rev. Lord William; see Cecil.
Gaselee, Gen. Sir Alfred, 1844–1918, vol. II
Gaselee, Sir Stephen, 1882–1943, vol. IV
Gash, Robert Walker, 1926–1986, vol. VIII
Gask, George Ernest, 1875–1951, vol. V
Gask, Rear-Adm. (S) Walter, 1870–1949, vol. IV
Gaskain, John Stuart Hinton, 1910–1971, vol. VII
Gaskell, Ven. Albert Fisher, 1874–1950, vol. IV
Gaskell, Surg. Vice-Adm. Sir Arthur, 1871–1952,
  vol. V
Gaskell, Rt Hon. Charles George Milnes,
  1842–1919, vol. II
Gaskell, Lady Constance M.; see Milnes Gaskell.
Gaskell, Evelyn Milnes, 1877–1931, vol. III
Gaskell, George Percival, 1868–1934, vol. III

Gaskell, Helen Mary, *died* 1940, vol. III
Gaskell, Henry Melville, 1879–1954, vol. V
Gaskell, Maj.-Gen. Herbert Stuart, 1882–1957, vol. V
Gaskell, Sir Holbrook, 1878–1951, vol. V
Gaskell, Col Joseph, 1849–1930, vol. III
Gaskell, Col Joseph Gerald, 1885–1959, vol. V
Gaskell, Walter Holbrook, 1847–1914, vol. I
Gaskell, William, 1874–1954, vol. V
Gaskin, Arthur J., 1862–1928, vol. II
Gasking, Mrs Ella Hudson, *died* 1966, vol. VI
Gaskoin, Charles Jacinth Bellairs, *died* 1955, vol. V
Gasquet, His Eminence Cardinal Francis Aidan, 1846–1929, vol. III
Gass, Ian Graham, 1926–1992, vol. IX
Gass, John Bradshaw, 1855–1939, vol. III
Gass, Sir Michael David Irving, 1916–1983, vol. VIII
Gass, Sir Neville Archibald, 1893–1965, vol. VI
Gasser, Herbert Spencer, 1888–1963, vol. VI
Gassman, Lewis, 1910–1998, vol. X
Gasson, Sir Lionel Bell, 1889–1977, vol. VII
Gastambide, Philippe, 1905–1984, vol. VIII
Gaster, Moses, 1856–1939, vol. III
Gastrell, Lt-Col Everard Huddleston, 1898–1960, vol. V
Gastrell, Sir William Houghton-, 1852–1935, vol. III
Gastrell, William Shaw Harriss, 1862–1948, vol. IV
Gasyonga II, Sir Charles Godfrey, 1910–1982, vol. VIII
Gatacre, Rear-Adm. Galfry George Ormond, 1907–1983, vol. VIII
Gatacre, Maj.-Gen. Sir John, 1841–1932, vol. III
Gatacre, Maj.-Gen. Sir William Forbes, 1843–1906, vol. I
Gatehouse, Maj.-Gen. Alexander Hugh, 1895–1964, vol. VI
Gatenby, James Brontë, 1892–1960, vol. V
Gater, Sir George Henry, 1886–1963, vol. VI
Gates, Caleb Frank, 1857–1946, vol. IV
Gates, Edward, *died* 1965, vol. VI
Gates, Ernest Everard, 1903–1984, vol. VIII
Gates, Sir Frank Campbell, 1862–1947, vol. IV
Gates, Horace Frederick Alfred, 1903–1962, vol. VI
Gates, Lewis Edwards, 1860–1924, vol. II
Gates, Percy, *died* 1940, vol. III
Gates, R(eginald) Ruggles, 1882–1962, vol. VI
Gates, Sidney Barrington, 1893–1973, vol. VII
Gates, Sylvester Govett, 1901–1972, vol. VII
Gates, Thomas Sovereign, Jr, 1906–1983, vol. VIII
Gates, Walter George, *died* 1936, vol. III
Gates, William Thomas George, 1908–1990, vol. VIII
Gatey, Joseph, 1855–1912, vol. I
Gathorne-Hardy, Hon. Alfred Erskine, 1845–1918, vol. II
Gathorne-Hardy, Col Hon. Charles Gathorne, 1841–1919, vol. II
Gathorne-Hardy, Gen. Hon. Sir Francis; *see* Gathorne-Hardy, Gen. Hon. Sir J. F.
Gathorne-Hardy, Geoffrey Malcolm, 1878–1972, vol. VII
Gathorne-Hardy, Lady Isobel, 1875–1963, vol. VI

Gathorne-Hardy, Gen. Hon. Sir (John) Francis, 1874–1949, vol. IV
Gathorne-Hardy, Hon. Robert, 1902–1973, vol. VII
Gati, Benerji D.; *see* Durga Gati.
Gatley, Clement Carpenter, 1881–1936, vol. III
Gatley, John, 1845–1934, vol. III
Gatliff, Gen. Albert Farrar, 1857–1927, vol. II
Gatling, Richard Jordan, 1818–1903, vol. I
Gatt, Hon. Camillo, vol. II
Gatt, Hon. Lorenzo, 1857–1938, vol. III
Gatti, Sir John M., 1872–1929, vol. III
Gattie, Alfred Warwick, 1856–1925, vol. II
Gattie, Maj.-Gen. Kenneth Francis Drake, 1890–1982, vol. VIII
Gattie, Vernon Rodney Montagu, 1885–1966, vol. VI
Gatty, Rev. Alfred, 1813–1903, vol. I
Gatty, Sir Alfred Scott S.; *see* Scott-Gatty.
Gatty, Nicholas Comyn, 1874–1946, vol. IV
Gatty, Sir Stephen Herbert, 1849–1922, vol. II
Gaudet, Col Frederick Mondelet, 1867–1947, vol. IV
Gaudin, Engr-Rear-Adm. Edouard, *died* 1945, vol. IV
Gaughran, Rt Rev. Laurence, 1842–1928, vol. II
Gaughren, Rt Rev. Matthew, 1843–1914, vol. I
Gaul, Walter Miller, 1867–1938, vol. III
Gaul, Rt Rev. William Thomas, *died* 1928, vol. II
Gauld, David, *died* 1936, vol. III
Gault, Brig. A(ndrew) Hamilton, 1882–1958, vol. V
Gault, Charles Alexander, 1908–1996, vol. X
Gault, James, 1850–1927, vol. II
Gault, Brig. Sir James Frederick 1902–1977, vol. VII
Gaumont, Léon Ernest, 1864–1946, vol. IV
Gaunt, Lt-Col Cecil Robert, 1863–1938, vol. III
Gaunt, Sir Edwin, 1818–1903, vol. I
Gaunt, Adm. Sir Ernest Frederick Augustus, 1865–1940, vol. III
Gaunt, Adm. Sir Guy Reginald Archer, 1870–1953, vol. V
Gaunt, Rev. Canon Howard Charles Adie, (Tom Gaunt), 1902–1983, vol. VIII
Gaunt, Mary, *died* 1942, vol. IV
Gaunt, Percy Reginald, 1875–1926, vol. II
Gaunt, Rev. Canon Tom; *see* Gaunt, Rev. Canon H. C. A.
Gaunt, Walter Henry, 1874–1951, vol. V
Gaunt, William, 1900–1980, vol. VII
Gaunt Suddards, Henry; *see* Suddards.
Gauntlett, Major Eric Gerald, 1885–1972, vol. VII
Gauntlett, Sir Frederic; *see* Gauntlett, Sir M. F.
Gauntlett, Sir (Mager) Frederic, 1873–1964, vol. VI
Gausden, Ronald, 1921–1997, vol. X
Gaussen, Maj.-Gen. Charles de Lisle, 1896–1971, vol. VII
Gaussen, Brig.-Gen. James Robert, 1871–1959, vol. V
Gaussen, Perceval David Campbell, 1862–1928, vol. II
Gauthier, Most Rev. Charles Hugh, 1843–1922, vol. II
Gauthier, Rt Rev. George, 1871–1940, vol. III
Gauthier-Villars, Henry, 1859–1931, vol. III
Gautier, C. Lucien, 1850–1924, vol. II

Gautier, Judith, *died* 1917, vol. II
Gauvain, (Catherine Joan) Suzette, (Mrs R. O. Murray), *died* 1980, vol. VII
Gauvain, Sir Henry, 1878–1945, vol. IV
Gauvain, Suzette; *see* Gauvain, C. J. S.
Gauvain, Timothy John Lund, 1942–1994, vol. IX
Gauvain, W., *died* 1910, vol. I
Gavan-Duffy, Hon. Sir Charles Leonard, 1882–1961, vol. VI
Gavan-Duffy, Thomas, 1867–1932, vol. III
Gavey, Clarence John, 1911–1982, vol. VIII
Gavey, Sir John, 1842–1923, vol. II
Gavin, Ethel, *died* 1918, vol. II
Gavin, Maj.-Gen. James Merricks Lewis, 1911–2000, vol. X
Gavin, Malcolm Ross, 1908–1989, vol. VIII
Gavin, Michael, 1843–1919, vol. II
Gavin, Sir William, 1886–1968, vol. VI
Gavin, William Aloysius, *died* 1948, vol. IV
Gavito, Vicente S.; *see* Sanchez-Gavito.
Gawan Taylor, Henry, 1855–1928, vol. II
Gawne, Ewan Moore, 1889–1978, vol. VII
Gawsworth, John, 1912–1970, vol. VI
Gawthorpe, Brig. John Bernard, 1891–1979, vol. VII
Gay, Maj.-Gen. Sir Arthur William, 1863–1944, vol. IV
Gay, Edwin Francis, 1867–1946, vol. IV
Gay, Maisie, 1883–1945, vol. IV
Gayda, Virginio, 1885–1944, vol. IV
Gaye, Sir Arthur Stretton, 1881–1960, vol. V
Gaye, Rev. Herbert Charles, *died* 1931, vol. III
Gayer, Arthur David, 1903–1951, vol. V
Gayer-Anderson, Major Robert Grenville, 1881–1945, vol. IV
Gayer-Anderson, Col Thomas Gayer, 1881–1960, vol. V
Gayford, Air Cdre Oswald Robert, 1893–1945, vol. IV
Gayley, Charles Mills, 1858–1932, vol. III
Gayre of Gayre and Nigg, Robert, 1907–1996, vol. X
Gaze, Alfred Harold, 1885–1954, vol. V
Geach, William Foster, 1859–1940, vol. III (A), vol. IV
Geake, Charles, 1867–1919, vol. II
Geake, Maj.-Gen. Clifford Henry, 1894–1982, vol. VIII
Gear, William, 1915–1997, vol. X
Geard, John Reginald, 1861–1934, vol. III
Geary, Major Benjamin Handley, 1891–1976, vol. VII
Geary, Lt-Col Hon. George Reginald, 1874–1954, vol. V
Geary, Lt-Gen. Sir Henry Le Guay, 1837–1918, vol. II
Geary, Sir William Nevill Montgomerie, 5th Bt, 1859–1944, vol. IV
Gebbie, Sir Frederick St John, 1871–1939, vol. III
Geddes, 1st Baron, 1879–1954, vol. V
Geddes, 2nd Baron, 1907–1975, vol. VII
Geddes of Epsom, Baron (Life Peer); Charles John Geddes, 1897–1983, vol. VIII
Geddes, Air Cdre Andrew James Wray, 1906–1988, vol. VIII

Geddes, Sir (Anthony) Reay (Mackay), 1912–1998, vol. X
Geddes, Rt Hon. Sir Eric Campbell, 1875–1937, vol. III
Geddes, Ewan, *died* 1935, vol. III
Geddes, George; *see* Geddes, W. G. M.
Geddes, Lt-Col George Hessing, 1864–1933, vol. III
Geddes, Irvine Campbell, 1882–1962, vol. VI
Geddes, Brig.-Gen. John Gordon, 1863–1919, vol. II
Geddes, Norman Bel, 1893–1958, vol. V
Geddes, Sir Patrick, 1854–1932, vol. III
Geddes, Sir Reay; *see* Geddes, Sir A. R. M.
Geddes, Col Robert James, 1858–1928, vol. II
Geddes, Rt Rev. William Archibald, 1894–1947, vol. IV
Geddes, Sir William Duguid, 1828–1900, vol. I
Geddes, William George Nicholson, 1913–1993, vol. IX
Geddie, John, 1848–1937, vol. III
Geddie, John Liddell, 1881–1969, vol. VI
Geddis, Sir William Duncan, 1896–1971, vol. VII
Geden, Alfred Shenington, 1857–1936, vol. III
Gedge, Rev. Edward Lionel, 1861–1932, vol. III
Gedge, Rev. Hugh Somerville, 1844–1923, vol. II
Gedge, Montagu Lathom, 1899–1958, vol. V
Gedge, Sydney, 1829–1923, vol. II
Gedye, George Eric Rowe, 1890–1970, vol. VI
Gedye, Nicholas George, 1874–1947, vol. IV
Gee, Col Ernest Edward, 1888–1959, vol. V
Gee, Lt-Col Frederick William, 1863–1930, vol. III
Gee, Geoffrey, 1910–1996, vol. X
Gee, Harry Percy, 1874–1962, vol. VI
Gee, Very Rev. Henry, *died* 1938, vol. III
Gee, Hubert George, 1909–1959, vol. V
Gee, Rev. Richard, 1817–1902, vol. I
Gee, Captain Robert, 1876–1960, vol. V
Gee, Samuel Jones, 1839–1911, vol. I
Gee, Timothy Hugh, 1936–1998, vol. X
Gee, William Winson Haldane, 1857–1928, vol. II
Geen, Burnard, 1882–1966, vol. VI
Geen, Harry, *died* 1939, vol. III
Geer, Ven. George Thomas, 1844–1918, vol. II
Geffen, John Lionel Henry, 1925–1975, vol. VII
Geijer, Eric Neville, *died* 1941, vol. IV
Geikie, Sir Archibald, 1835–1924, vol. II
Geikie, Rev. Cunningham, 1824–1906, vol. I
Geikie, James, 1839–1915, vol. I
Geikie-Cobb, Ivo; *see* Cobb.
Geikie-Cobb, Rev. William Frederick, 1857–1941, vol. IV
Geil, William Edgar, *died* 1925, vol. II
Geldart, Rev. Ernest, 1848–1929, vol. III
Geldart, Rev. James William, 1837–1914, vol. I
Geldart, William Martin, 1870–1922, vol. II
Gelder, Sir Alfred; *see* Gelder, Sir W. A.
Gelder, Sir (William) Alfred, 1855–1941, vol. IV
Gell, Alfred Antony Francis, 1945–1997, vol. X
Gell, Hon. Mrs Edith Mary, 1860–1944, vol. IV
Gell, Rt Rev. Frederick, *died* 1902, vol. I
Gell, Herbert George, 1856–1931, vol. III
Gell, Sir James, 1823–1905, vol. I
Gell, Philip Lyttelton, 1852–1926, vol. II
Gell, Rev. Canon William, 1859–1939, vol. III
Gell, William Charles Coleman, 1888–1969, vol. VI

Gell, William John, 1893–1961, vol. VI
Gellert, Leon, 1892–1977, vol. VII
Gellibrand, Maj.-Gen. Sir John, 1872–1945, vol. IV
Gellner, Ernest André, 1925–1995, vol. IX
Gelsthorpe, Rt Rev. (Alfred) Morris, 1892–1968, vol. VI
Gelsthorpe, Rt Rev. Morris; see Gelsthorpe, Rt Rev. A. M.
Gem, Rev. Hubert Arnold, died 1936, vol. III
Gemmell, Alan Robertson, 1913–1986, vol. VIII
Gemmell, Sir Arthur Alexander, 1892–1960, vol. V
Gemmell, George Harrison, 1860–1941, vol. IV
Gemmell, Samson, died 1913, vol. I
Gemmell, Lt-Col William Alexander Stewart, 1874–1932, vol. III
Gemmill, James Fairlie, died 1926, vol. II
Gemmill, Lt-Col William, 1878–1918, vol. III
Genée-Isitt, Dame Adeline, 1878–1970, vol. VI
Genese, Robert William, 1848–1928, vol. II
Genevoix, Maurice Charles Louis, 1890–1980, vol. VII
Genn, Leo John, 1905–1978, vol. VII
Genn, Captain Otto Hermann H.; see Hawke-Genn.
Gennadius, Joannes, 1844–1932, vol. III
Gennings, John Frederick, 1885–1955, vol. V
Genochio, Henry, 1862–1933, vol. III
Gent, Sir Edward; see Gent, Sir G. E. J.
Gent, Sir (Gerard) Edward (James), 1895–1948, vol. IV
Gent, John, 1844–1927, vol. II
Gentele, (Claes-) Göran Herman Arvid, 1920–1972, vol. VII
Gentele, Göran; see Gentele, C.-G. H. A.
Gentili, Most Rev. Charles, 1842–1917, vol. II
Gentle, Francis Steward, 1894–1962, vol. VI
Gentle, Sir Frederick William, 1892–1966, vol. VI
Gentle, Sir William Benjamin, 1864–1948, vol. IV
Gentles, Thomas A., 1867–1943, vol. IV
Gentner, Wolfgang, 1906–1980, vol. VII (AII)
Gentry, Jack Sydney Bates, 1899–1978, vol. VII
Gentry, Maj.-Gen. Sir William George, 1899–1991, vol. IX
Geoffrey-Lloyd, Baron (Life Peer); Geoffrey William Geoffrey-Lloyd, 1902–1984, vol. VIII
Geoffrion, Aimé, 1872–1946, vol. IV
Geoffrion, Victor, 1851–1923, vol. II
Geoghegan, Col Francis Edward, 1869–1945, vol. IV
Geoghegan, Hon. James, died 1951, vol. V
Geoghegan, Joseph, 1888–1948, vol. IV
Geoghegan, Col Norman Meredith, 1876–1962, vol. VI
Geoghegan, Brig.-Gen. Stannus, 1866–1929, vol. III
George, Rev. (Alfred) Raymond, 1912–1998, vol. X
George, Sir Anthony Hastings, 1886–1944, vol. IV
George, Ven. Christopher Owen, 1891–1977, vol. VII
George, Daniel, 1890–1967, vol. VI
George, Edward Claudius Scotney, 1865–1936, vol. III
George, Sir Edward James, died 1950, vol. IV
George, Sir Ernest, 1839–1922, vol. II
George, Frank Bernard, 1899–1974, vol. VII
George, Rev. Canon George Frank, 1873–1942, vol. IV

George, Griffith Owen, 1902–1994, vol. IX
George, Herbert Horace, 1890–1982, vol. VIII
George, Hereford B., 1838–1910, vol. I
George, Hugh Shaw, 1892–1967, vol. VI
George, Sir John Clarke, 1901–1972, vol. VII
George, Mary Dorothy, died 1971, vol. VII
George, Lady Megan L.; see Lloyd George.
George, Rev. Raymond; see George, Rev. A. R.
George, Air Vice-Marshal Sir Robert Allingham, 1896–1967, vol. VI
George, Robert Esmond Gordon; see Sencourt, R.
George, Rt Rev. Mgr Thomas, 1872–1943, vol. IV
George, Thomas Neville, 1904–1980, vol. VII
George, W. L., 1882–1926, vol. II
George, Senator Walter Franklin, 1878–1957, vol. V
George, Hon. William James, 1853–1931, vol. III
George, William R., 1866–1936, vol. III
George-Brown, Baron (Life Peer); George Alfred George-Brown, 1914–1985, vol. VIII
Georges, Sir (James) Olva, 1890–1976, vol. VII
Georges, Sir Olva; see Georges, Sir J. O.
Georges-Picot, Jacques Marie Charles, 1900–1987, vol. VIII
Gepp, Maj.-Gen. Sir Cyril; see Gepp, Maj.-Gen. Sir E. C.
Gepp, Maj.-Gen. Sir (Ernest) Cyril, 1879–1964, vol. VI
Gepp, Sir Herbert William, 1877–1954, vol. V
Gepp, Rev. Nicolas Parker, died 1921, vol. II
Geraghty, Sir William, 1917–1977, vol. VII
Gerahty, Sir Charles Cyril, 1888–1978, vol. VII
Gerald, William John, 1850–1923, vol. II
Gerard, 2nd Baron, 1851–1902, vol. I
Gerard, 3rd Baron, 1883–1953, vol. V
Gerard, 4th Baron, 1918–1992, vol. IX
Gerard, Amelia Louise, 1878–1970, vol. VI
Gerard, Bt Col Charles Robert Tolver Michael, 1894–1971, vol. VII
Gerard, Dorothea; see Longard de Longgarde, D.
Gerard, Geoffrey; see Gerard, W. G.
Gerard, Rt Rev. George Vincent, 1898–1984, vol. VIII
Gerard, Hon. James Watson, 1867–1951, vol. V
Gerard, (Jane) Emily, (Madame de Laszowska), 1849–1905, vol. I
Gerard, Father John, 1840–1912, vol. I
Gerard, Gen. Sir Montagu Gilbert, 1843–1905, vol. 1
Gerard, (William) Geoffrey, 1907–1994, vol. IX
Gerard-Dicconson, Hon. Robert Joseph; see Dicconson.
Gerardy, Jean, 1877–1929, vol. III
Géraud, Charles Joseph André, 1882–1974, vol. VII
Gerbrandy, Pieter S., 1885–1961, vol. VI
Gere, Charles March, 1869–1957, vol. V
Gere, John Arthur Giles, 1921–1995, vol. IX
Gerhard, Roberto Juan René, 1896–1970, vol. VI
Gerhardie, William Alexander, 1895–1977, vol. VII
Gerhardt, Elena, 1883–1961, vol. VI
Gericke van Herwijnen, Baron, died 1930, vol. III
Gérin, Winifred Eveleen, (Mrs John Lock), 1901–1981, vol. VIII
Germaine, Robert Arthur, died 1905, vol. I
German, Sir Edward, 1862–1936, vol. III
German, Major Sir James, 1879–1958, vol. V

German, Sir Ronald Ernest, 1905–1983, vol. VIII
German, William Manley, 1851–1933, vol. III
Germanos, Strenopoulos, 1872–1951, vol. V
Gernsheim, Helmut Erich Robert, 1913–1995, vol. IX
Gerome, Jean Leon, 1824–1904, vol. I
Gerothwohl, Maurice Alfred, 1877–1941, vol. IV
Gerrans, Henry Tresawna, 1858–1921, vol. II
Gerrard, Sir (Albert) Denis, 1903–1965, vol. VI
Gerrard, Alfred Horace, 1899–1998, vol. X
Gerrard, Basil Harding, 1919–1994, vol. IX
Gerrard, Charles Robert, died 1964, vol. VI
Gerrard, Sir Denis; see Gerrard, Sir A. D.
Gerrard, Air Cdre Eugene Louis, 1881–1963, vol. VI
Gerrard, Major Frederick Wernham, 1887–1974, vol. VII
Gerrard, Maj.-Gen. John Joseph, 1867–1938, vol. III
Gerry, Hon. Elbridge Thomas, 1837–1927, vol. II
Gershwin, George, 1898–1937, vol. III
Gertler, Mark, 1892–1939, vol. III
Gerty, Paymaster Captain Francis Hamilton, 1876–1955, vol. V
Gervais, Hon. Honoré Hippolyte Achille, 1864–1915, vol. I, vol. III
Gervers, Brig. Francis Richard Soutter, 1873–1971, vol. VII
Gervis, Henry, 1837–1924, vol. II
Gervis, Henry, 1863–1941, vol. IV
Gervis-Meyrick, Sir George Augustus Eliott Tapps; see Meyrick.
Gery, Henry Theodore W.; see Wade-Gery.
Gesell, Arnold, 1880–1961, vol. VI
Gethin, Sir Richard Charles Percy, 7th Bt, 1847–1921, vol. II
Gethin, Lt-Col Sir Richard Patrick St Lawrence, 9th Bt, 1911–1988, vol. VIII
Gethin, Col Sir Richard Walter St Lawrence, 8th Bt, 1878–1946, vol. IV
Gettins, Lt-Col Joseph Holmes, 1873–1954, vol. V
Getty, J(ean) Paul, 1892–1976, vol. VII
Geyer, Albertus Lourens, 1894–1969, vol. VI
Geyl, Pieter, 1887–1966, vol. VI
Ghale, Subedar Gaje; see Gaje Ghale.
Ghislain, Léon; see Carton de Wiart, L. C. G.
Ghormley, Vice-Adm. Robert Lee, 1883–1958, vol. V
Ghosal, Mrs Srimati Svarna Kumari Devi, 1857–1932, vol. III
Ghose, Sir Bipin Behary, 1868–1934, vol. III
Ghose, Sir Charu Chunder, 1874–1934, vol. III
Ghose, Sir Chunder Madhub, 1838–1918, vol. II
Ghose, Hemendra Prasad, 1876–1962, vol. VI
Ghose, Sir Rashbehary, 1845–1921, vol. II
Ghose, Sir Sarat Kumar, 1879–1963, vol. VI
Ghosh, Sir Jnan Chandra, 1894–1959, vol. V
Ghulam Mohammed, 1895–1956, vol. V
Ghuznavi, Hon. Alhadj Nawab Bahadur Sir Abdelkerim Abu Ahmed Kahan of Dilduar, 1872–1939, vol. III
Giacometti, Alberto, 1901–1966, vol. VI
Giamatti, (Angelo) Bartlett, 1938–1989, vol. VIII
Giamatti, Bartlett; see Giamatti, A. B.
Giannini, Amadeo Peter, 1870–1949, vol. IV

Giauque, William Francis, 1895–1982, vol. VIII
Gib, Gen. Sir William Anthony, 1827–1915, vol. I
Gibb, Sir Alexander, 1872–1958, vol. V
Gibb, Alistair Monteith, 1901–1955, vol. V
Gibb, Andrew Dewar, died 1974, vol. VII
Gibb, Andrew McArthur, 1927–1992, vol. IX
Gibb, Sir Claude Dixon, 1898–1959, vol. V
Gibb, Maj.-Gen. Sir Evan, 1877–1947, vol. IV
Gibb, George Dutton, 1920–1986, vol. VIII
Gibb, Sir George Stegmann, 1850–1925, vol. II
Gibb, Sir Hamilton Alexander Rosskeen, 1895–1971, vol. VII
Gibb, James, 1844–1910, vol. I
Gibb, Rev. James, 1857–1935, vol. III
Gibb, James A. T., 1842–1922, vol. II
Gibb, James Rattray, 1844–1946, vol. IV
Gibb, Rev. John, 1835–1915, vol. I
Gibb, Col John Hassard Stewart 1859–1933, vol. III
Gibb, Malcolm Couper, 1861–1938, vol. III
Gibb, Maurice Sylvester, 1878–1950, vol. IV
Gibb, Robert, 1845–1932, vol. III
Gibb, Robertson Fyffe, 1868–1944, vol. IV
Gibb, Lt-Col Ronald Charles, 1873–1946, vol. IV
Gibb, Thomas George, 1915–1980, vol. VII
Gibb, William Elphinstone, 1943–1988, vol. VIII
Gibb, William Eric, 1911–1992, vol. IX
Gibbard, George, 1886–1960, vol. V
Gibbard, Maj.-Gen. Thomas Wykes, 1865–1957, vol. V
Gibbens, Brian; see Gibbens, E. B.
Gibbens, (Edward) Brian, 1912–1985, vol. VIII
Gibbens, Frank Edward Hilary George, 1913–1987, vol. VIII
Gibbens, Trevor Charles Noel, 1912–1983, vol. VIII
Gibberd, Sir Frederick, 1908–1984, vol. VIII
Gibberd, George Frederick, died 1976, vol. VII
Gibbes, Cuthbert Chapman, 1850–1927, vol. II
Gibbes, Sir Edward Osborne-, 3rd Bt, 1850–1931, vol. III
Gibbes, Sir Philip Arthur Osborne-, 4th Bt, 1884–1940, vol. III
Gibbes, Reginald Prescott, 1867–1933, vol. III
Gibbings, Robert John, 1889–1958, vol. V
Gibbins, Elizabeth Mary, 1911–1992, vol. IX
Gibbins, Frederick William, 1861–1937, vol. III
Gibbins, Rev. Henry de Beltgens, 1865–1907, vol. I
Gibbins, Joseph, 1888–1965, vol. VI
Gibbins, Theodore, 1876–1952, vol. V
Gibbon, Col Charles Monk, 1877–1937, vol. III
Gibbon, Sir Douglas Stuart, 1882–1960, vol. V
Gibbon, Sir Gwilym; see Gibbon, Sir. I. G.
Gibbon, Sir (Ioan) Gwilym, 1874–1948, vol. IV
Gibbon, Brig.-Gen. James Aubrey, 1864–1947, vol. IV
Gibbon, Rev. James Morgan, died 1932, vol. III
Gibbon, Brig. John Houghton, 1878–1960, vol. V
Gibbon, Gen. Sir John Houghton, 1917–1997, vol. X
Gibbon, Monk; see Gibbon, W. M.
Gibbon, Perceval, 1879–1926, vol. II
Gibbon, Thomas Mitchell, died 1921, vol. II
Gibbon, Sir William Duff, 1837–1919, vol. II
Gibbon, Lt-Col William Duff, 1880–1955, vol. V
Gibbon, (William) Monk, 1896–1987, vol. VIII

Gibbons, Major Sir Alexander Doran, 7th Bt, 1873–1956, vol. V
Gibbons, Sir Charles, 6th Bt, 1828–1909, vol. I
Gibbons, Brig. Edward John, 1906–1990, vol. VIII
Gibbons, Major Edward Stephen, 1883–1918, vol. II
Gibbons, Cdre George, died 1959, vol. V
Gibbons, Sir George Christie, 1848–1918, vol. II
Gibbons, His Eminence Cardinal James, 1834–1921, vol. II
Gibbons, James Francis, 1890–1957, vol. V
Gibbons, James Samuel, 1850–1914, vol. I
Gibbons, Sir John Edward, 8th Bt, 1914–1982, vol. VIII
Gibbons, John Lloyd, 1837–1919, vol. II
Gibbons, Stella Dorothea, (Mrs A. B. Webb), 1902–1989, vol. VIII
Gibbons, Sir Thomas Clarke Pilling, 1868–1934, vol. III
Gibbons, Lt-Col Sir Walter, 1871–1933, vol. III
Gibbons, Sir William, 1841–1930, vol. III
Gibbons, Col William Ernest, 1898–1976, vol. VII
Gibbons, Sir William Kenrick, 1876–1957, vol. V
Gibbs, Dame Anstice Rosa, 1905–1978, vol. VII
Gibbs, Antony, 1842–1907, vol. I
Gibbs, Major Arthur Hamilton, died 1964, vol. VI
Gibbs, Cecil Armstrong, 1889–1960, vol. V
Gibbs, Charles, died 1943, vol. IV
Gibbs, Sir Charles Henry, 1854–1924, vol. II
Gibbs, Dennis Raleigh, 1922–1985, vol. VIII
Gibbs, Edward Mitchel, 1847–1935, vol. III
Gibbs, Sir Frank Stannard, 1895–1983, vol. VIII
Gibbs, Hon. Sir Geoffrey Cokayne, 1901–1975, vol. VII
Gibbs, George Howard, 1889–1969, vol. VI
Gibbs, Captain George Louis Downall, 1882–1956, vol. V
Gibbs, Air Marshal Sir Gerald Ernest, 1896–1992, vol. IX
Gibbs, Hon. Henry Lloyd, 1861–1907, vol. I
Gibbs, Rt Hon. Sir Humphrey Vicary, 1902–1990, vol. VIII
Gibbs, Col James Alec Charles, 1867–1930, vol. III
Gibbs, John Herbert, 1872–1962, vol. VI
Gibbs, Ven. Hon. Kenneth Francis, 1856–1935, vol. III
Gibbs, Brig. Lancelot Merivale, 1889–1966, vol. VI
Gibbs, Sir Martin St John Valentine, 1917–1992, vol. IX
Gibbs, Very Rev. Michael McCausland, 1900–1962, vol. VI
Gibbs, Hon. Michael Patrick, 1870–1943, vol. IV
Gibbs, Dame Molly Peel, 1912–1997, vol. X
Gibbs, Norman Henry, 1910–1990, vol. VIII
Gibbs, Oswald Moxley, 1927–1995, vol. IX
Gibbs, Sir Philip, 1877–1962, vol. VI
Gibbs, Rev. Thomas Crook, died 1914, vol. I
Gibbs, Hon. Vicary, 1853–1932, vol. III
Gibbs, Walter George, 1872–1929, vol. III
Gibbs, Lt-Col William, 1877–1963, vol. VI
Gibbs, William Edward, 1889–1934, vol. III
Gibbs-Smith, Charles Harvard, 1909–1981, vol. VIII
Gibbs-Smith, Very Rev. Oswin Harvard, 1901–1969, vol. VI
Giberne, Agnes, 1845–1939, vol. III

Giblin, Major Lyndhurst Falkiner, 1872–1951, vol. V
Giblin, Col Wilfrid Wanostrocht, 1872–1951, vol. V
Gibney, James, 1847–1908, vol. I (A), vol. III
Gibney, Rt Rev. Matthew, 1838–1925, vol. II
Gibson, Hon. Lord; Robert Gibson, 1886–1965, vol. VI
Gibson, Sir Ackroyd Herbert, 3rd Bt (cr 1926), 1893–1975, vol. VII
Gibson, Alan Frank, 1923–1988, vol. VIII
Gibson, Rt Rev. Alan George Sumner, 1856–1922, vol. II
Gibson, Alexander Boyce, 1900–1972, vol. VII
Gibson, Sir Alexander Drummond, 1926–1995, vol. IX
Gibson, Alexander George, 1875–1950, vol. IV
Gibson, Alexander James, 1876–1960, vol. V (A), vol. VI (AI)
Gibson, Andrew, 1864–1933, vol. III
Gibson, Arnold Hartley, 1878–1959, vol. V
Gibson, Arnold Mackenzie, died 1956, vol. V
Gibson, Sir Basil; see Gibson, Sir E. B.
Gibson, Charles Dana, 1867–1944, vol. IV
Gibson, Sir Charles Granville, 1880–1948, vol. IV
Gibson, Charles R., 1870–1931, vol. III
Gibson, Charles Stanley, 1884–1950, vol. IV
Gibson, Charles William, 1889–1977, vol. VII
Gibson, Sir Christopher Herbert, 2nd Bt (cr 1931), 1897–1962, vol. VI
Gibson, Sir Christopher Herbert, 3rd Bt (cr 1931), 1921–1994, vol. IX
Gibson, Clement William Osmund, 1878–1963, vol. VI
Gibson, Rear-Adm. Cuthbert Walter Sumner, 1890–1971, vol. VII
Gibson, Rev. (Sir) David Ackroyd, (4th Bt), 1922–1997, vol. X
Gibson, Vice-Adm. Sir Donald Cameron Ernest Forbes, 1916–2000, vol. X
Gibson, Sir Donald Evelyn Edward, 1908–1991, vol. IX
Gibson, Rt Rev. Edgar Charles Sumner, 1848–1924, vol. II
Gibson, Sir Edmund Currey, 1886–1974, vol. VII
Gibson, Hon. Edward Graves Mayne, 1873–1928, vol. II
Gibson, Elizabeth, 1869–1931, vol. III
Gibson, Sir (Ernest) Basil, 1877–1962, vol. VI
Gibson, Hon. Sir Frank Ernest, 1879–1965, vol. VI
Gibson, George, 1885–1953, vol. V
Gibson, George Alexander, 1854–1913, vol. I
Gibson, George Alexander, 1858–1930, vol. III
Gibson, George Herbert Rae, 1881–1932, vol. III
Gibson, Wing Comdr Guy Penrose, 1918–1944, vol. IV
Gibson, Harold, 1884–1961, vol. VI
Gibson, Harold Charles Lehrs, 1897–1960, vol. V
Gibson, Harold Leslie George, 1917–1994, vol. IX
Gibson, Harry Frederick C.; see Carew-Gibson.
Gibson, Harvery Dow, 1882–1950, vol. IV
Gibson, Sir Henry James, 1860–1950, vol. IV
Gibson, Sir Herbert, 1st Bt (cr 1926), 1851–1932, vol. III
Gibson, Sir Herbert, 1st Bt (cr 1931), 1863–1934, vol. III

Gibson, Herbert Mellor, 1896–1954, vol. V
Gibson, Hope, 1859–1928, vol. II
Gibson, Sir (Horace) Stephen, 1897–1963, vol. VI
Gibson, Rear-Adm. Isham Worsley, 1882–1950, vol. IV
Gibson, James, 1864–1943, vol. IV
Gibson, Rt Rev. James Byers, 1881–1952, vol. V
Gibson, Sir James Puckering, 1st Bt (cr 1909), 1849–1912, vol. I
Gibson, John Ashley, 1885–1948, vol. IV
Gibson, Rev. John Campbell, died 1919, vol. II
Gibson, John Constant, 1861–1939, vol. III
Gibson, Rt Hon. John George, 1846–1923, vol. II
Gibson, Rev. John George, 1859–1927, vol. II
Gibson, John Gibson, 1889–1970, vol. VI
Gibson, Sir John Hinshelwood, 1907–1985, vol. VIII
Gibson, Rev. John Monro, 1838–1921, vol. II
Gibson, Maj.-Gen. Sir John Mortson, 1842–1929, vol. III
Gibson, Rev. John Paul S. R., died 1964, vol. VI
Gibson, Sir John Watson, 1885–1947, vol. IV
Gibson, Joseph David, 1928–1992, vol. X
Gibson, Sir Kenneth Lloyd, 2nd Bt (cr 1926), 1888–1967, vol. VI
Gibson, Col Leonard Young, 1911–1993, vol. IX
Gibson, Sir Leslie Bertram, 1896–1952, vol. V
Gibson, Major Lewis, 1880–1935, vol. III
Gibson, Hon. Sir Marcus George, 1898–1987, vol. VIII
Gibson, Margaret Dunlop, died 1920, vol. II
Gibson, Very Rev. Matthew Sayer, died 1971, vol. VII
Gibson, Rt Hon. Sir Maurice White, 1913–1987, vol. VIII
Gibson, Captain Michael Bradford, 1929–1993, vol. IX
Gibson, Michael Joseph, 1876–1953, vol. V
Gibson, Myra Macindoe, 1886–1966, vol. VI
Gibson, Rt Rev. Percival William, 1893–1970, vol. VI
Gibson, Maj.-Gen. Ralph Burgess, 1894–1962, vol. VI
Gibson, Raymond Evelyn, 1878–1969, vol. VI
Gibson, Rev. Richard Hudson, died 1904, vol. I
Gibson, Robert; see Gibson, Hon. Lord.
Gibson, Sir Robert, 1864–1934, vol. III
Gibson, Rt Rev. Robert Atkinson, 1846–1919, vol. II
Gibson, Robert Clarence, 1892–1959, vol. V
Gibson, Robert John H.; see Harvey-Gibson.
Gibson, Sir Ronald George, 1909–1989, vol. VIII
Gibson, Sir Stephen; see Gibson, Sir H. S.
Gibson, Strickland, 1877–1958, vol. V
Gibson, Rt Rev. Theodore Sumner, 1885–1953, vol. V
Gibson, Thomas, 1875–1925, vol. II
Gibson, Thomas, 1915–1993, vol. IX
Gibson, Very Rev. Thomas B., 1847–1927, vol. II
Gibson, Walcot, 1864–1941, vol. IV
Gibson, Sir Walter Matthew, 1856–1940, vol. III
Gibson, Wilfrid, 1878–1962, vol. VI
Gibson, Hon. William, 1849–1914, vol. I
Gibson, Lt-Col William, 1887–1969, vol. VI
Gibson, Maj. William David, 1925–1998, vol. X

Gibson, William John, 1865–1944, vol. IV
Gibson, Air Vice-Marshal William Norman, 1915–1982, vol. VIII
Gibson, William Pettigrew, 1902–1960, vol. V
Gibson, William Ralph Boyce, 1869–1935, vol. III
Gibson, William Sumner, 1876–1946, vol. IV
Gibson, William Victor Halliday, 1884–1954, vol. V
Gibson, Sir William Waymouth, 1873–1971, vol. VII
Gibson-Carmichael, John Murray, 1860–1923, vol. II
Gibson-Craig, Sir Archibald Charles, 4th Bt, 1883–1914, vol. I
Gibson-Craig, Sir James Henry, 3rd Bt, 1841–1908, vol. I
Gibson-Craig-Carmichael, Sir (Archibald Henry) William, 14th Bt (and 7th Bt), 1917–1969, vol. VI
Gibson-Craig-Carmichael, Sir Eardley Charles William, 13th Bt (and 6th Bt), 1887–1939, vol. III
Gibson-Craig-Carmichael, Captain Sir Henry Thomas, 5th Bt (and 12th Bt), 1885–1926, vol. II
Gibson-Craig-Carmichael, Sir William; see Gibson-Craig-Carmichael, Sir A. H. W.
Gibson Fleming, Edward, 1885–1962, vol. VI
Gibsone, Maj.-Gen. William Waring Primrose, 1872–1957, vol. V
Gick, Sir William John, 1877–1948, vol. IV
Giddens, George, 1855–1920, vol. II
Giddings, Franklin Henry, 1855–1931, vol. III
Giddings, William John Peter, 1861–1938, vol. III (A), vol. IV
Giddy, Harry Douglas, 1887–1959, vol. V
Gide, André Paul Guillaume, 1869–1951, vol. V
Gide, Prof. Charles, 1847–1932, vol. III
Gideon, Col James Henry, 1862–1958, vol. V
Gidhour, Maharaja Bahadur Chandra Mauleshvar Prasad Singh, 1890–1937, vol. III
Gidhour, Maharajah Sir Ravneswar Prasad Singh, Bahadur of, 1860–1923, vol. II
Gidney, Sir Claude Henry, 1887–1968, vol. VI
Gidney, Lt-Col Sir Henry Albert John, 1873–1942, vol. IV
Gie, S. F. N., 1884–1945, vol. IV
Gielgud, Sir (Arthur) John, 1904–2000, vol. X
Gielgud, Sir John; see Gielgud, Sir A. J.
Gielgud, Lt-Col Lewis Evelyn, 1894–1953, vol. V
Gielgud, Val Henry, 1900–1981, vol. VIII
Gieseking, Walter Wilhelm, 1895–1956, vol. V
Giffard, Very Rev. Agnew Walter Giles, 1869–1947, vol. IV
Giffard, Adm. George Augustus, 1849–1925, vol. II
Giffard, George Campbell, 1853–1932, vol. III
Giffard, Gen. Sir George James, 1886–1964, vol. VI
Giffard, Maj.-Gen. Sir Gerald Godfray, 1867–1926, vol. II
Giffard, Hardinge Frank, died 1908, vol. I
Giffard, Sir Henry Alexander, 1838–1927, vol. II
Giffard, Walter Thomas Courtenay, 1839–1926, vol. II
Giffard, Col William Carter, 1859–1921, vol. II
Giffen, Edmund, 1902–1963, vol. VI
Giffen, Sir Robert, 1837–1910, vol. I
Gifford, 3rd Baron, 1849–1911, vol. I

Gifford, 4th Baron, 1857–1937, vol. III
Gifford, 5th Baron, 1899–1961, vol. VI
Gifford, Charles Edwin, 1843–1922, vol. II
Gifford, Ven. Edwin Hamilton, 1820–1905, vol. I
Gifford, (James) Maurice, 1922–1987, vol. VIII
Gifford, Maurice; see Gifford, J. M.
Gifford, Hon. Maurice Raymond, 1859–1910, vol. I
Gifford, Walter Sherman, 1885–1966, vol. VI
Gift, Theo.; see Boulger, D. H.
Giggall, Rt Hon. George Kenneth, 1914–1999, vol. X
Gigli, Beniamino, 1890–1957, vol. V
Gilbert, Albert, died 1927, vol. II
Gilbert, Sir Alfred, 1854–1934, vol. III
Gilbert, Brig.-Gen. Arthur Robert, 1863–1937, vol. III
Gilbert, Sir Bernard William, 1891–1957, vol. V
Gilbert, Carew Davies, died 1913, vol. I
Gilbert, Carl Joyce, 1906–1983, vol. VIII
Gilbert, Cass, 1859–1934, vol. III
Gilbert, Charles E. L., died 1937, vol. III
Gilbert, Rev. Charles Robert, 1851–1919, vol. II
Gilbert, Charles W.; see Web-Gilbert.
Gilbert, Edmund William, 1900–1973, vol. VII
Gilbert, Frederick, 1899–1989, vol. VIII
Gilbert, Mrs Grace Catherine Rose D.; see Davies-Gilbert.
Gilbert, Sir Henry; see Gilbert, Sir J. H.
Gilbert, Hugh Campbell, 1926–1998, vol. X
Gilbert, Sir Ian Anderson J.; see Johnson-Gilbert.
Gilbert, James Daniel, 1864–1941, vol. IV
Gilbert, Jean, died 1942, vol. IV
Gilbert, Sir John, 1817–1897, vol. I
Gilbert, John Cannon, 1908–2000, vol. X
Gilbert, John Orman, 1907–1995, vol. IX
Gilbert, Sir John Thomas, 1829–1898, vol. I
Gilbert, Sir John William, 1871–1934, vol. III
Gilbert, Sir (Joseph) Henry, 1817–1901, vol. I
Gilbert, Sir (Joseph) Trounsell, 1888–1975, vol. VII
Gilbert, Keith Reginald, 1914–1973, vol. VII
Gilbert, Brig. Leonard, 1889–1966, vol. VI
Gilbert, Lt-Col Leonard Erskine, 1874–1946, vol. IV
Gilbert, Rosa, (Lady Gilbert), (Rosa Mulholland), 1841–1921, vol. II
Gilbert, Hon. S. Parker, 1892–1938, vol. III
Gilbert, Adm. Thomas Drummond, 1870–1962, vol. VI
Gilbert, Thomas Ian J.; see Johnson-Gilbert.
Gilbert, Rev. Thomas Morrell, died 1928, vol. II
Gilbert, Sir Trounsell; see Gilbert, Sir J. T.
Gilbert, Walter, 1871–1946, vol. IV
Gilbert, William Gladstone, 1877–1964, vol. VI
Gilbert, Brig. Sir William Herbert Ellery, 1916–1987, vol. VIII
Gilbert, Sir William Schwenck, 1836–1911, vol. I
Gilbert-Carter, Sir Gilbert Thomas, 1848–1927, vol. II
Gilbert-Carter, Humphrey, 1884–1969, vol. VI
Gilbertson, Rev. Canon Arthur Deane, 1883–1964, vol. VI
Gilbertson, Sir Geoffrey, 1918–1991, vol. IX
Gilbertson, Rev. Lewis, 1857–1928, vol. II
Gilbey, Lt-Col Alfred, 1859–1927, vol. II
Gilbey, Sir Derek; see Gilbey, Sir W. D.

Gilbey, Sir (Henry) Walter, 2nd Bt, 1859–1945, vol. IV
Gilbey, Tresham, 1862–1947, vol. IV
Gilbey, Sir Walter, 1st Bt, 1831–1914, vol. I
Gilbey, Sir Walter; see Gilbey, Sir H. W.
Gilbey, Sir (Walter) Derek, 3rd Bt, 1913–1991, vol. IX
Gilchrist, Alexander Fitzmaurice, 1878–1956, vol. V
Gilchrist, Sir Andrew Graham, 1910–1993, vol. IX
Gilchrist, (Andrew) Rae, 1899–1995, vol. IX
Gilchrist, Archibald, 1877–1932, vol. III
Gilchrist, Archibald Daniel, 1877–1964, vol. VI
Gilchrist, Douglas Alston, died 1927, vol. II
Gilchrist, Sir Finlay; see Gilchrist, Sir J. F. E.
Gilchrist, Sir James Albert, 1884–1965, vol. VI
Gilchrist, Sir (James) Finlay (Elder), 1903–1987, vol. VIII
Gilchrist, John, 1929–1982, vol. VIII
Gilchrist, John Dow Fisher, 1866–1926, vol. II
Gilchrist, Percy Carlyle, 1851–1935, vol. III
Gilchrist, Philip Thomson, 1865–1956, vol. V
Gilchrist, Rae; see Gilchrist, A. R.
Gilchrist, Captain Robert Allister, 1921–1973, vol. VII
Gilchrist, Robert Murray, 1868–1917, vol. II
Gilchrist, Robert Niven, 1888–1972, vol. VII
Gilchrist, Lt-Col Walter Fellowes Cowan, 1879–1943, vol. IV
Gilchrist, William James, 1879–1955, vol. V
Gilchrist-Clark, Rev. William; see Clark-Maxwell, Rev. W. G.
Gildea, Col Sir James, 1838–1920, vol. II
Gildea, Rev. William, 1833–1925, vol. II
Gilder, Jeannette Leonard, 1849–1916, vol. II
Gilder, Joseph B., 1858–1936, vol. III (A), vol. IV
Gilder, Richard Watson, 1844–1909, vol. I
Gildersleeve, Basil Lanneau, 1831–1924, vol. II
Gildersleeve, Virginia Crocheron, 1877–1965, vol. VII
Gilding, Henry Percy, 1895–1973, vol. VII
Giles; see Giles, Carl Ronald.
Giles, Rev. Alan Stanley, 1902–1975, vol. VII
Giles, Sir Alexander Falconer, 1915–1989, vol. VIII
Giles, Sub-Lt Alfred Edward Boscawen, died 1917, vol. II
Giles, Arthur Edward, 1864–1935, vol. III
Giles, Bertram, 1874–1928, vol. II
Giles, Carl P.; see Prausnitz Giles.
Giles, Carl Ronald, 1916–1995, vol. IX
Giles, Sir Charles Tyrrell, 1850–1940, vol. III
Giles, Edward, 1849–1938, vol. III
Giles, Maj.-Gen. Edward Douglas, 1879–1966, vol. VI
Giles, Col Frank Lucas Netlam, 1879–1930, vol. III
Giles, G. C. T., died 1976, vol. VII
Giles, Geoffrey Reginald, 1936–1992, vol. IX
Giles, George Henry, 1904–1965, vol. VI
Giles, Major Godfrey Douglas, 1857–1941, vol. IV
Giles, Sir (Henry) Norman, 1905–1983, vol. VIII
Giles, Herbert Allen, 1845–1935, vol. III
Giles, John Laurent, 1901–1969, vol. VI
Giles, Lancelot, 1878–1934, vol. III
Giles, Lionel, 1875–1958, vol. V
Giles, Margaret M.; see Jenkin, Mrs Bernard.
Giles, Sir Norman; see Giles, Sir H. N.

Giles, Lt-Col Sir Oswald Bissill, 1888–1970, vol. VI
Giles, Peter, 1860–1935, vol. III
Giles, Peter Broome, 1850–1928, vol. II
Giles, Robert, 1846–1928, vol. II
Giles, Sir Robert Sidney, 1865–1944, vol. IV
Gilford, Hastings, 1861–1941, vol. IV
Gilham, Harold Sidney, 1897–1982, vol. VIII
Gilhooly, James Peter, 1847–1916, vol. II
Gilkes, Antony Newcombe, 1900–1977, vol. VII
Gilkes, Rev. Arthur Herman, died 1922, vol. II
Gilkes, Christopher Herman, 1898–1953, vol. V
Gilkison, Sir Alan Fleming, 1909–1990, vol. IX (AI)
Gilks, John Langton, 1880–1971, vol. VII
Gill, Alfred Henry, 1856–1914, vol. I
Gill, Allen, died 1933, vol. III
Gill, Andrew John Mitchell-, 1847–1921, vol. II
Gill, Sir Archibald Joseph, 1889–1976, vol. VII
Gill, Arthur Edmund, 1864–1932, vol. III
Gill, Austin, 1906–1990, vol. VIII
Gill, Sir Charles Frederick, 1851–1923, vol. II
Gill, Rt Rev. Charles Hope, 1861–1946, vol. IV
Gill, Colin Unwin, 1892–1940, vol. III
Gill, Conrad, 1883–1968, vol. VI
Gill, Cyril James, 1907–1990, vol. VIII
Gill, Cyril James, 1904–1994, vol. IX
Gill, Sir David, 1843–1914, vol. I
Gill, David Ian, 1928–1997, vol. X
Gill, Col Douglas Howard, 1877–1949, vol. IV
Gill, Eric, 1882–1940, vol. III
Gill, Rev. Ernest Compton, 1854–1912, vol. I
Gill, Ernest Walter Brudenell, 1883–1959, vol. V
Gill, Evan William Thistle, 1902–1990, vol. VIII
Gill, Air Cdre Hon. Frank; see Gill, Air Cdre Hon. T. F.
Gill, Sir Frank, 1866–1950, vol. IV
Gill, Frank Maxey, 1919–1990, vol. VIII
Gill, Frederick Gordon, 1881–1940, vol. III
Gill, Col Gordon Harry, 1882–1962, vol. VI
Gill, Sir Harry; see Gill, Sir. T. H.
Gill, Hubert Alexander, 1881–1954, vol. V
Gill, Ven. Hugh Stowell, 1830–1912, vol. I
Gill, Major James Herbert Wainwright, 1876–1951, vol. V
Gill, James Lester Willis, 1871–1939, vol. III
Gill, Maj.-Gen. John Galbraith, 1889–1981, vol. VIII
Gill, L. Upcott, 1846–1919, vol. II
Gill, MacDonald, 1884–1947, vol. IV
Gill, Air Cdre Napier John, 1890–1948, vol. IV
Gill, Robert Carey Chapple, 1875–1960, vol. V (A), vol. VI (AI)
Gill, Major Robert Harwar, 1877–1938, vol. III
Gill, Cdre Sir Roy, 1887–1967, vol. VI
Gill, Stanley, 1926–1975, vol. VII
Gill, Thomas, 1849–1923, vol. II
Gill, Air Cdre Hon. Thomas Francis, (Frank), 1917–1982, vol. VIII
Gill, Sir (Thomas) Harry, 1885–1955, vol. V
Gill, Thomas Patrick, 1858–1931, vol. III
Gill, Col William Smith, 1865–1957, vol. V
Gill-Carey, Chapple, 1897–1981, vol. VIII
Gill-Davies, Derek George, 1913–1974, vol. VII
Gillam, Gp Captain Denys Edgar, 1915–1991, vol. IX

Gillam, Brig.-Gen. Reynold Alexander, 1872–1942, vol. IV
Gillam, Major William Albert, 1870–1938, vol. III
Gillan, Sir Angus; see Gillan, Sir J. A.
Gillan, Lt-Col Sir George V. B., 1890–1974, vol. VII
Gillan, Sir (James) Angus, 1885–1981, vol. VIII
Gillan, Sir Robert Woodburn, 1867–1943, vol. IV
Gillanders, Jeannie Kathleen, 1896–1971, vol. VII
Gillanders, Hon. John Gordon, 1895–1946, vol. IV
Gillard, Francis George, 1908–1998, vol. X
Gillard, Hon. Sir Oliver James, 1906–1984, vol. VIII
Gillatt, Lt-Col John Maxwell, died 1937, vol. III
Gillen, Francis James, 1856–1912, vol. I
Gillen, Stanley James, 1911–1978, vol. VII
Gillespie, A. Lockhart, 1865–1904, vol. I
Gillespie, Charles Melville, 1866–1955, vol. V
Gillespie, Brig.-Gen. Ernest Carden Freeth, 1871–1942, vol. IV
Gillespie, Brig. Dame Helen Shiels, 1898–1974, vol. VII
Gillespie, Very Rev. Henry J., 1851–1936, vol. III
Gillespie, Ven. Henry Richard Butler, 1880–1943, vol. IV
Gillespie, Sir John, 1822–1901, vol. I
Gillespie, Very Rev. John, 1836–1912, vol. I
Gillespie, Peter, 1873–1929, vol. III
Gillespie, Sir Robert, died 1901, vol. I
Gillespie, Robert, 1897–1986, vol. VIII
Gillespie, Robert Alexander, 1848–1917, vol. II
Gillespie, Robert Dick, 1897–1945, vol. IV
Gillespie, Sir Robert Winton, died 1945, vol. IV
Gillespie, Col Rollo St John, 1872–1952, vol. V
Gillespie, Thomas Haining, 1876–1967, vol. VI
Gillespie, Maj.-Gen. William John, 1840–1931, vol. III
Gillespy, Rev. Francis Roebuck, 1880–1962, vol. VI
Gillett, Col Sir Alan; see Gillett, Col Sir W. A.
Gillett, Rev. Canon Charles Scott, 1880–1957, vol. V
Gillett, Charles William, 1901–1968, vol. VI
Gillett, Sir Edward Bailey, 1888–1978, vol. VII
Gillett, Lt-Col Edward Scott, 1877–1952, vol. V
Gillett, Eric, 1920–1987, vol. VIII
Gillett, Eric Walkey, 1893–1978, vol. VII
Gillett, Frederick Huntington, 1851–1935, vol. III
Gillett, Sir George Masterman, 1870–1939, vol. III
Gillett, Rev. Gresham F., 1867–1940, vol. III
Gillett, Sir Harold; see Gillett, Sir. S. H.
Gillett, Sir Michael Cavenagh, 1907–1971, vol. VII
Gillett, Adm. Owen Francis, 1863–1938, vol. III
Gillett, Maj.-Gen. Sir Peter Bernard, 1913–1989, vol. VIII
Gillett, Sir Stuart, 1903–1971, vol. VII
Gillett, Sir (Sydney) Harold, 1st Bt, 1890–1976, vol. VII
Gillett, Major William, 1839–1925, vol. II
Gillett, Col Sir (William) Alan, 1879–1959, vol. V
Gillette, William, 1857–1937, vol. III
Gillford, Lord; Richard Charles Meade, 1868–1905, vol. I
Gilliam, Laurence Duval, 1907–1964, vol. VI
Gilliat, Algernon Earle, 1884–1970, vol. VI
Gilliat, Rev. E., 1841–1915, vol. I

Gilliat, John Saunders, 1829–1912, vol. I
Gilliat, Lt-Col Sir Martin John, 1913–1993, vol. IX
Gilliat-Smith, Bernard Joseph, 1883–1973, vol. VII
Gilliat-Smith, Guy Basil, 1885–1933, vol. III
Gilliatt, Penelope Ann Douglass Conner, 1932–1993, vol. IX
Gilliatt, Roger William, 1922–1991, vol. IX
Gilliatt, Sir William, 1884–1956, vol. V
Gillibrand, Brig. Albert, 1884–1942, vol. IV
Gillick, Ernest George, died 1951, vol. V
Gillick, Mary, died 1965, vol. VI
Gillie, Dame Annis Calder, (Dame Annis Smith), 1900–1985, vol. VIII
Gillie, Blaise; see Gillie, F. B.
Gillie, (Francis) Blaise, 1908–1981, vol. VIII
Gillie, Rev. Robert Calder, 1865–1941, vol. IV
Gillies, Alexander, 1907–1977, vol. VII
Gillies, Sir Alexander, 1891–1982, vol. VIII
Gillies, Arthur Hunter Denholm, 1890–1953, vol. V
Gillies, Brig. Frederick George, 1881–1955, vol. V
Gillies, Gordon; see Gillies, M. G.
Gillies, Sir Harold Delf, 1882–1960, vol. V
Gillies, Hugh, 1903–1978, vol. V
Gillies, Captain James, 1873–1938, vol. III
Gillies, Rev. James Robertson, 1855–1938, vol. III
Gillies, John, 1895–1976, vol. VII
Gillies, Marshall Macdonald, 1901–1976, vol. VII
Gillies, (Maurice) Gordon, 1916–1997, vol. X
Gillies, Sir William George, 1898–1973, vol. VII
Gillies, William King, 1875–1952, vol. V
Gillies, Hon. William Neal, 1868–1928, vol. II
Gilligan, Albert, 1874–1939, vol. III
Gilligan, Arthur Edward Robert, 1894–1976, vol. VII
Gilligan, Frank William, 1893–1960, vol. V
Gilliglan, Major Edward Gibson, 1880–1947, vol. IV
Gillingham, Rev. Canon Frank Hay, 1875–1953, vol. V
Gillingham, Michael John, 1933–1999, vol. X
Gillingham, Rev. Canon Peter Llewellyn, 1914–1996, vol. X
Gillis, Bernard Benjamin, 1905–1996, vol. X
Gillis, Hon. Duncan, 1834–1903, vol. I
Gillis, William, 1859–1929, vol. III
Gillitt, Lt-Col William, 1879–1962, vol. VI
Gillman, Clement, 1882–1946, vol. IV
Gillman, Herbert Francis Webb, died 1918, vol. II
Gillman, Russell Davis, died 1910, vol. I
Gillman, Gen. Sir Webb, 1870–1933, vol. III
Gillmor, Rev. Fitzwilliam, 1867–1934, vol. III
Gillmore of Thamesfield, Baron (Life Peer); David Howe Gillmore, 1934–1999, vol. X
Gillmore, Air Vice-Marshal Alan David, 1905–1996, vol. X
Gillmore, Ven. Charles Albert, died 1939, vol. III
Gillon, Stair Agnew, 1877–1954, vol. V
Gillot, E. Louis, born 1867, vol. II
Gillot, Hon. Sir Samuel, 1838–1913, vol. I
Gillson, Brig.-Gen. Godfrey, 1867–1937, vol. III
Gillson, Lt-Col Robert Moore Thacker, 1878–1939, vol. III
Gillson, Thomas Huntington, 1917–1984, vol. VIII
Gilman, Sir Charles Rackham, 1833–1911, vol. I
Gilman, Charlotte Perkins, 1860–1935, vol. III

Gilman, Daniel Coit, 1831–1909, vol. I
Gilman, Edward Wilmot Francis, 1876–1955, vol. V
Gilman, Harold John Wilde, 1878–1919, vol. II
Gilman, Horace James, 1907–1976, vol. VII
Gilmartin, Hugh, 1923–1992, vol. IX
Gilmartin, Most Rev. Thomas P., 1861–1939, vol. III
Gilmer, Dame Elizabeth May, 1880–1960, vol. V
Gilmore, Hon. George Crosby, 1859–1937, vol. III
Gilmore, Dame Mary, 1865–1962, vol. VI
Gilmour, Andrew, 1898–1988, vol. VIII
Gilmour, David, died 1946, vol. IV
Gilmour, James Pinkerton, 1860–1941, vol. IV
Gilmour, Sir John, 1st Bt (cr 1897), 1845–1920, vol. II
Gilmour, Lt-Col Rt Hon. Sir John, 2nd Bt (cr 1897), 1876–1940, vol. III
Gilmour, Major John, 1884–1943, vol. IV
Gilmour, Sir John Little, 2nd Bt (cr 1926), 1899–1977, vol. VII
Gilmour, John Scott Lennox, 1906–1986, vol. VIII
Gilmour, Michael Hugh Barrie, 1904–1982, vol. VIII
Gilmour, Brig.-Gen. Sir Robert Gordon, 1st Bt (cr 1926), 1857–1939, vol. III
Gilmour, Lady Susan, 1870–1962, vol. VI
Gilmour, Thomas Lennox, 1859–1936, vol. III
Gilmour, William Ewing, 1854–1924, vol. II
Gilmour, William Henry, 1869–1942, vol. IV
Gilpin, Archibald, 1906–1959, vol. V
Gilpin, Sir Edmund Henry; see Gilpin, Sir Harry.
Gilpin, Brig.-Gen. Frederic Charles Almon, 1860–1950, vol. IV
Gilpin, Sir Harry, (Edmund Henry), 1876–1950, vol. IV
Gilpin, John, 1930–1983, vol. VIII
Gilpin, Peter Valentine, 1858–1928, vol. II
Gilpin, Rt Rev. William Percy, 1902–1988, vol. VIII
Gilpin-Brown, Adm. Frederick Dundas, 1866–1934, vol. III
Gilray, Colin Macdonald, 1885–1974, vol. VII
Gilray, Thomas, 1851–1920, vol. II
Gilroy, Rev. James, 1859–1931, vol. III
Gilroy, John T. Y., 1898–1985, vol. VIII
Gilroy, His Eminence Cardinal Sir Norman Thomas, 1896–1977, vol. VII
Gilroy Bevan, David; see Bevan, A. D. G.
Gilruth, John Anderson, 1871–1937, vol. III
Gilson, Lt-Col Charles Hugh, 1870–1930, vol. III
Gilson, Major Charles J. L. 1878–1943, vol. IV
Gilson, Etienne Henry, 1884–1978, vol. VII
Gilson, John Cary, 1912–1989, vol. VIII
Gilson, Julius Parnell, 1868–1929, vol. III
Gilson, Paul, 1865–1942, vol. IV
Gilson, Robert Cary, 1863–1939, vol. III
Gilstrap, Lt-Col John MacR.; see MacRae-Gilstrap.
Gilzean, Andrew, 1877–1957, vol. V
Gilzean-Reid, Sir Hugh; see Reid.
Gimblett, Charles Leonard, 1890–1957, vol. V
Gimlette, Lt-Col George Hart Desmond, 1855–1930, vol. III
Gimlette, Surg. Rear-Adm. Sir Thomas Desmond, 1857–1943, vol. IV

Gimson, Arthur Clive Stanford, 1919–1982, vol. VIII
Gimson, Christopher, 1886–1975, vol. VII
Gimson, Sir Franklin Charles, 1890–1975, vol. VII
Gimson, Col Thomas William, 1904–1979, vol. VII
Gingell, Overy Francis, 1916–1966, vol. VI
Gingold, Hermione, 1897–1987, vol. VIII
Gingras-Daly, Lt-Col Ludger Jules Olivier, 1876–1919, vol. II
Ginnell, Laurence, 1854–1923, vol. II
Ginner, Charles, 1878–1952, vol. V
Ginnett, Louis, died 1946, vol. IV
Ginsberg, Morris, 1889–1970, vol. VI
Ginsburg, Benedict William, 1859–1933, vol. III
Ginsburg, Christian David, 1831–1914, vol. I
Ginsburg, David, 1921–1994, vol. IX
Ginsbury, Norman, 1902–1991, vol. IX
Ginwala, Sir Padamji Pestonji, 1875–1962, vol. VI
Giolitti, Giovanni, 1842–1928, vol. II
Giordano, Umberto, 1867–1948, vol. IV
Giovanetti, Constantine William, 1868–1940, vol. III
Gipps, Sir Reginald Ramsay, 1831–1908, vol. I
Gipson, Lawrence Henry, 1880–1971, vol. VII
Girard, Robert George, 1859–1921, vol. II
Giraud, Surg.-Maj.-Gen. Charles Herve, died 1918, vol. II
Giraud, Gen. Henri Honoré, 1879–1949, vol. IV
Girault, Charles Louis, 1851–1932, vol. III
Girdlestone, Cuthbert Morton, 1895–1975, vol. VII
Girdlestone, Gathorne Robert, died 1950, vol. IV
Girdlestone, Rev. Robert Baker, 1836–1923, vol. II
Girdwood, Brig.-Gen. Austin Claude, 1875–1951, vol. V
Girdwood, Maj.-Gen. Sir Eric Stanley, 1876–1963, vol. VI
Girdwood, Gilbert P., 1832–1917, vol. II
Girdwood, John Graham, 1890–1981, vol. VIII
Giri, Varahagiri Venkata, 1894–1980, vol. VII
Giri de Teremala di Fogliano, Count Piero Mariano, 1885–1962, vol. VI
Girling, James Lawrence, 1901–1969, vol. VI
Girling, John Henry, died 1948, vol. IV
Girling, Maj.-Gen. Peter Howard, 1915–1991, vol. IX
Girling, William Henry, 1872–1958, vol. V
Girouard, Hon. Désiré, 1836–1911, vol. I
Girouard, Col Sir (Edouard) Percy Cranwill, 1867–1932, vol. III
Girouard, Hon. Jean, 1856–1940, vol. III (A), vol. IV
Girouard, Col Sir Percy; see Girouard, Col Sir E. P. C.
Girtin, Thomas, 1874–1960, vol. V
Gisborne, Henry Paterson, 1888–1953, vol. V
Gisborne, Lt-Col Lionel Guy, 1866–1928, vol. II
Gisborough, 1st Baron, 1856–1938, vol. III
Gisborough, 2nd Baron, 1889–1951, vol. V
Gish, Lillian Diana, 1893–1993, vol. IX
Gishford, Anthony Joseph, 1908–1975, vol. VII
Gissing, Algernon, 1860–1937, vol. III
Gissing, George, 1857–1903, vol. I
Gittings, Robert William Victor, 1911–1992, vol. IX
Gittins, Henry, 1858–1937, vol. III
Gittins, Robert John, 1895–1934, vol. III

Giuffrida-Ruggeri, Vincenzo, born 1872, vol. II
Given, Ernest Cranstoun, 1870–1961, vol. VI
Given, Rear-Adm. John Garnett Cranston, 1902–1988, vol. VIII
Given, Brig. Thomas Frederick, 1894–1952, vol. V
Givens, Hon. Thomas, 1864–1928, vol. II
Gjellerup, Karl Adolf, 1859–1919, vol. II
Gladding, Donald, 1888–1971, vol. VII
Gladstone, 1st Viscount, 1854–1930, vol. III
Gladstone of Hawarden, 1st Baron, 1852–1935, vol. III
Gladstone of Hawarden, Lady; (Maud Ernestine), died 1941, vol. IV
Gladstone, Sir Albert Charles, 5th Bt, 1886–1967, vol. VI
Gladstone, Charles Andrew, (6th Bt, but did not use the title), 1888–1968, vol. VI
Gladstone, Adm. Sir Gerald Vaughan, 1901–1978, vol. VII
Gladstone, Helen, 1849–1925, vol. II
Gladstone, Sir Hugh Steuart, 1877–1949, vol. IV
Gladstone, Sir John Evelyn, 4th Bt, 1855–1945, vol. IV
Gladstone, John Hall, 1827–1902, vol. I
Gladstone, Sir John Robert, 3rd Bt, 1852–1926, vol. II
Gladstone, Reginald John, 1865–1947, vol. IV
Gladstone, Robert, 1833–1919, vol. II
Gladstone, Samuel Steuart, 1837–1909, vol. I
Gladstone, Rev. Stephen Edward, 1844–1920, vol. II
Gladstone, Rt Hon. William Ewart, 1809–1898, vol. I
Gladstone, William Glynne Charles, 1885–1915, vol. I
Gladwyn, 1st Baron, 1900–1996, vol. X
Glaisher, James Whitbread Lee, 1848–1928, vol. II
Glaister, John, 1856–1932, vol. III
Glaister, John, 1892–1971, vol. VII
Glaister, Rev. William, died 1919, vol. II
Glancey, Rt Rev. Mgr Michael Francis, 1854–1925, vol. II
Glancy, Sir Bertrand James, 1882–1953, vol. V
Glancy, James Edward McAlinney, 1914–1980, vol. VII (AII)
Glancy, Sir Reginald Isidore Robert, 1874–1939, vol. III
Glanely, 1st Baron, 1868–1942, vol. IV
Glanfield, Sir Robert, 1862–1924, vol. II
Glantawe, 1st Baron, 1835–1915, vol. I
Glanusk, 1st Baron, 1858–1906, vol. I
Glanusk, 2nd Baron, 1864–1928, vol. II
Glanusk, 3rd Baron, 1891–1948, vol. IV
Glanusk, 4th Baron, 1917–1997, vol. X
Glanville, Mrs Edythe Mary, 1876–1959, vol. V
Glanville, Brig.-Gen. Francis, 1862–1938, vol. III
Glanville, Harold James, 1854–1930, vol. III
Glanville, Harold James Abbott, 1884–1966, vol. VI
Glanville, James Edward, 1891–1958, vol. V
Glanville, Stephen Ranulph Kingdon, 1900–1956, vol. V
Glanville, Sir William Henry, 1900–1976, vol. VII
Glascock, Lancelot Colin Bradford, 1875–1931, vol. III

Glascott, John Richard Donovan, 1877–1938, vol. III
Glaser, Dorothy, (Mrs O. C. Glaser); *see* Wrinch, D.
Glasfurd, Col Alexander Inglis Robertson, 1870–1942, vol. IV
Glasgow, 7th Earl of, 1833–1915, vol. I
Glasgow, 8th Earl of, 1874–1963, vol. VI
Glasgow, 9th Earl of, 1910–1984, vol. VIII
Glasgow, Brig.-Gen. Alfred Edgar, 1870–1950, vol. IV
Glasgow, Edwin, 1874–1955, vol. V
Glasgow, Ellen, 1874–1945, vol. IV
Glasgow, George, 1891–1958, vol. V
Glasgow, Mary Cecilia, 1905–1983, vol. VIII
Glasgow, Raymond Charles R.; *see* Robertson-Glasgow.
Glasgow, Maj.-Gen. Hon. Sir (Thomas) William, 1876–1955, vol. V
Glasgow, Maj.-Gen. Hon. Sir William; *see* Glasgow, Maj.-Gen. Hon. Sir T. W.
Glasgow, Brig.-Gen. William James Theodore, 1862–1944, vol. IV
Glasier, Major Frank Bedford, 1872–1940, vol. III
Glaspell, Susan, 1882–1948, vol. IV
Glass, David Victor, 1911–1978, vol. VII
Glass, Ven. Edward Brown, 1913–1995, vol. IX
Glass, Frederick James, 1881–1930, vol. III
Glass, George William, 1877–1967, vol. VI
Glass, James George Henry, 1843–1911, vol. I
Glass, Sir Leslie Charles, 1911–1988, vol. VIII
Glass, Ruth, 1912–1990, vol. VIII
Glass, William Mervyn, 1885–1965, vol. VI
Glasse, Alfred Onslow, 1889–1977, vol. VII
Glasse, John, 1848–1918, vol. II
Glasse, Thomas Henry, 1898–1994, vol. IX
Glassey, Alec Ewart, 1887–1970, vol. VI
Glassington, Charles William, 1857–1922, vol. II
Glasspole, Most Hon. Sir Florizel Augustus, 1909–2000, vol. X
Glauert, Hermann, 1892–1934, vol. III
Glazebrook, Francis Kirkland, 1903–1988, vol. VIII
Glazebrook, Hugh de T., 1855–1937, vol. III
Glazebrook, Rev. Michael George, 1853–1926, vol. II
Glazebrook, Philip Kirkland, 1880–1918, vol. II
Glazebrook, Reginald Field, 1899–1986, vol. VIII
Glazebrook, Sir Richard Tetley, 1854–1935, vol. III
Glazebrook, William Rimington, 1864–1954, vol. V
Glazier, Edward Victor Denis, 1912–1972, vol. VII
Glazounow, Alexander Constantinovich, 1865–1936, vol. III
Gleadell, Maj.-Gen. Paul, 1910–1988, vol. VIII
Gleadowe, George Edward Yorke, 1856–1903, vol. I
Gleadowe, Reginald Morier Yorke, 1888–1944, vol. IV
Gleadowe-Newcomen, Col Arthur Hills, 1853–1928, vol. II
Gleave, Ruth Marjory, 1926–1986, vol. VIII
Gledhill, Alan, 1895–1983, vol. VIII
Gledhill, David Anthony, 1934–1999, vol. X
Gledhill, Gilbert, 1889–1946, vol. IV
Gledstanes, Elsie, 1891–1982, vol. VIII
Gleed, Sir John Wilson, 1865–1946, vol. IV
Gleeson, Most Rev. Edmund, 1869–1956, vol. V
Glegg, Sir Alexander, 1848–1933, vol. III

Glegg, Edward Maxwell, 1849–1927, vol. II
Gleichen, Maj.-Gen. Lord (Albert) Edward Wilfred, 1863–1937, vol. III
Gleichen, Maj.-Gen. Lord Edward; *see* Gleichen, Maj.-Gen. Lord A. E. W.
Gleichen, Lady Feodora, 1861–1922, vol. II
Gleichen, Lady Helena, *died* 1947, vol. IV
Glen, Alexander, 1850–1913, vol. I
Glen, Sir Alexander, 1893–1972, vol. VII
Glen, Archibald, 1909–1996, vol. X
Glen, John Mackenzie, 1885–1976, vol. VII
Glen, Randolph Alexander, *died* 1934, vol. III
Glen-Coats, Sir Thomas Coats Glen, 2nd Bt; *see* Coats.
Glen-Coats, Sir Thomas Glen, 1st Bt, 1846–1922, vol. II
Glenarthur, 1st Baron, 1852–1928, vol. II
Glenarthur, 2nd Baron, 1883–1942, vol. IV
Glenarthur, 3rd Baron, 1909–1976, vol. VII
Glenavy, 1st Baron, 1851–1931, vol. III
Glenavy, 2nd Baron, 1885–1963, vol. VI
Glenavy, 3rd Baron, 1913–1980, vol. VII
Glenavy, 4th Baron, 1924–1984, vol. VIII
Glenconner, 1st Baron, 1859–1920, vol. II
Glenconner, 2nd Baron, 1899–1983, vol. VIII
Glenday, Dorothea Nonita, 1899–1982, vol. VIII
Glenday, Nonita; *see* Glenday, D. N.
Glenday, Roy Goncalves, 1889–1957, vol. V
Glenday, Sir Vincent Goncalves, 1891–1970, vol. VI
Glendenning, Raymond Carl, 1907–1974, vol. VII
Glendevon, 1st Baron, 1912–1996, vol. X
Glendinning, Edward Green, 1922–1984, vol. VIII
Glendinning, Henry, 1863–1938, vol. III
Glendinning, James Garland, 1919–1998, vol. X
Glendinning, John Clements, 1866–1949, vol. IV
Glendinning, Rt Hon. Robert Graham, 1844–1928, vol. II
Glendyne, 1st Baron, 1849–1930, vol. III
Glendyne, 2nd Baron, 1878–1967, vol. VI
Glenesk, 1st Baron, 1830–1908, vol. I
Glenister, Tony William Alphonse, 1923–1998, vol. X
Glenkinglas, Baron (Life Peer); Michael Antony Cristobal Noble, 1913–1984, vol. VIII
Glenn, Very Rev. Henry Patterson, 1858–1923, vol. II
Glenn, Robert George, 1844–1900, vol. I
Glenn, Air Vice-Marshal Robert William Lowry, 1901–1970, vol. VI
Glenn, William James, 1911–1984, vol. VIII
Glennie, Alan Forbes Bourne, 1903–1984, vol. VIII
Glennie, Brig. Edward Aubrey, 1889–1980, vol. VII
Glennie, Rev. Herbert John, 1860–1926, vol. II
Glennie, Adm. Sir Irvine Gordon, 1892–1980, vol. VII
Glennie, Vice-Adm. Robert Woodyear, 1868–1930, vol. III
Glenny, Alexander Thomas, 1882–1965, vol. VI
Glenny, William James, 1873–1963, vol. VI
Glenravel, 1st Baron, 1858–1937, vol. III
Glentanar, 1st Baron, 1849–1918, vol. II
Glentanar, 2nd Baron, 1894–1971, vol. VII
Glentoran, 1st Baron, 1880–1950, vol. IV
Glentoran, 2nd Baron, 1912–1995, vol. IX

Glentworth, Viscount; Edmond William Claude Gerard de Vere, 1894–1918, vol. II
Glin, 28th Knight of; *see* Fitz-Gerald, Desmond Windham Otho.
Glindoni, Henry Gillard, *died* 1913, vol. I
Gloag, Lt-Gen. Archibald Robertson, 1831–1914, vol. I
Gloag, John Edwards, 1896–1981, vol. VIII
Gloag, Paton James, 1823–1906, vol. I
Gloag, William Ellis; *see* Kincairney, Hon. Lord.
Gloag, William Murray, 1865–1934, vol. III
Glock, Sir William Frederick, 1908–2000, vol. X
Glossop, Clifford William Hudson, 1901–1975, vol. VII
Glossop, Rev. George Henry Pownall, 1858–1925, vol. II
Glossop, Vice-Adm. John Collings-Taswell, 1871–1934, vol. III
Gloster, Brig.-Gen. Gerald Meade, 1864–1928, vol. II
Glover, Derek Harding, 1916–1981, vol. VIII
Glover, Sir Douglas, 1908–1982, vol. VIII
Glover, Sir (Edward) Otho, 1876–1956, vol. V
Glover, Elizabeth Rosetta, (Lady Glover), *died* 1927, vol. II
Glover, Sir Ernest William, 1st Bt, 1864–1934, vol. III
Glover, George Wright, 1884–1918, vol. II
Glover, Sir Gerald Alfred, 1908–1986, vol. VIII
Glover, Maj.-Gen. Sir Guy de Courcy, 1887–1967, vol. VI
Glover, Halcott, *died* 1949, vol. IV
Glover, Harold, 1917–1988, vol. VIII
Glover, Sir Harold Matthew, 1885–1961, vol. VI
Glover, Henry Percy, *died* 1938, vol. III
Glover, James Alison, 1876–1963, vol. VI
Glover, James Grey, *died* 1908, vol. I
Glover, James Mackey, 1861–1931, vol. III
Glover, Gen. Sir James Malcolm, 1929–2000, vol. X
Glover, Sir John, 1829–1920, vol. II
Glover, Gp Captain John Neville, 1913–1995, vol. IX
Glover, Maj.-Gen. Malcolm, 1897–1970, vol. VI
Glover, Sir Otho; *see* Glover, Sir E. O.
Glover, Richard, 1837–1919, vol. II
Glover, Ronald Everett, *died* 1975, vol. VII
Glover, Terrot Reaveley, 1869–1943, vol. IV
Glover, Thomas, 1862–1942, vol. IV
Glover, Col William Reid, 1882–1959, vol. V
Glubb, Maj.-Gen. Sir Frederic Manley, 1857–1938, vol. III
Glubb, Lt-Gen. Sir John Bagot, 1897–1986, vol. VIII
Gluckman, Max, 1911–1975, vol. VII
Gluckmann, Grigory, 1898–1973, vol. VII
Gluckstein, Isidore Montague, 1890–1975, vol. VII
Gluckstein, Sir Louis Halle, 1897–1979, vol. VII
Gluckstein, Montague, 1854–1922, vol. II
Gluckstein, Major Montague, 1886–1958, vol. V
Gluckstein, Sir Samuel, 1880–1958, vol. V
Glueckauf, Eugen, 1906–1981, vol. VIII
Glunicke, Maj.-Gen. R. C. A., 1886–1963, vol. VI
Glyn, 1st Baron, 1885–1960, vol. V
Glyn, Sir Alan, 1918–1998, vol. X

Glyn, Hon. Alice Coralie, *died* 1928, vol. II
Glyn, Sir Anthony Geoffrey Leo Simon, 2nd Bt, 1922–1998, vol. X
Glyn, Sir Arthur Robert, 7th Bt (*cr* 1759), 1870–1942, vol. IV
Glyn, Mrs Clayton, (Elinor), *died* 1943, vol. IV
Glyn, Rt Rev. Hon. Edward Carr, 1843–1928, vol. II
Glyn, Elinor; *see* Glyn, Mrs Clayton.
Glyn, Sir Francis Maurice Grosvenor, 1901–1969, vol. VI
Glyn, Rev. Frederick Ware, *died* 1918, vol. II
Glyn, Col Geoffrey Carr, 1864–1933, vol. III
Glyn, Hon. George Edward Dudley Carr, 1896–1930, vol. III
Glyn, Sir Gervas Powell, 6th Bt (*cr* 1759), 1862–1921, vol. II
Glyn, Hilary Beaujolais, 1916–1995, vol. IX
Glyn, Lt-Gen. Sir John Plumptre Carr, 1837–1912, vol. I
Glyn, Sir Julius Richard, 1824–1905, vol. I
Glyn, Lewis Edmund, 1849–1919, vol. II
Glyn, Maurice George Carr, 1872–1920, vol. II
Glyn, Hon. Pascoe Charles, 1833–1904, vol. I
Glyn, Sir Richard Fitzgerald, 4th Bt (*cr* 1800) and 8th Bt (*cr* 1759), 1875–1960, vol. V
Glyn, Sir Richard George, 3rd Bt (*cr* 1800), 1831–1918, vol. II
Glyn, Col Sir Richard Hamilton, 5th Bt and 9th Bt, 1907–1980, vol. VII
Glyn, Lt-Gen. Richard Thomas, 1831–1900, vol. I
Glyn, Hon. Sidney Carr, 1835–1916, vol. II
Glyn Hughes, Hugh Llewelyn; *see* Hughes.
Glyn-Jones, Sir Hildreth, 1895–1980, vol. VII
Glyn-Jones, Sir William Samuel, 1869–1927, vol. II
Glynn, Air Cdre Arthur Samuel, 1885–1967, vol. VI
Glynn, Ernest E., *died* 1929, vol. III
Glynn, Sir Joseph Aloysius, 1869–1951, vol. V
Glynn, Hon. Patrick M'Mahon, 1855–1931, vol. III
Glynn, Prudence Loveday, (The Lady Windlesham), 1935–1986, vol. VIII
Glynn, Lt-Col Thomas George Powell, 1863–1949, vol. IV
Glynn, Thomas Robinson, *died* 1931, vol. III
Glynn Grylls, Rosalie; *see* Mander, Lady (Rosalie).
Glynton, Col Gerard Maxwell, *died* 1942, vol. IV
Gnien Is-Sultan, Paul Nicholas Apap-Pace-Bologna, 5th Marquis of, 1880–1955, vol. V
Goad, Sir Colin; *see* Goad, Sir E. C. V.
Goad, Sir (Edward) Colin (Viner), 1914–1998, vol. X
Goad, Harold Elsdale, 1878–1956, vol. V
Goad, Col Howard, 1857–1923, vol. II
Goadby, Hector Kenneth, 1902–1990, vol. VIII
Goadby, Sir Kenneth Weldon, 1873–1958, vol. V
Gobbi, Tito, 1915–1984, vol. VIII
Gobeil, Antoine, *born* 1854, vol. II
Goble, Leslie Herbert, 1901–1969, vol. VI
Goble, Air Vice-Marshal Stanley James, 1891–1948, vol. IV
Goble, Warwick, *died* 1943, vol. IV
Godber, 1st Baron, 1888–1976, vol. VII
Godber of Willington, Baron (Life Peer); Joseph Bradshaw Godber, 1914–1980, vol. VII
Godber, Geoffrey Chapman, 1912–1999, vol. X

Godbout, Hon. Joseph, 1851–1923, vol. III
Godbout, Hon. Joseph Adélard, 1892–1956, vol. V
Godby, Col Charles, 1863–1956, vol. V
Goddard, Baron (Life Peer); Rayner Goddard, 1877–1971, vol. VII
Goddard, Alexander, 1867–1956, vol. V
Goddard, Arabella, (Mrs Davison), 1836–1922, vol. II
Goddard, Arthur, 1853–1920, vol. II
Goddard, Rt Hon. Sir Daniel Ford, 1850–1922, vol. II
Goddard, Lt-Gen. Eric Norman, 1897–1992, vol. IX
Goddard, Ernest Hope, 1879–1939, vol. III
Goddard, Lt-Col Gerald Hamilton, 1873–1948, vol. IV
Goddard, Brig.-Gen. Henry Arthur, 1871–1955, vol. V
Goddard, Sir Holland; see Goddard, Sir. J. H.
Goddard, Maj.-Gen. John Desmond, 1919–1990, vol. VIII
Goddard, Sir (Joseph) Holland, died 1958, vol. V
Goddard, Air Marshal, Sir (Robert) Victor, 1897–1987, vol. VIII
Goddard, Thomas Herbert, 1885–1967, vol. VI
Goddard, Air Marshal Sir Victor; see Goddard, Air Marshal Sir R. V.
Godden, Ven. Max Leon, 1923–2000, vol. X
Godden, Rumer, (Margaret Rumer Haynes-Dixon), 1907–1998, vol. X
Godding, Insp.-Gen. Charles Cane, died 1939, vol. III
Gödel, Kurt, 1906–1978, vol. VII
Godfray, Col Sir James, 1816–1897, vol. I
Godfray, Brig.-Gen. John William, 1850–1921, vol. II
Godfrey, Brig. Arthur Harry Langham, 1896–1942, vol. IV
Godfrey, Captain Charles, died 1903, vol. I
Godfrey, Charles, 1873–1924, vol. II
Godfrey, Sir Dan, 1868–1939, vol. III
Godfrey, Derrick Edward Reid, 1918–1989, vol. VIII
Godfrey, Ernest Henry, 1862–1952, vol. V
Godfrey, Sir George Cochrane, 1871–1945, vol. IV
Godfrey, Vice-Adm. Harry Rowlandson, 1875–1947, vol. IV
Godfrey, Sir John Albert, 1889–1973, vol. VII
Godfrey, Sir John Ernest, 6th Bt, 1864–1935, vol. III
Godfrey, Sir John Fermor, 4th Bt, 1828–1900, vol. I
Godfrey, Adm. John Henry, 1888–1971, vol. VII
Godfrey, Hon. John M., 1871–1943, vol. IV
Godfrey, John Thomas, 1857–1911, vol. I
Godfrey, Sir Joseph Edward, 1858–1938, vol. III
Godfrey, Air Cdre Kenneth Walter, 1907–1979, vol. VII
Godfrey, Percy, 1859–1945, vol. IV
Godfrey, Robert Samuel, 1876–1953, vol. V
Godfrey, Lt-Col Stuart Hill, 1861–1941, vol. IV
Godfrey, Sir Walter, 1907–1976, vol. VII
Godfrey, Walter Hindes, 1881–1961, vol. VI
Godfrey, His Eminence Cardinal William, 1889–1963, vol. VI
Godfrey, Sir William Cecil, 5th Bt, 1857–1926, vol. II

Godfrey, Sir William Maurice, 7th Bt, 1909–1971, vol. VII
Godfrey, General Sir William Wellington, 1880–1952, vol. V
Godfrey-Faussett, Captain Sir Bryan Godfrey, 1863–1945, vol. IV
Godfrey-Faussett, Brig. Bryan Trevor, 1896–1970, vol. VI
Godfrey-Faussett, Brig.-Gen. Edmund Godfrey, 1868–1942, vol. IV
Godfrey Faussett, Lt-Col Owen Godfrey, 1866–1915, vol. I
Godkin, Edwin Lawrence, 1831–1902, vol. I
Godlee, Sir Rickman John, 1st Bt, 1849–1925, vol. II
Godley, Gen. Sir Alexander John, 1867–1957, vol. V
Godley, Alfred Denis, 1856–1925, vol. II
Godley, Hon. Eveline Charlotte, died 1951, vol. V
Godley, Brig.-Gen. Francis Clements, 1858–1941, vol. IV
Godley, Brig. Sir Francis William Crewe F.; see Fetherston-Godley.
Godley, Lt-Col Godfrey Archibald, 1871–1935, vol. III
Godley, Major Harry Crewe, 1861–1907, vol. I
Godley, John Cornwallis, 1861–1946, vol. IV
Godman, Dame Alice Mary, 1868–1944, vol. IV
Godman, Col Arthur Fitzpatrick, 1842–1930, vol. III
Godman, Air Cdre Arthur Lowthian, 1877–1956, vol. V
Godman, Col Charles Bulkeley, 1849–1941, vol. IV
Godman, Frederick Du Cane, 1834–1919, vol. II
Godman, Col John, 1886–1978, vol. VII
Godman, Major Laurence, 1880–1917, vol. II
Godman, Maj.-Gen. Richard Temple, 1832–1912, vol. I
Godman, Col Sherard Haughton, 1865–1938, vol. III
Godman Irvine, Rt Hon. Sir Bryant; see Irvine, Rt Hon. Sir B. G.
Godowsky, Leopold, 1870–1938, vol. III
Godsall, Walter Douglas, 1901–1964, vol. VI
Godsell, Sir William, 1838–1924, vol. II
Godson, Sir Augustus Frederick, 1835–1906, vol. I
Godson, Clement, 1845–1913, vol. I
Godwin, Dame Anne; see Godwin, Dame B. A.
Godwin, Sir Arthur, 1852–1921, vol. II
Godwin, Dame (Beatrice) Anne, 1897–1992, vol. IX
Godwin, Lt-Gen. Sir Charles Alexander Campbell, 1873–1951, vol. V
Godwin, Sir Harry, 1901–1985, vol. VIII
Godwin-Austen, Gen. Sir Alfred Reade, 1889–1963, vol. VI
Godwin-Austen, Henry Haversham, 1834–1923, vol. II
Goe, Rt Rev. Field Flowers, 1832–1910, vol. I
Goehr, Walter, 1903–1960, vol. V
Goenka, Rai Bahadur Sir Badridas, 1883–1973, vol. VII
Goenka, Rai Bahadur Sir Hariram, 1862–1935, vol. III
Goeppert Mayer, Maria; see Mayer.
Goethals, George Washington, 1858–1928, vol. II

Goetze, Sigismund Christian Hubert, 1866–1939, vol. III

Goff, Col Algernon Hamilton Stannus, 1863–1936, vol. III

Goff, Major Cecil Willie Trevor Thomas, 1860–1907, vol. I

Goff, Eric Noel Porter, 1902–1981, vol. VIII

Goff, Sir Ernest William Davis-, 3rd Bt, 1904–1980, vol. VII

Goff, Sir Herbert William Davis-, 2nd Bt, 1870–1923, vol. II

Goff, Sir Park, 1st Bt, 1871–1939, vol. III

Goff, Captain Reginald Stannus, 1882–1965, vol. VI

Goff, Rt Hon. Sir Reginald William, 1907–1980, vol. VII

Goff, Col Robert Charles, died 1922, vol. II

Goff, Thomas Clarence Edward, 1867–1949, vol. IV

Goff, Sir William Goff Davis-, 1st Bt, 1838–1917, vol. II

Goffe, Sir Herbert, 1870–1939, vol. III

Goffin, Comr Sir Dean; see Goffin, Comr Sir J. D.

Goffin, Comr Sir (John) Dean, 1916–1984, vol. VIII

Gogarty, Col Henry Edward, 1868–1955, vol. V

Gogarty, Oliver St John, 1878–1957, vol. V

Gohel, Sir Jayvantsinhji Kayaji, 1915–1995, vol. IX

Goitein, Hugh, 1896–1976, vol. VII

Gokhale, Hon. Gopal Krishna, 1866–1915, vol. I

Gold, Major Sir Archibald Gilbey, 1870–1935, vol. III

Gold, Sir Charles, 1837–1924, vol. II

Gold, Ernest, 1881–1976, vol. VII

Gold, Sir Harcourt Gilbey, 1876–1952, vol. V

Gold, Henry, 1835–1900, vol. I

Gold, James Herbert, 1885–1974, vol. VII

Gold, Sir Joseph, 1912–2000, vol. X

Gold, Victor, 1922–1985, vol. VIII

Goldberg, Arthur Joseph, 1908–1990, vol. VIII

Goldby, Frank, 1903–1997, vol. X

Golden, Grace Lydia, 1904–1993, vol. IX

Golden, Lt-Col Harold Arthur, 1896–1976, vol. VII

Goldfinch, Sir Arthur Horne, 1866–1945, vol. IV

Goldfinch, Sir Philip Henry Macarthur, 1884–1943, vol. IV

Goldfinger, Ernö, 1902–1987, vol. VIII

Goldfrap, Brig. Harold Wyn, 1884–1940, vol. III

Goldhawk, Rev. Ira G., died 1967, vol. VI

Goldie, Archibald Hayman Robertson, 1888–1964, vol. VI

Goldie, Barré Algernon Highmore, 1870–1949, vol. IV

Goldie, Rt Rev. Frederick, 1914–1980, vol. VII

Goldie, Rt Hon. Sir George Dashwood Taubman, 1846–1925, vol. II

Goldie, Major Kenneth Oswald, 1882–1938, vol. III

Goldie, Captain Mark Leigh, 1875–1915, vol. I

Goldie, Sir Noel Barré, 1882–1964, vol. VI

Goldie, Robert George, 1893–1971, vol. VII

Goldie-Taubman, Sir John Senhouse, 1838–1898, vol. I

Golding, Dame (Cecilie) Monica, 1902–1997, vol. X

Golding, Frank Yeates, 1867–1938, vol. III

Golding, F(rederick) Campbell, 1901–1984, vol. VIII

Golding, Rev. Harry, 1889–1969, vol. VI

Golding, Captain John, 1871–1943, vol. IV

Golding, John, 1931–1999, vol. X

Golding, Hon. Sir John Simon Rawson, 1921–1996, vol. X

Golding, Louis, 1895–1958, vol. V

Golding, Dame Monica; see Golding, Dame C. M.

Golding, Captain Thomas, 1860–1937, vol. III

Golding, Sir William Gerald, 1911–1993, vol. IX

Golding-Bird, Cuthbert Hilton, 1848–1939, vol. III

Golding-Bird, Rt Rev. Cyril Henry, 1876–1955, vol. V

Goldman, Charles Sydney, 1868–1958, vol. V

Goldman, Peter, 1925–1987, vol. VIII

Goldmann, Edwin E., 1862–1913, vol. I

Goldmann, Nahum, 1895–1982, vol. VIII

Goldmark, Karl, 1832–1915, vol. I

Goldney, Maj.-Gen. Claude Le Bas, 1887–1978, vol. VII

Goldney, Francis B.; see Bennett-Goldney.

Goldney, Sir Frederick Hastings, 3rd Bt, 1845–1940, vol. III

Goldney, Sir Gabriel, 1st Bt, 1813–1900, vol. I

Goldney, Col George Francis Bennett, 1879–1953, vol. V

Goldney, Sir Henry Hastings, 4th Bt, 1886–1974, vol. VII

Goldney, Hon. Sir John Tankerville, 1846–1920, vol. II

Goldney, Sir Prior, 2nd Bt, 1843–1925, vol. II

Goldney, Col Thomas Holbrow, 1847–1915, vol. I

Goldring, Douglas, 1887–1960, vol. V

Goldsbrough, George Ridsdale, 1881–1963, vol. VI

Goldsbrough, Giles Forward, died 1933, vol. III

Goldschmidt, Otto, 1829–1907, vol. I

Goldschmidt, Lt-Col Sidney George, 1869–1949, vol. IV

Goldsmid, Col Albert Edward Williamson, 1846–1904, vol. I

Goldsmid, Sir Frederic John, 1818–1908, vol. I

Goldsmid, Major Sir Henry Joseph d'A.; see d'Avigdor-Goldsmid.

Goldsmid, Maj.-Gen. Sir James Arthur d'A.; see d'Avigdor-Goldsmid.

Goldsmid, Sir Osmond Elim d'A.; see d'Avigdor-Goldsmid.

Goldsmid, Sidney Hoffnung, 1863–1930, vol. III

Goldsmid-Montefiore, Claude Joseph; see Montefiore.

Goldsmid-Stern-Salomons, Sir David Lionel; see Salomons.

Goldsmith, Sir Allen John Bridson, 1909–1976, vol. VII

Goldsmith, Edward, 1868–1951, vol. V

Goldsmith, Francis, 1874–1940, vol. III

Goldsmith, Frank, 1878–1967, vol. VI

Goldsmith, Rt Rev. Frederick, 1853–1932, vol. III

Goldsmith, Col George Mills, 1876–1937, vol. III

Goldsmith, Col Harry Dundas, 1878–1955, vol. V

Goldsmith, Herbert Symonds, 1873–1945, vol. IV

Goldsmith, Sir James Michael, 1933–1997, vol. X

Goldsmith, John Herman Thorburn, 1903–1987, vol. VIII

Goldsmith, John Mills, 1845–1912, vol. I

Goldsmith, Mac, 1902–1983, vol. VIII

Goldsmith, Rev. Malcolm George, 1849–1940, vol. III

Goldsmith, Vice-Adm. Sir Malcolm Lennon, 1880–1955, vol. V

Goldsmith, Col Perry Gladstone, 1874–1951, vol. V

Goldsmith, Maj.-Gen. Robert Frederick Kinglake, 1907–1995, vol. IX

Goldsmith, Rev. Sidney Willmer, 1869–1939, vol. III

Goldsmith, Captain Sir William Burgess, 1837–1912, vol. I

Goldsmith, William Noel, 1893–1975, vol. VII

Goldstein, Sydney, 1903–1989, vol. VIII

Goldstein, Baron W. van, 1831–1901, vol. I

Goldstone, David Israel, 1908–1992, vol. IX

Goldstone, Sir Frank Walter, 1870–1955, vol. V

Goldsworthy, Ian Francis, 1943–2000, vol. X

Goldsworthy, Captain Ivan Ernest Goodman, 1894–1970, vol. VI

Goldsworthy, Walter Tuckfield, 1837–1911, vol. I

Goldthorpe, Brian Lees, 1933–1992, vol. IX

Goldwater, Barry Morris, 1909–1998, vol. X

Goldwyn, Samuel, 1882–1974, vol. VII

Goligher, Hugh Garvin, 1873–1958, vol. V

Goligher, John Cedric, 1912–1998, vol. X

Goligher, William Alexander, 1870–1941, vol. IV

Golightly, Col Robert Edmund, 1856–1935, vol. III

Golla, Frederick Lucian, 1878–1968, vol. VI

Gollan, Sir Alexander, died 1902, vol. I

Gollan, Eliza Margaret; see Rita.

Gollan, Sir Henry Cowper, 1868–1949, vol. IV

Gollan, Herbert Roy, 1892–1968, vol. VI

Gollan, Spencer Herbert, 1860–1934, vol. III

Gollancz, Rev. Sir Hermann, 1852–1930, vol. III

Gollancz, Sir Israel, 1863–1930, vol. III

Gollancz, Sir Victor, 1893–1967, vol. VI

Gollin, Alfred, 1861–1946, vol. IV

Golombek, Harry, 1911–1995, vol. IX

Golsworthy, Arnold, 1865–1939, vol. III

Golt, Sidney, 1910–1995, vol. IX

Gomes, Sir Stanley Eugene, 1901–1985, vol. VIII

Gomez, Alice, died 1922, vol. II

Gomm, Francis Culling C.; see Carr-Gomm.

Gomm, Hubert William Culling C.; see Carr-Gomm.

Gomme, Arnold Wycombe, 1886–1959, vol. V

Gomme, Sir (George) Laurence, 1853–1916, vol. II

Gomme, Sir Laurence; see Gomme, Sir G. L.

Gomme-Duncan, Col Sir Alan Gomme; see Duncan.

Gompers, Samuel, 1850–1924, vol. II

Gompertz, Frank Priestly V.; see Vincent-Gompertz.

Gompertz, Sir Henry Hessey Johnston, 1867–1930, vol. III

Gompertz, Brig. Martin Louis Alan, 1886–1951, vol. V

Gonard, Samuel Alexandre, 1896–1975, vol. VII

Gondal, HH Maharaja of, 1865–1944, vol. IV

Gonner, Sir Edward Carter Kersey, 1862–1922, vol. II

Gonner, Rev. Eric Peter, died 1930, vol. III

Gonthier, George, 1869–1943, vol. IV

Gonzalez-Llubera, Ignacio Miguel, 1893–1962, vol. VI

Gonzi, Most Rev. Michael, 1885–1984, vol. VIII

Gooch, Sir Alfred Sherlock, 9th Bt (cr 1746), 1851–1899, vol. I

Gooch, Brian Sherlock, 1904–1968, vol. VI

Gooch, Charles Edmund, 1870–1937, vol. III

Gooch, Sir Daniel Fulthorpe, 3rd Bt (cr 1866), 1869–1926, vol. II

Gooch, Edwin George, 1889–1964, vol. VI

Gooch, George Gordon, 1893–1967, vol. VI (AII)

Gooch, George Peabody, 1873–1968, vol. VI

Gooch, Sir Henry Cubitt, 1871–1959, vol. V

Gooch, Sir Henry Daniel, 2nd Bt (cr 1866), 1841–1897, vol. I

Gooch, Henry Martyn, 1874–1957, vol. V

Gooch, Sir John Sherlock; see Gooch, Sir R. J. S.

Gooch, Brig. Richard Frank Sherlock, 1906–1973, vol. VII

Gooch, Sir (Richard) John Sherlock, 12th Bt (cr 1746), 1930–1999, vol. X

Gooch, Sir Robert Douglas, 4th Bt, 1905–1989, vol. VIII

Gooch, Col Sir Robert Eric Sherlock, 11th Bt (cr 1746), 1903–1978, vol. VII

Gooch, Sir Thomas Vere Sherlock, 10th Bt (cr 1746), 1881–1946, vol. IV

Good, Alan Paul, 1906–1953, vol. V

Good, Christopher Frank, died 1949, vol. IV

Good, Donal Bernard Waters, 1907–1993, vol. IX (AII)

Good, Air Vice-Marshal James Laurence Fuller F.; see Fuller-Good.

Good, James Winder, 1877–1930, vol. III

Good, Percy, died 1950, vol. IV

Good, Ronald D'Oyley, 1896–1992, vol. IX

Goodacre, Hugh George, 1865–1952, vol. V

Goodale, Cecil Paul, 1918–1992, vol. IX

Goodale, Sir Ernest William, 1896–1984, vol. VIII

Goodall, Alexander, 1876–1941, vol. IV

Goodall, Edward A., 1819–1908, vol. I

Goodall, Edward Basil Herbert, 1885–1936, vol. III

Goodall, Lt-Col Edwin, 1863–1944, vol. IV

Goodall, Frederick, 1822–1904, vol. I

Goodall, Rev. John William, died 1932, vol. III

Goodall, Joseph Strickland, 1874–1934, vol. III

Goodall, Rev. Norman, 1896–1985, vol. VIII

Goodall, Peter, 1920–1995, vol. IX

Goodall, Sir Reginald, 1901–1990, vol. VIII

Goodall, Rev. Canon Robert William, 1862–1938, vol. III

Goodall, Sir Stanley Vernon, 1883–1965, vol. VI

Gooday, John Francis Sykes, died 1915, vol. I

Goodbody, Col Cecil Maurice, 1874–1936, vol. III

Goodbody, Francis Woodcock, 1870–1938, vol. III

Goodbody, Gen. Sir Richard Wakefield, 1903–1981, vol. VIII

Goodchild, George, 1888–1969, vol. VI

Goodchild, George Frederick, 1871–1956, vol. V

Goodchild, Norman Walter, 1901–1970, vol. VI

Goodchild, Rt Rev. Ronald Cedric Osbourne, 1910–1998, vol. X

Goodchild, Lt-Col Sidney, 1903–1994, vol. IX

Goodchild, Sir William Alfred Cecil, 1885–1940, vol. III

Goodden, Abington, 1901–1978, vol. VII

Goodden, Rev. Edward Wyndham, 1847–1924, vol. II

Goodden, Col John Bernhard Harbin, 1876–1951, vol. V

Goode, Sir Charles Henry, 1827–1922, vol. II

Goode, Sir Richard Allmond Jeffrey, 1873–1953, vol. V
Goode, Samuel Walter, 1878–1935, vol. III
Goode, Sir William Allmond Codrington, 1907–1986, vol. VIII
Goode, Sir William Athelstane Meredith, *died* 1944, vol. IV
Gooden, Rev. Malcolm Cecil Whitridge, 1894–1969, vol. VI
Gooden, Stephen, 1892–1955, vol. V
Goodenough, Cecilia Phyllis, 1905–1998, vol. X
Goodenough, Ethel Mary, *died* 1946, vol. IV
Goodenough, Sir Francis William, 1872–1940, vol. III
Goodenough, Frederick Cranfurd, 1866–1934, vol. III
Goodenough, Kenneth Mackenzie, 1891–1985, vol. VIII
Goodenough, Rear-Adm. Michael Grant, 1904–1955, vol. V
Goodenough, Sir Richard Edmund, 2nd Bt, 1925–1996, vol. X
Goodenough, Samuel Kenneth Henry, 1930–1983, vol. VIII
Goodenough, Adm. Sir William Edmund, 1867–1945, vol. IV
Goodenough, Lt-Gen. Sir William Howley, 1833–1898, vol. I
Goodenough, Sir William Macnamara, 1st Bt, 1899–1951, vol. V
Gooderham, Col Sir Albert, 1861–1935, vol. III
Gooderham, Very Rev. Hector Bransby, 1901–1977, vol. VII
Gooderson, Richard Norman, 1915–1981, vol. VIII
Goodeve, Mrs Arthur, (Florence Everilda), *died* 1916, vol. II
Goodeve, Hon. Arthur Samuel, 1860–1920, vol. II
Goodeve, Sir Charles Frederick, 1904–1980, vol. VII
Goodeve, Florence Everilda; *see* Goodeve, Mrs Arthur.
Goodey, Tom, 1885–1953, vol. V
Goodfellow, Lt-Gen. Charles Augustus, 1836–1915, vol. I
Goodfellow, Maj.-Gen. Howard Courtney, 1898–1983, vol. VIII
Goodfellow, Keith Frank, 1926–1977, vol. VII
Goodfellow, Mark Aubrey, 1931–1999, vol. X
Goodfellow, Col Napier George Barras, 1878–1963, vol. VI
Goodfellow, Thomas Ashton, *died* 1937, vol. III
Goodfellow, Gen. W. W., 1833–1901, vol. I
Goodfellow, Sir William, 1880–1974, vol. VII
Goodhart, Arthur Lehman, 1891–1978, vol. VII
Goodhart, Sir Ernest Frederic, 2nd Bt, 1880–1961, vol. VI
Goodhart, Comdr Francis Herbert Heveningham, 1884–1917, vol. II
Goodhart, Gordon Wilkinson, 1882–1948, vol. IV
Goodhart, Sir James Frederic, 1st Bt, 1845–1916, vol. II
Goodhart, Sir John Gordon, 3rd Bt, 1916–1979, vol. VII
Goodhart, Leander McC.; *see* McCormick-Goodhart.

Goodhart-Rendel, Harry Stuart, 1887–1959, vol. V
Goodier, Most Rev. Alban, 1869–1939, vol. III
Goodier, Rev. Joseph Hulme, *died* 1920, vol. II
Goodings, Rt Rev. Allen, 1925–1992, vol. IX
Goodison, Robin Reynolds, 1912–1998, vol. X
Goodland, Col Herbert Tom, 1874–1956, vol. V
Goodlet, Brian Laidlaw, 1903–1961, vol. VI
Goodliffe, Francis Foster, *died* 1925, vol. II
Goodman, Baron (Life Peer); Arnold Abraham Goodman, 1913–1995, vol. IX
Goodman, Col Albert William, 1880–1937, vol. III
Goodman, Rev. Arthur Worthington, 1871–1951, vol. V
Goodman, Bruce Wilfred, 1906–1974, vol. VII
Goodman, Cyril, *died* 1938, vol. III
Goodman, Maj.-Gen. David; *see* Goodman, Maj.-Gen. J. D. W.
Goodman, Rev. George, 1821–1908, vol. I
Goodman, Hon. Sir Gerald Aubrey, 1862–1921, vol. II
Goodman, Brig.-Gen. Sir Godfrey Davenport, 1868–1957, vol. V
Goodman, Lt-Col Harry Russell, 1875–1936, vol. III
Goodman, Howard; *see* Goodman, R. H.
Goodman, John, 1862–1935, vol. III
Goodman, Maj.-Gen. (John) David (Whitlock), 1932–2000, vol. X
Goodman, Maude, *died* 1938, vol. III
Goodman, Rt Rev. Morse Lamb, 1917–1993, vol. IX
Goodman, Neville Marriott, 1898–1980, vol. VII
Goodman, Paul, 1875–1949, vol. IV
Goodman, Reginald Ernest, 1886–1968, vol. VI
Goodman, Robert Gwelo, *died* 1939, vol. III
Goodman, (Robert) Howard, 1928–1999, vol. X
Goodman, Sydney Charles Nichols, 1868–1936, vol. III
Goodman, Sir Victor Martin Reeves, 1899–1967, vol. VI
Goodman, Vyvian Edwin, 1889–1961, vol. VI
Goodman, Maj.-Gen. Walter Rutherfoord, 1899–1976, vol. VII
Goodman, Sir William George Toop, 1872–1961, vol. VI
Goodman, Hon. Sir William Meigh, 1847–1928, vol. II
Goodrich, Rev. A., 1840–1919, vol. II
Goodrich, Carter, 1897–1971, vol. VII
Goodrich, Edwin Stephen, 1868–1946, vol. IV
Goodrich, Henry E., 1887–1961, vol. VI
Goodrich, Adm. Sir James Edward Clifford, 1851–1925, vol. II
Goodrich, Dame Matilda, *died* 1972, vol. VII
Goodrich-Freer, A. M., *died* 1931, vol. III
Goodridge, Major Edwin, 1903–1969, vol. VI
Goodridge, Hon. Noel Herbert Alan, 1930–1997, vol. X
Goodridge, Rear-Adm. Walter Somerville, 1849–1929, vol. III
Goodsall, David Henry, *died* 1906, vol. I
Goodsell, Sir John William, 1906–1981, vol. VIII
Goodship, Harold Edwin, 1877–1951, vol. V
Goodson, Alan, 1927–1990, vol. VIII
Goodson, Sir Alfred Lassam, 1st Bt, 1867–1940, vol. III

Goodson, Lt-Col Sir Alfred Lassam, 2nd Bt, 1893–1986, vol. VIII
Goodson, Arthur, 1913–1975, vol. VII
Goodson, Katharine, died 1958, vol. V
Goodstein, Reuben Louis, 1912–1985, vol. VIII
Goodwin, Albert, died 1932, vol. III
Goodwin, Albert, 1906–1995, vol. IX
Goodwin, Aubrey, 1889–1964, vol. VI
Goodwin, Air Vice-Marshal Edwin Spencer, 1894–1991, vol. IX
Goodwin, Col Frank, 1857–1943, vol. IV
Goodwin, Engr-Rear-Adm. Frank Rheuben, 1875–1966, vol. VI
Goodwin, Geoffrey Lawrence, 1916–1995, vol. IX
Goodwin, Major George Alfred, 1857–1945, vol. IV
Goodwin, Engr Vice-Adm. Sir George Goodwin, 1862–1945, vol. IV
Goodwin, Harvey, 1850–1917, vol. II
Goodwin, Lt-Gen. Sir John; see Goodwin, Lt-Gen. Sir T. H. J. C.
Goodwin, Michael Felix James, 1916–1988, vol. VIII
Goodwin, Nathaniel Carl, 1857–1919, vol. II
Goodwin, Sir Reginald Eustace, 1908–1986, vol. VIII
Goodwin, Lt-Gen. Sir Richard Elton, 1908–1986, vol. VIII
Goodwin, Richard Murphey, 1913–1996, vol. X
Goodwin, Shirley, 1880–1927, vol. II
Goodwin, Sir Stuart Coldwell, 1886–1969, vol. VI
Goodwin, Lt-Col Thomas Frederick, 1904–1965, vol. VI
Goodwin, Lt-Gen. Sir (Thomas Herbert) John (Chapman), 1871–1960, vol. V
Goodwin, William, 1873–1953, vol. V
Goodwin, William Lawton, 1856–1941, vol. IV
Goodwin, Lt-Col William Richard, 1882–1930, vol. III
Goodwin, Col William Richard Power, 1875–1958, vol. V
Goodwin, Sir William V. S. Gradwell, 1865–1942, vol. IV
Goodwin-Tomkinson, Joseph; see Tomkinson.
Goodwyn, Rev. Canon Frederick Wildman, 1850–1931, vol. III
Goodwyn, Major Henry Edward, 1855–1929, vol. III
Goodwyn, Lt-Col Norton James, 1861–1906, vol. I
Goody, Most Rev. Launcelot John, 1908–1992, vol. IX
Goodyear, Francis Richard David, 1936–1987, vol. VIII
Goodyear, Robert Arthur Hanson, 1877–1948, vol. IV
Goodyear, William Henry, 1846–1923, vol. II
Goold, Baron (Life Peer); James Duncan Goold, 1934–1997, vol. X
Goold, Sir George Ignatius, 6th Bt, 1903–1967, vol. VI
Goold, Sir George Leonard, 7th Bt, 1923–1997, vol. X
Goold, Sir (George) Patrick, 5th Bt, 1878–1954, vol. V (A)
Goold, Sir James Stephen, 4th Bt, 1848–1926, vol. II

Goold-Adams, Major Sir Hamilton John, 1858–1920, vol. II
Goold-Adams, Col Sir Henry Edward Fane, 1860–1935, vol. III
Goold-Adams, Ven. John Michael, 1850–1922, vol. II
Goold-Adams, Richard John Moreton, 1916–1995, vol. IX
Goolden, Barbara, 1900–1990, vol. VIII
Goolden, Rear-Adm. Francis Hugh Walter, 1885–1950, vol. IV
Goolden, Richard Percy Herbert, 1895–1981, vol. VIII
Goonetilleke, Sir Oliver Ernest, 1892–1978, vol. VII
Goosman, Hon. Sir Stanley; see Goosman, Hon. Sir W. S.
Goosman, Hon. Sir (William) Stanley, 1890–1969, vol. VI
Goossens, Sir Eugene, 1893–1962, vol. VI
Goossens, Léon Jean, 1897–1988, vol. VIII
Gopathi Narayanaswami Chetty, Diwan Bahadur Sir, 1881–1945, vol. IV
Gopallawa, William, 1897–1981, vol. VIII
Gordine, Dora, 1906–1991, vol. IX
Gordon, Lord Adam Granville, 1909–1984, vol. VIII
Gordon, Lt-Col Adrian Charles, 1889–1917, vol. II
Gordon, Alban Goodwin, 1890–1947, vol. IV
Gordon, Alec Knyvet, 1870–1951, vol. V
Gordon, Hon. Sir Alexander, 1858–1942, vol. IV
Gordon, Alexander, 1886–1965, vol. VI
Gordon, Alexander Esmé, 1910–1993, vol. IX
Gordon, Lt-Gen. Sir Alexander Hamilton, 1859–1939, vol. III
Gordon, Sir Alexander John, 1917–1999, vol. X
Gordon, Alexander Morison, 1846–1913, vol. I
Gordon, Rev. Alexander Reid, 1872–1930, vol. III
Gordon, Lt-Col Rt Hon. Sir Alexander Robert Gisborne, 1882–1967, vol. VI
Gordon, Brig.-Gen. Alister Fraser, 1872–1917, vol. II
Gordon, Major Archibald Alexander, 1867–1949, vol. IV
Gordon, Sir (Archibald) Douglas, 1888–1966, vol. VI
Gordon, Sir Archibald McDonald, 1892–1974, vol. VII
Gordon, Rev. Hon. Arthur, 1854–1919, vol. II
Gordon of Ellon, Arthur John Lewis, 1847–1918, vol. II
Gordon, Aubrey Abraham, 1925–2000, vol. X
Gordon, Brig. Barbara Masson, 1913–1980, vol. VII
Gordon, Lt-Gen. Sir Benjamin Lumsden, 1833–1916, vol. II
Gordon, Surg.-Gen. Sir Charles Alexander, 1821–1899, vol. I
Gordon, Sir Charles Blair, 1867–1939, vol. III
Gordon, Sir Charles Edward, 7th Bt (cr 1706), 1835–1910, vol. I
Gordon, Rev. Charles W.; see Connor, Ralph.
Gordon, Christie Wilson, 1911–1979, vol. VII
Gordon, Christopher Martin P.; see Pirie-Gordon.
Gordon, Major Colin Lindsay, died 1940, vol. III
Gordon, Cora Josephine, died 1950, vol. IV

Gordon, Sir Cosmo (Edmund) Duff, 5th Bt (*cr* 1813), 1862–1931, vol. III
Gordon, Crawford, 1914–1967, vol. VI
Gordon, Very Rev. Daniel Miner, 1845–1925, vol. II
Gordon, Hon. Sir David John, 1865–1946, vol. IV
Gordon, Maj.-Gen. Desmond Spencer, 1911–1997, vol. X
Gordon, Donald, 1901–1969, vol. VI
Gordon, Donald James, 1915–1977, vol. VII
Gordon, Donald McDonald, 1921–1985, vol. VIII
Gordon, Sir Douglas; *see* Gordon, Sir A. D.
Gordon, Douglas; *see* Gordon, G. C. D.
Gordon, Sir Douglas Frederick D.; *see* Duff-Gordon.
Gordon, Hon. and Rev. Douglas H.; *see* Hamilton-Gordon.
Gordon, Douglas John, 1900–1959, vol. V
Gordon, Major Duncan Forbes, *born* 1849, vol. II
Gordon, Lt-Col Edward Hyde Hamilton-, *died* 1955, vol. V
Gordon, Rt Rev. Eric; *see* Gordon, Rt Rev. G. E.
Gordon, Eric V., 1896–1938, vol. III
Gordon, Esmé; *see* Gordon A. E.
Gordon, Col Esme Cosmo William C.; *see* Conway-Gordon.
Gordon, Lt-Col Evelyn Boscawen, 1877–1963, vol. VI
Gordon, Sir Eyre, 1884–1972, vol. VII
Gordon, Francis Frederick, 1866–1922, vol. II
Gordon, Lt-Col Francis Lewis, 1878–1920, vol. II
Gordon, Maj.-Gen. Hon. Sir Frederick, 1861–1927, vol. II
Gordon, Sir Garnet Hamilton, 1904–1975, vol. VII
Gordon, George, *died* 1914, vol. I
Gordon, George Angier, 1853–1929, vol. III
Gordon, Rt Rev. George Eric, 1905–1992, vol. IX
Gordon, Col George Grant, 1836–1912, vol. I
Gordon, Col George Grant, 1863–1926, vol. II
Gordon, Col George Hamilton, 1875–1961, vol. VI
Gordon, George Stuart, 1881–1942, vol. IV
Gordon, Lord Granville Armyne, 1856–1907, vol. I
Gordon, (Granville Cecil) Douglas, 1883–1930, vol. III
Gordon, Col Gwynnedd C.; *see* Conway-Gordon.
Gordon, Hampden Charles, *died* 1960, vol. V
Gordon, Harry Panmure, 1837–1902, vol. I
Gordon, Henry Erskine, 1849–1929, vol. III
Gordon, Captain Sir Henry Robert, 1886–1969, vol. VI
Gordon, Henry W.; *see* Wolrige-Gordon.
Gordon, Sir Henry William D., 6th Bt; *see* Duff-Gordon.
Gordon, Brig.-Gen. Herbert, 1869–1951, vol. V
Gordon, Herbert Ford, 1882–1963, vol. VI
Gordon, Sir Home Seton, 11th Bt (*cr* 1631), 1845–1906, vol. I
Gordon, Sir Home Seton Charles Montagu, 12th Bt (*cr* 1631), 1871–1956, vol. V
Gordon, Hugh Walker, 1897–1987, vol. VIII
Gordon, James Charles Maitland-, 1850–1915, vol. I
Gordon, Rt Rev. James Geoffrey, 1881–1938, vol. III

Gordon, Maj.-Gen. James Leslie, 1909–1985, vol. VIII
Gordon, James Scott, 1867–1946, vol. IV
Gordon, Jan, 1882–1944, vol. IV
Gordon, Rt Hon. John, 1849–1922, vol. II
Gordon, Lt-Col John, 1870–1938, vol. III
Gordon, Rt Hon. John Bowie, (Peter), 1921–1991, vol. IX
Gordon, Sir John Charles, 9th Bt, 1901–1982, vol. VIII
Gordon, Col John Charles Frederick, 1849–1923, vol. II
Gordon, Lt-Col John de la Hay, 1887–1959, vol. V
Gordon, Hon. John Edward, 1850–1915, vol. I
Gordon, Brig. John Evison, 1901–1977, vol. VII
Gordon, Rt Hon. John Fawcett, 1879–1965, vol. VI
Gordon, Col John Gordon W.; *see* Wolrige-Gordon.
Gordon, John Gunn Drummond, 1909–1992, vol. IX
Gordon, Hon. Sir John Hannah, 1850–1923, vol. II
Gordon, Gen. Sir John James Hood, 1832–1908, vol. I
Gordon, Brig. John Keily, 1883–1976, vol. VII
Gordon, Brig.-Gen. John Lewis Randolph, 1867–1953, vol. V
Gordon, John Rutherford, 1890–1974, vol. VII
Gordon, John William, 1853–1936, vol. III
Gordon, Maj.-Gen. Joseph Maria, 1856–1929, vol. III
Gordon, Kathleen Olivia, 1898–1985, vol. VIII
Gordon, Col Kenmure Alick Garth E.; *see* Evans-Gordon.
Gordon, Kenneth, 1897–1955, vol. V
Gordon, Brig.-Gen. Laurence George Frank, 1864–1943, vol. IV
Gordon, Captain Lewis, 1883–1915, vol. I
Gordon, Lewis, *died* 1935, vol. III
Gordon, Lt-Gen. Lewis C.; *see* Conway-Gordon.
Gordon, Sir Lionel Eldred Pottinger S. (3rd Bt); *see* Smith-Gordon.
Gordon, Sir Lionel Eldred Pottinger S. (4th Bt); *see* Smith-Gordon.
Gordon, Sir Lionel Eldred S.; *see* Smith-Gordon.
Gordon, Maj.-Gen. Lochinvar Alexander Charles, 1864–1927, vol. II
Gordon, Col Louis Augustus, 1857–1935, vol. III
Gordon, Dame Maria M. O.; *see* Ogilvie Gordon.
Gordon, Mervyn Henry, 1872–1953, vol. V
Gordon, Captain Oliver Loudon, 1896–1973, vol. VII
Gordon, Percival Hector, 1884–1975, vol. VII
Gordon, Rt Hon. Peter; *see* Gordon, Rt Hon. J. B.
Gordon, Peter Macie, 1919–2000, vol. X
Gordon, Col Philip Cecil Harcourt, 1864–1920, vol. II
Gordon, Lt-Col Ramsay Frederick Clayton, 1864–1943, vol. IV
Gordon, Reginald Hugh Lyall, 1863–1924, vol. II
Gordon, Richard J., 1881–1966, vol. VI
Gordon, Air Cdre Robert, 1882–1954, vol. V
Gordon, Robert Abercromby, *died* 1954, vol. V
Gordon, Sir Robert Charles, 8th Bt (*cr* 1706), 1862–1939, vol. III
Gordon, Sir Robert Glendonwyn, 9th Bt (*cr* 1625), 1824–1908, vol. I

Gordon, Captain Robert W.; *see* Wolrige Gordon.
Gordon, Robert Wilson, 1915–1993, vol. IX
Gordon, Captain Roderick Cosmo, 1902–1975, vol. VII
Gordon, Roland Graham, 1880–1958, vol. V
Gordon, Ronald Grey, 1889–1950, vol. IV
Gordon, Rupert Montgomery, 1893–1961, vol. VI
Gordon, Seton, 1886–1977, vol. VII
Gordon, Col Stannus Verner, 1846–1933, vol. III
Gordon, Strathearn, 1902–1983, vol. VIII
Gordon, Thomas Eagleson, *died* 1929, vol. III
Gordon, Gen. Sir Thomas Edward, 1832–1914, vol. I
Gordon, Sir Thomas Steward, 1882–1949, vol. IV
Gordon, Victor, 1884–1928, vol. II
Gordon, Vivian; *see* Bowden, V. G.
Gordon, Walter Maxwell, *died* 1951, vol. V
Gordon, Webster Boyle, 1859–1943, vol. IV
Gordon, Hon. Wesley Ashton, 1884–1943, vol. IV
Gordon, Sir William, 6th Bt (*cr* 1706), 1830–1906, vol. I
Gordon, Maj.-Gen. William, 1831–1909, vol. I
Gordon, Gen. William, 1824–1917, vol. II
Gordon, William, 1863–1929, vol. III
Gordon, Col William Alexander, 1869–1936, vol. III
Gordon, Col William Eagleson, 1866–1941, vol. IV
Gordon, Major Sir William Eden Evans, 1857–1913, vol. I
Gordon, Adm. William Everard Alphonso, 1817–1906, vol. I
Gordon, Col William Fanshawe Loudon, 1872–1931, vol. III
Gordon, Lt-Col William Howat Leslie, 1914–1997, vol. X
Gordon, William Smith, 1902–1967, vol. VI
Gordon, William Thomas, 1884–1950, vol. IV
Gordon Clark, Alfred Alexander, 1900–1958, vol. V
Gordon-Clark, Lt-Col Craufurd Alexander, 1864–1950, vol. IV
Gordon Clark, Henry Herbert, 1861–1951, vol. V
Gordon-Cumming, Major Sir Alexander Penrose, 5th Bt, 1893–1939, vol. III
Gordon-Cumming, Miss Constance Frederica, 1837–1924, vol. II
Gordon-Cumming, Sir William Gordon, 4th Bt, 1848–1930, vol. III
Gordon-Duff, Col Thomas Robert, 1911–1997, vol. X
Gordon-Finlayson, Air Vice-Marshal James Richmond, 1914–1990, vol. VIII
Gordon-Finlayson, Gen. Sir Robert, 1881–1956, vol. V
Gordon-Hall, Maj.-Gen. Frederick William, 1902–1990, vol. VIII
Gordon-Hall, Col Frederick William George, 1861–1942, vol. IV
Gordon-Hall, Lt-Col Gordon Charles William, 1875–1940, vol. III
Gordon-Ives, Col Gordon Maynard, 1837–1907, vol. I
Gordon Lennox, Rear-Adm. Sir Alexander Henry Charles, 1911–1987, vol. VIII
Gordon-Lennox, Col Lord Algernon Charles, 1847–1921, vol. II

Gordon-Lennox, Lady Algernon, (Blanche), *died* 1945, vol. IV
Gordon-Lennox, Lord Bernard Charles, 1878–1914, vol. I
Gordon-Lennox, Cosmo Charles, 1869–1921, vol. II
Gordon-Lennox, Lord Esme Charles, 1875–1949, vol. IV
Gordon Lennox, Lieut-Gen. Sir George Charles, 1908–1988, vol. VIII
Gordon-Lennox, Rt Hon. Lord Walter Charles, 1865–1922, vol. II
Gordon-Luhrs, Lt-Col Henry; *see* Luhrs.
Gordon-Smith, Sir Allan Gordon, 1881–1951, vol. V
Gordon-Smith, Frederic, 1886–1967, vol. VI
Gordon-Smith, Ralph, 1905–1993, vol. IX
Gordon-Smith, Richard, 1858–1918, vol. II
Gordon-Stables, William, 1840–1910, vol. I
Gordon-Taylor, Sir Gordon, *died* 1960, vol. V
Gordon-Walker, Baron (Life Peer); Patrick Chrestien Gordon Walker, 1907–1980, vol. VII
Gordon-Watson, Maj.-Gen. Sir Charles Gordon, 1874–1949, vol. IV
Gordon Watson, Hugh; *see* Watson.
Gore, Surg.-Gen. Albert H., 1839–1901, vol. I
Gore, Rev. Arthur, 1829–1913, vol. I
Gore, Col Arthur Francis Gore P. K.; *see* Pery-Knox-Gore.
Gore, Arthur (William Charles) Wentworth, 1868–1928, vol. II
Gore, Rt Rev. Charles, 1853–1932, vol. III
Gore, Col Charles Clitherow, 1839–1926, vol. II
Gore, Charles Henry, 1862–1945, vol. IV
Gore, Lt-Gen. Edward Arthur, 1839–1912, vol. I
Gore, Sir Francis Charles, 1846–1940, vol. III
Gore, Lt-Col Francis William George, 1855–1938, vol. III
Gore, Lt-Col Frederic Lawrence, 1884–1952, vol. V
Gore, George, 1826–1908, vol. I
Gore, Lt-Col J. C., 1852–1926, vol. II
Gore, John Ellard, 1845–1910, vol. I
Gore, John Francis, 1885–1983, vol. VIII
Gore, John Kearns, 1924–1980, vol. VII
Gore, Sir Ralph; *see* Gore, Sir St G. R.
Gore, Lt-Col Sir Ralph St George Brian, 11th Bt, 1908–1973, vol. VII
Gore, Sir Ralph St George Claude, 10th Bt, 1877–1961, vol. VI
Gore, Sir Richard Ralph St George, 13th Bt, 1954–1993, vol. IX
Gore, Col Robert Clements, 1867–1918, vol. II
Gore, Sir (St George) Ralph, 12th Bt, 1914–1973, vol. VII
Gore, Col Sir St John Corbet, 1859–1949, vol. IV
Gore, Hon. Seymour Fitzroy O.; *see* Ormsby-Gore.
Gore-Booth, Baron (Life Peer); Paul Henry Gore-Booth, 1909–1984, vol. VIII
Gore-Booth, Sir Angus Josslyn, 8th Bt, 1920–1996, vol. X
Gore-Booth, Eva Selina, *died* 1926, vol. II
Gore-Booth, Sir Henry William; *see* Booth.
Gore-Booth, Sir Josslyn Augustus Richard; *see* Booth.
Gore-Booth, Sir Michael Savile, 7th Bt, 1908–1987, vol. VIII
Gore-Browne, Col Sir Eric, 1885–1964, vol. VI

Gore-Browne, Sir Francis, 1860–1922, vol. II
Gore-Browne, Comdr Godfrey, 1863–1900, vol. I
Gore-Browne, Henry George, 1830–1912, vol. I
Gore-Browne, Lt-Col Sir Stewart, 1883–1967, vol. VI
Gore-Browne, Sir Thomas Anthony, 1918–1988, vol. VIII
Gore-Browne, Rt Rev. Wilfred, died 1928, vol. II
Gore-Langton, Hon. Chandos Graham T.; see Temple-Gore-Langton.
Gore-Langton, Comdr Hon. Evelyn Arthur Grenville T.; see Temple-Gore-Langton.
Gore-Langton, Major Gerald Wentworth, died 1937, vol. III
Gore-Langton, Hon. Henry Powell, 1854–1913, vol. I
Gorell, 1st Baron, 1848–1913, vol. I
Gorell, 2nd Baron, 1882–1917, vol. II
Gorell, 3rd Baron, 1884–1963, vol. VI
Gorell Barnes, Sir William Lethbridge, 1909–1987, vol. VIII
Gorer, Peter Alfred, 1907–1961, vol. VI
Gorgas, William Crawford, 1854–1920, vol. II
Gorges, Sir (Edmond) Howard (Lacam), 1872–1924, vol. II
Gorges, Brig.-Gen. Edmund Howard, 1868–1949, vol. IV
Gorges, Sir Howard; see Gorges, Sir E. H. L.
Gorham, Maurice Anthony Coneys, 1902–1975, vol. VII
Goring, Sir Craven Charles, 10th Bt, 1841–1897, vol. I
Goring, Captain Sir Forster Gurney, 12th Bt, 1876–1956, vol. V
Goring, Sir Harry Yelverton, 11th Bt, 1840–1911, vol. I
Göring, Field-Marshal Hermann Wilhelm, 1893–1946, vol. IV
Goring, Marius, 1912–1998, vol. X
Goring-Jones, Lt-Col Michael Durwas; see Jones.
Goring-Morris, Rex, 1926–1988, vol. VIII
Gorky, Maxim, (Alexei Maximovitch Pieshkov), 1868–1936, vol. III
Gorle, Major Harry Vaughan, 1868–1937, vol. III
Gorley Putt, Samuel; see Putt.
Gorman, Albert, 1883–1959, vol. V
Gorman, Arthur Pue, 1839–1906, vol. I
Gorman, Sir Eugene, 1891–1973, vol. VII
Gorman, John Peter, 1927–1996, vol. X
Gorman, Sir William, died 1964, vol. VI
Gorman, Ven. William Charles, 1826–1916, vol. II
Gormanston, 14th Viscount, 1837–1907, vol. I
Gormanston, 15th Viscount, 1879–1925, vol. II
Gormanston, 16th Viscount, 1914–1940, vol. III (A), vol. IV
Gormley, Baron (Life Peer); Joseph Gormley, 1917–1993, vol. IX
Goronwy-Roberts, Baron (Life Peer); Goronwy Owen Goronwy-Roberts, 1913–1981, vol. VIII
Gorringe, Lt-Gen. Sir George F., 1868–1945, vol. IV
Gorringe, Rev. Reginald Ernest Pennington, 1871–1959, vol. V
Gorst, Sir Eldon, 1861–1911, vol. I
Gorst, Elliot Marcet, 1885–1973, vol. VII

Gorst, Rev. Ernest Freeland, 1871–1942, vol. IV
Gorst, Mrs Harold, (Nina Cecilia Francesca), 1869–1926, vol. II
Gorst, Harold E., 1868–1950, vol. IV
Gorst, Rt Hon. Sir John Eldon, 1835–1916, vol. II
Gorst, Nina Cecilia Francesca; see Gorst, Mrs Harold.
Gort, 4th Viscount, 1819–1900, vol. I
Gort, 5th Viscount, 1849–1902, vol. I
Gort, 6th Viscount, 1886–1946, vol. IV
Gort, 7th Viscount, 1888–1975, vol. VII
Gort, 8th Viscount, 1916–1995, vol. IX
Gorton, Rt Rev. Neville Vincent, 1888–1955, vol. V
Gorton, Brig.-Gen. Reginald St George, 1866–1944, vol. IV
Gorvin, John Henry, 1886–1960, vol. V
Gos, Charles, 1885–1949, vol. IV
Goschen, 1st Viscount, 1831–1907, vol. I
Goschen, 2nd Viscount, 1866–1952, vol. V
Goschen, 3rd Viscount, 1906–1977, vol. VII
Goschen, Maj.-Gen. Arthur Alec, 1880–1975, vol. VII
Goschen, Charles Hermann, 1839–1915, vol. I
Goschen, Sir Edward Henry, 2nd Bt, 1876–1933, vol. III
Goschen, Hon. George Joachim, 1893–1916, vol. II
Goschen, Sir Harry, (William Henry Neville), 1865–1945, vol. IV
Goschen, Kenneth, 1882–1939, vol. III
Goschen, Rt Hon. Sir William Edward, 1st Bt, 1847–1924, vol. II
Goschen, Hon. Sir William Henry, 1870–1943, vol. IV
Goschen, Sir William Henry Neville; see Goschen, Sir Harry.
Gosford, 4th Earl of, 1841–1922, vol. II
Gosford, 5th Earl of, 1877–1954, vol. V
Gosford, 6th Earl of, 1911–1966, vol. VI
Gosling, Sir Arthur Hulin, 1901–1982, vol. VIII
Gosling, Sir Audley Charles, 1836–1913, vol. I
Gosling, Cecil, 1870–1944, vol. IV
Gosling, Col Charles, 1868–1917, vol. II
Gosling, Frederick; see Hamlyn, F.
Gosling, Col George, 1842–1915, vol. I
Gosling, Major George Edward, 1889–1938, vol. III
Gosling, Harry, 1861–1930, vol. III
Gosling, Herbert, 1841–1929, vol. III
Gosling, John Thomas, 1868–1933, vol. III
Gosling, Reginald George, 1899–1958, vol. V
Gosling, Richard Henry, 1853–1930, vol. III
Gosling, Major William Richard, 1891–1968, vol. VI
Gosnay, Maxwell, 1923–1986, vol. VIII
Goss, Alan; see Goss, W. A. B.
Goss, John, 1894–1953, vol. V
Goss, Leonard Cecil, 1925–1984, vol. VIII
Goss, Brig. Leonard George, 1895–1988, vol. VIII
Goss, Very Rev. Thomas Ashworth, 1912–1997, vol. X
Goss, (William) Alan (Belcher), 1908–1963, vol. VI
Goss-Custard, Reginald, 1877–1956, vol. V
Gossage, Alfred Milne, died 1948, vol. IV
Gossage, Air Marshal Sir Leslie, 1891–1949, vol. IV
Gosse, Alfred Hope, 1882–1956, vol. V
Gosse, Sir Edmund, 1849–1928, vol. II

Gosse, Sir James Hay, 1876–1952, vol. V
Gosse, Laura Sylvia, 1881–1968, vol. VI
Gosse, Philip, 1879–1959, vol. V
Gosselin, Rt Rev. Mgr Amédée, 1863–1941, vol. IV
Gosselin, L. L. T.; see Lenotre, G.
Gosselin, Sir Martin le Marchant Hadsley, 1847–1905, vol. I
Gosselin, Major Sir Nicholas, 1839–1917, vol. II
Gosselin-Grimshawe, Hellier Robert Hadsley, 1849–1924, vol. II
Gosset, Lt-Col Allen Butler, 1868–1948, vol. IV
Gosset, Ven. Charles Hilgrove, died 1923, vol. II
Gosset, Francis Russell, 1849–1930, vol. III
Gosset, Col Francis William, 1876–1931, vol. III
Gosset, Maj.-Gen. Sir Matthew William Edward, 1839–1909, vol. I
Gossip, Alex, 1862–1952, vol. V
Gossip, Rev. Arthur John, 1873–1954, vol. V
Gossling, Archibald George, 1878–1950, vol. IV
Gostling, Col Ernest Victor, 1872–1922, vol. II
Gostling, Maj.-Gen. Philip Le Marchant Stonhouse S.; see Stonhouse-Gostling.
Gotch, Francis, 1853–1913, vol. I
Gotch, John Alfred, 1852–1942, vol. IV
Gotch, Thomas Cooper, 1854–1931, vol. III
Gothard, Sir Clifford Frederic, 1893–1979, vol. VII
Gotley, George Rainald H.; see Henniker-Gotley.
Gotley, Roger Alwyn H.; see Henniker-Gotley.
Gott, Sir Benjamin S., died 1933, vol. III
Gott, Sir Charles Henry, 1866–1965, vol. VI
Gott, Rt Rev. John, 1830–1906, vol. I
Gott, Lt-Gen. William Henry Ewart, 1897–1942, vol. IV
Gottmann, Jean, 1915–1994, vol. IX
Gotto, Basil, 1866–1954, vol. V
Gotto, Brig. Christopher Hugh, 1888–1959, vol. V
Götz, Sir Frank Léon Aroha, 1892–1970, vol. VI (AII)
Goudeket, Mme Maurice; see Colette.
Goudge, Elizabeth de Beauchamp, 1900–1984, vol. VIII
Goudge, Rev. Henry Leighton, 1866–1939, vol. III
Goudge, James Alfred, 1862–1955, vol. V
Goudie, Hon. Sir George Louis, 1866–1949, vol. IV
Goudie, Hon. William Henry, 1916–2000, vol. X
Goudie, William John, 1868–1945, vol. IV
Goudy, Henry, 1848–1921, vol. II
Gouge, Sir Arthur, 1890–1962, vol. VI
Gough, 3rd Viscount, 1849–1919, vol. II
Gough, 4th Viscount, 1892–1951, vol. V
Gough, Col Alan Percy George, 1863–1930, vol. III
Gough, Rev. Preb. Alfred William, 1862–1931, vol. III
Gough, Sir (Arthur) Ernest, 1878–1974, vol. VII
Gough, Cecil Ernest Freeman, 1911–1998, vol. X
Gough, Col (Charles) Frederick (Howard), 1901–1977, vol. VII
Gough, Sir Charles John Stanley, 1832–1912, vol. I
Gough, Rev. Edwin Spencer, 1845–1927, vol. II
Gough, Sir Ernest; see Gough, Sir A. E.
Gough, Frederic Harrison, born 1863, vol. II
Gough, Col Frederick; see Gough, Col C. F. H.
Gough, Adm. Frederick William, 1824–1908, vol. I
Gough, Brig. Guy Francis, 1893–1988, vol. VIII
Gough, Harold Robert, 1889–1975, vol. VII

Gough, Lt-Col Henry Worsley Worsley-, 1874–1957, vol. V
Gough, Herbert John, 1890–1965, vol. VI
Gough, Gen. Sir Hubert de la Poer, 1870–1963, vol. VI
Gough, Lt-Col Hugh Augustus Keppel, 1871–1950, vol. IV
Gough, Gen. Sir Hugh Henry, 1833–1909, vol. I
Gough, Rt Rev. Hugh Rowlands, 1905–1997, vol. X
Gough, Maj.-Gen. Hugh Sutlej, 1848–1920, vol. II
Gough, Jethro, 1903–1979, vol. VII (AII)
Gough, John, 1910–1992, vol. IX
Gough, Brig.-Gen. John Edmond, 1871–1915, vol. I
Gough, William, 1876–1947, vol. IV
Gough-Calthorpe, Hon. Frederick Somerset; see Calthorpe.
Gough-Calthorpe, Admiral of the Fleet Hon. Sir Somerset Arthur; see Calthorpe.
Gouin, Hon. Sir Lomer, 1861–1929, vol. III
Goulburn, Brig.-Gen. Cuthbert Edward, 1860–1944, vol. IV
Goulburn, Maj.-Gen. Edward Henry, 1903–1980, vol. VII
Goulburn, Very Rev. Edward Meyrick, 1818–1897, vol. I
Gould, Hon. Sir Albert John, 1847–1936, vol. III
Gould, Alec Carruthers, 1870–1948, vol. IV
Gould, Sir Alfred Pearce, 1852–1922, vol. II
Gould, Barbara Ayrton, died 1950, vol. IV
Gould, Sir Basil John, 1883–1956, vol. V
Gould, Cecil Hilton Monk, 1918–1994, vol. IX
Gould, Charles, died 1909, vol. I
Gould, Edward, 1837–1922, vol. II
Gould, Edward Blencowe, 1847–1916, vol. II
Gould, Edwin, 1866–1933, vol. III
Gould, Eric Lush Pearce, 1886–1940, vol. III
Gould, Sir Francis Carruthers, 1844–1925, vol. II
Gould, Frederick, 1879–1971, vol. VII
Gould, Frederick James, 1855–1938, vol. III
Gould, George Jay, 1864–1923, vol. II
Gould, Rev. George Pearce, 1848–1921, vol. II
Gould, Gerald, 1885–1936, vol. III
Gould, Ven. Henry George, 1851–1914, vol. I
Gould, Herbert Ross, 1887–1954, vol. V
Gould, Howard Gould, 1871–1959, vol. V
Gould, James Childs, 1882–1944, vol. IV
Gould, James Nutcombe, died 1899, vol. I
Gould, Maj.-Gen. John Charles, 1915–1993, vol. IX
Gould, Nathaniel, 1857–1919, vol. II
Gould, Col Philip, 1870–1942, vol. IV
Gould, R(alph) Blair, 1904–1984, vol. VIII
Gould, Rev. Reginald Freestone, 1860–1939, vol. III
Gould, Sir Robert Macdonald, died 1971, vol. VII
Gould, Sir Ronald, 1904–1986, vol. VIII
Gould, Lt-Comdr Rupert Thomas, 1890–1948, vol. IV
Gould, Sabine B.; see Baring-Gould.
Gould, Sir Trevor Jack, 1906–1984, vol. VIII
Goulden, Charles Bernard, 1879–1953, vol. V
Goulden, Gontran Iceton, 1912–1986, vol. VIII
Goulden, Mark, died 1980, vol. VII
Goulden, Richard Reginald, died 1932, vol. III
Goulder, George Frederick, 1863–1942, vol. IV
Goulding, Sir Basil; see Goulding, Sir W. B.

Goulding, Sir (Ernest) Irvine, 1910–2000, vol. X
Goulding, Henry Raynor, 1859–1934, vol. III
Goulding, Sir Irvine; *see* Goulding, Sir E. I.
Goulding, Captain Sir Lingard; *see* Goulding, Captain Sir W. L. A.
Goulding, Lt-Col Terence Leslie Crawford P.; *see* Pierce-Goulding.
Goulding, Sir (William) Basil, 3rd Bt, 1909–1982, vol. VIII
Goulding, Rt Hon. Sir William Joshua, 1st Bt, 1856–1925, vol. II
Goulding, Captain Sir (William) Lingard Amphlett, 2nd Bt, 1883–1935, vol. III
Gouldsmith, Edmund, 1852–1932, vol. III
Gouldsmith, Rev. Herbert, *died* 1940, vol. III
Goument, Charles Ernest Vear, 1857–1941, vol. IV
Gour, Sir Hari Singh, 1866–1949, vol. IV
Gouraud, Gen. Henri, 1867–1946, vol. IV
Gourielli, Princess; *see* Rubinstein, Helena.
Gourlay, Charles, *died* 1926, vol. II
Gourlay, Harry Philp Heggie, 1916–1987, vol. VIII
Gourlay, Brig. Kenneth Ian, 1891–1970, vol. VI
Gourlay, William Robert, 1874–1938, vol. III
Gourley, Sir Edward Temperley, 1828–1902, vol. I
Govan, Raymond Eustace Grant, 1891–1940, vol. III
Gover, Brig. Charles Rhodes, 1881–1942, vol. IV
Gover, John Mahan, *died* 1947, vol. IV
Govett, Ven. Decimus Storry, 1827–1912, vol. I
Govett, Ven. Henry, 1819–1903, vol. I
Govett, John Romaine, 1897–1956, vol. V
Govindan Nair, Diwan Bahadur Chettur, 1881–1945, vol. IV (A), vol. V
Gow, Alexander, 1869–1955, vol. V
Gow, Alexander Edward, 1884–1952, vol. V
Gow, Andrew Carrick, 1848–1920, vol. II
Gow, Andrew Sydenham Farrar, 1886–1978, vol. VII
Gow, Charles, 1846–1929, vol. III
Gow, Rev. Henry, 1861–1938, vol. III
Gow, Ian Reginald Edward, 1937–1990, vol. VIII
Gow, Rev. James, 1854–1923, vol. II
Gow, Brig. John Wesley Harper, 1898–1986, vol. VIII
Gow, Leonard, 1859–1936, vol. III
Gow, Sir Leonard Maxwell H.; *see* Harper Gow.
Gow, Lt-Col Peter Fleming, 1885–1949, vol. IV
Gow, William, 1853–1919, vol. II
Gow, Very Rev. William Connell, 1909–1996, vol. X
Gow, William John, 1863–1933, vol. III
Gowan, Miss E. M., *died* 1934, vol. III
Gowan, Sir Hyde Clarendon, 1878–1938, vol. III
Gowan, Hon. Sir James Robert, 1815–1909, vol. I
Gowans, Surg. Rear-Adm. Francis Jollie, 1880–1952, vol. V
Gowans, Sir Gregory; *see* Gowans, Sir U. G.
Gowans, Hon. Lt-Col James, 1872–1936, vol. III (A), vol. IV
Gowans, Hon. Sir (Urban) Gregory, 1904–1994, vol. IX
Gowen, Rev. Herbert H., *died* 1960, vol. V (A), vol. VI (AI)
Gower, Major Lord Alistair St Clair Sutherland L.; *see* Leveson Gower.

Gower, Arthur Francis Gresham L.; *see* Leveson Gower.
Gower, Col Charles Cameron L.; *see* Leveson-Gower.
Gower, Frederick Neville Sutherland L.; *see* Leveson-Gower.
Gower, Sir George Granville L.; *see* Leveson Gower.
Gower, Most Rev. Godfrey Philip, 1899–1992, vol. IX
Gower, Granville Charles Gresham L.; *see* Leveson Gower.
Gower, Sir Henry Dudley Gresham L.; *see* Leveson Gower.
Gower, Sir (Herbert) Raymond, 1916–1989, vol. VIII
Gower, Ivon Llewellyn Owen, 1874–1955, vol. V
Gower, Jim; *see* Gower, L. C. B.
Gower, Laurence Cecil Bartlett, (Jim), 1913–1997, vol. X
Gower, Sir Patrick; *see* Gower, Sir R. P. M.
Gower, Col Philip L.; *see* Leveson Gower.
Gower, Sir Raymond; *see* Gower, Sir H. R.
Gower, Sir (Robert) Patrick (Malcolm), 1887–1964, vol. VI
Gower, Sir Robert Vaughan, 1880–1953, vol. V
Gower, Lord Ronald Sutherland-, 1845–1916, vol. II
Gower-Jones, Ven. Geoffrey, 1910–1982, vol. VIII
Gowers, Sir Ernest Arthur, 1880–1966, vol. VI
Gowers, Sir William Frederick, 1875–1954, vol. V
Gowers, Sir William Richard, 1845–1915, vol. I
Gowing, Ven. Ellis Norman, 1883–1960, vol. V
Gowing, Rt Rev. Eric Austin, 1913–1981, vol. VIII
Gowing, Sir Lawrence Burnett, 1918–1991, vol. IX
Gowing, Lionel Francis, 1859–1925, vol. II
Gowing, Margaret Mary, 1921–1998, vol. X
Gowing, Richard, 1831–1899, vol. I
Gowland, William, 1842–1922, vol. II
Gowland, Rev. William, 1911–1991, vol. IX
Gowlland, Lt-Col Edward Lake, 1876–1942, vol. IV
Gowlland, (George) Mark, 1943–1994, vol. IX
Gowlland, Mark; *see* Gowlland, G. M.
Gowrie, 1st Earl of, 1872–1955, vol. V
Goyder, George Armin, 1908–1997, vol. X
Graaff, Sir David Pieter de Villiers, 1st Bt, 1859–1931, vol. III
Graaff, Sir de Villiers, 2nd Bt, 1913–1999, vol. X
Graaff, Sir Jacobus Arnoldus Combrinck, *died* 1927, vol. II
Grabham, George Walter, 1882–1955, vol. V
Grabham, Michael Comport, 1840–1935, vol. III
Grace, David Mabe, 1945–1988, vol. VIII
Grace, Sir Gilbert; *see* Grace, Sir O. G.
Grace, Rev. Canon Harold Myers, 1888–1967, vol. VI
Grace, Harvey, 1874–1944, vol. IV
Grace, Adm. Henry Edgar, 1876–1937, vol. III
Grace, James E., 1850–1908, vol. I
Grace, John, 1886–1972, vol. VII
Grace, Sir John Te Herekiekie, 1905–1985, vol. VIII
Grace, Leo Bernard Aloysius, 1903–1969, vol. VI
Grace, Michael Anthony, 1920–1988, vol. VIII
Grace, Hon. Morgan Stanislaus, *died* 1903, vol. I

Grace, Sir (Oliver) Gilbert, 1896–1968, vol. VI
Grace, Sir Percy Raymond, 4th Bt, 1831–1903, vol. I
Grace, Sir Raymond Eustace, 6th Bt, 1903–1977, vol. VII
Grace, Col Sheffield Hamilton-, 1834–1915, vol. I
Grace, Ven. Thomas Samuel, 1850–1918, vol. II
Grace, Sir Valentine Raymond, 5th Bt, 1877–1945, vol. IV
Grace, Rear-Adm. Walter Keir Campbell, 1890–1964, vol. VI
Grace, Wilfrid Arnold, 1895–1964, vol. VI
Grace, William Gilbert, 1848–1915, vol. I
Gracey, Gen. Sir Douglas David, 1894–1964, vol. VI
Gracey, Captain George Frederick Handel, 1878–1958, vol. V
Gracey, Hugh Kirkwood, 1868–1929, vol. III
Gracey, Col Thomas, 1843–1921, vol. II
Gracias, HE Cardinal Valerian, 1900–1978, vol. VII
Gracie, Alan James, 1904–1973, vol. VII
Gracie, Sir Alexander, 1860–1930, vol. III
Gracie, George Handel H.; see Heath-Gracie.
Gracie, Captain Henry Stewart, 1901–1979, vol. VII
Grade, Baron (Life Peer); Lew Grade, 1906–1998, vol. X
Gradwell, Leo Joseph Anthony, 1899–1969, vol. VI
Gradwell, Robert Bernard George Ashhurst, 1858–1935, vol. III
Grady, John William, 1915–1982, vol. VIII
Graeme, Bruce, (Graham Montague Jeffries), 1900–1982, vol. VIII
Graeme, Sir Egerton Hood Murray H.; see Hamond-Graeme.
Graeme, Sir Graham Eden William H.; see Hamond-Graeme.
Graeme, Maj.-Gen. Ian Rollo, 1913–1993, vol. IX
Græme, Patrick Neale Sutherland, 1877–1958, vol. V
Græme-Sutherland, Alexander Malcolm, 1845–1908, vol. I
Graesser, Col Sir Alastair Stewart Durward, 1915–1993, vol. IX
Graff, Stephen John, 1842–1940, vol. III
Grafftey-Smith, Sir Anthony Paul, 1903–1960, vol. V
Grafftey-Smith, Sir Laurence Barton, 1892–1989, vol. VIII
Grafton, 7th Duke of, 1821–1918, vol. II
Grafton, 8th Duke of, 1850–1930, vol. III
Grafton, 9th Duke of, 1914–1936, vol. III
Grafton, 10th Duke of, 1892–1970, vol. VI
Grafton, Col Martin John, 1919–1991, vol. IX
Graham, Captain Alan Crosland, 1896–1964, vol. VI
Graham, Alastair, 1906–2000, vol. X
Graham, Captain Lord Alastair Mungo, 1886–1976, vol. VII
Graham, Alexander, 1861–1941, vol. IV
Graham, Allan James, died 1941, vol. IV
Graham, Andrew Guillemard, 1913–1981, vol. VIII
Graham, Angus, 1892–1979, vol. VII
Graham, Angus Charles, 1919–1991, vol. IX
Graham, Adm. Sir Angus Edward Malise Bontine C.; see Cunninghame Graham.

Graham, Anthony George M.; see Maxtone-Graham.
Graham, Sir Aubrey Gregor, 1867–1947, vol. IV
Graham, Sir Charles Spencer Richard, 6th Bt, 1919–1997, vol. X
Graham, Sir Cecil William Noble, 1872–1945, vol. IV
Graham, Comdr Charles Elphinstone Fleeming C.; see Cunninghame Graham.
Graham, Rt Rev. Charles Morice, 1834–1912, vol. I
Graham, Lt-Col Charles Percy, 1881–1961, vol. VI
Graham, Flt-Lt Charles Walter, 1893–1916, vol. II
Graham, Sir Clarence Johnston, 1st Bt (cr 1964), 1900–1966, vol. VI
Graham, Sir Claverhouse Frederick Charles, died 1924, vol. II
Graham, Clifford, 1937–1994, vol. IX
Graham, Constantine, 1882–1934, vol. III
Graham, Rear-Adm. Cosmo Moray, died 1946, vol. IV
Graham, Sir Crosland; see Graham, Sir J. C.
Graham, Brig.-Gen. Cuthbert Aubrey Lionel, 1882–1957, vol. V
Graham, David Alec, 1930–1991, vol. IX
Graham, Lt-Col David James, 1871–1929, vol. III
Graham, Donald, 1844–1901, vol. I
Graham, Maj.-Gen. Douglas Alexander Henry, 1893–1971, vol. VII
Graham, Rev. Douglas Leslie, 1909–1991, vol. IX
Graham, Brig. Lord (Douglas) Malise, 1883–1974, vol. VII
Graham, Douglas William, 1866–1936, vol. III
Graham, Duncan MacGregor, 1867–1942, vol. IV
Graham, Edward John, died 1918, vol. II
Graham, Maj.-Gen. Sir Edward Ritchie Coryton, 1858–1951, vol. V
Graham, Ennis; see Molesworth, Mary Louisa.
Graham, Rt Rev. Eric, 1888–1964, vol. VI
Graham, Sir Fergus; see Graham, Sir Frederick F.
Graham, Captain Francis, 1894–1918, vol. II
Graham, Sir Frederick, 1848–1923, vol. II
Graham, Maj.-Gen. Frederick Clarence Campbell, 1908–1988, vol. VIII
Graham, Sir (Frederick) Fergus, 5th Bt (cr 1783), 1893–1978, vol. VII
Graham, George, born 1838, vol. II
Graham, George, 1881–1949, vol. IV
Graham, George, 1882–1971, vol. VII
Graham, George Boughen, 1920–1994, vol. IX
Graham, Very Rev. George Frederick, 1877–1962, vol. VI
Graham, Sir George Goldie, 1892–1974, vol. VII
Graham, Rt Hon. George Perry, 1859–1943, vol. IV
Graham, Rev. George R., 1850–1927, vol. II
Graham, Sir Gerald, 1831–1899, vol. I
Graham, Gerald Sandford, 1903–1988, vol. VIII
Graham, Gilbert Maxwell Adair, 1883–1960, vol. V
Graham, (Godfrey) Michael, 1898–1972, vol. VII
Graham, Gordon, 1920–1997, vol. X
Graham, Major Sir Guy; see Graham, Major Sir R. G.
Graham, H. E.; see Hamilton, Col E. G.
Graham, Hamilton Maurice H.; see Howgrave-Graham.

Graham, Lt-Gen. Hamilton Maximillian Christian Williams, 1866–1934, vol. III
Graham, Harold, 1889–1963, vol. VI
Graham, Captain Harry J. C., 1874–1936, vol. III
Graham, Harry Robert, 1850–1933, vol. III
Graham, Captain Harry S. C., 1874–1936, vol. III
Graham, Lady Helen Violet, 1879–1945, vol. IV
Graham, Major Henry Archibald Roger, 1892–1970, vol. VI
Graham, Rev. Henry Burrans, 1909–1963, vol. VI
Graham, Rev. Henry Grey, 1843–1906, vol. I
Graham, Rt Rev. Henry Grey, 1874–1959, vol. V
Graham, Sir Henry John Lowndes, 1842–1930, vol. III
Graham, Air Vice-Marshal Henry Rudolph, 1910–1987, vol. VIII
Graham, Col Herman Witsius-Gore, 1859–1932, vol. III
Graham, Lt-Col Howard Boyd, 1891–1965, vol. VI (AII)
Graham, Lt-Gen. Howard Douglas, 1898–1986, vol. VIII
Graham, Hugh, died 1975, vol. VII
Graham, Sir James, 1856–1913, vol. I
Graham, Gen. Sir James; see Graham, Gen. Sir S. J.
Graham, James, 1870–1961, vol. VI
Graham, Maj.-Gen. Sir James Drummond, 1875–1958, vol. V
Graham, James Edward, died 1929, vol. III
Graham, James M.; see Maxtone Graham.
Graham, John, 1844–1918, vol. II
Graham, John, 1879–1958, vol. V
Graham, Rev. John; see Graham, Rev. Jonathan J. D.
Graham, Very Rev. John Anderson, 1861–1942, vol. IV
Graham, John Cameron, died 1929, vol. III
Graham, Sir John Frederick Noble, 2nd Bt (cr 1906), 1864–1936, vol. III
Graham, John Fuller, 1872–1946, vol. IV
Graham, Sir John Gibson, 1896–1964, vol. VI
Graham, Maj.-Gen. John Gordon, 1833–1911, vol. I
Graham, Sir John Hatt Noble, 1st Bt (cr 1906), 1837–1926, vol. II
Graham, Captain John Irvine, 1862–1947, vol. IV
Graham, Sir John James, 1847–1928, vol. II
Graham, John Macdonald, 1908–1982, vol. VIII
Graham, Ven. John Malcolm Alexander, died 1931, vol. III
Graham, Sir (John) Patrick, 1906–1993, vol. IX
Graham, Sir (John) Reginald (Noble), 3rd Bt (cr 1906), 1892–1980, vol. VII
Graham, John William, 1859–1932, vol. III
Graham, Rev. (Jonathan) John Drummond, died 1965, vol. VI
Graham, Joseph, 1828–1902, vol. I
Graham, Sir (Joseph) Crosland, 1866–1946, vol. IV
Graham, Kathleen Mary, 1903–2000, vol. X
Graham, Col Lancelot, 1864–1932, vol. III
Graham, Sir Lancelot, 1880–1958, vol. V
Graham, Brig. Lancelot Cecil Torbock, 1890–1962, vol. VI
Graham, Col Malcolm David, 1865–1941, vol. IV
Graham, Brig. Lord Malise; see Graham, Brig. Lord D. M.

Graham, Col Malise, 1884–1929, vol. III
Graham, Martha, 1894–1991, vol. IX
Graham, Michael; see Graham, G. M.
Graham, Michael, 1847–1925, vol. II
Graham, Maj.-Gen. Sir Miles William Arthur Peel, 1895–1976, vol. VII
Graham, Sir Montrose Stuart, 11th Bt (cr 1629), 1875–1939, vol. III
Graham, Sir Montrose Stuart, 12th Bt (cr 1629), 1904–1975, vol. VII
Graham, Norval Bantock, 1870–1944, vol. IV
Graham, P. Anderson, died 1925, vol. II
Graham, Sir Patrick; see Graham, Sir J. P.
Graham, Peter, 1836–1921, vol. II
Graham, Sir Ralph Wolfe, 13th Bt, 1908–1988, vol. VIII
Graham, Sir Reginald; see Graham, Sir J. R. N.
Graham, Major Sir (Reginald) Guy, 9th Bt (cr 1662), 1878–1940, vol. III
Graham, Sir Reginald Henry, 8th Bt (cr 1662), 1835–1920, vol. II
Graham, Sir Richard Bellingham, 10th Bt, 1912–1982, vol. VIII
Graham, Richard Brockbank, 1893–1957, vol. V
Graham, Sir Richard James, 4th Bt (cr 1783), 1859–1932, vol. III
Graham, Sir Robert, 1846–1929, vol. III
Graham, Sir Robert, 1876–1947, vol. IV
Graham, Robert Arthur, 1870–1940, vol. III
Graham, Col Robert Blackall, 1874–1944, vol. IV
Graham, Robert Bontine C.; see Cunninghame Graham.
Graham, Robert Henry, 1870–1956, vol. V
Graham, Robert James Douglas, died 1950, vol. IV (A)
Graham, Sir Robert James Stuart, 10th Bt (cr 1629), 1845–1917, vol. II
Graham, Col Robert M.; see Mould-Graham.
Graham, Air Vice-Marshal Ronald, 1896–1967, vol. VI
Graham, Rt Hon. Sir Ronald William, 1870–1949, vol. IV
Graham, Rose, 1875–1963, vol. VI
Graham, Gen. Sir (S.) James, 1837–1917, vol. II
Graham, Stanley Galbraith, 1895–1975, vol. VII
Graham, Stephen, 1884–1975, vol. VII
Graham, Sydney, 1879–1966, vol. VI
Graham, Maj.-Gen. Sir Thomas, 1842–1925, vol. II
Graham, Thomas Alexander Ferguson, 1840–1906, vol. I
Graham, Hon. Sir Thomas Lynedoch, 1860–1940, vol. III
Graham, Thomas Ottiwell, 1883–1966, vol. VI
Graham, Tom; see Graham, T. A. F.
Graham, Sir Wallace, 1848–1917, vol. II
Graham, Walter Armstrong, 1868–1949, vol. IV
Graham, Walter Gerald Cloete, 1906–1995, vol. IX
Graham, Adm. Walter Hodgson Bevan, 1849–1931, vol. III
Graham, Sir William, 1825–1907, vol. I
Graham, William, died 1911, vol. I
Graham, Sir William, 1861–1932, vol. III
Graham, Rt Hon. William, 1887–1932, vol. III
Graham, William, 1862–1943, vol. IV
Graham, William, 1896–1955, vol. V

Graham, William, 1894–1981, vol. VIII
Graham, Col William James, 1890–1971, vol. VII
Graham, William Murray, 1884–1956, vol. V
Graham, William Perceval Gore, 1861–1918, vol. II
Graham, Winifred, (Mrs Theodore Cory), *died* 1950, vol. IV
Graham Brown, Rt Rev. George Francis, 1891–1942, vol. IV
Graham Brown, Thomas, *died* 1965, vol. VI
Graham-Bryce, Dame Isabel, 1902–1997, vol. X
Graham-Campbell, Rt Rev. Archibald Rollo, 1903–1978, vol. VII
Graham-Campbell, David John, 1912–1994, vol. IX
Graham-Campbell, Sir Rollo Frederick, 1868–1946, vol. IV
Graham-Clarke, Captain Lionel Altham, 1867–1914, vol. I
Graham-Dixon, Charles; *see* Graham-Dixon, L. C.
Graham-Dixon, Leslie Charles, 1901–1986, vol. VIII
Graham Dow, Ronald; *see* Dow.
Graham-Green, Major Graham John, 1906–1985, vol. VIII
Graham-Harrison, Sir William Montagu, 1871–1949, vol. IV
Graham-Hodgson, Sir Harold Kingston; *see* Hodgson.
Graham-Little, Sir Ernest Gordon; *see* Little.
Graham-Montgomery, Sir Basil Templer; *see* Montgomery.
Graham-Montgomery, Rev. Sir Charles Percy; *see* Montgomery.
Graham-Moon, Sir Wilfred; *see* Moon.
Graham-Smith, George Stuart, *died* 1950, vol. IV
Graham Smith, Stanley, 1896–1989, vol. VIII
Graham-Stewart, Alexander, 1879–1944, vol. IV
Graham-Vivian, Preston; *see* Graham-Vivian, R. P.
Graham-Vivian, (Richard) Preston, 1896–1979, vol. VII
Grahame, Rt Hon. Sir George Dixon, 1873–1940, vol. III
Grahame, Lt-Col John Crum, 1870–1952, vol. V
Grahame, Kenneth, 1859–1932, vol. III
Grahame, Thomas George, 1861–1922, vol. II
Grahame-Thomson, Leslie; *see* MacDougall, L. G.
Grahame-White, Claude, 1879–1959, vol. V
Grain, Sir Peter, 1864–1947, vol. IV
Grainer, Ron, 1932–1981, vol. VIII
Grainger, Francis Edward; *see* Hill, Headon.
Grainger, (George) Percy Aldridge, 1882–1961, vol. VI
Grainger, Surg.-Gen. Thomas, 1862–1931, vol. III
Grainger-Stewart, Brig. Thomas, 1896–1979, vol. VII
Gramigna, Rt Rev. Fr Petronius, 1844–1917, vol. II
Granard, 8th Earl of, 1874–1948, vol. IV
Granard, 9th Earl of, 1915–1992, vol. IX
Grand, Keith Walter Chamberlain, 1900–1983, vol. VIII
Grand, Maj.-Gen. Laurence Douglas, 1898–1975, vol. VII
Grand, Sarah, *died* 1943, vol. IV
Grand' Combe, Félix de; *see* Boillot, Félix.
Grande, Julian, 1874–1946, vol. IV
Grandi, Count (di Mordano), Dino, 1895–1988, vol. VIII

Grane, Rev. William Leighton, 1855–1952, vol. V
Graner, Most Rev. Lawrence L., 1901–1982, vol. VIII
Granet, Col Edward John, 1858–1918, vol. II
Granet, Sir Guy; *see* Granet, Sir W. G.
Granet, Sir (William) Guy, 1867–1943, vol. IV
Grange-Bennett, Rev. Canon Ronald du Pré, 1901–1972, vol. VII
Granger, Frank Stephen, 1864–1936, vol. III
Granger, Sir (Hugh) Rupert, 1890–1959, vol. V
Granger, Sir Rupert; *see* Granger, Sir H. R.
Granger, Stewart, (James Lablache Stewart), 1913–1993, vol. IX
Granger, Col Thomas Arthur, *died* 1942, vol. IV
Granger, Sir Thomas Colpitts, 1852–1927, vol. II
Granit, Ragnar Arthur, 1900–1991, vol. IX
Grannum, Sir Edward Allan, 1869–1956, vol. V
Grannum, Edward Thomas, 1843–1922, vol. II
Grannum, Reginald Clifton, 1872–1946, vol. IV
Gransden, Sir Robert, 1893–1972, vol. VII
Grant, Rt Hon. Lord; William Grant, 1909–1972, vol. VII
Grant, Sir (Albert) William, 1891–1965, vol. VI
Grant, Alec Alan, 1932–1991, vol. IX
Grant, Sir Alexander, 1st Bt (*cr* 1924), 1864–1937, vol. III
Grant, Alexander, 1866–1941, vol. IV
Grant, Captain Alexander, 1872–1961, vol. VI
Grant, Col Alexander Brown, 1840–1921, vol. II
Grant, Alexander Ludovic, 1901–1986, vol. VIII
Grant, Alexander Thomas Kingdom, 1906–1988, vol. VIII
Grant, Adm. Alfred Ernest Albert, 1861–1933, vol. III
Grant, Sir (Alfred) Hamilton, 12th Bt (*cr* 1688), 1872–1937, vol. III
Grant, Alistair; *see* Grant, D. A. A.
Grant, Sir Allan John, 1875–1955, vol. V
Grant, Allan Wallace, 1911–1997, vol. X
Grant, Air Marshal Sir Andrew, 1890–1967, vol. VI
Grant, Andrew Francis Joseph, 1911–1992, vol. IX
Grant, Col Sir Arthur, 10th Bt (*cr* 1705), 1879–1931, vol. III
Grant, Sir Arthur Henry, 9th Bt (*cr* 1705), 1849–1917, vol. II
Grant, Arthur James, 1862–1948, vol. IV
Grant, Major Sir Arthur Lindsay, 11th Bt (*cr* 1705), 1911–1944, vol. IV
Grant, Engr Rear-Adm. Arthur Robert, 1870–1952, vol. V
Grant, Rev. (Arthur) Rowland (Harry), 1882–1961, vol. V
Grant, Bernard Alexander Montgomery, 1944–2000, vol. X
Grant, Cary, 1904–1986, vol. VIII
Grant, Rev. Cecil, 1870–1946, vol. IV
Grant, Sir Charles, 1836–1903, vol. I
Grant, Rt Rev. Charles Alexander, 1906–1989, vol. VIII
Grant, Charles Frederick, 1878–1966, vol. VI
Grant, Charles Graham, *died* 1935, vol. III
Grant, Col Charles James William, *died* 1932, vol. III
Grant, Gen. Sir Charles John Cecil, 1877–1950, vol. IV

Grant, Colin King, 1924–1981, vol. VIII
Grant, Corrie, 1850–1924, vol. II
Grant, Rev. Cyril Fletcher, *died* 1916, vol. II
Grant, Derek Aldwin, 1915–2000, vol. X
Grant, Douglas; *see* Grant, W. D. B.
Grant, Lt-Gen. Douglas Gordon Seafield St John, 1829–1907, vol. I
Grant, Douglas Marr Kelso, 1917–1995, vol. IX
Grant, Comdr Duncan, 1882–1955, vol. V
Grant, Sir Duncan Alexander, 13th Bt (*cr* 1688), 1928–1961, vol. VI
Grant, (Duncan) Alistair (Antoine), 1925–1997, vol. X
Grant, Duncan James Corrowr, 1885–1978, vol. VII
Grant, Adm. Sir (Edmund) Percy (Fenwick George), 1867–1952, vol. V
Grant, Edward, 1915–1997, vol. X
Grant, Lt-Col Edward James, 1854–1928, vol. II
Grant, Brig. Eneas Henry George, 1901–1994, vol. IX
Grant, Sir Ewan George M.; *see* Macpherson-Grant.
Grant, Maj.-Gen. Ferris Nelson, 1916–1991, vol. IX
Grant, Sir Francis Cullen, 12th Bt (*cr* 1705), 1914–1966, vol. VI
Grant, Francis Henry Symons, 1883–1963, vol. VI
Grant, Sir Francis James, 1863–1953, vol. V
Grant, Frank, 1890–1986, vol. VIII
Grant, Frederick, 1890–1954, vol. V
Grant, George, 1924–1984, vol. IX (AI)
Grant, Captain George Bertram M.; *see* Macpherson-Grant.
Grant, Sir George M.; *see* Macpherson-Grant.
Grant, Very Rev. George Monro, 1835–1902, vol. I
Grant, Gordon, 1907–1979, vol. VII
Grant, Sir Hamilton; *see* Grant, Sir A. H.
Grant, Lt-Gen. Harold George, 1884–1950, vol. IV
Grant, Adm. Sir Heathcoat Salusbury, 1864–1938, vol. III
Grant, Henry Eugene Walter, 1855–1934, vol. III
Grant, Gen. Sir Henry Fane, 1848–1919, vol. II
Grant, Adm. Henry William, 1870–1949, vol. IV
Grant, Col Hugh Gough, 1845–1922, vol. II
Grant, Maj.-Gen. Ian Cameron, 1891–1955, vol. V
Grant, Ian Dingwall, 1891–1962, vol. VI
Grant, Isabel Frances, 1887–1983, vol. VIII
Grant, Sir James Alexander, 1831–1920, vol. II
Grant, Sir James Augustus, 1st Bt (*cr* 1926), 1867–1932, vol. III
Grant, James Currie, 1914–1988, vol. VIII
Grant, Sir James Dundas-, 1854–1944, vol. IV
Grant, Sir James Monteith, 1903–1981, vol. VIII
Grant, James Pineo, 1922–1995, vol. IX
Grant, James Shaw, 1910–1999, vol. X
Grant, James William Hamilton, 1876–1934, vol. III
Grant, Joan, (Mrs Denys Kelsey), 1907–1989, vol. VIII
Grant, Rear-Adm. John, 1908–1996, vol. X
Grant, John Douglas, 1932–2000, vol. X
Grant, Col John Duncan, 1877–1967, vol. VI
Grant, John Leslie, 1890–1975, vol. VII
Grant, Sir John M.; *see* Macpherson-Grant.
Grant, Captain John Moreau, 1895–1986, vol. VIII
Grant, John Peter, 1860–1927, vol. II
Grant, John Peter, 1885–1963, vol. VI

Grant, John Sharp, 1909–1974, vol. VII
Grant, Rt Rev. Kenneth, 1900–1959, vol. V
Grant, Sir (Kenneth) Lindsay, 1899–1989, vol. VIII
Grant, Sir Kerr, 1878–1967, vol. VI
Grant, Leonard Bishopp, 1882–1974, vol. VII
Grant, Sir Lindsay; *see* Grant, Sir K. L.
Grant, Adm. Sir Lowther; *see* Grant, Adm. Sir W. L.
Grant, Sir Ludovic James, 11th Bt (*cr* 1688), 1862–1936, vol. III
Grant, Hon. MacCallum, *died* 1928, vol. II
Grant, Col Maurice Harold, *died* 1962, vol. VI
Grant, Neil Forbes, 1882–1970, vol. VI
Grant, Rear-Adm. Noel, 1868–1920, vol. II
Grant, Adm. Sir Percy; *see* Grant, Adm. Sir E. P. F. G.
Grant, Peter Forbes, 1921–1974, vol. VII
Grant, Peter John, 1926–1999, vol. X
Grant, Maj.-Gen. Sir Philip Gordon, 1869–1943, vol. IV
Grant, Lt-Gen. Sir Robert, 1837–1904, vol. I
Grant, Robert, 1842–1910, vol. I
Grant, Robert, 1852–1940, vol. III (A), vol. IV
Grant, Major Robert Francis Sidney, 1877–1927, vol. II
Grant, Sir Robert McVitie, 2nd Bt (*cr* 1924), 1894–1947, vol. IV
Grant, Sir Robert William L.; *see* Lyall Grant.
Grant, Brig.-Gen. Ronald Chas., 1864–1951, vol. V
Grant, Ronald Thomson, 1892–1989, vol. VIII
Grant, Rev. Rowland; *see* Grant, Rev. A. R. H.
Grant, Col Samuel Charles Norton, 1854–1939, vol. III
Grant, Lt-Gen. Seafield Falkland Murray Treasure, 1834–1910, vol. I
Grant, Air Vice Marshal Stanley Bernard, 1919–1987, vol. VIII
Grant, Lady Sybil, *died* 1955, vol. V
Grant, William; *see* Grant, Rt Hon. Lord.
Grant, Sir William; *see* Grant, Sir A. W.
Grant, William, 1863–1919, vol. II
Grant, Brig.-Gen. William, 1870–1939, vol. III
Grant, William, 1863–1946, vol. IV
Grant, Rt Hon. William, *died* 1949, vol. IV
Grant, (William) Douglas (Beattie), 1921–1969, vol. VI
Grant, William Lawson, 1872–1935, vol. III
Grant, Adm. Sir (William) Lowther, 1864–1929, vol. III
Grant, William Robert O.; *see* Ogilvie-Grant.
Grant, Willis, 1907–1981, vol. VIII
Grant-Dalton, Captain Charles, 1884–1952, vol. V
Grant-Dalton, Lt-Col Duncan, 1881–1969, vol. VI
Grant-Dalton, Adm. Hubert, 1862–1934, vol. III
Grant-Duff, Major Adrian, 1869–1914, vol. I
Grant-Duff, Sir Arthur Cuninghame, 1861–1948, vol. IV
Grant-Duff, Edith Florence, (Lady Grant-Duff), *died* 1937, vol. III
Grant-Duff, Sir Evelyn, 1863–1926, vol. II
Grant-Ferris, family name of Baron Harvington.
Grant-Lawson, Col Sir Peter; *see* Lawson.
Grant-Sturgis, Sir Mark Beresford Russell, 1884–1949, vol. IV
Grant-Suttie, Sir George; *see* Suttie.

Grant-Suttie, Sir (George) Philip; *see* Suttie.
Grant-Suttie, Col Hubert Francis; *see* Suttie.
Grant-Suttie, Sir Philip; *see* Suttie.
Grant Watson, Herbert Adolphus, 1881–1971, vol. VII
Grant-Wilson, Sir Wemyss, 1870–1953, vol. V
Grantchester, 1st Baron, 1893–1976, vol. VII
Grantchester, 2nd Baron, 1921–1995, vol. IX
Grantham, Sir Alexander William George Herder, 1899–1978, vol. VII
Grantham, Adm. Sir Guy, 1900–1992, vol. IX
Grantham, Vincent Alpe, 1889–1968, vol. VI
Grantham, Mrs Violet Hardisty, 1893–1983, vol. VIII
Grantham, Sir William, 1835–1911, vol. I
Grantham, William Wilson, 1866–1942, vol. IV
Grantley, 5th Baron, 1855–1943, vol. IV
Grantley, 6th Baron, 1892–1954, vol. V
Grantley, 7th Baron, 1923–1995, vol. IX
Granville, 3rd Earl, 1872–1939, vol. III
Granville, 4th Earl, 1880–1953, vol. V
Granville, 5th Earl, 1918–1996, vol. X
Granville of Eye, Baron (Life Peer); Edgar Louis Granville, 1898–1998, vol. X
Granville, Countess; (Rose Constance), 1890–1967, vol. VI
Granville, Alexander, 1874–1929, vol. III
Granville, Col Bernard, *died* 1933, vol. III
Granville, Captain Dennis, 1863–1929, vol. III
Granville, Sir Keith, 1910–1990, vol. VIII
Granville, Rev. Roger, 1848–1911, vol. I
Granville-Barker, Harley Granville, 1877–1946, vol. IV
Granville-Barker, Helen, *died* 1950, vol. IV
Granville-Sharp, Gilbert; *see* Sharp.
Granville-Smith, Stuart Hayne, 1901–1977, vol. VII
Granville-West, Baron (Life Peer); Daniel Granville-West, 1904–1984, vol. VIII
Grappelli, Stéphane, 1908–1997, vol. X
Gras, Norman Scott Brien, 1884–1956, vol. V
Grasar, Rt Rev. William Eric, 1913–1982, vol. VIII
Grasett, Lt-Gen. Sir (Arthur) Edward, 1888–1971, vol. VII
Grasett, Lt-Gen. Sir Edward; *see* Grasett, Lt-Gen. Sir A. E.
Grasett, Col Henry James, 1847–1930, vol. III
Gratiaen, Edward Frederick Noel, 1904–1973, vol. VII
Grattan, Col Henry William, 1872–1952, vol. V
Grattan, John Henry Grafton, 1878–1951, vol. V
Grattan, Col O'Donnel Colley, 1855–1929, vol. III
Grattan-Bellew, Sir Arthur John, 1903–1985, vol. VIII
Grattan-Bellew, Lt-Col Sir Charles Christopher, 4th Bt, 1887–1948, vol. IV
Grattan-Bellew, Sir Henry Christopher, 3rd Bt, 1860–1942, vol. IV
Grattan-Cooper, Rear Adm. Sidney, 1911–1999, vol. X
Grattan-Doyle, Sir Nicholas, 1862–1941, vol. IV
Grattidge, Captain Harry, 1890–1979, vol. VII
Gratton, Norman Murray Gladstone, 1886–1965, vol. VI
Gratwick, John, 1918–1997, vol. X
Gratwicke, George Frederick, 1850–1912, vol. I

Grau, Maurice, 1849–1907, vol. I
Grauer, Albert Edward, 1906–1961, vol. VI
Graul, Isidore, 1894–1962, vol. VI
Graumann, Sir Harry, 1868–1938, vol. III
Grave, Walter Wyatt, 1901–1999, vol. X
Gravely, Sir Walter B.; *see* Booth-Gravely.
Graves, 4th Baron, 1847–1904, vol. I
Graves, 5th Baron, 1847–1914, vol. I
Graves, 6th Baron, 1871–1937, vol. III
Graves, 7th Baron, 1877–1963, vol. VI
Graves, 8th Baron, 1911–1994, vol. IX
Graves, Alfred Perceval, 1846–1931, vol. III
Graves, Arnold F., 1847–1930, vol. III
Graves, Col Benjamin Chamney, 1845–1905, vol. I
Graves, Captain Sir Cecil George, 1892–1957, vol. V
Graves, Rt Rev. Charles, 1812–1899, vol. I
Graves, Rev. Charles Edward, 1839–1920, vol. II
Graves, Charles L., 1856–1944, vol. IV
Graves, Charles Patrick Ranke, 1899–1971, vol. VII
Graves, Clotilde Inez Mary, 1863–1932, vol. III
Graves, Rt Rev. Frederick Rogers, 1858–1940, vol. III (A), vol. IV
Graves, George, 1876–1949, vol. IV
Graves, Sir Hubert Ashton, 1894–1972, vol. VII
Graves, John George, 1865–1945, vol. IV
Graves, Marjorie, *died* 1961, vol. VI
Graves, Rev. Michael, 1855–1931, vol. III
Graves, Philip Perceval, 1876–1953, vol. V
Graves, Richard Massie, 1880–1960, vol. V
Graves, Robert Ernest, 1866–1922, vol. II
Graves, Robert Ranke, 1895–1985, vol. VIII
Graves, Sir Robert Windham, 1858–1934, vol. III
Graves, Rev. Walter Eccleston, *died* 1922, vol. II
Graves-Sawle, Sir Charles John; *see* Sawle.
Graveson, Ronald Harry, 1911–1991, vol. IX
Gravina, Conte Manfredi, 1883–1932, vol. III
Gray, Lady, (19th in line), 1841–1918, vol. II
Gray, 20th Lord, 1864–1919, vol. II
Gray, Lady (21st in line, shown as 22nd), 1866–1946, vol. IV
Gray, Master of; Hon. Lindsay Stuart Campbell-Gray, 1894–1945, vol. IV
Gray, Alan, 1855–1935, vol. III
Gray, Sir Albert, 1850–1928, vol. II
Gray, Albert Alexander, 1868–1936, vol. III
Gray, Sir Alexander, *died* 1933, vol. III
Gray, Sir Alexander, 1882–1968, vol. VI
Gray, Air Vice-Marshal Alexander, 1896–1980, vol. VII
Gray, Sir Alexander George, 1884–1968, vol. VI
Gray, Alexander Stuart, 1905–1998, vol. X
Gray, Andrew, 1847–1925, vol. II
Gray, Andrew Aitken, 1912–1997, vol. X
Gray, Sir Anthony; *see* Gray, Sir F. A.
Gray, Sir Archibald Montague Henry, 1880–1967, vol. VI
Gray, Arthur, 1852–1940, vol. III
Gray, Col Arthur Claypon Horner, 1878–1963, vol. VI
Gray, A(rthur) Herbert, 1868–1956, vol. V
Gray, Arthur Wellesley, 1876–1944, vol. IV
Gray, Basil, 1904–1989, vol. VIII
Gray, Charles Herbert, *died* 1982, vol. VIII
Gray, Charles Horace, 1911–1997, vol. X

Gray, Lt-Col Clive Osric Vere, 1882–1945, vol. IV
Gray, David, 1906–1976, vol. VII
Gray, David, 1927–1983, vol. VIII
Gray, David, 1914–1999, vol. X
Gray, Donald, 1893–1943, vol. IV
Gray, Douglas S., 1890–1959, vol. V
Gray, Rev. Edward Dundas McQueen, 1854–1932, vol. III
Gray, Edward Francis, 1871–1960, vol. V
Gray, Edward George, 1924–1999, vol. X
Gray, Rev. Edward Ker, 1842–1903, vol. I
Gray, Sir Ernest, 1857–1932, vol. III
Gray, Ethel, died 1962, vol. VI
Gray, Frances Ralph, died 1935, vol. III
Gray, Sir (Francis) Anthony, 1917–1992, vol. IX
Gray, Frank, 1880–1935, vol. III
Gray, Brig.-Gen. Frederick William Barton, 1867–1931, vol. III
Gray, Geoffrey Leicester, 1905–1994, vol. IX
Gray, George Buchanan, 1865–1922, vol. II
Gray, George Charles, 1897–1981, vol. VIII
Gray, Lt-Col George Douglas, died 1946, vol. IV
Gray, George Kruger, 1880–1943, vol. IV
Gray, Sir George Mervyn, 1910–1973, vol. VII
Gray, Hon. George Wilkie, 1844–1924, vol. II
Gray, Gordon, 1909–1982, vol. VIII
Gray, His Eminence Cardinal Gordon Joseph, 1910–1993, vol. IX
Gray, Rear-Adm. Gordon Thomas Seccombe, 1911–1997, vol. X
Gray, Harold James, 1907–1998, vol. X
Gray, Harold St George, 1872–1963, vol. VI
Gray, Sir Harold William Stannus, 1867–1951, vol. V
Gray, Rt Rev. Henry Allen, died 1939, vol. III
Gray, Sir Henry McIlree Williamson, 1870–1938, vol. III
Gray, Rev. Herbert Branston, 1851–1929, vol. III
Gray, Rev. Horace, 1874–1938, vol. III
Gray, Howard Alexander, 1870–1942, vol. IV
Gray, Ian, 1926–1983, vol. VIII
Gray, James, 1877–1968, vol. VI
Gray, Sir James, 1891–1975, vol. VII
Gray, James Andrew, 1890–1966, vol. VI
Gray, James Cooke, 1847–1902, vol. I
Gray, James Gordon, died 1934, vol. III
Gray, James Hugo, 1909–1941, vol. IV
Gray, James Hunter, 1867–1925, vol. II
Gray, James Neville, died 1959, vol. V
Gray, Maj.-Gen. John; see Gray, Maj.-Gen. R. J.
Gray, Rev. John, 1913–2000, vol. X
Gray, Lt-Col John Anselm Samuel, 1874–1950, vol. IV
Gray, Air Vice-Marshal John Astley, 1899–1987, vol. VIII
Gray, John Magnus, 1915–1993, vol. IX
Gray, Vice Adm. Sir John Michael Dudgeon, 1913–1998, vol. X
Gray, Sir John Milner, 1889–1970, vol. VI
Gray, Very Rev. John Rodger, 1913–1984, vol. VIII
Gray, Rt Rev. Joseph, 1919–1999, vol. X
Gray, Joseph Alexander, 1884–1966, vol. VI
Gray, Rev. Joseph Henry, 1856–1932, vol. III
Gray, Leonard Thomas Miller, 1893–1969, vol. VI

Gray, Louis Harold, 1905–1965, vol. VI
Gray, Mary Elizabeth, 1903–1983, vol. VIII
Gray, Maxwell, (Mary Gleed Tuttiett), 1847–1923, vol. II
Gray, Milner, 1871–1943, vol. IV
Gray, Milner Connorton, 1899–1997, vol. X
Gray, Nicol; see Gray, W. N.
Gray, Norah Neilson-, died 1931, vol. III
Gray, Sir Reginald, 1851–1935, vol. III
Gray, Maj.-Gen. (Reginald) John, 1916–1994, vol. IX
Gray, Robert Michael Ker, 1938–1996, vol. X
Gray, Robert Whytlaw W.; see Whytlaw-Gray.
Gray, Roger Ibbotson, 1921–1992, vol. IX
Gray, Ronald, 1868–1951, vol. V
Gray, Sir Samuel Brownlow, 1823–1910, vol. I
Gray, Stephen Alexander Reith, 1926–1982, vol. VIII
Gray, Sylvia Mary, 1909–1991, vol. IX
Gray, Theodore Grant, 1884–1964, vol. VI
Gray, Thomas, 1869–1932, vol. III
Gray, Trevor Robert, 1919–1985, vol. VIII
Gray, Vernon Foxwell, 1882–1978, vol. VII
Gray, Lt-Col Sir Vivian Beaconsfield, 1885–1948, vol. IV
Gray, Sir Walter, 1848–1918, vol. II
Gray, Sir William, 1823–1898, vol. I
Gray, Sir William, 2nd Bt, 1895–1978, vol. VII
Gray, Lt-Col William A.; see Anstruther-Gray.
Gray, Major William Bain, 1886–1949, vol. IV
Gray, Major William Birrell-, 1872–1940, vol. III
Gray, Rt Rev. William Crane, 1835–1919, vol. II
Gray, Sir William Cresswell, 1st Bt, 1867–1924, vol. II
Gray, Maj.-Gen. William du Gard, 1856–1932, vol. III
Gray, William Forbes, 1874–1950, vol. IV
Gray, Very Rev. William Henry, 1825–1908, vol. I
Gray, Ven. William James, 1874–1960, vol. V
Gray, William John, 1911–1985, vol. VIII
Gray, William John A.; see Anstruther-Gray.
Gray, Col William Lewis, 1864–1924, vol. II
Gray, William Macfarlane, 1910–1984, vol. VIII
Gray, (William) Nicol, 1908–1988, vol. VIII
Gray, Sir William Stevenson, 1928–2000, vol. X
Gray-Cheape, Lt-Col Hugh Annesley; see Cheape.
Gray Horton, Lt-Col W(illiam); see Horton.
Gray-Smith, James Maclaren, 1832–1900, vol. I
Grayburn, Sir Vandeleur Molyneux, 1881–1943, vol. IV
Graydon, Newenham Arthur Eustace, died 1914, vol. I
Grayfoot, Col Blenman Buhot, died 1916, vol. II
Grayson, Cecil, 1920–1998, vol. X
Grayson, Sir Denys Henry Harrington, 2nd Bt, 1892–1955, vol. V
Grayson, Lt-Col Sir Henry Mulleneux, 1st Bt, 1865–1951, vol. V
Grayson, Sir Ronald Henry Rudyard, 3rd Bt, 1916–1987, vol. VIII
Grayson, Sir Rupert Stanley Harrington, 4th Bt, 1897–1991, vol. IX
Grazebrook, Brig. George Charles, 1873–1930, vol. III

Grazebrook, Henry Broome Durley, 1884–1969, vol. VI

Grazebrook, Brig. Tom Neville, 1904–1967, vol. VI

Grazebrook, William, *died* 1955, vol. V

Greany, Surg.-Gen. John Philip, 1851–1919, vol. II

Greany, Captain John Wingate, 1892–1916, vol. II

Greatbatch, Sir Bruce, 1917–1989, vol. VIII

Greathed, Rear-Adm. Bernard Wilberforce, 1891–1961, vol. VI

Greatorex, Adm. Clement, 1869–1937, vol. III

Greaves, Rt Rev. Arthur Ivan, 1873–1959, vol. V

Greaves, Maj.-Gen. Bill; *see* Greaves, Maj.-Gen. C. G. B.

Greaves, Maj.-Gen. Charles Granville Barry, 1900–1982, vol. VIII

Greaves, Sir Ewart; *see* Greaves, Sir W. E.

Greaves, Gen. Sir George Richards, 1831–1922, vol. II

Greaves, Harold Richard Goring, 1907–1981, vol. VIII

Greaves, Sir John Bewley, 1890–1977, vol. VII

Greaves, Sir John Brownson, 1900–1965, vol. VI

Greaves, John Ernest, 1847–1945, vol. IV

Greaves, Robert William, 1909–1979, vol. VII

Greaves, Ronald Ivan Norreys, 1908–1990, vol. VIII

Greaves, Sir Western; *see* Greaves, Sir W. W.

Greaves, Sir (William) Ewart, 1869–1956, vol. V

Greaves, Sir William Herbert, 1857–1936, vol. III

Greaves, William Michael Herbert, 1897–1955, vol. V

Greaves, Sir (William) Western, 1905–1982, vol. VIII

Greaves-Lord, Sir Walter, 1878–1942, vol. IV

Grech, Herbert Felix, 1899–1982, vol. VIII

Grech-Biancardi, Lt-Col Nicola, 1850–1913, vol. I

Greely, Maj.-Gen. Adolphus Washington, 1844–1935, vol. III

Green, Alan, 1911–1991, vol. IX

Green, Sir Alan Michael, 1885–1958, vol. V

Green, Albert, 1874–1941, vol. IV

Green, Albert Edward, 1912–1999, vol. X

Green, Hon. Albert Ernest, 1869–1940, vol. III

Green, Alice Sophia Amelia, *died* 1929, vol. III

Green, Anna Katharine; *see* Rohlfs, Mrs Charles.

Green, Major Arthur Dowson, 1874–1914, vol. I

Green, Arthur Eatough, 1892–1984, vol. VIII

Green, Brig.-Gen. Arthur Frank Umfreville, 1878–1964, vol. VI

Green, Arthur George, 1864–1941, vol. IV

Green, Rt Rev. Arthur Vincent, 1857–1944, vol. IV

Green, Benny, 1927–1998, vol. X

Green, Col Bernard Charles, 1866–1925, vol. II

Green, Rev. Canon Bryan Stuart Westmacott, 1901–1993, vol. IX

Green, Cecil Alfred, 1908–1980, vol. VII

Green, Rt Rev. Charles Alfred Howell, 1864–1944, vol. IV

Green, Charles Edward, 1866–1920, vol. II

Green, Rev. Charles Edward Maddison, *died* 1911, vol. I

Green, Charles L.; *see* Leedham-Green.

Green, David, *died* 1918, vol. II

Green, Engr Rear-Adm. Sir (Donald) Percy, 1866–1950, vol. IV

Green, Brig.-Gen. Edgar Walter Butler, 1869–1938, vol. III

Green, Rev. Edmund Tyrrell-, 1864–1937, vol. III

Green, Sir Edward, 1st Bt (*cr* 1886), 1831–1923, vol. II

Green, Col Sir Edward Arthur Lycett, 3rd Bt (*cr* 1886), 1886–1941, vol. IV

Green, Sir (Edward) Lycett, 2nd Bt (*cr* 1886), 1860–1940, vol. III

Green, Sir (Edward) Stephen (Lycett), 4th Bt (*cr* 1886), 1910–1996, vol. X

Green, Ernest, 1885–1977, vol. VII

Green, Col Ernest Edward, 1878–1956, vol. V

Green, Miss Evelyn E.; *see* Everett-Green.

Green, Everard, 1844–1926, vol. II

Green, Sir Francis Haydn, 2nd Bt (*cr* 1901), 1871–1956, vol. V

Green, Francis Henry Knethell, 1900–1977, vol. VII

Green, Sir Frank, 1st Bt (*cr* 1901), 1835–1902, vol. I

Green, Sir Frederick, 1845–1927, vol. II

Green, Frederick Charles, 1891–1964, vol. VI

Green, Sir Frederick Daniel, 1869–1932, vol. III

Green, Frederick Ernest, 1867–1922, vol. II

Green, Frederick Lawrence, 1902–1953, vol. V

Green, Rev. Frederick Wastie, 1884–1953, vol. V

Green, Frederick William E.; *see* Edridge-Green.

Green, Geoffrey, 1918–1978, vol. VII

Green, Sir George, 1843–1916, vol. II

Green, George Alfred Lawrence, *died* 1949, vol. IV

Green, Sir George Arthur Haydn, 4th Bt (*cr* 1901, 1884–1959, vol. V

Green, George Comerford, *died* 1940, vol. III

Green, George Conrad, 1897–1976, vol. VII

Green, Sir George Ernest, 1892–1982, vol. VIII

Green, George Henry, 1881–1956, vol. V

Green, Maj. George Hugh, 1911–1993, vol. IX

Green, George Norman, 1906–1968, vol. VI

Green, Major Graham John G.; *see* Graham-Green.

Green, Lt-Col Harold Philip, 1877–1944, vol. IV

Green, Harry Norman, 1903–1967, vol. VI

Green, Henry, 1905–1973, vol. VII

Green, Brig.-Gen. Henry Clifford Rodes, 1872–1935, vol. III

Green, Henry Rupert, 1900–1988, vol. VIII

Green, Mrs Hetty Howland Robinson, 1835–1916, vol. II

Green, Hon. Howard Charles, 1895–1989, vol. VIII

Green, Rev. James, 1868–1948, vol. IV

Green, (James) Maurice (Spurgeon), 1906–1987, vol. VIII

Green, Rev. James Paul Weston, *born* 1876, vol. III

Green, John Alfred, 1867–1922, vol. II

Green, John Dennis Fowler, 1909–2000, vol. X

Green, Adm. Sir John Frederick Ernest, 1866–1948, vol. IV

Green, Sir John Little, 1862–1953, vol. V

Green, Joseph Frederick, 1855–1932, vol. III

Green, Joseph Reynolds, *died* 1914, vol. I

Green, Julian Hartridge, 1900–1998, vol. X

Green, Kathleen (Mary) Haydn, *died* 1944, vol. IV

Green, Hon. Sir Kenneth; *see* Green, Hon. Sir R. K.

Green, Maj.-Gen. Kenneth David, 1917–1987, vol. VIII

Green, Leonard, 1890–1963, vol. VI

Green, Captain Leonard Henry, 1885–1966, vol. VI
Green, Rev. Sir Leonard Henry Haydn, 3rd Bt (cr 1901), 1879–1958, vol. V
Green, Leslie William, 1912–1983, vol. VIII
Green, Sir Lycett; see Green, Sir E. L.
Green, Col Malcolm Scrimshire, 1824–1906, vol. I
Green, Maurice; see Green, J. M. S.
Green, Max Sullivan, 1864–1922, vol. II
Green, Brig. Michael Arthur, 1891–1971, vol. VII
Green, Paul Eliot, 1894–1981, vol. VIII
Green, Engr Rear-Adm. Sir Percy; see Green, Engr Rear-Adm. Sir D. P.
Green, Rev. Canon Peter, 1871–1961, vol. VI
Green, Sir Peter James Frederick, 1924–1996, vol. X
Green, P(hilip) M(arion) Kirby, 1905–1969, vol. VI
Green, Hon. Sir (Richard) Kenneth, 1907–1961, vol. VI
Green, Hon. Robert Francis, 1861–1946, vol. IV
Green, Roger Gilbert Lancelyn, 1918–1987, vol. VIII
Green, Roger James N.; see Northcote-Green.
Green, Roland, 1895–1972, vol. VII
Green, Ronald Bramble, 1895–1973, vol. VII
Green, Ronald Frank, 1905–1971, vol. VII
Green, Sam, 1907–1996, vol. X
Green, Rev. Samuel Walter, 1853–1926, vol. II
Green, Maj.-Gen. Sebert Francis St David's, 1868–1930, vol. III
Green, Sir Stephen; see Green, Sir E. S. L.
Green, Thomas Ernest, 1872–1937, vol. III
Green, Thomas Farrimond, 1899–1966, vol. VI
Green, Vincent, died 1958, vol. V
Green, Walford Davis, 1869–1941, vol. IV
Green, Walter Henry, 1878–1958, vol. V
Green, Brig.-Gen. Wilfrith Gerald Key, 1872–1937, vol. III
Green, Sir William, 1836–1897, vol. I
Green, Maj.-Gen. William, 1882–1947, vol. IV
Green, William, 1873–1952, vol. V
Green, William Allan McInnes, 1896–1972, vol. VII
Green, Rev. William Charles, 1832–1914, vol. I
Green, William Curtis, 1875–1960, vol. V
Green, Maj.-Gen. Sir William Henry Rodes, 1823–1912, vol. I
Green, William Kirby, 1876–1945, vol. IV
Green, Rev. William Spotswood, 1847–1919, vol. II
Green, Lt-Gen. Sir (William) Wyndham, 1887–1979, vol. VII
Green, Lt-Gen. Sir Wyndham; see Green, Lt-Gen. Sir W. W.
Green-Armytage, Lt-Col Vivian Bartley, 1882–1961, vol. VI
Green-Price, Sir John, 4th Bt, 1908–1964, vol. VI
Green-Price, Sir Richard Dansey, 2nd Bt, 1838–1909, vol. I
Green-Price, Major Sir Robert Henry, 3rd Bt, 1872–1962, vol. VI
Green-Wilkinson, Most Rev. Francis Oliver, 1913–1970, vol. VI
Green-Wilkinson, Lt-Gen. Frederick, 1825–1913, vol. I
Green-Wilkinson, Brig.-Gen. Lewis Frederic, 1865–1950, vol. IV

Greenacre, Sir Benjamin Wesley, 1832–1911, vol. I
Greenacre, Brig. Walter Douglas Campbell, 1900–1978, vol. VII
Greenall, Cyril Edward, died 1939, vol. III
Greenall, Thomas, 1857–1937, vol. III
Greenaway, Alan Pearce, 1913–1994, vol. IX
Greenaway, Sir Derek Burdick, 2nd Bt, 1910–1994, vol. IX
Greenaway, Sir Percy Walter, 1st Bt, 1874–1956, vol. V
Greenaway, Sir Thomas Moore, 1902–1980, vol. VII (AII)
Greenbank, Percy, 1878–1968, vol. VI
Greenbaum, Sidney, 1929–1996, vol. X
Greenberg, Leopold, 1885–1964, vol. VI
Greenberg, Leopold J., died 1931, vol. III
Greenborough, Sir John Hedley, 1922–1998, vol. X
Greene, 1st Baron, 1883–1952, vol. V
Greene, Benjamin Buck, 1808–1902, vol. I
Greene, Charles Henry, 1865–1942, vol. IV
Greene, (Charles) Raymond, 1901–1982, vol. VIII
Greene, Rt Hon. Sir Conyngham, 1854–1934, vol. III
Greene, Sir Edward Allan, 3rd Bt, 1882–1966, vol. VI
Greene, Col Hon. Edward Mackenzie, 1857–1944, vol. IV
Greene, Edward Reginald, 1904–1990, vol. VIII
Greene, Sir (Edward) Walter, 1st Bt, 1842–1920, vol. II
Greene, Eric Gordon, 1904–1966, vol. VI
Greene, Felix, 1909–1985, vol. VIII
Greene, Gen. Francis Vinton, died 1921, vol. II
Greene, Geoffrey Philip, 1868–1930, vol. III
Greene, George Arthur, 1853–1921, vol. II
Greene, George Ball, 1872–1945, vol. IV
Greene, Rev. Godfrey George, 1860–1929, vol. III
Greene, Sir Graham; see Greene, Sir W. G.
Greene, Graham, 1904–1991, vol. IX
Greene, H. Barrett, 1861–1927, vol. II
Greene, Harry Plunket, 1865–1936, vol. III
Greene, Henry David, 1843–1915, vol. I
Greene, Sir Hugh Carleton, 1910–1987, vol. VIII
Greene, Ian Rawdon, 1909–1992, vol. IX
Greene, Jerome Davis, 1874–1959, vol. V
Greene, Brig.-Gen. John, 1878–1956, vol. V
Greene, John Arch, died 1934, vol. III
Greene, John Arthur, 1879–1945, vol. IV
Greene, Dame Judith; see Anderson, Dame F. M.
Greene, Maurice Cherry, 1881–1959, vol. V
Greene, Raymond; see Greene, C. R.
Greene, Sir Raymond; see Greene, Sir W. R.
Greene, W. H. C.; see Clayton-Greene.
Greene, Sir Walter; see Greene, Sir E. W.
Greene, Hon. Sir Walter M.; see Massy-Greene.
Greene, Sir (Walter) Raymond, 2nd Bt, 1869–1947, vol. IV
Greene, Very Rev. William Conyngham, died 1910, vol. I
Greene, Sir (William) Graham, 1857–1950, vol. IV
Greene, William Pomeroy Crawford, 1884–1959, vol. V
Greene Kelly, Sir Henry, 1865–1934, vol. III
Greener, Lt-Col Herbert, 1862–1943, vol. IV
Greenewatt, Crawford Hallock, 1902–1993, vol. IX

Greenfield, Sir Cornelius Ewen MacLean, 1906–1980, vol. VII
Greenfield, Sir Harry, 1898–1981, vol. VIII
Greenfield, Brig. Hector Robert Hume, 1893–1975, vol. VII
Greenfield, Sir Henry Challen, 1885–1967, vol. VI
Greenfield, Herbert, 1869–1949, vol. IV (A), vol. V
Greenfield, John; see Field, John.
Greenfield, Hon. Julius MacDonald, 1907–1993, vol. IX
Greenfield, Brig.-Gen. Richard Menteith, 1856–1916, vol. II
Greenfield, Stanley Samuel, 1873–1956, vol. V
Greenfield, William Smith, 1846–1919, vol. II
Greenhalgh, Mrs Stobart; see Stobart, Mrs St Clair.
Greenham, Alfred Howard, 1895–1966, vol. VI
Greenham, Peter George, 1909–1992, vol. IX
Greenham, Robert Duckworth, 1906–1976, vol. VII
Greenhill, 1st Baron, 1887–1967, vol. VI
Greenhill, 2nd Baron, 1917–1989, vol. VIII
Greenhill of Harrow, Baron (Life Peer); Denis Arthur Greenhill, 1913–2000, vol. X
Greenhill, Sir George, 1847–1927, vol. II
Greenhill-Gardyne, Lt-Col Charles, 1831–1923, vol. II
Greenhough, Col Frederick Harry, 1871–1953, vol. V
Greenhow, William Thomas, 1831–1921, vol. II
Greenidge, Charles Wilton Wood, 1889–1972, vol. VII
Greening, Wilfred Peter, 1914–1999, vol. X
Greenish, Henry George, 1855–1933, vol. III
Greenland, Rev. William Kingscote, 1868–1957, vol. V
Greenleaves, Herbert Leslie, 1897–1975, vol. VII
Greenlees, Ian Gordon, 1913–1988, vol. VIII
Greenlees, James Robertson Campbell, 1878–1951, vol. V
Greenley, William Alfred, 1884–1949, vol. IV
Greenly, Edward, 1861–1951, vol. V
Greenly, Edward Howorth, 1837–1926, vol. II
Greenly, Lt-Col Sir John Henry Maitland, 1885–1950, vol. IV
Greenly, Maj.-Gen. Walter Howorth, 1875–1955, vol. V
Greenshields, James Naismith, 1853–1937, vol. III
Greenshields, R. A. E., died 1942, vol. IV
Greenslade, Brig. Cyrus, 1892–1985, vol. VIII
Greenslade, David Rex Willman, 1916–1977, vol. VII
Greenslade, Rev. Stanley Lawrence, 1905–1977, vol. VII
Greensmith, Edward William, 1909–1995, vol. IX
Greensmith, Edwin Lloydd, 1900–1993, vol. X (AI)
Greenstreet, Reginald Hawkins, 1858–1930, vol. III
Greenstreet, William John, 1861–1930, vol. III
Greenup, Rev. Albert William, 1866–1952, vol. V
Greenway, 1st Baron, 1857–1934, vol. III
Greenway, 2nd Baron, 1888–1963, vol. VI
Greenway, 3rd Baron, 1917–1975, vol. VII
Greenway, Maj.-Gen. Charles William, 1900–1968, vol. VI
Greenway, John Dee, 1896–1967, vol. VI
Greenwell, Allan, 1860–1944, vol. IV

Greenwell, Sir Bernard Eyre, 2nd Bt, 1874–1939, vol. III
Greenwell, Sir Francis, 1852–1931, vol. III
Greenwell, Captain Sir Peter McClintock, 3rd Bt, 1914–1978, vol. VII
Greenwell, Col Thomas George, 1894–1967, vol. VI
Greenwell, Sir Walpole Lloyd, 1st Bt, 1847–1919, vol. II
Greenwell, Rev. William, 1820–1918, vol. II
Greenwell, Col William Basil, 1881–1964, vol. VI
Greenwood, 1st Viscount, 1870–1948, vol. IV
Greenwood, 2nd Viscount, 1914–1998, vol. X
Greenwood, Viscountess; (Marjery), 1886–1968, vol. VI
Greenwood of Rossendale, Baron (Life Peer); Arthur William James Greenwood, (Anthony Greenwood), 1911–1982, vol. VIII
Greenwood, Rt Hon. Arthur, 1880–1954, vol. V
Greenwood, Col Charles Francis Hill, 1871–1944, vol. IV
Greenwood, Frederick, 1830–1909, vol. I
Greenwood, George David, 1881–1953, vol. V
Greenwood, Sir (Granville) George, 1850–1928, vol. II
Greenwood, Brig. Harold Gustave Francis, 1894–1978, vol. VII
Greenwood, Col Harry, 1881–1948, vol. IV
Greenwood, Henry Harold, 1873–1962, vol. VI
Greenwood, Hubert John, 1867–1932, vol. III
Greenwood, Jack Neville, 1922–1989, vol. VIII
Greenwood, Sir James Mantle, 1902–1969, vol. VI
Greenwood, (James) Russell, 1924–1993, vol. IX
Greenwood, Joan, 1921–1987, vol. VIII
Greenwood, John Arnold Charles, 1914–1992, vol. IX
Greenwood, John Eric, 1891–1975, vol. VII
Greenwood, John Frederic, 1885–1954, vol. V
Greenwood, John French, 1904–1968, vol. VI
Greenwood, John Neill, 1894–1981, vol. VIII
Greenwood, Major, 1880–1949, vol. IV
Greenwood, Peter Humphry, 1927–1995, vol. IX
Greenwood, Ranolf Nelson, 1889–1977, vol. VII
Greenwood, Robert, 1897–1981, vol. VIII
Greenwood, Robert Morrell, died 1947, vol. IV
Greenwood, Russell; see Greenwood, J. R.
Greenwood, Rev. Sydney, died 1926, vol. II
Greenwood, Thomas, 1851–1908, vol. I
Greenwood, Rt Rev. Tom, 1903–1974, vol. VII
Greenwsood, Walter, 1903–1974, vol. VII
Greenwood, William, 1875–1925, vol. II
Greenwood, William Frederick, 1861–1933, vol. III
Greenwood Wilson, John; see Wilson.
Greer, Rt Rev. David Hummell, 1844–1919, vol. II
Greer, Sir (Edmund) Wyly, 1862–1957, vol. V
Greer, Sir Francis Nugent, 1869–1925, vol. II
Greer, Brig.-Gen. Frederick Augustus, 1871–1958, vol. V
Greer, Rev. George Samuel, died 1921, vol. II
Greer, Sir Harry, 1876–1947, vol. IV
Greer, Sir Henry, 1855–1934, vol. III
Greer, Joseph, 1854–1922, vol. II
Greer, Richard Townsend, 1854–1942, vol. IV
Greer, Thomas Macgregor, 1853–1928, vol. II
Greer, Rt Rev. William Derrick Lindsay, 1902–1972, vol. VII

Greer, Sir Wyly; *see* Greer, Sir E. W.
Greeson, Surgeon Vice-Adm. Sir (Clarence) Edward, 1888–1979, vol. VII
Greeson, Surg. Vice-Adm. Sir Edward; *see* Greeson, Surg. Vice-Adm. Sir C. E.
Greet, Sir Philip Ben, 1857–1936, vol. III
Greeves, Rev. Derrick Amphlet, 1913–1991, vol. IX
Greeves, Rev. Frederic, 1903–1985, vol. VIII
Greeves, John Ernest, 1910–1987, vol. VIII
Greeves, R(eginald) Affleck, 1878–1966, vol. VI
Greeves, Maj.-Gen. Sir Stuart, 1897–1989, vol. VIII
Greffulhe, Comtesse, *died* 1952, vol. V
Greg, Lt-Col Alexander, 1867–1952, vol. V
Greg, Barbara, 1900–1983, vol. VIII
Greg, Col Ernest William, 1862–1934, vol. III
Greg, John Ronald, 1866–1950, vol. IV
Greg, Lionel Hyde, 1879–1945, vol. IV
Greg, Sir Robert Hyde, 1876–1953, vol. V
Greg, Sir Walter Wilson, 1875–1959, vol. V
Gregg, Miss; *see* Grier, Sydney C.
Gregg, Sir Cornelius Joseph, *died* 1959, vol. V
Gregg, Edward Andrew, 1881–1969, vol. VI
Gregg, Sir Henry, 1859–1928, vol. II
Gregg, Humphrey P.; *see* Procter-Gregg.
Gregg, Very Rev. James Fitzgerald, *died* 1905, vol. I
Gregg, James Reali, 1899–1978, vol. VII
Gregg, Most Rev. John Allen Fitzgerald, 1873–1961, vol. VI
Gregg, John Frank, 1912–1960, vol. V
Gregg, Milton Fowler, 1892–1978, vol. VII
Gregg, Sir Norman McAlister, *died* 1966, vol. VI
Gregge-Hopwood, Major Edward Byng George, 1880–1917, vol. II
Gregge-Hopwood, Edward Robert, 1846–1942, vol. IV
Grego, Joseph, 1843–1908, vol. I
Gregoire, His Eminence Cardinal Paul, 1911–1993, vol. IX
Gregor, James Wyllie, 1900–1980, vol. VII (AII)
Gregorie, Maj.-Gen. Charles Frederick, 1834–1918, vol. II
Gregorowski, Hon. Reinhold, 1856–1922, vol. II
Gregory, Hon. Alexander Frederick, 1843–1927, vol. II
Gregory, Arnold, 1924–1976, vol. VII
Gregory, Augusta, (Lady Gregory), *died* 1932, vol. III
Gregory, Hon. Sir Augustus Charles, 1819–1905, vol. I
Gregory, Rev. Benjamin, 1875–1950, vol. IV
Gregory, Charles, *died* 1920, vol. II
Gregory, Sir Charles Hutton, 1817–1898, vol. I
Gregory, Maj.-Gen. Charles Levinge, 1870–1944, vol. IV
Gregory, Vice-Adm. Sir David; *see* Gregory, Vice-Adm. Sir G. D. A.
Gregory, Rev. Edmund Ironside, 1835–1912, vol. I
Gregory, Edward John, 1850–1909, vol. I
Gregory, Eric Craven, 1887–1959, vol. V
Gregory, Captain Ernest Foster, 1873–1940, vol. III
Gregory, Rt Rev. Francis Ambrose, 1848–1927, vol. II
Gregory, Lt-Col Francis Brooke, 1862–1936, vol. III

Gregory, Frederick, 1831–1919, vol. II
Gregory, Frederick Gugenheim, 1893–1961, vol. VI
Gregory, Captain George, 1872–1929, vol. III
Gregory, Vice-Adm. Sir (George) David (Archibald), 1909–1975, vol. VII
Gregory, George Frederick, *born* 1839, vol. II
Gregory, Hon. Henry, 1860–1940, vol. III
Gregory, Sir Henry Stanley, 1890–1959, vol. V
Gregory, Sir Holman, 1864–1947, vol. IV
Gregory, Jackson, 1882–1943, vol. IV
Gregory, John Duncan, 1878–1951, vol. V
Gregory, Sir (John) Roger Burrow, 1861–1938, vol. III
Gregory, John Water, 1864–1932, vol. III
Gregory, Joshua C., 1875–1964, vol. VI
Gregory, Michael Anthony, 1925–1999, vol. X
Gregory, Padraic, 1886–1962, vol. VI
Gregory, Philip Herries, 1907–1986, vol. VIII
Gregory, Sir Philip Spencer, 1851–1918, vol. II
Gregory, Reginald Philip, 1879–1918, vol. II
Gregory, Sir Richard Arman, 1st Bt, 1864–1952, vol. V
Gregory, Very Rev. Robert, 1819–1911, vol. I
Gregory, Roderic Alfred, 1913–1990, vol. VIII
Gregory, Sir Roger; *see* Gregory, Sir J. R. B.
Gregory, Roland Charles Leslie, (Roy), 1916–1997, vol. X
Gregory, Roy; *see* Gregory, R. C. L.
Gregory, Sir Theodore, 1890–1970, vol. VI
Gregory, Theophilus Stephen, 1897–1975, vol. VII
Gregory, Thomas Sherwin P.; *see* Pearson-Gregory.
Gregory, William King, 1876–1970, vol. VI (AII)
Gregory Smith, George, 1865–1932, vol. III
Gregson, Edward Gelson, 1877–1942, vol. IV
Gregson, Ven. Francis Sitwell Knight, *died* 1926, vol. II
Gregson, Maj.-Gen. Guy Patrick, 1906–1988, vol. VIII
Gregson, Col Henry Guy Fulljames Savage, 1872–1949, vol. IV
Gregson, William Derek Hadfield, 1920–1998, vol. X
Gregson-Ellis, Maj.-Gen. Philip George Saxon, 1898–1956, vol. V
Greiffenhagen, Maurice, 1862–1931, vol. III
Greig, Sir Alexander, 1878–1950, vol. IV
Greig, Alexander Rodger, 1872–1947, vol. IV
Greig, Charles Alexis, 1880–1958, vol. V
Greig, David Middleton, *died* 1936, vol. III
Greig, Lt-Col Edward David Wilson, 1874–1950, vol. IV
Greig, Edward Hagerup, 1843–1907, vol. I
Greig, Col Frederick James, 1863–1931, vol. III
Greig, Sir James, *died* 1934, vol. III
Greig, James, 1861–1941, vol. IV
Greig, James, 1903–1991, vol. IX
Greig of Eccles, James Dennis, 1926–2000, vol. X
Greig, Rev. Lt-Col John Glennie, 1871–1958, vol. V
Greig, Rt Rev. John Harold, 1865–1938, vol. III
Greig, John Russell, 1889–1963, vol. VI
Greig, John Young Thomson, 1891–1963, vol. VI
Greig, Gp Captain Sir Louis, 1880–1953, vol. V
Greig, Maysie, (Mrs Jan Sopoushek), *died* 1971, vol. VII

Greig, Rear-Adm. Morice Gordon, 1914–1980, vol. VII
Greig, Sir Robert Blyth, 1874–1947, vol. IV
Greig, Captain Ronald Henry, 1876–1916, vol. II
Grein, J. T., 1862–1935, vol. III
Grenfell, 1st Baron, 1841–1925, vol. II
Grenfell, 2nd Baron, 1905–1976, vol. VII
Grenfell, Bernard Pyne, 1869–1926, vol. II
Grenfell, Lt-Col Cecil Alfred, 1864–1924, vol. II
Grenfell, Charles Seymour, 1839–1924, vol. II
Grenfell, Rt Hon. David Rhys, 1881–1968, vol. VI
Grenfell, Rev. George, 1849–1906, vol. I
Grenfell, Col Harold Maxwell, 1870–1929, vol. III
Grenfell, Vice-Adm. Harry Tremenheere, 1845–1906, vol. I
Grenfell, Henry Riversdale, 1824–1902, vol. I
Grenfell, Joyce Irene, 1910–1979, vol. VII
Grenfell, Hon. Julian Henry Francis, 1888–1915, vol. I
Grenfell, Sir Wilfred Thomason, 1865–1940, vol. III
Grenier, Gerard, died 1917, vol. II
Grenier, Gustave, born 1847, vol. II
Grenier, Joseph Richard, 1852–1926, vol. II
Grenside, Rev. William Bent, 1821–1913, vol. I
Grensted, Rev. Frederic Finnis, 1857–1919, vol. II
Grensted, Rev. Canon Laurence William, 1884–1964, vol. VI
Grente, HE Cardinal George, 1872–1959, vol. V
Grenville, Lt-Col Hon. Thomas George Breadalbane M.; see Morgan-Grenville.
Grenyer, Herbert Charles, 1913–1996, vol. X
Gresford Jones, Rt Rev. Edward Michael, 1901–1982, vol. VIII
Gresford Jones, Rt Rev. Michael; see Gresford Jones, Rt Rev. E. M.
Gresley, Sir Herbert Nigel, 1876–1941, vol. IV
Gresley, Sir Nigel, 12th Bt, 1894–1974, vol. VII
Gresley, Rear-Adm. Richard Nigel, 1850–1928, vol. II
Gresley, Sir Robert, 11th Bt, 1866–1936, vol. III
Gresley, Rev. Roger St John, died 1935, vol. III
Gresley, Sir William Frances, 13th Bt, 1897–1976, vol. VII
Gresson, Rt Hon. Sir Kenneth Macfarlane, 1891–1974, vol. VII
Gresson, Lt-Col Thomas Tinning, 1870–1921, vol. II
Gresson, William Jardine, died 1934, vol. III
Gresty, Hugh, 1899–1958, vol. V
Greswell, Air Cdre Jeaffreson Herbert, 1916–2000, vol. X
Greswell, Richard Egerton, 1916–1979, vol. VII
Greswell, Rev. William Henry Parr, died 1923, vol. II
Greswolde-Williams, Francis Wigley Greswolde, 1873–1931, vol. III
Gretton, 1st Baron, 1867–1947, vol. IV
Gretton, 2nd Baron, 1902–1982, vol. VIII
Gretton, 3rd Baron, 1941–1989, vol. VIII
Gretton, Major Frederic, died 1928, vol. II
Gretton, Brig. John Cunliffe, 1880–1953, vol. V
Gretton, Mary Sturge, died 1961, vol. VI
Gretton, Vice-Adm. Sir Peter William, 1912–1992, vol. IX
Greville, 2nd Baron, 1841–1910, vol. I

Greville, 3rd Baron, 1871–1952, vol. V
Greville, 4th Baron, 1912–1987, vol. VIII
Greville, Col Hon. Alwyn Henry Fulke, 1854–1929, vol. III
Greville, Major Charles Henry, 1889–1931, vol. III
Greville, Sir George, 1851–1937, vol. III
Greville, Hon. Louis George, 1856–1941, vol. IV
Greville, Dame Margaret Helen Anderson, (Hon. Mrs Ronald Greville), died 1942, vol. IV
Greville, Hon. Maynard, 1898–1960, vol. V
Greville, Hon. Mrs Ronald; see Greville, Dame M. H. A.
Greville, Hon. Ronald Henry Fulke, 1864–1908, vol. I
Greville, Hon. Sir Sidney Robert, 1866–1927, vol. II
Grew, Major Benjamin Dixon, 1892–1977, vol. VII
Grew, Edwin Sharpe, 1866–1950, vol. IV
Grew, Joseph Clark, 1880–1965, vol. VI
Grey, 4th Earl, 1851–1917, vol. II
Grey, 5th Earl, 1879–1963, vol. VI
Grey of Codnor, 5th Baron, 1903–1996, vol. X
Grey of Fallodon, 1st Viscount, 1862–1933, vol. III
Grey of Fallodon, Viscountess; (Pamela Adelaide Geneviève), 1871–1928, vol. II
Grey of Naunton, Baron (Life Peer); Ralph Francis Alnwick Grey, 1910–1999, vol. X
Grey de Ruthyn, 23rd (shown as 24th) Baron, 1858–1912, vol. I
Grey de Ruthyn, 24th Baron, 1862–1934, vol. III
Grey de Ruthyn, 25th Baron, 1883–1963, vol. VI
Grey, Annie, vol. III
Grey, Arthur, 1840–1911, vol. I
Grey, Col Arthur, 1855–1924, vol. II
Grey, Charles Frederick, 1903–1984, vol. VIII
Grey, Sir Charles George, 4th Bt (cr 1814), 1880–1957, vol. V
Grey, Charles Grey, 1875–1953, vol. V
Grey, Clifford, 1887–1941, vol. VII
Grey, Egerton Spenser, 1863–1950, vol. IV
Grey, Francis Temple, 1886–1941, vol. IV
Grey, Col Geoffrey Bridgman, 1911–1983, vol. VIII
Grey, Rt Hon. Sir George, 1812–1898, vol. I
Grey, Captain George Charles, 1918–1944, vol. IV
Grey, Sir George Duncan, 1868–1937, vol. III
Grey, Rev. Harry George, 1851–1925, vol. II
Grey, Sir (Harry) Martin, 5th Bt (cr 1814), 1882–1960, vol. V
Grey, Sir Henry Foley, 7th Bt (cr 1710), 1861–1914, vol. I
Grey, Sir John Foley, 8th Bt (cr 1710), 1893–1938, vol. III
Grey, Sir John Howarth, 1875–1960, vol. V
Grey, Col Leopold John Herbert, 1840–1921, vol. II
Grey, Sir Martin; see Grey, Sir H. M.
Grey, (Patrick) Ronald, 1927–1985, vol. VIII
Grey, Sir Paul Francis, 1908–1990, vol. VIII
Grey, Lt-Col Sir Raleigh, 1860–1936, vol. III
Grey, Major Robin, 1874–1922, vol. II
Grey, Sir Robin Edward Dysart, 6th Bt (cr 1814), 1886–1974, vol. VII
Grey, Ronald; see Grey, P. R.
Grey, Rowland; see Brown, Lilian Kate Rowland.
Grey, Samuel John, 1878–1942, vol. IV
Grey, Comdr Spenser Douglas Adair, 1889–1937, vol. III

Grey, Lt-Col William George, 1866–1953, vol. V
Grey, Maj.-Gen. Wulff Henry, *died* 1961, vol. VI
Grey, Zane, 1875–1939, vol. III
Grey-Egerton, Rev. Sir Brooke de Malpas; *see* Egerton.
Grey-Egerton, Sir Philip Henry Brian; *see* Egerton.
Grey-Egerton, Sir Philip Reginald le Belward, 14th Bt, 1885–1962, vol. VI
Grey-Smith, Sir Ross, 1901–1973, vol. VII
Grey-Turner, Elston, 1916–1984, vol. VIII
Grey Walter, William; *see* Walter.
Grey-Wilson, Sir William, 1852–1926, vol. II
Gribble, Bernard Finegan, 1872–1962, vol. VI
Gribble, Francis Henry, 1862–1946, vol. IV
Gribble, George James, 1846–1927, vol. II
Gribble, Col (Hon.) Howard Charles, 1886–1956, vol. V
Gribble, Leonard Reginald, 1908–1985, vol. VIII
Gribbon, Brig. Walter Harold, 1881–1944, vol. IV
Grice, Sir John, 1850–1935, vol. III
Grice, Col Walter Thomas, 1868–1926, vol. II
Grice-Hutchinson, George William, 1848–1906, vol. I
Gridley, 1st Baron, 1878–1965, vol. VI
Gridley, 2nd Baron, 1906–1996, vol. X
Gridley, John Crandon, 1904–1968, vol. VI
Grier, Anthony MacGregor, 1911–1989, vol. VIII
Grier, Brig.-Gen. Harry Dixon, 1863–1942, vol. IV
Grier, John Arthur Bolton, 1882–1946, vol. IV
Grier, Louis Monro, 1864–1920, vol. II
Grier, Lynda, 1880–1967, vol. VI
Grier, Patrick Arthur, 1918–1999, vol. X
Grier, Very Rev. Roy Macgregor, 1877–1940, vol. III
Grier, Sir Selwyn Macgregor, 1878–1946, vol. IV
Grier, Sydney C., 1868–1933, vol. III
Grierson, Sir Alexander Davidson, 9th Bt, 1858–1912, vol. I
Grierson, Sir Andrew, *died* 1936, vol. III
Grierson, Charles MacIver, 1864–1939, vol. III (A), vol. IV
Grierson, Rt Rev. Charles Thornton Primrose, 1857–1935, vol. III
Grierson, Edgar, 1884–1959, vol. V
Grierson, Francis, 1848–1927, vol. II
Grierson, Sir George Abraham, 1851–1941, vol. IV
Grierson, Sir Herbert John Clifford, 1866–1960, vol. V
Grierson, James Cullen, 1863–1919, vol. II
Grierson, Lt-Gen. Sir James Moncrieff, 1859–1914, vol. I
Grierson, John, 1898–1964, vol. VI
Grierson, John, 1898–1972, vol. VII
Grierson, Philip Francis H.; *see* Hamilton-Grierson.
Grierson, Sir Philip James Hamilton-, 1851–1927, vol. II
Grierson, Sir Richard Douglas, 11th Bt, 1912–1987, vol. VIII
Grierson, Sir Robert Gilbert White, 10th Bt, 1883–1957, vol. V
Grierson, William Wylie, *died* 1935, vol. III
Griesbach, Charles Ludolf, 1847–1907, vol. I
Griesbach, Maj.-Gen. Hon. William Antrobus, 1878–1945, vol. IV
Grieve, Rev. Alexander James, 1874–1952, vol. V

Grieve, Lt-Col Angus Alexander M.; *see* Macfarlane-Grieve.
Grieve, Christopher Murray, 1892–1978, vol. VII
Grieve, Captain Edward Leonard, 1880–1936, vol. III
Grieve, Edward William Lawrence, 1902–1960, vol. V (A)
Grieve, Sir (Herbert) Ronald (Robinson), 1896–1982, vol. VIII
Grieve, Rev. Canon James Gavin, 1880–1937, vol. III
Grieve, Percy; *see* Grieve, W. P.
Grieve, Robert, 1839–1906, vol. I
Grieve, Sir Robert, 1910–1995, vol. IX
Grieve, Robert G., 1881–1952, vol. V
Grieve, Sir Ronald; *see* Grieve, Sir H. R. R.
Grieve, Thomas Robert, 1909–1987, vol. VIII
Grieve, W. Percy; *see* Grieve, William P.
Grieve, Hon. Walter Baine, 1850–1921, vol. II
Grieve, Walter Graham, *died* 1937, vol. III
Grieve, William, 1885–1967, vol. VI
Grieve, William Alexander M.; *see* Macfarlane-Grieve.
Grieve, William Percival, (W. Percy), 1915–1998, vol. X
Grieves, Joseph Arthur, 1907–1976, vol. VII
Griffin, Alan Francis Rathbone, 1911–1965, vol. VI
Griffin, Alexander, 1883–1966, vol. VI
Griffin, Adm. Sir Anthony Templer Frederick Griffith, 1920–1996, vol. X
Griffin, Sir Arthur Cecil, 1888–1970, vol. VI
Griffin, Lt-Col Atholl Edwin, 1877–1956, vol. V
Griffin, His Eminence Cardinal Bernard W., 1899–1956, vol. V
Griffin, Sir Cecil; *see* Griffin, Sir L. C. L.
Griffin, Lt-Col Cecil Pender Griffith, 1864–1922, vol. II
Griffin, Sir Charles James, 1875–1962, vol. VI
Griffin, Air Vice-Marshal Charles Robert, 1919–1979, vol. VII
Griffin, Charles Thomas, *died* 1923, vol. II
Griffin, Brig.-Gen. Christopher Joseph, 1874–1957, vol. V
Griffin, Col Edgar Allen, 1907–1996, vol. X
Griffin, Lt-Gen. Edward Christian, 1836–1917, vol. II
Griffin, Sir Elton Reginald, 1906–1975, vol. VII
Griffin, Ernest Harrison, 1877–1936, vol. III
Griffin, Sir Francis Frederick, 1904–1982, vol. VIII
Griffin, Sir Henry Daly, 1864–1936, vol. III
Griffin, Major Henry Lysaght, 1866–1930, vol. III
Griffin, Sir Herbert John Gordon, 1889–1969, vol. VI
Griffin, Hester Wolferstan, (Mrs R. L. Griffin); *see* Chapman, Mrs H. W.
Griffin, Irene Marie, (Mrs F. D. Griffin); *see* Dunne, I. M.
Griffin, Maj.-Gen. John Arnold Atkinson, 1891–1972, vol. VII
Griffin, Sir John Bowes, 1903–1992, vol. IX
Griffin, Sir (Lancelot) Cecil Lepel, 1900–1964, vol. VI
Griffin, Sir Lepel Henry, 1840–1908, vol. I
Griffin, Martin Joseph, 1847–1921, vol. II

Griffin, Rear-Adm. Michael Howard, 1921–1995, vol. IX
Griffin, William Vincent, 1886–1958, vol. V
Griffis, Rev. William Elliot, 1843–1928, vol. II
Griffith, Alan Arnold, 1893–1963, vol. VI
Griffith, Arthur, 1872–1922, vol. II
Griffith, Hon. Arthur, *died* 1946, vol. IV
Griffith, Arthur Donald, 1882–1944, vol. IV
Griffith, Hon. Sir Arthur Frederick, 1913–1982, vol. VIII
Griffith, Major Arthur Lefroy Pritchard, 1886–1932, vol. III
Griffith, Arthur Stanley, 1875–1941, vol. IV
Griffith, Very Rev. Charles Edward Thomas, 1857–1934, vol. III
Griffith, Brig.-Gen. Charles Richard Jebb, 1867–1948, vol. IV
Griffith, Cyril Cobham, 1891–1972, vol. VII
Griffith, Rev. David, vol. II
Griffith, Lt-Col Edward Hugh, 1858–1936, vol. III
Griffith, Lt-Col Edward Waldegrave, 1871–1937, vol. III
Griffith, Sir Elis Arundell Ellis-, 2nd Bt (*cr* 1918), 1896–1934, vol. III
Griffith, Ven. Ellis Hughes, *died* 1938, vol. III
Griffith, Rt Hon. Sir Ellis Jones Ellis-, 1st Bt (*cr* 1918), 1860–1926, vol. II
Griffith, Brig. Eric Llewellyn Griffith G.; *see* Griffith-Williams.
Griffith, Sir Francis Charles, 1878–1942, vol. IV
Griffith, Francis Llewellyn, 1862–1934, vol. III
Griffith, Frank Kingsley, 1889–1962, vol. VI
Griffith, George Chetwynd, *died* 1906, vol. I
Griffith, George Herbert, 1877–1947, vol. IV
Griffith, Lt-Col George Richard, 1857–1920, vol. II
Griffith, Grosvenor Talbot, 1899–1981, vol. VIII
Griffith, Guy Thompson, 1908–1985, vol. VIII
Griffith, Rev. Henry Allday, 1875–1942, vol. IV
Griffith, Ven. Henry Wager, 1850–1932, vol. III
Griffith, Horace Major Brandford, 1863–1909, vol. I
Griffith, Hubert Freeling, 1896–1953, vol. V
Griffith, Hugh Emrys, 1912–1980, vol. VII
Griffith, Rev. James Shaw, 1875–1939, vol. III
Griffith, John Eaton, 1894–1985, vol. VIII
Griffith, Sir John Purser, 1848–1938, vol. III
Griffith, (Llewelyn) Wyn, 1890–1977, vol. VII
Griffith, Patrick Waldron Cobham, 1925–1980, vol. VII
Griffith, Lt-Col Sir Ralph Edwin Hotchkin, 1882–1963, vol. VI
Griffith, Ralph Thomas Hotchkin, 1826–1906, vol. I
Griffith, Sir Richard (John) Waldie-, 3rd Bt (*cr* 1858), 1850–1933, vol. III
Griffith, Rt Hon. Sir Samuel Walker, 1845–1920, vol. II
Griffith, Stewart Cathie, 1914–1993, vol. IX
Griffith, Thomas Wardrop, *died* 1946, vol. IV
Griffith, W. St Bodfan, 1876–1941, vol. IV
Griffith, Walter Spencer Anderson, 1854–1946, vol. IV
Griffith, William, 1868–1953, vol. V
Griffith, Sir William Brandford, 1858–1939, vol. III
Griffith, William Downes, *died* 1908, vol. I
Griffith, William L., 1864–1934, vol. III
Griffith, Wyn; *see* Griffith, L. W.

Griffith-Boscawen Rt Hon. Sir Arthur Sackville Trevor, 1865–1946, vol. IV
Griffith-Jones, Ebenezer, 1860–1942, vol. IV
Griffith-Jones, Sir Eric Newton, 1913–1979, vol. VII
Griffith-Jones, (John) Mervyn (Guthrie), 1909–1979, vol. VII
Griffith-Jones, Mervyn; *see* Griffith-Jones, J. M. G.
Griffith-Jones, Morgan Phillips, 1876–1939, vol. III
Griffith-Jones, Rev. William, 1895–1961, vol. VI
Griffith-Williams, Brig. Eric Llewellyn Griffith, 1894–1987, vol. VIII
Griffiths, Albert Edward, 1908–1970, vol. VI
Griffiths, Bruce Fletcher, 1924–1999, vol. X
Griffiths, Rev. Charles, 1847–1924, vol. II
Griffiths, Major Charles Du Plat R.; *see* Richardson-Griffiths.
Griffiths, Lt-Col Cyril Tracy, 1873–1934, vol. III
Griffiths, Surg. Rear-Adm. Cyril Verity, 1883–1959, vol. V
Griffiths, David, 1896–1977, vol. VII
Griffiths, Sir David Edward, *died* 1957, vol. V
Griffiths, Ven. David Henry, 1864–1926, vol. II
Griffiths, David Nathaniel, *died* 1961, vol. VI
Griffiths, Edward, 1929–1995, vol. IX
Griffiths, Ernest Howard, 1851–1932, vol. III
Griffiths, Sir (Ernest) Roy, 1926–1994, vol. IX
Griffiths, Ezer, 1888–1962, vol. VI
Griffiths, Brig. Felix Alexander Vincent C.; *see* Copland-Griffiths.
Griffiths, Lt-Gen. Francis Home, 1877–1961, vol. VI
Griffiths, George Arthur, 1880–1945, vol. IV
Griffiths, Lt-Col George Cruickshank, 1884–1949, vol. IV
Griffiths, George Hollier, 1839–1911, vol. I
Griffiths, Gilbert, 1901–1979, vol. VII
Griffiths, Captain Hubert Penry, 1894–1983, vol. VIII
Griffiths, Sir Hugh Ernest, 1891–1961, vol. VI
Griffiths, Rt Hon. James, 1890–1975, vol. VII
Griffiths, James Howard Eagle, 1908–1981, vol. VIII
Griffiths, Ven. John, *died* 1897, vol. I
Griffiths, John, *died* 1947, vol. IV
Griffiths, John Edward Seaton, 1908–1991, vol. IX
Griffiths, John G., 1845–1922, vol. II
Griffiths, Lt-Col Sir John Norton-, 1st Bt, 1871–1930, vol. III
Griffiths, John Samuel, *died* 1933, vol. III
Griffiths, Air Cdre John Swire, 1894–1969, vol. VI
Griffiths, John William Roger, 1921–1995, vol. IX (AII)
Griffiths, Col Joseph, *died* 1945, vol. IV
Griffiths, Sir Percival Joseph, 1899–1992, vol. IX
Griffiths, Engr Comdr Percy Frederick, 1873–1960, vol. V
Griffiths, Sir Peter N.; *see* Norton-Griffiths.
Griffiths, Sir Reginald Ernest, 1910–1991, vol. IX
Griffiths, Richard Cerdin, 1915–1985, vol. VIII
Griffiths, Sir Roy; *see* Griffiths, Sir E. R.
Griffiths, Brig.-Gen. Thomas, 1865–1947, vol. IV
Griffiths, Thomas, 1867–1955, vol. V
Griffiths, Trevor, 1913–1993, vol. IX
Griffiths, Vincent, 1831–1917, vol. II
Griffiths, Ward David, 1915–1988, vol. VIII

Griffiths, William, 1912–1973, vol. VII
Griffiths, William Russell, 1845–1910, vol. I
Griffiths, Sir William Thomas, 1895–1952, vol. V
Grigg, Rt Hon. Sir James; see Grigg, Rt Hon. Sir P. J.
Grigg, Rt Hon. Sir (Percy) James, 1890–1964, vol. VI
Grigg-Smith, Rev. Canon Thomas, died 1971, vol. VII
Griggs, Clare H., died 1950, vol. IV
Griggs, Frederick Landseer Maur, 1876–1938, vol. III
Griggs, Hon. John William, 1849–1927, vol. II, vol. III
Griggs, Sir Peter; see Griggs, Sir W. P.
Griggs, Sir (William) Peter, 1854–1920, vol. II
Grignard, (François Auguste) Victor, 1871–1935, vol. III
Grignard, Victor; see Grignard, F. A. V.
Grigorov, Mitko, 1920–1987, vol. VIII
Grigson, Geoffrey Edward Harvey, 1905–1985, vol. VIII
Grigson, (Heather Mabel) Jane, 1928–1990, vol. VIII
Grigson, Jane; see Grigson, H. M. J.
Grigson, Air Cdre John William Boldero, 1893–1943, vol. IV
Grigson, Sir Wilfrid Vernon, 1896–1948, vol. IV
Grigson, Rev. William Shuckforth, 1845–1930, vol. III
Grille, Sir Frederick Louis, 1889–1958, vol. V
Griller, Sidney Aaron, 1911–1993, vol. IX
Grillo, Ernesto N. G., 1877–1946, vol. IV
Grimble, Sir Arthur Francis, 1888–1956, vol. V
Grimble, Augustus, 1840–1925, vol. II
Grime, Arthur, died 1938, vol. III
Grime, Sir Harold Riley, 1896–1984, vol. VIII
Grimes, Ven. (Cecil) John, 1881–1976, vol. VII
Grimes, Ven. John; see Grimes, Ven. C. J.
Grimes, Mary Katharine, 1861–1921, vol. II
Grimes, William Francis, 1905–1988, vol. VIII
Grimley, Bertram Griffiths, 1867–1952, vol. V
Grimond, Baron (Life Peer); Joseph Grimond, 1913–1993, vol. IX
Grimm, Stanley, 1891–1966, vol. VI
Grimmer, Hon. W. C. Hazen, 1858–1945, vol. IV
Grimsdale, Harold Barr, 1866–1942, vol. IV
Grimsditch, Herbert Borthwick, 1898–1971, vol. VII
Grimshaw, Beatrice, died 1953, vol. V
Grimshaw, Captain Cecil Thomas Wrigley, 1875–1915, vol. I
Grimshaw, Most Rev. Francis Joseph, 1901–1965, vol. VI
Grimshaw, Thomas Wrigley, 1839–1900, vol. I
Grimshaw, Sir William Josiah, 1886–1958, vol. V
Grimshawe, Hellier Robert Hadsley G.; see Gosselin-Grimshawe.
Grimston of Westbury, 1st Baron, 1897–1979, vol. VII
Grimston, Col Lionel Augustus, 1868–1943, vol. IV
Grimston, Rev. Hon. Robert, 1860–1927, vol. V
Grimston, Brig.-Gen. Sir Rollo Estouteville, 1861–1916, vol. II
Grimston, Brig.-Gen. Sylvester Bertram, 1864–1924, vol. II

Grimston, William Hunter; see Kendal, W. H.
Grimthorpe, 1st Baron, 1816–1905, vol. I
Grimthorpe, 2nd Baron, 1856–1917, vol. II
Grimthorpe, 3rd Baron, 1891–1963, vol. VI
Grimwade, Hon. Frederick Sheppard, 1840–1910, vol. I
Grimwade, Geoffrey Holt, 1902–1961, vol. VI
Grimwade, Maj.-Gen. Harold William, 1869–1949, vol. IV
Grimwade, Sir Russell; see Grimwade, Sir W. R.
Grimwade, Sir (Wilfrid) Russell, 1879–1955, vol. V
Grimwood, Frank Southgate, 1904–1990, vol. VIII
Grimwood, Lt-Col James, 1873–1934, vol. III
Grindea, Miron, 1909–1995, vol. IX
Grindell-Matthews, Harry, 1880–1941, vol. IV
Grindle, Bernard Richard Theodore, 1879–1955, vol. V
Grindle, Sir Gilbert Edmund Augustine, 1869–1934, vol. III
Grindle, Captain John Annesley, 1900–1991, vol. IX
Grinke, Frederick Otto, 1911–1987, vol. VIII
Grinling, Charles Herbert, 1870–1906, vol. I
Grinling, Brig. Edward Johns, 1889–1963, vol. VI
Grinlinton, Frederick Henry, 1853–1938, vol. III
Grinlinton, Sir John Joseph, 1828–1912, vol. I
Grinsted, Harold, 1889–1955, vol. V
Gripenberg, Georg Achates, 1890–1975, vol. VII
Gripper, Col Hugh Thomas, 1867–1956, vol. V
Griscom, Sir Lloyd C., 1872–1959, vol. V
Grisdale, Rt Rev. John, born 1845, vol. II
Grisewood, Frederick Henry, 1888–1972, vol. VII
Grisewood, Harman Joseph Gerard, 1906–1996, vol. X
Grissell, Hartwell de la Garde, 1839–1907, vol. I
Grist, Frederic Edwin, 1883–1951, vol. V
Griswold, A(lfred) Whitney, 1906–1963, vol. VI
Griswold, Rev. H. D., 1860–1945, vol. IV
Griswold, Rt Rev. Sheldon M., 1861–1930, vol. III
Gritten, William George Howard, died 1943, vol. IV
Grobecker, Ven. Geoffrey Frank, 1922–1989, vol. VIII
Groener, Maria, 1883–1937, vol. III
Grogan, Brig.-Gen. Edward George, 1851–1944, vol. IV
Grogan, Col Sir Edward Ion Beresford, 2nd Bt, 1873–1927, vol. II
Grogan, Lt-Col George Meredyth, died 1942, vol. IV
Grogan, Brig.-Gen. George William St George, 1875–1962, vol. VI
Grogan, William Edward, 1863–1937, vol. III
Grohman, Vice-Adm. Harold Tom B.; see Baillie-Grohman.
Grohman, William A. B.; see Baillie-Grohman.
Gromyko, Andrei Andreevich, 1909–1989, vol. VIII
Gronchi, Giovanni, 1887–1978, vol. VII
Gronhaug, Arnold Conrad, 1921–1999, vol. X
Gronow, Albert George, 1878–1950, vol. IV
Gronow, Alun Gwilym, 1931–1989, vol. VIII
Groom, Gladys Laurence, (Mrs M. Cordellis), died 1948, vol. IV (A)
Groom, Hon. Sir Littleton Ernest, 1867–1936, vol. III

Groom, Percy, 1865–1931, vol. III
Groom, Sir Reginald; see Groom, Sir T. R.
Groom, Sir (Thomas) Reginald, 1906–1987, vol. VIII
Groom, Air Marshal Sir Victor Emmanuel, 1898–1990, vol. VIII
Groome, Francis Hindes, 1851–1902, vol. I
Groome, Adm. Robert Leonard, 1848–1917, vol. II
Gropius, Walter, 1883–1969, vol. VI
Gropper, William, 1897–1977, vol. VII
Grose, Frank Samuel, 1881–1941, vol. IV
Grose, Sir James Trevilly, 1872–1944, vol. IV
Grose-Hodge, Humfrey, 1891–1962, vol. VI
Gross, Anthony Imre Alexander, 1905–1984, vol. VIII
Gross, Edward John, 1844–1923, vol. II
Gross, Richard Oliver, 1882–1964, vol. VI
Grosschmid-Zsögöd, Géza Benjamin, 1918–1992, vol. IX
Grossmith, Caryll Archibald, 1895–1964, vol. VI
Grossmith, George, 1847–1912, vol. I
Grossmith, George, 1874–1934, vol. III
Grossmith, (Walter) Weedon, 1854–1919, vol. II
Grossmith, Weedon; see Grossmith, Walter W.
Grosvenor, Earl; Edward George Hugh Grosvenor, 1904–1909, vol. I
Grosvenor, Countess; (Sibell Mary), 1855–1929, vol. III
Grosvenor, Lord Arthur Hugh, 1860–1929, vol. III
Grosvenor, Mrs Beatrice Elizabeth Katherine, 1915–1985, vol. VIII
Grosvenor, Caroline, died 1940, vol. III
Grosvenor, Lord Edward Arthur, 1892–1929, vol. III
Grosvenor, Lord Gerald Richard, 1874–1940, vol. III
Grosvenor, Hon. Gilbert, 1881–1939, vol. III
Grosvenor, Gilbert Hovey, 1875–1966, vol. VI
Grosvenor, Lady Henry, (Rosamund Angharad), died 1941, vol. IV
Grosvenor, Lord Henry George, 1861–1914, vol. I
Grosvenor, Captain Lord Hugh William, 1884–1914, vol. II
Grosvenor, John Ernest, 1887–1963, vol. VI
Grosvenor, Hon. Richard Cecil, 1848–1919, vol. II
Grosvenor, Captain Robert Arthur, 1895–1953, vol. V
Grosvenor, Rosamund Angharad; see Grosvenor, Lady Henry.
Grosvenor, Vernon William, 1889–1961, vol. VI
Grotrian, Frederick Brent, died 1905, vol. I
Grotrian, Sir Herbert Brent, 1st Bt, 1870–1951, vol. V
Grotrian, Sir John Appelbe Brent, 2nd Bt, 1904–1984, vol. VIII
Grouard, Rt Rev. Mgr Emile, 1840–1931, vol. III
Grounds, George Ambrose, 1886–1983, vol. VIII
Grounds, Sir Roy Burman, 1905–1981, vol. VIII
Grounds, Stanley Paterson, 1904–1999, vol. X
Grousset, René, 1885–1952, vol. V
Grout, Rev. George W. G., 1837–1917, vol. II
Grout, Reginald George, 1901–1963, vol. VI
Grove, Agnes, (Lady Grove), 1864–1926, vol. II
Grove, Alfred John, 1888–1962, vol. VI
Grove, Archibald; see Grove, T. N. A.

Grove, Maj.-Gen. Sir Coleridge, 1839–1920, vol. II
Grove, Brig.-Gen. Edward Aickin William Stewart, 1852–1932, vol. III
Grove, Lt-Col Ernest William, 1870–1939, vol. III
Grove, Sir George, 1820–1900, vol. I
Grove, George Alexander, 1908–1971, vol. VII
Grove, Sir Gerald, 3rd Bt, 1886–1962, vol. VI
Grove, Henry Montgomery, 1867–1942, vol. IV
Grove, Col Reginald Parker, 1859–1942, vol. IV
Grove, (Thomas Newcomen) Archibald, died 1920, vol. II
Grove, Col Thomas Thackeray, 1879–1965, vol. VI
Grove, Sir Walter Felipe Philip, 4th Bt, 1927–1974, vol. VII
Grove, Sir Walter John, 2nd Bt, 1852–1932, vol. III
Grove-Hills, Col Edmond Herbert, 1864–1922, vol. II
Grove-White, Col James, 1852–1938, vol. III
Grove-White, Lt-Gen. Sir Maurice Fitzgibbon, 1887–1965, vol. VI
Grover, Sir Anthony Charles, 1907–1981, vol. VIII
Grover, Maj.-Gen. John Malcolm Lawrence, 1897–1979, vol. VII
Grover, Gen. Sir Malcolm Henry Stanley, 1858–1945, vol. IV
Grover, Montague Macgregor, 1870–1943, vol. IV
Groves, Sir Charles Barnard, 1915–1992, vol. IX
Groves, Charles Nixon, 1871–1950, vol. IV
Groves, Ernest William Hey, 1872–1944, vol. IV
Groves, Herbert Austen, 1880–1943, vol. IV
Groves, James Grimble, 1854–1914, vol. I
Groves, Sir John, 1828–1905, vol. I
Groves, Col John Edward Grimble, 1863–1948, vol. IV
Groves, Brig.-Gen. Percy Robert Clifford, died 1959, vol. V
Groves, Ronald, 1908–1991, vol. IX
Groves, Thomas Edward, 1884–1958, vol. V
Groves-Raines, Lt-Col Ralph Gore Devereux; see Raines.
Grozier, Edwin Atkins, 1859–1924, vol. II
Grubb, Col Alexander Henry Watkins, 1873–1933, vol. III
Grubb, Edward, 1854–1939, vol. III
Grubb, Lt-Col Herbert Watkins, 1875–1934, vol. III
Grubb, Sir Howard, 1844–1931, vol. III
Grubb, Sir Kenneth George, 1900–1980, vol. VII
Grubb, Violet Margaret, 1898–1985, vol. VIII
Grubbe, Adm. Sir Walter James H.; see Hunt-Grubbe.
Grubbe, Walter John, died 1926, vol. II
Gruber, Rudolph, 1868–1945, vol. IV
Grueber, Herbert Appold, 1846–1927, vol. II
Gruenther, Gen. Alfred Maximilian, 1899–1983, vol. VIII
Gruer, Harold George, 1886–1956, vol. V
Gruffydd, William John, 1881–1954, vol. V
Grumell, Ernest Sydney, 1885–1962, vol. VI
Grummitt, John Halliday, 1901–1974, vol. VII
Grundy, Cecil Reginald, 1870–1944, vol. II
Grundy, Sir Claude Herbert, 1891–1967, vol. VI
Grundy, Sir Cuthbert Cartwright, 1846–1946, vol. IV
Grundy, Air Marshal Sir Edouard Michael FitzFrederick, 1908–1987, vol. VIII

Grundy, Eustace Beardoe, 1849–1938, vol. III
Grundy, Francis, 1882–1953, vol. V
Grundy, Fred, 1905–1989, vol. VIII
Grundy, George Beardoe, *died* 1948, vol. IV
Grundy, John Brownsdon Clowes, 1902–1987, vol. VIII
Grundy, Rupert Francis Brooks, 1903–1988, vol. VIII
Grundy, Sydney, 1848–1914, vol. I
Grundy, Thomas Walter, 1864–1942, vol. IV
Grundy, Wilfred Walker, 1884–1936, vol. III
Grundy, William Mitchell, *died* 1960, vol. V
Grüneberg, Hans, 1907–1982, vol. VIII
Grunfeld, Henry, 1904–1999, vol. X
Gruning, John Frederick, 1870–1922, vol. II
Grutschnig, Karl, 1888–1965, vol. VI (AII)
Grylls, Charles John Tench Bedford, 1874–1946, vol. IV
Grylls, Rear-Adm. Henry John Bedford, 1903–1978, vol. VII
Grylls, Rosalie Glynn; *see* Mander, Lady (Rosalie).
Gryn, Rabbi Hugo Gabriel, 1930–1996, vol. X
Gsell, Most Rev. Francis Xavier, 1872–1960, vol. V
Guard, Lt-Col Frederic Henry Wickham, *died* 1927, vol. II
Gubbay, Henri Abraham, 1883–1940, vol. III
Gubbay, Moses Mordecai Simeon, 1876–1947, vol. IV
Gubbins, Sir Charles O'Grady, *died* 1911, vol. I
Gubbins, Maj.-Gen. Sir Colin McVean, 1896–1976, vol. VII
Gubbins, Frederick Bebb, 1818–1902, vol. I
Gubbins, John Harington, 1852–1929, vol. III
Gubbins, John R., 1839–1906, vol. I
Gubbins, Nathaniel; *see* Mott, Edward Spencer.
Gubbins, Lt-Col Richard Rolls, 1868–1918, vol. II
Gubbins, Lt-Col Stamer, 1882–1940, vol. III
Gubbins, Lt-Gen. Sir W. Launcelotte, 1849–1925, vol. II
Gubbins, Major William John Mounsey, 1907–1979, vol. VII
Gudenian, Haig, 1918–1985, vol. VIII
Gudgeon, Stanley Herbert, 1896–1966, vol. VI
Gudjonsson, Halldór; *see* Laxness, H. K.
Guðmundsson, Guðmundur I., 1909–1987, vol. IX (AI)
Guébhard, Madame; *see* Severine, Madame.
Guedalla, Philip, 1889–1944, vol. IV
Guedella, Mrs Herbert; *see* Hanbury, Lily.
Guerbel, Countess de; *see* Ward, Dame Genevieve.
Guerin, Hon. Edmund, 1858–1934, vol. III
Guerin, Hon. James John, 1856–1932, vol. III
Guérisse, Count Albert Marie Edmond, 1911–1989, vol. VII
Gueritz, Edward Peregrine, 1855–1938, vol. III
Guernsey, Lord; Heneage Greville Finch, 1883–1914, vol. I
Guess, George A., 1873–1954, vol. V
Guest, Baron (Life Peer); Christopher William Graham Guest, 1901–1984, vol. VIII
Guest, Air Marshal Sir Charles Edward Neville, 1900–1977, vol. VII
Guest, Lt-Col Hon. (Christian) Henry (Charles), 1874–1957, vol. V
Guest, Douglas Albert, 1916–1996, vol. X

Guest, Eric Ronald, 1904–1997, vol. X
Guest, Col Hon. Sir Ernest Lucas, 1882–1972, vol. VII
Guest, Captain Rt Hon. Frederick Edward, 1875–1937, vol. III
Guest, Lt-Col Hon. Henry; *see* Guest, Lt-Col Hon. C. H. C.
Guest, Henry Alan, 1920–1999, vol. X
Guest, John, 1867–1931, vol. III
Guest, Hon. Lionel George William, 1880–1935, vol. III
Guest, Montagu, 1839–1909, vol. I
Guest, Hon. Oscar Montague, 1888–1958, vol. V
Guest, Thomas Merthyr, 1838–1904, vol. I
Guest, Trevor George, 1928–1999, vol. X
Guest, William Campbell, 1864–1932, vol. III
Guest Williams, Rev. Samuel Blackwell, 1851–1920, vol. II
Gueterbock, Col Sir Paul Gottlieb Julius, 1886–1954, vol. V
Guggenheim, Edward Armand, 1901–1970, vol. VI
Guggisberg, Decima (Lady Guggisberg); *see* Moore Guggisberg.
Guggisberg, Brig.-Gen. Sir (Frederick) Gordon, 1869–1930, vol. III
Guggisberg, Brig.-Gen. Sir Gordon; *see* Guggisberg, Brig.-Gen. Sir F. G.
Gui, Vittorio, 1885–1975, vol. VII
Guibault, Joseph Alexandre, 1870–1940, vol. III (A), vol. IV
Guichard, Beatrice Catherine, (Beatrice Baskerville), 1878–1955, vol. V
Guider, James Adolphus, 1862–1943, vol. IV
Guidotti, Gastone, 1901–1982, vol. VIII
Guilbert, Yvette, 1865–1944, vol. IV
Guild David Alexander, 1884–1961, vol. VI
Guild, Surgeon Captain William John Forbes, 1908–1982, vol. VIII
Guilford, 8th Earl of, 1876–1949, vol. IV
Guilford, 9th Earl of, 1933–1999, vol. X
Guilford, Rev. Edward, 1853–1937, vol. III
Guillamore, 5th Viscount, 1841–1918, vol. II
Guillamore, 6th Viscount, 1847–1927, vol. II
Guillamore, 7th Viscount, 1860–1930, vol. III
Guillamore, 8th Viscount, 1867–1943, vol. IV
Guillamore, 9th Viscount, 1869–1955, vol. V
Guilland, Antoine, 1861–1938, vol. III
Guillaume, Rev. Alfred, 1888–1965, vol. VI
Guillaume, Charles Edouard, 1861–1938, vol. III
Guillebaud, Claude William, 1890–1971, vol. VII
Guillebaud, Walter Henry, 1890–1973, vol. VII
Guillemard, Francis Henry Hill, 1852–1933, vol. III
Guillemard, Hugh W.; *see* Wilkinson-Guillemard, W. H. J.
Guillemard, Sir Laurence Nunns, 1862–1951, vol. V
Guillum Scott, Sir John Arthur, 1910–1983, vol. VIII
Guilly, Rt Rev. Richard Lester, 1905–1996, vol. X
Guiney, John, 1868–1931, vol. III
Guiney, Louise Imogen, *died* 1920, vol. II
Guiney, Patrick, 1862–1913, vol. I
Guinness, Sir Alec, 1914–2000, vol. X
Guinness, Sir Algernon Arthur St Lawrence Lee, 3rd Bt, 1883–1954, vol. V
Guinness, Hon. (Arthur) Ernest, 1876–1949, vol. IV

Guinness, Arthur Eustace Seymour, 1867–1955, vol. V
Guinness, Hon. Sir Arthur Robert, 1846–1913, vol. I
Guinness, Sir Arthur Rundell, 1895–1951, vol. V
Guinness, Benjamin Lee, 1842–1900, vol. I
Guinness, Benjamin Seymour, 1868–1947, vol. IV
Guinness, Lt Eric Cecil, 1894–1920, vol. II
Guinness, Hon. Ernest; see Guinness, Hon. A. E.
Guinness, Rev. Henry Grattan, 1835–1910, vol. I
Guinness, Henry Samuel Howard, 1888–1975, vol. VII
Guinness, Henry Seymour, 1858–1945, vol. IV
Guinness, Col Henry William Newton, 1854–1925, vol. II
Guinness, Loel; see Guinness, T. L. E. B.
Guinness, Sir Reginald Robert Bruce, 1842–1909, vol. I
Guinness, Robert Darley, 1858–1938, vol. III
Guinness, Thomas Loel Evelyn Bulkeley, 1906–1988, vol. VIII
Guiringaud, Louis de, 1911–1982, vol. VIII
Guise, Sir Anselm William Edward, 6th Bt, 1888–1970, vol. VI
Guise, Sir John, 1914–1991, vol. IX
Guise, Sir William Francis George, 5th Bt, 1851–1920, vol. II
Guise-Moores, Col Charles Frederick; see Moores.
Guise-Moores, Maj.-Gen. Sir Guise, 1863–1942, vol. IV
Guitry, Lucien, 1860–1925, vol. II
Guitry, Sacha, 1885–1957, vol. V
Gujadhur, Hon. Sir Radhamohun, 1909–1988, vol. IX (AI)
Gulbenkian, Calouste Sarkis, 1869–1955, vol. V
Gulbenkian, Nubar Sarkis, 1896–1972, vol. VII
Gull, Sir Cameron; see Gull, Sir W. C.
Gull, Cyril Arthur Edward Ranger, 1876–1923, vol. II
Gull, Sir Michael Swinnerton Cameron, 4th Bt, 1919–1989, vol. VIII
Gull, Captain Sir Richard Cameron, 3rd Bt, 1894–1960, vol. V
Gull, Sir (William) Cameron, 2nd Bt, 1860–1922, vol. II
Gullan, Marjorie Isabel Morton, died 1959, vol. V
Gulland, George Lovell, 1862–1941, vol. IV
Gulland, John Alan, 1926–1990, vol. VIII
Gulland, John Masson, 1898–1947, vol. IV
Gulland, Rt Hon. John William, 1864–1920, vol. II
Gullett, Hon. Sir Henry Somer, 1878–1940, vol. III
Gullick, Joseph William, died 1909, vol. I
Gulliver, James Gerald, 1930–1996, vol. X
Gullstrand, Allvar, 1862–1930, vol. III
Gully, Hon. Edward Walford Karslake, 1870–1931, vol. III
Gumbleton, Rt Rev. Maxwell Homfray M.; see Maxwell-Gumbleton.
Gumbley, Douglas William Mew, 1880–1973, vol. VII
Gumley, Sir Louis Stewart, 1872–1941, vol. IV
Gummer, Ellis Norman, 1915–1999, vol. X
Gümrükçüoglu, Rohmi Kamil, 1927–1998, vol. X
Gun, William Townsend Jackson, 1876–1946, vol. IV
Gundelach, Finn Olav, 1925–1981, vol. VIII

Gundry, Rev. Canon Dudley William, 1916–1990, vol. VIII
Gundry, Philip George, 1877–1929, vol. III
Gundry, Richard Simpson, 1838–1924, vol. II
Gunesekera, Sir Frank Arnold, 1887–1952, vol. V
Gunlake, John Henry, 1905–1990, vol. VIII
Gunn, (Alan) Richard, 1936–1998, vol. X
Gunn, Major Alistair Dudley, 1884–1943, vol. IV
Gunn, Alistair Livingston, 1903–1970, vol. VI
Gunn, Battiscombe George, 1883–1950, vol. IV
Gunn, Bunty Moffat, 1923–1994, vol. IX (AII)
Gunn, Air Marshal Sir George Roy, 1910–1974, vol. VII
Gunn, Herbert Smith, 1904–1962, vol. VI
Gunn, Hugh, 1870–1931, vol. III
Gunn, Sir James, 1893–1964, vol. VI
Gunn, James Andrew, 1882–1958, vol. V
Gunn, Sir John, 1837–1918, vol. II
Gunn, Col John Alexander, 1878–1960, vol. VI (AI)
Gunn, Maj.-Gen. John Alexander, 1873–1966, vol. V (A), vol. VI
Gunn, John William Cormack, 1889–1941, vol. IV
Gunn, Neil M., 1891–1973, vol. VII
Gunn, Peter Nicholson, 1914–1995, vol. IX
Gunn, Richard; see Gunn, A. R.
Gunn, Robert Marcus, 1850–1909, vol. I
Gunnarsson, Gunnar, 1889–1975, vol. VII
Gunning, Brig.-Gen. Sir Charles Vere, 7th Bt, 1859–1950, vol. IV
Gunning, Sir Frederick Digby, 6th Bt, 1853–1906, vol. I
Gunning, Col George Hamilton, 1876–1936, vol. III
Gunning, Sir George William, 5th Bt, 1828–1903, vol. I
Gunning, John Edward Maitland, 1904–1992, vol. IX
Gunning, Col Orlando George, 1867–1917, vol. II
Gunning, Sir (Orlando) Peter, 1908–1964, vol. VI
Gunning, Sir Peter; see Gunning, Sir O. P.
Gunning, Sir Robert Charles, 8th Bt, 1901–1989, vol. VIII
Gunsaulus, Frank Wakeley, 1856–1921, vol. II
Gunsbourg, Raoul, 1859–1955, vol. V
Gunson, Sir James Henry, 1877–1963, vol. VI
Gunston, Major Sir Derrick Wellesley, 1st Bt, 1891–1985, vol. VIII
Gunston, Sir Richard Wellesley, 2nd Bt, 1924–1991, vol. IX
Gunter, Archibald Clavering, 1847–1907, vol. I
Gunter, Eustace Edward, 1873–1935, vol. III
Gunter, Lt-Col Francis Ernest, 1869–1936, vol. III
Gunter, Sir Geoffrey Campbell, 1879–1961, vol. VI
Gunter, Maj.-Gen. James, 1833–1908, vol. I
Gunter, Rt Hon. Raymond Jones, 1909–1977, vol. VII
Gunter, Sir Robert, 1st Bt, 1831–1905, vol. I
Gunter, Col Sir Robert Benyon Nevill, 2nd Bt, 1871–1917, vol. II
Gunter, Sir Ronald Vernon, 3rd Bt, 1904–1980, vol. VII
Günther, Albert Charles Lewis Gotthilf, 1830–1914, vol. I
Gunther, Charles Eugene, 1863–1931, vol. III
Gunther, Eustace Rolfe, 1902–1940, vol. III

Gunther, John, 1901–1970, vol. VI
Gunther, Sir John Thomson, 1910–1984, vol. VIII
Gunther, Robert Theodore, 1869–1940, vol. III
Gunther, Ven. William James, 1839–1918, vol. II
Guppy, Henry, 1861–1948, vol. IV
Guppy, Henry Brougham, 1854–1926, vol. II
Guppy, Ronald James, 1916–1977, vol. VII
Gupta, Bihari Lal, 1849–1916, vol. II
Gupta, J. N., 1870–1947, vol. IV (A), vol. V
Gupta, Sir Krishna Govinda, 1851–1926, vol. II
Gupta, Satyendra Nath, 1895–1956, vol. V
Gurd, Surg. Rear-Adm. Dudley Plunket, 1910–1987, vol. VIII
Gurden, Sir Harold Edward, 1903–1989, vol. VIII
Gurdon, Lt-Col Bertrand Evelyn Mellish, 1867–1949, vol. IV
Gurdon, Charles, 1855–1931, vol. III
Gurdon, Maj.-Gen. Edward Temple Leigh, 1896–1959, vol. V
Gurdon, Maj.-Gen. Evelyn Pulteney, 1833–1921, vol. II
Gurdon, Rt Rev. Francis, 1861–1929, vol. III
Gurdon, Lt-Col Philip Richard Thornhagh, 1863–1942, vol. IV
Gurdon, Rt Hon. Sir William Brampton, 1840–1910, vol. I
Gurion, David B.; see Ben-Gurion.
Gurnell, Engr Rear-Adm. Thompson, 1878–1965, vol. VI
Gurner, Sir (Cyril) Walter, 1888–1960, vol. V
Gurner, Henry Edward, 1853–1915, vol. I
Gurner, John Augustus, 1854–1937, vol. III
Gurner, Stanley Ronald Kershaw, 1890–1939, vol. III
Gurner, Vice-Adm. Victor Gallafent, 1869–1950, vol. IV
Gurner, Sir Walter; see Gurner, Sir C. W.
Gurney, (Ernest) Russell, 1879–1958, vol. V
Gurney, Sir Eustace, 1876–1927, vol. II
Gurney, Sir Henry Lovell Goldsworthy, 1898–1951, vol. V
Gurney, Rev. Henry Palin, 1847–1904, vol. I
Gurney, Sir Hugh, 1878–1968, vol. VI
Gurney, John Henry, 1848–1922, vol. II
Gurney, Martyn Pierre Cecil, 1861–1930, vol. III
Gurney, Norman William, 1880–1973, vol. VII
Gurney, Quintin Edward, 1883–1968, vol. VI
Gurney, Russell; see Gurney, E. R.
Gurney, Maj.-Gen. Russell, 1890–1947, vol. IV
Gurney, Sir Somerville Arthur, 1835–1917, vol. II
Gurney, Sir Walter Edwin, died 1924, vol. II
Gurney-Dixon, Sir Samuel, 1878–1970, vol. VI
Gurney-Salter, Emma, 1875–1967, vol. VI
Gurnhill, Rev. James, died 1928, vol. II
Gurowski, Major Count Dudley Beaumont, 1865–1939, vol. III
Gustafsson, Greta Lovisa; see Garbo, G.
Gutch, Sir John, 1905–1988, vol. VIII
Guthrie, Hon. Lord; Charles John Guthrie, 1849–1920, vol. II
Guthrie, Hon. Lord; Henry Wallace Guthrie, 1903–1970, vol. VI
Guthrie, Charles, died 1953, vol. V
Guthrie, Charles John; see Guthrie, Hon. Lord.

Guthrie, Captain Sir Connop, 1st Bt, 1882–1945, vol. IV
Guthrie, David Charles, 1861–1918, vol. II
Guthrie, Douglas James, 1885–1975, vol. VII
Guthrie, Sir Giles Connop McEacharn, 2nd Bt, 1916–1979, vol. VII
Guthrie, Henry Wallace; see Guthrie, Hon. Lord.
Guthrie, Hon. Hugh, 1866–1939, vol. III
Guthrie, Sir James, 1859–1930, vol. III
Guthrie, John Douglas Maude, 1856–1928, vol. II
Guthrie, Air Vice-Marshal Kenneth MacGregor, 1900–1993, vol. IX
Guthrie, Leonard George, 1858–1918, vol. II
Guthrie, Malcolm, 1903–1972, vol. VII
Guthrie, Mrs Murray, died 1945, vol. IV
Guthrie, Ramsay; see Bowran, Rev. J. G.
Guthrie, Robert Lyall, 1867–1937, vol. III
Guthrie, Robin Craig, 1902–1971, vol. VII
Guthrie, Hon. Sir Rutherford Campbell, 1899–1990, vol. VIII
Guthrie, Thomas Anstey, 1856–1934, vol. III
Guthrie, Thomas Maule, died 1943, vol. IV
Guthrie, Sir Tyrone; see Guthrie, Sir W. T.
Guthrie, Walter Murray, 1869–1911, vol. I
Guthrie, William, 1835–1908, vol. I
Guthrie, William Keith Chambers, 1906–1981, vol. VIII
Guthrie, Sir (William) Tyrone, 1900–1971, vol. VII
Guthrie-James, David, 1919–1986, vol. VIII
Guthrie-Smith, William Herbert, 1861–1940, vol. III
Gutierrez-Ponce, Don Ignacio, died 1942, vol. IV
Gutt, Camille, 1884–1971, vol. VII
Gutteridge, Harold Cooke, 1876–1953, vol. V
Gutteridge, Joyce Ada Cooke, 1906–1992, vol. IX
Guttery, Rev. Arthur Thomas, 1862–1920, vol. II
Guttery, Sir Norman Arthur, 1889–1962, vol. VI
Guttmann, Sir Ludwig, 1899–1980, vol. VII
Guttridge, George Herbert, 1898–1969, vol. VI
Guy, Comdr Basil John Douglas, 1882–1956, vol. V
Guy, Rt Rev. Basil Tudor, 1910–1975, vol. VII
Guy, Ven. Cuthbert Arnold, 1884–1954, vol. V
Guy, Rev. Douglas Sherwood, 1885–1934, vol. III
Guy, Sir Henry Lewis, 1887–1956, vol. V
Guy, Hon. James Allan, 1890–1980, vol. VII
Guy, John Crawford, 1861–1928, vol. II
Guy, Oswald Vernon, 1890–1973, vol. VII
Guy, Lt-Col Philip Langstaffe Ord, 1885–1952, vol. V
Guy, Lt-Col Robert Francis, 1878–1927, vol. II
Guy, Sydney Slater, 1884–1971, vol. VII
Guy, William, 1859–1950, vol. IV
Guy, William Henry, died 1968, vol. VI
Guymer, Maurice Juniper, 1914–1985, vol. VIII
Guymer, Robert, 1908–1981, vol. VIII
Guyomard, Rt Rev. John Alfred, 1884–1956, vol. V
Guyot, Y.; see Yves-Guyot.
Gwalior, HH Maharajah Sindhia of, 1876–1925, vol. II
Gwalior, Ruler of, 1916–1961, vol. VI
Gwandu, Emir of; Alhaji Haruna Muhammadu Basharu, 1913–1995, vol. X (AI)
Gwatkin, Frank Trelawny Arthur A.; see Ashton-Gwatkin.

Gwatkin, Maj.-Gen. Sir Frederick, 1885–1969, vol. VI
Gwatkin, Col Frederick Stapleton, 1849–1940, vol. III
Gwatkin, Rev. Henry Melvill, died 1916, vol. II
Gwatkin, Brig. Sir Norman Wilmshurst, 1899–1971, vol. VII
Gwatkin, Rev. Walter Henry Trelawny Ashton-, 1861–1945, vol. IV
Gwatkin, Maj.-Gen. Sir Willoughby Garnons, 1859–1925, vol. II
Gwatkin-Williams, Captain Rupert Stanley, died 1949, vol. IV
Gwenn, Edmund, 1877–1959, vol. V
Gwillim, Calvert Merton, died 1972, vol. VII
Gwillim, John Cole, died 1920, vol. II
Gwilt, Richard Lloyd, 1901–1972, vol. VII
Gwydyr, 4th Baron, 1810–1909, vol. I
Gwydyr, 5th Baron, 1841–1915, vol. I
Gwyer, Barbara Elizabeth, died 1974, vol. VII
Gwyer, Rt Rev. Herbert Linford, died 1960, vol. V
Gwyer, Sir Maurice Linford, 1878–1952, vol. V
Gwyn, Tatham, 1839–1915, vol. I
Gwyn-Thomas, Brig.-Gen. Gwyn, 1871–1946, vol. IV
Gwynn, Maj.-Gen. Sir Charles William, 1870–1963, vol. VI
Gwynn, Denis Rolleston, 1893–1971, vol. VII
Gwynn, Edward John, 1868–1941, vol. IV
Gwynn, Rev. John, 1827–1917, vol. II, vol. III
Gwynn, John Tudor, 1881–1956, vol. V
Gwynn, Rev. Robert Malcolm, 1877–1962, vol. VI
Gwynn, Stephen Lucius, 1864–1950, vol. IV
Gwynn, Col William Purnell, died 1940, vol. III
Gwynne, Comdr Alban Lewis, 1880–1942, vol. IV
Gwynne, Brig. Alfred Howel E.; see Evans-Gwynne.
Gwynne, Clement Wansbrough, 1883–1939, vol. III
Gwynne, H. A., 1865–1950, vol. IV
Gwynne, Hon. J. W., died 1902, vol. I
Gwynne, Rt Rev. Llewellyn Henry, 1863–1957, vol. V

Gwynne, Maj.-Gen. Nadolig Ximenes, 1832–1920, vol. II
Gwynne, Nevile Gwyn, 1868–1951, vol. V
Gwynne, Paul; see Slater, Ernest.
Gwynne, Brig.-Gen. Reginald John, 1863–1942, vol. IV
Gwynne, Lt-Col Sir Roland Vaughan, died 1971, vol. VII
Gwynne, Rupert Sackville, 1873–1924, vol. II
Gwynne-Evans, Sir Evan Gwynne, 2nd Bt, 1877–1959, vol. V
Gwynne-Evans, Sir Francis Loring, 4th Bt, 1914–1993, vol. IX
Gwynne-Evans, Sir Ian William, 3rd Bt, 1909–1985, vol. VIII
Gwynne-Evans, Sir William, 1st Bt, 1845–1927, vol. II
Gwynne-Hughes, John Williams; see Hughes.
Gwynne-James, Sir Arthur Gwynne; see James.
Gwynne-Jones, Allan, 1892–1982, vol. VIII
Gwynne-Jones, Howell, 1890–1946, vol. IV
Gwynne-Vaughan, David Thomas, 1871–1915, vol. I
Gwynne-Vaughan, Dame Helen Charlotte Isabella, 1879–1967, vol. VI
Gwyther, Ven. Arthur, died 1921, vol. II
Gwyther, Frank Edwin, died 1918, vol. II
Gwyther, Lt-Col Graham Howard, 1872–1934, vol. III
Gwyther, Reginald Duncan, 1887–1965, vol. VI
Gwyther, Very Rev. William Clements, 1866–1940, vol. III
Gye, Ernest Frederick, 1879–1955, vol. V
Gye, Percy, 1845–1916, vol. II
Gye, William Ewart, 1884–1952, vol. V
Gyee, Sir Maung, 1886–1971, vol. VII
Gyi, Sir Joseph Augustus Maung, 1872–1955, vol. V
Györgi, Albert S.; see Szent-Györgyi.
Gyp, Sybille Gabrielle Marie Antoinette de Riquetti de Mirabeau, Comtesse de Martel, died 1932, vol. III
Gzowski, Sir Casimir Stanislas, 1813–1898, vol. I

H

Haag, Carl, 1820–1915, vol. I
Haag, Norman C., 1871–1950, vol. IV
Haagner, Alwin Karl, 1880–1962, vol. VI
Haarhoff, T. J., 1892–1971, vol. VII
Haas, Paul, 1877–1960, vol. V
Haavelmo, Trygve, 1911–1999, vol. X
Habberton, John, 1842–1921, vol. II
Habdank-Woynicz; see Voynich, Wilfrid Michael.
Häberlin, Henry, 1868–1947, vol. IV
Habershon, Samuel Herbert, 1857–1915, vol. I
Hacault, Most Rev. Antoine, 1926–2000, vol. X
Hackenley, Most Rev. John, 1877–1943, vol. IV
Hacker, Arthur, 1858–1919, vol. II
Hacker, Louis Morton, 1899–1987, vol. VIII
Hacket-Thompson, Brig.-Gen. Frederick; see Thompson.
Hackett, Most Rev. Bernard, died 1932, vol. III

Hackett, Brian, 1911–1998, vol. X
Hackett, Cecil Arthur, 1908–2000, vol. X
Hackett, Felix E. W., 1882–1970, vol. VI (AII)
Hackett, Francis, 1883–1962, vol. VI
Hackett, Very Rev. Henry Monck Mason, 1849–1933, vol. III
Hackett, Hon. Sir John Winthrop, 1848–1916, vol. II
Hackett, Gen. Sir John Winthrop, 1910–1997, vol. X
Hackett, Sir Maurice Frederick, 1905–1980, vol. VII
Hackett, Col Robert Isaac Dalby, 1857–1925, vol. II
Hackett, Very Rev. T. Aylmer P., 1854–1928, vol. II
Hackett, Walter, 1876–1944, vol. IV
Hackett, Walter William, 1874–1964, vol. VI
Hackett, William Henry, 1853–1926, vol. II

Hackforth, Edgar, *died* 1952, vol. V
Hackforth, Reginald, 1887–1957, vol. V
Hacking, 1st Baron, 1884–1950, vol. IV
Hacking, 2nd Baron, 1910–1971, vol. VII
Hacking, Ven. Egbert, 1854–1936, vol. III
Hacking, Sir James, 1850–1929, vol. III
Hacking, Sir John, 1888–1969, vol. VI
Hackney, Rev. Walter, 1852–1938, vol. III
Hadath, Gunby, *died* 1954, vol. V
Hadcock, Sir (Albert) George, 1861–1936, vol. III
Hadcock, Sir George; *see* Hadcock, Sir A. G.
Hadden, Sir Charles Frederick, 1854–1924, vol. II
Hadden, J. Cuthbert, 1816–1914, vol. I
Hadden, Rev. Robert Henry, 1854–1909, vol. I
Hadden-Paton, Maj. Adrian Gerard Nigel, 1918–1991, vol. IX
Haddington, 11th Earl of, 1827–1917, vol. II
Haddington, 12th Earl of, 1894–1986, vol. VIII
Haddock, Edgar Augustus, 1859–1926, vol. II
Haddock, George Bahr, 1863–1930, vol. III
Haddock, Captain Herbert James, 1861–1946, vol. IV
Haddock, Rev. Jeremiah William, *died* 1913, vol. I
Haddock, Maurice Robert, 1909–1974, vol. VII
Haddon, Alfred Cort, 1855–1940, vol. III
Haddon, Archibald, *died* 1942, vol. IV
Haddon, Eric Edwin, 1908–1984, vol. VIII
Haddon, Frederick William, 1839–1906, vol. I
Haddon, Sir Richard Walker, 1893–1967, vol. VI
Haddon, Trevor, *died* 1941, vol. IV
Haddon-Cave, Sir (Charles) Philip, 1925–1999, vol. X
Haddon-Cave, Sir Philip; *see* Haddon-Cave, Sir C. P.
Haddon-Smith, Sir George Basil, 1861–1931, vol. III
Haddow, Sir Alexander, 1907–1976, vol. VII
Haddow, Alexander John, 1912–1978, vol. VII
Haddow, Sir Douglas; *see* Haddow, Sir T. D.
Haddow, Sir Renwick; *see* Haddow, Sir R. R.
Haddow, Sir (Robert) Renwick, 1891–1946, vol. IV
Haddow, Sir (Thomas) Douglas, 1913–1986, vol. VIII
Haddrill, Harry Victor, 1914–1983, vol. VIII
Haddy, Engr Rear-Adm. Frederick George, 1875–1950, vol. IV
Haden, Sir Francis Seymour, 1818–1910, vol. I
Haden, Francis Seymour, 1850–1918, vol. II
Haden, William Demmery, 1909–1999, vol. X
Haden-Guest, 1st Baron, 1877–1960, vol. V
Haden-Guest, 2nd Baron, 1902–1974, vol. VII
Haden-Guest, 3rd Baron, 1904–1987, vol. VIII
Haden-Guest, 4th Baron, 1913–1996, vol. X
Hadfield, Charles; *see* Hadfield, E. C. R.
Hadfield, Maj.-Gen. Charles Arthur, 1852–1938, vol. III
Hadfield, Charles Frederick, 1875–1965, vol. VI
Hadfield, (Ellis) Charles (Raymond), 1909–1996, vol. X
Hadfield, Sir Ernest, 1873–1947, vol. IV
Hadfield, Esmé Havelock, 1921–1992, vol. IX
Hadfield, Geoffrey, 1889–1968, vol. VI
Hadfield, James Arthur, 1882–1967, vol. VI
Hadfield, John Charles Heywood, 1907–1999, vol. X

Hadfield, Ven. John Collingwood, 1912–1993, vol. IX
Hadfield, Rt Rev. Octavius, *died* 1904, vol. I
Hadfield, Sir Robert A., 1st Bt, 1858–1940, vol. III
Hadfield, Walton John, *died* 1944, vol. IV
Hadland, Rev. Richard Phipps, *died* 1934, vol. III
Hadley, Arthur Edward, 1870–1954, vol. V
Hadley, Arthur Twining, 1856–1930, vol. III
Hadley, George Dickinson, 1908–1984, vol. VIII
Hadley, Sir Leonard Albert, 1911–1997, vol. X
Hadley, Patrick Arthur Sheldon, 1899–1973, vol. VII
Hadley, Wilfred James, 1862–1944, vol. IV
Hadley, William Sheldon, 1859–1927, vol. II
Hadley, William Waite *died* 1960, vol. V
Hadow, Lt-Col Arthur Lovell, 1877–1968, vol. VI
Hadow, Sir Austen; *see* Hadow, Sir F. A.
Hadow, Sir (Frederick) Austen, 1873–1932, vol. III
Hadow, Maj.-Gen. Frederick Edward, 1836–1915, vol. I
Hadow, Sir Gordon, 1908–1993, vol. IX
Hadow, Grace Eleanor, 1875–1940, vol. III
Hadow, Sir Henry; *see* Hadow, Sir W. H.
Hadow, Sir Michael; *see* Hadow, Sir R. M.
Hadow, Sir Raymond Patrick, 1879–1962, vol. VI
Hadow, Col Reginald Campbell, 1851–1919, vol. II
Hadow, Sir (Reginald) Michael, 1915–1993, vol. IX
Hadow, Sir Robert Henry, 1895–1963, vol. VI
Hadow, Sir (William) Henry, 1859–1937, vol. III
Hadrill, John Michael W.; *see* Wallace-Hadrill.
Hadwen, Walter Robert, 1854–1932, vol. III
Hadwick, Sir William, 1891–1951, vol. V
Haferkamp, Wilhelm, 1923–1995, vol. IX
Haffenden, Maj.-Gen. Donald James W.; *see* Wilson-Haffenden.
Haffkine, Waldemar Mordecai Wolff, 1860–1930, vol. III
Haffner, Albert Edward, 1907–1996, vol. X
Hagan, Very Rev. Edward J., 1879–1956, vol. V
Hagan, Rt Rev. Mgr John, *died* 1930, vol. III
Hagart-Speirs, Alexander Archibald; *see* Speirs.
Hagarty, Hon. Sir John Hawkins, 1816–1900, vol. I
Hagarty, Parker, 1859–1934, vol. III
Hagen, John Peter, 1908–1990, vol. VIII
Hagenbeck, Carl, 1844–1913, vol. I
Hagerty, James Campbell, (Jim Hagerty), 1909–1981, vol. VIII
Hagestadt, Leonard, 1907–1974, vol. VII
Haggard, Lt-Col Andrew Charles Parker, 1854–1923, vol. II
Haggard, Lt-Col Claude Mason, *died* 1909, vol. I
Haggard, Major Edward Arthur, 1860–1925, vol. II
Haggard, Sir Godfrey Digby Napier, 1884–1969, vol. VI
Haggard, Sir (Henry) Rider, 1856–1925, vol. II
Haggard, Lilias Margitson Rider, 1892–1968, vol. VI
Haggard, Sir Rider; *see* Haggard, Sir H. R.
Haggard, Adm. Sir Vernon Harry Stuart, 1874–1960, vol. V
Haggard, William; *see* Clayton, R. H. M.
Haggard, Sir William Henry Doveton, 1846–1926, vol. II
Haggart, Rt Rev. Alastair Iain Macdonald, 1915–1998, vol. X

Haggas, Sir James Ellison, 1849–1939, vol. III
Haggerston of Haggerston, Captain Sir Carnaby de Marie; see Haggerston of Haggerston, Captain Sir H. C. de M.
Haggerston of Haggerston, Sir Edward Charlton de Marie, 10th Bt, 1857–1925, vol. II
Haggerston of Haggerston, Captain Sir (Hugh) Carnaby de Marie, 11th Bt, 1906–1971, vol. VII
Haggerston of Haggerston, Sir John de Marie, 9th Bt, 1852–1918, vol. II
Haggerston, Sir Ralph Raphael Stanley de Marie, 12th Bt, 1912–1972, vol. VII
Haggitt, Very Rev. Percy Bolton, 1878–1957, vol. V
Hägglöf, Gunnar, 1904–1995, vol. IX
Hague, Anderson, died 1916, vol. II
Hague, Arnold, 1840–1918, vol. II
Hague, Bernard, 1893–1960, vol. V(A), vol. VI(AI)
Hague, Sir (Charles) Kenneth (Felix), 1901–1974, vol. VII
Hague, Rev. Dyson, died 1935, vol. III
Hague, Sir Harry, died 1960, vol. V
Hague, Harry, born 1922, vol. VIII
Hague, Sir Kenneth; see Hague, Sir C. K. F.
Hahn, Kurt Matthias Robert Martin, 1886–1974, vol. VII
Hahn, Otto, 1879–1968, vol. VI
Haider, Michael Lawrence, 1904–1986, vol. VIII
Haig, 1st Earl, 1861–1928, vol. II
Haig, Lt-Col Alan Gordon, 1877–1951, vol. V
Haig, Alexander, 1853–1924, vol. II
Haig, Captain Alexander Price, died 1940, vol. III
Haig, Lt-Col Arthur Balfour, 1840–1925, vol. II
Haig, Gen. Sir (Arthur) Brodie, 1886–1957, vol. V
Haig, Axel Herman, 1835–1921, vol. II
Haig, Gen. Sir Brodie; see Haig, Gen. Sir A. B.
Haig, Maj.-Gen. Charles Thomas, 1834–1907, vol. I
Haig, Col Claude Henry, 1874–1955, vol. V
Haig, Sir Harry Graham, 1881–1956, vol. V
Haig, Brig.-Gen. Neil Wolseley, 1868–1926, vol. II
Haig, Lt-Col Patrick Balfour, 1866–1949, vol. IV
Haig, Brig.-Gen. Roland Charles, 1873–1953, vol. V
Haig, Lt-Col Sir (Thomas) Wolseley, 1865–1938, vol. III
Haig, Lt-Col Sir Wolseley; see Haig, Lt-Col Sir T. W.
Haig, Lt-Col Wolseley de Haga, 1884–1960, vol. V
Haig-Brown, Rev. William, 1823–1907, vol. I
Haigh, Anthony; see Haigh, A. A. F.
Haigh, Arthur Elam, 1855–1905, vol. I
Haigh, (Austin) Anthony (Francis), 1907–1989, vol. VIII
Haigh, Hon. Col Bernard, 1876–1939, vol. III
Haigh, Bernard Parker, 1884–1941, vol. IV
Haigh, Charles, died 1913, vol. I
Haigh, Clifford, 1906–1999, vol. X
Haigh, Ernest Varley-, died 1948, vol. IV
Haigh, Engr Captain Francis Evans Percy, 1873–1934, vol. III
Haigh, Frank Fraser, 1891–1970, vol. VI
Haigh, Sir Fred, 1889–1954, vol. V
Haigh, Ven. Henry, 1837–1906, vol. I
Haigh, Rev. Henry, 1853–1917, vol. II
Haigh, Rt Rev. Mervyn George, 1887–1962, vol. VI

Haigh, Rev. William E., 1850–1932, vol. III
Haight, Gordon Sherman, 1901–1985, vol. VIII
Haile Sellassie, 1892–1975, vol. VII
Hailes, 1st Baron, 1901–1974, vol. VII
Hailes, Clements David Grierson, 1860–1929, vol. III
Hailey, 1st Baron, 1901–1974, vol. VII
Hailey, Hammett Reginald Clode, died 1960, vol. V
Hailsham, 1st Viscount, 1872–1950, vol. IV
Hailstone, Bernard, 1910–1987, vol. VIII
Hailwood, Augustine, 1875–1939, vol. III
Haimendorf, Christoph von F.; see Furer-Haimendorf
Hain, Sir Edward, 1851–1917, vol. II
Hain, Henry William Theodore, 1899–1972, vol. VII
Haine, Paymaster-Comdr Alec Ernest, 1885–1953, vol. V
Haine, Reginald Leonard, 1896–1982, vol. VIII
Haines, Sir Cyril Henry, 1895–1988, vol. VIII
Haines, F(rederick) Merlin, 1898–1963, vol. VI
Haines, Field-Marshal Sir Frederick Paul, 1819–1909, vol. I
Haines, Geoffrey Colton, 1899–1981, vol. VIII
Haines, Air Cdre Harold Alfred, 1899–1955, vol. V
Haines, Henry Haselfoot, died 1945, vol. IV
Haines, James, 1868–1936, vol. III
Haines, Maj.-Gen. James Laurence Piggott, 1896–1974, vol. VII
Haining, Gen. Sir Robert Hadden, 1882–1959, vol. V
Hains, Charles Brazier, 1882–1962, vol. VI
Hainsworth, Col John Raymond, 1900–1991, vol. IX
Hair, Gilbert, 1899–1965, vol. VI
Haire of Whiteabbey, Baron (Life Peer); John Edwin Haire, 1908–1966, vol. VI
Haire, Very Rev. James, died 1959, vol. V
Haire, Norman, 1892–1952, vol. V
Haire, Rev. William John, died 1932, vol. III
Haire-Forster, Very Rev. Arthur Newburgh, died 1932, vol. III
Haite, George Charles, 1855–1924, vol. II
Hajibhoy, Sir Mahomedbhoy, died 1926, vol. II
Hajihafiz Hidayet Hosain, Khan Bahadur, 1881–1935, vol. III
Hake, Guy Donne Gordon, 1887–1964, vol. VI
Hake, Sir Henry M., 1892–1951, vol. V
Hake, Henry Wilson, 1851–1930, vol. III
Hake, Herbert Denys, 1894–1975, vol. VII
Hake, William Augustus Gordon, 1811–1914, vol. I
Hakewill Smith, Maj.-Gen. Sir Edmund, 1896–1986, vol. VIII
Haking, Gen. Sir Richard Cyril Byrne, 1862–1945, vol. IV
Halahan, Air Vice-Marshal Frederick Crosby, died 1965, vol. VI
Halahan, Very Rev. John, died 1920, vol. II
Halahan, Gp Captain John Crosby, 1878–1967, vol. VI
Halas, John, 1912–1995, vol. IX
Halcrow, Sir William Thomson, 1883–1958, vol. V
Haldane, 1st Viscount, 1856–1928, vol. II
Haldane, Archibald Richard Burdon, 1900–1982, vol. VIII

Haldane, Lt-Col Charles Levenax, 1866–1934, vol. III
Haldane, Elizabeth Sanderson, 1862–1937, vol. III
Haldane, Henry Chicheley, 1872–1957, vol. V
Haldane, Gen. Sir J. Aylmer L., 1862–1950, vol. IV
Haldane, James Brodrick C.; see Chinnery-Haldane.
Haldane, Rt Rev. James Robert Alexander C.; see Chinnery-Haldane.
Haldane, Very Rev. John Bernard, 1881–1938, vol. III
Haldane, John Burdon Sanderson, 1892–1964, vol. VI
Haldane, John Rodger, 1882–1967, vol. VI
Haldane, John Scott, 1860–1936, vol. III
Haldane, Sir William Stowell, 1864–1951, vol. V
Haldar, Hiralal, 1865–1942, vol. IV
Haldeman, Donald Carmichael, 1860–1930, vol. III
Haldin, Henry Hyman, 1863–1931, vol. III
Haldin, Sir Philip Edward, 1880–1953, vol. V
Haldin-Davis, H., died 1949, vol. IV
Haldon, 2nd Baron, 1846–1903, vol. I
Haldon, 3rd Baron, 1869–1933, vol. III
Haldon, 4th Baron, 1896–1938, vol. III
Haldon, 5th Baron, 1854–1939, vol. III (A), vol. IV
Hale, Baron (Life Peer); (Charles) Leslie Hale, 1902–1985, vol. VIII
Hale, Arthur James, 1877–1970, vol. VI
Hale, Col Charles Henry, 1863–1921, vol. II
Hale, Col E. Matthew, died 1924, vol. II
Hale, Sir Edward, 1895–1978, vol. VII
Hale, Rev. Edward Everett, died 1909, vol. I
Hale, Frederick Marten, 1864–1931, vol. III
Hale, George Ellery, 1868–1938, vol. III
Hale, Lt-Col George Ernest, 1861–1933, vol. III
Hale, Herbert Edward John, 1927–1978, vol. VII
Hale, John Howard, 1863–1955, vol. V
Hale, Sir John Rigby, 1923–1999, vol. X
Hale, Comdr John William, 1907–1985, vol. VIII
Hale, Joseph, 1913–1985, vol. VIII
Hale, Kathleen; see Burke, K.
Hale, Kathleen, (Mrs Douglas McClean), 1898–2000, vol. X
Hale, Lionel Ramsay, 1909–1977, vol. VII
Hale, Col Sir Lonsdale Augustus, 1834–1914, vol. I
Hale, Maj.-Gen. Robert, 1834–1907, vol. I
Hale, Sarah J., died 1920, vol. II
Hale, Major Thomas Egerton, 1832–1909, vol. I
Hale, Brig.-Gen. Thomas Wyatt, 1864–1937, vol. III
Hale, W. Matthew, died 1929, vol. III
Hale, Sir William Edward, 1883–1967, vol. VI
Hale-White, Sir William, 1857–1949, vol. IV
Hales, A. G., 1870–1936, vol. III
Hales, Rev. Canon G. T. B.; see Brunwin-Hales.
Hales, Harold Keates, 1868–1942, vol. IV
Hales, Ven. John Percy, 1870–1952, vol. V
Hales, John Wesley, 1836–1914, vol. I
Halevy, Elie, 1870–1937, vol. III
Halevy, Ludovic, 1834–1908, vol. I
Haley, Francis Raymond, 1862–1931, vol. III
Haley, Kenneth Harold Dobson, 1920–1997, vol. X
Haley, Philip William Raymond Chatterton, 1917–1987, vol. VIII
Haley, Sir William John, 1901–1987, vol. VIII
Halford, Frank Bernard, 1894–1955, vol. V

Halford, Frederic Michael, 1844–1914, vol. I
Halford, Rt Rev. George Dowglas, 1865–1948, vol. IV
Halford, Jeannette, died 1950, vol. IV
Halford, Rev. Sir John Frederick, 4th Bt, 1830–1897, vol. I
Halford, Maj.-Gen. Michael Charles Kirkpatrick, 1914–1999, vol. X
Halford-MacLeod, Aubrey Seymour, 1914–2000, vol. X
Haliburton, 1st Baron, 1832–1907, vol. I
Haliburton, Hugh; see Robertson, J. L.
Halifax, 1st Earl of, 1881–1959, vol. V
Halifax, 2nd Earl of, 1912–1980, vol. VII
Halifax, Dowager Countess of; (Dorothy Evelyn Augusta), 1885–1976, vol. VII
Halifax, 2nd Viscount, 1839–1934, vol. III
Halkett, Baron; Hugh Colin Gustave George, 1861–1904, vol. I
Halkett, George Roland, 1855–1918, vol. II
Halkett, Brig.-Gen. Hugh Marjoribanks Craigie, 1880–1952, vol. V
Halkett, Lt-Col John Cornelius Craigie, 1830–1912, vol. I
Halkett, John Gilbert Hay, 1863–1937, vol. III
Halkett, Sir Peter Arthur, 8th Bt, 1834–1904, vol. I
Halkyard, Col Alfred, 1892–1964, vol. VI
Hall, 1st Viscount, 1881–1965, vol. VI
Hall, 2nd Viscount, 1913–1985, vol. VIII
Hall, Rev. Abraham Richard, 1851–1942, vol. IV
Hall, Adam; see Trevor, Elleston.
Hall, Alexander Cross, 1869–1920, vol. II
Hall, Alexander William, 1838–1919, vol. II
Hall, Alfred, 1873–1958, vol. V
Hall, Sir (Alfred) Daniel, 1864–1942, vol. IV
Hall, Rev. Alleyne Hall, 1845–1937, vol. III
Hall, Col Sir Angus William, 1834–1907, vol. I
Hall, Anmer; see Horne, A. B.
Hall, Sir Arnold Alexander, 1915–2000, vol. X
Hall, Rt Rev. Arthur Crawshay Alliston, 1847–1930, vol. III
Hall, Instr Rear-Adm. Sir Arthur Edward, 1885–1959, vol. V
Hall, Arthur Henderson, 1906–1983, vol. VIII
Hall, Arthur Henry, 1876–1949, vol. IV
Hall, Sir Arthur John, 1866–1951, vol. V
Hall, Arthur Lewis, 1872–1955, vol. V
Hall, Surg. Vice-Adm. Sir Basil; see Hall, Surg. Vice-Adm. Sir R. W. B.
Hall, Sir Basil Francis, 7th Bt (cr 1687), 1832–1909, vol. I
Hall, Benjamin Tom, 1864–1931, vol. III
Hall, Dame Catherine Mary, 1922–1996, vol. X
Hall, Cecil Charles, 1907–1987, vol. VIII
Hall, Rt Hon. Sir Charles, 1843–1900, vol. I
Hall, Rev. Charles Albert, 1872–1965, vol. VI
Hall, Sir Daniel; see Hall, Sir A. D.
Hall, Daniel George Edward, 1891–1979, vol. VII
Hall, David Oakley, 1935–1999, vol. X
Hall, Hon. David Robert, 1874–1945, vol. IV
Hall, Rt Rev. Denis Bartlett, 1899–1983, vol. VIII
Hall, Air Marshal Sir Donald Percy, 1930–1999, vol. X
Hall, Sir Douglas Bernard, 1st Bt (cr 1919), 1866–1923, vol. II

Hall, Maj.-Gen. Douglas Keith Elphinstone, 1869–1929, vol. III
Hall, Lt-Col Sir Douglas Montgomery Bernard, 2nd Bt (cr 1919), 1891–1962, vol. VI
Hall, Ven. Edgar Francis, 1888–1987, vol. VIII
Hall, Edna, (Lady Hall); see Clarke Hall, Edna.
Hall, Col Edward, 1872–1941, vol. IV
Hall, Edward, 1922–1991, vol. IX
Hall, Brig. Edward George, 1882–1968, vol. VI
Hall, Edward Laret, 1864–1947, vol. IV
Hall, Sir Edward M.; see Marshall-Hall.
Hall, Maj.-Gen. Edward Michael, 1915–1993, vol. IX
Hall, Edwin Geoffrey S.; see Sarsfield-Hall.
Hall, Edwin Stanley, 1881–1940, vol. III
Hall, Edwin Thomas, 1851–1923, vol. II
Hall, Col Ernest Frederic, 1856–1942, vol. IV
Hall, Ernest Thomas, 1871–1954, vol. V
Hall, Francis de Havilland, 1847–1929, vol. III
Hall, Brig.-Gen. Francis Henry, 1852–1919, vol. II
Hall, Francis J., 1857–1932, vol. III
Hall, Francis Woodall, 1918–2000, vol. X
Hall, Fred, 1855–1933, vol. III
Hall, Lt-Col Sir Frederick, 1st Bt (cr 1923), 1864–1932, vol. III
Hall, Frederick, 1860–1948, vol. IV
Hall, Sir Frederick Henry, 2nd Bt (cr 1923), 1899–1949, vol. IV
Hall, Frederick Thomas Duncan, 1902–1988, vol. VIII
Hall, Frederick William, died 1933, vol. III
Hall, Maj.-Gen. Frederick William G.; see Gordon-Hall.
Hall, Col Frederick William George G.; see Gordon-Hall.
Hall, G. W. L. M.; see Marshall-Hall.
Hall, Captain Geoffrey Fowler, 1888–1970, vol. VI
Hall, Geoffrey William, 1906–1974, vol. VII
Hall, George; see Hall, H. G.
Hall, George, 1879–1955, vol. V
Hall, George A., died 1945, vol. IV
Hall, Lt-Col George Clifford Miller, 1872–1930, vol. III
Hall, George Derek Gordon, 1924–1975, vol. VII
Hall, George Edmund, 1925–1980, vol. VII
Hall, Adm. Sir George Fowler K.; see King-Hall.
Hall, Rt Rev. (George) Noel (Lankester), 1891–1962, vol. VI
Hall, George Thompson, 1865–1948, vol. IV
Hall, Lt-Col Gordon Charles William G.; see Gordon-Hall.
Hall, Grahame; see Muncaster, Claude.
Hall, Granville Stanley, 1846–1924, vol. II
Hall, Hammond, 1857–1940, vol. III
Hall, Harold F.; see Fielding-Hall.
Hall, (Harold) George, 1920–1996, vol. X
Hall, (Harold) Peter, 1916–1986, vol. VIII
Hall, Major Harold Wesley, 1888–1964, vol. VI
Hall, Harry Reginald Holland, 1873–1930, vol. III
Hall, Sir Henry, died 1928, vol. II
Hall, Sir Henry, 1845–1936, vol. III
Hall, Ven. Henry Armstrong, 1853–1921, vol. II
Hall, Sir Henry John, 8th Bt (cr 1687), 1835–1913, vol. I
Hall, Henry Noble, 1872–1949, vol. IV

Hall, Col Henry Samuel, died 1923, vol. II
Hall, Henry Sinclair, 1848–1934, vol. III
Hall, Rev. Herbert, 1845–1921, vol. II
Hall, Herbert Austen, 1881–1968, vol. VI
Hall, Adm. Sir Herbert Goodenough K.; see King-Hall.
Hall, Sir Herbert Hall, 1879–1964, vol. VI
Hall, Rt Rev. Herbert William, 1889–1955, vol. V
Hall, Hubert, 1857–1944, vol. IV
Hall, Sir Hugh, 1848–1940, vol. III
Hall, Paymaster Rear-Adm. Hugh Seymour, 1869–1940, vol. III
Hall, I. Walker, 1868–1953, vol. V
Hall, James Henry, 1877–1942, vol. IV
Hall, Hon. Sir John, 1824–1907, vol. I
Hall, John, 1915–1966, vol. VI
Hall, Sir John, 1911–1978, vol. VII
Hall, John Basil, 1866–1926, vol. II
Hall, John Carey, 1844–1921, vol. II
Hall, John Edward Beauchamp, 1905–1989, vol. VIII
Hall, Surg. Rear-Adm. John Falconer, 1872–1946, vol. IV
Hall, Sir John Frederick, 1882–1959, vol. V
Hall, Brig.-Gen. John Hamilton, 1871–1953, vol. V
Hall, Sir John Hathorn, 1894–1979, vol. VII
Hall, Col Sir John Richard, 9th Bt (cr 1687), 1865–1928, vol. II
Hall, Rear-Adm. John Talbot Savignac, 1896–1964, vol. VI
Hall, John Thomas, 1896–1955, vol. V
Hall, Joseph, 1854–1927, vol. II
Hall, Joseph Compton, 1863–1937, vol. III
Hall, Lt-Gen. Julian, 1837–1911, vol. I
Hall, Julian Dudley, 1887–1961, vol. VI
Hall, Sir Julian Henry, 11th Bt (cr 1687), 1907–1974, vol. VII
Hall, Maj.-Gen. Kenneth, 1916–1987, vol. VIII
Hall, Kenneth Lambert, 1887–1979, vol. VII
Hall, Kenneth Ronald Lambert, 1917–1965, vol. VI
Hall, (Laura) Margaret; see MacDougall, Laura Margaret.
Hall, Captain Leonard Joseph, 1879–1953, vol. V
Hall, Brig.-Gen. Lewis Montgomery Murray, 1855–1928, vol. II
Hall, Lindsay Bernard, 1859–1935, vol. III
Hall, Sir Lionel Reid, 12th Bt (cr 1687), 1898–1975, vol. VII
Hall, Magdalen K.; see King-Hall.
Hall, Marie, 1884–1956, vol. V
Hall, Sir Martin Julian, 10th Bt (cr 1687), 1874–1958, vol. V
Hall, Lt-Col Montagu Heath, 1856–1928, vol. II
Hall, Sir Neville Reynolds, 13th Bt (cr 1687), 1900–1978, vol. VII
Hall, Rev. Newman, 1816–1902, vol. I
Hall, Rt Rev. Noel; see Hall, Rt Rev. G. N. L.
Hall, Sir Noel Frederick, 1902–1983, vol. VIII
Hall, Oliver, 1869–1957, vol. V
Hall, Owen, died 1907, vol. I
Hall, Percival Stanhope, 1879–1972, vol. VII
Hall, Percy, 1882–1955, vol. V
Hall, Peter; see Hall, H. P.
Hall, Philip, 1904–1982, vol. VIII
Hall, Col Philip de Havilland, 1885–1972, vol. VII

Hall, Miss Radclyffe, 1886–1943, vol. IV
Hall, Col Ralph Ellis Carr-, 1873–1963, vol. VI
Hall, Adm. Sir Reginald; see Hall, Adm. Sir W. R.
Hall, Reginald, 1931–1994, vol. IX
Hall, Richard James, died 1930, vol. III
Hall, Richard Nicklin, 1853–1914, vol. I
Hall, Robert, 1867–1949, vol. IV
Hall, Air Marshal Sir Robert Hamilton C.; see
  Clark-Hall.
Hall, Hon. Robert Newton, 1836–1917, vol. I
Hall, Surg. Vice-Adm. Sir (Robert William) Basil,
  1876–1951, vol. V
Hall, Sir Roger Evans, 1883–1969, vol. VI
Hall, Roger Wilby, 1907–1973, vol. VII
Hall, Ronald, 1900–1975, vol. VII
Hall, Ronald Acott, 1892–1966, vol. VI
Hall, Rt Rev. Ronald Owen, died 1975, vol. VII
Hall, Sir Samuel, 1841–1907, vol. I
Hall, Stewart S.; see Scott Hall.
Hall, Sydney Prior, 1842–1922, vol. II
Hall, Adm. Sydney Stewart, 1872–1955, vol. V
Hall, T. Walter, 1862–1953, vol. V
Hall, Thomas Donald Horn, 1885–1970, vol. VI
Hall, Thomas Sergeant, died 1915, vol. I
Hall, Trevor Henry, 1910–1991, vol. IX
Hall, Vernon Frederick, 1904–1998, vol. X
Hall, Lt-Col Walter D'Arcy, 1891–1980, vol. VII
Hall, Wilfrid John, 1892–1965, vol. VI
Hall, William Carby, 1864–1938, vol. III
Hall, Sir William Clarke, 1866–1932, vol. III
Hall, William Codrington Briggs, 1845–1914, vol. I
Hall, Rt Hon. William Glenvil, 1887–1962, vol. VI
Hall, Brig. Sir William Henry, 1906–1998, vol. X
Hall, Hon. William Lorimer, 1876–1958, vol. V
Hall, William M.; see Macalister-Hall.
Hall, Adm. Sir (William) Reginald, 1870–1943,
  vol. IV
Hall, William Telford, 1895–1985, vol. VIII
Hall, William Thomas, 1855–1938, vol. III
Hall Caine, Gordon Ralph, 1884–1962, vol. VI
Hall-Dalwood, Lt-Col John, died 1954, vol. V
Hall-Dare, Robert Westley, 1866–1939, vol. III
Hall-Davis, Sir Alfred George Fletcher, 1924–1979,
  vol. VII
Hall-Dempster, Col Reginald Hawkins, 1854–1922,
  vol. II
Hall-Edwards, John Francis, 1858–1926, vol. II
Hall-Jones, Hon. Sir William, 1851–1936, vol. III
Hall-Patch, Sir Edmund Leo, 1896–1975, vol. VII
Hall-Thompson, Maj. Lloyd; see Hall-Thompson,
  Maj. R. L.
Hall-Thompson, Adm. Percival Henry, 1874–1950,
  vol. IV
Hall-Thompson, Maj. (Robert) Lloyd, 1920–1992,
  vol. IX
Hall-Thompson, Lt-Col Rt Hon. S. H., 1885–1954,
  vol. V
Halladay, Eric, 1930–1997, vol. X
Hallam, (Arthur) Rupert, 1877–1955, vol. V
Hallam, Sir Clement Thornton, died 1965, vol. VI
Hallam, Rupert; see Hallam, A. R.
Hallam, Rt Rev. William Thomas Thompson,
  1878–1956, vol. V
Halland, Col Gordon Herbert Ramsay, 1888–1981,
  vol. VIII

Hallaran, Ven. Thomas Tuckey, died 1915, vol. I
Hallas, Eldred, 1870–1926, vol. II
Hallé, Charles E., 1846–1919, vol. II
Hallé, Wilma Maria Francisca, (Lady Hallé;
  Madame Norman Neruda), 1839–1911, vol. I
Hallen, Vet. Lt-Col James Herbert Brockencote,
  1829–1901, vol. I
Hallett, Cecil Walter, 1899–1994, vol. IX
Hallett, Vice Adm. Sir Charles H.; see Hughes
  Hallett.
Hallett, Rev. Canon Cyril, 1864–1942, vol. IV
Hallett, Sir Frederic G., 1860–1933, vol. III
Hallett, (George Eduard) Maurice, 1912–1998,
  vol. X
Hallett, Harold Foster, 1886–1966, vol. VI
Hallett, Holt S., died 1911, vol. I
Hallett, Sir Hugh Imbert Periam, 1886–1967,
  vol. VI
Hallett, Col James Wyndham H.; see
  Hughes-Hallett.
Hallett, Vice-Adm. John H.; see Hughes-Hallett.
Hallett, Leslie Charles H.; see Hughes-Hallett.
Hallett, Maurice; see Hallett, G. E. M.
Hallett, Sir Maurice Garnier, 1883–1969, vol. VI
Hallett, Rt Rev. Mgr Philip Edward, 1884–1948,
  vol. IV
Hallett, Vice-Adm. Sir Theodore John, 1878–1957,
  vol. V
Hallewell, Lt-Col Henry Lonsdale, 1852–1908, vol. I
Halliburton, Richard, 1900–1939, vol. III
Halliburton, William Dobinson, 1860–1931, vol. III
Halliday, Edward Irvine, 1902–1984, vol. VIII
Halliday, Gen. Francis Edward, 1834–1911, vol. I
Halliday, Frank Ernest, 1903–1982, vol. VIII
Halliday, Sir Frederick James, 1806–1901, vol. I
Halliday, Sir Frederick Loch, 1864–1937, vol. III
Halliday, Sir George Clifton, 1901–1987, vol. VIII
Halliday, Lt-Gen. George Thomas, 1841–1922,
  vol. II
Halliday, J., died 1962, vol. VI
Halliday, James; see Symington, David.
Halliday, Gen. John Gustavus, 1822–1917, vol. II
Halliday, Gen. Sir Lewis Stratford Tollemache,
  1870–1966, vol. VI
Halliday, Sir William Reginald, 1886–1966, vol. VI
Hallifax, Charles Joseph, died 1946, vol. IV
Hallifax, Adm. Sir David John, 1927–1992, vol. IX
Hallifax, Edwin Richard, 1874–1950, vol. IV
Hallifax, Rear-Adm. Guy Waterhouse, 1884–1941,
  vol. IV
Hallifax, Mrs Joanne Mary, 1900–1972, vol. VII
Hallifax, Vice-Adm. Ronald Hamilton Curzon,
  1885–1943, vol. IV
Hallilay, Lt-Col Herbert, died 1940, vol. III
Hallinan, Sir (Adrian) Lincoln, 1922–1997, vol. X
Hallinan, Sir Charles Stuart, 1895–1981, vol. VIII
Hallinan, Most Rev. Denis, 1849–1923, vol. II
Hallinan, Sir Eric, 1900–1985, vol. VIII
Hallinan, Sir Lincoln; see Hallinan, Sir A. L.
Hallinan, Major Thomas John, 1886–1960, vol. V
Halliwell, Brian, 1930–1999, vol. X
Halliwell, Leslie, 1929–1989, vol. VIII
Hallowes, Basil John Knight, 1884–1973, vol. VII
Hallowes, Col Francis William, 1866–1942, vol. IV
Hallowes, Frederick, 1907–1968, vol. VI

Hallowes, Maj.-Gen. Henry Jardine, 1838–1926, vol. II
Hallowes, Odette Marie Celine, 1912–1995, vol. IX
Hallows, Ralph Ingham, 1913–1990, vol. VIII
Hallows, Tim; see Hallows, R. I.
Hallpike, Charles Skinner, 1900–1979, vol. VII
Halls, Arthur Norman, (Michael), 1915–1970, vol. VI
Halls, Michael; see Halls, Arthur Norman.
Halls, Walter, 1871–1953, vol. V
Hallstein, Walter, 1901–1982, vol. VIII
Hallstrom, Sir Edward John Leeds, 1886–1970, vol. VI
Hallsworth, H. M., 1876–1953, vol. V
Hallsworth, Sir Joseph, 1884–1974, vol. VII
Hallward, Rev. Lancelot William, 1867–1951, vol. V
Hallward, Reginald, 1858–1948, vol. IV
Hallworth, Albert, 1898–1962, vol. VI
Halmos, Paul, 1911–1977, vol. VII
Halnon, Frederick James, 1881–1958, vol. V
Halpin, James, 1843–1909, vol. I
Halpin, Most Rev. Charles A., 1930–1994, vol. IX
Halpin, Kathleen Mary, 1903–1999, vol. X
Halsall, Rt Rev. Joseph Formby, 1902–1958, vol. V
Halsbury, 1st Earl of, 1823–1921, vol. II
Halsbury, 2nd Earl of, 1880–1943, vol. IV
Halsbury, 3rd Earl of, 1908–2000, vol. X
Halse, Most Rev. Reginald Charles, 1881–1962, vol. VI
Halse, Col Stanley Clarence, 1872–1961, vol. VI
Halsey, Captain Arthur, 1869–1957, vol. V
Halsey, Rt Hon. Sir Frederick; see Halsey, Rt Hon. Sir T. F.
Halsey, Sir Laurence Edward, 1871–1945, vol. IV
Halsey, Adm. Sir Lionel, 1872–1949, vol. IV
Halsey, Reginald John, 1902–1982, vol. VIII
Halsey, Captain Sir Thomas Edgar, 3rd Bt, 1898–1970, vol. VI
Halsey, Rt Hon. Sir (Thomas) Frederick, 1st Bt, 1839–1927, vol. II
Halsey, Lt-Col Sir Walter Johnston, 2nd Bt, 1868–1950, vol. IV
Halsey-Bircham, Sir Bernard Edward, 1869–1945, vol. IV
Halstead, Albert, 1867–1949, vol. IV (A)
Halstead, Major David, 1861–1937, vol. III
Halsted, Maj.-Gen. John Gregson, 1890–1980, vol. VII
Halton, Herbert Welch, 1863–1919, vol. II
Halward, Rt Rev. (Nelson) Victor, 1897–1953, vol. V
Halward, Rt Rev. Victor; see Halward, Rt Rev. N. V.
Haly, Maj.-Gen. Richard Hebden O'G.; see O'Grady-Haly.
Ham, Very Rev. Herbert, died 1964, vol. VI
Ham, James Milton, 1920–1997, vol. X
Ham, Rear-Adm. John Dudley Nelson, 1902–1994, vol. IX
Ham, Engr-Rear-Adm. John William, 1863–1931, vol. III
Ham, Wilbur Lincoln, 1883–1948, vol. IV
Hamber, Col Hon. Eric W., 1879–1960, vol. V
Hambidge, Jay, 1867–1924, vol. II

Hambleden, Viscountess (1st in line), 1828–1913, vol. I
Hambleden, 2nd Viscount, 1868–1928, vol. II
Hambleden, 3rd Viscount, 1903–1948, vol. IV
Hambleden, Dowager Viscountess; Patricia, 1904–1994, vol. IX
Hambling, Captain Sir Guy; see Hambling, Captain Sir H. G. M.
Hambling, Sir Herbert, 1st Bt, 1857–1932, vol. III
Hambling, Captain Sir (Herbert) Guy (Musgrave), 2nd Bt, 1883–1966, vol. VI
Hambly, Edmund Cadbury, 1942–1995, vol. IX
Hambly, Wilfrid Dyson, 1886–1962, vol. VI
Hambourg, Mark, 1879–1960, vol. V
Hambro, Captain Angus Valdemar, 1883–1957, vol. V
Hambro, Sir Charles Jocelyn, 1897–1963, vol. VI
Hambro, Sir Eric, 1872–1947, vol. IV
Hambro, Sir Everard Alexander, 1842–1925, vol. II
Hambro, Lt-Col Harold Everard, 1876–1952, vol. V
Hambro, Jocelyn Olaf, 1919–1994, vol. IX
Hambro, John Henry, 1904–1965, vol. VI
Hambro, Maj.-Gen. Sir Percy, 1870–1931, vol. III
Hambro, Ronald Olaf, 1885–1961, vol. VI
Hamburger, H. J., 1859–1924, vol. II
Hamel, Auguste-Charles, 1854–1923, vol. II
Hamel, Gustav, 1861–1922, vol. II
Hamer, Rev. Charles John, 1856–1943, vol. IV
Hamer, Sir George Frederick, 1885–1965, vol. VI
Hamer, Jean; see Rhys, J.
Hamer, John, 1910–1990, vol. VIII
Hamer, Captain Richard Lloyd, 1884–1951, vol. V
Hamer, Sam Hield, died 1941, vol. IV
Hamer, Sir William Heaton, died 1936, vol. III
Hamersley, Alfred St George, 1848–1929, vol. III
Hamerton, Bt Col Albert Ernest, 1873–1955, vol. V
Hames, Sir George Colvile H.; see Hayter Hames.
Hames, Jack Hamawi, 1920–1988, vol. VIII
Hamid, Khan Bahadur Dewan Sir Abdul, 1881–1973, vol. VII (AII)
Hamill, John Molyneux, 1880–1960, vol. V
Hamill, Sir Patrick, 1930–2000, vol. X
Hamill, Rev. Thomas Macafee, died 1919, vol. II
Hamilton, 13th Duke of, and Brandon, 10th Duke of, 1862–1940, vol. III
Hamilton, 14th Duke of, and Brandon, 11th Duke of, 1903–1973, vol. VII
Hamilton and Brandon, Duchess of; (Mary Louise Elizabeth), 1854–1934, vol. III
Hamilton, Marquess of; Captain James Albert Edward Hamilton, 1869–1913, vol. I
Hamilton of Dalzell, 1st Baron, 1829–1900, vol. I
Hamilton of Dalzell, 2nd Baron, 1872–1952, vol. V
Hamilton of Dalzell, 3rd Baron, 1911–1990, vol. VIII
Hamilton, Hon. Adam, 1880–1952, vol. V
Hamilton, Hon. Brig.-Gen. Alexander Beamish, 1860–1918, vol. II
Hamilton, Alexander Michell, 1872–1959, vol. V
Hamilton, Allan M'Lane, died 1919, vol. II
Hamilton, Allister McNicoll, 1895–1973, vol. VII
Hamilton, Andrew, 1862–1934, vol. III
Hamilton, Col Andrew Lorne, 1871–1951, vol. V
Hamilton, Anthony Norris, 1913–1991, vol. IX
Hamilton, (Anthony Walter) Patrick, 1904–1962, vol. VI

Hamilton, Sir Archibald; *see* Hamilton, Sir C. E. A. W.

Hamilton, Archibald, 1895–1974, vol. VII

Hamilton, (Arthur Douglas) Bruce, 1900–1974, vol. VII

Hamilton, Lt-Col Arthur Francis, 1880–1965, vol. VI

Hamilton, Arthur Plumptre Faunce, 1895–1977, vol. VII

Hamilton, Bruce; *see* Hamilton, A. D. B.

Hamilton, Gen. Sir Bruce Meade, 1857–1936, vol. III

Hamilton, Sir Bruce S.; *see* Stirling-Hamilton.

Hamilton, Charles Boughton, 1850–1927, vol. II

Hamilton, Sir (Charles) Denis, 1918–1988, vol. VIII

Hamilton, Sir Charles Edward, 1st Bt (*cr* 1892), 1845–1928, vol. II

Hamilton, Sir (Charles Edward) Archibald Watkin, 5th Bt (*cr* 1776) and 3rd Bt (*cr* 1819), 1876–1939, vol. III

Hamilton, Charles Gipps, 1857–1955, vol. V

Hamilton, Charles Harold St John; *see* Richards, Frank.

Hamilton, Rev. Charles James, 1840–1917, vol. II

Hamilton, Charles Keith Johnstone, 1890–1978, vol. VII

Hamilton, Hon. Charles William B.; *see* Baillie-Hamilton.

Hamilton, Sir (Charles) William (Feilden), 1899–1978, vol. VII

Hamilton, Cicely, 1872–1952, vol. V

Hamilton, Rev. Clarence Haselwood, 1877–1940, vol. III

Hamilton, Lt-Col Claud George Cole-, 1869–1957, vol. V

Hamilton, Rt Hon. Lord Claud John, 1843–1925, vol. II

Hamilton, Col Claud Lorn Campbell, 1874–1954, vol. V

Hamilton, Captain Lord Claud Nigel, 1889–1975, vol. VII

Hamilton, Col Claude de Courcy, 1861–1910, vol. I

Hamilton, Cosmo, *died* 1942, vol. IV

Hamilton, Cyril Robert Parke, 1903–1990, vol. VIII

Hamilton, Sir Daniel Mackinnon, 1860–1939, vol. III

Hamilton, David James, 1849–1909, vol. I

Hamilton, Captain David Monteith, 1874–1942, vol. IV

Hamilton, Sir Denis; *see* Hamilton, Sir C. D.

Hamilton, Col Douglas James; *see* Proby, Col D. J.

Hamilton, Sir Edward Archibald, 4th Bt (*cr* 1776) and 2nd Bt (*cr* 1819), 1843–1915, vol. I

Hamilton, Maj.-Gen. Sir Edward Owen Fisher, 1854–1944, vol. IV

Hamilton, Sir Edward Walter, 1847–1908, vol. I

Hamilton, Edwin, *died* 1919, vol. II

Hamilton, Edwin J., 1852–1946, vol. IV

Hamilton, Emily Moore, *died* 1972, vol. VII

Hamilton, Rt Rev. Eric Knightley Chetwode, 1890–1962, vol. VI

Hamilton, Eric Ronald, 1893–1967, vol. VI

Hamilton, Col Ernest Graham, *died* 1950, vol. IV

Hamilton, Lord Ernest William, 1858–1939, vol. III

Hamilton, Eugene L.; *see* Lee-Hamilton.

Hamilton, Rev. Francis Cole Lowry, *died* 1936, vol. III

Hamilton, Francis Hugh, 1927–1989, vol. IX (AI)

Hamilton, Sir Frederic Harding Anson, 7th Bt (*cr* 1647), 1836–1919, vol. II

Hamilton, Lord Frederic Spencer, 1856–1928, vol. II

Hamilton, Sir Frederic Howard, 1865–1956, vol. V

Hamilton, Adm. Sir Frederick Hew George D.; *see* Dalrymple-Hamilton.

Hamilton, Adm. Sir Frederick Tower, 1856–1917, vol. II

Hamilton, G. E., vol. II

Hamilton, Gavin Macaulay, 1880–1941, vol. IV

Hamilton, Brig. Gawaine Basil R.; *see* Rowan-Hamilton.

Hamilton, Col Gawin William Rowan-, 1844–1930, vol. III

Hamilton, Sir George Clements, 1st Bt (*cr* 1937), 1877–1947, vol. IV

Hamilton, George Douglas F.; *see* Findlay-Hamilton.

Hamilton, Rt Hon. Lord George Francis, 1845–1927, vol. II

Hamilton, Ven. George Hans, *died* 1905, vol. I

Hamilton, Sir George Rostrevor, 1888–1967, vol. VI

Hamilton, Lt-Col George Vaughan, 1851–1911, vol. I

Hamilton, Col Gilbert Claud, 1879–1943, vol. IV

Hamilton, Col Gilbert Henry Claude, 1853–1933, vol. III

Hamilton, Maj.-Gen. Godfrey John, 1912–1985, vol. VIII

Hamilton, Graeme Montagu, 1934–2000, vol. X

Hamilton, Rev. Hamilton Anne D.; *see* Douglas-Hamilton.

Hamilton, Hamish, 1900–1988, vol. VIII

Hamilton, Rt Rev. Heber James, 1862–1952, vol. V

Hamilton, Henry, *died* 1918, vol. II

Hamilton, Surg.-Gen. Sir Henry, 1851–1932, vol. III

Hamilton, Henry, 1896–1964, vol. VI

Hamilton, Col Henry Best Hans, 1850–1935, vol. III

Hamilton, Col Henry Blackburne, 1841–1920, vol. II

Hamilton, Rev. Herbert Alfred, 1897–1977, vol. VII

Hamilton, Sir Horace Perkins, 1880–1971, vol. VII

Hamilton, Maj.-Gen. Hubert Ion Wetherall, 1861–1914, vol. I

Hamilton, Hugh Brown, 1892–1960, vol. V

Hamilton, Rear-Adm. Hugh Dundas, 1882–1963, vol. VI

Hamilton, Brig. Hugh William Roberts, 1892–1959, vol. V

Hamilton, Iain Bertram, 1920–1986, vol. VIII

Hamilton, Iain Ellis, 1922–2000, vol. X

Hamilton, Gen. Sir Ian Standish Monteith, 1853–1947, vol. IV

Hamilton, Rev. J. M'Curdy, 1834–1915, vol. I

Hamilton, Very Rev. James, *died* 1925, vol. II

Hamilton, Sir James, 1857–1935, vol. III

Hamilton, Surg. Rear-Adm. James, 1899–1964, vol. VI

Hamilton, James, 1918–2000, vol. X

Hamilton, John C.; *see* Cole-Hamilton.

Hamilton, Rear-Adm. James de Courcy, 1860–1936, vol. III
Hamilton, James Fetherstonhaugh, 1850–1915, vol. I
Hamilton, James Gilbert Murdoch, 1907–1972, vol. VII
Hamilton, Brig. James Melvill, 1886–1972, vol. VII
Hamilton, Lt-Col James S.; see Stevenson-Hamilton.
Hamilton, James Whitelaw, 1860–1932, vol. III
Hamilton, James Winterbottom, 1849–1899, vol. I
Hamilton, John, 1851–1939, vol. III
Hamilton, John Almeric de Courcy, 1896–1973, vol. VII
Hamilton, John Angus Lushington Moore, died 1913, vol. I
Hamilton, Col John Archibald, 1869–1931, vol. III
Hamilton, Air Vice-Marshal John Beresford C.; see Cole-Hamilton.
Hamilton, John Gardiner, 1859–1912, vol. I
Hamilton, Brig.-Gen. John George Harry, 1869–1945, vol. IV
Hamilton, Adm. Sir John Graham, 1910–1994, vol. IX
Hamilton, John McLure, 1853–1936, vol. III
Hamilton, Maj.-Gen. John Robert Crosse, 1906–1985, vol. VIII
Hamilton, Captain Keith Randolph, 1871–1918, vol. II
Hamilton, Kismet Leland Brewer, 1883–1966, vol. VI
Hamilton, Hon. Leslie d'Henin, 1873–1914, vol. I
Hamilton, Hon. Liam; see Hamilton, Hon. W.
Hamilton, Lillias, died 1925, vol. II
Hamilton, Adm. Sir Louis Henry Keppel, 1890–1957, vol. V
Hamilton, Lord Malcolm Avendale D.; see Douglas-Hamilton.
Hamilton, Mary Agnes, died 1966, vol. VI
Hamilton, Sir Michael Aubrey, 1918–2000, vol. X
Hamilton, Col Hon. North de Coigny D.; see Dalrymple-Hamilton.
Hamilton, Col Sir North Victor Cecil D.; see Dalrymple-Hamilton.
Hamilton, Sir Orme R.; see Rowan-Hamilton.
Hamilton, Patrick; see Hamilton, A. W. P.
Hamilton, Sir Patrick George, 2nd Bt, 1908–1992, vol. IX
Hamilton, Patrick John Sinclair, 1934–1988, vol. VIII
Hamilton, Brig.-Gen. Percy Douglas, 1867–1936, vol. III
Hamilton, Percy Seymour D.; see Douglas-Hamilton.
Hamilton, Pryce Bowman, 1844–1918, vol. II
Hamilton, Adm. Sir Richard Vesey, 1829–1912, vol. I
Hamilton, Sir Robert Caradoc, 8th Bt (cr 1647), 1877–1959, vol. V
Hamilton, Very Rev. Robert James S.; see Shaw-Hamilton.
Hamilton, Very Rev. Robert Smyly Greer, 1861–1928, vol. II
Hamilton, Brig. Robert Sydney, 1871–1945, vol. IV
Hamilton, Sir Robert William, 1867–1944, vol. IV
Hamilton, Robert William, 1905–1995, vol. IX

Hamilton, Captain Sir Robert William Stirling-, 12th Bt, 1903–1982, vol. VIII
Hamilton, Lt-Col Roland, 1886–1953, vol. V
Hamilton, Sir Sydney; see Hamilton, Sir T. S. P.
Hamilton, Rt Hon. and Rev. Thomas, 1842–1925, vol. II
Hamilton, Maj.-Gen. Thomas de Courcy, 1825–1908, vol. I
Hamilton, Sir (Thomas) Sydney (Percival), 6th Bt (cr 1776) and 4th Bt (cr 1819), 1881–1966, vol. VI
Hamilton, Col Thomas William O'Hara, 1860–1918, vol. II
Hamilton, Walter, 1844–1899, vol. I
Hamilton, Walter, 1908–1988, vol. VIII
Hamilton, Sir William; see Hamilton, Sir C. W. F.
Hamilton, William Aitken Brown, 1909–1982, vol. VIII
Hamilton, Sir William Alexander B.; see Baillie-Hamilton.
Hamilton, Rear-Adm. William Des Vœux, 1852–1907, vol. I
Hamilton, William Donald, 1936–2000, vol. X
Hamilton, William Frederick, 1848–1922, vol. II
Hamilton, Brig.-Gen. William George, 1860–1940, vol. III
Hamilton, Rev. William Hamilton, 1886–1958, vol. V
Hamilton, Maj.-Gen. William Haywood, died 1955, vol. V
Hamilton, William James, 1903–1975, vol. VII
Hamilton, Hon. William, (Liam), 1928–2000, vol. X
Hamilton, Maj.-Gen. William Ralston Duncan, 1895–1969, vol. VI
Hamilton, Sir William Stirling, 10th Bt (cr 1673), 1830–1913, vol. I
Hamilton, Sir William Stirling-, 11th Bt (cr 1673), 1868–1946, vol. IV
Hamilton, William Winter, 1917–2000, vol. X
Hamilton-Dalrymple, Sir Hew Clifford; see Dalrymple.
Hamilton-Dalrymple, Sir Walter; see Dalrymple.
Hamilton-Gordon, Hon. and Rev. Douglas, 1824–1901, vol. I
Hamilton-Gordon, Lt-Col Edward Hyde; see Gordon.
Hamilton-Grace, Col Sheffield; see Grace.
Hamilton-Grierson, Philip Francis, 1883–1963, vol. VI
Hamilton-Grierson, Sir Philip James; see Grierson.
Hamilton Harding, George Trevor, 1895–1967, vol. VI
Hamilton-Hoare, Henry William, 1844–1931, vol. III
Hamilton-Jones, Maj.-Gen. John, 1926–1997, vol. X
Hamilton-King, Mrs Grace M., died 1980, vol. VII
Hamilton-Montgomery, Sir Basil Purvis-Russell; see Montgomery.
Hamilton-Russell, Hon. Claud Eustace, 1871–1948, vol. IV
Hamilton-Russell, Hon. Frederick Gustavus, 1867–1941, vol. IV
Hamilton-Russell, Hon. Gustavus Lascelles, 1907–1940, vol. III

Hamilton-Spencer-Smith, Sir Drummond Cospatric; *see* Spencer-Smith.
Hamilton-Spencer-Smith, Sir Thomas Cospatric; *see* Spencer-Smith.
Hamilton Stubber, Lt-Col John Henry, 1921–1986, vol. VIII
Hamley, Edmund Gilbert, 1818–1902, vol. I
Hamley, Col Francis Gilbert, 1851–1918, vol. II
Hamley, Herbert Russell, 1883–1949, vol. IV
Hamley, Joseph Osbertus, 1820–1911, vol. I
Hamling, William, 1912–1975, vol. VII
Hamlyn, Mrs Christine Louisa, 1855–1936, vol. III
Hamlyn, Frederick, 1846–1904, vol. I
Hamlyn, Rt Rev. N. Temple, 1864–1929, vol. III
Hamman, Lt-Col Jacob L., 1876–1948, vol. IV
Hammarskjöld, Dag Hjalmar Agne Carl, 1905–1961, vol. VI
Hammer, Armand, 1898–1990, vol. VIII
Hammer, Rev. Canon Raymond Jack, 1920–1994, vol. IX
Hammersley, Maj.-Gen. Frederick, 1858–1924, vol. II
Hammersley, Samuel Schofield, 1892–1965, vol. VI
Hammersley-Smith, Ralph Henry, 1880–1964, vol. VI
Hammerstein, Oscar, 1847–1919, vol. II
Hammerstein, Oscar, 2nd, 1895–1960, vol. V
Hammerton, Col George Herbert Leonard, 1875–1961, vol. VI
Hammerton, Sir John Alexander, 1871–1949, vol. IV
Hammet, Rear-Adm. James Lacon, 1849–1905, vol. I
Hammett, Sir Clifford James, 1917–1999, vol. X
Hammett, Dashiell; *see* Hammett, S. D.
Hammett, Harold George, 1906–1999, vol. X
Hammett, Richard C., 1880–1952, vol. V
Hammett, (Samuel) Dashiell, 1894–1961, vol. VI
Hammick, Dalziel Llewellyn, 1887–1966, vol. VI
Hammick, Ven. Ernest Austen, 1850–1920, vol. II
Hammick, Sir George Frederick, 4th Bt, 1885–1964, vol. VI
Hammick, Sir Murray, 1854–1936, vol. III
Hammick, Vice-Adm. Robert Frederick, 1843–1922, vol. II
Hammick, Brig. Robert Townsend, 1882–1947, vol. IV
Hammick, Sir St Vincent Alexander, 3rd Bt, 1839–1927, vol. II
Hammill, Captain Charles Ford, 1891–1980, vol. VII
Hammill, Captain John Schomberg, 1890–1959, vol. V
Hammond, Col Sir Arthur George, 1843–1919, vol. II
Hammond, Arthur Henry K.; *see* Knighton-Hammond.
Hammond, Maj.-Gen. Arthur Verney, 1892–1982, vol. VIII
Hammond, Aubrey Lindsay, 1893–1940, vol. III
Hammond, Basil Edward, 1842–1916, vol. II
Hammond, Catherine Elizabeth, 1909–1999, vol. X
Hammond, Rev. Charles Edward, 1837–1914, vol. I
Hammond, Chris, *died* 1900, vol. I

Hammond, Brig.-Gen. Dayrell Talbot, 1856–1942, vol. IV
Hammond, Dennis, 1913–1969, vol. VI
Hammond, Sir (Egbert) Laurie Lucas, 1873–1939, vol. III
Hammond, Brig.-Gen. Frederick Dawson, 1881–1952, vol. V
Hammond, Gertrude Demain, *died* 1952, vol. V
Hammond, Dame Joan Hood, 1912–1996, vol. X
Hammond, John, *died* 1907, vol. I
Hammond, Sir John, 1889–1964, vol. VI
Hammond, John Harold, *died* 1932, vol. III
Hammond, John Hays, 1855–1936, vol. III
Hammond, John Lawrence Le Breton, 1872–1949, vol. IV
Hammond, Rev. Joseph, 1839–1912, vol. I
Hammond, Kay, (Dorothy Katharine), 1909–1980, vol. VII
Hammond, Sir Laurie; *see* Hammond, Sir E. L. L.
Hammond, Rt Rev. Lempriere Durell, 1881–1965, vol. VI
Hammond, Captain Leslie Jennings Lucas, 1877–1943, vol. IV
Hammond, Lucy Barbara, 1873–1961, vol. VI
Hammond, Col Peter Henry, 1848–1933, vol. III
Hammond, Stanley Alfred Andrew, 1898–1981, vol. VIII
Hammond, Ven. Thomas Chatterton, 1877–1961, vol. VI
Hammond, Thomas Edwin, 1888–1943, vol. IV
Hammond, Walter R., 1903–1965, vol. VI
Hammond, Rev. William A., 1853–1931, vol. III
Hammond-Chambers, Robert Sharp Borgnis, 1855–1907, vol. I
Hammond Innes, Ralph, 1913–1998, vol. X
Hammonds, Rev. Edwin, *died* 1933, vol. III
Hamnett, Baron (Life Peer); Cyril Hamnett, 1906–1980, vol. VII
Hamnett, George, 1826–1904, vol. I
Hamon, Count Louis, 1866–1936, vol. III
Hamond, Sir Charles Frederick, 1817–1905, vol. I
Hamond-Graeme, Sir Egerton Hood Murray, 5th Bt, 1877–1969, vol. VI
Hamond-Graeme, Sir Graham Eden William, 4th Bt, 1845–1920, vol. II
Hamp, Arthur Edward, 1886–1951, vol. V
Hampden, 2nd Viscount, 1841–1906, vol. I
Hampden, 3rd Viscount, 1869–1958, vol. V
Hampden, 4th Viscount, 1900–1965, vol. VI
Hampden, 5th Viscount, 1902–1975, vol. VII
Hampden, Hon. Charles Edward H.; *see* Hobart-Hampden.
Hampden, Ernest Miles H.; *see* Hobart-Hampden.
Hampden, John, 1898–1974, vol. VII
Hamper, Rev. Richard John, 1928–1986, vol. VIII
Hampshire, Charles Herbert, 1885–1955, vol. V
Hampshire, Dugan Homfray, *died* 1942, vol. IV
Hampshire, Frederick William, 1863–1941, vol. IV
Hampshire, Sir (George) Peter, 1912–1981, vol. VIII
Hampshire, Sir Peter; *see* Hampshire, Sir G. P.
Hampson, Arthur Cecil, 1894–1972, vol. VII
Hampson, Sir Cyril Aubrey Charles, 12th Bt, 1909–1969, vol. VI

Hampson, Sir Dennys Francis, 11th Bt, 1897–1939, vol. III
Hampson, Elwyn Lloyd, 1916–1998, vol. X
Hampson, Sir George Francis, 10th Bt, 1860–1936, vol. III
Hampson, Sir Robert Alfred, 1852–1919, vol. II
Hampson, William, died 1926, vol. II
Hampton, 3rd Baron, 1848–1906, vol. I
Hampton, 4th Baron, 1883–1962, vol. VI
Hampton, 5th Baron, 1888–1974, vol. VII
Hampton, Lt-Col Bertie Cunynghame D.; see Dwyer-Hampton.
Hampton, Frederick, 1889–1958, vol. V
Hampton, Herbert, 1862–1929, vol. III
Hamson, Charles John, 1905–1987, vol. VIII
Hamson, Vincent Everard, 1888–1975, vol. VII
Hamsun, Knut, 1859–1952, vol. V
Hanafin, Lt-Col John Berchmans, 1882–1970, vol. VI
Hanauer, Rev. Canon James Edward, 1850–1938, vol. III
Hanbury, Rev. Hon. Arthur Allen B.; see Bateman-Hanbury.
Hanbury, Sir Cecil, 1871–1937, vol. III
Hanbury, Captain Hon. Charles Stanhope Melville B.; see Bateman-Hanbury.
Hanbury, Daniel, 1876–1948, vol. IV
Hanbury, Major Edward Reginald B.; see Bateman-Hanbury.
Hanbury, Evan, 1854–1918, vol. II
Hanbury, Frederick Janson, 1851–1938, vol. III
Hanbury, Lt-Col Sir Hanmer Cecil, 1916–1994, vol. IX
Hanbury, Harold Greville, 1898–1993, vol. IX
Hanbury, Sir James Arthur, 1832–1908, vol. I
Hanbury, Sir John Capel, 1908–1995, vol. IX
Hanbury, Lily, died 1908, vol. I
Hanbury, Lt-Col Lionel Henry, 1864–1954, vol. V
Hanbury, Noel, 1881–1935, vol. III
Hanbury, Brig.-Gen. Philip Lewis, 1879–1966, vol. VI
Hanbury, Brig. Richard Nigel, 1911–1971, vol. VII
Hanbury, Rt Hon. Robert William, 1845–1903, vol. I
Hanbury, Sir Thomas, 1832–1907, vol. I
Hanbury Tenison, Marika, 1938–1982, vol. VIII
Hanbury-Tracy, Major Hon. Algernon Henry Charles, 1871–1915, vol. I
Hanbury-Tracy, Hon. Frederick Stephen Archibald, 1848–1906, vol. I
Hanbury-Williams, Maj.-Gen. Sir John, 1859–1946, vol. IV
Hanbury-Williams, Sir John Coldbrook, 1892–1965, vol. VI
Hance, Lt-Gen. Sir Bennett; see Hance, Lt-Gen. Sir J. B.
Hance, Lt-Gen. Sir (James) Bennett, 1887–1958, vol. V
Hancock, Anthony Ilbert, 1906–1955, vol. V
Hancock, Anthony John, (Tony Hancock), 1924–1968, vol. VI
Hancock, Lt-Col Sir Cyril Percy, 1896–1990, vol. VIII
Hancock, Ernest, 1887–1950, vol. IV
Hancock, Ernest Legassicke, 1862–1932, vol. III

Hancock, Dame Florence May, 1893–1974, vol. VII
Hancock, Rev. Frederick, 1848–1920, vol. II
Hancock, George Charles, 1868–1938, vol. III
Hancock, Sir Henry Drummond, 1895–1965, vol. VI
Hancock, Sir Henry Tom, 1877–1957, vol. V
Hancock, John George, 1857–1940, vol. III
Hancock, Sir Keith; see Hancock, Sir W. K.
Hancock, Kingsley Montague, 1899–1969, vol. VI
Hancock, Col Mortimer Pawson, 1870–1939, vol. III
Hancock, Sir Patrick Francis, 1914–1980, vol. VII
Hancock, Comdr Reginald L., 1880–1919, vol. II
Hancock, Tony; see Hancock, A. J.
Hancock, Air Marshal Sir Valston Eldridge, 1907–1998, vol. X
Hancock, Rev. William Edward, died 1927, vol. II
Hancock, William Ilbert, 1873–1910, vol. I
Hancock, Sir (William) Keith, 1898–1988, vol. VIII
Hancox, Leslie Pascoe, 1906–1975, vol. VII
Hand, Rt Rev. George Sumner, died 1945, vol. IV
Hand, John Pierce, 1883–1933, vol. III
Hand, Hon. Learned, 1872–1961, vol. VI
Handfield-Jones, Montagu, 1855–1920, vol. II
Handfield-Jones, Ranald Montagu, 1892–1978, vol. VII
Handford, Sir John James William, 1881–1959, vol. V
Handford, Stanley Alexander, 1898–1978, vol. VII
Handley, Lt-Col Arthur, 1861–1927, vol. II
Handley, Richard Sampson, 1909–1984, vol. VIII
Handley, Tommy, 1896–1949, vol. IV
Handley, William Sampson, died 1962, vol. VI
Handley-Derry, Henry Forster, 1879–1966, vol. VI
Handley Page, Sir Frederick; see Page, Sir F. H.
Handley-Read, Edward Harry, died 1935, vol. III
Handman, Frederick William Adolph, 1876–1948, vol. IV
Handover, Lt-Col Sir Harry George, 1868–1948, vol. IV
Hands, C. E., died 1937, vol. III
Hands, David Richard Granville, 1943–2000, vol. X
Hands, Sir Harry, 1860–1948, vol. IV
Hands, Rev. John Compton, 1842–1928, vol. II, vol. III
Hands, Rev. Thomas, 1856–1926, vol. II
Hands, William Joseph, died 1947, vol. IV
Handy, Gen. Thomas Troy, 1892–1982, vol. VIII
Handyside, Surg. Rear-Adm. Sir Patrick Brodie, 1860–1939, vol. III
Hanes, Charles Samuel, 1903–1990, vol. VIII
Hanff, Helene, 1916–1997, vol. X
Hanford, Col John Compton, 1849–1911, vol. I
Hanforth, Thomas William, 1867–1948, vol. IV
Hanger, Sir Mostyn, 1908–1980, vol. VII
Hanham, Sir Henry Phelips, 11th Bt, 1901–1973, vol. VII
Hanham, Sir John Alexander, 9th Bt, 1854–1911, vol. I
Hanham, John Castleman S.; see Swinburne-Hanham.
Hanham, Sir John Ludlow, 10th Bt, 1898–1955, vol. V
Hanham, Leonard Edward, 1921–1998, vol. X
Hanington, Rev. Edward A. W., died 1917, vol. II
Hanitsch, Karl Richard, 1860–1940, vol. III

Hankey, 1st Baron, 1877–1963, vol. VI
Hankey, 2nd Baron, 1905–1996, vol. X
Hankey, Basil Howard Alers, *died* 1948, vol. IV
Hankey, Lt-Col Cyril, *died* 1945, vol. IV
Hankey, Very Rev. Cyril Patrick, 1886–1973, vol. VII
Hankey, Brig.-Gen. Edward Barnard, 1875–1959, vol. V
Hankey, Col George Trevor, 1900–1987, vol. VIII
Hankey, Hon. Henry Arthur Alers, 1914–1999, vol. X
Hankey, Mabel, *died* 1943, vol. IV
Hankey, Richard Lyons A.; *see* Alers Hankey.
Hankey, W. L.; *see* Lee-Hankey.
Hankin, Mrs Agnes Mary; *see* Field, M.
Hankin, Arthur Crommelin, 1859–1930, vol. III
Hankin, Arthur Maxwell, 1905–1972, vol. VII
Hankin, Ernest Hanbury, 1865–1939, vol. III
Hankin, Gen. George Crommelin, 1826–1902, vol. I
Hankin, St John, 1869–1909, vol. I
Hankins, George Alexander, 1895–1950, vol. IV
Hankinson, Charles James; *see* Holland, Clive.
Hankinson, Cyril Francis James, 1895–1984, vol. VIII
Hankinson, Sir Walter Crossfield, 1894–1984, vol. VIII
Hanley, Allan Hastings, 1863–1921, vol. II
Hanley, Denis Augustine, 1903–1980, vol. VII
Hanley, Gerald Anthony, 1916–1992, vol. IX
Hanley, James, 1901–1985, vol. VIII
Hanley, James Alec, 1886–1960, vol. V
Hanlon, Rt Rev. Henry, 1862–1937, vol. III
Hanlon, John Austin Thomas, 1905–1983, vol. VIII
Hanlon, Air Vice-Marshal Thomas James, 1916–1977, vol. VII
Hanmer, Lt-Col Sir Edward; *see* Hanmer, Lt-Col Sir G. W. E.
Hanmer, Lt-Col Sir (Griffin Wyndham) Edward, 7th Bt, 1893–1977, vol. VII
Hanmer, Adm. John Graham Job, 1836–1919, vol. II
Hanmer, Marguerite Frances, 1895–1975, vol. VII
Hanmer, Sir Wyndham Charles Henry, 6th Bt, 1867–1922, vol. II
Hann, Edmund Lawrence, 1881–1968, vol. VI
Hanna, George Boyle, 1877–1938, vol. III
Hanna, Hon. Henry, 1871–1946, vol. IV
Hanna, Marcus Alonzo, 1837–1904, vol. I
Hanna, Very Rev. Robert K., 1872–1947, vol. IV
Hanna, Hon. William John, 1862–1919, vol. II
Hannaford, Charles Arthur, 1887–1972, vol. VII
Hannaford, Charles E., 1863–1955, vol. V
Hannaford, Guy George, 1901–1976, vol. VII
Hannah, Air Marshal Sir Colin Thomas, 1914–1978, vol. VII
Hannah, Ian Campbell, 1874–1944, vol. IV
Hannah, Flt-Sgt John, 1921–1947, vol. IV
Hannah, Very Rev. John Julius, 1843–1931, vol. III
Hannah, Rev. Joseph Addison, 1867–1928, vol. II
Hannah, William George, 1868–1945, vol. IV
Hannan, Albert James, 1887–1965, vol. VI
Hannan, William, 1906–1987, vol. VIII
Hannay, Alexander Howard, 1889–1955, vol. V
Hannay, David, 1853–1934, vol. III

Hannay, Doris F., (Lady Fergusson Hannay); *see* Leslie, D.
Hannay, Brig.-Gen. Frederick R.; *see* Rainsford-Hannay.
Hannay, Col Frederick R.; *see* Rainsford-Hannay.
Hannay, Sir Hugh Augustus Macnish, 1878–1962, vol. VI
Hannay, James, 1842–1910, vol. I
Hannay, James Lennox, 1826–1903, vol. I
Hannay, Rev. James Owen, 1865–1950, vol. IV
Hannay, Mrs Jane Ewing, 1868–1938, vol. III
Hannay, Col Ramsay William R.; *see* Rainsford-Hannay
Hannay, Robert Kerr, 1867–1940, vol. III
Hannay, Maj.-Gen. Robert Strickland, 1871–1948, vol. IV
Hannay, Samuel Beveridge A.; *see* Armour-Hannay.
Hannay, Rt Rev. Thomas, 1887–1970, vol. VI
Hannay, Sir Walter Fergusson Leisrinck, 1904–1961, vol. VI
Hannay, Captain Walter Maxwell, 1873–1952, vol. V
Hannays, Sir Courtenay; *see* Hannays, Sir L. C.
Hannays, Sir (Leonard) Courtenay, 1892–1964, vol. VI
Hannen, Athene, (Mrs Nicholas Hannen); *see* Seyler, A.
Hannen, Lancelot, 1866–1942, vol. IV
Hannen, Nicholas James, 1881–1972, vol. VII
Hannen, Sir Nicholas John, 1842–1900, vol. I
Hannigan, Rt Rev. James, 1928–1994, vol. IX
Hanning, Hugh Peter James, 1925–2000, vol. X
Hannon, Ven. Arthur Gordon, 1891–1978, vol. VII
Hannon, Rt Rev. Daniel Joseph, 1884–1946, vol. IV
Hannon, Sir Patrick Joseph Henry, *died* 1963, vol. VI
Hannyngton, Col John Arthur, 1868–1918, vol. II
Hanotaux, Gabriel, 1853–1944, vol. IV
Hansard, Col Arthur Clifton, 1855–1927, vol. II
Hansell, Rev. Arthur Lloyd, 1865–1948, vol. IV
Hansell, Sir (Edward) William, 1856–1937, vol. III
Hansell, Henry Peter, 1863–1935, vol. III
Hansell, Sir William; *see* Hansell, Sir E. W.
Hansen, Alvin H., 1887–1975, vol. VII
Hansen, David Ernest, 1884–1972, vol. VII
Hansen, Hans, *died* 1947, vol. IV
Hansen, Harry, 1884–1977, vol. VII
Hansen, Brig. Percy Howard, 1890–1951, vol. V
Hansen, Sir Sven Wohlford, 1st Bt, 1876–1958, vol. V
Hansford, Col Sir Benjamin, 1863–1954, vol. V
Hansford, S(idney) Howard, 1899–1973, vol. VII
Hansford Johnson, Pamela; *see* Johnson, P. H.
Hansi, (Jacques Walz), *died* 1951, vol. V
Hanson, Albert Henry, 1913–1971, vol. VII
Hanson, Sir Anthony Leslie Oswald, 4th Bt (*cr* 1887), 1934–1996, vol. X
Hanson, Sir Charles Augustin, 1st Bt (*cr* 1918), 1846–1922, vol. II
Hanson, Major Sir Charles Edwin Bourne, 2nd Bt (*cr* 1918), 1874–1958, vol. V
Hanson, Sir (Charles) John, 3rd Bt (*cr* 1918), 1919–1996, vol. X
Hanson, Daniel, 1892–1953, vol. V
Hanson, (Emmeline) Jean, 1919–1973, vol. VII

Hanson, Sir Francis Stanhope, 1868–1910, vol. I
Hanson, Frederick Horowhenua Melrose, 1896–1979, vol. VII
Hanson, Sir Gerald Stanhope, 2nd Bt (cr 1887), 1867–1946, vol. IV
Hanson, Lt-Col Harry Ernest, 1873–1934, vol. III
Hanson, Jean; see Hanson, E. J.
Hanson, Sir John; see Hanson, Sir C. J.
Hanson, Sir Philip, 1871–1955, vol. V
Hanson, Sir Reginald, 1st Bt (cr 1887), 1840–1905, vol. I
Hanson, Rev. Preb. Richard, 1880–1963, vol. VI
Hanson, Hon. Richard Burpee, 1879–1948, vol. IV
Hanson, Sir Richard Leslie Reginald, 3rd Bt (cr 1887), 1905–1951, vol. V
Hanson, Rt Rev. Richard Patrick Crosland, 1916–1988, vol. VIII
Hanson, Rev. Robert Edward Vernon, 1866–1947, vol. IV
Hanson, Rupert Willoughby, 1873–1936, vol. III
Hanworth, 1st Viscount, 1861–1936, vol. III
Hanworth, 2nd Viscount, 1916–1996, vol. X
Hapgood, Henry James, 1855–1931, vol. III
Hapgood, Norman, 1868–1937, vol. III
Happell, Sir Alexander John, 1887–1968, vol. VI
Happell, Sir Arthur Comyn, 1891–1975, vol. VII
Happell, Brig. William Horatio, 1890–1971, vol. VII
Happold, Sir Edmund Frank Ley, 1930–1996, vol. X
Happold, Frank Charles, 1902–1991, vol. IX
Happold, Frederick Crossfield, 1893–1971, vol. VII
Harada, Rev. Tasuku, 1863–1940, vol. III
Haran, James Augustine, died 1940, vol. III (A), vol. IV
Haran, Timotheus, died 1904, vol. I
Harari, Sir Victor Pasha, 1857–1945, vol. IV
Harbach, Otto A., 1873–1963, vol. VI
Harben, Guy Philip, 1881–1949, vol. IV
Harben, Sir Henry, 1823–1911, vol. I
Harben, William Nathaniel, 1858–1919, vol. II
Harberton, 6th Viscount, 1836–1912, vol. I
Harberton, 7th Viscount, 1867–1944, vol. IV
Harberton, 8th Viscount, 1869–1956, vol. V
Harberton, 9th Viscount, 1908–1980, vol. VII
Harbison, Thomas James Stanislaus, 1864–1930, vol. III
Harbord, Sir Arthur, 1865–1941, vol. IV
Harbord, Rev. and Hon. (Charles) Derek (Gardner), 1902–1987, vol. VIII
Harbord, Brig.-Gen. Cyril Rodney, 1873–1958, vol. V
Harbord, Rev. and Hon. Derek; see Harbord, Rev. and Hon. C. D. G.
Harbord, Captain Eric Walter, 1879–1952, vol. V
Harbord, Frank William, died 1942, vol. IV
Harbord, Captain Maurice Assheton, 1874–1954, vol. V
Harbottle, Col Colin Clark, 1875–1933, vol. III
Harbottle, Frank, 1872–1923, vol. II
Harbottle, Sir John George, 1858–1920, vol. II
Harbottle, Brig. Michael Neale, 1917–1997, vol. X
Harbour, Brian Hugo, 1899–1974, vol. VII
Harby, Sir Frank Neville, 1888–1952, vol. V
Harcourt, 1st Viscount, 1863–1922, vol. II

Harcourt, 2nd Viscount, 1908–1979, vol. VII
Harcourt, Alfred, 1881–1954, vol. V
Harcourt, Aubrey, 1852–1904, vol. I
Harcourt, Augustus George V.; see Vernon Harcourt.
Harcourt, Adm. Sir Cecil Halliday Jepson, 1892–1959, vol. V
Harcourt, Evelyn, (Lady Harcourt); see Suart, Evelyn.
Harcourt, George, 1868–1947, vol. IV
Harcourt, Captain Guy Elliot, 1869–1936, vol. III
Harcourt, Henry, 1873–1933, vol. III
Harcourt, Sir John; see Harcourt, Sir R. J. R.
Harcourt, Leveson Francis V.; see Vernon-Harcourt.
Harcourt, Hon. Richard, 1849–1932, vol. III
Harcourt, Sir (Robert) John (Rolston), died 1969, vol. VI
Harcourt, Robert Vernon, 1878–1962, vol. VI
Harcourt, Rt Hon. Sir William George Granville Venables Vernon-, 1827–1904, vol. I
Harcourt-Smith, Sir Cecil; see Smith.
Harcourt-Smith, Air Vice-Marshal Gilbert, 1901–1968, vol. VI
Harcourt Williams, E. G.; see Williams.
Harcus, Rev. A(ndrew) Drummond, 1885–1964, vol. VI
Harcus, Rear Adm. Ronald Albert, 1921–1991, vol. IX
Hardaker, Alan, 1912–1980, vol. VII
Hardaker, Benjamin Rigby, 1890–1961, vol. VI
Hardcastle, Captain Alexander, 1872–1933, vol. III
Hardcastle, Edward, 1826–1905, vol. I
Hardcastle, Ven. Edward Hoare, 1862–1945, vol. IV
Hardcastle, Joseph Alfred, 1868–1917, vol. II
Hardcastle, Mary, 1901–1964, vol. VI
Hardcastle, Monica Alice, 1904–1966, vol. VI
Hardcastle, Engr-Captain Sydney Undercliffe, 1875–1960, vol. V
Harden, Sir Arthur, 1865–1940, vol. III
Harden, Donald Benjamin, 1901–1994, vol. IX
Harden, Maj. James Richard Edwards, 1916–2000, vol. X
Harden, Rt Rev. John Mason, died 1931, vol. III
Harders, Sir Clarence Waldemar, 1915–1997, vol. X
Hardie, Agnes; see Hardie, Mrs G. D.
Hardie, Ven. Archibald George, 1908–1997, vol. X
Hardie, Archibald William, 1911–1980, vol. VII
Hardie, Sir Charles Edgar Mathewes, 1910–1998, vol. X
Hardie, Charles Martin, 1858–1916, vol. II
Hardie, Colin Graham, 1906–1998, vol. X
Hardie, David, died 1939, vol. III
Hardie, Sir David, 1856–1945, vol. IV
Hardie, Frank; see Hardie, W. F. R.
Hardie, Mrs George Downie, (Agnes Hardie), died 1951, vol. V
Hardie, George Downie Blyth Crookston, died 1937, vol. III
Hardie, James Keir, 1856–1915, vol. I
Hardie, Maj.-Gen. John Leslie, 1882–1956, vol. V
Hardie, John William Somerville, 1912–1987, vol. VIII
Hardie, Martin, 1875–1952, vol. V

Hardie, Captain Maurice Linton, 1909–1972,
vol. VII
Hardie, Robert Purves, 1864–1942, vol. IV
Hardie, Steven James Lindsay, 1885–1969, vol. VI
Hardie, Rt Rev. William Auchterlonie, 1904–1980,
vol. VII
Hardie, William Francis Ross, 1902–1990, vol. VIII
Hardie, Most Rev. William George, 1878–1950,
vol. IV
Hardie, William Ross, 1862–1916, vol. II
Hardie Neil, James, 1875–1955, vol. V
Hardiman, Alfred Frank, 1891–1949, vol. IV
Hardiman, John Percy, 1874–1964, vol. VI
Harding of Petherton, 1st Baron, 1896–1989,
vol. VIII
Harding, Rt Rev. Alfred, 1852–1923, vol. II
Harding, Sir (Alfred) John, 1878–1953, vol. V
Harding, Anita Elizabeth, 1952–1995, vol. IX
Harding, Ann, 1902–1981, vol. VIII
Harding, Sir Charles O'Brien, 1859–1929, vol. III
Harding, Sir Christopher George Francis,
1939–1999, vol. X
Harding, Col Colin, 1863–1939, vol. III
Harding, Denys Wyatt, 1906–1993, vol. IX
Harding, Edward Archibald Fraser, 1903–1953,
vol. V
Harding, Sir Edward John, 1880–1954, vol. V
Harding, Rev. Edwin Elmer, died 1909, vol. I
Harding, Francis Egerton, 1856–1937, vol. III
Harding, George Frederick Morris, 1874–1964,
vol. VI
Harding, George Richardson, 1884–1976, vol. VII
Harding, George Trevor H.; see Hamilton Harding.
Harding, Gerald William Lankester, 1901–1979,
vol. VII
Harding, Gilbert Charles, 1907–1960, vol. V
Harding, Harold Ivan, 1883–1943, vol. IV
Harding, Sir Harold John Boyer, 1900–1986,
vol. VIII
Harding, Hugh Alastair, 1917–2000, vol. X
Harding, Sir John; see Harding, Sir A. J.
Harding, John Philip, 1911–1998, vol. X
Harding, Rev. John Taylor, 1835–1928, vol. II
Harding, Most Rev. Malcolm Taylor McAdam, died
1949, vol. IV
Harding, Lt-Col Maynard Ffolliott, died 1961,
vol. VI
Harding, Peter Thomas, 1930–1998, vol. X
Harding, Maj.-Gen. Reginald Peregrine, 1905–1981,
vol. VIII
Harding, Rosamond Evelyn Mary, 1898–1982,
vol. VIII
Harding, Air Vice-Marshal Ross Philip, 1921–1998,
vol. X
Harding, Rowe, 1901–1991, vol. IX
Harding, Sidnie M.; see Manton, S. M.
Harding, Walter; see Harding, T. W.
Harding, Col Thomas Walter, 1843–1927, vol. II
Harding, Walter Ambrose Heath, 1870–1942,
vol. IV
Harding, Warren Gamaliel, 1865–1923, vol. II
Harding, Lt-Col William, died 1945, vol. IV
Harding-Newman, Brig.-Gen. Edward; see Newman.
Harding-Newman, Maj.-Gen. John Cartwright,
1874–1935, vol. III

Hardinge, 3rd Viscount, 1857–1924, vol. II
Hardinge, 4th Viscount, 1905–1979, vol. VII
Hardinge, 5th Viscount, 1929–1984, vol. VIII
Hardinge of Penshurst, 1st Baron, 1858–1944,
vol. IV
Hardinge of Penshurst, 2nd Baron, 1894–1960,
vol. V
Hardinge of Penshurst, 3rd Baron, 1921–1997,
vol. X
Hardinge, Rt Hon. Sir Arthur Henry, 1859–1933,
vol. III
Hardinge, Sir Charles Edmund, 5th Bt, 1878–1968,
vol. VI
Hardinge, Sir Edmund Stracey, 4th Bt, 1833–1924,
vol. II
Hardinge, Hon. Henry Ralph, 1895–1915, vol. I
Hardinge, Sir Robert, 6th Bt, 1887–1973, vol. VII
Hardinge, Sir Robert Arnold, 7th Bt, 1914–1986,
vol. IX (AI)
Hardingham, Sir Robert Ernest, 1903–1991, vol. IX
Hardisty, Charles William, 1893–1973, vol. VII
Hardman, Amy Elizabeth, 1909–1990, vol. VIII
Hardman, David Rennie, 1901–1989, vol. VIII
Hardman, Air Chief Marshal Sir Donald Innes; see
Hardman, Air Chief Marshal Sir J. D. I.
Hardman, Sir Fred, 1914–1991, vol. IX
Hardman, James Arthur, 1929–1996, vol. X
Hardman, Air Chief Marshal Sir (James) Donald
Innes, 1899–1982, vol. VIII
Hardman, Rev. Oscar, 1880–1964, vol. VI
Hardman, Lt-Col Reginald Stanley, 1870–1936,
vol. III
Hardman-Jones, Vice-Adm. Everard John,
1881–1962, vol. VI
Hardwick, Charles Aubrey, 1885–1984, vol. VIII
Hardwick, Donald Ross, 1895–1977, vol. VII
Hardwick, Francis William, 1861–1934, vol. III
Hardwick, Rev. John Charlton, 1885–1953, vol. V
Hardwick, John Jessop, 1831–1917, vol. II
Hardwick, Michael John Drinkrow, 1924–1991,
vol. IX
Hardwick, Lt-Col Philip Edward, 1875–1919, vol. II
Hardwicke, 5th Earl of, 1836–1897, vol. I
Hardwicke, 6th Earl of, 1867–1904, vol. I
Hardwicke, 7th Earl of, 1840–1909, vol. I
Hardwicke, 8th Earl of, 1869–1936, vol. III
Hardwicke, 9th Earl of, 1906–1974, vol. VII
Hardwicke, Sir Cedric Webster, 1893–1964, vol. VI
Hardwicke, Herbert Junius, died 1921, vol. II
Hardy, Hon. Alfred Erskine G.; see
Gathorne-Hardy.
Hardy, Sir Alister Clavering, 1896–1985, vol. VIII
Hardy, Archibald C.; see Cozens-Hardy.
Hardy, Hon. Arthur Charles, 1872–1962, vol. VI
Hardy, Rev. Arthur Octavius, 1838–1910, vol. I
Hardy, Arthur Sherburne, 1847–1930, vol. III
Hardy, Rev. Canon Basil Augustus, 1901–1973,
vol. VII
Hardy, Major Sir Bertram, 3rd Bt, 1877–1953,
vol. V
Hardy, Gen. Sir Campbell Richard, 1906–1984,
vol. VIII
Hardy, Charles, 1874–1940, vol. III
Hardy, Col Hon. Charles Gathorne G.; see
Gathorne-Hardy.

Hardy, Charles Stewart, 1842–1914, vol. I
Hardy, Vice-Adm. Charles Talbot, 1877–1935, vol. III
Hardy, Dudley, 1867–1922, vol. II
Hardy, Rev. E. J., 1849–1920, vol. II
Hardy, Edgar Wrigley C.; see Cozens-Hardy.
Hardy, Sir Edward, 1887–1975, vol. VII
Hardy, Edward Arthur, 1884–1960, vol. V
Hardy, Col Edwin Greenwood, 1867–1944, vol. IV
Hardy, Major Eric John, 1884–1965, vol. VI
Hardy, Ernest George, 1852–1925, vol. II
Hardy, Evan A., 1890–1963, vol. VI
Hardy, Lt-Col Francis, 1875–1929, vol. III
Hardy, Francis, 1879–1977, vol. VII
Hardy, Maj.-Gen. Frederick, 1830–1916, vol. II
Hardy, Geoffrey Malcolm G.; see Gathorne-Hardy.
Hardy, George Alexander, 1851–1920, vol. II
Hardy, Brig. George Alfred, 1923–1990, vol. VIII
Hardy, Sir George Francis, died 1914, vol. I
Hardy, Gerald Holbech, 1852–1929, vol. III
Hardy, Godfrey Harold, 1877–1947, vol. IV
Hardy, Gordon Sidey, 1884–1936, vol. III
Hardy, Sir Harry, 1896–1984, vol. VIII
Hardy, Henry Harrison, 1882–1958, vol. V
Hardy, Herbert Ronald, 1900–1954, vol. V
Hardy, Lady Isobel G.; see Gathorne-Hardy.
Hardy, Iza Duffus, died 1922, vol. II
Hardy, Sir James Douglas, 1915–1986, vol. VIII
Hardy, Major Jocelyn Lee, 1894–1958, vol. V
Hardy, Sir (John) Francis G.; see Gathorne-Hardy.
Hardy, Rt Hon. Laurence, 1854–1933, vol. III
Hardy, Lt-Col Leonard Henry, 1882–1954, vol. V
Hardy, Oswald Henry, died 1940, vol. III
Hardy, Sir Reginald, 2nd Bt, 1848–1938, vol. III
Hardy, Richard Gillies, 1852–1923, vol. II
Hardy, Hon. Robert G.; see Gathorne-Hardy.
Hardy, Sir Rupert John, 4th Bt, 1902–1997, vol. X
Hardy, Air Cdre Stephen Haistwell, 1905–1945, vol. IV
Hardy, Rev. Theodore Bayley, 1866–1918, vol. II
Hardy, Thomas, 1840–1928, vol. II
Hardy, Co. Thomas Eben F.; see Forman Hardy.
Hardy, Maj.-Gen. Thomas Henry, 1863–1938, vol. III
Hardy, Thomas Lionel, 1887–1969, vol. VI
Hardy, Lt-Gen. William, 1822–1901, vol. I
Hardy, Sir William Bate, 1864–1934, vol. III
Hardy, William John, 1857–1919, vol. II
Hardy-Roberts, Brig. Sir Geoffrey Paul, 1907–1997, vol. X
Hare, Hon. Alan Victor, 1919–1995, vol. IX
Hare, Alfred Thomas, 1855–1945, vol. IV
Hare, Amy, died 1939, vol. III
Hare, Augustus John Cuthbert, 1834–1903, vol. I
Hare, Bt Lt-Col Charles Tristram Melville, 1879–1950, vol. IV
Hare, Christopher, died 1929, vol. III
Hare, Cyril; see Gordon Clark, Alfred Alexander.
Hare, Dora, (Hon. Mrs Richard Hare); see Gordine, D.
Hare, Dorothy Christian, died 1967, vol. VI
Hare, Edgar James, 1884–1969, vol. VI
Hare, Francis, 1858–1928, vol. II, vol. III
Hare, Col Frederick Stephen Christian, 1857–1931, vol. III

Hare, Geoffrey, 1940–1988, vol. VIII
Hare, Brig. George Ambrose, 1880–1948, vol. IV
Hare, Sir (George) Ralph Leigh, 3rd Bt (cr 1818), 1866–1933, vol. III
Hare, George Thompson, 1863–1906, vol. I
Hare, Henry Thomas, died 1921, vol. II
Hare, Rev. Hugh James, 1829–1909, vol. I
Hare, Maj.-Gen. James Francis, 1897–1970, vol. VI
Hare, Sir John, 1844–1921, vol. II
Hare, John Gilbert, 1869–1951, vol. V
Hare, John Hugh Montague, died 1935, vol. III
Hare, Rt Rev. John Tyrrell Holmes, 1912–1976, vol. VII
Hare, Julius, 1859–1932, vol. III
Hare, Kenneth, 1888–1962, vol. VI
Hare, Sir Lancelot, 1851–1922, vol. II
Hare, Patrick James, 1920–1982, vol. VIII
Hare, Sir Philip Leigh, 6th Bt (cr 1818), 1922–2000, vol. X
Hare, Sir Ralph; see Hare, Sir G. R. L.
Hare, Major Sir Ralph Leigh, 4th Bt (cr 1818), 1903–1976, vol. VII
Hare, Reginald Charles, died 1933, vol. III
Hare, Rear-Adm. Hon. Richard, 1836–1903, vol. I
Hare, Col Richard Charles, 1844–1917, vol. II
Hare, Hon. Richard Gilbert, 1907–1966, vol. VI
Hare, Robert Douglas, 1848–1929, vol. III
Hare, Brig.-Gen. Robert Hugh, 1867–1950, vol. IV
Hare, Brig.-Gen. Robert William, 1872–1953, vol. V
Hare, Robertson, 1891–1979, vol. VII
Hare, Ronald, 1899–1986, vol. VIII
Hare, St George, 1857–1933, vol. III
Hare, Maj.-Gen. Sir Steuart Welwood, 1867–1952, vol. V
Hare, Theodore Julius, 1839–1907, vol. I
Hare, Sir Thomas, 5th Bt (cr 1818), 1930–1993, vol. IX
Hare, Sir Thomas Leigh, 1st Bt (cr 1905), 1859–1941, vol. IV
Hare, Thomas Leman, died 1935, vol. III
Hare, Tom, 1895–1959, vol. V
Hare, William Loftus, 1868–1943, vol. IV
Hares, Ven. Archdeacon Walter P., 1877–1962, vol. VI
Harewood, 5th Earl of, 1846–1929, vol. III
Harewood, 6th Earl of, 1882–1947, vol. IV
Harford, Sir Arthur; see Harford, Sir G. A.
Harford, Charles Forbes, died 1925, vol. II
Harford, Rev. Edward John, died 1917, vol. II
Harford, Frederic Dundas, 1862–1931, vol. III
Harford, Rev. George, 1860–1921, vol. II
Harford, Sir (George) Arthur, 2nd Bt, 1897–1967, vol. VI
Harford, Col Henry Charles, 1850–1937, vol. III
Harford, Sir James Dundas, 1899–1993, vol. IX
Harford, Rev. John Battersby, 1857–1937, vol. III
Harford, Major Sir John Charles, 1st Bt, 1860–1934, vol. III
Hargest, Brig. James, 1891–1944, vol. IV
Hargrave, John Gordon, 1894–1982, vol. VIII
Hargreaves, Alfred, 1899–1978, vol. VII (AII)
Hargreaves, Anthony Dalzell, 1904–1959, vol. V
Hargreaves, Eric Lyde, 1898–1984, vol. VIII
Hargreaves, George Ronald, 1908–1962, vol. VI

Hargreaves, Sir Gerald de la Pryme, *died* 1972, vol. VII

Hargreaves, John, 1864–1926, vol. II

Hargreaves, John Henry, 1856–1934, vol. III

Hargreaves, Brig. Kenneth, 1903–1990, vol. VIII

Hargreaves, Lionel Stanley, 1882–1954, vol. V

Hargreaves, Sir Thomas, 1889–1966, vol. VI

Hargreaves, Sir Walter Ernest, 1865–1954, vol. V

Hargreaves, Maj.-Gen. William Herbert, 1908–1994, vol. IX

Hargrove, Rev. Joseph, 1843–1914, vol. I

Hari Kishan Kaul, Raja Pandit, 1869–1942, vol. IV

Hari Singhji Raja, Rao Bahadur, 1877–1933, vol. III

Harington, Gen. Sir Charles Harington, 1872–1940, vol. III

Harington, Sir Charles Robert, 1897–1972, vol. VII

Harington, Edward, 1863–1937, vol. III

Harington, (Edward Henry) Vernon, 1907–1995, vol. IX

Harington, Brig.-Gen. John, 1873–1943, vol. IV

Harington, Maj.-Gen. John, 1912–1989, vol. VIII

Harington, John Charles Dundas, 1903–1980, vol. VII

Harington, Sir Richard, 11th Bt, 1835–1911, vol. I

Harington, Sir Richard, 12th Bt, 1861–1931, vol. III

Harington, Sir Richard Dundas, 13th Bt, 1900–1981, vol. VIII

Harington, Vernon; *see* Harington, E. H. V.

Harington Hawes, Derrick Gordon, 1907–1986, vol. VIII

Harisinghji, Lt-Gen. Shri Sir, 1895–1961, vol. VI

Harker, Alfred, 1859–1939, vol. III

Harker, Mrs Allen, (Lizzie Harker), *died* 1933, vol. III

Harker, Brig. Arthur William Allen, 1890–1960, vol. V

Harker, Ven. Ernest Gardner, *died* 1928, vol. II

Harker, Gordon, 1885–1967, vol. VI

Harker, John Allen, 1870–1923, vol. II

Harker, Joseph Cunningham, 1855–1927, vol. II

Harker, Lizzie; *see* Harker, Mrs A.

Harker, Rowand, 1879–1946, vol. IV

Harkin, Brendan, 1920–1995, vol. X (AI)

Harkness, Sir Douglas Alexander Earsman, 1902–1980, vol. VII

Harkness, Lt-Col Hon. Douglas Scott, 1903–1999, vol. X

Harkness, Edward Burns, 1874–1957, vol. V

Harkness, Rev. Canon Edward Law, 1874–1931, vol. III

Harkness, Edward S., 1874–1940, vol. III

Harkness, Col Henry D'Alton, 1859–1934, vol. III

Harkness, Jack; *see* Harkness, John L.

Harkness, James, 1864–1923, vol. II

Harkness, John Leigh, (Jack), 1918–1994, vol. IX

Harkness, Sir Joseph Welsh Park, 1890–1962, vol. VI

Harkness, Captain Kenneth Lanyan, 1900–1990, vol. VIII

Harlan, John M., 1899–1971, vol. VII

Harland, Albert, 1869–1957, vol. V

Harland, Henry, 1861–1905, vol. I

Harland, Henry Peirson, 1876–1945, vol. IV

Harland, Ven. Lawrence Winston, 1905–1977, vol. VII

Harland, Rt Rev. Maurice Henry, 1896–1986, vol. VIII

Harland, Sydney Cross, 1891–1982, vol. VIII

Harland, William Arthur, 1926–1985, vol. VIII

Harlech, 2nd Baron, 1819–1904, vol. I

Harlech, 3rd Baron, 1855–1938, vol. III

Harlech, 4th Baron, 1885–1964, vol. VI

Harlech, 5th Baron, 1918–1985, vol. VIII

Harlech, Lady; (Beatrice Mildred Edith), 1891–1980, vol. VII

Harley, Alexander Hamilton, 1882–1951, vol. V

Harley, Rev. Alfred W. M., 1862–1941, vol. IV

Harley, Col George Ernest, 1844–1907, vol. I

Harley, Sir Harry, (Herbert Henry), 1877–1951, vol. V

Harley, Lt-Col Henry Kellett, 1868–1920, vol. II

Harley, Sir Herbert Henry; *see* Harley, Sir Harry.

Harley, John Hunter, 1865–1947, vol. IV

Harley, John Laker, 1911–1990, vol. VIII

Harley, Rev. Robert, 1828–1910, vol. I

Harley, Sir Stanley Jaffa, 1905–1979, vol. VII

Harley, Lt-Col Thomas William, 1876–1950, vol. IV

Harley, Sir Thomas Winlack, 1895–1991, vol. IX

Harley, Vaughan, 1863–1923, vol. II

Harlock, Maj.-Gen. Hugh George Frederick, 1900–1981, vol. VIII

Harlow, Christopher Millward, 1889–1972, vol. VII

Harlow, Frederick James, *died* 1965, vol. VI

Harlow, Vincent Todd, 1898–1961, vol. VI

Harman, Brig.-Gen. Alexander Ramsay, 1877–1954, vol. V

Harman, Lt-Gen. Sir (Antony Ernest) Wentworth, 1872–1961, vol. VI

Harman, Sir Cecil William Francis S. K.; *see* Stafford-King-Harman.

Harman, Sir Charles Anthony K.; *see* King-Harman.

Harman, Rt Hon. Sir Charles Eustace, 1894–1970, vol. VI

Harman, Sir (Clement) James, 1894–1975, vol. VII

Harman, Captain Douglas K.; *see* King-Harman.

Harman, Edward George, 1862–1921, vol. II

Harman, Ernest Henry, 1908–1989, vol. VIII

Harman, Major George Malcolm Nixon, 1872–1914, vol. I

Harman, Sir James; *see* Harman, Sir C. J.

Harman, John Bishop, 1907–1994, vol. IX

Harman, N. Bishop, 1869–1945, vol. IV

Harman, Lt-Col Richard, 1864–1905, vol. I

Harman, Captain (Robert) Douglas K.; *see* King-Harman.

Harman, Lt-Gen. Sir Wentworth; *see* Harman, Lt-Gen. Sir A. E. W.

Harman, Col Wentworth Henry K.; *see* King-Harman.

Harmar, Fairlie, *died* 1945, vol. IV

Harmar-Nicholls, Baron (Life Peer); Harmar Harmar-Nicholls, 1912–2000, vol. X

Harmer, Cyril Henry Carrington, 1903–1986, vol. VIII

Harmer, Sir Dudley; *see* Harmer, Sir J. D.

Harmer, Florence Elizabeth, *died* 1967, vol. VI

Harmer, Sir Frederic Evelyn, 1905–1995, vol. IX

Harmer, Frederic William, 1835–1923, vol. II

Harmer, Sir (John) Dudley, 1913–1991, vol. IX

Harmer, Rt Rev. John Reginald, 1857–1944, vol. IV
Harmer, Lewis Charles, 1902–1975, vol. VII
Harmer, Michael Hedley, 1912–1998, vol. X
Harmer, Sir Sidney Frederic, 1862–1950, vol. IV
Harmer, William Douglas, 1873–1962, vol. VI
Harmood-Banner, Sir George Knowles, 3rd Bt, 1918–1990, vol. VIII
Harmood-Banner, Major Sir Harmood, 2nd Bt, 1876–1950, vol. IV
Harmood-Banner, Sir John Sutherland, 1st Bt, 1847–1929, vol. II
Harmsworth, 1st Baron, 1869–1948, vol. IV
Harmsworth, 2nd Baron, 1903–1990, vol. VIII
Harmsworth, Sir Alfred Leicester St Barbe, 2nd Bt (cr 1918), 1892–1962, vol. VI
Harmsworth, Anthony; see Harmsworth, P. A. T. H.
Harmsworth, Sir (Arthur) Geoffrey (Annesley), 3rd Bt (cr 1918), 1904–1980, vol. VII
Harmsworth, Sir Geoffrey; see Harmsworth, Sir A. G. A.
Harmsworth, Sir Harold Cecil Aubrey, 1897–1952, vol. V
Harmsworth, Sir Hildebrand Alfred Beresford, 2nd Bt (cr 1922), 1901–1977, vol. VII
Harmsworth, Sir Hildebrand Aubrey, 1st Bt (cr 1922), died 1929, vol. III
Harmsworth, St John Bernard Vyvyan, 1912–1995, vol. IX
Harmsworth, Sir Leicester; see Harmsworth, Sir R. L.
Harmsworth, (Perceval) Anthony (Thomas Hildebrand), 1907–1968, vol. VI
Harmsworth, Sir (Robert) Leicester, 1st Bt (cr 1918), 1870–1937, vol. III
Harmsworth, Vyvyan George, 1881–1957, vol. V
Harnack, Adolf von, 1851–1930, vol. III
Harnam Singh, Hon. Raja Sir, 1851–1930, vol. III
Harness, Maj.-Gen. Arthur, 1838–1927, vol. II
Harnett, Air Cdre Edward St Clair, 1881–1964, vol. VI
Harnett, Walter Lidwell, 1879–1957, vol. V
Harnett, Rev. William Lee, 1864–1937, vol. III
Harney, Edward Augustine St Aubyn, died 1929, vol. III
Harniman, John Phillip, 1939–1999, vol. X
Harold, Bt Lt-Col Charles Henry Hasler, 1885–1938, vol. III
Harold, Eileen, 1909–1974, vol. VII
Harold, John, died 1916, vol. II
Haroon, Seth Haji Sir Abdoola, 1872–1942, vol. IV
Harper, Alan Henry, 1943–1997, vol. X
Harper, Alfred Alexander, 1907–1996, vol. X
Harper, Sir Arthur Grant, 1898–1982, vol. VIII
Harper, Bill; see Harper, F. A.
Harper, Charles G., 1863–1943, vol. IV
Harper, Sir Charles Henry, 1876–1950, vol. IV
Harper, Denis Rawnsley, 1907–1993, vol. IX
Harper, Sir Edgar, 1860–1934, vol. III
Harper, Frank Appleby (Bill), 1920–1983, vol. VIII
Harper, Sir George, 1843–1937, vol. III
Harper, George Clifford, 1900–1986, vol. VIII
Harper, George MacGowan, 1899–1976, vol. VII
Harper, George McLean, 1863–1947, vol. IV
Harper, George Milne, 1882–1943, vol. IV

Harper, Lt-Gen. Sir George Montague, 1865–1922, vol. II
Harper, Gerald, died 1929, vol. III
Harper, Harry, 1880–1960, vol. V
Harper, Ven. Henry William, died 1922, vol. II
Harper, Very Rev. James Walker, 1859–1938, vol. III
Harper, Vice-Adm. John Ernest Troyte, 1874–1949, vol. IV
Harper, Lt-Col John Robinson, 1867–1947, vol. IV
Harper, Joseph, 1914–1978, vol. VII
Harper, Sir Kenneth Brand, 1891–1961, vol. VI
Harper, Norman, 1904–1967, vol. VI
Harper, Norman Adamson, 1913–1982, vol. VIII
Harper, Lt-Col Reginald Tristram, 1876–1958, vol. V
Harper, Sir Richard Stephenson, 1902–1973, vol. VII
Harper, Very Rev. Walter, 1848–1930, vol. III
Harper, William Rainey, 1856–1906, vol. I
Harper Gow, Sir Maxwell; see Harper Gow, Sir L. M.
Harper Gow, Sir (Leonard) Maxwell, 1918–1996, vol. X
Harpham, Sir William, 1906–1999, vol. X
Harpignies, Henri Joseph, 1819–1916, vol. II
Harpley, Sydney Charles, 1927–1992, vol. IX
Harpole, James; see Abraham, J. J.
Harraden, Beatrice, 1864–1936, vol. III
Harragin, Alfred Ernest Albert, 1877–1941, vol. IV
Harragin, Sir Walter, 1890–1966, vol. VI
Harrap, George Godfrey, 1867–1938, vol. III
Harrap, (George) Paull (Munro), 1917–1985, vol. VIII
Harrap, Paull; see Harrap, G. P. M.
Harrap, Walter Godfrey, 1894–1967, vol. VI
Harrel, Rt Hon. Sir David, 1841–1939, vol. III
Harrel, William Vesey, 1866–1956, vol. V
Harrey, Cyril Ogden W.; see Wakefield-Harrey.
Harries, Arthur John, 1856–1922, vol. II
Harries, Sir Arthur Trevor, 1892–1959, vol. V
Harries, Rear-Adm. David Hugh, 1903–1980, vol. VII
Harries, Air Vice-Marshal Sir Douglas, 1893–1972, vol. VII
Harries, Frederick James, died 1934, vol. III
Harries, Robert Henry, 1859–1918, vol. II
Harries, Victor Percy, 1907–1977, vol. VII
Harriman, Averell; see Harriman, W. A.
Harriman, Edward Henry, died 1909, vol. I
Harriman, Sir George, died 1973, vol. VII
Harriman, Pamela, 1920–1997, vol. X
Harriman, (William) Averell, 1891–1986, vol. VIII
Harrington, 8th Earl of, 1844–1917, vol. II
Harrington, 9th Earl of, 1859–1928, vol. II
Harrington, 10th Earl of, 1887–1929, vol. III
Harrington, Charles, died 1943, vol. IV
Harrington, Ernest John, 1864–1944, vol. IV
Harrington, Col Hon. Gordon Sidney, 1883–1943, vol. IV
Harrington, Vice-Adm. Sir Hastings; see Harrington, Vice-Adm. Sir W. H.
Harrington, Sir John Lane, 1865–1927, vol. II
Harrington, Rt Hon. Sir Stanley, 1856–1949, vol. IV

Harrington, Thomas Joseph, 1875–1953, vol. V
Harrington, Timothy Charles, 1851–1910, vol. I
Harrington, Vice-Adm. Sir (Wilfred) Hastings, 1906–1965, vol. VI
Harriott, George Moss, 1858–1943, vol. IV
Harris, 4th Baron, 1851–1932, vol. III
Harris, 5th Baron, 1889–1984, vol. VIII
Harris, 6th Baron, 1920–1995, vol. IX
Harris, 7th Baron, 1916–1996, vol. X
Harris, Hon. Addison C., 1840–1916, vol. II
Harris, Sir Alan James, 1916–2000, vol. X
Harris, Albert Henry, 1885–1945, vol. IV
Harris, Sir Alexander; see Harris, Sir C. A.
Harris, Lt-Col Alexander Sutherland S.; see Sutherland-Harris.
Harris, Sir Anthony Travers Kyrle, 2nd Bt, 1918–1996, vol. X
Harris, Sir Archibald, 1883–1971, vol. VII
Harris, Sir Arthur Ambrose Hall, 1854–1939, vol. III
Harris, Marshal of the Royal Air Force, Sir Arthur Travers, Bt, 1892–1984, vol. VIII
Harris, Sir Austin Edward, 1870–1958, vol. V
Harris, Ven. Charles, died 1934, vol. III
Harris, Rev. Charles, 1865–1936, vol. III
Harris, Sir Charles, 1864–1943, vol. IV
Harris, Sir (Charles) Alexander, 1855–1947, vol. IV
Harris, Lt-Col Charles Beresford Maule, 1866–1932, vol. III
Harris, Sir Charles Felix, 1900–1974, vol. VII
Harris, Rear-Adm. Charles Frederick, 1887–1957, vol. V
Harris, Sir Charles Herbert S.; see Stuart-Harris.
Harris, Sir Charles Joseph William, 1901–1986, vol. VIII
Harris, Charles Reginald Schiller, 1896–1979, vol. VII
Harris, Colin Grendon, 1912–1992, vol. IX
Harris, Col Sir David, 1852–1942, vol. IV
Harris, David Fraser F.; see Fraser-Harris.
Harris, David R., died 1958, vol. V
Harris, Dame Diana R.; see Reader Harris.
Harris, Rev. Donald Bertram, 1904–1996, vol. X
Harris, Sir Douglas Gordon, 1883–1967, vol. VI
Harris, Edward, 1849–1933, vol. III
Harris, Edmund Leslie, 1928–1998, vol. X
Harris, (Emanuel) Vincent, 1876–1971, vol. VII
Harris, Evan Cadogan, 1906–1988, vol. VIII
Harris, Frank, 1856–1931, vol. III
Harris, Captain Hon. Frank Ernest, 1877–1951, vol. V
Harris, Frederic Walter, 1915–1979, vol. VII
Harris, Lt-Gen. Sir Frederick, 1891–1976, vol. VII
Harris, Rt Hon. Frederick Leverton, 1864–1926, vol. II
Harris, Frederick Rutherfoord, 1856–1920, vol. II
Harris, Frederick William, 1833–1917, vol. II
Harris, Geoffrey Herbert, 1914–1998, vol. X
Harris, Geoffrey Wingfield, 1913–1971, vol. VII
Harris, George, 1844–1922, vol. II
Harris, Major George Arthur, 1879–1935, vol. III
Harris, Sir George David, 1827–1920, vol. I
Harris, Maj.-Gen. George Francis Angelo, 1856–1931, vol. III

Harris, Rev. Canon George Herbert, 1885–1968, vol. VI
Harris, George Montagu, 1868–1951, vol. V
Harris, Col Gerald Noel Anstice, 1866–1952, vol. V
Harris, Harry, 1919–1994, vol. IX
Harris, Henry, died 1950, vol. IV
Harris, Henry Albert, 1886–1968, vol. VI
Harris, Sir Henry Percy, 1856–1941, vol. IV
Harris, (Henry) Wilson, 1883–1955, vol. V
Harris, Rev. Preb. Herbert, 1884–1971, vol. VII
Harris, Col Herbert Sextus, 1884–1932, vol. III
Harris, Lt-Gen. Sir Ian Cecil, 1910–1999, vol. X
Harris, Sir Jack Alexander S.; see Sutherland-Harris.
Harris, Air Vice-Marshal Jack Harris, 1903–1963, vol. VI
Harris, Sir James Charles, 1831–1904, vol. I
Harris, James Rendel, 1852–1941, vol. IV
Harris, Maj.-Gen. James Thomas, died 1914, vol. I
Harris, Joel Chandler, 1848–1908, vol. I
Harris, John Edward, 1910–1968, vol. VI
Harris, Sir John H., 1874–1940, vol. III
Harris, John Henry, 1875–1962, vol. VI
Harris, John Mitchell, 1856–1927, vol. II
Harris, John Redford Oberlin, 1877–1960, vol. V(A), vol. VI (AI)
Harris, Hon. Sir John Richards, 1868–1946, vol. IV
Harris, Hon. John William, 1849–1932, vol. III
Harris, Kenneth Edwin, 1900–1981, vol. VIII
Harris, Brig. Lawrence Anstie, 1896–1970, vol. VI
Harris, Leonard Charles, 1873–1953, vol. V
Harris, Leonard Tatham, died 1960, vol. V
Harris, Leslie J., 1898–1973, vol. VII
Harris, Sir Lewis Edward, 1900–1983, vol. VIII
Harris, Brig. Sir Lionel Herbert, 1897–1971, vol. VII
Harris, Lloyd, 1867–1925, vol. II
Harris, Margaret Frances, 1904–2000, vol. X
Harris, Mary Kathleen, 1885–1968, vol. VI
Harris, Sir Matthew, 1840–1917, vol. II
Harris, Nigel John, 1943–1996, vol. X
Harris, Noel Gordon, 1897–1963, vol. VI
Harris, Noël Hedley V.; see Vicars-Harris.
Harris, Norman Charles, 1887–1963, vol. VI
Harris, Rt Hon. Sir Percy Alfred, 1st Bt, 1876–1952, vol. V
Harris, Percy Graham, 1894–1945, vol. IV
Harris, Sir Percy W.; see Wyn-Harris.
Harris, Gen. Philip Henry Farrell, 1833–1913, vol. I
Harris, Reader, 1847–1909, vol. I
Harris, Richard, died 1906, vol. I
Harris, Richard Hancock William Henry, 1851–1927, vol. II
Harris, Sir Richard Olver, 1894–1955, vol. V
Harris, Robert, died 1919, vol. II
Harris, Robert, 1900–1995, vol. IX
Harris, Adm. Sir Robert Hastings, 1843–1926, vol. II
Harris, Robert John Cecil, 1922–1980, vol. VII
Harris, Robert Thornhill, 1865–1934, vol. III
Harris, Sir Ronald Montague Joseph, 1913–1995, vol. IX
Harris, Rev. Samuel Collard, 1869–1940, vol. III (A), vol. IV

Harris, Sidney, 1903–1976, vol. VII
Harris, Sir Sidney West, 1876–1962, vol. VI
Harris, Thomas Emlyn, 1894–1955, vol. V
Harris, Thomas Maxwell, 1903–1983, vol. VIII
Harris, Vincent; see Harris, E. V.
Harris, Walter B., 1866–1933, vol. III
Harris, Hon. Walter Edward, 1904–1999, vol. X
Harris, Sir Walter Henry, 1851–1922, vol. II
Harris, Wilfred John, 1869–1960, vol. V
Harris, William, 1864–1923, vol. II
Harris, William Barclay, 1911–2000, vol. X
Harris, Sir William Henry, 1883–1973, vol. VII
Harris, William James, 1835–1911, vol. I
Harris, Ven. William Stuart, died 1935, vol. III
Harris, Sir William Woolf, 1910–1988, vol. VIII
Harris, Wilson; see Harris, H. W.
Harris-Burland, John Burland, 1870–1926, vol. II
Harrison, Albert John, 1862–1941, vol. IV
Harrison, Albert Norman, 1901–1992, vol. IX
Harrison, Alexander, 1890–1988, vol. VIII
Harrison, Alfred Bayford, 1845–1918, vol. II
Harrison, Alick Robin Walsham, 1900–1969,
    vol. VI
Harrison, Sir Archibald Frederick, 1894–1976,
    vol. VII
Harrison, Archibald Walter, 1882–1946, vol. IV
Harrison, Brig.-Gen. Arthur Howarth Pryce,
    1871–1949, vol. IV
Harrison, Arthur Neville John, 1881–1973, vol. VII
Harrison, Austin, 1873–1928, vol. II
Harrison, Beatrice, died 1965, vol. VI
Harrison, Benjamin, 1833–1901, vol. I
Harrison, Sir (Bernard) Guy, 1885–1978, vol. VII
Harrison, Rev. Cecil Marriott, 1911–1986, vol. VIII
Harrison, Major Cecil Pryce, 1880–1938, vol. III
Harrison, Sir Cecil Reeves, 1856–1940, vol. III
Harrison, Cecil Stanley, 1902–1962, vol. VI
Harrison, Charles, 1835–1897, vol. I
Harrison, Charles, died 1943, vol. IV
Harrison, Charles Custis, 1844–1929, vol. III
Harrison, Col Charles Edward, 1852–1944, vol. IV
Harrison, Charles Victor, 1907–1996, vol. X
Harrison, Sir Charlton Scott Cholmeley,
    1881–1951, vol. V
Harrison, Col Cholmeley Edward Carl Branfill,
    1857–1937, vol. III
Harrison, Constance Cary, died 1920, vol. II
Harrison, Sir Cyril Ernest, 1901–1980, vol. VII
Harrison, Maj.-Gen. Desmond, 1896–1984,
    vol. VIII
Harrison, Douglas Creese, 1901–1997, vol. X
Harrison, Very Rev. Douglas Ernest William,
    1903–1974, vol. VII
Harrison, Lt-Col Edgar Garston, 1863–1947,
    vol. IV
Harrison, Sir Edward Richard, 1872–1960, vol. V
Harrison, Ven. Edward Stanley, 1889–1948, vol. IV
Harrison, Maj.-Gen. Eric George William Warde,
    1893–1987, vol. VIII
Harrison, Rt Hon. Sir Eric John, 1892–1974,
    vol. VII
Harrison, Ernest, 1877–1943, vol. IV
Harrison, Ernest, 1886–1981, vol. VIII
Harrison, Major Esme Stuart Erskine, 1864–1902,
    vol. I

Harrison, Sir Fowler; see Harrison, Sir J. F.
Harrison, Francis Capel, 1863–1938, vol. III
Harrison, Francis Llewelyn, 1905–1987, vol. VIII
Harrison, Fred, 1865–1954, vol. V
Harrison, Frederic, 1831–1923, vol. II
Harrison, Frederic James, died 1915, vol. I
Harrison, Lt-Col Sir Frederick, 1844–1914, vol. I
Harrison, Frederick, died 1926, vol. II
Harrison, Rev. Frederick, 1884–1958, vol. V
Harrison, Gabriel Harold, 1921–1974, vol. VII
Harrison, Sir Geoffrey Wedgwood, 1908–1990,
    vol. VIII
Harrison, Major George, 1885–1961, vol. VI
Harrison, George Anthony, 1930–1992, vol. IX
Harrison, Major George Arthur, 1876–1939, vol. III
Harrison, George Bagshawe, 1894–1991, vol. IX
Harrison, Brig.-Gen. George Hyde, 1877–1965,
    vol. VI
Harrison, George Leslie, 1887–1958, vol. V
Harrison, Gerald Joseph Cuthbert, 1895–1954,
    vol. V
Harrison, Brig.-Gen. Gilbert Harwood, 1866–1930,
    vol. III
Harrison, Sir Guy; see Harrison, Sir B. G.
Harrison, Brig. Harold Cecil, died 1940, vol. III
Harrison, Sir Harwood; see Harrison, Sir J. H.
Harrison, Sir Heath, 1st Bt (cr 1917), 1857–1934,
    vol. III
Harrison, Henry, 1867–1954, vol. V
Harrison, Captain Henry Neville Baskcomb-,
    1879–1915, vol. I
Harrison, Rear-Adm. Hubert Southwood,
    1898–1985, vol. VIII
Harrison, James, 1899–1959, vol. V
Harrison, James Fraser, 1890–1971, vol. VII
Harrison, Sir (James) Harwood, 1st Bt (cr 1961),
    1907–1980, vol. VII
Harrison, Sir James Humphreys, 1848–1933,
    vol. III
Harrison, James Jonathan, 1858–1923, vol. II
Harrison, Maj.-Gen. James Murray Robert,
    1880–1957, vol. V
Harrison, Maj.-Gen. Sir James William, 1912–1971,
    vol. VII
Harrison, Jane Ellen, 1850–1928, vol. II
Harrison, John, 1847–1922, vol. II
Harrison, Sir John, 1st Bt (cr 1922), 1856–1936,
    vol. III
Harrison, Sir John, 1866–1944, vol. IV
Harrison, John Audley, 1917–1992, vol. IX
Harrison, Sir John Burchmore, 1856–1926, vol. II
Harrison, Sir (John) Fowler, 2nd Bt (cr 1922),
    1899–1947, vol. IV
Harrison, John H.; see Heslop-Harrison.
Harrison, Maj.-Gen. John Martin Donald W.; see
    Ward-Harrison.
Harrison, John Vernon, 1892–1972, vol. VII
Harrison, John William H.; see Heslop-Harrison.
Harrison, Sir (John) Wyndham, 3rd Bt (cr 1922),
    1933–1955, vol. VII
Harrison, Joseph Richard, 1888–1957, vol. V
Harrison, Julius Allan Greenway, 1885–1963,
    vol. VI
Harrison, Kathleen, (Mrs J. H. Back), 1892–1995,
    vol. IX

Harrison, Laurence, 1897–1982, vol. VIII
Harrison, Lawrence Alexander, *died* 1937, vol. III
Harrison, Col Lawrence Whitaker, 1876–1964, vol. VI
Harrison, Lloyd Adnitt, 1911–1985, vol. VIII
Harrison, Bt Col Louis Kenneth, 1871–1951, vol. V
Harrison, Mary St Leger, 1852–1931, vol. III
Harrison, May, *died* 1959, vol. V
Harrison, Michael, 1876–1935, vol. III
Harrison, Lt-Col Norman, *died* 1949, vol. IV
Harrison, Philip, *died* 1933, vol. III
Harrison, Reginald, 1837–1908, vol. I
Harrison, Sir Reginald Carey, (Sir Rex), 1908–1990, vol. VIII
Harrison, Sir Rex; *see* Harrison, Sir Reginald C.
Harrison, Gen. Sir Richard, 1837–1931, vol. III
Harrison, Air Vice-Marshal Richard, 1893–1974, vol. VII
Harrison, Sir Richard John, 1920–1999, vol. X
Harrison, Richard Martin, 1935–1992, vol. IX
Harrison, Rev. Robert, 1841–1927, vol. II
Harrison, Brig.-Gen. Robert Arthur Gwynne, 1855–1943, vol. IV
Harrison, Robert Francis, 1858–1927, vol. II
Harrison, Robert Hichens Camden, *died* 1924, vol. II
Harrison, Robert Tullis, 1876–1950, vol. IV
Harrison, Ronald George, 1921–1982, vol. VIII
Harrison, Rosamond Mary, *died* 1948, vol. IV
Harrison, Ross G., 1870–1959, vol. V
Harrison, Ven. Talbot D.; *see* Dilworth-Harrison.
Harrison, Theophilus George, 1907–1996, vol. X
Harrison, Col Thomas Aylet, 1865–1935, vol. III
Harrison, Brig. Thomas Carleton, 1896–1962, vol. VI
Harrison, Sir Thomas Dalkin, 1885–1954, vol. V
Harrison, Lt-Col Thomas Elliot, 1862–1939, vol. III
Harrison, Thomas Fenwick, 1852–1916, vol. II
Harrison, Captain Walter Gordon, 1888–1951, vol. V
Harrison, Lt-Col Walter Lewis, *died* 1938, vol. III
Harrison, Wilfrid, 1909–1980, vol. VII
Harrison, William, *died* 1940, vol. III
Harrison, William English, *died* 1933, vol. III
Harrison, William Henry, 1880–1955, vol. V
Harrison, William Herbert, 1909–1975, vol. VII
Harrison, William Jerome, 1845–1909, vol. I
Harrison, William John, *died* 1943, vol. IV
Harrison, Sir William Montagu G.; *see* Graham-Harrison.
Harrison, Rt Rev. William Thomas, 1837–1920, vol. II
Harrison, Sir Wyndham; *see* Harrison, Sir J. W.
Harrison-Broadley, Henry Broadley; *see* Broadley.
Harrison-Church, Ronald James, 1915–1998, vol. X
Harrison-Smith, Sir Francis, *died* 1927, vol. II
Harrison-Topham, Lt-Col Thomas, 1864–1939, vol. III
Harrison-Wallace, Captain Henry Steuart Macnaghten, *died* 1963, vol. VI
Harriss, Charles Albert Edwin, 1862–1929, vol. III
Harrisson, Damer, 1852–1918, vol. II
Harrisson, Geoffry Harnett, *died* 1939, vol. III
Harrisson, Sydney Thirlwall, 1865–1953, vol. V
Harrisson, Tom, 1911–1976, vol. VII

Harrod, Frances M. D., 1866–1956, vol. V
Harrod, Maj.-Gen. Lionel Alexander Digby, 1924–1995, vol. IX
Harrod, Sir Roy Forbes, 1900–1978, vol. VII
Harrop, Angus John, 1900–1963, vol. VI
Harrop, Wilfrid Orrell, 1893–1969, vol. VI
Harrop, William Edward Montagu H.; *see* Hulton-Harrop.
Harrop, Maj.-Gen. William Harrington H.; *see* Hulton-Harrop.
Harrowby, 3rd Earl of, 1831–1900, vol. I
Harrowby, 4th Earl of, 1836–1900, vol. I
Harrowby, 5th Earl of, 1864–1956, vol. V
Harrowby, 6th Earl of, 1892–1987, vol. VIII
Harrower, John, 1857–1933, vol. III
Harrower, John Gordon, 1890–1936, vol. III
Harrowing, Sir John H., 1859–1937, vol. III
Harrowing, Lt-Col Wilkinson Wilberforce, 1898–1967, vol. VI
Harry, Philip A., *died* 1953, vol. V
Harry, Ralph Gordon, 1908–1984, vol. VIII
Harsant, Maj.-Gen. Arnold Guy, 1893–1977, vol. VII
Harsanyi, John Charles, 1920–2000, vol. X
Harsch, Joseph Close, 1905–1998, vol. X
Harston, Major Sir Ernest Sirdefield, 1891–1975, vol. VII
Hart of South Lanark, Baroness (Life Peer); Judith Constance Mary Hart, 1924–1991, vol. IX
Hart, Albert Bushnell, 1854–1943, vol. IV
Hart, Alfred H., *died* 1953, vol. V
Hart, Anthony Bernard, 1917–1999, vol. X
Hart, Arthur W.; *see* Woolley-Hart.
Hart, Sir Basil Henry L.; *see* Liddell Hart.
Hart, Bernard, 1879–1966, vol. VI
Hart, Bernard John W.; *see* Wilden-Hart.
Hart, Sir Bruce; *see* Hart, Sir E. B.
Hart, Sir Byrne, 1895–1989, vol. VIII
Hart, Cecil Augustus, 1902–1970, vol. VI
Hart, Charles Henry, 1847–1917, vol. II
Hart, Col Charles Joseph, 1851–1925, vol. II
Hart, Sir (Edgar) Bruce, 2nd Bt, 1873–1963, vol. VI
Hart, Lt-Col Eric George, 1878–1946, vol. IV
Hart, Ernest Abraham, 1836–1898, vol. I
Hart, Sir Ernest Sidney Walter, 1870–1957, vol. V
Hart, Sir Francis Edmund T.; *see* Turton-Hart.
Hart, Frank, 1878–1959, vol. V
Hart, Sir George Charles, 1901–1981, vol. VIII
Hart, Sir George Sankey, 1866–1937, vol. III
Hart, George Vaughan, 1841–1912, vol. I
Hart, George Vaughan, 1911–1996, vol. X
Hart, Heber Leonidas, *died* 1948, vol. IV
Hart, Henry George, 1843–1921, vol. II
Hart, Lt-Col Henry Travers, *died* 1948, vol. IV
Hart, Brig.-Gen. Sir Herbert Ernest, 1882–1968, vol. VI
Hart, Herbert Lionel Adolphus, 1907–1992, vol. IX
Hart, Sir Israel, 1835–1911, vol. I
Hart, Ivor Blashka, 1889–1962, vol. VI
Hart, Rt Rev. John Stephen, 1866–1952, vol. V
Hart, Moss, 1904–1961, vol. VI
Hart, Captain Raymond, 1913–1999, vol. X
Hart, Air Marshal Sir Raymund George, 1899–1960, vol. V

Hart, Gen. Sir Reginald Clare, 1848–1931, vol. III
Hart, Sir Robert, 1st Bt, 1835–1911, vol. I
Hart, Sir Robert, 3rd Bt, 1918–1970, vol. VI
Hart, Siriol; see Hugh-Jones, S. M. A.
Hart, Thomas Wheeler, 1875–1958, vol. V
Hart, Maj.-Gen. Trevor Stuart, 1926–2000, vol. X
Hart, Vincent, 1881–1939, vol. III
Hart, Rt Rev. Mgr William Andrew, 1904–1992, vol. IX
Hart, Sir William Edward, 1866–1942, vol. IV
Hart, Sir William Ogden, 1903–1977, vol. VII
Hart, Rev. William Roland R.; see Raven-Hart.
Hart-Davies, Thomas, 1849–1920, vol. II
Hart-Davis, Charles Henry, 1874–1958, vol. V
Hart-Davis, Sir Rupert Charles, 1907–1999, vol. X
Hart Dyke, Sir Derek William, 9th Bt, 1924–1987, vol. VIII
Hart-Synnot, Maj.-Gen. Arthur FitzRoy, 1884–1910, vol. I
Hart-Synnot, Brig.-Gen. Arthur Henry Seton, 1870–1942, vol. IV
Hart-Synnot, Ronald Victor Okes, 1879–1976, vol. VII
Harte, Bret; see Harte, F. B.
Harte, (Francis) Bret, 1839–1902, vol. I
Harte, Walter James, 1866–1954, vol. V
Harte, Wilma, 1916–1976, vol. VII
Harter, Maj.-Gen. James Francis, 1888–1960, vol. V
Harter, James Francis Hatfeild, 1854–1910, vol. I
Hartert, Ernst, 1859–1933, vol. III
Hartfall, Stanley Jack, 1899–1982, vol. VIII
Hartford, Captain George Bibby, 1883–1941, vol. IV
Hartford, Rev. Canon Richard Randall, 1904–1962, vol. VI
Hartgill, Maj.-Gen. William Clavering, 1888–1968, vol. VI
Hartigan, Lt-Gen. Sir James Andrew, 1876–1962, vol. VI
Hartill, Ven. Percy, 1892–1964, vol. VI
Harting, James Edmund, 1841–1928, vol. II
Harting, Pieter, 1892–1970, vol. VI
Hartington, Marquess of; William John Robert Cavendish, 1917–1944, vol. IV
Hartland, Edwin Sidney, 1848–1927, vol. II
Hartland, Sir Frederick Dixon D.; see Dixon-Hartland.
Hartland, George Albert, 1884–1944, vol. IV
Hartland, William John, 1909–1972, vol. VII
Hartland-Swann, Louis Herbert, 1878–1947, vol. IV
Hartley, Gen. Sir Alan Fleming, 1882–1954, vol. V
Hartley, Alfred, 1855–1933, vol. III
Hartley, Arthur Clifford, 1889–1960, vol. V
Hartley, Arthur Coulton, 1906–1994, vol. IX
Hartley, Col Bernard Charles, 1879–1960, vol. V
Hartley, Brian Joseph, 1907–1996, vol. X
Hartley, C. Gasquoine, (Mrs Arthur D. Lewis), 1869–1928, vol. II
Hartley, Sir Charles Augustus, 1825–1915, vol. I
Hartley, Christiana, died 1948, vol. IV
Hartley, Air Marshal Sir Christopher Harold, 1913–1998, vol. X
Hartley, Lt-Col Donald Reginald Cavendish, 1893–1970, vol. VI

Hartley, Edmund Baron, 1847–1919, vol. II
Hartley, Sir Frank, 1911–1997, vol. X
Hartley, Frederic St Aubyn, 1896–1969, vol. VI
Hartley, Brig.-Gen. Sir Harold, 1878–1972, vol. VII
Hartley, Harold T., 1851–1943, vol. IV
Hartley, Rev. John Thorneycroft, 1849–1935, vol. III
Hartley, Leslie Poles, 1895–1972, vol. VII
Hartley, Lewis Wynne, 1867–1931, vol. III
Hartley, Rev. Marshall, 1846–1928, vol. II
Hartley, Sir Percival, 1881–1957, vol. V
Hartley, Sir Percival Horton-Smith-, 1867–1952, vol. V
Hartley, Percival Hubert Graham Horton-Smith, 1896–1977, vol. VII
Hartley, Ven. Peter Harold Trahair, 1909–1994, vol. IX
Hartley, Sir Walter Noel, 1846–1913, vol. I
Hartley, Sir William Pickles, 1846–1922, vol. II
Hartline, Haldan Keffer, 1903–1983, vol. VIII
Hartling, Poul, 1914–2000, vol. X
Hartman, Dame (Gladys) Marea, 1920–1994, vol. IX
Hartman, Dame Marea; see Hartman, Dame G. M.
Hartmann, Karl Robert Eduard von, 1842–1906, vol. I
Hartmann, William, 1844–1926, vol. II
Hartnell, Air Vice-Marshal Geoffrey Clark, 1916–1981, vol. VIII
Hartnell, Sir Norman, 1901–1979, vol. VII
Hartnett, Sir Laurence John, 1898–1986, vol. VIII
Hartnoll, Comdr Henry James, 1890–1940, vol. III
Hartnoll, Sir Henry Sulivan, 1862–1935, vol. III
Hartog, Marcus, died 1923, vol. II
Hartog, Sir Philip Joseph, 1864–1947, vol. IV
Harton, Very Rev. Frederic Percy, 1889–1958, vol. V
Hartopp, Sir Charles Edward Cradock-, 5th Bt, 1858–1929, vol. III
Hartopp, Sir Charles (William Everard) Cradock-, 6th Bt, 1893–1930, vol. III
Hartopp, Sir Frederick Cradock-, 7th Bt, 1869–1937, vol. III
Hartopp, Sir George Francis Fleetwood Cradock-, 8th Bt, 1870–1949, vol. IV
Hartopp, Sir John Edmund Cradock-, 9th Bt, 1912–1996, vol. X
Hartopp, Lt-Comdr Sir Kenneth Alston C.; see Cradock-Hartopp.
Hartree, Douglas Rayner, 1897–1958, vol. V
Hartrick, Archibald Standish, 1864–1950, vol. IV
Hartridge, Gustavus, died 1923, vol. II
Hartridge, Hamilton, 1886–1976, vol. VII
Hartshorn, Rt Hon. Vernon, 1872–1931, vol. III
Hartshorne, Albert, 1839–1910, vol. I
Hartung, Ernst Johannes, 1893–1979, vol. VII
Hartvigson, Frits, 1841–1919, vol. II
Hartwell, Lady; Pamela Margaret Elizabeth Berry, 1914–1982, vol. VIII
Hartwell, Benjamin James, 1908–1999, vol. X
Hartwell, Sir Brodrick Cecil Denham Arkwright, 4th Bt, 1876–1948, vol. IV
Hartwell, Sir Brodrick William Charles Elwin, 5th Bt, 1909–1993, vol. IX
Hartwell, Sir Charles Herbert, 1904–1982, vol. VIII

Hartwell, Charles Leonard, 1873–1951, vol. V
Hartwell, Sir Francis Houlton, 3rd Bt, 1835–1900, vol. I
Hartwell, Maj.-Gen. John Redmond, 1887–1970, vol. VI
Harty, Agnes Helen, (Lady Harty), 1877–1959, vol. V
Harty, Maj.-Gen. Arthur Henry, 1890–1977, vol. VII
Harty, (Fredric) Russell, 1934–1988, vol. VIII
Harty, Sir Hamilton; see Harty, Sir Herbert H.
Harty, Sir Henry Lockington, 3rd Bt, 1826–1913, vol. I
Harty, Sir (Herbert) Hamilton, 1880–1941, vol. IV
Harty, Most Rev. J. M., 1867–1946, vol. IV
Harty, Sir Lionel Lockington, 4th Bt, 1864–1939, vol. III
Harty, Most Rev. Michael, 1922–1994, vol. IX (AII)
Harty, Sir Robert, 2nd Bt, 1815–1902, vol. I
Harty, Russell; see Harty, F. R.
Harty, Hon. William, died 1929, vol. III
Hartzell, Joseph Crane, 1842–1928, vol. II
Harvatt, Thomas, 1901–1984, vol. VIII
Harvey of Prestbury, Baron (Life Peer); Arthur Vere Harvey, 1906–1994, vol. IX
Harvey of Tasburgh, 1st Baron, 1893–1968, vol. VI
Harvey, Alexander, 1904–1987, vol. VIII
Harvey, Alexander Gordon Cummins, 1858–1922, vol. II
Harvey, Maj.-Gen. Alexander William Montgomery, 1881–1942, vol. IV
Harvey, Benjamin Hyde, 1908–1999, vol. X
Harvey, Lt-Col Cecil Walter Lewery, 1897–1958, vol. V
Harvey, Sir Charles, 2nd Bt (cr 1868, of Crown Point), 1849–1928, vol. II
Harvey, Lt-Col Charles Darley, 1881–1929, vol. III
Harvey, Sir (Charles) Malcolm B.; see Barclay-Harvey.
Harvey, Maj.-Gen. Sir Charles Offley, 1888–1969, vol. VI
Harvey, Sir Charles Robert Lambart Edward, 3rd Bt (cr 1868, of Crown Point), 1871–1954, vol. V
Harvey, Rev. Clement Fox, 1847–1917, vol. II
Harvey, Colin Stanley, 1924–2000, vol. X
Harvey, Conway, 1880–1943, vol. IV
Harvey, Cyril Pearce, 1900–1968, vol. VI
Harvey, Maj.-Gen. David, 1871–1958, vol. V
Harvey, Captain Edward M.; see Murray-Harvey.
Harvey, Sir Ernest Maes, 1872–1926, vol. II
Harvey, Sir Ernest Musgrave, 1st Bt (cr 1933), 1867–1955, vol. V
Harvey, Rev. Francis Clyde, died 1922, vol. II
Harvey, Col Francis George, 1872–1944, vol. IV
Harvey, Lt-Col Francis Henry, 1878–1960, vol. V
Harvey, Ven. Francis William, 1930–1986, vol. VIII
Harvey, Frederick William, died 1915, vol. I
Harvey, Col George, 1864–1928, vol. II
Harvey, Sir George, 1870–1939, vol. III
Harvey, Maj.-Gen. George Alfred Duncan, died 1957, vol. V
Harvey, Air Vice-Marshal Sir George David, 1905–1969, vol. VI

Harvey, Col Sir George Samuel Abercrombie, 1854–1930, vol. III
Harvey, Harold, died 1941, vol. IV
Harvey, Rear-Adm. Harold Lane, 1884–1960, vol. V
Harvey, Henry, 1899–1965, vol. VI
Harvey, Sir (Henry) Paul, 1869–1948, vol. IV
Harvey, Herbert Frost, 1875–1959, vol. V
Harvey, Hildebrand Wolfe, 1887–1970, vol. VI
Harvey, Hon. Horace, 1863–1949, vol. IV
Harvey, Ian Douglas, 1914–1987, vol. VIII
Harvey, Rev. James, 1859–1950, vol. IV
Harvey, James Graham, 1869–1950, vol. IV (A), vol. V
Harvey, John, 1841–1915, vol. I
Harvey, John Edmund Audley, 1851–1927, vol. II
Harvey, Sir John Martin-, 1863–1944, vol. IV
Harvey, Hon. Sir John Musgrave, 1865–1940, vol. III
Harvey, Lt-Col John Robert, 1861–1921, vol. II
Harvey, John Wilfred, 1889–1967, vol. VI
Harvey, Laurence, (Larushka Mischa Skikne), 1929–1973, vol. VII
Harvey, Leslie Arthur, 1903–1986, vol. VIII
Harvey, Air Marshal Sir Leslie Gordon, 1896–1972, vol. VII
Harvey, Rev. Moses, 1820–1901, vol. I
Harvey, Sir Paul; see Harvey, Sir H. P.
Harvey, Sir Percy Norman, 1887–1946, vol. IV
Harvey, Rachel; see Bloom, Ursula.
Harvey, Ven. Richard Charles Musgrave, 1864–1944, vol. IV
Harvey, Richard Jon Stanley, 1917–1986, vol. VIII
Harvey, Sir Richard Musgrave, 2nd Bt (cr 1933), 1898–1978, vol. VII
Harvey, Surg.-Gen. Robert, 1842–1901, vol. I
Harvey, Sir Robert, 1847–1930, vol. III
Harvey, Sir Robert Grenville, 2nd Bt (cr 1868, of Langley Park), 1856–1931, vol. III
Harvey, Sir Robert James Paterson, 1904–1965, vol. VI
Harvey, Maj.-Gen. Robert Napier, 1868–1937, vol. III
Harvey, Major Sir Samuel Emile, 1885–1959, vol. V
Harvey, Thomas, 1864–1940, vol. III
Harvey, Rt Rev. Thomas Arnold, 1878–1966, vol. VI
Harvey, Thomas Edmund, 1875–1955, vol. V
Harvey, Rev. Canon Treffry, 1853–1932, vol. III
Harvey, Lt-Col Valentine Vivyan, 1885–1930, vol. III
Harvey, Wilfred John, 1895–1971, vol. VII
Harvey, William, 1859–1927, vol. II
Harvey, William, 1874–1936, vol. III
Harvey, William Alfred, 1883–1946, vol. IV
Harvey, William Edwin, 1852–1914, vol. I
Harvey, Lt-Col William Frederick, 1873–1948, vol. IV
Harvey, William Leathem, died 1910, vol. I
Harvey, Lt-Col William Lueg, 1858–1937, vol. III
Harvey Evers, Henry; see Evers.
Harvey-Gibson, Robert John, 1860–1929, vol. III
Harvey-Jamieson, Lt-Col Harvey Morro, 1908–1999, vol. X

Harvey-Kelly, Captain Hubert Dunsterville; see Kelly.
Harvie Anderson, Margaret Betty; see Baroness Skrimshire.
Harvie-Brown, John A., 1844–1916, vol. II
Harvie-Clark, Ven. Sidney, 1905–1991, vol. IX
Harvie-Watt, Sir George Steven, 1st Bt, 1903–1989, vol. VIII
Harvington, Baron (Life Peer); Robert Grant Grant-Ferris, 1907 1997, vol. X
Harward, Col Arthur John Netherton, 1867–1938, vol. III
Harward, Charles Cuthbert, 1866–1933, vol. III
Harward, Lt-Gen. Thomas Netherton, 1829–1908, vol. I
Harwood, Antony; see Harwood, B. A.
Harwood, Basil, 1859–1949, vol. IV
Harwood, (Basil) Antony, 1903–1990, vol. VIII
Harwood, Charles Auguste de Lotbinière-, 1869–1954, vol. V
Harwood, Sir Edmund George, died 1964, vol. VI
Harwood, Elizabeth Jean, (Mrs J. A. C. Royle), 1938–1990, vol. VIII
Harwood, George, 1845–1912, vol. I
Harwood, Harold Marsh, died 1959, vol. V
Harwood, Henry Cecil, 1893–1964, vol. VI
Harwood, Adm. Sir Henry Harwood, 1888–1950, vol. IV
Harwood, Henry William Forsyth, 1856–1923, vol. II
Harwood, John Augustus, 1845–1929, vol. III
Harwood, Sir John James, 1832–1906, vol. I
Harwood, Sir Ralph Endersby, 1883–1951, vol. V
Hasan, Saiyid Ahmad, 1873–1936, vol. III
Haselden, Edward Christopher, 1903–1988, vol. VIII
Haselden, Rev. John, 1854–1937, vol. III
Haselden, William Kerridge, 1872–1953, vol. V
Haseldine, (Charles) Norman, 1922–1998, vol. X
Haseldine, Norman; see Haseldine, C. N.
Haselfoot, Captain Francis Edmund Blechynden, 1885–1938, vol. III
Hasell, Edward William, 1888–1972, vol. VII
Hasell, Rev. George Edmund, 1847–1932, vol. III
Haseltine, Herbert, 1877–1962, vol. VI
Haskard, Brig.-Gen. John McDougall, 1877–1967, vol. VI
Haskell, Arnold Lionel, 1903–1980, vol. VII
Haskell, Francis James Herbert, 1928–2000, vol. X
Haskell, Harold Noad, 1887–1955, vol. V
Haskell, Jacob Silas, 1857–1939, vol. III
Haskett-Smith, W. P.; see Smith.
Haskins, Charles Homer, 1870–1937, vol. III
Haskins, M. Louise, 1875–1957, vol. V
Haslam, Hon. Sir Alec Leslie, 1904–1997, vol. X
Haslam, Sir Alfred Seale, 1844–1927, vol. II
Haslam, Henry Cobden, 1870–1948, vol. IV
Haslam, Hon. Lt-Col Sir Humphrey; see Haslam, Hon. Lt-Col Sir R. H.
Haslam, J., 1842–1913, vol. I
Haslam, James, died 1937, vol. III
Haslam, Sir John, 1878–1940, vol. III
Haslam, John Fearby Campbell, 1888–1955, vol. V
Haslam, Lewis, 1856–1922, vol. II
Haslam, Robert Heywood, 1878–1954, vol. V

Haslam, Hon. Lt-Col Sir (Robert) Humphrey, 1882–1962, vol. VI
Haslam, Rev. Samuel Holker, died 1922, vol. II
Haslam, William Frederick, died 1932, vol. III
Haslegrave, Lt-Col Henry John, 1871–1956, vol. V
Haslegrave, Herbert Leslie, 1902–1999, vol. X
Haslegrave, John Ramsden, 1913–1980, vol. VII
Haslegrave, Neville Crompton, 1914–1998, vol. X
Haslehust, Ernest William, died 1949, vol. IV
Haslett, Dame Caroline, died 1957, vol. V
Haslett, Sir James Horner, 1832–1905, vol. I
Haslett, Very Rev. Thomas, died 1947, vol. IV
Haslett, Sir William John Handfield, 1866–1954, vol. V
Haslewood, Geoffrey Arthur Dering, 1910–1993, vol. IX
Haslip, Joan, 1912–1994, vol. IX
Hasluck, Rt Hon. Sir Paul Meernaa Caedwalla, 1905–1993, vol. IX
Hasluck, Paul Nooncree, 1854–1931, vol. III
Hassall, Arthur, 1853–1930, vol. III
Hassall, Christopher Vernon, 1912–1963, vol. VI
Hassall, Joan, 1906–1988, vol. VIII
Hassall, John, 1868–1948, vol. IV
Hassall, William Owen, 1912–1994, vol. IX
Hassam, Childe, 1859–1935, vol. III
Hassan, Hon. Sir Joshua Abraham, 1915–1997, vol. X
Hassanein, Sir Ahmed Mohamed Pasha, 1889–1946, vol. IV
Hassard, Sir John, 1831–1900, vol. I
Hassard, Rev. Richard Samuel, 1848–1921, vol. II
Hassard-Short, Adrian Hugh, 1879–1956, vol. V
Hassard-Short, Rev. Canon Frederick Winning, 1873–1953, vol. V
Hassé, Henry Ronald, 1884–1955, vol. V
Hassel, Odd, 1897–1981, vol. VIII
Hasselkus, John William, 1874–1951, vol. V
Hasted, Col Arthur Walter, 1864–1937, vol. III
Hasted, Lt-Col John Ord Cobbold, 1890–1942, vol. IV
Hasted, Maj.-Gen. William Freke, 1897–1977, vol. VII
Hastie, Edward, 1876–1947, vol. IV
Hastie, William, 1842–1903, vol. I
Hastilow, Cyril Alexander Frederick, 1895–1975, vol. VII
Hastings, 20th Baron, 1857–1904, vol. I
Hastings, 21st Baron, 1882–1956, vol. V
Hastings, Marchioness of; (Florence Cecilia), 1842–1907, vol. I
Hastings, Adm. Alexander Plantagenet, 1843–1925, vol. II
Hastings, Anne Wilson, died 1975, vol. VII
Hastings, Hon. Anthea, (Esther), 1924–1981, vol. VIII
Hastings, Basil Macdonald, 1881–1928, vol. II
Hastings, Bernard Ratcliffe, 1930–1989, vol. VIII
Hastings, Charles Godolphin William, 1854–1920, vol. II
Hastings, Rev. Edward, 1890–1980, vol. VII
Hastings, Maj.-Gen. Edward Spence, 1856–1932, vol. III
Hastings, Maj.-Gen. Francis Eddowes, 1843–1915, vol. I

Hastings, Lt-Gen. Francis William, 1825–1914, vol. I
Hastings, Frank, 1869–1940, vol. III (A), vol. IV
Hastings, Rev. Frederick, 1838–1937, vol. III
Hastings, Col Sir George, 1853–1943, vol. IV
Hastings, Graham, 1830–1922, vol. II
Hastings, Hubert De Cronin, 1902–1986, vol. VIII
Hastings, Rev. James, 1852–1922, vol. II
Hastings, Col John Henry, 1858–1940, vol. III
Hastings, Hon. Osmond William Toone Westenra, 1873–1933, vol. III
Hastings, Sir Patrick, 1880–1952, vol. V
Hastings, Paulyn Charles James Reginald Rawdon-, 1889–1915, vol. I
Hastings, Hon. Paulyn Francis Cuthbert R.; see Rawdon-Hastings.
Hastings, Lt-Col Robin Hood William Stewart, 1917–1990, vol. VIII
Hastings, Somerville, 1878–1967, vol. VI
Hastings, Thomas, 1860–1929, vol. III
Hastings, Lt-Col Wilfred Charles Norrington, 1873–1925, vol. II
Hastings, Col William Holland, 1884–1930, vol. III
Haston, Dougal, 1940–1977, vol. VII
Haswell, Brig. Chetwynd Henry, 1879–1956, vol. V
Haswell, Col John Francis, 1864–1949, vol. IV
Haswell, William A., 1854–1925, vol. II
Haszard, Col Gerald Fenwick, 1894–1967, vol. VI
Hatch of Lusby, Baron (Life Peer); John Charles Hatch, 1917–1992, vol. IX
Hatch, Sir Ernest Frederick George, 1st Bt, 1859–1927, vol. II
Hatch, Frederick Henry, 1864–1932, vol. III
Hatch, Lt-Col George Pelham, 1855–1923, vol. II
Hatch, George Washington, 1872–1963, vol. VI
Hatchard, Caroline, (Caroline Langford), 1883–1970, vol. VI
Hatchell, Maj.-Gen. George, 1838–1912, vol. I
Hatchell, Col Henry Melville, 1852–1933, vol. III
Hatchell, John, 1825–1902, vol. I
Hatcher, Captain James Olden, 1867–1936, vol. III
Hatfield, Rev. Cyril Northcote, 1882–1940, vol. III
Hatfield, Henry, 1854–1926, vol. II
Hatfield, Hon. Richard Bennett, 1931–1991, vol. IX
Hatfield, William Herbert, 1882–1943, vol. IV
Hathaway, Frank John, died 1942, vol. IV
Hathaway, Maj.-Gen. Harold George, 1860–1942, vol. IV
Hathaway, Dame Sibyl Mary, 1884–1974, vol. VII
Hatherell, William, 1855–1928, vol. II
Hatherton, 3rd Baron, 1842–1930, vol. III
Hatherton, 4th Baron, 1868–1944, vol. IV
Hatherton, 5th Baron, 1900–1969, vol. VI
Hatherton, 6th Baron, 1906–1973, vol. VII
Hatherton, 7th Baron, 1907–1985, vol. VIII
Hatt, Sir Harry Thomas, 1858–1934, vol. III
Hatten, Rev. Preb. John Charles Le Pelley, 1875–1943, vol. IV
Hattersley, Alan Frederick, 1893–1976, vol. VII
Hatton, Brig.-Gen. Edward Heneage F.; see Finch Hatton.
Hatton, Edwin Fullarton, 1858–1940, vol. III
Hatton, Frank, 1921–1978, vol. VII
Hatton, George, 1849–1933, vol. III

Hatton, Maj.-Gen. George Seton, 1899–1974, vol. VII
Hatton, Hon. Harold F.; see Finch-Hatton.
Hatton, John Leigh Smeathman, 1865–1933, vol. III
Hatton, Joseph, 1841–1907, vol. I
Hatton, Richard George, 1864–1926, vol. II
Hatton, Sir Ronald George, 1886–1965, vol. VI
Hatton, Thomas Fielding, 1931–1989, vol. VIII
Hatton, Maj.-Gen. Villiers, 1852–1914, vol. I
Hatzfeldt, Prince Francis (Edmond Joseph Gabriel Vit), 1853–1910, vol. I
Hatzfeldt-Wildenburg, Count Paul von, 1831–1901, vol. I
Hauff, Mrs Janet Alderson, 1913–1973, vol. VII
Haugh, Hon. Kevin O'Hanrahan, 1901–1969, vol. VI
Haughton, Benjamin, 1865–1924, vol. II
Haughton, Daniel Jeremiah, 1911–1987, vol. VIII
Haughton, Maj.-Gen. Henry Lawrence, 1883–1955, vol. V
Haughton, Lt-Col Henry Wilfred, 1862–1931, vol. III
Haughton, Surg. Rear-Adm. John Marsden, 1924–1992, vol. IX
Haughton, Col Samuel George Steele, 1883–1956, vol. V
Haughton, Col Samuel Gillmor, 1889–1959, vol. V
Haughton, Sidney Henry, 1888–1982, vol. VIII
Haulfryn Williams, John; see Williams.
Haultain, Hon. Sir Frederick William Gordon, 1857–1942, vol. IV
Haultain, Herbert Edward Terrick, 1869–1961, vol. VI
Haupt, Paul, 1858–1926, vol. II
Hauptmann, Gerhart Johann Robert, 1862–1946, vol. IV
Haussonville, Othenin Bernard Gabrielle de Cleron, Comte d', died 1924, vol. II
Havard, Sir Godfrey Thomas, 1885–1952, vol. V
Havard, Rt Rev. William Thomas, 1889–1956, vol. V
Havard-Williams, Peter, 1922–1995, vol. IX
Havell, Ernest B., 1861–1934, vol. III
Havelock, Sir Arthur Elibank, 1844–1908, vol. I
Havelock, Eric Henry Edwardes, 1891–1974, vol. VII
Havelock, Sir Thomas Henry, 1877–1968, vol. VI
Havelock-Allan, Sir Henry Marshman, 1st Bt, 1830–1897, vol. I
Havelock-Allan, Sir Henry Ralph Moreton, 3rd Bt, 1899–1975, vol. VII
Havelock-Allan, Sir Henry Spencer Moreton, 2nd Bt, 1872–1953, vol. V
Havenga, Hon. Nicolaas Christiaan, died 1957, vol. V
Haverfield, Francis John, 1860–1919, vol. II
Havergal, Henry MacLeod, 1902–1989, vol. VIII
Havers, Baron (Life Peer); Robert Michael Oldfield Havers, 1923–1992, vol. IX
Havers, Sir Cecil Robert, 1889–1977, vol. VII
Havers, Air Vice-Marshal Sir E. William, 1887–1979, vol. VII
Havers, Air Vice-Marshal Sir William; see Havers, Air Vice-Marshal Sir E. W.
Haversham, 1st Baron, 1835–1917, vol. II

Haviland, Denis William Garstin Latimer, 1910–2000, vol. X
Haviland, Rev. Edmund Arthur, 1874–1966, vol. VI
Haviland, Ven. Francis Ernest, *died* 1945, vol. IV
Havinden, Ashley Eldrid, 1903–1973, vol. VII
Haward, Edwin, 1884–1961, vol. VI
Haward, Sir Harry Edwin, 1863–1953, vol. V
Haward, J. Warrington, 1841–1921, vol. II
Haward, Lawrence, 1878–1957, vol. V
Haward, Sir Walter, 1882–1959, vol. V
Hawarden, 5th Viscount, 1842–1908, vol. I
Hawarden, 6th Viscount, 1890–1914, vol. I
Hawarden, 7th Viscount, 1877–1958, vol. V
Hawarden, 8th Viscount, 1926–1991, vol. IX
Haweis, Rev. Hugh Reginald, 1838–1901, vol. I
Hawes, Albert G. S., *died* 1897, vol. I
Hawes, Alexander Travers, 1851–1924, vol. II
Hawes, Col Benjamin Reddie, 1854–1941, vol. IV
Hawes, Charles George, 1890–1963, vol. VI
Hawes, Derrick Gordon H.; *see* Harington Hawes.
Hawes, Maj.-Gen. Leonard Arthur, 1892–1986, vol. VIII
Hawes, Sir Richard Brunel, 1893–1964, vol. VI
Hawes, Sir Ronald N.; *see* Nesbitt-Hawes.
Hawgood, John Arkas, 1905–1971, vol. VII
Hawk, William, 1851–1944, vol. IV
Hawke, 7th Baron, 1860–1938, vol. III
Hawke, 8th Baron, 1873–1939, vol. III
Hawke, 9th Baron, 1901–1985, vol. VIII
Hawke, 10th Baron, 1904–1992, vol. IX
Hawke, Sir Anthony; *see* Hawke, Sir E. A.
Hawke, Sir Anthony; *see* Hawke, Sir J. A.
Hawke, Sir (Edward) Anthony, 1895–1964, vol. VI
Hawke, John, 1846–1932, vol. III
Hawke, Sir (John) Anthony, 1869–1941, vol. IV
Hawke, Adm. Hon. Stanhope, 1863–1936, vol. III
Hawke-Genn, Captain Otto Hermann, 1875–1955, vol. V
Hawken, Rev. Charles Sydney, 1862–1930, vol. III
Hawken, Roger William Hercules, 1878–1947, vol. IV
Hawker, Albert Henry, 1911–1992, vol. IX
Hawker, Brig.-Gen. Claude Julian, 1867–1936, vol. III
Hawker, Sir Cyril; *see* Hawker, Sir F. C.
Hawker, Sir (Frank) Cyril, 1900–1991, vol. IX
Hawker, Sqdn Comdr Lanoe George, 1890–1916, vol. II
Hawker, Mary Elizabeth, 1848–1908, vol. I
Hawker, Sir Richard George, 1907–1982, vol. VIII
Hawkes, Arthur John, 1885–1952, vol. V
Hawkes, (Charles Francis) Christopher, 1905–1992, vol. IX
Hawkes, Charles John, 1880–1953, vol. V
Hawkes, Lt-Col Charles Pascoe, 1877–1956, vol. V
Hawkes, Christopher; *see* Hawkes, Charles F. C.
Hawkes, Lt-Col Corlis St Leger Gillman, 1871–1963, vol. VI
Hawkes, Frederic Clare, 1892–1974, vol. VII
Hawkes, Rt Rev. Frederick Ochterloney Taylor, 1878–1966, vol. VI
Hawkes, Maj.-Gen. Sir Henry Montague Pakington, 1855–1946, vol. IV
Hawkes, Lt-Gen. Henry Philip, 1834–1900, vol. I
Hawkes, Jacquetta, 1910–1996, vol. X

Hawkes, Leonard, 1891–1981, vol. VIII
Hawkes, Ven. Leonard Stephen, 1907–1969, vol. VI
Hawkes, Captain William Arthur, 1881–1962, vol. VI
Hawkesworth, Sir (Edward) Gerald, *died* 1949, vol. IV
Hawkesworth, Geoffrey, 1904–1969, vol. VI
Hawkesworth, Sir Gerald; *see* Hawkesworth, Sir E. G.
Hawkesworth, Lt-Gen. Sir John Ledlie Inglis, 1893–1945, vol. IV
Hawkesworth, Rear-Adm. Richard Arthur, 1890–1968, vol. VI
Hawkey, Sir (Alfred) James, 1st Bt, 1877–1952, vol. V
Hawkey, Rt Rev. (Ernest) Eric, 1909–1986, vol. IX (AI)
Hawkey, Rt Rev. Eric; *see* Hawkey, Rt Rev. Ernest E.
Hawkey, Sir James; *see* Hawkey, Sir A. J.
Hawkey, Sir Roger Pryce, 2nd Bt, 1905–1975, vol. VII
Hawkings, Sir (Francis) Geoffrey, 1913–1990, vol. VIII
Hawkings, Sir Geoffrey; *see* Hawkings, Sir F. G.
Hawkins, Maj.-Gen. Alexander Caesar, 1823–1916, vol. II
Hawkins, (Alexander) Desmond, 1908–1999, vol. X
Hawkins, Sir Anthony Hope, 1863–1933, vol. III
Hawkins, Sir Arthur Ernest, 1913–1999, vol. X
Hawkins, Arthur Vernon, *died* 1933, vol. III
Hawkins, Sir Benjamin, 1867–1930, vol. III
Hawkins, Brian Charles Keith, 1900–1962, vol. VI
Hawkins, Charles Caesar, 1864–1938, vol. III
Hawkins, (Clive) David B.; *see* Black-Hawkins.
Hawkins, David B.; *see* Black-Hawkins, C. D.
Hawkins, Desmond; *see* Hawkins, A. D.
Hawkins, Maj.-Gen. Edward Brian Barkley, *died* 1966, vol. VI
Hawkins, Rev. Edwards Comerford, 1872–1906, vol. I
Hawkins, Francis Henry, 1863–1936, vol. III
Hawkins, Frank Ernest, 1904–1996, vol. X
Hawkins, Adm. Sir Geoffrey Alan Brooke, 1895–1980, vol. VII
Hawkins, Maj.-Gen. George Ledsam Seymour, 1898–1978, vol. VII
Hawkins, Major Henry, 1876–1930, vol. III
Hawkins, Herbert Leader, 1887–1968, vol. VI
Hawkins, Herbert Pennell, 1859–1940, vol. III
Hawkins, Sir Howard Caesar, 8th Bt, 1956–1999, vol. X
Hawkins, Sir Humphry Villiers Caesar, 7th Bt, 1923–1993, vol. IX
Hawkins, Jack, 1910–1973, vol. VII
Hawkins, Rev. Sir John Caesar, 4th Bt, 1837–1929, vol. III
Hawkins, Sir John Scott Caesar, 5th Bt, 1875–1939, vol. III
Hawkins, Ven. John Stanley, 1903–1965, vol. VI
Hawkins, Leonard Cecil, 1897–1974, vol. VII
Hawkins, Sir Michael Babington Charles, 1914–1977, vol. VII
Hawkins, Percy, 1870–1949, vol. IV

Hawkins, Rt Rev. Ralph Gordon, 1911–1987, vol. VIII
Hawkins, Vice-Adm. Sir Raymond Shayle, 1909–1987, vol. VIII
Hawkins, Reginald Thomas, 1888–1978, vol. VII
Hawkins, Rev. Robert Henry, 1892–1989, vol. VIII
Hawkins, Col Thomas Henry, 1873–1944, vol. IV
Hawkins, Sir Villiers Geoffry Caesar, 6th Bt, 1890–1955, vol. V
Hawkins, Col Walter Francis, 1856–1936, vol. III
Hawkins, Lt-Col William, 1861–1932, vol. III
Hawkins, William Francis Spencer, 1896–1979, vol. VII
Hawks, Ellison, 1889–1971, vol. VII
Hawkshaw, John Clarke, 1841–1921, vol. II
Hawksley, Dorothy Webster, 1884–1970, vol. VI
Hawksley, Ernest B., died 1931, vol. III
Hawksley, Vice-Adm. James Rose Price, died 1955, vol. V
Hawksley, John Callis, 1903–1993, vol. IX
Hawksley, Brig.-Gen. Randal Plunkett Taylor, 1870–1961, vol. VI
Hawksley, Richard Walter Benson, 1915–1976, vol. VII
Hawksworth, Frederick William, 1884–1976, vol. VII
Hawksworth, William Thomas Martin, died 1935, vol. III
Hawley, Arthur, 1870–1952, vol. V
Hawley, Rev. Charles Cusac, 1851–1914, vol. I
Hawley, Major Sir David Henry, 7th Bt, 1913–1988, vol. VIII
Hawley, Sir Henry Cusack Wingfield, 6th Bt, 1876–1923, vol. II
Hawley, Sir Henry James, 4th Bt, 1815–1898, vol. I
Hawley, Sir Henry Michael, 5th Bt, 1848–1909, vol. I
Hawley, Maj.-Gen. William Hanbury, 1829–1917, vol. II
Hawley, Willis Chatman, 1864–1941, vol. IV
Haworth, Sir Arthur Adlington, 1st Bt, 1865–1944, vol. IV
Haworth, Sir (Arthur) Geoffrey, 2nd Bt, 1896–1987, vol. VIII
Haworth, Sir Geoffrey; see Haworth, Sir A. G.
Haworth, Rev. James, 1853–1942, vol. IV
Haworth, James, 1896–1976, vol. VII
Haworth, Very Rev. Kenneth William, 1903–1988, vol. VIII
Haworth, Lionel, 1912–2000, vol. X
Haworth, Lt-Col Sir Lionel Berkeley Holt, 1873–1951, vol. V
Haworth, Sir Norman; see Haworth, Sir W. N.
Haworth, Peter, 1891–1956, vol. V
Haworth, Robert Downs, 1898–1990, vol. VIII
Haworth, Sir (Walter) Norman, 1883–1950, vol. IV
Haworth, Very Rev. William, 1880–1960, vol. V
Haworth, Hon. Sir William Crawford, 1905–1984, vol. VIII
Haworth-Booth, Rear-Adm. Sir Francis Fitzgerald, 1864–1935, vol. III
Hawser, (Cyril) Lewis, 1916–1990, vol. VIII
Hawser, Lewis; see Hawser, C. L.
Hawtayne, George Hammond, 1832–1902, vol. I
Hawtayne, Lionel Edward, died 1920, vol. II

Hawthorn, Maj.-Gen. Douglas Cyril, 1897–1974, vol. VII
Hawthorn, Bt-Col Frank, died 1931, vol. III
Hawthorn, Brig.-Gen. George Montague Philip, 1873–1945, vol. IV
Hawthorne, Julian, 1846–1934, vol. III
Hawton, Sir John Malcolm Kenneth, 1904–1982, vol. VIII
Hawtrey, Sir Charles, 1858–1923, vol. II
Hawtrey, Brig. Henry Courtenay, 1882–1961, vol. VI
Hawtrey, Air Vice-Marshal John Gosset, 1901–1954, vol. V
Hawtrey, Sir Ralph George, 1879–1975, vol. VII
Hawtrey, Stephen Charles, 1907–1990, vol. VIII
Hay, Sir (Alan) Philip, 1918–1986, vol. VIII
Hay, Col (Alexander S.) Leith, 1818–1900, vol. I
Hay, Alfred, 1866–1932, vol. III
Hay, Hon. Alistair George, 1861–1929, vol. III
Hay, Major Hon. Arthur, 1855–1932, vol. III
Hay, Maj.-Gen. Arthur Kenneth, died 1949, vol. IV
Hay, Lt-Col Arthur Sidney, 1879–1940, vol. III
Hay, Sir Arthur Thomas Erroll, 10th Bt, 1909–1993, vol. IX
Hay, Athole S., 1861–1933, vol. III
Hay, Sir Bache McEvers Athole, 11th Bt (cr 1635), 1892–1966, vol. VI
Hay, Charles Edward Norman L.; see Leith-Hay.
Hay, Maj.-Gen. Charles John Bruce, 1877–1940, vol. III
Hay, Sir Charles John D.; see Dalrymple Hay.
Hay, Hon. Claude George Drummond, 1862–1920, vol. II
Hay, Clifford Henderson, 1878–1949, vol. IV
Hay, Sir David Allan, 1878–1957, vol. V
Hay, Denys, 1915–1994, vol. IX
Hay, Douglas, died 1949, vol. IV
Hay, Sir Duncan Edwyn, 10th Bt (cr 1635), 1882–1965, vol. VI
Hay, Ven. Edgar, 1863–1949, vol. IV
Hay, Lord Edward Douglas John, 1888–1944, vol. IV
Hay, Sir Edward Hamilton, 9th Bt (cr 1703), 1870–1936, did not prove his succession or use the title, and did not have an entry in Who's Who.
Hay, Maj.-Gen. Edward Owen, 1846–1946, vol. IV
Hay, Francis Edward Drummond-, 1868–1943, vol. IV
Hay, Frances Mary, (Mrs Roy Hay); see Perry, F. M.
Hay, Sir Francis Ringler Drummond-, 1830–1905, vol. I
Hay, Francis Stuart, 1863–1928, vol. II
Hay, Sir Frederick Baden-Powell, 10th Bt, 1900–1985, vol. VIII
Hay, George, died 1912, vol. I
Hay, Col Sir George Jackson, 1840–1921, vol. II
Hay, Col George Lennox, 1873–1946, vol. IV
Hay, Sir Harley Hugh D.; see Dalrymple-Hay.
Hay, Sir Hector Maclean, 7th Bt (cr 1703), 1821–1916, vol. II
Hay, Henry Hanby, 1849–1940, vol. III
Hay, Ian; see Beith, Maj.-Gen. J. H.
Hay, Col James, 1842–1915, vol. I

Hay, Col James Adam Gordon Richardson-Drummond-, 1863–1928, vol. II
Hay, Col James Charles Edward, 1889–1975, vol. VII
Hay, Sir James Lawrence, 1888–1971, vol. VII
Hay, James Paterson, 1863–1925, vol. II
Hay, Brig.-Gen. James Reginald Maitland Dalrymple, 1858–1924, vol. II
Hay, Sir James Shaw, 1839–1924, vol. II
Hay, Hon. Col John, 1838–1905, vol. I
Hay, Rt Hon. Lord John, 1827–1916, vol. II
Hay, John, 1873–1959, vol. V
Hay, John Albert, 1919–1998, vol. X
Hay, John Arthur Machray, 1887–1960, vol. V
Hay, John Binny, 1870–1939, vol. III
Hay, Rt Hon. Sir John Charles Dalrymple, 3rd Bt (cr 1798), 1821–1912, vol. I
Hay, Sir John George, 1883–1964, vol. VI
Hay, Captain John Primrose, 1878–1949, vol. IV
Hay, Paymaster Rear-Adm. Kenneth Sydney, 1872–1932, vol. III
Hay, Col Leith; see Hay, Col A. S. L.
Hay, Sir Lewis John Erroll, 9th Bt (cr 1663), 1866–1923, vol. II
Hay of Seaton, Major Malcolm Vivian, 1881–1962, vol. VI
Hay, Lady Margaret Katharine, 1918–1975, vol. VII
Hay, Marie, 1873–1938, vol. III
Hay, Mrs Mary Verena Campbell, 1875–1940, vol. III
Hay, Matthew, 1855–1932, vol. III
Hay, Noel Grant, 1910–1974, vol. VII
Hay, Peter Alexander, 1866–1952, vol. V
Hay, Sir Philip; see Hay, Sir A. P.
Hay, Lt-Gen. Sir Robert, 1889–1980, vol. VII
Hay, Maj.-Gen. Robert Arthur, 1920–1998, vol. X
Hay, Robert Edwin, (Roy), 1910–1989, vol. VIII
Hay, Sir Robert Hay-Drummond-, 1846–1926, vol. II
Hay, Lt-Gen. Sir Robert John, 1828–1910, vol. I
Hay, Rt Rev. Robert Milton, 1884–1973, vol. VII
Hay, Rt Rev. Robert Snowdon, 1867–1943, vol. IV
Hay, Brig. Ronald Bruce, 1887–1961, vol. VI
Hay, Sir Ronald Nelson, 11th Bt, 1910–1988, vol. VIII
Hay, Roy; see Hay, Robert E.
Hay, Lt-Col Sir Rupert; see Hay, Lt-Col Sir W. R.
Hay, Stephen Moffatt, 1857–1943, vol. IV
Hay, Thomas, died 1953, vol. V
Hay, Lt-Col Thomas William, 1882–1956, vol. V
Hay, Col Westwood Norman, 1871–1946, vol. IV
Hay, Will, 1888–1949, vol. IV
Hay, Sir William Archibald Dalrymple, 4th Bt (cr 1798), 1851–1929, vol. III
Hay, William Gosse, 1875–1945, vol. IV
Hay, Sir William Henry, 8th Bt (cr 1703), 1867–1927, vol. II, vol. IV
Hay, Lt-Col Sir (William) Rupert, 1893–1962, vol. VI
Hay-Dinwoody, Very Rev. Leofric Matthews, 1868–1936, vol. III
Hay-Drummond, Arthur William Henry, 1862–1953, vol. V
Hay-Drummond, Col Hon. Charles Rowley, 1836–1918, vol. II

Hay-Drummond-Hay, Sir Robert; see Hay.
Hay-Newton, Francis John Stuart, 1843–1913, vol. I
Hayashi, Gonsuke, 1861–1939, vol. III
Hayashi, Count Tadasu, 1850–1913, vol. I
Hayball, Frederick Ronald, 1914–1996, vol. X
Haycock, Alexander Wilkinson, 1882–1970, vol. VI
Haycock, Rev. Trevitt Reginald H.; see Hine-Haycock.
Haycock, Col Vaughan Randolph H.; see Hine-Haycock.
Haycocks, Norman, 1907–1982, vol. VIII
Haycraft, Colin Berry, 1929–1994, vol. IX
Haycraft, John Berry, died 1922, vol. II
Haycraft, John Berry, 1888–1969, vol. VI
Haycraft, John Stacpoole, 1926–1996, vol. X
Haycraft, Sir Thomas Wagstaffe, died 1936, vol. III
Hayday, Arthur, 1869–1956, vol. V
Hayday, Sir Frederick, 1912–1990, vol. VIII
Hayden, Arthur, 1868–1946, vol. IV
Hayden, Sir Henry Hubert, 1869–1923, vol. II
Hayden, John Patrick, 1863–1954, vol. V
Hayden, Luke Patrick, 1850–1897, vol. I
Hayden, Mary Teresa, died 1942, vol. IV
Hayden, Most Rev. William, 1868–1936, vol. III
Haydn Williams, Benjamin, 1902–1965, vol. VI
Haydon, Dame Anne, 1892–1966, vol. VI
Haydon, Arthur Lincoln, 1872–1954, vol. V
Haydon, Denis Arthur, 1930–1988, vol. VIII
Haydon, Maj.-Gen. Joseph Charles, 1899–1970, vol. VI
Haydon, Sir Robin; see Haydon, Sir W. R.
Haydon, Thomas Edmett, died 1952, vol. V
Haydon, Sir Walter Robert, (Sir Robin), 1920–1999, vol. X
Haydon-Lewis, Jack; see Lewis.
Hayek, Friedrich August von, 1899–1992, vol. IX
Hayes, Alfred, 1857–1936, vol. III
Hayes, Rev. Arthur Herbert, 1850–1933, vol. III
Hayes, Surg.-Lt-Col Aylmer Ellis, 1850–1900, vol. I
Hayes, Cdre Sir Bertram Fox, 1864–1941, vol. IV
Hayes, Carlton Joseph Huntley, 1882–1964, vol. VI
Hayes, Claude, 1852–1922, vol. II
Hayes, Sir Claude James, 1912–1996, vol. X
Hayes, Sir Edmund Francis, 5th Bt, 1850–1912, vol. I
Hayes, Edwin, 1819–1904, vol. I
Hayes, Lt-Col Edwin Charles, 1868–1942, vol. IV
Hayes, Maj.-Gen. Eric Charles, 1896–1951, vol. V
Hayes, Rev. Francis Carlile, died 1931, vol. III
Hayes, Frederick William, 1848–1914, vol. II
Hayes, Gerald Ravenscourt, 1889–1955, vol. V
Hayes, Gertrude, (Mrs E. M. Betts), 1872–1956, vol. V
Hayes, Helen, (Mrs Charles MacArthur), 1900–1993, vol. IX
Hayes, Hugh, died 1928, vol. II, vol. III
Hayes, Rt Rev. James Thomas, 1847–1904, vol. I
Hayes, John, vol. II
Hayes, Hon. John Blyth, 1868–1956, vol. V
Hayes, John Henry, 1889–1941, vol. IV
Hayes, Vice-Adm. Sir John Osler Chattock, 1913–1998, vol. X
Hayes, Lt-Col Joseph, 1864–1944, vol. IV
Hayes, Maurice Richard Joseph, died 1930, vol. III
Hayes, Michael, 1889–1976, vol. VII

Hayes, His Eminence Patrick Cardinal, 1867–1938, vol. III
Hayes, Very Rev. Richard, 1854–1938, vol. III
Hayes, Robert Edward, 1869–1931, vol. III
Hayes, Lt-Col Robert Hall, 1867–1946, vol. IV
Hayes, Rt Rev. Romuald, 1892–1945, vol. IV
Hayes, Sir Samuel Hercules, 1840–1901, vol. I
Hayes, Thomas Crawford, *died* 1909, vol. I
Hayes, Thomas William Henry, 1912–1989, vol. VIII
Hayes, Brig.-Gen. Wade Hampton, 1879–1956, vol. V
Hayes, Walter Leopold Arthur, 1924–2000, vol. X
Hayes, Captain William, 1891–1918, vol. II
Hayes, William, 1855–1940, vol. III
Hayes, William, 1913–1994, vol. IX
Hayford, John Fillmore, 1868–1925, vol. II, vol. III
Haygarth, Col Sir Joseph Henry, 1892–1969, vol. VI
Haygarth Jackson, Harold; *see* Jackson.
Hayhurst, William Hosken France-, 1873–1947, vol. IV
Hayhurst-France, Captain George Frederick Hayhurst, 1895–1940, vol. III
Hayler, Guy, 1850–1943, vol. IV
Hayley, Frederic Austin, 1881–1968, vol. VI
Hayman, Sir (Cecil George) Graham, 1893–1966, vol. VI
Hayman, Frank Harold, 1894–1966, vol. VI
Hayman, Sir Graham; *see* Hayman, Sir C. G. G.
Hayman, Rev. Henry, 1823–1904, vol. I
Hayman, Rev. Canon Henry Telford, 1853–1941, vol. IV
Hayman, Perceval Mills Cobham, 1883–1974, vol. VII
Hayman, Sir Peter Telford, 1914–1992, vol. IX
Hayman, Ven. Reginald John Edward, 1861–1927, vol. II
Hayman, Rev. Canon William Samuel, 1903–1993, vol. IX
Hayman-Joyce, Maj.-Gen. Hayman John, 1897–1958, vol. V
Haymes, Lt-Col Robert Leycester, 1870–1942, vol. IV
Hayne, Louis Brightwell, 1869–1926, vol. II
Haynes, Col Alleyne, 1859–1938, vol. III
Haynes, Alwyn Sidney, 1878–1963, vol. VI
Haynes, Col Charles Edward, 1855–1935, vol. III
Haynes, David Francis, (Frank), 1926–1998, vol. X
Haynes, Denys Eyre Lankester, 1913–1994, vol. IX
Haynes, Edmund Sidney Pollock, 1877–1949, vol. IV
Haynes, Edwin William George, 1911–1992, vol. IX
Haynes, Frank; *see* Haynes, D. F.
Haynes, Sir George Ernest, 1902–1983, vol. VIII
Haynes, Brig.-Gen. Kenneth Edward, 1871–1944, vol. IV
Haynes, Richard Septimus, 1857–1922, vol. II
Haynes, Robert, 1920–1976, vol. VII
Haynes, Robert Hall, 1931–1999, vol. X
Haynes, Hon. Samuel Johnson, 1852–1932, vol. III
Haynes, Rear-Adm. William Allen, 1913–1985, vol. VIII
Haynes-Dixon, Margaret Rumer; *see* Godden, Rumer.

Haynes-Rudge, Mrs Florence, *died* 1934, vol. III
Haynes-Williams, John, *died* 1908, vol. I
Hays, Arthur Garfield, 1881–1954, vol. V
Hays, Very Rev. Francis, 1870–1943, vol. IV
Hays, Sir Marshall, 1872–1948, vol. IV
Hays, Will H., 1879–1954, vol. V
Haysom, Sir George, 1862–1924, vol. II
Hayter, 1st Baron, 1848–1946, vol. IV
Hayter, 2nd Baron, 1871–1967, vol. VI
Hayter, Harrison, 1825–1898, vol. I
Hayter, Rev. Harrison Goodenough, 1855–1934, vol. III
Hayter, Brig. Ross John Finnis, 1875–1929, vol. III
Hayter, Stanley William, 1901–1988, vol. VIII
Hayter, Sir William Goodenough, 1869–1924, vol. II
Hayter, Sir William Goodenough, 1906–1995, vol. IX
Hayter, Rev. William Thomas Baring, 1858–1935, vol. III
Hayter Hames, Sir George Colvile, 1898–1968, vol. VI
Haythornthwaite, Rev. John Parker, 1862–1928, vol. II
Hayward, Sir Alfred, 1896–1988, vol. VIII
Hayward, Alfred Robert, 1875–1971, vol. VII
Hayward, Arthur Canler, 1870–1945, vol. IV
Hayward, Arthur Lawrence, 1885–1967, vol. VI
Hayward, Sir Charles William, 1892–1983, vol. VIII
Hayward, Rev. Edward, 1884–1974, vol. VII
Hayward, Sir Edward Waterfield, 1903–1983, vol. VIII
Hayward, Sir Edwin James, 1868–1929, vol. III
Hayward, Lt-Col Edwyn Walton, *died* 1933, vol. III
Hayward, Evan, 1876–1958, vol. V
Hayward, Sir Fred, 1876–1944, vol. IV
Hayward, Frederick Edward Godfrey, 1893–1961, vol. VI
Hayward, Maj.-Gen. George Victor, 1918–1999, vol. X
Hayward, Graham William, 1911–1976, vol. VII
Hayward, Maj.-Gen. Henry Blakeney, 1838–1930, vol. III
Hayward, Ven. Henry Rudge, *died* 1912, vol. I
Hayward, Ian Dudley, 1899–1964, vol. VI
Hayward, Sir Isaac James, 1884–1976, vol. VII
Hayward, Jane Elizabeth, 1946–2000, vol. X
Hayward, John Davy, 1905–1965, vol. VI
Hayward, Marjorie Olive, 1885–1953, vol. V
Hayward, Sir Maurice Henry Weston, 1868–1964, vol. VI
Hayward, Lt-Col Reginald Frederick Johnson, *died* 1970, vol. VI
Hayward, Sir Richard Arthur, 1910–1994, vol. IX
Hayward, Richard Frederick, 1879–1962, vol. VI
Hayward, Robert Baldwin, 1829–1903, vol. I
Hayward, Ronald George, 1917–1996, vol. X
Hayward, Sidney Pascoe, 1896–1961, vol. VI
Hayward, Tom Christopher, 1904–1975, vol. VII
Hayward, William Thornborough, 1854–1928, vol. II
Hayward, Sir William Webb, 1818–1899, vol. I
Haywood, Col Austin Hubert Wightwick, *died* 1965, vol. VI

Haywood, Horace Mason, *died* 1942, vol. IV
Hazan, Hon. Sir John Boris Roderick, 1926–1988, vol. VIII
Hazel, Alfred Ernest William, *died* 1944, vol. IV
Hazeldine, Evelyn Lilian; *see* Martinengo-Cesaresco, Countess.
Hazell, Sir Quinton, 1920–1996, vol. X
Hazell, W. Howard, 1869–1929, vol. III
Hazell, Walter, 1843–1919, vol. II
Hazell, Captain William, 1857–1927, vol. II
Hazeltine, Harold Dexter, 1871–1960, vol. V
Hazelton, Maj.-Gen. Percy Orr, 1871–1952, vol. V
Hazen, Hon. Sir Douglas; *see* Hazen, Hon. Sir J. D.
Hazen, Hon. Sir (John) Douglas, 1860–1937, vol. III
Hazlehurst, Rev. George Arthur, 1873–1940, vol. III
Hazlehurst, Thomas Francis, *died* 1918, vol. II
Hazlerigg, 1st Baron, 1878–1949, vol. IV
Hazlerigg, Lt-Col Thomas, 1877–1935, vol. III
Hazlerigg, Maj.-Gen. Thomas Maynard, 1840–1915, vol. I
Hazleton, Richard, 1880–1943, vol. IV
Hazlewood, Rt Rev. John, 1924–1998, vol. X
Hazlitt, William Carew, 1834–1913, vol. I
Head, 1st Viscount, 1906–1983, vol. VIII
Head, Lt-Col Alfred Searle, 1874–1952, vol. V
Head, Alice Maud, 1886–1981, vol. VIII
Head, Lt-Col Arthur Edward Maxwell, 1876–1921, vol. II
Head, Barclay Vincent, 1844–1914, vol. I
Head, Lt-Col Charles Octavius, 1869–1952, vol. V
Head, Ernest, 1871–1923, vol. II
Head, Francis Somerville Cameron C.; *see* Cameron-Head.
Head, Most Rev. Frederick Waldegrave, 1874–1941, vol. IV
Head, Rev. Canon George Frederick, 1836–1912, vol. I
Head, George Herbert, *died* 1927, vol. II
Head, Sir Henry, 1861–1940, vol. III
Head, James C.; *see* Cameron-Head.
Head, John Joshua, 1838–1925, vol. II
Head, Leslie Charles B.; *see* Broughton-Head.
Head, Robert, *died* 1957, vol. V
Head, Sir Robert Garnett, 3rd Bt, 1845–1907, vol. I
Head, Sir (Robert Pollock) Somerville, 4th Bt, 1884–1924, vol. II
Head, Sir Somerville; *see* Head, Sir R. P. S.
Headfort, 4th Marquess of, 1878–1943, vol. IV
Headfort, 5th Marquess of, 1902–1960, vol. V
Heading, Sir James Alfred, 1884–1969, vol. VI (AII)
Headington, Arthur Hutton, 1878–1917, vol. II
Headington, Kenneth George John, 1898–1960, vol. V
Headlam, Rt Rev. Arthur Cayley, 1862–1947, vol. IV
Headlam, Rev. Arthur William, 1826–1909, vol. I
Headlam, Cecil, 1872–1934, vol. III
Headlam, Lt-Col Rt Hon. Sir Cuthbert Morley, 1st Bt, 1876–1964, vol. VI
Headlam, Captain Sir Edward James, 1873–1943, vol. IV
Headlam, Francis John, 1829–1908, vol. I

Headlam, Air Vice-Marshal Frank, 1914–1976, vol. VII
Headlam, Gerald Erskine, 1877–1954, vol. V
Headlam, Brig.-Gen. Hugh Roger, 1877–1955, vol. V
Headlam, Maj.-Gen. Sir John Emerson Wharton, 1864–1946, vol. IV
Headlam, Maurice Francis, 1873–1956, vol. V
Headlam, Rev. Canon Morley Lewis Caulfield, 1868–1953, vol. V
Headlam, Rev. Stewart Duckworth, *died* 1924, vol. II
Headlam, Walter George, 1866–1908, vol. I
Headlam-Morley, Agnes, 1902–1986, vol. VIII
Headlam-Morley, Sir James Wycliffe, 1863–1929, vol. III
Headlam-Morley, Kenneth Arthur Sonntag, 1901–1982, vol. VIII
Headland, Isaac Taylor, 1859–1942, vol. IV
Headland, John, 1840–1927, vol. II
Headley, 4th Baron, 1845–1913, vol. I
Headley, 5th Baron, 1855–1935, vol. III
Headley, 6th Baron, 1901–1969, vol. VI
Headley, 7th Baron, 1902–1994, vol. IX
Headley, Ven. Charles Theophilus, 1870–1930, vol. III
Headley, Derek, 1908–1998, vol. X
Headridge, David, 1869–1938, vol. III
Heaf, Frederick Roland George, 1894–1973, vol. VII
Heakes, Air Vice-Marshal Francis Vernon, 1894–1989, vol. VIII
Heal, Sir Ambrose, 1872–1959, vol. V
Heal, Anthony Standerwick, 1907–1995, vol. IX
Heald, Sir Benjamin Herbert, 1874–1940, vol. III
Heald, Charles Brehmer, 1882–1974, vol. VII
Heald, Edith Shackleton, *died* 1976, vol. VII
Heald, Henry Townley, 1904–1975, vol. VII
Heald, Rt Hon. Sir Lionel Frederick, 1897–1981, vol. VIII
Heald, Nora Shackleton, *died* 1961, vol. VI
Heald, William, 1910–1980, vol. VII
Heale, Lt-Col Robert John Wingfield, 1876–1962, vol. VI
Healey, Col. Charles, 1856–1939, vol. III
Healey, Sir Charles Arthur C.; *see* Chadwyck-Healey.
Healey, Sir Charles Edward Heley C.; *see* Chadwyck-Healey.
Healey, Col Coryndon William Rutherford, 1864–1953, vol. V
Healey, Donald Mitchell, 1898–1988, vol. VIII
Healey, Sir Edward Randal C.; *see* Chadwyck-Healey.
Healey, Sir Gerald Edward C.; *see* Chadwyck-Healey.
Healey, Rt Rev. Kenneth, 1899–1985, vol. VIII
Healey, Oliver Nowell C.; *see* Chadwyck-Healey.
Healey-Kay, Patrick; *see* Dolin, Sir Anton.
Healy, Cahir, 1877–1970, vol. VI
Healy, Daniel, 1884–1962, vol. VI
Healy, Rev. George White, *died* 1943, vol. IV
Healy, Most Rev. John, 1841–1918, vol. II
Healy, Ven. John, 1850–1942, vol. IV
Healy, John Edward, *died* 1934, vol. III

Healy, Rt Rev. John F., 1900–1973, vol. VII
Healy, Maurice, 1859–1923, vol. II
Healy, Maurice, 1887–1943, vol. IV
Healy, Thomas Joseph, 1854–1925, vol. II
Healy, Timothy Michael, 1855–1931, vol. III
Hean, Hon. Alexander, 1859–1927, vol. II
Heane, Brig.-Gen. James, 1874–1954, vol. V
Heaney, Brig. George Frederick, 1897–1983, vol. VIII
Heaney, Henry Joseph, 1935–1999, vol. X
Heaney, Brig. Sheila Anne Elizabeth, 1917–1991, vol. IX
Heap, Sir Desmond, 1907–1998, vol. X
Heape, Walter, 1855–1929, vol. III
Heape, William Leslie, 1896–1972, vol. VII
Heard, Gerald; see Heard, H. F. G.
Heard, Henry Fitz Gerald, 1889–1971, vol. VII
Heard, Rev. Henry James, 1856–1931, vol. III
Heard, Adm. Hugh Lindsay Patrick, 1869–1954, vol. V
Heard, Brig. Leonard Ferguson, 1903–1976, vol. VII
Heard, Maj.-Gen. Richard, 1870–1950, vol. IV
Heard, Rev. Richard Grenville, died 1952, vol. V
Heard, Rev. William Augustus, 1847–1921, vol. II
Heard, His Eminence Cardinal William Theodore, 1884–1973, vol. VII
Hearle, Col Arthur Basset, 1884–1935, vol. III
Hearle, Francis Trounson, 1886–1965, vol. VI
Hearn, Sir Arthur Charles, 1877–1952, vol. V
Hearn, Rear-Adm. Frank Wright, 1919–1993, vol. IX
Hearn, Col George William Richard, 1893–1973, vol. VII
Hearn, Col Sir Gordon Risley, 1871–1953, vol. V
Hearn, John Whitcombe, 1885–1968, vol. VI
Hearn, Lafcadio, 1850–1904, vol. I
Hearn, Rt Rev. Robert Thomas, died 1952, vol. V
Hearn, Sir Walter Risley, 1853–1930, vol. III
Hearne, Sir Hector, 1892–1962, vol. VI
Hearnshaw, Fossey John Cobb, 1869–1946, vol. IV
Hearnshaw, Leslie Spencer, 1907–1991, vol. IX
Hearson, Air Cdre John Glanville, 1883–1964, vol. VI
Hearst, Hon. Sir William Howard, 1864–1941, vol. IV
Hearst, William Randolph, 1863–1951, vol. V
Hearst, William Randolph, Jr, 1908–1993, vol. IX
Heartz, Hon. Frank Richard, 1871–1955, vol. V
Heaslett, Rt Rev. Samuel, 1875–1947, vol. IV
Heath, Albert Edward, 1887–1956, vol. V
Heath, Ambrose, 1891–1969, vol. VI
Heath, Andrew, 1953–1996, vol. X
Heath, Archie Edward, 1887–1961, vol. VI
Heath, Arthur Douglas, died 1937, vol. III
Heath, Arthur Howard, 1856–1930, vol. III
Heath, Arthur Raymond, died 1943, vol. IV
Heath, Sir Barrie, 1916–1988, vol. VIII
Heath, Maj.-Gen. Sir Charles Ernest, 1854–1936, vol. III
Heath, Charles Joseph, 1856–1934, vol. III
Heath, Christopher, 1835–1905, vol. I
Heath, Cuthbert Eden, died 1939, vol. III
Heath, Col Edward, 1854–1927, vol. II
Heath, Col Edward Charles, 1873–1946, vol. IV

Heath, Francis George, 1843–1913, vol. I
Heath, Lt-Col Francis William, 1865–1936, vol. III
Heath, Sir Frank; see Heath, Sir H. F.
Heath, Col George Noah, 1881–1967, vol. VI
Heath, Maj.-Gen. Sir Gerard Moore, 1863–1929, vol. III
Heath, Maj.-Gen. Gerard William Egerton, 1897–1980, vol. VII
Heath, Harry Cecil, 1898–1972, vol. VII
Heath, Col Harry Heptinstall Rose, 1850–1922, vol. II
Heath, Sir (Henry) Frank, 1863–1946, vol. IV
Heath, Maj.-Gen. Henry Newport Charles, 1860–1915, vol. I
Heath, Adm. Sir Herbert Leopold, 1861–1954, vol. V
Heath, Sir James, 1st Bt, 1852–1942, vol. IV
Heath, Lt-Col John Macclesfield, 1843–1911, vol. I
Heath, Adm. Sir Leopold George, 1817–1907, vol. I
Heath, Lt-Gen. Sir Lewis Macclesfield, 1885–1954, vol. V
Heath, Air Marshal Sir Maurice Lionel, 1909–1998, vol. X
Heath, Oscar Victor Sayer, 1903–1997, vol. X
Heath, Robert Samuel, 1858–1931, vol. III
Heath, Brig.-Gen. Ronald Macclesfield, 1876–1942, vol. IV
Heath, Sir Thomas Little, 1861–1940, vol. III
Heath, Rear-Adm. William Andrew James, 1820–1903, vol. I
Heath-Caldwell, Maj.-Gen. Frederick Crofton, 1858–1945, vol. IV
Heath-Gracie, George Handel, 1892–1987, vol. VIII
Heath-Jones, Edgar, died 1949, vol. IV
Heathcoat Amory, Lady; see Wethered, J.
Heathcoat-Amory, Sir Ian Murray Heathcoat, 2nd Bt; see Amory.
Heathcoat-Amory, Major Sir John, 3rd Bt; see Amory.
Heathcoat-Amory, Sir John Heathcoat, 1st Bt, 1829–1914, vol. I
Heathcoat-Amory, Sir William, 5th Bt, 1901–1982, vol. VIII
Heathcote, Lt Alfred Spencer, died 1912, vol. I
Heathcote, Brig.-Gen. Charles Edensor, 1875–1947, vol. IV
Heathcote, Rt Rev. Sir Francis Cooke Caulfeild, 9th Bt, 1868–1961, vol. VI
Heathcote, Lt-Col Sir Gilbert Redvers, 8th Bt, 1854–1937, vol. III
Heathcote, John Norman, 1863–1946, vol. IV
Heathcote, Justinian Heathcote Edwards-, 1843–1928, vol. II
Heathcote, Sir Leonard Vyvyan, 10th Bt, 1885–1963, vol. VI
Heathcote, Reginald St Alban, 1888–1951, vol. V
Heathcote, Robert Evelyn Manners, 1884–1970, vol. VI
Heathcote, Rev. Sir William Arthur, 7th Bt, 1853–1924, vol. II
Heathcote, Sir William Perceval, 6th Bt, 1826–1903, vol. I
Heathcote-Drummond-Willoughby, Brig.-Gen. Hon. Charles Strathavon; see Willoughby.

Heathcote-Smith, Sir Clifford Edward, 1883–1963, vol. VI
Heathcote-Williams, Harold, 1896–1964, vol. VI
Heather, Very Rev. George Abraham, *died* 1907, vol. I
Heather, Henry James Shedlock, 1863–1939, vol. III(A), vol. IV
Heathershaw, James Thomas, 1871–1943, vol. IV
Heatley, David Playfair, 1867–1944, vol. IV
Heatly-Spencer, Col John, 1880–1946, vol. IV
Heaton, Rev. Eric William, 1920–1996, vol. X
Heaton, Sir Frederick; *see* Heaton, Sir J. F.
Heaton, Gwenllian Margaret, 1897–1979, vol. VII
Heaton, Herbert, 1890–1973, vol. VII
Heaton, Sir Herbert Henniker, 1880–1961, vol. VI
Heaton, Sir (John) Frederick, 1880–1949, vol. IV
Heaton, Sir John Henniker, 1st Bt, 1848–1914, vol. I
Heaton, Sir John Henniker, 2nd Bt, 1877–1963, vol. VI
Heaton, Sir (John Victor) Peregrine Henniker-, 3rd Bt, 1903–1971, vol. VII
Heaton, Sir Joseph John, 1860–1934, vol. III
Heaton, Joseph Rowland, 1881–1951, vol. V
Heaton, Sir Peregrine Henniker; *see* Heaton, Sir J. V. P. H.
Heaton, Ralph Neville, 1912–1994, vol. IX
Heaton, Raymond H.; *see* Henniker-Heaton.
Heaton, Rose Henniker, (Mrs Adrian Porter), 1884–1975, vol. VII
Heaton, Trevor Braby, 1886–1972, vol. VII
Heaton, William Haslam, *died* 1941, vol. IV
Heaton-Armstrong, Sir John Dunamace, 1888–1967, vol. VI
Heaton-Armstrong, William Charles, 1853–1917, vol. II
Heaton-Ellis, Lt-Col Sir Charles Henry Brabazon, 1864–1945, vol. IV
Heaton-Ellis, Vice-Adm. Sir Edward Henry Fitzhardinge, 1868–1943, vol. IV
Heaven, Rev. Hudson Grosett, 1826–1916, vol. II
Heaven, Joseph Robert, 1840–1911, vol. I
Heaviside, Arthur West, 1844–1923, vol. II
Heaviside, Oliver, 1850–1925, vol. II
Heawood, Edward, 1863–1949, vol. IV
Heawood, Geoffrey Leonard, 1893–1982, vol. VIII
Heawood, Percy John, 1861–1955, vol. V
Hebb, Donald Olding, 1904–1985, vol. VIII
Hebb, Rev. Harry Arthur, 1850–1934, vol. III
Hebb, Sir John Harry, 1878–1942, vol. IV
Hebb, R. G., *died* 1918, vol. II
Hebblethwaite, Percival, 1849–1922, vol. II
Hebblethwaite, Peter, 1930–1994, vol. IX
Hebblethwaite, Sidney Horace, 1914–1987, vol. VIII
Hebden, George Brentnall, 1886–1968, vol. VI
Hebel, John William, 1891–1934, vol. III
Heber-Percy, Algernon; *see* Percy.
Heberden, Charles Buller, 1849–1921, vol. II
Heberden, Surg. Captain George Alfred, 1860–1916, vol. II
Heberden, William Buller, 1838–1922, vol. II
Hebert, Godfrey Taunton, *died* 1957, vol. V
Hebert, Louis Philippe, 1850–1917, vol. II
Hebrard, Emile A., 1862–1927, vol. II
Hechle, James Herbert, 1864–1935, vol. III

Hecker, William Rundle, 1899–1983, vol. VIII
Heckle, Arnold, 1906–1982, vol. VIII
Heckstall-Smith, Major Brooke, 1869–1944, vol. IV
Heckstall-Smith, Hugh William, 1896–1973, vol. VII
Hector, Annie, (Mrs Alexander), 1825–1902, vol. I
Hector, Sir James, 1834–1907, vol. I
Hedderwick, Arthur Stuart, 1885–1939, vol. III
Hedderwick, Edwin Charles, 1850–1935, vol. III
Hedderwick, Thomas Charles Hunter, 1850–1918, vol. II
Heddle, (Bentley) John, 1941–1989, vol. VIII
Heddle, John; *see* Heddle, B. J.
Hedgcock, Frank Arthur, 1875–1954, vol. V
Hedgcock, Walter W., *died* 1932, vol. III
Hedgeland, Rev. Philip, 1825–1911, vol. I
Hedges, Alfred Paget, 1867–1929, vol. III
Hedges, Frederick Albert M.; *see* Mitchell-Hedges.
Hedges, John, 1847–1934, vol. III
Hedges, Sir John Francis, 1917–1983, vol. VIII
Hedges, Killingworth, *died* 1945, vol. IV
Hedges, Brig. Killingworth Michael Fentham, 1890–1969, vol. VI
Hedges, Robert Yorke, 1903–1963, vol. VI
Hedges, Sidney George, 1897–1974, vol. VII
Hedin, Sven Anders, 1865–1952, vol. V
Hedley, Col Sir Coote; *see* Hedley, Col Sir W. C.
Hedley, Hilda Mabel, 1918–1988, vol. VIII
Hedley, John, 1834–1916, vol. II
Hedley, Rt Rev. John Cuthbert, 1837–1915, vol. I
Hedley, John Prescott, 1876–1957, vol. V
Hedley, Lt-Col John Ralph, 1871–1917, vol. II
Hedley, Ralph, 1851–1913, vol. I
Hedley, Maj.-Gen. Robert Cecil Osborne, 1900–1973, vol. VII
Hedley, Walter, 1879–1951, vol. V
Hedley, Col Sir (Walter) Coote, 1865–1937, vol. III
Hedley-Whyte, Angus, 1897–1971, vol. VII
Hedstrom, Sir (John) Maynard, 1872–1951, vol. V
Hedstrom, Sir (John) Maynard, 1908–1983, vol. VIII
Hedstrom, Sir Maynard; *see* Hedstrom, Sir J. M.
Hedworth, Rev. Thomas, *died* 1950, vol. IV
Heelis, Frederick, 1868–1930, vol. III
Heenan, His Eminence Cardinal John Carmel, 1905–1975, vol. VII
Heenan, Sir Joseph William Allan, 1888–1951, vol. V
Heenan, Maurice, 1912–2000, vol. X
Heenan, Hon. Peter, 1875–1948, vol. IV
Heeney, Arnold Danford Patrick, 1902–1970, vol. VI
Heeps, William, 1929–1995, vol. IX
Hees, Hon. George Harris, 1910–1996, vol. X
Heffer, Eric Samuel, 1922–1991, vol. IX
Heffernan, Sir John Harold, 1834–1921, vol. II
Heffernan, Col Nesbitt Breillat, 1861–1930, vol. III
Hegan, Col Edward, 1855–1922, vol. II
Hegarty, Sir Daniel, 1849–1914, vol. I
Hegedus, Ferencz, 1881–1944, vol. IV
Heger, Paul, 1846–1925, vol. II
Heger, Robert, 1886–1978, vol. VII
Heggs, Gordon Barrett M.; *see* Mitchell-Heggs.
Hehir, Maj.-Gen. Sir Patrick, 1859–1937, vol. III
Heidegger, Martin, 1889–1976, vol. VII

Heidenstam, Karl Gustaf Verner von, 1859–1940, vol. III
Heifetz, Jascha, 1901–1987, vol. VIII
Heilbron, Sir Ian, 1886–1959, vol. V
Heilbronn, Hans Arnold, 1908–1975, vol. VII
Heilbuth, George Henry, *died* 1942, vol. IV
Heilgers, Lt-Col Frank Frederick Alexander, 1892–1944, vol. IV
Heilpern, Godfrey, 1911–1973, vol. VII
Hein, Sir (Charles Henri) Raymond, 1901–1983, vol. VIII
Hein, Sir Raymond; *see* Hein, Sir C. H. R.
Heinemann, William, 1863–1920, vol. II
Heinz, Henry John, II, 1908–1987, vol. VIII
Heinz, Howard, 1877–1941, vol. IV
Heinze, Sir Bernard Thomas, 1894–1982, vol. VIII
Heisenberg, Werner Karl, 1901–1976, vol. VII
Heiser, Rev. Canon F. B., *died* 1952, vol. V
Heiser, Victor George, 1873–1972, vol. VII
Heitland, M. (Margaret), 1860–1938, vol. III
Heitler, Walter Heinrich, 1904–1981, vol. VIII
Heitner, H. Jesse, 1893–1965, vol. VI
Hektoen, Ludvig, 1863–1951, vol. V
Helbert, Lt-Col Geoffrey Gladstone, *died* 1934, vol. III
Helder, Augustus, 1827–1906, vol. I
Hele, Sir Ivor Henry Thomas, 1912–1993, vol. IX
Hele, Thomas Shirley, 1881–1953, vol. V
Hele-Shaw, Henry Selby, 1854–1941, vol. IV
Helfrich, Adm. Conrad Emile Lambert, 1886–1962, vol. VI
Hellard, Frederick, 1850–1925, vol. II
Hellard, Col Robert Charles, 1851–1929, vol. III
Heller, Hans, 1905–1974, vol. VII
Heller, J. H. S.; *see* Heller, Hans.
Helleu, Paul-César, 1859–1927, vol. II
Hellier, John Banjamin, *died* 1924, vol. II
Hellings, Gen. Sir Peter William Cradock, 1916–1990, vol. VIII
Hellings, Robert Bailey, 1863–1947, vol. IV
Hellins, Rev. Edgar William James, 1872–1946, vol. IV
Helliwell, Maj.-Gen. John Percival, 1884–1948, vol. IV
Hellman, Lillian, 1907–1984, vol. VIII
Hellmuth, Rt Rev. Isaac, 1820–1901, vol. I
Hellyer, Arthur George Lee, 1902–1993, vol. IX
Helm, Sir (Alexander) Knox, 1893–1964, vol. VI
Helm, Rev. George Francis, 1882–1958, vol. V
Helm, Henry James, 1839–1918, vol. II
Helm, Sir Knox; *see* Helm, Sir A. K.
Helm, William Henry, 1860–1936, vol. III
Helme, Col Sir George Coope; *see* Mashiter, Col Sir G. C.
Helme, Sir Norval Watson, 1849–1932, vol. III
Helmer, Col Richard Alexis, 1864–1920, vol. II
Helmore, Sir James Reginald Carroll, 1906–1972, vol. VII
Helmore, Hon. Air Cdre William, 1894–1964, vol. VI
Helmsing, Most Rev. Charles Herman, 1908–1993, vol. IX
Helmsley, Viscountess; (Muriel Frances Talbot), *died* 1925, vol. II
Helpmann, Sir Robert Murray, 1909–1986, vol. VIII

Helps, Rev. Canon Arthur Leonard, 1872–1960, vol. V
Helsby, Baron (Life Peer); Laurence Norman Helsby, 1908–1978, vol. VII
Helsham, Rev. Edward, 1891–1955, vol. V
Hely, Brig. Alfred Francis, 1902–1990, vol. VIII
Hely, Air Cdre Arthur Hubert McMath, 1909–1996, vol. X
Hely, Air Vice-Marshal William Lloyd, 1909–1970, vol. VI (AII)
Hely-Hutchinson, Christopher Douglas, 1885–1958, vol. V
Hely-Hutchinson, Maurice Robert, 1887–1961, vol. VI
Hely-Hutchinson, May, (Hon. Lady Hely-Hutchinson), *died* 1938, vol. III
Hely-Hutchinson, Victor, 1901–1947, vol. IV
Hely-Hutchinson, Rt Hon. Sir Walter Francis, 1849–1913, vol. I
Helyar, Brig.-Gen. Arthur Beaumont, 1858–1933, vol. III
Helyar, Lt-Comdr Kenneth Cary, 1887–1941, vol. IV
Hembry, Henry William McQuitty, 1903–1961, vol. VI
Hemeon, Clarence Reid, 1897–1953, vol. V
Heming, George Booth, 1858–1938, vol. III
Heming, Captain Thomas Henry, 1856–1932, vol. III
Hemingford, 1st Baron, 1869–1947, vol. IV
Hemingford, 2nd Baron, 1904–1982, vol. VIII
Hemingway, Albert, 1902–1993, vol. IX
Hemingway, Charles Robert, 1860–1947, vol. IV
Hemingway, Ernest Miller, 1898–1961, vol. VI
Hemingway, Sir William, 1880–1967, vol. VI
Hemmant, George, 1880–1964, vol. VI
Hemmerde, Edward George, 1871–1948, vol. IV
Hemming, (Arthur) Francis, 1893–1964, vol. VI
Hemming, Sir Augustus William Lawson, 1841–1907, vol. I
Hemming, Gen. Edward Hughes, 1860–1943, vol. IV
Hemming, Francis; *see* Hemming, A. F.
Hemming, Maj.-Gen. Frederick Wilson, 1850–1934, vol. III
Hemming, George Wirgman, 1821–1905, vol. I
Hemming, Rev. George, 1859–1931, vol. III
Hemming, Lt-Col Henry Harold, 1893–1976, vol. VII
Hemming, Col Norman Mackenzie, 1868–1950, vol. IV
Hemming, Maj.-Gen. William Edward Gordon, 1899–1953, vol. V
Hempel, Frieda, *died* 1955, vol. V
Hemphill, 1st Baron, 1821–1908, vol. I
Hemphill, 2nd Baron, 1853–1919, vol. II
Hemphill, 3rd Baron, 1860–1930, vol. III
Hemphill, 4th Baron, 1901–1957, vol. V
Hemphill, Major Robert, 1888–1935, vol. III
Hemphill, Ven. Samuel, 1859–1927, vol. II
Hems, Arthur; *see* Hems, B. A.
Hems, (Benjamin) Arthur, 1912–1995, vol. IX
Hemsley, William, 1817–1906, vol. I
Hemsley, William Bottin, 1843–1924, vol. II
Hemsted, Captain John Rustat, 1881–1953, vol. V

Hemsted, Rupert William, 1876–1952, vol. V
Hemy, Charles Napier, 1841–1917, vol. II
Henare, Sir James Clendon Tau, 1911–1989, vol. VIII
Hench, Philip Showalter, 1896–1965, vol. VI
Henchley, Lt-Col Albert Richard, died 1938, vol. III
Henchmen, Hereward Humfry, 1874–1939, vol. III
Hendel, Charles William, 1890–1982, vol. VIII
Henderson, 1st Baron, 1891–1984, vol. VIII
Henderson of Ardwick, 1st Baron, died 1950, vol. IV
Henderson of Brampton, Baron (Life Peer); Peter Gordon Henderson, 1922–2000, vol. X
Henderson, Acheson Thompson, died 1909, vol. I
Henderson, Sir Alan Gerald Russell, 1886–1963, vol. VI
Henderson, Rev. Alexander, died 1937, vol. III
Henderson, Alexander, 1914–1954, vol. V
Henderson, Alexander Edward, 1844–1906, vol. I
Henderson, Rev. Alexander Roy, 1862–1950, vol. IV
Henderson, Amos, 1864–1922, vol. II
Henderson, Col Andrew, 1867–1951, vol. V
Henderson, Andrew Graham, 1882–1963, vol. VI
Henderson, Ann, 1921–1976, vol. VII
Henderson, Rev. Archibald, 1837–1927, vol. II
Henderson, Archibald, 1886–1962, vol. VI
Henderson, Archibald, 1877–1963, vol. VI
Henderson, Arthur; see Baron Rowley.
Henderson, Rt Hon. Arthur, 1863–1935, vol. III
Henderson, Arthur Edward, 1870–1956, vol. V
Henderson, Bernard William, 1871–1929, vol. III
Henderson, Brig.-Gen. Sir Brodie Haldane, 1869–1936, vol. III
Henderson, Charles Alexander, 1882–1956, vol. V
Henderson, Sir Charles James, 1882–1974, vol. VII
Henderson, Charles Lamond, 1896–1966, vol. VI
Henderson, Lt-Gen. Sir David, 1862–1921, vol. II
Henderson, Sir David Kennedy, 1884–1965, vol. VI
Henderson, David Patrick, 1865–1931, vol. III
Henderson, David Willis Wilson, 1903–1968, vol. VI
Henderson, Duncan, 1870–1934, vol. III
Henderson, Rt Rev. Edward Barry, 1910–1986, vol. VIII
Henderson, Ven. Edward Chance, 1916–1997, vol. X
Henderson, Edward Firth, 1917–1995, vol. IX
Henderson, Very Rev. Edward Lowry, 1873–1947, vol. IV
Henderson, Effie; see Albanesi, Mme.
Henderson, Hon. Eric Brand B.; see Butler-Henderson.
Henderson, Eugénie Jane Andrina, 1914–1989, vol. VIII
Henderson, Comdr Francis Barkley, 1859–1934, vol. III
Henderson, Vice-Adm. Frank Hannam, 1850–1918, vol. II
Henderson, Frank Young, 1894–1966, vol. VI
Henderson, Sir Frederick Ness, 1862–1944, vol. IV
Henderson, Rear-Adm. Geoffrey Archer, 1913–1985, vol. VIII
Henderson, Col George Burton, 1890–1940, vol. III
Henderson, George Cockburn, 1870–1944, vol. IV

Henderson, Very Rev. George David, 1888–1957, vol. V
Henderson, Col George Francis Robert, died 1903, vol. I
Henderson, George Gerald, 1862–1942, vol. IV
Henderson, Sir George Henry, 1889–1958, vol. V
Henderson, George Hugh, 1892–1949, vol. IV
Henderson, Rt Rev. George Kennedy Buchanan, 1921–1996, vol. X
Henderson, Adm. George Morris, 1851–1915, vol. I
Henderson, George William, 1854–1934, vol. III
Henderson, Sir Guy Wilmot McLintock, 1897–1987, vol. VIII
Henderson, Lt-Col Hon. Harold Greenwood, 1875–1922, vol. II
Henderson, Col Harry Dalton, 1858–1945, vol. IV
Henderson, Hector Bruce, 1895–1962, vol. VI
Henderson, Dame Henrietta Caroline, (Lady Henderson), died 1959, vol. V
Henderson, Lt-Col Henry Cockcroft P.; see Page-Henderson.
Henderson, Henry Ludwig, 1880–1963, vol. VI
Henderson, Herbert Stephen, 1870–1942, vol. IV
Henderson, Sir Hubert Douglas, 1890–1952, vol. V
Henderson, Rev. Ian, 1910–1969, vol. VI
Henderson, Ian Dalton, 1918–1995, vol. IX
Henderson, Sir Ian Leslie, 1901–1971, vol. VII
Henderson, Sir James, 1848–1914, vol. I
Henderson, Ven. James, 1840–1935, vol. III
Henderson, James, 1868–1945, vol. IV
Henderson, James, 1889–1963, vol. VI
Henderson, Sir James, 1882–1967, vol. VI
Henderson, James Bell, 1883–1975, vol. VII
Henderson, Sir James Blacklock, 1871–1950, vol. IV
Henderson, Sir James Thyne, 1901–1993, vol. IX
Henderson, John, 1862–1938, vol. III
Henderson, John, 1876–1949, vol. IV
Henderson, John, 1883–1965, vol. VI
Henderson, Sir John, 1888–1975, vol. VII
Henderson, John Cochrane, 1881–1946, vol. IV
Henderson, Sir John Craik, 1890–1971, vol. VII
Henderson, John Louis, 1907–1985, vol. VIII
Henderson, John M'Donald, 1846–1922, vol. II
Henderson, John Robertson, 1863–1925, vol. II
Henderson, John Scott, 1895–1964, vol. VI
Henderson, John Stuart Wilmot, 1919–1995, vol. IX
Henderson, Joseph Morris, 1863–1936, vol. III
Henderson, Keith, 1883–1982, vol. VIII
Henderson, Kenneth David Druitt, 1903–1988, vol. VIII
Henderson, Maj.-Gen. Kennett Gregg, 1836–1902, vol. I
Henderson, Kingsley Anketell, 1883–1942, vol. IV
Henderson, Lt-Col Malcolm, died 1923, vol. II
Henderson, Air Vice-Marshal Malcolm, 1891–1978, vol. VII
Henderson, Sir Malcolm Siborne, 1905–1981, vol. VIII
Henderson, Rt Hon. Sir Nevile Meyrick, died 1942, vol. IV
Henderson, Sir Neville Vicars, 1899–1986, vol. VIII
Henderson, Adm. Sir Nigel Stuart, 1909–1993, vol. IX
Henderson, Comdr Oscar, 1891–1969, vol. VI

Henderson, Rev. Patrick Arkley W.; *see* Wright-Henderson.
Henderson, Maj.-Gen. Patrick Hagart, 1876–1968, vol. VI
Henderson, Peter, 1904–1983, vol. VIII
Henderson, Maj.-Gen. Philip Durham, 1840–1918, vol. II
Henderson, Philip Prichard, 1906–1977, vol. VII
Henderson, R. B., 1880–1958, vol. V
Henderson, Ralph, 1897–1979, vol. VII
Henderson, Adm. Sir Reginald Friend Hannam, 1846–1932, vol. III
Henderson, Adm. Sir Reginald Guy Hannam, 1881–1939, vol. III
Henderson, Richard, 1854–1945, vol. IV
Henderson, Richard McNeil, 1886–1972, vol. VII
Henderson, Robert, 1842–1925, vol. II
Henderson, Robert Alistair, 1917–1999, vol. X
Henderson, Robert Candlish, 1874–1964, vol. VI
Henderson, Sir Robert Herriot, *died* 1932, vol. III
Henderson, Hon. Robert Hugh, 1862–1956, vol. V
Henderson, Captain Robert Ronald, 1876–1932, vol. III
Henderson, Maj.-Gen. Sir Robert Samuel Findlay, 1858–1924, vol. II
Henderson, Roy Galbraith, 1899–2000, vol. X
Henderson, Rupert Albert Geary, 1896–1986, vol. VIII
Henderson, T. F., 1844–1923, vol. II
Henderson, Thomas, 1870–1945, vol. IV
Henderson, Sir Thomas, 1874–1951, vol. V
Henderson, Thomas, 1867–1960, vol. V
Henderson, Captain Thomas Maxwell Stuart M.; *see* Milne-Henderson.
Henderson, Thomson, *died* 1960, vol. V
Henderson, Sir Trevor, 1862–1930, vol. III
Henderson, Velyien Ewart, 1877–1945, vol. IV
Henderson, Lt-Col Sir Vivian Leonard, 1884–1965, vol. VI
Henderson, Rev. W. J., 1843–1929, vol. III
Henderson, Vice-Adm. Wilfred, 1873–1930, vol. III
Henderson, Sir William, 1826–1904, vol. I
Henderson, Sir William, 1863–1940, vol. III
Henderson, Brig. William Alexander, 1882–1949, vol. IV, vol. V
Henderson, William Craig, 1873–1959, vol. V
Henderson, William Crichton, 1931–1992, vol. IX
Henderson, Very Rev. William George, 1819–1905, vol. I
Henderson, Adm. Sir William Hannam, 1845–1931, vol. III
Henderson, William James, 1855–1937, vol. III
Henderson, Sir William MacGregor, 1913–2000, vol. X
Henderson, William Ross, 1936–1998, vol. X
Henderson, William Walker, 1886–1960, vol. V
Henderson-Begg, Rev. Canon William, 1877–1934, vol. III
Henderson-Howat, Very Rev. Rudolph, 1896–1957, vol. V
Henderson-Scott, Lt-Col Archibald Malcolm, 1882–1967, vol. VI
Henderson-Smith, Mrs; *see* Klickmann, F.
Henderson-Stewart, Sir James, 1st Bt, 1897–1961, vol. VI

Hendley, Brig.-Gen. Charles Edward, 1863–1920, vol. II
Hendley, Maj.-Gen. Harold, 1861–1932, vol. III
Hendley, Col Thomas Holbein, 1847–1917, vol. II
Hendrey, Eiluned, (Mrs Graeme Hendrey); *see* Lewis Eiluned.
Hendrick, James, 1867–1949, vol. IV
Hendrie, Donald Stewart, 1909–1965, vol. VI
Hendrie, Herbert, 1887–1946, vol. IV
Hendrie, Col Sir John Strathearn, 1857–1923, vol. II
Hendriks, Sir Charles, (C. A. C. J. Hendriks), 1883–1960, vol. V
Hendry, Sir Alexander, 1867–1932, vol. III
Hendry, (Alexander) Forbes, 1908–1980, vol. VII
Hendry, Charles, 1870–1952, vol. V
Hendry, Forbes; *see* Hendry, A. F.
Hendry, James, 1885–1945, vol. IV
Hendry, Brig.-Gen. Patrick William, 1861–1952, vol. V
Hendry, Robert, 1876–1951, vol. V
Hendry, William Edward Russell, 1911–1965, vol. VI
Hendy, Arthur, 1874–1953, vol. V
Hendy, Frederick James Roberts, 1858–1933, vol. III
Hendy, Sir Philip, 1900–1980, vol. VII
Hendy, Roy, 1890–1959, vol. V
Heneage, 1st Baron, 1840–1922, vol. II
Heneage, 2nd Baron, 1866–1954, vol. V
Heneage, 3rd Baron, 1877–1967, vol. VI
Heneage, Sir Algernon Charles Fiesché, 1834–1915, vol. I
Heneage, Lt-Col Sir Arthur Pelham, 1881–1971, vol. VII
Heneage, Major Godfrey Clement Walker, 1868–1939, vol. III
Heneage, Lt-Col Hon. Henry Granville, 1868–1947, vol. IV
Henegan, Lt-Col John, 1865–1920, vol. II
Heneker, Gen. Sir William Charles Giffard, 1867–1939, vol. III
Heney, Thomas William, 1862–1928, vol. II
Henig, Sir Mark, 1911–1979, vol. VII
Henley, 3rd Baron, 1825–1899, vol. I
Henley, 4th Baron, 1849–1923, vol. II
Henley, 5th Baron, 1858–1925, vol. II
Henley, 6th Baron, 1877–1962, vol. VI
Henley, 7th Baron, 1914–1977, vol. VII
Henley, Brig.-Gen. Hon. Anthony Morton, *died* 1925, vol. II
Henley, Col Frank Le Leu, 1888–1941, vol. IV
Henley, Herbert James, 1882–1937, vol. III
Henley, Rear-Adm. Sir Joseph Charles Cameron, 1909–1999, vol. X
Henley, Vice-Adm. Joseph Charles Walrond, 1879–1968, vol. VI
Henley, Joseph John, 1821–1910, vol. I
Henley, Sir Thomas, 1860–1935, vol. III
Henley, William Ernest, 1849–1903, vol. I
Henman, Philip Sydney, 1900–1986, vol. VIII
Henn, Rt Rev. Henry, 1858–1931, vol. III
Henn, Sir Sydney Herbert Holcroft, 1861–1936, vol. III
Henn, Thomas Rice, 1814–1901, vol. I
Henn, Thomas Rice, 1901–1974, vol. VII

Henn, Col William Francis, 1892–1964, vol. VI
Henn-Collins, Hon. Sir Stephen Ogle, *died* 1958, vol. V
Hennell, Rev. Canon Michael Murray, 1918–1996, vol. X
Hennell, Col Sir Reginald, 1844–1925, vol. II
Henner, Jean Jacques, 1829–1905, vol. I
Hennessey, John Baboneau Nicklerlien, 1829–1910, vol. I
Hennessy, Sir John Wyndham P.; *see* Pope-Hennessy.
Hennessey, Robert Samuel Fleming, 1905–1989, vol. VIII
Hennessy, Hon. Sir Alfred Theodore, 1875–1963, vol. VI
Hennessy, Rt Hon. Sir David Valentine, 1855–1923, vol. II
Hennessy, Denis William, 1912–1990, vol. VIII
Hennessy, Maj.-Gen. Sir George Robertson, 1837–1905, vol. I
Hennessy, James P.; *see* Pope-Hennessy.
Hennessy, Lt-Col John, 1867–1954, vol. V
Hennessy, Col John Patrick Cumberlege, 1867–1933, vol. III
Hennessy, Maj.-Gen. Ladislaus Herbert Richard P.; *see* Pope-Hennessy.
Hennessy, Sir Patrick, 1898–1981, vol. VIII
Hennessy, Captain Richard, 1876–1953, vol. V
Hennessy, Richard M., 1854–1926, vol. II
Hennessy, Dame Una P.; *see* Pope-Hennessy.
Hennessy, William John, vol. II
Henniker, 5th Baron, 1842–1902, vol. I
Henniker, 6th Baron, 1872–1956, vol. V
Henniker, 7th Baron, 1883–1980, vol. VII
Henniker, Col Alan Major, 1870–1949, vol. IV
Henniker, Hon. Mrs Arthur, (Hon. Florence Ellen Hungerford Henniker-Major), 1885–1923, vol. II
Henniker, Adm. Sir Arthur John, 6th Bt; *see* Henniker-Hughan.
Henniker, Sir Brydges Powell, 4th Bt, 1835–1906, vol. I
Henniker, Sir Frederick Brydges Major, 5th Bt, 1862–1908, vol. I
Henniker, Brig. Sir Mark Chandos Auberon, 8th Bt, 1906–1991, vol. IX
Henniker, Lt-Col Sir Robert John Aldborough, 7th Bt, 1888–1958, vol. V
Henniker-Gotley, George Rainald, 1893–1974, vol. VII
Henniker-Gotley, Roger Alwyn, 1898–1985, vol. VIII
Henniker-Heaton, Sir (John Victor) Peregrine; *see* Heaton.
Henniker-Heaton, Raymond, 1874–1963, vol. VI
Henniker-Hughan, Adm. Sir Arthur John, 6th Bt, 1866–1925, vol. II
Henniker-Major, Maj.-Gen. Hon. Arthur Henry, 1855–1912, vol. I
Henniker-Major, Hon. Edward Minet, 1848–1924, vol. II
Henniker-Major, Hon. Florence Ellen Hungerford; *see* Henniker, Hon. Mrs Arthur.
Henniker-Major, Hon. Gerald Arthur George, 1872–1955, vol. V
Henning, Basil Duke, 1910–1990, vol. VIII

Henning, Walter Bruno, 1908–1967, vol. VI
Hennings, John Dunn, 1922–1985, vol. VIII
Hennings, Richard Owen, 1911–1993, vol. IX
Henri, Adrian Maurice, 1932–2000, vol. X
Henri, Robert, 1865–1929, vol. III
Henrici, Olaus M. F. E., 1840–1918, vol. II
Henrion, Frederic Henri Kay, 1914–1990, vol. VIII
Henriot, Emile, 1889–1961, vol. VI
Henriques, Sir Basil L. Q., 1890–1961, vol. VI
Henriques, Sir Cyril George Xavier, 1908–1982, vol. VIII
Henriques, Henry Straus Quixano, 1866–1925, vol. II
Henriques, Louis Fernando, 1916–1976, vol. VII
Henriques, Sir Philip Gutterez, 1867–1950, vol. IV
Henriques, Col Robert David Quixano, 1905–1967, vol. VI
Henrison, Dame (Anne) Rosina (Elizabeth), 1902–1989, vol. X (AI)
Henrison, Dame Rosina; *see* Henrison, Dame A. R. E.
Henry, Hon. Albert Royle, 1907–1981, vol. VIII
Henry, Alexander, *died* 1904, vol. I
Henry, Augustine, 1857–1930, vol. III
Henry, Sir Charles Solomon, 1st Bt (*cr* 1911), 1860–1919, vol. II
Henry, Cyril Bowdler, (C. Bowdler-Henry), 1893–1981, vol. VIII
Henry, Sir David, 1888–1963, vol. IV
Henry, Sir Denis Aynsley, 1917–2000, vol. X
Henry, Rt Hon. Sir Denis Stanislaus, 1st Bt (*cr* 1922), 1864–1925, vol. II
Henry, Sir Edward Richard, 1st Bt (*cr* 1918), 1850–1931, vol. III
Henry, (Ernest James) Gordon, 1919–1989, vol. VIII
Henry, Lt-Gen. George, 1846–1922, vol. II
Henry, George, 1858–1943, vol. IV
Henry, Hon. George Stewart, 1871–1958, vol. V
Henry, Gordon; *see* Henry, E. J. G.
Henry, Rt Rev. Henry, *died* 1908, vol. I
Henry, Rev. J. Edgar, 1841–1911, vol. I
Henry, Major James D.; *see* Douglas-Henry.
Henry, Sir James Holmes, 2nd Bt, 1911–1997, vol. X
Henry, James Macintyre, 1852–1929, vol. III
Henry, Sir John, 1858–1930, vol. III
Henry, Mitchell, 1826–1910, vol. I
Henry, Paul, *died* 1958, vol. V
Henry, Robert Francis Jack, 1902–1970, vol. VI
Henry, Robert Mitchell, 1873–1950, vol. IV
Henry, Maj.-Gen. St George Charles Henry, 1860–1909, vol. I
Henry, Seaghan P.; *see* Mac Enri, Seaghan P.
Henry, Thomas Cradock, 1910–1993, vol. IX
Henry, Col Vivian, 1868–1929, vol. III
Henry, William Alexander, 1863–1927, vol. II
Henry, Sir William Daniel, 1855–1934, vol. III
Henry, William Robert, 1915–1996, vol. X
Hensby, Frederick Charles, 1919–1982, vol. VIII
Henschel, Sir George, 1850–1934, vol. III
Henshall, John Henry, 1856–1928, vol. II
Henshaw, Rt Rev. Thomas, 1873–1938, vol. III
Hensley, Rev. Lewis, 1824–1905, vol. I
Hensley, Sir Robert Mitton, 1840–1912, vol. I

Henslow, Rev. George, 1835–1925, vol. II
Hensman, Col Henry Frank, 1839–1911, vol. I
Hensman, Howard, *died* 1916, vol. II
Henson, Rt Rev. Herbert Hensley, 1863–1947, vol. IV
Henson, John, 1879–1969, vol. VI
Henson, John James, 1868–1948, vol. IV
Henson, Leslie Lincoln, 1891–1957, vol. V
Henson, Ronald Alfred, 1915–1994, vol. IX
Hentschel, Christopher Carl, 1899–1986, vol. VIII
Hentschel, Carl, 1864–1930, vol. III
Henty, Hon. Sir Denham; *see* Henly, Hon. Sir N. H. D.
Henty, George Alfred, 1832–1902, vol. I
Henty, Hon. Sir (Norman Henry) Denham, 1903–1978, vol. VII
Henvey, Col Ralph, 1876–1945, vol. IV
Hepburn, Sir Archibald B.; *see* Buchan-Hepburn.
Hepburn, Audrey, 1929–1993, vol. IX
Hepburn, Col Bernard Richard, 1876–1939, vol. III
Hepburn, Bryan Audley St John, 1911–1991, vol. IX
Hepburn, Lt-Col David, *died* 1931, vol. III
Hepburn, Sir Harry Frankland, 1867–1931, vol. III
Hepburn, Sir John Karslake Thomas B.; *see* Buchan-Hepburn.
Hepburn, Malcolm Langton, 1866–1942, vol. IV
Hepburn, Hon. Mitchell F., 1896–1953, vol. V
Hepburn, Surg. Rear-Adm. Nicol Sinclair, 1913–2000, vol. X
Hepburn, Sir Ninian, B. A. J. B.; *see* Buchan-Hepburn.
Hepburn, Sir Thomas Henry, 1840–1917, vol. II
Hepburn, Thomas Nicoll Gabriel Setoun, 1861–1930, vol. III
Hepburn, William Andrew Hardie, 1898–1965, vol. VI
Hepburn-Ruston, Edda von Heemstra; *see* Hepburn, Audrey.
Hepburn-Stuart-Forbes-Trefusis, Hon. Henry Walter; *see* Trefusis.
Hepburn-Stuart-Forbes-Trefusis, Major Hon. John Frederick; *see* Trefusis.
Hepburne-Scott, Hon. Henry Robert, 1847–1914, vol. I
Hepburne-Scott, James Cospatrick; *see* Scott.
Hepenstal, Major Lambert John D.; *see* Dopping-Hepenstal.
Hepenstal, Col Maxwell Edward D.; *see* Dopping-Hepenstal.
Hepher, Rev. Canon Cyril, 1872–1931, vol. III
Heppel, Richard Purdon, 1913–1986, vol. VIII
Heppell, Ralph Gordon, 1910–1976, vol. VII
Heppenstall, (John) Rayner, 1911–1981, vol. VIII
Heppenstall, Rayner; *see* Heppenstall, J. R.
Hepper, Col Albert James, 1839–1915, vol. I
Hepper, Anthony Evelyn, 1923–1999, vol. X
Hepper, Sir Lawless, 1870–1935, vol. III
Hepple, Anne; *see* Dickinson, A. H.
Hepple, Norman; *see* Hepple, R. N.
Hepple, (Robert) Norman, 1908–1994, vol. IX
Heppleston, Alfred Gordon, 1915–1998, vol. X
Hepworth, Dame Barbara; *see* Hepworth, Dame J. B.

Hepworth, Dame (Jocelyn) Barbara, 1903–1975, vol. VII
Hepworth, Joseph, *died* 1945, vol. IV
Hepworth, Captain Melville Willis Campbell, 1849–1919, vol. II
Herapath, Lt-Col Edgar, 1853–1933, vol. III
Herapath, Col Lionel, 1880–1934, vol. III
Herbage, Julian Livingston-, 1904–1976, vol. VII
Herbert, Agnes, *died* 1960, vol. V
Herbert, Sir Alan Patrick, 1890–1971, vol. VII
Herbert, Hon. Alan Percy Harty Molyneux, *died* 1907, vol. I
Herbert, Sir Alfred, 1866–1957, vol. V
Herbert, Arnold; *see* Herbert, T. A.
Herbert, Sir Arthur James, 1820–1897, vol. I
Herbert, Sir Arthur James, 1855–1921, vol. II
Herbert, Hon. Auberon Edward William Molyneux, 1838–1906, vol. I
Herbert, Hon. Aubrey Nigel Henry Molyneux, 1880–1923, vol. II
Herbert, Lt-Col Charles, 1854–1919, vol. II
Herbert, Sir Charles Gordon, 1893–1970, vol. VI
Herbert, Christopher Alfred, 1913–1988, vol. VIII
Herbert, Lt-Col Claude, 1862–1937, vol. III
Herbert, Desmond Andrew, 1898–1976, vol. VII
Herbert, Brig.-Gen. Edmund Arthur, 1866–1946, vol. IV
Herbert, Sir Edward Dave Asher, 1892–1963, vol. VI
Herbert, Edward Maxwell K.; *see* Kenney-Herbert.
Herbert, Brig.-Gen. Edward Sidney, 1866–1936, vol. III
Herbert, Col. Edward William, 1855–1924, vol. II
Herbert, Lieut-Gen. Sir (Edwin) Otway, 1901–1984, vol. VIII
Herbert, Edwin Savory; *see* Baron Tangley.
Herbert of Lea, Lady; (Elizabeth), *died* 1911, vol. I
Herbert, Maj. George, 1892–1982, vol. VIII
Herbert, Col Hon. Sir George Sidney, 1st Bt (*cr* 1937), 1886–1942, vol. IV
Herbert, Lt-Col Herbert, 1865–1942, vol. IV
Herbert, Hilary A., *died* 1919, vol. II, vol. III
Herbert, Sir Jesse, 1851–1916, vol. II
Herbert, Jesse Basil, 1899–1972, vol. VII
Herbert, John Alexander, 1862–1948, vol. IV
Herbert, Lt-Col Sir John Arthur, 1895–1943, vol. IV
Herbert, Maj.-Gen. Lionel, 1860–1929, vol. III
Herbert, Hon. Mervyn Robert Howard Molyneux, 1882–1929, vol. III
Herbert, Hon. Sir Michael Henry, 1857–1903, vol. I
Herbert, Lieut-Gen. Sir Otway; *see* Herbert, Lieut-Gen. Sir E. O.
Herbert, Brig.-Gen. Otway Charles, 1877–1955, vol. V
Herbert, Rt Rev. Percy Mark, 1885–1968, vol. VI
Herbert, Air Cdre Philip Lee William, 1882–1936, vol. III
Herbert, Rt Hon. Sir Robert George Wyndham, 1831–1905, vol. I
Herbert, Roscoe, 1895–1975, vol. VII
Herbert, Captain Sir Sidney, 1st Bt (*cr* 1936), 1890–1939, vol. III
Herbert, Solomon, 1874–1940, vol. III
Herbert, Sydney, 1886–1967, vol. VI

Herbert, (Thomas) Arnold, *died* 1940, vol. III
Herbert, Violet Ida Evelyn; *see* Baroness Darcy de Knayth.
Herbert, Walter Elmes, 1902–1980, vol. VII
Herbert, William de Bracy, 1872–1928, vol. II
Herbert, Maj.-Gen. Hon. William Henry, 1834–1909, vol. I
Herbert, Maj.-Gen. William Norman, 1880–1949, vol. IV
Herbert-Smith, Charles, 1862–1944, vol. IV
Herbertson, Andrew John, *died* 1914, vol. I
Herbertson, James John William, 1883–1974, vol. VII
Herbison, Rt Hon. Margaret McCrone, 1907–1996, vol. X
Herbst, Major John Frederick, 1873–1961, vol. VI
Herchenroder, Sir Francis; *see* Herchenroder, Sir M. J. B. F.
Herchenroder, Sir Furcy Alfred, 1865–1932, vol. III
Herchenroder, (Marie Ferdinand) Philippe, 1893–1968, vol. VI
Herchenroder, Sir (Marie Joseph Barnabe) Francis, 1896–1982, vol. VIII
Herchenroder, Philippe; *see* Herchenroder, M. F. P.
Hercus, Sir Charles Ernest, 1888–1971, vol. VII
Hercy, Sir Francis Hugh George, 1868–1947, vol. IV
Herd, Harold, 1893–1976, vol. VII
Herdman, Hon. Sir Alexander Lawrence, 1869–1953, vol. V
Herdman, Major Sir Emerson Crawford, 1869–1949, vol. IV
Herdman, Sir Ernest; *see* Herdman, Sir R. E.
Herdman, Sir (Robert) Ernest, 1857–1952, vol. V
Herdman, Robert Duddingstone, 1863–1922, vol. II
Herdman, Sir William Abbott, 1858–1924, vol. II
Herdon, Maj.-Gen. Hugh Edward, *died* 1958, vol. V
Herdt, Louis A., 1872–1926, vol. II
Hereford, 16th Viscount, 1843–1930, vol. III
Hereford, 17th Viscount, 1865–1952, vol. V
Heren, Louis Philip, 1919–1995, vol. IX
Herford, Charles Harold, *died* 1931, vol. III
Herford, Ethilda B. Meakin, 1872–1956, vol. V
Herford, Geoffrey Vernon Brooke, 1905–2000, vol. X
Hergesheimer, Joseph, 1880–1954, vol. V
Heriot, Maj.-Gen. Mackay A. H. J., 1839–1918, vol. II
Heriot, Alexander John, 1914–1995, vol. IX
Heriot, Sir William M.; *see* Maitland-Heriot.
Heriot-Maitland, Brig.-Gen. James Dalgleish, 1814–1958, vol. V.
Heriot-Maitland, Maj.-Gen. Sir James Makgill; *see* Maitland.
Heritage, Brig. Francis Bede, 1877–1934, vol. III
Heritage, James Edgar, 1880–1957, vol. V
Heritage, Stanley James, *died* 1980, vol. VII
Heritage, Rev. Canon Thomas Charles, 1908–1995, vol. IX
Heriz, Captain Reginald Yorke, 1851–1910, vol. I
Herkless, Very Rev. Sir John, 1855–1920, vol. II
Herklots, Geoffrey Alton Craig, 1902–1986, vol. VIII
Herklots, Rev. Hugh Gerard Gibson, 1903–1971, vol. VII

Herkomer, Sir Hubert von, 1849–1914, vol. I
Herman, E., (Mrs M. Herman), *died* 1923, vol. II
Herman, George Ernest, 1849–1914, vol. I
Herman, Josef, 1911–2000, vol. X
Herman-Hodge, Rear-Adm. Hon. Claude Preston, 1888–1952, vol. V
Hermes, Gertrude Anna Bertha, 1901–1983, vol. VIII
Hermon-Hodge, Major Hon. Robert Edward Udny, 1882–1937, vol. III
Hern, William, *died* 1939, vol. III
Hernaman-Johnson, Francis, 1879–1949, vol. IV
Horno Soame, Sir Charles Buckworth; *see* Soame.
Herne-Soame, Sir Charles Burnett Buckworth-; *see* Soame.
Herniman, Ven. Ronald George, 1923–1998, vol. X
Heron, Hon. Col Alexander Robert, 1888–1949, vol. IV
Heron, (Cuthbert) George, 1911–1979, vol. VII
Heron, Lt-Col Davis, 1878–1941, vol. IV
Heron, Edward Thomas, 1867–1949, vol. IV
Heron, George; *see* Heron, C. G.
Heron, George Allan, 1845–1915, vol. I
Heron, Col Sir George Wykeham, 1880–1963, vol. VI
Heron, Rev. James, 1836–1918, vol. II
Heron, Patrick, 1920–1999, vol. X
Heron, Brig.-Gen. Sir Thomas, 1857–1931, vol. III
Heron-Allen, Edward, 1861–1943, vol. IV
Heron-Maxwell, Mrs Beatrice Maude Emilia, *died* 1927, vol. II
Heron-Maxwell, Captain Sir Ivor Walter, 8th Bt, 1871–1928, vol. II
Heron-Maxwell, Sir John Robert, 7th Bt, 1836–1910, vol. I
Heron-Maxwell, Sir Patrick Ivor, 9th Bt, 1916–1982, vol. VIII
Heron-Maxwell, Robert Charles, 1848–1938, vol. III
Herrera, Senator Luis Alberto de, 1873–1959, vol. V
Herreshoff, Nathanael Greene, 1848–1938, vol. III
Herrick, Frederick Charles, 1887–1970, vol. VI
Herrick, Col Henry, 1872–1928, vol. II
Herrick, Myron T., 1854–1929, vol. III
Herrick, Very Rev. Richard William, 1913–1981, vol. VIII
Herrick, Robert, 1868–1938, vol. III
Herrick, Major Robert Lysle Warren, 1895–1936, vol. III
Herridge, Geoffrey Howard, 1904–1997, vol. X
Herridge, Major Hon. William Duncan, 1888–1961, vol. VI
Herries, 11th Lord, 1837–1908, vol. I
Herries, Lady (12th in line), 1877–1945, vol. IV
Herries, Edward, 1821–1911, vol. I
Herries, Sir Michael Alexander Robert Young-, 1923–1995, vol. IX
Herries, Hon. Sir William Herbert, 1859–1923, vol. II
Herring, Major Alfred Cecil, 1888–1966, vol. VI
Herring, Lt-Gen. Hon. Sir Edmund Francis, 1892–1982, vol. VIII
Herring, George, 1832–1906, vol. I
Herring, Dame Mary Ranken, 1895–1981, vol. VIII
Herring, Percy Theodore, 1872–1967, vol. VI

Herring, Robert, 1903–1975, vol. VII
Herring, Brig.-Gen. Sydney Charles Edgar, 1882–1951, vol. V
Herring, Lt-Col William, 1839–1917, vol. II
Herring-Cooper, Lt-Col William Weldon, 1873–1953, vol. V
Herringham, Sir Wilmot Parker, 1855–1936, vol. III
Herrington, Hugh Geoffrey, 1900–1980, vol. VII
Herriot, Edonard, 1872–1957, vol. V
Herriot, James; see Wight, J. A.
Herriotts, John, died 1935, vol. III
Herron, Very Rev. David Craig, 1882–1955, vol. V
Herron, Henry, 1911–1996, vol. X
Herron, Hon. Sir Leslie James, 1902–1973, vol. VII
Herron, Sir Robert, 1836–1900, vol. I, vol. III
Herron, Ronald James, 1930–1994, vol. IX
Herron, Shaun, 1912–1989, vol. VIII
Herschel, Alexander Stewart, 1836–1907, vol. I
Herschel, Col John, 1837–1921, vol. II
Herschel, Rev. Sir John Charles William, 3rd Bt, 1869–1950, vol. IV
Herschel, Sir William James, 2nd Bt, 1833–1917, vol. II
Herschell, 1st Baron, 1837–1899, vol. I
Herschell, 2nd Baron, 1878–1929, vol. III
Herschell, Charles Richard, 1877–1962, vol. VI
Herschell, George, 1856–1914, vol. I
Hersey, John Richard, 1914–1993, vol. IX
Hershey, Alfred Day, 1908–1997, vol. X
Herter, Christian Archibald, 1895–1966, vol. VI
Hertford, 7th Marquess of, 1871–1940, vol. III
Hertford, 8th Marquess of, 1930–1997, vol. X
Hertslet, Sir Cecil, 1850–1934, vol. III
Hertslet, Sir Edward, 1824–1902, vol. I
Hertslet, Rev. Canon Edward Lewis Augustine, 1878–1936, vol. III
Hertslet, George Thomas, 1822–1906, vol. I
Hertslet, Harry Lester, 1856–1925, vol. II
Hertz, Alfred, 1872–1942, vol. IV
Hertz, Henry Felix, 1863–1932, vol. III
Hertz, Very Rev. Joseph Herman, 1872–1946, vol. IV
Hertz, William Axel, 1859–1950, vol. IV
Hertzberg, Maj.-Gen. Charles Sumner Lund, 1886–1944, vol. IV
Hertzberg, Maj.-Gen. Halfdan Fenton Harbo, 1884–1959, vol. V
Hertzog, Gen. Hon. James Barry Munnik, 1866–1942, vol. IV
Hervey, Arthur, 1855–1922, vol. II
Hervey, Gen. Charles Robert West, 1818–1903, vol. I
Hervey, Dudley Francis Amelius, 1849–1911, vol. I
Hervey, Lord Francis, 1846–1931, vol. III
Hervey, Rev. Frederick Alfred John, 1846–1910, vol. I
Hervey, Sir George William, 1845–1915, vol. I
Hervey, Henry Arthur William, 1832–1908, vol. I
Hervey, Lord Walter John, 1865–1948, vol. IV
Hervey-Bathurst, Major Sir Frederick Edward William; see Bathurst.
Hervey-Bathurst, Sir Frederick Peter Methuen; see Bathurst.
Hervieu, Paul Ernest, 1857–1915, vol. I

Herwarth von Bittenfeld, Hans Heinrich, 1904–1999, vol. X
Herzberg, Hon. Gerhard, 1904–1999, vol. X
Herzfeld, Ernst Emil, 1879–1948, vol. IV
Herzfeld, Gertrude Marianne Amalia, 1890–1981, vol. VIII
Herzig, Christopher, 1926–1993, vol. IX
Herzog, Chaim, 1918–1997, vol. X
Herzog, Rt Rev. Edward, 1841–1924, vol. II
Herzog, Frederick Joseph, 1890–1987, vol. VIII
Herzog, Chief Rabbi Isaac, 1888–1959, vol. V
Heseltine, Lt-Col Christopher, 1869–1944, vol. IV
Heseltine, Major Godfrey, 1871–1932, vol. III
Heseltine, Harry Nelson, died 1935, vol. III
Heseltine, John Postle, 1843–1929, vol. III
Heseltine, Michael, 1886–1952, vol. V
Hesilrige, Arthur George Maynard, 1863–1953, vol. V
Hesketh, 1st Baron, 1881–1944, vol. IV
Hesketh, 2nd Baron, 1916–1955, vol. V
Hesketh, Air Vice-Marshal Allan, died 1973, vol. VII
Hesketh, Charles Hesketh Fleetwood-, 1871–1947, vol. IV
Hesketh, (Charles) Peter (Fleetwood) Fleetwood-, 1905–1985, vol. VIII
Hesketh, Lt-Col George, 1878–1929, vol. III
Hesketh, Lt-Col James Arthur, 1863–1923, vol. II
Hesketh, Col Rawdon John Isherwood, 1872–1959, vol. V
Hesketh, Roger Fleetwood, 1902–1987, vol. VIII
Hesketh, Sir Thomas George Fermor-, 7th Bt, 1849–1924, vol. II
Heslop, Major Alfred Herbert, 1880–1929, vol. III
Heslop, Air Vice-Marshal Herbert William, 1898–1976, vol. VII
Heslop, Richard Oliver, 1842–1916, vol. II
Heslop, Major Thomas Bernard, 1891–1938, vol. III
Heslop-Harrison, John, 1920–1998, vol. X
Heslop-Harrison, John William, 1881–1967, vol. VI
Hespeler, Hon. Wilhelm, born 1850, vol. II
Hess, Ellen Elizabeth, 1908–1996, vol. X
Hess, Dame Myra, 1890–1965, vol. VI
Hess, Victor Francis, 1883–1964, vol. VI
Hess, Walter Rudolf, 1881–1973, vol. VII
Hess, Willy, 1859–1939, vol. III
Hesse, Hermann, 1877–1962, vol. VI
Hessey, Rev. Robert Falkner, 1826–1911, vol. I
Hessey, Brig.-Gen. William Francis, 1868–1939, vol. III
Hetherington, Alastair; see Hetherington, H. A.
Hetherington, (Arthur) Carleton, 1916–1995, vol. IX
Hetherington, Arthur Lonsdale, 1881–1960, vol. V
Hetherington, Carleton; see Hetherington, A. C.
Hetherington, Rear-Adm. Derick Henry Fellowes, 1911–1992, vol. IX
Hetherington, (Hector) Alastair, 1919–1999, vol. X
Hetherington, Sir Hector James Wright, 1888–1965, vol. VI
Hetherington, Ivystan, died 1917, vol. II
Hetherington, Sir Roger Gaskell, 1876–1952, vol. V
Hetherington, Roger le Geyt, 1908–1990, vol. VIII
Hetherington, Gp Captain Thomas Gerard, 1886–1951, vol. V
Hetherington, William Lonsdale, 1845–1911, vol. I

Hetherwick, Rev. Alexander, 1860–1939, vol. III
Hett, Major Francis Paget, *died* 1966, vol. VI
Hett, Geoffrey Seccombe, 1878–1949, vol. IV
Hett, Walter Stanley, 1882–1948, vol. IV
Heugh, Comdr John George, 1856–1915, vol. I
Heuston, Lt-Col Frederick Samuel, 1857–1914, vol. I
Heuston, Robert Francis Vere, 1923–1995, vol. IX
Heuvel, Frederick V.; *see* Vanden Heuvel.
Hevesy, George Charles de, 1885–1966, vol. VI
Hewan, Gethyn Elliot, 1916–1988, vol. VIII
Heward, Air Chief Marshal Sir Anthony Wilkinson, 1918 1995, vol. IX
Heward, Leslie Hays, 1897–1943, vol. IV
Hewart, 1st Viscount, 1870–1943, vol. IV
Hewart, 2nd Viscount, 1896–1964, vol. VI
Hewat, Aubrey Middleton, 1884–1976, vol. VII
Hewat, Air Cdre Harry Aitken, 1888–1970, vol. VI
Hewat, Col Sir John, 1863–1928, vol. II
Hewby, Louis John, 1871–1925, vol. II
Hewby, William Petch, 1866–1946, vol. IV
Hewer, Christopher Langton, 1897–1986, vol. VIII
Hewer, Humphrey Robert, 1903–1974, vol. VII
Hewer, Maj.-Gen. Reginald Kingscote, 1892–1970, vol. VI
Hewer, Thomas Frederick, 1903–1994, vol. IX
Hewetson, John T., 1872–1936, vol. III
Hewetson, Gen. Sir Reginald Hackett, 1908–1993, vol. IX
Hewett, Edbert Ansgar, 1860–1915, vol. I
Hewett, Edward Osborne, 1835–1897, vol. I
Hewett, Lt-Col Edward Vincent Osborne, 1867–1953, vol. V
Hewett, Sir (Frederick) Stanley, 1880–1954, vol. V
Hewett, Rear-Adm. George Hayley, 1855–1930, vol. III
Hewett, Captain George Stuart, 1863–1937, vol. III
Hewett, Captain Gilbert George Pearse, 1880–1966, vol. VI
Hewett, Sir Harold George, 4th Bt, 1858–1949, vol. IV
Hewett, Sir John George, 5th Bt, 1895–1990, vol. VIII
Hewett, Sir John Prescott, 1854–1941, vol. IV
Hewett, Col Murray Selwood, 1881–1939, vol. III
Hewett, Captain Robert Roy Scott, 1886–1967, vol. VI
Hewett, Sir Stanley; *see* Hewett, Sir F. S.
Hewins, Harold Preece, 1877–1956, vol. V
Hewins, Maurice Gravenor, 1897–1953, vol. V
Hewins, William Albert Samuel, 1865–1931, vol. III
Hewison, Robert, 1876–1959, vol. V
Hewit, Forrest, *died* 1956, vol. V
Hewitson, Captain Mark, 1897–1973, vol. VII
Hewitson, Rev. William, *died* 1932, vol. III
Hewitt, Abram S., 1822–1903, vol. I
Hewitt, Surg. Rear-Adm. Alfred James, *died* 1947, vol. IV
Hewitt, Captain Hon. Archibald Rodney, 1883–1915, vol. I
Hewitt, Cecil Rolph, (C. H. Rolph), 1901–1994, vol. IX
Hewitt, Brig. Charles Caulfield, 1883–1949, vol. IV
Hewitt, Surg.-Rear-Adm. David Walker, 1870–1940, vol. III

Hewitt, Lt-Col Dudley Riddiford, 1877–1971, vol. VII
Hewitt, Edgar Percy, *died* 1928, vol. II
Hewitt, Air Chief Marshal Sir Edgar Rainey L.; *see* Ludlow-Hewitt.
Hewitt, Hon. Edward, 1848–1931, vol. III
Hewitt, Sir Frederic William, 1857–1916, vol. II
Hewitt, Rev. Canon George Henry Gordon, 1912–1998, vol. X
Hewitt, Harold, 1908–1994, vol. IX
Hewitt, Adm. Henry Kent, 1887–1972, vol. VII
Hewitt, Sir John Francis, 1910–1979, vol. VII
Hewitt, Captain John Graham, 1902–1991, vol. IX
Hewitt, John Theodore, *died* 1954, vol. V
Hewitt, Lt-Col Sir Joseph, 1st Bt, 1865–1923, vol. II
Hewitt, Sir Joseph, 2nd Bt, 1907–1973, vol. VII
Hewitt, Air Vice-Marshal Joseph Eric, 1901–1985, vol. VIII
Hewitt, Margaret, 1928–1991, vol. IX
Hewitt, Richard Thornton, 1917–1994, vol. IX
Hewitt, Sir Thomas, *died* 1923, vol. II
Hewitt, William Graily, 1864–1952, vol. V
Hewlett, Baron (Life Peer); Thomas Clyde Hewlett, 1923–1979, vol. VII
Hewlett, Brig.-Gen. Ernest, 1879–1965, vol. VI
Hewlett, Paymaster Captain Graham, 1864–1937, vol. III
Hewlett, Maurice Henry, 1861–1923, vol. II
Hewlett, Sir Meyrick; *see* Hewlett, Sir W. M.
Hewlett, Richard Tanner, 1865–1940, vol. III
Hewlett, Thomas Henry, 1882–1956, vol. V
Hewlett, Sir (William) Meyrick, *died* 1944, vol. IV
Hewlett, William Oxenham, 1845–1912, vol. I
Hews, (Gordon) Rodney (Donald), 1917–1988, vol. VIII
Hews, Rodney; *see* Hews, G. R. D.
Hewson, Hon. Mrs Anne Elizabeth Mary Llywelyn, 1902–1963, vol. VI
Hewson, Sir Bushby; *see* Hewson, Sir J. B.
Hewson, George Henry Phillips, 1881–1972, vol. VII
Hewson, Sir (Joseph) Bushby, 1902–1976, vol. VII
Hext, Maj.-Gen. Frederick Maurice, 1901–1987, vol. VIII
Hext, Rear-Adm. Sir John, 1842–1924, vol. II
Hext, Brig.-Gen. Lyonel John, 1871–1934, vol. III
Hey, Donald Holroyde, 1904–1987, vol. VIII
Hey, James Stanley, 1909–2000, vol. X
Heycock, Baron (Life Peer); Llewelyn Heycock, 1905–1990, vol. VIII
Heycock, Charles Thomas, 1858–1931, vol. III
Heycock, Air Cdre George Francis Wheaton, 1909–1983, vol. VIII
Heydeman, Maj.-Gen. C. A., 1889–1967, vol. VI
Heydon, Charles Gilbert, 1845–1932, vol. III
Heydon, Hon. Louis Francis, 1848–1918, vol. II
Heydon, Sir Peter Richard, 1913–1971, vol. VII
Heyer, Georgette, 1902–1974, vol. VII
Heyes, Morris, *died* 1940, vol. III
Heyes, Sir Tasman Hudson Eastwood, 1896–1980, vol. VII (AII)
Heygate, Rev. Ambrose, 1852–1941, vol. IV
Heygate, Arthur Conolly Gage, 1862–1935, vol. III

Heygate, Sir Frederick Gage, 3rd Bt, 1854–1940, vol. III
Heygate, Sir George Lloyd, 5th Bt, 1936–1991, vol. IX
Heygate, Sir John Edward Nourse, 4th Bt, 1903–1976, vol. VII
Heygate, Captain Richard Lionel, 1859–1926, vol. II
Heygate, Col Robert Henry Gage, 1859–1923, vol. II
Heygate, Rev. William Augustine, 1847–1941, vol. IV
Heygate, William Unwin, 1825–1902, vol. I
Heyman, Allan, 1921–1998, vol. X
Heyman, Lt-Col Arthur Augustus Inglis, 1864–1931, vol. III
Heyman, Maj.-Gen. George Douglas Gordon Dufferin, 1905–1965, vol. VI
Heyman, Lt-Col Sir (Herman) Melville, 1859–1938, vol. III
Heyman, Sir Horace William, 1912–1998, vol. X
Heyman, Lt-Col Sir Melville; see Heyman, Lt-Col Sir H. M.
Heymanson, Sir Randal; see Heymanson, Sir S. H. R.
Heymanson, Sir (Sydney Henry) Randal, 1903–1984, vol. VIII
Heyner, Herbert, 1881–1954, vol. V
Heyrovský, Jaroslav, 1890–1967, vol. VI
Heys, Derek Isaac, 1911–1984, vol. VIII
Heys, John, 1899–1963, vol. VI
Heyse, Paul Johann Ludwig, 1830–1914, vol. I
Heysen, Sir Hans, 1877–1968, vol. VI
Heytesbury, 3rd Baron, 1862–1903, vol. I
Heytesbury, 4th Baron, 1863–1949, vol. IV
Heytesbury, 5th Baron, 1906–1971, vol. VII
Heyward, DuBose, 1885–1940, vol. III (A), vol. IV
Heywood, Sir Arthur Percival, 3rd Bt, 1849–1916, vol. II
Heywood, Rt Rev. Bernard O. F., 1871–1960, vol. V
Heywood, Bertram Charles Percival, 1864–1914, vol. II
Heywood, Maj.-Gen. Cecil Percival, 1880–1936, vol. III
Heywood, Charles Christopher, 1865–1948, vol. IV
Heywood, Francis Melville, 1908–1995, vol. IX
Heywood, Geoffrey Henry, 1903–1986, vol. VIII
Heywood, Sir (Graham) Percival, 4th Bt, 1878–1946, vol. IV
Heywood, Very Rev. Hugh Christopher Lempriere, 1896–1987, vol. VIII
Heywood, James Barnes, died 1924, vol. II
Heywood, Sir Oliver Kerr, 5th Bt, 1920–1992, vol. IX
Heywood, Sir Percival; see Heywood, Sir G. P.
Heywood, Rt Rev. Richard Stanley, 1867–1955, vol. V
Heywood, Maj.-Gen. Thomas George Gordon, 1886–1943, vol. IV
Heywood, Sir Thomas Percival, 2nd Bt, 1823–1897, vol. I
Heywood, Valentine, 1891–1963, vol. VI
Heywood, Wilfred Lanceley, 1900–1977, vol. VII
Heywood-Lonsdale, Lt-Col Arthur, 1900–1976, vol. VII

Heywood-Lonsdale, Arthur Pemberton, 1835–1897, vol. I
Heywood-Lonsdale, Lt-Col Henry Heywood, 1864–1930, vol. III
Heywood-Lonsdale, John Pemberton Heywood, 1869–1944, vol. IV
Heyworth, 1st Baron, 1894–1974, vol. VII
Heyworth, Brig.-Gen. Frederic James, 1863–1916, vol. II
Heyworth, Peter Lawrence Frederick, 1921–1991, vol. IX
Hezlet, Lt-Col Charles Owen, 1891–1965, vol. VI
Hezlet, Maj.-Gen. Robert Knox, 1879–1963, vol. VI
Hezlett, James, 1875–1963, vol. VI
Hiam, Sir Frederick, 1871–1938, vol. III
Hibbard, Howard, 1928–1984, vol. VIII
Hibben, John Grier, 1861–1933, vol. III
Hibberd, (Andrew) Stuard, 1893–1983, vol. VIII
Hibberd, Charles M.; see Maxwell-Hibberd
Hibberd, Sir Donald James, 1916–1982, vol. VIII
Hibberd, George, 1901–1989, vol. VIII
Hibberd, Stuart; see Hibberd, A. S.
Hibbert, Denys Heseltine, 1905–1977, vol. VII
Hibbert, Eleanor, 1906–1993, vol. IX
Hibbert, Rev. Preb. Francis Aidan, 1866–1933, vol. III
Hibbert, Francis Dennis, 1906–1975, vol. VII
Hibbert, Col Godfrey Leicester, 1864–1924, vol. II
Hibbert, Sir Henry Flemming, 1st Bt, 1850–1927, vol. II
Hibbert, Maj.-Gen. Hugh Brownlow, 1893–1988, vol. VIII
Hibbert, Adm. Hugh Thomas, 1863–1951, vol. V
Hibbert, John Geoffrey, 1890–1968, vol. VI
Hibbert, Rt Hon. Sir John Tomlinson, 1824–1908, vol. I
Hibbert, Brig. Oswald Yates, 1882–1966, vol. VI
Hibbert, Paul Edgar Tichborne, 1846–1929, vol. III
Hibbert, Walter, 1852–1935, vol. III
Hibbert, Hon. Wilfrid H.; see Holland-Hibbert.
Hibbert, William Nembhard, 1873–1936, vol. III
Hichens, Rev. Frederick Harrison, 1836–1921, vol. II
Hichens, John Knill Jope, 1836–1908, vol. I
Hichens, Lionel; see Hichens, W. L.
Hichens, Mrs Mary Hermione, 1894–1985, vol. VIII
Hichens, Robert Smythe, 1864–1950, vol. IV
Hichens, Rev. Thomas Sikes, died 1916, vol. II
Hichens, (William) Lionel, 1874–1940, vol. III
Hickes, Maj.-Gen. Lancelot Daryl, 1884–1965, vol. VI
Hickey, Captain Daniel, 1851–1935, vol. III
Hickey, Emily Henrietta, 1845–1924, vol. II
Hickey, Nancy Maureen, 1924–1986, vol. VIII
Hickford, Lawrence David, 1904–1978, vol. VII
Hickie, Brig.-Gen. Carlos Joseph, died 1959, vol. V
Hickie, Brig. George William Clement, 1897–1972, vol. VII
Hickie, Maj.-Gen. Sir William Bernard, 1865–1950, vol. IV
Hickin, Rev. Canon Henry Arthur, 1859–1938, vol. III
Hickin, Welton, 1876–1968, vol. VI
Hickinbotham, Rev. James Peter, 1914–1990, vol. VIII

Hickinbotham, Sir Tom, 1903–1983, vol. VIII
Hicking, Sir William Norton, 1st Bt, 1865–1947, vol. IV
Hickley, Adm. Cecil Spencer, 1865–1941, vol. IV
Hickley, Victor North, 1858–1923, vol. II
Hicklin, Denis Raymond, 1918–1998, vol. X
Hickling, Charles Frederick, 1902–1977, vol. VII
Hickling, Vice-Adm. Harold, 1892–1969, vol. VI
Hickling, Henry George Albert, 1883–1954, vol. V
Hickling, Lt-Col Horace Cyril Benjamin, 1879–1948, vol. IV
Hickman, Hon. Albert Edgar, 1875–1943, vol. IV
Hickman, Sir Alfred, 1st Bt, 1830–1910, vol. I
Hickman, Major Sir Alfred Edward, 2nd Bt, 1885–1947, vol. IV
Hickman, Sir (Alfred) Howard (Whitby), 3rd Bt, 1920–1979, vol. VII
Hickman, Captain Charlie Steward, 1868–1941, vol. IV
Hickman, Brig.-Gen. Harry Otho Devereux, 1860–1946, vol. IV
Hickman, Maj.-Gen. Henry Temple Devereux, 1888–1960, vol. V
Hickman, Sir Howard; see Hickman, Sir A. H. W.
Hickman, Maj.-Gen. Hugh Palliser, 1856–1930, vol. III
Hickman, Michael Ranulf, 1922–1999, vol. X
Hickman, Robert St John, 1867–1947, vol. IV
Hickman, Brig.-Gen. Thomas Edgecumbe, 1859–1930, vol. III
Hicks, Beatrice Janie, (Mrs Philip Hicks); see Whitby, B. J.
Hicks, Brig. Sir (Cedric) Stanton, 1892–1976, vol. VII
Hicks, David Nightingale, 1929–1998, vol. X
Hicks, Col Sir Denys Theodore, 1908–1987, vol. VIII
Hicks, Donald, 1902–1986, vol. VIII
Hicks, Rev. Canon Edward Barry, 1858–1939, vol. III
Hicks, Rt Rev. Edward Lee, 1843–1919, vol. II
Hicks, Sir (Edward) Seymour, 1871–1949, vol. IV
Hicks, Sir Edwin William, 1910–1984, vol. VIII
Hicks, (Ernest) George, 1879–1954, vol. V
Hicks, Rt Rev. (Frederick Cyril) Nugent, 1872–1942, vol. IV
Hicks, George; see Hicks, E. G.
Hicks, Rt Rev. George Bruno, 1878–1954, vol. V
Hicks, George Dawes, 1862–1941, vol. IV
Hicks, Henry, 1837–1899, vol. I
Hicks, Brig.-Gen. Henry T.; see Tempest-Hicks.
Hicks, Rev. Herbert S., died 1928, vol. II
Hicks, Howard Arthur, 1914–1989, vol. VIII
Hicks, Lt-Col James Hamilton, 1909–1985, vol. VIII
Hicks, John Donald, 1890–1972, vol. VII
Hicks, Sir John Richard, 1904–1989, vol. VIII
Hicks, Sir John Richard, 1904–1989, vol. IX (AI)
Hicks, Rt Rev. John Wale, 1840–1899, vol. I
Hicks, Lt Col Sir Maxwell, 1878–1959, vol. V
Hicks, Rt Rev. Nugent; see Hicks, Rt Rev. F. C. N.
Hicks, Brig. Philip Hugh Whitby, 1895–1967, vol. VI
Hicks, Reginald Jack, 1922–1980, vol. VII
Hicks, Robert Drew, 1850–1929, vol. III

Hicks, Sir Seymour; see Hicks, Sir E. S.
Hicks, Shadrach, died 1936, vol. III
Hicks, Brig. Sir Stanton; see Hicks, Brig. Sir C. S.
Hicks, Ursula Kathleen, (Lady Hicks), 1896–1985, vol. VIII
Hicks, Rev. Walter, 1868–1937, vol. III
Hicks, William Edward, 1852–1921, vol. II
Hicks, William Mitchinson, 1850–1934, vol. III
Hicks-Beach, Lady Victoria Alexandrina, 1879–1963, vol. VI
Hicks-Beach, William Frederick, 1841–1923, vol. II
Hicks-Beach, Major William Whitehead, 1907–1975, vol. VII
Hicks-Beach, Rt Hon. William Wither Bramston, 1826–1901, vol. I
Hickson, Geoffrey Fletcher, 1900–1978, vol. VII
Hickson, Lt-Gen. Sir Gerald Robert Stedall, 1879–1957, vol. V
Hickson, Sir Joseph, 1830–1897, vol. I
Hickson, Joseph William Andrew, died 1956, vol. V
Hickson, Mrs Murray; see Kitcat, M.
Hickson, Oswald Squire, 1877–1944, vol. IV
Hickson, Brig.-Gen. Robert Albert, 1848–1934, vol. III
Hickson, Robert Rowan Purdon, 1842–1923, vol. II
Hickson, Maj.-Gen. Sir Samuel, 1859–1928, vol. II
Hickson, Hon. Brig.-Gen. Samuel Arthur Einem, 1853–1932, vol. III
Hickson, Sydney John, 1859–1940, vol. III
Hidayat Hosain, M., 1887–1941, vol. IV
Hidayatallah, Hon. Khan Bahadur Shaikh (Sir) Ghulam Husain, died 1948, vol. IV
Hidayatullah, Mohammed, 1905–1992, vol. IX
Hide, Percy, 1874–1938, vol. III
Hieger, Izrael, 1901–1986, vol. VIII
Hiern, William Philip, 1839–1925, vol. II
Higgens, Charles, died 1920, vol. II
Higgin, Walter Wynnefield, 1889–1971, vol. VII
Higginbottom, Frederick James, 1859–1943, vol. IV
Higginbottom, S. W., died 1902, vol. I
Higgins, A., died 1903, vol. I
Higgins, Alec Wilfred, 1914–1997, vol. X
Higgins, Alexander Pearce, 1865–1935, vol. III
Higgins, Brig.-Gen. Charles Graeme, 1879–1961, vol. VI
Higgins, Sir Christopher Thomas, 1914–1998, vol. X
Higgins, Clement, 1844–1916, vol. II
Higgins, Edward John, 1864–1947, vol. IV
Higgins, Ellen C., died 1951, vol. V
Higgins, Hon. Sir Eoin; see Higgins, Hon. Sir J. P. B.
Higgins, Frank; see Higgins, W. F.
Higgins, Frederick P.; see Platt-Higgins.
Higgins, Frederick Robert, 1896–1941, vol. IV
Higgins, Sir George; see Higgins, Sir S. G.
Higgins, George Herbert, 1878–1937, vol. III
Higgins, Maj.-Gen. Harold John, 1894–1951, vol. V
Higgins, Hon. Henry Bournes, died 1929, vol. III
Higgins, Henry Vincent, 1855–1928, vol. II
Higgins, Hon. Sir John Patrick Basil, (Sir Eoin), 1927–1993, vol. IX
Higgins, John Comyn, 1882–1952, vol. V
Higgins, Rev. Canon John Denis P.; see Pearce-Higgins.

Higgins, Air Marshal Sir John Frederick Andrews, 1875–1948, vol. IV
Higgins, Sir John Michael, 1862–1937, vol. III
Higgins, Rt Rev. Joseph, 1838–1915, vol. I
Higgins, Rt Rev. Michael, 1863–1918, vol. II
Higgins, Reginald Edward, 1877–1933, vol. III
Higgins, Reynold Alleyne, 1916–1993, vol. IX
Higgins, Sir (Sydney) George, 1867–1947, vol. IV
Higgins, Air Cdre Thomas Charles Reginald, 1880–1953, vol. V
Higgins, Thomas Twistington, 1887–1966, vol. VI
Higgins, Rev. Canon Walter Norman, 1880–1957, vol. V
Higgins, (Wilfred) Frank, 1927–1993, vol. IX
Higgins Bernard, Lt-Col Francis Tyringham, died 1935, vol. III
Higginson, Captain Archibald Bertram Watson, died 1950, vol. IV
Higginson, Brig.-Gen. Cecil Pickford, 1866–1951, vol. V
Higginson, Charles James, 1871–1964, vol. VI
Higginson, Brig. Sir Frank, 1890–1958, vol. V
Higginson, Gen. Sir George Wentworth Alexander, 1826–1927, vol. II
Higginson, Maj.-Gen. Harold Whitla, 1873–1954, vol. V
Higginson, Col Theophilus, 1839–1903, vol. I
Higginson, Thomas Wentworth, 1823–1911, vol. I
Higgon, Col Laurence Hugh, 1884–1987, vol. VIII
Higgs, Col Frederick William, 1881–1924, vol. II
Higgs, Godfrey Walter, 1907–1986, vol. VIII
Higgs, Henry, 1864–1940, vol. III
Higgs, Rt Rev. Hubert Laurence, 1911–1992, vol. IX
Higgs, Sir (John) Michael (Clifford), 1912–1995, vol. IX
Higgs, Sir John Walter Yeoman, 1923–1986, vol. VIII
Higgs, Sir Michael; see Higgs, Sir J. M. C
Higgs, Captain Michael Arnold, 1927–1978, vol. VII
Higgs, Sydney Limbrey, 1892–1977, vol. VII
Higgs, Walter Frank, 1886–1961, vol. VI
Higgs, Hon. William Guy, 1862–1951, vol. V
Higgs-Walker, James Arthur, 1892–1979, vol. VII
High, Sir William, 1857–1934, vol. III
Higham, Anthony Richard Charles, 1907–1975, vol. VII
Higham, Lt-Col Bernard, 1880–1944, vol. IV
Higham, Charles Daniel, 1849–1935, vol. III
Higham, Sir Charles Frederick, 1876–1938, vol. III
Higham, John Sharp, 1857–1932, vol. III
Higham, Sir Thomas, 1847–1910, vol. I
Higham, Sir Thomas, 1866–1947, vol. IV
Higham, Thomas Farrant, 1890–1975, vol. VII
Highet, Gilbert Arthur, 1906–1978, vol. VII
Highet, Hugh Campbell, 1868–1929, vol. III
Highet, Sir Robert Swan, 1859–1934, vol. III
Highfield, John Somerville, 1871–1945, vol. IV
Highgate, Sir James Brown, 1920–1997, vol. X
Highmore, Sir Nathaniel Joseph, 1844–1924, vol. II
Highsmith, Patricia, 1921–1995, vol. IX
Hight, Sir James, 1870–1958, vol. V
Highton, Rear-Adm. Jack Kenneth, 1904–1988, vol. VIII

Highton, John Elborn, 1884–1937, vol. III
Highton, Mark Edward, 1888–1966, vol. VI
Higinbotham, Major George Mowat, 1866–1915, vol. I
Hignell, Harold, 1879–1943, vol. IV
Hignell, Sidney Robert, 1873–1939, vol. III
Hignett, Mrs Dorothy Eleanor Augusta, died 1946, vol. IV
Hilary, David Henry Jephson, 1932–1994, vol. IX
Hilbers, Ven. George Christopher, died 1918, vol. II
Hilbery, Rt Hon. Sir Malcolm, 1883–1965, vol. VI
Hilborne, Rev. Frederick Wilfred, 1901–1980, vol. VII
Hildebrand, Brig.-Gen. Arthur Blois Ross, 1870–1937, vol. III
Hildebrand, Arthur Hedding, 1843–1918, vol. II
Hilder, Lt-Col Frank, 1864–1951, vol. V
Hilder, Rev. Geoffrey Frank, 1906–1988, vol. VIII
Hilder, Rowland, 1905–1993, vol. IX
Hildesley, Alfred, 1873–1958, vol. V
Hilditch, Clarence Clifford, 1912–1974, vol. VII
Hilditch, Clifford Arthur, 1927–1991, vol. IX
Hilditch, Thomas Percy, 1886–1965, vol. VI
Hildred, Sir William Percival, 1893–1986, vol. VIII
Hildreth, Lt-Col Harold Crossley, 1876–1937, vol. III
Hildreth, Maj.-Gen. Sir (Harold) John (Crossley), 1908–1992, vol. IX
Hildreth, Maj.-Gen. Sir John; see Hildreth, Maj.-Gen. Sir H. J. C.
Hildyard, Rev. Christopher, 1901–1987, vol. VIII
Hildyard, Sir David Henry Thoroton, 1916–1997, vol. X
Hildyard, Gerard Moresby Thoroton, 1874–1956, vol. V
Hildyard, Brig.-Gen. Harold Charles Thoroton, 1872–1956, vol. V
Hildyard, Gen. Sir Henry John Thoroton, 1846–1916, vol. II
Hildyard, John Arundell, 1861–1935, vol. III
Hildyard, Gen. Sir Reginald John Thoroton, 1876–1965, vol. VI
Hiles, Sir Herbert, 1881–1968, vol. VI
Hiley, Sir (Ernest) Haviland, died 1943, vol. IV
Hiley, Sir Ernest Varvill, 1868–1949, vol. IV
Hiley, Sir Haviland; see Hiley, Sir E. H.
Hiley, Joseph, 1902–1989, vol. VIII
Hiley, Sir Thomas Alfred, 1905–1990, vol. IX (AI)
Hilgendorf, Sir Charles, 1908–1990, vol. VIII
Hilken, Captain Thomas John Norman, 1901–1969, vol. VI
Hill, 4th Viscount, 1863–1923, vol. II
Hill, 5th Viscount, 1866–1924, vol. II
Hill, 6th Viscount, 1876–1957, vol. V
Hill, 7th Viscount, 1904–1974, vol. VII
Hill of Luton, Baron (Life Peer); Charles Hill, 1904–1989, vol. VIII
Hill of Wivenhoe, Baron (Life Peer); Edward James Hill, 1899–1969, vol. VI
Hill, Adrian Keith Graham, 1895–1977, vol. VII
Hill, Sir Albert, 2nd Bt (cr 1917), 1877–1946, vol. IV
Hill, Alex, 1856–1929, vol. III
Hill, Rev. Alexander Currie, 1906–1983, vol. VIII
Hill, Sir Alexander Galloway E.; see Erskine-Hill.

Hill, Rt Hon. Alexander Staveley, 1825–1905, vol. I

Hill, Alfred, *died* 1945, vol. IV

Hill, Alfred Bostock, 1854–1932, vol. III

Hill, Alfred Francis, 1870–1960, vol. V

Hill, Alfred John, 1862–1927, vol. II

Hill, Rt Rev. Alfred Thomas, 1901–1969, vol. VI

Hill, Alan John Wills, 1912–1993, vol. IX

Hill, Annie; *see* Hill, Lady Arthur.

Hill, Rev. Canon Archdall, *died* 1936, vol. III

Hill, Archibald Vivian, 1886–1977, vol. VII

Hill, Captain Arthur, 1873–1913, vol. I

Hill, Arthur, 1854–1927, vol. II

Hill, Arthur, 1858–1927, vol. II

Hill, Lady Arthur, (Annie), *died* 1944, vol. IV

Hill, Captain Arthur Blundell George Sandys, 1837–1923, vol. II

Hill, (Arthur) Derek, 1916–2000, vol. X

Hill, Lord (Arthur) Francis (Henry), 1895–1953, vol. V

Hill, Arthur George, 1857–1923, vol. II

Hill, Lt-Col Arthur Hardie, 1887–1963, vol. VI

Hill, Sir Arthur Norman, 1st Bt (*cr* 1919), 1863–1944, vol. IV

Hill, Rt Hon. Lord Arthur William, 1846–1931, vol. III

Hill, Sir Arthur William, 1875–1941, vol. IV

Hill, Ven. Arundel Charles, 1845–1921, vol. II

Hill, Brig.-Gen. Augustus West, 1853–1922, vol. II

Hill, Sir Austin Bradford, 1897–1991, vol. IX

Hill, Maj.-Gen. Sir Basil Alexander, 1880–1960, vol. V

Hill, Brian, 1930–1995, vol. IX

Hill, Brig.-Gen. Cecil, 1861–1942, vol. IV

Hill, Charles Alexander, 1874–1948, vol. IV

Hill, Major Charles Glencairn, 1872–1915, vol. I

Hill, Charles Loraine, 1891–1976, vol. VII

Hill, Rev. Charles N.; *see* Noel-Hill.

Hill, Christopher Pascoe, 1903–1983, vol. VIII

Hill, Sir Claude Hamilton Archer, 1866–1934, vol. III

Hill, Sir Clement Lloyd, 1845–1913, vol. I

Hill, Clifford Francis, 1930–1979, vol. VII

Hill, Colin de Neufville, 1917–1989, vol. VIII

Hill, Constance, *died* 1929, vol. III

Hill, Sir Cyril Rowley; *see* Hill, Sir G. C. R.

Hill, Hon. David Jayne, 1850–1932, vol. III

Hill, Col David John Jackson, 1874–1938, vol. III

Hill, Sir Denis; *see* Hill, Sir J. D. N.

Hill, Derek; *see* Hill, A. D.

Hill, Dorothy, 1907–1997, vol. X

Hill, Rev. Canon Douglas George, 1912–1980, vol. VII

Hill, Douglas Rowland Holdsworth, 1904–1966, vol. VI

Hill, Douglas William, 1904–1985, vol. VIII

Hill, Captain Duncan C., 1900–1977, vol. VII

Hill, Edward Bernard Lewin, 1834–1915, vol. I

Hill, Rev. Edward F., 1858–1931, vol. III

Hill, Edward John, 1897–1965, vol. VI

Hill, Col (Edward) Roderick, 1904–1998, vol. X

Hill, Sir Edward Stock, 1834–1902, vol. I

Hill, Rev. Canon Edwin, 1843–1933, vol. III

Hill, Dame Elizabeth Mary, 1900–1996, vol. X

Hill, Sir Enoch, 1865–1942, vol. IV

Hill, Brig. Ernest Frederick John, 1879–1962, vol. VI

Hill, Ernest George, 1872–1917, vol. II

Hill, Ernest Saphir, 1891–1967, vol. VI

Hill, Col Eustace, 1869–1946, vol. IV

Hill, Eveline, (Mrs J. S. Hill), 1898–1973, vol. VII

Hill, Brig.-Gen. Felix Frederic, 1860–1940, vol. III

Hill, Lord Francis; *see* Hill, Lord A. F. H.

Hill, Sir Francis; *see* Hill, Sir J. W. F.

Hill, (Francis) John, 1915–1984, vol. VIII

Hill, Lt-Col Francis Robert, 1873–1956, vol. V

Hill, Major Francis Rowley, 1872–1939, vol. III

Hill, Lt-Col Frank William Rowland, 1875–1942, vol. IV

Hill, Brig.-Gen. Frederic William, 1866–1954, vol. V

Hill, Frederick George, 1865–1936, vol. III

Hill, Sir G. Rowland, 1855–1928, vol. II

Hill, Sir George Alfred Rowley, 9th Bt, 1899–1985, vol. VIII

Hill, George Birkbeck Norman, 1835–1903, vol. I

Hill, Sir (George) Cyril Rowley, 8th Bt (*cr* 1779), 1890–1980, vol. VII

Hill, Sir George Francis, 1867–1948, vol. IV

Hill, George Geoffrey David, 1911–1995, vol. IX

Hill, Sir George Rowley, 7th Bt (*cr* 1779), 1864–1954, vol. V

Hill, Col Gerald Victor Wilmot, 1887–1958, vol. V

Hill, Gerard Robert, 1872–1946, vol. IV

Hill, Gladys, 1894–1998, vol. X

Hill, Grace Livingston, (Mrs Thomas Franklin Hill), 1865–1947, vol. IV

Hill, Graham, 1929–1975, vol. VII

Hill, H. Lancelot H., 1883–1944, vol. IV

Hill, Harold G.; *see* Gardiner-Hill.

Hill, Harry, 1924–1993, vol. IX

Hill, Headon, (F. Grainger), *died* 1927, vol. II

Hill, Sir Henry Blyth, 6th Bt (*cr* 1779), 1867–1929, vol. III

Hill, Col Henry Cecil de la Montague, 1864–1931, vol. III

Hill, Rev. Henry Erskine, 1864–1939, vol. III

Hill, Henry Staveley S.; *see* Staveley-Hill.

Hill, Col Henry Warburton, 1877–1951, vol. V

Hill, Henry William, 1850–1926, vol. II

Hill, Lt-Col Hugh, 1875–1916, vol. II

Hill, Sir Ian George Wilson, 1904–1982, vol. VIII

Hill, Ivan Conrad, 1906–1998, vol. X

Hill, J. Arthur, 1872–1951, vol. V

Hill, J. Smith, 1866–1944, vol. IV

Hill, Sir James, 1st Bt (*cr* 1917), 1849–1936, vol. III

Hill, Sir James, 3rd Bt (*cr* 1917), 1905–1976, vol. VII

Hill, Sir James; *see* Hill, Sir S. J. A.

Hill, James Bastian, 1861–1927, vol. II

Hill, James J., 1838–1916, vol. II

Hill, James Meechan, 1899–1966, vol. VI

Hill, James Peter, 1873–1954, vol. V

Hill, James Stevens, 1854–1921, vol. II

Hill, Sir (James William) Francis, 1899–1980, vol. VII

Hill, John; *see* Hill, F. J.

Hill, Maj.-Gen. John, 1866–1935, vol. III

Hill, Rt Rev. John Charles, 1862–1943, vol. IV

Hill, Sir (John) Denis (Nelson), 1913–1982, vol. VIII
Hill, Sir John Edward Gray, 1839–1914, vol. I
Hill, John Frederick Rowland, 1905–1991, vol. IX
Hill, John Gibson, 1910–1975, vol. VII
Hill, Mrs John Stanley; see Hill, Eveline.
Hill, Col Joseph, 1850–1918, vol. II
Hill, Joseph, 1888–1947, vol. IV
Hill, Kenneth Robson, 1911–1973, vol. VII
Hill, Laurence Carr, 1890–1959, vol. V
Hill, Sir Leonard Erskine, 1866–1952, vol. V
Hill, Leonard R.; see Raven-Hill.
Hill, Maj.-Gen. Leslie Rowley, 1884–1975, vol. VII
Hill, Levi Clement, 1883–1961, vol. VI
Hill, Martin; see Hill, W. M.
Hill, Martin Spencer, 1893–1968, vol. VI
Hill, Matthew Davenport, 1872–1958, vol. V
Hill, Maurice; see Hill, P. M.
Hill, Sir Maurice, 1862–1934, vol. III
Hill, Maurice Neville, 1919–1966, vol. VI
Hill, Micaiah John Muller, 1856–1929, vol. III
Hill, Montague, died 1929, vol. III
Hill, Norman A.; see Ashton Hill.
Hill, Lt-Col Sir Norman Gray, 2nd Bt (cr 1919), 1894–1944, vol. IV
Hill, Norman Hammond, 1893–1984, vol. VIII
Hill, Octavia, 1838–1912, vol. I
Hill, Oliver, 1887–1968, vol. VI
Hill, Osman; see Hill, W. C. O.
Hill, Col Peter Edward, 1834–1919, vol. II
Hill, Philip Ernest, died 1944, vol. IV
Hill, (Philip) Maurice, 1892–1952, vol. V
Hill, Sir Quintin; see Hill, Sir T. St Q.
Hill, Ralph William, 1893–1966, vol. VI
Hill, Reginald Duke, 1866–1922, vol. II
Hill, Reginald Dykers Richardson, 1902–1973, vol. VII
Hill, Reginald Harrison, 1894–1976, vol. VII
Hill, Sir Reginald Herbert, 1888–1971, vol. VII
Hill, Reginald John James, 1905–1977, vol. VII
Hill, Vice-Adm. Hon. Sir Richard A. S., 1880–1954, vol. V
Hill, Sir Richard George Rowley, 10th Bt (cr 1779), 1925–1992, vol. IX
Hill, Surg. Vice-Adm. Sir Robert, 1865–1938, vol. III
Hill, Robert, 1899–1991, vol. IX
Hill, Maj.-Gen. Robert Charles C.; see Cottrell-Hill.
Hill, Sir Robert E.; see Erskine-Hill.
Hill, Robert Hughes, 1892–1963, vol. VI
Hill, Lt-Col Robert Montagu, 1872–1934, vol. III
Hill, Air Chief Marshal Sir Roderic Maxwell, 1894–1954, vol. V
Hill, Col Roderick; see Hill, Col E. R.
Hill, Rowland, 1883–1962, vol. VI
Hill, Brig. Rowland Clement Ridley, 1879–1967, vol. VI
Hill, Gen. Sir Rowley Sale S.; see Sale-Hill.
Hill, Sir Sidney Pearson, 1900–1968, vol. VI
Hill, Sir (Stanley) James (Allen), 1926–1999, vol. X
Hill, Sydney, 1902–1968, vol. VI
Hill, Thomas Arthur, 1854–1931, vol. III
Hill, Sir Thomas Eustace, died 1931, vol. III
Hill, Thomas George, 1876–1954, vol. V
Hill, Major Thomas Henry, 1844–1930, vol. III

Hill, Thomas Rowland, 1903–1967, vol. VI
Hill, Sir (Thomas St) Quintin, 1889–1963, vol. VI
Hill, Thomas William, 1866–1953, vol. V
Hill, Thomson; see Hill, W. T.
Hill, Victor Archibald Lord, 1905–1988, vol. VIII
Hill, Vincent Walker, died 1913, vol. I
Hill, Lt-Col Walter de Marchot, 1877–1927, vol. II
Hill, Maj.-Gen. Walter Pitts Hendy, 1877–1942, vol. IV
Hill, Engr Rear-Adm. Walter S.; see Scott-Hill.
Hill, Maj.-Gen. William, 1846–1903, vol. I
Hill, William, died 1928, vol. II
Hill, Col Sir William Alexander, 1846–1931, vol. III
Hill, Hon. William Caldwell, 1866–1939, vol. III
Hill, William Charles Osman, 1901–1975, vol. VII
Hill, William George John, 1876–1933, vol. III
Hill, William Henry, 1872–1957, vol. V
Hill, William Kirkpatrick, 1862–1944, vol. IV
Hill, (William) Martin, 1905–1976, vol. VII
Hill, William Sephton, 1926–1993, vol. IX
Hill, (William) Thomson, 1875–1959, vol. V
Hill, William Wills, 1881–1974, vol. VII
Hill-Trevor, Hon. George Edwyn; see Trevor.
Hill-Walker, Major Alan Richard, 1859–1944, vol. IV
Hill Watson, Hon. Lord; Laurence Hill Watson, 1895–1957, vol. V
Hill Watson, Laurence; see Hill Watson, Hon. Lord.
Hill-Wood, Captain Sir Basil Samuel Hill, 2nd Bt, 1900–1954, vol. V
Hill-Wood, Major Sir Samuel Hill, 1st Bt, 1872–1949, vol. IV
Hill-Wood, Sir Wilfred William Hill, 1901–1980, vol. VII
Hillaby, John, 1917–1996, vol. X
Hillard, Rev. Albert Ernest, 1865–1935, vol. III
Hillard, Frederick Arthur, 1868–1937, vol. III
Hillard, Richard Arthur Loraine, 1906–1996, vol. X
Hillard, Ronald Johnstone, 1903–1971, vol. VII
Hillary, Albert Ernest, 1868–1954, vol. V
Hillary, Michael, 1886–1976, vol. VII
Hiller, George François, 1916–1972, vol. VII
Hillgarth, Captain Alan Hugh, 1899–1978, vol. VII
Hillhouse, Percy Archibald, 1869–1942, vol. IV
Hillhouse, William, 1850–1910, vol. I
Hilliam, Maj.-Gen. Edward, 1863–1949, vol. IV
Hilliar, Harry William, died 1941, vol. IV
Hilliard, Christopher Richard, 1930–1985, vol. VIII
Hilliard, Edward, 1867–1940, vol. III
Hilliard, Harvey, died 1956, vol. V
Hilliard, Captain Maurice Alfred, 1863–1907, vol. I
Hilliard, Rt Rev. William George, died 1960, vol. V
Hillier, Alfred Peter, 1858–1911, vol. I
Hillier, Arthur, 1895–1986, vol. VIII
Hillier, Edward Guy, 1857–1924, vol. II
Hillier, Frank Norton, 1894–1959, vol. V
Hillier, Frederick James, 1869–1920, vol. II
Hillier, George Lacy, 1856–1941, vol. IV
Hillier, Sir Harold George, 1905–1985, vol. VIII
Hillier, Jack Ronald, 1912–1995, vol. IX
Hillier, Joseph Hillier, vol. II
Hillier, Tristram Paul, 1905–1983, vol. VIII
Hillier, Sir Walter Caine, 1849–1927, vol. II
Hillingdon, 1st Baron, 1830–1989, vol. I

Hillingdon, 2nd Baron, 1855–1919, vol. II
Hillingdon, 3rd Baron, 1891–1952, vol. V
Hillingdon, 4th Baron, 1922–1978, vol. VII
Hillingdon, 5th Baron, 1906–1982, vol. VIII
Hillis, Arthur Henry Macnamara, 1905–1997, vol. X
Hillis, Rev. Newell Dwight, 1858–1929, vol. III
Hillman, Ellis Simon, 1928–1996, vol. X
Hillman, G. B., 1867–1932, vol. III
Hills, Adam, 1880–1941, vol. IV
Hills, Sir Andrew Ashton Waller, 1st Bt, 1933–1955, vol. V
Hills, Col Edmond Herbert G.; see Grove-Hills.
Hills, Edwin Sherbon, 1906–1986, vol. VIII
Hills, Eustace Gilbert, died 1934, vol. III
Hills, Maj.-Gen. Sir John, 1834–1902, vol. I
Hills, Lt-Col John David, 1895–1975, vol. VII
Hills, Rt Hon. John Waller, 1867–1938, vol. III
Hills, Lawrence Donegan, 1911–1990, vol. VIII
Hills, Sir Reginald Playfair, 1877–1967, vol. VI
Hills-Johnes, Lt-Gen. Sir James, 1833–1919, vol. II
Hillyard, Comdr George Whiteside, 1864–1943, vol. IV
Hillyard, Patrick Cyril Henry, 1900–1991, vol. IX
Hilston, Sir Duncan, 1837–1913, vol. I
Hilton of Upton, Baron (Life Peer); Albert Victor Hilton, 1908–1977, vol. VII
Hilton, Cecil, 1884–1931, vol. III
Hilton, Conrad Nicholson, 1887–1979, vol. VII
Hilton, Sir Derek Percy, 1908–1986, vol. VIII
Hilton, Gwen, 1898–1971, vol. VII
Hilton, Harold Horsfall, 1869–1942, vol. IV
Hilton, James, 1900–1954, vol. V
Hilton, John, 1880–1943, vol. IV
Hilton, John Robert, 1908–1994, vol. IX
Hilton, Col Sir Peter, 1919–1995, vol. IX
Hilton, Reginald, 1895–1969, vol. VI
Hilton, Maj.-Gen. Richard, 1894–1978, vol. VII
Hilton, Sir Robert Stuart, 1870–1943, vol. IV
Hilton, Roger, 1911–1975, vol. VII
Hilton, William Samuel, 1926–1999, vol. X
Hilton-Sergeant, Maj.-Gen. Frederick Cavendish, 1898–1978, vol. VII
Hilton-Simpson, Melville William, 1881–1938, vol. III
Him, George, 1900–1982, vol. VIII
Himbury, Sir William Henry, died 1955, vol. V
Hime, Lt-Col Rt Hon. Sir Albert Henry, 1842–1919, vol. II
Hime, Maj.-Gen. Henry Charles Rupert, 1877–1945, vol. IV
Hime, Lt-Col Henry William Lovett, 1840–1929, vol. III
Himmelweit, Hildegard Therese, (Hilde), 1918–1989, vol. VIII
Himsworth, Eric, 1905–1991, vol. IX
Himsworth, Sir Harold Percival, 1905–1993, vol. IX
Hinchcliff, William Fryer, died 1931, vol. III
Hinchcliffe, Hon. Albert, 1860–1935, vol. III
Hinchcliffe, Sir (George) Raymond, 1900–1973, vol. VII
Hinchcliffe, Brig. John William, 1893–1975, vol. VII
Hinchcliffe, Sir Raymond; see Hinchcliffe, Sir G. R.
Hinchcliffe, Richard George, died 1942, vol. IV
Hinchey, Herbert John, 1908–1988, vol. VIII

Hinchley, John William, 1871–1931, vol. III
Hinchliff, Rev. Peter Bingham, 1929–1995, vol. IX
Hinchliffe, Sir (Albert) Henry (Stanley), 1893–1980, vol. VII
Hinchliffe, (Frank) Philip (Rideal), 1923–1976, vol. VII
Hinchliffe, Sir Henry; see Hinchliffe, Sir A. H. S.
Hinchliffe, Sir James Peace, 1861–1933, vol. III
Hinchliffe, Philip; see Hinchliffe, F. P. R.
Hinchliffe, William Algernon S.; see Simpson-Hinchliffe.
Hincks, Hon. Sir Cecil Stephen, 1894–1963, vol. VI
Hincks, Rev. Thomas, 1818–1899, vol. I
Hind, Arthur Mayger, 1880–1957, vol. V
Hind, C. Lewis, 1862–1927, vol. II
Hind, Sir Jesse William, 1866–1946, vol. IV
Hind, Rt Rev. John, 1879–1958, vol. V
Hind, Kenneth, 1920–1993, vol. IX
Hind, Maj.-Gen. Neville Godfray, 1892–1973, vol. VII
Hind, Richard Dacre A.; see Archer-Hind.
Hinde, Brig.-Gen. Alan, 1876–1950, vol. IV
Hinde, George Jennings, died 1918, vol. II
Hinde, George Langford, 1832–1910, vol. I
Hinde, Brig. Harold Montague, 1895–1965, vol. VI
Hinde, Rev. Herbert William, 1877–1955, vol. V
Hinde, Col John Henry Edward, 1847–1931, vol. III
Hinde, Lt-Col Reginald Graham, 1887–1971, vol. VII
Hinde, Maj.-Gen. Sir Robert; see Hinde, Maj.-Gen. Sir W. R. N.
Hinde, Sidney Langford, 1863–1930, vol. III
Hindemith, Maj.-Gen. (Hon.) Sir (William) Robert (Norris), 1900–1981, vol. VIII
Hindemith, Paul, 1895–1963, vol. VI
Hindenburg, Frau Herbert von; see Hay, Marie.
Hindenburg, Field-Marshal Paul von Beneckendorff und von, 1847–1934, vol. III
Hinderks, Hermann Ernst, born 1907, vol. VIII
Hindle, Edward, 1886–1973, vol. VII
Hindle, Sir Frederick, 1877–1953, vol. V
Hindle, Frederick George, 1848–1925, vol. II
Hindle, Wilfrid Hope, 1903–1967, vol. VI
Hindley, Sir Clement D. M., 1874–1944, vol. IV
Hindley, Brig. Geoffrey Bernard Sylvester, 1902–1980, vol. VII
Hindley, Henry Oliver Rait, 1906–1988, vol. VIII
Hindley, Ven. William George, died 1936, vol. III
Hindley-Smith, James Dury, 1894–1974, vol. VII
Hindlip, 2nd Baron, 1842–1897, vol. I
Hindlip, 3rd Baron, 1877–1931, vol. III
Hindlip, 4th Baron, 1906–1966, vol. VI
Hindlip, 5th Baron, 1912–1993, vol. IX
Hindmarsh, W(illiam) Russell, 1929–1973, vol. VII
Hinds, Benjamin, 1882–1952, vol. V
Hinds, John, 1862–1928, vol. II
Hindus, Maurice Gerschon, 1891–1969, vol. VI
Hine, George T., 1841–1916, vol. II
Hine, Harry, 1845–1941, vol. IV
Hine, Rt Rev. John Edward, 1857–1934, vol. III
Hine, Montague Leonard, 1883–1967, vol. IV
Hine, Reginald Leslie, 1883–1949, vol. IV
Hine-Haycock, Rev. Trevitt Reginald, 1861–1953, vol. V

Hine-Haycock, Col Vaughan Randolph, 1871–1937, vol. III
Hines, Sir Colin Joseph, 1919–1992, vol. X (AI)
Hines, Gerald; see Hines, V. G.
Hines, Robert Henry, 1931–1982, vol. VIII
Hines, (Vivian) Gerald, 1912–1987, vol. VIII
Hinge, Maj.-Gen. Harry Alexander, 1868–1948, vol. IV
Hingeston-Randolph, Rev. Francis Charles, 1833–1910, vol. I
Hingley, Anthony Capper Moore, 1908–1983, vol. VIII
Hingley, Sir Benjamin, 1st Bt, 1830–1905, vol. I
Hingley, Sir George Benjamin, 2nd Bt, 1850–1918, vol. II
Hingston, Lt-Col Clayton Alexander Francis, 1877–1969, vol. VI
Hingston, George, died 1925, vol. II
Hingston, Major Richard William George, 1887–1966, vol. VI
Hingston, Lt-Col Walter George, 1905–1992, vol. IX
Hingston, Hon. Sir William Hales, 1829–1907, vol. I
Hingston, Surg. Captain William Percival, 1879–1950, vol. IV
Hinks, Arthur Robert, 1873–1945, vol. IV
Hinkson, Henry Albert, 1865–1919, vol. II
Hinkson, Mrs Katharine Tynan; see Tynan, Katharine.
Hinkson, Pamela, died 1982, vol. VIII
Hinshelwood, Sir Cyril Norman, 1897–1967, vol. VI
Hinsley, His Eminence Cardinal Arthur, 1865–1943, vol. IV
Hinsley, Sir (Francis) Harry, 1918–1998, vol. X
Hinsley, Frederick Baden, 1900–1988, vol. VIII
Hinsley, Sir Harry; see Hinsley, Sir F. H.
Hinton of Bankside, Baron (Life Peer); Christopher Hinton, 1901–1983, vol. VIII
Hinton, A. Horsley, 1863–1908, vol. I
Hinton, Arthur, 1869–1941, vol. IV
Hinton, Mrs Arthur; see Goodson, K.
Hinton, Captain Eric Perceval, 1902–1970, vol. VI
Hinton, Geoffrey Thomas Searle, 1918–1980, vol. VII
Hinton, Lt-Col Godfrey Bingham, 1871–1918, vol. II
Hinton, Howard Everest, 1912–1977, vol. VII
Hinton, Martin Alister Campbell, 1883–1961, vol. VI
Hinton, Nicholas John, 1942–1997, vol. X
Hinton, Wilfred John, 1887–1949, vol. IV
Hinton-Cooper, Harold, 1891–1980, vol. VII
Hintz, Orton Sutherland, 1907–1985, vol. VIII
Hinwood, George Yorke, 1894–1960, vol. V
Hinxman, Lionel Wordsworth, 1855–1936, vol. III
Hiorns, Frederick Robert, 1876–1961, vol. VI
Hipkins, Alfred James, 1826–1903, vol. I
Hippisley, John, died 1898, vol. I
Hippisley, Richard John Bayntun, died 1956, vol. V
Hippisley, Col Richard Lionel, 1853–1936, vol. III
Hipwell, Col Alfred George, 1853–1939, vol. III
Hipwell, Hermine Hallam; see Vivenot, Baroness de.
Hipwell, Ven. Richard Senior, 1881–1962, vol. VI

Hipwood, Sir Charles, 1869–1946, vol. IV
Hirachand, Walchand, 1882–1953, vol. V
Hird, Rev. Arthur, 1883–1932, vol. III
Hird, Norman Leslie, 1886–1946, vol. IV
Hirohito, Emperor of Japan, (Emperor Showa), 1901–1989, vol. VIII
Hirsch, Maj.-Gen. Charles Ernest Rickards, 1903–1975, vol. VII
Hirsch, Emil G., 1851–1923, vol. II
Hirsch, Kurt August, 1906–1986, vol. VIII
Hirsch, Lt-Col Leonard, 1879–1942, vol. IV
Hirsch, Paul Adolf, 1881–1951, vol. V
Hirshfield, Baron (Life Peer); Desmond Barel Hirshfield, 1913–1993, vol. IX
Hirst, 1st Baron, 1863–1943, vol. IV
Hirst, Sir Amos Brook, 1878–1955, vol. V
Hirst, Sir Edmund Langley, 1898–1975, vol. VII
Hirst, Col Edward Audus, 1872–1937, vol. III
Hirst, Francis W., 1873–1953, vol. V
Hirst, Sir (Frank) Wyndham, died 1972, vol. VII
Hirst, Geoffrey Audus Nicholson, 1904–1984, vol. VIII
Hirst, George Henry, 1869–1933, vol. III
Hirst, George S. S., 1871–1912, vol. I
Hirst, John Malcolm, 1921–1997, vol. X
Hirst, Reginald John, 1880–1959, vol. V
Hirst, Rodney Julian, 1920–1999, vol. X
Hirst, William, 1873–1946, vol. IV
Hirst, William Alfred, 1870–1948, vol. IV
Hirst, Sir Wyndham; see Hirst, Sir F. W.
Hirtzel, Sir Arthur, 1870–1937, vol. III
Hiscock, Alfred James, died 1930, vol. III
Hiscocks, (Charles) Richard, 1907–1998, vol. X
Hiscocks, Edward Stanley, 1903–1973, vol. VII
Hiscocks, Richard; see Hiscocks, C. R.
Hiscox, Ralph, 1907–1970, vol. VI
Hislop, James, 1870–1932, vol. III
Hislop, Joseph, died 1977, vol. VII
Hislop, Margaret Ross, 1894–1972, vol. VII
Hislop, Thomas Charles Atkinson, 1888–1965, vol. VI
Hislop, Hon. Thomas William, 1850–1925, vol. II
Hiss, Alger, 1904–1996, vol. X
Hissey, James John, died 1921, vol. II
Hitch, Frederick Brook, 1877–1957, vol. V
Hitchcock, Sir Alfred Joseph, 1899–1980, vol. VII
Hitchcock, Lt-Gen. Sir Basil Ferguson Burnett-, 1877–1938, vol. III
Hitchcock, Edward Robert, 1929–1993, vol. IX
Hitchcock, Sir Eldred Frederick, 1887–1959, vol. V
Hitchcock, Ethan Allen, 1835–1909, vol. I
Hitchcock, Rev. Francis Ryan Montgomery, 1867–1951, vol. V
Hitchcock, Geoffrey Lionel Henry, 1915–1987, vol. VIII
Hitchcock, Rev. George Edward, 1862–1939, vol. III
Hitchcock, Henry-Russell, 1903–1987, vol. VIII
Hitchcock, Howard, 1866–1932, vol. III
Hitchcock, Rev. William Maunder, 1835–1921, vol. II
Hitchen, Rt Rev. Anthony, 1930–1988, vol. VIII
Hitchens, Harry Butler, 1910–1963, vol. VI
Hitchens, Ivon; see Hitchens, S. I.
Hitchens, (Sydney) Ivon, 1893–1979, vol. VII

Hitchin, Aylwin Drakeford, 1907–1996, vol. X
Hitching, Sir Thomas Henry B.; see Brooke-Hitching.
Hitching, Gp Captain John Phelp, 1899–1979, vol. VII
Hitchings, George Herbert, 1905–1998, vol. X
Hitchins, Col Charles Faunce, died 1959, vol. V
Hitchins, Col Charles Henry Macintire, 1860–1931, vol. III
Hitchins, Brig. Edward Norman Fortescue, 1884–1959, vol. V
Hitchins, Francis Eric, 1891–1983, vol. VIII
Hitchins, Captain Henry Luxmoore, 1885–1961, vol. VI
Hitchman, Sir Alan; see Hitchman, Sir E. A.
Hitchman, Sir (Edwin) Alan, 1903–1980, vol. VII
Hitler, Adolph, 1889–1945, vol. IV
Hives, 1st Baron, 1886–1965, vol. VI
Hives, 2nd Baron, 1913–1997, vol. X
Hives, Rt Rev. Harry Ernest, 1901–1974, vol. VII
Hjelt, Edvard Immanuel, 1855–1921, vol. II
Hjort, Johan, 1869–1948, vol. IV
Ho Tung, Sir Robert, 1862–1956, vol. V
Hoad, Maj.-Gen. Sir John Charles, 1856–1911, vol. I
Hoadley, Charles Archibald, 1887–1947, vol. IV
Hoadley, Jane, died 1946, vol. IV
Hoar, Arthur Stanley George, 1903–1972, vol. VII
Hoar, Hon. Ernest Knight, 1898–1979, vol. VII
Hoar, George F., 1826–1904, vol. I
Hoare, Alfred, 1850–1938, vol. III
Hoare, Sir Archer, 1876–1973, vol. VII
Hoare, Lt-Col Arthur Fanshawe, 1854–1925, vol. II
Hoare, Arthur Hervey, 1877–1953, vol. V
Hoare, Cecil Arthur, 1892–1984, vol. VIII
Hoare, Charles Richard, 1868–1933, vol. III
Hoare, Christopher Gurney, 1882–1973, vol. VII
Hoare, Brig.-Gen. Cuthbert Gurney, 1883–1969, vol. VI
Hoare, Rear-Adm. Dennis John, 1891–1979, vol. VII
Hoare, Rear-Adm. Desmond John, 1910–1988, vol. VIII
Hoare, Douglas, 1875–1947, vol. IV
Hoare, Edward Brodie, 1841–1911, vol. I
Hoare, Sir Edward O'Bryen, 7th Bt (cr 1784), 1898–1969, vol. VI
Hoare, Edward Ralphe Douro, 1894–1936, vol. III
Hoare, Edward Wallis, 1863–1920, vol. II, vol. III
Hoare, Maj.-Gen. Francis Richard Gurney, 1879–1959, vol. V
Hoare, Sir Frederick Alfred, 1st Bt, 1913–1986, vol. VIII
Hoare, Lt-Col Geoffrey Lennard, 1879–1960, vol. V
Hoare, Henry, 1866–1956, vol. V
Hoare, Sir Henry Hugh Arthur, 6th Bt (cr 1786), 1865–1947, vol. IV
Hoare, Henry Noel, 1877–1962, vol. VI
Hoare, Henry William H.; see Hamilton-Hoare.
Hoare, Hugh Edward, 1854–1929, vol. III
Hoare, Rev. John Gurney, 1847–1923, vol. II
Hoare, Rt Rev. Joseph, 1842–1927, vol. II
Hoare, Rt Rev. Joseph Charles, 1851–1906, vol. I
Hoare, Sir Joseph Wallis O'Bryen, 5th Bt (cr 1784), 1828–1904, vol. I

Hoare, Maj.-Gen. Lionel Lennard, 1881–1975, vol. VII
Hoare, Michael Richard, 1903–1970, vol. VI
Hoare, Oliver Vaughan Gurney, 1882–1957, vol. V
Hoare, Peter Arthur Marsham, 1869–1939, vol. III
Hoare, Sir Peter William, 7th Bt (cr 1786), 1898–1973, vol. VII
Hoare, Brig.-Gen. Reginald, 1865–1947, vol. IV
Hoare, Sir Reginald Hervey, died 1954, vol. V
Hoare, Rev. Richard Whitehead, 1840–1924, vol. II
Hoare, Major Robert Basil, 1870–1931, vol. III
Hoare, Col Robert Rawdon, 1897–1977, vol. VII
Hoare, Sir Samuel, 1st Bt (cr 1899), 1841–1915, vol. I
Hoare, Sir Samuel, 1896–1976, vol. VII
Hoare, Sir Sydney James O'Bryen, 6th Bt (cr 1784), 1860–1933, vol. III
Hoare, William Douro, 1862–1928, vol. II
Hobart, Lt-Col Sir (Claud) Vere Cavendish, 2nd Bt, 1870–1949, vol. IV
Hobart, Henry Metcalf, 1868–1946, vol. IV
Hobart, Brig. James Wilfred Lang Stanley, 1890–1970, vol. VI
Hobart, Maj.-Gen. Patrick Robert Chamier, 1917–1986, vol. VIII
Hobart, Maj.-Gen. Sir Percy Cleghorn Stanley, 1885–1957, vol. V
Hobart, Robert Charles Arthur Stanley, 1881–1955, vol. V
Hobart, Lt-Cmdr Sir Robert Hampden, 3rd Bt, 1915–1988, vol. VIII
Hobart, Sir Robert Henry, 1st Bt, 1836–1928, vol. II
Hobart, Lt-Col Sir Vere; see Hobart, Sir C. V. C.
Hobart-Hampden, Hon. Charles Edward, 1825–1913, vol. I
Hobart-Hampden, Ernest Miles, 1864–1949, vol. IV
Hobbes, John Oliver, 1867–1906, vol. I
Hobbins, Robert, died 1922, vol. II
Hobbins, Thomas Phillips, 1877–1959, vol. V
Hobbs, Lt-Col George Radley, 1853–1907, vol. I
Hobbs, Harold William, 1903–1976, vol. VII
Hobbs, Captain Horace Edwin, 1896–1935, vol. III
Hobbs, Jack; see Hobbs, Sir John B.
Hobbs, Sir John (Berry), (Jack), 1882–1963, vol. VI
Hobbs, Lt-Gen. Sir (Joseph John) Talbot, 1864–1938, vol. III
Hobbs, Maj.-Gen. Percy Eyre Francis, 1865–1939, vol. III
Hobbs, Brig.-Gen. Reginald Francis Arthur, 1878–1953, vol. V
Hobbs, Maj.-Gen. Reginald Geoffrey Stirling, 1908–1977, vol. VII
Hobbs, Lt-Gen. Sir Talbot; see Hobbs, Lt-Gen. Sir J. J. T.
Hobbs, William Alfred, 1912–1984, vol. VIII
Hobday, Alfred, 1870–1942, vol. IV
Hobday, Col Edmund Arthur Ponsonby, 1859–1931, vol. III
Hobday, Sir Frederick T. G., died 1939, vol. III
Hobday, Maj.-Gen. Thomas Francis, 1847–1938, vol. III
Hobden, Dennis Harry, 1920–1995, vol. IX
Hobhouse, 1st Baron, 1819–1904, vol. I
Hobhouse, Sir Arthur Lawrence, 1886–1965, vol. VI

Hobhouse, Sir Charles Chisholm, 6th Bt, 1906–1991, vol. IX
Hobhouse, Rt Hon. Sir Charles Edward Henry, 4th Bt, 1862–1941, vol. IV
Hobhouse, Sir Charles Parry, 3rd Bt, 1825–1916, vol. II
Hobhouse, Rt Rev. Edmund, 1817–1904, vol. I
Hobhouse, Edmund, 1860–1933, vol. III
Hobhouse, Edmund W. Neill, 1888–1973, vol. VII
Hobhouse, Rt Hon. Henry, 1854–1937, vol. III
Hobhouse, Sir John Richard, 1893–1961, vol. VI
Hobhouse, Leonard Trelawney, 1864–1929, vol. III
Hobhouse, Sir Reginald Arthur, 5th Bt, 1878–1947, vol. IV
Hobhouse, Rev. Walter, 1862–1928, vol. II
Hobkirk, Brig.-Gen. Clarence John, 1869–1949, vol. IV
Hobkirk, Col Elspeth Isabel Weatherley, 1903–1990, vol. VIII
Hobler, Air Vice-Marshal John Forde, 1907–1996, vol. X
Hobley, Charles William, 1867–1947, vol. IV
Hobley, John William Dixon, 1929–1994, vol. IX
Hobman, Joseph Burton, 1872–1953, vol. V
Hobson, Baron (Life Peer); Charles Rider Hobson, 1904–1966, vol. VI
Hobson, Sir Albert John, died 1923, vol. II
Hobson, Alec, 1899–1986, vol. VIII
Hobson, Alfred Dennis, 1901–1974, vol. VII
Hobson, Alice Mary, 1860–1954, vol. V
Hobson, Clement, 1877–1952, vol. V
Hobson, Ven. Edward Waller, 1851–1924, vol. II
Hobson, Rev. Edwin, 1847–1936, vol. III
Hobson, Ernest William, 1856–1933, vol. III
Hobson, Maj.-Gen. Frederic Taylor, 1840–1909, vol. I
Hobson, Frederick Greig, died 1961, vol. VI
Hobson, Geoffrey Dudley, 1882–1949, vol. IV
Hobson, Lt-Col Gerald Walton, 1873–1962, vol. VI
Hobson, Harold, 1891–1973, vol. VII
Hobson, Sir Harold, 1904–1992, vol. IX
Hobson, Harry Roy, died 1965, vol. VI
Hobson, Sir Henry Arthur, 1893–1968, vol. VI
Hobson, John Atkinson, 1858–1940, vol. III
Hobson, (John) Basil, 1905–1985, vol. VIII
Hobson, Rt Hon. Sir John Gardiner Sumner, 1912–1967, vol. VI
Hobson, John Lombard, died 1932, vol. III
Hobson, Lawrence John, 1921–1993, vol. IX
Hobson, Neville, 1886–1975, vol. VII
Hobson, Sir Oscar Rudolf, 1886–1961, vol. VI
Hobson, Sir Patrick, 1909–1970, vol. VI
Hobson, Rev. R., died 1914, vol. I
Hobson, Robert Lockhart, 1872–1941, vol. IV
Hobson, Sidney, 1887–1970, vol. VI
Hobson, Valerie Babette Louise, (Mrs J. Profumo), 1917–1998, vol. X
Hobson, William, 1911–1982, vol. VIII
Hoby, Major John Charles James, died 1938, vol. III
Hochoy, Sir Solomon, 1905–1983, vol. VIII
Hockaday, William Thomas, 1858–1933, vol. III
Hocken, Col Charles Augustus Frederick, 1870–1958, vol. V
Hocken, Hon. Horatio Clarence, 1857–1937, vol. III
Hocker, Alexander, died 1996, vol. X

Hocking, Frederick Denison Maurice, 1899–1996, vol. X
Hocking, Sir Henry Hicks, 1842–1907, vol. I
Hocking, Joseph, died 1937, vol. III
Hocking, Silas Kitto, 1850–1935, vol. III
Hocking, William John, 1864–1953, vol. V
Hockley, Ven. Guy Wittenoom, 1869–1946, vol. IV
Hockliffe, Ernest, 1863–1944, vol. IV
Hodd, Ven. Henry Norman, 1905–1973, vol. VII
Hodder, Lt-Col Andrew Edward, died 1938, vol. III
Hodder, Edwin, 1837–1904, vol. I
Hodder-Williams, Sir Ernest; see Hodder-Williams, Sir J. E.
Hodder-Williams, Sir (John) Ernest, 1876–1927, vol. II
Hodder-Williams, Ralph Wilfred, 1890–1961, vol. VI
Hodder-Williams, Robert Percy, 1880–1958, vol. V
Hodding, Col John, 1854–1919, vol. II
Hodgart, Matthew John Caldwell, 1916–1996, vol. X
Hodge, Alan, 1915–1979, vol. VII
Hodge, Albert H., 1875–1918, vol. II
Hodge, Alexander Mitchell, 1916–1997, vol. X
Hodge, Rear-Adm. Hon. Claude Preston H.; see Herman-Hodge.
Hodge, David, 1909–1991, vol. IX
Hodge, Rev. Canon Edward Grose, died 1928, vol. II
Hodge, Lt-Col Edward Humfrey Vere, 1883–1968, vol. VI
Hodge, Francis Edwin, 1883–1949, vol. IV
Hodge, Frederick Webb, 1864–1956, vol. V
Hodge, Harold, 1862–1937, vol. III
Hodge, Harry, 1872–1947, vol. IV
Hodge, Horace Emerton, 1940–1958, vol. V
Hodge, Humfrey G.; see Grose-Hodge.
Hodge, Lt-Col James Philip, 1879–1946, vol. IV
Hodge, Rt Hon. John, 1855–1937, vol. III
Hodge, John Douglass Vere, 1887–1973, vol. VII
Hodge, John Ernest, 1911–1989, vol. VIII
Hodge, Sir John Rowland, 2nd Bt, 1913–1995, vol. IX
Hodge, Merton; see Hodge, H. E.
Hodge, Major Hon. Robert Edward Udny H.; see Hermon-Hodge.
Hodge, Sir Rowland Frederic William, 1st Bt, 1859–1950, vol. IV
Hodge, Stephen Oswald Vere, 1891–1979, vol. VII
Hodge, Sir William Vallance Douglas, 1903–1975, vol. VII
Hodgen, Maj.-Gen. Gordon West, 1894–1968, vol. VI
Hodges, Rev. Alfred, 1853–1909, vol. I
Hodges, Arthur Harris, 1884–1941, vol. IV
Hodges, Lt-Col Aubrey Dallas Percival, 1861–1946, vol. IV
Hodges, Barbara K., 1893–1949, vol. IV
Hodges, Rt Rev. Edward Noel, 1849–1928, vol. II
Hodges, Rt Rev. Evelyn Charles, 1887–1980, vol. VII
Hodges, Frank, 1887–1947, vol. IV
Hodges, Ven. George, 1851–1922, vol. II
Hodges, Hon. Sir Henry Edward Agincourt, 1844–1919, vol. II

Hodges, Herbert Arthur, 1905–1976, vol. VII
Hodges, Kenneth Henry, 1915–1961, vol. VI
Hodges, Captain Michael, 1904–1977, vol. VII
Hodges, Adm. Sir Michael Henry, 1874–1951, vol. V
Hodges, Sir Reginald John, 1889–1973, vol. VII
Hodges, Rev. William Herbert, 1873–1948, vol. IV
Hodgett, Rev. Richard, 1884–1927, vol. II
Hodgetts, Charles Alfred, 1859–1952, vol. V
Hodgetts, Edward Arthur Brayley, 1859–1932, vol. III
Hodgins, Frank Egerton, died 1932, vol. III
Hodgins, Lt-Col Frederick Owen, 1887–1924, vol. II
Hodgins, Rev. Joseph Rogerson Edmond Cotter, died 1919, vol. II
Hodgins, Ven. Michael Minden, 1912–1998, vol. X
Hodgins, Thomas, 1828–1910, vol. I
Hodgins, Maj.-Gen. William Egerton, 1850–1930, vol. III
Hodgkin, Sir Alan Lloyd, 1914–1998, vol. X
Hodgkin, (Curwen) Eliot, 1905–1987, vol. VIII
Hodgkin, Dorothy Mary Crowfoot, 1910–1994, vol. IX
Hodgkin, Eliot; see Hodgkin, C. E.
Hodgkin, Lt-Col Harry Sidney, 1879–1943, vol. IV
Hodgkin, Henry Theodore, 1877–1933, vol. III
Hodgkin, Jonathan Edward, 1875–1953, vol. V
Hodgkin, Lucy Violet (Mrs John Holdsworth), 1869–1954, vol. V
Hodgkin, Robert Howard, 1877–1951, vol. V
Hodgkin, Thomas, 1831–1913, vol. I
Hodgkin, Thomas Lionel, 1910–1982, vol. VIII
Hodgkins, T., died 1909, vol. I
Hodgkinson, Rev. Canon Arthur Edward, 1913–1995, vol. IX (AII)
Hodgkinson, Col Charles, 1870–1939, vol. III
Hodgkinson, Rev. George Langton, 1837–1915, vol. I
Hodgkinson, Comdr Guy Beauchamp, 1903–1981, vol. VIII
Hodgkinson, Jonathan, 1886–1940, vol. III
Hodgkinson, Terence William Ivan, 1913–1999, vol. X
Hodgkinson, William Richard, 1851–1935, vol. III
Hodgson, Alfreda Rose, (Mrs Paul Blissett), 1940–1992, vol. IX
Hodgson, Sir Arthur, 1818–1902, vol. I
Hodgson, Arthur Brian, 1916–1999, vol. X
Hodgson, Arthur John, 1887–1971, vol. VII
Hodgson, Lt-Col Barnard Thornton, 1863–1939, vol. III
Hodgson, Sir Edward Highton, 1880–1955, vol. V
Hodgson, Sir Edward Matthew, 1820–1904, vol. I
Hodgson, Ernest Atkinson, 1886–1975, vol. VII
Hodgson, Rev. Francis Greaves, 1840–1920, vol. II
Hodgson, Rev. Francis Henry, 1848–1930, vol. III
Hodgson, Francis Henry Birkett, 1879–1935, vol. III
Hodgson, Rev. Francis Roger, died 1920, vol. II
Hodgson, Sir Frederic Mitchell, 1851–1925, vol. II
Hodgson, George Bryan, 1863–1926, vol. II
Hodgson, Sir Gerald Hassall, 1891–1971, vol. VII
Hodgson, Geraldine E., 1865–1937, vol. III
Hodgson, Lt-Col Greenwood, 1875–1950, vol. IV
Hodgson, Sir Harold (Kingston) Graham-, died 1960, vol. V

Hodgson, Rt Rev. Henry Bernard, 1856–1921, vol. II
Hodgson, Maj.-Gen. Sir Henry West, 1868–1930, vol. III
Hodgson, Herbert Henry, 1883–1967, vol. VI
Hodgson, James, 1925–1999, vol. X
Hodgson, Rev. James Muscutt, died 1923, vol. II
Hodgson, John Bury, 1912–2000, vol. X
Hodgson, Rear-Adm. John Coombe, 1881–1936, vol. III
Hodgson, (John) Stuart, 1877–1950, vol. IV
Hodgson, Rev. Leonard, 1889–1969, vol. VI
Hodgson, Sir Mark, 1880–1967, vol. VI
Hodgson, Norman, 1891–1963, vol. VI
Hodgson, Patrick Kirkman, 1884–1963, vol. VI
Hodgson, Phyllis, 1909–2000, vol. X
Hodgson, Ralph, 1871–1962, vol. VI
Hodgson, Ven. Robert, 1844–1917, vol. II
Hodgson, Robert Kirkman, 1850–1924, vol. II
Hodgson, Sir Robert MacLeod, 1874–1956, vol. V
Hodgson, Shadworth Hollway, 1832–1912, vol. I
Hodgson, Stuart; see Hodgson, J. S.
Hodgson, Ven. Thomas, died 1921, vol. II
Hodgson, Thomas Charles Birkett, 1907–1986, vol. VIII
Hodgson, Thomas Edward Highton, 1907–1985, vol. VIII
Hodgson, Brig. Walter Thornton, 1880–1957, vol. V
Hodgson, Rev. William, died 1919, vol. II
Hodgson, Sir William, 1854–1940, vol. III
Hodgson, Sir William, died 1945, vol. IV
Hodgson, William Archer, 1887–1965, vol. VI
Hodgson, William Earl, died 1910, vol. I
Hodgson, William Hope, 1877–1918, vol. II
Hodgson, Lt-Col William Roy, 1892–1958, vol. V
Hodgson, Mrs Willoughby, died 1949, vol. IV
Hodin, Josef Paul, 1905–1995, vol. IX
Hodkin, Rev. Canon Hedley, 1902–1995, vol. IX
Hodkinson, William, 1909–1991, vol. IX
Hodsdon, Sir James William Beeman, 1858–1928, vol. II
Hodsoll, Wing Comdr Sir (Eric) John, 1894–1971, vol. VII
Hodsoll, Wing Comdr Sir John; see Hodsoll, Wing Comdr Sir E. J.
Hodson, Baron (Life Peer); Francis Lord Charlton Hodson, 1895–1984, vol. VIII
Hodson, Sir Arnold Wienholt, 1881–1944, vol. IV
Hodson, Rt Rev. Augustine John, 1879–1961, vol. VI
Hodson, Cecil John, 1915–1985, vol. VIII
Hodson, Charles William, died 1910, vol. I
Hodson, Donald Manly, 1913–1988, vol. VIII
Hodson, Major Sir Edmond Adair, 5th Bt, 1893–1972, vol. VII
Hodson, Col Frederic Arthur, 1866–1925, vol. II
Hodson, Col George Benjamin, 1863–1916, vol. II
Hodson, Air Vice-Marshal George Stacey, 1899–1976, vol. VII
Hodson, Henry Vincent, 1906–1999, vol. X
Hodson, James Lansdale, 1891–1956, vol. V
Hodson, Joseph John, 1912–1983, vol. VIII
Hodson, Leslie Manfred Noel, 1902–1985, vol. VIII
Hodson, Rt Rev. Mark Allin, 1907–1985, vol. VIII

Hodson, Sir Robert Adair, 4th Bt, 1853–1921, vol. II
Hodson, Rt Rev. Robert Leighton, 1885–1960, vol. V
Hodson, Samuel John, *died* 1908, vol. I
Hodson, Thomas Callan, *died* 1953, vol. V
Hoehne, Most Rev. John, 1910–1978, vol. VII
Hoenig, Rose, *died* 1966, vol. VI
Hoerne, Augustus Frederic Rudolf, 1841–1918, vol. II
Hoernlé, R. F. Alfred, *died* 1943, vol. IV
Hoesch, Leopold Gustav Alexander von, 1881–1936, vol. III
Hoey, Frances Sarah, (Mrs Cashel Hoey), 1830–1908, vol. I
Hoey, Robert Alexander, 1883–1965, vol. VI
Hoey, William, 1849–1919, vol. II
Hoffding, Harold, 1843–1931, vol. III
Hoffe, Monckton, 1881–1951, vol. V
Hoffert, Hermann H., *born* 1860, vol. II
Hoffman, Anna Rosenberg, 1902–1983, vol. VIII
Hoffman, Michael Richard, 1939–1998, vol. X
Hoffman, Paul Gray, 1891–1974, vol. VII
Hoffman, Philip Christopher, 1878–1959, vol. V
Hoffman, Prof.; *see* Lewis, Angelo.
Hoffmeister, Maj.-Gen. Bertram Meryl, 1907–1999, vol. X
Hoffmeister, William, 1843–1910, vol. I
Hoffnung, Gerard, 1925–1959, vol. V
Hofmann, Josef, 1876–1957, vol. V
Hofmeyr, George Morgan, 1867–1928, vol. II, vol. III
Hofmeyr, Hon. Gysbert Reitz, 1871–1942, vol. IV
Hofmeyr, Hon. Jan Hendrik, 1845–1909, vol. I
Hofmeyr, Rt Hon. Jan Hendrik, 1894–1948, vol. IV
Hofstadter, Richard, 1916–1970, vol. VI
Hofstadter, Robert, 1915–1990, vol. VIII
Hog, Major Roger Thomas Alexander, 1893–1979, vol. VII
Hog, Steuart Bayley, 1864–1944, vol. IV
Hogan, Hon. Edmond John, 1884–1964, vol. VI
Hogan, Lt-Col Edward Vincent, 1874–1933, vol. III
Hogan, Air Vice-Marshal Henry Algernon Vickers, 1909–1993, vol. IX
Hogan, Henry Charles, 1860–1924, vol. II
Hogan, James Francis, 1855–1924, vol. II
Hogan, James H., 1883–1948, vol. IV
Hogan, Rt Rev. Mgr John F., 1858–1918, vol. II
Hogan, Hon. Sir Michael Joseph Patrick, 1908–1986, vol. VIII
Hogan, Patrick, 1891–1936, vol. III
Hogarth, Alfred Moore, 1876–1947, vol. IV
Hogarth, David George, 1862–1927, vol. II
Hogarth, Maj.-Gen. Donald Macdonald, 1879–1950, vol. IV (A), vol. V
Hogarth, Margaret Cameron, 1885–1980, vol. VII
Hogarth, Mary H. U., *died* 1935, vol. III
Hogarth, Robert George, 1868–1953, vol. V
Hogarth, William David, 1901–1965, vol. VI
Hogben, George, 1853–1920, vol. II
Hogben, Herbert Edward, 1905–1984, vol. VIII
Hogben, Lancelot, 1895–1975, vol. VII
Hogbin, Ven. George Henry, 1869–1937, vol. III
Hogbin, Henry Cairn, 1880–1966, vol. VI

Hogg, Lt-Gen. Sir Adam George Forbes, 1836–1908, vol. I
Hogg, Adam Spencer, 1870–1937, vol. III
Hogg, Hon. Alan, *died* 1934, vol. III
Hogg, Alexander Hubert Arthur, 1908–1989, vol. VIII
Hogg, Rev. Andrew Albert Victor, 1867–1927, vol. II
Hogg, Sir Anthony Henry L.; *see* Lindsay-Hogg.
Hogg, Sir Arthur Ramsay, 7th Bt, 1896–1995, vol. IX
Hogg, Sir Cecil; *see* Hogg, Sir J. C.
Hogg, Col Conrad Charles Henry, 1875–1950, vol. IV
Hogg, Cuthbert Stuart, 1911–1973, vol. VII
Hogg, David C., 1840–1914, vol. I
Hogg, Maj.-Gen. Douglas MacArthur, 1888–1965, vol. VI
Hogg, Edward Gascoigne, 1882–1971, vol. VII
Hogg, Sir Edward William L.; *see* Lindsay-Hogg.
Hogg, Sir Frederick Russell, 1836–1923, vol. II
Hogg, Maj.-Gen. George Crawford, 1842–1921, vol. II
Hogg, George Robert Disraeli, 1894–1977, vol. VII
Hogg, Sir Gilbert Pitcairn, 1884–1950, vol. IV
Hogg, Guy Weir, 1861–1943, vol. IV
Hogg, Wing Comdr Henry Robert William, 1886–1942, vol. IV
Hogg, Hope W., 1863–1912, vol. I
Hogg, Lt-Col Ian Graham, 1875–1914, vol. I
Hogg, Jabez, 1817–1899, vol. I
Hogg, Sir (James) Cecil, 1900–1973, vol. VII
Hogg, John Drummond, 1886–1937, vol. III
Hogg, Sir John Nicholson, 1912–1999, vol. X
Hogg, Rt Hon. Jonathan, 1847–1930, vol. III
Hogg, Sir Kenneth Weir, 6th Bt, 1894–1985, vol. VIII
Hogg, Sir Lindsay L.; *see* Lindsay-Hogg.
Hogg, Sir Malcolm Nicholson, 1883–1948, vol. IV
Hogg, Margaret, 1877–1975, vol. VII
Hogg, Norman, 1907–1975, vol. VII
Hogg, Brig. Oliver Frederick Gillilan, 1887–1979, vol. VII
Hogg, Percy Herbertson, 1898–1978, vol. VII
Hogg, Quintin, 1845–1903, vol. I
Hogg, Robert Henry, *died* 1949, vol. IV
Hogg, Brig.-Gen. Rudolph Edward Trower, 1877–1955, vol. V
Hogg, Sir Stuart Saunders, 1833–1921, vol. II
Hogg, William Edward, 1880–1968, vol. VI
Hogg, Sir William Lindsay L.; *see* Lindsay-Hogg.
Hogg, Lt-Col Willoughby Lugard, 1881–1969, vol. II
Hoggan, Maj.-Gen. John William, 1833–1900, vol. I
Hoggarth, Arthur Henry Graham, 1882–1964, vol. VI
Hoggatt, William, 1880–1961, vol. VI
Hogge, Col Charles, 1851–1911, vol. I
Hogge, James Myles, 1873–1928, vol. III
Hogge, Col John William, 1852–1910, vol. I
Hogger, Rear-Adm. Henry Charles, 1907–1982, vol. VIII
Hogshaw, Brig. John Harold, 1896–1968, vol. VI
Hogue, Hon. James Alexander, 1846–1920, vol. II
Hogue, Oliver Alfred John, 1910–1987, vol. VIII

Hohenlohe-Langenburg, Prince of; Ernest William Frederic Charles Maximilian, *died* 1913, vol. I
Hohler, Sir Gerald Fitzroy, 1862–1934, vol. III
Hohler, Henry Booth, 1835–1916, vol. II
Hohler, Sir Thomas Beaumont, 1871–1946, vol. IV
Hohler, Thomas Sidney A.; *see* Astell Hohler.
Holbech, Rev. Charles William, 1816–1901, vol. I
Holbech, Lt-Col Laurence, 1888–1963, vol. VI
Holbech, Ronald Herbert Acland, 1887–1956, vol. V
Holbech, Rt Rev. William Arthur, 1850–1930, vol. III
Holbech, Brian Harry, 1920–1982, vol. VIII
Holbein, Arthur Montague, 1897–1970, vol. VI
Holberton, Sir Edgar Joseph, 1874–1949, vol. IV
Holborow, Col William Hillier, 1841–1917, vol. II, vol. III
Holbrook, Col Sir Arthur Richard, 1850–1946, vol. IV
Holbrook, Col Sir Claude Vivian, 1886–1979, vol. VII
Holbrook, Rear-Adm. Leonard Stanley, 1882–1974, vol. VII
Holbrook, Comdr Norman Douglas, 1888–1976, vol. VII
Holbrooke, Josef, 1878–1958, vol. V
Holbrooke, Maj.-Gen. Philip Lancelot, 1872–1958, vol. V
Holburn, James, 1900–1988, vol. VIII
Holburn, John Goundry, 1843–1899, vol. I
Holcroft, Sir Charles, 1st Bt (*cr* 1905), 1831–1917, vol. II
Holcroft, Sir George Harry, 1st Bt (*cr* 1921), 1856–1951, vol. V
Holcroft, Sir Reginald Culcheth, 2nd Bt (*cr* 1921), 1899–1978, vol. VII
Holden, 1st Baron, 1833–1912, vol. I
Holden, 2nd Baron, 1867–1937, vol. III
Holden, 3rd Baron, 1898–1951, vol. V
Holden, Rev. Albert Thomas, 1866–1935, vol. III
Holden, Arthur, 1881–1964, vol. VI
Holden, Basil Munroe, 1913–1998, vol. X
Holden, Brig.-Gen. Sir Capel Lofft; *see* Holden, Brig.-Gen. Sir H. C. L.
Holden, Charles, 1875–1960, vol. V
Holden, Col Charles Walter, *died* 1939, vol. III
Holden, Sir David Charles Beresford, 1915–1998, vol. X
Holden, Captain Edward Charles Shuttleworth, 1865–1916, vol. II
Holden, Sir Edward Hopkinson, 1st Bt (*cr* 1909), 1848–1919, vol. II
Holden, Sir Edward Thomas, 1831–1926, vol. II
Holden, Hon. Sir Edward Wheewall, 1885–1947, vol. IV
Holden, Sir George, 2nd Bt (*cr* 1919), 1890–1937, vol. III
Holden, Sir George, 3rd Bt (*cr* 1919), 1914–1976, vol. VII
Holden, Harold Henry, 1885–1977, vol. VII
Holden, Sir Harry Cassie, 2nd Bt (*cr* 1909), 1877–1965, vol. VI
Holden, Rev. Henry, 1814–1909, vol. I
Holden, Brig.-Gen. Sir (Henry) Capel Lofft, 1856–1937, vol. III
Holden, Henry Smith, 1887–1963, vol. VI

Holden, Sir Isaac, 1st Bt (*cr* 1893), 1807–1897, vol. I
Holden, Sir Isaac Holden, 5th Bt (*cr* 1893), 1867–1962, vol. VI
Holden, Sir James Robert, 1903–1977, vol. VII
Holden, Rt Rev. John, 1882–1949, vol. IV
Holden, Sir John Henry, 1st Bt (*cr* 1919), 1862–1926, vol. II
Holden, Maj.-Gen. John Reid, 1913–1995, vol. IX
Holden, Rev. John Stuart, *died* 1934, vol. III
Holden, Kenneth Graham, 1910–1990, vol. VIII
Holden, Luther, 1815–1905, vol. I
Holden, Sir Michael Herbert Frank, 1913–1982, vol. VIII
Holden, Norman Edward, 1879–1946, vol. IV
Holden, Philip Edward, 1905–1987, vol. VIII
Holden, Rev. Robert, 1853–1926, vol. II
Holden, Maj.-Gen. William Corson, 1893–1955, vol. V
Holder, Douglas William, 1923–1977, vol. VII
Holder, Sir Frank Wilfred, 1897–1967, vol. VI
Holder, Hon. Sir Frederick William, 1850–1909, vol. I
Holder, Sir Henry Charles, 2nd Bt, 1874–1945, vol. IV
Holder, Rear-Adm. Henry Lowe, 1832–1924, vol. II
Holder, Sir John Charles, 1st Bt, 1838–1923, vol. II
Holder, Sir Eric Duncan, 3rd Bt, 1899–1986, vol. VIII
Holder, Rt Rev. Mgr Joseph, 1845–1917, vol. II
Holderness, Sir Ernest William Elsmie, 2nd Bt, 1890–1968, vol. VI
Holderness, Rt Rev. George Edward, 1913–1987, vol. VIII
Holderness, Sir Richard William, 3rd Bt, 1927–1998, vol. X
Holderness, Sir Thomas William, 1st Bt, 1849–1924, vol. II
Holdgate, Rev. William Wyatt, 1872–1949, vol. IV
Holdich, Gen. Sir Edward Alan, 1822–1909, vol. I
Holdich, Lt-Col Godfrey William Vanrennen, 1882–1921, vol. II
Holdich, Brig.-Gen. Harold Adrian, 1874–1964, vol. VI
Holdich, Col Sir Thomas Hungerford, 1843–1929, vol. III
Holding, Edgar Thomas, 1870–1952, vol. V
Holdsworth, Hon. Col Albert Amrytage, *died* 1932, vol. III
Holdsworth, Albert Edward, 1909–1993, vol. IX
Holdsworth, Lt Comdr (Arthur) John (Arundell), 1915–1999, vol. X
Holdsworth, Benjamin George, 1892–1943, vol. IV
Holdsworth, Sir Charles, 1863–1935, vol. III
Holdsworth, David, 1918–1978, vol. VII
Holdsworth, Sir Frank Wild, 1904–1969, vol. VI
Holdsworth, Brig.-Gen. George Lewis, 1862–1942, vol. IV
Holdsworth, Sir Herbert, 1890–1949, vol. IV
Holdsworth, Lt-Comdr John; *see* Holdsworth, Lt-Comdr A. J. A.
Holdsworth, Lt-Col John Joseph, 1844–1920, vol. II
Holdsworth, Lucy Violet; *see* Hodgkin, L. V.
Holdsworth, Mary, 1908–1978, vol. VII
Holdsworth, Max Ernest, 1895–1982, vol. VIII

Holdsworth, Sir William Searle, 1871–1944, vol. IV
Hole, Edwyn Cecil, *died* 1976, vol. VII
Hole, Francis George, 1904–1973, vol. VII
Hole, George Vincer, 1910–1988, vol. VIII
Hole, Lt-Col Hugh Marshall, 1865–1941, vol. IV
Hole, Robert Selby, 1875–1938, vol. III
Hole, S. Hugh F., 1862–1948, vol. IV
Hole, Very Rev. Samuel Reynolds, 1819–1904, vol. I
Hole, Tahu Ronald Charles Pearce, 1908–1985, vol. VIII
Hole, William, 1846–1917, vol. II
Holford, Baron (Life Peer); William Graham Holford, 1907–1975, vol. VII
Holford, Lt-Col Cecil Francis Lovell, 1900–1963, vol. VI
Holford, Rear-Adm. Frank Douglas, 1916–1991, vol. IX
Holford, Lt-Col Sir George Lindsay, 1860–1926, vol. II
Holford, Mrs Gwynne, (Mary Eleanor), *died* 1947, vol. IV
Holford, Lt-Col James Henry Edward, 1873–1936, vol. III
Holford, James Price William Gwynne, 1833–1916, vol. II
Holford, Surg. Rear-Adm. John Morley, 1909–1997, vol. X
Holford, Mary Eleanor; *see* Holford, Mrs Gwynne.
Holgate, Surg. Rear-Adm. (D) William, 1906–1993, vol. IX
Holgate, Hon. Harold Norman, 1933–1997, vol. X
Holiday, Sir Frederick Charles, 1843–1930, vol. III
Holiday, Henry, 1839–1927, vol. II
Hollamby, Edward Ernest, 1921–1999, vol. X
Hollams, Frederick William, 1848–1941, vol. IV
Hollams, Sir John, 1820–1910, vol. I
Holland, Alfred, 1900–1936, vol. III
Holland, Sir Alfred Herbert, 1878–1968, vol. VI
Holland, Sir Arthur, 1842–1928, vol. II
Holland, Lt-Gen. Sir Arthur Edward Aveling, 1862–1927, vol. II
Holland, Bernard Henry, 1856–1926, vol. II
Holland, Brian Arthur, 1935–1999, vol. X
Holland, Vice-Adm. Cedric Swinton, 1889–1950, vol. IV
Holland, Charles Thurstan, *died* 1941, vol. IV
Holland, Clive, (Charles James Hankinson), 1866–1959, vol. V
Holland, David George, 1925–1996, vol. X
Holland, Sir Eardley Lancelot, 1879–1967, vol. VI
Holland, Edgar William, 1899–1973, vol. VII
Holland, Sir Edward John, 1865–1939, vol. III
Holland, Sir (Edward) Milner, 1902–1969, vol. VI
Holland, Sir Erskine; *see* Holland, Sir T. E.
Holland, Fanny, (Mrs William Arthur Law), 1847–1931, vol. III
Holland, Rev. Francis James, 1828–1907, vol. I
Holland, Frank, 1899–1972, vol. VII
Holland, Frank William C.; *see* Crossley-Holland.
Holland, Sir George William Frederick, 1897–1962, vol. VI
Holland, Comdr Gerald Edward, 1860–1917, vol. II
Holland, Sir Guy Hope, 3rd Bt, 1918–1997, vol. X
Holland, Lt-Col Guy Lushington, *born* 1861, vol. II

Holland, Henry, 1859–1944, vol. IV
Holland, Henry Edmund, 1868–1933, vol. III
Holland, Rev. Henry Scott, 1847–1918, vol. II
Holland, Sir Henry Tristram, 1875–1965, vol. VI
Holland, Maj.-Gen. Henry William, 1825–1920, vol. II
Holland, Captain Herbert Christian, 1858–1916, vol. II
Holland, Rt Rev. Herbert St Barbe, 1882–1966, vol. VI
Holland, Hetty L.; *see* Lee-Holland.
Holland, Instr Captain Horace Herbert, *died* 1952, vol. V
Holland, Rear-Adm. Hubert Henry, 1873–1957, vol. V
Holland, Major Hugh, 1884–1922, vol. II
Holland, Sir Jim Sothern, 2nd Bt, 1911–1981, vol. VIII
Holland, Maj.-Gen. John Charles Francis, 1897–1956, vol. V
Holland, Rt Rev. John Tristram, 1912–1990, vol. VIII
Holland, Major John Vincent, 1889–1975, vol. VII
Holland, Col Lancelot, 1876–1943, vol. IV
Holland, Vice-Adm. Lancelot Ernest, 1887–1941, vol. IV
Holland, Leonard Duncan, 1874–1964, vol. VI
Holland, Hon. Lionel Raleigh, 1865–1936, vol. III
Holland, Sir Milner; *see* Holland, Sir E. M.
Holland, Sir (Reginald) Sothern, 1st Bt, 1876–1948, vol. IV
Holland, Richard, *died* 1942, vol. IV
Holland, Sir Robert Erskine, 1873–1965, vol. VI
Holland, Robert Henry Code, 1904–1974, vol. VII
Holland, Robert Wolstenholme, 1880–1962, vol. VI
Holland, Rt Hon. Sir Sidney George, 1893–1961, vol. VI
Holland, Sir Sothern; *see* Holland, Sir R. S.
Holland, Adm. Swinton Colthurst, 1844–1922, vol. II
Holland, Theodore, 1878–1947, vol. IV
Holland, Rt Rev. Thomas, 1908–1999, vol. X
Holland, Sir (Thomas) Erskine, 1835–1926, vol. II
Holland, Sir Thomas Henry, 1868–1947, vol. IV
Holland, Col Trevenen James, 1836–1910, vol. I
Holland, Vyvyan Beresford, 1886–1967, vol. VI
Holland, Rev. Preb. William Edward Sladen, 1873–1951, vol. V
Holland, William Jacob, 1848–1932, vol. III
Holland, Rev. William Lyall, 1846–1934, vol. III
Holland-Hibbert, Hon. Wilfrid, 1893–1961, vol. VI
Holland-Martin, Christopher John, 1910–1960, vol. V
Holland-Martin, Adm. Sir Deric Douglas Eric, 1906–1977, vol. VII
Holland-Martin, Edward, 1900–1981, vol. VIII
Holland-Pryor, Maj.-Gen. Sir Pomeroy; *see* Pryor.
Hollander, Bernard, 1864–1934, vol. III
Hollely, Sir Arthur Newton, *died* 1961, vol. VI
Hollenden, 1st Baron, 1845–1929, vol. III
Hollenden, 2nd Baron, 1885–1977, vol. VII
Hollenden, 3rd Baron, 1914–1999, vol. X
Holley, Maj.-Gen. Edmund Hunt, 1842–1919, vol. II
Holley, Robert William, 1922–1993, vol. IX
Holliday, Clifford, 1897–1960, vol. V

Holliday, Gilbert Leonard Gibson, 1910–1980, vol. VII
Holliday, Major Lionel Brook, 1880–1965, vol. VI
Holliman, John William, 1861–1937, vol. III
Hollingdrake, Sir Henry, 1872–1923, vol. II
Hollinghurst, Air Chief Marshal Sir Leslie Norman, 1895–1971, vol. VII
Hollings, Herbert John Butler, 1855–1922, vol. II
Hollings, Rev. Michael Richard, 1921–1997, vol. X
Hollingshead, John, 1827–1904, vol. I
Hollingsworth, Dorothy Frances, 1916–1994, vol. IX
Hollingsworth, Howard, 1871–1938, vol. III
Hollingsworth, John Ernest, 1916–1963, vol. VI
Hollington, Alfred Jordan, 1845–1926, vol. II
Hollingworth, Rev. Henry, 1841–1930, vol. III
Hollingworth, John, 1885–1976, vol. VII
Hollingworth, Sydney Ewart, 1899–1966, vol. VI
Hollins, Alfred, 1865–1942, vol. IV
Hollins, Arthur, 1876–1962, vol. VI
Hollins, Sir (Arthur) Meyrick, 2nd Bt, 1876–1938, vol. III
Hollins, Lt-Col Charles Ernest, 1875–1939, vol. III
Hollins, Sir Frank, 1st Bt, 1843–1924, vol. II
Hollins, Frank, 1907–1967, vol. VI
Hollins, Sir Frank Hubert, 3rd Bt, 1877–1963, vol. VI
Hollins, James Henry, died 1954, vol. V
Hollins, Sir Meyrick; see Hollins, Sir A. M.
Hollins, Samuel Thomas, 1881–1965, vol. VI
Hollinshead-Blundell, Henry B.; see Blundell-Hollinshead-Blundell.
Hollinshead-Blundell, Maj.-Gen. Richard B.; see Blundell-Hollinshead-Blundell.
Hollis, Sir (Alfred) Claud, 1874–1961, vol. VI
Hollis, Rt Rev. (Arthur) Michael, 1899–1986, vol. VIII
Hollis, Christopher; see Hollis, M. C.
Hollis, Sir Claud; see Hollis, Sir A. C.
Hollis, Rt Rev. Francis Septimus, 1884–1955, vol. V
Hollis, Rt Rev. George Arthur, 1868–1944, vol. IV
Hollis, Henry Park, 1858–1939, vol. III
Hollis, Hugh, 1910–1986, vol. VIII
Hollis, (James) Martin, 1938–1998, vol. X
Hollis, Sir Leslie Chasemore, 1897–1963, vol. VI
Hollis, Martin; see Hollis, J. M.
Hollis, (Maurice) Christopher, 1902–1977, vol. VII
Hollis, Sir Roger Henry, 1905–1973, vol. VII
Hollis, William Ainslie, 1839–1922, vol. II
Hollond, Henry Arthur, 1884–1974, vol. VII
Hollond, Maj.-Gen. Spencer Edmund, 1874–1950, vol. IV
Holloway, Baliol, 1883–1967, vol. VI
Holloway, Basil Edward, died 1947, vol. IV
Holloway, Maj.-Gen. Benjamin, 1861–1922, vol. II
Holloway, David Richard, 1924–1995, vol. IX
Holloway, Derrick Robert Le Blond, 1917–1997, vol. X
Holloway, Rt Hon. Edward James, 1880–1967, vol. VI
Holloway, Sir Ernest, 1887–1961, vol. VI
Holloway, Frederick William, 1873–1954, vol. V
Holloway, Gwendoline Elizabeth, 1893–1981, vol. VIII
Holloway, Sir Henry, 1857–1923, vol. II

Holloway, Sir Henry Thomas, 1876–1951, vol. V
Holloway, John, 1920–1999, vol. X
Holloway, Rev. John Ernest, 1881–1945, vol. IV
Holloway, Leonard Cloudesley, 1885–1966, vol. VI
Holloway, Maj.-Gen. Robin Hugh Ferguson, 1922–1998, vol. X
Holloway, Stanley, 1890–1982, vol. VIII
Hollowood, Albert Bernard, 1910–1981, vol. VIII
Holm, Alexander, 1878–1943, vol. IV
Holman, Sir Adrian, 1895–1974, vol. VII
Holman, Arthur Treve, 1893–1959, vol. V
Holman, Bernard Welpton, died 1964, vol. VI
Holman, Sir Constantine, 1829–1910, vol. I
Holman, Lt-Gen. Sir Herbert Campbell, 1869–1949, vol. IV
Holman, James Frederick, 1916–1974, vol. VII
Holman, Norman Frederick, 1914–1991, vol. IX
Holman, Percy, 1891–1978, vol. VII
Holman, Portia Grenfell, 1903–1983, vol. VIII
Holman, Col Richard Charles, 1861–1933, vol. III
Holman, Hon. William Arthur, 1871–1934, vol. III
Holman-Hunt, Hilary Lushington Holman, 1879–1949, vol. IV
Holman-Hunt, William, 1827–1910, vol. I
Holmden, Major Frank Alfred Amphlett, 1861–1935, vol. III
Holmden, Sir Osborn George, 1869–1945, vol. IV
Holme, Alan Thomas, 1872–1931, vol. III
Holme, Charles, 1848–1923, vol. II
Holme, C(harles) Geoffrey, 1887–1954, vol. V
Holme, Charles Henry, 1853–1928, vol. II
Holme, Constance, (Mrs Punchard), 1880–1955, vol. V
Holme, Ernest Rudolph, died 1952, vol. V
Holme, George A., 1848–1917, vol. II
Holme, Major Harold L., 1879–1931, vol. III
Holme, Sir Randle Fynes Wilson, 1864–1957, vol. V
Holme-Sumner, Captain Berkeley, 1872–1943, vol. IV
Holmes, Albert Edward, died 1953, vol. V
Holmes, Arthur, 1890–1965, vol. VI
Holmes, Arthur Bromley, 1849–1927, vol. II
Holmes, Sir Arthur William, 1877–1960, vol. V
Holmes, Ven. Bernard Edgar, 1860–1928, vol. II
Holmes, Brian, 1920–1993, vol. IX
Holmes, Burton, 1870–1958, vol. V
Holmes, Rev. Cecil Frederick Joy, 1877–1938, vol. III
Holmes, Sir Charles John, 1868–1936, vol. III
Holmes, Daniel Turner, 1863–1955, vol. V
Holmes, Sir (David) Ronald, 1913–1981, vol. VIII
Holmes, Doris Livesey, (Mrs Arthur Holmes; see Reynolds, D. L.
Holmes, Edmond Gore Alexander, 1850–1936, vol. III
Holmes, Edward Morell, 1843–1930, vol. III
Holmes, Eric Gordon, 1897–1972, vol. VII
Holmes, Eric Montagu Price, 1909–1983, vol. VIII
Holmes, Ven. Ernest Edward, 1854–1931, vol. III
Holmes, Ernest Hamilton, 1876–1957, vol. V
Holmes, Florence Mary, (Lady Holmes); see Rivington, Mme Hill.
Holmes, Geoffrey Shorter, 1928–1993, vol. IX
Holmes, Rt Rev. George, 1858–1912, vol. I

Holmes, George Augustus, 1861–1943, vol. IV
Holmes, Sir George Charles Vincent, 1848–1926, vol. II
Holmes, Rev. Canon George Edward Wilmot, 1869–1937, vol. III
Holmes, Ven. George Hedley, 1883–1972, vol. VII
Holmes, George John, 1874–1937, vol. III
Holmes, Comdr Gerard Robert Addison, 1881–1963, vol. VI
Holmes, Sir Gordon Morgan, *died* 1965, vol. VI
Holmes, Brig.-Gen. Hardress Gilbert, 1862–1922, vol. II
Holmes, Harold Kennard, 1875–1942, vol. IV
Holmes, Haywood Temple, 1865–1959, vol. V
Holmes, Lt-Col Henry, 1863–1933, vol. III
Holmes, Rev. Henry Comber, *died* 1920, vol. II
Holmes, Sir Henry Nicholas, 1868–1940, vol. III
Holmes, Sir Horace Edwin, 1888–1971, vol. VII
Holmes, Rt Hon. Hugh, 1840–1916, vol. II
Holmes, Sir Hugh Oliver, 1886–1955, vol. V
Holmes, James Macdonald, 1896–1966, vol. VI
Holmes, Paymaster Rear-Adm. John Dickonson, 1875–1947, vol. IV
Holmes, Rt Rev. John Garraway, *died* 1904, vol. I
Holmes, Rev. John Haynes, 1879–1964, vol. VI
Holmes, John Wentworth, 1925–1998, vol. X
Holmes, Rev. Joseph, 1820–1911, vol. I
Holmes, Hon. Julius Cecil, 1899–1968, vol. VI
Holmes, Brig. Kenneth Soar, 1912–1994, vol. IX
Holmes, Brig. Leonard Geoffrey, 1899–1985, vol. VIII
Holmes, Sir Leonard Stanistreet, 1884–1961, vol. VI
Holmes, Sir Maurice Andrew, 1911–1997, vol. X
Holmes, Sir Maurice Gerald, 1885–1964, vol. VI
Holmes, Maj.-Gen. Sir Noel Galway, 1891–1982, vol. VIII
Holmes, Hon. Oliver Wendell, 1841–1935, vol. III
Holmes, Air Vice-Marshal Peter Hamilton, 1912–1977, vol. VII
Holmes, Sir Richard Rivington, 1835–1911, vol. I
Holmes, Robert, 1861–1930, vol. III
Holmes, Col Robert Heuston, 1870–1952, vol. V
Holmes, Sir Robert William Arbuthnot, 1843–1910, vol. I
Holmes, Sir Ronald; *see* Holmes, Sir D. R.
Holmes, Sir Stanley, 1912–1987, vol. VIII
Holmes, Sir Stephen Lewis, 1896–1980, vol. VII
Holmes, Thomas, 1846–1918, vol. II
Holmes, Thomas Rice Edward, 1855–1933, vol. III
Holmes, Rev. Thomas Scott, 1852–1918, vol. II
Holmes, Sir Valentine, 1888–1956, vol. V
Holmes, Col William, 1862–1917, vol. II
Holmes, Lt-Gen. Sir William George, 1892–1969, vol. VI
Holmes, Rt Rev. William Hardy, 1873–1951, vol. V
Holmes-à-Court, Hon. Edward Alexander, 1845–1923, vol. II
Holmes à Court, Vice-Adm. Hon. Herbert Edward, 1869–1934, vol. III
Holmes à Court, (Michael) Robert (Hamilton), 1937–1990, vol. VIII
Holmes à Court, Robert; *see* Holmes à Court, M. R. H.
Holmes à Court, Col Rupert Edward, 1882–1958, vol. V

Holmes Sellors, Sir Thomas; *see* Sellors.
Holm-Patrick, 1st Baron, 1839–1898, vol. I
Holmpatrick, 2nd Baron, 1886–1942, vol. IV
HolmPatrick, 3rd Baron, 1928–1991, vol. IX
Holms, John Mitchell, 1863–1948, vol. IV
Holms, William Frederick, 1866–1950, vol. IV
Holmwood, Sir Herbert, 1856–1930, vol. III
Holmyard, Eric John, 1891–1959, vol. V
Holness, Col Harold James, 1882–1941, vol. IV
Holroyd, Sir Charles, 1861–1917, vol. II
Holroyd, Hon. Sir Edward Dundas, 1828–1916, vol. II
Holroyd, Michael, 1892–1953, vol. V
Holroyd, Sir Ronald, 1904–1973, vol. VII
Holroyd Pearce, Edward; *see* Baron Pearce.
Holroyd-Reece, John, 1897–1969, vol. VI
Holst, Axel, 1860–1931, vol. III
Holst, Gustav, 1874–1934, vol. III
Holst, Imogen Clare, 1907–1984, vol. VIII
Holt, Lt-Col Alwyn Vesey, 1887–1956, vol. V
Holt, Arthur Frederick, 1914–1995, vol. IX
Holt, Charles, 1899–1966, vol. VI
Holt, Christopher Robert Vesey, 1915–1997, vol. X
Holt, Sir Edward, 1st Bt (*cr* 1916), 1849–1928, vol. II
Holt, Sir Edward, 2nd Bt (*cr* 1916), 1883–1968, vol. VI
Holt, Very Rev. Edward John, 1867–1948, vol. IV (A), vol. V
Holt, Ernest James Henry, 1883–1972, vol. VII
Holt, Air Vice-Marshal Felton Vesey, 1886–1931, vol. III
Holt, Sir Follett, 1865–1944, vol. IV
Holt, Rt Hon. Harold Edward, 1908–1968, vol. VI
Holt, Harold Edward Sherwin, 1862–1932, vol. III
Holt, Henry, 1840–1926, vol. II
Holt, Sir Henry Gisborne, 1864–1944, vol. IV
Holt, Herbert, 1894–1978, vol. VII
Holt, Major Herbert Paton, 1890–1971, vol. VII
Holt, Sir Herbert S., 1856–1941, vol. IV
Holt, Jack; *see* Holt, John L.
Holt, James, 1899–1965, vol. VI
Holt, Sir James Arthur, 1899–1982, vol. VIII
Holt, James Maden, 1829–1911, vol. I
Holt, Sir James Richard, 1912–1990, vol. VIII
Holt, (James) Richard, 1931–1991, vol. IX
Holt, John Alphonse, 1906–1968, vol. VI
Holt, Sir John Anthony L.; *see* Langford-Holt.
Holt, Rear-Adm. John Bayley, 1912–1995, vol. IX
Holt, John Lapworth, (Jack), 1912–1995, vol. IX
Holt, L. Emmett, *died* 1924, vol. II
Holt, Lawrence During, 1882–1961, vol. VI
Holt, Martin Drummond Vesey, *died* 1956, vol. V
Holt, Maj.-Gen. Sir Maurice Percy Cue, 1862–1954, vol. V
Holt, Rev. Raymond Vincent, 1885–1957, vol. V
Holt, Vice-Adm. Reginald Vesey, 1884–1957, vol. V
Holt, Richard; *see* Holt, J. R.
Holt, Sir Richard Durning, 1st Bt (*cr* 1935), 1868–1941, vol. IV
Holt, Sir Stanley Silverwood, 1892–1973, vol. VII
Holt, Sir Vesey George Mackenzie, 1854–1923, vol. II
Holt, Victoria; *see* Hibbert, Eleanor.

Holt, Sir Vyvyan, 1896–1960, vol. V
Holt, Col William John, 1839–1913, vol. I
Holt, William R., *born* 1870, vol. II
Holt-Thomas, George, 1869–1929, vol. III
Holt-Wilson, Brig. Sir Eric Edward Boketon, 1875–1950, vol. IV
Holtby, Winifred, 1898–1935, vol. III
Holthouse, Edwin Hermus, 1855–1949, vol. IV
Holttum, Eric; *see* Holttum, R. E.
Holttum, Richard Eric, 1895–1990, vol. VIII
Holtz, Alfred Christian Carlsen, 1874–1948, vol. IV
Holtze, Maurice, 1840–1923, vol. II
Holwell, Captain Raymond Vernon Doherty-, 1882–1917, vol. II
Holyman, Sir Ivan Nello, 1896–1957, vol. V
Holyoake, George Jacob, 1817–1906, vol. I
Holyoake, Rt Hon. Sir Keith Jacka, 1904–1983, vol. VIII
Holyoake, Dame Norma Janet, 1909–1984, vol. VIII
Holzmann, Sir Maurice, 1835–1909, vol. I
Homan, Philip John Lindsay, 1916–1988, vol. VIII
Homans, George Caspar, 1910–1989, vol. IX (AI)
Hombersley, Ven. Arthur, 1855–1941, vol. IV
Homburg, Robert, 1848–1912, vol. I
Home, 12th Earl of, 1834–1918, vol. II
Home, 13th Earl of, 1873–1951, vol. V
Home, 14th Earl of; *see* Home of the Hirsel, Baron (Life Peer).
Home of the Hirsel, Baron (Life Peer); Alexander Frederick Douglas-Home, 1903–1995, vol. IX
Home, Sir Anthony Dickson, 1826–1914, vol. I
Home, Brig.-Gen. Sir Archibald Fraser, 1874–1953, vol. V
Home, Captain Archibald John Fitzwilliam M.; *see* Milne Home.
Home, Charles Cospatrick D.; *see* Douglas-Home.
Home, Sir David George, 13th Bt, 1904–1992, vol. IX
Home, David William M.; *see* Milne-Home.
Home, Ethel, *died* 1954, vol. V
Home, Col Frederick Jervis, 1839–1919, vol. II
Home, Lt-Col George, 1870–1956, vol. V
Home, Major George John Ninian L.; *see* Logan-Home.
Home, Gordon Cochrane, 1878–1969, vol. VI
Home, Sir James, 11th Bt, 1861–1931, vol. III
Home, Hon. James Archibald, 1837–1909, vol. I
Home, Col James Murray, 1866–1946, vol. IV
Home, Sir John, 12th Bt, 1872–1938, vol. III
Home, John Gavin M.; *see* Milne Holme.
Home, Sir John Hepburn Milne, 1876–1963, vol. VI
Home, Col Robert Elton, 1869–1943, vol. IV
Home, Walter, 1855–1936, vol. III
Home, Hon. William Douglas-, 1912–1992, vol. IX
Home, Maj.-Gen. Hon. William Sholto, 1842–1916, vol. II
Home Drummond, Lt-Col Henry Edward S.; *see* Stirling Home Drummond.
Homer, John Twigg, 1865–1934, vol. III
Homer, Louise, *died* 1947, vol. IV
Homer, Sidney, 1864–1953, vol. V
Homer, Winslow, 1836–1910, vol. I
Homewood, William Dennis, 1920–1989, vol. VIII
Homfray, Herbert Richards, 1864–1940, vol. III

Homfray, Captain John Glynne Richards, 1861–1934, vol. III
Homfray, Lt-Col John Robert Henry, 1868–1944, vol. IV
Homolle, Jean Théophile, 1848–1925, vol. II
Hone, Sir Brian William, 1907–1978, vol. VII
Hone, Rt Rev. Campbell Richard, 1873–1967, vol. VI
Hone, Sir Evelyn Dennison, 1911–1979, vol. VII
Hone, Elvie S., 1894–1955, vol. V
Hone, Frank Sandland, *died* 1951, vol. V
Hone, Maj.-Gen. Sir (Herbert) Ralph, 1896–1992, vol. IX
Hone, Joseph Maunsell, 1882–1959, vol. V
Hone, Nathaniel, *died* 1917, vol. II
Hone, Lt-Col Percy Frederick, 1878–1940, vol. III
Hone, Sir Ralph; *see* Hone, Sir H. R.
Honegger, Arthur, 1892–1955, vol. V
Honey, Sir de Symons Montagu George, 1872–1945, vol. IV
Honey, John William, 1862–1932, vol. III
Honey, William Bowyer, 1889–1956, vol. V
Honeyball, Mrs Olympia Lœtitia, 1876–1956, vol. V
Honeyman, Alexander Mackie, 1907–1988, vol. VIII
Honeyman, Sir George Gordon, 1898–1972, vol. VII
Honeyman, John, 1831–1914, vol. I
Honeyman, Tom John, 1891–1971, vol. VII
Honig, Frederick, 1912–2000, vol. X
Honner, Joseph, 1859–1940, vol. III
Honoré, Bertha; *see* Palmer, Mrs Poter.
Honour, Benjamin, 1888–1961, vol. VI
Honyman, Sir William Macdonald, 5th Bt, 1820–1911, vol. I
Honywood, Constance Mary, (Lady Honywood), *died* 1956, vol. V
Honywood, Sir Courtenay John, 9th Bt, 1880–1944, vol. IV
Honywood, Sir John William, 8th Bt, 1857–1907, vol. I
Honywood, Col Sir William Wynne, 10th Bt, 1891–1982, vol. VIII
Hood, 4th Viscount, 1838–1907, vol. I
Hood, 5th Viscount, 1868–1933, vol. III
Hood, 6th Viscount, 1910–1981, vol. VIII
Hood, 7th Viscount, 1914–1999, vol. X
Hood of Avalon, 1st Baron, 1824–1901, vol. I
Hood, Lt-Gen. Sir Alexander, 1888–1980, vol. VII
Hood, Sir (Alexander) Jarvie, 1860–1934, vol. III
Hood, Hon. Sir Alexander Nelson, 1854–1937, vol. III
Hood, Rev. Canon (Archibald) Frederic, 1895–1975, vol. VII
Hood, Captain Basil, 1864–1917, vol. II
Hood, Paymaster-Captain Basil Frederick, 1886–1941, vol. IV
Hood, Clifford Firoved, 1894–1978, vol. VII
Hood, David Wilson, 1874–1924, vol. II
Hood, Donald William Charles, 1847–1924, vol. II
Hood, Hon. Dorothy Violet, 1877–1965, vol. VI
Hood, Douglas; *see* Hood, J. D.
Hood, Maj.-Gen. Ernest Lionel Ouseley, 1915–1982, vol. VIII
Hood, Francis Campbell, 1895–1971, vol. VII
Hood, Rev. Canon Frederic; *see* Hood, Rev. Canon A. F.

Hood, George Percy J.; *see* Jacomb-Hood.
Hood, Rear-Adm. Hon. Horace Lambert Alexander, 1870–1916, vol. II
Hood, Sir Hugh Meggison, 1885–1952, vol. V
Hood, (James) Douglas, 1905–1981, vol. VIII
Hood, James Reaney, 1888–1968, vol. VI
Hood, Sir Jarvie; *see* Hood, Sir A. J.
Hood, Rev. John Charles Fulton, 1884–1964, vol. VI
Hood, Gen. John Cockburn, *died* 1901, vol. I
Hood, Sir Joseph, 1st Bt, 1863–1931, vol. III
Hood, Hon. Sir Joseph Henry, 1846–1922, vol. II
Hood, Hon. Maurice Henry Nelson, 1881–1915, vol. I
Hood, Lt-Col Hon. Neville Albert, 1872–1948, vol. IV
Hood, Rev. Norman Arthur, 1924–1990, vol. VIII
Hood, Sydney Walter, 1886–1960, vol. V
Hood, Col Sir Tom Fielden, 1904–1986, vol. VIII
Hood, Thomas, 1870–1949, vol. IV
Hood, Hon. Victor Albert Nelson, 1862–1929, vol. III
Hood, Sir William Acland, 8th Bt and 6th Bt, 1901–1990, vol. IX (AI)
Hood, William Francis, 1902–1980, vol. VII
Hooft, Willem Adolf V.; *see* Visser't Hooft.
Hook, Rt Rev. Cecil, 1844–1938, vol. III
Hook, Frederick Arthur, 1864–1935, vol. III
Hook, Henry, *died* 1905, vol. I
Hook, James Clarke, 1819–1907, vol. I
Hook, Very Rev. Norman, 1898–1976, vol. VII
Hook, Rt Rev. Ross Sydney, 1917–1996, vol. X
Hook, Sidney, 1902–1989, vol. VIII
Hooke, Rev. Daniel Burford, 1847–1933, vol. III
Hooke, Sir Lionel George Alfred, 1895–1974, vol. VII
Hooke, Samuel Henry, *died* 1968, vol. VI
Hooker, Sir Joseph Dalton, 1817–1911, vol. I
Hooker, Sir Leslie Joseph, 1901–1976, vol. VII
Hooker, Sir Stanley George, 1907–1984, vol. VIII
Hookey, James, 1839–1903, vol. I
Hookins, Rev. William, 1845–1917, vol. II
Hookway, Reginald John Samuel, 1920–1982, vol. VIII
Hoole, Alan Norman, 1942–2000, vol. X
Hoole, Sir Arthur Hugh, 1924–1998, vol. X
Hoole, Lt-Col James, 1850–1917, vol. II
Hooley, Maj.-Gen. St John Cutler, 1902–1985, vol. VIII
Hooley, Samuel Cutler, 1848–1929, vol. III
Hooley, Lt-Col Vernon Vavasour, 1862–1952, vol. V
Hooper, Sir Anthony Robin Maurice, 2nd Bt, 1918–1987, vol. VIII
Hooper, Arthur George, 1857–1940, vol. III
Hooper, Col Arthur Winsmore, 1869–1945, vol. IV
Hooper, Barrington, 1885–1960, vol. V
Hooper, Charles Arthur, 1889–1960, vol. V
Hooper, Ven. Charles German, 1911–1995, vol. IX
Hooper, Cyril Noel, 1884–1952, vol. V
Hooper, David, 1858–1947, vol. IV
Hooper, Edmund Huntly, 1845–1931, vol. III
Hooper, Sir Frederic Collins, 1st Bt, 1892–1963, vol. VI
Hooper, Rev. George, *born* 1866, vol. III

Hooper, Lt-Col Harry Uppington, *died* 1940, vol. III
Hooper, Howard Owen, 1911–1980, vol. VII
Hooper, Ian Mackay, 1902–1958, vol. V
Hooper, John, *died* 1907, vol. I
Hooper, John Robert Thomas, 1914–1975, vol. VII
Hooper, Sir Leonard James, 1914–1994, vol. IX
Hooper, Reginald Stewart, 1889–1945, vol. IV
Hooper, Major Richard Grenside, 1873–1940, vol. III
Hooper, Sir Robin William John, 1914–1989, vol. VIII
Hooper, Lt-Col Stuart Huntly, 1867–1915, vol. I
Hooper, Sydney Ernest, 1880–1966, vol. VI
Hooper, Rev. William, 1837–1922, vol. II
Hooper, William Henry, 1876–1946, vol. IV
Hooper, Col Sir William Roe, 1837–1921, vol. II
Hooper, Wynnard, 1853–1935, vol. III
Hoops, Albert Launcelot, 1876–1940, vol. III (A), vol. IV
Hooson, Tom Ellis, 1933–1985, vol. VIII
Hooton, Maj.-Gen. Alfred, 1870–1967, vol. VI
Hooton, John Charles, 1912–1980, vol. VII
Hoover, Calvin Bryce, 1897–1974, vol. VII
Hoover, Herbert, 1874–1964, vol. VI
Hoover, Herbert Clark, Jr, 1903–1969, vol. VI
Hoover, Herbert William, Jr, 1918–1997, vol. X
Hoover, John Edgar, 1895–1972, vol. VII
Hope, Adrian Elias, 1845–1919, vol. II
Hope, Adrian James Robert, 1874–1963, vol. VI
Hope, Maj.-Gen. Adrian Price Webley, 1911–1992, vol. IX
Hope, Col Adrian Victor Webley, 1873–1960, vol. V
Hope, Sir Alexander, 15th Bt (*cr* 1628), 1824–1918, vol. II
Hope, Anthony; *see* Hawkins, Sir A. H.
Hope, Sir Archibald Philip, 17th Bt, 1912–1987, vol. VIII
Hope, Ascott R.; *see* Moncrieff, Robert Hope.
Hope, Col Charles, 1850–1930, vol. III
Hope, Lord Charles Melbourne, 1892–1962, vol. VI
Hope, Sir (Charles) Peter, 1912–1999, vol. X
Hope, Collingwood, 1858–1949, vol. IV
Hope, Sir Edward Stanley, 1846–1921, vol. II
Hope, Edward William, 1854–1950, vol. IV
Hope, George Everard, 1886–1917, vol. II
Hope, Adm. Sir George Price Webley, 1869–1959, vol. V
Hope, Graham, *died* 1920, vol. II
Hope, Sir Harry, 1st Bt (*cr* 1932), 1865–1959, vol. V
Hope, Henry Walter, 1839–1913, vol. I
Hope, Sir Herbert James, 1851–1930, vol. III
Hope, Adm. Herbert Willes Webley, 1878–1968, vol. VI
Hope, Sir James, 2nd Bt (*cr* 1932), 1898–1979, vol. VII
Hope, James Kenneth, 1896–1983, vol. VIII
Hope, Jasper Edward, 1852–1917, vol. II
Hope, Captain John, 1843–1915, vol. I
Hope, Col John Andrew, 1890–1954, vol. V
Hope, Lt-Col Sir John Augustus, 16th Bt (*cr* 1628), 1869–1924, vol. II
Hope, John Deans, 1860–1949, vol. IV

Hope, Brig.-Gen. John Frederic Roundell, 1883–1970, vol. VI
Hope, John Owen Webley, 1875–1927, vol. II
Hope, Lt-Col John William, 1876–1942, vol. IV
Hope, John Wilson, 1856–1938, vol. III
Hope, Laura Elizabeth Rachel, *died* 1929, vol. III
Hope, Laurence Frank, 1918–1997, vol. X
Hope, Captain Laurence Nugent, 1890–1973, vol. VII
Hope, Col Lewis Anstruther, 1855–1929, vol. III
Hope, Lt-Col Sir Percy Mirehouse, 1886–1972, vol. VII
Hope, Sir Peter; *see* Hope, Sir C. P.
Hope, Hon. Richard Frederick, 1901–1964, vol. VI
Hope, Robert, *died* 1936, vol. III
Hope, Robert Charles, 1855–1926, vol. II
Hope, Sir Robert Holms-Kerr, 3rd Bt (*cr* 1932), 1900–1993, vol. IX
Hope, Sydney, 1905–1959, vol. V
Hope, Sir Theodore Cracraft, 1831–1915, vol. I
Hope, Col Thomas, 1848–1925, vol. II
Hope, Sir William, 14th Bt (*cr* 1628), 1819–1898, vol. I
Hope, Sir William Henry St John, 1854–1919, vol. II
Hope, Lt-Col William Henry Webley, 1871–1919, vol. II
Hope-Dunbar, Sir Basil Douglas, 7th Bt, 1907–1961, vol. VI
Hope-Dunbar, Sir Charles Dunbar, 6th Bt, 1873–1958, vol. V
Hope Gill, Cecil Gervase, 1894–1984, vol. VIII
Hope-Johnstone, John James, 1842–1912, vol. I
Hope-Jones, Sir Arthur, 1911–1984, vol. VIII
Hope-Jones, Ronald Christopher, 1920–2000, vol. X
Hope-Morley, Captain Hon. Claude Hope, 1887–1968, vol. VI
Hope-Vere, James Charles, 1858–1933, vol. III
Hope-Wallace, Philip Adrian, 191–1979, vol. VII
Hopewell, Alan Francis John, 1892–1957, vol. V
Hopewell-Ash, Edwin Lancelot; *see* Ash.
Hopewell-Smith, Arthur, 1865–1931, vol. III
Hopkin, Major Daniel, 1886–1951, vol. V
Hopkin, Sir David Armand, 1922–1997, vol. X
Hopkin-James, Rev. Lemuel John, 1874–1937, vol. III
Hopkins, Major Adrian Edmund, 1894–1967, vol. VI
Hopkins, Anthony Philip, 1937–1997, vol. X
Hopkins, Arthur, 1848–1930, vol. III
Hopkins, Arthur Antwis, 1855–1916, vol. II
Hopkins, Rev. Charles, 1834–1908, vol. I
Hopkins, Charles James William, 1887–1954, vol. V
Hopkins, Paymaster-in-Chief David Bertie Lyndsay, 1862–1925, vol. II
Hopkins, Douglas Edward, 1902–1992, vol. IX
Hopkins, Edward John, 1818–1901, vol. I
Hopkins, Everard, 1860–1928, vol. II
Hopkins, Adm. Sir Frank Henry Edward, 1910–1990, vol. VIII
Hopkins, Rt Rev. Frederick C., 1844–1923, vol. II
Hopkins, Sir Frederick Gowland, 1861–1947, vol. IV
Hopkins, Gerard Walter Sturgis, 1892–1961, vol. VI
Hopkins, Harold Horace, 1918–1994, vol. IX

Hopkins, Col Harold Leslie, 1897–1981, vol. VIII
Hopkins, Harry Geoffrey, 1918–1982, vol. VIII
Hopkins, Harry L., 1890–1946, vol. IV
Hopkins, Harry Sinclair, 1870–1953, vol. V
Hopkins, Henry Mayne Reid, 1867–1956, vol. V
Hopkins, Sir James Sidney Rawdon S.; *see* Scott-Hopkins.
Hopkins, John Castell, 1864–1923, vol. II
Hopkins, John Collier Frederick, 1898–1981, vol. VIII
Hopkins, Sir John Ommanney, 1834–1916, vol. II
Hopkins, John Richard, 1931–1998, vol. X
Hopkins, Sir John Wells Wainwright, 1st Bt, 1863–1946, vol. IV
Hopkins, Rev. Canon Leslie Freeman, 1914–1987, vol. VIII
Hopkins, Lt-Col Lewis Egerton, 1873–1945, vol. IV
Hopkins, Lionel Charles, 1854–1952, vol. V
Hopkins, Livingston, 1846–1927, vol. II
Hopkins, Very Rev. Noel Thomas, 1892–1969, vol. VI
Hopkins, Reginald Haydn, 1891–1965, vol. VI
Hopkins, Rt Hon. Sir Richard Valentine Nind, 1880–1955, vol. V
Hopkins, Robert Thurston, *died* 1958, vol. V
Hopkins, Maj.-Gen. Ronald Nicholas Lamond, 1897–1990, vol. VIII
Hopkins, Tighe, 1856–1919, vol. II
Hopkins, William Joseph, 1863–1927, vol. II
Hopkinson, Albert Cyril, 1911–1994, vol. IX
Hopkinson, Sir Alfred, 1851–1939, vol. III
Hopkinson, Rev. Arthur John, 1894–1953, vol. V
Hopkinson, Austin, 1879–1962, vol. VI
Hopkinson, Bertram, 1874–1918, vol. II
Hopkinson, Edward, 1859–1922, vol. II
Hopkinson, Emilius, 1869–1951, vol. V
Hopkinson, Sir Frederick Thomas, 1863–1947, vol. IV
Hopkinson, Maj.-Gen. Gerald Charles, 1910–1989, vol. VIII
Hopkinson, Gen. Henry, 1820–1899, vol. I
Hopkinson, Col Henry Charles Barwick Pasha, 1867–1946, vol. IV
Hopkinson, Sir Henry L., 1855–1936, vol. III
Hopkinson, Col (Henry) Somerset (Parnell), 1899–1988, vol. VIII
Hopkinson, Sir (Henry) Thomas, 1905–1990, vol. VIII
Hopkinson, John, 1849–1898, vol. I
Hopkinson, John, 1844–1919, vol. II
Hopkinson, Rev. John Henry, *died* 1957, vol. V
Hopkinson, Ralph Galbraith, 1913–1994, vol. IX
Hopkinson, Col Somerset; *see* Hopkinson, Col H. S. P.
Hopkinson, Sir Thomas; *see* Hopkinson, Sir H. T.
Hopley, Ven. Arthur, 1906–1981, vol. VIII
Hopley, Hon. William Musgrove, 1853–1919, vol. II
Hoppé, E. O., 1878–1972, vol. VII
Hoppe, Iver, 1920–1991, vol. IX
Hopper, Frederick Ernest, 1919–1997, vol. X
Hopper, Nora, 1871–1906, vol. I
Hopper, Robert John, 1910–1987, vol. VIII
Hopps, Air Vice-Marshal Frank Linden, *died* 1976, vol. VII

Hopps, John Page, 1834–1911, vol. I
Hopson, Sir Donald Charles, 1915–1974, vol. VII
Hopthrow, Brig. Harry Ewart, 1896–1992, vol. IX
Hopton, Ven. Charles Ernest, 1861–1946, vol. IV
Hopton, Lt-Gen. Sir Edward, 1837–1912, vol. I
Hopton, Col John Dutton, 1858–1934, vol. III
Hopton, Rev. Preb. Michael, 1838–1928, vol. II
Hopwood, Brig. Alfred Henry, died 1956, vol. V
Hopwood, Aubrey, 1863–1917, vol. II
Hopwood, Avery, died 1928, vol. II
Hopwood, Charles Augustus, 1847–1922, vol. II
Hopwood, Major Edward Byng George G.; see Gregge-Hopwood.
Hopwood, Edward Robert G.; see Gregge-Hopwood.
Hopwood, Frank Lloyd, 1884–1954, vol. V
Hopwood, Vice-Adm. Geoffrey, 1877–1947, vol. IV
Hopwood, Henry Silkstone, 1860–1914, vol. I
Hopwood, Brig.-Gen. Herbert Reginald, 1871–1938, vol. III
Hopwood, Brig. John Adam, 1910–1987, vol. VIII
Hopwood, Adm. Ronald Arthur, 1868–1949, vol. IV
Hopwood, Sir William, 1862–1936, vol. III
Horabin, Thomas Lewis, 1896–1956, vol. V
Horan, Rev. Charles Trevor, 1863–1932, vol. III
Horan, Rt Rev. Forbes Trevor, 1905–1996, vol. X
Horan, Gerald, 1879–1949, vol. IV
Horan, Henry Edward, 1890–1961, vol. VI
Horder, 1st Baron, 1871–1955, vol. V
Horder, 2nd Baron, 1910–1997, vol. X
Hordern, Anthony, 1889–1970, vol. VI (AII)
Hordern, Sir Archibald Frederick, 1889–1950, vol. IV
Hordern, Rev. Arthur Venables Calveley, 1866–1946, vol. IV
Hordern, Captain Edward Joseph Calveley, 1867–1944, vol. IV
Hordern, Brig.-Gen. Gwyn Venables, 1870–1945, vol. IV
Hordern, Rt Rev. Hugh Maudslay, 1868–1949, vol. IV
Hordern, Sir Michael Murray, 1911–1995, vol. IX
Hordern, Sir Samuel, 1876–1956, vol. V
Hordern, Samuel, 1909–1960, vol. V
Hore, Sir Adair; see Hore, Sir C. F. A.
Hore, Sir (Charles Fraser) Adair, 1874–1950, vol. IV
Hore, Col Charles Owen, 1860–1916, vol. II
Hore, Engr-Rear-Adm. Fred, 1863–1932, vol. III
Hore, Maj.-Gen. Walter Stuart, 1843–1918, vol. II
Hore-Belisha, 1st Baron, 1893–1957, vol. V
Hore-Ruthven, Col Hon. Malise; see Ruthven.
Horenstein, Jascha, 1899–1973, vol. VII
Horgan, John Joseph, 1881–1967, vol. VI
Horler, Sydney, 1888–1954, vol. V
Horlick, Sir Ernest Burford, 2nd Bt, 1880–1934, vol. III
Horlick, Sir James, 1st Bt, 1884–1921, vol. II
Horlick, Lt-Col Sir James Nockells, 4th Bt, 1886–1972, vol. VII
Horlick, Sir John James Macdonald, 5th Bt, 1922–1995, vol. IX
Horlick, Sir Peter James Cunliffe, 3rd Bt, 1908–1958, vol. V
Hormasji Bhiwandiwalla, Khan Bahadur Sir Dosabhai, died 1940, vol. III (A), vol. IV

Horn, Alan Bowes, 1917–1992, vol. IX
Horn, Sir Arthur Edwin, died 1943, vol. IV
Horn, David Bayne, 1851–1927, vol. II
Horn, David Bayne, 1901–1969, vol. VI
Horn, Gunnar, 1894–1946, vol. IV
Horn, Brig. Robert Victor Galbraith, 1886–1959, vol. V
Horn, William Austin, 1841–1922, vol. II
Horn-Elphinstone, Sir Graeme Hepburn D.; see Elphinstone.
Hornabrook, Ven. Charles Soward, died 1922, vol. II
Hornabrook, Rev. John, 1848–1937, vol. III
Hornaday, William Temple, 1854–1937, vol. III
Hornby, Maj.-Gen. Alan Hugh, 1894–1958, vol. V
Hornby, Albert Neilson, 1847–1925, vol. II
Hornby, C. H. St John, 1867–1946, vol. IV
Hornby, Charles Windham Leycester P.; see Penrhyn-Hornby.
Hornby, Brig.-Gen. Edmund John Phipps, 1857–1947, vol. IV
Hornby, Frank, 1863–1936, vol. III
Hornby, Frank Robert, 1911–1987, vol. VIII
Hornby, Sir Henry; see Hornby, Sir W. H.
Hornby, Sir (Henry) Russell, 2nd Bt, 1888–1971, vol. VI
Hornby, Rt Rev. Hugh Leycester, 1888–1965, vol. VI
Hornby, Rev. James John, 1826–1909, vol. I
Hornby, James William, 1924–1984, vol. VIII
Hornby, Michael Charles St John, 1899–1987, vol. VIII
Hornby, Brig.-Gen. Montague Leyland, 1870–1948, vol. IV
Hornby, Ven. Phipps John, 1853–1936, vol. III
Hornby, Adm. Robert Stewart Phipps, 1866–1956, vol. V
Hornby, Sir (Roger) Antony, 1904–1987, vol. VIII
Hornby, Sir Russell; see Hornby, Sir H. R.
Hornby, Rt Hon. Wilfrid Bird, 1851–1935, vol. III
Hornby, Ven. William, 1810–1899, vol. I
Hornby, Sir (William) Henry, 1st Bt, 1841–1928, vol. II
Hornby, Sir Windham, 1812–1899, vol. I
Hornby Steer, William Reed; see Steer.
Horncastle, Walter Radcliffe, 1850–1908, vol. I
Horndon, David, 1863–1938, vol. III
Horne, 1st Baron, 1861–1929, vol. III
Horne of Slamannan, 1st Viscount, 1871–1940, vol. III
Horne, Sir Alan Edgar, 2nd Bt, 1889–1984, vol. VIII
Horne, Alderson Burrell, 1863–1953, vol. V
Horne, Sir Allan; see Horne, Sir J. A.
Horne, Sir Andrew John, 1856–1924, vol. II
Horne, Rev. C. Silvester, 1865–1914, vol. I
Horne, (Charles) Kenneth, 1907–1969, vol. VI
Horne, Sir Edgar; see Horne, Sir W. E.
Horne, Edward Butler, 1881–1947, vol. IV
Horne, Col Edward William, 1857–1941, vol. IV
Horne, Frank Robert, 1904–1975, vol. VII
Horne, Frederic, 1863–1927, vol. II
Horne, Frederick Newman, 1863–1946, vol. IV
Horne, Maj.-Gen. Gerald Tom Warlters, 1898–1978, vol. VII

Horne, Herbert P., *died* 1916, vol. II
Horne, Sir (James) Allan, 1876–1944, vol. IV
Horne, Jobson; *see* Horne, W. J.
Horne, John, 1848–1928, vol. II
Horne, Kenneth; *see* Horne, C. K.
Horne, Lancelot Worthy, 1875–1924, vol. II
Horne, Leonard Thomas, 1860–1934, vol. III
Horne, Maynard, 1870–1944, vol. IV
Horne, Michael Rex, 1921–2000, vol. X
Horne, (Walter) Jobson, 1865–1953, vol. V
Horne, Sir (William) Edgar, 1st Bt, 1856–1941, vol. IV
Horne, Major William Guy, 1889–1974, vol. VII
Horne, Sir William Kenneth, 1883–1959, vol. V
Horne, William Ogilvie, *died* 1943, vol. IV
Hornel, Edward Atkinson, 1864–1933, vol. III
Hornell, Vice-Adm. Sir Robert Arthur, 1877–1949, vol. IV
Hornell, Sir William Woodward, 1878–1950, vol. IV
Horner, Andrew L., 1863–1916, vol. II
Horner, Arthur Lewis, 1894–1968, vol. VI
Horner, Arthur William, 1909–1999, vol. X
Horner, Rev. Bernard, 1873–1960, vol. V
Horner, Egbert Foster, 1864–1928, vol. II
Horner, Hallam; *see* Horner, L. J. H.
Horner, John, 1911–1997, vol. X
Horner, Sir John Francis Fortescue, 1842–1927, vol. II
Horner, (Lawrence John) Hallam, 1907–1989, vol. VIII
Horner, Norman Gerald, 1882–1954, vol. V
Horner, Mrs Sibyl Gertrude, 1895–1978, vol. VII
Horniblow, Brig.-Gen. Frank Herbert, 1860–1931, vol. III
Horniblow, Col Frederick, 1862–1945, vol. IV
Hornibrook, Sir Manuel Richard, 1893–1970, vol. VI (AII)
Horniman, Annie Elizabeth Fredericka, 1860–1937, vol. III
Horniman, Benjamin Guy, 1873–1948, vol. IV
Horniman, Emslie John, 1863–1932, vol. III
Horniman, Frederick John, 1835–1906, vol. I
Horniman, Rear-Adm. Henry, *died* 1956, vol. V
Horniman, Laurence Ivan, 1893–1963, vol. VI
Horniman, Roy, *died* 1930, vol. III
Horning, Eric Stephen Gurney, 1900–1959, vol. V
Horning, Lewis Emerson, 1858–1925, vol. II
Hornsby, Sir Bertram, *died* 1943, vol. IV
Hornsby, Frederick Middleton, 1874–1931, vol. III
Hornsby, Harker William, 1912–1971, vol. VII
Hornsby, Harry Reginald, 1907–1983, vol. VIII
Hornsby, Captain James Arthur, 1891–1972, vol. VII
Hornsby-Smith, Baroness (Life Peer); Margaret Patricia Hornsby-Smith, 1914–1985, vol. VIII
Hornsby-Wright, Lt-Col Guy Jefferys, 1872–1941, vol. IV
Hornung, Ernest William, 1866–1921, vol. II
Hornung, Lt-Col Sir John Derek, 1915–1978, vol. VII
Hornung, John Peter, 1861–1940, vol. III
Hornyold-Strickland, Henry, 1890–1975, vol. VII
Hornyold-Strickland, Hon. Mary Constance Elizabeth Christina, 1896–1970, vol. VI

Horobin, Sir Ian Macdonald, 1899–1976, vol. VII
Horobin, Norah Maud, 1898–1976, vol. VII
Horonitz, Vladimir, 1904–1989, vol. VIII
Horrabin, James Francis, 1884–1962, vol. VI
Horridge, John, 1893–1951, vol. V
Horridge, Sir Thomas Gardner, 1857–1938, vol. III
Horrobin, Walter, 1894–1967, vol. VI (AII)
Horrocks, Lt-Gen. Sir Brian Gwynne, 1895–1985, vol. VIII
Horrocks, Peter, *died* 1909, vol. I
Horrocks, Walter James Hodgson, 1897–1946, vol. IV
Horrocks, Col Sir William Heaton, 1859–1941, vol. IV
Horrox, Lewis, 1898–1975, vol. VII
Horsbrugh, Baroness (Life Peer); Florence Gertrude Horsbrugh, 1889–1969, vol. VI
Horsbrugh-Porter, Sir Andrew Marshall, 3rd Bt, 1907–1986, vol. VIII
Horsbrugh-Porter, Sir John Scott; *see* Porter.
Horsburgh, Benjamin, 1868–1935, vol. III (A), vol. IV
Horsefield, Rev. Frederic John, 1859–1933, vol. III
Horsefield, John Keith, 1901–1997, vol. X
Horsey, Captain Frank Lankester, 1884–1956, vol. V
Horsfall, Sir Donald; *see* Horsfall, Sir J. D.
Horsfall, Geoffrey Jonas, 1905–1985, vol. VIII
Horsfall, Jeremiah Garnett, 1840–1920, vol. II
Horsfall, Sir John Cousin, 1st Bt, 1846–1920, vol. II
Horsfall, Sir (John) Donald, 2nd Bt, 1891–1975, vol. VII
Horsfall, Thomas Coglan, 1841–1932, vol. III
Horsfall Turner, Harold, 1909–1981, vol. VIII
Horsfield, George, 1882–1956, vol. V
Horsfield, Brig. Herbert Eric, 1895–1981, vol. VIII
Horsfield, Lt-Col Richard Marshall, *died* 1940, vol. III
Horsford, Alan Arthur, 1927–1999, vol. X
Horsford, Cyril Arthur Bennett, 1876–1953, vol. V
Horsley, Major Bernard Hill, *died* 1940, vol. III
Horsley, Rt Rev. Cecil Douglas, 1903–1953, vol. V
Horsley, Gerald Callcott, 1862–1917, vol. II
Horsley, John Callcott, 1817–1903, vol. I
Horsley, Rev. John William, 1845–1921, vol. II
Horsley, Reginald Ernest, 1863–1926, vol. II
Horsley, Terence Beresford, 1904–1949, vol. IV
Horsley, Sir Victor Alexander Haden, 1857–1916, vol. II
Horsley, Col Walter Charles, 1855–1934, vol. III
Horsman, Dame Dorothea Jean, 1918–1994, vol. IX
Horsman, Sir Henry, 1887–1966, vol. VI
Horsnell, Horace, 1882–1949, vol. IV
Horstead, Rt Rev. Cecil; *see* Horstead, Rt Rev. J. L. C.
Horstead, Rt Rev. James Lawrence Cecil, 1898–1989, vol. VIII
Hort, Sir Arthur Fenton, 6th Bt, 1864–1935, vol. III
Hort, Edward Collett, 1868–1922, vol. II
Hort, Sir Fenton George, 7th Bt, 1896–1960, vol. V
Hort, Sir Fenton Josiah, 5th Bt, 1836–1902, vol. I
Hort, Greta, 1903–1967, vol. VI
Hort, Sir James Fenton, 8th Bt, 1926–1995, vol. IX
Horthy de Nagybanya, Adm. Nicholas Vitéz, 1868–1957, vol. V

Horton, Frank, 1878–1957, vol. V
Horton, Maj.-Gen. Frank Cyril, 1907–1989, vol. VIII
Horton, Sir Henry, 1870–1943, vol. IV
Horton, Major James, 1845–1925, vol. II
Horton, Lt-Col James H., 1871–1917, vol. II
Horton, Adm. Sir Max Kennedy, 1883–1951, vol. V
Horton, Percy Frederick, 1897–1970, vol. VI
Horton, Ralph Albert, 1885–1969, vol. VI
Horton, Rev. Reginald, 1852–1914, vol. I
Horton, Rev. Robert Forman, 1855–1934, vol. III
Horton, William, 1854–1944, vol. IV
Horton, Brig.-Gen. William Edward, 1868–1935, vol. III
Horton, Lt-Col W(illiam) Gray, 1897–1974, vol. VII
Horton-Smith, Lionel Graham Horton, 1871–1953, vol. V
Horton-Smith, Richard Horton, 1831–1919, vol. II
Horton-Smith-Hartley, Sir Percival; see Hartley.
Horton-Smith-Hartley, Percival Hubert Graham; see Hartley.
Horton-Starkie, Rev. Preb. Le Gendre George, 1859–1943, vol. IV
Horwill, Herbert William, 1864–1952, vol. V
Horwill, Sir Lionel Clifford, 1890–1972, vol. VII
Horwood, Hon. Owen Pieter Faure, 1916–1998, vol. X
Horwood, Hon. Sir William Henry, 1862–1945, vol. IV
Horwood, Brig.-Gen. Sir William Thomas Francis, 1868–1943, vol. IV
Hose, Charles, 1863–1929, vol. III
Hose, Edward Shaw, 1871–1946, vol. IV
Hose, Rt Rev. George Frederick, 1838–1922, vol. II
Hose, Sir (John) Walter, 1865–1958, vol. V
Hose, Robert John, 1863–1935, vol. III
Hose, Sir Walter; see Hose, Sir J. W.
Hosegood, Philip James, 1920–1987, vol. VIII
Hosford, John Percival, 1900–1991, vol. IX
Hosie, Sir Alexander, 1853–1925, vol. II
Hosie, Lt-Col Andrew, 1860–1931, vol. III
Hosie, Dorothea, (Lady Hosie), 1885–1959, vol. V
Hosie, Ian, 1905–1970, vol. VI
Hosie, James Findlay, 1913–1993, vol. IX
Hosier, Arthur Julius, 1877–1963, vol. VI
Hosier, John, 1928–2000, vol. X
Hosken, Clifford; see Keverne, Richard.
Hosken, Ernest Charles Heath, died 1934, vol. III
Hosker, Sir James Atkinson, 1857–1929, vol. III
Hoskin, Alan Simson, 1886–1945, vol. IV
Hoskin, John, 1836–1921, vol. II
Hoskin, Theo. Jenner Hooper, 1888–1954, vol. V
Hosking, Eric John, 1909–1991, vol. IX
Hosking, Ethelbert Bernard, 1890–1960, vol. V
Hosking, Hon. Sir John Henry, 1854–1928, vol. II
Hosking, Paymaster Rear-Adm. Richard Bosustow, 1869–1962, vol. VI
Hoskins, Sir Anthony Hiley, 1828–1901, vol. I
Hoskins, Maj.-Gen. Sir (Arthur) Reginald, 1871–1942, vol. IV
Hoskins, Sir Cecil Harold, 1899–1971, vol. VII
Hoskins, Maj.-Gen. Sir Reginald; see Hoskins, Maj.-Gen. Sir A. R.
Hoskins, William, died 1928, vol. II
Hoskins, William George, 1908–1992, vol. IX

Hoskyn, Col John Cunningham Moore, 1875–1941, vol. IV
Hoskyns, Ven. Benedict George, 1856–1935, vol. III
Hoskyns, Col Sir Chandos, 10th Bt, 1848–1914, vol. I
Hoskyns, Sir Chandos Wren, 14th Bt, 1923–1945, vol. IV
Hoskyns, Rt Rev. Sir Edwyn, 12th Bt, 1851–1925, vol. II
Hoskyns, Rev. Canon Sir Edwyn Clement, 13th Bt, 1884–1937, vol. III
Hoskyns, Sir John Chevallier, 15th Bt, 1926–1956, vol. V
Hoskyns, Rev. Sir John Leigh, 9th Bt, 1817–1911, vol. I
Hoskyns, Sir Leigh, 11th Bt, 1850–1923, vol. II
Hoskyns, Rear-Adm. Peyton, 1852–1919, vol. II
Hoskyns-Abrahall, Rt Rev. Anthony Leigh Egerton, 1903–1982, vol. VIII
Hoskyns-Abrahall, Bennet, 1858–1951, vol. V
Hoskyns-Abrahall, Sir Chandos; see Hoskyns-Abrahall, Sir T. C.
Hoskyns-Abrahall, Sir (Theo) Chandos, 1896–1975, vol. VII
Hoskyns-Festing, Major Arthur; see Festing.
Hosmer, James Kendall, 1834–1927, vol. II
Hossie, Major David Neil, 1890–1962, vol. VI
Hoste, Maj.-Gen. Dixon Edward, 1827–1905, vol. I
Hoste, Dixon Edward, 1861–1946, vol. IV
Hoste, Sir William Graham, 4th Bt, 1895–1915, vol. II
Hoste, Sir William Henry Charles, 3rd Bt, 1860–1902, vol. I
Hoster, Mrs Albert, 1864–1939, vol. III
Hotblack, Maj.-Gen. Frederick Elliot, 1887–1979, vol. VII
Hotblack, George Finch, 1883–1951, vol. V
Hotchin, Sir Claude, 1898–1977, vol. VII
Hotchkin, Stafford Vere, 1876–1953, vol. V
Hotham, 5th Baron, 1838–1907, vol. I
Hotham, 6th Baron, 1863–1923, vol. II
Hotham, 7th Baron, 1899–1967, vol. VI
Hotham, Adm. Sir Alan Geoffrey, 1876–1965, vol. VI
Hotham, Sir Charles Frederick, 1843–1925, vol. II
Hotham, Captain Henry Edward, 1855–1912, vol. I
Hotham, Brig.-Gen. John, 1851–1932, vol. III
Hotham, Rev. John Hallett, 1811–1901, vol. I
Hothfield, 1st Baron, 1844–1926, vol. II
Hothfield, 2nd Baron, 1873–1952, vol. V
Hothfield, 3rd Baron, 1897–1961, vol. VI
Hothfield, 4th Baron, 1916–1986, vol. VIII
Hothfield, 5th Baron, 1904–1991, vol. IX
Hotine, Brig. Martin, 1898–1968, vol. VI
Hotson, Sir Ernest; see Hotson, Sir J. E. B.
Hotson, Sir (John) Ernest (Buttery), 1877–1944, vol. IV
Hotson, Leslie, 1897–1992, vol. IX
Houblon, Mrs Doreen A.; see Archer Houblon.
Houblon, Col George Bramston Archer-, 1843–1913, vol. I
Houblon, Rev. Thomas Henry Archer, 1849–1933, vol. III
Houchen, Harry Owen, 1907–1981, vol. VIII
Houde, Camillien, 1889–1958, vol. V

Houfton, Sir John Plowright, 1857–1929, vol. III
Hough, Edwin Leadam, 1852–1928, vol. II
Hough, Graham Goulder, 1908–1990, vol. VIII
Hough, James Fisher, 1878–1960, vol. V
Hough, John Stanley, 1856–1928, vol. II
Hough, Rev. Lynn Harold, 1877–1971, vol. VII
Hough, Richard Alexander, 1922–1999, vol. X
Hough, Sydney Samuel, 1870–1923, vol. II
Hough, William, 1884–1962, vol. VI
Hough, Rt Rev. William Woodcock, 1859–1934, vol. III
Houghton of Sowerby, Baron (Life Peer); Arthur Leslie Noel Douglas Houghton, 1898–1996, vol. X
Houghton, Alanson Bigelow, 1863–1941, vol. IV
Houghton, Albert Morley, 1914–1987, vol. VIII
Houghton, Rev. Alfred Thomas, 1896–1993, vol. IX
Houghton, Arthur Amory, Jr, 1906–1990, vol. VIII
Houghton, Charles Thomas, 1892–1975, vol. VII
Houghton, Claude; see Oldfield, C. H.
Houghton, Rev. Edward James, 1838–1919, vol. II
Houghton, Rev. Edward John Walford, 1867–1955, vol. V
Houghton, Rt Rev. Frank, died 1972, vol. VII
Houghton, Rt Rev. Michael Alan, 1949–1999, vol. X
Houghton, Sir William Frederick, 1909–1971, vol. VII
Houghton, Rev. Canon William Reginald, 1910–1989, vol. VIII
Houghton, William Stanley, 1881–1913, vol. I
Houghton-Gastrell, Sir William; see Gastrell.
Houlden, George Houldsworth, 1902–1972, vol. VII
Houlder, Howard, 1858–1932, vol. III
Houldsworth, Sir Basil; see Houldsworth, Sir H. B.
Houldsworth, Sir (Harold) Basil, 2nd Bt (cr 1956), 1922–1990, vol. VIII
Houldsworth, Sir Henry Hamilton, 2nd Bt (cr 1887), 1867–1947, vol. IV
Houldsworth, Brig. Sir Henry Walter, 1896–1963, vol. VI
Houldsworth, Sir Hubert Stanley, 1st Bt (cr 1956), 1889–1956, vol. V
Houldsworth, J. H., died 1910, vol. I
Houldsworth, J. Hamilton, 1867–1941, vol. IV
Houldsworth, Sir Reginald Douglas Henry, 4th Bt, 1903–1989, vol. VIII
Houldsworth, Sir William Henry, 1st Bt (cr 1887), 1834–1917, vol. II
Houldsworth, Col Sir William Thomas Reginald, 3rd Bt (cr 1887), 1874–1960, vol. V
Hoult, (Eleanor) Norah, died 1984, vol. VIII
Hoult, Joseph, 1847–1917, vol. II
Houlton, Charlotte Leighton, 1882–1956, vol. V
Houlton, Sir Edward Victor Lewis, 1823–1899, vol. I
Houlton, Sir John Wardle, 1892–1973, vol. VII
Houndle, Henry Charles Herman Hawker, 1851–1919, vol. II
Hounsell, Maj.-Gen. Harold Arthur, 1897–1970, vol. VI
Hourigan, Thomas, 1904–1975, vol. VII
Housden, Rt Rev. James Alan George, 1904–1995, vol. IX
House, (Arthur) Humphry, 1908–1955, vol. V

House, Donald Victor, 1900–1992, vol. IX
House, Edward Mandell, 1858–1938, vol. III
House, George, 1892–1949, vol. IV
House, Harry Wilfred, 1895–1987, vol. VIII
House, Humphry; see House, A. H.
House, John William, 1919–1984, vol. VIII
Household, Geoffrey Edward West, 1900–1988, vol. VIII
Houseman, Alexander Randolph, 1920–1997, vol. X
Housman, Alfred Edward, 1859–1936, vol. III
Housman, Laurence, 1865–1959, vol. V
Houssay, Bernardo Alberto, 1887–1971, vol. VII
Houssaye, Henry, 1848–1911, vol. I
Houssemayne Du Boulay, Brig.-Gen. Noel Wilmot, 1861–1949, vol. IV
Houston, Sir Alexander Cruikshank, 1865–1933, vol. III
Houston, Arthur, 1833–1914, vol. I
Houston, Aubrey Claud D.; see Davidson-Houston.
Houston, Major Charles B.; see Blakiston-Houston.
Houston, Major Charles Elrington Duncan D.; see Davidson-Houston.
Houston, Dame Fanny Lucy, 1857–1936, vol. III
Houston, George, died 1947, vol. IV
Houston, John B.; see Blakiston-Houston.
Houston, Maj.-Gen. John B.; see Blakiston-Houston.
Houston, John R., 1856–1932, vol. III
Houston, Sir Robert Paterson, 1st Bt, 1853–1926, vol. II
Houston, Sir Thomas, died 1949, vol. IV
Houston, Lt-Col Wilfred Bennett D.; see Davidson-Houston.
Houston, William, 1846–1932, vol. III
Houston, William John Ballantyne, 1938–1991, vol. IX
Houston-Boswall-Preston, Thomas Alford, 1850–1918, vol. II
Houstoun, Robert Alexander, 1883–1975, vol. VII
Houstoun-Boswall, Sir George Lauderdale, 3rd Bt, 1847–1908, vol. I
Houstoun-Boswall, Sir George Reginald, 4th Bt, 1877–1915, vol. I
Houstoun-Boswall, Major Sir Gordon, 6th Bt, 1887–1961, vol. VI
Houstoun-Boswall, Sir Randolph; see Houstoun-Boswall, Sir T. R.
Houstoun-Boswall, Sir Thomas, 7th Bt, 1919–1982, vol. VIII
Houstoun-Boswall, Sir (Thomas) Randolph, 5th Bt, 1882–1953, vol. V
Houstoun-Boswall, Sir William Evelyn, 1892–1960, vol. V
Houthuesen, Albert Antony John, 1903–1979, vol. VII
Hovde, Frederick Lawson, 1908–1983, vol. VIII
Hovell, Very Rev. De Berdt, 1850–1905, vol. I
Hovell, Lt-Col Hugh De Berdt, 1863–1923, vol. II
Hovell, T. Mark, died 1925, vol. II
Hovil, Major Richard, died 1931, vol. III
How, Sir Friston Charles, 1897–1990, vol. VIII
How, Ven. Henry Walsham, 1856–1923, vol. II
How, Rt Rev. John Charles Halland, died 1961, vol. VI
How, Rev. John Hall, 1871–1938, vol. III
How, Walter Wybergh, 1861–1932, vol. III

How, Rt Rev. William Walsham, 1823–1897, vol. I
Howard de Walden, 7th Baron, 1830–1899, vol. I
Howard de Walden, 8th Baron, 1880–1946, vol. IV
Howard de Walden, 9th Baron, and Seaford, 5th
    Baron, 1912–1999, vol. X
Howard of Glossop, 2nd Baron, 1859–1924, vol. II
Howard of Glossop, 3rd Baron, 1885–1972, vol. VII
Howard of Glossop, Lady; (Winifred), died 1909,
    vol. I
Howard of Henderskelfe, Baron (Life Peer); George
    Anthony Geoffrey Howard, 1920–1984, vol. VIII
Howard of Penrith, 1st Baron, 1863–1939, vol. III
Howard of Penrith, 2nd Baron, 1905–1999, vol. X
Howard, Captain Alan Frederic William,
    1883–1971, vol. VII
Howard, Sir Albert, 1873–1947, vol. IV
Howard, Alexander Edward, 1909–1999, vol. X
Howard, Sir Algar Henry Stafford, 1880–1970,
    vol. VI
Howard, Andrée, 1910–1968, vol. VI
Howard, Sir (Andrew) Charles, died 1909, vol. I
Howard, Hon. Sir Arthur Jared Palmer, 1896–1971,
    vol. VII
Howard, Bronson, 1842–1908, vol. I
Howard, Sir Charles; see Howard, Sir A. C.
Howard, Brig. Sir Charles Alfred, 1878–1958,
    vol. V
Howard, Dame Christian; see Howard, Dame R. C.
Howard, Sir Douglas Frederick, 1897–1987,
    vol. VIII
Howard, Sir Ebenezer, 1850–1928, vol. II
Howard, Major Edmund, 1881–1960, vol. V
Howard, Sir (Edward) Stafford, 1851–1916, vol. II
Howard, Edwin Johnston, 1901–1971, vol. VII
Howard, Maj.-Gen. Sir Francis, 1848–1930, vol. III
Howard, Francis, 1874–1954, vol. V
Howard, Francis Alex, (Frankie Howerd),
    1922–1992, vol. IX
Howard, Col Francis James Leigh, 1870–1942,
    vol. IV
Howard, Major Frederic George, 1872–1915, vol. I
Howard, Sir Frederick, 1827–1915, vol. I
Howard, Frederick Richard, 1894–1977, vol. VII
Howard, Geoffrey, 1889–1973, vol. VII
Howard, Lt-Gen. Sir Geoffrey Weston, 1876–1966,
    vol. VI
Howard, Hon. Geoffrey William Algernon,
    1877–1935, vol. III
Howard, Captain George Augustus Hotham,
    1853–1931, vol. III
Howard, G(eorge) Wren, 1893–1968, vol. VI
Howard, Sir Gerald; see Howard, Sir S. G.
Howard, Maj.-Gen. Gordon Byron, 1895–1976,
    vol. VII
Howard, Lt Comdr Hon. Greville Reginald,
    1909–1987, vol. VIII
Howard, Captain Guy Robert, 1886–1918, vol. II
Howard, Sir (Harold Walter) Seymour, 1st Bt,
    1888–1967, vol. VI
Howard, Sir Harry, (Henry Rudolph Howard),
    1890–1970, vol. VI
Howard, Sir Henry, 1843–1921, vol. II
Howard, Rev. Henry, 1859–1933, vol. III
Howard, Lt-Col Hon. Henry Anthony Camillo,
    1913–1977, vol. VII

Howard, Col Henry Cecil Lloyd, 1882–1950,
    vol. IV
Howard, Henry Charles, 1850–1914, vol. I
Howard, Sir Henry Francis, 1809–1898, vol. I
Howard, Sir Henry Fraser, 1874–1943, vol. IV
Howard, Major Sir Henry George, 1883–1968,
    vol. VI
Howard, Henry Newman, 1861–1929, vol. III
Howard, Col Henry Richard Lloyd, 1853–1922,
    vol. II
Howard, Henry Rudolph; see Howard, Sir Harry.
Howard, Sir Herbert; see Howard, Sir S. H.
Howard, Hon. Hugh Melville, 1883–1919, vol. II
Howard, James Griffiths, 1927–1998, vol. X
Howard, John, died 1911, vol. I
Howard, John, died 1929, vol. III
Howard, Sir John Alfred Golding, 1901–1986,
    vol. VIII
Howard, Sir John Curtois, 1887–1970, vol. VI
Howard, John James, 1923–2000, vol. X
Howard, John Melbourne, 1913–1982, vol. VIII
Howard, Joseph, 1834–1923, vol. II
Howard, Keble; see Bell, John Keble.
Howard, Leon Alexander L.; see Lee Howard.
Howard, Leonard Henry, 1904–1993, vol. IX
Howard, Leslie, 1893–1943, vol. IV
Howard, Lady Mabel, 1878–1942, vol. IV
Howard, Hon. Mabel Bowden, died 1972, vol. VII
Howard, Marghanita; see Laski, M.
Howard, Hon. Oliver, 1875–1908, vol. I
Howard, Peter D., 1908–1965, vol. VI
Howard, Philip John Canning, 1853–1934, vol. III
Howard, Sir Richard Nicholas, 1832–1905, vol. I
Howard, Very Rev. Richard Thomas, 1884–1981,
    vol. VIII
Howard, Robert Jared Bliss, died 1921, vol. II
Howard, Robert Mowbray, 1854–1928, vol. II
Howard, Rev. Robert Wilmot, 1887–1960, vol. V
Howard, Robin Jarel Stanley, 1924–1989, vol. VIII
Howard, Rev. Canon Ronald Claude, 1902–1995,
    vol. IX
Howard, Dame (Rosemary) Christian, 1916–1999,
    vol. X
Howard, Roy Wilson, 1883–1964, vol. VI
Howard, Russell John, 1875–1942, vol. IV
Howard, Lt-Col Samuel Lloyd, 1827–1901, vol. I
Howard, Sir Seymour; see Howard, Sir H. W. S.
Howard, Sir Stafford; see Howard, Sir E. S.
Howard, Sir (Stanley) Herbert, 1888–1968, vol. VI
Howard, Sir (Stephen) Gerald, 1896–1973, vol. VII
Howard, Major Stephen Goodwin, 1867–1934,
    vol. III
Howard, T. Henry, 1849–1923, vol. II
Howard, Rev. Thomas Henry, died 1931, vol. III
Howard, Brig.-Gen. Thomas Nairne Scott
    Moncrieff, died 1960, vol. V
Howard, Tom Forrest, 1888–1953, vol. V
Howard, Trevor Wallace, 1913–1988, vol. VIII
Howard, Walter, 1866–1922, vol. II
Howard, Sir Walter Stewart, 1888–1992, vol. IX
Howard, Rev. Wilbert Francis, 1880–1952, vol. V
Howard, Captain William Gilbert, 1877–1960,
    vol. V
Howard, William McLaren, 1921–1990, vol. VIII
Howard, William Reginald, 1879–1966, vol. VI

Howard, Captain William Van Sittart, 1859–1937, vol. III
Howard-Brooke, Col Richard Edward Frederic, 1847–1918, vol. II
Howard-Johnston, Rear-Adm. Clarence Dinsmore, 1903–1996, vol. X
Howard-Jones, Maj.-Gen. Leonard Hamilton, 1905–1987, vol. VIII
Howard-Smith, Trevor Wallace; see Howard.
Howard-Vyse, Lt-Gen. Edward, 1826–1909, vol. I
Howard-Vyse, Lt-Gen. Sir Edward Dacre, 1905–1992, vol. IX
Howard-Vyse, Howard Henry, 1858–1927, vol. II
Howard-Vyse, Maj.-Gen. Sir Richard Granville Hylton, 1883–1962, vol. VI
Howard-Williams, W., 1879–1962, vol. VI
Howarth, Sir Alfred, 1867–1937, vol. III
Howarth, David Armine, 1912–1991, vol. IX
Howarth, Sir Edward, died 1953, vol. V
Howarth, Elijah, died 1938, vol. III
Howarth, Harry, 1916–1969, vol. VI
Howarth, Herbert Lomax, 1900–1974, vol. VII
Howarth, Osbert John Radclyffe, 1877–1954, vol. V
Howarth, Thomas Edward Brodie, 1914–1988, vol. VIII
Howarth, Walter Goldie, 1879–1962, vol. VI
Howarth, William James, died 1928, vol. II
Howat, Henry Taylor, 1911–1998, vol. X
Howat, Very Rev. Rudolph H.; see Henderson-Howat.
Howd, Isobel, 1928–2000, vol. X (AII)
Howden, Charles Robert Andrew, 1862–1936, vol. III
Howden, Captain Harry Leslie, 1896–1969, vol. VI
Howden, Robert, 1856–1940, vol. III
Howe, 3rd Earl, 1822–1900, vol. I
Howe, 4th Earl, 1861–1929, vol. III
Howe, 5th Earl, 1884–1964, vol. VI
Howe, 6th Earl, 1908–1984, vol. VIII
Howe, Allen, 1918–1998, vol. X
Howe, Adm. Hon. Sir Assheton Gore C.; see Curzon-Howe.
Howe, Rt Hon. Clarence Decatur, 1886–1960, vol. V
Howe, George Edward, 1925–1995, vol. IX
Howe, George Frederick, 1856–1937, vol. III
Howe, George William Osborn, 1875–1960, vol. V
Howe, Sir Gerard Lewis, 1899–1955, vol. V
Howe, Hon. James Henderson, 1839–1920, vol. II
Howe, John Allen, 1869–1952, vol. V
Howe, Julia Ward, 1819–1910, vol. I
Howe, Captain Leicester Charles Assheton St John C.; see Curzon-Howe.
Howe, Col Randall Charles Annesley, 1858–1930, vol. III
Howe, Sir Robert George, 1893–1981, vol. VIII
Howe, Sir Ronald Martin, 1896–1977, vol. VII
Howe, Air Cdre Thomas Edward Barham, 1886–1970, vol. VI
Howel-Jones, Lt-Col Walter, 1868–1948, vol. IV
Howell, Baron (Life Peer); Denis Herbert Howell, 1923–1998, vol. X
Howell, Col Arthur Anthony, 1862–1918, vol. II
Howell, Charles Alfred, 1905–1974, vol. VII
Howell, Hon. Clark, 1863–1936, vol. III

Howell, Conrad Meredyth Hinds, 1877–1960, vol. V
Howell, Very Rev. David, 1831–1903, vol. I
Howell, David Arnold, 1890–1953, vol. V
Howell, Dorothy, 1898–1982, vol. VIII
Howell, Sir Evelyn Berkeley, 1877–1971, vol. VII
Howell, Maj.-Gen. Frederick Duke Gwynne, 1881–1967, vol. VI
Howell, Rev. G., died 1918, vol. II
Howell, Lt-Col Geoffrey Llewellyn Hinds, 1875–1948, vol. IV
Howell, Col Harry Arthur Leonard, 1867–1937, vol. III
Howell, Hon. Hector Mansfield, 1842–1918, vol. II
Howell, Lt-Col Herbert Gwynne, 1879–1925, vol. II
Howell, John, 1871–1945, vol. IV
Howell, John Aldersey, 1888–1928, vol. II
Howell, Rt Rev. Kenneth Walter, 1909–1995, vol. IX
Howell, Mortimer Sloper, 1841–1925, vol. II
Howell, Paul Philip, 1917–1994, vol. IX
Howell, Brig.-Gen. Philip, 1877–1916, vol. II
Howell, Sir Walter Jack, 1854–1913, vol. I
Howell, Col Wilfrid Russell, 1865–1930, vol. III
Howell, William Gough, 1922–1974, vol. VII
Howell, William Gruffydd Rhys, 1904–1956, vol. V
Howell, William H., 1860–1945, vol. IV
Howell, Rev. Canon Willoughby John, died 1938, vol. III
Howell-Jones, Col John Hyndman, 1877–1941, vol. IV
Howell-Price, Lt-Col Owen Glendower, vol. II
Howells, Rt Rev. Adelakun Williamson, 1905–1963, vol. VI
Howells, Rt Rev. Adolphus Williamson, 1866–1938, vol. III
Howells, Christopher John, 1933–1984, vol. VIII
Howells, Derek William, 1928–1987, vol. VIII
Howells, George, 1871–1955, vol. V
Howells, Gilbert Haywood, 1897–1982, vol. VIII
Howells, Gwyn, 1918–1997, vol. X
Howells, Herbert Norman, 1892–1983, vol. VIII
Howells, William Dean, 1837–1920, vol. II
Howerd, Frankie; see Howard, F. A.
Howes, Lt-Gen. Albert Joseph, 1837–1914, vol. I
Howes, Arthur Burnaby, 1879–1963, vol. VI
Howes, Bobby, 1895–1972, vol. VII
Howes, Ernest James, 1895–1974, vol. VII
Howes, Frank Stewart, 1891–1974, vol. VII
Howes, George Bond, 1853–1905, vol. I
Howes, Henry William, 1896–1978, vol. VII
Howes, Rear-Adm. Peter Norris, 1916–1983, vol. VIII
Howes, Brig. Sidney Gerald, died 1961, vol. VI
Howes, Maj.-Gen. William, 1838–1924, vol. II
Howgill, Richard John Frederick, 1895–1975, vol. VII
Howgrave-Graham, Hamilton Maurice, 1882–1963, vol. VI
Howick of Glendale, 1st Baron, 1903–1973, vol. VII
Howie, Hon. Sir Archibald, 1879–1943, vol. IV
Howie, Sir James William, 1907–1995, vol. IX
Howie, Rev. Robert, 1836–1918, vol. II
Howie, Thomas McIntyre, 1926–1986, vol. VIII
Howison, George Holmes, 1834–1916, vol. II
Howitt, Sir Alfred Bakewell, 1879–1954, vol. V

Howitt, Alfred William, 1830–1908, vol. I
Howitt, Cecil; see Howitt, T. C.
Howitt, Charles Roberts, 1894–1969, vol. VI
Howitt, Frank Dutch, 1894–1954, vol. V
Howitt, Sir Harold Gibson, 1886–1969, vol. VI
Howitt, (Thomas) Cecil, 1889–1968, vol. VI
Howkins, Col Cyril Henry, 1876–1947, vol. IV
Howland, Hewitt Hanson, 1863–1944, vol. IV
Howland, Oliver Aiken, 1847–1904, vol. I
Howland, Robert Leslie, 1905–1986, vol. VIII
Howland, William Bailey, 1849–1917, vol. II
Howland, Hon. William Goldwin Carrington, 1915–1994, vol. IX
Howland, Hon. Sir William Pierce, 1811–1907, vol. I
Howles, Leonard, 1896–1957, vol. V
Howlett, Charles Edgar, 1854–1939, vol. III
Howlett, Edmund Henry, 1854–1930, vol. III
Howlett, Jack, 1912–1999, vol. X
Howlett, Rt Rev. Mgr Martin, 1863–1949, vol. IV
Howlett, Brig. Reginald, 1882–1942, vol. IV
Howlett, Reginald, 1908–1969, vol. VI
Howlett, Richard, 1841–1917, vol. II
Howley, Major Jasper Joseph, 1868–1915, vol. I
Howley, John F. W., 1866–1941, vol. IV
Howley, Most Rev. Michael Francis, 1843–1914, vol. I
Howley, Richard Joseph, died 1955, vol. V
Howley, William John Joseph, 1865–1948, vol. IV
Howley, William Richard, 1875–1941, vol. IV
Howman, Brig. Ross Cosens, 1899–1976, vol. VII
Howorth, Col Henry Godfrey, 1870–1947, vol. IV
Howorth, Sir Henry Hoyle, 1842–1923, vol. II
Howorth, Sir Rupert Beswicke, 1880–1964, vol. VI
Howsam, Air Vice-Marshal George Roberts, 1895–1988, vol. VIII
Howse, Derek; see Howse, H. D.
Howse, Francis, 1851–1925, vol. II
Howse, Sir Henry Greenway, 1841–1914, vol. I
Howse, Lt Comdr (Humphrey) Derek, 1919–1998, vol. X
Howse, Maj.-Gen. Hon. Sir Neville Reginald, 1863–1930, vol. III
Howson, G. W. S., died 1919, vol. II
Howson, Brig. Geoffrey, 1883–1961, vol. VI
Howson, Ven. George John, 1854–1943, vol. IV
Howson, Ven. James Francis, 1856–1934, vol. III
Howson, Hon. Comdr John, 1829–1907, vol. I
Howson, Captain John, 1871–1948, vol. IV
Howson, Rear-Adm. John, 1908–1992, vol. IX
Howson, Captain John Montagu, 1893–1959, vol. V
Howth, 4th Earl of, 1827–1909, vol. I
Hoy, Baron (Life Peer); James Hutchison Hoy, 1909–1976, vol. VII
Hoy, Rev. David, 1913–1997, vol. X
Hoy, Col Sir William Wilson, 1868–1930, vol. III
Hoyer-Millar, Dame (Evelyn Louisa) Elizabeth, 1910–1984, vol. VIII
Hoyes, Thomas, 1935–1997, vol. X
Hoyland, Harold Allan Dilke, 1885–1959, vol. V
Hoyland, John S., 1887–1957, vol. V
Hoyle, Arthur, born 1857, vol. III
Hoyle, Lt-Col Sir Emmanuel, 1st Bt, 1866–1939, vol. III
Hoyle, Ven. Frederick James, 1918–1994, vol. IX

Hoyle, George, 1900–1979, vol. VII
Hoyle, Hon. Henry Clement, 1852–1926, vol. II
Hoyle, J. Rossiter, 1856–1926, vol. II
Hoyle, John Clifford, 1901–1976, vol. VII
Hoyle, William Evans, died 1926, vol. II
Hoyles, Newman Wright, 1844–1928, vol. II
Hoysted, Col Desmond Murree Fitzgerald, 1874–1945, vol. IV
Hozier, Col Sir Henry Montague, 1838–1907, vol. I
Hozumi, Baron Nobushige, 1855–1926, vol. II, vol. III
Hrdlicka, Aleš, 1869–1943, vol. IV
Hsiung, Shih I, 1902–1991, vol. IX
Hsu Chen-Ping, Rt Rev. Francis, 1920–1974, vol. VII
Huban, Maj.-Gen. John Patrick, 1891–1957, vol. V
Hubback, Brig.-Gen. Arthur Benison, 1871–1948, vol. IV
Hubback, Vice-Adm. Sir (Arthur) Gordon Voules, 1902–1970, vol. VI
Hubback, David Francis, 1916–1991, vol. IX
Hubback, Mrs Eva M., 1886–1949, vol. IV
Hubback, Most Rev. George Clay, 1882–1955, vol. V
Hubback, Vice-Adm. Sir Gordon Voules; see Hubback, Vice-Adm. Sir A. G. V.
Hubback, Sir John Austen, 1878–1968, vol. VI
Hubbard, Charles Edward, 1900–1980, vol. VII
Hubbard, Elbert, 1859–1915, vol. I
Hubbard, (Eric) Hesketh, 1892–1957, vol. V
Hubbard, Hon. Evelyn, 1852–1934, vol. III
Hubbard, George, 1859–1936, vol. III
Hubbard, George William, 1870–1939, vol. III
Hubbard, Rt Rev. Harold Evelyn, 1883–1953, vol. V
Hubbard, Hesketh; see Hubbard, E. H.
Hubbard, Cdre Lancelot Fortescue; see Hubbard, Cdre R. L. F.
Hubbard, Louisa Maria, 1836–1906, vol. I
Hubbard, Percival Cyril, 1902–1961, vol. VI
Hubbard, Cdre (Robert) Lancelot Fortescue, 1887–1972, vol. VII
Hubbard, Bey Robert Richard, 1843–1926, vol. II, vol. III
Hubbard, Thomas Frederick, 1898–1961, vol. VI
Hubbard, William Egerton, died 1918, vol. II
Hubble, Sir Douglas Vernon, 1900–1981, vol. VIII
Hubble, Edwin Powell, 1889–1953, vol. V
Huberman, Bronislaw, 1882–1947, vol. IV
Hubrecht, J. B., 1883–1978, vol. VII
Hucker, Ernest George, 1908–1986, vol. VIII
Huckin, Victor Henry St John, 1880–1943, vol. IV
Huckle, Sir George; see Huckle, Sir H. G.
Huckle, Sir (Henry) George, 1914–1995, vol. IX
Hudd, Hon. Sir Herbert Sydney, 1881–1948, vol. IV
Hudd, Walter, 1898–1963, vol. VI
Huddie, Sir David Patrick, 1916–1998, vol. X
Huddleston, Sir Arthur James Croft, 1880–1948, vol. IV
Huddleston, Lady Diana De Vere, died 1905, vol. I
Huddleston, Most Rev. (Ernest Urban) Trevor, 1913–1998, vol. X
Huddleston, Captain Sir Ernest Whiteside, 1874–1959, vol. V
Huddleston, George, 1862–1944, vol. IV

Huddleston, Maj.-Gen. Sir Hubert Jervoise, 1880–1950, vol. IV
Huddleston, Sisley, 1883–1952, vol. V
Huddleston, Most Rev. Trevor; see Huddleston, Most Rev. E. U. T.
Huddleston, Tristram Frederick Croft, 1848–1936, vol. III
Huddleston, Captain Willoughby Baynes, 1866–1953, vol. V
Hu Dingyi, 1922–1994, vol. X (AI)
Hudleston, Ven. Cuthbert, died 1944, vol. IV
Hudleston, Air Chief Marshal Sir Edmund Cuthbert, 1908–1994, vol. IX
Hudleston, Lt-Gen. John Wallace, 1880–1961, vol. VI
Hudleston, Wilfred H., 1828–1909, vol. I
Hudleston, Col Wilfrid Edward, 1872–1952, vol. V
Hudon, Lt-Col Joseph Alfred George, 1858–1918, vol. II, vol. III
Hudson, 1st Viscount, 1886–1957, vol. V
Hudson, 2nd Viscount, 1924–1963 (this entry was not transferred to Who was Who).
Hudson, Albert Blellock, 1875–1947, vol. IV
Hudson, Alfred Arthur, died 1930, vol. III
Hudson, Arthur, 1861–1948, vol. IV
Hudson, Arthur Cyril, 1875–1962, vol. VI
Hudson, Col Arthur Ross, 1876–1963, vol. VI
Hudson, Rt Rev. Arthur William Goodwin, 1906–1985, vol. VIII
Hudson, Sir Austin Uvedale Morgan, 1st Bt, 1897–1956, vol. V
Hudson, Bernard, 1877–1957, vol. V
Hudson, Brig. Charles Edward, 1892–1959, vol. V
Hudson, Charles Thomas, 1828–1903, vol. I
Hudson, Lt-Col Charles Tilson, 1865–1948, vol. IV
Hudson, Maj.-Gen. Corrie, 1874–1958, vol. V
Hudson, Rev. Canon Cyril Edward, 1888–1960, vol. V
Hudson, Sir Edmund Peder, 1903–1978, vol. VII
Hudson, Edward, died 1936, vol. III
Hudson, Sir Edward Herbert, 1898–1966, vol. VI
Hudson, Eric Hamilton, 1902–1990, vol. VIII
Hudson, Sir Frank; see Hudson, Sir W. F.
Hudson, George Bickersteth, 1845–1912, vol. I
Hudson, Engr Rear-Adm. George William, 1861–1941, vol. IV
Hudson, H. Lindsay, (Harry Lindsay), died 1926, vol. II
Hudson, Harry Kynoch, 1867–1958, vol. V
Hudson, Gen. Sir Havelock, 1862–1944, vol. IV
Hudson, Sir Havelock Henry Trevor, 1919–1996, vol. X
Hudson, Lt-Col Henry Cecil Harland, 1885–1929, vol. III
Hudson, James Frank, 1872–1949, vol. IV
Hudson, James Hindle, 1881–1962, vol. VI
Hudson, Rev. Joseph, 1834–1919, vol. II
Hudson, Sir Leslie S., 1872–1946, vol. IV
Hudson, Manley Ottmer, 1886–1960, vol. V
Hudson, Mary Elizabeth, (Lady Hudson), 1867–1963, vol. VI
Hudson, Maurice William Petre, 1901–1992, vol. IX
Hudson, Rt Rev. Noel Baring, 1893–1970, vol. VI
Hudson, Col Percy, 1876–1955, vol. V
Hudson, Lt-Gen. Sir Peter, 1923–2000, vol. X

Hudson, Lt-Col Ralph Charles D.; see Donaldson-Hudson.
Hudson, Ralph Milbanke, 1849–1938, vol. III
Hudson, Rev. Robert, 1862–1936, vol. III
Hudson, Major Robert Arthur, 1880–1917, vol. II
Hudson, Sir Robert Arundell, 1864–1927, vol. II
Hudson, Robert George Spencer, 1895–1965, vol. VI
Hudson, Hon. Sir Robert James, 1885–1963, vol. VI
Hudson, Rowland Skeffington, 1900–1980, vol. VII
Hudson, R(upert) Vaughan, 1895–1967, vol. VI
Hudson, Sidney Rowland, 1897–1966, vol. VI
Hudson, Brig. Stanley Grey, 1902–1960, vol. V
Hudson, Stephen, died 1944, vol. IV
Hudson, Brig.-Gen. Thomas Roe Christopher, 1866–1940, vol. III
Hudson, Rev. Thomas William, 1861–1929, vol. III
Hudson, Sir William Brereton, 1843–1914, vol. I
Hudson, William Henry, 1841–1922, vol. II
Hudson, Walter, 1852–1935, vol. III
Hudson, Sir (Walter) Frank, 1875–1958, vol. V
Hudson, Walter Richard Austen, 1894–1970, vol. VI
Hudson, Rt Rev. Wilfrid John, 1904–1981, vol. VIII
Hudson, Lt-Col William, 1880–1967, vol. VI
Hudson, Sir William, 1896–1978, vol. VII
Hudson, William Henry, 1862–1918, vol. II
Hudson, William Henry Hoar, 1838–1915, vol. I
Hudson, William Meredith Fisher, 1916–1995, vol. IX
Hudson-Davies, Sir Alan Meredyth, 1901–1975, vol. VII
Hudson-Kinahan, Sir Edward Hudson; see Kinahan.
Hudson-Kinahan, Lt-Col George Frederick, 1879–1939, vol. III
Hudson-Kinahan, Sir Robert Henry; see Kinahan.
Hudson-Williams, Harri Llwyd, 1911–1998, vol. X
Hudson-Williams, Thomas, 1873–1961, vol. VI
Hudspeth, Major Henry Moore, 1886–1971, vol. VII
Hueffer, Oliver Madox, died 1931, vol. III
Huffam, Major James Palmer, 1897–1968, vol. VI
Hufton, Philip Arthur, 1911–1974, vol. VII
Hügel, Anatole, Baron von, 1854–1928, vol. II
Hügel, Friedrich, Baron von, 1852–1925, vol. II
Hugessen, Adrian Norton K.; see Knatchbull-Hugessen.
Hugessen, Herbert Thomas K.; see Knatchbull-Hugessen.
Hugessen, Sir Hughe Montgomery K.; see Knatchbull-Hugessen.
Huggard, Sir Walter Clarence, died 1957, vol. V
Huggett, Arthur St George Joseph McCarthy, 1897–1968, vol. VI
Huggett, Esther Margaret; see Killick, E. M.
Huggill, Henry Percy, 1886–1957, vol. V
Huggins, Brig.-Gen. Alfred, 1884–1959, vol. V
Huggins, Charles Brenton, 1901–1997, vol. X
Huggins, Sir George Frederick, died 1941, vol. IV
Huggins, Lt-Col Henry William, 1891–1965, vol. VI
Huggins, Sir John, 1891–1971, vol. VII
Huggins, Kenneth Herbert, 1908–1993, vol. IX
Huggins, Margaret Lindsay, (Lady Huggins), 1849–1915, vol. I
Huggins, Peter Jeremy William; see Brett, Jeremy.

Huggins, Lt-Col Ponsonby Glenn, 1857–1925, vol. II
Huggins, Sir William, 1824–1910, vol. I
Hugh-Jones, Evan Bonnor, 1890–1978, vol. VII
Hugh-Jones, Llewelyn Arthur, 1888–1970, vol. VI
Hugh-Jones, Siriol (Mary Aprille), (Siriol Hart), 1924–1964, vol. VI
Hughan, Adm. Sir Arthur John H.; see Henniker-Hughan.
Hughes, Baron (Life Peer); William Hughes, 1911–1999, vol. X
Hughes, Rt Rev. Albert Edward, 1878–1954, vol. V
Hughes, Albert Henry, 1917–1985, vol. VIII
Hughes, Sir Alfred, 9th Bt (cr 1773), 1825–1898, vol. I
Hughes, Alfred, 1860–1940, vol. III
Hughes, Alfred James, died 1947, vol. IV
Hughes, Andrew Anderson, 1915–1992, vol. IX
Hughes, Col Arbuthnott James, 1856–1945, vol. IV
Hughes, Brig. Archibald Cecil, 1886–1961, vol. VI
Hughes, Captain Arthur Beckett, 1873–1925, vol. II
Hughes, Arthur John, 1843–1910, vol. I
Hughes, Maj. Arthur John, 1914–1984, vol. VIII
Hughes, Arthur Montague D'Urban, 1873–1974, vol. VII
Hughes, Major Basil, 1878–1953, vol. V
Hughes, Maj.-Gen. Basil Perronet, 1903–1989, vol. VIII
Hughes, Brodie; see Hughes, E. B. C.
Hughes, Cecil Hugh Myddleton, died 1960, vol. V
Hughes, Charles Evans, 1862–1948, vol. IV
Hughes, Maj.-Gen. Charles Frederick, 1844–1932, vol. III
Hughes, Sir Collingwood, 10th Bt (cr 1773), 1854–1932, vol. III
Hughes, Collingwood, 1872–1963, vol. VI
Hughes, Col Cyril E., 1890–1958, vol. V
Hughes, David Arthur, 1905–1968, vol. VI
Hughes, David Edward, 1831–1900, vol. I
Hughes, David Leslie, 1912–1990, vol. VIII
Hughes, Air Vice-Marshal Desmond; see Hughes, Air Vice-Marshal F. D.
Hughes, Donald Wynn, 1911–1967, vol. VI
Hughes, Col Edmund Locock, 1880–1945, vol. IV
Hughes, Rev. Edward, died 1910, vol. I
Hughes, Edward, 1899–1965, vol. VI
Hughes, Edward David, 1906–1963, vol. VI
Hughes, Captain Edward Glyn de Styrap J.; see Jukes Hughes.
Hughes, Captain Edward Llewellyn, 1875–1955, vol. V
Hughes, Rev. Edward Marshall, 1913–1992, vol. IX
Hughes, Edward R., died 1908, vol. I
Hughes, Sir Edward Stuart Reginald, 1919–1999, vol. X
Hughes, Col Edward Talfourd, 1855–1943, vol. IV (A), vol. V
Hughes, Col Sir Edwin, 1832–1904, vol. I
Hughes, Elizabeth Phillipps, 1851–1925, vol. II
Hughes, Col Emilius, 1844–1926, vol. II
Hughes, Emmet John, 1920–1982, vol. VIII
Hughes, Emrys, 1894–1969, vol. VI
Hughes, (Ernest) Brodie (Cobbett), 1913–1989, vol. VIII
Hughes, Rev. Ernest Richard, 1883–1956, vol. V

Hughes, Rev. Ernest Selwyn, 1860–1942, vol. IV
Hughes, Evan, 1882–1951, vol. V
Hughes, Air Vice-Marshal (Frederick) Desmond, 1919–1992, vol. IX
Hughes, Maj.-Gen. Frederick Godfrey, 1857–1944, vol. IV
Hughes, Very Rev. Frederick Llewelyn, 1894–1967, vol. VI
Hughes, G. Bernard, died 1975, vol. VII
Hughes, Maj.-Gen. Garnet Burk, 1880–1937, vol. III
Hughes, George, 1937–1998, vol. X
Hughes, Col George Arthur, 1851–1926, vol. II
Hughes, Hon. George Edward, 1854–1937, vol. III
Hughes, George Lewis Hollingsworth, 1876–1932, vol. III
Hughes, George Ravensworth, 1888–1983, vol. VIII
Hughes, Brig. Gerald Birdwood V.; see Vaughan-Hughes.
Hughes, Gerald Stephen, 1878–1959, vol. V
Hughes, Captain Guy D'O.; see D'Oyly-Hughes.
Hughes, Guy Erskine, 1904–1980, vol. VII
Hughes, Rev. Harold, 1884–1950, vol. IV
Hughes, Hector, died 1970, vol. VI
Hughes, Maj.-Gen. Henry Bernard Wylde, 1887–1953, vol. V
Hughes, Henry Harold, died 1940, vol. III
Hughes, Rear-Adm. Henry Hugh, 1911–1986, vol. VIII
Hughes, Rev. Henry Maldwyn, 1875–1940, vol. III
Hughes, Brig.-Gen. Henry Thoresby, 1873–1947, vol. IV
Hughes, Rev. H(enry) Trevor, 1910–1988, vol. VIII
Hughes, Herbert, 1853–1917, vol. II
Hughes, Herbert Delauney, 1914–1995, vol. IX
Hughes, Major Herbert Francis, died 1939, vol. III
Hughes, H(ugh) L(lewelyn) Glyn, 1892–1973, vol. VII
Hughes, Rev. Hugh Price, 1847–1902, vol. I
Hughes, Hugh Robert, 1827–1911, vol. I
Hughes, Maj.-Gen. Ivor Thomas Percival, 1897–1962, vol. VI
Hughes, James John, 1874–1952, vol. V
Hughes, John, 1850–1932, vol. III
Hughes, Col John Arthur, 1860–1938, vol. III
Hughes, John David Ivor, 1885–1969, vol. VI
Hughes, Rt Rev. John George Hughes, 1935–1994, vol. IX
Hughes, Col John Gethin, 1866–1954, vol. V
Hughes, Captain John Grant Duncan-, 1882–1962, vol. VI
Hughes, Rt Rev. John Richard Worthington P.; see Poole Hughes.
Hughes, John Rowland, 1856–1937, vol. III
Hughes, John Turnbull, 1919–1977, vol. VII
Hughes, John Williams Gwynne-, 1858–1917, vol. II
Hughes, Joseph John, 1928–1976, vol. VII
Hughes, Rt Rev. Joshua Pritchard, 1847–1938, vol. III
Hughes, Katherine, died 1931, vol. III
Hughes, Rev. Levi Gethin, 1885–1953, vol. V
Hughes, Rev. Llewelyn Robert, died 1925, vol. II
Hughes, Mark; see Hughes, W. M.
Hughes, Dame Mary Ethel, died 1958, vol. V
Hughes, Mary Katherine H. P.; see Price Hughes.

Hughes, Myra Kathleen, *died* 1918, vol. II
Hughes, Rev. Nathaniel Thomas, 1834–1913, vol. I
Hughes, Paul Grant, 1928–1985, vol. VIII
Hughes, Sir Reginald Johnasson, 11th Bt (*cr* 1773), 1882–1945, vol. IV
Hughes, Reginald Richard M.; *see* Meyric Hughes.
Hughes, Ven. Richard, 1881–1962, vol. VI
Hughes, Richard Arthur Warren, 1900–1976, vol. VII
Hughes, Sir Richard Edgar, 13th Bt (*cr* 1773), 1897–1970, vol. VI
Hughes, Captain Robert Herbert Wilfrid, 1872–1936, vol, III
Hughes, Sir Robert Heywood, 12th Bt (*cr* 1773), 1865–1951, vol. V
Hughes, Sir Robert John, 1822–1904, vol. I
Hughes, Air Marshal Sir Rochford; *see* Hughes, Air Marshal Sir S. W. R.
Hughes, Ronw Moelwyn, 1897–1955, vol. V
Hughes, Hon. Lt-Gen. Hon. Sir Sam, 1853–1921, vol. II
Hughes, Rev. Samuel William, 1874–1954, vol. V
Hughes, Sean Francis, 1946–1990, vol. VIII
Hughes, Air Marshal Sir (Sidney Weetman) Rochford, 1914–1996, vol. X
Hughes, Spencer Leigh, 1858–1920, vol. II
Hughes, Sydney Herbert George, 1879–1962, vol. VI
Hughes, Talbot, 1869–1942, vol. IV
Hughes, Ted, 1930–1998, vol. X
Hughes, Sir Thomas, 1838–1923, vol. II
Hughes, Hon. Sir Thomas, 1863–1930, vol. III
Hughes, Sir Thomas, 1863–1942, vol. IV
Hughes, Thomas Cann, 1860–1948, vol. IV
Hughes, Mrs Thomas H. R., *died* 1930, vol. III
Hughes, Sir Thomas Harrison, 1st Bt (*cr* 1942), 1881–1958, vol. V
Hughes, Thomas Lewis, 1897–1980, vol. VII
Hughes, Thomas M'Kenny, *died* 1917, vol. II
Hughes, Rt Rev. Thomas Maurice, 1895–1981, vol. VIII
Hughes, Sir Thomas Raffles, 1856–1938, vol. III
Hughes, Rev. W. Worthington P.; *see* Poole-Hughes.
Hughes, Sir Walter Charleton, 1850–1922, vol. II
Hughes, Rev. Walter Octavius Marsh, *died* 1931, vol. III
Hughes, Walter Tatham, 1849–1917, vol. II
Hughes, Hon. Sir Wilfrid (Selwyn) Kent, 1895–1970, vol. VI
Hughes, Maj.-Gen. William Dillon, 1900–1999, vol. X
Hughes, William Henry, 1915–1990, vol. VIII
Hughes, Bt Col William Hesketh, 1872–1940, vol. III
Hughes, Rt Rev. William James, *died* 1979, vol. VII
Hughes, (William) Mark, 1932–1993, vol. IX
Hughes, Rt Hon. William Morris, 1864–1952, vol. V
Hughes, William Reginald Noel, 1913–1990, vol. VIII
Hughes, Sir William Templer, 1822–1897, vol. I
Hughes-Buller, Ralph Buller, 1871–1949, vol. IV
Hughes D'Aeth, Rear-Adm. Arthur Cloudesley Shovel, 1875–1956, vol. V

Hughes-Games, Ven. Joshua, 1831–1904, vol. I
Hughes Hallett, Vice Adm. Sir (Cecil) Charles, 1898–1985, vol. VIII
Hughes Hallett, Vice Adm. Sir Charles; *see* Hughes Hallett, Sir Cecil C.
Hughes-Hallett, Col James Wyndham, 1852–1927, vol. II
Hughes-Hallett, Vice-Adm. John, 1901–1972, vol. VII
Hughes-Hallett, Leslie Charles, 1887–1966, vol. VI
Hughes-Hunter, Sir Charles, 1st Bt (*cr* 1906), 1844–1907, did not have an entry in Who's Who,
Hughes-Hunter, Sir William Bulkeley Hughes, 2nd Bt, 1880–1951, vol. V
Hughes-Morgan, Major Sir David, 1st Bt; *see* Morgan.
Hughes-Morgan, Sir John Vernon, 2nd Bt, 1900–1969, vol. VI
Hughes-Onslow, Sir Geoffrey Henry, 1893–1971, vol. VII
Hughes-Onslow, Henry, 1871–1932, vol. III
Hughes-Parry, Robert, 1895–1986, vol. VIII
Hughes-Roberts, John Gwyndeg, 1894–1949, vol. IV
Hughes-Stanton, Blair Rowlands, 1902–1981, vol. VIII
Hughes-Stanton, Sir Herbert, 1870–1937, vol. III
Hughman, Sir (Ernest) Montague, 1876–1956, vol. V
Hughman, Sir Montague; *see* Hughman, Sir E. M.
Hugill, Rear-Adm. Réné Charles, 1883–1962, vol. VI
Hugo, Lt-Col Edward Victor, 1865–1951, vol. V
Hugo, Lt-Col James Henry, 1870–1943, vol. IV
Hugo, Lt-Col Sir John Mandeville, 1899–2000, vol. X
Huguenet, A. P., *died* 1910, vol. I
Huijsman, Nicolaas Basil Jacques, 1915–1995, vol. IX
Huish, Marcus Bourne, *died* 1921, vol. II
Huish, Sir Raymond Douglas, 1898–1970, vol. VI
Hulbert, Sir Charles, *died* 1932, vol. III
Hulbert, Rev. Charles Augustus, 1838–1919, vol. II
Hulbert, Dame Cicely; *see* Courtneidge, Dame Cicely.
Hulbert, Claude Noel, 1900–1964, vol. VI
Hulbert, Jack; *see* Hulbert, J. N.
Hulbert, John Norman, (Jack), 1892–1978, vol. VII
Hulbert, Wing Comdr Sir Norman John, 1903–1972, vol. VII
Hulett, Hon. Sir (James) Liege, 1838–1928, vol. II
Hulett, Hon. Sir Liege; *see* Hulett, Hon. Sir J. L.
Hulin de Loo, Georges Charles Nicolas Marie, 1862–1946, vol. IV
Hull, Arthur Eaglefield, 1876–1928, vol. II
Hull, Maj.-Gen. Sir Charles Patrick Amyatt, 1865–1920, vol. II
Hull, Cordell, 1871–1955, vol. V
Hull, Edward, 1829–1917, vol. II
Hull, Eleanor H., 1860–1935, vol. III
Hull, Hon. Henry Charles, 1860–1932, vol. III
Hull, Henry Mitchell, 1861–1946, vol. IV
Hull, Surg. Rear-Adm. Herbert Richard Barnes, 1886–1970, vol. VI
Hull, Sir Hubert, 1887–1976, vol. VII

Hull, Lt-Col Hubert Charles Edward, 1891–1939, vol. III
Hull, Sir Percy Clarke, *died* 1968, vol. VI
Hull, Field Marshal Sir Richard Amyatt, 1907–1989, vol. VIII
Hull, Comdr Thomas A., *died* 1904, vol. I
Hullah, John, 1876–1955, vol. V
Hullah-Brown, J., 1875–1973, vol. VII
Hulme, Hon. Sir Alan Shallcross, 1907–1989, vol. VIII
Hulme, Alfred Clive, 1911–1982, vol. VIII
Hulme, Edward Maslin, 1869–1951, vol. V
Hulme, Frederick Edward, 1841–1909, vol. I
Hulme, Henry Rainsford, 1908–1991, vol. IX
Hulme, Maj.-Gen. Jerrie Anthony, 1935–1995, vol. IX
Hulme, Rev. Thomas Ferrier, 1856–1942, vol. IV
Hulme-Moir, Rt Rev. Francis Oag, 1910–1979, vol. VII
Hulme Taylor, Col Jack, 1894–1970, vol. VI
Hulse, Sir Edward, 5th Bt, 1809–1899, vol. I
Hulse, Sir Edward Hamilton Westrow, 7th Bt, 1889–1915, vol. I
Hulse, Sir Edward Henry, 6th Bt, 1859–1903, vol. I
Hulse, Sir Hamilton, 8th Bt, 1864–1931, vol. III
Hulse, Sir (Hamilton) Westrow, 9th Bt, 1909–1996, vol. X
Hulse, Sir Westrow; *see* Hulse, Sir H. W.
Hulton, Sir Edward, 1st Bt (*cr* 1921), 1869–1925, vol. II
Hulton, Sir Edward George Warris, 1906–1988, vol. VIII
Hulton, Col Frederick Courtenay Longuet, 1864–1940, vol. III (A), vol. IV
Hulton, Sir Geoffrey Alan, 4th Bt (*cr* 1905), 1920–1993, vol. IX
Hulton, Rev. Henry Edward, 1839–1922, vol. II
Hulton, Lt-Col Henry Horne, 1882–1941, vol. IV
Hulton, John, 1915–1992, vol. IX
Hulton, Col John Meredith, 1882–1942, vol. IV
Hulton, Sir Roger Braddyll, 3rd Bt (*cr* 1905), 1891–1956, vol. V
Hulton, Sir William Rothwell, 2nd Bt (*cr* 1905), 1868–1943, vol. IV
Hulton, Sir William Wilbraham Blethyn, 1st Bt (*cr* 1905), 1844–1907, vol. I
Hulton-Harrop, William Edward Montagu, 1848–1916, vol. II
Hulton-Harrop, Maj.-Gen. William Harrington, 1906–1979, vol. VII
Humble, Joseph Graeme, 1913–1980, vol. VII
Humble-Burkitt, Col Bernard Maynard, 1864–1945, vol. IV
Humble-Crofts, Rev. William John, 1846–1924, vol. II
Humby, Lt-Col James Frederick, 1860–1943, vol. IV
Hume, Alexander Williamson, 1850–1925, vol. II, vol. III
Hume, Allan Octavian, 1829–1912, vol. I
Hume, Basil; *see* Hume, J. B.
Hume, His Eminence Cardinal Basil; *see* Hume, His Eminence Cardinal G. B.
Hume, Col Charles Vernon, 1860–1915, vol. I

Hume, Major Charles Westley, 1886–1981, vol. VIII
Hume, Fergus, 1859–1932, vol. III
Hume, George Alexander, 1860–1905, vol. I
Hume, His Eminence Cardinal (George) Basil, 1923–1999, vol. X
Hume, George Haliburton, 1845–1923, vol. II
Hume, Sir George Hopwood, 1866–1946, vol. IV
Hume, Sir (Hubert) Nutcombe, 1893–1967, vol. VI
Hume, James Gibson, 1860–1949, vol. IV, vol. V
Hume, John Basil, 1893–1974, vol. VII
Hume, Col John Edward, 1866–1939, vol. III
Hume, Brig.-Gen. John James Francis, 1858–1935, vol. III
Hume, Maj.-Gen. John Richard, 1831–1906, vol. I
Hume, Major Martin Andrew Sharp, 1847–1910, vol. I
Hume, Sir Nutcombe; *see* Hume, Sir H. N.
Hume, Brig. Reginald Vernon, 1898–1960, vol. V
Hume, Sir Robert, 1828–1909, vol. I
Hume, Thomas Andrew, 1917–1992, vol. IX
Hume, Sir William Errington, 1879–1960, vol. V
Hume, William Fraser, 1867–1949, vol. IV
Hume, Lt-Col William James Parke, 1866–1952, vol. V
Hume-Campbell, Sir John Home-Purves; *see* Campbell.
Hume-Cook, Hon. James, 1866–1942, vol. IV
Hume-Rothery, William, 1899–1968, vol. VI
Hume-Spry, Lt-Col Leighton; *see* Spry.
Hume-Williams, Rt Hon. Sir Ellis, 1st Bt, 1863–1947, vol. IV
Hume-Williams, Sir Roy Ellis, 2nd Bt, 1887–1980, vol. VII
Humfrey, Rev. John B.; *see* Blake-Humfrey.
Humfrey, Lt-Col Richard Edmond, 1881–1962, vol. VI
Hummel, Rt Rev. Francis Ignatius, 1870–1924, vol. II
Humphery, Lt-Col Sir John, 1872–1938, vol. III
Humphery, John Edward, 1873–1946, vol. IV
Humphery, Sir William Henry, 1st Bt, 1827–1909, vol. I
Humphrey, Marshal of the Royal Air Force Sir Andrew Henry, 1921–1977, vol. VII
Humphrey, Basil; *see* Humphrey, F. B.
Humphrey, Douglas, 1880–1945, vol. IV
Humphrey, (Frank) Basil, 1918–1994, vol. IX
Humphrey, George, 1889–1966, vol. VI
Humphrey, George Magoffin, 1890–1970, vol. VI
Humphrey, Herbert Alfred, 1868–1951, vol. V
Humphrey, Hubert Horatio, Jr, 1911–1978, vol. VII
Humphrey, John, 1862–1933, vol. III
Humphrey, John, 1879–1956, vol. V
Humphrey, Rev. John Henry, 1860–1934, vol. III
Humphrey, John Herbert, 1915–1987, vol. VIII
Humphrey, William Gerald, 1904–1995, vol. IX
Humphrey-Davy, Francis Herbert Mountjoy Nelson, *died* 1953, vol. V
Humphreys, Rev. Alfred Edward, 1843–1922, vol. II
Humphreys, Arthur L., 1865–1946, vol. IV
Humphreys, Arthur Raleigh, 1911–1988, vol. VIII
Humphreys, Cecil Lee Howard, 1893–1941, vol. IV
Humphreys, Christmas; *see* Humphreys, T. C.

Humphreys, Colin; *see* Humphreys, D. C.
Humphreys, Major Dashwood William Harrington, 1872–1917, vol. II
Humphreys, (David) Colin, 1925–1992, vol. IX
Humphreys, Lt-Gen. Sir (Edward) Thomas, 1878–1955, vol. V
Humphreys, Brig.-Gen. Gardiner, 1865–1942, vol. IV
Humphreys, George Alfred, *died* 1948, vol. IV
Humphreys, Maj.-Gen. George Charles, 1899–1991, vol. IX
Humphreys, Sir George William, 1863–1945, vol. IV
Humphreys, Gordon Noel, *died* 1966, vol. VI
Humphreys, Engr Rear-Adm. Sir Henry, *died* 1924, vol. II
Humphreys, Hubert, 1878–1967, vol. VI
Humphreys, Humphrey Francis, 1885–1977, vol. VII
Humphreys, John Henry, 1917–1993, vol. IX
Humphreys, John Lisseter, *died* 1929, vol. III
Humphreys, Captain Kenneth Noel, 1881–1955, vol. V
Humphreys, Sir Kenneth Owens, 1918–1981, vol. VIII
Humphreys, Kenneth William, 1916–1994, vol. IX
Humphreys, Sir Myles; *see* Humphreys, Sir. R. E. M.
Humphreys, Noel Algernon, 1837–1923, vol. II
Humphreys, Sir Olliver William, 1902–1996, vol. X
Humphreys, Sir (Raymond Evelyn) Myles, 1925–1998, vol. X
Humphreys, Very Rev. Robert, *died* 1917, vol. II
Humphreys, Robert Arthur, 1907–1999, vol. X
Humphreys, Lt-Gen. Sir Thomas; *see* Humphreys, Lt-Gen. Sir E. T.
Humphreys, Rt Hon. Sir Travers, 1867–1956, vol. V
Humphreys, (Travers) Christmas, 1901–1983, vol. VIII
Humphreys, Mrs W. Desmond; *see* Rita.
Humphreys-Davies, Brian, 1917–1971, vol. VII
Humphreys-Davies, (George) Peter, 1909–1985, vol. VIII
Humphreys-Davies, Peter; *see* Humphreys-Davies, G. P.
Humphreys-Owen, Arthur Charles, 1836–1905, vol. I
Humphries, Albert, 1872–1951, vol. V
Humphries, Sir Albert Edward, *died* 1935, vol. III
Humphries, George James, 1900–1981, vol. VIII
Humphries, Sir Herbert Henry, *died* 1938, vol. III
Humphries, Rev. Canon James Henry, 1890–1962, vol. VI
Humphries, Sir Sidney Richard White, 1857–1941, vol. IV
Humphries, Sydney S.; *see* Sidney-Humphries.
Humphris, Francis Howard, 1866–1947, vol. IV
Humphry, Alfred Paget, 1850–1916, vol. II
Humphry, Mrs C. E., *died* 1925, vol. II
Humphry, Laurence, 1856–1920, vol. II
Humphry, Maj.-Gen. Lawrence, 1875–1931, vol. III
Humphrys, Brig.-Gen. Charles Vesey, 1862–1944, vol. IV
Humphrys, Lt-Col Sir Francis Henry, 1879–1971, vol. VII

Humpidge, Kenneth Palmer, 1902–1987, vol. VIII
Huneker, James Gibbons, 1860–1921, vol. II
Hungarton, 1st Baron, 1890–1966, vol. VI
Hungerford, Sir (Alexander) Wilson, *died* 1969, vol. VI
Hungerford, Margaret Wolfe, *died* 1897, vol. I
Hungerford, Samuel James, 1872–1955, vol. V
Hungerford, Sir Wilson; *see* Hungerford, Sir A. W.
Hunkin, Rt Rev. Joseph Wellington, 1887–1950, vol. IV
Hunloke, Henry Philip, 1906–1978, vol. VII
Hunloke, Major Sir Philip, 1868–1947, vol. IV
Hunn, Sir Jack Kent, 1906–1997, vol. X
Hunn, Major Sydney Arthur, 1889–1942, vol. IV
Hunnings, Gordon, 1926–1986, vol. VIII
Hunsdon of Hunsdon, 1st Baron, 1854–1935, vol. III
Hunsdon of Hunsdon, 2nd Baron; *see* Aldenham, 4th Baron.
Hunt, Baron (Life Peer); Henry Cecil John Hunt, 1910–1998, vol. X
Hunt of Fawley, Baron (Life Peer); John Henderson Hunt, 1905–1987, vol. VIII
Hunt, Dame Agnes Gwendoline, 1866–1948, vol. IV
Hunt, Alan Henderson, 1908–1970, vol. VI
Hunt, Albert, 1863–1957, vol. V
Hunt, Rev. Canon Alfred, 1862–1937, vol. III
Hunt, Adm. Sir (Allen) Thomas, 1866–1943, vol. IV
Hunt, Arthur Surridge, 1871–1934, vol. III
Hunt, Atlee Arthur, 1864–1935, vol. III
Hunt, Cecil Arthur, 1873–1965, vol. VI
Hunt, Rev. David J. Stather, 1856–1929, vol. III
Hunt, Sir David Wathen Stather, 1913–1998, vol. X
Hunt, Rt Rev. Desmond Charles, 1918–1993, vol. IX
Hunt, Edmund Langley, 1868–1925, vol. II
Hunt, Major Edwin Watkin, 1869–1945, vol. IV
Hunt, Frank William, 1870–1955, vol. V
Hunt, Surg. Rear-Adm. Frederick George, 1894–1975, vol. VII
Hunt, Sir Frederick Seager, 1st Bt, 1837–1904, vol. I
Hunt, Brig. Frederick Welsley, 1871–1944, vol. IV
Hunt, Rear-Adm. Geoffrey Harry C.; *see* Carew Hunt.
Hunt, George Henry, 1853–1940, vol. III
Hunt, Captain George Percy Edward, *died* 1917, vol. II
Hunt, Col (George) Vivian, 1905–1979, vol. VII
Hunt, Major Gerald Ponsonby Sneyd, 1877–1918, vol. II
Hunt, Gerard L.; *see* Leigh-Hunt.
Hunt, Gilbert Adams, 1914–1995, vol. IX
Hunt, Rev. H. G. Bonavia, 1847–1917, vol. II
Hunt, Henry Ambrose, 1866–1946, vol. IV
Hunt, Rev. Henry de Vere, 1856–1919, vol. II
Hunt, Herbert James, 1899–1973, vol. VII
Hunt, Hilary Lushington Holman H.; *see* Holman-Hunt.
Hunt, Hubert Walter, 1865–1945, vol. IV
Hunt, Hugh Sydney, 1911–1993, vol. IX
Hunt, (Jack) Naylor, 1917–1986, vol. VIII
Hunt, James Simon Wallis, 1947–1993, vol. IX
Hunt, Sir John, 1859–1945, vol. IV

Hunt, John Francis, 1906–1979, vol. VII
Hunt, Sir John Joseph, *died* 1933, vol. III
Hunt, John Middlemass, 1858–1932, vol. III
Hunt, Lt-Col John Patrick, 1875–1938, vol. III
Hunt, Col John Philip, 1907–1970, vol. VI
Hunt, Joseph, 1854–1936, vol. III
Hunt, Sir Joseph Anthony, 1905–1982, vol. VIII
Hunt, Kevan, 1937–1999, vol. X
Hunt, Margaret, 1831–1912, vol. I
Hunt, Martita, 1900–1969, vol. VI
Hunt, Sir Peter John, 1933–1997, vol. X
Hunt, Gen. Sir Peter Mervyn, 1916–1988, vol. VIII
Hunt, Ralph Holmes V.; *see* Vernon-Hunt.
Hunt, Reginald Heber, 1891–1982, vol. VIII
Hunt, Lt-Col Reginald Seager, 1874–1942, vol. IV
Hunt, Richard Henry, 1912–1998, vol. X
Hunt, Sir Reuben James, 1888–1970, vol. VI
Hunt, Richard William, 1908–1979, vol. VII
Hunt, Maj.-Gen. Robert Augustus Carew, 1838–1935, vol. III
Hunt, Comdr Robert Gregory Maze Durrant, 1886–1937, vol. III
Hunt, Roger, 1935–1999, vol. X
Hunt, Captain Roland Cecil C.; *see* Carew Hunt.
Hunt, Roland Charles Colin, 1916–1999, vol. X
Hunt, Rowland, 1858–1943, vol. IV
Hunt, Stanley Herbert, *died* 1934, vol. III
Hunt, Adm. Sir Thomas; *see* Hunt, Adm. Sir A. T.
Hunt, Thomas, 1854–1929, vol. III
Hunt, Thomas Cecil, 1901–1980, vol. VII
Hunt, Lt-Col Thomas Edward C.; *see* Carew-Hunt.
Hunt, Rev. Thomas Hankey, 1842–1921, vol. III
Hunt, Rev. Thomas Henry, 1865–1941, vol. IV
Hunt, Vernon Arthur Moore, 1912–1983, vol. VIII
Hunt, Violet, *died* 1942, vol. IV
Hunt, Violet B.; *see* Brooke-Hunt.
Hunt, Col Vivian; *see* Hunt, Col G. V.
Hunt, Rt Rev. Warren; *see* Hunt, Rt Rev. William W.
Hunt, Rev. William, 1842–1931, vol. III
Hunt, Sir William Duffus, 1867–1939, vol. III
Hunt, Sir William Edgar, 1883–1969, vol. VI
Hunt, William Field, 1900–1981, vol. VIII
Hunt, William H.; *see* Holman-Hunt.
Hunt, Major William Morgan, 1881–1925, vol. II
Hunt, Rt Rev. (William) Warren, 1909–1994, vol. IX
Hunt-Grubbe, Adm. Sir Walter James, 1833–1922, vol. II
Hunte, Joseph Alexander, 1917–1983, vol. X (AI)
Hunter of Newington, Baron (Life Peer); Robert Brockie Hunter, 1915–1994, vol. IX
Hunter, Hon. Lord; William Hunter, 1865–1957, vol. V
Hunter, Adam, 1908–1991, vol. IX
Hunter, (Adam) Kenneth (Fisher), 1920–1996, vol. X
Hunter, Alan, 1912–1995, vol. IX
Hunter, Maj.-Gen. Sir Alan John, 1881–1942, vol. IV
Hunter, Alastair; *see* Hunter, M. I. A.
Hunter, Albert Edward, 1900–1969, vol. VI
Hunter, Sir Alexander Albert, 1920–1996, vol. X
Hunter, Andrew, 1876–1969, vol. VI
Hunter, Rev. Andrew Johnston, 1844–1914, vol. I

Hunter, Rev. Archer George, 1850–1939, vol. III
Hunter, Gen. Sir Archibald, 1856–1936, vol. III
Hunter, Archibald Macbride, 1906–1991, vol. IX
Hunter, Sir Bernard; *see* Hunter, Sir W. B.
Hunter, Lt-Col Cecil Stuart, 1882–1935, vol. III
Hunter, Brig.-Gen. Charles George Woodburn, 1871–1932, vol. III
Hunter, Sir Charles Roderick, 3rd Bt, 1858–1924, vol. II
Hunter, Colin, 1841–1904, vol. I
Hunter, Colin Graeme, 1913–1991, vol. IX
Hunter, Adm. Cuthbert, 1866–1952, vol. V
Hunter, Sir David, 1841–1914, vol. I
Hunter, Hon. David Stronach, 1926–1991, vol. IX
Hunter, Donald, 1898–1978, vol. VII
Hunter, Captain Douglas William, *died* 1918, vol. II
Hunter, Sir Ellis, 1892–1961, vol. VI
Hunter, Sir (Ernest) John, 1912–1983, vol. VIII
Hunter, Col Evan Austin, 1887–1954, vol. V
Hunter, G(eorge) Sherwood, 1882–1920, vol. II
Hunter, Sir George, 1860–1930, vol. III
Hunter, Sir George Burton, 1845–1937, vol. III
Hunter, Maj.-Gen. George Douglas, 1860–1922, vol. II
Hunter, Brig.-Gen. George Gillett, 1864–1930, vol. III
Hunter, Gordon, 1863–1929, vol. III
Hunter, Guy, 1911–1992, vol. IX
Hunter, Hamilton, 1845–1923, vol. II
Hunter, Henry Charles Vicars, 1861–1934, vol. III
Hunter, Henry Hamilton, 1875–1944, vol. IV
Hunter, Air Cdre Henry John Francis, 1893–1966, vol. VI
Hunter, Brig. Henry Noel Alexander, 1881–1964, vol. VI
Hunter, Sir Herbert; *see* Hunter, Sir J. H.
Hunter, Col Sir Herbert Patrick, 1880–1968, vol. VI
Hunter, Ian Basil, 1900–1975, vol. VII
Hunter, James de Graaff, 1881–1967, vol. VI
Hunter, Captain James Edward, 1834–1932, vol. III
Hunter, Sir John; *see* Hunter, Sir E. J.
Hunter, John, 1833–1914, vol. I
Hunter, Rev. John, 1849–1917, vol. II
Hunter, Sir John, 1863–1936, vol. III
Hunter, Rt Rev. John, 1897–1965, vol. VI
Hunter, Sir John Adams, 1890–1962, vol. VI
Hunter, John B., 1890–1951, vol. V
Hunter, John George, 1888–1964, vol. VI
Hunter, Maj.-Gen. John Gunning, 1859–1926, vol. II
Hunter, Sir (John) Herbert, 1864–1930, vol. III
Hunter, Hon. John McEwan, 1863–1940, vol. III (A), vol. IV
Hunter, Sir (John) Mark (Somers), 1865–1932, vol. III
Hunter, Lt-Col John Muir, 1844–1920, vol. II
Hunter, Joseph, 1875–1935, vol. III
Hunter, Maj. Joseph Charles, 1894–1983, vol. VIII
Hunter, Kenneth; *see* Hunter, A. K. F.
Hunter, Rt Rev. Leslie Stannard, 1890–1983, vol. VIII
Hunter, Louis, 1899–1986, vol. VIII
Hunter, Louis Lucien, 1889–1959, vol. V
Hunter, Sir Mark; *see* Hunter, Sir J. M. S.
Hunter, (Mark Ian) Alastair, 1909–1983, vol. VIII

Hunter, Matthew, *died* 1941, vol. IV
Hunter, Captain Michael John, 1891–1951, vol. V
Hunter, Norman Charles, 1908–1971, vol. VII
Hunter, Rev. Peter Hay, 1854–1909, vol. I
Hunter, Peter Sinclair, 1883–1954, vol. V
Hunter, Philip Vassar, 1883–1956, vol. V
Hunter, Sir Robert, 1844–1913, vol. I
Hunter, Robert Lewin, 1852–1942, vol. IV
Hunter, Samuel Robert, 1877–1948, vol. IV
Hunter, Summers, 1856–1940, vol. III
Hunter, Sir Summers, 1890–1963, vol. VI
Hunter, Sir Thomas, 1850–1919, vol. II
Hunter, Sir Thomas, 1872–1953, vol. V
Hunter, Lt-Col Thomas, 1873–1965, vol. VI
Hunter, Sir Thomas Alexander, 1876–1953, vol. V
Hunter, Sir Thomas Anderson, *died* 1958, vol. V
Hunter, Thomas Briggs, *died* 1957, vol. V
Hunter, Trevor Havard, *died* 1960, vol. V
Hunter, Walter King, 1867–1947, vol. IV
Hunter, William; *see* Hunter, Hon. Lord.
Hunter, William, 1861–1937, vol. III
Hunter, William, *died* 1967, vol. VI
Hunter, William Alexander, 1844–1898, vol. I
Hunter, Sir (William) Bernard, 1868–1924, vol. II
Hunter, Sir William Bulkeley Hughes H.; *see* Hughes-Hunter.
Hunter, William George, 1869–1950, vol. IV (A)
Hunter, Sir William Guyer, 1829–1902, vol. I
Hunter, Sir William Henry, 1849–1917, vol. II
Hunter, Sir William Wilson, 1840–1900, vol. I
Hunter-Blair, Rt Rev. Sir David, 5th Bt, 1853–1939, vol. III
Hunter-Blair, Captain Sir Edward, 6th Bt, 1858–1945, vol. IV
Hunter Blair, Sir James, 7th Bt, 1889–1985, vol. VIII
Hunter Blair, Peter, 1912–1982, vol. VIII
Hunter-Blair, Maj.-Gen. Walter Charles, 1860–1938, vol. III
Hunter-Rodwell, Sir Cecil; *see* Rodwell.
Hunter-Tod, Air Marshal Sir John Hunter, 1917–2000, vol. X
Hunter-Weston, Lt-Gen. Sir Aylmer, 1864–1940, vol. III
Hunter-Weston, Lt-Col Gould, 1823–1904, vol. I
Hunting, (Charles) Patrick (Maule), 1910–1993, vol. IX
Hunting, Clive; *see* Hunting, L. C.
Hunting, (Gerald) Lindsay, 1891–1966, vol. VI
Hunting, Lindsay; *see* Hunting, G. L.
Hunting, (Lindsay) Clive, 1925–2000, vol. X
Hunting, Patrick; *see* Hunting, C. P. M.
Hunting, Sir Percy Llewellyn, 1885–1973, vol. VII
Hunting, Richard Haigh, 1927–1988, vol. VIII
Huntingdon, 14th Earl of, 1868–1939, vol. III
Huntingdon, 15th Earl of, 1901–1990, vol. VIII
Huntingfield, 3rd Baron, 1818–1897, vol. I
Huntingfield, 4th Baron, 1842–1915, vol. I
Huntingfield, 5th Baron, 1883–1969, vol. VI
Huntingfield, 6th Baron, 1915–1994, vol. IX
Huntingford, Lt-Col Walter Legh, 1882–1933, vol. III
Huntington, Archer Milton, 1870–1955, vol. V
Huntington, Major Arthur William, 1871–1933, vol. III

Huntington, Sir Charles Philip, 1st Bt, 1833–1906, vol. I
Huntington, Sir Charles Philip, 3rd Bt, 1888–1928, vol. II
Huntington, Emily Mabel, *died* 1948, vol. IV
Huntington, Henry Edwards, 1850–1927, vol. II
Huntington, Sir Henry Leslie, 2nd Bt, 1885–1907, vol. I
Huntington-Whiteley, Sir Herbert; *see* Whiteley.
Huntington-Whiteley, Captain Sir (Herbert) Maurice, 2nd Bt, 1896–1975, vol. VII
Huntington-Whiteley, Captain Sir Maurice; *see* Huntington-Whiteley, Captain Sir H. M.
Huntley, Arthur Geoffrey, 1897–1980, vol. VII (AII)
Huntly, 11th Marquess of, 1847–1937, vol. III
Huntly, 12th Marquess of, 1908–1987, vol. VIII
Huntly, Frances E.; *see* Mayne, Ethel Colburn.
Hunton, Sidney W., *died* 1941, vol. IV
Hunton, Gen. Sir Thomas Lionel, 1885–1970, vol. VI
Hurcomb, 1st Baron, 1883–1975, vol. VII
Hurd, Baron (Life Peer); Anthony Richard Hurd, 1901–1966, vol. VI
Hurd, Sir Archibald, *died* 1959, vol. V
Hurd, Derrick Guy Edmund, 1928–1986, vol. VIII
Hurd, Sir Percy Angier, *died* 1950, vol. IV
Hurdon, Elizabeth, *died* 1941, vol. IV
Hurlbatt, Ethel, *died* 1934, vol. III
Hurle, Col Edward Forbes Cooke-, 1866–1923, vol. II
Hurle, John A. Cooke-, 1863–1941, vol. IV
Hurley, Ven. Alfred Vincent, 1896–1986, vol. VIII
Hurley, Captain Frank, (James Francis Hurley), 1890–1962, vol. VI
Hurley, Sir Hugh; *see* Hurley, Sir W. H.
Hurley, James Francis; *see* Hurley, Captain Frank.
Hurley, Sir John Garling, 1906–1990, vol. VIII
Hurley, Col Lionel James, 1879–1955, vol. V
Hurley, Sir (Thomas Ernest) Victor, 1888–1958, vol. V
Hurley, Sir Victor; *see* Hurley, Sir T. E. V.
Hurley, Sir (Wilfred) Hugh, 1910–1984, vol. VIII
Hurll, Alfred William, 1905–1991, vol. IX
Hurndall, Brig. Frank Brereton, 1883–1968, vol. VI
Hurok, Sol, 1888–1974, vol. VII
Hurrell, Col Geoffrey Taylor, 1900–1989, vol. VIII
Hurrell, Ian Murray, 1914–1989, vol. VIII
Hurrell, Ven. William Philip, 1860–1952, vol. V
Hurren, Samuel, 1875–1953, vol. V
Hurry, Jamieson Boyd, 1857–1930, vol. III
Hurry, Leslie, 1909–1978, vol. VII
Hurst, Sir Alfred William, 1884–1975, vol. VII
Hurst, Sir Arthur Frederick, 1879–1944, vol. IV
Hurst, Bertram Lawrance, 1875–1943, vol. IV
Hurst, Sir Cecil James Barrington, 1870–1963, vol. VI
Hurst, Charles Chamberlain, 1870–1947, vol. IV
Hurst, Christopher Salkeld, 1886–1963, vol. VI
Hurst, Sir Donald; *see* Hurst, Sir J. H. D.
Hurst, Edward Weston, 1900–1980, vol. VII
Hurst, Fannie, *died* 1968, vol. VI
Hurst, Frank Arnold, 1883–1967, vol. VI
Hurst, Sir Gerald Berkeley, 1877–1957, vol. V
Hurst, Gilbert Harrison John, 1872–1930, vol. III
Hurst, Hal, 1865–1938, vol. III

Hurst, Harold Edwin, 1880–1978, vol. VII
Hurst, Col Herbert Clarence, 1884–1951, vol. V
Hurst, James Edgar, 1893–1959, vol. V
Hurst, Sir (James Henry) Donald, 1895–1980, vol. VII
Hurst, John Gibbard, *died* 1931, vol. III
Hurst, Leonard Henry, 1889–1981, vol. VIII
Hurst, Margery, 1913–1989, vol. VIII
Hurst, Robert, 1915–1996, vol. X
Hurst, Robert H., *died* 1905, vol. I
Hurst, William M.; *see* Martin-Hurst.
Hurstfield, Joel, 1911–1980, vol. VII
Hurt, Francis Cecil Albert, 1878–1930, vol. III
Hurt, Captain Henry Albert le Fowne, 1881–1969, vol. VI
Hurth, Peter Joseph, 1857–1935, vol. III
Hurwitz, Alter Max, 1899–1970, vol. VI
Husain, Abul Basher M.; *see* Mahmud Husain.
Husain, Hon. Mian Sir, Fazl-i-, 1877–1936, vol. III
Husain, Zakir, 1897–1969, vol. VI
Husband, Sir Charles; *see* Husband, Sir H. C.
Husband, Sir (Henry) Charles, 1908–1983, vol. VIII
Husband, Rev. John, 1841–1909, vol. I
Husband, Thomas Fair, 1862–1921, vol. II
Huskinson, Edward, 1877–1941, vol. IV
Huskinson, Air Cdre Patrick, 1897–1966, vol. VI
Huskinson, Richard King; *see* King, Richard.
Huskisson, Major Alfred, 1892–1984, vol. VIII
Huskisson, Col Samuel George, 1837–1911, vol. I
Huskisson, Maj.-Gen. William, 1859–1946, vol. IV
Huskisson, Lt-Col William Gordon, 1877–1949, vol. IV
Huson, Thomas, 1844–1920, vol. II
Hussain, Wajahat, 1894–1945, vol. IV
Hussein bin Onn, Datuk, 1922–1990, vol. VIII
Hussein bin Talal, 1935–1999, vol. X
Hussey, Col Arthur Herbert, 1863–1923, vol. II
Hussey, Christopher Edward Clive, 1899–1970, vol. VI
Hussey, Dyneley, 1893–1972, vol. VII
Hussey, Edward Windsor, 1855–1952, vol. V
Hussey, Eric Robert James, 1885–1958, vol. V
Hussey, Sir George Alfred Ernest, 1864–1950, vol. IV
Hussey, Very Rev. (John) Walter (Atherton), 1909–1985, vol. VIII
Hussey, Captain Thomas Edgar Cyril, 1884–1958, vol. V
Hussey, Very Rev. Walter; *see* Hussey, Very Rev. J. W. A.
Hussey, Major William Clive, *died* 1929, vol. III
Hussey-Walsh, Valentine John; *see* Walsh.
Hussey-Walsh, Lt-Col William, 1863–1925, vol. II
Huston, Major Desmond Wellesley William Desmond Mountjoy C.; *see* Chapman-Huston.
Huston, Maj.-Gen. John, 1901–1969, vol. VI
Huston, John, 1906–1987, vol. VIII
Hutber, Patrick, 1928–1980, vol. VII
Hutchen, Frank, 1870–1942, vol. IV
Hutchen, Lt-Col James William, 1880–1943, vol. IV
Hutcheon, Sir Alexander Byres, 1891–1956, vol. V
Hutcheson, Captain Bellenden Seymour, 1883–1954, vol. V
Hutcheson, John, 1870–1959, vol. V

Hutchings, Sir Alan, 1880–1951, vol. V
Hutchings, Andrew William Seymour, 1907–1996, vol. X
Hutchings, Arthur James Bramwell, 1906–1989, vol. VIII
Hutchings, Charles Henry, 1869–1946, vol. IV
Hutchings, Geoffrey Balfour, 1904–1982, vol. VIII
Hutchings, Harold Varlo, 1885–1948, vol. IV
Hutchings, Hugh Houston, 1869–1937, vol. III
Hutchings, Captain John Fenwick, 1885–1968, vol. VI
Hutchings, Norman Edwin, 1899–1960, vol. V
Hutchings, Sir Robert Howell, 1897–1976, vol. VII
Hutchings, Ven. William Henry, 1835–1912, vol. I
Hutchins, Sir David Ernest, 1850–1920, vol. II
Hutchins, Frank Ernest, 1922–1988, vol. VIII
Hutchins, George D'Oyly, 1866–1949, vol. IV
Hutchins, Ven. George Francis, 1909–1977, vol. VII
Hutchins, Harry Burns, 1847–1930, vol. III
Hutchins, Horace Albert, *died* 1923, vol. III
Hutchins, Sir Philip Perceval, 1838–1928, vol. II
Hutchins, Captain Ronald Edward, 1912–1998, vol. X
Hutchins, Robert Maynard, 1899–1977, vol. VII
Hutchinson, Brig. Alan George Caldwell, 1879–1947, vol. IV
Hutchinson, Rev. Canon Archibald Campbell, 1883–1981, vol. VIII
Hutchinson, Arthur, 1866–1937, vol. III
Hutchinson, Arthur Cyril William, 1889–1969, vol. VI
Hutchinson, Arthur Stuart Menteth, 1879–1971, vol. VII
Hutchinson, Sir Arthur Sydney, 1896–1981, vol. VIII
Hutchinson, Col Charles Alexander Robert, 1872–1928, vol. II
Hutchinson, Sir Charles Fred., 1850–1907, vol. I
Hutchinson, Maj.-Gen. Charles Scrope, 1826–1912, vol. I
Hutchinson, Rev. Christopher Blick, 1828–1910, vol. I
Hutchinson, Christopher Clarke, 1854–1914, vol. I
Hutchinson, Christopher Douglas H.; *see* Hely-Hutchinson.
Hutchinson, Rear-Adm. Christopher Haynes, 1906–1990, vol. VIII
Hutchinson, Claude Mackenzie, 1869–1941, vol. IV
Hutchinson, Rev. Canon Deryck Reeves, 1911–1971, vol. VII
Hutchinson, Col Edward Douglas B. S.; *see* Browne-Synge-Hutchinson.
Hutchinson, Sir Edward Synge-, 4th Bt, 1830–1906, vol. I
Hutchinson, Rev. Francis Ernest, 1871–1947, vol. IV
Hutchinson, Maj.-Gen. Francis Hope Grant, 1870–1931, vol. III
Hutchinson, Col Francis Patrick, 1858–1944, vol. IV
Hutchinson, Frederick Heap, 1892–1975, vol. VII
Hutchinson, Rev. Canon Frederick William, 1870–1964, vol. VI
Hutchinson, Geoffrey Clegg; *see* Baron Ilford.
Hutchinson, Lt-Col George Higginson F.; *see* Ford-Hutchinson.

Hutchinson, George Thomas, 1880–1948, vol. IV
Hutchinson, Sir George Thompson, 1857–1931, vol. III
Hutchinson, George William G.; *see* Grice-Hutchinson.
Hutchinson, Lt-Gen. Henry Doveton, 1847–1924, vol. II
Hutchinson, Rev. Henry Neville, 1856–1927, vol. II
Hutchinson, Sir Herbert John, 1889–1971, vol. VII
Hutchinson, Horatio Gordon, 1859–1932, vol. III
Hutchinson, Lt-Col Hugh Moore, 1874–1924, vol. II
Hutchinson, Col James Bird, 1844–1921, vol. II
Hutchinson, John, *died* 1916, vol. II
Hutchinson, John, 1884–1972, vol. VII
Hutchinson, Sir Jonathan, 1828–1913, vol. I
Hutchinson, Jonathan, 1859–1933, vol. III
Hutchinson, Sir Joseph Burtt, 1902–1988, vol. VIII
Hutchinson, Hon. Sir Joseph Turner, 1850–1924, vol. II
Hutchinson, Sir Lewis Bede, 1899–1975, vol. VII
Hutchinson, Maurice Robert H.; *see* Hely-Hutchinson.
Hutchinson, May H., (Hon. Lady Hutchinson); *see* Hely-Hutchinson.
Hutchinson, Ormond, 1896–1978, vol. VII
Hutchinson, Ray Coryton, 1907–1975, vol. VII
Hutchinson, St John, 1884–1942, vol. IV
Hutchinson, Sir Sydney Hutton Cooper, 1852–1929, vol. III
Hutchinson, Teasdale H., 1837–1928, vol. II
Hutchinson, Col Thomas Massie, 1877–1952, vol. V
Hutchinson, Vere Stuart Menteth, 1891–1932, vol. III
Hutchinson, Victor H.; *see* Hely-Hutchinson.
Hutchinson, Rt Hon. Sir Walter Francis H.; *see* Hely-Hutchinson.
Hutchinson, Walter Victor, 1887–1950, vol. IV
Hutchinson, Maj.-Gen. William Francis Moore, 1841–1917, vol. II
Hutchinson, William H., *died* 1965, vol. VI
Hutchinson, William James, 1919–1985, vol. VIII
Hutchinson, Rev. William P. H., 1810–1910, vol. I
Hutchison of Montrose, 1st Baron, 1873–1950, vol. IV
Hutchison, A(lan) Michael Clark, 1914–1993, vol. IX
Hutchison, Gen. Sir Alexander Richard Hamilton, 1871–1930, vol. III
Hutchison, Lt-Gen. Sir Balfour Oliphant, 1889–1967, vol. VI
Hutchison, Bruce; *see* Hutchison, W. B.
Hutchison, Brig. Colin Ross Marshall, 1893–1943, vol. IV
Hutchison, Hon. Sir Douglas; *see* Hutchison, Sir J. D.
Hutchison, Brig. Sir Eric Alexander Ogilvy, 2nd Bt (*cr* 1923), 1897–1972, vol. VII
Hutchison, Sir George Aitken Clark, 1873–1928, vol. II
Hutchison, George Andrew, 1841–1913, vol. I
Hutchison, George William, 1882–1947, vol. IV
Hutchison, Lt-Col Graham Seton, 1890–1946, vol. IV
Hutchison, Col Henry Oliphant, 1883–1935, vol. III
Hutchison, Isobel Wylie, *died* 1982, vol. VIII

Hutchison, Sir James, 1867–1946, vol. IV
Hutchison, Hon. Sir (James) Douglas, 1894–1981, vol. VIII
Hutchison, James Holmes, 1912–1987, vol. VIII
Hutchison, Sir James Riley Holt, 1st Bt (*cr* 1956), 1893–1979, vol. VII
Hutchison, James Seller, 1904–1986, vol. VIII
Hutchison, John, *died* 1910, vol. I
Hutchison, Sir John Colville, 1890–1965, vol. VI
Hutchison, Adm. John de Mestre, 1862–1932, vol. III
Hutchison, Sir Kenneth; *see* Hutchison, Sir W. K.
Hutchison, Very Rev. Michael Balfour, *born* 1844, vol. II
Hutchison, Sir Peter, 2nd Bt (*cr* 1939), 1907–1998, vol. X
Hutchison, Sir Robert, 1st Bt (*cr* 1939), 1871–1960, vol. V
Hutchison, Robert Gemmell, *died* 1936, vol. III
Hutchison, Sidney Charles, 1912–2000, vol. X
Hutchison, Sir Thomas, 1st Bt (*cr* 1923), 1866–1925, vol. II
Hutchison, Thomas Oliver, 1931–1998, vol. X
Hutchison, William, *died* 1924, vol. II
Hutchison, William, 1926–1976, vol. VII
Hutchison, (William) Bruce, 1901–1992, vol. IX
Hutchison, William Gordon Douglas, 1904–1975, vol. VII
Hutchison, Sir (William) Kenneth, 1903–1989, vol. VIII
Hutchison, William McPhee, 1924–1998, vol. X
Hutchison, Sir William Oliphant, 1889–1970, vol. VI
Huth, Alfred Henry, 1850–1910, vol. I
Huth, Edward, 1847–1935, vol. III
Hutch, Louis, 1821–1905, vol. I
Hutin, Marcel, 1869–1950, vol. IV
Hutson, Most Rev. Edward, *died* 1936, vol. III
Hutson, Ven. Eyre, *born* 1830, vol. II
Hutson, Sir Eyre, 1864–1936, vol. III
Hutson, Sir Francis Challenor, 1895–1992, vol. IX
Hutson, Maj.-Gen. Henry Porter Wolseley, 1893–1991, vol. IX
Hutson, Sir John, 1859–1950, vol. IV
Hutson, Thomas, 1896–1952, vol. V
Hutt, Sir (Alexander McDonald) Bruce, 1904–1978, vol. VII
Hutt, Sir Bruce; *see* Hutt, Sir A. McD. B.
Hutt, Rev. Henry Robert Mackenzie, 1870–1933, vol. III
Hutt, William Harold, 1899–1988, vol. VIII
Hutten, Baroness von, 1874–1957, vol. V
Hutton, Captain Alfred, 1840–1910, vol. I
Hutton, Alfred Eddison, 1865–1947, vol. IV
Hutton, Air Vice-Marshal Arthur Francis, 1900–1979, vol. VII
Hutton, Arthur Hill, 1859–1922, vol. II
Hutton, Rev. Arthur Wollaston, 1848–1912, vol. I
Hutton, (David) Graham, 1904–1988, vol. VIII
Hutton, Edward, 1875–1969, vol. VI
Hutton, Lt-Gen. Sir Edward Thomas Henry, 1848–1923, vol. II
Hutton, Rear-Adm. FitzRoy Evelyn Patrick, 1894–1975, vol. VII

Hutton, Captain Frederick Wollaston, 1836–1905, vol. I
Hutton, Rev. George Clark, 1825–1908, vol. I
Hutton, George Morland, *died* 1901, vol. I
Hutton, Major Gilbert Montgomerie, 1865–1911, vol. I
Hutton, Graham; *see* Hutton, D. G.
Hutton, Rev. Henry Wollaston, 1835–1916, vol. I
Hutton, Isabel Emslie, (Lady Hutton), *died* 1960, vol. V
Hutton, James Arthur, 1862–1955, vol. V
Hutton, Sir John, 1842–1903, vol. I
Hutton, John, 1847–1921, vol. II
Hutton, Rev. John Alexander, 1868–1947, vol. IV
Hutton, John Campbell, 1906–1978, vol. VII
Hutton, John Henry, 1885–1968, vol. VI
Hutton, Sir Leonard, 1916–1990, vol. VIII
Hutton, Maurice, 1856–1940, vol. III
Hutton, Maurice, 1914–1986, vol. VIII
Hutton, Sir Maurice Inglis, 1904–1970, vol. VI
Hutton, Sir Noël Kilpatrick, 1907–1984, vol. VIII
Hutton, Maj.-Gen. Reginald Antony, 1899–1983, vol. VIII
Hutton, Rear-Adm. Reginald Maurice James, 1899–1973, vol. VII
Hutton, Richard Holt, 1826–1897, vol. I
Hutton, Robert Crompton, 1897–1978, vol. VII
Hutton, Robert Salmon, 1876–1970, vol. VI
Hutton, Samuel King, 1877–1961, vol. VI
Hutton, Stamford, 1866–1941, vol. IV
Hutton, Lt-Gen. Sir Thomas Jacomb, 1890–1981, vol. VIII
Hutton, Thomas Winter, 1887–1973, vol. VII
Hutton, Maj.-Gen. Walter Morland, 1912–1994, vol. IX
Hutton, William, 1871–1933, vol. III
Hutton, William, 1902–1983, vol. VIII
Hutton, Very Rev. William Holden, 1860–1930, vol. III
Hutton, William Kilpatrick, 1870–1937, vol. III
Hutton-Wilson, Col Arthur Harry, 1873–1955, vol. V
Hutty, Sir Fred Harvey, 1903–1974, vol. VII
Huxham, Harold James, 1889–1961, vol. VI
Huxham, Henry William Walter, 1908–1982, vol. VIII
Huxham, Hon. John, *died* 1949, vol. IV
Huxley, Aldous Leonard, 1894–1963, vol. VI
Huxley, Anthony Julian, 1920–1992, vol. IX
Huxley, Elspeth Josceline, (Mrs Gervas Huxley), 1907–1997, vol. X
Huxley, Gervas, 1894–1971, vol. VII
Huxley, Sir Julian Sorell, 1887–1975, vol. VII
Huxley, Leonard, 1860–1933, vol. III
Huxley, Sir Leonard George Holden, 1902–1988, vol. VIII
Huxley, Mrs Lindsey Kathleen, 1894–1945, vol. IV
Huxley, Michael Heathorn, 1899–1979, vol. VII
Huxstep, Emily Mary, 1906–1995, vol. IX
Huxtable, Rev. John; *see* Huxtable, Rev. W. J. F.
Huxtable, Lt-Col Robert Beveridge, 1867–1920, vol. II
Huxtable, Rev. (William) John (Fairchild), 1912–1990, vol. VIII
Huybers, Jessie; *see* Couvreur, Mme Jessie.

Huyghe, René, 1906–1997, vol. X
Huyshe-Eliot, Hon. Reginald Hyshe, 1868–1920, vol. II
Huysmans, Joris Karl, 1848–1907, vol. I
Hyams, Edward, 1910–1975, vol. VII
Hyamson, Albert Montefiore, 1875–1954, vol. V
Hyamson, Derek Joseph, 1914–1971, vol. VII
Hyamson, Moses, 1862–1949, vol. IV
Hyat-Khan, Hon. Lt-Col Sirdar Sir Sikander, 1892–1942, vol. IV
Hyatali, Sir Isaac Emanuel, 1917–2000, vol. X
Hyatt, Stanley Portal, 1877–1914, vol. I
Hyatt King, Alexander; *see* King.
Hyatt-Woolf, Charles, 1863–1938, vol. III
Hydari, Rt Hon. Sir Akbar, 1869–1942, vol. IV
Hydari, Sir Muhammad Saleh Akbar, 1894–1948, vol. IV
Hyde, Lord; George Herbert Arthur Edward Hyde Villiers, 1906–1935, vol. III
Hyde, Lady; (Marion Féoderovna Louise), 1900–1970, vol. VI
Hyde, Sir Charles, 1st Bt, 1876–1942, vol. IV
Hyde, Sir Clarendon Golding, 1858–1934, vol. III
Hyde, Lt-Col Dermot Owen, 1877–1928, vol. II
Hyde, Donald Frizell, 1909–1966, vol. VI
Hyde, Douglas, 1860–1949, vol. IV
Hyde, Edward Wyllys, 1843–1930, vol. III
Hyde, Adm. Sir Francis; *see* Hyde, Adm. Sir G. F.
Hyde, Francis Edwin, 1908–1978, vol. VII
Hyde, Frederick, 1870–1939, vol. III
Hyde, Adm. Sir (George) Francis, 1877–1937, vol. III
Hyde, H(arford) Montgomery, 1907–1989, vol. VIII
Hyde, Sir Harry, *died* 1957, vol. V
Hyde, Henry Armroid, 1885–1976, vol. VII
Hyde, Rev. Henry Barry, 1854–1932, vol. III
Hyde, Rev. Canon Henry Edward, 1884–1941, vol. IV
Hyde, James Hazen, 1876–1959, vol. V (A), vol. VI (AI)
Hyde, James Wilson, 1841–1918, vol. II
Hyde, John Bean, 1928–1985, vol. VIII
Hyde, Lt-Col John Irvine L.; *see* Lang-Hyde.
Hyde, Vice-Adm. Richard, 1872–1931, vol. III
Hyde, Sir Robert Robertson, 1878–1967, vol. VI
Hyde, Walter, *died* 1951, vol. V
Hyde, Walter Henry, 1864–1953, vol. V
Hyde, William, 1889–1945, vol. IV
Hyde, William De Witt, 1858–1917, vol. II
Hyde, William Leonard, 1914–2000, vol. X (AII)
Hyde-Clarke, (Ernest) Meredyth, 1950–1972, vol. VII
Hyde-Clarke, Meredyth; *see* Hyde-Clarke, E. M.
Hyde-Lees, Rev. Harold Montagu, 1890–1963, vol. VI
Hyde-Page, Lt-Gen. George, 1823–1908, vol. I
Hyde Parker, Sir William Stephen; *see* Parker.
Hyde White, Wilfrid, 1903–1991, vol. IX
Hyderabad (Deccan), HH the Nizam of, 1866–1911, vol. I
Hyderabad, Nizam of, 1886–1967, vol. VI
Hyett, Sir Francis Adams, 1844–1941, vol. IV
Hyett, John Edward, *died* 1936, vol. III
Hyland, Maj.-Gen. Frederick Gordon, 1888–1962, vol. VI

Hyland, Hon. Sir Herbert John Thornhill, *died* 1970, vol. VI
Hylton, 2nd Baron, 1829–1899, vol. I
Hylton, 3rd Baron, 1862–1945, vol. IV
Hylton, 4th Baron, 1898–1967, vol. VI
Hylton, Jack, 1892–1965, vol. VI
Hylton-Foster, Rt Hon. Sir Harry Braustyn Hylton, 1905–1965, vol. VI
Hyman, Hon. Charles Smith, 1854–1926, vol. II
Hyman, Joe, 1921–1999, vol. X
Hymans, Paul, 1865–1941, vol. IV
Hynard, Sir William George, 1881–1953, vol. V
Hynd, Henry, 1900–1985, vol. VIII
Hynd, John Burns, 1902–1971, vol. VII
Hyndley, 1st Viscount, 1883–1963, vol. VI
Hyndman, Henry Mayers, 1842–1921, vol. II
Hyndman-Jones, Sir William Henry, 1847–1926, vol. II
Hyne, Engr-Rear-Adm. Arthur Edward, 1874–1956, vol. V
Hyne, Charles John Cutcliffe Wright, 1865–1944, vol. IV

Hyne, Sir Ragnar, 1893–1966, vol. VI
Hynes, Arthur Cecil, 1873–1940, vol. III
Hynes, Group Captain George Bayard, 1887–1938, vol. III
Hynes, John William, *died* 1930, vol. III
Hynes, Sir Lincoln Carruthers, 1912–1977, vol. VII
Hynes, Captain William Bayard, 1889–1968, vol. VI
Hyslop, Rev. Archibald Richard Frith, 1866–1926, vol. II
Hyslop, Lt-Col Francis, *died* 1944, vol. IV
Hyslop, Brig.-Gen. Henry Hugh Gordon, 1873–1932, vol. III
Hyslop, Col James, 1856–1917, vol. II
Hyslop, James Morton, 1908–1984, vol. VIII
Hyslop, James Telfer, 1916–1997, vol. X
Hyslop, Sir Murray; *see* Hyslop, Sir R. M.
Hyslop, Sir (Robert) Murray, *died* 1935, vol. III
Hyslop, Theo Bulkeley, *died* 1933, vol. III
Hyslop, Sir Thomas, 1859–1919, vol. II
Hyslop, Lt-Col William Campbell, 1860–1915, vol. I
Hytten, Torleiv, 1890–1980, vol. VII

I

Iago-Trelawny, Maj.-Gen. John, *died* 1909, vol. I
Ibañez, Vicente Blasco, 1867–1928, vol. II
Ibberson, Dora, 1890–1962, vol. VI
Ibbetson, Hon. Sir Denzil Charles Jelf, 1847–1908, vol. I
Ibbotson, Lancelot William Cripps, 1909–1998, vol. X
Ibbotson, Sir William, 1886–1956, vol. V
Ibert, Jacques, 1890–1962, vol. VI
Ibiam, Sir Francis Akanu, 1906–1995, vol. IX
Ibrahim, Sir (Shettima) Kashim, 1910–1990, vol. X (AI)
Ibsen, Henrik, 1828–1906, vol. I
Idar, Maharaja of, *died* 1931, vol. III
Iddesleigh, 2nd Earl of, 1845–1927, vol. II
Iddesleigh, 3rd Earl of, 1901–1970, vol. VI
Idelson, Vladimir Robert, *died* 1954, vol. V
Idington, Hon. John, 1840–1928, vol. II
Idris; *see* Mee, Arthur.
Idris, Thomas Howell Williams, 1842–1925, vol. II
Idun, Sir Samuel Okai Q.; *see* Quashie-Idun.
Ievers, Rear-Adm. John Augustine, 1912–1995, vol. IX
Ievers, Maj.-Gen. Osburne, *died* 1963, vol. VI
Ievers, Robert Wilson, *died* 1905, vol. I
Ife, HH Aderemi I, The Oni of Ife; Sir Titus Martins Adesoji Tadeniawo Aderemi, 1889–1980, vol. VII
Iftikhar-Ud-Din, Fakir Sayad, *died* 1914, vol. II
Igglesden, Sir Charles, 1861–1949, vol. IV
Iggulden, Sir Douglas Percy, 1907–1977, vol. VII
Iggulden, Brig.-Gen. Herbert Augustus, 1861–1937, vol. III
Ignatieff, George, 1913–1989, vol. VIII
Ignatius, Father, (Joseph Leycester Lyne), 1837–1908, vol. I

Ihaka, Ven. Sir Kingi Matutaera, 1921–1993, vol. IX
Ikin, Rutherford Graham, 1903–1989, vol. VIII
Ikramullah, Mohammad, 1903–1963, vol. VI
Ilbert, Sir Courtenay Peregrine, 1841–1924, vol. II
Ilchester, 5th Earl of, 1847–1905, vol. I
Ilchester, 6th Earl of, 1874–1959, vol. V
Ilchester, 7th Earl of, 1905–1964, vol. VI
Ilchester, 8th Earl of, 1887–1970, vol. VI
Ilderton, Col Charles Edward, 1841–1905, vol. I
Iles, Col Frederic Arthur, 1874–1966, vol. VI
Iles, John Henry, *died* 1951, vol. V
Iles, Air Vice-Marshal Leslie Millington, 1894–1974, vol. VII
Ilford, Baron (Life Peer); Geoffrey Clegg Hutchinson, 1893–1974, vol. VII
Iliff, Rt Rev. Geoffrey Durnford, 1867–1946, vol. IV
Iliff, Neil Atkinson, 1916–1973, vol. VII
Iliff, Sir William Angus Boyd, 1898–1972, vol. VII
Iliffe, 1st Baron, 1877–1960, vol. V
Iliffe, 2nd Baron, 1908–1996, vol. X
Iliffe, Barrie John, 1925–1997, vol. X
Iliffe, Frederick, 1847–1928, vol. II
Ilkeston, 1st Baron, 1840–1913, vol. I
Ilkeston, 2nd Baron, 1867–1952, vol. V
Illing, Vincent C., *died* 1969, vol. VI
Illingworth, 1st Baron, 1865–1942, vol. IV
Illingworth, Alfred, 1827–1907, vol. I
Illingworth, Sir Charles Frederick William, 1899–1991, vol. IX
Illingworth, Captain Sir (Cyril) Gordon, *died* 1959, vol. V
Illingworth, Dudley Holden, 1876–1958, vol. V
Illingworth, Captain Sir Gordon; *see* Illingworth, Captain Sir C. G.
Illingworth, Rev. John Richardson, *died* 1915, vol. I

Illingworth, Leslie Gilbert, 1902–1979, vol. VII
Illingworth, Percy Holden, 1869–1915, vol. I
Illingworth, Rear Adm. Philip Holden Crothers, 1916–1987, vol. VIII
Illingworth, Ronald Stanley, 1909–1990, vol. VIII
Ilott, Sir John Moody Albert, 1884–1973, vol. VII
Ilsley, Most Rev. Edward, 1838–1926, vol. II
Ilsley, Rt Hon. James Lorimer, 1894–1967, vol. VI
Ilyushin, Sergei Vladimirovich, 1894–1977, vol. VII
Image, Selwyn, 1849–1930, vol. III
Imam, Bahksh Khan, Mazari Sir, Mir Nawab, *died* 1903, vol. I
Imbert-Terry, Sir Andrew Henry Bouhier, 4th Bt, 1945–1985, vol. VIII
Imbert-Terry, Lt-Col Claude Henry Maxwell, 1880–1942, vol. IV
Imbert-Terry, Major Sir Edward Henry Bouhier, 3rd Bt, 1920–1978, vol. VII
Imbert-Terry, Captain Frederic Bouhier; *see* Terry.
Imbert-Terry, Lt-Col Sir Henry Bouhier, 2nd Bt, 1885–1962, vol. VI
Imbert-Terry, Sir Henry Machu, 1st Bt, 1854–1938, vol. III
Imeson, Kenneth Robert, 1908–1994, vol. IX
Imms, Augustus Daniel, 1880–1949, vol. IV
Imms, George, 1911–1995, vol. IX
Imperiali, Marquis Guglielmo, 1858–1944, vol. IV
Impey, Col Eugene Clutterbuck, 1830–1904, vol. I
Impey, Lt-Col Lawrence, 1862–1944, vol. IV
Impey, William Henry Lockington, 1856–1905, vol. I
Imrie, Lt-Col Hew Francis Blair, 1873–1942, vol. IV
Imrie, Sir John Dunlop, 1891–1981, vol. VIII
im Thurn, Sir Everard, 1852–1932, vol. III
Im Thurn, Vice-Adm. John Knowles, 1881–1956, vol. V
Inayat-Khan, Pir-o-Murshid, 1882–1927, vol. II
Inayat Masih, Rt Rev.; *see* Masih.
Ince, Brig. Cecil Edward Ronald, 1897–1988, vol. VIII
Ince, Charles Percy, 1875–1952, vol. V
Ince, Edward Lindsay, 1891–1941, vol. IV
Ince, Captain Edward Watkins W.; *see* Whittington-Ince.
Ince, Evelyn Grace, *died* 1941, vol. IV
Ince, Sir Godfrey Herbert, 1891–1960, vol. V (A), vol. VI (AI)
Ince, Wesley Armstrong, 1893–1990, vol. IX (AI)
Ince, Rev. William, 1825–1910, vol. I
Inch, Rev. Alex. S., 1863–1932, vol. III
Inch, Sir John Ritchie, 1911–1993, vol. IX
Inchcape, 1st Earl of, 1852–1932, vol. III
Inchcape, 2nd Earl of, 1887–1939, vol. III
Inchcape, 3rd Earl of, 1917–1994, vol. IX
Inches, Cyrus Fiske, 1883–1956, vol. V
Inches, Lt-Col Edward James, 1877–1934, vol. III
Inches, Sir Robert Kirk, 1840–1918, vol. II
Inchiquin, 14th Baron, 1839–1900, vol. I
Inchiquin, 15th Baron, 1864–1929, vol. III
Inchiquin, 16th Baron, 1897–1968, vol. VI
Inchiquin, 17th Baron of, 1900–1982, vol. VIII
Inchyra, 1st Baron, 1900–1989, vol. VIII
Incledon-Webber, Brig.-Gen. Adrian Beare, 1876–1946, vol. IV

Incledon-Webber, Lt-Col Godfrey Sturdy, 1904–1986, vol. VIII
Incze, Jenö, 1901–1969, vol. VI
Ind, Charles Francis, 1905–1940, vol. III
Ind, Edward Murray, 1853–1915, vol. I
Inderwick, Frederic Andrew, 1836–1904, vol. I
Indore, HH Maharaj-dhiraj Sir Shivaji Rao Holkar Bahadur, 1860–1908, vol. I
Indore, Maj.-Gen. HH Maharaja of, 1908–1961, vol. VI
Indore, Ex-Maharaja of; HH Tukoji Rao Holkar, 1890–1978, vol. VII
Infield, Henry John, *died* 1921, vol. II
Ing, Col George Harold Absell, 1880–1957, vol. V
Ing, Harry Raymond, 1899–1974, vol. VII
Ingall, Douglas Heber, 1891–1968, vol. VI
Ingalls, John James, 1833–1900, vol. I
Inge, Mary Caroline, (Mrs W. F. Inge), *died* 1961, vol. VI
Inge, Mrs W. F.; *see* Inge, Mary Caroline.
Inge, William, 1829–1903, vol. I
Inge, Very Rev. William Ralph, 1860–1954, vol. V
Ingelow, Jean, 1820–1897, vol. I
Ingersoll, Ralph McAllister, 1900–1985, vol. VIII
Ingestre, Viscount; Charles John Alton Chetwynd Chetwynd-Talbot, 1882–1915, vol. I
Ingham, Albert Edward, 1900–1967, vol. VI
Ingham, Brig.-Gen. Charles St Maur, *died* 1936, vol. III
Ingham, Rt Rev. Ernest Graham, 1851–1926, vol. II
Ingham, John Henry, 1910–1992, vol. IX
Ingham, Robert Wood, 1846–1928, vol. II
Ingham, Major Samuel, 1893–1950, vol. IV
Ingham, Stanley Ainsworth, 1920–1991, vol. IX
Ingilby, Sir Henry Day, 2nd Bt, 1826–1911, vol. I
Ingilby, Sir Joslan William Vivian, 5th Bt, 1907–1974, vol. VII
Ingilby, Sir William, 3rd Bt, 1829–1918, vol. II
Ingilby, Sir William Henry, 4th Bt, 1874–1950, vol. IV
Ingle, Charles Fiennes, 1908–1983, vol. VIII
Ingle, Rt Rev. George Ernest, 1895–1964, vol. VI
Ingle-Finch, Peter; *see* Finch.
Ingleby, 1st Viscount, 1897–1966, vol. VI
Ingleby, Holcombe, 1854–1926, vol. III
Ingleby Mackenzie, Surg. Vice-Adm. Sir Alexander; *see* Ingleby Mackenzie, Surg. Vice-Adm. Sir K. A.
Ingleby Mackenzie, Surg. Vice-Adm. Sir (Kenneth) Alexander, 1892–1961, vol. VI
Inglefield, Rear-Adm. Sir Edward Fitzmaurice, 1861–1945, vol. IV
Inglefield, Maj.-Gen. Francis Seymour, 1855–1930, vol. III
Inglefield, Adm. Sir Frederick Samuel, 1854–1921, vol. II
Inglefield, Sir Gilbert Samuel, 1909–1991, vol. IX
Inglefield, Col Sir John Frederick C.; *see* Crompton-Inglefield.
Inglefield, Brig. Lionel Dalton, 1881–1953, vol. V
Inglefield, Brig.-Gen. Norman Bruce, 1855–1912, vol. I
Inglefield-Watson, Captain Sir Derrick William Inglefield; *see* Watson.
Ingles, Ven. Charles Leycester, 1856–1930, vol. III

Ingles, Rev. Charles William Chamberlayne, 1869–1954, vol. V
Ingles, Rev. David, 1836–1921, vol. II
Ingles, Brig.-Gen. John Darnley, 1872–1957, vol. V
Ingleson, Philip, 1892–1985, vol. VIII
Inglewood, 1st Baron; William Morgan Fletcher-Vane, 1909–1989, vol. VIII
Inglis, Sir (Albemarle) Percy, 1841–1932, vol. III
Inglis, Allan, 1906–1984, vol. VIII
Inglis, Captain Arthur McCulloch, 1884–1919, vol. II
Inglis, Brian St John, 1916–1993, vol. IX
Inglis, Sir Charles Edward, 1875–1952, vol. V
Inglis, Lt-Col Charles Elliot, 1878–1936, vol. III
Inglis, Sir Claude Cavendish, 1883–1974, vol. VII
Inglis, Maj.-Gen. Sir Drummond; see Inglis, Maj.-Gen. Sir J. D.
Inglis, Air Vice-Marshal Francis Frederic, 1899–1969, vol. VI
Inglis, Maj.-Gen. George Henry, 1902–1979, vol. VII
Inglis, Rev. George John, 1900–1965, vol. VI
Inglis, Col Henry Alves, 1859–1924, vol. II
Inglis, Sir Hugh Arbuthnot, 1890–1948, vol. IV
Inglis, Hon. James, 1845–1908, vol. I
Inglis, Sir James Charles, 1851–1911, vol. I
Inglis, Rev. James W., 1861–1943, vol. IV
Inglis, Lt-Col John, 1882–1967, vol. VI
Inglis, John Alexander, 1873–1941, vol. IV
Inglis, Maj.-Gen. Sir (John) Drummond, 1895–1985, vol. VIII
Inglis, Vice-Adm. Sir John Gilchrist Thesiger, 1906–1972, vol. VII
Inglis, John Kenneth Harold, 1877–1935, vol. III
Inglis, Lindsay Merritt, 1894–1966, vol. VI
Inglis of Glencorse, Sir Maxwell Ian Hector, 9th Bt, 1903–1974, vol. VII
Inglis, Sir Percy; see Inglis, Sir A. P.
Inglis, Robert Alexander, 1918–1995, vol. IX
Inglis, Sir Robert John Mathison, 1881–1962, vol. VI
Inglis, Lt-Col Sir Robert William, 1843–1923, vol. II
Inglis, Col Russell Tracy-, 1875–1937, vol. III
Inglis, William Arbuthnot, 1853–1936, vol. III
Ingold, Sir Christopher Kelk, 1893–1970, vol. VI
Ingoldby, Eric, 1892–1986, vol. VIII
Ingpen, Arthur Robert, died 1917, vol. II
Ingpen, Lt-Col Percy Leigh, 1874–1930, vol. III
Ingpen, Roger, died 1936, vol. III
Ingram, Captain Alexander Gordon, 1883–1929, vol. III
Ingram, Archibald Kenneth, 1882–1965, vol. VI
Ingram, Rt Rev. and Rt Hon. Arthur Foley Winnington, 1858–1946, vol. IV
Ingram, Rev. Arthur John, died 1931, vol. III
Ingram, Ven. Arthur John W.; see Winnington-Ingram.
Ingram, Sir Bruce Stirling, 1877–1963, vol. VI
Ingram, Rev. Edward Henry Winnington-, 1849–1930, vol. III
Ingram, Edward Maurice Berkeley, 1890–1941, vol. IV
Ingram, Sir Herbert, 2nd Bt, 1875–1958, vol. V
Ingram, Sir Herbert, 3rd Bt, 1912–1980, vol. VII

Ingram, John H., 1849–1916, vol. II
Ingram, John Kells, 1823–1907, vol. I
Ingram, Lt-Col John O'Donnell, 1870–1939, vol. III
Ingram, John Thornton, 1899–1972, vol. VII
Ingram, Dame Kathleen Annie; see Raven, Dame K.
Ingram, Hon. Mrs Meynell, (Emily Charlotte), 1840–1904, vol. I
Ingram, Reginald Pepys W.; see Winnington-Ingram.
Ingram, Thomas Allan, 1870–1922, vol. II
Ingram, Captain Thomas Lewis, 1875–1916, vol. II
Ingram, W. Ayerst, 1855–1913, vol. I
Ingram, William, 1865–1943, vol. IV
Ingram, Very Rev. William Clavell, 1834–1901, vol. I
Ingram, Sir William James, 1st Bt, 1847–1924, vol. II
Ingram-Johnson, Rev. Rowland Theodore, 1877–1964, vol. VI
Ingrams, Leonard St Clair, 1900–1953, vol. V
Ingrams, William Harold, 1897–1973, vol. VII
Ingrem, Rev. Charles, 1854–1937, vol. III
Inigo-Jones, Captain Henry Richmund, 1899–1978, vol. VII
Inkson, Col Edgar Thomas, 1872–1947, vol. IV
Inman, 1st Baron, 1892–1979, vol. VII
Inman, Arnold, 1867–1951, vol. V
Inman, Arthur Conyers, 1879–1926, vol. II
Inman, Rev. Canon Edward, died 1924, vol. II
Inman, Peter Donald, 1916–1987, vol. VIII
Inman, Rt Rev. Thomas George Vernon, 1904–1989, vol. VIII
Innes, Alexander Taylor, 1833–1912, vol. I
Innes, Alfred M.; see Mitchell-Innes.
Innes, Sir Andrew Lockhart, 1898–1960, vol. V
Innes, Arthur Donald, died 1938, vol. III
Innes, Lt-Col Sir Berowald; see Innes, Lt-Col Sir R. G. B.
Innes, Captain Cecil M; see Mitchell-Innes.
Innes, Sir Charles Alexander, 1874–1959, vol. V
Innes, Sir Charles Alexander, 1902–1963, vol. VI
Innes of Coxton, Sir Charles Kenneth Gordon, 11th Bt, 1910–1990, vol. VIII
Innes, Donald Esme, 1888–1961, vol. VI
Innes, Edward Alfred M.; see Mitchell-Innes.
Innes, Fergus Munro, 1903–1994, vol. IX
Innes, Guy Edward Mitchell, 1882–1953, vol. V
Innes, Hammond; see Hammond Innes, Ralph.
Innes, Sir James, 13th Bt, 1846–1919, vol. II
Innes, Lt-Col James Archibald, 1875–1948, vol. IV
Innes, Sir James Bourchier, 14th Bt, 1883–1950, vol. IV
Innes, James John M'Leod, 1830–1907, vol. I
Innes, Rt Hon. Sir James R.; see Rose-Innes.
Innes, Captain James William Guy, 1873–1939, vol. III
Innes, Sir John, 12th Bt, 1840–1912, vol. I
Innes, John, 1888–1961, vol. VI
Innes, Surg.-Gen. Sir John Harry Ker, 1820–1907, vol. I
Innes, John Robert, 1863–1948, vol. IV
Innes, Michael; see Stewart, J. I. M.
Innes, Sir Patrick R.; see Rose-Innes.

Innes, Sir Peter David, 1881–1961, vol. VI

Innes, Hon. Reginald Heath L.; *se* Long Innes.

Innes, Rev. Reginald John Simpson M.; *see* Mitchell-Innes.

Innes, Robert Mann, 1926–1994, vol. IX

Innes, Robert T. A., 1861–1933, vol. III

Innes, Lt-Col Sir (Ronald Gordon) Berowald, 16th Bt, 1907–1988, vol. VIII

Innes of Learney, Col. Thomas, 1814–1912, vol. I

Innes of Learney, Sir Thomas, 1893–1971, vol. VII

Innes, Sir Walter James, 15th Bt, 1903–1978, vol. VII

Innes, William Arnold, 1902–1973, vol. VII

Innes-Ker, Lord Alastair Robert, 1880–1936, vol. III

Innes-Ker, Major Lord Robert Edward, 1885–1958, vol. V

Innes-Noad, Sidney Reginald, *died* 1931, vol. III

Innes-Wilson, Col. Campbell Aubrey Kenneth, 1905–1978, vol. VII

Inness, George, 1854–1926, vol. II

Inness, Air Cdre William Innes Cosmo, 1916–1986, vol. VIII

Inness, William James Deacon, 1877–1948, vol. IV

Innis, Harold Adams, 1894–1952, vol. V

Inniss, Sir Clifford de Lisle, 1910–1998, vol. X

Inonu, Gen. Ismet, 1884–1973, vol. VII

Inouyé, Marquis Kaoru, 1835–1915, vol. I

Inouyé, Marquis Katsunoske, 1861–1929, vol. III

Insall, Gp Captain Gilbert Stuart Martin, 1894–1972, vol. VII

Insch, James Ferguson, 1911–1994, vol. IX

Insh, George Pratt, 1883–1956, vol. V (A), vol. VI (AI)

Inskip, Sir Arthur Cecil, 1894–1951, vol. V

Inskip, Hampden; *see* Inskip, J. H.

Inskip, J. Henry, *died* 1947, vol. IV

Inskip, (John) Hampden, 1924–1991, vol. IX

Inskip, Rt Rev. James Theodore, 1868–1949, vol. IV

Inskip, Sir John Hampden, 1879–1960, vol. V

Inskip, Rev. Oliver Digby, *died* 1934, vol. III

Inskip, Maj.-Gen. Roland Debenham, 1885–1971, vol. VII

Instone, Sir Samuel, 1878–1937, vol. III

Insull, Samuel, 1859–1938, vol. III

Inverchapel, 1st Baron, 1882–1951, vol. V

Inverclyde, 1st Baron, 1829–1901, vol. I

Inverclyde, 2nd Baron, 1861–1905, vol. I

Inverclyde, 3rd Baron, 1864–1919, vol. II

Inverclyde, 4th Baron, 1897–1957, vol. V

Inverforth, 1st Baron, 1865–1955, vol. V

Inverforth, 2nd Baron, 1897–1975, vol. VII

Inverforth, 3rd Baron, 1932–1982, vol. VIII

Invernairn, 1st Baron, 1856–1936, vol. III

Inverurie, Lord; Ian Douglas Montagu Keith Falconer, 1877–1897, vol. I

Inwards, Richard, 1840–1937, vol. III

Ionesco, Eugène, 1912–1994, vol. IX

Ionescu, George Ghita, 1913–1996, vol. X

Ionides, Basil, 1884–1950, vol. IV

Ipswich, Viscount; William Henry Alfred Fitzroy, 1884–1918, vol. II

Irby, Hon. Cecil Saumarez, 1862–1935, vol. III

Iredell, Air Vice-Marshal Sir Alfred William, 1879–1967, vol. VI

Iredell, Charles Edward, 1877–1961, vol. VI

Iredell, Lt-Gen. Francis Shrubb, 1837–1924, vol. II

Ireland, Alleyne; *see* Ireland, W. A.

Ireland, Arthur Joseph, 1874–1931, vol. III

Ireland, Frank, 1909–1983, vol. VIII

Ireland, Frank Edward, 1913–2000, vol. X

Ireland, Lt-Col Gerald Blakeney de C.; *see* de Courcy-Ireland.

Ireland, Most Rev. John, 1838–1918, vol. II

Ireland, John, 1879–1962, vol. VI

Ireland, Col Sir Robert Megaw, 1849–1919, vol. II

Ireland, (Walter) Alleyne, *died* 1951, vol. V

Iremonger, Col Edgar Assheton, 1862–1953, vol. V

Iremonger, Very Rev. Frederic Athelwold, 1878–1952, vol. V

Iremonger, Major Harold Edward William, *died* 1937, vol. III

Iremonger, Thomas Lascelles Isa Shandon Valiant, 1916–1998, vol. X

Irens, Alfred Norman, 1911–1996, vol. X

Ireson, Rev. Canon Gordon Worley, 1906–1994, vol. IX

Irgens, Johannes, 1869–1939, vol. III

Irish, Sir Ronald Arthur, 1913–1993, vol. IX

Iron, Air Cdre Douglas, 1893–1983, vol. VIII

Ironmonger, Sir (Charles) Ronald, 1914–1984, vol. VIII

Ironmonger, Sir Ronald; *see* Ironmonger, Sir C. R.

Irons, Ralph; *see* Schreiner, Olive.

Ironside, 1st Baron, 1880–1959, vol. V

Ironside, Christopher, 1913–1992, vol. IX

Ironside, Sir Henry George Outram B.; *see* Bax-Ironside.

Ironside, Redvers Nowell, 1899–1968, vol. VI

Ironside, Robin, 1912–1965, vol. VI

Irvin, Sir John Hannell, 1874–1952, vol. V

Irvin, Captain William Dion, 1870–1965, vol. V

Irvine, Lt-Col Acheson Gosford, *born* 1837, vol. II

Irvine, Alexander, 1863–1941, vol. IV

Irvine, Alexander Forbes, 1881–1922, vol. II

Irvine, Brig.-Gen. Alfred Ernest, 1876–1962, vol. VI

Irvine, Lt-Col Andrew Alexander, 1871–1939, vol. III

Irvine, Rt Hon. Sir Arthur James, 1909–1978, vol. VII

Irvine, Rt Hon. Sir Bryant Godman, 1909–1992, vol. IX

Irvine, Captain Charles Alexander Lindsay, 1876–1965, vol. VI

Irvine, Col Francis Stephen, 1873–1962, vol. VI

Irvine, Rt Rev. Gerard Addington D'A; *see* D'Arcy-Irvine.

Irvine, Lt-Col Gerard Beatty, 1863–1947, vol. IV

Irvine, Surg. Captain Gerard Sutherland, 1913–1997, vol. X

Irvine, Sir James Colquhoun, 1877–1952, vol. V

Irvine, James Mercer, *died* 1945, vol. IV

Irvine, Maj.-Gen. John, 1914–1997, vol. X

Irvine, Lt-Col Richard Abercrombie, *died* 1946, vol. IV

Irvine, Sir Robin Orlando Hamilton, 1929–1996, vol. X

Irvine, Adm. Sir St George Caufield D'Arcy-, 1883–1916, vol. II

Irvine, Rev. Thomas Thurstan, 1913–1985, vol. VIII
Irvine, William Fergusson, 1869–1962, vol. VI
Irvine, Hon. Sir William Hill, 1858–1943, vol. IV
Irvine, William Tait, 1925–1980, vol. VII
Irvine-Fortescue, Col Archer, 1880–1959, vol. V
Irvine-Jones, Douglas Vivian, 1904–1974, vol. VII
Irvine Smith, Thomas, 1908–1985, vol. VIII
Irving of Dartford, Baron (Life Peer); Sydney Irving, 1918–1989, vol. VIII
Irving, Sir Æmilius, 1823–1913, vol. I
Irving, Lt-Col Andrew B.; see Bell-Irving.
Irving, Captain Charles Edward, 1871–1955, vol. V
Irving, Sir Charles Graham, 1924–1995, vol. IX
Irving, Charles John, 1831–1917, vol. II
Irving, David Blair, 1903–1986, vol. VIII
Irving, David Daniel, 1854–1924, vol. II
Irving, David Jarvis M.; see Mill Irving.
Irving, Dorothea, (Mrs Henry Irving), died 1933, vol. III
Irving, Rear-Adm. Sir Edmund George, 1910–1990, vol. VIII
Irving, Ven. Edward Arthur, 1850–1943, vol. IV
Irving, Mrs H. B.; see Irving, Dorothea.
Irving, Harry Munroe Napier Hetherington, 1905–1993, vol. IX
Irving, Sir Henry, 1838–1905, vol. I
Irving, Henry Brodribb, 1870–1919, vol. II
Irving, Sir Henry Turner, 1833–1923, vol. II
Irving, Herbert Cavan, 1854–1930, vol. III
Irving, James Jardine B.; see Bell-Irving.
Irving, James Tutin, 1902–1992, vol. IX
Irving, John, 1920–1996, vol. X
Irving, John B.; see Bell-Irving.
Irving, Kelville Ernest, 1877–1953, vol. V
Irving, Laurence Henry Forster, 1897–1988, vol. VIII
Irving, Laurence Sydney Brodribb, 1871–1914, vol. I
Irving, Martin Howy, 1831–1912, vol. I
Irving, Sir Miles, 1876–1962, vol. VI
Irving, Hon. Paulus Æmilius, 1857–1916, vol. II
Irving, Rev. Robert, 1840–1922, vol. II
Irving, Robert Augustine, 1913–1991, vol. IX
Irving, Captain Sir Robert Beaufin, 1877–1954, vol. V
Irving, Robert Lock Graham, 1877–1969, vol. VI
Irving, Sir Stanley Gordon, 1886–1970, vol. VI
Irving, Rev. Thomas Henry, 1856–1926, vol. II
Irving, William John, 1892–1967, vol. VI
Irwin, Alfred, 1865–1951, vol. V
Irwin, Sir Alfred Macdonald Bulteel, 1853–1921, vol. II
Irwin, Ven. Charles King, 1837–1915, vol. I
Irwin, Rt Rev. Charles King, 1874–1960, vol. V
Irwin, Rev. Clarke Huston, 1858–1934, vol. III
Irwin, Cyril James, 1881–1962, vol. VI
Irwin, Col De la Cherois Thomas, 1843–1928, vol. II
Irwin, Francis Charles, 1928–1990, vol. VIII
Irwin, Sir George, 1832–1899, vol. I
Irwin, George Robert, 1855–1933, vol. III
Irwin, Henry, 1841–1922, vol. II
Irwin, Henry Raikes Alexander, 1858–1937, vol. III
Irwin, Sir James Campbell, 1906–1990, vol. VIII
Irwin, Col Sir (James) Murray, 1858–1938, vol. III

Irwin, Sir John, 1857–1935, vol. III
Irwin, Rev. John, died 1932, vol. III
Irwin, John Conran, 1917–1997, vol. X
Irwin, Lt-Gen. John Staples, 1846–1917, vol. II
Irwin, Joseph Boyd, 1895–1968, vol. VI
Irwin, Leighton Francis, 1892–1962, vol. VI
Irwin, Margaret, died 1967, vol. VI
Irwin, Margaret Hardinge, died 1940, vol. III
Irwin, Col Sir Murray; see Irwin, Col. Sir J. M.
Irwin, Lt-Gen. Noel Mackintosh Stuart, 1892–1972, vol. VII
Irwin, Raymond, 1902–1976, vol. VII
Irwin, Robert, died 1941, vol. IV
Irwin, Robert Christopher, 1865–1937, vol. III
Irwin, Ven. Ronald John Beresford, 1880–1930, vol. III
Irwin, Sir Samuel Thompson, 1877–1961, vol. VI
Irwin, Maj.-Gen. Stephen Fenemore, 1895–1964, vol. VI
Irwin, Thomas Lennox, 1846–1918, vol. II
Irwin, William Henry, 1907–1974, vol. VII
Irwin, William Knox, 1883–1973, vol. VII
Isaac, Very Rev. Abraham, died 1906, vol. I
Isaac, Alfred James, 1919–1997, vol. X
Isaac, Charles Leonard, died 1944, vol. IV
Isaac, Rev. Gerald Moore, died 1940, vol. III
Isaac, Joseph Charles, 1859–1939, vol. III
Isaac, Sir Neil, 1915–1987, vol. VIII
Isaac, Lt-Col Thomas William Talbot, 1880–1930, vol. III
Isaacs, Alick, 1921–1967, vol. VI
Isaacs, Edward Maurice, 1881–1953, vol. V
Isaacs, Evelyn M.; see Lawrence, E. M.
Isaacs, Rev. Frederick Walter, 1858–1935, vol. III
Isaacs, Rt Hon. George Alfred, 1883–1979, vol. VII
Isaacs, Godfrey Charles, died 1925, vol. II
Isaacs, Sir Henry Aaron, 1830–1909, vol. I
Isaacs, Rt Hon. Sir Isaac Alfred, 1855–1948, vol. IV
Isaacs, Jacob, 1896–1973, vol. VII
Isaacs, Sir Kendal George Lamon, 1925–1996, vol. X
Isaacs, Susan Sutherland, 1885–1948, vol. IV
Isaacson, Frederick Wootton, 1836–1898, vol. I
Isaacson, Richard, 1950–1998, vol. X
Isaacson, Sir Robert Spencer, 1907–1972, vol. VII
Isacke, Maj.-Gen. Hubert, 1872–1943, vol. IV
Isbister, William James, 1866–1950, vol. IV
Iselin, Charles Oliver, died 1932, vol. III
Isemonger, Frederick Charles, 1876–1960, vol. V
Isham, Sir Charles Edmund, 10th Bt, 1819–1903, vol. I
Isham, Sir Gyles, 12th Bt, 1903–1976, vol. VII
Isham, Lt-Col Ralph Heyward, 1890–1955, vol. V
Isham, Sir Vere, 11th Bt, 1862–1941, vol. IV
Isherwood, Albert Arthur Mangnall, 1889–1957, vol. V
Isherwood, Col Charles Edward Ramsbottom, 1849–1934, vol. III
Isherwood, Christopher William Bradshaw-, 1904–1986, vol. VIII
Isherwood, Rt Rev. Harold, 1907–1989, vol. VIII
Isherwood, Lt-Col James, died 1929, vol. III
Isherwood, John Henry Bradshaw-, 1841–1924, vol. II

Isherwood, Sir Joseph William, 1st Bt, 1870–1937, vol. III
Isherwood, Sir William, 2nd Bt, 1898–1946, vol. IV
Ishibashi, Kazunori, *died* 1928, vol. II
Isitt, Dame Adeline G.; *see* Genée-Isitt.
Isitt, Air Vice-Marshal Sir Leonard Monk, 1891–1976, vol. VII
Isle, William Herbert Mosley, 1896–1973, vol. VII
Isles, Keith Sydney, 1902–1977, vol. VII
Islington, 1st Baron, 1866–1936, vol. III
Ismail, Sir Miras M., 1883–1959, vol. V
Ismail Sait, Khan Bahadur Fukhr-ut-tujjar Sir Hajee, 1859–1934, vol. III
Ismay, 1st Baron, 1887–1965, vol. VI
Ismay, Sir George, 1891–1984, vol. VIII
Ismay, James Hainsworth, 1867–1930, vol. III
Ismay, Joseph Bruce, 1862–1937, vol. III
Ismay, Sir Stanley, 1848–1914, vol. I
Ismay, Thomas Henry, 1837–1899, vol. I
Ismay, Rev. William, 1846–192, vol. II
Isola; *see* Teeling, Mrs Bartle.
Ispahani, Mirza Abol Hassan, 1902–1981, vol. VIII
Israel, John William, 1850–1926, vol. II
Israels, Joseph, 1824–1911, vol. I
Israr, Hon. Sir Maulvi Mohammad Israr Hasan Khan, 1865–1934, vol. III
Isserlis, Alexander Reginald, 1922–1986, vol. VIII
Isserstedt, Hans S.; *see* Schmidt-Isserstedt.
Issigonis, Sir Alec Arnold Constantine, 1906–1988, vol. VIII
Ithel Jones, Rev. John; *see* Jones.
Ito, Prince Hirobumi, 1838–1909, vol. I
Ito, Admiral of the Fleet Count Yuko, 1843–1914, vol. I

Iturbi, José, 1895–1980, vol. VII
Ivatt, Henry George, 1886–1972, vol. VII
Iveagh, 1st Earl of, 1847–1927, vol. II
Iveagh, 2nd Earl of, 1874–1967, vol. VI
Iveagh, 3rd Earl of, 1937–1992, vol. IX
Iveagh, Countess of; (Gwendolen), *died* 1966, vol. VI
Ivelaw-Chapman, Air Chief Marshal Sir Ronald, 1899–1978, vol. VII
Ivens, Rev. Charles Llewelyn, 1854–1931, vol. III
Ivens, Richard, *died* 1931, vol. III
Ivens, Rev. William Edmunds, 1845–1910, vol. I
Iverach, Rev. James, 1839–1922, vol. II
Iversen, Johannes, 1904–1971, vol. VII
Ives, Arthur Glendinning Loveless, 1904–1991, vol. IX
Ives, George Cecil, 1867–1950, vol. IV
Ives, Col Gordon Maynard G.; *see* Gordon-Ives.
Ives, Harry William Maclean, 1867–1941, vol. IV
Ives, Robert, 1906–1985, vol. VIII
Ivimey, John William, 1868–1961, vol. VI
Ivimey, Julia B., (Mrs Fairfax Ivimey); *see* Matthews, J. B.
Ivins, Derek; *see* Ivins, J. D.
Ivins, John Derek, 1923–1986, vol. VIII
Iwi, Edward Frank, 1904–1966, vol. VI
Iyengar, S. Kasturi Ranga, 1859–1923, vol. II
Izard, Ven. Herbert Crawford, 1869–1934, vol. III
Izat, Alexander, 1844–1920, vol. II
Izat, Sir (James) Rennie, 1886–1962, vol. VI
Izat, John, 1879–1966, vol. VI
Izat, Sir Rennie; *see* Izat, Sir J. R.
Izycki de Notto, Sir Matthew, 1899–1952, vol. V

J

Jack, Adolphus Alfred, 1868–1946, vol. IV
Jack, Alexander G. Mackenzie, 1851–1927, vol. II
Jack, Brig.-Gen. Archibald, 1874–1939, vol. III
Jack, Sir Daniel Thomson, 1901–1984, vol. VIII
Jack, Brig. Evan Maclean, 1873–1951, vol. V
Jack, Col Herbert Rowett Henry, 1863–1932, vol. III
Jack, James, 1910–1987, vol. VIII
Jack, Brig.-Gen. James Lochhead, 1880–1962, vol. VI
Jack, John Louttit, 1878–1954, vol. V
Jack, Mackenzie; *see* Jack, A. G. M.
Jack, Richard, 1866–1952, vol. V
Jack, Sir Robert Ernest, *died* 1962, vol. VI
Jack, Robert Logan, 1845–1921, vol. II
Jack, Hon. Sir Roy Emile, 1914–1977, vol. VII
Jack, William, 1834–1924, vol. II
Jack, William Robert, 1866–1927, vol. II
Jacklin Air Vice-Marshal Edward Ward Seymour, 1917–1969, vol. VI
Jackling, Sir Roger William, 1913–1986, vol. VIII
Jackman, Mgr Canon Arthur, 1878–1945, vol. IV
Jackman, Air Marshal Sir Douglas, 1902–1991, vol. IX
Jackman, Frank Downer, 1901–1981, vol. VIII

Jackman, William T., 1871–1951, vol. V
Jacks, Graham Vernon, 1901–1977, vol. VII
Jacks, Hector Beaumont, 1903–1994, vol. IX
Jacks, Lawrence Pearsall, 1860–1955, vol. V
Jacks, Maurice Leonard, 1894–1964, vol. VI
Jacks, Thomas Lavington, 1884–1966, vol. VI
Jacks, William, 1841–1907, vol. I
Jackson, 1st Baron, 1893–1954, vol. V
Jackson of Burnley, Baron (Life Peer); Willis Jackson, 1904–1970, vol. VI
Jackson of Lodsworth, Baroness (Life Peer); Barbara Mary Jackson, 1914–1981, vol. VIII
Jackson, Abraham Valentine Williams, 1862–1937, vol. III
Jackson, Adrian Alexander W.; *see* Ward-Jackson.
Jackson, Albert Edward, 1865–1930, vol. III
Jackson, Brig. Alexander Cosby Fishburn, 1903–2000, vol. X
Jackson, Alexander Young, 1882–1974, vol. VII
Jackson, Sir Anthony Henry Mather M.; *see* Mather-Jackson.
Jackson, Col Arnold Nugent Strode S.; *see* Strode-Jackson.
Jackson, Arthur, 1853–1938, vol. III
Jackson, Sir Arthur, *died* 1940, vol. III

Jackson, Maj.-Gen. Arthur James, 1923–1987, vol. VIII
Jackson, B. Leslie, *born* 1866, vol. III
Jackson, Sir Barry Vincent, 1879–1961, vol. VI
Jackson, Lt-Col Basil A.; *see* Archer-Jackson.
Jackson, Basil Rawdon, 1892–1957, vol. V
Jackson, Benjamin Daydon, 1846–1927, vol. II
Jackson, Rev. Blomfield, 1839–1905, vol. I
Jackson, Air Chief Marshal Sir Brendan James, 1935–1998, vol. X
Jackson, Rev. Brice Lee, 1864–1941, vol. IV
Jackson, Hon. Cecil Gower, 1872–1920, vol. II
Jackson, Brig. Cecil Vivian Staveley, 1887–1964, vol. VI
Jackson, Charles d'Orville Pilkington, 1887–1973, vol. VII
Jackson, Sir Charles James, 1849–1923, vol. II
Jackson, Major Charles Lionel Atkins W.; *see* Ward-Jackson.
Jackson, Sir Christopher Mather M., 5th Bt (*cr* 1869); *see* Mather-Jackson, Sir G. C. M.
Jackson, Colin; *see* Jackson, G. C.
Jackson, Sir Cyril, 1863–1924, vol. II
Jackson, Rev. Canon Cyril, 1897–1969, vol. VI
Jackson, Daniel, 1858–1931, vol. III
Jackson, Daphne Frances, 1936–1991, vol. IX
Jackson, Derek Ainslie, 1906–1982, vol. VIII
Jackson, Sir Donald Edward, 1892–1981, vol. VIII
Jackson, Sir Edward Arthur Mather-, 4th Bt (*cr* 1869), 1899–1956, vol. V
Jackson, Edward Francis, 1915–1989, vol. VIII
Jackson, Sir Edward St John, 1886–1961, vol. VI
Jackson, Rev. Canon Edwin B.; *see* Brook-Jackson.
Jackson, Egbert Joseph William, *died* 1975, vol. VII
Jackson, Eric Stead, 1909–1991, vol. IX
Jackson, Sir Ernest; *see* Jackson, Sir J. E.
Jackson, Lt-Col Ernest Somerville, 1872–1943, vol. IV
Jackson, F. Ernest, *died* 1945, vol. IV
Jackson, Rt Rev. Fabian Menteath Elliot, 1902–1978, vol. VII
Jackson, Rev. Forbes, *died* 1913, vol. I
Jackson, Col Sir Francis (James) Gidlow, 1889–1979, vol. VII
Jackson, Rt Hon. Sir (Francis) Stanley, 1870–1947, vol. IV
Jackson, Major Sir Francis Walter Fitton, 1881–1936, vol. III
Jackson, Rev. Canon Frank Hilton, 1870–1960, vol. V
Jackson, Col Frank Lawson John, 1919–1976, vol. VII
Jackson, Frank Stather, 1853–1922, vol. II
Jackson, Major Frank Whitford, 1886–1955, vol. V
Jackson, Most Rev. Frederic; *see* Jackson, Most Rev. G. F. C.
Jackson, Major Frederick George, *died* 1938, vol. III
Jackson, Frederick Hamilton, 1848–1923, vol. II
Jackson, Frederick Hume, 1918–1994, vol. IX
Jackson, Rt Hon. Frederick Huth, 1863–1921, vol. II
Jackson, Sir Frederick John, 1860–1929, vol. III
Jackson, Frederick John F.; *see* Foakes-Jackson.

Jackson, Sir Geoffrey Holt Seymour, 1915–1987, vol. VIII
Jackson, Brig.-Gen. Geoffrey Meinertzhagen, 1869–1946, vol. IV
Jackson, George, 1843–1931, vol. III
Jackson, Rev. George, 1864–1945, vol. IV
Jackson, (George) Colin, 1921–1981, vol. VIII
Jackson, Most Rev. George Frederic Clarence, 1907–1990, vol. VIII
Jackson, Maj.-Gen. George Hanbury, 1876–1958, vol. V
Jackson, Major Sir George Julius, 3rd Bt (*cr* 1902), 1883–1956, vol. V
Jackson, Lt-Col George Scott, *died* 1946, vol. IV
Jackson, Gerald Breck, 1916–2000, vol. X
Jackson, Sir Gilbert Hollinshead Blomfield, 1875–1956, vol. V
Jackson, Sir Gordon; *see* Jackson, Sir R. G.
Jackson, Gordon Cameron, 1923–1990, vol. VIII
Jackson, Gordon Noel, 1913–1999, vol. X
Jackson, Lt-Col Guy, 1903–1960, vol. V
Jackson, Harold Gordon, 1888–1950, vol. IV
Jackson, Captain Harold Gordon, *died* 1950, vol. IV
Jackson, H(arold) Haygarth, 1896–1972, vol. VII
Jackson, Sir Harold Warters, 1883–1972, vol. VII
Jackson, Harry, 1892–1976, vol. VII
Jackson, Harry W., 1855–1930, vol. III
Jackson, Harvey, 1900–1982, vol. VIII
Jackson, Henry, 1839–1921, vol. II
Jackson, Sir Henry, 1st Bt (*cr* 1935), 1875–1937, vol. III
Jackson, Admiral of the Fleet Sir Henry Bradwardine, 1855–1929, vol. III
Jackson, Gen. Sir Henry Cholmondeley, 1879–1972, vol. VII
Jackson, Rev. Henry Latimer, 1851–1926, vol. II
Jackson, Captain Henry Leigh, 1886–1956, vol. V
Jackson, Captain Henry Mather-, 1894–1928, vol. II
Jackson, Sir Henry Mather-, 3rd Bt (*cr* 1869), 1855–1942, vol. IV
Jackson, Sir Henry Moore, 1849–1908, vol. I
Jackson, Sir Herbert, 1863–1936, vol. III
Jackson, Herbert, 1909–1989, vol. VIII
Jackson, Brig.-Gen. Herbert Kendall, 1859–1938, vol. III
Jackson, Maj.-Gen. Sir Herbert William, 1861–1931, vol. III
Jackson, Maj.-Gen. Herbert William, 1872–1940, vol. III
Jackson, Holbrook, 1874–1948, vol. IV
Jackson, Hugh Marrison Gower, 1870–1934, vol. III
Jackson, Col Hugh Milbourne, 1858–1940, vol. III
Jackson, Sir Hugh Nicholas, 2nd Bt (*cr* 1913), 1881–1979, vol. VII
Jackson, Maj.-Gen. James, 1866–1957, vol. V
Jackson, James Barry; *see* Barry, Michael.
Jackson, Ven. James M'Creight, 1841–1913, vol. I
Jackson, Sir John, 1851–1919, vol. II
Jackson, Sir John, 1865–1933, vol. III
Jackson, John, 1887–1958, vol. V
Jackson, John Arthur, 1862–1937, vol. III
Jackson, John Brinckerhoff, 1862–1920, vol. II
Jackson, Sir (John) Ernest, 1876–1941, vol. IV
Jackson, John Hughlings, 1835–1911, vol. I

Jackson, Sir John Montrésor, 6th Bt (*cr* 1815), 1914–1980, vol. VII
Jackson, Sir John Peter Todd, 1868–1945, vol. IV
Jackson, John Wharton, 1902–1986, vol. VIII
Jackson, John Whitfield-, 1847–1910, vol. I
Jackson, Joseph, 1924–1987, vol. VIII
Jackson, Joseph Cooksey, 1879–1938, vol. III
Jackson, Sir Keith George, 4th Bt (*cr* 1815), 1842–1916, vol. II
Jackson, Kenneth Hurlstone, 1909–1991, vol. IX
Jackson, Col Lambert Cameron, 1875–1953, vol. V
Jackson, Laura Riding, 1901–1991, vol. IX
Jackson, Lawrence Colvile, *died* 1905, vol. I
Jackson, Hon. Sir Lawrence Walter, 1913–1993, vol. IX
Jackson, Brig.-Gen. Lionel Warren de Vere S.; *see* Sadleir-Jackson.
Jackson, Maj.-Gen. Sir Louis Charles, 1856–1946, vol. IV
Jackson, Maunsell Bowers, *died* 1922, vol. II
Jackson, Morton Strode, 1848–1913, vol. I
Jackson, Nicholas L.; *see* Lane-Jackson.
Jackson, Rev. Percival, 1845–1929, vol. III
Jackson, Sir Percy Richard, 1869–1941, vol. IV
Jackson, Sir Ralph, 1872–1943, vol. IV
Jackson, Air Vice-Marshal Sir Ralph Coburn, 1914–1991, vol. IX
Jackson, Raymond Allen, (JAK), 1927–1997, vol. X
Jackson, Reginald Nevill, 1887–1937, vol. III
Jackson, Sir Richard Hoyle, 1869–1944, vol. IV
Jackson, Col Richard John Laurence, 1908–1989, vol. VIII
Jackson, Sir Richard Leofric, 1902–1975, vol. VII
Jackson, Richard Meredith, 1903–1986, vol. VIII
Jackson, Lt-Col Richard Rolt Brash, 1874–1943, vol. IV
Jackson, Richard Stephens, 1850–1938, vol. III
Jackson, Maj.-Gen. Robert Edward, 1886–1948, vol. IV
Jackson, Robert Edwin, 1826–1909, vol. I
Jackson, Robert Frederick, 1880–1951, vol. V
Jackson, Comdr Sir Robert Gillman Allen, 1911–1991, vol. IX
Jackson, Robert H., 1892–1954, vol. V
Jackson, Sir Robert Montrésor, 5th Bt (*cr* 1815), 1876–1940, vol. III
Jackson, Col Sir Robert Whyte Melville, 1860–1928, vol. II
Jackson, Sir Robert William, 1826–1921, vol. II
Jackson, Rt Rev. Robert Wyse, 1908–1976, vol. VII
Jackson, Sir (Ronald) Gordon, 1924–1991, vol. IX
Jackson, Sir Russell; *see* Jackson, Sir W. D. R.
Jackson, Col Samuel, 1845–1911, vol. I
Jackson, Samuel Macauley, 1851–1912, vol. I
Jackson, Samuel Phillips, 1830–1904, vol. I
Jackson, Rt Hon. Sir Stanley; *see* Jackson, Sir F. S.
Jackson, Col Sydney Charles Fishburn, 1863–1928, vol. II
Jackson, Sir Thomas, 1st Bt (*cr* 1902), 1841–1915, vol. I
Jackson, Adm. Sir Thomas, 1868–1945, vol. IV
Jackson, Brig.-Gen. Sir Thomas Daare, 2nd Bt (*cr* 1902), 1876–1954, vol. V
Jackson, Sir Thomas Graham, 1st Bt (*cr* 1913), 1835–1924, vol. II

Jackson, Adm. Sir Thomas Sturges, 1842–1934, vol. III
Jackson, Thomas Vincent, *died* 1901, vol. I
Jackson, Rt Rev. Vibert, 1874–1963, vol. VI
Jackson, Lt-Col Vivian Archer, 1882–1943, vol. IV
Jackson, Sir (Walter David) Russell, 4th Bt (*cr* 1902), 1890–1956, vol. V
Jackson, Sir Wilfrid Edward Francis, 1883–1971, vol. VII
Jackson, Maj.-Gen. William, 1830–1912, vol. I
Jackson, William Alexander, 1905–1964, vol. VI
Jackson, Gen. Sir William Godfrey Fothergill, 1917–1999, vol. X
Jackson, William Henry, *died* 1920, vol. II
Jackson, Rear-Adm. William Lindsay, 1889–1962, vol. VI
Jackson, Sir William M.; *see* Mather-Jackson.
Jackson, William Unsworth, 1926–1999, vol. X
Jackson, Rev. William V.; *see* Vincent-Jackson.
Jackson, Rev. William Walrond, 1838–1931, vol. III
Jackson-Stops, Gervase Frank Ashworth, 1947–1995, vol. IX
Jacob, Albert Edward, 1858–1929, vol. III
Jacob, Mrs Arthur, (Violet Jacob), *died* 1946, vol. IV
Jacob, Maj.-Gen. Arthur Le Grand, 1867–1942, vol. IV
Jacob, Lt-Col Arthur Leslie, 1870–1944, vol. IV
Jacob, Ven. Bernard Victor, 1921–1992, vol. IX
Jacob, Field-Marshal Sir Claud William, 1863–1948, vol. IV
Jacob, Rt Rev. Edgar, 1844–1920, vol. II
Jacob, Edward Fountaine, 1852–1912, vol. I
Jacob, Ernest Fraser, 1894–1971, vol. VII
Jacob, Lt-Gen. Sir (Edward) Ian (Claud), 1899–1993, vol. IX
Jacob, Sir George Harold L.; *see* Lloyd-Jacob.
Jacob, Gordon Percival Septimus, 1895–1984, vol. VIII
Jacob, Lt-Col Harold Fenton, 1866–1936, vol. III
Jacob, Lieut-Gen. Sir Ian; *see* Jacob, Lieut-Gen. Sir E. I. C.
Jacob, Sir Isaac Hai, (Sir Jack), 1908–2000, vol. X
Jacob, Sir Jack; *see* Jacob, Sir I. H.
Jacob, John Hier, 1884–1964, vol. VI
Jacob, Sir Lionel Montague, 1853–1934, vol. III
Jacob, Naomi, 1884–1964, vol. VI
Jacob, Rhoda Hannah, 1900–1979, vol. VII
Jacob, Sir (Samuel) Swinton, 1841–1917, vol. II
Jacob, Sir Swinton; *see* Jacob, Sir S. S.
Jacob, Col Sydney Long, 1845–1911, vol. I
Jacob, Violet; *see* Jacob, Mrs Arthur.
Jacob, Lt-Col Walter Henry Bell, 1871–1925, vol. II
Jacob, Maj.-Gen. William, 1837–1917, vol. II
Jacob, Rev. William, *died* 1940, vol. III
Jacob, Very Rev. William Ungoed, 1910–1990, vol. VIII
Jacobi, Georges, 1840–1906, vol. I
Jacobs, Arthur David, 1922–1996, vol. X
Jacobs, Brig. John Conrad S.; *see* Saunders-Jacobs.
Jacobs, Joseph, 1854–1916, vol. II
Jacobs, Sir Piers, 1933–1999, vol. X
Jacobs, Sir Roland Ellis, 1891–1981, vol. VIII
Jacobs, Sir Wilfred Ebenezer, 1919–1994, vol. X (AI)

Jacobs, William Wymark, 1863–1943, vol. IV
Jacobs-Bond, Carrie; see Bond.
Jacobs-Larkcom, Eric Herbert Larkcom, 1895–1982, vol. VIII
Jacobsen, Arne, 1902–1971, vol. VII
Jacobsen, Frithjof Halfdan, 1914–1999, vol. X
Jacobsen, Thomas Owen, 1864–1941, vol. IV
Jacobson, Baron (Life Peer); Sydney Jacobson, 1908–1988, vol. VIII
Jacobson, Ernest Nathaniel Joseph, 1877–1947, vol. IV
Jacobsson, Per, 1894–1963, vol. VI
Jacobsthal, Paul Ferdinand, 1880–1957, vol. V
Jacoby, Felix, 1876–1959, vol. V
Jacoby, Sir James Alfred, 1852–1909, vol. I
Jacomb, Rear-Adm. Humphrey Benson, 1891–1969, vol. VI
Jacomb-Hood, George Percy, 1857–1929, vol. III
Jacques, Baron (Life Peer); John Henry Jacques, 1905–1995, vol. IX
Jacques, Rev. Kinton, 1837–1915, vol. I
Jacques, Brig. Leslie Innes, 1897–1959, vol. V
Jacques, Reginald; see Jacques, T. R.
Jacques, Robin, 1920–1995, vol. IX
Jacques, (Thomas) Reginald, 1894–1969, vol. VI
Jacquot, Général d'Armée Pierre Elie, 1902–1984, vol. VIII
Jacson, Rev. Owen Fitzherbert, 1861–1935, vol. III
Jadunath Mazoomdar, Rai Bahadur, Vedanta Bachaspati, 1859–1932, vol. III
Jaeger, John Conrad, 1907–1979, vol. VII
Jaeger, Werner W., 1888–1961, vol. VI
Jafar, Rafa Sir Saiyid Abu, died 1927, vol. II
Ja'far El Askeri, General, 1885–1936, vol. III
Jaffé, (Andrew) Michael, 1923–1997, vol. X
Jaffé, Michael; see Jaffé, A. M.
Jaffe, Sir Otto, 1846–1929, vol. III
Jaffer, Sir Ebrahim Haroon, 1881–1930, vol. III
Jaffray, Sir John, 1st Bt, 1818–1901, vol. I
Jaffray, Sir John Henry, 3rd Bt, 1893–1916, vol. II
Jaffray, Hon. Robert, 1832–1914, vol. I
Jaffray, Sir William, 2nd Bt, 1852–1914, vol. I
Jaffray, Sir William Edmund, 4th Bt, 1895–1953, vol. V
Jaffray, Rev. William Stevenson, 1867–1941, vol. IV
Jaffrey, Francis, 1861–1919, vol. II
Jaffrey, Sir Thomas, 1st Bt, 1861–1953, vol. V
Jagan, Cheddi, 1918–1997, vol. X
Jagatsingh, Hon. Sir Keharsingh, (Hon. Sir Kher), 1931–1985, vol. VIII
Jagatsingh, Hon. Sir Kher; see Jagatsingh, Hon. Sir Keharsingh.
Jaggard, Captain William, died 1947, vol. IV
Jagger, Charles Sargeant, 1885–1934, vol. III
Jagger, David, died 1958, vol. V
Jagger, Rev. James Edwin, died 1937, vol. III
Jagger, John, 1872–1942, vol. IV
Jago, Thomas Sampson, 1835–1915, vol. I
Jago, William, 1854–1938, vol. III
Jagoe, Rt Rev. John Arthur, 1889–1962, vol. VI
Jahn, Gunnar, 1883–1971, vol. VII
Jahn, Hermann Arthur, 1907–1979, vol. VII
Jaipur, Maharaja of, 1861–1922, vol. II
Jaipur, Maharaja of, 1911–1970, vol. VI

Jaisalmer, Maharajahdhiraj of, 1882–1949, vol. IV (A), vol. V
JAK; see Jackson, R. A.
Jakeway, Sir Derek; see Jakeway, Sir F. D.
Jakeway, Sir (Francis) Derek, 1915–1993, vol. IX
Jacobovits, Baron (Life Peer); Immanuel Jakobovits, 1921–1999, vol. X
Jakobson, Roman, 1896–1982, vol. VIII
Jalland, Arthur Edgar, 1889–1958, vol. V
Jalland, Rev. Trevor Gervase, 1896–1975, vol. VII
Jalland, William Herbert Wainwright, 1922–2000, vol. X
Jamal Sir Abdul Karim Abdul Shakur, 1862–1924, vol. II
Jamer, Herman Watson, 1904–1972, vol. VII
James of Hereford, 1st Baron, 1828–1911, vol. I
James of Rusholme, Baron (Life Peer); Eric John Francis James, 1909–1992, vol. IX
James, Abraham Thomas, 1883–1940, vol. III
James, Alexander, 1850–1932, vol. III
James, Alfred Henry, 1868–1941, vol. IV
James, Brig.-Gen. Alfred Henry Cotes, 1873–1947, vol. IV
James, Antony B.; see Brett-James, E. A.
James, Wing Comdr Sir Archibald William Henry, 1893–1980, vol. VII
James, Arthur, 1871–1959, vol. V
James, Rev. Canon Arthur Dyfrig, 1902–1980, vol. VII
James, Rt Hon. Sir Arthur Evan, 1916–1976, vol. VII
James, Arthur Godfrey, 1876–1959, vol. V
James, Sir Arthur Gwynne Gwynne-, 1885–1936, vol. III
James, Captain Arthur Keedwell Harvey; see Craven, Arthur Scott.
James, Arthur L.; see Lloyd James.
James, Rev. Arthur Oswel, 1849–1932, vol. III
James, Maj.-Gen. Sir Bernard; see James, Maj.-Gen. Sir W. B.
James, Col Bernard Ramsden, 1864–1938, vol. III
James, Lt-Col Boucher Charlewood, 1882–1930, vol. III
James, Col Cecil Polglase, 1879–1943, vol. IV
James, Charles Ashworth, died 1937, vol. III
James, Charles Canniff, 1863–1916, vol. II
James, Lt-Col Charles Henry, 1863–1944, vol. IV
James, Charles Holloway, 1893–1953, vol. V
James, Engr Rear-Adm. Charles John, 1862–1943, vol. IV
James, Hon. Sir Claude Ernest Weymouth, died 1961, vol. VI
James, Lt-Col Hon. Cuthbert, 1872–1930, vol. III
James, Brig.-Gen. Cyril Henry Leigh, died 1946, vol. IV
James, David G.; see Guthrie-James.
James, David Gwilym, 1905–1968, vol. VI
James, Sir David John, 1887–1967, vol. VI
James, David Pelham; see Guthrie-James, D.
James, David William Francis, 1929–1995, vol. IX (AII)
James, Ven. Denis, 1895–1965, vol. VI
James, Air Vice-Marshal Edgar, 1915–1996, vol. X
James, Lt-Col Edmund Henry Salt, 1874–1952, vol. V

James, Edmund Janes, 1855–1925, vol. II
James, Edmund Purcell S.; Skone James.
James, Rev. Edward, 1828–1913, vol. I
James, Edward, 1885–1971, vol. VII
James, Sir Edward Albert, 5th Bt, 1862–1942, vol. IV
James, Sir Edward Burnet, 1857–1927, vol. II
James, Rev. Edwin Oliver, 1888–1972, vol. VII
James, (Eliot) Antony B.; see Brett-James.
James, (Ernest) Gethin, 1925–1995, vol. IX
James, Florence, 1857–1929, vol. III
James, Sir Francis; see James, Sir J. F. W.
James, Francis Edward, died 1920, vol. II
James, F(rank) Cyril, 1903–1973, vol. VII
James, Sir Frederick Ernest, 1891–1971, vol. VII
James, Sir Frederick Seton, 1870–1934, vol. III
James, Captain Sir Fullarton, 6th Bt, 1864–1955, vol. V
James, Sir Gavin Fullarton, 4th Bt, 1859–1937, vol. III
James, George William Blomfield, died 1968, vol. VI
James, Georgina Giselle, 1951–2000, vol. X
James, Gethin; see James, E. G.
James, Mrs Helena Constance R.; see Romanne-James.
James, Henry, 1843–1916, vol. II
James, Sir Henry Evan Murchison, 1846–1923, vol. II
James, Henry Leonard, 1919–1998, vol. X
James, Very Rev. Henry Lewis, 1864–1949, vol. IV
James, Henry Rosher, 1862–1931, vol. III
James, Col Herbert, 1859–1943, vol. IV
James, Rev. Herbert Armitage, 1844–1931, vol. III
James, Lt-Col Herbert Ellison Rhodes, died 1939, vol. III
James, Lt-Col Herbert Lionel, 1863–1946, vol. IV
James, Ivor Benjamin Hugh, 1882–1963, vol. VI
James, Sir Jack; see James, Sir John H.
James, Gen. Sir John, 1832–1901, vol. I
James, John, 1906–1996, vol. X
James, John Anthony, 1913–1987, vol. IX (AI)
James, John Arthur, 1853–1917, vol. II
James, Ven. John D., 1862–1938, vol. III
James, John Egbert, 1876–1965, vol. VI
James, Sir John Ernest, died 1963, vol. VI
James, Sir (John) Francis (William), 1879–1950, vol. IV
James, Very Rev. John Gwynno, 1912–1967, vol. VI
James, Sir John Hastings, (Sir Jack), 1906–1980, vol. VI
James, Sir John Kingston Fullarton, 3rd Bt, 1852–1933, vol. III
James, John Morrice Cairns; see Baron Saint Brides.
James, John Richings, 1912–1980, vol. VII
James, John William, 1907–1975, vol. VII
James, John Wynford George, 1911–1990, vol. VIII
James, Rev. Lemuel John H.; see Hopkin-James.
James, Lewis Cairns, 1865–1946, vol. IV
James, Lionel, 1868–1948, vol. IV
James, Col Lionel, 1871–1955, vol. V
James, Brig. Manley Angell, 1896–1975, vol. VII
James, Rt Rev. Melville Charles, 1877–1957, vol. V

James, Montague Rhodes, 1862–1936, vol. III
James, Col Murray Ray de Bruyne, 1870–1939, vol. III
James, Noel David Glaves, 1911–1993, vol. IX
James, Norah C., 1901–1979, vol. VII
James, Peter Maunde Coram, 1922–1993, vol. IX
James, Philip Brutton, 1901–1974, vol. VII
James, Philip Gaved, 1904–1978, vol. VII
James, Lt-Col Ralph Ernest Haweis, 1875–1964, vol. VI
James, Reginald Hugh Lloyd L.; see Langford-James.
James, Reginald William, 1891–1964, vol. VI
James, Richard Bush, 1889–1970, vol. VI
James, Richard Lewis Malcolm, 1897–1972, vol. VI
James, Hon. Robert, 1873–1960, vol. V
James, Robert Leoline, 1905–1982, vol. VIII
James, Sir Robert Vidal R.; see Rhodes James.
James, Rolfe Arnold S.; see Scott-James.
James, Lt-Col Sydney Price, died 1946, vol. IV
James, Ven. Sydney Rhodes, 1855–1934, vol. III
James, Thomas David, 1871–1955, vol. V
James, Thomas Geraint Illtyd, 1900–1996, vol. X
James, Thomas Maurice, 1890–1962, vol. VI
James, Vice-Adm. Thomas Norman, 1878–1965, vol. VI
James, Thurstan Trewartha, 1903–1975, vol. VII
James, Lt-Col Tristram Bernard Wordsworth, 1883–1939, vol. III
James, Hon. Sir Walter Hartwell, 1863–1943, vol. IV
James, Lt-Col Walter Haweis, 1847–1927, vol. II
James, Rev. Walter Hill, 1828–1910, vol. I
James, William, 1842–1910, vol. I
James, Maj.-Gen. Sir (William) Bernard, 1865–1940, vol. III
James, William Dodge, 1854–1912, vol. I
James, William Garnet, 1895–1977, vol. VII
James, William Henry E.; see Ewart James.
James, Adm. Sir William Milbourne, 1881–1973, vol. VII
James, William Owen, 1900–1978, vol. VII
James, Col William Reginald Wallwyn, 1860–1925, vol. II
James, William Thomas, 1892–1982, vol. VIII
James, William Warwick, 1874–1965, vol. VI
James, Winifred Lewellin, (Mrs Henry de Jan), died 1941, vol. IV
Jameson, Adam, 1860–1907, vol. I
Jameson, Alexander Hope, 1874–1952, vol. V
Jameson, Rt Hon. Andrew, 1855–1941, vol. IV
Jameson, Andrew; see Ardwall, Hon. Lord.
Jameson, Cecil Stuart, born 1883, vol. VI
Jameson, Ven. Francis Bernard, 1889–1960, vol. V (A), vol. VI (AI)
Jameson, Brig. Frank Robert Wordsworth, 1893–1965, vol. VI
Jameson, Surgeon-Gen. James, 1837–1904, vol. I
Jameson, James Alexander, 1885–1961, vol. VI
Jameson, John, died 1920, vol. II
Jameson, Lt-Col John Bland, died 1954, vol. V
Jameson, Lt-Col John Eustace-, 1853–1919, vol. II
Jameson, John Franklin, 1859–1937, vol. III
Jameson, John Gordon, 1878–1955, vol. V

Jameson, Rt Hon. Sir Leander Starr, 1st Bt, 1853–1917, vol. II

Jameson, (Margaret) Storm, 1891–1986, vol. VIII

Jameson, Noel Rutherford, 1892–1971, vol. VII

Jameson, Air Cdre Patrick Geraint, 1912–1996, vol. X

Jameson, Surg.-Captain Robert Dundonald, 1869–1938, vol. III

Jameson, Storm; see Jameson, M. S.

Jameson, Maj.-Gen. Thomas Henry, 1894–1985, vol. VIII

Jameson, William George, 1851–1939, vol. III

Jameson, Rear-Adm. Sir William Scarlett, 1899–1966, vol. VI

Jameson, Sir (William) Wilson, 1885–1962, vol. VI

Jameson, Sir Wilson; see Jameson, Sir W. W.

Jamiat Rai, Diwan, Rai Bahadur, Diwan Bahadur, 1861–1941, vol. IV

Jamieson, Rt Hon. Lord; Douglas Jamieson, 1880–1952, vol. V

Jamieson, Alexander, 1873–1937, vol. III

Jamieson, Sir Archibald Auldjo, 1884–1959, vol. V

Jamieson, Hon. Donald Campbell, 1921–1986, vol. VIII

Jamieson, Douglas; see Jamieson, Rt Hon. Lord.

Jamieson, Vice-Adm. Douglas Y.; see Young-Jamieson.

Jamieson, Edgar George, 1882–1958, vol. V

Jamieson, George, 1843–1920, vol. II

Jamieson, Lt-Col Harvey Morro H.; see Harvey-Jamieson.

Jamieson, Sir James William, 1867–1946, vol. IV

Jamieson, John Kay, 1873–1948, vol. IV

Jamieson, John Kenneth, 1910–1999, vol. X

Jamieson, R. Kirkland, 1881–1950, vol. IV

Jamieson, Stanley Wyndham, 1885–1970, vol. VI

Jamieson, William Allan, 1839–1916, vol. II

Jamison, Evelyn Mary, 1877–1972, vol. VII

Jamison, James Hardie, 1913–1996, vol. X

Jamison, Robin Ralph, 1912–1991, vol. IX

Jan, Winifred Lewellin de; see James, W. L.

Jane, Frank William, 1901–1963, vol. VI

Jane, Fred. T., 1870–1916, vol. II

Janes, Emily, died 1928, vol. II

Janes, Sir Herbert Charles, 1884–1977, vol. VII

Janes, Rev. Maxwell Osborne, 1902–1981, vol. VIII

Janes, Norman Thomas, 1892–1980, vol. VII

Janet, Pierre, 1859–1947, vol. IV

Janion, Edwin Manifold, 1863–1952, vol. V

Janion, Rear-Adm. Sir Hugh Penderel, 1923–1994, vol. IX

Janisch, Noel, died 1930, vol. III

Janjira, HH Nawab, 1862–1922, vol. II

Jannaris, Anthony, 1852–1909, vol. I

Janner, Baron (Life Peer); Barnett Janner, 1892–1982, vol. VIII

Janner, Lady; Elsie Sybil Janner, 1905–1994, vol. IX

Jansen, Ernest George, 1881–1959, vol. V

Jansen, Peter Johan, 1940–1998, vol. X

Janson, Stanley Eric, 1908–1974, vol. VII

Jansz, Sir Eric; see Jansz, Sir H. E.

Jansz, Sir (Herbert) Eric, 1890–1976, vol. VII

Janvrin, Vice-Adm. Sir (Hugh) Richard Benest, 1915–1993, vol. IX

Janvrin, Vice-Adm. Sir Richard; see Janvrin, Vice-Adm. Sir H. R. B.

Janvrin, Rev. William Langston Benest, 1853–1927, vol. II

Jaora State, Lt-Col HH Fakhr-ud-Daulah Nawab Sir Mohammad Iftikhar Ali Khan Bahadur Saulat Jang, 1883–1947, vol. IV

Japp, Francis Robert, 1848–1925, vol. II

Japp, Sir Henry, 1869–1939, vol. III

Jaques-Dalcroze, Emile, 1865–1950, vol. IV

Jaquet, Sir Robert Glover, 1856–1937, vol. III

Jardine, Sir Alexander, 10th Bt (cr 1672), 1868–1942, vol. IV

Jardine, Brig. Christian West B.; see Bayne-Jardine.

Jardine, Christopher Willoughby, 1911–1982, vol. VIII

Jardine, Maj.-Gen. Sir Colin Arthur, 3rd Bt (cr 1916), 1892–1957, vol. V

Jardine, David Jardine, 1847–1922, vol. II

Jardine, Sir Douglas James, 1888–1946, vol. IV

Jardine, Douglas Robert, 1900–1958, vol. V

Jardine, Sir Ernest, 1st Bt (cr 1919), 1859–1947, vol. IV

Jardine, Brig. Sir Ian Liddell, 4th Bt, 1923–1982, vol. VIII

Jardine, James, 1846–1909, vol. I

Jardine, Brig.-Gen. James Bruce, 1870–1955, vol. V

Jardine, James Willoughby, 1879–1945, vol. IV

Jardine, Sir John, 1st Bt (cr 1916), 1844–1919, vol. II

Jardine, Sir John, 2nd Bt (cr 1919), 1884–1965, vol. VI

Jardine, John, 1881–1974, vol. VII

Jardine, Major Sir John Eric Birdwood, 2nd Bt (cr 1916), 1890–1924, vol. II

Jardine, John Frederick James, 1926–1990, vol. VIII

Jardine, Captain Sir John William Buchanan-, 3rd Bt (cr 1885), 1900–1969, vol. VI

Jardine, Lionel Westropp, 1895–1980, vol. VII

Jardine, Malcolm Robert, 1869–1947, vol. IV

Jardine, Michael James, 1915–1988, vol. VIII

Jardine, Sir Robert, 1st Bt (cr 1885), 1825–1905, vol. I

Jardine, Robert, 1862–1932, vol. III

Jardine, Robert Frier, 1894–1982, vol. VIII

Jardine, Sir Robert William Buchanan, 2nd Bt (cr 1885), 1868–1927, vol. II

Jardine, Sir William, 9th Bt (cr 1672), 1865–1915, vol. I

Jardine of Applegirth, Col Sir William Edward, 11th Bt, 1917–1986, vol. VIII

Jardine, William Ellis, 1867–1944, vol. IV

Jardine-Brown, Robert, 1905–1972, vol. VII

Jardine Paterson, Lt Col Arthur James, 1918–1988, vol. VIII

Jardine Paterson, Sir John Valentine, 1920–2000, vol. X

Jarman, Charles, 1893–1947, vol. IV

Jarman, Rev. Canon Cyril Edgar, 1892–1978, vol. VII

Jarman, Derek; see Jarman, M. D.

Jarman, John Robert, 1844–1922, vol. II

Jarman, Air Cdre Lance Michael E.; *see* Elworthy-Jarman.
Jarman, (Michael) Derek, 1942–1994, vol. IX
Jarmay, Sir John Gustav, 1856–1944, vol. IV
Jarrad, Sir Vivian Everard Donne, *died* 1938, vol. III
Jarratt, Sir Arthur William, 1894–1958, vol. V
Jarratt, Sir William Smith, 1871–1966, vol. VI
Jarrell, Randall, 1914–1965, vol. VI
Jarrett, Sir Clifford George, 1909–1995, vol. IX
Jarrett, Sir Francis Moncreiff K.; *see* Kerr-Jarrett.
Jarrett, George William Symonds, 1880–1960, vol. V
Jarrett, Col Henry Sullivan, 1839–1919, vol. II
Jarrett, James Henry, 1895–1943, vol. IV
Jarrett, Norman Rowlstone, 1889–1982, vol. VIII
Jarrold, (Herbert) John, 1906–1979, vol. VII
Jarrold, John; *see* Jarrold, H. J.
Jarvie, John Gibson, 1883–1964, vol. VI
Jarvis, Sir Adrian; *see* Jarvis, Sir A. A.
Jarvis, Alan Hepburn, 1915–1972, vol. VII
Jarvis, Very Rev. Alfred Charles Eustace, 1876–1957, vol. V
Jarvis, Ven. Alfred Clifford, 1908–1981, vol. VIII
Jarvis, Sir (Arnold) Adrian, 2nd Bt, 1904–1965, vol. VI
Jarvis, Lt-Col Arthur Leonard Fitzgerald, 1852–1927, vol. II
Jarvis, Lt-Col Arthur Murray, 1863=n1930, vol. III
Jarvis, Lt-Col Charles Francis Cracroft, *died* 1957, vol. V
Jarvis, Major Claude Scudamore, 1879–1953, vol. V
Jarvis, Mrs Doris Annie, *born* 1912, vol. VIII
Jarvis, Edward Blackwell, 1873–1950, vol. IV
Jarvis, Hon. Eric William George, 1907–1987, vol. VIII
Jarvis, Very Rev. Ernest David, 1888–1964, vol. VI
Jarvis, Rev. Francis Amcotts, *died* 1937, vol. III
Jarvis, Hugh John, 1930–1993, vol. IX
Jarvis, Sir John, 1st Bt, 1876–1950, vol. IV
Jarvis, Sir John Layton, 1887–1968, vol. VI
Jarvis, Maj.-Gen. Samuel Peters, 1820–1905, vol. I
Jarvis, Col Sir Weston, 1855–1939, vol. III
Jarvis, William Rose, 1885–1943, vol. IV
Jaspar, Henri, 1870–1939, vol. III
Jasper, Cyril Charles, 1923–1987, vol. VIII
Jasper, Very Rev. Ronald Claud Dudley, 1917–1990, vol. VIII
Jaspers, Karl, 1883–1969, vol. VI
Jast, L. Stanley, 1868–1944, vol. IV
Jastrow, Morris, Jr, 1861–1921, vol. II
Jatia, Sir Onkar Mull, 1882–1938, vol. III
Jaujard, Jacques, 1895–1967, vol. VI (AII)
Jaurès, Jean Léon, 1859–1914, vol. I
Javal, Paul C.; *see* Cremieu-Javal.
Jawahir Singh, Sardar Bahadur Sir Sardar, *died* 1947, vol. IV
Jay, Baron (Life Peer); Douglas Patrick Thomas Jay, 1907–1996, vol. X
Jay, Major Charles Douglas, *died* 1941, vol. IV
Jay, Edith Katharine Spicer; *see* Prescott, E. Livingston.
Jay, Rev. Canon Eric George, 1907–1989, vol. VIII
Jay, Harriett, 1863–1932, vol. III

Jay, Thomas, 1887–1962, vol. VI
Jay, William Samuel, *died* 1933, vol. III
Jayakar, Rt Hon. Mukund R., *died* 1959, vol. V
Jayasundera, Sir Ukwatte, 1896–1962, vol. VI
Jayatilaka, Sir Don Baron, 1868–1944, vol. IV
Jayes, Percy Harris, 1915–1997, vol. X
Jayetileke, Sir Edward George Perera, 1888–1975, vol. VII
Jayewardene, E. W., *died* 1932, vol. III
Jayewardene, Junius Richard, 1906–1996, vol. X
Jayne, Col Arthur Alfred, 1878–1934, vol. III
Jayne, Rt Rev. Francis John, 1845–1921, vol. II
Jayne, Ronald Garland, 1877–1951, vol. V
Jays, Tom, 1868–1947, vol. IV
Jeaffreson, John Cordy, 1831–1901, vol. I
Jeakes, Rev. James, 1829–1915, vol. I
Jeanneret, Charles-Edouard; *see* Le Corbusier.
Jeanneret, François Charles Archile, 1890–1967, vol. VI
Jeanniot, Pierre Georges, 1848–1934, vol. III
Jeans, Sir Alexander Grigor, 1849–1924, vol. II
Jeans, Sir Alick, (Alexander Grigor), 1912–1972, vol. VII
Jeans, Allan, 1877–1961, vol. VI
Jeans, Hon. Maj.-Gen. Charles Gilchrist, 1854–1920, vol. II
Jeans, Frank, 1878–1933, vol. III
Jeans, Isabel, 1891–1985, vol. VIII
Jeans, J. Stephen, 1846–1913, vol. I
Jeans, Sir James Hopwood, 1877–1946, vol. IV
Jeans, Sir Richard Walter, 1846–1924, vol. II
Jeans, Ronald, *died* 1973, vol. VII
Jeans, Major Thomas Kilvington, 1885–1962, vol. VI
Jeans, Surg. Rear-Adm. Thomas Tendron, *died* 1938, vol. III
Jeans, Ursula, *died* 1973, vol. VII
Jeans, William, *died* 1916, vol. II
Jebb, Eglantyne Mary, 1889–1978, vol. VII
Jebb, Geraldine Emma May, *died* 1959, vol. V
Jebb, Brig.-Gen. Gladwyn Dundas, 1877–1947, vol. IV
Jebb, Col (Joshua Henry) Miles, 1875–1935, vol. III
Jebb, Col Miles; *see* Jebb, Col J. H. M.
Jebb, Richard, 1874–1953, vol. V
Jebb, Sir Richard Claverhouse, 1841–1905, vol. I
Jeckell, George Allen, 1880–1950, vol. IV (A), vol. V
Jedlizka, Marie; *see* Jeritza, M.
Jee, Joseph, *died* 1899, vol. I
Jeejeebhoy, Sir Byramjee, 1881–1946, vol. IV
Jeelof, Gerrit, 1927–1996, vol. X
Jeeves, William John, *died* 1932, vol. III
Jeffcoat, Col Algernon Cautley, 1877–1963, vol. VI
Jeffcoat, Captain Henry Jamieson Powell, *died* 1901, vol. I
Jeffcoate, Sir Norman; *see* Jeffcoate, Sir T. N. A.
Jeffcoate, Sir (Thomas) Norman (Arthur), 1907–1992, vol. IX
Jeffcott, Henry Homan, *died* 1937, vol. III
Jefferis, Maj.-Gen. Sir Millis Rowland, 1899–1963, vol. VI
Jeffers, Le Roy, 1878–1926, vol. II
Jeffers, William Martin, 1876–1953, vol. V

Jefferson, Frederick Thomas, 1854–1920, vol. II
Jefferson, Sir Geoffrey, 1886–1961, vol. VI
Jefferson, Captain Henry, 1865–1937, vol. III
Jefferson, Lt-Col Sir John Alexander D.; *see* Dunnington-Jefferson.
Jefferson, Joseph, 1829–1905, vol. I
Jefferson, Rt Rev. Robert, 1881–1968, vol. VI
Jefferson, Wood G., *died* 1912, vol. I
Jeffery, Cecil Albert, 1888–1970, vol. VI (AII)
Jeffery, Edward Turner, 1843–1927, vol. II, vol. III
Jeffery, George Barker, 1891–1957, vol. V
Jeffery, George H. Everett, *died* 1935, vol. III
Jeffery, George Henry Padget, 1907–1987, vol. VIII
Jeffery, Lilian Hamilton, 1915–1986, vol. VIII
Jeffery, Rev. Samuel, *died* 1934, vol. III
Jeffery, Walter, 1861–1922, vol. II
Jeffery, Col Walter Hugh, 1878–1957, vol. V
Jefferys, Charles William, 1869–1951, vol. V
Jeffes, Maurice, *died* 1954, vol. V
Jefford, Vice-Adm. James Wilfred, 1901–1980, vol. VII
Jeffrey, Very Rev. George Johnstone, 1881–1961, vol. VI
Jeffrey, Maj.-Gen. Hugh Crozier, 1914–1976, vol. VII
Jeffrey, Sir John, 1871–1947, vol. IV
Jeffrey, Rev. Norman Stuart, *died* 1919, vol. II
Jeffrey, Robert, 1884–1956, vol. V
Jeffrey, William, 1896–1946, vol. IV
Jeffrey-Waddell, John, 1876–1941, vol. IV
Jeffreys, 1st Baron, 1878–1960, vol. V
Jeffreys, 2nd Baron, 1932–1986, vol. VIII
Jeffreys, Anthony Henry, 1896–1984, vol. VIII
Jeffreys, Rt Hon. Arthur Frederick, 1848–1906, vol. I
Jeffreys, Adm. Edmund Frederick, 1846–1925, vol. II
Jeffreys, Sir Harold, 1891–1989, vol. VIII
Jeffreys, Maj.-Gen. Henry Byron, 1854–1949, vol. IV
Jeffreys, Montagu Vaughan Castelman, 1900–1985, vol. VIII
Jeffreys, Brig.-Gen. Patrick Douglas, 1848–1922, vol. II
Jeffreys, Rev. Tom Reginald Frederic, 1871–1938, vol. III
Jeffreys, W. Rees, 1871–1954, vol. V
Jeffreys Jones, David; *see* Jones.
Jeffries, Charles H., 1864–1936, vol. III
Jeffries, Sir Charles Joseph, 1895–1972, vol. VII
Jeffries, Graham Montague; *see* Graeme, Bruce.
Jeffries, Hon. Sir Shirley Williams, 1886–1963, vol. VI
Jeffries, Brig. William Francis, 1891–1969, vol. VI
Jeffs, Ernest Harry, 1885–1973, vol. VII
Jeffs, Gp Captain (George) James (Horatio), 1900–1996, vol. X
Jeffs, Harry, 1860–1938, vol. III
Jeffs, Gp Captain James; *see* Jeffs, Gp Captain G. J. H.
Jeger, George, 1903–1971, vol. VII
Jeger, Santo Wayburn, 1898–1953, vol. V
Jehanghir, Sir Cowasjee, 1st Bt, 1853–1934, vol. III
Jehanghir, Sir Cowasjee, 2nd Bt, 1879–1962, vol. VI

Jehangir, Sir Hirji, 3rd Bt, 1915–2000, vol. X
Jehangir, Vakil Hon. Khan Bahadur Sardar Sir Rustom, *died* 1933, vol. III
Jehu, Ivor Stewart, 1908–1960, vol. V
Jehu, Thomas John, 1871–1943, vol. IV
Jejeebhoy, Sir Jamsetjee, (Manockjee Cursetjee), 3rd Bt, 1851–1898, vol. I
Jejeebhoy, Sir Jamsetjee, (Cowasjee Cursetjee), 4th Bt, 1852–1908, vol. I
Jejeebhoy, Sir Jamsetjee, 6th Bt, 1909–1968, vol. VI
Jejeebhoy, Sir Jamsetjee; *see* Jejeebhoy, Sir R. C. C. J.
Jejeebhoy, Sir (Rustomjee Cowasjee Cursetjee) Jamsetjee, 5th Bt, 1878–1931, vol. III
Jekyll, Agnes, (Lady Jekyll), 1861–1937, vol. III
Jekyll, Gertrude, 1843–1932, vol. III
Jekyll, Col Sir Herbert, 1846–1932, vol. III
Jelf, Sir Arthur Richard, 1837–1917, vol. II
Jelf, Sir Arthur Selborne, 1876–1947, vol. IV
Jelf, Sir Ernest Arthur, 1868–1949, vol. IV
Jelf, Rev. George Edward, 1834–1908, vol. I
Jelf, Herbert William, 1882–1943, vol. IV
Jelf, Col Richard Henry, 1844–1913, vol. I
Jelf, Maj.-Gen. Richard William, 1904–1994, vol. IX
Jelf, Brig.-Gen. Rudolf George, 1873–1958, vol. V
Jelf, Col Wilfrid Wykeham, 1880–1933, vol. III
Jellett, Very Rev. Henry, *died* 1901, vol. I
Jellett, Henry, 1872–1948, vol. IV
Jellett, Col John Hewitt, 1859–1938, vol. III
Jellett, John Holmes, 1905–1971, vol. VII
Jellett, William Morgan, *died* 1936, vol. III
Jellicoe, 1st Earl, 1859–1935, vol. III
Jellicoe, Rear-Adm. Christopher Theodore, 1903–1977, vol. VII
Jellicoe, Sir Geoffrey Alan, 1900–1996, vol. X
Jellicoe, Brig.-Gen. Richard Carey, 1875–1962, vol. VI
Jellicorse, Rev. William, *died* 1920, vol. II
Jellinek, Lionel, 1898–1979, vol. VII
Jencken, Maj.-Gen. Francis John, 1858–1943, vol. IV
Jenkin, Mrs Bernard, (Margaret M. Giles), 1868–1949, vol. IV
Jenkin, Charles Frewen, 1865–1940, vol. III
Jenkin, Henry Archibald Tregarthen, 1886–1951, vol. V
Jenkin, Engr Rear-Adm. John Harry, 1866–1933, vol. III
Jenkin, Mary Elizabeth, 1892–1979, vol. VII
Jenkin, Thomas James, 1885–1965, vol. VI
Jenkin, Sir William Norman Prentice, 1899–1983, vol. VIII
Jenkin-Jones, Charles Mark, 1885–1971, vol. VII
Jenkin Pugh, Rev. Canon Thomas; *see* Pugh.
Jenkings, Adm. Albert Baldwin, 1846–1942, vol. IV
Jenkins, Baron (Life Peer); David Llewelyn Jenkins, 1899–1969, vol. VI
Jenkins, Rev. Canon Alfred Thomas, 1893–1960, vol. V
Jenkins, Arthur, *died* 1946, vol. IV
Jenkins, A(rthur) Robert, 1908–1989, vol. VIII
Jenkins, Charles Elliott Edward, 1859–1946, vol. IV
Jenkins, Rev. Canon Claude, 1877–1959, vol. V
Jenkins, Clive; *see* Jenkins, D. C.

Jenkins, David, 1848–1915, vol. I
Jenkins, Rev. David, *died* 1926, vol. II
Jenkins, Ven. David, 1876–1960, vol. V
Jenkins, (David) Clive, 1926–1999, vol. X
Jenkins, Rev. David Erwyd, *died* 1937, vol. III
Jenkins, Dennis Frederick M.; *see* Martin-Jenkins.
Jenkins, Douglas, 1880–1961, vol. VI
Jenkins, Edward, 1838–1910, vol. I
Jenkins, Sir (Edward) Enoch, 1895–1960, vol. V
Jenkins, Major Edward Vaughan, 1879–1941, vol. IV
Jenkins, Sir Enoch; *see* Jenkins, Sir E. E.
Jenkins, Evan David Thomas, 1882–1960, vol. V
Jenkins, Sir Evan Meredith, 1896–1985, vol. VIII
Jenkins, Lt-Col Francis, 1877–1927, vol. II
Jenkins, Brig.-Gen. Francis Conway, 1888–1933, vol. III
Jenkins, Col Sir Francis Howell, 1832–1906, vol. I
Jenkins, Frank L.; *see* Lynn-Jenkins.
Jenkins, Garth John, 1933–1995, vol. IX
Jenkins, Sir George Frederick, 1878–1957, vol. V
Jenkins, Sir George Henry, 1843–1911, vol. I
Jenkins, George Kirkhouse, *died* 1957, vol. V
Jenkins, Gilbert Henry, 1875–1957, vol. V
Jenkins, Sir Gilmour; *see* Jenkins, Sir T. G.
Jenkins, Harold, 1909–2000, vol. X
Jenkins, Herbert, *died* 1923, vol. II
Jenkins, Lt-Col Herbert Harold, 1877–1932, vol. III
Jenkins, Herbert Riches, 1880–1944, vol. IV
Jenkins, Huntly E., *died* 1923, vol. II
Jenkins, Mrs Inez Mary Mackay, 1895–1981, vol. VIII
Jenkins, Sir James, 1818–1912, vol. I
Jenkins, John, *born* 1852, vol. III
Jenkins, Hon. John Greeley, 1851–1923, vol. II
Jenkins, John Lewis, 1857–1912, vol. I
Jenkins, Ven. (John) Owen, 1906–1988, vol. VIII
Jenkins, Joseph Barclay, 1870–1950, vol. IV
Jenkins, Rt Hon. Sir Lawrence Hugh, 1858–1928, vol. II
Jenkins, Leslie Augustus Westover, 1910–1978, vol. VII
Jenkins, Brig.-Gen. Noble Fleming, 1860–1927, vol. II
Jenkins, Sir Owain Trevor, 1907–1996, vol. X
Jenkins, Ven. Owen; *see* Jenkins, Ven. J. O.
Jenkins, Peter George James, 1934–1992, vol. IX
Jenkins, Robert Christmas Dewar, 1900–1978, vol. VII
Jenkins, Robert Thomas, 1881–1969, vol. VI
Jenkins, Romilly James Heald, 1907–1969, vol. VI
Jenkins, Lt-Col Stephen Reginald Martin, 1915–1991, vol. IX
Jenkins, Very Rev. Thomas Edward, 1902–1996, vol. X
Jenkins, Vivian Evan, 1918–1997, vol. X
Jenkins, Sir (Thomas) Gilmour, 1894–1981, vol. VIII
Jenkins, Walter Allen, 1891–1958, vol. V
Jenkins, Sir Walter St David, 1874–1951, vol. V
Jenkins, Sir William, 1871–1944, vol. IV
Jenkins, Sir William, 1904–1983, vol. VIII
Jenkins, Sir William Albert, *died* 1968, vol. VI
Jenkins, William Frank, 1889–1980, vol. VII
Jenkins, William Henry Philips, 1842–1916, vol. II

Jenkins, Sir William John, 1892–1957, vol. V
Jenkins, Rev. William Owen, 1863–1919, vol. II
Jenkinson, Sir Anthony Banks, 13th Bt, 1912–1989, vol. VIII
Jenkinson, Sir (Charles) Hilary, *died* 1961, vol. VI
Jenkinson, Sir Edward George, 1835–1919, vol. II
Jenkinson, Francis Broxholm Grey, 1846–1902, vol. I
Jenkinson, Francis John Henry, 1853–1923, vol. II
Jenkinson, Sir George Banks, 12th Bt, 1851–1915, vol. I
Jenkinson, Major George Seymour Charles, 1858–1907, vol. I
Jenkinson, Sir Hilary; *see* Jenkinson, Sir C. H.
Jenkinson, John Edward, 1858–1937, vol. III (A), vol. IV
Jenkinson, Sir Mark Webster, *died* 1935, vol. III
Jenks, Clarence Wilfred, 1909–1973, vol. VII
Jenks, Rev. David, 1866–1935, vol. III
Jenks, Edward, 1861–1939, vol. III
Jenks, Sir Maurice, 1st Bt, 1872–1946, vol. IV
Jenks, Sir Richard Atherley, 2nd Bt, 1906–1993, vol. IX
Jenks, Very Rev. Walter, 1864–1935, vol. III
Jenkyns, Sir Henry, 1838–1899, vol. I
Jenner, Lt-Col Sir Albert Victor, 3rd Bt, 1862–1954, vol. V
Jenner, George Francis Birt, *born* 1840, vol. II
Jenner, Rt Rev. Henry Lascelles, 1820–1898, vol. I
Jenner, Katherine Lee, *died* 1936, vol. III
Jenner, Lt-Col Leopold Christian Duncan, 1869–1953, vol. V
Jenner, Sir Walter Kentish William, 2nd Bt, 1860–1948, vol. IV
Jenner, Sir William, 1st Bt, 1815–1898, vol. I
Jenner-Fust, Herbert, 1806–1904, vol. I
Jenney, Col Archibald Offley, 1864–1946, vol. IV
Jenney, Brig. Reginald Charles Napier, 1906–1960, vol. V
Jennings, Sir Albert Victor, 1896–1993, vol. IX
Jennings, Antony; *see* Jennings, B. A.
Jennings, Arnold Harry, 1915–1994, vol. IX
Jennings, Sir Arthur Oldham, 1855–1934, vol. III
Jennings, Arthur Seymour, *born* 1860, vol. II
Jennings, (Bernard) Antony, 1939–1990, vol. VIII
Jennings, Christopher; *see* Jennings, R. E. C.
Jennings, (Edgar) Owen, 1899–1985, vol. VIII
Jennings, Edward Charles, 1877–1955, vol. V
Jennings, Col Edward Lawrence Frederick, 1850–1931, vol. III
Jennings, Rev. Edward Linck, *died* 1940, vol. III
Jennings, Gertrude E., *died* 1958, vol. V
Jennings, Henry Cecil, 1908–1983, vol. VIII
Jennings, Brig.-Gen. Herbert Alexander Kaye, 1862–1921, vol. II
Jennings, Herbert Spencer, 1868–1947, vol. IV
Jennings, Sir Ivor; *see* Jennings, Sir W. I.
Jennings, James George, 1866–1921, vol. II
Jennings, James George, 1866–1941, vol. IV
Jennings, Lt-Col James Willes, 1866–1954, vol. V
Jennings, Rev. Canon John Andrew, 1855–1923, vol. II
Jennings, John Charles, 1903–1990, vol. VIII
Jennings, Sir John Rogers, 1820–1897, vol. I
Jennings, Leonard, *died* 1956, vol. V

Jennings, Owen; see Jennings, E. O.
Jennings, Hon. Sir Patrick Alfred, 1831–1897, vol. I
Jennings, Paul Francis, 1918–1989, vol. VIII
Jennings, Percival Henry, 1903–1995, vol. IX
Jennings, Sir Raymond Winter, 1897–1995, vol. IX
Jennings, Col Richard, 1856–1935, vol. III
Jennings, (Richard Edward) Christopher, 1911–1982, vol. VIII
Jennings, Col Robert Henry, 1852–1918, vol. II
Jennings, Gen. Sir Robert Melvill, 1841–1922, vol. II
Jennings, Sir Roland, 1894–1968, vol. VI
Jennings, Sir (William) Ivor, 1903–1965, vol. VI
Jennings, William Thomas, 1854–1923, vol. II
Jenour, Sir (Arthur) Maynard (Chesterfield), 1905–1992, vol. IX
Jenour, Brig.-Gen. Arthur Stawell, 1867–1938, vol. III
Jenour, Sir Maynard; see Jenour, Sir A. M. C.
Jensen, Ernest T., 1873–1950, vol. IV
Jensen, Johannes Hans Daniel, 1906–1973, vol. VII
Jensen, Sir John Klunder, 1884–1970, vol. VI
Jephcott, Alfred Roger, 1853–1932, vol. III
Jephcott, Hon. Sir Bruce Reginald, 1929–1987, vol. VIII
Jephcott, Sir Harry, 1st Bt, 1891–1978, vol. VII
Jephson, Sir Alfred, 1841–1900, vol. I
Jephson, Arthur Jermy Mounteney, 1858–1908, vol. I
Jephson, Rev. Arthur W., 1853–1935, vol. III
Jephson, Harriet Julia, (Lady Jephson), died 1930, vol. III
Jephson, Brig. Maurice Denham, 1890–1968, vol. VI
Jephson, Sir Stanhope William, 4th Bt, 1810–1900, vol. I
Jephson-Jones, Brig. Robert Llewellyn, 1905–1985, vol. VIII
Jeppe, Sir Julius, 1859–1929, vol. III
Jepson, Edgar, 1863–1938, vol. III
Jepson, Richard Pomfret, 1918–1980, vol. VII
Jepson, Captain Rowland Walter, 1888–1954, vol. V
Jepson, Selwyn, 1899–1989, vol. VIII
Jepson, Stanley, 1894–1976, vol. VII
Jerdan, Rev. Charles, 1843–1926, vol. II
Jerichow, Herbert Peter Andreas, 1889–1967, vol. VI
Jeritza, Maria, 1887–1982, vol. VIII
Jermyn, Sir Alfred, 1845–1921, vol. II
Jermyn, Rt Rev. Hugh Willoughby, 1820–1903, vol. I
Jerne, Niels Kaj, 1911–1994, vol. IX
Jerningham, Charles Edward Wynne, 1854–1921, vol. II
Jerningham, Sir Henry William Stafford, 11th Bt, 1867–1935, vol. III
Jerningham, Sir Hubert Edward Henry, 1842–1914, vol. I
Jerome, Maj.-Gen. Henry Edward, 1830–1901, vol. I
Jerome, Col Henry Joseph Walker, 1854–1943, vol. IV
Jerome, Jerome Klapka, 1859–1927, vol. II
Jerome, Lucien Joseph, 1870–1943, vol. IV

Jerome, Thomas Stroud, died 1917, vol. II
Jerome, William J. Smith, 1839–1929, vol. III
Jerram, Rev. Arnold Escombe, died 1934, vol. III
Jerram, Sir Bertrand; see Jerram, Sir C. B.
Jerram, Sir (Cecil) Bertrand, 1891–1971, vol. VII
Jerram, Lt-Col Charles Frederic, 1882–1969, vol. VI
Jerram, Adm. Sir Martyn; see Jerram, Adm. Sir T. H. M.
Jerram, Maurice William, 1922–1981, vol. VIII
Jerram, Maj.-Gen. Richard Martyn, 1928–1993, vol. IX
Jerram, Rear-Adm. Sir Rowland Christopher, 1890–1981, vol. VIII
Jerram, Brig. Roy Martyn, 1895–1974, vol. VII
Jerram, Adm. Sir (Thomas Henry) Martyn, 1858–1933, vol. III
Jerrard, Brig. Charles Ian, 1900–1977, vol. VII
Jerred, Sir Walter Tapper, 1864–1918, vol. II
Jerrold, Douglas, 1893–1964, vol. VI
Jerrold, Laurence, 1873–1918, vol. II
Jerrold, Mary, 1877–1955, vol. V
Jerrold, Walter Copeland, 1865–1929, vol. III
Jersey, 7th Earl of, 1845–1915, vol. I
Jersey, 8th Earl of, 1873–1923, vol. II
Jersey, 9th Earl of, 1910–1998, vol. X
Jersey, Dowager Countess of; (Margaret Elizabeth), 1849–1945, vol. IV
Jervis, Charles Elliott, 1907–1999, vol. X
Jervis, Charles Walter Lionel, 1914–1989, vol. VIII
Jervis, Sir Henry (Felix) Jervis-White-, 5th Bt, 1859–1947, vol. IV
Jervis, Col Herbert Swynfen, 1878–1965, vol. VI
Jervis, Captain Hon. John Cyril Carnegie, 1898–1929, vol. III
Jervis, Col Sir John Henry Jervis-White-, 4th Bt, 1857–1943, vol. IV
Jervis, John Johnstone, 1882–1969, vol. VI
Jervis, Col Nicholas Gordon Mainwaring, 1881–1943, vol. IV
Jervis, Lt-Col Hon. St Leger Henry, 1863–1952, vol. V
Jervis, Hon. William Monk, 1827–1909, vol. I
Jervis, Lt-Col William Swynfen Whitehall P.; see Parker-Jervis.
Jervis Read, Simon Holcombe; see Read.
Jervis-Smith, Rev. Frederick J., 1848–1911, vol. I
Jervis-White-Jervis, Sir Henry; see Jervis, Sir H. F. J. W.
Jervis-White-Jervis, Col Sir John Henry; see Jervis.
Jervois, Sir William Francis Drummond, 1821–1897, vol. I
Jervoise, Sir Arthur Henry Clarke-, 3rd Bt, 1856–1902, vol. I
Jervoise, Sir Dudley Alan Lestock Clarke-, 7th Bt, 1876–1933, vol. III
Jervoise, Rear-Adm. Edmund Purefoy Ellis, 1861–1950, vol. IV
Jervoise, Sir Eustace James Clarke, 6th Bt, 1870–1916, vol. II
Jervoise, Francis Henry Tristram, 1872–1959, vol. V
Jervoise, Sir Harry Samuel Cumming Clarke, 5th Bt, 1832–1911, vol. I
Jervoise, Sir Henry Clarke, 4th Bt, 1831–1908, vol. I

Jerwood, Rev. Thomas Frederick, *died* 1926, vol. II
Jesper, Col Norman McKay, 1896–1968, vol. VI
Jesperson, Otto, 1860–1943, vol. IV
Jess, Lt-Gen. Sir Carl Herman, 1884–1948, vol. IV
Jesse, F. Tennyson, *died* 1958, vol. V
Jesse, Col John Leonard, 1876–1944, vol. IV
Jesse, Richard Henry, 1853–1921, vol. II, vol. III
Jesse, William, 1870–1945, vol. IV
Jessel, 1st Baron, 1866–1950, vol. IV
Jessel, 2nd Baron, 1904–1990, vol. VIII
Jessel, Albert Henry, 1864–1917, vol. VII
Jessel, Sir Charles James, 1st Bt, 1860–1928, vol. II
Jessel, David Charles George, 1924–1985, vol. VIII
Jessel, Sir George, 2nd Bt, 1891–1977, vol. VII
Jessel, Dame Penelope, 1920–1996, vol. X
Jessel, Sir Richard Hugh, 1896–1979, vol. VII
Jesson, Charles, *born* 1862, vol. II
Jesson, Major Thomas Edward, 1883–1958, vol. V
Jessop, Col Charles Thorp, 1858–1915, vol. I
Jessop, Frederic Hubert, 1882–1969, vol. VI
Jessop, Gilbert Laird, 1874–1955, vol. V
Jessop, Lt-Comdr John de Burgh, 1885–1924,
    vol. II
Jessop, Joseph Chasser, 1892–1972, vol. VII
Jessop, Thomas Edmund, 1896–1980, vol. VII
Jessop, Thomas Richard, 1837–1903, vol. I
Jessop, Walter Hamilton Hylton, 1853–1917, vol. II
Jessopp, Rev. Augustus, 1823–1914, vol. I
Jessup, Frank William, 1909–1990, vol. VIII
Jessup, Philip Caryl, 1897–1986, vol. VIII
Jette, Sir Louis Amable, 1836–1920, vol. II
Jeudwine, Rev. George Wynne, 1849–1933, vol. III
Jeudwine, Lt-Gen. Sir Hugh Sandham, 1862–1942,
    vol. IV
Jeudwine, Lt-Col Wilfrid Wynne, 1877–1943,
    vol. IV
Jeune, Rt Hon. Sir Francis Henry; *see* St Helier,
    Baron.
Jeune, John Frederic Symons-, 1849–1925, vol. II
Jevons, Frank Byron, 1858–1936, vol. III
Jevons, Herbert Stanley, 1875–1955, vol. V
Jevons, Shirley Byron, *died* 1928, vol. II
Jewell, Maurice Frederick Stewart, 1885–1978,
    vol. VII
Jewell, Peter Arundel, 1925–1998, vol. X
Jewesbury, Reginald Charles, 1878–1971, vol. VII
Jewett, Sarah Orne, 1849–1909, vol. I
Jewkes, John, 1902–1988, vol. VIII
Jewson, Dorothy, 1884–1964, vol. VI
Jewson, Percy William, 1881–1962, vol. VI
Jex-Blake, Arthur John, *died* 1957, vol. V
Jex-Blake, Henrietta, *died* 1953, vol. V
Jex-Blake, Katharine, 1860–1951, vol. V
Jex-Blake, Sophia Louisa, 1840–1912, vol. I
Jex-Blake, Very Rev. Thomas William, 1832–1915,
    vol. I
Jeyes, Samuel Henry, *died* 1911, vol. I
Jeypore, Samasthanam, Maharaja Sri Sri Sri
    Ramachendra Deo of, 1893–1931, vol. III
Jha, Sir Mahamahopadhyaya Ganganath, *born*
    1871, vol. I
Jhalawar, HH Maharaj Rana Sir Bhawani Singh
    Bahadur of, 1874–1929, vol. III
Jhalawar, Lieut HH Maharaj Rana Sir Shri Rajendra
    Singh Ji Dev Bahadur of, 1900–1943, vol. IV

Jibowu, Hon. Sir Olumuyiwa, 1899–1959, vol. V
Jillett, Raymond Leslie, 1925–1983, vol. VIII
Jiménez de Aréchaga, Eduardo, 1918–1994, vol. X
    (AI)
Jiménez (Mantacon), Juan Ramón, 1881–1958,
    vol. V
Jind, Brig. HH Farzand-i-Dilband Rasikh-ul-Itikad
    Daulat-i-Inglishia, Raja-i-Rajgan Maharaja Sir
    Ranbir Singh Rajendra Bahadur, 1879–1948,
    vol. IV
Jinkin, Paymaster Rear-Adm. Robert Alfred,
    1876–1944, vol. IV
Jinks, John Leonard, 1929–1987, vol. VIII
Jinnah, Mahomed Ali, 1876–1948, vol. IV
Jivanjee, Sir Yusufali Alibhal Karimjee, 1882–1966,
    vol. VI
Joachim, Harold Henry, 1868–1938, vol. III
Joachim, Joseph, 1831–1907, vol. I
Joad, Cyril Edwin Mitchinson, 1891–1953, vol. V
Job, William Carson, 1864–1943, vol. IV
Jobberns, Very Rev. Joseph Brewer, 1868–1936,
    vol. III
Jobling, Geoffrey Lionel, 1889–1965, vol. VI
Jobson, Brig.-Gen. Alexander, 1875–1933, vol. III
Jocelyn, Ada Maria; *see* Roden, Dowager Countess
    of.
Jocelyn, Captain Arthur Cecil, 1880–1959, vol. V
Jocelyn, Henry David, 1933–2000, vol. X
Jocelyn, Col Julian Robert John, 1852–1929, vol. III
Jödahl, Ole Erik, 1910–1982, vol. VIII
Jodhpur, Maharaja of, 1880–1911, vol. I
Jodhpur, Maharaja of, 1898–1918, vol. II
Jodhpur, Maharaja of, 1903–1947, vol. IV
Jodhpur, Maharaja of, 1923–1952, vol. V
Jodl, Friedrich, 1849–1914, vol. I
Jodrell, Sir Alfred, 4th Bt, 1847–1929, vol. III
Jodrell, Dorothy Lynch R.; *see* Ramsden-Jodrell.
Jodrell, Col Sir Edward Thomas Davenant C.; *see*
    Cotton-Jodrell.
Jodrell, Lt-Col Henry Ramsden, *died* 1950, vol. IV
Jodrell, Sir Neville Paul, 1858–1932, vol. III
Joel, Hon. Sir Asher Alexander, 1912–1998, vol. X
Joel, Dudley Jack Barnato, 1904–1941, vol. IV
Joel, Harry Joel, (Jim), 1894–1992, vol. IX
Joel, Jack Barnato, 1862–1940, vol. III
Joel, Jim; *see* Joel, H. J.
Joel, Lt-Col Solomon Barnato, *died* 1931, vol. III
Joel, Woolf, *died* 1898, vol. I
Joelson, Ferdinand Stephen, 1893–1979, vol. VII
Joffre, Marshal Joseph Jacques Césaire, 1852–1931,
    vol. III
Jogendra Singh, Sir Sardar, 1877–1946, vol. IV
Joglekar, Rao Bahadur Ramchandra Narayan,
    1858–1928, vol. II, vol. III
Johannson, Arwid, 1862–1935, vol. III
John XXIII, His Holiness Pope, (Angelo Giuseppe
    Roncalli), 1881–1963, vol. VI
John, Arthur Walwyn, 1912–1991, vol. IX
John, Augustus Edwin, 1878–1961, vol. VI
John, Brynmor Thomas, 1934–1988, vol. VIII
John, Adm. of the Fleet Sir Caspar, 1903–1984,
    vol. VIII
John, David Dilwyn, 1901–1995, vol. IX
John, De Witt, 1915–1985, vol. VIII
John, Edward Thomas, 1857–1931, vol. III

John, Sir Edwin, 1856–1935, vol. III
John, Sir Goscombe; see John, Sir W. G.
John, Rev. Griffith, 1831–1912, vol. I
John, Michael M.; see Morley-John.
John, Robert Michael, 1924–1980, vol. VII
John, Sir Rupert Godfrey, 1916–1996, vol. X
John, Rt Rev. Thomas Charles, 1871–1936, vol. III
John, William, 1878–1955, vol. V
John, Sir (William) Goscombe, 1860–1952, vol. V
John-Mackie, Baron (Life Peer); John John-Mackie, 1909–1994, vol. IX
John O'London; see Whitten, Wilfred.
John Paul I, His Holiness Pope, (Albino Luciani), 1912–1978, vol. VII
Johnes, Herbert Johnes L.; see Lloyd-Johnes.
Johnes, Lt-Gen. Sir James H.; see Hills-Johnes.
Johns, Alan Wesley, 1931–1995, vol. IX
Johns, Alun Morris, died 1990, vol. VIII
Johns, Sir Arthur William, 1873–1937, vol. III
Johns, Charles Rowland, 1882–1961, vol. VI
Johns, Rev. Claude Hermann Walter, 1857–1920, vol. II
Johns, Fred, 1868–1932, vol. III
Johns, Horace John, 1890–1961, vol. VI
Johns, John Francis, 1885–1967, vol. VI
Johns, Peter Magrath, 1914–1983, vol. VIII
Johns, Richard Henry, 1878–1960, vol. V
Johns, Rev. Thomas, died 1915, vol. I
Johns, Lt-Col Whitfield Glanville, 1877–1941, vol. IV
Johns, Col Sir William Arthur, 1858–1918, vol. II
Johns, Captain William Earl, 1893–1968, vol. VI
Johnson, Alan C.; see Campbell-Johnson.
Johnson, Alan Woodworth, 1917–1982, vol. VIII
Johnson, Alexander, died 1913, vol. I
Johnson, Alice Neville Vowe, died 1938, vol. III
Johnson, Gen. Sir Allen Bayard, 1829–1907, vol. I
Johnson, Col Allen Victor, 1871–1939, vol. III
Johnson, Alvin Saunders, 1874–1971, vol. VII
Johnson, Amy, died 1941, vol. IV
Johnson, (Arthur) Basil (Noel), 1861–1950, vol. IV
Johnson, Rev. Arthur Henry, 1845–1927, vol. II
Johnson, Col Arthur Morrell, 1887–1946, vol. IV
Johnson, Sir Arthur Palmer, 1865–1944, vol. IV
Johnson, Rev. Aubrey Rodway, 1901–1985, vol. VIII
Johnson, B. S., (Bryan Stanley William Johnson), 1933–1973, vol. VII
Johnson, Basil; see Johnson, A. B. N.
Johnson, Sir Benjamin Sands, 1865–1937, vol. III
Johnson, Bernard, 1868–1935, vol. III
Johnson, Bernard Richard Millar, 1905–1959, vol. V
Johnson, Bertha Jane, 1846–1927, vol. II
Johnson, Borough; see Johnson, E. B.
Johnson, Bryan Stanley William; see Johnson, B. S.
Johnson, Carol Alfred, 1903–2000, vol. X
Johnson, Cecil W.; see Webb-Johnson.
Johnson, Dame Celia, (Dame Celia Fleming), 1908–1982, vol. VIII
Johnson, Ven. Charles, 1850–1927, vol. II
Johnson, Charles, 1870–1961, vol. VI
Johnson, Gen. Sir Charles Cooper, 1827–1905, vol. I
Johnson, Adm. Charles Duncan, 1869–1930, vol. III

Johnson, Charles Edward, 1832–1913, vol. I
Johnson, Charles Plumptre, 1853–1938, vol. III
Johnson, Brig. Charles Reginald, 1876–1953, vol. V
Johnson, Charles William Heaton, 1896–1964, vol. VI
Johnson, Christopher Hollis, 1904–1978, vol. VII
Johnson, Claude Goodman, 1864–1926, vol. II
Johnson, Maj.-Gen. Cyril Maxwell R.; see Ross-Johnson.
Johnson, Rear-Adm. (S) Cyril Sheldon, 1882–1954, vol. V
Johnson, Cyrus, 1848–1925, vol. II
Johnson, Daniel Cowan, 1915–1969, vol. VI
Johnson, David Hugh Nevil, 1920–1999, vol. X
Johnson, David John, 1938–2000, vol. X
Johnson, Rt Hon. Sir David Powell C.; see Croom-Johnson.
Johnson, (Denis) Gordon, 1911–1995, vol. IX
Johnson, Dennis R.; see Ross-Johnson.
Johnson, Donald McIntosh, 1903–1978, vol. VII
Johnson, Hon. Dame Doris Louise, 1921–1983, vol. VIII
Johnson, Dorothy, 1890–1977, vol. VII
Johnson, Maj.-Gen. Dudley Graham, 1884–1975, vol. VII
Johnson, Sir (Edward) Gordon, 5th Bt (cr 1755), 1867–1957, vol. V
Johnson, Rt Rev. Edward Ralph, died 1911, vol. I
Johnson, Hon. Sir Elliot; see Johnson, Hon. Sir W. E.
Johnson, Eric Alfred George, 1911–1994, vol. IX
Johnson, Eric Seymour Thewlis, 1897–1978, vol. VII
Johnson, Eric Townsend, 1875–1942, vol. IV
Johnson, (Ernest) Borough, died 1949, vol. IV
Johnson, Sir Ernest James, 1881–1962, vol. VI
Johnson, Eyvind, 1900–1976, vol. VII
Johnson, Francis H.; see Hernaman-Johnson.
Johnson, Rev. Frank, died 1927, vol. II
Johnson, Maj.-Gen. Frank Ernest, 1861–1945, vol. IV
Johnson, Lt-Col Sir Frank William Frederick, 1866–1943, vol. IV
Johnson, Sir Frederic Charles, 1890–1972, vol. VII
Johnson, Lt-Col Frederic L.; see Luttman-Johnson.
Johnson, Major Frederick Colpoys Ormsby, 1858–1932, vol. III
Johnson, Maj.-Gen. Frederick Francis, 1852–1931, vol. III
Johnson, Major Frederick Henry, 1890–1917, vol. II
Johnson, Very Rev. Frederick Wells, vol. III
Johnson, Sir George, 1867–1947, vol. IV
Johnson, George Arthur, 1903–1972, vol. VII
Johnson, Maj.-Gen. Sir George Frederick, 1903–1980, vol. VII
Johnson, George H., died 1933, vol. III
Johnson, Hon. Sir George H., 1872–1936, vol. III
Johnson, George Lindsay, 1853–1943, vol. IV
Johnson, George Macness, 1853–1935, vol. III
Johnson, Air Marshal George Owen, 1896–1980, vol. VII
Johnson, George William, 1857–1926, vol. II
Johnson, Gordon; see Johnson, D. G.
Johnson, Sir Gordon; see Johnson, Sir E. G.
Johnson, Sir Gordon; see Johnson, Sir J. N. G.

Johnson, Brig. Guy Allen Colpoys Ormsby, 1886–1957, vol. V
Johnson, Guy Francis, *died* 1969, vol. VI
Johnson, H. C. Brooke, 1873–1949, vol. IV
Johnson, Harold Cottam, 1903–1973, vol. VII
Johnson, Harold Daintree, 1910–1980, vol. VII
Johnson, Captain Harry Cecil, 1877–1915, vol. I
Johnson, Harry Gordon, 1923–1977, vol. VII
Johnson, Col Harry Hall, 1892–1973, vol. VII
Johnson, Engr Rear-Adm. Harry Herbert, 1875–1961, vol. VI
Johnson, Ven. Hayman, 1912–1993, vol. IX
Johnson, Sir Henry Allen Beaumont, 5th Bt (*cr* 1818), 1887–1965, vol. VI
Johnson, Brig.-Gen. Sir Henry Allen William, 4th Bt (*cr* 1818), 1855–1944, vol. IV
Johnson, Sir Henry Cecil, 1906–1988, vol. VIII
Johnson, Rt Rev. Henry Frank, 1834–1908, vol. I
Johnson, Henry Harrold, 1869–1940, vol. III (A), vol. IV
Johnson, Sir Henry James, 1851–1917, vol. II
Johnson, Henry Langhorne, 1874–1945, vol. IV
Johnson, Henry Leslie, 1904–1991, vol. IX
Johnson, Henry Powell C.; *see* Croom-Johnson.
Johnson, Herbert, 1856–1949, vol. IV
Johnson, Herschel V., 1894–1966, vol. VI
Johnson, Very Rev. Hewlett, 1874–1966, vol. VI
Johnson, Hiram Warren, 1866–1945, vol. IV
Johnson, Howard Sydney, 1910–2000, vol. X
Johnson, Major Hugh Spencer, *died* 1962, vol. VI
Johnson, Rev. James, *died* 1911, vol. I
Johnson, Rt Rev. James, *died* 1917, vol. II
Johnson, James, 1908–1995, vol. IX
Johnson, John, 1850–1910, vol. I
Johnson, John, 1882–1956, vol. V
Johnson, John Charles S.; *see* Sperrin-Johnson.
Johnson, Sir John Henry, 1826–1909, vol. I
Johnson, Sir (John Nesbitt) Gordon, 1885–1955, vol. V
Johnson, Sir John Paley, 6th Bt (*cr* 1755), 1907–1975, vol. VII
Johnson, Hon. John W. Fordham, 1866–1938, vol. III
Johnson, Rt Rev. Joseph Horsfall, 1847–1928, vol. II, vol. III
Johnson, Lionel Pigot, 1867–1902, vol. I
Johnson, Louis Arthur, 1891–1966, vol. VI
Johnson, Sir (Louis) Stanley, 1869–1937, vol. III
Johnson, Lyndon Baines, 1908–1973, vol. VII
Johnson, Most Rev. Martin Michael, 1899–1975, vol. VII
Johnson, Lt-Col Maurice Eustace Stanley, 1879–1937, vol. III
Johnson, Michael Howard, 1930–1994, vol. IX
Johnson, Sir Nelson King, 1892–1954, vol. V
Johnson, Owen, 1878–1952, vol. V
Johnson, Pamela Hansford, (Lady Snow), 1912–1981, vol. VIII
Johnson, Patrick, 1904–1996, vol. X
Johnson, Lt-Col Pelham; *see* Johnson, Lt-Col T. P.
Johnson, Sir Philip Bulmer, 1887–1964, vol. VI
Johnson, R. Brimley, 1867–1932, vol. III
Johnson, Ralph Hudson, 1933–1993, vol. IX
Johnson, Raymond, *died* 1944, vol. IV

Johnson, Hon. Sir Reginald Powell C.; *see* Croom-Johnson.
Johnson, Rex, 1921–1995, vol. IX
Johnson, Brig.-Gen. Richard Francis, 1852–1938, vol. III
Johnson, Richard Stringer, 1907–1981, vol. VIII
Johnson, Sir Robert Arthur, 1874–1938, vol. III
Johnson, Sir Robert Stewart, 1872–1951, vol. V
Johnson, Robert Underwood, 1853–1937, vol. III
Johnson, Robert White, 1912–1995, vol. IX
Johnson, Sir Robin Eliot, 7th Bt (*cr* 1818), 1929–1989, vol. IX (AI)
Johnson, Sir Ronald Ernest Charles, 1913–1996, vol. X
Johnson, Brig.-Gen. Ronald Marr, 1873–1925, vol. II
Johnson, Rev. Rowland Theodore I.; *see* Ingram-Johnson.
Johnson, Sir Samuel George, 1831–1909, vol. I
Johnson, Samuel Waite, *died* 1912, vol. I
Johnson, Seymour Shepherd, 1875–1962, vol. VI
Johnson, Sir Sidney Midlane, 1885–1960, vol. V
Johnson, Sir Stanley; *see* Johnson, Sir L. S.
Johnson, Stanley W.; *see* Webb-Johnson.
Johnson, Stephen Keymer, 1899–1936, vol. III
Johnson, Lt-Col T. Pelham, 1871–1918, vol. II
Johnson, Thomas, 1863–1954, vol. V
Johnson, Thomas Frank, *died* 1972, vol. VII
Johnson, Lt-Col Thomas Gordon Blois-, 1867–1918, vol. II
Johnson, Rt Rev. Thomas Sylvester Claudius, 1873–1955, vol. V
Johnson, Tom Loftin, 1854–1911, vol. I
Johnson, Tom Richard, *died* 1935, vol. III
Johnson, Sir Victor Philipse Hill, 6th Bt (*cr* 1818), 1905–1986, vol. VIII
Johnson, Sir Walter, 1845–1912, vol. I
Johnson, Sir Walter Burford, 1885–1951, vol. V
Johnson, Lt-Col Walter R.; *see* Russell-Johnson.
Johnson, Wilfrid A.; *see* Athelstan-Johnson.
Johnson, Rev. Wilfrid Harry Cowper, 1879–1967, vol. VI
Johnson, William, 1849–1919, vol. II
Johnson, William, 1903–1993, vol. IX
Johnson, Rt Rev. William Anthony, 1832–1909, vol. I
Johnson, Sir William Clarence, 1899–1982, vol. VIII
Johnson, Rev. William Cowper, *died* 1916, vol. II
Johnson, Hon. William Dartnell, 1872–1948, vol. IV
Johnson, Hon. Sir (William) Elliot, 1862–1932, vol. III
Johnson, William Evelyn Patrick, 1902–1976, vol. VII
Johnson, Sir William George, 4th Bt (*cr* 1755), 1830–1908, vol. I
Johnson, William Harold Barrett, 1916–1992, vol. IX
Johnson, Rt Rev. William Herbert, 1889–1960, vol. V
Johnson, William Joseph, 1892–1971, vol. VII
Johnson, Rt Hon. Sir William Moore, 1st Bt (*cr* 1909), 1828–1918, vol. II
Johnson, Ven. William Percival, *died* 1928, vol. II

Johnson-Ferguson, Sir Edward; *see* Johnson-Ferguson, Sir J. E.

Johnson-Ferguson, Sir Edward Alexander James, 2nd Bt, 1875–1953, vol. V

Johnson-Ferguson, Sir (Jabez) Edward, 1st Bt, 1849–1929, vol. III

Johnson-Ferguson, Sir Neil Edward, 3rd Bt, 1905–1992, vol. IX

Johnson-Gilbert, Sir Ian Anderson, 1891–1974, vol. VII

Johnson-Gilbert, Thomas Ian, 1923–1998, vol. X

Johnson-Marshall, Percy Edwin Alan, 1915–1993, vol. IX

Johnson-Marshall, Sir Stirrat Andrew William, 1912–1981, vol. VIII

Johnson-Walsh, Sir Hunt Henry Allen; *see* Walsh.

Johnston, Hon. Lord; Henry Johnston, 1844–1931, vol. III

Johnston, Alastair McPherson; *see* Dunpark, Hon. Lord.

Johnston, Alexander, 1867–1951, vol. V

Johnston, Sir Alexander, 1905–1994, vol. IX

Johnston, Alice Crawford, 1902–1976, vol. VII

Johnston, Andrew, 1835–1922, vol. II

Johnston, A(nthony) G(ordon) Knox, 1909–1972, vol. VII

Johnston, Archibald Gilchrist, 1931–1985, vol. VIII

Johnston, Betty Joan, (Lady Johnston), 1916–1994, vol. IX

Johnston, Brian Alexander, 1912–1994, vol. IX

Johnston, Carruthers Melvill, 1909–1970, vol. VI

Johnston, Sir Charles, 1st Bt (*cr* 1916), 1848–1933, vol. III

Johnston, Col Charles Arthur, 1867–1926, vol. II

Johnston, Lt-Col Charles Evelyn, 1878–1922, vol. II

Johnston, Ven. Charles Francis Harding, 1842–1925, vol. II

Johnston, Charles Hampton, 1919–1981, vol. VIII

Johnston, Sir Charles Hepburn, 1912–1986, vol. VIII

Johnston, Christopher Nicholson; *see* Sands, Hon. Lord.

Johnston, Rear-Adm. Clarence Dinsmore H.; *see* Howard-Johnston.

Johnston, David, 1836–1899, vol. I

Johnston, Col David Seton, 1886–1960, vol. V

Johnston, Denis; *see* Johnston, W. D.

Johnston, Hon. Lord; Douglas Harold Johnston, 1907–1985, vol. VIII

Johnston, Col Sir Duncan Alexander, 1847–1931, vol. III

Johnston, Edward, 1872–1944, vol. IV

Johnston, Sir Edward Alexander, 1929–1991, vol. IX

Johnston, Edward Hamilton, 1885–1942, vol. IV

Johnston, Wing Comdr Ernest Henry, 1885–1938, vol. III

Johnston, Francis Alexander, 1864–1958, vol. V

Johnston, Brig.-Gen. Francis Earl, 1871–1917, vol. II

Johnston, Rt Rev. Francis Featherstonhaugh, 1891–1963, vol. VI

Johnston, Lt-Col Francis Gawen Dillon, 1875–1945, vol. IV

Johnston, Frederick, 1859–1937, vol. III

Johnston, Frederick Mair, 1903–1973, vol. VII

Johnston, Sir Frederick William, 1872–1947, vol. IV

Johnston, Frederick William, 1899–1981, vol. VIII

Johnston, Sir Gaston, 1874–1965, vol. VI (AII)

Johnston, Sir George, 10th Bt, 1845–1921, vol. II

Johnston, George Alexander, 1888–1983, vol. VIII

Johnston, George Douglas, 1886–1971, vol. VII

Johnston, George Francis, 1860–1943, vol. IV

Johnston, George Jameson, 1866–1926, vol. II

Johnston, Maj.-Gen. George Jameson, 1868–1949, vol. IV

Johnston, Brig.-Gen. George Napier, 1867–1947, vol. IV

Johnston, Grace L. Keith, *died* 1929, vol. III

Johnston, Sir Harold Featherston, 1875–1959, vol. V

Johnston, Sir Harry Hamilton, 1858–1927, vol. II

Johnston, Henry; *see* Johnston, Hon. Lord.

Johnston, Col Henry Halcro, 1856–1939, vol. III

Johnston, Henry Joseph, 1858–1906, vol. I

Johnston, Hugh Anthony Stephen, 1913–1967, vol. VI

Johnston, Rev. Hugh William, *died* 1918, vol. II

Johnston, Rt Hon. Sir James, 1849–1924, vol. II

Johnston, Maj.-Gen. James Alexander Deans, 1911–1988, vol. VIII

Johnston, Rev. James B., 1862–1953, vol. V

Johnston, James Osborne, 1921–1978, vol. VII

Johnston, Rt Rev. James Steptoe, 1843–1924, vol. II, vol. III

Johnston, Maj.-Gen. James Thomason, 1860–1938, vol. III

Johnston, James Wellwood, 1900–1958, vol. V

Johnston, Sir John, 1873–1952, vol. V

Johnston, John Alexander Hope, 1871–1938, vol. III

Johnston, Major John Alexander Weir, 1879–1957, vol. V

Johnston, Sir John Barr, 1843–1919, vol. II

Johnston, John Douglas Hartley, 1935–2000, vol. X (AII)

Johnston, John Lawson, 1839–1900, vol. I

Johnston, Rev. John Octavius, 1852–1923, vol. II

Johnston, Joseph, 1890–1972, vol. VII

Johnston, Joseph Wilson-, 1876–1933, vol. III

Johnston, Kenneth Robert Hope, 1905–1998, vol. X

Johnston, Malcolm Campbell-; *see* Campbell-Johnston.

Johnston, Mary, 1870–1936, vol. III

Johnston, Michael Errington, 1916–1992, vol. IX

Johnston, Ninian Rutherford Jamieson, 1912–1990, vol. VIII

Johnston, Col Osmond Moncreiff, 1848–1934, vol. III

Johnston, Patrick Murdoch, 1911–1981, vol. VIII

Johnston, Col Percy Herbert, 1851–1932, vol. III

Johnston, Peter Hope, 1915–1982, vol. VIII

Johnston, Philip Mainwaring, 1865–1936, vol. III

Johnston, R. M'Kenzie, 1856–1930, vol. III

Johnston, Reginald Eden, 1847–1922, vol. II

Johnston, Sir Reginald Fleming, 1874–1938, vol. III

Johnston, Major Robert, 1872–1950, vol. IV

Johnston, Brig. Robert, 1879–1956, vol. V

Johnston, Major Robert Douglas, 1882–1959, vol. V

Johnston, Robert Mackenzie, *died* 1918, vol. II

Johnston, Robert Matteson, 1867–1920, vol. II
Johnston, Robert William Fairfield, 1895–1991, vol. IX
Johnston, Ronald Carlyle, 1907–1990, vol. VIII
Johnston, Samuel, *born* 1835, vol. II
Johnston, Rev. Samuel Alfred, 1864–1940, vol. III
Johnston, Rt Hon. Thomas, 1881–1965, vol. VI
Johnston, Sir Thomas Alexander, 11th Bt, 1857–1950, vol. IV
Johnston, Sir Thomas Alexander, 12th Bt, 1888–1959, vol. V
Johnston, Sir Thomas Alexander, 13th Bt, 1916–1984, vol. VIII
Johnston, Thomas Baillie, 1883–1960, vol. V
Johnston, Thomas Harvey, 1881–1951, vol. V
Johnston, Brig.-Gen. Thomas Kelly Evans, 1860–1936, vol. III
Johnston, Thomas Kenneth, 1878–1953, vol. V
Johnston, Maj.-Gen. Walter Edward Wilson-, 1878–1948, vol. IV
Johnston, William, 1829–1902, vol. I
Johnston, Col William, 1843–1914, vol. I
Johnston, Sir William, 9th Bt, 1849–1917, vol. II
Johnston, William, 1890–1976, vol. VII
Johnston, Rt Rev. William, 1914–1986, vol. VIII
Johnston, Sir William Campbell, 1860–1938, vol. III
Johnston, (William) Denis, 1901–1984, vol. VIII
Johnston, Sir William Ernest George, 1884–1951, vol. V
Johnston, Lt-Col William Hamilton Hall, *died* 1952, vol. V
Johnston, Lt-Col William James, 1870–1937, vol. III
Johnston, William John, 1869–1940, vol. III (A), vol. IV
Johnston, Rev. William Murdoch, 1847–1905, vol. I
Johnston, Sir William Wallace Stewart, 1887–1962, vol. VI
Johnston-Saint, Captain Peter Johnston, *died* 1974, vol. VII
Johnston-Stewart of Physgill, Adm. Robert Hathorn, 1858–1940, vol. III
Johnstone, Alan Stewart, 1905–1990, vol. VIII
Johnstone, Hon. Sir Alan Vanden-Bempde-, 1858–1932, vol. III
Johnstone, Sir Alexander Howat, 1876–1956, vol. V
Johnstone, Air Vice-Marshal Alexander Vallance Riddell, 1916–2000, vol. X
Johnstone, Alfred; *see* Johnstone, J. A.
Johnstone, Lt-Col Bede, 1877–1942, vol. IV
Johnstone, Vice-Adm. Charles, 1843–1927, vol. II
Johnstone, David Kirkpatrick, 1926–1993, vol. IX
Johnstone, Major David Patrick, 1876–1951, vol. V
Johnstone, Sir Donald Campbell, 1857–1920, vol. II
Johnstone, Mrs Dorothy Christian Liddle, 1915–1981, vol. VIII
Johnstone, Brig.-Gen. Francis Buchanan, 1863–1947, vol. IV
Johnstone, Sir Frederic Allan George, 10th Bt, 1906–1994, vol. IX
Johnstone, Sir Frederic John William, 8th Bt, 1841–1913, vol. I
Johnstone, Frederick John, 1841–1934, vol. III

Johnstone, Rev. George Alexander, 1868–1932, vol. III
Johnstone, Lt-Col George Charles Keppel, 1841–1912, vol. I
Johnstone, Sir George Frederic Thomas Tankerville, 9th Bt, 1876–1952, vol. V
Johnstone, Gerald Ewart, 1906–1973, vol. VII
Johnstone, Rt Hon. Harcourt, 1895–1945, vol. IV
Johnstone, Hilda, 1882–1961, vol. VI
Johnstone, Col Hope, 1868–1939, vol. III
Johnstone, J. Alfred, 1861–1941, vol. IV
Johnstone, James Arthur, 1913–1989, vol. VIII
Johnstone, Major James Henry L'Estrange, 1865–1906, vol. I
Johnstone, Maj.-Gen. James Robert, 1859–1932, vol. III
Johnstone, James William Douglas, 1855–1925, vol. II
Johnstone, Lt John Andrew, 1893–1915, vol. II
Johnstone, John Heywood, 1850–1904, vol. I
Johnstone, John James H.; *see* Hope-Johnstone.
Johnstone, Joseph, 1860–1931, vol. III
Johnstone, Kenneth Roy, 1902–1978, vol. VII
Johnstone, Lewis Martin, 1870–1960, vol. V
Johnstone, Col Montague George, 1848–1928, vol. II
Johnstone, Morris Mackintosh O.; *see* Ord Johnstone.
Johnstone, Maj.-Gen. Ralph E.; *see* Edgeworth-Johnstone.
Johnstone, Ralph William, *died* 1915, vol. I
Johnstone, Maj.-Gen. Reginald Forster, 1904–1976, vol. VII
Johnstone, Robert, 1861–1944, vol. IV
Johnstone, Rev. Robert Cuthbert, 1857–1934, vol. III
Johnstone, Robert Edgeworth, 1900–1994, vol. IX
Johnstone, Sir Robert J., 1872–1938, vol. III
Johnstone, Maj.-Gen. Robert Maxwell, 1914–1990, vol. VIII
Johnstone, Sir Robert Stewart, 1855–1936, vol. III
Johnstone, Robert William, 1879–1969, vol. VI
Johnstone, Very Rev. Thomas McGimpsey, 1876–1961, vol. VI
Johnstone, Thomas Muir, 1924–1983, vol. VIII
Johnstone, Lt-Col Sir Walter E.; *see* Edgeworth-Johnstone.
Johnstone-Burt, Charles Kingsley, 1891–1973, vol. VII
Johnstone-Douglas, Arthur Henry; *see* Douglas.
Johnstone-Wallace, Denis Bowes, 1894–1960, vol. V
Johore, Sultan of, 1873–1959, vol. V
Johore, Sultan of, 1894–1981, vol. VIII
Joicey, 1st Baron, 1846–1936, vol. III
Joicey, 2nd Baron, 1880–1940, vol. III
Joicey, 3rd Baron, 1881–1966, vol. VI
Joicey, 4th Baron, 1925–1993, vol. IX
Joicey, Major James, 1836–1912, vol. I
Joicey, James John, 1870–1932, vol. III
Joicey-Cecil, Lord John Packenham; *see* Cecil.
Joint, Sir (Edgar) James, 1902–1981, vol. VIII
Joint, Sir James; *see* Joint, Sir E. J.
Jokai, Maurus, 1825–1904, vol. I
Joliot-Curie, Jean Frédéric, 1900–1958, vol. V
Joll, Cecil Augustus, *died* 1945, vol. IV

Joll, James Bysse, 1918–1994, vol. IX
Jolley, Maj.-Gen. Norman Kempe, 1894–1951, vol. V
Jollie, Ethel M.; *see* Colquhoun, E. M.
Jollie, Mrs Tawse; *see* Colquhoun, Ethel M.
Jolliffe, Arthur Ernest, 1871–1944, vol. IV
Jolliffe, John Edward Austin, 1891–1964, vol. VI
Jolliffe, John William, 1924–1985, vol. VIII
Jolliffe, Richard Orlando, 1876–1932, vol. III
Jolliffe, Lt-Col Thomas William, 1873–1944, vol. IV
Jolliffe, Captain Hon. William Sydney Hylton, 1841–1912, vol. I
Jolly, Gen. Sir Alan, 1910–1977, vol. VII
Jolly, Anthony Charles, 1932–1992, vol. IX
Jolly, Lt-Gen. Sir Gordon Gray, *died* 1962, vol. VI
Jolly, Hugh Reginald, 1918–1986, vol. VIII
Jolly, James, 1902–1968, vol. VI
Jolly, James Hornby, 1887–1972, vol. VII
Jolly, John Catterall, 1887–1950, vol. IV
Jolly, Rev. Canon Reginald Bradley, 1885–1972, vol. VII
Jolly, Thomas Riley, 1849–1929, vol. III
Jolly, William Adam, *died* 1939, vol. III
Jolly, William Alfred, *died* 1955, vol. V
Jolly, Rear-Adm. Sir William E. H., 1887–1961, vol. VI
Jolowicz, Herbert Felix, 1890–1954, vol. V
Joly, Charles Jasper, 1864–1906, vol. I
Joly, John, *died* 1933, vol. III
Joly, John Swift, *died* 1943, vol. IV
Joly de Lotbinière, Maj.-Gen. Alain Chartier, 1862–1944, vol. IV
Joly de Lotbinière, Lt-Col Sir Edmond, 1903–1994, vol. IX
Joly de Lotbinière, Hon. Sir Henry Gustave, 1829–1908, vol. I
Joly de Lotbinière, Brig.-Gen. Henri Gustave, 1868–1960, vol. V
Joly de Lotbinière, Seymour; *see* de Lotbinière.
Jon, Montague; *see* Dovener, J. M.
Jonas, Harry Marshall, 1866–1939, vol. III
Jones, Abel John, *died* 1949, vol. IV
Jones, Captain Adrian, 1845–1938, vol. III
Jones, Brig. Alan Harvey, 1910–1975, vol. VII
Jones, Alan Payan P.; *see* Pryce-Jones.
Jones, Alan Trevor, 1901–1979, vol. VII
Jones, (Albert) Arthur, 1915–1991, vol. IX
Jones, Rev. Sir Albert E.; *see* Evans-Jones.
Jones, Rt Hon. Alec; *see* Jones, Rt Hon. T. A.
Jones, Alfred; *see* Jones, E. A.
Jones, (Alfred) Ernest, *died* 1958, vol. V
Jones, Alfred Gîlpin, 1824–1906, vol. I
Jones, Sir Alfred Lewis, 1846–1909, vol. I
Jones, Lt-Col Alfred Stowell, 1832–1920, vol. II
Jones, Allan G.; *see* Gwynne-Jones.
Jones, Sir Andrew; *see* Jones, Sir W. J. A.
Jones, Maj.-Gen. Anthony George Clifford, 1923–1999, vol. X
Jones, Arnold Hugh Martin, 1904–1970, vol. VI
Jones, Arthur; *see* Jones, Albert A.
Jones, Rt Hon. Arthur Creech, 1891–1964, vol. VI
Jones, Lt-Col Arthur Daniel D.; *see* Derviche-Jones.
Jones, Arthur Davies, 1897–1980, vol. VII
Jones, Arthur Griffith M.; *see* Maitland-Jones.

Jones, Sir Arthur Probyn P.; *see* Probyn-Jones.
Jones, Arthur R.; *see* Rocyn-Jones.
Jones, Very Rev. Arthur Stuart D.; *see* Duncan-Jones.
Jones, Brig. Arthur Thomas C.; *see* Cornwall-Jones.
Jones, Hon. Sir Austin Ellis Lloyd, 1884–1967, vol. VI
Jones, Austin Ernest D.; *see* Duncan-Jones.
Jones, Sir Barry; *see* Jones, Sir T. B.
Jones, Maj.-Gen. Basil Douglas, 1903–1992, vol. IX
Jones, Rev. Basil M., *died* 1925, vol. II
Jones, Rev. Canon Benjamin, 1865–1955, vol. V
Jones, Benjamin George, 1914–1989, vol. VIII
Jones, Captain Benjamin Henry, *died* 1949, vol. IV
Jones, Benjamin Howell, *died* 1913, vol. I
Jones, Benjamin Rowland R.; *see* Rice-Jones.
Jones, Sir (Bennett) Melvill, 1887–1975, vol. VII
Jones, Bernard Mouat, 1882–1953, vol. V
Jones, Sir Bertram Hyde, 1879–1961, vol. VI
Jones, Bobby; *see* Jones, Robert Tyre.
Jones, Brian Leslie, 1930–1999, vol. X
Jones, Major Bryan John, 1874–1918, vol. II
Jones, Sir Brynmor, 1903–1989, vol. VIII
Jones, Rev. Bulkeley Owen, 1824–1914, vol. I
Jones, Sir Cadwaladr Bryner, 1872–1954, vol. V
Jones, Cecil Artimus E.; *see* Evan-Jones.
Jones, Cecil Charles, 1872–1943, vol. IV
Jones, Chapman; *see* Jones, H. C.
Jones, Charles Alfred, 1848–1934, vol. III
Jones, Charles Edward, 1852–1932, vol. III
Jones, Charles Edward Irvine, 1899–1951, vol. V
Jones, Sir Charles Ernest, 1892–1953, vol. V
Jones, Charles Evan William, 1879–1951, vol. V
Jones, Charles Henry, 1857–1936, vol. III
Jones, Lt-Col Charles Herbert, 1865–1953, vol. V
Jones, Charles Hugh LePailleur, *died* 1949, vol. IV
Jones, Charles Jerome, 1847–1929, vol. III
Jones, Major Charles Llewelyn W.; *see* Wynne-Jones.
Jones, Sir Charles Lloyd, 1878–1958, vol. V
Jones, Charles Mark J.; *see* Jenkin-Jones.
Jones, Gen. Sir Charles Phibbs, 1906–1988, vol. VIII
Jones, Sir (Charles) Sydney, 1872–1947, vol. IV
Jones, Rev. Canon Cheslyn Peter Montague, 1918–1987, vol. VIII
Jones, Chester, 1854–1922, vol. II
Jones, Sir Clement Wakefield, 1880–1963, vol. VI
Jones, Clifford T., 1873–1948, vol. IV
Jones, Clinton; *see* Jones, J. C.
Jones, Constance; *see* Jones, E. E. C.
Jones, Col Conwyn M.; *see* Mansel-Jones.
Jones, Sir Crawford Douglas D.; *see* Douglas-Jones.
Jones, Sir Cyril Edgar, 1891–1970, vol. VI
Jones, Rev Cyril L.; *see* Leslie-Jones.
Jones, Lt-Col Sir Cyril Vivian, 1882–1961, vol. VI
Jones, Cyril Walter L.; *see* Lloyd Jones.
Jones, Rev. Daniel, *died* 1934, vol. III
Jones, Daniel, 1881–1967, vol. VI
Jones, Daniel, 1908–1985, vol. VIII
Jones, Rev. David, 1848–1909, vol. I
Jones, David, 1895–1974, vol. VII
Jones, Rev. Canon David A.; *see* Akrill-Jones.
Jones, Rt Hon. Sir David Brynmor, 1852–1921, vol. II

Jones, David Elwyn L.; *see* Lloyd Jones.
Jones, Sir (David) Fletcher, 1895–1977, vol. VII
Jones, David Jeffreys, 1909–1981, vol. VIII
Jones, Very Rev. David John, 1870–1949, vol. IV
Jones, David Lewis, 1889–1953, vol. V
Jones, Ven. David Morgan, 1874–1950, vol. IV
Jones, David Morgan, 1915–2000, vol. X
Jones, D(avid) Prys, 1913–1982, vol. VIII
Jones, David Thomas, 1866–1931, vol. III
Jones, David Thomas, *died* 1963, vol. VI
Jones, Sir David Thomas R.; *see* Rocyn-Jones.
Jones, David Trevor L.; *see* Lloyd-Jones.
Jones, Captain Desmond V.; *see* Vincent-Jones.
Jones, Rev. Donald, 1857–1925, vol. II
Jones, Douglas Vivian I.; *see* Irvine-Jones.
Jones, Dudley William Carmalt, 1874–1957, vol. V
Jones, E. Alfred, 1872–1943, vol. IV
Jones, E. E. Constance, *died* 1922, vol. II
Jones, Sir E. Wynne C.; *see* Cemlyn-Jones.
Jones, Ebenezer G.; *see* Griffith-Jones.
Jones, Edgar H.; *see* Heath-Jones.
Jones, Edgar Montague, 1866–1938, vol. III
Jones, Sir Edgar Rees, 1878–1962, vol. VI
Jones, Edgar Stafford, 1909–1992, vol. IX
Jones, Edmund Angus, 1903–1983, vol. VIII
Jones, Sir Edmund Britten, 1888–1953, vol. V
Jones, Rev. Edmund Osborne, 1858–1931, vol. III
Jones, Edward; *see* Jones, J. E.
Jones, Sir Edward Coley B.; *see* Burne-Jones.
Jones, Sir Edward Martin F.; *see* Furnival Jones.
Jones, Rt Rev. Edward Michael G.; *see* Gresford
    Jones.
Jones, Edward Norton, 1902–1983, vol. VIII
Jones, Col Sir Edward P.; *see* Pryce-Jones.
Jones, Rear-Adm. Edward Pitcairn, 1850–1908,
    vol. I
Jones, Sir Edward R.; *see* Redmayne-Jones.
Jones, Edward Taylor, 1872–1961, vol. VI
Jones, Rt Hon. Sir Edward Warburton, 1912–1993,
    vol. IX
Jones, Edward William M.; *see* Milner-Jones.
Jones, Edwin, 1841–1900, vol. I
Jones, Eifion, 1912–1995, vol. IX
Jones, Elfryn, 1913–1983, vol. VIII
Jones, Eli Stanley, 1884–1973, vol. VII
Jones, Elwyn; *see* Baron Elwyn-Jones.
Jones, Sir Elwyn; *see* Jones, Sir W. E. E.
Jones, Emlyn Bartley, 1920–1999, vol. X
Jones, Emrys; *see* Jones, J. E.
Jones, Sir Emrys; *see* Jones, Sir W. E.
Jones, Enid, (Lady Jones); *see* Bagnold, E.
Jones, Eric Kyffin, 1876–1977, vol. VII
Jones, Sir Eric Malcolm, 1907–1986, vol. VIII
Jones, Sir Eric Newton G.; *see* Griffith-Jones.
Jones, Ernest; *see* Jones, A. E.
Jones, Ernest; *see* Jones, W. E.
Jones, Ernest L.; *see* Lancaster-Jones.
Jones, Ernest Turner, 1897–1981, vol. VIII
Jones, Ernest W.; *see* Whitley-Jones.
Jones, Eryl O.; *see* Owen-Jones.
Jones, Captain Sir Evan, *died* 1949, vol. IV
Jones, Evan Bonnor H.; *see* Hugh-Jones.
Jones, Evan Bowen, 1869–1940, vol. III
Jones, Evan David, 1903–1987, vol. VIII

Jones, Sir Evan Davies, 1st Bt (*cr* 1917),
    1859–1949, vol. IV
Jones, Major Evan Rowland, 1840–1920, vol. II
Jones, Vice-Adm. Everard John H.; *see*
    Hardman-Jones.
Jones, F. W. D.; *see* Doyle-Jones.
Jones, Sir Felix E. A.; *see* Aylmer-Jones.
Jones, Sir Fletcher; *see* Jones, Sir D. F.
Jones, Francis, 1845–1925, vol. II
Jones, Maj. Francis, 1908–1993, vol. IX
Jones, Sir Francis Adolphus, 1861–1947, vol. IV
Jones, Francis Edgar, 1914–1988, vol. VIII
Jones, Frank, 1873–1961, vol. VI
Jones, Lt-Col Frank Aubrey, 1873–1916, vol. II
Jones, Ven. Frank Emlyn, *died* 1935, vol. III
Jones, Frank Ernest, *died* 1974, vol. VII
Jones, F(rank) Llewellyn-, 1907–1997, vol. X
Jones, Rt Rev. Frank Melville, 1866–1941, vol. IV
Jones, Frank Newling, *died* 1942, vol. IV
Jones, (Frederic) Wood, 1879–1954, vol. V
Jones, Hon. Frederick, 1884–1966, vol. VI
Jones, Frederick Archibald L.; *see* Leslie-Jones.
Jones, Frederick Elwyn; *see* Baron Elwyn-Jones.
Jones, Frederick Herbert P.; *see* Page-Jones.
Jones, Frederick James, 1874–1943, vol. IV
Jones, Sir Frederick John, 1st Bt (*cr* 1919),
    1854–1936, vol. III
Jones, Frederick L.; *see* Llewellyn-Jones.
Jones, Frederick Theodore, 1885–1968, vol. VI
Jones, Col Frederick William C.; *see* Caton-Jones.
Jones, Frederick William F.; *see* Farey-Jones.
Jones, Ven. Geoffrey G.; *see* Gower-Jones.
Jones, George, 1844–1921, vol. II
Jones, Air Marshal Sir George, 1896–1992, vol. IX
Jones, George Arthur, 1889–1962, vol. VI
Jones, George Basil Harris, 1896–1946, vol. IV
Jones, Sir (George) Basil T.; *see* Todd-Jones.
Jones, Vice-Adm. George Clarence, 1895–1946,
    vol. IV
Jones, Sir George L.; *see* Legh-Jones.
Jones, George Lewis, 1907–1971, vol. VII
Jones, George Mallory, 1873–1940, vol. III
Jones, George Morgan Edwardes, 1858–1936,
    vol. III
Jones, George William, 1860–1942, vol. IV
Jones, Sir George William Henry, *died* 1956, vol. V
Jones, Geraint Dyfed Barri, 1936–1999, vol. X
Jones, Geraint Iwan, 1917–1998, vol. X
Jones, Gerallt; *see* Jones, R. G.
Jones, Cdre Gerald N., 1885–1958, vol. V
Jones, Rev. Gilbert Basil, 1894–1958, vol. V (A),
    vol. VI (AI)
Jones, Sir Glyn Smallwood, 1908–1992, vol. IX
Jones, Sir Gordon Pearce, 1927–1999, vol. X
Jones, Griffith Winston Guthrie, 1914–1996, vol. X
Jones, Rev. Gustavus John, 1848–1929, vol. III
Jones, Maj.-Gen. Guy Carleton, 1864–1950, vol. IV
Jones, Maj.-Gen. Sir Guy S.; *see* Salisbury-Jones.
Jones, Gwilym Arthur, 1887–1957, vol. V
Jones, Gwilym Peredur, 1892–1975, vol. VII
Jones, (Gwilym) Wyn, 1926–1993, vol. IX
Jones, Gwyn, 1907–1999, vol. X
Jones, G(wyneth) Ceris, 1906–1987, vol. VIII
Jones, H. Chapman, 1854–1932, vol. III
Jones, Sir Harold Spencer, 1890–1960, vol. V

Jones, Harry, 1866–1925, vol. II
Jones, Harry, 1905–1986, vol. VIII
Jones, Col Harry Balfour, 1866–1952, vol. V
Jones, Harry Davies Campbell, 1863–1935, vol. III
Jones, Sir Harry Ernest, 1911–1998, vol. X
Jones, Harry O.; *see* Orton-Jones.
Jones, Henry, (Cavendish), 1831–1899, vol. I
Jones, Sir Henry, 1852–1922, vol. II
Jones, Sir Henry, 1862–1926, vol. II
Jones, Henry Albert, *died* 1945, vol. IV
Jones, Lt-Gen. Henry Albert H., *died* 1944, vol. IV
Jones, Henry Arthur, 1851–1929, vol. III
Jones, Rev. Henry David, 1842–1925, vol. II
Jones, Very Rev. Henry Donald Maurice S.; *see* Spence-Jones.
Jones, Henry Festing, 1851–1928, vol. II
Jones, Sir Henry Frank Harding, 1906–1987, vol. VIII
Jones, Sir Henry Haydn, 1863–1950, vol. IV
Jones, Ven. Henry James Church, 1870–1941, vol. IV
Jones, Henry Lewis, 1857–1915, vol. I
Jones, Henry M.; *see* Macnaughton-Jones.
Jones, Sir Henry M.; *see* Morris-Jones, Sir J. H.
Jones, Captain Henry Michael, *died* 1916, vol. II
Jones, Bt Col Henry Morris P.; *see* Pryce-Jones.
Jones, Captain Henry Richmund I.; *see* Inigo-Jones.
Jones, Sir Henry S.; *see* Stuart-Jones.
Jones, Brig.-Gen. Herbert Arthur, *died* 1955, vol. V
Jones, Very Rev. Herbert Arthur, *died* 1969, vol. VI
Jones, Rt Rev. Herbert Edward, 1861–1920, vol. II
Jones, Air Cdre Herbert George, 1884–1979, vol. VII
Jones, Rt Rev. Herbert Gresford, 1870–1958, vol. V
Jones, Herbert Lee Jackson, 1870–1936, vol. III
Jones, Herbert Riversdale M.; *see* Mansel-Jones.
Jones, Sir Hildreth G.; *see* Glyn-Jones.
Jones, Howard Parker, 1863–1924, vol. II
Jones, Gen. Sir Howard Sutton, 1835–1912, vol. I
Jones, Rev. Howard W.; *see* Watkin-Jones.
Jones, Howell G.; *see* Gwynne-Jones.
Jones, Rev. Hubert C.; *see* Cunliffe-Jones.
Jones, Ven. Hugh, 1815–1897, vol. I
Jones, Rev. Hugh; *see* Jones, Rev. R. W. H.
Jones, Hugh E.; *see* Emlyn-Jones.
Jones, Hugh Ferguson, 1913–1979, vol. VII
Jones, Air Marshal Sir Humphrey E.; *see* Edwardes Jones.
Jones, Humphrey Lloyd, 1910–1983, vol. VIII
Jones, Humphrey Stanley Herbert, *died* 1902, vol. I
Jones, Ven. Humphrey Tudor Morrey, *died* 1936, vol. III
Jones, Huw M.; *see* Morris-Jones.
Jones, Hywel Glyn, 1948–1999, vol. X
Jones, Ian C.; *see* Chester Jones.
Jones, Ian E.; *see* Edwards-Jones.
Jones, Idris Deane, 1899–1947, vol. IV
Jones, Ifano, 1865–1955, vol. V
Jones, Maj.-Gen. Inigo Richmund, 1848–1914, vol. I
Jones, Isaac, 1883–1968, vol. VI
Jones, Ivan Ellis, 1903–1984, vol. VIII
Jones, Ivor R.; *see* Roberts-Jones.
Jones, J. Clinton, 1848–1936, vol. III
Jones, J. Morgan, 1873–1946, vol. IV

Jones, Jack, 1884–1970, vol. VI
Jones, Sir James, 1895–1962, vol. VI
Jones, James, 1921–1977, vol. VII
Jones, Sir James Duncan, 1914–1995, vol. IX
Jones, James Edmund, 1866–1939, vol. III
Jones, Sir James Edward, 1843–1922, vol. II
Jones, James Idwal, 1900–1982, vol. VIII
Jones, James Ilston, 1911–1976, vol. VII
Jones, Gp Captain James Ira Thomas, 1896–1960, vol. V
Jones, Lt-Col James Walker, 1887–1933, vol. III
Jones, Ven. James William Percy, 1881–1980, vol. VII
Jones, James William W.; *see* Webb-Jones.
Jones, John Arthur, 1867–1939, vol. III
Jones, Sir John Bowen Bowen-, 1st Bt (*cr* 1911), 1840–1925, vol. II
Jones, Rt Rev. John Charles, 1904–1956, vol. V
Jones, John Cyril, 1899–1990, vol. VIII
Jones, Rev. John Daniel, 1865–1942, vol. IV
Jones, John David Rheinallt, 1884–1953, vol. V
Jones, Paymaster Rear-Adm. John Edward, 1866–1948, vol. IV
Jones, (John) Edward, 1914–1998, vol. X
Jones, Sir John Edward L.; *see* Lennard-Jones.
Jones, John Emlyn E.; *see* Emlyn-Jones.
Jones, (John) Emrys, 1914–1991, vol. IX
Jones, Maj.-Gen. John H.; *see* Hamilton-Jones.
Jones, John Harry, 1881–1973, vol. VII
Jones, John Henry, 1894–1962, vol. VI
Jones, Sir (John) Henry M.; *see* Morris-Jones.
Jones, Rev. John Hugh Watkins, 1862–1937, vol. III
Jones, Col John Hyndman H.; *see* Howell-Jones.
Jones, John Iorwerth, *born* 1901, vol. VIII
Jones, Rev. J(ohn) Ithel, 1911–1980, vol. VII (AII)
Jones, Rev. John James, *died* 1934, vol. III
Jones, Col Sir John James, 1845–1938, vol. III
Jones, John Joseph, 1873–1941, vol. IV
Jones, John Joseph Casimer, 1839–1929, vol. III
Jones, Sir (John) Kenneth (Trevor), 1910–1995, vol. IX
Jones, John Kenyon Netherton, 1912–1977, vol. VII
Jones, John L.; *see* Lees-Jones.
Jones, Sir John Lewis, 1923–1998, vol. X
Jones, Ven. John Lloyd-, 1848–1934, vol. III
Jones, (John) Mervyn (Guthrie) G.; *see* Griffith-Jones.
Jones, John Morgan, 1903–1989, vol. VIII
Jones, Sir John Morris-, 1864–1929, vol. III
Jones, Brig. John Murray R.; *see* Rymer-Jones.
Jones, Sir John P.; *see* Prichard-Jones.
Jones, John Richard, 1881–1955, vol. V
Jones, (John) Share, *died* 1950, vol. IV
Jones, Rev. Preb. John Stephen Langton, 1889–1992, vol. IX
Jones, John Viriamu, 1856–1901, vol. I
Jones, John Walter, 1892–1973, vol. VII
Jones, Air Chief Marshal Sir John Whitworth, 1896–1981, vol. VIII
Jones, Joseph, *died* 1948, vol. IV
Jones, Joseph, 1890–1979, vol. VII
Jones, Rev. Josiah Towyn, 1858–1925, vol. II
Jones, Dame Katharine Henrietta, 1888–1967, vol. VI

Jones, Keith M.; *see* Miller Jones.
Jones, Kennedy; *see* Jones, W. K.
Jones, Sir Kenneth; *see* Jones, Sir J. K. T.
Jones, Captain Kingsmill Williams, 1875–1918, vol. II
Jones, Air Marshal Sir Laurence Alfred, 1933–1995, vol. IX
Jones, Lawrence, *died* 1949, vol. IV
Jones, Sir Lawrence Evelyn, 5th Bt (*cr* 1831), 1885–1969, vol. VI
Jones, Sir Lawrence John, 4th Bt (*cr* 1831), 1857–1954, vol. V
Jones, Leonard Ivan S.; *see* Stranger-Jones.
Jones, Leslie, 1917–1994, vol. IX
Jones, Maj.-Gen. Leslie Cockburn, 1870–1960, vol. V
Jones, Rev. Lewis, 1842–1928, vol. II
Jones, Maj.-Gen. Lewis, 1862–1935, vol. III
Jones, Sir Lewis, 1884–1968, vol. VI
Jones, Lewis; *see* Jones, G. L.
Jones, Lewis; *see* Jones, W. L.
Jones, Leycester Hudson L.; *see* Leslie-Jones.
Jones, Lionel P.; *see* Powys-Jones.
Jones, Rt Rev. Llewellyn, 1840–1918, vol. II
Jones, Llewellyn Archer A.; *see* Atherley-Jones.
Jones, Col Llewellyn Murray, 1871–1946, vol. IV
Jones, Llewellyn Rodwell, 1881–1947, vol. IV
Jones, Llewelyn Arthur H.; *see* Hugh-Jones.
Jones, Maj.-Gen. Llewelyn W.; *see* Wansbrough-Jones.
Jones, Very Rev. Llewelyn W.; *see* Wynne-Jones.
Jones, Rev. Lloyd Timothy, *died* 1920, vol. II
Jones, Brig.-Gen. Lumley Owen Williames, 1876–1918, vol. II
Jones, Sir Lyman Melvin, 1843–1917, vol. II
Jones, Mrs Mabel Mary Cheveley; *see* Rayner, M. M. C.
Jones, Martin, 1897–1979, vol. VII
Jones, Marvin, *died* 1976, vol. VII
Jones, Dame Mary Latchford Kingsmill, *died* 1968, vol. VI
Jones, Rev. Maurice, 1863–1957, vol. V
Jones, Maurice; *see* Jones, S. M.
Jones, Sir Melvill; *see* Jones, Sir B. M.
Jones, Mervyn; *see* Jones, T. M.
Jones, Michael Barry, 1932–1996, vol. X
Jones, Lt-Col Michael Durwas Goring-, 1866–1919, vol. II
Jones, Rt Rev. Michael G.; *see* Gresford Jones, Rt Rev. E. M.
Jones, Montagu H.; *see* Handfield-Jones.
Jones, Brig.-Gen. Morey Q.; *see* Quayle-Jones.
Jones, Morgan, 1885–1939, vol. III
Jones, Morgan; *see* Jones, J. M.
Jones, Morgan Philips G.; *see* Griffith-Jones.
Jones, Noel Andrew Stephen, 1940–1995, vol. IX
Jones, Norman Edward, 1904–1972, vol. VII
Jones, Rt Rev. Norman Sherwood, 1911–1951, vol. V
Jones, Norman Stewart C.; *see* Carey Jones.
Jones, Norman William, 1923–1993, vol. IX
Jones, Norvela, (Mrs Michael Jones); *see* Forster, N.
Jones, Captain Oscar Philip, 1898–1980, vol. VII
Jones, Captain Owen, 1866–1941, vol. IV

Jones, Owen Daniel, 1861–1951, vol. V
Jones, Sir Owen Haddon W.; *see* Wansbrough-Jones.
Jones, Owen Thomas, 1878–1967, vol. VI
Jones, Parry William John, 1891–1963, vol. VI
Jones, Patrick Nicholas Hill, 1864–1934, vol. III
Jones, Sir Pendrill Charles V.; *see* Varrier-Jones.
Jones, Penrhyn Grant, 1878–1945, vol. IV
Jones, Major Percy Arnold Lloyd-, 1876–1916, vol. II
Jones, Maj.-Gen. Percy George C.; *see* Calvert-Jones.
Jones, Rev. Percy Herbert, 1864–1941, vol. IV
Jones, Percy Mansell, 1889–1968, vol. VI
Jones, Hon. Percy Sydney T.; *see* Twentyman-Jones.
Jones, Sir Peter (Fawcett) Benton, 3rd Bt (*cr* 1919), 1911–1972, vol. VII
Jones, Peter Howard, 1911–1975, vol. VII
Jones, Sir Philip; *see* Jones, Sir T. P.
Jones, Philip Asterley, 1914–1978, vol. VII
Jones, Sir Philip B.; *see* Burne-Jones.
Jones, Sir Philip Frederick, 1912–1983, vol. VIII
Jones, Philip Mark, 1928–2000, vol. X
Jones, Col Philip Reginald B.; *see* Bence-Jones.
Jones, Sir Philip Sydney, 1836–1918, vol. II
Jones, Sir Pryce P.; *see* Pryce-Jones.
Jones, Sir Pryce Victor P.; *see* Pryce-Jones.
Jones, Ranald Montagu H.; *see* Handfield-Jones.
Jones, Raymond R.; *see* Ray-Jones.
Jones, Reginald Ernest, 1904–1993, vol. IX
Jones, Reginald Trevor, 1888–1974, vol. VII
Jones, Reginald Victor, 1911–1997, vol. X
Jones, Sir Reginald W.; *see* Watson-Jones.
Jones, Rev. Richard Charles Stuart, *died* 1941, vol. IV
Jones, Rev. Canon Richard E.; *see* Evan-Jones.
Jones, Richard Francis L.; *see* Lloyd Jones.
Jones, Lt-Col Richard Godfrey, 1855–1934, vol. III
Jones, Air Vice-Marshal Richard Ian, 1916–1993, vol. IX
Jones, Maj.-Gen. Richard K.; *see* Keith-Jones.
Jones, Richard S.; *see* Stanton-Jones.
Jones, Rev. Richard Thomas, *died* 1917, vol. II
Jones, Rt Rev. Richard William, *died* 1953, vol. V
Jones, Sir Robert, 1st Bt (*cr* 1926), 1858–1933, vol. III
Jones, Sir Robert Armstrong-, 1857–1943, vol. IV
Jones, Robert Edmond, 1887–1954, vol. V
Jones, (Robert) Gerallt, 1934–1999, vol. X
Jones, Robert L.; *see* Lloyd-Jones.
Jones, Brig. Robert Llewellyn J.; *see* Jephson-Jones.
Jones, Robert Noble, 1864–1942, vol. IV
Jones, Maj.-Gen. Robert Owen, 1837–1926, vol. II
Jones, Air Marshal Sir R(obert) Owen, 1901–1972, vol. VII
Jones, Robert Thomas, *died* 1940, vol. III
Jones, Robert Tyre, (Bobby), 1902–1971, vol. VII
Jones, Robert Walter, 1890–1951, vol. V
Jones, Rev. (Robert William) Hugh, 1911–1993, vol. IX
Jones, Sir Roderick, 1877–1962, vol. VI
Jones, Maj.-Gen. Roderick Idrisyn, 1895–1970, vol. VI
Jones, Ronald Christopher H.; *see* Hope-Jones.

Jones, Comdr Ronald L.; *see* Langton-Jones.
Jones, Brig. Ronald M.; *see* Montague-Jones.
Jones, Ronald Owen Lloyd A.; *see* Armstrong-Jones.
Jones, Royston Oscar, 1925–1974, vol. VII
Jones, Rufus M., 1863–1948, vol. IV
Jones, Rev. S. M.; *see* Martin-Jones.
Jones, S. Maurice, *died* 1932, vol. III
Jones, Sir Samuel Bankole-, 1911–1981, vol. VIII
Jones, Sir Samuel Owen, 1905–1985, vol. VIII
Jones, Share; *see* Jones, J. S.
Jones, Air Cdre Shirley Ann, *died* 1997, vol. X
Jones, Siriol (Mary Aprille) H.; *see* Hugh-Jones.
Jones, Rev. Spencer John, 1857–1943, vol. IV
Jones, Stanley Wilson, 1888–1962, vol. VI
Jones, Stuart Lloyd, 1917–1998, vol. X
Jones, Sir Sydney; *see* Jones, Sir C. S.
Jones, Sydney, 1911–1990, vol. VIII
Jones, Sydney T.; *see* Tapper-Jones.
Jones, Hon. Sydney Twentyman, 1849–1913, vol. I
Jones, Sir (Tom) Barry, 2nd Bt (*cr* 1917), 1888–1952, vol. V
Jones, Col Theophilus Percy, 1866–1934, vol. III
Jones, Rev. Canon Thomas, 1839–1927, vol. II
Jones, Sir Thomas, 1870–1945, vol. IV
Jones, Thomas, 1870–1955, vol. V
Jones, Captain Thomas Alban, 1869–1945, vol. IV
Jones, Sir Thomas Artemus, *died* 1943, vol. IV
Jones, Thomas Boughton B.; *see* Bovell-Jones.
Jones, Thomas E.; *see* Elder-Jones.
Jones, Rt Rev. Thomas Edward, 1903–1972, vol. VII
Jones, Sir Thomas George, 1881–1948, vol. IV
Jones, Thomas Gwynn, 1871–1949, vol. IV
Jones, Thomas Isaac M.; *see* Mardy Jones.
Jones, Rev. Thomas Jesse, *died* 1930, vol. III
Jones, Sir Thomas M.; *see* Miller-Jones.
Jones, (Thomas) Mervyn, 1910–1989, vol. VIII
Jones, Sir (Thomas) Philip, 1931–2000, vol. X
Jones, Thomas Rees, 1863–1938, vol. III
Jones, Thomas Ridge, 1840–1924, vol. II
Jones, Thomas Rupert, 1819–1911, vol. I
Jones, Rt Rev. Thomas Sherwood, 1872–1972, vol. VII
Jones, Thomas William; *see* Baron Maelor.
Jones, Timothy Fraser, 1931–1996, vol. X
Jones, Tom, 1908–1985, vol. VIII
Jones, Tom, 1908–1990, vol. VIII
Jones, Tom Neville W.; *see* Wynne-Jones.
Jones, Sir Tracy French Gavin, 1872–1953, vol. V
Jones, Rt Hon. (Trevor) Alec, 1924–1983, vol. VIII
Jones, Vernon Stanley V.; *see* Vernon-Jones.
Jones, Sir Vincent L.; *see* Lloyd-Jones.
Jones, Sir Vincent Strickland, 1874–1967, vol. VI
Jones, W. Lewis, 1866–1922, vol. II
Jones, Walter, 1846–1924, vol. II
Jones, Sir Walter Benton, 2nd Bt (*cr* 1919), 1880–1967, vol. VI
Jones, Lt-Col Walter Dally, 1855–1926, vol. II
Jones, Lt-Col Walter H.; *see* Howel-Jones.
Jones, Captain Walter Henry Clulee, 1899–1932, vol. III
Jones, W(alter) Idris, 1900–1971, vol. VII
Jones, Walter L.; *see* Lindley-Jones.

Jones, Lt-Col Walter Thomas Cresswell, 1874–1923, vol. II
Jones, Wendell Phillips, 1866–1944, vol. IV
Jones, William, *died* 1915, vol. I
Jones, Sir William, 1888–1961, vol. VI
Jones, William Brittain, 1834–1912, vol. I
Jones, Rev. William David, 1909–1976, vol. VII
Jones, Very Rev. William Edward, 1897–1974, vol. VII
Jones, Sir (William) Elwyn (Edwards), 1904–1989, vol. VIII
Jones, Sir (William) Emrys, 1915–2000, vol. X
Jones, William Ernest, 1867–1957, vol. V (A)
Jones, (William) Ernest, 1895–1973, vol. VII
Jones, William Everard Tyldesley, 1874–1938, vol. III
Jones, Rev. William G.; *see* Griffith-Jones.
Jones, William Garmon, 1884–1937, vol. III
Jones, Hon. Sir William H.; *see* Hall-Jones.
Jones, William Henry, 1873–1944, vol. IV
Jones, Sir William Henry H.; *see* Hyndman-Jones.
Jones, William Henry Samuel, 1876–1963, vol. VI
Jones, Sir William Hollingworth Quayle, 1854–1925, vol. II
Jones, Rev. William Hudson M.; *see* Macnaughton-Jones.
Jones, William Hugh, 1866–1960, vol. V
Jones, William Jenkyn, 1867–1934, vol. III
Jones, Sir William John, 1866–1938, vol. III
Jones, Sir (William John) Andrew, 1889–1971, vol. VII
Jones, (William) Kennedy, 1865–1921, vol. II
Jones, William Llewellyn, 1881–1950, vol. IV
Jones, Hon. Sir William Lloyd M.; *see* Mars-Jones.
Jones, William Morris, 1889–1963, vol. VI
Jones, Lt-Col William Nathaniel, 1858–1934, vol. III
Jones, William Neilson, 1883–1974, vol. VII
Jones, William Richard, 1880–1970, vol. VI
Jones, William Ronald Rees; *see* Rhys, Keidrych.
Jones, Rt Rev. William S.; *see* Stanton-Jones.
Jones, Sir William Samuel G.; *see* Glyn-Jones.
Jones, William Stephen, 1913–1981, vol. VIII
Jones, William Sydney, 1888–1959, vol. V
Jones, William Thorpe, 1864–1932, vol. III
Jones, William Tinnion, 1927–1981, vol. VIII
Jones, William Tudor, 1865–1946, vol. IV
Jones, Most Rev. William West, 1838–1908, vol. I
Jones, Rt Rev. William Wynn, 1900–1950, vol. IV
Jones, Sir William Y.; *see* Yarworth-Jones.
Jones, Wyn; *see* Jones, G. W.
Jones, Wyndraeth Humphreys M.; *see* Morris-Jones.
Jones, Wood; *see* Jones, F. W.
Jones-Davies, Henry, 1870–1955, vol. V
Jones Mitton, Col George, 1860–1949, vol. IV
Jones-Parry, Sir Ernest, 1908–1992, vol. IX
Jones-Parry, Rear-Adm. John Parry, 1829–1920, vol. II
Jones-Roberts, Kate Winifred, 1889–1971, vol. VII
Jones-Vaughan, Maj.-Gen. Hugh Thomas, 1841–1916, vol. II
Jonnart, Celestin Auguste, 1857–1927, vol. II
Jonsson, Einar, 1874–1954, vol. V
Jonzen, Karin, 1914–1998, vol. X
Jooste, Gerhardus Petrus, 1904–1990, vol. VIII

Jope, Edward Martyn, 1915–1996, vol. X
Jopling, Louise, 1843–1933, vol. III
Jopling-Rowe, Louise; *see* Jopling, Louise.
Jopp, Col John, 1940–1923, vol. II
Jopson, Sir Keith; *see* Jopson, Sir R. K.
Jopson, Norman Brooke, 1890–1969, vol. VI
Jopson, Sir (Reginald) Keith, 1898–1957, vol. V
Jordan, King Hussein of; *see* Hussein bin Talal.
Jordan, Alfred Charles, 1872–1956, vol. V
Jordan, Most Rev. Anthony, 1901–1982, vol. VIII
Jordan, David Harold, 1924–1998, vol. X
Jordan, David Starr, 1851–1931, vol. III
Jordan, Douglas Arthur, 1918–1999, vol. X
Jordan, Edwin Oakes, 1866–1926, vol. II, vol. III
Jordan, Elizabeth, *died* 1947, vol. IV
Jordan, Sir Frederick Richard, 1881–1949, vol. IV
Jordan, Rev. George, 1876–1936, vol. III
Jordan, Heinrich Ernst Karl, 1861–1959, vol. V
Jordan, Helen; *see* Ashton, H.
Jordan, Henry, 1919–1994, vol. IX
Jordan, Herbert William, 1874–1947, vol. IV
Jordan, Rev. Preb. Hugh, 1906–1984, vol. VIII
Jordan, Humfrey Robertson, 1885–1963, vol. VI
Jordan, Rev. Canon James Henry, 1882–1959, vol. V
Jordan, Jeremiah, *died* 1911, vol. I
Jordan, Rt Hon. Sir John Newell, 1852–1925, vol. II
Jordan, Maj.-Gen. Joseph, 1826–1899, vol. I
Jordan, Karl; *see* Jordan, H. E. K.
Jordan, Louis Arnold, 1892–1964, vol. VI
Jordan, Rev. Louis Henry, 1855–1923, vol. II
Jordan, Philip Furneaux, 1902–1951, vol. V
Jordan, Air Marshal Sir Richard Bowen, 1902–1994, vol. IX
Jordan, Lt-Col Richard Price, 1869–1963, vol. VI
Jordan, Sara M., (Mrs Penfield Mower), 1884–1959, vol. V
Jordan, Rev. W. G., 1852–1939, vol. III
Jordan, Wilbur Kitchener, 1902–1980, vol. VII
Jordan, William Edward, 1869–1938, vol. III
Jordan, William George, 1864–1928, vol. II
Jordan, Rt Hon. Sir William Joseph, *died* 1959, vol. V
Jordan Lloyd, Dorothy, 1889–1946, vol. IV
Jordan Malkin, Harold; *see* Malkin.
Jordan-Moss, Norman, 1920–1998, vol. X
Jorden, John M., *died* 1907, vol. I
Jorisch, Norah; *see* Lofts, N.
Jorre de St Jorre, Danielle Marie-Madeleine, 1941–1997, vol. X
Jory, Norman Adams, 1896–1965, vol. VI
Jory, Philip John, 1892–1973, vol. VII
Josa, Ven. Fortunato Pietro Luigi, 1851–1922, vol. II
Joscelyne, Rt Rev. Albert Ernest, 1866–1945, vol. IV
Jose, Captain Arthur Wilberforce, 1863–1934, vol. III
Jose, Very Rev. George Herbert, 1868–1956, vol. V
Jose, Sir Ivan Bede, 1893–1969, vol. VI (AII)
Joseph, Baron (Life Peer); Keith Sinjohn Joseph, 1918–1994, vol. IX
Joseph, Delissa, 1859–1927, vol. II

Joseph, Sir Francis L'Estrange, 1st Bt, 1870–1951, vol. V
Joseph, Sir (Herbert) Leslie, 1908–1992, vol. IX
Joseph, Horace William Brindley, 1867–1943, vol. IV
Joseph, Sir Leslie; *see* Joseph, Sir H. L.
Joseph, Sir Maxwell, 1910–1982, vol. VIII
Joseph, Michael, 1897–1958, vol. V
Joseph, Hon. Mrs Michael; *see* Hastings, Hon. Anthea.
Joseph, Rev. Morris, 1848–1930, vol. III
Joseph, Sir Norman; *see* Joseph, Sir S. N.
Joseph, Sir Samuel George, 1888–1944, vol. IV
Joseph, Sir (Samuel) Norman, 1908–1974, vol. VII
Josephs, Wilfred, 1927–1997, vol. X
Joshi, Rev. Canon D. L., 1864–1923, vol. II
Joshi, Narayan Malhar, 1879–1955, vol. V
Joske, Hon. Sir Percy Ernest, 1895–1981, vol. VIII
Joslin, David Maelgwyn, 1925–1970, vol. VI
Joslin, Ivy Collin, 1900–1986, vol. VIII
Joslin, Maj.-Gen. Stanley William, 1899–1982, vol. VIII
Josling, John Francis, 1910–1993, vol. IX
Josselyn, Col John, 1872–1943, vol. IV
Jossett, Lawrence Leon Louis, 1910–1995, vol. IX
Joubert de la Ferte, Air Chief Marshal Sir Philip Bennet, *died* 1965, vol. VI
Joughin, Sir Michael, 1926–1996, vol. X
Jouhaux, Léon, 1879–1954, vol. V
Joulain, Rt Rev. Henry, 1852–1919, vol. II
Joules, Horace, 1902–1977, vol. VII
Jourdain, Lt-Col Charles Edward Arthur, 1869–1918, vol. II
Jourdain, Eleanor Frances, *died* 1924, vol. II
Jourdain, Rev. Francis C. R., *died* 1940, vol. III
Jourdain, Lt-Col Henry Francis Newdigate, 1872–1968, vol. VI
Jourdain, Sir Henry John, 1835–1901, vol. I
Jourdan, Rev. George Viviliers, *died* 1955, vol. V
Jowers, Reginald Francis, 1861–1934, vol. III
Jowett, Edmund, 1858–1936, vol. III
Jowett, Rt Hon. Frederick William, 1864–1944, vol. IV
Jowett, Rev. John Henry, 1864–1923, vol. II
Jowett, Percy Hague, 1882–1955, vol. V
Jowett, Ronald Edward, 1901–1986, vol. VIII
Jowitt, 1st Earl, 1885–1957, vol. V
Jowitt, Frederick McCulloch, 1868–1919, vol. II
Jowitt, Harold, 1893–1963, vol. VI
Jowsey, Col Thomas, 1853–1934, vol. III
Joy, Albert B.; *see* Bruce-Joy.
Joy, David, *died* 1903, vol. I
Joy, Edith Katharine Spicer; *see* Prescott, E. Livingston.
Joy, Sir George Andrew, 1896–1974, vol. VII
Joy, George William, 1844–1925, vol. II
Joy, Henry Holmes, *died* 1934, vol. III
Joy, Michael Gerard Laurie, 1916–1993, vol. IX
Joyce, Alec Houghton, 1894–1982, vol. VIII
Joyce, Archibald, 1873–1963, vol. VI
Joyce, Rt Rev. Edward Michael, 1907–1964, vol. VI
Joyce, Eileen Alannah, 1912–1991, vol. IX
Joyce, Rev. Frederick Wayland, 1852–1934, vol. III
Joyce, Rt Rev. Gilbert Cunningham, 1866–1942, vol. IV

Joyce, Maj.-Gen. Hayman John H.; *see* Hayman-Joyce.
Joyce, James, 1882–1941, vol. IV
Joyce, Rev. James Barclay, *died* 1934, vol. III
Joyce, John Hall, 1906–1982, vol. VIII
Joyce, Rt Hon. Sir Matthew Ingle, 1839–1930, vol. III
Joyce, Patrick Weston, 1827–1914, vol. I
Joyce, Lt-Col Pierce Charles, *died* 1965, vol. VI
Joyce, Rt Rev. Mgr T. J., *died* 1947, vol. IV
Joyce, Thomas Athol, 1878–1942, vol. IV
Joyce, Thomas Heath, 1850–1925, vol. II
Joyner, Robert Batson, 1844–1919, vol. II
Joynt, Evelyn Gertrude, 1919–1991, vol. IX
Joynt, John William, 1852–1933, vol. III
Joynt, Rev. Robert Charles, 1856–1938, vol. III
Jubb, Edwin Charles, 1883–1978, vol. VII
Juda, Hans Peter, 1904–1975, vol. VII
Judd, Alfred, *died* 1932, vol. III
Judd, Charles Wilfred, 1896–1974, vol. VII
Judd, Sir George, 1840–1909, vol. I
Judd, George William, *born* 1854, vol. II
Judd, Harold Godfrey, 1878–1961, vol. VI
Judd, John Basil Thomas, 1909–1983, vol. VIII
Judd, John Wesley, 1840–1916, vol. II
Judd, Thomas Langley, 1880–1945, vol. IV
Judd, Walter Albert, 1861–1931, vol. III
Jude, Sir Norman Lane, 1905–1975, vol. VII
Judge, Edward Thomas, 1908–1992, vol. IX
Judge, Mark Hayler, 1847–1927, vol. II
Judge, Captain Spencer Francis, 1861–1911, vol. I
Judges, Arthur Valentine, 1898–1973, vol. VII
Judkins, Rev. Eimer, 1855–1940, vol. III
Judson, Harry Pratt, 1849–1927, vol. II
Jugmohandas Varjivandas, Sir, 1869–1934, vol. III
Juin, Alphonse Pierre, 1888–1967, vol. VI
Jukes, E(rnest) Martin, 1909–1982, vol. VIII
Jukes, John Andrew, 1917–1997, vol. X
Jukes, John Edwin Clapham, 1878–1955, vol. V
Jukes, Richard Starr, 1906–1987, vol. VIII

Jukes-Browne, Alfred John, 1851–1914, vol. I
Jukes Hughes, Captain Edward Glyn de Styrap, 1883–1966, vol. VI
Juler, Frank Anderson, 1880–1962, vol. VI
Juler, Henry Edward, *died* 1921, vol. II
Julian, Ernest Laurence, *died* 1915, vol. I
Julian, Sir Ivor; *see* Julian, Sir K. I.
Julian, Rev. John, 1839–1913, vol. I
Julian, Sir (Kenneth) Ivor, 1895–1971, vol. VII
Julian, Maj.-Gen. Sir Oliver Richard Archer, 1863–1925, vol. II
Julius, Most Rev. Churchill, 1847–1938, vol. III
Julius, Sir George Alfred, 1873–1946, vol. IV
Julius, Very Rev. John Awdry, 1874–1956, vol. V
Jullian, Camille, 1859–1933, vol. III
Julyan, Sir Penrose Goodchild, 1816–1907, vol. I
Julyan, Lt-Col William Leopold, 1888–1972, vol. VII
Juma, Sa'ad, *born* 1916
Junagadh, Nawab Saheb of, 1900–1959, vol. V
Junagarh, HH Sir Rasul Khanji Muhabat Khanji, Nawab of, *died* 1911, vol. I
Jung, Carl Gustav, 1875–1961, vol. VI
Jungwirth, Sir John; *see* Jungwirth, Sir W. J.
Jungwirth, Sir (William) John, 1897–1981, vol. VIII
Junor, Sir John, 1919–1997, vol. X
Jupp, Rev. Canon, *died* 1911, vol. I
Jupp, Clifford Norman, 1919–1989, vol. VIII
Jury, Col Edward Cotton, 1881–1966, vol. VI
Jury, Sir William Frederick, 1870–1944, vol. IV
Jusserand, Jean Adrien Antoine Jules, 1855–1932, vol. III
Just, Sir Hartmann, 1854–1929, vol. III
Justham, David Gwyn, 1923–1991, vol. IX
Justice, Maj.-Gen. Henry Annesley, 1832–1908, vol. I
Justice, James Norval Harald R.; *see* Robertson-Justice.
Justice, Maj.-Gen. William Clive, 1835–1908, vol. I
Juta, Sir Henry Hubert, 1857–1930, vol. III

K

Kaberry of Adel, Baron (Life Peer); Donald Kaberry, 1907–1991, vol. IX
Kadoorie, Baron (Life Peer); Lawrence Kadoorie, 1899–1993, vol. IX
Kadoorie, Sir Ellis, 1865–1922, vol. II
Kadoorie, Sir Elly, 1867–1944, vol. IV
Kadoorie, Sir Horace, 1902–1995, vol. IX
Kagan, Baron (Life Peer); Joseph Kagan, 1915–1995, vol. IX
Kagwa, Sir Apolo, *died* 1927, vol. II
Kahan, Barbara Joan, 1920–2000, vol. X
Kahle, Paul Ernest, 1875–1964, vol. VI
Kahn, Baron (Life Peer); Richard Ferdinand Kahn, 1905–1989, vol. VIII
Kahn, Franz Daniel, 1926–1998, vol. X
Kahn-Freund, Sir Otto, 1900–1979, vol. VII
Khan, Otto Hermann, 1867–1934, vol. III
Kaine, Hon. John Charles, 1854–1921, vol. II
Kaiser, Henry J., 1882–1967, vol. VI

Kaiser Shamsher Jang Bahadur Rana, HH Commanding-Gen. Sir, 1892–1964, vol. VI
Kalat, Wali of, *died* 1931, vol. III
Kalat, HH Sir Beglar Begi Nawab Bahadur Mir Azam Jan, *died* 1933, vol. III
Kaldor, Baron (Life Peer); Nicholas Kaldor, 1908–1986, vol. VIII
Kalergi, Richard N. C.; *see* Coudenhove-Kalergi.
Kalinin, Mikhail Ivanovich, 1875–1946, vol. IV
Kalisch, Alfred, 1863–1933, vol. III
Kalisher, Michael David Lionel, 1941–1996, vol. X
Kallas, Madame Aino Julia Maria, *died* 1956, vol. V
Kallas, Oskar Philipp, 1868–1946, vol. IV
Kalmus, Herbert Thomas, 1881–1963, vol. VI
Kamâl, Gazi Mustafa; *see* Atatürk, K.
Kamal-ud-Din, Khwaja, 1870–1932, vol. III
Kamat, B. S., 1871–1945, vol. IV
Kambal, Miralai (Col) Beshir Bey, 1855–1919, vol. II

Kamphausen, Adolf Hermann Heinrich, 1829–1909, vol. I
Kandathil, Most Rev. Augustine, 1874–1956, vol. V
Kandel, Isaac Leon, 1881–1965, vol. VI
Kane, Albert Edmond, 1867–1949, vol. IV
Kane, Edward William, died 1934, vol. III
Kane, Adm. Sir Henry Coey, 1843–1917, vol. II
Kane, Jack, 1911–1999, vol. X
Kane, Robert Romney, 1842–1902, vol. I
Kane, Captain Robert Romney Godred, 1888–1918, vol. II
Kane, William Francis de Vismes, 1840–1918, vol. II
Kania, Hon. Sir Harilal Jekisundas, 1890–1951, vol. V
Kanika, Raja of, 1881–1948, vol. IV
Kantaraj Urs, Sir Mysore, 1870–1923, vol. II
Kanthack, Alfred Antunes, 1863–1898, vol. I
Kanthack, Francis Edgar, 1872–1961, vol. VI
Kantorovich, Leonid Vitaljevich, 1912–1986, vol. VIII
Kantorowich, Roy Herman, 1916–1996, vol. X
Kantorowicz, Hermann, 1877–1940, vol. III
Kapadia, Shaporji Aspaniarji, 1857–1941, vol. IV
Kapitza, Peter Leonidovich, 1894–1984, vol. VIII
Kaplan, Joseph, 1902–1991, vol. IX
Kapp Edmond X., 1890–1978, vol. VII
Kapp, Gisbert, died 1922, vol. II
Kapp, Helen, 1907–1978, vol. VII
Kapp, Reginald Otto, 1885–1966, vol. VI
Kappel, Frederick Russell, 1902–1994, vol. IX
Kapurthala, HH Maharajah Raja-i-Rajgan of, 1872–1949, vol. IV
Karajan, Herbert von; see von Karajan.
Karamanlis, Konstantinos, 1907–1998, vol. X
Karanja, Hon. Josphat Njuguna, 1931–1994, vol. IX
Karasek, Franz, 1924–1986, vol. VIII
Karanjia, Sir Behram Narosji, 1876–1957, vol. V
Karauli, HH Maharaja Dhiraj Sir Bhanwar Pal, Deo Bahadur, Yadukul Chandra Bhal, 1864–1927, vol. II
Karauli, Maharaja of, HH Maharaja Sir Bhom Pal Deo Bahadur Yadukul Chandra Bhal, 1866–1947, vol. IV
Karimjee, Sir Tayabali Hassanali Alibhoy, 1897–1987, vol. VIII
Kark, Mrs Evelyn Florence, (Lucie Clayton), 1928–1997, vol. X
Karkaria, R. P., 1869–1919, vol. II
Karloff, Boris (William Henry Pratt), 1887–1969, vol. VI
Karmel, Alexander David, 1904–1998, vol. X
Karmel, David, 1907–1982, vol. VIII
Karminski, Rt Hon. Sir Seymour Edward, 1902–1974, vol. VII
Karn, Frederick James, 1862–1940, vol. III
Karn, Valerie Ann, 1939–1999, vol. X
Karney, Rt Rev. Arthur Baillie Lumsdaine, 1874–1963, vol. VI
Karp, David, 1922–1999, vol. X
Karr, Sir Henry S.; see Seton-Karr.
Karr, Heywood Walter S.; see Seton-Karr.
Karrer, Paul, 1889–1971, vol. VII
Karsavina, Tamara, (Mrs H. J. Bruce), 1885–1978, vol. VII

Karslake, Lt-Gen. Sir Henry, 1879–1942, vol. IV
Karslake, Lt-Col John Burgess Preston, 1868–1942, vol. IV
Karslake, Sir William Wollaston, 1834–1913, vol. I
Karve, Dattatreya Gopal, 1898–1967, vol. VI
Kashmir and Jammu, Lt-Gen. HH Maharaja of, 1850–1925, vol. II
Kasimbazar, Maharaja of, 1860–1929, vol. III
Kassanis, Basil, 1911–1985, vol. VIII
Kastler, Alfred, 1902–1984, vol. VIII
Kästner, Erich, 1899–1974, vol. VII
Kastner, L. E., died 1940, vol. III
Kastner, Leslie James, 1911–1996, vol. X
Katchen, Julius, 1926–1969, vol. VI
Katenga, Bridger Winston, 1926–1975, vol. VII
Kater, Sir Gregory Blaxland, 1912–1978, vol. VII
Kater, Hon. Sir Norman William, 1874–1965, vol. VI
Kato, Viscount Takaaki, 1860–1926, vol. II
Kato, Adm. Baron Tomosaburo, 1859–1923, vol. II
Kato, Tadao, 1916–1996, vol. X
Katrak, Khan Bahadur Sir Kavasji Hormusji, died 1946, vol. IV
Katsina, Emir of; see Nagogo, Alhaji Hon. Sir Usuman.
Katsura, Gen. Marquess Taro, 1847–1913, vol. I
Katz, Milton, 1907–1995, vol. IX
Katz, Mindru, 1925–1978, vol. VII
Katzin, Olga, 1896–1987, vol. VIII
Kauffer, Edward McKnight, died 1954, vol. V
Kaufman, George Simon, 1889–1961, vol. VI
Kaufmann, Rev. Moritz, 1839–1920, vol. II
Kaula, Sir Ganga, 1877–1970, vol. VI
Kaulbach, Ven. James Albert, 1839–1913, vol. II
Kaulback, Ronald John Henry, 1909–1995, vol. IX
Kauntze, William Henry, 1887–1947, vol. IV
Kautsky, Karl, 1854–1938, vol. III
Kavan, Anna, died 1968, vol. VI
Kavanagh, Lt-Gen. Sir Charles Toler McMurrough, 1864–1950, vol. IV
Kavanagh, Col Sir Dermot M.; see McMorrough Kavanagh.
Kavanagh, Lt-Col Edward James, 1881–1940, vol. III
Kavanagh, Patrick, 1905–1967, vol. VI
Kavanagh, Rt Hon. Walter MacMurrough, 1856–1922, vol. II
Kawamata, Katsuji, 1905–1986, vol. VIII
Kay, Archibald, 1860–1935, vol. III
Kay, Arthur, died 1939, vol. III
Kay, Arthur William, 1904–1970, vol. VI
Kay, Brian Wilfrid, 1921–1997, vol. X
Kay, Sir Brook, 4th Bt, 1820–1907, vol. I
Kay, Air Vice-Marshal Cyril Eyton, 1902–1993, vol. IX
Kay, Rev. D. Miller, died 1930, vol. III
Kay, Rt Hon. Sir Edward Ebenezer, 1822–1897, vol. I
Kay, Ernest, 1915–1994, vol. IX
Kay, Harold Isherwood, 1893–1938, vol. III
Kay, Sir Herbert, 1879–1957, vol. V
Kay, Herbert Davenport, 1893–1976, vol. VII
Kay, James, 1858–1942, vol. IV
Kay, Sir James Reid, 1885–1965, vol. VI
Kay, John Menzies, 1920–1995, vol. IX

Kay, Sir Joseph Aspden, 1884–1958, vol. V
Kay, Katharine Cameron, *died* 1965, vol. VI
Kay, Ven. Kenneth, 1902–1958, vol. V
Kay, Patrick Healey-; *see* Dolin, Sir Anton.
Kay, Sir Robert Newbald, 1869–1947, vol. IV
Kay, Sydney Entwisle, 1888–1978, vol. VII
Kay, Thomas, *died* 1938, vol. III
Kay, Sir William, 1868–1955, vol. V
Kay, Very Rev. William, 1894–1980, vol. VII
Kay, Sir William Algernon, 5th Bt, 1837–1914, vol. I
Kay, Lt-Col Sir William Algernon Ireland, 6th Bt, 1876–1918, vol. II
Kay, Maj.-Gen. William Heape, 1871–1929, vol. III
Kay, Col William Martin, 1871–1948, vol. IV (A), vol. V
Kay-Mouat, John Richard, 1881–1952, vol. V
Kay-Shuttleworth, Edward James, 1890–1917, vol. II
Kay-Shuttleworth, Hon. Lawrence Ughtred, 1887–1917, vol. II
Kaye, Lt-Col Sir Cecil, 1868–1935, vol. III
Kaye, Sir Cecil Edmund L.; *see* Lister-Kaye.
Kaye, Cecil William, 1865–1941, vol. IV
Kaye, Danny, (Daniel Kominski), 1913–1987, vol. VIII
Kaye, Sir David Alexander Gordon, 4th Bt, 1919–1994, vol. IX
Kaye, Col Douglas Robert Beaumont, 1909–1996, vol. X
Kaye, Sir Emmanuel, 1914–1999, vol. X
Kaye, George William Clarkson, 1880–1941, vol. IV
Kaye, Captain and Flt Comdr Sir Henry Gordon, 2nd Bt, 1889–1965, vol. V
Kaye, Lt-Col James Levett, 1861–1917, vol. II
Kaye, Sir John Christopher Lister L.; *see* Lister-Kaye.
Kaye, Sir John Pepys L.; *see* Lister-Kaye.
Kaye, Sir Joseph H., 1st Bt, 1856–1923, vol. II
Kaye, Sir Kenelm Arthur L.; *see* Lister-Kaye.
Kaye, Levett Mackenzie, 1869–1941, vol. IV
Kaye, Sir Lister L.; *see* Lister-Kaye.
Kaye, Ven. Martin, 1919–1977, vol. VII
Kaye, Col Ralph Arthur, 1863–1933, vol. III
Kaye, Robert Walter, 1871–1957, vol. V
Kaye, Sir Stephen Henry Gordon, 3rd Bt, 1917–1983, vol. VIII
Kaye, Ven. William Frederick John, *died* 1913, vol. I
Kaye, Sir William Squire Barker, 1831–1901, vol. I
Kaye-Smith, Sheila, *died* 1956, vol. V
Kayle, Wing Comdr Joseph Robert, 1914–2000, vol. X
Kays, Brig.-Gen. Horace Francis, 1861–1945, vol. IV
Kays, Brig.-Gen. Walpole Swinton, 1858–1941, vol. IV
Kayser, Charles William, 1870–1947, vol. IV
Kazanjian, Varaztad Hovhannes, 1879–1974, vol. VII
Keable, Robert, 1887–1927, vol. II
Kealy, Sir (Edward) Herbert, 1873–1953, vol. V
Kealy, Sir Herbert; *see* Kealy, Sir E. H.
Kean, Captain Abraham, 1855–1945, vol. IV

Kean, Arnold Wilfred Geoffrey, 1914–2000, vol. X
Kean, Oscar, 1875–1961, vol. VI
Kean, Thomas Alban, 1894–1968, vol. VI (AII)
Keane, Augustus Henry, 1833–1912, vol. I
Keane, Charles Alexander, *died* 1931, vol. III
Keane, Most Rev. David, 1871–1945, vol. IV
Keane, Major Gerald Joseph, 1880–1943, vol. IV
Keane, Lt-Col Sir John, 5th Bt, 1873–1956, vol. V
Keane, John Fryer Thomas, 1854–1937, vol. III
Keane, Mary Nesta, (Molly), (Mrs Robert Keane), 1904–1996, vol. X
Keane, Sir Michael, 1874–1937, vol. III
Keane, Molly; *see* Keane, M. N.
Keane, Lt-Col Richard Henry, 1881–1925, vol. II
Kearney, Very Rev. Alexander Major, *died* 1912, vol. I
Kearney, Count Cecil; *see* Kearney, R. C. J. P.
Kearney, Elfric Wells Chalmers, 1881–1966, vol. VI
Kearney, Sir Francis Edgar, 1870–1938, vol. III
Kearney, Robert Cecil Joseph Patrick, (Count Cecil-Kearney), *died* 1911, vol. I
Kearns, Sir Frederick Matthias, 1921–1983, vol. VIII
Kearns, Sir (Henry Ward) Lionel, 1891–1962, vol. VI
Kearns, Howard George Henry, 1902–1986, vol. VIII
Kearns, Sir Lionel; *see* Kearns, Sir H. W. L.
Kearns, Rev. John Willis, *died* 1962, vol. VI
Kearns, Major Reginald Arthur Ernest Holmes, *died* 1918, vol. II
Kearns, Col Thomas Joseph, 1861–1920, vol. II
Kearon, Air Cdre Norman Walter, 1913–1981, vol. VIII
Kearsley, Brig.-Gen. Sir Harvey; *see* Kearsley, Brig.-Gen. Sir R. H.
Kearsley, Brig.-Gen. Sir (Robert) Harvey, 1880–1956, vol. V
Kearton, Baron (Life Peer); Christopher Frank Kearton, 1911–1992, vol. IX
Kearton, Cherry, 1871–1940, vol. III
Kearton, Richard, 1862–1928, vol. II
Kearton, William Johnston, 1893–1978, vol. VII
Keary, Charles Francis, *died* 1917, vol. II
Keary, Lt-Gen. Sir Henry D'Urban, 1857–1937, vol. III
Keary, Peter, 1865–1915, vol. I
Keating, Donald Norman, 1924–1995, vol. IX
Keating, Most Rev. Frederick William, 1859–1928, vol. II
Keating, Brig. Harold John Buckler, 1893–1970, vol. VI (AII)
Keating, John, (Seán Céitinn), 1889–1977, vol. VII
Keating, Rev. John Fitzstephen, 1850–1911, vol. I
Keating, Hon. John Henry, 1872–1940, vol. III
Keating, Joseph, 1871–1934, vol. III
Keating, Rev. Joseph Ignatius, 1865–1939, vol. III
Keating, Matthew, 1869–1937, vol. III
Keating, Paul John Geoffrey, 1924–1980, vol. VII
Keatinge, Sir Edgar Mayne, 1905–1998, vol. X
Keatinge, Gerald Francis, 1872–1965, vol. VI
Keatinge, Henry Pottinger, 1860–1928, vol. II
Keatinge, Maurice Walter, 1868–1935, vol. III
Keatinge, Gen. Richard Harte, 1825–1904, vol. I
Keatinge, Richard Herbert, 1911–1968, vol. VI

Keatinge, Rt Rev. William Lewis, 1869–1934, vol. III
Keay, Herbert O., 1875–1958, vol. V
Keay, James Donald, *died* 1933, vol. III
Keay, Lt-Col John, *died* 1943, vol. IV
Keay, Sir John, 1894–1964, vol. VI
Keay, John Seymour, 1839–1909, vol. I
Keay, Sir Lancelot Herman, 1883–1974, vol. VII
Keay, Ronald William John, 1920–1998, vol. X
Keble, Col Alfred Ernest Conquer, 1869–1940, vol. III
Kebty-Fletcher, John Robert, 1868–1918, vol. II
Keck, Thomas Charles Leycester P.; *see* Powys-Keck.
Kedarnath Das, Sir, 1867–1936, vol. III
Keddie, Henrietta, (Sarah Tytler), 1827–1914, vol. I
Keddie, Col Herbert William Graham, 1873–1943, vol. IV
Kedourie, Elie, 1926–1992, vol. IX
Kedward, Rev. Roderick Morris, 1881–1937, vol. III
Keeble, Sir Frederick William, 1870–1952, vol. V
Keeble, Lillah, (Lady Keeble); *see* McCarthy, L.
Keeble, Thomas Whitfield, 1918–1994, vol. IX
Keefe, Sir Ronald Barry, 1901–1967, vol. VI
Keefer, Thomas Coltrin, 1821–1915, vol. I
Keegan, Denis Michael, 1924–1993, vol. IX
Keegan, Lt-Col Herbert Leo, 1888–1937, vol. III
Keel, James Frederick, 1871–1954, vol. V
Keel, Jonathan Edgar, 1895–1979, vol. VII
Keelan, Percival Stanley, 1875–1950, vol. IV (A)
Keele, Cyril Arthur, 1905–1987, vol. VIII
Keeley, Thomas Clews, 1894–1988, vol. VIII
Keeling, (Cyril) Desmond (Evans), 1921–1979, vol. VII
Keeling, Desmond; *see* Keeling, C. D. E.
Keeling, Edward Allis, 1885–1975, vol. VII
Keeling, Sir Edward Herbert, *died* 1954, vol. V
Keeling, Sir Hugh Trowbridge, *died* 1955, vol. V
Keeling, Surg. Rear-Adm. John, 1921–2000, vol. X
Keeling, Sir John Henry, 1895–1978, vol. VII
Keeling, Thomas, 1882–1963, vol. VI
Keeling, Rev. William Hulton, 1840–1916, vol. II
Keeling, Rev. William Theodore, 1871–1946, vol. IV
Keely, Eric Philipps, 1899–1988, vol. VIII
Keen, Archibald, 1860–1932, vol. III
Keen, Arthur, *died* 1915, vol. I
Keen, Austin, *died* 1922, vol. II
Keen, Sir Bernard Augustus, 1890–1981, vol. VIII
Keen, Frank Noel, 1869–1957, vol. II
Keen, Frederick Grinham; *see* Kerr, Frederick.
Keen, Col Sir Frederick John, 1834–1902, vol. I
Keen, Col Frederick Stewart, 1874–1949, vol. IV
Keen, Gregory Bernard, 1844–1930, vol. III
Keen, Col John Fred, 1881–1949, vol. IV
Keen, Brig. Patrick Houston, 1877–1954, vol. V
Keen, Patrick John, 1911–1983, vol. VIII
Keen, Col. Sidney, 1868–1941, vol. IV
Keen, Lt-Col William John, *died* 1958, vol. V
Keen, William Williams, 1837–1932, vol. III
Keenan, Margaret Helen, 1869–1939, vol. III
Keenan, Hon. Sir Norbert, 1866–1954, vol. V
Keenan, William, *died* 1955, vol. V

Keene, Air Vice-Marshal Allan Lancelot Addison P.; *see* Perry-Keene.
Keene, Col Alfred, 1855–1918, vol. II
Keene, Charles James, 1850–1917, vol. II
Keene, Sir Charles Robert, 1891–1977, vol. VII
Keene, Henry George, 1825–1915, vol. I
Keene, Most Rev. James Bennett, 1849–1919, vol. II
Keene, James Robert, 1838–1913, vol. I
Keene, Mary Frances Lucas, *died* 1977, vol. VII
Keene, Vice-Adm. Philip R.; *see* Ruck Keene.
Keene, William, 1851–1920, vol. II
Keene, Adm. William George Elmhirst Ruck, 1867–1935, vol. III
Keenleyside, Hugh Llewellyn, 1989–1992, vol. IX
Keenlyside, Francis Hugh, 1911–1990, vol. VIII
Keens, Philip Francis, 1903–1989, vol. VIII
Keens, Sir Thomas, 1870–1953, vol. V
Keep, Arthur Corrie, 1861–1940, vol. III
Keeping, Charles William James, 1924–1988, vol. VIII
Keesey, Walter Monckton, 1887–1970, vol. VI
Keesing, Felix Maxwell, 1902–1961, vol. VI
Keetley, Charles Robert Bell, *died* 1909, vol. I
Keeton, George Haydn, 1878–1949, vol. IV
Keeton, George Williams, 1902–1989, vol. VIII
Keeton, Haydn, 1847–1921, vol. II
Keevil, Col Sir Ambrose, 1893–1973, vol. VII
Kefauver, Estes, 1903–1963, vol. VI
Keflegzi, Gabre-Mascal, 1917–1969, vol. VI
Keggin, Air Vice-Marshal Harold, 1909–1989, vol. VIII
Kegie, James, 1913–1984, vol. VIII
Kehoe, Miles, *died* 1907, vol. I
Keighley, Col Charles Marsh, 1847–1911, vol. I
Keighley, Frank, 1900–1981, vol. VIII
Keighley, Lt-Col Vernon Aubrey Scott, 1874–1939, vol. III
Keighly-Peach, Captain Charles Lindsey, 1902–1995, vol. IX
Keighly-Peach, Adm. Charles William, 1865–1943, vol. IV
Keightley, Gen. Sir Charles Frederic, 1901–1974, vol. VII
Keightley, Sir Samuel Robert, 1859–1949, vol. IV
Keigwin, Richard Prescott, 1883–1972, vol. VII
Keilin, David, *died* 1963, vol. VI
Keiller, Brian Edwin, 1901–1977, vol. VII
Keily, Maj.-Gen. Frederick Peter Charles, 1870–1938, vol. III
Keily, Rt Rev. John, 1854–1928, vol. II
Keir, Sir David Lindsay, 1895–1973, vol. VII
Keir, Lt-Gen. Sir John Lindesay, 1856–1937, vol. III
Keir, Thelma C.; *see* Cazalet-Keir.
Keir, Surg. Rear-Adm. William Wallace, 1876–1949, vol. IV
Keirstead, Burton Seely, 1907–1973, vol. VII
Keirstead, Wilfred Currier, 1871–1944, vol. IV
Keith of Avonholm, Baron (Life Peer); James Keith, 1886–1964, vol. VI
Keith, Alexander Milne, 1886–1967, vol. VI
Keith, Rev. Canon Archibald Leslie, 1871–1956, vol. V
Keith, Sir Arthur, 1866–1955, vol. V

Keith, Arthur Berriedale, 1879–1944, vol. IV
Keith, David; *see* Steegmuller, Francis.
Keith, Edward John, 1908–1968, vol. VI
Keith, George Skene, 1819–1910, vol. I
Keith, Sir Henry Shanks, 1852–1944, vol. IV
Keith, Col James, 1842–1919, vol. II
Keith, James, 1879–1953, vol. V
Keith, John Lucien, 1895–1988, vol. VIII
Keith, Leslie; *see* Johnston, Grace L. Keith.
Keith, Robert Farquharson, 1912–1988, vol. VIII
Keith, Skene, 1858–1919, vol. II
Keith, Trevor, 1921–1988, vol. VIII
Keith, Sir William John, 1873–1937, vol. III
Keith-Jones, Maj.-Gen. Richard, 1913–1992, vol. IX
Keith-Lucas, Bryan, 1912–1996, vol. X
Keith-Lucas, David, 1911–1997, vol. X
Keith-Roach, Edward, 1885–1954, vol. V
Kekedo, Dame Mary Angela, 1919–1993, vol. X (AI)
Kekewich, Rt Hon. Sir Arthur, 1832–1907, vol. I
Kekewich, Sir George William, 1841–1921, vol. II
Kekewich, Rear-Adm. Piers Keane, 1889–1967, vol. VI
Kekewich, Maj.-Gen. Robert George, 1854–1914, vol. I
Kekewich, Sir Trehawke Herbert, 1st Bt, 1851–1932, vol. III
Kekwick, Alan, 1909–1974, vol. VII
Kekwick, Ralph Ambrose, 1908–2000, vol. X
Kelcey, Air Vice-Marshal Alick F.; *see* Foord-Kelcey.
Kelf-Cohen, Reuben, 1895–1981, vol. VIII
Kelham, Brig.-Gen. Henry Robert, 1853–1931, vol. III
Kelk, Sir John William, 2nd Bt, 1851–1923, vol. II
Kell, Joseph; *see* Burgess, Anthony.
Kell, Maj.-Gen. Sir Vernon George Waldegrave, 1873–1942, vol. IV
Kelland, Gilbert James, 1924–1997, vol. X
Kelland, Sir John; *see* Kelland, Sir P. J. L.
Kelland, Sir (Percy) John (Luxton), *died* 1958, vol. V
Kellar, Robert James, *died* 1980, vol. VII
Kellas, A. M., *died* 1921, vol. II
Kellaway, Charles Halliley, 1889–1952, vol. V
Kellaway, Rt Hon. Frederick George, 1870–1933, vol. III
Kelleher, Stephen B., 1875–1917, vol. II
Keller, Adolf, 1872–1963, vol. VI
Keller, Andrew, 1925–1999, vol. X
Keller, Helen Adams, 1880–1968, vol. VI
Keller, Hon. John; *see* Keller, Hon. L. J. W.
Keller, Hon. (Laurence) John Walter, 1885–1959, vol. V
Keller, René Jacques, 1914–1997, vol. X
Keller, Maj.-Gen. Rodney Frederick Leopold, 1900–1954, vol. V
Kellett, Adelaide Maud, *died* 1945, vol. IV
Kellett, Alfred Henry, 1904–1995, vol. IX (AII)
Kellett, Sir Brian Smith, 1922–1994, vol. IX
Kellett, Lt-Col Edward Orlando, 1902–1943, vol. IV
Kellett, Ernest Edward, 1864–1950, vol. IV
Kellett, Maj.-Gen. Gerald, 1905–1973, vol. VII
Kellett, Sir Henry de Castres, 3rd Bt, 1851–1924, vol. II

Kellett, Sir Henry de Castres, 4th Bt, 1882–1966, vol. VI
Kellett, Sir Henry de Castres, 5th Bt, 1914–1966, vol. VI
Kellett, Col John Philip, 1890–1959, vol. V
Kellett, Maj.-Gen. Richard Orlando, 1864–1931, vol. III
Kellett, Sir Stanley Everard, 6th Bt, 1911–1983, vol. VIII
Kelley, Major Sir Frederic Arthur, 1863–1926, vol. II
Kelley, Howard G., 1858–1928, vol. II
Kelley, Richard, 1904–1984, vol. VIII
Kellie, Lawrence, 1862–1932, vol. III
Kelliher, Sir Henry Joseph, 1896–1991, vol. IX
Kellock, Hon. Roy Lindsay, 1893–1975, vol. VII
Kellock, Thomas Herbert, 1863–1922, vol. II
Kellock, Thomas Oslaf, 1923–1993, vol. IX
Kellogg, Frank Billings, 1856–1937, vol. III
Kellor, Alexander James, 1905–1982, vol. VIII
Kellow, Kathleen; *see* Hibbert, Eleanor.
Kelly, Annie Elizabeth, *died* 1946, vol. IV
Kelly, Major Arthur Dillon Denis, The O'Kelly, 1853–1936, vol. III
Kelly, Brig.-Gen. Arthur James, 1857–1930, vol. III
Kelly, Sir Arthur John, 1898–1983, vol. VIII
Kelly, Charles, 1815–1905, vol. I
Kelly, Rev. Charles H., 1833–1911, vol. I
Kelly, Col Courtenay Russell, 1872–1945, vol. IV
Kelly, Sir Dalziel; *see* Kelly, Sir G. D.
Kelly, Sir David Victor, 1891–1959, vol. V
Kelly, Rt Rev. Denis, 1852–1924, vol. II
Kelly, Denis; *see* Kelly, R. D. L.
Kelly, Edward Festus, 1854–1939, vol. III
Kelly, Brig. Edward Henry, 1883–1963, vol. VI
Kelly, Dame Elisabeth Hariott, 1878–1962, vol. VI
Kelly, Francis, 1868–1939, vol. III
Kelly, Maj.-Gen. Francis Henry, 1859–1937, vol. III
Kelly, Francis Michael, 1879–1945, vol. IV
Kelly, Frederick Septimus, 1881–1916, vol. II
Kelly, Brig. George Alexander, 1888–1973, vol. VII
Kelly, Maj.-Gen. George Charles, 1880–1938, vol. III
Kelly, Sir (George) Dalziel, 1891–1953, vol. V
Kelly, Sir Gerald Festus, 1879–1972, vol. VII
Kelly, Major Henry, *died* 1960, vol. V
Kelly, Brig.-Gen. Henry Edward Theodore, 1870–1932, vol. III
Kelly, Sir Henry G.; *see* Greene Kelly.
Kelly, Rev. Herbert Hamilton, 1860–1950, vol. IV
Kelly, Adm. Sir Howard; *see* Kelly, Adm. Sir W. A. H.
Kelly, Howard Atwood, 1858–1943, vol. IV
Kelly, Captain Hubert Dunsterville Harvey-, 1891–1917, vol. II
Kelly, Hon. Hugh Thomas, 1858–1945, vol. IV
Kelly, Captain James Alphonse Mari Joseph Patrick, 1875–1909, vol. I
Kelly, Most Rev. James Butler Knill, *born* 1832.
Kelly, Rev. James Davenport, 1828–1912, vol. I
Kelly, James Gerald, 1897–1942, vol. IV
Kelly, Col James Graves, 1843–1923, vol. II
Kelly, John, vol. II
Kelly, Admiral of the Fleet Sir John Donald, 1871–1936, vol. III

Kelly, Rev. John Norman Davidson, 1909–1997, vol. X
Kelly, Lt-Col John Sherwood-, 1880–1931, vol. III
Kelly, Major John Upton, 1882–1943, vol. IV
Kelly, John William, 1885–1966, vol. VI
Kelly, Kenneth Linden, 1913–1985, vol. VIII
Kelly, Sir Malachy, 1850–1916, vol. II
Kelly, Mark Jamestown, 1848–1916, vol. II
Kelly, Mervin J., 1894–1971, vol. VII
Kelly, Most Rev. Michael, 1850–1940, vol. III
Kelly, Sir Patrick Aloysius, 1880–1966, vol. VI
Kelly, Lt-Surg. Peter Burrowes, 1888–1920, vol. II
Kelly, Brig.-Gen. Philip James Vandeleur, *died* 1948, vol. IV
Kelly, Hon. Sir Raymond; *see* Kelly, Hon. Sir W. R.
Kelly, Richard Barrett Talbot, 1896–1971, vol. VII
Kelly, Sir Richard Denis, (The O'Kelly Mor), 1815–1897, vol. I
Kelly, Richard Denis Lucien, 1916–1990, vol. VIII
Kelly, Richard John, *died* 1931, vol. III
Kelly, Brig.-Gen. Richard Makdougall Brisbane Francis, 1857–1915, vol. I
Kelly, R. Talbot, 1861–1934, vol. III
Kelly, Robert Alsop, 1881–1950, vol. IV
Kelly, Sir Robert Ernest, 1879–1944, vol. IV
Kelly, Sir Robert McErlean, 1902–1971, vol. VII
Kelly, Sir Samuel, *died* 1937, vol. III
Kelly, Sir Stanley Anthony Hill, 1869–1949, vol. IV
Kelly, Sir Theo; *see* Kelly, Sir W. T.
Kelly, Rev. Thomas, *died* 1926, vol. II
Kelly, Sir Thomas, 1862–1947, vol. IV
Kelly, Thomas Dwyer, 1880–1949, vol. IV
Kelly, Lt-Col Thomas Francis Henry, 1899–1940, vol. III
Kelly, Air Vice-Marshal Thomas James, 1890–1967, vol. VI
Kelly, Col Tom, 1869–1965, vol. VI
Kelly, William, *died* 1944, vol. IV
Kelly, Adm. Sir (William Archibald) Howard, 1873–1952, vol. V
Kelly, Rt Rev. William Bernard, 1855–1921, vol. II
Kelly, Lt-Gen. Sir William Freeman, 1847–1914, vol. I
Kelly, Captain William Henry, 1873–1941, vol. IV
Kelly, Hon. Sir (William) Raymond, 1898–1956, vol. V
Kelly, Sir William Theodore, (Sir Theo), 1907–1998, vol. X
Kelly, William Thomas, 1874–1944, vol. IV
Kelly-Kenny, Gen. Sir Thomas, 1840–1914, vol. I
Kelman, Rev. John, 1864–1929, vol. III
Kelsey, Emanuel, 1905–1985, vol. VIII
Kelsey, Joan; *see* Grant, J.
Kelsey, Julian George, 1922–1995, vol. IX
Kelsey, Vice-Adm. Marcel Harcourt Attwood, 1894–1964, vol. VI
Kelsick, Osmund Randolph, 1922–1992, vol. X (AI)
Kelso, Maj.-Gen. John Edward U.; *see* Utterson-Kelso.
Kelson, William Henry, 1862–1940, vol. III
Keltie, Sir John Scott, 1840–1927, vol. II
Kelvin, 1st Baron, 1824–1907, vol. I
Kelway, Albert Clifton, 1865–1952, vol. V
Kelway, Col George Trevor, 1899–1990, vol. VIII
Kelynack, Theo N., 1866–1944, vol. IV

Kem, 1906–1988, vol. VIII
Kemball, Gen. Sir Arnold Burrowes, 1820–1908, vol. I
Kemball, Col Arnold Henry Grant, 1861–1917, vol. II
Kemball, Charles, 1923–1998, vol. X
Kemball, Lt-Col Charles Arnold, 1860–1943, vol. IV
Kemball, Christopher Gurdon, 1899–1969, vol. VI
Kemball, Maj.-Gen. Sir George Vero, 1859–1941, vol. IV
Kemball-Cook, Sir Basil Alfred; *see* Cook.
Kemmer, Nicholas, 1911–1998, vol. X
Kemmis, Lt-Col William, 1861–1932, vol. III
Kemmis Betty, Vice-Adm. Arthur, 1877–1961, vol. VI
Kemmis Betty, Lt-Col Paget, 1876–1948, vol. IV
Kemnal, Sir James, 1864–1927, vol. II
Kemp, Hon. Sir (Albert) Edward, 1858–1929, vol. III
Kemp, (Athole) Stephen (Horsford), 1917–1995, vol. IX
Kemp, Charles, 1897–1983, vol. VIII
Kemp, Charles Edward, 1901–1986, vol. VIII
Kemp, Rear-Adm. Cuthbert Francis, 1913–1999, vol. X
Kemp, Dixon, 1839–1899, vol. I
Kemp, Hon. Sir Edward; *see* Kemp, Hon. Sir A. E.
Kemp, Sir Ernest, 1870–1938, vol. III
Kemp, Rev. Frederick James, 1885–1943, vol. IV
Kemp, Brig.-Gen. Geoffrey Chicheley, 1868–1936, vol. III
Kemp, Maj.-Gen. Geoffrey Chicheley, 1890–1976, vol. VII
Kemp, Henry Thomas, 1852–1943, vol. IV
Kemp, Sir John, 1883–1955, vol. V
Kemp, Sir Joseph Horsford, 1874–1950, vol. IV
Kemp, Sir Kenneth Hagar, 12th Bt, 1853–1936, vol. III
Kemp, Sir Kenneth McIntrye, 1883–1949, vol. IV
Kemp, Sir Leslie Charles, 1890–1988, vol. VIII
Kemp, Sir Norman Wright, *died* 1937, vol. III
Kemp, Oliver, 1916–1996, vol. X
Kemp, Lt-Comdr Peter Kemp, 1904–1992, vol. IX
Kemp, Stanley Wells, 1882–1945, vol. IV
Kemp, Stephen, 1849–1918, vol. II
Kemp, Stephen; *see* Kemp, A. S. H.
Kemp, Thomas R., 1836–1905, vol. I
Kemp, Adm. Thomas Webster, 1866–1928, vol. II
Kemp-Welch, Lucy Elizabeth, *died* 1958, vol. V
Kemp-Welch, Margaret, *died* 1968, vol. VI
Kemp-Welch, Brig.-Gen. Martin, 1885–1951, vol. V
Kempe, Sir Alfred Bray, 1849–1922, vol. II
Kempe, Charles Eamer, 1837–1907, vol. I
Kempe, Rev. Edward Wood, 1844–1918, vol. II
Kempe, Lt-Col Frederick Hawke, *died* 1954, vol. V
Kempe, Harry Robert, 1852–1935, vol. III
Kempe, Sir John Arrow, 1846–1928, vol. II
Kempe, Rev. John Edward, 1810–1907, vol. I
Kempe, Rudolf, 1910–1976, vol. VII
Kempff, Wilhelm Walter Friedrich, 1895–1991, vol. IX
Kempling, William Bailey, *died* 1941, vol. IV
Kempson, Rt Rev. Edwin Hone, 1862–1931, vol. III
Kempson, Eric William Edward, *died* 1948, vol. IV

Kempster, Christopher Richard, 1869–1948, vol. IV
Kempster, Col Francis James, 1855–1925, vol. II
Kempster, Lt-Col Herbert William, *died* 1944, vol. IV
Kempster, John Westbeech, 1864–1947, vol. IV
Kempster, Hon. Michael Edmund Ivor, 1923–1998, vol. X
Kempthorne, Lt-Col Gerard Ainslie, 1876–1939, vol. III
Kempthorne, Rt Rev. John Augustine, 1864–1946, vol. IV
Kempthorne, Rt Rev. Leonard Stanley, 1886–1963, vol. VI
Kempton, Charles Leslie, *died* 1965, vol. VI
Kemsley, 1st Viscount, 1883–1968, vol. VI
Kemsley, 2nd Viscount, 1909–1999, vol. X
Kemsley, Col Sir Alfred Newcombe, 1896–1987, vol. VIII (A)
Kemsley, Col Sir Colin Norman T.; *see* Thornton-Kemsley.
Kenchington, Brig. Arthur George, 1890–1966, vol. VI
Kendal, Dame Madge Grimston, 1849–1935, vol. III
Kendal, Sir Norman, 1880–1966, vol. VI
Kendal, William Hunter, 1843–1917, vol. II
Kendall, Anthony Colin, 1898–1967, vol. VI
Kendall, Arthur Wallis, 1904–1975, vol. VII
Kendall, Sir Charles Henry Bayley, 1878–1935, vol. III
Kendall, Captain Charles James Cope, 1864–1943, vol. IV
Kendall, Denis; *see* Kendall, W. D.
Kendall, Edward Calvin, 1886–1972, vol. VII
Kendall, Col Ernest Arthur, 1876–1938, vol. III
Kendall, Guy, 1876–1960, vol. V
Kendall, H. Bickerstaffe, 1844–1919, vol. II
Kendall, Henry, 1897–1962, vol. VI
Kendall, Rev. Henry Ewing, 1888–1963, vol. VI
Kendall, Henry Way, 1926–1999, vol. X
Kendall, James, 1889–1978, vol. VII
Kendall, John David, 1893–1936, vol. III
Kendall, Rev. John Francis, 1862–1931, vol. III
Kendall, Major John Kaye, *died* 1952, vol. V
Kendall, Katherine Githa; *see* Sowerby, K. G.
Kendall, Sir Maurice George, 1907–1983, vol. VIII
Kendall, Percy Fry, 1856–1936, vol. III
Kendall, Maj.-Gen. Roy, 1897–1963, vol. VI
Kendall, Lt-Col Sydney Robert Gordon, 1879–1959, vol. V
Kendall, (William) Denis, 1903–1995, vol. IX
Kendall, William Henry, *died* 1951, vol. V
Kendall, William Leslie, 1923–2000, vol. X
Kendall-Carpenter, John MacGregor Kendall, 1925–1990, vol. VIII
Kenderdine, Sir Charles Halstaff, 1866–1936, vol. III
Kendon, Donald Henry, 1895–1985, vol. VIII
Kendon, Frank, 1893–1959, vol. V
Kendrew, Maj.-Gen. Sir Douglas Anthony, 1910–1989, vol. VIII
Kendrew, Hubert, 1894–1966, vol. VI
Kendrew, Sir John Cowdery, 1917–1997, vol. X
Kendrew, Wilfrid George, *died* 1962, vol. VI
Kendrick, Albert Frank, 1872–1954, vol. V

Kendrick, John Bebbington Bernard, 1905–1995, vol. IX
Kendrick, Sydney Percy, 1874–1955, vol. V
Kendrick, Sir Thomas Downing, 1895–1979, vol. VII
Kenealy, Alexander, 1864–1915, vol. I
Kenealy, Most Rev. Anselm E. J., 1864–1943, vol. IV
Kenealy, Arabella, *died* 1938, vol. III
Kenealy, Noel Byron, *died* 1918, vol. II
Kenilworth, 1st Baron, 1866–1953, vol. V
Kenilworth, 2nd Baron, 1894–1971, vol. VII
Kenilworth, 3rd Baron; *see* Siddeley, J. T. D.
Kenmare, 4th Earl of, 1825–1905, vol. I
Kenmare, 5th Earl of, 1860–1941, vol. IV
Kenmare, 6th Earl of, 1891–1943, vol. IV
Kenmare, 7th Earl of, 1896–1952, vol. V
Kenna, Col Paul Aloysius, 1862–1915, vol. I
Kennaby, Very Rev. Noel Martin, 1905–1994, vol. IX
Kennan, George, 1845–1924, vol. II
Kennan, John Melville, 1904–1960, vol. V
Kennan, Thomas Brereton, 1891–1965, vol. VI
Kennard, Adam Steinmetz, 1833–1915, vol. I
Kennard, Major Arthur Molloy, 1867–1917, vol. II
Kennard, Rt Rev. Mgr Charles H., 1840–1920, vol. II
Kennard, Sir Coleridge Arthur Fitzroy, 1st Bt, 1885–1948, vol. IV
Kennard, Col Edmund Hegan, *died* 1912, vol. I
Kennard, Sir George Arnold Ford, 3rd Bt, 1915–1999, vol. X
Kennard, Col Henry Gerard, *died* 1946, vol. IV
Kennard, Sir Howard William, 1878–1955, vol. V
Kennard, Sir Lawrence Ury Charles, 2nd Bt, 1912–1967, vol. VI
Kennard, Martyn Thomas, 1859–1920, vol. II
Kennard, Captain Willoughby Arthur, 1881–1918, vol. II
Kennaway, Alexander, 1923–2000, vol. X (AII)
Kennaway, Sir Ernest Laurence, 1881–1958, vol. V
Kennaway, Sir John, 4th Bt, 1879–1956, vol. V
Kennaway, Rt Hon. Sir John Henry, 3rd Bt, 1837–1919, vol. II
Kennaway, Sir Walter, 1835–1920, vol. II
Kennedy, Hon. Lord; Neil J. D. Kennedy, 1855–1918, vol. II
Kennedy, Sir Albert Henry, 1906–1991, vol. IX
Kennedy, Alex. Mills, *died* 1960, vol. V
Kennedy, Alexander, 1909–1960, vol. V
Kennedy, Sir Alexander Blackie William, 1847–1928, vol. II
Kennedy, Sir Alexander McAusland, 1860–1939, vol. III
Kennedy, Maj.-Gen. Alfred Alexander, 1870–1926, vol. II
Kennedy, Alfred Ravenscroft, 1879–1943, vol. IV
Kennedy, Lt-Col Andrew Campbell, 1872–1941, vol. IV
Kennedy, Rev. Archibald Cowan, 1892–1966, vol. VI
Kennedy, Archibald Edmund C.; *see* Clark-Kennedy.
Kennedy, Brig. Archibald Gordon M.; *see* Mackenzie-Kennedy.

Kennedy, Rev. Archibald Robert Stirling, 1859–1938, vol. III
Kennedy, Aubrey Leo, 1885–1965, vol. VI
Kennedy, Bart, 1861–1930, vol. III
Kennedy, Brig.-Gen. Charles Henry, 1860–1916, vol. II
Kennedy, Sir Charles Malcolm, 1831–1908, vol. I
Kennedy, Charles Rann, 1871–1950, vol. IV
Kennedy, Sir Clyde David Allen, 1912–1991, vol. X (AI)
Kennedy, Daisy, 1893–1981, vol. VIII
Kennedy, David Matthew, 1905–1996, vol. X
Kennedy, Sir Derrick Edward de Vere, 6th Bt, 1904–1976, vol. VII
Kennedy, Sir Donald; see Mackenzie-Kennedy, Sir H. C. D. C.
Kennedy, Douglas Neil, 1893–1988, vol. VIII
Kennedy, Eamon, 1921–2000, vol. X (AII)
Kennedy, Maj.-Gen. Sir Edward Charles William M.; see Mackenzie-Kennedy.
Kennedy, Major Francis Malcolm Evory, 1869–1945, vol. IV
Kennedy, Adm. Francis William, 1862–1939, vol. III
Kennedy, Frank Robert, 1895–1971, vol. VII
Kennedy, Frederick Charles, 1849–1916, vol. II
Kennedy, Rev. Geoffrey Anketell Studdert, died 1929, vol. III
Kennedy, George, 1838–1916, vol. II, vol. III
Kennedy, Lt-Col Sir (George) Ronald (Derrick), 7th Bt, 1927–1988, vol. VIII
Kennedy, Gilbert George, 1844–1909, vol. I
Kennedy, Rev. Harry Angus Alexander, 1866–1934, vol. III
Kennedy, Hartley, 1852–1938, vol. III
Kennedy, Henry Albert, 1877–1965, vol. VI
Kennedy, Brig.-Gen. Henry Brewster Percy Lion, died 1953, vol. V
Kennedy, Sir (Henry Charles) Donald (Cleveland) M.; see Mackenzie-Kennedy.
Kennedy, Very Rev. Herbert Brownlow, 1863–1939, vol. III
Kennedy, Horas Tristram, 1917–1997, vol. X
Kennedy, Howard Angus, 1861–1938, vol. III
Kennedy, Brig.-Gen. Hugh, 1864–1930, vol. III
Kennedy, Hugh, 1879–1936, vol. III
Kennedy, Hon. Sir James Arthur, 1882–1954, vol. V
Kennedy, James Cowie, 1914–1989, vol. VIII
Kennedy, Col James Crawford, 1879–1944, vol. IV
Kennedy, Sir James Edward, 5th Bt, 1898–1974, vol. VII
Kennedy, Rev. James Houghton, died 1924, vol. II
Kennedy, Rev. John, 1813–1900, vol. I
Kennedy, Brig.-Gen. John, 1878–1921, vol. II
Kennedy, Rev. John, died 1931, vol. III
Kennedy, Maj.-Gen. Sir John, 1878–1948, vol. IV
Kennedy, Sir John Charles, 3rd Bt, 1856–1923, vol. II
Kennedy, John Fitzgerald, 1917–1963, vol. VI
Kennedy, Sir John Gordon, 1836–1912, vol. I
Kennedy, Rev. John Joseph, born 1882, vol. III
Kennedy, Sir John Macfarlane, 1879–1954, vol. V
Kennedy, Col John Murray, 1841–1928, vol. II
Kennedy, Maj.-Gen. Sir John Noble, 1893–1970, vol. VI

Kennedy, John Norman, 1927–1985, vol. VIII
Kennedy, Sir John Ralph Bayly, 4th Bt, 1896–1968, vol. VI
Kennedy, John Robert, 1871–1956, vol. V
Kennedy, Lt-Col John Ross, 1905–1942, vol. IV
Kennedy, John Stodart, 1912–1993, vol. IX
Kennedy, John William James Clark-, 1875–1939, vol. III
Kennedy, Joseph Patrick, 1888–1969, vol. VI
Kennedy, Rt Rev. Kenneth William Stewart, died 1943, vol. IV
Kennedy, Kevin, 1937–2000, vol. X
Kennedy, Captain Macdougall Ralston, 1878–1924, vol. II
Kennedy, Margaret, (Lady Davies), died 1967, vol. VI
Kennedy, Michael, 1859–1932, vol. III
Kennedy, Sir Michael Kavanagh, 1824–1898, vol. I
Kennedy, Milward; see Burge, M. R. K.
Kennedy, Rev. Mortimer Egerton, 1853–1929, vol. III
Kennedy, Myles, 1862–1928, vol. II
Kennedy, Captain Myles Arthur Claude, 1885–1918, vol. II
Kennedy, Myles Burton, 1861–1914, vol. I
Kennedy, Myles Storr Nigel, 1889–1964, vol. VI
Kennedy, Neil J. D.; see Kennedy, Hon. Lord.
Kennedy, Bt-Col Norman, 1881–1960, vol. V
Kennedy, Patrick James, 1864–1947, vol. IV
Kennedy, Robert, 1865–1913, vol. I
Kennedy, Robert, 1865–1924, vol. II
Kennedy, Hon. Sir Robert, 1887–1974, vol. VII
Kennedy, Robert Francis, 1925–1968, vol. VI
Kennedy, Robert Gregg, 1851–1920, vol. II
Kennedy, Sir Robert John, 1851–1936, vol. III
Kennedy, Lt-Col Sir Ronald; see Kennedy, Lt-Col Sir G. R. D.
Kennedy, Vice-Adm. Theobald Walter, 1871–1934, vol. III
Kennedy, Rev. Thomas, 1828–1913, vol. I
Kennedy, Rt Hon. Thomas, 1876–1954, vol. V
Kennedy, Lt-Col Thomas Francis Archibald W.; see Watson-Kennedy.
Kennedy, Sir Thomas Sinclair, 1884–1951, vol. V
Kennedy, Vincent, 1876–1943, vol. IV
Kennedy, William, 1866–1936, vol. III
Kennedy of Knockgray, Lt-Col William Hew Clark-, 1879–1961, vol. VI
Kennedy, Lt-Col William Magill, 1868–1923, vol. II
Kennedy, William Paul McClure, 1879–1963, vol. VI
Kennedy, William Quarrier, 1903–1979, vol. VII
Kennedy, Rt Hon. Sir William Rann, 1846–1915, vol. I
Kennedy, Adm. Sir William Robert, 1838–1916, vol. II
Kennedy, Lt-Col Willoughby Pitcairn, 1850–1928, vol. II
Kennedy-Cooke, Brian, 1894–1963, vol. VI
Kennedy-Cox, Sir Reginald Kennedy, died 1966, vol. VI
Kennedy-Craufurd-Stuart, Lt-Col Charles; see Stuart.
Kennedy-Purvis, Adm. Sir Charles Edward, died 1946, vol. IV

Kenner, George Wallace, 1922–1978, vol. VII
Kenner, James, 1885–1974, vol. VII
Kennet, 1st Baron, 1879–1960, vol. V
Kennet, Lady; (Kathleen), *died* 1947, vol. IV
Kennett, Lt-Col Brackley Herbert Barrington B.; *see* Barrington-Kennett.
Kennett, Rev. Robert Hatch, 1864–1932, vol. III
Kennett-Barrington, Sir Vincent Hunter Barrington, 1844–1903, vol. I
Kenney, Col Arthur Herbert, 1855–1923, vol. II
Kenney, James C. F.; *see* Fitzgerald-Kenney.
Kenney, John; *see* Kenney, W. J.
Kenney, Reginald, 1912–1986, vol. VIII
Kenney, (William) John, 1904–1992, vol. IX
Kenney-Herbert, Edward Maxwell, 1845–1916, vol. II
Kenning, Sir George, 1880–1956, vol. V
Kennington, Eric Henri, *died* 1960, vol. V
Kennington, T. B., *died* 1916, vol. II
Kennion, Rt Rev. George Wyndham, 1845–1922, vol. II
Kennion, Lt-Col Roger Lloyd, 1866–1942, vol. IV
Kennon, Vice-Adm. Sir James Edward Campbell, 1925–1991, vol. IX
Kenny, Arthur William, 1918–1998, vol. X
Kenny, Augustus Leo, 1863–1946, vol. IV
Kenny, Courtney Stanhope, 1847–1930, vol. III
Kenny, Douglas Timothy, 1923–1996, vol. X
Kenny, Elizabeth, 1886–1952, vol. V
Kenny, Joseph Edward, 1845–1900, vol. I
Kenny, Matthew J., 1861–1942, vol. IV
Kenny, Michael, 1941–1999, vol. X
Kenny, Sir Patrick John, 1914–1987, vol. VIII
Kenny, Sean, 1932–1973, vol. VII
Kenny, Gen. Sir Thomas K.; *see* Kelly-Kenny.
Kenny, Brig. Vincent Raymond, 1882–1966, vol. VI
Kenny, Rt Hon. William, 1846–1921, vol. II
Kenny, Maj.-Gen. William Wallace, 1854–1929, vol. III
Kenrick, Frank Boteler, 1874–1951, vol. V
Kenrick, Sir George Cranmer, 1863–1939, vol. III
Kenrick, Brig.-Gen. George Edmund Reginald, 1871–1935, vol. III
Kenrick, Sir George Hamilton, 1850–1939, vol. III
Kenrick, George Harry Blair, *died* 1952, vol. V
Kenrick, Brig. Harry Selwyn, 1898–1979, vol. VII
Kenrick, John Arthur, 1829–1926, vol. II
Kenrick, Rt Hon. William, 1831–1919, vol. II
Kensington, 5th Baron, 1863–1900, vol. I
Kensington, 6th Baron, 1873–1938, vol. III
Kensington, 7th Baron, 1904–1981, vol. VIII
Kensington, Sir Alfred, 1855–1918, vol. II
Kensington, Brig. Edgar Claude, 1879–1967, vol. VI
Kensington, William Charles, 1845–1922, vol. II
Kenswood, 1st Baron, 1887–1963, vol. VI
Kent, Albert Frank Stanley, 1863–1958, vol. V
Kent, Arthur William, 1913–1998, vol. X
Kent, Charles; *see* Kent, W. C. M.
Kent, Rev. Charles, 1857–1929, vol. III
Kent, Charles Kenneth Stafford, 1892–1963, vol. VI
Kent, Charles Weller, 1864–1952, vol. V
Kent, Chris Shotter, 1887–1954, vol. V
Kent, Rear-Adm. Derrick George, 1920–1983, vol. VIII
Kent, Dorothy Miriam, 1920–1988, vol. VIII

Kent, Geoffrey Charles, 1922–1992, vol. IX
Kent, Sir Harold Simcox, 1903–1998, vol. X
Kent, Rev. Harry Arnold, 1880–1962, vol. VI
Kent, Lt-Gen. Henry, 1825–1921, vol. II
Kent, Col Herbert Vaughan, 1863–1944, vol. IV
Kent, Hon. James M., 1872–1939, vol. III
Kent, Col Sir John; *see* Kent, Col Sir W. J.
Kent, John Philip Cozens, 1928–2000, vol. X
Kent, Keneth; *see* Kent, C. K. S.
Kent, Sir Percy Edward, (Sir Peter Kent), 1913–1986, vol. VIII
Kent, Percy Horace Braund, 1876–1963, vol. VI
Kent, Sir Peter, *see* Kent, Sir Percy E.
Kent, Rockwell, 1882–1971, vol. VII
Kent, Ronald Clive, 1916–2000, vol. X
Kent, Brig. Sidney Harcourt, 1915–1999, vol. X
Kent, Sir Stephenson Hamilton, 1873–1954, vol. V
Kent, Thomas Parkes, *died* 1923, vol. II
Kent, Sir Walter George, 1858–1938, vol. III
Kent, (William) Charles (Monk), 1823–1902, vol. I
Kent, Col Sir (William) John, 1877–1960, vol. V
Kent, William Richard Gladstone, 1884–1963, vol. VI
Kent-Lemon, Brig. Arthur Leslie, 1889–1970, vol. VI
Kentish, Brig.-Gen. Reginald John, 1876–1956, vol. V
Kentner, Louis Philip, 1905–1987, vol. VIII
Kenward, Rev. Herbert, *died* 1954, vol. V
Kenwood, Lt-Col Henry Richard, 1862–1945, vol. IV
Kenworthy, Cecil, 1918–2000, vol. X
Kenworthy, John Dalzell, 1858–1954, vol. V
Kenyatta, Hon. Mzee Jomo, 1889–1978, vol. VII
Kenyon, 4th Baron, 1864–1927, vol. II
Kenyon, 5th Baron, 1917–1993, vol. IX
Kenyon, Alec Hindle, 1905–1982, vol. VIII
Kenyon, Arthur William, *died* 1969, vol. VI
Kenyon, Barnet, 1853–1930, vol. III
Kenyon, Sir Bernard, 1940–1977, vol. VII
Kenyon, Clifford, 1896–1979, vol. IX (AI)
Kenyon, Edith C., *died* 1925, vol. II
Kenyon, Maj.-Gen. Edward Ranulph, 1854–1937, vol. III
Kenyon, Sir Frederic George, 1863–1952, vol. V
Kenyon, Hon. George Thomas, 1840–1908, vol. I
Kenyon, Sir Harold Vaughan, 1875–1959, vol. V
Kenyon, Hugh, 1910–1981, vol. VIII
Kenyon, James, 1846–1924, vol. II
Kenyon, John George, 1843–1914, vol. I
Kenyon, John Philipps, 1927–1996, vol. X
Kenyon, Joseph, 1885–1961, vol. VI
Kenyon, Dame Kathleen Mary, 1906–1978, vol. VII
Kenyon, Maj.-Gen. Lionel Richard, 1867–1952, vol. V
Kenyon, Myles Noel, 1886–1960, vol. V
Kenyon, Sir Norris Vaughan, 1903–1958, vol. V
Kenyon, Robert Lloyd, 1848–1931, vol. III
Kenyon, Hon. and Rev. William Trevor, 1847–1930, vol. III
Kenyon-Slaney, Col Francis Gerald, 1858–1938, vol. III
Kenyon-Slaney, Major Philip Percy, 1896–1928, vol. II

Kenyon-Slaney, Major Robert Orlando Rodolph, 1892–1965, vol. VI
Kenyon-Slaney, Sybil Agnes, 1888–1970, vol. VI
Kenyon-Slaney, Maj.-Gen. Walter Rupert, 1851–1936, vol. III
Kenyon-Slaney, Rt Hon. William Slaney, 1847–1908, vol. I
Keogh, Lt-Gen. Sir Alfred, 1857–1936, vol. III
Keogh, Col James Blair, 1871–1944, vol. IV
Keogh, Joseph Wiseman, *died* 1947, vol. IV
Keogh, Martin Jerome, 1855–1928, vol. II, vol. III
Keogh, Michael Frederick, 1866–1940, vol. III
Keogh, Most Rev. Thomas, 1884–1969, vol. VI
Keohane, Kevin William, 1923–1996, vol. X
Keown, Anna Gordon, *died* 1957, vol. V
Keown, Eric Oliver Dilworth, 1904–1963, vol. VI
Keown-Boyd, Sir Alexander William, 1884–1954, vol. V
Keppel, Adm. Sir Colin Richard, 1862–1947, vol. IV
Keppel, Hon. Sir Derek, 1863–1944, vol. IV
Keppel, Col Edward George, 1847–1934, vol. III
Keppel, Frederick Paul, 1875–1943, vol. IV
Keppel, Lt-Col Hon. George, 1865–1947, vol. IV
Keppel, Sir George Roos-, 1866–1921, vol. II
Keppel, Hon. Sir Henry, 1809–1904, vol. I
Keppel, Rear-Adm. Leicester Chantrey, *died* 1917, vol. II
Keppel, Captain Hon. Rupert Oswald Derek, 1886–1964, vol. VI
Keppel-Compton, Robert Herbert, 1900–1989, vol. VIII
Keppie, John, 1862–1945, vol. IV
Ker, Lord Alastair Robert I.; *see* Innes-Ker.
Ker, Major Allan Ebenezer, *died* 1958, vol. V
Ker, Sir Arthur Milford, 1853–1915, vol. I
Ker, Charles, 1860–1940, vol. III
Ker, Maj.-Gen. Charles Arthur, 1875–1962, vol. VI
Ker, Lt-Col Douglas Rous E.; *see* Edwardes-Ker.
Ker, Frederick Innes, *died* 1977, vol. VII
Ker, James Campbell, 1878–1961, vol. VI
Ker, James Inglis, *died* 1936, vol. III
Ker, Ven. John, 1848–1913, vol. I
Ker, Hon. John Errington, 1860–1918, vol. II
Ker, K(eith) R(eginald) Welbore, 1913–1984, vol. VIII
Ker, Neil Ripley, 1908–1982, vol. VIII
Ker, Mrs Phyllis de Burgh; *see* Lett, Phyllis.
Ker, Richard William Blackwood, 1850–1942, vol. IV
Ker, Major Lord Robert Edward I.; *see* Innes-Ker.
Ker, William Paton, 1855–1923, vol. II
Ker, William Pollock, 1864–1945, vol. IV
Kerans, Comdr John Simon, 1915–1985, vol. VIII
Kerby, Air Vice-Marshal Harold Spencer, 1893–1963, vol. VI
Kerby, Captain Henry Briton, 1914–1971, vol. VII
Kerensky, Oleg Alexander, 1905–1984, vol. VIII
Kerin, Col Michael William, 1856–1912, vol. I
Kerle, Rt Rev. Ronald Clive, 1915–1997, vol. X
Kerley, Sir Peter James, 1900–1979, vol. VII
Kerly, Sir Duncan Mackenzie, 1863–1938, vol. III
Kermack, Stuart Grace, 1888–1981, vol. VIII
Kermack, William Ogilvy, 1898–1970, vol. VI

Kermode, Air Vice-Marshal Alfred Cotterill, 1897–1973, vol. VII
Kermode, Rev. Sir Derwent William, 1898–1960, vol. V
Kern, Jerome, 1885–1945, vol. IV
Kernahan, Coulson, 1858–1943, vol. IV
Kernahan, Mrs Coulson, *died* 1941, vol. IV
Kernoff, Harry, 1900–1974, vol. VII
Kernot, W. C., 1845–1909, vol. I
Kerouac, Jack, (Jean-Louis), 1922–1969, vol. VI
Kerr, Sir Alastair B.; *see* Blair Kerr, Sir W. A.
Kerr, Col Alex. Ferrier K.; *see* Kidston-Kerr.
Kerr, Andrew Stevenson, 1918–1994, vol. IX
Kerr, Mrs Anne Patricia, (Mrs R. W. Kerr), 1925–1973, vol. VII
Kerr, Archibald Brown, 1907–1990, vol. VIII
Kerr, Desmond Moore, 1930–1998, vol. X
Kerr, Donald Frederick, 1915–1997, vol. X
Kerr, Douglas James Acworth, 1894–1960, vol. V
Kerr, Rev. F. W., 1881–1945, vol. IV
Kerr, Francis Robert Newsam, 1916–1995, vol. IX
Kerr, Captain Frank Robison, 1889–1977, vol. VII
Kerr, Col Frederic Walter, 1867–1914, vol. I
Kerr, Frederick, 1858–1933, vol. III
Kerr, Sir Hamilton William, 1st Bt, 1903–1974, vol. VII
Kerr, Maj.-Gen. Sir (Harold) Reginald, 1897–1974, vol. VII
Kerr, Henry W., 1857–1936, vol. III
Kerr, Lt-Col Sir Howard; *see* Kerr, Lt-Col Sir L. W. H.
Kerr, James, *died* 1941, vol. IV
Kerr, Hon. James Kirkpatrick, 1841–1916, vol. II
Kerr, James Lennox, 1899–1963, vol. VI
Kerr, James Rutherford, 1878–1942, vol. IV
Kerr, Rev. John, *died* 1907, vol. I
Kerr, John, 1830–1916, vol. II
Kerr, John, *born* 1852, vol. II
Kerr, Rev. John, 1852–1920, vol. II
Kerr, Sir John Graham, 1869–1957, vol. V
Kerr, Sir John Henry, 1871–1934, vol. III
Kerr, (John Martin) Munro, 1868–1960, vol. V
Kerr, Rt Hon. Sir John Robert, 1914–1991, vol. IX
Kerr, Lt-Col Sir (Louis William) Howard, 1894–1977, vol. VII
Kerr, Lt-Col Mark Ancrum, 1859–1941, vol. IV
Kerr, Adm. Mark Edward Frederic, 1864–1944, vol. IV
Kerr, Gen. Lord Mark Ralph George, 1817–1900, vol. I
Kerr, Munro; *see* Kerr, J. M. M.
Kerr, Philip Walter, *died* 1941, vol. IV
Kerr, Lord Ralph Drury, 1837–1916, vol. II
Kerr, Rev. Ralph Francis, 1874–1932, vol. III
Kerr, Maj.-Gen. Sir Reginald; *see* Kerr, Maj.-Gen. Sir H. R.
Kerr, Robert, 1823–1904, vol. I
Kerr, Robert Bird, 1867–1951, vol. V
Kerr, Robert Malcolm, 1821–1902, vol. I
Kerr, Robert Reid, 1914–1995, vol. IX
Kerr, Brig.-Gen. Robert S.; *see* Scott-Kerr.
Kerr, Col Rowan Scrope R.; *see* Rait Kerr.
Kerr, Sir Russell James, 1863–1952, vol. V
Kerr, Russell Whiston, 1921–1983, vol. VIII
Kerr, Thomas, 1818–1907, vol. I

Kerr, Admiral of the Fleet Lord Walter Talbot, 1839–1927, vol. II
Kerr, Captain William, 1877–1918, vol. II
Kerr, Sir William, 1895–1959, vol. V
Kerr, Captain William Alexander, *died* 1919, vol. II
Kerr, Sir William Alexander B., (Sir Alastair); *see* Blair Kerr.
Kerr, Rev. William Goodwin, 1862–1934, vol. III
Kerr, Adm. Sir William Munro, 1876–1959, vol. V
Kerr, William Richard, 1853–1943, vol. IV
Kerr, Rt Rev. William Shaw, 1873–1960, vol. V
Kerr, William Warren, 1864–1949, vol. IV
Kerr-Dineen, Rev. Canon Frederick George, 1915–1988, vol. VIII
Kerr-Jarrett, Sir Francis Moncreiff, 1885–1968, vol. VI
Kerr-Muir, Ronald John, 1910–1974, vol. VII
Kerr-Pearse, Major Beauchamp Albert Thomas, 1871–1934, vol. III
Kerr-Smiley, Peter Kerr, 1879–1943, vol. IV
Kerrich, Lt-Col Walter Edmund, 1860–1938, vol. III
Kerridge, Sir Robert James, 1901–1979, vol. VII
Kerrigan, Daniel Patrick, 1909–1971, vol. VII
Kerrin, Very Rev. Richard Elual, 1898–1988, vol. VIII
Kerrison, Lt-Col Edmund Roger Allday, 1855–1944, vol. IV
Kerrison, Roger, 1842–1924, vol. II
Kerry, Earl of; Henry Maurice John Petty-Fitzmaurice, 1913–1933, vol. III
Kersey, Major Henry Maitland, 1859–1941, vol. IV
Kersh, Cyril, 1925–1993, vol. IX
Kersh, Gerald, 1911–1968, vol. VI
Kershaw, 1st Baron, 1881–1961, vol. VI
Kershaw, 2nd Baron, 1904–1961, vol. VI
Kershaw, 3rd Baron, 1906–1962, vol. VI
Kershaw, Harold Slaney, 1882–1969, vol. VI
Kershaw, Henry Aiden, 1927–1995, vol. IX
Kershaw, John Felix, 1873–1927, vol. II
Kershaw, Rev. John Frederick, 1853–1935, vol. III
Kershaw, Sir Leonard William, 1864–1949, vol. IV
Kershaw, Sir Lewis Addin, 1845–1899, vol. I
Kershaw, Sir Louis James, 1869–1947, vol. IV
Kershaw, Sir Noel Thomas, 1863–1930, vol. III
Kershaw, Philip Charles Stones, 1910–1986, vol. VIII
Kershaw, Raymond Newton, 1898–1981, vol. VIII
Kershaw, S. Wayland, *died* 1914, vol. I
Kershaw, Thomas Herbert, 1851–1913, vol. I
Kershaw, William Edgar, 1911–1998, vol. X
Kerss, William, 1931–1997, vol. X
Kertesz, Istvan, 1929–1973, vol. VII
Kerwin, Hon. Patrick, 1899–1963, vol. VI
Kessel, Lipmann, 1914–1986, vol. VIII
Kessell, Ernest, 1868–1948, vol. IV
Kestell-Cornish, Rt Rev. George Kestell, 1856–1925, vol. II
Kestell-Cornish, Rt Rev. Robert Kestell, 1824–1909, vol. I
Kestelman, Morris, 1905–1998, vol. X
Kesteven, 2nd Baron, 1851–1915, vol. I
Kesteven, 3rd Baron, 1891–1915, vol. I
Kesteven, Sir Charles Henry, *died* 1923, vol. II
Keswick, David Johnston, 1901–1976, vol. VII

Keswick, Major Henry, 1870–1928, vol. II
Keswick, Sir John Henry, 1906–1982, vol. VIII
Keswick, William, 1835–1912, vol. I
Keswick, Sir William Johnston, 1903–1990, vol. VIII
Ketchen, Maj.-Gen. Huntly Douglas Brodie, 1872–1959, vol. V
Ketchen, Maj.-Gen. Isaac, 1839–1920, vol. II
Ketchum, Philip A. C., 1899–1964, vol. VI
Kethley, Andrew Horace Victor P.; *see* Pitt-Kethley.
Kettering, Charles Franklin, 1876–1958, vol. V
Kettle, Edgar Hartley, 1882–1936, vol. III
Kettle, Marguerite Henrietta, 1887–1939, vol. III
Kettle, Roy Henry Richard, 1924–1996, vol. X
Kettle, Rupert Edward Cooke, 1854–1908, vol. I
Kettle, Sir Russell, 1887–1968, vol. VI
Kettle, Thomas Michael, 1880–1916, vol. II
Kettlewell, Arthur Bradley, 1871–1945, vol. IV
Kettlewell, Bernard; *see* Kettlewell, H. B. D.
Kettlewell, (Henry) Bernard (Davis), 1907–1979, vol. VII
Kettlewell, Rev. Percy W. H., 1868–1950, vol. IV
Kettlewell, Richard Wildman, 1910–1994, vol. IX
Ketton-Cremer, Robert Wyndham, 1906–1969, vol. VI
Kevenhoerster, Most Rev. John Bernard, 1869–1949, vol. IV
Keverne, Richard, 1882–1950, vol. IV
Keville, Sir Errington; *see* Keville, Sir W. E.
Keville, Sir (William) Errington, 1901–1992, vol. IX
Kewish, John Douglas, 1907–1989, vol. VIII
Kewley, Rev. James William, 1846–1935, vol. III
Kewley, Ven. John, 1860–1941, vol. IV
Key, Major Sir Aston C.; *see* Cooper-Key.
Key, Maj.-Gen. Berthold Wells, 1895–1986, vol. VIII
Key, Rt Rev. Bransby Lewis, 1838–1901, vol. I
Key, Carl Axel Helmer, 1864–1938, vol. III (A), vol. IV
Key, Sir Charles Edward, 1900–1978, vol. VII
Key, Rt Hon. Charles William, *died* 1964, vol. VI
Key, Maj.-Gen. (Clement) Denis, 1915–1994, vol. IX
Key, Maj.-Gen. Denis; *see* Kemp, Maj.-Gen. C. D.
Key, Captain Edmund Moore Cooper C.; *see* Cooper-Key.
Key, Edward Emmerson, 1917–1976, vol. VII
Key, Ellen, 1849–1926, vol. II
Key, Rev. Sir John Kingsmill Causton, 3rd Bt, 1853–1926, vol. II
Key, Rt Rev. John Maurice, 1905–1984, vol. VIII
Key, Sir Kingsmill Grove, 2nd Bt, 1815–1899, vol. I
Key, Sir Kingsmill James, 4th Bt, 1864–1932, vol. III
Key, Sir Neill C.; *see* Cooper-Key.
Keyes, 1st Baron, 1872–1945, vol. IV
Keyes, Comdr Adrian St Vincent, 1882–1926, vol. II
Keyes, Frances Parkinson, (Mrs Henry Wilder Keyes), 1885–1970, vol. VI
Keyes, Brig.-Gen. Sir Terence Humphrey, 1877–1939, vol. III
Keymer, Sir Daniel Thomas, 1857–1933, vol. III
Keymer, Rev. Nathaniel, 1844–1922, vol. II

Keynes, 1st Baron, 1883–1946, vol. IV
Keynes, Lady; (Lydia Lopokova), 1892–1981, vol. VIII
Keynes, Sir Geoffrey Langdon, 1887–1982, vol. VIII
Keynes, John Neville, 1852–1949, vol. IV
Keys, Sir (Alexander George) William, 1923–2000, vol. X
Keys, David Reid, 1856–1939, vol. III
Keys, Ivor Christopher Banfield, 1919–1995, vol. IX
Keys, Rear-Adm. (S) John Anthony, 1863–1955, vol. V
Keys, Sir William; see Keys, Sir A. G. W.
Keys, William Herbert, 1923–1990, vol. VIII
Keyser, Agnes, (Sister Agnes), died 1941, vol. IV
Keyser, Arthur Louis, died 1924, vol. II
Keyser, Charles Edward, 1847–1929, vol. III
Keyser, Col Frederick Charles, 1841–1920, vol. II
Keyser, Lionel Edward, 1878–1955, vol. V
Keyserling, Count Hermann, 1880–1946, vol. IV
Khachaturyan, Aram Ilych, 1903–1978, vol. VII
Khairpur, HH Mir Sir Faiz Mohammad Khan Talpur, Mir of, died 1909, vol. I
Khairpur State, HH Mir Imam Baksh Khan, Ruler of, died 1921, vol. II
Khairpur State, HH Mir Ali Nawaz Khan, Ruler of, died 1935, vol. III
Khalil, Mohammed Bey, 1895–1950, vol. IV (A), vol. V
Khama, Sir Seretse M., 1921–1980, vol. VII
Khan, Vice-Adm. Afzal Rahman, 1921–1983, vol. VIII
Khan, Gen. Agha Muhammad Y.; see Yahya Khan.
Khan, Hon. Chaudin Sir Muhammad Z.; see Zafrulla Khan.
Khan, Brig. Fazalur Rahman, 1914–1980, vol. VII
Khan, Ghaanfar Ali, 1875–1959, vol. V
Khan, Major Sir Khan Hashmatullah, died 1936, vol. III (A), vol. IV
Khan, Nawab Sir Khan-i-Zaman, died 1936, vol. III
Khan, Liaquat Ali, 1895–1951, vol. V
Khan, Field-Marshal Mohammad Ayub, died 1974, vol. VII
Khan, Sir Mohammed Y.; see Yamin Khan.
Khan, Raja Sir Muhammud Nazim, died 1938, vol. III
Khan, Pir-o-Murshid I.; see Inayat-Khan.
Khan, Sir Shafa'at Ahmad, 1893–1947, vol. IV
Kher, Shri Bal Gangadhar, 1888–1957, vol. V
Khouini, Hamadi, 1943–1994, vol. IX
Khrushchev, Nikita Sergeyevich, 1894–1971, vol. VII
Khundkar, Sir Nurul Azeem, 1890–1947, vol. IV
Khurshid Jah, Bahadur Sir, Nawab, died 1902, vol. I
Kibblewhite, Ebenezer Job, 1846–1924, vol. II
Kidd, Beatrice Ethel, 1867–1958, vol. V
Kidd, Benjamin, 1858–1916, vol. II
Kidd, Rev. Beresford James, 1864–1948, vol. IV
Kidd, Lt-Col Bertram Graham Balfour, 1875–1943, vol. IV
Kidd, Frank S., 1878–1934, vol. III
Kidd, Franklin, 1890–1974, vol. VII
Kidd, Frederic William, 1890–1971, vol. VII
Kidd, Henry, 1862–1923, vol. II
Kidd, James, 1872–1928, vol. II

Kidd, John, 1821–1910, vol. I
Kidd, Lt-Col John Franklin, died 1933, vol. III
Kidd, Rt Rev. John Thomas, 1868–1950, vol. IV (A), vol. V
Kidd, Rev. Joseph Henry, 1877–1930, vol. III
Kidd, Dame Margaret Henderson; see Macdonald, Dame M. H.
Kidd, Percy M., 1851–1942, vol. IV
Kiddle, Adm. Sir Edward Buxton, 1866–1933, vol. III
Kiddle, Col Frederick, 1871–1936, vol. III
Kiddle, Captain Kerrison, 1876–1949, vol. IV
Kiddy, Arthur William, 1868–1950, vol. IV
Kidman, Sir Sidney, 1857–1935, vol. III
Kidman, Thomas Walter, 1915–1996, vol. X
Kidn, Hon. Sir Buri William, 1945–1994, vol. IX
Kidner, Brig. William Elworthy, 1884–1969, vol. VI
Kidron, Abraham, 1919–1982, vol. VIII
Kidson, Edward, 1882–1939, vol. III
Kidson, Fenn, 1874–1965, vol. VI
Kidson, Harold Percy, 1887–1971, vol. VII
Kidston, George Jardine, 1873–1954, vol. V
Kidston, Robert, died 1924, vol. II
Kidston, Hon. William, 1849–1919, vol. II
Kidston-Kerr, Col Alex. Ferrier, 1840–1926, vol. II
Kiek, Rev. Edward S., 1883–1959, vol. V
Kielberg, Sir Michael K.; see Kroyer-Kielberg.
Kielhorn, Franz, 1840–1908, vol. I
Kier, Olaf, 1899–1986, vol. VIII
Kierkels, Most Rev. Leo Peter, 1882–1957, vol. V
Kiesinger, Kurt Georg, 1904–1988, vol. VIII
Kiggell, Lt-Gen. Sir Launcelot Edward, 1862–1954, vol. V
Kiki, Hon. Sir (Albert) Maori, 1931–1993, vol. IX
Kiki, Hon. Sir Maori; see Kiki, Hon. Sir A. M.
Kikuchi, Baron Dairoku, 1855–1917, vol. II
Kilbracken, 1st Baron, 1847–1932, vol. III
Kilbracken, 2nd Baron, 1877–1950, vol. IV
Kilbrandon, Baron (Life Peer); Charles James Dalrymple Shaw, 1906–1989, vol. VIII
Kilbride, Dennis, 1848–1924, vol. II
Kilburn, Bertram Edward D.; see Dunbar Kilburn.
Kilburn, John Maurice, 1885–1965, vol. VI
Kilburne, George Goodwin, 1839–1924, vol. II
Kilby, Reginald George, died 1949, vol. IV
Kilényi, Edward A., 1911–2000, vol. X
Kiley, James Daniel, 1865–1953, vol. V
Kilfedder, Sir James Alexander, 1928–1995, vol. IX
Kilgour, Rev. Robert, 1867–1942, vol. IV
Kilham Roberts, Denys, 1903–1976, vol. VII
Kilkelly, Surg.-Lt-Col Charles Randolph, 1861–1953, vol. V
Killam, Albert Clements, 1849–1908, vol. I
Killanin, 1st Baron; see Morris and Killanin.
Killanin, 2nd Baron, 1867–1927, vol. II
Killanin, 3rd Baron, 1914–1999, vol. X
Killby, Leonard Gibbs, 1883–1975, vol. VII
Killearn, 1st Baron, 1880–1964, vol. VI
Killearn, 2nd Baron, 1919–1996, vol. X
Killen, Rev. William Dool, 1806–1902, vol. I
Killey, Homer Charles, 1915–1976, vol. VII
Killian, Most Rev. Andrew, 1872–1939, vol. III
Killian, James Rhyne, Jr, 1904–1988, vol. VIII

Killick, Brig. Sir Alexander Herbert, 1894–1975, vol. VII
Killick, Sir Anthony Bernard, 1901–1966, vol. VI
Killick, Esther Margaret, (Mrs A. St G. Huggett), 1902–1960, vol. V
Killick, John Spencer, 1878–1952, vol. V
Killick, Paul Victor St John, 1916–1998, vol. X
Killik, Sir Stephen Henry Molyneux, 1861–1938, vol. III
Killin, Robert, 1870–1943, vol. IV
Kilmaine, 4th Baron, 1843–1907, vol. I
Kilmaine, 5th Baron, 1878–1946, vol. IV
Kilmaine, 6th Baron, 1902–1978, vol. VII
Kilmany, Baron (Life Peer); William John St Clair Anstruther-Gray, 1905–1985, vol. VIII
Kilmarnock, 6th Baron, 1903–1975, vol. VII
Kilmartin, Terence Kevin, 1922–1991, vol. IX
Kilmorey, 3rd Earl of, 1842–1915, vol. I
Kilmorey, 4th Earl of, 1883–1961, vol. VI
Kilmorey, 5th Earl of, 1915–1977, vol. VII
Kilmuir, 1st Earl of, 1900–1967, vol. VI
Kilner, Group Captain Cecil Francis, 1883–1925, vol. II
Kilner, Lt-Col Charles Harold, 1864–1936, vol. III
Kilner, Cyril, 1910–1985, vol. VIII
Kilner, Rt Rev. Francis Charles, died 1921, vol. II
Kilner, Major Sir Hew Ross, 1892–1953, vol. V
Kilner, T(homas) Pomfret, 1890–1964, vol. VI
Kilpatrick, Florence Antoinette, died 1968, vol. VI
Kilpatrick, Rev. George Dunbar, 1910–1989, vol. VIII
Kilpatrick, George Gordon Dinwiddie, 1888–1975, vol. VII
Kilpatrick, Sir James MacConnell, 1902–1960, vol. V
Kilpatrick, Sir William John, 1906–1985, vol. VIII
Kilpin, Sir Ernest Fuller, 1854–1931, vol. III
Kilroy, Dame Alix; see Meynell, Dame Alix.
Kilvert, Sir Harry Vernon, 1862–1924, vol. II
Kim, Tan Jiak, died 1917, vol. II
Kimalel, Shadrack Kiptenai, 1930–1980, vol. VII
Kimball, Katharine, 1866–1949, vol. IV
Kimball, Major Lawrence, 1900–1971, vol. VII
Kimball, LeRoy Elwood, 1888–1962, vol. VI
Kimbell, Rev. Ralph Raymond, 1884–1964, vol. VI
Kimber, Augustus Charles Edmund, died 1930, vol. III
Kimber, Derek Barton, 1917–1995, vol. IX
Kimber, Lt-Col Edmund Gibbs, 1870–1954, vol. V
Kimber, Gurth, 1906–1978, vol. VII
Kimber, Sir Henry, 1st Bt, 1834–1923, vol. II
Kimber, Sir Henry Dixon, 2nd Bt, 1862–1950, vol. IV
Kimber, Sir Sidney Guy, 1873–1949, vol. IV
Kimberley, 1st Earl of, 1826–1902, vol. I
Kimberley, 2nd Earl of, 1848–1932, vol. III
Kimberley, 3rd Earl of, 1883–1941, vol. IV
Kimberley, Paul, died 1964, vol. VI
Kimens, Richard Edward, 1872–1950, vol. IV
Kimmins, Captain Anthony Martin, 1901–1964, vol. VI
Kimmins, Lt-Gen. Sir Brian Charles Hannam, 1899–1979, vol. VII
Kimmins, Charles William, died 1948, vol. IV
Kimmins, Dame Grace Thyrza, died 1954, vol. V

Kimpton, Lawrence Alpheus, 1910–1977, vol. VII
Kinahan, Charles Henry Grierson, 1915–1995, vol. IX
Kinahan, Sir Edward Hudson Hudson-, 2nd Bt, 1865–1938, vol. III
Kinahan, Lt-Col George Frederick H.; see Hudson-Kinahan.
Kinahan, Adm. Sir Harold Richard George, 1893–1980, vol. VII
Kinahan, Sir Robert George Caldwell, (Sir Robin), 1916–1997, vol. X
Kinahan, Sir Robert Henry Hudson-, 3rd Bt, 1872–1949, vol. IV
Kinahan, Sir Robin; see Kinahan, Sir R. G. C.
Kinane, Most Rev. Jeremiah, 1884–1959, vol. V
Kincaid, Charles Augustus, 1870–1954, vol. V
Kincaid, Maj.-Gen. William, 1831–1909, vol. I
Kincaid, Col William Francis Henry Style, 1861–1945, vol. IV
Kincaid-Lennox, Charles Spencer Bateman-Hanbury, 1827–1912, vol. I
Kincaid-Smith, Brig.-Gen. Kenneth John, 1871–1949, vol. IV
Kincaid-Smith, Lt-Col Malcolm, 1874–1938, vol. III
Kincairney, Hon. Lord; William Ellis Gloag, 1828–1909, vol. I
Kinch, Anthony Alec, 1926–1999, vol. X
Kinch, Edward, 1848–1920, vol. II
Kinder, Claude William, 1852–1936, vol. III
Kindersley, 1st Baron, 1871–1954, vol. V
Kindersley, 2nd Baron, 1899–1976, vol. VII
Kindersley, Lt-Col Archibald Ogilvie Lyttelton, 1869–1955, vol. V
Kindersley, Lt-Col Claude Richard Henry, 1911–1993, vol. IX
Kindersley, David Guy, 1915–1995, vol. IX
Kindersley, Rt Rev. George Aelred, 1860–1934, vol. III
Kindersley, Major Guy Molesworth, 1877–1956, vol. V
Kindersley, Major James Benjamin, 1893–1939, vol. III
King, Sir Albert, 1905–1995, vol. X (AI)
King, Very Rev. Albert Edward, 1865–1938, vol. III
King, Albert Leslie, 1911–1999, vol. X
King, Albert Theodore, 1885–1939, vol. III
King, Sir Alexander Boyne, 1888–1973, vol. VII
King, Sir Alexander Freeman, 1851–1942, vol. IV
King, Alexander Hyatt, (Alec), 1911–1995, vol. IX
King, Lt-Col Alexander James, 1863–1943, vol. IV
King, Sir Alexander William, 6th Bt (cr 1815), 1892–1969, vol. VI
King, Alfred Hazell, 1896–1956, vol. V
King, Alfred John, 1859–1920, vol. II
King, Brig.-Gen. Algernon D'Aguilar, 1862–1945, vol. IV
King, Alison Elsie, 1913–1992, vol. IX
King, Sir Anthony Highmore, 1890–1977, vol. VII
King, Sir Archibald John, 1887–1961, vol. VI
King, Sir (Arthur) Henry (William), 1889–1966, vol. VI
King, Arthur Thomas, 1845–1922, vol. II
King, Maj.-Gen. Augustus Henry, 1831–1899, vol. I
King, Basil Charles, 1915–1985, vol. VIII
King, Sir Carleton Moss, 1878–1954, vol. V

459

King, Cecil, 1881–1942, vol. IV
King, Cecil Edward, 1912–1981, vol. VIII
King, Cecil Harmsworth, 1901–1987, vol. VIII
King, Maj.-Gen. Charles, 1844–1933, vol. III
King, Charles A., *died* 1936, vol. III
King, Sir Charles Albert, 1853–1922, vol. II
King, Col Charles Dickson, 1860–1933, vol. III
King, Major Charles Edward Stuart, 1869–1934, vol. III
King, Lt-Gen. Sir Charles John Stuart, 1890–1967, vol. VI
King, Charles Macintosh, 1836–1920, vol. II
King, Charles Montague, 1872–1956, vol. V
King, Sir Charles Simeon, 3rd Bt (*cr* 1821), 1840–1921, vol. II
King, Charles Thomas, *died* 1932, vol. III
King, Brig.-Gen. Sir Charles Wallis, 1861–1943, vol. IV
King, Sir (Clifford) Robertson, 1895–1976, vol. VII
King, Colin Henry Harmsworth, 1931–1977, vol. VII
King, Rev. Cuthbert, 1889–1981, vol. VIII
King, Cyril Lander, *died* 1972, vol. VII
King, David Wylie, *died* 1945, vol. IV
King, Douglas James Edward, 1919–1992, vol. IX
King, Col Sir Dudley Gordon Alan D.; *see* Duckworth-King.
King, Earl Judson, 1901–1962, vol. VI
King, Rt Rev. Edward, 1829–1910, vol. I
King, E(dward) J(ohn) Boswell, *died* 1975, vol. VII
King, Adm. Edward Leigh Stuart, 1889–1971, vol. VII
King, Col Sir Edwin James, 1877–1952, vol. V
King, Ernest Gerald, *died* 1955, vol. V
King, Fleet Admiral Ernest Joseph, 1878–1956, vol. V
King, Dame Ethel Locke, 1864–1956, vol. V
King, Evelyn Mansfield, 1907–1994, vol. IX
King, Gen. Sir Frank Douglas, 1919–1998, vol. X
King, Frank Gordon, 1915–1988, vol. VIII
King, Engr Rear-Adm. Frank Victor, 1889–1961, vol. VI
King, Frederic, 1853–1933, vol. III
King, Sir (Frederic) Truby, 1858–1938, vol. III
King, Frederick Ernest, 1905–1999, vol. X
King, Sir Geoffrey Stuart, 1894–1981, vol. VIII
King, Lt-Col Sir George, 1840–1909, vol. I
King, Mrs George, (Sister Janet Wells); *see* King, Janet.
King, George, *died* 1922, vol. II
King, Sir George Adolphus, 5th Bt (*cr* 1815), 1864–1954, vol. V
King, Sir George Anthony, 1858–1928, vol. II
King, George Edward Fenton, 1887–1962, vol. VI
King, George Falconer, *died* 1929, vol. III
King, Sir George Henry James D.; *see* Duckworth-King.
King, George Kemp, 1880–1920, vol. II
King, Rt Rev. George Lanchester, 1860–1941, vol. IV
King, Major Gerald Hartley, 1882–1940, vol. III
King, Lt-Col Giffard Hamilton Macarthur, 1885–1956, vol. V (A), vol. VI (AI)
King, Sir Gilbert, 4th Bt (*cr* 1815), 1846–1920, vol. II

King, Gilbert Walter, 1871–1937, vol. III
King, Mrs Grace M. H.; *see* Hamilton-King.
King, Harold, 1887–1956, vol. V
King, Maj.-Gen. Harold Francis Sylvester, 1895–1974, vol. VII
King, Lt-Col Harold Holmes, 1884–1961, vol. VI
King, Mrs Harriet Eleanor Baillie Hamilton, *died* 1920, vol. II
King, Haynes, 1831–1904, vol. I
King, Sir Henry; *see* King, Sir A. H. W.
King, Sir Henry Clark, 1857–1920, vol. II
King, Cdre Rt Hon. Henry Douglas, 1877–1930, vol. III
King, Rev. Henry Hugh, 1869–1918, vol. II
King, Sir (Henry) Seymour, 1st Bt (*cr* 1932), 1852–1933, vol. III
King, Hubert John, 1915–1988, vol. VIII
King, Hugh Charles, 1872–1937, vol. III
King, Humphrey Hastings, 1880–1950, vol. IV
King, Ivor Edward, 1889–1983, vol. VIII
King, Rev. J. Harper, *died* 1933, vol. III
King, Jack; *see* King, J. G. M.
King, Sir James, 1st Bt (*cr* 1888), 1830–1911, vol. I
King, James Edward, *died* 1933, vol. III
King, James Foster, 1862–1947, vol. IV
King, Sir James Granville Le Neve, 3rd Bt, 1898–1989, vol. VIII
King, Brig.-Gen. James Gurwood K.; *see* King-King.
King, James H., 1873–1955, vol. V
King, James Lawrence, 1922–2000, vol. X
King, Janet, (Mrs George King), *died* 1911, vol. I
King, Jeffrey William Hitchen, 1906–1995, vol. IX
King, Jock; *see* King, John G. M.
King, John Baragwanath, *died* 1939, vol. III
King, John Charles, 1847–1918, vol. II
King, John George Maydon, (Jock), 1908–1992, vol. IX
King, John Hampden, 1865–1945, vol. IV
King, Most Rev. John Henry, 1880–1965, vol. VI
King, (John) Oliver (Letts), 1914–2000, vol. X
King, Rev. John Richard, 1835–1907, vol. I
King, Sir John Richard D.; *see* Duckworth-King.
King, Sir John Westall, 2nd Bt (*cr* 1888), 1863–1940, vol. III
King, Joseph, 1860–1943, vol. IV
King, Joseph, 1914–1989, vol. IX (AI)
King, Sir Kelso, 1853–1943, vol. IV
King, Kenneth Charles, 1911–1970, vol. VI
King, Lt-Col Lancelot Noel Friedrick Irving, 1878–1947, vol. IV
King, Laurence Edward, 1907–1981, vol. VIII
King, Leonard William, 1869–1919, vol. II
King, Sir Louis, 1904–1972, vol. VII
King, Louis Vessot, 1886–1956, vol. V
King, Sir Lucas White, 1856–1925, vol. II
King, Martin Luther, Jr, 1929–1968, vol. VI
King, Maurice John, 1880–1952, vol. V
King, Merton, *died* 1939, vol. III
King, Michael, 1934–1990, vol. IX (AI)
King, Sir Norman, 1880–1963, vol. VI
King, Bt Col Norman Carew, 1871–1953, vol. V
King, Oliver, 1855–1923, vol. II, vol. III
King, Oliver; *see* King, J. O. L.

King, Sir Peter Alexander, 7th Bt (*cr* 1815), 1928–1973, vol. VII
King, Philip, 1904–1979, vol. VII
King, Preston, 1862–1943, vol. IV
King, Ralph Malcolm MacDonald, 1911–1997, vol. X
King, Richard, (Richard King Huskinson), 1879–1947, vol. IV
King, Richard Ashe, 1839–1932, vol. III
King, Sir Richard Brian Meredith, 1920–1998, vol. X
King, Very Rev. Richard George Salmon, *died* 1958, vol. V
King, Rear-Adm. Richard Matthew, 1883–1969, vol. VI
King, Maj.-Gen. Robert Charles Moss, 1904–1983, vol. VIII
King, Sir Robertson; see King, Sir C. R.
King, Sir Seymour; see King, Sir H. S.
King, Sir Sydney Percy, 1916–1991, vol. IX
King, Thomas, 1842–1903, vol. I
King, Thomas Mulhall, 1842–1914, vol. I
King, Thomas William, 1881–1936, vol. III
King, Sir Truby; see King, Sir F. T.
King, Col Walter Gawen, 1851–1935, vol. III
King, Air Vice-Marshal Walter MacIan, 1910–1999, vol. X
King, Sir Wilfred Creyke, *died* 1943, vol. IV
King, William Benjamin Basil, 1859–1928, vol. II
King, William Bernard Robinson, 1889–1963, vol. VI
King, Maj.-Gen. William Birchall Macaulay, 1878–1950, vol. IV
King, William Charles Holland, 1884–1973, vol. VII
King, William Cyril Campbell, 1891–1963, vol. VI
King, William Frederick, 1854–1916, vol. II
King, William Joseph Harding, 1869–1933, vol. III
King, Rt Hon. W(illiam) L(yon) Mackenzie, 1874–1950, vol. IV
King, Sir William Oliver Evelyn M.; *see* Meade-King.
King, Rev. William Templeton, 1849–1933, vol. III
King, Yeend, 1855–1924, vol. II
King-Farlow, Sir Sydney Nettleton, 1864–1957, vol. V
King-Hall, Baron (Life Peer); William Stephen Richard King-Hall, 1893–1966, vol. VI
King-Hall, Adm. Sir George Fowler, 1850–1939, vol. III
King-Hall, Adm. Sir Herbert Goodenough, 1862–1936, vol. III
King-Hall, Magdalen, (Mrs Patrick Perceval-Maxwell), 1904–1971, vol. VII
King-Harman, Sir Charles Anthony, 1851–1939, vol. III
King-Harman, Captain (Robert) Douglas, 1891–1978, vol. VII
King-Harman, Col Wentworth Henry, 1840–1919, vol. II
King-King, Brig.-Gen. James Gurwood, 1863–1939, vol. III
King-Martin, Brig. John Douglas, 1915–1993, vol. IX
King-Wood, William, 1867–1921, vol. II

Kingan, William Sinclair, 1876–1946, vol. IV
Kingcome, Engr Vice-Adm. Sir John, 1890–1950, vol. IV
Kingdom, Thomas, 1881–1957, vol. V
Kingdom, Thomas Doyle, 1910–1990, vol. VIII
Kingdon, Sir Donald, 1883–1961, vol. VI
Kingdon, Rt Rev. Hollingworth Tully, 1835–1907, vol. I
Kingdon-Ward, F., 1885–1958, vol. V
Kingham, James Frederick, 1925–1995, vol. IX
Kingham, Sir Robert Dixon, 1883–1966, vol. VI
Kinghorn, Col Harry Jackson, 1867–1947, vol. IV
Kinglake, Robert Alexander, 1843–1915, vol. I
Kings Norton, Baron (Life Peer); Harold Roxbee Cox, 1902–1997, vol. X
Kingsale, 33rd Baron, 1855–1931, vol. III
Kingsale, 34th Baron, 1882–1969, vol. VI
Kingsburgh, Rt Hon. Lord, 1836–1919, vol. II
Kingsbury, Allan Neave, 1888–1965, vol. VI
Kingscote, Lady Emily Marie, 1836–1910, vol. I
Kingscote, Mrs Howard; see Cleeve, Lucas.
Kingscote, Col Sir Robert Nigel FitzHardinge, 1830–1908, vol. I
Kingscote, Thomas Arthur Fitzhardinge, 1845–1935, vol. III
Kingsford, A. Beresford, *died* 1944, vol. IV
Kingsford, Charles Lethbridge, 1862–1926, vol. II
Kingsford, Adm. Henry Coare, 1858–1941, vol. IV
Kingsford, Reginald John Lethbridge, 1900–1978, vol. VII
Kingsford-Smith, Air Cdre Sir Charles Edward, 1897–1935, vol. III
Kingsley, Brig. Harold Evelyn William Bell, 1885–1970, vol. VI
Kingsley, Hyman Herbert, 1897–1956, vol. V
Kingsley, J(ohn) Donald, 1908–1972, vol. VII
Kingsley, Sir Patrick Graham Toler, 1908–1999, vol. X
Kingsley, Col William Henry Bell, 1835–1901, vol. I
Kingsmill, Lt-Col Andrew de Portal, 1881–1956, vol. V
Kingsmill, Adm. Sir Charles Edmund, 1855–1935, vol. III
Kingsmill, Hugh, (Hugh Kingsmill Lunn), 1889–1949, vol. IV
Kingsmill, Sir Walter, 1864–1935, vol. III
Kingsmill, Lt-Col Walter B., 1876–1957, vol. V
Kingsmill, Lt-Col William Henry, 1905–1971, vol. VII
Kingsnorth, Engr Rear-Adm. Sir Arthur Frederick, 1864–1947, vol. IV
Kingston, 9th Earl of, 1874–1946, vol. IV
Kingston, 10th Earl of, 1897–1948, vol. IV
Kingston, Rt Hon. Charles Cameron, 1850–1908, vol. I
Kingston, Most Rev. George Frederick, 1889–1950, vol. IV
Kingston, George Henry, 1866–1933, vol. III
Kingston, Gertrude, *died* 1937, vol. III
Kingston-McCloughry, Air Vice-Marshal Edgar James, 1896–1972, vol. VII
Kingstone, Arthur Courtney, 1874–1938, vol. III
Kingstone, Brig. James Joseph, *died* 1966, vol. VI
Kington, Captain William Miles, 1876–1914, vol. I

Kington-Blair-Oliphant, Lt-Col Philip Lawrence, 1867–1918, vol. II
Kingzett, Charles Thomas, 1852–1935, vol. III
Kininmonth, Sir William Hardie, 1904–1988, vol. VIII
Kinkead, Richard John, *died* 1928, vol. II
Kinley, John, *died* 1957, vol. V
Kinloch, Sir Alexander, 10th Bt (*cr* 1686), 1830–1912, vol. I
Kinloch, Maj.-Gen. Alexander Angus Airlie, 1838–1919, vol. II
Kinloch, Sir Alexander Davenport, 12th Bt, 1902–1982, vol. VIII
Kinloch, Brig.-Gen. Sir David Alexander, 11th Bt (*cr* 1686), 1856–1944, vol. IV
Kinloch, Sir George, 3rd Bt (*cr* 1873), 1880–1948, vol. IV
Kinloch, J. Parlane, *died* 1932, vol. III
Kinloch, James Laird, 1878–1952, vol. V
Kinloch, Sir John, 4th Bt (*cr* 1873), 1907–1992, vol. IX
Kinloch, Sir John George Smyth, 2nd Bt (*cr* 1873), 1849–1910, vol. I
Kinloch-Cooke, Sir Clement, 1st Bt, *died* 1944, vol. IV
Kinloss, Baroness (11th in line, styled 8th), 1852–1944, vol. IV
Kinloss, Master of; Rev. Hon. Luis Chandos Francis Temple Morgan-Grenville, 1889–1944, vol. IV
Kinmonth, John Bernard, 1916–1982, vol. VIII
Kinnaird, 11th Lord, 1847–1923, vol. II
Kinnaird, 12th Lord, 1880–1972, vol. VII
Kinnaird, 13th Lord, 1912–1997, vol. X
Kinnaird, Master of; Hon. Douglas Arthur Kinnaird, 1879–1914, vol. I
Kinnaird, Hon. Emily, *died* 1947, vol. IV
Kinnaird, Hon. Patrick, 1898–1948, vol. IV
Kinnear, 1st Baron, 1833–1917, vol. II
Kinnear, Alfred, *died* 1912, vol. I
Kinnear, Hon. Helen Alice, 1894–1970, vol. VI
Kinnear, John Boyd, 1828–1920, vol. II
Kinnear, Nigel Alexander, 1907–2000, vol. X
Kinnear, Sir Norman Boyd, 1882–1957, vol. V
Kinnear, Sir Walter Samuel, 1872–1953, vol. V
Kinnell, Rev. Gordon, 1891–1971, vol. VII
Kinnoull, 13th (shown as 12th) Earl of, 1855–1916, vol. II
Kinnoull, 14th Earl of, 1902–1938, vol. III
Kino, Major Algernon Roderick, 1880–1924, vol. II
Kinross, 1st Baron, 1837–1905, vol. I
Kinross, 2nd Baron, 1870–1939, vol. III
Kinross, 3rd Baron, 1904–1976, vol. VI
Kinross, 4th Baron, 1906–1985, vol. VIII
Kinross, Albert, 1870–1929, vol. III
Kinross, John, *died* 1931, vol. III
Kinross, John Blythe, 1904–1989, vol. VIII
Kinsey, Sir Joseph James, 1852–1936, vol. III
Kinsey, Joseph Ronald, 1921–1983, vol. VIII
Kinsley, Albert, 1852–1945, vol. IV
Kinsley, Rev. James, 1922–1984, vol. VIII
Kinsman, Frederick Joseph, 1868–1944, vol. IV
Kinsman, Col Gerald Richard Vivian, 1876–1963, vol. VI
Kintore, 9th Earl of, (incorrectly shown as 10th), 1852–1930, vol. III

Kintore, 10th Earl of, 1879–1966, vol. VI
Kintore, Countess of (11th in line), 1874–1974, vol. VII
Kintore, 12th Earl of, 1908–1989, vol. VIII
Kinvig, Robert Henry, 1893–1969, vol. VI
Kiparsky, Valentin Julius Alexander, 1904–1983, vol. IX
Kipling, John Lockwood, 1837–1911, vol. I
Kipling, (Joseph) Rudyard, 1865–1936, vol. III
Kipling, Rudyard; *see* Kipling, J. R.
Kippen, William James, *died* 1928, vol. II
Kippenberger, Maj.-Gen. Sir Howard Karl, 1897–1957, vol. V
Kipping, Frederic Stanley, 1863–1949, vol. IV
Kipping, Sir Norman Victor, 1901–1979, vol. VII
Kipps, William John, 1866–1938, vol. III
Kiralfy, Imre, *died* 1919, vol. II
Kirby, Sir Alfred, 1840–1900, vol. I
Kirby, Brig.-Gen. Arthur Durham, 1867–1948, vol. IV
Kirby, Sir Arthur Frank, 1899–1983, vol. VIII
Kirby, Bertie Victor, 1887–1953, vol. V
Kirby, Adm. Francis George, 1854–1951, vol. V
Kirby, Gp Captain Frank Howard, 1871–1956, vol. V
Kirby, George, 1845–1937, vol. III
Kirby, Sir (Horace) Woodburn, 1853–1932, vol. III
Kirby, Jack Howard, 1913–1989, vol. VIII
Kirby, Sir James Norman, 1899–1971, vol. VII
Kirby, Air Cdre John Lawrence, 1899–1980, vol. VII
Kirby, Col Norbone, 1863–1922, vol. II
Kirby, Maj.-Gen. Stanley Woodburn, 1895–1968, vol. VI
Kirby, Brig.-Gen. Stuart Rodger, 1873–1959, vol. V
Kirby, Walter, 1891–1981, vol. VIII
Kirby, William Forsell, 1844–1912, vol. I
Kirby, Sir Woodburn; *see* Kirby, Sir H. W.
Kirchhoffer, Hon. John Nesbitt, 1848–1914, vol. I
Kirchner, Bernard Joseph, 1894–1982, vol. VIII
Kirk, Adam Kennedy, 1893–1975, vol. VII
Kirk, Adm. Alan Goodrich, 1888–1963, vol. VI
Kirk, Alexander Comstock, 1888–1979, vol. VII
Kirk, Sir Amos Child, 1856–1928, vol. II
Kirk, Geoffrey William, 1907–1975, vol. VII
Kirk, Grayson Louis, 1903–1997, vol. X
Kirk, Harry B., *died* 1948, vol. IV
Kirk, Sir Henry Alexander, 1847–1929, vol. III
Kirk, James Balfour, 1893–1984, vol. VIII
Kirk, Sir John, 1832–1922, vol. II
Kirk, Sir John, 1847–1922, vol. II
Kirk, John, 1881–1959, vol. V
Kirk, John Henry, 1907–1995, vol. IX
Kirk, Rt Rev. Kenneth Escott, 1886–1954, vol. V
Kirk, Lucy Phoebe, 1890–1961, vol. VI
Kirk, Dame (Lucy) Ruth, *died* 2000, vol. X
Kirk, Rt Hon. Norman Eric, 1923–1974, vol. VII
Kirk, Rev. Paul Thomas Radford-Rowe, *died* 1962, vol. VI
Kirk, Sir Peter Michael, 1928–1977, vol. VII
Kirk, Dame Ruth; *see* Kirk, Dame L. R.
Kirk, Thomas Sinclair, 1869–1940, vol. III
Kirkaldy, Adam Willis, 1867–1931, vol. III
Kirkaldy, Harold Stewart, 1902–1976, vol. VII
Kirkaldy, John Francis, 1908–1990, vol. VIII

Kirkbride, Sir Alec Seath, 1897–1978, vol. VII
Kirkby, Lt-Col Henry McKenzie, 1877–1952, vol. V
Kirkby, Rt Rev. Sydney James, 1879–1935, vol. III
Kirkconnell, Watson, 1895–1977, vol. VII
Kirke, Claud Cecil Augustus, 1875–1959, vol. V
Kirke, Henry, 1842–1925, vol. II
Kirke, Percy St George, died 1966, vol. VI
Kirke, Gen. Sir Walter Mervyn St George, 1877–1949, vol. IV
Kirkhope, Lt-Col Kenneth Macleay, 1877–1950, vol. IV
Kirkland, Edward Chase, 1894–1975, vol. VII
Kirkland, James Hampton, 1859–1939, vol. III
Kirkland, Joseph Lane, 1922–1999, vol. X
Kirkland, Rev. Canon Thomas James, 1884–1965, vol. VI
Kirkley, 1st Baron, 1863–1935, vol. III
Kirkley, Sir (Howard) Leslie, 1911–1989, vol. VIII
Kirkley, Sir Leslie; see Kirkley, Sir H. L.
Kirkman, Frederick Bernulf Beever, 1869–1945, vol. IV
Kirkman, Maj.-Gen. John Mather, 1898–1964, vol. VI
Kirkman, Gen. Sir Sidney Chevalier, 1895–1982, vol. VIII
Kirkman, Hon. Thomas, 1843–1919, vol. II
Kirkness, Lewis Hawker, 1881–1950, vol. IV
Kirkpatrick, Very Rev. Alexander Francis, 1849–1940, vol. III
Kirkpatrick, Lt-Col Alexander Ronald Yvone, 1868–1950, vol. IV
Kirkpatrick, Hon. Andrew Alexander, 1848–1928, vol. II
Kirkpatrick, Maj.-Gen. Charles, 1879–1955, vol. V
Kirkpatrick, Sir Charles Sharpe, 9th Bt, 1874–1937, vol. III
Kirkpatrick, Sir Cyril Reginald Sutton, 1872–1957, vol. V
Kirkpatrick, Francis, 1840–1921, vol. II
Kirkpatrick, Frederick Alex., 1861–1953, vol. V
Kirkpatrick, Hon. Sir George Airey, 1841–1899, vol. I
Kirkpatrick, Gen. Sir George Macaulay, 1866–1950, vol. IV
Kirkpatrick, Lt-Col Henry, 1871–1958, vol. V
Kirkpatrick, Lt-Col Henry Pownall, 1862–1919, vol. II
Kirkpatrick, Rev. Canon Herbert Francis, 1888–1971, vol. VII
Kirkpatrick, Air Vice-Marshal Herbert James, 1910–1977, vol. VII
Kirkpatrick, Col Ivone, 1860–1936, vol. III
Kirkpatrick, Sir Ivone Augustine, died 1964, vol. VI
Kirkpatrick, Sir James, 8th Bt, 1841–1899, vol. I
Kirkpatrick, Sir James Alexander, 10th Bt, 1918–1954, vol. V
Kirkpatrick, John, 1835–1926, vol. II
Kirkpatrick, Col Roger, 1859–1933, vol. III
Kirkpatrick, T. Percy C., 1869–1954, vol. V
Kirkpatrick, Major William, 1863–1941, vol. IV
Kirkpatrick, William, 1886–1947, vol. IV
Kirkpatrick, William MacColin, 1878–1953, vol. V
Kirkpatrick, Brig.-Gen. William Johnston, 1851–1931, vol. III

Kirkpatrick-Caldecot, Ivone, 1867–1951, vol. V
Kirkup, Brig. Philip, 1893–1959, vol. V
Kirkup, Thomas, 1844–1912, vol. I
Kirkup, Thomas Henry, 1864–1951, vol. V
Kirkwood, 1st Baron, 1872–1955, vol. V
Kirkwood, 2nd Baron, 1903–1970, vol. VI
Kirkwood, Col Carleton Hooper Morrison, 1860–1937, vol. III
Kirkwood, Lt-Col James George, 1872–1955, vol. V
Kirkwood, Major John Hendley Morrison, 1877 1924, vol. II
Kirkwood, Kenneth, 1919–1997, vol. X
Kirkwood, Sir Robert Lucien Morrison, 1904–1984, vol. VIII
Kirkwood, Sir Walter Guy Coffin, 1856–1935, vol. III
Kirkwood, William Montague Hammett, 1850–1926, vol. II
Kirsop, (Arthur) Michael (Benjamin), 1931–1995, vol. IX
Kirsop, Michael; see Kirsop, A. M. B.
Kirstein, Lincoln Edward, 1907–1996, vol. X
Kirton, Col Hugh, 1910–1997, vol. X
Kirton, Robert James, 1901–1988, vol. VIII
Kirwan, Sir (Archibald) Laurence (Patrick), 1907–1999, vol. X
Kirwan, Lt-Gen. Sir Bertram Richard, 1871–1960, vol. V
Kirwan, Rev. Ernest Cecil, 1867–1936, vol. III
Kirwan, Lt-Col Ernest William O'Gorman, 1887–1965, vol. VI
Kirwan, Geoffrey Dugdale, 1896–1970, vol. VI
Kirwan, Hon. Sir John Waters, 1866–1949, vol. IV
Kirwan, Sir Laurence; see Kirwan, Sir A. L. P.
Kirwan, Lionel M.; see Maitland-Kirwan.
Kirwan-Taylor, Harold George, 1895–1981, vol. VIII
Kisch, (Alastair) Royalton, 1919–1995, vol. IX
Kisch, Barthold Schlesinger, 1882–1961, vol. VI
Kisch, Sir Cecil Hermann, 1884–1961, vol. VI
Kisch, Brig. Frederick Hermann, 1888–1943, vol. IV
Kisch, Harold, died 1959, vol. V
Kisch, Hermann Michael, 1850–1942, vol. IV
Kisch, John Marcus, 1916–1992, vol. IX
Kisch, Royalton; see Kisch, A. R.
Kishangarh, Lt-Col HH Umdai Rajhae Buland Makan Maharajadhiraj Maharaj Sir Madan Singh Bahadur, 1884–1926, vol. II
Kishun Pershad, Raja-i-Rajayan Maharajah Bahadur, Yamin-us-Saltanat, Sir, 1864–1940, vol. III
Kissan, Edgar Duguid, died 1932, vol. III
Kissen, Hon. Lord; Manuel Kissen, 1912–1981, vol. VIII
Kissen, Manuel; see Kissen, Hon. Lord.
Kissin, Baron (Life Peer); Harry Kissin, 1912–1997, vol. X
Kistiakowsky, George Bogdan, 1900–1982, vol. VIII
Kitcat, Mabel, (Mrs S. A. P. Kitcat), died 1922, vol. II
Kitchen, Frederick Bruford, 1912–1995, vol. IX
Kitchen, Sir Geoffrey, 1906–1978, vol. VII
Kitchen, Percy Inman, 1883–1963, vol. VI
Kitchener of Khartoum, 1st Earl, 1850–1916, vol. II

Kitchener of Khartoum, 2nd Earl, 1846–1937, vol. III
Kitchener, Francis Elliott, 1838–1915, vol. I
Kitchener, Lt-Gen. Sir Frederick Walter, 1858–1912, vol. I
Kitchin, Ven. Arthur, 1855–1928, vol. II
Kitchin, Arthur James Warburton, 1870–1957, vol. V
Kitchin, Clifford Henry Benn, 1895–1967, vol. VI
Kitchin, Darcy Butterworth, 1863–1939, vol. III
Kitchin, Finlay Lorimer, died 1934, vol. III
Kitchin, Frederick Harcourt, 1867–1932, vol. III
Kitchin, Very Rev. George William, 1827–1912, vol. I
Kitchin, John, 1869–1951, vol. V
Kitchin, John Leslie Harlow, 1924–1982, vol. VIII
Kitchin, Shepherd Braithwaite, died 1944, vol. IV
Kitching, Rt Rev. Arthur Leonard, 1875–1960, vol. V
Kitching, Elsie, 1870–1955, vol. V
Kitching, Maj.-Gen. George, 1910–1999, vol. X
Kitching, John Alwyne, 1908–1996, vol. X
Kitching, Theodore Hopkins, 1866–1930, vol. III
Kitching, Wilfred, 1893–1977, vol. VII
Kite, Frederick William, 1856–1940, vol. III
Kite, Rev. Joseph Bertram, 1857–1939, vol. III
Kitiyakara, Prince Nakkhatra Mangala, 1898–1953, vol. V
Kitson, Sir Albert Ernest, 1868–1937, vol. III
Kitson, Alexander Harper, 1921–1997, vol. X
Kitson, Col Charles Edward, 1874–1928, vol. II
Kitson, Charles Herbert, 1874–1944, vol. IV
Kitson, Geoffrey Herbert, 1896–1974, vol. VII
Kitson, Sir George Vernon, 1899–1980, vol. VII
Kitson, Maj.-Gen. Sir Gerald Charles, 1856–1950, vol. IV
Kitson, Vice-Adm. Sir Henry Karslake, 1877–1952, vol. V
Kitson, Captain James Buller, 1883–1976, vol. VII
Kitson, Hon. James Clifford, 1892–1942, vol. IV
Kitson, Col James Edward, 1848–1912, vol. I
Kitson, Michael William Lely, 1926–1998, vol. X
Kitson, Sydney Decimus, 1871–1937, vol. III
Kitson, William Henry, 1886–1952, vol. V
Kitson Clark, George Sidney Roberts, 1900–1975, vol. VII
Kittermaster, F. R., 1899–1972, vol. VII
Kittermaster, Sir Harold Baxter, 1879–1939, vol. III
Kitto, Rt Hon. Sir Frank Walters, 1903–1994, vol. IX
Kitto, Humphrey Davy Findley, 1897–1982, vol. VIII
Kitto, John Vivian, 1875–1953, vol. V
Kittoe, Lt-Col Montagu Francis Markham Sloane, died 1967, vol. VI
Kitton, Frederic George, 1856–1904, vol. I
Kitts, Sir Francis Joseph, 1914–1979, vol. VII
Kittson, Rev. Henry, 1848–1925, vol. II, vol. III
Klaestad, Helge, 1885–1965, vol. VI
Klecki, Paul; see Kletzi, P.
Kleczkowski, Alfred Alexander Peter, 1908–1970, vol. VI
Kleffens, Eelco Nicolaas van, 1894–1983, vol. VIII
Kleiber, Erich, 1890–1956, vol. V
Klein, Edward Emanuel, 1844–1925, vol. II

Klein, Abbé Felix, 1862–1954, vol. V
Klein, Herman, 1856–1934, vol. III
Klein, Sydney Turner, 1853–1934, vol. III
Kleindienst, Richard Gordon, 1923–2000, vol. X
Kleinwort, Sir Alexander Drake, 1st Bt, 1858–1935, vol. III
Kleinwort, Sir Alexander Santiago, 2nd Bt, 1892–1983, vol. VIII
Kleinwort, Sir Cyril Hugh, 1905–1980, vol. VII
Kleinwort, Ernest Greverus, 1901–1977, vol. VII
Kleinwort, Herman Greverus, 1856–1942, vol. IV
Kleinwort, Sir Kenneth Drake, 3rd Bt, 1935–1994, vol. IX
Klemperer, Otto, 1885–1973, vol. VII
Kletzi, Paul, (Paul Klecki), 1900–1973, vol. VII
Klickmann, Flora, (Mrs Henderson-Smith), died 1958, vol. V
Klien, Walter, 1928–1991, vol. IX
Klijnstra, Gerrit Dirk Ale, 1912–1976, vol. VII
Klinck, Leonard Sylvanus, 1877–1969, vol. VI
Klinghoffer, Clara, 1900–1970, vol. VI
Klopsch, Louis, died 1910, vol. I
Klotz, Otto, 1852–1923, vol. II
Klugh, Ven. Leonard, 1859–1943, vol. IV
Klyne, William, 1913–1977, vol. VII
Knaggs, Col Henry Thomas, 1863–1946, vol. IV
Knaggs, Col Morton Herbert, 1871–1948, vol. IV
Knaggs, Robert Lawford, died 1945, vol. IV
Knaggs, Sir Samuel William, 1856–1924, vol. II
Knapp, Sir Arthur Rowland, died 1954, vol. V
Knapp, Charles Welbourne, 1848–1916, vol. II
Knapp, Brig.-Gen. Kempster Kenmure, 1866–1948, vol. IV
Knapp, Marion Domville, 1870–1963, vol. VI
Knapp, Valentine, 1861–1935, vol. III
Knapp, William Ireland, 1835–1908, vol. I
Knapp-Fisher, Arthur Bedford, 1888–1965, vol. VI
Knapp-Fisher, Sir Edward Francis, 1864–1940, vol. III
Knaresborough, 1st Baron, 1845–1929, vol. III
Knatchbull, Brig.-Gen. George Wyndham Chichester, 1862–1943, vol. IV
Knatchbull, Major Reginald Norton, 1872–1917, vol. II
Knatchbull, Sir Wyndham, 12th Bt, 1844–1917, vol. II
Knatchbull-Hugessen, Hon. Adrian Norton, 1891–1976, vol. VII
Knatchbull-Hugessen, Herbert Thomas, 1835–1922, vol. II
Knatchbull-Hugessen, Sir Hughe Montgomery, 1886–1971, vol. VII
Kneale, Sydney James, 1895–1975, vol. VII
Kneale, William Calvert, 1906–1990, vol. VIII
Knebworth, Viscount; Edward Anthony James Lytton, 1903–1933, vol. III
Knebworth, Viscount; Alexander Edward John Lytton, 1910–1942, vol. IV
Knecht, Edmund, 1861–1925, vol. II
Kneeland, Abner W., 1853–1928, vol. II
Kneen, John Joseph, 1873–1938, vol. III
Kneen, Thomas, died 1916, vol. II
Kneen, William, 1862–1921, vol. II
Kneipp, Hon. Sir George; see Kneipp, Hon. Sir J. P. G.

Kneipp, Hon. Sir (Joseph Patrick) George, 1922–1993, vol. IX
Knell, Rt Rev. Eric Henry, 1903–1987, vol. VIII
Knibbs, Sir George Handley, 1858–1929, vol. III
Knight, A. Charles, *died* 1958, vol. V
Knight, Most Rev. Alan John, 1902–1979, vol. VII
Knight, Rt Rev. Albion Williamson, 1859–1936, vol. III
Knight, Alfred Ernest, 1861–1934, vol. III
Knight, Sir Allan Walton, 1910–1998, vol. X
Knight, Rev. Angus Clifton, 1873–1931, vol. III
Knight, Archibald Patterson, *died* 1935, vol. III
Knight, Arthur Harold John, 1903–1963, vol. VI
Knight, Rt Rev. Arthur Mesac, 1964–1939, vol. III
Knight, (Arthur) Rex, 1903–1963, vol. VI
Knight, Bert Cyril James Gabriel, 1904–1981, vol. VIII
Knight, Charles, 1863–1941, vol. IV
Knight, Charles, 1901–1990, vol. VIII
Knight, Charles Andrew R. B.; *see* Rouse-Boughton-Knight.
Knight, Charles Joseph, 1863–1950, vol. IV
Knight, Captain Charles William Robert, 1884–1957, vol. V
Knight, Clara Millicent, *died* 1950, vol. IV
Knight, Clifford, 1909–1959, vol. V
Knight, Edward Frederick, 1852–1925, vol. II
Knight, Eric, 1897–1943, vol. IV
Knight, Eric Ayshford, 1863–1944, vol. IV
Knight, Eric John Percy Crawford L; *see* Lombard Knight.
Knight, Esmond Pennington, 1906–1987, vol. VIII
Knight, Sir Frederic Winn, 1812–1897, vol. I
Knight, Geoffrey Cureton, 1906–1994, vol. IX
Knight, Geoffrey Egerton, 1921–1997, vol. X
Knight, Sir George, 1874–1951, vol. V
Knight, (George Richard) Wilson, 1897–1985, vol. VIII
Knight, Gerald Hocken, 1908–1979, vol. VII
Knight, Gilfred Norman, 1891–1978, vol. VII
Knight, Air Vice-Marshal Glen Albyn Martin, 1903–1990, vol. VIII
Knight, Harold, 1874–1961, vol. VI
Knight, Sir Henry Edmund, 1833–1917, vol. II
Knight, Sir Henry Foley, 1886–1960, vol. V
Knight, Rt Rev. Henry Joseph Corbett, *died* 1920, vol. II
Knight, Brig.-Gen. Henry Lewkenor, 1874–1945, vol. IV
Knight, Henry Lougher, 1907–1986, vol. VIII
Knight, Rev. Herbert Theodore, 1869–1934, vol. III
Knight, Holford, 1877–1936, vol. III
Knight, Jasper Frederick, 1909–1972, vol. VII
Knight, John Broughton, 1863–1937, vol. III
Knight, John Buxton, 1842–1908, vol. I
Knight, Captain John Peake, 1890–1916, vol. II
Knight, Jonathan; *see* Knight, B. C. J. G.
Knight, Joseph, 1829–1907, vol. I
Knight, Joseph, 1838–1909, vol. I
Knight, Dame Laura, 1877–1970, vol. VI
Knight, Rt Rev. Leslie Albert, 1890–1950, vol. IV (A), vol. V
Knight, Very Rev. Marcus, 1903–1988, vol. VIII
Knight, Nicholas, 1861–1942, vol. IV
Knight, Nora; *see* Swinburne Johnson, Elinore

Knight, Percy, 1891–1968, vol. VI
Knight, Rex; *see* Knight, A. R.
Knight, Richard James, 1915–2000, vol. X
Knight, Rt Rev. Samuel Kirshbaum, 1868–1932, vol. III
Knight, Chief Engr T. H., *died* 1918, vol. II
Knight, William Anderson, 1861–1915, vol. I, vol. III
Knight, William Angus, 1836–1916, vol. II
Knight, William Arnold, 1915–1996, vol. X
Knight, William Francis Jackson, 1895–1964, vol. VI
Knight, William George, *died* 1938, vol. III
Knight, William George, 1858–1943, vol. IV
Knight, William Lowry Craig, 1889–1955, vol. V
Knight, William Stanley Macbean, 1869–1950, vol. IV
Knight, Wilson; *see* Knight, G. R. W.
Knight, Maj.-Gen. Sir Wyndham Charles, 1863–1942, vol. IV
Knight-Adkin, Harry Kenrick, 1851–1927, vol. II
Knight-Adkin, Rev. Walter Kenrick, 1880–1957, vol. V
Knight Dix, Dorothy; *see* Waddy, D. K.
Knightley, Lady; (Louisa Mary), 1842–1913, vol. I
Knightley, Sir Charles Valentine, 5th Bt, 1853–1932, vol. III
Knightley, Rev. Sir Henry Francis, 6th Bt, 1854–1938, vol. III
Knightley, Captain Percy Frank, 1874–1942, vol. IV
Knightley, Rev. Sir Valentine, 4th Bt, 1812–1898, vol. I
Knighton, William, *died* 1900, vol. I
Knighton-Hammond, Arthur Henry, 1875–1970, vol. VI
Knights, Henry Newton, *died* 1959, vol. V
Knights, Lionel Charles, 1906–1997, vol. X
Knights, Maj.-Gen. Robert William, 1912–1975, vol. VII
Knill, Sir Ian S.; *see* Stuart-Knill.
Knill, Sir John, 2nd Bt, 1856–1934, vol. III
Knill, Sir John Kenelm Stuart, 4th Bt, 1913–1998, vol. X
Knill, Sir Stuart, 1st Bt, 1824–1898, vol. I
Knipe, Sir Leslie Francis, 1913–1992, vol. IX
Knittel, John Herman Emanuel, 1891–1970, vol. VI
Knobel, Edward Ball, 1841–1930, vol. III
Knoblock, Edward, 1874–1945, vol. IV
Knocker, Sir Edward Wollaston Nadir, 1838–1907, vol. I
Knollys, 1st Viscount, 1837–1924, vol. II
Knollys, 2nd Viscount, 1895–1966, vol. VI
Knollys, Rev. Archibald A., 1851–1940, vol. III
Knollys, Hon. Charlotte; *see* Knollys, Hon. E. C.
Knollys, Sir Courtenay (Clement), 1849–1905, vol. I
Knollys, Sir Courtney; *see* Knollys, Sir C. C.
Knollys, Hon. (Elizabeth) Charlotte, 1835–1930, vol. III
Knollys, Rev. Erskine William, 1842–1923, vol. II
Knollys, Col Sir Henry, 1840–1930, vol. III
Knollys, Major Louis Frederic, 1847–1922, vol. II
Knollys, William Edward, 1843–1910, vol. I
Knoop, Douglas, 1883–1948, vol. IV
Knopf, Alfred A., 1892–1984, vol. VIII
Knott, Rev. Alfred Ernest, 1869–1951, vol. V

Knott, Cargill Gilston, 1856–1922, vol. II
Knott, Frank Alexander, 1889–1962, vol. VI
Knott, Lt-Gen. Sir Harold Edwin, 1903–1974, vol. VII
Knott, Sir James, 1st Bt, 1855–1934, vol. III
Knott, John, 1853–1921, vol. II
Knott, John Espenett, died 1959, vol. V
Knott, Sir John Laurence, 1910–1999, vol. X
Knott, Ralph, 1878–1929, vol. III
Knott, Stratton Collings, 1856–1904, vol. I
Knott, Sir Thomas Garbutt, 2nd Bt, 1879–1949, vol. IV
Knottesford-Fortescue, Laurence; see Fortescue.
Knowelden, John, 1919–1997, vol. X
Knowland, William Fife, 1908–1974, vol. VII
Knowles, Arthur, 1858–1929, vol. III
Knowles, Arthur Richard, 1899–1960, vol. V
Knowles, Maj.-Gen. Sir Charles Benjamin, 1835–1924, vol. II
Knowles, Sir Charles George Frederick, 4th Bt, 1832–1918, vol. II
Knowles, Rev. David; see Knowles, Rev. Michael Clive.
Knowles, Rt Rev. Donald Rowland, 1898–1977, vol. VII
Knowles, Air Vice-Marshal Edgar, 1907–1977, vol. VII
Knowles, Rt Rev. Edwin Hubert, 1874–1962, vol. VI
Knowles, Frances Ivens; see Knowles, M. H. F. I.
Knowles, Rev. Francis, 1830–1916, vol. II
Knowles, Sir Francis Gerald William, 6th Bt, 1915–1974, vol. VII
Knowles, Sir Francis Howe Seymour, 5th Bt, 1886–1953, vol. V
Knowles, Frank, 1865–1934, vol. III
Knowles, Frederick Arthur, 1872–1922, vol. II
Knowles, Rear-Adm. George Herbert, 1881–1961, vol. VI
Knowles, Sir George Shaw, 1882–1947, vol. IV
Knowles, George Sheridan, 1863–1931, vol. III
Knowles, John, 1898–1977, vol. VII
Knowles, Lt-Col John George, died 1919, vol. II
Knowles, Joshua Kenneth, 1903–1974, vol. VII
Knowles, Ven. Kenneth Davenport, 1874–1944, vol. IV
Knowles, Sir Lees, 1st Bt (cr 1903), 1857–1928, vol. II
Knowles, Sir Leonard Joseph, 1916–1999, vol. X (AII)
Knowles, Lilian Charlotte Anne, died 1926, vol. II
Knowles, Mabel Winifred, (May Wynne), 1875–1949, vol. IV
Knowles, (Mary Hannah) Frances Ivens, died 1944, vol. IV
Knowles, Maurice Baxendale, 1893–1988, vol. VIII
Knowles, Rev. Michael Clive, (Rev. David Knowles), 1896–1974, vol. VII
Knowles, Lt-Col Robert, 1883–1936, vol. III
Knowles, Robert Millington, 1843–1924, vol. II
Knowles, William Henry, 1857–1943, vol. IV
Knowling, Hon. George, 1841–1923, vol. II
Knowling, Rev. Richard John, 1851–1919, vol. II
Knowlson, Thomas Sharper, 1867–1947, vol. IV
Knox, Rt Hon. Sir Adrian, 1863–1932, vol. III

Knox, Alfred Dilwyn, died 1943, vol. IV
Knox, Maj.-Gen. Sir Alfred William Fortescue, 1870–1964, vol. VI
Knox, Rev. Andrew, 1849–1915, vol. I
Knox, Col Arthur Francis Gore P. K. G.; see Pery-Knox-Gore.
Knox, Major Arthur Rice, 1863–1917, vol. II
Knox, Lt-Gen. Sir Charles Edmond, 1846–1938, vol. III
Knox, Collie, died 1977, vol. VII
Knox, Rt Rev. Edmund Arbuthnott, 1847–1937, vol. III
Knox, (Edmund Francis) Vesey, 1865–1921, vol. II
Knox, Edmund George Valpy, 1881–1971, vol. VII
Knox, Sir Edward, 1819–1901, vol. I
Knox, Sir Edward Ritchie, 1889–1973, vol. VII
Knox, Brig. Sir Errol Galbraith, 1889–1949, vol. IV
Knox, Sir Geoffrey George, 1884–1958, vol. V
Knox, Sir George Edward, 1845–1922, vol. II
Knox, Brig. Hon. Sir George Hodges, 1885–1960, vol. V
Knox, Lt-Col George Stuart, 1871–1945, vol. IV
Knox, Lt-Col Sir Hamish James Stuart, died 1940, vol. III
Knox, Gen. Sir Harry Hugh Sidney, 1873–1971, vol. VII
Knox, Henry Murray Owen, 1909–1986, vol. VIII
Knox, Brig.-Gen. Henry Owen, 1874–1955, vol. V
Knox, Rev. Canon Ian Carroll, 1932–1997, vol. X
Knox, Sir James, 1850–1926, vol. II
Knox, Sir James, 1862–1938, vol. III
Knox, His Eminence Cardinal James Robert, 1914–1983, vol. VIII
Knox, Jean Marcia; see Swaythling, J. M.
Knox, John Crawford, 1891–1964, vol. VI
Knox, Joseph Alan Cruden, 1911–1984, vol. VIII
Knox, Sir Malcolm; see Knox, Sir T. M.
Knox, Rt Hon. Sir Ralph Henry, 1836–1913, vol. I
Knox, Lt-Col Richard, 1848–1918, vol. II
Knox, Robert, died 1928, vol. II
Knox, Robert, 1904–2000, vol. X
Knox, Sir Robert Uchtred Eyre, 1889–1965, vol. VI
Knox, Sir Robert Wilson, 1890–1973, vol. VII
Knox, Rt Rev. Mgr Ronald Arbuthnott, 1888–1957, vol. V
Knox, Lt-Col Stuart George, 1869–1956, vol. V
Knox, Sir (Thomas) Malcolm, 1900–1980, vol. VII
Knox, Vesey; see Knox, E. F. V.
Knox, Walter Ernest, 1894–1970, vol. VI
Knox, Rev. Wilfred Lawrence, died 1950, vol. IV
Knox, Hon. William, 1850–1913, vol. I
Knox, Maj.-Gen. Sir William George, 1847–1916, vol. II
Knox Johnston, Anthony Gordon; see Johnston.
Knox Little, Rev. William John, 1839–1918, vol. II
Knox-Shaw, Charles Thomas, 1854–1939, vol. III
Knox-Shaw, Harold, 1885–1970, vol. VI
Knox-Shaw, Thomas, 1886–1972, vol. VII
Knubley, Rev. Edward Ponsonby, 1850–1931, vol. III
Knudsen, Sir Karl Fredrik, 1872–1937, vol. III
Knudsen, Martin, 1871–1949, vol. IV
Knudsen, Semon Emil, 1912–1998, vol. X
Knuthsen, Sir Louis Francis Roebuck, died 1957, vol. V

Knutsford, 1st Viscount, 1825–1914, vol. I
Knutsford, 2nd Viscount, 1855–1931, vol. III
Knutsford, 3rd Viscount, 1855–1935, vol. III
Knutsford, 4th Viscount, 1888–1976, vol. VII
Knutsford, 5th Viscount, 1920–1986, vol. VIII
Knyvett, Alexander Vansittart, 1848–1911, vol. I
Knyvett, Rt Rev. Carey Frederick, 1885–1967, vol. VI
Knyvett, Seymour Henry, 1849–1915, vol. I
Koch, Lauge, 1892–1964, vol. VI
Koch, Ludwig, 1881–1974, vol. VII
Koch, Robert, 1843–1910, vol. I
Kodàly, Zoltán, 1882–1967, vol. VI
Kodama, Lt-Gen. Baron Gentaro, 1855–1906, vol. I
Kodicek, Egon Hynek, 1908–1982, vol. VIII
Koe, Maj.-Gen. Frederick William Brooke, 1862–1935, vol. III
Koe, Brig.-Gen. Lancelot Charles, died 1941, vol. IV
Koebel, Major Frederick Ernest, 1881–1940, vol. III
Koebel, W. H., 1872–1923, vol. II
Koechlin, Raymond, 1860–1931, vol. III
Koechlin-Smythe, Patricia Rosemary, 1928–1996, vol. X
Koelle, Vice-Adm. Sir Harry Philpot, 1901–1980, vol. VII
Koenig, Gén. d'Armée Marie-Pierre, 1898–1970, vol. VI
Koenigsberger, Franz, 1907–1979, vol. VII
Koeppler, Sir Henry, (Sir Heinz), 1912–1979, vol. VII
Koestler, Arthur, 1905–1983, vol. VIII
Kohan, Major Charles Mendel, 1884–1974, vol. VII
Kohan, Robert Mendel, 1883–1967, vol. VI
Kohler, Irene, 1912–1996, vol. X
Kohler, Joy David, 1908–1990, vol. VIII
Kohler, Kaufmann, 1843–1926, vol. II
Kohlsaat, Herman H., 1853–1924, vol. II, vol. III
Kohnstam, George, 1920–1997, vol. X
Kohoban-Wickreme, Alfred Silva, 1914–1989, vol. IX (AI)
Koizumi, Yakumo; see Hearn, L.
Kokkinakis, Theodoros G.; see Athenagoras, T.
Kokoschka, Oskar, 1886–1980, vol. VII
Kolane, John Teboho, 1926–1999, vol. X (AII)
Kolbuszewski, Janusz, 1915–1984, vol. VIII
Kole, Nene Sir Emmanuel Mate, 1860–1939, vol. III
Kolhapur, Maharaja of, 1874–1922, vol. II
Kolhapur, Maharaja of, 1897–1940, vol. III
Kolhapur, Maharaja of, 1910–1983, vol. VIII
Kollengode, Raja Sir Vengarad of, 1873–1940, vol. III
Koller, Pius Charles, 1904–1979, vol. VII
Kominski, Daniel; see Kaye, Danny.
Komisarjevsky, Theodore, died 1954, vol. V
Komura, Marquis Jutaro, 1855–1911, vol. I
Kon, George Armand Robert, 1892–1951, vol. V
Konig, Frederick Adolphus, 1867–1940, vol. III
Konody, Paul G., 1872–1933, vol. III
Konovalov, Sergey, 1899–1982, vol. VIII
Konstam, Edwin Max., 1870–1956, vol. V
Konstam, Geoffrey Lawrence Samuel, 1899–1962, vol. VI
Koo, Vi Kyuin Wellington, 1888–1985, vol. VIII

Koop, Albert James, 1877–1945, vol. IV
Koopmans, Tjalling Charles, 1910–1985, vol. VIII
Kopal, Zdeněk, 1914–1993, vol. IX
Koppel, Percy Alexander, 1876–1932, vol. III
Korda, Sir Alexander, 1893–1956, vol. V
Körner, Stephan, 1913–2000, vol. X
Korngold, Erich Wolfgang, 1897–1957, vol. V
Korsah, Sir Arku; see Korsah, Sir K. A.
Korsah, Sir (Kobina) Arku, 1894–1967, vol. VI
Kortright, Sir Cornelius Hendrichsen, 1817–1897, vol. I
Kortright, Henry Somers, 1870–1942, vol. IV
Kosinski, Jerzy Nikodem, 1933–1991, vol. IX
Kossuth, Francis, 1841–1914, vol. I
Kostelanetz, André, 1901–1980, vol. VII
Kosterlitz, Hans Walter, 1903–1996, vol. X
Kosygin, Alexei Nikolaevich, 1904–1980, vol. VII
Kotah, Lt-Col HH Maharajahdiraj Maharaj Mahimahendra Maharaorajaji Shri Sir Umed Singh Bahadur, 1873–1941, vol. IV
Kotelawala, Col Rt Hon. Sir John Lionel, 1897–1980, vol. VII
Kotewall, Sir Robert Hormus, 1880–1949, vol. IV
Kothari, Sir Jehangir Hormasji, died 1934, vol. III
Kothavala, Tehmasp Tehmul, 1893–1977, vol. VII
Kotval, Peshotan Sohrabji, 1868–1949, vol. IV (A)
Kotze, Sir John Gilbert, 1849–1940, vol. III
Kotzé, Sir Robert Nelson, 1870–1953, vol. V
Kouropatkin, Alexei Nicholaevitch, 1848–1921, vol. II
Koussevitzky, Serge, 1874–1951, vol. V
Kozygin, Alexei Nikolaevich; see Kosygin, A. N.
Kraay, Colin Mackennal, 1918–1982, vol. VIII
Krabbé, Col Clarence Brehmer, 1886–1985, vol. VIII
Krabbé, Paymaster-Rear-Adm. Frederick James, 1860–1933, vol. III
Kramrisch, Stella, died 1993, vol. IX
Kratovil, Bohuslav G., 1901–1972, vol. VII
Kraus, Adolf, 1849–1928, vol. II, vol. III
Kraus, Otakar, 1909–1980, vol. VII
Krause, Frederick Edward Traugott, 1868–1959, vol. V
Krause, Lotte, (Madame Otto Krause); see Lehmann, Lotte.
Krausse, Alexis Sidney, 1859–1904, vol. I
Krebs, Sir Hans Adolf, 1900–1981, vol. VIII
Kreisler, Fritz, 1875–1962, vol. VI
Kremer, Michael, 1907–1988, vol. VIII
Krestin, David, died 1991, vol. IX
Kretser, Edward de, 1854–1925, vol. II
Kreuger, Ivar, 1880–1932, vol. III
Kreyer, Brig. Hubert Stanley, 1890–1949, vol. IV
Krips, Josef, 1902–1974, vol. VII
Krishna, Sri, 1896–1984, vol. VIII
Krishna Menon, Vengalil Krishnan, 1896–1974, vol. VII
Krishna Rau, Sir Mysore Nanjundiah, 1877–1958, vol. V
Krishna Shumshere, Jung Bahadur Rana, General, 1900–1977, vol. VII
Krishnama Chariar, Sir Vangal Thiruvenkatachari, 1881–1964, vol. VI
Krishnamurti, Jiddu, 1895–1986, vol. VIII
Krishnan, Cheruvari, 1868–1927, vol. II

Krishnan, Sir Kariamanikkam Srinivasa, 1898–1961, vol. VI
Krishnan Nair, Dewan Bahadur Sir M., 1870–1938, vol. III
Krishnaswami Ayyar, Diwan Bahadur Sir Alladi, 1883–1953, vol. V
Kristensen, Thorkil, 1899–1989, vol. VIII
Krogh, August, 1874–1949, vol. IV
Kroll, Wilhelm, 1869–1939, vol. III
Kronberger, Hans, 1920–1970, vol. VI
Kropotkin, Prince Peter Alexeievitch, 1842–1921, vol. II
Kroyer-Kielberg, Sir (F.) Michael, 1882–1958, vol. V
Krug, Julius A., 1907–1970, vol. VI
Kruger, Stephen J. Paul, 1825–1904, vol. I
Krusin, Sir Stanley Marks, 1908–1998, vol. X
Kubelik, Jan, 1880–1940, vol. III
Kubelik, Rafael, 1914–1996, vol. X
Kubrick, Stanley, 1928–1999, vol. X
Küchemann, Dietrich, 1911–1976, vol. VII
Kuenen, Johannes Petrus, 1866–1922, vol. II
Kuenssberg, Ekkehard von, 1913–2000, vol. X
Kuhe, William, 1823–1912, vol. I
Kuhn, Heinrich Gerhard, 1904–1994, vol. IX
Kuhn, Richard, 1900–1967, vol. VI
Kuiper, Gerard Peter, 1905–1973, vol. VII
Kukday, Col Sir Krishnaji Vishnoo, 1870–1958, vol. V (A), vol. VI (AI)
Kuklos; see Wray, W. Fitzwater.
Kuneralp, Zeki, 1914–1998, vol. X
Kuprin, Aleksandr Ivonovich, 1870–1938, vol. III
Kuroki, General Count, 1844–1923, vol. II
Kurongku, Most Rev. Sir Peter, 1930–1996, vol. X
Kurosawa, Akira, 1910–1998, vol. X
Kurti, Nicholas, 1908–1998, vol. X
Kurz, Otto, 1908–1975, vol. VII
Kusch, Polykarp, 1911–1993, vol. IX
Kusel, Baron de, 1848–1917, vol. II
Küssner, Amalia, died 1932, vol. III
Kutch, Maharao of; Lt-Col HH Maharaja Dhiraj Mirza Maharao Shri Sir Vijayaraji, Savai Bahadur, 1885–1948, vol. IV
Kutch, HH Maharaja Dhiraj Mirzan Maharao Shri Khengarji Sawai Bahadur Maharao of, 1866–1942, vol. IV

Kutlehr, Raja Ram Pal of, 1849–1927, vol. II, vol. III
Kutscher, Hans, 1911–1993, vol. IX
Kuwait, Emir of, 1895–1965, vol. VI
Kuyper, A., 1837–1920, vol. II
Kuypers, Henricus Gerardus Jacobus Maria, 1925–1989, vol. VIII
Kuznets, Simon, 1901–1985, vol. VIII
Kwakye, Emmanuel Bamfo, 1933–1993, vol. IX
Kwan, Sir Cho-Yiu, 1907–1971, vol. VII
Kwan Sai Kheong, 1920–1981, vol. VIII
Kyd, Sir David Hope, 1862–1933, vol. III
Kyd, James Gray, 1882–1968, vol. VI
Kyd, John Normansell, 1864–1931, vol. III
Kydd, Ronald Robertson, 1920–1972, vol. VII
Kyffin-Taylor, Brig.-Gen. Gerald; see Taylor.
Kyle, Elizabeth, (Agnes Mary Robertson Dunlop), died 1982, vol. VIII
Kyle, Emily Escher, died 1958, vol. V
Kyle, Henry Greville, died 1956, vol. V
Kyle, Lt-Col Robert, 1862–1942, vol. IV
Kyle, Air Chief Marshal Sir Wallace Hart, 1910–1988, vol. VIII
Kyle, William Galloway, 1875–1967, vol. VI
Kyllachy, Hon. Lord; William Mackintosh, 1842–1918, vol. II
Kylsant, 1st Baron, 1863–1937, vol. III
Kynaston, George Henry, 1850–1906, vol. I
Kynaston, Rev. Herbert, 1835–1910, vol. I
Kynaston, Walter Roger Owen, 1874–1935, vol. III
Kynch, George James, 1915–1987, vol. VIII
Kyne, Most Rev. John Anthony, 1904–1966, vol. VI
Kynnaird, Viscount; Sigismondo Maria Giuseppe Rospigliosi, 1886–1918, vol. II
Kynnersley, Charles Walter Sneyd-, 1849–1904, vol. I
Kynoch, John Alexander, died 1931, vol. III
Kynoch, Sir John Wheen, 1878–1946, vol. IV
Kynsey, Sir William Raymond, 1840–1904, vol. I
Kyrke, Lt-Col Henry Vernon Venables, 1881–1933, vol. III
Kyrle, Ven. Rowland Tracy Ashe M.; see Money-Kyrle.
Kyte, George William, 1864–1940, vol. III (A), vol. IV

L

Labarthe, André, 1902–1967, vol. VI
Labia, Princess Ida, died 1961, vol. VI
La Billois, Hon. Charles H., 1856–1928, vol. II
Laborde, Edward Daniel, 1863–1928, vol. II
Labori, Fernand, 1860–1917, vol. II
Labouchere, Sir George Peter, 1905–1999, vol. X
Labouchere, Rt Hon. Henry Du Pré, 1831–1912, vol. I
Labouisse, Henry Richardson, 1904–1987, vol. VIII
La Brooy, Justin Theodore, 1857–1944, vol. IV
Laby, Thomas Howell, 1880–1946, vol. IV
Lacaita, Charles Carmichael, 1853–1933, vol. III
Lace, John Henry, died 1918, vol. II

Lacey, Alfred Travers, 1892–1966, vol. VI
Lacey, Ven. Clifford George, 1921–1997, vol. X
Lacey, Daniel; see Lacey, W. D.
Lacey, Sir Francis Eden, 1859–1946, vol. IV
Lacey, Frank, 1919–1996, vol. X
Lacey, Gerald, 1887–1979, vol. VII
Lacey, Janet, 1903–1988, vol. VIII
Lacey, Sir Ralph Wilfred, 1900–1965, vol. VI
Lacey, Rev. Thomas Alexander, 1853–1931, vol. III
Lacey, Walter Graham, 1894–1974, vol. VII
Lacey, (William) Daniel, 1923–1985, vol. VIII
Lachaise, Gaston, 1882–1935, vol. III
Lachance, Arthur, 1868–1945, vol. IV

Lachman, Harry, 1886–1975, vol. VII
Lachs, Henry Lazarus, 1927–2000, vol. X
Lachs, Manfred, 1914–1993, vol. IX
Lack, David, 1910–1973, vol. VII
Lack, Harry Lambert, 1867–1943, vol. IV
Lack, Henry Martyn, 1909–1979, vol. VII
Lack, Sir Henry Reader, 1832–1908, vol. I
Lack, Victor John Frederick, 1893–1988, vol. VIII
Lackey, Rt Rev. Edwin Keith, 1930–1993, vol. X (AI)
Lackey, Hon. Sir John, 1830–1903, vol. I
Lackie, William Walter, 1869–1945, vol. IV
Lacon, Sir Edmund Beecroft Francis Heathcote, 5th Bt, 1870–1911, vol. I
Lacon, Sir Edmund Broughton Knowles, 4th Bt, 1842–1899, vol. I
Lacon, Sir George Haworth Ussher, 6th Bt, 1881–1950, vol. IV
Lacon, Sir George Vere Francis, 7th Bt, 1909–1980, vol. VII
Lacon, Captain Henry Edmund, 1849–1924, vol. II
Lacoste, Hon. Sir Alexandre, 1842–1923, vol. II
La Cour, Leonard Francis, 1907–1984, vol. VIII
Lacy, Captain Ernest Edward, 1865–1946, vol. IV
Lacy, Francis Brandon, 1872–1954, vol. V
Lacy, Frederick St John, 1862–1935, vol. III
Lacy, Sir Hugh Maurice Pierce, 3rd Bt, 1943–1998, vol. X
Lacy, Sir Maurice John Pierce, 2nd Bt, 1900–1965, vol. VI
Lacy, Sir Pierce Thomas, 1st Bt, 1872–1956, vol. V
Lacy, Rt Rev. Richard, 1841–1929, vol. III
Ladd, George Trumbull, 1842–1921, vol. II
Lade, Hon. Henry Augustus M.; see Milles-Lade.
La Dell, Edwin, 1914–1970, vol. VI
Laemmle, Carl, 1867–1939, vol. III
La Fárge, John, 1835–1910, vol. I
La Farge, Oliver, 1901–1963, vol. VI
Laferla, Albert Victor, 1887–1943, vol. IV
Laferté, Hon. Hector, 1885–1971, vol. VII
Laffan, Bertha Jane; see Laffan, Mrs Robert Stuart de Courcy.
Laffan, Col Henry David, 1858–1931, vol. III
Laffan, Robert George Dalrymple, 1887–1972, vol. VII
Laffan, Mrs Robert Stuart de Courcy, (Bertha Jane Laffan), died 1912, vol. I
Laffan, Rev. Robert Stuart de Courcy, 1853–1927, vol. II
Laffan, William M., 1848–1909, vol. I
Lafleche, Maj.-Gen. Léo-Richer, died 1956, vol. V
Lafleur, Paul Theodore, died 1924, vol. II
La Follette, Robert M., jun., 1895–1953, vol. V
La Follette, Robert Marion, 1855–1925, vol. II
Lafone, Rear-Adm. Albert Sumner, 1863–1933, vol. III
Lafone, Alfred, 1821–1911, vol. I
Lafone, Major Edgar Mortimore, died 1938, vol. III
Lafone, Harold Carlisle, 1879–1938, vol. III
Lafone, Ven. Henry Pownall Malins, 1867–1955, vol. V
Lafont, Rev. Eugène, 1837–1908, vol. I
Lafontaine, Henri Marie, 1854–1943, vol. IV
La Fontaine, Lt-Col Sydney Hubert, 1885–1964, vol. VI

La Force, Auguste de Caumont, Duc de, 1878–1961, vol. VI
Lagden, Godfrey William, 1906–1989, vol. VIII
Lagden, Sir Godfrey Yeatman, 1851–1934, vol. III
Lagerkvist, Pär Fabian, 1891–1974, vol. VII
Lagerlof, Selma, 1858–1940, vol. III
Lagesen, Air Marshal Sir Philip Jacobus, 1923–1994, vol. IX
Lagos, Oba of, died 1964, vol. VI
LaGuardia, Fiorello Henry, 1882–1947, vol. IV
Lahej, Sultan of, Sir Abdul Karim Fadthli Bin Ali, died 1947, vol. IV
Laidlaw, Sir George, 1883–1969, vol. VI
Laidlaw, James, 1847–1913, vol. I
Laidlaw, Rev. John, 1832–1906, vol. I
Laidlaw, Sir Patrick Playfair, 1881–1940, vol. III
Laidlaw, Sir Robert, 1856–1915, vol. I
Laidlaw, Robert, 1897–1964, vol. VI
Laidlaw, Rt Hon. Thomas Kennedy, 1864–1943, vol. IV
Laidlaw, William Allison, 1898–1983, vol. VIII
Laidlay, William James, 1846–1912, vol. I
Lailey, Barnard, died 1944, vol. IV
Lailey, Guy Patrick Barnard, 1888–1946, vol. IV
Lailey, John Raymond N.; see Nicholson-Lailey.
Laine, Sir Abraham James, 1876–1948, vol. IV
Laing, Alfred Martin, 1875–1949, vol. IV
Laing, Andrew, died 1931, vol. III
Laing, Austen, 1923–1992, vol. IX
Laing, Bertram Mitchell, died 1960, vol. V
Laing, Frederick Ninian Robert, 1856–1931, vol. III
Laing, Air Vice-Marshal Sir George, 1884–1956, vol. V
Laing, Sir James, 1823–1901, vol. I
Laing, Sir John William, 1879–1978, vol. VII
Laing, Malcolm Alfred, 1846–1917, vol. II
Laing, Malcolm Buchanan, 1890–1974, vol. VII
Laing, Percy Lyndon, 1909–1979, vol. VII
Laing, Ronald David, 1927–1989, vol. VIII
Laing, Samuel, 1812–1897, vol. I
Laing, Col Stanley van Buren, 1884–1962, vol. VI
Lainson, Major Alexander John, 1869–1931, vol. III
Laird, David, 1833–1914, vol. I
Laird, Edgar Ord (Michael), 1915–1992, vol. IX
Laird, John, 1887–1946, vol. IV
Laird, John Robert, (Robin), 1909–1991, vol. IX
Laird, Brig. Kenneth Macgregor, 1880–1954, vol. V
Laird, Michael; see Laird, E. O.
Laird, Sir Patrick Ramsay, 1888–1967, vol. VI
Laird, Robin; see Laird, J. R.
Laird, Thomas Patrick, 1860–1927, vol. II
Laird, Sir William, died 1901, vol. I
Laird, William, 1881–1962, vol. VI
Laistner, Max Ludwig Wolfram, 1890–1959, vol. V
Laithwaite, Eric Roberts, 1921–1997, vol. X
Laithwaite, Sir Gilbert; see Laithwaite, Sir J. G.
Laithwaite, Sir (John) Gilbert, 1894–1986, vol. VIII
Lajtha, Laszlo George, 1920–1995, vol. IX
Lake, Sir Arthur Johnstone, 8th Bt, 1849–1924, vol. II
Lake, Captain Sir Atwell Henry, 9th Bt, 1891–1972, vol. VII
Lake, Sir Atwell King, 6th Bt, 1834–1897, vol. I

Lake, Adm. Atwell Peregrine Macleod, 1842–1915, vol. I
Lake, Col Ernest Atwell Winter, 1886–1945, vol. IV
Lake, Col Harry William, *died* 1940, vol. III
Lake, Rev. Henry Ashton, 1847–1929, vol. III
Lake, Kirsopp, 1872–1946, vol. IV
Lake, Lt-Col Morice Challoner, 1885–1943, vol. IV
Lake, Brig.-Gen. Noel Montagu, 1852–1932, vol. III
Lake, Norman C., 1888–1966, vol. VI
Lake, Lt-Gen. Sir Percy Henry Noel, 1855–1940, vol. III
Lake, Richard, 1861–1949, vol. IV
Lake, Sir Richard Stuart, 1860–1950, vol. IV
Lake, Sir St Vincent Atwell, 7th Bt, 1862–1916, vol. II
Lakeman, Enid, 1903–1995, vol. IX
Laker, Albert, 1875–1948, vol. IV
Lakin, Charles Ernest, 1878–1972, vol. VII
Lakin, Cyril Harry Alfred, 1893–1948, vol. IV
Lakin, Sir Henry, 3rd Bt, 1904–1979, vol. VII
Lakin, John Edmund Douglas, 1920–1977, vol. VII
Lakin, Maj.-Gen. John Henry Foster, 1878–1943, vol. IV
Lakin, Sir Michael Henry, 1st Bt, 1846–1931, vol. III
Lakin, Sir Richard, 2nd Bt, 1873–1955, vol. V
Laking, Sir Francis Henry, 1st Bt, 1847–1914, vol. I
Laking, Sir Guy Francis, 2nd Bt, 1875–1919, vol. II
Laking, Sir Guy Francis William, 3rd Bt, 1904–1930, vol. III
Lal, Kanhaiya Lal, 1866–1945, vol. IV
Lal, Shavax Ardeshir, 1899–1987, vol. VIII
Lalaing, Count de, 1856–1919, vol. II
Lalique, René, 1860–1945, vol. IV (A), vol. V
Lall, I. C., 1863–1922, vol. II
Lall, Panna; *see* Panna Lall.
Lall, Sir Shankar, 1901–1951, vol. V
Lally, Miss Gwen, *died* 1963, vol. VI
Lalouette, Marie Joseph Gerard, 1912–1992, vol. IX
Lamarche, Rt Rev. Charles, 1870–1940, vol. III
Lamarque, Walter Geoffrey, 1913–1979, vol. VII
Lamb, Sir Albert (Sir Larry), 1929–2000, vol. X
Lamb, Major Algernon Joseph Rutherfurd, 1891–1941, vol. IV
Lamb, Sir Archibald, 3rd Bt, 1845–1921, vol. II
Lamb, Arthur Moore, 1873–1946, vol. IV
Lamb, Rev. Benjamin, *died* 1925, vol. II
Lamb, Col Sir Charles Anthony, 4th Bt, 1857–1948, vol. IV
Lamb, David C., 1866–1951, vol. V
Lamb, Col David Ogilvy Wight, 1885–1942, vol. IV
Lamb, Edmund, 1863–1925, vol. II
Lamb, Ernest Horace, 1878–1946, vol. IV
Lamb, Frank de Villiers, 1880–1962, vol. VI
Lamb, Harold Norman, 1922–1998, vol. X
Lamb, Sir Harry Harling, 1857–1948, vol. IV
Lamb, Henry, 1883–1960, vol. V
Lamb, Sir Horace, 1849–1934, vol. III
Lamb, Sir John, 1871–1952, vol. V
Lamb, Rev. John, 1886–1974, vol. VII
Lamb, John, 1922–1991, vol. IX
Lamb, Sir John Cameron, 1845–1915, vol. I

Lamb, Sir John Edward Stewart, 1892–1954, vol. V
Lamb, Sir Joseph Quinton, 1873–1949, vol. IV
Lamb, Hon. Kenneth Henry Lowry, 1923–1995, vol. IX
Lamb, Sir Larry; *see* Lamb, Sir A.
Lamb, Sir Lionel Henry, 1900–1992, vol. IX
Lamb, Lynton Harold, 1907–1977, vol. VII
Lamb, Percy, 1896–1973, vol. VII
Lamb, Sir Richard Amphlett, 1858–1923, vol. II
Lamb, Lt-Col Roger Montague Radcliffe, 1881–1937, vol. III
Lamb, Sir Thomas, *died* 1943, vol. IV
Lamb, Sir Walter Rangeley Maitland, 1882–1961, vol. VI
Lamb, Captain William John, 1906–1993, vol. IX
Lambarde, Brig.-Gen. Francis Fane, 1868–1948, vol. IV
Lambart, Brig.-Gen. Edgar Alan, 1857–1930, vol. III
Lambart, Lt-Col Sir Gustavus Francis, 1st Bt, 1848–1926, vol. II
Lambart, Julian Harold Legge, 1893–1982, vol. VIII
Lambart, Hon. Lionel John Olive, 1873–1940, vol. III
Lambart, Sir Oliver Francis, 2nd Bt, 1913–1986, vol. VIII
Lambart, Richard, 1875–1924, vol. II
Lambe, Adm. of the Fleet Sir Charles Edward, 1900–1960, vol. V
Lambe, Air Vice-Marshal Sir Charles Laverock, *died* 1953, vol. V
Lambe, Philip Agnew, 1897–1968, vol. VI
Lambert, 1st Viscount, 1866–1958, vol. V
Lambert, 2nd Viscount, 1909–1989, vol. VIII
Lambert, 3rd Viscount, 1912–1999, vol. X
Lambert, Agnes, *died* 1917, vol. II
Lambert, Alfred Uvedale Miller, *died* 1928, vol. II
Lambert, Arthur Bradley, 1858–1929, vol. III
Lambert, Sir Arthur William, 1876–1948, vol. IV
Lambert, Bertram, 1881–1963, vol. VI
Lambert, Rev. Brooke, 1834–1901, vol. I
Lambert, Adm. Sir Cecil Foley, 1864–1928, vol. II
Lambert, Ven. Charles Edmund, 1872–1954, vol. V
Lambert, Charles Ernest, 1900–1974, vol. VII
Lambert, Ven. Charles Henry, 1894–1983, vol. VIII
Lambert, Engr. Rear-Adm. Charles William, 1891–1961, vol. VI
Lambert, Constant, 1905–1951, vol. V
Lambert, Rear-Adm. Sir David Sidney, 1885–1966, vol. VI
Lambert, Brig.-Gen. Edward Parry, 1865–1932, vol. III
Lambert, Sir Edward Thomas, 1901–1994, vol. IX
Lambert, Eric Thomas Drummond, 1909–1996, vol. X
Lambert, Ernest, 1874–1951, vol. V
Lambert, Dame Florence Barrie, 1871–1957, vol. V
Lambert, Francis Henry, 1867–1929, vol. III
Lambert, Francis L., 1838–1925, vol. II
Lambert, Frank, 1884–1973, vol. VII
Lambert, Rev. Frederick Fox, *died* 1920, vol. II
Lambert, Sir George Bancroft, 1873–1945, vol. IV
Lambert, Sir George Thomas, 1837–1918, vol. II
Lambert, George Washington, 1873–1930, vol. III

Lambert, Sir Greville Foley, 9th Bt, 1900–1988, vol. VIII
Lambert, Col Guy Lenox B.; *see* Bence-Lambert.
Lambert, Guy William, 1889–1983, vol. VIII
Lambert, Maj.-Gen. Harold Roger, 1896–1980, vol. VII
Lambert, Sir Henry Charles Miller, 1868–1935, vol. III
Lambert, Jack Walter, 1917–1986, vol. VIII
Lambert, Vet.-Col James Drummond, 1835–1905, vol. I
Lambert, Sir John, 1838–1916, vol. II
Lambert, Ven. Joseph Malet, 1853–1931, vol. III
Lambert, Hon. Margaret Barbara, 1906–1995, vol. IX
Lambert, Maurice, 1901–1964, vol. VI
Lambert, Olaf Francis, 1925–1993, vol. IX
Lambert, Richard Cornthwaite, *died* 1939, vol. III
Lambert, Richard Stanton, 1894–1981, vol. VIII
Lambert, Robert, 1908–1971, vol. VII
Lambert, Rear-Adm. Robert Cathcart Kemble, 1874–1950, vol. IV
Lambert, Surgeon Vice-Adm. Roger John William, 1928–1984, vol. VIII
Lambert, Royston James, 1932–1982, vol. VIII
Lambert, Thomas Howard, 1926–1997, vol. X
Lambert, Col Thomas Stanton, 1871–1921, vol. II
Lambert, Victor Albert George, 1897–1971, vol. VII
Lambert, Victor Francis, 1899–1981, vol. VIII
Lambert, Brig.-Gen. Walter John, 1876–1944, vol. IV
Lambert, Lt-Col Walter Miller, 1843–1924, vol. II
Lambert, Maj.-Gen. William, 1836–1907, vol. I
Lambert, Maj.-Gen. William Harold, 1905–1978, vol. VII
Lambert, Rev. William Henry, 1833–1924, vol. II
Lambie, Charles George, 1891–1961, vol. VI
Lambkin, Col Francis, 1858–1912, vol. I
Lamble, Ven. George Edwin, 1877–1939, vol. III
Lamboll, Alan Seymour, 1923–1994, vol. IX
Lambooy, Maj.-Gen. Albert Percy, 1899–1976, vol. VII
Lamborn, Edmund Arnold Greening, 1877–1950, vol. IV
Lamborn, Harry George, 1915–1982, vol. VIII
Lambotte, Paul, 1862–1939, vol. III
Lambourne, 1st Baron, 1847–1928, vol. II
Lambrick, Hugh Trevor, 1904–1982, vol. VIII
Lambton, Viscount; John Roderick Geoffrey Francis Edward Lambton, 1920–1941, vol. IV
Lambton, Lt-Gen. Arthur, 1836–1908, vol. I
Lambton, Arthur, 1869–1935, vol. III
Lambton, Brig.-Gen. Hon. Charles, 1857–1949, vol. IV
Lambton, Lt-Col Francis W., 1834–1921, vol. II
Lambton, Hon. George, 1860–1945, vol. IV
Lambton, Lt-Col George Charles, 1872–1927, vol. II
Lambton, Maj.-Gen. Hon. Sir William, 1863–1936, vol. III
Lamburn, Richmal Crompton, 1890–1969, vol. VI
Lambury, 1st Baron, 1896–1967, vol. VI
Lamert, Sidney Streatfield, 1875–1963, vol. VI
Lamerton, Leonard Frederick, 1915–1999, vol. X

Laming, Rev. Canon Frank Fairbairn, 1908–1989, vol. VIII
Laming, Major Henry Thornton, 1863–1934, vol. III
Laming, Richard Valentine, 1887–1959, vol. V
Lamington, 2nd Baron, 1860–1940, vol. III
Lamington, 3rd Baron, 1896–1951, vol. V
Lammie, Col George, 1891–1946, vol. IV
Lamonby, Isaac Wannop, 1886–1938, vol. III
Lamond, Frederic, 1868–1948, vol. IV
Lamond, Henry, 1869–1934, vol. III
Lamond, Sir William, 1887–1974, vol. VII
Lamont, Very Rev. Daniel, *died* 1950, vol. IV
Lamont, Daniel Scott, 1851–1905, vol. I
Lamont, Sir James, 1st Bt, 1828–1913, vol. I
Lamont, Lt-Col John Charles, 1864–1945, vol. IV
Lamont, Hon. John Henderson, 1865–1936, vol. III
Lamont, Brig.-Gen. John William Fraser, 1872–1956, vol. V
Lamont, Sir Norman, 2nd Bt, 1869–1949, vol. IV
Lamont, Thomas William, 1870–1948, vol. IV
Lamont, William Dawson, 1901–1982, vol. VIII
La Mothe, Frederick Malcolm, 1864–1947, vol. IV
Lamotte, Brig.-Gen. Frank Grimshaw Lagier, 1864–1938, vol. III
Lamotte, Major George Moorsom Lagier, 1869–1935, vol. III
Lampard, Martin Robert, 1926–2000, vol. X
Lampard-Vachell, Benjamin Garnet, 1892–1965, vol. VI
Lampe, Rev. Geoffrey William Hugo, 1912–1980, vol. VII
Lampen, Rev. Charles Dudley, 1859–1943, vol. IV
Lampen, Graham Dudley, 1899–1960, vol. V
Lampen, Rev. Canon Herbert Dudley, 1868–1941, vol. IV
Lampen, Lt-Gen. Lewis Charles, 1878–1946, vol. IV
Lampitt, Leslie Herbert, 1887–1957, vol. V
Lamplough, Augustus Osborne, 1877–1930, vol. III
Lamplough, Maj.-Gen. Charles Robert Wharram, 1896–1981, vol. VIII
Lamplugh, George William, 1859–1926, vol. II
Lamplugh, Rt Rev. Kenneth Edward Norman, 1901–1979, vol. VII
Lamplugh, Maj.-Gen. Stephen, 1900–1983, vol. VIII
Lampson, Sir Curtis George, 3rd Bt, 1890–1971, vol. VII
Lampson, Curtis Walter, 1875–1952, vol. V
Lampson, Sir George Curtis, 2nd Bt, 1833–1899, vol. I
Lampson, Rt Hon. Godfrey Lampson Tennyson L.; *see* Locker-Lampson.
Lampson, Jane L.; *see* Locker-Lampson.
Lampson, Comdr Oliver Stillingfleet L.; *see* Locker-Lampson.
Lamrock, Brig.-Gen. John, 1859–1935, vol. III
Lamsdorff, Count Wladimir, 1844–1907, vol. I
Lamy, Etienne Marie Victor, 1845–1919, vol. II
Lancashire, George Herbert, 1866–1945, vol. IV
Lancaster, Col Claude Granville, 1899–1977, vol. VII
Lancaster, Brig. Edmund Henry, 1881–1975, vol. VII
Lancaster, Dame Jean, 1909–1996, vol. X

Lancaster, Joan Cadogan; *see* Lancaster Lewis, J. C.
Lancaster, John Roy, 1871–1951, vol. V
Lancaster, Vice-Adm. Sir John Strike, 1903–1992, vol. IX
Lancaster, Joseph Torry, 1892–1966, vol. VI
Lancaster, Sir Osbert, 1908–1986, vol. VIII
Lancaster, Percy, 1878–1950, vol. IV
Lancaster, Sir Robert Fisher, 1885–1945, vol. IV
Lancaster, Sir William John, 1841–1929, vol. III
Lancaster, William Joseph Cosens, 1851–1922, vol. II
Lancaster-Jones, Ernest, 1891–1945, vol. IV
Lancaster Lewis, Joan Cadogan, 1918–1992, vol. IX
Lancaster-Ranking, Maj.-Gen. Robert Philip; *see* Ranking.
Lancastre, Countess of; (Adeline Louise Maria); *see* Cardigan and Lancastre.
Lance, Rev. Edwin Mildred, 1862–1935, vol. III
Lance, Lt-Gen. Sir Frederick, 1837–1913, vol. I
Lance, Rev. Preb. John Du Boulay, 1907–1991, vol. IX
Lancelot, Rev. John Bennett, 1864–1944, vol. IV
Lanchester, Elsa, 1902–1986, vol. VIII
Lanchester, Frank, 1870–1960, vol. V
Lanchester, Frederick William, 1868–1946, vol. IV
Lanchester, Henry Vaughan, 1863–1953, vol. V
Lanciani, Commendatore Rodolfo, 1846–1929, vol. III
Lanctot, Charles, 1863–1946, vol. IV
Land, Edwin Herbert, 1909–1991, vol. IX
Land, Frank William, 1911–1990, vol. VIII
Land, Roger Burton, 1940–1988, vol. VIII
Landa, Hon. Abram, 1902–1989, vol. IX (AI)
Landale, David, 1868–1935, vol. III
Landale, David Fortune, 1905–1970, vol. VI
Landale, Russell Talbot, 1911–1984, vol. VIII
Landau, Dorothea, (Mrs C. Da Fano), *died* 1941, vol. IV
Landau, Lev Davidovich, 1908–1968, vol. VI
Landau, Muriel Elsie, (Mrs Samuel Sacks), 1895–1972, vol. VII
Landau, Rom, 1899–1974, vol. VII
Lander, Cecil Howard, 1881–1949, vol. IV
Lander, Frank Patrick Lee, 1906–1981, vol. VIII
Lander, Rt Rev. Gerard Heath, 1861–1934, vol. III
Lander, Rt Rev. Richard Brook, *died* 1937, vol. III
Landey, Very Rev. Theophilus Patrick, *died* 1935, vol. III
Landis, James McCauley, 1899–1964, vol. VI
Landon, Alfred Mossman, 1887–1987, vol. VIII
Landon, Lt-Col Charles Richard Henry Palmer, 1879–1940, vol. III
Landon, Maj.-Gen. Sir Frederick William Bainbridge, 1860–1937, vol. III
Landon, Maj.-Gen. Herman James Shelley, 1859–1948, vol. IV
Landon, Col James William Bainbridge, 1890–1966, vol. VI
Landon, Gp Captain Joseph Herbert Arthur, *died* 1935, vol. III
Landon, Perceval, 1869–1927, vol. II
Landon, Philip Aislabie, 1888–1961, vol. VI
Landor, A. Henry Savage, *died* 1924, vol. II
Landouzy, Louis Joseph, *died* 1917, vol. II
Landowski, Paul, 1875–1961, vol. VI

Landry, Col Hon. Auguste Charles Philippe Robert, 1846–1919, vol. II
Landry, Hon. David V., 1866–1929, vol. III
Landry, Maj.-Gen. Joseph Phillippe, 1870–1926, vol. II
Landry, Hon. Sir Pierre Armand, 1846–1916, vol. II
Landsteiner, Karl, 1868–1943, vol. IV
Lane, Sir Allen Lane Williams, 1902–1970, vol. VI
Lane, Annie E.; *see* Lane, Mrs John.
Lane, Sir Arbuthnot; *see* Lane, Sir W. A.
Lane, Charles Macdonald, 1882–1956, vol. V
Lane, Maj.-Gen. Sir Charles Reginald Cambridge, 1890–1964, vol. VI
Lane, Maj.-Gen. Charles Stuart, 1831–1913, vol. I
Lane, Sir Charlton Adelbert Gustavus, 1890–1962, vol. VI
Lane, Col Clayton Turner, 1842–1920, vol. II
Lane, Sir David William Stennis Stuart, 1922–1998, vol. X
Lane, Edward Arthur, 1909–1963, vol. VI
Lane, Dame Elizabeth Kathleen, 1905–1988, vol. VIII
Lane, Very Rev. Ernald, 1836–1913, vol. I
Lane, Ernest Frederick Cambridge, 1882–1958, vol. V
Lane, Ernest Olaf, 1916–1976, vol. VII
Lane, Brig. Frank, 1888–1963, vol. VI
Lane, Frank Laurence, 1912–1993, vol. IX
Lane, Col George Howard M.; *see* Moore-Lane.
Lane, Harry George, 1881–1957, vol. V
Lane, Sir Harry Philip Parnell, 1870–1927, vol. II
Lane, Brig.-Gen. Henry Arthur, 1868–1930, vol. III
Lane, Rear-Adm. Henry Gerald Elliot, 1875–1946, vol. IV
Lane, H(enry) J(errold) Randall, 1898–1975, vol. VII
Lane, Henry Murray, 1833–1913, vol. I
Lane, Rev. Henry Tydd, 1846–1939, vol. III
Lane, Herbert Allardyce, 1883–1959, vol. V
Lane, Brig.-Gen. Herbert Edward Bruce, 1862–1950, vol. IV
Lane, Sir Hugh Percy, 1875–1915, vol. I
Lane, Brig. Hugh Robert Charles, 1885–1953, vol. V
Lane, James Ernest, *died* 1926, vol. II
Lane, Jane, (Mrs Andrew Dakers), *died* 1978, vol. VII
Lane, John, 1854–1925, vol. II
Lane, John, 1924–1992, vol. IX
Lane, Mrs John, (Annie E. Lane), *died* 1927, vol. II
Lane, John Henry Hervey Vincent, 1867–1917, vol. II
Lane, John Macdonald, 1840–1927, vol. II
Lane, Lupino, 1892–1959, vol. V
Lane, Col Maitland Moore-, 1841–1915, vol. I
Lane, Margaret, 1907–1994, vol. IX
Lane, Rhona Arbuthnot, *died* 1953, vol. V
Lane, Richard Ouseley Blake, 1842–1914, vol. I
Lane, Maj.-Gen. Sir Ronald Bertram, 1847–1937, vol. III
Lane, Ronald Epey, 1897–1995, vol. IX
Lane, Col Samuel Willington, 1860–1948, vol. IV
Lane, Rear-Adm. Walter Frederick Boyt, 1909–1988, vol. VIII

Lane, Sir (William) Arbuthnot, 1st Bt, 1856–1943, vol. IV
Lane, Sir William Arbuthnot, 2nd Bt, 1897–1972, vol. VII
Lane, Lt-Col William Byam, 1866–1945, vol. IV
Lane-Fox, Baroness (Life Peer); Felicity Lane-Fox, 1918–1988, vol. VIII
Lane-Fox, Col Francis Gordon Ward, 1899–1989, vol. VIII
Lane-Jackson, Nicholas, 1849–1937, vol. III
Lane-Notter, Col J.; see Notter.
Lane Poole, Charles Edward, 1885–1970, vol. VI (AII)
Lane Poole, Vice Adm. Sir Richard Hayden Owen, 1883–1971, vol. VII
Lane-Poole, Stanley, 1854–1931, vol. III
Lane-Roberts, Cedric Sydney, died 1959, vol. V
Lanesborough, 6th Earl of, 1839–1905, vol. I
Lanesborough, 7th Earl of, 1865–1929, vol. III
Lanesborough, 8th Earl of, 1868–1950, vol. IV
Lanesborough, 9th Earl of, 1918–1998, vol. X
Lang of Lambeth, 1st Baron, 1864–1945, vol. IV
Lang, Air Vice-Marshal Albert Frank, 1895–1977, vol. VII
Lang, Alexander, 1848–1930, vol. III
Lang, (Alexander) Matheson, died 1948, vol. IV
Lang, Andrew, 1844–1912, vol. I
Lang, Archibald Orr, 1880–1957, vol. V
Lang, Col Arthur Moffatt, 1832–1916, vol. II
Lang, Col Bertram John, 1878–1975, vol. VII
Lang, Charles Dowson, 1845–1930, vol. III
Lang, Charles Russell, 1862–1940, vol. III
Lang, David Marshall, 1924–1991, vol. IX
Lang, Col Elliott Brownlow, 1862–1955, vol. V
Lang, Hon. Sir Frederic William, 1852–1937, vol. III
Lang, Lt-Col Godfrey George, 1867–1923, vol. II
Lang, Rev. Gordon, 1893–1981, vol. VIII
Lang, Henry George, 1919–1997, vol. X
Lang, Sir John Gerald, 1896–1984, vol. VIII
Lang, Very Rev. John Marshall, 1834–1909, vol. I
Lang, John Russell, 1902–1993, vol. IX
Lang, Hon. John Thomas, 1876–1975, vol. VII
Lang, Rt Rev. Leslie Hamilton, 1889–1974, vol. VII
Lang, Lt-Col Lionel Edward, 1885–1956, vol. V
Lang, Very Rev. Marshall B., 1868–1954, vol. V
Lang, Matheson; see Lang, A. M.
Lang, Rt Rev. Norman Macleod, 1875–1956, vol. V
Lang, Patrick Keith, 1863–1961, vol. VI
Lang, Sir Peter Redford Scott, 1850–1926, vol. II
Lang, Robert Buntin, 1906–1970, vol. VI
Lang, Sir Robert Hamilton, 1836–1913, vol. I
Lang, William, 1852–1937, vol. III
Lang, Sir William Biggart, 1868–1942, vol. IV
Lang, William Dickson, 1878–1966, vol. VI
Lang, William Henry, died 1960, vol. V
Lang, William Lindsay Holmes, 1888–1928, vol. II
Lang, William Marshall F.; see Farquharson-Lang.
Lang, Col William Robert, died 1925, vol. II
Lang-Coath, Howell Lang, 1878–1949, vol. IV
Lang-Hyde, Lt-Col John Irvine, 1859–1940, vol. III
Langbridge, Rev. Frederick, 1849–1922, vol. II
Langbridge, Rosamond Grant, died 1964, vol. VI
Langdale, Henry Joseph, died 1923, vol. II
Langdale, Lt-Col Philip Joseph, died 1950, vol. IV

Langdon, Adolph Max, died 1949, vol. IV
Langdon, Rev. Alfred, died 1925, vol. II
Langdon, Alfred Gordon, 1915–1988, vol. VIII
Langdon, (Augustus) John, 1913–1992, vol. IX
Langdon, George, 1867–1957, vol. V
Langdon, Col Harry, 1855–1925, vol. II
Langdon, John; see Langdon, A. J.
Langdon, Michael, 1920–1991, vol. IX
Langdon, Stephen Herbert, 1876–1937, vol. III
Langdon, Hon. Thomas, 1832–1914, vol. I
Langdon, Air Cdre William Frederick, 1898–1976, vol. VII
Langdon-Brown, Sir Walter, 1870–1946, vol. IV
Langdon-Davies, Bernard Noël, 1876–1952, vol. V
Langdon-Davies, John, 1897–1971, vol. VII
Langdon-Down, Barbara; see Littlewood Barbara, (Lady Littlewood).
Lange, Christian Lous, 1869–1938, vol. III
Langelier, Hon. Charles, 1852–1920, vol. II
Langelier, Sir François Charles Stanislas, 1838–1915, vol. I
Langerman, Sir Jan Willem Stuckeris, 1853–1931, vol. III
Langevin, Hon. Sir Hector Louis, 1826–1906, vol. I
Langevin, Most Rev. Louis Philip Adelard, 1855–1915, vol. I
Langford, 4th Baron, 1848–1919, vol. II
Langford, 5th Baron, 1894–1922, vol. II
Langford, 6th Baron, 1849–1931, vol. III
Langford, 7th Baron, 1885–1952, vol. V
Langford, 8th Baron, 1870–1953, vol. V
Langford, Caroline; see Hatchard, C.
Langford, John Alfred, 1823–1903, vol. I
Langford, Surgeon Martyn Henry, died 1918, vol. II
Langford-Holt, Sir John Anthony, 1916–1993, vol. IX
Langford-James, Reginald Hugh Lloyd, 1876–1961, vol. VI
Langford-Sainsbury, Air Vice-Marshal Thomas Audley, 1897–1972, vol. VII
Langham, Sir Charles Arthur; see Langham, Sir H. C. A.
Langham, Sir Cyril Leigh Macrae, 1885–1950, vol. IV
Langham, Col Frederick George, 1863–1946, vol. IV
Langham, Sir (Herbert) Charles Arthur, 13th Bt, 1870–1951, vol. V
Langham, Sir Herbert Hay, 12th Bt, 1840–1909, vol. I
Langham, Sir John Charles Patrick, 14th Bt, 1894–1972, vol. VII
Langhorne, Maj.-Gen. Algernon Philip Yorke, 1882–1945, vol. IV
Langhorne, Brig.-Gen. Harold Stephen, 1866–1932, vol. III
Langhorne, Brig. James Archibald Dunboyne, 1879–1950, vol. IV
Langker, Sir Erik, 1899–1982, vol. VIII
Langler, Sir Alfred, 1865–1928, vol. II
Langley, Alexander, 1871–1952, vol. V
Langley, Comdr Arthur Sydney, 1881–1964, vol. VI
Langley, Batty, 1834–1914, vol. I
Langley, Beatrice, (Mrs Basil Tozer), 1872–1958, vol. V

Larking, Lt-Col Sir (Charles) Gordon, 1893–1978, vol. VII
Larking, Col Cuthbert, 1842–1910, vol. I
Larking, Captain Dennis Augustus Hugo, 1876–1970, vol. VI
Larking, Lt-Col Sir Gordon; see Larking, Lt-Col Sir C. G.
Larking, Sir John, 1857–1931, vol. III
Larking, Lt-Col Reginald Nesbitt Wingfield, 1868–1943, vol. IV
Larkins, Laurence Brouncker Southey, 1891–1953, vol. V
Larkworthy, Falconer, 1833–1928, vol. II
Larminie, Margaret Rivers, (Mrs M. R. Tragett), 1885–1964, vol. VI
Larmor, Alexander, died 1936, vol. III
Larmor, Sir Graham; see Larmor, Sir J. G.
Larmor, Sir (John) Graham, 1897–1968, vol. VI
Larmor, Sir Joseph, 1857–1942, vol. IV
Larmour, Sir Edward Noel, (Sir Nick), 1916–1999, vol. X
Larmour, Sir Nick; see Larmour, Sir E. N.
Larnach, James Walker, 1849–1919, vol. II
Larnder, Col Eugene William, 1864–1941, vol. IV
La Rochelle, Michael Gautron, 1868–1934, vol. III
La Rocque, Rt Rev. Paul, 1846–1926, vol. II
Larpent, Sir George Albert de Hochepied, 3rd Bt, 1846–1899, vol. I
Larpent, Maj.-Gen. Lionel Henry Planta de H.; see de Hochepied Larpent.
Larsen, Cyril Anthony, 1919–1993, vol. IX
Larsen, Roy Edward, 1899–1979, vol. VII
Larson, Frederick H., 1913–1994, vol. X (AI)
Lartigue, Alexander Raphael C.; see Cools-Lartigue.
Lartigue, Sir Louis C.; see Cools-Lartigue.
Larue, Rt Rev. Stephen, 1865–1935, vol. III
Larymore, Major Henry Douglas, 1867–1946, vol. IV
Lasbrey, Rt Rev. Bertram, died 1976, vol. VII
Lascelles, Rt Hon. Sir Alan Frederick, 1887–1981, vol. VIII
Lascelles, Sir Alfred George, 1857–1952, vol. V
Lascelles, Daniel Richard, 1908–1985, vol. VIII
Lascelles, Sir Daniel William, 1902–1967, vol. VI
Lascelles, Bt Major Hon. Edward Cecil, 1887–1935, vol. III
Lascelles, Edward Charles Ponsonby, 1884–1956, vol. V
Lascelles, Lt-Col Edward ffrancis Ward, died 1959, vol. V
Lascelles, Sir Francis William, 1890–1979, vol. VII
Lascelles, Frank, died 1934, vol. III
Lascelles, Rt Hon. Sir Frank Cavendish, 1841–1920, vol. II
Lascelles, Hon. Frederick Canning, 1848–1928, vol. II
Lascelles, Hon. George Edwin, 1826–1911, vol. I
Lascelles, Lt-Col George Reginald, 1864–1939, vol. III
Lascelles, Hon. Gerald William, 1849–1928, vol. II
Lascelles, Maj.-Gen. Henry Anthony, 1912–2000, vol. X
Lascelles, Rev. Hon. James Walter, 1831–1901, vol. I
Lascelles, Mary Madge, 1900–1995, vol. IX

Lascelles, Rev. Maurice G., 1860–1940, vol. III
Lascelles, Captain Walter Charles, 1867–1911, vol. I
Lash, Zebulun Aiton, 1846–1920, vol. II
Lash, Rt Rev. William Quinlan, 1905–1986, vol. VIII
Lashmore, Engr Rear-Adm. Harry, 1868–1945, vol. IV
Lasker, Emanuel, 1868–1941, vol. IV
Laskey, Sir Denis Seward, 1916–1987, vol. VIII
Laskey, Francis Seward, 1886–1972, vol. VII
Laski, Harold J., 1893–1950, vol. IV
Laski, Marghanita, (Mrs J. E. Howard), 1915–1988, vol. VIII
Laski, Nathan, 1863–1941, vol. IV
Laski, Neville Jonas, 1890–1969, vol. VI
Laskin, Rt Hon. Bora, 1912–1984, vol. VIII
Lasky, Jesse L., 1880–1958, vol. V
Laslett, Henry James, 1844–1914, vol. I
Lasok, Dominik, 1921–2000, vol. X
Lassalle, Jean Louis, 1847–1909, vol. I
Lassetter, Brig.-Gen. Harry Beauchamp, 1860–1926, vol. II
Last, Hugh Macilwain, died 1957, vol. V
Last, Raymond Jack, 1903–1993, vol. IX
Last, William Isaac, 1857–1911, vol. I
Laszlo de Lombos, Philip Alexius, 1869–1937, vol. III
Latchford, Francis Robert, 1854–1938, vol. III
Latey, John, 1842–1902, vol. I
Latey, Rt Hon. Sir John Brinsmead, 1914–1999, vol. X
Latey, William, 1885–1976, vol. VII
Latham, 1st Baron, 1888–1970, vol. VI
Latham, Albert George, 1864–1940, vol. III
Latham, Alexander Mere, 1862–1934, vol. III
Latham, Charles, 1868–1917, vol. II
Latham, Hon. Sir Charles George, 1882–1968, vol. VI
Latham, Edward Bryan, 1895–1980, vol. VII
Latham, Brig. Francis, 1883–1958, vol. V
Latham, Gustavus Henry, 1888–1975, vol. VII
Latham, Rev. Henry, 1821–1902, vol. I
Latham, Sir (Herbert) Paul, 2nd Bt, 1905–1955, vol. V
Latham, Ven. James King, 1847–1932, vol. III
Latham, Rt Hon. Sir John Greig, 1877–1964, vol. VI
Latham, Sir Joseph, 1905–1988, vol. VIII
Latham, Sir Paul; see Latham, Sir H. P.
Latham, Peter Wallwork, 1832–1923, vol. II
Latham, Robert Clifford, 1912–1995, vol. IX
Latham, Russell, 1896–1964, vol. VI
Latham, Sir Thomas Paul, 1st Bt, 1855–1931, vol. III
Latham, William, died 1915, vol. I
Lathan, George, 1875–1942, vol. IV
La Thangue, H. H., died 1929, vol. III
Lathbury, Daniel Conner, 1831–1922, vol. II
Lathbury, Gen. Sir Gerald William, 1906–1978, vol. VII
Lathlain, Sir William Francis, 1862–1936, vol. III
Lathom, 1st Earl of, 1837–1898, vol. I
Lathom, 2nd Earl of, 1864–1910, vol. I
Lathom, 3rd Earl of, 1895–1930, vol. III
Lathrop, Lorin Andrews, died 1929, vol. III

Lathrop, Mother Mary Alphonsa; *see* Lathrop, R. H.
Lathrop, Rose Hawthorne, (Mother Mary Alphonsa Lathrop), 1851–1926, vol. II, vol. III
Latifi, Almá, 1879–1959, vol. V
Latimer, Sir Courtenay, 1880–1944, vol. IV
Latimer, Frederick William, 1845–1910, vol. I
Latimer, Rev. William Thomas, *died* 1919, vol. II
Latner, Albert Louis, 1912–1992, vol. IX
Laton, Col Stephen F.; *see* Frewen-Laton.
La Touche, Sir James John Digges, 1844–1921, vol. II
Latouche, John; *see* Crawfurd, Oswald.
La Touche, Robert Percy O'Connor, 1846–1921, vol. II
Latourette, Kenneth Scott, 1884–1968, vol. VI
Latrobe, William Sanderson, 1870–1943, vol. IV
La Trobe-Bateman, Rev. William Fairbairn; *see* Bateman.
Latta, Sir Andrew Gibson, *died* 1953, vol. V
Latta, Sir John, 1st Bt, 1867–1946, vol. IV
Latta, Robert, 1865–1932, vol. III
Latta, Hon. Samuel John, 1866–1946, vol. IV
Latter, Algernon, 1870–1944, vol. IV
Latter, Arthur Malcolm, 1875–1961, vol. VI
Latter, Maj.-Gen. John Cecil, 1896–1972, vol. VII
Latter, Leslie William, 1921–1998, vol. X
Latter, Oswald Hawkins, 1864–1948, vol. IV
Lattey, Rev. Cuthbert Charles, 1877–1954, vol. V
Lattimer, Robert Binney, 1863–1929, vol. III
Lattimore, Owen, 1900–1989, vol. VIII
Lattin, Francis Joseph, 1905–1986, vol. VIII
Latto, Douglas, 1913–1999, vol. X
Latulipe, Rt Rev. E. A., 1859–1922, vol. II
Latymer, 5th Baron, 1852–1923, vol. II
Latymer, 6th Baron, 1876–1949, vol. IV
Latymer, 7th Baron, 1901–1987, vol. VIII
Laucke, Hon. Sir Condor Louis, 1914–1993, vol. IX
Laudenbach, Pierre; *see* Fresnay, P.
Lauder, Charles James, *died* 1920, vol. II
Lauder, Sir George Andrew Dick-, 12th Bt, 1917–1981, vol. VIII
Lauder, Sir George William Dalrymple Dick-, 10th Bt, 1852–1936, vol. III
Lauder, Sir Harry MacLennan, 1870–1950, vol. IV
Lauder, Major James La Fayette, 1889–1934, vol. III
Lauder, Lt-Col Sir John North Dalrymple Dick-, 11th Bt, 1883–1958, vol. V
Lauder, Sir Thomas North Dick-, 9th Bt, 1846–1919, vol. II
Lauderdale, 13th Earl of, 1840–1924, vol. II
Lauderdale, 14th Earl of, 1868–1931, vol. III
Lauderdale, 15th Earl of, 1891–1953, vol. V
Lauderdale, 16th Earl of, 1904–1968, vol. VI
Laughlin, Irwin, 1871–1941, vol. IV
Laughton, Col Arthur Frederick, 1840–1915, vol. I
Laughton, Charles, 1899–1962, vol. VI
Laughton, Eric, 1911–1988, vol. VIII
Laughton, Lt-Gen. George Arnold, 1830–1912, vol. I
Laughton, George Christian, 1887–1952, vol. V
Laughton, Very Rev. John George, 1891–1965, vol. VI
Laughton, Sir John Knox, 1830–1915, vol. I

Laughton, Major Joseph Vinters, 1862–1948, vol. IV
Laughton-Scott, Edward Hey, 1926–1978, vol. VII
Laurence, Frederick Andrew, 1843–1912, vol. I
Laurence, Adm. Sir Noel Frank, *died* 1970, vol. VI
Laurence, Sir Perceval Maitland, 1854–1930, vol. III
Laurence, Reginald Vere, 1876–1934, vol. III
Laurie, Rev. Albert Ernest, 1866–1937, vol. III
Laurie, Arthur Pillans, 1861–1949, vol. IV
Laurie, Col Sir Claude Villiers Emilius, 4th Bt (*cr* 1834), 1855–1930, vol. III
Laurie, Rev. Sir Emilius; *see* Laurie, Rev. Sir J. R. L. E.
Laurie, Lt-Col George Halliburton Foster Peel V.; *see* Vere-Laurie.
Laurie, James Stuart, 1831–1904, vol. I
Laurie, John B., 1865–1934, vol. III
Laurie, Lt-Col Sir John Dawson, 1st Bt (*cr* 1942), 1872–1954, vol. V
Laurie, Maj.-Gen. Sir John Emilius, 6th Bt, 1892–1983, vol. VIII
Laurie, Rev. Sir (John Robert Laurie) Emilius, 3rd Bt (*cr* 1834), 1823–1917, vol. II
Laurie, Lt-Gen. John Wimburn, 1835–1912, vol. I
Laurie, Malcolm Vyvyan, 1901–1973, vol. VII
Laurie, Brig. Sir Percy Robert, 1880–1962, vol. VI
Laurie, Ranald Macdonald, 1869–1927, vol. II
Laurie, Robert Douglas, 1874–1953, vol. V
Laurie, Col Robert Peter, 1835–1905, vol. I
Laurie, Maj.-Gen. Rufus Henry, 1892–1961, vol. VI
Laurie, Simon Somerville, 1829–1909, vol. I
Laurie, Col Vernon Stewart, 1896–1981, vol. VIII
Laurie, Sir Wilfrid Emilius, 5th Bt (*cr* 1834), 1859–1936, vol. III
Laurier, Rt Hon. Sir Wilfrid, 1841–1919, vol. II
Laurvig, Count Preben Ferdinand A.; *see* Ahlefeldt-Laurvig.
Lauterpacht, Sir Hersch, 1897–1960, vol. V
Lauwerys, Joseph Albert, 1902–1981, vol. VIII
Laval, Pierre, 1883–1945, vol. IV
Lavarack, Lt-Gen. Sir John Dudley, 1885–1957, vol. V
Lavedan, Henri, 1859–1940, vol. III
Lavelle, Rev. Canon Alexander Bannerman, 1899–1964, vol. VI
Laver, James, 1899–1975, vol. VII
Laver, William Adolphus, 1866–1940, vol. III (A), vol. IV
Laver, William Scott, 1909–1988, vol. VIII
Laverack, Frederick Joseph, 1871–1928, vol. II
Lavergne, Joseph, 1847–1922, vol. II
Lavergne, Hon. Louis, 1845–1931, vol. III
Lavers, Sydney Charles Robert, 1898–1972, vol. VII
Lavery, Cecil, 1894–1967, vol. VI
Lavery, Sir John, 1856–1941, vol. IV
Lavin, Mary, (Mrs M. MacDonald Scott), 1912–1996, vol. X
Lavington, Cyril Michael, 1912–1990, vol. VIII
Lavington, Michael; *see* Lavington, C. M.
Lavington Evans, Leonard Glyde; *see* Evans.
Lavis, Rt Rev. Sidney Warren, *died* 1965, vol. VI
Lavisse, Ernest, 1842–1922, vol. II

Lavoipierre, Jacques Joseph Maurice, 1909–1987, vol. VIII
Lavrin, Janko John, 1887–1986, vol. VIII
Law, Albert, 1872–1956, vol. V
Law, Lt-Col Alfred, 1871–1928, vol. II
Law, Sir Alfred Joseph, 1860–1939, vol. III
Law, Alfred Noel, *born* 1895, vol. VIII
Law, Sir Algernon, 1856–1943, vol. IV
Law, Anastasia, (Mrs Nigel Law), 1886–1976, vol. VII
Law, Rt Hon. Andrew Bonar, 1858–1923, vol. II
Law, Sir Archibald Fitzgerald, 1853–1921, vol. II
Law, Arthur, 1876–1933, vol. III
Law, Sir Charles Ewan, 1884–1974, vol. VII
Law, Edward, 1853–1930, vol. III
Law, Major Sir Edward FitzGerald, 1846–1908, vol. I
Law, Sir Eric John Ewan, 1913–1988, vol. VIII
Law, Ernest, 1854–1930, vol. III
Law, Francis Towry Adeane, 1835–1901, vol. I
Law, Frank William, 1898–1987, vol. VIII
Law, Graham Couper, 1923–1996, vol. X
Law, Harry Davis, 1930–1990, vol. VIII
Law, Henry Duncan Graves, 1883–1964, vol. VI
Law, Herbert Henry, 1862–1943, vol. IV
Law, Hugh Alexander, *died* 1943, vol. IV
Law, Col Hugh Francis d'Assisi Stuart, 1897–1984, vol. VIII
Law, Margaret Dorothy, *died* 1980, vol. VII
Law, Mary, 1889–1919, vol. II
Law, Ralph Hamilton, 1915–1967, vol. VI
Law, Raja Reshee Case, 1852–1935, vol. III
Law, Rev. Robert, 1860–1919, vol. II
Law, Brig.-Gen. Robert Theophilus Hewitt, 1855–1949, vol. IV
Law, Samuel Horace, 1873–1940, vol. III (A), vol. IV
Law, Sir Sydney, 1861–1949, vol. IV
Law, Rev. Thomas, 1854–1910, vol. I
Law, Thomas Pakenham, 1834–1905, vol. I
Law, Maj.-Gen. Victor Edward, 1842–1910, vol. I
Law, William Arthur, 1844–1913, vol. I
Law, Mrs William Arthur; *see* Holland, Fanny.
Law, Rev. William Smalley, 1865–1937, vol. III
Law-Smith, Sir (Richard) Robert, 1914–1992, vol. IX
Law-Smith, Sir Robert; *see* Law-Smith, Sir Richard R.
Lawder, Rear-Adm. Keith Macleod, 1893–1986, vol. VIII
Lawes, Edward Thornton Hill, 1869–1921, vol. II
Lawes, Sir John Bennet, 1st Bt, 1814–1899, vol. I
Lawes, Sir John Claud Bennet, 4th Bt, 1898–1979, vol. VII
Lawes Wittewronge, Sir Charles Bennet, 2nd Bt, 1843–1911, vol. I
Lawes-Wittewronge, Sir John Bennet, 3rd Bt, 1872–1931, vol. III
Lawford, John Bowring, 1858–1934, vol. III
Lawford, Lt-Gen. Sir Sydney Turing Barlow, 1865–1953, vol. V
Lawford, Captain (S) Vincent Adrian, 1871–1959, vol. V
Lawler, Wallace Leslie, 1912–1972, vol. VII
Lawless, Col Hon. Edward, 1841–1921, vol. II

Lawless, Hon. Emily, *died* 1913, vol. I
Lawless, Henry Hamilton, *died* 1913, vol. I
Lawless, Surg. Lt-Col Sir Warren Roland Crooke-, 1863–1931, vol. III
Lawley, Hon. Alethea Jane Wiel, *died* 1929, vol. III
Lawley, Edgar Ernest, *died* 1977, vol. VII
Lawlor, Very Rev. Hugh Jackson, 1860–1938, vol. III
Lawlor, John, 1906–1975, vol. VII
Lawlor, John James, 1918–1999, vol. X
Lawn, James Gunson, 1868–1952, vol. V
Lawrance, Major Sir Arthur Salisbury, 1880–1965, vol. VI
Lawrance, Rt Hon. Sir John Compton, 1832–1912, vol. I
Lawrance, Very Rev. Walter John, 1840–1914, vol. I
Lawrance, William Thomas, *died* 1932, vol. III
Lawrence, 2nd Baron, 1846–1913, vol. I
Lawrence, 3rd Baron, 1878–1947, vol. IV
Lawrence, 4th Baron, 1908–1968, vol. VI
Lawrence of Kingsgate, 1st Baron, 1855–1927, vol. II
Lawrence, Albert, 1893–1961, vol. VI
Lawrence, Alexander John, 1837–1905, vol. I
Lawrence, Sir Alexander Waldemar, 4th Bt (*cr* 1858), 1874–1939, vol. III
Lawrence, Hon. (Alfred) Clive, 1876–1926, vol. II
Lawrence, Alfred Kingsley, *died* 1975, vol. VII
Lawrence, (Arabella) Susan, 1871–1947, vol. IV
Lawrence, Arnold Walter, 1900–1991, vol. IX
Lawrence, Rev. Arthur Evelyn B.; *see* Barnes-Lawrence.
Lawrence, Aubrey Trevor, 1875–1930, vol. III
Lawrence, Bernard Edwin, 1901–1988, vol. VIII
Lawrence, Lt-Col Bryan Turner Tom, 1873–1949, vol. IV
Lawrence, C. E., 1870–1940, vol. III
Lawrence, Ven. Charles D'Aguilar, 1847–1935, vol. III
Lawrence, Hon. Clive; *see* Lawrence, Hon. A. C.
Lawrence, David Herbert, 1885–1930, vol. III
Lawrence, Sir Edward, 1825–1909, vol. I
Lawrence, Sir Edwin D.; *see* Durning-Lawrence.
Lawrence, Ernest Orlando, 1901–1958, vol. V
Lawrence, Evelyn M., (Mrs Nathan Isaacs), 1892–1987, vol. VIII
Lawrence, Sir Frederick, 1889–1981, vol. VIII
Lawrence, Sir (Frederick) Geoffrey, 1902–1967, vol. VI
Lawrence, Major Freeling Ross, 1872–1914, vol. I
Lawrence, Sir Geoffrey; *see* Lawrence, Sir F. G.
Lawrence, Geoffrey Charles, 1915–1994, vol. IX
Lawrence, Lt-Col George Henniker, 1868–1932, vol. III
Lawrence, Gertrude, (Mrs Richard Stoddard Aldrich), 1898–1952, vol. V
Lawrence, Sir Guy Kempton, 1914–2000, vol. X
Lawrence, Sir Henry Eustace Waldemar, 5th Bt (*cr* 1858), 1905–1967, vol. VI
Lawrence, Sir Henry Hayes, 2nd Bt (*cr* 1858), 1864–1898, vol. I
Lawrence, Lt-Col Henry Rundle, 1878–1949, vol. IV
Lawrence, Sir Henry Staveley, 1870–1949, vol. IV

Lawrence, Sir Henry Waldemar, 3rd Bt (*cr* 1858), 1845–1908, vol. I
Lawrence, Captain Henry Walter Neville, 1891–1959, vol. V
Lawrence, Gen. Hon. Sir Herbert Alexander, 1861–1943, vol. IV
Lawrence, Herbert Cecil B.; *see* Barnes-Lawrence.
Lawrence, Col Hugh Duncan, 1862–1946, vol. IV
Lawrence, Sir James Clarke, 1st Bt (*cr* 1869), 1820–1897, vol. I
Lawrence, Sir James John Trevor, 2nd Bt (*cr* 1867), 1831–1913, vol. I
Lawrence, Sir (James) Taylor, 1888–1944, vol. IV
Lawrence, Sir John Waldemar, 6th Bt (*cr* 1858), 1907–1999, vol. X
Lawrence, Sir Joseph, 1st Bt (*cr* 1918), 1848–1919, vol. II
Lawrence, Margery, (Mrs Arthur Towle), *died* 1969, vol. VI
Lawrence, Marjorie Florence, *died* 1979, vol. VII
Lawrence, Hon. Dame Maude Agnes, 1864–1933, vol. III
Lawrence, Rt Hon. Sir Paul Ogden, 1861–1952, vol. V
Lawrence, Penelope, *died* 1932, vol. III
Lawrence, Lt-Col Sir (Percy) Roland (Bradford), 2nd Bt (*cr* 1906), 1886–1950, vol. IV
Lawrence, Peter Frederick, 1937–1976, vol. VII
Lawrence, Lt-Col Richard Travers, 1890–1973, vol. VII
Lawrence, Robert Daniel, 1892–1968, vol. VI
Lawrence, Sir Robert Leslie Edward, 1915–1984, vol. VIII
Lawrence, Roger Bernard, *died* 1925, vol. II
Lawrence, Lt-Col Sir Roland; *see* Lawrence, Lt-Col Sir P. R. B.
Lawrence, Sir Russell; *see* Lawrence, Sir W. R.
Lawrence, Samuel Chave, 1894–1980, vol. VII
Lawrence, Susan; *see* Lawrence, A. S.
Lawrence, Sydney, 1905–1976, vol. VII
Lawrence, Sydney Boyle, *died* 1951, vol. V
Lawrence, Sir Taylor; *see* Lawrence, Sir J. T.
Lawrence, Air Vice-Marshal Thomas Albert, 1895–1992, vol. IX
Lawrence, Thomas Edward; *see* Shaw, T. E.
Lawrence, Rev. Thomas Joseph, 1849–1919, vol. II
Lawrence, Vernon, 1899–1971, vol. VII
Lawrence, Sir Walter, 1872–1939, vol. III
Lawrence, Sir Walter Roper, 1st Bt (*cr* 1906), 1857–1940, vol. III
Lawrence, Sir William, 1818–1897, vol. I
Lawrence, Rt Rev. William, 1850–1941, vol. IV
Lawrence, Sir William, 4th Bt, 1913–1986, vol. VIII
Lawrence, Maj.-Gen. William Alexander, 1843–1924, vol. II
Lawrence, William Frederic, 1844–1935, vol. III
Lawrence, William John, 1862–1940, vol. III
Lawrence, Sir William Matthew Trevor, 3rd Bt (*cr* 1867), 1870–1934, vol. III
Lawrence, William Robert, 1942–1996, vol. X
Lawrence, Sir (William) Russell, 1903–1976, vol. VII
Lawrence-Archer, Col James Henry, 1871–1948, vol. IV

Lawrence-Wilson, Harry Lawrence, 1920–1986, vol. VIII
Lawrie, Allan James, 1873–1926, vol. II
Lawrie, Sir Archibald Campbell, 1837–1914, vol. I
Lawrie, Maj.-Gen. Charles Edward, 1864–1953, vol. V
Lawrie, Captain Edward McConnell Wyndham, 1882–1933, vol. III
Lawrie, James Haldane, 1907–1979, vol. VII
Lawrie, John, 1861–1935, vol. III
Laws, Bernard Courtney, *died* 1947, vol. IV
Laws, Courtney Alexander, 1934–1996, vol. X
Laws, Gp Captain Frederick Charles Victor, 1887–1975, vol. VII
Laws, Rev. George Edward, *died* 1923, vol. II
Laws, Lt-Col Henry William, 1876–1954, vol. V
Laws, John William, 1921–1999, vol. X
Laws, Robert, 1851–1934, vol. III
Laws, Samuel Charles, 1879–1963, vol. VI
Lawson, 1st Baron, 1881–1965, vol. VI
Lawson, Abercrombie Anstruther, *died* 1927, vol. II
Lawson, Alexander, 1852–1921, vol. II
Lawson, Brig.-Gen. Algernon, 1869–1929, vol. III
Lawson, Andrew Sherlock, 1855–1914, vol. I
Lawson, Sir Arnold, 1867–1947, vol. IV
Lawson, Arthur Ernest, 1863–1933, vol. III
Lawson, Sir Arthur Tredgold, 1st Bt (*cr* 1900), 1844–1915, vol. I
Lawson, Charles, 1916–1989, vol. VIII
Lawson, Sir Charles Allen, 1838–1915, vol. I
Lawson, Sir Digby, 2nd Bt (*cr* 1900), 1880–1959, vol. V
Lawson, Frederick Henry, 1897–1983, vol. VIII
Lawson, Rev. Frederick Pike, *died* 1920, vol. II
Lawson, Major Frederick Washington, 1869–1924, vol. II
Lawson, Sir George, 1838–1898, vol. I
Lawson, George McArthur, 1906–1978, vol. VII
Lawson, H. S., 1876–1918, vol. II
Lawson, Lt-Col Harold Andrew Balvaird, 1899–1985, vol. VIII
Lawson, Sir Harry Sutherland Wightman, 1875–1952, vol. V
Lawson, Sir Henry Brailsford, 1898–1978, vol. VII
Lawson, Henry Hertzberg, 1867–1922, vol. II
Lawson, Sir Henry Joseph, 3rd Bt (*cr* 1841), 1877–1947, vol. IV
Lawson, Lt-Gen. Sir Henry Merrick, 1859–1933, vol. III
Lawson, Major Sir Hilton, 4th Bt (*cr* 1831), 1895–1959, vol. V
Lawson, Hugh McDowall, 1912–1997, vol. X
Lawson, Air Vice-Marshal Ian Douglas Napier, 1917–1998, vol. X
Lawson, Hon. James Earl, 1891–1950, vol. IV
Lawson, Sir John, 2nd Bt (*cr* 1841), 1829–1910, vol. I
Lawson, John, 1893–1977, vol. VII
Lawson, Sir John Grant, 1st Bt (*cr* 1905), 1856–1919, vol. II
Lawson, Hon. Sir Neil, 1908–1996, vol. X
Lawson, Col Sir Peter Grant, 2nd Bt (*cr* 1905), 1903–1973, vol. VII
Lawson, Sir Ralph Henry, 4th Bt (*cr* 1841), 1905–1975, vol. VII

Lawson, Rear-Adm. Robert Neale, 1873–1945, vol. IV
Lawson, Thomas William, 1857–1925, vol. II
Lawson, Victor F., 1850–1925, vol. II
Lawson, Sir Wilfrid, 2nd Bt (cr 1831), 1829–1906, vol. I
Lawson, Sir Wilfrid, 3rd Bt (cr 1831), 1862–1937, vol. III
Lawson, Sir William Halford, 1899–1971, vol. VII
Lawson, Sir William Howard, 5th Bt, 1907–1990, vol. VIII
Lawson, William Norton, 1830–1911, vol. I
Lawson, Rev. William Thomas, died 1937, vol. III
Lawson, Dick Clare, 1913–1987, vol. VIII
Lawson-Tancred, Major Sir Thomas Selby, 9th Bt, 1870–1945, vol. IV
Lawther, Barry Charles Alfred, 1888–1974, vol. VII
Lawther, Sir William, 1889–1976, vol. VII
Lawton, Alastair; see Lawton, J. A.
Lawton, Frank, 1904–1969, vol. VI
Lawton, Frank Dickinson, 1915–1983, vol. VIII
Lawton, Sir Frank Ewart, 1915–2000, vol. X
Lawton, Frank Warburton, 1881–1966, vol. VI
Lawton, (John) Alistair, 1929–2000, vol. X
Lawton, Ven. John Arthur, 1913–1995, vol. IX
Lawton, Kenneth Keith Fullerton, 1924–1985, vol. VIII
Lawton, Louis David, 1936–1993, vol. IX
Lawton, Philip Charles Fenner, 1912–1993, vol. IX
Laxness, Halldór Kiljan, 1902–1998, vol. X
Lay, Arthur Hyde, 1865–1934, vol. III
Lay, Brig. William Oswald, 1892–1952, vol. V
Layard, Austen Havelock, 1895–1956, vol. V
Layard, Sir Charles Peter, 1849–1915, vol. I
Layard, Edgar Leopold, 1824–1900, vol. I
Layard, George Somes, 1857–1925, vol. II
Layard, Raymond de Burgh Money, 1859–1941, vol. IV
Laybourne, Rear-Adm. Alan Watson, 1898–1977, vol. VII
Laybourne-Smith, Louis, 1880–1965, vol. VI
Laycock, Brig.-Gen. Sir Joseph Frederick, 1867–1952, vol. V
Laycock, Sir Leslie Ernest, 1903–1981, vol. VIII
Laycock, Maj.-Gen. Sir Robert Edward, 1907–1968, vol. VI
Layden, Sir John, 1926–1996, vol. X
Laye, Evelyn, 1900–1996, vol. X
Laye, Maj.-Gen. Joseph Henry, 1849–1938, vol. III
Layfield, Sir Frank Henry Burland Willoughby, 1921–2000, vol. X
Layh, Lt-Col Herbert Thomas Christoph, 1885–1964, vol. VI
Layland-Barratt, Sir Francis; see Barratt.
Layland-Barratt, Captain Sir Francis Henry Godolphin, 2nd Bt, 1896–1968, vol. VI
Layman, Captain Herbert Francis Hope, 1899–1989, vol. VIII
Layng, Rev. Thomas Malcolm, 1892–1958, vol. V
Layng, Rev. William Wright, 1845–1936, vol. III
Layton, 1st Baron, 1884–1966, vol. VI
Layton, Major Edward, 1857–1913, vol. I
Layton, 2nd Baron, 1912–1989, vol. VIII
Layton, Lt-Col Basil Douglas Bailey, 1907–1986, vol. VIII

Layton, Edwin J., 1850–1929, vol. III
Layton, Adm. Sir Geoffrey, 1884–1964, vol. VI
Layton, Paul Henry, 1905–1989, vol. VIII
Layton, Captain Perceval Norman, 1872–1943, vol. IV
Layton, Thomas Arthur, 1910–1988, vol. VIII
Layton, Thomas Bramley, 1882–1964, vol. VI
Layton, William Grazebrook, 1868–1949, vol. IV
Lazarovich-Hrebelianovich, HH Princess, (Eleanor Calhoun), died 1957, vol. V
Lazarus, Sir Peter Esmond, 1926–1995, vol. IX
Lazarus, Robert Stephen, 1909–1991, vol. IX
Lazarus, Ruth, (Mrs David V. Glass); see Glass, R.
Lazarus-Barlow, Walter Sydney, died 1950, vol. IV
Lazell, Henry George Leslie, 1903–1982, vol. VIII
Lazenby, Frederick George, 1876–1943, vol. IV
Lazier, Stephen Franklin, 1841–1916, vol. II
Lea, Arthur Sheridan, died 1915, vol. I
Lea, Edward Thomas, 1852–1938, vol. III
Lea, Frederick Charles, died 1952, vol. V
Lea, Sir Frederick Measham, 1900–1984, vol. VIII
Lea, George Harris, 1843–1915, vol. I
Lea, Lt-Gen. Sir George Harris, 1912–1990, vol. VIII
Lea, Lt-Col Harold Futvoye, 1867–1940, vol. III
Lea, Henry Charles, 1852–1909, vol. I
Lea, Hugh Cecil, 1869–1926, vol. II
Lea, John, 1871–1958, vol. V
Lea, Sir Julian; see Lea, Sir T. J.
Lea, Measham, 1869–1963, vol. VI
Lea, Lt-Col Percy Gerald Parker, 1875–1945, vol. IV
Lea, Col Samuel Job, 1851–1919, vol. II
Lea, Sir Sydney; see Lea, Sir T. S.
Lea, Sir Thomas, 1st Bt, 1841–1902, vol. I
Lea, Sir Thomas Claude Harris, 3rd Bt, 1901–1985, vol. VIII
Lea, Sir (Thomas) Julian, 4th Bt, 1934–1990, vol. VIII
Lea, Sir (Thomas) Sydney, 2nd Bt, 1867–1946, vol. IV
Lea-Cox, Maj.-Gen. Maurice, 1898–1974, vol. VII
Leach, Rt Hon. Sir (Alfred Henry) Lionel, 1883–1960, vol. V
Leach, Archibald A.; see Grant, Cary.
Leach, Arthur Francis, 1851–1915, vol. I
Leach, Arthur Gordon, 1885–1978, vol. VII
Leach, Bernard Howell, 1887–1979, vol. VII
Leach, Charles, 1847–1919, vol. II
Leach, Charles Harold, 1901–1975, vol. VII
Leach, Maj.-Gen. Sir Edmund, 1836–1923, vol. II
Leach, Rev. Edmund Foxcroft, 1851–1939, vol. III
Leach, Sir Edmund Ronald, 1910–1989, vol. VIII
Leach, Gen. Sir Edward Pemberton, 1847–1913, vol. I
Leach, Frank Burton, 1881–1961, vol. VI
Leach, Frederick, 1843–1916, vol. II
Leach, Lt-Col Sir George Archibald, 1820–1913, vol. I
Leach, Brig.-Gen. Harold Pemberton, 1851–1930, vol. III
Leach, Rev. Henry, died 1921, vol. II
Leach, Henry, 1874–1942, vol. IV
Leach, Brig.-Gen. Henry Edmund Burleigh, 1870–1936, vol. III

Leach, Sir John, 1848–1927, vol. II
Leach, Captain John Catterall, 1894–1941, vol. IV
Leach, Rt Hon. Sir Lionel; see Leach, Rt Hon. Sir A. H. L.
Leach, Norman, 1912–1996, vol. X
Leach, Col Reginald Pemberton, 1855–1929, vol. III
Leach, Rear-Adm. Robert Owen, 1832–1920, vol. II
Leach, Sir Ronald George, 1907–1996, vol. X
Leach, Thomas Stephen, 1896–1973, vol. VII
Leach, William, 1870–1949, vol. IV
Leachman, Col Gerard Evelyn, 1880–1920, vol. II
Leacock, Sir Dudley Gordon, 1880–1954, vol. V
Leacock, Stephen Butler, 1869–1944, vol. IV
Lead, Major Sir William Chollerton, died 1942, vol. IV
Leadam, Isaac Saunders, died 1913, vol. I
Leadbetter, James Stevenson, 1867–1939, vol. III
Leadbitter, Edward, 1919–1996, vol. X
Leadbitter, Sir Eric Cyril Egerton, 1891–1971, vol. VII
Leadbitter, Jasper Michael, 1912–1989, vol. VIII
Leader, Barbara; see Blackburn, E. B.
Leader, Maj.-Gen. Henry Peregrine, 1865–1934, vol. III
Leader, William Nicholas, 1851–1931, vol. III
Leaf, Cecil Huntington, 1864–1910, vol. I
Leaf, Major Henry Meredith, 1862–1931, vol. III
Leaf, Walter, 1852–1927, vol. II
Leah, Samuel Dawson, 1844–1916, vol. II
Leahy, Arthur Herbert, 1857–1928, vol. II
Leahy, Engr Rear-Adm. James Palmer, 1871–1940, vol. III
Leahy, Lt-Col John Patrick Daunt, 1869–1935, vol. III
Leahy, Brig. Thomas Bernard Arthur, 1878–1947, vol. IV
Leahy, Major Thomas Joseph Carroll, 1889–1942, vol. IV
Leahy, Fleet Adm. William Daniel, 1875–1959, vol. V
Leak, Hector, 1887–1976, vol. VII
Leake, Lt-Col Arthur Martin-, 1874–1953, vol. V
Leake, Vice-Adm. Francis M.; see Martin-Leake.
Leake, George, 1856–1902, vol. I
Leake, Henry Dashwood Stucley, 1876–1970, vol. VI
Leake, Hugh Martin-, 1878–1977, vol. VII
Leake, Col Jonas William, 1873–1934, vol. III
Leake, Percy Dewe, died 1949, vol. IV
Leake, Sidney Henry, 1892–1973, vol. VII
Leakey, Maj.-Gen. Arundell Rea, 1915–1999, vol. X
Leakey, Felix William, 1922–1999, vol. X
Leakey, Louis Seymour Bazett, 1903–1972, vol. VII
Leakey, Mary Douglas, 1913–1996, vol. X
Leale, Rev. Sir John, 1892–1969, vol. VI
Leamy, Edmund, 1848–1904, vol. I
Lean, Air Vice-Marshal Daniel Alexander Ronald, 1927–1982, vol. VIII
Lean, Sir David, 1908–1991, vol. IX
Lean, (Edward) Tangye, 1911–1974, vol. VII
Lean, Florence; see Marryat, F.
Lean, Captain John Trevor, 1903–1961, vol. VI
Lean, Maj.-Gen. Kenneth Edward, 1859–1921, vol. II
Lean, Tangye; see Lean, E. T.

Leane, Col Edwin Thomas, 1867–1928, vol. II
Leane, Brig.-Gen. Sir Raymond Lionel, 1878–1962, vol. VI
Lear, Cyril James, 1911–1987, vol. VIII
Lear, Ven. Francis, 1823–1914, vol. I
Learmont, Captain Percy Hewitt, 1894–1983, vol. VIII
Learmonth, Agnes Moore L.; see Livingstone-Learmonth.
Learmonth, Lt-Col (Francis) Leger (Christian) Livingstone-, 1875–1930, vol. III
Learmonth, Adm. Sir Frederick Charles, 1866–1941, vol. IV
Learmonth, Frederick Valiant Cotton L.; see Livingstone-Learmonth.
Learmonth, Sir James Rögnvald, 1895–1967, vol. VI
Learmonth, Brig.-Gen. John Eric Christian L.; see Livingstone-Learmonth.
Learmonth, Lt-Col Leger Livingstone-; see Learmonth, Lt-Col F. L. C. L.
Learoyd, Wing Comdr Roderick Alastair Brook, 1913–1996, vol. X
Learoyd-Cockburn, Col Charles Douglas, 1859–1946, vol. IV
Leary, Leonard Poulter, 1891–1990, vol. VIII
Leask, George Alfred, 1878–1950, vol. IV (A)
Leask, Air Vice-Marshal Kenneth Malise St Clair Graeme, 1896–1974, vol. VII
Leatham, Major Bertram Henry, 1881–1915, vol. I
Leatham, Vice-Adm. Eustace La Trobe, 1870–1935, vol. III
Leatham, Adm. Sir Ralph, 1886–1954, vol. V
Leathart, Air Cdre James Anthony, 1915–1998, vol. X
Leathem, John Gaston, 1906–1984, vol. VIII
Leathem, Walter Henry, 1894–1967, vol. VI
Leather, Col Francis Holdsworth, 1864–1929, vol. III
Leather, John Walter, 1860–1934, vol. III
Leather, Lt-Col Kenneth John Walters, 1878–1963, vol. VI
Leatherland, Baron (Life Peer); Charles Edward Leatherland, 1898–1992, vol. IX
Leathers, 1st Viscount, 1883–1965, vol. VI
Leathers, 2nd Viscount, 1908–1996, vol. X
Leathes, John Beresford, 1864–1956, vol. V
Leathes, Maj.-Gen. Reginald Carteret de Mussenden, 1909–1987, vol. VIII
Leathes, Rev. Stanley, 1830–1900, vol. I
Leathes, Sir Stanley Mordaunt, 1861–1938, vol. III
Leaver, Noel Harry, 1889–1951, vol. V
Leavey, John Anthony, 1915–1999, vol. X
Leavis, Frank Raymond, 1895–1978, vol. VII
Le Bargy, Charles Gustave, 1858–1936, vol. III
Le Bas, Edward, 1904–1966, vol. VI
Le Bas, Sir Hedley Francis, 1868–1926, vol. II
Le Bas, Air Vice-Marshal Michael Henry, 1916–1988, vol. VIII
Lebeter, Fred, 1903–1988, vol. IX (AI)
Leblanc, Rt Rev. Camille André, 1898–1993, vol. IX
Le Blanc, Rt Rev. Edouard, 1870–1935, vol. III
Le Blanc, Sir Pierre Evariste, 1854–1918, vol. II

Le Blond, Elizabeth Alice Frances, (Mrs Aubrey Le Blond), *died* 1934, vol. III
Lebour, George Alexander Louis, 1847–1918, vol. II
Le Braz, Anatole, 1859–1926, vol. II
Le Breton, Clement Martin, 1852–1927, vol. II
Le Breton, Col Sir Edward Philip, 1883–1961, vol. VI
Le Breton-Simmons, Col George Francis Henry, 1864–1930, vol. III
Lebrun, Albert, 1871–1950, vol. IV
Le Brun, Paymaster Captain William Henry, *died* 1942, vol. IV
Leburn, Gilmour; *see* Leburn, W. G.
Leburn, (William) Gilmour, 1913–1963, vol. VI
Lebus, Sir Herman Andrew Harris, 1884–1957, vol. V
Le Chatelier, Henry Louis, 1850–1936, vol. III
Leche, Sir John Hurleston, 1889–1960, vol. V
Lechmere, Sir Edmund Arthur, 4th Bt, 1865–1937, vol. III
Lechmere, Captain Sir Ronald Berwick Hungerford, 5th Bt, 1886–1965, vol. VI
Leck, David Calder, 1857–1927, vol. II
Leckie, John, 1911–1992, vol. IX
Leckie, Col John Edwards, 1872–1950, vol. IV
Leckie, Joseph Alexander, 1866–1938, vol. III
Leckie, Joseph Hannay, 1865–1935, vol. III
Leckie, Air Marshal Robert, 1890–1975, vol. VII
Leckonby, William Douglas, 1907–1989, vol. VIII
Lecky, Captain Arthur Macaulay, 1881–1933, vol. III
Lecky, Col Frederick Beauchamp, 1858–1928, vol. II
Lecky, Captain Halton Stirling, 1878–1940, vol. III
Lecky, Maj.-Gen. Robert St Clair, 1863–1940, vol. III
Lecky, Sir Thomas, 1828–1907, vol. I
Lecky, Rt Hon. William Edward Hartpole, 1838–1903, vol. I
Leclerc, Maj.-Gen. Pierre Edouard, 1893–1982, vol. VIII
Leclercq, Auguste B.; *see* Bouche-Leclercq.
Leclézio, Sir Eugène Pierre Jules, 1832–1915, vol. II
Leclezio, Hon. Sir Henry, *died* 1929, vol. III
Leclézio, Sir Jules, 1877–1951, vol. V
Lecocq, Charles, 1832–1918, vol. III
LeComber, Peter George, 1941–1992, vol. IX
Lecomte, Georges, 1867–1958, vol. V
Leconfield, 2nd Baron, 1830–1901, vol. I
Leconfield, 3rd Baron, 1872–1952, vol. V
Leconfield, 4th Baron, 1877–1963, vol. VI
Leconfield, 5th Baron, 1883–1967, vol. VI
Le Corbusier, (Charles-Edouard Jeanneret), 1887–1965, vol. VI
Le Cornu, Col Charles Philip, 1829–1911, vol. I
le Couteur, Frank, *died* 1950, vol. IV
Ledeboer, John Henry, 1853–1930, vol. III
Ledgard, Sir Henry, 1853–1946, vol. IV
Ledgard, Rev. Ralph Gilbert, *died* 1939, vol. III
Ledgard, Reginald Armitage, 1883–1949, vol. IV
Ledger, Air Vice-Marshal Arthur Percy, 1897–1970, vol. VI
Ledger, Claude Kirwood, 1888–1974, vol. VII
Ledger, Edward, *died* 1921, vol. II

Ledger, Sir Frank; *see* Ledger, Sir J. F.
Ledger, Sir Joseph Francis, (Sir Frank), 1899–1993, vol. IX
Ledingham, Col George Alexander, 1890–1978, vol. VII
Ledingham, Sir John Charles Grant, 1875–1944, vol. IV
Ledingham, John Marshall, 1916–1993, vol. IX
Ledingham, Mrs Una Christina, 1900–1965, vol. VI
Ledlie, James Crawford, 1860–1928, vol. II
Ledlie, Reginald Cyril Bell, 1898–1966, vol. VI
Ledóchowski, Wlodimir Halka, Count, 1866–1942, vol. IV
Leduc, Paul, 1889–1971, vol. VII
Ledward, Gilbert, 1888–1960, vol. V
Ledward, Richard Thomas Davenport, 1915–1963, vol. VI
Ledwidge, Sir Bernard; *see* Ledwidge, Sir W. B. J.
Ledwidge, Sir (William) Bernard (John), 1915–1998, vol. X
Lee of Asheridge, Baroness (Life Peer); Janet Bevan, (Jennie Lee), 1904–1988, vol. VIII
Lee of Fareham, 1st Viscount, 1868–1947, vol. IV
Lee of Newton, Baron (Life Peer); Frederick Lee, 1906–1984, vol. VIII
Lee, Rev. Albert, 1852–1935, vol. III
Lee, Lt-Col Sir (Albert) George, 1879–1967, vol. VI
Lee, Maj.-Gen. Alec Wilfred, 1896–1973, vol. VII
Lee, Alfred Morgan, 1901–1975, vol. VII
Lee, Arthur Jones, 1920–1993, vol. IX
Lee, Arthur Michael, 1913–1983, vol. VIII
Lee, Lt-Col Arthur Neale, 1877–1954, vol. V
Lee, Air Vice-Marshal Arthur Stanley Gould, 1894–1975, vol. VII
Lee, Col Arthur Vaughan Hanning V.; *see* Vaughan-Lee.
Lee, Mrs Asher; *see* Lee, Mollie Carpenter.
Lee, Auriol, 1880–1941, vol. IV
Lee, Bremner Patrick, 1864–1937, vol. III
Lee, Hon. Charles Alfred, 1842–1926, vol. II
Lee, Charles Guy V.; *see* Vaughan-Lee.
Lee, Adm. Sir Charles Lionel V.; *see* Vaughan-Lee.
Lee, Sir Desmond; *see* Lee, Sir H. D. P.
Lee, Rev. Donald Rathbone, 1911–1988, vol. VIII
Lee, Edgar, 1851–1908, vol. I
Lee, Sir Edward, 1833–1909, vol. I
Lee, Edward Owen, 1891–1950, vol. IV
Lee, Rev. Canon Edwin Maywood O'Hara, 1859–1942, vol. IV
Lee, Ernest Markham, 1874–1956, vol. V
Lee, Fitzhugh, *died* 1905, vol. I
Lee, Brig.-Gen. Francis, 1866–1932, vol. III
Lee, Frank, 1867–1941, vol. IV
Lee, Rt Hon. Sir Frank Godbould, 1903–1971, vol. VII
Lee, Frank Herbert, *born* 1869, vol. V
Lee, Rev. Frederick George, 1832–1902, vol. I
Lee, Lt-Col Sir George; *see* Lee, Lt-Col Sir A. G.
Lee, Lt-Gen. George Leonard, 1860–1939, vol. III
Lee, (George) Russell, 1912–1995, vol. IX
Lee, Sir (George) Wilton, 1904–1986, vol. VIII
Lee, Gilbert Henry Clifton, 1911–1991, vol. IX
Lee, Gordon Ambrose de Lisle, 1864–1927, vol. II
Lee, Lt-Col H. R.; *see* Romer-Lee.

Lee, Harry Wilmot, 1848–1914, vol. I
Lee, Sir Henry Austin, 1847–1918, vol. II
Lee, Sir (Henry) Desmond (Pritchard), 1908–1993, vol. IX
Lee, Col Tun Sir Henry Hau Shik, 1901–1988, vol. VIII
Lee, Maj.-Gen. Henry Herbert, 1838–1920, vol. II
Lee, Henry William, 1865–1932, vol. III
Lee, Herbert William, 1865–1940, vol. III
Lee, Ivy Ledbetter, 1877–1934, vol. III
Lee, James Paris, 1831–1904, vol. I
Lee, Rev. James Wideman, 1849–1919, vol. II
Lee, John, 1867–1928, vol. II
Lee, John Thomas Cyril, 1927–1999, vol. X
Lee, Joseph Johnston, 1876–1954, vol. V (A)
Lee, Sir Kenneth, 1st Bt, died 1967, vol. VI
Lee, Laurie, 1914–1997, vol. X
Lee, Lawford Y.; see Yate-Lee.
Lee, Lennox B., 1864–1949, vol. IV
Lee, Malcolm Kenneth, 1943–1999, vol. X
Lee, Manfred B., died 1971, vol. VII
Lee, May B.; see Stott, May, (Lady Stott).
Lee, Mollie Carpenter, (Mrs Asher Lee), died 1973, vol. VII
Lee, Col Reginald Tilson, 1878–1940, vol. III
Lee, Rev. Richard, died 1922, vol. II
Lee, Richard Henry, died 1923, vol. II
Lee, Maj.-Gen. Sir Richard Phillips, 1865–1953, vol. V
Lee, Robert Warden, 1868–1958, vol. V
Lee, Roger Malcolm, 1902–1972, vol. VII
Lee, S. Richmond, (Mrs John W. Richmond Lee); see Yorke, Curtis.
Lee, Russell; see Lee, G. R.
Lee, Sir Sidney, 1859–1926, vol. II
Lee, Brig. Stanlake Swinton, 1890–1952, vol. V
Lee, Sydney, 1866–1949, vol. IV
Lee, Vernon; see Paget, Violet.
Lee, Hon. Sir Walter Henry, 1874–1963, vol. VI
Lee, Rt Rev. William, 1875–1948, vol. IV
Lee, William Alexander, 1886–1971, vol. VII
Lee, Sir William Allison, 1907–1996, vol. X
Lee, William Frederick, 1857–1930, vol. III
Lee, William Stevens, 1871–1965, vol. VI
Lee, Rev. William Walker, 1909–1979, vol. VII
Lee, Sir Wilton; see Lee, Sir G. W.
Lee-Barber, Rear-Adm. John, 1905–1995, vol. IX
Lee-Dillon, Hon. Harry Lee Stanton, 1874–1923, vol. II
Lee-Elliott, David Lee, 1869–1956, vol. V
Lee-Hamilton, Eugene Jacob, 1845–1907, vol. I
Lee-Hankey, W., 1869–1952, vol. V
Lee-Holland, Hetty, died 1954, vol. V
Lee-Howard, Leon Alexander, 1914–1978, vol. VII
Lee Lander, Frank Patrick; see Lander.
Lee Potter, Air Marshal Sir Patrick Brunton, 1904–1982, vol. VIII
Lee Steere, Sir Ernest Augustus, 1866–1957, vol. V
Lee-Warner, Lt-Col Harry Granville, 1883–1932, vol. III
Lee Warner, Philip Henry, 1877–1925, vol. II
Lee-Warner, Sir William, 1846–1914, vol. I
Leebody, John R., 1840–1927, vol. II
Leece, Rev. Charles Henry, died 1930, vol. III
Leech, Arthur John, 1873–1940, vol. III

Leech, Sir Bosdin Thomas, 1836–1912, vol. I
Leech, Clifford, 1909–1977, vol. VII
Leech, Air Vice-Marshal David Bruce, 1934–1994, vol. IX
Leech, Ernest Bosdin, 1875–1950, vol. IV
Leech, George William, 1894–1966, vol. VI
Leech, Henry Brougham, 1843–1921, vol. II
Leech, John, 1857–1942, vol. IV
Leech, Sir Joseph William, 1865–1940, vol. III
Leech, Priestley, died 1936, vol. III
Leech, Samuel Chetwynd, 1872–1931, vol. III
Leech, Sir Stephen, 1864–1925, vol. II
Leech, (Sir) William Charles, 1900–1990, vol. VIII
Leech, William John, 1881–1968, vol. VI
Leech, William Thomas, 1869–1953, vol. V
Leech-Porter, Maj.-Gen. John Edmund, 1896–1979, vol. VII
Leechman, Hon. Lord; James Graham Leechman, 1906–1986, vol. VIII
Leechman, Barclay, 1901–1984, vol. VIII
Leedale, Harry Heath, 1914–1991, vol. IX
Leeder, S. H., died 1930, vol. III
Leedham, Air Cdre Hugh, 1889–1947, vol. IV
Leedham-Green, Charles, died 1931, vol. III
Leeds, 10th Duke of, 1862–1927, vol. II
Leeds, 11th Duke of, 1901–1963, vol. VI
Leeds, 12th Duke of, 1884–1964, vol. VI
Leeds, Duchess of; (Katherine), died 1952, vol. V
Leeds, Sir Edward Templer, 5th Bt, 1859–1924, vol. II
Leeds, Edward Thurlow, 1877–1955, vol. V
Leeds, Sir George Graham Mortimer, 7th Bt, 1927–1983, vol. VIII
Leeds, Comdr Sir Reginald Arthur St John, 6th Bt, 1899–1970, vol. VI
Leeds, Lt-Col Thomas Louis, 1869–1926, vol. II
Leeds, William Henry Arthur St John, 1864–1917, vol. II
Leefe, Gen. John Beckwith, 1849–1922, vol. II
Leek, James, 1892–1978, vol. VII
Leeke, Rev. Edward Tucker, 1841–1925, vol. II
Leeke, George, died 1939, vol. III
Leeke, Rt Rev. John Cox, 1843–1919, vol. II
Leeke, Col Ralph, 1849–1943, vol. IV
Leeke, Ven. Thomas Newton, 1854–1933, vol. III
Leeland, John Roger, 1930–1990, vol. VIII
Leen, Very Rev. Edward, 1885–1944, vol. IV
Leen, Rt Rev. James, 1888–1949, vol. IV
Leeper, Alexander, 1848–1934, vol. III
Leeper, Alexander Wigram Allen, 1887–1935, vol. III
Leeper, Rev. Canon Arthur Lindsay, 1883–1942, vol. IV
Leeper, Sir Reginald Wildig Allen, 1888–1968, vol. VI
Leeper, Richard Kevin, 1894–1987, vol. VIII
Lees, Air Marshal Sir Alan, 1895–1973, vol. VII
Lees, Anthony David, 1917–1992, vol. IX
Lees, Sir Arthur Henry James, 5th Bt (cr 1804), 1863–1949, vol. IV
Lees, Arthur John, 1867–1956, vol. V
Lees, Mrs Charles; see Lees, Sarah Anne.
Lees, Charles Archibald, 1869–1943, vol. IV
Lees, Sir Charles Archibald Edward Ivor, 7th Bt (cr 1804), 1902–1963, vol. VI

Lees, Sir Charles Cameron, 1837–1898, vol. I
Lees, Col Charles Henry Brownlow, 1871–1941, vol. IV
Lees, Charles Herbert, 1864–1952, vol. V
Lees, Sir Clare; see Lees, Sir W. C.
Lees, David, died 1934, vol. III
Lees, David, 1910–1986, vol. VIII
Lees, David Bridge, died 1915, vol. I
Lees, Rear-Adm. Dennis Marescaux, 1900–1973, vol. VII
Lees, Donald Hector, died 1953, vol. V
Lees, Edith Mabel Lucy, 1878–1956, vol. V
Lees, Sir Elliott, 1st Bt (cr 1897), 1860–1908, vol. I
Lees, George Martin, 1898–1955, vol. V
Lees, Rev. George Robinson, 1860–1944, vol. IV
Lees, Sir Harcourt James, 4th Bt (cr 1804), 1840–1917, vol. II
Lees, Rev. Harold Montagu H.; see Hyde-Lees.
Lees, Most Rev. Harrington Clare, 1870–1929, vol. III
Lees, Sir Hereward; see Lees, Sir W. H. C.
Lees, Jack, died 1941, vol. IV
Lees, Very Rev. Sir James Cameron, 1834–1913, vol. I
Lees, James Ferguson, 1872–1935, vol. III
Lees, Sir Jean Marie Ivor, 6th Bt (cr 1804), 1875–1957, vol. V
Lees, Sir John M'Kie, 1843–1926, vol. II
Lees, Col Sir John Victor Elliott, 3rd Bt (cr 1897), 1887–1955, vol. V
Lees, Lt-Col Lawrence Werner Wyld, 1887–1976, vol. VII
Lees, Oswald Campbell, 1857–1945, vol. IV
Lees, Col Roderick Livingstone, 1864–1936, vol. III
Lees, Roland James, 1917–1985, vol. VIII
Lees, Air Marshal Sir Ronald Beresford, 1910–1991, vol. IX
Lees, Samuel, 1885–1940, vol. III
Lees, Sarah Anne, 1842–1935, vol. III
Lees, Stanley Lawrence, 1911–1980, vol. VII
Lees, Sir Thomas Evans Keith, 2nd Bt (cr 1897), 1886–1915, vol. I
Lees, Thomas Orde Hastings, 1846–1924, vol. II
Lees, Walter Kinnear P.; see Pyke-Lees.
Lees, Sir (William) Clare, 1st Bt (cr 1937), 1874–1951, vol. V
Lees, Sir (William) Hereward (Clare), 2nd Bt (cr 1937), 1904–1976, vol. VII
Lees-Jones, John, 1887–1966, vol. VI
Lees-Milne, James, 1908–1997, vol. X
Lees Read, Bertie, 1903–1960, vol. V
Lees-Smith, Rt Hon. Hastings Bertrand, 1878–1941, vol. IV
Leese, Sir Alexander William, 4th Bt, 1909–1979, vol. VII
Leese, Charles William, 1876–1969, vol. VI
Leese, John Arthur, 1930–1991, vol. IX
Leese, Sir Joseph Francis, 1st Bt, 1845–1914, vol. I
Leese, Lt-Gen. Sir Oliver William Hargreaves, 3rd Bt, 1894–1978, vol. VII
Leese, Sir William Hargreaves, 2nd Bt, 1868–1937, vol. III
Leeson, Rt Rev. Spencer, 1892–1956, vol. V
Leeson-Marshall, Markham Richard, 1859–1939, vol. III

Leete, Alfred Chew, 1882–1933, vol. III
Leete, Frederick Alexander, died 1941, vol. IV
Leete, Leslie William Thomas, 1909–1976, vol. VII
Leetham, Lt-Col Sir Arthur, 1859–1933, vol. III
LeFanu, Dame Elizabeth; see Maconchy, Dame E.
Le Fanu, George Ernest Hugh, 1874–1965, vol. VI
Le Fanu, Most Rev. Henry Frewen, 1870–1946, vol. IV
Le Fanu, Adm. Sir Michael, 1913–1970, vol. VI
Le Fanu, Thomas Philip, 1858–1945, vol. IV
Le Fanu, William Richard, 1861–1925, vol. II
Lefeaux, Leslie, 1886–1962, vol. VI
Le Feuvre, Amy, died 1929, vol. III
Le Fèvre, Raymond James Wood, 1905–1986, vol. VIII
Leffingwell, Russell Cornell, 1878–1960, vol. V
Leffler, Gösta M.; see Mittag-Leffler.
le Fleming, Sir Andrew Fleming Hudleston; see Fleming.
Le Fleming, Sir (Ernest) Kaye, 1872–1946, vol. IV
le Fleming, Sir Frank Thomas, 10th Bt, 1887–1971, vol. VII
Le Fleming, Sir Kaye; see Le Fleming, Sir E. K.
le Fleming, Sir Quentin John, 12th Bt, 1949–1995, vol. X (AI)
Le Fleming, Maj.-Gen. Roger Eustace, 1895–1962, vol. VI
Le Fleming, Stanley Hughes, 1855–1939, vol. III
Le Fleming, Sir William Hudleston, 9th Bt, 1861–1945, vol. IV
le Fleming, Sir William Kelland, 11th Bt, 1922–1988, vol. VIII
Lefroy, A. H. F., 1852–1919, vol. II
Lefroy, Sir Anthony Langlois Bruce, 1881–1958, vol. V
Lefroy, Bt Major Bertram Perceval, 1878–1915, vol. I
Lefroy, Captain Cecil Maxwell-, 1876–1931, vol. III
Lefroy, Rev. Charles Edward Cotterell, died 1940, vol. III
Lefroy, Sir Edward Henry Bruce, 1887–1966, vol. VI
Lefroy, Rev. Frederick Anthony, 1846–1920, vol. II
Lefroy, Rt Rev. George Alfred, 1854–1919, vol. II
Lefroy, Major H., died 1935, vol. III
Lefroy, Harold Maxwell-, 1877–1925, vol. II
Lefroy, Hon. Sir Henry Bruce, 1854–1930, vol. III
Lefroy, Walter John Magrath, 1870–1955, vol. V
Lefroy, Very Rev. William, 1836–1909, vol. I
Lefroy, William Chambers, 1849–1915, vol. I
Lefschetz, Solomon, 1884–1972, vol. VII
Le Gallais, Sir Richard Lyle, 1916–1983, vol. VIII
Le Gallais, Theodore, 1852–1903, vol. I
Le Gallienne, Eva, 1899–1991, vol. IX
Le Gallienne, Richard, 1866–1947, vol. IV
Legard, Albert George, 1845–1922, vol. II
Legard, Bt-Col Alfred Digby, 1878–1939, vol. III
Legard, Sir Algernon Willoughby, 12th Bt, 1842–1923, vol. II
Legard, Rev. Cecil Henry, 1843–1918, vol. II
Legard, Sir Charles, 11th Bt, 1846–1901, vol. I
Legard, Brig.-Gen. D'Arcy, 1873–1953, vol. V
Legard, Sir Digby Algernon Hall, 13th Bt, 1876–1961, vol. VI
Legard, Col Sir James Digby, 1846–1935, vol. III

Legard, Captain Sir Thomas Digby, 14th Bt, 1905–1984, vol. VIII
Legat, Charles Edward, 1876–1966, vol. VI
Legat, Harold, died 1960, vol. V
Legentilhomme, Général Paul Louis, 1884–1975, vol. VII
Léger, Alexis; see Léger, M.-R. A. A. St-L.
Léger, Rt Hon. Jules, 1913–1980, vol. VII
Léger, (Marie-René Auguste) Alexis Saint-Léger, 1887–1975, vol. VII
Léger, His Eminence Cardinal Paul-Émile, 1904–1991, vol. IX
Le Geyt, Maj.-Gen. Philip Harrison, 1834–1922, vol. II
Legg, Allan Aubrey R.; see Rowan-Legg.
Legg, Captain Sir George Edward Wickham, 1870–1927, vol. II
Legg, John Wickham, 1843–1921, vol. II
Legg, Leopold George Wickham, 1877–1962, vol. VI
Legg, Ven. Richard Wickham, 1867–1952, vol. V
Legg, Thomas Percy, 1872–1930, vol. III
Leggate, John Mortimer, 1904–1985, vol. VIII
Leggate, Hon. William Muter, 1879–1955, vol. V
Leggatt, Charles Ashley Scott, 1861–1935, vol. III
Leggatt, Maj.-Gen. Charles St Quentin Outen Fullbrook-, 1889–1972, vol. VII
Leggatt, Captain Charles William Stares, 1864–1954, vol. V
Leggatt, Col Hon. Sir William Watt, 1894–1968, vol. VI
Legge, Rt Rev. Hon. Augustus, 1839–1913, vol. I
Legge, Hon. Charles Gounter, 1842–1907, vol. I
Legge, Dominica; see Legge, M. D.
Legge, Francis Cecil, 1873–1940, vol. III
Legge, Col Hon. Sir Harry Charles, 1852–1924, vol. II
Legge, Col Hon. Heneage, 1845–1911, vol. I
Legge, Rev. James, 1815–1897, vol. I
Legge, Lt-Gen. James Gordon, 1863–1947, vol. IV
Legge, James Granville, 1861–1940, vol. III
Legge, (Mary) Dominica, 1905–1986, vol. VIII
Legge, Rear-Adm. Montague George Bentinck, 1883–1951, vol. V
Legge, Lt-Col Norton, 1860–1900, vol. I
Legge, Brig.-Gen. Reginald Francis, died 1955, vol. V
Legge, Robin Humphrey, 1862–1933, vol. III
Legge, Maj.-Gen. Stanley Ferguson, 1900–1977, vol. VII
Legge, Sir Thomas Morison, 1863–1932, vol. III
Legge, Brig.-Gen. William Kaye, 1869–1946, vol. IV
Legge-Bourke, Major Sir (Edward Alexander) Henry, (Sir Harry), 1914–1973, vol. VII
Legge-Bourke, Major Sir Harry; see Legge-Bourke, Major Sir E. A. H.
Leggett, Col Archibald Herbert, 1877–1936, vol. III
Leggett, B. J., 1890–1968, vol. VI (AII)
Leggett, Douglas Malcolm Aufrère, 1912–1994, vol. IX
Leggett, Major Sir Edward Humphrey Manisty, 1871–1947, vol. IV
Leggett, Major Eric Henry Goodwin, 1880–1916, vol. II

Leggett, Sir Frederick William, 1884–1983, vol. VIII
Leggett, Henry Aufrere, 1874–1950, vol. IV
Leggett, Vice-Adm. Oliver Elles, 1876–1946, vol. IV
Leggo, Sir Jack Frederick, 1916–1983, vol. VIII
Legh, Edmund Willoughby, 1874–1943, vol. IV
Legh, Maj. Hon. Sir Francis Michael, 1919–1984, vol. VIII
Legh, Major Hon. Gilbert, 1858–1939, vol. III
Legh, Col Harry Shuldham S.; see Shuldham-Legh.
Legh, Lt-Col Hon. Sir Piers Walter, 1890–1955, vol. V
Legh-Jones, Sir George, 1890–1960, vol. V
Legouis, Emile, 1861–1937, vol. III
Le Grand, Gen. Frederick Gasper, 1836–1905, vol. I
Legrand, Rt Rev. Joseph, 1853–1937, vol. III
Le Grave, Rev. William, 1843–1922, vol. II
Le Grice, Charles Henry, 1870–1942, vol. IV
Le Grice, Very Rev. F(rederick) Edwin, 1911–1992, vol. IX
Legris, Hon. Joseph Hormidas, 1850–1932, vol. III
Legros, Alphonse, 1837–1911, vol. I
Lehar, Franz, 1870–1948, vol. IV
Lehfeldt, Robert Alfred, 1868–1927, vol. II
Lehman, Hon. Herbert H., 1878–1963, vol. VI
Lehmann, Adolf Ludwig Ferdinand, 1863–1937, vol. III
Lehmann, Beatrix, 1903–1979, vol. VII
Lehmann, Hermann, 1910–1985, vol. VIII
Lehmann, John Frederick, 1907–1987, vol. VIII
Lehmann, Liza, (Elizabeth Nina Mary Frederika), (Mrs Herbert Bedford), 1862–1918, vol. II
Lehmann, Lotte, 1888–1976, vol. VII
Lehmann, Rosamond Nina, 1901–1990, vol. VIII
Lehmann, Rudolf, 1819–1905, vol. I
Lehmann, Rudolf Chambers, 1856–1929, vol. III
Le Hunte, Sir George Ruthven, 1852–1925, vol. II
Lei Wang-Kee, Most Rev. Peter, 1922–1974, vol. VII
Leicester, 2nd Earl of, 1822–1909, vol. I
Leicester, 3rd Earl of, 1848–1941, vol. IV
Leicester, 4th Earl of, 1880–1949, vol. IV
Leicester, 5th Earl of, 1908–1976, vol. VII
Leicester, 6th Earl of, 1909–1994, vol. IX
Leicester, Sir Charles Byrne Warren, 9th Bt, 1896–1968, vol. VI
Leicester, James, 1915–1976, vol. VII
Leicester, Lt-Col John Cyril Holdich, 1872–1949, vol. IV
Leicester, Sir Peter Fleming Frederic, 8th Bt, 1863–1945, vol. IV
Leicester-Warren, Cuthbert, 1877–1954, vol. V
Leicester-Warren, Lt-Col John Leighton Byrne, 1907–1975, vol. VII
Leigh, 2nd Baron, 1824–1905, vol. I
Leigh, 3rd Baron, 1855–1938, vol. III
Leigh, 4th Baron, 1908–1979, vol. VII
Leigh, Alan de Verd, 1891–1961, vol. VI
Leigh, (Archibald) Denis, 1915–1998, vol. X
Leigh, Arthur George, 1909–1968, vol. VI
Leigh, Major Chandos, 1873–1915, vol. I
Leigh, Charles Edward A.; see Austen-Leigh.
Leigh, Christopher Thomas Bowes, 1905–1971, vol. VII

Leigh, Denis; *see* Leigh, A. D.
Leigh, Hon. Sir Edward Chandos, 1832–1915, vol. I
Leigh, Egerton, 1843–1928, vol. II
Leigh, Lt-Col Henry Percy Poingdestre, 1851–1928, vol. II
Leigh, Hon. and Very Rev. James Wentworth, 1838–1923, vol. II
Leigh, Sir John, 1st Bt, 1884–1959, vol. V
Leigh, Sir John, 2nd Bt, 1909–1992, vol. IX
Leigh, John Blundell, 1858–1931, vol. III
Leigh, Lt-Col John Cecil Gerard, 1889 1965, vol. VI
Leigh, Sir Joseph, 1841–1908, vol. I
Leigh, Rev. Neville Egerton, 1852–1929, vol. III
Leigh, Sir Neville Egerton, 1922–1994, vol. IX
Leigh, Col Oswald Mosley, 1864–1949, vol. IV
Leigh, Ralph Alexander, 1915–1987, vol. VIII
Leigh, Reginald Gerard, 1880–1962, vol. VI
Leigh, Richard Arthur A., *see* Austen-Leigh.
Leigh, Roger, 1840–1924, vol. II
Leigh, Hon. Rupert, 1856–1919, vol. II
Leigh, Thomas Bowes, 1867–1947, vol. IV
Leigh, Vivien, 1913–1967, vol. VI
Leigh-Bennett, Henry Currie, 1852–1903, vol. I
Leigh-Bennett, Percy Raymond, 1887–1964, vol. VI
Leigh-Hunt, Gerard, 1873–1945, vol. IV
Leigh-Mallory, Rev. Herbert Leigh, 1856–1943, vol. IV
Leigh-Mallory, Air Chief Marshal Sir Trafford Leigh, 1892–1944, vol. IV
Leigh-Pemberton, Sir Edward, 1823–1910, vol. I
Leigh-Pemberton, John, 1911–1997, vol. X
Leigh-Wood, Lt-Col Sir James, *died* 1949, vol. IV
Leigh-Wood, Roger, 1906–1987, vol. VIII
Leighton of St Mellons, 1st Baron, 1896–1963, vol. VI
Leighton of St Mellons, 2nd Baron, 1922–1998, vol. X
Leighton, Arthur Edgar, 1873–1961, vol. VI
Leighton, Major Bertie Edward Parker, 1875–1952, vol. V
Leighton, Major Sir Bryan Baldwin Mawddwy, 9th Bt, 1868–1919, vol. II
Leighton, Clare, 1899–1989, vol. VIII
Leighton, Edmund Blair, 1853–1922, vol. II
Leighton, Gerald, 1868–1953, vol. V
Leighton, John, 1822–1912, vol. I
Leighton, Captain John Albert, 1881–1945, vol. IV
Leighton, Kenneth, 1929–1988, vol. VIII
Leighton, Margaret, 1922–1976, vol. VII
Leighton, Marie Connor, *died* 1941, vol. IV
Leighton, Bt Col Sir Richard Tihel, 10th Bt, 1893–1957, vol. V
Leighton, Robert, *died* 1934, vol. III
Leighton, Sir Robert, 1884–1959, vol. V
Leighton, Ronald, 1930–1994, vol. IX
Leighton, Stanley, 1837–1901, vol. I
Leighton-Boyce, Guy Gilbert, 1920–1989, vol. VIII
Leiningen, HSH Prince Ernest Leopold Victor Charles Auguste Joseph Emich, 1830–1904, vol. I
Leinsdorf, Erich, 1912–1993, vol. IX
Leinster, 6th Duke of, 1887–1922, vol. II
Leinster, 7th Duke of, 1892–1976, vol. VII
Leiper, Robert Thomson, 1881–1969, vol. VI

Leiper, William, 1839–1916, vol. II
Leir, Rear-Adm. Ernest W., 1883–1971, vol. VII
Leir-Carleton, Maj.-Gen. Richard Langford, 1841–1933, vol. III
Leishman, Alan Ross, *died* 1937, vol. III
Leishman, Sir James, *died* 1939, vol. III
Leishman, James Blair, 1902–1963, vol. VI
Leishman, John G. A., 1857–1924, vol. II
Leishman, Maj.-Gen. John Thomas, 1835–1920, vol. II
Leishman, Rev. Thomas, 1825–1904, vol. I
Leishman, Lt-Gen. Sir William Boog, 1865–1926, vol. II
Leisk, James Rankine, 1876–1948, vol. IV
Leitch, Archibald, 1878–1931, vol. III
Leitch, Isabella, 1890–1980, vol. VII (AII)
Leitch, Hon. James, *born* 1850, vol. II
Leitch, Lt-Col John Wilson, 1873–1935, vol. III
Leitch, Rev. Matthew, *died* 1922, vol. II
Leitch, Sir Walter, 1867–1945, vol. IV
Leitch, Sir William, 1880–1965, vol. VI
Leitch, William Andrew, 1915–1999, vol. X
Leiter, Joseph, 1868–1932, vol. III
Leiter, Levi Zeigler, 1834–1904, vol. I
Leith of Fyvie, 1st Baron, 1847–1925, vol. II
Leith, Lt-Col Sir Alexander, 1st Bt, 1869–1956, vol. V
Leith, Captain George Piercy, 1877–1945, vol. IV
Leith, Gordon, 1879–1941, vol. IV
Leith of Fyvie, Sir Ian F.; *see* Forbes-Leith of Fyvie, Sir R. I. A.
Leith, Captain Lockhart, 1876–1940, vol. III
Leith, Robert Fraser Calder, 1854–1936, vol. III
Leith, Major Thomas, 1830–1920, vol. II
Leith-Buchanan, Sir Alexander Wellesley George Thomas, 5th Bt, 1866–1925, vol. II
Leith-Buchanan, Sir George Hector, 4th Bt, 1833–1903, vol. I
Leith-Buchanan, Sir George Hector Macdonald, 6th Bt, 1889–1973, vol. VII
Leith-Hay, Charles Edward Norman, 1858–1939, vol. III
Leith-Ross, Sir Frederick William, 1887–1968, vol. VI
Leithead, James Douglas, 1911–1998, vol. X
Leitrim, 5th Earl of, 1879–1952, vol. V
Lejeune, Caroline Alice, (Mrs E. Roffe Thompson), 1897–1973, vol. VII
Lejeune, Maj.-Gen. Francis St David Benwell, 1899–1984, vol. VIII
Le Jeune, Henry, 1819–1904, vol. I
Leland, Charles Godfrey, 1824–1903, vol. I
Leland, Col Francis William George, 1877–1943, vol. IV
Leland, Captain Herbert John Collett, 1873–1931, vol. III
Lelean, Percy Samuel, 1871–1956, vol. V
Leleux, Sydney Wallis, 1862–1941, vol. IV
Leloir, Luis Federico, 1906–1987, vol. VIII
Lelong, Lucien, 1889–1958, vol. V
Lely, Sir Frederic Styles Philpin, 1846–1934, vol. III
Lely, John Mountney, 1839–1907, vol. I
Lemaire, Ernest Joseph, 1874–1945, vol. IV

Lemaire, Most Rev. Ishmael Samuel Mills, *died* 1984, vol. VIII
Le Maistre, Charles, *died* 1953, vol. V
Le Maitre, Sir Alfred Sutherland, 1896–1959, vol. V
Le Maitre, Ella Katharine Irving, 1896–1960, vol. V
Lemaitre, François Elie Jules, 1853–1915, vol. I
Leman, Count Georges, 1851–1920, vol. II
Le Marchant, Sir Denis, 3rd Bt, 1870–1922, vol. II
Le Marchant, Sir Denis, 5th Bt, 1906–1987, vol. VIII
Le Marchant, Brig.-Gen. Sir Edward Thomas, 4th Bt, 1871–1953, vol. V
Le Marchant, Adm. Evelyn Robert, *died* 1949, vol. IV
Le Marchant, Sir Henry Denis, 2nd Bt, 1839–1915, vol. I
Le Marchant, Lt-Col Louis St Gratien, 1866–1914, vol. I
Le Marchant, Sir Spencer, 1931–1986, vol. VIII
Lemare, Edwin H., 1866–1934, vol. III
Le Marinel, Very Rev. Matthew, 1883–1963, vol. VI
Lemass, Edwin Stephen, 1890–1970, vol. VI
Lemass, Peter Edmund, 1850–1928, vol. II, vol. III
Lemass, Seán Francis, 1899–1971, vol. VI
Le Masurier, Sir Robert Hugh, 1913–1996, vol. X
le May, Reginald Stuart, 1885–1972, vol. VII
Le May, Gp Captain William Kent, 1911–1978, vol. VII
Lemberg, (Max) Rudolf, 1896–1975, vol. VII
Lemberg, Rudolf; *see* Lemberg, M. R.
Le Messurier, Col Augustus, 1837–1916, vol. II
Le Messurier, Henry William, 1848–1931, vol. III
Le Mesurier, Col Cecil Brooke, 1831–1913, vol. I
Le Mesurier, Captain Charles Edward, *died* 1917, vol. II
Le Mesurier, Captain Edward Kirby, 1903–1980, vol. VII
Le Mesurier, Wing Comdr Eric Clive, 1915–1943, vol. IV
Le Mesurier, Col Frederick Augustus, 1839–1926, vol. II
Le Mesurier, Sir Havilland, 1866–1931, vol. III
Le Mesurier, Lt-Col Herbert Grenville, 1873–1940, vol. III
Lemieux, Auguste, 1874–1956, vol. V
Lemieux, Sir François Xavier, 1851–1933, vol. III
Lemieux, Louis Joseph, *born* 1870, vol. IV
Lemieux, Most Rev. (Marie-) Joseph, 1902–1994, vol. IX
Lemieux, Rodolphe, 1866–1937, vol. III
Lemmon, Cyril Whitefield, 1901–1993, vol. IX
Lemmon, David Hector, 1931–1998, vol. X
Lemmon, Col Sir Thomas Warne, 1838–1928, vol. II
Lemnitzer, Gen. Lyman Louis, 1899–1988, vol. VIII
Le Moine, Jucherean de St Denis, 1850–1922, vol. II
Le Moine, Sir James MacPherson, 1825–1912, vol. I
Lemon, Arthur Henry, 1864–1933, vol. III
Lemon, Brig. Arthur Leslie K.; *see* Kent-Lemon.
Lemon, Sir Ernest John Hutchings, 1884–1954, vol. V
Lemon, Lt-Col Frederick Joseph, 1879–1952, vol. V
Lemon, Sir James, 1833–1923, vol. II

Lemonius, Lt-Col Gerard Maclean, *died* 1950, vol. IV
Lemonnier, Adm. André Georges, 1896–1963, vol. VI
Lempfert, Rudolph Gustave Karl, 1875–1957, vol. V
Lempriere, Lt-Col Henry Anderson, 1867–1914, vol. I
Lempriere, Rev. Philip Charles, 1890–1949, vol. IV (A), vol. V
Lempriere, Reginald Raoul, 1851–1931, vol. III
Lenanton, Carola Mary Anima, (Lady Lenanton); *see* Oman, C. M. A.
Lenanton, Sir Gerald, 1896–1952, vol. V
Lenbach, T. von, *died* 1904, vol. I
Lendon, Alfred Austin, 1856–1935, vol. III
Lendon, Penry Bruce, 1882–1914, vol. I
Lendrum, Alan Chalmers, 1906–1994, vol. IX
Le Neve Foster, Fermian; *see* Foster.
Lenfestey, Giffard Hocart, 1872–1943, vol. IV
Lenfestey, Col Leopold d'Estreville, 1875–1948, vol. IV
Leng, Christopher David, 1861–1921, vol. II
Leng, Sir Hilary Howard, 1862–1936, vol. III
Leng, Sir John, 1828–1906, vol. I
Leng, Sir William Christopher, 1825–1902, vol. I
Lenglen, Suzanne, *died* 1938, vol. III
Lenihan, Brian Joseph, 1930–1995, vol. IX
Lenman, Rt Rev. Thomas, 1883–1959, vol. V
Lenn, Paymaster Captain Frank, 1868–1932, vol. III
Lennard, Sir Fiennes B.; *see* Barrett-Lennard.
Lennard, Lt-Col Sir Henry Arthur Hallam Farnaby, 2nd Bt (*cr* 1880), 1859–1928, vol. II
Lennard, Lt-Col John B.; *see* Barrett-Lennard.
Lennard, Sir John Farnaby, 1st Bt (*cr* 1880), 1816–1899, vol. I
Lennard, Reginald Vivian, 1885–1967, vol. VI
Lennard, Sir Richard Barrett-; *see* Lennard, Sir T. R. F. B.
Lennard, Sir Richard Fiennes Barrett-, 4th Bt (*cr* 1801), 1861–1934, vol. III
Lennard, Lt-Col Sir Stephen Arthur Hallam Farnaby, 3rd Bt (*cr* 1880), 1899–1980, vol. VII
Lennard, Sir Thomas Barrett-, 2nd Bt (*cr* 1801), 1826–1919, vol. II
Lennard, Sir Thomas Barrett-, 3rd Bt (*cr* 1801), 1853–1923, vol. II
Lennard, Sir Thomas J., 1861–1938, vol. III
Lennard, Sir (Thomas) Richard (Fiennes) Barrett-, 5th Bt (*cr* 1801), 1898–1977, vol. VII
Lennard-Jones, Sir John Edward, 1894–1954, vol. V
Lennie, Robert Aim, 1889–1961, vol. VI
Lennon, Dennis; *see* Lennon, J. D.
Lennon, (George) Gordon, 1911–1996, vol. X
Lennon, Gordon; *see* Lennon, George G.
Lennon, Most Rev. James Gerard, 1923–1989, vol. VIII
Lennon, (John) Dennis, 1918–1991, vol. IX
Lennon, Most Rev. Patrick, 1914–1990, vol. VIII
Lennon, Hon. William, 1849–1938, vol. III
Lennox, Rear Adm. Sir Alexander Henry Charles G.; *see* Gordon Lennox.
Lennox, Col Lord Algernon Charles G.; *see* Gordon-Lennox.
Lennox, Lady Algernon G.; *see* Gordon-Lennox.

Lennox, Lord Bernard Charles G.; *see* Gordon-Lennox.

Lennox, Charles Spencer Bateman-Hanbury K.; *see* Kincaid-Lennox.

Lennox, Cosmo Charles G.; *see* Gordon-Lennox.

Lennox, Lord Esme Charles G.; *see* Gordon-Lennox.

Lennox, Lt-Gen. Sir George Charles G.; *see* Gordon Lennox.

Lennox, Rt Hon. Lord Walter Charles G.; *see* Gordon-Lennox.

Lennox, Sir Wilbraham Oates, 1830–1897, vol. I

Lenny, Most Rev. Francis, 1928–1978, vol. VII (AII)

Lenotre, G., 1857–1935, vol. III

Lenox-Conyngham, Col Sir Gerald Ponsonby, 1866–1956, vol. V

Lenox-Conyngham, Sir William Fitzwilliam, 1824–1906, vol. I

Lenski, Lois, 1893–1974, vol. VII

Lentaigne, Sir John, *died* 1915, vol. I

Lentaigne, Maj.-Gen. Walter David Alexander, 1899–1955, vol. V

Lenton, (Aylmer) Ingram, 1927–1994, vol. IX

Lenton, Rev. Charles H., 1873–1951, vol. V

Lenton, Ingram; *see* Lenton, A. I.

Lenton, Jessie; *see* Pope, J.

Leny, Bt Lt-Col R. L. Macalpine-, 1870–1941, vol. IV

Leo XIII, His Holiness Pope, (Vincent Joachim Pecci), 1810–1903, vol. I

Leo, Dame Sister Mary, 1896–1989, vol. IX (AI)

Leon, Sir George Edward, 2nd Bt, 1875–1947, vol. IV

Leon, Henri Marcel, 1855–1932, vol. III

Leon, Henry Cecil, 1902–1976, vol. VII

Leon, Sir Herbert Samuel, 1st Bt, 1850–1926, vol. II

Leon, Paul, 1874–1962, vol. VI

Leon, Philip, 1895–1974, vol. VII

Leon, Sir Ronald George, 3rd Bt, 1902–1964, vol. VI

Leon, Samuel, 1848–1933, vol. III

Leonard, Baron (Life Peer); John Denis Leonard, 1909–1983, vol. VIII

Leonard, George Hare, 1863–1941, vol. IV

Leonard, James W., *died* 1909, vol. I

Leonard, John William, *died* 1910, vol. I

Leonard, Rt Rev. Martin Patrick Grainge, 1889–1963, vol. VI

Leonard, Patrick Marcellinus, 1821–1901, vol. I

Leonard, Sir Reginald Byron, 1907–1986, vol. VIII

Leonard, Lt-Col Reuben Wells, 1860–1930, vol. III

Leonard, Robert Galloway Louis, 1878–1957, vol. V

Leonard, Samuel Henry, 1854–1929, vol. III

Leonard, Sir Walter McEllister, 1915–1985, vol. VIII

Leonard, William, 1887–1969, vol. VI

Leonard, Rt Rev. William Andrew, 1848–1930, vol. III

Leonard, Col William Hugh, 1876–1960, vol. V

Leonard-Williams, Air Vice-Marshal Harold Guy, 1911–1994, vol. IX

Leoncavallo, Ruggiero, 1858–1919, vol. II

Leoni, Franco, 1864–1949, vol. IV

Leontief, Wassily, 1906–1999, vol. X

Le Page, Engr-Rear-Adm. George Wilfred, 1883–1940, vol. III

Lepailleur, Rt Rev. Alfred, 1886–1952, vol. V

le Patourel, Herbert Augustus, 1875–1934, vol. III

Le Patourel, Brig. Herbert Wallace, 1916–1979, vol. VII

Le Patourel, John Herbert, 1909–1981, vol. VIII

Le Pelley, Lt-Col Edward Carey, 1870–1942, vol. IV

Lepicier, Cardinal Alexis Henry Marie, 1863–1936, vol. III

Lepine, Louis, 1846–1933, vol. III

Le Poer Trench, Hon. Frederick, 1835–1913, vol. I

Le Poer Trench, Lt-Col Frederick Amelius, 1857–1942, vol. IV

Le-Poer-Trench, Col Hon. William, 1837–1920, vol. II

Le Quesne, Charles Thomas, 1885–1954, vol. V

Le Quesne, Ferdinand Simeon, 1863–1950, vol. IV

Le Queux, William Tufnell, 1864–1927, vol. II

Leray, Mgr Joseph M. M., 1854–1929, vol. III

Lermon, Norman, 1915–1989, vol. VIII

Lerner, Alan Jay, 1918–1986, vol. VIII

Lerner, Max, 1902–1992, vol. IX

Le Rossignol, Col Alfred Ernest, 1869–1951, vol. V

Le Rossignol, James Edward, 1866–1959, vol. V

Le Rossignol, Walter Aubin, *died* 1945, vol. IV

Le Rougetel, Sir John Helier, 1894–1975, vol. VII

Le Roy, Édouard Louis Emmanuel Julien, 1870–1954, vol. V

Le Roy-Lewis, Col Herman, 1860–1931, vol. III

Le Sage, Sir John Merry, 1837–1926, vol. II

Lescaze, William, 1896–1969, vol. VI

Lescher, Joseph Francis, 1842–1923, vol. II

Lescher, Thomas Edward, 1877–1938, vol. III

Leschititzky, Theodore, 1830–1915, vol. I

Leslie, Lt-Col Archibald Stewart, 1873–1928, vol. II

Leslie, Col Archibald Young, *died* 1913, vol. I

Leslie, Sir Bradford, 1831–1926, vol. II

Leslie, Lt-Col Sir Bradford, 1867–1936, vol. III

Leslie, Lt-Col Charles, *died* 1930, vol. III

Leslie, Sir Charles Henry, 7th Bt (*cr* 1625), 1848–1905, vol. I

Leslie, David Clement, 1924–1993, vol. IX

Leslie, Doris, (Lady Fergusson Hannay), 1891–1982, vol. VIII

Leslie, Edward Henry John, 1880–1966, vol. VI

Leslie, Sir Francis Galloway, 1902–1971, vol. VII

Leslie, Frank Matthews, 1935–2000, vol. X

Leslie, Frank, (Miriam Florence Folline, Baroness de Bazus), 1851–1914, vol. I

Leslie, Maj.-Gen. George Arthur James, 1867–1936, vol. III

Leslie, Rear-Adm. George Cunningham, 1920–1988, vol. VIII

Leslie, George Dunlop, 1835–1921, vol. II

Leslie, Hon. George Waldegrave-, 1825–1904, vol. I

Leslie, Gilbert Frank, 1909–1995, vol. IX

Leslie, Harald Robert; *see* Birsay, Hon. Lord.

Leslie, Henrietta, (Mrs Harrie Schütze), *died* 1946, vol. IV

Leslie, Sir (Henry John) Lindores, 9th Bt (*cr* 1625), 1920–1967, vol. VI

Leslie, Ian William Murray, 1905–1987, vol. VIII
Leslie, James Campbell, *died* 1974, vol. VII
Leslie, Rt Hon. James Graham, 1868–1949, vol. IV
Leslie, Sir John, 1st Bt (*cr* 1876), 1822–1916, vol. II
Leslie, Col Sir John, 2nd Bt (*cr* 1876), 1857–1944, vol. IV
Leslie, Lt-Col John, 1888–1965, vol. VI
Leslie, John D.; *see* Dean-Leslie.
Leslie, Lt-Col John Henry, 1858–1943, vol. IV
Leslie, Very Rev. John Herbert, 1867–1934, vol. III
Leslie, Sir (John Randolph) Shane, 3rd Bt (*cr* 1876), 1885–1971, vol. VII
Leslie, John Robert, 1873–1955, vol. V
Leslie, Col John Robert Sloan, 1871–1943, vol. IV
Leslie, Lt-Col John Tasman Waddell, 1861–1911, vol. I
Leslie, Hon. John Wayland, 1909–1991, vol. IX
Leslie, John William St Lawrance, *died* 1934, vol. III
Leslie, Sir Lindores; *see* Leslie, Sir H. J. L.
Leslie, Miriam Florence Folline; *see* Leslie, Frank.
Leslie, Sir Norman Alexander, 1870–1945, vol. IV
Leslie, Wing Comdr Sir Norman Roderick Alexander David, 8th Bt (*cr* 1625), 1889–1937, vol. III
Leslie, Robert, 1885–1951, vol. V
Leslie, Robert Murray, 1866–1921, vol. II
Leslie, Maj.-Gen. Robert Walter Dickson, 1883–1957, vol. V
Leslie, Samuel Clement, 1898–1980, vol. VII
Leslie, Seymour Argent Sandford, 1902–1953, vol. V
Leslie, Sir Shane; *see* Leslie, Sir J. R. S.
Leslie, Gen. Sir Walter Stewart, 1876–1947, vol. IV
Leslie of Warthill, William A.; *see* Arbuthnot-Leslie.
Leslie-Ellis, Lt-Col Henry, 1852–1919, vol. II
Leslie-Jones, Rev. Cyril, 1873–1932, vol. III
Leslie-Jones, Frederick Archibald, 1874–1946, vol. IV
Leslie-Jones, Leycester Hudson, *died* 1935, vol. III
Leslie Melville, Lt-Col Hon. Ian, 1894–1967, vol. VI
Leslie-Roberts, H(ugh); *see* Roberts.
Le Souef, Albert Sherbourne, 1877–1951, vol. V
Le Souëf, W. H. Dudley, *died* 1924, vol. II
Lessard, Maj.-Gen. François Louis, 1860–1927, vol. II
Lesser, Henry, *died* 1966, vol. VI
Lesser, Most Rev. Norman Alfred, 1902–1985, vol. VIII
Lesser, Sidney Lewis, 1912–1993, vol. IX
Lessing, Edward Albert, 1890–1964, vol. VI
Lessing, Rudolf, 1878–1964, vol. VI
Lesslie, Brig.-Gen. William Breck, 1868–1942, vol. IV
Lessore, Frederick, 1879–1951, vol. V
Lessore, Helen, 1907–1994, vol. IX
Lessore, Thérèse, *died* 1945, vol. IV
Lester, Engr-Rear-Adm. Arthur Ellis, 1878–1956, vol. V
Lester, Rev. Henry Arthur, *died* 1922, vol. II
Lester, Sean, 1888–1959, vol. V
Lester, Rev. T. Major, *died* 1903, vol. I
Lester-Garland, Lester V., *died* 1944, vol. IV
Lestor of Eccles, Baroness, (Life Peer); Joan Lestor, 1931–1998, vol. X

Lestrade, Gérard Paul, 1897–1962, vol. VI
Le Strange, Charles Alfred, 1892–1933, vol. III
L'Estrange, Constance; *see* Collier, C.
Le Strange, Guy, 1854–1933, vol. III
Le Strange, Hamon, 1840–1918, vol. II
L'Estrange, Lawrence Percy Farrer, 1912–1990, vol. VIII
Le Strange, Roland, 1869–1919, vol. II
Lesueur, Daniel, *died* 1921, vol. II
L'Etang, Hugh Joseph Charles James, 1917–1996, vol. X
Letch, Sir Robert, 1899–1962, vol. VI
Letchworth, Rev. Arnold, 1840–1923, vol. II
Letchworth, Sir Edward, 1833–1917, vol. II
Letchworth, Rev. Henry Howard, 1836–1921, vol. II
Letchworth, Thomas Edwin, 1906–1973, vol. VII
Lethaby, William Richard, 1857–1931, vol. III
Letham, James, 1907–1972, vol. VII
Lethbridge, Alan Bourchier, 1878–1923, vol. II
Lethbridge, Col Alfred, 1884–1968, vol. VI
Lethbridge, Lt-Col Sir Alfred Swaine, 1844–1917, vol. II
Lethbridge, Col Ernest Astley Edmund, 1864–1943, vol. IV
Lethbridge, Lt-Col Francis Washington, 1867–1939, vol. III
Lethbridge, Captain Sir Hector Wroth, 6th Bt, 1898–1978, vol. VII
Lethbridge, Maj.-Gen. John Sydney, 1897–1961, vol. VI
Lethbridge, Marion Eva, 1879–1959, vol. V
Lethbridge, Sir Roper, 1840–1919, vol. II
Lethbridge, Thomas Charles, 1901–1971, vol. VII
Lethbridge, Sir Wroth Acland, 4th Bt, 1831–1902, vol. I
Lethbridge, Sir Wroth Periam Christopher, 5th Bt, 1863–1950, vol. IV
Lethem, Sir Gordon James, 1886–1962, vol. VI
Le Tocq, Eric George, 1918–1996, vol. X
Letourneau, Séverin, 1871–1949, vol. IV
Letson, Maj.-Gen. Harry Farnham Germaine, 1896–1992, vol. IX
Lett, Eva, *died* 1945, vol. IV
Lett, Rev. Henry William, 1838–1920, vol. II
Lett, Sir Hugh, 1st Bt, 1876–1964, vol. VI
Lett, Phyllis, (Mrs Phyllis de Burgh Ker), *died* 1962, vol. VI
Letton, Charles Thomas, 1878–1949, vol. IV
Letts, Charles Trevor, 1905–1996, vol. X
Letts, Edmund Albert, 1852–1918, vol. II
Letts, Malcolm Henry Ikin, 1882–1957, vol. V
Letts, Rev. Reginald, 1857–1940, vol. III
Letts, Sir William Malesbury, 1873–1957, vol. V
Letts, Winifred M., 1882–1972, vol. VII
Leuba, James Henri, 1868–1946, vol. IV
Leuchars, Col Hon. Sir George, 1868–1924, vol. II
Leuchars, Sir William Douglas, 1920–1991, vol. IX
Leuckert, Jean Elizabeth, (Mrs Harry Leuckert); *see* Muir, J. E.
Leudesdorf, Charles, 1853–1924, vol. II
Leupena, Sir Tupua, 1922–1996, vol. X
Leutwiler, Fritz, 1924–1997, vol. X
Leuty, Thomas Richmond, 1853–1911, vol. I
Levame, Mgr Albert, 1881–1958, vol. V
Levander, F. W., *died* 1916, vol. II

Leveen, Jacob, 1891–1980, vol. VII

Leven, 11th Earl of, **and Melville,** 10th Earl of, 1835–1906, vol. I

Leven, 12th Earl of, **and Melville,** 11th Earl of, 1886–1913, vol. I

Leven, 13th Earl of, **and Melville,** 12th Earl of, 1890–1947, vol. IV

Lever, Baron (Life Peer); Leslie Maurice Lever, 1905–1977, vol. VII

Lever of Manchester, Baron (Life Peer); Harold Lever, 1914–1995, vol. IX

Lever, Col Sir Arthur Levy, 1st Bt (*cr* 1911), 1860–1924, vol. II

Lever, Sir Ernest Harry, 1890–1970, vol. VI

Lever, Sir Hardman; *see* Lever, Sir S. H.

Lever, Richard Hayley, 1876–1958, vol. V(A), vol. VI (AI)

Lever, Sir (Samuel) Hardman, 1st Bt (*cr* 1920), 1869–1947, vol. IV

Lever, Sir Tresham Joseph Philip, 2nd Bt (*cr* 1911), 1900–1975, vol. VII

Leverhulme, 1st Viscount, 1851–1925, vol. II

Leverhulme, 2nd Viscount, 1888–1949, vol. IV

Leverhulme, 3rd Viscount, 1915–2000, vol. X

Leversedge, Leslie Frank, 1904–1996, vol. X

Leverson, Col George Francis, *died* 1938, vol. III

Leverson, Lt-Col George Riland Francis, 1886–1936, vol. III

Leverson, Col Julian John, 1853–1941, vol. IV

Levertoff, Rev. Paul Philip, 1878–1954, vol. V

Leveson, Adm. Sir Arthur Cavenagh, 1868–1929, vol. III

Leveson Gower, Major Lord Alastair St Clair Sutherland-, 1890–1921, vol. II

Leveson Gower, Arthur Francis Gresham, 1851–1922, vol. II

Leveson-Gower, Col Charles Cameron, 1866–1951, vol. V

Leveson Gower, Frederick Neville Sutherland, 1874–1959, vol. V

Leveson Gower, Sir George Granville, 1858–1951, vol. V

Leveson Gower, Granville Charles Gresham, 1865–1948, vol. IV

Leveson Gower, Sir Henry Dudley Gresham, 1873–1954, vol. V

Leveson Gower, Col Philip, *died* 1939, vol. III

Levesque, Most Rev. Louis, 1908–1998, vol. X

Lévesque, Hon. René, 1922–1987, vol. VIII

Levett, Major Berkeley John Talbot, 1863–1941, vol. IV

Levett, Ernest Laurence, *died* 1916, vol. II

Levett, Theophilus Basil Percy, 1856–1929, vol. III

Levett-Yeats, Gerald Aylmer, 1863–1938, vol. III

Levey, Lady; *see* Brophy, B. A.

Levey, Charles Joseph, 1846–1920, vol. II

Levey, George Collins, 1835–1919, vol. II

Levi, Edward Hirsch, 1911–2000, vol. X

Levi, Peter Chad Tigar, 1931–2000, vol. X

Levi, Sylvain, 1863–1935, vol. III

Levi, T. Arthur, 1874–1954, vol. V

Levick, Claude Blaxland, 1896–1953, vol. V

Levick, Surg.-Comdr G. Murray, *died* 1956, vol. V

Levick, Sir Hugh Gwynne, 1870–1937, vol. III

Levick, Thomas Henry Carlton, 1867–1957, vol. V

Levien, Jerome William John, 1893–1961, vol. VI

Levien, John Mewburn, 1863–1953, vol. V

Levin, Nyman, 1906–1965, vol. VI

Levin, Richard. 1910–2000, vol. X

Levine, Abraham, 1870–1949, vol. IV

Levinge, Sir Edward Vere, 1867–1954, vol. V

Levinge, Major Sir Richard Vere Henry, 1911–1984, vol. VIII

Levinge, Sir Richard William, 10th Bt, 1878–1914, vol. I

Levinstein, Herbert, *died* 1956, vol. V

Levis, Maj.-Gen. Derek George, 1911–1993, vol. IX

Lévis Mirepoix, Antoine, Duc de, 1884–1981, vol. VIII

Levison, Sir Leon, 1881–1936, vol. III

Levita, Lt-Col Sir Cecil Bingham, 1867–1953, vol. V

Levitt, Walter Montague, 1900–1983, vol. VIII

Levy, Aaron Harold, *died* 1977, vol. VII

Levy, Sir Albert, *died* 1937, vol. III

Levy, Sir Arthur, 1855–1938, vol. III

Levy, Benn Wolfe, 1900–1973, vol. VII

Levy, Sir Bruce; *see* Levy, Sir E. B.

Levy, Hon. Sir Daniel, 1873–1937, vol. III

Levy, Sir (Enoch) Bruce, 1892–1985, vol. VIII

Levy, Sir Ewart Maurice, 2nd Bt, 1897–1996, vol. X

Levy, George Joseph, 1927–1996, vol. X

Levy, Hermann, 1881–1949, vol. IV

Levy, Hyman, 1889–1975, vol. VII

Levy, J. Langley, 1870–1945, vol. IV

Levy, Joseph Hiam, 1838–1913, vol. I

Levy, Joshua Moses, 1854–1922, vol. II

Levy, Sir Maurice, 1st Bt, 1859–1933, vol. III

Levy, Reuben, 1891–1966, vol. VI

Levy, Richard Francis, 1892–1968, vol. VI

Levy, Stanley Isaac, 1890–1968, vol. VI

Levy, Thomas, *died* 1953, vol. V

Levy, Major Walter Henry, 1876–1923, vol. II

Lewanika III, Sir Mwanawina; *see* Barotseland, Litunga of.

Lewenhaupt, Count Carl, 1835–1906, vol. I

Lewer, Ethel, 1861–1946, vol. IV

Lewer, Surg.-Maj.-Gen. Robert, *died* 1914, vol. I

Lewers, Arthur Hamilton Nicholson, *died* 1934, vol. III

Lewes, Earl of; Henry John Montacute Nevill, 1948–1965, vol. VI

Lewes, Brig.-Gen. Charles George, 1869–1938, vol. III

Lewes, Maj.-Gen. H. C., 1838–1907, vol. I

Lewes, John Hext, 1903–1992, vol. IX

Lewes, Col Price Kinnear, 1870–1943, vol. IV

Lewes, Captain Price Vaughan, 1865–1914, vol. I

Lewes, Sir Samuel William Sayer, 1824–1907, vol. I

Lewes, Captain Thomas Powell, 1860–1940, vol. III

Lewes, Vivian Byam, 1852–1915, vol. I

Lewey, Sir Arthur Werner, 1894–1973, vol. VII

Lewin, Baron (Life Peer); Adm. of the Fleet Terence Thornton Lewin, 1920–1999, vol. X

Lewin, Brig.-Gen. Arthur Corrie, 1874–1952, vol. V

Lewin, Captain Duncan; *see* Lewin, Captain E. D. G.

Lewin, Captain (Edgar) Duncan (Goodenough), 1912–1983, vol. VIII
Lewin, Maj.-Gen. Ernest Ord, 1879–1950, vol. IV
Lewin, George Arthur, 1867–1941, vol. IV
Lewin, Rev. George Harrison R.; *see* Ross-Lewin.
Lewin, (George) Ronald, 1914–1984, vol. VIII
Lewin, Brig.-Gen. Henry Frederick Elliott, 1872–1946, vol. IV
Lewin, Octavia Margaret Sophia, *died* 1955, vol. V
Lewin, Percy Evans, 1876–1955, vol. V
Lewin, Ven. Richard S. R.; *see* Ross-Lewin.
Lewin, Rev. Robert O'Donelan R.; *see* Ross-Lewin.
Lewin, Ronald; *see* Lewin, G. R.
Lewin, Lt-Col Thomas Herbert, 1839–1916, vol. II
Lewin, Walpole Sinclair, 1915–1980, vol. VII
Lewin, William Charles James; *see* Terriss, William.
Lewis, Ada Travers, *died* 1931, vol. III
Lewis, Mrs Agnes Smith, 1843–1926, vol. II
Lewis, Sir Alfred Edward, 1868–1940, vol. III
Lewis, A(lfred) Neville; *see* Lewis, Neville.
Lewis, Sir Allen Montgomery, 1909–1993, vol. IX
Lewis, Sir Andrew Jopp Williams, 1875–1952, vol. V
Lewis, Adm. Sir Andrew Mackenzie, 1918–1993, vol. IX
Lewis, Angelo, 1839–1919, vol. II
Lewis, Sir Anthony Carey, 1915–1983, vol. VIII
Lewis, Sir Arthur; *see* Lewis, Sir W. A.
Lewis, Arthur Cyril Wentworth, 1885–1928, vol. II
Lewis, Lt-Col Arthur Francis O.; *see* Owen-Lewis.
Lewis, Arthur Griffith Poyer, 1848–1909, vol. I
Lewis, Arthur Hornby, 1843–1926, vol. II
Lewis, Arthur King, 1867–1954, vol. V
Lewis, Arthur William John, 1917–1998, vol. X
Lewis, Sir Aubrey Julian, 1900–1975, vol. VII
Lewis, B. Roland, 1884–1959, vol. V
Lewis, Barnet, *died* 1929, vol. III
Lewis, Bernard, 1905–1999, vol. X
Lewis, Brig.-Gen. Bridges George, 1857–1925, vol. II
Lewis, Bunnell, 1824–1908, vol. I
Lewis, C. Gasquoine; *see* Hartley, C. G.
Lewis, Cecil Arthur, 1898–1997, vol. X
Lewis, Cecil D.; *see* Day-Lewis.
Lewis, Ven. Charles Gerwyn Rice, *died* 1964, vol. VI
Lewis, Ven. Christopher Gwynne, 1895–1963, vol. VI
Lewis, Brig. Sir Clinton Gresham, 1885–1978, vol. VII
Lewis, Clive Staples, 1898–1963, vol. VI
Lewis, Cyril Alexander O.; *see* Owen-Lewis.
Lewis, Cyril Arthur Liddon, 1873–1943, vol. IV
Lewis, D. Morgan, 1851–1937, vol. III
Lewis, David, 1849–1897, vol. I
Lewis, Col David Francis, 1855–1927, vol. II
Lewis, Very Rev. David Gareth, 1931–1997, vol. X
Lewis, David John, 1893–1982, vol. VIII
Lewis, David Malcolm, 1928–1994, vol. IX
Lewis, David Thomas, 1909–1992, vol. IX
Lewis, Dominic Bevan Wyndham, *died* 1969, vol. VI
Lewis, Lt Donald Swain, 1886–1916, vol. II
Lewis, Mrs Dorothy; *see* Lewis, Mrs M. D.
Lewis, Sir Duncan O.; *see* Orr-Lewis.

Lewis, Edgar Samuel, 1853–1922, vol. II
Lewis, E(dward) Daly, 1908–1977, vol. VII
Lewis, Rev. Edward Lincoln, 1865–1939, vol. III
Lewis, Maj.-Gen. Edward Mann, 1863–1949, vol. IV
Lewis, Sir Edward Roberts, 1900–1980, vol. VII
Lewis, Eiluned, *died* 1979, vol. VII
Lewis, Hon. Sir Elliott; *see* Lewis, Hon. Sir N. E.
Lewis, Emily Catherine, *died* 1965, vol. VI
Lewis, Eric William Charles, 1914–1981, vol. VIII
Lewis, Major Ernest Albert, 1873–1937, vol. III
Lewis, Ernest Harry, 1877–1951, vol. V
Lewis, Essington, 1881–1961, vol. VI
Lewis, Very Rev. Evan, 1818–1901, vol. I
Lewis, Francis John, 1875–1955, vol. V
Lewis, Rev. Frank Ernest, *died* 1929, vol. III
Lewis, Frederic Henry, 1865–1940, vol. III
Lewis, Brig.-Gen. Frederick Gustav, 1873–1967, vol. VI
Lewis, Sir Frederick Orr O.; *see* Orr-Lewis.
Lewis, Lt-Col George Alfred, 1869–1961, vol. VI
Lewis, Sir George Henry, 1st Bt, 1833–1911, vol. I
Lewis, Sir George James Ernest, 3rd Bt, 1910–1945, vol. IV
Lewis, Sir George James Graham, 2nd Bt, 1868–1927, vol. II
Lewis, George P.; *see* Pitt-Lewis.
Lewis, Gerald Champion, 1863–1939, vol. III
Lewis, Gilbert Newton, 1875–1946, vol. IV
Lewis, Gwynedd Margaret, 1911–1993, vol. IX
Lewis, Harold, 1856–1924, vol. II
Lewis, Maj.-Gen. Harold Victor, 1887–1945, vol. IV
Lewis, (Harry) Sinclair, 1885–1951, vol. V
Lewis, Sir Hawthorne; *see* Lewis, Sir W. H.
Lewis, Rev. Henry, 1857–1914, vol. I
Lewis, Sir Henry, 1847–1923, vol. II
Lewis, Col Henry, 1847–1925, vol. II
Lewis, Henry, 1889–1968, vol. VI
Lewis, Maj.-Gen. Henry Augustus, 1879–1966, vol. VI
Lewis, Henry David, 1875–1936, vol. III
Lewis, Captain Henry Edward, 1889–1979, vol. VII
Lewis, Henry Gethin, 1899–1986, vol. VIII
Lewis, Rt Hon. Sir Herbert; *see* Lewis, Rt Hon. Sir J. H.
Lewis, Sir Herbert David William, 1872–1931, vol. III
Lewis, Col Herman Le R.; *see* Le Roy-Lewis.
Lewis, Howell Elvet, 1860–1953, vol. V
Lewis, Hugh, *died* 1937, vol. III
Lewis, Hywel David, 1910–1992, vol. IX
Lewis, Sir Ian Malcolm, 1925–1990, vol. VIII
Lewis, Isaac, 1849–1927, vol. II
Lewis, (Isaiah) Leonard, 1909–1994, vol. IX
Lewis, Ivor Evan Gerwyn, 1904–1977, vol. VII
Lewis, J(ack) Haydon, 1904–1971, vol. VII
Lewis, Rev. Canon James Abraham, 1874–1946, vol. IV
Lewis, Brig. James Charles W.; *see* Windsor Lewis.
Lewis, Rev. James Dawson, 1845–1905, vol. I
Lewis, James Hamilton, *died* 1939, vol. III
Lewis, James Henry, 1856–1924, vol. II
Lewis, Jane, (Lady Lewis), *died* 1939, vol. III
Lewis, Joan; *see* Lancaster Lewis, J. C.
Lewis, Hon. John, 1842–1923, vol. II

Lewis, Lt-Col John, 1859–1937, vol. III
Lewis, John, 1851–1943, vol. IV
Lewis, John, 1912–1969, vol. VI
Lewis, John Christopher, 1842–1918, vol. II
Lewis, Sir (John) Duncan O.; *see* Orr-Lewis.
Lewis, John F., 1876–1963, vol. VI
Lewis, John Hardwicke, 1840–1927, vol. II
Lewis, Rt Hon. Sir (John) Herbert, 1858–1933, vol. III
Lewis, John Llewellyn, 1880–1969, vol. VI
Lewis, Maj.-Gen. John Michael Hardwicke, 1919–1999, vol. X
Lewis, John Penry, 1854–1923, vol. II
Lewis, Rev. John Price, 1857–1930, vol. III
Lewis, John Spedan, 1885–1963, vol. VI
Lewis, Sir John Todd, 1901–1977, vol. VII
Lewis, Most Rev. John Travers, 1825–1901, vol. I
Lewis, Ven. John Wilfred, 1909–1984, vol. VIII
Lewis, Very Rev. Julius, *died* 1920, vol. II
Lewis, Sir Kenneth, 1916–1997, vol. X
Lewis, Maj.-Gen. Kenneth Frank Mackay, 1897–1993, vol. IX
Lewis, Leonard; *see* Lewis, I. L.
Lewis, Leonard John, 1909–1999, vol. X
Lewis, Rt Rev. Lewis, 1821–1905, vol. I
Lewis, Lucas Reginald, 1883–1931, vol. III
Lewis, Mabel Terry, (Mrs R. C. Batley), *died* 1957, vol. V
Lewis, Malcolm Meredith, 1891–1955, vol. V
Lewis, Mary; *see* Milne, Mrs Leslie.
Lewis, Mrs (Mary) Dorothy, 1894–1975, vol. VII
Lewis, Mary W.; *see* Wolseley-Lewis.
Lewis, Michael Arthur, 1890–1970, vol. VI
Lewis, Michael Samuel, 1937–1994, vol. IX
Lewis, Morris Michael, 1898–1971, vol. VII
Lewis, Hon. Sir (Neil) Elliott, 1858–1935, vol. III
Lewis, Neville, 1895–1972, vol. VII
Lewis, Norman Bache, 1896–1988, vol. VIII
Lewis, Oswald, 1887–1966, vol. VI
Lewis, Percival Cecil, 1912–1983, vol. VIII
Lewis, Percy G., 1862–1935, vol. III
Lewis, Col Percy John Tonson, 1861–1910, vol. I
Lewis, (Percy) Wyndham, 1884–1957, vol. V
Lewis, Peter Edwin, 1912–1976, vol. VII
Lewis, Richard, 1914–1990, vol. VIII
Lewis, Lt-Col Richard Charles, *died* 1914, vol. I
Lewis, Maj.-Gen. Sir Richard George, 1895–1965, vol. VI
Lewis, Maj.-Gen. Robert Stedman, 1898–1987, vol. VIII
Lewis, Captain Roger Curzon, 1909–1994, vol. IX
Lewis, Ronald Howard, 1909–1990, vol. VIII
Lewis, Sir Samuel, 1843–1903, vol. I
Lewis, Saunders, 1893–1983, vol. VIII
Lewis, Sinclair; *see* Lewis, H. S.
Lewis, Col Somers Reginald, 1843–1931, vol. III
Lewis, Stanley Radcliffe, 1878–1964, vol. VI
Lewis, Thomas, *died* 1928, vol. II
Lewis, Sir Thomas, 1881–1945, vol. IV
Lewis, Thomas, 1868–1953, vol. V
Lewis, Thomas, 1873–1962, vol. VI
Lewis, Thomas Arthur, 1881–1923, vol. II
Lewis, Col Thomas Lewis Hampton, 1834–1912, vol. I
Lewis, Sir Thomas Williams, 1852–1926, vol. II

Lewis, Vernon Arthur, *died* 1950, vol. IV
Lewis, Sir Walter Llewellyn, 1849–1930, vol. III
Lewis, Walter Samuel, 1894–1962, vol. VI
Lewis, Wilfrid Bennett, 1908–1987, vol. VIII
Lewis, Sir Wilfrid Hubert Poyer, 1881–1950, vol. IV
Lewis, Rev. Canon William, *died* 1922, vol. II
Lewis, Sir (William) Arthur, 1915–1991, vol. IX
Lewis, William B.; *see* Bevan-Lewis.
Lewis, William Cudmore McCullagh, *died* 1956, vol. V
Lewis, William Edmund Ames, 1912–1988, vol. VIII
Lewis, William George, 1844–1926, vol. II
Lewis, Sir (William) Hawthorne, 1888–1970, vol. VI
Lewis, William Henry, 1866–1948, vol. IV
Lewis, William Henry, 1869–1963, vol. VI
Lewis, William James, 1847–1926, vol. II
Lewis, William Waller; *see* Waller, Lewis.
Lewis, Sir Willmott Harsant, 1877–1950, vol. IV
Lewis, Wilmarth Sheldon, 1895–1979, vol. VII
Lewis, Wyndham; *see* Lewis, P. W.
Lewis-Crosby, Very Rev. Ernest Henry, *died* 1961, vol. VI
Lewis-Dale, Henry Angley, 1876–1938, vol. III
Lewisham, Viscount; William Legge, 1913–1942, vol. IV
Lewisohn, Frederick, 1878–1951, vol. V
Lewison, Peter George Hornby, 1911–1992, vol. IX
Le Witt, Jan, 1907–1991, vol. IX
Lewtas, Lt-Col John, *died* 1920, vol. II
Lewthwaite, Raymond, 1894–1972, vol. VII
Lewthwaite, Sir William, 1st Bt, 1853–1927, vol. II
Lewthwaite, Sir William, 2nd Bt, 1882–1933, vol. III
Lewthwaite, Sir William Anthony, 3rd Bt, 1912–1993, vol. IX
Lewton-Brian, Lawrence, 1879–1922, vol. II
Lewy, Casimir, 1919–1991, vol. IX
Ley, Arthur Harris, 1903–1993, vol. IX
Ley, Arthur Herbert, 1879–1938, vol. III
Ley, Sir Francis, 1st Bt, 1846–1916, vol. II
Ley, Sir Francis Douglas, 4th Bt, 1907–1995, vol. IX
Ley, Sir Gerald Gordon, 3rd Bt, 1902–1980, vol. VII
Ley, Sir Gordon; *see* Ley, Sir H. G.
Ley, Henry George, 1887–1962, vol. VI
Ley, Sir (Henry) Gordon, 2nd Bt, 1874–1944, vol. IV
Ley, Adm. James Clement, 1869–1946, vol. IV
Ley, James William Thomas, *died* 1943, vol. IV
Ley, William Henry, 1847–1919, vol. II
Leyborne-Popham, Francis William, 1862–1907, vol. I
Leycester, William Hamilton, 1864–1925, vol. II
Leyds, Willem Johannes, 1859–1940, vol. III
Leyel, Mrs C. F., (Hilda Winifred), *died* 1957, vol. V
Leyland, Christopher John, 1849–1926, vol. II
Leyland, Sir Edward N.; *see* Naylor-Leyland.
Leyland, Captain Sir Herbert Scarisbrick N.; *see* Naylor-Leyland.
Leyland, John, *died* 1924, vol. II

Leyland, Norman Harrison, 1921–1981, vol. VIII
Leyland, Peter; see Pyke-Lees, W. K.
Leyland, Sir Vivyan Edward N.; see Naylor-Leyland.
Leys, Sir Cecil; see Leys, Sir W. C.
Leys, John Kirkwood, 1847–1909, vol. I
Leys, Sir (William) Cecil, 1877–1950, vol. IV
Leyser, Karl Joseph, 1920–1992, vol. IX
Leyton, Albert Sidney Frankau, 1869–1921, vol. II
Leyton, Nevil; see Leyton, R. N. A.
Leyton, Otto, 1873–1938, vol. III
Leyton, (Robert) Nevil (Arthur), born 1910, vol. VIII
Li Ching Fong, 1854–1934, vol. III
Li, Choh-Ming, 1912–1991, vol. IX
Liakat Ali, Sir Syed, 1878–1947, vol. IV
Liaqat Hyat Khan, Nawab Sir, 1887–1948, vol. IV
Liardet, Maj-Gen. Sir Claude Francis, 1881–1966, vol. VI
Liardet, Maj.-Gen. Henry Maughan, 1906–1996, vol. X
Lias, Rev. John James, 1834–1923, vol. II
Lias, William John, died 1941, vol. IV
Libbert, Laurence Joseph, 1933–1985, vol. VIII
Libby, Willard Frank, 1908–1980, vol. VII
Liberty, Sir Arthur Lasenby, 1843–1917, vol. II
Liberty, Captain Ivor Stewart-, 1887–1952, vol. V
Lichfield, 3rd Earl of, 1856–1918, vol. II
Lichfield, 4th Earl of, 1883–1960, vol. V
Lichine, David, 1910–1972, vol. VII
Lichine, Mme David; see Riabouchinska, Tatiana.
Lichnowsky, Princess Mechtilde, 1879–1958, vol. V
Lichtenberger, Rt Rev. Arthur Carl, 1900–1968, vol. VI
Lichtenburg, Captain John Wills, 1872–1912, vol. I
Lichtenstein, Roy, 1923–1997, vol. X
Lickley, Sir Robert Lang, 1912–1998, vol. X
Lidbury, Sir Charles, 1880–1978, vol. VII
Lidbury, Sir David John, 1884–1973, vol. VII
Lidbury, Ernest Alan, 1862–1948, vol. IV
Lidbury, Sir John Towersey, 1912–1994, vol. IX
Liddall, Sir Walter Sydney, 1884–1963, vol. VI
Liddell, Adolphus George Charles, 1846–1920, vol. II
Liddell, Lt-Col Arthur Robert, 1872–1966, vol. VI
Liddell, Charles, 1856–1922, vol. II
Liddell, Gen. Sir Clive Gerard, 1883–1956, vol. V
Liddell, Colin, 1862–1916, vol. II, vol. III
Liddell, Donald Woollven, 1917–1996, vol. X
Liddell, Rev. Edward, died 1914, vol. I
Liddell, Edward George Tandy, 1895–1981, vol. VIII
Liddell, Sir Frederick Francis, 1865–1950, vol. IV
Liddell, Guy Maynard, 1892–1958, vol. V
Liddell, Harry, died 1931, vol. III
Liddell, Very Rev. Henry George, 1811–1898, vol. I
Liddell, (John) Robert, 1908–1992, vol. IX
Liddell, Major John Stewart, died 1934, vol. III
Liddell, Laurence Ernest, 1916–1985, vol. VIII
Liddell, Lionel Charles, 1868–1942, vol. IV
Liddell, Mark Harvey, 1866–1936, vol. III
Liddell, Maximilian Friedrich, 1887–1968, vol. VI
Liddell, Peter John, 1921–1979, vol. VII
Liddell, Robert; see Liddell, J. R.
Liddell, Sir Robert Morris, 1870–1928, vol. II

Liddell, T. Hodgson, 1860–1925, vol. II
Liddell, Maj.-Gen. Sir William Andrew, 1865–1949, vol. IV
Liddell Hart, Sir Basil Henry, 1895–1970, vol. VI
Lidderdale, Sir David William Shuckburgh, 1910–1998, vol. X
Lidderdale, Rt Hon. William, 1832–1902, vol. I
Liddiard, Mabel, 1882–1962, vol. VI
Liddiard, Richard England, 1917–1993, vol. IX
Liddle, Sir Donald Ross, 1906–1989, vol. VIII
Liddle, Henry Weddell, 1885–1956, vol. V
Liddle, Robert W., 1864–1917, vol. II
Lidgett, Rev. John Scott, 1854–1953, vol. V
Lidiard, Sir Herbert, 1864–1941, vol. IV
Lidstone, George James, 1870–1952, vol. V
Lie, Jonas, 1833–1908, vol. I
Lie, Trygve Halvdan, 1896–1968, vol. VI
Lieber, B. Franklin, died 1915, vol. I
Liebling, George, died 1946, vol. IV
Lienhop, Sir John Henry, 1898–1967, vol. VI (AII)
Liesching, Sir Percivale, 1895–1973, vol. VII
Lifar, Serge, 1905–1986, vol. VIII
Lifford, 5th Viscount, 1837–1913, vol. I
Lifford, 6th Viscount, 1844–1925, vol. II
Lifford, 7th Viscount, 1880–1954, vol. V
Lifford, 8th Viscount, 1900–1987, vol. VIII
Ligertwood, Sir George Coutts, 1888–1967, vol. VI
Liggins, Sir Edmund Naylor, 1909–1991, vol. IX
Light, Sir Edgar William, 1885–1969, vol. VI
Lightbody, Philip Frazer, 1880–1936, vol. III
Lightbody, William Paterson Hay, 1893–1962, vol. VI
Lightbound, Rt Rev. Aloysius Anselm, died 1973, vol. VII
Lightbown, Sir David Lincoln, 1932–1995, vol. IX
Lightfoot, Ben, 1888–1966, vol. VI
Lightfoot, Rev. John, 1853–1917, vol. II
Lightfoot, Rev. John Alfred, 1861–1928, vol. II
Lightfoot, Nicholas Morpeth Hutchinson, 1902–1962, vol. VI
Lightfoot, Ven. Reginald Prideaux, 1836–1906, vol. I
Lightfoot, Robert Henry, 1883–1953, vol. V
Lightfoot, Ven. Thomas Fothergill, 1831–1904, vol. I
Lightfoot Boston, Sir Henry Josiah; see Boston.
Lighthall, William Douw, 1857–1954, vol. V
Lighthill, Sir James; see Lighthill, Sir M. J.
Lighthill, Sir (Michael) James, 1924–1998, vol. X
Lightley, Rev. John W., 1867–1948, vol. IV
Lightman, Harold, 1906–1998, vol. X
Lighton, Sir (Christopher) Robert, 7th Bt, 1848–1929, vol. III
Lighton, Sir Christopher Robert, 8th Bt, 1897–1993, vol. IX
Lighton, Sir Robert; see Lighton, Sir C. R.
Lightstone, Herbert, 1878–1942, vol. IV
Lightwood, Reginald, 1898–1985, vol. VIII
Liley, Sir (Albert) William, 1929–1983, vol. VIII
Liley, Sir William; see Liley, Sir A. W.
Lilford, 5th Baron, 1863–1945, vol. IV
Lilford, 6th Baron, 1869–1949, vol. IV
Lilienthal, David Eli, 1899–1981, vol. VIII
Lilley, Rev. Canon Alfred Leslie, 1860–1948, vol. IV

Lilley, Cecil William, 1878–1953, vol. V
Lilley, Sir Charles, 1830–1897, vol. I
Lilley, Ernest Lewis, 1876–1948, vol. IV
Lilley, Francis James Patrick, 1907–1971, vol. VII
Lilley, Captain James Lindsay, 1871–1923, vol. II
Lilley, Thomas, 1902–1959, vol. V
Lillico, Hon. Sir Alexander, 1872–1966, vol. VI
Lillico, William Lionel James, 1880–1948, vol. IV
Lillicrap, Sir Charles Swift, 1887–1966, vol. VI
Lillicrap, Harry George, 1913–2000, vol. X
Lillie, Beatrice Gladys, (Lady Peel), 1894–1989, vol. VIII
Lillie, Rev. Handley William Russell, 1902–1967, vol. VI
Lillie, Very Rev. Henry Alexander, 1911–1986, vol. VIII
Lillie, John Adam, 1884–1983, vol. VIII
Lillingston, Rev. Canon Arthur Blackwell Goulburn, 1864–1943, vol. IV
Lilly, Malcolm Douglas, 1936–1998, vol. X
Lilly, Walter Elsworthy, 1867–1940, vol. III
Lilly, William Samuel, 1840–1919, vol. II
Lima, Sir Bertram Lewis, 1883–1919, vol. II
Lima, Most Rev. Mgr Joaquim Rodriques, 1875–1936, vol. III
Limann, Hilla, 1934–1998, vol. X
Limbdi, Thakore Saheb Shri Daulatsinhji Jaswantsinhji Bahadur, 1868–1940, vol. III
Limbert, Roy, died 1954, vol. V
Limentani, Prof. Uberto, 1913–1989, vol. VIII
Limerick, 4th Earl of, 1863–1929, vol. III
Limerick, 5th Earl of, 1888–1967, vol. VI
Limerick, Countess of; (Mary Imelda Josephine), died 1943, vol. IV
Limerick, Dowager Countess of; (Angela Olivia Pery), 1897–1981, vol. VIII
Limpenny, Engr-Rear-Adm. Charles Joseph, 1881–1952, vol. V
Limpus, Adm. Sir Arthur Henry, 1863–1931, vol. III
Limri, Thakur Saheb Sir, 1859–1907, vol. I
Lin Yutang, 1895–1976, vol. VII
Lincoln, Sir Anthony Handley, 1911–1993, vol. IX
Lincoln, Hon. Sir Anthony Leslie Julian, 1920–1991, vol. IX
Lincoln, F(redman) Ashe, 1907–1998, vol. X
Lincoln, Joseph, 1870–1944, vol. IV
Lincoln, Air Cdre Philip Lionel, 1892–1981, vol. VIII
Lincolnshire, 1st Marquess of, 1843–1928, vol. II
Lind, Hon. Sir Albert Eli, 1878–1964, vol. VI
Lind-af-Hageby, Emelie Augusta Louise, 1878–1963, vol. VI
Lind-Smith, Gerard Gustave, 1903–1982, vol. VIII
Lindars, Barnabas; see Lindars, Rev. F. C.
Lindars, Rev. Frederick Chevallier, (Barnabas), 1923–1991, vol. IX
Lindbergh, Col Charles Augustus, 1902–1974, vol. VII
Lindell, John Henry Stockton, 1908–1973, vol. VII
Lindemann, Lt-Col Charles Lionel, 1885–1970, vol. VI
Lindgren, Baron (Life Peer); George Samuel Lindgren, 1900–1971, vol. VII

Lindley, Baron (Life Peer); Nathaniel Lindley, 1828–1921, vol. II
Lindley, Sir Arnold Lewis George, 1902–1995, vol. IX
Lindley, Charles Gustaf, 1865–1957, vol. V
Lindley, Rt Hon. Sir Francis Oswald, 1872–1950, vol. IV
Lindley, Sir Frank; see Lindley, Sir M. F.
Lindley, Rear-Adm. George Robert, 1850–1918, vol. II
Lindley, James Bryant, 1851–1940, vol. III
Lindley, Maj.-Gen. Hon. John Edward, 1860 1925, vol. II
Lindley, Sir (Mark) Frank, 1881–1951, vol. V
Lindley, Hon. Walter Barry, 1861–1944, vol. IV
Lindley, Sir William Heerlein, 1853–1917, vol. II
Lindley-Jones, Walter, 1863–1930, vol. III
Lindner, Doris Lexey Margaret, 1896–1979, vol. VII
Lindner, Ingram Joseph, died 1959, vol. V
Lindner, Peter Moffat, 1852–1949, vol. IV
Lindo, Sir (Henry) Laurence, 1911–1980, vol. VII
Lindo, Sir Laurence; see Lindo, Sir H. L.
Lindon, John Benjamin, 1884–1960, vol. V
Lindon, Sir Leonard Charles Edward, 1896–1978, vol. VII
Lindop, Audrey Beatrice Noël E.; see Erskine-Lindop.
Lindop, Col Carl Arthur Boys, 1899–1968, vol. VI
Lindow, Lt-Col Isaac William B.; see Burns-Lindow.
Lindrum, Walter, 1898–1960, vol. V
Lindsay, 11th Earl of, 1832–1917, vol. II
Lindsay, 12th Earl of, 1867–1939, vol. III
Lindsay, 13th Earl of, 1872–1943, vol. IV
Lindsay, 14th Earl of, 1901–1985, vol. VIII
Lindsay, 15th Earl of, 1926–1989, vol. VIII
Lindsay of Birker, 1st Baron, 1879–1952, vol. V
Lindsay of Birker, 2nd Baron, 1909–1994, vol. IX
Lindsay, Alexander Martin, 1844–1906, vol. I
Lindsay, Sir Benjamin, died 1939, vol. III
Lindsay, Caroline Blanche Elizabeth, (Lady Lindsay), died 1912, vol. I
Lindsay, Sir Charles William, 1856–1939, vol. III
Lindsay, Sir Coutts, 2nd Bt, 1824–1913, vol. I
Lindsay, Col Creighton Hutchinson, 1877–1941, vol. IV
Lindsay, Sir Darcy, 1865–1941, vol. IV
Lindsay, Sir Daryl; see Lindsay, Sir E. D.
Lindsay, David, 1856–1922, vol. II
Lindsay, Maj.-Gen. Edward Stewart, 1905–1990, vol. VIII
Lindsay, Ernest Charles, 1883–1943, vol. IV
Lindsay, Sir (Ernest) Daryl, 1889–1976, vol. VII
Lindsay, Maj.-Gen. George Mackintosh, 1880–1956, vol. V
Lindsay, Harry; see Hudson, H. Lindsay.
Lindsay, Sir Harry Alexander Fanshawe, 1881–1963, vol. VI
Lindsay, Col Henry Arthur Peyton, 1868–1926, vol. II
Lindsay, Col Henry Edzell Morgan, 1857–1935, vol. III
Lindsay, Lt-Col Henry Gore, 1830–1914, vol. I
Lindsay, Howard, 1889–1968, vol. VI

Lindsay, Major Sir Humphrey B.; *see* Broun Lindsay.
Lindsay, Ian Gordon, 1906–1966, vol. VI
Lindsay, Jack, 1900–1990, vol. VIII
Lindsay, Rev. James, *died* 1923, vol. II
Lindsay, James Alexander, 1856–1931, vol. III
Lindsay, Lt-Col James Howard, *died* 1940, vol. III
Lindsay, Hon. James Louis, 1906–1997, vol. X
Lindsay, Sir John, 1860–1927, vol. II
Lindsay, John Allan, 1865–1942, vol. IV
Lindsay, John Vliet, 1921–2000, vol. X
Lindsay, Kenneth Martin, 1897–1991, vol. IX
Lindsay, Leonard Cecil Colin, 1857–1941, vol. IV
Lindsay, Lionel Arthur, 1861–1945, vol. IV
Lindsay, Sir Lionel Arthur, 1874–1961, vol. VI
Lindsay of Dowhill, Sir Martin Alexander, 1st Bt, 1905–1981, vol. VIII
Lindsay, Nicholas Vachel; *see* Lindsay, Vachel.
Lindsay, Norman Alfred William, 1879–1969, vol. VI
Lindsay, Maj.-Gen. Peter; *see* Lindsay, Maj.-Gen. E. S.
Lindsay, Philip, 1906–1958, vol. V
Lindsay, Rt Hon. Sir Ronald Charles, 1877–1945, vol. IV
Lindsay, Ven. Thomas Enraght, *died* 1947, vol. IV
Lindsay, Thomas Martin, 1843–1914, vol. I
Lindsay, Ven. Thomas Somerville, 1854–1933, vol. III
Lindsay, Vachel, 1879–1931, vol. III
Lindsay, Wallace M., 1858–1937, vol. III
Lindsay, Walter Charles, 1866–1929, vol. III
Lindsay, Maj.-Gen. Sir Walter Fullerton Lodovic, 1855–1930, vol. III
Lindsay, Sir William, 1907–1986, vol. VIII
Lindsay, William Alexander, 1846–1926, vol. II
Lindsay, William Arthur, 1866–1936, vol. III
Lindsay, Maj.-Gen. William Bethune, 1880–1933, vol. III
Lindsay, Sir William O'Brien, 1909–1975, vol. VII
Lindsay-Fynn, Sir Basil Mortimer, 1901–1988, vol. VIII
Lindsay-Hogg, Sir Anthony Henry, 2nd Bt, 1908–1968, vol. VI
Lindsay-Hogg, Sir Edward William, 4th Bt, 1910–1999, vol. X
Lindsay-Hogg, Sir Lindsay, 1st Bt, 1853–1923, vol. II
Lindsay-Hogg, Sir William Lindsay, 3rd Bt, 1930–1987, vol. VIII
Lindsay-Rea, Robert; *see* Rea.
Lindsell, Henry Martin, 1846–1925, vol. II
Lindsell, Herbert George, 1903–1973, vol. VII
Lindsell, Col Robert Frederick, 1856–1914, vol. I
Lindsell, Lt-Gen. Sir Wilfrid Gordon, 1884–1973, vol. VII
Lindsey, 11th Earl of, 1815–1899, vol. I
Lindsey, 12th Earl of, 1861–1938, vol. III
Lindsey, 13th Earl of, and **Abingdon,** 8th Earl of, 1887–1963, vol. VI
Lindt, Auguste Rudolph, 1905–2000, vol. X
Line, Ven. Henry, *died* 1938, vol. III
Lineham, Joseph, 1869–1952, vol. V
Linehan, John, 1865–1935, vol. III
Linehan, Patrick Aloysius, 1904–1973, vol. VII

Linehan, William, 1892–1955, vol. V
Lines, Albert Walter, 1914–1976, vol. VII
Lines, Rt Rev. Edwin S., 1845–1927, vol. II
Lines, Vincent, 1909–1968, vol. VI
Lines, Walter, 1882–1972, vol. VII
Linfield, Sir Arthur George, *died* 1974, vol. VII (AII)
Linfield, Frederick Caesar, *died* 1939, vol. III
Linfoot, Edward Hubert, 1905–1982, vol. VIII
Ling, Arthur George, 1913–1995, vol. IX (AII)
Ling, Arthur Robert, 1861–1937, vol. III
Ling, Brig. Christopher George, 1880–1953, vol. V
Ling, Maj.-Gen. Fergus Alan Humphrey, 1914–1995, vol. IX
Ling, George Herbert, 1874–1942, vol. IV
Lingeman, Eric Ralph, 1898–1966, vol. VI
Lingen, 1st Baron, 1819–1905, vol. I
Lingham, Brig. John, 1897–1976, vol. VII
Link, Edwin Albert, 1904–1981, vol. VIII
Linklater, Eric, 1899–1974, vol. VII
Linklater, John Edmund, 1848–1917, vol. II
Linklater, Nelson Valdemar, 1918–1997, vol. X
Linklater, Rev. Robert, 1839–1915, vol. I
Links, Mary, (Mrs J. G. Links); *see* Lutyens, Mary.
Linlithgow, 1st Marquess of, 1860–1908, vol. I
Linlithgow, 2nd Marquess of, 1887–1952, vol. V
Linlithgow, 3rd Marquess of, 1912–1987, vol. VIII
Linnell, Air Marshal Sir Francis John, 1892–1944 vol. IV
Linnell, John Wycliffe, 1878–1967, vol. VI
Linnell, Wilfred Herbert, 1894–1983, vol. VIII
Linnett, John Wilfrid, 1913–1975, vol. VII
Linnett, Michael Joseph, 1926–1996, vol. X
Linsley, Ven. Stanley Frederick, 1903–1974, vol. VII
Linstead, Sir Hugh Nicholas, 1901–1987, vol. VIII
Linstead, Sir Patrick; *see* Linstead, Sir R. P.
Linstead, Sir (Reginald) Patrick, 1902–1966, vol. VI
Lintern, Bernard Francis, 1908–1979, vol. VII
Lintern, Reep, 1902–1967, vol. VI
Linthorne, Sir Richard Roope, 1864–1935, vol. III
Linton, Sir Andrew, 1893–1971, vol. VII
Linton, David Leslie, 1906–1971, vol. VII
Linton, Elizabeth Lynn, 1822–1898, vol. I
Linton, Sir James Dromgole, 1840–1916, vol. II
Linton, Rt Rev. James Henry, 1879–1958, vol. V
Linton, Ralph, 1893–1953, vol. V
Linton, Sir Richard, 1879–1959, vol. V
Linton, Robert George, 1882–1960, vol. V
Lintott, Major Alfred Lord, *died* 1940, vol. III
Lintott, Henry John, 1877–1965, vol. VI
Lintott, Sir Henry John Bevis, 1908–1995, vol. IX
Linzee, Captain Robert Gordon Hood, 1900–1973, vol. VII
Lion, Flora, *died* 1958, vol. V
Lion, Leon M., 1879–1947, vol. IV
Lipatti, Dinu, 1917–1950, vol. IV
Lipfriend, Alan, 1916–1996, vol. X
Lipinsky, Sigmund, 1873–1940, vol. III
Lipman, Vivian David, 1921–1990, vol. VIII
Lipmann, Fritz Albert, 1899–1986, vol. VIII
Lippincott, Craige, 1846–1911, vol. I
Lippmann, Walter, 1889–1974, vol. VII
Lipscomb, Maj.-Gen. Christopher Godfrey, 1907–1982, vol. VIII

Lipscomb, Air Vice-Marshal Frederick Elvy, 1902–1992, vol. IX
Lipsett, Maj.-Gen. Louis James, 1874–1918, vol. II
Lipson, Daniel Leopold, 1886–1963, vol. VI
Lipson, Ephraim, 1888–1960, vol. V
Lipson, Henry Solomon, 1910–1991, vol. IX
Lipton, Marcus, 1900–1978, vol. VII
Lipton, Sir Thomas Johnstone, 1st Bt, 1850–1931, vol. III
Lisburne, 6th Earl of, 1862–1899, vol. I
Lisburne, 7th Earl of, 1892–1965, vol. VI
Lish, Joseph J., *died* 1923, vol. II
Lisle, 5th Baron, 1811–1898, vol. I
Lisle, 6th Baron, 1840–1919, vol. II
Lisle, 7th Baron, 1903–1997, vol. X
Lisle, Aubrey Edwin O.; *see* Orchard-Lisle.
Lismer, Arthur, 1885–1969, vol. VI
Lismore, 2nd Viscount, 1815–1898, vol. I
Lissack, Victor Jack, 1930–1981, vol. VIII
Lissmann, Hans Werner, 1909–1995, vol. IX
Lister, 1st Baron, 1827–1912, vol. I
Lister, Arthur, 1905–1975, vol. VII
Lister, Sir Ashton, 1845–1929, vol. III
Lister, Hon. Charles Alfred, 1887–1915, vol. I
Lister, Charles Ashton, 1871–1965, vol. VI
Lister, Sir (Charles) Percy, 1897–1983, vol. VIII
Lister, Sir Frederick; *see* Lister, Sir T. F.
Lister, Lt-Col Frederick Hamilton, 1880–1971, vol. VII
Lister, Sir (Frederick) Spencer, 1876–1939, vol. III
Lister, Lt-Col Harry Laidman, 1902–1982, vol. VIII
Lister, Col James Fraser, *died* 1944, vol. IV
Lister, John, 1931–1989, vol. VIII
Lister, Joseph Jackson, *died* 1927, vol. II
Lister, Laurier, 1907–1986, vol. VIII
Lister, Sir Percy; *see* Lister, Sir C. P.
Lister, Hon. Sir Reginald, 1865–1912, vol. I
Lister, Sir Spencer; *see* Lister, Sir F. S.
Lister, Hon. Thomas, 1878–1904, vol. I
Lister, Thomas, 1892–1967, vol. VI
Lister, Thomas David, 1869–1924, vol. II
Lister, Sir (Thomas) Frederick, *died* 1966, vol. VI
Lister, Thomas Liddell, 1922–1985, vol. VIII
Lister, Rev. Thomas Llewellyn, *died* 1926, vol. II
Lister, Sir Thomas Villiers, 1832–1902, vol. I
Lister, Tom, 1887–1945, vol. IV
Lister, Dame Unity Viola, 1913–1998, vol. X
Lister, Sir William Tindall, 1868–1944, vol. IV
Lister-Kaye, Sir Cecil Edmund, 4th Bt, 1854–1931, vol. III
Lister-Kaye, Sir John Christopher Lister, 7th Bt, 1913–1982, vol. VIII
Lister-Kaye, Sir John Pepys, 3rd Bt, 1853–1924, vol. II
Lister-Kaye, Sir Kenelm Arthur, 5th Bt, 1892–1955, vol. V
Lister-Kaye, Sir Lister, 6th Bt, 1873–1962, vol. VI
Liston, David Joel, 1914–1990, vol. VIII
Liston, James Malcolm, 1909–1996, vol. X
Liston, Most Rev. James Michael, 1881–1976, vol. VII
Liston, Lt-Col William Glen, 1873–1950, vol. IV
Liston-Foulis, Sir Archibald Charles; *see* Foulis.
Liston-Foulis, Sir William; *see* Foulis.
Listowel, 3rd Earl of, 1833–1924, vol. II

Listowel, 4th Earl of, 1866–1931, vol. III
Listowel, 5th Earl, 1906–1997, vol. X
Litauer, Stefan, 1892–1959, vol. V
Litchfield, Captain F. Shirley; *see* Speer, Rear-Adm. F. Shirley L.
Litchfield, Frederick, 1850–1930, vol. III
Litchfield, Jack Watson, 1909–2000, vol. X
Litchfield, John Shirley Sandys, 1903–1993, vol. IX
Litchfield-Speer, Rear-Adm. F. Shirley; *see* Speer.
Lithgow, Sir James, 1st Bt, 1883–1952, vol. V
Lithgow, Michael John, 1920–1963, vol. VI
Lithgow, Samuel, 1860–1937, vol. III
Lithihy, Sir John, 1852–1936, vol. III
Litster, William James, 1869–1930, vol. III
Litten, Maurice Sidney, 1919–1979, vol. VII
Litterick, Thomas, 1929–1981, vol. VIII
Little, Alan Neville, 1934–1986, vol. VIII
Little, Sir Alexander; *see* Little, Sir R. A.
Little, Andrew George, 1863–1945, vol. IV
Little, Mrs Archibald, *died* 1926, vol. II
Little, Archibald John, 1838–1908, vol. I
Little, Gen. Arthur Greenway, 1875–1948, vol. IV
Little, Rev. Arthur Wentworth Roberts, 1880–1932, vol. III
Little, Col Charles Blakeway, 1859–1929, vol. III
Little, Adm. Sir Charles James Colebrooke, 1882–1973, vol. VII
Little, David, 1867–1947, vol. IV
Little, David John, *died* 1984, vol. VIII
Little, Hon. Sir Douglas Macfarlan, 1904–1990, vol. VIII
Little, Sir Ernest Gordon Graham-, *died* 1950, vol. IV
Little, Ernest Muirhead, 1854–1935, vol. III
Little, George Jerningham Knightley, 1886–1966, vol. VI
Little, George Leon, *died* 1941, vol. IV
Little, Lt-Gen. Henry Alexander, 1837–1908, vol. I
Little, Engr-Rear-Adm. Henry Augustus, 1883–1954, vol. V
Little, James, *died* 1916, vol. II
Little, Rev. James, 1868–1946, vol. IV
Little, James Stanley, 1856–1940, vol. III
Little, John Carruthers, 1874–1957, vol. V
Little, John Eric Russell, 1913–1998, vol. X
Little, Sir Joseph Ignatius, *died* 1902, vol. I
Little, Kenneth Lindsay, 1908–1991, vol. IX
Little, Brig-Gen. Malcolm Orme, 1857–1931, vol. III
Little, Robert, *died* 1944, vol. IV
Little, Sir (Rudolf) Alexander, 1895–1977, vol. VII
Little, Rev. William John K.; *see* Knox Little.
Little, William Morison, 1909–1984, vol. VIII
Littleboy, Col Charles Norman, 1894–1966, vol. VI
Littledale, Harold, 1853–1930, vol. III
Littlehailes, Richard, 1878–1950, vol. IV
Littlejohn, Harvey, *died* 1927, vol. II
Littlejohn, Sir Henry Duncan, 1828–1914, vol. I
Littlejohn, Robert, *died* 1920, vol. II
Littlejohn, William Still, 1859–1933, vol. III
Littlejohn Cook, George Steveni, 1919–1998, vol. X
Littlejohns, Captain Astle Scott, 1875–1939, vol. III
Littler, Captain Charles Augustus, *died* 1916, vol. II
Littler, Sir Emile, 1903–1985, vol. VIII
Littler, Rev. Harold Davies, 1887–1948, vol. IV

Littler, Prince, 1901–1973, vol. VII
Littler, Sir Ralph Daniel Makinson, 1835–1908, vol. I
Littler, William Brian, 1908–1999, vol. X
Littleton, Alfred Henry, 1845–1914, vol. I
Littleton, Rev. Hon. Cecil James, 1850–1912, vol. I
Littleton, Hon. Charles Christopher Josceline, 1872–1950, vol. IV
Littlewood, Barbara, (Lady Littlewood), 1909–1995, vol. IX
Littlewood, Rear-Adm. Charles, 1902–1984, vol. VIII
Littlewood, Bt-Col Harry, 1861–1921, vol. II
Littlewood, James, 1885–1968, vol. VI
Littlewood, James, 1922–1998, vol. X
Littlewood, John Edensor, 1885–1977, vol. VII
Littlewood, Samuel Robinson, 1875–1963, vol. VI
Littlewood, Sir Sydney Charles Thomas, 1895–1967, vol. VI
Litvinov, Maxim, 1876–1951, vol. V
Liveing, Lt-Col Charles Hawker, 1872–1934, vol. III
Liveing, Edward, 1832–1919, vol. II
Liveing, Edward George Downing, 1895–1963, vol. VI
Liveing, George Downing, 1827–1924, vol. II
Liveing, Robert, 1834–1919, vol. II
Livens, Horace Mann, 1862–1936, vol. III
Livermore, Sir Harry, 1908–1989, vol. VIII
Liverpool, 1st Earl of (cr 1905, 2nd creation), 1846–1907, vol. I
Liverpool, 2nd Earl of, 1870–1941, vol. IV
Liverpool, 3rd Earl of, 1878–1962, vol. VI
Liverpool, 4th Earl of, 1887–1969, vol. VI
Liversidge, Archibald, 1847–1927, vol. II
Livesay, Brig.-Gen. Robert O'Hara, 1876–1946, vol. IV
Livesey, Sir Harry, 1860–1932, vol. III
Livesey, Rev. Herbert, 1892–1970, vol. VI
Livesey, James, 1831–1925, vol. II
Livesey, Roger, 1906–1976, vol. VII
Livings, Henry, 1929–1998, vol. X
Livingston, Charles, 1857–1937, vol. III
Livingston, Brig.-Gen. Guy, 1881–1950, vol. IV
Livingston, Henry Brockholst, 1895–1968, vol. VI
Livingston, James Barrett, 1906–1991, vol. IX
Livingston, Sir Noel Brooks, 1882–1954, vol. V
Livingston, Air Marshal Sir Philip Clermont, 1893–1982, vol. VIII
Livingston-Herbage, Julian; see Herbage.
Livingstone, Dame Adelaide Lord, died 1970, vol. VI
Livingstone, Sir Alexander Mackenzie, 1880–1950, vol. IV
Livingstone, Archibald Macdonald, died 1972, vol. VII
Livingstone, Ven. Arthur Guinness, 1840–1902, vol. I
Livingstone, Maj.-Gen. Sir Hubert Armine Anson, 1865–1940, vol. III
Livingstone, James, 1912–1991, vol. IX
Livingstone, James Livingstone, 1900–1988, vol. VIII
Livingstone, Matthew, 1837–1917, vol. II
Livingstone, Rev. Richard John, 1828–1907, vol. I

Livingstone, Sir Richard Winn, 1880–1960, vol. V
Livingstone, Rev. Robert George, 1838–1935, vol. III
Livingstone, Stuart Moodie, died 1902, vol. I
Livingstone, William P., died 1950, vol. IV (A)
Livingstone-Learmonth, Agnes Moore, 1877–1936, vol. III
Livingstone-Learmonth, Lt-Col (Francis) Leger (Christian); see Learmonth.
Livingstone-Learmonth, Frederick Valiant Cotton, 1862–1945, vol. IV
Livingstone-Learmonth, Brig.-Gen. John Eric Christian, 1876–1936, vol. III
Ljungberg, Göta, died 1955, vol. V
Llandaff, 1st Viscount, 1826–1913, vol. I
Llangattock, 1st Baron, 1837–1912, vol. I
Llangattock, 2nd Baron, 1870–1916, vol. II
Llewellin, 1st Baron, 1893–1957, vol. IV
Llewellin, George Herbert, 1871–1946, vol. IV
Llewellyn, Sir David Richard, 1st Bt, 1879–1940, vol. III
Llewellyn, Sir David Treharne, 1916–1992, vol. IX
Llewellyn, Col Evan Henry, 1847–1914, vol. I
Llewellyn, Brig.-Gen. Evan Henry, 1871–1948, vol. IV
Llewellyn, Sir (Frederick) John, 1915–1988, vol. VIII
Llewellyn, Col Sir Godfrey; see Llewellyn, Col Sir R. G.
Llewellyn, Sir Harry; see Llewellyn, Sir Henry M.
Llewellyn, Sir Henry Morton, (Sir Harry), 3rd Bt (cr 1922), 1911–1999, vol. X
Llewellyn, Col Sir Hoel, 1871–1945, vol. IV
Llewellyn, Sir John; see Llewellyn, Sir F. J.
Llewellyn, John Charles, 1908–1990, vol. VIII
Llewellyn, Rev. John Francis Morgan, 1921–1995, vol. IX
Llewellyn, Lt-Col John Malet, died 1945, vol. IV
Llewellyn, Captain Llewellyn Evan Hugh, 1879–1970, vol. VI
Llewellyn, Lt-Col Sir Michael Rowland Godfrey, 2nd Bt (cr 1959), 1921–1994, vol. IX
Llewellyn, Lt-Col Sir Rhys, 2nd Bt, 1910–1978, vol. VII
Llewellyn, Richard; see Lloyd, R. D. V. L.
Llewellyn, Richard Llewelyn Jones, died 1934, vol. III
Llewellyn, Col Sir (Robert) Godfrey, 1st Bt (cr 1959), 1893–1986, vol. VIII
Llewellyn, Robert William, 1848–1910, vol. I
Llewellyn, Sir (Samuel Henry) William, 1863–1941, vol. IV
Llewellyn, Sir William; see Llewellyn Sir S. H. W.
Llewellyn-Jones, Frank; see Jones, F. Ll.
Llewellyn-Jones, Frederick, 1866–1941, vol. IV
Llewelyn, Sir John Talbot Dillwyn-, 1st Bt, 1836–1927, vol. II
Llewelyn, Sir Leonard Wilkinson, 1874–1924, vol. II
Llewelyn, Brig. Sir Michael Dillwyn-V.; see Venables-Llewelyn.
Llewelyn, Sir Robert Baxter, 1845–1919, vol. II
Llewelyn, W. Craven, died 1966, vol. VI
Llewelyn-Davies, Baron (Life Peer); Richard Llewelyn-Davies, 1912–1981, vol. VIII

Llewelyn-Davies of Hastoe, Baroness (Life Peer); Patricia Llewelyn-Davies, 1915–1997, vol. X
Llewelyn-Williams, David, 1870–1949, vol. IV
Llewhellin, Col George Elliot, 1874–1940, vol. III
Lloyd, 1st Baron, 1879–1941, vol. IV
Lloyd, 2nd Baron, 1912–1985, vol. VIII
Lloyd of Hampstead, Baron (Life Peer); Dennis Lloyd, 1915–1992, vol. IX
Lloyd of Kilgerran, Baron (Life Peer); Rhys Gerran Lloyd, 1907–1991, vol. IX
Lloyd, Sir Alan Hubert, 1883–1948, vol. IV
Lloyd, Rev. Albert Henry, died 1941, vol. IV
Lloyd, Antony Charles, 1916–1994, vol. IX
Lloyd, Arnold de Gorges; see Lloyd, W. A. de G.
Lloyd, Rev. Arthur, 1851–1911, vol. I
Lloyd, Captain Arthur Athelwold, 1864–1940, vol. III
Lloyd, Rev. Arthur Gittins, 1865–1931, vol. III
Lloyd, Brig.-Gen. Arthur Henry Orlando, 1864–1944, vol. IV
Lloyd, Rt Rev. Arthur Selden, 1857–1936, vol. III
Lloyd, Rt Rev. Arthur Thomas, died 1907, vol. I
Lloyd, Captain Arthur Wynell, 1883–1967, vol. VI
Lloyd, Bernard Dean, 1923–1987, vol. VIII
Lloyd, Bertram Arthur, 1884–1948, vol. IV
Lloyd, (Charles) Christopher, 1906–1986, vol. VIII
Lloyd, Charles Ellis, died 1939, vol. III
Lloyd, Lt-Col Charles Geoffrey, 1884–1953, vol. V
Lloyd, Charles Harford, 1849–1919, vol. II
Lloyd, Col Charles Robert, 1882–1930, vol. III
Lloyd, Charles William, 1915–1999, vol. X
Lloyd, Christopher; see Lloyd, Charles C.
Lloyd, Maj.-Gen. Cyril, 1906–1989, vol. VIII
Lloyd, Cyril Edward, 1876–1963, vol. VI
Lloyd, Rt Rev. Daniel Lewis, 1843–1899, vol. I
Lloyd, David John, 1886–1951, vol. V
Lloyd, Denis Thelwall, 1924–1998, vol. X
Lloyd, Dorothy J.; see Jordan Lloyd.
Lloyd, Edward, 1845–1927, vol. II
Lloyd, Edward Honoratus, 1860–1930, vol. III
Lloyd, Edward Mayow Hastings, 1889–1968, vol. VI
Lloyd, Col Edward Prince, 1887–1970, vol. VI
Lloyd, Comdr Edward William, 1855–1945, vol. IV
Lloyd, Eric Ivan, 1892–1954, vol. V
Lloyd, Major Sir (Ernest) Guy (Richard) 1st Bt, 1890–1987, vol. VIII
Lloyd, Ernest Sampson, 1870–1945, vol. IV
Lloyd, Lt-Col Fitzwarren, 1859–1923, vol. II
Lloyd, Lt-Gen. Sir Francis, 1853–1926, vol. II
Lloyd, Francis Ernest, 1868–1947, vol. IV
Lloyd, Francis Nelson, 1907–1974, vol. VII
Lloyd, Maj.-Gen. Francis Thomas, 1838–1912, vol. I
Lloyd, Col Frederic Percy L.; see Lousada Lloyd.
Lloyd, Brig.-Gen. Frederick Charles, 1860–1957, vol. V
Lloyd, Col Frederick Lindsay, 1866–1940, vol. III
Lloyd, Geoffrey William; see Baron Geoffrey-Lloyd.
Lloyd, George Butler, 1854–1930, vol. III
Lloyd, Col George Evan, 1855–1900, vol. I
Lloyd, Rt Rev. George Exton, 1861–1940, vol. III
Lloyd, George Walter Selwyn, 1913–1998, vol. X
Lloyd, George Whitelocke, 1830–1910, vol. I

Lloyd, Glyn, 1919–1991, vol. IX
Lloyd, Major Sir Guy; see Lloyd, Major Sir E. G. R.
Lloyd, Guy Vaughan, 1901–1975, vol. VII
Lloyd, Maj.-Gen. Herbert William, 1883–1957, vol. V
Lloyd, Dame Hilda Nora; see Rose, Dame H. N.
Lloyd, Brig.-Gen. Horace Giesler, 1872–1936, vol. III
Lloyd, Sir Horatio, 1829–1920, vol. II
Lloyd, Howard, 1837–1920, vol. II
Lloyd, Sir Howard Watson, 1868–1955, vol. V
Lloyd, Air Chief Marshal Sir Hugh Pughe, 1894–1981, vol. VIII
Lloyd, Captain Sir Humphrey Clifford, 1893–1966, vol. VI
Lloyd, Huw Ifor, 1893–1977, vol. VII
Lloyd, Sir Idwal Geoffrey, 1878–1946, vol. IV
Lloyd, Ifor Bowen, 1902–1990, vol. VIII
Lloyd, Rev. Iorwerth Grey, 1844–1920, vol. II
Lloyd, Air Cdre Ivor Thomas, 1896–1966, vol. VI
Lloyd, J. A. R., died 1956, vol. V
Lloyd, James Monteith, 1911–1995, vol. X (AI)
Lloyd, Rt Rev. John, 1847–1915, vol. I
Lloyd, Sir John Buck, 1874–1952, vol. V
Lloyd, Lt-Col Sir John Conway, 1878–1954, vol. V
Lloyd, John Davies Knatchbull, 1900–1978, vol. VII
Lloyd, Sir John Edward, 1861–1947, vol. IV
Lloyd, Col John Edward, 1894–1965, vol. VI
Lloyd, Sir John Hall S.; see Seymour-Lloyd.
Lloyd, Brig.-Gen. John Hardress, 1874–1952, vol. V
Lloyd, Brig.-Gen. John Henry, 1872–1941, vol. IV
Lloyd, John Owen, 1914–1982, vol. VIII
Lloyd, Sir (John) Peter (Daniel), 1915–1996, vol. X
Lloyd, (John) Selwyn (Brooke); see Baron Selwyn-Lloyd.
Lloyd, Ven. John Walter, 1879–1951, vol. V
Lloyd, Jordan, died 1913, vol. I
Lloyd, Rev. Joseph, died 1938, vol. III
Lloyd, Air Vice-Marshal Kenneth Buchanan, 1897–1973, vol. VII
Lloyd, Col Langford Newman, 1873–1956, vol. V
Lloyd, Llewelyn Southworth, 1876–1956, vol. V
Lloyd, Sir Marteine Owen Mowbray, 2nd Bt, 1851–1933, vol. III
Lloyd, Martin, 1908–1989, vol. VIII
Lloyd, Col Sir Morgan George, 1843–1917, vol. II
Lloyd, Nathaniel, 1867–1933, vol. III
Lloyd, Norman, 1895–1983, vol. VIII
Lloyd, Maj.-Gen. Sir Owen Edward Pennefather, 1854–1941, vol. IV
Lloyd, Col Pen; see Lloyd, Col Philip H.
Lloyd, Sir Peter; see Lloyd, Sir J. P. D.
Lloyd, Col Philip Henry, (Pen), 1905–1979, vol. VII
Lloyd, Lt-Col Reginald Broughton, 1881–1975, vol. VII
Lloyd, Richard Dafydd Vivian Llewellyn, (Richard Llewellyn), 1906–1983, vol. VIII
Lloyd, Major Richard Ernest, 1875–1935, vol. III
Lloyd, Maj.-Gen. Richard Eyre, 1906–1991, vol. IX
Lloyd, Rickard William, 1859–1933, vol. III
Lloyd, Col Robert Oliver, 1849–1921, vol. II
Lloyd, Sir Robert Owen, 1894–1970, vol. VI
Lloyd, Adm. Rodney Maclaine, 1841–1911, vol. I

Lloyd, Rev. Canon Roger Bradshaigh, *died* 1966, vol. VI
Lloyd, Samuel Cook, 1854–1929, vol. III
Lloyd, Brig.-Gen. Samuel Eyre Massy, 1867–1952, vol. V
Lloyd, Selwyn; *see* Baron Selwyn-Lloyd.
Lloyd, Seton Howard Frederick, 1902–1996, vol. X
Lloyd, Stuart, vol. III
Lloyd, T. Alwyn, 1881–1960, vol. V
Lloyd, Theodore Howard, 1872–1959, vol. V
Lloyd, Col Thomas, 1853–1916, vol. II
Lloyd, Rt Rev. Thomas, 1857–1935, vol. III
Lloyd, Col Thomas Edward John, 1856–1937, vol. III
Lloyd, Maj.-Gen. Thomas Francis, 1839–1921, vol. II
Lloyd, Brig. Thomas Ifan, 1903–1981, vol. VIII
Lloyd, Sir Thomas Ingram Kynaston, 1896–1968, vol. VI
Lloyd, Lt-Col Thomas Owen, 1866–1945, vol. IV
Lloyd, Tom, *died* 1910, vol. I
Lloyd, Col Wilford Neville, 1855–1935, vol. III
Lloyd, Maj.-Gen. Wilfrid Lewis, 1896–1944, vol. IV
Lloyd, William, 1874–1948, vol. IV
Lloyd, (William) Arnold de Gorges, 1904–1982, vol. VIII
Lloyd, William Ernest, *died* 1975, vol. VII
Lloyd, Rt Hon. Sir William Frederick, 1864–1937, vol. III
Lloyd, William Harris, 1836–1923, vol. II
Lloyd, Wilson, 1835–1908, vol. I
Lloyd, Wynne Llewelyn, 1910–1973, vol. VII
Lloyd-Anstruther, Lt-Col Robert Hamilton; *see* Anstruther.
Lloyd-Baker, Granville Edwin Lloyd, 1841–1924, vol. II
Lloyd-Baker, Olive Katherine Lloyd, 1902–1975, vol. VII
Lloyd-Blood, Lancelot Ivan Neptune; *see* Blood.
Lloyd Davies, J(ohn) Robert, 1913–1999, vol. X
Lloyd-Davies, Oswald Vaughan, 1905–1987, vol. VIII
Lloyd Davies, Trevor Arthur, 1909–1998, vol. X
Lloyd-Eley, John, 1923–1998, vol. X
Lloyd-Evans, Annie; *see* Evans.
Lloyd George of Dwyfor, 1st Earl, 1863–1945, vol. IV
Lloyd George of Dwyfor, 2nd Earl, 1889–1968, vol. VI
Lloyd George of Dwyfor, Countess; (Frances Louise), 1888–1972, vol. VII
Lloyd George, Lady Megan Arvon, 1902–1966, vol. VI
Lloyd-Jacob, Sir George Harold, 1897–1969, vol. VI
Lloyd James, Arthur, 1884–1943, vol. IV
Lloyd-Johnes, Herbert Johnes, 1900–1983, vol. VIII
Lloyd Jones, Cyril Walter, 1881–1981, vol. VIII
Lloyd Jones, David Elwyn, 1920–1991, vol. IX
Lloyd-Jones, David Trevor, 1917–1998, vol. X
Lloyd-Jones, Sir (Harry) Vincent, 1901–1986, vol. VIII
Lloyd-Jones, Ven. John; *see* Jones.
Lloyd-Jones, Major Percy Arnold; *see* Jones.
Lloyd Jones, Richard Francis, 1908–1975, vol. VII

Lloyd-Jones, Robert, 1931–1999, vol. X
Lloyd-Jones, Sir Vincent; *see* Lloyd-Jones, Sir H. V.
Lloyd-Mostyn, Hon. Henry Richard Howel, 1857–1938, vol. III
Lloyd-Mostyn, Maj.-Gen. Hon. Sir Savage, 1835–1914, vol. I
Lloyd Owen, David Charles, *died* 1925, vol. II
Lloyd Phillips, Ivan, 1910–1984, vol. VIII
Lloyd-Roberts, George Charles, 1918–1986, vol. VIII
Lloyd-Roberts, Sir Richard, 1885–1956, vol. V
Lloyd Webber, William Southcombe, 1914–1982, vol. VIII
Lloyd-Williams, Dorothy Sylvia, 1901–1977, vol. VII
Lloyd-Williams, Hugh, 1889–1968, vol. VI
Lloyd-Williams, Comdr Hugh, 1900–1977, vol. VII
Lloyd-Williams, Captain James Evan, 1888–1969, vol. VI
Lloyd-Williams, Katharine Georgina, 1896–1973, vol. VII
Llubera, Ignacio Miguel G.; *see* Gonzalez-Llubera.
Llucen; *see* Cullen, Rev. John.
Llwyd, Very Rev. John Plummer Derwent, 1861–1933, vol. III
Lo, Kenneth Hsiao Chien, 1913–1995, vol. IX
Lo, Hon. Sir Man-kam, 1893–1959, vol. V
Lo Feng-Luh, Sir Chih Chen, 1850–1903, vol. I
Loane, Miss M., *died* 1922, vol. II
Lobb, Howard Leslie Vicars, 1909–1993, vol. IX
Lobb, John, 1840–1921, vol. II
Lobban, Charles Henry, 1881–1963, vol. VI
Lobjoit, Sir William George, 1859–1939, vol. III
Lobnitz, Sir Frederick, 1863–1932, vol. III
Loch, 1st Baron, 1827–1900, vol. I
Loch, 2nd Baron, 1873–1942, vol. IV
Loch, 3rd Baron, 1916–1982, vol. VIII
Loch, 4th Baron, 1920–1991, vol. IX
Loch, Sir Charles Stewart, 1849–1923, vol. II
Loch, Maj.-Gen. Granville George, 1870–1950, vol. IV
Loch, Lt-Col Granville Henry, 1859–1929, vol. III
Loch, Col John Carysfort, 1877–1974, vol. VII
Loch, Lt-Gen. Sir Kenneth Morley, 1890–1961, vol. VI
Loch, Maj.-Gen. Stewart Gordon, 1873–1952, vol. V
Loch, Lt-Col William, 1845–1912, vol. I
Lochee, 1st Baron, 1845–1911, vol. I
Lochhead, James, *died* 1940, vol. III
Lochhead, John, *died* 1921, vol. II
Lochhead, William, 1864–1927, vol. II
Lochore, Sir James, 1874–1953, vol. V
Lock, B. Fossett, 1847–1922, vol. II
Lock, Air Vice-Marshal Basil Goodhand, 1923–1989, vol. VIII
Lock, (Cecil) Max, 1909–1988, vol. VIII
Lock, Lt-Comdr Sir Duncan; *see* Lock, Lt-Comdr Sir J. D.
Lock, Flt Lt Eric Stanley, 1919–1942, vol. IV
Lock, Brig.-Gen. Frederic Robert Edward, 1867–1945, vol. IV
Lock, Rev. John Bascombe, 1849–1921, vol. II
Lock, Lt-Comdr Sir (John) Duncan, 1918–1999, vol. X

Locke, John Howard, 1923–1998, vol. X
Lock, Max; see Lock, C. M.
Lock, Maj.-Gen. Sir Robert Ferguson, 1879–1957, vol. V
Lock, Robert Heath, 1879–1915, vol. I
Lock, Rev. Walter, 1846–1933, vol. III
Lock, Winifred; see Gérin, W.
Locke, Arthur, 1872–1932, vol. III
Locke, Arthur D'Arcy, (Bobby Locke), 1917–1987, vol. VIII
Locke, Bobby; see Locke, A. D'A.
Locke, Charles Holland, 1887–1980, vol. VII (AII)
Locke, George Herbert, 1870–1937, vol. III
Locke, George T., 1872–1968, vol. VI
Locke, William John, 1863–1930, vol. III
Locke King, Dame Ethel; see King, Dame E. L.
Locker, William Algernon, 1863–1930, vol. III
Locker-Lampson, Rt Hon. Godfrey Lampson Tennyson, 1875–1946, vol. IV
Locker-Lampson, (Hannah) Jane, died 1915, vol. I
Locker-Lampson, Jane; see Locker-Lampson, H. J.
Locker-Lampson, Comdr Oliver Stillingfleet, 1880–1954, vol. V
Lockett, Air Cdre Charles Edward Stuart, 1910–1966, vol. VI
Lockett, Richard Jeffery, 1907–1980, vol. VII
Lockhart, Sir Allan Robert E.; see Eliott Lockhart.
Lockhart, Sir Charles Ramsdale, 1892–1954, vol. V
Lockhart, Sir Graeme Alexander Sinclair, 10th Bt (cr 1636), 1820–1904, vol. I
Lockhart, Sir Graeme Duncan Power S.; see Sinclair-Lockhart.
Lockhart, Sir James Haldane Stewart, 1858–1937, vol. III
Lockhart, Sir John Beresford S.; see Sinclair-Lockhart.
Lockhart, John Gilbert, 1891–1960, vol. V
Lockhart, John Harold Bruce, 1889–1956, vol. V
Lockhart, John Macgregor B.; see Bruce Lockhart.
Lockhart, Maj.-Gen. Leslie Keith, 1897–1966, vol. VI
Lockhart, Sir Muir Edward S.; see Sinclair-Lockhart.
Lockhart, Lt-Col Percy Clare E.; see Eliott-Lockhart.
Lockhart, Rab Brougham B.; see Bruce Lockhart.
Lockhart, Gen. Sir Rob MacGregor Macdonald, 1893–1981, vol. VIII
Lockhart, Sir Robert Cook, 1861–1943, vol. IV
Lockhart, Robert Douglas, 1894–1987, vol. VIII
Lockhart, Sir Robert Duncan S.; see Sinclair-Lockhart.
Lockhart, Sir Robert Hamilton B.; see Bruce Lockhart.
Lockhart, Sidney Alexander, 1914–1969, vol. VI
Lockhart, Sir Simon Macdonald, 5th Bt (cr 1806), 1849–1919, vol. II
Lockhart, Stephen Alexander, 1905–1989, vol. VIII
Lockhart, William Ewart, 1846–1900, vol. I
Lockhart-Mummery, Sir Hugh Evelyn, 1918–1988, vol. VIII
Lockhart-Mummery, John Percy, 1875–1957, vol. V
Lockie, John, 1863–1906, vol. I
Lockitt, Charles Henry, 1877–1964, vol. VI
Lockley, Ronald Mathias, 1903–2000, vol. X

Lockroy, Edouard, 1838–1913, vol. I
Lockroy, Etienne Auguste Edouard Simon; see Lockroy, Edouard.
Lockspeiser, Sir Ben, 1891–1990, vol. VIII
Lockton, Charles Langton, 1856–1932, vol. III
Lockwood, Charles Barrett, died 1914, vol. I
Lockwood, Sir Francis, 1847–1897, vol. I
Lockwood, Francis William, 1908–1955, vol. V
Lockwood, James Horace, 1888–1972, vol. VII
Lockwood, Lt-Col John Cutts, 1890–1983, vol. VIII
Lockwood, Sir John Francis, 1903–1965, vol. VI
Lockwood, Sir Joseph Flawith, 1904–1991, vol. IX
Lockwood, Margaret Mary, 1916–1990, vol. VIII
Lockwood, Walter Sydney Douglas, 1895–1989, vol. VIII
Lockyer, Air Vice-Marshal Clarence Edward Williams, 1892–1963, vol. VI
Lockyer, Cuthbert H. J., 1867–1957, vol. V
Lockyer, Captain Hughes Campbell, 1866–1941, vol. IV
Lockyer, Sir (Joseph) Norman, 1836–1920, vol. II
Lockyer, Sir Nicholas Colston, 1855–1933, vol. III
Lockyer, Sir Norman; see Lockyer, Sir J. N.
Lockyer, William James Stewart, 1868–1936, vol. III
Locmaria, Marquis du P.; see Parc-Locmaria.
Locock, Sir Charles Bird, 3rd Bt, 1878–1965, vol. VI
Locock, Sir Guy Harold, 1883–1958, vol. V
Locock, Col Herbert, 1847–1910, vol. I
Loder, Sir Edmund Giles, 2nd Bt, 1849–1920, vol. II
Loder, Major Eustace, 1867–1914, vol. I
Loder, Lt-Col Giles Harold, 1884–1966, vol. VI
Loder, Sir Giles Rolls, 3rd Bt, 1914–1999, vol. X
Loder, Sir Louis Francis, 1896–1972, vol. VII
Loder, Reginald Bernhard, 1864–1931, vol. VII
Loder-Symonds, Captain F. C.; see Symonds.
Loder-Symonds, Vice-Adm. Frederick Parland; see Symonds.
Lodge, Alfred, 1854–1937, vol. III
Lodge, Alfred, 1893–1957, vol. V
Lodge, Eleanor Constance, 1869–1936, vol. III
Lodge, Lt-Col Francis Cecil, 1868–1951, vol. V
Lodge, Frank Adrian, 1861–1947, vol. IV
Lodge, Henry Cabot, 1850–1924, vol. II
Lodge, Henry Cabot, 1902–1985, vol. VIII
Lodge, John, 1890–1954, vol. V
Lodge, Sir Oliver Joseph, 1851–1940, vol. III
Lodge, Oliver William Foster, 1878–1955, vol. V
Lodge, Sir Richard, 1855–1936, vol. III
Lodge, Sir Ronald Francis, 1889–1960, vol. V
Lodge, Rupert Clendon, 1886–1961, vol. VI
Lodge, Thomas, 1882–1958, vol. V
Lodge, Sir Thomas, 1909–1997, vol. X
Lodge, Thomas Arthur, 1888–1967, vol. VI
Lodge, Thomas Cecil S.; see Skeffington-Lodge.
Lodge, Tom Stewart, 1909–1987, vol. VIII
Lodwick, John Alan Patrick, 1916–1959, vol. V
Lodwick, Captain John Thornton, 1882–1915, vol. I
Loeb, Jacques, 1859–1924, vol. II
Loeb, James, 1867–1933, vol. III
Loehris, Sir Clive, 1902–1992, vol. IX
Loewe, Frederick, 1901–1988, vol. VIII
Loewe, Herbert Martin James, 1882–1940, vol. III

Loewen, Gen. Sir Charles Falkland, 1900–1986, vol. VIII
Loewenstein-Wertheim, HSH Princess, 1866–1927, vol. II
Loewenstein-Wertheim-Freudenberg, Hubertus Friedrich, Prince of, 1906–1984, vol. VIII
Loewenthal, Sir John, 1914–1979, vol. VII
Loewi, Otto, 1873–1961, vol. VI
Loewy, Raymond Fernand, 1893–1986, vol. VIII
Lofthouse, Rt Rev. Joseph, 1855–1933, vol. III
Lofthouse, Rt Rev. Joseph, 1880–1962, vol. VI
Lofthouse, Samuel Hill Smith, 1843–1915, vol. I
Lofthouse, Rev. William Frederick, 1871–1965, vol. VI
Loftie, Rev. Arthur Gershom, 1843–1922, vol. II
Loftie, Rev. William John, 1839–1911, vol. I
Lofting, Hugh John, 1886–1947, vol. IV
Lofts, Norah, (Mrs Robert Jorisch), 1904–1983, vol. VIII
Loftus, Rt Hon. Lord Augustus William Frederick Spencer, 1817–1904, vol. I
Loftus, Cissie; see M'Carthy, Marie Cecilia.
Loftus, Col Ernest Achey, 1884–1987, vol. VIII
Loftus, Montague Egerton, 1860–1934, vol. III
Loftus, Pierse Creagh, 1877–1956, vol. V
Logan, Sir Charles Bowman, 1837–1907, vol. I
Logan, Brig.-Gen. David Finlay Hosken, 1862–1923, vol. II
Logan, David Gilbert, 1871–1964, vol. VI
Logan, Sir Douglas William, 1910–1987, vol. VIII
Logan, Lt-Col Edward Townshend, died 1915, vol. I
Logan, Sir Ewen Reginald, 1868–1945, vol. IV
Logan, Brig.-Gen. Francis Douglas, 1875–1947, vol. IV
Logan, Hon. Hance James, 1869–1944, vol. IV
Logan, Lt-Col Harry Tremaine, 1887–1971, vol. VII
Logan, James, 1927–1993, vol. IX
Logan, Lt-Col John, 1907–1987, vol VIII
Logan, John William, 1845–1925, vol. II
Logan, Col Robert, 1863–1935, vol. III
Logan, Thomas Moffat, 1904–1981, vol. VIII
Logan, Sir William Marston, 1889–1968, vol. VI
Logan-Home, Major George John Ninian, 1855–1936, vol. III
Loggin, George Nicholas, 1882–1955, vol. V
Logie, William Alexander, 1866–1933, vol. III
Login, Rear-Adm. Spencer Henry Metcalfe Login, 1851–1909, vol. I
Logsdail, William, 1859–1944, vol. IV
Logsdon, Geoffrey Edward, 1914–1982, vol. VIII
Logue, Lionel, 1880–1953, vol. V
Logue, His Eminence Cardinal Michael, 1840–1924, vol. II
Loharu, Hon. Nawab Sir Amir-ud-Din Ahmed Khan Bahadur, 1860–1937, vol. III
Lohr, Hervey, 1856–1927, vol. II
Löhr, Marie, 1890–1975, vol. VII
Loisy, Alfred, 1857–1940, vol. III
Lomas, Surg.-Captain Ernest Courtney, 1864–1921, vol. II
Lomas, Ernest Gabriel, 1878–1947, vol. IV
Lomas, Harry, 1916–1980, vol. VII
Lomas, Herbert, 1887–1961, vol. VI
Lomas, John, 1846–1927, vol. II
Lomas, Kenneth, 1922–2000, vol. X

Lomas, Sophie Crawford, died 1929, vol. III
Lomas-Walker, Sir G. Bernard, 1881–1960, vol. V
Lomax, Maj.-Gen. Cyril Ernest Napier, 1893–1973, vol. VII
Lomax, Sir John, 1864–1936, vol. III
Lomax, John A., 1857–1923, vol. II
Lomax, Sir John Garnett, 1896–1987, vol. VIII
Lomax, Michael Roger T.; see Trappes-Lomax.
Lomax, Maj.-Gen. Samuel Holt, 1855–1915, vol. I
Lomax, Brig. Thomas Byrnand T.; see Trappes-Lomax.
Lombard Knight, Eric John Percy Crawford, 1907–1987, vol. VIII
Lombe, Vice-Adm. Sir Edward Malcolm E.; see Evans-Lombe.
Lombroso, Cesare, 1836–1909, vol. I
Londesborough, 1st Earl of, 1834–1900, vol. I
Londesborough, 2nd Earl of, 1864–1917, vol. II
Londesborough, 3rd Earl of, 1892–1920, vol. II
Londesborough, 4th Earl of, 1894–1937, vol. III
Londesborough, 6th Baron, 1876–1963, vol. VI
Londesborough, 7th Baron, 1885–1967, vol. VI
Londesborough, 8th Baron, 1901–1968, vol. VI
London, Sir (Edgar) Stanford, 1861–1943, vol. IV
London, Sir George Ernest, 1889–1957, vol. V
London, Heinz, 1907–1970, vol. VI
London, Hugh Stanford, 1884–1959, vol. V
London, Jack, 1876–1916, vol. II
London, Sir Stanford; see London, Sir E. S.
Londonderry, 6th Marquess of, 1852–1915, vol. I
Londonderry, 7th Marquess of, 1878–1949, vol. IV
Londonderry, 8th Marquess of, 1902–1955, vol. V
Londonderry, Dowager Marchioness of; (Edith Helen), 1879–1959, vol. V
Loney, Sidney Luxton, 1860–1939, vol. III
Long, 2nd Viscount, 1911–1944, vol. IV
Long, 3rd Viscount, 1892–1967, vol. VI
Long, (Adrian) Douglas, 1925–1990, vol. VIII
Long, Lt-Col Albert de Lande, 1880–1956, vol. V
Long, Alfred James, 1890–1952, vol. V
Long, Brig.-Gen. Sir Arthur, 1866–1941, vol. VI
Long, Arthur Tilney, 1871–1946, vol. IV
Long, Basil Kellett, 1878–1944, vol. IV
Long, Basil Somerset, 1881–1937, vol. III
Long, Sir Bertram, 1889–1975, vol. VII
Long, Charles Wigram, 1842–1911, vol. I
Long, Douglas; see Long, A. D.
Long, Edward Charles, 1860–1940, vol. III
Long, Edward Ernest, died 1956, vol. V
Long, Ernest, 1898–1982, vol. VIII
Long, Captain Eustace Ruffel Drake, 1883–1941, vol. IV
Long, Air Vice-Marshal Francis William, 1899–1983, vol. VIII
Long, Gabrielle; see Long, M. G.
Long, Gavin Merrick, 1901–1968, vol. VI
Long, George Bathurst, 1855–1917, vol. II
Long, Sir George Henry, 1818–1900, vol. I
Long, Rt Rev. George Merrick, 1874–1930, vol. III
Long, Gerald, 1923–1998, vol. X
Long, Sir James, 1862–1928, vol. II
Long, John Luther, 1861–1927, vol. II
Long, Kathleen Ida, 1896–1968, vol. VI
Long, (Margaret) Gabrielle, 1888–1952, vol. V

Long, Pamela Marjorie, (Mrs John Nichols), 1930–1999, vol. X
Long, Ven. Robert, *died* 1907, vol. I
Long, Robert Edward Crozier, 1872–1938, vol. III
Long, Sir Ronald, 1902–1987, vol. VIII
Long, Maj.-Gen. Sidney Selden, 1863–1940, vol. III
Long, Sydney, (Sid Long), 1878–1955, vol. V
Long, Sydney Herbert, 1870–1939, vol. III
Long, Lt-Col Walter, 1879–1917, vol. II
Long, Col Walter Edward Lionel, 1884–1960, vol. V
Long, Lt-Col Wilfred James, 1871–1954, vol. V
Long, Lt-Col William, 1843–1926, vol. II
Long, William Henry, 1900–1969, vol. VI
Long, Lt-Col William Hoare Bourchier, 1868–1943, vol. IV
Long, Rev. William Joseph, 1866–1952, vol. V
Long Innes, Hon. Reginald Heath, 1869–1947, vol. IV
Longard de Longgarde, Dorothea, 1855–1915, vol. I
Longbotham, Hugh Ashley, 1880–1938, vol. III
Longbotham, Samuel, 1908–1988, vol. VIII
Longbottom, Arthur William, 1883–1943, vol. IV
Longbottom, Sir Benjamin, 1876–1930, vol. III
Longbourne, Brig.-Gen. Francis Cecil M. M.; *see* More-Molyneux-Longbourne.
Longcroft, Air Vice-Marshal Sir Charles Alexander Holcombe, 1883–1958, vol. V
Longcroft, James George Stoddart, 1929–1994, vol. IX
Longden, Major Alfred Appleby, *died* 1954, vol. V
Longden, Clifford; *see* Longden, H. C.
Longden, Fred, 1894–1952, vol. V
Longden, Sir Gilbert James Morley, 1902–1997, vol. X
Longden, (Harry) Clifford, 1869–1953, vol. V
Longden, Maj.-Gen. Harry Leicester, 1900–1981, vol. VIII
Longden, Henry Alfred, 1909–1997, vol. X
Longden, Vice-Adm. Horace Walker, 1877–1953, vol. V
Longden, Robert Paton, 1903–1940, vol. III
Longe, Desmond Evelyn, 1914–1990, vol. VIII
Longe, Col Francis Bacon, 1856–1922, vol. II
Longfellow, Ernest Wadsworth, 1845–1921, vol. II
Longfield, Captain John Percival, 1885–1915, vol. I
Longford, 5th Earl of, 1864–1915, vol. I
Longford, 6th Earl of, 1902–1961, vol. VI
Longford, Joseph Henry, 1849–1925, vol. II
Longford, Rev. William Wingfield, 1882–1964, vol. VI
Longhurst, Col Arthur Lyster, 1872–1952, vol. V
Longhurst, Cyril, 1879–1948, vol. IV
Longhurst, Sir Henry Bell, 1835–1926, vol. II
Longhurst, Henry Carpenter, 1909–1978, vol. VII
Longhurst, Margaret Helen, 1882–1958, vol. V
Longhurst, Ven. William Belsey, 1847–1939, vol. III
Longhurst, William Henry, 1819–1904, vol. I
Longhurst, Rev. William Henry Roberts, 1838–1943, vol. IV
Longland, Austin Charles, 1888–1972, vol. VII
Longland, Cedric James, 1914–1991, vol. IX
Longland, Sir David Walter, 1909–1988, vol. VIII
Longland, Sir Jack; *see* Longland, Sir J. L.

Longland, Sir John Laurence, (Sir Jack), 1905–1993, vol. IX
Longland, Rev. Sydney Ernest, 1873–1957, vol. V
Longley, Sir Henry, 1833–1899, vol. I
Longley, James Wilberforce, 1849–1922, vol. II
Longley, Maj.-Gen. Sir John Raynsford, 1867–1953, vol. V
Longley, Sir Norman, 1900–1994, vol. IX
Longley, Stanislaus Soutten, 1894–1966, vol. VI
Longley-Cook, Vice-Adm. Eric William, 1898–1983, vol. VIII
Longman, Charles James, 1852–1934, vol. III
Longman, Sir Hubert Harry, 1st Bt, 1856–1940, vol. III
Longman, Mark Frederic Kerr, 1916–1972, vol. VII
Longman, Thomas Norton, 1849–1930, vol. III
Longman, William, 1882–1967, vol. VI
Longmore, Air Chief Marshal Sir Arthur Murray, 1885–1970, vol. VI
Longmore, Col Sir Charles Elton, 1855–1930, vol. III
Longmore, Lt-Col Charles Moorsom, 1882–1933, vol. III
Longmore, Brig. John Alexander, 1899–1973, vol. VII
Longmore, Brig.-Gen. John Constantine Gordon, 1870–1958, vol. V
Longmore, Philip Elton, 1884–1954, vol. V
Longmore, William James Maitland, 1919–1988, vol. VIII
Longmuir, Very Rev. James Boyd, 1907–1973, vol. VII
Longmuir, Robert Findlay, 1864–1942, vol. IV
Longridge, Rev. George, 1857–1936, vol. III
Longridge, Lt-Col Theodore, 1860–1940, vol. III
Longrigg, Roger Erskine, 1929–2000, vol. X
Longrigg, Brig. Stephen Hemsley, 1893–1979, vol. VII
Longson, Edward Harold, 1872–1941, vol. IV
Longstaff, Cedric Llewellyn, 1876–1950, vol. IV
Longstaff, George Blundell, 1849–1921, vol. II
Longstaff, Mrs George Blundell; *see* Longstaff, M. J.
Longstaff, Gilbert Conrad, 1884–1964, vol. VI
Longstaff, Sir John, 1862–1941, vol. IV
Longstaff, Llewellyn Wood, 1841–1918, vol. II
Longstaff, Mary Jane, (Mrs George Longstaff), *died* 1935, vol. III
Longstaff, Tom George, 1875–1964, vol. VI
Longstaffe, Amyas Philip, 1868–1914, vol. I
Longstreth-Thompson, Francis, 1890–1973, vol. VII
Longueville, Thomas, 1844–1922, vol. II
Longworth, Francis Travers Dames, 1834–1898, vol. I
Longworth, Sir Fred, 1890–1973, vol. VII
Longworth, Nicholas, 1869–1931, vol. III
Longworth, Rt Rev. Tom, 1891–1977, vol. VII
Lonsdale, 5th Earl of, 1857–1944, vol. IV
Lonsdale, 6th Earl of, 1867–1953, vol. V
Lonsdale, Allister, 1926–1977, vol. VII
Lonsdale, Lt-Col Arthur H.; *see* Heywood-Lonsdale.
Lonsdale, Arthur Pemberton H.; *see* Heywood-Lonsdale.
Lonsdale, Frederick, 1881–1954, vol. V
Lonsdale, Rev. Henry, *died* 1926, vol. II

Lonsdale, Lt-Col Henry Heywood H.; *see* Heywood-Lonsdale.
Lonsdale, James Rolston, 1865–1921, vol. II
Lonsdale, Rev. John Gylby, 1818–1907, vol. I
Lonsdale, John Pemberton Heywood H.; *see* Heywood-Lonsdale.
Lonsdale, Dame Kathleen, 1903–1971, vol. VII
Looker, Sir Cecil Thomas, 1913–1988, vol. IX (AI)
Looker, Herbert William, 1871–1951, vol. V
Loombe, Claude Evan, 1905–1978, vol. VII
Loomis, Maj.-Gen. Sir Frederick Oscar Warren, 1870–1937, vol. III
Loomis, Roger Sherman, 1887–1966, vol. VI
Loosley, George; *see* Loosley, S. G. H.
Loosley, (Stanley) George (Henry), 1910–1991, vol. IX
Lopes, George, 1857–1910, vol. I
Lopes, Sir Henry Yarde Buller, 4th Bt; *see* Roborough, 1st Baron.
Lopes, Rt Hon. Sir (Lopes) Massey, 3rd Bt, 1818–1908, vol. I
Lopes, Rt Hon. Sir Massey; *see* Lopes, Rt Hon. Sir L. M.
Lopokova, Lydia; *see* Keynes, Lady.
Loraine, John Alexander, 1924–1988, vol. VIII
Loraine, Sir Lambton, 11th Bt, 1838–1917, vol. II
Loraine, Rev. Nevison, *died* 1917, vol. II
Loraine, Rt Hon. Sir Percy Lyham, 12th Bt, 1880–1961, vol. VI
Loraine, Robert, 1876–1935, vol. III
Loram, Charles Templeman, 1879–1940, vol. III (A), vol. IV
Lorant, Stefan, 1901–1997, vol. X
Lord, Sir Ackland Archibald, 1901–1982, vol. VIII
Lord, Cyril, 1911–1984, vol. VIII
Lord, Sir Frank, 1894–1974, vol. VII
Lord, Rev. Fred Townley, 1893–1962, vol. VI
Lord, Herbert Owen, 1854–1928, vol. II
Lord, Col John Ernest Cecil, 1870–1949, vol. IV
Lord, John Herent, 1928–1994, vol. IX
Lord, John King, 1848–1926, vol. II
Lord, John Robert, 1874–1931, vol. III
Lord, Sir Percy, 1903–1968, vol. VI
Lord, Sir Riley, 1838–1920, vol. II
Lord, Captain S(ydney) Riley, 1884–1959, vol. V
Lord, Sir Walter G.; *see* Greaves-Lord.
Lord, Maj.-Gen. Wilfrid Austin, 1902–1982, vol. VIII
Lorden, Sir John William, 1862–1944, vol. IV
Loreburn, 1st Earl, 1846–1923, vol. II
Lorenz, Konrad Zacharias, 1903–1989, vol. VIII
Lorimer, Lt-Col David Lockhart Robertson, 1876–1962, vol. VI
Lorimer, Emily Overend, (Mrs D. L. R. Lorimer), 1881–1949, vol. IV
Lorimer, George Horace, 1868–1937, vol. III
Lorimer, Henry Dubs, 1879–1933, vol. III
Lorimer, Hew Martin, 1907–1993, vol. IX
Lorimer, John Campbell, *died* 1922, vol. II
Lorimer, John Gordon, 1870–1914, vol. I
Lorimer, John Henry, 1856–1936, vol. III
Lorimer, Norma, *died* 1948, vol. IV
Lorimer, Sir Robert Stodart, 1864–1929, vol. III
Lorimer, Sir William, 1844–1922, vol. II
Lorimer, William Laughton, 1885–1967, vol. VI

Loring, Andrew; *see* Lathrop, L. A.
Loring, Vice-Adm. Ernest Kindersley, 1869–1945, vol. IV
Loring, Francis; *see* Gwynne-Evans, Sir F. L.
Loring, Frederick George, 1869–1951, vol. V
Loring, James Adrian, 1918–1990, vol. VIII
Loring, Sir (John) Nigel, 1896–1979, vol. VII
Loring, Sir Nigel; *see* Loring, Sir J. N.
Loring, William, 1865–1915, vol. I
Loring, Col William, 1872–1935, vol. III
Lorne, Marion, 1888–1968, vol. VI
Lornie, James, 1876–1959, vol. V
Lorrain, Rt Rev. Narcisse Zephyrin, 1842–1915, vol. I
Lort Phillips, Lt-Col John Frederick, 1854–1926, vol. II
Lort-Williams, Sir John Rolleston, 1881–1966, vol. VI
Lory, Frederic Burton Pendarves, 1875–1954, vol. V
Losey, Joseph, 1909–1984, vol. VIII
Loss, Joe; *see* Loss, Joshua A.
Loss, Joshua Alexander, (Joe Loss), 1909–1990, vol. VIII
Lote, Thomas Alfred, *born* 1863, vol. II
Loten, Harold Ivens, 1887–1980, vol. VII
Loth, David, *born* 1899, vol. VIII
Lothian, 9th Marquess of, 1833–1900, vol. I
Lothian, 10th Marquess of, 1874–1930, vol. III
Lothian, 11th Marquess of, 1882–1940, vol. III
Lothian, Sir Arthur Cunningham, 1887–1962, vol. VI
Loti, Pierre, 1850–1923, vol. II
Loton, Sir Ernest Thorley, 1895–1973, vol. VII
Loton, Sir William Thorley, 1839–1924, vol. II
Lott, Bernard Maurice, 1922–1996, vol. X
Lott, Air Vice-Marshal Charles George, 1906–1989, vol. VIII
Lott, Frank Melville, 1896–1982, vol. VIII
Lott, Air Vice-Marshal George; *see* Lott, Air Vice-Marshal C. G.
Loubet, Émile François, 1838–1929, vol. III
Louch, Ven. Thomas, 1848–1927, vol. II
Loucks, Rev. Edwin, 1829–1919, vol. II
Loud, Arthur Bertram, 1863–1931, vol. III
Loudan, Mouat, 1868–1925, vol. II
Loudon, James, 1841–1916, vol. II
Loudon, Sir John, 1881–1948, vol. IV
Loudon, John, *died* 1966, vol. VI
Loudon, John Hugo, 1905–1996, vol. X
Loudoun, 11th Earl of, 1855–1920, vol. II
Loudoun, Countess of (12th in line), 1883–1960, vol. V
Loudoun, Donaldson, 1909–1980, vol. VII
Loudoun, Maj.-Gen. Robert Beverley, 1922–1998, vol. X
Lough, John, 1913–2000, vol. X
Lough, Brig. John Robertson Stewart, 1887–1970, vol. VI
Lough, Lt-Gen. Reginald Dawson Hopcraft, 1885–1958, vol. V
Lough, Rt Hon. Thomas, 1850–1922, vol. II
Loughborough, Lord; Francis Edward Scudamore St Clair Erskine, 1892–1929, vol. III

Loughborough, Maj.-Gen. Arthur Harold, 1883–1967, vol. VI
Loughead, Peter, 1950–1995, vol. IX (AII)
Lougheed, Hon. Sir James Alexander, 1854–1925, vol. II
Lougheed, Lt-Col Samuel Forster, 1860–1932, vol. III
Lougher, Sir Lewis, 1871–1955, vol. V
Loughlin, Dame Anne, 1894–1979, vol. VII
Loughlin, Charles William, 1914–1993, vol. IX
Loughnane, Farquhar McGillivray, 1885–1948, vol. IV
Loughnane, Norman Gerald, 1883–1955, vol. V
Louis, Sir Charles, 4th Bt, 1818–1900, vol. I
Louis, Sir Charles, 5th Bt, 1859–1949, vol. IV
Louis, Henry, 1855–1939, vol. III
Louis, John Jeffry, Jr, 1925–1995, vol. IX
Louisson, Hon. Charles, 1842–1924, vol. II
Lounsbury, Thomas Raynesford, 1838–1915, vol. I
Lousada, Duc de; Comdr Francis Clifford de Lousada, 1842–1916, vol. II
Lousada, Sir Anthony Baruh, 1907–1994, vol. IX
Lousada Lloyd, Col Frederic Percy, 1853–1930, vol. III
Louth, 14th Baron, 1868–1941, vol. IV
Louth, 15th Baron, 1892–1950, vol. IV
Loutit, John Freeman, 1910–1992, vol. IX
Louw, Hon. Eric Hendrik, 1890–1968, vol. VI
Louys, Pierre, 1870–1925, vol. II
Lovat, 14th Baron, 1871–1933, vol. III
Lovat, 17th Baron, 1911–1995, vol. IX
Lovat, Master of; Hon. Simon Augustine Fraser, 1939–1994, vol. IX
Lovat, Leonard Scott, 1926–1996, vol. X
Lovat-Fraser, James Alexander, 1868–1938, vol. III
Love, Augustus Edward Hough, 1863–1940, vol. III
Love, Charles Marshall, 1945–1993, vol. IX
Love, Sir Clifton; see Love, Sir J. C.
Love, Enid Rosamond, (Mrs G. C. F. Whitaker), 1911–1979, vol. VII
Love, James Kerr, 1858–1942, vol. IV
Love, Sir (Joseph) Clifton, 1868–1951, vol. V
Love, Sir (Makere Rangiatea) Ralph, 1907–1994, vol. IX
Love, Sir Ralph; see Love, Sir M. R. R.
Love, Richard Archibald, 1873–1941, vol. IV
Love, Robert, 1867–1934, vol. III
Love, Robert John McNeill, 1891–1974, vol. VII
Loveday, Alexander, 1888–1962, vol. VI
Loveday, Arthur Frederic, 1878–1968, vol. VI
Loveday, Rt Rev. David Goodwin, 1896–1985, vol. VIII
Loveday, Rev. Eric Stephen, 1904–1947, vol. IV
Loveday, George Arthur, 1909–1981, vol. VIII
Loveday, Thomas, 1875–1966, vol. VI
Lovegrove, Edwin William, 1868–1956, vol. V
Lovejoy, Arthur Oncken, 1873–1962, vol. VI
Lovel, Raymond William, 1912–1969, vol. VI
Lovelace, 2nd Earl of, 1839–1906, vol. I
Lovelace, 3rd Earl of, 1865–1929, vol. III
Lovelace, 4th Earl of, 1905–1964, vol. VI
Lovelace, Countess of; (Mary Caroline), died 1941, vol. IV
Lovelace, Lt-Col Alec, 1907–1981, vol. VIII
Loveland, Richard Loveland, 1841–1923, vol. II

Lovell, Arnold Henry, 1926–1990, vol. VIII
Lovell, Sir Francis Henry, 1844–1916, vol. II
Lovell, Henry Willoughby, 1866–1939, vol. III
Lovell, Mark; see Tollemache, David.
Lovell, Reginald, 1897–1972, vol. VII
Lovell, Stanley Hains, 1906–1985, vol. VIII
Lovell, William George, 1868–1944, vol. IV
Lovely, Percy Thomas, 1894–1975, vol. VII
Lovemore, Wing Comdr Robert Baillie, died 1978, vol. VII
Loveridge, Arthur John, 1904–1975, vol. VII
Loveridge, Charles William, 1869–1957, vol. V
Loveridge, Joan Mary, 1912–1987, vol. VIII
Loveridge, Sir John Henry, 1912–1994, vol. IX
Loveridge, Walter David, 1867–1940, vol. III (A), vol. IV
Loverseed, John Frederick 1881–1928, vol. II
Lovett, Col Alfred Crowdy, 1862–1919, vol. II
Lovett, Maj.-Gen. Beresford, 1839–1926, vol. II
Lovett, Rt Rev. Ernest Neville, 1869–1951, vol. V
Lovett, Sir (Harrington) Verney, 1864–1945, vol. IV
Lovett, Rev. Canon John Percival Willoughby, 1880–1968, vol. VI
Lovett, Maj.-Gen. Osmond de Turville, 1898–1982, vol. VIII
Lovett, Rev. Richard, 1851–1904, vol. I
Lovett, Robert Abercrombie, 1895–1986, vol. VIII
Lovett, Sir Verney; see Lovett, Sir H. V.
Lovett-Cameron, Rev. Charles Leslie, 1843–1927, vol. II
Loveys, Walter Harris, 1920–1969, vol. VI
Lovibond, Joseph Williams, 1833–1918, vol. II
Lovick, Albert Ernest Fred, 1912–1996, vol. X
Low, Hon. Lord; Alexander Low, 1845–1910, vol. I
Low, A. M., 1888–1956, vol. V
Low, Sir A. Maurice, 1860–1929, vol. III
Low, Gen. Alexander, 1817–1904, vol. I
Low, Alexander, 1868–1950, vol. IV
Low, Alexander; see Low, Hon. Lord.
Low, Sir Austin; 1862–1956, vol. V
Low, Sir Charles Ernest, 1869–1941, vol. IV
Low, Charles Rathbone, 1837–1918, vol. II
Low, Sir David Alexander Cecil, 1891–1963, vol. VI
Low, David Allan, 1857–1937, vol. III
Low, David Morrice, 1890–1972, vol. VII
Low, Sir Francis, 1893–1972, vol. VII
Low, Frank Harrison, 1854–1912, vol. I
Low, Sir Frederick, 1856–1917, vol. II
Low, George Carmichael, 1872–1952, vol. V
Low, George Macritchie, 1849–1922, vol. II
Low, Harold, 1863–1932, vol. III
Low, Sir Henry Telfer, 1880–1964, vol. VI
Low, Sir Hugh, 1824–1905, vol. I
Low, Sir James, 1st Bt, 1849–1923, vol. II
Low, John Laing, 1869–1929, vol. III
Low, Mabel Bruce, died 1972, vol. VII
Low, Lt-Col Robert Balmain, 1864–1927, vol. II
Low, Robert Bruce, 1846–1922, vol. II
Low, Robert Cranston, 1879–1949, vol. IV
Low, Gen. Sir Robert Cunliffe, 1838–1911, vol. I
Low, Hon. Seth, 1850–1916, vol. II
Low, Sir Sidney, 1857–1932, vol. III
Low, Sir Stephen Philpot, 1883–1955, vol. V
Low, Col Stuart, 1888–1942, vol. IV

Low, Vincent Warren, *died* 1942, vol. IV
Low, Sir Walter John Morrison-, 2nd Bt, 1899–1955, vol. V
Low, Ven. Walter Percival, 1876–1960, vol. V
Low, Will Hicok, 1853–1932, vol. III
Low, William Alexander, *died* 1970, vol. VI
Low, Rev. William Leslie, 1840–1929, vol. III
Low, William Malcolm, 1835–1923, vol. II
Low, William S.; *see* Stuart-Low.
Lowdon, Andrew Gilchrist Ross, 1911–1965, vol. VI
Lowdon, John, 1881–1963, vol. VI
Lowe, Sir (Albert) George, 1901–1967, vol. VI
Lowe, Alexander Francis, 1861–1929, vol. III
Lowe, Arthur, 1915–1982, vol. VIII
Lowe, Lt-Col Arthur Cecil, 1868–1917, vol. II
Lowe, Arthur Labron, 1861–1928, vol. II
Lowe, Charles, *died* 1931, vol. III
Lowe, Sir Charles John, 1880–1969, vol. VI
Lowe, Gp Captain Cyril Nelson, 1891–1983, vol. VIII
Lowe, David, 1868–1947, vol. IV
Lowe, Sir David, 1899–1980, vol. VII
Lowe, David Nicoll, 1909–1999, vol. X
Lowe, Douglas Gordon Arthur, 1902–1981, vol. VIII
Lowe, Sir Drury Curzon D., *see* Drury-Lowe.
Lowe, Duncan; *see* Lowe, J. D.
Lowe, Air Vice-Marshal Sir Edgar Noel, 1905–1992, vol. IX
Lowe, Rev. Edward Clarke, 1823–1912, vol. I
Lowe, Edward Cronin, 1880–1958, vol. V
Lowe, Edwin Ernest, 1877–1958, vol. V
Lowe, Elias Avery, 1879–1969, vol. VI
Lowe, Mrs Eveline M., *died* 1956, vol. V
Lowe, Sir (Francis) Gordon, 2nd Bt, 1884–1972, vol. VII
Lowe, Major Francis Manley, 1859–1934, vol. III
Lowe, Sir Francis Reginald Gordon, 3rd Bt, 1931–1986, vol. VIII
Lowe, Rt Hon. Sir Francis William, 1st Bt, 1852–1929, vol. III
Lowe, Sir George; *see* Lowe, Sir A. G.
Lowe, Sir Gordon; *see* Lowe, Sir F. G.
Lowe, Rev. Herbert Hampson, 1865–1945, vol. IV
Lowe, Herbert John, 1892–1960, vol. V
Lowe, Rear-Adm. John, 1838–1930, vol. III
Lowe, Rev. John, 1899–1960, vol. V
Lowe, (John) Duncan, 1948–1998, vol. X
Lowe, John Eric Charles, 1907–1998, vol. X
Lowe, Rev. Joseph, *died* 1920, vol. II
Lowe, Sir Lionel Harold Harvey, 1897–1960, vol. V
Lowe, Percy Roycroft, 1870–1948, vol. IV
Lowe, Robson, 1905–1997, vol. X
Lowe, Rouxville Mark, 1881–1957, vol. V
Lowe, Ven. Sidney Edward, 1882–1968, vol. VI
Lowe, Vice-Adm. Sidney Robert D.; *see* Drury-Lowe.
Lowe, Lt-Col Thomas Alfred, 1888–1967, vol. VI
Lowe, Maj.-Gen. William Henry Muir, 1861–1944, vol. IV
Lowe, Very Rev. William James, 1853–1931, vol. III
Lowe-Brown, William Lowe, 1876–1956, vol. V
Lowell, Abbott Lawrence, 1856–1943, vol. IV

Lowell, Army, 1874–1925, vol. II
Lowell, Percival, 1855–1916, vol. II
Lowell, Robert Traill Spence, Jr, 1917–1977, vol. VII
Lowenfeld, Margaret Frances Jane, 1890–1973, vol. VII
Lowenstein, Otto Egon, 1906–1999, vol. X
Lowenthal, Charles Frederick, *died* 1933, vol. III
Lowery, Harry, 1896–1967, vol. VI
Lowes, John Livingston, 1867–1945, vol. IV
Loweth, Sidney Harold, 1893–1977, vol. VII
Loweth, Walter Ernest, 1892–1968, vol. VI
Lowinger, Victor Alexander, 1879–1957, vol. V
Lowinsky, Thomas Esmond, 1892–1947, vol. IV
Lowis, Cecil Champain, 1866–1948, vol. IV
Lowis, Frank Currie, 1872–1963, vol. VI
Lowis, Lt-Col Penton Shakspear, 1870–1931, vol. III
Lowles, Sir Geoffrey; *see* Lowles, Sir J. G. N.
Lowles, Sir (John) Geoffrey (Nelson), 1898–1962, vol. VI
Lowman, Rev. Canon Edward Sydney Charles, 1908–1974, vol. VII
Lowndes, Alan, 1921–1978, vol. VII
Lowndes, Frederic Sawrey Archibald, *died* 1940, vol. III
Lowndes, Rt Hon. Sir George Rivers, 1862–1943, vol. IV
Lowndes, Marie; *see* Belloc, Marie Adelaide.
Lowndes, Mary E., 1863–1947, vol. IV
Lowndes, Brig. Montacute William Worrall S.; *see* Selby-Lowndes.
Lowndes, Maj.-Gen. Thomas, *died* 1927, vol. II
Lowndes, William Selby-, 1836–1920, vol. II
Lowndes, Col William Selby-, 1871–1951, vol. V
Lowrey, Sir Joseph, 1859–1936, vol. III
Lowry, Baron (Life Peer); Robert Lynd Erskine Lowry, 1919–1999, vol. X
Lowry, Rev. Walter, 1868–1959, vol. V
Lowry, Sir Arthur, 1868–1938, vol. III
Lowry, Charles, 1857–1922, vol. II
Lowry, Charles Gibson, 1880–1951, vol. V
Lowry, Henry Dawson, 1869–1906, vol. I
Lowry, Hugh Avant, 1913–1982, vol. VIII
Lowry, Col James, 1856–1937, vol. III
Lowry, Laurence Stephen, 1887–1976, vol. VII
Lowry, Adm. Sir Robert Swinburne, 1854–1920, vol. II
Lowry, Lt-Gen. Robert William, 1824–1905, vol. I
Lowry, Thomas Martin, 1874–1936, vol. III
Lowry, Rt Hon. William, *died* 1949, vol. IV
Lowry-Corry, Adm. Hon. Armar, 1836–1919, vol. II
Lowry-Corry, Lt-Col Sir Henry Charles, 1887–1973, vol. VII
Lowry-Corry, Col Hon. Henry William, 1845–1927, vol. II
Lowry-Corry, Brig.-Gen. Noel Armar, 1867–1935, vol. III
Lowsley, Col Herbert de Lisle P.; *see* Pollard-Lowsley.
Lowsley-Williams, George, 1869–1937, vol. III
Lowson, Sir Denys Colquhoun Flowerdew, 1st Bt, 1906–1975, vol. VII
Lowson, James Gray Flowerdew, 1860–1942, vol. IV

Lowth, Lt-Col Frank Robert, 1850–1931, vol. III
Lowth, Thomas, 1858–1931, vol. III
Lowther, Viscount; Anthony Edward Lowther, 1896–1949, vol. IV
Lowther, Captain Hon. Anthony George, 1925–1981, vol. VIII
Lowther, Maj.-Gen. Sir Cecil; see Lowther, Maj.-Gen. Sir H. C.
Lowther, Lt-Col Sir Charles Bingham, 4th Bt (cr 1824), 1880–1949, vol. IV
Lowther, Major Hon. Christopher William, 1887–1935, vol. III
Lowther, Claude, 1872–1929, vol. III
Lowther, Rt Hon. Sir Gerard Augustus, 1st Bt (cr 1914), 1858–1916, vol. II
Lowther, Maj.-Gen. Sir (Henry) Cecil, 1869–1940, vol. III
Lowther, Sir Henry Crofton, 1858–1939, vol. III
Lowther, Rt Hon. James, 1840–1904, vol. I
Lowther, John Arthur, 1910–1942, vol. IV
Lowther, Col John George, 1885–1977, vol. VII
Lowther, Hon. William, 1821–1912, vol. I
Lowther, Lt-Col Sir William Guy, 5th Bt, 1912–1982, vol. VIII
Lowther-Crofton, Vice-Adm. Edward George, 1873–1942, vol. IV
Lowthian, Caroline; see Prescott, C.
Lowthian, George Henry, 1908–1986, vol. VIII
Loxam, John Gordon, 1927–2000, vol. X
Loyd, Archie Kirkman, 1847–1922, vol. II
Loyd, Arthur Thomas, 1882–1944, vol. IV
Loyd, Gen. Sir Charles; see Loyd, Gen. Sir H. C.
Loyd, Edward Henry, 1861–1938, vol. III
Loyd, Gen. Sir (Henry) Charles, 1891–1973, vol. VII
Loyd, Lewis Vivian, 1852–1908, vol. I
Loyd, Llewellyn Foster, 1861–1939, vol. III
Loyd, Lady Mary, died 1936, vol. III
Loyd, Rt Rev. Philip Henry, 1884–1952, vol. V
Loyn, Henry Royston, 1922–2000, vol. X
Lu, Gwei-Djen, 1904–1991, vol. IX
Luard, Maj.-Gen. Charles Camac, 1867–1947, vol. IV
Luard, Lt-Col Charles Eckford, 1869–1927, vol. II
Luard, Maj.-Gen. Charles Edward, 1939–1908, vol. I
Luard, (David) Evan (Trant), 1926–1991, vol. IX
Luard, Major Edward Bourryau, 1870–1916, vol. II
Luard, Evan; see Luard, D. E. T.
Luard, Adm. John Scott, 1865–1936, vol. III
Luard, Lowes Dalbiac, died 1944, vol. IV
Luard, Comdr William Blaine, 1897–1979, vol. VII
Luard, Adm. Sir William Garnham, 1820–1910, vol. I
Lubbock, Sir Alan, 1897–1990, vol. VIII
Lubbock, Arthur Nevile, 1869–1939, vol. III
Lubbock, Basil, 1876–1944, vol. IV
Lubbock, Cecil 1872–1956, vol. V
Lubbock, Christopher William Stuart, 1920–2000, vol. X
Lubbock, Edgar, 1847–1907, vol. I
Lubbock, Frederic, 1844–1927, vol. II
Lubbock, Geoffrey, 1873–1932, vol. III
Lubbock, Brig.-Gen. Guy, 1870–1956, vol. V
Lubbock, Hon. Harold Fox-Pitt, 1888–1918, vol. II

Lubbock, Henry James, 1838–1910, vol. I
Lubbock, Hon. Maurice Fox Pitt, 1900–1957, vol. V
Lubbock, Montagu, 1842–1925, vol. II
Lubbock, Sir Nevile, 1839–1914, vol. I
Lubbock, Hon. Norman, 1861–1926, vol. II
Lubbock, Percy, 1879–1965, vol. VI
Lubbock, Roy, 1892–1985, vol. VIII
Lubbock, Samuel Gurney, died 1958, vol. V
Lubbock, Lady Sybil Marjorie, 1879–1943, vol. IV
Lubienski, Count Louis B.; see Bodenham-Lubienski.
Lubitsch, Ernst, 1892–1947, vol. IV
Lucan, 4th Earl of, 1830–1914, vol. I
Lucan, 5th Earl of, 1860–1949, vol. IV
Lucan, 6th Earl of, 1898–1964, vol. VI
Lucas of Chilworth, 1st Baron, 1896–1967, vol. VI
Lucas of Crudwell, 8th Baron, and Dingwall, 5th Lord, 1876–1916, vol. II
Lucas of Crudwell, Baroness (9th in line), and Dingwall, Lady (6th in line), 1880–1958, vol. V
Lucas of Crudwell, Baroness (10th in line), and Dingwall, Lady (13th in line), 1919–1991, vol. IX
Lucas, Col Alfred George, 1854–1941, vol. IV
Lucas, Captain Armytage Anthony, died 1950, vol. IV
Lucas, Rev. Arthur, 1851–1921, vol. II
Lucas, Sir Arthur, 1845–1922, vol. II
Lucas, Arthur, 1863–1932, vol. III
Lucas, Sir Arthur Charles, 2nd Bt, 1853–1915, vol. I
Lucas, Bryan K.; see Keith-Lucas.
Lucas, Brig.-Gen. Cecil Courtenay, 1883–1957, vol. V
Lucas, Rear-Adm. Charles Davis, 1834–1914, vol. I
Lucas, Charles James, 1853–1928, vol. II
Lucas, Sir Charles Prestwood, 1853–1931, vol. III
Lucas, Claude Arthur, 1894–1974, vol. VII
Lucas, Colin Anderson, 1906–1984, vol. VIII
Lucas, Maj.-Gen. Cuthbert Henry Tindall, 1879–1958, vol. V
Lucas, David K.; see Keith-Lucas.
Lucas, Donald William, 1905–1985, vol. VIII
Lucas, Hon. Sir Edward, 1857–1950, vol. IV
Lucas, Sir Edward Lingard, 3rd Bt, 1860–1936, vol. III
Lucas, Edward Verrall, 1868–1938, vol. III
Lucas, Edward William, 1864–1940, vol. III
Lucas, Rev. Egbert de Grey, 1878–1958, vol. V
Lucas, Col Francis Alfred, 1850–1918, vol. II
Lucas, Francis Herman, 1878–1920, vol. II
Lucas, Hon. Frank Archibald William, 1881–1959, vol. V
Lucas, Frank Laurence, 1894–1967, vol. VI
Lucas, Brig.-Gen. Frederic George, 1866–1922, vol. II
Lucas, Maj.-Gen. Geoffrey, 1904–1982, vol. VIII
Lucas, Henry Frederick Lucas, died 1943, vol. IV
Lucas, Hon. Isaac Benson, 1867–1940, vol. III
Lucas, Rt Rev. James Richard, 1867–1938, vol. III
Lucas, Major Sir Jocelyn Morton, 4th Bt, 1889–1980, vol. VII
Lucas, Ven. John Michael, 1921–1992, vol. IX
Lucas, John Seymour, 1849–1923, vol. II
Lucas, Keith, 1879–1916, vol. II
Lucas, Marie Elizabeth Seymour, 1855–1921, vol. II

Lucas, Percy Belgrave, 1915–1998, vol. X
Lucas, Brig. Reginald Hutchinson, 1888–1956, vol. V
Lucas, Reginald Jafray, 1865–1914, vol. I
Lucas, Richard Clement, *died* 1915, vol. I
Lucas, St John Welles, 1879–1934, vol. III
Lucas, Sir Thomas, 1st Bt, 1822–1902, vol. I
Lucas, Col Thomas John Rashleigh, 1858–1929, vol. III
Lucas, Wilfrid Irvine, 1905–1973, vol. VII
Lucas, William Henry, 1867–1937, vol. III
Lucas, Rt Rev. William Vincent, 1883–1945, vol. IV
Lucas-Shadwell, William, 1852–1915, vol. I
Lucas-Tooth, Sir (Archibald) Leonard (Lucas), 2nd Bt, 1884–1918, vol. II
Lucas-Tooth, Sir Leonard; *see* Lucas-Tooth, Sir A. L. L.
Lucas-Tooth, Sir Robert Lucas, 1st Bt, 1844–1915, vol. I
Lucceshi, Andrea Carlo, 1860–1925, vol. II
Luce, Rev. Arthur Aston, 1882–1977, vol. VII
Luce, Hon. Clare Boothe, 1903–1987, vol. VIII
Luce, Adm. Sir David; *see* Luce, Adm. Sir J. D.
Luce, Rev. Edward, 1851–1917, vol. II
Luce, Rev. Canon Harry Kenneth, 1897–1972, vol. VII
Luce, Henry Robinson, 1898–1967, vol. VI
Luce, Adm. John, 1870–1932, vol. III
Luce, Adm. Sir (John) David, 1906–1971, vol. VII
Luce, Morton, 1849–1943, vol. IV
Luce, Reginald William, 1893–1971, vol. VII
Luce, Maj.-Gen. Sir Richard Harman, 1867–1952, vol. V
Luce, Sir William Henry Tucker, 1907–1977, vol. VII
Lucet, Charles Ernest, 1910–1990, vol. VIII
Lucey, Most Rev. Cornelius, *died* 1982, vol. VIII
Lucey, Rear-Adm. Martin Noel, 1920–1992, vol. IX
Lucey, Col Walter Francis, 1880–1962, vol. VI
Luciani, Albino; *see* John Paul I.
Lucie-Smith, Sir Alfred van W., 1854–1947, vol. IV
Lucie-Smith, Sir John Alfred, 1888–1969, vol. VI
Luck, Col Brian John Michael, 1874–1948, vol. IV
Luck, Captain Cyril Montagu, 1872–1944, vol. IV
Luck, Gen. Sir George, 1840–1916, vol. II
Luck, Richard, 1847–1920, vol. II
Lucker, Sydney Charles, 1897–1977, vol. VII
Luckes, Eva C. E., *died* 1919, vol. II
Luckham, Major Arthur Albert, 1883–1957, vol. V
Luckham, Ven. William Arthur Grant, 1857–1921, vol. II
Luckhoo, Hon. Sir Edward Victor, 1912–1998, vol. X
Luckhoo, Hon. Sir Joseph Alexander, 1917–1990, vol. IX (AI)
Luckhoo, Sir Lionel Alfred, 1914–1997, vol. X
Luckner, Felix, Count, 1881–1966, vol. VI
Luckock, Maj.-Gen. Russell Mortimer, 1877–1950, vol. IV
Lucraft, Frederick Hickman, 1894–1981, vol. VIII
Lucy, Major Sir Brian Fulke Cameron-Ramsay-F.; *see* Fairfax-Lucy.
Lucy, Sir Henry, 1845–1924, vol. II

Lucy, Sir Henry William Cameron-Ramsay-F.; *see* Fairfax-Lucy.
Lucy, Captain Sir Montgomerie F.; *see* Fairfax-Lucy, Captain Sir H. M. R.
Ludbrook, Samuel Lawrence, 1895–1976, vol. VII
Ludby, Max, 1858–1943, vol. IV
Luddington, James Little, 1853–1935, vol. III
Ludlow, 1st Baron, 1827–1899, vol. I
Ludlow, 2nd Baron, 1865–1922, vol. II
Ludlow, Lady; (Alice Sedgwick), *died* 1945, vol. IV
Ludlow, Brig.-Gen. Edmund Ranald Owen, 1864–1929, vol. III
Ludlow, Col Edmund Samuel, 1840–1906, vol. I
Ludlow, Sir Henry, 1834–1903, vol. I
Ludlow, John Malcolm, 1821–1911, vol. I
Ludlow, Sir Richard Robert, 1882–1956, vol. V
Ludlow, Brig.-Gen. Sir Walter Robert, 1857–1941, vol. IV
Ludlow-Hewitt, Air Chief Marshal Sir Edgar Rainey, 1886–1973, vol. VII
Ludovici, Captain Anthony M., 1882–1971, vol. VII
Ludwig, Emil, 1881–1948, vol. IV
Lueger, Karl, 1844–1910, vol. I
Luff, Arthur Pearson, 1855–1938, vol. III
Luff, Richard Edmund Reife, 1887–1969, vol. VI
Luff, Richard William Peter, 1927–1993, vol. IX
Luft, Rev. Canon Hyam Mark, 1913–1986, vol. VIII
Luft, Rev. Canon Mark; *see* Luft, Rev. Canon H. M.
Lugard, 1st Baron, 1858–1945, vol. IV
Lugard, Lady; (Flora), *died* 1929, vol. III
Lugard, Rt Hon. Sir Edward, 1810–1898, vol. I
Lugard, Major Edward James, 1865–1957, vol. V
Lugard, Col Edward John, 1845–1911, vol. I
Lugg, Gp Captain Sidney, 1906–1972, vol. VII
Luhrs, Lt-Col Henry Gordon-, 1880–1954, vol. V
Luke, 1st Baron, 1873–1943, vol. IV
Luke, 2nd Baron, 1905–1996, vol. X
Luke, Sir Charles Manley, 1857–1941, vol. IV
Luke, Lt-Col Edward Vyvyan, 1861–1908, vol. I
Luke, Hon. Sir Emile Fashole, *born* 1895, vol. VII (AII)
Luke, Eric Howard Manley, 1894–1987, vol. VIII
Luke, Sir Harry Charles, 1884–1969, vol. VI
Luke, Sir John Pearce, 1858–1931, vol. III
Luke, Sir Kenneth George, 1898–1971, vol. VII
Luke, Peter Ambrose Cyprian, 1919–1995, vol. IX
Luke, Sir Stephen Elliot Vyvyan, 1905–1988, vol. VIII
Luke, Stephen Paget Walter Vyvyan, 1845–1929, vol. III
Luke, Brig.-Gen. Thomas Mawe, 1872–1952, vol. V
Luke, William Edgell, 1909–1987, vol. VIII
Luke, William Joseph, 1862–1934, vol. III
Luker, Col Roland, 1878–1947, vol. IV
Lukin, Maj.-Gen. Sir Henry Timson, 1860–1925, vol. II
Lukin, Hon. Lionel Oscar, 1868–1944, vol. IV
Lukin, Brig.-Gen. Robert Clarence Wellesley, 1870–1955, vol. VI
Lukis, Surg.-Gen. Hon. Sir Charles Pardey, 1857–1918, vol. II
Lukis, Maj.-Gen. Wilfrid Boyd Fellowes, 1896–1969, vol. VI

Luling, Sylvia; *see* Thompson, S.
Lumb, Sir Charles Frederick, 1846–1911, vol. I
Lumb, Col Frederick George Edward, 1877–1958, vol. V
Lumby, Lt-Col Arthur Friedrich Rawson, 1890–1943, vol. IV
Lumby, Sir Henry, 1909–1989, vol. VIII
Lumby, John Henry, *died* 1948, vol. IV
Lumholtz, Carl, 1851–1922, vol. II
Lumière, Louis, 1864–1948, vol. IV
Lumley, Sir Dudley Owen, 1895–1964, vol. VI
Lumley, Air Cdr Eric Alfred, 1891–1979, vol. VII
Lumley, Col Francis Douglas, 1857–1925, vol. II
Lumley, Lyulph, *died* 1944, vol. IV
Lumley, Brig.-Gen. Hon. Osbert Victor George Atheling, 1862–1923, vol. II
Lumley, Theodore, *died* 1922, vol. II
Lumley-Smith, Major Sir Thomas Gabriel Lumley, 1879–1961, vol. VI
Lumsdaine, Edwin Robert John S.; *see* Sandys-Lumsdaine.
Lumsden, Col Bruce John David, 1907–1965, vol. VI
Lumsden, Col Dugald M'Tavish, 1851–1915, vol. I
Lumsden, E. S., 1883–1948, vol. IV
Lumsden, Maj.-Gen. Herbert, 1897–1945, vol. IV
Lumsden, Sir James Robert, 1884–1970, vol. VI
Lumsden, Sir John, 1869–1944, vol. IV
Lumsden, Dame Louisa Innes, 1840–1935, vol. III
Lumsden, Gen. Sir Peter Stark, 1829–1918, vol. II
Lumsden, Thomas William, 1874–1953, vol. V
Lumsden, Rear-Adm. Walter, 1865–1947, vol. IV
Lunawada, Rajah of, 1860–1929, vol. III
Lund, Henrik, 1879–1935, vol. III
Lund, Niels M., 1863–1916, vol. II
Lund, Lt-Gen. Sir Otto Marling, 1891–1956, vol. V
Lund, Sir Thomas George, 1906–1981, vol. VIII
Lundgren, Captain Albert Edvin, 1878–1942, vol. IV
Lundon, Thomas, 1883–1951, vol. V
Lunham, Col Sir Ainslie, *died* 1930, vol. III
Lunn, Sir Arnold, 1888–1974, vol. VII
Lunn, Sir George, 1861–1939, vol. III
Lunn, Sir Henry Simpson, 1859–1939, vol. III
Lunn, Hugh Kingsmill; *see* Kingsmill, Hugh.
Lunn, Louise Kirkby, 1873–1930, vol. III
Lunn, William, 1872–1942, vol. IV
Lunt, Alfred, 1892–1977, vol. VII
Lunt, Rt Rev. Francis Evered, 1900–1982, vol. VIII
Lunt, Rt Rev. Geoffrey Charles Lester, *died* 1948, vol. IV
Lunt, Rev. Canon Ronald Geoffrey, 1913–1994, vol. IX
Lupton, Arnold, *died* 1930, vol. III
Lupton, Arthur Sinclair, 1877–1949, vol. IV
Lupton, Charles, 1855–1935, vol. III
Lupton, John, 1869–1946, vol. IV
Lurgan, 3rd Baron, 1858–1937, vol. III
Lurgan, 4th Baron, 1902–1984, vol. VIII
Lurgan, 5th Baron, 1911–1991, vol. IX
Luria, Salvador Edward, 1912–1991, vol. IX
Luscombe, Sir John Henry, 1848–1937, vol. III
Luscombe, Norman Percival, 1902–1976, vol. VII
Luscombe, Ven. Popham Street, *died* 1927, vol. II
Lush, Sir Archibald James, 1900–1976, vol. VII

Lush, Rt Hon. Sir Charles Montague, 1853–1930, vol. III
Lush, Maurice Stanley, 1896–1990, vol. VIII
Lush-Wilson, Sir Herbert W., 1850–1941, vol. IV
Lushington, Alfred Wyndham, *died* 1920, vol. II
Lushington, Major Sir Arthur Patrick Douglas, 5th Bt, 1861–1937, vol. III
Lushington, Rev. Franklyn de Winton, 1868–1941, vol. IV
Lushington, Sir Godfrey, 1832–1907, vol. I
Lushington, Maj.-Gen. Godfrey Edward W.; *see* Wildman-Lushington.
Lushington, Sir Henry, 3rd Bt, 1802–1897, vol. I
Lushington, Sir Henry, 4th Bt, 1826–1898, vol. I
Lushington, Sir Henry Edmund Castleman, 7th Bt, 1909–1988, vol. VIII
Lushington, Sir Herbert Castleman, 6th Bt, 1879–1968, vol. VI
Lushington, Brig.-Gen. Stephen, 1864–1940, vol. III
Lushington, Sydney George, 1859–1909, vol. I
Lushington, Vernon, 1832–1912, vol. I
Lusk, Sir Andrew, 1st Bt, 1810–1909, vol. I
Lusk, William C., 1875–1944, vol. IV
Lustgarten, Edgar, 1907–1978, vol. VII
Lusty, Sir Robert Frith, 1909–1991, vol. IX
Luther, Col Anthony John, 1864–1937, vol. III
Luther, Rev. George Minchin, *died* 1911, vol. I
Luthuli, Albert John Mvumbi, 1899–1967, vol. VI
Lutoslawski, Wincenty, 1863–1955, vol. V
Lutosławski, Witold, 1913–1994, vol. IX
Luttig, Hendrik Gerhardus, 1907–1975, vol. VII
Luttman, Willie Lewis, 1874–1930, vol. III
Luttman-Johnson, Lt-Col Frederic, 1845–1917, vol. II
Luttrell, Alexander Fownes, 1855–1944, vol. IV
Luttrell, George Fownes, 1826–1910, vol. I
Luttrell, Hugh Courtenay Fownes, 1857–1918, vol. II
Lutwyche, Hudson Latham, 1856–1925, vol. II
Lutyens, (Agnes) Elisabeth, (Mrs Edward Clark), 1906–1983, vol. VIII
Lutyens, Sir Edwin Landseer, 1869–1944, vol. IV
Lutyens, Elisabeth; *see* Lutyens, A.
Lutyens, Lady Emily, 1874–1964, vol. VI
Lutyens, Mary, (Mrs J. G. Links), 1908–1999, vol. X
Lützow, Count, *died* 1916, vol. II
Luwum, Most Rev. Janani, 1924–1977, vol. VII
Luxford, Major Rev. John Aldred, *died* 1921, vol. II
Luxford, John Hector, 1890–1971, vol. VII
Luxmoore, Rt Hon. Sir (Arthur) Fairfax (Charles Coryndon), 1876–1944, vol. IV
Luxmoore, Rt Hon. Sir Fairfax; *see* Luxmoore, Rt Hon. Sir A. F. C. C.
Luxmoore, Henry Elford, *died* 1926, vol. II
Luxton, Brig. Daniel Aston, 1891–1960, vol. V (A)
Luxton, Rt Rev. George Nasmith, 1901–1970, vol. VI
Luxton, Sir Harold, 1888–1957, vol. V
Luxton, William John, 1909–1992, vol. IX
Luzzatti, Luigi, 1841–1927, vol. II
Lwoff, André Michel, 1902–1994, vol. IX
Luyt, Sir Richard Edmonds, 1915–1994, vol. IX
Lyal, David Hume, 1892–1965, vol. VI
Lyall, Rt Hon. Sir Alfred Comyn, 1835–1911, vol. I

Lyall, Archibald Laurence, 1904–1964, vol. VI
Lyall, Dame Beatrix Margaret, *died* 1948, vol. IV
Lyall, Charles Elliott, 1877–1942, vol. IV
Lyall, Sir Charles James, 1845–1920, vol. II
Lyall, David Robert, 1841–1917, vol. II
Lyall, Edna; *see* Bayly, Ada Ellen.
Lyall, Major Edward, 1869–1929, vol. III
Lyall, Frank Frederick, 1872–1950, vol. IV
Lyall, George, 1883–1959, vol. V
Lyall, Col Graham Thomson, 1892–1941, vol. IV
Lyall, Sir James Broadwood, 1838–1916, vol. II
Lyall, Lt-Col Robert Adolphus, 1876–1948, vol. IV
Lyall Grant, Sir Robert William, 1875–1955, vol. V
Lyautey, Marshal Hubert, 1854–1934, vol. III
Lycett, Brig. Cyril Vernon Lechmere, 1894–1978, vol. VII
Lyddon, Vice-Adm. Sir Horace Collier, 1912–1968, vol. VI
Lyddon, Col William George, 1871–1944, vol. IV
Lyde, Lionel William, 1863–1947, vol. IV
Lydekker, Richard, 1849–1915, vol. I
Lydford, Air Marshal Sir Harold Thomas, 1898–1979, vol. VII
Lye, Lt-Col Robert Cobbe, 1865–1917, vol. II
Lyell, 1st Baron, 1850–1926, vol. II
Lyell, 2nd Baron, 1913–1943, vol. IV
Lyell, Hon. Charles Henry, 1875–1918, vol. II
Lyell, Col David, 1866–1940, vol. III
Lyell, Denis David, 1871–1946, vol. IV
Lyell, Sir Maurice Legat, 1901–1975, vol. VII
Lyell, William Darling, 1860–1925, vol. II
Lygon, Major Hon. Henry, 1884–1936, vol. III
Lygon, Lt-Col Hon. Robert, 1879–1952, vol. V
Lyle of Westbourne, 1st Baron, 1882–1954, vol. V
Lyle of Westbourne, 2nd Baron, 1905–1976, vol. VII
Lyle, Sir Alexander Park, 1st Bt (*cr* 1929), 1849–1933, vol. III
Lyle, Sir Archibald Moir Park, 2nd Bt (*cr* 1929), 1884–1946, vol. IV
Lyle, Charles, 1851–1929, vol. III
Lyle, Col George Samuel Bateson, 1865–1943, vol. IV (A)
Lyle, Sir Harold, 1873–1927, vol. II
Lyle, Henry Samuel, 1857–1916, vol. II
Lyle, Herbert Willoughby, *died* 1956, vol. V
Lyle, Col Hugh Thomas, 1858–1942, vol. IV
Lyle, Sir Ian D., 1907–1978, vol. VII
Lyle, James Duncan, 1887–1972, vol. VII
Lyle, John Cromie, 1862–1947, vol. IV
Lyle, Sir Oliver, 1890–1961, vol. VI
Lyle, Robert, 1905–1966, vol. VI
Lyle, Robert Charles, 1887–1943, vol. IV
Lyle, Sir Robert Park, 1st Bt (*cr* 1915), 1859–1923, vol. II
Lyle, Robert Patton Ranken, 1870–1950, vol. IV
Lyle, Samuel, *died* 1941, vol. IV
Lyle, Thomas Keith, 1903–1987, vol. VIII
Lyle, Thomas McElderry, 1886–1962, vol. VI
Lyle, Sir Thomas Ranken, 1860–1944, vol. IV
Lyle, William, 1871–1949, vol. IV
Lyle-Samuel, Alexander, 1883–1942, vol. IV
Lymer, Brig. Rymel Watts, 1909–1972, vol. VII
Lymington, Viscount; Oliver Kintzing Wallop, 1923–1984, vol. VIII
Lynam, Alfred Edmund, 1873–1956, vol. V

Lynam, Edward William O'Flaherty, *died* 1950, vol. IV
Lynam, Jocelyn Humphrey Rickman, 1902–1978, vol. VII
Lynch, Col Arthur 1861–1934, vol. III
Lynch, Col Charles Joseph, *born* 1878, vol. III
Lynch, Col David A., 1880–1944, vol. IV
Lynch, Rev. Prebendary Donald MacLeod, 1911–2000, vol. X
Lynch, Finian, 1889–1966, vol. VI
Lynch, Francis Joseph, 1909–1980, vol. VII
Lynch, George, 1868–1928, vol. II
Lynch, George William Augustus, *died* 1940, vol. III
Lynch, G(erald) Roche, 1880–1957, vol. V
Lynch, Hannah, *died* 1904, vol. I
Lynch, Henry Finnis Blosse, 1862–1913, vol. I
Lynch, Sir Henry Joseph, 1878–1958, vol. V
Lynch, John, 1917–1999, vol. X
Lynch, John Gilbret Bohun, 1884–1928, vol. II
Lynch, Sir John Patrick, 1858–1921, vol. II
Lynch, Patrick, *died* 1947, vol. IV
Lynch, Hon. Patrick Joseph, 1867–1944, vol. IV
Lynch, Rt Hon. Sir Phillip Reginald, 1933–1984, vol. VIII
Lynch, Richard Irwin, 1850–1924, vol. II
Lynch, Captain Vincent James, 1892–1961, vol. VI
Lynch, William Joseph, 1853–1937, vol. III
Lynch-Blosse, Sir David Edward, 16th Bt, 1925–1971, vol. VII
Lynch-Blosse, Sir Henry, 15th Bt, 1884–1969, vol. VI
Lynch-Blosse, Sir Robert Cyril; *see* Blosse.
Lynch-Blosse, Sir Robert Geoffrey; *see* Blosse.
Lynch-Robinson, Sir Christopher Henry, 2nd Bt, 1884–1958, vol. V
Lynch-Robinson, Sir Niall Bryan, 3rd Bt, 1918–1996, vol. X
Lynch-White, Lt-Col Robert, 1875–1940, vol. III
Lynd, Robert, 1879–1949, vol. IV
Lynd, Sylvia, 1888–1952, vol. V
Lynde, Carleton John, 1872–1971, vol. VII
Lynden-Bell, Maj.-Gen. Sir Arthur Lynden, 1867–1943, vol. IV
Lynden-Bell, Col Edward Horace Lynden, 1858–1922, vol. II
Lyndhurst, Lady; (Georgina), *died* 1901, vol. I
Lyne, Arthur W., 1884–1971, vol. VII
Lyne, Joseph Leycester; *see* Ignatius, Father.
Lyne, Rev. Leonard Augustus, *died* 1919, vol. II
Lyne, Maj.-Gen. Lewis Owne, 1899–1970, vol. VI
Lyne, Air Vice-Marshal Michael Dillon, 1919–1997, vol. X
Lyne, Robert Francis, 1885–1957, vol. V
Lyne, Robert Nunez, 1864–1961, vol. VI
Lyne, Rear-Adm. Sir Thomas John Spence, 1870–1955, vol. V
Lyne, Hon. Sir William John, 1844–1913, vol. I
Lynen, Feodor Felix Konrad, 1911–1979, vol. VII
Lynes, Rear-Adm. Charles Edward, 1875–1977, vol. VII
Lynes, Rear-Adm. Hubert, 1874–1942, vol. IV
Lynham, John E. A., 1882–1946, vol. IV
Lynn, Col Graham Rigby, *died* 1966, vol. VI
Lynn, Rev. Joseph, 1887–1956, vol. V

Lynn, Ralph, 1882–1962, vol. VI
Lynn, Sir Robert, 1873–1945, vol. IV
Lynn, Stanley B.; *see* Balfour-Lynn.
Lynn, Wilfred, 1905–1994, vol. IX
Lynn, William H., *died* 1915, vol. I
Lynn-Jenkins, Frank, 1870–1927, vol. II
Lynn-Thomas, Sir John, 1861–1939, vol. III
Lynskey, Sir George Justin, 1888–1957, vol. V
Lynx, Larry; *see* Sarl, Arthur J.
Lyon, Sir Alexander, 1850–1927, vol. II
Lyon, Alexander Ward, 1931–1993, vol. IX
Lyon, Lt-Col Charles, 1865–1944, vol. IV
Lyon, Brig.-Gen. Charles Harry, 1878–1959, vol. V
Lyon, Brig. Cyril Arthur, 1880–1955, vol. V
Lyon, Hon. Sir David B.; *see* Bowes-Lyon.
Lyon, David Murray, 1888–1956, vol. V
Lyon, Brig.-Gen. Francis, 1867–1953, vol. V
Lyon, Hon. Francis B.; *see* Bowes-Lyon.
Lyon, Maj.-Gen. Sir Francis James Cecil B.; *see* Bowes-Lyon.
Lyon, Captain Geoffrey Francis B.; *see* Bowes-Lyon.
Lyon, Adm. Sir George Hamilton D'Oyly, 1883–1947, vol. IV
Lyon, Adm. Herbert, 1856–1919, vol. II
Lyon, Hugh; *see* Lyon, P. H. B.
Lyon, Brig. Surg. Lt-Col Isidore Bernadotte, 1839–1911, vol. I
Lyon, Kenneth, 1886–1956, vol. V
Lyon, Laurance, 1875–1932, vol. III
Lyon, Malcolm Douglas, 1898–1964, vol. VI
Lyon, Hon. Michael Claude Hamilton B.; *see* Bowes-Lyon.
Lyon, Percy Comyn, 1862–1952, vol. V
Lyon, (Percy) Hugh (Beverley), 1893–1986, vol. VIII
Lyo, Lt-Col Ralph Edward, 1865–1930, vol. III
Lyon, Rev. Ralph John, *died* 1914, vol. I
Lyon, Robert, 1894–1978, vol. VII
Lyon, Captain Ronald George B.; *see* Bowes Lyon.
Lyon, Stanley Douglas, 1917–1991, vol. IX
Lyon, Thomas Glover, 1855–1915, vol. I
Lyon, Thomas Henry, 1825–1914, vol. I
Lyon, Thomas Stewart, 1866–1946, vol. IV
Lyon, Ursula Mary, *died* 1961, vol. VI
Lyon, Ven. William John, 1883–1961, vol. VI
Lyon Dean, William John; *see* Dean.
Lyons of Brighton, Baron (Life Peer); Braham Jack Dennis Lyons, 1918–1978, vol. VII
Lyons, A. Neil, 1880–1940, vol. III
Lyons, Abraham Montagu, 1894–1961, vol. VI
Lyons, Sir Algernon McLennan, 1833–1908, vol. I
Lyons, Hon. Dame Enid Muriel, 1897–1981, vol. VIII
Lyons, Eric Alfred, 1912–1980, vol. VII
Lyons, Francis Stewart Leland, 1923–1983, vol. VIII
Lyons, Hamilton, 1918–1992, vol. IX
Lyons, Col Sir Henry George, 1864–1944, vol. IV
Lyons, James, 1887–1983, vol. VIII
Lyons, Most Rev. John, 1878–1958, vol. V
Lyons, Sir Joseph, *died* 1917, vol. II
Lyons, Rt Hon. Joseph Aloysius, 1879–1939, vol. III

Lyons, Mrs Miriam Isabel, 1880–1968, vol. VI
Lyons, Most Rev. Patrick, 1875–1949, vol. IV
Lyons, Most Rev. Patrick Francis, 1903–1967, vol. VI
Lyons, Brig. Richard Clarke, 1893–1981, vol. VIII
Lyons, Sir Rudolph, 1912–1991, vol. IX
Lyons, Terence Patrick, 1919–1992, vol. IX
Lyons, Thomas, 1896–1985, vol. VIII
Lyons, Sir William, 1901–1985, vol. VIII
Lyons, Rt Hon. William Henry Holmes, 1843–1924, vol. II
Lyons-Montgomery, Col Hugh Frederick, 1856–1931, vol. III
Lys, Christian; *see* Brebner, P. J.
Lys, Rev. Francis John, 1863–1947, vol. IV
Lysaght, Desmond Royse, 1903–1970, vol. VI
Lysaght, Gerald Stuart, 1869–1951, vol. V
Lysaght, Hon. Horace George, 1873–1918, vol. II
Lysaght, Sidney Royse, *died* 1941, vol. IV
Lysaght, William Royse, 1858–1945, vol. IV
Lysons, Sir Daniel, 1816–1898, vol. I
Lyster, Anthony St George, 1888–1971, vol. VII
Lyster, Adm. Sir (Arthur) Lumley (St George), 1888–1957, vol. V
Lyster, Cecil Rupert Chaworth, 1859–1920, vol. II
Lyster, Lt-Gen. Harry Hammon, 1830–1922, vol. II
Lyster, Very Rev. Henry Cameron, 1862–1932, vol. III
Lyster, Rt Rev. John, 1850–1911, vol. I
Lyster, Adm. Sir Lumley; *see* Lyster, Adm. Sir A. L. St G.
Lyster, Robert Arthur, *died* 1955, vol. V
Lyster, Thomas William, 1855–1922, vol. II
Lyte, Sir Henry Churchill Maxwell-, 1848–1940, vol. III
Lythgoe, Ian Gordon, 1914–2000, vol. X
Lythgoe, Sir James, 1891–1972, vol. VII
Lythgoe, Richard James, 1896–1940, vol. III
Lyttelton, Rt Hon. Alfred, 1857–1913, vol. I
Lyttelton, Hon. Mrs Alfred, (Dame Edith Lyttelton), *died* 1948, vol. IV
Lyttle, John Gordon, 1933–1991, vol. IX
Lyttelton, Rt Rev. Hon. Arthur Temple, 1852–1903, vol. I
Lyttelton, Rev. Hon. Charles Frederick, 1887–1931, vol. III
Lyttelton, Dame Edith Sophie; *see* Lyttelton, Hon. Mrs Alfred.
Lyttelton, Rev. Hon. Edward, 1855–1942, vol. IV
Lyttelton, Hon. George William, 1883–1962, vol. VI
Lyttelton, Hon. George William Spencer, 1847–1913, vol. I
Lyttelton, Gen. Rt Hon. Sir Neville Gerald, 1845–1931, vol. III
Lyttelton, Raymond Arthur, 1911–1995, vol. IX
Lyttelton, Hon. Robert Henry, 1854–1939, vol. III
Lyttelton, Comdr Stephen Clive, 1887–1959, vol. V
Lyttelton-Annesley, Lt-Gen. Sir Arthur Lyttelton, 1837–1926, vol. II
Lytton, 2nd Earl of, 1876–1947, vol. IV
Lytton, 3rd Earl of, 1879–1951, vol. V
Lytton, 4th Earl of, 1900–1985, vol. VIII

Lytton, Countess of; (Edith), 1841–1936, vol. III
Lytton, Lady Constance Georgina, 1869–1923, vol. II
Lytton, Sir Henry Alfred, 1867–1936, vol. III
Lytton Sells, Arthur Lytton, 1895–1978, vol. VII
Lyveden, 2nd Baron, 1824–1900, vol. I

Lyveden, 3rd Baron, 1857–1926, vol. II
Lyveden, 4th Baron, 1892–1969, vol. VI
Lyveden, 5th Baron, 1888–1973, vol. VII
Lyveden, 6th Baron, 1915–1999, vol. X
Lywood, Air Vice-Marshal Oswyn George William Gifford, 1895–1957, vol. V

M

Maartens, Maarten, 1858–1915, vol. I
Maas, Paul, 1880–1964, vol. VI
Maasdorp, Hon. Sir Andries Ferdinand Stockenström, 1847–1931, vol. III
Maasdorp, Christian George, 1848–1926, vol. II
Maass, Otto, 1890–1961, vol. VI
Mabane, 1st Baron, 1895–1969, vol. VI
Mabbott, John David, 1898–1988, vol. VIII
Maberly, Col Charles Evan, 1854–1920, vol. II
Mabie, Hamilton Wright, died 1917, vol. II
Mabson, Richard Rous, 1846–1933, vol. III
Maby, (Alfred) Cedric, 1915–2000, vol. X
Maby, Cedric; see Maby, A. C.
Maby, Sir Charles George, 1888–1967, vol. VI
McAdam, Sir Ian William James, 1917–1999, vol. X
Macadam, Sir Ivison Stevenson, 1894–1974, vol. VII
Macadam, Sir Peter, 1921–1997, vol. X
McAdam, Robert, 1906–1978, vol. VII
Macadam, Col Walter, 1865–1930, vol. III
M'Adam, Walter, 1866–1935, vol. III
McAdam, William, 1886–1952, vol. V
MacAdam, William, 1885–1976, vol. VII
McAdam, William Alexander, 1889–1961, vol. VI
McAdam Clark, James; see Clark, James McAdam.
McAdden, Sir Stephen James, 1907–1979, vol. VII
McAdoo, Most Rev. Henry Robert, 1916–1998, vol. X
McAdoo, William Gibbs, 1863–1941, vol. IV
Macafee, Charles Horner Greer, 1898–1978, vol. VII
Macafee, Col John Leeper Anketell, 1915–1974, vol. VII
McAleer, Hugh K., died 1941, vol. IV
Macaleese, Daniel, 1840–1900, vol. I
MacAlevey, Maj.-Gen. Gerald Esmond, 1894–1969, vol. VI
Macalister, Alexander, 1844–1919, vol. II
Macalister, Charles John, died 1943, vol. IV
MacAlister, Sir Donald, 1st Bt, 1854–1934, vol. III
Macalister, George Hugh Kidd, 1879–1930, vol. III
Macalister, Sir Ian, 1878–1957, vol. V
MacAlister, Sir John Young Walker, 1856–1925, vol. II
McAlister, Mary A., (Mrs J. Alexander McAlister), died 1976, vol. VII
Macalister, Robert Alexander Stewart, 1870–1950, vol. IV
Macalister, Sir Robert Lachlan, 1890–1967, vol. VI
McAlister, Samuel, 1896–1971, vol. VII
McAlister, William James, 1877–1937, vol. III
Macalister-Hall, William, 1872–1938, vol. III
McAllen, Captain Thomas Wilfred, 1888–1957, vol. V

McAllister, Alister; see Wharton, Anthony.
McAllister, Gilbert, 1906–1964, vol. VI
McAllister, Sir Reginald Basil, born 1900, vol. VIII
Macallum, Archibald Byron, 1858–1934, vol. III
McAlpin, Malcolm Caird, 1876–1930, vol. III
McAlpine of Moffat, Baron (Life Peer); Robert Edwin McAlpine, 1907–1990, vol. VIII
McAlpine, Sir Alfred David, 1881–1944, vol. IV
McAlpine, Sir (Alfred) Robert, 3rd Bt, 1907–1968, vol. VI
McAlpine, Archibald Douglas; see McAlpine, D.
McAlpine, Douglas, 1890–1981, vol. VIII
MacAlpine, Sir George Watson, 1850–1920, vol. II
McAlpine, Hon. Sir John Kenneth, 1906–1984, vol. VIII
MacAlpine, J(ohn) Warren, died 1956, vol. V
McAlpine, Sir Malcolm; see McAlpine, Sir T. M.
McAlpine, Sir Robert; see McAlpine, Sir A. R.
McAlpine, Sir Robert, 1st Bt, 1847–1934, vol. III
McAlpine, Sir Robert, 2nd Bt, 1868–1934, vol. III
McAlpine, Sir Robin, 1906–1993, vol. IX
McAlpine, Sir Thomas George Bishop, 4th Bt, 1901–1983, vol. VIII
McAlpine, Sir (Thomas) Malcolm, 1877–1967, vol. VI
Malcalpine-Leny, Bt Lt-Col R. L.; see Leny.
Macan, Sir Arthur Vernon, 1843–1908, vol. I
Macan, Reginald Walter, 1848–1941, vol. IV
Macan, Col Thomas Townley, 1860–1934, vol. III
Macan-Markar, Hadji Sir Mohamed, 1879–1952, vol. V (A), vol. VI (AI)
McAnally, Rev. Charles Mortimer, 1854–1938, vol. III
McAnally, Sir Henry William Watson, 1870–1952, vol. V
Macandie, George Lionel, 1877–1968, vol. VI
MacAndrew, 1st Baron, 1888–1979, vol. VII
MacAndrew, 2nd Baron, 1919–1989, vol. VIII
Macandrew, Sir Henry Cockburn, 1832–1898, vol. I
Macandrew, Maj.-Gen. Henry John Milnes, 1866–1919, vol. II
MacAndrew, Lt-Col James Orr, 1899–1979, vol. VII
Macann, Lt-Col Arthur Ernest Henry, 1898–1944, vol. IV
Macara, Sir (Charles) Douglas, 3rd Bt, 1904–1982, vol. VIII
Macara, Sir Charles Wright, 1st Bt, 1845–1929, vol. III
Macara, Sir Douglas; see Macara, Sir C. D.
McAra, Sir Thomas W., 1864–1942, vol. IV
Macara, Sir William Cowper, 2nd Bt, 1875–1931, vol. III

M'Ardle, John Stephen, 1859–1928, vol. II
McArdle, Michael John Francis, 1909–1989, vol. VIII
McArdle, Sean; see McArdle, M. J. F.
Macardle, Sir Thomas Callan, 1856–1925, vol. II
M'Arthur, Alexander, 1814–1909, vol. I
M'Arthur, Charles, 1844–1910, vol. I
MacArthur, Mrs Charles; see Hayes, Helen.
Macarthur, Charles Ramsay, 1922–2000, vol. X
MacArthur, (David) Wilson, 1903–1981, vol. VIII
McArthur, Donald Neil, 1892–1965, vol. VI
MacArthur, General of the Army Douglas, 1880–1964, vol. VI
McArthur, Hon. Sir Gordon Stewart, 1896–1965, vol. VI
Macarthur, Sir Ian Hannay, 1906–1975, vol. VII
Macarthur, Rt Rev. James, 1848–1922, vol. II
McArthur, Col Sir Malcolm Hugh, 1912–1985, vol. VIII
Macarthur, Mary Reid, 1880–1921, vol. II
MacArthur, Neil, 1886–1973, vol. VII
MacArthur, Sir Oliphant; see MacArthur, Sir W. O.
McArthur, Hon. Sir Stewart; see McArthur, Hon. Sir W. G. S.
M'Arthur, William Alexander, 1857–1923, vol. II
McArthur, Hon. Sir (William Gilbert) Stewart, 1861–1935, vol. III
McArthur, William Lyon, 1870–1946, vol. IV
MacArthur, Sir (William) Oliphant, 1871–1953, vol. V
MacArthur, Lt-Gen. Sir William Porter, 1884–1964, vol. VI
MacArthur, Wilson; see MacArthur, D. W.
Macarthur-Onslow, Maj.-Gen. Sir Denzil, 1904–1984, vol. VIII
Macarthur Onslow, Brig.-Gen. George Macleay, 1875–1931, vol. III
Macarthur-Onslow, Maj.-Gen. Hon. James William, 1867–1946, vol. IV
Macartney, Sir Alexander Miller, 5th Bt, 1869–1960, vol. V
Macartney, Allan; see Macartney, W. J. A.
Macartney, Carlile Aylmer, 1895–1978, vol. VII
Macartney, Sir Edward Henry, 1863–1956, vol. V
Macartney, Sir George, 1867–1945, vol. IV
Macartney, Sir Halliday; see Macartney, Sir S. H.
Macartney, Lt-Col Henry Dundas Keith, 1880–1932, vol. III
Macartney, Sir John, 3rd Bt, 1832–1911, vol. I
Macartney, John William Ellison-, 1818–1904, vol. I
Macartney, John William Merton, 1850–1925, vol. II
Macartney, Sir Mervyn Edmund, died 1932, vol. III
Macartney, Sir (Samuel) Halliday, 1833–1906, vol. I
Macartney, Rt Hon. Sir William Grey Ellison-, 1852–1924, vol. II
Macartney, Sir William Isaac, 4th Bt, 1867–1942, vol. IV
Macartney, (William John) Allan, 1941–1998, vol. X
Macartney-Filgate, John Victor Openshaw, 1897–1964, vol. VI
Macaskie, Charles Frederick Cunningham, 1888–1969, vol. VI

Macaskie, Nicholas Lechmere Cunningham, 1881–1967, vol. VI
Macaskie, Stuart Cunningham, 1853–1903, vol. I
Macassey, Rev. Ernest Livingston, died 1947, vol. IV
Macassey, Sir Lynden Livingston, 1876–1963, vol. VI
M'Aulay, Alexander, 1863–1931, vol. III
Macaulay, Rev. Alexander Beith, 1871–1950, vol. IV
Macaulay, Sir Alfred Newton, 1864–1939, vol. III
McAulay, Allan; see Stewart, Charlotte.
Macaulay, Lt Col Archibald Duncan Campbell, 1897–1982, vol. VIII
Macaulay, Dame (Emily) Rose, 1881–1958, vol. V
Macaulay, Francis Sowerby, 1862–1937, vol. III
Macaulay, Frederic Julius, 1830–1912, vol. I
Macaulay, Sir Hamilton, 1901–1986, vol. VIII
Macaulay, G. C., 1852–1915, vol. I
Macaulay, James, 1817–1902, vol. I
Macaulay, Very Rev. James J., 1870–1951, vol. V
Macaulay, James Morison, 1889–1955, vol. V
Macaulay, Janet Stewart Alison, 1909–2000, vol. X
Macaulay, Rev. John Heyrick, died 1914, vol. I
McAulay, (John) Roy (Vincent), 1933–1987, vol. VIII
Macaulay, Hon. Leopold, 1887–1979, vol. VII
Macaulay, Dame Rose; see Macaulay, Dame E. R.
McAulay, Roy; see McAulay, J. R. V.
Macaulay, Thomas Bassett, 1860–1942, vol. IV
Macaulay, William Herrick, 1853–1936, vol. III
Macaulay, William J. B., 1892–1964, vol. VI
Macaulay-Owen, Peter, 1906–1962, vol. VI
Macauley, Brig. Gen. Sir George Bohun, 1869–1940, vol. III
McAuliffe, Gen. Anthony Clement, 1898–1975, vol. VII
McAuliffe, Sir Henry T., 1867–1951, vol. V
McAvity, Lt-Col Thomas Malcolm, 1889–1944, vol. IV
Macbain, Alexander, 1855–1907, vol. I
McBain, Alexander Richardson, 1887–1971, vol. VII
M'Bain, James Anderson Dickson, 1869–1938, vol. III
McBain, James William, 1882–1953, vol. V
McBain, Rev. John, 1871–1936, vol. III
McBarnet, Alexander Cockburn, 1867–1934, vol. III
M'Barnet, Lt-Col Alexander Edward, 1865–1932, vol. III
McBean, Col Alexander, 1854–1937, vol. III
McBean, Angus Rowland, 1904–1990, vol. VIII
Macbean, Maj.-Gen. Forbes, 1857–1919, vol. II
Macbean, Gen. George Scougal, died 1903, vol. I
Macbean, Captain John Albert Emmanuel, 1865–1900, vol. I
Macbean, Reginald Gambier, 1859–1942, vol. IV
Macbeath, Alexander, 1888–1964, vol. VI
Macbeath, Rev. John, died 1967, vol. VI
McBeath, Rear-Adm. John Edwin Home, 1907–1982, vol. VIII
McBeath, Sir William George, 1865–1931, vol. III
McBee, Silas, 1853–1924, vol. II
Macbeth, Alexander Killen, 1889–1957, vol. V
MacBeth, George Mann, 1932–1992, vol. IX

Macbeth, Rev. John, 1841–1924, vol. II
Macbeth, Percy, 1877–1938, vol. III
Macbeth, Robert Walker, 1848–1910, vol. I
Macbeth-Raeburn, Henry Raeburn; see Raeburn.
McBey, James, 1883–1959, vol. V
MacBride, Alexander, 1859–1955, vol. V
MacBride, Ernest William, 1866–1940, vol. III
MacBride, Geoffrey Ernest Derek, 1917–1975, vol. VII
McBride, Neil, 1910–1974, vol. VII
M'Bride, Hon. Sir Peter, 1867–1923, vol. II
M'Bride, Peter, 1854–1946, vol. IV
McBride, Rt Hon. Sir Philip Albert Martin, 1892–1982, vol. VIII
M'Bride, Sir Richard, 1870–1917, vol. II
McBride, Robert, died 1934, vol. III
Macbride, Robert Knox, 1844–1905, vol. I
MacBridge, Seán, 1904–1988, vol. VIII
McBride, Wilbert George, 1879–1943, vol. IV
McBride, Vice-Adm. Sir William, 1895–1959, vol. V
MacBrien, Maj.-Gen. Sir James Howden, 1878–1938, vol. III
McBryde, Hon. Duncan Elphinstone, 1853–1920, vol. II
McBurney, Charles Brian Montagu, 1914–1979, vol. VII
McCabe, Alasdair, died 1972, vol. VII
MacCabe, Brian Farmer, 1914–1992, vol. IX
M'Cabe, Sir Daniel, 1852–1919, vol. II
MacCabe, Sir Francis Xavier Frederick, 1833–1914, vol. I
McCabe, Joseph, 1867–1955, vol. V
McCabe, Most Rev. Thomas, 1902–1983, vol. VIII
Maccaffrey, Rt Rev. Mgr James, 1875–1935, vol. III
McCahearty, Ven. Reginald George Henry, died 1966, vol. VI
MacCaig, Norman Alexander, 1910–1996, vol. X
McCall, Sir Alexander, died 1973, vol. VII
McCall, Charles James, 1907–1989, vol. VIII
McCall, Charles William Home, 1877–1958, vol. V
Maccall, Hon. Maj.-Gen. Henry Blackwood, 1845–1921, vol. II
McCall, Adm. Sir Henry William Urquhart, 1895–1980, vol. VII
McCall, Lt-Col Hugh William, 1878–1957, vol. V
M'Call, Hon. Sir John, 1860–1919, vol. II
M'Call, Brig.-Gen. John P.; see Pollok-M'Call.
McCall, Kenneth Murray, 1912–1987, vol. VIII
McCall, Sir Robert Alfred, 1849–1934, vol. III
McCall, Robert Clark, 1906–1970, vol. VI
McCall, Robin Home, 1912–1991, vol. IX
McCall, Rt Rev. Theodore Bruce, 1911–1969, vol. VI
McCall, William, 1851–1929, vol. III
MacCallan, Arthur Ferguson, died 1955, vol. V
McCallum, Archibald Duncan Dugald, 1914–1993, vol. IX
McCallum, Colin Whitton; see Coborn, Charles.
McCallum, Major Sir Duncan, 1888–1958, vol. V
McCallum, Brig. Frank, 1900–1983, vol. VIII
McCallum, Col Sir Henry Edward, 1852–1919, vol. II
McCallum, Ian; see McCallum, John.

MacCallum, James Dalgleish Kellie, 1845–1932, vol. III
McCallum, John, (Ian), 1920–1995, vol. IX
McCallum, Rev. John Donaldson, 1856–1930, vol. III
McCallum, Major John Dunwoodie Martin, 1883–1967, vol. VI
M'Callum, Sir John Mills, 1847–1920, vol. II
MacCallum, Sir Mungo William, 1854–1942, vol. IV
MacCallum, Sir Peter, 1885–1975, vol. VII
McCallum, Ronald Buchanan, 1898–1973, vol. VII
McCallum, Sir William Alexander, 1883–1959, vol. V
MacCalman, Douglas Robert, 1903–1957, vol. V
M'Calmont, Col Barklie Cairns, 1860–1929, vol. III
M'Calmont, Harry Leslie Blundell, 1861–1902, vol. I
McCalmont, Maj.-Gen. Sir Hugh, 1845–1924, vol. II
M'Calmont, James Martin, 1847–1913, vol. I
McCalmont, Brig.-Gen. Sir Robert Chaine Alexander, 1881–1953, vol. V
M'Cammond, Sir William, 1831–1898, vol. I
McCance, Sir Andrew, 1889–1983, vol. VIII
McCance, Robert Alexander, 1898–1993, vol. IX
McCandlish, Douglas, 1883–1954, vol. V
McCandlish, Maj.-Gen. John Edward Chalmers, 1901–1974, vol. VII
McCandlish, Lt-Col Patrick Dalmahoy, 1871–1942, vol. IV
McCann, Sir Charles Francis Gerald, 1880–1951, vol. V
McCann, Frederick John, died 1941, vol. IV
McCann, Hugh James, 1916–1986, vol. VIII
M'Cann, James, died 1904, vol. I
McCann, Most Rev. James, 1897–1983, vol. VIII
McCann, John, 1910–1972, vol. VII
McCann, His Eminence Cardinal Owen, 1907–1994, vol. IX
McCann, Rt Rev. Philip Justin, 1882–1959, vol. V
McCann, Pierce, died 1919, vol. II
M'Cann, Thomas S., 1868–1942, vol. IV
McCannell, Otway, 1883–1969, vol. VI
McCardie, Sir Henry Alfred, 1869–1933, vol. III
McCarrison, Maj.-Gen. Sir Robert, 1878–1960, vol. V
McCarroll, James Joseph, 1889–1937, vol. III
McCarroll, Col James Neil, 1873–1951, vol. V
McCarron, Edward Patrick, died 1970, vol. VI
M'Cartan, Michael, 1851–1902, vol. I
McCartan, Patrick, 1878–1963, vol. VI
McCarthy, Adolf Charles, 1922–1995, vol. X(AI)
MacCarthy, Sir Desmond, 1877–1952, vol. V
McCarthy, Adm. Sir Desmond; see McCarthy, Adm. Sir E. D. B.
McCarthy, Donal John, 1922–1997, vol. X
McCarthy, Adm. Sir (Edward) Desmond (Bewley), 1893–1966, vol. VI
McCarthy, Most Rev. Edward Joseph, 1850–1931, vol. III
McCarthy, Sir Edwin, 1896–1980, vol. VII
McCarthy, Dame (Emma) Maud, 1858–1949, vol. IV
McCarthy, Sir Frank, died 1924, vol. II
M'Carthy, James Desmond, 1839–1923, vol. II

McCarthy, Rt Rev. James W., 1853–1943, vol. IV
M'Carthy, Jeremiah, *died* 1924, vol. II
M'Carthy, Most Rev. John, 1858–1950, vol. IV
McCarthy, John Haydon, 1914–1984, vol. VIII
McCarthy, John William, 1854–1935, vol. III
McCarthy, Joseph R., 1909–1957, vol. V
M'Carthy, Justin, 1830–1912, vol. I
M'Carthy, Justin Huntly, 1861–1936, vol. III
McCarthy, Hon. Leighton Goldie, 1869–1952, vol. V
McCarthy, Sir Leslie Ernest Vivian, 1885–1970, vol. VI
McCarthy, Lillah, (Lady Keeble), 1875–1960, vol. V
M'Carthy, Marie Cecilia, 1876–1943, vol. IV
McCarthy, Mary, (Mrs James West), 1912–1989, vol. VIII
McCarthy, Dame Maud; *see* McCarthy, Dame E. M.
McCarthy, Michael John Fitzgerald, *died* 1928, vol. II
MacCarthy, Brig.-Gen. Morgan John, 1867–1939, vol. III
McCarthy, Sir Mortimer Eugene, 1890–1967, vol. VI
McCarthy, Ralph, 1906–1976, vol. VII
M'Carthy, Robert Henry, *died* 1927, vol. II
McCarthy, Tim, *died* 1928, vol. II
McCarthy, Lt-Col W. H. Leslie, 1885–1962, vol. VI
Maccarthy, Rt Rev. Welbore, *died* 1925, vol. II
MacCarthy-Morrogh, Lt-Col Donald Florence, 1869–1932, vol. III
McCarthy-O'Leary, Brig. Heffernan William Denis; *see* O'Leary.
Maccartie, Lt-Col Frederick Fitzgerald, 1851–1916, vol. II
McCartney, James Elvins, 1891–1969, vol. VI
McCaughey, Sir (David) Roy, 1898–1971, vol. VII
M'Caughey, Sir Roy; *see* McCaughey, Sir D. R.
M'Caughey, Hon. Sir Samuel, *died* 1919, vol. II
McCaul, Ethel Rosalie Ferrier, 1867–1931, vol. III
McCauley, Ven. George James, *died* 1917, vol. II
McCauley, Air Marshal Sir John Patrick Joseph, 1899–1989, vol. VIII
M'Causland, Lt-Gen. Edwin Loftus, *died* 1923, vol. II
McCausland, Lucius Perronet T.; *see* Thompson-McCausland.
McCausland, Rt Hon. Maurice Marcus, 1872–1938, vol. III
M'Causland, Sir Richard Bolton, 1810–1900, vol. I
McCausland, Maj. Gen. William Henry, 1836–1916, vol. II
McCaw, George Tyrrell, 1870–1942, vol. IV
McCaw, Hon. Sir Kenneth Malcolm, 1907–1989, vol. IX(AI)
MacCaw, Sir Vivian, 1883–1936, vol. III
MacCaw, William John MacGeagh, *died* 1928, vol. II
McCawley, Thomas William, 1881–1925, vol. II
McCay, Lt-Col David, 1873–1948, vol. IV
M'Cay, Lt-Gen. Hon. Sir James Whiteside, 1864–1930, vol. III
McCay, Lt-Gen. (Hon.) Sir Ross Cairns, 1895–1969, vol. VI

McCheane, Col Montague William Hiley, 1872–1955, vol. V
MacChesney, Brig.-Gen. Nathan William, 1878–1954, vol. V
McClaughry, Air Vice-Marshal Wilfred Ashton, 1894–1943, vol. IV
McClean, (Donald Francis) Stuart, 1909–1960, vol. V
McClean, Sir Francis Kennedy, 1876–1955, vol. V
M'Clean, Frank, 1837–1904, vol. I
McClean, Rt Rev. Gerard; *see* McClean, Rt Rev. J. G.
McClean, Rt Rev. (John) Gerard, 1914–1978, vol. VII
McClean, Kathleen, (Mrs Douglas McClean); *see* Hale, K.
McClean, Rev. Richard Arthur, 1862–1948, vol. IV
McClean, Stuart; *see* McClean, D. F. S.
McCleary, George Frederick, 1867–1962, vol. VI
McCleary, Robert, 1869–1936, vol. III
McCleery, Rt Hon. Sir William Victor, 1887–1957, vol. V
M'Clelan, Hon. Abner Reid, 1831–1917, vol. II
McClellan, Frank Campbell, 1871–1957, vol. V
McClellan, George B., 1865–1940, vol. III
M'Clellan, Rev. John B., *died* 1916, vol. II
McClellan, John William Tyndale, 1865–1948, vol. IV
McClelland, Rev. Henry Simpson, 1882–1961, vol. VI
McClelland, Hugh Charles, 1893–1966, vol. VI
M'Clelland, John Alexander, 1870–1920, vol. II
McClelland, Sir Peter Hannay, 1856–1924, vol. II
McClelland, William, 1889–1968 (this entry was not transferred to Who was Who).
McClelland, William, 1873–1971, vol. VII
McClemens, John Henry, 1905–1975, vol. VII
Macclement, William Thomas, 1861–1938, vol. III
McClenaghan, Ven. Henry St George, 1865–1950, vol. IV
McClenaghan, Herbert Eric St George, 1896–1955, vol. V
Macclesfield, 7th Earl of, 1888–1975, vol. VII
Macclesfield, 8th Earl of, 1914–1992, vol. IX
McClintic, Katharine, (Mrs Guthrie McClintic); *see* Cornell, K.
M'Clintock, Lt-Col Arthur George, 1878–1936, vol. III
M'Clintock, Arthur George Florence, 1856–1930, vol. III
M'Clintock, Major Augustus, 1866–1912, vol. I
McClintock, Very Rev. Francis George le Poer, *died* 1924, vol. II
M'Clintock, Sir Francis Leopold, 1819–1907, vol. I
McClintock, Bt Col John Knox, 1864–1936, vol. III
McClintock, Vice-Adm. John William Leopold, 1874–1929, vol. III
McClintock, Lt-Col Robert Lyle, 1874–1943, vol. IV
McClintock, Brig.-Gen. William Kerr, 1858–1940, vol. III
McCloughry, Air Vice-Marshal Edgar James K.; *see* Kingston-McCloughry.
McCloy, John Jay, 1895–1989, vol. VIII
McCloy, John Moorcroft, 1874–1943, vol. IV

M'Clure, Alexander Logan, 1860–1932, vol. III
McClure, David, 1926–1998, vol. X
M'Clure, Rev. Edmund, *died* 1922, vol. II
McClure, George Buchanan, 1887–1955, vol. V
McClure, Ivor Herbert, *died* 1981, vol. VIII
McClure, J. Campbell, 1873–1934, vol. III
M'Clure, James Gore King, 1848–1932, vol. III
McClure, Sir John David, 1860–1922, vol. II
McClure, Samuel S., 1857–1949, vol. IV
MacClure, Victor, 1887–1963, vol. VI
McClure, Sir William Kidston, 1877–1939, vol. III
McClure-Smith, Hugh Alexander, 1902–1961, vol. VI
McCluskey, Alexander, 1908–1959, vol. V
McCluskie, Samuel Joseph, 1932–1995, vol. IX
M'Clymont, Rt Rev. James A., 1848–1927, vol. II
McClymont, Lt-Col Robert Arthur, 1874–1949, vol. IV
MacColl, Sir Albert Edward, 1882–1951, vol. V
McColl, Sir Alexander Lowe, 1878–1962, vol. VI
McColl, Angus John, 1854–1902, vol. I
MacColl, Dugald Sutherland, 1859–1948, vol. IV
McColl, Col George Guthrie, 1858–1938, vol. III
MacColl, James Eugene, 1908–1971, vol. VII
M'Coll, Hon. James Hiers, 1844–1929, vol. III
MacColl, Rev. Malcolm, 1831–1907, vol. I
MacColl, Norman, 1843–1905, vol. I
MacColl, René, 1905–1971, vol. VII
McCollum, Elmer Verner, 1879–1967, vol. VI
McColvin, Lionel Roy, 1896–1976, vol. VII
McComas, Robert Bond, 1862–1938, vol. III
McComb, James Ellis, 1909–1982, vol. VIII
McComb, Col Robert Brophy, 1855–1925, vol. II, vol. III
McComb, Rev. Samuel, 1864–1938, vol. III
McCombe, Francis William Walker, 1894–1969, vol. VI
McCombe, Lt-Col Gault, 1885–1970, vol. VI (AII)
McCombe, Brig. John Smith, 1885–1959, vol. V
McCombie, Major Hamilton, 1880–1962, vol. VI
McCombie, Col William McCombie D.; *see* Duguid-McCombie.
McCombs, Hon. Sir Terence Henderson, 1905–1982, vol. VIII
McConachie, George William Grant, 1909–1965, vol. VI
M'Conaghey, Lt-Col Allen, 1864–1925, vol. II
McConaghy, Hugh, 1877–1943, vol. IV
McConaghy, Col John Gerald, 1879–1942, vol. IV
McCone, John Alex, 1902–1991, vol. IX
McConnach, James, 1896–1955, vol. V
McConnan, Sir Leslie James, 1887–1954, vol. V
McConnel, Maj.-Gen. Douglas Fitzgerald, 1893–1961, vol. VI
McConnel, John Wanklyn, 1855–1922, vol. II
McConnell, Baron (Life Peer); Robert William McConnell, 1922–2000, vol. X
McConnell, Adams Andrew, 1884–1973, vol. VII
McConnell, Albert Joseph, 1903–1993, vol. IX
McConnell, Gerard Hamilton, 1913–1982, vol. VIII
McConnell, Sir Joseph, 2nd Bt, 1877–1942, vol. IV
M'Connell, Robert, *died* 1942, vol. IV
M'Connell, Sir Robert John, 1st Bt, 1853–1927, vol. II

McConnell, Comdr Sir Robert Melville Terence, 3rd Bt, 1902–1987, vol. VIII
McConnell, Sir Thomas Edward, 1868–1938, vol. III
M'Connell, W. R., 1837–1906, vol. I
McConnell, William Samuel, 1904–1982, vol. VIII
MacConochie, John Angus, 1908–1992, vol. IX
McCorkell, Sir Dudley Evelyn Bruce, 1883–1960, vol. V
McCorkill, Hon. John Charles, 1854–1920, vol. II
MacCormac, Henry, *died* 1950, vol. IV
Mac Cormac, Sir William, 1st Bt, 1836–1901, vol. I
McCormack, Arthur Gerard, 1911–1992, vol. IX
McCormack, Arthur John, 1866–1936, vol. III
MacCormack, Charles Joseph, 1861–1952, vol. V
Maccormack, Rt Rev. Francis Joseph, 1833–1909, vol. I
McCormack, John, Count, 1884–1945, vol. IV
McCormack, Most Rev. John, 1921–1996, vol. X
McCormack, John William, 1891–1980, vol. VII
McCormack, Rt Rev. Joseph, 1887–1958, vol. V
McCormack, Percy Hicks, 1890–1980, vol. VII
McCormack, Robert John Murray, 1922–1981, vol. VIII
McCormack, Hon. William, 1879–1947, vol. IV
MacCormick, Sir Alexander, 1856–1947, vol. IV
McCormick, Lt-Col Andrew Louis Charles, 1869–1943, vol. IV
McCormick, Anne O'Hare, *died* 1954, vol. V
M'Cormick, Arthur David, 1860–1943, vol. IV
McCormick, Ven. George Fitzherbert, *died* 1935, vol. III
McCormick, Gerald Bernard, *died* 1966, vol. VI
McCormick, Rev. James, *died* 1921, vol. II
McCormick, Major James Hanna, 1875–1955, vol. V
MacCormick, John MacDonald, 1904–1961, vol. VI
McCormick, Rt Rev. John Newton, 1863–1939, vol. III (A), vol. IV
McCormick, Rev. Joseph, 1834–1914, vol. I
McCormick, Very Rev. Joseph Gough, 1874–1924, vol. II
MacCormick, Brig. Kenneth, 1891–1963, vol. VI
McCormick, Adm. Lynde Dupuy, 1895–1956, vol. V
M'Cormick, Robert, *died* 1919, vol. II
McCormick, Robert Rutherford, 1880–1955, vol. V
McCormick, Rev. William Patrick Glyn, 1877–1940, vol. III
M'Cormick, Sir William Symington, 1859–1930, vol. III
McCormick-Goodhart, Leander, 1884–1965, vol. VI
McCorquodale of Newton, 1st Baron, 1901–1971, vol. VII
McCorquodale, Dame Barbara (Hamilton); *see* Cartland, Dame B. H.
McCosh, Andrew Kirkwood, 1880–1967, vol. VI
McCosh, Robert, 1885–1959, vol. V
McCourt, Hon. William, *died* 1913, vol. I
McCourt, William Rupert, 1884–1947, vol. IV
McCowan, Sir David, 1st Bt, 1860–1937, vol. III
McCowan, Sir David James Cargill, 2nd Bt, 1897–1965, vol. VI
McCowan, Sir Hew Cargill, 3rd Bt, 1930–1998, vol. X
McCowan, Lt-Col William Hew, 1878–1958, vol. V

McCowen, Oliver Hill, 1870–1942, vol. IV
M'Coy, Sir Frederick, 1823–1899, vol. I
McCoy, Captain James Abernethy, 1900–1955, vol. V
Maccoy, Sir John, 1843–1935, vol. III
McCoy, William Frederick, *died* 1976, vol. VII
McCoy, William Taylor, 1866–1929, vol. III
McCracken, Esther Helen, 1902–1971, vol. VII
McCracken, Lt-Gen. Sir Frederick William Nicholas, 1859–1949, vol. IV
Maccracken, Henry Mitchell, 1840–1919, vol. II
MacCracken, Henry Noble, 1880–1970, vol. VI
McCracken, William, *died* 1948, vol. IV
McCrae, Alister Geddes, 1909–1996, vol. X
M'Crae, Sir George, 1860–1928, vol. II
McCraith, Sir Douglas, 1878–1952, vol. V
McCraith, Sir James William, 1853–1928, vol. II
M'Craith, Sir John Tom, 1847–1919, vol. II
McCraith, Col Patrick James Danvers, 1916–1998, vol. X
McCraken, Sir Robert, 1846–1924, vol. II
McCray, Sir Lionel Joseph, 1908–1984, vol. VIII
McCrea, Rev. Alexander, 1879–1963, vol. VI
McCrea, Brig.-Gen. Alfred Coryton, 1864–1942, vol. IV
McCrea, Charles, 1877–1952, vol. V
McCrea, Major Frederick Bradford, 1833–1914, vol. I
McCrea, Hugh Moreland, *died* 1941, vol. IV
McCrea, Sir William Hunter, 1904–1999, vol. X
McCready, Hugh Latimer, 1876–1950, vol. IV
McCreery, (Henry Edwin) Lewis, 1920–1998, vol. X
McCreery, Lewis; *see*McCreery, H. E. L.
McCreery, Gen. Sir Richard Loudon, 1898–1967, vol. VI
M'Crie, Charles Greig, 1836–1910, vol. I
McCrie, John Gibb, 1902–1977, vol. VII
McCrindle, Major John Ronald, 1894–1977, vol. VII
McCrindle, Sir Robert Arthur, 1929–1998, vol. X
McCrone, Robert Watson, 1893–1982, vol. VIII
McCrossan, Mary, *died* 1934, vol. III
McCrostie, Hugh Cecil, 1897–1970, vol. VI
McCuaig, Maj.-Gen. George Eric, 1885–1958, vol. V
McCubbin, Very Rev. David, 1929–1999, vol. X
McCubbin, Frederick, 1855–1917, vol. II
McCubbin, Lt-Col Thomas, *died* 1925, vol. II, vol. III
McCullagh, Rt Hon. Sir Crawford, 1st Bt, 1868–1948, vol. IV
McCullagh, Sir Crawford; *see* McCullagh, Sir J. C.
M'Cullagh, Francis, 1874–1956, vol. V
MacCullagh, Sir James Acheson, 1854–1918, vol. II
McCullagh, Sir (Joseph) Crawford, 2nd Bt, 1907–1974, vol. VII
McCullagh, McKim; *see* McCullagh, W.McK. H.
McCullagh, (William) McKim (Herbert), 1889–1964, vol. VI
McCullers, Carson, (Mrs Carson Smith McCullers), 1917–1967, vol. VI
McCulloch, Allan Riverstone, 1885–1925, vol. II
McCulloch, Maj.-Gen. Sir Andrew Jameson, 1876–1960, vol. V

McCulloch, Derek Ivor Breashur, 1897–1967, vol. VI
M'Culloch, George, 1848–1907, vol. I
M'Culloch, Rev. James Duff, 1836–1926, vol. II
MacCulloch, Rev. Canon John Arnott, 1868–1950, vol. IV
McCulloch, Joseph, 1893–1961, vol. VI
McCulloch, Sir Malcolm McLeod, 1894–1969, vol. VI
McCulloch, Norman George, 1882–1965, vol. VI
McCulloch, Brig.-Gen. Robert Henry Frederick, 1869–1946, vol. IV
M'Culloch, Hon. William, *died* 1909, vol. I
McCulloch, William Edward, 1896–1963, vol. VI
McCullough, Donald; *see* McCullough, W. D. H.
McCullough, Thomas Warburton, 1901–1989, vol. VIII
McCullough, (William) Donald (Hamilton), 1901–1978, vol. VII
MacCunn, Captain Fergus, 1890–1941, vol. IV
MacCunn, Hamish, 1868–1916, vol. II
McCunn, Major James, 1894–1967, vol. VI
MacCunn, John, 1846–1929, vol. III
McCunn, Peter Alexander, 1922–1992, vol. IX
McCurdy, Rt Hon. Charles Albert, 1870–1941, vol. IV
MacCurdy, Edward Alexander Coles, 1871–1957, vol. V
McCurdy, Hon. Fleming Blanchard, 1875–1952, vol. V
M'Curdy, J. F., 1847–1935, vol. III
MacCurdy, John Thomson, 1886–1947, vol. IV
McCusker, Harold; *see* McCusker, J. H.
McCusker, Sir James Alexander, 1913–1995, vol. X(AI)
McCusker, (James) Harold, 1940–1990, vol. VIII
M'Cutcheon, George Barr, 1866–1928, vol. II
McCutcheon, Katharine Howard, 1875–1956, vol. V
McCutcheon, Hon. (Malcolm) Wallace, 1906–1969, vol. VI
McCutcheon, Sir Osborn; *see* McCutcheon, Sir W. O.
McCutcheon, Hon. Wallace; *see* McCutcheon, Hon. M. W.
McCutcheon, Sir (Walter) Osborn, 1899–1983, vol. VIII
McDavid, Sir Edwin Frank, 1895–1980, vol. VII
McDavid, Sir Herbert Gladstone, 1898–1966, vol. VI
McDavid, James Wallace, 1887–1964, vol. VI
McDermid, Rev.Canon Richard Thomas Wright, 1929–1994, vol. IX
MacDermot, The, (Charles Edward), 1862–1947, vol. IV
MacDermot, The, (Charles John), 1899–1979, vol. VII
MacDermot, The, (Sir Dermot MacDermot), 1906–1989, vol. VIII
MacDermot, The, (Rt Hon. Hugh Hyacinth O'Rorke), 1834–1904, vol. I
MacDermot, Charles Edward; *see* MacDermot, The.
MacDermot, Charles John; *see* MacDermot, The.
MacDermot, Sir Dermot; *see* MacDermot, The.
MacDermot, Captain Ffrench, Fitzgerald, (The Macdermot-Roe), 1848–1917, vol. II

515

MacDermot, Rev. Henry Myles Fleetwood, 1837–1918, vol. II
MacDermot, Rt Hon. Hugh Hyacinth O'Rorke; see MacDermot, The.
MacDermot, Niall, 1916–1996, vol. X
MacDermot, Terence William Leighton, 1896–1966, vol. VI
MacDermot-Roe, The; see MacDermot, Captain Ffrench F.
MacDermott, Baron (Life Peer); John Clarke MacDermott, 1896–1979, vol. VII
M'Dermott, Edward R., 1847–1932, vol. III
McDermott, Geoffrey Lyster, 1912–1978, vol. VII
Mac Dermott, Rev. George Martius, 1863–1939, vol. III
McDermott, John Frederick, 1906–1958, vol. V
Macdermott, Patrick, 1859–1942, vol. IV
M'Dermott, Peter Joseph, 1858–1922, vol. II
Macdiarmid, Sir Allan Campbell, 1880–1945, vol. IV
Macdiarmid, Duncan Stewart, 1873–1954, vol. V
Macdiarmid, Hon. Finlay George, 1869–1933, vol. III
McDiarmid, Hugh; see Grieve, C. M.
Macdiarmid, Niall Campbell, 1919–1978, vol. VII
Macdona, Brian Fraser, 1901–1971, vol. VII
Macdona, John Cumming, 1836–1907, vol. I
McDonagh, James Eustace Radclyffe, 1881–1965, vol. VI
Macdonagh, Michael, 1860–1946, vol. IV
Macdonald, 6th Baron, 1853–1947, vol. IV
Macdonald, 7th Baron, 1909–1970, vol. VI
Macdonald of Earnscliffe, Baroness (1st in line), 1836–1920, vol. II
Macdonald of Gwaenysgor, 1st Baron, 1888–1966, vol. VI
Macdonald, Adam Davidson, 1895–1978, vol. VII
Macdonald, Lt-Gen. Alastair M'Ian, 1830–1910, vol. I
Macdonald, Alexander, died 1921, vol. II
Macdonald, Alexander, 1878–1939, vol. III
Macdonald, Most Rev. Alexander, 1858–1941, vol. IV
MacDonald, Alexander, 1894–1954, vol. V
McDonald, Alexander, 1903–1968, vol. VI
McDonald, Sir Alexander Forbes, 1911–1981, vol. VIII
McDonald, Alexander Gordon (Alex), 1921–1992, vol. IX
McDonald, Alexander Hugh, 1908–1979, vol. VII
Macdonald of Sleat, Sir (Alexander) Somerled (Angus Bosville), 16th Bt (cr 1625), 1917–1958, vol. V
Macdonald of the Isles, Sir Alexander Wentworth Macdonald Bosville, 14th Bt (cr 1625), 1865–1933, vol. III
Macdonald, Alistair, 1912–1991, vol. IX
Macdonald, Alistair Archibald, 1927–1998, vol. X
Macdonald, Alistair Huistean, 1925–1999, vol. X
McDonald, Alistair Ian, 1921–1995, vol. IX
Macdonald, Rev. Allan John Macdonald, 1887–1959, vol. V
Macdonald, Allan Ronald, 1906–1984, vol. VIII
M'Donald, Sir Andrew, 1836–1919, vol. II
Macdonald, Hon. Andrew Archibald, 1829–1912, vol. I
Macdonald, Most Rev. Andrew Joseph, 1871–1950, vol. IV
Macdonald, Most Rev. Angus, 1844–1900, vol. I
Macdonald, Angus Alexander, 1904–1965, vol. VI
Macdonald, Hon. Angus Lewis, died 1954, vol. V
Macdonald, Angus Roderick, 1858–1944, vol. IV
Macdonald, Angus Stewart, 1935–1996, vol. X
McDonald, Air Comdt Ann Smith, 1914–1972, vol. VII
Macdonald, Anne, died 1958, vol. V
MacDonald, Anne Elizabeth Campbell Bard, (Betty MacDonald), 1908–1958, vol. V
Macdonald, Archibald James Florence, 1904–1983, vol. VIII
Macdonald, Sir Archibald John, 4th Bt (cr 1813), 1871–1919, vol. II
Macdonald, Sir Archibald Keppel, 3rd Bt (cr 1813), 1820–1901, vol. I
Macdonald, Col Archibald William, 1869–1939, vol. III
Macdonald, Sir Arthur, 1887–1953, vol. V
Macdonald, Lt-Col Arthur Cameron, died 1940, vol. III
MacDonald, Gen. Sir Arthur Leslie, 1919–1995, vol. IX
McDonald, Air Marshal Sir Arthur William Baynes, 1903–1996, vol. X
Macdonald, Augustine Colin, 1837–1919, vol. II
MacDonald, Betty; see MacDonald, A. E. C. B.
McDonald, Bouverie Francis Primrose, 1861–1931, vol. III
Macdonald of Sleat, Miss Celia Violet Bosville, 1889–1976, vol. VII
M'Donald, Hon. Charles, died 1925, vol. II
Macdonald, Charles Blair, 1855–1939, vol. III
McDonald, Sir Charles George, 1892–1970, vol. VI
Macdonald, Charles James Black, 1864–1930, vol. III
MacDonald, Col Charles Joseph, 1862–1947, vol. IV
Macdonald, Lt-Col Charles Leslie, 1881–1939, vol. III
Macdonald, Col Clarence Reginald, 1876–1962, vol. VI
Macdonald, Rt Hon. Sir Claude Maxwell, 1852–1915, vol. I
Macdonald, Coll, 1924–1983, vol. VIII
Macdonald, Daniel Alexander, 1858–1937, vol. III
MacDonald, David Keith Chalmers, 1920–1963, vol. VI
Macdonald, Adm. David R.; see Robertson-Macdonald.
Macdonald, Donald, died 1932, vol. III
McDonald, Sir Donald, 1849–1934, vol. III
McDonald, Hon. Donald, born 1865, vol. III
Macdonald, Maj.-Gen. Sir Donald Alexander, 1845–1920, vol. II
Macdonald, Rev. Donald Bruce, 1872–1962, vol. VI
Macdonald, Donald Farquhar, 1906–1988, vol. VIII
Macdonald, Rev. Donald Farquhar Macleod, 1915–1995, vol. IX
Macdonald, Donald Hardman, 1908–1990, vol. VIII
Macdonald, Air Vice-Marshal Donald Malcolm Thomas, 1909–1988, vol. VIII

Macdonald, Major Donald R., 1884–1934, vol. III
MacDonald, Douglas George, 1930–1989, vol. VIII
MacDonald, Rev. Duncan, 1885–1941, vol. IV
McDonald, Sir Duncan, 1921–1997, vol. X
Macdonald, Rev. Duncan Black, 1863–1943, vol. IV
Macdonald, Edward Mortimer, 1865–1940, vol. III
Macdonald, Dame Ethel, *died* 1941, vol. IV
Macdonald, Rev. Frederic William, 1842–1928, vol. II
Macdonald, Rev. Frederick Charles, *died* 1936, vol. III
Macdonald, Rev. Frederick William, 1848–1928, vol. II
Macdonald, George, 1824–1905, vol. I
Macdonald, Sir George, 1862–1940, vol. III
Macdonald, George, 1903–1967, vol. VI
MacDonald, George Alan, 1909–1985, vol. VIII
Macdonald, George Grant, 1921–2000, vol. X
Macdonald, Hon. Godfrey Evan Hugh, 1879–1915, vol. I
Macdonald of the Isles, Sir Godfrey Middleton Bosville, 15th Bt (*cr* 1625), 1887–1951, vol. V
McDonald, Graeme Patrick Daniel, 1930–1997, vol. X
MacDonald, Greville, 1856–1944, vol. IV
McDonald, Brig.-Gen. Harold French, 1885–1943, vol. IV
Macdonald, Maj.-Gen. Harry, 1886–1976, vol. VII
Macdonald, Maj.-Gen. Sir Hector Archibald, 1853–1903, vol. I
Macdonald, Hector Munro, 1865–1935, vol. III
Macdonald, Sir Herbert George de Lorme, 1902–1991, vol. IX
Macdonald, Hugh, 1885–1958, vol. V
M'Donald, Hugh Campbell, 1869–1921, vol. II
Macdonald, Hon. Sir Hugh John, 1850–1929, vol. III
Macdonald, Ian Wilson, 1907–1989, vol. VIII
Macdonald, Ishbel Allan; *see* Peterkin, I. A.
Macdonald, James, 1852–1913, vol. I
Macdonald, James, 1877–1954, vol. V
Macdonald, James, 1898–1963, vol. VI
McDonald, Sir James, 1899–1989, vol. VIII
Macdonald, James Alexander, 1862–1923, vol. II
Macdonald, Hon. James Alexander, 1858–1939, vol. III (A), vol. IV
Macdonald, James Alexander, 1908–1997, vol. X
Macdonald, Maj.-Gen. James Balfour, 1898–1959, vol. V
MacDonald, James E. H., *died* 1932, vol. III
McDonald, Sir James Gordon, 1867–1942, vol. IV
Macdonald, James Harold, 1878–1955, vol. V
MacDonald, Rt Hon. James Ramsay, 1866–1937, vol. III
Macdonald, Maj.-Gen. Sir James Ronald Leslie, 1862–1927, vol. II
Macdonald, James Smith, 1873–1923, vol. II
MacDonald, James Stuart, 1878–1952, vol. V
MacDonald, John, 1843–1928, vol. II
Macdonald, John, *died* 1940, vol. III
McDonald, Sir John, 1874–1964, vol. VI
Macdonald, Col John Andrew, 1837–1916, vol. II
Macdonald, Rt Hon. John Archibald Murray, 1854–1939, vol. III
Macdonald, John Blake, 1829–1902, vol. I

Macdonald, Air Cdre John Charles, 1910–2000, vol. X
Macdonald, Sir John Denis, 1826–1908, vol. I
Macdonald, Maj.-Gen. John Frederick Matheson, 1907–1979, vol. VII
McDonald, Hon. Sir John Gladstone Black, 1898–1977, vol. VII
Macdonald, Rt Hon. Sir John Hay Athole; *see* Kingsburgh, Rt Hon. Lord.
MacDonald, Most Rev. John Hugh, 1881–1965, vol. VI
Macdonald, John Robert, 1879–1965, vol. VI
Macdonald, John Ronald Moreton, 1873–1921, vol. II
Macdonald, John Smyth, 1867–1941, vol. IV
Macdonald, Rev. John Somerled, 1871–1956, vol. V
Macdonald, John William, 1882–1934, vol. III
Macdonald, Lt-Col Kenneth Lachlan, 1867–1938, vol. III
MacDonald, Sir Kenneth Mackenzie, 1879–1954, vol. V
Macdonald, Mrs L. M., (L. M. Montgomery), 1874–1942, vol. IV
MacDonald, Rt Hon. Malcolm John, 1901–1981, vol. VIII
Macdonald, Dame Margaret Henderson, (Dame Margaret Kidd), 1900–1989, vol. VIII
Macdonald, Sir Murdoch, 1866–1957, vol. V
McDonald, Niel, 1886–1968, vol. VI
Macdonald, Col Norman, 1890–1948, vol. IV
Macdonald, Patrick Donald, 1909–1987, vol. VIII
Macdonald, Sir Percy, *died* 1957, vol. V
Macdonald, Percy Stuart, 1890–1945, vol. IV
Macdonald, Captain Sir Peter Drummond, 1895–1961, vol. VI
Macdonald, Sir Peter George, 1898–1983, vol. VIII
MacDonald, Pirie, 1867–1942, vol. IV
MacDonald, Ranald, 1868–1931, vol. III
Macdonald, Ranald Mackintosh, 1860–1928, vol. II
Macdonald, Sir Reginald John, 1820–1899, vol. I
Macdonald, Lt-Col Reginald Percy, *born* 1856, vol. II
MacDonald, Robert, *died* 1971, vol. VII
McDonald, Sir (Robert) Ross, 1888–1964, vol. VI
Macdonald, Lt-Col Roderick William, 1881–1959, vol. V
MacDonald, Ronald, 1860–1933, vol. III
Macdonald, Ronald John, 1919–1999, vol. X
McDonald, Sir Ross; *see* McDonald, Sir Robert R.
Macdonald of Sleat, Sir Somerled; *see* Macdonald of Sleat, Sir A. S. A. B.
Macdonald, Air Vice-Marshal Somerled Douglas, 1899–1979, vol. VII
Macdonald, Maj.-Gen. Stuart, 1861–1939, vol. III
MacDonald, Sydney Gray, 1879–1946, vol. IV
Macdonald, Rt Rev. Thomas Brian, 1911–1997, vol. X
Macdonald, Air Vice-Marshal Thomas Conchar, 1909–1996, vol. X
MacDonald, Hon. Sir Thomas Lachlan, 1898–1980, vol. VII
McDonald, Thomas Muirhead, 1952–1995, vol. IX
McDonald, Thomas Pringle, 1901–1969, vol. VI
M'Donald, Rev. Walter, 1854–1920, vol. II

McDonald, Sir Warren D'Arcy, 1901–1965, vol. VI
Macdonald, William, 1875–1935, vol. III
Macdonald, Captain William Balfour, 1870–1937, vol. III
Macdonald, Sir William Christopher, 1831–1917, vol. II
McDonald, Hon. Sir William John Farquhar, 1911–1995, vol. X(AI)
MacDonald, Air Chief Marshal Sir William Laurence Mary, 1908–1984, vol. VIII
Macdonald, William Marshall, 1872–1956, vol. V
Macdonald, William Rae, 1843–1923, vol. II
Macdonald-Buchanan, Major Sir Reginald Narcissus, 1898–1981, vol. VIII
MacDonald Scott, Mary, (Mrs Michael MacDonald Scott); see Lavin, Mary
Macdonald-Smith, Sydney, 1908–1994, vol. IX
Macdonald-Tyler, Sir Henry Hewey Francis, 1877–1962, vol. VI
McDonaugh, James, 1912–1998, vol. X
McDonell, Æneas Ranald, 1875–1941, vol. IV
MacDonell of Glengarry, Air Cdre (Aeneas Ranald) Donald, 1913–1999, vol. X
Macdonell, Angus Claude, 1861–1924, vol. II
Macdonell, Lt-Gen. Sir Archibald Cameron, 1864–1941, vol. IV
Macdonell, Archibald Gordon, 1895–1941, vol. IV
Macdonell, Maj.Gen. Hon. Archibald Hayes, 1868–1939, vol. III
Macdonell, Arthur Anthony, 1854–1930, vol. III
MacDonell of Glengarry, Air Cdre Donald; see MacDonell of Glengarry, Air Cdre A. R. D.
MacDonell, Edgar Errol Napier, 1874–1928, vol. II
Macdonell, Rt Hon. Sir Hugh Guion, 1832–1904, vol. I
Macdonell, Sir John, 1846–1921, vol. II
Macdonell, Rt Hon. Sir Philip James, 1873–1940, vol. III
Macdonell, 1st Baron, 1844–1925, vol. II
McDonnell, Col Hon. Angus, 1881–1966, vol. VI
M'Donnell, Col Francis, 1828–1904, vol. I
Macdonnell, Henry, 1839–1922, vol. II
McDonnell, Col John, 1851–1928, vol. II
Macdonnell, Very Rev. John Cotter, died 1902, vol. I
MacDonnell, John de Courcy, 1869–1915, vol. I
MacDonnell, Mark Antony, 1854–1906, vol. I
MacDonnell, Mervyn Sorley, 1880–1949, vol. IV
McDonnell, Sir Michael Francis Joseph, 1882–1956, vol. V
Macdonnell, Hon. Norman Scarth, 1886–1938, vol. III
M'Donnell, Richard Grant Peter Purcell, died 1927, vol. II
McDonnell, Hon Sir Schomberg Kerr, 1861–1915, vol. I
Macdonnell, Col William, 1831–1919, vol. II, vol. III
Macdonnell, Rt Rev. William Andrew, 1853–1920, vol. II
Macdonogh, Lt-Gen. Sir George Mark Watson, 1865–1942, vol. IV
McDouall, John Crichton, 1912–1979, vol. VII
McDouall, Brig.-Gen. Robert, 1871–1941, vol. IV
M'Douall, William, 1855–1924, vol. II

M'Douall, Thomas William Houldsworth, 1885–1931, vol. III
M'Dougald, John, 1848–1919, vol. II
Macdougall, Maj.-Gen. Alastair Ian, 1888–1972, vol. VII
MacDougall, Brig.-Gen. Alexander, 1878–1927, vol. II
MacDougall, Alexander James, 1872–1953, vol. V
MacDougall, Sir Alexander Maclean, 1878–1953, vol. V
McDougall, Alexander Patrick, died 1959, vol. V
McDougall, Archibald, 1903–1984, vol. VIII
MacDougall of MacDougall, Madam; (Coline Helen Elizabeth), 1904–1990, vol. VIII
MacDougall, Brig. David Mercer, 1904–1991, vol. IX
McDougall, Dugald Gordon, 1867–1944, vol. IV
M'Dougall, Ernest Hugh, 1877–1908, vol. I
McDougall, Frank Lidgett, 1884–1958, vol. V
Macdougall, Gordon Walters, died 1947, vol. IV
MacDougall, Air Cdre Ian Neil, 1920–1987, vol. VIII
MacDougall, Maj.-Gen. James Charles, 1863–1927, vol. II
McDougall, James Currie, 1890–1957, vol. V
MacDougall, Sir James Patten, 1849–1919, vol. II
M'Dougall, Sir John, 1844–1917, vol. II
McDougall, John Bowes, 1890–1967, vol. VI
McDougall, John Henry Gordon, 1889–1969, vol. VI
M'Dougall, John Lorn, 1838–1909, vol. I
MacDougall, Laura Margaret, (Lady MacDougall), 1910–1995, vol. IX
MacDougall, Leslie Grahame, 1896–1974, vol. VII
McDougall, Sir Malcolm, 1899–1970, vol. VI
Macdougall, Margaret, died 1943, vol. IV
MacDougall, Sir Raibeart MacIntyre, 1892–1949, vol. IV
McDougall, Richard Sedgwick, 1904–1983, vol. VIII
McDougall, Sir Robert, 1871–1938, vol. III
McDowall, Robert John Stewart, 1892–1990, vol. VIII
Macdougall, Robert Stewart, 1862–1947, vol. IV
MacDougall, Lt-Col Stewart, 1854–1916, vol. II
Macdougall, Hon. William, 1822–1905, vol. I
McDougall, William, 1871–1938, vol. III
Macdougall, William Brown, died 1936, vol. III
M'Dowall, Rev. Charles Robert Loraine, 1872–1950, vol. IV
McDowall, Robert William, 1914–1987, vol. VIII
McDowall, Roger Gordon, 1886–1972, vol. VII
McDowall, Rev. Stewart Andrew, 1882–1935, vol. III
M'Dowall, Thomas William, died 1936, vol. III
McDowell, Lt-Col Arnott Edward Connell, 1883–1944, vol. IV
MacDowell, Col Charles Carlyle, died 1959, vol. V
McDowell, Coulter; see McDowell, M. R. C.
McDowell, Donald Keith, 1867–1940, vol. III
M'Dowell, Surg.-Col Edmund Greswold, 1831–1907, vol. I
Macdowell, Edward, 1861–1908, vol. I
McDowell, Sir Frank Schofield, 1889–1982, vol. VIII

McDowell, Sir Henry McLorinan, 1910–2000, vol. X
McDowell, John, 1874–1936, vol. III
McDowell, (Martin Rastall) Coulter, 1932–1993, vol. IX
MacDowell, Lt-Col Thain Wendell, 1890–1960, vol. V
McDowell, William Fraser, 1858–1937, vol. III
MacDuff, John Levy, 1905–1963, vol. VI
Mace, Cecil Alec, 1894–1971, vol. VII
Mace, Comdr Frederick William, 1872–1960, vol. I
MacEacharn, Hon. Sir Malcolm Donald, 1852–1910, vol. I
McEachern, Malcolm, died 1945, vol. IV
M'Eachran, Duncan, 1841–1926, vol. II, vol. III
M'Elderry, Robert Knox, 1869–1949, vol. IV
McElderry, Samuel Burnside Boyd, 1885–1984, vol. VIII
McEleney, Most Rev. John, 1895–1986, vol. VIII
McElheran, Robert Benjamin, died 1939, vol. III
McElhone, Frank, 1929–1982, vol. VIII
McElligott, Edward John, died 1946, vol. IV
McElligott, James, 1893–1974, vol. VII
McElligott, Neil Martin, 1915–1989, vol. VIII
McElroy, Neil H., 1904–1972, vol. VII
McElroy, Robert, 1872–1959, vol. V
McElroy, Roy Granville, 1907–1994, vol. IX
McElwaine, Sir Percy Alexander, 1884–1969, vol. VI
Mac Enri, (Henry), Seaghan P., died 1930, vol. III
McEntee, 1st Baron, 1871–1953, vol. V
MacEntee, Seán, 1889–1984, vol. VIII
McEntegart, Air Vice-Marshal Bernard, 1891–1954, vol. V
MacEoin, Lt-Gen. Seán, 1893–1973, vol. VII
M'Evay, Most Rev. Fergus Patrick, 1852–1911, vol. I
MacEvilly, Most Rev. John, 1817–1902, vol. I
McEvoy, Ambrose, 1878–1927, vol. II
M'Evoy, Charles, 1879–1929, vol. III
McEvoy, John Alexander, 1882–1935, vol. III
McEvoy, Air Chief Marshal Sir Theodore Newman, 1904–1991, vol. IX
MacEwan, David, 1830–1910, vol. I
MacEwan, David, 1846–1927, vol. II
MacEwan, Very Rev. James, died 1911, vol. I
MacEwan, Peter, 1856–1917, vol. II
M'Ewan, Rt Hon. William, 1827–1913, vol. I
McEwan Younger, Sir William; see Younger, Sir W. M.
MacEwen, Sir Alexander Malcolm, 1875–1941, vol. IV
MacEwen, Alexander R., 1851–1916, vol. II
MacEwen, Alexander Robert, 1894–1946, vol. IV
MacEwen, Brig.-Gen. Douglas Lilburn, 1867–1941, vol. IV
M'Ewen, Ewen, 1916–1993, vol. IX
McEwen, Sir James Francis Lindley, 4th Bt, 1960–1983, vol. VIII
McEwen, Sir James Napier Finnie, 2nd Bt, 1924–1971, vol. VII
McEwen, Rev. James Stevenson, 1910–1993, vol. IX
McEwen, Rt Hon. Sir John, 1900–1980, vol. VII
MacEwen, John A. C., died 1944, vol. IV

McEwen, Sir John Blackwood, 1868–1948, vol. IV
McEwen, Sir John Helias Finnie, 1st Bt, 1894–1962, vol. VI
MacEwen, Malcolm, 1911–1996, vol. X
MacEwen, Brig.-Gen. Maurice Lilburn, 1869–1943, vol. IV
Macewen, Air Vice-Marshal Sir Norman Duckworth Kerr, 1881–1953, vol. V
McEwen, Robert Finnis, 1861–1926, vol. II
McEwen, Sir Robert Lindley, 3rd Bt, 1926–1980, vol. VII
MacEwen, Sir William, 1848–1924, vol. II
McEwin, Hon. Sir (Alexander) Lyell, 1897–1988, vol. VIII
McEwin, Hon. Sir Lyell; see McEwin, Hon. Sir A. L.
Macey, John Percival, 1906–1987, vol. VIII
MacFadden, Arthur William James, 1869–1933, vol. III
McFadden, Hon. David Henry, 1856–1935, vol. III
M'Fadden, Edward, 1862–1922, vol. II
McFadden, Gertrude Violet, died 1963, vol. VI
McFadyean, Sir Andrew, 1887–1974, vol. VII
McFadyean, Sir John, 1853–1941, vol. IV
Macfadyen, Allan, 1860–1907, vol. I
Macfadyen, Air Marshal Sir Douglas, 1902–1968, vol. VI
Macfadyen, Rev. Dugald, 1867–1936, vol. III
Macfadyen, Sir Eric, 1879–1966, vol. VI
M'Fadyen, John Edgar, 1870–1933, vol. III
Macfadyen, William Allison, 1865–1924, vol. II
McFadzean, Baron (Life Peer); William Hunter McFadzean, 1903–1996, vol. X
McFadzean of Kelvinside, Baron (Life Peer); Francis Scott McFadzean, 1915–1992, vol. IX
McFall, David Bernard, 1919–1988, vol. VIII
Macfall, Haldane, 1860–1928, vol. II
Macfall, John Edward Whitley, 1873–1938, vol. III
Macfarlan, Brig.-Gen. Frederic Alexander, 1866–1954, vol. V
Macfarlan, Hon. Sir James Ross, 1872–1955, vol. V
McFarland, Arthur, 1893–1966, vol. VI
McFarland, Sir Basil Alexander Talbot, 2nd Bt, 1898–1986, vol. VIII
McFarland, Bryan Leslie, 1900–1963, vol. VI
MacFarland, Sir John Henry, 1851–1935, vol. III
MacFarland, Robert Arthur Henry, died 1922, vol. II
Macfarlane, Rt Rev. Angus, 1843–1912, vol. I
McFarlane, Sir Charles Stuart, 1895–1958, vol. V
Macfarlane, Col David Mason, 1862–1930, vol. III
Macfarlane, Donald, 1882–1946, vol. IV
MacFarlane, Donald, 1910–1991, vol. IX
Macfarlane, Sir Donald Horne, 1830–1904, vol. I
Macfarlane, Very Rev. Dugald, 1869–1956, vol. V
Macfarlane, Brig.-Gen. Duncan Alwyn, 1857–1941, vol. IV
MacFarlane, Lt-Gen. Sir (Frank) Noel Mason-, 1889–1953, vol. V
Macfarlane, George James, 1855–1933, vol. III
Macfarlane, George Lewis; see Ormidale, Hon. Lord.
Macfarlane, Hon. James, 1844–1914, vol. I
Macfarlane, Sir James, 1857–1944, vol. IV
Macfarlane, James Waddell, 1877–1952, vol. V

McFarlane, James Walter, 1920–1999, vol. X
Macfarlane, Sir James Wright, 1908–1992, vol. IX
Macfarlane, Janet Alston, died 1980, vol. VII
Macfarlane, Lt-Gen. Sir Noel Mason-; see Macfarlane, Lt-Gen. Sir F. N. M.
McFarlane, Brig. Percy Muir, 1880–1946, vol. IV
Macfarlane, Robert Campbell, 1892–1963, vol. VI
Macfarlane, Robert Gwyn, 1907–1987, vol. VIII
Macfarlane, Hon. Sir Robert Mafeking, 1901–1981, vol. VIII
McFarlane, Major Ronald, 1860–1915, vol. I
McFarlane, Stuart Gordon, 1885–1970, vol. VI
Macfarlane, Thomas, 1834–1907, vol. I
Macfarlane, William Dove, died 1932, vol. III
Macfarlane-Grieve, Lt-Col Angus Alexander, 1891–1970, vol. VI
Macfarlane-Grieve, William Alexander, 1844–1917, vol. II
MacFarquhar, Sir Alexander, 1903–1987, vol. VIII
Macfarren, Walter Cecil, 1826–1905, vol. I
McFee, William, 1881–1966, vol. VI
MacFeely, Most Rev. Anthony C., 1909–1986, vol. VIII
McFerran, Lt-Col Edwin Millar Gilliland, 1873–1962, vol. VI
McFetrich, Cecil, 1911–1988, vol. VIII
Macfetridge, Ven. Charles, died 1920, vol. II
Macfetridge, William C., 1878–1957, vol. V
Macfie, Alec Lawrence, 1898–1980, vol. VII
Macfie, Brig.-Gen. Andrew Laurie, 1860–1936, vol. III
Macfie, Maj.-Gen. John Mandeville, 1891–1985, vol. VIII
Macfie, John William Scott, 1879–1948, vol. IV
Macfie, Ronald Campbell, died 1931, vol. III
Macfie, Col William, 1840–1912, vol. I
McGann, Lt-Col H. H., died 1943, vol. IV
McGarry, Hon. Thomas William, 1871–1935, vol. III
McGarvey, Daniel, 1919–1977, vol. VII
McGavin, Maj.-Gen. Sir Donald Johnstone, 1876–1960, vol. V
McGavin, Lawrie Hugh, 1868–1932, vol. III
McGaw, Andrew Kidd, 1873–1956, vol. V
McGaw, Rev. Joseph Thoburn, 1836–1905, vol. I
McGaw, William Rankin, 1900–1974, vol. VII
MacGeagh, Col Sir Henry Davies Foster, 1883–1962, vol. VI
McGee, James Dwyer, 1903–1987, vol. VIII
McGee, Rt Rev. Joseph, 1904–1983, vol. VIII
McGeer, Gerald Grattan, 1888–1947, vol. IV
Macgeorge, Col Henry King, 1865–1940, vol. III
Macgeorge, W. S. died 1931, vol. III
McGeough, Most Rev. Joseph F., 1903–1970, vol. VI
Macgeough Bond, Sir Walter Adrian, 1857–1945, vol. IV
McGhee, Henry George, 1898–1959, vol. V
McGhie, Hamish; see McGhie, J. I.
McGhie, James Ironside, (Hamish), 1915–1992, vol. IX
McGhie, Maj.-Gen. John, 1914–1985, vol. VIII
MacGibbon, Rev. James, 1865–1922, vol. II
McGibbon, John E. G., died 1959, vol. V
M'Giffert, Arthur Cushman, 1861–1933, vol. III

McGill, Maj.-Gen. Allan, 1914–1989, vol. VIII
MacGill, Major Campbell Gerald Hertslet, 1876–1922, vol. II
McGill, Air Vice-Marshal Frank Scholes, 1894–1980, vol. VII (AII)
MacGill, Adm. Thomas, 1850–1926, vol. II
McGilligan, Denis Brian, 1921–1995, vol. IX
MacGillivray, Hon. Angus, 1842–1918, vol. II
MacGillivray of MacGillivray, Angus, 1865–1947, vol. IV
MacGillivray of MacGillivray, Angus Robertson, 1892–1955, vol. V
MacGillivray, Charles Watson, 1851–1932, vol. III
MacGillivray, Donald, 1862–1931, vol. III
MacGillivray, Sir Donald Charles, 1906–1966, vol. VI
MacGillivray, Evan James, 1873–1955, vol. V
Macgillivray, James Pittendrigh, 1856–1938, vol. III
Macgillivray, John, 1855–1930, vol. III
Macgillivray, John Walker, 1884–1961, vol. VI
MacGillivray, William, 1823–1917, vol. II
McGillivray, Hon. William Alexander, 1918–1984, vol. VIII
McGillycuddy, Denis Donough Charles, (The McGillycuddy of the Reeks), 1852–1921, vol. II
McGillycuddy, John Patrick, (The McGillycuddy of the Reeks), 1909–1959, vol. V
McGillycuddy, Lt-Col Ross Kinloch, (The McGillycuddy of the Reeks), 1882–1950, vol. IV
M'Gilp, Major Clyde, 1885–1918, vol. II
McGilvray, James William, 1938–1995, vol. X(AI)
McGilvray, Sir William, 1887–1956, vol. V
M'Ginness, Brig-Gen. John R., 1840–1918, vol. II
McGinnety, Frank Edward, 1907–1973, vol. VII
MacGinnis, Francis Robert, 1924–1993, vol. IX
McGirr, John Joseph Gregory, 1879–1949, vol. IV
McGivern, Cecil, 1907–1963, vol. VI
Macgivern, Rt Rev. Thomas, died 1900, vol. I
McGlashan, Rear-Adm. Sir Alexander Davidson, 1901–1976, vol. VII
McGlashan, Archibald A., 1888–1980, vol. VII
McGlashan, Sir George Tait, 1885–1968, vol. VI
MacGlashan, John, 1874–1948, vol. IV
McGlashan, Maxwell Len, 1924–1997, vol. X
McGlinn, Brig.-Gen. John Patrick, 1869–1946, vol. IV
McGonigal, Rt Hon. Sir Ambrose Joseph, 1917–1979, vol. VII
McGonigal, John, 1870–1943, vol. IV
MacGonigal, Maurice, 1900–1979, vol. VII
M'Gonigle, Rev. William Alexander, 1849–1939, vol. III
Macgougan, John, 1913–1998, vol. X
McGougan, Malcolm, 1905–1976, vol. VII
M'Goun, Archibald, 1853–1921, vol. II
McGovern, John, 1887–1968, vol. VI
McGovern, Sir Patrick Silvesta, 1895–1975, vol. VII
M'Govern, Thomas, died 1904, vol. I
McGovern, William Montgomery, 1897–1964, vol. VI
McGowan, 1st Baron, 1874–1961, vol. VI
McGowan, 2nd Baron, 1906–1966, vol. VI
McGowan, Ven. Frank, 1895–1968, vol. VI
Macgowan, Gault, 1894–1970, vol. VI
McGowan, Rt Rev. Henry, 1891–1948, vol. IV

Macgowan, Rev. William Stuart, 1864–1939, vol. III
McGowen, Hon. James Sinclair Taylor, 1855–1922, vol. II
MacGranahan, Very Rev. James, 1855–1940, vol. III(A), vol. IV
McGrath, Sir Charles; see McGrath, Sir J. C.
McGrath, Sir Charles Gullan, 1910–1984, vol. VIII
McGrath, John Cornelius, 1905–1985, vol. VIII
M'Grath, Sir Joseph, 1858–1923, vol. II
McGrath, Sir (Joseph) Charles, 1875–1951, vol. V
McGrath, Most Rev. Michael Joseph, 1882–1961, vol. VI
McGrath, Patrick Gerard, 1916–1994, vol. IX
McGrath, Hon. Sir Patrick Thomas, 1868–1929, vol. III
McGrath, Peter William, 1931–1990, vol. VIII
McGrath, Raymond, 1903–1977, vol. VII
McGrath, Rosita, (Mrs Arthur T. McGrath); see Forbes, Joan R.
McGrath, Captain William, 1917–1942, vol. IV
M'Grath, William Martin, died 1912, vol. I
McGraw, Curtis Whittlesey, 1895–1953, vol. V
McGregor of Durris, Baron (Life Peer); Oliver Ross McGregor, 1921–1997, vol. X
MacGregor, Alasdair Alpin, 1899–1970, vol. VI
MacGregor, Sir (Alasdair Duncan) Atholl, 1883–1945, vol. IV
Macgregor, Alastair Goold, 1919–1972, vol. VII
MacGregor, Alexander Brittan, 1909–1965, vol. VI
McGregor, Hon. Alexander John, 1864–1946, vol. IV
Macgregor, Sir Alexander Stuart Murray, 1881–1967, vol. VI
MacGregor, Alexander Stewart, 1848–1906, vol. I
MacGregor, Air Vice-Marshal Andrew, 1897–1983, vol. VIII
MacGregor, Sir Atholl; see MacGregor, Sir Alasdair D. A.
Macgregor, Col Charles Reginald, 1847–1902, vol. I(A)
MacGregor, Sir Colin Malcolm, 1901–1982, vol. VIII
Macgregor, Sir Cyril Patrick M'Connell, 5th Bt (cr 1828), 1887–1958, vol. V
Macgregor, David Hutchison, 1877–1953, vol. V
MacGregor, David Sliman, 1864–1952, vol. V
Macgregor, Duncan, 1892–1984, vol. VIII
Macgregor, Rev. Duncan Campbell, 1858–1943, vol. IV
MacGregor, Edward Ian Roy, 1911–1989, vol. VIII
Macgregor, Eric Dickson, 1886–1950, vol. IV
MacGregor, Sir Evan, 1842–1926, vol. II
MacGregor, Geddes; see MacGregor, J. G.
Macgregor, Rev. George Hogarth Carnaby, 1892–1963, vol. VI
McGregor, Sir George Innes, 1899–1976, vol. VII
M'Gregor, Hon. Gregor, 1848–1913, vol. I
MacGregor, Gregor, 1869–1919, vol. II
MacGregor of MacGregor, Gylla Constance Susan, (Hon. Lady MacGregor of MacGregor), died 1980, vol. VII
McGregor, Air Marshall Sir Hector Douglas, 1910–1973, vol. VII
Macgregor, Col Henry Grey, 1838–1925, vol. II
McGregor, Ian Alexander, 1921–1998, vol. X

McGregor, Sir Ian Kinloch, 1912–1998, vol. X
MacGregor, Very Rev. James, 1832–1910, vol. I
M'Gregor, Rt Rev. Mgr James, 1860–1928, vol. II
Macgregor, James, 1889–1953, vol. V
Macgregor, James Cochran Stevenson, 1897–1949, vol. IV
Macgregor, Sir James Comyn, 1861–1935, vol. III
McGregor, James Drummond, 1838–1919, vol. II
McGregor, Hon. James Duncan, 1860–1935, vol. III
MacGregor, James Gordon, 1852–1913, vol. I
McGregor, James Reid, 1896–1984, vol. VIII
McGregor, Sir James Robert, 1889–1973, vol. VII
MacGregor, Lt-Col John, died 1932, vol. III
Macgregor, John, 1877–1967, vol. VI
Macgregor, (John) Geddes, 1909–1998, vol. X
Macgregor, John Julius, 1869–1948, vol. IV
MacGregor, John Marshall, 1879–1936, vol. III
Macgregor, John Roy, 1913–1997, vol. X
McGregor, Kenneth, 1903–1984, vol. VIII
Macgregor, Lewis Richard, 1886–1973, vol. VII
MacGregor of MacGregor, Sir Malcolm, 5th Bt (cr 1795), 1873–1958, vol. V
MacGregor, Malcolm Evan, 1889–1933, vol. III
Macgregor, Maj.-Gen. Malcolm John Robert, 1840–1914, vol. I
Macgregor, Lt-Col Philip Arthur, 1877–1934, vol. III
Macgregor, Robert, 1847–1922, vol. II
MacGregor, Robert Anderson, 1888–1953, vol. V
MacGregor, Robert Barr, 1896–1979, vol. VII
MacGregor, Lt-Col Robert Forrester Douglas, 1885–1960, vol. V
Macgregor, Sir Robert James McConnell, 6th Bt (cr 1828), 1890–1963, vol. VI
MacGregor, Hon. Robert Malcolm, 1876–1924, vol. II
MacGregor, Robert Menzies, 1882–1946, vol. IV
MacGregor, Robert Roy, 1847–1922, vol. II
Macgregor, W. Y., 1855–1923, vol. II
MacGregor, Rt Hon. Sir William, 1847–1919, vol. II
MacGregor, William Cunningham, 1862–1934, vol. III
Macgregor, William Duncan, 1878–1974, vol. VII
Macgregor, Sir William Gordon, 4th Bt (cr 1828), 1846–1905, vol. I
Macgregor, Very Rev. William Malcolm, 1861–1944, vol. IV
Macgregor Mitchell, Hon. Lord; Robert Macgregor Mitchell, died 1938, vol. III
Macgregor-Morris, John Turner, 1872–1959, vol. V
McGrigor, Lt-Col Sir Charles Colquhoun, 4th Bt, 1893–1946, vol. IV
M'Grigor, Brig.Gen. Charles Roderic Robert, 1860–1927, vol. II
M'Grigor, Captain Sir James Rhoderick Duff, 3rd Bt, 1857–1924, vol. II
McGrigor, Adm. of the Fleet Sir Rhoderick Robert, 1893–1959, vol. V
M'Guckin, Barton, 1853–1913, vol. I
MacGuckin, Charles John Graham, died 1934, vol. III
McGuffie, Kenneth Cunningham, 1913–1972, vol. VII
McGuffin, Samuel, 1863–1952, vol. V

McGuigan, His Eminence Cardinal James Charles, 1894–1974, vol. VII
MacGuigan, Hon. Mark Rudolph, 1931–1998, vol. X
M'Guinness, Bingham, vol. III
McGuinness, Brig. Edward, 1883–1958, vol. V
McGuinness, James Henry, 1912–1987, vol. VIII
McGuinness, Joseph, died 1922, vol. II
McGuinness, Norah Allison, died 1980, vol. VII (AII)
McGuire, (Dominic) Paul, 1903–1978, vol. VII (AII)
McGuire, Paul; see McGuire, D. P.
McGuire, Robert Ely, 1901–1991, vol. IX
McGuire, Most Rev. Terence Bernard, 1881–1957, vol. V
McGuire, Thomas Horace, 1849–1923, vol. II
McGurk, Colin Thomas, 1922–2000, vol. X
McGurk, Harry, 1936–1998, vol. X
McGusty, Victor William Tighe, 1887–1981, vol. VIII
MccGwire, Maj.-Gen. Edward Thomas St Lawrance, 1830–1917, vol. II
MccGwire, Lt-Col John Edward, died 1950, vol. IV
Machain, Monsieur, 1839–1910, vol. I
McHardy, Maj.-Gen. Alexander Anderson, 1868–1958, vol. V
McHardy, Lt-Col Sir Alexander Burness, 1842–1917, vol. II
McHardy, Rev. Archibald, 1890–1973, vol. VII
M'Hardy, Malcolm Macdonald, 1852–1913, vol. I
McHardy, William Duff, 1911–2000, vol. X
Macharg, Sir Andrew Simpson, 1871–1959, vol. V
Machell, James Octavius, 1837–1902, vol. I
Machell, Percy Wilfrid, 1862–1916, vol. II
Machell, Lady Valda, 1868–1951, vol. V
Machen, Arthur, 1863–1947, vol. IV
Machin, Arnold, 1911–1999, vol. X
Machin, George, 1922–1989, vol. VIII
Machin, Sir Stanley, 1861–1939, vol. III
Machray, Most Rev. Robert, 1831–1904, vol. I
Machray, Robert, 1857–1946, vol. IV
Machray, Robert, 1906–1968, vol. VI
Machtig, Sir Eric Gustav, 1889–1973, vol. VII
Machugh, Rt Rev. Charles, 1855–1926, vol. II
M'Hugh, Edward, died 1900, vol. I
McHugh, Mary Patricia, 1915–1992, vol. IX
M'Hugh, Patrick Aloysius, 1858–1909, vol. I
Machugh, Lt-Col Robert Joseph, died 1925, vol. II
McIllree, John Henry, 1849–1925, vol. II
McIlquham, Sir Gilbert, 1863–1953, vol. V
MacIlreith, R. T., died 1943, vol. IV
McIlroy, Dame (Anne) Louise, 1877–1968, vol. VI
McIlroy, Dame Louise; see McIlroy, Dame A. L.
McIlroy, Robert, died 1911, vol. I
McIlroy, William Ewart Clarke, 1893–1963, vol. VI
McIlveen, Brig. Sir Arthur William, died 1979, vol. VII (AII)
McIlvenna, Maj.-Gen. John Antony, 1919–1997, vol. X
McIlwain, Charles Howard, 1871–1968, vol. VI(AII)
McIlwain, Henry, 1912–1992, vol. IX
MacIlwaine, Alexander Gillilan Johnson, 1887–1942, vol. IV

MacIlwaine, John Bedell Stanford, 1857–1945, vol. IV
MacIlwaine, John Elder, 1874–1930, vol. III
McIlwaine, Hon. Sir Robert, 1871–1943, vol. IV
McIlwraith, Arthur Renwick, 1914–1994, vol. IX
M'Ilwraith, Jean H., died 1938, vol. III
McIlwraith, Sir Malcolm, 1865–1941, vol. IV
M'Ilwraith, Hon. Sir Thomas, 1835–1900, vol. I
McIlwraith, William, 1924–1968, vol. VI
McIndoe, Sir Archibald Hector, 1900–1960, vol. V
Macinerney, Michael Chartres, 1850–1929, vol. III
McInerney, Hon. Sir Murray Vincent, 1911–1988, vol. VIII
M'Inerney, Lt-Col Timothy Marcus, 1869–1929, vol. III
MacInnes, Rev. Alexander M. F., 1866–1934, vol. III
MacInnes, Rt Rev. Angus Campbell, 1901–1977, vol. VII
MacInnes, Charles Malcolm, 1891–1971, vol. VII
MacInnes, Charles Stephen, 1872–1952, vol. V
MacInnes, Colin, 1914–1976, vol. VII
MacInnes, Rt Rev. Duncan, 1897–1970, vol. VI
Macinnes, Lt-Col Duncan Sayre, 1870–1918, vol. II
MacInnes, Helen Clark, 1907–1985, vol. VIII
McInnes, James, 1901–1974, vol. VII
MacInnes, Miles, 1830–1909, vol. I
MacInnes, Rt Rev. Rennie, 1870–1931, vol. III
MacInnes, Robert Ian Aonas, 1902–1972, vol. VII
MacInnes, William Alexander, 1892–1977, vol. VII
MacInnes Shaw, Sir Douglas; see Shaw, Sir A. D. M.
McInnis, Lt-Col Edward Bowater, 1846–1927, vol. II
M'Inroy, Col Charles, 1838–1919, vol. II
McIntosh, Alastair James, 1913–1973, vol. VII
McIntosh, Alexander Morrison, 1877–1944, vol. IV
McIntosh, Sir Alister Donald, 1906–1978, vol. VII
McIntosh, Annie, 1871–1951, vol. V
McIntosh, Arthur Johnston, 1890–1956, vol. V
Macintosh, Douglas Clyde, 1877–1948, vol. IV(A), vol. V
MacIntosh, Duncan William, 1904–1966, vol. VI
Macintosh, Edward Hyde, 1895–1970, vol. VI
MacIntosh, Frank Campbell, 1909–1992, vol. IX
McIntosh, George, 1889–1949, vol. IV
McIntosh, Hon. Hugh Donald, 1876–1942, vol. IV
McIntosh, Ian Donald, 1908–1975, vol. VII
Macintosh, John Macintosh, died 1913, vol. I
McIntosh, Hon. Sir Malcolm, 1888–1960, vol. V
McIntosh, Sir Malcolm Kenneth, 1945–2000, vol. X
McIntosh, Robert, 1894–1972, vol. VII
Macintosh, Sir Robert Reynolds, 1897–1989, vol. VIII
Macintosh, Sir William, 1863–1929, vol. III
M'Intosh, William Carmichael, 1838–1931, vol. III
MacIntyre, Sir Alexander, 1879–1952, vol. V
Macintyre, Angus Donald, 1935–1994, vol. IX
Macintyre, David Lowe, 1895–1967, vol. VI
McIntyre, Rev. David Martin, 1859–1938, vol. III
Macintyre, Maj.-Gen. Donald, 1831–1903, vol. I
McIntyre, Donald, 1891–1954, vol. V
Macintyre, Sir Donald, 1891–1978, vol. VII
Macintyre, Maj.-Gen. Donald Charles Frederick, 1859–1938, vol. III

McIntyre, F(rederick) Donald (Livingstone), 1905–1981, vol. VIII
MacIntyre, Ian, 1869–1946, vol. IV
Macintyre, Captain Ian Agnew Patteson, 1893–1967, vol. VI
McIntyre, Rev. Canon James, 1888–1978, vol. VII
McIntyre, Cardinal James Francis Aloysius, 1886–1979, vol. VII
McIntyre, James Gordon; see Sarn, Hon. Lord.
M'Intyre, Hon. Sir John, 1832–1904, vol. I
Macintyre, John, 1859–1928, vol. II
M'Intyre, Most Rev. John, 1855–1934, vol. III
McIntyre, Air Vice-Marshal Sir John, died 1950, vol. IV.
M'Intyre, John M'Intyre, 1842–1930, vol. III
McIntyre, Air Commodore Kenneth John, 1908–1989, vol. VIII
McIntyre, Sir Laurence Rupert, 1912–1981, vol. VIII
Macintyre, Margaret, died 1943, vol. IV
McIntyre, Raymond, died 1933, vol. III
McIntyre, Robert Douglas, 1913–1998, vol. X
Macintyre, Very Rev. Ronald George, 1863–1954, vol. V
McIntyre, Stuart Charles, 1912–1989, vol. VIII
McIntyre, William Keverall, 1882–1969, vol. VI
McIntyre, Surgeon Rear-Adm. William Percival Edwin, 1903–1986, vol. VIII
MacIver, Alan Squarey, 1894–1975, vol. VII
MacIver, Arthur Milne, 1905–1972, vol. VII
MacIver, Major Sir Charles, 1866–1935, vol. III
MacIver, David, 1840–1907, vol. I
MacIver, David R.; see Randall-MacIver.
M'Iver, Sir Lewis, 1st Bt, 1846–1920, vol. II
MacIver, Robert Morrison, 1882–1970, vol. VI
McIver, William, 1871–1930, vol. III
McIvor, Freda K., (Mrs I. McIvor); see Corbet, F. K.
Mack, Alan Frederick, 1920–1989, vol. VIII
Mack, Alan Osborne, 1918–1994, vol. IX
Mack, Rear-Adm. Frederick Robert Joseph, 1897–1959, vol. V
Mack, Sir Henry; see Mack, Sir W. H. B.
Mack, Sir Hugh, 1832–1920, vol. II
Mack, Hon. Jason Miller, 1843–1927, vol. II
Mack, John David, died 1957, vol. V
Mack, Rear-Adm. Philip John, 1892–1943, vol. IV
Mack, Hon. Sir Ronald William, 1904–1968, vol. VI
Mack, Sir William George, 1904–1979, vol. VII
Mack, Sir (William) Henry (Bradshaw), 1894–1974, vol. VII
McKaig, Col Sir John Bickerton, 1883–1962, vol. VI
McKaig, Adm. Sir (John) Rae, 1922–1996, vol. X
McKaig, Adm. Sir Rae; see McKaig, Adm. Sir J. R.
Mackail, Denis George, 1892–1971, vol. VII
Mackail, John William, 1859–1945, vol. IV
Mackain of Ardnamurchan, Rev. William James, 1854–1936, vol. III
Mackarness, Ven. Charles Coleridge, 1850–1918, vol. II
Mackarness, Cuthbert George Milford, 1890–1962, vol. VI
Mackarness, Frederic Coleridge, 1854–1920, vol. II

Mackawee, Khan Bahadur Sir Mohamed Abdul Kader, 1875–1954, vol. V(A)
Mackay, Hon. Lord; Alexander Morrice Mackay, 1875–1955, vol. V
Mackay, Æneas James George, 1839–1911, vol. I
Mackay, Alastair, 1911–1999, vol. X
McKay, Sir Alex, (Sir Alick Benson McKay), 1909–1983, vol. VIII
Mackay, Alexander Grant, 1860–1920, vol. II
Mackay, Hon. Col Alexander Howard, 1848–1929, vol. III
McKay, Maj.-Gen. Alexander Matthew, 1921–1999, vol. X
Mackay, Alexander Morrice; see Mackay, Hon. Lord.
McKay, Sir Alick Benson; see McKay, Sir Alex.
McKay, Andrew Foggo, 1923–1979, vol. VII
McKay, Archibald Charles, 1929–1995, vol. IX(AII)
Mackay, A(rthur) Stewart, 1909–1998, vol. X
McKay, Sir Charles Holly, 1896–1972, vol. VII
MacKay, Donald G., 1870–1958, vol. V
MacKay, Donald MacCrimmon, 1922–1987, vol. VIII
McKay, Hon. Sir Donald Norman, 1908–1988, vol. VIII
MacKay, Ebenezer, 1864–1920, vol. II
Mackay, Edward Fairbairn, 1868–1953, vol. V
Mackay, Eric, 1851–1898, vol. I
McKay, Maj.-Gen. Eric McLachlan, 1921–1995, vol. IX
Mackay, Ernest John Henry, 1880–1943, vol. IV
McKay, Very Rev. Frederick; see McKay, Very Rev. J. F.
Mackay, George, died 1949, vol. IV
Mackay, Hon. George Hugh, 1872–1961, vol. VI
McKay, Sir George Mills, 1869–1937, vol. III
Mackay, Sir (George Patrick) Gordon, 1914–1998, vol. X
Mackay, Gillian Helen, (Mrs Walter Tallis), 1923–1984, vol. VIII
Mackay, Sir Gordon; see Mackay, Sir G. P. G.
Mackay, Helen M. M., 1891–1965, vol. VI
Mackay, Rev. Henry Falconar Barclay, died 1936, vol. III
McKay, Col Henry Kellock, 1850–1930, vol. III
Mackay, Henry Martyn, 1868–1930, vol. III
Mackay, Ian Keith, 1909–1985, vol. VIII
MacKay, Ira Allen, 1875–1934, vol. III
Mackay, Lt-Gen. Sir Iven Giffard, 1882–1966, vol. VI
M'Kay, James, 1862–1931, vol. III
Mackay, Maj.-Gen. Hon. James Alexander Kenneth, 1859–1935, vol. III
Mackay, James Francis, 1855–1933, vol. III
McKay, Very Rev. (James) Frederick, 1907–2000, vol. X
Mackay, Sir James Mackerron, 1907–1985, vol. VIII
McKay, Sir James Wilson, 1912–1992, vol. IX
Mackay, Jessie, 1864–1938, vol. III
Mackay, Rev. John, died 1938, vol. III
McKay, Ven. John, 1870–1942, vol. IV
McKay, John, 1885–1964, vol. VI
Mackay, John, 1914–1999, vol. X

Mackay, Ven. John Alexander, 1838–1923, vol. II
Mackay, John Alexander, 1889–1983, vol. VIII
Mackay, Lt-Col John F., *died* 1930, vol. III
Mackay, Hon. John Keiller, 1888–1970, vol. VI
Mackay, John Martin, 1899–1970, vol. VI
Mackay, Rev. John Robertson, 1865–1939, vol. III
Mackay, John Sturgeon, 1843–1914, vol. I
Mackay, John William, 1831–1902, vol. I
McKay, John William, 1883–1936, vol. III
Mackay, John Yule, 1860–1930, vol. III
Mackay, Brig. Kenneth, 1901–1974, vol. VII
Mackay, Rev. Canon Malcolm, 1873–1953, vol. V
McKay, Margaret, 1911–1996, vol. X
Mackay, Mary; *see* Corelli, Marie.
Mackay, Hon. Robert, 1840–1916, vol. II
Mackay, Robert John, 1859–1935, vol. III
Mackay, Very Rev. Roderick John, 1874–1956,
    vol. V
Mackay, Ronald William Gordon, 1902–1960,
    vol. V
McKay, Rev. Roy, 1900–1993, vol. IX
M'Kay, Hon. Thomas, 1839–1912, vol. I
Mackay, William Æneas, 1871–1929, vol. III
Mackay, Lt-Col William Bertie, 1863–1938, vol. III
Mackay, Sir William Calder, 1896–1990, vol. VIII
M'Kay, William D., 1844–1924, vol. II
Mackay Lewis, Maj.-Gen. Kenneth Frank; *see*
    Lewis.
Mackay-Tallack, Sir Hugh, 1912–1989, vol. VIII
McKeag, Major William, 1897–1972, vol. VII
M'Kean, Col Alexander Chalmers, 1895–1933,
    vol. III
M'Kean, Captain George Burdon, 1890–1926,
    vol. II
McKean, Air Vice-Marshal Sir Lionel Douglas
    Dalzell, 1886–1963, vol. VI
Mackean, Rev. Canon William Herbert, 1877–1960,
    vol. V
M'Kechnie, Alexander Balfour, 1860–1930, vol. III
M'Kechnie, Dugald, 1845–1912, vol. I
McKechnie, Hector, 1899–1966, vol. VI
McKechnie, Sir James, *died* 1931, vol. III
McKechnie, James, 1911–1964, vol. VI
McKechnie, William Sharp, 1863–1930, vol. III
McKechnie, Sir William Wallace, *died* 1947, vol. IV
McKee, Air Marshal Sir Andrew, 1901–1988,
    vol. VIII
McKee, Sir Dermot St Oswald, 1904–1980, vol. VII
McKee, Major Hugh Kennedy, 1896–1957, vol. V
McKee, Captain James, 1886–1934, vol. III
McKee, J(ohn) Ritchie, 1900–1964, vol. VI
McKee, Rev. Robert Alexander, 1847–1926, vol. II
McKee, Col Samuel Hanford, 1875–1942, vol. IV
McKee, William Desmond, 1926–1982, vol. VIII
McKee, William Henry, 1881–1956, vol. V
McKeefry, His Eminence Cardinal Peter Thomas
    Bertram, 1899–1973, vol. VII
Mackeen, Hon. David, 1839–1916, vol. II
McKeever, Ronald Fraser, 1914–1981, vol. VIII
MacKeigan, Hon. Ian Malcolm, 1915–1996, vol. X
Mackeith, Malcolm Henry, 1895–1942, vol. IV
Mac Keith, Ronald Charles, 1908–1977, vol. VII
McKell, Rt Hon. Sir William John, 1891–1985,
    vol. VIII

Mackellar, Hon. Sir Charles Kinnaird, 1844–1926,
    vol. II
McKelvey, Sir John Lawrance, 1881–1939, vol. III
McKelvey, Air Cdre John Wesley, 1914–2000,
    vol. X
MacKelvie, Col Maxwell, 1877–1933, vol. III
Mackelvie, Col Thomas, 1867–1952, vol. V
Macken, Frederic Raymond, 1903–1987, vol. VIII
McKendrick, Archibald, 1876–1960, vol. V (A),
    vol. VI (AI)
M'Kendrick, John Gray, 1841–1926, vol. II
MacKenna, Sir Bernard Joseph Maxwell, (Sir
    Brian), 1905–1989, vol. VIII
MacKenna, Sir Brian; *see* MacKenna, Sir Bernard
    J. M.
McKenna, Harold, 1879–1946, vol. IV
MacKenna, Sir James, 1872–1940, vol. III
McKenna, Brig. James Charles, 1879–1943, vol. IV
M'Kenna, Sir Joseph Neale, 1819–1906, vol. I
McKenna, Rt Rev. Patrick, 1869–1942, vol. IV
McKenna, Rt Hon. Reginald, 1863–1943, vol. IV
MacKenna, Robert Merttins Bird, 1903–1984,
    vol. VIII
Mackenna, Robert William, 1874–1930, vol. III
McKenna, Siobhán, 1923–1986, vol. VIII
McKenna, Stephen, 1888–1967, vol. VI
Mackennal, Rev. Alexander, 1835–1904, vol. I
Mackennal, Sir Bertram, 1863–1931, vol. III
Mackennal, Ven. William Leavers, 1881–1947,
    vol. IV
Mackenzie, Hon. Lord; Charles Kincaid Mackenzie,
    1857–1938, vol. III
Mackenzie, Agnes Mure, 1891–1955, vol. V
MacKenzie, Alasdair Francis, 1910–1971, vol. VII
Mackenzie, Alasdair Roderick, 1903–1970, vol. VI
Mackenzie, Alastair Oswald Morison, 1858–1949,
    vol. IV
Mackenzie, Alastair Stewart, (Sandy), 1930–1986,
    vol. VIII
McKenzie, Alex, 1869–1951, vol. V
Mackenzie, Sir Alexander, 1842–1902, vol. I
Mackenzie, Sir Alexander, 1860–1943, vol. IV
Mackenzie, Alexander, 1915–1982, vol. VIII
McKenzie, Sir Alexander, 1896–1992, vol. IX
Mackenzie, Sir Alexander Campbell, 1847–1935,
    vol. III
Mackenzie, Lt-Col Alexander Dalziel; *see*
    Mackenzie, Lt-Col D. W. A. D.
Mackenzie, Col Alexander Francis, 1861–1935,
    vol. III
Mackenzie, Sir (Alexander George Anthony) Allan,
    4th Bt (*cr* 1890), 1913–1993, vol. IX
Mackenzie, Alexander George Robertson,
    1879–1963, vol. VI
Mackenzie, Alexander Herbert, 1867–1952, vol. V
Mackenzie, Sir Alexander M.; *see* Muir-Mackenzie.
Mackenzie, Alexander Marshall, 1848–1933, vol. III
Mackenzie, Col Sir Alfred Robert Davidson,
    1835–1921, vol. II
Mackenzie, Sir Allan; *see* Mackenzie, Sir Alexander
    G. A. A.
Mackenzie, Sir Allan Russell, 2nd Bt (*cr* 1890),
    1850–1906, vol. I
M'Kenzie, Lt-Col Archibald Ernest Graham,
    1878–1918, vol. II

Mackenzie, Sir Arthur George Ramsay, 11th Bt (*cr* 1673), 1865–1935, vol. III
Mackenzie, Arthur Henderson, 1880–1936, vol. III
Mackenzie, Arthur Stanley, 1865–1938, vol. III
Mackenzie, Austin, 1856–1935, vol. III
Mackenzie, Captain Cecil James Granville, 1889–1959, vol. V
Mackenzie, Chalmers Jack, 1888–1984, vol. VIII
Mackenzie, Lt-Col Charles, 1869–1953, vol. V
Mackenzie, Major Charles Fraser, *died* 1955, vol. V
Mackenzie, Charles Kincaid; *see* Mackenzie, Hon. Lord.
Mackenzie, Sir Clutha Nantes, 1895–1966, vol. VI
MacKenzie, Sir Colin, 1877–1938, vol. III
Mackenzie, Rear-Adm. Colin, 1872–1968, vol. VI
Mackenzie, Maj. Colin Dalzell, 1919–1999, vol. X
Mackenzie, Colin Hercules, 1898–1986, vol. VIII
Mackenzie, Maj.-Gen. Sir Colin John, 1861–1956, vol. V
Mackenzie, Sir Compton, 1883–1972, vol. VII
M'Kenzie, Dan, *died* 1935, vol. III
MacKenzie, David Alexander, 1922–1989, vol. VIII
Mackenzie, Brig. David Alexander Laurance, 1897–1976, vol. VII
Mackenzie, David James, 1855–1925, vol. II
Mackenzie, David James Masterton, 1905–1994, vol. IX
Mackenzie, Donald Alexander, 1873–1936, vol. III
M'Kenzie, Donald Duncan, 1859–1927, vol. II
McKenzie, Donald Francis, 1931–1999, vol. X
Mackenzie, Lt-Col (Douglas William) Alexander Dalziel, 1889–1955, vol. V
Mackenzie, Brig-Gen. Sir Duncan, 1859–1932, vol. III
Mackenzie, Sir Duncan George, 1883–1965, vol. VI
Mackenzie, Col Edward Leslie, 1870–1947, vol. IV
Mackenzie, Sir Edward Montague Compton; *see* Mackenzie, Sir C.
Mackenzie, Col Edward Philippe, 1842–1929, vol. III
Mackenzie, Col Eric Dighton, 1891–1972, vol. VII
Mackenzie, Faith Compton, (Lady Mackenzie), *died* 1960, vol. V
Mackenzie, Col Sir Felix Calvert, 1826–1902, vol. I
Mackenzie, Rev. Francis Scott, 1884–1970, vol. VI
MacKenzie, Fraser, 1905–1978, vol. VII
Mackenzie, Frederick A., 1869–1931, vol. III
Mackenzie, Lt-Col Frederick Finch, 1849–1934, vol. III
Mackenzie, Ven. Gaden Crawford, *died* 1920, vol. II
Mackenzie, George, 1881–1950, vol. IV
Mackenzie, Brig.-Gen. George Birnie, 1872–1952, vol. V
Mackenzie, Col George Frederick Campbell, 1855–1909, vol. I
Mackenzie, Sir George Sutherland, 1844–1910, vol. I
MacKenzie, Rt Hon. Gregor; *see* MacKenzie, Rt Hon. J. G.
Mackenzie, H. Millicent, 1863–1942, vol. IV
Mackenzie, Col Harry Malcolm, *died* 1947, vol. IV
M'Kenzie, Rev. Harry Ward, 1850–1941, vol. IV
Mackenzie, Sir Hector David, 8th Bt (*cr* 1703, of Gairloch), 1893–1958, vol. V

Mackenzie, Lt-Col Hector G. Gordon, 1869–1930, vol. III
Mackenzie, Sir Hector William Gavin, 1856–1929, vol. III
Mackenzie, Helen Margaret, *died* 1966, vol. VI
Mackenzie, Lt-Col Herbert John, 1878–1941, vol. IV
Mackenzie, Hugh, 1861–1940, vol. III
M'Kenzie, Hon. Hugh, 1853–1942, vol. IV
Mackenzie, Sir Hugh, 1888–1959, vol. V
Mackenzie, Vice-Adm. Sir Hugh Stirling, 1913–1996, vol. X
Mackenzie, Rt Hon. Ian Alistair, 1890–1949, vol. IV
Mackenzie, J. Hamilton, 1875–1926, vol. II
Mackenzie, J. J., 1865–1922, vol. II
Mackenzie, Sir James, 1853–1925, vol. II
Mackenzie, Rev. James Cameron, *died* 1931, vol. III
Mackenzie, Sir James Dixon, 7th Bt (*cr* 1703, of Scatwell), 1830–1900, vol. I
MacKenzie, Brig. James Dunbar, 1889–1947, vol. IV
MacKenzie, Rt Hon. (James) Gregor, 1927–1992, vol. IX
Mackenzie, Sir (James) Kenneth Douglas, 8th Bt (*cr* 1703, of Scatwell), 1859–1930, vol. III
Mackenzie, Sir (James) Moir, 1886–1963, vol. VI
MacKenzie, James Sargent Porteous, 1916–2000, vol. X
Mackenzie, James Young, 1914–1971, vol. VII
Mackenzie, Lt-Col John, 1876–1949, vol. IV
McKenzie, Very Rev. John, 1883–1955, vol. V
McKenzie, John, 1915–1986, vol. VIII
MacKenzie, Lt-Col John Alexander, 1881–1960, vol. V
Mackenzie, Brig. John Alexander, 1915–1995, vol. IX
Mackenzie, John Alexander S.; *see* Shaw-Mackenzie.
McKenzie, John Grant, 1882–1963, vol. VI
Mackenzie, John Gurney, 1907–1975, vol. VII
Mackenzie, Col John Hugh, 1876–1963, vol. VI
Mackenzie of Mornish, Captain John Hugh Munro, 1925–2000, vol. X
Mackenzie, John Moncrieff Ord, 1911–1985, vol. VIII
Mackenzie, Maj.-Gen. John Percival, 1884–1961, vol. VI
McKenzie, Sir John Robert, 1876–1955, vol. V
Mackenzie, John Stuart, 1860–1935, vol. III
Mackenzie, Sir John William Pitt M.; *see* Muir-Mackenzie.
Mackenzie, Keith Roderick Turing, 1921–1990, vol. VIII
Mackenzie, Rt Rev. Kenneth, 1863–1945, vol. IV
Mackenzie, Surg. Vice-Adm. Sir (Kenneth) Alexander I.; *see* Ingleby Mackenzie.
Mackenzie, Rt Rev. Kenneth Donald, 1876–1966, vol. VI
Mackenzie, Sir Kenneth Douglas; *see* Mackenzie, Sir J. K. D.
Mackenzie, Kenneth Edward, 1910–1995, vol. IX
Mackenzie, Rear-Adm. Kenneth Harry Litton, 1889–1970, vol. VI
Mackenzie, Kenneth James Joseph, 1867–1924, vol. II

Mackenzie, Col Kenneth James Loch, *died* 1903, vol. I
Mackenzie, Kenneth James M.; *see* Muir Mackenzie.
Mackenzie, Sir Kenneth John, 7th Bt (*cr* 1703, of Gairloch), 1861–1929, vol. III
Mackenzie, Kenneth Roderick, 1908–1991, vol. IX
Mackenzie, Sir Kenneth Smith, 6th Bt (*cr* 1703, of Gairloch), 1832–1900, vol. I
MacKenzie, Kenneth William Stewart, 1915–1999, vol. X
Mackenzie, Sir Leslie, 1862–1935, vol. III
Mackenzie, Sir (Lewis) Roderick Kenneth, 9th Bt (*cr* 1703, of Scatwell), 1902–1972, vol. VII
McKenzie, Malcolm George, 1917–1979, vol. VII
McKenzie, Marian, *died* 1927, vol. II
Mackenzie, Maxwell Weir, 1907–1991, vol. IX
Mackenzie, Melville Douglas, 1889–1972, vol. VII
Mackenzie, Michael Alexander, 1866–1949, vol. IV
Mackenzie, Sir Moir; *see* Mackenzie, Sir J. M.
Mackenzie, Montague M.; *see* Muir-Mackenzie.
MacKenzie, Nicol Finlayson, 1857–1943, vol. IV
MacKenzie, Norman Archibald MacRae, 1894–1986, vol. VIII
MacKenzie, Peter Alexander Cameron; *see* Serra Largo, Count de.
Mackenzie, Col Sir Robert Campbell, 1856–1945, vol. IV
Mackenzie, Sir Robert Cecil M.; *see* Muir-Mackenzie.
McKenzie, Hon. Robert Donald, 1865–1928, vol. II, vol. III
Mackenzie, Sir Robert Evelyn, 12th Bt, 1906–1990, vol. VIII
Mackenzie, Sir Robert Henry M.; *see* Muir Mackenzie
Mackenzie, Col Robert Holden, vol. II
Mackenzie, Robert Jameson, 1857–1912, vol. I
Mackenzie, Lt-Col Sir Robert Smythe M.; *see* Muir-Mackenzie.
McKenzie, (Robert) Tait, 1867–1938, vol. III
McKenzie, Robert Trelford, 1917–1981, vol. VIII
Mackenzie, Maj.-Gen. Roderick, 1830–1916, vol. II
Mackenzie, Sir Roderick; *see* Mackenzie, Sir L. R. K.
Mackenzie, Sir Roderick Campbell, 10th Bt, 1954–1981, vol. VIII
Mackenzie, Captain Sir Roderick Edward François McQuhae, 11th Bt, 1894–1986, vol. VIII
Mackenzie, Ronald Pierson, 1864–1930, vol. III
Mackenzie, Sandy; *see* Mackenzie, A. S.
McKenzie, Tait; *see* McKenzie, R. T.
Mackenzie, Hon. Sir Thomas, 1854–1930, vol. III
McKenzie, Thomas, 1891–1954, vol. V
Mackenzie, Thomas William, 1875–1939, vol. III
Mackenzie, Col Sir Victor Audley Falconer, 3rd Bt (*cr* 1890), 1882–1944, vol. IV
Mackenzie, W. G., vol. II
Mackenzie, Sir William, 1849–1923, vol. II
Mackenzie, William Andrew, 1870–1942, vol. IV
Mackenzie, William Cook, 1862–1952, vol. V
Mackenzie, William Dalziel, 1840–1928, vol. II
Mackenzie, William Douglas, 1859–1936, vol. III
MacKenzie, William Forbes, 1907–1980, vol. VII
Mackenzie, William James Millar, 1909–1996, vol. X

Mackenzie, William Lyon, *died* 1938, vol. III
Mackenzie, William Mackay, 1871–1952, vol. V
Mackenzie, Major William Roderick Dalziel, 1864–1952, vol. V
Mackenzie, Lt-Col William Scobie, *died* 1926, vol. II
Mackenzie, Col William Shand, 1876–1944, vol. IV
Mackenzie Crooks, Air Vice-Marshal Lewis, 1909–1992, vol. IX
Mackenzie-Kennedy, Brig. Archibald Gordon, 1904–1987, vol. VIII
Mackenzie-Kennedy, Sir Donald; *see* Mackenzie-Kennedy, Sir H. C. D. C.
Mackenzie-Kennedy, Maj.-Gen. Sir Edward Charles William, *died* 1932, vol. III
Mackenzie-Kennedy, Sir (Henry Charles) Donald (Cleveland), 1889–1965, vol. VI
Mackenzie King, Rt Hon. William Lyon; *see* King.
Mackenzie-Rogan, Lt-Col John, 1855–1932, vol. III
Mackenzie-Stuart, Baron (Life Peer); Alexander John Mackenzie Stuart, 1924–2000, vol. X
M'Keown, Hon. Harrison Andrew, 1863–1932, vol. III
Mackeown, John Ainslie, 1902–1984, vol. VIII
McKeown, Robert John, 1869–1925, vol. II
McKeown, Thomas, 1912–1988, vol. VIII
McKeown, Walter, 1866–1925, vol. II
McKercher, Sir William Gourley, *died* 1937, vol. III
MacKereth, Sir Gilbert, 1893–1962, vol. VI
McKergow, Lt-Col Robert Wilson, 1866–1947, vol. IV
McKerihan, Sir (Clarence) Roy, 1896–1969, vol. VI
McKerihan, Sir Roy; *see* McKerihan, Sir C. R.
M'Kerlie, Sir John Graham, 1814–1900, vol. I
McKerral, Andrew, 1876–1967, vol. VI
McKerrell, Brig-Comdr Augustus de Ségur, 1863–1916, vol. II
McKerron, Sir Patrick Alexander Bruce, 1896–1964, vol. VI
McKerron, Robert Gordon, 1862–1937, vol. III
McKerron, Robert Gordon, 1900–1973, vol. VII
McKerrow, Ronald Brunlees, 1872–1940, vol. III
Mackeson, Brig. Sir Harry Ripley, 1st Bt, 1905–1964, vol. VI
Mackessack, George Ross, 1851–1935, vol. III
Mackessack, Lt-Col Kenneth, 1902–1982, vol. VIII
Mackesy, Col Charles Ernest Randolph, 1861–1925, vol. II
Mackesy, Maj.-Gen. Pierse Joseph, 1883–1956, vol. V
Mackesy, Lt-Gen. William Henry, 1837–1914, vol. I
Mackeurtan, Harold Graham, 1884–1942, vol. IV
McKew, Rev. Robert, *died* 1944, vol. IV
Mackey, Archibald John, 1844–1936, vol. III
Mackey, Brig.-Gen. Hugh James Alexander, 1876–1927, vol. II
Mackey, Hon. Sir John Emanuel, 1865–1924, vol. II
Mackey, William Arthur, 1906–1990, vol. VIII
McKibbin, Col Alan John, 1892–1958, vol. V
McKibbin, Major Thomas, 1879–1943, vol. IV
Mackichan, Rev. D., 1851–1932, vol. III
Mackie, Alexander, 1876–1955, vol. V
Mackie, Alfred William White, 1877–1951, vol. V
Mackie, Brig. Andrew Hugh, 1897–1968, vol. VI
Mackie, Charles, *died* 1940, vol. III(A), vol. IV

Mackie, Charles H., 1862–1920, vol. II
McKie, Douglas, 1896–1967, vol. VI
Mackie, Edwin Gordon, 1896–1980, vol. VII
Mackie, Bt Col F. Percival, 1875–1944, vol. IV
Mackie, Rev. George M., 1854–1922, vol. II
McKie, Helen Madeleine, died 1957, vol. V
Mackie, Sir Horatio George Arthur, 1868–1940, vol. III
Mackie, Sir James, 1838–1898, vol. I
Mackie, James Richard, 1896–1981, vol. VIII
McKie, Lt-Col John, 1857–1934, vol. III
Mackie, John, 1862–1939, vol. III
Mackie, John, Beveridge, 1848–1919, vol. II
McKie, Rt Rev. John David, 1909–1994, vol. IX
Mackie, John Duncan, 1887–1978, vol. VII
Mackie, John Hamilton, 1898–1958, vol. V
Mackie, John Leslie, 1917–1981, vol. VIII
Mackie, John Lindsay, 1864–1956, vol. V
Mackie, Sir Maitland, 1912–1996, vol. X
Mackie, Sir Peter Jeffrey, 1st Bt, 1855–1924, vol. II
Mackie, Peter Robert McLeod, died 1959, vol. V
Mackie, Sir Richard, 1851–1923, vol. II
Mackie, Thomas Jones, 1888–1955, vol. V
Mackie, Col Tom Darke, 1883–1941, vol. IV
McKie, William Murray, 1866–1932, vol. III
McKie, Sir William Neil, 1901–1984, vol. VIII
McKie Reid, Col Andrew; see Reid.
Mackilligin, Robert Springett, 1890–1972, vol. VII
MacKillop, Douglas, 1891–1959, vol. V
McKillop, Edgar Ravenswood, 1895–1987, vol. VIII
McKillop, James, 1844–1913, vol. I
M'Killop, William, died 1909, vol. I
McKim, Ven. Charles W., 1867–1934, vol. III
McKim, Rt Rev. John, 1852–1936, vol. III
Mackinder, Rt Hon. Sir Halford John, 1861–1947, vol. IV
Mackinder, William, 1880–1930, vol. III
McKinlay, Adam Storey, died 1950, vol. IV
Mackinlay, Antoinette, (Mrs John Mackinlay); see Sterling, A.
MacKinlay, Sir Bruce, 1912–1999, vol. X
Mackinlay, Lt-Col George, 1847–1928, vol. II
Mackinlay, Sir George Mason, 1906–1973, vol. VII
Mackinlay, Jean Sterling, died 1958, vol. V
Mackinlay, Malcolm Sterling, 1876–1952, vol. V
M'Kinley, William, 1842–1901, vol. I
McKinnell, James Jesse, 1869–1950, vol. IV
Mackinney, Frederick Walker, 1871–1950, vol. IV
McKinney, Judith, (Mrs J. P. McKinney); see Wright, J.
McKinney, Sir William, 1897–1979, vol. VII
Mackinnon, Rev. Albert Glenthorne Tait, 1871–1939, vol. III
Mackinnon, Lt-Col Alexander Charles Broughton, 1878–1942, vol. IV
Mackinnon, Angus, 1911–1987, vol. VIII
Mackinnon, Archibald Donald, 1864–1937, vol. III
Mackinnon of Mackinnon, Comdr Arthur Avalon, 1893–1964, vol. VI
Mackinnon, Donald, died 1914, vol. I
Mackinnon, Hon. Donald, 1859–1932, vol. III
Mackinnon, Hon. Donald Alexander, 1863–1928, vol. II
MacKinnon, Donald MacKenzie, 1913–1994, vol. IX

Mackinnon, Doris Livingston, died 1956, vol. V
Mackinnon, Duncan, 1909–1984, vol. VIII
Mackinnon, Rear-Adm. Edmund Julius Gordon, 1880–1940, vol. III
MacKinnon of MacKinnon, Francis Alexander, 1848–1947, vol. IV
MacKinnon, Rt Hon. Sir Frank Douglas, 1871–1946, vol. IV
MacKinnon, Gena; see MacKinnon, Georgina R. D.
MacKinnon, Georgina Russell Davidson, (Gena MacKinnon), 1885–1973, vol. VII
McKinnon, Hector Brown, 1890–1981, vol. VIII
MacKinnon, Gen. Sir Henry; see MacKinnon, Gen. Sir W. H.
Mackinnon, Lt-Col Henry William Alexander, 1842–1905, vol. I
Mackinnon, James, 1860–1945, vol. IV
McKinnon, Sir James, 1894–1971, vol. VII
MacKinnon, James Alexander Rudolf, 1888–1955, vol. V
Mackinnon, John, 1886–1958, vol. V
Mackinnon, Kenneth Wulsten, 1906–1964, vol. VI
Mackinnon, Col Lachlan, 1886–1973, vol. VII
Mackinnon, Vice-Adm. Lachlan Donald Ian, 1882–1948, vol. IV
Mackinnon, Sir Lauchlan Charles, 1848–1925, vol. II
Mackinnon, Murdoch, 1865–1944, vol. IV
McKinnon, Neil Nairn, 1909–1988, vol. VIII
Mackinnon, Sir Percy Graham, 1872–1956, vol. V
M'Kinnon, Rev. W., 1843–1925, vol. II, vol. III
McKinnon, Maj.-Gen. Walter Sneddon, 1910–1998, vol. X
Mackinnon, Sir William Alexander, 1830–1897, vol. I
MacKinnon, Gen. Sir (William) Henry, 1852–1929, vol. III
Mackinnon, Lt-Col William Thomas Morris, died 1957, vol. V
McKinstry, Sir Archibald, 1877–1952, vol. V
McKinstry, Captain Edward Robert, 1861–1943, vol. IV
Mackintosh, Hon. Lord; Charles Machintosh, 1888–1978, vol. VII
Mackintosh of Halifax, 1st Viscount, 1891–1964, vol. VI
Mackintosh of Halifax, 2nd Viscount, 1921–1980, vol. VII
Mackintosh, The; Alfred Donald Mackintosh, 1851–1938, vol. III
Mackintosh, The; see Mackintosh of Mackintosh, Vice-Adm. L. D.
Mackintosh, Rt Rev. Mgr Alexander, 1854–1922, vol. II
Mackintosh, Sir Alexander, 1858–1948, vol. IV
Mackintosh, Alfred Donald; see Mackintosh, The.
Mackintosh, Allan Roy, 1936–1995, vol. IX
MacKintosh, Sir Angus MacKay, 1915–1986, vol. VIII
Mackintosh, Sir Ashley Watson, 1868–1937, vol. III
Mackintosh, Charles; see Mackintosh, Hon. Lord.
Mackintosh, (Charles Ernest Whistler) Christopher, 1903–1974, vol. VII
Mackintosh, Charles Rennie, 1869–1928, vol. II

Mackintosh, Christopher; see Mackintosh, Charles E. W. C.

Mackintosh, David Forbes, 1900–1988, vol. VIII

Mackintosh, Most Rev. Donald, died 1943, vol. IV

Mackintosh, Most Rev. Donald A., 1845–1919, vol. II

Mackintosh, Donald James, 1862–1947, vol. IV

Mackintosh, Duncan Robert, 1902–1991, vol. IX

Mackintosh, Eric Donald, 1906–1978, vol. VII

Mackintosh, Col Ernest Elliot Buckland, 1880–1957, vol. V

Mackintosh, Col George, 1860–1954, vol. V

Mackintosh, Rev. Hugh Ross, 1870–1936, vol. III

Mackintosh, (Hugh) Stewart, 1903–1989, vol. VIII

Mackintosh, James, 1858–1944, vol. IV

Mackintosh, James Macalister, 1891–1966, vol. VI

Mackintosh, John, 1833–1907, vol. I

Mackintosh, John Pitcairn, 1929=n1978, vol. VII

Mackintosh, Captain Sir Kenneth Lachlan, 1902–1979, vol. VII

Mackintosh of Mackintosh, Vice-Adm. Lachlan Donald, (The Mackintosh), 1896–1957, vol. V

Mackintosh of Mackintosh, Lt-Comdr Lachlan Ronald Duncan, 1928–1995, vol. IX

Mackintosh, Rev. Robert, 1858–1933, vol. III

Mackintosh, Stanley Hugh, 1883–1967, vol. VI

Mackintosh, Stewart; see Mackintosh, H. S.

Mackintosh, William; see Kyllachy, Hon. Lord.

Mackintosh, William Archibald, 1895–1970, vol. VI(AII)

Mackintosh, Rev. William Lachlan, 1858–1926, vol. II

McKisack, Sir Audley, 1903–1966, vol. VI

M'Kisack, Henry Lawrence, 1859–1928, vol. II

McKisack, May, 1900–1981, vol. VIII

McKissock, Sir Wylie, 1906–1994, vol. IX

McKittrick, Thomas Harrington, 1889–1970, vol. VI

Macklen, Victor Harry Burton, 1919–1993, vol. IX

Mackley, Garnet Hercules, 1883–1986, vol. VIII

Mackley, George Edward, 1900–1983, vol. VIII

Macklin, Sir (Albert) Noel (Campbell), died 1946, vol. IV

Macklin, Albert Romer, 1863–1921, vol. II

Macklin, Sir (Albert) Sortain (Romer), 1890–1976, vol. VII

Macklin, Sir Bruce Roy, 1917–2000, vol. X(AII)

Macklin, Sir James, 1864–1944, vol. IV

Macklin, Sir Noel; see Macklin, Sir A. N. C.

Macklin, Sir Sortain; see Macklin, Sir A. S. R.

Macklin, T. Eyre, 1867–1943, vol. IV

Mackness, Rev. George, 1834–1914, vol. I

Mackness, Lt-Comdr George John, 1892–1970, vol. VI

Mackness, William Robert, 1879–1963, vol. VI

Macknight, Dodge, 1860–1950, vol. IV(A)

Macknight, Dame Ella Annie Noble, 1904–1997, vol. X

Macknight, Lt-Col John James Thow, 1876–1965, vol. VI

Macknight, Thomas, 1829–1899, vol. I

Mackworth, Sir Arthur William, 6th Bt, 1842–1914, vol. I

Mackworth, Comdr Sir David Arthur Geoffrey, 9th Bt, 1912–1998, vol. X

Mackworth, Vice-Adm. Geoffrey, 1879–1952, vol. V

Mackworth, Col Sir Harry Llewellyn, 8th Bt, 1878–1952, vol. V

Mackworth, Sir Humphrey, 7th Bt, 1871–1948, vol. IV

Mackworth, John Dolben, 1887–1939, vol. III

Mackworth, Air Vice-Marshal Philip Herbert, 1897–1958, vol. V

Mackworth-Praed, Sir Herbert Bulkley; see Praed.

Mackworth-Young, Gerard; see Young.

Mackworth-Young, (Gerard) William, 1926–1984, vol. VIII

Mackworth-Young, Sir Robert Christopher, (Sir Robin), 1920–2000, vol. X

Mackworth-Young, Sir Robin; see Mackworth-Young, Sir Robert C.

Maclachlan, Alan Bruce, 1874–1955, vol. V

Maclachlan, Lt-Col Alexander Fraser Campbell, 1875–1918, vol. II

McLachlan, Angus Henry, 1908–1996, vol. X

McLachlan, Charles, 1931–1990, vol. VIII

Maclachlan, Adm. Crawford, 1867–1952, vol. V

McLachlan, Donald Harvey, 1908–1971, vol. VII

McLachlan, Duncan Clark, 1853–1929, vol. III

McLachlan, Herbert, 1876–1958, vol. V

McLachlan, Air Vice-Marshal Ian Dougald, 1911–1991, vol. IX

McLachlan, Maj.-Gen. James Douglas, 1869–1937, vol. III

Maclachlan of Maclachlan, John, 1859–1942, vol. IV

McLachlan, Peter John, 1936–1999, vol. X

M'Lachlan, Robert, 1837–1904, vol. I

MacLachlan, Robert Boyd, 1880–1975, vol. IV

Maclachlan, Brig.-Gen. Ronald Campbell, 1872–1917, vol. II

Maclachlan, Sir T. J. Leigh, 1864–1946, vol. IV

Maclachlan, Thomas Banks, died 1952, vol. V

Maclachlan, Thomas Kay, 1895–1972, vol. VII

Maclachlan, Col Thomas Robertson, 1870–1921, vol. II

McLagan, Archibald Gibson, 1853–1928, vol. II

Maclagan, Sir Douglas, 1812–1900, vol. I

Maclagan, Sir Edward Douglas, 1864–1952, vol. V

Maclagan, Sir Eric Robert Dalrymple, 1879–1951, vol. V

Maclagan, Maj.-Gen. Ewen George S.; see Sinclair-Maclagan.

Maclagan, John, 1846–1929, vol. III

Maclagan, Noel Francis, 1904–1987, vol. VIII

Maclagan, Col Robert Smeiton, 1860–1931, vol. III

Maclagan, Most Rev. William Dalrymple, 1826–1910, vol. I

Maclagan, William Gauld, 1903–1972, vol. VII

McLaggan, Sir Douglas; see McLaggan, Sir J. D.

McLaggan, Sir (John) Douglas, 1893–1967, vol. VI

McLaglen, Victor, 1886–1959, vol. V

Maclaine of Lochbuie, Kenneth Douglas Lorne, 1880–1935, vol. III

Maclaine of Lochbuie, Murdoch Gillian, 1845–1909, vol. I

M'Laren, Hon. Lord; John M'Laren, 1831–1910, vol. I

M'Laren, Rev. Alexander, 1826–1910, vol. I

MacLaren, Andrew, 1883–1975, vol. VII

Maclaren, Archibald Campbell, 1871–1944, vol. IV
MacLaren, Brig.-Gen. Charles Henry, 1878–1962, vol. VI
McLaren, Sir Charles Northrop, 1898–1955, vol. V
MacLaren of MacLaren, Donald, 1910–1966, vol. VI
M'Laren, Rev. Douglas, 1866–1956, vol. V
M'Laren, Hon. Francis Walter Stafford, 1886–1917, vol. II
McLaren, Sir Hamish Duncan, 1898–1990, vol. VIII
McLaren, Henry, 1883–1943, vol. IV
McLaren, Hugh Cameron, 1913–1986, vol. VIII
Maclaren, Ian; see Watson, Rev. John.
McLaren, Ian; see McLaren, J. W.
McLaren, Jack, 1887–1954, vol. V
Maclaren, James Anderson, 1866–1926, vol. II
McLaren, Sir John, 1850–1920, vol. II
M'Laren, John; see M'Laren, Hon. Lord.
McLaren, Sir John Gilbert, 1871–1958, vol. V
Maclaren, John James, died 1926, vol. II
McLaren, John Watt, 1906–1982, vol. VIII
Maclaren, Major Kenneth, 1860–1924, vol. II
McLaren, Martin, 1914–1979, vol. VII
McLaren, Moray, 1901–1971, vol. VII
MacLaren, Col Murray, 1861–1942, vol. IV
McLaren, Robert, 1856–1940, vol. III
McLaren, Ross Scott, 1906–1975, vol. VII
M'Laren, Walter Stowe Bright, 1853–1912, vol. I
McLaren, Rev. William David, 1856–1921, vol. II
McLarty, Hon. Sir (Duncan) Ross, 1891–1962, vol. VI
McLarty, Hon. Norman Alexander, 1889–1945, vol. IV
McLarty, Hon. Sir Ross; see McLarty, Hon. Sir D. R.
Maclauchlan, Hugh Simon, died 1899, vol. I
McLaughlan, Rear-Adm. Ian David, 1919–1996, vol. X
McLaughlan, Roy James Philip, 1898–1982, vol. VIII
MacLaughlin, Lt-Col Alexander John Maunsell, 1854–1932, vol. III
M'Laughlin, Andrew Cunningham, 1861–1947, vol. IV
MacLaughlin, Col Arthur Maunsell, died 1954, vol. V
McLaughlin, Charles Redmond, 1909–1979, vol. VII
McLaughlin, Mrs (Florence) Patricia (Alice), 1916–1996, vol. X
McLaughlin, George Vincent, 1922–1987, vol. VIII
McLaughlin, Sir Henry, 1876–1927, vol. II
M'Laughlin, Lt-Col Hubert James, 1860–1915, vol. I
McLaughlin, Rev. John Fletcher, 1863–1933, vol. III
McLaughlin, Mrs Patricia; see McLaughlin, Mrs F. P. A.
McLaughlin, Rear-Adm. Patrick Vivian, 1901–1969, vol. VI
M'Laurin, Duncan, 1848–1921, vol. II
MacLaurin, Hon. Sir Henry Normand, 1835–1914, vol. I
McLaurin, Engr-Rear-Adm. John, died 1955, vol. V
Maclaurin, Richard Cockburn, 1870–1920, vol. II
Maclaverty, Edward Hyde East, 1847–1922, vol. II
Maclay, 1st Baron, 1857–1951, vol. V

Maclay, 2nd Baron, 1899–1969, vol. VI
Maclay, Hon. Walter Symington, 1901–1964, vol. VI
Maclean, Baron (Life Peer); Charles Hector Fitzroy Maclean, 1916–1990, vol. VIII
McLean, Major Sir Alan, 1875–1959, vol. V
Maclean, Alexander, 1867–1940, vol. III
Maclean, Surg. Rear-Adm. Alexander, 1868–1945, vol. IV
Maclean, Sir Alexander, 1872–1948, vol. IV
Maclean of Ardgour, Alexander John Hew, 1880–1930, vol. III
Maclean, Rev. Alexander Miller, 1865–1925, vol. II
Maclean, Alexander Morvaren, 1872–1936, vol. III
Maclean, Alick; see Maclean, Alexander Morvaren.
Maclean, Alistair, 1922–1987, vol. VIII
M'Lean, Hon. Allan, 1840–1911, vol. I
Maclean, Allan, 1858–1918, vol. II
McLean, Andrew Sinclair, 1919–1981, vol. VIII
MacLean, Angus, 1863–1948, vol. IV
MacLean, Hon. Angus; see MacLean, Hon. J. A.
Maclean, Angus Alexander, 1854–1943, vol. IV
MacLean, Col Archibald Campbell Holms, 1883–1970, vol. VI
Maclean, Most Rev. Arthur John, 1858–1943, vol. IV
McLean, Calvin Stowe, 1888–1970, vol. VI
Maclean, Catherine Macdonald, died 1960, vol. V
Maclean, Brig.-Gen. Charles Alexander Hugh, 1874–1947, vol. IV
MacLean, Col Charles Allan, 1892–1978, vol. VII
Maclean, Charles Donald, 1843–1916, vol. II
McLean, Lt-Col Charles Herbert, 1877–1940, vol. III(A), vol. IV
Maclean, Maj.-Gen. Charles Smith, 1836–1921, vol. II
McLean, Col Charles Wesley Weldon, 1882–1962, vol. VI
Maclean, Vice-Adm. Colin Kenneth, died 1935, vol. III
MacLean, Air Vice-Marshal Cuthbert Trelawder, 1886–1969, vol. VI
M'Lean, Donald, died 1915, vol. I
Maclean, Rt Hon. Sir Donald, 1864–1932, vol. III
Maclean, Captain Donald Charles Hugh, 1875–1909, vol. I
MacLean, Captain Donald Murdo, 1899–1991, vol. IX
Maclean, Sir Douglas; see Maclean, Sir R. D. D.
McLean, Edward B., died 1941, vol. IV
Maclean, Sir Ewen John, died 1953, vol. V
Maclean, Sir Fitzroy Donald, 10th Bt, 1835–1936, vol. III
Maclean of Dunconnel, Sir Fitzroy Hew, 1st Bt (cr 1957), 1911–1996, vol. X
McLean, Sir Francis Charles, 1904–1998, vol. X
Maclean, Sir Francis William, 1844–1913, vol. I
Maclean, Frederick Gurr, 1848–1915, vol. I
M'Lean, Hon. Sir George, 1834–1917, vol. II
Maclean, George Edwin, 1850–1938, vol. III
Maclean, Brig. Gordon Forbes, 1897–1982, vol. VIII
Maclean, Gordon Thompson, 1884–1943, vol. IV
Maclean, Kaid, Gen. Sir Harry Aubrey deVere, 1848–1920, vol. II

Maclean, Lt-Col Henry Donald Neil, 1872–1926, vol. II
McLean, Lt-Col Henry John, 1868–1931, vol. III
MacLean, Hugh, 1879–1957, vol. V
McLean, Maj.-Gen. Hon. Hugh Havelock, 1854–1938, vol. III
Maclean, Ian Albert Druce, 1902–1986, vol. VIII
Maclean of Pennycross, Rear-Adm. Iain Gilleasbuig, 1902–1988, vol. VIII
MacLean, Ida Smedley, died 1944, vol. IV
MacLean, James A., 1868–1945, vol. IV
Maclean, James Borrowman, 1881–1940, vol. III
Maclean, James Mackenzie, 1835–1906, vol. I
McLean, Col James Reynolds, 1872–1921, vol. II
McLean, John, 1893–1978, vol. VII
MacLean, John Alexander, 1903–1992, vol. IX
McLean, John Alexander Lowry, 1921–1997, vol. X
MacLean, Hon. (John) Angus, 1914–2000, vol. X
Maclean, Lt-Col John Bayne, 1862–1950, vol. IV
Maclean, John Cassilis Birkmyre, 1849–1925, vol. II
MacLean, Hon. John Duncan, 1873–1948, vol. IV
Maclean, Col John Francis, 1901–1986, vol. VIII
Maclean, John Kennedy, 1874–1933, vol. III
McLean, John Reid, 1856–1935, vol. III
McLean, John Roll, 1848–1916, vol. II
McLean, Lt-Gen. Sir Kenneth Graeme, 1896–1987, vol. VIII
Maclean, Lachlan Frederick Copeland, 1885–1957, vol. V
Maclean, Magnus, died 1937, vol. III
McLean, Mary, died 1949, vol. IV
Maclean, Neil, died 1953, vol. V
MacLean, Neil Adam, 1885–1944, vol. IV
McLean, Lt-Col Neil Loudon Desmond, 1918–1986, vol. VIII
M'Lean, Norman, 1865–1947, vol. IV
Maclean, Very Rev. Norman, 1869–1952, vol. V
McLean, Sir Robert, 1884–1964, vol. VI
Maclean, Sir Robert Alexander, 1908–1999, vol. X
McLean, Robert Colquhoun, 1890–1981, vol. VIII
Maclean, Sir (Robert Donald) Douglas, 1852–1929, vol. III
M'Lean, Simon James, 1871–1946, vol. IV
Maclean, William Campbell, died 1898, vol. I
Maclean, William Findlay, 1854–1929, vol. III
McLean, Sir William Hannah, 1877–1967, vol. VI
McLean, Rev. Col William Richard James, 1858–1932, vol. III
McLean, Sir William Ross, 1901–1965, vol. VI
Macleane, Rev. Douglas, 1856–1925, vol. II
Maclear, Rev. George Frederick, 1833–1902, vol. I
Maclear, Lt-Col Harry, 1872–1916, vol. II
Maclear, Adm. John Pearse, 1838–1907, vol. I
McLearn, Sir William, 1837–1918, vol. II
McLeavy, Baron (Life Peer); Frank McLeavy, 1899–1976, vol. VII
Macleay, Col Alexander Caldcleugh, 1843–1907, vol. I
McLeay, Hon. George, 1892–1955, vol. V
Macleay, Sir (James William) Ronald, 1870–1943, vol. IV
McLeay, Hon. Sir John, 1893–1982, vol. VIII
Macleay, John Thomson, 1870–1955, vol. V
MacLeay, Oswell Searight, 1905–1982, vol. VIII

Macleay, Sir Ronald; see Macleay, Sir J. W. R.
MacLehose of Beoch, Baron (Life Peer); Crawford Murray MacLehose, 1917–2000, vol. X
Maclehose, James, 1857–1943, vol. IV
Maclehose, Norman M., 1859–1931, vol. III
MacLeish, Archibald, 1892–1982, vol. VIII
McLeish, Donald Alexander Stewart, 1893–1958, vol. V(A)
M'Leish, Col Duncan, 1851–1920, vol. II
M'Lellan, Alexander Matheson, 1872–1957, vol. V
MacLellan, Alexander Stephen, 1886–1966, vol. VI
M'Lellan, C. M. S., 1865–1916, vol. II
McLellan, David, 1904–1982, vol. VIII
McLellan, Eric Burns, 1918–1992, vol. IX
MacLellan, George Douglas Stephen, 1922–1999, vol. X
MacLellan, Sir (George) Robin (Perronet), 1915–1991, vol. IX
McLellan, James Kidd, 1914–1981, vol. VIII
MacLellan, Sir Robin; see MacLellan, Sir G. R. P.
McLellan, Lt-Col William, died 1934, vol. III
MacLellan, William Turner, died 1945, vol. IV
MacLennan, Maj.-Gen. Alastair, 1912–2000, vol. X
MacLennan, Alexander, 1872–1953, vol. V
M'Lennan, Lt-Col Bartlett, 1868–1918, vol. II
Maclennan, Farquhar Stuart, died 1925, vol. II
MacLennan, Sir Hector, 1905–1978, vol. VII
MacLennan, Hugh; see McLennan, J. H.
Maclennan, Sir Ian Morrison Ross, 1909–1986, vol. VIII
McLennan, Sir Ian Munro, 1909–1998, vol. X
M'Lennan, Sir John Cunningham, 1867–1935, vol. III
M'Lennan, John Ferguson, 1855–1917, vol. II
MacLennan, (John) Hugh, 1907–1990, vol. VIII
McLennan, John Stewart, 1853–1939, vol. III
Maclennan, Kenneth, 1872–1952, vol. V
MacLennan, Sir Robert Laing, 1888–1977, vol. VII
MacLennan of MacLennan, Ronald George, 1925–1989, vol. VIII
M'Lennan, William, 1856–1904, vol. I
Macleod of Borve, Baroness (Life Peer); Evelyn Hester Macleod, 1915–1999, vol. X
MacLeod of Fuinary, Baron (Life Peer); Very Rev. George Fielden MacLeod, Bt, 1895–1991, vol. IX
McLeod, Sir Alan Cumbrae Rose, 1904–1981, vol. VIII
MacLeod, Alexander Cameron, 1899–1971, vol. VII
McLeod, Hon. Alexander Donald, 1872–1938, vol. III
Macleod, Allan, 1887–1955, vol. V
Macleod, Adm. Angus, 1847–1920, vol. II
MacLeod, Angus, 1906–1991, vol. IX
MacLeod, Aubrey Seymour H.; see Halford-MacLeod.
MacLeod, Cameron; see MacLeod, A. C.
McLeod, Sir Charles Campbell, 1st Bt (cr 1925), 1858–1936, vol. III
Macleod, Maj.-Gen. Charles William, 1881–1944, vol. IV
M'Leod, Clement Henry, died 1917, vol. II
Macleod, Very Rev. Donald, died 1916, vol. II
M'Leod, Hon. Donald, died 1918, vol. II, vol. III

MacLeod, Air Vice-Marshal Donald Francis Graham, 1917–1993, vol. IX
M'Leod, Gen. Sir Donald James Sim, 1845–1922, vol. II
McLeod, Lt-Gen. Sir (Donald) Kenneth, 1885–1958, vol. V
MacLeod, Douglas Hamilton, 1901–1970, vol. VI
MacLeod, Duncan, 1876–1949, vol. IV
McLeod, Sir Ezekiel, 1840–1920, vol. II
Macleod, Fiona; see Sharp, William.
MacLeod of MacLeod, Dame Flora, 1878–1976, vol. VII
Macleod, Frederick Henry, died 1938, vol. III
MacLeod, Sir Frederick Larkins, 1858–1936, vol. III
McLeod, George William Buckham, 1868–1947, vol. IV
M'Leod, Hon. Harry Fulton, 1871–1920, vol. II
M'Leod, Herbert, 1841–1923, vol. II
MacLeod, Sir (Hugh) Roderick, 1929–1993, vol. IX
Macleod, Rt Hon. Iain Norman, 1913–1970, vol. VI
MacLeod, Captain Sir Ian Francis Norman, 3rd Bt (cr 1924), 1921–1944, vol. IV
Macleod, James John, 1841–1919, vol. II
MacLeod, Sir James MacIver, 1866–1944, vol. IV
McLeod, (James) Walter, 1887–1978, vol. VII
Macleod, Rev. John, 1840–1898, vol. I
Macleod, John, 1839–1927, vol. II
Macleod, John, 1891–1969, vol. VI(AII)
MacLeod, Sir John, 1913–1984, vol. VIII
Macleod, John James Rickard, 1876–1935, vol. III
MacLeod, Sir John Lorne, 1873–1946, vol. IV
MacLeod, Sir John Mackintosh, 1st Bt (cr 1924), 1857–1934, vol. III
MacLeod, Sir (John Mackintosh) Norman, 2nd Bt (cr 1924), 1891–1939, vol. III
MacLeod, John MacLeod Hendrie, 1870–1954, vol. V
MacLeod, Col John Norman, 1865–1932, vol. III
Macleod, Joseph Todd Gordon, 1903–1984, vol. VIII
Macleod, Col Kenneth, 1840–1922, vol. II
McLeod, Lt-Gen. Sir Kenneth; see McLeod, Lt-Gen. Sir D. K.
Macleod, Lewis Rose, 1875–1941, vol. IV
MacLeod, Maj.-Gen. Malcolm Neynoe, 1882–1969, vol. VI
MacLeod, Maj.-Gen. Minden Whyte-Melville, 1896–1981, vol. VIII
McLeod, Sir Murdoch Campbell, 2nd Bt (cr 1925), 1893–1950, vol. IV
Macleod, Rev. Norman, 1838–1911, vol. I
Macleod, Lt-Col Norman, 1872–1960, vol. V
MacLeod, Sir Norman; see MacLeod, Sir J. M. N.
Macleod, Sir Norman Cranstoun, 1866–1945, vol. IV
M'Leod, Norman F., 1856–1921, vol. II
Macleod of Macleod, Norman Magnus, 1839–1929, vol. III
Macleod of Macleod, Sir Reginald, 1847–1935, vol. III
McLeod, Lt-Col Reginald George M'Queen, 1859–1910, vol. I
Macleod, Robert Duncan, died 1973, vol. VII
Macleod, Col Robert Lockhart Ross, 1863–1943, vol. IV

MacLeod, Sir Roderick; see MacLeod, Sir H. R.
Macleod, Rev. Roderick Charles, 1852–1934, vol. III
Macleod, Col Roderick William, 1851–1932, vol. III
McLeod, Gen. Sir Roderick William, 1905–1980, vol. VII
Macleod, Roderick Willoughby, 1858–1931, vol. III
Macleod, Simon John Fraser, 1857–1938, vol. III
McLeod, Walter; see McLeod, J. W.
Macleod, Inspector-Gen. William, died 1904, vol. I
Macleod, Very Rev. William Arthur, 1867–1932, vol. III
McLeod, Brig.-Gen. William Kelty, 1862–1928, vol. II
Macleod, Captain William Simon Fraser, 1888–1940, vol. III
Macleod-Smith, Alastair Macleod, 1916–1999, vol. X
McLetchie, James Leslie, 1909–1965, vol. VI
Mac Liammóir, Micheál, 1899–1978, vol. VII
McLintock, Sir Thomson, 2nd Bt, 1905–1953, vol. V
McLintock, Sir William, 1st Bt, 1873–1947, vol. IV
McLintock, William Francis Porter, 1887–1960, vol. V
McLintock, Sir William Traven, 3rd Bt, 1931–1987, vol. VIII
Macloone, James, died 1934, vol. III
McLoughlin, Edward Patrick, died 1956, vol. V
McLoughlin, Maj.-Gen. George Somers, 1867–1943, vol. IV
McLuhan, (Herbert) Marshall, 1911–1980, vol. VII
McLuhan, Marshall; see McLuhan, H. M.
Maclure, Lt-Col Alan Francis, 1873–1929, vol. III
Maclure, Very Rev. Edward Craig, 1833–1906, vol. I
Maclure, Sir John Edward Stanley, 2nd Bt, 1869–1938, vol. III
Maclure, Sir John William, 1st Bt, 1835–1901, vol. I
Maclure, Lt-Col Sir John William Spencer, 3rd Bt, 1899–1980, vol. VII
MacLysaght, Edward Anthony, 1887–1986, vol. VIII
McMahon, Col Sir (Arthur) Henry, 1862–1949, vol. IV
McMahon, Col Bernard William Lynedoch, 1865–1928, vol. II
McMahon, Gen. Charles Alexander, 1830–1904, vol. I
Macmahon, Cortlandt, died 1954, vol. V
MacMahon, Ella, died 1956, vol. V
McMahon, Gregan, 1874–1941, vol. IV
McMahon, Lt-Col Sir Eyre, 6th Bt, 1860–1935, vol. III
McMahon, Col Sir Henry; see McMahon, Col Sir A. H.
M'Mahon, Major Sir Horace Westropp, 5th Bt, 1863–1932, vol. III
Macmahon, Hugh, 1836–1911, vol. I
MacMahon, Maj.-Gen. Hugh Francis Edward, 1880–1939, vol. III
Macmahon, Rt Hon. James, 1865–1954, vol. V
McMahon, Rt Rev. Mgr John, 1844–1932, vol. III
M'Mahon, Sir Lionel, 4th Bt, 1856–1926, vol. II

McMahon, Lt-Col Norman Reginald, 1866–1914, vol. I
McMahon, Sir Patrick; see McMahon, Sir W. P.
Macmahon, Lt-Gen. Peadar, 1893–1975, vol. VII
MacMahon, Percy Alexander, 1854–1929, vol. III
McMahon, Rt Hon. Sir William, 1908–1988, vol. VIII
McMahon, Sir (William) Patrick, 7th Bt, 1900–1977, vol. VII
M'Mahon, Sir William Samuel, 3rd Bt, 1839–1905, vol. I
Macmanaway, Rt Rev. James, died 1947, vol. IV
MacManaway, Rev. James Godfrey, 1898–1951, vol. V
McManus, Dermot Aloysius, 1944–2000, vol. X
MacManus, Emily Elvira Primrose, 1886–1978, vol. VII
MacManus, John Leslie Edward, 1920–1998, vol. X
Macmanus, Joseph Edward, died 1921, vol. II
McManus, Maurice, 1906–1982, vol. VIII
MacManus, Seumas, died 1960, vol. V
McMaster, Hon. Andrew R., 1876–1937, vol. III
Macmaster, Sir Donald, 1st Bt, 1846–1922, vol. II
McMaster, Sir Fergus, 1879–1950, vol. IV(A), vol. V
McMaster, Sir Frederick Duncan, 1873–1954, vol. V
McMaster, Gordon James, 1960–1997, vol. X
McMaster, Ian, 1898–1978, vol. VII
Macmaster, James, died 1933, vol. III
McMaster, John Bach, 1852–1932, vol. III
McMaster, Col John Maxwell, 1855–1937, vol. III
McMaster, Robert Maxwell, 1892–1936, vol. III
McMaster, Stanley Raymond, 1926–1992, vol. IX
M'Means, Lt-Col Hon. Lendrum, 1859–1941, vol. IV(A), vol. V
MacMechan, Archibald M'Kellar, 1862–1933, vol. III
McMeekan, Brig. Gilbert Reader, 1900–1982, vol. VIII
McMeekin, Lt-Gen. Sir Terence Douglas Herbert, 1918–1984, vol. VIII
McMenemey, William Henry, 1905–1977, vol. VII
MacMichael, Sir Harold Alfred, 1882–1969, vol. VI
McMichael, Sir John, 1904–1993, vol. IX
Macmichael, Neil, 1871–1949, vol. IV
MacMichael, Nicholas Hugh, 1933–1985, vol. VIII
McMichael, Robert Clark, 1878–1957, vol. V
M'Michael, Solon William, 1848–1923, vol. II
McMicking, Major Gilbert, 1862–1942, vol. IV
McMicking, Col Harry, 1867–1944, vol. IV
McMicking, Maj.-Gen. Neil, 1894–1963, vol. VI
Macmillan of Ovenden, Viscount; Maurice Victor Macmillan, 1921–1984, vol. VIII
Macmillan, Baron (Life Peer); Hugh Pattison Macmillan, 1873–1952, vol. V
McMillan, Alec, died 1919, vol. II
Macmillan, Lt-Col Alexander, 1871–1929, vol. III
Macmillan, Archibald Morven, 1880–1954, vol. V
McMillan, Rev. Charles D. H., died 1919, vol. II
Macmillan, Chrystal, died 1937, vol. III
Macmillan, Daniel, 1886–1965, vol. VI
McMillan, Sir Daniel Hunter, 1846–1933, vol. III
M'Millan, Hon. Donald, 1835–1914, vol. I
Macmillan, Rev. Donald, 1855–1927, vol. II

Macmillan, Donald, 1919–1982, vol. VIII
McMillan, Col Donald, 1906–1995, vol. IX
MacMillan, Donald Baxter, 1874–1970, vol. VI
McMillan, Duncan, 1914–1993, vol. IX
Macmillan, Very Rev. Ebenezer, 1881–1944, vol. IV
McMillan, Edwin Mattison, 1907–1991, vol. IX
MacMillan, Sir Ernest Campbell, 1893–1973, vol. VII
Macmillan, Sir Frederick, 1851–1936, vol. III
Macmillan, George A., 1855–1936, vol. III
MacMillan of MacMillan, Gen. Sir Gordon Holmes Alexander, 1897–1986, vol. VIII
MacMillan, Harvey Reginald, 1885–1976, vol. VII
Macmillan, Rev. Hugh, 1833–1903, vol. I
MacMillan, James, 1898–1985, vol. VIII
McMillan, James Athole, 1896–1977, vol. VII
Macmillan, Sir (James) Wilson, 1906–1989, vol. VIII
McMillan, John, 1873–1939, vol. III
Macmillan, Rt Rev. Mgr John, 1899–1957, vol. V
Macmillan, Rt Rev. John Victor, 1877–1956, vol. V
MacMillan, Sir Kenneth, 1929–1992, vol. IX
Macmillan, Malcolm K., 1913–1978, vol. VII
McMillan, Margaret, 1860–1931, vol. III
Macmillan, Maurice Crawford, 1853–1936, vol. III
Macmillan, Rt Hon. Maurice Victor; see Macmillan of Ovenden, Viscount.
Macmillan, Michael, 1853–1925, vol. II
Macmillan, Norman, 1892–1976, vol. VII
Macmillan, Rev. Robert Alexander Cameron, 1883–1917, vol. II
McMillan, Sir Robert Furse, 1858–1931, vol. III
McMillan, Thomas McLellan, 1919–1980, vol. VII
McMillan, W. H., died 1947, vol. IV
MacMillan, W. J. P., 1881–1957, vol. V
Macmillan, Wallace, 1913–1992, vol. IX
M'Millan, Hon. Sir William, 1850–1926, vol. II
McMillan, William, 1887–1977, vol. VIII
McMillan, William Bentley, 1871–1922, vol. II
Macmillan, William Miller, 1885–1974, vol. VII
McMillan, Sir William Northrup, 1872–1925, vol. II
Macmillan, Sir Wilson; see Macmillan, Sir J. W.
McMinnies, John Gordon, 1919–1998, vol. X
MacMonnies, Frederick William, 1863–1937, vol. III
McMordie, Julia, died 1942, vol. IV
M'Mordie, Robert James, 1849–1914, vol. I
M'Morine, Ven. John Ker, died 1912, vol. I
Macmorran, Alexander, 1852–1933, vol. III
McMorran, Donald Hanks, 1904–1965, vol. VI
McMorran, Helen Isabella, 1898–1985, vol. VIII
Macmorran, Kenneth Mead, 1883–1973, vol. VII
McMorrough Kavanagh, Col Sir Dermot, 1890–1958, vol. V
MacMullan, Charles W. Kirkpatrick, 1889–1973, vol. VII
McMullan, Henry Wallace, 1909–1988, vol. VIII
McMullan, Sir Thomas Wallace, 1864–1945, vol. IV
McMullen, Alexander Percy, 1875–1961, vol. VI
Macmullen, Gen. Sir (Cyril) Norman, 1877–1944, vol. IV
McMullen, Col Denis, 1902–1973, vol. VII
McMullen, Maj.-Gen. Sir Donald Jay, 1891–1967, vol. VI

MacMullen, Maj.-Gen. Hugh Tennent, 1892–1946, vol. IV

McMullen, Rear-Adm. Morrice Alexander, 1909–1990, vol. VIII

Macmullen, Gen. Sir Norman; see Macmullen, Gen. Sir C. N.

McMullen, Lt-Col Osmond Robert, died 1946, vol. IV

M'Mullen, William Halliburton, 1876–1958, vol. V

McMullin, Hon. Sir Alister Maxwell, 1900–1984, vol. VIII

MacMunn, Charles Alexander, 1852–1911, vol. I

MacMunn, Lt-Gen. Sir George Fletcher, 1869–1952, vol. V

McMunn, Maj.-Gen. James Robert, 1866–1945, vol. IV

MacMurchy, Helen, 1862–1953, vol. V

McMurdo, Captain Arthur Montagu, 1861–1914, vol. I

McMurray, Hon. Edward James, 1878–1969, vol. VI

McMurray, James Hamish, died 1950, vol. IV

Macmurray, John, 1891–1976, vol. VII

McMurray, Thomas Porter, 1887–1949, vol. IV

M'Murrich, James Playfair, 1859–1939, vol. III

McMurtrie, Francis Edwin, 1884–1949, vol. IV

M'Murtrie, Very Rev. John, 1831–1912, vol. I

McMurtrie, Gp Captain Richard Angus, 1909–1994, vol. IX

Macnab, Col Allan James, 1864–1947, vol. IV

Macnab of Macnab, Archibald Corrie, 1886–1970, vol. VI

McNab, Hon. Archibald Peter, 1864–1945, vol. IV

Macnab, Brig.-Gen. Colin Lawrance, 1870–1918, vol. II

Macnab, Brig. Sir Geoffrey Alex Colin, 1899–1995, vol. IX

Macnab, George Henderson, 1904–1967, vol. VI

Macnab of Barachastlain, Iain, 1890–1967, vol. VI

Macnab, Brig. John Francis, 1906–1980, vol. VII

M'Nab, Hon. Robert, 1864–1917, vol. II

Macnab, William, 1858–1941, vol. IV

McNabb, Surg.-Rear-Adm. Sir Daniel Joseph Patrick, 1862–1937, vol. III

Macnabb, Sir Donald Campbell, 1832–1913, vol. I

Macnabb, Lt-Col Donald John Campbell, 1864–1936, vol. III

MacNachtan, Col Neil Ferguson, 1850–1928, vol. II

Macnaghten, Baron (Life Peer); Edward Macnaghten, 1830–1913, vol. I

Macnaghten, Sir Antony, 10th Bt, 1899–1972, vol. VII

Macnaghten, Sir Arthur Douglas, 7th Bt, 1897–1916, vol. II

Macnaghten, Col Charles Melville, 1879–1931, vol. III

Macnaghten, Hon. Sir Edward Charles, 5th Bt, 1859–1914, vol. I

Macnaghten, Sir Edward Henry, 6th Bt, 1896–1916, vol. II

Macnaghten, Brig.-Gen. Ernest Brander, 1872–1948, vol. IV

Macnaghten, Hon. Sir Francis Alexander, 8th Bt, 1863–1951, vol. V

Macnaghten, Rt Hon. Sir Francis Edmund Workman-, 3rd Bt, 1828–1911, vol. I

Macnaghten, Hon. Sir Frederic Fergus, 9th Bt, 1867–1955, vol. V

Macnaghten, Sir Henry Pelham Wentworth, 1880–1949, vol. IV

Macnaghten, Rev. Henry Alexander, 1850–1928, vol. II

Macnaghten, Hugh Vibart, died 1929, vol. III

Macnaghten, Rt Hon. Sir Malcolm, 1869–1955, vol. V

Macnaghten, Sir Melville Leslie, 1853–1921, vol. II

Macnaghten, Robin Donnelly, 1927–1999, vol. X

Macnaghten, Steuart, 1873–1952, vol. V

Macnaghten, Terence Charles, 1872–1944, vol. IV

McNair, 1st Baron, 1885–1975, vol. VII

McNair, 2nd Baron, 1915–1989, vol. VIII

McNair, Arthur James, 1887–1964, vol. VI

McNair, Arthur Wyndham, 1872–1965, vol. VI

McNair, Sir Douglas; see McNair, Sir G. D.

M'Nair, Lt-Gen. Edward John, 1838–1921, vol. II

McNair, Captain Eric Archibald, died 1918, vol. II

McNair, Sir (George) Douglas, 1887–1967, vol. VI

McNair, Air Vice-Marshal James Jamieson, 1917–1990, vol. VIII

McNair, John, 1887–1968, vol. VI

M'Nair, Major John Frederick Adolphus, 1828–1910, vol. I

McNair, Brig. John Kirkland, 1893–1973, vol. VII

Macnair, Peter, 1868–1929, vol. III

Macnair, Sir Robert Hill, 1877–1959, vol. V

McNair, Thomas Jaffrey, 1927–1994, vol. IX

McNair, Sir William Lennox, 1892–1979, vol. VII

McNair-Wilson, Sir Michael; see McNair-Wilson, Sir R. M. C.

McNair-Wilson, Sir (Robert) Michael (Conal), 1930–1993, vol. IX

McNairn, Edward Somerville, 1907–1975, vol. VII

McNally, Most Rev. John Thomas, 1871–1952, vol. V

McNalty, Brig.-Gen. Arthur George Preston, 1871–1958, vol. V

MacNalty, Sir Arthur Salusbury, 1880–1969, vol. VI

M'Nalty, Lt-Col George William, 1837–1912, vol. I

Macnamara, Arthur, 1829–1906, vol. I

McNamara, Lt-Gen. Sir Arthur Edward, 1877–1949, vol. IV

MacNamara, Arthur James, 1885–1962, vol. VI

Macnamara, Eric Danvers, died 1934, vol. III

McNamara, Air Vice-Marshal Frank Hubert, 1894–1961, vol. VI

McNamara, George, 1881–1953, vol. V

Macnamara, Col John Robert Jermain, 1905–1944, vol. IV

McNamara, Most Rev. Kevin, 1926–1987, vol. VIII

Macnamara, N. C., died 1918, vol. II

Macnamara, Neil Cameron, 1891–1968, vol. VI

Macnamara, Rear-Adm. Sir Patrick, 1886–1957, vol. V

Macnamara, Rt Hon. Thomas James, 1861–1931, vol. III

Macnamara, Walter Henry, 1851–1920, vol. II

M'Namara, Surg.-Gen. William Henry, 1846–1915, vol. I

McNamara Ryan, Patrick John; see Ryan.

Mac-Namee, Rt Rev. James Joseph, 1876–1966, vol. VI
McNarney, Gen. Joseph Taggart, 1893–1972, vol. VII
M'Naught, William Gray, 1849–1918, vol. II
McNaught, William, 1883–1953, vol. V
McNaught, William Kirkpatrick, 1845–1919, vol. II
Macnaughtan, Sarah, *died* 1916, vol. II
Macnaughton, Allan Wight, 1859–1937, vol. III
McNaughton, Gen. Hon. Andrew George Latta, 1887–1966, vol. VI
McNaughton, Brig. Forbes Lankester, 1891–1959, vol. V
McNaughton, Sir George Matthew, 1893–1966, vol. VI
Macnaughton, Rev. John, 1858–1943, vol. IV
Macnaughton-Jones, Henry, *died* 1918, vol. II
Macnaughton-Jones, Rev. William Hudson, *died* 1941, vol. IV
Macneal, Sir Hector Murray, 1879–1966, vol. VI
McNee, Sir John William, 1887–1984, vol. VIII
MacNeece, Maj.-Gen. James Gaussen, 1856–1919, vol. II
MacNeece, William Foster; *see* Foster, Air Vice-Marshal W. F. MacN.
McNeely, Most Rev. William, 1888–1963, vol. VI
MacNeice, (Frederick) Louis, 1907–1963, vol. VI
McNeice, Rt Rev. John Frederick, *died* 1942, vol. IV
MacNeice, Louis; *see* MacNeice, F. L.
McNeice, Sir Percy; *see* McNeice, Sir T. P. F.
McNeice, Sir (Thomas) Percy (Fergus), 1901–1998, vol. X
McNeil, Anne, 1902–1984, vol. VIII
McNeil, Charles, 1881–1964, vol. VI
M'Neil, Daniel, 1853–1918, vol. II
McNeil, Rt Hon. Hector, 1907–1955, vol. V
McNeil, Sir Hector, 1904–1978, vol. VII
MacNeil, Hermon Atkins, 1866–1947, vol. IV(A)
McNeil, John Struthers, 1907–1993, vol. IX
McNeil, Kenneth Gordon, 1902–1970, vol. VI
M'Neil, Most Rev. Neil, 1851–1934, vol. III
McNeil, Engr Rear-Adm. Percival Edwin, 1883–1951, vol. V
Macneil of Barra, Robert Lister, (The Macneil of Barra), 1889–1970, vol. VI
M'Neile, Rev. Alan Hugh, 1871–1933, vol. III
McNeile, Lt-Col Cyril, 1888–1937, vol. III
McNeile, Robert Arbuthnot, 1913–1985, vol. VIII
McNeill, Maj.-Gen. Alister Argyll Campbell, 1884–1971, vol. VII
M'Neill, Brig.-Gen. Angus John, 1874–1950, vol. IV
McNeill, Sir David Bruce, 1922–1990, vol. VIII
Macneill, Eoin; *see* Macneill, John.
McNeill, Florence Marian, 1885–1973, vol. VII
McNeill, (Gordon) Keith, 1953–1998, vol. X
McNeill, Sir Hector, 1892–1952, vol. V
McNeill, James, 1869–1938, vol. III
McNeill, Sir James Charles, 1916–1987, vol. VIII
MacNeill, Maj.-Gen. James Graham Robert Douglas, 1842–1904, vol. I
McNeill, Sir James McFadyen, 1892–1964, vol. VI
M'Neill, Rev. John, 1854–1933, vol. III
Macneill, Rev. John, 1874–1937, vol. III
Macneill, John, (Eoin Macneill), 1867–1945, vol. IV

M'Neill, Maj.-Gen. Sir John Carstairs, 1831–1904, vol. I
Macneill, John Gordon Swift, 1849–1926, vol. II
McNeill, Maj.-Gen. John Malcolm, 1909–1996, vol. X
McNeill, Keith; *see* McNeill, G. K.
M'Neill, Captain Malcolm, 1866–1917, vol. II
McNeill, Sir Malcolm, 1839–1919, vol. II
Macneill, Murray, 1877–1951, vol. V
McNeill, Robert Norman, *died* 1956, vol. V
McNeill-Moss, Major Geoffrey, *died* 1954, vol. V
McNerney, Joshua William, 1872–1944, vol. IV
McNess, Sir Charles, 1853–1938, vol. III
Macnicol, Nicol, 1870–1952, vol. V
McNicoll, Vice-Adm. Sir Alan Wedel Ramsay, 1908–1987, vol. VIII
McNicoll, Brig.-Gen. Sir Walter Ramsay, 1877–1947, vol. IV
McNish, Col George, 1866–1943, vol. IV
McNulty, Rev. C. T. Bernard, 1875–1939, vol. III
McNulty, Rt Rev. John, 1879–1943, vol. IV
Macnutt, Ernest Augustus, 1876–1955, vol. V
Macnutt, Rev. Canon Frederick Brodie, 1873–1949, vol. IV
McNutt, Hon. Peter, 1834–1919, vol. II
MacNutt, Hon. Thomas, 1850–1927, vol. II
Maconachie, Sir Richard Roy, 1885–1962, vol. VI
Maconchy, Dame Elizabeth, (Dame Elizabeth LeFanu), 1907–1994, vol. IX
Maconchy, Brig.-Gen. Ernest William Stuart King, 1860–1945, vol. IV
Maconchy, Captain Frederick Campbell, 1868–1943, vol. IV
Maconochie, Archibald White, 1855–1926, vol. II
Maconochie, Charles Cornelius, 1852–1930, vol. III
Maconochie, Sir Evan, 1868–1927, vol. II
Maconochie, Sir Robert Henry, 1883–1962, vol. VI
MacOrlan, Pierre, 1882–1970, vol. VI
Macoun, James Melville, 1862–1920, vol. II
Macoun, John, 1831–1921, vol. II
Macoun, Michael John, 1914–1997, vol. X
McOwan, George, 1894–1972, vol. VII
M'Owan, Islay, 1871–1948, vol. IV
MacOwan, Michael Charles Henry, 1906–1980, vol. VII
M'Peake, James Young, 1868–1924, vol. II
McPetrie, Sir James Carnegie, 1911–1991, vol. IX
McPetrie, James Stuart, 1902–1990, vol. VIII
Macphail, Alexander, 1872–1938, vol. III
Macphail, Col Alexander, 1870–1949, vol. IV
Macphail, Sir Andrew, 1864–1938, vol. III
Macphail, Rev. Earle Monteith, 1861–1937, vol. III
Macphail, James Robert Nicolson, *died* 1933, vol. III
McPhail, Walter, *died* 1941, vol. IV
Macphail, Rev. William Merry, 1857–1916, vol. II
M'Phedran, Alexander, *died* 1934, vol. III
McPhee, Hon. Sir John Cameron, 1878–1952, vol. V
Macpherson of Drumochter, 1st Baron, 1888–1965, vol. VI
Macpherson, Alan, 1857–1930, vol. III
McPherson, Brig. Alan Bruce, 1887–1978, vol. VII
Macpherson, Brig. Alan David, (Cluny Macpherson), 1887–1969, vol. VI

Macpherson, Albert Cameron, (Cluny Macpherson), 1854–1932, vol. III
Macpherson, Alexander Calderwood, 1939–1999, vol. X
Macpherson, Brig.-Gen. Alexander Duncan, 1877–1944, vol. IV
Macpherson of Pitmain, Lt-Col Alexander Kilgour, 1888–1974, vol. VII
Macpherson, Lt-Col Archibald Duncan, 1872–1928, vol. II
Macpherson, Sir Arthur George, 1828–1921, vol. II
Macpherson, Arthur George Holdsworth, 1873–1942, vol. IV
Macpherson, Arthur Holte, 1867–1953, vol. V
Macpherson, Hon. Campbell Leonard, 1907–1973, vol. VII
Macpherson, Charles, 1870–1927, vol. II
Macpherson, Charles Gordon Welland, 1846–1910, vol. I
McPherson, Sir Clive, 1884–1958, vol. V
Macpherson, Lt-Col Cluny, 1879–1966, vol. VI
MacPherson, Rt Rev. Colin, 1917–1990, vol. VIII
Macpherson, Colin, 1927–1988, vol. VIII
Macpherson, Colin Francis, 1884–1970, vol. VI
McPherson, Col David William, 1869–1923, vol. II
MacPherson, Donald, 1894–1989, vol. VIII
McPherson, Donald George, 1914–1973, vol. VII
Macpherson, Sir Duncan James, 1855–1936, vol. III
Macpherson, Ewan Francis, died 1941, vol. IV
Macpherson, Ewen, 1872–1962, vol. VI
McPherson, Ewen Alexander, 1879–1954, vol. V
Macpherson, Rev. Ewen George Fitzroy, 1863–1926, vol. II
Macpherson, Brig.-Gen. Ewen Henry Davidson, (Cluny Macpherson), 1836–1900, vol. I
Macpherson, Fiona Mary, 1940–2000, vol. X
Macpherson, George, 1851–1924, vol. II
Macpherson, George Philip Stewart, 1903–1981, vol. VIII
Macpherson, Hector, died 1924, vol. II
Macpherson, Rev. Hector, 1888–1956, vol. V
McPherson, Henry Alexander, 1855–1939, vol. III
M'Pherson, Sir Hugh, 1870–1960, vol. V, vol. VI
Macpherson, Ian, 1936–1994, vol. IX
Macpherson, Lt-Col James, 1876–1938, vol. III
McPherson, Bt Col James, 1876–1963, vol. VI
Macpherson, James, 1911–1982, vol. VIII
Macpherson, James Simpson, 1863–1935, vol. III
Macpherson, Sir John, 1857–1942, vol. IV
Macpherson, Sir John Molesworth, 1853–1914, vol. I
Macpherson, Sir John Stuart, 1898–1971, vol. VII
Macpherson, Sir Keith Duncan, 1920–1993, vol. IX
Macpherson, Rear-Adm. Kenneth Douglas Worsley, 1883–1962, vol. VI
MacPherson, Malcolm, 1904–1971, vol. VII
MacPherson, Major Hon. Murdoch Alexander, 1891–1966, vol. VI
Macpherson, Sir Norman Macgregor, died 1947, vol. IV
Macpherson, Roderick Ewen, 1916–2000, vol. X
Macpherson, Stewart, died 1941, vol. IV
Macpherson, Sir Stewart; see Macpherson, Sir T. S.
MacPherson, Stewart Myles, 1908–1995, vol. IX
McPherson, Sir Thomas, died 1947, vol. IV

Macpherson, Sir (Thomas) Stewart, 1876–1949, vol. IV
Macpherson, Rev. Thomas William, 1863–1936, vol. III
Macpherson, Sir William, 1836–1909, vol. I
Macpherson, William Charles, 1855–1936, vol. III
Macpherson, Maj.-Gen. Sir William Grant, 1858–1927, vol. II
McPherson, Hon. Sir William Murray, 1865–1932, vol. III
Macpherson, Very Rev. William Stuart, 1901–1978, vol. VII
Macpherson-Grant, Sir Ewan George, 6th Bt, 1907–1983, vol. VIII
Macpherson-Grant, Sir George, 5th Bt, 1890–1951, vol. V
Macpherson-Grant, Captain George Bertram, died 1932, vol. III
Macpherson-Grant, Sir John, 4th Bt, 1863–1914, vol. I
McPhillips, Captain Hon. Albert Edward, 1861–1938, vol. III
McQuade, John, 1912–1984, vol. VIII
McQuaid, Most Rev. John Charles, 1895–1973, vol. VII
Macquaker, Sir Thomas, 1851–1938, vol. III
MacQuarrie, Josiah H., 1897–1971, vol. VII
McQuarrie, William Garland, 1876–1943, vol. IV
Macqueen, Angus, 1910–1995, vol. IX
Macqueen, James, 1853–1936, vol. III
MacQueen, Maj.-Gen. John Henry, 1893–1980, vol. VII
M'Queen, Lt-Gen. Sir John Withers, 1836–1909, vol. I
McQueen, Maj.-Gen. Keith John, 1923–2000, vol. X
Macqueen-Pope, Walter James, 1888–1960, vol. V
McQuesten, Hon. Thomas Baker, 1882–1948, vol. IV
M'Quhae, Captain John Mackenzie, 1847–1901, vol. I
McQuibban, Lewis, 1866–1944, vol. IV
Macquisten, Frederick Alexander, 1870–1940, vol. III
MacQuitty, James Lloyd, 1912–1999, vol. X
Macquoid, Brig.-Gen. Charles Edward Every Francis Kirwan, 1869–1945, vol. IV
Macquoid, Gilbert Samuel, 1854–1940, vol. III
Macquoid, Katharine Sarah, 1824–1917, vol. II
Macquoid, Percy, 1852–1925, vol. II
Macquoid, Thomas Robert, 1820–1912, vol. I
Macrae, Maj.-Gen. Albert Edward, 1886–1958, vol. V
McRae, Maj.-Gen. Hon. Alexander Duncan, 1874–1946, vol. IV
Macrae, Col Alexander William, 1858–1920, vol. II
Macrae, Angus, 1893–1975, vol. VII
Macrae, Charles Colin, 1843–1922, vol. II
Macrae, Christopher, 1910–1990, vol. VIII
Macrae, Sir Colin George, 1844–1925, vol. II
MacRae of Feoirlinn, Col Sir Colin William, 1869–1952, vol. V
MacRae, Donald Gunn, 1921–1997, vol. X
MacRae, Donald Mackenzie, 1869–1955, vol. V
McRae, Col Henry Napier, 1851–1915, vol. I
Macrae, Herbert Alexander, 1886–1967, vol. VI

535

Macrae, Hugh, 1880–1965, vol. VI
Macrae, Maj.-Gen. Ian Macpherson, 1882–1956, vol. V
Macrae, Col John Cecil, 1881–1940, vol. III
MacRae, Very Rev. John Eric, 1870–1947, vol. IV
Macrae, Col Sir Robert Andrew Alexander Scarth, 1915–1999, vol. X
Macrae, Robert Scarth Farquhar, 1877–1926, vol. II
Macrae, Col Roderick, 1850–1915, vol. I
Macrae, Russell Duncan, 1888–1956, vol. V
McRae, William, 1878–1952, vol. V
MacRae-Gilstrap, Lt-Col John, 1861–1937, vol. III
Macran, Henry Stewart, died 1937, vol. III
Macray, Rev. William Dunn, 1826–1916, vol. II
McRea, Sir Charles James Hugh, 1874–1951, vol. V
Macready, Gen. Rt Hon. Sir (Cecil Frederick) Nevil, 1st Bt, 1862–1946, vol. IV
Macready, Lt-Gen. Sir Gordon Nevil, 2nd Bt, 1891–1956, vol. V
Macready, Brig. John, 1887–1957, vol. V
Macready, Gen. Rt Hon. Sir Nevil; see Macready, Gen. Rt Hon. Sir C. F. N.
MacRedmond, Rt Rev. Thomas, 1838–1904, vol. I
MacRitchie, Farquhar, 1902–1988, vol. VIII
McRobert, Brig. Leslie Harrison, 1898–1981, vol. VIII
MacRitchie, David, 1851–1925, vol. II
MacRobert, Sir Alasdair Workman, 2nd Bt, 1912–1938, vol. III
M'Robert, Sir Alexander, 1st Bt, 1854–1922, vol. II
MacRobert, Rt Hon. Alexander Munro, 1873–1930, vol. III
McRobert, Sir George Reid, 1895–1976, vol. VII
MacRobert, Sir Iain Workman, 4th Bt, 1917–1941, vol. IV
MacRobert, Norman Murie, 1899–1972, vol. VII
MacRobert, Rachel W., (Lady MacRobert), died 1954, vol. V
MacRobert, Sir Roderic Alan, 3rd Bt, 1915–1941, vol. IV
MacRobert, Thomas Murray, 1884–1962, vol. VI
Macrorie, Vice-Adm. Arthur Kenneth, 1874–1947, vol. IV
Macrorie, Rt Rev. William Kenneth, 1831–1905, vol. I
Macrory, Edmund, died 1904, vol. I
MacRory, His Eminence Cardinal Joseph, 1861–1945, vol. IV
Macrory, Sir Patrick Arthur, 1911–1993, vol. IX
Macrossan, Hugh Denis, 1881–1940, vol. III
Macrossan, Hon. Neal William, 1889–1955, vol. V
McShane, John J., 1882–1972, vol. VII
McSheehy, Maj.-Gen. Oswald William, 1884–1975, vol. VII
Mac-Sherry, Most Rev. Hugh, 1852–1940, vol. III
McShine, Hon. Sir Arthur Hugh, 1906–1983, vol. IX(AI)
McSparran, James, 1892–1970, vol. VI
MacSweeney, Rev. Patrick M., 1873–1935, vol. III
McSweeny, George, 1865–1923, vol. II, vol. III
McSwiney, Bryan Austin, 1894–1947, vol. IV
McSwiney, Col Edward Frederick Henry, 1858–1907, vol. I
McSwiney, Col Herbert Frederick Cyril, 1886–1963, vol. VI

MacSwiney, Terrence Joseph, 1880–1920, vol. II
MacTaggart, Sir Andrew McCormick, 1888–1978, vol. VII
Mactaggart, Col Charles, 1861–1930, vol. III
Mactaggart, Sir Ian Auld, 3rd Bt, 1923–1987, vol. VIII
Mactaggart, Sir John Auld, 1st Bt, 1867–1956, vol. V
Mactaggart, Sir John Auld, 2nd Bt, 1898–1960, vol. V
M'Taggart, John M'Taggart Ellis, 1866–1925, vol. II
McTaggart, Lt-Col Maxwell Fielding, 1874–1936, vol. III
McTaggart, Robert, 1945–1989, vol. VIII
McTaggart, Captain W. B., died 1919, vol. II
M'Taggart, William, 1835–1910, vol. I
MacTaggart, Sir William, 1903–1981, vol. VIII
MacTaggart-Stewart, Sir Edward Orde; see Stewart.
MacTier, Sir (Reginald) Stewart, 1905–1984, vol. VIII
MacTier, Sir Stewart; see MacTier, Sir R. S.
McTiernan, Rt Hon. Sir Edward Aloysius, 1892–1990, vol. VIII
M'Turk, Michael, 1843–1915, vol. I
M'Vail, Sir David Caldwell, 1845–1917, vol. II
McVail, John Christie, 1849–1926, vol. II
Macveagh, Jeremiah, 1870–1932, vol. III
M'Vean, Col Donald Archibald Dugald, 1870–1937, vol. III
McVeigh, Rt Hon. Sir Herbert Andrew, 1908–1977, vol. VII
McVey, Arthur Michael, 1879–1964, vol. VI
McVey, Sir Daniel, 1892–1972, vol. VII
MacVicar, Hon. John, 1859–1928, vol. II, vol. III
M'Vicker, Sir Robert, 1822–1897, vol. I
McVie, John, 1888–1967, vol. VI
M'Vittie, Surg.-Gen. Charles Edwin, died 1916, vol. II
McVittie, Lt-Col Charles Edwin, 1870–1933, vol. III
McVittie, Maj.-Gen. Charles Harold, 1908–1988, vol. VIII
McVittie, George Cunliffe, 1904–1988, vol. VIII
McVittie, Col Robert Henry, 1872–1949, vol. IV
McVittie, Wilfrid Wolters, 1906–1980, vol. VII
Macwatt, Maj.-Gen. Sir Charles; see Macwatt, Maj.-Gen. Sir R. C.
MacWatt, Hay, 1855–1920, vol. II
Macwatt, John, 1857–1938, vol. III
Macwatt, Maj.-Gen. Sir (Robert) Charles, 1865–1945, vol. IV
McWatters, Sir Arthur Cecil, 1880–1965, vol. VI
McWeeney, Edmond J., 1864–1925, vol. II, vol. III
McWeeney, Henry Charles, 1867–1935, vol. III
McWhae, Brig. Douglas Murray, 1884–1969, vol. VI
M'Whae, Hon. Sir John, 1858–1927, vol. II
McWhan, John, 1885–1943, vol. IV
McWhinnie, Donald, 1920–1987, vol. VIII
McWhinnie, Hugh, died 1923, vol. II
McWhirter, (Alan) Ross, 1925–1975, vol. VII
Macwhirter, Clara Elizabeth Littlewort, died 1971, vol. VII
MacWhirter, John, 1839–1911, vol. I
McWhirter, Robert, 1904–1994, vol. IX

McWhirter, Ross; see McWhirter, A. R.
McWhirter, William Allan, 1888–1955, vol. V
MacWhite, Michael, 1883–1958, vol. V
M'William, Andrew, died 1922, vol. II
McWilliam, Edward; see McWilliam, F. E.
McWilliam, (Frederick) Edward, 1909–1992, vol. IX
McWilliam, Sir John, 1910–1974, vol. VII
MacWilliam, John Alexander, 1857–1937, vol. III
McWilliam, William Nicholson, 1897–1987, vol. VIII
Macy, George, 1900–1956, vol. V
Madan, Falconer, 1851–1935, vol. III
Madan, Rev. Nigel, 1840–1915, vol. I
Madariaga, Don Salvador de, 1886–1978, vol. VII
Maddan, James Gracie, 1873–1966, vol. VI
Maddan, Martin, 1920–1973, vol. VII
Madden, Adm. Sir Alexander Cumming Gordon, 1895–1964, vol. VI
Madden, Archibald Maclean, 1864–1928, vol. II
Madden, Charles Dodgson, 1833–1910, vol. I
Madden, Admiral of the Fleet Sir Charles Edward, 1st Bt, 1862–1935, vol. III
Madden, Rear-Adm. Colin Duncan, 1915–2000, vol. X
Madden, Rt Hon. Dodgson Hamilton, 1840–1928, vol. II
Madden, Hon. Sir Frank, 1847–1921, vol. II
Madden, Frank Cole, 1873–1929, vol. III
Madden, Frederic William, 1839–1904, vol. I
Madden, Lt-Col George Colquhoun, 1856–1912, vol. I
Madden, Hon. Sir John, 1844–1918, vol. II
Madden, Lt-Col John Clements Waterhouse, 1870–1935, vol. III
Madden, Samuel Fitzgerald, 1878–1934, vol. III
Madden, Ven. T. J., 1853–1915, vol. I
Madden, Thomas More, 1844–1902, vol. I
Madden, Hon. Walter, 1848–1925, vol. II
Madden, William Thomas, 1877–1967, vol. VI
Madden, Wyndham D'Arcy, 1885–1968, vol. VI
Maddex, Sir George Henry, 1895–1982, vol. VIII
Maddick, Edmund Distin, died 1939, vol. III
Maddick, George John, 1849–1942, vol. IV
Maddison, Rev. Arthur Roland, 1843–1912, vol. I
Maddison, Fred, 1856–1937, vol. III
Maddison, Vincent Albert, 1915–1998, vol. X
Maddison, Rev. William, 1853–1920, vol. II
Maddock, Rt Rev. David Rokeby, 1915–1984, vol. VIII
Maddock, Lt-Col Edward Cecil Gordon, 1876–1952, vol. V
Maddock, Sir Ieuan, 1917–1988, vol. VIII
Maddock, Sir Simon, 1869–1927, vol. II
Maddocks, George, 1896–1980, vol. VII
Maddocks, Sir Henry, 1871–1931, vol. III
Maddocks, Henry Hollingdrake, 1898–1969, vol. VI
Maddocks, William Henry, 1921–1992, vol. IX
Maddox, Ernest Edmund, 1860–1933, vol. III
Maddox, Sir (John) Kempson, 1901–1990, vol. VIII
Maddox, Sir Kempson; see Maddox, Sir J. K.
Maddox, Lt-Col Ralph Henry, 1864–1935, vol. III
Maddox, Samuel, 1930–1979, vol. VII
Maddox, Stuart Lockwood, 1866–1942, vol. IV
Maddrell, Rev. Thomas Fisher, 1861–1932, vol. III
Maddy, Rev. H. W., 1829–1909, vol. I

Madeley, Earl of; Richard George Archibald John Lucien Hungerford Crew-Milnes, 1911–1922, vol. II
Maden, Henry, 1892–1960, vol. V
Maden, Sir John Henry, 1862–1920, vol. II
Madgavkar, Sir Govind Dinanath, 1871–1948, vol. IV
Madge, Charles Henry, 1912–1996, vol. X
Madge, Rev. Francis Thomas, 1849–1933, vol. III
Madge, Captain Sir Frank William, 2nd Bt, 1897–1962, vol. VI
Madge, Sidney Joseph, 1874–1961, vol. VI
Madge, Sir William Thomas, 1st Bt, 1845–1927, vol. II
Madgwick, Sir Robert Bowden, 1905–1979, vol. VII (AII)
Madhava, Rae, V. P., died 1934, vol. III(A), vol. IV
Madigan, Cecil Thomas, 1889–1947, vol. IV
Madigan, Sir Russel Tullie, 1920–1999, vol. X
Madill, Surg. Rear-Adm. Thomas, 1895–1962, vol. VI
Madoc, Lt-Col Henry William, died 1937, vol. III
Madoc, Maj.-Gen. Reginald William, 1907–1986, vol. VIII
Madocks, Brig.-Gen. William Robarts Napier, 1871–1946, vol. IV
Madrid, Duke of; see Carlos, Don.
Madsen, Sir John Percival Vissing, 1879–1969, vol. VI
Maegraith, Brian Gilmore, 1907–1989, vol. VIII
Maelor, Baron (Life Peer), Thomas William Jones, 1898–1984, vol. VIII
Maenan, 1st Baron, 1854–1951, vol. V
Maeterlinck, Count Maurice Polydore Marie Bernard, 1862–1949, vol. IV
Maflin, Major George Hamilton, vol. II
Magan, Lt-Col Arthur Tilson Shaen, 1880–1965, vol. VI
Magarey, Sir (James) Rupert, 1914–1990, vol. VIII
Magarey, Sir Rupert; see Magarey, Sir J. R.
Magauran, Wilfrid Henry Bertram, 1898–1964, vol. VI
Magee, Allan Angus, 1881–1961, vol. VI
Magee, Sir Cuthbert Gaulter, died 1963, vol. VI
Magee, Hon. James, born 1846, vol. III
Magee, Reginald Arthur Edward, 1914–1989, vol. VIII
Mageean, Most Rev. Daniel, 1882–1962, vol. VI
Magenis, Maj.-Gen. Henry Cole, 1838–1906, vol. I
Magennis, Rt Rev. Edward, died 1906, vol. I
Magennis, Edward, died 1938, vol. III
Magennis, William, 1869–1946, vol. IV
Mager, Sydney, 1877–1952, vol. V
Maggs, Joseph Herbert, 1875–1964, vol. VI
Magheramorne, 2nd Baron, 1861–1903, vol. I
Magheramorne, 3rd Baron, 1863–1946, vol. IV
Magheramorne, 4th Baron, 1865–1957, vol. V
Magian, Anthony John Capper, 1878–1956, vol. V
Magill, Andrew Philip, died 1941, vol. IV
Magill, Air Vice-Marshal Graham Reese, 1915–1998, vol. X
Magill, Sir Ivan Whiteside, 1888–1986, vol. VIII
Magill, Col Sir James, 1850–1936, vol. III
Magill, Walter Alexander, 1879–1950, vol. IV

Maginess, Rt Hon. William Brian, 1901–1967, vol. VI
Maginness, Edmund John, 1857–1938, vol. III
Maginness, Sir Greville Simpson, 1888–1961, vol. VI
Maglione, His Eminence Cardinal Luigi, 1877–1944, vol. IV
Magnani, Anna, 1918–1973, vol. VII
Magnay, Brig. Arthur Douglas, 1893–1964, vol. VI
Magnay, Major Sir Christopher Boyd William, 3rd Bt, 1884–1960, vol. V
Magnay, Harold Swindale, 1904–1971, vol. VII
Magnay, Thomas, 1876–1949, vol. IV
Magnay, Sir William, 2nd Bt, 1855–1917, vol. II
Magner, Jeremiah John, 1891–1973, vol. VII
Magnes, Judah Leon, 1877–1948, vol. IV
Magniac, Brig.-Gen. Sir Charles Lane, 1873–1953, vol. V
Magniac, Major Hubert, died 1909, vol. I
Magniac, Oswald Cecil, died 1939, vol. III
Magniac, Rear-Adm. Vernon St Clair Lane, 1908–1994, vol. IX
Magnus, Henry Adolph, 1909–1967, vol. VI
Magnus, Hilary Barrow, 1909–1987, vol. VIII
Magnus, Katie, (Lady Magnus), 1844–1924, vol. II
Magnus, Laurie, 1872–1933, vol. V
Magnus, Sir Philip, 1st Bt, 1842–1933, vol. III
Magnus, Samuel Woolf, 1910–1992, vol. IX
Magnus-Allcroft, Sir Philip, 2nd Bt, 1906–1988, vol. VIII
Magor, Maj. Edward Walter Moyle, 1911–1995, vol. IX
Magowan, Sir John Hall, 1893–1951, vol. V
Magowan, Joseph Irvine, 1901–1977, vol. VII
Magrane, Col John Plunkett, 1896–1963, vol. VI
Magrath, Maj.-Gen. Beauchamp Henry Whittingham, 1832–1920, vol. II
Magrath, Charles Alexander, 1860–1949, vol. IV
Magrath, Harry William, died 1969, vol. VI
Magrath, Rev. John Richard, 1839–1930, vol. III
Maguiness, Rev. John Thomas, died 1920, vol. II
Maguinness, William Stuart, 1903–1982, vol. VIII
Maguire, Sir Alexander Herbert, 1876–1947, vol. IV
Maguire, Conor A., 1889–1971, vol. VII
Maguire, Very Rev. Edward, 1822–1913, vol. I
Maguire, Frank; see Maguire, M. F.
Maguire, Maj.-Gen. Frederick Arthur, 1888–1953, vol. V(A)
Maguire, James Rochfort, 1855–1925, vol. II
Maguire, Most Rev. John A., 1851–1920, vol. II
Maguire, Meredith Francis, (Frank Maguire), 1929–1981, vol. VIII
Maguire, Robert, 1857–1915, vol. I
Maguire, Rt Rev. Robert Kenneth, 1923–2000, vol. X(AII)
Maguire, William Joseph, died 1934, vol. III
Mahadeva, Sir Arunachalam, born 1885, vol. VI
Mahaffy, Alexander Francis, 1891–1962, vol. VI
Mahaffy, Arthur William, 1869–1919, vol. II
Mahaffy, Rev. Gilbert, died 1916, vol. II
Mahaffy, Sir John Pentland, 1839–1919, vol. II
Mahaffy, Robert Pentland, 1871–1943, vol. IV
Mahaim, Ernest A. J., 1865–1938, vol. III(A), vol. IV

Mahalanobis, Prasanta Chandra, 1893–1972, vol. VII
Mahalanobis, S. C., 1867–1953, vol. V
Mahan, Rear Adm. Alfred T., 1840–1914, vol. I
Mahdi Husain, Khan, Wahud-ud-Daula, Azod-ul-Mulk, Nawab Mirza, Khan Bahadur, born 1834, vol. II
Maher, Charles Ernest, 1896–1961, vol. VI
Maher, Maj.-Gen. Sir James, 1858–1928, vol. II
Maheshwari, Panchanan, 1904–1966, vol. VI
Maheu, René G., 1905–1975, vol. VII
Mahir, Thomas Edward, 1915–1970, vol. VI
Mahler, Kurt, 1903–1988, vol. VIII
Mahmud Husain, Syed Abul Basher, 1916–1982, vol. IX(AI)
Mahmudabad, Maharaja of, 1877–1931, vol. III
Mahomed, Ismail, 1931–2000, vol. X
Mahon, Lt-Col Bryan MacMahon, 1890–1949, vol. IV
Mahon, Gen. Rt Hon. Sir Bryan Thomas, 1862–1930, vol. III
Mahon, Edward Elphinstone, 1851–1912, vol. I
Mahon, Sir George Edward John, 6th Bt, 1911–1987, vol. VIII
Mahon, Sir Gerald MacMahon, 1904–1982, vol. VIII
Mahon, Rt Rev. Gerald Thomas, 1922–1992, vol. IX
Mahon, Harold J. D., 1873–1938, vol. III
Mahon, Captain Henry P.; see Pakenham-Mahon.
Mahon, Hon. Hugh, 1858–1931, vol. III
Mahon, John FitzGerald, 1858–1942, vol. IV
Mahon, Peter, 1909–1980, vol. X(AI)
Mahon, Ralph Bodkin, 1862–1943, vol. IV(A)
Mahon, Maj.-Gen. Reginald Henry, 1859–1929, vol. III
Mahon, Simon, 1914–1986, vol. VIII
Mahon, Sir William Henry, 5th Bt, 1856–1926, vol. II
Mahoney, Charles, 1903–1968, vol. VI
Mahoney, Sir John Andrew, 1883–1966, vol. VI
Mahoney, Merchant Michael, 1886–1946, vol. IV
Mahony, Francis Joseph, 1915–2000, vol. X
Mahony, Lt-Col John Keefer, 1911–1990, vol. VIII
Mahony, Rt Rev. Mgr John Mathew, 1862–1918, vol. II
Mahony, Major Michael Joseph, died 1927, vol. II
Mahony, Peirce Gun, 1878–1914, vol. I
Mahood, James, 1876–1950, vol. IV
Mahtab, Maharajadhiraja Bahadur Sir Uday Chand, 1905–1984, vol. VIII
Maiden, Joseph Henry, 1859–1925, vol. II
Maidment, Kenneth John, 1910–1990, vol. VIII
Maillard, Staff Surgeon William J., died 1903, vol. I
Maillart, Ella Kini, 1903–1997, vol. IX
Maillol, Aristide, 1861–1944, vol. IV
Main, Rev. Archibald, 1876–1947, vol. IV
Main, David, 1861–1941, vol. IV
Main, David Duncan, 1856–1934, vol. III
Main, Frank Fiddes, 1905–1994, vol. IX (AII)
Main, Lt-Comdr Frank Morgan, died 1924, vol. II
Main, Henry, 1888–1949, vol. IV
Main, Brig. John Walter, 1900–1971, vol. VII
Main, Col Thomas Ryder, 1850–1934, vol. III

Maindron, Maurice Georges Rene, 1857–1911, vol. I

Mainds, Allan Douglass, 1881–1945, vol. IV

Maine, Rev. Basil Stephen, 1894–1972, vol. VII

Maine, Henry Cecil Sumner, 1886–1968, vol. VI

Maingot, Rodney Honor, 1893–1982, vol. VIII

Maini, Sir Amar Nath, 1911–1999, vol. X

Mainland, William Faulkner, 1905–1988, vol. VIII

Mainprise, Maj.-Gen. Cecil Wilmot, 1873–1951, vol. V

Mainprise, Captain William Thomas, died 1902, vol. I

Mainstone, Madeleine Françoise, 1925–1979, vol. VII

Mainwaring, Albert James, 1891–1941, vol. IV

Mainwaring, Charles Francis Kynaston, 1877–1949, vol. IV

Mainwaring, Col Charles Salusbury, 1845–1920, vol. II

Mainwaring, Brig. Guy Rowland, 1885–1956, vol. V

Mainwaring, Sir Harry Stapleton, 5th Bt, 1878–1934, vol. III

Mainwaring, Brig. Hugh Salusbury Kynaston, 1906–1976, vol. VII

Mainwaring, Sir Philip Tatton, 4th Bt, 1838–1906, vol. I

Mainwaring, Hon. Maj.-Gen. Rowland Broughton, 1850–1926, vol. II

Mainwaring, Col Sir Watkin Randle Kynaston, 1875–1944, vol. IV

Mainwaring, Hon. William Frederick Barton Massey-, 1845–1907, vol. I

Mainwaring, Gen. William George, 1823–1905, vol. I

Mainwaring, William Henry, 1884–1971, vol. VII

Mainwaring-Bowen, Arthur Charles, 1922–1980, vol. VII

Mair, Alexander, 1870–1927, vol. II

Mair, Alexander, 1912–1995, vol. IX

Mair, Alexander W., died 1928, vol. II

Mair, Charles, 1838–1927, vol. II

Mair, George Herbert, 1887–1926, vol. II

Mair, Brig.-Gen. George Tagore, 1873–1941, vol. IV

Mair, Rev. John, 1822–1902, vol. I

Mair, John Bagrie, 1857–1927, vol. II

Mair, Lucy Philip, 1901–1986, vol. VIII

Mair, Col Robert John Byford, 1868–1940, vol. III

Mair, Dame Sarah Elizabeth Siddons, 1846–1941, vol. IV

Mair, Very Rev. William, 1830–1920, vol. II

Mairet, Ethel, 1872–1952, vol. V

Mairis, Gen. Geoffrey, 1834–1917, vol. II

Mais, Baron (Life Peer); Alan Raymond Mais, 1911–1993, vol. IX

Mais, Hon. Sir Hugh; see Mais, Hon. Sir R. H.

Mais, Hon. Sir (Robert) Hugh, 1907–1996, vol. X

Mais, Stuart Petre Brodie, 1885–1975, vol. VII

Maisky, Ivan Mikhailovich, 1884–1975, vol. VII

Maistre, Le Roy de, (Roy de Maistre), 1894–1968, vol. VI

Maitland, Viscount; Ivor Colin James Maitland, 1915–1943, vol. IV

Maitland, Sir Adam, 1885–1949, vol. IV

Maitland, Rev. Adam Gray, died 1928, vol. II

Maitland, Agnes Catherine, 1849–1906, vol. I

Maitland, Sir Alexander, 1877–1965, vol. VI

Maitland, Sir Alexander Keith, 8th Bt, 1920–1963, vol. VI

Maitland, Rt Hon. Sir Arthur Herbert Drummond Ramsay S.; see Steel-Maitland.

Maitland, Dalrymple, 1848–1919, vol. II

Maitland, Maj.-Gen. David M. C.; see Makgill-Crichton-Maitland.

Maitland, Col Eardley, 1833–1911, vol. I

Maitland, Air-Cdre Edward Maitland, 1880–1921, vol. II

Maitland, Frederic William, 1850–1906, vol. I

Maitland, Lt-Col Sir (George) Ramsay, 7th Bt, 1882–1960, vol. V

Maitland, Lt-Col Hon. George Thomas, 1841–1910, vol. I

Maitland, Sir Herbert Lethington, 1868–1923, vol. II

Maitland, Hugh Bethune, 1895–1972, vol. VII

Maitland, J. A. F.; see Fuller-Maitland.

Maitland, Brig.-Gen. James Dalgleish H.; see Heriot-Maitland.

Maitland, Maj.-Gen. Sir James Makgill Heriot-, 1837–1902, vol. I

Maitland, Sir James S.; see Steel-Maitland.

Maitland, Sir John, 6th Bt, 1879–1949, vol. IV

Maitland, Comdr Sir John Francis Whitaker, 1903–1977, vol. VII

Maitland, Sir John Nisbet, 5th Bt, 1850–1936, vol. III

Maitland, Sir Keith Richard Felix Ramsay-Steel; see Steel-Maitland.

Maitland, Col Mark Edward Makgill Crichton, 1882–1972, vol. VII

Maitland, Maj.-Gen. Pelham James, 1847–1935, vol. III

Maitland, Air Vice-Marshal Percy Eric, 1895–1985, vol. VIII

Maitland, Lt-Col Sir Ramsay; see Maitland, Lt-Col Sir G. R.

Maitland, Lt-Col Reginald Charles Frederick, 1882–1939, vol. III

Maitland, Sir Richard John, 9th Bt, 1952–1994, vol. IX

Maitland, Thomas Gwynne, died 1948, vol. IV

Maitland, Victor Kennard, 1897–1950, vol. IV

Maitland, William F.; see Fuller-Maitland.

Maitland, William James, 1847–1919, vol. II

Maitland, William Whitaker, 1864–1926, vol. II

Maitland-Gordon, James Charles; see Gordon.

Maitland-Heriot, Sir William, 1856–1939, vol. III

Maitland-Jones, Arthur Griffith, 1890–1957, vol. V

Maitland-Kirwan, Lionel, 1849–1927, vol. II

Maitland-Makgill-Crichton, Sir Andrew; see Crichton.

Maitland-Makgill-Crichton, Brig. Henry Coventry; see Crichton.

Maitland-Titterton, Major David Maitland, 1904–1988, vol. VIII

Maizels, Montague, 1899–1976, vol. VII

Majdalany, Fred, 1913–1967, vol. VI

Majendie, Brig.-Gen. Bernard J., 1875–1959, vol. V

Majendie, James Henry Alexander, 1871–1932, vol. III
Majendie, Sir Vivian Dering, 1836–1898, vol. I
Majendie, Maj.-Gen. Vivian Henry Bruce, 1886–1960, vol. V
Majendie, Rev. William Richard Stuart, 1869–1932, vol. III
Majithia, Sir Surendra Singh, 1895–1983, vol. IX(AI)
Major, Albany Featherstonehaugh, 1858–1925, vol. II
Major, Sir Alfred, died 1907, vol. I
Major, Alfred George, 1879–1940, vol. III(A), vol. IV
Major, Maj.-Gen. Hon. Arthur Henry H.; see Henniker-Major.
Major, Charles, 1856–1913, vol. I
Major, Sir Charles Henry, 1860–1933, vol. III
Major, Charles Immanuel Forsyth, 1843–1923, vol. II
Major, Col Charles Thomas, 1869–1938, vol. III
Major, Edith Helen, 1867–1951, vol. V
Major, Hon. Edward Minet H.; see Henniker-Major.
Major, Ernest Harry, 1876–1941, vol. IV
Major, Francis William, 1863–1923, vol. II
Major, Hon. Gerald Arthur George H.; see Henniker-Major.
Major, Rev. Henry Dewsbury Alves, 1871–1961, vol. VI
Major, James Perrins, 1878–1964, vol. VI(AII)
Major, Kathleen, 1906–2000, vol. X
Majury, Maj.-Gen. James Herbert Samuel, 1921–1996, vol. X
Makarios III, Archbishop, 1913–1977, vol. VII
Makdougall, Hugh James Elibank S.; see Scott Makdougall.
Makgill, Sir George, 11th Bt, 1868–1926, vol. II
Makgill, Robert Haldane, 1870–1946, vol. IV
Makgill-Crichton-Maitland, Maj.-Gen. David, 1841–1907, vol. I
Makin, Frank, 1918–1984, vol. VIII
Makin, Hon. Norman John Oswald, 1889–1982, vol. VIII
Makino, Nobuaki, Count, 1861–1949, vol. IV
Makins, Sir (Alfred) John (Ware), 1894–1972, vol. VII
Makins, Brig.-Gen. Sir Ernest, 1869–1959, vol. V
Makins, Captain Geoffry, 1877–1915, vol. I
Makins, Sir George Henry, 1853–1933, vol. III
Makins, Sir John; see Makins, Sir A. J. W.
Makins, Sir Paul Augustine, 2nd Bt, 1871–1939, vol. III
Makins, Sir Paul Vivian, 4th Bt, 1913–1999, vol. X
Makins, Col Sir William Thomas, 1st Bt, 1840–1906, vol. I
Makins, Lt-Col Sir William Vivian, 3rd Bt, 1903–1969, vol. VI
Makinson, Joseph, 1836–1914, vol. I
Makower, Ernest Samuel, 1876–1946, vol. IV
Makower, Walter, 1879–1945, vol. IV
Malabari, Behramji Merwanji, 1854–1912, vol. I
Malalasekera, Gunapala Piyasena, 1899–1973, vol. VII
Malamud, Bernard, 1914–1986, vol. VIII

Malan, Gp Captain Adolph Gysbert, 1910–1963, vol. VI
Malan, Hon. Daniel François, 1874–1959, vol. V
Malan, Rt Hon. François Stephanus, 1871–1941, vol. IV
Malaviya, Pandit Madan Mohan, 1861–1946, vol. IV
Malbrán, Manuel E., 1876–1942, vol. IV
Malcolm of Poltalloch, 1st Baron, 1833–1902, vol. I
Malcolm, Angus Christian Edward, 1908–1971, vol. VII
Malcolm, Lt-Col Arthur William Alexander, 1903–1989, vol. VIII
Malcolm, Charles Adolf, 1879–1948, vol. IV
Malcolm, Sir David Peter Michael, 11th Bt, 1919–1995, vol. IX
Malcolm, Sir Dougal Orme, 1877–1955, vol. V
Malcolm, Dugald, 1917–2000, vol. X
Malcolm, Col Edward Donald, 1837–1930, vol. III
Malcolm, Sir George, 1818–1897, vol. I
Malcolm, George, 1876–1941, vol. IV
Malcolm, Col George Alexander, 1872–1933, vol. III
Malcolm of Poltalloch, Lt-Col George Ian, 1903–1976, vol. VII
Malcolm, George John, 1917–1997, vol. X
Malcolm, Hon. George John Huntly, 1865–1930, vol. III
Malcolm, George William, 1870–1933, vol. III
Malcolm, Gerald; see Malcolm, W. G.
Malcolm, Harcourt Gladstone, 1875–1936, vol. III
Malcolm, Brig.-Gen. Henry Huntly Leith, 1860–1938, vol. III
Malcolm, Sir Ian Zachary, 1868–1944, vol. IV
Malcolm, Sir James, 8th Bt, 1823–1901, vol. I
Malcolm, Hon. James, 1880–1935, vol. III
Malcolm, Sir James William, 9th Bt, 1862–1927, vol. II
Malcolm, John, 1873–1954, vol. V
Malcolm, John D., 1857–1937, vol. III
Malcolm, Kenneth Robert, 1908–1984, vol. VIII
Malcolm, Sir Michael Albert James, 1898–1976, vol. VII
Malcolm, Maj.-Gen. Sir Neill, 1869–1953, vol. V
Malcolm, Lt-Col Pulteney, 1861–1940, vol. III
Malcolm, Robert Carmichael, 1868–1941, vol. IV
Malcolm, Ronald, died 1949, vol. IV
Malcolm, (William) Gerald, 1916–1996, vol. X
Malcolmson, John Grant, died 1902, vol. I
Malcolmson, Maj.-Gen. John Henry Porter, 1832–1920, vol. II
Malcolmson, Kenneth Forbes, 1911–1995, vol. IX
Malcolmson, Vernon Austen, 1872–1947, vol. IV
Malden, Charles Edward, 1845–1926, vol. II
Malden, Edmund Claud, 1890–1962, vol. VI
Malden, Air Vice-Marshal (Francis) David (Stephen) S.; see Scott-Malden
Malden, Very Rev. Richard Henry, 1879–1951, vol. V
Male, Emile, 1862–1954, vol. V
Male, Peter John Ellison, 1920–1996, vol. X
Malenkov, Georgi Maximilianovich, 1902–1988, vol. VIII
Maler Kotla, Nawab of, 1881–1947, vol. IV
Malet, Sir Charles St Lo, 6th Bt, 1906–1918, vol. II

Malet, Rt Hon. Sir Edward Baldwin, 4th Bt, 1837–1908, vol. I
Malet, Sir Edward St Lo, 5th Bt, 1872–1909, vol. I
Malet, Col Sir Edward William St Lo, 8th Bt, 1908–1990, vol. VIII
Malet, Guilbert Edward Wyndham, 1839–1918, vol. II
Malet, Sir Harry Charles, 7th Bt, 1873–1931, vol. III
Malet, Sir Henry Charles Eden, 3rd Bt, 1835–1904, vol. I
Malet, John C., died 1901, vol. I
Malet, Lucas; see Harrison, Mary St Leger.
Malet de Carteret, Captain Charles Edward, died 1942, vol. IV
Malet de Carteret, Lt-Col Edouard Charles, 1838–1914, vol. I
Malet de Carteret, Reginald, 1865–1935, vol. III
Malherbe, Ernst G., 1895–1982, vol. VIII
Malik Khuda Bakhsh Khan Tiwana, Nawab Sir, died 1930, vol. III
Malik Mohammed Umar Hayat Khan (Tiwana), Maj.-Gen. Hon. Sir, 1874–1944, vol. IV
Malik, Bidhubhusan, 1895–1981, vol. IX(AI)
Malik, Sardar Bahadur Sir Teja Singh, died 1953, vol. V
Malik, Sardar Hardit Singh, 1894–1985, vol. VIII
Malik, Yakov Alexandrovich, 1906–1980, vol. VII
Malim, Comdr David Wentworth, 1914–1985, vol. VIII
Malim, Frederic Blagden, 1872–1966, vol. VI
Malin, Peter; see Conner, Rearden.
Maling, George Allan, 1889–1929, vol. III
Maling, Captain Irwin Charles, 1841–1918, vol. II
Malinovsky, Marshal Rodion Yakovlevich, 1898–1967, vol. VI
Malinowski, Bronislaw, 1884–1942, vol. IV
Malins, Sir Edward, 1841–1922, vol. II
Malipiero, G. Francesco, 1882–1973, vol. VII
Malkin, Harold Jordan, 1898–1978, vol. VII
Malkin, Herbert Charles, 1836–1913, vol. I
Malkin, Sir (Herbert) William, 1883–1945, vol. IV
Malkin, Sir William; see Malkin, Sir H. W.
Malko, Nicolai, 1888–1961, vol. VI
Mallabar, Herbert John, 1871–1956, vol. V
Mallabar, Sir John Frederick, 1900–1988, vol. VIII
Mallaby, Col Aubertin Walter Sothern, 1899–1945, vol. IV
Mallaby, Sir George; see Mallaby, Sir H. G. C.
Mallaby, Sir (Howard) George (Charles), 1902–1978, vol. VII
Mallaby, Rev. John Jackson, died 1929, vol. III
Mallaby-Deeley, Sir Anthony Meyrick, 3rd Bt, 1923–1962, vol. VI
Mallaby-Deeley, Sir Guy Meyrick Mallaby, 2nd Bt, 1897–1946, vol. IV
Mallaby-Deeley, Sir Harry Mallaby, 1st Bt, 1863–1937, vol. III
Malladra, Alessandro, 1868–1944, vol. IV
Mallalieu, Sir Edward Lancelot, (Sir Lance), 1905–1979, vol. VII
Mallalieu, Frederick William, 1860–1932, vol. III
Mallalieu, Sir Joseph Percival William, 1908–1980, vol. VII
Mallalieu, Sir Lance; see Mallalieu, Sir E. L.

Mallalieu, Sir William; see Mallalieu, Sir J. P. W.
Mallam, Lt-Col Rev. George Leslie, 1895–1978, vol. VII
Mallarmé, Stéphane, 1842–1898, vol. I
Malle, Louis, 1932–1995, vol. IX
Mallen, Sir Leonard Ross, 1902–1980, vol. VII (AII)
Malleson, Lady Constance, (Colette O'Niel), 1895–1975, vol. VII
Malleson, Col George Bruce, 1825–1898, vol. I
Malleson, Herbert Cecil, died 1935, vol. III
Malleson, Miles; see Malleson, W. M.
Malleson, Maj.-Gen. Sir Wilfrid, 1866–1946, vol. IV
Malleson, Comdr Wilfrid St Aubyn, died 1975, vol. VII
Malleson, (William) Miles, 1888–1969, vol. VI
Mallet, Sir Bernard, 1859–1932, vol. III
Mallet, Sir Charles Edward, 1862–1947, vol. IV
Mallet, Sir Claude Coventry, 1860–1941, vol. IV
Mallet, Hooper Pelgué, 1901–1985, vol. VIII
Mallet, Sir Ivo; see Mallet, Sir W. I.
Mallet, John William, 1832–1912, vol. I
Mallet, Rt Hon. Sir Louis du Pan, 1864–1936, vol. III
Mallet, Matilde de Obarrio, (Lady Mallet), 1872–1964, vol. VI
Mallet, Sir Victor Alexander Louis, 1893–1969, vol. VI
Mallet, Sir (William) Ivo, 1900–1988, vol. VIII
Mallett, Edward, 1888–1950, vol. IV
Mallett, Ven. Peter, 1925–1996, vol. X
Mallett, Richard, 1910–1972, vol. VII
Mallett, Sir Rowland, 1869–1947, vol. IV
Malley, Cecil Patrick, 1902–1981, vol. VIII
Malley, William Bernard, 1889–1966, vol. VI
Mallik, Devendra Nath, 1866–1941, vol. IV
Mallik, Manmath C., died 1853, vol. III
Mallin, Rev. Canon Stewart Adam Thomson, 1924–2000, vol. X
Mallinson, Albert, 1870–1946, vol. IV
Mallinson, Dennis Hainsworth, 1921–1993, vol. IX
Mallinson, Sir Dyson, 1852–1929, vol. III
Mallinson, Lt-Col Henry, 1879–1940, vol. III
Mallinson, Sir Paul; see Mallinson, Sir W. P.
Mallinson, Col Sir Stuart Sidney, 1888–1981, vol. VIII
Mallinson, Sir William, 1st Bt, died 1936, vol. III
Mallinson, Sir William James, 2nd Bt, 1879–1944, vol. IV
Mallinson, Sir William John, 4th Bt, 1942–1995, vol. IX
Mallinson, Sir (William) Paul, 3rd Bt, 1909–1989, vol. VIII
Malloch, George Reston, died 1953, vol. V
Malloch, James, 1860–1932, vol. III
Mallock, Brig. Arthur Richard Ogilvie, 1885–1972, vol. VII
Mallock, Major Charles Herbert, 1878–1917, vol. II
Mallock, Henry Reginald A., died 1933, vol. III
Mallock, Richard, 1843–1900, vol. I
Mallock, Lt-Col Thomas Raymond, died 1934, vol. III
Mallock, William Hurrell, 1849–1923, vol. II
Mallon, James Joseph, 1875–1961, vol. VI

Mallorie, Air Vice-Marshal Paul Richard, 1923–1999, vol. X
Mallory, Rev. Herbert Leigh L.; see Leigh-Mallory.
Mallory, Air Chief Marshal Sir Trafford Leigh L.; see Leigh-Mallory.
Mallowan, Dame Agatha; see Christie, Dame A. M. C.
Mallowan, Sir Max Edgar Lucien, 1904–1978, vol. VII
Malmesbury, 4th Earl of, 1842–1899, vol. I
Malmesbury, 5th Earl of, 1872–1950, vol. IV
Malmesbury, 6th Earl of, 1907–2000, vol. X
Malone, Surg. Rear-Adm. Albert Edward, died 1970, vol. VI
Malone, Lt-Col Cecil John L'Estrange, 1890–1965, vol. VI
Malone, Sir Clement, 1883–1967, vol. VI
Malone, Hon. Sir Denis Eustace Gilbert, 1922–2000, vol. X
Malone, Denis George Withers, 1906–1983, vol. VIII
Malone, Herbert, 1893–1962, vol. VI
Malone, Leah, (Mrs L'Estrange Malone), died 1951, vol. V
Malone, Major Sir Patrick Bernard, 1857–1939, vol. III
Malory, Shaun; see Russell, Reginald James Kingston.
Malott, Deane Waldo, 1898–1996, vol. X
Malouin, Arthur Cyrille Albert, 1857–1930, vol. III
Malraux, André, 1901–1976, vol. VII
Maltby, Maj.-Gen. (Christopher) Michael, 1891–1980, vol. VII
Maltby, Lt-Comdr Gerald Rivers, 1851–1922, vol. II
Maltby, Henry Francis, 1880–1963, vol. VI
Maltby, John Newcombe, 1928–1998, vol. X
Maltby, Maj.-Gen. Michael; see Maltby, Maj.-Gen. C. M.
Maltby, Air Vice-Marshal Sir Paul Copeland, 1892–1971, vol. VII
Maltby, Sir Thomas Karran, 1891–1976, vol. VII
Malthus, Col Sydenham, 1831–1916, vol. II
Maltwood, Katharine E., 1878–1961, vol. VI
Malvern, 1st Viscount, 1883–1971, vol. VII
Malvern, 2nd Viscount, 1922–1978, vol. VII
Malvern, Harry Ladyman, 1908–1982, vol. VIII
Mamhead, 1st Baron, 1871–1945, vol. IV
Mamoulian, Rouben, 1897–1987, vol. VIII
Man, Maj.-Gen. Christopher Mark Morrice, 1914–1989, vol. VIII
Man, Edward Garnet, 1837–1920, vol. II
Man, Edward Horace, 1846–1929, vol. III
Man, Col Hubert William, died 1956, vol. V
Man, Col John Alexander; see Stuart, Col. J. A. M.
Man, Captain Joseph, 1867–1951, vol. V
Man, Morgan Charles Garnet, 1915–1986, vol. VIII
Man, Maj.-Gen. Patrick Holberton, 1913–1979, vol. VII
Manby, Sir Alan Reeve, 1848–1925, vol. II
Manby, Mervyn Colet, 1915–1994, vol. IX
Manby, Percy Alan Farrer, 1877–1940, vol. III
Mance, Brig.-Gen. Sir H. Osborne, 1875–1966, vol. VI
Mance, Sir Henry Christopher, 1840–1926, vol. II
Mance, Sir Henry Stenhouse, 1913–1981, vol. VIII

Manchester, 9th Duke of, 1877–1947, vol. IV
Manchester, 10th Duke of, 1902–1977, vol. VII
Manchester, 11th Duke of, 1929–1985, vol. VIII
Manchester, Sir William Edwin, 1869–1956, vol. V
Mancinelli, Luigi, 1848–1921, vol. II
Mancroft, 1st Baron, 1872–1942, vol. IV
Mancroft, 2nd Baron, 1914–1987, vol. VIII
Mander, Sir Charles Arthur, 2nd Bt, 1884–1951, vol. V
Mander, Sir Charles Tertius, 1st Bt, 1852–1929, vol. III
Mander, Sir Frederick, 1883–1964, vol. VI
Mander, Maj.-Gen. Frederick Day, 1842–1939, vol. III
Mander, Sir Geoffrey Le Mesurier, 1882–1962, vol. VI
Mander, Captain John Harold, 1869–1927, vol. II
Mander, Lionel Henry Miles, 1888–1946, vol. IV
Mander, Raymond Josiah Gale, 1911–1983, vol. VIII
Mander, Lady; (Rosalie), (R. Glynn Grylls), 1905–1988, vol. VIII
Manders, Horace Craigie, 1882–1963, vol. VI
Manders, Richard, 1854–1931, vol. III
Manderson, Maj.-Gen. George Rennie, 1834–1918, vol. II
Manderville, Rt Rev. Gay Lisle Griffith, 1894–1969, vol. VI
Mandi, Lt-Col Raja (Sir) Joginder Sen Bahadur of, 1904–1986, vol. VIII
Mandleberg, Sir G. Charles, 1860–1932, vol. III
Mandleberg, J. Harold, 1885–1973, vol. VII
Mandleberg, Brig. Lennard Charles, 1893–1975, vol. VII
Mandlik, Sir Narayan Vishvanath, 1870–1948, vol. IV
Manfield, Harry, 1855–1923, vol. II
Manfield, Sir Philip, 1819–1899, vol. I
Mangan, Rt Rev. John, 1852–1917, vol. II
Mangham, Sydney, 1886–1962, vol. VI
Mangiagalli, Riccardo P.; see Pick-Mangiagalli.
Mangin, Ven. Robert Rattray, 1863–1944, vol. IV
Mangin, Sir Thorleif Rattray Orde, 1896–1950, vol. IV
Mangles, Maj.-Gen. Cecil, 1842–1906, vol. I
Mangles, Brig.-Gen. Roland Henry, 1874–1948, vol. IV
Mangles, Ross Lowis, 1833–1905, vol. I
Mangles, Major Walter James, 1862–1929, vol. III
Manhood, Harold Alfred, 1904–1991, vol. IX
Manifold, Hon. Sir Chester; see Manifold, Hon. Sir T. C.
Manifold, Maj.-Gen. Sir Courtenay Clarke, 1864–1957, vol. V
Manifold, Maj.-Gen. Sir Graham; see Manifold, Maj.-Gen. Sir M. G. E. B.
Manifold, Maj.-Gen. John Alexander, 1884–1960, vol. V
Manifold, Lt-Col John Forster, 1857–1933, vol. III
Manifold, Maj.-Gen. Sir (Michael) Graham Egerton Bowman-, 1871–1940, vol. III
Manifold, Hon. Sir (Thomas) Chester, 1897–1979, vol. VII
Manifold, Hon. Sir Walter Synnot, 1849–1928, vol. II

Manion, Hon. Robert James, 1881–1943, vol. IV
Manipur, HH Sir Chura Chand Singh Maharajah of, 1886–1941, vol. IV
Manisty, Rear-Adm. Sir Eldon; see Manisty, Rear-Adm. Sir H. W. E.
Manisty, Rear-Adm. Sir (Henry Wilfred) Eldon, 1876–1960, vol. V
Manisty, Herbert Francis, 1853–1939, vol. III
Mankiewicz, Joseph Leo, 1909–1993, vol. IX
Mankowitz, (Cyril) Wolf, 1924–1998, vol. X
Mankowitz, Wolf; see Mankowitz, C. W.
Manktelow, Sir (Arthur) Richard, 1899–1977, vol. VII
Manktelow, Sir Richard; see Manktelow, Sir A. R.
Manley, Edgar Booth, 1897–1959, vol. V
Manley, Gordon, 1902–1980, vol. VII
Manley, Rt Hon. Michael Norman, 1924–1997, vol. X
Manley, Norman Washington, 1893–1969, vol. VI
Mann, Sir Alan Harbury, 1914–1970, vol. VI(AII)
Mann, Alexander, died 1908, vol. I
Mann, Arthur Henry, 1876–1972, vol. VII
Mann, Bruce Leslie Home D.; see Douglas-Mann.
Mann, Rt Rev. Cameron, 1851–1932, vol. III
Mann, Cathleen, (Mrs J. R. Follett), died 1959, vol. V
Mann, Sir Donald, 1853–1934, vol. III
Mann, Sir Duncombe; see Mann, Sir T. D.
Mann, Sir Edward, 1st Bt, 1854–1943, vol. IV
Mann, Sir (Edward) John, 2nd Bt, 1883–1971, vol. VII
Mann, Eileen Alannah; see Joyce, E. A.
Mann, Mrs Fairman; see Mann, Mary E.
Mann, Francis; see Mann, Frederick A.
Mann, Frederick Alexander (Francis), 1907–1991, vol. IX
Mann, Frederick George, 1897–1982, vol. VIII
Mann, Hon. Sir Frederick Wollaston, 1869–1958, vol. V
Mann, Rev. George Albert Douglas, 1914–1983, vol. VIII
Mann, Harold Hart, 1872–1961, vol. VI
Mann, Harrington, 1864–1937, vol. III
Mann, Heinrich, 1871–1950, vol. IV
Mann, Rt Rev. Mgr Horace K., 1859–1928, vol. II
Mann, Dame Ida Caroline, 1893–1983, vol. VIII
Mann, J. Dixon, died 1912, vol. I
Mann, Jacob, 1888–1940, vol. III(A), vol. IV
Mann, Sir James Gow, 1897–1962, vol. VI
Mann, Maj.-Gen. James Robert, 1823–1915, vol. I
Mann, James Scrimgeour, 1883–1946, vol. IV
Mann, Jean, 1889–1964, vol. VI
Mann, Sir John, 1863–1955, vol. V
Mann, Sir John, died 1957, vol. V
Mann, Sir John; see Mann, Sir E. J.
Mann, Rt Rev. John Charles, 1880–1967, vol. VI
Mann, Julia de Lacy, 1891–1985, vol. VIII
Mann, Keith Cranston, 1903–1972, vol. VII
Mann, Keith John Sholto D.; see Douglas-Mann
Mann, Ludovic MacLellan, died 1955, vol. V
Mann, Mary E., died 1929, vol. III
Mann, Rt Hon. Sir Michael, 1930–1998, vol. X
Mann, Rt Rev. Peter Woodley, 1924–1999, vol. X
Mann, Ronald, 1908–1987, vol. VIII

Mann, Thaddeus Robert Rudolph, 1908–1993, vol. IX
Mann, Thomas, 1875–1955, vol. V
Mann, Sir (Thomas) Duncombe, 1857–1949, vol. IV
Mann, Tom, 1856–1941, vol. IV
Mann, Major William Edgar, 1885–1969, vol. VI
Mann, Air Cdre William Edward George, 1899–1966, vol. VI
Mann, William Somervell, 1924–1989, vol. VIII
Mannering, Rev. Ernest, 1882–1977, vol. VII
Mannering, Rev. Canon Leslie George, 1883–1974, vol. VII
Manners, 3rd Baron, 1852–1927, vol. II
Manners, 4th Baron, 1897–1972, vol. VII
Manners, Lord Cecil Reginald John, 1868–1945, vol. IV
Manners, Charles, 1857–1935, vol. III
Manners, Brig. Charles Molyneux Sandys, 1885–1954, vol. V
Manners, Lord Edward William John, 1864–1903, vol. I
Manners, Ernest John, 1877–1944, vol. IV
Manners, Rear-Adm. Sir Errol, 1883–1953, vol. V
Manners, Sir George Espec John, 1860–1939, vol. III
Manners, J. Hartley, 1870–1928, vol. II
Manners, Major Lord Robert William Orlando, 1870–1917, vol. II
Manners-Smith, Francis St George, died 1941, vol. IV
Manners-Sutton, Francis Henry Astley, 1869–1916, vol. II
Mannheim, Hermann, 1889–1974, vol. VII
Mannheim, Karl, 1893–1947, vol. IV
Mannheim, Lucie, 1905–1976, vol. VII
Mannin, Ethel, 1900–1984, vol. VIII
Manning, Miss, died 1905, vol. I
Manning, Bernard Lord, 1892–1941, vol. IV
Manning, Brian O'Donoghue, 1891–1964, vol. VI
Manning, Charles Anthony Woodward, 1894–1978, vol. VII
Manning, Cecil Aubrey Gwynne, 1892–1985, vol. VIII
Manning, Air Cdre Edye Rolleston, 1889–1957, vol. V
Manning, Dame (Elizabeth) Leah, 1886–1977, vol. VII
Manning, Frederick Allan, 1904–1991, vol. IX
Manning, Frederick Edwin Alfred, 1897–1987, vol. VIII
Manning, Air Cdre Frederick John, 1912–1988, vol. VIII
Manning, Sir George, 1887–1976, vol. VII
Manning, Sir Henry Edward, 1877–1963, vol. VI
Manning, Sir (James) Kenneth, 1907–1976, vol. VII
Manning, John Westley, 1866–1954, vol. V
Manning, Sir Kenneth; see Manning, Sir J. K.
Manning, Dame Leah; see Manning, Dame E. L.
Manning, Olivia Mary, (Mrs R. D. Smith), 1915–1980, vol. VII
Manning, Richard Joseph, 1883–1979, vol. VII
Manning, Thomas Henry, 1911–1998, vol. X
Manning, W. Westley, died 1954, vol. V

Manning, Brig.-Gen. Sir William Henry, 1863–1932, vol. III
Manning, Sir William Patrick, 1845–1915, vol. I
Manning, Rt Rev. William Thomas, 1866–1949, vol. IV
Manningham-Buller, Lt-Col Sir Mervyn Edward, 3rd Bt, 1876–1956, vol. V
Manningham-Buller, Sir Morton Edward; see Buller.
Mannix, Most Rev. Daniel, 1864–1963, vol. VI
Mannooch, Geoffrey Herbert, 1890–1959, vol. V
Manns, Sir August, 1825–1907, vol. I
Manohar Lal, Hon. Sir, 1880–1949, vol. IV
Mansbridge, Albert, 1876–1952, vol. V
Mansbridge, Very Rev. Harold Chad, 1917–1980, vol. VII
Mansel, Col Alfred, 1852–1918, vol. II
Mansel, Sir Courtenay Cecil, 13th Bt (shown as 11th Bt), 1880–1933, vol. III (the 12th and 13th Bts are wrongly numbered in their entries).
Mansel, Sir Edward Berkeley, 12th Bt (shown as 10th Bt), 1839–1908, vol. I
Mansel, George, died 1914, vol. I
Mansel, Col George Clavell, 1861–1910, vol. I
Mansel, Rev. Canon James Seymour Denis, 1907–1995, vol. IX
Mansel, Sir John Philip Ferdinand, 14th Bt, 1910–1947, vol. IV
Mansel, Major Rhys Clavell, 1891–1969, vol. VI
Mansel-Jones, Col Conwyn, 1871–1942, vol. IV
Mansel-Jones, Herbert Riversdale, 1836–1907, vol. I
Mansel-Pleydell, Lt-Col Edmund Morton, 1850–1914, vol. I
Mansel-Pleydell, John Clavell, 1817–1902, vol. I
Mansel-Pleydell, Rev. John Colvile Morton, 1851–1938, vol. III
Mansell, Vice-Adm. Sir (George) Robert, 1868–1936, vol. III
Mansell, Lt-Col George William, 1904–1983, vol. VIII
Mansell, Lt-Col Sir John Herbert, 1864–1933, vol. III
Mansell, Air Vice-Marshal Reginald Baynes, 1896–1945, vol. IV
Mansell, Vice-Adm. Sir Robert; see Mansell, Vice-Adm. Sir G. R.
Mansell-Moullin, Charles William, 1851–1940, vol. III
Mansergh, Vice-Adm. Sir Aubrey; see Mansergh, Vice-Adm. Sir C. A. L.
Mansergh, Vice-Adm. Sir (Cecil) Aubrey (Lawson), 1898–1990, vol. VIII
Mansergh, Cornewall Lewis, 1863–1935, vol. III
Mansergh, Gen. Sir (Eric Carden) Robert, 1900–1970, vol. VI
Mansergh, Fanny; see Moody, F.
Mansergh, James, 1834–1905, vol. I
Mansergh, Adm. Sir Maurice James, 1896–1966, vol. VI
Mansergh, Nicholas; see Mansergh, P. N. S.
Mansergh, (Philip) Nicholas (Seton), 1910–1991, vol. IX
Mansergh, Gen. Sir Robert; see Mansergh, Gen. Sir E. C. R.
Mansergh, Southcote; see Manners, Charles.

Mansfield and Mansfield, 4th Earl of, 1806–1898, vol. I
Mansfield and Mansfield, 5th Earl of, 1860–1906, vol. I
Mansfield and Mansfield, 6th Earl of, 1864–1935, vol. III
Mansfield and Mansfield, 7th Earl of, 1900–1971, vol. VII
Mansfield, Hon. Sir Alan James, 1902–1980, vol. VII (AII)
Mansfield, Sir Alfred, 1870–1940, vol. III
Mansfield, Sir Charles Edward, 1828–1907, vol. I
Mansfield, Cyril James, 1861–1916, vol. II
Mansfield, F. J., 1872–1946, vol. IV
Mansfield, Henry, 1914–1979, vol. VII
Mansfield, Maj.-Gen. Sir Herbert, 1855–1939, vol. III
Mansfield, Horace Rendall, 1863–1914, vol. I
Mansfield, Vice-Adm. Sir John Maurice, 1893–1949, vol. IV
Mansfield, Orlando Augustine, 1863–1936, vol. III
Mansfield, Philip Theodore, 1892–1975, vol. VII
Mansfield, Purcell James, 1889–1968, vol. VI
Mansfield, Richard, 1857–1907, vol. I
Mansfield, Robert William, 1850–1911, vol. I
Mansfield, Walter, 1870–1916, vol. II
Mansfield, Wilfrid Stephen, 1894–1968, vol. VI
Mansfield, William Thomas, died 1939, vol. III(A), vol. IV
Mansfield Cooper, Sir William, 1903–1992, vol. IX
Manship, Paul, 1885–1966, vol. VI
Mansion, John Edmond, 1870–1942, vol. IV
Manson, Edward, 1849–1919, vol. II
Manson, Henry James, 1869–1952, vol. V
Manson, James Alexander, 1851–1921, vol. II
Manson, James Bolivar, 1879–1945, vol. IV
Manson, John, 1842–1923, vol. II
Manson, Sir Patrick, 1844–1922, vol. II
Manson, Robert George, 1893–1969, vol. VI
Manson, Rev. Thomas Walter, 1893–1958, vol. V
Manson, Rev. William, 1882–1958, vol. V
Manson-Bahr, Sir Philip, 1881–1966, vol. VI
Mant, (Arthur) Keith, 1919–2000, vol. X
Mant, Sir Cecil George, 1906–1990, vol. VIII
Mant, Keith; see Mant, A. K.
Mant, Sir Reginald Arthur, 1870–1942, vol. IV
Mantegazza, Paul, 1831–1910, vol. I
Mantell, Col Patrick Riners, 1862–1936, vol. III
Mantle, Lee, 1851–1934, vol. III
Mantle, Philip Jaques, 1901–1989, vol. VIII
Manton, 1st Baron (cr 1922), 1873–1922, vol. II
Manton, 2nd Baron, 1899–1968, vol. VI
Manton, G. Grenville, died 1932, vol. III
Manton, Sir Henry, 1835–1924, vol. II
Manton, Irene, 1904–1988, vol. VIII
Manton, Brig. Lionel, 1887–1961, vol. VI
Manton, Sidnie M., (Mrs J. P. Harding), 1902–1979, vol. VII
Mantoux, Paul Joseph, 1877–1956, vol. V
Manuel, Archibald Clark, 1901–1976, vol. VII
Manuel, Joseph Thomas, 1909–1990, vol. VIII
Manuel, Stephen, 1880–1954, vol. V
Manuwa, Chief Hon. Sir Samuel Layinka Ayodeji, 1903–1975, vol. VII

Manvell, Rev. Arnold Edward William, 1868–1927, vol. II
Manvell, (Arnold) Roger, 1909–1987, vol. VIII
Manvell, Roger; see Manvell, A. R.
Manvers, 3rd Earl, 1825–1900, vol. I
Manvers, 4th Earl, 1854–1926, vol. II
Manvers, 5th Earl, 1888–1940, vol. III
Manvers, 6th Earl, 1881–1955, vol. V
Manville, Sir Edward, 1862–1933, vol. III
Manwaring, George Ernest, 1882–1939, vol. III
Manzù, Giacomo, 1908–1991, vol. IX
Manzoni, Sir Herbert John Baptista, 1899–1972, vol. VII
Maori; see Inglis, Hon. J.
Maple, Sir John Blundell, 1st Bt, 1845–1903, vol. I
Maplesden, Rev. Arthur William, 1864–1932, vol. III
Mapleson, Henry, 1851–1927, vol. II
Maplestone, Philip Alan, died 1969, vol. VI
Mapother, Edward, 1881–1940, vol. III
Mapother, Edward Dillon, 1835–1908, vol. I
Mapp, Charles, 1903–1978, vol. VII
Mapp, Henry William, 1871–1955, vol. V
Mappin, Sir Charles Thomas Hewitt, 4th Bt, 1909–1941, vol. IV
Mappin, Sir Frank, 2nd Bt, 1846–1920, vol. II
Mappin, Sir Frank Crossley, 6th Bt, 1884–1975, vol. VII
Mappin, Sir Frederick Thorpe, 1st Bt, 1821–1910, vol. I
Mappin, Sir Samuel Wilson, 5th Bt, 1854–1942, vol. IV
Mappin, Sir Wilson, 3rd Bt, 1848–1925, vol. II
Mapson, Leslie William, 1907–1970, vol. VI
Mar, 27th (styled 33rd) Earl of, 1836–1930, vol. III
Mar, 28th (styled 34th) Earl of, 1868–1932, vol. III
Mar, 29th Earl of, 1891–1965, vol. VI
Mar, 30th Earl of, 1914–1975, vol. VII
Mar, Master of: see Garioch, Lord.
Mar, 12th Earl of, and Kellie, 14th Earl of, 1865–1955, vol. V
Mar, 13th Earl of, and Kellie, 15th Earl of, 1921–1993, vol. IX
Mar, Helen, died 1940, vol. III(A), vol. IV
Mara, Timothy Nicholas, 1948–1997, vol. X
Marais, Colin B.; see Bain-Marais.
Marais, Rev. Johannes Izak, 1848–1919, vol. II
Maraj, James Ajodhya, 1930–1999, vol. X
Maratib Ali, Sir Syed, 1883–1961, vol. VI
'Marc'; see Boxer, C. M. E.
Marcel, Gabriel, 1889–1973, vol. VII
Marcet, William, died 1900, vol. I
March, Sir Derek Maxwell, 1930–1992, vol. IX
March, George Edward, 1834–1922, vol. II
March, George Frederick, 1893–1985, vol. VIII
March, Henry Arthur, 1905–1988, vol. VIII
March, Rt Rev. John, 1863–1940, vol. III
March, Gen. Payton Conway, 1864–1955, vol. V
March, Samuel, 1861–1935, vol. III
Marchamley, 1st Baron, 1855–1925, vol. II
Marchamley, 2nd Baron, 1886–1949, vol. IV
Marchamley, 3rd Baron, 1922–1994, vol. IX
Marchand, Geoffrey Isidore Charles, died 1965, vol. VI
Marchand, Gen. Jean Baptiste, 1863–1934, vol. III

Marchant, Maj.-Gen. Alfred Edmund, 1863–1924, vol. II
Marchant, Bessie, (Mrs J. A. Comfort), 1862–1941, vol. IV
Marchant, Catherine; see Cookson, Dame C.
Marchant, Edgar Cardew, 1864–1960, vol. V
Marchant, Edgar Vernon, 1915–1997, vol. X
Marchant, Edgar Walford, 1876–1962, vol. VI
Marchant, Ernest Cecil, 1902–1979, vol. VII
Marchant, Sir Herbert Stanley, 1906–1990, vol. VIII
Marchant, Sir James, 1867–1956, vol. V
Marchant, James Robert Vernam, 1853–1936, vol. III
Marchant, Sir Stanley, 1883–1949, vol. IV
Marchant, Brig.-Gen. Thomas Harry Saunders, 1875–1952, vol. V
Marchant, William Sydney, 1894–1953, vol. V
Marchbank, John, 1883–1946, vol. IV
Marchbank, James, 1862–1947, vol. IV
Marchesi, Blanche, 1863–1940, vol. III
Marchesi, Mathilde, 1826–1913, vol. I
Marchmont, Arthur Williams, 1852–1923, vol. II
Marchwood, 1st Viscount, 1876–1955, vol. V
Marchwood, 2nd Viscount, 1912–1979, vol. VII
Marcil, Hon. Charles, 1860–1937, vol. III
Marcks, Violet Olivia C.; see Cressy-Marcks.
Marcon, Rev. Walter Hubert, died 1937, vol. III
Marconi, Marchese; Guglielmo Marconi, 1874–1937, vol. III
Marcosson, Isaac Frederick, 1876–1961, vol. VI
Marcotte, Rev. Francis Xavier, 1883–1967, vol. VI
Marcus, Frank Ulrich, 1928–1996, vol. X
Marcus, Michael, 1894–1960, vol. V(A), vol. VI(AI)
Marcuse, Herbert, 1898–1979, vol. VII
Marden, John Louis, 1919–1999, vol. X
Marden, Orison Swett, 1850–1924, vol. II
Marden, Maj.-Gen. Sir Thomas Owen, 1866–1951, vol. V
Marder, Arthur Jacob, 1910–1980, vol. VII
Mardon, Lt-Col (John) Kenric La Touche, 1905–1993, vol. IX
Mardon, Lt-Col Kenric; see Mardon, Lt-Col J. K. La T.
Mardy Jones, Thomas Isaac, 1879–1970, vol. VI
Mare, Captain Philip Armitage, 1891–1951, vol. V
Marek, Kurt W., 1915–1972, vol. VII
Marengo, Kimon Evan; see Kem.
Marescaux, Captain Alfred Edward Hay, died 1942, vol. IV
Marescaux, Vice-Adm. Gerald Charles Adolphe, 1860–1920, vol. II
Marett, Sir Robert Hugh Kirk, 1907–1981, vol. VIII
Marett, Robert Ranulph, 1866–1943, vol. IV
Margadale, 1st Baron, 1906–1996, vol. X
Margai, Sir Albert Michael, 1910–1980, vol. VII
Margai, Rt Hon. Sir Milton Augustus Strieby, 1895–1964, vol. VI
Margerison, Sir Lawrence, 1872–1958, vol. V
Margesson, 1st Viscount, 1890–1965, vol. VI
Margesson, Col Evelyn William, 1865–1944, vol. IV
Margesson, Sir Mortimer R., 1861–1947, vol. IV

Margesson, Captain Wentworth Henry Davies, 1869–1950, vol. IV
Margesson, Lt-Col William George, 1821–1911, vol. I
Margetson, Alfred James, 1877–1944, vol. IV
Margetson, Maj. Sir Philip Reginald, 1894–1985, vol. VIII
Margetson, W. H., 1861–1940, vol. III
Margetson, Very Rev. William James, 1874–1946, vol. IV
Margetts, Frederick Chilton, 1905–1989, vol. VIII
Margoliouth, David Samuel, 1858–1940, vol. III
Margoliouth, Rev. G., 1853–1924, vol. II
Margoliouth, Herschel Maurice, 1887–1959, vol. V
Margrett, Charles Henry, 1863–1941, vol. IV
Marillier, Frank William, 1855–1928, vol. II
Marillier, Henry Currie, 1865–1951, vol. V
Marin, John C., 1870–1953, vol. V
Marindin, Maj.-Gen. Arthur Henry, 1868–1947, vol. IV
Marindin, Col Cecil Colvile, 1879–1932, vol. III
Marindin, Sir Francis Arthur, 1838–1900, vol. I
Marion, Léo Edmond, 1899–1979, vol. VII
Maris, Matthew, 1839–1917, vol. II
Maritain, Jacques, 1882–1973, vol. VII
Marix, Air Vice-Marshal Reginald Lennox George, 1889–1966, vol. VI
Marjolin, Robert Ernest, 1911–1986, vol. VIII
Marjoribanks, Hon. Coutts, 1860–1924, vol. II
Marjoribanks, Dudley Sinclair, 1858–1929, vol. III
Marjoribanks, Edward, 1900–1932, vol. III
Marjoribanks, (Edyth) Leslia, 1927–1993, vol. IX
Marjoribanks, Sir George John, 1856–1931, vol. III
Marjoribanks, Leslia; see Marjoribanks, E. L.
Marjoribanks, Sir Norman Edward, 1872–1939, vol. III
Mark, J. M., died 1948, vol. IV
Mark, Sir John, 1832–1909, vol. I
Mark-Wardlaw, Rear-Adm. Alexander Livingston Penrose, 1891–1975, vol. VII
Mark-Wardlaw, Rear-Adm. William Penrose, 1887–1952, vol. V
Markall, Most Rev. Francis, 1905–1992, vol. IX
Markar, Hadji Sir Mohamed M.; see Macan-Markar.
Markby, Sir William, 1829–1914, vol. I
Markelius, Sven Gottfrid, 1889–1972, vol. VII
Marker, Edwin Henry Simon, 1888–1973, vol. VII
Marker, Col Raymond John, 1867–1914, vol. I
Marker, Richard, 1835–1916, vol. II
Markham, Adm. Sir Albert Hastings, 1841–1918, vol. II
Markham, Rt Rev. Algernon A., 1869–1949, vol. IV
Markham, Sir Arthur Basil, 1st Bt, 1866–1916, vol. II
Markham, Rt Rev. Bernard, 1907–1984, vol. VIII
Markham, Sir Charles, 2nd Bt, 1899–1952, vol. V
Markham, Brig.-Gen. Charles John, 1862–1927, vol. II
Markham, Sir Clements Robert, 1830–1916, vol. II
Markham, Lt-Gen. Sir Edwin, 1833–1918, vol. II
Markham, Edwin, 1852–1940, vol. III
Markham, Sir Frank; see Markham, Sir S. F.
Markham, Sir Henry Vaughan, 1897–1946, vol. IV

Markham, Roy, 1916–1979, vol. VII
Markham, Sir (Sydney) Frank, 1897–1975, vol. VII
Markham, Violet Rosa, (Mrs J. Carruthers), died 1959, vol. V
Markievicz, Constance Georgine, 1868–1927, vol. II
Marklew, Ernest, 1874–1939, vol. III
Marks, 1st Baron, 1858–1938, vol. III
Marks of Broughton, 1st Baron, 1888–1964, vol. VI
Marks of Broughton, 2nd Baron, 1920–1998, vol. X
Marks, Alexander Hammett, 1880–1954, vol. V
Marks, Barnett Samuel, 1827–1916, vol. II
Marks, Major Claud Laurie, 1863–1910, vol. I
Marks, David Woolf, 1811–1909, vol. I
Marks, Derek John, 1921–1975, vol. VII
Marks, Eric Astor David; see Marshall, Eric.
Marks, Ernest Samuel, 1872–1947, vol. IV
Marks, Frederick William, 1886–1942, vol. IV
Marks, Geoffrey, 1864–1938, vol. III
Marks, Harry Hananel, 1855–1916, vol. II
Marks, Hon. Sir Henry, 1861–1938, vol. III
Marks, Henry Stacy, 1829–1898, vol. I
Marks, Sir John Hedley Douglas, 1916–1982, vol. VIII
Marks, Kenneth, 1920–1988, vol. VIII
Marks, Leslie, 1889–1956, vol. V
Marks, Oliver, 1866–1940, vol. III
Marks, Captain Percy D'Evelyn, 1883–1968, vol. VI
Markus, Erika; see Markus, Rika
Markus, Rika, (Rixi), 1910–1992, vol. IX
Markus, Rixi; see Markus, Rika
Markwick, Col Ernest Elliott, 1853–1925, vol. II
Marlar, Edward Alfred Geoffrey, 1901–1978, vol. VII
Marlay, Charles Brinsley, 1831–1912, vol. I
Marlborough, 9th Duke of, 1871–1934, vol. III
Marlborough, 10th Duke of, 1897–1972, vol. VII
Marler, Hon. Sir Herbert, 1876–1940, vol. III
Marler, Leslie Sydney, 1900–1981, vol. VIII
Marler, Sydney; see Marler, L. S.
Marler, William de Montmollkin, 1849–1929, vol. III
Marley, 1st Baron, 1884–1952, vol. V
Marley, 2nd Baron, 1913–1990, vol. VIII
Marley, Brig. Cuthbert David, 1897–1960, vol. V
Marley, James, 1893–1954, vol. V
Marling, Sir Charles Murray, 1862–1933, vol. III
Marling, Lt-Col Sir John Stanley Vincent, 4th Bt, 1910–1977, vol. VII
Marling, Col Sir Percival Scrope, 3rd Bt, 1861–1936, vol. III
Marling, Sir William Henry, 2nd Bt, 1835–1919, vol. II
Marlow, Arthur Herbert, 1893–1964, vol. VI
Marlow, Col Benjamin William, 1863–1943, vol. IV
Marlow, Ewart, 1895–1965, vol. VI
Marlow, Frederick William, 1877–1936, vol. III
Marlow, Louis; see Wilkinson, L. U.
Marlow, Roger Douglas Frederick, 1912–1986, vol. VIII
Marlow, Roy George, 1931–1988, vol. VIII
Marlow, Sydney Raymond, 1896–1945, vol. IV
Marlowe, Anthony Alfred Harmsworth, 1904–1965, vol VI
Marlowe, Thomas, 1868–1935, vol. III

Marnan, John Fitzgerald, 1908–1990, vol. VIII
Marnham, Francis John, 1853–1941, vol. IV
Marnham, Harold, 1911–1987, vol. VIII
Marnham, John Ewart, 1916–1985, vol. VIII
Marnham, Sir Ralph, 1901–1984, vol. VIII
Marnoch, Col Sir John, 1867–1936, vol. III
Marochetti, Baron, 1894–1952, vol. V
Marples, Baron (Life Peer); Alfred Ernest Marples, 1907–1978, vol. VII
Marples, Brian John, 1907–1997, vol. X
Marples, George, 1869–1939, vol. III
Marquand, Rt Hon. Hilary Adair, 1901–1972, vol. VII
Marquand, John Phillips, 1893–1960, vol. V
Marquand, Reginald, 1874–1931, vol. III
Marr, Alexander, 1876–1938, vol. III
Marr, Allan James, 1907–1989, vol. VIII
Marr, Sir Charles William Clanan, 1880–1960, vol. V
Marr, Francis Alleyne, 1894–1942, vol. IV
Marr, Hamilton Clelland, 1870–1936, vol. III
Marr, Sir James, 1st Bt, 1854–1932, vol. III
Marr, James William Slesser, 1902–1965, vol. VI
Marr, John Edward, 1857–1933, vol. III
Marr, Col John Lynn, 1877–1931, vol. III
Marrable, Brig.-Gen. Arthur George, 1863–1925, vol. II
Marrable, Mrs, died 1916, vol. II
Marrack, Rear-Adm. Hugh Richard, 1888–1972, vol. VII
Marrack, John Richardson, 1886–1976, vol. VII
Marre, Sir Alan Samuel, 1914–1990, vol. VIII
Marriage, Herbert James, 1872–1946, vol. IV
Marriage, John Goodbody, 1929–1984, vol. VIII
Marrian, Guy Frederic, 1904–1981, vol. VIII
Marrie, J. J.; see Creasey, John.
Marrinan, Patrick Aloysius, 1877–1940, vol. III
Marriner, Lt-Col Bryan Lister, 1888–1943, vol. IV
Marriott, Col Alfred Sinclair, 1876–1943, vol. IV
Marriott, Charles, 1869–1957, vol. V
Marriott, Charles Bertrand, 1868–1946, vol. IV
Marriott, Sir Charles Hayes, 1834–1910, vol. I
Marriott, Captain Charles John Bruce, 1861–1936, vol. III
Marriott, Cyril Herbert Alfred, 1897–1977, vol. VII
Marriott, Eric Llewellyn, 1888–1945, vol. IV
Marriott, Ernest, 1882–1918, vol. II
Marriott, Francis, 1876–1957, vol. V
Marriott, Frederick, 1860–1941, vol. IV
Marriott, Sir Hayes, 1873–1929, vol. III
Marriott, Ven. Henry, 1870–1952, vol. V
Marriott, Herbert, 1865–1935, vol. III
Marriott, Hugh Leslie, 1900–1983, vol. VIII
Marriott, Rev. Sir Hugh Randolph Cavendish S.; see Smith-Marriott.
Marriott, James William, 1884–1953, vol. V
Marriott, Brig.-Gen. John, 1861–1953, vol. V
Marriott, Sir John Arthur Ransome, 1859–1945, vol. IV
Marriott, Maj.-Gen. Sir John Charles Oakes, 1895–1978, vol. VII
Marriott, John Hayes, 1909–1982, vol. VIII
Marriott, John Miles, 1935–1997, vol. X
Marriott, Captain John Peter Ralph, 1879–1938, vol. III

Marriott, Sir John Richard Wyldbore S.; see Smith-Marriott.
Marriott, Very Rev. John Thomas, died 1924, vol. II
Marriott, Marjorie Jane; see Speed, M. J.
Marriott, Patrick Arthur, 1899–1980, vol. VII
Marriott, Sir Ralph George Cavendish S.; see Smith-Marriott.
Marriott, Major Reginald Adams, 1857–1930, vol. III
Marriott, Richard D'Arcy, 1911–1985, vol. VIII
Marriott, Major Richard George Armine, 1867–1924, vol. II
Marriott, Richard Michael Harris, 1926–1975, vol. VII
Marriott, Brig. Sir Robert Ecklin, 1887–1984, vol. VIII
Marriott, Rev. Stephen Jack, 1886–1964, vol. VI
Marriott, William, 1848–1916, vol. II
Marriott, Sir William Henry S.; see Smith-Marriott.
Marriott, Sir William John S.; see Smith-Marriott.
Marriott, William Mason, 1889–1960, vol. V
Marriott, Sir William S.; see Smith-Marriott.
Marriott, Rt Hon. Sir William Thackeray, 1834–1903, vol. I
Marriott-Dodington, Brig.-Gen. Wilfred; see Dodington.
Marris, Adam Denzil, 1906–1983, vol. VIII
Marris, Eric Denyer, 1891–1976, vol. VII
Marris, Rev. Nisbet Colquhoun, died 1937, vol. III
Marris, Sir William Sinclair, 1873–1945, vol. IV
Marrs, Robert, 1884–1951, vol. V
Marryat, Very Rev. Charles, 1827–1907, vol. I
Marryat, Florence, (Mrs Francis Lean), 1838–1899, vol. I
Marryshow, Hon. Theophilus Albert, 1887–1958, vol. V
Mars-Jones, Hon. Sir William Lloyd, 1915–1999, vol. X
Marsack, Sir Charles Croft, 1892–1987, vol. VIII
Marsden, Alexander Edwin, 1832–1902, vol. I
Marsden, Allen Gatenby, 1893–1988, vol. VIII
Marsden, Captain Arthur, 1883–1960, vol. V
Marsden, Arthur Whitcombe, 1911–1997, vol. X
Marsden, (Charles) David, 1938–1998, vol. X
Marsden, David; see Marsden, C. D.
Marsden, Ven. E(dwyn) Lisle, 1886–1960, vol. V
Marsden, Col Sir Ernest, 1889–1970, vol. VI
Marsden, Captain George, 1874–1916, vol. II
Marsden, Sir John Denton, 1st Bt, 1873–1944, vol. IV
Marsden, Sir John Denton, 2nd Bt, 1913–1985, vol. VIII
Marsden, Leslie Alfred, 1921–1987, vol. VIII
Marsden, Sir Nigel John Denton, 3rd Bt, 1940–1997, vol. X
Marsden, Percy, 1888–1955, vol. V
Marsden, R. Sydney, 1856–1919, vol. II
Marsden, Rt Rev. Samuel Edward, 1832–1912, vol. I
Marsden, Terence Barclay, 1932–1981, vol. VIII
Marsden, Sir Thomas Rogerson, died 1927, vol. II
Marsden, Wilfred Alexander, 1878–1949, vol. IV
Marsden, Lt-Col William, 1841–1925, vol. II
Marsh, Ven. Bazil Roland, 1921–1997, vol. X

Marsh, Col Cunliffe Hebbert, 1878–1938, vol. III
Marsh, David Charles, 1917–1983, vol. VIII
Marsh, Rt Rev. Donald Ben, 1903–1973, vol. VII
Marsh, Dame Edith Ngaio; *see* Marsh, Dame Ngaio.
Marsh, Maj.-Gen. Edward Bertram, 1890–1976, vol. VII
Marsh, Sir Edward Howard, 1872–1953, vol. V
Marsh, Col Frank, 1855–1943, vol. IV
Marsh, Frank Burr, 1880–1940, vol. III(A), vol. IV
Marsh, Brig.-Gen. Frank Graham, 1875–1957, vol. V
Marsh, Maj.-Gen. Frank Hale Berwick, 1841–1923, vol. II
Marsh, Rev. Fred Shipley, 1886–1953, vol. V
Marsh, George Fletcher Riley, 1895–1984, vol. VIII
Marsh, Henry, 1850–1939, vol. III
Marsh, Rt Rev. Henry Hooper, 1898–1995, vol. IX
Marsh, (Henry) John, 1913–1992, vol. IX
Marsh, Howard, 1839–1915, vol. I
Marsh, James Ernest, 1860–1938, vol. III
Marsh, Lt-Col Jeremy-Taylor, 1872–1944, vol. IV
Marsh, John; *see* Marsh, H. J.
Marsh, Rev. John, 1904–1994, vol. IX
Marsh, Margaret Munnerlyn Mitchell, (Mrs John Robert Marsh), *died* 1949, vol. IV
Marsh, Michael John Waller, 1921–1983, vol. VIII
Marsh, Dame Ngaio, 1899–1982, vol. VIII
Marsh, Othniel Charles, 1831–1899, vol. I
Marsh, Sir Percy William, 1881–1969, vol. VI
Marsh, Richard, *died* 1915, vol. I
Marsh, Richard, 1851–1933, vol. III
Marsh, Rev. Sidney Frank, 1860–1936, vol. III
Marsh, Thomas Robertson, 1847–1929, vol. III
Marsh, Sir William Henry, 1827–1906, vol. I
Marsh, William Thomas, 1897–1985, vol. VIII
Marsh, William Waller, 1877–1959, vol. V
Marsh Smith, Reginald Norman, 1891–1975, vol. VII
Marshall, 1st Baron, 1865–1936, vol. III
Marshall of Goring, Baron (Life Peer); Walter Charles Marshall, 1932–1996, vol. X
Marshall of Leeds, Baron (Life Peer); Frank Shaw Marshall, 1915–1990, vol. VIII
Marshall, Alfred, 1842–1924, vol. II
Marshall, Sir Anthony, 1826–1911, vol. I
Marshall, Archibald, 1866–1934, vol. III
Marshall, Archibald Cook, 1890–1959, vol. V
Marshall, Sir Archie Pellow, 1899–1966, vol. VI
Marshall, Arthur; *see* Marshall, C. A. B.
Marshall, Arthur, 1873–1968, vol. VI
Marshall, Arthur C.; *see* Calder-Marshall.
Marshall, Sir Arthur Harold, 1870–1956, vol. V
Marshall, Arthur Hedley, 1904–1994, vol. IX
Marshall, Col Sir Arthur Wellington, 1841–1918, vol. II
Marshall, Bruce, 1899–1987, vol. VIII
Marshall, (Charles) Arthur (Bertram), 1910–1989, vol. VIII
Marshall, Charles Devereux, 1867–1918, vol. II
Marshall, Charles Frederic, 1864–1940, vol. III
Marshall, Brig. Charles Frederick Keilk, 1888–1953, vol. V
Marshall, Charles Jennings, 1890–1954, vol. V
Marshall, Charles Robertshaw, 1869–1952, vol. V
Marshall, D. H., 1848–1932, vol. III

Marshall, (Davis) Edward, 1869–1933, vol. III
Marshall, Comdr Sir Douglas, 1906–1976, vol. VII
Marshall, Hon. Duncan M'Lean, 1872–1946, vol. IV
Marshall, Edward, *see* Marshall, D. E.
Marshall, Rev. Edward Thory, 1842–1933, vol. III
Marshall, Elizabeth Middleton O.; *see* Ord Marshall.
Marshall, Emma, 1828–1899, vol. I
Marshall, Eric, (Eric Astor David Marks), 1891–1961, vol. VI
Marshall, Eric Stewart, 1879–1963, vol. VI
Marshall, Frances; *see* St Aubyn, Alan.
Marshall, Francis Hugh Adam, 1878–1949, vol. IV
Marshall, Maj.-Gen. Francis James, 1876–1942, vol. IV
Marshall, Frank, 1886–1952, vol. V
Marshall, Frank James, 1877–1944, vol. IV
Marshall, Fred, 1883–1962, vol. VI
Marshall, Fredda, (Mrs Herbert Marshall); *see* Brilliant, F.
Marshall, Frederic, *died* 1910, vol. I
Marshall, Lt-Gen. Sir Frederick, 1829–1900, vol. I
Marshall, Frederick Henry, 1878–1955, vol. V
Marshall, Engr-Adm. Frederick William, 1870–1956, vol. V
Marshall, Sir Geoffrey, 1887–1982, vol. VIII
Marshall, George Balfour, 1863–1928, vol. II
Marshall, Hon. George Catlett, 1880–1959, vol. V
Marshall, Maj.-Gen. George Frederick Leycester, 1843–1934, vol. III
Marshall, Maj.-Gen. Sir George Henry, 1843–1909, vol. I
Marshall, George Leslie, *died* 1964, vol. VI
Marshall, George Wicks, 1916–1987, vol. VIII
Marshall, George William, 1839–1905, vol. I
Marshall, Major George William, 1867–1940, vol. III
Marshall, Rt Rev. Guy, 1909–1978, vol. VII
Marshall, Sir Guy Anstruther Knox, 1871–1959, vol. V
Marshall, Col Hannath Douglas, 1872–1944, vol. IV
Marshall, Hedley; *see* Marshall, A. H.
Marshall, Hedley Herbert, 1909–1982, vol. VIII
Marshall, Henry D., *died* 1906, vol. I
Marshall, Major Henry Seymour, 1879–1937, vol. III
Marshall, Rt Rev. Henry Vincent, 1884–1955, vol. V
Marshall, Sir Herbert; *see* Marshall, Sir J. H.
Marshall, Herbert Brough Falcon, 1890–1966, vol. VI
Marshall, Herbert Menzies, 1841–1913, vol. I
Marshall, Herbert Percival James, 1906–1991, vol. IX
Marshall, Horace, *died* 1944, vol. IV
Marshall, Howard Percival, 1900–1973, vol. VII
Marshall, Hugh, 1868–1913, vol. I
Marshall, Hugh John Cole, 1873–1947, vol. IV
Marshall, Brig.-Gen. Hugh John Miles, 1867–1946, vol. IV
Marshall, Sir Hugo Frank, 1905–1986, vol. VIII
Marshall, J. Fitz, 1859–1932, vol. III
Marshall, Sir James, 1894–1979, vol. VII
Marshall, Sir James Brown, 1853–1922, vol. II

Marshall, James Cole, 1876–1952, vol. V
Marshall, Rev. James M'Call, 1838–1926, vol. II
Marshall, James Rissik, 1886–1959, vol. V
Marshall, John, 1845–1915, vol. I
Marshall, John, 1860–1951, vol. V
Marshall, John, 1895–1970, vol. VI
Marshall, Captain John Dodds, 1878–1931, vol. III
Marshall, John Edwin, 1864–1937, vol. III
Marshall, John Frederick, 1874–1949, vol. IV
Marshall, Sir John Hubert, 1876–1958, vol. V
Marshall, John Robert Neil, 1922–1990, vol. VIII
Marshall, Rt Hon. Sir John Ross, 1912–1988, vol. VIII
Marshall, Maj.-Gen. John Stuart, 1883–1944, vol. IV
Marshall, Rev. John Turner, 1850–1923, vol. II
Marshall, Brig.-Gen. John Willoughby Astell, 1854–1921, vol. II
Marshall, John Wilson, died 1923, vol. II
Marshall, Sir (Joseph) Herbert, 1851–1918, vol. II
Marshall, Rev. Joseph William, 1835–1915, vol. I
Marshall, Kenneth McLean, 1874–1954, vol. V
Marshall, Rev. Laurence Henry, 1882–1953, vol. V
Marshall, Lumley Arnold, 1852–1942, vol. IV
Marshall, Markham Richard L.; see Leeson-Marshall.
Marshall, Martin John, 1914–1998, vol. X
Marshall, Neil; see Marshall, J. R. N.
Marshall, Lt-Col Noel George Lambert, 1852–1926, vol. II
Marshall, Brig. Norman, 1886–1942, vol. IV
Marshall, Norman, 1901–1980, vol. VII
Marshall, Norman Bertram, 1915–1996, vol. X
Marshall, Captain Oswald Percival, 1857–1939, vol. III
Marshall, Patrick, 1869–1950, vol. IV(A)
Marshall, Percy Edwin Alan J.; see Johnson-Marshall
Marshall, Captain Robert, 1863–1910, vol. I
Marshall, Robert, 1889–1975, vol. VII
Marshall, Sir Robert Braithwaite, 1920–2000, vol. X
Marshall, Sir Robert C.; see Calder-Marshall.
Marshall, Robert Ian, 1899–1970, vol. VI
Marshall, Robert Smith, 1902–1976, vol. VII
Marshall, Maj.-Gen. Roger Sydenham, 1913–1994, vol. IX
Marshall, Maj.-Gen. Roy Stuart, 1917–1987, vol. VIII
Marshall, Septimus, 1876–1962, vol. VI
Marshall, Sheina Macalister, 1896–1977, vol. VII
Marshall, Sir Sidney, 1882–1973, vol. VII
Marshall, Sir Stirrat Andrew William J.; see Johnson-Marshall.
Marshall, Brig.-Gen. Thomas Edward, 1865–1946, vol. IV
Marshall, Col Sir Thomas Horatio, 1833–1917, vol. II
Marshall, Thomas Humphrey, 1893–1981, vol. VIII
Marshall, Thomas Riley, 1854–1925, vol. II
Marshall, Thurgood, 1908–1993, vol. IX
Marshall, Major W. R., died 1916, vol. II
Marshall, Cdre William, 1873–1930, vol. III
Marshall, Rev. William, 1875–1955, vol. V
Marshall, William, 1912–1995, vol. IX

Marshall, William Hibbert, 1866–1929, vol. III
Marshall, William Lawrence Wright, died 1939, vol. III
Marshall, Sir William Marchbank, 1875–1967, vol. VI
Marshall, Lt-Gen. Sir William Raine, 1865–1939, vol. III
Marshall, Lt-Col William Thomas, 1854–1920, vol. II
Marshall, William Thomas, 1907–1975, vol. VII
Marshall-Cornwall, Gen. Sir James Handyside, 1887–1985, vol. VIII
Marshall-Hall, Sir Edward, 1858–1927, vol. II
Marshall-Hall, G. W. L., 1862–1915, vol. I
Marshall-Reynolds, Clyde Albert, 1898–1977, vol. VII
Marsham, Brig. Francis William Bullock-, 1883–1971, vol. VII
Marsham, George, 1849–1927, vol. II
Marsham, Dame Joan; see Marsham, Hon. Mrs S.
Marsham, Rev. Hon. John, 1842–1926, vol. II
Marsham, Robert H. Bullock-, 1833–1913, vol. I
Marsham, Hon. Mrs Sydney, died 1972, vol. VII
Marsham, Thomas Nelson, 1923–1989, vol. VIII
Marsham-Townshend, Hon. Robert, 1834–1914, vol. I
Marsillac, Jacques J. B. de, 1879–1962, vol. VI
Marsland, Edward Abson, 1923–1996, vol. X
Marson, Air Vice-Marshal John, 1906–1988, vol. VIII
Marston, Archibald Daniel, 1891–1962, vol. VI
Marston, Sir Charles, 1867–1946, vol. IV
Marston, Edward, 1825–1914, vol. I
Marston, Freda, 1895–1949, vol. IV
Marston, Hedley Ralph, 1900–1965, vol. VI
Marston, Surg.-Gen. Jeffery Allen, 1831–1911, vol. I
Marston, Reginald St Clair, 1886–1943, vol. IV
Marston, Robert Bright, 1853–1927, vol. II
Martel, Comtesse de; see Gyp, Sybille.
Martel, Brig.-Gen. Sir Charles Philip, 1861–1945, vol. IV
Martel, Lt-Gen. Sir Giffard Le Quesne, 1889–1958, vol. V
Martell, Edward Drewett, 1909–1989, vol. IX(AI)
Martell, Vice-Adm. Sir Hugh Colenso, 1912–1998, vol. X
Martelli, Ernest Wynne, died 1917, vol. II
Martelli, Maj.-Gen. Sir Horace de Courcy, 1877–1959, vol. V
Martello Tower; see Norman, Comdr F. M.
Marten, Hon. Sir Alfred George, 1839–1906, vol. I
Marten, Sir Amberson Barrington, 1870–1962, vol. VI
Marten, Sir (Clarence) Henry (Kennett), 1872–1948, vol. IV
Marten, Eric Charles, 1899–1948, vol. IV
Marten, Vice-Adm. Sir Francis Arthur, 1879–1950, vol. IV
Marten, Ven. George Henry, 1876–1966, vol. VI
Marten, Rt Hon. Sir (H.) Neil, 1916–1985, vol. VIII
Marten, Sir Henry; see Marten, Sir C. H. K.
Marten, John Thomas, 1872–1929, vol. III
Marti, Karl, 1855–1925, vol. II
Martin, Sir Albert, died 1943, vol. IV

Martin, Col Albert Edward, 1876–1936, vol. III
Martin, Sir Albert Victor, 1897–1968, vol. VI
Martin, Sir Alec, 1884–1971, vol. VII
Martin, Very Rev. Alexander, 1857–1946, vol. IV
Martin, Alfred James, 1875–1959, vol. V
Martin, Lt-Gen. Sir Alfred Robert, 1853–1926, vol. II
Martin, Andrew, 1906–1985, vol. VIII
Martin, Sir Andrew; see Martin, Sir R. A. St G.
Martin, Hon. Archer, 1865–1941, vol. IV
Martin, Arthur Anderson, died 1916, vol. II
Martin, Arthur Campbell, 1875–1963, vol. VI
Martin, Arthur John, 1883–1942, vol. IV
Martin, Arthur Patchett, 1851–1902, vol. I
Martin, (Basil) Kingsley, 1897–1969, vol. VI
Martin, Vice-Adm. Sir Benjamin Charles Stanley, 1891–1957, vol. V
Martin, Bradley, 1841–1913, vol. I
Martin, Sir Carlaw; see Martin, Sir T. C.
Martin, Sir Charles Carnegie, 1901–1969, vol. VI
Martin, Charles Emanuel, 1891–1977, vol. VII
Martin, Charles F., 1868–1953, vol. V
Martin, Sir Charles James, 1866–1955, vol. V
Martin, Charlie; see Martin, J. C.
Martin, Chester, 1882–1958, vol. V
Martin, Christopher, 1866–1933, vol. III
Martin, Christopher John H.; see Holland-Martin.
Martin, Col Claude Buist, 1869–1950, vol. IV
Martin, Rt Rev. Clifford Arthur, 1895–1977, vol. VII
Martin, Cornwallis Philip Wykeham-, 1855–1924, vol. II
Martin, Col Cunliffe, 1834–1917, vol. II
Martin, Brig. Cyril Gordon, 1891–1980, vol. VII
Martin, Cyril Hubert, 1867–1940, vol. III(A), vol. IV
Martin, Daisy Maud, died 1964, vol. VI
Martin, Sir David Christie, 1914–1976, vol. VII
Martin, Rear-Adm. Sir David James, 1933–1990, vol. VIII
Martin, Adm. Sir Deric Douglas Eric H.; see Holland-Martin.
Martin, Rt Rev. Donald, 1873–1938, vol. III
Martin, Douglas Whitwell, 1906–1989, vol. VIII
Martin, Lt-Col Edward Cuthbert De R.; see De Renzy-Martin.
Martin, Brig.-Gen. Edward Fowell, 1875–1950, vol. IV
Martin, Edward H.; see Holland-Martin.
Martin, Captain Edward Harington, died 1921, vol. II
Martin, Edward Kenneth, 1883–1980, vol. VII
Martin, Edward Pritchard, 1844–1910, vol. I
Martin, Brig. Edwyn Sandys Dawes, 1894–1954, vol. V
Martin, Emma; see Marshall, E.
Martin, Sir Ernest, 1872–1957, vol. V
Martin, Col Ernest Edmund, 1869–1925, vol. II
Martin, Frank, 1890–1974, vol. VII
Martin, (Fred) Russell (Beauchamp), 1887–1981, vol. VIII
Martin, Frederick, 1882–1950, vol. IV
Martin, Frederick George Stephen, 1890–1981, vol. VIII
Martin, Frederick John, 1891–1964, vol. VI

Martin, Frederick Morris, 1923–1985, vol. VIII
Martin, Frederick Royal, 1919–1997, vol. X
Martin, Frederick Townsend, 1849–1914, vol. I
Martin, Col George Blake Napier, 1847–1917, vol. II
Martin, Sir George Clement, 1844–1916, vol. II
Martin, Rev. George Currie, 1865–1937, vol. III
Martin, George Peter, 1823–1910, vol. I
Martin, Sir George William, 1884–1976, vol. VII
Martin, Col Gerald Hamilton, 1879–1952, vol. V
Martin, Glenn Luther, 1886–1955, vol. V
Martin, Granville Edward B.; see Bromley-Martin.
Martin, Air Marshal Sir Harold Brownlow Morgan, 1918–1988, vol. VIII
Martin, Captain Harry Cutfield, 1852–1932, vol. III
Martin, Helen, (Lady Martin); see Faucit, H.
Martin, Rev. Henry, 1844–1919, vol. II
Martin, Rev. Henry, 1844–1923, vol. II
Martin, Henry, 1889–1964, vol. VI
Martin, Rt Rev. Henry David, 1889–1971, vol. VII
Martin, Col Henry Graham, 1872–1955, vol. V
Martin, Henry Robert Charles, 1889–1942, vol. IV
Martin, Brig.-Gen. Herbert, 1857–1931, vol. III
Martin, Howard, died 1924, vol. II
Martin, Hubert, died 1938, vol. III
Martin, Rev. Hugh, 1890–1964, vol. VI
Martin, Lt-Gen. Hugh Gray, 1887–1969, vol. VI
Martin, Humphrey Trice, died 1931, vol. III
Martin, Sir James, 1861–1935, vol. III
Martin, Sir James, 1893–1981, vol. VIII
Martin, James Arthur, 1903–1989, vol. IX(AI)
Martin, Major James Evans Baillie, 1859–1931, vol. III
Martin, Maj.-Gen. James Fitzgerald, 1876–1958, vol. V
Martin, James Hamilton, 1841–1937, vol. III
Martin, Maj.-Gen. James Mansergh Wentworth, 1902–1986, vol. VIII
Martin, James Purdon, 1893–1984, vol. VIII
Martin, James Rea, 1877–1951, vol. V
Martin, John, 1847–1944, vol. IV
Martin, John, 1884–1949, vol. IV
Martin, John Christopher, (Charlie), 1926–1999, vol. X
Martin, Brig. John Crawford, 1896–1963, vol. VI
Martin, Brig. John Douglas K.: see King-Martin.
Martin, John Francis Ryde, 1943–1999, vol. X
Martin, John Hanbury, 1892–1983, vol. VIII
Martin, Sir (John) Leslie, 1908–2000, vol. X
Martin, Sir John Miller, 1904–1991, vol. IX
Martin, John Powell, 1925–1997, vol. X
Martin, Maj.-Gen. John Simson Stuart, 1888–1973, vol. VII
Martin, Hon. Joseph, 1852–1923, vol. II
Martin, Joseph Samuel, 1845–1911, vol. I
Martin, Maj.-Gen. Kevin John, 1890–1958, vol. V
Martin, Kingsley; see Martin, B. K.
Martin, Leonard Charles James, 1920–1987, vol. VIII
Martin, Leonard Cyril, 1886–1976, vol. VII
Martin, Sir Leslie; see Martin, Sir J. L.
Martin, Sir Leslie Harold, 1900–1983, vol. VIII
Martin, Louis Claude, 1891–1981, vol. VIII
Martin, Hon. Maurice, 1872–1937, vol. III
Martin, Nicholas Henry, 1906–1981, vol. VIII

Martin, Hon. Sir Norman Angus, 1893–1978, vol. VII
Martin, Olaus Macleod, 1890–1981, vol. VIII
Martin, Olive F., 1887–1967, vol. VI
Martin, Patrick William, 1916–2000, vol. X
Martin, Hon. Paul Joseph James, 1903–1992, vol. IX
Martin, Percy F., 1861–1941, vol. IV
Martin, Peter Lewis, 1918–1998, vol. X
Martin, Rev. Philip Montague, 1913–1981, vol. VIII
Martin, Philippa Parry, 1897–1981, vol. VIII
Martin, Most Rev. Pierre, 1910–1987, vol. VIII
Martin, Reginald James, 1892–1970, vol. VI
Martin, Col Reginald Victor, 1889–1973, vol. VII
Martin, Rt Hon. Sir Richard, 1st Bt (*cr* 1885), 1831–1901, vol. I
Martin, Sir Richard, *died* 1922, vol. II
Martin, Rev. Richard, 1836–1927, vol. II
Martin, Sir Richard Biddulph, 1st Bt (*cr* 1905), 1838–1916, vol. II
Martin, Sir Richard Byam, 5th Bt, (*cr* 1791), 1841–1910, vol. I
Martin, Sir Richard Edward Rowley, 1847–1907, vol. I
Martin, Col Sir (Robert) Andrew (St George), 1914–1993, vol. IX
Martin, Lt-Col Sir Robert Edmund, 1874–1961, vol. VI
Martin, Robert M. Holland, 1872–1944, vol. IV
Martin, Col Rowland Hill, 1848–1919, vol. II
Martin, Rupert Claude, 1905–1991, vol. IX
Martin, Hon. Russell; *see* Martin, Hon. F. R. B.
Martin, Samuel Frederick Radcliffe, 1918–2000, vol. X(AII)
Martin, Sidney, 1860–1927, vol. II
Martin, Sir Sidney Launcelot, 1918–1991, vol. IX
Martin, Stapleton, 1846–1922, vol. II
Martin, Sir Theodore, 1816–1909, vol. I
Martin, Very Rev. Thomas, 1856–1942, vol. IV
Martin, Thomas, 1893–1971, vol. VII
Martin, Sir Thomas Acquin, 1850–1906, vol. I
Martin, Thomas Ballantyne, 1901–1995, vol. IX
Martin, Sir (Thomas) Carlaw, 1850–1920, vol. II
Martin, Col Thomas Morgan, 1854–1928, vol. II
Martin, Thomas Shannon, 1891–1954, vol. V
Martin, Victoria Claflin Woodhull, 1838–1927, vol. II
Martin, Violet, 1862–1915, vol. I
Martin, W. A. P., 1827–1916, vol. II
Martin, Captain W. R., *died* 1913, vol. I
Martin, Willem, 1876–1954, vol. V
Martin, Sir William, 1856–1924, vol. II
Martin, Paymaster Rear-Adm. William Ernest Russell, 1867–1946, vol. IV
Martin, William Gregory W.; *see* Wood-Martin.
Martin, William Henry Blyth, 1862–1946, vol. IV
Martin, William Henry Porteous, 1886–1939, vol. III
Martin, Hon. William Lee, 1870–1950, vol. IV
Martin, William McChesney, Jr, 1906–1998, vol. X
Martin, William Pethebridge, 1859–1933, vol. III
Martin-Bird, Col Sir Richard Dawnay, 1910–1992, vol. IX
Martin du Gard, Roger, 1881–1958, vol. V

Martin-Harvey, Sir John; *see* Harvey.
Martin-Hurst, William, 1876–1941, vol. IV
Martin-Jenkins, Dennis Frederick, 1911–1991, vol. IX
Martin-Jones, Rev. S., 1872–1941, vol. IV
Martin-Leake, Lt-Col Arthur; *see* Leake.
Martin-Leake, Vice-Adm. Francis, 1869–1928, vol. II
Martin-Leake, Hugh; *see* Leake.
Martindale, Sir Arthur Henry Temple, 1854–1942, vol. IV
Martindale, Col Benjamin Hay, 1824–1904, vol. I
Martindale, Rev. Cyril Charlie, 1879–1963, vol. VI
Martindale, Ven. Henry, 1879–1946, vol. IV
Martindale, Hilda, 1875–1952, vol. V
Martindale, Louisa, *died* 1966, vol. VI
Martindell, Herbert Edward West, 1866–1933, vol. III
Martineau, Alfred, *died* 1903, vol. I
Martineau, Edith, 1842–1909, vol. I
Martineau, Lt-Col Ernest, 1861–1951, vol. V
Martineau, George, 1835–1919, vol. II
Martineau, Rev. Canon George Edward, 1905–1969, vol. VI
Martineau, James, 1805–1900, vol. I
Martineau, Paul Gideon, 1858–1934, vol. III
Martineau, Sir Philip Hubert, 1862–1944, vol. IV
Martineau, Rt Rev. Robert Arnold Schürhoff, 1913–1999, vol. X
Martineau, Sir Wilfrid, 1889–1964, vol. VI
Martineau, Sir William, 1865–1950, vol. IV
Martinengo-Cesaresco, Countess; Evelyn Lilian Hazeldine, *died* 1931, vol. III
Martinez Zuviria, Gen. Gustavo, 1915–1994, vol. IX
Martino, Commendatore Eduardo de, *died* 1912, vol. I
Martins, Armando; *see* Martins, V. A.
Martins, (Virgilio) Armando, 1914–1988, vol. VIII
Martinson, Rt Rev. Ezra Douglas, 1885–1968, vol. VI
Martinson, Harry Edmond, 1904–1978, vol. VII
Marton, Col George Blucher Heneage, 1839–1905, vol. I
Marton, Lt-Col Richard Oliver, 1872–1945, vol. IV
Martonmere, 1st Baron, 1907–1989, vol. VIII
Marty, Cardinal François, 1904–1994, vol. IX
Martyn, Col Anthony Wood, 1864–1955, vol. V
Martyn, Brig.-Gen. Arundel, 1868–1945, vol. IV
Martyn, Brig. Athelstan Markham, 1881–1956, vol. V
Martyn, David Forbes, 1906–1970, vol. VI
Martyn, Edward, 1859–1923, vol. II
Martyn, Sir Henry Linnington, 1888–1947, vol. IV
Martyn, Joan, 1899–1989, vol. VIII
Martyn, Rev. Richard James, 1846–1913, vol. I
Martyn, Selwyn Rawlings, 1892–1956, vol. V
Martyr, Lt-Col Cyril Godfrey, 1860–1936, vol. III
Martyr, (Joseph) Weston, 1885–1966, vol. VI
Martyr, Richard Edward, 1857–1940, vol. III
Marvin, Francis Sydney, 1863–1943, vol. IV
Marwick, Sir Brian Allan, 1908–1992, vol. IX
Marwick, Ewan, 1952–1993, vol. IX
Marwick, Hugh, 1881–1965, vol. VI
Marwick, Sir James David, 1826–1908, vol. I
Marwood, Sidney Lionel, 1891–1981, vol. VIII

Marwood, Sir William Francis, 1863–1935, vol. III
Marwood-Elton, Lt-Col William, 1865–1931, vol. III
Marx, Enid Crystal Dorothy, 1902–1998, vol. X
Marx, Adm. John Locke, 1852–1939, vol. III
Mary Leo, Sister; *see* Leo, Dame Sister Mary
Maryon, Herbert, 1874–1965, vol. VI
Maryon-Wilson, George Maryon; *see* Wilson.
Maryon-Wilson, Rev. Canon Sir (George) Percy (Maryon), 12th Bt, 1898–1965, vol. VI
Maryon-Wilson, Sir Hubert Guy Maryon, 13th Bt, 1888–1978, vol. VII
Maryon-Wilson, Rev. Canon Sir Percy; *see* Maryon-Wilson, Rev. Canon Sir G. P. M.
Maryon-Wilson, Sir Spencer Pocklington Maryon; *see* Wilson.
Marzban, Jehangier B., 1848–1928, vol. II
Marzban, Pherozeshah Jehangir, 1876–1933, vol. III
Marzials, Sir Frank Thomas, 1840–1912, vol. I
Masani, Sir Rustom Pestonji, 1876–1966, vol. VI
Masaryk, Jan Garrigue, 1886–1948, vol. IV
Masaryk, Thomas Garrigue, 1850–1937, vol. III
Mascagni, Pietro, 1863–1945, vol. IV
Mascall, Rev. Canon Eric Lionel, 1905–1993, vol. IX
Mascall, Col Maurice Edward, 1882–1958, vol. V
Maschwitz, Eric, 1901–1969, vol. VI
Masefield, John, 1878–1967, vol. VI
Masefield, Col Robert Taylor, 1839–1922, vol. II
Masey, Albert, *died* 1910, vol. I
Masham, 1st Baron, 1815–1906, vol. I
Masham, 2nd Baron, 1857–1917, vol. II
Masham, 3rd Baron, 1867–1924, vol. II
Masham, William George, 1843–1916, vol. II
Mashiter, Col Sir George Coope, 1843–1927, vol. II
Masih, Rt Rev. Inayat, 1918–1980, vol. VII
Maskell, Alfred Ogle, *died* 1912, vol. I
Maskell, Ernest John, 1895–1958, vol. V
Maskelyne, John Nevil, 1839–1917, vol. II
Maskelyne, Mervyn Herbert Nevil Story, 1823–1911, vol. I
Maskew, Rev. Arthur Fairclough, 1854–1938, vol. III
Mason, Alan Kenneth, 1920–1990, vol. VIII
Mason, Alfred Edward Woodley, 1865–1948, vol. IV
Mason, Alfred John, 1853–1918, vol. II
Mason, Arnold Henry, 1885–1963, vol. VI
Mason, Rev. Arthur James, 1851–1928, vol. II
Mason, Arthur Malcolm, 1915–1998, vol. X
Mason, Sir Arthur Wier, 1860–1924, vol. II
Mason, Brewster, 1922–1987, vol. VIII
Mason, Charlotte Maria Shaw, 1842–1923, vol. II
Mason, Sir Dan Hurdis, 1911–1982, vol. VIII
Mason, Sir David, 1862–1940, vol. III
Mason, David Marshall, 1865–1945, vol. IV
Mason, Vice-Adm. Dennis Howard, 1916–1996, vol. X
Mason, Rev. Edmund Robert, *died* 1922, vol. II
Mason, Eudo Colecestra, 1901–1969, vol. VI
Mason, Vice-Adm. Sir Frank Trowbridge, 1900–1988, vol. VIII
Mason, Frank H., 1876–1965, vol. VI
Mason, Sir George Charles, 1855–1904, vol. I
Mason, Rev. George Edward, 1847–1928, vol. II

Mason, Maj.-Gen. Harry Macan, 1850–1929, vol. III
Mason, Rev. Henry Alfred, 1851–1939, vol. III
Mason, Hon. Henry Greathead Rex, 1885–1975, vol. VII
Mason, Col Hubert Oliver Browne B.; *see* Browne-Mason.
Mason, Rev. James, 1840–1912, vol. I
Mason, James, 1909–1984, vol. VIII
Mason, Lt-Col James Cooper, 1875–1923, vol. II
Mason, James Francis, 1861–1929, vol. III
Mason, John H., 1875–1951, vol. V
Mason, Joseph, 1866–1933, vol. III
Mason, Lt-Col Kenneth, 1887–1976, vol. VII
Mason, Ven. Lancelot, 1905–1990, vol. VIII
Mason, Sir Laurence, 1886–1970, vol. VI
Mason, Leonard Ralph, 1910–1974, vol. VII
Mason, Marianne Harriet, *died* 1932, vol. III
Mason, Michael; *see* Mason, R. M.
Mason, Michael Henry, 1900–1982, vol. VIII
Mason, Sir Paul, 1904–1978, vol. VII
Mason, Lt-Col Percival Lawrence, 1857–1938, vol. III
Mason, Philip, 1906–1999, vol. X
Mason, Major Philip Granville, 1872–1915, vol. I
Mason, Richard, 1919–1997, vol. X
Mason, Rev. Canon Richard John, 1929–1997, vol. X
Mason, (Richard) Michael, 1917–1977, vol. VII
Mason, Rev. Richard Swann S.; *see* Swann-Mason.
Mason, Robert, 1857–1927, vol. II
Mason, Robert Heath, 1918–1969, vol. VI
Mason, Robert Whyte, 1905–1984, vol. VIII
Mason, Brig. Searle Dwyer, 1892–1953, vol. V
Mason, Stewart Carlton, 1906–1983, vol. VIII
Mason, Sydney, 1920–1995, vol. IX
Mason, Sir Thomas, *died* 1924, vol. II
Mason, Thomas Godfrey, 1890–1959, vol. V(A)
Mason, Adm. Thomas Henry, 1811–1900, vol. I
Mason, Walt, 1862–1939, vol. III
Mason, Lt-Col Walter, 1863–1937, vol. III
Mason, Walter W.; *see* Wynne Mason.
Mason, William, 1872–1961, vol. VI
Mason-Macfarlane, Lt-Gen. Sir Noel; *see* Macfarlane.
Masood, Sir Syed Ross, 1889–1937, vol. III
Maspero, Sir Gaston Camille Charles, 1846–1916, vol. II
Massenet, Jules Emile Frédéric, 1842–1912, vol. I
Massereene, 11th Viscount, **and Ferrard,** 4th Viscount, 1842–1905, vol. I
Massereene, 12th Viscount, **and Ferrard,** 5th Viscount, 1873–1956, vol. VI
Massereene, 13th Viscount, **and Ferrard,** 6th Viscount, 1914–1992, vol. IX
Massey, Sir Arthur, 1894–1980, vol. VII
Massey, Dame Christina Allen, *died* 1932, vol. III
Massey, Daniel Raymond, 1933–1998, vol. X
Massey, Rev. Edwyn Reynolds, 1847–1923, vol. II
Massey, Gerald, 1828–1907, vol. I
Massey, Gertrude, 1868–1957, vol. V
Massey, Sir Harrie Stewart Wilson, 1908–1983, vol. VIII
Massey, Rev. John Cooke, 1842–1928, vol. II
Massey, Raymond, 1896–1983, vol. VIII

Massey, Rt Hon. Vincent, 1887–1967, vol. VI
Massey, William Edmund Devereux, 1901–1991, vol. IX
Massey, Rt Hon. William Ferguson, 1856–1925, vol. II
Massey, William Henry, died 1940, vol. III
Massey-Mainwaring, Hon. William Frederick Barton; see Mainwaring.
Massiah, Sir Grey; see Massiah, Sir H. G.
Massiah, Sir (Hallam) Grey, 1888–1972, vol. VII
Massie, Grant, 1896–1964, vol. VI
Massie, John, 1842–1925, vol. II
Massie, Major John Hamon, 1872–1914, vol. I
Massie, Lt-Col Robert Allwright, 1890–1966, vol. VI
Massie, Brig.-Gen. Roger Henry, 1869–1927, vol. II
Massie, Adm. Thomas Leeke, 1802–1898, vol. I
Massigli, René, 1888–1988, vol. VIII
Massine, Lénide, 1896–1979, vol. VII
Massingberd, Mrs, died 1897, vol. I
Massingberd, Field-Marshal Sir Archibald Armar M.; see Montgomery-Massingberd.
Massingberd, Stephen Langton, 1869–1925, vol. II
Massingham, Harold John, 1888–1952, vol. V
Massingham, Henry William, 1860–1924, vol. II
Masson, David, 1822–1907, vol. I
Masson, Sir David Orme, 1858–1937, vol. III
Masson, Hon. Col Sir David Parkes, 1847–1915, vol. I
Masson, Flora, died 1937, vol. III
Masson, Frederic, 1847–1923, vol. II
Masson, Sir Irvine; see Masson, Sir J. I. O.
Masson, Sir (James) Irvine (Orme), 1887–1862, vol. VI
Masson, John, died 1927, vol. II
Masson, Sir John Robertson, 1898–1965, vol. VI
Masson, Rosaline, died 1949, vol. IV
Massy, 6th Baron, 1835–1915, vol. I
Massy, 7th Baron, 1864–1926, vol. II
Massy, 8th Baron, 1894–1958, vol. V
Massy, Brig. Charles Walter, 1887–1973, vol. VII
Massy, Brig.-Gen. Edward Charles, 1868–1946, vol. IV
Massy, Col Godfrey, 1863–1944, vol. IV
Massy, Col Harry Stanley, 1855–1920, vol. II
Massy, Lt-Gen. Hugh Royds Stokes, 1884–1965, vol. VI
Massy, Col Percy Hugh Hamon, 1857–1939, vol. III
Massy, Col William George, 1857–1941, vol. IV
Massy, Lt-Gen. William Godfrey Dunham, 1838–1906, vol. I
Massy-Beresford, John George, 1856–1923, vol. II
Massy-Dawson, Captain Francis Evelyn, 1872–1939, vol. III
Massy-Greene, Hon. Sir Walter, 1874–1952, vol. V
Massy-Westropp, Col John, 1860–1951, vol. V
Mastel, Royston John, 1917–1998, vol. X
Master, Alfred, 1883–1978, vol. VII
Master, Lt-Col Arthur Gilbert, 1867–1942, vol. IV
Master, Captain Charles Edward Hoskins, 1878–1960, vol. V
Master, Charles Gilbert, died 1903, vol. I
Master, Rev. Harold C.; see Chester-Master.
Master, Lt-Col Richard C.; see Chester-Master.

Master, Thomas William Chester C; see Chester-Master.
Master, Col William Alfred C.; see Chester-Master.
Masterman, Arthur Thomas, 1869–1941, vol. IV
Masterman, Rt Hon. Charles Frederick Gurney, 1873–1927, vol. II
Masterman, Sir Christopher Hughes, 1889–1982, vol. VIII
Masterman, Air Cdre Edward Alexander Dimsdale, 1880–1957, vol. V
Masterman, Sir John Cecil, 1891–1977, vol. VII
Masterman, Rt Rev. John Howard Bertram, 1867–1933, vol. III
Masterman, William, 1846–1903, vol. I
Masters, Albert Edward Hefford, 1902–1968, vol. VI
Masters, Col Alexander, 1848–1936, vol. III
Masters, Rt Rev. Brian John, 1932–1998, vol. X
Masters, C. H., 1852–1931, vol. III
Masters, David, died 1965, vol. VI
Masters, Edgar Lee, 1869–1950, vol. IV
Masters, Sir Frederick, 1872–1947, vol. IV
Masters, Rev. Canon James Herbert, 1863–1942, vol. IV
Masters, Rev. James Hoare, died 1918, vol. II
Masters, John, 1914–1983, vol. VIII
Masters, Maxwell T., 1833–1907, vol. I
Masters, Hon. Robert, 1879–1967, vol. VI
Masters, Very Rev. Thomas Heywood, 1865–1939, vol. III
Masters, Rev. William Caldwall, 1843–1924, vol. II
Masterson, Major James Edward I., 1862–1935, vol. III
Masterson, Most Rev. Mgr Joseph, 1899–1953, vol. V
Masterton, William, 1913–1971, vol. VII
Masterton-Smith, Sir James Edward, 1878–1938, vol. III
Mastin, John, 1865–1932, vol. III
Maston, Charles James, 1912–1986, vol. VIII
Matania, Chevalier Fortunino, 1881–1963, vol. VI
Matcham, Col William Eyre E.; see Eyre-William.
Matchan, Leonard Joseph, 1911–1987, vol. VIII
Mather, Arthur Stanley, 1842–1929, vol. III
Mather, Rev. Frederic Vaughan, 1824–1914, vol. I
Mather, Rt Rev. Herbert, 1840–1922, vol. II
Mather, James Marshall, 1851–1916, vol. II
Mather, John Chadwick, 1904–1961, vol. VI
Mather, Sir Kenneth, 1911–1990, vol. VIII
Mather, Leonard Charles, 1909–1991, vol. IX
Mather, Loris Emerson, 1886–1976, vol. VII
Mather, Richard, 1886–1964, vol. VI
Mather, Thomas, died 1937, vol. III
Mather, Rt Hon. Sir William, 1838–1920, vol. II
Mather, Col William, 1888–1966, vol. VI
Mather, William Allan, 1885–1961, vol. VI
Mather, Sir William Loris, 1913–1998, vol. X
Mather-Jackson, Sir Anthony Henry Mather, 6th Bt, 1899–1983, vol. VIII
Mather-Jackson, Sir Christopher; see Mather-Jackson, Sir G. C. M.
Mather-Jackson, Sir Edward Arthur; see Jackson.
Mather-Jackson, Sir (George) Christopher (Mather), 5th Bt, 1896–1976, vol. VII
Mather-Jackson, Sir Henry; see Jackson.

Mather-Jackson, Sir William, 7th Bt, 1902–1985, vol. VIII
Mathers, 1st Baron, 1886–1965, vol. VI
Mathers, Edward Peter, 1850–1924, vol. II
Mathers, Edward Powys, 1892–1939, vol. III
Mathers, Frederick Francis, 1871–1947, vol. IV
Mathers, Helen, 1853–1920, vol. II
Mathers, Thomas Graham, 1859–1927, vol. II
Matheson, Captain Alexander Francis, 1905–1976, vol. VII
Matheson, Sir Alexander Perceval, 3rd Bt, 1861–1929, vol. III
Matheson, Angus, 1912–1962, vol. VI
Matheson, Annie, 1853–1924, vol. II
Matheson, Lt-Col Archibald, 1876–1936, vol. III
Matheson, Arthur Alexander, 1919–1981, vol. VIII
Matheson, Lt-Col Hon. Arthur James, 1845–1913, vol. I
Matheson, Cdre Sir Charles George, 1876–1948, vol. IV
Matheson, Charles Louis, 1851–1921, vol. II
Matheson, Sir Donald, 1832–1901, vol. I
Matheson, Donald, died 1901, vol. I
Matheson, Donald Alexander, 1860–1935, vol. III
Matheson, Donald Capell, 1880–1948, vol. IV
Matheson, Donald Macleod, 1896–1979, vol. VII
Matheson, Lt-Col Duncan, 1850–1930, vol. III
Matheson, Very Rev. Frederick William, 1882–1942, vol. IV
Matheson, Rev. George, 1842–1906, vol. I
Matheson, John, 1873–1944, vol. IV
Matheson, Rt Rev. John A., 1901–1950, vol. IV
Matheson, Sir Kenneth James, 2nd Bt, 1854–1920, vol. II
Matheson, M. Cecile, died 1950, vol. IV
Matheson, Percy Ewing, 1859–1946, vol. IV
Matheson, Rt Hon. Sir Robert Edwin, 1845–1926, vol. II
Matheson, Sir Roderick Mackenzie Chisholm, 4th Bt, 1861–1944, vol. IV
Matheson, Most Rev. Samuel Pritchard, 1852–1942, vol. IV
Matheson of Matheson, Sir Torquhil Alexander, 6th Bt, 1925–1993, vol. IX
Matheson, Gen. Sir Torquhil George, 5th Bt, 1871–1963, vol. VI
Mathew, Rev. Anthony Gervase, 1905–1976, vol. VII
Mathew, Sir Charles, 1903–1968, vol. VI
Mathew, Charles James, 1872–1923, vol. II
Mathew, Maj.-Gen. Sir Charles Massy, 1866–1932, vol. III
Mathew, Most Rev. David, 1902–1975, vol. VII
Mathew, Francis, 1907–1965, vol. VI
Mathew, Frank, 1865–1924, vol. II
Mathew, Lt-Gen. George, 1879–1958, vol. V
Mathew, George Felton, 1846–1931, vol. III
Mathew, Rt Hon. Sir James Charles, 1830–1908, vol. I
Mathew, Rev. John, died 1929, vol. III
Mathew, Robert, 1911–1966, vol. VI
Mathew, Theobald, 1866–1939, vol. III
Mathew, Sir Theobald, 1898–1964, vol. VI
Mathew, Theobald David, 1942–1998, vol. X

Mathew-Lannowe, Brig.-Gen. Edmund Byam; see Lannowe.
Mathews, Rev. (Arthur) Kenneth, 1906–1992, vol. IX
Mathews, Basil Joseph, 1879–1951, vol. V
Mathews, Sir Charles Willie, 1st Bt, 1850–1920, vol. II
Mathews, Denis Owen, 1901–1984, vol. VIII
Mathews, Ernest, 1847–1930, vol. III
Mathews, George Ballard, 1861–1922, vol. II
Mathews, Gregory Macalister, 1876–1949, vol. IV
Mathews, Henry Edmund, 1868–1947, vol. IV
Mathews, Henry Mends, 1903–1982, vol. VIII
Mathews, Henry Montague Segundo, 1860–1941, vol. IV
Mathews, Rev. Kenneth; see Mathews, Rev. A.K.
Mathews, Sir Lloyd William, 1850–1901, vol. I
Mathews, Shailer, 1863–1941, vol. IV
Mathews, Dame Vera Elvira Sibyl Maria Laughton, 1888–1959, vol. V
Mathews, Rev. William Arnold, 1839–1925, vol. II
Mathewson, Sir Alexander Robert, 1907–1968, vol. VI
Mathias, Alfred Ernest, 1880–1963, vol. VI
Mathias, Charles Ronald, 1877–1949, vol. IV
Mathias, Col Henry Harding, 1850–1914, vol. I
Mathias, Brig. Leonard William Henry, 1890–1972, vol. VII
Mathias, Lewis James, 1864–1945, vol. IV
Mathias, Lionel Armine, 1907–1991, vol. IX
Mathias, Most Rev. Louis, 1887–1965, vol. VI
Mathias, Sir Richard, 1st Bt, 1863–1942, vol. IV
Mathias, Sir Richard Hughes, 2nd Bt, 1905–1991, vol. IX
Mathias, Ronald Cavill, 1912–1968, vol. VI
Mathias, William Delamotte, 1877–1940, vol. III
Mathias, William James, 1934–1992, vol. IX
Mathieson, Hon. John A., 1863–1947, vol. IV
Mathieson, William Allan Cunningham, 1916–1999, vol. X
Mathieson, William Gordon, 1902–1981, vol. VIII
Mathieson, William Law, 1868–1938, vol. III
Mathieu, Most Rev. Mgr Olivier Elzear, 1853–1929, vol. III
Mathieu-Perez, Sir Joseph Leon; see Perez.
Mathys, Sir (Herbert) Reginald, 1908–1977, vol. VII
Mathys, Sir Reginald; see Mathys, Sir H. R.
Matilal, Bimal Krishna, 1935–1991, vol. IX
Matisse, Henri, 1869–1954, vol. V
Matley, Charles Alfred, 1866–1947, vol. IV
Matsudaira, Tsuneo, 1877–1949, vol. IV
Matsui, Rt Rev. Peter Yonetaro, 1869–1946, vol. IV
Matsumura, Jinzo, 1856–1928, vol. II, vol. III
Matt, Albert E., 1864–1941, vol. IV
Mattei, Marchese Alfred, 1853–1930, vol. III
Mattei, Tito, 1841–1914, vol. I
Matters, Sir Francis; see Matters, Sir R. F.
Matters, Leonard Warburton, 1881–1951, vol. V
Matters, Sir (Reginald) Francis, 1895–1975, vol. VII
Matthai, George, 1887–1947, vol. IV
Matthai, John, 1886–1959, vol. V
Matthay, Tobias, 1858–1945, vol. IV
Matthew, Colin; see Matthew, H. C. G.

Matthew, Edwin, *died* 1950, vol. IV
Matthew, Frederic David, 1838–1918, vol. II
Matthew, (Henry) Colin Gray, 1941–1999, vol. X
Matthew, John Godfrey, 1881–1947, vol. IV
Matthew, Col John Smart, 1864–1935, vol. III
Matthew, Reginald Walter, 1879–1928, vol. II
Matthew, Sir Robert Hogg, 1906–1975, vol. VII
Matthew, Thomas Urquhart, 1909–1962, vol. VI
Matthews, Baron (Life Peer); Victor Collin
 Matthews, 1919–1995, vol. IX
Matthews, Alfred Edward, 1869–1960, vol. V
Matthews, Sir (Alfred) Herbert (Henry), 1870–1958,
 vol. V
Matthews, Sir Arthur, 1886–1971, vol. VII
Matthews, Arthur Ratcliff, 1866–1932, vol. III
Matthews, Brander, 1852–1929, vol. III
Matthews, Sir Bromhead; *see* Matthews, Sir J. B.
Matthews, Sir Bryan Harold Cabot, 1906–1986,
 vol. VIII
Matthews, Ven. Cecil Lloyd, 1881–1962, vol. VI
Matthews, David, 1868–1960, vol. V
Matthews, David Napier, 1911–1997, vol. X
Matthews, Denis James, 1919–1988, vol. VIII
Matthews, Drummond Hoyle, 1931–1997, vol. X
Matthews, Major Durham, 1876–1950, vol. IV
Matthews, Edith Marcia, 1883–1946, vol. IV
Matthews, Rev. Edward Walter, 1846–1933, vol. III
Matthews, Ernest, 1904–1995, vol. X(AI)
Matthews, Ernest Lewis, 1871–1941, vol. IV
Matthews, Ernest Romney, 1873–1930, vol. III
Matthews, Maj.-Gen. Francis Raymond Gage,
 1903–1976, vol. VII
Matthews, Brig.-Gen. Frank Broadwood,
 1857–1940, vol. III
Matthews, Frank Herbert, 1861–1909, vol. I
Matthews, Ven. Frederick Albert John, 1913–1985,
 vol. VIII
Matthews, Gilbert, 1890–1969, vol. VI
Matthews, Col Godfrey Estcourt, 1866–1917, vol. II
Matthews, Gordon Richards, 1908–2000, vol. X
Matthews, Maj.-Gen. Harold Halford, 1877–1940,
 vol. III
Matthews, Sir (Harold Lancelot) Roy, 1901–1981,
 vol. VIII
Matthews, Harry G.; *see* Grindell-Matthews.
Matthews, Sir Herbert; *see* Matthews, Sir A. H. H.
Matthews, Horatio Keith, 1917–1994, vol. IX
Matthews, Ven. Hubert John, 1889–1971, vol. VII
Matthews, Sir James Henry John, 1887–1981,
 vol. VIII
Matthews, Rt Rev. James Joseph Edmund,
 1871–1939, vol. III
Matthews, James Robert, 1889–1978, vol. VII
Matthews, Jessie, 1907–1981, vol. VIII
Matthews, Sir (John) Bromhead, 1864–1934, vol. III
Matthews, John Charles, 1872–1946, vol. IV
Matthews, Joseph Bridges, *died* 1928, vol. II
Matthews, Julia B., (Mrs Fairfax Ivimey), *died*
 1948, vol. IV
Matthews, L(eonard) Harrison, 1901–1986, vol. VIII
Matthews, Maj.-Gen. Michael, 1930–1993, vol. IX
Matthews, Norman Derek, 1922–1976, vol. VII
Matthews, Rev. Norman Gregory, 1904–1964,
 vol. VI

Matthews, Pamela Winifred, (Mrs Peter Matthews),
 1914–1999, vol. X
Matthews, Paul Taunton, 1919–1987, vol. VIII
Matthews, Percy John, 1895–1964, vol. VI
Matthews, Rt Rev. Ralph Vernon, 1928–1983,
 vol. VIII
Matthews, Richard Bonnar, 1915–1997, vol. X
Matthews, Richard Ellis Ford, 1921–1995, vol. IX
Matthews, Hon. Robert Charles, 1871–1952, vol. V
Matthews, Robert Lee, 1876–1950, vol. IV
Matthews, Ronald Sydney, 1922–1995, vol. IX
Matthews, Sir Ronald Wilfred, 1885–1959, vol. V
Matthews, Sir Roy; *see* Matthews, Sir H. L. R.
Matthews, Sir Russell, 1896–1987, vol. VIII
Matthews, Rt Rev. Seering John, 1900–1978,
 vol. VII
Matthews, Sir Stanley (John), 1915–2000, vol. X
Matthews, Sir Thomas, 1849–1930, vol. III
Matthews, Thomas Stanley, 1901–1991, vol. IX
Matthews, Rt Rev. Timothy John, 1907–1991,
 vol. IX
Matthews, Sir Trevor Jocelyn, 1882–1954, vol. V
Matthews, Col Valentine, 1855–1921, vol. II
Matthews, Lt-Col Walter Hudson, 1864–1929,
 vol. III
Matthews, Very Rev. Walter Robert, 1881–1973,
 vol. VII
Matthews, Sir William, 1844–1922, vol. II
Matthews, William, 1905–1975, vol. VII
Matthews, William E., 1862–1938, vol. III
Matthews, William Kleesmann, 1901–1958, vol. V
Matthews, Sir William Thomas, 1888–1968, vol. VI
Matthey, Col Edward, 1836–1918, vol. II
Matthey, George, *died* 1913, vol. I
Matthiessen, Francis Otto, 1902–1950, vol. IV(A),
 vol. V
Mattingly, Garrett, 1900–1962, vol. VI
Mattingly, Harold, 1884–1964, vol. VI
Mattinson, Sir Miles, 1854–1944, vol. IV
Matturi, Sahr Thomas, 1925–1987, vol. VIII
Maturin, Father Basil William, 1847–1915, vol. I
Matz, Bertram Waldrom, 1865–1925, vol. II
Maubert, Louis, 1875–1949, vol. IV
Mauchline, Lord; Ian Huddleston Abney-Hastings,
 1918–1944, vol. IV
Mauchline, Rev. John, 1902–1984, vol. VIII
Maud, Captain Charles Carus, 1875–1914, vol. I
Maud, Constance Elizabeth, *died* 1929, vol. III
Maud, Col Harry, 1867–1948, vol. IV
Maud, Rt Rev. John Primatt, 1860–1932, vol. III
Maud, Brig.-Gen. Philip, 1870–1947, vol. IV
Maud, W. T., *died* 1903, vol. I
Maud, Lt-Col William Hartley, 1868–1948, vol. IV
Maude of Stratford-upon-Avon, Baron (Life Peer);
 Angus Edmund Upton Maude, 1912–1993,
 vol. IX
Maude, Col Alan Hamer, 1885–1979, vol. VII
Maude, Aylmer, 1858–1938, vol. III
Maude, Ven. Charles Bulmer, 1848–1927, vol. II
Maude, Charles John, 1847–1910, vol. I
Maude, Brig. Christian George, 1884–1971,
 vol. VII
Maude, Cyril, 1862–1951, vol. V
Maude, Edith Caroline, 1865–1922, vol. II
Maude, Evan Walter, 1919–1980, vol. VII

Maude, Sir (Evelyn) John, 1883–1963, vol. VI
Maude, Col Francis Cornwallis, 1828–1900, vol. I
Maude, Col Frederic Natusch, 1854–1933, vol. III
Maude, Sir Frederick Francis, 1821–1897, vol. I
Maude, Lt-Gen. Sir Frederick Stanley, 1864–1917, vol. II
Maude, Isabel Winifred Maud Emery; see Emery, Winifred.
Maude, Sir John; see Maude, Sir E. J.
Maude, John Cyril, 1901–1986, vol. VIII
Maude, Major Ralph Walter, 1873–1922, vol. II
Maude, Sir Walter, 1862–1943, vol. IV
Maude-Roxby, John Henry, 1919–1989, vol. VIII
Maudling, Rt Hon. Reginald, 1917–1979, vol. VII
Maudslay, Alfred Percival, 1850–1931, vol. III
Maudslay, Algernon, 1873–1948, vol. IV
Maudslay, Cecil Winton, 1880–1969, vol. VI
Maudslay, Major Sir (James) Rennie, 1915–1988, vol. VIII
Maudslay, Major Sir Rennie; see Maudslay, Major Sir J. R.
Maudslay, Walter Henry, 1844–1927, vol. II
Maudsley, Henry, 1835–1918, vol. II
Maudsley, Sir Henry Carr, 1859–1944, vol. IV
Maufe, Sir Edward Brantwood, 1883–1974, vol. VII
Maufe, Herbert Brantwood, 1879–1946, vol. IV
Maufe, Captain T. Harold Broadbent, 1898–1942, vol. IV
Mauger, Hon. Samuel, 1857–1936, vol. III
Maugham, 1st Viscount, 1866–1958, vol. V
Maugham, 2nd Viscount, 1916–1981, vol. VIII
Maugham, Reginald Charles Fulke, 1866–1956, vol. V
Maugham, Robin; see Maugham, 2nd Viscount
Maugham, Somerset; see Maugham, W. S.
Maugham, (William) Somerset, 1874–1965, vol. VI
Maughan, Sir David, 1873–1955, vol. V
Maughan, Janet Leith; see Story, J. L.
Maughan, Lt-Col Francis Gilfrid, died 1938, vol. III
Maul, Rev. John Frederic, 1849–1915, vol. I
Maula Bakhsh, Nawab Maula Bakhsh Khan Bahadur of Batala, 1862–1949, vol. IV
Maule, Col Henry Noel St John, 1873–1953, vol. V
Maule, Major Hugh Patrick Guarin, 1873–1940, vol. III
Maule, Sir Robert, 1852–1931, vol. III
Maulvi Haji, Rahim Bakhsh, died 1935, vol. III
Maund, Air Vice-Marshal Arthur Clinton, 1891–1942, vol. IV
Maund, Rt Rev. John Arthur Arrowsmith, 1909–1998, vol. X
Maund, Rear-Adm. Loben Edward Harold, 1892–1957, vol. V
Maunder, Annie Scott Dill, (Mrs Walter Maunder), 1868–1947, vol. IV
Maunder, Edward Walter, 1851–1928, vol. II
Maundrell, Captain Arthur Goodall, 1884–1972, vol. VII
Maung Kin, Hon. Sir, 1872–1924, vol. II
Maung Me, 1871–1952, vol. V
Maung Pe, 1858–1924, vol. II
Maunsell, Lt-Col Francis Richard, 1861–1936, vol. III
Maunsell, Brig.-Gen. Frederick Guy, 1864–1929, vol. III

Maunsell, Gen. Sir Frederick Richard, 1828–1916, vol. II
Maunsell, Col George William, 1859–1937, vol. III
Maunsell, Mark Stuart Ker, 1910–1980, vol. VII
Maunsell, Brig. Raymund John, 1903–1976, vol. VII
Maunsell, Richard Edward Lloyd, died 1944, vol. IV
Maunsell, Robert Charles Butler, 1872–1930, vol. III
Maunsell, Maj.-Gen. Sir Thomas, 1822–1908, vol. I
Maunsell, Surg.-Gen. Thomas, 1839–1937, vol. III
Mauny-Talvande, Countess de; (Lady Mary Elizabeth Agnes Byng), died 1946, vol. IV
Maurault, Rt Rev. Mgr Olivier, 1886–1968, vol. VI
Maurel, Victor, 1848–1923, vol. II
Mauriac, François, 1885–1970, vol. VI
Maurice, Lt-Col Albert Jafa, 1864–1943, vol. IV
Maurice, Lt-Col David Blake, 1866–1925, vol. II
Maurice, Maj.-Gen. Sir Frederick; see Maurice, Maj.-Gen. Sir J. F.
Maurice, Maj.-Gen. Sir Frederick Barton, 1871–1951, vol. V
Maurice, Col George Thelwall Kindersley, 1867–1950, vol. IV
Maurice, Col Godfrey Kindersley, 1887–1949, vol. IV
Maurice, Henry Gascoyen, 1874–1950, vol. IV
Maurice, Maj.-Gen. Sir (John) Frederick, 1841–1912, vol. I
Maurois, André, 1885–1967, vol. VI
Maurras, Charles, 1868–1952, vol. V
Maury, Amy-Gaston B.; see Bonet Maury.
Mavor, James, 1854–1925, vol. II
Mavor, Air Marshal Sir Leslie Deane, 1916–1991, vol. IX
Mavor, O. H.; see Bridie, James.
Mavrogordato, John George, 1905–1987, vol. VIII
Mavrogordato, John Nicolas, 1882–1970, vol. VI
Maw, William Henry, 1838–1924, vol. II
Maw, William Nawton, 1869–1946, vol. IV
Mawbey, Adm. Henry Lancelot, 1870–1933, vol. III
Mawby, Sir Maurice Alan Edgar, 1904–1977, vol. VII
Mawby, Raymond Llewellyn, 1922–1990, vol. VIII
Mawer, Sir Allen, 1879–1942, vol. IV
Mawer, Air Cdre Allen Henry, 1921–1989, vol. VIII
Mawhinny, Col Robert John Watt, died 1953, vol. V
Mawhood, Mary; see Clare, M.
Mawson, Cecil Allerton Greville, 1876–1950, vol. IV
Mawson, Sir Douglas, 1882–1958, vol. V
Mawson, Thomas H., died 1933, vol. III
Max-Müller, Rt Hon. Friedrich, 1823–1900, vol. I
Max-Muller, Sir William Grenfell, 1867–1945, vol. IV
Maxim, Sir Hiram Stevens, 1840–1916, vol. II
Maxse, Ernest George Berkeley, 1863–1943, vol. IV
Maxse, Adm. Frederick Augustus, 1833–1900, vol. I
Maxse, Gen. Sir Ivor, 1862–1958, vol. V
Maxse, Leopold James, 1864–1932, vol. III
Maxse, Dame Marjorie, 1891–1975, vol. VII
Maxton, James, 1885–1946, vol. IV
Maxtone-Graham, Anthony George, 1854–1930, vol. III
Maxtone Graham, James, 1863–1940, vol. III

Maxwell, Hon. Lord; Peter Maxwell, 1919–1994, vol. IX
Maxwell, Sir Alexander, 1880–1963, vol. VI
Maxwell, Alexander Hyslop, 1864–1957, vol. V
Maxwell, Sir Alexander Hyslop, 1896–1971, vol. VII
Maxwell, Allan Victor, 1887–1975, vol. VII
Maxwell, Col Sir Arthur, 1875–1935, vol. III
Maxwell, Arthur Crawford, 1909–1964, vol. VI
Maxwell, Col (Arthur) Terence, 1905–1991, vol. IX
Maxwell, Maj.-Gen. Sir Aymer, 1891–1971, vol. VII
Maxwell, Sir Aymer, 8th Bt, 1911–1987, vol. VIII
Maxwell, Beatrice II.; see Heron Maxwell.
Maxwell, Hon. Bernard Constable, 1848–1938, vol. III
Maxwell, Bertram Wayburn, 1891–1972, vol. VII
Maxwell, Constantia Elizabeth, 1885–1962, vol. VI
Maxwell, Vice-Adm. Hon. Sir Denis Crichton, 1892–1970, vol. VI
Maxwell, Denis Oliver, 1906–1971, vol. VII
Maxwell, Donald, 1877–1936, vol. III
Maxwell, Douglas Rider, 1885–1967, vol. VI
Maxwell, Lt-Col F. D., 1862–1910, vol. I
Maxwell, Col Francis Aylmer, 1871–1917, vol. II
Maxwell of Ardwell, Col Frederick Gordon, 1905–1997, vol. X
Maxwell, Sir Frederic Mackenzie, 1860–1931, vol. III
Maxwell, Gavin, 1914–1969, vol. VI
Maxwell, Col Geoffrey Archibald Prentice, 1885–1953, vol. V
Maxwell, Sir George; see Maxwell, Sir W. G.
Maxwell, George Arnot, died 1935, vol. III
Maxwell, Wing-Comdr Gerald Constable, 1895–1959, vol. V
Maxwell, Gerald Verner, 1877–1965, vol. VI
Maxwell, Hamilton, 1830–1923, vol. II
Maxwell, Rt Rev. Harold Alexander, 1897–1975, vol. VII
Maxwell, Col Hon. Henry Edward, 1857–1919, vol. II
Maxwell, Lt-Col Henry St Patrick, 1850–1928, vol. II
Maxwell, Rt Hon. Sir Herbert Eustace, 7th Bt (cr 1681), 1845–1937, vol. III
Maxwell, Herbert William, 1888–1979, vol. VII
Maxwell, (Ian) Robert, 1923–1991, vol. IX
Maxwell, Sir Ivor Walter H.; see Heron-Maxwell.
Maxwell, James, 1905–1956, vol. V
Maxwell, Major James Andrew Colvile W.; see Wedderburn-Maxwell.
Maxwell, Sir James Crawford, 1869–1932, vol. III
Maxwell, James Laidlaw, 1873–1951, vol. V
Maxwell, Brig.-Gen. James McCall, 1865–1945, vol. IV
Maxwell, James Robert, 1902–1970, vol. VI
Maxwell, Sir John, 1875–1946, vol. IV
Maxwell, John, 1905–1962, vol. VI
Maxwell, Sir John, 1882–1968, vol. VI
Maxwell, Gen. Rt Hon. Sir John Grenfell, 1859–1929, vol. III
Maxwell, Sir John Maxwell Stirling-, 10th Bt (cr 1682), 1866–1956, vol. V
Maxwell, Sir John Robert H.; see Heron-Maxwell.
Maxwell, Joseph, 1896–1967, vol. VI

Maxwell, Surgeon Rear-Adm. Joseph Archibald, 1890–1980, vol. VII
Maxwell, Brig.-Gen. Laurence Lockhart, 1868–1954, vol. V
Maxwell, Lawrence, 1853–1927, vol. II, vol. III
Maxwell, Magdalen Perceval, (Mrs Patrick Perceval-Maxwell); see King-Hall, M.
Maxwell, Mary Elizabeth; see Braddon, M. E.
Maxwell, Maurice William, 1910–1982, vol. VIII
Maxwell, Maxwell Hyslop, died 1937, vol. III
Maxwell, Patrick, 1909–1991, vol. IX
Maxwell, Sir Patrick Ivor H.; see Heron-Maxwell.
Maxwell, Perriton, died 1947, vol. IV(A)
Maxwell, Sir Reginald Maitland, 1882–1967, vol. VI
Maxwell, Brig. Richard Hobson, 1899–1965, vol. VI
Maxwell, Richard Ponsonby, 1853–1928, vol. II
Maxwell, Robert; see Maxwell, I. R.
Maxwell, Robert Charles H.; see Heron-Maxwell.
Maxwell, Col Rt Hon. Robert David Perceval, 1870–1932, vol. III
Maxwell, Lt-Gen. Sir Ronald Charles, 1852–1924, vol. II
Maxwell, Sir Robert Hugh, 1906–1994, vol. IX
Maxwell, Hon. Somerset Arthur, 1905–1942, vol. IV
Maxwell, Col Terence; see Maxwell, Col A. T.
Maxwell, Thomas Doveton, died 1946, vol. IV
Maxwell, Rear-Adm. Thomas Heron, 1912–1997, vol. X
Maxwell, Wellwood, 1857–1933, vol. III
Maxwell, Rear-Adm. Sir Wellwood George Courtenay, 1882–1965, vol. VI
Maxwell, Captain Sir William, died 1928, vol. II
Maxwell, Sir William, 1841–1929, vol. III
Maxwell, Sir William, 1870–1947, vol. IV
Maxwell, Sir William, died 1947, vol. IV
Maxwell, William, 1873–1957, vol. V
Maxwell, Captain William Babington, 1866–1938, vol. III
Maxwell, Sir William Edward, 1846–1897, vol. I
Maxwell, Lt-Col William Ernest, 1898–1951, vol. V
Maxwell, Sir William Francis, 4th Bt (cr 1804), 1844–1924, vol. II
Maxwell, Lt-Col William Frederick, 1878–1940, vol. III
Maxwell, Sir (William) George, 1871–1959, vol. V
Maxwell, Rev. William Gilchrist C.; see Clark-Maxwell.
Maxwell, Adm. William Henry, 1840–1920, vol. II
Maxwell, William Henry, 1852–1921, vol. II
Maxwell, William Jardine Herries, 1852–1933, vol. III
Maxwell, William Wayland, 1925–1986, vol. VIII
Maxwell-Anderson, Captain Sir Maxwell Hendry; see Anderson.
Maxwell-Carpendale, Major Frederic; see Carpendale.
Maxwell-Gumbleton, Rt Rev. Maxwell Homfray, 1872–1952, vol. V
Maxwell-Hibberd, Charles, 1853–1935, vol. III
Maxwell-Lefroy, Harold; see Lefroy.
Maxwell-Lyte, Sir Henry Church; see Lyte.
Maxwell-Scott, Rear-Adm. Malcolm; see Scott.
Maxwell Scott, Sir Michael Fergus, 13th Bt, 1921–1989, vol. VIII

Maxwell-Scott, Maj.-Gen. Sir Walter Joseph Constable, 1st Bt, 1875–1954, vol. V

Maxwell Stuart, Arthur Constable, 1845–1942, vol. IV

Maxwell-Stuart, Herbert Constable, 1842–1921, vol. II

Maxwell-Willshire, Sir Arthur Reginald Thomas; see Willshire.

Maxwell-Willshire, Sir Gerard Arthur; see Willshire.

May, 1st Baron, 1871–1946, vol. IV

May, 2nd Baron, 1904–1950, vol. IV

May, Rt Rev. Alston James Weller, 1869–1940, vol. III

May, Captain Arthur Dekewer Livius, 1875–1943, vol. IV

May, Sir Arthur William, 1854–1925, vol. II

May, Aylmer William, 1874–1950, vol. IV

May, Barry, 1869–1948, vol. IV

May, Bennett, 1846–1937, vol. III

May, Surgeon Vice-Adm. Sir Cyril; see May, Surgeon Vice-Adm. Sir R. C.

May, Edward Hooper, 1831–1914, vol. I

May, Maj.-Gen. Sir Edward Sinclair, 1856–1936, vol. III

May, Sir Francis Henry, 1860–1922, vol. II

May, Major Frederick, (Fred May), 1891–1976, vol. VII

May, Sir Gould, died 1944, vol. IV

May, Harry Blight, 1908–1991, vol. IX

May, Col Henry Allan Roughton, 1863–1930. vol. III

May, Rear-Adm. Henry John, 1853–1904, vol. I

May, Maj.-Gen. James, 1837–1903, vol. I

May, James Lewis, 1873–1961, vol. VI

May, John, 1912–1992, vol. IX

May, John Cecil, 1890–1959, vol. V

May, Lt-Col John Cyril, 1874–1943, vol. IV

May, Rt Hon. Sir John Douglas, 1923–1997, vol. X

May, Sir Kenneth Spencer, 1914–2000, vol. X

May, Otto, died 1946, vol. IV

May, Paul, 1907–1996, vol. X

May, Percy, 1886–1974, vol. VII

May, Peter Barker Howard, 1929–1994, vol. IX

May, Phil, 1864–1903, vol. I

May, Gen. Sir Reginald Seaburne, 1879–1958, vol. V

May, Richard William Legerton, 1902–1967, vol. VI

May, Surgeon Vice-Adm. Sir (Robert) Cyril, 1897–1979, vol. VII

May, Rev. Thomas Henry, 1851–1932, vol. III

May, Major Thomas James, 1864–1952, vol. V

May, W. Charles, 1853–1931, vol. III

May, William, 1863–1932, vol. III

May, Col William Allan, 1850–1937, vol. III

May, Admiral of the Fleet Sir William Henry, 1849–1930, vol. III

May, Rt Hon. William Morrison, 1909–1962, vol. VI

May, Major William Southall Reid, 1864–1937, vol. III

Mayall, Sir (Alexander) Lees, 1915–1992, vol. IX

Mayall, Sir Lees; see Mayall, Sir A. L.

Mayall, Robert Cecil, 1893–1962, vol. VI

Maybin, Sir Alexander, 1889–1941, vol. IV

Maybray-King, Baron (Life Peer); Horace Maybray Maybray-King, 1901–1986, vol. VIII

Maybrick, Michael, 1844–1913, vol. I

Maybury, Bernard Constable, 1888–1953, vol. V

Maybury, Brig.-Gen. Sir Henry Percy, 1864–1943, vol. IV

Maycock, Alan Lawson, 1898–1968, vol. VI

Maycock, Rev. Francis Hugh, 1903–1980, vol. VII

Maycock, Rev. Herbert William, 1863–1939, vol. III

Maycock, Sir William d'Auvergne, 1911–1987, vol. VIII

Maycock, Sir Willoughby Robert Dottin, 1849–1922, vol. II

Maydon, Hon. John George, 1857–1919, vol. II

Maydon, Lt-Comdr Stephen Lynch Conway, 1913–1971, vol. VII

Mayeda, Marquis Toshinari, 1885–1942, vol. IV

Mayer, Col Edward Rudolph, 1902–1973, vol. VII

Mayer, John, 1904–1967, vol. VI

Mayer, Maria Goeppert, 1906–1972, vol. VII

Mayer, René, 1895–1972, vol. VII

Mayer, Sir Robert, 1879–1985, vol. VIII

Mayer, Sylvain, 1863–1948, vol. IV

Mayer Brown, Howard; see Brown, H. M.

Mayers, Very Rev. George Samuel, died 1952, vol. V

Mayers, Norman, 1895–1986, vol. VIII

Mayers, Thomas Henry, 1907–1970, vol. VI

Mayes, William, 1874–1960, vol. V

Mayfield, Ven. Guy, 1905–1976, vol. VII

Maygar, Lt-Col Leslie Cecil, 1871–1917, vol. II

Mayhew, Baron (Life Peer); Christopher Paget Mayhew, 1915–1997, vol. X

Mayhew, Rev. Arnold, 1873–1939, vol. III

Mayhew, Arthur Innes, 1878–1948, vol. IV

Mayhew, Sir Basil Edgar, 1883–1966, vol. VI

Mayhew, Captain George Henry, 1901–1973, vol. VII

Mayhew, Lt-Col Sir John, 1884–1954, vol. V

Mayle, Norman Leslie, 1899–1980, vol. VII

Maynard, Maj.-Gen. Sir Charles Clarkson Martin, 1870–1945, vol. IV

Maynard, Charles Gordon, 1889–1970, vol. VI

Maynard, Constance Louisa, 1849–1935, vol. III

Maynard, Dudley Christopher, 1874–1941, vol. IV

Maynard, Air Vice-Marshal Forster Herbert Martin, 1893–1976, vol. VII

Maynard, Brig.-Gen. Francis Herbert, 1881–1979, vol. VII

Maynard, Lt-Col Frederic P., died 1921, vol. II

Maynard, Harry Russell, 1873–1954, vol. V

Maynard, Rev. Henry Langston, 1865–1940, vol. III

Maynard, Sir (Herbert) John, 1865–1943, vol. IV

Maynard, Joan; see Maynard, V. J.

Maynard, Sir John; see Maynard, Sir H. J.

Maynard, John Percy Gordon, died 1918, vol. II

Maynard, Air Chief Marshal Sir Nigel Martin, 1921–1998, vol. X

Maynard, Richard de Kirklevington, 1892–1969, vol. VI

Maynard, (Vera) Joan, 1921–1998, vol. X

Mayne, Arthur Brinley, 1893–1948, vol. IV

Mayne, Gen. Sir (Ashton Gerard Oswald) Mosley, 1889–1955, vol. V

Mayne, Brig.-Gen. Charles Robert Graham, 1874–1944, vol. IV
Mayne, Cuthbert Joseph, 1902–1972, vol. VII
Mayne, Ethel Colburn, died 1941, vol. IV
Mayne, Very Rev. Frank, died 1929, vol. III
Mayne, Lt-Col George Nisbet, 1854–1932, vol. III
Mayne, Gerald Outram, 1919–1980, vol. VII
Mayne, Horace Ardran, 1876–1958, vol. V
Mayne, Captain Jasper Graham, 1859–1936, vol. III
Mayne, Rev. Jonathan, 1838–1912, vol. I
Mayne, Jonathan Webster Coryton, 1868–1940, vol. III
Mayne, Ven. Joseph, 1843–1927, vol. II
Mayne, Gen. Sir Mosley; see Mayne, Gen. Sir A. G. O. M.
Mayne, Major Otway, 1855–1939, vol. III
Mayne, Col Richard Charles Graham, 1852–1939, vol. III
Mayne, Very Rev. William Cyril, 1877–1962, vol. VI
Mayneord, William Valentine, 1902–1988, vol. VIII
Mayo, 7th Earl of, 1851–1927, vol. II
Mayo, 8th Earl of, 1859–1939, vol. III
Mayo, 9th Earl of, 1890–1962, vol. VI
Mayo, Arthur, 1840–1920, vol. II
Mayo, Rev. Charles Herbert, 1845–1929, vol. III
Mayo, Charles Horace, 1865–1939, vol. III
Mayo, Charles William, 1898–1968, vol. VI
Mayo, Rev. Cuthbert Edward, 1860–1934, vol. III
Mayo, Dame Eileen Rosemary, 1906–1994, vol. IX
Mayo, Sir Herbert, 1885–1972, vol. VII
Mayo, Isabella, (Mrs John Mayo), 1843–1914, vol. I
Mayo, Rev. John Augustus, died 1941, vol. IV
Mayo, Katherine, 1868–1940, vol. III
Mayo, Robert Hobart, 1890–1957, vol. V
Mayo, William James, 1861–1939, vol. III
Mayo-Robson, Sir Arthur William; see Robson.
Mayoh, Raymond Blanchflower, 1925–1995, vol. IX(AII)
Mayor, John Eyton Bickersteth, 1825–1910, vol. I
Mayor, Rev. Joseph Bickersteth, 1828–1916, vol. II
Mayor, Robert John Grote, 1869–1947, vol. IV
Mayou, M. Stephen, 1876–1934, vol. III
Mayrs, Edward Brice Cooper, 1891–1964, vol. VI
Mays, Raymond, 1899–1980, vol. VII (AII)
Mays-Smith, Sir Alfred, 1861–1931, vol. III
Mayston, Very Rev. Richard John Forrester, 1907–1963, vol. VI
Mayston, Engr Rear-Adm. Robert, 1851–1936, vol. III
Mayurbhanj, Maharaja of, born 1901, vol. VI
Maze, Sir Frederick William, died 1959, vol. V
Maze, Paul Lucien, 1887–1979, vol. VII
Mbanefo, Sir Louis Nwachukwu, 1911–1977, vol. VII
Mboya, Tom, (Thomas Joseph), 1930–1969, vol. VI
Meaby, Kenneth Tweedale, 1883–1965, vol. VI
Meachen, George Norman, 1876–1955, vol. V
Mead, Sir Cecil, 1900–1979, vol. VII
Mead, (Elsie) Stella, died 1981, vol. VIII
Mead, Frederick, 1847–1945, vol. IV
Mead, George Edward, 1849–1932, vol. III
Mead, George Robert Stow, 1863–1933, vol. III
Mead, John Phillips, 1886–1951, vol. V
Mead, Lloyd; see Mead, W. H. L.

Mead, Margaret, 1901–1978, vol. VII
Mead, Maj.-Gen. Owen Herbert, 1892–1942, vol. IV
Mead, Percy James, 1871–1923, vol. II
Mead, Rev. Richard Gawler, 1833–1909, vol. I
Mead, Stella; see Mead, E. S.
Mead, Brig. Stephen, 1882–1972, vol. VII
Mead, (William Howard) Lloyd, 1905–1987, vol. VIII
Meade, (Charles Alan) Gerald, 1905–1985, vol. VIII
Meade, Elizabeth Thomasina; see Meade, L. T.
Meade, Sir Geoffrey; see Meade, Sir R. G. A.
Meade, Gerald; see Meade, C. A. G.
Meade, Major Harry Edward, 1884–1952, vol. V
Meade, James Edward, 1907–1995, vol. IX
Meade, Gen. John Michael de Courcy, 1831–1909, vol. I
Meade, Rt Hon. Joseph Michael, 1839–1900, vol. I
Meade, L. T., 1854–1914, vol. I
Meade, Lt-Col Malcolm John, 1854–1933, vol. III
Meade, Sir (Richard) Geoffrey (Austin), 1902–1992, vol. IX
Meade, Hon. Sir Robert Henry, 1835–1898, vol. I
Meade, Rev. Hon. Sidney, 1839–1917, vol. II
Meade, Rt Rev. William Edward, 1832–1912, vol. I
Meade-Fetherstonhaugh, Adm. Hon. Sir Herbert, 1875–1964, vol. VI
Meade-King, Sir William Oliver Evelyn, 1858–1940, vol. III
Meaden, Lt-Col Alban Anderson, 1876–1934, vol. III
Meaden, Surg.-Captain Edward Henry, 1864–1943, vol. IV
Meaden, Rt Rev. John Alfred, 1892–1987, vol. VIII
Meadon, Ernest John, 1911–1970, vol. VI
Meadon, Sir Percival Edward, 1878–1959, vol. V
Meadowcroft, Lancelot Vernon, 1884–1952, vol. V
Meadows, Alice Maud, died 1913, vol. I
Meadows, Robert, 1902–1998, vol. X
Meadows, Surg.-Maj.-Gen. Robert Wyatt, 1832–1911, vol. I
Meadows, Swithin Pinder, 1902–1993, vol. IX
Meadus, Engr-Captain Harry Howard, 1856–1934, vol. III
Meadus, Engr-Captain William Henry, 1862–1947, vol. IV
Meagher, Michael, 1846–1927, vol. II
Meagher, Hon. Nicholas Hogan, 1842–1932, vol. III
Meagher, Hon. Richard Denis, 1866–1931, vol. III
Meagher, Sir Thomas, 1902–1979, vol. VII
Meakin, Annette M. B., died 1959, vol. V
Meakin, Budgett, 1866–1906, vol. I
Meakin, Henry William, 1847–1939, vol. III
Meakin, Walter, 1878–1940, vol. III
Meakin, Brig. Jonathan Campbell, 1882–1959, vol. V
Meale, Arthur; see Meale, J. A.
Meale, (John) Arthur, 1880–1932, vol. III
Mealing, Sir Kenneth William, 1895–1968, vol. VI
Meaney, Sir Patrick Michael, 1925–1992, vol. IX
Meany, George, 1894–1980, vol. VII
Meara, Rev. Henry George Jephson, died 1921, vol. II
Meares, John Willoughby, 1871–1946, vol. IV
Meares, Lt-Col Mervyn, 1880–1930, vol. III

Meares, Maj.-Gen. William Lewis D.; *see* Devenish-Meares.
Mearns, Andrew Daniel, 1857–1925, vol. II
Mears, Sir Edward Grimwood, 1869–1963, vol. VI
Mears, Sir Frank Charles, 1880–1953, vol. V
Mears, Brig. Gerald Grimwood, 1896–1979, vol. VII
Mears, Sir Grimwood; *see* Mears, Sir E. G.
Mears, Margaret Mary, (Lady Mears); *see* Tempest, M. M.
Mears, Thomas Lambert, *died* 1918, vol. II, vol. III
Mears, Lt-Col Trevor Irvine Nevitt, 1875–1937, vol. III
Mease, Very Rev. Charles William O'Hara, 1856–1922, vol. II
Measham, Paymaster Rear-Adm. Herbert Stanley, 1875–1954, vol. V
Measham, Richard John Rupert, 1885–1976, vol. VII
Measom, Sir George Samuel, 1818–1901, vol. I
Measures, Wing Comdr Arthur Harold, 1882–1969, vol. VI
Measures, Harry Bell, 1862–1940, vol. III
Measures, Sir Philip Herbert, 1893–1961, vol. VI
Meath, 12th Earl of, 1841–1929, vol. III
Meath, 13th Earl of, 1869–1949, vol. IV
Meath, 14th Earl of, 1910–1998, vol. X
Mechan, Sir Henry, *died* 1943, vol. IV
Mecredy, Sir James, 1854–1938, vol. III
Mecredy, Richard James, 1861–1924, vol. II
Medawar, Sir Peter Brian, 1915–1987, vol. VIII
Medd, Patrick William, 1919–1995, vol. IX
Medd, Rev. Peter Goldsmith, 1929–1908, vol. I
Medd, Wilfrid, 1877–1956, vol. V
Medforth, Marguerite Elizabeth, 1879–1966, vol. VI
Medhurst, Air Chief Marshal Sir Charles Edward Hastings, 1896–1954, vol. V
Medill, Brig. Percy Montomery, 1882–1963, vol. VI
Medland, Hubert Moses, 1881–1964, vol. VI
Medley, Charles Douglas, 1870–1963, vol. VI
Medley, (Charles) Robert (Owen), 1905–1994, vol. IX
Medley, Dudley Julius, 1861–1953, vol. V
Medley, Brig. Edgar J., 1893–1972, vol. VII
Medley, Sir John Dudley Gibbs, 1891–1962, vol. VI
Medley, Robert; *see* Medley, C. R. O.
Medlicott, Sir Frank, 1903–1972, vol. VII
Medlicott, Henry Benedict, 1829–1905, vol. I
Medlicott, Col Henry Edward, 1882–1948, vol. IV
Medlicott, Rev. Canon Robert Sumner, *died* 1941, vol. IV
Medlicott, William Norton, *died* 1923, vol. II
Medlicott, William Norton, 1900–1987, vol. VIII
Medlycott, Sir Edward Bradford, 4th Bt, 1832–1902, vol. I
Medlycott, Rev. Sir Hubert James, 6th Bt, 1841–1920, vol. II
Medlycott, Sir Hubert Mervyn, 7th Bt, 1874–1964, vol. VI
Medlycott, Sir (James) Christopher, 8th Bt, 1907–1986, vol. VIII
Medlycott, Sir Mervyn Bradford, 5th Bt, 1837–1908, vol. I
Medtner, Nicholas, 1879–1951, vol. V
Medwin, Robert Joseph G.; *see* Gardner-Medwin

Mee, Arthur, 1860–1926, vol. II
Mee, Arthur, 1875–1943, vol. IV
Mee, Ellen Catherine, 1894–1981, vol. VIII
Meech, Sir John Valentine, 1907–1971, vol. VII
Meech, Thomas Cox, *died* 1940, vol. III
Meechie, Brig. Helen Guild, 1938–2000, vol. X
Meecham, Bert, 1886–1964, vol. VI
Meehan, Francis Edward, 1868–1946, vol. IV
Meehan, Patrick Aloysius, 1852–1913, vol. I
Meek, Alexander, 1865–1949, vol. IV
Meek, Lt-Col Arthur Stanley, 1883–1955, vol. V
Meek, Charles Kingsley, 1885–1965, vol. VI
Meek, Sir David Burnett, 1885–1964, vol. VI
Meek, Charles Innes, 1920–1999, vol. X
Meek, Col James, 1861–1939, vol. III
Meek, William Alfred, 1850–1929, vol. III
Meeking, Lt-Col Charles, 1839–1912, vol. I
Meeks, Hon. Sir Alfred William, 1849–1932, vol. III
Meenan, James Nahor, 1879–1950, vol. IV (A), vol. V
Meere, Sir Frank, (Francis Anthony), 1895–1985, vol. VIII
Meeres, Col Charles Stuart, 1861–1935, vol. III
Meers, James Blackader, 1850–1933, vol. III
Mees, Charles Edward Kenneth, 1882–1960, vol. V
Meeson, Dora, (Mrs George J. Coates), *died* 1955, vol. V
Meeson, Engr-Comdr Edward Hickman Tucker, 1877–1916, vol. II
Meff, Sir William, 1861–1935, vol. III
Megaw, Arthur Stanley, *died* 1961, vol. VI
Megaw, Rt Hon. Sir John, 1909–1997, vol. X
Megaw, Maj.-Gen. Sir John Wallace Dick, 1874–1958, vol. V
Megaw, Robert Dick, *died* 1947, vol. IV
Meghnad Saha, 1893–1956, vol. V
Megrah, Maurice Henry, 1896–1985, vol. VIII
Mégroz, Rodolphe Louis, 1891–1968, vol. VI
Meharry, Rev. J. B., *died* 1916, vol. II
Mehta, Khan Bahadur, Sir Bezonji Dalabhoy, *died* 1927, vol. II
Mehta, Hon. Sir Homi, 1871–1948, vol. IV
Mehta, Jivraj Narayan, 1887–1978, vol. VII
Mehta, Sir Mangaldas Vijbhukandas, *died* 1945, vol. IV
Mehta, Sir Manubhai Nandshankar, 1868–1946, vol. IV
Mehta, Sir Phirozshah Merwanji, *died* 1915, vol. I
Mehta, Roostumjee Dhunjeebhoy, 1849–1930, vol. III
Mehta Shuja-ul-Mulk, Sir, *died* 1936, vol. III (A), vol. IV
Mehta, Sir Sorabji Bezonji, *died* 1938, vol. III
Meier, Frederic Alfred, 1887–1954, vol. V
Meiggs, Russell, 1902–1989, vol. VIII
Meighen, Rt Hon. Arthur, 1874–1960, vol. V
Meighen, Maj.-Gen. Frank Stephen, 1870–1946, vol. IV
Meikle, Alexander, 1905–1980, vol. VII
Meikle, Andrew, 1847–1922, vol. II
Meikle, Captain Archibald Robert, 1886–1958, vol. V
Meikle, Henry William, 1880–1958, vol. V
Meikle, Lt-Col James Hamilton, 1876–1941, vol. IV

Meiklejohn, Col John Forbes, 1889–1966, vol. VI
Meiklejohn, John Miller Dow, 1836–1902, vol. I
Meiklejohn, Major Matthew Fontaine Maury, 1870–1913, vol. I
Meiklejohn, Surg. Rear-Adm. Norman Sinclair, 1879–1961, vol. VI
Meiklejohn, Ven. Robert, 1889–1974, vol. VII
Meiklejohn, Sir Roderick Sinclair, 1876–1962, vol. VI
Meiklejohn, Maj.-Gen. Sir William Hope, 1845–1909, vol. I
Meiklereid, Sir (Ernest) William, 1899–1965, vol. VI
Meiklereid, Sir William; see Meiklereid, Sir E. W.
Meillet, Paul Jules Antoine, 1866–1936, vol. III
Mein, Major Desbrisay Blundell, 1889–1937, vol. III
Meinertzhagen, Daniel, 1915–1991, vol. IX
Meinertzhagen, Sir Ernest Louis, 1854–1933, vol. III
Meinertzhagen, Sir Peter, 1920–1999, vol. X
Meinertzhagen, Col Richard, 1878–1967, vol. VI
Meir, Golda, 1898–1978, vol. VII
Meiss, Millard, 1904–1975, vol. VII
Meissas, Gaston, vol. II
Mekie, David Eric Cameron, 1902–1989, vol. VIII
Mekie, Eoin Cameron, 1906–1977, vol. VII
Melas, Michael Constantine, 1902–1967, vol. VI
Melba, Dame Nellie, 1861–1931, vol. III
Melcher, Frederic Gershom, 1879–1963, vol. VI
Melchett, 1st Baron, 1868–1930, vol. III
Melchett, 2nd Baron, 1898–1949, vol. IV
Melchett, 3rd Baron, 1925–1973, vol. VII
Melchett, Lady; (Violet), died 1945, vol. IV
Melchior, Lauritz L. H., 1890–1973, vol. VII
Melchior-Bonnet, Christian, 1904–1995, vol. X(AI)
Meldola, Raphael, 1849–1915, vol. I
Meldon, Sir Albert, 1845–1924, vol. II
Meldon, Lt-Col James Austin, 1869–1931, vol. III
Meldon, Lt-Col Philip Albert, 1874–1942, vol. IV
Meldrum, Andrew, 1909–1995, vol. IX
Meldrum, Charles, 1821–1901, vol. I
Meldrum, David Storrar, 1864–1940, vol. III
Meldrum, Sir Peter Lowrie, 1910–1965, vol. VI
Meldrum, Brig.-Gen. William, 1865–1964, vol. VI
Melhado, Carlos, 1852–1922, vol. II
Melhuish, Sir Charles W., 1860–1946, vol. IV
Meline, Felix Jules, 1838–1925, vol. II
Melitus, Paul Gegory, 1858–1924, vol. II
Mellanby, Alexander Lawson, 1871–1951, vol. V
Mellanby, Sir Edward, 1884–1955, vol. V
Mellanby, John, 1878–1939, vol. III
Mellanby, Kenneth, 1908–1993, vol. IX
Mellanby, May, (Lady Mellanby), 1882–1978, vol. VII
Mellanby, Molly, 1893–1962, vol. VI
Melland, Charles Herbert, 1872–1953, vol. V
Melland, Norman, 1865–1933, vol. III
Meller, Grahame Temple, 1905–1965, vol. VI
Meller, Sir Richard James, 1872–1940, vol. III
Mellersh, Arthur, 1857–1938, vol. III
Mellersh, Air Vice-Marshal Sir Francis John Williamson, 1898–1955, vol. V
Mellersh, Air Vice-Marshal Francis Richard Lee, 1922–1996, vol. X
Melles, Major William Eugene, 1883–1953, vol. V

Melling, Cecil Thomas, 1899–1998, vol. X
Mellis, Rev. James, 1843–1925, vol. II
Mellis, Col William Andrew, 1848–1925, vol. II
Mellish, Baron (Life Peer); Robert Joseph Mellish, 1913–1998, vol. X
Mellish, Rev. Edward Noel, 1880–1962, vol. VI
Mellish, Lt-Col Henry, 1856–1927, vol. II
Mellish, Humphrey, 1862–1937, vol. III
Mellish, Robert Walter, 1869–1938, vol. III
Melliss, Maj.-Gen. Sir Charles John, 1862–1936, vol. III
Melliss, Col Sir Howard, 1847–1921, vol. II
Mellon, Andrew William, 1855–1937, vol. III
Mellon, Paul, 1907–1999, vol. X
Mellon, Rt Rev. William H., 1877–1952, vol. V
Mellone, Sydney Herbert, died 1956, vol. V
Mellor, Lt-Col Abel, 1880–1967, vol. VI
Mellor, Francis Hamilton, 1854–1925, vol. II
Mellor, Sir Frank, 1863–1941, vol. IV
Mellor, Sir George, died 1947, vol. IV
Mellor, Brig.-Gen. Sir Gilbert, 1872–1947, vol. IV
Mellor, Wing-Comdr Harry Manners, 1903–1941, vol. IV
Mellor, Brig. James Frederick McLean, 1912–1997, vol. X
Mellor, Sir James Robert, 1839–1926, vol. II
Mellor, John Edward, 1852–1925, vol. II
Mellor, Sir John Francis, 3rd Bt, 1925–1990, vol. VIII
Mellor, John James, 1830–1916, vol. II
Mellor, Sir John Paget, 1st Bt, 1862–1929, vol. III
Mellor, Sir John Serocold Paget, 2nd Bt, 1893–1986, vol. VIII
Mellor, Brig. John Seymour, 1883–1962, vol. VI
Mellor, Rt Hon. John William, 1835–1911, vol. I
Mellor, Joseph William, died 1938, vol. III
Mellor, Col Robert Ramsden, 1870–1951, vol. V
Mellor, Captain William, 1874–1928, vol. II
Mellor, William, 1888–1942, vol. III
Mellowes, Liam; see Mellowes, W. J.
Mellowes, William Joseph, (Liam), died 1922, vol. II
Melly, George Henry, 1860–1927, vol. II
Melrose, James, 1841–1922, vol. II
Melrose, James, 1828–1929, vol. III
Melrose, John, 1853–1927, vol. II
Melrose, Sir John, 1860–1938, vol. III
Melvill, Maj.-Gen. Charles William, 1878–1925, vol. II
Melvill, Philip Sandys, 1827–1906, vol. I
Melvill, Sir William Henry, 1827–1911, vol. I
Melville, 5th Viscount, 1835–1904, vol. I
Melville, 6th Viscount, 1843–1926, vol. II
Melville, 7th Viscount, 1873–1935, vol. III
Melville, 8th Viscount, 1909–1971, vol. VII
Melville, Alan, 1910–1983, vol. VIII
Melville, Archibald Ralph, 1912–1982, vol. VIII
Melville, Arthur, 1855–1904, vol. I
Melville, Beresford Valentine, 1857–1931, vol. III
Melville, Col Charles Henderson, 1863–1943, vol. IV
Melville, Maj.-Gen. Charles William Francis, 1877–1949, vol. IV
Melville, Rev. David, 1813–1904, vol. I
Melville, Lt-Col Edward Patrick Alexander, 1880–1936, vol. III

Melville, Sir Eugene, 1911–1986, vol. VIII
Melville, Frances Helen, 1873–1962, vol. VI
Melville, Sir George, 1842–1924, vol. II
Melville, Lt-Col Harry George, 1869–1918, vol. II
Melville, Sir Harry Work, 1908–2000, vol. X
Melville, Henry Edward, 1883–1976, vol. VII
Melville, Lt-Col Hon. Ian L.; see Leslie Melville.
Melville, James, 1908–1984, vol. VIII
Melville, Sir James Benjamin, 1885–1931, vol. III
Melville, Rev. Leslie, 1838–1908, vol. I
Melville, Leslie Melville B.; see Balfour-Melville.
Melville, Lewis; see Benjamin, L. S.
Melville, Robert Dundonald, 1872–1927, vol. II
Melville, William, 1852–1918, vol. II
Melville, Rev. William Gardner, 1863–1939, vol. III
Melvin, George Spencer, 1887–1949, vol. IV
Melvin, Air Cdre James Douglas, 1914–1987, vol. VIII
Melvin, John Turcan, 1916–1999, vol. X
Melvin, Sir Martin John, 1st Bt, 1879–1952, vol. V
Menardos, Simos, 1872–1933, vol. III
Menary, Surg.-Captain John, 1865–1941, vol. IV
Menaul, Air Vice-Marshal Stewart William Blacker, 1915–1987, vol. VIII
Mencken, H. L., 1880–1956, vol. V
Mende, Erich, 1916–1998, vol. X
Mendel, William, 1854–1917, vol. II
Mendelsohn, Eric, 1887–1953, vol. V
Mendelson, John Jakob, 1917–1978, vol. VII
Mendelssohn, Kurt Alfred Georg, 1906–1980, vol. VII
Mendes, Catulle, 1841–1909, vol. I
Mendès France, Pierre, 1907–1982, vol. VIII
Mendl, Sir Charles, 1871–1958, vol. V
Mendl, Sir Sigismund Ferdinand, 1866–1945, vol. IV
Mendoza, Maurice, 1921–2000, vol. X
Mends, Hon. Brig.-Gen. Horatio Reginald, 1851–1933, vol. III
Mends, Sir William Robert, 1812–1897, vol. I
Meneces, Maj.-Gen. Ambrose Neponucene Trelawny, 1904–1979, vol. VII
Menendez, Sir (Manuel) Raymond, 1864–1952, vol. V
Menéndez y Pelayo, Marcelino, 1856–1912, vol. I
Menendez, Sir Raymond; see Menendez, Sir M. R.
Mengelberg, Rudolf, 1892–1959, vol. V
Menges, Herbert, 1902–1972, vol. VII
Menges, Isolde, 1893–1976, vol. VII
Meninsky, Bernard, 1891–1950, vol. IV
Menneer, Stephen Snow, 1910–1996, vol. X
Mennell, George Gillies, 1878–1959, vol. V
Mennell, James Beaver, 1880–1957, vol. V
Mennell, Peter, 1918–1981, vol. VIII
Mennell, Zebulon, 1876–1959, vol. V
Menninger, William C., 1899–1966, vol. VI
Menon, Sir Konkoth R.; see Ramunni Menon.
Menon, Rao Bahadur Vapal Pangunni, 1894–1966, vol. VI
Menon, Vengalil Krishnan K.; see Krishna Menon.
Menpes, Mortimer, died 1938, vol. III
Mensforth, Sir Eric, 1906–2000, vol. X
Mensforth, Sir Holberry, 1871–1951, vol. V
Menson, Sir Charles William T.; see Tachie-Menson.

Menteth, Lt-Col Sir James Frederick Stuart-, 4th Bt, 1846–1926, vol. II
Menteth, Sir James Stuart-, 3rd Bt, 1841–1918, vol. II
Menteth, Sir William Frederick Stuart-, 5th Bt, 1874–1952, vol. V
Menuhin, Baron (Life Peer), Yehudi Menuhin, 1916–1999, vol. X
Menzies, Alexander John Pople, 1863–1943, vol. IV
Menzies, Rev. Allan, 1845–1916, vol. II
Menzies, Captain Arthur John Alexander, died 1918, vol. II
Menzies, Col Charles T., 1858–1943, vol. IV
Menzies, Rt Hon. Sir Douglas Ian, 1907–1974, vol. VII
Menzies, Sir Frederick Norton Kay, 1875–1949, vol. IV
Menzies, George Kenneth, 1869–1954, vol. V
Menzies, James Acworth, died 1921, vol. II
Menzies, Sir Laurence James, 1906–1983, vol. VIII
Menzies, Marie Ney, 1895–1981, vol. VIII
Menzies, Sir Neil James, 8th Bt, 1855–1910, vol. I
Menzies, Dame Pattie Maie, 1899–1995, vol. IX
Menzies, Sir Peter Thomson, 1912–1998, vol. X
Menzies, Sir Robert, 7th Bt, 1817–1903, vol. I
Menzies, Sir Robert, 1891–1967, vol. VI
Menzies, Rt Hon. Sir Robert Gordon, 1894–1978, vol. VII
Menzies of Menzies, Ronald Steuart, 1884–1961, vol. VI
Menzies, Maj.-Gen. Sir Stewart Graham, 1890–1968, vol. VI
Menzies, Maj.-Gen. Thomas, 1893–1969, vol. VI
Menzies, Thomas Graham, 1869–1958, vol. V
Menzies, Tom Alexander, 1877–1950, vol. IV (A)
Menzies, Sir Walter, 1856–1913, vol. I
Menzies, William George S.; see Steuart-Menzies.
Menzies, William Gladstone, 1879–1938, vol. III
Menzies Anderson, Sir Gilmour, 1914–1977, vol. VII
Menzler, Frederick August Andrew, 1888–1968, vol. VI
Mercadier, Elie, 1844–1916, vol. II
Mercer, Alexander Warren, 1871–1943, vol. IV
Mercer, Major Cecil William, 1885–1960, vol. V
Mercer, Maj.-Gen. Sir David, 1864–1920, vol. II
Mercer, David, 1928–1980, vol. VII
Mercer, Col Edward Gilbert, 1873–1926, vol. II
Mercer, Maj.-Gen. Sir Frederic; see Mercer, Maj.-Gen. Sir H. F.
Mercer, George Gibson, 1873–1964, vol. VI
Mercer, Maj.-Gen. Sir (Harvey) Frederic, 1858–1936, vol. III
Mercer, Col Herbert, 1862–1944, vol. IV
Mercer, Howard, 1896–1973, vol. VII
Mercer, James, 1883–1932, vol. III
Mercer, John Charles Kenneth, 1917–1999, vol. X
Mercer, Rt Rev. John Edward, died 1922, vol. II
Mercer, John Swan, 1867–1947, vol. IV
Mercer, Laurence, 1863–1932, vol. III
Mercer, Rev. Samuel Alfred Browne, 1879–1969, vol. VI
Mercer, Stephen Pascal, 1891–1944, vol. IV
Mercer, Sir Walter, 1890–1971, vol. VII
Mercer, Sir William Hepworth, 1855–1932, vol. III
Mercer, Rev. William Marsden, 1858–1939, vol. III

Mercer-Nairne, Major Lord Charles George Francis, 1874–1914, vol. I
Merchant, Livingston Tallmadge, 1903–1976, vol. VII
Merchant, Vivien, 1929–1982, vol. VIII
Merchant, Wilfred, 1912–1965, vol. VI
Merchant, Rev. William Moelwyn, 1913–1997, vol. X
Mercie, Jean Marius Antonin, 1845–1916, vol. II
Mercieca, Hon. Sir Arturo, 1878–1969, vol. VI
Mercier, Charles Arthur, 1852–1919, vol. II
Mercier, His Eminence Cardinal Desiré, 1851–1926, vol. II
Mercier, Hon. Honoré, 1875–1937, vol. III
Mercier, Winifred Louise, 1878–1934, vol. III
Meredith, Arthur, 1856–1915, vol. I
Meredith, Arthur C., died 1938, vol. III (A)
Meredith, Air Vice-Marshal Sir Charles Warburton, 1896–1977, vol. VII
Meredith, George, 1828–1909, vol. I
Meredith, George Patrick, 1904–1978, vol. VII
Meredith, George Thomas, 1907–1959, vol. V
Meredith, Sir Herbert Ribton, 1890–1959, vol. V
Meredith, Hubert Angelo, 1884–1965, vol. VI
Meredith, Hugh Owen, 1878–1964, vol. VI
Meredith, Sir James Creed, 1842–1912, vol. I
Meredith, James Creed, died 1942, vol. IV
Meredith, Leonard Arthur De Lacy, 1888–1971, vol. VII
Meredith, Rt Rev. Lewis Evan, 1900–1968, vol. VI
Meredith, Margaret, died 1964, vol. VI (AII)
Meredith, Rev. Canon Ralph Creed, 1887–1970, vol. VI
Meredith, Rev. Richard, died 1928, vol. II, vol. III
Meredith, Richard, 1867–1957, vol. V
Meredith, Rt Hon. Richard Edmund, 1855–1916, vol. II
Meredith, Richard Martin, 1847–1934, vol. III
Meredith, Sir Vincent, 1st Bt, 1850–1929, vol. III
Meredith, Sir Vincent Robert Sissons, 1877–1965, vol. VI
Meredith, William Appleton, 1848–1916, vol. II
Meredith, Rev. William Macdonald, 1848–1931, vol. III
Meredith, William Maxse, 1865–1937, vol. III
Meredith, Hon. Sir William Ralph, 1840–1923, vol. II
Meredith, Col William Rice, 1882–1964, vol. VI
Meredyth, Captain Arthur Gwynn Moreton, 1862–1955, vol. V
Meredyth, Paymaster Rear-Adm. Charles Edward Hughes, 1861–1949, vol. IV
Meredyth, Sir Edward Henry John, 10th Bt (cr 1660), 1828–1904, vol. I
Meredyth, Sir George Augustus Jérvis, 11th Bt (cr 1660), 1832–1907, vol. I
Meredyth, Sir Henry Bayly, 5th Bt (cr 1795), 1863–1923, vol. II
Merer, Air Vice-Marshal John William Frederick, 1899–1964, vol. VI
Merewether, Sir Edward Marsh, 1858–1938, vol. III
Merewether, Edward Rowland Alworth, 1892–1970, vol. VI
Merewether, Lt-Col John Walter Beresford, 1867–1942, vol. IV

Merewether, Rev. Wyndham Arthur Scinde, 1852–1928, vol. II
Merezhkovski, Dmitri Sergeievich, 1865–1941, vol. IV (A), vol. V
Meritt, Benjamin Dean, 1899–1989, vol. VIII
Merivale, Dame Gladys; see Cooper, Dame Gladys.
Merivale, Herman Charles, 1839–1906, vol. I
Merk, William Rudolph Henry, 1852–1925, vol. II
Mermagen, Air Cdre Herbert Waldemar, 1912–1998, vol. X
Mermagen, Patrick Hassell Frederick, 1911–1984, vol. VIII
Merrells, Thomas Ernest, 1891–1987, vol. VIII
Merrett, Sir Charles Edward, 1863–1948, vol. IV
Merrett, Charles Edwin, 1923–1994, vol. IX
Merrett, Sir Herbert, 1886–1959, vol. V
Merriam, John Campbell, 1869–1945, vol. IV
Merriam, Sir Laurence Pierce Brooke, 1894–1966, vol. VI
Merrick, Major George Charleton, 1872–1913, vol. I
Merrick, Sir John Edward-Siegfried, 1888–1968, vol. VI
Merrick, Leonard, 1864–1939, vol. III
Merricks, Frank, 1866–1936, vol. III
Merrifield, Leonard Stanford, 1880–1943, vol. IV
Merrill, Elmer Truesdell, 1860–1936, vol. III
Merriman, 1st Baron, 1880–1962, vol. VI
Merriman, Basil Mandeville, 1911–1999, vol. X
Merriman, Gen. Charles James, 1831–1906, vol. I
Merriman, Rev. Charles Victor, died 1931, vol. III
Merriman, Henry Seton, 1862–1903, vol. I
Merriman, James Henry Herbert, 1915–1997, vol. X
Merriman, Rt Hon. John Xavier, 1841–1926, vol. II
Merriman, P. J., 1877–1943, vol. IV
Merriman, Lt-Col Reginald Gordon, 1866–1938, vol. III
Merriman, Roger Bigelow, 1876–1945, vol. IV
Merriman, Sir Walter Thomas, 1882–1972, vol. VII
Merriman, Col William, 1838–1917, vol. II
Merrington, Rev. Ernest Northcroft, 1876–1953, vol. V
Merrison, Sir Alec; see Merrison, Sir Alexander W.
Merrison, Sir Alexander Walter, (Sir Alec Merrison), 1924–1989, vol. VIII
Merritt, Anna Lea, 1844–1930, vol. III
Merrivale, 1st Baron, 1855–1939, vol. III
Merrivale, 2nd Baron, 1883–1951, vol. V
Merry, Archibald William, died 1933, vol. III
Merry, Rev. William Walter, 1835–1918, vol. II
Merry del Val, Marquis de, 1864–1943, vol. IV
Merry del Val, His Eminence Cardinal Raphael, 1865–1930, vol. III
Mersey, 1st Viscount, 1840–1929, vol. III
Mersey, 2nd Viscount, 1872–1956, vol. V
Mersey, 3rd Viscount, 1906–1979, vol. VII
Merthyr, 1st Baron, 1837–1914, vol. I
Merthyr, 2nd Baron, 1866–1932, vol. III
Merthyr, 3rd Baron, 1901–1977, vol. VII
Merton, Patrick Anthony, 1920–2000, vol. X
Merton, Sir Thomas Ralph, 1888–1969, vol. VI
Merton, Air Chief Marshal Sir Walter Hugh, 1905–1986, vol. VIII
Merz, Charles, 1893–1977, vol. VII
Merz, Charles Hesterman, 1874–1940, vol. III

Merz, John Theodore, 1840–1922, vol. II
Mess, Henry Adolphus, 1884–1944, vol. IV
Messager, André, 1853–1929, vol. III
Messager, Hope, (Mme André Messager); see Temple, Hope.
Messel, Oliver Hilary Sambourne, 1904–1978, vol. VII
Messel, Rudolph, 1848–1920, vol. II
Messent, Philip Glynn, 1862–1925, vol. II
Messent, Sir Philip Santo, 1895–1976, vol. VII
Messer, Adam Brunton, died 1919, vol. II
Messer, Allan Ernest, 1865–1954, vol. V
Messer, Lt-Col Arthur Albert, 1863–1934, vol. III
Messer, Sir Frederick, 1886–1971, vol. VII
Messer, Malcolm, 1901–1984, vol. VIII
Messervy, Albert, 1908–1985, vol. VIII
Messervy, Gen. Sir Frank Walter, 1893–1974, vol. VII
Messervy, Sir Godfrey; see Messervy, Sir R. G. C.
Messervy, Sir (Roney) Godfrey (Collumbell), 1924–1995, vol. IX
Messiaen, Olivier, 1908–1992, vol. IX
Messina, Count, Don Francesco (di Paola), born 1848, vol. III
Messiter, Lt-Col Charles Bayard, 1870–1940, vol. III
Messiter, Air Cdre Herbert Lindsell, 1902–1994, vol. IX
Meston, 1st Baron, 1865–1943, vol. IV
Meston, 2nd Baron, 1894–1984, vol. VIII
Meston, Rev. William, 1871–1933, vol. III
Mestrovic, Ivan, 1883–1962, vol. VI
Metalious, Grace, 1924–1964, vol. VI
Metaxa, Count Andrea, 1844–1921, vol. II
Metaxa, Vice-Adm. Count Frederick Cosmeto, 1847–1910, vol. I
Metaxas, Dimitry George, died 1928, vol. II
Metcalf, Maurice Rupert, 1905–1972, vol. VII
Metcalfe, Sir Aubrey; see Metcalfe, Sir H. A. F.
Metcalfe, Sir Charles Herbert Theophilus, 6th Bt, 1853–1928, vol. II
Metcalfe, Maj.-Gen. Charles Theophilus Evelyn, 1856–1912, vol. I
Metcalfe, Captain Christopher Powell, 1873–1935, vol. III
Metcalfe, Rev. Edmund Lionel, died 1941, vol. IV
Metcalfe, Major Edward Dudley, died 1957, vol. V
Metcalfe, Brig.-Gen. Francis Edward, 1878–1934, vol. III
Metcalfe, Sir Frederic William, 1886–1965, vol. VI
Metcalfe, Sir George, 1848–1931, vol. III
Metcalfe, Henry Wray, 1864–1937, vol. III
Metcalfe, Herbert, 1887–1940, vol. III
Metcalfe, Sir (Herbert) Aubrey (Francis), 1883–1957, vol. V
Metcalfe, Lt-Col Herbert Charles, 1864–1940, vol. III
Metcalfe, James, 1863–1930, vol. III
Metcalfe, Air Cdre Joan, 1923–2000, vol. X
Metcalfe, Maj.-Gen. John Francis, 1908–1975, vol. VII
Metcalfe, Percy, 1895–1970, vol. VI
Metcalfe, Sir Ralph Ismay, 1896–1977, vol. VII
Metcalfe, Brig.-Gen. Sydney Fortescue, 1870–1948, vol. IV

Metcalfe, Sir Theophilus John, 8th Bt, 1916–1979, vol. VII
Metcalfe, Sir Theophilus John Massie, 7th Bt, 1866–1950, vol. IV
Metcalfe, Thomas Llewellyn, 1870–1922, vol. II
Metcalfe, Rev. W. M., 1840–1916, vol. II
Metcalfe-Smith, Lt-Col Bertram, 1863–1944, vol. IV
Metchnikoff, Élie, 1845–1916, vol. II
Metford, Col Sir Francis Killigrew Seymour, 1863–1946, vol. IV
Methold, Sir Henry Tindal, 1869–1952, vol. V
Methuen, 3rd Baron, 1845–1932, vol. III
Methuen, 4th Baron, 1886–1974, vol. VII
Methuen, 5th Baron, 1891–1975, vol. VII
Methuen, 6th Baron, 1925–1994, vol. IX
Methuen, Sir Algernon Methuen Marshall, 1st Bt, 1856–1924, vol. II
Methven, Sir Harry Finlayson, 1886–1968, vol. VI
Methven, Sir John; see Methven, Sir M. J.
Methven, John Cecil Wilson, 1885–1968, vol. VI
Methven, Sir (Malcolm) John, 1926–1980, vol. VII
Metson, Gilbert Harold, 1907–1981, vol. VIII
Mettam, A. E., died 1917, vol. II
Meuleman, Most Rev. Brice, 1862–1924, vol. II
Meux, Admiral of the Fleet Hon. Sir Hedworth, 1856–1929, vol. III
Mewburn, Maj.-Gen. Hon. Sydney Chilton, 1863–1956, vol. V
Mews, Arthur, 1864–1947, vol. IV
Mexborough, 4th Earl of, 1810–1899, vol. I
Mexborough, 5th Earl of, 1843–1916, vol. II
Mexborough, 6th Earl of, 1868–1945, vol. IV
Mexborough, 7th Earl of, 1906–1980, vol. VII
Mexborough, Countess of; (Anne), died 1943, vol. IV
Meyendorff, Alexander, 1869–1964, vol. VI
Meyer, Alfred, 1895–1990, vol. VIII
Meyer, Arthur, 1845–1924, vol. II
Meyer, Sir Carl Ferdinand, 1st Bt, 1851–1922, vol. II
Meyer, Lt-Col Charles Hardwick Louw, 1859–1942, vol. IV
Meyer, Eugene, 1875–1959, vol. V
Meyer, Sir Frank Cecil, 2nd Bt, 1886–1935, vol. III
Meyer, Rev. Frederick Brotheron, 1847–1929, vol. III
Meyer, George von Lengerke, 1858–1918, vol. II
Meyer, Heinerich Carl, 1896–1972, vol. VII
Meyer, Jack; see Meyer, R. J. O.
Meyer, John Mount Montague, 1915–1979, vol. VII
Meyer, Kuno, 1859–1919, vol. II, vol. III
Meyer, Louis, 1871–1915, vol. I
Meyer, Sir Manasseh, 1831–1930, vol. III
Meyer, Michael Leverson, 1921–2000, vol. X
Meyer, Sir Oscar Gwynne, 1910–1981, vol. VIII
Meyer, Paul, 1840–1917, vol. II
Meyer, Sir Robert, 1858–1935, vol. III
Meyer, Rollo John Oliver, (Jack), 1905–1991, vol. IX
Meyer, Sir William Stevenson, 1860–1922, vol. II
Meyerheim, Robert Gustav, died 1920, vol. II
Meyerhof, Otto Fritz, 1884–1951, vol. V
Meyerstein, Edward Harry William, 1889–1952, vol. V

Meyerstein, Sir Edward William, 1863–1942, vol. IV
Meyjes, Anthony Cornelius, died 1929, vol. III
Meyler, Lt-Col Hugh Mowbray, 1875–1929, vol. III
Meynell, Alice Christiana Gertrude, 1847–1922, vol. II
Meynell, Dame Alix Hester Marie, (Lady Meynell), 1903–1999, vol. X
Meynell, Edgar, 1859–1923, vol. II
Meynell, Edgar John, 1825–1901, vol. I
Meynell, Esther Hallam, (E. Hallam Moorhouse), died 1955, vol. V
Meynell, Everard, 1882–1926, vol. II
Meynell, Sir Everard Charles, 1885–1956, vol. V
Meynell, Sir Francis, 1891–1975, vol. VII
Meynell, Francis Hugo Lindley, 1880–1941, vol. IV
Meynell, Rev. Francis William, 1851–1932, vol. III
Meynell, Hon. Frederick George Lindley, 1846–1910, vol. I
Meynell, Brig.-Gen. Godfrey, 1870–1943, vol. IV
Meynell, Laurence Walter, 1899–1989, vol. VIII
Meynell, Viola, died 1956, vol. V
Meynell, Wilfrid, 1852–1948, vol. IV
Meyner, Robert Baumle, 1908–1990, vol. VIII
Meynink, John Fitzsimmons, 1887–1972, vol. VII
Meyric Hughes, Reginald Richard, 1915–1962, vol. VI
Meyrick, Edward, 1854–1938, vol. III
Meyrick, Brig.-Gen. Sir Frederick Charlton, 2nd Bt (cr 1880), 1862–1932, vol. III
Meyrick, Rev. Frederick J., 1871–1945, vol. IV
Meyrick, Sir George Augustus Eliott Tapps-Gervis-, 4th Bt (cr 1791), 1855–1928, vol. II
Meyrick, Lt-Col Sir George David Eliott Tapps Gervis-, 6th Bt, 1915–1988, vol. VIII
Meyrick, Major Sir George Llewelyn Tapps-Gervis-, 5th Bt (cr 1791), 1885–1960, vol. V
Meyrick, James Joseph, 1834–1925, vol. II
Meyrick, Adm. Sir Sidney Julius, 1879–1973, vol. VII
Meyrick, Col Sir Thomas C.; see Charlton-Meyrick.
Meyrick, Col Sir Thomas Frederick, 3rd Bt, 1899–1983, vol. VIII
Meyrick, Walter Henry, 1880–1950, vol. IV
Meysey-Thompson, Captain Sir Algar de Clifford Charles, 3rd Bt, 1885–1967, vol. VI
Meysey-Thompson, Captain Hon. Claude Henry, 1887–1915, vol. I
Meysey-Thompson, Ernest Claude, 1859–1944, vol. IV
Meysey-Thompson, Hubert Charles, 1883–1956, vol. V
Meysey-Thompson, Col Richard Frederick, 1847–1926, vol. II
Mézières, Alfred Jean François, died 1915, vol. I
Miall, Louis Compton, 1842–1921, vol. II
Micallef, Sir Richard, 1846–1933, vol. III
Michael, Albert Davidson, 1836–1927, vol. II
Michael, David Parry Martin, 1910–1986, vol. VIII
Michael, Rev. J. Hugh, 1878–1959, vol. V
Michael, Gen. James, 1828–1907, vol. I
Michaelis, Sir Archie, 1889–1975, vol. VII
Michaelis, Sir Maximillian, died 1932, vol. III
Michaels, Michael Israel, 1908–1992, vol. IX
Michalopoulos, André, born 1897, vol. IX(AI)

Michalowski, Jerzy, 1909–1993, vol. IX
Michel, Louise, 1830–1905, vol. I
Michelham, 1st Baron, 1851–1919, vol. II
Michelham, 2nd Baron, 1900–1984, vol. VIII
Michelham, Lady; (Aimée Geraldine), died 1927, vol. II
Michelin, Reginald Townend, 1903–1998, vol. X
Michelin, William Plunkett, 1872–1943, vol. IV
Michell, Alan, 1913–1985, vol. VIII
Michell, Anthony George Maldon, died 1959, vol. V
Michell, Rev. Francis Rodon, 1839–1920, vol. II
Michell, Francis Victor, 1908–1985, vol. VIII
Michell, George Babington, 1864–1936, vol. III
Michell, Rev. Gilbert Arthur, 1883–1960, vol. V
Michell, Harry Denis, 1923–1971, vol. VII
Michell, Humphrey, 1883–1970, vol. VI
Michell, John, 1836–1921, vol. II
Michell, John Henry, died 1940, vol. III
Michell, Comdr Kenneth, 1887–1967, vol. VI
Michell, Hon. Sir Lewis Loyd, 1842–1928, vol. II
Michell, Sir Robert Carminowe, 1876–1956, vol. V
Michell, Roland Lyons Nosworthy, 1847–1931, vol. III
Michell, Walter Cecil, 1864–1939, vol. III
Michelli, Sir James, 1853–1935, vol. III
Michelmore, Maj.-Gen. Sir Godwin; see Michelmore, Maj.-Gen. Sir W. G.
Michelmore, Sir Walter Harold Strachan, 1908–1988, vol. VIII
Michelmore, Maj.-Gen. Sir (William) Godwin, 1894–1982, vol. VIII
Michelson, Albert Abraham, 1852–1931, vol. III
Michelson, Christian, 1857–1925, vol. II
Michener, Rt Hon. (Daniel) Roland, 1900–1991, vol. IX
Michener, James Albert, 1907–1997, vol. X
Michener, Rt Hon. Roland; see Michener, Rt Hon. D. R.
Michie, Alexander, 1833–1902, vol. I
Michie, Sir Archibald, 1810–1899, vol. I
Michie, Charles Watt, 1907–1982, vol. VIII
Michie, James, 1867–1943, vol. IV
Michie, James Coutts, 1861–1919, vol. II
Michie, James Kilgour, 1887–1967, vol. VI
Michie, John, 1853–1934, vol. III
Michie, John Lundie, 1882–1946, vol. IV
Michie, Robert James, 1856–1928, vol. II
Micholls, E. Montefiore, 1852–1926, vol. II
Micklem, Major Charles, 1882–1955, vol. V
Micklem, Maj.-Gen. Edward, 1840–1934, vol. III
Micklem, Comdr Sir (Edward) Robert, 1891–1952, vol. V
Micklem, Col Henry Andrew, 1872–1963, vol. VI
Micklem, Brig.-Gen. John, 1889–1952, vol. V
Micklem, Nathaniel, 1853–1954, vol. V
Micklem, Rev. Nathaniel, 1888–1976, vol. VII
Micklem, Very Rev. Philip Arthur, 1876–1965, vol. VI
Micklem, Brig. Ralph, 1884–1977, vol. VII
Micklem, Comdr Sir Robert; see Micklem, Comdr Sir E. R.
Micklethwait, Frances Mary Gore, 1867–1950, vol. IV
Micklethwait, Hon. Ivy Mary, (Hon. Mrs Micklethwait), 1895–1967, vol. IV

Micklethwait, Rear-Adm. St John Aldrich, 1901–1977, vol. VII
Micklethwait, St John Gore, 1870–1951, vol. V
Micklethwait, Sir Robert Gore, 1902–1992, vol. IX
Micks, Sir Robert, 1825–1902, vol. I
Micks, Robert Henry, 1895–1970, vol. VI
Micks, William Lawson, 1851–1928, vol. II
Middlebro, William Sora, 1868–1948, vol. IV
Middlebrook, Sir Harold, 2nd Bt, 1887–1971, vol. VII
Middlebrook, Sir William, 1st Bt, 1851–1936, vol. III
Middlemas, Noel Allan, 1892–1967, vol. VI
Middlemiss, Charles Stewart, 1859–1945, vol. IV
Middlemiss, Sir Howard; see Middlemiss, Sir J. H.
Middlemiss, Sir (John) Howard, 1916–1983, vol. VIII
Middleditch, Edward, 1923–1987, vol. VIII
Middlemore, Sir John Throgmorton, 1st Bt, 1844–1925, vol. II
Middlemore, Sir William Hawkslow, 2nd Bt, 1908–1987, vol. VIII
Middleton, 9th Baron, 1844–1922, vol. II
Middleton, 10th Baron, 1847–1924, vol. II
Middleton, 11th Baron, 1887–1970, vol. VI
Middleton, A. Safroni, died 1950, vol. IV
Middleton, Sir Arthur Edward, 7th Bt, 1838–1933, vol. III
Middleton, Sir Arthur Edward, 1891–1953, vol. V
Middleton, Sir Charles Arthur, 8th Bt, 1873–1942, vol. IV
Middleton, Drew, 1914–1990, vol. VIII
Middleton, Edgar, 1894–1939, vol. III
Middleton, Sir Frederick Dobson, 1825–1898, vol. I
Middleton, Sir George, 1876–1938, vol. III
Middleton, Sir George Humphrey, 1910–1998, vol. X
Middleton, Sir George Proctor, 1905–1987, vol. VIII
Middleton, George Walker, 1898–1971, vol. VII
Middleton, Adm. Gervase Boswell, 1893–1961, vol. VI
Middleton, Hubert Stanley, 1890–1959, vol. V
Middleton, Sir John, 1870–1954, vol. V
Middleton, Sir John Page, 1851–1954, vol. III
Middleton, Kenneth William Bruce, 1905–1995, vol. IX
Middleton, Lambert William, 1877–1941, vol. IV
Middleton, Sir Lawrence Monck, 10th Bt, 1912–1999, vol. X
Middleton, Lucy Annie, 1894–1983, vol. VIII
Middleton, Noel, 1875–1955, vol. V
Middleton, Peggy Arline, 1916–1974, vol. VII
Middleton, Reginald Empson, 1844–1925, vol. II
Middleton, Richard William Evelyn, 1846–1905, vol. I
Middleton, Ronald George, 1913–1999, vol. X
Middleton, Sir Stephen Hugh, 9th Bt, 1909–1993, vol. IX
Middleton, Sir Thomas, 1863–1943, vol. IV
Middleton, William Aberdein, 1876–1940, vol. III
Midgley, Eric Atkinson, 1913–2000, vol. X
Midgley, Rt Hon. Harry, died 1957, vol. V
Midgley, Lt-Col Stephen, 1871–1954, vol. V
Midgley, Wilson, 1887–1954, vol. V
Midlane, Albert, 1825–1909, vol. I

Midleton, 1st Earl of, 1856–1942, vol. IV
Midleton, 2nd Earl of, 1888–1979, vol. VII
Midleton, 8th Viscount, 1830–1907, vol. I
Midleton, 11th Viscount, 1903–1988, vol. VIII
Midwinter, Captain Sir Edward Colpoys, 1872–1947, vol. IV
Midwood, Lt-Col Harrison, 1857–1944, vol. IV
Miers, Rear-Adm. Sir Anthony Cecil Capel, 1906–1985, vol. VIII
Miers, Sir Henry Alexander, 1858–1942, vol. IV
Mies van der Rohe, Ludwig, 1886–1969, vol. VI
Mieville, Arthur Leonard, 1879–1976, vol. VII
Mieville, Sir Eric Charles, 1896–1971, vol. VII
Miéville, Sir Walter Frederick, 1855–1929, vol. III
Mifflin, Lloyd, 1846–1921, vol. II
Mifsud, Edward Robert, 1875–1970, vol. VI
Mifsud, Hon. Sir Ugo Pasquale, 1889–1942, vol. IV
Migdale, Hon. Lord; James Frederick Gordon Thomson, 1897–1983, vol. VIII
Migeod, Frederick William Hugh, 1872–1952, vol. V
Mighell, Sir Norman Rupert, 1894–1955, vol. V
Mignault, Pierre Basile, 1854–1945, vol. IV
Mignot, Rev. Peter Thomas, 1863–1935, vol. III
Mijatovich, Chedomille, 1842–1932, vol. III
Mikardo, Ian, 1908–1993, vol. IX
Mikes, George, 1912–1987, vol. VIII
Mikkelsen, Captain Ejnar, 1880–1971, vol. VII
Mikoyan, Anastas Ivanovich, 1895–1978, vol. VII
Milbank, Sir Frederick Acclom, 1st Bt, 1820–1898, vol. I
Milbank, Major Sir Frederick Richard Powlett, 3rd Bt, 1881–1964, vol. VI
Milbank, Maj. Sir Mark Vane, 4th Bt, 1907–1984, vol. VIII
Milbank, Sir Powlett Charles John, 2nd Bt, 1852–1918, vol. II
Milbanke, Sir John Charles Peniston, 11th Bt, 1902–1947, vol. IV
Milbanke, Sir John Peniston, 10th Bt, 1872–1915, vol. I
Milbanke, Sir Peniston, 9th Bt, 1847–1899, vol. I
Milbanke, Ralph, 1852–1903, vol. I
Milbanke, Sir Ralph Mark, 12th Bt, 1907–1949, vol. IV
Milborne-Swinnerton-Pilkington, Major Sir Arthur William; see Pilkington.
Milborne-Swinnerton-Pilkington, Sir Thomas Edward; see Pilkington.
Milburn, Captain Booker, 1888–1941, vol. IV
Milburn, Charles Henry, 1860–1948, vol. IV
Milburn, Sir Charles Stamp, 2nd Bt, 1878–1917, vol. II
Milburn, James Booth, 1860–1923, vol. II
Milburn, Sir John Davison, 1st Bt, 1851–1907, vol. I
Milburn, Sir John Nigel, 4th Bt, 1918–1985, vol. VIII
Milburn, Sir Leonard John, 3rd Bt, 1884–1957, vol. V
Milburn, Very Rev. Robert Leslie Pollington, 1907–2000, vol. X
Milchsack, Lisalotte, (Dame Lilo Milchsack), 1905–1992, vol. IX
Mildmay of Flete, 1st Baron, 1861–1947, vol. IV

Mildmay of Flete, 2nd Baron, 1909–1950, vol. IV
Mildmay, Sir Anthony St John-, 8th Bt, 1894–1947, vol. IV
Mildmay, Rev. Sir (Aubrey) Neville St John-, 10th Bt, 1865–1955, vol. V
Mildmay, Sir Gerald Anthony Shaw-Lefevre St John-, 7th Bt, 1860–1929, vol. III
Mildmay, Sir Henry Bouverie Paulet St John-, 5th Bt, 1810–1902, vol. I
Mildmay, Sir Henry Gerald St John-, 9th Bt, 1926–1949, vol. IV
Mildmay, Major Sir Henry Paulet St John, 6th Bt, 1853–1916, vol. II
Mildmay, Lt-Col Herbert Alexander St John-, 1836–1922, vol. II
Mildmay, Rev. Sir Neville St John-; see Mildmay, Rev. Sir A. N. St J.
Mildmay, Major Wyndham Paulet St John-, 1855–1934, vol. III
Mildren, Col William Frederick, 1874–1948, vol. IV
Miles, Baron (Life Peer); Bernard James Miles, 1907–1991, vol. IX
Miles, Alexander, 1865–1953, vol. V
Miles, Alfred Henry, 1848–1929, vol. III
Miles, Alfred Henry, 1855–1933, vol. III
Miles, Sir (Arnold) Ashley, 1904–1988, vol. VIII
Miles, Major Arthur Tremayne, 1889–1934, vol. III
Miles, Sir Ashley; see Miles, Sir A. A.
Miles, Basil Raymond, 1906–1984, vol. VIII
Miles, Sir Cecil Leopold, 3rd Bt, 1873–1898, vol. I
Miles, Lt-Gen. Charles George Norman, 1884–1958, vol. V
Miles, Col Charles Napier, 1854–1918, vol. II
Miles, Sir Charles Watt, 1901–1970, vol. VI
Miles, Sir Charles William, 5th Bt, 1883–1966, vol. VI
Miles, Maj.-Gen. Eric Grant, 1891–1977, vol. VII
Miles, Eustace, 1868–1948, vol. IV
Miles, Rev. Frederic James, 1869–1962, vol. VI
Miles, Frederick George, 1903–1976, vol. VII
Miles, Geoffrey, 1922–2000, vol. X
Miles, Adm. Sir Geoffrey John Audley, 1890–1986, vol. VIII
Miles, George Edward, 1852–1942, vol. IV
Miles, George Herbert, 1880–1955, vol. V
Miles, Gordon, 1891–1959, vol. V
Miles, Sir Henry Robert William, 4th Bt, 1843–1915, vol. I
Miles, Lt-Gen. Sir Herbert Scott Gould, 1850–1926, vol. II
Miles, Herbert William, 1898–1987, vol. VIII
Miles, Sir John Charles, 1870–1963, vol. VI
Miles, Rev. Joseph Henry, died 1935, vol. III
Miles, Dame Margaret, 1911–1994, vol. IX
Miles, Maurice Edward, 1908–1985, vol. VIII
Miles, Maxine Frances Mary, 1901–1984, vol. VIII
Miles, Lt-Gen. Nelson Appleton, 1839–1925, vol. II
Miles, Brig.-Gen. Philip John, 1864–1948, vol. IV
Miles, Philip Napier, 1865–1935, vol. III
Miles, Brig. Reginald, 1892–1943, vol. IV
Miles, Richard, 1893–1976, vol. VII
Miles, Surgeon Rear-Adm. Stanley, 1911–1987, vol. VIII
Miles, Captain Wilfrid, 1885–1962, vol. VI

Miles, William Ernest, 1869–1947, vol. IV
Miley, Col James Aloysius, 1846–1919, vol. II
Milford, 1st Baron, 1874–1962, vol. VI
Milford, 2nd Baron, 1902–1993, vol. IX
Milford, 3rd Baron, 1929–1999, vol. X
Milford, Rev. Canon Campbell Seymour, 1896–1981, vol. VIII
Milford, Maj.-Gen. Edward James, died 1972, vol. VII
Milford, Brig. Ernest William, 1898–1944, vol. IV
Milford, Sir Humphrey Sumner, 1877–1952, vol. V
Milford, Rev. Canon Theodore Richard, 1895–1987, vol. VIII
Milford Haven, 1st Marquess of, 1854–1921, vol. II
Milford Haven, 2nd Marquess of, 1892–1938, vol. III
Milford Haven, 3rd Marquess of, 1919–1970, vol. VI
Milhaud, Darius, 1892–1974, vol. VII
Milkomane, G. A. M.; see Sava, George
Mill, Rear-Adm. Ernest, 1906–1988, vol. VIII
Mill, Hugh Robert, 1861–1950, vol. IV
Mill, Laura Margaret Dorothea, 1897–1990, vol. VIII
Mill, Thomas, 1878–1941, vol. IV
Mill, William Allin, 1902–1968, vol. VI
Mill, William Claude Frederick V. B.; see Vaudrey-Barker-Mill.
Mill Irving, David Jarvis, 1904–1978, vol. VII
Millais, Sir Everett, 2nd Bt, 1856–1897, vol. I
Millais, Sir Geoffroy William, 4th Bt, 1863–1941, vol. IV
Millais, Sir John Everett, 3rd Bt, 1888–1920, vol. II
Millais, John Guille, 1865–1931, vol. III
Millais, Sir Ralph Regnault, 5th Bt, 1905–1992, vol. IX
Milland, Raymond Alton, 1907–1986, vol. VIII
Millar, A. H., 1847–1927, vol. II
Millar, Alexander, 1867–1944, vol. IV
Millar, Edric William Hoyer, 1880–1963, vol. VI
Millar, Eric George, 1887–1966, vol. VI
Millar, Dame (Evelyn Louisa) Elizabeth II.; see Hoyer-Millar.
Millar, Frederick Charles James, died 1899, vol. I
Millar, Henry James, 1878–1960, vol. V
Millar, Ian Alastair D.; see Duncan Millar
Millar, Sir Jackson, 1888–1958, vol. V
Millar, Sir James Duncan, 1871–1932, vol. III
Millar, James Gardner, 1855–1917, vol. II
Millar, John, 1905–1978, vol. VII
Millar, John Alexander Stevenson, 1854–1938, vol. III
Millar, John Hepburn, 1864–1929, vol. III
Millar, Robert, 1850–1908, vol. I
Millar of Orton, Maj.-Gen. Robert Kirkpatrick, 1901–1981, vol. VIII
Millar, Sir Ronald Graeme, 1919–1998, vol. X
Millar, William Malcolm, 1913–1996, vol. X
Millar-Craig, Hamish, 1918–1989, vol. VIII
Millard, Charles Killick, 1870–1952, vol. V
Millard, Ven. Ernest Norman, 1899–1969, vol. VI
Millard, Evelyn, died 1941, vol. IV
Millard, Raymond Spencer, 1920–1997, vol. X
Millard, Col Reginald Jeffery, 1868–1943, vol. IV
Millard, Thomas, 1884–1935, vol. III

Millay, Edna St Vincent, 1892–1950, vol. IV
Millbourn, Rev. Arthur Russell, 1892–1973, vol. VII
Millbourn, Sir Eric; see Millbourn, Sir P. E.
Millbourn, Sir (Philip) Eric, 1902–1982, vol. VIII
Millbourn, Sir Ralph, 1862–1942, vol. IV
Miller, Sir Alastair George Lionel Joseph, 6th Bt (cr 1788), 1893–1964, vol. VI
Miller, Sir Alexander Edward, 1828–1903, vol. I
Miller, Alexander Gordon, 1843–1929, vol. III
Miller, Alexander James Nicol, 1911–1974, vol. VII
Miller, Alexander Ronald, 1915–1996, vol. X
Miller, Alexander Thomas, 1875–1942, vol. IV
Miller, Brig.-Gen. Alfred Douglas, 1864–1933, vol. III
Miller, Rear-Adm. Andrew John, 1926–1986, vol. VIII
Miller, Archibald Elliot Haswell, 1887–1979, vol. VII
Miller, A(rthur) Austin, 1900–1968, vol. VI
Miller, Arthur Hallowes, 1880–1956, vol. V
Miller, Arthur William Kaye, 1849–1914, vol. I
Miller, Maj.-Gen. Austin T., 1888–1947, vol. IV
Miller, Charles A. Duff, 1854–1909, vol. I
Miller, Vice-Adm. Charles Blois, 1867–1926, vol. II
Miller, Lt-Col Charles Darley, 1868–1951, vol. V
Miller, Maj.-Gen. Charles Harvey, 1894–1974, vol. VII
Miller, Charles Hewitt, 1875–1939, vol. III
Miller, Sir (Charles John) Hubert, 8th Bt (cr 1705), 1858–1940, vol. III
Miller, Cincinnatus Heine; see Miller, Joaquin.
Miller, Brig.-Gen. David, 1857–1934, vol. III
Miller, Maj.-Gen. David Edwin, 1931–1996, vol. X
Miller, Sir Dawson, 1867–1942, vol. IV
Miller, Sir Denison Samuel King, 1860–1923, vol. II
Miller, Desmond Campbell, 1914–1986, vol. VIII
Miller, Donald C.; see Crichton-Miller
Miller, Sir Douglas; see Miller, Sir I. D.
Miller, Douglas Gordon, 1881–1956, vol. V
Miller, Sir Douglas Sinclair, 1906–1996, vol. X
Miller, Edmund Morris, 1881–1964, vol. VI
Miller, Hon. Sir Edward, 1848–1932, vol. III
Miller, Edward, 1915–2000, vol. X
Miller, Lt-Col Edward Darley, 1865–1930, vol. III
Miller, Emanuel, 1894–1970, vol. VI
Miller, Sir Eric; see Miller, Sir H. E.
Miller, Sir Ernest, 1879–1939, vol. III
Miller, Sir Ernest Henry John, 10th Bt (cr 1705), 1897–1960, vol. V
Miller, Lt-Gen. Sir Euan Alfred Bews, 1897–1985, vol. VIII
Miller, Florence Fenwick, 1854–1935, vol. III
Miller, Rev. Francis Broughton Anson, 1855–1934, vol. III
Miller, Sir (Francis) Henry, 1865–1936, vol. III
Miller, Sir Francis N.; see Norie-Miller.
Miller, Adm. Francis Spurstow, 1863–1954, vol. V
Miller, Air Chief Marshal Frank Robert, 1908–1998, vol. X
Miller, Fred, 1863–1924, vol. II
Miller, Frederick Robert, died 1967, vol. VI
Miller of Glenlee, Sir (Frederick William) Macdonald, 7th Bt (cr 1788), 1920–1991, vol. IX

Miller, Col Sir Geoffry C.; see Christie-Miller.
Miller, George, 1833–1909, vol. I
Miller, George, 1842–1923, vol. II
Miller, Maj.-Gen. George Murray, 1829–1911, vol. I
Miller, Brig. George Patrick Rose-, 1897–1984, vol. VIII
Miller, George Waterston, 1874–1955, vol. V
Miller, Gerald Cedar, 1894–1982, vol. VIII
Miller, Gilbert Heron, 1884–1969, vol. VI
Miller, Sir Gordon William, 1844–1906, vol. I
Miller, Gray, 1885–1947, vol. IV
Miller, Captain Grenville Acton, died 1951, vol. V
Miller, Sir (Hans) Eric, 1882–1958, vol. V
Miller, Harold Tibbatts, 1873–1948, vol. IV
Miller, Henry, 1859–1927, vol. II
Miller, Sir Henry; see Miller, Sir F. H.
Miller, Henry George, 1913–1976, vol. VII
Miller, Sir Henry Holmes, 9th Bt (cr 1705), 1865–1952, vol. V
Miller, Hon. Sir Henry John, 1830–1918, vol. II
Miller, Henry Valentine, 1891–1980, vol. VII
Miller, Sir Holmes; see Miller, Sir J. H.
Miller, Mrs Horrie; see Durack, Dame M.
Miller, Sir Hubert; see Miller, Sir C. J. H.
Miller, Rear-Adm. Hugh, 1880–1972, vol. VII
Miller, Hugh C.; see Crichton-Miller.
Miller, Brig. Hugh de Burgh, 1874–1951, vol. V
Miller, Hugh Rodolph, 1875–1953, vol. V
Miller, Sir (Ian) Douglas, 1900–1996, vol. X
Miller, Maj.-Gen. James, 1835–1929, vol. III
Miller, James, died 1947, vol. IV
Miller, James, 1875–1958, vol. V
Miller, Sir James, 1905–1977, vol. VII
Miller, James, 1893–1987, vol. VIII
Miller, James Gordon, 1874–1950, vol. IV
Miller, Bt Col Sir James MacBride, 1896–1977, vol. VII
Miller, Sir James Percy, 2nd Bt (cr 1874), 1864–1906, vol. I
Miller, Joaquin, 1842–1913, vol. I
Miller, John, 1911–1975, vol. VII
Miller, Sir John Alexander, 3rd Bt (cr 1874), 1867–1918, vol. II
Miller, Lt-Comdr John Bryan Peter Duppa-, 1903–1994, vol. IX
Miller, John Duncan, 1902–1977, vol. VII
Miller, Sir John Francis C.; see Compton Miller
Miller, Very Rev. John Harry, 1869–1940, vol. III
Miller, Sir John Holmes, 11th Bt (cr 1705), 1925–1995, vol. X(AI)
Miller, Sir John Ontario, 1857–1943, vol. IV
Miller, Sir John Wilson Edington, 1894–1957, vol. V
Miller, Maj.-Gen. Joseph Esmond, 1914–1990, vol. VIII
Miller, Sir (Joseph) Holmes, 1919–1986, vol. VIII
Miller, Brig. Laurence Walter, 1882–1958, vol. V
Miller, Leonard; see Merrick, L.
Miller, Sir Leslie Creery, 1862–1925, vol. II
Miller, Dame Mabel, died 1978, vol. VII
Miller of Glenlee, Sir Macdonald; see Miller of Glenlee, Sir F. W. M.
Miller, Merton Howard, 1923–2000, vol. X
Miller, Mrs Millie, 1923–1977, vol. VII

Miller, Rev. Norman, *died* 1980, vol. VII
Miller, Rev. Norman James, *died* 1932, vol. III
Miller, Rev. Canon Paul William, 1918–2000, vol. X
Miller, Peter Francis Nigel, 1924–1997, vol. X
Miller, Rev. Peter Watters, 1890–1976, vol. VII
Miller, Philip Homan, *died* 1928, vol. II
Miller, Ralph William Richardson, 1892–1958, vol. V
Miller, Reginald Henry, *died* 1948, vol. IV
Miller, René F.; *see* Fülop-Miller.
Miller, Sir Richard Hope, 1904–1989, vol. VIII
Miller, Richard King, 1945–1992, vol. IX
Miller, Rt Rev. Robert, 1866–1931, vol. III
Miller, Robert Brown, 1905–1963, vol. VI
Miller, Robert Sydney, 1901–1980, vol. VII (AII)
Miller, Sir Roderick William, 1911–1971, vol. VII
Miller, Ronald, 1910–1990, vol. VIII
Miller, Comdr Ronald S.; *see* Scott-Miller.
Miller, Rudolph Valdemar Thor C.; *see* Castle-Miller.
Miller, Samuel Vandeleur C.; *see* Christie-Miller.
Miller, Sinclair, 1885–1961, vol. VI
Miller, Sir Stanley N.; *see* Norie-Miller.
Miller, Stearnhall, 1813–1897, vol. I
Miller, Sir Steven James Hamilton, 1915–1996, vol. X
Miller, Stewart Crichton, 1934–1999, vol. X
Miller, Sydney Richardson C.; *see* Christie-Miller.
Miller, Thomas Butt, 1859–1915, vol. I
Miller, Willet G., *died* 1925, vol. II
Miller, Sir William, 1828–1900, vol. I
Miller, Rt Hon. William, 1834–1912, vol. I
Miller, Rev. William, 1838–1923, vol. II
Miller, William, 1864–1945, vol. IV
Miller, Major William Archibald, *died* 1925, vol. II
Miller, William Christopher, 1898–1976, vol. VII
Miller, Sir William Frederic, 5th Bt (*cr* 1788), 1868–1948, vol. IV
Miller, William Lash, 1866–1940, vol. III
Miller, Col William Miles, 1891–1946, vol. IV
Miller, Comdr William Ronald, 1918–1991, vol. IX
Miller, William Thomas, 1865–1930, vol. III
Miller, William Thomas, 1880–1963, vol. VI
Miller-Cunningham, Sir George, 1867–1945, vol. IV
Miller Jones, Hon. Mrs; *see* Askwith, Hon. B. E.
Miller Jones, Keith, 1899–1978, vol. VII
Miller-Jones, Sir Thomas, 1874–1944, vol. IV
Millerand, Alexandre, 1859–1943, vol. IV
Millers, Harold Cuthbert Townley, 1903–1968, vol. VI
Milles, Carl, 1875–1955, vol. V
Milles-Lade, Hon. Henry Augustus, 1867–1937, vol. III
Millet, Francis Davis, 1846–1912, vol. I
Millett, George Prideaux, 1863–1950, vol. IV
Millevoye, Lucien, 1850–1918, vol. II
Milligan, Lucien, 1850–1918, vol. II
Milligan, Rt Hon. Lord; William Rankine Milligan, 1898–1975, vol. VII
Milligan, Very Rev. George, 1860–1934, vol. III
Milligan, John Williamson, 1875–1965, vol. VI
Milligan, Patrick Ward, 1910–1978, vol. VII
Milligan, Samuel, 1874–1954, vol. V

Milligan, Lt-Col Stanley Lyndall, 1887–1968, vol. VI
Milligan, Stephen David Wyatt, 1948–1994, vol. IX
Milligan, Veronica Jean Kathleen, 1926–1989, vol. IX(AI)
Milligan, Sir William, 1864–1929, vol. III
Milligan, Rt Hon. William Rankine; *see* Milligan, Rt Hon. Lord.
Milligan, Wyndham Macbeth Moir, 1907–1999, vol. X
Millikan, Robert Andrews, 1868–1953, vol. V
Milliken, Alexander, 1841–1914, vol. I
Milliken, Brig. Robert Cecil, 1883–1959, vol. V
Millin, Albert, 1893–1964, vol. VI
Millin, Sarah Gertrude, *died* 1968, vol. VI
Milling, Air Marshal Sir Denis C.; *see* Crowley-Milling.
Milling, Geoffrey, 1901–1983, vol. VIII
Millingen, Alexander van, 1840–1915, vol. I
Millington, Air Cdre Edward Geoffrey Lyall, 1914–1988, vol. VIII
Millington, Air Cdre Geoffrey; *see* Millington, Air Cdre E. G. L.
Millington, Powell; *see* Synge, Major Mark.
Millington-Drake, Sir Eugen John Henry Vanderstegen, 1889–1972, vol. VII
Millington-Drake, James Mackay Henry, 1928–1983, vol. VIII
Millis, Charles Howard Goulden, 1894–1984, vol. VIII
Millis, Sir Leonard William Francis, 1908–1986, vol. VIII
Milln, Rear-Adm. William Bryan Scott, 1915–1979, vol. VII
Millott, Norman, 1912–1990, vol. VIII
Mills, 1st Viscount, 1890–1968, vol. VI
Mills, 2nd Viscount, 1919–1988, vol. VIII
Mills, Maj.-Gen. Alan Oswald Gawler, 1914–1992, vol. IX
Mills, Hon. Algernon Henry, 1856–1922, vol. II
Mills, Maj. Anthony David, 1918–1993, vol. IX
Mills, Arthur, 1887–1955, vol. V
Mills, Rev. Arthur Everard, 1863–1929, vol. III
Mills, Arthur John, 1868–1956, vol. V
Mills, Maj.-Gen. Sir Arthur Mordaunt, 1879–1964, vol. VI
Mills, Arthur Stewart Hunt, 1897–1968, vol. VI
Mills, Bertram Wagstaff, 1873–1938, vol. III
Mills, Charles A., vol. II
Mills, (Charles) Ernest, 1916–1983, vol. VIII
Mills, Hon. Charles Houghton, 1844–1923, vol. II
Mills, Darius Ogden, 1825–1910, vol. I
Mills, David, 1831–1903, vol. I
Mills, Lady Dorothy R. M., *died* 1959, vol. V
Mills, Edmund James, 1840–1921, vol. II
Mills, Edward, 1849–1933, vol. III
Mills, Edward David, 1915–1998, vol. X
Mills, Eric, 1892–1961, vol. VI
Mills, Ernest; *see* Mills, C. E.
Mills, Sir Ernest Arnold, *died* 1949, vol. IV
Mills, Sir Frederick, 1st Bt, 1865–1953, vol. V
Mills, Major Sir (Frederick Leighton) Victor, 2nd Bt, 1893–1955, vol. V
Mills, Captain Hon. Geoffrey Edward, 1875–1917, vol. II

Mills, Brig.-Gen. George Arthur, 1855–1927, vol. II
Mills, Air Chief Marshal Sir George Holroyd, 1902–1971, vol. VII
Mills, George Percival, 1883–1952, vol. V
Mills, Maj.-Gen. Graham; see Mills, Maj.-Gen. W. G. S.
Mills, Harry Woosnam, 1873–1925, vol. II
Mills, Rev. Canon Henry Holroyd, 1860–1947, vol. IV
Mills, Herbert Horatio, 1917–1987, vol. VIII
Mills, Col Herbert James, 1836–1927, vol. II
Mills, Iain Campbell, 1940–1997, vol. X
Mills, Ivor, 1929–1996, vol. X
Mills, J. Saxon, died 1929, vol. III
Mills, James, 1840–1924, vol. II
Mills, Sir James, 1847–1936, vol. III
Mills, Col James Edgar, 1878–1937, vol. III
Mills, James Philip, 1890–1960, vol. V
Mills, John; see Mills, L. J.
Mills, Col Sir John Digby, 1879–1972, vol. VII
Mills, John Edmund, died 1951, vol. V
Mills, John Frobisher, 1859–1929, vol. III
Mills, John Norton, 1914–1977, vol. VII
Mills, John Robert, 1916–1998, vol. X
Mills, John Spencer, 1917–1976, vol. VII
Mills, (John) Vivian G., 1887–1987, vol. VIII
Mills, Joseph Trueman, 1836–1924, vol. II
Mills, (Laurence) John, 1920–1994, vol. IX
Mills, Lawrence Heyworth, born 1837, vol. II
Mills, Leonard Sidney, 1914–2000, vol. X
Mills, Air Marshal Sir Nigel Holroyd, 1932–1991, vol. IX
Mills, Hon. Ogden L., 1884–1937, vol. III
Mills, Maj.-Gen. Percy Strickland, died 1973, vol. VII
Mills, Sir Peter McLay, 1921–1993, vol. IX
Mills, Air Vice-Marshal Reginald Percy, 1885–1968, vol. VI
Mills, Sir Richard, 1830–1906, vol. I
Mills, Richard Charles, 1886–1952, vol. V
Mills, Robert Watkin, 1856–1930, vol. III
Mills, Stephen, 1857–1948, vol. IV
Mills, Brig. Stephen Douglas, 1892–1984, vol. VIII
Mills, T. Wesley, died 1915, vol. I
Mills, Major Sir Victor; see Mills, Major Sir F. L. V.
Mills, Vivian G.; see Mills, J. V. G.
Mills, Wilbur Daigh, 1909–1992, vol. IX
Mills, Rev. William, died 1922, vol. II
Mills, Sir William, 1856–1932, vol. III
Mills, Maj.-Gen. (William) Graham (Stead), 1917–1992, vol. IX
Mills, William Haslam, 1874–1930, vol. III
Mills, William Hobson, 1873–1959, vol. V
Mills, Rt Rev. William Lennox, died 1917, vol. II
Mills-Owens, Richard Hugh, 1910–1987, vol. VIII
Mills-Roberts, Robert Herbert, 1862–1935, vol. III
Millspaugh, Arthur Chester, 1883–1955, vol. V
Millspaugh, Rt Rev. Frank Rosebrook, 1848–1916, vol. II
Millward, William, 1909–1994, vol. IX
Milman, Archibald John Scott, died 1902, vol. I
Milman, Lt-Col Sir Derek, 9th Bt, 1918–1999, vol. X

Milman, Sir Dermot Lionel Kennedy, 8th Bt, 1912–1990, vol. VIII
Milman, Sir Francis, 5th Bt, 1872–1946, vol. IV
Milman, Sir Francis John, 4th Bt, 1842–1922, vol. II
Milman, Lt-Gen. Sir George Bryan, 1822–1915, vol. I
Milman, Brig.-Gen. Sir Lionel Charles Patrick, 7th Bt, 1877–1962, vol. VI
Milman, Lt-Col Octavius Rodney Everard, 1882–1971, vol. VII
Milman, Sir William Ernest, 6th Bt, 1875–1962, vol. VI
Milmo, Sir Helenus Patrick Joseph, 1908–1988, vol. VIII
Miln, Mrs George Crichton, 1864–1933, vol. III
Miln, Louise Jordan; see Miln, Mrs George Crichton.
Milne, 1st Baron, 1866–1948, vol. IV
Milne, Alan Alexander, 1882–1956, vol. V
Milne, Alan Hay, 1869–1919, vol. II
Milne, Alexander, died 1903, vol. I
Milne, Alexander Boland, 1842–1904, vol. I
Milne, Alexander George, 1891–1981, vol. VIII
Milne, Alexander Taylor, 1906–1994, vol. IX
Milne, Rt Rev. Andrew Jamieson, 1831–1906, vol. I
Milne, Andrew McNicoll, 1937–1995, vol. IX
Milne, Sir (Archibald) Berkeley, 2nd Bt, 1855–1938, vol. III
Milne, Archibald George, 1910–1980, vol. VII
Milne, Arthur; see Milne, E. A.
Milne, Arthur Dawson, 1867–1932, vol. III
Milne, Sir Berkeley; see Milne, Sir A. B.
Milne, Charles, died 1960, vol. V
Milne, Christian Hoyer Millar, 1870–1945, vol. IV
Milne, David, 1876–1954, vol. V
Milne, Sir David, 1896–1972, vol. VII
Milne, Denys Gordon, (Tiny), 1926–2000, vol. X
Milne, Maj.-Gen. Douglas Graeme, 1919–1996, vol. X
Milne, Rev. Edgar Astley, 1862–1945, vol. IV
Milne, (Edward) Arthur, 1896–1950, vol. IV
Milne, Edward James, 1915–1983, vol. VIII
Milne, Lt-Col George, 1857–1939, vol. III
Milne, George Torrance, 1862–1943, vol. IV
Milne, J. Maclauchlan, died 1957, vol. V
Milne, James, 1865–1951, vol. V
Milne, Sir James, 1883–1958, vol. V
Milne, James, 1921–1986, vol. VIII
Milne, Sir James Allan, 1896–1966, vol. VI
Milne, James L.; see Lees-Milne.
Milne, James Mathewson, 1883–1959, vol. V
Milne, John, 1850–1913, vol. I
Milne, John Alexander, 1872–1955, vol. V
Milne, Sir John Sydney W.; see Wardlaw-Milne.
Milne, Joseph Grafton, 1867–1951, vol. V
Milne, Kenneth John, 1880–1929, vol. III
Milne, Kenneth Lancelot, 1915–1995, vol. X(AI)
Milne, Mrs Leslie, (Mary Lewis), 1860–1952, vol. V
Milne, Malcolm Davenport, 1915–1991, vol. IX
Milne, Maurice, 1916–1998, vol. X
Milne, Norman, 1915–2000, vol. X
Milne, Oswald Partridge, 1881–1968, vol. VI
Milne, Lt-Col Richard Lewis, 1832–1906, vol. I

Milne, Col Thomas, 1882–1959, vol. V
Milne, Tiny; *see* Milne, D. G.
Milne, William Proctor, 1881–1967, vol. VI
Milne, Sir William Robertson, *died* 1959, vol. V
Milne-Bailey, Walter, *died* 1935, vol. III
Milne Henderson, Captain Thomas Maxwell Stuart, 1888–1968, vol. VI
Milne Home, Captain Archibald John Fitzwilliam, 1909–1993, vol. IX
Milne-Home, David William, 1873–1918, vol. II
Milne Home, John Gavin, 1916–2000, vol. X
Milne-Redhead, Lt-Col Richard Henry, 1862–1944, vol. IV
Milne-Thomson, Col Alexander, *died* 1944, vol. IV
Milne-Thomson, Louis Melville, 1891–1974, vol. VII
Milne-Watson, Sir David, 1st Bt, *died* 1945, vol. IV
Milne-Watson, Sir (David) Ronald, 2nd Bt, 1904–1982, vol. VIII
Milne-Watson, Sir Michael, 3rd Bt, 1910–1999, vol. X
Milne-Watson, Sir Ronald; *see* Milne-Watson, Sir D. R.
Milner, 1st Viscount, 1854–1925, vol. II
Milner, Viscountess; (Violet Georgina), *died* 1958, vol. V
Milner of Leeds, 1st Baron, 1889–1967, vol. VI
Milner, Elizabeth Eleanor, *died* 1953, vol. V
Milner, Frank, 1875–1944, vol. IV
Milner, Frank Leopold, 1870–1946, vol. IV
Milner, Fred, *died* 1939, vol. III
Milner, Frederic, 1905–1957, vol. V
Milner, Rt Hon. Sir Frederick George, 7th Bt, 1849–1931, vol. III
Milner, George, 1829–1914, vol. I
Milner, George Andrew, 1927–1986, vol. VIII
Milner, Sir (George Edward) Mordaunt, 9th Bt, 1911–1995, vol. IX
Milner, Brig.-Gen. George Francis, 1862–1921, vol. II
Milner, James Donald, 1874–1927, vol. II
Milner, John Giddings, 1900–1985, vol. VIII
Milner, Engr-Rear-Adm. John William, *died* 1953, vol. V
Milner, Marcus Henry, 1864–1939, vol. III
Milner, Sir Mordaunt; *see* Milner, Sir G. E. M.
Milner, Samuel Roslington, 1875–1958, vol. V
Milner, Thomas Stuart, 1909–1969, vol. VI
Milner, William Aldam, 1854–1931, vol. III
Milner, Sir William Frederick Victor Mordaunt, 8th Bt, 1893–1960, vol. V
Milner-Barry, E. L., *died* 1917, vol. II
Milner-Barry, Sir Philip Stuart, 1906–1995, vol. IX
Milner-Jones, Edward William, 1853–1942, vol. IV
Milner-White, Very Rev. Eric, 1884–1963, vol. VI
Milner-White, Sir Henry, 1854–1922, vol. II
Milnes, Alfred, 1849–1921, vol. II
Milnes, Nora, 1882–1972, vol. VII
Milnes, W. H., 1865–1957, vol. V
Milnes-Coates, Captain Sir Clive; *see* Coates.
Milnes Coates, Sir Robert Edward James Clive, 3rd Bt, 1907–1982, vol. VIII
Milnes Gaskell, Lady Constance, 1885–1964, vol. VI
Milnes Walker, Robert; *see* Walker, R. M.
Miloslavsky, Dimitry T.; *see* Tolstoy, D.

Milroy, Hugh, 1840–1919, vol. II
Milroy, John Alexander, *died* 1934, vol. III
Milroy, Thomas Hugh, 1869–1950, vol. IV
Milsom, Hilda Maud, *died* 1972, vol. VII
Milson, Rev. Frederick William, 1912–1984, vol. VIII
Milstein, Nathan, 1904–1992, vol. IX
Milthorpe, Frederick Leon, 1917–1985, vol. VIII
Milton, Ernest, 1890–1974, vol. VII
Milton, Sir Frank, 1906–1976, vol. VII
Milton, Sir William Henry, 1854–1930, vol. III
Milvain, Sir Thomas, 1844–1916, vol. II
Milverton, 1st Baron, 1885–1978, vol. VII
Milward, Sir Anthony Horace, 1905–1981, vol. VIII
Milward, Sir Christopher Annakin, 1834–1906, vol. I
Milward, Maj.-Gen. Sir Clement Arthur, 1877–1951, vol. V
Milward, John Frederic, 1908–1982, vol. VIII
Milward, Col Victor, *died* 1901, vol. I
Mimpriss, Trevor Walter, 1905–1989, vol. VIII
'Min'; *see* Minhinnick, Sir G. E. G., vol. IX
Mina; *see* Reiach, H.
Minchin, Lt-Col Alfred Beckett, 1870–1939, vol. III
Minchin, Lt-Col Charles Frederick, 1862–1943, vol. IV
Minchin, Charles Owen, 1844–1930, vol. III
Minchin, E. A., 1866–1915, vol. I
Minchin, Maj.-Gen. Frederick Falkiner, 1860–1922, vol. II
Minchin, George M., *died* 1914, vol. I
Minchin, Harry Christopher, 1861–1941, vol. IV
Minchin, James George Cotton, *died* 1933, vol. III
Minchin, Col William Cyril, 1856–1924, vol. II
Minchinton, Walter Edward, 1921–1996, vol. X
Mines, George Ralph, 1886–1914, vol. I
Minett, Francis Colin, 1890–1953, vol. V
Minford, Hugh, *died* 1950, vol. IV
Minford, Rt Hon. Nathaniel Owens, 1912–1975, vol. VII
Mingana, Alphonse, 1881–1937, vol. III
Minhinnick, Sir Gordon Edward George, 1902–1992, vol. IX
Minio-Paluello, Lorenzo, 1907–1986, vol. VIII
Minion, Stephen, 1908–1990, vol. VIII
Minney, Rubeigh James, 1895–1979, vol. VII
Minnis, Samuel Ellison, 1882–1971, vol. VII
Minnitt, Robert John, 1913–2000, vol. X
Minns, Captain Allan Noel, 1891–1921, vol. II
Minns, Sir Ellis Hovell, 1874–1953, vol. V
Minogue, Hon. Sir John (Patrick), 1909–1989, vol. VIII
Minoprio, Frank Charles, 1870–1951, vol. V
Minor, Clark Haynes, 1878–1967, vol. VI
Minorsky, Vladimir, 1877–1966, vol. VI
Minot, Charles Sedgwick, 1852–1914, vol. I
Minot, George Richards, 1885–1950, vol. IV
Minshull-Ford, Maj.-Gen. John Randle; *see* Ford.
Minter, Sir Frederick Albert, 1887–1976, vol. VII
Minter, Percy, 1866–1955, vol. V
Minto, 4th Earl of, 1847–1914, vol. I
Minto, 5th Earl of, 1891–1975, vol. VII
Minto, John, 1863–1935, vol. III
Minton, (Francis) John, 1917–1957, vol. V
Minton, John; *see* Minton, F. J.

Miraj, (Junior), Chief of; Sir Shrimant Madhavrao Harihar, *alias* Baba Saheb Patwardhan, *died* 1950, vol. IV (A), vol. V
Miralles Moya, Enric, 1955–2000, vol. X
Mirbeau, Octave, 1850–1917, vol. II
Mirehouse, Lt-Col Richard Walter Byrd, 1849–1914, vol. I
Mirehouse, William Edward, 1844–1925, vol. II
Mirepoix, Antoine, Duc de L.; *see* Lévis Mirepoix.
Miró, Joan, 1893–1983, vol. VIII
Miron, Wilfrid Lyonel, 1913–2000, vol. X
Mirrielees, Sir Frederick James, 1851–1914, vol. I
Mirrlees, Maj.-Gen. William Henry Buchanan, 1892–1964, vol. VI
Mirza Ali Akbar Khan, 1880–1934, vol. III
Mirza, Maj.-Gen. Iskander, 1899–1969, vol. VI
Misa, Brig. Lawrence Edward, 1896–1968, vol. VI
Miskin, Sir James William, 1925–1993, vol. IX
Misra, Sir Lakshmipati, 1888–1964, vol. VI
Missen, Leslie Robert, 1897–1983, vol. VIII
Missenden, Sir Eustace James, 1886–1973, vol. VII
Mistinguett, (Jeanne Bourgeois), 1875–1956, vol. V
Mistral, Frédéric, 1830–1914, vol. I
Mitcham, Heather, 1941–1993, vol. IX
Mitchell, Alan Alexander McCaskill, 1882–1941, vol. IV
Mitchell, Alexander, 1871–1934, vol. III
Mitchell, Alexander Ferrier, 1822–1899, vol. I
Mitchell, Andrew, 1843–1915, vol. I
Mitchell, Andrew Park, 1894–1975, vol. VII
Mitchell, Sir Angus Sinclair, 1884–1961, vol. VI
Mitchell, Rt Rev. Anthony, 1868–1917, vol. II
Mitchell, Arnold, *died* 1944, vol. IV
Mitchell, Sir Arthur, 1826–1909, vol. I
Mitchell, Arthur Brownlow, 1865–1942, vol. IV
Mitchell, Arthur James, 1893–1967, vol. VI
Mitchell, Bertram, 1898–1978, vol. VII
Mitchell, Lt-Col Brian Granville Blayney, 1900–1983, vol. VIII
Mitchell, Charles, *died* 1957, vol. V
Mitchell, Charles Ainsworth, 1867–1948, vol. IV
Mitchell, Sir Charles Bullen Hugh, *died* 1899, vol. I
Mitchell, Brig.-Gen. Charles Hamilton, 1872–1941, vol. IV
Mitchell, Major Charles Johnstone, 1879–1918, vol. II
Mitchell, Hon. Charles Richmond, 1872–1942, vol. IV
Mitchell, Charles W., *died* 1903, vol. I
Mitchell, Lt-Col Colin Campbell, 1925–1996, vol. X
Mitchell, Craig, 1896–1975, vol. VII
Mitchell, Sir David George, 1879–1963, vol. VI
Mitchell, Edmund, 1861–1917, vol. II
Mitchell, Edward Card, 1853–1914, vol. I
Mitchell, Sir Edward Fancourt, 1855–1941, vol. IV
Mitchell, Edward Rosslyn, 1879–1965, vol. VI
Mitchell, Edwin Laurence, 1883–1960, vol. V
Mitchell, Adm. Francis Herbert, 1876–1946, vol. IV
Mitchell, Maj.-Gen. Francis Neville, 1904–1954, vol. V
Mitchell, Frank; *see* Mitchell, G. F.
Mitchell, Sir Frank Herbert, 1878–1951, vol. V
Mitchell, Frank William Drew, 1845–1936, vol. III
Mitchell, Air Vice-Marshal Frederick George Stewart, 1901–1974, vol. VII

Mitchell, Rt Rev. Frederick Julian, 1901–1979, vol. VII
Mitchell, George, 1867–1937, vol. III
Mitchell, George Archibald Grant, 1906–1993, vol. IX
Mitchell, Sir George Arthur, 1860–1948, vol. IV
Mitchell, George Francis, (Frank), 1912–1997, vol. X
Mitchell, George Hoole, 1902–1976, vol. VII
Mitchell, Sir George Irvine, 1911–1978, vol. VII
Mitchell, Mrs George J., (Maggie Richardson), *died* 1953, vol. V
Mitchell, George Winter, 1865–1935, vol. III
Mitchell, Gladys Maude Winifred, 1901–1983, vol. VIII
Mitchell, Sir Godfrey Way, 1891–1982, vol. VIII
Mitchell, Graham Russell, 1912–1984, vol. VIII
Mitchell, Sir Hamilton, 1910–1989, vol. VIII
Mitchell, Harold Charles, 1896–1991, vol. IX
Mitchell, Harold John, 1877–1941, vol. IV
Mitchell, Col Sir Harold Paton, 1st Bt, 1900–1983, vol. VIII
Mitchell, Rev. Harry, 1847–1933, vol. III
Mitchell, Helen Porter; *see* Melba, Dame Nellie.
Mitchell, Sir Henry, 1823–1898, vol. I
Mitchell, Henry McCormick, 1870–1935, vol. III
Mitchell, Henry Tai, 1877–1944, vol. IV
Mitchell, Henry Thomas, 1870–1946, vol. IV
Mitchell, Sir Herbert Edward, 1861–1936, vol. III
Mitchell, James Clyde, 1918–1995, vol. IX(AII)
Mitchell, J. Campbell, 1865–1922, vol. II
Mitchell, Very Rev. James, 1830–1911, vol. I
Mitchell, James, 1865–1941, vol. IV
Mitchell, Hon. Sir James, 1866–1951, vol. V
Mitchell, Sir James, 1905–1968, vol. VI
Mitchell, James Alexander, 1849–1905, vol. I
Mitchell, James Alexander Hugh, 1939–1985, vol. VIII
Mitchell, James Leslie, 1901–1935, vol. III
Mitchell, Very Rev. James Robert Mitford, 1843–1914, vol. I
Mitchell, John, 1860–1923, vol. II
Mitchell, Sir John, *died* 1934, vol. III
Mitchell, John Ames, 1845–1918, vol. II
Mitchell, John David Bawden, 1917–1980, vol. VII
Mitchell, Lt-Col John Douglas, 1881–1955, vol. V
Mitchell, Sir John Edwin, 1865–1931, vol. III
Mitchell, John Fowler, 1886–1984, vol. VIII
Mitchell, John Malcolm, 1879–1940, vol. III
Mitchell, John Richard Anthony, (Tony), 1928–1991, vol. IX
Mitchell, Rev. John Thomas, *died* 1947, vol. IV
Mitchell, Rt Rev. Joseph, 1859–1931, vol. III
Mitchell, Joseph Stanley, 1909–1987, vol. VIII
Mitchell, Sir Kenneth Grant, 1885–1966, vol. VI
Mitchell, Leslie Herbert, 1914–1989, vol. VIII
Mitchell, Margaret; *see* Marsh, Margaret Munnerlyn Mitchell.
Mitchell, Sir Mark Ledingham, 1902–1977, vol. VII
Mitchell, Sir Miles Ewart, 1875–1955, vol. V
Mitchell, Norman Frederick, 1900–1972, vol. VII
Mitchell, Oliver Worden, 1898–1963, vol. VI
Mitchell, Sir Peter Chalmers, 1864–1945, vol. IV
Mitchell, Peter Dennis, 1920–1992, vol. IX

Mitchell, Maj.-Gen. Sir Philip Euen, 1890–1964, vol. VI
Mitchell, Philip George Mylne, 1875–1954, vol. V
Mitchell, Richard Arthur Henry, 1843–1905, vol. I
Mitchell, Major Robert, 1855–1933, vol. III
Mitchell, Major Robert, 1873–1939, vol. III
Mitchell, Robert, 1913–1996, vol. X
Mitchell, Very Rev. Robert Andrew, *died* 1949, vol. IV
Mitchell, Maj.-Gen. Robert Imrie, 1916–1993, vol. IX
Mitchell, Robert Lyell, 1910–1982, vol. VIII
Mitchell, Robert Macgregor; *see* Macgregor Mitchell, Hon. Lord.
Mitchell, Robert William Span, 1840–1909, vol. I
Mitchell, Hon. Dame Roma Flinders, 1913–2000, vol. X
Mitchell, Sir (Seton) Steuart (Crichton), 1902–1990, vol. VIII
Mitchell, Silas Weir, 1829–1914, vol. I
Mitchell, Stephen, 1884–1951, vol. V
Mitchell, Sir Steuart; *see* Mitchell, Sir Seton S. C.
Mitchell, Sir Thomas, 1844–1919, vol. II
Mitchell, Col Thomas, 1839–1921, vol. II
Mitchell, Sir Thomas, 1869–1959, vol. V
Mitchell, Col Thomas John, 1882–1966, vol. VI
Mitchell, Thomas Walker, 1869–1944, vol. IV
Mitchell, Tony; *see* Mitchell, J. R. A.
Mitchell, Victor Evelyn, 1865–1932, vol. III
Mitchell, Dame Wendy, 1932–1999, vol. X
Mitchell, Col Wilfrid James, 1871–1953, vol. V
Mitchell, William, 1838–1914, vol. I
Mitchell, William, *died* 1937, vol. III
Mitchell, Sir William, 1861–1962, vol. VI
Mitchell, Captain William Edward Clifton, *born* 1875, vol. III
Mitchell, William Eric Marcus, 1897–1990, vol. VIII
Mitchell, Sir William Foot, 1859–1947, vol. IV
Mitchell, Air Chief Marshal Sir William Gore Sutherland, 1888–1944, vol. IV
Mitchell, William H., 1853–1929, vol. III
Mitchell, Sir William Lane, 1861–1940, vol. III
Mitchell, Sir William Wilson, 1840–1915, vol. I
Mitchell, Yvonne, 1925–1979, vol. VII
Mitchell-Cotts, Sir Campbell; *see* Cotts, Sir W. C. M.
Mitchell-Gill, Andrew John; *see* Gill.
Mitchell-Hedges, Frederick Albert, 1882–1959, vol. V
Mitchell-Heggs, Gordon Barrett, 1904–1975, vol. VII
Mitchell-Innes, Alfred, 1864–1950, vol. IV
Mitchell-Innes, Captain Cecil, 1866–1949, vol. IV
Mitchell-Innes, Edward Alfred, 1863–1932, vol. III
Mitchell-Innes, Rev. Reginald John Simpson, 1848–1930, vol. III
Mitchell-Thomson, Sir Mitchell, 1st Bt, 1846–1918, vol. II
Mitchelson, Sir Archibald, 1st Bt, 1878–1945, vol. IV
Mitchelson, Hon. Sir Edwin, 1846–1934, vol. III
Mitchenson, Francis Joseph Blackett, (Joe), 1911–1992, vol. IX
Mitchenson, Joe; *see* Mitchenson, F. J. B.
Mitcheson, Sir George Gibson, 1883–1955, vol. V

Mitcheson, James Cecil, 1898–1979, vol. VII
Mitcheson, John Moncaster Ley, 1893–1966, vol. VI
Mitchiner, Philip Henry, 1888–1952, vol. V
Mitchinson, Rt Rev. John, 1833–1918, vol. II
Mitchison, Baron (Life Peer); Gilbert Richard Mitchison, 1890–1970, vol. VI
Mitchison, Naomi Margaret, 1897–1999, vol. X
Mitchison, Rev. Richard Stovin, 1850–1936, vol. III
Mitford, Bertram, *died* 1914, vol. I
Mitford, Maj.-Gen. Bertram Reveley, 1863–1936, vol. III
Mitford, Hon. Clement Bertram Ogilvy F.; *see* Freeman-Mitford
Mitford, Jessica Lucy, (Mrs Jessica Treuhaft) 1917–1996, vol. X
Mitford, Nancy, (Hon. Mrs Peter Rodd), 1904–1973, vol. VII
Mitford, Maj.-Gen. Reginald Colville William Reveley, 1839–1925, vol. II
Mitford, Captain Robert Osbaldeston-, 1846–1924, vol. II
Mitford, Robert Sidney, 1849–1931, vol. III
Mitford, Rupert Leo Scott B.; *see* Bruce-Mitford.
Mitford, Terence Bruce, 1905–1978, vol. VII
Mitford, Major Hon. Thomas David Freeman-, 1909–1945, vol. IV
Mitford, Col William Kenyon, 1857–1943, vol. IV
Mitford-Barberton, Ivan Graham; *see* Barberton.
Mitford-Slade, Col Cecil Townley, 1903–1986, vol. VIII
Mitha, Hon. Sardar Sir Suleman Cassum, vol. VII
Mitman, Frederick Snyder, 1900–1989, vol. VIII
Mitra, Sir Bhupendra Nath, 1875–1937, vol. III
Mitra, Sir Dhirendra Nath, 1891–1966, vol. VI
Mitra, S. M., 1856–1925, vol. II
Mitra, Sisir Kumar, 1890–1963, vol. VI
Mitrany, David, 1888–1975, vol. VII
Mitropoulos, Dimitri, 1896–1960, vol. V
Mittag-Leffler, Gösta, 1846–1927, vol. II
Mittelholzer, Edgar Austin, 1909–1965, vol. VI
Mitter, Rt Hon. Sir Binof Chandra, 1872–1930, vol. III
Mitter, Sir Brojendra Lal, 1875–1950, vol. IV
Mitter, Sir Provash Chandra, 1875–1934, vol. III
Mitterrand, François Maurice Marie, 1916–1996, vol. X
Mitton, Rev. Charles Leslie, 1907–1998, vol. X
Mitton, Geraldine Edith, (Lady Scott), *died* 1955, vol. V
Mitton, Col George J.; *see* Jones Mitton.
Mitton, H. Eustace, 1871–1946, vol. IV
Mitton, Rev. Henry Arthur, 1837–1918, vol. II
Mitton, Rev. Welbury Theodore, 1862–1933, vol. III
Mivart, Frederick St George, *died* 1925, vol. II
Mivart, St George Jackson, 1827–1900, vol. I
Mobbs, Sir (Arthur) Noel, 1880–1959, vol. V
Mobbs, Sir Noel; *see* Mobbs, Sir A. N.
Moberly, Brig. Archibald Henry, 1879–1960, vol. V
Moberly, Sir Arthur Norman, 1873–1934, vol. III
Moberly, Lt-Gen. Sir Bertrand Richard, 1877–1963, vol. VI
Moberly, Charles Noel, 1880–1969, vol. VI
Moberly, Charlotte Anne Elizabeth, 1846–1937, vol. III

Moberly, Brig.-Gen. Frederick James, 1867–1952, vol. V

Moberly, Brig. Hugh Stephenson, 1873–1947, vol. IV

Moberly, Rev. Robert Campbell, 1845–1903, vol. I

Moberly, Rt Rev. Robert Hamilton, 1884–1978, vol. VII

Moberly, Sir Walter Hamilton, 1881–1974, vol. VII

Moberly, Winifred Horsbrugh, 1875–1928, vol. II

Mocatta, Sir Alan Abraham, 1907–1990, vol. VIII

Mockett, Sir Vere, 1885–1977, vol. VII

Mockford, Julian, 1898–1950, vol. IV

Mockler, Col Percy Rice, 1860–1927, vol. II

Mockler-Ferryman, Lt-Col Augustus Ferryman, 1856–1930, vol. III

Mockler-Ferryman, Col Eric Edward, 1896–1978, vol. VII

Modi, Sir Jivanji Jamshedji, 1854–1933, vol. III

Modjeska-Chlapowska, Helena, 1844–1909, vol. I

Mody, Sir Homi Peroshaw, 1881–1969, vol. VI

Moe, Henry Allen, 1894–1975, vol. VII

Moens, Gen. Sir Arthur William Hamilton May, 1879–1939, vol. III

Moens, Hon. Lt-Col Seaburne Godfrey Arthur May, 1876–1956, vol. V

Moeran, Edward Warner, 1903–1997, vol. X

Moeran, Ernest John, 1894–1950, vol. IV

Moffat, Alfred, 1868–1950, vol. IV

Moffat, David H., 1839–1911, vol. I

Moffat, Graham, 1866–1951, vol. V

Moffat, Hon. Howard Unwin, 1869–1951, vol. V

Moffat, John, 1879–1966, vol. VI(AII), vol. VII

Moffat, John, 1891–1973, vol. VII

Moffat, Rev. John Smith, 1835–1918, vol. II

Moffat, Sir John Smith, 1905–1985, vol. VIII

Moffat, Rennie John, 1891–1978, vol. VII

Moffat, Robert Unwin, 1866–1947, vol. IV

Moffatt, Alexander, 1863–1921, vol. II

Moffatt, Rev. James, 1870–1944, vol. IV

Moffatt, Paul McGregor, died 1963, vol. VI

Moffet, Stanley Ormerod, 1886–1960, vol. V

Moffett, John Perry, 1909–1972, vol. VII

Moffett, Sir Thomas William, 1830–1908, vol. I

Mogg, Lt-Col Graham Beauchamp Coxeter R.; see Rees-Mogg.

Mogg, Rev. Henry Herbert, 1850–1929, vol. III

Mogg, Rev. Canon Joseph William, 1882–1970, vol. VI(AII)

Mogg, Engr Rear-Adm. William George, 1860–1929, vol. III

Moggridge, Adm. Arthur Yerbury, 1858–1946, vol. IV

Moggridge, Ernest Grant, 1863–1925, vol. II

Moggridge, Lt-Col Harry Weston, 1879–1960, vol. V

Mohamed, Hon. Sir Abdool Razack, 1906–1978, vol. VII

Mohamed Akbar Khan, Lt-Col Nawab Sir, 1885–1952, vol. V

Mohan Singh, Sardar Bahadur Sardar, 1897–1961, vol. VI

Mohsin-ul-Mulk, Nawab, 1837–1907, vol. I

Moinet, Rev. Charles, 1842–1913, vol. I

Moir, Brig.-Gen. Alan James Gordon, 1873–1940, vol. III

Moir, Alan John, 1903–1982, vol. VIII

Moir, Captain Sir Arrol, 2nd Bt, 1894–1957, vol. V

Moir, Byres, 1853–1928, vol. II

Moir, Vice-Adm. Dashwood Fowler, 1880–1942, vol. IV

Moir, Sir Ernest Ian Royds, 3rd Bt, 1925–1998, vol. X

Moir, Sir Ernest William, 1st Bt, 1862–1933, vol. III

Moir, Rt Rev. Francis Oag H.; see Hulme-Moir.

Moir, (George) Guthrie, 1917–1993, vol. IX

Moir, Guthrie; see Moir, George G.

Moir, James, died 1915, vol. I

Moir, Col James Philip, 1872–1934, vol. III

Moir, James Reid, 1879–1944, vol. IV

Moir, John Chassar, 1900–1977, vol. VII

Moir, John William, died 1940, vol. III

Moir, Percival John, 1893–1980, vol. VII

Moir, Sir Thomas Eyebron, 1874–1932, vol. III

Moir, Rear-Adm. William Mitchell, 1873–1942, vol. IV

Moir Carey, David Macbeth; see Carey, D. M. M.

Moira, Gerald, died 1959, vol. V

Moiseiwitsch, Benno, 1890–1963, vol. VI

Mok, Rt Rev. Shau Tsang, 1866–1943, vol. IV

Mokama, Hon. Moleleki Didwell, 1933–1997, vol. X

Molamure, Sir (Alexander) Francis, 1886–1951, vol. V

Molamure, Sir Francis; see Molamure, Sir A. F.

Mold, Brig. Gilbert Leslie, 1893–1963, vol. VI

Mole, Sir Charles Johns, 1886–1962, vol. VI

Mole, Brig. Gerard Herbert Leo, 1897–1944, vol. IV

Mole, Harold Frederic, 1866–1917, vol. II

Moles, Rt Hon. Thomas, 1871–1937, vol. III

Molesworth, 8th Viscount, 1829–1906, vol. I

Molesworth, 9th Viscount, 1867–1947, vol. IV

Molesworth, 10th Viscount, 1869–1961, vol. VI

Molesworth, 11th Viscount, 1907–1997, vol. X

Molesworth, Brig. Alec Lindsay Mortimer, 1881–1939, vol. III

Molesworth, Col Arthur Ludovic, 1860–1939, vol. III

Molesworth, Major Edward Algernon, died 1939, vol. III

Molesworth, Brig.-Gen. Edward Hogarth, 1854–1943, vol. IV

Molesworth, Lt-Gen. George Noble, 1890–1968, vol. VI

Molesworth, Sir Guilford Lindsey, 1828–1925, vol. II

Molesworth, Hender Delves, 1907–1978, vol. VII

Molesworth, Col Herbert Ellicombe, 1872–1941, vol. IV

Molesworth, Hickman, 1842–1907, vol. I

Molesworth, Hugh Wilson, 1870–1959, vol. V

Molesworth, Sir Lewis William, 11th Bt, 1853–1912, vol. I

Molesworth, Mrs Mary Louisa, 1839–1921, vol. II

Molesworth, Col Richard Pigot, 1868–1946, vol. IV

Molesworth, Col William, 1865–1951, vol. V

Molesworth-St Aubyn, Sir Hugh, 13th Bt, 1865–1942, vol. IV

Molesworth-St Aubyn, Rev. Sir St A. Hender, 12th Bt, 1833–1913, vol. I

Molesworth-St Aubyn, Lt-Col Sir Arscott; *see* Molesworth-St Aubyn, Lt-Col Sir J. A.

Molesworth-St Aubyn, Sir John, 14th Bt, 1899–1985, vol. VIII

Molesworth-St Aubyn, Lt-Col Sir (John) Arscott, 15th Bt, 1926–1998, vol. X

Molin, C. Hjalmar V., 1868–1954, vol. V

Moline, Rev. Robert Percy, *died* 1935, vol. III

Moline, Most Rev. Robert William Haines, 1889–1979, vol. VII

Molineux, Rev. Arthur Ellison, *died* 1919, vol. II

Molineux, Rev. Charles Hurlock, *died* 1927, vol. II

Moll, Rev. William Edmund, 1856–1932, vol. III

Mollan, Maj.-Gen. Francis Robert Henry, 1893–1982, vol. VIII

Mollan, Lt-Col William Campbell, 1820–1910, vol. I

Moller, Marjorie, 1899–1981, vol. VIII

Mollett, Sir John, 1892–1952, vol. V

Mollison, James Alan, 1905–1959, vol. V

Mollison, James W., *died* 1927, vol. II

Mollison, William Loudon, 1851–1929, vol. III

Mollison, William Mayhew, 1878–1967, vol. VI

Mollo, Victor, 1909–1987, vol. VIII

Molloy, Bernard Charles, 1842–1916, vol. II

Molloy, Col Edward, 1842–1905, vol. I

Molloy, Rt Rev. Mgr Gerald, 1834–1906, vol. I

Molloy, Ven. John, *died* 1915, vol. I

Molloy, Joseph Fitzgerald, 1858–1908, vol. I

Molloy, Leonard Greenham Star, *died* 1937, vol. III

Molohan, Michael John Brew, 1906–1980, vol. VII

Moloney, Sir Cornelius Alfred, 1848–1913, vol. I

Moloney, Henry J., 1887–1965, vol. VI

Molony, Rev. Brian Charles, 1892–1963, vol. VI

Molony, Col Charles Mills, 1836–1901, vol. I

Molony, Edmund Alexander, 1866–1942, vol. IV

Molony, Rev. Henry William Eliott, *died* 1919, vol. II

Molony, Rt Rev. Herbert James, 1865–1939, vol. III

Molony, Sir Hugh Francis, 2nd Bt, 1900–1976, vol. VII

Molony, Sir Joseph Thomas, 1907–1978, vol. VII

Molony, Rt Hon. Sir Thomas Francis, 1st Bt, 1865–1949, vol. IV

Molotov, Vyacheslav Mikhailovich, 1890–1986, vol. VIII

Molson, Baron (Life Peer); Arthur Hugh Elsdale Molson, 1903–1991, vol. IX

Molson, Lt-Col Herbert, 1875–1938, vol. III

Molson, Major John Elsdale, 1863–1925, vol. II

Molteno, Hon. Sir James Tennant, 1865–1936, vol. III

Molteno, Percy Alport, 1861–1937, vol. III

Molteno, Vice-Adm. Vincent Barkly, 1872–1952, vol. V

Molyneux, Major Edward Mary Joseph, 1866–1913, vol. I

Molyneux, Sir Ernest, 10th Bt, 1865–1940, vol. III

Molyneux, Rt Rev. Frederick Merivale, 1885–1948, vol. IV

Molyneux, Maj.-Gen. George Hand M.; *see* More-Molyneux.

Molyneux, John Anthony, (Tony), 1923–1982, vol. VIII

Molyneux, Rev. Sir John Charles, 9th Bt, 1843–1928, vol. II

Molyneux, Sir John Harry, 1882–1968, vol. VI

Molyneux, Sir Percy, 1870–1937, vol. III

Molyneux, Major Philip Lucas, 1893–1939, vol. III

Molyneux, Major Hon. Sir Richard F., 1873–1954, vol. V

Molyneux, Adm. Sir Robert Henry M.; *see* More-Molyneaux.

Molyneux, Tony; *see* Molyneux, J. A.

Molyneux, Wilfred, 1910–1994, vol. IX

Molyneux-Seel, Major Edward, 1862–1939, vol. III

Momber, Captain Edward Marie Felix, *died* 1917, vol. II

Momerie, Rev. Alfred Williams, 1848–1900, vol. I

Momigliano, Arnaldo Dante, 1908–1987, vol. VIII

Momin, Khan Bahadur Mohammad Abdul, 1876–1946, vol. IV

Mommsen, Theodor, 1817–1903, vol. I

Monaco, Prince of, Albert Honoré Charles, 1848–1922, vol. II

Monaghan, Rt Rev. James, 1914–1994, vol. IX

Monahan, Rt Rev. Alfred Edwin, 1877–1945, vol. IV

Monahan, George Henry, 1873–1944, vol. IV

Monahan, James Henry Francis, 1912–1985, vol. VIII

Monahan, Most Rev. Peter Joseph, 1882–1947, vol. IV

Monahan, Hon. Sir Robert Vincent, 1898–1975, vol. VII

Monash, Gen. Sir John, 1865–1931, vol. III

Moncheur, Ludovic, 2nd Baron, 1857–1940, vol. III

Monck, 5th Viscount, 1849–1927, vol. II

Monck, 6th Viscount, 1905–1982, vol. VIII

Monck, Hon. Charles Henry Stanley, 1876–1914, vol. I

Monck, Sir John Berkeley, 1883–1964, vol. VI

Monck, Nugent; *see* Monck, W. N. B.

Monck, Lt-Gen. Hon. Richard, 1829–1904, vol. V

Monck, (Walter) Nugent (Bligh), 1878–1958, vol. I

Monckton of Brenchley, 1st Viscount, 1891–1965, vol. VI

Monckton of Brenchley, Dowager Viscountess; *see* Ruthven of Freeland, Lady.

Monckton, Arthur, 1845–1917, vol. II

Monckton, Edward Philip, 1840–1916, vol. II

Monckton, Francis, 1844–1926, vol. II

Monckton, Col Hon. Horace Manners, 1824–1904, vol. I

Monckton, Sir John Braddick, 1832–1902, vol. I

Monckton, Lionel, 1862–1924, vol. II

Monckton, Reginald Francis Percy, 1896–1975, vol. VII

Moncreiff, 2nd Baron, 1840–1909, vol. I

Moncreiff, 3rd Baron, 1843–1913, vol. I

Moncreiff, 4th Baron, 1872–1942, vol. IV

Moncreiff, Rt Rev. Francis Hamilton, 1906–1984, vol. VIII

Moncreiff, Hon. Frederick Charles, 1847–1929, vol. III

Moncreiff, Hon. James William, 1845–1920, vol. II

Moncreiffe of that Ilk, Sir David Gerald, 10th Bt, 1922–1957, vol. V

Moncreiffe of that Ilk, Sir Iain; see Moncreiffe of that Ilk, Sir R. I. K.
Moncreiffe, Comdr Sir John Robert Guy, 9th Bt, 1884–1934, vol. III
Moncreiffe, Sir Robert Drummond, 8th Bt, 1856–1931, vol. III
Moncreiffe of that Ilk, Sir (Rupert) Iain (Kay), 11th Bt, 1919–1985, vol. VIII
Moncrief, Rev. Archibald, 1845–1938, vol. III
Moncrieff, Rt. Hon. Lord; Alexander Moncrieff, died 1949, vol. IV
Moncrieff, Sir Alan Aird, 1901–1971, vol. VII
Moncrieff, Adm. Sir Alan Kenneth S.; see Scott-Moncrieff.
Moncrieff, Col Sir Alexander, 1829–1906, vol. I
Moncrieff, Rt Hon. Alexander; see Moncrieff, Rt Hon. Lord.
Moncrieff, Alexander Bain, 1845–1928, vol. II
Moncrieff, Charles Kenneth S.; see Scott Moncrieff.
Moncrieff, Sir Colin Campbell S.; see Scott-Moncrieff.
Moncrieff, Lt-Gen. George Hay, 1836–1918, vol. II
Moncrieff, Maj.-Gen. Sir George Kenneth S.; see Scott-Moncrieff.
Moncrieff, Joanna Constance S.; see Scott-Moncrieff.
Moncrieff, Lt-Col John Mitchell, 1865–1931, vol. III
Moncrieff, Robert Hope, 1846–1927, vol. II
Moncrieff, William George S.; see Scott-Moncrieff.
Moncrieff, William S.; see Scott-Moncrieff
Moncur, George, 1868–1946, vol. IV
Mond, Ludwig, 1839–1909, vol. I
Mond, Sir Robert Ludwig, 1867–1938, vol. III
Monday, Horace Reginald, 1907–1996, vol. X
Mondor, Henri Jean, 1885–1962, vol. VI
Monet, Claude, 1840–1926, vol. II
Monet, Dominique, 1865–1923, vol. II
Moneta, Ernesto Teodoro, 1833–1918, vol. II
Money, Sir Alonzo, died 1900, vol. I
Money, Maj.-Gen. Sir Arthur Wigram, 1866–1951, vol. V
Money, Vice-Adm. Brien Michael, 1880–1939, vol. III
Money, Col Charles Gilbert Colvin, 1852–1928, vol. II
Money, Brig.-Gen. Ernest Douglas, 1866–1952, vol. V
Money, Rev. Canon Frank Reginald, 1905–1968, vol. VI
Money, Brig.-Gen. Gordon Lorn Campbell, 1848–1929, vol. III
Money, Brig. Harold Douglas Kyrie, 1896–1965, vol. VI
Money, Maj.-Gen. Herbert Cecil, 1857–1939, vol. III
Money, Sir Leo (George) Chiozza, 1870–1944, vol. IV
Money, Brig.-Gen. Noel Ernest, 1867–1941, vol. IV
Money, Col Reginald Angel, 1897–1984, vol. VIII
Money, Col Robert Cotton, 1861–1954, vol. V
Money, Maj.-Gen. Robert Cotton, 1888–1985, vol. VIII
Money, Walter, 1836–1926, vol. II
Money, William James, died 1910, vol. I

Money-Kyrle, Ven. Rowland Tracy Ashe, died 1928, vol. II
Moneypenny, Frederick William, 1859–1912, vol. I
Moneypenny, Sir Frederick William, 1859–1932, vol. III
Monger, George William, 1937–1992, vol. IX
Monie, Rev. Peter William, 1877–1946, vol. IV
Monier-Williams, Clarence Faithfull, 1893–1974, vol. VII
Monier-Williams, Major Craufurd Victor, 1888–1922, vol. II
Monier-Williams, Sir Monier, 1819–1899, vol. I
Monier-Williams, Monier Faithfull, 1849–1928, vol. II
Monier-Williams, Montagu Sneade Faithfull, 1860–1931, vol. III
Moniz, Egas Antonio Caetano de Abren Freire, 1874–1955, vol. V
Moniz de Aragão, José Joaquim de Lima e Silva, 1887–1974, vol. VII (AII)
Monk, Albert Ernest, 1900–1975, vol. VII
Monk, Beatrice Marsh; see Monk, M. B. M.
Monk, Charles James, 1824–1900, vol. I
Monk, Hon. Frederick Debartzch, 1856–1914, vol. I
Monk, Mark James, 1858–1929, vol. III
Monk, (Mary) Beatrice Marsh, died 1962, vol. VI
Monk Bretton, 1st Baron, 1825–1897, vol. I
Monk Bretton, 2nd Baron, 1869–1933, vol. III
Monkhouse, Allan Noble, 1858–1936, vol. III
Monkhouse, Sir Edward Bertram, 1890–1959, vol. V
Monkhouse, Francis John, 1914–1975, vol. VII
Monkhouse, John Parry, 1899–1968, vol. VI
Monkhouse, Brig.-Gen. William Percival, 1871–1935, vol. III
Monks, Air Vice-Marshal Alfred Thomas, 1908–1972, vol. VII
Monks, Constance Mary, 1911–1989, vol. VIII
Monkswell, 2nd Baron, 1845–1909, vol. I
Monkswell, 3rd Baron, 1875–1964, vol. VI
Monnet, Jean Omer Marie Gabriel, 1888–1979, vol. VII
Mönnig, Hermann Otto, 1897–1978, vol. VII
Monnington, Sir Thomas; see Monnington, Sir W. T.
Monnington, Rev. Thomas Pateshall, died 1937, vol. III
Monnington, Sir (Walter) Thomas, 1902–1976, vol. VII
Monod, Gustave Jean Philippe, 1878–1932, vol. III
Monod, Jacques Lucien, 1910–1976, vol. VII
Monod, Théodore, 1836–1921, vol. II
Monod, Théodore André, 1902–2000, vol. X
Monod, Wilfred, 1867–1943, vol. IV
Monro, Alexander, 1847–1916, vol. II
Monro, Alexander, 1890–1953, vol. V
Monro, Alexander William, 1875–1960, vol. V
Monro, Gen. Sir Charles Carmichael, 1st Bt, 1860–1929, vol. III
Monro, David Binning, 1836–1905, vol. I
Monro, Maj.-Gen. David Carmichael, 1886–1960, vol. V, vol. VI
Monro, Edwin George, 1875–1954, vol. V
Monro, George, 1876–1951, vol. V
Monro, Harold Edward, 1879–1932, vol. III

Monro, Sir Horace Cecil, 1861–1949, vol. IV
Monro, James, 1838–1920, vol. II
Monro, Hon. Mary Caroline, (Hon. Lady Monro), 1879–1972, vol. VII
Monro, Col Seymour Charles Hale, 1856–1906, vol. I
Monro, Thomas Kirkpatrick, 1865–1958, vol. V
Monroe, Elizabeth, (Mrs Humphrey Neame), 1905–1986, vol. VIII
Monroe, Rev. Horace Granville, 1872–1933, vol. III
Monroe, Hubert Holmes, 1920–1982, vol. VIII
Monroe, Vice-Adm. Hubert Seeds, 1877–1966, vol. VI
Monroe, James Harvey, 1884–1944, vol. IV
Monroe, Rt Hon. John, 1839–1899, vol. I
Monroe, John George, 1913–1991, vol. IX
Monroe, Paul, 1869–1947, vol. IV
Monroe, Hon. Walter S., 1871–1952, vol. V
Monroe, Will S., 1863–1939, vol. III(A), vol. IV
Monsarrat, Keith Waldegrave, 1872–1968, vol. VI
Monsarrat, Nicholas John Turney, 1910–1979, vol. VII
Monsell, 1st Viscount, 1881–1969, vol. VI
Monsell, 2nd Viscount, 1905–1993, vol. IX
Monsey, Yvonne, (Mrs Derek Monsey); see Mitchell, Yvonne.
Monslow, Baron (Life Peer); Walter Monslow, 1895–1966, vol. VI
Monson, 8th Baron, 1830–1900, vol. I
Monson, 9th Baron, 1868–1940, vol. III
Monson, 10th Baron, 1907–1958, vol. V
Monson, Rt Hon. Sir Edmund John, 1st Bt, 1834–1909, vol. I
Monson, Sir Edmund St John Debonnaire John, 3rd Bt, 1883–1969, vol. VI
Monson, Sir George Louis Esmé John, 4th Bt, 1888–1969, vol. VI
Monson, Sir Leslie; see Monson, Sir W. B. L.
Monson, Sir Maxwell William Edmund John, 2nd Bt, 1882–1936, vol. III
Monson, Sir (William Bonnar) Leslie, 1912–1993, vol. IX
Montagu of Beaulieu, 1st Baron, 1832–1905, vol. I
Montagu of Beaulieu, 2nd Baron, 1866–1929, vol. III
Montagu, Ainsley Marshall Rendall, 1891–1977, vol. VII
Montagu, (Alexander) Victor (Edward Paulet), 1906–1995, vol. IX
Montagu, Ashley; see Montagu, M. F. A.
Montagu, Lord Charles William Augustus, 1860–1939, vol. III
Montagu, Col Edward, 1861–1941, vol. IV
Montagu, Rt Hon. Edwin Samuel, 1879–1924, vol. II
Montagu, Sir Ernest William Sanders, 1862–1952, vol. V
Montagu, Hon. Ewen Edward Samuel, 1901–1985, vol. VIII
Montagu, Captain Frederick James Osbaldeston, 1878–1957, vol. V
Montagu, Gen. Sir Horace William, 1823–1916, vol. II
Montagu, (Hon.) Ivor (Goldsmid Samuel), 1904–1984, vol. VIII
Montagu, James Drogo, died 1958, vol. V

Montagu, Hon. Lilian Helen, 1873–1963, vol. VI
Montagu, (Montague Francis) Ashley, 1905–2000, vol. X
Montagu, Rt Hon. Lord Robert, 1825–1902, vol. I
Montagu, Hon. Robert Henry D. S.; see Douglas-Scott-Montagu.
Montagu, Victor; see Montagu, A. V. E. P.
Montagu, Rear-Adm. Hon. Victor Alexander, 1841–1915, vol. I
Montagu-Douglas-Scott, Lord Charles Thomas; see Scott.
Montagu-Douglas-Scott, Lt-Col Lord Francis George; see Scott
Montagu-Douglas-Scott, Lord George William; see Scott.
Montagu-Douglas-Scott, Col Lord Henry Francis; see Scott.
Montagu-Douglas-Scott, Lord Herbert Andrew; see Scott.
Montagu-Douglas-Scott, Lt-Col Lord William Walter; see Scott.
Montagu-Pollock, Sir George Seymour; see Pollock.
Montagu-Pollock, Sir Montagu Frederick; see Pollock.
Montagu-Pollock, Sir William Horace, 1903–1993, vol. IX
Montagu-Stuart-Wortley, Maj.-Gen. Hon. Edward James; see Stuart-Wortley.
Montagu-Stuart-Wortley, Lt-Gen. Hon. Sir Richard; see Stuart-Wortley.
Montague of Oxford, Baron (Life Peer); Michael Jacob Montague, 1932–1999, vol. X
Montague, Charles Edward, 1867–1928, vol. II
Montague, Francis Arnold, 1904–1991, vol. IX
Montague, Francis Charles, 1858–1935, vol. III
Montague, Major Furry Ferguson, 1884–1950, vol. IV(A)
Montague, Leslie Clarence, 1901–1986, vol. VIII
Montague, Lt-Gen. Hon. Percival John, 1882–1966, vol. VI
Montague, Maj.-Gen. William Edward, 1838–1906, vol. I
Montague-Barlow, Rt Hon. Sir Anderson; see Montague-Barlow, Rt Hon. Sir C. A.
Montague-Barlow, Rt Hon. Sir (Clement) Anderson, 1868–1951, vol. V
Montague-Jones, Brig. Ronald, 1909–1996, vol. X
Montague-Smith, Patrick Wykeham, 1920–1986, vol. VIII
Montalba, Clara, died 1929, vol. III
Montale, Eugenio, 1896–1981, vol. VIII
Montanaro, Col Arthur Forbes, 1862–1914, vol. I
Montanaro, Brig. Gerald Charles Stokes, 1916–1979, vol. VII
Montand, Simone Henriette Charlotte; see Signoret, S.
Monteagle of Brandon, 2nd Baron, 1849–1926, vol. II
Monteagle of Brandon, 3rd Baron, 1883–1934, vol. III
Monteagle of Brandon, 4th Baron, 1852–1937, vol. III
Monteagle of Brandon, 5th Baron, 1887–1946, vol. IV
Monteath, Alexander McLaurin, 1859–1933, vol. III

Monteath, Sir David Taylor, 1887–1961, vol. VI
Monteath, Harry Henderson, 1885–1962, vol. VI
Monteath, Sir James, 1847–1929, vol. III
Monteath, John, 1878–1955, vol. V
Monteath, Robert Campbell, 1907–1985, vol. VIII
Monteath, Sir Ruthven Grey, 1864–1949, vol. IV
Montefiore, Claude Joseph Goldsmid-, 1858–1938, vol. III
Montefiore, Edmund Sebag-, 1869–1929, vol. III
Montefiore, Sir Francis Abraham, 1st Bt, 1860–1935, vol. III
Montefiore, Sir Joseph Sebag-, 1822–1903, vol. I
Monteith, Charles Montgomery, 1921–1995, vol. IX
Monteith, Col John, 1852–1928, vol. II
Monteith, Brig. John Cassels, 1915–1983, vol. VIII
Monteith, Jos. D., 1865–1934, vol. III
Monteith, Lt-Col Michael; see Monteith, Lt-Col R. C. M.
Monteith, Nelson, 1862–1949, vol. IV
Monteith, Lt-Col (Robert Charles) Michael, 1914–1993, vol. IX
Montessori, Maria, 1870–1952, vol. V
Monteux, Pierre, 1875–1964, vol. VI
Montford, Paul Raphael, 1868–1938, vol. III
Montgomerie, Lt-Col Alexander, 1882–1932, vol. III
Montgomerie, Alexander, 1879–1958, vol. V
Montgomerie, Harvey Hugh, 1888–1965, vol. VI
Montgomerie, James, 1873–1962, vol. VI
Montgomerie, Adm. John Eglinton, 1825–1902, vol. I
Montgomerie, Rear-Adm. Robert Archibald James, 1855–1908, vol. I
Montgomerie, Samuel Hynman, 1856–1915, vol. I
Montgomery of Alamein, 1st Viscount, 1887–1976, vol. VII
Montgomery, Sir Alexander, 5th Bt (cr 1808), 1859–1939, vol. III
Montgomery, Sir Basil Purvis-Russell Hamilton-, 8th Bt (cr 1801), 1884–1964, vol. VI
Montgomery, Sir Basil Templer Graham-, 5th Bt (cr 1801), 1852–1928, vol. II
Montgomery, Bo Gabriel de, Count, 1894–1969, vol. VI
Montgomery, Sir (Charles) Hubert, 1876–1942, vol. IV
Montgomery, Rev. Sir Charles Percy Graham-, 6th Bt (cr 1801), 1855–1930, vol. III
Montgomery, Brig. Ernest John, 1901–1972, vol. VII
Montgomery, Florence Sophia, 1843–1923, vol. II
Montgomery, Sir Frank Percival, 1892–1972, vol. VII
Montgomery, George Allison, 1898–1969, vol. VI
Montgomery, George H. A., 1874–1951, vol. V
Montgomery, George Lightbody, 1905–1993, vol. IX
Montgomery, Captain George Rodgers, 1910–1997, vol. X
Montgomery, Sir Graham Graham, 3rd Bt (cr 1801), 1823–1901, vol. I
Montgomery, Harold Robert, 1884–1958, vol. V
Montgomery, Henry Greville, 1864–1951, vol. V
Montgomery, Rt Rev. Henry Hutchinson, 1847–1932, vol. III
Montgomery, Sir Henry James

Purvis-Russell-Hamilton, 7th Bt (cr 1801), 1859–1947, vol. IV
Montgomery, Lt-Col Henry Keith Purvis-Russell-, 1896–1954, vol. V
Montgomery, Sir Hubert; see Montgomery, Sir C. H.
Montgomery, Sir Hugh Conyngham Gaston, 4th Bt (cr 1808), 1847–1915, vol. I
Montgomery, Rt Hon. Hugh de Fellenberg, 1844–1924, vol. II
Montgomery, Col Hugh Frederick L.; see Lyons-Montgomery.
Montgomery, Maj.-Gen. Hugh Maude de Fellenberg, 1870–1954, vol. V
Montgomery, Ian, 1913–1971, vol. VII
Montgomery, Col James Alexander Lawrence, 1849–1940, vol. III
Montgomery, Sir James Gordon Henry Graham, 4th Bt (cr 1801), 1850–1902, vol. I
Montgomery, John, 1858–1937, vol. III
Montgomery, Col John Willoughby Verner, 1867–1968, vol. VI
Montgomery, K. L.; see Montgomery, Kathleen, and Montgomery, Letitia.
Montgomery, Kathleen, died 1960, vol. V
Montgomery, L. M.; see Macdonald, Mrs L. M.
Montgomery, Leslie Alexander; see Doyle, Lynn.
Montgomery, Letitia, died 1930, vol. III
Montgomery, Sir Matthew Walker, 1859–1933, vol. III
Montgomery of Blessingbourne, Captain Peter Stephen, 1909–1988, vol. VIII
Montgomery, Maj.-Gen. Robert Arthur, 1848–1931, vol. III
Montgomery, Maj.-Gen. Sir Robert Arundel Kerr, 1862–1951, vol. V
Montgomery, Robert Ernest, 1878–1962, vol. VI
Montgomery, Robert Eustace, 1880–1932, vol. III
Montgomery, Robert Mortimer, died 1948, vol. IV
Montgomery, Walter Basil Graham, 1881–1928, vol. II
Montgomery, Major William Alexander, died 1932, vol. III
Montgomery, William Barr, 1865–1936, vol. III
Montgomery, Maj.-Gen. William Edward, 1847–1927, vol. II
Montgomery, William Hugh, 1866–1958, vol. V
Montgomery Campbell, Rt Rev. and Rt Hon. Henry Colville, 1887–1970, vol. VI
Montgomery-Campbell, Brig-Gen. Herbert, 1861–1937, vol. III
Montgomery-Cuninghame, Sir Andrew; see Cuninghame, Sir W. A. M. M. O. M.
Montgomery-Cuninghame, Sir Thomas Andrew Alexander; see Cuninghame.
Montgomery-Cuninghame, Sir William James; see Cuninghame.
Montgomery-Massingberd, Field Marshal Sir Archibald Armar, 1871–1947, vol. IV
Montgomery-Moore, Gen. Sir Alexander George, 1833–1919, vol. II
Montgomery-Smith, Col Edwin Charles, 1869–1963, vol. VI
Montgomery White, Cyril; see White.
Montgorge, Alexis Jean; see Gabin, J.
Montherlant, Henry de, 1896–1972, vol. VII

Montini, Giovanni Battista; *see* Paul VI.
Montizambert, Frederick, 1843–1929, vol. III
Montresor, Miss F. F., *died* 1934, vol. III
Montrose, 5th Duke of, 1852–1925, vol. II
Montrose, 6th Duke of, 1878–1954, vol. V
Montrose, 7th Duke of, 1907–1992, vol. IX
Monty, Hon. Rodolphe, 1874–1928, vol. II
Moodie, Alexander Reid, 1886–1968, vol. VI
Moodie, Donald, 1892–1963, vol. VI
Moodie, William, 1886–1960, vol. V
Moody, Lt-Col Arthur Hatfield, 1875–1926, vol. II
Moody, Arthur Seymour, 1891–1976, vol. VII
Moody, Charles Harry, 1874–1965, vol. VI
Moody, Adm. Sir Clement, 1891–1960, vol. V
Moody, Madame Fanny, (Mrs Southcote Mansergh), 1866–1945, vol. IV
Moody, Sir George Edward James, 1859–1939, vol. III
Moody, Helen Wills; *see* Roark, H. W.
Moody, Sir James Matthew, *died* 1915, vol. I
Moody, John C., 1884–1962, vol. VI
Moody, Maj.-Gen. Sir John Macdonald, 1839–1921, vol. II
Moody, John Percivale, 1906–1993, vol. IX
Moody, Col Richard Stanley Hawks, 1854–1930, vol. III
Moody, Robert Ley, 1909–1970, vol. VI
Moody, Sydney, 1889–1979, vol. VII
Moody, Theodore William, 1907–1984, vol. VIII
Moody, William H., 1853–1917, vol. II
Moody-Stuart, Sir Alexander, 1899–1971, vol. VII
Mookerjee, Sir Asutosh, 1864–1924, vol. II
Mookerjee, Sir Birendra Nath, 1899–1982, vol. X(AI)
Mookerjee, Sir Rajendra Nath, 1854–1936, vol. III
Mookerji, Radha Kumud, 1884–1963, vol. VI
Moon, Maj.-Gen. Alan Neilson, 1906–1981, vol. VIII
Moon, Col Alfred, 1861–1943, vol. IV
Moon, Arthur, 1882–1961, vol. VI
Moon, Sir (Arthur) Wilfred Graham-, 4th Bt (*cr* 1855), 1905–1954, vol. V
Moon, Sir Cecil Ernest, 2nd Bt (*cr* 1887), 1867–1951, vol. V
Moon, Sir Edward, 5th Bt, 1911–1988, vol. VIII
Moon, Rev. Sir Edward Graham, 2nd Bt (*cr* 1855), 1825–1904, vol. I
Moon, Sir (Edward) Penderel, 1905–1987, vol. VIII
Moon, Edward Robert Pacy, 1858–1949, vol. IV
Moon, Sir Ernest Robert, 1854–1930, vol. III
Moon, Sir Francis Sidney Graham, 3rd Bt (*cr* 1855), 1855–1911, vol. I
Moon, George Washington, 1823–1909, vol. I
Moon, Harold Philip, 1910–1982, vol. VIII
Moon, Henry E., *died* 1920, vol. II
Moon, Sir John Arthur, 4th Bt (*cr* 1887), 1905–1979, vol. VII
Moon, Sir Penderel; *see* Moon, Sir E. P.
Moon, Sir Peter James Scott, 1928–1991, vol. IX
Moon, Philip Burton, 1907–1994, vol. IX
Moon, Sir Richard, 1st Bt (*cr* 1887), 1815–1899, vol. I
Moon, Sir Richard, 3rd Bt (*cr* 1887), 1901–1961, vol. VI
Moon, Robert Oswald, 1865–1953, vol. V

Moon, Lieut Rupert Vance, 1892–1986, vol. VIII
Moon, Walter, 1871–1954, vol. V
Moon, Sir Wilfred Graham-; *see* Moon, Sir A. W. G.
Mooney, His Eminence Cardinal Edward, 1882–1958, vol. V
Mooney, George Stuart, 1900–1965, vol. VI(AII)
Mooney, Herbert C., *died* 1948, vol. IV
Mooney, Herbert Francis, 1897–1964, vol. VI
Mooney, Sir John, 1874–1934, vol. III
Moor, Rev. Edward, 1880–1953, vol. V
Moor, Rt Hon. Sir Frederick Robert, 1853–1927, vol. II
Moor, George Raymond Dallas, 1896–1918, vol. II
Moor, Sir Ralph Denham Rayment, 1860–1909, vol. I
Moor, Samuel Albert, *died* 1944, vol. IV
Moorcroft, William, 1872–1945, vol. IV
Moore, Sir Alan Hilary, 2nd Bt (*cr* 1919), 1882–1959, vol. V
Moore, Ven. Alexander Duff, 1872–1942, vol. IV
Moore, Gen. Sir Alexander George M.; *see* Montgomery-Moore.
Moore, Rev. Alfred Edgar, *died* 1924, vol. II
Moore, Captain Alldin Usborne, 1878–1942, vol. IV
Moore, Antony Ross, 1918–2000, vol. X
Moore, Adm. Sir Archibald Gordon Henry Wilson, 1862–1934, vol. III
Moore, Archie Murrell Acheson, 1904–1979, vol. VII
Moore, Arthur Collin, 1866–1952, vol. V
Moore, Ven. Arthur Crompton, *died* 1954, vol. V
Moore, Arthur Edward, 1872–1951, vol. V
Moore, Hon. Arthur Edward, 1876–1963, vol. VI
Moore, Count Arthur John, 1849–1904, vol. I
Moore, Rev. Arthur John, 1853–1919, vol. II
Moore, Maj.-Gen. Arthur Thomas, 1830–1913, vol. I
Moore, Col Arthur Trevelyan, *died* 1948, vol. IV
Moore, Arthur William, 1853–1909, vol. I
Moore, Adm. Sir Arthur William, 1847–1934, vol. III
Moore, Col Athelstan, 1879–1918, vol. II
Moore, Beatrice Esther, *died* 1953, vol. V
Moore, Benjamin, *died* 1922, vol. II
Moore, Bobby; *see* Moore, Robert.
Moore, Brian, 1921–1999, vol. X
Moore, Maj.-Gen. Charles Alfred, 1839–1925, vol. II
Moore, Charles Gordon, 1884–1957, vol. V
Moore, Adm. Charles Henry Hodgson, 1858–1920, vol. II
Moore, Col Charles Hesketh Grant, 1868–1942, vol. IV
Moore, Sir Charles James S.; *see* Stevenson-Moore.
Moore, Charles Joseph Henry O'Hara, 1880–1965, vol. VI
Moore, Charles Thomas John, 1827–1900, vol. I
Moore, Clarence L., 1869–1953, vol. V
Moore, Maj.-Gen. Claude Douglas Hamilton, 1875–1928, vol. II
Moore, Rev. Mgr Clement Harington, 1845–1905, vol. I
Moore, Rev. Courtenay, 1840–1922, vol. II
Moore, Rev. Daniel, 1809–1899, vol. I

Moore, Rev. David Keys, 1854–1935, vol. III
Moore, Maj.-Gen. Denis Grattan, 1909–1987, vol. VIII
Moore, Doris Langley, 1903–1989, vol. VIII
Moore, Dorothea Mary, *died* 1933, vol. III
Moore, Rev. Edward, 1835–1916, vol. II
Moore, Rt Rev. Edward Alfred Livingstone, 1870–1944, vol. IV
Moore, Sir Edward Cecil, 1st Bt (*cr* 1923), 1851–1923, vol. II
Moore, Rt Rev. Edward Francis Butler, 1906–1997, vol. X
Moore, Col Edward James, 1862–1925, vol. II
Moore, Ven. Edward Marsham, *died* 1921, vol. II
Moore, Sir Edward Stanton, 2nd Bt (*cr* 1923), 1910–1992, vol. IX
Moore, Eldon, 1901–1954, vol. V
Moore, Eric Olawolu, 1878–1944, vol. IV
Moore, Eva, (Mrs Henry V. Esmond), *died* 1955, vol. V
Moore, Evelyn, (Mrs Stuart Moore); *see* Underhill, E.
Moore, Rev. E(velyn) Garth, 1906–1990, vol. VIII
Moore, Col Francis, 1879–1938, vol. III
Moore, Lt-Col Francis Hamilton, 1876–1952, vol. V
Moore, Maj.-Gen. Francis Malcolm, 1897–1974, vol. VII
Moore, Francis William, 1849–1927, vol. II
Moore, Frank Frankfort, 1855–1931, vol. III
Moore, Sir Fred Denby, 1863–1951, vol. V
Moore, Frederick Craven, 1871–1943, vol. IV
Moore, Maj.-Gen. Frederick David, 1902–1997, vol. X
Moore, Lt-Col Frederick Grattan, 1877–1955, vol. V
Moore, Frederick Thomas, 1913–1983, vol. VIII
Moore, Sir Frederick William, 1857–1949, vol. IV
Moore, Geoffrey Ernest, 1916–1989, vol. VIII
Moore, Geoffrey Herbert, 1920–1999, vol. X
Moore, Col George A., 1869–1955, vol. V
Moore, George Arbuthnot, 1857–1923, vol. II
Moore, George Augustus, 1852–1933, vol. III
Moore, Rear-Adm. George Dunbar, 1893–1979, vol. VII
Moore, George Edgar, 1907–1996, vol. X
Moore, George Edward, 1873–1958, vol. V
Moore, George Foot, 1851–1931, vol. III
Moore, George Herbert, 1903–1993, vol. IX
Moore, Lt-Col Sir George Montgomery John, 1844–1911, vol. I
Moore, Gerald, 1899–1987, vol. VIII
Moore, Gordon Charles, 1928–1998, vol. X
Moore, Grace; *see* Parera, G. M.
Moore, Brig. Guy Newton, 1893–1984, vol. VIII
Moore, Harold, 1878–1972, vol. VII
Moore, Col Harold Arthur, 1880–1945, vol. IV
Moore, Brig. Harold Edward, 1888–1968, vol. VI
Moore, Sir Harold John de Courcy, 1877–1976, vol. VII
Moore, Sir Harrison; *see* Moore, Sir W. H.
Moore, Harry, 1887–1960, vol. V
Moore, Harry Thornton, 1908–1981, vol. VIII
Moore, Captain Hartley Russell Gwennap, 1881–1953, vol. V
Moore, Lt-Gen. Sir Henry, 1829–1915, vol. I
Moore, Henry, 1898–1986, vol. VIII

Moore, Henry Charles, 1862–1933, vol. III
Moore, Rev. Henry Dodwell, 1838–1919, vol. II
Moore, Henry F., 1887–1954, vol. V
Moore, Henry Ian, 1905–1976, vol. VII
Moore, Henry John, 1872–1950, vol. V
Moore, Rev. Henry Kingsmill, *died* 1943, vol. IV
Moore, Sir Henry Monck-Mason, 1887–1964, vol. VI
Moore, Adm. Sir Henry Ruthven, 1886–1978, vol. VII
Moore, Rev. Herbert Augustine, *died* 1937, vol. III
Moore, Col Herbert Tregosse Gwennap, 1875–1958, vol. V
Moore, Rear-Adm. Humfrey John Bradley, 1898–1985, vol. VIII
Moore, James Lennox Irwin, 1866–1953, vol. V
Moore, James M., 1871–1932, vol. III
Moore, Gen. Sir (James Newton) Rodney, 1905–1985, vol. VIII
Moore, Jocelyn A. M., (Mrs David Symon), 1904–1979, vol. VII
Moore, Maj.-Gen. Sir John, 1864–1940, vol. III
Moore, John Bassett, 1860–1947, vol. IV
Moore, John Cecil, 1907–1967, vol. VI
Moore, Hon. Sir John Cochrane, 1915–1998, vol. X
Moore, Sir John Samuel, 1831–1916, vol. II
Moore, Sir John Voce, 1826–1904, vol. I
Moore, Rev. John Walter Barnwell, 1886–1969, vol. VI
Moore, Rev. John Walter Brady, *died* 1938, vol. III
Moore, Sir John William, 1845–1937, vol. III
Moore, Joseph Henry Hamilton, 1852–1933, vol. III
Moore, Kathleen Ella, 1874–1969, vol. VI
Moore, Kenneth Alfred Edgar, 1894–1976, vol. VII
Moore, Sir Leopold Frank, 1868–1945, vol. IV
Moore, Louis Herbert, 1860–1918, vol. II
Moore, Marianne Craig, 1887–1972, vol. VII
Moore, Mary, 1861–1931, vol. III
Moore, Mary Emily MacLeod; *see* Rees, Mrs Leonard.
Moore, Col Maurice George, 1854–1939, vol. III
Moore, Col Maxtone, 1876–1950, vol. IV
Moore, Major Montagu Seymour, 1896–1966, vol. VI
Moore, Maj.-Gen. Hon. Sir Newton James, 1870–1936, vol. III
Moore, Noel Temple, 1833–1903, vol. I
Moore, Sir Norman, 1st Bt (*cr* 1919), 1847–1922, vol. II
Moore, Rev. Obadiah, 1848–1923, vol. II
Moore, Percival, 1886–1964, vol. VI
Moore, Very Rev. Peter Clement, 1924–2000, vol. X
Moore, Pierce Langrishe, 1873–1944, vol. IV
Moore, Ralph Westwood, 1906–1953, vol. V
Moore, Ramsey Bignall, 1880–1969, vol. VI
Moore, Reginald, 1910–1968, vol. VI
Moore, Sir Richard Greenslade, 1878–1966, vol. VI
Moore, Lt-Col Richard St Leger, 1848–1921, vol. II
Moore, Rev. Robert, 1863–1935, vol. III
Moore, Rev. and Rt Hon. Robert, 1886–1960, vol. V
Moore, Robert, 1915–1998, vol. X
Moore, Robert Ernest, 1863–1934, vol. III
Moore, Robert Foster, 1877–1963, vol. VI

Moore, Robert Frederick, (Bobby), 1941–1993, vol. IX
Moore, Very Rev. Robert Henry, 1872–1964, vol. VI
Moore, Col Robert Reginald Heber, 1858–1942, vol. IV
Moore, Gen. Sir Rodney; see Moore, Gen. Sir. J. N. R.
Moore, Roy, 1908–1992, vol. IX
Moore, Hon. Samuel Wilkinson, 1854–1935, vol. III
Moore, Stanford, 1913–1982, vol. VIII
Moore, Vice-Adm. Stephen St Leger, 1884–1955, vol V
Moore, Thomas, 1858–1920, vol. II
Moore, Thomas, 1903–1983, vol. VIII
Moore, Lt-Col Sir Thomas Cecil Russell, 1st Bt (cr 1956), 1886–1971, vol. VII
Moore, Sir Thomas O'Connor, 11th Bt (cr 1681), 1845–1926, vol. II
Moore, Thomas Sturge, 1870–1944, vol. IV
Moore, Thomas Warren, 1872–1937, vol. III
Moore, Tom Sidney, 1881–1966, vol. VI
Moore, Vice-Adm. W. Usborne, 1849–1918, vol. II
Moore, Hon. William, 1817–1914, vol. II
Moore, Rev. Canon William, died 1943, vol. IV
Moore, Rt Hon. Sir William, 1st Bt (cr 1932), 1864–1944, vol. IV
Moore, Hon. William, 1817–1914, vol. I
Moore, W(illiam) Arthur, 1880–1962, vol. VI
Moore, Rev. William B.; see Bramley-Moore.
Moore, William H., 1848–1923, vol. II
Moore, Sir (William) Harrison, 1867–1935, vol. III
Moore, William Harvey, 1891–1961, vol. VI
Moore, William Monro, 1880–1936, vol. III
Moore, Rt Rev. William Richard, 1858–1930, vol. III
Moore, Sir William Samson, 2nd Bt (cr 1932), 1891–1978, vol. VII
Moore-Coulson, Maj.-Gen. Samuel, 1908–1983, vol. VIII
Moore Darling, Rev. Canon Edward, 1884–1968, vol. VI
Moore-Guggisberg, Decima, (Lady Moore-Guggisberg), died 1964, vol. VI
Moore-Lane, Col George Howard, 1844–1905, vol. I
Moore-Lane, Col Maitland; see Lane.
Moore-Park, Carton, 1877–1956, vol. V
Moorehead, Alan McCrae, 1910–1983, vol. VIII
Moores, Col Charles Frederick Guise-, 1873–1938, vol. III
Moores, Maj.-Gen. Sir Guise G.; see Guise-Moores.
Moores, Sir John, 1896–1993, vol. IX
Moorhead, Maj.-Gen. Charles Dawson, 1894–1965, vol. VI
Moorhead, Thomas Gillman, 1878–1960, vol. V
Moorhouse, E. Hallam; see Meynell, Esther H.
Moorhouse, Lt-Col Sir Harry Claude, 1872–1934, vol. III
Moorhouse, Rt Rev. James, 1826–1915, vol. I
Mooring, Sir (Arthur) George (Rixson), 1908–1969, vol. VI
Mooring, Sir George; see Mooring, Sir A. G. R.
Moorman, Frederic William, 1872–1919, vol. II
Moorman, Rt Rev. John Richard Humpidge, 1905–1989, vol. VIII

Moorman, Mary Caroline, 1905–1994, vol. IX
Moorshead, Engr-Rear-Adm. Herbert Brooks, 1870–1955, vol. V
Moorsom, Maj.-Gen. Charles John, 1837–1908, vol. I
Moorsom, Lt-Col Henry Martin, 1839–1921, vol. II
Moorsom, James Marshall, died 1918, vol. II
Moos, Sorab Nanabhoy, 1890–1974, vol. VII
Mootham, Sir Orby Howell, 1901–1995, vol. IX
Moran, 1st Baron, 1882–1977, vol. VII
Moran, Frances Elizabeth, 1893–1977, vol. VII
Moran, Joseph Michael, 1925–1978, vol. VII
Moran, Patrick Alfred Pierce, 1917–1988, vol. VIII
Moran, His Eminence Cardinal Patrick Francis, 1830–1911, vol. I
Moran, Thomas, 1899–1987, vol. VIII
Moran, Rev. Canon Walter Isidore, 1865–1958, vol. V
Morand, Paul, 1889–1975, vol. VII
Morant, Captain Edgar Robert, 1874–1931, vol. III
Morant, Adm. Sir George Digby, 1837–1921, vol. II
Morant, Brig.-Gen. Hubert Horatio Shirley, 1870–1946, vol. IV
Morant, Dame Mary Maud, (Sister Mary Regis), 1903–1985, vol. VIII
Morant, Sir Robert Laurie, 1863–1920, vol. II
Moraud, Hon. Lucien, died 1951, vol. V
Moravia, Alberto, 1907–1990, vol. VIII
Moray, 15th Earl of, 1840–1901, vol. I
Moray, 16th Earl of, 1842–1909, vol. I
Moray, 17th Earl of, 1855–1930, vol. III
Moray, 18th Earl of, 1892–1943, vol. IV
Moray, 19th Earl of, 1894–1974, vol. VII
Moray, Edward Bruce D., see Dawson-Moray.
Moray, Captain William Augustus Stirling Home Drummond, 1852–1939, vol. III
Moray Williams, Barbara, (Barbara Arnason), 1911–1975, vol. VII
Morcom, Rev. Canon Anthony John, 1916–1997, vol. X
Morcom, John Brian, 1925–1997, vol. X
Morcom, Lt-Col Reginald Keble, 1877–1961, vol. VI
Morcom, William Boase, 1846–1910, vol. I
Morcom, Sir William John, 1859–1934, vol. III
Morcos-Asaad, Fikry Naguib, 1930–1998, vol. X
Mordaunt, Sir Charles, 10th Bt, 1836–1897, vol. I
Mordaunt, Elinor, died 1942, vol. IV
Mordaunt, Sir Henry, 12th Bt, 1867–1939, vol. III
Mordaunt, Lt-Col Sir Nigel John, 13th Bt, 1907–1979, vol. VII
Mordaunt, Sir Osbert L'Estrange, 11th Bt, 1884–1934, vol. III
Mordecai, Sir John Stanley, 1903–1986, vol. VIII
Mordell, Louis Joel, 1888–1972, vol. VII
Morden, Lt-Col Walter Grant, 1880–1932, vol. III
Mordey, William M., 1856–1938, vol. III
More, Lt-Col James Carmichael, 1883–1959, vol. V
More, Sir Jasper, 1907–1987, vol. VIII
More, John William, 1879–1959, vol. V
More, Kenneth Gilbert, 1914–1982, vol. VIII
More, Paul Elmer, 1864–1937, vol. III
More, Richard Edwardes, 1879–1936, vol. III
More, Brig.-Gen. Robert Henry, died 1951, vol. V
More, Robert Jasper, died 1903, vol. I

More-Molyneux, Maj.-Gen. George Hand, 1851–1903, vol. I
More-Molyneux, Adm. Sir Robert Henry, 1838–1904, vol. I
More-Molyneux-Longbourne, Brig.-Gen. Francis Cecil, 1883–1963, vol. VI
More-O'Ferrall, Dominic; *see* O'Ferrall.
Morecambe, Eric; *see* Bartholomew, J. E.
Moreau, Emile Edouard, 1856–1937, vol. III
Moreing, Adrian Charles, 1892–1940, vol. III
Moreing, Captain Algernon Henry, 1889–1974, vol. VII
Morel, Edmund Dene, 1873–1924, vol. II
Morel, Sir Thomas, 1847–1903, vol. I
Moreland, Rt Rev. William Hall, 1861–1946, vol. IV
Moreland, William Harrison, 1868–1938, vol. III
Morell, Sir Stephen Joseph, 1869–1944, vol. IV
Moresby, Adm. John, 1830–1922, vol. II
Moresby, Walter Halliday, *died* 1951, vol. V
Moreton, Lord; Henry Haughton Reynolds-Moreton, 1857–1920, vol. II
Moreton, Hon. Algernon Howard, 1880–1951, vol. V
Moreton, Rev. Arthur Cyprian, 1866–1936, vol. III
Moreton, Rev. Canon Harold Albert Victor, 1889–1966, vol. VI
Moreton, Hon. Sir Richard Charles, 1846–1928, vol. II
Morey, Very Rev. Dom Adrian, 1904–1989, vol. VIII
Morfee, Air Vice-Marshal Arthur Laurence, *born* 1897, vol. VIII
Morfill, William Richard, 1834–1909, vol. I
Morford, Maj.-Gen. Albert Clarence St C.; *see* St Clair-Morford.
Morford, Howard Frederick, 1894–1963, vol. VI
Morgan, Alexander, 1860–1946, vol. IV
Morgan, Col Alexander Braithwaite, 1866–1930, vol. III
Morgan, Col Sir Alexander Brooke, 1837–1911, vol. I
Morgan, Alfred Kedington, 1868–1928, vol. II
Morgan, Alun Michael, 1915–1981, vol. VIII
Morgan, Angela, *died* 1957, vol. V
Morgan, Lt-Col Anthony Hickman, 1858–1924, vol. II
Morgan, Hon. Sir Arthur, 1856–1916, vol. II
Morgan, Sir Arthur Croke, *died* 1955, vol. V
Morgan, Sir Arthur E., 1886–1956, vol. V
Morgan, Arthur Eustace, 1886–1972, vol. VII
Morgan, Sir Benjamin Howell, *died* 1937, vol. III
Morgan, Major Cecil Buckley, 1860–1918, vol. II
Morgan, Cecil Lloyd, 1882–1965, vol. VI
Morgan, Rev. Chandos Clifford Hastings Mansel, 1920–1993, vol. IX
Morgan, Adm. Sir Charles Eric, 1889–1951, vol. V
Morgan, Sir Charles Langbridge, 1855–1940, vol. III
Morgan, Charles Langbridge, 1894–1958, vol. V
Morgan, Col Claude Kyd, 1871–1934, vol. III
Morgan, Clement Yorke, 1903–1960, vol. V
Morgan, Sir Clifford Naunton, 1901–1986, vol. VIII
Morgan, Conwy Lloyd, 1852–1936, vol. III
Morgan, Cyril Dion, 1917–1994, vol. IX

Morgan, D. J., 1844–1918, vol. II
Morgan, Major Sir David Hughes-, 1st Bt (*cr* 1925), 1871–1941, vol. IV
Morgan, Rev. David Lewis, (Dewi), 1916–1993, vol. IX
Morgan, David Loftus, 1904–1976, vol. VII
Morgan, Very Rev. David Watcyn, *died* 1940, vol. III
Morgan, Lt-Col David Watts, 1867–1933, vol. III
Morgan, Dennis, 1928–1987, vol. VIII
Morgan, Rev. Dewi; *see* Morgan, Rev. David L.
Morgan, Rt Rev. Edmund Robert, 1888–1979, vol. VII
Morgan, Hon. Sir Edward James Ranembe, 1900–1977, vol. VII
Morgan, Ellis, 1916–1998, vol. X
Morgan, Col Emmanuel Maria, 1853–1929, vol. III
Morgan, Sir Ernest Dunstan, 1896–1979, vol. IX(AI)
Morgan, Col Farrar Robert Horton, 1893–1978, vol. VII
Morgan, Col Frank Stanley, 1893–1992, vol. IX
Morgan, Sir Frank William, 1887–1974, vol. VII
Morgan, Hon. Frederic Courtenay, 1834–1909, vol. I
Morgan, Lt-Gen. Sir Frederick Edgworth, 1894–1967, vol. VI
Morgan, Col Frederick James, 1862–1931, vol. III
Morgan, Rear-Adm. Frederick Robert William, 1861–1910, vol. I
Morgan, Captain Frederick Thomas de Mallet, 1889–1959, vol. V
Morgan, Rev. G. Campbell, 1863–1945, vol. IV
Morgan, Engr Rear-Adm. Geoffrey, 1889–1956, vol. V
Morgan, George, 1853–1943, vol. IV
Morgan, George, 1867–1957, vol. V
Morgan, George Ernest, 1861–1934, vol. III
Morgan, George Hay, 1866–1931, vol. III
Morgan, Rt Hon. Sir George Osborne, 1st Bt (*cr* 1892), 1826–1897, vol. I
Morgan, Geraint; *see* Morgan, W.G. O.
Morgan, Sir Gilbert Thomas, 1872–1940, vol. III
Morgan, Gladys Mary, *died* 1957, vol. V
Morgan, Graham, 1903–1987, vol. VIII
Morgan, Guy Leslie Llewellyn, 1902–1987, vol. VIII
Morgan, Gwenda, 1908–1991, vol. IX
Morgan, Harington, *died* 1914, vol. I
Morgan, Maj.-Gen. Harold de Riemer, 1888–1964, vol. VI
Morgan, Rev. Harold Dunbar, *died* 1945, vol. IV
Morgan, Col Harrison Ross Lewin, 1842–1914, vol. I
Morgan, Ven. Harry J., 1871–1947, vol. IV
Morgan, Heaton Andrew Kenneth, 1889–1962, vol. VI
Morgan, Henry, 1875–1944, vol. IV
Morgan, Rev. Henry Arthur, 1830–1912, vol. I
Morgan, Henry James, 1842–1913, vol. I
Morgan, Sir Herbert Edward, 1880–1951, vol. V
Morgan, Hilda, (Mrs Charles Morgan); *see* Vaughan, H.
Morgan, Brig.-Gen. Sir Hill Godfrey, 1862–1923, vol. II

Morgan, Hopkin, 1849–1933, vol. III
Morgan, H(opkin) Trevor; see Morgan, Trevor.
Morgan, Captain Horace Leslie, 1888–1973, vol. VII
Morgan, Hugh Travers, 1919–1988, vol. VIII
Morgan, Hyacinth Bernard Wenceslaus, 1885–1956, vol. V
Morgan, Hywel Glyn, 1899–1966, vol. VI
Morgan, Irvonwy, 1907–1982, vol. VIII
Morgan, Very Rev. J., died 1904, vol. I
Morgan, James, 1882–1968, vol VI
Morgan, James Conwy, 1910–1977, vol. VII
Morgan, Rev. John, died 1924, vol. II
Morgan, John, died 1938, vol. III
Morgan, John, 1892–1940, vol. III
Morgan, Most Rev. John, 1886–1957, vol. V
Morgan, Sir John David, 1874–1939, vol. III
Morgan, John Hammond, 1847–1924, vol. II
Morgan, Brig.-Gen. John Hartman, 1876–1955, vol. V
Morgan, John Lewis, 1919–2000, vol. X
Morgan, John Lloyd, 1861–1944, vol. IV
Morgan, John Pierpont, 1837–1913, vol. I
Morgan, John Pierpont, 1867–1943, vol. IV
Morgan, John T., 1824–1907, vol. I
Morgan, Sir John Vernon H.; see Hughes-Morgan.
Morgan, Sir Kenyon Pascoe V.; see Vaughan-Morgan.
Morgan, Col Kevern Ivor, 1894–1971, vol. VII
Morgan, Leslie James Joseph, 1922–1988, vol. VIII
Morgan, Montagu Travers, 1889–1974, vol. VII
Morgan, Brig. Morgan Cyril, 1891–1960, vol. V
Morgan, Sir Morien Bedford, 1912–1978, vol. VII
Morgan, Oswald Gayer, 1889–1981, vol. VIII
Morgan, Rear-Adm. Sir Patrick John, 1917–1989, vol. VIII
Morgan, Paul Robert James, 1898–1974, vol. VII
Morgan, Peter Trevor Hopkins, 1919–1995, vol. IX
Morgan, Lt-Gen. Reginald Hallward, 1871–1948, vol. IV
Morgan, Richard Cope, 1827–1908, vol. I
Morgan, Rev. Richard James Basil P.; see Paterson-Morgan.
Morgan, Robert Harry, 1880–1960, vol. V
Morgan, R(obert) Orlando, 1865–1956, vol. V
Morgan, Brig.-Gen. Rosslewin Westropp, 1879–1947, vol. IV
Morgan, Lt-Col Stuart Williams, 1867–1922, vol. II
Morgan, Sydney Cope, 1887–1967, vol. VI
Morgan, Thomas Hunt, 1866–1945, vol. IV
Morgan, Trevor, 1892–1976, vol. VII
Morgan, Adm. Sir Vaughan, 1891–1969, vol. VI
Morgan, Sir Walter, 1821–1906, vol. I
Morgan, Walter, 1886–1960, vol. V
Morgan, Walter J., died 1924, vol. II
Morgan, Sir Walter Vaughan, 1st Bt (cr 1906), 1831–1916, vol. II
Morgan, Air Cdre Wilfred W.; see Wynter-Morgan.
Morgan, Rev. William, 1862–1928, vol. II
Morgan, William, 1870–1945, vol. IV
Morgan, Gen. Sir William Duthie, 1891–1977, vol. VII
Morgan, Rev. Preb. William Edgar, 1888–1968, vol. VI

Morgan, William Geraint Oliver, 1920–1995, vol. IX
Morgan, Major William Henry, 1883–1966, vol. VI
Morgan, Rt Hon. William James, 1914–1999, vol. X
Morgan, William Matheson, 1906–1972, vol. VII
Morgan, William Pritchard, 1844–1924, vol. II
Morgan, William Stanley, 1908–1986, vol. VIII
Morgan-Brown, Rev. Nigel Mackenzie, 1859–1932, vol. III
Morgan-Grenville, Lt-Col Hon. Thomas George Breadalbane, 1891–1965, vol. VI
Morgan Jones, John; see Jones.
Morgan-Owen, Maj.-Gen. Llewellyn Isaac Gethin, 1879–1960, vol. V
Morgan-Powell, Samuel, 1878–1962, vol. VI
Morgenthau, Henry, 1856–1946, vol. IV
Morgenthau, Henry, Jr, 1891–1967, vol. VI
Mori, Haruki, 1911–1988, vol. IX(AI)
Moriarty, Rt Rev. Ambrose James, 1870–1949, vol. IV
Moriarty, Cecil Charles Hudson, 1877–1958, vol. V
Moriarty, Captain Henry Augustus, 1815–1906, vol. I
Moriarty, Rt Hon. John Francis, died 1915, vol. I
Morice, Beaumont, died 1937, vol. III
Morice, Sir George, Pasha, died 1904, vol. I
Morin, Leopold Frédéric Germain, 1861–1946, vol. IV
Morine, Sir Alfred Bishop, 1857–1944, vol. IV
Morini, Erica, 1904–1995, vol. IX
Morison, Rt Hon. Lord; Thomas Brash Morison, died 1945, vol. IV
Morison, Alexander Blackhall, 1850–1927, vol. II
Morison, Cecil Graham Traquair, 1881–1965, vol. VI
Morison, Donald, 1857–1924, vol. II
Morison, Hector, 1850–1939, vol. III
Morison, Sir John, 1893–1958, vol. V
Morison, Lt-Col John, 1879–1971, vol. VII
Morison, John Lyle, 1875–1952, vol. V
Morison, John Millcr Woodburn, 1875–1951, vol. V
Morison, Engr-Rear-Adm. Richard Barns, 1871–1932, vol. III
Morison, Sir Ronald Peter, 1900–1976, vol. VII
Morison, Rutherford, 1853–1939, vol. III
Morison, Samuel Eliot, 1887–1976, vol. VII
Morison, Stanley, 1889–1967, vol. VI
Morison, Sir Theodore, 1863–1936, vol. III
Morison, Rt Hon. Thomas Brash; see Morison, Rt Hon. Lord.
Morison, Sir William Thomson, 1860–1931, vol. III
Morita, Akio, 1921–1999, vol. X
Moritz, Rudolph, 1878–1940, vol. III
Moritz, Siegmund, 1855–1932, vol. III
Morkill, William Lucius, 1858–1936, vol. III
Morland, Andrew John, 1896–1957, vol. V
Morland, Egbert Coleby, 1874–1955, vol. V
Morland, Captain Henry, 1876–1966, vol. VI (AII)
Morland, Sir Oscar Charles, 1904–1980, vol. VII
Morland, Gen. Sir Thomas Lethbridge Napier, 1865–1925, vol. II
Morland, William Vane, 1884–1962, vol. VI
Morle, Philip Bartlett, 1876–1956, vol. V
Morley, 3rd Earl of, 1843–1905, vol. I

Morley, 4th Earl of, 1877–1951, vol. V
Morley, 5th Earl of, 1878–1962, vol. VI
Morley of Blackburn, 1st Viscount, 1838–1923,
  vol. II
Morley, Agnes H.; *see* Headlam-Morley.
Morley, Sir Alexander Francis, 1908–1971, vol. VII
Morley, Rt Hon. Arnold, 1849–1916, vol. II
Morley, Arthur, 1881–1946, vol. IV
Morley, Arthur, 1876–1962, vol. VI
Morley, Austin, 1898–1970, vol. VI
Morley, Cecil Denis, 1911–1999, vol. X
Morley, Charles, *died* 1916, vol. II
Morley, Charles, 1847–1917, vol. II
Morley, Charles, 1885–1955, vol. V
Morley, Christopher, 1890–1957, vol. V
Morley, Captain Hon. Claude Hope H.; *see*
  Hope-Morley.
Morley, Edith Julia, 1875–1964, vol. VI
Morley, Edward Williams, 1838–1923, vol. II
Morley, Eric Douglas, 1918–2000, vol. X
Morley, Sir George, 1873–1942, vol. IV
Morley, Air Vice-Marshal George Henry,
  1907–1971, vol. VII
Morley, Sir Godfrey William Rowland, 1909–1987,
  vol. VIII
Morley, Harry, 1881–1943, vol. IV
Morley, Henry Forster, 1855–1943, vol. IV
Morley, Henry Seaward, 1897–1960, vol. V
Morley, Sir James Wycliffe H.; *see*
  Headlam-Morley.
Morley, John, *died* 1974, vol. VII
Morley, John, 1924–1994, vol. IX
Morley, Kenneth Arthur Sonntag H.; *see*
  Headlam-Morley.
Morley, Lt-Col Lyddon Charteris, 1877–1954,
  vol. V
Morley, Ralph, 1882–1955, vol. V
Morley, Robert, 1857–1941, vol. IV
Morley, Robert Adolf Wilton, 1908–1992, vol. IX
Morley, Rt Rev. Samuel, 1841–1923, vol. II
Morley, Very Rev. William Fenton, 1912–1995,
  vol. IX
Morley-John, Michael, 1923–1993, vol. IX
Morling, Col Leonard Francis, 1904–1994, vol. IX
Morling, Norton Arthur, 1909–1994, vol. IX
Mornement, Bt Col Edward, 1867–1956, vol. V
Moro, Aldo, 1916–1978, vol. VII
Moro, Peter, 1911–1998, vol. X
Morony, Thomas Henry, 1879–1961, vol. VI
Morony, Gen. Sir Thomas Lovett, 1926–1989,
  vol. VIII
Morphett, Lt-Col George Charles, 1878–1968,
  vol. VI
Morphew, Col Edward Maudsley, 1867–1947,
  vol. IV
Morphy, Hugh Boulton, 1860–1932, vol. III
Morpurgo, Jack Eric, 1918–2000, vol. X
Morrah, Mrs Dermot; *see* Morrah, Ruth.
Morrah, Dermot Michael Macgregor, 1896–1974,
  vol. VII
Morrah, Herbert Arthur, *died* 1939, vol. III
Morrah, Ruth, (Mrs Dermot Morrah), 1899–1990,
  vol. VIII
Morrell, Rear-Adm. Arthur, *died* 1915, vol. I
Morrell, Arthur Claude, 1894–1978, vol. VII

Morrell, Captain Sir Arthur Routley Hutson,
  1878–1968, vol. VI
Morrell, Charles, 1842–1913, vol. I
Morrell, Mrs G. Herbert, (Emily Alicia Morrell),
  died 1938, vol. III
Morrell, George Herbert, 1845–1906, vol. I
Morrell, Col (Herbert) William (James), 1915–1995,
  vol. IX
Morrell, James George, 1923–2000, vol. X
Morrell, Rt Rev. James Herbert Lloyd, 1907–1996,
  vol. X
Morrell, Philip, 1870–1943, vol. IV
Morrell, R. M., *died* 1912, vol. I
Morrell, Col William; *see* Morrell, Col H. W. J.
Morrell, William Bowes, 1913–1981, vol. VIII
Morren, Sir William Booth Rennie, 1890–1972,
  vol. VII
Morrice, Humphrey Alan Walter, 1906–1959,
  vol. V
Morrice, Rev. James Cornelius, 1874–1953, vol. V
Morrice, Rev. John David, 1849–1938, vol. III
Morrice, Lt-Col Lewis Edward, 1862–1933, vol. III
Morrill, Thomas James, 1886–1969, vol. VI
Morris, 1st Baron, 1858–1935, vol. III
Morris, 2nd Baron, 1903–1975, vol. VII
Morris and Killanin, 1st Baron, 1827–1901, vol. I
Morris of Borth-y-Gest, Baron (Life Peer); John
  William Morris, 1896–1979, vol. VII
Morris of Grasmere, Baron (Life Peer); Charles
  Richard Morris, 1898–1990, vol. VIII
Morris of Kenwood, 1st Baron, 1893–1954, vol. V
Morris, Alfred, 1874–1945, vol. IV
Morris, Air Cdre Alfred Drummond W.; *see*
  Warrington-Morris.
Morris, Most Rev. (Alfred) Edwin, 1894–1971,
  vol. VII
Morris, Air Vice-Marshal Sir (Alfred) Samuel,
  1889–1964, vol. VI
Morris, Brig. Arthur de Burgh, 1902–1978, vol. VII
Morris, Rt Rev. Arthur Harold, 1898–1977, vol. VII
Morris, Col Arthur Henry, 1861–1939, vol. III
Morris, Brig. Arthur Henry Musgrave, 1904–1972,
  vol. VII
Morris, Col Arthur Hugh, 1872–1941, vol. IV
Morris, Col Augustus William, 1845–1906, vol. I
Morris, Benjamin Stephen, 1910–1990, vol. VIII
Morris, C. J., *see* Morris, John.
Morris, Sir Cedric Lockwood, 9th Bt, 1889–1982,
  vol. VIII
Morris, Charles, *died* 1929, vol. III
Morris, Charles Alfred, 1898–1983, vol. VIII
Morris, Charles Arthur, *died* 1942, vol. IV
Morris, (Charles) Greville, 1861–1922, vol. II
Morris, Lt-Col Charles Reade Monroe, 1882–1936,
  vol. III
Morris, Charles Sculthorpe, 1875–1949, vol. IV
Morris, Col Charles Temple, 1876–1956, vol. V
Morris, Colin John Owen Rhonabwy, 1910–1981,
  vol. VIII
Morris, Major Cyril Clarke Boville, 1882–1950,
  vol. IV
Morris, Sir Daniel, 1844–1933, vol. III
Morris, David Edward, 1915–1990, vol. VIII
Morris, Denis Edward, 1907–1999, vol. X

Morris, Air Marshal Sir Douglas Griffith, 1908–1990, vol. VIII

Morris, Brig.-Gen. Edmund Merritt, 1868–1939, vol. III

Morris, Edmund Montague, 1871–1913, vol. I

Morris, Commissary-Gen. Sir Edward, 1833–1923, vol. II

Morris, Edward Allan, 1910–1997, vol. X

Morris, Edward Ellis, 1843–1902, vol. I

Morris, Edward Gilbert, 1884–1943, vol. IV

Morris, Air Cdre Edward James, 1915–1999, vol. X

Morris, Edward Robert, 1862–1934, vol. III

Morris, Most Rev. Edwin; see Morris, Most Rev. A. E.

Morris, Gen. Sir Edwin Logie, 1889–1970, vol. VI

Morris, Rev. Ernest Edwin, 1856–1924, vol. II

Morris, Sir Ernest William, died 1937, vol. III

Morris, Sir Francis, 1859–1944, vol. IV

Morris, Geoffrey Grant, 1888–1938, vol. III

Morris, Sir Geoffrey N.; see Newman-Morris.

Morris, Geoffrey O'C.; see O'Connor-Morris.

Morris, Sir George, 1833–1912, vol. I

Morris, Col George Abbott, 1879–1957, vol. V

Morris, Sir George Cecil, 6th Bt (cr 1806), 1852–1940, vol. IV

Morris, Lt-Col Hon. George Henry, 1872–1915, vol. I

Morris, Captain George Horace Guy, 1897–1979, vol. VII

Morris, Sir George Lockwood, 8th Bt (cr 1806), 1859–1947, vol. IV

Morris, Brig.-Gen. George Mortimer, 1868–1954, vol. V

Morris, Sir George Parker; see Morris, Sir Parker.

Morris, Greville; see Morris, C. G.

Morris, Guy Wilfrid, 1884–1956, vol. V

Morris, Sir Gwilym; see Morris, Sir T. G.

Morris, Gwilym Ivor, 1911–1965, vol. VI

Morris, Gwyn Rhyse Francis, 1910–1982, vol. VIII

Morris, Sir Harold Spencer, 1876–1967, vol. VI

Morris, Harrison Smith, 1856–1948, vol. IV

Morris, Harry Frank Grave, 1907–1982, vol. VIII

Morris, Sir Henry, 1st Bt (cr 1909), 1844–1926, vol. II

Morris, Sir Herbert Edward, 7th Bt (cr 1806), 1884–1947, vol. IV

Morris, Brig. Herbert Edwin Abrahall, 1894–1969, vol. VI

Morris, Herbert Picton, 1856–1946, vol. IV

Morris, Ian; see Morris, W. I. C.

Morris, Ira Nelson, died 1942, vol. IV

Morris, Ivor Gray, born 1911, vol. X(AI)

Morris, Rt Rev. James, 1876–1957, vol. V

Morris, James Archibald, 1857–1942, vol. IV

Morris, (James) Peter, 1926–1998, vol. X

Morris, John, (C. J. Morris), 1895–1980, vol. VII

Morris, Rev. John C., 1870–1940, vol. III

Morris, John David, 1895–1972, vol. VII

Morris, Hon. Sir John Demetrius, 1902–1956, vol. V

Morris, Maj.-Gen. John Edward Longworth, 1909–1988, vol. VIII

Morris, Sir John Henry, 1828–1912, vol. I

Morris, John Humphrey Carlile, 1910–1984, vol. VIII

Morris, Maj.-Gen. John Ignatius, 1842–1902, vol. I

Morris, Rev. (John) Marcus (Harston), 1915–1989, vol. VIII

Morris, Sir John N.; see Newman-Morris.

Morris, Major John Patrick, 1894–1962, vol. VI

Morris, Brig. John Sidney, 1890–1961, vol. VI

Morris, John Turner M.; see Macgregor-Morris.

Morris, Sir Keith Douglas, 1908–1981, vol. VIII

Morris, Hon. Sir Kenneth James, 1903–1978, vol. VII

Morris, Lawrence Henry, 1902–1969, vol. VI

Morris, Air Marshal Sir Leslie D.; see Dalton-Morris

Morris, Sir Lewis, 1833–1907, vol. I

Morris, Sir Malcolm Alexander, 1849–1924, vol. II

Morris, Malcolm John, 1913–1972, vol. VII

Morris, Rev. Marcus; see Morris, Rev. J. M. H.

Morris, May, died 1938, vol. III

Morris, Nigel Godfrey, 1908–1996, vol. X

Morris, Noah, died 1947, vol. IV

Morris, Sir Owen T.; see Temple-Morris.

Morris, Sir Parker, 1891–1972, vol. VII

Morris, Percy, 1893–1967, vol. VI

Morris, Peter; see Morris, J. P.

Morris, Philip Richard, 1833–1902, vol. I

Morris, Sir Philip Robert, 1901–1979, vol. VII

Morris, Quentin Mathew, 1930–1989, vol. VIII

Morris, Ralph Clarence, 1889–1959, vol. V

Morris, Reginald Owen, 1886–1948, vol. IV

Morris, Rex G.; see Goring-Morris.

Morris, Sir Rhys Hopkin, 1888–1956, vol. V

Morris, Rev. Richard, died 1923, vol. II

Morris, Richard John, 1860–1936, vol. III

Morris, Richard Murchison, 1898–1979, vol. VII

Morris, Maj.-Gen. Robert, 1840–1914, vol. I

Morris, Sir Robert Armine, 4th Bt (cr 1806), 1848–1927, vol. II

Morris, Sir Robert Byng, 10th Bt, 1913–1999, vol. X

Morris, R(obert) Schofield, 1898–1964, vol. VI

Morris, Air Vice-Marshal Ronald James Arthur, 1915–2000, vol. X

Morris, Rev. Rupert Hugh, 1844–1918, vol. II

Morris, Samuel, 1846–1920, vol. II

Morris, Air Vice-Marshal Sir Samuel; see Morris, Air Vice-Marshal Sir A. S.

Morris, Sir Samuel Meeson, 1857–1937, vol. III

Morris, Rev. Silas, 1862–1923, vol. II

Morris, Captain Sir Tankerville Robert Armine, 5th Bt (cr 1806), 1892–1937, vol. III

Morris, Most Rev. Thomas, 1914–1997, vol. X

Morris, Sir (Thomas) Gwilym, 1913–1982, vol. VIII

Morris, Lt-Col Thomas Henry, 1848–1927, vol. II

Morris, Thomas Joseph, 1876–1953, vol. V

Morris, Timothy Denis, 1935–1996, vol. X

Morris, Rev. Canon Walter Edmund Harston, 1872–1968, vol. VI

Morris, Walter Frederick, 1914–1999, vol. X

Morris, William Alexander, 1905–1979, vol. VII

Morris, William Alfred, 1912–1973, vol. VII

Morris, Col Sir William George, 1847–1935, vol. III

Morris, Sir William Gerard, 1909–1984, vol. VIII

Morris, William Ian Clinch, 1907–1995, vol. IX

Morris, William O'Connor, 1824–1904, vol. I
Morris, Col William P.; see Pollok Morris.
Morris, William Russell, 1853–1936, vol. III
Morris, Sir Willie, 1919–1982, vol. VIII
Morris-Airey, Harold, 1880–1927, vol. II
Morris-Eyton, Lt-Col Charles Reginald, 1890–1961, vol. VI
Morris-Eyton, Lt-Col Robert Charles Gilfrid, 1921–1990, vol. VIII
Morris Johns, Alun; see Johns.
Morris-Jones, Sir Henry; see Morris-Jones, Sir J. H.
Morris-Jones, Huw, 1912–1989, vol. VIII
Morris-Jones, Ifor Henry, 1922–1999, vol. X
Morris-Jones, Sir John; see Jones.
Morris-Jones, Sir (John) Henry, 1884–1972, vol. VII
Morris-Jones, Wyndraeth Humphreys, 1918–1999, vol. X
Morrisby, Major Hon. Arthur, 1847–1925, vol. II
Morrish, Arthur Gabriel, 1869–1936, vol. III
Morrish, Rev. Francis, 1852–1937, vol. III
Morrish, Rear-Adm. William Douglas Travers, 1882–1958, vol. V
Morrison, 1st Baron, 1881–1953, vol. V
Morrison, 2nd Baron, 1914–1997, vol. X
Morrison of Lambeth, Baron (Life Peer); Herbert Stanley Morrison, 1888–1965, vol. VI
Morrison, Agnes Brysson, 1867–1934, vol. III
Morrison, Maj.-Gen. Albert Edward, 1901–1989, vol. VIII
Morrison, Alexander, 1868–1941, vol. IV
Morrison, Alexander, 1917–1982, vol. VIII
Morrison, Alexander Thomas, 1886–1954, vol. V
Morrison, Archibald Cameron, 1870–1948, vol. IV
Morrison, Arthur, 1863–1945, vol. IV
Morrison, Arthur Andrew, 1858–1934, vol. III
Morrison, Arthur Cecil Lockwood, 1881–1960, vol. V
Morrison, Hon. Aulay MacAulay, 1863–1942, vol. IV
Morrison, Brig.-Gen. Colquhoun Grant, 1860–1916, vol. II
Morrison, David, died 1936, vol. III
Morrison, Maj.-Gen. Sir Edward Whipple Bancroft, 1867–1925, vol. II
Morrison, Col F. L., 1863–1917, vol. II
Morrison, Col Frank Stanley, 1881–1969, vol. VI
Morrison, George Alexander, 1869–1956, vol. V
Morrison, George Ernest, 1862–1920, vol. II
Morrison, Very Rev. George Herbert, 1866–1928, vol. II
Morrison, Herbert Needham, 1891–1963, vol. VI
Morrison, Hugh, 1868–1931, vol. III
Morrison, Hugh Smith, 1858–1929, vol. III
Morrison, Air Vice-Marshal Ian Gordon, 1914–1997, vol. X
Morrison, Most Rev. James, 1861–1950, vol. IV
Morrison, James, 1900–1987, vol. VIII
Morrison, Major James Archibald, 1873–1934, vol. III
Morrison, Rt Rev. James Dow, 1844–1934, vol. III
Morrison, James Thomas Jackman, died 1933, vol. III
Morrison, James Victor, 1917–1990, vol. VIII
Morrison, Col John, died 1919, vol. II
Morrison, John Sinclair, 1913–2000, vol. X

Morrison, Joseph Albert Colquhoun, 1882–1964, vol. VI
Morrison, Julia Minnie, died 1942, vol. IV
Morrison, Sir Murray; see Morrison, Sir W. M.
Morrison, Sir Nicholas Godfrey, 1918–1981, vol. VIII
Morrison, Rt Hon. Sir Peter Hugh, 1944–1995, vol. IX
Morrison, R. E., born 1851, vol. II
Morrison, Rear-Adm. Thomas Kenneth, 1911–1983, vol. VIII
Morrison, Walter, 1836–1921, vol. II
Morrison, Sir William, 1877–1951, vol. V
Morrison, Rev. William Douglas, 1852–1943, vol. IV
Morrison, Sir (William) Murray, 1873–1948, vol. IV
Morrison-Bell, Sir (Arthur) Clive, 1st Bt (cr 1923), 1871–1956, vol. V
Morrison-Bell, Sir Charles Reginald Francis, 3rd Bt (cr 1905), 1915–1967, vol. VI
Morrison-Bell, Sir Charles William, 1st Bt (cr 1905), 1833–1914, vol. I
Morrison-Bell, Sir Claude William Hedley, 2nd Bt (cr 1905), 1867–1943, vol. IV
Morrison-Bell, Sir Clive; see Morrison-Bell, Sir A. C.
Morrison-Bell, Lt-Col Ernest FitzRoy, 1871–1960, vol. V
Morrison-Bell, Lt-Col Eustace Widdrington, 1874–1947, vol. IV
Morrison-Low, Sir Walter John; see Low.
Morrison-Scott, Sir Terence Charles Stuart, 1908–1991, vol. IX
Morrisroe, Rt Rev. Patrick, 1869–1946, vol. IV
Morrocco, Alberto, 1917–1998, vol. X
Morrogh, Lt-Col Donald Florence MacC.; see MacCarthy-Morrogh.
Morrogh, Brig. Walter Francis, 1891–1954, vol. V
Morrogh Bernard, Rt Rev. Mgr Canon Eustace Anthony, 1893–1972, vol. VII
Morrow, Albert, 1863–1927, vol. II
Morrow, Sir (Arthur) William, 1903–1977, vol. VII
Morrow, Dwight Whitney, 1873–1931, vol. III
Morrow, Forbes St John, 1860–1949, vol. IV
Morrow, George, 1870–1955, vol. V
Morrow, Cdre James Cairns, 1905–1963, vol. VI
Morrow, Very Rev. John Love, died 1940, vol. III
Morrow, Sir William; see Morrow, Sir A. W.
Morrow, Very Rev. William Edward Reginald, 1869–1950, vol. IV
Morse, Vice-Adm. Sir Anthony; see Morse, Vice-Adm. Sir J. A. V.
Morse, Sir Arthur, 1892–1967, vol. VI
Morse, Charles, 1860–1945, vol. IV
Morse, David Abner, 1907–1990, vol. VIII
Morse, Sir George Henry, 1857–1931, vol. III
Morse, Hosea Ballou, 1855–1934, vol. III
Morse, Vice-Adm. Sir (John) Anthony (Vere), 1892–1960, vol. V
Morse, L. Lapper, 1853–1913, vol. I
Morse, Rev. Wallace Ransom, 1860–1932, vol. III
Morse, William Ewart, 1878–1952, vol. V
Morse, Withrow, 1880–1951, vol. V
Morse-Boycott, Rev. Desmond, 1892–1979, vol. VII

Morshead, Edmund Doidge Anderson, *died* 1912, vol. I
Morshead, Lt-Col Henry Treise, 1882–1931, vol. III
Morshead, Leonard Frederick, 1868–1936, vol. III
Morshead, Lt-Gen. Sir Leslie James, 1889–1959, vol. V
Morshead, Sir Owen Frederick, 1893–1977, vol. VII
Morshead, Lt-Col Rupert Henry A.; *see* Anderson-Morshead.
Morshead, Sir Warwick Charles, 3rd Bt, 1824–1905, vol. I
Morson, A(lbert) Clifford, 1881–1975, vol. VII
Morson, Walter Augustus Ormsby, 1851–1921, vol. II
Mort, David Llewellyn, 1888–1963, vol. VI
Mort, Rt Rev. John Ernest Llewelyn, 1915–1997, vol. X
Morten, Edward, 1845–1929, vol. III
Morten, Frederick Joseph, 1888–1960, vol. V
Morten, Honnor, *died* 1913, vol. I
Mortensen, Theodor, 1868–1952, vol. V
Morter, Col Sidney Pelham, 1869–1933, vol. III
Mortimer, Chapman; *see* Chapman-Mortimer, W. C.
Mortimer, Sir Charles Edward, 1886–1974, vol. VII
Mortimer, Rev. Christian, *died* 1916, vol. II
Mortimer, Emile Samuel, 1853–1935, vol. III
Mortimer, Francis James, 1875–1944, vol. IV
Mortimer, George Frederick Lloyd, 1866–1928, vol. II
Mortimer, Gerald James, 1918–1997, vol. X
Mortimer, Lt-Col James, *died* 1916, vol. II
Mortimer, John Desmond, *died* 1942, vol. IV
Mortimer, Penelope Ruth, 1918–1999, vol. X
Mortimer, Brig. Philip, 1882–1963, vol. VI
Mortimer, Sir Ralph George Elpinstone, 1869–1955, vol. V
Mortimer, Raymond, 1895–1980, vol. VII
Mortimer, Rt Rev. Robert Cecil, 1902–1976, vol. VII
Mortimer, Air Vice-Marshal Roger, 1914–1992, vol. IX
Mortimer, William Charles C.; *see* Chapman-Mortimer.
Mortimer, William Egerton, 1878–1940, vol. III
Mortimer, Col Sir William Hugh, 1846–1921, vol. II
Mortimore, Lt-Col Claude Alick, 1875–1927, vol. II
Mortimore, Frederick William, 1858–1928, vol. II
Mortished, Ronald James Patrick, 1891–1957, vol. V
Mortlock, Rev. Canon Charles Bernard, 1888–1967, vol. VI
Mortlock, Rev. Canon E., 1859–1945, vol. IV
Mortlock, Herbert Norman, 1926–1995, vol. IX
Morton, 20th Earl of, 1844–1935, vol. III
Morton, 21st Earl of, 1907–1976, vol. VII
Morton of Henryton, Baron (Life Peer); Fergus Dunlop Morton, 1887–1973, vol. VII
Morton of Shuna, Baron (Life Peer); Hugh Drennan Baird Morton, 1930–1995, vol. IX
Morton, Alastair; *see* Morton, S. A.
Morton, Sir Alpheus Cleophas, 1840–1923, vol. II
Morton, Anthony; *see* Creasey, John.
Morton, Rev. Arthur, 1915–1996, vol. X
Morton, Arthur Henry Aylmer, 1836–1913, vol. I

Morton, Gen. Boyce William Dunlop, 1829–1919, vol. II
Morton, Sir Brian, 1912–1991, vol. IX
Morton, Charles, 1819–1904, vol. I
Morton, Charles Alexander, 1860–1929, vol. III
Morton, Sir Charles Henry, 1852–1939, vol. III
Morton, Air Cdre Crichton Charles, 1912–1996, vol. X
Morton, Lt-Col David Simson, *died* 1937, vol. III
Morton, Major Sir Desmond John Falkiner, 1891–1971, vol. VII
Morton, Digby; *see* Morton, H. D.
Morton, Edward, *died* 1922, vol. II
Morton, Brig.-Gen. Edward, 1871–1949, vol. IV
Morton, Edward John Chalmers, 1856–1902, vol. I
Morton, Edward Reginald, 1867–1944, vol. IV
Morton, Frank, 1906–1999, vol. X
Morton, Sir George, 1870–1953, vol. V
Morton, Sir George Bond, 1893–1954, vol. V
Morton, Lt-Gen. Sir Gerald de Courcy, 1845–1906, vol. I
Morton, George F., 1882–1975, vol. VII
Morton, Guy Mainwaring, 1896–1968, vol. VI
Morton, Major Harold Trestrail, 1894–1972, vol. VII
Morton, Rev. Harry Osborne, 1925–1988, vol. VIII
Morton, (Henry) Digby, 1906–1983, vol. VIII
Morton, Henry Vollam, 1892–1979, vol. VII
Morton, Hugh, 1883–1941, vol. IV
Morton, Col Hugh Murray, 1873–1946, vol. IV
Morton, J. B.; *see* Morton, J. C. A. B. M.
Morton, Sir James, 1867–1943, vol. IV
Morton, James Elliot Vowler, 1861–1924, vol. II
Morton, James H., 1881–1918, vol. II
Morton, John Cameron Andrieu Bingham Michael, (J. B. Morton), 1893–1979, vol. VII
Morton, John Percival, 1911–1985, vol. VIII
Morton, Levi Parsons, 1824–1920, vol. II
Morton, Michael, *died* 1931, vol. III
Morton, Sir Ralph John, 1896–1985, vol. VIII
Morton, Richard Alan, 1899–1977, vol. VII
Morton, Rev. Robert, 1847–1932, vol. III
Morton, Sir Stanley William Gibson, 1911–1975, vol. VII
Morton, (Stephen) Alastair, 1913–1992, vol. IX
Morton, Air Vice-Marshal Terence Charles St Clessie, 1893–1968, vol. VI
Morton, Thomas Corsan, 1859–1928, vol. II
Morton, Sir Wilfred; *see* Morton, Sir W. W.
Morton, William Blair, 1868–1949, vol. IV
Morton, William Cuthbert, 1875–1971, vol. VII
Morton, Sir William David, 1926–1993, vol. IX
Morton, William Ernest, 1902–1981, vol. VIII
Morton, Sir (William) Wilfred, 1906–1981, vol. VIII
Morton Boyd, John; *see* Boyd.
Morvi, HH Thakur Saheb Sir Waghji Ravaji, 1858–1922, vol. II
Morvi State, ex-Ruler of, 1876–1957, vol. V
Moscheles, Felix, 1833–1917, vol. II
Moseley, Charles Herbert Harley, 1857–1933, vol. III
Moseley, Geoffrey, 1882–1953, vol. V
Moseley, Herbert Harvey, 1873–1959, vol. V
Moseley, Sydney Alexander, 1888–1961, vol. VI

Mosely, Alfred, 1855–1917, vol. II
Mosely, Sir Archie Gerard, 1883–1951, vol. V
Moser, Oswald, 1874–1916, vol. II
Moser, Robert Oswald, *died* 1953, vol. V
Moses, Sir Charles Joseph Alfred, 1900–1988, vol. VIII
Moses, James J. H., 1873–1946, vol. IV
Moses, Kenneth, 1931–1992, vol. IX
Moshier, H. H., 1889–1918, vol. II
Mosley, Sir Alexander, 1847–1927, vol. II
Mosley, Lady Cynthia Blanche, *died* 1933, vol. III
Mosley, Rt Rev. Henry, 1868–1948, vol. IV
Mosley, Brig. Henry Samuel, 1879–1975, vol. VII
Mosley, Sir Oswald, 4th Bt, 1848–1915, vol. I
Mosley, Sir Oswald, 5th Bt, 1873–1928, vol. II
Mosley, Sir Oswald Ernald, 6th Bt, 1896–1980, vol. VII
Moss, Abraham, 1899–1964, vol. VI
Moss, Alfred Allinson, 1912–1990, vol. VIII
Moss, Sir Charles, 1840–1912, vol. I
Moss, Charles Edward, 1872–1930, vol. III
Moss, David Francis, 1927–1992, vol. IX
Moss, Sir Edward; *see* Moss, Sir H. E.
Moss, Edward Herbert St George, 1918–1995, vol. IX
Moss, Col Edward Lawton, 1880–1975, vol. VII
Moss, Sir Eric de Vere, 1896–1981, vol. VIII
Moss, Captain Ernest William, 1876–1915, vol. I
Moss, Geoffrey; *see* McNeill-Moss, Major G.
Moss, Sir George Sinclair, 1882–1959, vol. V
Moss, Rev. Henry Whitehead, 1841–1917, vol. II
Moss, Sir (Horace) Edward, *died* 1912, vol. I
Moss, John, 1890–1976, vol. VII
Moss, Sir John Edwards E.; *see* Edwards-Moss.
Moss, Sir John Herbert Theodore E.; *see* Edwards-Moss.
Moss, Kenneth Neville, 1891–1942, vol. IV
Moss, Lewis S., *died* 1903, vol. I
Moss, Brig.-Gen. Lionel Boyd B.; *see* Boyd-Moss.
Moss, Hon. Matthew Lewis, 1863–1946, vol. IV
Moss, Norman J.; *see* Jordan-Moss.
Moss, Rev. Richard Waddy, 1850–1935, vol. III
Moss, Robert, *died* 1973, vol. VII
Moss, Rosalind Louisa Beaufort, 1890–1990, vol. VIII
Moss, Samuel, 1858–1918, vol. II
Moss, Sir Thomas E.; *see* Edwards-Moss.
Moss, Trevor Simpson, 1921–1996, vol. X
Moss, Wilfred, 1867–1938, vol. III
Moss-Blundell, Lt-Col Bryan Seymour; *see* Blundell.
Moss-Blundell, Henry Seymour; *see* Blundell.
Mosscockle, Rita Francis, *died* 1943, vol. IV
Mosse, Lt-Col Arthur Henry Eyre, 1877–1943, vol. IV
Mosse, Charles Benjamin, 1830–1912, vol. I
Mosse, Robert Lee, 1877–1963, vol. VI
Mosse, Rev. William George, 1859–1929, vol. III
Mosses, William, 1858–1943, vol. IV
Mossman, Robert Cockburn, 1870–1940, vol. III
Mossop, Major Albert Isaac, *died* 1936, vol. III
Mossop, Sir Allan George, 1887–1965, vol. VI
Mossop, Joseph Upjohn, 1872–1928, vol. II, vol. III
Mossop, Leonard, 1869–1933, vol. III
Moston, Henry Ernest, 1881–1962, vol. VI
Mostyn, 3rd Baron, 1856–1929, vol. III

Mostyn, 4th Baron, 1885–1965, vol. VI
Mostyn, 5th Baron, 1920–2000, vol. X
Mostyn, Sir Basil Antony Trevor, 13th Bt, 1902–1956, vol. V
Mostyn, Most Rev. Francis, 1860–1939, vol. III
Mostyn, Hon. Henry Richard Howel L.; *see* Lloyd-Mostyn.
Mostyn, Rev. Hon. Hugh Wynne, 1838–1930, vol. III
Mostyn, Sir Jeremy John Anthony, 14th Bt, 1933–1988, vol. VIII
Mostyn, Sir Pyers Charles, 10th Bt, 1895–1917, vol. II
Mostyn, Sir Pyers Edward, 12th Bt, 1928–1955, vol. V
Mostyn, Captain Sir Pyers George Joseph, 11th Bt, 1893–1937, vol. III
Mostyn, Sir Pyers William, 9th Bt, 1846–1912, vol. I
Mostyn, Maj.-Gen. Hon. Sir Savage L.; *see* Lloyd-Mostyn.
Mostyn, Tom, 1864–1930, vol. III
Mostyn-Owen, Lt-Col Roger Arthur; *see* Owen.
Mote, Harold Trevor, 1919–1995, vol. IX
Moten, Brig. Murray John, 1899–1953, vol. V
Motherwell, Hon. William Richard, 1860–1943, vol. IV
Moti Chand, Raja Sir, *died* 1934, vol. III
Motilal, Raja Bahadur Sir Bansilal, *died* 1935, vol. IV
Motion, Andrew Richard, 1857–1933, vol. III
Motion, Robert Russa, 1867–1940, vol. III (A), vol. IV
Motion, Major Thomas Augustus, *died* 1942, vol. IV
Mott, Sir Adrian Spear, 2nd Bt, 1889–1964, vol. VI
Mott, Sir Basil, 1st Bt, 1859–1938, vol. III
Mott, Edward Spencer, 1844–1910, vol. I
Mott, Sir Frederick Walker, 1853–1926, vol. II
Mott, John Raleigh, 1865–1955, vol. V
Mott, Sir Nevill Francis, 1905–1996, vol. X
Mott, Norman Gilbert, 1910–1987, vol. VIII
Mott, Hon. Maj.-Gen. Stanley Fielder, 1873–1959, vol. V
Mott-Radclyffe, Sir Charles Edward, 1911–1992, vol. IX
Mottershead, Peter Michael Hall, 1926–1985, vol. VIII
Mottistone, 1st Baron, 1868–1947, vol. IV
Mottistone, 2nd Baron, 1899–1963, vol. VI
Mottistone, 3rd Baron, 1905–1966, vol. VI
Mottl, Felix, 1856–1911, vol. I
Motton, Paymaster-Rear-Adm. Frederick George, *died* 1935, vol. III
Mottram, James Cecil, 1880–1945, vol. IV
Mottram, Maj.-Gen. John Frederick, 1930–1998, vol. X
Mottram, Ralph Hale, 1883–1971, vol. VII
Mottram, Sir Richard, 1848–1914, vol. I
Mottram, Sir Thomas Harry, 1859–1937, vol. III
Mottram, Vernon Henry, 1882–1976, vol. VII
Mottram, Rev. William, 1836–1921, vol. II
Motz, Hans, 1909–1987, vol. VIII
Mouat, Sir James, 1815–1899, vol. I
Mouat, John Richard K.; *see* Kay-Mouat.

Moubray, John James, 1857–1928, vol. II
Mould, James, 1893–1958, vol. V
Mould, John, 1890–1964, vol. VI
Mould, Percy, *died* 1923, vol. II
Mould, Sam Carter, 1880–1963, vol. VI
Mould, Col William Thomas, 1865–1935, vol. III
Mould-Graham, Col Robert, 1895–1979, vol. VII
Moulden, Sir Frank Beaumont, 1876–1932, vol. III
Moule, Rev. Arthur Christopher, 1873–1957, vol. V
Moule, Ven. Arthur Evans, 1836–1918, vol. II
Moule, Charles Walter, 1834–1921, vol. II
Moule, Edward Christopher, 1902–1945, vol. IV
Moule, Rt Rev. George Evans, 1828–1912, vol. I
Moule, Rt Rev. Handley Carr Glyn, 1841–1920, vol. II
Moule, Horace Frederick D'Oyly, 1843–1925, vol. II
Moule, Ven. Walter Stephen, *died* 1949, vol. IV
Moule-Evans, David, 1905–1988, vol. VIII
Moullin, Charles William M.; *see* Mansell-Moullin.
Moullin, Eric Balliol, 1893–1963, vol. VI
Moulsdale, Rev. Stephen Richard Platt, 1872–1944, vol. IV
Moult, Thomas Moult, 1885–1974, vol. VII
Moulton, Baron (Life Peer); John Fletcher Moulton, 1844–1921, vol. II
Moulton, Hon. Hugh Fletcher, 1876–1962, vol. VI
Moulton, Rev. James Hope, 1863–1917, vol. II
Moulton, Maj.-Gen. James Louis, 1906–1993, vol. IX
Moulton, Louise Chandler, *died* 1908, vol. I
Moulton, Richard Green, 1849–1924, vol. II
Moulton, Rev. William Fiddian, 1835–1898, vol. I
Moulton-Barrett, Brig.-Gen. Edward Alfred, 1859–1932, vol. III
Mound, Trevor Ernest John, 1930–1998, vol. X
Mounet, Jean Sully, 1841–1916, vol. II
Mounsey, Sir George Augustus, 1879–1966, vol. VI
Mounsey, John Edward, 1879–1929, vol. III
Mounsey, John Little, 1852–1933, vol. III
Mounsey, John Patrick David, 1914–1999, vol. X
Mounsey, Rt Rev. William Robert Rupert, 1867–1952, vol. V
Mount, Lt-Col Sir Alan Henry Lawrence, 1881–1955, vol. V
Mount, Ven. Francis John, 1831–1903, vol. I
Mount, Sir James William Spencer, 1908–1994, vol. IX
Mount, Sir William Arthur, 1st Bt, 1866–1930, vol. III
Mount, William George, 1824–1906, vol. I
Mount, Sir William Malcolm, 2nd Bt, 1904–1993, vol. IX
Mount Edgcumbe, 4th Earl of, 1832–1917, vol. II
Mount Edgcumbe, 5th Earl of, 1865–1944, vol. IV
Mount Edgcumbe, 6th Earl of, 1873–1965, vol. VI
Mount Edgcumbe, 7th Earl of, 1903–1982, vol. VIII
Mount Stephen, 1st Baron, 1829–1921, vol. II
Mount Stephen, Lady; (Gian), *died* 1933, vol. III
Mount Temple, 1st Baron, 1867–1939, vol. III
Mountain, Arthur Reginald, 1877–1940, vol. III
Mountain, Lt-Col Sir Brian Edward Stanley, 2nd Bt, 1899–1977, vol. VII
Mountain, Sir Edward Mortimer, 1st Bt, 1872–1948, vol. IV

Mountain, John Francis, 1895–1965, vol. VI
Mountain, Surgeon Rear-Adm. (D) William Leonard, 1908–1980, vol. VII
Mountbatten of Burma, 1st Earl, 1900–1979, vol. VII
Mountbatten of Burma, Countess; (Edwina Cynthia Annette), 1901–1960, vol. V
Mountbatten, Major Lord; Leopold Arthur Louis, 1889–1922, vol. II
Mountcashell, 5th Earl, 1826–1898, vol. I
Mountcashell, 6th Earl, 1829–1915, vol. I
Mountevans, 1st Baron, 1881–1957, vol. V
Mountevans, 2nd Baron, 1918–1974, vol. VII
Mountfield, Alexander Stuart, 1902–1984, vol. VIII
Mountfield, Stuart; *see* Mountfield, A. S.
Mountford, Arnold Robert, 1922–1993, vol. IX
Mountford, Edward William, 1855–1908, vol. I
Mountford, Sir James Frederick, 1897–1979, vol. VII
Mountford, Lewis James, 1871–1944, vol. IV
Mountgarret, 13th Viscount, 1816–1900, vol. I
Mountgarret, 14th Viscount, 1844–1912, vol. I
Mountgarret, 15th Viscount, 1875–1918, vol. II
Mountgarret, 16th Viscount, 1903–1966, vol. VI
Mountifield, Engr Rear-Adm. James, 1871–1957, vol. V
Mountmorres, 6th Viscount, 1872–1936, vol. III
Mountmorres, 7th Viscount, 1879–1951, vol. V
Mountstephen, Sir William H., 1868–1946, vol. IV
Mountseven, Col Francis Hender, 1844–1935, vol. III
Mourant, Arthur Ernest, 1904–1994, vol. IX
Mousley, Edward Opotiki, 1886–1965, vol. VI
Moverley, Rt Rev. Gerald, 1922–1996, vol. X
Mowat, Col Sir Alfred Law, 2nd Bt, 1890–1968, vol. VI
Mowat, Rev. Canon John Dickson, *died* 1955, vol. V
Mowat, Sir John Gunn, 1st Bt, 1859–1935, vol. III
Mowat, Brig.-Gen. Magnus, 1875–1953, vol. V
Mowat, Hon. Sir Oliver, 1820–1903, vol. I
Mowat, Robert Anderson, 1843–1925, vol. II
Mowat, Robert Balmain, 1883–1941, vol. IV
Mowatt, Lt-Col Charles Ryder John, 1872–1943, vol. IV
Mowatt, Rt Hon. Sir Francis, 1837–1919, vol. II
Mowbray, 24th Baron, Segrave, 25th Baron, and Stourton, 21st Baron, 1867–1936, vol. III
Mowbray, 25th Baron, Segrave, 26th Baron, and Stourton, 22nd Baron, 1895–1965, vol. VI
Mowbray, Rev. Sir Edmund George Lionel, 4th Bt, 1859–1919, vol. II
Mowbray, Sir George Robert, 5th Bt, 1899–1969, vol. VI
Mowbray, Major John Leslie, 1875–1916, vol. II
Mowbray, Rt Hon. Sir John Robert, 1st Bt, 1815–1899, vol. I
Mowbray, Sir Reginald Ambrose, 3rd Bt, 1852–1916, vol. II
Mowbray, Robert, 1877–1947, vol. IV
Mowbray, Sir Robert Gray Cornish, 2nd Bt, 1850–1916, vol. II
Mower, Brian Leonard, 1934–1993, vol. IX
Mower, Sara M.; *see* Jordan, S. M.
Mowle, William Stewart, 1867–1935, vol. III

Mowlem, Rainsford, 1902–1986, vol. VIII
Mowll, Rt Rev. Edward Worsfold, 1881–1964, vol. VI
Mowll, Most Rev. Howard West Kilvinton, 1890–1958, vol. V
Mowrer, Edgar Ansel, 1892–1977, vol. VII
Moxham, Sir Harry Cuthbertson, 1879–1965, vol. VI
Moxon, Col Charles Carter, 1866–1924, vol. II
Moxon, Sir John, died 1943, vol. IV
Moxon, Rev. Canon Reginald Stewart, died 1950, vol. IV
Moxon, Ven. Robert Julius, vol. II
Moxon, Rev. Preb. Thomas Allen, 1877–1943, vol. IV
Moya, Hidalgo; see Moya, J. H.
Moya, (John) Hidalgo, 1920–1994, vol. IX
Moyer, L. Clare, 1887–1958, vol. V
Moyers, Sir George, 1836–1916, vol. II
Moyes, Rt Rev. John Stoward, 1884–1972, vol. VII
Moyes, William Henry, died 1926, vol. II
Moylan, David; see Moylan, J. D. F.
Moylan, (John) David (FitzGerald), 1915–1996, vol. X
Moylan, Sir John Fitzgerald, 1882–1967, vol. VI
Moyle, Baron (Life Peer); Arthur Moyle, 1894–1974, vol. VII
Moynan, R. T., 1856–1906, vol. I
Moyne, 1st Baron, 1880–1944, vol. IV
Moyne, 2nd Baron, 1905–1992, vol. IX
Moynihan, 1st Baron, 1865–1936, vol. III
Moynihan, 2nd Baron, 1906–1965, vol. IV
Moynihan, 3rd Baron, 1936–1991, vol. IX
Moynihan, Most Rev. Denis, 1885–1975, vol. VII
Moynihan, Sir Noël Henry, 1916–1994, vol. IX
Moynihan, Rodrigo, 1910–1990, vol. VIII
Moyse, Charles E., 1852–1924, vol. II
Moysey, Maj.-Gen. Charles John, 1840–1922, vol. II
Moysey, Edward Luttrell, 1877–1970, vol. VI
Moysey, Henry Luttrell, 1849–1918, vol. II
Mozley, Lt-Col Edward Newman, 1875–1950, vol. IV
Mozley, Rev. John Kenneth, 1883–1946, vol. IV
Mtekateka, Rt Rev. Josiah, 1903–1995, vol. IX
Muchmore, Alfred, 1893–1962, vol. VI
Mucklow, Graham Fernie, 1894–1973, vol. VII
Mudaliar, Diwan Bahadur Sir Arcot Lakshmanaswami, 1887–1974, vol. VII
Mudaliar, Diwan Bahadur Sir Arcot Ramaswami, 1887–1976, vol. VII
Mudaliar, Dewan Bahadur V. Shanmuga, 1874–1953, vol. V
Mudaliyar, Rao Bahadur C. Jumbulingam, died 1906, vol. I
Muddiman, Sir Alexander Phillips, 1875–1928, vol. II
Muddock, J. E. Preston, died 1934, vol. III
Mudford, W. H., 1839–1916, vol. II
Mudge, Brig.-Gen. Arthur, 1871–1958, vol. V
Mudhol, Lt Meherban Raja Sir Malojirao Vyankatrao Raje Ghorpade, 1884–1937, vol. III
Mudholkar, Hon. Rao Bahadur Rangnath Narsinh, 1857–1921, vol. II
Mudie, Sir Francis; see Mudie, Sir R. F.
Mudie, Sir (Robert) Francis, 1890–1976, vol. VII

Mudie, Brig. Thomas Couper, 1880–1948, vol. IV
Mudie-Smith, Richard, 1877–1916, vol. II
Muecke, Francis Frederick, 1879–1945, vol. IV
Mueller, Dame Anne Elisabeth, 1930–2000, vol. X
Mueller, Sir Ferdinand von, 1825–1897, vol. I
Muggeridge, Douglas Thomas, 1928–1985, vol. VIII
Muggeridge, Henry Thomas, 1864–1942, vol. IV
Muggeridge, Malcolm; see Muggeridge, T. M.
Muggeridge, (Thomas) Malcolm, 1903–1990, vol. VIII
Mugliston, Francis Hugh, 1886–1932, vol. III
Muhammad, Valiyaveettil Abdulaziz Seyid, 1923–1985, vol. VIII
Muhammad Amir Hasan Khan, 1849–1903, vol. I
Muhammad Fakhr-ud-Din, Khan Bahadur Sir Saiyed, died 1933, vol. III
Muhammad Iqbal, Sheikh Sir, 1876–1938, vol. III
Muhammad Rafiq, Sir, died 1929, vol. III
Muhammed Aslam Khan, Hon. Col Nawab, died 1914, vol. I
Muhrman, Henry, 1854–1916, vol. II
Muil, Maj.-Gen. David John, 1898–1982, vol. VIII
Muir, Air Cdre Adam, 1908–1986, vol. VIII
Muir, Alec Andrew, 1909–1997, vol. X
Muir, Sir (Alexander) Kay, 2nd Bt, 1868–1951, vol. V
Muir, Col Archibald Huleatt Huntly, 1886–1948, vol. IV
Muir, Augustus; see Muir, C. A. C.
Muir, (Charles) Augustus (Carlow), 1892–1989, vol. VIII
Muir, Col Charles Wemyss, 1850–1920, vol. II
Muir, Sir David John, 1916–1986, vol. VIII
Muir, Sir Edward Francis, 1905–1979, vol. VII
Muir, Sir Edward Grainger, 1906–1973, vol. VII
Muir, Edwin, 1887–1959, vol. V
Muir, Ernest, 1880–1974, vol. VII
Muir, Frank, 1920–1998, vol. X
Muir, Gordon; see Muir, W. A. G.
Muir, James, 1875–1945, vol. IV
Muir, James, died 1960, vol. V
Muir, Jean Elizabeth (Mrs Harry Leuckert), 1928–1995, vol. IX
Muir, Sir John, 1st Bt, 1828–1903, vol. I
Muir, John, 1838–1914, vol. I
Muir, Lt-Col John Balderstone, died 1955, vol. V
Muir, John Cochran, 1902–1981, vol. VIII
Muir, John Gerald Grainger, 1918–1990, vol. VIII
Muir, Sir John Harling, 3rd Bt, 1910–1994, vol. IX
Muir, John William, 1879–1931, vol. III
Muir, Sir Kay; see Muir, Sir A. K.
Muir, Kenneth Arthur, 1907–1996, vol. X
Muir, Matthew Moncrieff Pattison, 1848–1931, vol. III
Muir, Rt Rev. Pearson M'Adam, 1846–1924, vol. II
Muir, Percival Horace, 1894–1979, vol. VII
Muir, Ramsay, 1872–1941, vol. IV
Muir, Sir Richard David, 1857–1924, vol. II
Muir, Sir Robert, 1864–1959, vol. V
Muir, Ronald James Samuel, 1899–1960, vol. V
Muir, Ronald John K.; see Kerr-Muir.
Muir, Sir Thomas, 1844–1934, vol. III
Muir, Ward, 1878–1927, vol. II
Muir, Sir William, 1819–1905, vol. I
Muir, William, 1844–1929, vol. III

Muir, (William Archibald) Gordon, 1931–1981, vol. VIII
Muir, Lt-Col Wingate Wemyss, 1879–1966, vol. VI
Muir Beddall, Hugh Richard; see Beddall.
Muir-Mackenzie, 1st Baron, 1845–1930, vol. III
Muir-Mackenzie, Sir Alexander, 3rd Bt, 1840–1909, vol. I
Muir-Mackenzie, Sir John William Pitt, 1854–1916, vol. II
Muir Mackenzie, Kenneth James, 1882–1932, vol. III
Muir-Mackenzie, Montague Johnstone, 1847–1919, vol. II
Muir-Mackenzie, Sir Robert Cecil, 5th Bt, 1891–1918, vol. II
Muir Mackenzie, Sir Robert Henry, 6th Bt, 1917–1970, vol. VI
Muir-Mackenzie, Lt-Col Sir Robert Smythe, 4th Bt, 1841–1918, vol. II
Muirhead, Alexander, died 1920, vol. II
Muirhead, Alexander, 1859–1935, vol. III
Muirhead, Lt-Col Anthony John, 1890–1939, vol. III
Muirhead, Charles Alexander, 1888–1967, vol. VI
Muirhead, David, died 1930, vol. III
Muirhead, Sir David Francis, 1918–1999, vol. X
Muirhead, Findlay, 1860–1935, vol. III
Muirhead, James Fullarton, 1853–1934, vol. III
Muirhead, Lt-Col James Ingram, 1893–1964, vol. VI
Muirhead, John, 1863–1927, vol. II
Muirhead, John Henry, 1855–1940, vol. III
Muirhead, Sir John Spencer, 1889–1972, vol. VII
Muirhead, (Litellus) Russell, 1896–1976, vol. VII
Muirhead, Peter Haig, died 1958, vol. V
Muirhead, Russell; see Muirhead, L. R.
Muirshiel, 1st Viscount, 1905–1992, vol. IX
Mukerjee, Most Rev. Arabinda Nath, 1892–1970, vol. VI (AII)
Mukerjee, Radhakamal, 1889–1968, vol. VI
Mukerjee, Air Marshal Subroto, 1911–1960, vol. V
Mukerji, Sir Lal Gopal, 1874–1942, vol. IV
Mukerji, Sir Manmatha Nath, 1874–1942, vol. IV
Mukerji, Rai Bahadur P. N., 1882–1965, vol. VI
Mukle, May, 1880–1963, vol. VI
Mulcahy, Hon. Edward, 1850–1927, vol. II
Mulcahy, Maj.-Gen. Sir Francis Edward, 1857–1940, vol. III
Mulcahy, Gen. Richard, 1886–1971, vol. VII
Muldoon, John, 1865–1938, vol. III
Muldoon, Rt Hon. Sir Robert David, 1921–1992, vol. IX
Mules, Sir Charles; see Mules, Sir H. C.
Mules, Rt Rev. Charles Oliver, 1837–1927, vol. II
Mules, Sir (Horace) Charles, 1856–1939, vol. III
Mulford, Clarence Edward, 1883–1956, vol. V
Mulhall, John Archibald, 1899–1971, vol. VII
Mulhall, Michael G., 1836–1900, vol. I
Mulhern, Most Rev. Edward C., 1863–1943, vol. IV
Mulholland, Hon. Alfred John, 1856–1938, vol. III
Mulholland, Hon. (Andrew) Edward (Somerset), 1882–1914, vol. I
Mulholland, Gp Captain Denis Osmond, 1891–1949, vol. IV

Mulholland, Hon. Edward; see Mulholland, Hon. A. E. S.
Mulholland, Hon. (Godfrey) John (Arthur Murray Lyle), 1892–1948, vol. IV
Mulholland, Rt Hon. Sir Henry George Hill, 1st Bt, 1888–1971, vol. VII
Mulholland, Hon. John; see Mulholland, Hon. G. J. A. M. L.
Mulholland, Hon. Mrs John, (Olivia Vernon), 1902–1984, vol. VIII
Mulholland, Hon. Olivia Vernon; see Mulholland, Hon. Mrs John.
Mulholland, Rosa; see Gilbert, Rosa, (Lady Gilbert).
Mulholland, W., 1843–1907, vol. I
Mulholland, Sir Walter; see Mulholland, Sir W. W.
Mulholland, Sir (William) Walter, 1887–1971, vol. VII
Mulji, Rao Sahib Sir Vasanji Trikamji, 1866–1925, vol. II, vol. III
Mulla, Rt Hon. Sir Dinshah Fardunji, 1868–1934, vol. III
Mullally, Gerald Thomas, 1887–1969, vol. VI
Mullaly, Maj.-Gen. Sir Herbert, 1860–1932, vol. III
Mullaly, Joseph John, 1853–1936, vol. III
Mullan, Charles Heron, 1912–1996, vol. X
Mullan, Charles Seymour, 1893–1969, vol. VI
Mullen, Benjamin Henry, 1862–1925, vol. II
Mullen, Lt-Col John Lawrence William F.; see Ffrench-Mullen.
Mullen, Lt-Col Leslie Miltiades, 1882–1943, vol. IV
Mulleneux, Captain Hugh Bowring, 1878–1947, vol. IV
Mulleneux-Grayson, Louise Mary, (Lady Mulleneux-Grayson); see Dale, Louise.
Mullens, Sir Harold Hill, 1900–1980, vol. VII
Mullens, Sir John Ashley, 1869–1937, vol. III
Mullens, Maj.-Gen. Richard Lucas, 1871–1952, vol. V
Mullens, Sir William John Herbert de Wette, 1909–1975, vol. VII
Müller, Rt Hon. Friedrich M.; see Max-Müller.
Muller, Col George Herbert, 1856–1932, vol. III
Muller, Hermann Joseph, 1890–1967, vol. VI
Muller, Hon. Hilgard, 1914–1985, vol. VIII
Müller, Hugo, died 1915, vol. I
Muller, J. P., 1866–1938, vol. III
Muller, Lt-Col John, 1883–1942, vol. IV
Muller, Oswald Valdemar, 1868–1900, vol. I
Müller, W. Max, 1862–1919, vol. II
Muller, Walter Angus, 1898–1970, vol. VI
Muller, Sir William Grenfell M.; see Max-Muller.
Mulley, Baron (Life Peer); Frederick William Mulley, 1918–1995, vol. IX
Mullick, Sir Basanta Kumar, 1868–1931, vol. III
Mulligan, Col Hugh Waddell, 1901–1982, vol. VIII
Mulligan, James, 1847–1937, vol. III
Mulligan, Most Rev. Patrick, 1912–1991, vol. IX
Mulliken, Robert Sanderson, 1896–1986, vol. VIII
Mullin, Daniel, born 1860, vol. III
Mulliner, Ven. Harold George, 1897–1946, vol. IV
Mullinger, James Bass, died 1917, vol. II
Mullings, Sir Clement Tudway, 1874–1962, vol. VI
Mullings, Frank Coningsby, 1881–1953, vol. V
Mullins, Arthur, 1895–1963, vol. VI
Mullins, Brian Percival, 1920–1990, vol. VIII

Mullins, Major Charles Herbert, *died* 1916, vol. II
Mullins, Claud, 1887–1968, vol. VI
Mullins, Gen. George James Herbert, *died* 1943, vol. IV
Mullins, Lt-Col George Lane, 1862–1918, vol. II
Mullins, Hon. John Lane, 1857–1939, vol. III
Mullins, Leonard, 1918–1997, vol. X
Mulock, Air Cdre Redford Henry, 1886–1961, vol. VI
Mulock, Rt Hon. Sir William, 1844–1944, vol. IV
Mulvany, Charles Mathew, 1867–1945, vol. IV
Mulvany, T. R., 1839–1907, vol. I
Mulvany, Most Rev. Thomas, *died* 1943, vol. IV
Mulvey, Anthony, 1882–1957, vol. V
Mulvey, Thomas, 1863–1935, vol. III
Mumford, A. Harold, 1864–1939, vol. III
Mumford, Sir Albert Henry, 1903–1989, vol. VIII
Mumford, Henry Plevy, 1862–1941, vol. IV
Mumford, L(awrence) Quincy, 1903–1982, vol. VIII
Mumford, Lewis, 1895–1990, vol. VIII
Mumford, Rt Rev. Peter, 1922–1992, vol. IX
Mummery, Sir Hugh Evelyn L.; *see* Lockhart-Mummery.
Mummery, John Howard, 1847–1926, vol. II
Mummery, John Percy L.; *see* Lockhart-Mummery.
Mumtazud Dowlah Muhammad Faiyaz Ali Khan; *see* Faiyaz Ali Khan.
Mun, Adrien Albert Marie, Comte de, 1841–1914, vol. I
Munby, Alan Noel Latimer, 1913–1974, vol. VII
Munby, Lt-Col Aldwin Montgomery, 1882–1939, vol. III
Munby, Lt-Col Joseph Ernest, 1881–1962, vol. VI
Muncaster, 5th Baron, 1834–1917, vol. II
Muncaster, Claude, 1903–1974, vol. VII
Muncey, Rev. Edward Howard Parker, 1886–1954, vol. V
Munch, Charles, 1891–1968, vol. VI
Mundahl, Henry Smethurst, 1865–1938, vol. III
Munday, Charles Frederick, 1868–1948, vol. IV
Munday, John A., 1863–1932, vol. III
Munday, Luther, 1857–1922, vol. II
Munday, Maj.-Gen. Richard Cleveland, 1867–1952, vol. V
Munday, Sir William Luscombe, 1865–1952, vol. V
Mundelein, Cardinal George William, 1872–1939, vol. III
Mundella, Rt Hon. Anthony John, 1825–1897, vol. I
Mundy, Alfred Edward Miller, 1849–1920, vol. II
Mundy, Adm. Godfrey Harry Brydges, 1860–1928, vol. II
Mundy, John Cloudesley, 1900–1971, vol. VII
Mundy, Sir Otto, 1887–1958, vol. V
Mundy, Talbot, 1879–1940, vol. III
Munford, James, 1852–1932, vol. III
Muni, Paul, 1895–1967, vol. VI
Munir Bey, Sir Mehmed, 1890–1957, vol. V
Munn, Rt Rev. Eric George, 1903–1968, vol. VI
Munn, Mrs Marguerite; *see* Bryant, M.
Munn, Lt-Col Reginald George, *died* 1947, vol. IV
Munn, Rear-Adm. William James, 1911–1989, vol. VIII
Munnings, Sir Alfred J., 1878–1959, vol. V
Munro, Sir Alan Whiteside, 1898–1968, vol. VI

Munro, Maj.-Gen. Archibald Campbell, 1886–1961, vol. VI
Munro, Sir Arthur Herman, 14th Bt (*cr* 1634), 1893–1972, vol. VII
Munro, Sir Arthur Talbot, 13th Bt (*cr* 1634), 1866–1953, vol. V
Munro, Sir Campbell, 3rd Bt (*cr* 1825), 1823–1913, vol. I
Munro, C(harles) K.; *see* MacMullan, C. W. K.
Munro, Charles Rowcliffe, 1902–1995, vol. X(AI)
Munro, Air Vice-Marshal Sir David, 1878–1952, vol. V
Munro, Lt-Col David Campbell Duncan, 1885–1974, vol. VII
Munro, Captain Donald John, 1865–1952, vol. V
Munro, Sir George Hamilton, 12th Bt (*cr* 1634), 1864–1945, vol. IV
Munro, Sir Gordon; *see* Munro, Sir R. G.
Munro, Lt-Gen. Gustavus Francis, 1835–1908, vol. I
Munro, Sir Hector, 11th Bt (*cr* 1634), 1849–1935, vol. III
Munro, Sir Henry, 1842–1921, vol. II
Munro, Sir Hugh Thomas, 4th Bt (*cr* 1825), 1856–1919, vol. II
Munro, Ian Arthur Hoyle, 1923–1997, vol. X
Munro, Sir Ian Talbot, 15th Bt (*cr* 1634), 1929–1996, vol. X
Munro, John, *died* 1930, vol. III
Munro, John Arthur Ruskin, 1864–1944, vol. IV
Munro, John Bennet Lorimer, 1905–1993, vol. IX
Munro, Leo, 1878–1957, vol. V
Munro, Sir Leslie Knox, 1901–1974, vol. VII
Munro, Col Lewis, 1859–1927, vol. II
Munro, Neil, 1864–1930, vol. III
Munro, Patrick, 1883–1942, vol. IV
Munro of Foulis, Captain Patrick, 1912–1995, vol. IX
Munro, Sir (Richard) Gordon, 1895–1967, vol. VI
Munro, Robert, 1835–1920, vol. II
Munro, Sir Robert Lindsay, 1907–1995, vol. IX
Munro, Robert Wilson, 1915–1985, vol. VIII
Munro, Sir Thomas, 2nd Bt (*cr* 1825), 1819–1901, vol. I
Munro, Sir Thomas, 1866–1923, vol. II
Munro, Thomas Arthur Howard, 1905–1966, vol. VI
Munro, Sir (Thomas) Torquil (Alfonso), 5th Bt, 1901–1985, vol. VIII
Munro, Sir Torquil; *see* Munro, Sir T. T. A.
Munro, William, 1900–1992, vol. IX
Munro, William Bennett, 1875–1957, vol. V
Munro, William Thow, 1884–1948, vol. IV
Munro-Lucas-Tooth, Sir Hugh Vere Huntly Duff, 1st Bt, 1903–1985, vol. VIII
Munroe, Sir Harry C.; *see* Courthope-Munroe.
Munroe, Lt-Col Hon. Hugh Edwin, 1879–1947, vol. IV
Munrow, David John, 1942–1976, vol. VII
Munrow, William Davis, 1903–1986, vol. VIII
Munsey, Frank Andrew, 1854–1925, vol. II
Munster, 2nd Earl of, 1824–1901, vol. I
Munster, 3rd Earl of, 1859–1902, vol. I
Munster, 4th Earl of, 1862–1928, vol. II
Munster, 5th Earl of, 1906–1975, vol. VII

Munster, 6th Earl of, 1899–1983, vol. VIII
Munster, 7th Earl of, 1926–2000, vol. X
Munster, Countess of; (Wilhelmina), 1830–1906, vol. I
Münster Derneburg, Prince, 1820–1902, vol. I
Münsterberg, Hugo, 1863–1916, vol. II
Munthe, Axel, 1857–1949, vol. IV
Muntz, Alan; see Muntz, F. A. I.
Muntz, (Frederick) Alan (Irving), 1899–1985, vol. VIII
Muntz, Frederick Ernest, 1845–1920, vol. II
Muntz, Sir Gerard Albert, 2nd Bt, 1864–1927, vol. II
Muntz, Sir Gerard Philip Graves, 3rd Bt, 1917–1940, vol. III (A), vol. IV
Muntz, Godric; see Muntz, T. G. A.
Muntz, Hope; see Muntz, I. H.
Muntz, (Isabelle) Hope, 1907–1981, vol. VIII
Muntz, Sir Philip Albert, 1st Bt, 1839–1908, vol. I
Muntz, Thomas Godric Aylett, 1906–1986, vol. VIII
Murchie, Lt-Gen. John Carl, 1895–1966, vol. VI
Murchie, John Ivor, 1928–1999, vol. X
Murchison, Sir (Charles) Kenneth, 1872–1952, vol. V
Murchison, Sir Kenneth; see Murchison, Sir C. K.
Murchison, Very Rev. Thomas Moffat, 1907–1984, vol. VIII
Murdoch, Air Marshal Sir Alister Murray, 1912–1984, vol. VIII
Murdoch, Charles, 1902–1962, vol. VI (AII)
Murdoch, Charles, 1925–1979, vol. VII
Murdoch, Charles Stewart, 1838–1908, vol. I
Murdoch, Charles Townshend, 1837–1898, vol. I
Murdoch, Hector B.; see Burn-Murdoch.
Murdoch, Dame Iris; see Murdoch, Dame J. I.
Murdoch, Dame (Jean) Iris, (Dame Iris Bayley), 1919–1999, vol. X
Murdoch, James, 1856–1921, vol. II
Murdoch, Lt-Col Sir James Anderson, 1867–1939, vol. III
Murdoch, Rev. Canon James McGibbon B.; see Burn-Murdoch.
Murdoch, Maj.-Gen. Sir John Francis B.; see Burn-Murdoch.
Murdoch, John Smith, 1863–1945, vol. IV
Murdoch, Sir Keith Arthur, 1886–1952, vol. V
Murdoch, Richard Bernard, 1907–1990, vol. VIII
Murdoch, Robert, (Robin), 1911–1994, vol. IX
Murdoch, Robin; see Murdoch, Robert
Murdoch, Hon. Thomas, 1868–1946, vol. IV
Murdoch, W. G. Blaikie, 1880–1934, vol. III
Murdoch, W. G. Burn; see Burn-Murdoch.
Murdoch, Sir Walter, 1874–1970, vol. VI
Murdoch, William, 1888–1942, vol. IV
Murdoch, William Lloyd, 1855–1911, vol. I
Murdoch, William Ridley Morton, 1917–2000, vol. X(AII)
Murdock, Kenneth Ballard, 1895–1975, vol. VII
Mure, Geoffrey Reginald Gilchrist, 1893–1979, vol. VII
Mure, William, 1898–1977, vol. VII
Mure, William John, 1845–1924, vol. II
Murfree, Mary Noailles, died 1922, vol. II, vol. III
Murie, James, 1830–1925, vol. II

Muriel, Rev. Herbert Claude, 1867–1939, vol. III
Murison, Alexander Falconer, 1847–1934, vol. III
Murison, Alfred Ross, 1891–1968, vol. VI
Murison, Maj.-Gen. Charles Alexander Phipps, 1894–1981, vol. VIII
Murison, Sir (James) William, 1872–1945, vol. IV
Murison, Sir William; see Murison, Sir J. M.
Murland, William, 1855–1926, vol. II
Murless, Sir (Charles Francis) Noel, 1910–1987, vol. VIII
Murless, Sir Noel; see Sir C. F. N.
Murley, Sir Reginald Sydney, 1916–1997, vol. X
Murnaghan, Francis Dominic, 1893–1976, vol. VII
Murnaghan, George, 1847–1929, vol. III
Murnaghan, James Augustine, 1881–1973, vol. VII
Murphy, Sir Alexander Paterson, 1892–1976, vol. VII
Murphy, Alfred John, 1901–1980, vol. VII
Murphy, Hon. Charles, 1863–1935, vol. III
Murphy, Brig.-Gen. Cyril Francis de Sales, 1882–1961, vol. VI
Murphy, Hon. Denis, 1870–1947, vol. IV
Murphy, Sir Dermod Art Pelly, 1914–1975, vol. VII
Murphy, Rt Hon. Edward Sullivan, 1880–1945, vol. IV
Murphy, Sir Ellis; see Murphy, Sir O. E. J.
Murphy, Emily F., died 1933, vol. III
Murphy, Emmett Patrick, 1887–1960, vol. V
Murphy, Hon. Frank, 1890–1949, vol. IV
Murphy, Air Vice-Marshal Frederick John, 1892–1969, vol. VI
Murphy, George Fitzgerald, 1850–1920, vol. II
Murphy, Col George Francis, 1883–1962, vol. VI
Murphy, Sir George Francis, 2nd Bt (cr 1912), 1881–1963, vol. VI
Murphy, Col George Patterson, 1883–1938, vol. III
Murphy, Lt-Col Gerald Patrick, 1888–1978, vol. VII
Murphy, Harold Lawson, 1882–1942, vol. IV
Murphy, Most Rev. Henry, 1912–1973, vol. VII
Murphy, Rev. Hugh Davis, 1849–1927, vol. II
Murphy, Rt Hon. James, 1826–1901, vol. I
Murphy, James Francis, 1893–1949, vol. IV
Murphy, Sir James Joseph, 1st Bt (cr 1903), 1843–1922, vol. II
Murphy, James Keogh, 1869–1916, vol. II
Murphy, Very Rev. Jeremiah Matthias, died 1955, vol. V
Murphy, Very Rev. John, vol. II
Murphy, John, 1871–1930, vol. III (A), vol. IV
Murphy, Rev. John, 1876–1949, vol. IV
Murphy, Most Rev. John Aloysius, 1905–1995, vol. IX
Murphy, Rt Rev. John Baptist Tuohill, 1854–1926, vol. II
Murphy, John Harvey, 1862–1924, vol. II
Murphy, John Patrick, 1831–1907, vol. I
Murphy, (John) Pelly, 1909–1979, vol. VII
Murphy, Lionel Keith, 1922–1986, vol. VIII
Murphy, Martin, 1832–1926, vol. II
Murphy, Martin Joseph, 1862–1919, vol. II
Murphy, Sir Michael, 1st Bt (cr 1912), 1845–1925, vol. II
Murphy, Neville Richard, 1890–1971, vol. VII

Murphy, Sir (Oswald) Ellis (Joseph), 1895–1980, vol. VII (AII)
Murphy, Patrick Charles, 1868–1925, vol. II
Murphy, Pelly; see Murphy, J. P.
Murphy, Maj.-Gen. Richard, 1896–1971, vol. VII
Murphy, Richard Holmes, 1915–1994, vol. IX
Murphy, Robert Daniel, 1894–1978, vol. VII
Murphy, Sir Shirley Forster, 1848–1923, vol. II
Murphy, Stephen Dunlop, 1921–1990, vol. VIII
Murphy, Sir Stephen James, died 1950, vol. IV
Murphy, Rev. William, 1872–1943, vol. IV
Murphy, Sir William Lindsay, 1887–1965, vol. VI
Murphy, William Lombard, died 1943, vol. IV
Murphy, William Martin, 1844–1919, vol. II
Murphy, William Parry, 1892–1987, vol. VIII
Murphy, Col William Reed, 1849–1927, vol. II
Murrant, Sir Ernest Henry, 1889–1974, vol. VII
Murray, Rt Hon. Lord; Charles David Murray, 1866–1936, vol. III
Murray of Elibank, 1st Baron, 1870–1920, vol. II
Murray of Gravesend, Baron (Life Peer); Albert James Murray, 1930–1980, vol. VII
Murray of Newhaven, Baron (Life Peer); Keith Anderson Hope Murray, 1903–1993, vol. IX
Murray, Abijah, died 1912, vol. I
Murray, Adam George, 1893–1966, vol. VI
Murray, Alan James Ruthven-, 1900–1959, vol. V
Murray of Blackbarony, Sir Alan John Digby, 14th Bt (cr 1628), 1909–1978, vol. VII
Murray, Alastair Campbell, 1895–1957, vol. V
Murray, Albert E., 1849–1924, vol. II
Murray, Albert Victor, 1890–1967, vol. VI
Murray, Col Alexander, 1850–1910, vol. I
Murray, Alexander Davidson, 1840–1907, vol. I
Murray, Alexander Henry Hallam, 1854–1934, vol. III
Murray, Major Alexander Penrose, 1863–1926, vol. II
Murray, Sir Alexander Robertson, 1872–1956, vol. V
Murray, Alexander Stuart, 1841–1904, vol. I
Murray, Sir Alistair; see Murray, Sir R. A.
Murray, Alma, 1854–1945, vol. IV
Murray, Col Andrew, 1837–1915, vol. I
Murray, Hon. Andrew David, 1863–1901, vol. I
Murray, Sir Andrew Hunter Arbuthnot, 1903–1977, vol. VII
Murray, Angus, 1919–1982, vol. VIII
Murray, Sir Angus Johnston, died 1968, vol. VI
Murray, Maj.-Gen. Anthony Hepburn, 1840–1917, vol. II
Murray, Gen. Sir Archibald James, 1860–1945, vol. IV
Murray, Lt-Col Arthur Alexander W.; see Wolfe-Murray.
Murray, Lt-Col Arthur E.; see Erskine-Murray.
Murray, Adm. Arthur John Layard, 1886–1959, vol. V
Murray, Col Arthur Mordaunt, 1852–1920, vol. II
Murray, Brian, 1933–1993, vol. IX
Murray, Rear-Adm. Sir Brian Stewart, 1921–1991, vol. IX
Murray, Catherine Joan Suzette; see Gauvain, C. J. S.
Murray, Cecil James Boyd, 1910–1991, vol. IX

Murray, Charles, 1864–1941, vol. IV
Murray, Lt-Col Charles Crawford, 1863–1939, vol. III
Murray, Rt Hon. Charles David; see Murray, Rt Hon. Lord.
Murray, Charles de Bois, 1891–1974, vol. VII
Murray, Gp-Captain Charles Geoffrey, 1880–1962, vol. VI
Murray, Rt Rev. Charles Herbert, 1899–1950, vol. IV
Murray, Charles James, 1851–1929, vol. III
Murray, Charles Oliver, died 1924, vol. II
Murray, Charles Stewart, 1858–1903, vol. I
Murray, Charles Wadsworth, 1894–1945, vol. IV
Murray, Col Sir (Charles) Wyndham, 1844–1928, vol. II
Murray, Colin Alexander, 1847–1913, vol. I
Murray, Colin Robert Baillie, 1892–1979, vol. VII
Murray, Lt-Col Cyril Francis Tyrell, 1863–1929, vol. III
Murray, David, 1842–1928, vol. II
Murray, Sir David, 1849–1933, vol. III
Murray, David Christie, 1847–1907, vol. I
Murray, Col David Keith, 1865–1952, vol. V
Murray, David King; see Birnam, Hon. Lord.
Murray, David Leslie, 1888–1962, vol. VI
Murray of Blackbarony, Sir Digby, 11th Bt (cr 1628), 1829–1906, vol. I
Murray, Donald, 1862–1923, vol. II
Murray, Sir Donald Frederick, 1924–1998, vol. X
Murray, Col Donald Norman Watson, 1876–1945, vol. IV
Murray, Rev. Canon Edmund Theodore, 1877–1969, vol. VI
Murray, Edward C.; see Croft-Murray.
Murray, Paymaster Rear-Adm. Edward F., 1877–1933, vol. III
Murray, Lt-Col Sir Edward Robert, 13th Bt (cr 1626), 1875–1958, vol. V
Murray, Sir Evelyn; see Murray, Sir G. E. P.
Murray, Everitt George Dunne, 1890–1964, vol. VI
Murray, Brig. Francis Mackenzie, 1880–1958, vol. V
Murray, Sir (Francis) Ralph (Hay), 1908–1983, vol. VIII
Murray, Col Frank, 1864–1917, vol. II
Murray, Ven. Frederic Richardson, 1845–1925, vol. II
Murray, Rev. Frederick William, died 1913, vol. I
Murray, Sir George, 1865–1942, vol. IV
Murray, Brig. Sir (George David) Keith, 1898–1965, vol. VI
Murray, Sir (George) Evelyn (Pemberton), 1880–1947, vol. IV
Murray, (George) Gilbert (Aimé), 1866–1957, vol. V
Murray, Hon. George Henry, 1861–1929, vol. III
Murray, Rt Hon. Sir George Herbert, 1849–1936, vol. III
Murray, Hon. Sir George John Robert, 1863–1942, vol. IV
Murray, George McIntosh, 1900–1970, vol. VI
Murray, George Raymond B.; see Beasley-Murray
Murray, George Redmayne, died 1939, vol. III
Murray, George Robert Milne, 1858–1911, vol. I

Murray, Sir George Sheppard, 1851–1928, vol. II
Murray, George William Welsh, 1885–1966, vol. VI
Murray, Most Rev. Gerald, *died* 1951, vol. V
Murray, Gilbert; *see* Murray, G. G. A.
Murray, Gladstone; *see* Murray, W. E. G.
Murray, Greig; *see* Murray, J. G.
Murray, Lt-Col Henry William, 1883–1966, vol. VI
Murray, Lt-Col Herbert Edward, 1889–1951, vol. V
Murray, Sir Herbert Harley, 1829–1904, vol. I
Murray, Herbert Leith, 1880–1932, vol. III
Murray, Rear-Adm. Herbert Patrick William George, 1880–1958, vol. V
Murray, Gen. Sir Horatius, 1903–1989, vol. VIII
Murray, Howard, 1859–1930, vol. III
Murray, Lt-Col Howard, 1876–1934, vol. III
Murray, Sir Hubert; *see* Murray, Sir J. H. P.
Murray, Hubert Leonard, 1886–1963, vol. VI
Murray, Hubert Montague, 1855–1907, vol. I
Murray, Sir Hugh, 1861–1941, vol. IV
Murray, Ian, 1899–1974, vol. VII
Murray, Sir (Jack) Keith, 1889–1979, vol. VII
Murray, Rt Rev. James, 1828–1909, vol. I
Murray, James, 1865–1914, vol. I
Murray, Sir James, 1850–1932, vol. III
Murray, James Alexander, 1873–1950, vol. IV
Murray, Sir James Augustus Henry, 1837–1915, vol. I
Murray, James Dalton, 1911–1984, vol. VIII
Murray, James Dixon, 1887–1965, vol. VI
Murray, James Greig, 1919–1987, vol. VIII
Murray, James Patrick, 1906–1993, vol. IX
Murray, James Whiteford, *died* 1941, vol. IV
Murray, Lt-Gen. Sir James Wolfe, 1853–1919, vol. II
Murray, Captain James Wolfe, 1880–1930, vol. III
Murray, Sir John, 1841–1914, vol. I
Murray, Sir John, 1851–1928, vol. II
Murray, John, 1883–1937, vol. III
Murray, John, 1863–1943, vol. IV
Murray, John, 1871–1954, vol. V
Murray, John, 1879–1964, vol. VI
Murray, Sir John, 1884–1967, vol. VI
Murray, Engr Captain John Adam, 1860–1948, vol. IV
Murray, John Arnaud Robin Grey, 1909–1993, vol. IX
Murray of Blackbarony, Sir John Digby, 12th Bt (*cr* 1628), 1867–1938, vol. III
Murray, John George, 1864–1953, vol. V
Murray, Lt-Col John Hanna, *died* 1959, vol. V
Murray, Sir (John) Hubert (Plunkett), 1861–1940, vol. III
Murray, Gen. Sir John Irvine, 1826–1902, vol. I
Murray, Sir John Murray, 1888–1976, vol. VII
Murray, Rev. John Oswald, 1869–1943, vol. IV
Murray, Rev. John Owen Farquhar, 1858–1944, vol. IV
Murray, John Pears, 1866–1947, vol. IV (A), vol. V
Murray, Sir (John) Stanley, 1884–1971, vol. VII
Murray, Katherine Maud Elisabeth, 1909–1998, vol. X
Murray, Brig. Sir Keith; *see* Murray, Brig. Sir G. D. K.
Murray, Sir Keith; *see* Murray, Sir J. K.

Murray, Keith Day Pearce, 1892–1981, vol. VIII
Murray, Keith William, 1860–1922, vol. II
Murray of Blackbarony, Sir Kenelm Bold, 13th Bt (*cr* 1628), 1898–1959, vol. V
Murray, Col Kenelm Digby, 1839–1915, vol. I
Murray, Col Kenelm Digby Bold, 1879–1947, vol. IV
Murray, Sir Kenneth, 1891–1979, vol. VII
Murray, Rear-Adm. Leonard Warren, 1896–1971, vol. VII
Murray, Lt-Col Sir Malcolm Donald, 1867–1938, vol. III
Murray, (Malcolm) Patrick, 1905–1979, vol. VII
Murray, Margaret Alice, 1863–1963, vol. VI
Murray, Margaret Mary Alberta, *died* 1974, vol. VII
Murray, Sir Norman McIver, *died* 1934, vol. III
Murray, Sir Oswyn Alexander Ruthven, 1873–1936, vol. III
Murray, Patrick; *see* Murray, M. P.
Murray, Sir Patrick Ian Keith, 10th Bt (*cr* 1673), 1904–1962, vol. VI
Murray, Sir Patrick Keith, 8th Bt (*cr* 1673), 1835–1921, vol. II
Murray, Peter, 1915–2000, vol. X
Murray, Peter John, 1920–1992, vol. IX
Murray, Philip, 1886–1952, vol. V
Murray, Sir Ralph; *see* Murray, Sir F. R. H.
Murray, Richard, 1865–1925, vol. II
Murray, Sir Robert, 1846–1924, vol. II
Murray, Robert, 1870–1950, vol. IV
Murray, Sir (Robert) Alistair, 1896–1973, vol. VII
Murray, Col Robert Davidson, 1851–1920, vol. II
Murray, Rev. Canon Robert Henry, *died* 1947, vol. IV
Murray, Robert Howson, 1882–1960, vol. V
Murray, Maj.-Gen. Robert Hunter, 1847–1925, vol. II
Murray, Rear-Adm. Ronald Gordon, 1898–1975, vol. VII
Murray, Ronald Ormiston, 1912–1995, vol. IX
Murray, Major Hon. Ronald Thomas Graham, 1875–1934, vol. III
Murray, Sir Rowland William Patrick, 14th Bt (*cr* 1630), 1910–1994, vol. X(AI)
Murray, Col Shadwell John, 1867–1940, vol. III
Murray, Sir Stanley; *see* Murray, Sir J. S.
Murray, Lt-Col Stewart George Cromartie, 1884–1932, vol. III
Murray, T. C., 1873–1959, vol. V
Murray, T. Douglas, 1841–1911, vol. I
Murray, Brig. Terence Desmond, 1891–1961, vol. VI
Murray, Thomas J., 1880–1936, vol. III
Murray, Hon. Sir Thomas Keir, 1854–1936, vol. III
Murray, Brig.-Gen. Sir Valentine, 1867–1942, vol. IV
Murray, Violet Cecil, 1885–1961, vol. VI
Murray, Rev. W. Rigby, *died* 1914, vol. I
Murray, Walter Charles, 1866–1946, vol. IV
Murray, Lt-Col Walter Graham, 1868–1937, vol. III
Murray, Major William, 1865–1923, vol. II
Murray, William Alexander, 1889–1935, vol. III
Murray, Lt-Col William Atholl, 1879–1953, vol. V
Murray, (William Ewart) Gladstone, 1893–1970, vol. VI

Murray, Rev. William Hill, 1843–1911, vol. I
Murray, Brig.-Gen. William Hugh Eric, 1858–1915, vol. I
Murray, Sir William Keith, 9th Bt (*cr* 1673), 1872–1956, vol. V
Murray, Sir William Patrick Keith, 11th Bt (*cr* 1673), 1939–1977, vol. VII
Murray, Sir William Robert, 12th Bt (*cr* 1626), 1840–1904, vol. I
Murray, William Staite, 1881–1962, vol. VI
Murray, Col Sir Wyndham; *see* Murray, Col Sir C. W.
Murray-Aynsley, Sir Charles Murray, 1893–1967, vol. VI
Murray Baillie, Lt-Col Frederick David, 1862–1924, vol. II
Murray-Brown, Gilbert Alexander, 1893–1981, vol. VIII
Murray-Harvey, Captain Edward, 1886–1967, vol. VI
Murray-Philipson, Hylton Ralph; *see* Philipson.
Murray-Smith, Lt-Col Arthur, 1868–1943, vol. IV
Murray-Threipland, Col William, 1866–1942, vol. IV
Murray-White, Col Richard Stephen; *see* White.
Murrell, Frank Edric Joseph, 1874–1931, vol. III
Murrell, William, 1853–1912, vol. I
Murrell, William Lee, 1893–1971, vol. VII
Murrie, Sir William Stuart, 1903–1994, vol. IX
Murrill, Herbert Henry John, 1909–1952, vol. V
Murrough, John Patrick, 1822–1901, vol. I
Murrow, Edward Roscoe, 1908–1965, vol. VI
Murry, John Middleton, 1889–1957, vol. V
Murshedabad, Nawab Bahadur of, 1846–1906, vol. I
Murshidabad, Nawab Bahadur of, 1875–1959, vol. V (A)
Murton, Sir Walter, 1836–1927, vol. II
Muscat, HH The Sultan of, *died* 1913, vol. I
Muschamp, Rt Rev. Cecil Emerson Barron, 1902–1984, vol. VIII
Muschamp, Sidney, *died* 1929, vol. III
Muscio, Bernard, 1887–1926, vol. II
Muscroft, Harold Colin, 1924–1999, vol. X
Muselier, Vice-Am. d'Escadre Emile Henry, 1882–1965, vol. VI
Musgrave, Hon. Anthony, 1849–1912, vol. I
Musgrave, Brig.-Gen. Arthur David, 1874–1931, vol. III
Musgrave, Sir Charles, 14th Bt (*cr* 1611), 1913–1970, vol. VI
Musgrave, Charles Edwin, 1861–1923, vol. II
Musgrave, Sir Christopher George, 1855–1929, vol. III
Musgrave, Lt-Col Sir Christopher Norman, 6th Bt (*cr* 1782), 1892–1956, vol. V
Musgrave, Clifford, 1904–1982, vol. VIII
Musgrave, Sir Courtenay; *see* Musgrave, Sir N. C.
Musgrave, Sir Cyril; *see* Musgrave, Sir F. C.
Musgrave, Dennis Charles, 1921–1999, vol. X
Musgrave, Ernest Illingworth, 1901–1957, vol. V
Musgrave, Sir (Frank) Cyril, 1900–1986, vol. VIII
Musgrave, Major Herbert, 1876–1918, vol. II
Musgrave, Herbert Wenman W.; *see* Wykeham-Musgrave.

Musgrave, Sir James, 1st Bt (*cr* 1897), 1829–1904, vol. I
Musgrave, John, 1920–2000, vol. X
Musgrave, Sir (Nigel) Courtenay, 13th Bt (*cr* 1611), 1896–1957, vol. V
Musgrave, Noel Henry, 1903–1971, vol. VII
Musgrave, Sir Richard George, 12th Bt (*cr* 1611), 1872–1926, vol. II
Musgrave, Sir Richard James, 7th Bt (*cr* 1782), 1922–2000, vol. X
Musgrave, Sir Richard John, 5th Bt (*cr* 1782), 1850–1930, vol. III
Musgrave, Rev. Vernon, *died* 1906, vol. I
Musgrave, James, 1862–1935, vol. III
Mushin, William Woolf, 1910–1993, vol. IX
Musker, Sir John Harold, 1906–1992, vol. IX
Muskerry, 4th Baron, 1854–1929, vol. III
Muskerry, 5th Baron, 1874–1952, vol. V
Muskerry, 6th Baron, 1875–1954, vol. V
Muskerry, 7th Baron, 1874–1966, vol. VI
Muskerry, 8th Baron, 1907–1988, vol. VIII
Muskett, Arthur Edmund, 1900–1984, vol. VIII
Muskie, Edmund Sixtus, 1914–1996, vol. X
Muspratt, Edmund Knowles, 1833–1923, vol. II
Muspratt, Brig.-Gen. Francis Clifton, 1864–1944, vol. IV
Muspratt, Sir Max, 1st Bt, 1872–1934, vol. III
Muspratt, Gen. Sir Sydney Frederick, 1878–1972, vol. VII
Muspratt-Williams, Lt-Col Charles Augustus, 1861–1925, vol. II
Musselwhite, Ven. William Ralph, 1887–1956, vol. V
Mussen, Sir Gerald, 1872–1960, vol. V
Mussen, Surgeon Rear-Adm. Robert Walsh, 1900–1985, vol. VIII
Mussenden, Maj.-Gen. William, 1836–1910, vol. I
Mussolini, Benito, 1883–1945, vol. IV
Musson, Maj.-Gen. Alfred Henry, 1900–1995, vol. IX
Musson, Maj.-Gen. Arthur Ingram, 1877–1961, vol. VI
Musson, Dame Ellen Mary, 1867–1960, vol. V
Musson, Francis William, 1894–1962, vol. VI
Musson, Samuel Dixon, 1908–1992, vol. IX
Musters, Col John Nevile C.; *see* Chaworth-Musters.
Musters, John Patricius Chaworth, 1860–1921, vol. II
Musto, Sir Arnold Albert, 1883–1977, vol. VII
Mustoe, Nelson Edwin, *died* 1976, vol. VII
Musurus Pasha, Stephen, 1841–1907, vol. I
Mutch, Air Cdre James Richard, 1905–1973, vol. VII
Mutch, Nathan, 1886–1982, vol. VIII
Muther, Richard, 1860–1909, vol. I
Muthiah Chettiar, Sir M. C. T., 1887–1929, vol. III
Mutter, Rev. Cecil G., 1876–1942, vol. IV
Muzammilullah Khan, Khan Bahadur Nawab Sir Muhammad, *died* 1938, vol. III
Mwendwa, Hon. Maluki Kitili, 1929–1985, vol. VIII
Myburgh, Brig. Philip Stafford, 1893–1963, vol. VI
Myddelton, Lt-Col Ririd, 1902–1988, vol. VIII
Myddelton, Robert Edward, 1866–1949, vol. IV

Myer, Lt-Col George Val., 1883–1959, vol. V
Myer, Horatio, 1850–1916, vol. II
Myer, Dame (Margery) Merlyn Baillieu, 1900–1982, vol. VIII
Myer, Dame Merlyn Baillieu; see Myer, Dame M. M. B.
Myer, Sir Norman, 1897–1956, vol. V
Myers, Hon. Sir Arthur, 1867–1926, vol. II
Myers, Arthur Wallis, 1878–1939, vol. III
Myers, Asher Isaac, 1848–1902, vol. I
Myers, Bernard, 1872–1957, vol. V
Myers, Rev. Canon Charles, 1856–1948, vol. IV
Myers, Charles Samuel, 1873–1946, vol. IV
Myers, David Milton, 1911–1999, vol. X
Myers, Sir Dudley Borron, 1861–1944, vol. IV
Myers, Brig. Edmund Charles Wolf, 1906–1997, vol. X
Myers, Most Rev. Edward, 1875–1956, vol. V
Myers, Frederic W. H., 1843–1901, vol. I
Myers, Harry Eric 1914–1996, vol. X
Myers, Sir James Eckersley, 1890–1958, vol. V
Myers, Sir Kenneth Ben, 1907–1998, vol. X
Myers, Leo Hamilton, 1881–1944, vol. IV
Myers, Leonard William, died 1962, vol. VI
Myers, Mark, 1930–1990, vol. VIII
Myers, Rt Hon. Sir Michael, 1873–1950, vol. IV
Myers, Tom, 1872–1949, vol. IV
Myers, William Henry, 1854–1933, vol. III
Myerson, Aubrey Selwyn, 1926–1986, vol. VIII

Myint, Hla, 1920–1989, vol. VIII
Myles, Captain Edgar Kinghorn, 1894–1977, vol. VII
Myles, Sir Thomas, 1857–1937, vol. III
Myles, Surg.-Captain Thomas William, 1878–1933, vol. III
Mylks, Gordon Wright, 1874–1957, vol. V
Mylne, Rev. Alan Moultrie, 1886–1944, vol. IV
Mylne, Rt Rev. Louis George, 1843–1921, vol. II
Mynett, George Kenneth, 1913–1984, vol. VIII
Mynors, Rev. Aubrey Baskerville, 1865–1937, vol. III
Mynors, Sir Humphrey Charles Baskerville, 1st Bt, 1903–1989, vol. VIII
Mynors, Sir Roger Aubrey Baskerville, 1903–1989, vol. VIII
Myrander; see Stevenson, James Alexander.
Myrdal, Alva, 1902–1986, vol. VIII
Myrdal, Gunnar; see Myrdal, K. G.
Myrdal, (Karl) Gunnar, 1898–1987, vol. VIII
Myrddin-Evans, Sir Guildhaume, 1894–1964, vol. VI
Myres, Sir John Linton, 1869–1954, vol. V
Myres, John Nowell Linton, 1902–1989, vol. VIII
Myres, Nowell; see Myres, J. N. L.
Mysore, HH Maharaja of, 1884–1940, vol. III
Mysore, HH Maharaja of, 1919–1974, vol. VII
Mysore, Yuvaraja of, 1888–1940, vol. III
Mytton, Sir Thomas Henry, 1878–1966, vol. VI

N

Nabarro, David Nunes, 1874–1958, vol. V
Nabarro, Sir Gerald David Nunes, 1913–1973, vol. VII
Nabarro, Sir John David Nunes, 1915–1998, vol. X
Nabha, HH Rajah, 1843–1911, vol. I
Nabokov, Vladimir, 1899–1977, vol. VII
Nadesan, Sir S. P.; see Pararajasingam, Sir S.
Nadia, Maharaja of, 1890–1928, vol. II
Naef, Sir Conrad James, 1871–1954, vol. V
Naegeli, Otto, died 1938, vol. III (A), vol. IV
Naesmith, Sir Andrew, 1888–1961, vol. VI
Naesmyth, Sir Douglas Arthur Bradley, 8th Bt, 1905–1928, vol. II
Naesmyth, Sir James Tolmé, 7th Bt, 1864–1922, vol. II
Naesmyth, Sir Michael George, 6th Bt, 1828–1907, vol. I
Nagar, Raja Sir Sikander Khan of, died 1940, vol. III
Nageon de Lestang, Sir Clement; see Nageon de Lestang, Sir M. C. E. C.
Nageon de Lestang, Sir (Marie Charles Emmanuel) Clement, 1910–1986, vol. VIII
Nagogo, Alhaji Hon. Sir Usuman, died 1981, vol. VIII
Nahum, Jack Messoud Eric di Victor, 1906–1959, vol. V
Naidu, Mme Sarojini, died 1949, vol. IV
Nailor, Peter, 1928–1996, vol. X

Naipaul, Shivadhar Srinivasa, 1945–1985, vol. VIII
Nair, Rt Hon. Sir Chettur Madhavan, 1879–1970, vol. VI (AII)
Nair, Sir Chettur S.; see Sankaran Nair.
Nairac, Hon. Sir André Lawrence, 1905–1981, vol. VIII
Nairac, Sir Edouard; see Nairac, Sir G. E.
Nairac, Sir (George) Edouard, 1876–1960, vol. V (A), vol. VI (AI)
Nairn, Bryce James Miller, 1903–1978, vol. VII
Nairn, Sir Douglas Leslie Spencer-, 2nd Bt, 1906–1970, vol. VI
Nairn, Sir George; see Nairn, Sir M. G.
Nairn, George Alexander Stokes, 1889–1974, vol. VII
Nairn, Rev. John Arbuthnot, 1874–1957, vol. V
Nairn, Air Vice-Marshal Kenneth Gordon, 1898–1988, vol. IX(AI)
Nairn, Sir Michael, 2nd Bt, 1874–1952, vol. V
Nairn, Sir Michael Barker, 1st Bt, 1838–1915, vol. I
Nairn, Sir (Michael) George, 3rd Bt, 1911–1984, vol. VIII
Nairn, Major Sir Robert S.; see Spencer-Nairn.
Nairn, Walter Maxwell, died 1958, vol. V
Nairne, Lady, (12th in succession) 1912–1995, vol. IX
Nairne, Rev. Alexander, 1863–1936, vol. III
Nairne, Gen. Sir Charles Edward, 1836–1899, vol. I
Nairne, Major Lord Charles George Francis M.; see Mercer-Nairne.

Nairne, Brig.-Gen. Edward Spencer Hoare, 1869–1958, vol. V
Nairne, Sir Gordon; see Nairne, Sir J. G.
Nairne, Rev. John Domett, 1846–1929, vol. III
Nairne, Sir (John) Gordon, 1st Bt, 1861–1945, vol. IV
Nairne, Sir Perceval Alleyn, 1841–1921, vol. II
Naisby, John Vickers, 1894–1983, vol. VIII
Naish, Albert Ernest, 1871–1964, vol. VI
Naish, Rear-Adm. George Oswald, 1904–1960, vol. V
Naish, Lt-Comdr George Prideaux Brabant, 1909–1977, vol. VII
Naish, John Paull, died 1964, vol. VI
Naish, Redmond, born 1848, vol. II
Naismith, Lt-Col William John, 1847–1926, vol. II
Nalder, Hon. Sir Crawford David, 1910–1994, vol. IX
Nalder, Leonard Fielding, 1888–1958, vol. V
Nalder, Maj.-Gen. Reginald Francis Heaton, 1895–1978, vol. VII
Naldrett, Edward James, died 1930, vol. III
Nall, J(ohn) Spencer, 1887–1970, vol. VI
Nall, Col Sir Joseph, 1st Bt, 1887–1958, vol. V
Nally, Will, 1914–1965, vol. VI
Namier, Sir Lewis Bernstein, 1888–1960, vol. V
Nan Kivell, Sir Rex de Charambac, 1899–1977, vol. VII
Nanak Chand, Masheerud-dowla Rai Bahadur, 1860–1920, vol. II, vol. III
Nanavati, Sir Manilal B., 1877–1967, vol. VI
Nanavatty, Col Sir Byramji Hormasji, 1861–1937, vol. III
Nance, Surg.-Captain Sir Arthur Stanley, 1860–1938, vol. III
Nance, Francis James, 1915–1995, vol. IX
Nance, Rev. James Trengove, 1852–1942, vol. IV
Nand Lal, Diwan Bahadur Pandit, 1857–1926, vol. II
Nandris, Grigore, 1895–1968, vol. VI
Nanjundayya, H. Velpanuru, 1860–1920, vol. II
NanKivell, Sir Rex de Charambac; see Nan Kivell.
Nannetti, Joseph Patrick, 1851–1915, vol. I
Nansen, Fridtjof, 1861–1930, vol. III
Nanson, Edward John, 1850–1936, vol. III
Nanson, Group Captain Eric Roper-Curzon, 1883–1960, vol. V
Nanson, Hon. John Leighton, 1863–1916, vol. II
Nantel, Hon. Wilfrid Bruno, 1857–1940, vol. III (A), vol. IV
Nanton, Sir Augustus Meredith, 1860–1925, vol. II
Nanton, Brig.-Gen. Herbert Colbourne, 1863–1935, vol. III
Naoroji, Dadabhai, 1825–1917, vol. II
Naper, Captain William Lenox, 1879–1942, vol. IV
Napier, 10th Lord, and Ettrick, 1st Baron, 1819–1898, vol. I
Napier, 11th Lord, and Ettrick, 2nd Baron, 1846–1913, vol. I
Napier, 12th Lord, and Ettrick, 3rd Baron, 1876–1941, vol. IV
Napier, 13th Lord, and Ettrick, 4th Baron, 1900–1954, vol. V
Napier of Magdala, 2nd Baron, 1845–1921, vol. II
Napier of Magdala, 3rd Baron, 1849–1935, vol. III

Napier of Magdala, 4th Baron, 1861–1948, vol. IV
Napier of Magdala, 5th Baron, 1904–1987, vol. VIII
Napier, Hon. Sir Albert Edward Alexander, 1881–1973, vol. VII
Napier, Albert Napier Williamson, 1894–1969, vol. VI
Napier, Col Alexander, 1851–1928, vol. II
Napier, Captain Sir Alexander Lennox Milliken, 11th Bt (cr 1627), 1882–1954, vol. V
Napier, Sir Archibald Lennox Milliken, 10th Bt (cr 1627), 1855–1907, vol. I
Napier, Arthur Sampson, 1853–1916, vol. II
Napier, Barbara Langmuir, 1914–1991, vol. IX
Napier, Charles Frederick, 1862–1932, vol. III
Napier, Charles Goddard, 1889–1978, vol. VII
Napier, Adm. Charles Lionel, 1861–1934, vol. III
Napier, Col Charles Scott, 1899–1946, vol. IV
Napier, Major Egbert, 1867–1916, vol. II
Napier, Lt-Col Hon. George Campbell, 1845–1914, vol. I
Napier, Lt-Col Hon. Henry Dundas, 1864–1941, vol. IV
Napier, Ian Patrick Robert, 1895–1977, vol. VII
Napier, Brig. John Lenox Clavering, 1898–1966, vol. VI
Napier, Hon. Sir (John) Mellis, 1882–1976, vol. VII
Napier, Col Hon. John Scott, 1848–1938, vol. III
Napier, Sir Joseph William Lennox, 4th Bt, 1895–1986, vol. VIII
Napier, Lionel Everard, 1888–1957, vol. V
Napier, Hon. Mark Francis, 1852–1919, vol. II
Napier, Hon. Sir Mellis; see Napier, Hon. Sir J. M.
Napier, Rev. Michael Scott, 1929–1996, vol. X
Napier, Sir Robert Archibald, 12th Bt (cr 1627), 1889–1965, vol. VI
Napier, Sir Robin Surtees, 5th Bt (cr 1867), 1932–1994, vol. IX
Napier, Thomas Bateman, 1854–1933, vol. III
Napier, Vice-Adm. Sir Trevylyan Dacres Willes, 1867–1920, vol. II
Napier, Brig. Vernon Monro Colquhoun, 1881–1957, vol. V
Napier, Brig. Vivian John Lennox, 1898–1990, vol. VIII
Napier, Sir Walter John, 1857–1945, vol. IV
Napier, Col William, 1861–1920, vol. II, vol. III
Napier, Sir William Archibald, 13th Bt, 1915–1990, vol. VIII
Napier, William Heathcote Unwin, died 1959, vol. V
Napier, Maj.-Gen. William John, 1863–1925, vol. II
Napier, Sir William Lennox, 3rd Bt (cr 1867), 1867–1915, vol. I
Napier, Adm. William Rawdon, 1877–1951, vol. V
Napier-Clavering, Col Charles Warren, 1858–1931, vol. III
Napier-Clavering, Maj.-Gen. Noel Warren, 1888–1964, vol. VI
Napley, Sir David, 1915–1994, vol. IX
Napoleon, Prince Louis, 1864–1932, vol. III
Napoleon, HIH Prince (Victor Jerome Frederic), 1862–1926, vol. II
Napper, Jack Hollingworth, 1904–1978, vol. VII
Narain, Sir Sathi, 1919–1989, vol. IX(AI)
Narang, Sir Gokul Chand, 1878–1970, vol. VI

Narasimha Gopalaswami Ayyangar, Sir, 1882–1953, vol. V
Narasimha Sarma, Rao Bahadur Sir Bayya, 1867–1932, vol. III
Naratomdas, Sir Harkisandas, 1849–1908, vol. I
Narayan, Rudy, 1938–1998, vol. X
Narayan Kissen Sen, 1861–1935, vol. III
Narbeth, John Harper, 1863–1944, vol. IV
Narborough, Rt Rev. Dudley Vaughan; *see* Narborough, Rt Rev. F. D. V.
Narborough, Rt Rev. (Frederick) Dudley Vaughan, 1895–1966, vol. VI
Narendra, Krishna, Sir, Maharaja Bahadur, 1822–1903, vol. I
Nares, Maj.-Gen. Eric Paytherus, 1892–1947, vol. IV
Nares, Sir George Strong, 1831–1915, vol. I
Nares, Vice-Adm. John Dodd, 1877–1957, vol. V
Nares, Owen Ramsay, *died* 1943, vol. IV
Nariman, Sir Temulji Bhicaji, 1848–1940, vol. III
Narracott, Arthur Henson, 1905–1967, vol. VI
Narsingarh, Sahib Bahadur of, 1887–1924, vol. II
Nash, Rev. Adam James Glendinning, *died* 1920, vol. II
Nash, Rev. Alexander, 1845–1924, vol. II
Nash, Alfred William, 1886–1942, vol. IV
Nash, (Denis Frederic) Ellison, 1913–2000, vol. X
Nash, Ellison; *see* Nash, D. F. E.
Nash, Eveleigh, 1873–1956, vol. V
Nash, Captain Geoffrey Stewart Fleetwood, 1883–1936, vol. III
Nash, George Howard, 1881–1950, vol. IV
Nash, Gilbert John, 1905–1974, vol. VII
Nash, Rev. Glendinning, *died* 1915, vol. I
Nash, Brig.-Gen. Henry Edmund Palmer, 1869–1949, vol. IV
Nash, Rt Rev. James Okey, 1862–1943, vol. IV
Nash, Rev. James Palmer, 1842–1915, vol. I
Nash, John Brady, *born* 1857, vol. II
Nash, John Kevin Tyrie Llewellyn, 1922–1981, vol. VIII
Nash, John Northcote, 1893–1977, vol. VII
Nash, Joseph, *died* 1922, vol. II
Nash, Kenneth Twigg, 1918–1981, vol. VIII
Nash, Kevin; *see* Nash, J. K. T. L.
Nash, Col Llewellyn Thomas Manly, 1861–1928, vol. II
Nash, Norman E. Keown, 1885–1966, vol. VI
Nash, Ogden, 1902–1971, vol. VII
Nash, Paul, 1889–1946, vol. IV
Nash, Maj.-Gen. Sir Philip Arthur Manley, 1875–1936, vol. III
Nash, Rev. Robert Seymour, 1822–1904, vol. I
Nash, Thomas Arthur Manly, 1905–1993, vol. IX
Nash, Vaughan, 1861–1932, vol. III
Nash, Sir Vincent, 1865–1942, vol. IV
Nash, Rt Hon. Sir Walter, 1882–1968, vol. VI
Nash, Major William Fleetwood, 1861–1915, vol. I
Nash, William Harry, 1848–1929, vol. III
Nash-Williams, Victor Erle, 1897–1955, vol. V
Nashimoto, Morimasa, Prince, 1874–1951, vol. V
Nasim Ali, Sir Syed, *died* 1946, vol. IV
Nasir, Rt Rev. Eric Samuel, 1916–1987, vol. VIII
Nasir-El-Mulk, Abdul Kassim Khan, 1858–1927, vol. II

Nasmith, Rear Adm. David Arthur D.; *see* Dunbar-Nasmith.
Nasmith, Adm. Sir Martin Eric Dunbar-, *died* 1965, vol. VI
Nasmyth, Thomas Goodall, *died* 1937, vol. III
Nason, Col Fortescue John, 1859–1952, vol. V
Nason, Rev. George Stephen, 1901–1975, vol. VII
Nason, Lt-Col Henry Hyde Williamson, 1857–1929, vol. III
Nasser, Gamal Abdel, 1918–1970, vol. VI
Natali, Lorenzo, 1922–1989, vol. VIII
Nath, Rao Bahadur Bhagavatula V.; *see* Viswa Nath
Nathan, 1st Baron, 1889–1963, vol. VI
Nathan, Lady; (Eleanor Joan Clara), 1892–1972, vol. VII
Nathan, Charles, 1891–1949, vol. IV
Nathan, Sir Charles Samuel, 1870–1936, vol. III
Nathan, Daniel; *see* Dannay, Frederic.
Nathan, Col Sir Frederic Lewis, 1861–1933, vol. III
Nathan, George Jean, 1882–1958, vol. V
Nathan, Sir Gustavus, 1835–1902, vol. I
Nathan, Kandiah Shanmuga, 1930–1990, vol. VIII
Nathan, Manfred, 1875–1945, vol. IV
Nathan, Lt-Col Rt Hon. Sir Matthew, 1862–1939, vol. III
Nathan, Sir Maurice Arnold, 1914–1982, vol. VIII
Nathan, Sir Nathaniel, 1843–1916, vol. II
Nathan, Sir Robert, 1866–1921, vol. II
Nathan, Major Walter Simeon, 1867–1940, vol. III
Nathans, Daniel, 1928–1999, vol. X
Nathubhai, Tribhovandas Mangaldas, 1856–1920, vol. II
Nation, Brig.-Gen. John James Henry, 1874–1946, vol. IV
Nation, Sir John Louis, 1825–1906, vol. I
Nation, William Hamilton Codrington, 1843–1914, vol. I
Natta, Giulio, 1903–1979, vol. VII
Nattrass, Frederick John, 1891–1979, vol. VII
Naughton, Most Rev. James, 1864–1950, vol. IV
Nauticus; *see* Clowes, Sir W. L.
Navarro, Mary Anderson de, 1859–1940, vol. III
Naville, Henri Edouard, 1844–1926, vol. II
Nawanagar, Maharaja Jamsaheb of, 1872–1933, vol. III
Nawanagar, Maharaja Jam Saheb of, 1895–1966, vol. VI
Naylor, Very Rev. Alfred Thomas Arthur, 1889–1966, vol. VI
Naylor, Arthur Holden, 1897–1983, vol. VIII
Naylor, Rev. Canon Basil; *see* Naylor, Rev. Canon C. B.
Naylor, Rev. Canon Charles Basil, 1911–1988, vol. VIII
Naylor, (Gordon) Keith, 1933–1990, vol. VIII
Naylor, Henry Darnley, 1872–1945, vol. IV
Naylor, James Richard, 1842–1922, vol. II
Naylor, Keith; *see* Naylor, G. K.
Naylor, Margaret Ailsa; *see* Naylor, Margot.
Naylor, Margot, (Margaret Ailsa), 1907–1972, vol. VII
Naylor, Maj.-Gen. Robert Francis Brydges, 1889–1971, vol. VII
Naylor, Thomas Ellis, 1868–1958, vol. V

Naylor, Thomas Humphrey, 1890–1966, vol. VI
Naylor, Ven. William Herbert, 1846–1918, vol. II
Naylor-Leyland, Sir (Albert) Edward (Herbert), 2nd Bt, 1890–1952, vol. V
Naylor-Leyland, Sir Edward; see Naylor-Leyland, Sir A. E. H.
Naylor-Leyland, Captain Sir Herbert Scarisbrick, 1st Bt, 1864–1899, vol. I
Naylor-Leyland, Sir Vivyan Edward, 3rd Bt, 1924–1987, vol. VIII
Naz, Sir Virgile, 1825–1901, vol. I
Nazimuddin, (Sir) Al-Haj Khwaja, 1894–1964, vol. VI
Neagle, Dame Anna, (Dame (Florence) Marjorie Wilcox), 1904–1986, vol. VIII
Neal, Arthur, 1862–1933, vol. III
Neal, Harold, 1897–1972, vol. VI
Neal, John, 1889–1962, vol. VI
Neal, Mary C. S., died 1944, vol. IV
Neal, Sir Phené; see Neal, Sir W. P.
Neal, Sir (William) Phené, 1st Bt, 1860–1942, vol. IV
Neale, Sir Alan Derrett, 1918–1995, vol. IX
Neale, Rev. Edgar, 1872–1937, vol. III
Neale, Edward A., 1858–1943, vol. IV
Neale, Folliott Sandford, 1901–1972, vol. VII
Neale, Lt-Col Sir Gordon; see Neale, Lt-Col Sir W. G.
Neale, Sir Henry James Vansittart-, 1842–1923, vol. II
Neale, Sir John Ernest, 1890–1975, vol. VII
Neale, Lt-Col Sir (Walter) Gordon, 1880–1966, vol. VI
Neales, Very Rev. Scovil, 1864–1936, vol. III
Neame, Lt-Col Arthur Laurence Cecil, 1883–1948, vol. IV
Neame, Captain Douglas Mortimer Lewes, 1901–1988, vol. VIII
Neame, Elizabeth; see Monroe, Elizabeth.
Neame, Gwendolyn Mary, (Lady Neame); see Desmond, Astra.
Neame, Humphrey, died 1968, vol. VI
Neame, Lawrence Elwin, died 1964, vol. VI
Neame, Lt-Gen. Sir Philip, 1888–1978, vol. VII
Neame, Sir Thomas, 1885–1973, vol. VII
Neat, Captain (S) Edward Hugh, 1864–1948, vol. IV
Neatby, Edwin Awdas, 1858–1933, vol. III
Neate, Horace Richard, 1891–1966, vol. VI
Neathercoat, Ernest Tom, 1880–1950, vol. IV
Neave, Airey Middleton Sheffield, 1916–1979, vol. VII
Neave, Sir Arundell Thomas Clifton, 6th Bt, 1916–1992, vol. IX
Neave, James Stephen, 1898–1970, vol. VI
Neave, Sheffield, 1853–1936, vol. III
Neave, Sheffield Airey, 1879–1961, vol. VI
Neave, Major Sir Thomas Lewis Hughes, 5th Bt, 1874–1940, vol. III
Nedd, Sir Archibald; see Nedd, Sir R. A.
Nedd, Sir (Robert) Archibald, 1916–1992, vol. X(AI)
Neden, Sir Wilfred John, 1893–1978, vol. VII
Needham, Col Alfred Owen, 1883–1951, vol. V
Needham, Alicia Adelaide, died 1945, vol. IV

Needham, Col Charles, 1844–1934, vol. III
Needham, Sir Christopher Thomas, 1866–1944, vol. IV
Needham, Dorothy Mary Moyle, 1896–1987, vol. VIII
Needham, Major Hon. Francis Edward, 1886–1955, vol. V
Needham, Francis Jack, 1842–1924, vol. II
Needham, Sir Frederick, 1832–1924, vol. II
Needham, Sir George William, 1843–1928, vol. II
Needham, Gwei-Djen Lu-; see Lu, G.-D.
Needham, Maj.-Gen. Henry, 1876–1965, vol. VI
Needham, James Ernest, died 1937, vol. III
Needham, John, 1909–1990, vol. VIII
Needham, Comr John Edward Dunmore, 1917–1983, vol. VIII
Needham, Rev. Canon John Stafford, 1875–1942, vol. IV
Needham, Joseph; see Needham, N. J. T. M.
Needham, Joseph, 1853–1920, vol. II
Needham, Col Joseph George, died 1939, vol. III
Needham, (Noël) Joseph (Terence Montgomery), 1900–1995, vol. IX
Needham, Sir Raymond Walter, 1877–1965, vol. VI
Needham, Bt Col Sir Richard Arthur, 1877–1949, vol. IV
Neef, Walter, 1857–1905, vol. I
Neel, Edmund, 1841–1933, vol. III
Neel, Louis Boyd, 1905–1981, vol VIII
Neelands, Abram Rupert, died 1971, vol. VII
Neeld, Sir Algernon William, 2nd Bt, 1846–1900, vol. I
Neeld, Lt-Col Sir Audley Dallas, 3rd Bt, 1849–1941, vol. IV
Neeld, Rear-Adm. Reginald Rundell, 1850–1939, vol. III
Neely, Major George Henry, 1885–1934, vol. III
Neely, Air Vice-Marshal John Conrad, 1901–1989, vol. VIII
Neep, Edward John Cecil, 1900–1980, vol. VII
Neerunjun, Sir Rampersad, 1906–1967, vol. VI
Neff, Erroll Aubrey, 1887–1942, vol. IV
Negus, Arthur George, 1903–1985, vol. VIII
Negus, Sir Victor Ewings, 1887–1974, vol. VII
Nehru, Shri Jawaharlal, 1889–1964, vol. VI
Nehru, Pandit Motilal, 1861–1931, vol. III
Neil, Albert Michael; see Lyons, A. Neil.
Neil, Edwin Lee, 1872–1934, vol. III
Neil, Eric, 1918–1990, vol. VIII
Neil, James H.; see Hardie Neil.
Neil, Rev. John, 1853–1928, vol. II
Neil, Robert Alexander, 1852–1901, vol. I
Neil, Rev. William, 1909–1979, vol. VII
Neilans, Alison R. N., 1884–1942, vol. IV
Neild, Rev. Canon Alfred, 1865–1941, vol. V
Neill, Alexander Sutherland, 1883–1973, vol. VII
Neill, Charles Ernest, 1873–1931, vol. III
Neill, Derrick James, 1922–2000, vol. X
Neill, Col Duncan Ferguson Dempster, 1868–1938, vol. III
Neill, Col Sir Frederick Austin, 1891–1967, vol. VI
Neill, James Scott, 1889–1958, vol. V
Neill, Col James William S.; see Smith-Neill.
Neill, Rt Rev. Stephen Charles, 1900–1984, vol. VIII

Neill, Sir Thomas, 1856–1937, vol. III
Neill, Sir William Frederick, 1889–1960, vol. V
Neilson, Alexander, 1868–1929, vol. III
Neilson, Francis, 1867–1961, vol. VI
Neilson, George, 1858–1923, vol. II
Neilson, Henry John, 1862–1949, vol. IV
Neilson, Col James, 1838–1903, vol. I
Neilson, Lt-Col John Beaumont, 1885–1957, vol. V
Neilson, Lt-Col John Fraser, 1884–1962, vol. VI
Neilson, John Shaw, 1872–1942, vol. IV
Neilson, Julia, (Mrs Fred Terry), died 1957, vol. V
Neilson, Nigel Fraser, 1919–2000, vol. X
Neilson, Richard Alvin, 1937–1997, vol. X
Neilson, Richard Gillies, 1876–1956, vol. V
Neilson, Col Walter Gordon, 1876–1927, vol. II
Neilson, William Allan, 1869–1946, vol. IV
Neilson, Hon. William Arthur, 1925–1989, vol. VIII
Neilson-Gray, Norah; see Gray.
Neilson-Terry, Phyllis, 1892–1977, vol. VII
Neish, Arthur Charles, 1916–1973, vol. VII
Neish, Sir Charles Henry Lawrence, 1857–1934, vol. III
Neish, Edward William, died 1938, vol. III
Neitenstein, Frederick William, 1850–1921, vol. II
Neligan, Desmond West Edmund, 1906–1993, vol. IX
Neligan, Rt Rev. Moore Richard, died 1922, vol. II
Nelke, Paul, 1860–1925, vol. II
Nell, Sir Harry, 1882–1958, vol. V
Nelles, Brig.-Gen. Charles Macklem, 1863–1936, vol. III
Nelles, Adm. Percy Walker, 1892–1951, vol. V
Nelson, 3rd Earl, 1823–1913, vol. I
Nelson, 4th Earl, 1857–1947, vol. IV
Nelson, 5th Earl, 1860–1951, vol. V
Nelson, 6th Earl, 1890–1957, vol. V
Nelson, 7th Earl, 1894–1972, vol. VII
Nelson, 8th Earl, 1905–1981, vol. VIII
Nelson of Stafford, 1st Baron, 1887–1962, vol. VI
Nelson of Stafford, 2nd Baron, 1917–1995, vol. IX
Nelson, Sir Amos, 1860–1947, vol. IV
Nelson, Sir Arthur Edward, 1875–1950, vol. IV
Nelson, Bertram, 1905–1984, vol. VIII
Nelson, Campbell Louis, 1910–1991, vol. IX
Nelson, Charles Gilbert, 1880–1962, vol. VI
Nelson, Rev. Canon Charles Moseley, 1843–1919, vol. II
Nelson, Rt Rev. Cleland Kinloch, 1852–1917, vol. II
Nelson, Lieut David, 1886–1918, vol. II
Nelson, Donald Marr, 1888–1959, vol. V
Nelson, Brig.-Gen. Edgar F., 1859–1933, vol. III
Nelson, Edward Milles, died 1938, vol. III
Nelson, Sir Edward Montague, 1841–1919, vol. II
Nelson, Air Cdre Eric Douglas Mackinlay, 1912–1996, vol. X
Nelson, Maj.-Gen. Sir (Eustace) John (Blois), 1912–1993, vol. IX
Nelson, Sir Frank, 1883–1966, vol. VI
Nelson, Geoffrey Sheard, 1909–1984, vol. VIII
Nelson, Henry Ince, 1897–1981, vol. VIII
Nelson, Gp Captain Hugh, 1890–1948, vol. IV
Nelson, Rt Hon. Sir Hugh Muir, 1835–1906, vol. I
Nelson, Sir James Hope, 2nd Bt, 1883–1960, vol. V
Nelson, Maj.-Gen. Sir John; see Nelson, Maj.-Gen. Sir E. J. B.

Nelson, John Howard, 1925–1979, vol. VII
Nelson, Col John Joseph Harper, 1882–1961, vol. VI
Nelson, Major John Weddall, 1878–1935, vol. III
Nelson, Captain Maurice Henry Horatio, 1864–1942, vol. IV
Nelson, Rear-Adm. Hon. Maurice Horatio, 1832–1914, vol. I
Nelson, Col Percy Reginald, 1884–1939, vol. III
Nelson, Rt Rev. Richard Henry, 1859–1931, vol. III
Nelson, Rt Rev. Robert, 1913–1959, vol. V
Nelson, Robert Frederick William Robertson, 1888–1932, vol. III
Nelson, Sir William, 1st Bt, 1851–1922, vol. II
Nelson, William Henry, 1880–1948, vol. IV
Nelson, Sir William Vernon Hope, 3rd Bt, 1914–1991, vol. IX
Nelson-Ward, Adm. Philip, 1866–1937, vol. III
Nelthorpe, Col Oliver S.; see Sutton Nelthorpe.
Nelthorpe, Robert Nassau S.; see Sutton-Nelthorpe.
Nemetz, Hon. Nathaniel Theodore, 1913–1997, vol. X
Nemon, Oscar, 1906–1985, vol. VIII
Nendick, David Alan Challoner, 1932–1997, vol. X
Nenk, David Moerel, 1916–1960, vol. V
Nepal, Maharaja Chandra Shum Shere Jung Bahadur Rana, 1863–1929, vol. III
Nepal, Maharaja Bhim Shum Shere Jung Bahadur Rana, 1865–1932, vol. III
Nepal, Ex-Maharaja of, 1875–1952, vol. V
Nepal, Maharaja Mohan Shamsher Jang Bahadur Rana, 1885–1967, vol. VI
Nepean, Sir Charles Evan Molyneux Yorke, 5th Bt, 1867–1953, vol. V
Nepean, Edith, died 1960, vol. V
Nepean, Sir Evan Colville, 1836–1908, vol. I
Nepean, Rev. Sir Evan Yorke, 4th Bt, 1825–1903, vol. I
Nepean, Col Herbert Dryden Home Yorke, 1893–1956, vol. V
Nepean, Brig.-Gen. Herbert Evan Charles, 1865–1951, vol. V
Nepean, Comdr St Vincent, 1844–1915, vol. I
Neruda, Pablo, 1904–1973, vol. VII
Nervi, Pier Luigi, 1891–1979, vol. VII
Nesbit, E(dith), (Mrs Hubert Bland), 1858–1924, vol. II
Nesbit, Paris, 1852–1927, vol. II
Nesbitt, Rev. Allan James, died 1918, vol. II
Nesbitt, Cathleen Mary, 1888–1982, vol. VIII
Nesbitt, Maj.-Gen. Frederick George B.; see Beaumont-Nesbitt.
Nesbitt, Major Randolph Cosby, 1867–1956, vol. V
Nesbitt, Lt-Col Richard Atholl, 1838–1905, vol. I
Nesbitt, Robert Chancellor, died 1944, vol. IV
Nesbitt, Hon. Wallace, 1858–1930, vol. III
Nesbitt-Hawes, Sir Ronald, 1895–1969, vol. VI
Ness, Air Marshal Sir Charles Ernest, 1924–1994, vol. IX
Ness, E. Wilhelmina; see Ness, Mrs P.
Ness, J. A., died 1931, vol. III
Ness, Mrs Patrick, (E. Wilhelmina Ness), died 1962, vol. VI
Ness, Robert Barclay, died 1954, vol. V
Nessi, Pio B.; see Baroja Nessi.

Nestle, (Christof) Eberhard, 1851–1913, vol. I
Nestle, Eberhard; see Nestle, C. E.
Nethersole, Lt-Col Frederick Ralph, died 1933, vol. III
Nethersole, Sir Michael, 1859–1920, vol. II
Nethersole, Sir Michael Henry Braddon, 1891–1965, vol. VI
Nethersole, Olga, 1870–1951, vol. V
Netherthorpe, 1st Baron, 1908–1980, vol. VII
Netherthorpe, 2nd Baron, 1936–1982, vol. VIII
Netherwood, A., died 1930, vol. III
Nettlefold, Sir Thomas Sydney, 1879–1956, vol. V
Nettleship, Edward, 1845–1913, vol. I
Nettleship, John Trivett, 1841–1902, vol. I
Nettleton, Wing Comdr John Dering, 1917–1943, vol. IV
Nettleton, Martin Barnes, 1911–1964, vol. VI
Neubauer, Adolf, 1832–1907, vol. I
Neuberger, Albert, 1908–1996, vol. X
Neumann, Sir Cecil Gustavus Jacques; see Newman.
Neumann, Sir Sigmund, 1st Bt, 1857–1916, vol. II
Nevada, Mignon, died 1971, vol. VII
Nevares, Celso, born 1850, vol. II
Neve, Arthur, 1858–1919, vol. II
Neve, David Lewis, 1920–1992, vol. IX
Neve, Eric Read, 1887–1958, vol. V
Neve, Ernest Frederic, 1861–1946, vol. IV
Neven-Spence, Col Sir Basil Hamilton Hebden, 1888–1974, vol. VII
Nevile, Christopher, 1891–1962, vol. VI
Nevile, Henry Nicholas, 1920–1996, vol. X
Nevile, Sir Sydney Oswald, 1873–1969, vol. VI
Nevill, Air Vice-Marshal Sir Arthur de Terrotte, 1899–1985, vol. VIII
Nevill, Col Charles William, 1907–1973, vol. VII
Nevill, Lady Dorothy Fanny, died 1913, vol. I
Nevill, Edmund Neville, died 1940, vol. III
Nevill, Rev. Edmund Robert, 1862–1933, vol. III
Nevill, Lord George Montacute, 1856–1920, vol. II
Nevill, Ven. Henry Ralph, 1821–1900, vol. I
Nevill, Henry Rivers, 1876–1939, vol. III
Nevill, Captain Hugh Lewis, 1877–1915, vol. I
Nevill, Ralph Henry, 1865–1930, vol. III
Nevill, Hon. Ralph Pelham, 1832–1914, vol. I
Nevill, Lord Richard Plantagenet, 1864–1939, vol. III
Nevill, Lord Rupert Charles Montacute, 1923–1982, vol. VIII
Nevill, Most Rev. Samuel Tarratt, born 1837, vol. II
Nevill, Rev. Thomas Seymour, 1901–1980, vol. VII
Nevill, Rev. Valentine Paul, 1882–1954, vol. V
Nevill, Comdr Walter Howard, 1887–1956, vol. V
Nevill, Sir Walter Palmer, 1854–1929, vol. III
Neville, Brig. Alfred Geoffrey, 1891–1955, vol. V
Neville, Arthur William, 1884–1948, vol. IV
Neville, Bertie Aylmer Crampton, 1882–1973, vol. VII
Neville, Edith, 1874–1951, vol. V
Neville, Lt-Col Sir Edmund; see Neville, Lt-Col Sir J. E. H.
Neville, (Eric) Graham, 1933–1999, vol. X
Neville, Eric Harold, 1889–1961, vol. VI
Neville, Francis Henry, 1847–1915, vol. I
Neville, Adm. Sir George, 1850–1923, vol. II
Neville, Graham; see Neville, E. G.

Neville, Rev. Hon. Grey, 1857–1920, vol. II
Neville, Henry; see Neville, T. H. G.
Neville, Henry Allen Dugdale, 1880–1952, vol. V
Neville, Lt-Col Sir (James) Edmund (Henderson), 2nd Bt, 1897–1982, vol. VIII
Neville, Kenneth Percival Rutherford, 1876–1957, vol. V
Neville, Nigel Charles Alfred, 1849–1923, vol. II
Neville, Captain Philip Lloyd, 1888–1976, vol. VII
Neville, Sir Ralph, 1848–1918, vol. II
Neville, Sir Reginald James Neville, 1st Bt, 1863–1950, vol. IV
Neville, Sir Richard Lionel John Baines, 3rd Bt, 1921–1994, vol. IX
Neville, Maj.-Gen. Sir Robert Arthur Ross, 1896–1987, vol. VIII
Neville, Royce Robert, 1914–1997, vol. X
Neville, Thomas Henry Gartside, (Henry Neville), 1837–1910, vol. I
Neville, Col William Candler, 1859–1926, vol. II
Neville-Rolfe, Eustace, 1845–1908, vol. I
Nevin, Richard; see Nevin, T. R.
Nevin, Robert Wallace, 1907–1980, vol. VII
Nevin, Samuel, died 1979, vol. VII
Nevin, (Thomas) Richard, 1916–2000, vol. X
Nevins, Allan, 1890–1971, vol. VII
Nevinson, Christopher Richard Wynne, 1889–1946, vol. IV
Nevinson, Henry Woodd, 1856–1941, vol. IV
Nevinson, Margaret Wynne, died 1932, vol. III
New, Charles George Morley, 1879–1957, vol. V
New, Edmund Hort, 1871–1931, vol. III
New, Sir Henry Francis, 1859–1931, vol. III
New, Rev. James Marr, 1855–1931, vol. III
Newall, 1st Baron, 1886–1963, vol. VI
Newall, Dame Bertha Surtees, 1877–1932, vol. III
Newall, Hugh Frank, 1857–1944, vol. IV
Newall, Norman Dakeyne, 1888–1952, vol. V
Newall, Col Stuart, 1843–1920, vol. II
Newark, Francis Headon, 1907–1976, vol. VII
Newberry, Percy Edward, 1869–1949, vol. IV
Newbery, Arthur, died 1930, vol. III
Newbery, Francis H., died 1946, vol. IV
Newbigging, Brig.-Gen. William Patrick Eric, 1871–1940, vol. III
Newbigin, Rt Rev. (James Edward) Lesslie, 1909–1998, vol. X
Newbigin, Rt Rev. Lesslie; see Newbigin, Rt Rev. J. E. L.
Newbigin, Marion I., died 1934, vol. III
Newbold, Sir Charles Demorée, 1909–1993, vol. IX
Newbold, Lt-Col Charles Joseph, died 1946, vol. IV
Newbold, Sir Douglas, 1894–1945, vol. IV
Newbold, John Turner Walton, 1888–1943, vol. IV
Newbolt, Captain (Arthur) Francis, 1893–1966, vol. VI
Newbolt, Captain Francis; see Newbolt, Captain A. F.
Newbolt, Sir Francis George, 1863–1940, vol. III
Newbolt, Sir Henry John, 1862–1938, vol. III
Newbolt, Rev. Michael Robert, 1874–1956, vol. V
Newbolt, Rev. William Charles Edmund, 1844–1930, vol. III
Newborough, 4th Baron, 1873–1916, vol. II
Newborough, 5th Baron, 1878–1957, vol. V

Newborough, 6th Baron, 1877–1965, vol. VI
Newborough, 7th Baron, 1917–1998, vol. X
Newbould, Alfred Ernest, 1873–1952, vol. V
Newbould, Sir (Babington) Bennett, 1867–1937, vol. III
Newbould, Sir Bennett; see Newbould, Sir Babington B.
Newboult, Sir Alexander Theodore, 1896–1964, vol. VI
Newburgh, 8th Earl of, 1818–1908, vol. I
Newburgh, 9th (shown as 10th) Earl of, 1862–1941, vol. IV
Newburgh, Countess of (10th in line), 1889 1977, vol. VII
Newburgh, 11th Earl of, 1907–1986, vol. VIII
Newby, Percy Howard, 1918–1997, vol. X
Newcastle, 7th Duke of, 1864–1928, vol. II
Newcastle, 8th Duke of, 1866–1941, vol. IV
Newcastle, 9th Duke of, 1907–1988, vol. VIII
Newcastle, 10th Duke of, 1920–1988, vol. VIII
Newcastle, Duchess of; (Kathleen Florence May), died 1955, vol. V
Newcomb, Lt-Col Clive, 1882–1968, vol. VI
Newcomb, Simon, 1835–1909, vol. I
Newcomb, Wilfrid Davison, 1889–1971, vol. VII
Newcombe, Edmund Leslie, 1859–1931, vol. III
Newcombe, Major Edward Osborn Armstrong, 1874–1941, vol. IV
Newcombe, Maj.-Gen. Henry William, 1875–1963, vol. VI
Newcombe, Luxmoore, 1880–1952, vol. V
Newcombe, Col Stewart Francis, 1878–1956, vol. V
Newcomen, Col Arthur Hills G.; see Gleadowe-Newcomen.
Newcomen, Gleadowe Henry Turner, 1877–1932, vol. III
Newdegate, Anne Emily Newdigate-, (Lady Newdigate-Newdegate), died 1924, vol. II
Newdegate, Sir Edward Newdigate, 1825–1902, vol. I
Newdegate, Sir Francis Alexander Newdigate, 1862–1936, vol. III
Newdigate, Bernard Henry, 1869–1944, vol. IV
Newdigate, Lt-Gen. Sir Henry Richard Legge, 1832–1908, vol. I
Newdigate-Newdegate, A. E.; see Newdegate.
Newe, Rt Hon. Gerard Benedict, 1907–1982, vol. VIII
Newell, Arthur Franklin, 1885–1976, vol. VII
Newell, Gordon Ewart, 1908–1968, vol. VI
Newell, Harold, died 1937, vol. III
Newell, Lt-Col Herbert Andrews, 1869–1934, vol. III
Newell, Hugh Hamilton, 1878–1941, vol. IV
Newell, Rev. Canon John Philip Peter, 1911–1980, vol. VII
Newell, Kenneth Wyatt, 1925–1990, vol. VIII
Newell, Philip Staniforth, 1903–1990, vol. VIII
Newell, William Homan, 1819–1901, vol. I
Newenham, Brig.-Gen. Henry Edward Berkeley, 1866–1934, vol. III
Newey, John Henry Richard, 1923–1994, vol. IX
Newham, Lt-Col Hugh Basil Greaves, 1874–1959, vol. V
Newhouse, Ven. John; see Newhouse, Ven. R. J. D.

Newhouse, Ven. (Robert) John (Darrell), 1911–2000, vol. X
Newhouse, Rev. Robert Perceval, died 1933, vol. III
Newill, Ven. Edward Joseph, 1877–1954, vol. V
Newitt, Dudley Maurice, 1894–1980, vol. VII
Newland, Col Edmund Walcott, 1858–1937, vol. III
Newland, Maj.-Gen. Sir Foster Reuss, 1862–1943, vol. IV
Newland, Captain H. Osman, died 1920, vol. II
Newland, Sir Henry Simpson, 1873–1969, vol. VI
Newland-Pedley, Frederick, died 1944, vol. IV
Newlands, 1st Baron, 1825–1906, vol. I
Newlands, 2nd Baron, 1851–1929, vol. III
Newlands, Alexander, 1870–1938, vol. III
Newlands, Harry Scott, 1884–1933, vol. III
Newlands, Hon. Sir John, 1864–1932, vol. III
Newlands, John, 1857–1937, vol. III
Newley, Anthony; see Newley, G. A.
Newley, Edward Frank, 1913–1994, vol. IX
Newley, (George) Anthony, 1931–1999, vol. X'
Newling, (Alfred) John, 1896–1957, vol. V
Newling, John; see Newling, A. J.
Newman, Albert Gordon, 1894–1956, vol. V
Newman, Lt-Col (Augustus) Charles, 1904–1972, vol. VII
Newman, Bernard, 1897–1968, vol. VI
Newman, Bertram, 1886–1962, vol. VI
Newman, Sir Cecil Gustavus Jacques, 2nd Bt (cr 1912), 1891–1955, vol. V
Newman, Lt-Col Charles; see Newman, Lt-Col A. C.
Newman, Charles Edward Kingsley, 1900–1989, vol. VIII
Newman, Maj.-Gen. Charles Richard, 1875–1954, vol. V
Newman, Cyril Wilfred Francis, 1937–2000, vol. X
Newman, David, 1853–1924, vol. II
Newman, Edward, 1858–1946, vol. IV
Newman, Edward Braxton, 1842–1916, vol. II
Newman, Brig.-Gen. Edward Harding-, 1872–1955, vol. V
Newman, Captain Edward John Kendall, 1860–1941, vol. IV
Newman, Major Edward William Polson, 1887–1967, vol. VI
Newman, Ernest, 1868–1959, vol. V
Newman, Lt-Col Ernest Alan Robert, 1867–1943, vol. IV
Newman, Ven. Ernest Frederick, 1859–1928, vol. II
Newman, Francis William, 1805–1897, vol. I
Newman, Frank Herbert, 1875–1948, vol. IV
Newman, Sir George, 1870–1948, vol. IV
Newman, Sir Gerard Robert Henry Sigismund, 3rd Bt, 1927–1987, vol. VIII
Newman, Graham Reginald, 1924–1992, vol. IX
Newman, Harold Lancelot, 1878–1949, vol. IV
Newman, Maj.-Gen. Hubert Thomas, 1895–1965, vol. VI
Newman, Sir Jack, 1902–1996, vol. X
Newman, Maj.-Gen. John Cartwright H.; see Harding-Newman.
Newman, Sir John Robert Pretyman, 1871–1947, vol. IV
Newman, Maxwell Herman Alexander, 1897–1984, vol. VIII

Newman, Philip Harker, 1911–1994, vol. IX
Newman, Philip Harry, 1840–1927, vol. II
Newman, Sir Ralph Alured, 5th Bt (*cr* 1836), 1902–1968, vol. VI
Newman, Rev. Canon Richard, 1871–1961, vol. VI
Newman, Col Richard Ernest Upton, 1883–1956, vol. V
Newman, Robert Lydston, 1865–1937, vol. III
Newman, Ronald William, 1921–1987, vol. VIII
Newman, Sidney Thomas Mayow, 1906–1971, vol. VII
Newman, Sydney Cecil, 1917–1997, vol. X
Newman, Thomas Prichard, 1846–1915, vol. I
Newman, Trevor Clyde, 1882–1955, vol. V
Newman, William Henry, 1865–1947, vol. IV
Newman-Morris, Sir Geoffrey, 1909–1981, vol. VIII
Newman-Morris, Sir John, 1879–1957, vol. V
Newmarch, Alexander, 1869–1935, vol. III
Newmarch, Bernard James, 1856–1929, vol. III
Newmarch, Francis Welles, 1853–1918, vol. II
Newmarch, Maj.-Gen. George, 1833–1912, vol. I
Newmarch, Sir Oliver Richardson, 1834–1920, vol. II
Newmarch, Rosa Harriet, 1857–1940, vol. III
Newnes, Sir Frank Hillyard, 2nd Bt, 1876–1955, vol. V
Newnes, Sir George, 1st Bt, 1851–1910, vol. I
Newnham, Ernest Percy, 1870–1943, vol. IV
Newnham, Hubert Ernest, 1886–1970, vol. VI
Newnham, Captain Ian Frederick Montague, 1911–1993, vol. IX
Newnham, Rt Rev. Jervois Arthur, 1852–1941, vol. IV
Newnham, Ven. Obadiah Samuel, 1848–1932, vol. III
Newnham, William Harry Christopher, 1859–1941, vol. IV
Newnham-Davis, Lt-Col Nathaniel, 1854–1917, vol. II
Newns, Sir (Alfred) Foley (Francis Polden), 1909–1998, vol. X
Newns, Sir Foley; *see* Newns, Sir A. F. F. P.
Newns, George Henry, 1908–1985, vol. VIII
Newport, Surg. Captain Alexander Charles William, 1874–1948, vol. IV
Newsam, Sir Frank Aubrey, 1893–1964, vol. VI
Newsam, Richard William, 1918–1983, vol. VIII
Newsholme, Sir Arthur, 1857–1943, vol. IV
Newsom, Col Augustus Charles, 1866–1936, vol. III
Newsom, Rev. George Ernest, 1871–1934, vol. III
Newsom, George Harold, 1909–1992, vol. IX
Newsom, Rear-Adm. John Bertram, 1902–1971, vol. VII
Newsom, Sir John Hubert, 1910–1971, vol. VII
Newson, Sir Percy Wilson, 1st Bt, 1874–1950, vol. IV
Newson-Smith, Sir Frank Edwin, 1st Bt, 1879–1971, vol. VII
Newson-Smith, Sir John Kenneth, 2nd Bt, 1911–1997, vol. X
Newstead, Robert, 1859–1947, vol. IV
Newsum, Sir Clement Henry, 1865–1947, vol. IV
Newte, Horace Wykeham Can, *died* 1949, vol. IV
Newth, Brig. Arthur Leslie Walter, 1897–1978, vol. VII

Newth, David Richmond, 1921–1988, vol. VIII
Newton, 1st Baron, 1828–1898, vol. I
Newton, 2nd Baron, 1857–1942, vol. IV
Newton, 3rd Baron, 1888–1960, vol. V
Newton, 4th Baron, 1915–1992, vol. IX
Newton, Sir Alan, 1887–1949, vol. IV
Newton, Alfred, 1829–1907, vol. I
Newton, Sir Alfred James, 1st Bt (*cr* 1900), 1849–1921, vol. II
Newton, Algernon, 1880–1968, vol. VI
Newton, Arthur, 1858–1942, vol. IV
Newton, Arthur Percival, 1873–1942, vol. IV
Newton, Sir Basil Cochrane, 1889–1965, vol. VI
Newton, Bernard St John, 1890–1977, vol. VII
Newton, Charles Edmund, 1831–1908, vol. I
Newton, Sir Charles Henry, 1882–1973, vol. VII
Newton, Captain Denzil Onslow Cochrane, 1880–1915, vol. I
Newton, Douglas Anthony, (Tony), 1915–1993, vol. IX
Newton, Sir Edgar Henry, 2nd Bt (*cr* 1924), 1893–1971, vol. VII
Newton, Sir Edward, 1832–1897, vol. I
Newton, Edwin Tulley, 1840–1930, vol. III
Newton, Eric, 1893–1965, vol. VI
Newton, Ernest, 1856–1922, vol. II
Newton, Sir Francis James, 1857–1948, vol. IV
Newton, Francis John Stuart H.; *see* Hay-Newton.
Newton, Lt-Col Frank Graham, 1877–1962, vol. VI
Newton, George Percival, 1868–1951, vol. V
Newton, Giles Fendall, 1891–1974, vol. VII
Newton, Sir Gordon; *see* Newton, Sir L. G.
Newton, Sir Harry Kottingham, 2nd Bt (*cr* 1900), 1875–1951, vol. V
Newton, Rt Rev. Henry, 1866–1947, vol. IV
Newton, Lt-Col Henry, 1880–1959, vol. V
Newton, Henry Chance, 1854–1931, vol. III
Newton, Sir Henry William, 1842–1914, vol. I
Newton, Sir Hibbert Alan Stephen; *see* Newton, Sir Alan.
Newton, Hibbert Henry, 1861–1927, vol. II
Newton, Rev. Horace, 1841–1920, vol. II
Newton, Sir Hubert, 1904–1989, vol. VIII
Newton, Ivor, 1892–1981, vol. VIII
Newton, John, 1864–1916, vol. II
Newton, John David, 1921–2000, vol. X
Newton, John Mordaunt, 1913–1986, vol. VIII
Newton, Rev. Joseph Fort, 1880–1950, vol. IV
Newton, Sir (Leslie) Gordon, 1907–1998, vol. X
Newton, Lily, 1893–1981, vol. VIII
Newton, Col Sir Louis Arthur, 1st Bt (*cr* 1924), 1867–1945, vol. IV
Newton, Rev. Richard Heber, 1840–1914, vol. I
Newton, Robert, 1905–1956, vol. V
Newton, Robert, 1908–1983, vol. VIII
Newton, Robert Henry, 1864–1943, vol. IV
Newton, Robert Milnes, 1821–1900, vol. I
Newton, Maj.-Gen. Thomas Cochrane, 1885–1976, vol. VII
Newton, Tony; *see* Newton, D. A.
Newton, Sir Wilberforce Stephen, 1890–1956, vol. V
Newton, Sir William, *died* 1915, vol. I
Newton, William George, 1859–1920, vol. II
Newton, William Godfrey, 1885–1949, vol. IV

Newton, William Henry, 1904–1949, vol. IV
Newton, William James Oliver, 1884–1952, vol. V
Newton-Brady, Sir Andrew, 1849–1918, vol. II
Newton-Butler, Lord; John Brinsley Danvers, 1893–1912, vol. I
Newton-Robinson, Charles Edmund, 1853–1913, vol. I
Ney, Marie; *see* Menzies, M. N.
Neylan, Sir Daniel, 1866–1943, vol. IV
Neylan, Lt-Col John Nolan, *died* 1936, vol. III
Ngata, Hon. Sir Apirana Turupa, 1874–1950, vol. IV
Niall, Sir Horace Lionel Richard, 1904–1994, vol. IX
Niarchos, Stavros Spyros, 1909–1996, vol. X
Niblack, Rear-Adm. Albert P., 1859–1929, vol. III
Niblett, Adm. Harry Seawell Frank, 1852–1939, vol. III
Niblett, Robert Henry, 1859–1918, vol. II
Niblock, Henry, (Pat), 1911–1996, vol. X
Niblock, Pat; *see* Niblock, H.
Niccol, Kathleen Agnes; *see* Leo, Dame Sister M.
Nichol, Col Charles Edward, 1859–1939, vol. III
Nichol, Muriel Edith, 1893–1983, vol. IX(AI)
Nichol, Robert, 1890–1925, vol. II
Nichol, Robert John, *died* 1946, vol. IV
Nichol, Hon. Walter Cameron, 1866–1928, vol. II
Nicholas, Sir Alfred James, 1900–1984, vol. VIII
Nicholas, Sir Harry; *see* Nicholas, Sir Herbert R.
Nicholas, Herbert George, 1911–1998, vol. X
Nicholas, Sir Herbert Richard, (Sir Harry), 1905–1997, vol. X
Nicholas, Captain John, 1851–1920, vol. II
Nicholas, Montagu Richmond, 1905–1964, vol. VI
Nicholas, Reginald Owen Mercer, 1903–1981, vol. VIII
Nicholas, Col Stephen Henry Edmund, 1870–1948, vol. IV
Nicholas, Sir Walter Powell, 1868–1926, vol. II
Nicholas, Rev. William, 1838–1912, vol. I
Nicholetts, Air Marshal Sir Gilbert Edward, 1902–1983, vol. VIII
Nicholl, Sir Allan Hume, *died* 1941, vol. IV
Nicholl, Rear-Adm. Angus Dacres, 1896–1977, vol. VII
Nicholl, Maj.-Gen. Sir Christopher Rice Havard, 1836–1928, vol. II
Nicholl, Sir Edward, 1862–1939, vol. III
Nicholl, George Frederick, *died* 1913, vol. I
Nicholl, Air Vice-Marshal Sir Hazelton Robson, 1882–1956, vol. V
Nicholl, John Storer, 1888–1958, vol. V
Nicholls, Agnes; *see* Harty, A. H.
Nicholls, Albert George, 1870–1946, vol. IV
Nicholls, Arthur, 1880–1974, vol. VII
Nicholls, Rev. Arthur Bell, 1816–1906, vol. I
Nicholls, Bertram, 1883–1974, vol. VII
Nicholls, Rear-Adm. Brian B.; *see* Brayne-Nicholls.
Nicholls, Pastor Sir Douglas Ralph, 1906–1988, vol. VIII
Nicholls, Rear-Adm. (Francis) Brian (Price) B.; *see* Brayne-Nicholls.
Nicholls, Frederick, 1871–1952, vol. V
Nicholls, George, 1864–1943, vol. IV

Nicholls, Rt Hon. George Heaton, 1876–1959, vol. V
Nicholls, Harry, 1852–1926, vol. II
Nicholls, Harry, 1915–1975, vol. VII
Nicholls, Hon. Sir Henry Alfred Alford, 1851–1926, vol. II
Nicholls, Hon. Sir Herbert, 1868–1940, vol. III
Nicholls, John Ralph, 1889–1970, vol. VI
Nicholls, Sir John Walter, 1909–1970, vol. VI
Nicholls, Maj.-Gen. Sir Leslie, (Burtonshaw), 1895–1975, vol. VII
Nicholls, Lucius, 1885–1969, vol. VI
Nicholls, Sir Marriott Fawckner, 1898–1969, vol. VI
Nicholls, Surg. Vice-Adm. Sir Percival Thomas, 1877–1959, vol. V
Nicholls, Richard Howell, 1868–1946, vol. IV
Nicholls, Sir Robert Dove, 1889–1970, vol. VI
Nicholls, Col Stephen Charles Phillips, 1883–1959, vol. V
Nicholls, Rt Rev. Vernon Sampson, 1917–1996, vol. X
Nicholls, William, 1882–1970, vol. VI
Nicholls, Lt-Col William Ashley, 1883–1941, vol. IV
Nicholls, Gen. Sir William Charles, 1854–1935, vol. III
Nicholls, Sir William Edgar, 1858–1932, vol. III
Nichols, Arthur Eastwood, 1891–1959, vol. V
Nichols, Beverley, 1898–1983, vol. VIII
Nichols, Catherine Maude, *died* 1923, vol. II
Nichols, Clement Roy, 1909–1997, vol. X
Nichols, Sir Edward Henry, 1911–1992, vol. IX
Nichols, Edward Leamington, 1854–1937, vol. III
Nichols, George Herbert Fosdike, *died* 1933, vol. III
Nichols, Herbert John, 1895–1959, vol. V
Nichols, John; *see* Nichols, K. J. H.
Nichols, Joseph Cowie, *died* 1954, vol. V
Nichols, (Kenneth) John (Heastey) 1923–1996, vol. X
Nichols, Pamela Marjorie, (Mrs John Nichols); *see* Long, P. M.
Nichols, Peter, 1928–1989, vol. VIII
Nichols, Sir Philip Bouverie Bowyer, 1894–1962, vol. VI
Nichols, Robert Malise Bowyer, 1893–1944, vol. IV
Nichols, Roy Franklin, 1896–1973, vol. VII
Nichols, Rt Rev. William Ford, 1849–1924, vol. II
Nicholson, 1st Baron, 1845–1918, vol. II
Nicholson, Anthony Thomas Cuthbertson, 1929–1999, vol. X
Nicholson, Sir Arthur, 1842–1929, vol. III
Nicholson, Bt Col Arthur Falkner, 1885–1954, vol. V
Nicholson, Arthur Pole, 1869–1940, vol. III
Nicholson, Sir Arthur William, 1852–1932, vol. III
Nicholson, Sir Arthur William, 1903–1981, vol. VIII
Nicholson, Ben, 1894–1982, vol. VIII
Nicholson, Bertram, 1875–1943, vol. IV
Nicholson, Captain Bertram William Lothian, 1879–1958, vol. V
Nicholson, Gen. Sir Cameron Gordon Graham, 1898–1979, vol. VII
Nicholson, Maj.-Gen. Sir Cecil Lothian, 1865–1933, vol. III

Nicholson, Sir Charles, 1st Bt (*cr* 1859), 1808–1903, vol. I
Nicholson, Sir Charles, 2nd Bt (*cr* 1859), 1867–1949, vol. IV
Nicholson, Charles Ernest, 1868–1954, vol. V
Nicholson, Rear-Adm. Charles Hepworth, 1891–1966, vol. VI
Nicholson, Sir Charles Norris, 1st Bt (*cr* 1912), 1857–1918, vol. II
Nicholson, Hon. Sir David Eric, 1904–1997, vol. X
Nicholson, Douglas; *see* Nicholson, F. D.
Nicholson, Adm. Sir Douglas Romilly Lothian, 1867–1946, vol. IV
Nicholson, Lt-Col Edmund James Houghton, 1870–1955, vol. V
Nicholson, Comdr Edward Hugh Meredith, 1876–1956, vol. V
Nicholson, (Edward) Rupert, 1909–2000, vol. X
Nicholson, Edward Williams Byron, 1849–1912, vol. I
Nicholson, Maj.-Gen. Francis Lothian, 1884–1953, vol. V
Nicholson, Sir Frank, 1875–1952, vol. V
Nicholson, Frank Carr, *died* 1962, vol. VI
Nicholson, (Frank) Douglas, 1905–1984, vol. VIII
Nicholson, Sir Frederick Augustus, 1846–1936, vol. III
Nicholson, Major Geoffrey, 1894–1976, vol. VII
Nicholson, George Crosfield Norris, 1884–1915, vol. I
Nicholson, George Gibb, 1875–1948, vol. IV
Nicholson, Brig.-Gen. George Harvey, 1862–1942, vol. IV
Nicholson, Sir Godfrey, 1st Bt (*cr* 1958), 1901–1991, vol. IX
Nicholson, Brig.-Gen. Graham Henry Whalley, 1869–1946, vol. IV
Nicholson, Adm. Sir Gresham; *see* Nicholson, Adm. Sir R. S. G.
Nicholson, Harold, 1883–1949, vol. IV
Nicholson, Harry Oliphant, 1870–1941, vol. IV
Nicholson, Henry Alleyne, 1844–1899, vol. I
Nicholson, Adm. Sir Henry Frederick, 1835–1914, vol. I
Nicholson, Horace Watson, 1883–1935, vol. III
Nicholson, Major Hugh Blomfield, *died* 1957, vol. V
Nicholson, Ivor Percy, *died* 1937, vol. II
Nicholson, Sir John Charles, 3rd Bt, 1904–1986, vol. VIII
Nicholson, Brig. John Gerald, 1906–1979, vol. VII
Nicholson, Sir John Gibb, 1879–1959, vol. V
Nicholson, John Henry, 1889–1972, vol. VII
Nicholson, (John) Leonard, 1916–1990, vol. VIII
Nicholson, Rev. John Malcolm, 1908–1983, vol. VIII
Nicholson, Sir John Norris, 2nd Bt (*cr* 1912), 1911–1993, vol. IX
Nicholson, Hon. John Paton, 1922–1985, vol. VIII
Nicholson, Sir John Rumney, 1866–1939, vol. III
Nicholson, Brig.-Gen. John Sanctuary, 1863–1924, vol. II
Nicholson, John Wilfred, 1893–1949, vol. IV
Nicholson, John William, *died* 1955, vol. V
Nicholson, Joseph Shield, 1850–1927, vol. II
Nicholson, Joseph Sinclair, 1882–1968, vol. VI

Nicholson, Leonard; *see* Nicholson, J. L.
Nicholson, Lewis Frederick, 1918–1999, vol. X
Nicholson, Lt-Col Mark Alleyne, 1885–1952, vol. V
Nicholson, Meredith, 1866–1947, vol. IV
Nicholson, Nick; *see* Nicholson, L. F.
Nicholson, Norman Cornthwaite, 1914–1987, vol. VIII
Nicholson, Maj.-Gen. Octavius Henry Lothian, 1877–1938, vol. III
Nicholson, Otho William, 1891–1978, vol. VII
Nicholson, Rev. Ralph, 1856–1930, vol. III
Nicholson, Major Randolph, 1894–1928, vol. II
Nicholson, Adm. Sir (Randolph Stewart) Gresham, 1892–1975, vol. VII
Nicholson, Reginald, 1869–1946, vol. IV
Nicholson, Reginald Popham, 1874–1950, vol. IV
Nicholson, Reynold Alleyne, 1868–1945, vol. IV
Nicholson, Sir Richard, 1828–1913, vol. I
Nicholson, Captain Richard Lindsay, 1882–1940, vol. III
Nicholson, Rupert; *see* Nicholson, E. R.
Nicholson, Adm. Stuart, 1865–1936, vol. III
Nicholson, Maj.-Gen. Stuart James, 1836–1917, vol. II
Nicholson, Sir Sydney Hugo, 1875–1947, vol. IV
Nicholson, Sir Walter Frederic, 1876–1946, vol. IV
Nicholson, Col Walter Norris, 1877–1964, vol. VI
Nicholson, Sir William, 1865–1944, vol. IV
Nicholson, Adm. Sir William Coldingham Masters, 1863–1932, vol. III
Nicholson, William Ewart, 1890–1983, vol. VIII
Nicholson, Rt Hon. William Graham, 1862–1942, vol. IV
Nicholson, Gen. Sir William Gustavus, 1845–1909, vol. I
Nicholson, Sir William Newzam Prior, 1872–1949, vol. IV
Nicholson, Adm. Wilmot Stuart, 1872–1947, vol. IV
Nicholson-Lailey, John Raymond, 1900–1979, vol. VII
Nickalls, Captain Guy, 1866–1935, vol. III
Nickalls, Guy Oliver, 1899–1974, vol. VII
Nickalls, Sir Patteson, 1836–1910, vol. I
Nickerson, Albert Lindsay, 1911–1994, vol. IX
Nickerson, Maj.-Gen. William Henry Snyder, 1875–1954, vol. V
Nicklin, Hon. Sir Francis; *see* Nicklin, Hon. Sir G. F. R.
Nicklin, Hon. Sir (George) Francis (Reuben), 1895–1978, vol. VII
Nicklin, Robert Shenstone, 1901–1975, vol. VII
Nickolls, Lewis Charles, 1899–1970, vol. VI
Nickson, Francis, 1929–1999, vol. X
Nickson, Rt Rev. George, 1864–1949, vol. IV
Nickson, Col John Edgar, 1899–1969, vol. VI
Nicol, Abioseh; *see* Nicol, D. S. H. W.
Nicol, Rev. Anderson, 1906–1972, vol. VII
Nicol, Brig. Cameron Macdonald, 1891–1965, vol. VI
Nicol, Claude Scott, 1914–1984, vol. VIII
Nicol, Davidson Sylvester Hector Willoughby, 1924–1994, vol. IX
Nicol, Donald Ninian, 1843–1903, vol. I
Nicol, Erskine, 1825–1904, vol. I
Nicol, Henry, 1821–1905, vol. I

Nicol, Jacob, *died* 1958, vol. V
Nicol, James Lauder, 1889–1971, vol. VII
Nicol, John, 1838–1920, vol. II
Nicol, Hon. Brig.-Gen. Lewis Loyd, 1858–1935, vol. III
Nicol, Rev. Thomas, 1846–1916, vol. II
Nicol, Thomas, 1900–1983, vol. VIII
Nicol, Sir Thomas Drysdale, 1878–1961, vol. VI
Nicol, William Allardyce, 1909–1989, vol. VIII
Nicolas, Nicholas Harris, 1830–1905, vol. I
Nicolay, Col Bernard Underwood, 1873–1960, vol. V, vol. VI
Nicolet, Gabriel, 1856–1921, vol. II
Nicoll, Allardyce; *see* Nicoll, J. R. A.
Nicoll, Gordon, *died* 1959, vol. V
Nicoll, Gen. Henry, 1816–1907, vol. I
Nicoll, James Gibson, 1870–1949, vol. IV
Nicoll, James H., 1865–1921, vol. II
Nicoll, Sir John Fearns, 1899–1981, vol. VIII
Nicoll, John Ramsay Allardyce, 1894–1976, vol. VII
Nicoll, Maurice, 1884–1953, vol. V
Nicoll, Lt-Col Peter Strachan, 1864–1942, vol. IV
Nicoll, Ronald Ewart, 1921–1991, vol. IX
Nicoll, Sir William, 1860–1908, vol. I
Nicoll, Sir William Robertson, 1851–1923, vol. II
Nicolle, Edmund Toulmin, 1868–1929, vol. III
Nicolle, John Macarthur, 1885–1964, vol. VI
Nicolle, Maurice, 1862–1932, vol. III
Nicolls, Arthur Edward Jefferys, *died* 1963, vol. VI
Nicolls, Sir Basil Edward, 1893–1965, vol. VI
Nicolls, Brig.-Gen. Edmund Gustavus, 1858–1932, vol. III
Nicolls, Edward Hugh Dyneley, 1871–1963, vol. VI
Nicolls, Ven Gerald Edward, 1862–1937, vol. III
Nicolls, Maj.-Gen. Oliver Henry Atkins, 1834–1920, vol. II
Nicolson, Sir Arthur John Frederick William, 11th Bt (*cr* 1629), 1882–1952, vol. V
Nicolson, Sir Arthur Thomas Bennet Robert, 10th Bt (*cr* 1629), 1842–1917, vol. II
Nicolson, David, 1844–1932, vol. III
Nicolson, Sir David Lancaster, 1922–1996, vol. X
Nicolson, Wing Comdr Eric James Brindley, 1917–1945, vol. IV
Nicolson, Sir Frederick William Erskine, 10th Bt (*cr* 1637), 1815–1899, vol. I
Nicolson, Hon. Sir Harold George, 1886–1968, vol. VI
Nicolson, Sir (Harold) Stanley, 12th Bt, 1883–1961, vol. VI
Nicolson, Sir John William, 1895–1965, vol. VI
Nicolson, Sir Kenneth, 1891–1964, vol. VI
Nicolson, Lionel Benedict, 1914–1978, vol. VII
Nicolson, Lt-Gen. Malcolm Hassels, 1843–1904, vol. I
Nicolson, Malise Allen, 1921–1995, vol. IX
Nicolson, Sir Stanley; *see* Nicolson, Sir H. S.
Nicoresti, Carol Adolph C.; *see* Cofman-Nicoresti.
Nidditch, Peter Harold, 1928–1983, vol. VIII
Niebuhr, Reinhold, 1892–1971, vol. VII
Niecks, Frederick, 1845–1924, vol. II
Niehaus, Charles Henry, 1855–1935, vol. III
Nield, Sir Basil Edward, 1903–1996, vol. X
Nield, Rt Hon. Sir Herbert, 1862–1932, vol. III
Nield, Sir William Alan, 1913–1994, vol. IX

Nielson, Hon. Niel, 1869–1930, vol. III
Niemeyer, Sir Otto Ernst, 1883–1971, vol. VII
Niemöller, Rev. (Friedrich Gustav Emil) Martin, 1892–1984, vol. VIII
Niemöller, Rev. Martin; *see* Niemöller, Rev. F. G. E. M.
Nietzsche, Friedrich Wilhelm, 1844–1900, vol. I
Nightingale, Sir Charles Athelstan, 16th Bt, 1902–1977, vol. VII
Nightingale, Edward Humphrey, 1904–1996, vol. X
Nightingale, Sir Edward Manners, 14th Bt, 1888–1953, vol. V
Nightingale, Florence, 1820–1910, vol. I
Nightingale, Sir Geoffrey Slingsby, 15th Bt, 1904–1972, vol. VII
Nightingale, Sir Henry Dickonson, 13th (styled 9th) Bt, 1830–1911, vol. I
Nightingale, Maj.-Gen. Manners Ralph Willmot, 1871–1956, vol. V
Nightingale of Cromarty, Michael David, 1927–1998, vol. X
Nightingale, Percy Herbert, 1907–1981, vol. VIII
Nightingale, Thomas Slingsby, 1866–1918, vol. II
Nihalsingh, Rev. Canon Solomon, 1852–1916, vol. II
Nihill, Sir Barclay; *see* Nihill, Sir J. H. B.
Nihill, Sir (John Harry) Barclay, 1892–1975, vol. VII
Nijland, Albertus Antonie, 1868–1936, vol. III
Niland, D'Arcy Francis, *died* 1967, vol. VI
Niles, Emory Hamilton, 1892–1976, vol. VII
Nilkanth, Rao Bahadur Sir Ramanbhai Mahipatram, *died* 1928, vol. II
Nilsson, Mme Christine, (Comtesse de Miranda), 1843–1921, vol. II
Nilsson, Lars-Åke, 1943–1996, vol. X
Nimitz, Fleet Adm. Chester William, 1885–1966, vol. VI
Nimmo, Sir Adam, *died* 1939, vol. III
Nimmo, Derek Robert, 1930–1999, vol. X
Nimmo, Surg. Rear-Adm. Frank Hutton, 1872–1954, vol. V
Nimmo, Henry, 1885–1954, vol. V
Nimmo, Hon. Sir John Angus, 1909–1997, vol. X
Nimmo, Sir Robert, 1894–1979, vol. VII
Nimmo, Maj.-Gen. Thomas Rose, 1831–1904, vol. I
Nimptsch, Uli, 1897–1977, vol. VII
Nind, William Walker, 1882–1964, vol. VI
Ninis, Rev. Richard Duncan, 1867–1940, vol. III
Ninnes, Bernard, 1899–1971, vol. VII
Ninnis, Insp.-Gen. Belgrave, *died* 1922, vol. II
Nipher, Francis Eugene, 1847–1926, vol. II
Nisbet, Brig.-Gen. Francis Courtenay, 1869–1953, vol. V
Nisbet, Hugh Bryan, 1902–1969, vol. VI
Nisbet, Hume, *born* 1849, vol. II
Nisbet, James Wilkie, 1903–1974, vol. VII
Nisbet, John, 1853–1914, vol. I
Nisbet, John Ferguson, 1851–1899, vol. I
Nisbet, Rev. Matthew Alexander, 1838–1919, vol. II
Nisbet, Noel L., 1887–1956, vol. V
Nisbet, Pollok Sinclair, *born* 1848, vol. II
Nisbet, Robert Buchan, 1857–1942, vol. IV
Nisbet, Col Robert Parry, 1839–1916, vol. II
Nisbet, Col Thomas, 1882–1956, vol. V

Nisbet-Hamilton Ogilvy, Mrs; *see* Ogilvy.
Nisbett, Lt-Col George Dalrymple More, 1850–1922, vol. II
Nisbett, George Hinde, 1866–1940, vol. III
Nisse, Bertram Sydney, *died* 1946, vol. IV
Nissen, Karl Iversen, 1906–1995, vol. IX
Nissen, Lt-Col Peter Norman, 1871–1930, vol. III
Nissim, Charles, 1845–1918, vol. II
Nitch, Cyril Alfred Rankin, *died* 1969, vol. VI
Niven, Sir (Cecil) Rex, 1898–1993, vol. IX
Niven, Charles, *died* 1923, vol. II
Niven, David; *see* Niven, J. D. G.
Niven, Frederick John, 1878–1944, vol. IV
Niven, James, 1851–1925, vol. II
Niven, (James) David (Graham), 1910–1983, vol. VIII
Niven, Sir John, 1877–1947, vol. IV
Niven, Margaret Graeme, 1906–1997, vol. X
Niven, Sir Rex; *see* Niven, Sir C. R.
Niven, Very Rev. T. B. W., 1834–1914, vol. I
Niven, Col Thomas Murray, 1900–1987, vol. VIII
Niven, William, *died* 1921, vol. II
Niven, Sir William Davidson, 1842–1917, vol. II
Niven, William Dickie, 1879–1965, vol. VI
Nixon, Alfred, 1858–1928, vol. II
Nixon, Maj.-Gen. Arundel James, 1849–1925, vol. II
Nixon, Sir (Charles) Norman, 1891–1978, vol. VII
Nixon, Sir Christopher John, 1st Bt, 1849–1914, vol. I
Nixon, Major Sir Christopher John Louis Joseph, 3rd Bt, 1918–1978, vol. VII
Nixon, Sir Christopher William, 2nd Bt, 1877–1945, vol. IV
Nixon, Sir Edwin Vandervord, 1876–1955, vol. V
Nixon, Sir Frank Horsfall, 1890–1966, vol. VI
Nixon, Ven. George Robinson, *died* 1963, vol. VI
Nixon, Rear-Adm. Harry Desmond, 1920–1986, vol. VIII
Nixon, Henry, 1874–1939, vol. III
Nixon, Rev. Howard, *died* 1936, vol. III
Nixon, Howard Millar, 1909–1983, vol. VIII
Nixon, Job, 1891–1938, vol. III
Nixon, John Alexander, 1874–1951, vol. V
Nixon, Sir John Carson, 1887–1958, vol. V
Nixon, Gen. Sir John Eccles, 1857–1921, vol. II
Nixon, John William, *died* 1949, vol. IV
Nixon, Rev. Sir Kenneth Michael John Basil, 4th Bt, 1919–1997, vol. X
Nixon, Rev. Leigh Hunter, 1871–1941, vol. IV
Nixon, Sir Norman; *see* Nixon, Sir C. N.
Nixon, Richard Milhous, 1913–1994, vol. IX
Nixon, Rev. Robin Ernest, 1931–1978, vol. VII
Nixon, Wilfrid Ernest, 1892–1970, vol. VI
Nixon, William Charles Wallace, 1903–1966, vol. VI
Nizamat Jung; *see* Ahmad, Maulvi Sir N.
Nkrumah, Kwame, 1909–1972, vol. VII
Noad, Lewis, 1865–1950, vol. IV
Noad, Sir Kenneth Beeson, 1900–1987, vol. IX(AI)
Noad, Sidney Reginald L.; *see* Innes-Noad.
Noakes, Ven. Edward Spencer, *died* 1944, vol. IV
Noakes, Col Geoffrey William, 1913–1989, vol. VIII
Noakes, Sidney Henry, 1905–1993, vol. IX

Noal, Comdr Richard John, 1870–1950, vol. IV
Nobbs, Percy Erskine, 1875–1966, vol. VI
Nobes, Peter John, 1935–1997, vol. X
Noble, Comdr Rt Hon. Sir Allan Herbert Percy, 1908–1982, vol. VIII
Noble, Sir Andrew, 1st Bt (*cr* 1902), 1831–1915, vol. I
Noble, Sir Andrew Napier, 2nd Bt, 1904–1987, vol. VIII
Noble, Col Sir Arthur, 1908–1982, vol. VIII
Noble, Dennis, 1898–1966, vol. VI
Noble, Edward, 1857–1941, vol. IV
Noble, Frederick Arnold W.; *see* Williamson-Noble.
Noble, Sir George John William, 2nd Bt (*cr* 1902), 1859–1937, vol. III
Noble, Sir Humphrey Brunel, 4th Bt (*cr* 1902), 1892–1968, vol. VI
Noble, J. Campbell, 1846–1913, vol. I
Noble, John, 1837–1898, vol. I
Noble, Sir John Henry Brunel, 1st Bt (*cr* 1923), 1865–1938, vol. III
Noble, Kenneth Albert, 1912–1998, vol. X
Noble, Maj. Sir Marc Brunel, 5th Bt (*cr* 1902), 1927–1991, vol. IX
Noble, Michael Alfred, 1935–1983, vol. VIII
Noble, Michael Antony Cristobal; *see* Baron Glenkinglas.
Noble, Adm. Sir Percy Lockhart Harnam, 1880–1955, vol. V
Noble, Sir Peter Scott, 1899–1987, vol. VIII
Noble, Philip Ernest, *died* 1931, vol. III
Noble, Robert, 1857–1917, vol. II
Noble, Robert More Hilary, 1909–1984, vol. VIII
Noble, Sir Saxton William Armstrong, 3rd Bt (*cr* 1902), 1863–1942, vol. IV
Noble, Thomas Tertius, 1867–1953, vol. V
Noble, Thomas Paterson, 1887–1959, vol. V
Noble, Rev. Walter James, 1879–1962, vol. VI
Noble, Sir William, 1861–1943, vol. IV
Noble, William James, 1855–1914, vol. I
Noble, Rev. William Mackreth, 1845–1929, vol. III
Noble, Wilson, 1854–1917, vol. II
Noblett, Bt Lt-Col Louis Hemington, 1869–1948, vol. IV
Nock, Arthur Darby, 1902–1963, vol. VI
Nock, Rt Rev. Frank Foley, 1916–1989, vol. VIII
Nock, Sir Norman Lindfield, 1899–1990, vol. VIII
Nockolds, Stephen Robert, 1909–1990, vol. VIII
Nodzu, Michitsura, Marshal Marquess, 1841–1908, vol. I
Noel, Andre Espitalier-, 1898–1950, vol. IV (A), vol. V
Noel, Lady Augusta, 1838–1902, vol. I
Noel, Hon. Charles Hubert Francis, 1885–1947, vol. V
Noël, Sir Claude; *see* Noël, Sir M. E. C.
Noel, Rev. Conrad le Despenser Roden, 1869–1942, vol. IV
Noel, Lt-Col Hon. Edward, 1852–1917, vol. II
Noel, Ernest, 1831–1931, vol. III
Noel, Evan Baillie, 1879–1928, vol. II
Noel, Adm. Francis Charles Methuen, 1852–1925, vol. II
Noel, Rear-Adm. Gambier John Byng; 1914–1995, vol. IX

Noel, Admiral of the Fleet Sir Gerard Henry Uctred, 1845–1918, vol. II
Noel, Rt Hon. Gerard James, 1823–1911, vol. I
Noel, Bt Col Harold Ernest, 1884–1941, vol. IV
Noel, Rev. Canon John Monk, 1840–1921, vol. II
Noël, Sir (Martial Ernest) Claude, 1912–1985, vol. VIII
Noel-Baker, Baron (Life Peer); Philip John Noel-Baker, 1889–1982, vol. VIII
Noel-Buxton, 1st Baron, 1869–1948, vol. IV
Noel-Buxton, 2nd Baron, 1917–1980, vol. VII
Noel-Buxton, Lady; (Lucy Edith), died 1960, vol. V
Noel-Hill, Rev. Charles, 1848–1911, vol. I
Noel-Paton, family name of Baron Ferrier.
Noel-Walker, Sir Edward; see Walker.
Noghi, Gen. Count Mare-Suke, 1849–1912, vol. I
Nokes, George Augustus; see Sekon, G. A.
Nokes, Gerald Dacre, 1899–1971, vol. VII
Nolan, Lt-Col Andrew Bellew, 1867–1932, vol. III
Nolan, Very Rev. Mgr Edmond, 1857–1931, vol. III
Nolan, James Joseph, 1869–1939, vol. III
Nolan, John J., 1888–1952, vol. V
Nolan, Col John Philip, died 1912, vol. I
Nolan, Michael James, 1859–1944, vol. IV
Nolan, Sir Robert Howard, died 1923, vol. II
Nolan, Sir Sidney Robert, 1917–1992, vol. IX
Nöldeke, Theodor, 1836–1930, vol. III
Nolhac, Pierre de, 1859–1936, vol. III
Nollet, Edouard, 1865–1941, vol. IV
Nolloth, Rev. Charles Frederick, 1850–1932, vol. III
Nolloth, Rev. Henry Edward, 1846–1929, vol. III
Nonweiler, Terence Reginald Forbes, 1925–1999, vol. X
Nonweiler, Maj.-Gen. Wilfrid Ivan, 1900–1953, vol. V
Noon, Firoz Khan, 1893–1970, vol. VI
Noon, Nawab Sir Malik Mohamed Hayat, 1875–1941, vol. IV
Noone, Paul, 1939–1989, vol. VIII
Noott, Col Cuthbert Cecil, 1870–1933, vol. III
Nops, Walter, 1850–1918, vol. II
Nops, Sir Wilfrid Walter, 1884–1948, vol. IV
Norbury, 4th Earl of, 1862–1943, vol. IV
Norbury, 5th Earl of, 1893–1955, vol. V
Norbury, 6th Earl of, 1939–2000, vol. X
Norbury, Edwin Arthur, 1849–1918, vol. II
Norbury, Insp.-Gen. Sir Henry Frederick, 1839–1925, vol. II
Norbury, Sir Henry Frederick Oswald, 1880–1948, vol. IV
Norbury, Captain Herbert Reginald, 1876–1967, vol. VI
Norbury, Lionel Edward Close, 1882–1967, vol. VI
Norbury, Col Thomas Coningsby, 1829–1899, vol. I
Norcock, Vice-Adm. Charles James, 1847–1933, vol. III
Norcott, Col Charles Hawtrey Bruce, 1849–1931, vol. III
Nordau, Max Simon, 1849–1923, vol. II
Nordenskiold, Baron Adolphe Eric, 1832–1901, vol. I
Nordenskjöld, Otto, 1869–1928, vol. II
Nordhoff, Heinrich, 1899–1968, vol. VI
Nordica, Lillian, 1859–1914, vol. I

Nordmeyer, Hon. Sir Arnold Henry, 1901–1989, vol. VIII
Norfolk, 15th Duke of, 1847–1917, vol. II
Norfolk, 16th Duke of, 1908–1975, vol. VII
Norfolk, Lavinia Duchess of, 1916–1995, vol. IX
Norfolk, Rear-Adm. George Anthony Francis, 1907–1966, vol. VI
Norie, Maj.-Gen. Charles Edward Manley, 1866–1929, vol. III
Norie, Maj.-Gen. Evelyn Medows, 1833–1913, vol. I
Norie-Miller, Sir Francis, 1st Bt, 1859–1947, vol. IV
Norie-Miller, Sir Stanley, 2nd Bt, 1888–1973, vol. VII
Nörlund, Niels Erik, 1885–1981, vol. VIII
Norman, 1st Baron, 1871–1950, vol. IV
Norman, Lady; Priscilla Cecilia Maria Norman, 1899–1991, vol. IX
Norman, (Alexander) Vesey (Bethune), 1930–1998, vol. X
Norman, Vice-Adm. Alfred Headley, 1881–1973, vol. VII
Norman, Rev. Alfred Merle, 1831–1918, vol. II
Norman, Arthur William, 1850–1928, vol. II
Norman, Sir Charles, 1892–1976, vol. VII
Norman, Rev. Charles Frederick, 1829–1913, vol. I
Norman, Charles Kensit, 1857–1937, vol. III
Norman, Maj.-Gen. Charles Wake, 1891–1974, vol. VII
Norman, Brig.-Gen. Claude Lumsden, 1876–1967, vol. VI
Norman, Brig. Compton Cardew, 1877–1955, vol. V
Norman, Duncan Thomas, 1889–1972, vol. VII
Norman, Edward, 1847–1923, vol. II
Norman, Sir Edward James, 1900–1983, vol. VIII
Norman, Rt Rev. Edward Kinsella Norman, 1916–1987, vol. VIII
Norman, Comdr F. M., 1833–1918, vol. II
Norman, Sir Francis Booth, 1830–1901, vol. I
Norman, Sir Frederick, 1857–1936, vol. III
Norman, Frederick, 1897–1968, vol. VI
Norman, Vice-Adm. Sir Geoffrey; see Norman, Vice-Adm. Sir. H. G.
Norman, Col. Harold Hugh, 1875–1933, vol. III
Norman, Rt Hon. Sir Henry, 1st Bt, 1858–1939, vol. III
Norman, Henry Gordon, 1890–1967, vol. VI
Norman, Sir (Henry) Nigel St Valery, 2nd Bt, 1897–1943, vol. IV
Norman, Lt-Gen. Sir Henry Radford, 1818–1899, vol. I
Norman, Sir Henry Wylie, 1826–1904, vol. I
Norman, Herman Cameron, 1872–1955, vol. V
Norman, Vice-Admiral Sir (Horace) Geoffrey, 1896–1992, vol. IX
Norman, Brig. Hugh Ronald, 1905–1979, vol. VII
Norman, Mark Richard, 1910–1994, vol. IX
Norman, Sir Nigel; see Norman, Sir H. N. St V.
Norman, Philip, died 1931, vol. III
Norman, Sir Richard Oswald Chandler, 1932–1993, vol. IX
Norman, Sir Robert Wentworth, 1912–1997, vol. X
Norman, Ronald Collet, 1873–1963, vol. VI
Norman, Vesey; see Norman, A. V. B.

Norman, Surg.-Vice-Adm. Sir William Henry, 1855–1934, vol. III
Norman, Col William Wylie, 1860–1935, vol. III
Norman, Willoughby Rollo, 1909–1997, vol. X
Norman Barnett, Lt-Col Henry, died 1952, vol. V
Norman-Walker, Sir Hugh Selby, 1916–1985, vol. VIII
Norman-Walker, Col John Norman, 1872–1951, vol. V
Normanbrook, 1st Baron, 1902–1967, vol. VI
Normanby, 3rd Marquess of, 1846–1932, vol. III
Normanby, 4th Marquis of, 1912–1994, vol. IX
Normand, Baron (Life Peer); Wilfrid Guild Normand, 1884–1962, vol. VI
Normand, Alexander Robert, 1880–1958, vol. V
Normand, Sir Charles William Blyth, 1889–1982, vol. VIII
Normand, Mrs Ernest, (Henrietta Rae), 1859–1928, vol. II
Normand, Captain Patrick Hill, 1876–1943, vol. IV
Normand, Robert Casley, 1897–1962, vol. VI
Normanton, 4th Earl of, 1865–1933, vol. III
Normanton, 5th Earl of, 1910–1967, vol. VI
Normanton, Helena Florence, 1883–1957, vol. V
Normanton, Sir Tom, 1917–1997, vol. X
Norreys, Lord; Montagu Charles Francis Towneley-Bertie, 1860–1919, vol. II
Norrie, 1st Baron, 1893–1977, vol. VII
Norrie, Beatrice, died 1933, vol. III
Norrie, Col Edward Creer, 1885–1958, vol. V
Norrington, Sir Arthur Lionel Pugh, 1899–1982, vol. VIII
Norrington, Lt-Col Reginald Lewis, died 1960, vol. V
Norris, Dame Ada May, 1901–1989, vol. VIII
Norris, Alan Hedley, 1913–1981, vol. VIII
Norris, Sir Alfred Henry, 1894–1989, vol. VIII
Norris, Arthur Gilbert, 1889–1962, vol. VI
Norris, Arthur Herbert, 1875–1953, vol. V
Norris, Charles Arthur, 1874–1941, vol. IV
Norris, Vice-Adm. Sir Charles Fred Wivell, 1900–1989, vol. VIII
Norris, Charles Gilman, died 1945, vol. IV
Norris, Adm. David Thomas, 1875–1937, vol. III
Norris, Donald Craig, died 1968, vol. VI
Norris, Rev. Edward John, 1860–1940, vol. III
Norris, Edward Samuel, 1832–1908, vol. I
Norris, Francis Edward Boshear, died 1966, vol. VI
Norris, Rt Rev. Francis Lushington, 1864–1945, vol. IV
Norris, Maj.-Gen. Sir (Frank) Kingsley, 1893–1984, vol. VIII
Norris, George Michael, 1841–1922, vol. II
Norris, Henry, 1852–1954, vol. V
Norris, Col Henry Crawley, 1841–1914, vol. I
Norris, Lt-Col Henry Everard DuCane, 1869–1960, vol. V
Norris, Col Sir Henry George, 1865–1934, vol. III
Norris, Herbert, died 1950, vol. IV
Norris, Herbert Walter, 1904–1991, vol. IX
Norris, Rt Rev. Ivor Arthur, 1901–1969, vol. VI
Norris, Very Rev. John, 1843–1911, vol. I
Norris, John Alexander, 1872–1962, vol. VI
Norris, John Freeman, 1842–1904, vol. I
Norris, Sir John Gerald, 1903–1990, vol. VIII

Norris, Kathleen, 1880–1966, vol. VI
Norris, Maj.-Gen. Sir Kingsley; see Norris, Maj.-Gen. Sir F. K.
Norris, Oswald Thomas, 1883–1973, vol. VII
Norris, Richard Hill, 1886–1970, vol. VI
Norris, Lt-Col Richard Joseph, 1854–1935, vol. III
Norris, Captain Stephen Hugh, 1903–1944, vol. IV
Norris, Rev. Canon Walter Edward, 1905–1971, vol. VII
Norris, William Edward, 1847–1925, vol. II
Norris, Very Rev. William Foxley, 1859–1937, vol. III
Norrish, Ronald George Wreyford, 1897–1978, vol. VII
Norritt, Sir James Henry, 1889–1963, vol. VI
Norstad, Gen. Lauris, 1907–1988, vol. VIII
North, 11th Baron, 1836–1932, vol. III
North, 12th Baron, 1860–1938, vol. III
North, 13th Baron, 1917–1941, vol. IV
North, Lord; Francis George North, 1902–1940, vol. III
North, Rt Hon. Sir Alfred Kingsley, 1900–1981, vol. VIII
North, Brig.-Gen. Bordrigge North, 1862–1936, vol. III
North, Rev. Christopher Richard, 1888–1975, vol. VII
North, Col Dudley, 1840–1917, vol. II
North, Adm. Sir Dudley Burton Napier, 1881–1961, vol. VI
North, Hon. Dudley William John, 1891–1936, vol. III
North, Col Edward, 1856–1927, vol. II
North, Lt-Col Edward Bunbury, 1869–1944, vol. IV
North, Major Edward Tempest Tunstall, 1900–1942, vol. IV
North, Rt Hon. Sir Ford, 1830–1913, vol. I
North, Brig. Francis Roger, 1894–1978, vol. VII
North, Frederic Dudley, 1866–1921, vol. II
North, Frederick Keppel, 1860–1948, vol. IV
North, Sir George Cecil, 1895–1971, vol. VII
North, Brig. Harold Napier, 1883–1957, vol. V
North, Sir Harry, 1866–1920, vol. II
North, Herbert L., 1871–1941, vol. IV
North, Howard; see Trevor, E.
North, Major John, 1894–1973, vol. VII
North, John Dudley, 1893–1968, vol. VI
North, John William, 1842–1924, vol. II
North, Lt-Col Sir Jonathan, 1855–1939, vol. III
North, North, 1824–1910, vol. I
North, Roger, 1901–1985, vol. VIII
North, Roland Arthur Charles, 1889–1961, vol. VI
North, Walter Meyrick, died 1900, vol. I
North, William Albert, 1881–1946, vol. IV
Northam, Sir Reginald, died 1967, vol. VI
Northampton, 4th Marquess of, 1818–1897, vol. I
Northampton, 5th Marquess of, 1851–1913, vol. I
Northampton, 6th Marquess of, 1885–1978, vol. VII
Northbourne, 2nd Baron, 1846–1923, vol. II
Northbourne, 3rd Baron, 1869–1932, vol. III
Northbourne, 4th Baron, 1896–1982, vol. VIII
Northbrook, 1st Earl of, 1826–1904, vol. I
Northbrook, 2nd Earl of, 1850–1929, vol. III
Northbrook, Countess of; (Florence Anita Eyre), died 1946, vol. IV

Northbrook, 4th Baron, 1882–1947, vol. IV
Northbrook, 5th Baron, 1915–1990, vol. VIII
Northchurch, Baroness (Life Peer); *see* Davidson, Dowager Viscountess.
Northcliffe, 1st Viscount, 1865–1922, vol. II
Northcote, 1st Baron, 1846–1911, vol. I
Northcote, Lady; (Alice), *died* 1934, vol. III
Northcote, Rev. Hon. Arthur Francis, 1852–1943, vol. IV
Northcote, Sir Ernest Augustus, 1850–1915, vol. I
Northcote, Sir Geoffry Alexander Stafford, 1881–1948, vol. IV
Northcote, Rev. Hon. John Stafford, 1850–1920, vol. II
Northcote, Lady Rosalind Lucy Stafford, *died* 1950, vol. IV
Northcote-Green, Roger James, 1912–1990, vol. VIII
Northcott, Rev. Cecil; *see* Northcott, Rev. W. C.
Northcott, Gen. Sir John, 1890–1966, vol. VI
Northcott, Captain Ralph William Frank, 1907–1976, vol. VII
Northcott, Richard A., 1871–1931, vol. III
Northcott, Rev. William, 1854–1924, vol. II
Northcott, Rev. (William) Cecil, 1902–1987, vol. VIII
Northcroft, Sir Erima Harvey, 1884–1953, vol. V
Northcroft, Ernest George Drennan, 1896–1976, vol. VII
Northedge, Frederick Samuel, 1918–1985, vol. VIII
Northen, Lt-Col Arthur, 1873–1964, vol. VI
Northesk, 10th Earl of, 1865–1921, vol. II
Northesk, 11th Earl of, 1901–1963, vol. VI
Northesk, 12th Earl of, 1895–1975, vol. VII
Northesk, 13th Earl of, 1926–1994, vol. IX
Northey, Sir Armand Hunter Kennedy Wilbraham, 1897–1964, vol. VI
Northey, Maj.-Gen. Sir Edward, 1868–1953, vol. V
Northey, Lt-Col Herbert Hamilton, 1870–1938, vol. III
Northey, Captain William, 1876–1914, vol. I
Northfield, Douglas William Claridge, *died* 1976, vol. VII
Northland, Viscount; Thomas Uchter Caulfield Knox, 1882–1915, vol. I
Northmore, Sir John Alfred, 1865–1958, vol. V
Northrop, Cyrus, 1834–1922, vol. II
Northrop, Filmer Stuart Cuckow, 1893–1992, vol. IX
Northrop, John Howard, 1891–1987, vol. VIII
Northrup, William Barton, *died* 1925, vol. II
Northumberland, 6th Duke of, 1810–1899, vol. I
Northumberland, 7th Duke of, 1846–1918, vol. II
Northumberland, 8th Duke of, 1880–1930, vol. III
Northumberland, 9th Duke of, 1912–1940, vol. III
Northumberland, 10th Duke of, 1914–1988, vol. VIII
Northumberland, 11th Duke of, 1953–1995, vol. IX
Northumberland, Duchess of; (Helen Magdalen), *died* 1965, vol. VI
Northwick, Lady; (Elizabeth Augusta), 1832–1912, vol. I
Norton, 1st Baron, 1814–1905, vol. I
Norton, 2nd Baron, 1846–1926, vol. II
Norton, 3rd Baron, 1872–1933, vol. III

Norton, 4th Baron, 1885–1944, vol. IV
Norton, 5th Baron, 1854–1945, vol. IV
Norton, 6th Baron, 1886–1961, vol. VI
Norton, 7th Baron, 1915–1993, vol. IX
Norton, Major Alfred Edward Marston, 1869–1922, vol. II
Norton, Arthur Trehern, 1841–1912, vol. I
Norton, Brig.-Gen. Cecil Burrington, 1868–1953, vol. V
Norton, Sir Charles; *see* Norton, Sir W. C.
Norton, Lt-Col Charles Edward, 1861–1931, vol. III
Norton, Charles Eliot, 1827–1908, vol. I
Norton, Brig.-Gen. Charles Ernest Graham, 1869–1953, vol. V
Norton, Charles William, 1870–1946, vol. IV
Norton, Sir Clifford John, 1891–1990, vol. VIII
Norton, Maj.-Gen. Cyril Henry, 1898–1983, vol. VIII
Norton, David, 1851–1929, vol. III
Norton, David Evans, 1863–1946, vol. IV
Norton, Edward, 1841–1923, vol. II
Norton, Lt-Gen. Edward Felix, 1884–1954, vol. V
Norton, Sir Evan Augustus, 1901–1967, vol. VI
Norton, George Frederic, *died* 1946, vol. IV
Norton, Col Gilbert Paul, 1882–1962, vol. VI
Norton, Ven. Hugh Ross, 1890–1969, vol. VI
Norton, Rt Rev. John F., 1891–1963, vol. VI
Norton, Ven. John George, 1840–1924, vol. II
Norton, Rt Rev. John Henry, 1855–1923, vol. II
Norton, Mary, 1903–1992, vol. IX
Norton, Richard, 1872–1918, vol. II
Norton, Robert, 1838–1926, vol. II
Norton, Robert Frederick, 1854–1929, vol. III
Norton, Roger Edward, 1897–1978, vol. VII
Norton, Thomas, 1845–1935, vol. III
Norton, Sir (Walter) Charles, 1896–1974, vol. VII
Norton, Wilfrid, *died* 1973, vol. VII
Norton, William, *died* 1963, vol. VI
Norton-Griffiths, Lt-Col Sir John; *see* Griffiths.
Norton-Griffiths, Sir Peter, 2nd Bt, 1905–1983, vol. VIII
Norval, Sir James, 1862–1936, vol. III
Norway, Arthur Hamilton, 1859–1938, vol. III
Norway, Nevil Shute, 1899–1960, vol. V
Norwich, 1st Viscount, 1890–1954, vol. V
Norwood, Sir Charles John Boyd, 1871–1966, vol. VI
Norwood, Christopher Bonnewell Burton, 1932–1972, vol. VII
Norwood, Sir Cyril, 1875–1956, vol. V
Norwood, Rev. Frederick William, *died* 1958, vol. V
Norwood, Gilbert, 1880–1954, vol. V
Norwood, Captain John, 1876–1914, vol. I
Norwood, Rev. Reginald, 1874–1928, vol. II, vol. III
Norwood, William Stuart, *died* 1944, vol. IV
Noser, Most Rev. Adolf, 1900–1981, vol. VIII
Nossiter, Bernard Daniel, 1926–1992, vol. IX
Nosworthy, Lt-Gen. Sir Francis Poitiers, 1887–1971, vol. VII
Nosworthy, Harold George, 1908–1997, vol. X
Nosworthy, Sir John Reeve, 1915–1990, vol. VIII
Nosworthy, Richard, 1860–1946, vol. IV
Nosworthy, Sir Richard Lysle, 1885–1966, vol. VI
Nosworthy, Hon. Sir William, 1867–1946, vol. IV
Notcutt, Henry Clement, 1865–1935, vol. III

Notestein, Wallace, 1878–1969, vol. VI
Notley, Captain Sir Franke Bartlett Stuart, 1865–1939, vol. III
Nott, Charles Robert Harley, 1904–1997, vol. X
Nott, Frederic Trevor, 1885–1950, vol. IV
Nott, Comdr Sir James Grenvile P.; see Pyke-Nott.
Nott, Kathleen Cecilia, 1905–1999, vol. X
Nott, Very Rev. Michael John, 1916–1988, vol. VIII
Nott-Bower, Sir Edmund Ernest, 1853–1933, vol. III
Nott-Bower, Sir Guy; see Nott-Bower, Sir W. G.
Nott-Bower, Sir John Reginald Hornby, 1892–1972, vol. VII
Nott-Bower, Captain Sir (John) William, 1849–1939, vol. III
Nott-Bower, Captain Sir William; see Nott-Bower, Captain Sir J. W.
Nott-Bower, Sir (William) Guy, 1890–1977, vol. VII
Notten-Pole, Sir Cecil Pery Van; see Pole.
Notter, Col J. Lane-, died 1923, vol. II
Nottidge, Sir William Rolfe, 1889–1966, vol. VI
Nottingham, Rev. Edward Emil, 1866–1921, vol. II
Nougués, Jean, died 1932, vol. III
Nourse, William John Chichele, died 1937, vol. III
Novar, 1st Viscount, 1860–1934, vol. III
Novar, Viscountess; (Helen Hermione), 1865–1941, vol. IV
Nove, Alexander, 1915–1994, vol. IX
Novello, Ivor, 1893–1951, vol. V
Novikoff, Mme Olga, 1848–1925, vol. II
Novy, Frederick G., 1864–1957, vol. V
Nowell, Arthur T., 1861–1940, vol. III
Nowell, Charles, 1890–1954, vol. V
Nowell, Air Cdre Henry Edward, 1903–1967, vol. VI
Nowell, Ralph Machattie, 1903–1973, vol. VII
Nowell, William, 1880–1968, vol. VI
Nowell, Rev. William Edward, died 1929, vol. III
Nowell-Rostron, Rev. Sydney, 1883–1948, vol. IV
Nowell-Smith, Simon Harcourt, 1909–1996, vol. X
Noxon, William Courtland, died 1943, vol. IV
Noyce, Sir Frank, 1878–1948, vol. IV
Noyes, Alfred, 1880–1958, vol. V
Noyes, Gen. Sir Cyril Dupré, 1885–1946, vol. IV
Noyes, Ralph Norton, 1923–1998, vol. X
Nuffield, 1st Viscount, 1877–1963, vol. VI
Nugee, Rev. Francis Edward, died 1930, vol. III
Nugee, Francis John, 1891–1966, vol. VI
Nugent, 1st Baron, 1895–1973, vol. VII
Nugent of Guildford, Baron (Life Peer); George Richard Hodges Nugent, 1907–1994, vol. IX
Nugent, Albert Beauchamp, died 1938, vol. III
Nugent, Algernon John FitzRoy, 1865–1922, vol. II
Nugent, Sir Charles, 5th Bt (cr 1795), 1847–1927, vol. II
Nugent, Sir Charles Butler Peter Hodges, 1827–1899, vol. I
Nugent, Col Charles Hugh Hodges, 1868–1924, vol. II
Nugent of Bellême, David James Douglas, 1917–1988, vol. VIII
Nugent, Sir Edmund Charles, 3rd Bt (cr 1806), 1839–1928, vol. II
Nugent, Brig.-Gen. Frank B.; see Burnell-Nugent.
Nugent, Col George Colbourne, 1864–1915, vol. I

Nugent, Sir (George) Guy (Bulwer), 4th Bt (cr 1806), 1892–1970, vol. VI
Nugent, Sir Guy; see Nugent, Sir G. G. B.
Nugent of Clonlost, Guy Patrick Douglas John, 1915–1944, vol. IV
Nugent, Sir Horace Dickinson, 1858–1924, vol. II
Nugent, Sir Hugh Charles, 6th Bt, 1904–1983, vol. VIII
Nugent, Hon. John, 1843–1900, vol. I
Nugent, John Dillon, died 1940, vol. III
Nugent, Maj.-Gen. John Fagan Henslowe, 1889–1975, vol. VII
Nugent, Sir John Nugent, 3rd Bt (cr 1831 of Cloncoskoran), 1849–1929, vol. III
Nugent, Maj.-Gen. Sir Oliver Stewart Wood, 1860–1926, vol. II
Nugent, Vice-Adm. Raymond Andrew, 1870–1959, vol. V
Nugent, Hon. Richard Anthony, 1842–1912, vol. I
Nugent, Col Robert Arthur, 1853–1926, vol. II
Nugent, Rt Hon. Sir Roland Thomas, 1st Bt (cr 1961), 1886–1962, vol. VI
Nugent, Sir Walter Richard, 4th Bt (cr 1831 of Donore), 1865–1955, vol. V
Nugent, Col Walter Vyvian, 1880–1963, vol. VI
Nugent, Captain Hon. William Andrew, 1876–1915, vol. I
Nulty, Rt Rev. Thomas, died 1898, vol. I
Nunan, Sir Joseph, 1873–1934, vol. III
Nunan, William, 1880–1955, vol. V
Nunburnholme, 1st Baron, 1833–1907, vol. I
Nunburnholme, 2nd Baron, 1875–1924, vol. II
Nunburnholme, 3rd Baron, 1904–1974, vol. VII
Nunburnholme, 4th Baron, 1928–1998, vol. X
Nunburnholme, 5th Baron, 1935–2000, vol. X
Nunn, Rev. Henry Drury Cust, died 1922, vol. II
Nunn, Jean Josephine, 1916–1982, vol. VIII
Nunn, Col Joshua Arthur, 1853–1908, vol. I
Nunn, Sir Percy, 1870–1944, vol. IV
Nunn, Thomas William, 1825–1909, vol. I
Nunn, Vice-Adm. Wilfrid, died 1956, vol. V
Nunn, William, 1879–1971, vol. VII
Nunns, Hector Matthew, 1905–1979, vol. VII
Nureyev, Rudolf Hametovich, 1938–1993, vol. IX
Nursaw, William George, 1903–1994, vol. IX
Nurse, Ven. Charles Euston, 1909–1981, vol. VIII
Nurse, George Edward, 1873–1945, vol. IV
Nussey, Col Albert Henry Mortimer, 1880–1944, vol. IV
Nussey, Sir Thomas Moore, 2nd Bt, 1898–1971, vol. VII
Nussey, Sir Willans, 1st Bt, 1868–1947, vol. IV
Nuthall, Brig.-Gen. Charles Edwin, 1862–1943, vol. IV
Nuthall, Col Henry John, 1834–1914, vol. I
Nutt, Albert Boswell, 1898–1978, vol. VII
Nutt, Alfred Trübner, 1856–1910, vol. I
Nutt, Alfred Young, 1847–1924, vol. II
Nutt, Arthur Edgar W.; see Woodward-Nutt.
Nutt, Francis George, 1878–1954, vol. V
Nutt, Maj.-Gen. Harold Rothery, 1876–1953, vol. V
Nutt, Col Herbert John, 1861–1940, vol. III
Nutt, Col James Anson Francis, died 1924, vol. II
Nuttall, Sir Edmund, 1st Bt, 1870–1923, vol. II

Nuttall, Lt-Col Sir (Edmund) Keith, 2nd Bt, 1901–1941, vol. IV
Nuttall, Ellis, 1890–1951, vol. V
Nuttall, Most Rev. Enos, 1842–1916, vol. II
Nuttall, Rev. Frank, 1870–1943, vol. IV
Nuttall, George Henry Falkiner, 1862–1937, vol. III
Nuttall, Harry, 1849–1924, vol. II
Nuttall, Sir James, 1891–1962, vol. VI
Nuttall, Sir James Mansfield, 1827–1897, vol. I
Nuttall, Lt-Col Sir Keith; see Nuttall, Sir E. K.
Nuttall, Thomas Downham, 1877–1934, vol. III
Nuttall, Captain William Ewart, 1876–1939, vol. III
Nuttall, Major William Francis D.; see Dixon-Nuttall.
Nutting, Rt Hon. Sir Anthony; see Nutting, Rt Hon. Sir H. A.
Nutting, Arthur Ronald Stansmore, 1888–1964, vol. VI

Nutting, Air Vice-Marshal Charles William, 1889–1964, vol. VI
Nutting, Rt Hon. Sir (Harold) Anthony, 3rd Bt, 1920–1999, vol. X
Nutting, Sir Harold Stansmore, 2nd Bt, 1882–1972, vol. VII
Nutting, Jack, 1924–1998, vol. X
Nutting, Sir John Gardiner, 1st Bt, 1852–1918, vol. II
Nye, Engr Captain Alfred John, 1855–1932, vol. III
Nye, Lt-Gen. Sir Archibald Edward, 1895–1967, vol. VI
Nye, Sir Geoffrey Walter, 1902–1976, vol. VII
Nyerere, Julius Kambarage, 1922–1999, vol. X
Nygaardsvold, John, 1879–1952, vol. V
Nyholm, Sir Ronald Sydney, 1917–1971, vol. VII
Nys, Ernest, 1851–1920, vol. II
Nystrom, Anton, 1842–1931, vol. III

O

Oak-Rhind, Edwin Scoby, 1883–1963, vol. VI
Oakden, Sir Ralph, 1871–1953, vol. V
Oake, George Robert, 1903–1969, vol. VI
Oakeley, Sir Atholl; see Oakeley, Sir E. A.
Oakeley, Sir Charles John, 5th Bt, 1862–1938, vol. III
Oakeley, Sir Charles Richard Andrew, 6th Bt, 1900–1959, vol. V
Oakeley, Sir Charles William Atholl, 4th Bt, 1828–1915, vol. I
Oakeley, Sir (Edward) Atholl, 7th Bt, 1900–1987, vol. VIII
Oakeley, Sir Herbert Stanley, 1830–1903, vol. I
Oakeley, Hilda Diana, 1867–1950, vol. IV
Oakeley, Mary, 1913–1997, vol. X
Oakes, Sir Augustus Henry, 1839–1919, vol. II
Oakes, Sir Cecil, 1884–1959, vol. V
Oakes, Hon. Charles William, 1861–1928, vol. II
Oakes, Ven. George Spencer, 1855–1932, vol. III
Oakes, Sir Harry, 1st Bt (cr 1939), 1874–1943, vol. IV
Oakes, Sir Reginald Louis, 4th Bt (cr 1815), 1847–1927, vol. II
Oakes, Col Richard, 1876–1944, vol. IV
Oakes, Sir Sydney, 2nd Bt (cr 1939), 1927–1966, vol. VI
Oakeshott, Maj.-Gen. John Field Fraser, 1899–1957, vol. V
Oakeshott, Keith Robertson, 1920–1974, vol. VII
Oakeshott, Michael Joseph, 1901–1990, vol. VIII
Oakeshott, Sir Walter Fraser, 1903–1987, vol. VIII
Oakey, John Martin, 1888–1963, vol. VI
Oakley, Alfred James, 1880–1959, vol. V
Oakley, Rev. Austin, 1890–1977, vol. VII
Oakley, Cyril Leslie, 1907–1975, vol. VII
Oakley, Harry Ekermans, 1866–1943, vol. IV
Oakley, Sir Henry, 1823–1912, vol. I
Oakley, Lt-Col Henry John Percy, 1878–1942, vol. IV
Oakley, John, died 1945, vol. IV
Oakley, Sir John Hubert, 1867–1946, vol. IV

Oakley, Kenneth Page, 1911–1981, vol. VIII
Oakley, Philip Douglas, 1883–1958, vol. V
Oakley, Thomas, 1879–1936, vol. III
Oakley, Wilfrid George, 1905–1998, vol. X
Oaksey, 1st Baron; see under Trevethin, 3rd Baron and Oaksey, 1st Baron.
Oakshott, Baron (Life Peer); Hendrie Dudley Oakshott, 1904–1975, vol. VII
Oaten, Edward Farley, 1884–1973, vol. VII
Oates, Francis Hamer, 1866–1923, vol. II
Oates, Frederick Arthur Harman, died 1928, vol. II
Oates, John Claud Trewinard, 1912–1990, vol. VIII
Oates, Lt-Col William Coape, 1862–1942, vol. IV
Oatley, Sir Charles William, 1904–1996, vol. X
Oatley, Sir George Herbert, 1863–1950, vol. IV
Obaidulla Khan, Nowabzada Hafiz Mohamad Bahadur, 1878–1924, vol. II
O'Beirne, Cornelius Banahan, 1915–1992, vol. IX
O'Beirne, Hugh James, 1866–1916, vol. II
Oberg, Olof David August, 1893–1975, vol. VII
Oberon, Merle, (Estelle Merle O'Brien Thompson), 1911–1979, vol. VII
Obert de Thieusies, Vicomte Alain, 1888–1979, vol. VII
Obey, André, 1892–1975, vol. VII
Obeyesekere, Hon. Sir Christoffel; see Obeyesekere, Hon. Sir S. C.
Obeyesekere, Sir James Peter, 1879–1968, vol. VI
Obeyesekere, Hon. Sir (Solomon) Christoffel, 1848–1926, vol. II, vol. III
Obre, Henry, 1855–1922, vol. II
O'Briain, Art Patrick, 1872–1949, vol. IV
O'Briain, Hon. Barra, 1901–1988, vol. VIII
O'Brien, 1st Baron, 1842–1914, vol. I
O'Brien of Lothbury, Baron (Life Peer); Leslie Kenneth O'Brien, 1908–1995, vol. IX
O'Brien, Arthur John Rushton, 1883–1940, vol. III
O'Brien, Lt-Col Aubrey John, 1870–1930, vol. III
O'Brien, Brian, died 1973, vol. VII
O'Brien, Brig. Brian Palliser Tiegue, 1898–1966, vol. VI

O'Brien, Bryan Justin, 1902–1978, vol. VII
O'Brien, Lt-Col Sir Charles Richard Mackey, 1859–1935, vol. III
O'Brien, Christopher Michael, 1861–1935, vol. III
O'Brien, Most Rev. Cornelius, 1843–1906, vol. I
O'Brien, Daniel Joseph, *died* 1949, vol. IV
O'Brien, Sir David Edmond, 6th Bt, 1902–1982, vol. VIII
O'Brien, Dermod, 1865–1945, vol. IV
O'Brien, Hon. Donough, 1879–1953, vol. V
O'Brien, Brig.-Gen. Edmund Donough John, 1858–1945, vol. IV
O'Brien, Lt-Col Edward, 1872–1965, vol. VI
O'Brien, Edward Joseph Harrington, 1890–1941, vol. IV
O'Brien, Ernest Edward, 1869–1932, vol. III
O'Brien, Sir (Frederick) Lucius, 1896–1974, vol. VII
O'Brien, George, 1892–1973, vol. VII
O'Brien, Sir George Thomas Michael, 1844–1906, vol. I
O'Brien, Henry, *born* 1836, vol. III
O'Brien, Lt-Col Hon. Henry Barnaby, 1887–1969, vol. VI
O'Brien, James Francis Xavier, 1828–1905, vol. I
O'Brien, John, 1895–1947, vol. V
O'Brien, Sir John Edmond Noel, 5th Bt, 1899–1969, vol. VI
O'Brien, Sir John Terence Nicolls, 1830–1903, vol. I
O'Brien, Kate, 1897–1974, vol. VII
O'Brien, Kendal Edmund, 1849–1909, vol. I
O'Brien, Sir Lucius; *see* O'Brien, Sir F. L.
O'Brien, Very Rev. Lucius H., 1842–1913, vol. I
O'Brien, Most Rev. Michael, 1877–1952, vol. V
O'Brien, Michael, 1883–1958, vol. V
O'Brien, Rt Rev. Mgr Michael Joseph, 1913–1978, vol. VII
O'Brien, Lt-Col Hon. Murrough, 1866–1934, vol. III
O'Brien, Oswald, 1928–1997, vol. X
O'Brien, Owen, 1920–1987, vol. VIII
O'Brien, Patrick, 1853–1917, vol. II
O'Brien, Patrick Joseph, *died* 1911, vol. I
O'Brien, Richard Alfred, 1878–1970, vol. VI
O'Brien, Richard Barry, 1847–1918, vol. II
O'Brien, Sir Robert Rollo Gillespie, 4th Bt, 1901–1952, vol. V
O'Brien, Sir Timothy Carew, 3rd Bt, 1861–1948, vol. IV
O'Brien, Sir Tom, 1900–1970, vol. VI
O'Brien, Turlough Aubrey, 1907–1997, vol. X
O'Brien, Rt Hon. William, 1832–1899, vol. I
O'Brien, William, 1852–1928, vol. II
O'Brien-Butler, Pierce Essex, 1858–1954, vol. V
O'Brien Twohig, Brig. Joseph Patrick, 1905–1973, vol. VII
O'Brien-Twohig, Col Michael Joseph, 1893–1971, vol. VII
O'Bryan, Sir Norman, 1894–1968, vol. VI
O'Byrne, Count John, 1834–1905, vol. I
O'Byrne, John, 1884–1954, vol. V
O'Callaghan, The; *see* O'Callaghan-Westropp, Col George.

O'Callaghan, Col Denis Moriarty, 1861–1926, vol. II
O'Callaghan, Maj.-Gen. Sir Desmond Dykes Tynte, 1843–1931, vol. III
O'Callaghan, Most Rev. Eugene, 1888–1973, vol. VII
O'Callaghan, Sir Francis Langford, 1839–1909, vol. I
O'Callaghan, Adm. George William Douglass, *died* 1900, vol. I
O'Callaghan, Adm. Michael Pelham, 1850–1937, vol. III
O'Callaghan, Robert Alexander, *died* 1903, vol. I
O'Callaghan, Most Rev. Thomas Alphonsus, 1839–1916, vol. II
O'Callaghan, Timothy Patrick Moriarty, 1886–1961, vol. VI
O'Callaghan-Westropp, Col George, (The O'Callaghan), 1864–1944, vol. IV
O'Carroll, Joseph Francis, 1855–1942, vol. IV
O'Carroll Scott, Maj.-Gen. Anthony Gerald; *see* Scott.
O'Casey, Sean, 1880–1964, vol. VI
Ochoa, Severo, 1905–1993, vol. IX
Ochs, Adolph S., 1858–1935, vol. III
Ochterlony, Sir Charles Francis, 5th Bt, 1891–1964, vol. VI
Ochterlony, Sir David Ferguson, 3rd Bt, 1848–1931, vol. III
Ochterlony, Sir Matthew Montgomerie, 4th Bt, 1880–1946, vol. IV
Ockrent, Michael Robert, 1946–1999, vol. X
O'Clery, Count, (The O'Clery), 1849–1913, vol. I
O'Collins, Most Rev. Sir James Patrick, 1892–1983, vol. VIII
O'Connell, Sir Bernard Thomas, 1909–1981, vol. VIII
O'Connell, Daniel Patrick, 1924–1979, vol. VII
O'Connell, Sir Daniel Ross, 3rd Bt, 1861–1905, vol. I
O'Connell, Captain Donal Bernard, 1893–1971, vol. VII
O'Connell, Rev. Frederick William, 1876–1929, vol. III
O'Connell, Captain James Ross, 1863–1925, vol. II
O'Connell, Rev. Sir John Robert, 1868–1943, vol. IV
O'Connell, Captain Sir Maurice James Arthur, 5th Bt, 1889–1949, vol. IV
O'Connell, Sir Morgan Donal Conail, 6th Bt, 1923–1989, vol. VIII
O'Connell, Sir Morgan Ross, 4th Bt, 1862–1919, vol. II
O'Connell, Sir Peter Reilly, *died* 1927, vol. II
O'Connell, Thomas J., 1882–1969, vol. VI
O'Connell, Hon. W. B., *died* 1903, vol. I
O'Connell, His Eminence Cardinal William Henry, 1859–1944, vol. IV
O'Connor, Arthur, 1844–1923, vol. II
O'Connor, Arthur John, 1888–1950, vol. IV (A), vol. V
O'Connor, Col Arthur Patrick, 1856–1920, vol. II
O'Connor, Rt Hon. Charles Andrew, 1854–1928, vol. II
O'Connor, Charles Gerald, 1890–1949, vol. IV (A)

O'Connor, Charles Yelverton, 1843–1902, vol. I
O'Connor, Most Rev. Denis, *died* 1911, vol. I
O'Connor, Lt-Gen. Sir Denis Stuart Scott, 1907–1988, vol. VIII
O'Connor, Rev. Edward Dominic, 1874–1954, vol. V
O'Connor, Francis Brian, 1932–2000, vol. X
O'Connor, Frank, 1903–1966, vol. VI
O'Connor, Lt-Col Sir Frederick; *see* O'Connor, Lt-Col Sir W. F. T.
O'Connor, George Bligh, 1883–1957, vol. V
O'Connor, Col Henry Willis-, 1886–1957, vol. V
O'Connor, James, 1836–1910, vol. I
O'Connor, Rt Hon. Sir James, 1872–1931, vol. III
O'Connor, James Malachy, 1886–1974, vol. VII
O'Connor, John, 1850–1928, vol. II
O'Connor, Sir Kenneth Kennedy, 1896–1985, vol. VIII
O'Connor, Rt Rev. Kevin, 1929–1993, vol. IX
O'Connor, Maj.-Gen. Sir Luke, 1832–1915, vol. I
O'Connor, Lt-Col Patrick Fenelon, 1850–1939, vol. III
O'Connor, Rt Rev. Patrick Joseph, *died* 1932, vol. III
O'Connor, Richard Edward, 1851–1912, vol. I
O'Connor, Gen. Sir Richard Nugent, 1889–1981, vol. VIII
O'Connor, Sir Terence James, 1891–1940, vol. III
O'Connor, Thomas Arthur Leslie S.; *see* Scott O'Connor.
O'Connor, Rt Hon. Thomas Power, 1848–1929, vol. III
O'Connor, Vincent Clarence Scott, *died* 1945, vol. IV
O'Connor, Lt-Col Sir (William) Frederick (Travers), 1870–1943, vol. IV
O'Connor-Morris, Geoffrey, 1886–1964, vol. VI
O'Conor, Rt Hon. Charles Owen, (The O'Conor Don), 1838–1906, vol. I
O'Conor, Rt Hon. Denis Charles Joseph, (The O'Conor Don), 1869–1917, vol. II
O'Conor, James Edward, 1843–1917, vol. II
O'Conor, Sir John, 1863–1927, vol. II
O'Conor, Norreys Jephson, 1885–1958, vol. V
O'Conor, Owen Phelim, (The O'Conor Don), 1870–1943, vol. IV
O'Conor Don, The; *see* O'Conor, Rt Hon. C. O.
O'Conor Don, The; *see* O'Conor, Rt Hon. D. C. J.
O'Conor Don, The; *see* O'Conor, O. P.
O'Conor-Eccles, Miss, *died* 1911, vol. I
Ó Dálaigh, Cearbhall, 1911–1978, vol. VII
Oddie, John William, 1839–1923, vol. II
Oddin-Taylor, Harry Willoughby, 1886–1967, vol. VI
Oddy, Sir John James, 1867–1921, vol. II
O'Dea, Rt Rev. Thomas, 1858–1923, vol. II
O'Dea, William, 1870–1936, vol. III (A), vol. V
O'Dea, William Thomas, 1905–1981, vol. VIII
O'Deirg, Tomás, (Thomas Derrig), 1897–1956, vol. V
O'Dell, Andrew Charles, 1909–1966, vol. VI
Odell, Noel Ewart, 1890–1987, vol. VIII
Odell, Thomas Alexander, 1847–1909, vol. I
Odets, Clifford, 1906–1963, vol. VI
Odey, George William, 1900–1985, vol. VIII

Odgers, Sir Charles Edwin, 1870–1964, vol. VI
Odgers, James Rowland, 1914–1985, vol. VIII
Odgers, Lindsey Noel Blake, 1892–1979, vol. VII
Odgers, Walter Blake, 1880–1969, vol. VI
Odgers, William Blake, 1849–1924, vol. II
Odhams, Ernest Lynch, 1880–1947, vol. IV
Odle, Dorothy M.; *see* Richardson, D. M.
Odling, Charles William, 1847–1932, vol. III
Odling, Thomas Francis, *died* 1906, vol. I
Odling, William, 1829–1921, vol. II
Odling, Maj.-Gen. William, 1909–1997, vol. X
Odlum, Doris Maude, 1890–1985, vol. VIII
Odlum, Maj.-Gen. Victor Wentworth, 1880–1971, vol. VII
O'Dogherty, Engr-Rear-Adm. Francis Blake, *died* 1952, vol. V
O'Doherty, Most Rev. Eugene, 1896–1979, vol. VII
O'Doherty, Rt Rev. J. Keys, *died* 1907, vol. I
O'Doherty, Philip, 1871–1926, vol. II
O'Doherty, Rt Rev. Thomas, 1877–1936, vol. III
O'Doherty, William, 1868–1905, vol. I
Odom, Rev. William, 1846–1933, vol. III
O'Donnell, Charles James, 1850–1934, vol. III
O'Donnell, Elliott, *died* 1965, vol. VI
O'Donnell, Maj.-Gen. Eric Hugh, 1893–1950, vol. IV
O'Donnell, Frank Hugh Macdonald, 1848–1916, vol. II
O'Donnell, Maj.-Gen. Hugh, 1858–1917, vol. II
O'Donnell, Rev. Michael J., 1881–1944, vol. IV
O'Donnell, His Eminence Cardinal Patrick, 1856–1927, vol. II
O'Donnell, Most Rev. Patrick Mary, 1897–1980, vol. VII (AII)
O'Donnell, Peador, 1893–1986, vol. VIII
O'Donnell, Sir Samuel Perry, 1874–1946, vol. IV
O'Donnell, Thomas, 1872–1943, vol. IV
O'Donnell, Maj.-Gen. Sir Thomas Joseph, 1858–1947, vol. IV
O'Donoghue, Charles Henry, 1885–1961, vol. VI
O'Donoghue, David J., 1866–1917, vol. II, vol. III
O'Donoghue, Geoffrey Charles Patrick, (The O'Donoghue of the Glens), 1859–1935, vol. III
O'Donoghue, Geoffrey Charles Patrick Randal, (The O'Donoghue of the Glens), 1896–1974, vol. VII
O'Donoghue, John Kingston, 1894–1976, vol. VII
O'Donoghue, Col Montague Ernest, 1859–1943, vol. IV
O'Donoghue, Richard John Langford, 1889–1972, vol. VII
O'Donoghue, Thomas Henry, 1886–1957, vol. V
O'Donoghue of the Glens, The; *see* O'Donoghue, G. C. P.
O'Donoghue of the Glens, The; *see* O'Donoghue, G. C. P. R.
O'Donohoe, Sir James, *died* 1933, vol. III
O'Donovan, The; *see* O'Donovan, Brig. M. J. W.
O'Donovan, The; *see* O'Donovan, M. W.
O'Donovan, John, 1858–1927, vol. II
O'Donovan, Michael; *see* O'Connor, Frank.
O'Donovan, Brig. Morgan John Winthrop, (The O'Donovan), 1893–1969, vol. VI
O'Donovan, Morgan William, (The O'Donovan), 1861–1940, vol. III
O'Donovan, William James, *died* 1955, vol. V

O'Dowd, Sir James Cornelius, 1829–1903, vol. I
O'Dowda, Lt-Gen. Sir James Wilton, 1871–1961, vol. VI
O'Driscoll, Florence, *died* 1939, vol. III
O'Duffy, Eimar Ultan, 1893–1935, vol. III
O'Duffy, Gen. Eoin, 1892–1944, vol. IV
O'Dwyer, Rt Rev. Edward Thomas, 1842–1917, vol. II
O'Dwyer, Sir Michael Francis, 1864–1940, vol. III
O'Dwyer, Robert, 1862–1949, vol. IV
O'Dwyer, Surg.-Gen. Thomas Francis, *died* 1919, vol. II
O'Dwyer, Una, (Lady O'Dwyer), 1872–1956, vol. V
O'Dwyer, William, 1890–1964, vol. VI
Oehlers, Sir George Edward Noel, 1908–1968, vol. VI
Oelrichs, Hermann, 1850–1906, vol. I
Oelsner, Herman, 1871–1923, vol. II
Oesterley, Rev. William O. E., 1866–1950, vol. IV
O'Faolain, Sean, 1900–1991, vol. IX
O'Farrell, Sir Edward, 1856–1926, vol. II
O'Farrell, Sir George Plunkett, 1845–1911, vol. I
O'Farrell, Rt Rev. Michael, 1865–1928, vol. II
O'Feeney, Sean; *see* Ford, John.
O'Ferrall, Dominic More-, 1854–1942, vol. IV
O'Ferrall, Rt Rev. Ronald Stanhope More, 1890–1973, vol. VII
Offaly, Earl of; Thomas FitzGerald, 1974–1997, vol. X
O'Fiaich, His Eminence Cardinal Tomás Séamus, 1923–1990, vol. VIII
Officer, Sir (Frank) Keith, 1889–1969, vol. VI
Officer, Sir Keith; *see* Officer, Sir F. K.
Officer, Maj.-Gen. William James, 1903–1989, vol. VIII
Officer Brown, Sir (Charles) James; *see* Brown, Sir C. J. O.
Offler, Hilary Seton, 1913–1991, vol. IX
Offner, Richard, 1889–1965, vol. VI
Offor, Richard, 1882–1964, vol. VI
Offord, (Albert) Cyril, 1906–2000, vol. X
Offord, Cyril; *see* Offord, A. C.
O'Flaherty, Liam, 1896–1984, vol. VIII
O'Flynn, Brig. Dennis John Edwin, 1907–1985, vol. VIII
O'Flynn, Surg. Rear-Adm. Joseph Aloysius, 1889–1976, vol. VII
Ogden, Sir Alwyne George Neville, 1889–1981, vol. VIII
Ogden, Charles Kay, 1889–1957, vol. V
Ogden, Eric, 1923–1997, vol. X
Ogden, Frank Collinge, 1907–1989, vol. VIII
Ogden, Fred, 1871–1933, vol. III
Ogden, Sir George Chester, 1913–1983, vol. VIII
Ogden, George Washington, 1871–1966, vol. VI
Ogdon, John Andrew Howard, 1937–1989, vol. VIII
Ogg, David, 1887–1965, vol. VI
Ogg, Col George Sim, 1866–1935, vol. III
Ogg, Sir William Gammie, 1891–1979, vol. VII
Ogg, Col William Mortimer, 1873–1958, vol. V
Ogilby, Col Robert James Leslie, 1880–1964, vol. VI
Ogilvie, Alan Grant, 1887–1954, vol. V
Ogilvie, Hon. Albert George, 1891–1939, vol. III
Ogilvie, Sir Alec Drummond, 1913–1997, vol. X

Ogilvie, Alexander, 1882–1962, vol. VI
Ogilvie, Sir Andrew Muter John, 1858–1924, vol. II
Ogilvie, Sir Charles MacIvor Grant, 1891–1967, vol. VI
Ogilvie, Lt-Col Duncan, 1873–1941, vol. IV
Ogilvie, Col Edward Collingwood, 1867–1950, vol. IV
Ogilvie, Sir Francis Grant, 1858–1930, vol. III
Ogilvie, Sir Frederick Wolff, 1893–1949, vol. IV
Ogilvie, George, 1852–1918, vol. II
Ogilvie, Lt-Col Sir George Drummond, 1882–1966, vol. VI
Ogilvie, Glencairn Stuart, 1858–1932, vol. III
Ogilvie, Lt-Col Gordon, 1878–1958, vol. V
Ogilvie, Sir Heneage; *see* Ogilvie, Sir W. H.
Ogilvie, Rt Rev. James Nicoll, 1860–1926, vol. II
Ogilvie, Mary Helen, (Lady Ogilvie), 1900–1990, vol. VIII
Ogilvie, Robert Maxwell, 1932–1981, vol. VIII
Ogilvie, Lt-Col Sholto Stuart, 1884–1961, vol. VI
Ogilvie, Col Thomas, 1871–1944, vol. IV
Ogilvie, Maj.-Gen. Sir Walter Holland, 1869–1936, vol. III
Ogilvie, Sir (William) Heneage, 1887–1971, vol. VII
Ogilvie, William Henry, 1869–1963, vol. VI
Ogilvie-Farquharson, Mrs; *see* Farquharson.
Ogilvie-Forbes, Sir George Arthur D.; *see* Forbes.
Ogilvie Gordon, Dame Maria M., *died* 1939, vol. III
Ogilvie-Grant, William Robert, 1863–1924, vol. II
Ogilvy, Major Angus Howard Reginald, 1860–1906, vol. I
Ogilvy, Brig. David, 1881–1949, vol. IV
Ogilvy, Sir David John Wilfrid, 13th Bt, 1914–1992, vol. IX
Ogilvy, David Mackenzie, 1911–1999, vol. X
Ogilvy, Gilbert Francis Molyneux, 1868–1953, vol. V
Ogilvy, Sir Gilchrist Nevill, 11th Bt, 1892–1914, vol. I
Ogilvy, Henry Thomas Nisbet Hamilton, 1837–1909, vol. I
Ogilvy, Sir Herbert Kinnaird, 12th Bt, 1865–1956, vol. V
Ogilvy, Captain J. H. C., 1872–1901, vol. I
Ogilvy, Mary Georgiana Constance Nisbet-Hamilton; *see* Ogilvy, Mrs N.-H.
Ogilvy, Mrs Nisbet-Hamilton, (Mary Georgiana Constance), *died* 1920, vol. II
Ogilvy, Sir Reginald Howard Alexander, 10th Bt, 1832–1910, vol. I
Ogilvy, Col William Lewis Kinloch, 1840–1900, vol. I
Ogilvy-Dalgleish, Wing Comdr James William, 1888–1969, vol. VI
Ogilvy-Wedderburn, Sir John Andrew, 11th and 5th Bt, 1866–1956, vol. V
Ogilvy-Wedderburn, Comdr Sir (John) Peter, 12th and 6th Bt, 1917–1977, vol. VII
Ogilvy-Wedderburn, Comdr Sir Peter; *see* Ogilvy-Wedderburn, Comdr Sir J. P.
Oglander, Brig.-Gen. Cecil Faber A.; *see* Aspinall-Oglander.
Ogle, Col Sir Edmund Ashton, 8th Bt, 1857–1940, vol. III
Ogle, Lt-Col Edmund Chaloner, 1878–1935, vol. III

Ogle, Maj.-Gen. Frederic Amelius, 1841–1931, vol. III
Ogle, Sir Henry Asgill, 7th Bt, 1850–1921, vol. II
Ogle, Newton Charles, 1850–1912, vol. I
Ogle, William, 1827–1905, vol. I
Ogle-Skan, Peter Henry, 1915–1992, vol. IX
Ogmore, 1st Baron, 1903–1976, vol. VII
O'Gorman, The; see O'Gorman, Col N. P.
O'Gorman, Brian Stapleton, 1910–1991, vol. IX
O'Gorman, Col Charles John, 1872–1930, vol. III
O'Gorman, Rt Rev. John A., 1866–1935, vol. III
O'Gorman, Mervyn, 1871–1958, vol. V
O'Gorman, Col Nicholas Purcell, (The O'Gorman), 1845–1935, vol. III
O'Gorman, Lt-Col Patrick Wilkins, 1860–1950, vol. IV
O'Gowan, Maj.-Gen. Robert W.; see Wanless-O'Gowan.
O'Grady, The; see O'Grady, W. de R.
O'Grady, Donald de Courcy, 1881–1943, vol. IV
O'Grady, Guillamore, 1879–1952, vol. V
O'Grady, Brig.-Gen. Henry de Courcy, 1873–1949, vol. IV
O'Grady, Sir James, 1866–1934, vol. III
O'Grady, Lt-Col John de Courcy, 1856–1920, vol. II
O'Grady, Standish, 1846–1928, vol. II
O'Grady, Lt-Col Standish de Courcy, 1872–1920, vol. II
O'Grady, William de Rienzi, (The O'Grady), 1852–1932, vol. III
O'Grady, Rev. William Waller, 1844–1921, vol. II
O'Grady-Haly, Maj.-Gen. Richard Hebden, 1841–1911, vol. I
Ogston, Sir Alexander, 1844–1929, vol. III
Ogston, Alexander George, 1911–1996, vol. X
Ogston, Brig.-Gen. Charles, 1877–1944, vol. IV
Ogston, Frank, 1846–1917, vol. II
Ogundipe, Brig. Babafemi Olatunde, 1924–1971, vol. VII
O'Hagan, 2nd Baron, 1878–1900, vol. I
O'Hagan, 3rd Baron, 1882–1961, vol. VI
O'Hagan, Thomas, 1855–1939, vol. III
O'Halloran, Sir Charles Ernest, 1924–1993, vol. IX
O'Halloran, Cornelius Hawkins, 1890–1963, vol. VI
O'Halloran, George Finley, 1862–1937, vol. III
O'Halloran, Joseph Sylvester, 1842–1920, vol. II
O'Halloran, Michael Joseph, 1933–1999, vol. X
O'Halloran, Rev. Richard, died 1925, vol. II
O'Hanlon, Rt Rev. Mgr James, 1840–1921, vol. II
O'Hara, Major Charles Kean, 1860–1947, vol. IV
O'Hara, Rear-Adm. Derek, 1927–1986, vol. VIII
O'Hara, Air Vice-Marshal Derek Ive, 1928–1998, vol. X
O'Hara, Col Errill Robert, died 1956, vol. V
O'Hara, Francis Charles Trench, 1870–1954, vol. V
O'Hara, Frank, 1917–1985, vol. VIII
O'Hara, Most Rev. Gerald Patrick, 1895–1963, vol. VI
O'Hara, Rt Rev. Henry Stewart, 1843–1923, vol. II
O'Hara, Col James, 1865–1928, vol. II
O'Hara, John Bernard, 1862–1927, vol. II
O'Hara, John Henry, 1905–1970, vol. VI
O'Hara, Valentine J., 1875–1941, vol. IV
O'Hare, Patrick, 1849–1917, vol. II

O'Hare, Patrick Joseph, 1883–1961, vol. VI
O'Hegarty, Patrick Sarsfield, 1879–1955, vol. V
O'Higgins, Kevin Christopher, 1892–1927, vol. II
Ohlenschlager, Comdr Norman Albert Gustave, 1890–1938, vol. III
Ohlin, Bertil Gotthard, 1899–1979, vol. VII
Ohlson, Sir Erik, 1st Bt, 1873–1934, vol. III
Ohlson, Sir Eric James, 2nd Bt, 1911–1983, vol. VIII
Ohnet, Georges, 1848–1918, vol. II
Oistrakh, David Fyodorovich, 1908–1974, vol. VII
Ojukwu, Sir Odumegwu, 1909–1966, vol. VI
OK; see Novikoff, O.
O'Kane, Rt Rev. Bernard, died 1939, vol. III
Oke, Harris Rendell, 1891–1940, vol. III
Okeden, Richard Godfrey Christian P.; see Parry-Okeden.
Okeden, William Edward P.; see Parry-Okeden.
O'Keefe, Hon. David John, 1864–1943, vol. IV
O'Keefe, Hon. Michael, 1865–1926, vol. II
O'Keeffe, Francis Arthur, 1856–1909, vol. I
O'Keeffe, Georgia, 1887–1986, vol. VIII
O'Keeffe, James George, died 1937, vol. III
O'Keeffe, Maj.-Gen. Sir Menus William, 1859–1944, vol. IV
O'Keeffe, Stephen Martin Lanigan, 1878–1948, vol. IV
Okell, Charles Cyril, 1888–1939, vol. III
Okell, Rt Rev. Frank Jackson, 1887–1950, vol. IV
O'Kelly, The; see Kelly, Major A. D. D.
O'Kelly, The; see Kelly, Sir R. D.
O'Kelly, Edward Peter, died 1914, vol. I
O'Kelly, James Joseph, 1845–1916, vol. II
O'Kelly, John Joseph, died 1957, vol. V
O'Kelly, Sean Thomas, 1882–1966, vol. VI
O'Kelly de Gallagh et Tycooly, Count Gerald Edward, 1890–1968, vol. VI
Okeover, Haughton Charles, 1825–1912, vol. I
Okeover, Col Sir Ian Peter Andrew Monro W.; see Walker-Okeover.
Okey, Thomas, 1852–1935, vol. III
O'Kinealy, Lt-Col Frederick, 1865–1940, vol. III
Okoro, Godfrey; see Benin, Oba of.
Oku, Field-Marshal Count Yasukata, 1845–1930, vol. III
Okuma, Prince Shigenobu, 1838–1922, vol. II
Okyar, Bay Fethi, died 1943, vol. IV
Olabegi II, The Olowo of Owo, (Sir Olateru), 1910–1999, vol. X
Olcott, Col Henry Steel, died 1907, vol. I
Oldcastle, John; see Meynell, Wilfred.
Oldershaw, John, 1850–1938, vol. III
Oldershaw, William James Norman, 1856–1926, vol. II
Oldfield, Col Arthur Radulphus, 1872–1940, vol. III
Oldfield, Rev. Charles, died 1908, vol. I
Oldfield, Col Christopher George, 1863–1944, vol. IV
Oldfield, Claude Houghton, died 1961, vol. VI
Oldfield, Sir Francis Du Pre, 1869–1928, vol. II
Oldfield, Rev. George Biscoe, 1840–1932, vol. III
Oldfield, Maj.-Gen. John Rawdon Hodge, died 1940, vol. III
Oldfield, John Richard Anthony, 1899–1999, vol. X
Oldfield, Major John William, 1886–1955, vol. V

Oldfield, Josiah, *died* 1953, vol. V
Oldfield, Maj.-Gen. Sir Louis, 1872–1949, vol. IV
Oldfield, Sir Maurice, 1915–1981, vol. VIII
Oldfield, Sir Richard Charles, 1828–1918, vol. II
Oldfield, Richard Charles, 1909–1972, vol. VII
Oldfield, Bt Lt-Col Richard William, 1891–1933, vol. III
Oldfield, William Henry, *died* 1961, vol. VI
Oldfield, Rev. William John, 1857–1934, vol. III
Oldfield-Davies, Alun Bennett, 1905–1988, vol. VIII
Oldham, Alan Trevor, 1904–1971, vol. VII
Oldham, Ven. Algernon Langston, *died* 1916, vol. II
Oldham, Rev. Canon Arthur Charles Godolphin, 1905–1998, vol. X
Oldham, Charles Evelyn Arbuthnot William, 1869–1949, vol. IV
Oldham, Charles H., *died* 1926, vol. II
Oldham, Sir Ernest Fitzjohn, 1870–1926, vol. II
Oldham, Col Sir Henry Hugh, 1840–1922, vol. II
Oldham, Henry Yule, 1862–1951, vol. V
Oldham, James Bagot, 1899–1977, vol. VII
Oldham, Joseph Houldsworth, 1874–1969, vol. VI
Oldham, Richard Dixon, 1858–1936, vol. III
Oldham, William Benjamin, 1845–1916, vol. II
Oidman, Cecil Bernard, 1894–1969, vol. VI
Oldman, Col Sir Hugh Richard Deare, 1914–1988, vol. VIII
Oldman, Maj.-Gen. Richard Deare Furley, 1877–1943, vol. IV
Oldmeadow, Ernest James, 1867–1949, vol. IV
Oldrieve, William Thomas, 1853–1922, vol. II
Oldroyd, George, 1886–1951, vol. V
Oldroyd, James Gardner, 1921–1982, vol. VIII
Oldroyd, Sir Mark, 1843–1927, vol. II
Olds, Irving Sands, 1887–1963, vol. VI
O'Leary, Daniel, 1878–1954, vol. V
O'Leary, Rev. De Lacy Evans, 1872–1957, vol. V
O'Leary, Brig. Heffernan William Denis McCarthy-, 1885–1948, vol. IV
O'Leary, Most Rev. Henry Joseph, 1879–1938, vol. III
O'Leary, Rt Hon. Sir Humphrey Francis, 1886–1953, vol. V
O'Leary, John, 1830–1907, vol. I
O'Leary, Rt Rev. Louis James, 1877–1930, vol. III
O'Leary, Major Michael J., 1888–1961, vol. VI
O'Leary, Patrick Albert; *see* Guérisse, Count A. M. E.
O'Leary, Brig.-Gen. Tom Evelyn, 1862–1924, vol. II
Oliphant, Ernest Henry Clark, 1862–1936, vol. III
Oliphant, Captain Henry Gerard Laurence, 1879–1955, vol. V
Oliphant, John Ninian, 1887–1960, vol. V
Oliphant, Sir Lancelot, 1881–1965, vol. VI
Oliphant, Mrs Laurence, 1846–1937, vol. III
Oliphant, Gen. Sir Laurence James, 1846–1914, vol. I
Oliphant, Sir Marcus Laurence Elwin, (Sir Mark), 1901–2000, vol. X
Oliphant, Margaret Oliphant Wilson, 1828–1897, vol. I
Oliphant, Sir Mark; *see* Oliphant, Sir Marcus L. E.
Oliphant, Patrick James, 1914–1979, vol. VII

Oliphant, Lt-Col Philip Lawrence; *see* Kington-Blair-Oliphant, P. L.
Oliphant, Rosamond; *see* Oliphant, Mrs Laurence.
Oliphant-Sheffield, Robert Stoney, 1864–1937, vol. III
Olive, George William, *died* 1963, vol. VI
Olive, Sir James William, 1856–1942, vol. IV
Oliveira, Mrs A. J. E.; *see* Tubb, Carrie.
Oliveira, Francisco Regis de, *died* 1916, vol. II
Oliver, Major Alfred Alexander, 1874–1965, vol. VI
Oliver, Sir Arthur Maule, 1871–1937, vol. III
Oliver, Rev. Arthur West, 1858–1941, vol. IV
Oliver, Dame Beryl, 1882–1972, vol. VII
Oliver, Charles A., 1861–1945, vol. IV
Oliver, Lt-Col Sir (Charles) Frederick, *died* 1939, vol. III
Oliver, Charles Nicholson Jewel, 1848–1920, vol. II, vol. III
Oliver, Charles Pye, 1861–1951, vol. V
Oliver, Daniel, 1830–1916, vol. II
Oliver, Dennis Stanley, 1926–1996, vol. X
Oliver, Wing-Comdr Douglas Austin, 1887–1939, vol. III
Oliver, Very Rev. Edmund Henry, 1882–1935, vol. III
Oliver, Edwin, *died* 1950, vol. IV
Oliver, Sir Ernest; *see* Oliver, Sir F. E.
Oliver, Hon. Dame Florence C.; *see* Cardell-Oliver, Hon. Dame A. F. G.
Oliver, Francis Alfred, 1866–1944, vol. IV
Oliver, Francis Wall, 1864–1951, vol. V
Oliver, Hon. Frank, 1853–1933, vol. III
Oliver, Lt-Col Sir Frederick; *see* Oliver, Lt-Col Sir C. F.
Oliver, Sir (Frederick) Ernest, 1900–1994, vol. IX
Oliver, Frederick Scott, 1864–1934, vol. III
Oliver, Adm. Sir Geoffrey Nigel, 1898–1980, vol. VII
Oliver, George, 1841–1915, vol. I
Oliver, Rev. George, 1848–1920, vol. II
Oliver, George Harold, 1888–1984, vol. VIII
Oliver, Henry Alfred, 1854–1935, vol. III
Oliver, Admiral of the Fleet Sir Henry Francis, 1865–1965, vol. VI
Oliver, Henry John Callard, 1915–1978, vol. VII
Oliver, James, 1857–1941, vol. IV
Oliver, Brig. James Alexander, 1906–1990, vol. VIII
Oliver, Gp Captain John Oliver William, 1911–1997, vol. X
Oliver, John Orlando Hercules Norman, 1822–1901, vol. I
Oliver, John Rathbone, 1872–1943, vol. IV
Oliver, Maj.-Gen. John Ryder, 1834–1909, vol. I
Oliver, Sir John William Lambton, 1873–1952, vol. V
Oliver, Laurence Herbert, 1881–1962, vol. VI
Oliver, Leslie Claremont, 1909–1990, vol. VIII
Oliver, Col Lionel Grant, 1858–1936, vol. III
Oliver, Martin Hugh, 1916–1987, vol. VIII
Oliver, Mary Louise, (Lady Oliver), 1868–1950, vol. IV
Oliver, Matthew William Baillie, *died* 1926, vol. II
Oliver, Philip Milner, 1884–1954, vol. V
Oliver, Raymond, 1921–1976, vol. VII

Oliver, Richard Alexander Cavaye, 1904–1998, vol. X
Oliver, Rev. Richard John Deane, *died* 1942, vol. IV
Oliver, Vice-Adm. Robert Don, 1895–1980, vol. VII
Oliver, Sir Roland Giffard, 1882–1967, vol. VI
Oliver, Stephen Michael Harding, 1950–1992, vol. IX
Oliver, Sir Thomas, 1853–1942, vol. IV
Oliver, Thomas, 1871–1946, vol. IV
Oliver, Victor, 1898–1964, vol. VI
Oliver, Walter Reginald Brook, 1883–1957, vol. V
Oliver, William, 1836–1917, vol. II
Oliver, William, *died* 1962, vol. VI
Oliver, Col William James, 1860–1937, vol. III
Oliver, Lt-Gen. Sir William Pasfield, 1901–1981, vol. VIII
Oliver-Bellasis, Captain Richard, 1900–1964, vol. VI
Olivey, Sir Walter Rice, 1831–1922, vol. II
Olivier, 1st Baron, 1859–1943, vol. IV
Olivier, Baron (Life Peer); Laurence Kerr Olivier, 1907–1989, vol. VIII
Olivier, C. F., *died* 1940, vol. III (A), vol. IV
Olivier, Rev. Dacres, 1831–1919, vol. II
Olivier, Edith, *died* 1948, vol. IV
Olivier, George B.; *see* Borg Olivier.
Olivier, Henry, 1914–1994, vol. X(AII)
Olivier, Rev. Henry Eden, 1866–1936, vol. III
Olivier, Herbert Arnould, 1861–1952, vol. V
Olivier, Martin John, 1900–1959, vol. V
Olivier, Captain Sidney Richard, 1870–1932, vol. III
Ollard, Lt-Col John William Arthur, 1893–1961, vol. VI
Ollard, Rev. Sidney Leslie, 1875–1949, vol. IV
Ollerenshaw, Robert, 1882–1948, vol. IV
Ollis, William David, 1924–1999, vol. X
Ollivant, Alfred, 1874–1927, vol. II
Ollivant, Brig-Gen. Alfred Henry, 1871–1919, vol. II
Ollivant, Sir Charles; *see* Ollivant, Sir E. C. K.
Ollivant, Sir (Edward) Charles (Kyall), 1846–1928, vol. II
Ollivant, Col John Spencer, 1872–1937, vol. III
Ollivier, Olivier Emile, 1825–1913, vol. I
Olmsted, Rt Rev. Charles Sanford, 1853–1918, vol. II
Olmsted, Rt Rev. Charles Tyler, 1842–1924, vol. II
Olney, Hon. Sir Herbert Horace, 1875–1957, vol. V
Olney, Richard, 1835–1917, vol. II
O'Loghlen, Hon. Sir Bryan, 3rd Bt, 1928–1905, vol. I
O'Loghlen, Sir Charles Hugh Ross, 5th Bt, 1881–1951, vol. V
O'Loghlen, Sir Michael, 4th Bt, 1866–1934, vol. III
O'Loghlin, Hon. James Vincent, 1852–1925, vol. II
Olorenshaw, Leslie, 1912–1972, vol. VII
O'Loughlin, Hon. Laurence, 1854–1927, vol. II
O'Loughlin, Very Rev. Robert Stuart, 1852–1925, vol. II
Olphert, Sir John, 1844–1917, vol. II
Olphert, Captain Wybrants, 1879–1938, vol. III
Olpherts, Sir William, 1822–1902, vol. I
Olsen, Björn Magnusson, 1850–1919, vol. II
Olson, Sven Olof, 1916–1977, vol. VII
Olsson, Julius, 1864–1942, vol. IV

Olufosoye, Most Rev. Timothy Omotayo, 1918–1992, vol. IX
Oluwasanmi, Hezekiah Adedunmola, 1919–1983, vol. VIII
Oluwole, Rt Rev. Isaac, *died* 1932, vol. III
Olver, Col Sir Arthur, 1875–1961, vol. VI
O'Mahony, The; *see* O'Mahony, P. C. de L.
O'Mahony, John, (Sean), *died* 1934, vol. III
O'Mahony, Pierce Charles de Lacy, (The O'Mahony), 1850–1930, vol. III
O'Máille, Tomás, *died* 1938, vol. III
O'Malley, Rt Hon. Brian Kevin, 1930–1976, vol. VII
O'Malley, Maj.-Gen. David Vincent, 1891–1955, vol. V
O'Malley, Sir Edward Loughlin, 1842–1932, vol. III
O'Malley, Hon. King, *died* 1953, vol. V
O'Malley, Lewis Sydney Steward, 1874–1941, vol. IV
O'Malley, Mary Dolling, (Lady O'Malley); *see* Bridge, Ann.
O'Malley, Sir Owen St Clair, 1887–1974, vol. VII
O'Malley, William, 1853–1939, vol. III
O'Malley, Col William Arthur D'Oyly, 1853–1925, vol. II
Oman, Carola Mary Anima, (Lady Lenanton), 1897–1978, vol. VII
Oman, Charles Chichele, 1901–1982, vol. VIII
Oman, Sir Charles William Chadwick, 1860–1946, vol. IV
Oman, John Campbell, 1841–1911, vol. I
Oman, John Wood, 1860–1939, vol. III
O'Mara, Joseph, 1866–1927, vol. II
O'Meagher, Col John Kevin, 1866–1946, vol. IV
O'Meara, Captain Bulkeley Ernest Adolphus, 1867–1916, vol. II
O'Meara, Lt-Col Charles Albert Edmond, 1868–1923, vol. II
O'Meara, Rev. Daniel, 1877–1929, vol. III
O'Meara, Francis, 1886–1941, vol. IV
O'Meara, Maj.-Gen. Francis Joseph, 1900–1967, vol. VI
O'Meara, Stephen, 1854–1918, vol. II
O'Meara, Rev. Thomas Robert, 1864–1930, vol. III
O'Meara, Lt-Col Walter Alfred John, 1863–1939, vol. III
Ommanney, Brig.-Gen. Albert Edward, 1849–1930, vol. III
Ommanney, Charles Henry, 1852–1915, vol. I
Ommanney, Lt-Col Charles Vernon, 1872–1952, vol. V
Ommanney, Col Edward Lacon, 1834–1914, vol. I
Ommanney, Adm. Sir Erasmus, 1814–1904, vol. I
Ommanney, Francis Downes, 1903–1980, vol. VII
Ommanney, Sir Montague Frederick, 1842–1925, vol. II
Ommanney, Adm. Sir Nelson; *see* Ommanney, Adm. Sir R. N.
Ommanney, Adm. Sir (Robert) Nelson, 1854–1938, vol. III
Omolulu, Olumide Olusanya, 1925–1967, vol. VI
Omond, George William Thomson, 1846–1929, vol. III
Omond, Robert Traill, 1858–1914, vol. I
Omont, Henri, 1857–1940, vol. III (A), vol. IV

O'Morchoe, Captain Arthur Donel MacMurrogh, (The O'Morchoe), 1892–1966, vol. VI
O'Morchoe, Rev. Thomas Arthur, (The O'Morchoe), 1865–1921, vol. II
Onassis, Aristotle Socrates, 1906–1975, vol. VII
O'Neil, Most Rev. Alexander Henry, 1907–1997, vol. X
O'Neil, Bryan Hugh St John, 1905–1954, vol. V
O'Neil, Hon. Sir Desmond Henry, 1920–1999, vol. X
O'Neil, Rt Rev. Henry, 1843–1915, vol. I
O'Neill, 2nd Baron, 1839–1928, vol. II
O'Neill, 3rd Baron, 1907–1944, vol. IV
O'Neill of the Maine, Baron (Life Peer); Terence Marne O'Neill, 1914–1990, vol. VIII
O'Neill, Alan Albert, 1916–1991, vol. IX
O'Neill, Hon. Arthur Edward Bruce, 1876–1914, vol. I
O'Neill, Sir Arthur Eugene, 1877–1950, vol. IV
O'Neill, Charles, 1849–1918, vol. II
O'Neill, Hon. Sir Con Douglas Walter, 1912–1988, vol. VIII
O'Neill, Denis Edmund, 1908–1981, vol. VIII
O'Neill, Eugene Gladstone, 1888–1953, vol. V
O'Neill, Col Eugene Joseph, 1875–1962, vol. VI
O'Neill, Rev. George, 1863–1947, vol. IV
O'Neill, Herbert Charles, died 1953, vol. V
O'Neill, Most Rev. Hugh John, 1898–1955, vol. V
O'Neill, Rev. John, 1880–1947, vol. IV
O'Neill, Sir John; see O'Neill, Sir M. J.
O'Neill, Joseph, 1886–1953, vol. V
O'Neill, Sir (Matthew) John, 1914–1976, vol. VII
O'Neill, Michael, 1909–1976, vol. VII
O'Neill, Most Rev. Michael Cornelius, 1898–1983, vol. VIII
O'Neill, Norman, 1875–1934, vol. III
O'Neill, Patrick, died 1938, vol. III
O'Neill, Most Rev. Patrick, 1891–1958, vol. V
O'Neill, Col Patrick Laurence, 1876–1962, vol. VI
O'Neill, Rt Rev. Peter Austin, 1841–1911, vol. I
O'Neill, Hon. Robert Torrens, 1845–1910, vol. I
O'Neill, Thomas Philip, Jr, 1912–1994, vol. IX
O'Neill, Col William Henry Slingsby, 1854–1931, vol. III
O'Nial, Surg.-Gen. John, 1827–1919, vol. II, vol. III
Onians, Richard Broxton, 1899–1986, vol. VIII
O'Niel, Colette; see Malleson, Lady Constance.
Onion, Francis Leo, 1903–1983, vol. VIII
Onions, Alfred, 1858–1921, vol. III
Onions, Berta, (Mrs Oliver Onions); see Ruck, B.
Onions, Charles Talbut, 1873–1965, vol. VI
Onions, Oliver, 1873–1961, vol. VI
Onkar Singh, Maj.-Gen. Sir Apji, 1872–1951, vol. V
Onnes, (Heike) Kamerlingh, 1853–1926, vol. II
Onnes, Kamerlingh; see Onnes, H. K.
Onraet, Rene Henry de S., 1887–1952, vol. V
Onsager, Lars, 1903–1976, vol. VII
Onslow, 4th Earl of, 1853–1911, vol. I
Onslow, 5th Earl of, 1876–1945, vol. IV
Onslow, 6th Earl of, 1913–1971, vol. VII
Onslow, Sir Alexander Campbell, 1842–1908, vol. I
Onslow, Brig.-Gen. Cranley Charlton, 1869–1940, vol. III
Onslow, Denzil Roberts, 1839–1908, vol. I

Onslow, Maj.-Gen. Sir Denzil M.; see Macarthur-Onslow.
Onslow, Sir Geoffrey Henry H.; see Hughes-Onslow.
Onslow, Brig.-Gen. George Macleay M.; see Macarthur Onslow.
Onslow, Maj.-Gen. George Thorp, 1858–1921, vol. II
Onslow, Henry H.; see Hughes-Onslow.
Onslow, Hon. Mrs Huia, died 1932, vol. III
Onslow, Maj.-Gen. Hon. James William M.; see Macarthur-Onslow.
Onslow, Muriel Wheldale; see Onslow, Hon. Mrs Huia.
Onslow, Captain Richard Francis John, died 1942, vol. IV
Onslow, Adm. Sir Richard George, 1904–1975, vol. VII
Onslow, Sir Richard Wilmot, 7th Bt, 1906–1963, vol. VI
Onslow, Sir Roger Warin Beaconsfield, 6th Bt, 1880–1931, vol. III
Onslow, Sibella Macarthur, 1871–1943, vol. IV
Onslow, William George, 1908–1983, vol. VIII
Onslow, Maj.-Gen. Sir William Henry, 1863–1929, vol. III
Onslow, Sir William Wallace Rhoderic, 5th Bt, 1845–1916, vol. II
Onyon, Engr-Captain William, 1862–1953, vol. V
Oonvala, Mancherahaw Framji, 1851–1914, vol. I
Openshaw, Sir James, 1871–1935, vol. III
Openshaw, Mary; see Binstead, Mary.
Openshaw, Thomas Horrocks, 1856–1929, vol. III
Openshaw, William Harrison, 1912–1981, vol. VIII
Opher, William David, 1903–1983, vol. VIII
Opie, Evelyn Arnold, 1905–1990, vol. VIII
Opie, Peter Mason, 1918–1982, vol. VIII
Opie, Redvers, 1900–1984, vol. VIII
Opie, Roger Gilbert, 1927–1998, vol. X
Opie, Air Vice-Marshal William Alfred, 1901–1977, vol. VII
Oppé, Adolph Paul, 1878–1957, vol. V
Oppenheim, Tan Sri Sir Alexander, 1903–1997, vol. X
Oppenheim, E(dward) Phillips, 1866–1946, vol. IV
Oppenheim, Ernest Ferdinand, 1875–1939, vol. III
Oppenheim, Henry, 1835–1912, vol. I
Oppenheim, Lassa Francis Lawrence, 1858–1919, vol. II
Oppenheim, Lt-Col Lawrie Charles Frith, 1871–1923, vol. II
Oppenheimer, Albert Martin, 1872–1945, vol. IV
Oppenheimer, Sir Bernard, 1st Bt, 1866–1921, vol. II
Oppenheimer, Sir Charles, 1836–1900, vol. I
Oppenheimer, Charles, 1875–1961, vol. VI
Oppenheimer, Sir Ernest, 1880–1957, vol. V
Oppenheimer, Sir Francis Charles, 1870–1961, vol. VI
Oppenheimer, Harry Frederick, 1908–2000, vol. X
Oppenheimer, Joseph, born 1876, vol. VI
Oppenheimer, Julius Robert, 1904–1967, vol. VI
Oppenheimer, Sir Michael, 2nd Bt, 1892–1933, vol. III
Oppenheimer, Sir Philip Jack, 1911–1995, vol. IX

Oppenheimer, Raymond Harry, 1905–1984, vol. VIII

Opper, Frederick Burr, 1857–1937, vol. III (A), vol. IV

Opperman, Hon. Sir Hubert Ferdinand, 1904–1996, vol. X

Orage, Alfred Richard, 1873–1934, vol. III

Oram, Baron (Life Peer); Albert Edward Oram, 1913–1999, vol. X

Oram, Dame Elizabeth; see Oram, Dame S. E.

Oram, Engr Vice-Adm. Sir Henry John, 1858–1939, vol. III

Oram, Sir Matthew Henry, 1885–1969, vol. VI

Oram, Richard Edward Sprague, 1830–1909, vol. I

Oram, Samuel, 1913–1991, vol. IX

Oram, Dame (Sarah) Elizabeth, 1860–1946, vol. IV

Orange, Beatrice, died 1955, vol. V

Orange, George James, 1871–1925, vol. II

Orange, Sir Hugh William, 1866–1956, vol. V

Orange, William, 1833–1916, vol. II

Oranmore and Browne, 2nd Baron, 1819–1900, vol. I

Oranmore and Browne, 3rd Baron, 1861–1927, vol. II

Orbach, Maurice, 1902–1979, vol. VII

Orchard, Henry Ben, died 1937, vol. III

Orchard, Jonathan, 1853–1938, vol. III

Orchard, Peter Francis, 1927–1993, vol. IX

Orchard, Hon. Richard Beaumont, 1871–1942, vol. IV

Orchard, W(illiam) Arundel, died 1961, vol. VI

Orchard, Rev. William Edwin, 1877–1955, vol. V

Orchard-Lisle, Aubrey Edwin, 1908–1989, vol. VIII

Orchardson, Sir William Quiller, 1835–1910, vol. I

Orchha, Maharaja, Sir Pratap Singh Bahadur, 1854–1930, vol. III

Orchin, Frederick Joseph, 1885–1971, vol. VII

Orczy, Baroness, (Mrs Montague Barstow), died 1947, vol. IV

Ord, Bernhard Boris, died 1961, vol. VI

Ord, Ven. Charles Edward B.; see Blackett Ord.

Ord, Col Frederick Cusac, 1851–1938, vol. III

Ord, William Miller, 1834–1902, vol. I

Ord Johnstone, Morris Mackintosh, 1907–1978, vol. VII

Ord Marshall, Elizabeth Middleton, died 1931, vol. III

Orde, Alan Colin.; see Campbell Orde.

Orde, Sir Arthur John Campbell-Orde, 4th Bt, 1865–1933, vol. III

Orde, Sir Charles William, 1884–1980, vol. VII

Orde, John Fosbery, 1870–1932, vol. III

Orde, Sir John William Powlett Campbell-, 3rd Bt, 1827–1897, vol. I

Orde, Sir Julian Walter, 1861–1929, vol. III

Orde, Sir Percy Lancelot, 1888–1975, vol. VII

Orde, Brig. Reginald John, 1893–1975, vol. VII

Orde, Roden Horace Powlett, 1867–1941, vol. IV

Orde, Major Sir Simon Arthur Campbell-, 5th Bt, 1907–1969, vol. VI

Orde Browne, Sir Granville St John, 1883–1947, vol. IV

Ordish, Thomas Fairman, 1855–1924, vol. II

O'Regan, Hon. Sir Barry; see O'Regan, Hon. Sir J. B.

O'Regan, Hon. Sir (John) Barry, 1915–1996, vol. X(AI)

O'Reilly, The; see O'Reilly, M. G.

O'Reilly, Rt Rev. James, 1856–1928, vol. II

O'Reilly, Sir Lennox Arthur Patrick, 1880–1949, vol. IV

O'Reilly, Myles George, (The O'Reilly), 1830–1911, vol. I

O'Reilly, William Edmund, 1873–1934, vol. III

O'Reily, Most Rev. John, 1846–1915, vol. I

O'Rell, Max, 1848–1903, vol. I

Orenstein, Maj.-Gen. Alexander Jeremiah, 1879–1972, vol. VII

Orford, 5th Earl of, 1854–1931, vol. III

Organe, Sir Geoffrey Stephen William, 1908–1989, vol. VIII

Orgill, Tyrrell Churton, 1884–1975, vol. VII

O'Riain, 'Liam P.; see Ryan, William Patrick.

Oriel, George Harold, 1894–1939, vol. III (A), vol. IV

Oriel, John Augustus, 1896–1968, vol. VI

Origo, Marchesa Iris, 1902–1988, vol. VIII

O'Riordan, Conal Holmes O'Connell, 1874–1948, vol. IV

O'Riordan, Rt Rev. Mgr Michael, 1857–1919, vol. II

Orkney, 7th Earl of, 1867–1951, vol. V

Orkney, 8th Earl of, 1919–1998, vol. X

Orleans, Duc d'; Louis Philippe Robert, 1869–1926, vol. II

Orlebar, Sir Michael Keith Orlebar S.; see Simpson-Orlebar

Orloff, Nicholas, died 1915, vol. I

Ormandy, Eugene, 1899–1985, vol. VIII

Ormandy, William Reginald, 1870–1941, vol. IV

Ormathwaite, 2nd Baron, 1827–1920, vol. II

Ormathwaite, 3rd Baron, 1859–1937, vol. III

Ormathwaite, 4th Baron, 1863–1943, vol. IV

Ormathwaite, 5th Baron, 1868–1944, vol. IV

Ormathwaite, 6th Baron, 1912–1984, vol. VIII

Orme, Edith Temple, died 1960, vol. V

Orme, Lt-Col Frank Leslie, 1898–1968, vol. VI

Orme, Frederick George, died 1954, vol. V

Orme, Gilbert Edward, 1874–1945, vol. IV

Orme, Ion Hunter Touchet G.; see Garnett-Orme.

Orme, John Samuel, 1916–1984, vol. VIII

Orme, William Bryce, 1871–1962, vol. VI

Ormerod, Rt Hon. Sir Benjamin, 1890–1974, vol. VII

Ormerod, Major Sir Berkeley; see Ormerod, Major Sir C. B.

Ormerod, Major Sir (Cyril) Berkeley, 1897–1983, vol. VIII

Ormerod, Eleanor Anne, 1828–1901, vol. I

Ormerod, Frank Cunliffe, 1894–1967, vol. VI

Ormerod, George Milner, 1879–1936, vol. III

Ormerod, Henry Arderne, 1886–1964, vol. VI

Ormerod, Herbert Eliot, 1831–1911, vol. I

Ormerod, Joseph Arderne, 1848–1925, vol. II

Ormerod, Richard Caton, 1915–1981, vol. VIII

Ormidale, Hon. Lord; George Lewis Macfarlane, 1854–1941, vol. IV

Ormiston, Thomas, 1878–1937, vol. III

Ormiston, Lt-Col Thomas Lane, 1867–1954, vol. V

Ormond, Arthur William, 1871–1964, vol. VI

Ormond, Maj.-Gen. Daniel Mowat, 1885–1974, vol. VII
Ormond, E. W., 1863–1930, vol. III
Ormond, Ernest Charles, 1896–1962, vol. VI
Ormond, Sir Herbert John, 1867–1934, vol. III
Ormond, Sir John Davies Wilder, 1905–1995, vol. X(AI)
Ormonde, 3rd Marquess of, 1844–1919, vol. II
Ormonde, 4th Marquess of, 1849–1943, vol. IV
Ormonde, 5th Marquess of, 1890–1949, vol. IV
Ormonde, 6th Marquess of, 1893–1971, vol. VII
Ormonde, 7th Marquess of, 1899–1997, vol. X
Ormrod, Peter, 1869–1923, vol. II
Ormrod, Rt Hon. Sir Roger Fray Greenwood, 1911–1992, vol. IX
Ormsby, Rev. Edwin Robert, 1845–1915, vol. I
Ormsby, Rt Rev. George Albert, 1843–1924, vol. II
Ormsby, Sir Lambert Hepenstal, 1850–1923, vol. II
Ormsby, Lt-Gen. Robert Daly, 1879–1946, vol. IV
Ormsby, Rev. Thomas, 1871–1942, vol. IV
Ormsby, Lt-Col Vincent Alexander, 1865–1917, vol. II
Ormsby-Gore, Hon. Seymour Fitzroy, 1863–1950, vol. IV
Ornstein, John Isidore Maurice, 1854–1919, vol. II
O'Rorke, Rev. Benjamin Garniss, 1875–1918, vol. II
O'Rorke, E. Brian, 1901–1974, vol. VII
O'Rorke, Lt-Col Frederick Charles, *died* 1976, vol. VII
O'Rorke, Lt-Col George Mackenzie, 1883–1958, vol. V
O'Rorke, Hon. Sir (George) Maurice, 1830–1916, vol. II
O'Rorke, Hon. Sir Maurice; *see* O'Rorke, Hon. Sir G. M.
O'Rorke, Rt Rev. Mowbray Stephen, 1869–1953, vol. V
Orowan, Egon, 1902–1989, vol. VIII
Orpen, R. Caulfeild, 1863–1938, vol. III
Orpen, Rt Rev. Raymond d'Audemar, 1837–1930, vol. III
Orpen, Major Redmond Newenham Morris, 1864–1940, vol. III (A), vol. IV
Orpen, Richard Theodore, 1869–1926, vol. II
Orpen, Major Sir William, 1878–1931, vol. III
Orpen-Palmer, Brig.-Gen. Harold Bland Herbert, 1876–1941, vol. IV
Orpen-Palmer, Col Reginald Arthur Herbert, 1877–1943, vol. IV
Orphoot, Burnett Napier Henderson, 1880–1964, vol. VI
Orr, Rt Hon. Sir Alan Stewart, 1911–1991, vol. IX
Orr, Col Alexander Stewart, 1861–1914, vol. I
Orr, Arthur A., *died* 1949, vol. IV
Orr, Charles Roger, *died* 1938, vol. III
Orr, Sir Charles William James, 1870–1945, vol. IV
Orr, Christine Grant Millar, *died* 1963, vol. VI
Orr, Major Frank George, 1881–1945, vol. IV
Orr, Col Gerald Maxwell, 1876–1934, vol. III
Orr, James, 1844–1913, vol. I
Orr, James, 1841–1920, vol. II
Orr, James Peter, 1867–1949, vol. IV
Orr, Jean Fergus Henderson, 1920–1997, vol. X

Orr, Most Rev. John, 1874–1938, vol. III
Orr, John, 1885–1966, vol. VI
Orr, Major John Boyd, 1871–1915, vol. I
Orr, John Boyd; *see* Baron Boyd Orr.
Orr, John Charles, 1858–1941, vol. IV
Orr, Sir John Henry, 1918–1995, vol. IX
Orr, John Washington, 1901–1984, vol. VIII
Orr, John Wellesley, 1878–1956, vol. V
Orr, Maj.-Gen. John William, 1829–1916, vol. II
Orr, Capt. Lawrence Percy Story, 1918–1990, vol. VIII
Orr, Major Michael Harrison, 1859–1926, vol. II
Orr, Robert Low, 1854–1944, vol. IV
Orr, Sir Samuel, 1886–1972, vol. VII
Orr, Thomas, 1857–1937, vol. III
Orr, William James, 1873–1963, vol. VI
Orr, William M'Fadden, 1866–1934, vol. III
Orr-Ewing, Baron (Life Peer); (Charles) Ian Orr-Ewing, 1912–1999, vol. X
Orr-Ewing, Sir Archibald Ernest, 3rd Bt, 1853–1919, vol. II
Orr-Ewing, Charles Lindsay, 1860–1903, vol. I
Orr Ewing, Sir Ian Leslie, 1893–1958, vol. V
Orr-Ewing, Major James Alexander, 1857–1900, vol. I
Orr Ewing, Brig.-Gen. Sir Norman Archibald, 4th Bt, 1880–1960, vol. V
Orr-Ewing, Sir William, 2nd Bt, 1848–1903, vol. I
Orr-Lewis, Sir Duncan; *see* Orr-Lewis, Sir J. D.
Orr-Lewis, Sir Frederick Orr, 1st Bt, 1866–1921, vol. II
Orr-Lewis, Sir (John) Duncan, 2nd Bt, 1898–1980, vol. VII
Orrin, Herbert Charles, 1878–1963, vol. VI
Orrock, James, 1829–1913, vol. I
Orsborn, Albert William Thomas, 1886–1967, vol. VI
Orsman, W. J., 1838–1923, vol. II
Ortcheson, Sir John, 1905–1977, vol. VII
Orton, Charles William P.; *see* Previté-Orton.
Orton, Maj.-Gen. Sir Ernest Frederick, 1874–1960, vol. V
Orton, George Harrison, 1873–1947, vol. IV
Orton, Harold, 1898–1975, vol. VII
Orton, James Herbert, 1884–1953, vol. V
Orton, Kennedy Joseph Previté, 1872–1930, vol. III
Orton, Brig. Sidney Bernard, 1881–1933, vol. III
Orton-Jones, Harry, 1894–1976, vol. VII
Orwell, George, (Eric Blair), *died* 1950, vol. IV
Orwin, Charles Stewart, 1876–1955, vol. V
Osbaldeston-Mitford, Captain Robert; *see* Mitford.
Osborn, Sir Algernon Kerr Butler, 7th Bt, 1870–1948, vol. IV
Osborn, Sir Danvers Lionel Rouse, 8th Bt, 1916–1983, vol. VIII
Osborn, E. B., *died* 1938, vol. III
Osborn, Sir Francis; *see* Osborn, Sir N. F. B.
Osborn, Sir Frederic James, 1885–1978, vol. VII
Osborn, Henry Fairfield, 1857–1935, vol. III
Osborn, Margaret, 1906–1985, vol. VIII
Osborn, Sir Melmoth, 1833–1899, vol. V
Osborn, Sir (N.) Francis (B.), 1872–1954, vol. V
Osborn, Major Philip Barlow, 1870–1909, vol. I
Osborn, Samuel, 1848–1936, vol. III
Osborn, Sir Samuel, 1864–1952, vol. V

Osborn, Theodore George Bentley, 1887–1973, vol. VII
Osborn, Brig.-Gen. William Lushington, 1871–1951, vol. V
Osborne, Col Arthur de Vere-W.; *see* Willoughby-Osborne.
Osborne, Sir Basil, 1907–1987, vol. VIII
Osborne, Rev. Charles Edward, 1856–1936, vol. III
Osborne, Maj.-Gen. Rev. Coles Alexander, 1896–1994, vol. IX
Osborne, Sir Cyril, 1898–1969, vol. VI
Osborne, Lt-Gen. Edmund Archibald, 1885–1969, vol. VI
Osborne, Edward, 1861–1939, vol. III
Osborne, Vice-Adm. Edward Oliver Brudenell Seymour, 1883–1956, vol. V
Osborne, Rt Rev. Edward William, 1845–1926, vol. II
Osborne, Captain F. Creagh-, *died* 1943, vol. IV
Osborne, Sir Francis, 15th Bt, 1856–1948, vol. IV
Osborne, Lord Francis Granville Godolphin, 1864–1924, vol. II
Osborne, Sir George Francis, 16th Bt, 1894–1960, vol. V
Osborne, Col Henry Campbell, 1874–1949, vol. IV
Osborne, Rev. (Henry James) Reginald, *died* 1952, vol. V
Osborne, Rev. James Denham, 1854–1934, vol. III
Osborne, John, 1911–1984, vol. VIII
Osborne, John James, 1929–1994, vol. IX
Osborne, Captain John Warde, 1851–1936, vol. III
Osborne, Surg. Rear-Adm. (D) Leslie Bartlet, 1900–1989, vol. VIII
Osborne, Lithgow, 1892–1980, vol. VII
Osborne, Malcolm, 1880–1963, vol. VI
Osborne, Maj.-Gen. Osborne Herbert D.; *see* Delano-Osborne.
Osborne, Rev. Reginald; *see* Osborne, Rev. H. J. R.
Osborne, Robert Ernest, 1861–1939, vol. III
Osborne, Rosabelle, *died* 1958, vol. V
Osborne, William Alexander, 1873–1967, vol. VI
Osborne-Gibbes, Sir Edward; *see* Gibbes.
Osborne-Gibbes, Sir Philip Arthur; *see* Gibbes.
Osbourne, Brig.-Gen. George Nowell Thomas S.; *see* Smyth-Osbourne.
Osbourne, Air Cdre Sir Henry Percy S.; *see* Smyth-Osbourne.
Osbourne, Lloyd, 1868–1947, vol. IV
Osburn, Lt-Col Arthur, *died* 1952, vol. V
Osburn, Comdr Francis, 1834–1917, vol. II
Osgood, Sir (Frederic) Stanley, 1872–1952, vol. V
Osgood, Sir Stanley; *see* Osgood, Sir F. S.
O'Shaughnessy, Patrick Joseph, 1872–1920, vol. II
O'Shaughnessy, Richard, 1842–1918, vol. II
O'Shaughnessy, Rt Hon. Sir Thomas Lopdell, 1850–1933, vol. III
O'Shea, Alexander Paterson, 1902–1990, vol. VIII
O'Shea, Sir Henry, 1858–1926, vol. II, vol. III
O'Shea, Henry George, 1838–1905, vol. I
O'Shea, Lucius Trant, *died* 1920, vol. II
O'Shea, Most Rev. Thomas, 1870–1954, vol. V
O'Shea, Lt-Col Timothy, 1856–1921, vol. II
O'Shee, James John, 1866–1946, vol. IV
O'Shee, Lt-Col Richard Alfred Poer, 1867–1942, vol. IV

Osler, Sir Edmund Boyd, 1845–1924, vol. II
Osler, Featherston, 1838–1924, vol. II
Osler, Col Stratton Harry, 1882–1930, vol. III
Osler, Sir William, 1st Bt, 1849–1919, vol. II
Osley, Arthur Sidney, 1917–1987, vol. VIII
Osman, Sir (Abdool) Raman (Mahomed), 1902–1992, vol. IX(AII)
Osman, Louis, 1914–1996, vol. X
Osman, Sir Raman; *see* Osman, Sir A. R. M.
Osmaston, Bertram Beresford, 1868–1961, vol. VI
Osmaston, Col Cecil Alvend FitzHerbert, 1866–1949, vol. IV
Osmond, Wing-Comdr Edward, 1890–1946, vol. IV
Osmond, Mervyn Victor, 1912–1998, vol. X
Osmond, Sir Paul; *see* Osmond, Sir S. P.
Osmond, Sir (Stanley) Paul, 1917–2000, vol. X
Osmond, Thomas Edward, 1884–1985, vol. VIII
Osmond, Brig. William Robert Fiddes, 1890–1952, vol. V
Osmond-Clarke, Sir Henry, 1905–1986, vol. VIII
Ossiannilsson, Karl Gustav, 1875–1970, vol. VI (AII)
Ossit; *see* Deslandes, Baronne M.
Ostberg, Ragnar, 1866–1945, vol. IV
Ostenso, Martha, 1900–1963, vol. VI
Ostler, Hon. Sir Henry Hubert, 1876–1944, vol. IV
Ostrer, Isidore, *died* 1975, vol. VII
Ostrorog, Count Leon, 1867–1932, vol. III
O'Sullevan, Col John Joseph, 1879–1936, vol. III
O'Sullivan, Most Rev. Charles, 1862–1927, vol. II
O'Sullivan, Cornelius, 1841–1907, vol. I
O'Sullivan, Col Daniel, 1853–1946, vol. IV (A)
O'Sullivan, Dennis Neil, 1899–1973, vol. VII
O'Sullivan, Hon. Edward William, 1846–1910, vol. I
O'Sullivan, Eugene, 1879–1942, vol. IV
O'Sullivan, Maj.-Gen. Hugh Dermod Evan, 1874–1958, vol. V
O'Sullivan, Rt Rev. James, 1834–1915, vol. I
O'Sullivan, John M., 1881–1948, vol. IV
O'Sullivan, Most Rev. Joseph Anthony, 1886–1972, vol. VII
O'Sullivan, Ven. Leopold, *died* 1919, vol. II
O'Sullivan, Sir Neil, 1900–1968, vol. VI
O'Sullivan, Richard, 1888–1963, vol. VI
O'Sullivan, Seumas, (James Sullivan Starkey), 1879–1958, vol. V
O'Sullivan, Hon. Thomas, 1856–1953, vol. V
O'Sullivan, Timothy, *died* 1950, vol. IV
O'Sullivan-Beare, Daniel Robert, 1865–1921, vol. II
Oswald, Arthur Louis, 1858–1931, vol. III
Oswald, Col Christopher Percy, 1875–1966, vol. VI
Oswald, Eugene, *died* 1912, vol. I
Oswald, Felix, 1866–1958, vol. V
Oswald, Henry Robert, *died* 1940, vol. III
Oswald, James Francis, 1838–1908, vol. I
Oswald, Maj.-Gen. Marshall St John, 1911–1991, vol. IX
Oswald, Brig.-Gen. Oswald Charles Williamson, 1863–1938, vol. III
Oswald, Richard Alexander, 1841–1921, vol. II
Oswald, Col St Clair, 1858–1938, vol. III
Oswald, Thomas, 1904–1990, vol. VIII
Oswald, William Digby, 1880–1916, vol. II

Ottaway, Christopher Wyndham, 1910–1978, vol. VII
Ottaway, Eric Carlton, 1904–1967, vol. VI
Otter, Rt Rev. Anthony, 1896–1986, vol. VIII
Otter, Sir John Lonsdale, 1852–1932, vol. III
Otter, Robert Edward, *died* 1932, vol. III
Otter, Air Vice-Marshal Victor Charles, 1914–1996, vol. X
Otter, Gen. Sir William Dillon, 1843–1929, vol. III
Otter-Barry, Rt Rev. Hugh Van Lynden, 1887–1971, vol. VII
Otter-Barry, William Whitmore, 1878–1973, vol. VII
Otterson, Henry, 1846–1929, vol. III
Ottley, Agnes May, 1899–1990, vol. VIII
Ottley, Rear-Adm. Sir Charles Langdale, 1858–1932, vol. III
Ottley, Rev. Edward Bickersteth, 1853–1910, vol. I
Ottley, Rev. Feilding Hay, 1877–1958, vol. V
Ottley, Rev. Henry Bickersteth, *died* 1932, vol. III
Ottley, Col Sir John Walter, 1841–1931, vol. III
Ottley, Rev. Robert Lawrence, 1856–1933, vol. III
Ottley, Warner Herbert Taylor, 1889–1980, vol. VII (AII)
Otto, Rudolf, 1869–1937, vol. III
Otway, Rt Hon. Sir Arthur John, 3rd Bt, 1822–1912, vol. I
Oudendyk, Dame Margaret, 1876–1971, vol. VII
Oudendyk, William J., 1874–1953, vol. V
Ouida, 1839–1908, vol. I
Ouimet, Hon. Joseph Alderic, 1848–1916, vol. II, vol. III
Ould, Hermon, 1885–1951, vol. V
Ould, Robert F.; *see* Fielding-Ould.
Ouless, Walter William, 1848–1933, vol. III
Oulsnam, Sir Harrison; *see* Oulsnam, Sir S. H. Y.
Oulsnam, Sir (Samuel) Harrison (Yardley), 1898–1972, vol. VII
Oulton, George N., *died* 1928, vol. II
Oulton, Rev. John Ernest Leonard, 1886–1957, vol. V
Oulton, Air Vice-Marshal Wilfred Ewart, 1911–1997, vol. X
Oulton, William Harold Stowe, 1869–1941, vol. IV
Oury, Libert, 1868–1939, vol. III
Ouseley, Brig.-Gen. Ralph Glynn, 1866–1931, vol. III
Outcault, Richard Felton, 1863–1928, vol. II
Outen, Roland Thomas, 1900–1957, vol. V
Outerbridge, Sir Joseph, 1843–1933, vol. III
Outerbridge, Col Hon. Sir Leonard Cecil, 1888–1986, vol. VIII
Outeriño, Felix C; *see* Candela Outeriño.
Outhwaite, Ernest, 1875–1931, vol. III
Outhwaite, R. L., 1868–1930, vol. III
Outram, Comdr Edmund, 1858–1937, vol. III
Outram, Sir Francis Boyd, 2nd Bt, 1836–1912, vol. I
Outram, Major Sir Francis Davidson, 4th Bt, 1867–1945, vol. IV
Outram, Lt-Col Harold William Sydney, *died* 1944, vol. IV
Outram, Sir James, 3rd Bt, 1864–1925, vol. II
Outtrim, Hon. Alfred Richard, 1845–1925, vol. II
Outtrim, Frank Leon, 1847–1917, vol. II

Ouvry, Ernest Carrington, 1866–1951, vol. V
Ovans, Major Hugh Lambert, 1881–1946, vol. IV
Ovenden, Very Rev. Charles T., 1846–1924, vol. II
Ovenden, Harry, 1876–1974, vol. VII
Ovens, Hon. Brig.-Gen. Gerald Hedley, 1856–1933, vol. III
Ovens, Maj.-Gen. Patrick John, 1922–1994, vol. IX
Ovens, Col Robert Montgomery, 1868–1950, vol. IV
Overbury, Sir Robert Leslie, 1887–1955, vol. V
Overend, Douglas, 1914–1981, vol. VIII
Overend, Thomas George, 1846–1915, vol. I
Overend, Walker, *died* 1926, vol. II, vol. III
Overman, Henry Jacob, 1862–1933, vol. III
Overstreet, Harry Allen, 1875–1970, vol. VI
Overton, Sir Arnold Edersheim, 1893–1975, vol. VII
Overton, Charles Ernest, 1865–1933, vol. III
Overton, Rev. Frederick Arnold, 1862–1935, vol. III
Overton, George Leonard, 1875–1948, vol. IV
Overton, Sir Hugh Thomas Arnold, 1923–1991, vol. IX
Overton, Rev. John Henry, 1835–1903, vol. I
Overton, Robert, 1859–1924, vol. II
Overtoun, 1st Baron, 1843–1908, vol. I
Overy, Sir Thomas Stuart, 1893–1973, vol. VII
Ovey, Sir Esmond, 1879–1963, vol. VI
Ovey, Lt-Col Richard Lockhart, 1878–1946, vol. IV
Owen, Sir Alfred George Beech, 1908–1975, vol. VII
Owen, Alun Davies, 1925–1994, vol. IX
Owen, Col Arthur Allen, 1842–1917, vol. II
Owen, Arthur Charles H.; *see* Humphreys-Owen.
Owen, Sir (Arthur) David Kemp, 1904–1970, vol. VI
Owen, Sir (Arthur) Douglas, 1904–1977, vol. VII
Owen, Col Arthur Lewis S.; *see* Scott-Owen.
Owen, Basil Wilberforce Longmore, *died* 1943, vol. IV
Owen, Sir Cecil; *see* Owen, Sir W. C.
Owen, Brig.-Gen. Charles C.; *see* Cunliffe-Owen.
Owen, Lt-Col Charles Harold Wells, 1872–1936, vol. III
Owen, Maj.-Gen. Charles Henry, 1830–1921, vol. II
Owen, Very Rev. Charles Mansfield, 1852–1940, vol. III
Owen, Col Charles Richard Blackstone, 1870–1954, vol. V
Owen, Brig.-Gen. Charles Samuel, 1879–1959, vol. V
Owen, Lt-Col Charles William, 1853–1922, vol. II
Owen, Collinson, 1882–1956, vol. V
Owen, David Charles L.; *see* Lloyd Owen.
Owen, David Elystan, 1912–1987, vol. VIII
Owen, Sir David John, 1874–1941, vol. IV
Owen, Sir David Kemp; *see* Owen, Sir A. D. K.
Owen, Most Rev. Derwyn Trevor, 1876–1947, vol. IV
Owen, Sir Douglas, 1850–1920, vol. II
Owen, Sir Douglas; *see* Owen, Sir A. D.
Owen, Sir Dudley Herbert C.; *see* Cunliffe-Owen.
Owen, Edmund, *died* 1915, vol. I
Owen, Edward Cunliffe, 1857–1918, vol. II
Owen, Rev. Edward Cunliffe, *died* 1937, vol. III
Owen, Edwin Augustine, 1887–1973, vol. VII

Owen, Eric Hamilton, 1903–1989, vol. VIII
Owen, Evan Roger, *died* 1930, vol. III
Owen, Lt-Col F. C.; *see* Cunliffe-Owen.
Owen, Frank, 1905–1979, vol. VII
Owen, Rev. G., *died* 1914, vol. I
Owen, George Douglas, 1887–1965, vol. VI
Owen, George Elmslie, 1899–1964, vol. VI
Owen, George Sherard, 1892–1976, vol. VII
Owen, Rev. George Vale, 1869–1931, vol. III
Owen, Lt-Col Sir Goronwy, 1881–1963, vol. VI
Owen, Grace, 1873–1965, vol. VI
Owen, Gwilym, 1880–1940, vol. III (A), vol. IV
Owen, Gwilym Ellis Lane, 1922–1982, vol. VIII
Owen, H. F.; *see* Owen, F.
Owen, Harold, 1872–1930, vol. III
Owen, Harrison, 1890–1966, vol. VI (AII)
Owen, Maj.-Gen. Harry, 1911–1998, vol. X
Owen, Henry, *died* 1919, vol. II
Owen, Col Henry Mostyn, 1858–1927, vol. II
Owen, Captain Hilary Dorsett, 1894–1980, vol. VII
Owen, Sir (Herbert) Isambard, 1850–1927, vol.II
Owen, Sir Hugh, 1835–1916, vol. II
Owen, Sir Hugh Charles, 3rd Bt, 1826–1909, vol. I
Owen, Sir Hugo C.; *see* Cunliffe-Owen.
Owen, Sir Isambard; *see* Owen, Sir H. I.
Owen, Rev. Ithel George, 1863–1941, vol. IV
Owen, Sir James George, 1869–1939, vol. III
Owen, Jean A., (Mrs Owen Visger), *died* 1922, vol. II
Owen, Rt Rev. John, 1854–1926, vol. II
Owen, John, *died* 1949, vol. IV
Owen, Sir John Arthur, 4th Bt, 1892–1973, vol. VII
Owen, John Benjamin Brynmor, 1910–1998, vol. X
Owen, Col John Edward, 1928–1989, vol. VIII
Owen, Gen. Sir John Fletcher, 1839–1924, vol. II
Owen, John Glendwr, 1914–1977, vol. VII
Owen, Maj.-Gen. John Ivor Headon, 1922–1999, vol. X
Owen, John Simpson, 1912–1995, vol. IX
Owen, Rev. John Smith, *died* 1922, vol. II
Owen, Joslyn Grey, 1928–1992, vol. IX
Owen, Sir Langer Meade Loftus, 1862–1935, vol. III
Owen, Leonard, 1890–1965, vol. VI
Owen, Sir Leonard; *see* Owen, Sir W. L.
Owen, Leonard Victor Davies, 1888–1952, vol. V
Owen, Rt Rev. Leslie, 1886–1947, vol. IV
Owen, Lt-Col Lindsay Cunliffe, *died* 1941, vol. IV
Owen, Maj.-Gen. Llewellyn Isaac Gethin M.; *see* Morgan-Owen.
Owen, Lloyd, 1903–1966, vol. VI
Owen, Mary Alicia, 1858–1935, vol. III
Owen, O. Morgan, *died* 1930, vol. III
Owen, Owen William, 1863–1930, vol. III
Owen, Paul Robert, 1920–1990, vol. VIII
Owen, Col Percy Thomas, 1864–1936, vol. III
Owen, Peter Granville, 1918–1986, vol. VIII
Owen, Peter M.; *see* Macaulay-Owen.
Owen, Most Rev. Reginald Herbert, 1887–1961, vol. VI
Owen, Rear-Adm. Richard Arthur James, 1910–1997, vol. X
Owen, Robert; *see* Owen, P. R.
Owen, Robert Davies, 1898–1988, vol. VIII

Owen, Lt-Col Robert Haylock, 1862–1927, vol. II
Owen, Lt-Col Roger Arthur Mostyn-, 1888–1947, vol. IV
Owen, Lt-Col Roger Carmichael Robert, 1866–1941, vol. IV
Owen, Ronald Allan, 1920–1982, vol. VIII
Owen, Sir Ronald Hugh, 1910–1988, vol. VIII
Owen, Rosamond Dale; *see* Oliphant, Mrs Laurence.
Owen, Rowland Hubert, 1903–1995, vol. IX
Owen, Sackville Herbert Edward Gregg, 1880–1960, vol. V
Owen, Sidney George, 1858–1940, vol. III
Owen, Sidney James, 1827–1912, vol. I
Owen, Lt-Col Sydney Lloyd, *born* 1872, vol. II
Owen, Thomas, 1840–1898, vol. I
Owen, Thomas Arfon, 1933–2000, vol. X
Owen, Sir Thomas David, 1854–1921, vol. II
Owen, Thomas Joseph, 1903–1986, vol. VIII
Owen, Rev. Thomas M. Bulkeley B.; *see* Bulkeley-Owen.
Owen, Cdre Trevor Lewis, 1895–1980, vol. VII
Owen, Ven. Walter Edwin, 1879–1945, vol. IV
Owen, Will, 1869–1957, vol. V
Owen, Sir William, 1834–1912, vol. I
Owen, William, 1837–1918, vol. II
Owen, Sir (William) Cecil, 1872–1959, vol. V
Owen, Rt Hon. Sir William Francis Langer, 1899–1972, vol. VII
Owen, Captain William Henry, 1857–1931, vol. III
Owen, William Hugh, 1886–1957, vol. V
Owen, William James, 1901–1981, vol. VIII
Owen, Sir (William) Leonard, 1897–1971, vol. VII
Owen, William Stevenson, 1834–1909, vol. I
Owen-Jones, Eryl; *see* Owen-Jones, J. E.
Owen-Jones, (John) Eryl, 1912–2000, vol. X
Owen-Lewis, Lt-Col Arthur Francis, 1868–1926, vol. II
Owen-Lewis, Cyril Alexander, 1871–1905, vol. I
Owen-Smyth, Charles Edward, 1851–1925, vol. II
Owens, Captain Sir Arthur Lewis, *died* 1967, vol. VI
Owens, Sir Charles John, 1845–1933, vol. III
Owens, Ernest Stanley, 1916–1983, vol. VIII
Owens, Frank Arthur Robert, 1912–1995, vol. IX
Owens, Most Rev. Richard, *died* 1909, vol. I
Owens, Richard Hugh M.; *see* Mills-Owens.
Owens, Sir Robert Arthur, 1921–1999, vol. X
Owens, Col Robert Leonce, 1862–1937, vol. III
Owens, Tom Paterson, 1888–1968, vol. VI
Owens, Hon. William, 1840–1917, vol. II
Owles, Captain Garth Henry Fyson, 1896–1975, vol. VII
Owles, Thomas Arthur, 1890–1966, vol. VI
Owsley, John William, 1840–1929, vol. III
Owst, Gerald Robert, 1894–1962, vol. VI
Oxborrow, Brig. Claud Catton, 1898–1972, vol. VII
Oxenbridge, 1st Viscount, 1829–1898, vol. I
Oxenden, Sir Percy Dixwell Nowell Dixwell-, 10th Bt, 1838–1924, vol. II
Oxenham, Elsie Jeannette, *died* 1960, vol. V
Oxenham, John, *died* 1941, vol. IV
Oxford, Sir Kenneth Gordon, 1924–1998, vol. X
Oxford and Asquith, 1st Earl of, 1852–1928, vol. II

Oxford and Asquith, Countess of; (Emma Alice Margaret) (Margot), 1864–1945, vol. IV
Oxfuird, 12th Viscount, 1899–1986, vol. VIII
Oxland, Air Vice-Marshal Robert Dickinson, 1889–1959, vol. V
Oxley, Sir Alfred James R.; see Rice-Oxley.
Oxley, Adm. Charles Lister, 1841–1920, vol. II
Oxley, Douglas George R.; see Rice-Oxley.
Oxley, John Stewart, 1861–1935, vol. III
Oxley, Brig.-Gen. Reginald Stewart, 1863–1951, vol. V

Oxley, Maj.-Gen. Walter Hayes, 1891–1978, vol. VII
Oyama, Iwao, Field-Marshal Prince, 1842–1916, vol. II
Oyebode, Rt Rev. David Richard, 1898–1960, vol. V
Ozanne, Sir Edward Chepmell, 1852–1929, vol. III
Ozanne, James William, died 1931, vol. III
Ozanne, John Henry, 1850–1902, vol. I
Ozanne, Maj.-Gen. William Maingay, 1891–1966, vol. VI

P

Pace, Rev. Edward George, 1881–1953, vol. V
Pace, George Gaze, 1915–1975, vol. VII
Pace, Most Rev. Pietro, 1831–1914, vol. I
Pacelli, Eugene; see Pius XII.
Pachmann, Vladimir de, 1848–1933, vol. III
Pächt, Otto Ernest, 1902–1988, vol. VIII
Pack, Arthur Dennis Henry Heber R.; see Reynell-Pack.
Pack, Captain Stanley Walter Croucher, 1904–1977, vol VII
Pack-Beresford, Denis R., 1864–1942, vol. IV
Packard, Lt-Gen. Sir (Charles) Douglas, 1903–1999, vol. X
Packard, Lt-Gen. Sir Douglas; see Packard, Lt-Gen. Sir C. D.
Packard, Sir Edward, 1843–1932, vol. III
Packard, Lt-Col Henry Norrington, 1870–1916, vol. II
Packard, Vance Oakley, 1914–1996, vol. X
Packe, Sir Edward Hussey, 1878–1946, vol. IV
Packe, Lt-Col Frederick Edward, 1879–1953, vol. V
Packe, Hussey, 1846–1908, vol. I
Packer, Sir (Douglas) Frank (Hewson), 1906–1974, vol. VII
Packer, Sir Frank; see Packer, Sir D. F. H.
Packer, Col Harry Dixon, 1872–1947, vol. IV
Packer, Adm. Sir Herbert Annesley, 1894–1962, vol. VI
Packer, Joy, (Lady Packer), 1905–1977, vol. VII
Packman, Lt-Col Kenneth Chalmers, 1899–1969, vol. VI
Paddison, Sir George Frederick, died 1927, vol. II
Paddock, Rt Rev. Robert L., vol III
Paddon, Lt John Frederick, 1856–1913, vol. I
Paddon, Lt-Col Sir Stanley Somerset Wreford, 1881–1963, vol. VI
Paddon, Rev. William Francis Locke, died 1922, vol. II
Padel, Charles Frederick Christian, 1872–1958, vol. V
Paderewski, Ignace Jean, 1860–1941, vol. IV
Padfield, Rev. William Herbert Greenland, 1875–1956, vol. III
Padley, Walter Ernest, 1916–1984, vol. VIII
Padley, Wilfred, 1910–1968, vol. VI
Padmore, Lady (Thomas); see Culhane, Rosalind.
Padmore, Sir Thomas, 1909–1996, vol. X
Padwick, Francis Herbert, 1856–1945, vol. IV

Padwick, Surgeon-Captain Harold Boultbee, 1889–1972, vol. VII
Padwick, Philip Hugh, 1876–1958, vol. V
Pae, David, 1864–1948, vol. IV
Paffard, Rear-Adm. Ronald Wilson, 1904–1994, vol. IX
Pafford, John Henry Pyle, 1900–1996, vol. X
Pagan, Brig.-Gen. Alexander William, 1878–1949, vol. IV
Pagan, Very Rev. John, 1830–1909, vol. I
Pagan, Brig. Sir John Ernest, 1914–1986, vol. VIII
Pagden, Arthur Sampson, 1858–1942, vol. IV
Page, Sir Alexander Warren, 1914–1993, vol. IX
Page, Ven. Alfred Charles, 1912–1988, vol. VIII
Page, Col Alfred John, 1912–1987, vol. VIII
Page, Sir Archibald, 1875–1949, vol. IV
Page, Very Rev. Arnold Henry, 1851–1943, vol. IV
Page, Sir Arthur, 1876–1958, vol. V
Page, Bertram Samuel, (Tony), 1904–1993, vol. IX
Page, (Charles) James, 1925–1981, vol. VIII
Page, Sir (Charles) Max, 1882–1963, vol. VI
Page, Lt-Col Cuthbert Frederick Graham, 1880–1919, vol. II
Page, Sir Denys Lionel, 1908–1978, vol. VII
Page, Rt Hon. Sir Earle Christmas Grafton, 1880–1961, vol. VI
Page, Edward, 1877–1937, vol. III
Page, Brig. (Edwin) Kenneth, 1898–1995, vol. IX
Page, Ernest, 1848–1930, vol. III
Page, Lt-Col F., died 1917, vol. II
Page, Frederick, died 1919, vol. II
Page, Sir Frederick Handley, 1885–1962, vol. VI
Page, Lt-Gen. George H., see Hyde-Page.
Page, Gertrude, (Mrs Dobbin), died 1922, vol. II
Page, Rt Hon. Sir Graham; see Page, Rt Hon. Sir R. G.
Page, Major Harold Hillis, 1888–1942, vol. IV
Page, Harold James, 1890–1972, vol. VII
Page, Harry Marmaduke, 1860–1942, vol. IV
Page, Sir Harry Robertson, 1911–1985, vol. VIII
Page, Herbert William, 1845–1926, vol. II
Page, Hon. James, 1860–1921, vol. II
Page, James; see Page, C. J.
Page, John Lloyd Warden, 1858–1916, vol. II
Page, Kenneth; see Page, E. K.
Page, Sir Leo Francia, 1890–1951, vol. V
Page, Maj.-Gen. Lionel Frank, 1884–1944, vol. IV
Page, Sir Max; see Page, Sir C. M.

Page, Norman John, 1920–1985, vol. VIII
Page, Robert Palgrave, 1867–1947, vol. IV
Page, Rt Hon. Sir (Rodney) Graham, 1911–1981,
    vol. VIII
Page, Russell, 1906–1985, vol. VIII
Page, Sidney John, 1892–1973, vol. VII
Page, Lt-Col Stanley Hatch, 1874–1962, vol. VI
Page, Thomas Ethelbert, 1850–1936, vol. III
Page, Thomas Nelson, 1853–1922, vol. II
Page, Sir Thomas Spurgeon, 1879–1958, vol. V
Page, Thomas Walker, 1866–1937, vol. III
Page, Tony; see Page. B. S.
Page, Walter Hines, 1855–1918, vol. II
Page, William, 1861–1934, vol. III
Page, William Frank, 1894–1980, vol. VII
Page, William Morton, 1883–1950, vol. IV
Page, William Walter Keightly, 1878–1962, vol. VI
Page-Henderson, Lt-Col Henry Cockcroft,
    1856–1942, vol. IV
Page-Jones, Frederick Herbert, 1903–1972, vol. VII
Page-Roberts, Very Rev. William; see Roberts.
Page Wood, Sir David John Hatherley, 7th Bt,
    1921–1955, vol. V
Pagenstecher, Hermann, 1844–1932, vol. III
Paget of Northampton, Baron (Life Peer); Reginald
    Thomas Paget, 1908–1990, vol. VIII
Paget, Lt-Col Albert Edward Sydney Louis,
    1879–1917, vol II
Paget, Adm. Sir Alfred Wyndham, 1852–1918,
    vol. II
Paget, Gen. Rt Hon. Sir Arthur Henry Fitzroy,
    1851–1928, vol. II
Paget, Gen. Sir Bernard Charles Tolver, 1887–1961,
    vol. VI
Paget, Lt-Col Sir Cecil Walter, 2nd Bt (cr 1897),
    1874–1936, vol. III
Paget, Major Eden Wilberforce, 1865–1955, vol. V
Paget, Very Rev. Edward Clarence, 1851–1927,
    vol. II
Paget, Most Rev. Edward Francis, 1886–1971,
    vol. VII
Paget, Sir Ernest; see Paget, Sir G. E.
Paget, Rt Rev. Francis, 1851–1911, vol. I
Paget, Sir (George) Ernest, 1st Bt (cr 1897),
    1841–1923, vol. II
Paget, Major George Thomas Cavendish,
    1853–1939, vol. III
Paget, Col Harold, 1849–1933, vol. III
Paget, Lt-Comdr Henry Edward Clarence,
    1860–1940, vol. III
Paget, Rt Rev. Henry Luke, 1853–1937, vol. III
Paget, Henry Marriott, 1856–1936, vol. III
Paget, Captain J. Otho, 1860–1934, vol. III
Paget, Sir James, 1st Bt (cr 1871), 1814–1899, vol I
Paget, Captain Sir James Francis, 3rd Bt (cr 1871),
    1890–1972, vol. VII
Paget, John, 1811–1898, vol. I
Paget, Sir John Rahere, 2nd Bt (cr 1871),
    1848–1938, vol. III
Paget, Sir John Starr, 3rd Bt (cr 1886), 1914–1992,
    vol. IX
Paget, Dame Leila; see Paget, Dame L. M. L. W.
Paget, Dame (Louise Margaret) Leila (Wemyss),
    1881–1958, vol. V
Paget, Mary, (Lady Paget), died 1919, vol. II

Paget, Dame (Mary) Rosalind, 1855–1948, vol. IV
Paget, Paul Edward, 1901–1985, vol. VIII
Paget, Rt Hon. Sir Ralph Spencer, 1864–1940,
    vol. III
Paget, Sir Richard Arthur Surtees, 2nd Bt (cr 1886),
    1869–1955, vol. V
Paget, Rt Hon. Sir Richard Horner, 1st Bt (cr 1886),
    1832–1908, vol. I
Paget, Dame Rosalind; see Paget, Dame M. R.
Paget, Sidney Edward, 1860–1908, vol. I
Paget, Stephen, 1855–1926, vol. II
Paget, Major Thomas Guy Frederick, 1886–1952,
    vol. V
Paget, Lord Victor William, 1889–1952, vol. V
Paget, Violet, 1856–1935, vol. III
Paget, Walburga, (Lady Paget), 1839–1929, vol. III
Paget, Brig.-Gen. Wellesley Lynedoch Henry,
    1858–1918, vol. II
Paget, William Edmund, 1879–1928, vol. II
Paget-Cooke, Sir Henry, 1861–1923, vol. II
Paget-Cooke, Oliver Dayrell Paget, 1891–1954,
    vol. V
Pagnol, Marcel, 1895–1974, vol. VII
Paice, Rev. Arthur, 1857–1923, vol. II
Paige, Lt-Col Cyril Penrose, 1882–1958, vol. V
Paige, Col Douglas, 1886–1958, vol. V
Paige, Rear-Adm. Richard Collings, 1911–1998,
    vol. X
Pain, Arthur Bernard, 1904–1973, vol. VII
Pain, Rt Rev. Arthur Wellesley, 1841–1920, vol. II
Pain, Barry Eric Odell, 1864–1928, vol. II
Pain, Sir Charles John, 1873–1961, vol. VI
Pain, Brig.-Gen. Sir (George) William (Hacket),
    1855–1924, vol. II
Pain, Sir William; see Pain, Sir G. W. H.
Paine, Lt-Col Albert Ingraham, 1874–1949, vol. IV
Paine, Brig. Douglas Duke, 1892–1960, vol. V (A)
Paine, George, 1918–1992, vol. IX
Paine, Rear-Adm. Sir Godfrey Marshall,
    1871–1932, vol. III
Paine, Sir (Herbert) Kingsley, 1883–1972, vol. VII
Paine, Hubert S.; see Scott-Paine.
Paine, Major James Henry, 1870–1918, vol. II
Paine, Brig.-Gen. John Jackson, 1864–1936, vol. III
Paine, Sir Kingsley; see Paine, Sir H. K.
Paine, Sir Thomas, 1822–1908, vol. I
Paine, Thomas Otten, 1921–1992, vol. IX
Paine, William Worship, 1861–1946, vol. IV
Paine, Wyatt W.; see Wyatt-Paine.
Painleve, Paul, 1863–1933, vol. III
Painter, Brig.-Gen. Arnaud Clarke, 1863–1945,
    vol. IV
Painter, Sir Frederic George, 1844–1926, vol. II
Painter, Brig. Gordon Whistler Arnaud, 1893–1960,
    vol. V
Painter, Robert John, 1927–1972, vol. VII
Paish, Frank Walter, 1898–1988, vol. VIII
Paish, Sir George, 1867–1957, vol. V
Paisley, John Lawrence, 1909–1987, vol. VIII
Paisley, Robert. 1919–1996, vol. X
Pakeman, Sir John, 1860–1946, vol. IV
Pakeman, Robert J., died 1906, vol. I
Pakenham, Hon. Sir Francis John, 1832–1905, vol. I
Pakenham, Col George de la Poer Beresford,
    1875–1960, vol. V

627

Pakenham, Col Hercules Arthur, *died* 1937, vol. III
Pakenham, Lt-Gen. Thomas Henry, 1826–1913, vol. I
Pakenham, Adm. Sir William Christopher, 1861–1933, vol. III
Pakenham-Mahon, Captain Henry, 1851–1922, vol. II
Pakenham-Walsh, Ernst, 1875–1964, vol. VI
Pakenham-Walsh, Rt Rev. Herbert Pakenham, 1871–1959, vol. V (A)
Pakenham-Walsh, Maj.-Gen. Ridley P., 1888–1966, vol. VI
Pakes, Ernest John, 1899–1988, vol. VIII
Pal, Benjamin Peary, 1906–1989, vol. VIII
Palacio Valdés, Armando, 1853–1938, vol. III
Paladini, Carlo, 1864–1922, vol. II, vol. III
Palairet, Lionel Charles Hamilton, 1870–1933, vol. II
Palairet, Sir Michael, 1882–1956, vol. V
Palamountain, Edgar William Irwin, 1917–1990, vol. VIII
Palanpur, Nawab of, 1852–1918, vol. II
Palanpur, Nawab of, 1883–1957, vol. V
Paléologue, Maurice, 1859–1944, vol. IV
Paley, Col Alan Thomas, 1876–1950, vol. IV
Paley, Maj.-Gen. Sir (Alexander George) Victor, 1903–1976, vol. VII
Paley, Frederick John, 1859–1924, vol. II
Paley, Maj.-Gen. Sir Victor, *see* Paley, Maj.-Gen. Sir A. G. V.
Palfrey, William John Henry, 1906–1979, vol. VII
Palgrave, Francis Turner, 1824–1897, vol. I
Palgrave, Sir Reginald Francis Douce, 1829–1904, vol. I
Palgrave, Sir Robert Harry Inglis, 1827–1919, vol. II
Palin, Col Gilbert Walter, 1862–1946, vol. IV
Palin, John Henry, vol. III
Palin, Maj.-Gen. Sir Philip Charles, 1864–1937, vol. III
Palin, Lt-Col Randle Harry, 1873–1950, vol. IV
Palin, Ven. William, 1893–1967, vol. VI
Palin, William Mainwaring, 1862–1947, vol. IV
Paling, Gerald Richard, 1895–1966, vol. VI
Paling, Rt Hon. Wilfred, 1883–1971, vol. VII
Paling, William Thomas, 1892–1992, vol. IX
Palit, Sir Tarak Nath, *died* 1914, vol. I
Palitana, Thakur Saheb Sir, Mansinghji Sursinghji, 1863–1905, vol. I
Palk, Major Hon. Lawrence Charles Walter, 1870–1916, vol. II
Palles, Rt Hon. Christopher, 1831–1920, vol. II
Palliez, Bernard Maurice Alexandre V.; *see* Vernier-Palliez.
Pallin, Lt-Col Samuel Farrer Godfrey, 1878–1930, vol. III
Pallin, Col William Alfred, 1873–1956, vol. V
Pallis, Alex., 1851–1935, vol. III
Palliser, Adm. Sir Arthur Francis Eric, *died* 1956, vol. V
Palliser, Charles Frederick Wray Bury, 1854–1934, vol. III
Palliser, Adm. Henry St Leger Bury, 1839–1907, vol. I
Palliser, Herbert William, 1883–1963, vol. VI

Pallot, Rev. Elias George, 1876–1954, vol. VI
Palme, Olof; *see* Palme, S. O. J.
Palme, (Sven) Olof (Joachim), 1927–1986, vol. VIII
Palmella, 5th Duke of, 1897–1969, vol. VI
Palmer, 1st Baron, 1858–1948, vol. IV
Palmer, 2nd Baron, 1882–1950, vol. IV
Palmer, 3rd Baron, 1916–1990, vol. VIII
Palmer, Alan; *see* Palmer, C. A. S.
Palmer, Col Albert John, *died* 1940, vol. III
Palmer, Alexander Croydon, 1887–1963, vol. VI
Palmer, Captain Alexander Edward Guy, 1886–1926, vol. II
Palmer, Alexander Mitchell, 1872–1936, vol. III
Palmer, Col Aleyn Zouch, 1882–1934, vol. III
Palmer, Alfred, 1852–1936, vol. III
Palmer, Sir Alfred Molyneux, 3rd Bt (*cr* 1886), 1853–1935, vol. III
Palmer, Sir Anthony Frederick Mark, 4th Bt (*cr* 1886), 1914–1941, vol. IV
Palmer, Sir Archdale Robert, 4th Bt (*cr* 1791), 1838–1905, vol. I
Palmer, Arthur, 1841–1897, vol. I
Palmer, Sir Arthur Hunter, 1819–1898, vol. I
Palmer, Arthur Montague Frank, 1912–1994, vol. IX
Palmer, Captain Arthur Percy, 1872–1915, vol. I
Palmer, Gen. Sir Arthur Power, 1840–1904, vol. I
Palmer, Charles Alan Salier, 1913–1990, vol. VIII
Palmer, Sir (Charles) Eric, *died* 1948, vol. IV
Palmer, Charles Felix, *died* 1919, vol. II
Palmer, Charles Frederick, 1869–1920, vol. II
Palmer, Charles George, 1847–1940, vol. III
Palmer, Col Charles Henry Dayrell, 1872–1939, vol. III
Palmer, Ven. Charles Jasper, 1863–1931, vol. III
Palmer, Sir Charles Mark, 1st Bt (*cr* 1886), 1822–1907, vol. I
Palmer, Gen. Sir (Charles) Patrick (Ralph), 1933–1999, vol. X
Palmer, Rev. Charles Samuel, 1830–1921, vol. II
Palmer, Charles William, 1945–2000, vol. V
Palmer, Lt-Col Claude Bowes, 1868–1949, vol. IV
Palmer, Clement Charlton, 1871–1944, vol. IV
Palmer, Brig.-Gen. Cyril Eustace, 1870–1939, vol. III
Palmer, Sir Edward Geoffrey Broadley, 10th Bt (*cr* 1660), 1864–1925, vol. II
Palmer, Edward Timothy, 1878–1947, vol. IV
Palmer, Rt Rev. Edwin James, 1869–1954, vol. V
Palmer, Sir Elwin Mitford, 1852–1906, vol. I
Palmer, Sir Eric; *see* Palmer, Sir C. E.
Palmer, Eustace Exall, 1878–1931, vol. III
Palmer, Sir Francis Beaufort, 1845–1917, vol. II
Palmer, Francis Noel, *died* 1961, vol. VI
Palmer, Sir Frederick, 1862–1934, vol. III
Palmer, Frederick, 1873–1958, vol. V
Palmer, Sir Frederick Archdale, 6th Bt (*cr* 1791), 1857–1933, vol. III
Palmer, Frederick Bernard, 1862–1947, vol. IV
Palmer, Lt-Col Frederick Carey Stuckley S.; *see* Sambourne-Palmer.
Palmer, Frederick Stephen, *died* 1926, vol. II
Palmer, Frederick William, 1891–1955, vol. V
Palmer, Lt-Col Sir Geoffrey Frederick Neill, 11th Bt (*cr* 1660), 1893–1951, vol. V

Palmer, Maj.-Gen. Geoffrey Woodroffe, 1891–1952, vol. V

Palmer, Rear-Adm. George, 1829–1917, vol. II

Palmer, Maj.-Gen. George Erroll P., *see* Prior-Palmer.

Palmer, George Henry, 1871–1945, vol. IV

Palmer, Rev. George Herbert, 1846–1926, vol. II

Palmer, Sir George Hudson, 5th Bt (*cr* 1791), 1841–1919, vol. II

Palmer, Brig.-Gen. George Llewellen, 1856–1932, vol. III

Palmer, Sir George Robson, 2nd Bt (*cr* 1886), 1849–1910, vol. I

Palmer, Rev. George Thomas, *died* 1908, vol. I

Palmer, Rt Hon. George William, 1851–1913, vol. I

Palmer, Gerald Eustace Howell, 1904–1984, vol. VIII

Palmer, Godfrey Mark, 1878–1933, vol. III

Palmer, Col Hon. Sir Gordon William Nottage, 1918–1989, vol. VIII

Palmer, Brig.-Gen. Harold Bland Herbert O.; *see* Orpen-Palmer.

Palmer, Rev. Henry, 1835–1931, vol. III

Palmer, Henry Alleyn, 1893–1965, vol. VI

Palmer, Col Henry Ingham Evered, 1862–1943, vol. IV

Palmer, Henry John, 1853–1903, vol. I

Palmer, Rev. Henry John, 1861–1936, vol. III

Palmer, Herbert Edward, 1880–1961, vol. VI

Palmer, Sir (Herbert) Richmond, 1877–1958, vol. V

Palmer, Horace Stanley, 1904–1968, vol. VI

Palmer, Howard; *see* Palmer, W. H.

Palmer, James L., *died* 1961, vol. VI

Palmer, James Lynwood, *died* 1941, vol. IV

Palmer, Rev. James Nelson, *died* 1908, vol. I

Palmer, Sir John Archdale, 7th Bt (*cr* 1791), 1894–1963, vol. VI

Palmer, John Leslie, 1885–1944, vol. IV

Palmer, Rev. Joseph Blades, 1849–1930, vol. III

Palmer, Ven. Joseph John Beauchamp, 1866–1942, vol. IV

Palmer, Leonard Robert, 1906–1984, vol. VIII

Palmer, Leslie Robert, 1910–1992, vol. IX

Palmer, Hon. Lewis; *see* Palmer, Hon. W. J. L.

Palmer, Rev. Sir Lewis Henry, 9th Bt (*cr* 1660), 1818–1909, vol. I

Palmer, Adm. Norman Craig, 1866–1926, vol. II

Palmer, Brig. Sir Otho Leslie P.; *see* Prior-Palmer.

Palmer, Gen. Sir Patrick; *see* Palmer, Gen. Sir C. P. R.

Palmer, Maj.-Gen. Peter Garwood, 1914–1979, vol. VII

Palmer, Philip, 1867–1940, vol. III

Palmer, Maj.-Gen. Philip Francis, 1903–1992, vol. IX

Palmer, Mrs Potter, (Bertha Honoré), *died* 1918, vol. II

Palmer, Ralph Charlton, 1839–1923, vol. II

Palmer, Col Reginald Arthur Herbert O.; *see* Orpen-Palmer.

Palmer, Reginald Howard Reed, 1898–1970, vol. VI

Palmer, Sir Richmond; *see* Palmer, Sir H. R.

Palmer, Maj.-Gen. Robert John, 1891–1957, vol. V

Palmer, Lt-Col Roderick George F.; *see* Fenwick-Palmer.

Palmer, Sir Roger William Henry, 5th Bt (*cr* 1777), 1832–1910, vol. I

Palmer, Sutton, 1854–1933, vol. III

Palmer, Sir Sydney Bacon, 1890–1954, vol. V

Palmer, Sir Walter, 1st Bt (*cr* 1904), 1858–1910, vol. I

Palmer, Sir William, 1883–1964, vol. VI

Palmer, (William) Howard, 1865–1923, vol. II

Palmer, Hon. (William Jocelyn) Lewis, 1894–1971, vol. VII

Palmer, William John, 1909–1993, vol. IX

Palmer, Lt-Col William Legh, 1868–1955, vol. V

Palmer, Col William Llewellen, 1883–1954, vol. V

Palmes, Rev. George, 1851–1927, vol. II

Palmes, Col Philip, 1856–1914, vol. I

Palmgren, Selim, 1878–1951, vol. V

Palmour, Sir Charles John Geoffrey, 1877–1948, vol. IV

Palmstierna, Baron Erik Kule, 1877–1959, vol. V

Paltridge, Sir Shane Dunne, 1910–1966, vol. VI

Paluello, Lorenzo M.; *see* Minio-Paluello.

Pam, Major Albert, 1875–1955, vol. V

Pamphlett, Engr Rear-Adm. William Frederic, *died* 1940, vol. III

Panagal, Rajah of, 1866–1928, vol. II

Panapa, Rt Rev. Wiremu Netana, 1898–1970, vol. VI

Panckridge, Sir Hugh Rahere, 1885–1942, vol. IV

Panckridge, Surg. Vice-Adm. Sir Robert; *see* Panckridge, Surg. Vice-Adm. Sir W. R. S.

Panckridge, Surg. Vice-Adm. Sir (William) Robert (Silvester), 1901–1990, vol. VIII

Pandey, Ishwari Raj, 1934–1995, vol. X(AI)

Pandit, Mrs Ranjit S.; *see* Pandit, V. L.

Pandit, Vijaya Lakshmi, (Mrs Ranjit S. Pandit), 1900–1990, vol. VIII

Pandya, Jagannath Bhavanishanker, 1891–1942, vol. IV

Panet, Brig.-Gen. Alphonse Eugene, 1867–1950, vol. IV

Panet, Maj.-Gen. Henri Alexandre, 1869–1951, vol. V

Panet, Brig. Henri de Lotbinière, 1896–1985, vol. VIII

Paneth, Friedrich Adolf, 1887–1958, vol. V

Panikkar, Kavalam Madhava, 1895–1963, vol. VI

Pank, Col Cecil Henry, 1876–1957, vol. V

Pank, Sir John Lovell, 1846–1922, vol. II

Pankhurst, Albert Stanley, 1897–1975, vol. VII

Pankhurst, Dame Christabel, 1880–1958, vol. V

Pankhurst, Emmeline, 1858–1928, vol. II

Pankhurst, (Estelle) Sylvia, 1882–1960, vol. V

Pankhurst, Air Vice-Marshal Leonard Thomas, 1902–1996, vol. X

Pankhurst, Sylvia; *see* Pankhurst, E. S.

Panna Lall, 1883–1967, vol. VI (AII)

Pannall, Major J. Charles, 1879–1960, vol. V

Pannell, Baron (Life Peer); Thomas Charles Pannell, 1902–1980, vol. VII

Pannell, Norman Alfred, 1901–1976, vol. VII

Pannett, Charles Aubrey, 1884–1969, vol. VI

Pannirselvam, Sir Arogyaswami Thamaraiselvam, Avargal, *died* 1940, vol. III

Panofsky, Erwin, 1892–1968, vol. VI

Pant, Apasaheb Balasaheb, 1912–1992, vol. IX

Pantcheff, Theodore Xenophon Henry, 1920–1989, vol. VIII
Panter, Air Vice-Marshal Arthur Edward, 1889–1969, vol. VI
Panter-Downes, Mollie Patricia, (Mrs Clare Robinson), 1906–1997, vol. X
Pantin, Most Rev. Anthony, 1929–2000, vol. X
Pantin, Carl Frederick Abel, 1899–1967, vol. VI
Pantin, William Abel, 1902–1973, vol. VII
Panton, Alexander Hugh, 1877–1951, vol. V
Panton, Edward Brooks Henderson, 1873–1929, vol. III
Panton, Mrs Jane Ellen, 1848–1923, vol. II
Panton, Col John Gerald, 1861–1915, vol. I
Panton, Sir Philip Noel, died 1950, vol. IV
Panufrik, Sir Andrzej, 1914–1991, vol. IX
Panzera, Lt-Col Francis William, 1851–1917, vol. II
Pao, Sir Yue-Kong, 1918–1991, vol. IX
Papadopoulos, Achilles Symeon, 1923–1996, vol. X
Papalexopoulo, Rear-Adm. Dimitri, died 1959, vol. V
Papandreou, Andreas George, 1919–1996, vol. X
Pape, Archibald Gabriel, 1876–1927, vol. II
Pape, Sir George Augustus, 1903–1987, vol. VIII
Pape, Hector; see Pape, J. H. C.
Pape, (Jonathan) Hector (Carruthers), 1918–1993, vol. IX
Papillon, Lt-Col Pelham Rawstorn, 1864–1940, vol. III
Papillon, Rev. Thomas Leslie, 1841–1926, vol. II
Papini, Giovanni, 1881–1956, vol. V
Papprill, Rev. Frederick, 1859–1924, vol. II
Papworth, Rev. Sir Harold Charles, 1888–1967, vol. VI
Paradis, Hon. Philippe, 1868–1933, vol. III
Paramore, Richard Horace, 1876–1965, vol. VI
Paranjpye, Sir Raghunath Purushottam, 1876–1966, vol. VI
Pararajasingam, Sir Sangarapillai, 1896–1983, vol. IX(AI)
Parbury, George Mark, 1908–1988, vol. VIII
Parc-Locmaria, Marquis du, Alain, 1892–1973, vol. VII
Pardo-Bazán, Countess Emilia, 1852–1921, vol. II
Pardoe, Col Frank Lionel, 1880–1948, vol. IV
Pardoe, Geoffrey Keith Charles, 1928–1996, vol. X
Pardoe, John George, 1871–1965, vol. VI
Pardoe-Thomas, Bertie, 1866–1937, vol. III
Pare, Rev. Canon Clive Frederick, 1908–1973, vol. VII
Pare, Rev. Philip Norris, 1910–1992, vol. IX
Parekh, Sir Gokuldas Kahandas, 1847–1925, vol. II
Parent, Most Rev. Charles Eugène, 1902–1982, vol. VIII
Parent, Hon. George, 1879–1942, vol. IV
Parent, Hon. Simon Napoleon, 1855–1920, vol. II
Pareparambil, Rt Rev. Aloysius, 1847–1919, vol. II
Parera, Grace Moore, died 1947, vol. IV
Pares, Surg. Lt-Col Basil, 1869–1943, vol. IV
Pares, Sir Bernard, 1867–1949, vol. IV
Pares, Rev. Canon Norman, 1857–1936, vol. III
Pares, Peter, 1908–1992, vol. IX
Pares, Richard, 1902–1958, vol. V
Paret, Bishop William, 1826–1911, vol. I
Parfit, Rev. Joseph Thomas, 1870–1953, vol. V

Parfitt, James John, 1857–1926, vol. II
Parfitt, Rt Rev. Thomas Richards, 1911–1984, vol. VIII
Pargeter, Edith Mary, 1913–1995, vol. IX
Pargiter, Baron (Life Peer); George Albert Pargiter, 1897–1982, vol. VIII
Pargiter, Frederick Eden, 1852–1927, vol. II
Pargiter, Maj.-Gen. Robert Beverley, 1889–1984, vol. VIII
Parham, Rt Rev. Arthur Groom, 1883–1961, vol. VI
Parham, Adm. Sir Frederick Robertson, 1901–1991, vol. IX
Parham, Hedley John, 1892–1978, vol. VII
Parham, Maj.-Gen. Hetman Jack, 1895–1974, vol. VII
Parikian, Manoug, 1920–1987, vol. VIII
Paris, Maj.-Gen. Sir Archibald, 1861–1937, vol. III
Paris, Sir Edward Talbot, 1889–1985, vol. VIII
Paris, Gaston Bruno Paulin, 1839–1903, vol. I
Paris, John, 1912–1985, vol. VIII
Pariser, Sir Maurice Philip, 1906–1968, vol. VI
Pariset, Georges, 1865–1927, vol. II
Parish, Alan Raymond, 1925–1985, vol. VIII
Parish, Arthur John, 1861–1942, vol. IV
Parish, Sir David Elmer W.; see Woodbine Parish.
Parish, Frank, 1824–1906, vol. I
Parish, Rev. John William, 1857–1937, vol. III
Parish, Ven. William Okes, 1859–1940, vol. III
Parish, Lt-Col Woodbine, 1862–1938, vol. III
Park, Alexander Dallas, 1882–1971, vol. VII
Park, Sir Archibald Richard, 1888–1959, vol. V
Park, Carton M.,; see Moore-Park.
Park, Maj.-Gen. Cecil William, 1856–1913, vol. I
Park, George Maclean, 1914–1994, vol. IX
Park, James, 1857–1946, vol. IV
Park, Col James Smith, 1854–1921, vol. II
Park, John, died 1913, vol. I
Park, Air Chief Marshal Sir Keith Rodney, 1892–1975, vol. VII
Park, Sir Maitland Hall, 1862–1921, vol. II
Park, Rev. Philip Lees, 1860–1925, vol. II
Park, Trevor, 1927–1995, vol. IX
Park, Rev. William, 1844–1925, vol. II
Park, William, 1909–1982, vol. VIII
Park, William H., 1863–1939, vol. III
Park, Rev. William Robert, 1880–1961, vol. VI
Park, Col William Urquart, 1846–1917, vol. II
Parke, Ernest, 1860–1944, vol. IV
Parke, Herbert William, 1903–1986, vol. VIII
Parke, Mary, 1908–1989, vol. VIII
Parke, Lt-Col Roger Kennedy, 1848–1911, vol. I
Parke, Sir William, 1822–1897, vol. I
Parker of Waddington, Baron (Life Peer); Robert John Parker, 1857–1918, vol. II
Parker of Waddington, Baron (Life Peer); Hubert Lister Parker, 1900–1972, vol. VII
Parker, Sir Alan; see Parker, Sir W. A.
Parker, Agnes Miller, 1895–1980, vol. IX(AI)
Parker, Albert, 1892–1980, vol. VII
Parker, Alexander Augustine, 1908–1989, vol. VIII
Parker, Hon. Alexander Edward, 1864–1958, vol. V
Parker, Lt-Col Alfred Chevallier, 1874–1935, vol. III
Parker, Sir Alfred Livingston, 1875–1935, vol. III

Parker, Rear-Adm. (S) Alfred Ramsay, *died* 1951, vol. V

Parker, Alwyn, 1877–1951, vol. V

Parker, Dom Anselm Edward Stanislaus, 1880–1962, vol. VI

Parker, Brig.-Gen. Arthur, 1867–1941, vol. IV

Parker, Bertie Patterson, 1871–1930, vol. III

Parker, Cecil, 1897–1971, vol. VII

Parker, Hon. Cecil Thomas, 1845–1931, vol. III

Parker, Charles Arthur, 1863–1938, vol. III

Parker, Charles Sandbach, 1864–1920, vol. II

Parker, Rt Hon. Charles Stuart, 1829–1910, vol. I

Parker, Charles Thomas, 1859–1944, vol. IV

Parker, Christopher John, 1859–1932, vol. III

Parker, Rt Rev. Clement George St Michael, 1900–1980, vol. VII

Parker, Clifford Frederick, 1920–1996, vol. X

Parker, Rt Hon. Dame Dehra Kerr, *died* 1963, vol. VI

Parker, Dorothy, (Mrs Alan Campbell), 1893–1967, vol. VI

Parker, Rear-Adm. Douglas Granger, 1919–2000, vol. X

Parker, Sir Douglas William Leigh, 1900–1988, vol. VIII

Parker, Adm. Edmond Hyde, 1868–1951, vol. V

Parker, Sir Edmund; *see* Parker, Sir W. E.

Parker, Hon. Edmund William, 1857–1943, vol. IV

Parker, Edward Harper, 1849–1926, vol. II

Parker, Rt Rev. Edward Melville, 1855–1925, vol. II, vol. III

Parker, Eric; *see* Parker, R. E.

Parker, Eric, 1870–1955, vol. V

Parker, Rev. Ernest Julius, 1872–1942, vol. IV

Parker, Hon. Francis, 1851–1931, vol. III

Parker, Captain Francis Maitland Wyborn, 1876–1915, vol. I

Parker, Col Frederic James, 1861–1944, vol. IV

Parker, Geoffrey, 1917–1985, vol. VIII

Parker, Geoffrey Edward, 1902–1973, vol. VII

Parker, Adm. George, 1827–1904, vol. I

Parker, George, 1853–1937, vol. III

Parker, Sir George Arthur, 1843–1900, vol. I

Parker, George Howard, 1864–1955, vol. V

Parker, Sir George Phillips, 1863–1943, vol. IV

Parker, Rt Hon. Sir Gilbert, 1st Bt (*cr* 1915), 1862–1932, vol. III

Parker, Gordon; *see* Parker, H. G.

Parker, Hampton Wildman, 1897–1968, vol. VI

Parker, Col Harold, 1881–1939, vol. III

Parker, Harold, 1873–1962, vol. VI

Parker, Sir Harold, 1895–1980, vol. VII

Parker, Harper, 1864–1929, vol. III

Parker, Sir Henry; *see* Parker, Sir S. H.

Parker, (Henry) Gordon, 1892–1980, vol. VII

Parker, Henry Michael Denne, 1894–1971, vol. VII

Parker, Col Henry William Manwaring, *died* 1948, vol. IV

Parker, Adm. Henry Wise, 1875–1940, vol. III

Parker, Horatio William, 1863–1919, vol. II

Parker, Lt-Col Hon. Hubert Stanley Wyborn, 1883–1966, vol. VI

Parker, James, 1863–1948, vol. IV

Parker, James Gordon, 1869–1948, vol. IV

Parker, John, 1875–1952, vol. V

Parker, John, 1906–1987, vol. VIII

Parker, Sir John Edward, 1904–1985, vol. VIII

Parker, Hon. John Holford, 1886–1955, vol. V

Parker, Lt-Col John Oxley, 1886–1979, vol. VII

Parker, Col John William Robinson, 1857–1938, vol. III

Parker, John Williams, 1885–1961, vol. VI

Parker, Rev. Joseph, 1830–1902, vol. I

Parker, Joseph, 1831–1924, vol. II

Parker, Louis N., 1852–1944, vol. IV

Parker, Sir Karl Theodore, 1895–1992, vol. IX

Parker, Kenneth Albert Lamport, 1912–1995, vol. IX

Parker, Dame Marjorie Alice Collett, *died* 1991, vol. IX

Parker, Matthew Archibald, 1871–1953, vol. V

Parker, Sir Melville, 6th Bt (*cr* 1797), 1824–1903, vol. I

Parker, Rt Rev. Michael; *see* Parker, Rt Rev. C. G. St M.

Parker, Maj.-Gen. Neville Fraser, 1841–1916, vol. II

Parker, Owen, 1860–1936, vol. III

Parker, Vice-Adm. Patrick Edward, 1881–1941, vol. IV

Parker, Percy Livingstone, 1867–1925, vol. II

Parker, Hon. Reginald, 1854–1942, vol. IV

Parker, Rev. Reginald Boden, 1901–1993, vol. IX

Parker, Captain Reginald Francis, 1871–1946, vol. IV

Parker, Richard Barry, *died* 1947, vol. IV

Parker, Col Richard Cecil Oxley, 1894–1959, vol. V

Parker, (Richard) Eric, 1925–1982, vol. VIII

Parker, Robert, 1847–1937, vol. III

Parker, Brig.-Gen. Robert Gabbett, 1875–1927, vol. II

Parker, Robert Lewis, 1862–1948, vol. IV

Parker, Rear-Adm. Robert William, 1902–1985, vol. VIII

Parker, Roger Henry, 1889–1973, vol. VII

Parker, Ronald William, 1909–1996, vol. X

Parker, Rushton, 1847–1932, vol. III

Parker, Brig.-Gen. St John William Topp, *died* 1943, vol. IV

Parker, Sir (Stephen) Henry, 1846–1927, vol. II

Parker, Rt Rev. Thomas Leo, 1887–1975, vol. VII

Parker, Rev. Thomas Maynard, 1906–1985, vol. VIII

Parker, Sir (Walter) Edmund, 1908–1981, vol. VIII

Parker, Captain Walter Henry, 1869–1935, vol. III

Parker, Brig.-Gen. Walter Mansel, 1875–1962, vol. VI

Parker, Wilfred Henry, 1888–1938, vol. III

Parker, Rt Rev. Wilfrid, 1883–1966, vol. VI

Parker, Rev. Canon William, 1871–1952, vol. V

Parker, Sir (William) Alan, 4th Bt, 1916–1990, vol. VIII

Parker, Rt Rev. William Alonzo, 1897–1982, vol. VIII

Parker, Sir William Biddulph, 2nd Bt (*cr* 1844), 1824–1902, vol. I

Parker, William Frye, 1855–1919, vol. II

Parker, Rev. William Hasell, *died* 1935, vol. III

Parker, Rev. Sir William Hyde, 10th Bt (*cr* 1681), 1863–1931, vol. III
Parker, Sir William Lorenzo, 3rd Bt (*cr* 1844), 1889–1971, vol. VII
Parker, William Newton, *died* 1923, vol. II
Parker, Engr-Captain William Ramsey, 1862–1943, vol. IV
Parker, Sir William Stephen Hyde, 11th Bt (*cr* 1681), 1892–1951, vol. V
Parker-Bowles, Dame Ann, 1918–1987, vol. VIII
Parker-Jervis, Lt-Col William Swynfen Whitehall, 1879–1936, vol. III
Parkes, Sir Alan Sterling, 1900–1990, vol. VIII
Parkes, Sir Basil Arthur, 1907–1993, vol. IX
Parkes, Edward, 1890–1953, vol. V
Parkes, Sir Edward Ebenezer, 1848–1919, vol. II
Parkes, Ernest William, 1873–1941, vol. IV
Parkes, Sir Fred, 1881–1962, vol. VI
Parkes, Geoffrey, 1902–1982, vol. VIII
Parkes, Major Harry Reeves, 1873–1949, vol. IV (A), vol. V
Parkes, Rev. James William, 1896–1981, vol. VIII
Parkes, Kineton, 1865–1938, vol. III
Parkes, Louis C., *died* 1942, vol. IV
Parkes, Norman James, 1912–1991, vol. X
Parkes, Oscar, 1885–1958, vol. V
Parkes, Sir Roderick Wallis, 1909–1972, vol. VII
Parkes, Sir Sydney, 1879–1961, vol. VI
Parkes, Col William Henry, 1864–1933, vol. III
Parkhill, Hon. Sir Archdale; *see* Parkhill, Hon. Sir R. A.
Parkhill, Hon. Sir (Robert) Archdale, 1879–1947, vol. IV
Parkhurst, Raymond Thurston, 1898–1993, vol. IX
Parkin, Benjamin Theaker, 1906–1969, vol. VI
Parkin, Rev. George, 1846–1933, vol. III
Parkin, Sir George Robert, 1846–1922, vol. II
Parkin, Lt-Col Henry, 1858–1937, vol. III
Parkin, Sir Ian Stanley Colston, 1896–1971, vol. VII
Parkington, Sir John Roper, 1845–1924, vol. II
Parkington, Thomas Robert, 1866–1942, vol. IV
Parkinson, Sir (Albert) Lindsay, 1870–1936, vol. III
Parkinson, Sir (Arthur Charles) Cosmo, 1884–1967, vol. VI
Parkinson, Rev. Charles Meredith Octavius, 1852–1936, vol. III
Parkinson, Sir Cosmo; *see* Parkinson, Sir A. C. C.
Parkinson, Cyril Northcote, 1909–1993, vol. IX
Parkinson, David Hardress, 1918–1993, vol. IX
Parkinson, Desmond Frederick, 1920–1995, vol. IX
Parkinson, Desmond John, 1913–1996, vol. X
Parkinson, Frank, 1887–1946, vol. IV
Parkinson, Brig. George Singleton, 1880–1953, vol. V
Parkinson, Maj.-Gen. Graham Beresford, 1896–1979, vol. VII
Parkinson, Hargreaves, 1896–1950, vol. IV
Parkinson, Sir Harold, 1894–1974, vol. VII
Parkinson, Rt Rev. Mgr Henry, 1852–1924, vol. II
Parkinson, John, 1872–1947, vol. IV
Parkinson, Sir John, 1885–1976, vol. VII
Parkinson, John Allen, 1870–1941, vol. IV
Parkinson, John Porter, 1863–1930, vol. III
Parkinson, John Wilson Henry, 1877–1923, vol. II

Parkinson, Joseph Ernest, 1883–1962, vol. VI
Parkinson, Sir Kenneth Wade, 1908–1981, vol. VIII
Parkinson, Sir Lindsay; *see* Parkinson, Sir A. L.
Parkinson, Dame Nancy Broadfield, 1904–1974, vol. VII
Parkinson, Norman, 1913–1990, vol. VIII
Parkinson, Thomas Harry, 1907–1996, vol. X
Parkinson, Sir Thomas Wright, 1863–1935, vol. III
Parkinson, Wilfrid, 1887–1965, vol. VI
Parkinson, William Edward, 1871–1927, vol. II
Parkinson Smith, Ronald; *see* Parkinson, N.
Parks, Sir Alan Guyatt, 1920–1982, vol. VIII
Parks, Elizabeth; *see* Robins, E.
Parks, Sir John, 1844–1919, vol. II
Parks, Rev. Leighton, 1852–1938, vol. III
Parks, William Arthur, 1868–1936, vol. III
Parkyn, Very Rev. Nathaniel Lindon, *died* 1931, vol. III
Parkyn, William Samuel, 1875–1949, vol. IV
Parkyns, Sir Thomas Mansfield Forbes, 7th Bt, 1853–1926, vol. II
Parlby, Joshua, 1889–1975, vol. VII
Parlett, Sir Harold George, 1869–1945, vol. IV
Parlett, Harry Edgar, *died* 1931, vol. III
Parmar, Rt Rev. Philip, 1909–1970, vol. VI
Parmelee, James Grannis, 1875–1953, vol. V
Parmelee, William Grannis, 1833–1921, vol. II
Parminter, Brig. Reginald Horace Roger, 1893–1967, vol. VI
Parmoor, 1st Baron, 1852–1941, vol. IV
Parmoor, 2nd Baron, 1882–1977, vol. VII
Parmoor, 3rd Baron, 1885–1977, vol. VII
Parnall, Robert Boyd Cochrane, 1912–1976, vol. VII
Parnall, Engr-Rear-Adm. Walter Rudolph, *died* 1954, vol. V
Parnell, Col Hon. Arthur, 1841–1914, vol. I
Parnell, Ven. Arthur Henry, *died* 1935, vol. III
Parnell, John Howard, 1843–1923, vol. II
Parnell, Lt-Gen. John William, 1860–1931, vol. III
Parnell, Valentine Charles, 1894–1972, vol. VII
Parnis, Alexander Edward Libor, 1911–1994, vol. IX
Parnwell, Sidney Arthur, 1880–1944, vol. IV
Parodi, Ernest Victor, 1870–1944, vol. IV
Parr, Adm. Alfred Arthur Chase, 1849–1914, vol. I
Parr, Cecil Francis, 1847–1928, vol. II
Parr, Cecil William Chase, *died* 1943, vol. IV
Parr, Hon. Sir (Christopher) James, 1869–1941, vol. IV
Parr, Col Clements, 1865–1935, vol. III
Parr, George Herbert Edmeston, 1890–1969, vol. VI
Parr, Maj.-Gen. Sir Harington Owen, 1867–1928, vol. II
Parr, Maj.-Gen. Sir Henry Hallam, 1847–1914, vol. I
Parr, Hon. Sir James; *see* Parr, Hon. Sir C. J.
Parr, Rev. John, *died* 1935, vol. III
Parr, Joseph Charlton, 1837–1920, vol. II
Parr, Louisa, *died* 1903, vol. I
Parr, Martin Willoughby, 1892–1985, vol. VIII
Parr, Olive Katharine, (Beatrice Chase), 1874–1955, vol. V
Parr, Raymond Cecil, 1884–1965, vol. VI

Parr, Sir Robert, 1894–1979, vol. VII
Parr, Sir Robert John, 1862–1931, vol. III
Parr, Roger Charlton, 1874–1958, vol. V
Parr, Stanley, 1917–1985, vol. VIII
Parr, Thomas Henning, 1864–1937, vol. III
Parratt, Sir Walter, 1841–1924, vol. II
Parrett, John, 1947–1992, vol. IX
Parrington, Francis Rex, 1905–1981, vol. VIII
Parrington, Rex; see Parrington, F. R.
Parrish, Alfred Sherwen, 1931–1990, vol. VIII
Parrish, Anne, (Mrs Josiah Titzell), died 1957, vol. V
Parrish, Maxfield, 1870–1966, vol. VI
Parrock, Richard Arthur, 1869–1938, vol. III
Parrott, Sir Cecil Cuthbert, 1909–1984, vol. VIII
Parrott, Sir Edward; see Parrott, Sir J. E.
Parrott, Sir (James) Edward, 1863–1921, vol. II
Parrott, William, 1843–1905, vol. I
Parry, Very Rev. Albert William, died 1950, vol. IV
Parry, Rear-Adm. Cecil Ramsden Langworthy, 1901–1977, vol. VII
Parry, Charles de Courcy, 1869–1948, vol. IV
Parry, Sir (Charles) Hubert (Hastings), 1st Bt, 1848–1918, vol. II
Parry, Claude Frederick, 1896–1980, vol. VII
Parry, Clive, 1917–1982, vol. VIII
Parry, Captain Cuthbert Morris, 1907–1980, vol. VII
Parry, Sir David Hughes, 1893–1973, vol. VII
Parry, Adm. Sir Edward; see Parry, Adm. Sir W. E.
Parry, Sir Edward Abbott, 1863–1943, vol. IV
Parry, Most Rev. Edward Archibald, died 1943, vol. IV
Parry, Major Ernest G.; see Gambier-Parry.
Parry, Sir Ernest J.; see Jones Parry.
Parry, Sir (Frank) Hugh (Nigel), 1911–1992, vol. IX
Parry, Sir (Frederick) Sydney, 1861–1941, vol. IV
Parry, Lt-Col Henry Jules, 1867–1944, vol. IV
Parry, Hon. Sir Henry W.; see Wynn Parry.
Parry, Engr Rear-Adm. Herbert Lyell, 1875–1963, vol. VI
Parry, Ven. Herbert Thomas, 1869–1940, vol. III
Parry, Sir Hubert; see Parry, Sir C. H. H.
Parry, Sir Hugh; see Parry, Sir F. H. N.
Parry, Adm. Sir John Franklin, 1863–1926, vol. II
Parry, John Horace, 1914–1982, vol. VIII
Parry, Rear-Adm. John Parry J.; see Jones-Parry.
Parry, Joseph, 1841–1903, vol. I
Parry, Rev. Kenneth Loyd, 1884–1962, vol. VI
Parry, Lt-Col Llewelyn England Sidney, 1856–1929, vol. III
Parry, Maj.-Gen. Michael Denman G.; see Gambier-Parry.
Parry, Rt Rev. Oswald Hutton, 1868–1936, vol. III
Parry, Rev. Reginald St John, 1858–1935, vol. III
Parry, Vice-Adm. Reginald St Pierre, 1879–1939, vol. III
Parry, Air Vice-Marshal Rey Griffith, 1889–1969, vol. VI
Parry, Brig. Sir Richard G.; see Gambier-Parry.
Parry, Robert, 1933–2000, vol. X
Parry, Robert H.; see Hughes-Parry.
Parry, Sir Sidney; see Parry, Sir F. S.

Parry, Sir Thomas, 1904–1985, vol. VIII
Parry, Lt-Col Thomas Henry, 1881–1939, vol. III
Parry, Thomas Robert G.; see Gambier-Parry.
Parry, Col William, 1867–1935, col. III
Parry, Hon. William Edward, 1878–1952, vol. V
Parry, Adm. Sir (William) Edward, 1893–1972, vol. VII
Parry, William John, 1842–1927, vol. II
Parry-Evans, Rev. Joseph David Samuel, 1876–1936, vol. III
Parry-Okeden, Richard Godfrey Christian, 1900–1978, vol. VII
Parry-Okeden, William Edward, 1840–1926, vol. II
Parry Pryce, Ven. Thomas, died 1953, vol. V
Parry-Williams, Sir Thomas Herbert, 1887–1975, vol. VII
Pars, Leopold Alexander, 1896–1985, vol. VIII
Parselle, Air Vice-Marshal Thomas Alford Boyd, 1911–1979, vol. VII
Parsey, Edward Moreland, 1900–1976, vol. VII
Parshall, Horace Field, 1865–1932, vol. III
Parshall, Horace Field, 1903–1986, vol. VIII
Parsloe, Charles Guy, 1900–1985, vol. VIII
Parsloe, Guy; see Parsloe, C. G.
Parson, Col George, 1879–1950, vol. IV (A)
Parsons, Sir Alan Lethbridge; see Parsons, Sir Alfred A. L.
Parsons, Albert, 1865–1938, vol. III
Parsons, Sir (Alfred) Alan Lethbridge, 1882–1964, vol. VI
Parsons, Alfred William, 1847–1920, vol. II
Parsons, Lt-Col Alfred Woodis, 1878–1954, vol. V
Parsons, Hon. Sir Angas; see Parsons, Hon. Sir H. A.
Parsons, Sir Anthony Derrick, 1922–1996, vol. X
Parsons, Maj.-Gen. Sir Arthur Edward Broadbent, 1884–1966, vol. VI
Parsons, Beatrice, died 1955, vol. V
Parsons, Lt-Col Cecil, 1870–1935, vol. III
Parsons, Maj.-Gen. Sir Charles, 1855–1923, vol. II
Parsons, Hon. Sir Charles Algernon, 1854–1931, vol. III
Parsons, Mrs Clement, (Florence Mary Parsons), 1864–1934, vol. III
Parsons, Lt-Gen. Cunliffe McNeile, 1865–1923, vol. II
Parsons, Lt-Col Durie, 1872–1945, vol. IV
Parsons, Major Edward Howard Thornbrough, 1868–1946, vol. IV
Parsons, Rt Rev. Edward Lambe, 1868–1960, vol. V (A)
Parsons, Florence Mary; see Parsons, Mrs Clement.
Parsons, Frank Bett, 1902–1948, vol. IV
Parsons, Major Frederick George, 1856–1904, vol. I
Parsons, Col Frederick George, 1856–1933, vol. III
Parsons, Frederick Gymer, 1863–1943, vol. IV
Parsons, Hon. Geoffry Lawrence, 1874–1956, vol. V
Parsons, Geoffrey Penwill, 1929–1995, vol. IX
Parsons, George Richard, 1898–1961, vol. VI
Parsons, Godfrey Valentine Hope, 1894–1948, vol. IV
Parsons, Maj.-Gen. Sir Harold Daniel Edmund, 1863–1925, vol. II
Parsons, Harold George, died 1905, vol. I

Parsons, Henry Franklin, 1846–1913, vol. I
Parsons, Hon. Sir (Herbert) Angas, 1872–1945, vol. IV
Parsons, Sir Herbert James Francis, 1st Bt, 1870–1940, vol. III
Parsons, Ian Macnaghten, 1906–1980, vol. VII
Parsons, J. W., 1859–1937, vol. III
Parsons, Col Sir John; see Parsons, Col Sir P. J.
Parsons, Sir John Herbert, died 1957, vol. V
Parsons, John Inglis, 1857–1928, vol. II
Parsons, John Randal, 1884–1967, vol. VI
Parsons, Brig. Johnston Lindsey Rowlett, 1876–1935, vol. III
Parsons, Kenneth Charles, 1921–1999, vol. X
Parsons, Rev. Canon Laurence Edmund, 1883–1972, vol. VII
Parsons, Lt-Gen. Sir Lawrence Worthington, 1850–1923, vol. II
Parsons, Sir Leonard Gregory, 1879–1950, vol. IV
Parsons, Sir Maurice Henry, 1910–1978, vol. VII
Parsons, Patricia, (Mrs J. D. Parsons); see Beer, P.
Parsons, Col Sir (Percy) John, 1881–1954, vol. V
Parsons, Philip Harry, died 1920, vol. II
Parsons, Rev. Hon. Randal, 1848–1936, vol. III
Parsons, Hon. Richard Clere, 1851–1923, vol. II
Parsons, Rev. Canon Richard Edward, 1888–1971, vol. VII
Parsons, Rt Rev. Richard Godfrey, 1882–1948, vol. IV
Parsons, William Barclay, 1859–1932, vol. III
Parsons, Col William Forster, 1879–1959, vol. V
Parsons, Engr Rear-Adm. William Roskilly, 1865–1954, vol. V
Parsons-Smith, Basil Thomas, 1882–1954, vol. V
Parsons-Smith, (Basil) Gerald, 1911–1995, vol. IX
Parsons-Smith, Gerald; see Parsons-Smith, B. G.
Part, Sir Antony Alexander, 1916–1990, vol. VIII
Part, Lt-Col Sir Dealtry Charles, died 1961, vol. VI
Partabgarh, Maharawat of, 1857–1929, vol. III
Partington, Rev. Canon Ellis Foster E.; see Edge-Partington.
Partington, James Riddick, 1886–1965, vol. VI
Partington, Wilfred, 1888–1955, vol. V
Parton, Cyril John, 1880–1953, vol. V
Parton, Ernest, died 1933, vol. III
Partridge, Ann St John, died 1936, vol. III
Partridge, Rt Rev. Arthur; see Partridge, Rt Rev. W. A.
Partridge, Sir Bernard, 1861–1945, vol. IV
Partridge, Sir Cecil, 1873–1937, vol. III
Partridge, Edward Hincks, 1901–1962, vol. VI
Partridge, Eric Honeywood, 1894–1979, vol. VII
Partridge, Ernest, 1895–1974, vol. VII
Partridge, Sir (Ernest) John, 1908–1982, vol. VIII
Partridge, Very Rev. Francis, 1846–1906, vol. I
Partridge, Rt Rev. Frank, 1877–1941, vol. IV
Partridge, Harry Cowderoy, 1925–1990, vol. VIII
Partridge, Sir John; see Partridge, Sir E. J.
Partridge, Maurice William, 1913–1973, vol. VII
Partridge, Miles; see Partridge S. M.
Partridge, (Stanley) Miles, 1913–1992, vol. IX
Partridge, Col Sydney George, 1881–1957, vol. V
Partridge, Rt Rev. (William) Arthur, 1912–1992, vol. IX
Partridge, William Ordway, 1861–1930, vol. III

Pascal, Rt Rev. Albert, 1848–1920, vol. II
Pascal, Gabriel, 1894–1954, vol. V
Pascal, Jean Louis, 1837–1920, vol. II, vol. III
Pascal, Roy, 1904–1980, vol. VII
Pascall, Charles, 1853–1931, vol. III
Paschalis, Neoptolemus, 1880–1946, vol. V
Pascoe, Sir Edwin Hall, 1878–1949, vol. IV
Pascoe, Sir (Frederick) John, 1893–1963, vol. VI
Pascoe, Sir John; see Pascoe, Sir F. J.
Pask, Edgar Alexander, 1912–1966, vol. VI
Paske-Smith, Montague Bentley Talbot, died 1946, vol. IV
Paskin, Sir (Jesse) John, 1892–1972, vol. VII
Paskin, Sir John; see Paskin, Sir J. J.
Pasley, Maj.-Gen. Gilbert James, 1834–1910, vol. I
Pasley, Maj.-Gen. Joseph Montagu Sabine, 1898–1978, vol. VII
Pasley, Sir Rodney Marshall Sabine, 4th Bt, 1899–1982, vol. VIII
Pasley, Major Sir Thomas Edward Sabine, 3rd Bt, 1863–1947, vol. IV
Pasley, Thomas Hamilton Sabine, 1861–1927, vol. II
Pasmore, (Edwin John) Victor, 1908–1998, vol. X
Pasmore, Victor; see Pasmore, E. J. V.
Pasolini, Pierpaolo, 1922–1975, vol. VII
Pasquill, Frank, 1914–1994, vol. IX
Pass, (Alfred) Douglas, 1885–1970, vol. VI
Pass, Douglas; see Pass, A. D.
Pass, Rev. Herman Leonard, 1875–1938, vol. III
Passant, Ernest James, 1890–1959, vol. V
Passey, Richard Douglas, 1888–1971, vol. VII
Passfield, 1st Baron, 1859–1947, vol. IV
Passfield, Lady; (Beatrice); see Webb, Mrs Sidney.
Passingham, Col Augustus Mervyn Owen A.; see Anwyl-Passingham.
Passmore, John Reginald Jutsum, 1878–1965, vol. VI
Passmore, Rt Rev. Nicholas Wilfrid, 1907–1976, vol. VII
Pasternak, Boris Leonidovich, 1890–1960, vol. V
Pasteur, Louis V.-R.; see Vallery-Radot Pasteur.
Pasteur, William, died 1943, vol. IV
Paston-Bedingfeld, Sir Henry Edward, 8th Bt, 1860–1941, vol. IV
Paston-Bedingfeld, Sir Henry George, 7th Bt, 1830–1902, vol. I
Paston Brown, Dame Beryl, 1909–1997, vol. X
Paston-Cooper, Sir Astley Paston, 3rd Bt, 1824–1904, vol. I
Paston-Cooper, Sir Charles Naunton Paston, 4th Bt, 1867–1941, vol. IV
Pastor, Antonio Ricardo, 1894–1971, vol. VII
Pasture, 4th Marquis de la, 1836–1916, vol. II
Pasture, 5th Marquis de la, 1886–1962, vol. VI
Patch, Lt-Gen. Alexander McCarrell, 1889–1945, vol. IV
Patch, Sir Edmund Leo H.; see Hall-Patch.
Patch, Brig.-Gen. Francis Robert, 1868–1947, vol. IV
Patch, Air Chief Marshal Sir Hubert Leonard, 1904–1987, vol. VIII
Patch, Col Robert, 1842–1927, vol. II
Patchell, William Henry, 1862–1932, vol. III
Patchett, Terry, 1940–1996, vol. X

Patchett, William, *died* 1915, vol. I
Pate, Henry Reginald, 1880–1942, vol. IV
Patel, Ambalal Bhailalbhai, 1898–1987, vol. VIII
Patel, Khan Bahadur Burjorji D., *died* 1931, vol. III
Patenaude, Esioff Léon, 1875–1963, vol. VI
Pater, John Edward, 1911–1989, vol. VIII
Paterson, A., 1865–1944, vol. IV
Paterson, Col Adrian Gordon, 1888–1940, vol. III
Paterson, Albert Rutherford, 1885–1959, vol. V
Paterson, Sir Alexander, 1884–1947, vol. IV
Paterson, Alexander Brown, 1917–1980, vol. VII
Paterson, Alexander Nisbet, 1862–1947, vol. IV
Paterson, Sir (Alexander) Swinton, 1893–1980, vol. VII
Paterson, Alfred Croom, 1875–1933, vol. III
Paterson, Andrew Barton, 1864–1941, vol. IV
Paterson, Andrew Melville, 1862–1919, vol. II
Paterson, Rev. Archibald, *died* 1932, vol. III
Paterson, Arthur Henry, 1862–1928, vol. II
Paterson, Lt Col Arthur James J.; *see* Jardine Paterson.
Paterson, Arthur Spencer, 1900–1983, vol. VIII
Paterson, Lt-Col Arthur William Sibbald, 1878–1937, vol. III
Paterson, Aylmer John Noel, 1902–1977, vol. VII
Paterson, Sir Clifford Copland, 1879–1948, vol. IV
Paterson, Donald Hugh, 1890–1968, vol. VI
Paterson, Emily Murray, *died* 1934, vol. III
Paterson, Brig.-Gen. Ewing, 1873–1950, vol. IV
Paterson, Col George Frederick Joseph, 1885–1949, vol. IV
Paterson, George McLeod, 1891–1953, vol. V
Paterson, Sir George Mutlow, 1906–1996, vol. X
Paterson, Graham, *died* 1938, vol. III
Paterson, Surg.-Maj.-Gen. Henry Foljambe, 1836–1920, vol. II
Paterson, Lt-Col Henry Francis William, 1880–1943, vol. IV
Paterson, Herbert John, 1868–1940, vol. III
Paterson, Maj.-Gen. Herbert MacGregor, 1898–1979, vol. VII
Paterson, Sqdn-Ldr Ian Veitch, 1911–1994, vol. X(AI)
Paterson, James, 1854–1932, vol. III
Paterson, Rev. James Alexander, 1851–1915, vol. I
Paterson, (James Edmund) Neil, 1915–1995, vol. IX
Paterson, James Ralston Kennedy, 1897–1981, vol. VIII
Paterson, James Veitch, 1866–1943, vol. IV
Paterson, Jennifer Mary, 1928–1999, vol. X
Paterson, John Allan, 1909–1991, vol. IX
Paterson, John Mower Alexander, 1920–2000, vol. X
Paterson, John Sidney, 1899–1965, vol. VI
Paterson, Sir John Valentine J.; *see* Jardine Paterson.
Paterson, John Waugh, 1869–1958, vol. V
Paterson, John Wilson, 1887–1970, vol. VI
Paterson, Marcus, 1870–1932, vol. III
Paterson, Mary Muirhead, *died* 1941, vol. IV
Paterson, Neil; *see* Paterson, J. E. N.
Paterson, Nicholas Julian, *died* 1934, vol. III
Paterson, Noel Kennedy, 1905–1984, vol. VIII
Paterson, Lt-Col Norman Fitzherbert, 1843–1925, vol. II

Paterson, Col Philip Joseph, 1874–1930, vol. III
Paterson, Captain Quentin Hunter, 1888–1975, vol. VII
Paterson, Ralston; *see* Paterson, J. R. K.
Paterson, Sir Reginald G. C., 1875–1939, vol. III
Paterson, Robert Lancelot, 1918–1995, vol. IX
Paterson, Gen. Robert Ormiston, 1878–1941, vol. IV
Paterson, Brig.-Gen. Robert Walter, 1876–1936, vol. III
Paterson, Col Stanley, 1860–1950, vol. IV
Paterson, Stronach, 1886–1957, vol. V
Paterson, Sir Swinton; *see* Paterson, Sir A. S.
Paterson, Maj.-Gen. Thomas George Ferguson, 1876–1942, vol. IV
Paterson, Thomas Wilson, *born* 1851, vol. II
Paterson, William, 1815–1903, vol. I
Paterson, Sir William, 1874–1956, vol. V
Paterson, William Bromfield, *died* 1924, vol. II
Paterson, William G. R., 1878–1954, vol. V
Paterson, William James Macdonald, 1911–1976, vol. VII
Paterson, Very Rev. William Paterson, 1860–1939, vol. III
Paterson-Morgan, Rev. Richard James Basil, 1879–1966, vol. VI
Pateshall, Col Henry Evan Pateshall, 1879–1948, vol. IV
Patey, David Howard, 1899–1977, vol. VII
Patey, Adm. Sir George Edwin, 1859–1935, vol. III
Patiala, Lt-Gen. HH Maharaja Dhiraj of, 1891–1938, vol. III
Patiala, Lt-Gen. HH Maharajadhiraj of, 1913–1974, vol. VII
Patna, HH Maharaja of, 1912–1975, vol. VII
Paton, Maj. Adrian Gerard Nigel H.; *see* Hadden-Paton.
Paton, Alan Stewart, 1903–1988, vol. VIII
Paton, Col Alexander, 1897–1985, vol. VIII
Paton, Alexander Allan, *died* 1934, vol. III
Paton, Sir Alfred Vaughan, 1861–1930, vol. III
Paton, Sir Angus; *see* Paton, Sir T. A. L.
Paton, Brig. Charles Morgan, 1896–1979, vol. VII
Paton, Rev. Canon David Macdonald, 1913–1992, vol. IX
Paton, Diarmid Noel, 1859–1928, vol. II
Paton, Florence Beatrice, *died* 1976, vol. VII
Paton, Frederick Noel, 1861–1914, vol. I
Paton, G., *died* 1906, vol. I
Paton, Maj.-Gen. George, 1841–1931, vol. III
Paton, George Campbell Henderson, 1905–1984, vol. VIII
Paton, George Pearson, 1882–1975, vol. VII
Paton, Sir George Whitecross, 1902–1985, vol. VIII
Paton, Sir George William, 1859–1934, vol. III
Paton, Harold William, 1900–1986, vol. VIII
Paton, Herbert James, 1887–1969, vol. VI
Paton, Hugh, 1853–1927, vol. II
Paton, James, 1843–1921, vol. II
Paton, James Bowie, *died* 1940, vol. III (A), vol. IV
Paton, Sir James Wallace, 1863–1948, vol. IV
Paton, Maj.-Gen. John, 1867–1943, vol. IV
Paton, John, 1886–1976, vol. VII
Paton, John Brown, 1830–1911, vol. I
Paton, John Gibson, 1824–1907, vol. I

635

Paton, John Lewis, 1863–1946, vol. IV
Paton, Sir Joseph Noël, 1821–1901, vol. I
Paton, Sir Leonard Cecil, 1892–1986, vol. VIII
Paton, Leslie, 1872–1943, vol. IV
Paton, Rev. Lewis Bayles, 1864–1932, vol. III
Paton, Robert Thomson, 1856–1929, vol. III
Paton, Robert Young, 1894–1973, vol. VII
Paton, Sir Stuart Henry, 1900–1987, vol. VIII
Paton, Sir (Thomas) Angus (Lyall), 1905–1999, vol. X
Paton, Rev. William, 1886–1943, vol. IV
Paton, William Calder, 1886–1979, vol. VII
Paton, Vice-Adm. William Douglas, 1874–1952, vol. V
Paton, Sir William Drummond Macdonald, 1917–1993, vol. IX
Patrick, Rt Hon. Lord; William Donald Patrick, 1889–1967, vol. VI
Patrick, Adam, 1883–1970, vol. VI
Patrick, Major Charles Kennedy Cochran-, 1896–1933, vol. III
Patrick, (Colin) Mark, 1893–1942, vol. IV
Patrick, David, 1849–1914, vol. I
Patrick, (James) McIntosh, 1907–1998, vol. X
Patrick, Rev. John, 1850–1933, vol. III
Patrick, Brig. John, 1898–1985, vol. VIII
Patrick, John Bowman, 1916–1999, vol. X
Patrick, McIntosh; see Patrick, J. M.
Patrick, Mark; see Patrick, C. M.
Patrick, Mary Mills, 1850–1940, vol. III
Patrick, Sir Neil James Kennedy C.; see Cochran-Patrick.
Patrick, Nigel Dennis Wemyss, 1913–1981, vol. VIII
Patrick, Sir Paul Joseph, 1888–1975, vol. VII
Patrick, Rt Hon. William Donald; see Patrick, Rt Hon. Lord.
Patro Garu, Rao Bahadur Sir Annepu Parasuramadas, 1875–1946, vol. IV
Patron, Sir Joseph, 1896–1981, vol. VIII
Patron, Joseph Armand, 1856–1922, vol. II
Patry, Edward, died 1940, vol. III
Pattani, Sir Prabhashanker Dalpatram, 1862–1938, vol. III
Patten, Charles J., 1870–1948, vol. IV
Patten, Rev. John Alexander, 1883–1952, vol. V
Patten, Tom, 1926–1999, vol. X
Pattenson, Arthur Eric Tylden, 1888–1955, vol. V
Pattenson, Major Arthur Henry T.; see Tylden-Pattenson.
Pattenson, Lt-Col Edwin Cooke Tylden-, 1871–1940, vol. III
Patterson, Alexander Blakeley, 1842–1919, vol. II
Patterson, Rev. Alexander Hamilton, 1851–1943, vol. IV
Patterson, Annie W., died 1934, vol. III
Patterson, Arthur, 1906–1996, vol. X
Patterson, Maj.-Gen. Arthur Gordon, 1917–1996, vol. X
Patterson, Rt Rev. Cecil John, 1908–1992, vol. IX
Patterson, Colin, 1933–1998, vol. X
Patterson, Daniel Wells, 1871–1932, vol. III
Patterson, David Clarke, 1879–1948, vol. IV
Patterson, Eric James, 1891–1972, vol. VII
Patterson, Geoffrey Crosbie, 1912–1984, vol. VIII

Patterson, George, 1846–1925, vol. II, vol. III
Patterson, Hugh Foggan, 1924–1999, vol. X
Patterson, Hon. James Colebrooke, 1839–1929, vol. III
Patterson, James Kennedy, 1833–1922, vol. II
Patterson, Rt Rev. James Laird, 1822–1902, vol. I
Patterson, Jocelyn, 1900–1965, vol. VI
Patterson, John Edward, died 1919, vol. II
Patterson, Sir John Robert, 1892–1976, vol. VII
Patterson, Rear-Adm. Julian Francis Chichester, 1884–1972, vol. VII
Patterson, Rev. Melville Watson, 1873–1944, vol. IV
Patterson, Norman, 1879–1909, vol. I
Patterson, Norman, 1877–1950, vol. IV
Patterson, Sir Reginald Stewart, 1878–1930, vol. III
Patterson, Sir Robert Lloyd, 1836–1906, vol. I
Patterson, Robert Porter, 1891–1952, vol. V
Patterson, Lt-Col Sir Stewart Blakeley Agnew, 1872–1942, vol. IV
Patterson, Thomas Redden, 1898–1972, vol. VII
Patterson, Thomas Stewart, 1872–1949, vol. IV
Patterson, Lt-Col Thomas W., 1844–1902, vol. I
Patterson, Adm. Sir Wilfrid Rupert, 1893–1954, vol. V
Patteson, John Coleridge, 1896–1954, vol. V
Patti, Mme Adelina, (Baroness Rolf Cederström), 1843–1919, vol. II
Pattinson, Arthur Edward, 1868–1939, vol. III
Pattinson, Hon. Sir Baden, 1899–1978, vol. IX(AI)
Pattinson, George Norman, 1887–1966, vol. VI
Pattinson, John Mellor, 1899–1999, vol. X
Pattinson, Rev. Canon Joseph Alfred, 1861–1919, vol. II
Pattinson, Air Marshal Sir Lawrence Arthur, 1890–1955, vol. V
Pattinson, Peter Lawrence F.; see Foden Pattinson.
Pattinson, Sir Robert, 1872–1954, vol. V
Pattinson, Samuel, 1870–1942, vol. IV
Pattison, Andrew Seth Pringle; see Seth, Andrew.
Pattison, Bruce, 1908–1996, vol. X
Pattison, Harold Arthur Langston, 1897–1966, vol. VI
Pattisson, Jacob Luard, 1841–1915, vol. I
Pattisson, Adm. John Robert Ebenezer, 1844–1928, vol. II
Patton, Arnold Gordon, 1892–1960, vol. V
Patton, Rev. Francis Landey, 1843–1932, vol. III
Patton, Gen. George Smith, Jr, 1885–1945, vol. IV
Patton, Col Henry Bethune, 1835–1915, vol. I
Patton, Rt Rev. Henry Edmund, 1867–1943, vol. IV
Patton, Thomas William Saunderson, 1914–1993, vol. IX
Patton, Walter Scott, 1876–1960, vol. V
Pattrick, Michael; see Pattrick, W. M. T.
Pattrick, (William) Michael (Thomas), 1913–1980, vol. VII
Pattullo, Hon. Thomas Dufferin, 1873–1956, vol. V
Pattullo, William Ogilvy, 1924–1975, vol. VII
Patwardhan, Baba Saheb; see Miraj (Junior), Chief of.
Pau, Gen. Paul Mary Cæsar Gerald, 1848–1932, vol. III
Pauer, Max, 1866–1945, vol. IV

Paul VI, His Holiness Pope, (Giovanni Battista Montini), 1897–1978, vol. VII
Paul, Alfred Wallis, 1847–1912, vol. I
Paul, Sir Aubrey Edward Henry Dean, 5th Bt (cr 1821), 1869–1961, vol. VI
Paul, Sir Brian Kenneth, 6th Bt (cr 1821), 1904–1972, vol. VII
Paul, Cedar, died 1972, vol. VII
Paul, Charles Kegan, 1828–1902, vol. I
Paul, Sir (Charles) Norman, 1883–1959, vol. V
Paul, Very Rev. David, 1845–1929, vol. III
Paul, David Manuel, 1927–1993, vol. IX
Paul, Col Denis, 1865–1944, vol. IV
Paul, Elliot Harold, 1891–1958, vol. V
Paul, Eric Barlow, 1919–1968, vol. VI
Paul, Rev. F. J., died 1941, vol. IV
Paul, Francis Kinnier, 1911–1965, vol. VI
Paul, Frank Thomas, 1851–1941, vol. IV
Paul, Rev. G. W., 1820–1911, vol. I
Paul, Rt Rev. Geoffrey John, 1921–1983, vol. VIII
Paul, Sir (George) Graham, 1887–1960, vol. V
Paul, Sir George Morison, 1839–1926, vol. II
Paul, Brig.-Gen. Gerard Robert Clark, 1861–1913, vol. I
Paul, Sir Graham; see Paul, Sir George G.
Paul, Sir Gregory Charles, 1830–1900, vol. I
Paul, Sir Harisankar, 1888–1951, vol. V
Paul, Herbert Woodfield, 1853–1935, vol. III
Paul, Sir James Balfour, 1846–1931, vol. III
Paul, Rev. Sir Jeffrey; see Paul, Rev. Sir W. E. J.
Paul, Lt-Col John William Balfour, 1873–1957, vol. V
Paul, Leslie Allen, 1905–1985, vol. VIII
Paul, Leslie Douglas, 1903–1970, vol. VI
Paul, Maurice Eden, 1865–1944, vol. IV
Paul, Sir Norman; see Paul, Sir C. N.
Paul, Engr-Rear-Adm. Oliver Richard, 1868–1955, vol. V
Paul, Paul, 1865–1937, vol. III
Paul, Sir Robert Joshua, 3rd Bt (cr 1794), 1820–1898, vol. I
Paul, Captain Sir Robert Joshua, 5th Bt (cr 1794), 1883–1955, vol. V
Paul, Roderick Sayers, 1935–1998, vol. X
Paul, Stuart, 1879–1961, vol. VI
Paul, Maj.-Gen. Walter Reginald, 1882–1953, vol. V
Paul, Rev. Sir (William Edmund) Jeffrey, 6th Bt (cr 1794), 1885–1961, vol. VI
Paul, Sir William Joshua, 4th Bt (cr 1794), 1851–1912, vol. I
Paul-Boncour, Joseph, 1873–1972, vol. VII
Paulet, Major Charles Standish, 1873–1953, vol. V
Paulin, Sir David, 1847–1930, vol. III
Paulin, George Henry, 1888–1962, vol. VI
Paulin, Sir William Thomas, 1848–1931, vol. III
Pauline, Sister; see Young, Hilda Beatrice.
Pauling, Linus Carl, 1901–1994, vol. IX
Paull, Sir Gilbert James, 1896–1984, vol. VIII
Paull, Harry Major, 1854–1934, vol. III
Paull, Richard James, 1862–1937, vol. III
Paulson, Godfrey Martin Ellis, 1908–1990, vol. VIII
Paulton, James Mellor, 1857–1923, vol. II
Pauncefort-Duncombe, Sir Everard; see Duncombe, Sir E. P. D. P.

Pauncefote, 1st Baron, 1828–1902, vol. I
Paur, Emil, 1855–1932, vol. III
Paus, Christopher L., 1881–1963, vol. VI
Pavière, Sydney Herbert, 1891–1971, vol. VII
Pavitt, Laurence Anstice, 1914–1989, vol. VIII
Pavlides, Sir Paul George, 1897–1977, vol. VII
Pavlides, Stelios, 1892–1968, vol. VI (AII)
Pavry, Faredun Cursetji, 1877–1943, vol. IV
Pavy, Emily Dorothea, died 1967, vol. VI
Pavy, Frederick William, 1829–1911, vol. I
Pawan, Joseph Lennox, 1887–1957, vol. V
Pawel-Rammingen, Baron Luitbert Alexander George Lionel Alphons, 1843–1932, vol. III
Pawle, Brig. Hanbury, 1886–1972, vol. VII
Pawley, Ven. Bernard Clinton, 1911–1981, vol. VIII
Pawsey, Sir Charles Ridley, 1894–1972, vol. VII
Pawsey, Joseph Lade, 1908–1962, vol. VI
Pawson, Albert Guy, 1888–1986, vol. VIII
Pawson, Henry Cecil, 1897–1978, vol. VII
Pawson, Ven. Wilfrid Denys, 1905–1959, vol. V
Paxton, Air Vice-Marshal Sir Anthony Lauderdale, 1896–1957, vol. V
Paxton, Sir Thomas, 1st Bt, died 1930, vol. III
Payen-Payne, de Vincheles, 1866–1945, vol. IV
Payn, James, 1830–1898, vol. I
Payne, Col Alexander Vaughan, 1857–1943, vol. IV
Payne, Anson; see Payne, J. A.
Payne, Arthur Robert, 1926–1976, vol. VII
Payne, Ben Iden, 1881–1976, vol. VII
Payne, Charles, 1871–1948, vol. IV
Payne, Charles Frederick, 1875–1966, vol. VI
Payne, Charles Robert Salusbury, 1859–1942, vol. IV
Payne, Vice-Adm. Christopher Russell, 1874–1952, vol. V
Payne, Rev. David Bruce, 1827–1913, vol. I
Payne, de Vincheles P.; see Payen-Payne.
Payne, Col Edward Henry, 1868–1941, vol. IV
Payne, Edward John, 1844–1904, vol. I
Payne, Rev. Ernest Alexander, 1902–1980, vol. VII
Payne, Rev. Francis Reginald Chassereau, 1876–1961, vol. VI
Payne, Maj.-Gen. George Lefevre, 1911–1992, vol. IX
Payne, Henry, 1871–1945, vol. IV
Payne, Henry A., 1868–1940, vol. III
Payne, Sir Henry Arthur, 1873–1931, vol. III
Payne, Col Herbert Chidgey Brine, 1862–1945, vol. IV
Payne, Hon. Herbert James Mockford, 1866–1944, vol. IV
Payne, Humfry Gilbert Garth, 1902–1936, vol. III
Payne, Jack Marsh, 1929–1988, vol. VIII
Payne, (John) Anson, 1917–1987, vol. VIII
Payne, John Bruce, died 1928, vol. II
Payne, John Horne, 1837–1920, vol. II
Payne, Joseph Frank, 1840–1910, vol. I
Payne, Lt-Col Leslie Herbert, 1888–1942, vol. IV
Payne, Sir Reginald Withers, 1904–1980, vol. VII
Payne, Maj.-Gen. Richard Lloyd, 1854–1921, vol. II
Payne, Sir Robert Frederick, 1908–1985, vol. VIII
Payne, Major Robert Leslie, 1880–1942, vol. IV
Payne, Sylvia May, 1880–1976, vol. VII
Payne, Walter, died 1949, vol. IV
Payne, Sir William Labatt, 1890–1962, vol. VI

Payne-Gallwey, Sir Ralph William Frankland; *see* Gallwey.
Payne-Gallwey, Sir Reginald Frankland; *see* Gallwey.
Payne-Gallwey, Captain William Thomas Frankland; *see* Gallwey.
Paynter, Col Camborne Haweis, 1864–1949, vol. IV
Paynter, Brig.-Gen. Sir George Camborne Beauclerk, 1880–1950, vol. IV
Paynter, Air Cdre Noel Stephen, 1898–1998, vol. X
Paynter, (Thomas) William, 1903–1984, vol. VIII
Paynter, William; *see* Paynter, T. W.
Payton, Sir Charles Alfred, 1843–1926, vol. II
Payton, Rev. Wilfred Ernest Granville, 1913–1989, vol. VIII
Payton, Wilfrid Hugh, 1892–1965, vol. VI
Paz, Octavio, 1914–1998, vol. X
Peabody, George Foster, 1852–1938, vol. III
Peace, Albert Lister, 1844–1912, vol. I
Peace, Captain Alfred Geoffrey, 1885–1940, vol. III
Peace, Sir Walter, 1840–1917, vol. II
Peacey, Rt Rev. Basil William, 1889–1969, vol. VI
Peacey, Rev. J. R., 1896–1971, vol. VII
Peach, Benjamin Neeve, 1842–1926, vol. II
Peach, Captain Charles Lindsay K,; *see* Keighly-Peach.
Peach, Adm. Charles William K.; *see* Keighly-Peach.
Peach, Denis Alan, 1928–2000, vol. X
Peach, Major Edmund, 1865–1902, vol. I
Peach, Lawrence du Garde, 1890–1974, vol. VII
Peachey, Captain Allan Thomas George Cumberland, 1896–1967, vol. VI
Peacock, Alexander David, *died* 1976, vol. VII
Peacock, Hon. Sir Alexander James, 1861–1933, vol. III
Peacock, Rev. Charles Alfred, 1868–1944, vol. IV
Peacock, David Henry, 1889–1978, vol. VII
Peacock, Edward Eden, 1850–1909, vol. I
Peacock, Sir Edward Robert, 1871–1962, vol. VI
Peacock, Major Ferdinand Mansel, 1861–1908, vol. I
Peacock, Frederick Hood, 1886–1969, vol. VI
Peacock, Major Frederick William, 1859–1924, vol. II
Peacock, Sir Geoffrey Arden, 1920–1991, vol. IX
Peacock, (John) Roydon, 1902–1982, vol. VIII
Peacock, Joseph Henry, 1918–1992, vol. IX
Peacock, Sir Kenneth Swift, 1902–1968, vol. VI
Peacock, Matthew Henry, 1856–1929, vol. III
Peacock, Millie, (Lady Peacock), *died* 1948, vol. IV
Peacock, Sir Peter, 1872–1948, vol. IV
Peacock, Col Pryce, 1868–1956, vol. V
Peacock, Ralph, *died* 1946, vol. IV
Peacock, Sir Robert, 1859–1926, vol. II
Peacock, Ronald, 1907–1993, vol. IX
Peacock, Roydon; *see* Peacock, J. R.
Peacock, Sir Thomas, *died* 1959, vol. V
Peacock, Rev. W. Arthur, 1905–1968, vol. VI
Peacock, Sir Walter, 1871–1956, vol. V
Peacock, Rev. Canon Wilfrid Morgan, 1890–1970, vol. VI
Peacock, William Henry, 1881–1946, vol. IV
Peacocke, Rt Rev. Cuthbert Irvine, 1903–1994, vol. IX

Peacocke, Emilie Hawkes, 1883–1964, vol. VI
Peacocke, Most Rev. Joseph Ferguson, 1835–1916, vol. II
Peacocke, Rt Rev. Joseph Irvine, 1866–1962, vol. VI
Peacocke, Col Thomas George, 1865–1939, vol. III
Peacocke, Col William, 1848–1931, vol. III
Peake, Hon. Archibald Henry, 1859–1920, vol. II
Peake, Sir Arthur Copson, 1854–1934, vol. III
Peake, Arthur Samuel, 1865–1929, vol. III
Peake, Sir Charles Brinsley Pemberton, 1897–1958, vol. V
Peake, Brig. Edward Robert Luxmoore, 1894–1964, vol. VI
Peake, Sir Francis, 1889–1984, vol. VIII
Peake, Frederick Gerard, 1886–1970, vol. VI
Peake, George Herbert, 1859–1950, vol. IV
Peake, Sir Harald, 1899–1978, vol. VII
Peake, Harold John Edward, 1867–1946, vol. IV
Peake, Brig.-Gen. Malcolm, 1865–1917, vol. II
Peake, Mervyn, 1911–1968, vol. VI
Peake, Thomas, 1868–1945, vol. IV
Peaker, Alfred Pearson, 1896–1973, vol. VII
Peaker, Frederick, 1867–1942, vol. IV
Peal, Lt-Col Edward Raymond, 1884–1967, vol. VI
Pear, Tom Hatherley, 1886–1972, vol. VII
Pearce, Baron (Life Peer); Edward Holroyd Pearce, 1901–1990, vol. VIII
Pearce, C. Maresco, 1874–1964, vol. VI
Pearce, Charles E., *died* 1924, vol. II
Pearce, Sir (Charles) Frederick (Byrde), 1892–1964, vol. VI
Pearce, Charles William, 1856–1928, vol. II
Pearce, Clifford James, 1916–1985, vol. VIII
Pearce, Col Cyril Harvey, 1878–1943, vol. IV
Pearce, Rt Rev. Edmund Courtenay, 1870–1935, vol. III
Pearce, Sir Edward Charles, 1862–1928, vol. II
Pearce, E(dward) Ewart, 1898–1963, vol. VI
Pearce, Sir Eric Herbert, 1905–1997, vol. X
Pearce, Ernest Alfred John, 1868–1943, vol. IV
Pearce, Rt Rev. Ernest Harold, 1865–1930, vol. III
Pearce, Major Francis Barrow, 1866–1926, vol. II
Pearce, Sir Frank James, 1878–1946, vol. IV
Pearce, Sir Frederick; *see* Pearce, Sir C. F. B.
Pearce, Air Cdre Frederick Laurence, 1898–1975, vol. VII
Pearce, Sir George Alfred, 1894–1971, vol. VII
Pearce, Rt Hon. Sir George Foster, 1870–1952, vol. V
Pearce, Harold Seward, 1880–1961, vol. VI
Pearce, Henry, 1869–1925, vol. II
Pearce, Hon. James Edward Holroyd, 1934–1985, vol. VIII
Pearce, John Dalziel Wyndham, 1904–1994, vol. IX
Pearce, John Trevor Archdall, 1916–2000, vol. X
Pearce, Kenneth Leslie, 1910–1988, vol. VIII
Pearce, Sir Leonard; *see* Pearce, Sir S. L.
Pearce, Malcolm Arthur Fraser, 1898–1979, vol. VII (AII)
Pearce, Hon. Richard Bruce Holroyd, 1930–1987, vol. VIII
Pearce, Sir Robert, 1840–1922, vol. II
Pearce, Rev. Robert John, 1841–1920, vol. II
Pearce, Seward, 1866–1951, vol. V

Pearce, Sir (Standen) Leonard, 1873–1947, vol. IV
Pearce, Thomas Ernest, 1883–1941, vol. IV
Pearce, Sir William, 1853–1932, vol. III
Pearce, Rev. William Fletcher, 1869–1935, vol. III
Pearce, Sir William George, 2nd Bt, 1861–1907, vol. I
Pearce, William Harvey, 1920–1982, vol. VIII
Pearce-Higgins, Rev. Canon John Denis, 1905–1985, vol. VIII
Pearce-Serocold, Brig.-Gen. Eric, 1870–1926, vol. II
Pearce-Serocold, Oswald, 1865–1951, vol. V
Peard, Frances Mary, died 1923, vol. II
Peard, Rear-Adm. Sir Kenyon Harry Terrell, 1902–1994, vol. IX
Pearkes, Maj.-Gen. Hon. George Randolph, 1888–1984, vol. VIII
Pearl, Amy Lea, (Mrs F. Warren Pearl), 1880–1964, vol. VI
Pearl, Mrs F. Warren; see Pearl, Amy Lea.
Pearl, Raymond, 1879–1940, vol. III (A), vol. IV
Pearless, Brig.-Gen. Charles William, 1872–1940, vol. III
Pearman, Rev. Augustus John, died 1909, vol. I
Pearman, Sir James Eugene, 1904–1994, vol. IX
Pearman-Smith, Sir William Joseph, 1863–1939, vol. III
Pears, Charles, 1873–1958, vol. V
Pears, Adm. Sir Edmund Radcliffe, 1862–1941, vol. IV
Pears, Sir Edwin, 1835–1919, vol. II
Pears, Harold Snowden, 1926–1982, vol. VIII
Pears, Major M. L., died 1916, vol. II
Pears, Sir Peter Neville Luard, 1910–1986, vol. VIII
Pears, Sidney John, 1900–1972, vol. VII
Pears, Rear-Adm. Steuart Arnold, 1894–1978, vol. VII
Pears, Sir Steuart Edmund, 1875–1931, vol. III
Pearsall, Phyllis Isobel, 1906–1996, vol. X
Pearsall, William Booth, 1845–1913, vol. I
Pearsall, William Harold, 1891–1964, vol. VI
Pearse, Albert William, 1857–1951, vol. V
Pearse, Captain Alfred, died 1933, vol. III
Pearse, Major Beauchamp Albert Thomas K.; see Kerr-Pearse.
Pearse, Gen. George Godfrey, 1827–1905, vol. I
Pearse, H. H. S., died 1905, vol. I
Pearse, Col Hugh Wodehouse, 1855–1919, vol. II
Pearse, James, 1871–1962, vol. VI
Pearse, Sir John Slocombe, 1870–1949, vol. IV
Pearse, Rev. Mark Guy, 1842–1930, vol. III
Pearse, Ronald Livian, 1880–1960, vol. V
Pearse, Lt-Col Sydney Arthur, died 1937, vol. III
Pearse, Thomas Lawrence S.; see Smith-Pearse.
Pearse, Rev. Thomas Northmore Hart S.; see Smith-Pearse.
Pearse, Brig.-Gen. Tom Harry Finch, 1864–1947, vol. IV
Pearson, Baron (Life Peer); Colin Hargreaves Pearson, 1899–1980, vol. VII
Pearson, Hon. Lord; Charles John Pearson, 1843–1910, vol. I
Pearson, Brig. Alastair Stevenson, 1915–1996, vol. X
Pearson, Rt Rev. Alfred, 1848–1909, vol. I
Pearson, Gen. Sir Alfred Astley, 1850–1937, vol. III

Pearson, Alfred Chilton, 1861–1935, vol. III
Pearson, Rev. Andrew Forret Scott, 1886–1952, vol. V
Pearson, Andrew Russell; see Pearson, Drew.
Pearson, Sir Arthur; see Pearson, Sir C. A.
Pearson, Arthur, 1897–1980, vol. VII
Pearson, Arthur Ashley, 1847–1933, vol. III
Pearson, Aylmer Cavendish, 1876–1926, vol. II
Pearson, Hon. (Bernard) Clive, 1887–1965, vol. VI
Pearson, Bertram Lamb, 1893–1984, vol. VIII
Pearson, Burton, 1872–1937, vol. III
Pearson, Charles Child, 1875–1955, vol. V
Pearson, Charles John; see Pearson, Hon. Lord
Pearson, Sir Charles Knight, 1834–1909, vol. I
Pearson, Charles Yelverton, 1857–1947, vol. IV
Pearson, Claude Edmund, 1903–1971, vol. VII
Pearson, Hon. Clive; see Pearson, Hon. B. C.
Pearson, Colin Bateman, 1889–1974, vol. VII
Pearson, Sir (Cyril) Arthur, 1st Bt, 1866–1921, vol. II
Pearson, David Morris, 1915–1985, vol. VIII
Pearson, Sir Denning; see Pearson, Sir J. D.
Pearson, Drew, (Andrew Russell Pearson), 1897–1969, vol. VI
Pearson, Sir Edward Ernest, 1874–1925, vol. II
Pearson, Egon Sharpe, 1895–1980, vol. VII
Pearson, Ethel Maud, (Lady Pearson), 1870–1959, vol. V
Pearson, Sir Francis Fenwick, 1st Bt, 1911–1991, vol. IX
Pearson, Frederick John, 1866–1932, vol. III
Pearson, George Sherwin Hooke, 1875–1941, vol. IV
Pearson, Col George Thomson, 1876–1946, vol. IV
Pearson, Gerald Lionel, 1918–1978, vol. VII
Pearson, Sir Glen Gardner, 1907–1976, vol. VII
Pearson, Henry Harold Welch, 1870–1916, vol. II
Pearson, Sir Herbert Grayhurst, 1878–1958, vol. V
Pearson, Air Cdre Herbert Macdonald, 1908–1992, vol. IX
Pearson, Hesketh, 1887–1964, vol. VI
Pearson, Hugh Drummond, 1873–1922, vol. II
Pearson, Adm. Sir Hugo Lewis, 1843–1912, vol. I
Pearson, Sir (James) Denning, 1908–1992, vol. IX
Pearson, James Douglas, 1911–1997, vol. X
Pearson, James Rae, 1871–1951, vol. V
Pearson, Sir (James) Reginald, 1897–1984, vol. VIII
Pearson, Vice-Adm. John Lewis, 1879–1965, vol. VI
Pearson, John Loughborough, 1817–1897, vol. I
Pearson, Joseph, 1881–1971, vol. VII
Pearson, Karl, 1857–1936, vol. III
Pearson, Rt Hon. Lester Bowles, 1897–1972, vol. VII
Pearson, Lionel Godfrey, 1879–1953, vol. V
Pearson, Sir Louis Frederick, 1863–1943, vol. IV
Pearson, Louise Kirkby; see Lunn, L. K.
Pearson, Rev. Marchant, 1871–1956, vol. V
Pearson, Col Michael Brown, 1840–1923, vol. II
Pearson, Sir Neville Arthur, 2nd Bt, 1898–1982, vol. VIII
Pearson, Lt-Col Noel Gervis, 1884–1958, vol. V
Pearson, Norman Charles, 1909–1992, vol. IX
Pearson, Octavius Henry, 1839–1914, vol. I
Pearson, Sir Ralph Sneyd, 1874–1958, vol. V

Pearson, Sir Reginald; *see* Pearson, Sir J. R.
Pearson, Richard Francis Malachy, 1872–1956, vol. V
Pearson, Sir Robert Barclay, 1871–1954, vol. V
Pearson, Robert Hooper, 1866–1918, vol. II
Pearson, Rupert Samuel Bruce, 1904–1974, vol. VII
Pearson, Sidney Vere, 1875–1950, vol. IV
Pearson, Thomas Bailey, 1864–1927, vol. II
Pearson, Rt Rev. Thomas Bernard, 1907–1987, vol. VIII
Pearson, Thomas William, 1872–1957, vol. V
Pearson, Rt Rev. Thomas Wulstan, 1870–1938, vol. III
Pearson, Brig.-Gen. Vere Lorraine Nuttall, 1880–1939, vol. III
Pearson, Col Walter Bagot, 1872–1954, vol. V
Pearson, Major Wilfred John, 1884–1957, vol. V
Pearson, William, *died* 1907, vol. I
Pearson, William, 1882–1976, vol. VII
Pearson, William George, *died* 1963, vol. VI
Pearson, William Thomas Shipston, 1917–1990, vol. VIII
Pearson-Gregory, Thomas Sherwin, 1851–1935, vol. III
Peart, Baron (Life Peer); (Thomas) Frederick Peart, 1914–1988, vol. VIII
Peart, Col Charles Lubé, 1876–1957, vol. V
Peart, Donald Richard, 1909–1981, vol. VIII
Peart, Ernest Grafford, 1918–1982, vol. VIII
Peart, Joseph Norriss, 1900–1942, vol. IV
Peary, Robert Edwin, 1856–1920, vol. II
Pease, Sir Alfred Edward, 2nd Bt (*cr* 1882), 1857–1939, vol. III
Pease, Arthur, 1837–1898, vol. I
Pease, Sir Arthur Francis, 1st Bt (*cr* 1920), 1866–1927, vol. II
Pease, Sir Edward, 3rd Bt (*cr* 1882), 1880–1963, vol. VI
Pease, Edward R., 1857–1955, vol. V
Pease, Col Henry Thomas, 1862–1943, vol. IV
Pease, Joseph Gerald, 1863–1928, vol. II
Pease, Sir Joseph Whitwell, 1st Bt (*cr* 1882), 1828–1903, vol. I
Pease, Lt-Gen. Leonard Thales, 1857–1936, vol. III
Pease, Sir Richard Arthur, 2nd Bt (*cr* 1920), 1890–1969, vol. VI
Pease, Col Sir Thales, 1835–1919, vol. II
Pease, William Edwin, 1865–1926, vol. II
Peasgood, Osborne Harold, 1902–1962, vol. VI
Peat, Charles Urie, 1892–1979, vol. VII
Peat, Sir George, 1893–1945, vol. IV
Peat, Sir Harry William Henry, 1878–1959, vol. V
Peat, Lt-Comdr Percy Sutcliffe, 1889–1936, vol. III
Peat, Stanley, 1902–1969, vol. VI
Peat, Sir William Barclay, 1852–1936, vol. III
Peate, Iorwerth Cyfeiliog, 1901–1982, vol. VIII
Pecci, Vincent Joachim; *see* Leo XIII.
Pechell, Sir Alexander B., 7th Bt; *see* Brooke-Pechell, Sir Augustus A.
Pechell, Sir George Samuel Brooke-, 5th Bt, 1819–1897, vol. I
Pechell, Lt-Col Sir Paul, 8th Bt, 1889–1972, vol. VII
Pechell, Sir Ronald Horace, 9th Bt, 1918–1984, vol. VIII

Pechell, Sir Samuel George Brooke-, 6th Bt, 1852–1904, vol. I
Pechey, Archibald Thomas, 1876–1961, vol. VI
Peck, Vice-Adm. Ambrose Maynard, *died* 1963, vol. VI
Peck, Antony Dilwyn, 1914–1987, vol. VIII
Peck, Arthur Leslie, 1902–1974, vol. VII
Peck, Maj.-Gen. Arthur Wharton, 1869–1948, vol. IV
Peck, Col Cyrus Wesley, 1871–1956, vol. V
Peck, Lt-Col Edward George, *died* 1939, vol. III
Peck, Maj.-Gen. Henry Richardson, 1874–1965, vol. VI
Peck, Sir James Wallace, 1875–1964, vol. VI
Peck, Jasper Augustine, 1905–1980, vol. VII
Peck, Sir John Howard, 1913–1995, vol. IX
Peck, Very Rev. Michael David Saville, 1914–1968, vol. VI
Peck, Air-Marshal Sir Richard Hallam, 1893–1952, vol. V
Peck, Maj.-Gen. Sydney Capel, 1871–1949, vol. IV
Peck, Sir William, 1862–1925, vol. II
Peck, Winifred Frances, (Lady Peck), *died* 1962, vol. VI
Peckitt, Reginald Godfrey, *died* 1937, vol. III
Peckover, 1st Baron, 1830–1919, vol. II
Pedder, Vice-Adm. Sir Arthur Reid, 1904–1995, vol. IX
Pedder, John, 1850–1929, vol. III
Pedder, Sir John, 1869–1956, vol. V
Peddie, Baron (Life Peer); James Mortimer Peddie, 1907–1978, vol. VII
Peddie, Coventry Dick, 1863–1950, vol. IV
Peddie, Maj.-Gen. Graham, 1905–1987, vol. VIII
Peddie, John Ronald, 1887–1979, vol. VII
Peddie, John Taylor, 1879–1947, vol. IV
Peddie, Robert Allan, 1921–1998, vol. X
Peddie, Ronald, 1905–1986, vol. VIII
Peddie, William, 1861–1946, vol. IV
Peddie-Waddell, Alexander; *see* Waddell.
Peden, Hon. Sir John Beverley, 1871–1946, vol. IV
Pedersen, Charles John, 1904–1989, vol. VIII
Pedler, Sir Alexander, 1849–1918, vol. II
Pedler, Sir Frederick Johnson, 1908–1991, vol. IX
Pedler, Margaret, *died* 1948, vol. IV
Pedley, Arthur Charles, 1859–1943, vol. IV
Pedley, Frederick N.; *see* Newland-Pedley.
Pedley, John Edward, 1891–1972, vol. VII
Pedley, Richard Rodman, 1912–1973, vol. VII
Pedley, Robin, 1914–1988, vol. VIII
Pedley, Brig.-Gen. Stanhope Humphrey, 1865–1938, vol. III
Peebles, Allan Charles Chiappini, 1907–1974, vol. VII
Peebles, Lt-Col Arthur Stansfield, 1872–1933, vol. III
Peebles, Brig.-Gen. Evelyn Chiappini, 1865–1937, vol. III
Peebles, Major Herbert Walter, 1877–1955, vol. V
Peebles, James Ross, 1909–1967, vol. VI
Peech, Alan James, 1905–1997, vol. X
Peech, James, 1878–1935, vol. III
Peech, Neil Malcolm, 1908–1997, vol. X
Peek, Sir Cuthbert Edgar, 2nd Bt, 1855–1901, vol. I

Peek, Sir Francis Henry Grenville, 4th Bt, 1915–1996, vol. X
Peek, Sir Henry William, 1st Bt, 1825–1898, vol. I
Peek, Sir Wilfrid, 3rd Bt, 1884–1927, vol. II
Peel, 1st Earl, 1867–1937, vol. III
Peel, 2nd Earl, 1901–1969, vol. VI
Peel, 1st Viscount, 1829–1913, vol. I
Peel, Lady Adelaide Margaret; see Peel, Lady Delia.
Peel, Rev. Albert, 1887–1949, vol. IV
Peel, Algernon Robert, 1862–1920, vol. II
Peel, Lt-Col Arthur, 1882–1938, vol. III
Peel, Hon. (Arthur) George (Villiers), 1868–1956, vol. V
Peel, Sir Arthur Robert, 1861–1952, vol. V
Peel, Lt-Col Basil Gerard, 1881–1954, vol. V
Peel, Beatrice Gladys, (Lady Peel); see Lillie, B. G.
Peel, Charles Lawrence Kinloch, 1883–1954, vol. V
Peel, Sir Charles Lennox, 1823–1999, vol. I
Peel, Mrs Charles S., died 1934, vol. III
Peel, Lady Delia, (Adelaide Margaret), 1889–1981, vol. VIII
Peel, Brig.-Gen. Edward John Russell, 1869–1939, vol. III
Peel, Sir Edward Townley, 1884–1961, vol. VI
Peel, Edwin Arthur, 1911–1992, vol. IX
Peel, Captain Sir (Francis Richard) Jonathan, 1897–1979, vol. VII
Peel, Rt Hon. Sir Frederick, 1823–1906, vol. I
Peel, Hon. George; see Peel, Hon. A. G. V.
Peel, (Gerald) Graham, 1877–1937, vol. III
Peel, Graham; see Peel, Gerald G.
Peel, Col Herbert Haworth, 1866–1956, vol. V
Peel, Horace, 1857–1940, vol. III
Peel, Major Hugh Edmund Ethelston, 1871–1950, vol. IV
Peel, Jack Armitage, 1921–1993, vol. IX
Peel, James, 1811–1906, vol. I
Peel, Sir Jonathan; see Peel, Sir F. R. J.
Peel, Rev. Hon. Maurice Berkeley, 1873–1917, vol. II
Peel, Sir Mervyn Lloyd, 1856–1929, vol. III
Peel, Sir Robert, 4th Bt (cr 1800), 1867–1925, vol. II
Peel, Sir Robert, 5th Bt (cr 1800), 1898–1934, vol. III
Peel, Sir Robert, 6th Bt (cr 1800), 1920–1942, vol. IV
Peel, Robert, 1881–1969, vol. VI
Peel, Col Robert Francis, 1874–1924, vol. II
Peel, Roland Tennyson, 1892–1945, vol. IV
Peel, Ronald Francis Edward Waite, 1912–1985, vol. VIII
Peel, Col Hon. Sir Sidney Cornwallis, 1st Bt (cr 1936), 1870–1938, vol. III
Peel, Sir Theophilus, 1st Bt (cr 1897), 1837–1911, vol. I
Peel, Walter, 1868–1949, vol. IV
Peel, Sir William, 1875–1945, vol. IV
Peel, William Croughton, 1870–1957, vol. V
Peel, Rt Rev. William George, 1854–1916, vol. II
Peel Yates, Lt-Gen. Sir David, 1911–1978, vol. VII
Peeler, Joseph, 1930–1997, vol. X
Peers, Sir Charles Reed, 1868–1952, vol. V
Peers, Edgar Allison, died 1952, vol. V
Peers, Robert, 1888–1972, vol. VII

Peers, Roger Ernest, 1906–1968, vol. VI
Peet, Hubert William, 1886–1951, vol. V
Peet, Thomas Eric, 1882–1934, vol. III
Pegasus; see Lawrence, B. T. T.
Pegg, Arthur John, 1906–1978, vol. VII
Pegg, Rev. Canon Henry F.; see Foster Pegg.
Pegler, Alfred Ernest, 1924–1998, vol. X
Pegler, James Basil Holmes, 1912–1992, vol. IX
Pegler, Louis Hemington, 1852–1927, vol. II
Pegram, A. Bertram, 1873–1941, vol. IV
Pegram, Vice-Adm. Frank Henderson, 1890–1944, vol. IV
Pegram, Frederick, 1870–1937, vol. III
Pegram, Henry, 1862–1937, vol. III
Peierls, Sir Rudolf Ernst, 1907–1995, vol. IX
Peile, Rev. Arthur Lewis Babington, 1830–1911, vol. I
Peile, Henry, died 1935, vol. III
Peile, Sir James Braithwaite, 1833–1906, vol. I
Peile, Ven. James Hamilton Francis, 1863–1940, vol. III
Peile, John, 1838–1910, vol. I
Peile, Vice-Adm. Sir Lancelot Arthur Babington, 1905–1989, vol. VIII
Peile, Col Schofield Patten, 1859–1940, vol. III
Peile, Col Solomon Charles Frederick, 1855–1932, vol. III
Peirce, Lt-Col Harold Ernest, 1892–1979, vol. VII
Peiris, Hon. Sir James, 1856–1930, vol. III
Peiris, Mahapitage Velin Peter, 1898–1988, vol. VIII
Peirs, Hugh John Chevallier, 1886–1943, vol. IV
Peirse, Sir Henry Bernard de la Poer B.; see Beresford-Peirse.
Peirse, Sir Henry Campbell de la Poer B.; see Beresford-Peirse.
Peirse, Sir Henry Monson de la Poer B.; see Beresford-Peirse.
Peirse, Lt-Gen. Sir Noel Monson de la Poer B.; see Beresford-Peirse.
Peirse, Air Chief Marshal Sir Richard Edmund Charles, 1892–1970, vol. VI
Peirse, Adm. Sir Richard H., 1860–1940, vol. III
Peirse, Rev. Richard Windham de la Poer B.; see Beresford-Peirse.
Peirse, Rev. Canon Windham de la Poer B.; see Beresford-Peirse.
Peirson, David Edward Herbert, 1915–1976, vol. VII
Peirson, Garnet Frank, 1911–1963, vol. VI
Pelham, Sir Clinton; see Pelham, Sir G. C.
Pelham, Major Hon. Dudley Roger Hugh, 1872–1953, vol. V
Pelham, Sir (Edward) Henry, 1876–1949, vol. IV
Pelham, Adm. Frederick Sidney, 1854–1931, vol. III
Pelham, Sir (George) Clinton, 1898–1984, vol. VIII
Pelham, Sir Henry; see Pelham, Sir E. H.
Pelham, Henry Francis, 1846–1907, vol. I
Pelham, Rt Rev. Herbert S., 1881–1944, vol. IV
Pelham, James T.; see Thursby-Pelham.
Pelham, Rev. John Barrington, 1848–1941, vol. IV
Pelham, Rev. Sidney, 1849–1926, vol. II
Pelham, Hon. Thomas Henry William, 1847–1916, vol. II

Pelham Browne, Cynthia; *see* Stockley, C.
Pelham Burn, Brig.-Gen. Henry; *see* Burn.
Pelham-Clinton, Lord Edward William; *see* Clinton.
Pelham Welby, Charles Cornwallis Anderson, 1876–1959, vol. V
Pell, Albert, 1820–1907, vol. I
Pell, Major Albert Julian, 1863–1916, vol. II
Pell, Major Beauchamp Tyndall, 1866–1914, vol. I
Pellatt, Sir Henry Mill, 1860–1939, vol. III
Pelletier, Sir Charles Alphonse Pantaléon, 1837–1911, vol. I
Pelletier, Hector Rooney, 1911–1976, vol. VII
Pelletier, Lt-Col J. M. J. Pantaleon, 1860–1924, vol. II
Pelletier, Hon. Louis Philippe, 1857–1921, vol. II
Pelletier, Wilfrid, 1896–1982, vol. VIII
Pellew, Lancelot Vivian, 1899–1970, vol. VI
Pelling, Henry Mathison, 1920–1997, vol. X
Pelliot, Paul, 1878–1945, vol. IV
Pellizzi, Camillo, 1896–1979, vol. VII (AII)
Pelloe, Rev. Canon John Parker, 1905–1983, vol. VIII
Pelly, Major Sir Alwyne; *see* Pelly, Major Sir H. A.
Pelly, Air Chief Marshal Sir Claude Bernard Raymond, 1902–1972, vol. VII
Pelly, Cornelius James, 1908–1985, vol. VIII
Pelly, Rev. Douglas Raymond, 1865–1943, vol. IV
Pelly, Lt-Col Edmund Godfrey, 1889–1939, vol. III
Pelly, Sir Harold, 4th Bt, 1863–1950, vol. IV
Pelly, Major Sir (Harold) Alwyne, 5th Bt, 1893–1981, vol. VIII
Pelly, Adm. Sir Henry Bertram, 1867–1942, vol. IV
Pelly, Maj. Sir John Alwyne, 6th Bt, 1918–1993, vol. IX
Pelly, Captain John Noel, 1888–1945, vol. IV
Pelly, Lt-Col John Stannus, 1859–1938, vol. III
Pelly, Sir Kenneth Raymond, 1893–1973, vol. VII
Pelly, Rear-Adm. Peter Douglas Herbert Raymond, 1904–1980, vol. VII
Pelly, Rev. Raymond P., 1841–1911, vol. I
Pelly, Brig.-Gen. Raymond Theodore, 1881–1952, vol. V
Pelly, Rev. Canon Richard Lawrence, 1886–1976, vol. VII
Pember, Edward Henry, 1833–1911, vol. I
Pember, Francis William, 1862–1954, vol. V
Pemberton, Rev. Desmond Valdo, 1927–1996, vol. X
Pemberton, Sir Edward Leigh; *see* Leigh-Pemberton, Sir E.
Pemberton, Horatio Nelson, 1902–1967, vol. VI
Pemberton, John L.; *see* Leigh-Pemberton.
Pemberton, John Stapylton Grey, 1860–1940, vol. III
Pemberton, Sir Max, 1863–1950, vol. IV
Pemberton, Maj.-Gen. Robert Charles Boileau, 1934–1914, vol. I
Pemberton, T(homas) Edgar, 1849–1905, vol. I
Pemberton, Rev. Thomas Percy, *died* 1921, vol. II
Pemberton, William Shakespear C.; *see* Childe-Pemberton.
Pemberton, Maj.-Gen. Sir Wykeham Leigh, 1833–1918, vol. II
Pemberton-Pigott, Alan Desmond Frederick, 1916–1972, vol. VII

Pembleton, Edgar Stanley, 1888–1968, vol. VI
Pembrey, John Cripps, 1831–1918, vol. II
Pembrey, Marcus Seymour, 1868–1934, vol. III
Pembroke, 14th Earl of, and Montgomery, 11th Earl of, 1853–1913, vol. I
Pembroke, 15th Earl of, and Montgomery, 12th Earl of, 1880–1960, vol. V
Pembroke, 16th Earl of, and Montgomery, 13th Earl of, 1906–1969, vol. VI
Pembroke, Mary Countess of; Mary Dorothea Herbert, 1903–1995, vol. IX
Penberthy, John, 1858–1927, vol. II
Pendarves, William Cole, 1841–1929, vol. III
Pendavis, Ven. Whylock, *died* 1924, vol. II
Pendenys, Arthur; *see* Humphreys, Arthur L.
Pender, 1st Baron, 1882–1949, vol. IV
Pender, 2nd Baron, 1907–1965, vol. VI
Pender, Major Henry Denison Denison, 1884–1967, vol. VI
Pender, Sir James, 1st Bt, 1841–1921, vol. II
Pender, Major James, 1860–1936, vol. III
Pender, Sir John Denison Denison-, 1855–1929, vol. III
Pender, Bt Col William Stanhope, 1889–1948, vol. IV
Pendered, Mary Lucy, 1858–1940, vol. III (A), vol. IV
Penderel-Brodhurst, James George Joseph, 1859–1934, vol. III
Pendlebury, Charles, 1854–1941, vol. IV
Pendlebury, Herbert Stringfellow, 1870–1953, vol. V
Pendlebury, John Devitt Stringfellow, 1904–1941, vol. IV
Pendleton, Alan O'Bryan George William, 1837–1916, vol. II
Pendred, Air Marshal Sir Lawrence Fleming, 1899–1986, vol. VIII
Pendred, Loughnan St Lawrence, 1870–1953, vol. V
Penfield, Wilder Graves, 1891–1976, vol. VII
Penfold, Surg. Rear-Adm. Ernest Alfred, 1866–1956, vol. V
Penfold, Very Rev. John Brookes Vernon, 1864–1922, vol. II
Penfold, Captain Marchant Hubert, 1873–1961, vol. VI
Penfold, Lt-Col Sir Stephen, 1842–1925, vol. II
Pengelley, Gen. George Farquharson, 1843–1929, vol. III
Pengelly, Herbert Staddon, 1892–1963, vol. VI
Pengelly, William Lister, 1892–1983, vol. VIII
Pengilly, Sir Alexander, 1868–1965, vol. VI
Penhaligon, David Charles, 1944–1986, vol. VIII
Peniakoff, Lt-Col Vladimir, 1897–1951, vol. V
Penlake, Richard; *see* Salmon, Percy R.
Penley, Belville S., 1861–1940, vol. III
Penley, William Sydney, 1851–1912, vol. I
Penman, David, *died* 1961, vol. VI
Penman, Most Rev. David John, 1936–1989, vol. VIII
Penman, Gerard Giles, 1899–1982, vol. VIII
Penman, Howard Latimer, 1909–1984, vol. VIII
Penman, John, 1913–1994, vol. IX
Penn, Sir Arthur Horace, 1886–1960, vol. V

Penn, Lt-Col Sir Eric, 1916–1993, vol. IX
Penn, John, 1848–1903, vol. I
Penn, Will C., died 1968, vol. VI
Pennant, Hon. Alan George Sholto D.; see Douglas-Pennant.
Pennant, Hon. Charles D.; see Douglas-Pennant.
Pennant, Adm. Hon. Sir Cyril Eustace D.; see Douglas-Pennant.
Pennant, Captain Hon. George Henry D.; see Douglas-Pennant.
Pennant, Hon. Violet Blanche D.; see Douglas-Pennant.
Pennefather, Sir (Alfred) Richard, 1845–1918, vol. II
Pennefather, Harold Wilfrid Armine F.; see Freese-Pennefather.
Pennefather, Sir John de Fonblanque, 1st Bt, 1856–1933, vol. III
Pennefather, Sir Richard; see Pennefather, Sir A. R.
Pennefather, Rev. Preb. Somerset Edward, 1848–1917, vol. II
Pennefather-Evans, Brig. Brian, 1897–1954, vol. V
Pennefather-Evans, Lt-Col Granville, died 1963, vol. VI
Pennell, Arthur, 1852–1926, vol. II
Pennell, Sir Charles Henry, 1805–1898, vol. I
Pennell, Charles Henry, born 1848, vol. III
Pennell, Elizabeth Robins, died 1936, vol. III
Pennell, Henry Cholmondeley-, 1837–1915, vol. I
Pennell, Captain Henry Singleton, 1874–1907, vol. I
Pennell, Rev. Canon (James Henry) Leslie, 1906–1996, vol. X
Pennell, Joseph, 1860–1926, vol. II
Pennell, Kenneth Eustace Lee, 1890–1948, vol. IV
Pennell, Rev. Canon Leslie; see Pennell, Rev. Canon J. H. L.
Pennell, Montague Mattinson, 1916–1981, vol. VIII
Pennell, Lt-Col Richard, 1885–1963, vol. VI
Pennell, Vernon Charles, 1889–1976, vol. VII
Pennethorne, Rev. Gregory Walton, 1837–1915, vol. I
Penney, Baron (Life Peer); William George Penney, 1909–1991, vol. IX
Penney, Air Cdre Howard Wright, 1903–1970, vol. VI
Penney, José Campbell, 1893–1976, vol. VII
Penney, Maj.-Gen. Sir Ronald Campbell; see Penney, Maj.-Gen. Sir W. R. C.
Penney, Scott Moncrieff, 1857–1932, vol. III
Penney, Rev. William Campbell, died 1945, vol. IV
Penney, Maj.-Gen. Sir (William) Ronald Campbell, 1896–1964, vol. VI
Pennington, Hon. Alan Joseph, 1837–1913, vol. I
Pennington, Anne Elizabeth, 1934–1981, vol. VIII
Pennington, Brig.-Gen. Arthur Watson, 1867–1927, vol. II
Pennington, Lt-Gen. Sir Charles Richard, 1838–1910, vol. I
Pennington, Frederick, 1819–1914, vol. I
Pennington, Lt-Col Hubert Stanley Whitmore, died 1949, vol. IV
Pennington, Hon. John Warburton, 1870–1945, vol. IV
Pennington, Sydney Content Boeth, 1869–1937, vol. III

Pennington-Ramsden, Major Sir (Geoffrey) William, 7th Bt, 1904–1986, vol. VIII
Pennington-Ramsden, Sir William; see Pennington-Ramsden, Sir G. W.
Pennison, Clifford Francis, 1913–1995, vol. IX
Pennock, Baron (Life Peer); Raymond William Pennock, 1920–1993, vol. IX
Pennoyer, Richard Edmands, 1885–1968, vol. VI
Penny, Rev. Alfred, 1845–1935, vol. III
Penny, Major Arthur Taylor, 1871–1915, vol. I
Penny, Edmund, 1852–1919, vol. II
Penny, Fanny Emily, died 1939, vol. III
Penny, Col Frederick Septimus, 1869–1955, vol. V
Penny, Sir James Downing, 1886–1978, vol. VII
Penny, Joseph Noel Bailey, 1916–1998, vol. X
Pennybacker, Joseph Buford, 1907–1983, vol. VIII
Pennycuick, Hon. Alexander, 1844–1906, vol. I
Pennycuick, Charles Edward Ducat, died 1903, vol. I
Pennycuick, Brig. James Alexander Charles, 1890–1966, vol. VI
Pennycuick, Col John, 1841–1911, vol. I
Pennycuick, Rt Hon. Sir John, 1899–1982, vol. VIII
Pennyman, Rev. Preb. William Geoffrey, died 1942, vol. IV
Pennymore, Lt-Col Percy George, 1869–1940, vol. III (A), vol. IV
Penoyre, John, 1870–1954, vol. V
Penrhyn, 2nd Baron, 1836–1907, vol. I
Penrhyn, 3rd Baron, 1864–1927, vol. II
Penrhyn, 4th Baron, 1894–1949, vol. IV
Penrhyn, 5th Baron, 1865–1967, vol. VI
Penrhyn, Rev. Oswald Henry Leycester, 1828–1918, vol. II
Penrhyn-Hornby, Charles Windham Leycester, 1873–1966, vol. VI
Penrice, Geoffrey, 1923–1994, vol. IX
Penrose, Brig.-Gen. Cooper, 1855–1927, vol. II
Penrose, Edith Tilton, 1914–1996, vol. X
Penrose, Dame Emily, 1858–1942, vol. IV
Penrose, Francis Cranmer, 1817–1903, vol. I
Penrose, Francis George, 1857–1932, vol. III
Penrose, J. Doyle, 1862–1932, vol. III
Penrose, James Edward, 1850–1936, vol. III
Penrose, Maj.-Gen. John Hubert, 1916–2000, vol. X
Penrose, Lionel Sharples, 1898–1972, vol. VII
Penrose, Sir Penrose Charles, 1822–1902, vol. I
Penrose, Sir Roland Algernon, 1900–1984, vol. VIII
Penrose-Welsted, Col Reginald Hugh, 1891–1966, vol. VI
Penruddock, Sir Clement Frederick, 1905–1988, vol. VIII
Penson, Sir Henry; see Penson, Sir T. H.
Penson, John Hubert, 1893–1979, vol. VII
Penson, Dame Lillian Margery, 1896–1963, vol. VI
Penson, Sir (Thomas) Henry, 1864–1955, vol. V
Penston, Norah Lillian, 1903–1974, vol. VII
Pentecost, David Henry, 1938–2000, vol. X
Pentecost, Rev. George F., 1841–1920, vol. II
Pentin, Rev. Herbert, 1873–1965, vol. VI
Pentland, 1st Baron, 1860–1925, vol. II
Pentland, 2nd Baron, 1907–1984, vol. VIII
Pentland, Norman, 1912–1972, vol. VII
Pentney, Richard George, 1922–1990, vol. VIII
Penton, Maj.-Gen. Arthur Pole, 1854–1920, vol. II
Penton, Brig. Bertie Cyril, 1880–1962, vol. VI

Penton, Cyril Frederick, 1886–1960, vol. V
Penton, Sir Edward, 1875–1967, vol. VI
Penton, Frederick Thomas, 1851–1929, vol. III
Penton, Col Richard Hugh, 1863–1934, vol. III
Pentreath, Rev. Canon Arthur Godolphin Guy
 Carleton, 1902–1985, vol. VIII
Pentreath, Ven. Edwyn Sandys Wetmore,
 1846–1913, vol. I
Penzance, 1st Baron, 1816–1899, vol. I
Penzer, Norman Mosley, 1892–1960, vol. V
Pepler, Sir George Lionel, 1882–1959, vol. V
Peploe, Denis Frederic Neil, 1914–1993, vol. IX
Peploe, Rev. Hanmer William W.; see
 Webb-Peploe.
Peploe, Mrs J. R.; see Stevenson, D. E.
Peploe, S. J., died 1935, vol. III
Pepper, Augustus Joseph, died 1935, vol. III
Pepper, Claude Denson, 1900–1989, vol. VIII
Pepper, Brig. Ernest Cecil, 1899–1981, vol. VIII
Pepper, Sir Francis Henry, died 1936, vol. III
Pepper, George Wharton, 1867–1961, vol. VI
Peppercorn, Trevor Edward, 1904–1984, vol. VIII
Pepperell, Elizabeth Maud, (E. M. Brewin),
 1914–1971, vol. VII
Peppiatt, Sir Kenneth Oswald, 1893–1983, vol. VIII
Peppiatt, Sir Leslie Ernest, 1891–1968, vol. VI
Pepys, Rev. Charles Sidney, 1875–1927, vol. II
Pepys, Rt Rev. George Christopher Cutts,
 1914–1974, vol. VII
Pepys, George Digby, 1868–1957, vol. V
Pepys, Col Gerald Leslie, 1879–1936, vol. III
Pepys, Rev. Herbert George, 1830–1918, vol. II
Pepys, Lady (Mary) Rachel, 1905–1992, vol. IX
Pepys, Lady Rachel; see Pepys, Lady M. R.
Pepys, Walter Evelyn, 1885–1966, vol. VI
Perak, HH Sultan of, died 1916, vol. II
Perak, HH Sultan of, 1887–1948, vol. IV
Perceval, Col Charles C., 1866–1937, vol. III
Perceval, Col Christopher Peter Westby,
 1890–1967, vol. VI
Perceval, Brig.-Gen. Claude John, 1864–1932,
 vol. III
Perceval, Maj.-Gen. Sir Edward Maxwell,
 1861–1955, vol. V
Perceval, Sir Westby Brook, 1854–1928, vol. II
Perceval-Maxwell, Magdalen, (Mrs Patrick
 Perceval-Maxwell); see King-Hall, M.
Percival, Allen Dain, 1925–1992, vol. IX
Percival, Sir Anthony Edward, 1910–1994, vol. IX
Percival, Archibald Stanley, 1862–1935, vol. III
Percival, Lt-Gen. Arthur Ernest, 1887–1966, vol. VI
Percival, Major Arthur Jex-Blake, 1870–1914, vol. I
Percival, Edgar Wikner, 1897–1984, vol. VIII
Percival, Francis William, died 1929, vol. III
Percival, George Hector, 1901–1983, vol. VIII
Percival, Col Sir Harold Franz Passawer,
 1876–1944, vol. IV
Percival, Harold Stanley, 1868–1914, vol. I
Percival, Rt Hon. Sir Ian; see Percival, Rt Hon. Sir
 W. I.
Percival, Rt Rev. John, 1834–1918, vol. II
Percival, John, died 1949, vol. IV
Percival, Sir John Hope, 1870–1954, vol. V
Percival, Rev. Preb. Launcelot Jefferson,
 1869–1941, vol. IV

Percival, Philip Edward, 1872–1939, vol. III
Percival, Robert Clarendon, 1908–1995, vol. X(AI)
Percival, Sir Tom, 1877–1933, vol. III
Percival, Rt Hon. Sir (Walter) Ian, 1921–1998,
 vol. X
Percival, Rev. Wilfred Ernest Holtzendorff,
 1861–1935, vol. III
Percy, Earl; Henry Algernon George, 1871–1909,
 vol. I
Percy of Newcastle, 1st Baron, 1887–1958, vol. V
Percy, Algernon Heber-, 1845–1911, vol. I
Percy, Lord Algernon Malcolm Arthur, 1851–1933,
 vol. III
Percy, Charles, died 1929, vol. III
Percy, Esmé; see Percy, S. E.
Percy, Sir James Campbell, 1869–1928, vol. II
Percy, Maj.-Gen. Sir Jocelyn, 1871–1952, vol. V
Percy, Lord Richard Charles, 1921–1989, vol. VIII
Percy, (Saville) Esmé, 1887–1957, vol. V
Percy, Col Lord William Richard, 1882–1963,
 vol. VI
Percy-Chapman, Major William, 1850–1932, vol. III
Perdue, Rt Rev. Richard Gordon, 1910–1998,
 vol. X
Perdue, Hon. William Egerton, 1850–1933, vol. III
Peregrine, Rev. David Wilkie, 1859–1940, vol. III
Peregrine, Gwilym Rhys, 1924–1998, vol. X
Pereira, Adeodato Anthony, 1889–1965, vol. VI
Pereira, Arthur Leonard, 1906–1999, vol. X
Pereira, Maj.-Gen. Sir Cecil Edward, 1869–1942,
 vol. IV
Pereira, Frederick Linwood Clinton, 1880–1958,
 vol. V
Pereira, Brig.-Gen. George Edward, 1865–1923,
 vol. II
Pereira, Helio Gelli, 1918–1994, vol. IX
Pereira, Rt Rev. Henry Horace, 1845–1926, vol. II
Pereira, Sir Horace Alvarez de Courcy, 1879–1963,
 vol. VI
Pereira, Marguerite Scott, 1921–1987, vol. VIII
Pereira, Pedro T.; see Theotonio Pereira.
Pereira, Richard Lionel, 1880–1960, vol. V
Perelman, Sidney Joseph, 1904–1979, vol. VII
Peren, Sir Geoffrey Sylvester, 1892–1980, vol. VII
Perez, Sir Joseph Leon Mathieu-, 1896–1967,
 vol. VI
Perfect, Captain Herbert Mosley, 1867–1928, vol. II
Perham, Dame Margery, 1895–1982, vol. VIII
Perier, Jean Paul Pierre C.; see Casimir-Perier.
Peries, Sir Albert; see Peries, Sir P. P. A. F.
Peries, Sir (Pattiya Pathirannahalgae) Albert
 (Frederick), 1900–1967, vol. VI
Perini, Rt Rev. Paul, 1867–1932, vol. III
Peritz, Rev. Ismar J., 1863–1950, vol. IV (A),
 vol. V
Perkin, Arthur George, 1861–1937, vol. III
Perkin, Sir Athol; see Perkin, Sir E. A. O.
Perkin, (Edwin) Graham, 1929–1975, vol. VII
Perkin, Sir (Emil) Athol (Owen), 1889–1951, vol. V
Perkin, Frederick Mollwo, 1869–1928, vol. II
Perkin, Graham; see Perkin, E. G.
Perkin, Sir William Henry, 1838–1907, vol. I
Perkin, William Henry, 1860–1929, vol. III
Perkins, Gen. Sir Æneas, 1834–1901, vol. I
Perkins, Alan Hubert Banbury, 1898–1977, vol. VII

Perkins, Sir (Albert) Edward, 1908–1977, vol. VII
Perkins, Lt-Col Alfred Edward, *born* 1863, vol. II
Perkins, Col Alfred Thrale, 1843–1934, vol. III
Perkins, Major Alfred Thrale, 1869–1935, vol. III
Perkins, Brig.-Gen. Arthur Ernest John, *died* 1921, vol. II
Perkins, Bernard James, 1928–1996, vol. X
Perkins, Surg. Vice-Adm. Sir Derek Duncombe S.; *see* Steele-Perkins.
Perkins, Dexter, 1889–1984, vol. VIII
Perkins, Dudley; *see* Perkins, G. D. G.
Perkins, Sir Edward; *see* Perkins, Sir A. E.
Perkins, Col Sir Edwin King, 1855–1937, vol. III
Perkins, Rev. E(rnest) Benson, 1881–1974, vol. VII
Perkins, Frances, *died* 1965, vol. VI
Perkins, Francis Layton, 1912–1994, vol. IX
Perkins, Rev. Francis Leonard, 1865–1932, vol. III
Perkins, Sir Frederick, 1826–1902, vol. I
Perkins, Rev. Canon Frederick Howard, *died* 1977, vol. VII
Perkins, Frederick William, *died* 1938, vol. III
Perkins, George, *died* 1979, vol. VII
Perkins, (George) Dudley (Gwynne), 1911–1986, vol. VIII
Perkins, Col George Forder, 1884–1972, vol. VII
Perkins, George Walbridge, 1862–1920, vol. II
Perkins, Harry Innes, *died* 1924, vol. II
Perkins, Air Vice-Marshal Irwyn Morse, 1920–1996, vol. X
Perkins, J. H. Raymond R.; *see* Roze, Raymond.
Perkins, James Alfred, 1911–1998, vol. X
Perkins, Rev. Jocelyn Henry Temple, 1870–1962, vol. VI
Perkins, John Bryan W.; *see* Ward-Perkins.
Perkins, Lt-Col John Charles Campbell, 1866–1916, vol. II
Perkins, Joseph John, *died* 1928, vol. II
Perkins, Air Vice-Marshal Maxwell Edmund Massy, 1907–1985, vol. VIII
Perkins, Norman Stuart, 1904–1972, vol. VII
Perkins, Sir Robert; *see* Perkins, Sir W. R. D.
Perkins, Surg.-Captain Robert Clerk, *died* 1916, vol. I, vol. II
Perkins, Robert Cyril Layton, 1866–1955, vol. V
Perkins, Robert George, 1850–1922, vol. II
Perkins, Thomas Luff, 1867–1940, vol. III
Perkins, Walter Frank, 1865–1946, vol. IV
Perkins, Sir (Walter) Robert (Dempster), 1903–1988, vol. VIII
Perkins, Rev. William, 1843–1922, vol. II
Perkins, William Jackson, *died* 1939, vol. III
Perkins, William Turner, *died* 1927, vol. II
Perks, Clifford; *see* Perks, J. C.
Perks, (John) Clifford, 1915–1994, vol. IX
Perks, Sir Malcolm; *see* Perks, Sir R. M. M.
Perks, Sir (Robert) Malcolm (Mewburn), 2nd Bt, 1892–1979, vol. VII
Perks, Sir Robert William, 1st Bt, 1849–1934, vol. III
Perks, Sydney, *died* 1944, vol. IV
Perley, Rt Hon. Sir George Halsey, 1857–1938, vol. III
Perlo, Rt Rev. G. O. Filippo, 1873–1948, vol. IV
Perlo, Rt Rev. P. G. Gabriele, 1879–1948, vol. IV
Pernet, George, 1861–1940, vol. III

Perodeau, Hon. Narcisse, 1851–1932, vol. III
Perowne, Rt Rev. Arthur William Thomson, 1867–1948, vol. IV
Perowne, Rear-Adm. Benjamin Cubitt, 1921–1992, vol. IX
Perowne, Rev. Edward Henry, 1826–1906, vol. I
Perowne, Dame Freya; *see* Stark, Dame Freya.
Perowne, Rt Rev. John James Stewart, 1823–1904, vol. I
Perowne, Sir John Victor Thomas Woolrych Tait, 1897–1951, vol. V
Perowne, Maj.-Gen. Lancelot Edgar Connop Mervyn, 1902–1982, vol. VIII
Perowne, Stewart Henry, 1901–1989, vol. VIII
Perowne, Ven. Thomas John, 1868–1954, vol. V
Perowne, Ven. Thomas Thomason, *died* 1913, vol. I
Perram, George James, 1848–1939, vol. III
Perrault, Hon. Joseph Edouard, 1874–1948, vol. IV
Perreau, Brig.-Gen. Arthur Montagu, 1870–1953, vol. V
Perreau, Col Charles Noel, 1874–1952, vol. V
Perree, Walter Francis, 1871–1950, vol. IV
Perren, Edward Arthur, 1900–1978, vol. VII
Perrett, His Honour John, 1906–1992, vol. IX
Perrier, Edmond, 1844–1921, vol. II
Perrin, Alice, 1867–1934, vol. III
Perrin, Harold Ernest, 1877–1948, vol. IV
Perrin, Harry Crane, 1865–1953, vol. V
Perrin, Sir Michael Willcox, 1905–1988, vol. VIII
Perrin, William Gordon, 1874–1931, vol. III
Perrin, Rt Rev. William Willcox, 1848–1934, vol. III
Perring, Engr Rear-Adm. Harold Hepworth, 1885–1949, vol. IV
Perring, Col Sir John, 1870–1948, vol. IV
Perring, Rev. Sir Philip, 4th Bt, 1828–1920, vol. II
Perring, Sir Ralph Edgar, 1st Bt, 1905–1998, vol. X
Perring, Sir William, 1866–1937, vol. III
Perring, William George Arthur, 1898–1951, vol. V
Perrins, Charles William Dyson, 1864–1958, vol. V
Perrins, Wesley, 1905–1990, vol. VIII
Perris, Ernest A., *died* 1961, vol. VI
Perris, George Herbert, 1866–1920, vol. II
Perron, Hon. Joseph Léonide, 1872–1930, vol. III
Perrott, Arthur Finch, 1892–1969, vol. VI
Perrott, Sir Donald Cyril Vincent, 1902–1985, vol. VIII
Perrott, Sir Herbert Charles, 6th Bt, 1849–1922, vol. II
Perrott, Samuel Wright, 1870–1964, vol. VI
Perrott, Maj.-Gen. Sir Thomas, 1851–1919, vol. II
Perry, 1st Baron, 1878–1956, vol. V
Perry, Alan Cecil, 1892–1971, vol. VII
Perry, Hon. Sir (Alan) Clifford, 1907–1983, vol. VIII
Perry, Sir Allan, 1860–1929, vol. III
Perry, Rev. Arthur John, *died* 1926, vol. II
Perry, Maj.-Gen. Aylesworth Bowen, 1860–1956, vol. V
Perry, Bliss, 1860–1954, vol. V
Perry, Charles Bruce, 1903–1996, vol. X
Perry, Hon. Sir Clifford; *see* Perry, Hon. Sir A. C.
Perry, Sir Cooper; *see* Perry, Sir E. C.
Perry, Edward William, 1891–1971, vol. VII
Perry, Sir (Edwin) Cooper, 1856–1938, vol. III

Perry, Ernest George, 1908–1998, vol. X
Perry, Lt-Col Ernest Middleton, 1878–1963, vol. VI
Perry, Frances Mary, 1907–1993, vol. IX
Perry, Lt-Col Francis Frederic, 1854–1940, vol. III
Perry, Sir Frank Tennyson, 1887–1965, vol. VI
Perry, Frederick John, 1909–1995, vol. IX
Perry, Ven. George Gresley, 1820–1897, vol. I
Perry, Rev. George Henry, 1854–1935, vol. III
Perry, Sir Gerald Raoul de C.; *see* de Courcy-Perry.
Perry, Maj.-Gen. Henry Marrian, 1884–1955,
vol. V
Perry, Maj.-Gen. Sir Hugh Whitchurch, 1861–1938,
vol. III
Perry, Rt Rev. James De Wolf, 1871–1947, vol. IV
Perry, John, 1850–1920, vol. II
Perry, Hon. John, 1845–1922, vol. II
Perry, Rear-Adm. John Laisné, *died* 1917, vol. II
Perry, John Tavenor, 1842–1915, vol. I
Perry, Kenneth Murray Allan, 1909–1984, vol. VIII
Perry, Rev. Nathaniel Irwin, 1867–1931, vol. III
Perry, Peter George, 1923–1994, vol. IX
Perry, Ralph Barton, 1876–1957, vol. V
Perry, Robert Grosvenor, 1873–1949, vol. IV
Perry, Lt-Col Robert Stanley Grosvenor,
1909–1987, vol. VIII
Perry, Roger, 1940–1995, vol. IX
Perry, Samuel Frederick, 1877–1954, vol. V
Perry, Rev. Stephen Nugent, 1861–1941, vol. IV
Perry, Sir (Thomas) Wilfred, 1899–1979, vol. VII
Perry, Sir Wilfred; *see* Perry, Sir T. W.
Perry, Rev. William, *died* 1948, vol. IV
Perry, Sir William, 1863–1956, vol. V
Perry, Sir William, 1885–1968, vol. VI
Perry, William James, *died* 1949, vol. IV
Perry, Sir William Payne, 1858–1931, vol. III
Perry-Keene, Air Vice-Marshal Allan Lancelot
Addison, 1898–1987, vol. VIII
Perse, St John; *see* Léger, M.-R. A. St-L.
Pershing, Gen. John Joseph, 1860–1948, vol. IV
Persse, Burton Walter, 1854–1935, vol. III
Pert, Maj.-Gen. Claude Ernest, 1898–1982,
vol. VIII
Pertab Singhji, Gen. Sir, 1845–1922, vol. II
Perth, 14th Earl of, **and Melfort,** 6th Earl of,
1807–1902, vol. I
Perth, 15th Earl of, 1871–1937, vol. III
Perth, 16th Earl of, 1876–1951, vol. V
Pertinax; *see* Géraud, C. J. A.
Pertwee, Rev. Arthur, *died* 1919, vol. II
Pertwee, Captain Herbert Guy, 1893–1978, vol. VII
Pertwee, Roland, *died* 1963, vol. VI
Perugini, Charles Edward, 1839–1918, vol. II
Perugini, Kate, *died* 1929, vol. III
Perugini, Mark Edward, *died* 1948, vol. IV
Pery-Knox-Gore, Col Arthur Francis Gore,
1880–1954, vol. V
Peshall, Rev. Charles John Eyre, 1881–1957, vol. V
Peshall, Samuel Frederick, 1882–1977, vol. VII
Pestangi, Jehangir Khan Bahadur, *died* 1914, vol. I
Pétain, Philippe, 1856–1951, vol. V
Petavel, James William, 1870–1945, vol. IV
Petavel, Sir Joseph Ernest, 1873–1936, vol. III
Petch, Sir Louis, 1913–1981, vol. VIII
Petch, Norman James, 1917–1992, vol. IX
Peter, Bernard Hartley, 1885–1970, vol. VI

Peter, Sir John Charles, 1863–1939, vol. III
Peterkin, Col Alfred, 1854–1929, vol. III
Peterkin, Lt-Col Charles Duncan, 1887–1962,
vol. VI
Peterkin, Rt Rev. George William, 1841–1916,
vol. II
Peterkin, Ishbel Allan, 1903–1982, vol. VIII
Peters, Hon. Arthur, 1854–1908, vol. I
Peters, Arthur, *died* 1956, vol. V
Peters, Rev. Canon Arthur E. G., 1866–1943,
vol. IV
Peters, Adm. Sir Arthur Malcolm, 1888–1979,
vol. VII
Peters, Augustus Dudley, 1892–1973, vol. VII
Peters, Bernard George, 1903–1967, vol. VI
Peters, Sir Byron; *see* Peters, Sir L. B.
Peters, Edwin Arthur, *died* 1945, vol. IV
Peters, Ellis; *see* Pargeter, E.
Peters, Captain Frederic Thornton, *died* 1942,
vol. IV
Peters, Sir George Henry, 1853–1931, vol. III
Peters, John, 1929–1988, vol. VIII
Peters, Major John Weston Parsons, 1864–1924,
vol. II, vol. III
Peters, Kenneth Jamieson, 1923–2000, vol. X
Peters, Sir (Lindsley) Byron, 1867–1939, vol. III
Peters, Raymond Harry, 1918–1995, vol. X(AI)
Peters, Sir Rudolph Albert, 1889–1982, vol. VIII
Peters, Sidney John, 1885–1976, vol. VII
Peters, Sir William, 1889–1964, vol. VI
Peters, Maj.-Gen. William Henry Brooke,
1842–1913, vol. I
Petersen, Sir William, 1856–1925, vol. II
Peterson, Alexander Duncan Campbell, 1908–1988,
vol. VIII
Peterson, Sir Arthur Frederick, 1859–1922, vol. II
Peterson, Sir Arthur William, 1916–1986, vol. VIII
Peterson, Brig.-Gen. Frederick Hopewell,
1864–1925, vol. II
Peterson, John Carlos Kennedy, 1876–1955, vol. V
Peterson, John Magnus, 1902–1978, vol. VII
Peterson, Margaret, 1883–1933, vol. III
Peterson, Sir Maurice Drummond, 1889–1952,
vol. V
Peterson, Sir William, 1856–1921, vol. II
Peterson, Lt-Col William Gordon, 1888–1930,
vol. III
Petfield, Sir Arthur Henry, 1912–1974, vol. VII
Pethebridge, Col Sir Samuel Augustus, 1862–1918,
vol. II
Petheram, Sir William Comer, 1835–1922, vol. II
Petherick, Captain Cyril Hamley, 1893–1944,
vol. IV
Petherick, Maurice, 1894–1985, vol. VIII
Pethick-Lawrence, 1st Baron, 1871–1961, vol. VI
Pethybridge, Frank, 1924–1989, vol. VIII
Petigara, Khan Bahadur Kavasji Jamshedji,
1877–1941, vol. IV
Petit, Sir Dinshaw Manockjee, 1st Bt, 1823–1901,
vol. I
Petit, Sir Dinshaw Manockjee, 2nd Bt, 1873–1933,
vol. III
Petit, Sir Dinshaw Manockjee, 3rd Bt, 1901–1983,
vol. VIII

Petit, Sir Dinshaw Manockjee, 4th Bt, 1934–1998, vol. X
Petit, Rt Rev. John Edward, 1895–1973, vol. VII
Petit, Rev. Paul, 1856–1941, vol. IV
Petley, Eaton Wallace, 1850–1913, vol. I
Petman, Charles Earle Bevan, 1866–1939, vol. III
Peto, Sir Basil, 1st Bt (*cr* 1927), 1862–1945, vol. IV
Peto, Major (Basil Arthur) John, 1900–1954, vol. V
Peto, Brig. Sir Christopher Henry Maxwell, 3rd Bt (*cr* 1927), 1897–1980, vol. VII
Peto, Dorothy Olivia Georgiana, 1886–1974, vol. VII
Peto, Comdr Sir Francis; *see* Peto, Comdr Sir H. F. M.
Peto, Sir Geoffrey Kelsall, 1878–1956, vol. V
Peto, Gladys Emma, 1890–1977, vol. VII
Peto, Sir Henry, 2nd Bt (*cr* 1855), 1840–1938, vol. III
Peto, Comdr Sir (Henry) Francis (Morton), 3rd Bt (*cr* 1855), 1889–1978, vol. VII
Peto, Lt-Col Sir (James) Michael, 2nd Bt (*cr* 1927), 1894–1971, vol. VII
Peto, Major John; *see* Peto, Major B. A. J.
Peto, Mrs Mechtilde; *see* Lichnowsky, Princess Mechtilde.
Peto, Lt-Col Sir Michael; *see* Peto, Lt-Col Sir J. M.
Petre, 14th Baron, 1858–1908, vol. I
Petre, 15th Baron, 1864–1908, vol. I
Petre, 16th Baron, 1890–1914, vol. I
Petre, 17th Baron, 1914–1989, vol. VIII
Petre, Hon. Albert Henry, 1832–1917, vol. II
Petre, Major Edward Henry, 1881–1941, vol. IV
Petre, Edward Oswald Gabriel T.; *see* Turville-Petre.
Petre, Francis Loraine, 1852–1925, vol. II
Petre, Francis William, 1847–1918, vol. II
Petre, Sir George Glynn, 1822–1905, vol. I
Petre, Major Henry Aloysius, 1884–1962, vol. VI
Petre, Col Henry Cecil, 1861–1939, vol. III
Petre, Maud D. M., *died* 1942, vol. IV
Petre, Lt-Col Oswald Henry Philip T.; *see* Turville-Petre.
Petre, Maj.-Gen. Roderic Loraine, 1887–1971, vol. VII
Petre, Rear-Adm. Walter Reginald Glynn, 1873–1942, vol. IV
Petri, Egon, 1881–1962, vol. VI
Petrides, Sir Philip Bertie, 1881–1956, vol. V
Petrie, Ven. Alan Julian, 1888–1947, vol. IV
Petrie, Alfred Alexander Webster, 1884–1962, vol. VI
Petrie, Cecilia, (Lady Petrie), 1901–1987, vol. VIII
Petrie, Sir Charles, 1st Bt, 1853–1920, vol. II
Petrie, Sir Charles Alexander, 3rd Bt, 1895–1977, vol. VII
Petrie, Lt-Col Charles Louis Rowe, 1866–1922, vol. II
Petrie, Sir (Charles) Richard (Borthwick), 4th Bt, 1921–1988, vol. VIII
Petrie, Sir David, 1879–1961, vol. VI
Petrie, Edward James, 1907–1983, vol. VIII
Petrie, Sir Edward Lindsay Haddon, 2nd Bt, 1881–1927, vol. II
Petrie, Sir Flinders; *see* Petrie, Sir W. M. F.

Petrie, Ven. Frederick Herbert, 1875–1948, vol. IV
Petrie, Graham, 1859–1940, vol. III
Petrie, (Jessie) Cecilia, (Lady Petrie); *see* Petrie, C.
Petrie, Joan Caroline, (Lady Bathurst), 1920–1999, vol. X
Petrie, Col Ricardo Dartnel, 1861–1925, vol. II
Petrie, Sir Richard; *see* Petrie, Sir C. R. B.
Petrie, Sir (William Matthew) Flinders, 1853–1942, vol. IV
Petter, Sir Ernest Willoughby, 1873–1954, vol. V
Petticrew, Rev. Francis, *died* 1909, vol. I
Pettigrew, Sir Andrew Hislop, 1857–1942, vol. IV
Pettigrew, James Bell, 1834–1908, vol. I
Pettingell, Sir William Walter, 1914–1987, vol. VIII
Petty, Hon. Sir Horace Rostill, 1904–1982, vol. VIII
Pevsner, Sir Nikolaus Bernhard Leon, 1902–1983, vol. VIII
Peyrefitte, (Pierre-) Roger, 1907–2000, vol. X
Peyrefitte, Roger; *see* Peyrefitte, P-R.
Peyton, Sir Algernon, 7th Bt, 1889–1962, vol. VI
Peyton, Sir Algernon Francis, 6th Bt, 1855–1916, vol. II
Peyton, Francis, 1823–1905, vol. I
Peyton, Guy Wynne Alfred, 1862–1950, vol. IV
Peyton, Sidney Augustus, 1891–1982, vol. VIII
Peyton, Rev. Thomas Thornhill, 1856–1927, vol. II
Peyton, Gen. Sir William Eliot, 1866–1931, vol. III
Pfeiffer, Alois, 1924–1987, vol. VIII
Pfeiffer, Rudolf, 1889–1979, vol. VII
Pfeil, Leonard Bessemer, 1898–1969, vol. VI
Pflimlin, Pierre, 1907–2000, vol. X
Phair, Rev. Ernest Edward Maxwell, 1870–1915, vol. I
Phair, Rt Rev. John Percy, 1876–1967, vol. VI
Phalp, Geoffrey Anderson, 1915–1986, vol. VIII
Phayre, Lt-Gen. Sir Arthur, 1856–1940, vol. III
Phear, Arthur George, 1867–1959, vol. V
Phear, Sir John Budd, 1825–1905, vol. I
Phear, Rev. Samuel George, 1829–1918, vol. II
Phelan, Edward Joseph, 1888–1967, vol. VI
Phelan, Major Ernest Cyril, vol. II
Phelan, Maj.-Gen. Frederick Ross, 1885–1970, vol. VI (AII)
Phelan, Rt Rev. Patrick, 1860–1925, vol. II
Phelips, William Robert, 1846–1919, vol. II
Phelps, Lt-Gen. Arthur, 1837–1920, vol. II
Phelps, Brig.-Gen. Arthur, 1867–1940, vol. III
Phelps, Charles Frederick, 1934–2000, vol. X
Phelps, Most Rev. Francis Robinson, 1863–1938, vol. III
Phelps, Rev. Lancelot Ridley, 1853–1936, vol. III
Phelps, William Lyon, 1865–1943, vol. IV
Phelps, William Peyton, 1865–1942, vol. IV
Phelps Brown, Sir Ernest Henry; *see* Brown, Sir E. H. P.
Phemister, James, 1893–1986, vol. VIII
Phemister, Thomas Crawford, 1902–1982, vol. VIII
Phibbs, Sir Charles, 1878–1964, vol. VI
Philbin, Most Rev. William J., 1907–1991, vol. IX
Philbrick, Arthur James, 1866–1941, vol. IV
Philbrick, Frederick Adolphus, 1836–1910, vol. I
Philby, Harry St John Bridger, 1885–1960, vol. V
Philby, Captain Ralph Montague, 1884–1969, vol. VI
Philip, Very Rev. Adam, 1856–1945, vol. IV

Philip, Alexander, 1911–1979, vol. VII
Philip, Anne Glenday, 1878–1952, vol. V
Philip, Charles Lyall, 1881–1951, vol. V
Philip, James Charles, 1873–1941, vol. IV
Philip, Sir (James) Randall, 1900–1957, vol. V
Philip, John Robert, 1927–1999, vol. X
Philip, Sir Randall; see Philip, Sir J. R.
Philip, Sir Robert William, 1857–1939, vol. III
Philip, William Marshall, 1872–1932, vol. III
Philip, Sir William Shearer, 1891–1975, vol. VII (AII)
Philipe, Maj.-Gen. Arthur Terence de R.; see de Rhé-Philipe.
Philipp, John, 1869–1938, vol. III (A), vol. IV
Philipps, Sir Charles Edward Gregg, 1st Bt (cr 1887), 1840–1928, vol. II
Philipps, Lt-Col Sir Grismond Picton, 1898–1967, vol. VI
Philipps, Hon. Hanning; see Philipps, Hon. R. H.
Philipps, Captain Sir Henry Erasmus Edward, 2nd Bt (cr 1887), 1871–1938, vol. III
Philipps, Maj.-Gen. Sir Ivor, 1861–1940, vol. III
Philipps, Rev. Sir James Erasmus, 12th Bt (cr 1621), 1824–1912, vol. I
Philipps, Hon. James Perrott, 1905–1984, vol. VIII
Philipps, Sir John Erasmus Gwynne Alexander, 3rd Bt (cr 1887), 1915–1948, vol. IV
Philipps, Lady Marion Violet, 1908–1995, vol. IX
Philipps, Sir Richard Foley F., 4th Bt (cr 1887); see Foley-Philipps.
Philipps, Hon. (Richard) Hanning, 1904–1998, vol. X
Philipps, Tracy, 1890–1959, vol. V
Philips, Austin; see Philips, J. A. D.
Philips, Lt-Col Burton Henry, 1858–1927, vol. II
Philips, Francis Charles, 1849–1921, vol. II
Philips, John Austin Drury, 1875–1947, vol. IV
Philips, Lt-Col John Lionel, 1878–1975, vol. VII
Philips, Brig.-Gen. Lewis Francis, 1870–1935, vol. III
Philipson, Sir George Hare, 1836–1918, vol. II
Philipson, Hilton, 1892–1941, vol. IV
Philipson, Mrs Hilton, (Mabel Russell), 1887–1951, vol. V
Philipson, Hylton, 1866–1935, vol. III
Philipson, Hylton Ralph Murray-, 1902–1934, vol. III
Philipson, Oliphant James, 1905–1987, vol. VIII
Philipson, Robert, 1860–1916, vol. II
Philipson, Sir Robert James, (Sir Robin), 1916–1992, vol. IX
Philipson, Sir Robin; see Philipson, Sir R. J.
Philipson-Stow, Sir Edmond Cecil, 4th Bt, 1912–1982, vol. VIII
Philipson-Stow, Sir Elliot Philipson; see Stow.
Philipson-Stow, Sir Frederic Lawrence; see Stow.
Philipson-Stow, Sir Frederic Samuel; see Stow.
Philipson-Stow, Robert Frederic; see Stow.
Phillimore, 1st Baron, 1845–1929, vol. III
Phillimore, 2nd Baron, 1879–1947, vol. IV
Phillimore, 3rd Baron, 1939–1990, vol. VIII
Phillimore, 4th Baron, 1911–1994, vol. IX
Phillimore, Sir Augustus, 1822–1997, vol. I
Phillimore, Rt Hon. Sir Henry Josceline, 1910–1974, vol. VII

Phillimore, John Swinnerton, 1873–1926, vol. II
Phillimore, Col Reginald Henry, 1879–1964, vol. VI
Phillimore, Adm. Sir Richard Fortescue, 1864–1940, vol. III
Phillimore, Ven. Hon. Stephen Henry, 1881–1956, vol. V
Phillimore, Captain Valentine Egerton Bagot, 1875–1945, vol. IV
Phillimore, William P. W., 1853–1913, vol. I
Phillip, Colin Bent, 1855–1932, vol. III
Phillipps, Maj.-Gen. Henry Pye, 1836–1927, vol. II
Phillipps, Henry Vivian, died 1955, vol. V
Phillipps, Sir Herbert; see Phillipps, Sir W. H.
Phillipps, Lt-Gen. Picton, 1869–1928, vol. II
Phillipps, William Douglas, died 1932, vol. III
Phillipps, Sir (William) Herbert, 1847–1935, vol. III
Phillipps-Wolley, Sir Clive, 1854–1918, vol. II
Phillips, Baroness (Life Peer); Norah Phillips, 1910–1992, vol. IX
Phillips of Ellesmere, Baron (Life Peer); David Chilton Phillips, 1924–1999, vol. X
Phillips, Col Alan Andrew, 1889–1972, vol. VII
Phillips, Alban William Housego, 1914–1975, vol. VII
Phillips, Alison; see Phillips, W. A.
Phillips, Arthur, 1907–1991, vol. IX
Phillips, Sir Beaumont; see Phillips, Sir F. B.
Phillips, Sir Benjamin Samuel F.; see Faudel-Phillips.
Phillips, Rt Rev. Charles, 1847–1906, vol. I
Phillips, Sir Charles; see Phillips, Sir E. C.
Phillips, Charles Garrett, 1916–1994, vol. IX
Phillips, Maj.-Gen. Charles George, 1889–1982, vol. VIII
Phillips, Charles James, 1852–1930, vol. III
Phillips, Sir Claude, 1846–1924, vol. II
Phillips, Douglas Herbert Charles, 1924–1990, vol. VIII
Phillips, Maj.-Gen. Sir Edward, 1889–1973, vol. VII
Phillips, Sir (Edward) Charles, 1888–1974, vol. VII
Phillips, Major Edward Hawtin, 1876–1914, vol. I
Phillips, Edwin William, 1918–1997, vol. X
Phillips, Eleanor Addison, 1874–1952, vol. V
Phillips, Col Eric Charles Malcolm, 1883–1957, vol. V
Phillips, Ernest, 1870–1956, vol. V
Phillips, Rear-Adm. Esmonde; see Phillips, Rear-Adm. P. E.
Phillips, Very Rev. Evan Owen, died 1897, vol. I
Phillips, Maj.-Gen. Sir Farndale, 1905–1961, vol. VI
Phillips, Rev. Forbes Alexander, 1866–1917, vol. II
Phillips, Francis, 1835–1925, vol. II
Phillips, Frank Coles, 1902–1982, vol. VIII
Phillips, Sir Frederick, 1884–1943, vol. IV
Phillips, Sir (Frederick) Beaumont, 1890–1957, vol. V
Phillips, Frederick William, 1879–1956, vol. V
Phillips, Col Geoffrey Francis, 1880–1968, vol. VI
Phillips, George, 1876–1948, vol. IV
Phillips, Surg. Rear-Adm. George, 1902–1980, vol. VII
Phillips, Major George Edward, died 1902, vol. I
Phillips, Sir George Faudel F.; see Faudel-Phillips.
Phillips, Brig.-Gen. George Fraser, 1863–1921, vol. II

Phillips, George Godfrey, 1900–1965, vol. VI
Phillips, Bt Lt-Col George Ingleton, 1866–1936, vol. III
Phillips, Rev. Godfrey Edward, 1878–1963, vol. VI
Phillips, Gordon, 1890–1952, vol. V
Phillips, Rev. Gordon Lewis, 1911–1982, vol. VIII
Phillips, Captain H. C. B., *died* 1906, vol. I
Phillips, Harold Ernest, 1877–1941, vol. IV
Phillips, Henry Bettesworth, 1866–1950, vol. IV
Phillips, Vice-Adm. Sir Henry Clarmont, *died* 1968, vol. VI
Phillips, Rev. Henry Frederick, *died* 1914, vol. I
Phillips, Major Henry Jacob Vaughan, *died* 1914, vol. I
Phillips, Sir Herbert, 1878–1957, vol. V
Phillips, Brig.-Gen. Herbert de Touffreville, 1862–1933, vol. III
Phillips, Herbert Moore, 1908–1987, vol. VIII
Phillips, Hubert, 1891–1964, vol. VI
Phillips, Hugh Richard, 1873–1932, vol. III
Phillips, Ven. Hugh Stowell, 1865–1940, vol. III
Phillips, Ivan L.; *see* Lloyd Phillips.
Phillips, J. S. Ragland, 1850–1919, vol. II
Phillips, James Falkner, *died* 1933, vol. III
Phillips, John, *died* 1917, vol. II
Phillips, Sir John, 1855–1928, vol. II
Phillips, Col John Alfred Steele, 1882–1960, vol. V
Phillips, Rev. Canon John Bertram, 1906–1982, vol. VIII
Phillips, Major John Charles S.; *see* Spencer-Phillips.
Phillips, John Fleetwood Stewart, 1917–1998, vol. X
Phillips, Rev. John Francis, 1860–1934, vol. III
Phillips, John Francis, 1911–1998, vol. X
Phillips, Lt-Col John Frederick L.; *see* Lort Phillips.
Phillips, John George Crispin, 1938–1982, vol. VIII
Phillips, John George P.; *see* Porter-Phillips.
Phillips, Sir John Grant, 1911–1986, vol. VIII
Phillips, John Guest, 1933–1987, vol. VIII
Phillips, John Henry Hood, 1902–1977, vol. VII
Phillips, Rt Rev. John Henry Lawrence, 1910–1985, vol. VIII
Phillips, Very Rev. John Leoline, 1879–1947, vol. IV
Phillips, Sir John Randal, 1857–1945, vol. IV
Phillips, Sir (John) Raymond, 1915–1982, vol. VIII
Phillips, Rev. Lawrence Arthur, 1870–1949, vol. IV
Phillips, Lawrence Barnett, 1842–1922, vol. II
Phillips, Leonard George, 1890–1975, vol. VII
Phillips, Maj.-Gen. Sir Leslie Gordon, 1892–1966, vol. VI
Phillips, Sir Leslie Walter, 1894–1983, vol. VIII
Phillips, Sir Lionel, 1st Bt, 1855–1936, vol. III
Phillips, Captain Sir Lionel Francis, 2nd Bt, 1914–1944, vol. IV
Phillips, Sir Lionel Lawson Faudel F.; *see* Faudel-Phillips.
Phillips, Llewellyn Powell, 1871–1927, vol. II
Phillips, Mrs McGrigor, (Dorothy Una Ratcliffe), *died* 1967, vol. VI
Phillips, Mandeville Blackwood, 1848–1929, vol. III
Phillips, Air Cdre Manfred Norman, 1912–1986, vol. VIII
Phillips, Marion, 1881–1932, vol. III
Phillips, Montague Fawcett, 1885–1969, vol. VI

Phillips, Morgan Hector, 1885–1953, vol. V
Phillips, Morgan Walter, 1902–1963, vol. VI
Phillips, Lt-Col Noel Clive, 1883–1961, vol. VI
Phillips, Father Oliver Rodie V.; *see* Vassall-Phillips.
Phillips, Maj.-Gen. Owen Forbes, 1882–1966, vol. VI
Phillips, Owen Hood, 1907–1986, vol. VIII
Phillips, Patrick Edward, 1907–1976, vol. VII
Phillips, Patrick Laurence, 1912–1980, vol. VII
Phillips, Sir Percival, 1877–1937, vol. III
Phillips, Sir Philip David, 1897–1970, vol. VI
Phillips, Rear-Adm. (Philip) Esmonde, 1888–1960, vol. V
Phillips, Sir Raymond; *see* Phillips, Sir J. R.
Phillips, Reginald Arthur, 1913–1988, vol. VIII
Phillips, Reginald William, 1854–1926, vol. II
Phillips, Surg. Rear-Adm. Rex Philip, 1913–1995, vol. IX
Phillips, Robert Randal, 1878–1967, vol. VI
Phillips, Air Cdre Ronald Lancelot, 1909–1956, vol. V
Phillips, Sir Rowland Ricketts, 1904–1976, vol. VII
Phillips, Rt Rev. Samuel Charles, 1881–1974, vol. VII
Phillips, Rev. Sidney, 1840–1917, vol. II
Phillips, Sidney, *died* 1951, vol. V
Phillips, Sidney Hill, 1882–1962, vol. VI
Phillips, Stephen, 1864–1915, vol. I
Phillips, Rev. Stephen, *died* 1919, vol. II
Phillips, Sydney William Charles, 1908–1991, vol. IX
Phillips, Rev. Theodore Evelyn Reece, 1868–1942, vol. IV
Phillips, Maj.-Gen. Thomas, 1837–1913, vol. I
Phillips, Rev. Thomas, 1868–1936, vol. III
Phillips, Lt-Col Thomas Richmond, 1866–1963, vol. VI
Phillips, Rear-Adm. Thomas Tyacke, 1832–1920, vol. II
Phillips, Sir Thomas Williams, 1883–1966, vol. VI
Phillips, Ven. Thompson, *died* 1909, vol. I
Phillips, Adm. Sir Tom Spencer Vaughan, 1888–1941, vol. IV
Phillips, Wallace Banta, 1886–1952, vol. V
Phillips, (Walter) Alison, 1864–1950, vol. IV
Phillips, Bt-Col Walter Ernest, 1858–1911, vol. I
Phillips, Walter R., 1855–1930, vol. III
Phillips, William, 1867–1941, vol. IV
Phillips, William, 1878–1968, vol. VI
Phillips, Lt-Col William Eric, 1893–1964, vol. VI
Phillips, William James, *died* 1963, vol. VI
Phillips, William Lambert Collyer, 1858–1924, vol. II
Phillips, Sir William Watkin, 1870–1933, vol. III
Phillips Brocklehurst, Charles Douglas Fergusson, 1904–1977, vol. VII
Phillipson, Andrew Tindal, 1910–1977, vol. VII
Phillipson, Coleman, 1875–1958, vol. V
Phillipson, John Tindal, 1865–1929, vol. III
Phillipson, Sir Sydney, 1892–1966, vol. VI
Phillott, Constance, *died* 1931, vol. III
Phillott, Lt-Col Douglas Craven, 1860–1930, vol. III
Phillpotts, Adelaide Eden; *see* Phillpotts, M. A. E.
Phillpotts, Arthur Stephens, 1844–1920, vol. II

Phillpotts, Dame Bertha Surtees; *see* Newall, Dame B. S.
Phillpotts, Christopher Louis George, 1915–1985, vol. VIII
Phillpotts, Eden, 1862–1960, vol. V
Phillpotts, Adm. Edward Montgomery, 1871–1952, vol. V
Phillpotts, James Surtees, 1839–1930, vol. III
Phillpotts, Lt-Col Louis Murray, 1870–1916, vol. II
Phillpotts, (Mary) Adelaide Eden, (Mrs Nicholas Ross), 1896–1993, vol. X(AI)
Phillpotts, Owen Surtees, 1870–1932, vol. III
Phillpotts, Sir Ralegh Buller, 1871–1950, vol. IV
Philp, Hon. Sir Robert, 1851–1922, vol. II
Philp, Lt-Col Robert, 1896–1980, vol. VII
Philp, Sir Roslyn Foster Bowie, 1895–1965, vol. VI
Philpot, Frederick Freeman, *died* 1916, vol. II
Philpot, Glyn Warren, 1884–1937, vol. III
Philpot, Joseph Henry, 1850–1939, vol. III
Philpot, Oliver Lawrence Spurling, 1913–1993, vol. IX
Philpot, Robert, 1849–1913, vol. I
Philpott, Rev. John Nigel, 1859–1932, vol. III
Philpott, Air Vice-Marshal Peter Theodore, 1915–1988, vol. VIII
Philps, (Alan) Seymour, 1906–1956, vol. V
Philps, Frank Richard, 1914–1995, vol. IX
Philps, Seymour; *see* Philps, A. S.
Phimister, Rev. Alexander, *died* 1921, vol. II
Phin, Sir John, 1881–1955, vol. V
Phippen, Hon. Frank Hedley, 1862–1932, vol. III
Phipps, Alan Thomas, 1944–1999, vol. X
Phipps, Brig. Charles Constantine, 1889–1958, vol. V
Phipps, Lt-Col Charles Edward, 1864–1946, vol. IV
Phipps, Col Charles Foskett, 1871–1931, vol. III
Phipps, Charles Nicholas Paul, 1845–1913, vol. I
Phipps, Rev. Constantine Osborne, 1861–1921, vol. II
Phipps, Sir Edmund Bampfylde, 1869–1947, vol. IV
Phipps, Sir Edmund Constantine Henry, 1840–1911, vol. I
Phipps, Rt Hon. Sir Eric Clare Edmund, 1875–1945, vol. IV
Phipps, Rev. Frederick, 1858–1934, vol. III
Phipps, Gerald Hastings, 1882–1973, vol. VII
Phipps, Hon. Harriet Lepel, *died* 1922, vol. II
Phipps, Henry, 1839–1930, vol. III
Phipps, Maj.-Gen. Herbert Clive, 1898–1975, vol. VII
Phipps, Dame Jessie Wilton, 1855–1934, vol. III
Phipps, John Constantine, 1910–1986, vol. VIII
Phipps, Col John Hare, 1871–1936, vol. III
Phipps, Paul, 1880–1953, vol. V
Phipps, Vice-Adm. Sir Peter, 1909–1989, vol. VIII
Phipps, Ven. Richard, 1865–1934, vol. III
Phipps, Captain William Duncan, 1882–1967, vol. VI
Phipson, Col Edward Selby, 1884–1973, vol. VII
Phoenix, George, 1863–1935, vol. III
Phythian, John Ernest, 1858–1935, vol. III
Phythian-Adams, Rev. Canon William John Telia Phythian, 1888–1967, vol. VI
Piaget, Jean, 1896–1980, vol. VII
Piaggio, Henry Thomas Herbert, 1884–1967, vol. VI

Piatigorsky, Gregor, 1903–1976, vol. VII
Piatti, Alfredo, 1822–1901, vol. I
Pibworth, Charles James, 1878–1958, vol. V
Picachy, His Eminence Cardinal Lawrence Trevor, 1916–1992, vol. IX
Picard, Émile, 1856–1941, vol. IV
Picasso, Pablo Ruiz, 1881–1973, vol. VII
Piccard, Auguste Antoine, 1884–1962, vol. VI
Piccaver, Alfred, 1889–1958, vol. V
Picciotto, Cyril Moses, 1888–1940, vol. III
Pick, Surg. Rear.-Adm. Bryan Pickering, 1879–1959, vol. V
Pick, Charles Samuel, 1917–2000, vol. X
Pick, Frank, 1878–1941, vol. IV
Pick, Thomas Pickering, 1841–1919, vol. II
Pick-Mangiagalli, Riccardo, 1882–1949, vol. IV
Pickard, Alexander, 1897–1972, vol. VII
Pickard, Benjamin, 1842–1904, vol. I
Pickard, Sir Cyril Stanley, 1917–1992, vol. IX
Pickard, Lt-Col Jocelyn Arthur Adair, 1885–1962, vol. VI
Pickard, Gp Captain Percy Charles, 1915–1944, vol. IV
Pickard, Col Ransom, 1867–1953, vol. V
Pickard, Sir Robert Howson, 1874–1949, vol. IV
Pickard, Rt Rev. Stanley Chapman, 1910–1988, vol. VIII
Pickard-Cambridge, Sir Arthur Wallace, 1873–1952, vol. V
Pickard-Cambridge, Rev. Octavius, 1828–1917, vol. II
Pickard-Cambridge, William Adair, 1879–1957, vol. V
Pickavance, Gerald; *see* Pickavance, T. G.
Pickavance, (Thomas) Gerald, 1915–1991, vol. IX
Picken, Andrew, 1886–1938, vol. III
Picken, David Kennedy, 1879–1956, vol. V
Picken, Ralph Montgomery Fullarton, 1884–1955, vol. V
Pickerill, Dame Cecily Mary Wise, *born* 1903, vol. VIII
Pickerill, Henry Percy, *died* 1956, vol. V
Pickering, Col Charles James, 1880–1951, vol. V
Pickering, Derek; *see* Pickering, F. D.
Pickering, Edward Charles, 1846–1919, vol. II
Pickering, Bt Col Emil William, 1882–1942, vol. IV
Pickering, Frederick Derwent, (Derek Pickering), 1909–1989, vol. VIII
Pickering, Frederick Pickering, 1909–1981, vol. VIII
Pickering, Sir George Hunter, 1877–1971, vol. VII
Pickering, Sir George White, 1904–1980, vol. VII
Pickering, Herbert Kitchener, 1915–1992, vol. IX
Pickering, Ian George Walker, 1915–1984, vol. VIII
Pickering, J. L., *died* 1912, vol. I
Pickering, John Robertson, 1925–1995, vol. IX
Pickering, Loring, 1888–1959, vol. V (A)
Pickering, Percival Spencer Umfreville, 1858–1920, vol. II
Pickering, Brig. Ralph Emerson, 1898–1962, vol. VI
Pickering, Wilfred Francis, 1915–1980, vol. VII
Pickering, Captain William, 1856–1933, vol. III
Pickering, William Alexander, 1840–1907, vol. I
Pickering, William Henry, 1858–1912, vol. I
Pickersgill, Frederick Richard, 1820–1900, vol. I
Pickersgill, William Clayton, 1846–1901, vol. I

Pickett, Rev. Henry John, *died* 1931, vol. III
Pickett, Jacob, 1835–1922, vol. II
Pickett, Rev. James, 1853–1918, vol. II
Pickett, Thomas, 1912–1997, vol. X
Pickford, Sir Alfred Donald, 1872–1947, vol. IV
Pickford, Sir Anthony Frederick Ingham, 1885–1970, vol. VI
Pickford, Frank, 1917–1984, vol. VIII
Pickford, Mary, 1893–1979, vol. VII
Pickford, Hon. Mary Ada, *died* 1934, vol. III
Pickford, Ralph William, 1903–1986, vol. VIII
Pickles, Edward Llewellyn, 1884–1949, vol. IV
Pickles, Sir John Sydney, 1898–1972, vol. VII
Pickles, Wilfred, 1904–1978, vol. VII
Pickles, William Norman, 1885–1969, vol. VI
Pickmere, Edward Ralph, *died* 1941, vol. IV
Pickop, Rev. James, 1847–1919, vol. II
Pickthall, Marmaduke William, 1875–1936, vol. III
Pickthall, Col Wallace Edward Colin, 1891–1948, vol. IV
Pickthorn, Sir Charles William Richards, 3rd Bt, 1927–1995, vol. IX
Pickthorn, Rt Hon. Sir Kenneth William Murray, 1st Bt, 1892–1975, vol. VII
Pickup, Sir Arthur, 1878–1960, vol. V
Pickwoad, Col Edwin Hay, 1853–1932, vol. III
Pickworth, Sir Frederick, 1890–1959, vol. V
Picot, Francis Raymond, 1893–1971, vol. VII
Picot, Lt-Col Francis Slater, 1859–1939, vol. III
Picot, Lt-Col Henry Philip, 1857–1937, vol. III
Picot, Jacques Marie Charles G.; *see* Georges-Picot.
Picton, Ven. Arnold Stanley, 1899–1962, vol. VI
Picton, Glyn; *see* Picton, J. G.
Picton, Jacob Glyndwr, (Glyn), 1912–1998, vol. X
Picton, James Allanson, 1832–1910, vol. I
Picton, Col Reginald Ernest, 1863–1932, vol. III
Picton-Turbervill, Edith, *died* 1960, vol. V
Pidcock, Air Vice-Marshal Geoffrey Arthur Henzell, 1897–1976, vol. VII
Piddington, Albert Bathurst, 1862–1945, vol. IV
Pidduck, Frederick Bernard, 1885–1952, vol. V
Pidsley, Brig. Wilfrid Gould, 1892–1967, vol. VI
Pielou, Douglas Percival, 1887–1927, vol. II
Pienaar, Maj.-Gen. Daniel Hermanus, 1893–1942, vol. IV
Pierce, Bedford, 1861–1932, vol. III
Pierce, Rev. Charles Frederick, 1877–1936, vol. III
Pierce, Rev. Francis Dormer, *died* 1923, vol. II
Pierce, Francis William, 1915–1999, vol. X
Pierce, Hugh Humphrey, 1931–1998, vol. X
Pierce, Sir John, 1863–1949, vol. IV
Pierce, Rt Rev. Reginald James, 1909–1992, vol. IX
Pierce, Robert, 1884–1968, vol. VI
Pierce, Stephen Rowland, 1896–1966, vol. VI
Pierce-Goulding, Lt-Col Terence Leslie Crawford, 1918–1987, vol. VIII
Piercy, 1st Baron, 1886–1966, vol. VI
Piercy, 2nd Baron, 1918–1981, vol. VIII
Piercy, Benjamin Herbert, 1870–1941, vol. IV
Piercy, Norman Augustus Victor, 1891–1953, vol. V
Piercy, Hon. Penelope Katherine, 1916–1997, vol. X
Pieris, Sir Paulus Edward Deraniyagala, 1874–1959, vol. V
Pierpoint, Robert, 1845–1932, vol. III

Pierre, Hon. Charles Henry, 1878–1937, vol. III
Pierre, Sir Henry; *see* Pierre, Sir J. H.
Pierre, Sir (Joseph) Henry, 1904–1984, vol. VIII
Piers, Sir Charles Pigott, 9th Bt, 1870–1945, vol. IV
Piers, Sir Charles Robert Fitzmaurice, 10th Bt, 1903–1996, vol. X
Piers, Sir Eustace Fitz-Maurice, 8th Bt, 1840–1913, vol. I
Pierse, Rev. Garrett, 1882–1932, vol. III
Pierson, Reginald Kirshaw, 1891–1948, vol. IV
Pierson, Warren Lee, 1896–1978, vol. VII
Pierssené, Sir Stephen Herbert, 1899–1966, vol. VI
Pieshkov, Alexei Maximovitch; *see* Gorky, Maxim.
Piggott, Maj.-Gen. Francis James Claude, 1910–1996, vol. X
Piggott, Maj.-Gen. Francis Stewart Gilderoy, 1883–1966, vol. VI
Piggott, Sir Francis Taylor, 1852–1925, vol. II
Piggott, Sir George Bettesworth, 1867–1952, vol. V
Piggott, Sir Henry Howard, 1871–1951, vol. V
Piggott, Col Joseph Clive, 1892–1975, vol. VII
Piggott, Julian Ito, 1888–1965, vol. VI
Piggott, Stuart, 1910–1996, vol. X
Piggott, Sir Theodore Caro, 1867–1944, vol. IV
Piggott, Rev. William Charter, *died* 1943, vol. IV
Pigot, Sir George, 5th Bt, 1850–1934, vol. III
Pigot, John H., 1863–1928, vol. II
Pigot, Brig.-Gen. Sir Robert, 6th Bt, 1882–1977, vol. VII
Pigot, Maj.-Gen. Sir Robert Anthony, 7th Bt, 1915–1986, vol. VIII
Pigot, Thomas Herbert, 1921–1998, vol. X
Pigot, Rev. William Melville, 1842–1916, vol. II
Pigott, Alan Desmond Frederick P.; *see* Pemberton-Pigott.
Pigott, Maj.-Gen. Alan John Keefe, 1892–1969, vol. VI
Pigott, Major Sir Berkeley, 4th Bt, 1894–1982, vol. VIII
Pigott, Sir Charles Robert, 3rd Bt, 1835–1911, vol. I
Pigott, Sir Digby; *see* Pigott, Sir T. D.
Pigott, Brig. Frank Borkman, 1894–1971, vol. VII
Pigott, Lt-Col Grenville Edmund, 1870–1942, vol. IV
Pigott, Rt Rev. Harold Grant, 1894–1979, vol. VII
Pigott, Harry, *died* 1974, vol. VII
Pigott, John Robert Wilson, 1850–1928, vol. II
Pigott, Gp Captain (Joseph) Ruscombe (Wadham) S.; *see* Smyth-Pigott.
Pigott, Air Vice-Marshal Michael Joseph, 1904–1990, vol. VIII
Pigott, Montague Horatio Mostyn Turtle, 1865–1927, vol. II
Pigott, Sir Paynton, 1840–1915, vol. I
Pigott, Richard, 1861–1931, vol. III
Pigott, Col Robert Edward Pemberton, 1866–1943, vol. IV
Pigott, Gp Captain Ruscombe S.; *see* Smyth-Pigott.
Pigott, Sir Stephen J., 1880–1955, vol. V
Pigott, Sir (Thomas) Digby, 1840–1927, vol. II
Pigott, William; *see* Wales, Hubert.
Pigott, Vice-Adm. William Harvey, 1848–1924, vol. II
Pigott-Brown, Captain Sir John Hargreaves, 2nd Bt, 1913–1942, vol. IV

Pigou, Arthur Cecil, 1877–1959, vol. V
Pigou, Very Rev. Francis, 1832–1916, vol. II
Pike, Andrew Hamilton, 1903–1984, vol. VIII
Pike, Cecil Frederick, 1898–1968, vol. VI
Pike, Lt-Col Cuthbert Joseph, 1868–1947, vol. IV
Pike, Douglas Henry, 1908–1974, vol. VII
Pike, Col Ebenezer John Lecky, 1884–1965, vol. VI
Pike, Edmund William, 1838–1910, vol. I
Pike, Vice-Adm. Frederick Owen, 1851–1921, vol. II
Pike, Air Cdre James Maitland Nicholson, 1916–1999, vol. X
Pike, John Milton, 1872–1940, vol. III (A), vol. IV
Pike, Rt Rev. St John Surridge, 1909–1992, vol. IX
Pike, Joseph, died 1929, vol. III
Pike, Leonard Henry, 1885–1961, vol. VI
Pike, Most Rev. Robert Bonsall, 1905–1973, vol. VII
Pike, Sir Theodore Ouseley, 1904–1987, vol. VIII
Pike, Marshal of the Royal Air Force Sir Thomas Geoffrey, 1906–1983, vol. VIII
Pike, Rt Rev. Victor Joseph, 1907–1986, vol. VIII
Pike, Lt-Gen. Sir William Gregory Huddlestone, 1905–1992, vol. IX
Pike, Maj.-Gen. Sir William Watson, 1860–1941, vol. IV
Pilcher, Lt-Col Alan Humphrey, 1898–1957, vol. V
Pilcher, Vice-Adm. Cecil Horace, 1877–1953, vol. V
Pilcher, Rt Rev. Charles Venn, 1879–1961, vol. VI
Pilcher, Sir (Charlie) Dennis, 1906–1994, vol. IX
Pilcher, Sir Dennis; see Pilcher, Sir C. D.
Pilcher, Maj.-Gen. Edgar Montagu, 1865–1947, vol. IV
Pilcher, George, 1882–1962, vol. VI
Pilcher, Sir Gonne St Clair, 1890–1966, vol. VI
Pilcher, Sir John Arthur, 1912–1990, vol. VIII
Pilcher, Robert Stuart, 1882–1961, vol. VI
Pilcher, Robin Sturtevant, 1902–1994, vol. IX
Pilcher, Maj.-Gen. Thomas David, 1858–1928, vol. II
Pilditch, Sir Denys, 1891–1975, vol. VII
Pilditch, James George Christopher, 1929–1995, vol. IX
Pilditch, Sir Philip Edward, 1st Bt, 1861–1948, vol. IV
Pilditch, Sir Philip Harold, 2nd Bt, 1890–1949, vol. IV
Pilditch, Sir Philip John Frederick, 3rd Bt, 1919–1954, vol. V
Pile, Gen. Sir Frederick Alfred, 2nd Bt, 1884–1976, vol. VII
Pile, Sir George Clarke, 1821–1906, vol. I
Pile, Sir George Laurie, 1857–1948, vol. IV
Pile, Sir John Devereux, 1918–1982, vol. VIII
Pile, Sir Thomas Devereux, 1st Bt, 1856–1931, vol. III
Pile, Sir William Dennis, 1919–1997, vol. X
Pilgrim, David; see Saunders, H. A. St G.
Pilgrim, Guy Ellcock, 1875–1943, vol. IV
Pilkington, Baron (Life Peer); Harry (William Henry) Pilkington, 1905–1983, vol. VIII
Pilkington, Sir Alastair; see Pilkington, Sir L. A. B.
Pilkington, Sir Antony Richard, 1935–2000, vol. X
Pilkington, Major Sir Arthur William
Milborne-Swinnerton-, 13th Bt, 1898–1952, vol. V
Pilkington, Lt-Col Charles Raymond, 1875–1938, vol. III
Pilkington, Charles Vere, 1905–1983, vol. VIII
Pilkington, Rev. Canon Evan Matthias, 1916–1987, vol. VIII
Pilkington, Sir George Augustus, 1848–1916, vol. II
Pilkington, Harry Seymour Hoyle, 1869–1954, vol. V
Pilkington, Major Sir Henry, 1849–1930, vol. III
Pilkington, Col Henry Lionel, 1857–1914, vol. I
Pilkington, Col Herbert Edward, 1877–1956, vol. V
Pilkington, Lawrence Herbert Austin, 1911–2000, vol. X
Pilkington, Sir Lionel Alexander Bethune, (Sir Alastair), 1920–1995, vol. IX
Pilkington, Col Lionel Edward, died 1952, vol. V
Pilkington, Sir Lionel Milborne Swinnerton, 11th Bt, 1835–1901, vol. I
Pilkington, M. Evelyn, 1879–1955, vol. V
Pilkington, Margaret, 1891–1974, vol. VII
Pilkington, Captain Sir Richard Antony, 1908–1976, vol. VII
Pilkington, Robert Rivington, died 1942, vol. IV
Pilkington, Sir Thomas Edward Milborne-Swinnerton-, 12th Bt, 1857–1944, vol. IV
Pilkington, Sir William Handcock, 1859–1905, vol. I
Pilkington, Col William Norman, 1877–1935, vol. III
Pilkington Jackson, Charles d'Orville; see Jackson.
Pillai, Sir (Narayana) Raghavan, 1898–1992, vol. IX
Pillai, Sir Raghavan; see Pillai, Sir N. R.
Pillans, Charles Eustace, 1850–1919, vol. II, vol. III
Pillar, Sir William Thomas, 1924–1999, vol. X
Pilleau, Maj.-Gen. Gerald Arthur, 1896–1964, vol. VI
Pilleau, Major Henry Charles, 1866–1914, vol. I
Pilley, Charles, 1885–1937, vol. III
Pilley, John Gustave, 1899–1968, vol. VI
Pilling, Sir Guy; see Pilling, Sir H. G.
Pilling, Sir (Henry) Guy, 1886–1953, vol. V
Pilling, Tom Sharpley, 1921–1977, vol. VII
Pillsbury, Harry N., 1872–1906, vol. I
Pilot, Rev. William, 1841–1913, vol. I
Pilson, Major Arthur Forde, 1865–1929, vol. III
Pilsudski, Joseph Clemens, 1867–1935, vol. III
Pilter, Sir John George, 1848–1935, vol. III
Pilter, Col William Frederick, 1831–1915, vol. I
Pim, Sir Alan William, died 1958, vol. V
Pim, Frederic William, 1839–1925, vol. II
Pim, Brig. George Adrien, 1888–1965, vol. VI
Pim, Howard, died 1934, vol. III
Pim, Rev. John, died 1932, vol. III
Pim, Rt Hon. Jonathan, 1858–1949, vol. IV
Pim, Captain Sir Richard Pike, 1900–1987, vol. VIII
Pimlott, John Alfred Ralph, 1909–1969, vol. VI
Pinault, Col Louis Felix, 1852–1906, vol. I
Pinay, Antoine, 1891–1994, vol. IX
Pinchard, Rev. Arnold Theophilus Biddulph, died 1934, vol. III
Pinches, Theophilus Goldridge, 1856–1934, vol. III

Pinchin, Arthur John Scott, *died* 1936, vol. III
Pinchin, Ernest Alfred, 1874–1929, vol. III
Pinching, Sir Horace Henderson, 1857–1935, vol. III
Pinchot, Gifford, 1865–1946, vol. IV
Pinckard, George Henry, *died* 1950, vol. IV
Pinckney, Charles Percy, 1901–1982, vol. VIII
Pinckney, John Robert Hugh, 1876–1964, vol. VI
Pinder, Ven. Charles, 1921–1999, vol. X
Pindling, Rt Hon. Sir Lynden Oscar, 1930–2000, vol. X
Pine, John Bradley, 1913–1989, vol. VIII
Pine, Leslie Gilbert, 1907–1987, vol. VIII
Pine Coffin, Major John Edward, 1866–1919, vol. II
Pine-Coffin, Gen. Roger, 1847–1921, vol. II
Pineau, Christian Paul Francis, 1904–1995, vol. IX
Pinero, Sir Arthur Wing, 1855–1934, vol. III
Piney, Alfred, 1896–1965, vol. VI
Ping, Aubrey Charles, 1905–1978, vol. VII
Pinhey, Lt-Col Sir Alexander Fleetwood, 1861–1916, vol. II
Pinhorn, Col Henry Quinten, 1862–1929, vol. III
Pininfarina, Battista, 1895–1966, vol. VI
Pink, Col Francis John, 1857–1934, vol. III
Pink, Sir Harold Rufus, 1858–1952, vol. V
Pink, Ven Hubert Arthur Stanley, 1905–1976, vol. VII
Pink, Sir Ivor Thomas Montague, 1910–1966, vol. VI
Pink, Ralph Bonner, 1912–1984, vol. VIII
Pink, Air Cdre Richard Charles Montagu, 1888–1932, vol. III
Pink, Sir Thomas, 1855–1926, vol. II
Pink, Sir William, 1829–1906, vol. I
Pinker, Rev. Martin Wallis, 1893–1980, vol. VII (AII)
Pinkerton, John, 1845–1908, vol. I
Pinkerton, John Macpherson, 1941–1988, vol. VIII
Pinkerton, Robert Hamilton, 1855–1938, vol. III
Pinkham, Lt-Col Sir Charles, 1853–1938, vol. III
Pinkham, Rt Rev. William Cyprian, 1844–1928, vol. II
Pinkney, Col Edmund Walker Renny, 1876–1940, vol. III
Pinnell, Leonard George, 1896–1979, vol. VII
Pinney, Charles Robert, 1883–1945, vol. IV
Pinney, Maj.-Gen. Sir Reginald John, 1863–1943, vol. IV
Pinnington, Geoffrey Charles, 1919–1995, vol. IX
Pinnock, Frank Frewin, 1902–1977, vol. VII
Pinsent, Dame Ellen Frances, 1866–1949, vol. IV
Pinsent, Gerald Hume Saverie, 1888–1976, vol. VII
Pinsent, Col John Ryland, 1888–1957, vol. V
Pinsent, Sir Richard Alfred, 1st Bt, 1852–1948, vol. IV
Pinsent, Roger Philip, 1916–1997, vol. X
Pinsent, Sir Roy, 2nd Bt, 1883–1978, vol. VII
Pinto, Vivian de Sola, 1895–1969, vol. VI
Piper, Arthur William, 1865–1936, vol. III
Piper, Bright Harold, (Peter), 1918–1993, vol. IX
Piper, Sir David Towry, 1918–1990, vol. VIII
Piper, Harold Bayard, 1894–1953, vol. V
Piper, Henry Mansell, 1890–1949, vol. IV
Piper, John Edwin, 1854–1938, vol. III
Piper, John Egerton Christmas, 1903–1992, vol. IX
Piper, Peter; *see* Piper, B. H.

Piper, Stephen Harvey, 1887–1963, vol. VI
Piper, Air Marshal Sir Thomas William; *see* Piper, Air Marshal Sir Tim.
Piper, Air Marshal Sir Tim, (Thomas William), 1911–1978, vol. VII
Pipes, Hon. William Thomas, 1850–1908, vol. I
Pipkin, Broughton; *see* Pipkin, C. H. B.
Pipkin, (Charles Harry) Broughton, 1913–1995, vol. IX
Pipon, Maj.-Gen. Henry, 1843–1924, vol. II
Pipon, Vice-Adm. Sir James Murray, 1882–1971, vol. VII
Pipon, John Pakenham, 1849–1899, vol. I
Pipon, Gen. Philip Gosset, 1824–1905, vol. I
Pipon, Philip James Griffiths, 1874–1960, vol. V
Pippard, Alfred John Sutton, 1891–1969, vol. VI
Pippett, Roger Samuel, 1895–1962, vol. VI
Pirandello, Luigi, 1867–1936, vol. III
Piratin, Philip, 1907–1995, vol. IX
Pirbhai, Diwan Sir E.; *see* Eboo Pirbhai.
Pirbright, 1st Baron, 1840–1903, vol. I
Pire, Rev. Père Dominique-Georges, 1910–1969, vol. VI
Pirenne, Henri, 1862–1935, vol. III
Pirie, Alexander Howard, 1875–1944, vol. IV
Pirie, Anne Gillespie, (Mrs J. H. Pirie); *see* Shaw, A. G.
Pirie, Major Arthur Murray, 1869–1917, vol. II
Pirie, Maj.-Gen. Charles Patrick William, 1859–1933, vol. III
Pirie, Duncan Vernon, 1858–1931, vol. III
Pirie, Rev. George, 1843–1904, vol. I
Pirie, Sir George, 1863–1946, vol. IV
Pirie, Air Chief Marshal Sir George Clark, 1896–1980, vol. VII
Pirie, Henry Ward, 1922–1995, vol. IX
Pirie, Norman Wingate, 1907–1997, vol. X
Pirie, Psyche, 1918–1995, vol. IX
Pirie-Gordon of Buthlaw, Christopher Martin, 1911–1980, vol. VII
Pirow, Hon. Oswald, *died* 1959, vol. V
Pirquet, Clemens, Freiherr von, 1874–1929, vol. III
Pirrie, 1st Viscount, 1847–1924, vol. II
Pirrie, Viscountess; (Margaret), *died* 1935, vol. III
Pirrie, Col Francis William, 1867–1948, vol. IV
Pisani, Salvator Aloysius, 1828–1908, vol. I
Pissarro, Lucien, 1863–1944, vol. IV
Piston, Walter, 1894–1976, vol. VII
Pitblado, Sir David Bruce, 1912–1997, vol. X
Pitcher, *see* Binstead, A. M.
Pitcher, Col Duncan George, *born* 1839, vol. II
Pitcher, Air Cdre Duncan le Geyt, 1877–1944, vol. IV
Pitcher, William J. C., 1858–1925, vol. II
Pitchford, Denys James W.; *see* Watkins-Pitchford.
Pitchford, Lt-Col Herbert W.; *see* Watkins-Pitchford.
Pitchford, John Hereward, 1904–1995, vol. IX
Pitchford, John W.; *see* Watkins-Pitchford.
Pitchforth, Harry, 1917–1996, vol. X
Pitchforth, (Roland) Vivian, 1895–1982, vol. VIII
Pitchforth, Vivian; *see* Pitchforth, R. V.
Pite, Arthur Beresford, 1861–1934, vol. III
Pite, Arthur Goodhart, 1896–1938, vol. III
Pite, William Alfred, 1860–1949, vol. IV

Pithie, Michael, 1846–1915, vol. I
Pitkeathly, Sir James Scott, 1882–1949, vol. IV
Pitman, Hon. Lord; James Campbell Pitman, 1864–1941, vol. IV
Pitman, Alfred, 1862–1952, vol. V
Pitman, Charles Edward, 1845–1933, vol. III
Pitman, Charles Murray, 1872–1948, vol. IV
Pitman, Captain Charles Robert Senhouse, 1890–1975, vol. VII
Pitman, Clement Fothergill, 1894–1973, vol. VII
Pitman, Edwin James George, 1897–1993, vol. IX
Pitman, Frederick Islay, 1863–1942, vol. IV
Pitman, Sir Henry Alfred, 1808–1908, vol. I
Pitman, Sir Hubert, 1901–1986, vol. VIII
Pitman, Sir (Isaac) James, 1901–1985, vol. VIII
Pitman, Sir James; see Pitman, Sir I. J.
Pitman, James Campbell; see Pitman, Hon. Lord.
Pitman, John Sitwell, 1860–1938, vol. III
Pitman, Captain Robert, 1836–1921, vol. II
Pitman, Maj.-Gen. Thomas Tait, 1868–1941, vol. IV
Pitt of Hampstead, Baron (Life Peer); David Thomas Pitt, 1913–1994, vol. IX
Pitt, Douglas F.; see Fox-Pitt.
Pitt, Dame Edith Maud, 1906–1966, vol. VI
Pitt, Frances, 1888–1964, vol. VI
Pitt, Captain Francis Joseph, 1840–1929, vol. III
Pitt, George Newton, 1853–1929, vol. III
Pitt, Henry Arthur, 1872–1955, vol. V
Pitt, Percy, 1870–1932, vol. III
Pitt, Col Robert Brindley, 1888–1974, vol. VII
Pitt, Captain Stanley Talbot Dean, 1853–1936, vol. III
Pitt, Terence John, 1937–1986, vol. VIII
Pitt, Col William, died 1933, vol. III
Pitt, Maj.-Gen. William Augustus Fitzgerald Lane F.; see Fox-Pitt.
Pitt-Kethley, Andrew Horace Victor, 1879–1955, vol. V
Pitt-Lewis, George, 1845–1906, vol. I
Pitt-Pitts, Ven. W. A., 1890–1940, vol. III
Pitt-Rivers, Augustus Henry Lane F.; see Fox-Pitt-Rivers.
Pitt-Rivers, George Henry Lane Fox, 1890–1966, vol. VI
Pitt-Rivers, Rosalind Venetia, 1907–1990, vol. VIII
Pitt-Taylor, Gen. Sir Walter William, 1878–1950, vol. IV
Pitt-Watson, Very Rev. James, 1893–1962, vol. VI
Pittam, Robert Raymond, 1919–1991, vol. IX
Pittar, Barry, 1880–1948, vol. IV
Pittar, Sir Thomas John, 1846–1924, vol. II
Pittendrigh, Rev. George, 1857–1930, vol. III
Pitter, Ruth, 1837–1992, vol. IX
Pitti, Sir Thyagaraya Chetti Garum, Diwan Bahadur, died 1925, vol. II, vol. III
Pittman, Osmund, 1874–1958, vol. V
Pittom, L(ois) Audrey, 1918–1990, vol. VIII
Pitts, Arthur Thomas, 1881–1939, vol. III
Pitts, Hon. James Stewart, 1847–1914, vol. I
Pitts, Captain Percy, 1876–1937, vol. III
Pitts, Thomas, 1857–1919, vol. II
Pitts, Rev. Thomas, died 1929, vol. III
Pitts, Ven. W. A. P.; see Pitt-Pitts.
Pitts, William Ewart, 1900–1980, vol. VII

Pitts-Chambers, Sir Newman; see Chambers.
Pitts-Tucker, Robert St John, 1909–1993, vol. IX
Pius X, His Holiness Pope, (Giuseppe Sarto), 1835–1914, vol. I
Pius XI, His Holiness Pope, (Achille Ambrogio Damiano Ratti), 1857–1939, vol. III
Piux XII, His Holiness Pope, (Eugene Pacelli), 1876–1958, vol. V
Pixley, Col Francis W., 1852–1933, vol. III
Pixley, Sir Neville Drake, 1905–1993, vol. IX
Pixley, Norman Stewart, 1898–1989, vol. IX(AI)
Pizey, Adm. Sir Charles Thomas Mark, 1899–1993, vol. IX
Place, Rear-Adm. Basil Charles Godfrey, 1921–1994, vol. IX
Place, Major (Charles) Godfrey (Morris), 1886–1931, vol. III
Place, Col Charles Otley, 1875–1955, vol. V
Place, Major Godfrey; see Place, Major C. G. M.
Placzek, Mrs A. K.; see Struther, Jan.
Plaidy, Jean; see Hibbert, Eleanor.
Plaister, Sir Sydney, 1909–1991, vol. IX
Plamenatz, John Petrov, 1912–1975, vol. VII
Planck, Max Karl Ernst Ludwig, 1858–1947, vol. IV
Plant, Baron (Life Peer); Cyril Thomas Howe Plant, 1910–1986, vol. VIII
Plant, Sir Arnold, 1898–1978, vol. VII
Plant, Edmund Carter, 1842–1902, vol. I
Plant, Maj.-Gen. Eric Clive Pegus, 1890–1950, vol. IV
Plant, George Frederick, 1877–1954, vol. V
Plant, Morton F., died 1918, vol. II
Plante, Mgr J. Omer, 1867–1948, vol. IV
Plarr, Victor Gustave, 1863–1929, vol. III
Plaskett, Harry Hemley, 1893–1980, vol. VII
Plaskett, John Stanley, 1865–1941, vol. IV
Platnauer, Maurice, 1887–1974, vol. VII
Platt, Baron (Life Peer); Robert Platt, 1900–1978, vol. VII
Platt, Benjamin Stanley, 1903–1969, vol. VI
Platt, Christopher; see Platt, D. C. M.
Platt, (Desmond) Christopher (Martin), 1934–1989, vol. VIII
Platt, Major Eric James Walter, 1871–1946, vol. IV
Platt, Comdr Francis Cuthbert, 1885–1941, vol. IV
Platt, Sir Frank, 1890–1955, vol. V
Platt, Sir (Frank) Lindsey, 2nd Bt (cr 1958), 1919–1998, vol. X
Platt, Rev. Frederic, 1859–1955, vol. V
Platt, Sir Harry, 1st Bt, 1886–1986, vol. VIII
Platt, Col Henry, 1842–1914, vol. I
Platt, J. Arthur, 1860–1925, vol. II
Platt, James Westlake, 1897–1972, vol. VII
Platt, Kenneth Harry, 1909–1985, vol. VIII
Platt, Sir Lindsey; see Platt, Sir F. L.
Platt, Hon. Sir Peter, 2nd Bt (cr 1959), 1924–2000, vol. X
Platt, Samuel R., died 1902, vol. I
Platt, Sir Thomas Comyn-, 1875–1961, vol. VI
Platt, Gen. Sir William, 1885–1975, vol. VII
Platt, Rev. William James, 1893–1993, vol. IX
Platt-Higgins, Frederick, 1840–1910, vol. I
Platts, Frederick William, 1865–1941, vol. IV
Platts, Col Matthew George, 1886–1969, vol. VI

Platts, Thomas, 1843–1919, vol. II
Platts, W. Carter, 1864–1944, vol. IV
Platzer, Wilfried, 1909–1981, vol. VIII
Plaxton, Ven. Cecil Andrew, 1902–1993, vol. IX
Player, Denis Sydney, 1913–1994, vol. IX
Playfair, 1st Baron, 1818–1898, vol. I
Playfair, 2nd Baron, 1849–1939, vol. III
Playfair, Maj.-Gen. Archibald Lewis, 1838–1915, vol. I
Playfair, Arthur Lambert, *died* 1939, vol. III
Playfair, Arthur Wyndham, 1869–1918, vol. II
Playfair, Sir Edward Wilder, 1909–1999, vol. X
Playfair, George Macdonald Home, 1850–1917, vol. II
Playfair, Maj.-Gen. Ian Stanley Ord, 1894–1972, vol. VII
Playfair, Hon. Lyon George Henry Lyon, 1888–1915, vol. I
Playfair, Sir Nigel, 1874–1934, vol. III
Playfair, Sir Patrick, 1852–1915, vol. I
Playfair, Air Marshal Sir Patrick Henry Lyon, 1889–1974, vol. VII
Playfair, Rev. Patrick M., 1858–1924, vol. II
Playfair, Sir Robert Lambert, 1828–1899, vol. I
Playfair, William Smoult, 1835–1903, vol. I
Playford, Hon. Thomas, 1837–1915, vol. I
Playford, Hon. Sir Thomas, 1896–1981, vol. VIII
Playne, Air Cdre Basil Alfred, 1885–1944, vol. IV
Pleasance, Donald, 1919–1995, vol. IX.
Pleass, Sir Clement John, 1901–1988, vol. VIII
Pledge, Henry, *died* 1949, vol. IV (A), vol. V
Pledge, Humphrey Thomas, 1903–1960, vol. V, vol. VI
Pleeth, William, 1916–1999, vol. X
Plender, 1st Baron, 1861–1946, vol. IV
Plender, Lady; (Mabel Agnes), *died* 1970, vol. VI
Plenderleath, Captain Claude William Manners, 1863–1937, vol. III
Plenderleith, Air Vice-Marshal Brian William, 1927–1978, vol. VII
Plenderleith, Harold James, 1898–1997, vol. X
Plenderleith, Thomas Donald, 1921–1995, vol. X(AI)
Pless, HSH Daisy, (Mary Theresa Olivia), Princess of, *died* 1943, vol. IV
Pleven, René Jean, 1901–1993, vol. IX
Pleydell, Lt-Col Edmund Morton M.; *see* Mansel-Pleydell.
Pleydell, John Clavell M.; *see* Mansel-Pleydell.
Pleydell, Rev. John Colvile Morton M.; *see* Mansel-Pleydell.
Pleydell-Bouverie, Rev. Hon. Bertrand, 1845–1926, vol. II
Pleydell-Bouverie, Hon. Duncombe, 1842–1909, vol. I
Pleydell-Bouverie, Col Hon. Stuart, 1877–1947, vol. IV
Pleydell-Railston, Lt-Col Henry George Moreton, 1885–1936, vol. III
Pliatzky, Sir Leo, 1919–1999, vol. X
Plimmer, Sir Clifford Ulric, 1905–1988, vol. VIII
Plimmer, Henry George, *died* 1918, vol. II
Plimmer, Robert Henry Aders, 1877–1955, vol. V
Plimsoll, Sir James, 1917–1987, vol. VIII

Plomer, William Charles Franklyn, 1903–1973, vol. VII
Plomer, Col William Harry Percival, 1861–1937, vol. III
Plomley, (Francis) Roy, 1914–1985, vol. VIII
Plomley, Roy; *see* Plomley, F. R.
Plow, Maj.-Gen. Hon. Edward Chester, 1904–1988, vol. VIII
Plowden, Lady, (Bridget Horatia Plowden), 1910–2000, vol. X
Plowden, Alfred Chichele, 1844–1914, vol. I
Plowden, Anna Bridget, 1938–1997, vol. X
Plowden, Brig. Bryan Edward Chicheley, 1892–1965, vol. VI
Plowden, Cecil Ward Chicheley, 1864–1944, vol. IV
Plowden, Lt-Col Charles Terence Chichele, 1883–1956, vol. V
Plowden, Sir Henry Meredyth, 1840–1920, vol. II
Plowden, Rear-Adm. Richard Anthony Aston, *died* 1941, vol. IV
Plowden, Roger Edmund Joseph, 1879–1946, vol. IV
Plowden, Sir Trevor John Chichele C.; *see* Chichele-Plowden.
Plowden, Sir William Chichele, 1832–1915, vol. I
Plowden, William Francis, 1853–1914, vol. I
Plowden-Wardlaw, Rev. James Tait, 1873–1963, vol. VI
Plowman, Sir Anthony; *see* Plowman, Sir J. A.
Plowman, Sir Claude, 1895–1954, vol. V
Plowman, Clifford Henry Fitzherbert, 1889–1948, vol. IV
Plowman, Sir George Thomas, 1858–1943, vol. IV
Plowman, Sir (John) Anthony, 1905–1993, vol. IX
Plowman, Mark, (Max Plowman), 1883–1941, vol. IV
Plowman, Max; *see* Plowman, Mark.
Plucknett, Theodore Frank Thomas, 1897–1965, vol. VI
Plugge, Lt-Col Arthur, 1878–1934, vol. III
Plugge, Captain Leonard Frank, 1889–1981, vol. VIII
Plumb, Rt Rev. C. E., 1864–1930, vol. III
Plumbe, William John Conway, 1910–1979, vol. VII
Plume, William Thomas, 1869–1962, vol. VI
Plumer, 1st Viscount, 1857–1932, vol. III
Plumer, 2nd Viscount, 1890–1944, vol. IV
Plumer, Hon. Eleanor Mary, 1885–1967, vol. VI
Plumley, Rev. Jack Martin, 1910–1999, vol. X
Plummer, Baroness (Life Peer); Beatrice Plummer, 1903–1972, vol. VII
Plummer, Rev. Alfred, 1841–1926, vol. II
Plummer, Alfred, 1896–1978, vol. VII
Plummer, Rev. Charles, 1851–1927, vol. II
Plummer, Charles Henry Scott, 1859–1948, vol. IV
Plummer, Sir Edgar Stroud, 1873–1940, vol. III
Plummer, Rev. Francis Bowes, 1851–1932, vol. III
Plummer, Henry Crozier, 1875–1946, vol. IV
Plummer, John Archibald Temple, 1877–1943, vol. IV
Plummer, Sir Leslie Arthur, 1901–1963, vol. VI
Plummer, Norman Swift, 1907–1978, vol. VII
Plummer, Sir Walter Richard, 1858–1917, vol. II

Plummer, William Edward, 1849–1928, vol. II
Plumptre, Adelaide M., (Mrs H. P. Plumptre), *died* 1948, vol. IV
Plumptre, Mrs H. P.; *see* Plumptre, A. M.
Plumptre, Reginald Charles Edward, 1848–1929, vol. III
Plumtree, Air Vice-Marshal Eric, 1919–1990, vol. VIII
Plunket, 5th Baron, 1864–1920, vol. II
Plunket, 6th Baron, 1899–1938, vol. III
Plunket, 7th Baron, 1923–1975, vol. VII
Plunket, Hon. and Most Rev. Benjamin J., 1870–1947, vol. IV
Plunket, Hon. Emmeline Mary, 1835–1924, vol. II
Plunkett, Brig.-Gen. Edward Abadie, 1870–1926, vol. II
Plunkett, Rt Hon. Sir Francis Richard, 1835–1907, vol. I
Plunkett, George Noble, Count, 1851–1948, vol. IV
Plunkett, Lt-Col George Tindall, 1842–1922, vol. II
Plunkett, Rt Hon. Sir Horace Curzon, 1854–1932, vol. III
Plunkett, Brig. James Joseph, 1893–1990, vol. VIII
Plunkett-Ernle-Erle-Drax, Adm. Hon. Sir Reginald Aylmer Ranfurly, 1880–1967, vol. VI
Plurenden, Baron (Life Peer); Rudy Sternberg, 1917–1978, vol. VII
Plymen, Francis Joseph, 1879–1960, vol. V
Plymouth, 1st Earl of, 1857–1923, vol. II
Plymouth, 2nd Earl of, 1889–1943, vol. IV
Po, Sir San Crombie, 1870–1946, vol. IV
Poananga, Maj.-Gen. Brian Matauru, 1924–1995, vol. IX
Poate, Sir Hugh Raymond Guy, 1884–1961, vol. VI
Pobedonosteff, Constantini Petrovitch, 1827–1907, vol. I
Pochin, Sir Edward Eric, 1909–1990, vol. VIII
Pochin, Horace Wilmer, 1903–1961, vol. VI
Pochin, Victor Robert, 1879–1972, vol. VII
Pochkhanawala, Sir Sorabji Nusserwanji, 1881–1937, vol. III
Pockley, Francis Antill, 1857–1941, vol. IV
Pocklington, Geoffrey Richard, 1879–1958, vol. V
Pocklington, Henry Cabourn, 1870–1952, vol. V
Pocock, Carmichael Charles Peter, (Michael Pocock), 1920–1979, vol. VII
Pocock, Sir Charles Guy Coventry, 4th Bt, 1863–1921, vol. II
Pocock, Childe, 1854–1934, vol. III
Pocock, Sir George Francis Coventry, 3rd Bt, 1830–1915, vol. I
Pocock, Guy Noël, 1880–1955, vol. V
Pocock, Col Herbert Innes, 1861–1947, vol. IV
Pocock, Hugh Shellshear, 1894–1987, vol. VIII
Pocock, Kenneth Walter, (Peter), 1913–2000, vol. X
Pocock, Michael; *see* Pocock, C. C. P.
Pocock, Peter; *see* Pocock, K. W.
Pocock, Most Rev. Philip Francis, 1906–1984, vol. VIII
Pocock, Brig. Philip Frederick, 1871–1941, vol. IV
Pocock, Reginald Innes, 1863–1947, vol. IV
Pocock, Captain Roger, 1865–1941, vol. IV
Pocock, Sir Sidney Job, 1855–1931, vol. III
Pode, Sir (Edward) Julian, 1902–1968, vol. VI
Pode, Sir Julian; *see* Pode, Sir E. J.

Podmore, Edward Boyce, 1860–1928, vol. II
Podmore, Frank, 1856–1910, vol. I
Poe, Adm. Sir Edmund Samuel, 1849–1921, vol. II
Poe, Lt-Col Sir Hutcheson; *see* Poe, Lt-Col Sir W. H.
Poe, Col John, 1873–1941, vol. IV
Poe, Lt-Col Sir (William) Hutcheson, 1st Bt, 1848–1934, vol. III
Poë, Col William Skeffington, 1878–1958, vol. V
Poë Domvile, Sir Hugo Compton Domvile, 2nd Bt, 1889–1959, vol. V
Poel, William, 1852–1934, vol. III
Poett, Maj.-Gen. Joseph Howard, 1858–1929, vol. III
Poett, Gen. Sir (Joseph Howard) Nigel, 1907–1991, vol. IX
Poett, Gen. Sir Nigel; *see* Poett, Gen. Sir. J. H. N.
Pogany, Willy, (William Andrew), 1882–1955, vol. V
Poincaré, Jules Henri, 1854–1912, vol. I
Poincaré, Raymond, 1860–1934, vol. III
Pointer, Joseph, 1875–1914, vol. I
Poire, Emmanuel; *see* D'Ache, Caran.
Poiret, Paul, 1879–1944, vol. IV
Poirier, Hon. Pascal, 1852–1932, vol. III
Polack, Rudolph, 1842–1917, vol. II
Poland, Rear-Adm. Allan, 1888–1984, vol. VIII
Poland, Vice-Adm. Sir Albert Lawrence, 1895–1967, vol. VI
Poland, Sir Harry Bodkin, 1829–1928, vol. II
Poland, Vice-Adm. James Augustus, 1832–1918, vol. II
Poland, John, 1855–1937, vol. III
Poland, Comdr John Roberts, 1893–1961, vol. VI
Polanyi, Michael, 1891–1976, vol. VII
Pole, Alexander Edward, 1848–1909, vol. I
Pole, Sir Cecil Pery Van Notten-, 4th Bt (*cr* 1791), 1863–1948, vol. IV
Pole, Major David Graham, *died* 1952, vol. V
Pole, Sir Edmund Reginald Talbot de la, 10th Bt (*cr* 1628), 1844–1912, vol. I
Pole, Sir Felix John Clewett, 1877–1956, vol. V
Pole, Sir Frederick Arundell de la, 11th Bt (*cr* 1628), 1850–1926, vol. II
Pole, Brig.-Gen. Harry Anthony C.; *see* Chandos-Pole.
Pole, Col Sir John Gawen C.; *see* Carew Pole.
Pole, Lt-Col John C.; *see* Chandos-Pole.
Pole, William, 1814–1900, vol. I
Pole-Evans, Illtyd Buller, 1879–1968, vol. VI
Poley, Thomas W.; *see* Weller-Poley.
Polhill, Rev. Arthur Twisleton, *died* 1935, vol. III
Polignano, 6th Duke of, 1835–1920, vol. II
Poling, Daniel Alfred, 1884–1968, vol. IV
Polk, Hon. Frank L., 1871–1943, vol. IV
Pollard, Alan Faraday Campbell, 1877–1948, vol. IV
Pollard, Albert Frederick, 1869–1948, vol. IV
Pollard, Captain Alfred Oliver, 1893–1960, vol. V (A), vol. VI (AI)
Pollard, Alfred William, 1859–1944, vol. IV
Pollard, Arthur Tempest, 1854–1934, vol. III
Pollard, Maj.-Gen. Barry; *see* Pollard, Maj.-Gen. C. B.
Pollard, Rt Rev. Benjamin, 1890–1967, vol. VI

Pollard, Bilton, 1855–1931, vol. III
Pollard, Lt-Gen. Charles, 1826–1911, vol. I
Pollard, Maj.-Gen. (Charles) Barry, 1927–2000, vol. X
Pollard, Paymaster Rear-Adm. Sir Charles Fleetwood, 1868–1938, vol. III
Pollard, Sir (Charles) Herbert, 1898–1990, vol. VIII
Pollard, Claude, died 1957, vol. V
Pollard, Rear-Adm. Edwin John, 1833–1909, vol. I
Pollard, Lt-Col George Chambers, died 1954, vol. V
Pollard, Sir George Herbert, 1864–1937, vol. III
Pollard, Rear-Adm. George Northmore Arthur, 1847–1920, vol. II
Pollard, Graham; see Pollard, H. G.
Pollard, (Henry) Graham, 1903–1976, vol. VII
Pollard, Sir Herbert; see Pollard, Sir C. H.
Pollard, Geoffrey Samuel, 1926–1985, vol. VIII
Pollard, Major Hugh B. C., died 1966, vol. VI
Pollard, Maj.-Gen. James Hawkins-Whitshed, 1866–1942, vol. IV
Pollard, Lt-Gen. Sir Reginald George, 1903–1978, vol. VII
Pollard, Sidney, 1925–1998, vol. X
Pollard-Lowsley, Col Herbert de Lisle, 1877–1936, vol. III
Pollard-Urquhart, Lt-Col Francis Edward Romulus, 1848–1915, vol. I
Pollen, Arthur Joseph Hungerford, 1866–1937, vol. III
Pollen, Captain Francis Gabriel Hungerford, 1862–1944, vol. IV
Pollen, Henry Court W.; see Willock-Pollen.
Pollen, John, 1848–1923, vol. II
Pollen, John Hungerford, 1820–1902, vol. I
Pollen, Rev. John Hungerford, 1858–1925, vol. II
Pollen, Sir John Launcelot Hungerford, 6th Bt, 1884–1959, vol. V
Pollen, Sir Richard, 5th Bt, 1878–1930, vol. III
Pollen, Sir Richard Hungerford, 4th Bt, 1846–1918, vol. II
Pollen, Lt-Col Stephen Hungerford, died 1935, vol. III
Pollen, Sir Walter Michael Hungerford, 1894–1968, vol. VI
Polley, Denis William, 1921–1983, vol. VIII
Pollitt, George Paton, 1878–1964, vol. VI
Pollitt, Gerald Paton, 1877–1943, vol. IV
Pollitt, Harry, 1890–1960, vol. V
Pollitt, Col Sir William, 1842–1908, vol. I
Pollitzer, Sir Frank Joseph Coleman, 1869–1944, vol. IV
Pollock, Sir Adrian Donald Wilde, 1867–1943, vol. IV
Pollock, Maj.-Gen. Arthur Jocelyn Coleman, 1891–1968, vol. VI
Pollock, Lt-Col Arthur Williamson Alsager, 1853–1923, vol. II
Pollock, Rt Rev. Bertram, 1863–1943, vol. IV
Pollock, Rev. Charles Archibald Edmund, 1858–1910, vol. IV
Pollock, Hon. Sir Charles Edward, 1823–1997, vol. I
Pollock, Maj.-Gen. Charles Edward, died 1929, vol. III

Pollock, Courtenay Edward Maxwell, died 1943, vol. IV
Pollock, David Linton, 1906–1991, vol. IX
Pollock, Hon. Surg. Comdr Sir Donald; see Pollock, Hon. Surg. Comdr Sir J. D.
Pollock, Sir Edward James, 1841–1930, vol. III
Pollock, Ellen Clara, 1902–1997, vol. IX
Pollock, Rt Hon. Sir Frederick, 3rd Bt (cr 1866), 1845–1937, vol. III
Pollock, Sir (Frederick) John, 4th Bt (cr 1866), 1878–1963, vol. VI
Pollock, Sir Frederick Richard, 1827–1899, vol. I
Pollock, Sir George, 1901–1991, vol. IX
Pollock, George Frederick, 1821–1915, vol. I
Pollock, Sir George Seymour Montagu-, 4th Bt, 1900–1985, vol. VIII
Pollock, Guy Cameron, 1878–1957, vol. V
Pollock, Harry Frederick, 1857–1901, vol. I
Pollock, Henry Brodhurst, 1883–1958, vol. V
Pollock, Hon. Sir Henry Edward, 1864–1953, vol. V
Pollock, Rev. Herbert Charles, 1852–1910, vol. I
Pollock, Rt Hon. Hugh McDowell, 1852–1937, vol. III
Pollock, J. Arthur, died 1922, vol. II
Pollock, James Edward, 1819–1910, vol. I
Pollock, James Huey Hamill, 1893–1982, vol. VIII
Pollock, Rev. Jeremy Taylor, 1850–1916, vol. II
Pollock, Sir John; see Pollock, Sir F. J.
Pollock, Lt-Col John Alsager, 1882–1941, vol. IV
Pollock, Maj.-Gen. John Archibald Henry, 1856–1949, vol. IV
Pollock, John Denton, 1926–1995, vol. IX
Pollock, Hon. Surg. Comdr Sir (John) Donald, 1st Bt (cr 1939), 1868–1962, vol. VI
Pollock, Martin Rivers, 1914–1999, vol. X
Pollock, Sir Montagu Frederick Montagu-, 3rd Bt (cr 1872), 1864–1938, vol. III
Pollock, Robert Erskine, 1849–1915, vol. I
Pollock, Sir Ronald Evelyn, 1891–1974, vol. VII
Pollock, Walter Herries, 1850–1926, vol. II
Pollock, William Barr Inglis, 1878–1953, vol. V
Pollock, Sir William Horace M.; see Montagu-Pollock.
Pollock, William Rivers, 1859–1909, vol. I
Pollok, Rev. Allan, 1829–1918, vol. II
Pollok, Maj.-Gen. Robert Valentine, 1884–1979, vol. VII
Pollok-M'Call, Brig.-Gen. John Buchanan, 1870–1951, vol. V
Pollok Morris, Col William, 1867–1936, vol. III
Polo de Bernabe, Don Luis, 1854–1929, vol. III
Polson, Cyril John, 1901–1986, vol. VIII
Polson, Milson George, 1917–1977, vol. VII
Polson, Col Sir Thomas Andrew, 1865–1946, vol. IV
Polson, Hon. Sir William John, 1875–1960, vol. V
Poltimore, 2nd Baron, 1837–1908, vol. I
Poltimore, 3rd Baron, 1859–1918, vol. II
Poltimore, 4th Baron, 1882–1965, vol. VI
Poltimore, 5th Baron, 1883–1967, vol. VI
Poltimore, 6th Baron, 1888–1978, vol. VII
Polunin, Nicholas, 1909–1997, vol. X
Polunin, Oleg, 1914–1985, vol. VIII
Polwarth, 8th (styled 6th) Lord, 1838–1920, vol. II
Polwarth, 9th Lord, 1864–1944, vol. IV

Polwarth, Master of; Hon. Walter Thomas Hepburne-Scott, 1890–1942, vol. IV
Polybe, *see* Reinach, Joseph.
Pomare, Hon. Sir Maui, 1876–1930, vol. III
Pomeroy, F. W., *died* 1924, vol. II
Pomfret, Surgeon Rear-Adm. Arnold Ashworth, 1900–1984, vol. VIII
Pompidou, Georges Jean Raymond, 1911–1974, vol. VII
Ponce, Don Ignacio G.; *see* Gutierrez-Ponce.
Poncet, André F.; *see* François-Poncet.
Pond, Sir Desmond Arthur, 1919–1986, vol. VIII
Pond, James Burton, 1838–1903, vol. I
Poniatowski, Prince Louis Leopold Charles Marie André, 1864–1954, vol. V
Pons, Lily, 1898–1976, vol. VII
Ponsford, Brian David, 1938–1989, vol. VIII
Ponsonby of Shulbrede, 1st Baron, 1871–1946, vol. IV
Ponsonby of Shulbrede, 2nd Baron, 1904–1976, vol. VII
Ponsonby of Shulbrede, 3rd Baron, 1930–1990, vol. VIII
Ponsonby, Arthur Gordon, 1892–1978, vol. VII
Ponsonby, Hon. Bertie Brabazon, 1885–1967, vol. VI
Ponsonby, Col Sir Charles Edward, 1st Bt, 1879–1976, vol. VII
Ponsonby, Hon. Cyril Myles Brabazon, 1881–1915, vol. I
Ponsonby, Hon. Edwin Charles William, 1851–1939, vol. III
Ponsonby, Sir George Arthur, 1878–1969, vol. VI
Ponsonby, Hon. Gerald, 1829–1908, vol. I
Ponsonby, Rev. Gordon; *see* Ponsonby, Rev. S. G.
Ponsonby, Brig. Henry Chambré, 1883–1953, vol. V
Ponsonby, Maj.-Gen. Sir John, 1866–1952, vol. V
Ponsonby, Col Justinian Gordon, *died* 1929, vol. III
Ponsonby, Rev. Maurice George Jesser, 1880–1943, vol. IV
Ponsonby, Myles Walter, 1924–1999, vol. X
Ponsonby, Noel Edward, 1891–1928, vol. II
Ponsonby, Rev. (Stewart) Gordon, *died* 1938, vol. III
Ponsonby, Thomas Brabazon, *died* 1946, vol. IV
Ponsonby, Captain William Rundall, 1874–1919, vol. II
Ponsonby-Fane, Rt Hon. Sir Spencer Cecil Brabazon, 1824–1915, vol. I
Pontecorvo, Guido, 1907–1999, vol. X
Pontifex, Sir Charles, 1831–1912, vol. I
Pontin, Sir Frederick William, (Sir Fred), 1906–2000, vol. X
Ponting, Herbert George, *died* 1935, vol. III
Ponting, Brig. Theophilus John, 1886–1972, vol. VII
Pontoppidan, Henrik, 1857–1943, vol. IV
Pontypridd, 1st Baron, 1840–1927, vol. II
Pool, Arthur George, 1905–1963, vol. VI
Pool, Augustus Frank, 1872–1955, vol. V
Pool, Bernard Frank, 1896–1977, vol. VII
Pool, William Arthur, 1889–1969, vol. VI
Poole, 1st Baron, 1911–1993, vol. IX
Poole, Brig.-Gen. Arthur James, 1872–1956, vol. V
Poole, Austin Lane, 1889–1963, vol. VI

Poole, Major Cecil Charles, 1902–1956, vol. V
Poole, Charles Edward L.; *see* Lane Poole.
Poole, Edgar Girard Croker, 1891–1940, vol. III
Poole, Ernest, 1880–1950, vol. IV (A), vol. V
Poole, Rev. Frederic John, 1852–1923, vol. II
Poole, Maj.-Gen. Sir Frederick Cuthbert, 1869–1936, vol. III
Poole, Lt-Gen. Gerald Robert, 1868–1937, vol. III
Poole, Granville, 1885–1962, vol. VI
Poole, Henry, 1873–1928, vol. II
Poole, Brig. Ivan Maxwell Conway, 1878–1963, vol. VI
Poole, Sir James, 1827–1903, vol. I
Poole, John Hewitt Jellett, 1893–1976, vol. VII
Poole, Rev. Canon Joseph Weston, 1909–1989, vol. VIII
Poole, Maj.-Gen. Leopold Thomas, 1888–1965, vol. VI
Poole, Sir Lionel Pinnock, 1894–1967, vol. VI
Poole, Reginald Lane, 1857–1939, vol. III
Poole, Sir Reginald Ward Edward Lane, 1864–1941, vol. IV
Poole, Vice-Adm. Sir Richard Hayden Owen L.; *see* Lane-Poole.
Poole, Stanley L.; *see* Lane-Poole.
Poole, Lt-Col Sir Thomas G., 1859–1937, vol. III
Poole, Hon. Thomas Slaney, 1873–1927, vol. II
Poole, Maj.-Gen. William Henry Evered, 1902–1969, vol. VI
Poole, Wordsworth, 1868–1902, vol. I
Poole Hughes, Rt Rev. John Richard Worthington, 1916–1988, vol. VIII
Poole-Hughes, Rev. W. Worthington, 1865–1928, vol. II
Pooler, Ven. Lewis Arthur, 1858–1924, vol. II
Pooley, Charles Blois, 1881–1938, vol. III
Pooley, Sir Ernest Henry, 1st Bt, 1876–1966, vol. VI
Pooley, Frederick Bernard, 1916–1998, vol. X
Poore, Dennis; *see* Poore, R. D.
Poore, Sir Edward, 5th Bt, 1894–1938, vol. III
Poore, Maj.-Gen. Francis Harwood, 1841–1928, vol. II
Poore, George Vivian, 1843–1904, vol. I
Poore, Adm. Sir Richard, 4th Bt, 1853–1930, vol. III
Poore, Brig.-Gen. Robert Montagu, 1866–1938, vol. III
Poore, Major Roger Alvin, 1870–1917, vol. II
Poore, Roger Dennistoun, (Dennis), 1916–1987, vol. VIII
Pope, Col Albert Augustus, 1843–1909, vol. I
Pope, Alfred, 1842–1934, vol. III
Pope, Andrew Lancelot, (Lance), 1912–1993, vol. IX
Pope, Arthur Upham, 1881–1969, vol. VI
Pope, Arthur William Uglow, 1858–1927, vol. II
Pope, Sir Barton; *see* Pope, Sir S. B.
Pope, Dudley Bernard Egerton, 1925–1997, vol. X
Pope, Lt-Col Edward Alexander, 1875–1919, vol. II
Pope, Sir Ernle; *see* Pope, Sir J. E.
Pope, Frank Aubrey, 1893–1962, vol. VI
Pope, Sir George Reginald, 1902–1982, vol. VIII
Pope, Rev. George Uglow, 1820–1908, vol. I
Pope, Col Harold, 1873–1938, vol. III

Pope, Rev. Henry John, 1836–1912, vol. I
Pope, Rev. Hugh, 1869–1946, vol. IV
Pope, James Alister, 1883–1954, vol. V
Pope, Jessie, (Mrs Babington Lenton), *died* 1941, vol. IV
Pope, Vice-Adm. Sir (John) Ernle, 1921–1998, vol. X
Pope, Rev. (John) Russell, 1909–1985, vol. VIII
Pope, John van Someren, 1850–1932, vol. III
Pope, Sir Joseph, 1854–1926, vol. II
Pope, Lance; *see* Pope, A. L.
Pope, Lt-Gen. Maurice Arthur, 1889–1978, vol. VII
Pope, Mildred Katherine, 1872–1956, vol. V
Pope, Col Philip Edward, 1842–1916, vol. II
Pope, Rev. Richard William Massy, 1849–1923, vol. II
Pope, Brig. Ronald James, 1924–1976, vol. VII
Pope, Rev. Russell; *see* Pope, Rev. J. R.
Pope, Samuel, 1826–1901, vol. I
Pope, Samuel, *died* 1935, vol. III
Pope, Sir (Sidney) Barton, 1905–1983, vol. VIII
Pope, Maj.-Gen. Sydney Buxton, 1879–1955, vol. V
Pope, Thomas Michael, 1875–1930, vol. III
Pope, Maj.-Gen. Vyvyan Vavasour, 1891–1941, vol. IV
Pope, Walter James M.; *see* Macqueen-Pope.
Pope, Sir William Jackson, 1870–1939, vol. III
Pope, Lt-Col William Wippell, 1857–1926, vol. II
Pope, Wilson, 1866–1953, vol. V
Pope-Hennessy, James, 1916–1974, vol. VII
Pope-Hennessy, Sir John Wyndham, 1913–1994, vol. IX
Pope-Hennessy, Maj.-Gen. Ladislaus Herbert Richard, 1875–1942, vol. IV
Pope-Hennessy, Dame Una, *died* 1949, vol. IV
Popham, Arthur Ewart, 1889–1970, vol. VI
Popham, Francis William L.; *see* Leyborne-Popham.
Popham, Sir Henry Bradshaw, 1881–1947, vol. IV
Popham, Air Chief Marshal Sir (Henry) Robert (Moore) Brooke-, 1878–1953, vol. V
Popham, Margaret Evelyn, 1894–1982, vol. VIII
Popham, Mervyn Reddaway, 1927–2000, vol. X
Popham, Air Chief Marshal Sir Robert Brooke-; *see* Popham, Air Chief Marshal Sir H. R. M. B.
Popham, Col Robert Stewart, 1876–1949, vol. IV
Popják, George Joseph, 1914–1998, vol. X
Popkess, Captain Athelstan, 1893–1967, vol. VI
Popper, Sir Karl Raimund, 1902–1994, vol. IX
Popplewell, Baron (Life Peer); Ernest Popplewell, 1899–1977, vol. VII
Popplewell, Patrick John Lyon, 1937–1983, vol. VIII
Porbandar, HH Maharaja of, 1901–1982, vol. VIII
Porcelli, Col Baron Alfred, 1849–1937, vol. III
Porcelli, Lt-Col Baron Ernest George Macdonald di S Andrea, 1886–1965, vol. VI
Porch, Col Edward Albert, 1879–1937, vol. III
Porcher, Michael Somerville, 1921–1994, vol. IX
Porges, Waldo William, 1899–1976, vol. VII
Porral, Albert, 1846–1918, vol. II
Porritt, Baron (Life Peer); Arthur Espie Porritt, 1900–1994, vol. IX
Porritt, Arthur, 1872–1947, vol. IV
Porritt, Lt-Col Austin Townsend, 1875–1956, vol. V
Porritt, Benjamin Dawson, 1884–1940, vol. III

Porritt, Edward, 1860–1921, vol. II
Porritt, Captain Richard W., 1910–1940, vol. III
Portal, 1st Viscount, 1885–1949, vol. IV
Portal of Hungerford, 1st Viscount, 1893–1971, vol. VII
Portal of Hungerford, Baroness (2nd in line), 1923–1990, vol. VIII
Portal, Brig.-Gen. Sir Bertram Percy, 1866–1949, vol. IV
Portal, Sir Francis Spencer, 5th Bt, 1903–1984, vol. VIII
Portal, Melville, 1819–1904, vol. I
Portal, Adm. Sir Reginald Henry, 1894–1983, vol. VIII
Portal, Sir Spencer John, 4th Bt, 1864–1955, vol. V
Portal, Sir William Wyndham, 2nd Bt, 1850–1931, vol. III
Portal, Sir Wyndham Spencer, 1st Bt, 1822–1905, vol. I
Portarlington, 5th Earl of, 1858–1900, vol. I
Portarlington, 6th Earl of, 1883–1959, vol. V
Portelli, Rt Rev. Angelo, *born* 1852, vol. II
Porteous, Alexander, 1855–1932, vol. III
Porteous, Alexander James Dow, 1896–1981, vol. VIII
Porteous, Col Charles Arkcoll, 1839–1929, vol. III
Porteous, Douglas Archibald, 1891–1974, vol. VII
Porteous, Lt-Col John James, 1857–1948, vol. IV
Porteous, Norman, 1881–1940, vol. III
Porteous, Col Patrick Anthony, 1918–2000, vol. X
Porter, Baron (Life Peer); Samuel Lowry Porter, 1877–1956, vol. V
Porter, Surg.-Col Alexander, 1841–1918, vol. II
Porter, Sir Alexander, 1853–1926, vol. II
Porter, Sir Alfred de Bock, 1840–1908, vol. I
Porter, Alfred Ernest, 1896–1987, vol. VIII
Porter, Rev. Alfred Stephenson, 1841–1914, vol. I
Porter, Alfred William, 1863–1939, vol. III
Porter, Rt Hon. Sir Andrew Marshall, 1st Bt (*cr* 1902), 1837–1919, vol. II
Porter, Annie, (Mrs H. B. Fantham), *died* 1963, vol. VI
Porter, Barry; *see* Porter, G. B.
Porter, Cecil George, 1887–1938, vol. III
Porter, Air Vice-Marshal Cedric Ernest Victor, 1893–1975, vol. VII
Porter, Charles, 1873–1952, vol. V
Porter, Rev. Charles Fleetwood, 1830–1914, vol. I
Porter, Cole, 1893–1964, vol. VI
Porter, Brig.-Gen. Cyril Lachlan, 1872–1951, vol. V
Porter, Rt Rev. David Brownfield, 1906–1993, vol. IX
Porter, Dorothea Noelle Naomi, (Thea), 1927–2000, vol. X
Porter, Edward, 1880–1960, vol. V
Porter, Edward Guss, 1859–1929, vol. III
Porter, Eric Richard, 1928–1995, vol. IX
Porter, Frederick, 1871–1949, vol. IV (A)
Porter, Gene Stratton-, 1868–1924, vol. II
Porter, Col Geoffrey M., 1854–1944, vol. IV
Porter, George, 1884–1973, vol. VII
Porter, George Barrington, (Barry), 1939–1996, vol. X

Porter, Sir George Swinburne, 3rd Bt (*cr* 1889), 1908–1974, vol. VII
Porter, Sir Haldane; *see* Porter, Sir W. H.
Porter, Harold, 1879–1938, vol. III
Porter, Sir Harry Edwin Bruce B.; *see* Bruce-Porter.
Porter, Helen Kemp, 1899–1987, vol. VIII
Porter, Major Herbert Alfred, 1872–1939, vol. III (A), vol. IV
Porter, Rev. James, *died* 1900, vol. I
Porter, Sir James, *died* 1935, vol. III
Porter, John, 1838–1922, vol. II
Porter, John Bonsall, 1861–1944, vol. IV
Porter, Maj.-Gen. John Edmund L.; *see* Leech-Porter.
Porter, John Fletcher, 1873–1927, vol. II
Porter, Captain John Grey Archdale, 1886–1917, vol. II
Porter, John Porter, 1855–1939, vol. III
Porter, Sir John Scott Horsbrugh-, 2nd Bt (*cr* 1902), 1871–1953, vol. V
Porter, Joseph William Geoffrey, 1920–1983, vol. VIII
Porter, Katherine Anne, 1890–1980, vol. VII
Porter, Keith Ridley Douglas, 1913–1977, vol. VII
Porter, Sir Leslie Alexander Selim, 1854–1932, vol. III
Porter, Sir Ludovic Charles, 1869–1928, vol. II
Porter, Hon. Sir Murray Victor, 1909–1993, vol. IX
Porter, Sir Neale, *died* 1905, vol. I
Porter, Raymond Alfred James, 1896–1988, vol. VIII
Porter, Major Reginald Whitworth, *died* 1902, vol. I
Porter, Maj.-Gen. Sir Robert, 1858–1928, vol. II
Porter, Sir Robert Evelyn, 1913–1983, vol. VIII
Porter, Robert P., 1852–1917, vol. II
Porter, Rev. Robert Waltham, *died* 1927, vol. II
Porter, Rodney Robert, 1917–1985, vol. VIII
Porter, Rose Henniker, (Mrs Adrian Porter); *see* Heaton, R. H.
Porter, Rt Hon. Samuel Clarke, 1875–1956, vol. V
Porter, Stanley; *see* Porter, W. S.
Porter, Thea; *see* Porter, D. N. N.
Porter, Brig.-Gen. Thomas Cole, 1851–1938, vol. III
Porter, Thomas Cunningham, 1860–1933, vol. III
Porter, Col Thomas William, 1844–1920, vol. II
Porter, (Walter) Stanley, 1909–2000, vol. X
Porter, Sir (William) Haldane, 1867–1944, vol. IV
Porter, Sir William Henry, 2nd Bt (*cr* 1889), 1862–1935, vol. III
Porter, William Ninnis, *died* 1929, vol. III
Porter, William Smith, 1855–1927, vol. II
Porter, Hon. William Thomas, 1877–1928, vol. II
Porter Goff, Eric Noel; *see* Goff.
Porter-Phillips, John George, *died* 1946, vol. IV
Porteus, Rev. Canon Thomas Cruddas, 1876–1948, vol. IV
Portland, 6th Duke of, 1857–1943, vol. IV
Portland, 7th Duke of, 1893–1977, vol. VII
Portland, 8th Duke of, 1888–1980, vol. VIII
Portland, 9th Duke of, 1897–1990, vol. VIII
Portland, 11th Earl of, 1919–1997, vol. X
Portlock, Rear-Adm. Ronald Etridge, 1908–1983, vol. VIII
Portman, 2nd Viscount, 1829–1919, vol. II

Portman, 3rd Viscount, 1860–1923, vol. II
Portman, 4th Viscount, 1864–1929, vol. III
Portman, 5th Viscount, 1898–1942, vol. IV
Portman, 6th Viscount, 1868–1946, vol. IV
Portman, 7th Viscount, 1875–1948, vol. IV
Portman, 8th Viscount, 1903–1967, vol. VI
Portman, 9th Viscount, 1934–1999, vol. X
Portman, Hon. Edward William Berkeley, 1856–1911, vol. I
Portman, Hon. Edwin Berkeley, 1830–1921, vol. II
Portman, Eric, 1903–1969, vol. VI
Portman, Guy Maurice Berkeley, 1890–1961, vol. VI
Portman-Dalton, Seymour Berkeley, 1838–1912, vol. I
Porto-Riche, Georges de, 1849–1930, vol. III
Portsea, 1st Baron, 1860–1948, vol. IV
Portsmouth, 6th Earl of, 1856–1917, vol. II
Portsmouth, 7th Earl of, 1859–1925, vol. II
Portsmouth, 8th Earl of, 1861–1943, vol. IV
Portsmouth, 9th Earl of, 1898–1984, vol. VIII
Portsmouth, Percy, 1874–1953, vol. V
Portway, Col Donald, 1887–1979, vol. VII
Poskitt, Frederick Richard, 1900–1983, vol. VIII
Poskitt, Rt Rev. Henry John, 1888–1950, vol. IV
Post, Emily, (Mrs Price Post), *died* 1960, vol. V
Post, Col Kenneth Graham, 1908–1998, vol. X
Post, Mrs Price; *see* Post, Emily.
Post, Rear-Adm. Simon Edward, 1910–1965, vol. VI
Postan, Sir Michael Moïssey, 1899–1981, vol. VIII
Postgate, John Percival, 1853–1926, vol. II
Postgate, Raymond William, 1896–1971, vol. VII
Postgate, Richard Seymour, 1908–1991, vol. IX
Postill, Ronald, 1907–1980, vol. VII
Postlethwaite, John Rutherfoord Parkin, 1883–1956, vol. V
Potez, Andrew Louis, 1920–1977, vol. VII
Po Tha, Sir Maung, *died* 1933, vol. III
Pothecary, Major Walter Frank, 1882–1958, vol. V
Potier, Gilbert George, 1915–1969, vol. VI
Pott, Anthony Percivall, 1904–1963, vol. VI
Pott, Col Douglas, 1888–1974, vol. VII
Pott, Francis Lister Hawks, 1864–1947, vol. IV
Pott, Sir (George) Stanley, 1870–1951, vol. V
Pott, Gladys Sydney, 1867–1961, vol. VI
Pott, H(enry) Percivall, 1908–1964, vol. VI
Pott, Rear-Adm. Herbert, 1886–1945, vol. IV
Pott, Sir Leslie, 1903–1985, vol. VIII
Pott, Sir Stanley; *see* Pott, Sir G. S.
Potter, Sir Alan Graeme, 1891–1969, vol. VI
Potter, Albert Knight, 1864–1948, vol. IV
Potter, Arthur Kingscote, 1905–1998, vol. X
Potter, Beatrice; *see* Webb, Mrs Sidney.
Potter, Ven. Beresford, 1853–1931, vol. III
Potter, Carlyle Thornton, *died* 1962, vol. VI
Potter, Lt-Col Claud Furniss, 1881–1965, vol. VI
Potter, Col Colin Kynaston, 1877–1964, vol. VI
Potter, Cora Urquhart, *died* 1936, vol. III
Potter, Cyril H., 1877–1941, vol. IV
Potter, David Morris, 1910–1971, vol. VII
Potter, Dennis Christopher George, 1935–1994, vol. IX
Potter, Douglas Charles Loftus, 1903–1983, vol. VIII

Potter, Frank, 1856–1919, vol. II
Potter, Frederick Felix, 1882–1955, vol. V
Potter, George Richard, 1900–1981, vol. VIII
Potter, Harold, 1896–1951, vol. V
Potter, Rt Rev. Henry Codman, 1834–1908, vol. I
Potter, Sir Henry Steven, 1904–1976, vol. VII
Potter, Brig.-Gen. Herbert Cecil, 1875–1964, vol. VI
Potter, Howard Vincent, 1888–1970, vol. VI (AII)
Potter, Sir Ian; see Potter, Sir W. I.
Potter, Mrs J. Brown; see Potter, Cora Urquhart.
Potter, Lt-Col James Archer, 1875–1962, vol. VI
Potter, Jeremy; see Potter, R. J.
Potter, John, 1873–1940, vol. III
Potter, John Alexander, 1851–1929, vol. III
Potter, Rev. John Hasloch, 1847–1935, vol. III
Potter, Sir (Joseph) Raymond (Lynden), 1916–1993, vol. IX
Potter, Marian Anderson, (Mary), 1900–1981, vol. VIII
Potter, Mrs Mary; see Potter, Marian A.
Potter, Rev. Michael Cressé, 1858–1948, vol. IV
Potter, Air Marshal Sir Patrick Brunton L.; see Lee Potter.
Potter, Sir Raymond; see Potter, Sir J. R. L.
Potter, Rev. Reginald Joseph William Henry, 1877–1941, vol. IV
Potter, Ven. Richard Harry, 1861–1931, vol. III
Potter, (Ronald) Jeremy, 1922–1997, vol. X
Potter, Rupert Barnadiston, 1899–1970, vol. VI
Potter, Simeon, 1898–1976, vol. VII
Potter, Stephen, 1900–1969, vol. VI
Potter, Thomas Bayley, 1817–1898, vol. I
Potter, Timothy William, 1944–2000, vol. X
Potter, Col William Allen, died 1953, vol. V
Potter, Sir (William) Ian, 1902–1994, vol. IX
Pottinger, Lt-Gen. Brabazon Henry, 1840–1913, vol. I
Pottinger, David, 1843–1938, vol. III
Pottinger, Don; see Pottinger, J. I. D.
Pottinger, Lt-Col Eldred Thomas, 1840–1905, vol. I
Pottinger, George; see Pottinger, W. G.
Pottinger, Sir Henry, 3rd Bt, 1834–1909, vol. I
Pottinger, John Inglis Drever, (Don Pottinger), 1919–1986, vol. VIII
Pottinger, Lt-Col Robert Southey, 1870–1943, vol. IV
Pottinger, (William) George, 1916–1998, vol. X
Pottle, Frederick Albert, 1897–1987, vol. VIII
Potts, Archie, 1914–1991, vol. IX
Potts, Lt-Col Edmund Thurlow, 1878–1948, vol. IV
Potts, Edward Logan Johnston, 1915–1984, vol. VIII
Potts, Brig.-Gen. Frederick, 1866–1945, vol. IV
Potts, George, 1877–1948, vol. IV
Potts, John, died 1938, vol. III
Potts, Kenneth Hampson, 1921–1990, vol. VIII
Potts, Peter, 1935–1996, vol. X
Potts, Thomas Edmund, 1908–1993, vol. IX
Potts, William Alexander, 1866–1939, vol. III
Pouishnoff, Leff, 1891–1959, vol. V
Poulenc, Francis, 1899–1963, vol. VI
Poulett, 6th Earl, 1827–1899, vol. I
Poulett, 7th Earl, 1883–1918, vol. II
Poulett, 8th Earl, 1909–1973, vol. VII

Pouliot, Joseph Camille, 1865–1935, vol. III
Poultney, Alfred Henry, died 1906, vol. I
Poulton, Lt-Col Arthur Faulconer, 1858–1935, vol. III
Poulton, Sir Edward Bagnall, 1856–1943, vol. IV
Poulton, Edward Lawrence, 1865–1937, vol. III
Poulton, Edward Palmer, 1883–1939, vol. III
Poulton, Elgan Nathaniel George, 1881–1944, vol. IV
Poulton, Lt-Col Henry Mortimer, 1898–1973, vol. VII
Poulton, Rev. Canon John Frederick, 1925–1987, vol. VIII
Pouncey, Denys Duncan Rivers, 1906–1999, vol. X
Pouncey, Philip Michael Rivers, 1910–1990, vol. VIII
Pound, Admiral of the Fleet Sir (Alfred) Dudley (Pickman Rogers), 1877–1943, vol. IV
Pound, Sir Allen Leslie, 3rd Bt, 1888–1952, vol. V
Pound, Sir Derek Allen, 4th Bt, 1920–1980, vol. VII
Pound, Admiral of the Fleet Sir Dudley; see Pound, Admiral of the Fleet Sir A. D. P. R.
Pound, Ezra Weston Loomis, 1885–1972, vol. VII
Pound, Sir John, 1st Bt, 1829–1915, vol. I
Pound, Sir (John) Lulham, 2nd Bt, 1862–1937, vol. III
Pound, Sir Lulham; see Pound, Sir J. L.
Pound, Roscoe, 1870–1964, vol. VI
Pounder, Rafton John, 1933–1991, vol. IX
Pounds, Charles Courtice, 1862–1927, vol. II
Pounsett, Clement Aubrey, 1900–1968, vol. VI
Pountney, Arthur Meek, 1873–1940, vol. III
Povah, Rev. John Walter, 1883–1961, vol. VI
Powditch, Alan Cecil Robert, 1912–1997, vol. X
Powel, Thomas, 1845–1922, vol. II
Powell, Agnes B.; see Baden-Powell.
Powell, Alan Richard, 1894–1975, vol. VII
Powell, Sir Allan; see Powell, Sir G. A.
Powell, Anthony Dymoke, 1905–2000, vol. X
Powell, Rev. Canon Arnold Cecil, 1882–1963, vol. VI
Powell, Arthur, 1864–1926, vol. II
Powell, Arthur, 1853–1930, vol. III
Powell, Arthur Barrington, 1918–1995, vol. IX
Powell, Arthur Geoffrey, 1915–1982, vol. VIII
Powell, Rev. Astell Drayner, 1851–1934, vol. III
Powell, Col Atherton Ffolliott, 1858–1941, vol. IV
Powell, Major Baden Fletcher Smyth B.; see Baden-Powell.
Powell, Baden Henry B.; see Baden-Powell.
Powell, Cecil Frank, 1903–1969, vol. VI
Powell, Maj.-Gen. Sir Charles Herbert, 1857–1943, vol. IV
Powell, Ven. Dacre Hamilton, 1843–1912, vol. I
Powell, David, 1914–1995, vol. IX
Powell, Lt-Col David Watson, 1878–1935, vol. III
Powell, Dilys; see Powell, E. D.
Powell, Brig. Donald, 1896–1942, vol. IV
Powell, Lt-Col Sir Douglas, 2nd Bt (cr 1897), 1874–1932, vol. III
Powell, E. Alexander, 1879–1957, vol. V
Powell, Rt Rev. Edmund Nathanael, 1859–1928, vol. II
Powell, Edward, 1907–1982, vol. VIII

Powell, Brig.-Gen. Edward Weyland Martin, 1869–1954, vol. V
Powell, (Elizabeth) Dilys, 1901–1995, vol. IX
Powell, Ellis Thomas, 1869–1922, vol. II
Powell, Rt Hon. Enoch; see Powell, Rt Hon. J. E.
Powell, Lt-Col Evelyn George Harcourt, 1883–1961, vol. VI
Powell, Sir Francis, 1833–1914, vol. I
Powell, Adm. Sir Francis, 1849–1927, vol. II
Powell, Francis Edward, died 1938, vol. III
Powell, Sir Francis Sharp, 1st Bt (cr 1892), 1827–1911, vol. I
Powell, Frank John, 1891–1971, vol. VII
Powell, Frank Smyth B.; see Baden-Powell.
Powell, Frederick York, 1850–1904, vol. I
Powell, Geoffrey Charles Hamilton, 1920–1999, vol. X
Powell, Sir (George) Allan, died 1948, vol. IV
Powell, Vice-Adm. George Bingham, 1871–1952, vol. V
Powell, George Herbert, 1856–1924, vol. II
Powell, Sir George Smyth B.; see Baden-Powell.
Powell, Gillian Margot, 1934–1989, vol. VIII
Powell, Rt Rev. Grandage Edwards, 1882–1948, vol. IV
Powell, Harry Allan Rose, (Tim), 1912–1993, vol. IX
Powell, Helena Langhorne, 1862–1942, vol. IV
Powell, Henry Arthur, 1868–1944, vol. IV
Powell, Col Henry Lloyd, 1866–1941, vol. IV
Powell, Herbert Marcus, 1906–1991, vol. IX
Powell, Rear-Adm. James, 1887–1971, vol. VII
Powell, Col James Leslie Grove, 1853–1925, vol. II
Powell, Col John, 1876–1936, vol. III
Powell, Lt-Col John, 1856–1938, vol. III
Powell, Gp-Captain John Alexander, 1909–1944, vol. IV
Powell, John Alfred, 1923–1996, vol. X
Powell, Rt Hon. John Blake, died 1923, vol. II
Powell, Rt Hon. (John) Enoch, 1912–1998, vol. X
Powell, Lawrence Fitzroy, 1881–1975, vol. VII
Powell, Sir Leonard; see Powell, Sir R. L.
Powell, Lewis Franklin, Jr, 1907–1998, vol. X
Powell, Llewelyn, 1870–1934, vol. III
Powell, Michael Latham, 1905–1990, vol. VIII
Powell, Rev. Morgan Jones, 1863–1947, vol. IV
Powell, Dame Muriel, 1914–1978, vol. VII
Powell, Percival Herbert, died 1958, vol. V
Powell, Lt-Col Philip Lionel William, 1882–1959, vol. V
Powell, Raphael, 1904–1965, vol. VI
Powell, Ray Edwin, 1887–1973, vol. VII
Powell, Richard, 1889–1961, vol. VI
Powell, Richard Albert Brakell, 1892–1957, vol. V
Powell, Sir Richard Douglas, 1st Bt (cr 1897), 1842–1925, vol. II
Powell, Major Sir Richard George Douglas, 3rd Bt (cr 1897), 1909–1980, vol. VII
Powell, Robert Lane B.; see Bayne-Powell.
Powell, Sir (Robert) Leonard, 1853–1938, vol. III
Powell, Robert William, 1909–1998, vol. X
Powell, Roger, 1896–1990, vol. VIII
Powell, Ronald Arthur, 1888–1966, vol. VI
Powell, Samuel M.; see Morgan-Powell.
Powell, Sidney, 1894–1964, vol. VI

Powell, Maj.-Gen. Sidney Henry, 1866–1945, vol. IV
Powell, Tim; see Powell, H. A. R.
Powell, Victor George Edward, 1929–1997, vol. X
Powell, Warington B.; see Baden-Powell.
Powell, Lt-Col William Bowen, 1868–1940, vol. III
Powell, Rev. William Hawkshaw, 1842–1930, vol. III
Powell, Col William Jackson, 1881–1961, vol. VI
Powell-Cotton, Percy Horace Gordon, 1866–1940, vol. III
Powell-Price, John Cadwgan, 1888–1964, vol. VI
Power, Sir Adam Clayton, 6th Bt (cr 1836), 1844–1903, vol. I
Power, Albert G., 1883–1945, vol. IV
Power, Admiral of the Fleet Sir Arthur John, 1889–1960, vol. V
Power, Vice-Adm. Sir Arthur Mackenzie, 1921–1984, vol. VIII
Power, Beryl Millicent le Poer, 1891–1974, vol. VII
Power, Charles Gavan, 1888–1968, vol. VI
Power, Sir D'Arcy, 1855–1941, vol. IV
Power, Air Vice-Marshal d'Arcy, 1889–1958, vol. V
Power, Eileen, 1889–1940, vol. III
Power, Sir Elliott Derrick le Poer, 5th Bt (cr 1836), 1872–1902, vol. I
Power, Eugene Barnum, 1905–1993, vol. IX
Power, Sir George, 7th Bt (cr 1836), 1846–1928, vol. II
Power, Ven. George Edmund, died 1950, vol. IV (A), vol. V
Power, Gerald, 1891–1967, vol. VI
Power, Lt-Col Gervase Bushe, 1883–1974, vol. VII
Power, Harold Septimus, died 1951, vol. V
Power, Henry, died 1911, vol. I
Power, Hubert, born 1860, vol. II
Power, Sir Ivan McLannahan Cecil, 2nd Bt (cr 1924), 1903–1954, vol. V
Power, Sir James Douglas Talbot, 4th Bt (cr 1841), 1884–1914, vol. I
Power, Sir James Talbot, 5th Bt (cr 1841), 1851–1916, vol. II
Power, Sir John Cecil, 1st Bt (cr 1924), 1870–1950, vol. IV
Power, John Danvers, 1858–1927, vol. II
Power, Sir John Elliott Cecil, 4th Bt (cr 1836), 1870–1900, vol. I
Power, Sir John Patrick McLannahan, 3rd Bt, (cr 1924), 1928–1984, vol. VIII
Power, Sir John Talbot, 3rd Bt (cr 1841), 1845–1901, vol. I
Power, Mrs (John) Wyse, died 1941, vol. IV
Power, Adm. Sir Laurence Eliot, 1864–1927, vol. II
Power, Hon. Lawrence Geoffrey, 1841–1921, vol. II
Power, Adm. Sir Manley Laurence, 1904–1981, vol. VIII
Power, Rev. Patrick, 1862–1951, vol. V
Power, Patrick Joseph, 1850–1913, vol. I
Power, Patrick Joseph Mahon, 1826–1913, vol. I
Power, Sir Samuel Murray, 1863–1933, vol. III
Power, Gen. Thomas Sarsfield, 1905–1970, vol. VI
Power, Sir Thomas Talbot, 6th Bt (cr 1841), 1863–1930, vol. III
Power, William, 1873–1951, vol. V

Power, Sir William Henry, 1842–1916, vol. II
Power, Sir William Richard, 1861–1945, vol. IV
Power, Major William Sayer, 1859–1940, vol. III
Power, Mrs Wyse; see Power, Mrs John W.
Powers, Hon. Sir Charles, 1853–1939, vol. III
Powers, George Wightman, 1864–1932, vol. III
Powerscourt, 7th Viscount, 1836–1904, vol. I
Powerscourt, 8th Viscount, 1880–1947, vol. IV
Powerscourt, 9th Viscount, 1905–1973, vol. VII
Powicke, Frederick James, 1854–1935, vol. III
Powicke, Sir (Frederick) Maurice, 1879–1963,
    vol. VI
Powicke, Sir Maurice; see Powicke, Sir F. M.
Powis, 4th Earl of, 1862–1952, vol. V
Powis, 5th Earl of, 1889–1974, vol. VII
Powis, 6th Earl of, 1904–1988, vol. VIII
Powis, 7th Earl of, 1925–1993, vol. IX
Powles, Col (Charles) Guy, 1872–1951, vol. V
Powles, Col Guy; see Powles, Col C. G.
Powles, Sir Guy Richardson, 1905–1994, vol. IX
Powles, Lewis Charles, 1860–1942, vol. IV
Powlett, Adm. Armund Temple, 1841–1925, vol. II
Powlett, Vice-Adm. Frederick Armand, 1873–1963,
    vol. VI
Powlett, Col Percy William, 1837–1910, vol. I
Powlett, Vice-Adm. Sir Peveril Barton Reibey
    Wallop W.; see William-Powlett.
Powlett, Rear-Adm. Philip Frederick, 1906–1991,
    vol. IX
Powley, Albert E., 1868–1937, vol. III
Powley, Edward B., 1887–1968, vol. VI
Pownall, Lt-Col Sir Assheton, 1877–1953, vol. V
Pownall, Adm. Charles Pipon B.; see
    Beaty-Pownall.
Pownall, George Henry, 1850–1916, vol. II
Pownall, Lt-Gen. Sir Henry Royds, 1887–1961,
    vol. VI
Pownall, John Cecil Glossop, 1891–1967, vol. VI
Pownall, Mary, died 1937, vol. III
Powter, John, 1881–1930, vol. III
Powys, Albert Reginad, 1881–1936, vol. III
Powys, John Cowper, 1872–1963, vol. VI
Powys, Llewelyn, 1884–1939, vol. III
Powys, Theodore Francis, died 1953, vol. V
Powys-Jones, Lionel, 1894–1966, vol. VI
Powys-Keck, Thomas Charles Leycester, 1871–1931,
    vol. III
Poy; see Fearon, Percy Hutton.
Poynder, Lt-Col Frederic Sinclair, 1893–1943,
    vol. IV
Poynter, Sir Ambrose Macdonald, 2nd Bt,
    1867–1923, vol. II
Poynter, Sir Edward John, 1st Bt, 1836–1919,
    vol. II
Poynter, (Frederick) Noel (Lawrence), 1908–1979,
    vol. VII
Poynter, Sir Hugh Edward, 3rd Bt, 1882–1968,
    vol. VI
Poynter, Noel; see Poynter, F. N. L.
Poynting, John Henry, 1852–1914, vol. I
Poynton, Hon. Alexander, 1853–1935, vol. III
Poynton, Arthur Blackburne, 1867–1944, vol. IV
Poynton, Sir (Arthur) Hilton, 1905–1996, vol. X
Poynton, Frederic John, 1869–1943, vol. IV
Poynton, Sir Hilton; see Poynton, Sir A. H.

Poyntz, Rev. Newdigate, 1842–1931, vol. III
Poyser, Sir (Arthur Hampden) Ronald (Wastell),
    1884–1957, vol. V
Poyser, Arthur Horatio, 1849–1923, vol. II
Poyser, Sir Kenneth Elliston, died 1943, vol. IV
Poyser, Col Richard, 1842–1919, vol. II
Poyser, Sir Ronald; see Poyser, Sir A. H. R. W.
Pozzi, Jean Samuel, 1849–1918, vol. II
Pozzoni, Mgr Dominico, 1861–1924, vol. II
Pradhan, Sir Govindrao Balwantrao, 1874–1943,
    vol. IV
Praed, Sir Herbert Bulkley Mackworth-, 1st Bt,
    1841–1921, vol. II
Praed, Rosa Caroline Mackworth, 1851–1935,
    vol. III
Praeger, Robert Lloyd, 1865–1953, vol. V
Praeger, S. Rosamond, died 1954, vol. V
Praga, Alfred, died 1949, vol. IV
Pragnell, Sir George, 1863–1916, vol. II
Pragnell, Col Thomas Wykeham, 1883–1957,
    vol. V
Prain, Alexander Moncur, 1908–1989, vol. VIII
Prain, Lt-Col Sir David, 1857–1944, vol. IV
Prain, John Murray, 1902–1985, vol. VIII
Prain, Sir Ronald Lindsay, 1907–1991, vol. IX
Prain, Vyvyen Alice, 1895–1983, vol. VIII
Prance, Basil Camden, 1884–1948, vol. IV
Prance, Brig. Robert Courtnay, 1882–1966, vol. VI
Prang, Louis, 1824–1909, vol. I
Prasad, Ganesh, 1876–1935, vol. III
Prasad, Jagat, 1879–1957, vol. V
Prasad, Sir Jwala, 1875–1933, vol. III
Prasad, Rajendra, 1884–1963, vol. VI
Prasada, Krishna, 1894–1982, vol. IX(AI)
Prater, Stanley Henry, 1890–1960, vol. V
Pratley, Clive William, 1929–1996, vol. X
Pratt, Anthony Malcolm G.; see Galliers-Pratt.
Pratt, Col (Arthur) Spencer, 1855–1933, vol. III
Pratt, Sir Bernard; see Pratt, Sir E. B.
Pratt, Rear-Adm. Charles Bernard, 1907–1973,
    vol. VII
Pratt, David Doig, 1894–1962, vol. VI
Pratt, Maj.-Gen. Douglas Henry, 1892–1958, vol. V
Pratt, Sir (E.) Bernard, 1889–1975, vol. VII
Pratt, Edward Millard, 1865–1949, vol. IV
Pratt, Edward Roger Murray, 1847–1921, vol. II
Pratt, Edwin John, 1883–1964, vol. VI
Pratt, Brig.-Gen. (Ernest) St George, 1863–1918,
    vol. II
Pratt, (Ewart) George, 1917–1999, vol. X
Pratt, Col Fendall William Harvey, 1892–1960,
    vol. V
Pratt, Very Rev. Francis; see Pratt, Very Rev.
    J. F. I.
Pratt, Rev. Canon Francis William, 1900–1971,
    vol. VII
Pratt, Frederick Greville, 1869–1949, vol. IV
Pratt, George; see Pratt, E. G.
Pratt, Col Henry Marsh, 1838–1919, vol. II
Pratt, Sir Henry Sheldon, 1873–1954, vol. V
Pratt, Hugh MacDonald, 1900–1993, vol. IX
Pratt, John, 1880–1935, vol. III
Pratt, Very Rev. (John) Francis (Isaac), 1913–1992,
    vol. IX
Pratt, John Lhind, 1885–1960, vol. V

Pratt, Sir John Thomas, 1876–1970, vol. VI
Pratt, Sir John William, 1873–1952, vol. V
Pratt, Joseph, 1843–1929, vol. III
Pratt, Peter Lynn, 1927–1995, vol. IX
Pratt, Brig. Reginald S.; *see* Sutton-Pratt.
Pratt, Rev. Ronald Arthur Frederick, 1886–1983, vol. VIII
Pratt, Brig.-Gen. St George; *see* Pratt, Brig.-Gen. E. St G.
Pratt, Col Spencer; *see* Pratt, Col A. S.
Pratt, William Henry; *see* Karloff, Boris.
Pratt, Surg.-Gen. William Simson, 1849–1917, vol. II
Pratt-Tynte, Fortescue Joseph; *see* Tynte.
Pratten, Herbert Edward, 1865–1928, vol. II
Pratz, Claire de, *died* 1934, vol. III
Prausnitz Giles, Carl, 1876–1963, vol. VI
Praz, Mario, 1896–1982, vol. VIII
Prebensen, Per Preben, 1896–1961, vol. VI
Preece, Sir Arthur Henry, 1867–1951, vol. V
Preece, Engr Vice-Adm. Sir George, *died* 1945, vol. IV
Preece, John Richard, 1843–1917, vol. II
Preece, Sir William Henry, 1834–1913, vol. I
Preedy, Rev. Arthur, *died* 1929, vol. III
Preedy, Digby C.; *see* Cotes-Preedy.
Preedy, George R.; *see* Long, M. G.
Preedy, Kenelm, *died* 1945, vol. IV
Preeston, Lt-Col Noel Percival Richard, 1880–1937, vol. III
Préfontaine, Hon. Joseph Raymond Fournier, 1850–1905, vol. I
Preller, Charles S. Du Riche, 1844–1929, vol. III
Prelog, Vladimir, 1906–1998, vol. X
Prelooker, Jaakoff, 1860–1935, vol. III
Prem, Dhani Ram, 1904–1979, vol. VII
Premadasa, Hon. Ranasinghe, 1924–1993, vol. IX
Premchand, Sir Kikabhai, 1883–1953, vol. V
Preminger, Otto Ludwig, 1906–1986, vol. VIII
Prempeh II, Otumfuo Sir Osei Agyeman, 1892–1970, vol. VI
Prendergast, Anthony; *see* Prendergast, C. A
Prendergast, Brig.-Gen. Charles Gordon, 1864–1930, vol. III
Prendergast, (Christopher) Anthony, 1931–1998, vol. X
Prendergast, Brig.-Gen. Donald Guy, 1861–1938, vol. III
Prendergast, Hon. George Michael, 1854–1937, vol. III
Prendergast, Maj.-Gen. Guy Annesley, 1834–1919, vol. II
Prendergast, Gen. Sir Harry North Dalrymple, 1834–1913, vol. I
Prendergast, Hon. Sir James, 1828–1921, vol. II
Prendergast, Hon. James Emile Pierre, 1858–1945, vol. IV
Prendergast, Sir John Vincent, 1912–1993, vol. IX
Prendergast, Adm. Sir Robert John, 1864–1946, vol. IV
Prendergast, W. Dowling, 1862–1933, vol. III
Prendergast, William, 1868–1933, vol. III
Prenderville, Arthur de, *died* 1919, vol. II
Prendiville, Most Rev. Redmond, 1900–1968, vol. VI

Prentice, Bertram, 1867–1938, vol. III
Prentice, Frank Douglas, 1898–1962, vol. VI
Prentice, Brig.-Gen. Robert Emile Shepherd, 1872–1953, vol. V
Prentice, Sir William David Russell, *died* 1933, vol. III
Prescott, Caroline, (Mrs Cyril Prescott), *died* 1943, vol. IV
Prescott, Charles Barrow Clarke, 1870–1932, vol. III
Prescott, Charles John, 1857–1946, vol. IV
Prescott, Sir Charles William Beeston, 6th Bt (*cr* 1794), 1877–1955, vol. V
Prescott, Mrs Cyril; *see* Prescott, Caroline.
Prescott, E. Livingston, *died* 1901, vol. I
Prescott, Sir George Lionel Lawson Bagot, 5th Bt (*cr* 1794), 1875–1942, vol. IV
Prescott, Lt-Col Henry Cecil, 1882–1960, vol. V
Prescott, Hilda F. M., 1896–1972, vol. VII
Prescott, James Arthur, 1890–1987, vol. VIII
Prescott, James C., 1894–1964, vol. VI
Prescott, Ven. John Eustace, *died* 1920, vol. II
Prescott, Richard Gordon Bathgate, 1896–1963, vol. VI
Prescott, Sir Richard Stanley, 2nd Bt (*cr* 1938), 1899–1965, vol. VI
Prescott, Stanley; *see* Prescott, W. R. S.
Prescott, Sir Stanley Lewis, 1910–1978, vol. VII
Prescott, Col Sir William Henry, 1st Bt (*cr* 1938), 1874–1945, vol. IV
Prescott, (William Robert) Stanley, 1912–1962, vol. VI
Prescott-Davies, N., 1862–1915, vol. I
Prescott-Decie, Brig.-Gen. Cyril; *see* Decie.
Prescott-Westcar, Lt-Col Sir William Villiers Leonard, 7th Bt (*cr* 1794), 1882–1959, vol. V
Presgrave, Col Edward Robert John, 1855–1919, vol. II
Presland, John David, 1930–1993, vol. IX
Presland, John, (Gladys Bendit), *died* 1975, vol. VII
Press, Robert, 1915–1984, vol. VIII
Pressburger, Emeric, 1902–1988, vol. VIII
Pressly, David Leith, 1855–1922, vol. II
Prest, Alan Richmond, 1919–1984, vol. VIII
Prest, Major Edward Papillon, 1864–1932, vol. III
Prest, Stanley Faber, 1858–1931, vol. III
Prestage, Edgar, 1869–1951, vol. V
Prestige, Rev. Canon George Leonard, 1889–1955, vol. V
Prestige, Major Sir John Theodore, 1884–1962, vol. VI
Preston, Alan, 1929–1988, vol. VIII
Preston, Hon. Mrs Angela C.; *see* Campbell-Preston.
Preston, Arthur, 1864–1948, vol. IV
Preston, Major Arthur John, 1842–1930, vol. III
Preston, Rt Rev. Arthur Llewellyn, *died* 1936, vol. III
Preston, Aston Zachariah, 1925–1986, vol. VIII
Preston, Bryan Wentworth, 1905–1965, vol. VI
Preston, Col D'Arcy Brownlow, 1860–1932, vol. III
Preston, Lt-Col Sir Edward Hulton, 5th Bt, 1888–1963, vol. VI
Preston, Francis Noel Dykes, 1888–1957, vol. V
Preston, Frank Sansome, 1875–1970, vol. VI

Preston, Sir Frederick George Panizzi, *died* 1949, vol. IV
Preston, F(rederick) Leslie, 1903–1994, vol. IX
Preston, Rev. George, 1840–1913, vol. I
Preston, George Dawson, 1896–1972, vol. VII
Preston, George Frederic, *died* 1939, vol. III
Preston, Sir Harry John, 1860–1936, vol. III
Preston, Henry Edward, 1857–1924, vol. II
Preston, Herbert Sansome, *died* 1935, vol. III
Preston, Sir Jacob, 4th Bt, 1887–1918, vol. II
Preston, Lt-Col Jenico Edward, 1855–1940, vol. III
Preston, Joseph Henry, 1911–1985, vol. VIII
Preston, Sir Kenneth Huson, 1901–1995, vol. IX
Preston, Kerrison, 1884–1974, vol. VII
Preston, Leslie; *see* Preston, F. L.
Preston, Adm. Sir Lionel George, 1875–1971, vol. VII
Preston, Sir Peter Sansome, 1922–1996, vol. X
Preston, Reginald Dawson, 1908–2000, vol. X
Preston, Lt-Col Hon. Richard Martin Peter, 1884–1965, vol. VI
Preston of Ardchattan, Robert Modan Thorne C.; *see* Campbell-Preston.
Preston, Sir Ronald Douglas Hildebrand, 7th Bt, 1916–1999, vol. X
Preston, Col Rupert Lionel, 1902–1982, vol. VIII
Preston, Sidney, 1850–1938, vol. III
Preston, Thomas, 1860–1900, vol. I
Preston, Thomas, 1834–1901, vol. I
Preston, Col Thomas, 1886–1966, vol. VI
Preston, Thomas Alford H. B.; *see* Houston-Boswall-Preston.
Preston, Sir Thomas Hildebrand, 6th Bt, 1886–1976, vol. VII
Preston, Sir Walter Reuben, 1875–1946, vol. IV
Preston, William, 1874–1941, vol. IV
Preston, Sir William Edward, 1865–1939, vol. III
Preston, Lt-Col William John Phaelim, 1873–1943, vol. IV
Preston-Thomas, Herbert, *died* 1909, vol. I
Prestt, Ian, 1929–1995, vol. IX
Pretorius, Major Philip Jacobus, *died* 1945, vol. IV
Pretty, Eric Ernest Falk, 1891–1967, vol. VI
Pretty, Air Marshal Sir Walter Philip George, 1909–1975, vol. VII
Pretyman, Rt Hon. Ernest George, 1860–1931, vol. III
Pretyman, Frederic Henry, 1875–1939, vol. III
Pretyman, Wing-Comdr George Frederick, 1891–1937, vol. III
Pretyman, Maj.-Gen. Sir George Tindal, 1845–1917, vol. II
Pretyman, Sir Walter Frederick, 1901–1988, vol. VIII
Prevett, Comdr Harry, 1900–1972, vol. VII
Previté-Orton, Charles William, 1877–1947, vol. IV
Prevost, Sir Augustus, 1st Bt (*cr* 1903), 1837–1913, vol. I
Prevost, Sir Charles, 3rd Bt (*cr* 1805), 1831–1902, vol. I
Prevost, Sir Charles Thomas Keble, 4th Bt (*cr* 1805), 1866–1939, vol. III
Prevost, Francis; *see* Battersby, H. F. P.
Prevost, Captain Sir George James Augustine, 5th Bt, 1910–1985, vol. VIII

Prevost, Marcel, 1862–1941, vol. IV
Prey, Hermann, 1929–1998, vol. X
Preziosi, Count Luigi, *died* 1965, vol. VI
Price, Col Adolphus James, 1846–1937, vol. III
Price, Albert Thomas, 1903–1978, vol. VII
Price, Allen, 1905–1970, vol. VI
Price, Sir Archibald Grenfell, 1892–1977, vol. VII
Price, Arnold Justin, 1919–1987, vol. VIII
Price, Aubrey Joseph, 1899–1978, vol. VII
Price, Bartholomew, 1818–1898, vol. I
Price, Hon. Brig.-Gen. Bartholomew George, 1870–1947, vol. IV
Price, Byron, 1891–1981, vol. VIII
Price, Maj.-Gen. Cedric Rhys George, 1905–1987, vol. VIII
Price, Maj.-Gen. Charles Basil, 1889–1975, vol. VII
Price, Charles Edward, *died* 1934, vol. III
Price, Sir Charles Frederick Rugge-, 7th Bt (*cr* 1804), 1868–1953, vol. V
Price, Brig.-Gen. Charles Henry Uvedale, 1862–1942, vol. IV
Price, Lt-Col Sir Charles James Napier Rugge-, 8th Bt (*cr* 1804), 1902–1966, vol. VI
Price, Sir (Charles) Keith (Napier) Rugge-, 9th Bt (*cr* 1804), 1936–2000, vol. X
Price, Captain Charles Lempriere, 1877–1914, vol. I
Price, Sir (Charles) Roy, 1893–1976, vol. VII
Price, Sir Charles Rugge-, 6th Bt (*cr* 1804), 1841–1927, vol. II
Price, Major Sir Charles William Mackay, 1872–1954, vol. V
Price, Rev. Clement, 1858–1937, vol. III
Price, Rev. Cyril, *died* 1943, vol. IV
Price, Col Cyril Uvedale, 1868–1956, vol. V
Price, Hon. Sir David William T.; *see* Tudor Price.
Price, Maj.-Gen. Denis Walter, 1908–1966, vol. VI
Price, Dennis, 1915–1973, vol. VII
Price, Dorothy Stopford, 1890–1954, vol. V
Price, Rt Rev. Dudley William Mackay, 1899–1971, vol. VII
Price, (Edith) Mary, 1897–1980, vol. VII
Price, Rev. Canon Edward Hyde B.; *see* Blackwood-Price.
Price, Edwin Lessware, 1874–1935, vol. III
Price, Ernest Griffith, 1870–1962, vol. VI
Price, Rev. Ernest Jones, 1882–1952, vol. V
Price, Sir Francis Caradoc Rose, 5th Bt (*cr* 1815), 1880–1949, vol. IV
Price, Frank Corbyn, *born* 1862, vol. III
Price, Sir Frederick; *see* Price, Sir J. F.
Price, Frederick George Hilton, 1842–1909, vol. I
Price, Frederick William, *died* 1957, vol. V
Price, G. Ward, *died* 1961, vol. VI
Price, Gabriel, 1879–1934, vol. III
Price, George Basil, *died* 1939, vol. III
Price, Brig.-Gen. George Dominic, 1867–1943, vol. IV
Price, Comdr George Edward, 1842–1926, vol. II
Price, Gwilym Ivor, 1899–1981, vol. VIII
Price, H. L., 1899–1943, vol. IV
Price, Harold Louis, 1917–1986, vol. VIII
Price, Harry, 1881–1948, vol. IV
Price, Henry Alfred, 1911–1982, vol. VIII
Price, Henry Habberley, 1899–1984, vol. VIII

Price, Sir Henry Philip, 1st Bt (*cr* 1953), 1877–1963, vol. VI
Price, Captain Henry Ryan, 1912–1986, vol. VIII
Price, Captain Henry Talbot, 1839–1915, vol. I
Price, Herbert Spencer, 1892–1976, vol. VII
Price, Rt Rev. Hetley; *see* Price, Rt Rev. S. H.
Price, Very Rev. Hilary Martin Connop, 1912–1998, vol. X
Price, Rt Rev. Horace MacCartie Eyre, 1863–1941, vol. IV
Price, Major Hubert Davenport, 1890–1958, vol. V
Price, Comdr Hugh Perceval, 1901–1983, vol. VIII
Price, Sir James Frederick George, 1873–1957, vol. V
Price, Sir (James) Robert, 1912–1999, vol. X
Price, John Cadwgan P.; *see* Powell-Price.
Price, Sir (John) Frederick, 1839–1927, vol. II
Price, Sir John G.; *see* Green-Price.
Price, John Lister Willis, 1915–1995, vol. IX
Price, John Lloyd, 1882–1941, vol. IV
Price, (John) Maurice, 1922–1995, vol. IX
Price, John Playfair, 1905–1988, vol. VIII
Price, Rev. John Willis, 1872–1940, vol. III
Price, (Joseph) Thomas, 1902–1973, vol. VII
Price, Julius Mendes, *died* 1924, vol. II
Price, Sir Keith, 1879–1956, vol. V
Price, Sir Keith Rugge-; *see* Price, Sir C. K. N. R.
Price, Langford Lovell F. R., 1862–1950, vol. IV
Price, Sir Leslie Victor, 1920–1996, vol. X
Price, (Lilian) Nancy (Bache), 1880–1970, vol. VI
Price, Marjorie Muriel, 1907–1946, vol. IV
Price, Mary; *see* Price, E. M.
Price, Maurice; *see* Price, J. M.
Price, Morgan Philips, 1885–1973, vol. VII
Price, Nancy; *see* Price, L. N. B.
Price, Norman Stewart, 1907–1988, vol. VIII
Price, Lt-Col Owen Glendower H.; *see* Howell-Price.
Price, Peter S.; *see* Stanley Price.
Price, Col Sir Rhys Howell, 1872–1943, vol. IV
Price, Sir Richard Dansey G.; *see* Green-Price.
Price, Richard John Lloyd, 1843–1923, vol. II
Price, Robert; *see* Price, W. R.
Price, Sir Robert; *see* Price, Sir J. R.
Price, Major Sir Robert Henry G.; *see* Green-Price.
Price, Sir Robert John, 1854–1926, vol. II
Price, Very Rev. Robert Peel, 1905–1981, vol. VIII
Price, Brig. Rollo Edward Crwys, 1916–1995, vol. IX
Price, Sir Rose, 4th Bt (*cr* 1815), 1878–1901, vol. I
Price, Sir Rose Francis, 6th Bt (*cr* 1815), 1910–1979, vol. VII
Price, Sir Rose Lambart, 3rd Bt (*cr* 1815), 1837–1899, vol. I
Price, Sir Roy; *see* Price, Sir C. R.
Price, S. Warren, *died* 1944, vol. IV
Price, Seymour James, 1886–1959, vol. V
Price, Rt Rev. (Stuart) Hetley, 1922–1977, vol. VII
Price, Hon. Thomas, 1852–1909, vol. I
Price, Col Thomas, 1842–1911, vol. I
Price, Thomas; *see* Price, J. T.
Price, Brig.-Gen. Thomas Herbert Francis, 1869–1945, vol. IV
Price, Thomas Phillips, 1844–1932, vol. III
Price, Sir Thomas Rees, 1848–1916, vol. II

Price, Brig. Thomas Reginald, 1894–1978, vol. VII
Price, Brig.-Gen. Thomas Rose Caradoc, 1875–1949, vol. IV
Price, Thomas Slater, 1875–1949, vol. IV
Price, Mrs Vincent; *see* Browne, C. E.
Price, Major Vincent Walter, 1890–1976, vol. VII
Price, Walter Harrington C.; *see* Crawfurd-Price.
Price, Walter Robert, 1926–1987, vol. VIII
Price, Wilfrid, 1879–1961, vol. VI
Price, Willard De Mille, 1887–1983, vol. VIII
Price, Sir William, 1867–1924, vol. II
Price, Sir William, *died* 1938, vol. III
Price, Hon. Brig.-Gen. William, 1864–1952, vol. V
Price, William Charles, 1909–1993, vol. IX
Price, William George, 1934–1999, vol. X
Price, Lt-Col William Herbert, 1877–1963, vol. VI
Price, Rev. William James, *died* 1928, vol. II
Price, William James, 1884–1973, vol. VII
Price, William Thomas, 1895–1982, vol. VIII
Price-Davies, Brig. Charles Stafford, 1892–1959, vol. V
Price-Davies, Maj.-Gen. Llewelyn Alberic Emilius, 1878–1965, vol. VI
Price Hughes, Mary Katherine H., 1853–1948, vol. IV
Price Thomas, Sir Clement, 1893–1973, vol. VII
Price-White, Lt-Col David Archibald, 1906–1978, vol. VII
Prichard, Rev. Alfred George, 1869–1945, vol. IV
Prichard, Arthur William, *died* 1926, vol. II
Prichard, Brig.-Gen. Charles Stewart, 1861–1942, vol. IV
Prichard, Harold Arthur, 1871–1947, vol. IV
Prichard, Herbert William, 1873–1951, vol. V
Prichard, Major (Hesketh Vernon) Hesketh, 1876–1922, vol. II
Prichard, Lt-Col Hubert Cecil, 1865–1942, vol. IV
Prichard, Sir John, 1887–1971, vol. VII
Prichard, Katharine Susannah, *died* 1969, vol. VI
Prichard, Sir Montague Illtyd, 1915–1991, vol. IX
Prichard, Sir Norman George Mollet, 1895–1972, vol. VII
Prichard, Rev. Canon Thomas Estlin, 1910–1975, vol. VII
Prichard, Brig. Walter Clavel Herbert, 1883–1965, vol. VI
Prichard-Jones, Sir John, 1st Bt, 1845–1917, vol. II
Prickard, Arthur Octavius, 1843–1939, vol. III
Prickard, Thomas Francis Vaughan, 1879–1973, vol. VII
Prickett, Brig. Charles Henry, 1881–1958, vol. V
Prickman, Air Cdre Thomas Bain, 1902–1992, vol. IX
Priday, Christopher Bruton, 1926–1992, vol. IX
Prideaux, Sir Francis; *see* Prideaux, Sir J. F. E.
Prideaux, Lt-Col Francis Beville, 1871–1938, vol. III
Prideaux, Sir John Francis, 1911–1993, vol. IX
Prideaux, Sir (Joseph) Francis (Engledue), 1884–1959, vol. V
Prideaux, Walter Arbuthnot, 1910–1995, vol. IX
Prideaux, Rev. Canon Walter Archibald, 1882–1965, vol. VI
Prideaux, Rev. Walter Cross, 1845–1912, vol. I
Prideaux, Sir Walter Sherburne, 1846–1928, vol. II

Prideaux, Col William Francis, 1840–1914, vol. I
Prideaux-Brune, Charles Glynn, 1821–1907, vol. I
Prideaux-Brune, Col Charles Robert, 1848–1936, vol. III
Prideaux-Brune, Sir Humphrey Ingelram, 1886–1979, vol. VII
Pridham, Vice-Adm. Sir (Arthur) Francis, 1886–1975, vol. VII
Pridham, Vice-Adm. Sir Francis; see Pridham, Vice-Adm. Sir A. F.
Pridham, Col Geoffrey Robert, 1872–1951, vol. V
Pridham-Wippell, Adm. Sir Henry Daniel, 1885–1952, vol. V
Pridie, Sir Eric Denholm, 1896–1978, vol. VII
Pridmore, Albert Edward, 1864–1927, vol. II
Pridmore, Walter George, 1864–1943, vol. IV
Priebsch, Robert, 1866–1935, vol. III
Priest, Alfred, 1874–1929, vol. III
Priest, Maj.-Gen. Robert Cecil, died 1966, vol. VI
Priestland, Gerald Francis, 1927–1991, vol. IX
Priestley, Sir Arthur, 1864–1933, vol. III
Priestley, Briggs, 1832–1907, vol. I
Priestley, Charles Henry Brian, 1915–1998, vol. X
Priestley, Sir Gerald William, 1888–1978, vol. VII
Priestley, Lt-Col Harold Edgar, died 1941, vol. IV
Priestley, Henry, 1884–1961, vol. VI
Priestley, Henry James, 1883–1932, vol. III
Priestley, Herbert Ingram, 1875–1944, vol. IV
Priestley, Mrs J. B.; see Hawkes, Jacquetta.
Priestley, John Boynton, 1894–1984, vol. VIII
Priestley, Sir Joseph Child, 1862–1941, vol. IV
Priestley, Joseph Hubert, 1883–1944, vol. IV
Priestley, Sir Raymond Edward, 1886–1974, vol. VII
Priestley, Sir William Edwin Briggs, 1859–1932, vol. III
Priestman, Bertram, 1868–1951, vol. V
Priestman, Harold Eddey, 1888–1956, vol. V
Priestman, Howard, 1865–1931, vol. III
Priestman, Sir John, 1st Bt, died 1941, vol. IV
Priestman, Maj.-Gen. John Hedley Thornton, 1885–1964, vol. VI
Prime, Derek Arthur, 1932–1990, vol. VIII
Prime-Stevenson, Edward Irenaeus; see Stevenson.
Primo de Rivera, Duke of, died 1964, vol. VI
Primrose, Sir Alasdair Neil, 4th Bt, 1935–1986, vol. VIII
Primrose, Alexander, 1861–1944, vol. IV
Primrose, Vice-Adm. George Anson, 1849–1930, vol. III
Primrose, Rt Hon. Sir Henry William, 1846–1923, vol. II
Primrose, Sir John Ure, 1st Bt, 1847–1924, vol. II
Primrose, Sir John Ure, 1900–1974, vol. VII
Primrose, Sir John Ure, 3rd Bt, 1908–1984, vol. VIII
Primrose, Rt Hon. Neil James Archibald, 1882–1917, vol. II
Primrose, William, 1904–1982, vol. VIII
Primrose, Sir William Louis, 2nd Bt, 1880–1953, vol. V
Prince, Sir Alexander William, 1870–1933, vol. III
Prince, Anthony; see Prince, C. T.
Prince, (Celestino) Anthony, 1921–1993, vol. IX
Prince, Edward Ernest, 1858–1936, vol. III

Prince, Henry Ashworth, 1921–2000, vol. X
Prince, J.-E., 1851–1923, vol. II, vol. III
Prince, John Dyneley, 1868–1945, vol. IV
Prince, Leslie Barnett, 1901–1985, vol. VIII
Prince, Lt-Col Peregrine, 1882–1935, vol. III
Prince, Lt-Col Robert, died 1945, vol. IV
Prince-Smith, Sir Prince, 2nd Bt, 1869–1940, vol. III
Prince-Smith, Sir William, 3rd Bt, 1898–1964, vol. VI
Prinetti, Marchese Giulio, 1851–1908, vol. I
Pring, David Andrew Michael, 1922–1991, vol. IX
Pring, Hon. Robert Darlow, 1853–1922, vol. II
Pringle, Rev. Arthur, 1866–1933, vol. III
Pringle, Lt-Col David, died 1936, vol. III (A), vol. IV
Pringle, Derek Hair, 1926–1995, vol. IX
Pringle, G. L. Kerr, died 1961, vol. VI
Pringle, Sir George, 1825–1911, vol. I
Pringle, George Taylor, 1890–1955, vol. V
Pringle, Brig. Hall Grant, 1876–1942, vol. IV
Pringle, Harold, died 1935, vol. III
Pringle, James Alexander, 1874–1935, vol. III
Pringle, James Hogarth, died 1941, vol. IV
Pringle, Sir James Scott, 1876–1951, vol. V
Pringle, Sir John, 1848–1923, vol. II
Pringle, Rev. John Christian, 1872–1938, vol. III
Pringle, John James, died 1922, vol. II
Pringle, John Mackay, 1888–1955, vol. V
Pringle, John Martin Douglas, 1912–1999, vol. X
Pringle, J(ohn) Seton Michael, 1909–1975, vol. VII
Pringle, Col Sir John Wallace, 1863–1938, vol. III
Pringle, John William Sutton, 1912–1982, vol. VIII
Pringle, Captain Lionel Graham, 1880–1915, vol. I
Pringle, Mia Lilly Kellmer, 1920–1983, vol. VIII
Pringle, Sir Norman Hamilton, 9th Bt, 1903–1961, vol. VI
Pringle, Sir Norman Robert, 8th Bt, 1871–1919, vol. II
Pringle, Maj.-Gen. Sir Robert, 1855–1926, vol. II
Pringle, Robert William, 1920–1996, vol. X
Pringle, Seton Sidney, 1879–1955, vol. V
Pringle, William Henderson, 1877–1967, vol. VI
Pringle, William Mather Rutherford, 1874–1928, vol. II
Pringle-Pattison, Andrew Seth; see Seth, Andrew.
Prinsep, Anthony Leyland, 1888–1942, vol. IV
Prinsep, Lt-Gen. Arthur Haldimand, 1840–1915, vol. I
Prinsep, Col Evelyn Siegfried MacLeod, 1892–1973, vol. VII
Prinsep, Hon. Sir Henry Thoby, 1836–1914, vol. I
Prinsep, Valentine Cameron, 1838–1904, vol. I
Prinz, Gerhard, 1929–1983, vol. VIII
Prioleau, John Randolph Hamilton, 1882–1954, vol. V
Prior, A. C. Vincent, 1881–1954, vol. V
Prior, Rev. Alfred Hall, died 1937, vol. III
Prior, Arthur Norman, 1914–1969, vol. VI
Prior, Sir (Charles) Geoffrey, died 1972, vol. VII
Prior, Col Hon. Edward Gawler, 1853–1920, vol. II
Prior, Edward Schroder, 1852–1932, vol. III
Prior, Sir Geoffrey; see Prior, Sir C. G.
Prior, George Thurland, 1862–1936, vol. III
Prior, Maj.-Gen. George Upton, 1843–1919, vol. II
Prior, Sir Henry Carlos, 1890–1967, vol. VI

Prior, Melton, 1845–1910, vol. I
Prior, Oliver Herbert Phelps, 1871–1934, vol. III
Prior, Comdr Redvers Michael, *died* 1964, vol. VI
Prior, Samuel Henry, 1869–1933, vol. III
Prior, Ven. William Henry, 1883–1969, vol. VI
Prior-Palmer, Maj.-Gen. George Erroll, 1903–1977, vol. VII
Prior-Palmer, Brig. Sir Otho Leslie, 1897–1986, vol. VIII
Priston, Rev. Stewart Browne, 1880–1960, vol. V
Pritchard, Baron (Life Peer); Derek Wilbraham Pritchard, 1910–1995, vol. IX
Pritchard, Sir Albert Edward, 1859–1937, vol. III
Pritchard, Sir Asa Hubert, 1891–1990, vol. VIII
Pritchard, Brig.-Gen. Aubrey Gordon, 1869–1943, vol. IV
Pritchard, Sir Charles Bradley, 1837–1903, vol. I
Pritchard, Brig. Charles Hilary Vaughan; *see* Vaughan, Brig. C. H. V.
Pritchard, Brig.-Gen. Clive Gordon, 1871–1948, vol. IV
Pritchard, Sir Edward Evan E.; *see* Evans-Pritchard.
Pritchard, Eric; *see* Pritchard, G. E. C.
Pritchard, Eric Alfred Blake, 1889–1962, vol. VI
Pritchard, Sir Fred Eills, 1899–1982, vol. VIII
Pritchard, Frederick Hugh Dalzel, 1905–1983, vol. VIII
Pritchard, (George) Eric (Campbell), *died* 1943, vol. IV
Pritchard, Maj.-Gen. Gordon Arthur Thomas, 1902–1957, vol. V
Pritchard, Lt-Gen. Sir Gordon Douglas, 1835–1912, vol. I
Pritchard, Sir Harry Goring, 1868–1962, vol. VI
Pritchard, Maj.-Gen. Harry Lionel, 1871–1953, vol. V
Pritchard, Lt-Col Hugh Robert Norman, 1879–1967, vol. VI
Pritchard, Hugh Wentworth, 1903–1999, vol. X
Pritchard, Col Hurlock Galloway, 1836–1909, vol. I
Pritchard, Ivor Mervyn, *died* 1948, vol. IV (A), vol. V
Pritchard, John Joseph, 1916–1979, vol. VII
Pritchard, Captain John Laurence, 1885–1968, vol. VI
Pritchard, Sir John Michael, 1921–1989, vol. VIII
Pritchard, Leslie Francis Gordon, 1918–1977, vol. VII
Pritchard, Robert Albion, *died* 1916, vol. II
Pritchard, Urban, 1845–1925, vol. II
Pritchard, Rev. William Charles, 1856–1931, vol. III
Pritchett, John Suckling, *died* 1941, vol. IV
Pritchett, Sir Theodore Beal, 1890–1969, vol. VI
Pritchett, Sir Victor Sawdon, 1900–1997, vol. X
Pritt, Denis Nowell, 1887–1972, vol. VII
Prittie, Hon. Terence Cornelius Farmer, 1913–1985, vol. VII
Privett, Frank John, 1874–1937, vol. III
Probert, Arthur Reginald, 1909–1975, vol. VII
Probert, Rev. Lewis, 1841–1908, vol. I
Probert, Rhys Price, 1921–1980, vol. VII
Proby, Col Douglas James, 1856–1931, vol. III
Proby, Granville, 1883–1947, vol. IV

Proby, Major Sir Richard George, 1st Bt, 1886–1979, vol. VII
Probyn, Rt Hon. Sir Dighton Macnaghten, 1833–1924, vol. II
Probyn, Air Cdre Harold Melsome, 1891–1992, vol. IX
Probyn, Sir Lesley Charles, 1834–1916, vol. II
Probyn, Sir Leslie, 1862–1938, vol. III
Probyn, Lt-Col Percy John, *died* 1940, vol. III
Probyn-Jones, Sir Arthur Probyn, 2nd Bt, 1892–1951, vol. V
Probyn-Williams, Robert James, 1866–1952, vol. V
Procter, Rev. Arthur Herbert, 1890–1973, vol. VII
Procter, Rev. Charles James, *died* 1925, vol. II
Procter, Dod, *died* 1972, vol. VII
Procter, Ernest, *died* 1935, vol. III
Procter, Evelyn Emma Stefanos, 1897–1980, vol. VII
Procter, Henry Adam, 1883–1955, vol. V
Procter, Sir Henry Edward Edleston, 1866–1928, vol. II
Procter, Henry Richardson, 1848–1927, vol. II
Procter, Lt-Col James, 1884–1955, vol. V
Procter, Joan Beauchamp, 1897–1931, vol. III
Procter, Very Rev. John, 1849–1911, vol. I
Procter, Rev. John Mathias, 1835–1917, vol. II
Procter, Sir William, 1871–1951, vol. V
Procter-Gregg, Humphrey, 1895–1980, vol. VII
Proctor, Adam E., 1864–1913, vol. I
Proctor, Alexander Phimister, 1862–1950, vol. IV (A), vol. V
Proctor, Col Alfred Henry, *died* 1950, vol. IV
Proctor, Captain Andrew Weatherley Beauchamp, *died* 1921, vol. II
Proctor, David Victor, 1930–2000, vol. X
Proctor, Sir Dennis; *see* Proctor, Sir P. D.
Proctor, Sir (George) Philip, 1902–1986, vol. VIII
Proctor, Rev. Henry, *died* 1940, vol. III
Proctor, Ian Douglas Ben, 1918–1992, vol. IX
Proctor, Mary, *died* 1957, vol. V
Proctor, Sir Philip; *see* Proctor, Sir G. P.
Proctor, Sir Philip Bridger, 1870–1940, vol. III
Proctor, Sir (Philip) Dennis, 1905–1983, vol. VIII
Proctor, Surg. Rear-Adm. Richard Louis Gibbon, 1900–1969, vol. VI
Proctor, Sir Roderick Consett, 1914–1991, vol. IX
Proctor, William Thomas, 1896–1967, vol. VI
Proctor-Beauchamp, Col Sir Horace George; *see* Beauchamp.
Proctor-Beauchamp, Rev. Sir Ivor Cuthbert; *see* Beauchamp.
Proctor-Beauchamp, Rev. Sir Montagu Harry; *see* Beauchamp.
Proctor-Beauchamp, Sir Reginald William; *see* Beauchamp.
Proctor-Sims, Ernest William; *see* Sims.
Proe, Thomas, 1852–1922, vol. II
Proes, Lt-Col Ernest Marinus, 1871–1940, vol. III
Profeit, Col Charles William, 1870–1937, vol. III
Profumo, Albert Peter Anthony, 1879–1940, vol. III
Profumo, Valerie Babette Louise; *see* Hobson, V. B. L.
Prokofieff, Serge Sergeyevich, 1891–1953, vol. V
Prokosch, Frederic, 1908–1989, vol. VIII
Prole, Lozania; *see* Bloom, Ursula.

Proom, Maj. William Arthur, 1916–2000, vol. X
Proops, Marjorie; *see* Proops, R. M.
Proops, (Rebecca) Marjorie, *died* 1996, vol. X
Propert, Rev. P. S. G., 1861–1940, vol. III
Propper, Arthur, 1910–1992, vol. IX
Propsting, Hon. William Bispham, 1861–1937, vol. III
Prosser, (Albert) Russell (Garness), 1915–1988, vol. VIII
Prosser, Rt Rev. Charles Keith Kipling, 1897–1954, vol. V
Prosser, Rt Rev. David Lewis, *died* 1950, vol. IV
Prosser, David Russell, 1889–1974, vol. VII
Prosser, Ernest Albert, *died* 1933, vol. III
Prosser, Francis Richard W.; *see* Wegg-Prosser.
Prosser, Rev. Henry Paul, *died* 1932, vol. III
Prosser, Sir John, 1857–1945, vol. IV
Prosser, Russell; *see* Prosser, A. R. G.
Prosser, Seward, 1871–1942, vol. IV
Prosser, Thomas Vivian, 1908–1987, vol. VIII
Prothero, Adm. Arthur William Edward, 1850–1931, vol. III
Prothero, Sir George Walter, 1848–1922, vol. II
Prothero, Vice-Adm. Reginald Charles, 1849–1927, vol. II
Protheroe, Ven. James Havard, *died* 1903, vol. I
Protheroe, Maj.-Gen. Montagu, 1841–1905, vol. I
Protheroe-Beynon, Major Godfrey Evan Schaw, 1872–1958, vol. V
Protheroe-Smith, Lt-Col Sir Hugh Bateman, 1872–1961, vol. VI
Proud, Sir George, 1910–1976, vol. VII
Proud, Air Cdre Harold John Granville Ellis, 1906–1995, vol. IX
Proud, Sir John Seymour, 1907–1998, vol. X
Proudfoot, Alexander, 1878–1957, vol. V
Proudfoot, Bruce Falconer, 1903–1993, vol. IX
Proudfoot, Col Frank Grégoire, 1869–1940, vol. III
Proudfoot, James, 1908–1971, vol. IV
Proudfoot, William, 1932–1990, vol. VIII
Proudman, Joseph, 1888–1975, vol. VII
Prout, Ebenezer, 1835–1909, vol. I
Prout, Henry Goslee, *died* 1927, vol. II, vol. III
Prout, Margaret F.; *see* Fisher Prout.
Prout, Sir William Thomas, *died* 1939, vol. III
Provand, Andrew Dryburgh, 1839–1915, vol. I
Provis, Edward, 1849–1941, vol. IV
Provis, Sir Samuel Butler, 1845–1926, vol. II
Prowde, Oswald Longstaff, 1882–1949, vol. IV
Prower, Brig. John Mervyn, 1885–1968, vol. VI
Prowse, Arthur Bancks, 1856–1925, vol. II
Prowse, Daniel Woodley, 1834–1914, vol. I
Prowse, Richard Orton, 1862–1949, vol. IV
Prowse, Richard Thomas, 1835–1921, vol. II
Prudden, T. Mitchell, 1849–1924, vol. II
Prude, Agnes George; *see* de Mille, A. G.
Pruden, Arthur George, 1860–1936, vol. III
Prunty, Francis Thomas Garnet, 1910–1979, vol. VII
Prunty, Garnet; *see* Prunty, F. T. G.
Pryce, Daniel Merlin, 1902–1976, vol. VII
Pryce, Edward Calcott, 1885–1972, vol. VII
Pryce, Frederick Norman, 1888–1953, vol. V
Pryce, Howard Lloyd, *died* 1932, vol. III
Pryce, Very Rev. John, *died* 1903, vol. I

Pryce, Ven. Lewis Hugh Oswald, 1873–1930, vol. III
Pryce, Rev. R. Vaughan, 1834–1917, vol. II
Pryce, Richard, *died* 1942, vol. IV
Pryce, Very Rev. Shadrach, *died* 1914, vol. I
Pryce, Ven. Thomas P.; *see* Parry Pryce.
Pryce-Jones, Alan Payan, 1908–2000, vol. X
Pryce-Jones, Col Sir Edward; *see* Pryce-Jones, Col Sir P. E.
Pryce-Jones, Bt Col Henry Morris, 1878–1952, vol. V
Pryce-Jones, Sir Pryce, 1834–1920, vol. II
Pryce-Jones, Col Sir (Pryce) Edward, 1st Bt, 1861–1926, vol. II
Pryce-Jones, Sir Pryce Victor, 2nd Bt, 1887–1963, vol. VI
Pryde, David Johnstone, 1890–1959, vol. V
Pryde, George Smith, 1899–1961, vol. VI
Pryde, James, 1869–1941, vol. IV
Pryde, James Richmond Northridge, 1894–1980, vol. VII
Pryer, Major Alfred Amos, 1891–1943, vol. IV
Pryke, Sir David Dudley, 3rd Bt, 1912–1998, vol. X
Pryke, Sir Dudley; *see* Pryke, Sir W. R. D.
Pryke, Rev. William Emmanuel, 1843–1920, vol. II
Pryke, Sir William Robert, 1st Bt, 1847–1932, vol. III
Pryke, Sir (William Robert) Dudley, 2nd Bt, 1882–1959, vol. V
Pryn, Surg. Rear-Adm. Sir William Wenmoth, 1859–1942, vol. IV
Prynne, Edward A. Fellowes, 1854–1921, vol. II
Prynne, Rev. George Rundle, 1818–1903, vol. I
Prynne, Brig. Harold Gordon Lusby, 1899–1976, vol. VII
Prynne, Col Harold Vernon, *died* 1954, vol. V
Prynne, Maj.-Gen. Michael Whitworth, 1912–1977, vol. VII
Pryor, Arthur Vickris, 1846–1927, vol. II
Pryor, Grafton Deen, 1883–1947, vol. IV
Pryor, Maurice Arthur, 1911–1969, vol. VI
Pryor, Rev. Michael, 1857–1929, vol. III
Pryor, Norman Selwyn, 1896–1982, vol. VIII
Pryor, Maj.-Gen. Sir Pomeroy Holland-, 1866–1955, vol. V
Pryor, Robert Nelson, 1921–1979, vol. VII
Pryor, S. J., 1865–1924, vol. II
Pryor, Lt-Col Walter Marlborough, 1880–1962, vol. VI
Prys, Rev. Owen, 1857–1934, vol. III
Prys Jones, David; *see* Jones, D. P.
Pryse, Sir Edward John Webley-Parry-, 2nd Bt, 1862–1918, vol. II
Pryse, Gerald Spencer, 1882–1956, vol. V
Pryse, Sir Lewes Thomas Loveden, 3rd Bt, 1864–1946, vol. IV
Pryse, Sir Pryse, 1st Bt, 1838–1906, vol. I
Pryse, Sir Pryse Loveden S.; *see* Saunders-Pryse.
Pryse-Rice, Dame Margaret Ker, *died* 1948, vol. IV
Pryse-Saunders, Sir George Rice, 4th Bt, 1870–1948, vol. IV
Ptolemy, William John, 1850–1920, vol. II
Puccini, Giacomo, 1858–1924, vol. II
Puckey, Sir Walter Charles, 1899–1983, vol. VIII
Puckle, Sir Frederick Hale, 1889–1966, vol. VI

Puckle, Lt-Col Frederick Kaye, 1880–1959, vol. V
Puckle, Lt-Col John, 1869–1917, vol. II
Puckle, Richard Kaye, 1830–1917, vol. II
Puckridge, Geoffrey Martin, 1895–1974, vol. VII
Puddester, Sir John Charles, 1881–1947, vol. IV
Puddicombe, Anne Adalisa, (Mrs Beynon Puddicombe); *see* Raine, Allen.
Pudner, Anthony Serle, 1917–1980, vol. VII
Pudney, John Sleigh, 1909–1977, vol. VII
Pudsey, Lt-Col Denison, 1876–1940, vol. III (A), vol. IV
Pudukota, Raja of, 1875–1928, vol. II
Pudumjee, Nowrojee, 1841–1930, vol. III
Puech, Albert G., 1859–1929, vol. III
Puech, Denys, 1854–1942, vol. IV
Pugh, Sir Alun; *see* Pugh, Sir J. A.
Pugh, Sir Arthur, 1870–1955, vol. V
Pugh, Lt-Col David Charles, 1859–1929, vol. III
Pugh, Rt Rev. Edward; *see* Pugh, Rt Rev. W. E. A.
Pugh, Ven. Edward William Wynn, *died* 1950, vol. IV
Pugh, Edwin William, 1874–1930, vol. III
Pugh, Harold Valentine, 1899–1996, vol. X
Pugh, Sir (John) Alun, 1894–1971, vol. VII
Pugh, Rev. Canon John Richards, 1885–1961, vol. VI
Pugh, Leslie Mervyn, 1905–1978, vol. VII
Pugh, Leslie Penrhys, 1895–1983, vol. VIII
Pugh, Maj.-Gen. Lewis Owain, 1907–1981, vol. VIII
Pugh, Lewis Pugh, 1837–1908, vol. I
Pugh, Lewis Pugh Evans, 1865–1940, vol. III
Pugh, Surg. Rear-Adm. Patterson David Gordon, 1920–1993, vol. IX
Pugh, Ralph Bernard, 1910–1982, vol. VIII
Pugh, Roger Courtenay Beckwith, 1917–1999, vol. X
Pugh, Rev. Canon T(homas) Jenkin, 1903–1980, vol. VII
Pugh, Rt Rev. William Edward Augustus, 1909–1986, vol. VIII
Pugh, Sir William John, 1892–1974, vol. VII
Pugh, William Thomas Gordon, *died* 1945, vol. IV
Pugno, Raoul, 1852–1914, vol. I
Pugsley, Sir Alfred Grenvile, 1903–1998, vol. X
Pugsley, Rear Adm. Anthony Follett, 1901–1990, vol. VIII
Pugsley, Sir Reuben James, 1886–1975, vol. VII
Pugsley, Hon. William, 1850–1925, vol. II
Pulay, George, 1923–1981, vol. VIII
Pulbrook, Sir Eustace Ralph, 1881–1953, vol. V
Puleston, Sir John Henry, 1830–1908, vol. I
Pulford, Air Vice-Marshal Conway Walter Heath, *died* 1942, vol. IV
Pulford, Col Russell Richard, 1845–1920, vol. II
Pulitzer, Joseph, 1847–1911, vol. I
Pulitzer, Ralph, 1879–1939, vol. III
Pullan, Ayrton George Popplewell, 1879–1973, vol. VII
Pullan, Ayrton John Seaton, 1906–1967, vol. VI
Pullan, John Marshall, 1915–1998, vol. X
Pullan, Rev. Leighton, 1865–1940, vol. III
Pullar, Hubert Norman, 1914–1988, vol. VIII
Pullar, Sir Robert, 1828–1912, vol. I
Pullar, Rufus D., 1861–1917, vol. II

Pullein, John, *died* 1948, vol. IV
Pullein-Thompson, Mrs Joanna; *see* Cannan, J.
Pulleine, Rt Rev. John James, 1841–1913, vol. I
Pullen, Rev. Henry William, 1836–1903, vol. I
Pullen, Sir Reginald; *see* Pullen, Sir W. R. J.
Pullen, William le Geyt, 1855–1922, vol. II
Pullen, Sir (William) Reginald (James), 1922–1996, vol. X
Pullen-Burry, Bessie, 1858–1937, vol. III
Puller, Rev. Frederick William, 1843–1938, vol. III
Pulley, Col Charles, 1851–1925, vol. II
Pulley, Sir Charles Thornton, 1864–1947, vol. IV
Pulley, Sir Joseph, 1st Bt, 1822–1901, vol. I
Pulliblank, Engr-Rear-Adm. John Blackler, 1879–1951, vol. V
Pullicino, Anthony Alfred, 1917–1986, vol. VIII
Pullicino, Sir Philip, 1889–1960, vol. V
Pullin, Victor Edward, *died* 1956, vol. V
Pulling, Alexander, 1857–1942, vol. IV
Pulling, Rev. Edward Herbert, 1859–1928, vol. II
Pulling, Martin John Langley, 1906–1988, vol. VIII
Pullinger, Frank, 1866–1920, vol. II
Pullinger, Henry Robert, 1884–1970, vol. VI
Pullinger, John Elphick, 1930–2000, vol. X
Pullinger, Thomas Charles Willis, 1867–1945, vol. IV
Pullman, Major Alfred Hopewell, *died* 1942, vol. IV
Pulsford, Rev. Edward John, 1878–1952, vol. V
Pulteney, Lt-Gen. Sir William Pulteney, 1861–1941, vol. IV
Pulvertaft, Robert James Valentine, 1897–1990, vol. VIII
Pumpelly, Raphael, 1837–1923, vol. II
Pumphrey, Richard Julius, 1906–1967, vol. VI
Punch, Arthur Lisle, *died* 1964, vol. VI
Punchard, Constance, (Mrs F. B. Punchard); *see* Holme, C.
Punchard, Rev. Elgood George, 1844–1917, vol. II
Punnett, Reginald Crundall, 1875–1967, vol. VI
Pupin, Michael Idvorsky, 1858–1935, vol. III
Purbrick, Reginald, 1877–1950, vol. IV
Purcell, Albert Arthur, 1872–1935, vol. III
Purcell, Denis; *see* Purcell, J. D.
Purcell, Edward Mills, 1912–1997, vol. X
Purcell, Sir Gilbert Kenelm Treffry, 1867–1934, vol. III
Purcell, Rev. Handfield Noel, *died* 1925, vol. II
Purcell, Harry, 1919–1998, vol. X
Purcell, Hubert Kennett, 1884–1962, vol. VI
Purcell, (John) Denis, 1913–1990, vol. VIII
Purcell, Sir John Samuel, 1839–1924, vol. II
Purcell, Pierce Francis, 1881–1968, vol. VI
Purcell, Major Raymond John Hugo, 1885–1928, vol. II
Purcell, Ronald Herbert, 1904–1969, vol. VI
Purcell, Victor, 1896–1965, vol. VI
Purcell, Rev. Canon William Ernest, 1909–1999, vol. X
Purcell, Ven. William Henry Samuel, 1912–1994, vol. IX
Purcell-Buret, Captain Theobald John Claud, 1879–1974, vol. VII
Purchas, Rev. Canon Alban Charles Theodore, 1890–1976, vol. VII
Purchase, Sir Bentley; *see* Purchase, Sir W. B.

Purchase, Edward James, *died* 1924, vol. II
Purchase, Henry George, 1873–1945, vol. IV
Purchase, Sir (William) Bentley, 1890–1961, vol. VI
Purchase, Sir William Henry, 1860–1924, vol. II
Puchon, William Sydney, 1879–1942, vol. IV
Purdie, Rev. Albert Bertrand, 1888–1976, vol. VII
Purdie, Edna, 1894–1968, vol. VI
Purdie, Thomas, 1843–1916, vol. II
Purdie, Wendy C.; *see* Campbell-Purdie.
Purdom, Charles Benjamin, 1883–1965, vol. VI
Purdom, Thomas Hunter, 1853–1923, vol. II
Purdon, Lt-Col David William, 1853–1948, vol. IV (A), vol. V
Purdon, Maj.-Gen. William Brooke, *died* 1950, vol. IV
Purdy, Lt-Col John Smith, 1872–1936, vol. III
Purdy, Richard Little, 1904–1990, vol. VIII
Purdy, Robert John, 1916–1998, vol. X
Purefoy, Richard Dancer, *died* 1919, vol. II
Purefoy, Adm. Richard Purefoy FitzGerald, 1862–1943, vol. IV
Purefoy, Wilfred Bagwell, 1862–1930, vol. III
Purey-Cust, Very Rev. Arthur Perceval; *see* Cust.
Purey-Cust, Adm. Sir Herbert Edward; *see* Cust.
Purey-Cust, Brig. Richard Brownlow, 1888–1958, vol. V
Purey Cust, Rev. Canon William Arthur; *see* Cust.
Purnell, Anthony Guy, 1944–1989, vol. VIII
Purnell, Charlotte, *died* 1944, vol. IV
Purnell, Christopher James, 1878–1959, vol. V
Purnell, David Cuthbert, 1932–1979, vol. VII
Purohit, Sir Gopinath Sahitya Bhusan, 1863–1935, vol. III
Purse, Benjamin Ormond, 1876–1950, vol. IV
Purseglove, John William, 1912–1991, vol. IX
Purser, Maj.-Gen. Arthur William, 1884–1953, vol. V
Purser, Frederick, 1840–1910, vol. I
Purser, John Mallet, 1839–1929, vol. III
Purser, Louis Claude, 1854–1932, vol. III
Pursey, Comdr Harry, 1891–1980, vol. VII
Purssell, Richard Stanley, 1882–1954, vol. V
Purucker, Gottfried von; *see* Purucker, H. L. G. von.
Purucker, (Hobart Lorenz) Gottfried von, 1874–1942, vol. IV
Purves, James Grant, 1911–1984, vol. VIII
Purves, James Liddell, 1843–1910, vol. I
Purves, Laidlaw; *see* Purves, W. L.
Purves, Sir Raymond Edgar, 1910–1973, vol. VII
Purves, Robert Egerton, 1859–1943, vol. IV
Purves, Col Sir Thomas Fortune, 1871–1950, vol. IV
Purves, William Donald Campbell Laidlaw, 1888–1964, vol. VI
Purves, (William) Laidlaw, *died* 1917, vol. II
Purves-Stewart, Sir James; *see* Stewart.
Purvis, Brig.-Gen. Alexander Burridge, 1854–1928, vol. II

Purvis, Rt Hon. Arthur Blaikie, 1890–1941, vol. IV
Purvis, Adm. Sir Charles Edward K.; *see* Kennedy-Purvis.
Purvis, Sir Robert, 1844–1920, vol. II
Purvis, Tom, *died* 1959, vol. V
Purvis-Russell-Montgomery, Lt-Col Henry Keith; *see* Montgomery.
Pusey, Philip Francis B.; *see* Bouverie-Pusey.
Putnam, George Haven, 1844–1930, vol. III
Putnam, Herbert, 1861–1955, vol. V
Putnam, Sir Thomas, 1862–1936, vol. III
Putt, Gorley; *see* Putt, S. G.
Putt, S(amuel) Gorley, 1913–1995, vol. IX
Puttanna Chetty, Sir Krishnarajapur Palligondé, 1856–1938, vol. III
Puttick, Lt-Gen. Sir Edward, 1890–1976, vol. VII
Puxley, Henry Lavallin, 1834–1909, vol. I
Pyatt, Rt Rev. William Allan, 1916–1991, vol. X(AI)
Pybus, Sir John; *see* Pybus, Sir P. J.
Pybus, Sir (Percy) John, 1st Bt, *died* 1935, vol. III
Pycraft, W. P., 1868–1942, vol. IV
Pye, Sir David Randall, 1886–1960, vol. V
Pye, Joseph Patrick, *died* 1920, vol. II
Pye, Col William Edmund, 1872–1949, vol. IV
Pye-Smith, Arnold, 1847–1933, vol. III
Pye-Smith, Philip Henry, *died* 1914, vol. I
Pye-Smith, Rutherfoord John, 1848–1921, vol. II
Pyke, Air Cdre Alan, 1911–1977, vol. VII
Pyke, Cyril John, 1892–1976, vol. VII
Pyke, Joseph, 1884–1955, vol. V
Pyke, Lionel Edward, 1854–1899, vol. I
Pyke, Sir Louis Frederick, 1907–1988, vol. VIII
Pyke, Magnus Alfred, 1908–1992, vol. IX
Pyke, Rev. R., 1873–1965, vol. VI
Pyke-Lees, Walter Kinnear, 1909–1978, vol. VII
Pyke-Nott, Comdr Sir James Grenvile, 1897–1972, vol. VII
Pyle, Cyril Alfred, *died* 1994, vol. IX
Pyle, Howard, 1853–1912, vol. I
Pym, Barbara Mary Crampton, 1913–1980, vol. VII
Pym, Sir Charles Evelyn, 1879–1971, vol. VII
Pym, Charles Guy, 1841–1918, vol. II
Pym, Francis, 1849–1927, vol. II
Pym, Col Frederick Harry Norris, 1868–1944, vol. IV
Pym, Leslie Ruthven, 1884–1945, vol. IV
Pym, Rev. Thomas Wentworth, 1885–1945, vol. IV
Pyman, Frank Lee, 1882–1944, vol. IV
Pyman, Gen. Sir Harold English, 1908–1971, vol. VII
Pyman, Lancelot Frank Lee, 1910–1996, vol. X
Pyne, Brig. Henry George, 1887–1945, vol. IV
Pyne, James Kendrick, 1852–1938, vol. III
Pyne, Hon. Robert Allan, 1855–1931, vol. III
Pyne, Sir Salter; *see* Pyne, Sir T. S.
Pyne, Thomas, 1843–1935, vol. III
Pyne, Sir (Thomas) Salter, 1860–1921, vol. II
Pyrah, Leslie Norman, 1899–1995, vol. IX.

Q

Qadir, Khan Bahadur Sheikh Sir Abdul, 1874–1951, vol. V
Quail, Jesse, *died* 1939, vol. III
Quain, Sir Richard, 1st Bt, 1816–1898, vol. I
Qualtrough, Sir Joseph Davidson, 1885–1960, vol. V
Quaranta di San Severino, Baron Bernardo, 1870–1934, vol. III
Quarles, Donald Aubrey, 1894–1959, vol. V
Quarmby, Sir John, 1868–1943, vol. IV
Quaroni, Pietro, 1898–1971, vol. VII
Quarrell, Arthur George, 1910–1983, vol. VIII
Quarrington, Rev. Edwin Fowler, *died* 1922, vol. II
Quartermaine, Sir Allan Stephen, 1888–1978, vol. VII
Quartermaine, Leon, 1876–1967, vol. VI
Quashie-Idun, Sir Samuel Okai, 1902–1966, vol. VI
Quasimodo, Salvatore, 1901–1968, vol. VI
Quass, Phineas, *died* 1961, vol. VI
Quastel, Juda Hirsch, 1899–1987, vol. VIII
Quayle, Sir Anthony; *see* Quayle, Sir J. A.
Quayle, Bronte Clucas, 1919–1986, vol. VIII
Quayle, Sir (John) Anthony, 1913–1989, vol. VIII
Quayle, Richard William, 1901–1973, vol. VII
Quayle, Thomas, 1884–1963, vol. VI
Quayle-Jones, Brig.-Gen. Morey, 1855–1946, vol. IV
Queen, Rt Rev. Carman John, 1912–1974, vol. VII
Queen, Ellery; *see* Dannay, Frederic and Lee, Manfred B.
Queenborough, 1st Baron, 1861–1949, vol. IV
Queensberry, 9th Marquess of, 1844–1900, vol. I (A)
Queensberry, 10th Marquess of, 1868–1920, vol. II
Queensberry, 11th Marquess of, 1896–1954, vol. V
Quekett, Sir Arthur Scott, 1881–1945, vol. IV
Quénet, Hon. Sir Vincent Ernest, 1906–1983, vol. VIII
Quenington, Viscount; Michael Hugh Hicks-Beach, 1877–1916, vol. II
Quennell, Charles Henry Bourne, 1872–1935, vol. III
Quennell, Marjorie, *died* 1972, vol. VII
Quennell, Sir Peter Courtney, 1905–1993, vol. IX
Quennell, Rev. William, 1839–1908, vol. I
Querido, Israël, 1874–1932, vol. III
Queripel, Hon. Col Alfred Ernest, 1870–1921, vol. II
Queripel, Col Leslie Herbert, 1881–1962, vol. VI
Quex; *see* Nichols, George Herbert Fosdike.
Quibell, 1st Baron, 1879–1962, vol. VI
Quick, Hon. Sir John, 1852–1932, vol. III
Quick, Norman, 1922–1997, vol. X
Quick, Rev. Oliver Chase, 1885–1944, vol. IV
Quick, Richard, *died* 1939, vol. III
Quick-Smith, George William, 1905–1986, vol. VIII
Quicke, Captain Noel Arthur Godolphin, 1888–1943, vol. IV
Quickswood, 1st Baron, 1869–1956, vol. V

Quidde, Ludwig, 1858–1941, vol. IV
Quig, Alexander Johnstone, 1892–1962, vol. VI
Quigley, Arthur Grainger, *died* 1945, vol. IV
Quigley, Hugh, 1895–1979, vol. VII
Quigley, Most Rev. James Edward, 1854–1916, vol. II
Quill, Albert William, *died* 1908, vol. I
Quill, Lt-Col Berkeley Crosbie, 1852–1932, vol. III
Quill, Col Raymond Humphrey, 1897–1987
Quill, Maj.-Gen. Richard Henry, 1848–1924, vol. II
Quiller-Couch, Sir Arthur Thomas, 1863–1944, vol. IV
Quilter, Sir Cuthbert; *see* Quilter, Sir W. C.
Quilter, Sir Cuthbert; *see* Quilter, Sir W. E. C.
Quilter, Harry, 1851–1907, vol. I
Quilter, Sir (John) Raymond (Cuthbert), 3rd Bt, 1902–1959, vol. V
Quilter, Sir Raymond; *see* Quilter, Sir J. R. C.
Quilter, Roger, 1877–1953, vol. V
Quilter, Sir (William) Cuthbert, 1st Bt, 1841–1911, vol. I
Quilter, Sir (William Eley) Cuthbert, 2nd Bt, 1873–1952, vol. V
Quin, Rt Rev. George Alderson, 1914–1990, vol. VIII
Quin, Sir Stephen, 1860–1944, vol. IV
Quin, Maj.-Gen. Thomas James, 1842–1919, vol. II
Quin, Captain Hon. Valentine Maurice W.; *see* Wyndham-Quin.
Quinan, Gen. Sir Edward Pellew, 1885–1960, vol. V
Quinan, Kenneth Bingham, 1878–1948, vol. IV
Quince, Tom; *see* Marriott, E.
Quine, Rev. John, 1857–1940, vol. III
Quine, Willard Van Orman, 1908–2000, vol. X
Quinlan, Maj.-Gen. Henry, 1906–2000, vol. X
Quinlan, Hon. Timothy Francis, 1861–1927, vol. II
Quinn, Most Rev. Austin, 1892–1974, vol. VII
Quinn, Harley; *see* Thorley, Wilfrid.
Quinn, James, 1870–1951, vol. V
Quinn, John, 1870–1924, vol. II, vol. III
Quinn, Sir Patrick, 1855–1936, vol. III
Quinnell, Cecil Watson, 1868–1932, vol. III
Quinnell, Air Cdre John Charles, 1891–1983, vol. VIII
Quinton, Hon. Herman William, 1896–1952, vol. V
Quinton, Richard Frith, 1849–1934, vol. III
Quirk, Lt-Col Douglas, 1887–1941, vol. IV
Quirk, Rev. James Francis, 1850–1927, vol. II
Quirk, Rt Rev. Canon John Nathaniel, 1849–1924, vol. II
Quirk, Col John Owen, 1847–1928, vol. II
Quirk, Rev. Canon Robert, 1883–1949, vol. IV
Quirk, Roger Nathaniel, 1909–1964, vol. VI
Quirk, Ronald Charles, 1908–1973, vol. VII
Quist, Sir Emmanuel Charles, *died* 1959, vol. V
Quraishi, Khan Bahadur Nawab, *born* 1878, vol. VI
Qvist, George, 1910–1981, vol. VIII

R

Rabagliati, Andrea Carlo Francisco, 1843–1930, vol. III
Rabagliati, Herman Victor, 1883–1962, vol. VI
Raban, Brig.-Gen. Sir Edward, 1850–1927, vol. II
Rabett, Brig. Reginald Lee Rex, 1887–1966, vol. VI
Rabi, Isidor Isaac, 1898–1988, vol. VIII
Rabin, Yitzhak, 1922–1995, vol. IX
Rabino, H. Louis, 1877–1950, vol. IV, vol. V
Raborn, Vice-Adm. William Francis, Jr, 1905–1990, vol. VIII
Rabukawaqa, Sir Joshua Rasilau, 1917–1992, vol. IX
Raby, Frederic James Edward, 1888–1966, vol. VI
Raby, Henry James, 1827–1907, vol. I
Raby, Joseph Thomas, 1853–1916, vol. II
Raby, Sir Victor Harry, 1897–1990, vol. VIII
Race, Robert Russell, 1907–1984, vol. VIII
Rachmaninoff, Sergei Vassilievitch, 1873–1943, vol. IV
Rackham, Arthur, 1867–1939, vol. III
Rackham, Bernard, 1876–1964, vol. VI
Rackham, Clara Dorothea, 1875–1966, vol. VI
Rackham, Harris, 1868–1944, vol. IV
Raczynski, Count Edward, 1891–1993, vol. IX
Radcliffe, 1st Viscount, 1899–1977, vol. VII
Radcliffe, Alexander Nelson, 1856–1944, vol. IV
Radcliffe, Very Rev. Bennett Samuel, died 1943, vol. IV
Radcliffe, Brig.-Gen. Sir Charles D.; see Delme-Radcliffe.
Radcliffe, Sir Clifford Walter, 1888–1965, vol. VI
Radcliffe, Sir David, 1834–1907, vol. I
Radcliffe, Sir Everard; see Radcliffe, Sir J. B. E. H.
Radcliffe, Sir Everard Joseph, 5th Bt, 1884–1969, vol. VI
Radcliffe, Francis Reynolds Yonge, 1851–1924, vol. II
Radcliffe, Sir Frederick Morton, 1861–1953, vol. V
Radcliffe, Brig.-Gen. Frederick Walter, 1873–1934, vol. III
Radcliffe, Geoffrey Reynolds Yonge, 1886–1959, vol. V
Radcliffe, Ven. Harry Sydney, 1867–1949, vol. IV
Radcliffe, Henry, died 1921, vol. II
Radcliffe, Hugh John Reginald Joseph, 1911–1993, vol. IX
Radcliffe, Major Jasper Fitzgerald, 1867–1916, vol. II
Radcliffe, Rev. John Ed., 1846–1919, vol. II
Radcliffe, Sir (Joseph Benedict) Everard (Henry), 6th Bt, 1910–1975, vol. VII
Radcliffe, Sir Joseph Edward, 4th Bt, 1858–1949, vol. IV
Radcliffe, Sir Joseph Percival Pickford, 3rd Bt, 1824–1908, vol. I
Radcliffe, Col Nathaniel Robert, 1870–1930, vol. III
Radcliffe, Percy, 1916–1991, vol. IX
Radcliffe, Gen. Sir Percy Pollexfen de Blaquiere, 1874–1934, vol. III
Radcliffe, Col Philip John Joseph, 1863–1943, vol. IV

Radcliffe, Sir Pollexfen; see Radcliffe, Sir W. P.
Radcliffe, Sir Ralph Hubert John D.; see Delme-Radcliffe.
Radcliffe, Lt-Gen. Robert Parker, 1819–1907, vol. I
Radcliffe, Vice-Adm. Stephen Herbert, 1874–1939, vol. III
Radcliffe, William, 1856–1938, vol. III
Radcliffe, Sir (William) Pollexfen, 1822–1897, vol. I
Radcliffe, Wyndham Ivor, died 1927, vol. II
Radcliffe-Brown, Alfred Reginald, 1881–1955, vol. V
Radcliffe-Cooke, Charles Wallwyn; see Cooke.
Radclyffe, Lt-Col Charles Edward, 1864–1915, vol. I
Radclyffe, Sir Charles Edward M.; see Mott-Radclyffe.
Radclyffe, Major (Charles Robert) Eustace, 1873–1953, vol. V
Radclyffe, Major Eustace; see Radclyffe, Major C. R. E.
Radden, Horace Gray, 1903–1966, vol. VI
Radford, Arthur, 1888–1963, vol. VI
Radford, Adm. Arthur William, 1896–1973, vol. VII
Radford, Basil, 1897–1952, vol. V
Radford, Sir Charles Horace, 1854–1916, vol. II
Radford, (Courtenay Arthur) Ralegh, 1900–1998, vol. X
Radford, Air Cdre Dudley Spencer, 1910–1984, vol. VIII
Radford, Edmund Ashworth, 1881–1944, vol. IV
Radford, Edward, 1831–1920, vol. II
Radford, Sir George Heynes, 1851–1917, vol. II
Radford, Rt Rev. Lewis Bostock, 1869–1937, vol. III
Radford, Col Oswald Claude, 1850–1924, vol. II
Radford, Ralegh; see Radford, C. A. R.
Radford, Robert, 1874–1933, vol. III
Radford, Sir Ronald Walter, 1916–1995, vol. IX
Radhakrishnan, Sir Sarvepalli, 1888–1975, vol. VII
Radhanpur, Nawab Sahib of, 1889–1936, vol. III
Radice, Mrs A. H., (Sheila Radice), died 1960, vol. V
Radice, Edward Albert, 1907–1996, vol. X
Radice, Evasio Hampden, 1866–1909, vol. I
Radice, Fulke Rosavo, 1888–1987, vol. VIII
Radice, Italo de Lisle, 1911–2000, vol. X
Radice, Sheila; see Radice, Mrs A. H.
Radin, Max, 1880–1950, vol. IV (A), vol. V
Radley, Sir Gordon; see Radley, Sir W. G.
Radley, Brig. Hugh Poynton, 1891–1943, vol. IV
Radley, Oswald Alfred, 1887–1977, vol. VII
Radley, Sir (William) Gordon, 1898–1970, vol. VI
Radnor, 5th Earl of, 1841–1900, vol. I
Radnor, 6th Earl of, 1868–1930, vol. III
Radnor, 7th Earl of, 1895–1968, vol. VI
Rado, Richard, 1906–1989, vol. VIII
Radstock, 3rd Baron, 1833–1913, vol. I
Radstock, 4th Baron, 1859–1937, vol. III
Radstock, 5th Baron, 1867–1953, vol. V
Radzinowicz, Sir Leon, 1906–1999, vol. X

Rae, Sir Alexander, 1849–1924, vol. II
Rae, Sir Alexander (Montgomery) Wilson, 1896–1978, vol. VII
Rae, Allan Alexander Sinclair, 1925–1999, vol. X
Rae, Lt-Col Cecil, 1880–1945, vol. IV
Rae, Brig. Cecil Alexander, 1889–1966, vol. VI
Rae, Cecil Douglas, 1882–1942, vol. IV
Rae, Charles Robert Angus, 1922–1990, vol. VIII
Rae, Duncan McFadyen, 1888–1964, vol. VI
Rae, George Bentham Leathart, 1884–1958, vol. V
Rae, Henrietta; *see* Normand, Mrs Ernest.
Rae, Henry Edward Grant, 1925–1999, vol. X
Rae, Sir (Henry) Norman, 1860–1928, vol. II
Rae, Sir James, 1879–1957, vol. V
Rae, Captain Sir James Robert, 1859–1928, vol. II
Rae, Sir James Stanley, 1881–1956, vol. V
Rae, John, 1845–1915, vol. I
Rae, Sir Norman; *see* Rae, Sir H. N.
Rae, Sir Robert, 1894–1971, vol. VII
Rae, Robert Wright, 1914–1995, vol. X (AI)
Rae, Air Vice-Marshal Ronald Arthur R.; *see* Ramsay Rae.
Rae, William, 1840–1907, vol. I
Rae, Lt-Col William, 1883–1973, vol. VII
Rae, William Fraser, 1835–1905, vol. I
Rae Smith, Sir Alan, 1885–1961, vol. VI
Raeburn, Agnes M., *died* 1955, vol. V
Raeburn, Sir Colin, 1894–1970, vol. VI
Raeburn, Sir Edward Alfred, 3rd Bt, 1919–1977, vol. VII
Raeburn, Sir Ernest Manifold, 1878–1922, vol. II
Raeburn, Henry Raeburn Macbeth-, 1860–1947, vol. IV
Raeburn, Walter Augustus Leopold, 1897–1972, vol. IV
Raeburn, Sir William Hannay, 1st Bt, 1850–1934, vol. III
Raeburn, Sir William Norman, 2nd Bt, 1877–1947, vol. IV
Raemaekers, Louis, 1869–1956, vol. V
Rafael, Gideon, 1913–1999, vol. X
Raffaelli, J. F., 1850–1924, vol. II
Raffan, Peter Wilson, 1863–1940, vol. III
Rafferty, Rt Rev. Mgr Kevin Lawrence, 1933–1996, vol. X
Rafferty, Michael Harvey, 1877–1953, vol. V
Raffety, Frank Walter, 1875–1946, vol. IV
Raffety, Harold Vezey, 1873–1948, vol. IV
Raffles, Rev. Thomas Stamford, 1853–1926, vol. II
Raffles-Flint, Ven. Stamford Raffles, 1847–1925, vol. II
Raffray, Sir Philippe, 1888–1975, vol. VII
Rafter, Sir Charles Haughton, *died* 1935, vol. III
Raftery, Peter Albert, 1929–1996, vol. X
Ragg, Rt Rev. Harry Richard, 1889–1967, vol. VI
Ragg, Sir Hugh Hall, 1882–1963, vol. VI
Ragg, Ven. Lonsdale, 1866–1945, vol. IV
Ragg, Air Vice-Marshal Robert Linton, 1901–1973, vol. VII
Ragg, Rev. William Henry Murray, 1861–1944, vol. IV
Raggatt, Sir Harold George, 1900–1968, vol. VI
Raghava Rau, G. Pantulu, 1862–1921, vol. II
Raghavendra Rao, E., *died* 1942, vol. IV

Raghunath Das, Diwan Bahadur Sir Chaube, 1849–1923, vol. II
Raghunath Rao Dinkar, Rao Raja, Mashir-i-Khas Bahadur, Madar-ul-Moham, *born* 1858, vol. II
Raglan, 3rd Baron, 1857–1921, vol. II
Raglan, 4th Baron, 1885–1964, vol. VI
Rahilly, Captain Denis Edward, 1887–1966, vol. VI
Rahim, Sir Abdur, 1867–1952, vol. V
Rahimtoola, Sir Fazal Ibrahim, 1895–1977, vol. VII
Rahimtoola, Habib Ibrahim, 1912–1991, vol. IX
Rahimtoola, Sir Ibrahim, 1862–1942, vol. IV
Rahman, Shaikh Abdur, 1903–1979, vol. VII
Rahman, Sir Ahmed Fazlur, *died* 1945, vol. IV (A), vol. V
Rahman, Sheikh Mujibur, 1920–1975, vol. VII
Rahman Putra, Tunku (Prince) Abdul; *see* Abdul Rahman Putra.
Raikes, Captain Arthur E. H., 1867–1915, vol. I
Raikes, Arthur Stewart, 1856–1925, vol. II
Raikes, Vice-Adm. Cecil Dacre Staveley, 1874–1947, vol. IV
Raikes, Maj.-Gen. Charles Lewis, 1837–1919, vol. II
Raikes, Col David Taunton, 1897–1966, vol. VI
Raikes, Ernest Barkley, 1863–1931, vol. III
Raikes, Francis Edward, 1870–1922, vol. II
Raikes, Francis William, *died* 1906, vol. I
Raikes, Lt-Col Frederick Duncan, 1848–1915, vol. I
Raikes, Maj.-Gen. Sir Geoffrey Taunton, 1884–1975, vol. VII
Raikes, Maj.-Gen. George Leonard, 1878–1949, vol. IV
Raikes, Henry St John Digby, 1863–1943, vol. IV
Raikes, Sir (Henry) Victor (Alpin MacKinnon), 1901–1986, vol. VIII
Raikes, Humphrey Rivaz, *died* 1955, vol. V
Raikes, Col Lawrence Taunton, 1882–1932, vol. III
Raikes, Adm. Sir Robert Henry Taunton, 1885–1953, vol. V
Raikes, Gen. Robert Napier, 1813–1909, vol. I
Raikes, Sir Victor; *see* Raikes, Sir H. V. A. M.
Raikes, Rev. Walter Allan, 1852–1928, vol. II
Railing, Sir Harry, 1878–1963, vol. VI
Railing, Max John, 1868–1942, vol. IV
Railston, Lt-Col Henry George Moreton P.; *see* Pleydell-Railston.
Railton, Herbert, 1857–1910, vol. I
Railton, James, 1863–1949, vol. IV
Railton, Brig. Dame Mary, 1906–1992, vol. IX
Railton, Ven. Nathaniel Gerard, 1886–1948, vol. IV
Railton, Reid Antony, 1895–1977, vol. VII
Raimond, C. E.; *see* Robins, Elizabeth.
Rainals, Sir Harry Thomas Alfred, 1816–1899, vol. I
Rainbird, George Meadus, 1905–1986, vol. VIII
Raine, Allen, 1836–1908, vol. I
Raine, (Harcourt) Neale, 1923–1994, vol. IX
Raine, Neale; *see* Raine, H. N.
Raine, Sir Walter, 1874–1938, vol. III
Raines, Gen. Sir Julius Augustus Robert, 1827–1909, vol. I
Raines, Lt-Col Ralph Gore Devereux Groves-, 1877–1953, vol. V
Rainey, Lt-Col John Wakefield, 1881–1967, vol. VI
Rainey, Reginald Charles, 1913–1990, vol. VIII

Rainey, William, 1852–1936, vol. III
Rainey-Robinson, Col Robert Maximilian, 1861–1932, vol. III
Rainier, Adm. John Harvey, 1847–1915, vol. I
Rains, Claude, 1889–1967, vol. VI
Rainsford, Col Marcus Edward Read, 1853–1933, vol. III
Rainsford, Surg. Rear-Adm. Seymour Grome, 1900–1994, vol. IX
Rainsford, Col Stephen Dickson, 1853–1920, vol. II
Rainsford, Col William John Read, 1852–1932, vol. III
Rainsford-Hannay, Brig.-Gen. Frederick, 1854–1950, vol. IV
Rainsford-Hannay, Col Frederick, 1878–1959, vol. V
Rainsford-Hannay, Col Ramsay William, 1844–1933, vol. III
Rainville, Hon. Henri B., 1852–1937, vol. III
Rainwater, James; see Rainwater, L. J.
Rainwater, (Leo) James, 1917–1986, vol. VIII
Rainy, Adam Rolland, 1862–1911, vol. I
Rainy, Sir George, 1875–1946, vol. IV
Rainy, Rev. Robert, 1826–1906, vol. I
Raisman, Sir (Abraham) Jeremy, 1892–1978, vol. VII
Raisman, Sir Jeremy; see Raisman, Sir A. J.
Raison, Rev. Herbert Chaplin, 1889–1952, vol. V
Raistrick, Harold, 1890–1971, vol. VII
Rait, Lt-Col Arthur John, 1839–1902, vol. I
Rait, Helen Anna Macdonald, died 1955, vol. V
Rait, Sir Robert Sangster, 1874–1936, vol. III
Rait Kerr, Col Rowan Scrope, 1891–1961, vol. VI
Raitt, Maj.-Gen. Sir Herbert Aveling, 1858–1935, vol. III
Rajadhyaksha, Ganpat Sakharam, 1896–1955, vol. V
Rajagopala, Sir Chariyar, Perungavur, 1862–1927, vol. II
Rajagopalachari, Sir Shrinivas Prasonna, 1883–1963, vol. VI
Rajagopalacharya, Chakravarti, 1878–1972, vol. VII
Rajah, Arumugam Ponnu, 1911–1999, vol. X
Rajapakse, Sir Lalita Abhaya, 1900–1976, vol. VII
Rajgarh, HH Rajah Bir Indra of, died 1936, vol. III
Rajkot, Thakore Saheb Shri Dharmendrasinhji Lakhaji Raj, 1910–1940, vol. III
Rajkot, Thakore Saheb Sir Lakhaji Raj Bawaji Raj, 1885–1930, vol. III
Rajpipla, Raja of, 1862–1915, vol. I
Rajpipla, Maharaja of, died 1951, vol. V
Rajwade, Maj.-Gen. Ganpatrao Raghunath Raja, Mushir-i-Khas Bahadur, Shaukat-Jung, 1884–1945, vol. IV
Rake, Alfred Mordey, 1906–1978, vol. VII
Raleigh, Cecil, died 1914, vol. I
Raleigh, Nigel Hugh C.; see Curtis-Raleigh.
Raleigh, Hon. Sir Thomas, 1850–1920, vol. II
Raleigh, Sir Walter Alexander, 1861–1922, vol. II
Ralfs, Maj.-Gen. Bertram George, 1905–1977, vol. VII
Ralli, Augustus John, 1875–1954, vol. V
Ralli, Constantine S.; see Scaramanga-Ralli.
Ralli, Sir Lucas Eustratio, 1st Bt, 1846–1931, vol. III

Ralli, Pandeli, 1845–1928, vol. II
Ralli, Sir Strati, 2nd Bt, 1876–1964, vol. VI
Ralph, Col Alfred Colyer, 1869–1932, vol. III
Ralph, Annabella, 1884–1962, vol. VI
Ralph, Helen Douglas Guest, 1892–1961, vol. VI
Ralph, Herbert Walter, 1885–1955, vol. V
Ralph, Ronald Seton, 1895–1985, vol. VIII
Ralph, William, 1841–1928, vol. II, vol. III
Ralphs, Sir (Frederick) Lincoln, 1909–1978, vol. VII
Ralphs, Sir Lincoln; see Ralphs, Sir F. L.
Ralston, Alexander Gerard, 1860–1932, vol. III
Ralston, Col Alexander Windeyer, 1885–1971, vol. VII
Ralston, Col Hon. James Layton, 1881–1948, vol. IV
Ralston, Maj.-Gen. William Henry, 1837–1914, vol. I
Ram, Abel John, 1842–1920, vol. II
Ram, Sir Granville; see Ram, Sir L. A. J. G.
Ram, Jagjivan, 1908–1986, vol. VIII
Ram, Rai Bahadur Sir Lala G.; see Ganga Ram.
Ram, Sir (Lala) Shri, 1884–1963, vol. VI
Ram, Sir (Lucius Abel John) Granville, 1885–1952, vol. V
Ram, Rev. Robert Digby, 1844–1925, vol. II
Ram, Sir Shri; see Ram, Sir L. S.
Ram, Rev. Stephen Adye Scott, 1864–1928, vol. II
Ram, William Francis Willett, 1907–1968, vol. VI
Ram Chandra, 1889–1987, vol. VIII
Ramachandra Rao, Dewan Bahadur Sir M., 1868–1936, vol. III
Ramaciotti, Maj.-Gen. Gustave, 1861–1927, vol. II
Ramage, Cathleen Mary; see Nesbitt, C. M.
Ramage, Captain Cecil Beresford, 1895–1988, vol. VIII
Ramage, Sir Richard Ogilvy, 1896–1971, vol. VII
Ramakrishna, T., born 1854, vol. II
Raman, Sir (Chandrasekhara) Venkata, 1888–1970, vol. VI
Raman, Sir Venkata; see Raman, Sir C. V.
Ramanathan, Sir Ponnambalam, 1851–1930, vol. III
Ramasany Mudaliyar, Raja Sir Savalai, 1840–1911, vol. I
Ramaswami Aiyar, Sir Chetpat Pattabhirama, 1879–1966, vol. VI
Rambaut, Arthur Alcock, 1859–1923, vol. II
Rambert, Dame Marie (Dame Marie Dukes), 1888–1982, vol. VIII
Ramée, Marie Louise De la; see Ouida.
Ramelson, Baruch, (Bert), 1910–1994, vol. IX
Ramelson, Bert; see Ramelson, Baruch.
Ramgoolam, Rt Hon. Sir Seewoosagur, 1900–1985, vol. VIII
Rammingen, Baron Luitbert Alexander George Lionel Alphons P.; see Pawel-Rammingen.
Rampal, Jean-Pierre Louis, 1922–2000, vol. X
Rampal Singh, Raja, 1867–1909, vol. I
Rampolla, His Eminence Cardinal Mariano, 1843–1913, vol. I
Rampton, Sir Jack Leslie, 1920–1994, vol. IX
Rampur, Nawab Sir Sayed Mohammad Hamid Ali Khan Bahadur, 1875–1930, vol. III
Rampur, Maj.-Gen. HH the Nawab, 1906–1966, vol. VI

Ramsay, Maj.-Gen. Sir Alan Hollick, 1895–1973, vol. VII

Ramsay, Alexander, 1822–1909, vol. I

Ramsay, Rev. Alexander, 1857–1935, vol. III

Ramsay, Sir Alexander, 1887–1969, vol. VI

Ramsay, Sir Alexander Burnett, 6th Bt (cr 1806), 1903–1965, vol. VI

Ramsay, Sir Alexander Entwisle, 4th Bt (cr 1806), 1837–1902, vol. I

Ramsay, Adm. Hon. Sir Alexander Robert Maule, 1881–1972, vol. VII

Ramsay, Allen Beville, 1872–1955, vol. V

Ramsay, Andrew Maitland, 1859–1946, vol. IV

Ramsay, Captain Archibald Henry Maule, died 1955, vol. V

Ramsay, Lt-Col Arthur Dennys Gilbert, 1872–1939, vol. III

Ramsay, Adm. Sir Bertram Home, 1883–1945, vol. IV

Ramsay, Hon. Charles Maule, 1859–1936, vol. III

Ramsay, Clyde Archibald, 1914–1974, vol. VII

Ramsay, Maj.-Gen. Frank William, 1875–1954, vol. V

Ramsay, Rev. Frederick Ernest, died 1913, vol. I

Ramsay, Sir George Dalhousie, 1828–1920, vol. II

Ramsay, George Gilbert, 1839–1921, vol. II

Ramsay, Gilbert Anderson, 1880–1915, vol. I

Ramsay, Graham Colville, 1889–1959, vol. V

Ramsay, Henry Havelock, 1863–1929, vol. III

Ramsay, Henry Thomas, 1907–1997, vol. X

Ramsay, Sir Herbert, 5th Bt (cr 1806), 1868–1924, vol. II

Ramsay, Maj.-Gen. Herbert Maynard, 1843–1917, vol. II

Ramsay, Comdr Hugh Malcolm, 1884–1975, vol. VII

Ramsay, Rev. Ivor Erskine St Clair, 1902–1956, vol. V

Ramsay, J. Grant, 1856–1940, vol. III

Ramsay, James, 1905–1959, vol. V

Ramsay, J(ames) Arthur, 1909–1988, vol. VIII

Ramsay, Sir James Douglas, 11th Bt (cr 1666), 1878–1959, vol. V

Ramsay, Lt-Col James Gordon, 1880–1952, vol. V

Ramsay, Sir James Henry, 10th Bt (cr 1666), 1832–1925, vol. II

Ramsay, Cdre Sir James Maxwell, 1916–1986, vol. VIII

Ramsay, Lt-Col Sir John, 1862–1942, vol. IV

Ramsay, Sir John, 1872–1944, vol. IV

Ramsay, Maj.-Gen. Sir John George, 1856–1920, vol. II

Ramsay, Dom Leander; see Ramsay, H. H.

Ramsay, Louis Eveleigh Bawtree C.; see Cobden-Ramsay.

Ramsay, Mabel Lieda, died 1954, vol. V

Ramsay, Sir Malcolm Graham, 1871–1946, vol. IV

Ramsay, Sir Neis Alexander, 12th Bt, 1909–1986, vol. VIII

Ramsay, Norman James Gemmill, 1916–1999, vol. X

Ramsay, The Lady Patricia, (Victoria Patricia Helena Elizabeth), 1886–1974, vol. VII

Ramsay, Hon. Sir Patrick William Maule, 1879–1962, vol. VI

Ramsay, Robert Anstruther, 1887–1975, vol. VII

Ramsay, Rt Rev. Ronald Erskine, 1882–1954, vol. V

Ramsay, Thomas Anderson, 1920–1998, vol. X

Ramsay, Thomas Bridgehill Wilson, 1887–1956, vol. V

Ramsay, Sir Thomas Meek, 1907–1995, vol. IX

Ramsay, Sir William, 1852–1916, vol. II

Ramsay, Sir William Clark, 1901–1973, vol. VII

Ramsay, Sir William Mitchell, 1851–1939, vol. III

Ramsay-Fairfax, Lt-Col William George Astell, 1876–1946, vol. IV

Ramsay-Fairfax, Sir William George Herbert Taylor; see Fairfax.

Ramsay-Fairfax-Lucy, Major Sir Brian Fulke Cameron; see Fairfax-Lucy.

Ramsay-Fairfax-Lucy, Sir Henry William Cameron; see Fairfax-Lucy.

Ramsay Rae, Air Vice-Marshal Ronald Arthur, 1910–1994, vol. IX

Ramsay-Steel-Maitland, Sir Keith Richard Felix; see Steel-Maitland.

Ramsbotham, Rt Rev. John Alexander, 1906–1989, vol. VIII

Ramsbottom, Edmund Cecil, 1881–1959, vol. V

Ramsbottom, John, 1885–1974, vol. VII

Ramsbottom, John William, 1883–1966, vol. VI

Ramsden, 1st Baron, 1883–1955, vol. V

Ramsden, Brig. Sir Arthur Maxwell, 1894–1957, vol. V

Ramsden, Sir Caryl Oliver Imbert, 8th Bt, 1915–1987, vol. VIII

Ramsden, Charles Frederick Ingram, 1888–1958, vol. V

Ramsden, Sir Geoffrey Charles Frescheville, 1893–1990, vol. VIII

Ramsden, George Taylor, 1879–1936, vol. III

Ramsden, Lady Guendolen; see Ramsden, Lady H. G.

Ramsden, Lady (Helen) Guendolen, 1846–1910, vol. I

Ramsden, Col Herbert Frecheville Smyth, 1856–1931, vol. III

Ramsden, John Charles Francis, 1835–1910, vol. I

Ramsden, Sir John Frecheville, 6th Bt, 1877–1958, vol. V

Ramsden, John Watkinson, 1880–1943, vol. IV

Ramsden, Sir John William, 5th Bt, 1831–1914, vol. I

Ramsden, Lt-Col Josslyn Vere, 1876–1952, vol. V

Ramsden, Omar, 1873–1939, vol. III

Ramsden, Sally; see Ramsden Sarah.

Ramsden, Sarah, (Sally), 1910–1995, vol. IX

Ramsden, Lt-Col Vincent Basil, 1888–1936, vol. III

Ramsden, Walter, died 1947, vol. IV

Ramsden, Sir William, 1857–1928, vol. II

Ramsden, Maj.-Gen. William Havelock Chaplin, 1888–1969, vol. VI

Ramsden, Major Sir William P.; see Pennington-Ramsden.

Ramsden-Jodrell, Dorothy Lynch, died 1958, vol. V

Ramsey of Canterbury, Baron (Life Peer); Rt Rev. and Rt Hon. Arthur Michael Ramsey, 1904–1988, vol. VIII

Ramsey, Sir Alfred Ernest, 1920–1999, vol. X

Ramsey, Alicia, *died* 1933, vol. III
Ramsey, Arthur Stanley, 1867–1954, vol. V
Ramsey, Adm. Sir Charles Gordon, 1882–1966, vol. VI
Ramsey, Col Colin Worthington Pope, 1883–1926, vol. II
Ramsey, Rt Rev. Ian Thomas, 1915–1972, vol. VII
Ramsey, Rt Rev. Kenneth Venner, 1909–1990, vol. VIII
Ramsey, Leonard Gerald Gwynne, 1913–1990, vol. VIII
Ramsey, Robert John, 1921–1986, vol. VIII
Ramsey, Stanley Churchill, 1882–1968, vol. VI
Ramson, Ven. John Luce, 1870–1944, vol. IV
Ramunni Menon, Sir Konkoth, 1872–1949, vol. IV
Ranalow, Frederick Baring, 1873–1953, vol. V
Ranasinha, Sir Arthur Godwin, 1898–1976, vol. VII (AII)
Ranbir Singh, Raja Sir, *died* 1916, vol. II
Rance, Gerald Francis, 1927–2000, vol. X
Rance, Maj.-Gen. Sir Hubert Elvin, 1898–1974, vol. VII
Rand, Benjamin, 1856–1934, vol. III
Rand, Ivan Cleveland, 1884–1969, vol. VI
Randall, Sir Alec Walter George, 1892–1977, vol. VII
Randall, Gp Captain Charles Russell Jekyl, 1879–1956, vol. V
Randall, Harry, 1860–1932, vol. III
Randall, Harry Enos, 1899–1976, vol. VII
Randall, Sir Henry Edward, 1847–1930, vol. III
Randall, Henry John, 1877–1964, vol. VI
Randall, Henry John, 1894–1967, vol. VI
Randall, J(ames) G(arfield), 1881–1953, vol. V
Randall, Rt Rev. James Leslie, *died* 1922, vol. II
Randall, John, 1810–1910, vol. I
Randall, Sir John Turton, 1905–1984, vol. VIII
Randall, John William, 1891–1979, vol. VII
Randall, Sir Richard John, 1906–1982, vol. VIII
Randall, Very Rev. Richard William, 1824–1906, vol. I
Randall, Terence George, 1904–1979, vol. VII
Randall, William Edward, 1920–1997, vol. X
Randall Lane, Henry Jerrold; *see* Lane.
Randall-MacIver, David, 1873–1945, vol. IV
Randegger, Alberto, 1832–1911, vol. I
Randell, Major Charles Edmund, 1893–1961, vol. VI
Randell, David, 1854–1912, vol. I
Randell, Hon. George, 1830–1912, vol. I
Randell, John Bulmer, 1918–1982, vol. VIII
Randell, Wilfrid L., 1874–1952, vol. V
Randle, Herbert Niel, 1880–1973, vol. VII
Randles, Sir John Scurrah, 1857–1945, vol. IV
Randles, Rev. Marshall, 1826–1904, vol. I
Randolph, Lt-Col Algernon Forbes, 1865–1953, vol. V
Randolph, Rev. Berkeley William, 1858–1925, vol. II
Randolph, Cyril George, 1899–1985, vol. VIII
Randolph, Mrs Evelyn St L.; *see* St Leger, E.
Randolph, Rev. Francis Charles H.; *see* Hingeston-Randolph.
Randolph, George Boscawen, 1864–1951, vol. V

Randolph, Adm. Sir George Granville, 1818–1907, vol. I
Randolph, John Hugh Edward, 1913–2000, vol. X
Randolph, Rt Rev. John Hugh Granville, 1866–1936, vol. III
Randolph, Joseph Randolph, 1867–1936, vol. III
Randolph, Rev. Michael Richard Spencer, 1925–1997, vol. X
Randolph, Peter, 1920–1971, vol. VII
Randolph, Ven. Thomas Berkeley, 1904–1987, vol. VIII
Randolph-Rose, Walter Clerk, 1884–1938, vol. III
Randrup, Michael, 1913–1984, vol. VIII
Ranfurly, 5th Earl of, 1856–1933, vol. III
Ranfurly, 6th Earl of, 1913–1988, vol. VIII
Ranganathan, Shiyali Ramamrita, 1892–1972, vol. VII
Ranger, Sir Douglas, 1916–1997, vol. X
Ranger, James, 1889–1975, vol. VII
Ranger, Sir Washington, 1848–1929, vol. III
Rangnekar, Hon. Sir Saiba Shankar, 1878–1949, vol. IV
Ranjitsinhji, Kumar Shri; *see* Nawanagar, Maharaja Jamsaheb of.
Rank, 1st Baron, 1888–1972, vol. VII
Rank, James Voase, 1881–1952, vol. V
Rank, Joseph, *died* 1943, vol. IV
Rank, Joseph McArthur, 1918–1999, vol. X
Rankeillour, 1st Baron, 1870–1949, vol. IV
Rankeillour, 2nd Baron, 1897–1958, vol. V
Rankeillour, 3rd Baron, 1899–1967, vol. VI
Ranken, William Bruce Ellis, 1881–1941, vol. IV
Rankin, Sir Alick Michael, 1935–1999, vol. X
Rankin, Lt-Col Allan Coats, 1877–1959, vol. V
Rankin, Dame Annabelle Jane Mary, *died* 1986, vol. VIII
Rankin, Archibald Aloysius, 1871–1951, vol. V
Rankin, Lt-Col (Arthur) Niall (Talbot), 1904–1965, vol. VI
Rankin, Brig.-Gen. Charles Herbert, 1873–1946, vol. IV
Rankin, Ethel Mary, 1893–1956, vol. V
Rankin, Rt Hon. Sir George Claus, 1877–1946, vol. IV
Rankin, Guthrie, 1854–1919, vol. II
Rankin, Maj.-Gen. Henry Charles Deans, 1888–1965, vol. VI
Rankin, Sir Hugh Charles Rhys, 3rd Bt, 1899–1988, vol. VIII
Rankin, Sir James, 1st Bt (*cr* 1898), 1842–1915, vol. I
Rankin, James Deans, 1918–2000, vol. X
Rankin, James Stuart, *died* 1960, vol. V
Rankin, John, 1845–1928, vol. II
Rankin, John, *died* 1973, vol. VII
Rankin, John Elliott, 1882–1960, vol. V
Rankin, John Eric, 1905–1976, vol. VII
Rankin, John Mitchell, 1924–1980, vol. VII
Rankin, Lt-Col Niall; *see* Rankin, Lt-Col A. N. T.
Rankin, Rev. Oliver Shaw, 1885–1954, vol. V
Rankin, Lt-Col Sir Reginald, 2nd Bt (*cr* 1898), 1871–1931, vol. III
Rankin, Sir Robert, 1st Bt (*cr* 1937), 1877–1960, vol. V
Rankin, Thomas, 1884–1959, vol. V

Rankin, William Brian, 1915–1976, vol. VII
Rankine, Alexander Oliver, 1881–1956, vol. V
Rankine, Sir John, 1846–1922, vol. II
Rankine, Sir John Dalzell, 1907–1987, vol. VIII
Rankine, Sir Richard Sims Donkin, 1875–1961, vol. VI
Rankine, Col Robert, 1868–1941, vol. IV
Ranking, Lt-Col George Speirs Alexander, 1852–1934, vol. III
Ranking, Robert Duncan, 1915–1994, vol. IX
Ranking, Maj.-Gen. Robert Philip Lancaster-, 1896–1961, vol. VI
Rankl, Karl, 1898–1968, vol. VI
Ranksborough, 1st Baron, 1852–1921, vol. II
Ransford, Col Sir Alister John, 1895–1974, vol. VII
Ransford, Ella, died 1968, vol. VI
Ransford, Rev. Robert Bolton, 1840–1914, vol. I
Ransom, Hon. Sir Alfred; see Ransom, Hon. Sir E. A.
Ransom, Rear-Adm. (S) Alfred Charles, 1871–1953, vol. V
Ransom, Charles Frederick George, 1911–1986, vol. VIII
Ransom, Hon. Sir (Ethelbert) Alfred, 1868–1943, vol. IV
Ransom, Herbert Charles, 1881–1960, vol. V
Ransom, William Henry, 1824–1907, vol. I
Ransome, Maj.-Gen. Algernon Lee, 1883–1969, vol. VI
Ransome, Arthur, 1834–1922, vol. II
Ransome, Arthur, 1884–1967, vol. VI
Ransome, Edward Coleby, 1864–1939, vol. III
Ransome, Sir Gordon Arthur, 1910–1978, vol. VII
Ransome, James, 1865–1944, vol. IV
Ransome, Maj.-Gen. Robert St George Tyldesley, 1903–1982, vol. VIII
Ransome, Stafford, 1860–1931, vol. III
Ranson, Col Wilson, 1870–1937, vol. III
Rapallo, Rt Rev. Edward, 1914–1984, vol. VIII
Raper, Agnes Madeline, died 1948, vol. IV
Raper, Alfred Baldwin, 1889–1941, vol. IV
Raper, Maj.-Gen. Allan Graeme, 1843–1906, vol. I
Raper, Vice-Adm. Sir George; see Raper, Vice-Adm. Sir R. G.
Raper, Henry Stanley, died 1951, vol. V
Raper, Sir John Hugh Francis, 1889–1955, vol. V
Raper, Sir Robert George, 1827–1901, vol. I
Raper, Vice-Adm. Sir (Robert) George, 1915–1990, vol. VIII
Raper, Robert William, 1842–1915, vol. I
Raphael, Chaim, 1908–1994, vol. IX
Raphael, Francis Charles, 1871–1945, vol. IV
Raphael, Geoffrey George, 1893–1969, vol. VI
Raphael, Sir Herbert Henry, 1st Bt, 1859–1924, vol. II
Raphael, John N. (Percival), 1868–1917, vol. II
Raphael, Ralph Alexander, 1921–1998, vol. X
Rapp, Sir Thomas Cecil, 1893–1984, vol. VIII
Rappoport, Angelo Solomon, 1871–1950, vol. IV
Rapson, Edward James, 1861–1937, vol. III
Ras Mekonen, Sir, 1852–1906, vol. I
Rasch, Sir Carne; see Rasch, Sir F. C.
Rasch, Sir Frederic Carne, 1st Bt, 1847–1914, vol. I
Rasch, Sir (Frederic) Carne, 2nd Bt, 1880–1963, vol. VI

Rasch, Brig. Guy Elland Carne, 1885–1955, vol. V
Rasch, Sir Richard Guy Carne, 3rd Bt, 1918–1996, vol. X
Raschen, George Herman, 1889–1964, vol. VI
Rash, Dora Eileen A.; see Wallace, Doreen.
Rashbrook, Engr Rear-Adm. Henry Samuel, 1856–1942, vol. IV
Rashdall, Very Rev. Hastings, 1858–1924, vol. II
Rashleigh, Sir Colman Battie, 3rd Bt, 1846–1907, vol. I
Rashleigh, Sir Colman Battie Walpole, 4th Bt, 1873–1951, vol. V
Rashleigh, Sir Harry Evelyn Battie, 5th Bt, 1923–1984, vol. VIII
Rashleigh, Rev. John Kendall, 1847–1933, vol. III
Rashleigh, Major Philip, 1881–1949, vol. IV
Rashleigh, Captain Vernon Stanhope, 1879–1946, vol. IV
Rashleigh, Rev. William, 1867–1937, vol. III
Rasminsky, Louis, 1908–1998, vol. X
Rasmussen, Knud, 1879–1933, vol. III
Rasmussen, Steen Eiler, 1898–1990, vol. VIII
Rason, Hon. Sir Cornthwaite Hector, 1858–1927, vol. II
Rason, Ernest Goldfinch, vol. II
Rassam, Hormuzd, 1826–1910, vol. I
Rastall, Robert Heron, 1871–1950, vol. IV
Rasul, Syed Alay, 1931–1987, vol. VIII
Ratcliff, Rev. Canon Edward Craddock, 1896–1967, vol. VI
Ratcliff, Robert Frederick, died 1943, vol. IV
Ratcliffe, Arthur, 1882–1963, vol. VI
Ratcliffe, Dorothy Una; see Phillips, Mrs McGrigor.
Ratcliffe, Henry Butler, died 1929, vol. III
Ratcliffe, John Ashworth, 1902–1987, vol. VIII
Ratcliffe, Reginald, 1908–1982, vol. VIII
Ratcliffe, Samuel Kerkham, 1868–1958, vol. V
Ratcliffe-Ellis, Sir Thomas Ratcliffe, 1842–1925, vol. II
Rathbone, Basil, 1892–1967, vol. VI
Rathbone, Eleanor, died 1946, vol. IV
Rathbone, Hugh Reynolds, died 1940, vol. III
Rathbone, John Francis Warre, 1909–1995, vol. IX
Rathbone, John Rankin, 1910–1940, vol. III
Rathbone, Monroe Jackson, 1900–1976, vol. VII
Rathbone, Very Rev. Norman Stanley, 1914–1995, vol. IX
Rathbone, Philip Richardson, 1913–1988, vol. VIII
Rathbone, William Gair, 1849–1919, vol. II
Rathborne, Air Cdre Charles Edward Harry, died 1943, vol. IV
Rathcavan, 1st Baron, 1883–1982, vol. VIII
Rathcavan, 2nd Baron, 1909–1994, vol. IX
Rathcreedan, 1st Baron, 1850–1930, vol. III
Rathcreedan, 2nd Baron, 1905–1990, vol. VIII
Rathdonnell, 2nd Baron, 1848–1929, vol. III
Rathdonnell, 3rd Baron, 1881–1937, vol. III
Rathdonnell, 4th Baron, 1914–1959, vol. V
Rathmore, 1st Baron, 1838–1919, vol. II
Rathom, John Revelstoke, 1868–1923, vol. II
Ratlam, Maj.-Gen. HH Maharaja Sir Sajjan Singhji, 1880–1947, vol. IV
Ratsey, Col Harold Edward, 1861–1953, vol. V
Ratten, Victor Richard, 1878–1962, vol. VI
Rattenbury, John Ernest, 1870–1963, vol. VI

Rattenbury, Robert Mantle, 1901–1970, vol. VI
Ratteray, Hon. Sir George Oswald, 1903–1980, vol. VII
Rattey, Engr-Rear-Adm. William, 1871–1939, vol. III
Ratti, Achille Ambrogio Damiano; *see* Pius XI.
Rattigan, Frank; *see* Rattigan, W. F. A.
Rattigan, Sir Henry Adolphus Byden, 1864–1920, vol. II
Rattigan, Sir Terence Mervyn, 1911–1977, vol. VII
Rattigan, (William) Frank (Arthur), 1879–1952, vol. V
Rattigan, Sir William Henry, 1842–1904, vol. I
Rattray, Rear-Adm. Sir Arthur Rullion, 1891–1966, vol. VI
Rattray, Brig.-Gen. Charles, 1868–1943, vol. IV
Rattray, Lt-Col Haldane Burney, 1870–1917, vol. II
Rattray, Lt-Gen. Sir James C.; *see* Clerk-Rattray.
Rattray, Col John Grant, 1867–1944, vol. IV
Rattray, Col Paul Robert Burn Clerk, 1859–1937, vol. III
Rattray, Robert Fleming, *died* 1967, vol. VI
Rattray, Captain Robert Sutherland, 1881–1938, vol. III
Rattray, Simon; *see* Trevor, E.
Rattray, Wellwood, 1849–1902, vol. I
Rattray Taylor, Gordon; *see* Taylor.
Ratter, John, 1908–1985, vol. VIII
Ratwatte, Sir Jayatilaka Cudah, *died* 1940, vol. III (A), vol. V
Rau, Sir Benegal Rama, 1889–1969, vol. VI
Rau, Bhimanakunté Hanumanta, 1855–1922, vol. II
Rau, Sir Narsing, 1887–1953, vol. V
Rau, Sir Raghavendra, 1889–1942, vol. IV
Ravel, Maurice, 1875–1937, vol. III
Raven, Rev. Berney Wodehouse, *died* 1911, vol. I
Raven, Rev. Charles Earle, 1885–1964, vol. VI
Raven, Edward, 1874–1952, vol. V
Raven, Rev. Edward Earle, 1889–1951, vol. V
Raven, Rev. John James, 1833–1906, vol. I
Raven, Rear-Adm. John Stanley, 1910–1987, vol. VIII
Raven, Dame Kathleen, (Dame Kathleen Annie Ingram), 1910–1999, vol. X
Raven, Martin Owen, 1888–1976, vol. VII
Raven, Ronald William, 1904–1991, vol. IX
Raven, Sir Vincent Litchfield, 1859–1934, vol. III
Raven-Hart, Rev. William Roland, *died* 1919, vol. II
Raven-Hill, Leonard, 1867–1942, vol. IV
Ravenel, Mazyck P., *died* 1946, vol. IV
Ravenhill, Lt-Col Edgar Evelyn, 1859–1907, vol. I
Ravenhill, Brig.-Gen. Frederick Thornhill, 1865–1935, vol. III
Ravenhill, Col Harry Stuart, 1872–1930, vol. III
Ravenhill, Rev. Henry Everett, 1831–1913, vol. I
Ravenscroft, Edward William, 1831–1911, vol. I
Ravensdale, Baroness (2nd in line), 1896–1966, vol. VI
Ravensdale, Thomas Corney, 1905–1990, vol. VIII
Ravenshaw, Lt-Col Charles Withers, 1851–1935, vol. III
Ravenshaw, Maj.-Gen. Hurdis Secundus Lalande, 1869–1920, vol. II
Ravenshear, Ewart Watson, 1893–1959, vol. V
Ravenstein, Ernest George, 1834–1913, vol. I

Ravensworth, 2nd Earl, 1821–1903, vol. I
Ravensworth, 3rd Earl, 1833–1904, vol. I
Ravensworth, 5th Baron, 1837–1919, vol. II
Ravensworth, 6th Baron, 1869–1932, vol. III
Ravensworth, 7th Baron, 1902–1950, vol. IV
Raverat, Gwendolen Mary, 1885–1957, vol. V
Ravilious, Eric, *died* 1942, vol. IV
Raw, Brig. Cecil Whitfield, 1900–1969, vol. VI
Raw, Lt-Col Nathan, 1866–1940, vol. III
Raw, Rupert George, 1912–1988, vol. VIII
Raw, Vice-Adm. Sir Sydney Moffatt, 1898–1967, vol. VI
Rawcliffe, Gordon Hindle, 1910–1979, vol. VII
Rawden-Smith, Rupert Rawden, 1912–1985, vol. VIII
Rawdon, Rev. J. Hamer, *died* 1916, vol. II
Rawdon-Hastings, Paulyn Charles James Reginald; *see* Hastings.
Rawdon-Hastings, Hon. Paulyn Francis Cuthbert, 1856–1907, vol. I
Rawdon Smith, Edward Rawdon, 1890–1957, vol. V
Rawle, Francis, 1846–1930, vol. III
Rawling, Brig.-Gen. Cecil Godfrey, 1870–1917, vol. II
Rawling, Ven. John, 1869–1955, vol. V
Rawlings, Adm. Sir Bernard; *see* Rawlings, Adm. Sir H. B. H.
Rawlings, Edmund Charles, 1854–1917, vol. II
Rawlings, Francis Ian Gregory, 1895–1969, vol. VI
Rawlings, Gertrude Burford, *died* 1939, vol. III
Rawlings, Adm. Sir (Henry) Bernard (Hughes), 1889–1962, vol. VI
Rawlings, Rear-Adm. Henry Clive, 1883–1965, vol. VI
Rawlings, Justly John Gabriel, 1868–1950, vol. IV
Rawlings, Margaret, 1906–1996, vol. X
Rawlings, Marjorie Kinnan, 1896–1953, vol. V
Rawlins, Maj.-Gen. Alexander Macdonell, 1838–1916, vol. II
Rawlins, Lt-Col Arthur Kennedy, 1868–1943, vol. IV
Rawlins, Evelyn Charles Donaldson, 1884–1971, vol. VII
Rawlins, Francis Hay, 1850–1920, vol. II
Rawlins, Morna Lloyd, 1882–1969, vol. VI
Rawlins, Percy Lionel Edwin, 1902–1977, vol. VII
Rawlins, Maj.-Gen. Stuart Blundell, 1897–1955, vol. V
Rawlins, Col Stuart William Hughes, 1880–1927, vol. II
Rawlins, William Donaldson, 1846–1920, vol. II
Rawlinson, 1st Baron, 1864–1925, vol. II
Rawlinson, Lt-Col Sir Alfred, 3rd Bt, 1867–1934, vol. III
Rawlinson, Rt Rev. Alfred Edward John, 1884–1960, vol. V
Rawlinson, Sir (Alfred) Frederick, 4th Bt, 1900–1969, vol. VI
Rawlinson, Sir Anthony Keith, 1926–1986, vol. VIII
Rawlinson, Rev. Bernard Stephen, 1865–1953, vol. V
Rawlinson, Lt-Col Charles Brooke, 1866–1919, vol. II
Rawlinson, Charles William, *died* 1910, vol. I
Rawlinson, Francis William, 1856–1944, vol. IV

Rawlinson, Sir Frederick; see Rawlinson, Sir A. F.
Rawlinson, Rev. Canon George, 1812–1902, vol. I
Rawlinson, Hugh George, 1880–1957, vol. V
Rawlinson, Rt Hon. John Frederick Peel, 1860–1926, vol. II
Rawlinson, Sir Joseph, 1897–1971, vol. VII
Rawlinson, Sir Robert, 1810–1898, vol. I
Rawlinson, Lt-Col Spencer Richard, 1848–1903, vol. I
Rawnsley, Col Claude, 1862–1944, vol. IV
Rawnsley, Edward Preston, 1851–1934, vol. III
Rawnsley, Col Gerald Thomas, 1865–1942, vol. IV
Rawnsley, Rev. Hardwicke Drummond, 1851–1920, vol. II
Rawnsley, Kenneth, 1926–1992, vol. IX
Raworth, Benjamin Alfred, 1849–1919, vol. II
Raws, Lt-Col Sir Lennon; see Raws, Lt-Col Sir W. L.
Raws, Lt-Col Sir (William) Lennon, 1878–1958, vol. V
Rawson, Sir Cooper, 1876–1946, vol. IV
Rawson, Brig. Creswell Duffield, 1883–1964, vol. VI
Rawson, Elizabeth Donata, 1934–1988, vol. VIII
Rawson, Frank, 1856–1928, vol. II
Rawson, Maj.-Gen. Geoffrey Grahame, 1887–1979, vol. VII
Rawson, Harry, 1862–1930, vol. III
Rawson, Adm. Sir Harry Holdsworth, 1843–1910, vol. I
Rawson, Col Herbert Edward, 1852–1924, vol. II
Rawson, Sir Rawson William, 1812–1899, vol. I
Rawson, Col Richard Hamilton, 1863–1918, vol. II
Rawson, Sir Stanley Walter, 1891–1973, vol. VII
Rawson-Shaw, William, 1860–1932, vol. III
Rawsthorne, Alan, 1905–1971, vol. VII
Rawstorne, Rt Rev. Atherton Gwillym, 1855–1936, vol. III
Rawstorne, Brig. George Streynsham, 1895–1962, vol. VI
Rawstorne, Lawrence, 1842–1938, vol. III
Rawstorne, Ven. Robert Atherton, 1824–1902, vol. I
Ray, Rt Rev. Chandu, born 1912, vol. VIII
Ray, Cyril, 1908–1991, vol. IX
Ray, Frederick Ivor, 1899–1983, vol. VIII
Ray, Gordon Norton, 1915–1986, vol. VIII
Ray, Maharaja Rao Sir Jogendra Narayan, died 1946, vol. IV
Ray, Maj.-Gen. Kenneth, 1894–1956, vol. V
Ray, Major MacCarthy Emmet, 1867–1906, vol. I
Ray, Mahendranath, 1862–1925, vol. II
Ray, Matthew Burrow, died 1950, vol. IV
Ray, Sir Prafulla Chandra, 1861–1944, vol. IV
Ray, Prithwis Chandra, 1870–1927, vol. II
Ray, Reginald Edwin Anthony, 1891–1972, vol. VII
Ray, Robin, 1935–1998, vol. X
Ray, Satyajit, 1921–1992, vol. IX
Ray, Sidney Herbert, 1858–1939, vol. III
Ray, Ted, 1905–1977, vol. VII
Ray, Sir William, 1876–1937, vol. III
Ray-Jones, Raymond, 1886–1942, vol. IV
Raybould, Clarence, 1886–1972, vol. VI
Raybould, Sidney Griffith, 1903–1977, vol. VII
Rayburn, Sam, 1882–1961, vol. VI
Rayleigh, 3rd Baron, 1842–1919, vol. II

Rayleigh, 4th Baron, 1875–1947, vol. IV
Rayleigh, 5th Baron, 1908–1988, vol. VIII
Rayment, Instr Captain Guy Varley, 1878–1951, vol. V
Raymer, Rev. Robert Richmond, 1870–1948, vol. IV
Raymond, Air Vice-Marshal Adélard, 1889–1962, vol. VI
Raymond, E. T.; see Thompson, Edward Raymond.
Raymond, Ernest, 1888–1974, vol. VII
Raymond, Col Francis, 1854–1945, vol. IV
Raymond, George, died 1929, vol. III
Raymond, George Lansing, 1839–1929, vol. III
Raymond, Harold, 1887–1975, vol. VII
Raymond, Lt-Col Maurice Claud, 1884–1959, vol. V
Raymond, Sir Stanley Edward, 1913–1988, vol. VIII
Raymond, Walter, 1852–1931, vol. III
Raymont, John Edwin George, 1915–1979, vol. VII
Raymont, Thomas, 1864, 1953, vol. V
Rayne, Sir Edward, 1922–1992, vol. IX
Rayner, Baron (Life Peer); Derek George Rayner, 1926–1998, vol. X
Rayner, Frank, 1866–1945, vol. IV
Rayner, Henry, 1841–1926, vol. II
Rayner, Vice-Adm. Herbert Sharples, 1911–1976, vol. VII
Rayner, Mabel Mary Cheveley, (Mrs W. N. Jones), died 1948, vol. IV
Rayner, Neville, 1914–1988, vol. VIII
Rayner, Brig. Sir Ralph, died 1977, vol. VII
Rayner, Sir Thomas Crossley, 1860–1914, vol. I
Raynes, Harold Ernest, 1882–1964, vol. VI
Raynes, John Richard, 1881–1944, vol. IV
Raynes, Rev. Raymond Richard Elliott, 1903–1958, vol. V
Raynes, William Robert, 1871–1966, vol. VI
Raynham, Eustace Frederick, died 1939, vol. III
Raynor, Geoffrey Vincent, 1913–1983, vol. VIII
Raynor, Rev. Philip Edwin, 1857–1930, vol. III
Raynor, Sir William Pick, 1854–1972, vol. II
Raynsford, Lt-Col Richard Montague, 1877–1965, vol. VI
Raza Ali, Sir Syed, 1882–1949, vol. IV
Razak bin Hussein, Hon. Tun Haji Abdul; see Abdul Razak.
Razzall, Leonard Humphrey, 1912–1999, vol. X
Rea, 1st Baron, 1873–1948, vol. IV
Rea, 2nd Baron, 1900–1981, vol. VIII
Rea, Lady; (Lorna), 1897–1978, vol. VII
Rea, Alec Lionel, 1878–1953, vol. V
Rea, Cecil W., died 1935, vol. III
Rea, Edward Hugh, died 1901, vol. I
Rea, George Grey, 1858–1931, vol. III
Rea, Major John George Grey, 1886–1955, vol. V
Rea, Robert Lindsay-, 1881–1971, vol. VII
Rea, Rt Hon. Russell, 1846–1916, vol. II
Read, Alan Ernest Alfred, 1926–1993, vol. IX
Read, Alexander Llewellyn, 1877–1942, vol. IV
Read, Alfred Burgess, 1899–1973, vol. VII
Read, Sir Alfred Henry, 1871–1955, vol. V
Read, Col Alfred Howard, 1893–1977, vol. VII
Read, Gen. Sir Antony; see Read, Gen. Sir J. A. J.
Read, Arthur Avery, 1868–1943, vol. IV

Read, Vice-Adm. Arthur Duncan, 1889–1976, vol. VII
Read, Bertie L.; see Lees Read.
Read, Carveth, 1848–1931, vol. III
Read, Charles; see Read, Cyril N.
Read, Sir Charles David, 1902–1957, vol. V
Read, Sir (Charles) Hercules, 1857–1929, vol. III
Read, Clare Sewell, 1826–1905, vol. I
Read, Conyers Read, 1881–1959, vol. V
Read, Cyril Norman, (Charles), 1925–1987, vol. VIII
Read, Edward Harry H.; see Handley-Read.
Read, Ernest, 1879–1965, vol. VI
Read, Francis Charles Jennings, 1875–1958, vol. V
Read, Grantly Dick-, 1890–1959, vol. V
Read, Brig.-Gen. Hastings, 1852–1928, vol. II
Read, Rt Rev. Henry Cecil, 1890–1963, vol. VI
Read, Sir Herbert Edward, 1893–1968, vol. VI
Read, Herbert Harold, 1889–1970, vol. VI
Read, Sir Herbert James, 1863–1949, vol. IV
Read, Sir Hercules; see Read, Sir C. H.
Read, John, 1884–1963, vol. VI
Read, Gen. Sir (John) Antony (Jervis), 1913–2000, vol. X
Read, (Sir) John Cecil, (styled 9th Bt cr 1641), 1820–1899, vol. I
Read, John Erskine, 1888–1973, vol. VII
Read, John Gordon, 1886–1958, vol. V
Read, Lt-Gen. Sir John Hugh Sherlock, 1917–1987, vol. VIII
Read, Margaret Helen, 1889–1991, vol. IX
Read, Opie, 1852–1939, vol. III (A), vol. IV
Read, Col Randulph Offley C.; see Crewe-Read.
Read, Col Richard Valentine, 1892–1964, vol. VI
Read, Simon Holcombe Jervis, 1922–1989, vol. VIII
Read, Thomas Talmage, 1893–1974, vol. VII
Read, Walter William, 1855–1907, vol. I
Read, William Henry McLeod, 1819–1909, vol. I
Read, (Sir) William Vero, (styled 10th Bt cr 1641), born 1839 (this entry was not transferred to Who Was Who).
Reade, Aleyn Lyell, 1876–1953, vol. V
Reade, Lt-Col Charles James, 1863–1912, vol. I, vol. III
Reade, Sir Clyde Nixon, 12th Bt, 1906–1982, vol. IX (AI)
Reade, Sir George Compton, 9th Bt, 1845–1908, vol. I
Reade, Rev George Edwin Pearsall, 1841–1937, vol. III
Reade, Sir George Franklin, 10th Bt, 1869–1923, vol. II
Reade, Herbert Taylor, 1828–1897, vol. I
Reade, Herbert Vincent, 1870–1929, vol. III
Reade, John, 1837–1919, vol. II
Reade, Surg. Maj.-Gen. Sir John By Cole, 1832–1914, vol. I
Reade, Sir John Stanhope, 11th Bt, 1896–1958, vol. V
Reade, Maj.-Gen. Raymond Northland Revell, 1861–1943, vol. IV
Reade, Robert Henry, died 1913, vol. I
Reader, Dame Audrey Tattie Hinchcliff, 1903–1989, vol. VIII

Reader, Ralph; see Reader, W. H. R.
Reader, (William Henry) Ralph, 1903–1982, vol. VIII
Reader Harris, Dame Diana; see Reader Harris, Dame. M. D.
Reader Harris, Dame (Muriel) Diana, 1912–1996, vol. X
Readett-Bayley, Sir H. Dennis, 1878–1940, vol. III
Readhead, Sir James, 1st Bt, died 1930, vol. III
Readhead, Sir James Halder, 2nd Bt, 1879–1940, vol. III
Readhead, James Templeman, (3rd Bt), 1910–1988, vol. VIII
Reading, 1st Marquess of, 1860–1935, vol. III
Reading, 2nd Marquess of, 1889–1960, vol. V
Reading, 3rd Marquess of, 1916–1980, vol. VII
Reading, Marchioness of; (Stella); Baroness Swanborough (Life Peer), 1894–1971, vol. VII
Reading, Marchioness of; (Eva Violet), 1895–1973, vol. VII
Reading, Maj.-Gen. Arnold Hughes Eagleton, 1896–1975, vol. VII
Reading, Sir Claude Hill, 1874–1946, vol. IV
Reading, Joseph Lewis, 1907–1980, vol. VII
Reading, Martin Luther, 1869–1943, vol. IV
Readman, Maj.-Gen. Edgar Platt, 1893–1980, vol. VII
Readwin, Edgar Seeley, 1915–1992, vol. IX
Ready, Gen. Sir Felix Fordati, 1872–1940, vol. III
Reakes, Charles John, 1865–1943, vol. IV
Reakes, George Leonard, 1889–1961, vol. VI
Real, Patrick, 1847–1928, vol. II
Reardon-Smith, Sir William; see Smith.
Reardon-Smith, Sir Willie; see Smith.
Reason, Richard Edmund, 1903–1987, vol. VIII
Reaume, Hon. Joseph Octave, 1856–1933, vol. III
Reavell, Arthur; see Reavell, J. A.
Reavell, (James) Arthur, 1872–1973, vol. VII
Reavell, Sir William, 1866–1948, vol. IV
Reay, 11th Lord, 1839–1921, vol. II
Reay, 12th Lord, 1870–1921, vol. II
Reay, 13th Lord, 1905–1963, vol. VI
Reay, Basil; see Reay, S. B.
Reay, Hon. Brig.-Gen. Charles Tom, 1857–1933, vol. III
Reay, George Adam, 1901–1971, vol. VII
Reay, Margaret Edith, 1876–1959, vol. V
Reay, (Stanley) Basil, 1909–1987, vol. VIII
Reay, Rev. Thomas Osmotherley, 1834–1914, vol. I
Rebbeck, Denis, 1914–1994, vol. IX
Rebbeck, Rear Adm. Sir Edward; see Rebbeck, Sir L. E.
Rebbeck, Sir Frederick Ernest, 1877–1964, vol. VI
Rebbeck, Rear-Adm. Sir (Leopold) Edward, 1901–1983, vol. VIII
Rébora, Piero, 1889–1963, vol. VI
Rebsch, Brig. William Knowles, 1885–1940, vol. III
Reckitt, Sir Harold James, 2nd Bt, 1868–1930, vol. III
Reckitt, Sir James, 1st Bt, 1833–1924, vol. II
Reckitt, Sir Philip Bealby, 3rd Bt, 1873–1944, vol. IV
Recknell, George Hugh, 1893–1975, vol. VII
Reclus, Jacques Elisée, 1830–1905, vol. I
Record, Edgar W., 1873–1943, vol. IV

Redcliffe-Maud, Baron (Life Peer); John Primatt Redcliffe Redcliffe-Maud, 1906–1982, vol. VIII

Reddaway, (Arthur Frederick) John, 1916–1990, vol. VIII

Reddaway, (George Frank) Norman, 1918–1999, vol. X

Reddaway, John; *see* Reddaway, A. F. J.

Reddaway, Norman; *see* Reddaway, G. F. N.

Reddaway, William Fiddian, 1872–1949, vol. IV

Reddick, Ven. Percy George, 1896–1978, vol. VII

Reddie, Brig.-Gen. Anthony Julian, 1873–1960, vol. V

Reddie, Cecil, 1858–1932, vol. III

Reddie, Charles Frederick, *died* 1931, vol. III

Reddie, Lt-Col Sir John Murray, 1872–1954, vol. V

Redding, Rt Rev. Donald Llewellyn, 1898–1969, vol. VI

Redding, John Magnus, 1889–1930, vol. III

Reddish, Sir Halford Walter Lupton, 1898–1978, vol. VII

Reddy, Sir C. Ramalinga, 1880–1951, vol. V

Reddy, Michael, *died* 1919, vol. II

Reddy, Neelam Sanjiva, 1913–1996, vol. X

Rede, Captain Roger L'Estrange Murray, *died* 1930, vol. III

Redesdale, 1st Baron, 1837–1916, vol. II

Redesdale, 2nd Baron, 1878–1958, vol. V

Redesdale, 3rd Baron, 1880–1962, vol. VI

Redesdale, 4th Baron, 1885–1963, vol. VI

Redesdale, 5th Baron, 1932–1991, vol. IX

Redfearn, Sir Herbert, 1915–1988, vol. VIII

Redfern, Sir (Arthur) Shuldham, 1895–1985, vol. VIII

Redfern, Sir Shuldham; *see* Redfern, Sir A. S.

Redfern, Rev. Thomas, 1853–1924, vol. II

Redfern, Thomas William, 1859–1924, vol. II

Redford, Arthur, 1896–1961, vol. VI

Redford, Sir Edward Pigott William, 1850–1933, vol. III

Redford, George Alexander, *died* 1916, vol. II

Redgrave, Sir Michael Scudamore, 1908–1985, vol. VIII

Redgrave, William Archibald, 1903–1986, vol. VIII

Redhead, Brian, 1929–1994, vol. IX

Redhead, Edward Charles, 1902–1967, vol. VI

Redhead, Captain Mahon, 1871–1940, vol. III

Redhead, Lt-Col Richard Henry M.; *see* Milne-Redhead.

Redington, Rt Hon. Christopher Talbot, 1847–1899, vol. I

Redington, Frank Mitchell, 1906–1984, vol. VIII

Redl, Lt-Col Ernest Arthur Frederick, 1869–1954, vol. V

Redlich, Rev. Canon Edwin Basil, 1878–1960, vol. V

Redlich, Hans Ferdinand, 1903–1968, vol. VI

Redman, Rev. Alfred, *died* 1927, vol. II

Redman, Brig. Arthur Stanley, 1879–1963, vol. VI

Redman, George Herbert, 1882–1959, vol. V

Redman, Lt-Gen. Sir Harold, 1899–1986, vol. VIII

Redman, Sir (Herbert) Vere, 1901–1975, vol. VII

Redman, Roderick Oliver, 1905–1975, vol. VII

Redman, Sir Vere; *see* Redman, Sir H. V.

Redmayne, Baron (Life Peer); Martin Redmayne, 1910–1983, vol. VIII

Redmayne, Sir Richard Augustine Studdert, 1865–1955, vol. V

Redmayne-Jones, Sir Edward, 1877–1963, vol. VI

Redmond, Sir James, 1918–1999, vol. X

Redmond, John Edward, 1856–1918, vol. II

Redmond, Lt-Gen. John Patrick Sutton, *died* 1902, vol. I

Redmond, Sir Joseph Michael, *died* 1921, vol. II

Redmond, Martin, 1937–1997, vol. X

Redmond, Captain William Archer, 1886–1932, vol. III

Redmond, Major William Hoey Kearney, 1861–1917, vol. II

Redpath, Anne, 1895–1965, vol. VI

Redpath, Rev. Henry Adeney, 1848–1908, vol. I

Redpath, Robert, 1871–1960, vol. V

Redshaw, Sir Leonard, 1911–1989, vol. VIII

Redshaw, Seymour Cunningham, 1906–1995, vol. IX

Redwood, Sir Boverton, 1st Bt, 1846–1919, vol. II

Redwood, Most Rev. Francis Mary, 1839–1935, vol. III

Redwood, Rev. Canon Frederick Arthur, 1891–1964, vol. VI

Redwood, Hugh; *see* Redwood, W. A. H.

Redwood, Sir Thomas Boverton, 2nd Bt, 1906–1974, vol. VII

Redwood, (William Arthur) Hugh, 1883–1963, vol. VI

Ree, Sir Frank, *died* 1914, vol. I

Reece, Sir Alan; *see* Reece, Sir L. A.

Reece, B(razilla) Carroll, 1889–1961, vol. VI

Reece, Courtenay Walton, 1899–1984, vol. VIII

Reece, Francis Bertram, 1888–1971, vol. VII

Reece, Sir Gerald, 1897–1985, vol. VIII

Reece, John H.; *see* Holroyd-Reece.

Reece, Sir (Louis) Alan, 1906–1984, vol. VIII

Reece, Surg.-Col Richard James, 1862–1924, vol. II

Reed, Sir (Albert) Ralph, 1884–1958, vol. V

Reed, Sir Alfred Hamish, 1875–1975, vol. VII

Reed, Sir Andrew, 1837–1914, vol. I

Reed, Sir Arthur Conrad, 1881–1961, vol. VI

Reed, Arthur William, 1873–1957, vol. V

Reed, Austin Leonard, 1873–1954, vol. V

Reed, Bellamy Alexander C.; *see* Cash-Reed.

Reed, Sir Carol, 1906–1976, vol. VII

Reed, Col Charles, 1879–1958, vol. V

Reed, Clinton Austin, 1876–1954, vol. V

Reed, Douglas, 1895–1976, vol. VII

Reed, Edward, 1902–1953, vol. V

Reed, Sir Edward James, 1830–1906, vol. I

Reed, Edward Tennyson, 1860–1933, vol. III

Reed, Rt Rev. Ernest Samuel, 1909–1970, vol. VI

Reed, Hon. Sir Geoffrey Sandford, 1892–1970, vol. VI (AII)

Reed, Maj.-Gen. Hamilton Lyster, 1869–1931, vol. III

Reed, Haythorne, 1873–1934, vol. III

Reed, Henry, 1914–1986, vol. VIII

Reed, Henry Ashman, 1866–1935, vol. III

Reed, Col Henry Robert Baynes, 1880–1939, vol. III

Reed, Herbert Langford, 1889–1954, vol. V

Reed, Herbert Parker, *died* 1920, vol. II

Reed, Sir (Herbert) Stanley, 1872–1969, vol. VI

Reed, Lt-Col John Arthur Wemyss, 1864–1939, vol. III
Reed, Hon. Sir John Ranken, 1864–1955, vol. V
Reed, Sir John Seymour B.; see Blake-Reed.
Reed, Col Sir Joseph, 1867–1942, vol. IV
Reed, Joseph Martin, 1857–1932, vol. III
Reed, Langford; see Reed, H. L.
Reed, Rev. Martin, 1856–1926, vol. II
Reed, Maurice Ernest, 1908–1975, vol. VII
Reed, Michael, 1912–1985, vol. VIII
Reed, Sir Nigel Vernon, 1913–1997, vol. X
Reed, Oliver; see Reed, R. O.
Reed, Philip Dunham, 1899–1989, vol. VIII
Reed, Sir Ralph; see Reed, Sir A. R.
Reed, Sir Reginald Charles, 1909–1982, vol. VIII
Reed, (Robert) Oliver, 1938–1999, vol. X
Reed, Rev. Samuel, 1844–1932, vol. III
Reed, Sir Stanley; see Reed, Sir H. S.
Reed, Stanley William, 1911–1996, vol. X
Reed, Thomas Brackett, 1839–1902, vol. I
Reed, Most Rev. Thomas Thornton, 1902–1995, vol. X (AI)
Reed, William Henry, 1877–1942, vol. IV
Reekie, Henry Enfield, 1907–2000, vol. X
Rees, Arthur J., died 1942, vol. IV
Rees, Arthur Morgan, 1912–1998, vol. X
Rees, Sir Beddoe, died 1931, vol. III
Rees, Sir (Charles William) Stanley, 1907–2000, vol. X
Rees, Ven. David John, 1862–1924, vol. II
Rees, David Morgan, 1904–1980, vol. VII
Rees, Dame Dorothy Mary, born 1898, vol. VIII
Rees, E(dgar) Philip, 1896–1964, vol. VI
Rees, Lt-Col Evan Thomas, 1883–1955, vol. V
Rees, (Florence) Gwendolen, 1906–1994, vol. IX
Rees, Gwendolen; see Rees, F. G.
Rees, Sir Frederick; see Rees, Sir J. F.
Rees, Sir Frederick Tavinor, 1890–1976, vol. VII
Rees, Prof. Garnet, 1912–1990, vol. VIII
Rees, Geraint; see Rees, R. G.
Rees, Goronwy; see Rees, M. G.
Rees, Griffith Caradoc, 1868–1924, vol. II
Rees, Haydn; see Rees, T. M. H.
Rees, Rev. Henry, 1844–1924, vol. II
Rees, Howell, 1847–1933, vol. III
Rees, Brig.-Gen. Hubert Conway, 1882–1948, vol. IV
Rees, Sir Hugh E.; see Ellis-Rees.
Rees, Sir (James) Frederick, 1883–1967, vol. VI
Rees, Sir John David, 1st Bt, 1854–1922, vol. II
Rees, Engr-Captain John David, 1861–1951, vol. V
Rees, Lt-Col John Gordon, 1884–1963, vol. VI
Rees, John Rawlings, 1890–1969, vol. VI
Rees, (John) Tudor, died 1956, vol. V
Rees, Sir Josiah, 1821–1899, vol. I
Rees, Llewellyn; see Rees, W. L.
Rees, Leonard, 1856–1932, vol. III
Rees, Mrs Leonard, (Mary Emily MacLeod Moore), died 1960, vol. V
Rees, Gp Captain Lionel Wilmot Brabazon, 1884–1955, vol. V
Rees, Sir Milsom, 1866–1952, vol. V
Rees, (Morgan) Goronwy, 1909–1979, vol. VII
Rees, Richard Geraint, 1907–1986, vol. VIII
Rees, (Richard John) William, 1917–1998, vol. X

Rees, Sir Richard Lodowick Edward Montagu, 2nd Bt, 1900–1970, vol. VI
Rees, Sir Stanley; see Rees, Sir C. W. S.
Rees, Rev. Thomas, 1869–1926, vol. II
Rees, Thomas Ifor, 1890–1977, vol. VII
Rees, Thomas James, 1875–1957, vol. V
Rees, Rev. Thomas Morgan, 1850–1937, vol. III
Rees, (Thomas Morgan) Haydn, 1915–1995, vol. IX
Rees, Maj.-Gen. Thomas Wynford, died 1959, vol. V
Rees, Rt Rev. Timothy, 1874–1939, vol. III
Rees, Tudor; see Rees, J. T.
Rees, Ven. Vaughan William Treharne, 1879–1948, vol. IV
Rees, (Walter) Llewellyn, 1901–1994, vol. IX
Rees, William, 1887–1978, vol. VII
Rees, Rev. William Goodman Edwards, died 1936, vol. III
Rees, Adm. William Stokes, 1853–1929, vol. III
Rees-Davies, Sir Colin, 1867–1933, vol. III
Rees-Davies, Sir William; see Davies.
Rees-Davies, William Rupert, 1916–1992, vol. IX
Rees-Mogg, Lt-Col Graham Beauchamp Coxeter, 1881–1949, vol. IV
Rees-Reynolds, Col Alan Randall, 1909–1982, vol. VIII
Rees-Thomas, Ruth, (Mrs William Rees-Thomas); see Darwin, R.
Rees-Thomas, William, 1887–1978, vol. VII
Reese, Frederick Focke, 1854–1924, vol. II
Reese, Surg. Rear-Adm. (John) Mansel, 1906–1997, vol. X
Reese, (John) Terence, 1913–1996, vol. X
Reese, Mansel; see Reese, J. M.
Reese, Terence; see Reese, J. T.
Reeve, Ada, 1874–1966, vol. VI
Reeve, Rt Rev. (Arthur) Stretton, 1907–1981, vol. VIII
Reeve, Charles Arthur, 1857–1936, vol. III
Reeve, Sir (Charles) Trevor, 1915–1993, vol. IX
Reeve, Charles William, 1879–1965, vol. VI
Reeve, Rev. Edward Henry Lisle, died 1936, vol. III
Reeve, Henry Fenwick, 1854–1920, vol. II
Reeve, Maj.-Gen. John Talbot Wentworth, 1891–1983, vol. VIII
Reeve, Mrs Marjorie Frances, 1899–1998, vol. X
Reeve, Raymond Roope, 1875–1952, vol. V
Reeve, Russell, 1895–1970, vol. VI
Reeve, Simms, 1826–1919, vol. II
Reeve, Rt Rev. Stretton; see Reeve, Rt Rev. A. S.
Reeve, Sir Trevor; see Reeve, Sir C. T.
Reeve, Rt Rev. William Day, 1844–1925, vol. II
Reeves, Amber; see Blanco White, A.
Reeves, Rt Rev. Ambrose; see Reeves, Rt Rev. R. A.
Reeves, Vice-Adm. Edward, 1869–1954, vol. V
Reeves, Edward Ayearst, 1862–1945, vol. IV
Reeves, Helen, (Mrs Henry Reeves); see Mathers, Helen.
Reeves, Henry Albert, died 1914, vol. I
Reeves, Col Henry Spencer Edward, 1843–1914, vol. I
Reeves, James, 1909–1978, vol. VII
Reeves, Col John, 1854–1904, vol. I
Reeves, John Sims, 1822–1900, vol. I

Reeves, Joseph, 1888–1969, vol. VI
Reeves, Rt Rev. (Richard) Ambrose, 1899–1980, vol. VII
Reeves, Hon. Sir William Conrad, 1838–1902, vol. I
Reeves, Hon. William Pember, 1857–1932, vol. III
Reeves-Smith, Sir George, *died* 1941, vol. IV
Refalo, Sir Michelangelo, 1876–1923, vol. II
Reford, John Hope, 1873–1957, vol. V
Regan, Charles Tate, 1878–1943, vol. IV
Regan, Col James Louis, 1888–1948, vol. IV
Regener, Erich, 1881–1955, vol. V
Regester, William, 1848–1929, vol. III
Regg, Ven. Thomas Richard, *died* 1930, vol. III
Regis, Sister Mary; *see* Morant, Dame Mary Maud.
Regis de Oliveira, Raul, *died* 1942, vol. IV
Regnart, Sir Horace Grece, 1841–1912, vol. I
Regnier, Henri François Joseph de, 1864–1936, vol. III
Rehan, Ada, 1860–1916, vol. II
Reiach, Alan, 1910–1992, vol. IX
Reiach, Herbert, 1873–1921, vol. II
Reich, Emil, 1854–1910, vol. I
Reichenbach, Henry-Béat de F.; *see* de Fischer-Reichenbach.
Reichardt, Charles Henry, 1851–1903, vol. I
Reichel, Sir Harry Rudolf, 1856–1931, vol. III
Reichel, Rev. Oswald Joseph, 1840–1923, vol. II
Reichstein, Tadeus, 1897–1996, vol. X
Reid, Baron (Life Peer); James Scott Cumberland Reid, 1890–1975, vol. VII
Reid, Surg.-Gen. Sir Adam Scott, 1848–1918, vol. II
Reid, Captain Alec Stratford C.; *see* Cunningham-Reid.
Reid, Alexander, 1843–1919, vol. II
Reid, Lt-Col Alexander, 1863–1927, vol. II
Reid, Sir Alexander James, 1889–1968, vol. VI
Reid, Maj.-Gen. Sir Alexander John Forsyth, 1846–1913, vol. I
Reid, Col Alexander Kirkwood, 1884–1948, vol. IV
Reid, Alfred Henry, 1845–1931, vol. III
Reid, Col A(ndrew) McKie, 1893–1973, vol. VII
Reid, Sir Archdall; *see* Reid, Sir G. A. O'B.
Reid, Archibald Cameron, 1915–1994, vol. IX
Reid, Archibald David, 1844–1908, vol. I
Reid, Sir Archibald Douglas, 1871–1924, vol. II
Reid, Arthur Beatson, 1888–1965, vol. VI
Reid, Sir Arthur Hay Stewart, 1851–1930, vol. III
Reid, Beryl, 1920–1996, vol. X
Reid, Sir Charles, 1819–1901, vol. I
Reid, Charles, 1892–1961, vol. VI
Reid, Sir Charles Carlow, 1879–1961, vol. VI
Reid, Charles William, 1895–1983, vol. VIII
Reid, Dame Clarissa Guthrie, *died* 1933, vol. III
Reid, Clement, *died* 1916, vol. II
Reid, Sir David Douglas, 1st Bt (*cr* 1936), 1872–1939, vol. III
Reid, Lt-Col David Elder, 1864–1930, vol. III
Reid, Maj.-Gen. Denys Whitehorn, 1897–1970, vol. VI
Reid, Desmond Arthur, 1918–1983, vol. VIII
Reid, Donald Darnley, 1914–1977, vol. VII
Reid, Sir Douglas Neilson, 2nd Bt (*cr* 1922), 1898–1971, vol. VII

Reid, Rev. Canon Douglas William John, 1934–2000, vol. X
Reid, Sir Edward, 1819–1912, vol. I
Reid, Edward Douglas Whitehead, 1883–1930, vol. III
Reid, Sir Edward James, 2nd Bt (*cr* 1897), 1901–1972, vol. VII
Reid, Rt Rev. Edward Thomas Scott, 1871–1938, vol. III
Reid, Edward Waymouth, 1862–1948, vol. IV
Reid, Col Ellis Ramsay, 1850–1918, vol. II
Reid, Ven. Ernest Gordon, 1884–1966, vol. VI
Reid, Forrest, 1876–1947, vol. IV
Reid, Francis Alexander, 1915–1987, vol. VIII
Reid, Col Francis Maude, 1849–1922, vol. II
Reid, Brig. Sir Francis Smith, 1900–1970, vol. VI
Reid, Frank Aspinall, 1875–1961, vol. VI
Reid, Very Rev. G. R. S., 1871–1964, vol. VI
Reid, Sir George, 1841–1913, vol. I
Reid, George, 1854–1925, vol. II
Reid, George Agnew, 1860–1947, vol. IV
Reid, Sir (George) Archdall O'Brien, 1860–1929, vol. III
Reid, Col George Eric, *died* 1938, vol. III
Reid, Rt Hon. Sir George Houstoun, 1845–1918, vol. II
Reid, George Ogilvy, 1851–1928, vol. II
Reid, Hon. Sir George Oswald, 1903–1993, vol. IX
Reid, Air Vice-Marshal Sir (George) Ranald Macfarlane, 1893–1991, vol. IX
Reid, George Smith, 1904–1985, vol. VIII
Reid, Sir George Thomas, 1881–1966, vol. VI
Reid, Very Rev. George Thomson Henderson, 1910–1990, vol. VIII
Reid, Gordon Stanley, 1923–1989, vol. VIII
Reid, Harold Alexander, 1891–1974, vol. VII
Reid, Lt-Col Harry Avery, 1877–1947, vol. IV
Reid, Rt Rev. Harry Seymour, *died* 1943, vol. IV
Reid, Col Hector Gowans, 1881–1966, vol. VI
Reid, Helen Richmond Young, 1869–1941, vol. IV
Reid, Helen Rogers, (Mrs Ogden Reid), 1882–1970, vol. VI
Reid, Rev. Henry M. B., 1856–1927, vol. II
Reid, Sir Henry Valentine Rae, 4th Bt (*cr* 1823), 1845–1903, vol. I
Reid, Lt-Col Herbert Cartwright, 1864–1950, vol. IV
Reid, Vice-Adm. Howard Emerson, 1897–1962, vol. VI
Reid, Sir Hugh, 1st Bt (*cr* 1922), 1860–1935, vol. III
Reid, Sir Hugh Gilzean-, 1836–1911, vol. I
Reid, Col Ivo; *see* Reid, Col P. F. I.
Reid, James, 1839–1908, vol. I
Reid, Sir James, 1st Bt (*cr* 1897), 1849–1923, vol. II
Reid, Rev. James, 1877–1963, vol. VI
Reid, James, 1921–1999, vol. X
Reid, James Robert, 1838–1908, vol. I
Reid, James Smith, 1846–1926, vol. II
Reid, Very Rev. James Watson, *died* 1904, vol. I
Reid, Sir John, 1861–1933, vol. III
Reid, John, 1874–1934, vol. III
Reid, John, 1906–1990, vol. VIII
Reid, John Alexander, 1895–1969, vol. VI

Reid, Hon. John Dowsley, 1859–1929, vol. III
Reid, Lt-Col John Garnet, 1878–1939, vol. III
Reid, Sir John James Andrew, 1925–1994, vol. IX
Reid, Adm. Sir (John) Peter (Lorne), 1903–1973, vol. VII
Reid, John Robertson, 1851–1926, vol. II
Reid, John Robson, 1925–1992, vol. IX
Reid, Sir John Thyne, 1903–1984, vol. VIII
Reid, Sir John Watt, 1823–1909, vol. I
Reid, Rev. Kenneth Lyle, 1873–1937, vol. III
Reid, Col Lestock Hamilton, 1857–1936, vol. III
Reid, Louis Arnaud, 1895–1986, vol. VIII
Reid, Sir Marshall Frederick, 1864–1925, vol. II
Reid, May, 1882–1980, vol. VII
Reid, Ogden, 1882–1947, vol. IV
Reid, Mrs Ogden; see Reid, Helen Rogers.
Reid, Patrick Robert, 1910–1990, vol. VIII
Reid, Col (Percy Fergus) Ivo, 1911–1994, vol. IX
Reid, Col Percy Lester, 1882–1968, vol. VI
Reid, Adm. Sir Peter; see Reid, Adm. Sir J. P. L.
Reid, Rachel Robertson, 1876–1952, vol. V
Reid, Air Vice-Marshal Sir Ranald; see Reid, Air Vice-Marshal Sir G. R. M.
Reid, Lt-Col Richard, died 1918, vol. II
Reid, Robert, 1922–1980, vol. VII
Reid, Sir Robert Basil, 1921–1993, vol. IX
Reid, Robert Douglas, 1898–1983, vol. VIII
Reid, Robert Lawrence, 1858–1916, vol. II
Reid, Sir Robert Niel, 1883–1964, vol. VI
Reid, Robert Payton, 1859–1945, vol. IV
Reid, Robert Whyte, 1885–1929, vol. III
Reid, Robert William, died 1939, vol. III
Reid, Samuel, 1854–1919, vol. II
Reid, Stephen, 1873–1948, vol. IV
Reid, Stuart J., died 1927, vol. II
Reid, Thomas, 1881–1963, vol. VI
Reid, Thomas Bertram Wallace, 1901–1981, vol. VIII
Reid, Sir (Thomas) Wemyss, 1842–1905, vol. I
Reid, Walter, died 1917, vol. II
Reid, Col Walter Richard, 1880–1959, vol. V
Reid, Sir Wemyss; see Reid, Sir T. W.
Reid, Hon. Whitelaw, 1837–1912, vol. I
Reid, Major Sir William, died 1934, vol. III
Reid, William, died 1965, vol. VI
Reid, Sir William, 1906–1985, vol. VIII
Reid, William Allan, 1865–1952, vol. V
Reid, Rev. William Cawley, died 1933, vol. III
Reid, William Clarke, 1909–1956, vol. V
Reid, William David, 1883–1964, vol. VI
Reid, Sir William Duff, 1869–1924, vol. II
Reid, William Edwin Charles, 1870–1947, vol. IV
Reid, Sir William James, 1871–1939, vol. III
Reid, William Paton, 1854–1932, vol. III
Reid, William Sydney, 1880–1960, vol. V
Reid-Adam, Randle, 1912–1982, vol. VIII
Reid Dick, Sir W(illiam), 1879–1961, vol. VI
Reidy, Joseph Patrick Irwin, 1907–1991, vol. IX
Reigate, Baron (Life Peer); John Kenyon Vaughan-Morgan, 1905–1995, vol. IX
Reilly, Baron (Life Peer); Paul Reilly, 1912–1990, vol. VIII
Reilly, Lt-Col Sir Bernard Rawdon, 1882–1966, vol. VI
Reilly, Brian Thomas, 1924–1988, vol. VIII

Reilly, Col Charles Cooper, 1862–1926, vol. II
Reilly, Sir Charles Herbert, 1874–1948, vol. IV
Reilly, Sir D'Arcy; see Reilly, Sir H. D. C.
Reilly, Sir (D'Arcy) Patrick, 1909–1999, vol. X
Reilly, E. Albert, 1868–1943, vol. IV
Reilly, Sir (Henry) D'Arcy (Cornelius), 1876–1948, vol. IV
Reilly, Joseph, 1889–1965, vol. VI
Reilly, Noel Marcus Prowse, (Peter), 1902–1991, vol. IX
Reilly, Sir Patrick; see Reilly, Sir D. P.
Reilly, Peter ; see Reilly, N. M. P.
Reilly, Very Rev. Thomas, died 1921, vol. II
Reinach, Joseph, 1856–1921, vol. II
Reinach, Salomon, 1858–1932, vol. III
Reindorp, Rt Rev. George Edmund, 1911–1990, vol. VIII
Reines, Frederick, 1918–1998, vol. X
Reinhardt, Max, 1873–1943, vol. IV
Reinold, Arnold William, 1843–1921, vol. II
Reinold, Vice-Adm. Harold Owen, 1877–1962, vol. VI
Reisner, George Andrew, 1867–1942, vol. IV
Reiss, Lt-Col Alec, 1871–1932, vol. III
Reiss, Charles, 1873–1949, vol. IV
Reiss, Sir John Anthony Ewart, 1909–1989, vol. VIII
Reiss, John Henry, 1918–1998, vol. X
Reiss, Richard Leopold, 1883–1959, vol. V
Reith, 1st Baron, 1889–1971, vol. VII
Reith, Rev. David, 1842–1909, vol. I
Reitlinger, Gerald Roberts, 1900–1978, vol. VII
Reitz, Col Deneys, 1882–1944, vol. IV
Reitz, Hon. Francis William, 1844–1934, vol. III
Réjane, Madame, (Gabrielle Réju), 1857–1920, vol. II
Relf, Ernest Frederick, 1888–1970, vol. VI
Relly, Gavin Walter Hamilton, 1926–1999, vol. X
Relph, George, 1888–1960, vol. V
Relton, Arthur John, 1856–1946, vol. IV
Relton, Frederick Ernest, 1883–1963, vol. VI
Relton, Rev. Herbert Maurice, 1882–1971, vol. VII
Relton, Stanley, 1923–1998, vol. X
Remarque, Erich Maria, 1898–1970, vol. VI
Remer, John Rumney, 1883–1948, vol. IV
Remez, Aharon, 1919–1994, vol. IX
Remington, Geoffrey Cochrane, 1897–1968, vol. VI
Remizov, Alexei, 1877–1957, vol. V
Remnant, 1st Baron, 1863–1933, vol. III
Remnant, 2nd Baron, 1895–1967, vol. VI
Remnant, Ernest, 1872–1941, vol. IV
Remnant, Hon. Peter Farquharson, 1897–1968, vol. VI
Remsen, Ira, 1846–1927, vol. II
Renals, Sir Herbert, 3rd Bt, 1919–1961, vol. VI
Renals, Sir James Herbert, 2nd Bt, 1870–1927, vol. II, vol. III
Renals, Sir Joseph, 1st Bt, 1843–1908, vol. I
Renard, Samuel, died 1924, vol. II
Renaud, Maj.-Gen. Ernest James, died 1967, vol. VI
Renaud, Madeleine, 1900–1994, vol. IX
Renault, Louis, 1843–1918, vol. II
Renault, Mary (Mary Challans), 1905–1983, vol. VIII
Rendall, Archibald, 1921–1989, vol. VIII

Rendall, Athelstan, 1871–1948, vol. IV
Rendall, Rev. Gerald Henry, 1851–1945, vol. IV
Rendall, Montague John, 1862–1950, vol. IV
Rendall, Peter Godfrey, 1909–1998, vol. X
Rendall, Philip Stanley, 1895–1983, vol. VIII
Rendall, Richard Antony, 1907–1957, vol. V
Rendall, Vernon Horace, 1869–1960, vol. V
Rendel, 1st Baron, 1834–1913, vol. I
Rendel, Sir Alexander Meadows, 1829–1918, vol. II
Rendel, George Wightwick, 1833–1902, vol. I
Rendel, Sir George William, 1889–1979, vol. VII
Rendel, Harry Stuart G.; see Goodhart-Rendel.
Rendell, Rev. Arthur Medland, 1842–1918, vol. II
Rendell, Rev. James Robson, 1850–1926, vol. II
Rendell, Col Walter Frederic, 1888–1951, vol. V
Rendell, Sir William, 1908–1995, vol. IX
Rendell, William Reginald, 1868–1948, vol. IV
Rendle, Alfred Barton, 1865–1938, vol. III
Rendlesham, 5th Baron, 1840–1911, vol. I
Rendlesham, 6th Baron, 1868–1938, vol. III
Rendlesham, 7th Baron, 1874–1943, vol. IV
Rendlesham, 8th Baron, 1915–1999, vol. X
Renfrew, Rt Rev. Charles McDonald, 1929–1992, vol. IX
Renfrew, Thomas, 1901–1975, vol. VII
Renier, Gustaaf Johannes, 1892–1962, vol. VI
Renison, Sir Patrick Muir, 1911–1965, vol. VI
Renison, Most Rev. Robert John, 1875–1957, vol. V
Rennell, 1st Baron, 1858–1941, vol. IV
Rennell, 2nd Baron, 1895–1978, vol. VII
Rennenkampff, Gen.-Lt Paul Charles von, 1854–1918, vol. II
Rennert, Guenther, 1911–1978, vol. VII
Rennie, Sir Alfred Baillie, 1896–1987, vol. VIII
Rennie, Charles Robert, 1880–1969, vol. VI
Rennie, Compton Alexander, 1915–1987, vol. VIII
Rennie, Edward Henry, 1852–1927, vol. II
Rennie, Sir Ernest Amelius, 1868–1935, vol. III
Rennie, Francis Pepys, 1872–1946, vol. IV
Rennie, Col George Arthur Paget, 1872–1951, vol. V
Rennie, Col George Septimus, died 1930, vol. III
Rennie, Sir Gilbert McCall, 1895–1981, vol. VIII
Rennie, Lt-Col Horace Watt, died 1943, vol. IV
Rennie, James, 1814–1903, vol. I
Rennie, John, died 1960, vol. V (A)
Rennie, Major John George, 1865–1920, vol. II
Rennie, Sir John Ogilvy, 1914–1981, vol. VIII
Rennie, Sir Richard Temple, 1839–1905, vol. I
Rennie, Maj.-Gen. Robert, 1862–1949, vol. IV
Rennie, Col Samuel James, 1855–1935, vol. III
Rennie, Maj.-Gen. Tom Gordon, 1900–1945, vol. IV
Rennie, William, died 1957, vol. V
Renny, Brig. George Douglas, 1908–1971, vol. VII
Renny, Gen. Henry, 1815–1900, vol. I
Renny, Col Lewis Frederick, 1877–1955, vol. V
Renny, Maj.-Gen. Sidney Mercer, 1861–1921, vol. II
Renny-Tailyour, Col Thomas Francis Bruce, 1863–1937, vol. III
Renoir, Jean, 1894–1979, vol. VII
Renold, Sir Charles Garonne, 1883–1967, vol. VI
Renouf, Vice-Adm. Edward de Faye, 1888–1972, vol. VII

Renouf, Sir Francis Henry, 1918–1998, vol. X
Renouf, Sir Peter le Page, 1822–1897, vol. I
Renouf, Winter Charles, 1868–1954, vol. V
Renouvin, Pierre, 1893–1974, vol. VII
Renowden, Very Rev. Charles Raymond, 1923–2000, vol. X
Renshaw, Arthur Henry, 1851–1918, vol. II
Renshaw, Sir Charles Bine, 1st Bt, 1848–1918, vol. II
Renshaw, Sir (Charles) Stephen (Bine), 2nd Bt, 1883–1976, vol. VII
Renshaw, Hon. John Brophy, 1909–1987, vol. VIII
Renshaw, John W., 1877–1955, vol. V
Renshaw, Sir Stephen; see Renshaw, Sir C. S. B.
Renshaw, Walter Charles, 1840–1922, vol. II
Rentell, Henry William Sidney, 1864–1927, vol. II, vol. III
Renton, Major (Alexander) Leslie, 1868–1947, vol. IV
Renton, Sir Alexander Wood, 1861–1933, vol. III
Renton, Lady; Claire Cicely Renton, 1923–1986, vol. VIII
Renton, Gordon Pearson, 1928–2000, vol. X
Renton, James Crawford, died 1919, vol. II
Renton, Brig. James Malcolm Leslie, 1898–1972, vol. VII
Renton, Major Leslie; see Renton, Major A. L.
Rentoul, Sir Gervais, 1884–1946, vol. IV
Rentoul, James Alexander, 1854–1919, vol. II
Rentoul, Rt Rev. John Laurence, 1846–1926, vol. II
Renwick, 1st Baron, 1904–1973, vol. VII
Renwick, Hon. Sir Arthur, 1837–1910, vol. I
Renwick, Sir Eustace Deuchar, 3rd Bt (cr 1921), 1902–1973, vol. VII
Renwick, Sir George, 1st Bt (cr 1921), 1850–1931, vol. III
Renwick, George Russell, 1901–1984, vol. VIII
Renwick, Major Gustav Adolph, 1883–1956, vol. V
Renwick, Sir Harry Benedetto, 1st Bt, 1861–1932, vol. III
Renwick, James Harrison, 1926–1994, vol. IX
Renwick, Sir John, 1901–1983, vol. VIII
Renwick, Sir John Robert, 2nd Bt (cr 1921), 1877–1946, vol. IV
Renwick, William Lindsay, 1889–1970, vol. VI
Renzis, Francesco de, Baron, died 1900, vol. I
Repington, Lt-Col Charles A'Court-, 1858–1925, vol. II
Repington, Charles Henry Wyndham A'C.; see A'Court Repington.
Repplier, Agnes, 1858–1950, vol. IV
Reso, Sidney Joseph, 1935–1992, vol. IX
Restieaux, Rt Rev. Cyril Edward, 1910–1996, vol. X
Restler, Sir James William, died 1918, vol. II
Reston, Clifford Arthur, 1928–1979, vol. VII
Reszke, Jean de, 1853–1925, vol. II
Rettie, Middleton, died 1910, vol. I
Retie, Lt-Col William John Kerr, 1868–1939, vol. III
Retzius, Magnus Gustaf, 1842–1919, vol. II
Reuter, Baron de; Auguste Julius Clemens Herbert, 1852–1915, vol. I
Reuter, Baron de; Paul Julius, 1816–1899, vol. I
Reuter, (Gerd Edzard) Harry, 1921–1992, vol. IX
Reuter, Harry; see Reuter, G. E. H.

Reuther, Walter Philip, 1907–1970, vol. VI
Revans, Sir John, 1911–1988, vol. VIII
Revel, John Daniel, 1884–1967, vol. VI
Revell, Alfred Edgar, 1877–1932, vol. III
Revell, Daniel Graisberry, 1869–1954, vol. V
Revell-Smith, Maj.-Gen. William Revell, 1894–1956, vol. V
Revelstoke, 1st Baron, 1828–1897, vol. I
Revelstoke, 2nd Baron, 1863–1929, vol. III
Revelstoke, 3rd Baron, 1864–1934, vol. III
Revelstoke, 4th Baron, 1911–1994, vol. IX
Reventlow, Count Eduard, 1883–1963, vol. VI
Revic, Donald, 1927–1989, vol. VIII
Reville, Rt Rev. Mgr Stephen, 1844–1916, vol. II
Revington, Air Cdre Arthur Pethick, 1901–1986, vol. VIII
Rew, Lt-Col Horace Edward, 1899–1967, vol. VI
Rew, Sir (R.) Henry, 1858–1929, vol. III
Rewa, Bandhvesh Ex-Maharaja of, Sir Gulab Singh Bahadur, 1903–1950, vol. IV
Rewah, HH Maharaja Venkat Raman Singh Bahadur, 1876–1918, vol. II
Rewcastle, Cuthbert Snowball, 1888–1962, vol. VI
Rewse, Rev. Gilbert Flesher S.; see Smith-Rewse.
Rewse, Col Henry Whistler, S.; see Smith-Rewse.
Rex, Marcus, 1886–1971, vol. VII
Rex, Hon. Sir Robert Richmond, 1909–1992, vol. IX
Rey, Lt-Col Sir Charles Fernand, 1877–1968, vol. VI
Rey, Jean, 1902–1983, vol. VIII
Reyes, Narciso Gallardo, 1914–1996, vol. X
Reymont, Wladislaw Stanislaw, 1867–1925, vol. II
Reynard, Helene, 1875–1947, vol. IV
Reynard, Matthew Andrew, 1878–1946, vol. IV
Reynard, Robert Froding, 1857–1926, vol. II
Reynardson, Col Charles Birch-, 1845–1919, vol. II
Reynardson, Lt-Col Henry T. Birch, 1892–1972, vol. VII
Reynaud, Paul, 1878–1966, vol. VI
Reyne, Rear-Adm. Sir Cecil Nugent, 1881–1958, vol. V
Reyne, Lt-Col Gerard van Rossum, 1886–1940, vol. III
Reynell, Douglas, 1877–1949, vol. IV
Reynell, Walter Rupert, 1885–1948, vol. IV
Reynell-Pack, Arthur Denis Henry Heber, 1860–1937, vol. III
Reynolds, Col Alan Randall R.; see Rees-Reynolds.
Reynolds, Lt-Col Alan Boyd, 1879–1940, vol. III
Reynolds, Alan Lowe, 1897–1977, vol. VII
Reynolds, Sir Alfred, 1850–1931, vol. III
Reynolds, Alfred Charles, 1884–1969, vol. VI
Reynolds, Alice; see Cullen, A.
Reynolds, Rev. Bernard, 1850–1930, vol. III
Reynolds, Air Marshal Sir Bryan Vernon, 1902–1965, vol. VI
Reynolds, Cedric Lawton, 1888–1958, vol. V
Reynolds, Charles Henry, 1844–1908, vol. I
Reynolds, Clyde Albert M.; see Marshall-Reynolds.
Reynolds, Lt-Col Denys Walter, 1884–1940, vol. III
Reynolds, Doris Livesey, (Mrs Arthur Holmes), 1899–1985, vol. VIII
Reynolds, Major Douglas, 1881–1916, vol. II
Reynolds, Edward, 1874–1944, vol. IV

Reynolds, Emerson; see Reynolds, J. E.
Reynolds, Eric Vincent, 1904–1992, vol. IX
Reynolds, Ernest Septimus, 1861–1926, vol. II
Reynolds, Sir Francis Jubal, 1857–1924, vol. II
Reynolds, Frank, 1876–1953, vol. V
Reynolds, Frank Arrowsmith, 1916–1994, vol. IX
Reynolds, Frank Neon, 1895–1952, vol. V
Reynolds, Sir Frank Umhlali, 1852–1930, vol. III
Reynolds, George McClelland, 1865–1940, vol. III
Reynolds, Rt Hon. Gerald William, 1927–1969, vol. VI
Reynolds, Adm. Harry Campbell, 1853–1949, vol. IV
Reynolds, Captain Henry, 1881–1948, vol. IV
Reynolds, Henry Osborne, 1883–1947, vol. IV
Reynolds, Herbert John, 1832–1916, vol. II
Reynolds, J. H., 1842–1927, vol. II
Reynolds, James, 1908–1999, vol. X
Reynolds, (James) Emerson, 1844–1920, vol. II
Reynolds, Lt-Col James Henry, 1844–1932, vol. III
Reynolds, Col Sir James Philip, 1st Bt, 1865–1932, vol. III
Reynolds, Sir Jeffrey Fellowes Crofts, 1893–1966, vol. VI
Reynolds, John Arthur, 1925–1990, vol. VIII
Reynolds, Lt-Col Sir John Francis Roskell, 2nd Bt, 1899–1956, vol. V
Reynolds, John Henry, 1874–1949, vol. IV
Reynolds, John Richardson, 1873–1934, vol. III
Reynolds, Leighton Durham, 1930–1999, vol. X
Reynolds, Sir Leonard William, 1874–1946, vol. IV
Reynolds, Mrs Louis Baillie, died 1939, vol. III
Reynolds, Louis George Stanley, died 1945, vol. IV
Reynolds, Osborne, 1842–1912, vol. I
Reynolds, Paul Kenneth Baillie, 1896–1973, vol. VII
Reynolds, Major Sir Percival Reuben, 1876–1965, vol. VI
Reynolds, Major Philip Guy, 1871–1936, vol. III
Reynolds, Quentin James, 1902–1965, vol. VI
Reynolds, Reginald Francis, died 1936, vol. III
Reynolds, Reginald Philip Neri, 1867–1936, vol. III
Reynolds, Richard Samuel, Jr, 1908–1980, vol. VII
Reynolds, Maj.-Gen. Roger Clayton, 1895–1983, vol. VIII
Reynolds, Russell John, 1880–1964, vol. VI
Reynolds, Seymour John Romer, 1911–1987, vol. VIII
Reynolds, Sidney Hugh, 1867–1949, vol. IV
Reynolds, Stephen, 1881–1919, vol. II
Reynolds, Warwick, 1880–1926, vol. II
Reynolds, William George Waterhouse, 1860–1928, vol. II
Reynolds, William Vaughan, 1908–1988, vol. VIII
Reynolds-Ball, Eustace Alfred, died 1928, vol. II
Reynolds-Stephens, Sir William, 1862–1943, vol. IV,HH
Rhayader, 1st Baron, 1862–1939, vol. III
Rhead, George Woolliscroft, 1855–1920, vol. II
Rheam, Henry Meynell, 1859–1920, vol. II
Rhigini, Madame de; see Russell, Ella.
Rhind, Donald, 1899–1982, vol. VIII
Rhind, Lt-Col Sir Duncan; see Rhind, Lt-Col Sir T. D.
Rhind, Edwin Scoby O.; see Oak-Rhind.

Rhind, John Massey, 1868–1936, vol. III
Rhind, Lt-Col Sir (Thomas) Duncan, 1871–1927, vol. II
Rhind, William Birnie, *died* 1933, vol. III
Rhine, Joseph Banks, 1895–1980, vol. VII
Rhoades, James, 1841–1923, vol. II
Rhoads, Cornelius Packard, 1898–1959, vol. V
Rhodes, Baron (Life Peer); Hervey Rhodes, 1895–1987, vol. VIII
Rhodes, Sir Campbell, 1874–1941, vol. IV
Rhodes, Rt Hon. Cecil John, 1853–1902, vol. I
Rhodes, Rev. Canon Cecil, 1910–1990, vol. VIII
Rhodes, Charles Kenneth, 1889–1941, vol. IV
Rhodes, Sir Christopher George, 3rd Bt, 1914–1964, vol. VI
Rhodes, Rev. Clifford Oswald, 1911–1985, vol. VIII
Rhodes, Hon. Edgar Nelson, 1877–1942, vol. IV
Rhodes, Sir Edward, 1870–1959, vol. V
Rhodes, Major Elmhirst, 1858–1931, vol. III
Rhodes, Col Francis William, 1851–1905, vol. I
Rhodes, Sir Frederick Edward, 4th Bt, 1843–1911, vol. I
Rhodes, Geoffrey William, 1928–1974, vol. VII
Rhodes, George, 1851–1924, vol. II
Rhodes, Sir George Wood, 1st Bt, 1860–1924, vol. II
Rhodes, Brig.-Gen. Sir Godfrey Dean, 1886–1971, vol. VII
Rhodes, Harold, 1885–1964, vol. VI
Rhodes, Harold Vale, 1886–1970, vol. VI
Rhodes, Harold William, 1889–1956, vol. V
Rhodes, Col Hon. Sir Heaton; *see* Rhodes, Col Hon. Sir R. H.
Rhodes, Helen, *died* 1936, vol. III
Rhodes, Rev. Herbert A., 1869–1956, vol. V
Rhodes, James Ford, 1848–1927, vol. II
Rhodes, Lt-Col Sir John Phillips, 2nd Bt, 1884–1955, vol. V
Rhodes, Kathlyn Mary, *died* 1962, vol. VI
Rhodes, Marion, 1907–1998, vol. X
Rhodes, Col Hon. Sir (Robert) Heaton, 1861–1956, vol. V
Rhodes, Col Stephen, 1885–1966, vol. VI
Rhodes, Stephen, 1918–1989, vol. VIII
Rhodes, Walter Harpham, 1888–1962, vol. VI
Rhodes James, Sir Robert Vidal, 1933–1999, vol. X
Rhondda, 1st Viscount, 1856–1918, vol. II
Rhondda, Viscountess (2nd in line), *died* 1958, vol. V
Rhondda, Viscountess; (Sybil), *died* 1941, vol. IV
Rhydderch, Sir William Edmund Hodges, 1890–1961, vol. VI
Rhyl, Baron (Life Peer); (Evelyn) Nigel (Chetwode) Birch, 1906–1981, vol. VIII
Rhymes, Rev. Canon Douglas Alfred, 1914–1996, vol. X
Rhys, Ernest, 1859–1946, vol. IV
Rhys, Jean, (Mrs Jean Hamer), 1894–1979, vol. VII
Rhys, Rt Hon. Sir John, 1840–1915, vol. I
Rhys, Keidrych, 1915–1987, vol. VIII
Rhys-Roberts, Thomas Esmôr Rhys, 1910–1975, vol. VII
Rhys Williams, Sir Brandon Meredith, 2nd Bt, 1927–1988, vol. VIII

Rhys Williams, Juliet Evangeline, (Lady Rhys Williams), 1898–1964, vol. VI
Rhys-Williams, Lt-Col Sir Rhys; *see* Williams.
Riabouchinska, Tatiana, (Mme Lichine), 1916–2000, vol. X
Riach, Col William, 1873–1942, vol. IV
Riall, Air Cdre Arthur Bookey, 1911–1984, vol. VIII
Ribbentrop, Joachim von, 1893–1946, vol. IV
Ribblesdale, 4th Baron, 1854–1925, vol. II
Riberi, His Eminence Cardinal Antonio, 1897–1967, vol. VI
Ribot, Alexandre F., 1842–1923, vol. II
Ribton, Sir George, 4th Bt, 1842–1901, vol. I
Ricardo, Lt-Col Ambrose St Quintin, 1866–1923, vol. II
Ricardo, Adm. Arthur David, 1861–1931, vol. III
Ricardo, Col Francis Cecil, 1852–1924, vol. II
Ricardo, Halsey Ralph, 1854–1928, vol. II
Ricardo, Sir Harry Ralph, 1885–1974, vol. VII
Ricardo, Major Harry William Ralph, 1860–1945, vol. IV
Ricardo, Lt-Col Henry George, 1860–1940, vol. III
Ricardo, Col Horace, 1850–1935, vol. III
Ricardo, Col Percy Ralph, 1855–1907, vol. I
Ricci, Luigi, *died* 1915, vol. I
Rice, Alexander Hamilton, 1875–1956, vol. V
Rice, Alice Hegan, *died* 1942, vol. IV
Rice, (Benjamin) Lewis, 1837–1927, vol. II
Rice, Cale Young, 1872–1943, vol. IV (A), vol. V
Rice, Rt Hon. Sir Cecil Arthur S.; *see* Spring-Rice.
Rice, David Talbot, 1903–1972, vol. VII
Rice, Dominick S.; *see* Spring-Rice.
Rice, Air Vice-Marshal Sir Edward Arthur Beckton, 1893–1948, vol. IV
Rice, Sir Edward Bridges, 1819–1902, vol. I
Rice, Elmer, 1892–1967, vol. VI
Rice, Adm. Sir Ernest, 1840–1927, vol. II
Rice, Sir Frederick Gill, 1866–1935, vol. III
Rice, George Ritchie, 1881–1982, vol. VIII
Rice, George Samuel, 1866–1950, vol. IV
Rice, Col Henry James, 1894–1964, vol. VI
Rice, James, 1874–1936, vol. III
Rice, Joseph, M., 1857–1934, vol. III
Rice, Lewis; *see* Rice, B. L.
Rice, Dame Margaret Ker P.; *see* Pryse-Rice.
Rice, Percy Christopher, 1877–1963, vol. VI
Rice, Peter Ronan, 1935–1992, vol. IX
Rice, Roderick Alexander, 1922–1984, vol. VIII
Rice, Lt-Col Sidney Mervyn, 1873–1959, vol. V
Rice, Maj.-Gen. Sir Spring Robert, 1858–1929, vol. III
Rice, Stephen Edward S.; *see* Spring-Rice.
Rice, Thomas Edmund, *died* 1941, vol. IV
Rice, Walter Francis, *died* 1941, vol. IV
Rice, Wilfred Eric, 1898–1979, vol. VII
Rice, Sir William George, 1861–1936, vol. III
Rice, Rev. William Ignatius, 1883–1955, vol. V
Rice, Hon. and Rev. William Talbot, 1861–1945, vol. IV
Rice, Comdr William Victor, *died* 1932, vol. III
Rice-Jones, Benjamin Rowland, 1888–1978, vol. VII
Rice-Oxley, Sir Alfred James, 1856–1941, vol. IV
Rice-Oxley, Douglas George, 1885–1972, vol. VII

Rich, Adena M., (Mrs Kenneth F. Rich), *died* 1967, vol. VI

Rich, Alfred William, 1856–1922, vol. II

Rich, Sir Almeric Edmund Frederic, 5th Bt, 1859–1948, vol. IV

Rich, Sir Almeric Frederic Conness, 6th Bt, 1897–1983, vol. VIII

Rich, Sir Charles Henry Stuart, 4th Bt, 1859–1913, vol. I

Rich, Charles T., 1869–1940, vol. III

Rich, Edmund Milton, 1875–1954, vol. V

Rich, Col Edmund Tillotson, 1874–1937, vol. III

Rich, Edward Charles, 1895–1959, vol. V

Rich, Edwin Ernest, 1904–1979, vol. VII

Rich, Vice-Adm. Frederick St George, 1852–1914, vol. I

Rich, Rt Hon. Sir George Edward, 1863–1956, vol. V

Rich, Maj.-Gen. Henry Hampden, 1891–1976, vol. VII

Rich, Jacob Morris, 1897–1987, vol. VIII

Rich, Rev. John, 1826–1913, vol. I

Rich, John Rowland, 1928–1995, vol. IX

Rich, Mrs Kenneth F.; *see* Rich, Adena M.

Rich, Rev. Leonard James, *died* 1920, vol. II

Rich, Rowland William, 1901–1981, vol. VIII

Rich, Roy, 1912–1970, vol. VI

Richard, Ven. Robert Henry, 1869–1929, vol. III

Richard, Timothy, 1845–1919, vol. II

Richards, Albert Edwin George, 1856–1942, vol. IV

Richards, Albert Elswood, 1848–1918, vol. II

Richards, Alfred Newton, 1876–1966, vol. VI

Richards, Archibald Banks, 1911–1996, vol. X

Richards, Audrey Isabel, 1899–1984, vol. VIII

Richards, Bertrand; *see* Richards, E. B. B.

Richards, Catherine Margaret, 1940–1993, vol. IX

Richards, Ceri Giraldus, 1903–1971, vol. VII

Richards, Charles Anthony Langdon, 1911–1996, vol. X

Richards, Brig. Collen Edward Melville, *died* 1971, vol. VII

Richards, Rev. Daniel, 1892–1989, vol. VIII

Richards, Dickinson Woodruff, Jr, 1895–1973, vol. VII

Richards, Edgar Lynton, (Tony Richards), 1912–1983, vol. VIII

Richards, Sir Edmund Charles, 1889–1955, vol. V

Richards, (Edmund) Bertrand (Bamford), 1913–2000, vol. X

Richards, Hon. Sir Edward Trenton, 1908–1991, vol. IX

Richards, Edward Windsor, *died* 1921, vol. II

Richards, Elfyn John, 1914–1995, vol. IX

Richards, Sir Erle; *see* Richards, Sir H. E.

Richards, Major Francis Howe, 1890–1937, vol. III

Richards, Francis John, 1901–1965, vol. VI

Richards, Frank, 1875–1961, vol. VI

Richards, Frank Roydon, 1899–1978, vol. VII

Richards, Franklin Thomas Grant, 1872–1948, vol. IV

Richards, Fred C., *died* 1932, vol. III

Richards, Sir Frederick William, 1833–1912, vol. I

Richards, Hon. Sir Frederick William, 1869–1957, vol. V

Richards, Rear-Adm. G. E., 1852–1927, vol. II

Richards, Rev. George Chatterton, 1867–1951, vol. V

Richards, George Edward Fugl, 1891–1974, vol. VII

Richards, Maj.-Gen. George Warren, 1898–1978, vol. VII

Richards, Gertrude Mary, *died* 1944, vol. IV

Richards, Gilbert Stanley Nowell, 1912–1980, vol. VII

Richards, Sir Gordon, 1904–1986, vol. VIII

Richards, Gordon Waugh, 1930–1998, vol. X

Richards, Very Rev. Gwnfryn, 1902–1992, vol. IX

Richards, Lt-Col Harold Arthur David, 1874–1947, vol. IV

Richards, Harold Meredith, *died* 1942, vol. IV

Richards, Henry Caselli, 1884–1947, vol. IV

Richards, Henry Charles, 1851–1905, vol. I

Richards, Sir (Henry) Erle, 1861–1922, vol. II

Richards, Sir Henry George, 1860–1928, vol. II

Richards, Sir Henry Maunsell, 1869–1957, vol. V

Richards, Henry William, 1865–1956, vol. V

Richards, Herbert Arthur, 1866–1957, vol. V

Richards, Herbert Paul, 1848–1916, vol. II

Richards, Hugh Augustine, 1884–1949, vol. IV

Richards, Brig. Hugh Upton, 1894–1983, vol. VIII

Richards, Rt Rev. Isaac, 1859–1936, vol. III

Richards, Ivor Armstrong, 1893–1979, vol. VII

Richards, Sir James Maude, 1907–1992, vol. IX

Richards, Engr-Captain John Arthur, 1865–1949, vol. IV

Richards, John Arthur, 1918–1995, vol. IX

Richards, John Eugene, 1885–1951, vol. V

Richards, John Gower Meredith, 1900–1968, vol. VI

Richards, Very Rev. John Harold, 1869–1952, vol. V

Richards, John Henry, 1818–1901, vol. I

Richards, John Morgan, 1841–1918, vol. II

Richards, Rt Rev. John Richards, 1901–1990, vol. VIII

Richards, Sir Joseph, 1888–1968, vol. VI

Richards, Rev. Leyton, 1879–1948, vol. IV

Richards, Maurice John, 1894–1969, vol. VI

Richards, Michael, 1915–1994, vol. IX

Richards, Michael Anthony, 1926–1997, vol. X

Richards, Hon. Mrs Noel Olivier, 1892–1969, vol. VI (AIII)

Richards, Sir Norman Grantham Lewis, 1905–1977, vol. VII

Richards, Owain Westmacott, 1901–1984, vol. VIII

Richards, Owen, 1873–1949, vol. IV

Richards, Percy Andrew Ellis, 1868–1937, vol. III

Richards, Raymond, 1906–1978, vol. VII

Richards, Reginald James, *died* 1950, vol. IV

Richards, Lt-Comdr Richard Meredyth, 1920–1999, vol. X

Richards, Robert, 1884–1954, vol. V

Richards, Rt Rev. Ronald Edwin, 1908–1994, vol. X (AI)

Richards, Rupert Peel, 1872–1941, vol. IV

Richards, Col Samuel Smith Crosland, 1841–1918, vol. II

Richards, Major Sidney, vol. III

Richards, Stephen Elswood, 1878–1950, vol. IV (A)

Richards, Theodore William, 1868–1928, vol. II, vol. III

Richards, Rt Hon. Thomas, 1859–1931, vol. III
Richards, Thomas Frederick, 1863–1942, vol. IV
Richards, Tony; see Richards, E. L.
Richards, Whitmore Lionel, 1869–1954, vol. V
Richards, William, 1863–1939, vol. III
Richards, Air Cdre William Edward Victor, 1897–1964, vol. VI
Richards, William James, 1915–1978, vol. VII
Richards, William John, 1903–1976, vol. VII
Richards, Maj.-Gen. William Watson, 1892–1961, vol. VI
Richardson, Very Rev. Alan, 1905–1975, vol. VII
Richardson, Sir Albert Edward, 1880–1964, vol. VI
Richardson, Air Marshal Sir (Albert) Victor (John), 1884–1960, vol. V
Richardson, Sir Albion Henry Herbert, died 1950, vol. IV
Richardson, Sir Alexander, 1864–1928, vol. II
Richardson, Alexander Stewart, 1897–1989, vol. VIII
Richardson, Maj.-Gen. Alexander Whitmore Colquhoun, 1887–1964, vol. VI
Richardson, Alfred, died 1934, vol. III
Richardson, Arnold Edwin Victor, 1883–1949, vol. IV
Richardson, Arthur, 1860–1936, vol. III
Richardson, Arthur, 1897–1980, vol. VII (AII)
Richardson, Arthur Johnstone, 1862–1940, vol. III
Richardson, Cecil Antonio, (Tony), 1928–1991, vol. IX
Richardson, Charles Arthur, 1918–1972, vol. VII
Richardson, Gen. Sir Charles Leslie, 1908–1994, vol. IX
Richardson, Brig. Charles Walter Philipps, 1905–1993, vol. IX
Richardson, Lt-Gen. Sir Charles William Grant, 1868–1929, vol. III
Richardson, Cyril Albert, 1891–1966, vol. VI
Richardson, Maj.-Gen. David Turnbull, 1886–1957, vol. V
Richardson, Air Marshal Sir (David) William, 1932–1993, vol. IX
Richardson, Dorothy M., (Mrs Alan Odle), died 1957, vol. V
Richardson, Sir Earl; see Richardson, Sir L. E. G.
Richardson, Sir Edward Austin Stewart-, 15th Bt (cr 1630), 1872–1914, vol. I
Richardson, Edward Gick, 1896–1960, vol. V
Richardson, E(dward) Ryder, 1901–1961, vol. VI
Richardson, Ven. Edward Shaw, 1862–1921, vol. II
Richardson, Lt-Col Edwin Hautonville, 1863–1948, vol. IV
Richardson, Sir Egerton Rudolf, 1912–1988, vol. IX (AI)
Richardson, Elliot Lee, 1920–1999, vol. X
Richardson, Emily Moore; see Hamilton, E. M.
Richardson, Foster, died 1942, vol. IV
Richardson, Major Francis James, 1866–1917, vol. II
Richardson, Sir Frank; see Richardson, Sir H. F.
Richardson, Frank, 1870–1917, vol. II
Richardson, Maj.-Gen. Frank McLean, 1904–1996, vol. X
Richardson, Frederic Stuart, 1855–1934, vol. III

Richardson, Rev. Canon Frederick, 1885–1967, vol. VI
Richardson, Frederick Denys, 1913–1983, vol. VIII
Richardson, Rev. George Leyburn, 1867–1934, vol. III
Richardson, Lt-Gen. Sir George Lloyd Reily, 1847–1931, vol. III
Richardson, Maj.-Gen. Sir George Spafford, 1868–1938, vol. III
Richardson, Sir George Wigham, 3rd Bt, 1895–1981, vol. VIII
Richardson, Col Gerald, 1907–1974, vol. VII
Richardson, Graham Edmund, 1913–1992, vol. IX
Richardson, Major Guy; see Richardson, Major T. G. F.
Richardson, Harold Owen Wilson, 1907–1982, vol. VIII
Richardson, Harry, 1891–1966, vol. VI
Richardson, Harry Linley, 1878–1947, vol. IV
Richardson, Sir Henry; see Richardson, Sir J. H. S.
Richardson, Henry Gerald, died 1974, vol. VII
Richardson, Henry Handel, died 1946, vol. IV
Richardson, Henry Marriott, 1876–1936, vol. III
Richardson, Lt-Col Henry Sacheverell Carleton, 1883–1958, vol. V
Richardson, Hon. Horace Frank, 1854–1935, vol. III
Richardson, Sir (Horace) Frank, 1901–1983, vol. VIII
Richardson, Horace Vincent, 1913–2000, vol. X
Richardson, Hugh Edward, 1905–2000, vol. X
Richardson, Major Sir Ian Rorie Hay S.; see Stewart-Richardson.
Richardson, Ven. James Banning, 1843–1923, vol. II
Richardson, Col James Jardine, 1873–1942, vol. IV
Richardson, James Nicholson, 1846–1921, vol. II
Richardson, Ven. John, 1817–1904, vol. I
Richardson, Engr-Rear-Adm. John, 1862–1928, vol. II
Richardson, Major John, 1859–1935, vol. III
Richardson, Rt Rev. John, 1894–1978, vol. VII
Richardson, Most Rev. John Andrew, 1868–1938, vol. III
Richardson, Maj.-Gen. John Booth, 1838–1923, vol. II
Richardson, Maj.-Gen. John Dalyell, 1880–1954, vol. V
Richardson, John David Benbow, 1919–1997, vol. X
Richardson, John Eric, 1916–1998, vol. X
Richardson, Ven. John Farquhar, 1905–1991, vol. IX
Richardson, Ven. John Gray, 1849–1924, vol. II
Richardson, John Henry, 1890–1970, vol. VI
Richardson, Sir (John) Henry (Swain), 1889–1980, vol. VII
Richardson, John I., 1836–1913, vol. I
Richardson, Very Rev. John Macdonald, 1880–1964, vol. VI
Richardson, Joseph, 1830–1902, vol. I
Richardson, Maj.-Gen. Joseph Fletcher, 1822–1900, vol. I
Richardson, Joseph Hall, 1857–1945, vol. IV
Richardson, Josephine 1923–1994, vol. IX

Richardson, Josephus Hargreaves, 1856–1932, vol. III

Richardson, Kenneth Albert, 1926–1994, vol. IX

Richardson, Leopold John Dixon, 1893–1979, vol. VII

Richardson, Captain Leslie, 1885–1934, vol. III

Richardson, Sir Leslie Lewis, 2nd Bt, 1915–1985, vol. VIII

Richardson, Sir Lewis, 1st Bt (cr 1924), 1873–1934, vol. III

Richardson, Lewis Fry, 1881–1953, vol. V

Richardson, Linetta de Castelvecchio, died 1975, vol. VII

Richardson, Sir (Lionel) Earl (George), 1921–1990, vol. VIII

Richardson, Maggie; see Mitchell, Mrs G. J.

Richardson, Maurice Robert, 1884–1950, vol. IV

Richardson, Gp Capt. Michael Oborne, 1908–1994, vol. IX

Richardson, Brig.-Gen. Morris Ernald, 1878–1929, vol. III

Richardson, Lt-Col Neil Graham Stewart-, 1881–1934, vol. III

Richardson, Sir Owen Willans, 1879–1959, vol. V

Richardson, Philip John Sampey, 1875–1963, vol. VI

Richardson, Lt-Col Sir Philip Wigham, 1st Bt (cr 1929), 1865–1953, vol. V

Richardson, Ralph, 1845–1933, vol. III

Richardson, Sir Ralph David, 1902–1983, vol. VIII

Richardson, Rev. Raymond William, 1909–1968, vol. VI

Richardson, Robert, 1862–1943, vol. IV

Richardson, Bt Lt-Col Robert Airth, 1864–1936, vol. III

Richardson, Robert Augustus, 1912–1996, vol. X

Richardson, Rev. Canon Robert Douglas, 1893–1989, vol. VIII

Richardson, Maj.-Gen. Roland, 1896–1973, vol. VII

Richardson, Ronald Frederick, 1913–1991, vol. IX

Richardson, Spencer William, 1869–1927, vol. II

Richardson, Sir Thomas, 1846–1906, vol. I

Richardson, Thomas, 1868–1928, vol. II

Richardson, Thomas, died 1956, vol. V

Richardson, Major (Thomas) Guy (Fenton), 1885–1966, vol. VI

Richardson, Sir Thomas William, 1865–1947, vol. IV

Richardson, Maj.-Gen. Thomas William, 1895–1968, vol. VI

Richardson, Tony; see Richardson, C. A.

Richardson, Air Marshal Sir Victor; see Richardson, Air Marshal Sir A. V. J.

Richardson, Violet Roberta S.; see Stewart-Richardson.

Richardson, William, 1916–1999, vol. X

Richardson, Air Marshal Sir William; see Richardson, Air Marshal Sir D. W.

Richardson, William Eric, 1915–1995, vol. IX

Richardson, Rt Rev. William Moore, 1844–1915, vol. I

Richardson, Sir William Robert, 1909–1986, vol. VIII

Richardson, William Rowson, 1892–1978, vol. VII

Richardson, Maj.-Gen. William Stewart, died 1901, vol. I

Richardson, Sir William Wigham, 2nd Bt (cr 1929), 1893–1973, vol. VII

Richardson, Col Sir Wodehouse Dillon, 1854–1929, vol. III

Richardson-Bunbury, Sir Mervyn William; see Bunbury.

Richardson-Cox, Major Eustace, 1862–1935, vol. III

Richardson-Drummond-Hay, Col James Adam Gordon; see Hay.

Richardson-Griffiths, Major Charles Du Plat, 1855–1925, vol. II

Riche, Georges de P.; see Porto-Riche.

Richepin, Jean, 1849–1926, vol. II

Riches, Sir Derek Martin Hurry, 1912–1997, vol. X

Riches, Sir Eric William, 1897–1987, vol. VIII

Riches, Gen. Sir Ian Hurry, 1908–1996, vol. X

Riches, Rt Rev. Kenneth, 1908–1999, vol. X

Riches, Lindsay Gordon, 1904–1972, vol. VII

Riches, Tom Hurry, 1846–1911, vol. I

Richet, Charles Robert, 1850–1935, vol. III

Richey, Lt-Col George Henry Mills, 1867–1949, vol. IV

Richey, James Alexander, 1874–1931, vol. III

Richey, Sir James Bellett, 1834–1902, vol. I

Richey, James Ernest, 1886–1968, vol. VI

Richmond, 7th Duke of, and Gordon, 2nd Duke of, 1845–1928, vol. II

Richmond, 8th Duke of, and Gordon, 3rd Duke of, 1870–1935, vol. III

Richmond, 9th Duke of, and Gordon, 4th Duke of, 1904–1989, vol. VIII

Richmond and Gordon, Duchess of; (Hilda Madeleine), died 1971, vol. VII

Richmond, Sir Alan James, 1919–1997, vol. X

Richmond, Sir Arthur Cyril, 1879–1968, vol. VI

Richmond, Brig. Arthur Eaton, 1892–1961, vol. VI

Richmond, Sir Bruce Lyttelton, 1871–1964, vol. VI

Richmond, Rt Hon. Sir Clifford Parris, 1914–1997, vol. X

Richmond, Sir Daniel; see Richmond, Sir R. D.

Richmond, Sir David, 1843–1908, vol. I

Richmond, Douglas Close, 1839–1930, vol. III

Richmond, Sir Frederick Henry, 1st Bt, 1873–1953, vol. V

Richmond, Rev. George Edward, 1859–1935, vol. III

Richmond, Adm. Sir Herbert W., 1871–1946, vol. IV

Richmond, Herbert William, 1863–1948, vol. IV

Richmond, Sir Ian, 1902–1965, vol. VI

Richmond, James, 1849–1914, vol. I

Richmond, Sir John Christopher Blake, 1909–1990, vol. VIII

Richmond, Sir John Frederick, 2nd Bt, 1924–2000, vol. X

Richmond, Sir John Ritchie, 1869–1963, vol. VI

Richmond, Lawrence, 1885–1968, vol. VI

Richmond, Leonard, died 1965, vol. VI

Richmond, Maurice Wilson, 1860–1919, vol. II

Richmond, Vice-Adm. Sir Maxwell, 1900–1986, vol. VIII

Richmond, Oliffe Legh, 1881–1977, vol. VII

Richmond, Sir (Robert) Daniel, 1878–1948, vol. IV

Richmond, Rev. Thomas Knyvett, *died* 1901, vol. I
Richmond, Rev. Wilfrid John, 1848–1938, vol. III
Richmond, Col Wilfrid Stanley, 1881–1962, vol. VI
Richmond, Sir William Blake, 1842–1921, vol. II
Richnell, Donovan Thomas, 1911–1994, vol. IX
Richter, Eugen, 1838–1906, vol. I
Richter, Gisela M. A., 1882–1972, vol. VII
Richter, Hans, 1843–1916, vol. II
Richter, Hon. Sir Harold, 1906–1979, vol. VII
Richter, Herbert Davis, 1874–1955, vol. V
Richter, Jean Paul, 1847–1937, vol. III
Richter, Mrs Jean Paul; *see* Richter, Louise Marie.
Richter, Louise Marie, *died* 1938, vol. III
Richter, Sviatoslav Theofilovich, 1915–1997, vol. X
Rickaby, Father Joseph, 1845–1932, vol. III
Rickard, Sir Arthur, 1868–1948, vol. IV
Rickard, Charles Ernest, 1880–1961, vol. VI
Rickard, Rev. Herbert, *died* 1926, vol. II
Rickard, Jessie Louisa, *died* 1963, vol. VI
Rickard, Thomas Arthur, 1864–1953, vol. V
Rickard, Mrs Victor; *see* Rickard, J. L.
Rickards, Arthur George, 1848–1924, vol. II
Rickards, David Ayscough, 1912–1973, vol. VII
Rickards, George William, 1877–1943, vol. IV
Rickards, Maj.-Gen. Gerald Arthur, 1886–1972,
vol. VII
Rickards, Rev. Marcus Samuel Cam, 1840–1928,
vol. II
Rickards, Oscar Stanley Norman, 1893–1986,
vol. VIII
Rickenbacker, Edward Vernon, 1890–1973, vol. VII
Ricketson, Staniforth, 1891–1967, vol. VI
Rickett, Arthur C.; *see* Compton-Rickett.
Rickett, Sir Denis Hubert Fletcher, 1907–1997,
vol. X
Rickett, Harold Robert Norman, 1909–1969, vol. VI
Rickett, Rt Hon. Sir Joseph C.; *see*
Compton-Rickett.
Rickett, Sir Raymond Mildmay Wilson, 1927–1996,
vol. X
Ricketts, Maj.-Gen. Abdy Henry Gough,
1905–1993, vol. IX
Ricketts, (Anne) Theresa, (Lady Ricketts),
1919–1998, vol. X
Ricketts, Major Arthur, 1874–1968, vol. VI
Ricketts, Charles, 1866–1931, vol. III
Ricketts, Sir Claude Albert Frederick, 6th Bt,
1880–1937, vol. III
Ricketts, Rt Rev. Clement Mallory, 1885–1961,
vol. VI
Ricketts, Sir Frederick William Rodney, 5th Bt,
1857–1925, vol. II
Ricketts, George Henry Mildmay, 1827–1914, vol. I
Ricketts, George William, 1864–1927, vol. II
Ricketts, Gordon Randolph, 1918–1968, vol. VI
Ricketts, Lt-Col Percy Edward, 1868–1940, vol. III
Ricketts, Theresa; *see* Ricketts, A. T.
Rickford, Braithwaite; *see* Rickford, R. B. K.
Rickford, Richard Braithwaite Keevil, 1914–1990,
vol. VIII
Rickman, Lt-Col Arthur Wilmot, 1874–1925, vol. II
Rickman, Captain William Edward, 1855–1927,
vol. II
Rickmers, W. Rickmer, 1873–1965, vol. VI
Ricks, Sir John Plowman, 1910–1991, vol. IX

Riddel, Vice-Adm. Daniel MacNab, *died* 1941,
vol. IV
Riddel, James, 1857–1928, vol. II
Riddell, 1st Baron, 1865–1934, vol. III
Riddell, Sir (Alexander) Oliver, 1844–1918, vol. II
Riddell, Rt Rev. Arthur, 1836–1907, vol. I
Riddell, Athol George, 1917–1974, vol. VII
Riddell, Maj.-Gen. Charles James Buchanan,
1817–1903, vol. I
Riddell, Charlotte Eliza Lawson, (Mrs J. H.
Riddell), 1832–1906, vol. I
Riddell, Cuthbert David Giffard, 1868–1937, vol. III
Riddell, Brig.-Gen. Sir Edward Pius Arthur,
1875–1957, vol. V
Riddell, Col Edward Vansittart Dick, 1873–1942,
vol. IV
Riddell, Florence, *died* 1960, vol. V
Riddell, Captain George Hutton, 1878–1915, vol. I
Riddell, Mrs J. H.; *see* Riddell, C. E. L.
Riddell, Rev. John Gervase, 1896–1955, vol. V
Riddell, John Robertson, 1874–1941, vol. IV
Riddell, Col John Scott, 1864–1929, vol. III
Riddell, Sir John Walter Buchanan-, 11th Bt (*cr*
1628), 1849–1924, vol. II
Riddell, Sir Oliver; *see* Riddell, Sir A. O.
Riddell, Sir Rodney Stuart, 4th Bt (*cr* 1778),
1838–1907, vol. I
Riddell, Roland William, (Ronald), 1913–1984,
vol. VIII
Riddell, Ronald; *see* Riddell, Roland W.
Riddell, Victor Horsley, *died* 1976, vol. VII
Riddell, Walter Alexander, 1881–1963, vol. VI
Riddell, Sir Walter Robert Buchanan-, 12th Bt (*cr*
1628), 1879–1934, vol. III
Riddell, William John Brownlow, 1899–1976,
vol. VII
Riddell, William Renwick, 1852–1945, vol. IV
Riddell-Blount, Edward Francis; *see* Blount.
Riddell-Webster, John Alexander, 1921–1999, vol. X
Riddell-Webster, Gen. Sir Thomas Sheridan,
1886–1974, vol. VII
Riddet, William, 1896–1958, vol. V
Riddick, Col John Galloway, 1879–1964, vol. VI
Ridding, Rt Rev. George, 1828–1904, vol. I
Riddle, Sir Ernest Cooper, 1873–1939, vol. III
Riddle, Sir George, 1875–1944, vol. IV
Riddle, John Wallace, 1864–1941, vol. IV
Riddoch, George, 1888–1947, vol. IV
Riddoch, Ian; *see* Riddoch, J. H.
Riddoch, John Haddow, (Ian), 1909–1991, vol. IX
Riddoch, John William, 1893–1969, vol. VI
Riddoch, William, 1862–1942, vol. IV
Ride, Sir Lindsay Tasman, 1898–1977, vol. VII
Rideal, Sir Eric Keightley, 1890–1974, vol. VII
Rideal, Samuel, *died* 1929, vol. III
Ridealgh, Mabel, 1898–1989, vol. VIII
Ridehalgh, Arthur, 1907–1971, vol. VII
Rideing, William Henry, 1853–1919, vol. II
Rideout, Maj.-Gen. Arthur Kennedy, 1835–1913,
vol. I
Rideout, Maj.-Gen. Francis Goring, 1839–1913,
vol. I
Rideout, Percy Rodney, 1868–1956, vol. V
Rider, Engr Rear-Adm. Sydney, *died* 1943, vol. IV
Rider, Thomas Francis, 1843–1922, vol. II

Ridge, Pett; *see* Ridge, W. P.
Ridge, (William) Pett, 1857–1930, vol. III
Ridgers, John Nalton Sharpe, 1910–1999, vol. X
Ridgeway, Rt Rev. Charles John, 1841–1927, vol. II
Ridgeway, Rev. Charles Spencer-Churchill FitzGerald, (F. Gerald Ridgeway), 1872–1958, vol. V
Ridgeway, Brig. David Graeme, 1879–1950, vol. IV
Ridgeway, Major Edward William Crawfurd, *died* 1917, vol. II
Ridgeway, F. Gerald; *see* Ridgeway, Rev. C. S.-C. F.
Ridgeway, Rt Rev. Frederick Edward, 1848–1921, vol. II
Ridgeway, Rt Hon. Sir (Joseph) West, 1844–1930, vol. III
Ridgeway, Col Richard Kirby, 1848–1924, vol. II
Ridgeway, Ven. S., 1872–1951, vol. V
Ridgeway, Rt Hon. Sir West; *see* Ridgeway, Rt Hon. Sir J. W.
Ridgeway, Sir William, 1853–1926, vol. II
Ridgway, Gen. Matthew Bunker, 1895–1993, vol. IX
Ridgway, Brig.-Gen. Richard Thomas Incledon, 1868–1939, vol. III
Riding, George Albert, 1888–1982, vol. VIII
Ridley, 1st Viscount, 1842–1904, vol. I (A)
Ridley, 2nd Viscount, 1874–1916, vol. II
Ridley, 3rd Viscount, 1902–1964, vol. VI
Ridley of Liddesdale, Baron (Life Peer); Nicholas Ridley, 1929–1993, vol. IX
Ridley, Alice, (Lady Ridley), *died* 1945, vol. IV
Ridley, Arnold, 1896–1984, vol. VIII
Ridley, Brig.-Gen. Charles Parker, 1855–1937, vol. III
Ridley, Wing Comdr Claude Alward, 1896–1942, vol. IV
Ridley, Rt Hon. Sir Edward, 1843–1928, vol. II
Ridley, Edward Alexander Keane, 1904–2000, vol. X
Ridley, Col Edward Davenport, 1883–1934, vol. III
Ridley, Frederick Thomas, 1903–1977, vol. VII
Ridley, George, 1886–1944, vol. IV
Ridley, Guy, 1885–1947, vol. IV
Ridley, Henry Nicholas, 1855–1956, vol. V
Ridley, Hon. Sir Jasper Nicholas, 1887–1951, vol. V
Ridley, Maurice Roy, 1890–1969, vol. VI
Ridley, Nicholas Charles, 1863–1937, vol. III
Ridley, Philip Waller, 1921–1996, vol. X
Ridley, Samuel Forde, 1864–1944, vol. IV
Ridley, Sir Sidney, 1902–1993, vol. IX
Ridley, Rt Rev. William, 1836–1911, vol. I
Ridley, William Arnold; *see* Ridley, A.
Ridout, Maj.-Gen. Sir Dudley Howard, 1866–1941, vol. IV
Ridpath, Sir Henry, 1873–1950, vol. IV
Ridsdale, Arthur Francis, *died* 1935, vol. III
Ridsdale, Sir Aurelian; *see* Ridsdale, Sir E. A.
Ridsdale, Rt Rev. Charles Henry, 1873–1952, vol. V
Ridsdale, Sir (Edward) Aurelian, 1864–1923, vol. II
Ridsdale, Sir William, 1890–1957, vol. V
Rie, Dame Lucie, 1902–1995, vol. IX
Riefler, Winfield William, 1897–1974, vol. VII
Rieger, Sir Clarence Oscar Ferrero, 1897–1978, vol. VII

Riesenfeld, Hugo, 1884–1939, vol. III (A), vol. IV
Rietchel, Julius, *died* 1963, vol. VI
Rieu, Charles Pierre Henri, 1820–1902, vol. I
Rieu, Emile Victor, 1887–1972, vol. VII
Rieu, Sir (Jean) Louis, 1872–1964, vol. VI
Rieu, Sir Louis; *see* Rieu, Sir J. L.
Rifaat, Kamal Eldin Mahmoud, 1921–1977, vol. VII
Rigby, Cuthbert, 1850–1935, vol. III
Rigby, Herbert Cecil, 1917–1986, vol. VIII
Rigby, Lt-Col Sir (Hugh) John Macbeth, 2nd Bt, 1914–1999, vol. X
Rigby, Col Sir Hugh Mallinson, 1st Bt, 1870–1944, vol. IV
Rigby, Sir Ivo Charles Clayton, 1911–1987, vol. VIII
Rigby, Rt Hon. Sir John, 1834–1903, vol. I
Rigby, Sir John; *see* Rigby, Sir H. J. M.
Rigby, Norman Leslie, 1920–1996, vol. X
Rigby, Reginald Francis, 1919–1999, vol. X
Rigby, Brig. Thomas, 1897–1969, vol. VI
Rigg, Caroline E., *died* 1929, vol. III
Rigg, Sir Edward, 1850–1933, vol. III
Rigg, Harry Sibson Leslie, 1915–1976, vol. VII
Rigg, Herbert Addington, *died* 1924, vol. II
Rigg, James Harrison, 1821–1909, vol. I
Rigg, John, 1858–1943, vol. IV
Rigg, Major Richard, 1877–1942, vol. IV
Rigg, Sir Theodore, 1888–1972, vol. VII
Rigg, Ven. William Harrison, 1877–1966, vol. VI
Riggall, Major Arthur Horton, 1867–1929, vol. III
Riggall, Lt-Col Harold William, 1882–1930, vol. III
Riggall, Robert Marmaduke, 1881–1970, vol. VI
Riggs, Kate Douglas, (Mrs George Christopher Riggs); *see* Wiggin, K. D.
Righton, Thomas Edward Corrie Burns, *died* 1899, vol. I
Rignold, Hugo Henry, 1905–1976, vol. VII
Riis, Jacob A., *died* 1914, vol. I
Riley, Athelstan, 1858–1945, vol. IV
Riley, Ben, 1866–1946, vol. IV
Riley, Rt Rev. Charles Lawrence, 1888–1971, vol. VII
Riley, Most Rev. Charles Owen Leaver, 1854–1929, vol. III
Riley, Frederick Fox, *died* 1934, vol. III
Riley, Maj.-Gen. Sir Guy; *see* Riley, Maj.-Gen. Sir H. G.
Riley, Lt-Col Hamlet Lewthwaite, 1882–1932, vol. III
Riley, Harry Lister, 1899–1986, vol. VIII
Riley, Maj.-Gen. Sir (Henry) Guy, 1884–1964, vol. VI
Riley, James Whitcomb, 1849–1916, vol. II
Riley, Maj. John Roland Christopher, 1925–1998, vol. X
Riley, Norman Denbigh, 1890–1979, vol. VII
Riley, Sir Ralph, 1924–1999, vol. X
Riley, Brig. Rupert Farquhar, 1873–1941, vol. IV
Riley, William, 1866–1961, vol. VI
Riley, William Edward, 1852–1937, vol. III
Riley, Engr Rear-Adm. William Henry, *died* 1926, vol. II
Rilot, Charles Frederick, 1864–1942, vol. IV
Rimbault, Brig. Geoffrey Acworth, 1908–1991, vol. IX

Rimington, Alexander Wallace, 1854–1918, vol. II
Rimington, Claude, 1902–1993, vol. IX
Rimington, Maj.-Gen. Joseph Cameron, 1864–1942, vol. IV
Rimington, Maj.-Gen. Sir Michael Frederic, 1858–1928, vol. II
Rimington-Wilson, Reginald Henry Rimington; see Wilson.
Rimmer, Edward Johnson, 1883–1962, vol. VI
Rimmer, Frederick William, 1914–1998, vol. X
Rind, Col Alexander Thomas Seton Abercromby, 1847–1925, vol. II
Rind, Lt-Col George Burnet Abercrombie, 1880–1958, vol. V
Rinder, Frank, 1863–1937, vol. III
Rinehart, Mary Roberts, died 1958, vol. V
Rinfret, Hon. Gabriel-Edouard, 1905–1994, vol. X (AI)
Rinfret, Rt Hon. Thibaudeau, 1879–1962, vol. VI
Ring, George Alfred, died 1927, vol. II
Ring, Sir Lindsay Roberts, 1914–1997, vol. X
Ring, Rev. Timothy J., 1858–1941, vol. IV
Ringer, Sydney, 1835–1910, vol. I
Ringham, Reginald, 1894–1973, vol. VII
Ringwood, Alfred Edward, 1930–1993, vol. IX
Rink, George Arnold, 1902–1983, vol. VIII
Rink, Margaret Joan; see Suttill, M. J.
Rintoul, Andrew, 1908–1984, vol. VIII
Riordan, Very Rev. Father James John, 1896–1959, vol. V
Riordan, Most Rev. Patrick William, 1841–1914, vol. I
Rios Urruti, Fernando de los, born 1879, vol. IV
Ripley, Lt-Col B., 1880–1958, vol. V
Ripley, Sir Edward, 2nd Bt (cr 1880), 1840–1903, vol. I
Ripley, Sir Frederick, 1st Bt (cr 1897), 1846–1907, vol. I
Ripley, Sir Frederick Hugh, 2nd Bt (cr 1897), 1878–1945, vol. IV
Ripley, Sir Geoffrey Arnold, 3rd Bt (cr 1897), 1883–1954, vol. V
Ripley, Gladys, (Mrs E. A. Dick), 1908–1955, vol. V
Ripley, Sir Henry William Alfred, 3rd Bt (cr 1880), 1879–1956, vol. V
Ripley, Sydney William Leonard, 1909–1991, vol. IX
Ripley, Rev. William Nottidge, died 1912, vol. I
Ripman, Walter, 1869–1947, vol. IV
Ripon, 1st Marquess of, 1827–1909, vol. I
Ripon, 2nd Marquess of, 1852–1923, vol. II
Ripper, Walter Eugene, 1908–1965, vol. VI
Ripper, William, 1853–1937, vol. III
Rippon of Hexham, (Life Peer); (Aubrey) Geoffrey (Frederick) Rippon, 1924–1997, vol. X
Riquetti de Mirabeau, Sybille Gabrielle Marie Antoinette de; see Gyp, Sybille.
Riseley, George, 1845–1932, vol. III
Rishbeth, John, 1918–1991, vol. IX
Rishworth, Frank Sharman, 1876–1960, vol. V
Risk, (Charles) John, 1926–1985, vol. VIII
Risk, John; see Risk, C. J.
Risk, Captain Richard Henry Litle, 1857–1933, vol. III

Risk, William Symington, 1909–1996, vol. X
Risley, Sir Herbert Hope, 1851–1911, vol. I
Risley, Sir John Shuckburgh, 1867–1957, vol. V
Risness, Eric John, 1927–2000, vol. X
Rissik, Hon. Johann Friedrich Bernhardt, died 1925, vol. II
Risson, Maj.-Gen. Sir Robert Joseph Henry, 1901–1992, vol. IX
Ristori, Madame, 1822–1906, vol. I
Rita, (Mrs W. Desmond Humphreys), died 1938, vol. III
Ritchard, Cyril, 1898–1977, vol. VII
Ritchie of Dundee, 1st Baron, 1838–1906, vol. I
Ritchie of Dundee, 2nd Baron, 1866–1948, vol. IV
Ritchie of Dundee, 3rd Baron, 1902–1975, vol. VII
Ritchie of Dundee, 4th Baron, 1908–1978, vol. VII
Ritchie, Sir Adam Beattie, 1881–1957, vol. V
Ritchie, Alexander Brown, 1865–1936, vol. III
Ritchie, Alexander Charles Otway, 1928–2000, vol. X
Ritchie, Ven. Andrew Binny, 1880–1956, vol. V
Ritchie, Anne Isabella, (Lady Ritchie), 1837–1919, vol. II
Ritchie, Anthony Elliot, 1915–1997, vol. X
Ritchie, Maj.-Gen. Sir Archibald Buchanan, 1869–1955, vol. V
Ritchie, Arthur David, 1891–1967, vol. VI
Ritchie, Rev. Canon Charles Henry, 1887–1958, vol. V
Ritchie, Charles John, 1871–1950, vol. IV
Ritchie, Charles Stewart Almon, 1906–1995, vol. IX
Ritchie, David; see Ritchie, H. D.
Ritchie, David George, 1853–1903, vol. I
Ritchie, Rev. David Lakie, 1864–1951, vol. V
Ritchie, Sir Douglas; see Ritchie, Sir J. D.
Ritchie, Douglas Ernest, 1905–1967, vol. VI
Ritchie, Douglas Malcolm, 1941–1993, vol. IX
Ritchie, Sir George, 1849–1921, vol. II
Ritchie, Hon. Sir George, 1864–1944, vol. IV
Ritchie, Major Hon. Harold, 1876–1918, vol. II
Ritchie, Harry; see Ritchie, Henry P.
Ritchie, Henry Parker, (Harry), 1919–1988, vol. VIII
Ritchie, Captain Henry Peel, 1876–1958, vol. V
Ritchie, (Horace) David, 1920–1993, vol. IX
Ritchie, Hugh, 1864–1948, vol. IV
Ritchie, James, 1864–1923, vol. II
Ritchie, James, 1882–1958, vol. V
Ritchie, Sir James Edward Thomson, 2nd Bt, 1902–1991, vol. IX
Ritchie, Sir James Martin, 1874–1951, vol. V
Ritchie, (James) Martin, 1917–1993, vol. IX
Ritchie, Rear-Adm. James Stuart McLaren, 1884–1955, vol. V
Ritchie, Sir James Thomson, 1st Bt (cr 1903), 1835–1912, vol. I
Ritchie, James Walter, 1920–1998, vol. X
Ritchie, Sir James William, 1st Bt cr 1918 (styled 2nd Bt), 1868–1937, vol. III
Ritchie, Maj.-Gen. John, 1834–1919, vol. II
Ritchie, Sir John, died 1947, vol. IV
Ritchie, John, 1882–1959, vol. V
Ritchie, John, 1913–1988, vol. VIII
Ritchie, Sir (John) Douglas, 1885–1983, vol. VIII
Ritchie, Sir John Neish, 1904–1977, vol. VII

Ritchie, Captain Sir Lewis Anselmo, 1886–1967, vol. VI
Ritchie, Martin; see Ritchie, J. M.
Ritchie, Gen. Sir Neil Methuen, 1897–1983, vol. VIII
Ritchie, R. L. Græme, 1880–1954, vol. V
Ritchie, Sir Richmond Thackeray Willoughby, 1854–1912, vol. I
Ritchie, Lt-Col Thomas Fraser, 1875–1931, vol. III
Ritchie, Sir Thomas Malcolm, 1894–1971, vol. VII
Ritchie, Maj.-Gen. Walter Henry Dennison, 1901–1984, vol. VIII
Ritchie, William, 1854–1931, vol. III
Ritchie, Col William Buchanan, 1877–1937, vol. III
Ritchie, William George Brookfield, 1875–1949, vol. IV
Ritchie, William Thomas, 1873–1945, vol. IV
Ritchie-Calder, Baron (Life Peer); Peter Ritchie Ritchie-Calder, 1906–1982, vol. VIII
Ritchie-Scott, Alexander, 1874–1962, vol. VI
Ritson, Sir Edward Herbert, 1892–1981, vol. VIII
Ritson, Lt-Col John Anthony Sydney, 1887–1957, vol. V
Ritson, Rev. John Holland, 1868–1953, vol. V
Ritson, Joshua, 1874–1955, vol. V
Ritson, Lady Kitty, 1887–1969, vol. VI
Ritson, Muriel, 1885–1980, vol. VII
Ritson, Col William Henry, 1867–1942, vol. IV
Ritter, Gustave Albert, died 1914, vol. I
Ritter, His Eminence Cardinal Joseph Elmer, 1892–1967, vol. VI
Rivalland, Sir Michel Jean Joseph Laval, 1910–1970, vol. VI
Rivard, Adjutor, 1868–1945, vol. IV
Rivaz, Hon. Sir Charles Montgomery, 1845–1926, vol. II
Rivaz, Col Vincent, 1842–1924, vol. II
Riverdale, 1st Baron, 1873–1957, vol. V
Riverdale, 2nd Baron, 1901–1998, vol. X
Rivers, Lady; (Emmeline Laura), died 1918, vol. II
Rivers, Alfred Peter, 1906–1979, vol. VII
Rivers, Very Rev. Arthur Richard, 1857–1940, vol. III (A), vol. IV
Rivers, Augustus Henry Lane F. P.; see Fox-Pitt-Rivers.
Rivers, George Henry Lane Fox P.; see Pitt-Rivers.
Rivers, Georgia; see Clark, Marjorie.
Rivers, Rosalind Venetia P.; see Pitt-Rivers.
Rivers, William Halse R., 1864–1922, vol. II
Rivers Pollock, William; see Pollock.
Rives, Amélia, (Princess Pierre Troubetskoy), 1863–1945, vol. IV
Rivet, Albert Lionel Frederick, 1915–1993, vol. IX
Rivet, Raoul, 1896–1957, vol. V
Rivett, Sir (Albert Cherbury) David, 1885–1961, vol. VI
Rivett, Sir David; see Rivett, Sir A. C. D.
Rivett, Louis Carnac, 1888–1947, vol. IV
Rivett-Carnac, Charles James, 1853–1935, vol. III
Rivett-Carnac, Sir Claud James, 4th Bt, 1877–1909, vol. I
Rivett-Carnac, Rev. Sir George, 6th Bt, 1850–1932, vol. III
Rivett-Carnac, Sir Henry George Crabbe, 7th Bt, 1889–1972, vol. VII

Rivett-Carnac, Vice-Adm. James William, 1891–1970, vol. VI
Rivett-Carnac, Col John Henry, 1838–1923, vol. II
Rivett-Carnac, Col Percy Temple, 1852–1932, vol. III
Rivett-Carnac, Sir William Percival, 5th Bt, 1847–1924, vol. II
Rivett-Drake, Brig. Dame Jean Elizabeth, 1909–1999, vol. X
Rivière, A. Joseph, 1859–1946, vol. IV
Riviere, Briton, 1840–1920, vol. II
Riviere, Clive, 1872–1929, vol. III
Riviere, Hugh Goldwin, 1869–1956, vol. V
Rivington, Albert Gibson, 1883–1950, vol. IV
Rivington, Rev. Cecil Stansfeld, 1853–1934, vol. III
Rivington, Charles Robert, 1846–1928, vol. II
Rivington, Mme Hill, (Lady Holmes), died 1957, vol. V
Rivington, Gerald Chippindale, 1893–1977, vol. VII
Rivington, Rev. Thurston, 1848–1929, vol. III
Rivington, William John, 1845–1914, vol. I
Rix, Rt Rev. George Alexander, died 1945, vol. IV
Roach, Alfred Thomas, 1899–1946, vol. IV
Roach, Edward K.; see Keith-Roach.
Roach, Rt Rev. Frederick, 1856–1922, vol. II
Roach, Air Vice-Marshal Harold Jace, 1896–1977, vol. VII
Roach, Harry Robert, 1906–1979, vol. VII
Road, Sir Alfred, 1891–1972, vol. VII
Roaf, Herbert Eldon, 1881–1952, vol. V
Roark, Helen Wills, 1905–1998, vol. X
Rob, John Vernon, 1915–1971, vol. VII
Robartes, Hon. Thomas Charles Reginald A.; see Agar-Robartes.
Robarts, Abraham John, 1838–1926, vol. II
Robarts, Basil, 1915–1997, vol. X
Robarts, David John, 1906–1989, vol. VIII
Robarts, Eric Kirkby, 1908–1992, vol. IX
Robarts, John, 1872–1954, vol. V
Robathan, Rev. Canon Frederick Norman, 1896–1986, vol. VIII
Robb, Alexander, died 1934, vol. III
Robb, Alfred Arthur, 1873–1936, vol. III
Robb, Andrew McCance, 1887–1968, vol. VI
Robb, Sir Douglas; see Robb, Sir G. D.
Robb, Maj.-Gen. Sir Frederick Spencer, 1858–1948, vol. IV
Robb, Sir (George) Douglas, 1899–1974, vol. VII
Robb, Hon. James Alexander, 1859–1929, vol. III
Robb, James Christie, 1924–1999, vol. X
Robb, Air Chief Marshal Sir James Milne, died 1968, vol. VI
Robb, Rt Hon. John Hanna, 1873–1956, vol. V
Robb, Hon. John Morrow, 1876–1942, vol. IV
Robb, Leonard Arthur, 1891–1964, vol. VII (AI)
Robb, Michael Antony Moyse, 1914–1977, vol. VII
Robb, Nesca Adeline, 1905–1976, vol. VII
Robb, Ven. Percy Douglas, 1902–1976, vol. VII
Robb, William, 1885–1982, vol. VIII
Robb, William George, 1872–1940, vol. III
Robberds, Rt Rev. Walter John Forbes, 1863–1944, vol. IV
Robbins, Baron (Life Peer); Lionel Charles Robbins, 1898–1984, vol. VIII
Robbins, Alan Pitt, 1888–1967, vol. VI

Robbins, Sir Alfred Farthing, 1856–1931, vol. III
Robbins, Alfred Gordon, 1883–1944, vol. IV
Robbins, Dennis; *see* Robbins, J. D.
Robbins, Edgar Carmichael, 1911–1988, vol. VIII
Robbins, Sir Edmund, 1847–1922, vol. II
Robbins, Harold, 1916–1997, vol. X
Robbins, Jerome, 1918–1998, vol. X
Robbins, John Dennis, 1915–1986, vol. VIII
Robbins, Rowland Richard, *died* 1960, vol. V
Robbins, Brig. Thomas, 1893–1981, vol. VIII
Robens of Woldingham, Baron (Life Peer); Alfred
  Robens, 1910–1999, vol. X
Roberge, Guy, 1915–1991, vol. IX
Roberson, Rev. Henry, 1858–1934, vol. III
Robert, Henri, 1863–1936, vol. III
Roberthall, Baron (Life Peer); Robert Lowe
  Roberthall, 1901–1988, vol. VIII
Roberton, Sir Hugh S., 1874–1952, vol. V
Roberton, Rev. Ivor Johnstone, 1865–1948, vol. IV
Roberton, Violet Mary Craig, 1888–1954, vol. V
Roberts, 1st Earl, 1832–1914, vol. I
Roberts, Countess (2nd in line), 1870–1944, vol. IV
Roberts, Countess (3rd in line), 1875–1955, vol. V
Roberts, Albert, 1911–1992, vol. IX
Roberts, Aled Owen, 1889–1949, vol. IV
Roberts, Rev. Alexander, 1826–1901, vol. I
Roberts, Lt-Col Sir Alexander Fowler, 1882–1961,
  vol. VI
Roberts, Hon. Alexander William, 1857–1938,
  vol. III
Roberts, Sir Alfred, 1823–1899, vol. I
Roberts, Ven. Alfred, 1853–1937, vol. III
Roberts, Sir Alfred, 1897–1963, vol. VI
Roberts, Allan, 1943–1990, vol. VIII
Roberts, Allan Arbuthnot Lane, 1884–1967, vol. VI
Roberts, Angus, 1893–1937, vol. III
Roberts, Arthur, 1852–1933, vol. III
Roberts, Rev. Arthur Betton, 1880–1961, vol. VI
Roberts, Sir Arthur Cornelius, 1869–1946, vol. IV
Roberts, Arthur James Rooker, 1882–1943, vol. IV
Roberts, Arthur Loten, 1906–2000, vol. X
Roberts, Rt Rev. Basil Coleby, 1887–1957, vol. V
Roberts, Rev. Bleddyn Jones, 1906–1977, vol. VII
Roberts, Brian Birley, 1912–1978, vol. VII
Roberts, Brian Richard, 1906–1988, vol. VIII
Roberts, Sir Bryan Clieve, 1923–1996, vol. X
Roberts, Bryn, 1897–1964, vol. VI
Roberts, Carl Eric Bechhofer, 1894–1949, vol. IV
Roberts, Cecil Edric Mornington, 1892–1976,
  vol. VII
Roberts, Cedric Sydney L.; *see* Lane-Roberts.
Roberts, Chalmers; *see* Roberts, H. C.
Roberts, Ven. Charles Frederic, *died* 1942, vol. IV
Roberts, Col Charles Fyshe, 1837–1914, vol. I
Roberts, Sir Charles George Douglas, 1860–1943,
  vol. IV
Roberts, Charles Henry, 1865–1959, vol. V
Roberts, Charles Hubert, *died* 1929, vol. III
Roberts, Hon. Charles James, 1846–1925, vol. II
Roberts, Rev. Charles Philip, 1842–1918, vol. II
Roberts, Charles Stuart, 1918–1989, vol. VIII
Roberts, Colin Henderson, 1909–1990, vol. VIII
Roberts, Cyril, 1871–1949, vol. IV
Roberts, Cyril Alfred, 1908–1988, vol. VIII
Roberts, Sir David Arthur, 1924–1987, vol. VIII

Roberts, Sir David Charles, 1859–1940, vol. III
Roberts, Ven. David Egryn, *died* 1935, vol. III
Roberts, Rt Rev. (David) John, 1919–2000, vol. X
Roberts, David Lloyd, *died* 1920, vol. II
Roberts, David Thomas, *died* 1903, vol. I
Roberts, Denis; *see* Roberts, E. F. D.
Roberts, Denys K.; *see* Kilham-Roberts.
Roberts, Rev. E. Berwyn, 1869–1951, vol. V
Roberts, Col Edward, 1841–1904, vol. I
Roberts, Very Rev. Edward Albert Trevillian,
  1877–1968, vol. VI
Roberts, Rev. Edward Dale, 1848–1927, vol. II
Roberts, Edward E.; *see* Emrys-Roberts.
Roberts, Rev. Canon Edward Eric, 1911–2000,
  vol. X
Roberts, (Edward Frederick) Denis, 1927–1990,
  vol. VIII
Roberts, Ellis, 1860–1930, vol. III
Roberts, Emrys Owain, 1910–1990, vol. VIII
Roberts, Rt Rev. Eric Matthias, 1914–1997, vol. X
Roberts, Ernest Alfred Cecil, 1912–1994, vol. IX
Roberts, Sir Ernest Handforth Goodman,
  1890–1969, vol. VI
Roberts, Rev. Ernest Marling, 1873–1929, vol. III
Roberts, Rev. Ernest Stewart, 1847–1912, vol. I
Roberts, Francis Noel, 1893–1969, vol. VI
Roberts, Maj.-Gen. Frank Crowther, 1891–1982,
  vol. VIII
Roberts, Sir Frank Kenyon, 1907–1998, vol. X
Roberts, Hon. Frederick Hugh Sherston,
  1872–1899, vol. I
Roberts, Rt Hon. Frederick Owen, 1876–1941,
  vol. IV
Roberts, Frederick Thomas, *died* 1918, vol. II
Roberts, Geoffrey Dorling, 1886–1967, vol. VI
Roberts, Air Cdre Sir Geoffrey Newland,
  1906–1995, vol. IX
Roberts, Brig. Sir Geoffrey Paul H.; *see*
  Hardy-Roberts.
Roberts, Sir George, 1st Bt (*cr* 1930), 1859–1950,
  vol. IV
Roberts, George Augustus, 1875–1962, vol. VI
Roberts, George Charles L.; *see* Lloyd-Roberts.
Roberts, Col Sir George Fossett, 1870–1954, vol. V
Roberts, Rt Hon. George Henry, 1869–1928, vol. II
Roberts, George Lawrence, 1904–1967, vol. VI
Roberts, Maj.-Gen. (George) Philip (Bradley),
  1906–1997, vol. X
Roberts, George Quinlan, 1860–1943, vol. IV
Roberts, Sir George William Kelly, 1907–1964,
  vol. VI
Roberts, Gervase Henry, *died* 1944, vol. IV
Roberts, Sir Gilbert, 1899–1978, vol. VII
Roberts, Captain Gilbert Howland, 1900–1986,
  vol. VIII
Roberts, Air Vice Marshal Glynn S.; *see* Silyn
  Roberts.
Roberts, Goronwy; *see* Baron Goronwy-Roberts.
Roberts, Very Rev. Griffith, 1845–1943, vol. IV
Roberts, Harold, 1884–1950, vol. IV
Roberts, Harold, 1879–1959, vol. V
Roberts, Rev. Harold, 1896–1982, vol. VIII
Roberts, Sir Harold Charles West, 1892–1983,
  vol. VIII
Roberts, Harry, 1871–1946, vol. IV

Roberts, (Henry) Chalmers, *died* 1949, vol. IV
Roberts, Henry David, 1870–1951, vol. V
Roberts, Lt-Col Henry Roger Crompton-, 1863–1925, vol. II
Roberts, Herbert Ainslie, 1864–1932, vol. III
Roberts, Brig.-Gen. Hereward Llewelyn, 1864–1947, vol. IV
Roberts, Sir Howard; *see* Roberts, Sir J. R. H.
Roberts, Col Sir Howland, 5th Bt (*cr* 1809), 1845–1917, vol. II
Roberts, Hugh Douglas, 1869–1942, vol. IV
Roberts, Hugh Gordon, 1885–1961, vol. VI
Roberts, Hugh Leslie-, 1860–1949, vol. IV
Roberts, Hugh Lloyd, *died* 1906, vol. I
Roberts, Isaac, 1829–1904, vol. I
Roberts, Rev. J. J., 1840–1914, vol. I
Roberts, Sir James, 1st Bt (*cr* 1909), 1848–1935, vol. III
Roberts, Hon. James, 1881–1967, vol. VI
Roberts, James Alexander, 1876–1945, vol. IV
Roberts, Sir James Denby, 2nd Bt (*cr* 1909), 1904–1973, vol. VII
Roberts, James Ernest Helme, *died* 1948, vol. IV
Roberts, James Frederick, 1847–1911, vol. II
Roberts, Sir (James Reginald) Howard, 1891–1975, vol. VII
Roberts, Lt-Col Sir James Reid, 1861–1941, vol. IV
Roberts, Dame Jean, *died* 1988, vol. VIII
Roberts, Dame Joan Howard, 1907–1990, vol. VIII
Roberts, Sir John, 1861–1917, vol. II
Roberts, Sir John, 1845–1934, vol. III
Roberts, Captain John, 1867–1943, vol. IV
Roberts, Sir John, 1876–1966, vol. VI
Roberts, Rt Rev. John; *see* Roberts, Rt Rev. D. J.
Roberts, John Alexander Fraser, 1899–1987, vol. VIII
Roberts, John Bryn, 1843–1931, vol. III
Roberts, Rev. John Edward, 1866–1929, vol. III
Roberts, John Eric, 1907–1998, vol. X
Roberts, Air Vice-Marshal John Frederick, 1913–1996, vol. X
Roberts, John Gwyndeg H.; *see* Hughes-Roberts.
Roberts, Maj.-Gen. John Hamilton, 1891–1962, vol. VI
Roberts, John Harvey Polmear, 1935–1994, vol. IX
Roberts, John Keith, 1897–1944, vol. IV
Roberts, John Reginald, 1893–1971, vol. VII
Roberts, Sir John Reynolds, 1834–1917, vol. II
Roberts, John Varley, 1841–1920, vol. II
Roberts, Kate Winifred J.; *see* Jones-Roberts.
Roberts, Kenneth, 1885–1957, vol. V
Roberts, Lancelot, *died* 1950, vol. IV (A), vol. V
Roberts, Sir Leslie, *died* 1976, vol. VII
Roberts, Llewelyn, 1881–1939, vol. III
Roberts, Major Marmaduke Torin Cramer-, 1880–1939, vol. III
Roberts, Captain Marshall Owen, 1878–1931, vol. III
Roberts, Martin, 1853–1926, vol. II, vol. III
Roberts, Michael, 1902–1948, vol. IV
Roberts, Michael, 1908–1996, vol. X
Roberts, Michael Hilary Arthur, 1927–1983, vol. VIII
Roberts, Brig. Michael Rookherst, 1894–1977, vol. VII

Roberts, Morley, 1857–1942, vol. IV
Roberts, Norman Stafford, 1926–1993, vol. IX
Roberts, Sir Norman Stanley, 1893–1972, vol. VII
Roberts, Gen. Sir Ouvry Lindfield, 1898–1986, vol. VIII
Roberts, Sir Owen, 1835–1915, vol. I
Roberts, Owen Glynne, 1880–1947, vol. IV
Roberts, Owen Josephus, 1875–1955, vol. V
Roberts, Patrick Maxwell, 1895–1937, vol. III
Roberts, Paul Ernest, 1873–1949, vol. IV
Roberts, Peter Burman Moir, 1874–1956, vol. V
Roberts, Sir Peter Geoffrey, 3rd Bt, 1912–1985, vol. VIII
Roberts, Lt-Comdr Peter Scawen Watkinson, 1917–1979, vol. VII
Roberts, Maj.-Gen. Philip; *see* Roberts, Maj.-Gen. G. P. B.
Roberts, Rachel, 1927–1980, vol. VII
Roberts, Sir Randal Howland, 4th Bt (*cr* 1809), 1837–1899, vol. I
Roberts, Reginald Arthur, 1874–1940, vol. III
Roberts, Reginald Hugh, 1883–1955, vol. V
Roberts, Very Rev. Richard, 1874–1945, vol. IV
Roberts, Richard Arthur, 1851–1943, vol. IV
Roberts, Rear-Adm. Richard Douglas, 1916–1995, vol. IX
Roberts, Richard Ellis, 1879–1953, vol. V
Roberts, Rev. Richard Gwylfa, 1871–1935, vol. III
Roberts, Ven. Richard Henry, *died* 1970, vol. VI
Roberts, Sir Richard L.; *see* Lloyd-Roberts.
Roberts, Richard Owen, 1876–1929, vol. III
Roberts, Robert A.; *see* Alun Roberts.
Roberts, Robert David Valpo, 1906–1973, vol. VII
Roberts, Robert Davies, 1851–1911, vol. I
Roberts, Rev. Canon Robert Edwin, 1878–1940, vol. III
Roberts, Robert Herbert M.; *see* Mills-Roberts.
Roberts, Robert Lewis, 1875–1956, vol. V
Roberts, Robert Silyn, *died* 1930, vol. III
Roberts, Rev. Roger Lewis, 1911–1990, vol. VIII
Roberts, Rev. Canon Roland Harry William, 1894–1951, vol. V
Roberts, Roy Ernest James, 1928–1993, vol. IX
Roberts, Samuel, 1852–1913, vol. I
Roberts, Rt Hon. Sir Samuel, 1st Bt (*cr* 1919), 1852–1926, vol. II
Roberts, Sir Samuel, 2nd Bt (*cr* 1919), 1882–1955, vol. V
Roberts, Dame Shelagh Marjorie, 1924–1992, vol. IX
Roberts, Sidney Morton Pearson, 1860–1930, vol. III
Roberts, Sir Stephen Henry, 1901–1971, vol. VII
Roberts, Lt-Col Stephen Richard Harricks, 1874–1943, vol. IV
Roberts, Stuart; *see* Roberts, C. S.
Roberts, Sir Sydney Castle, 1887–1966, vol. VI
Roberts, T. Stanley, *died* 1935, vol. III
Roberts, Thomas Arnold, 1911–1990, vol. VIII
Roberts, Most Rev. Thomas d'Esterre, 1893–1976, vol. VII
Roberts, Sir Thomas Edwards, 1851–1926, vol. II
Roberts, Thomas Esmôr Rhys R.; *see* Rhys-Roberts.
Roberts, Thomas Francis, 1860–1919, vol. II

Roberts, Col Sir Thomas Langdon Howland, 6th Bt (*cr* 1809), 1898–1979, vol. VII
Roberts, Sir Thomas Lee, 1848–1924, vol. II
Roberts, Tom, 1856–1931, vol. III
Roberts, W. J., *died* 1943, vol. IV
Roberts, Sir Walter St Clair Howland, 1893–1978, vol. VII
Roberts, Walter Stewart S.; *see* Stewart-Roberts.
Roberts, Sir Walworth Howland, 1855–1924, vol. II
Roberts, Wilfrid Hubert Wace, 1900–1991, vol. IX
Roberts, Sir William, 1830–1899, vol. I
Roberts, William, 1862–1940, vol. III
Roberts, Sir William, 1884–1971, vol. VII
Roberts, William, 1895–1980, vol. VII
Roberts, Rev. William Corbett, 1873–1953, vol. V
Roberts, Rev. William Henry, 1844–1921, vol. II
Roberts, Col William Henry, 1848–1926, vol. II
Roberts, Brig. William Henry, 1882–1954, vol. V
Roberts, William Lee Henry, 1871–1928, vol. II
Roberts, Rev. William Masfen, *died* 1927, vol. II
Roberts, Very Rev. William Page-, 1836–1928, vol. II
Roberts, William Poulter, 1874–1937, vol. III
Roberts, Col William Quincey, 1912–1980, vol. VII
Roberts, Rev. William Ralph Westropp, 1850–1935, vol. III
Roberts, William Rhys, 1858–1929, vol. III
Roberts, Col William Richter, 1888–1975, vol. VII
Roberts, William Stewart, *died* 1937, vol. III
Roberts, Ven Windsor, 1898–1962, vol. VI
Roberts-Austen, Sir William Chandler, 1843–1902, vol. I
Roberts-Jones, Ivor, 1913–1996, vol. X
Roberts-Wray, Sir Kenneth Owen, 1899–1983, vol. VIII
Roberts-Wray, Captain Thomas Henry; *see* Wray.
Robertshaw, Vice-Adm. Sir Ballin Illingworth, 1902–1971, vol. VII
Robertshaw, Sir Charles, 1874–1960, vol. V
Robertshaw, Wilfrid, 1893–1974, vol. VII
Robertson, Baron (Life Peer); James Patrick Bannerman Robertson, 1845–1909, vol. I
Robertson, Hon. Lord; Thomas Graham Robertson, 1881–1944, vol. IV
Robertson of Oakridge, 1st Baron, 1896–1974, vol. VII
Robertson, Alan, 1920–1989, vol. VIII
Robertson, Alan, 1920–1997, vol. X
Robertson, Alan Murray, 1914–1984, vol. VIII
Robertson, Alasdair Stewart Struan-Robertson, 1863–1910, vol. I
Robertson, Rear-Adm. Albert John, 1884–1954, vol. V
Robertson, Alec; *see* Robertson, A. T. P. A. C.
Robertson, Rev. Alexander, 1846–1933, vol. III
Robertson, Alexander, *died* 1970, vol. VI
Robertson, Sir Alexander, 1896–1970, vol. VI
Robertson, Sir Alexander, 1908–1990, vol. VIII
Robertson, Brig.-Gen. Alexander Brown, 1878–1951, vol. V
Robertson, Alexander Thomas Parke Anthony Cecil, (Alec Robertson), 1892–1982, vol. VIII
Robertson, Algar Ronald Ward, 1902–1975, vol. VII
Robertson, Andrew, *died* 1977, vol. VII
Robertson, Anne Strachan, *died* 1997, vol. X

Robertson, Rt Rev. Archibald, 1853–1931, vol. III
Robertson, Archibald Wallace, 1895–1966, vol. VI
Robertson, Cdre A(rthur) Ian, 1898–1961, vol. VI
Robertson, Sir Benjamin, 1864–1953, vol. V
Robertson, Sir Carrick Hey, 1879–1963, vol. VI
Robertson, Catherine Christian, 1886–1985, vol. VIII
Robertson, Maj.-Gen. Cecil Bruce, 1897–1977, vol. VII
Robertson, Rev. Charles, *died* 1921, vol. II
Robertson, Charles, 1874–1968, vol. VI
Robertson, Sir Charles Grant, 1869–1948, vol. IV
Robertson, Adm. Charles Hope, 1856–1942, vol. IV
Robertson, Lt-Col Charles Lonsdale, 1867–1943, vol. IV
Robertson, Very Rev. Charles R., 1873–1946, vol. IV
Robertson, Charles Robert Suttie, 1920–1999, vol. X
Robertson, Col Colin MacLeod, 1870–1951, vol. V
Robertson, Maj.-Gen. David, *died* 1913, vol. I
Robertson, Rev. David, 1838–1916, vol. II
Robertson, David, *died* 1925, vol. II
Robertson, David, 1875–1941, vol. IV
Robertson, David, *died* 1952, vol. V
Robertson, Sir David, 1890–1970, vol. VI
Robertson, David Lars Manwaring, 1917–1999, vol. X
Robertson, Sir Dennis Holme, 1890–1963, vol. VI
Robertson, Lt-Col Sir Donald, 1847–1930, vol. III
Robertson, Maj.-Gen. Donald Elphinston, 1879–1953, vol. V
Robertson, Donald James, 1926–1970, vol. VI
Robertson, Col Donald Murdoch, 1859–1938, vol. III
Robertson, Donald Struan, 1885–1961, vol. VI
Robertson, Douglas Moray Cooper Lamb Argyll, 1837–1909, vol. I
Robertson, Douglas William, 1898–1993, vol. IX
Robertson, E. Arnot, (Lady Turner), 1903–1961, vol. VI
Robertson, Edith Anne, 1883–1973, vol. VII
Robertson, Air Cdre Edmund Digby Maxwell, 1887–1956, vol. V
Robertson, Edward, 1879–1964, vol. VI
Robertson, Eric Desmond, 1914–1987, vol. VIII
Robertson, Francis Calder F.; *see* Ford-Robertson.
Robertson, Sir Frederick Alexander, 1854–1918, vol. II
Robertson, Frederick Ewart, 1847–1912, vol. I
Robertson, Sir Frederick Wynne, 1885–1964, vol. VI
Robertson, George, 1883–1956, vol. V
Robertson, George Matthew, 1864–1932, vol. III
Robertson, George Paterson, 1911–1982, vol. VIII
Robertson, Sir George Scott, 1852–1916, vol. II
Robertson, George Scott, 1893–1948, vol. IV
Robertson, Sir George Stuart, 1872–1967, vol. VI
Robertson, Hon. Gideon Decker, 1874–1933, vol. III
Robertson, Lt-Col Gordon McMahon, 1891–1932, vol. III
Robertson, Lt-Col Graham; *see* Robertson, Lt-Col J. H. G.
Robertson, Granville Douglas, 1891–1951, vol. V

Robertson, (Harold) Rocke, 1912–1998, vol. X
Robertson, Sir Helenus Robert, 1841–1919, vol. II
Robertson, Sir Henry Beyer, 1862–1948, vol. IV
Robertson, Henry Robert, 1839–1921, vol. II
Robertson, Herbert, 1849–1916, vol. II
Robertson, Lt-Gen. Sir Horace Clement Hugh, 1894–1960, vol. V
Robertson, Sir Howard Morley, 1888–1963, vol. VI
Robertson, Engr-Comdr Hugh, *died* 1940, vol. III (A)
Robertson, Ian Gow, 1910–1983, vol. VIII
Robertson, Ian Macbeth, 1918–1992, vol. IX
Robertson, Very Rev. James, 1837–1920, vol. II
Robertson, Rev. James, 1840–1920, vol. II
Robertson, Rev. James, 1855–1929, vol. III
Robertson, James, *died* 1938, vol. III
Robertson, James, 1912–1991, vol. IX
Robertson, Rev. James Alex., 1880–1955, vol. V
Robertson, Sir James Anderson, 1906–1990, vol. VIII
Robertson, Lt-Col James Archibald St George Fitzwarenne D.; *see* Despencer-Robertson.
Robertson, Brig.-Gen. James Campbell, 1878–1951, vol. V
Robertson, James Cassels, 1921–1978, vol. VII
Robertson, Lt-Col James Currie, 1870–1923, vol. II
Robertson, James Edwin, 1840–1915, vol. I
Robertson, Col James F.; *see* Forbes-Robertson.
Robertson, James Geddes, 1910–2000, vol. X
Robertson, Lt-Col (James Herbert) Graham, *died* 1956, vol. V
Robertson, Maj.-Gen. James Howden, 1915–1987, vol. VIII
Robertson, Sir James Jackson, 1893–1970, vol. VI
Robertson, Group Captain James Leask, 1882–1945, vol. IV
Robertson, James Logie, *died* 1922, vol. II
Robertson, Col James Peter, 1822–1916, vol. II
Robertson, James Wilson, 1857–1930, vol. III
Robertson, Sir James Wilson, 1899–1983, vol. VIII
Robertson, Jean, 1928–1996, vol. X
Robertson, Jean F.; *see* Forbes-Robertson.
Robertson, Rev. John, 1852–1913, vol. I
Robertson, Col John, 1837–1915, vol. I
Robertson, Rev. John, *died* 1925, vol. II
Robertson, John, 1867–1926, vol. II
Robertson, Sir John, 1862–1936, vol. III
Robertson, John, *died* 1937, vol. III
Robertson, Col John, 1878–1951, vol. V
Robertson, John, 1913–1987, vol. VIII
Robertson, John Archibald Campbell, 1912–1962, vol. VI
Robertson, John Arthur Thomas, 1873–1942, vol. IV
Robertson, Maj.-Gen. John Carnegie, 1917–1994, vol. IX
Robertson, Rev. John Charles, 1868–1931, vol. III
Robertson, John Charles, 1864–1956, vol. V
Robertson, John F.; *see* Forbes-Robertson.
Robertson, John G., 1867–1933, vol. III
Robertson, John Henry; *see* Connell, John.
Robertson, Captain John Hercules, 1864–1943, vol. IV
Robertson, John James, 1898–1955, vol. V
Robertson, John McKellar, 1883–1939, vol. III

Robertson, Rt Hon. John Mackinnon, 1856–1933, vol. III
Robertson, John Monteath, 1900–1989, vol. VIII
Robertson, Col John Richard Hugh, 1912–1977, vol. VII
Robertson, John Williamson, 1900–1969, vol. VI
Robertson, Sir Johnston F.; *see* Forbes-Robertson.
Robertson, Laurence, *died* 1945, vol. IV
Robertson, Lindesay John, 1861–1929, vol. III
Robertson, Sir MacPherson, 1860–1945, vol. IV
Robertson, Rt Hon. Sir Malcolm Arnold, 1877–1951, vol. V
Robertson, Margaret Ethel, 1861–1943, vol. IV
Robertson, Muriel, 1883–1973, vol. VII
Robertson, Comdt Dame Nancy Margaret, 1909–2000, vol. X
Robertson, Noel Farnie, 1923–1999, vol. X
Robertson, Norman Alexander, 1904–1968, vol. VI
Robertson, Norman Charles, 1908–1956, vol. V
Robertson, Maj.-Gen. Sir Philip Rynd, 1866–1936, vol. III
Robertson, Rae, 1893–1956, vol. V
Robertson, Sir Robert, 1869–1949, vol. IV
Robertson, Robert, 1909–1996, vol. X
Robertson, Robert Alexander, 1922–1992, vol. IX
Robertson, Robert Burns, 1861–1938, vol. III
Robertson, Robert Spelman, 1870–1955, vol. V
Robertson, Robin Haskew, 1898–1952, vol. V
Robertson, Rocke; *see* Robertson, H. R.
Robertson, Ronald Foote, 1920–1991, vol. IX
Robertson, Stuart, *died* 1958, vol. V
Robertson, Thomas, *died* 1906, vol. I
Robertson, Thomas, 1842–1925, vol. II
Robertson, Thomas Atholl, *died* 1955, vol. V
Robertson, Thomas Dixon Marr Trotter, 1856–1913, vol. I
Robertson, Thomas Graham; *see* Robertson, Hon. Lord.
Robertson, Thomas Logan, 1901–1969, vol. VI
Robertson, Thorburn Brailsford, 1884–1930, vol. III
Robertson, Tom, 1850–1947, vol. IV
Robertson, Vernon Alec Murray, 1890–1971, vol. VII
Robertson, W. Graham, 1866–1948, vol. IV
Robertson, Major W. M., *died* 1902, vol. I
Robertson, Walter James, 1869–1942, vol. IV
Robertson, Watson A.; *see* Askew-Robertson.
Robertson, Wheatley Alexander, 1885–1964, vol. VI
Robertson, Sir William, 1856–1923, vol. II
Robertson, Rev. William, 1847–1936, vol. III
Robertson, Lt-Col William, 1865–1949, vol. IV
Robertson, William Albert, 1885–1942, vol. IV
Robertson, Sir William Charles Fleming, *died* 1937, vol. III
Robertson, William Chrystal, 1850–1922, vol. II
Robertson, William Francis, 1882–1939, vol. III
Robertson, William Haggerston A.; *see* Askew Robertson.
Robertson, Rev. William Lewis, 1860–1947, vol. IV
Robertson, William Nathaniel, *died* 1938, vol. III
Robertson, Field-Marshal Sir William Robert, 1st Bt, 1860–1933, vol. III
Robertson, William Walter Samuel, 1906–1989, vol. VIII

Robertson-Aikman, Col Thomas S. G. H.; *see* Aikman.

Robertson-Eustace, Major Charles Legge Eustace, 1867–1908, vol. I

Robertson-Eustace, Majority Edith, *died* 1957, vol. V

Robertson-Eustace, Robert William Barrington, 1870–1935, vol. III

Robertson-Glasgow, Raymond Charles, 1901–1965, vol. VI

Robertson-Justice, James Norval Harald, 1905–1975, vol. VII

Robertson-Macdonald, Adm. David, 1817–1910, vol. I

Robertson Scott, John William, 1866–1962, vol. VI

Robeson, Ven. Hemming, *died* 1912, vol. I

Robeson, Paul Le Roy, 1898–1976, vol. VII

Robey, Edward George Haydon, 1899–1983, vol. VIII

Robey, Sir George, 1869–1954, vol. V

Robichaud, Most Rev. Norbert, 1905–1979, vol. VII (AII)

Robidoux, Joseph Emery, 1843–1929, vol. III

Robieson, Sir William, 1890–1977, vol. VII

Robin, Maj.-Gen. Sir Alfred William, 1860–1935, vol. III

Robin, Rt Rev. Bryan Percival, 1887–1969, vol. VI

Robins, 1st Baron, 1884–1962, vol. VI

Robins, Rev. Arthur, 1834–1899, vol. 1

Robins, Daniel Gerard, 1942–1989, vol. VIII

Robins, Denise Naomi, 1897–1985, vol. VIII

Robins, Rt Rev. Edwin Frederick, 1870–1951, vol. V

Robins, Elizabeth, (Mrs George Richmond Parks; C. E. Raimond), 1862–1952, vol. V

Robins, G. M.; *see* Reynolds, Mrs Louis Baillie.

Robins, Very Rev. Henry Charles, 1882–1960, vol. V

Robins, Sir Reginald Edwin, 1891–1971, vol. VII

Robins, Robert Henry, 1921–2000, vol. X

Robins, Ven. William Aubrey, 1868–1949, vol. IV

Robins, Rev. William Henry, 1847–1923, vol. II

Robins, William Palmer, 1882–1959, vol. V

Robinson, 1st Baron, 1883–1952, vol. V

Robinson, Albert, 1878–1943, vol. IV

Robinson, Rev. Canon Albert Gossage, 1863–1948, vol. IV

Robinson, Maj.-Gen. Alfred Eryk, 1894–1978, vol. VII

Robinson, Sir Alfred Theodore Vaughan, 1879–1945, vol. IV

Robinson, Andrew, 1858–1929, vol. III

Robinson, Rev. Archibald, *died* 1902, vol. I

Robinson, Sir Arnet, 1898–1975, vol. VII

Robinson, Arnold; *see* Robinson, F. A.

Robinson, Sir Arnold Percy, 1879–1960, vol. V

Robinson, Hon. Sir Arthur, 1872–1945, vol. IV

Robinson, Arthur, 1862–1948, vol. IV

Robinson, Arthur, 1864–1948, vol. IV

Robinson, Sir Arthur; *see* Robinson, Sir W. A.

Robinson, Sir (Arthur) Douglas, 1878–1939, vol. III

Robinson, Arthur Hildyard, 1859–1939, vol. III

Robinson, Arthur Leyland, 1887–1959, vol. V

Robinson, Rev. Arthur William, 1856–1928, vol. II

Robinson, Sir Austin; *see* Robinson, Sir E. A. G.

Robinson, Air Vice-Marshal Bruce, 1912–1998, vol. X

Robinson, Rev. Cecil Lowes, 1869–1936, vol. III

Robinson, Charles, 1870–1937, vol. III

Robinson, Charles Edmund N.; *see* Newton-Robinson.

Robinson, Adm. Charles Grey, 1850–1934, vol. III

Robinson, Rev. Charles Henry, 1861–1925, vol. II

Robinson, Rev. Charles Kirkby, 1826–1909, vol. I

Robinson, Charles Napier, 1849–1936, vol. III

Robinson, Charles Stanley, 1887–1969, vol. VI

Robinson, Maj.-Gen. Sir Charles Walker, 1836–1924, vol. II

Robinson, Sir Christopher Henry L.; *see* Lynch-Robinson.

Robinson, Rt Rev. Christopher James Gossage, 1903–1988, vol. VIII

Robinson, Mrs Clare; *see* Panter-Downes, M. P.

Robinson, Hon. Clifford William, 1866–1944, vol. IV

Robinson, Sir Clifton, 1849–1910, vol. I

Robinson, Clifton Eugene Bancroft, 1926–1996, vol. X

Robinson, Rear-Adm. Sir Cloudesley Varyl, 1883–1959, vol. V

Robinson, Courtenay Denis Carew, 1887–1958, vol. V

Robinson, Rt Rev. Cuthbert Cooper, 1893–1971, vol. VII

Robinson, Sir David, 1904–1987, vol. VIII

Robinson, Captain David Lubbock, 1882–1943, vol. IV

Robinson, David Moore, 1880–1958, vol. V

Robinson, David Morrant, 1910–1977, vol. VII

Robinson, Cdre David Samuel, 1888–1972, vol. VII

Robinson, Sir Douglas; *see* Robinson, Sir A. D.

Robinson, Sir Douglas Innes, 6th Bt (*cr* 1823), 1863–1944, vol. IV

Robinson, Sir Dove-Myer, 1901–1989, vol. VIII

Robinson, Sir (Edward) Austin (Gossage), 1897–1993, vol. IX

Robinson, Rev. Edward Colles, 1877–1956, vol. V

Robinson, Edward G., 1893–1973, vol. VII

Robinson, Edward Kay, 1857–1928, vol. II

Robinson, Sir Edward Stanley Gotch, *died* 1976, vol. VII

Robinson, Edwin Arlington, 1869–1935, vol. III

Robinson, Eric, 1908–1974, vol. VII

Robinson, Rear-Adm. Eric Gascoigne, 1882–1965, vol. VI

Robinson, Col Ernest, 1877–1935, vol. III

Robinson, Sir (Ernest) Stanley, 1905–1977, vol. VII

Robinson, Sir Ernest William, 5th Bt (*cr* 1823), 1862–1924, vol. II

Robinson, (Esmé Stuart) Lennox, 1886–1958, vol. V

Robinson, Forbes; *see* Robinson, P. F.

Robinson, Sir Foster Gotch, 1880–1967, vol. VI

Robinson, Frank Arnold, 1907–1988, vol. VIII

Robinson, Frederic Cayley-, 1862–1927, vol. II

Robinson, Sir Frederic Lacy, 1840–1911, vol. I

Robinson, Sir Frederick Arnold, 3rd Bt (*cr* 1854), 1855–1901, vol. I

Robinson, Sir (Frederick) Percival, 1887–1949, vol. IV

Robinson, Major Sir Frederick Villiers Laud, 10th Bt (*cr* 1660), 1880–1975, vol. VII
Robinson, Frederick William, 1830–1901, vol. I
Robinson, George Drummond, 1864–1950, vol. IV
Robinson, Sir George Gilmour, 1894–1985, vol. VIII
Robinson, Surg.-Gen. George Winsor, 1854–1929, vol. III
Robinson, Gerald Philip, 1858–1942, vol. IV
Robinson, Sir Gerald William Collingwood, 4th Bt (*cr* 1819), 1857–1903, vol. I
Robinson, Gilbert Wooding, 1888–1950, vol. IV
Robinson, Gleeson Edward, *died* 1978, vol. VII
Robinson, Godfrey, 1897–1961, vol. VI
Robinson, Lt-Col Godfrey Walker, 1863–1930, vol. III
Robinson, Maj.-Gen. Guy St George, 1887–1973, vol. VII
Robinson, Sir Harold Ernest, 1905–1979, vol. VII
Robinson, Sir Harold Francis C.; *see* Cartmel-Robinson.
Robinson, Harold George Robert, 1924–1995, vol. IX
Robinson, Harold Roper, 1889–1955, vol. V
Robinson, Sir Harry Perry, 1859–1930, vol. III
Robinson, Lt-Col Sir Heaton Forbes, 1873–1946, vol. IV
Robinson, Rt Rev. Hector Gordon, 1899–1965, vol. VI
Robinson, Henry, *died* 1901, vol. I
Robinson, Rev. Henry, 1849–1918, vol. II
Robinson, Rt Hon. Sir Henry Augustus, 1st Bt (*cr* 1920), 1857–1927, vol. II
Robinson, Henry Betham, 1860–1918, vol. II
Robinson, Henry Goland, 1896–1960, vol. V
Robinson, Captain Henry Harold, *died* 1919, vol. II
Robinson, Henry Morton, 1898–1961, vol. VI
Robinson, Maj.-Gen. Henry R.; *see* Rowan-Robinson.
Robinson, Rear-Adm. Sir Henry Russell, 1856–1942, vol. IV
Robinson, Rev. Henry Wheeler, 1872–1945, vol. IV
Robinson, Hon. Hercules Edward Joseph, 1895–1915, vol. I
Robinson, Sir (Hugh) Malcolm, 1857–1933, vol. III
Robinson, James, 1884–1956, vol. V
Robinson, Joan Violet, 1903–1983, vol. VIII
Robinson, Hon. Sir John, 1839–1903, vol. I
Robinson, Sir John, 1839–1929, vol. III
Robinson, Hon. John Alexander, 1862–1929, vol. III
Robinson, John Armstrong, 1925–1998, vol. X
Robinson, Rt Rev. John Arthur Thomas, 1919–1983, vol. VIII
Robinson, Sir John Beverley, 4th Bt (*cr* 1854), 1848–1933, vol. III
Robinson, Sir John Beverley, 6th Bt (*cr* 1854), 1885–1954, vol. V
Robinson, Sir John Beverley, 7th Bt (*cr* 1854), 1913–1988, vol. VIII
Robinson, Sir John Beverley Beverley, 5th Bt (*cr* 1854), 1895–1948, vol. IV
Robinson, Sir John Charles, 1824–1913, vol. I
Robinson, Sir John Edgar, 1895–1978, vol. VII
Robinson, John Foster, 1909–1988, vol. VIII
Robinson, John George, 1856–1943, vol. IV

Robinson, Sir John Holdsworth, 1855–1927, vol. II
Robinson, Rev. John J., *died* 1916, vol. II
Robinson, John Lovell, 1849–1939, vol. III
Robinson, Col John Poole Bowring, 1881–1966, vol. VI
Robinson, John Robert, 1850–1910, vol. I
Robinson, John William Dudley, 1886–1967, vol. VI
Robinson, Joseph, 1905–1970, vol. VI
Robinson, Rev. Canon Joseph, 1927–1999, vol. X
Robinson, Very Rev. Joseph Armitage, 1858–1933, vol. III
Robinson, Sir Joseph Benjamin, 1st Bt (*cr* 1908), 1840–1929, vol. III
Robinson, Sir Joseph Benjamin, 2nd Bt (*cr* 1908), 1887–1954, vol. V
Robinson, Joseph John, 1858–1939, vol. III
Robinson, Kathleen Marian, (Mrs Vincent F. Sherry), 1911–1998, vol. X
Robinson, Rt Hon. Sir Kenneth, 1911–1996, vol. X
Robinson, Kenneth Dean, 1909–1987, vol. VIII
Robinson, Laurence Milner, 1885–1957, vol. V
Robinson, Lennox; *see* Robinson, E. S. L.
Robinson, Leonard Nicholas, 1869–1955, vol. V
Robinson, Sir Leslie Harold, 1903–1974, vol. VII
Robinson, Lloyd; *see* Robinson, T. L.
Robinson, Rev. Ludovick Stewart, 1864–1923, vol. II
Robinson, Lt-Col Macleod Bawtree, 1858–1935, vol. III
Robinson, Sir Malcolm; *see* Robinson, Sir H. M.
Robinson, Gp Captain Marcus, 1912–1999, vol. X
Robinson, Air Cdre Maurice Wilbraham Sandford, 1910–1977, vol. VII
Robinson, Sir Montague Arnet; *see* Robinson, Sir Arnet.
Robinson, Sir Niall Bryan L.; *see* Lynch-Robinson.
Robinson, Nigel Francis Maltby, 1906–1985, vol. VIII
Robinson, Very Rev. Norman, 1905–1973, vol. VII
Robinson, Sir Norman De Winton, 1890–1972, vol. VII
Robinson, Rev. Norman Hamilton Galloway, 1912–1978, vol. VII
Robinson, Oliver John, 1908–1996, vol. X
Robinson, Maj.-Gen. Oliver Long, 1867–1947, vol. IV
Robinson, Most Rev. Mgr Paschal, 1870–1948, vol. IV
Robinson, Sir Percival; *see* Robinson, Sir F. P.
Robinson, Percival James, 1879–1944, vol. IV
Robinson, Brig.-Gen. Percy Morris, 1873–1949, vol. IV
Robinson, (Peter) Forbes, 1926–1987, vol. VIII
Robinson, Rev. Canon Reginald Henry, 1881–1970, vol. VI
Robinson, Sir Richard Atkinson, 1849–1928, vol. II
Robinson, Sir Richard Harcourt, 5th Bt (*cr* 1819), 1828–1910, vol. I
Robinson, Sir Robert, 1886–1975, vol. VII
Robinson, Col Robert Maximilian R.; *see* Rainey-Robinson.
Robinson, Robert Thomson, 1867–1926, vol. II
Robinson, Ronald Edward, 1920–1999, vol. X

Robinson, Ronald Henry Ottywell Betham, 1896–1973, vol. VII
Robinson, Samuel, 1870–1958, vol. V
Robinson, Samuel, 1893–1967, vol. VI
Robinson, Sidney, 1863–1956, vol. V
Robinson, Stanford, 1904–1984, vol. VIII
Robinson, Sir Stanley; *see* Robinson, Sir E. S.
Robinson, Stanley Scott, 1913–1997, vol. X
Robinson, Col Stapylton Chapman Bates, 1855–1927, vol. II
Robinson, Brig.-Gen. Stratford Watson, 1871–1962, vol. VI
Robinson, Sydney Allen, 1905–1978, vol. VII
Robinson, Sir Sydney Maddock, 1865–1948, vol. IV
Robinson, Sir Sydney Walter, 1876–1950, vol. IV
Robinson, Theodore Henry, 1881–1964, vol. VI
Robinson, Sir Thomas, 1827–1897, vol. I
Robinson, Sir Thomas, 1855–1927, vol. II
Robinson, Sir Thomas, *died* 1953, vol. V
Robinson, Lt-Col Sir Thomas Bilbe, 1853–1939, vol. III
Robinson, Thomas Lloyd, 1912–1996, vol. X
Robinson, Sir Thomas William, 1864–1946, vol. IV
Robinson, Tom, *died* 1916, vol. II
Robinson, Ursula; *see* Bloom, U.
Robinson, Sir Victor Lloyd, 1899–1966, vol. VI
Robinson, Vincent Joseph, 1829–1910, vol. I
Robinson, Rt Rev. Mgr Walter Croke, 1839–1914, vol. I
Robinson, Rt Rev. Walter Wade, 1919–1975, vol. VII
Robinson, Maj.-Gen. Wellesley Gordon Walker, 1839–1908, vol. I
Robinson, Sir William, 1836–1912, vol. I
Robinson, Sir William, *died* 1932, vol. III
Robinson, William, 1838–1935, vol. III
Robinson, Sir William, 1879–1961, vol. VI
Robinson, William Albert, *died* 1949, vol. IV
Robinson, Brig.-Gen. William Arthur, 1864–1929, vol. III
Robinson, Sir (William) Arthur, 1874–1950, vol. IV
Robinson, Maj.-Gen. William Arthur, 1908–1982, vol. VIII
Robinson, Sir William Cleaver Francis, 1835–1897, vol. I
Robinson, William Cornforth, 1861–1931, vol. III
Robinson, William Edward, 1863–1927, vol. II
Robinson, Rev. W(illiam) Gordon, 1903–1977, vol. VII
Robinson, William Heath, 1872–1944, vol. IV
Robinson, Sir William Henry, *died* 1940, vol. III
Robinson, Sir William Henry, 1874–1964, vol. VI
Robinson, Maj.-Gen. William Henry Banner, 1863–1922, vol. II
Robinson, William Leefe, 1895–1918, vol. II
Robinson, William Oscar James, 1909–1968, vol. VI
Robinson, William Sugden, 1881–1968, vol. VI
Robinson-Douglas, William Douglas; *see* Douglas.
Robiquet, Jean, 1874–1960, vol. V (A), vol. VI (AI)
Robison, Lionel MacDowall, 1886–1967, vol. VI
Robison, Robert, 1883–1941, vol. IV
Robjent, Frederick Pring, 1859–1938, vol. III
Robjohns, Sydney, 1878–1954, vol. V
Robles, Alfonso G.; *see* García Robles.

Robley, Maj.-Gen. Horatio Gordon, 1840–1930, vol. III
Roblin, Hon. Sir Rodmond Palen, 1853–1937, vol. III
Roborough, 1st Baron, 1859–1938, vol. III
Roborough, 2nd Baron, 1903–1992, vol. IX
Robotham, Hon. Sir Lascelles Lister, 1923–1996, vol. X
Robson, Baron (Life Peer); William Snowdon Robson, 1852–1918, vol. II
Robson of Kiddington, Baroness (Life Peer); Inga-Stina Robson, 1919–1999, vol. X
Robson, Air Vice-Marshal Adam Henry, 1892–1980, vol. VII
Robson, Albert Henry, *died* 1939, vol. III
Robson, Sir Arthur William Mayo-, 1853–1933, vol. III
Robson, Denis Hicks, 1904–1983, vol. VIII
Robson, Edward Robert, 1835–1917, vol. II
Robson, Dame Flora, 1902–1984, vol. VIII
Robson, Vice-Adm. Sir Geoffrey; *see* Robson, Vice-Adm. Sir W. G. A.
Robson, George, 1842–1911, vol. I
Robson, Hon. Harold Burge, 1888–1964, vol. VI
Robson, Sir Henry, 1848–1911, vol. I
Robson, Henry Naunton, 1861–1925, vol. II
Robson, Lt-Col Henry William Cumine, 1886–1942, vol. IV
Robson, Sir Herbert Thomas, 1874–1935, vol. III
Robson, Hugh Amos, 1871–1945, vol. IV
Robson, Sir Hugh Norwood, 1917–1977, vol. VII
Robson, Captain Humphrey Maurice, 1889–1940, vol. III
Robson, James, 1890–1981, vol. VIII
Robson, James Jeavons, 1918–1989, vol. VIII
Robson, Rev. John, 1836–1908, vol. I
Robson, John Henry Matthews, 1870–1945, vol. IV
Robson, John Michael, 1900–1982, vol. VIII
Robson, Juliette Louise; *see* Alvin, J. L.
Robson, Sir Kenneth, 1909–1978, vol. VII
Robson, Col Lancelot, 1855–1936, vol. III
Robson, Lawrence Fendick, 1916–1992, vol. IX
Robson, Sir Lawrence William, 1904–1982, vol. VIII
Robson, Leonard Charles, 1894–1964, vol. VI
Robson, Nigel John, 1926–1993, vol. IX
Robson, Philip Appleby, 1871–1951, vol. V
Robson, Robert, 1845–1928, vol. II
Robson, Sir Thomas Buston, 1896–1991, vol. IX
Robson, Thomas Snowdon, 1922–1992, vol. IX
Robson, William, 1893–1975, vol. VII
Robson, William Alexander, 1895–1980, vol. VII
Robson, Vice-Adm. Sir (William) Geoffrey (Arthur), 1902–1989, vol. VIII
Robson, Rev. William Henry Fairfax, 1834–1913, vol. I
Robson, William Michael, 1912–1998, vol. X
Robson, William Wallace, 1923–1993, vol. IX
Robson Brown, Sir William, *died* 1975, vol. VII
Robson-Scott, William Douglas, 1901–1980, vol. VII
Roby, Arthur Godfrey, 1862–1944, vol. IV
Roby, Henry John, 1830–1915, vol. I
Roch, Col Horace Sampson, 1876–1960, vol. V
Roch, Walter Francis, 1880–1965, vol. VI
Rochdale, 1st Baron, 1866–1945, vol. IV

Rochdale, 1st Viscount, 1906–1993, vol. IX
Roche, Baron (Life Peer); Alexander Adair Roche, 1871–1956, vol. V
Roche, Alexander, 1861–1921, vol. II
Roche, Alexander Ernest, 1896–1963, vol. VI
Roche, Hon. Alexis Charles Burke, 1853–1914, vol. I
Roche, Augustine, died 1915, vol. I
Roche, Sir David Vandeleur, 2nd Bt, 1833–1908, vol. I
Roche, Most Rev. Edward Patrick, 1874–1950, vol. IV (A)
Roche, Frederick Lloyd, 1931–1992, vol. IX
Roche, Sir George, 1850–1932, vol. III
Roche, Col Henry John, 1864–1944, vol. IV
Roche, Most Rev. James J., 1870–1956, vol. V
Roche, John, 1848–1914, vol. I
Roche, Sir Standish Deane O'Grady, 3rd Bt, 1845–1914, vol. I
Roche, Sir Standish O'Grady, 4th Bt, 1911–1977, vol. VII
Roche, Hon. Thomas Gabriel, 1909–1998, vol. X
Roche, Col Hon. Ulick de Rupe Burke, 1856–1919, vol. II
Roche, Hon. William, 1842–1925, vol. II
Roche, William, 1880–1942, vol. IV
Roche, Hon. William James, 1860–1937, vol. III
Rochefort, Henri, 1831–1913, vol. I
Rochefort-Lucay, Marquis de, Victor Henri; see Rochefort, Henri.
Rochester, 1st Baron, 1876–1955, vol. V
Rocheta, Manuel Farrajota, 1906–1989, vol. IX (AI)
Rochford, James Donald Henry, 1921–1986, vol. VIII
Rochfort, Maj.-Gen. Sir Alexander Nelson, 1850–1916, vol. II
Rochfort, Sir Cecil Charles B.; see Boyd-Rochfort.
Rochfort, Captain George Arthur B.; see Boyd-Rochfort.
Rochfort-Boyd, Col Charles Augustus, 1850–1940, vol. III
Rochfort-Boyd, Lt-Col Henry Charles, 1877–1917, vol. II
Rocke, Col Cyril Edmund Alan, 1876–1968, vol. VI
Rocke, Maj.-Gen. James Harwood, 1829–1913, vol. I
Rocke, John Roy Mansfield, 1918–1993, vol. IX
Rocke, Col Walter Leslie, 1862–1932, vol. III
Rockefeller, John Davison, 1839–1937, vol. III
Rockefeller, John Davison, Jr, 1874–1960, vol. V
Rockefeller, John Davison, 3rd, 1906–1978, vol. VII
Rockefeller, Nelson Aldrich, 1908–1979, vol. VII
Rockhill, William Woodville, 1854–1914, vol. I
Rockley, 1st Baron, 1865–1941, vol. IV
Rockley, 2nd Baron, 1901–1976, vol. VII
Rockley, Lady; (Alicia-Margaret), died 1941, vol. IV
Rockliff, Percy, 1869–1958, vol. V
Rocyn-Jones, Arthur, died 1972, vol. VII
Rocyn-Jones, Sir David Thomas, 1872–1953, vol. V
Rod, Edouard, 1857–1910, vol. I
Rodd, Hon. Nancy, (Hon. Mrs Peter Rodd); see Mitford, N.
Rodda, Diwan Bahadur Shrinivas Konher, 1851–1929, vol. III
Roddan, Gilbert McMicking, 1906–1990, vol. VIII

Roddick, Sir Thomas George, 1846–1923, vol. II
Roddie, Lt-Col William Stewart, 1878–1961, vol. VI
Roddy, Col Henry Hugh, 1866–1932, vol. III
Roden, 5th Earl of, 1823–1897, vol. I
Roden, 6th Earl of, 1842–1910, vol. I
Roden, 7th Earl of, 1845–1915, vol. I
Roden, 8th Earl of, 1883–1956, vol. V
Roden, 9th Earl of, 1909–1993, vol. IX
Roden, Countess of; (Ada Maria), 1860–1931, vol. III
Roden, Sir Robert Blair, 1860–1939, vol. III
Rodenberg, Julius, 1831–1914, vol. I
Roderick, Rev. Charles Edward Morys, 1910–1993, vol. IX
Rodes Green, Brig.-Gen. Henry Clifford; see Green.
Rodger, Adam Keir, 1855–1946, vol. IV
Rodger, Alec, (Thomas Alexander), 1907–1982, vol. VIII
Rodger, Sir Alexander, died 1950, vol. IV
Rodger, Allan George, 1902–1996, vol. X
Rodger, Sir John Pickersgill, 1851–1910, vol. I
Rodger, Thomas Alexander; see Rodger, Alec.
Rodger, Thomas Ferguson, 1907–1978, vol. VII
Rodger, T(homas) Ritchie, 1878–1968, vol. VI
Rodger, Sir William Glendinning, 1912–1990, vol. VIII
Rodgers, Air Cdre Alexander Mitchell, 1906–1973, vol. VII
Rodgers, Mrs Barbara Noel, 1912–1992, vol. IX
Rodgers, David John, 1890–1975, vol. VII
Rodgers, George, 1925–2000, vol. X
Rodgers, Gerald Fleming, 1917–1990, vol. VIII
Rodgers, Rt Rev. Harold Nickinson, died 1947, vol. IV
Rodgers, Sir John Charles, 1st Bt, 1906–1993, vol. IX
Rodgers, Sir (John Fairlie) Tobias, 2nd Bt, 1940–1997, vol. X
Rodgers, Richard, 1902–1979, vol. VII
Rodgers, Sir Tobias; see Rodgers, Sir J. F. T.
Rodgers, William Robert, 1909–1969, vol. VI
Rodham, Brig. Cuthbert Harold Boyd, 1900–1973, vol VII
Rodham, Rear-Adm. (S) Harold, 1873–1947, vol. IV
Rodin, Auguste, 1840–1917, vol. II
Rodman, Adm. Hugh, 1859–1940, vol. III
Rodney, 7th Baron, 1857–1909, vol. I
Rodney, 8th Baron, 1891–1973, vol. VII
Rodney, 9th Baron, 1920–1992, vol. IX
Rodney, Hon. James Henry Bartie, 1893–1933, vol. III
Rodocanachi, Emmanuel Michel, 1855–1932, vol. III
Rodrigo, Joseph Lionel Christie, born 1895, vol. VII
Rodrigo, Sir Philip; see Rodrigo, Sir S. T. P.
Rodrigo, Sir (Senapathige Theobald) Philip, born 1899, vol. VII
Rodway, James, 1848–1926, vol. II
Rodway, Leonard, 1853–1936, vol. III
Rodwell, Sir Cecil Hunter-, 1874–1953, vol. V
Rodwell, Brig.-Gen. Ernest Hunter, 1858–1937, vol. III
Rodwell, Air Cdre Robert John, 1897–1970, vol. VI

Rodzianko, Col Paul, *died* 1965, vol. VI
Rodzinski, Arthur, 1894–1958, vol. V
Roe, 1st Baron, 1832–1923, vol. II
Roe, Sir Alliot Verdon-, 1877–1958, vol. V
Roe, Sir Charles Arthur, 1841–1927, vol. II
Roe, Brig.-Gen. Cyril Harcourt, 1864–1928, vol. II
Roe, Francis Reginald, 1869–1942, vol. IV
Roe, Fred, *died* 1947, vol. IV
Roe, Frederic Gordon, 1894–1985, vol. VIII
Roe, Frederick Charles, 1894–1958, vol. V
Roe, Rt Rev. Gordon; *see* Roe, Rt Rev. W. G.
Roe, Harold Riley, 1883–1963, vol. VI
Roe, Humphrey Verdon, 1878–1949, vol. IV
Roe, Rev. Robert Gordon, 1860–1927, vol. II
Roe, Rev. Robert James, *died* 1921, vol. II
Roe, Brig. William C.; *see* Carden Roe.
Roe, Dep. Surg.-Gen. William Carden, 1834–1922, vol. II
Roe, Lt-Col William Francis, 1871–1925, vol. II
Roe, Maj.-Gen. Sir William Gordon, 1904–1969, vol. VI
Roe, Rt Rev. (William) Gordon, 1932–1999, vol. X
Roe-Thompson, Edwin Reginald, 1894–1970, vol. VI
Roebuck, Alfred, 1889–1962, vol. VI
Roerich, Nicholas K., 1874–1947, vol. IV
Roff, William George, 1858–1926, vol. II
Roffey, Edgar Stuart, 1875–1957, vol. V
Roffey, Sir (George) Walter, 1870–1940, vol. III
Roffey, Sir James, *died* 1912, vol. I
Roffey, Sir Walter; *see* Roffey, Sir G. W.
Rogan, Lt-Col John M.; *see* Mackenzie-Rogan.
Rogan, Rev. William Henry, 1908–1987, vol. VIII
Roger, Alastair Forbes, 1916–1980, vol. VII
Roger, Sir Alexander, 1878–1961, vol. VI
Roger, Captain Archibald, *born* 1842, vol. II
Rogers, Arthur Kenyon, 1868–1936, vol. III
Rogers, Sir Arthur Stanley, 1883–1953, vol. V
Rogers, Arthur William, 1872–1946, vol. IV
Rogers, Benjamin, 1837–1923, vol. II
Rogers, Bertram Mitford Heron, 1860–1953, vol. V
Rogers, Betty Evelyn, (Mrs P. E. Rogers); *see* Box, B. E.
Rogers, Bruce, 1870–1957, vol. V
Rogers, Charles Coltman Coltman, 1854–1929, vol. III
Rogers, Rev. Charles Fursdon, 1848–1928, vol. II
Rogers, Charles Gilbert, *died* 1937, vol. III
Rogers, Claude Maurice, 1907–1979, vol. VII
Rogers, Rev. Clement Francis, 1866–1949, vol. IV
Rogers, Brig. Edgar William, 1892–1973, vol. VII
Rogers, Edmund Dawson, 1823–1910, vol. I
Rogers, Rev. Edward, 1909–1997, vol. X
Rogers, Edwin John, 1858–1951, vol. V
Rogers, Ven. Evan James Gwyn, 1914–1982, vol. VIII
Rogers, Captain Francis Caryer Campbell, 1883–1915, vol. I
Rogers, Francis Edward Newman, 1868–1925, vol. II
Rogers, Frederick, 1846–1915, vol. I
Rogers, Rev. Frederick Arundel, 1876–1944, vol. IV
Rogers, George Henry Roland, 1906–1983, vol. VIII

Rogers, Ven. George Herbert, *died* 1926, vol. II
Rogers, George Theodore, 1919–1999, vol. X
Rogers, Col George William, 1843–1917, vol. II
Rogers, Graham, 1907–1973, vol. VII
Rogers, Rev. Guy; *see* Rogers, Rev. T. G.
Rogers, Ven. Gwyn; *see* Rogers, Ven. E. J. G.
Rogers, Sir Hallewell, 1864–1931, vol. III
Rogers, Lt-Col Henry, 1876–1931, vol. III
Rogers, Henry Augustus, 1918–1999, vol. X
Rogers, Sir Henry Montagu, 1855–1931, vol. III
Rogers, Lt-Col Henry Schofield, 1869–1955, vol. V
Rogers, Henry Wade, 1853–1926, vol. II
Rogers, Herbert Lionel, 1871–1950, vol. IV
Rogers, Howard John, 1943–1987, vol. VIII
Rogers, Hugh Charles Innes, 1904–1991, vol. IX
Rogers, Lt-Col Hugh Henry, 1858–1932, vol. III
Rogers, Rear-Adm. Hugh Hext, 1883–1955, vol. V
Rogers, Brig.-Gen. Hugh Stuart, 1878–1952, vol. V
Rogers, Rev. James Guinness, 1822–1911, vol. I
Rogers, John, *died* 1945, vol. IV
Rogers, John, 1878–1975, vol. VII
Rogers, Lt-Col Sir John Godfrey, 1850–1922, vol. II
Rogers, Lt-Col John Middleton, 1864–1945, vol. IV
Rogers, Brig. Joseph Bartlett, *died* 1940, vol. III
Rogers, Lambert Charles, 1897–1961, vol. VI
Rogers, Maj.-Gen. Sir Leonard, 1868–1962, vol. VI
Rogers, Leonard James, 1862–1933, vol. III
Rogers, Lindsay, 1891–1970, vol. VI (AII)
Rogers, Mark, 1848–1933, vol. III
Rogers, Muriel Augusta Gillian C.; *see* Coltman-Rogers.
Rogers, Murray Rowland Fletcher, 1899–1991, vol. IX
Rogers, Neville William, 1908–1985, vol. VIII
Rogers, Maj.-Gen. Norman Annesley C.; *see* Coxwell-Rogers.
Rogers, Hon. Norman McLeod, 1894–1940, vol. III
Rogers, Sir Percival Halse, 1883–1945, vol. IV
Rogers, Rev. Percy, 1826–1910, vol. I
Rogers, Sir Philip, 1914–1990, vol. VIII
Rogers, Philip Graham, *died* 1958, vol. V
Rogers, Sir Philip James, 1908–1994, vol. IX
Rogers, Hon. Robert, 1864–1936, vol. III
Rogers, Lt-Gen. Sir Robert Gordon, 1832–1906, vol. I
Rogers, Sir Robert Hargreaves, 1850–1924, vol. II
Rogers, Robert Vashon, 1843–1911, vol. I
Rogers, Robert William, 1864–1930, vol. III
Rogers, Roland, 1847–1927, vol. II
Rogers, Thomas Arthur, 1897–1965, vol. VI
Rogers, Thomas Edward, 1912–1999, vol. X
Rogers, Thomas Englesby, 1817–1912, vol. I
Rogers, Rev. (Travers) Guy, 1876–1967, vol. VI
Rogers, Major Vivian Barry, 1887–1965, vol. VI
Rogers, William Penn Adair, 1879–1935, vol. III
Rogerson, John, 1917–1990, vol. VIII
Rogerson, Captain John Edwin, 1865–1925, vol. II
Rogerson, Col Sidney, 1894–1968, vol. VI
Roget, F. F., 1859–1938, vol. III
Rogosinski, Werner Wolfgang, 1894–1964, vol. VI
Rohan, Duchesse de, (dowager); Herminie de Verteillac, *died* 1926, vol. II
Rohde, Eleanour Sinclair, *died* 1950, vol. IV

Rohlfs, Mrs Charles, (Anna Katharine Rohlfs), 1846–1935, vol. III
Rohmer, Sax, *died* 1959, vol. V
Roijen, Jan Herman Van, 1905–1991, vol. IX
Roland, Nicholas; *see* Walmsley, A. R.
Roles, Francis Crosbie, 1867–1931, vol. III
Rolfe, Douglass Horace B.; *see* Boggis-Rolfe.
Rolfe, Eustace N.; *see* Neville-Rolfe.
Rolfe, Rev. Harry Roger, 1851–1924, vol. II
Rolfe, Rear-Adm. Henry Cuthbert Norris, 1908–1997, vol. X
Rolfe, Captain Herbert Neville, 1854–1942, vol. IV
Rolfe, William James, 1827–1910, vol. I
Roll, Sir Cecil Ernest, 3rd Bt, 1878–1938, vol. III
Roll, Sir Frederick James, 2nd Bt, 1873–1933, vol. III
Roll, Grahame Winfield, *died* 1942, vol. IV
Roll, Sir James, 1st Bt, 1846–1927, vol. II
Roll, Rev. Sir James William Cecil, 4th Bt, 1912–1998, vol. X
Rolland, Brig.-Gen. Alexander, 1871–1939, vol. III
Rolland, Very Rev. Sir Francis William, 1878–1965, vol. VI
Rolland, Major George Murray, 1869–1910, vol. I
Rolland, Romain, 1866–1944, vol. IV
Rolland, Brig.-Gen. Stewart Erskine, 1846–1927, vol. II
Rolland, Vice-Adm. William Rae, 1817–1904, vol. I
Rollason, Ernest Clarence, 1908–1972, vol. VII
Rolle, Hon. Mark George Kerr, 1835–1907, vol. I
Roller, Major George C., 1856–1941, vol. IV
Rolleston, Charles Ffranck, 1833–1913, vol. I
Rolleston, Francis Joseph, 1873–1946, vol. IV
Rolleston, Sir Humphry Davy, 1st Bt, 1862–1944, vol. IV
Rolleston, Iris Brenda, 1880–1948, vol. IV
Rolleston, John Davy, 1873–1946, vol. IV
Rolleston, Sir John Fowke Lancelot, 1848–1919, vol. II
Rolleston, Adm. John Philip, 1859–1936, vol. III
Rolleston, Col Sir Lancelot, 1847–1941, vol. IV
Rolleston, Thomas William, 1857–1920, vol. II
Rolleston, Sir William Gustavus Stanhope, 1862–1944, vol. IV
Rolleston, Col William Lancelot, 1905–1974, vol. VII
Rollett, Herbert, 1872–1932, vol. III
Rolling, Col Bernard Ismay, 1883–1937, vol. III
Rollins, John Wenlock, *died* 1940, vol. III
Rollit, Sir Albert Kaye, 1842–1922, vol. II
Rollo, 10th Lord, 1835–1916, vol. II
Rollo, 11th Lord, 1860–1946, vol. IV
Rollo, 12th Lord, 1889–1947, vol. IV
Rollo, 13th Lord, 1915–1997, vol. X
Rollo, Hon. Bernard Francis, 1868–1935, vol. III
Rollo, Hon. Eric Norman, 1861–1930, vol. III
Rollo, Lt-Col George, 1881–1944, vol. IV
Rollo, Gen. Hon. Sir Robert, 1814–1907, vol. I
Rollo, Rev. William, 1859–1949, vol. IV
Rolls, Hon. Charles Stewart, 1877–1910, vol. I
Rolls, Captain Sir John Courtown Edward S.; *see* Shelley-Rolls.
Rolo, Cyril Felix, 1918–2000, vol. X
Rolo, Sir Robert, 1869–1944, vol. IV
Rolph, Cecil Hewitt; *see* Hewitt, C. R.

Rolph, Sir Gordon Burns, 1893–1959, vol. V
Rolt, Bernard, 1874–1937, vol. III
Rolt, Very Rev. Cecil Henry, 1865–1926, vol. II
Rolt, James, 1860–1938, vol. III
Rolt, Lionel Thomas Caswall, 1910–1974, vol. VII
Rolt, Brig.-Gen. Stuart Peter, 1862–1933, vol. III
Rolt, Vivian, 1874–1933, vol. III
Romains, Jules, 1885–1972, vol. VII
Romanes, Ethel, *died* 1927, vol. II
Romanes, Mrs George; *see* Romanes, Ethel.
Romanis, William Hugh Cowie, 1889–1972, vol. VII
Romanne-James, Helena Constance, (Mrs H. C. Aylen), *died* 1966, vol. VI
Romanos, Athos, 1858–1940, vol. III
Rome, Brig.-Charles Leslie, 1878–1936, vol. III
Rome, Brig.-Gen. Claude Stuart, 1875–1956, vol. V
Rome, Maj.-Gen. Francis David, 1905–1985, vol. VIII
Rome, Thomas, 1852–1938, vol. III
Romer, Baron (Life Peer); Mark Lemon Romer, 1866–1944, vol. IV
Romer, Carrol, 1883–1951, vol. V
Romer, Gen. Sir Cecil Francis, 1869–1962, vol. VI
Romer, Rt Hon. Sir Charles Robert Ritchie, 1897–1969, vol. VI
Romer, Frank, 1871–1939, vol. III
Romer, Lt-Col Frederick Charles, 1854–1915, vol. I
Romer, Rt Hon. Sir Robert, 1840–1918, vol. II
Romer, Thomas Ansdell, 1848–1917, vol. II
Romer-Lee, Lt-Col H., 1874–1955, vol. V
Romeril, Herbert George, 1881–1963, vol. VI
Romilly, 3rd Baron, 1866–1905, vol. I
Romilly, 4th Baron, 1899–1983, vol. VIII
Romilly, Col Bertram Henry Samuel, 1878–1940, vol. III
Romilly, Eric Carnegie, (Frederic Carnegie Romilly), 1886–1953, vol. IV
Romilly, Frederic Carnegie; *see* Romilly, E. C.
Romilly, Col Frederick William, 1854–1935, vol. III
Romilly, George, *died* 1933, vol. III
Romilly, Samuel Henry, 1849–1940, vol. III
Romiti, William, 1850–1936, vol. III
Romney, 4th Earl of, 1841–1905, vol. I
Romney, 5th Earl of, 1864–1933, vol. III
Romney, 6th Earl of, 1892–1975, vol. VII
Ronald, E. B.; *see* Barker, Ronald Ernest.
Ronald, Sir Landon, 1873–1938, vol. III
Ronald, Sir Nigel Bruce, 1894–1973, vol. VII
Ronalds, Andrew John, 1897–1978, vol. VII
Ronaldson, James Bruce, 1886–1952, vol. V
Ronaldson, Brig.-Gen. Robert William Hawthorn, 1864–1946, vol. IV
Ronaldson, Thomas Martine, 1881–1942, vol. IV
Ronan, Very Rev. Myles V., 1877–1959, vol. IV
Ronan, Rt Hon. Stephen, 1848–1925, vol. II
Ronayne, Thomas, 1848–1925, vol. II
Roncalli, Angelo Giuseppe; *see* John XXIII.
Roney, Sir Ernest, 1871–1952, vol. V
Roocroft, Col William Mitchell, 1859–1943, vol. IV
Rood, Felix Stephen, 1883–1933, vol. III
Rook, Air Vice-Marshal Sir Alan Filmer, *died* 1960, vol. V
Rook, John Allan Fynes, 1926–1987, vol. VIII
Rook, Sir William James, 1885–1958, vol. V

Rooke, Charles Eustace, 1892–1947, vol. IV
Rooke, Lt-Col Everard Home, 1875–1936, vol. III
Rooke, Col Harry William, 1842–1921, vol. II
Rooke, Ven. Henry, 1829–1926, vol. II
Rooke, Herbert K., 1872–1944, vol. IV
Rooke, Thomas Matthews, 1842–1942, vol. IV
Rooke, Maj.-Gen. William, 1836–1919, vol. II
Rooker, John Kingsley, 1887–1951, vol. V
Rooks, Maj.-Gen. Lowell W., 1893–1973, vol. VII
Rookwood, 1st Baron, 1826–1902, vol. I
Room, Thomas Gerald, 1902–1986, vol. VIII
Roome, Gen. Frederick, 1829–1907, vol. I
Roome, Engr-Rear-Adm. George W., 1865–1945,
  vol. IV
Roome, Henry Delacombe, 1882–1930, vol. III
Roome, Rear-Adm. Henry Stewart, 1896–1981,
  vol. VI
Roome, Maj.-Gen. Sir Horace Eckford, 1887–1964,
  vol. VI
Rooney, Denis Michael Hall, 1919–1994, vol. IX
Rooney, Rt Rev. John, died 1927, vol. II
Rooney, Maj.-Gen. Sir Owen Patrick James,
  1900–1972, vol. VII
Roos, Gustaf Ehrenreich, 1838–1928, vol. II
Roos-Keppel, Sir George; see Keppel.
Roose, (Edward Charles) Robson, 1848–1905, vol. I
Roosevelt, (Anna) Eleanor, (Mrs F. D. Roosevelt),
  1884–1962, vol. VI
Roosevelt, Eleanor; see Roosevelt, A. E.
Roosevelt, Franklin Delano, 1882–1945, vol. IV
Roosevelt, Col Kermit, died 1943, vol. IV
Roosevelt, Robert Barnewell, 1829–1906, vol. I
Roosevelt, Col Theodore, 1858–1919, vol. II
Roosevelt, Theodore, 1887–1944, vol. IV
Root, Hon. Elihu, 1845–1937, vol. III
Root, Frederick James, 1906–1982, vol. VIII
Rootes, 1st Baron, 1894–1964, vol. VI
Rootes, 2nd Baron, 1917–1992, vol. IX
Rootes, Sir Reginald Claud, 1896–1977, vol. VII
Rooth, Henry Goodwin, 1861–1928, vol. II
Rooth, Ivar, 1888–1972, vol. VII
Rooth, John, 1864–1930, vol. III
Rootham, Cyril Bradley, 1875–1938, vol. III
Rootham, Jasper St John, 1910–1990, vol. VIII
Roots, Rt Rev. Logan Herbert, 1870–1945, vol. IV
Roots, William Lloyd, 1911–1971, vol. VII
Rope, Ellen Mary, died 1934, vol. III
Roper, Brig.-Gen. Alexander William, 1862–1940,
  vol. III
Roper, Hon. Sir Clinton Marcus, 1921–1994,
  vol. IX
Roper, Edgar Stanley, 1878–1953, vol. V
Roper, Captain Edward Gregson, 1910–1983,
  vol. VIII
Roper, Edward Ridgill, 1885–1974, vol. VII
Roper, Freeman, 1862–1925, vol. II
Roper, Garnham, 1862–1940, vol. III
Roper, Sir Harold, 1891–1971, vol. VII
Roper, Henry Basil, 1846–1918, vol. II
Roper, Maj.-Gen. Henry Ernest, 1923–1982,
  vol. VIII
Roper, Most Rev. John Charles, 1858–1940, vol. III
Roper, John Charles Abercromby, 1915–1998,
  vol. X
Roper, Philip Hampden, 1906–1956, vol. V

Ropes, Arthur Reed, 1859–1933, vol. III
Ropner, Sir (Emil Hugo Oscar) Robert, 3rd Bt (cr
  1904), 1893–1962, vol. VI
Ropner, Sir Guy; see Ropner, Sir W. G.
Ropner, Sir John Henry, 2nd Bt (cr 1904),
  1860–1936, vol. III
Ropner, John Raymond, 1903–1996, vol. X
Ropner, Leonard, 1873–1937, vol. III
Ropner, Col Sir Leonard, 1st Bt (cr 1952),
  1895–1977, vol. VII
Ropner, Col Sir Robert, 1st Bt (cr 1904),
  1838–1924, vol. II
Ropner, Sir Robert; see Ropner, Sir E. H. O. R.
Ropner, Sir Robert Desmond, 1908–1977, vol. VII
Ropner, Sir (William) Guy, 1896–1971, vol. VII
Rops, Henry D.; see Daniel-Rops.
Roques, Frederick William, 1898–1964, vol. VI
Roques, Mario Louis Guillaume, 1875–1961,
  vol. VI
Rorie, Col David, 1867–1946, vol. IV
Rorie, James, 1838–1911, vol. I
Rorimer, James J., 1905–1966, vol. VI
Rorison, Very Rev. Vincent Lewis, 1851–1910,
  vol. I
Rorke, Rev. Joseph, died 1932, vol. III
Rorke, Kate, (Mrs Douglas Cree), died 1945,
  vol. IV
Rosa, John Nogueira, 1903–1977, vol. VII
Rosay, Françoise, 1891–1974, vol. VII
Rosbotham, Sir Samuel Thomas, 1864–1950,
  vol. IV
Roscoe, (Edward) John (Townsend), 1913–1984,
  vol. VIII
Roscoe, Edward Stanley, 1849–1932, vol. III
Roscoe, Frank, 1870–1942, vol. IV
Roscoe, Rt Hon. Sir Henry Enfield, 1833–1915,
  vol. I
Roscoe, Rev. John, 1861–1932, vol. III
Roscoe, John; see Roscoe, E. J. T.
Roscoe, Kenneth Harry, 1914–1970, vol. VI
Roscoe, Air Cdre Peter Henry, 1912–1987, vol. VIII
Rose, Sir Alan Edward Percival, 1899–1975,
  vol. VII
Rose, Sir Alec Richard, 1908–1991, vol. IX
Rose, Rt Rev. Alfred Carey Wollaston, died 1971,
  vol. VII
Rose, Algernon Sidney, died 1934, vol. III
Rose, Archibald; see Rose, C. A. W.
Rose, Hon. Lt-Col Sir Arthur; see Rose, Hon.
  Lt-Col Sir H. A.
Rose, Captain Arthur Martin Thomas, 1918–1987,
  vol. VIII
Rose, Bernard William George, 1916–1996, vol. X
Rose, (Charles) Archibald (Walker), 1879–1961,
  vol. VI
Rose, Sir Charles Day, 1st Bt (cr 1909), 1847–1913,
  vol. I
Rose, Sir Charles Henry, 3rd Bt (cr 1909),
  1912–1966, vol. VI
Rose, Clifford Alan, 1929–1983, vol. VIII
Rose, Sir Cyril Stanley, 3rd Bt (cr 1872),
  1874–1915, vol. I
Rose, Sir David James Gardiner, 1923–1969,
  vol. VI
Rose, Edward, 1849–1904, vol. I

Rose, Edward, 1845–1910, vol. I
Rose, Gen. Edward Lee, 1841–1903, vol. I
Rose, (Edward) Michael, 1913–1986, vol. VIII
Rose, Eliot Joseph Benn, (Jim), 1909–1999, vol. X
Rose, Lt-Col Ernest Albert, 1879–1976, vol. VII
Rose, Sir Francis Cyril, 4th Bt (cr 1872), 1909–1979, vol. VII
Rose, Francis Leslie, 1909–1988, vol. VIII
Rose, Frank Atcherley, 1873–1935, vol. III
Rose, Vice-Adm. Sir Frank Forrester, 1878–1955, vol. V
Rose, Frank Herbert, 1857–1928, vol. II
Rose, Sir Frank Stanley, 2nd Bt (cr 1909), 1877–1914, vol. I
Rose, Frederick, died 1932, vol. III
Rose, Frederick Campbell, 1865–1946, vol. IV
Rose, Geoffrey Arthur, 1926–1993, vol. IX
Rose, Geoffrey Keith, 1889–1959, vol. V
Rose, George Pringle, 1855–1918, vol. II
Rose, Graham John, 1928–1995, vol. IX
Rose, Brig.-Gen. Henry Metcalfe, 1848–1909, vol. I
Rose, Herbert Jennings, 1883–1961, vol. VI
Rose, Dame Hilda Nora, 1891–1982, vol. VIII
Rose, Horace Arthur, 1867–1933, vol. III
Rose, Lt-Col Hugh, 1863–1946, vol. IV
Rose, Sir Hugh, 2nd Bt (cr 1935) 1902–1976, vol. VII
Rose, Major Hugh Alexander Leslie, died 1918, vol. II
Rose, Lt-Col Sir (Hugh) Arthur, 1st Bt (cr 1935), 1875–1937, vol. III
Rose, Hugh Edward, 1869–1945, vol. IV
Rose, Major James, 1820–1909, vol. I
Rose, Jim; see Rose, E. J. B.
Rose, John, 1841–1926, vol. II
Rose, John Donald, 1911–1976, vol. VII
Rose, John Holland, 1855–1942, vol. IV
Rose, Brig.-Gen. John Latham, 1867–1931, vol. III
Rose, Col John Markham, 1865–1942, vol. IV
Rose, Michael; see Rose, E. M.
Rose, Percy Jesse, 1878–1959, vol. V
Rose, Sir Philip Frederick, 2nd Bt (cr 1874), 1843–1919, vol. II
Rose, Captain Sir Philip Humphrey Vivian, 3rd Bt, 1903–1982, vol. VIII
Rose, Reginald Leslie S.; see Smith-Rose.
Rose, Col Richard Aubrey De Burgh, 1877–1962, vol. VI
Rose, Stuart; see Rose, T. S.
Rose, Captain Thomas Allen, 1874–1914, vol. I
Rose, Sir Thomas Kirke, 1865–1953, vol. V
Rose, (Thomas) Stuart, 1911–1993, vol. IX
Rose, Walter Clerk R.; see Randolph-Rose.
Rose, Sir William, 2nd Bt (cr 1872), 1846–1902, vol. I
Rose, William, 1847–1910, vol. I
Rose, William, 1894–1961, vol. VI
Rose, William John, 1885–1968, vol. VI
Rose-Innes, Rt Hon. Sir James, 1855–1942, vol. IV
Rose-Innes, Sir Patrick, 1853–1924, vol. II
Rose-Miller, Brig. George Patrick; see Miller.
Rosebery, 5th Earl of, 1847–1929, vol. III
Rosebery, 6th Earl of, 1882–1974, vol. VII
Rosedale, Captain Rev. Honyel Gough, 1863–1928, vol. II

Rosenbach, Abraham S. Wolf, 1876–1952, vol. V
Rosenfeld, Léon, 1904–1974, vol. VII
Rosenhain, Walter, 1875–1934, vol. III
Rosenhead, Louis, 1906–1984, vol. VIII
Rosenheim, Baron (Life Peer); Max Leonard Rosenheim, 1908–1972, vol. VII
Rosenheim, Otto, 1871–1955, vol. V
Rosenman, Samuel Irving, 1896–1973, vol. VII
Rosenthal, Maj.-Gen. Sir Charles, 1875–1954, vol. V
Rosenthal, Erwin Isak Jacob, 1904–1991, vol. IX
Rosenthal, Harold David, 1917–1988, vol. VIII
Rosenthal, Moriz, 1862–1946, vol. IV
Roseveare, Sir Martin Pearson, 1898–1985, vol. VIII
Roseveare, Rt Rev. Reginald Richard, 1902–1972, vol. VII
Roseveare, Rev. Richard Polgreen, 1865–1924, vol. II
Roseveare, Richard Victor Harley, 1897–1968, vol. VI
Roseveare, William Nicholas, 1864–1948, vol. IV
Rosewater, Hon. Edward, 1841–1906, vol. I
Rosewater, Victor, 1871–1940, vol. III (A), vol. IV
Roseway, Sir David; see Roseway, Sir G. D.
Roseway, Sir (George) David, 1890–1969, vol. VI
Rosier, Air Chief Marshal Sir Frederick Ernest, 1915–1998, vol. X
Rosing, Vladimir, died 1963, vol. VI
Roskell, John Smith, 1913–1998, vol. X
Roskill, Baron (Life Peer); Eustace Wentworth Roskill, 1911–1996, vol. X
Roskill, Sir Ashton Wentworth, 1902–1991, vol. IX
Roskill, John, died 1940, vol. III
Roskill, Oliver Wentworth, 1906–1994, vol. IX
Roskill, Captain Stephen Wentworth, 1903–1982, vol. VIII
Rosling, Sir Edward, 1863–1946, vol. IV
Roslyn, Louis Frederick, 1878–1940, vol. III
Rosman, Alice Grant, died 1961, vol. VI
Rosmead, 1st Baron, 1824–1897, vol. I
Rosmead, 2nd Baron, 1866–1933, vol. III
Rosmer, Milton, 1882–1971, vol. VII
Ross of Marnock, Baron (Life Peer); William Ross, 1911–1988, vol. VIII
Ross of Newport, Baron (Life Peer); Stephen Sherlock Ross, 1926–1993, vol. IX
Ross, Adrian; see Ropes, A. R.
Ross, Brig. Alan Campbell, 1878–1937, vol. III
Ross, Alan Strode Campbell, 1907–1980, vol. VII
Ross, Alexander, 1845–1923, vol. II
Ross, Rev. Alexander, 1888–1965, vol. VI
Ross, Brig.-Gen. Alexander, 1880–1973, vol. VII
Ross, Sir Alexander, 1907–1994, vol. IX
Ross, Alexander Carnegie, 1859–1940, vol. III (A), vol. IV
Ross, Alexander David, 1883–1966, vol. VI
Ross, Lt-Gen. Sir Alexander George, 1840–1910, vol. I
Ross, Rev. Alexander George Gordon, died 1938, vol. III
Ross, Alexander Howard, 1880–1965, vol. VI
Ross, Alfred William, 1914–1991, vol. IX
Ross, Allan Dawson, 1909–1982, vol. VIII
Ross, Andrew, 1849–1925, vol. II

Ross, Sir Archibald David Manisty, 1911–1996, vol. X

Ross, Archibald Hugh Houstoun, 1896–1969, vol. VI

Ross, Sir Archibald John Campbell, 1867–1931, vol. III

Ross, Brig.-Gen. Arthur Edward, 1870–1952, vol. V

Ross, Rt Rev. Arthur Edwin, 1869–1923, vol. II

Ross, Lt-Col Arthur Murray, 1879–1933, vol. III

Ross, Barnaby; see Dannay, Frederic and Lee, Manfred B.

Ross, Hon. Sir Bruce; see Ross, Hon. Sir D. B.

Ross, Maj.-Gen. Charles, 1864–1930, vol. III

Ross of that Ilk, Charles Campbell, yr, 1901–1966, vol. VI

Ross, Charles Griffith, 1885–1950, vol. IV

Ross, Sir Charles Henry Augustus Frederick Lockhart, 9th Bt (cr 1672), 1872–1942, vol. IV

Ross, (Claud) Richard, 1924–1996, vol. X

Ross, Sir David; see Ross, Sir W. D.

Ross, Rev. David Morison, 1852–1927, vol. II

Ross, Sir David Palmer, 1842–1904, vol. I

Ross, Sir Denison; see Ross, Sir E. D.

Ross, Hon. Sir (Dudley) Bruce, 1892–1984, vol. VIII

Ross, Edward Alsworth, 1866–1951, vol. V

Ross, Sir Edward Charles, 1836–1913, vol. I

Ross, Sir (Edward) Denison, 1871–1940, vol. III

Ross, Edward Rowlandson, 1868–1941, vol. IV

Ross, Rt Rev. Mgr Canon Francis, 1873–1945, vol. IV

Ross, Hon. Frank Mackenzie, 1891–1971, vol. VII

Ross, Sir Frederick William L.; see Leith Ross.

Ross, Col George, 1853–1926, vol. II

Ross, Rev. George Alexander Johnston, 1865–1937, vol. III

Ross, Rear-Adm. George Campbell, 1900–1993, vol. IX

Ross, George Edward Aubert, 1847–1931, vol. III

Ross, George Mabyn, 1883–1954, vol. V

Ross, Rear-Adm. George Parish, 1875–1942, vol. IV

Ross, George Robert Thomson, 1874–1959, vol. V

Ross, Col George Whitehill, 1878–1952, vol. V

Ross, Hon. Sir George William, 1841–1914, vol. I

Ross, Hon. Dame (Grace) Hilda, 1884–1959, vol. V

Ross, Col Harry, 1869–1938, vol. III

Ross, Lt-Col Henry, 1877–1958, vol. V

Ross, Sir Henry James, 1893–1973, vol. VII

Ross, Hon. Dame Hilda; see Ross, Hon. Dame G. H.

Ross, Howard Salter, 1872–1955, vol. V

Ross, Major Hugh Alexander, 1880–1918, vol. II

Ross, Lt-Col Hugh Cairns Edward, 1884–1940, vol. III

Ross, Hugh Campbell, 1875–1926, vol. II

Ross, Captain Hugo Donald, 1880–1960, vol. V

Ross, Sir Ian C.; see Clunies-Ross.

Ross, Ven. James, 1836–1902, vol. I

Ross, James, 1848–1913, vol. I

Ross, James, died 1953, vol. V

Ross, James, 1913–1996, vol. X

Ross, James Alexander, 1911–1997, vol. X

Ross, Maj.-Gen. James George, 1861–1956, vol. V

Ross, Sir James Paterson, 1st Bt (cr 1960), 1895–1980, vol. VII

Ross, Sir James Stirling, 1877–1961, vol. VI

Ross, James Stiven, 1892–1975, vol. VII

Ross, Janet Anne, 1842–1927, vol. II

Ross, Gen. Sir John, 1829–1905, vol. I

Ross, Rev. John, 1842–1915, vol. I

Ross, Sir John, 1834–1927, vol. II

Ross, Sir John, 1838–1931, vol. III

Ross, Rt Hon. Sir John, 1st Bt (cr 1919), 1854–1935, vol. III

Ross, John, 1893–1967, vol. VI

Ross, Major John Alexander, 1893–1917, vol. II

Ross, Brig. John Ellis, 1893–1965, vol. VI

Ross, Sir John Foster George; see Ross-of-Bladensburg.

Ross, John Kenneth Murray, 1856–1939, vol. III

Ross, John M. E., 1870–1925, vol. II

Ross, Maj.-Gen. John Munro, 1877–1959, vol. V

Ross, Sir John Sutherland, 1877–1959, vol. V

Ross, Rev. John Trelawny T.; see Trelawny-Ross.

Ross, Joseph Thorburn, 1849–1903, vol. I

Ross, Kenneth Brebner, 1901–1973, vol. VII

Ross, Rev. Kenneth Needham, 1908–1970, vol. VI

Ross, Leonard Q.; see Rosten, L. C.

Ross, Sir Lewis Nathan, 1911–1991, vol. IX

Ross, Malcolm Keir, 1910–1993, vol. IX

Ross, Martin; see Martin, Violet.

Ross, Rear-Adm. Maurice James, 1908–1996, vol. X

Ross, Rev. Neil, 1871–1943, vol. IV

Ross, Mrs Nicholas; see Phillpotts, M. A. E.

Ross, Norah Cecil; see Runge, N. C.

Ross, Norman Stilliard, 1919–1990, vol. IX (AI)

Ross, Peter McGregor, 1919–1974, vol. VII

Ross, Philip Dansken, 1858–1949, vol. IV

Ross, Reginald James Blair, born 1871, vol. II

Ross, Richard; see Ross, C. R.

Ross, Robert, 1893–1969, vol. VI

Ross, Robert Baldwin, 1869–1918, vol. II

Ross, Brig.-Gen. Robert James, 1865–1943, vol. IV

Ross, Maj.-Gen. Robert Knox, 1893–1951, vol. V

Ross, Air Cdre Robert Peel, 1888–1963, vol. VI

Ross, Roderick, 1863–1943, vol. IV

Ross, Col Sir Ronald, 1857–1932, vol. III

Ross, Lt-Col Sir Ronald Deane, 2nd Bt (cr 1919), 1888–1958, vol. V

Ross, Comdr Ronald Douglas, 1920–1994, vol. IX

Ross, Rev. Spence, 1843–1929, vol. III

Ross, Stanley Graham, 1888–1980, vol. VII

Ross, Thomas Arthur, 1875–1941, vol. IV

Ross, Rev. Thomas Harry, 1863–1943, vol. IV

Ross, Sir Thomas Mackenzie, died 1927, vol. II

Ross of Cromarty, Brig.-Gen. Sir Walter Charteris, 1857–1928, vol. II

Ross, Col Walter John Macdonald, 1914–1982, vol. VIII

Ross, Hon. William, 1825–1912, vol. I

Ross, Hon. William, 1850–1925, vol. II

Ross, William Alexander, 1891–1977, vol. VII

Ross, Captain William Alston, 1875–1944, vol. IV

Ross, Hon. William Benjamin, 1854–1929, vol. III

Ross, Sir (William) David, 1877–1971, vol. VII

Ross, Hon. William Donald, 1869–1947, vol. IV

Ross, William Henry, 1862–1944, vol. IV

Ross, William Munro, 1858–1914, vol. I (A), vol. III
Ross, Hon. William Roderick, 1869–1928, vol. II, vol. III
Ross-Brown, James William, *died* 1938, vol. III
Ross-Frames, Col Percival, 1863–1947, vol. IV
Ross-Johnson, Maj.-Gen. Cyril Maxwell, 1868–1934, vol. III
Ross-Johnson, Dennis, 1860–1941, vol. IV
Ross-Lewin, Rev. George Harrison, 1846–1913, vol. I
Ross-Lewin, Ven. Richard S., 1848–1921, vol. II
Ross-Lewin, Rev. Robert O'Donelan, 1850–1922, vol. II
Ross-of-Bladensburg, Sir John Foster George, 1848–1926, vol. II
Ross Skinner, Lt-Col Harry Crawley, 1896–1972, vol. VII
Ross-Taylor, Sir Joshua, 1878–1959, vol. V
Ross Taylor, Walter, 1877–1958, vol. V
Ross-Taylor, Walter, 1912–1983, vol. VIII
Ross Williamson, Hugh, 1901–1978, vol. VII
Ross Williamson, Reginald Pole, 1907–1966, vol. VI
Rosse, 4th Earl of, 1840–1908, vol. I
Rosse, 5th Earl of, 1873–1918, vol. II
Rosse, 6th Earl of, 1906–1979, vol. VII
Rosselli, (Ignace Adolphe) Jacques, 1907–1974, vol. VII
Rosselli, Jacques; *see* Rosselli, I. A. J.
Rosser, Rachel Mary, 1941–1998, vol. X
Rossetti, Harold Ford, 1909–1983, vol. VIII
Rossetti, William Michael, 1829–1919, vol. II
Rossillon, Rt Rev. Peter, 1874–1947, vol. IV
Rossiter, James Leonard, 1887–1963, vol. VI
Rossiter, Hon. Sir John Frederick, 1913–1988, vol. VIII
Rossiter, Leonard, 1926–1984, vol. VIII
Rosslyn, 5th Earl of, 1869–1939, vol. III
Rosslyn, 6th Earl of, 1917–1977, vol. VII
Rossmore, 5th Baron, 1853–1921, vol. II
Rossmore, 6th Baron, 1892–1958, vol. V
Rostal, Max, 1905–1991, vol. IX
Rostand, Edmond, 1868–1918, vol. II
Rostand, Jean, 1894–1977, vol. VII
Rosten, Leo Calvin, (Leonard Q. Ross), 1908–1997, vol. X
Rostern, Joseph, 1862–1930, vol. III
Rostovtzeff, Michael I., 1870–1952, vol. V
Rostron, Captain Sir Arthur Henry, 1869–1940, vol. III
Rostron, Sir Frank, 1900–1991, vol. IX
Rostron, Rev. Sydney N.; *see* Nowell-Rostron.
Rotch, Abbott Lawrence, 1861–1912, vol. I
Roth, Cecil, 1899–1970, vol. VI
Roth, George Kingsley, 1903–1960, vol. V
Roth, Leon, 1896–1963, vol. VI
Roth, Paul Bernard, 1882–1962, vol. VI
Roth, Brig.-Gen. Reuter Emerich, 1858–1924, vol. II
Roth, Air Cdre Victor Henry Batten, 1904–1979, vol. VII
Rotha, Paul, 1907–1984, vol. VIII
Rothband, Sir Henry Lesser, 1st Bt, *died* 1940, vol. III (A), vol. IV

Rothenstein, Sir John Knewstub Maurice, 1901–1992, vol. IX
Rothenstein, Michael, 1908–1993, vol. IX
Rothenstein, Sir William, 1872–1945, vol. IV
Rothera, Sir Percy, 1877–1940, vol. III
Rotherham, 1st Baron, 1849–1927, vol. II
Rotherham, 2nd Baron, 1876–1950, vol. IV
Rotherham, Arthur, *died* 1946, vol. IV
Rotherham, Air Vice-Marshal John Kevitt, 1910–1998, vol. X
Rothermere, 1st Viscount, 1868–1940, vol. III
Rothermere, 2nd Viscount, 1898–1978, vol. VII
Rothermere, 3rd Viscount, 1925–1998, vol. X
Rotherwick, 1st Baron, 1881–1958, vol. V
Rotherwick, 2nd Baron, 1912–1996, vol. X
Rothery, Guy Cadogan, 1863–1940, vol. III (A), vol. IV
Rothery, William Gurney, 1858–1930, vol. III
Rothery, William H.; *see* Hume-Rothery.
Rothes, 19th Earl of, 1877–1927, vol. II
Rothes, 20th Earl of, 1902–1975, vol. VII
Rothko, Mark, 1903–1970, vol. VI
Rothman, Sydney, 1897–1995, vol. IX
Rothnie, Sir Alan Keir, 1920–1997, vol. X
Rothschild, 1st Baron, 1840–1915, vol. I
Rothschild, 2nd Baron, 1868–1937, vol. III
Rothschild, 3rd Baron, 1910–1990, vol. VIII
Rothschild, Alfred Charles de, 1842–1918, vol. II
Rothschild, Anthony Gustav de, 1887–1961, vol. VI
Rothschild, Baron Ferdinand James de, 1839–1898, vol. I
Rothschild, Baron Henri de, 1872–1947, vol. IV
Rothschild, Baron Robert, 1911–1998, vol. X
Rothschild, James A. de, *died* 1957, vol. V
Rothschild, Leopold de, 1845–1917, vol. II
Rothschild, Lionel Nathan de, 1882–1942, vol. IV
Rothschild, Hon. Nathaniel Charles, 1877–1923, vol. II
Rothwell, Harry, 1902–1980, vol. VII
Rothwell, James Herbert, 1881–1944, vol. IV
Rothwell, Brig. Richard Sutton, 1882–1962, vol. VI
Rothwell, Sheila Gwendoline, 1935–1997, vol. X
Rothwell, Lt-Col William Edward, 1879–1937, vol. III
Rotter, Rear-Adm. (S) Charles John Ehrhardt, 1871–1948, vol. IV
Rotter, Godfrey, 1879–1969, vol. VI
Rotton, Sir John Francis, 1837–1926, vol. II
Rotton, Brig.-Gen. John Guy, 1867–1940, vol. III
Rouault, Georges, 1871–1958, vol. V
Roughead, William, 1870–1952, vol. V
Roughton, Edmund W., 1861–1913, vol. I
Roughton, Francis John Worsley, 1899–1972, vol. VII
Roughton, Noel James, 1885–1953, vol. V
Rougier, George Ronald, 1900–1976, vol. VII
Rouillard, Frederic Melchoir Louis, 1866–1933, vol. III
Rouleau, His Eminence Cardinal Raymond Marie, 1866–1931, vol. III
Roullier, Jean Georges, 1898–1974, vol. VII
Roulston, Air Cdre Jack Fendick, 1913–1973, vol. VII
Roumania, Queen Elizabeth of; *see* Sylva, Carmen.
Round, Charles James, 1885–1945, vol. IV

Round, Francis Richard, 1845–1920, vol. II
Round, Rt Hon. James, 1842–1916, vol. II
Round, John Horace, 1854–1928, vol. II
Round-Turner, Vice-Adm. Charles Wolfran, *died* 1953, vol. V
Roundell, Charles Savile, 1827–1906, vol. I
Roundell, Christopher Foulis, 1876–1958, vol. V
Roundell, Richard Foulis, 1872–1940, vol. III
Roundway, 1st Baron, 1854–1925, vol. II
Roundway, 2nd Baron, 1880–1944, vol. IV
Rounsevell, Hon. William Benjamin, 1842–1923, vol. II
Rountree, Gilbert Harry, 1907–1962, vol. VI
Rountree, Harry, 1878–1950, vol. IV
Rountree, Rev. James Peter, 1846–1929, vol. III
Roupell, Lt-Col Ernest Percy Stuart, 1870–1938, vol. III
Roupell, Brig. George Rowland Patrick, 1892–1974, vol. VII
Rous, (Francis) Peyton, 1879–1970, vol. VI
Rous, Peyton; *see* Rous, F. P.
Rous, Sir Stanley Ford, 1895–1986, vol. VIII
Rous, Lt-Gen Hon. Sir William Edward, 1939–1999, vol. X
Rous, William John, 1833–1914, vol. I
Rouse, Sir Alexander Macdonald, 1878–1966, vol. VI
Rouse, Sir Anthony Gerald Roderick, 1911–1994, vol. IX
Rouse, Arthur Frederick, 1910–1984, vol. VIII
Rouse, Edward Clive, 1901–1997, vol. X
Rouse, Harold Lindsay, 1887–1959, vol. V
Rouse, Col Hubert, 1864–1945, vol. IV
Rouse, William Henry Denham, 1863–1950, vol. IV
Rouse-Boughton, Sir Charles Henry; *see* Boughton.
Rouse-Boughton, Sir Edward Hotham; *see* Boughton.
Rouse-Boughton, Sir William St Andrew; *see* Boughton.
Rouse-Boughton-Knight, Charles Andrew, 1859–1947, vol. IV
Rousseau, Arthur, 1871–1934, vol. III
Rousseau, Pierre Marie W.; *see* Waldeck-Rousseau.
Roussin, Leander Gaspard, 1870–1936, vol. III
Routh, Amand J. McC., 1853–1927, vol. II
Routh, Augustus Crosbie, 1892–1982, vol. VIII
Routh, Edward John, 1831–1907, vol. I
Routh, Co. Guy Montgomery, 1882–1963, vol. VI
Routh, Harold Victor, 1878–1951, vol. V
Routh, Vice-Adm. Henry Peter, 1851–1944, vol. IV
Routh, Robert Gordon, 1869–1964, vol. VI
Routhier, Hon. Sir Adolphe Basile, 1839–1919, vol. II
Routledge, Rev. C. F., 1838–1904, vol. I
Routledge, Rev. Canon Graham; *see* Routledge, Rev. Canon K. G.
Routledge, Rev. Canon (Kenneth) Graham, 1927–1989, vol. VIII
Routledge, Robert M., *died* 1907, vol. I
Routledge, Scoresby, 1859–1939, vol. III
Routley, Rev. Erik Reginald, 1917–1982, vol. VIII
Routley, Frederick William, 1879–1951, vol. V
Routley, Thomas Clarence, 1889–1963, vol. VI
Roux, François C.; *see* Charles-Roux.
Row, Canchi Sarvothama, *born* 1856, vol. II
Row, Hon. Sir John Alfred, 1905–1993, vol. IX

Row, Kodikal S.; *see* Sanjiva Row.
Row, Comdr Sir Philip John, *died* 1990, vol. VIII
Row, Paymaster Rear-Adm. Philip John Hawkins Lander, 1870–1932, vol. III
Row, Brig. Robert Amos, 1888–1959, vol. V (A)
Rowallan, 1st Baron, 1856–1933, vol. III
Rowallan, 2nd Baron, 1895–1977, vol. VII
Rowallan, 3rd Baron, 1919–1993, vol. IX
Rowan, Carl Thomas, 1925–2000, vol. X
Rowan, John, *died* 1948, vol. IV
Rowan, Sir Leslie; *see* Rowan, Sir T. L.
Rowan, Lt-Col Percy Stewart, 1882–1931, vol. III
Rowan, Ven. Robert Philip, 1870–1946, vol. IV
Rowan, Sir (Thomas) Leslie, 1908–1972, vol. VII
Rowan-Hamilton, Brig. Gawaine Basil, 1884–1947, vol. IV
Rowan-Hamilton, Col Gawin William; *see* Hamilton.
Rowan-Hamilton, Sir Orme, 1877–1949, vol. IV
Rowan-Legg, Allan Aubrey, 1912–1998, vol. X
Rowan-Robinson, Maj.-Gen. Henry, 1873–1947, vol. IV
Rowan-Thomson, Sir William, 1867–1929, vol. III
Rowand, Alexander, 1868–1936, vol. III
Rowatt, Hugh Howard, 1861–1938, vol. III
Rowatt, Thomas, 1879–1950, vol. IV
Rowbotham, Edgar Stanley, 1890–1979, vol. VII
Rowbotham, Sir Hanson; *see* Rowbotham, Sir S. H.
Rowbotham, Rev. John Frederick, 1859–1925, vol. II
Rowbotham, Sir (Samuel) Hanson, 1880–1946, vol. IV
Rowbotham, Sir Thomas, 1851–1939, vol. III
Rowcroft, Maj.-Gen. Sir Bertram; *see* Rowcroft, Maj.-Gen. Sir E. B.
Rowcroft, Maj.-Gen. Sir (Eric) Bertram, 1891–1963, vol. VI
Rowcroft, Major Ernest Cave, 1866–1916, vol. II
Rowcroft, Maj.-Gen. George Cleland, 1831–1922, vol. II
Rowden, Aldred William, *died* 1919, vol. II
Rowe, Albert Percival, *died* 1976, vol. VII
Rowe, Rev. Alfred William, *died* 1921, vol. II
Rowe, Charles Henry, 1869–1925, vol. II
Rowe, Charles Henry, *died* 1943, vol. IV
Rowe, Charles William Dell, 1893–1954, vol. V
Rowe, Edward Rowe F.; *see* Fisher-Rowe.
Rowe, Eric George, 1904–1987, vol. VIII
Rowe, Frederick Maurice, 1891–1946, vol. IV
Rowe, Sir Henry Peter, 1916–1992, vol. IX
Rowe, Col Herbert Mayow F.; *see* Fisher-Rowe.
Rowe, Sir Jeremy, 1928–1996, vol. X
Rowe, John Clifford, 1872–1944, vol. IV
Rowe, Ven. John Tetley, *died* 1915, vol. I
Rowe, Louise J.; *see* Jopling, Louise.
Rowe, Sir Michael Edward, 1901–1978, vol. VII
Rowe, Norbert Edward, 1898–1995, vol. IX
Rowe, Norman Francis, 1908–1990, vol. VIII
Rowe, Norman Lester, 1915–1991, vol. IX
Rowe, Rt Rev. Peter Trimble, 1856–1942, vol. IV
Rowe, Sir Reginald P. P., *died* 1945, vol. IV
Rowe, Lt-Col Richard Herbert, 1883–1933, vol. III
Rowe, S. Grant, 1861–1928, vol. II
Rowe, Chief Engr William, *died* 1924, vol. II
Rowe, William Hugh Cecil, *died* 1939, vol. III(A), vol. IV

710

Rowe-Dutton, Sir Ernest, 1891–1965, vol. VI
Rowell, Sir Andrew Herrick, 1890–1973, vol. VII
Rowell, Sir Herbert Babington, 1860–1921, vol. II
Rowell, Sir (Herbert Babington) Robin, 1894–1981, vol. VIII
Rowell, Col James, 1851–1940, vol. III
Rowell, Sir John Joseph, 1916–1996, vol. X (AII)
Rowell, John Soulsby, 1846–1916, vol. II
Rowell, Hon. Newton Wesley, 1867–1941, vol. IV
Rowell, Percy Fitz-Patrick, 1874–1940, vol. III
Rowell, Sir Reginald Kaye, 1888–1964, vol. VI
Rowell, Sir Robin; see Rowell, Sir H. B. R.
Rowell, Lt-Gen. Sir Sydney Fairbairn, 1894–1975, vol. VII
Rowell, Thomas Irvine, 1840–1932, vol. III
Rowett, Geoffrey Charles, 1925–1986, vol. VIII
Rowett, John Quiller, 1876–1924, vol. II
Rowland, Rev. Alfred, 1840–1925, vol. II
Rowland, Christopher John Salter, 1929–1967, vol. VI
Rowland, Deborah Molly, 1913–1986, vol. VIII
Rowland, Ernest Daniel, 1858–1933, vol. III
Rowland, Francis George, 1883–1957, vol. V
Rowland, Frank Mortimer, 1866–1932, vol. III
Rowland, Sir Frederick, 1st Bt, 1874–1959, vol. V
Rowland, Herbert Grimley, 1905–1991, vol. IX
Rowland, Air Marshal Sir James Anthony, 1922–1999, vol. X
Rowland, Sir John, 1877–1941, vol. IV
Rowland, Sir John Edward Maurice, 1882–1969, vol. VI
Rowland, Sir John Thomas Podger, 1878–1933, vol. III
Rowland, John William, 1852–1925, vol. II
Rowland, Sir Leonard Bromfield, 1862–1939, vol. III
Rowland, Col Michael Carmichael, 1862–1947, vol. IV
Rowland, Col Thomas, 1831–1914, vol. I
Rowland, Sir Wentworth Lowe, 2nd Bt, 1909–1970, vol. VI
Rowland, Sir William, 1858–1945, vol. IV
Rowland-Brown, Lilian Kate; see Brown.
Rowlands, Sir Alun; see Rowlands, Sir R. A.
Rowlands, Sir Archibald, 1892–1953, vol. V
Rowlands, Rev. David, 1836–1907, vol. I
Rowlands, Ernest Brown B.; see Bowen-Rowlands.
Rowlands, Sir Gwilym, 1878–1949, vol. IV
Rowlands, Horace, 1869–1954, vol. V
Rowlands, Gen. Sir Hugh, 1829–1909, vol. I
Rowlands, James, 1851–1920, vol. II
Rowlands, John Wilfred, 1869–1948, vol. IV
Rowlands, Maldwyn Jones, 1918–1995, vol. X (AI)
Rowlands, Moses John, 1876–1932, vol. III
Rowlands, Sir (Richard) Alun, 1885–1977, vol. VII
Rowlands, Robert Pugh, 1874–1933, vol. III
Rowlands, Rowland, died 1935, vol. III
Rowlands, W. S., died 1939, vol. III
Rowlands, William Bowen, died 1906., vol. I
Rowlandson, Edmund James, 1882–1962, vol. VI
Rowlandson, Sir Graham; see Rowlandson, Sir S. G.
Rowlandson, Sir (Stanley) Graham, 1908–1986, vol. VIII
Rowlatt, Charles James, 1894–1959, vol. V
Rowlatt, Sir Frederick Terry, 1865–1950, vol. IV

Rowlatt, Sir John, 1898–1956, vol. V
Rowlatt, Rt Hon. Sir Sidney Arthur Taylor, 1862–1945, vol. IV
Rowledge, A. J., died 1957, vol. V
Rowlette, Robert James, 1873–1944, vol. IV
Rowley, Baron (Life Peer); Arthur Henderson, 1893–1968, vol. VI
Rowley, Alec, 1892–1958, vol. V
Rowley, Adm. Charles John, 1832–1919, vol. II
Rowley, Lt-Col Charles Samuel, 6th Bt (cr 1786), 1891–1962, vol. VI
Rowley, Brig.-Gen. Frank George Mathias, 1866–1949, vol. IV
Rowley, Rev. Sir George Charles Augustus, 4th Bt (cr 1836), 1869–1924, vol. II
Rowley, Sir George Charles Erskine, 3rd Bt (cr 1836), 1844–1922, vol. II
Rowley, George Fydell, 1851–1933, vol. III
Rowley, Captain Sir George William, 5th Bt (cr 1836), 1896–1953, vol. V
Rowley, Rev. Harold Henry, 1890–1969, vol. VI
Rowley, Hercules Douglas Edward, 1859–1945, vol. IV
Rowley, Hon. Hercules Langford, 1828–1904, vol. I
Rowley, Captain Howard Fiennes Julius, 1868–1948, vol. IV
Rowley, Hon. Hugh, 1833–1908, vol. I
Rowley, Ven. Hugh Edward, died 1938, vol. III
Rowley, John Charles, 1919–2000, vol. X
Rowley, John Hewitt, 1917–1986, vol. VIII
Rowley, John Vincent d'Alessio, 1907–1996, vol. X
Rowley, Sir Joshua Francis, 7th Bt (cr 1786), 1920–1997, vol. X
Rowley, Sir Joshua Thellusson, 5th Bt (cr 1786), 1838–1931, vol. III
Rowley, Sir William Joshua, 6th Bt (cr 1836), 1891–1971, vol. VII
Rowley, Rev. William Walter, 1812–1907, vol. I
Rowley-Conwy, Rear-Adm. Rafe Grenville; see Conwy.
Rowling, Rt Hon. Sir Wallace Edward, 1927–1995, vol. IX
Rowntree, Arnold Stephenson, 1872–1951, vol. V
Rowntree, Arthur, 1861–1949, vol. IV
Rowntree, Benjamin Seebohm, 1871–1954, vol. V
Rowntree, Cecil, died 1943, vol. IV
Rowntree, Ernest William, 1877–1936, vol. III
Rowntree, Joseph, 1836–1925, vol. II
Rowntree, Sir Norman Andrew Forster, 1912–1991, vol. IX
Roworth, Edward, 1880–1964, vol. VI
Rowse, Alfred Leslie, 1903–1996, vol. X
Rowse, Herbert James, died 1963, vol. VI
Rowse, William Crapo, 1883–1961, vol. VI
Rowsell, Mary Catharine, vol. II
Rowsell, Philip Foale, 1864–1946, vol. IV
Rowsell, Rev. Walter Frederick, 1837–1924, vol. II
Rowson, Edmund, died 1951, vol. V
Rowson, Guy, died 1937, vol. III
Rowson, Lionel Edward Aston, 1914–1989, vol. VIII
Rowton, 1st Baron, 1838–1903, vol. I
Roxbee Cox, family name of Baron Kings Norton.
Roxburgh, Alexander Bruce, died 1953, vol. V
Roxburgh, Archibald Cathcart, 1886–1954, vol. V

Roxburgh, Eleanor Mary Ann, (Lady Roxburgh), *died* 1929, vol. III
Roxburgh, Francis, 1850–1935, vol. III
Roxburgh, Air Vice-Marshal Henry Lindsay, 1909–1989, vol. VIII
Roxburgh, Sir James; *see* Roxburgh, Sir T. J. Y.
Roxburgh, Sir John Archibald, 1854–1937, vol. III
Roxburgh, John Fergusson, 1888–1954, vol. V
Roxburgh, Sir Ronald Francis, 1889–1981, vol. VIII
Roxburgh, Sir (Thomas) James (Young), 1892–1974, vol. VII
Roxburgh, Sir Thomas Laurence, 1853–1945, vol. IV
Roxburgh, 8th Duke of, 1876–1932, vol. III
Roxburgh, 9th Duke of, 1913–1974, vol. VII
Roxburgh, Duchess of; (Anne Emily), *died* 1923, vol. II
Roxby, Rev. Edmund Lally, 1844–1912, vol. I
Roxby, Captain Herbert, 1848–1905, vol. I
Roxby, John Henry M.; *see* Maude-Roxby.
Roxby, Percy Maude, 1880–1947, vol. IV
Roy, Sir Asoka Kumar, 1886–1982, vol. VIII
Roy, Sir Bijoy Prosad S.; *see* Singh Roy.
Roy, Camille, 1870–1943, vol. IV
Roy, Catherine Murray, *died* 1976, vol. VII
Roy, Charles T., 1854–1897, vol. I
Roy, Donald Whatley, 1881–1960, vol. V
Roy, Ferdinand, 1873–1948, vol. IV
Roy, Sir Ganen, 1872–1943, vol. IV
Roy, James Alexander, *died* 1973, vol. VII
Roy, Brig.-Gen. John William Gascoigne, 1863–1941, vol. IV
Roy, Lt-Col Joseph Edensor Gascoigne, 1872–1935, vol. III
Roy, His Eminence Cardinal Maurice, 1905–1985, vol. VIII
Roy, Maurice Paul Mary, *born* 1899, vol. VIII
Roy, Most Rev. Paul Eugene, 1859–1926, vol. II
Roy, Comdr Robert Stewart, 1878–1924, vol. II
Roy, Sir Satyendra Nath, 1888–1955, vol. V
Royall, Kenneth Claiborne, 1894–1971, vol. VII
Royalton, Kisch, Alastair; *see* Kisch.
Royce, Sir (Frederick) Henry, 1st Bt, 1863–1933, vol. III
Royce, Sir Henry; *see* Royce, Sir F. H.
Royce, William Stapleton, 1857–1924, vol. II
Royde Smith, Naomi Gwladys, *died* 1964, vol. VI
Royden, 1st Baron, 1871–1950, vol. IV
Royden, (Agnes) Maude, (Mrs G. W. H. Shaw), 1876–1956, vol. V
Royden, Sir Ernest Bland, 3rd Bt, 1873–1960, vol. V
Royden, Sir John Ledward, 4th Bt, 1907–1976, vol. VII
Royden, Maude; *see* Royden, A. M.
Royden, Sir Thomas Bland, 1st Bt, 1831–1917, vol. II
Royds, Vice-Adm. Sir Charles William Rawson, 1876–1931, vol. III
Royds, Col Sir Clement Molyneaux, 1842–1916, vol. II
Royds, Sir Edmund, 1860–1946, vol. IV
Royds, Rev. F. C., 1825–1913, vol. I
Royds, Rev. Gilbert Twemlow, 1845–1933, vol. III

Royds, Adm. Sir Percy Molyneaux Rawson, 1874–1955, vol. V
Royds, William Massy, 1879–1951, vol. V
Roylance, Robert Walker, 1882–1962, vol. VI
Royle, Baron (Life Peer); Charles Royle, 1896–1975, vol. VII
Royle, Arnold, 1837–1919, vol. II
Royle, Rev. Canon Arthur, 1895–1973, vol. VII
Royle, Charles, 1872–1863, vol. VI
Royle, Elizabeth Jean, (Mrs J. A. C. Royle); *see* Harwood, E. J.
Royle, Sir George, 1861–1949, vol. IV
Royle, Adm. Sir Guy Charles Cecil, 1885–1954, vol. V
Royle, Rear-Adm. Henry Lucius Fanshawe, 1849–1906, vol. I
Royle, Joseph Ralph Edward John, 1844–1929, vol. III
Royle, Joseph Kenneth, 1924–1990, vol. VIII
Royle, Sir Lancelot Carrington, 1898–1978, vol. VII
Royle, Col Reginald George, 1887–1938, vol. III
Royle, Thomas Wright, 1882–1969, vol. VI
Royle, Rev. Vernon Peter Fanshawe Archer, 1854–1929, vol. III
Royston, Viscount; Philip Simon Prospero Lindley Rupert Yorke, 1938–1973, vol. VII
Royston, Brig.-Gen. John Robinson, 1860–1942, vol. IV
Royston, Rt Rev. Peter Sorenson, 1830–1915, vol. I
Roze, Marie, 1846–1926, vol. II
Roze, Raymond, 1875–1920, vol. II
Roze-Perkins, J. H. Raymond; *see* Roze, Raymond.
Rubbra, Arthur Alexander, 1903–1982, vol. VIII
Rubbra, Edmund, 1901–1986, vol. VIII
Rube, Charles, 1852–1914, vol. I
Rubens, Paul Alfred, 1875–1917, vol. II
Rubie, Rev. Alfred Edward, 1863–1948, vol. IV
Rubie, Lt-Col Claude Blake, 1888–1939, vol. III
Rubie, John Fonthill, *died* 1907, vol. I
Rubin, Kenneth Warnell Reginald, 1920–2000, vol. X
Rubinstein, Arthur, 1887–1982, vol. VIII
Rubinstein, Harold Frederick, 1891–1975, vol. VII
Rubinstein, Helena, (Princess Gourielli), 1871–1965, vol. VI
Rubner, Ben, 1921–1998, vol. X
Rubra, Edward John, 1902–1974, vol. VII
Ruck, Berta, (Mrs Oliver Onions), 1878–1978, vol. VII
Ruck, Maj.-Gen. Sir Richard Matthews, 1851–1935, vol. III
Ruck Keene, Vice-Adm. Philip, 1897–1977, vol. VII
Ruck Keene, Adm. William George Elmhirst, 1867–1935, vol. III
Rucker, Sir Arthur Nevil, 1895–1991, vol. IX
Rücker, Sir Arthur William, 1848–1915, vol. I
Ruckstull, Frederick Wellington, 1853–1942, vol. IV
Rudd, Surg. Rear-Adm. Eric Thomas Sutherland, 1902–1977, vol. VII
Rudd, G(eoffrey) Burkitt (Whitcomb), 1908–1975, vol. VII
Rudd, Col Thomas William, 1869–1943, vol. IV
Ruddell, Ven. Joseph, 1866–1941, vol. IV
Rudden, James, 1911–2000, vol. X

Rudderham, Rt Rev. Joseph Edward, 1899–1979, vol. VII
Ruddle, Lt-Col Sir (George) Kenneth (Fordham), 1903–1979, vol. VII
Ruddle, Lt-Col Sir Kenneth; *see* Ruddle, Lt-Col Sir G. K. F.
Ruddock, Ven. David, *died* 1920, vol. II
Ruddock, Richard, 1837–1908, vol. I
Ruddock, Thomas Emerson, 1873–1932, vol. III
Rudé, George Frederick Elliot, 1910–1993, vol. IX
Rudgard, Rev. R. W., *died* 1933, vol. III
Rudgard, Ven. Richard Cuthbert, 1901–1985, vol. VIII
Rudge, Florence H.; *see* Haynes-Rudge.
Rudini, Antonio Starrabba, Marquis di, 1839–1908, vol. I
Rudkin, Brig.-Gen. Charles Mark Clement, 1872–1957, vol. V
Rudkin, George Drury, 1879–1929, vol. III
Rudkin, Brig.-Gen. William Charles Eric, 1875–1930, vol. III
Rudler, Frederick William, 1840–1915, vol. I
Rudler, Gustave, 1872–1957, vol. V
Rudmose-Brown, Robert Neal, 1879–1957, vol. V
Rudmose-Brown, Thomas Brown, 1878–1942, vol. IV
Rudolf, Rev. Edward de Montjoie, 1852–1933, vol. III
Rudolf, Robert Dawson, 1865–1941, vol. IV
Rudolf, Robert de Montjoie, 1856–1932, vol. III
Rudolph, Felix; *see* Scatcherd, F. R.
Rueff, Jacques, 1896–1978, vol. VII
Ruegg, Alfred Henry, *died* 1941, vol. IV
Ruegger, Paul J., 1897–1988, vol. VIII
Ruete, Hans Hellmuth, 1914–1987, vol. VIII
Ruff, Howard, *died* 1928, vol. II
Ruff, William Willis, 1914–1992, vol. IX
Ruffer, Sir Marc Armand, 1859–1917, vol. II
Ruffside, 1st Viscount, 1879–1958, vol. V
Rugambwa, His Eminence Cardinal Laurean, 1912–1997, vol. X
Rugby, 1st Baron, 1877–1969, vol. VI
Rugby, 2nd Baron, 1913–1990, vol. VIII
Rugg, Sir (Edward) Percy, 1906–1986, vol. VIII
Rugg, Sir Percy; *see* Rugg, Sir E. P.
Rugge-Price, Sir Charles; *see* Price.
Rugge-Price, Sir Charles Frederick; *see* Price.
Rugge-Price, Lt-Col Sir Charles James Napier; *see* Price.
Rugge-Price, Sir Charles Keith Napier; *see* Price.
Ruggeri, Vincenzo G.; *see* Giuffrida-Ruggeri.
Ruggles, Maj.-Gen. John, 1827–1919, vol. II
Ruggles-Brise, Archibald Weyland, 1853–1939, vol. III
Ruggles-Brise, Col Sir Edward Archibald, 1st Bt, 1882–1942, vol. IV
Ruggles-Brise, Sir Evelyn John, 1857–1935, vol. III
Ruggles-Brise, Captain Guy Edward, 1914–2000, vol. X
Ruggles-Brise, Maj.-Gen. Sir Harold Goodeve, 1864–1927, vol. II
Ruggles Brise, Col Sir Samuel; *see* Brise.
Rugman, Sir Francis Dudley, 1894–1946, vol. IV
Ruiz Soler, Antonio, (Antonio), 1921–1996, vol. X

Rukidi III, HH Sir George David Kamurasi, 1906–1966, vol. VI
Rule, David Charles, 1937–2000, vol. X
Rule, Frank Gordon, 1882–1965, vol. VI
Rule, Mollie, 1899–1965, vol. VI
Rumball, Air Vice-Marshal Sir Aubrey; *see* Rumball, Air Vice-Marshal Sir C. A.
Rumball, Air Vice-Marshal Sir (Campion) Aubrey, 1904–1975, vol. VII
Rumble, Sir Bertram Thomas, 1875–1949, vol. IV
Rumble, Captain John Bertram, 1928–1996, vol. X
Rumbold, Sir Algernon; *see* Rumbold, Sir H. A. F.
Rumbold, Sir Anthony; *see* Rumbold, Sir H. A. C.
Rumbold, Captain Charles E. A. L., 1872–1943, vol. IV
Rumbold, Rev. Canon Charles Robert, *died* 1973, vol. VII
Rumbold, Etheldred, (Lady Rumbold), 1879–1964, vol. VI
Rumbold, Rt Hon. Sir Horace, 8th Bt, 1829–1913, vol. I
Rumbold, Sir (Horace) Algernon (Fraser), 1906–1993, vol. IX
Rumbold, Sir (Horace) Anthony (Claude), 10th Bt, 1911–1983, vol. VIII
Rumbold, Rt Hon. Sir Horace George Montagu, 9th Bt, 1869–1941, vol. IV
Rumbold, Col William Edwin, 1870–1947, vol. IV
Rumboll, Arthur Charles, 1869–1935, vol. III
Rumford, R. Kennerley, 1870–1957, vol. V
Ruml, Beardsley, 1894–1960, vol. V
Rumney, Abraham Wren, 1863–1942, vol. IV
Rumsey, Almaric, 1825–1899, vol. I
Rumsey, Harry Victor, 1898–1971, vol. VII
Rumsey, Robert Murray, 1849–1922, vol. II
Runcie, Baron (Life Peer); Rt Rev. and Rt Hon. Robert Kennedy Alexander Runcie, 1921–2000, vol. X
Runciman, 1st Baron, 1847–1937, vol. III
Runciman of Doxford, 1st Viscount, 1870–1949, vol. IV
Runciman of Doxford, 2nd Viscount, 1900–1989, vol. VIII
Runciman of Doxford, Viscountess, (Hilda), 1869–1956, vol. V
Runciman, Hon. Sir James Cochran Stevenson (Hon. Sir Steven), 1903–2000, vol. X
Runciman, Philip, *died* 1953, vol. V
Runciman, Hon. Sir Steven; *see* Runciman, Hon. Sir J. C. S.
Runcorn, Baron (Life Peer); Dennis Forwood Vosper, 1916–1968, vol. VI
Runcorn, Keith; *see* Runcorn, S. K.
Runcorn, (Stanley) Keith, 1922–1995, vol. IX
Rundall, Lt-Col Charles Frank, 1871–1951, vol. V
Rundall, Sir Francis Brian Anthony, 1908–1987, vol. VIII
Rundall, Gen. Francis Hornblow, 1823–1908, vol. I
Rundall, Col Frank Montagu, 1851–1930, vol. III
Rundall, Matthew Adkins, 1856–1935, vol. III
Rundle, David John, 1938–1987, vol. VIII
Rundle, Col George Richard Tyrrell, 1860–1947, vol. IV
Rundle, Gen. Sir (Henry Macleod) Leslie, 1856–1934, vol. III

Rundle, Gen. Sir Leslie; see Rundle, Gen. Sir H. M. L.
Rundle, Rear-Adm. Mark, 1871–1958, vol. V
Runge, Rev. Charles Herman Schmettau, 1889–1970, vol. VI
Runge, Norah Cecil, (Mrs Thomas A. Ross), 1884–1978, vol. VII
Runge, Sir Peter Francis, 1909–1970, vol. VI
Runnett, Henry Brian, 1935–1970, vol. VI
Runtz, Sir John Johnson, 1842–1922, vol. II
Ruoff, Theodore Burton Fox, 1910–1990, vol. VIII
Rupp, Rev. (Ernest) Gordon, 1910–1986, vol. VIII
Rupp, Rev. Gordon; see Rupp, Rev. E. G.
Rusby, Lloyd; see Rusby, N. L.
Rusby, Norman Lloyd, 1905–1988, vol. VIII
Ruse, Harold Stanley, 1905–1974, vol. VII
Rush, (Edward Antisell) Michael (Stanistreet), 1933–1988, vol. VIII
Rush, Michael; see Rush, E. A. M. S.
Rushbrook Williams, Laurence Frederick; see Williams.
Rushbrooke, Vice-Adm. Edmund Gerard Noel, 1892–1972, vol. VII
Rushbrooke, G(eorge) Stanley, 1915–1995, vol. IX
Rushbrooke, Rev. James Henry, 1870–1947, vol. IV
Rushbrooke, Stanley; see Rushbrooke, G. S.
Rushbrooke, William George, 1849–1926, vol. II
Rushbury, Sir Henry George, 1889–1968, vol. VI
Rushcliffe, 1st Baron, 1872–1949, vol. IV
Rushmore, Frederick Margetson, 1869–1933, vol. III
Rusholme, 1st Baron, 1890–1977, vol. VII
Rushout, Sir Charles Hamilton, 4th Bt, 1868–1931, vol. III
Rushton, Sir Arnold, 1870–1930, vol. III
Rushton, Vice-Adm. Edward Astley Astley-, 1879–1935, vol. III
Rushton, Frederick Alan, 1905–1982, vol. VIII
Rushton, George R., died 1948, vol. IV
Rushton, Maj. Harold Petit, 1895–1968, vol. VI
Rushton, Martin Amsler, 1903–1970, vol. VI
Rushton, Sir Reginald Fielding, died 1979, vol. VII
Rushton, William Albert Hugh, 1901–1980, vol. VII
Rushton, William George, 1937–1996, vol. X
Rushton, William S., 1850–1924, vol. II
Rushworth, Geoffrey Harrington, 1899–1969, vol. VI
Rusk, Dean, 1909–1994, vol. IX
Rusk, Robert Robertson, 1879–1972, vol. VII
Ruska, Ernst August Friedrich, 1906–1988, vol. VIII
Ruskin, John, 1819–1900, vol. I
Russ, Sidney, 1879–1963, vol. VI
Russel, James, 1858–1939, vol. III
Russell, 2nd Earl, 1865–1931, vol. III
Russell, 3rd Earl, 1872–1970, vol. VI
Russell, 4th Earl, 1921–1987, vol. VIII
Russell, Countess; (Elizabeth Mary), died 1941, vol. IV
Russell, 1st Baron, 1834–1920, vol. II
Russell, Hon. Lord; Albert Russell, 1884–1975, vol. VII
Russell, Baron (Life Peer); Charles Russell, 1832–1900, vol. I

Russell, Baron (Life Peer); Frank Russell, 1867–1946, vol. IV
Russell of Killowen, Baron (Life Peer); Charles Ritchie Russell, 1908–1986, vol. VIII
Russell of Liverpool, 2nd Baron, 1895–1981, vol. VIII
Russell, Alan, 1910–1986, vol. VIII
Russell, Albert; see Russell, Hon. Lord.
Russell, Captain Sir Alec Charles, 2nd Bt (cr 1916), 1894–1938, vol. III
Russell, Alexander, 1861–1943, vol. IV
Russell, Alexander David, 1864–1934, vol. III
Russell, Col Alexander Fraser, 1856–1938, vol. III
Russell, Hon. Sir (Alexander) Fraser, 1876–1952, vol. V
Russell, Lord Alexander George, 1821–1907, vol. I
Russell, Col Sir Alexander James Hutchison, 1882–1958, vol. V
Russell, Alexander Smith, 1888–1972, vol. VII
Russell, Brig.-Gen. Hon. Alexander Victor Frederick Villiers, 1874–1965, vol. VI
Russell, Sir Alexander West, 1879–1961, vol. VI
Russell, Alfred Ernest, 1870–1944, vol. IV
Russell, Rev. Alfred Francis, died 1936, vol. III
Russell, Sir Alison, 1875–1948, vol. IV
Russell, Maj.-Gen. Sir Andrew Hamilton, 1868–1960, vol. V
Russell, Sir Archibald Edward, 1904–1995, vol. IX
Russell, Archibald George Blomefield, 1879–1955, vol. V
Russell, Hon. Arthur, 1861–1907, vol. I
Russell, Sir Arthur Edward Ian Montagu, 6th Bt (cr 1812), 1878–1964, vol. VI
Russell, Audrey; see Russell, M. A.
Russell, Gen. Sir Baker Creed, 1837–1911, vol. I
Russell, Ben Harold, 1891–1979, vol. VII
Russell, Hon. Benjamin, 1849–1935, vol. III
Russell, Brian Fitzgerald, 1904–1994, vol. IX
Russell, Hon. Sir Charles, 1st Bt (cr 1916), 1863–1928, vol. II
Russell, Charles Alfred, 1855–1926, vol. II
Russell, Charles Barrett, 1823–1911, vol. I
Russell, Rev. Charles Dickinson, died 1915, vol. I
Russell, Rev. Charles Frank, 1882–1951, vol. V
Russell, Charles Gilchrist, 1840–1916, vol. II
Russell, Sir Charles Ian, 3rd Bt (cr 1916), 1918–1997, vol. X
Russell, Sir (Charles) Lennox (Somerville), 1872–1960, vol. V
Russell, Charles Pearce, 1887–1961, vol. VI
Russell, Charles Scott, 1912–1971, vol. VII
Russell, Charles Taze, (Pastor Russell), 1852–1916, vol. II
Russell, Hon. Claud Eustace H.; see Hamilton-Russell.
Russell, Sir Claud Frederick William, 1871–1959, vol. V
Russell, Hon. Cyril, 1866–1920, vol. II
Russell, Sir David, 1872–1956, vol. V
Russell, Dilys (Mrs Leonard Russell); see Powell, (E.) D.
Russell, Dorothy Stuart, 1895–1983, vol. VIII
Russell, Lt-Gen. Sir Dudley, 1896–1978, vol. VII
Russell, Lt-Col Edmund Stuart Eardley Wilmot E.; see Eardley-Russell.

Russell, Rev. Edward Augustine, 1916–1997, vol. X
Russell, Rev. Edward Francis, 1844–1925, vol. II
Russell, Hon. Edward John, 1879–1925, vol. II
Russell, Sir (Edward) John, 1872–1965, vol. VI
Russell, Sir Edward Lechmere, 1818–1904, vol. I
Russell, Sir (Edward) Lionel, 1903–1983, vol. VIII
Russell, Edward Stuart, 1887–1954, vol. V
Russell, Edward Walter, 1904–1994, vol. IX
Russell, Madame Ella, 1864–1935, vol. III
Russell, Sir Evelyn Charles Sackville, 1912–1992, vol. IX
Russell, Hon. (Francis Albert) Rollo, 1849–1914, vol. I
Russell, Maj.-Gen. Frank Shirley, 1840–1912, vol. I
Russell, Hon. Sir Fraser; see Russell, Hon. Sir A. F.
Russell, Hon. Frederick Gustavus H.; see Hamilton-Russell.
Russell, Frederick Vernon, 1870–1942, vol. IV
Russell, Sir Frederick Stratten, 1897–1984, vol. VIII
Russell, Sir George, 4th Bt, 1828–1898, vol. I
Russell, Sir George Arthur Charles, 5th Bt (cr 1812), 1868–1944, vol. IV
Russell, George Clifford Dowsett, 1901–1970, vol. VI
Russell, Sir George Michael, 7th Bt (cr 1812), 1908–1993, vol. IX
Russell, Maj.-Gen. George Neville, 1899–1971, vol. VII
Russell, Rev. George Stanley, died 1957, vol. V
Russell, George William, 1867–1935, vol. III
Russell, Rt Hon. George William Erskine, 1853–1919, vol. II
Russell, Adm. Gerald Walter, 1850–1928, vol. II
Russell, Sir Gordon; see Russell, Sir S. G.
Russell, Hon. Frederick Gustavus H.; see Hamilton-Russell.
Russell, Sir Guthrie; see Russell, Sir T. G.
Russell, Col Guy Hamilton, 1882–1958, vol. V
Russell, Adm. Hon. Sir Guy Herbrand Edward, 1898–1977, vol. VII
Russell, Gyrth, 1892–1970, vol. VI
Russell, Hamer, died 1941, vol. IV
Russell, Harold G. Bedford, 1886–1957, vol. V
Russell, Harold John Hastings, 1868–1926, vol. II
Russell, Henry, 1813–1900, vol. I
Russell, Henry Blythe Westrap, 1868–1912, vol. I
Russell, Henry Chamberlain, 1836–1907, vol. I
Russell, Henry Norris, 1877–1957, vol. V
Russell, Henry Stanway, 1910–1985, vol. VIII
Russell, Rear-Adm. Sir (Henshaw) Robert, 1875–1957, vol. V
Russell, Air Vice-Marshal Herbert Bainbrigge, 1895–1963, vol. VI
Russell, Herbert John, 1890–1949, vol. IV
Russell, Sir Herbert William Henry, 1869–1944, vol. IV
Russell, Lt-Col Horatio Douglas, 1874–1931, vol. III
Russell, James, 1839–1923, vol. II
Russell, Sir James Alexander, 1846–1918, vol. II
Russell, James Burn, 1837–1905, vol. I
Russell, Rt Rev. James Curdie, 1830–1925, vol. II
Russell, James George, 1848–1918, vol. II
Russell, Captain James Reginald, 1893–1920, vol. II
Russell, James Samuel Risien, died 1939, vol. III

Russell, Sir John; see Russell, Sir E. J.
Russell, John Archibald, 1816–1899, vol. I
Russell, Air Vice-Marshal John Bernard, 1916–1978, vol. VII
Russell, Air Cdre John Cannan, 1896–1956, vol. V
Russell, Maj.-Gen. John Cecil, 1839–1909, vol. I
Russell, John Eaton Nevill, 1911–1970, vol. VI
Russell, John Francis Robert V.; see Vaughan-Russell.
Russell, Maj.-Gen. John Joshua, 1862–1941, vol. IV
Russell, Rt Rev. John Keith, 1916–1979, vol. VII
Russell, John Lawson, 1917–1992, vol. IX
Russell, Sir John Weir, 1893–1978, vol. VII
Russell, Sir John Wriothesley, 1914–1984, vol. VIII
Russell, Sir Lennox; see Russell, Sir C. L. S.
Russell, Leonard, 1906–1974, vol. VII
Russell, Leonard James, 1884–1971, vol. VII
Russell, Hon. Leopold Oliver, 1907–1989, vol. VIII
Russell, Lilian M., 1875–1949, vol. IV
Russell, Sir Lionel; see Russell, Sir E. L.
Russell, Louis Pitman, 1850–1914, vol. I
Russell, Mabel; see Philipson, Mrs H.
Russell, Martin Guthrie, 1914–1996, vol. X
Russell, Rev. Matthew, 1834–1912, vol. I
Russell, Maj. Gen. Sir Michael William, 1860–1949, vol. IV
Russell, (Muriel) Audrey, 1906–1989, vol. VIII
Russell, Brig. Nelson, 1897–1971, vol. VII
Russell, Hon. Sir Odo William Theophilus Villiers, 1870–1951, vol. V
Russell, Patrick Wimberley D.; see Dill-Russell.
Russell, Sir Peter Nicol, died 1905, vol. I
Russell, Col Reginald Edmund Maghlin, 1879–1950, vol. IV
Russell, Reginald James Kingston, 1883–1943, vol. IV
Russell, Reginald Pemberton, 1860–1917, vol. II
Russell, Richard Drew, 1903–1981, vol. VIII
Russell, Richard John, 1872–1943, vol. IV
Russell, Col Richard Tyler, 1875–1940, vol. III
Russell, Ritchie; see Russell, W. R.
Russell, Robert, 1843–1910, vol. I
Russell, Rear-Adm. Sir Robert; see Russell, Rear-Adm. Sir H. R.
Russell, Sir Robert Edwin, 1890–1972, vol. VII
Russell, Robert Tor, 1888–1972, vol. VII
Russell, Hon. Rollo; see Russell, Hon. F. A. R.
Russell, Sir Ronald Stanley, 1904–1974, vol. VII
Russell, Rosalind, (Mrs F. Brisson), 1911–1976, vol. VII
Russell, Sir Spencer Thomas, 1923–1995, vol. X
Russell, Captain Stuart Hugh Minto, 1909–1943, vol. IV
Russell, Sir (Sydney) Gordon, 1892–1980, vol. VII
Russell, Thomas, 1830–1904, vol. I
Russell, Sir (Thomas) Guthrie, 1887–1963, vol. VI
Russell, Rt Hon. Sir Thomas Wallace, 1st Bt, 1841–1920, vol. II
Russell, Sir Thomas Wentworth, 1879–1954, vol. V
Russell, Col Valentine Cubitt, 1896–1976, vol. VII
Russell, Rev. Vernon William, 1861–1953, vol. V
Russell, Hon. Victor Alexander Frederick Villiers, 1874–1965, vol. VI
Russell, Sir Walter Westley, 1867–1949, vol. IV

Russell, Sir William, 3rd Bt (*cr* 1832), 1865–1915, vol. I
Russell, William, 1868–1931, vol. III
Russell, William, 1859–1937, vol. III (A), vol. IV
Russell, William, 1852–1940, vol. III
Russell, William Clark, 1844–1911, vol. I
Russell, Sir William Fleming, *died* 1925, vol. II
Russell, Sir William Howard, 1820–1907, vol. I
Russell, William James, 1830–1910, vol. I
Russell, Col William Kelson, 1873–1949, vol. IV
Russell, (William) Ritchie, 1903–1980, vol. VII
Russell, William Robert, 1913–1994, vol. IX
Russell, Captain Sir William Russell, 1838–1913, vol. I
Russell, Captain Wilmot Peregrine Maitland, 1874–1950, vol. IV
Russell-Astley, Bertram Frankland F.; *see* Astley.
Russell-Astley, Henry Jacob Delaval F.; *see* Astley.
Russell-Brown, Col Claude, 1873–1939, vol. III
Russell-Johnson, Lt-Col Walter, 1888–1940, vol. III
Russell-Smith, Dame Enid Mary Russell, 1903–1989, vol. VIII
Russell-Wells, Sir Sydney, 1869–1924, vol. II
Russia, Grand Duke Michael of, 1861–1929, vol. III
Russo, Sir Peter George, *born* 1899, vol. VIII
Russon, Sir Clayton; *see* Russon, Sir W. C.
Russon, Sir (William) Clayton, 1895–1968, vol. VI
Rust, William, 1903–1949, vol. IV
Rust, William Thomas Cutler, 1874–1937, vol. III
Rustomjee, Heerjeebhoy Manackjee, *died* 1904, vol. I
Ruston, Rev. Canon (Cuthbert) Mark, 1916–1990, vol. VIII
Ruston, Lt-Col Joseph Seward, 1869–1939, vol. III
Ruston, Rev. Canon Mark; *see* Ruston, Rev. Canon C. M.
Ruston, Col Reginald Seward, 1867–1963, vol. VI
Ruth, Rev. Thomas E., 1875–1956, vol. V
Ruthen, Sir Charles Tamlin, 1871–1926, vol. II
Rutherfoord, Captain J. B., *born* 1864, vol. II
Rutherford, 1st Baron, 1871–1937, vol. III
Rutherford, Hon. Alexander Cameron, 1857–1941, vol. IV
Rutherford, Andrew, 1929–1998, vol. X
Rutherford, Col Charles, 1858–1922, vol. II
Rutherford, Very Rev. Claud Anselm, 1886–1952, vol. V
Rutherford, Sir David Carter, 1868–1948, vol. IV
Rutherford, Sir Ernest Victor Buckley, *died* 1929, vol. III
Rutherford, George, 1818–1904, vol. I
Rutherford, Gideon Campbell, 1888–1971, vol. VII
Rutherford, (Gordon) Malcolm, 1939–1999, vol. X
Rutherford, James Rankin, 1882–1967, vol. VI
Rutherford, Sir John, 1st Bt (*cr* 1916), 1854–1932, vol. III
Rutherford, Sir John George, 1886–1967, vol. VI
Rutherford, John Gunion, 1857–1923, vol. II
Rutherford, Sir John Hugo, 2nd Bt (*cr* 1923), 1887–1942, vol. IV
Rutherford, John Rutherford, 1904–1957, vol. V
Rutherford, Malcolm; *see* Rutherford, G. M.
Rutherford, Vice-Adm. Malcolm Graham, 1941–1997, vol. X
Rutherford, Dame Margaret, 1892–1972, vol. VII

Rutherford, Mark; *see* White, William Hale.
Rutherford, Sir Robert, 1854–1930, vol. III
Rutherford, Sir Thomas George, 1886–1957, vol. V
Rutherford, Brig.-Gen. Thomas John, 1893–1975, vol. VII
Rutherford, Vickerman Henzell, 1860–1934, vol. III
Rutherford, Sir Watson; *see* Rutherford, Sir William W.
Rutherford, William, 1839–1899, vol. I
Rutherford, Rev. William Gunion, 1853–1907, vol. I
Rutherford, William John, 1868–1930, vol. III
Rutherford, Sir (William) Watson, 1st Bt (*cr* 1923), 1853–1927, vol. II
Rutherfurd, Andrew, 1835–1906, vol. I
Rutherfurd, James Hunter, 1864–1927, vol. II
Rutherfurd, Maj.-Gen. Thomas Walter, 1832–1918, vol. II
Rutherston, Albert Daniel, 1881–1953, vol. V
Ruthnaswamy, Miriadas, 1885–1977, vol. VII (AII)
Ruths, Johannes, 1879–1935, vol. III
Ruthven of Freeland, 9th Lord, 1838–1921, vol. II
Ruthven of Freeland, 10th (wrongly shown as 9th) Lord, 1870–1956, vol. V
Ruthven of Freeland, Lady (11th in line), (The Dowager Viscountess Monckton of Brenchley), 1896–1982, vol. VIII
Ruthven, Col Hon. (Christian) Malise Hore, 1880–1969, vol. VI
Ruthven, Col Hon. Malise Hore-; *see* Ruthven, Col. Hon. C. M. H.
Ruthven-Murray, Alan James; *see* Murray.
Rutkowski, Sir Miecislas de, 1853–1941, vol. IV
Rutland, 7th Duke of, 1818–1906, vol. I
Rutland, 8th Duke of, 1852–1925, vol. II
Rutland, 9th Duke of, 1886–1940, vol. III
Rutland, 10th Duke of, 1919–1999, vol. X
Rutland, Duchess of; (Violet), *died* 1937, vol. III
Rutland, Charles, 1858–1943, vol. IV
Rutledge, Hon. Sir Arthur, 1843–1917, vol. II
Rutledge, Sir Guy; *see* Rutledge, Sir. J. G.
Rutledge, Sir (John) Guy, 1872–1930, vol. III
Rutledge, Wiley, 1894–1949, vol. IV
Ruttan, Robert F., 1856–1930, vol. III
Rutter, Frank V. P., 1876–1937, vol. III
Rutter, Sir Frederick William Pascoe, 1859–1949, vol. IV
Rutter, Herbert Hugh, 1905–1975, vol. VII
Rutter, Air Vice-Marshal Norman Colpoy Simpson, 1909–1998, vol. X
Rutter, Owen, 1889–1944, vol. IV
Rutter, W(illiam) Arthur, 1890–1980, vol. VII
Ruttle, Henry Samuel, 1906–1995, vol. IX
Ruttledge, David Knox, 1865–1931, vol. III
Ruttledge, Hugh, 1884–1961, vol. VI
Ruttledge, Lt-Col Thomas Geoffrey, 1882–1958, vol. V
Ruvigny and Raineval, 9th Marquis of, 1868–1921, vol. II
Ruvigny and Raineval, 10th Marquis of, 1903–1941, vol. IV
Ruxton, Major U. FitzHerbert, 1873–1954, vol. V
Ryall, Sir Charles, *died* 1922, vol. II
Ryalls, Hon. Captain Harry Douglas, 1887–1964, vol. VI

Ryan, Alfred Patrick, 1900–1972, vol. VII
Ryan, Sir Andrew, 1876–1949, vol. IV
Ryan, Arthur James, 1900–1990, vol. VIII
Ryan, Sir Charles Lister, 1831–1920, vol. II
Ryan, Brig.-Gen. Charles Montgomerie, 1867–1935, vol. III
Ryan, Maj.-Gen. Sir Charles Snodgrass, 1853–1926, vol. II
Ryan, Cornelius John, 1920–1974, vol. VII
Ryan, Curteis Norwood, 1891–1969, vol. VI
Ryan, Captain Cyril Percy, 1875–1940, vol. III
Ryan, Major Denis George Jocelyn, 1885–1927, vol. II
Ryan, Sir Derek Gerald, 3rd Bt, 1922–1990, vol. VIII
Ryan, Most Rev. Dermot, 1924–1985, vol. VIII
Ryan, Edward Joseph, 1845–1923, vol. II
Ryan, Col Eugene, 1873–1951, vol. V
Ryan, Most Rev. Finbar, 1882–1975, vol. VII
Ryan, Adm. Frank Edward Cavendish, 1865–1945, vol. IV
Ryan, Bt Major George Julian, 1878–1915, vol. I
Ryan, Sir Gerald Ellis, 2nd Bt, 1888–1947, vol. IV
Ryan, Sir Gerald Hemmington, 1st Bt, died 1937, vol. III
Ryan, Hugh, 1873–1931, vol. III
Ryan, Most Rev. Hugh Edward, 1888–1977, vol. VII
Ryan, James, 1892–1970, vol. VI
Ryan, (James) Stewart, 1913–1990, vol. VIII
Ryan, John, 1894–1975, vol. VIII
Ryan, Rt Rev. John A., 1869–1945, vol. IV
Ryan, John Francis, 1894–1978, vol. VII
Ryan, Rt Rev. Joseph Francis, 1897–1990, vol. VIII
Ryan, Mary, 1873–1961, vol. VI
Ryan, Mervyn Frederick, died 1952, vol. V
Ryan, Patrick Francis William, 1873–1939, vol. III
Ryan, Patrick John McNamara, 1919–1978, vol. VII
Ryan, Most Rev. Richard, 1881–1957, vol. V
Ryan, Lt-Col Rupert Sumner, 1884–1952, vol. V
Ryan, Stewart; see Ryan, J. S.
Ryan, Sir Thomas, 1879–1934, vol. III
Ryan, Thomas, born 1911, vol. VIII
Ryan, Thomas Joseph, 1876–1921, vol. II
Ryan, Wing-Comdr William John, 1883–1959, vol. V
Ryan, William Patrick, died 1942, vol. IV
Rybczynski, Tadeusz Mieczyslaw, 1923–1998, vol. X
Ryburn, Rev. Hubert James, 1897–1988, vol. IX (AI)
Ryckman, Hon. Edmond Baird, 1866–1934, vol. III
Rycroft, Sir Benjamin William, 1902–1967, vol. VI
Rycroft, Charlotte Susanna, (Mrs W. N. Wenban-Smith), 1941–1990, vol. VIII
Rycroft, Bt Major Julian Neil Oscar, 1892–1928, vol. II
Rycroft, Sir Nelson Edward Oliver, 6th Bt, 1886–1958, vol. V
Rycroft, Sir Richard Nelson, 5th Bt, 1859–1925, vol. II
Rycroft, Sir Richard Newton, 7th Bt, 1918–1999, vol. X
Rycroft, Maj.-Gen. Sir William Henry, 1861–1925, vol. II

Rydbeck, Olof, 1913–1995, vol. X (AI)
Ryde, John Walter, 1898–1961, vol. VI
Ryde, Walter Cranley, 1856–1938, vol. III
Ryden, Kenneth, 1917–1994, vol. IX
Ryder of Warsaw, Baroness (Life Peer); Sue Ryder, 1923–2000, vol. X
Ryder, Rev. Alexander Roderick, 1852–1919, vol. II
Ryder, Charles Foster, died 1942, vol. IV
Ryder, Col Charles Henry Dudley, 1868–1945, vol. IV
Ryder, Lady Frances, 1888–1965, vol. VI
Ryder, Col Francis John, 1866–1920, vol. II
Ryder, Sir Gerard, 1909–1973, vol. VII
Ryder, Peter Hugh Dudley, 1913–1993, vol. IX
Ryder, Captain Robert Edward Dudley, 1908–1986, vol. VIII
Rydge, Sir Norman Bede, 1900–1980, vol. VII
Rydon, (Henry) Norman, 1912–1991, vol. IX
Rydon, Norman; see Rydon, H. N.
Rye, Frank Gibbs, 1874–1948, vol. IV
Rye, Reginald Arthur, 1876–1945, vol. IV
Rye, Walter, 1843–1929, vol. III
Ryerson, Maj.-Gen. George Sterling, 1854–1926, vol. II
Rylah, Hon. Sir Arthur Gordon, 1909–1974, vol. VII
Ryland, Sir (Albert) William (Cecil), 1913–1988, vol. VIII
Ryland, Charles Ivor Phipson Smith, 1898–1929, vol. III
Ryland, Sir Charles Mortimer Tollemache S.; see Smith-Ryland.
Ryland, Edward Charles, 1864–1941, vol. IV
Ryland, Frederick, 1854–1902, vol. I
Ryland, Henry, died 1924, vol. II
Ryland, John, 1900–1991, vol. IX
Ryland, Sir William; see Ryland, Sir A. W. C.
Rylands, George Humphrey Wolferstan, 1902–1999, vol. X
Rylands, Louis Gordon, 1862–1942, vol. IV
Rylands, Sir Peter; see Rylands, Sir W. P.
Rylands, Sir (William) Peter, 1st Bt, 1868–1948, vol. IV
Ryle, Arthur Johnston, 1857–1915, vol. I
Ryle, George Bodley, 1902–1978, vol. VII
Ryle, Gilbert, 1900–1976, vol. VII
Ryle, Herbert, 1881–1966, vol. VI
Ryle, Rt Rev. Herbert Edward, 1856–1925, vol. II
Ryle, John Alfred, 1889–1950, vol. IV
Ryle, Rt Rev. John Charles, 1816–1900, vol. I
Ryle, Kenneth Sherriff, 1912–1993, vol. IX
Ryle, Sir Martin, 1918–1984, vol. VIII
Ryle, Reginald John, 1854–1922, vol. II
Rylett, Rev. Harold, 1851–1936, vol. III
Ryley, Air Vice-Marshal Douglas William Robert, 1905–1985, vol. VIII
Ryley, Madeleine Lucette, 1868–1934, vol. III
Ryman, Brenda Edith, (Mrs Harry Barkley), 1922–1983, vol. VIII
Rymer, Sir Joseph Sykes, 1841–1923, vol. II
Rymer-Jones, Brig. John Murray, 1897–1993, vol. IX
Rymill, Hon. Sir Arthur Campbell, 1907–1989, vol. VIII

Rymill, John Riddoch, 1905–1968, vol. VI
Ryner, Harry, 1872–1964, vol. VI

Ryrie, Maj.-Gen. Hon. Sir Granville de Laune, 1865–1937, vol. III

S

Sabatier, Paul, 1858–1928, vol. II
Sabatier, Paul, 1854–1941, vol. IV (A), vol. V
Sabatini, Rafael, 1875–1950, vol. IV
Sabben-Clare, Ernest Elwin, 1910–1993, vol. IX
Sabelli, Humbert Anthony, 1878–1961, vol. VI
Sabin, Albert Bruce, 1906–1993, vol. IX
Sabin, Arthur Knowles, 1879–1959, vol. V
Sabin, Howard Westcott, 1916–1996, vol. X
Sabine, Neville Warde, 1910–1994, vol. IX
Sabiti, Most Rev. Erica, 1903–1988, vol. VIII
Sacher, Harry, 1881–1971, vol. VII
Sacher, Michael Moses, 1917–1986, vol. VIII
Sachin, Nawab of, 1886–1930, vol. III
Sachs, Maj.-Gen. Albert, 1904–1976, vol. VII
Sachs, Edwin O., 1870–1919, vol. II
Sachs, Rt Hon. Sir Eric, 1898–1979, vol. VII
Sachs, Nelly Leonie, 1891–1970, vol. VI
Sachse, Sir Frederic Alexander, 1878–1957, vol. V
Sackett, Alfred Barrett, 1895–1977, vol. VII
Sacks, Muriel Elsie, (Mrs Samuel Sacks); see
    Landau, M. E.
Sackville, 2nd Baron, 1827–1908, vol. I
Sackville, 3rd Baron, 1867–1928, vol. II
Sackville, 4th Baron, 1870–1962, vol. VI
Sackville, 5th Baron, 1901–1965, vol. VI
Sackville, Major Lionel Charles Stopford,
    1891–1920, vol. II
Sackville, Lady Margaret, 1881–1963, vol. VI
Sackville, Col Nigel Victor S.; see Stopford
    Sackville.
Sackville, Sackville George Stopford, 1840–1926,
    vol. II
Sackville-West, Hon. Victoria Mary, (Vita),
    1892–1962, vol. VI
Sackville-West, Hon. Vita; see Sackville-West, Hon.
    Victoria M.
Sacre, Rev. Arthur Joseph, 1862–1931, vol. III
Sackwood, Mark, 1926–2000, vol. X
Sadasiva Aiyar, Sir Theagaraja Aiyar, died 1927,
    vol. II
Sadat, Mohamed Anwar El; see El-Sadat, M. A.
Sadd, Sir Clarence Thomas Albert, 1883–1962,
    vol. VI
Sadhu, Rai Tarak Nath, 1875–1937, vol. III
Sadleir, Michael, 1888–1957, vol. V
Sadleir-Jackson, Brig.-Gen. Lionel Warren de Vere,
    1876–1932, vol. III
Sadler, Adm. Arthur Hayes, 1863–1952, vol. V
Sadler, Arthur Lindsay, 1882–1970, vol. VI
Sadler, Herbert Charles, 1872–1948, vol. IV
Sadler, Lt-Col Sir James Hayes, 1851–1922, vol. II
Sadler, Sir Michael Ernest, 1861–1943, vol. IV
Sadler, Col Sir Samuel Alexander, 1842–1911,
    vol. I
Sadler, Walter Dendy, 1854–1923, vol. II
Sadlier, Rt Rev. William Charles, 1867–1935,
    vol. III

Sadul Singh, Col Rao Bahadur, Thakur, Sir,
    1881–1937, vol. III
Safford, Sir Archibald, 1892–1961, vol. VI
Safford, Col Arthur Hunt, 1873–1933, vol. III
Safford, Frank, died 1929, vol. III
Safonoff, Wassily, 1852–1918, vol. II
Sagrada, Rt Rev. V. Emanuel, 1860–1939, vol. III
Sahni, Birbal, 1891–1949, vol. IV
Sahni, Rai Bahadur Daya Ram, 1879–1939, vol. III
Sailana, Raja of, 1864–1919, vol. II
Sailana, Raja of, 1891–1961, vol. VI
Sainer, Leonard, 1909–1991, vol. IX
Sainsbury, Rev. Charles, 1837–1915, vol. I
Sainsbury, Baron (Life Peer); Alan John Sainsbury,
    1902–1998, vol. X
Sainsbury, Richard Eric, 1909–1991, vol. IX
Sainsbury, Sir Robert, 1906–2000, vol. X
Sainsbury, Air Vice-Marshal Thomas Audley L.; see
    Langford-Sainsbury.
Saint, Charles Frederick Morris, 1886–1973,
    vol. VII
Saint, Sir John; see Saint, Sir S. J.
Saint, Lawrence Bradford, 1885–1961, vol. VI
Saint, Captain Peter Johnson J.; see Johnston-Saint.
Saint, Sir (Sidney) John, 1897–1987, vol. VIII
Saint, Stafford Eric, 1904–1988, vol. VIII
Saint, Sir Thomas Wakelin, 1861–1928, vol. II
St Albans, 10th Duke of, 1840–1898, vol. I
St Albans, 11th Duke of, 1870–1934, vol. III
St Albans, 12th Duke of, 1874–1964, vol. VI
St Albans, 13th Duke of, 1915–1988, vol. VIII
St Albans, Duchess of; (Grace), died 1926, vol. II
St Aldwyn, 1st Earl, 1837–1916, vol. II
St Aldwyn, 2nd Earl, 1912–1992, vol. IX
St Aubyn, Alan, died 1920, vol. II
St Aubyn, Hon. Edward Stuart, 1858–1915, vol. I
St Aubyn, Geoffrey Peter, born 1858, vol. II
St Aubyn, Sir Hugh M.; see Molesworth-St Aubyn.
St Aubyn, Sir (John) Arscott M.; see Molesworth-St
    Aubyn.
St Aubyn, Sir John M.; see Molesworth-St Aubyn.
St Aubyn, Captain Hon. Lionel Michael,
    1878–1965, vol. VI
St Aubyn, Rev. Sir St A. Hender M.; see
    Molesworth-St Aubyn.
St Audries, 1st Baron, 1853–1917, vol. II
St Audries, 2nd Baron, 1893–1971, vol. VII
Saint Aulaire, Comte de, 1866–1954, vol. V
Saint Brides, Baron (Life Peer); John Morrice Cairns
    James, 1916–1989, vol. VIII
Saint-Clair, George; see Coudurier de Chassaigne,
    Joseph.
St Clair, Maj.-Gen. George James Paul, 1885–1955,
    vol. V
St Clair, Col James Latimer Crawshay, 1850–1940,
    vol. III

St Clair, Hon. Lockhart Matthew, 1855–1930, vol. III
St Clair, William; see Ford, William.
St Clair, Lt-Col William Augustus Edmond, 1854–1923, vol. II
St Clair, William Graeme, 1849–1930, vol. III
St Clair, Adm. William Home Chisholme, 1841–1905, vol. I
St Clair, Major William Lockhart, 1883–1920, vol. II
St Clair-Ford, Captain Sir Aubrey, 6th Bt, 1904–1991, vol. IX
St Clair-Ford, Maj.-Gen. Sir Peter, 1905–1989, vol. VIII
St Clair-Morford, Maj.-Gen. Albert Clarence, 1893–1945, vol. IV
St Cyres, Viscount; Stafford Harry Northcote, 1869–1926, vol. II
St Davids, 1st Viscount, 1860–1938, vol. III
St Davids, 2nd Viscount, 1917–1991, vol. IX
St Davids, Viscountess; (Elizabeth Frances), 1884–1974, vol. VII
Saint-Denis, Michel Jacques, 1897–1971, vol. VII
St George, 6th Marquis of, born 1875, vol. III
St George, Sir Denis Howard, 8th Bt, 1902–1989, vol. VIII
St George, Air Vice-Marshal Douglas Fitzclarence, 1919–1985, vol. VIII
St George, Frederick Ferris Bligh, 1908–1970, vol. VI
St George, Sir George Bligh, 9th Bt, 1908–1995, vol. X (AI)
Saint-George, Henry, 1866–1917, vol. II
St George, Sir John, 5th Bt, 1851–1938, vol. III
St George, Sir Robert Alan, 7th Bt, 1900–1983, vol. VIII
St George, Sir Theophilus John, 6th Bt, 1856–1943, vol. IV
St Germans, 5th Earl of, 1835–1911, vol. I
St Germans, 6th Earl of, 1890–1922, vol. II
St Germans, 7th Earl of, 1867–1942, vol. IV
St Germans, 8th Earl of, 1870–1960, vol. V
St Germans, 9th Earl of, 1914–1988, vol. VIII
St Helens, 1st Baron, 1912–1980, vol. VII
St Helier, 1st Baron, 1843–1905, vol. I
St Helier, Lady; (Mary), died 1931, vol. III
St John of Bletso, 17th Baron, 1876–1920, vol. II
St John of Bletso, 18th Baron, 1877–1934, vol. III
St John of Bletso, 19th Baron, 1917–1976, vol. VII
St John of Bletso, 20th Baron, 1918–1978, vol. VII
St John, Alfred, 1857–1939, vol. III
St John, Lt-Col Sir Beauchamp; see St John, Lt-Col Sir H. B.
St John, Charles Edward, 1857–1935, vol. III
St John, Col Edmund Farquhar, 1879–1945, vol. IV
St John, Vice-Adm. Francis Gerald, 1869–1947, vol. IV
St John, Sir Frederick Robert, 1831–1923, vol. II
St John, Geoffrey Robert, 1889–1972, vol. VII
St John, Brig.-Gen. George Francis William, 1861–1937, vol. III
St John, Lt-Col Sir (Henry) Beauchamp, 1874–1954, vol. V
St John, Adm. Henry Craven, died 1909, vol. I
St John, Henry Percy, 1854–1921, vol. II

St John, Hon. Joseph Wesley, 1854–1907, vol. I
St John, Mabel; see Cooper, H. St J.
St John, Rev. Maurice William Ferdinand, 1827–1914, vol. I
St John, Lt-Col Oliver Charles Beauchamp, 1907–1976, vol. VII
St John, Maj.-Gen. Richard Stukeley, 1876–1959, vol. V
St John, Maj.-Gen. Roger Ellis Tudor, 1911–1998, vol. X
St John, Hon. Rowland Tudor, 1882–1948, vol. IV
St John, Sir Spencer, 1825–1910, vol. I
St John-Brooks, Ralph Terence, 1884–1963, vol. VI
St John-Mildmay, Sir Anthony; see Mildmay.
St John-Mildmay, Sir Gerald Anthony Shaw-Lefevre; see Mildmay.
St John-Mildmay, Sir Henry Bouverie Paulet; see Mildmay.
St John-Mildmay, Sir Henry Gerald; see Mildmay.
St John-Mildmay, Rev. Sir Neville; see Mildmay.
St John-Mildmay, Major Wyndham Paulet; see Mildmay.
St John Perse; see Léger, Marie-René Alexis Saint-Léger.
St Johnston, Sir Eric; see St Johnston, Sir T. E.
St Johnston, Sir Reginald, 1881–1950, vol. IV
St Johnston, Sir (Thomas) Eric, 1911–1986, vol. VIII
St Joseph, John Kenneth Sinclair, 1912–1994, vol. IX
St Just, 1st Baron, 1870–1941, vol. IV
St Just, 2nd Baron, 1922–1984, vol. VIII
St Laurent, Rt Hon. Louis Stephen, 1882–1973, vol. VII
St Lawrence, Julian Charles G.; see Gaisford-St Lawrence.
St Leger, Evelyn, died 1944, vol. IV
St Leger, Col Henry Hungerford, 1833–1925, vol. II
St Leger, Col Stratford Edward, 1878–1935, vol. III
St Leger Searle, Rear-Adm. Malcolm Walter; see Searle, Rear-Adm. M. W. St L.
St Leonards, 2nd Baron, 1847–1908, vol. I
St Leonards, 3rd Baron, 1890–1972, vol. VII
St Leonards, 4th Baron, 1950–1985, vol. VIII
St Levan, 1st Baron, 1829–1908, vol. I
St Levan, 2nd Baron, 1857–1940, vol. III
St Levan, 3rd Baron, 1895–1978, vol. VII
St Maur, Lord Ernest, 1847–1922, vol. II
St Maur, Lord Percy, 1847–1907, vol. I
St Oswald, 2nd Baron, 1857–1919, vol. II
St Oswald, 3rd Baron, 1893–1957, vol. V
St Oswald, 4th Baron, 1916–1984, vol. VIII
St Oswald, 5th Baron, 1919–1999, vol. X
St Quintin, William Herbert, 1851–1933, vol. III
Saint-Saens, Camille, 1835–1921, vol. II
St Vigeans, Hon. Lord; David Anderson, 1862–1948, vol. IV
St Vincent, 5th Viscount, 1855–1908, vol. I
St Vincent, 6th Viscount, 1859–1940, vol. III
St Vincent Ferreri, 7th Marquis of, 1880–1945, vol. IV
Sainthill, Loudon, 1919–1969, vol. VI
Sainton, Charles Prosper, 1861–1914, vol. I
Saintsbury, George Edward Bateman, 1845–1933, vol. III

Saionji, Prince, *died* 1940, vol. III
Sait, Edward M'Chesney, 1881–1943, vol. IV
Saiyid, Fazl Ali, Sir, 1886–1959, vol. V
Sakharov, Andrei Dimitrievich, 1921–1989, vol. VIII
Saklatvala, Sir Nowroji, 1875–1938, vol. III
Saklatvala, Shapurji, 1874–1936, vol. III
Saklatvala, Sir Sorabji Dorabji, *died* 1948, vol. IV (A), vol. V
Sakzewski, Sir Albert, 1905–1991, vol. IX
Sala, Antoni, 1893–1945, vol. IV
Salam, Abdus, 1926–1996, vol. X
Salaman, Charles Kensington, 1814–1901, vol. I
Salaman, Malcolm Charles, 1855–1940, vol. III
Salaman, Myer Head, 1902–1994, vol. IX
Salaman, Redcliffe Nathan, 1874–1955, vol. V
Salandra, Antonio, 1853–1931, vol. III
Salas, Rafael Montinola, 1928–1987, vol. VIII
Salazar, Antonio de Oliveira, 1889–1970, vol. VI
Salberg, Major Frank James, 1884–1964, vol. VI
Sale, Charles Vincent, 1868–1943, vol. IV
Sale, Geoffrey Stead, 1907–1987, vol. VIII
Sale, George S., 1831–1922, vol. II
Sale, John Lewis, 1885–1973, vol. VII
Sale, Col Matthew Townsend, 1841–1913, vol. I
Sale, Richard, 1919–1987, vol. VIII
Sale, Sir Stephen George, 1852–1934, vol. III
Sale, Stephen Leonard, 1889–1958, vol. V
Sale, Ven. Thomas Rawlinson, 1865–1939, vol. III
Sale, Brig. Walter Morley, 1903–1976, vol. VII
Sale-Hill, Gen. Sir Rowley Sale, 1839–1916, vol. II
Saleeby, Caleb Williams, 1878–1940, vol. III
Sales, William Henry, 1903–1991, vol. IX
Salis-Schwabe, Maj.-Gen. George, 1843–1907, vol. I
Salisbury, 3rd Marquess of, 1830–1903, vol. I
Salisbury, 4th Marquess of, 1861–1947, vol. IV
Salisbury, 5th Marquess of, 1893–1972, vol. VII
Salisbury, Lt-Col Alfred George Grazier, 1885–1942, vol. IV
Salisbury, Sir Edward James, 1886–1978, vol. VII
Salisbury, Francis, 1850–1922, vol. II
Salisbury, Francis Owen, (Frank), 1874–1962, vol. VI
Salisbury, Frank; *see* Salisbury, Francis O.
Salisbury, Harrison Evans, 1908–1993, vol. IX
Salisbury-Jones, Maj.-Gen. Sir (Arthur) Guy, 1896–1985, vol. VIII
Salisbury-Jones, Maj.-Gen. Sir Guy; *see* Salisbury-Jones, Maj.-Gen. Sir A. G.
Salk, Jonas Edward, 1914–1995, vol. IX
Salles, Georges Adolphe, 1889–1966, vol. VI
Salmon, Baron (Life Peer); Cyril Barnet Salmon, 1903–1991, vol. IX
Salmon, Alec; *see* Salmon, W. A.
Salmon, Alfred, 1868–1928, vol. II
Salmon, Amedee Victor, 1857–1919, vol. II
Salmon, Balliol, 1868–1953, vol. V
Salmon, Barnett Alfred, 1895–1965, vol. VI
Salmon, Lt-Col Hon. Charles Carty, *died* 1917, vol. II
Salmon, Cyril, 1924–1981, vol. VIII
Salmon, Air Vice-Marshal Sir Cyril John Roderic; *see* Salmon, Air Vice-Marshal Sir Roderic.
Salmon, Edward, 1865–1955, vol. V
Salmon, Ven. Edwin Arthur, 1832–1899, vol. I

Salmon, Sir Eric Cecil Heygate, 1896–1946, vol. IV
Salmon, Frederick John, 1882–1964, vol. VI
Salmon, Geoffrey Isidore Hamilton, 1908–1990, vol. VIII
Salmon, Col Geoffrey Nowell, 1871–1954, vol. V
Salmon, Rev. George, 1819–1904, vol. I
Salmon, Rev. Preb. Harold Bryant, 1891–1965, vol. VI
Salmon, Harry, 1881–1950, vol. IV
Salmon, Sir Isidore, 1876–1941, vol. IV
Salmon, John Cuthbert, 1844–1917, vol. II
Salmon, Sir Julian, 1903–1978, vol. VII
Salmon, Dame Nancy Marion; *see* Snagge, Dame N.
Salmon, Neil Lawson, 1921–1989, vol. VIII
Salmon, Admiral of the Fleet Sir Nowell, 1835–1912, vol.I
Salmon, Percy R., 1872–1959, vol. V
Salmon, Air Vice-Marshal Sir Roderic, 1911–1985, vol. VIII
Salmon, Sir Samuel Isidore, 1900–1980, vol. VII
Salmon, Thomas David, 1916–1997, vol. X
Salmon, Col William Alexander, (Alec), 1910–2000, vol. X
Salmond, Air Chief Marshal Sir Geoffrey; *see* Salmond, Air Chief Marshal Sir W. G. H.
Salmond, Hubert George, 1889–1946, vol. IV
Salmond, Captain Hubert Mackenzie, 1874–1947, vol. IV
Salmond, Marshal of the Royal Air Force Sir John Maitland, 1881–1968, vol. VI
Salmond, Sir John William, 1862–1924, vol. II
Salmond, Robert Williamson Asher, 1883–1953, vol. V
Salmond, Rev. Stewart Dingwall Fordyce, 1838–1905, vol. I
Salmond, Rev. William, 1835–1917, vol. II
Salmond, Maj.-Gen. Sir William, 1840–1933, vol. III
Salmond, Air Chief Marshal Sir (William) Geoffrey (Hanson), 1878–1933, vol. III
Salmone, H. Anthony, 1860–1904, vol. I
Salomon, Sir Walter Hans, 1906–1987, vol. VIII
Salomons, Sir David Lionel Goldsmid-Stern-, 2nd Bt, 1851–1925, vol. II
Salomons, Hon. Sir Julian Emanuel, 1836–1909, vol. I
Saloway, Sir Reginald Harry, 1905–1959, vol. V
Salt, Sir Anthony Houlton, 6th Bt (*cr* 1869), 1931–1991, vol. IX
Salt, Dame Barbara, 1904–1975, vol. VII
Salt, Sir David Shirley, 5th Bt (*cr* 1869), 1930–1978, vol. VII
Salt, Sir Edward William, 1881–1970, vol. VI
Salt, Emmaline Juanita, 1910–1986, vol. VIII
Salt, Rev. Enoch, 1845–1919, vol. II
Salt, Maj.-Gen. Harold Francis, 1879–1971, vol. VII
Salt, Henry Edwin, *died* 1970, vol. VI
Salt, Henry Stephens, 1851–1939, vol. III
Salt, Sir John William Titus, 4th Bt (*cr* 1869), 1884–1953, vol. V
Salt, Sir Shirley Harris, 3rd Bt (*cr* 1869), 1857–1920, vol. II
Salt, Sir Thomas, 1st Bt (*cr* 1899), 1830–1904, vol. I

Salt, Sir Thomas Anderdon, 2nd Bt (*cr* 1899), 1863–1940, vol. III
Salt, Lt-Col Sir Thomas Henry, 3rd Bt (*cr* 1899), 1905–1965, vol. VI
Salter, 1st Baron, 1881–1975, vol. VII
Salter, Alfred, 1873–1945, vol. IV
Salter, Sir Arthur Clavell, 1859–1928, vol. II
Salter, Emma G.; *see* Gurney-Salter.
Salter, Frank Reyner, 1887–1967, vol. VI
Salter, Rev. Herbert Edward, 1863–1951, vol. V
Salter, Vice-Admiral Jocelyn Stuart Cambridge, 1901–1989, vol. VIII
Salter, Mortyn de Carle Sowerby, 1880–1923, vol. II
Salter Davies, Ernest, 1872–1955, vol. V
Salter Davies, Roy Dicker; *see* Davies.
Saltmarsh, Sir (Edward) George, 1869–1931, vol. III
Saltmarsh, Sir George; *see* Saltmarsh, Sir E. G.
Saltmarsh, John, 1848–1916, vol. II
Saltmarshe, Col Philip, 1853–1941, vol. IV
Saltoun, 18th Lord, 1851–1933, vol. III
Saltoun, 19th Lord, 1886–1979, vol. VII
Saltoun, Master of; Hon. Alexander Simon Fraser, 1921–1944, vol. IV
Saltus, Edgar Evertson, 1858–1921, vol. II
Saltzman, Charles Eskridge, 1903–1994, vol. IX
Salusbury, Charles Vanne, 1887–1969, vol. VI
Salusbury, Frederic George Hamilton Piozzi, 1895–1957, vol. V
Salusbury-Trelawny, Sir John William; *see* Trelawny.
Salusbury-Trelawny, Sir John William Robin Maurice; *see* Trelawny.
Salusbury-Trelawny, Sir William Lewis; *see* Trelawny.
Salvage, Sir Samuel Agar, 1876–1946, vol. IV
Salvemini, Gaetano, 1873–1957, vol. V
Salvesen, Rt Hon. Lord; Edward Theodore Salvesen, 1857–1942, vol. IV
Salvesen, Edward Theodore; *see* Rt Hon. Lord Salvesen.
Salvidge, Rt Hon. Sir Archibald Tutton James, 1863–1928, vol. II
Salvin, Gerard Thornton, 1878–1921, vol. II
Salvin, Henry; *see* Salvin, M. H.
Salvin, (Marmaduke) Henry, 1849–1924, vol. II
Salvin, Osbert, 1835–1898, vol. I
Salvini, Comdr Tommaso, *died* 1915, vol. I
Salwey, Rev. Herbert, 1842–1929, vol. III
Salwey, Rev. John, 1867–1943, vol. IV
Salzman, Louis Francis, 1878–1971, vol. VII
Samaldas, Sir Lalubhai, 1863–1936, vol. III
Samarth, Narayan Madhav, *died* 1926, vol. II
Sambell, Most Rev. Geoffrey Tremayne, 1914–1980, vol. VII
Sambon, Louis Westenra, *died* 1931, vol. III
Samborne-Palmer, Lt-Col Frederick Carey Stuckley, 1868–1950, vol. IV
Sambourne, Edward Linley, 1845–1910, vol. I
Sambrook, Gordon Hartley, 1930–1996, vol. X
Sambrook, Henry Fabian, 1886–1935, vol. III
Samman, Lt-Col Charles Thomas, 1865–1939, vol. III
Samman, Sir Henry, 1st Bt, 1849–1928, vol. II

Samman, Sir Henry, 2nd Bt, 1881–1960, vol. V
Samman, Peter Derrick, 1914–1992, vol. IX
Sammarco, Giuseppe Mario, 1873–1930, vol. III
Sammons, Albert E., 1886–1957, vol. V
Sammons, Herbert, 1896–1967, vol. VI
Sammut, Oscar, 1879–1959, vol. V
Sampayo, Sir Thomas Edward de, 1855–1927, vol. II
Sampson, Alexander Whitehead, 1859–1932, vol. III
Sampson, Col Sir Aubrey W.; *see* Wools-Sampson.
Sampson, Charles Henry, 1859–1936, vol. III
Sampson, Rev. Canon Christopher Bolckow, 1903–1967, vol. VI
Sampson, George, 1873–1950, vol. IV
Sampson, Rev. Gerald Victor, 1864–1928, vol. II
Sampson, Hon. Henry William, 1872–1938, vol. III
Sampson, Herbert E., 1871–1962, vol. VI
Sampson, Jack; *see* Sampson, Jacob Albert.
Sampson, Jacob Albert, (Jack Sampson), 1905–1976, vol. VII
Sampson, John, 1859–1925, vol. II
Sampson, Major Patrick, 1881–1922, vol. II
Sampson, Ralph Allen, 1866–1939, vol. III
Sampson, Hon. Victor, 1855–1940, vol. II, vol. III
Sampson, Rear Adm. William Thomas, 1840–1902, vol. I
Sampson-Way, Maj.-Gen. Nowell FitzUpton; *see* Way.
Sams, Sir Hubert Arthur, 1875–1957, vol. V
Samson, Col Arthur Oliver, 1888–1955, vol. V
Samson, Charles Leopold, 1853–1923, vol. II
Samson, Air Cdre Charles Rumney, 1883–1931, vol. III
Samson, Sir (Edward) Marlay, 1869–1949, vol. IV
Samson, Sir Frederick; *see* Samson, Sir W. F.
Samson, John, 1848–1905, vol. I
Samson, Lt-Col Louis Lort Rhys, 1866–1944, vol. IV
Samson, Sir Marlay; *see* Samson, Sir E. M.
Samson, Otto William, 1900–1976, vol. VII
Samson, Sir (William) Frederick, 1892–1974, vol. VII
Samthar, Maharaja of, 1865–1936, vol. III
Samuel, 1st Viscount, 1870–1963, vol. VI
Samuel, 2nd Viscount, 1898–1978, vol. VII
Samuel of Wych Cross, Baron (Life Peer); Harold Samuel, 1912–1987, vol. VIII
Samuel, Alexander L.; *see* Lyle-Samuel.
Samuel, Sir Edward Levien, 2nd Bt (*cr* (1898), 1862–1937, vol. III
Samuel, Sir Edward Louis, 3rd Bt (*cr* 1898), 1896–1961, vol. VI
Samuel, Col Frederick Dudley, 1877–1951, vol. V
Samuel, Harold, 1879–1937, vol. III
Samuel, Rt Hon. Sir Harry Simon, 1853–1934, vol. III
Samuel, Herbert Dawkin, 1904–1984, vol. VIII
Samuel, Howel Walter, 1881–1953, vol. V
Samuel, John Augustus, 1887–1965, vol. VI
Samuel, Sir John Oliver Cecil, 4th Bt (*cr* 1898), 1916–1962, vol. VI
Samuel, Sir John Smith, 1870–1934, vol. III
Samuel, Jonathan, 1853–1917, vol. II
Samuel, Marcus, 1873–1942, vol. IV
Samuel, Rev. Richard W.; *see* Wood-Samuel.

Samuel, Samuel, 1855–1934, vol. III
Samuel, Hon. Sir Saul, 1st Bt (*cr* 1898),
1820–1900, vol. I
Samuel, Sir Stuart Montagu, 1st Bt (*cr* 1912),
1856–1926, vol. II
Samuels, Rt Hon. Arthur Warren, 1852–1925, vol. II
Samuels, Albert Edward, 1900–1982, vol. VIII
Samuels, Sir Alexander, 1905–1986, vol. VIII
Samuels, Herbert David, 1880–1947, vol. IV
Samuels, Moss T.; *see* Turner-Samuels.
Samuelson, Berhard Martin, 1874–1921, vol. II
Samuelson, Rt Hon. Sir Bernhard, 1st Bt,
1820–1905, vol. I
Samuelson, Cecil Llewellyn, 1882–1950, vol. IV
Samuelson, Sir Francis, 3rd Bt, 1861–1946, vol. IV
Samuelson, Sir Francis Henry Bernard, 4th Bt,
1890–1981, vol. VIII
Samuelson, Godfrey Blundell, 1863–1941, vol. IV
Samuelson, Sir Henry Bernhard, 2nd Bt, 1845–1937,
vol. III
Samuelson, Sir Herbert, 1865–1952, vol. V
Samut, Lt-Col Achilles, 1859–1935, vol. III
Samwell, Ven. Frederick William, 1861–1925,
vol. II
San Giovanni, 12th Baron, 1866–1934, vol. III
San Giuliano, Antonino Paterno Castello, Marquis
of, 1852–1914, vol. I
San Vincenzo Ferreri, 8th Marquis, 1911–1988,
vol. IX (AI)
Sanchez-Gavito, Vicente, 1910–1976, vol. VII
Sanctuary, Rev. Charles Lloyd, 1854–1934, vol. III
Sand, Alec, 1901–1945, vol. IV
Sandall, Col Thomas Edward, 1869–1930, vol. III
Sandars, Lt-Col Edward Carew, 1869–1944, vol. IV
Sandars, George Edward Russell, 1901–1985,
vol. VIII
Sandars, John Drysdale, 1860–1922, vol. II
Sandars, John Eric William Graves, 1906–1974,
vol. VII
Sandars, Rt Hon. John Satterfield, 1853–1934,
vol. III
Sandars, Vice-Adm. Sir (Reginald) Thomas,
1904–1975, vol. VII
Sandars, Vice-Adm. Sir Thomas; *see* Sandars,
Vice-Adm. Sir R. T.
Sanday, Rev. William, 1843–1920, vol. II
Sandbach, Maj.-Gen. Arthur Edmund, 1859–1928,
vol. II
Sandbach, Francis Edward, 1874–1946, vol. IV
Sandbach, (Francis) Henry, 1903–1991, vol. IX
Sandbach, Henry; *see* Sandbach, F. H.
Sandbach, John Brown, *died* 1951, vol. V
Sandberg, Christer Peter, 1876–1941, vol. IV
Sandberg, Nils Percy Patrick, 1881–1934, vol. III
Sandbrook, John Arthur, 1876–1942, vol. IV
Sandburg, Carl, 1878–1967, vol. VI
Sandeman, Albert George, 1833–1923, vol. II
Sandeman, Christopher, 1882–1951, vol. V
Sandeman, Condie, 1866–1933, vol. III
Sandeman, Col Donald George, 1884–1965, vol. VI
Sandeman, Edward, 1862–1959, vol. V
Sandeman, Rear-Adm. Henry George Glas,
1868–1928, vol. II
Sandeman, John Glas, 1836–1921, vol. II

Sandeman, Sir Nairne Stewart, 1st Bt, 1876–1940,
vol. III
Sanders, Alan, 1878–1969, vol. VI
Sanders, Air Chief Marshal Sir Arthur Penrose
Martyn, 1898–1974, vol. VII
Sanders, Rev. Charles Evatt, 1846–1927, vol. II
Sanders, Sir Charles John Ough, 1865–1938, vol. III
Sanders, Christopher Cavania, 1905–1991, vol. IX
Sanders, Sir Edgar Christian, 1871–1942, vol. IV
Sanders, Rev. Ernest Arthur Blackwell, 1858–1917,
vol. II
Sanders, Ven. Frederick Arthur, 1856–1930, vol. III
Sanders, Brig. Geoffrey Percival, 1880–1952, vol. V
Sanders, Brig. Gen. George Herbert, 1868–1935,
vol. III
Sanders, Brig.-Gen. Gerard Arthur Fletcher,
1869–1941, vol. IV
Sanders, Col Gilbert Edward, 1863–1955, vol. V
Sanders, Sir Harold George, 1898–1985, vol. VIII
Sanders, Henry Arthur, 1868–1956, vol. V (A),
vol. VI (AI)
Sanders, Rev. Henry Martyn, 1869–1963, vol. VI
Sanders, Rev. Canon Henry S., 1864–1920, vol. II
Sanders, Sir John Owen, 1892–1954, vol. V
Sanders, Sir Percy Alan, 1881–1962, vol. VI
Sanders, Rev. S. J. W., 1846–1915, vol. I
Sanders, Terence Robert Beaumont, 1901–1985,
vol. VIII
Sanders, Thomas W., 1855–1926, vol. II
Sanders, Engr Rear-Adm. William Cory,
1868–1933, vol. III
Sanders, Captain William Stephen, 1871–1941,
vol. IV
Sanderson, 1st Baron (*cr* 1905), 1841–1923, vol. II
Sanderson, 1st Baron (*cr* 1930), 1868–1939, vol. III
Sanderson of Ayot, 1st Baron, 1894–1971, vol. VII
Sanderson, Air Marshal Sir (Alfred) Clifford,
1898–1976, vol. VII
Sanderson, Lt-Col Aymor Eden, 1886–1932, vol. III
Sanderson, Sir Bryan; *see* Sanderson, Sir F. P. B.
Sanderson, Sir Charles Claxton, 1864–1929, vol. III
Sanderson, Air Marshal Sir Clifford; *see* Sanderson,
Air Marshal Sir A. C.
Sanderson, Rev. Edward, *died* 1930, vol. III
Sanderson, Rev. Edward Manners, 1847–1932,
vol. III
Sanderson, Sir Frank Bernard, 1st Bt, 1880–1965,
vol. VI
Sanderson, Sir (Frank Philip) Bryan, 2nd Bt,
1910–1992, vol. IX
Sanderson, Frederick William, 1857–1922, vol. II
Sanderson, Harold Arthur, *died* 1932, vol. III
Sanderson, Sir Harold Leslie, 1890–1966, vol. VI
Sanderson, Col Henry Bristow, 1840–1915, vol. I
Sanderson, Sir John, 1868–1945, vol. IV
Sanderson, John Ellerslie, 1922–1985, vol. VIII
Sanderson, Sir John Scott B.; *see*
Burdon-Sanderson.
Sanderson, Air Vice-Marshal Keith Fred,
1932–1994, vol. IX
Sanderson, Kenneth Francis Villiers, 1895–1973,
vol. VII
Sanderson, Rt Hon. Sir Lancelot, 1863–1944,
vol. IV
Sanderson, Captain Lancelot, 1889–1984, vol. VIII

Sanderson, Oswald, 1863–1926, vol. II
Sanderson, Sir Percy, 1842–1919, vol. II
Sanderson, Robert, 1881–1943, vol. IV
Sanderson, Rev. Robert Edward, 1828–1913, vol. I
Sanderson, Sibyl, 1865–1903, vol. I
Sanderson, Wilfrid Ernest, 1878–1935, vol. III
Sanderson, Rt Rev. Wilfrid Guy, 1905–1988, vol. VIII
Sanderson, William Allendale, 1913–1961, vol. VI
Sanderson, Col William Denziloe, 1868–1941, vol. IV
Sanderson, William Waite, 1868–1944, vol. IV
Sanderson-Wells, John Sanderson, 1872–1955, vol. V
Sanderson-Wells, Thomas Henry, 1871–1958, vol. V
Sandes, Alfred James Terence F.; see Fleming-Sandes.
Sandes, Lt-Col Edward Warren Caulfeild, 1880–1973, vol. VII
Sandes, Elise, 1851–1934, vol. III
Sandford, 1st Baron, 1887–1959, vol. V
Sandford, Arthur Wellesley, 1858–1939, vol. III
Sandford, Rt Rev. Charles Waldegrave, 1828–1903, vol. I
Sandford, Brig. Daniel Arthur, 1882–1972, vol. VII
Sandford, Ven. Ernest Grey, 1839–1910, vol. I
Sandford, Ven. Folliott George, 1861–1945, vol. IV
Sandford, Sir Folliott Herbert, 1906–1986, vol. VIII
Sandford, Captain Francis Hugh, 1887–1926, vol. II
Sandford, Brig. Francis Rossall, 1898–1962, vol. VI
Sandford, Sir George Ritchie, 1892–1950, vol. IV
Sandford, Herbert Henry, 1916–1999, vol. X
Sandford, Hon. Sir (James) Wallace, 1879–1958, vol. V
Sandford, Kenneth Stuart, 1899–1971, vol. VII
Sandford, Thomas Frederick, 1886–1963, vol. VI
Sandford, Hon. Sir Wallace; see Sandford, Hon. Sir J. W.
Sandford Smith, Richard Henry, 1909–2000, vol. X
Sandham, E., died 1944, vol. IV
Sandham, Henry, 1842–1910, vol. I
Sandhurst, 1st Viscount, 1855–1921, vol. II
Sandhurst, 3rd Baron, 1857–1933, vol. III
Sandhurst, 4th Baron, 1892–1964, vol. VI
Sandie, Brig. John Grey, 1897–1975, vol. VII
Sandiford, Charles Thomas, 1840–1919, vol. II
Sandiford, Peter, 1882–1941, vol. IV
Sandilands, Sir Francis Edwin Prescott, 1913–1995, vol. IX
Sandilands, George Sommerville, 1889–1961, vol. VI
Sandilands, Brig. Harold Richard, 1876–1961, vol. VI
Sandilands, Brig.-Gen. Henry George, 1864–1930, vol. III
Sandilands, Maj.-Gen. James Walter, 1874–1959, vol. V
Sandison, Sir Alfred, died 1906, vol. I
Sandlands, Paul Ernest, 1878–1962, vol. VI
Sandon, Frank, 1890–1979, vol. VII
Sandover, Sir (Alfred) Eric, 1897–1983, vol. VIII
Sandover, Sir Eric; see Sandover, Sir A. E.
Sandrey, John Gordon, 1903–1988, vol. VIII
Sands, Hon. Lord; Christopher Nicholson Johnston, 1857–1934, vol. III

Sands, Ven. Havilland Hubert Allport, 1896–1970, vol. VI
Sands, Rev. Hubert, 1855–1922, vol. II
Sands, Sir James Patrick, 1859–1925, vol. II
Sands, Percy Cooper, 1883–1971, vol. VII
Sands, Sir Stafford Lofthouse, 1913–1972, vol. VII
Sands, William Southgate, 1853–1924, vol. II
Sandwich, 8th Earl of, 1839–1916, vol. II
Sandwich, 9th Earl of, 1874–1962, vol. VI
Sandwich, 10th Earl of; see Montagu, A. V. E. P.
Sandwith, Fleming Mant, 1853–1918, vol. II
Sandwith, Major Ralph Leslie, 1859–1920, vol. II
Sandwith, Thomas Backhouse, 1831–1900, vol. I
Sandys, 4th Baron, 1840–1904, vol. I
Sandys, 5th Baron, 1855–1948, vol. IV
Sandys, 6th Baron, 1876–1961, vol. VI
Sandys, Duncan Edwin; see Baron Duncan-Sandys.
Sandys, Hon. Edmund Arthur Marcus, 1860–1914, vol. I
Sandys, Lt-Col Edward Seton, 1872–1953, vol. V
Sandys, Frederick, 1832–1904, vol. I
Sandys, Captain George John, 1875–1937, vol. III
Sandys, George Owen, 1884–1973, vol. VII
Sandys, Sir John Edwin, 1844–1922, vol. II
Sandys, Julian George Winston, 1936–1997, vol. X
Sandys, Oliver, died 1964, vol. VI
Sandys, Col Thomas Myles, 1837–1911, vol. I
Sandys, Brig.-Gen. William Bain Richardson, 1868–1946, vol. IV
Sandys-Lumsdaine, Edwin Robert John, 1864–1933, vol. III
Saner, Col John Arthur, 1864–1952, vol. V
Sanford, Col Edward Charles Ayshford, 1859–1923, vol. II
Sanford, Lt-Gen. George Edward Langham Somerset, 1840–1901, vol. I
Sangar, Owen Jermy, 1893–1972, vol. VII
Sanger, Sir Ernest, 1875–1939, vol. III
Sanger, Gerald Fountaine, 1898–1981, vol. VIII
Sanger, William, 1873–1948, vol. IV
Sangster, Sir Donald Burns, 1911–1967, vol. VI
Sangster, John Laing, 1922–1993, vol. IX
Sangster, John Young, 1896–1977, vol. VII
Sangster, Leith, died 1962, vol. VI
Sangster, Margaret Elizabeth, 1838–1912, vol. I
Sangster, Maj.-Gen. Patrick Barclay, 1872–1951, vol. V
Sangster, Rev. William Edwin Robert, 1900–1960, vol. V
Sanguinetti, Frederick Shedden, 1847–1906, vol. I
Sanjiva Row, Kodikal, 1890–1951, vol. V
Sankaran Nair, Sir Chettur, 1857–1934, vol. III
Sankey, 1st Viscount, 1866–1948, vol. IV
Sankey, Guy Richard, 1944–2000, vol. X
Sankey, Col Harold Bantock, 1895–1954, vol. V
Sankey, Ira David, 1840–1908, vol. I
Sankey, Captain Matthew Henry Phineas Riall, 1853–1925, vol. III
Sankey, Sir Richard Hieram, 1829–1908, vol. I
Sankey, Col Sir Stuart, 1854–1940, vol. III
Sansar Chandra Sen, Rao Bahadur, 1846–1909, vol. I
Sansbury, Rt Rev. (Cyril) Kenneth, 1905–1993, vol. IX

Sansbury, Rev. Canon Graham Rogers, 1909–1980, vol. VII
Sansbury, Rt Rev. Kennth; see Sansbury, Rt Rev. C. K.
Sansom, Andrew William, 1937–1992, vol. IX
Sansom, Arthur Ernest, 1838–1907, vol. I
Sansom, Col Charles Henry, 1886–1949, vol. IV
Sansom, Charles Lane, 1862–1951, vol. V
Sansom, Lt-Gen. Ernest William, born 1890, vol. VIII
Sansom, Sir George Bailey, 1883–1965, vol. VI
Sansom, George Samuel, 1888–1980, vol. VII
Sansom, William, 1912–1976, vol. VII
Sant, Raja of, 1881–1946, vol. IV
Sant, James, 1820–1916, vol. II
Sant, Captain Mowbray Lees, 1863–1943, vol. IV
Sant-Cassia, 7th Count, 1889–1947, vol. IV
Santa Cruz, Marqués de; José Fernandez Villaverde y Roca de Togores, 1902–1988, vol. VIII
Santa Cruz, Victor Rafael Andrés, 1913–1990, vol. VIII
Santayana, George, 1863–1952, vol. V
Santi, Philip Robert William de, died 1942, vol. IV
Santley, Sir Charles, 1834–1922, vol. II
Santos-Dumont, Alberto, 1873–1932, vol. III
Sao, Sir Moung, 1847–1926, vol. II
Sao Kin Maung, 1883–1936, vol. III
Sapara-Williams, Hon. Christopher Alexander, 1854–1915, vol. II
Sapellnikoff, Wassily, 1868–1941, vol. IV (A), vol. V
Sapper; see McNeile, Lt-Col Cyril.
Sapper, Laurence Joseph, 1922–1989, vol. VIII
Sapru, Rt Hon. Sir Tej Bahadur, died 1949, vol. IV
Sapsworth, Captain Charles Howard, 1883–1958, vol. V
Sapte, Ven. John Henry, 1821–1906, vol. I
Sara, Rt Rev. Edmund Willoughby, 1891–1965, vol. VI
Saragat, Giuseppe, 1898–1988, vol. VIII
Sarajčič, Ivo, 1915–1994, vol. IX
Sarasate, Pablo Martin Meliton de, 1844–1908, vol. I
Saravanamuttu, Sir Ratnajoti, died 1949, vol. IV
Sarawak, Rajah of, 1829–1917, vol. II
Sarawak, Rajah of; see Brooke, Sir C. V.
Sarawak, HH Ranee Margaret Alice Lilly of, died 1936, vol. III
Sarbah, John Mensah, 1864–1910, vol. I
Sardou, Victorien, 1831–1908, vol. I
Sarel, Rear-Adm. Colin Alfred Molyneux, 1880–1954, vol. V
Sarel, Col George Benedict Molyneux, died 1953, vol. V
Sarel, Rev. Sydney Lancaster, died 1950, vol. IV
Sarel, William Samuel, 1861–1933, vol. III
Sarell, Philip Charles, 1866–1942, vol. IV
Sargan, John Denis, 1924–1996, vol. X
Sargant, Rt Hon. Sir Charles Henry, 1856–1942, vol. IV
Sargant, Sir Edmund; see Sargant, Sir H. E.
Sargant, Sir (Henry) Edmund, 1906–1998, vol. X
Sargant, Ethel, 1863–1918, vol. II
Sargant, Thomas, 1905–1988, vol. VIII
Sargant, Walter Lee, died 1956, vol. V

Sargant, William Walters, 1907–1988, vol. VIII
Sargant-Florence, Mary, 1857–1954, vol. V
Sargeant, Sir Alfred Read, 1873–1949, vol. IV
Sargeaunt, Bertram Edward, 1877–1978, vol. VII
Sargeaunt, Henry Anthony, 1907–1997, vol. X
Sargeaunt, John, 1857–1922, vol. II
Sargeaunt, Margaret Joan, 1903–1978, vol. VII
Sargent, Rev. Canon Alexander, 1895–1989, vol. VIII
Sargent, Arthur J., 1871–1947, vol. IV
Sargent, Sir Charles, 1821–1900, vol. I
Sargent, Rt Rev. Christopher Birdwood Roussel, 1906–1943, vol. IV
Sargent, Sir Donald; see Sargent, Sir S. D.
Sargent, Rt Rev. Douglas Noel, 1907–1979, vol. VII
Sargent, Sir Frank Leyden, 1871–1940, vol. III
Sargent, Sir (Harold) Orme (Garton), 1884–1962, vol. VI
Sargent, Maj.-Gen. Harry Neptune, 1866–1946, vol. IV
Sargent, Sir (Henry) Malcolm (Watts), 1895–1967, vol. VI
Sargent, Very Rev. John Paine, 1838–1919, vol. II
Sargent, Sir John Philip, 1888–1972, vol. VII
Sargent, John Singer, 1856–1925, vol. II
Sargent, Sir Malcolm; see Sargent, Sir H. M. W.
Sargent, Sir Orme; see Sargent, Sir H. O. G.
Sargent, Sir Percy, 1873–1933, vol. III
Sargent, Sir (Sidney) Donald, 1906–1984, vol. VIII
Sargison, Phillip Harold, 1920–1989, vol. VIII
Sargood, Hon. Lt-Col Sir Frederick Thomas, 1834–1903, vol. I
Sargood, Lilian Mary, 1879–1945, vol. IV
Sargood, Sir Percy Rolfe, 1865–1940, vol. III
Sargood, Richard, 1888–1979, vol. VII
Sarila, Maharaja of, 1898–1983, vol. VIII
Sarjant, Reginald Josiah, died 1965, vol. VI
Sarjeant, Frederick Arthur, 1861–1933, vol. III
Sark, Dame of; see Hathaway, Dame S. M.
Sarkar, Sir Jadunath, 1870–1958, vol. V
Sarkodee-Adoo, Julius, 1908–1971, vol. VII
Sarl, Arthur J., died 1946, vol. IV
Sarle, Sir Allen Lanyon, 1828–1903, vol. I
Sarle, Charles Spenser, died 1936, vol. III
Sarma, Rao Bahadur Sir Bayya N.; see Narasimha Sarma.
Sarma, Sir (Ramaswami) Srinivasa, 1890–1957, vol. V
Sarma, Sir Srinivasa; see Sarma, Sir R. S.
Sarnoff, David, 1891–1971, vol. VII
Sarolea, Charles, 1870–1953, vol. V
Saroyan, William, 1908–1981, vol. VIII
Sarrailh, Jean, 1891–1964, vol. VI
Sarraute, Nathalie, 1900–1999, vol. X
Sarsfield-Hall, Edwin Geoffrey, 1886–1975, vol. VII
Sarson, Col John Edward, 1844–1940, vol. III
Sarto, Giuseppe; see Pius X.
Sartoris, Alfred Urbain, 1826–1909, vol. I
Sartoris, Francis Charles, 1857–1923, vol. II
Sartorius, Maj.-Gen. Euston Henry, 1844–1925, vol. II
Sartorius, Col George, 1840–1912, vol. I
Sartorius, Maj.-Gen. Reginald William, 1841–1907, vol. I
Sartre, Jean-Paul, 1905–1980, vol. VII

Sarup, Anand, HH Sahabji Maharaj Sir, 1881–1937, vol. III
Sarvadhikary, Sir Deva Prasad, 1862–1935, vol. III
Sarzano, 11th Marquis of, 1847–1920, vol. II
Sasse, Captain Cecil Duncan, 1891–1934, vol. III
Sassoon, Arthur Abraham David, 1840–1912, vol. I
Sassoon, Sir Edward Albert, 2nd Bt (*cr* 1890), 1856–1912, vol. I
Sassoon, Sir Edward Elias, 2nd Bt (*cr* 1909), 1853–1924, vol. II
Sassoon, Sir (Ellice) Victor, 3rd Bt (*cr* 1909), 1881–1961, vol. VI
Sassoon, Eugenie Louise Judith, 1854–1943, vol. IV
Sassoon, Sir Jacob Elias, 1st Bt (*cr* 1909), 1844–1916, vol. II
Sassoon, Joseph S., 1855–1918, vol. II
Sassoon, Meyer Elias, 1855–1924, vol. II
Sassoon, Rt Hon. Sir Philip Albert Gustave David, 3rd Bt (*cr* 1890), 1888–1939, vol. III
Sassoon, Siegfried, 1886–1967, vol. VI
Sassoon, Sir Victor; *see* Sassoon, Sir E. V.
Sastri, Sir Calamur Viravalli Kumaraswami, 1870–1934, vol. III
Sastri, Rt Hon. Valangiman Sankaranarayana Srinivasa, 1869–1946, vol. IV
Satchell, Edward William John, 1916–1998, vol. X
Sato, Eisaku, 1901–1975, vol. VII (AII)
Satow, Rt Hon. Sir Ernest Mason, 1843–1929, vol. III
Satow, Sir Harold Eustace, 1876–1969, vol. VI
Satow, Hugh Ralph, 1877–1967, vol. VI
Satow, Captain Lawrence de W., 1865–1948, vol. IV
Satow, Samuel Augustus Mason, 1847–1925, vol. II
Satterlee, Rt Rev. Henry Yates, 1843–1908, vol. I
Satterly, Air Vice-Marshal Harold Vivian, 1907–1982, vol. VIII
Satterly, John, 1879–1963, vol. VI
Satterthwaite, Rev. Charles James, 1834–1910, vol. I
Satterthwaite, Lt-Col Clement Richard, 1884–1953, vol. V
Satterthwaite, Col Edward, 1857–1932, vol. III
Satterthwaite, Lt-Col Richard George, 1920–1993, vol. IX
Sauber, Robert, 1868–1936, vol. III
Saudi Arabia, HM King of, 1905–1975, vol. VII
Sauer, Hon. J. W., *died* 1913, vol. I
Sauerwein, Jules Auguste, 1880–1967, vol. VI
Saugman, Christian Ditlev Trappaud, 1895–1976, vol. VII
Saul, Bazil Sylvester W.; *see* Wingate-Saul.
Saul, Sir Ernest Wingate W.; *see* Wingate-Saul.
Saul, Air Vice-Marshal Richard Ernest, *died* 1965, vol. VI
Saulles, G. W. de, *died* 1903, vol. I
Saumarez, Lt-Col Richard James, 1864–1943, vol. IV
Saundby, Robert, 1849–1918, vol. II
Saundby, Air Marshal Sir Robert Henry Magnus Spencer, 1896–1971, vol. VII
Saunders, Col Alan, 1886–1964, vol. VI
Saunders, Sir Alan Arthur, *died* 1957, vol. V
Saunders, Sir Alexander Morris C.; *see* Carr-Saunders.

Saunders, Arthur Leslie, 1862–1935, vol. III
Saunders, Basil, 1925–1998, vol. X
Saunders, Benjamin James, 1856–1938, vol. III
Saunders, Lt-Col Cecil Howie, 1881–1954, vol. V
Saunders, Sir Charles Edward, 1867–1937, vol. III
Saunders, Sir Charles James Renault, 1857–1931, vol. III
Saunders, Rt Rev. Charles John Godfrey, 1888–1973, vol. VII
Saunders, Christopher Thomas, 1907–2000, vol. X
Saunders, Lt-Col Cyril, 1875–1935, vol. III
Saunders, Edward, 1848–1910, vol. I
Saunders, Captain Edward Aldbrough, 1873–1934, vol. III
Saunders, Edward Arthur, 1866–1947, vol. IV
Saunders, Sir Edwin, 1814–1901, vol. I
Saunders, Major Frederick John, 1876–1916, vol. II
Saunders, Sir Frederick Richard, 1838–1910, vol. I
Saunders, George, 1823–1913, vol. I
Saunders, George, 1859–1922, vol. II
Saunders, Major George Frederick Cullen, 1869–1934, vol. III
Saunders, Sir George Rice P.; *see* Pryse-Saunders.
Saunders, Captain Harold Cecil Rich, 1882–1919, vol. II
Saunders, Sir Harold Leonard, 1885–1965, vol. VI
Saunders, Ven. Harry Patrick, 1913–1967, vol. VI
Saunders, Henry George Boulton, 1914–1984, vol. VIII
Saunders, Hilary Aidan St George, 1898–1951, vol. V
Saunders, Howard, 1835–1907, vol. I
Saunders, Air Chief Marshal Sir Hugh William Lumsden, 1894–1987, vol. VIII
Saunders, John O'Brien, *died* 1903, vol. I
Saunders, John Tennant, 1888–1965, vol. VI
Saunders, Maj.-Gen. Kenneth, 1920–1994, vol. IX
Saunders, Maj.-Gen. Macan, 1884–1956, vol. V
Saunders, Margaret B.; *see* Baillie-Saunders.
Saunders, Margaret Marshall, 1861–1947, vol. IV
Saunders, Michael Lawrence, 1944–1996, vol. X
Saunders, Sir Owen Alfred, 1904–1993, vol. IX
Saunders, Reginald George Francis, 1882–1947, vol. IV
Saunders, Col Robert Joseph Pratt, 1841–1908, vol. I
Saunders, Samuel Edgar, 1857–1933, vol. III
Saunders, Thomas Bailey, 1860–1928, vol. II
Saunders, Rev. Thomas Bekenn Avening, 1870–1950, vol. IV
Saunders, William, 1836–1914, vol. I
Saunders-Davies, Rt Rev. David Henry, 1894–1975, vol. VII
Saunders-Jacobs, Brig. John Conrad, 1900–1986, vol. VIII
Saunders-Pryse, Sir Pryse Loveden, 5th Bt, 1896–1962, vol. VI
Saunderson, Col Rt Hon. Edward James, 1837–1906, vol. I
Saurat, Denis, 1890–1958, vol. V
Sausmarez, Sir Havilland Walter de, 1st Bt, 1861–1941, vol. IV
Sauter, George, 1866–1937, vol. III
Sauve, Hon. Arthur, 1875–1944, vol. IV

Sauvé, Rt Hon. Jeanne Mathilde, 1922–1993, vol. IX
Sauveur, Albert, 1863–1939, vol. III
Sauzier, Anatole, 1849–1920, vol. II, vol. III
Sauzier, Sir (André) Guy, 1910–1998, vol. X
Sauzier, Sir Guy; see Sauzier, Sir A. G.
Sava, George, (George Alexis Milkomanovich Milkomane), 1903–1996, vol. X
Savage, Albert Walter, 1898–1993, vol. IX
Savage, Sir Alfred William Lungley, 1903–1980, vol. VII
Savage, Anthony, 1920–1989, vol. VIII
Savage, Col Arthur Johnson, 1874–1933, vol. III
Savage, Sir (Edward) Graham, 1886–1981, vol. VIII
Savage, Rev. Edwin Sidney, 1862–1947, vol. IV
Savage, Ernest A., 1877–1966, vol. VI
Savage, Rev. Canon Ernest Bickersteth, 1849–1915, vol. I
Savage, Rev. Francis Forbes, died 1932, vol. III
Savage, Sir Geoffrey Herbert, 1893–1953, vol. V
Savage, Sir George Henry, 1842–1921, vol. II
Savage, Col George Robert Rollo, 1849–1930, vol. III
Savage, Rt Rev. Gordon David, 1915–1990, vol. VIII
Savage, Sir Graham; see Savage, Sir E. G.
Savage, Henry, 1854–1912, vol. I
Savage, Very Rev. Henry Edwin, died 1939, vol. III
Savage, John Percival, 1895–1970, vol. VI
Savage, Rt Hon. Michael Joseph, 1872–1940, vol. III
Savage, Lt-Col Morris Boscawen, 1879–1958, vol. V
Savage, Raymond, 1884–1964, vol. VI
Savage, Rt Rev. Thomas Joseph, 1900–1966, vol. VI
Savage, Sir William George, 1872–1961, vol. VI
Savage, Col William Henry, 1863–1951, vol. V
Savage-Armstrong, Major Francis Savage Nesbitt, 1880–1917, vol. II
Savage-Armstrong, George Francis, 1845–1906, vol. I
Savary, Alfred William, 1831–1918, vol. II
Savary, Ven. T. W., 1878–1948, vol. IV
Savatard, Louis Charles Arthur, 1874–1962, vol. VI
Savery, Frank, 1883–1965, vol. VI
Savery, Sir S. Servington, died 1938, vol. III
Savi, Ethel Winifred, died 1954, vol. V
Savige, Lt-Gen. Sir Stanley George, 1890–1954, vol. V
Savile, 2nd Baron, 1853–1931, vol. III
Savile, Lady Anne; see Loewenstein-Wertheim, HSH Princess.
Savile, Brig. Clare Ruxton Uvedale, 1881–1949, vol. IV
Savile, Rev. E. S. Gordon, 1866–1937, vol. III
Savile, Hon. George, 1871–1937, vol. III
Savile, Bt Col George Walter Wrey, 1860–1936, vol. III
Savile, Col Henry Bourchier Osborne, 1819–1917, vol. II
Savile, Sir Leopold Halliday, 1870–1953, vol. V
Savile, Robert Stewart, 1863–1945, vol. IV
Savile, Lt-Col Robert Vesey, 1873–1947, vol. IV
Savile, Brig.-Gen. Walter Clare, 1857–1928, vol. II

Savill, Agnes Forbes, 1875–1964, vol. VI
Savill, Lt-Col Alfred Cecil, 1897–1943, vol. IV
Savill, Sir Edwin, 1868–1947, vol. IV
Savill, Sir Eric Humphrey, 1895–1980, vol. VII
Savill, Ven. Leonard, 1869–1959, vol. V
Savill, Lt-Col Sydney Rowland, 1891–1967, vol. VI
Savill, Thomas Dixon, 1856–1910, vol. I
Saville, (Leonard) Malcolm, 1901–1982, vol. VIII
Saville, Malcolm; see Saville, L. M.
Savin, Lewis Herbert, 1901–1983, vol. VIII
Savorgnan, Count de; see Brazza, P. P. F. C. de.
Savory, Rev. Sir Borradaile, 2nd Bt, 1855–1906, vol. I
Savory, Sir Douglas Lloyd, 1878–1969, vol. VI
Savory, Rev. Edmund, died 1912, vol. I
Savory, Vice-Adm. Herbert Whitmore, 1857–1918, vol. II
Savory, Sir Joseph, 1st Bt, 1843–1921, vol. II
Savory, Major Kenneth Stevens, 1894–1939, vol. III
Savory, Lt-Gen. Sir Reginald Arthur, 1894–1980, vol. VII
Savory, Sir Reginald Charles Frank, 1908–1989, vol. VIII
Savory, Sir William Borradaile, 3rd Bt, 1882–1961, vol. VI
Saw, Hon. Athelstan John Henton, 1868–1929, vol. III
Saw, Ruth Lydia, 1901–1986, vol. VIII
Sawantwadi, Raja of, 1897–1937, vol. III
Saward, Maj.-Gen. Michael Henry, 1840–1928, vol. II
Saward, Sidney Carman, 1889–1967, vol. VI
Sawbridge, Henry Raywood, 1907–1990, vol. VIII
Sawbridge, Rear-Adm. Henry Richard, 1885–1956, vol. V
Sawbridge, Rev. John Sikes, died 1925, vol. II
Sawers, Maj.-Gen. James Maxwell, 1920–1988, vol. VIII
Sawers, Maj.-Gen. Max; see Sawers, Maj.-Gen. J. M.
Sawicki, Roman Mieczyslaw, 1930–1990, vol. VIII
Sawistowski, Henryk, 1925–1984, vol. VIII
Sawkins, Harold, 1888–1957, vol. V
Sawle, Sir Charles Brune Graves, 2nd Bt, 1816–1903, vol. I
Sawle, Sir Charles John Graves-, 4th Bt, 1851–1932, vol. III
Sawle, Col Sir Francis Aylmer Graves, 3rd Bt, 1849–1903, vol. I
Sawrey-Cookson, Sydney Spencer, 1876–1933, vol. III
Sawyer, Charles, 1887–1979, vol. VII
Sawyer, Col Charles Edward, 1848–1931, vol. III
Sawyer, Ethel V.; see Vaughan-Sawyer.
Sawyer, George Alexander, died 1944, vol. IV
Sawyer, Rev. Harold Athelstane Parry, 1865–1939, vol. III
Sawyer, Maj.-Gen. Henry Thomas, 1871–1955, vol. V
Sawyer, Sir James, 1844–1919, vol. II
Sawyer, James Edward Hill, 1874–1953, vol. V
Sawyer, John Stanley, 1916–2000, vol. X
Sawyer, Maj.-Gen. Richard Henry Stewart, 1857–1926, vol. II
Sawyer, Robert Henry, 1832–1905, vol. I

Sawyer, Sir William Phillips, 1844–1908, vol. I
Sawyerr, Rev. Canon Harry Alphonso Ebun, 1909–1986, vol. VIII
Saxby, Jessie Margaret Edmondston, 1842–1940, vol. III (A), vol. IV
Saxe-Weimar, HH Prince (William Augustus) Edward of, 1823–1902, vol. I
Saxl, Fritz, 1890–1948, vol. IV
Saxon Snell, Alfred Walter, 1860–1949, vol. IV
Saxton, John Arthur, 1914–1980, vol. VII
Saxton, Rev. William Isaac, 1891–1975, vol. VII
Sayce, Rev. Archibald Henry, 1845–1933, vol. III
Sayce, Col George Edward, 1857–1940, vol. III
Sayce, George Ethelbert, 1875–1953, vol. V
Saye and Sele, 17th (styled 14th) Baron, 1830–1907, vol. I
Saye and Sele, 18th Baron, 1858–1937, vol. III
Saye and Sele, 19th Baron, 1884–1949, vol. IV
Saye and Sele, 20th Baron, 1885–1968, vol. VI
Saye, Air Vice-Marshal Geoffrey Ivon Laurence, 1907–1959, vol. V
Sayer, Brig. Arthur Penrice, 1885–1962, vol. VI
Sayer, Ettie, *died* 1923, vol. II
Sayer, Vice-Adm. Sir Guy Bourchier, 1903–1985, vol. VIII
Sayer, Captain Humphrey, 1889–1943, vol. IV
Sayer, Captain Maxwell Barcham, 1874–1928, vol. II
Sayers, Dorothy Leigh, 1893–1957, vol. V
Sayers, Sir Edward George, 1902–1985, vol. VIII
Sayers, Eric Colin, 1916–1991, vol. IX
Sayers, Sir Frederick, 1885–1977, vol. VII
Sayers, James, 1912–1993, vol. IX
Sayers, John Edward, 1911–1969, vol. VI
Sayers, Dame Lucile Newell, *died* 1959, vol. V
Sayers, (Matthew Herbert) Patrick, 1908–2000, vol. X
Sayers, Patrick; *see* Sayers, M. H. P.
Sayers, Richard Sidney, 1908–1989, vol. VIII
Sayers, William Charles Berwick, 1881–1960, vol. V
Sayle, Robert, 1889–1971, vol. VII
Sayles, George Osborne, 1901–1994, vol. IX
Saywell, Rev. Preb. George Frederick, 1882–1956, vol. V
Sbarretti, His Eminence Cardinal Donatus, 1856–1939, vol. III
Scaddan, Hon. John, 1876–1934, vol. III
Scadding, Rt Rev. Charles, 1861–1914, vol. I
Scadding, John Guyett, 1907–1999, vol. X
Scafe, Gen. Charles, 1844–1918, vol. II
Scafe, Lt-Col William Ernest, 1878–1951, vol. V
Scales, Francis Shillington, *died* 1927, vol. II
Scallan, Eugene Kevin, 1893–1966, vol. VI
Scallon, Gen. Sir Robert Irvin, 1857–1939, vol. III
Scammell, Lt-Col Alfed George, 1878–1941, vol. IV
Scamp, Sir (Athelstan) Jack, 1913–1977, vol. VII
Scamp, Sir Jack; *see* Scamp, Sir A. J.
Scanlan, Most Rev. Mgr James Donald, 1899–1976, vol. VII
Scanlan, Thomas, *died* 1930, vol. III
Scanlen, Hon. Sir Thomas Charles, 1834–1912, vol. I
Scannell, Rev. Thomas Bartholomew, 1854–1917, vol. II

Scaramanga-Ralli, Constantine, 1854–1934, vol. III
Scarborough, Harold, 1909–1988, vol. VIII
Scarbrough, 10th Earl of, 1857–1945, vol. IV
Scarbrough, 11th Earl of, 1896–1969, vol. VI
Scarbrough, John Impey, 1846–1929, vol. III
Scarfe, Francis Harold, 1911–1986, vol. VIII
Scarff, Robert Wilfred, 1899–1970, vol. VI
Scarfoglio, Carlo, 1887–1969, vol. VI
Scarisbrick, Sir Charles, 1839–1923, vol. II
Scarisbrick, Sir Everard Talbot, 2nd Bt, 1896–1955, vol. V
Scarisbrick, Sir Tom Talbot Leyland, 1st Bt, 1874–1933, vol. III
Scarles, Sir Edward John, 1871–1947, vol. IV
Scarlett, Air Vice-Marshal Francis Rowland, 1875–1934, vol. III
Scarlett, Maj.-Gen. Hon. Gerald, 1885–1957, vol. V
Scarlett, Lt-Col Henry A.; *see* Ashley-Scarlett.
Scarlett, Lt-Col James Alexander, 1877–1925, vol. II
Scarlett, Hon. John Leopold Campbell, 1916–1994, vol. IX
Scarlett, Sir Peter William Shelley Yorke, 1905–1987, vol. VIII
Scarr, John Geoffrey Fearnley, 1910–1982, vol. VIII
Scarsdale, 2nd Viscount, 1898–1977, vol. VII
Scarsdale, 3rd Viscount, 1924–2000, vol. X
Scarsdale, 4th Baron, 1831–1916, vol. II
Scarth, Sir Charles, 1846–1921, vol. II
Scarth of Breckness, Col Henry William, 1899–1972, vol. VII
Scarth, Rev. John, 1826–1909, vol. I
Scarth, Lt-Col Robert, 1894–1966, vol. VI
Scatcherd, Felicia Rudolphina, *died* 1927, vol. II
Sceales, Col George Adinston M'Laren, 1878–1956, vol. V
Scebarras, Sir Fillipo, *died* 1928, vol. II
Scerri, Arthur J., 1921–1980, vol. VII
Schacht, Hjalmar Horace Greely, 1877–1970, vol. VI
Schacht, Joseph, 1902–1969, vol. VI
Schaeffer, Claude Frederic Armand, 1898–1982, vol. VIII
Schafer, Sir Edward Albert S.; *see* Sharpey-Schafer.
Schafer, Edward Peter S.; *see* Sharpey-Schafer.
Schalch, Col Vernon Ansdell, 1849–1935, vol. III
Schapiro, Leonard Bertram, 1908–1983, vol. VIII
Schapiro, Meyer, 1904–1996, vol. X
Schärf, Adolf, 1890–1965, vol. VI
Scharff, Robert Francis, 1858–1934, vol. III
Scharlieb, Dame Mary Ann Dacomb, 1845–1930, vol. III
Scharrer, Irene, *died* 1971, vol. VII
Schaw, Maj.-Gen. Henry, 1829–1902, vol. I
Schawlow, Arthur Leonard, 1921–1999, vol. X
Schechter, Solomon, *died* 1915, vol. I
Schelfhaut, Mgr Philip, 1850–1921, vol. II
Schelling, Ernest, *died* 1939, vol. III
Schembri, Carmelo, 1922–1997, vol. X
Scherer, Jacques, 1912–1997, vol. X
Scherger, Air Chief Marshal Sir Frederick Rudolph Williams, 1904–1984, vol. VIII
Schermbrucker, Lt-Col Hon. Frederic, *died* 1904, vol. I

Schiaparelli, Mme Elsa, *died* 1975, vol. VII
Schick, Béla, 1877–1967, vol. VI
Schierwater, Harry Turner, 1876–1952, vol. V
Schiff, Sir Ernest Frederick, 1840–1918, vol. II
Schild, Heinz Otto, 1906–1984, vol. VIII
Schiller, Ferdinand Canning Scott, 1864–1937, vol. III
Schiller, Ferdinand Philip Maximilian, 1868–1946, vol. IV
Schiller, Karl, 1911–1994, vol. IX
Schilling, Richard Selwyn Francis, 1911–1997, vol. X
Schilsky, Eric, 1898–1974, vol. VII
Schindler, Gen. Albert Houtum, *died* 1916, vol. II
Schipa, Tito, 1890–1965, vol. VI
Schlapp, Otto, 1859–1939, vol. III
Schlapp, Walter, 1898–1966, vol. VI
Schlesinger, Arthur Meier, 1888–1965, vol. VI
Schlesinger, Bernard Edward, 1896–1984, vol. VIII
Schlesinger, Frank, 1871–1943, vol. IV
Schleswig-Holstein, HH Major Prince Christian Victor of, 1867–1900, vol. I
Schleswig-Holstein, HRH Gen. Prince Frederick Christian Charles Augustus of, 1831–1917, vol. II
Schletter, Col Percy, 1855–1922, vol. II
Schley, Rear-Adm. Winfield Scott, 1839–1911, vol. I
Schlich, Sir William, 1840–1925, vol. II
Schlink, Sir Herbert Henry, 1883–1962, vol. VI
Schloesser, C. W. Adolph, 1830–1913, vol. I
Schmidt, Carl Friedrich, 1875–1948, vol. IV
Schmidt, Nathaniel, 1862–1939, vol. III (A), vol. IV
Schmidt-Isserstedt, Hans, 1900–1973, vol. VII
Schmiedel, Paul Wilhelm, 1851–1935, vol. III
Schmitt, Marchese Albert Félix; *see* Della Torre Alta.
Schmitt, Bernadotte Everly, 1886–1969, vol. VI
Schmitthoff, Clive Macmillan, 1903–1990, vol. VIII
Schmoller, Hans Peter, 1916–1985, vol. VIII
Schnabel, Artur, 1882–1951, vol. V
Schnadhorst, Francis, 1840–1900, vol. I
Schneider, Charles Eugene, 1868–1942, vol. IV
Schneider, Sir Gualterus Stewart, 1864–1938, vol. III
Schneider, Sir John William, 1824–1903, vol. I
Schneider, Rt Hon. Sir Lancelot Raymond A.; *see* Adams-Schneider.
Schnittke, Alfred, 1934–1998, vol. X
Schnyder, Félix, 1910–1992, vol. IX
Schober, Johannes, 1874–1932, vol. III
Schoenberg, Arnold; *see* Schönberg, A.
Schofield, Alfred, 1913–1994, vol. IX
Schofield, Alfred Norman, 1903–1973, vol. VII
Schofield, Alfred Taylor, 1846–1929, vol. III
Schofield, Bertram, 1896–1998, vol. X
Schofield, Vice-Adm. Brian Betham, 1895–1984, vol. VIII
Schofield, Rt Rev. Charles de Veber, 1871–1936, vol. III
Schofield, (Edward) Guy, 1902–1990, vol. VIII
Schofield, Lt-Col Frederick William, 1856–1949, vol. IV
Schofield, Guy; *see* Schofield, E. G.
Schofield, Lt-Col Harry Norton, 1865–1931, vol. III

Schofield, Herbert, 1883–1963, vol. VI
Schofield, Ivor Frederick Wentworth, 1904–1979, vol. VII
Schofield, J. W., *died* 1944, vol. IV
Schofield, Sidney, 1911–1992, vol. IX
Schofield, W. Elmer, 1867–1944, vol. IV
Schofield, Wentworth, 1891–1957, vol. V
Scholder, Charles Albert, 1861–1918, vol. II
Scholderer, (Julius) Victor, 1880–1971, vol. VII
Scholderer, Victor; *see* Scholderer, J. V.
Scholefield, Arthur, 1853–1930, vol. III
Scholefield, Charles Edward, 1902–1993, vol. IX
Scholefield, Guy Hardy, 1877–1963, vol. VI
Scholefield, Sir Joshua, *died* 1950, vol. IV
Scholes, Alwyn Denton, 1910–1997, vol. X
Scholes, Frank Victor Gordon, 1885–1954, vol. V
Scholes, G. E., *died* 1968, vol. VI
Scholes, Joseph, 1889–1983, vol. VIII
Scholes, Percy Alfred, 1877–1958, vol. V
Scholey, Harry, 1872–1945, vol. IV
Scholfield, Alwyn Faber, 1884–1969, vol. VI
Scholfield, Brig.-Gen. George Peabody, 1868–1952, vol. V
Scholte, Lieut-Col Frederick Lewellen, 1890–1984, vol. VIII
Schomberg, Rev. Edward St George, 1882–1952, vol. V
Schomberg, Gen. Sir George Augustus, 1821–1907, vol. I
Schomberg, Brig. Harold St George, 1886–1954, vol. V
Schomberg, Lt-Gen. Herbert St George, 1845–1915, vol. I
Schomberg, Col Reginald Charles Francis, *died* 1958, vol. V
Schon, Baron (Life Peer); Frank Schon, 1912–1995, vol. IX
Schönberg, Arnold, 1874–1951, vol. V
Schonell, Sir Fred Joyce, 1900–1969, vol. VI
Schöner, Josef A., 1904–1978, vol. VII
Schonland, Sir Basil Ferdinand Jamieson, 1896–1972, vol. VII
Schonland, Selmar, 1860–1940, vol. III
Schooles, Sir Henry Pipon, *died* 1913, vol. I
Schooling, Frederick, 1851–1936, vol. III
Schooling, John Holt, 1859–1927, vol. II
Schooling, Sir William, 1860–1936, vol. III
Schorr, Friedrich, 1888–1953, vol. V
Schorstein, Gustave, *died* 1906, vol. I
Schott, George Adolphus, 1868–1937, vol. III
Schotz, Benno, 1891–1984, vol. VIII
Schram, Emil, 1893–1987, vol. VIII
Schreiber, Col Acton Lemuel, 1865–1951, vol. V
Schreiber, Maj.-Gen. Brymer Francis, 1835–1907, vol. I
Schreiber, Sir Collingwood, 1831–1918, vol. II
Schreiber, Brig. Derek, 1904–1972, vol. VII
Schreiber, Lt-Gen. Sir Edmond Charles Acton, 1890–1972, vol. VII
Schreiber, Gaby, *died* 1991, vol. IX
Schreiber, Ricardo Rivera, 1892–1969, vol. VI
Schreiner, Olive Emilie Albertina, 1855–1920, vol. II
Schreiner, S. C. Cronwright; *see* Cronwright, S. C.

Schreiner, Rt Hon. William Philip, 1857–1919, vol. II
Schröder, Baron Bruno, 1867–1940, vol. III
Schroder, Ernest Melville, 1901–1993, vol. IX
Schroder, Helmut William Bruno, 1901–1969, vol. VI
Schröder, Sir John Henry William, 1st Bt, 1825–1910, vol. I
Schröder, Sir Walter, 1855–1942, vol. IV
Schroder, Captain William Henry, 1867–1945, vol. IV
Schrödinger, Erwin, 1887–1961, vol. VI
Schryver, Samuel Barnett, 1869–1929, vol. III
Schüddekopf, Albert Wilhelm, 1861–1916, vol. II
Schuler, Gottlieb Frederick Henry, 1854–1926, vol. II
Schultz, Donald Lorimer, 1926–1987, vol. VIII
Schultz, Sir Joseph Leopold, (Sir Leo), 1900–1991, vol. IX
Schultz, Sir Leo; see Schultz, Sir J. L.
Schultz, Theodore W., 1902–1998, vol. X
Schumacher, Ernst F(riedrich), 1911–1977, vol. VII
Schuman, Robert, 1886–1963, vol. VI
Schumann, Elisabeth, 1885–1952, vol. V
Schumann, Maurice, 1911–1998, vol. X
Schunck, Henry Edward, 1820–1903, vol. I
Schurman, Jacob Gould, 1854–1942, vol. IV
Schuschnigg, Kurt von, 1897–1977, vol. VII
Schuster, 1st Baron, 1869–1956, vol. V
Schuster, Sir Arthur, 1851–1934, vol. III
Schuster, Ernest Joseph, 1850–1924, vol. II
Schuster, Sir Felix, 1st Bt, 1854–1936, vol. III
Schuster, Sir (Felix) James (Moncrieff), 3rd Bt, 1913–1996, vol. X
Schuster, Sir (Felix) Victor, 2nd Bt, 1885–1962, vol. VI
Schuster, Sir George Ernest, 1881–1982, vol. VIII
Schuster, Sir James; see Schuster, Sir F. J. M.
Schuster, Sir Victor; see Schuster, Sir F. V.
Schutt, William John, 1868–1933, vol. III
Schütze, Gladys Henrietta, (Mrs Harrie Schütze); see Leslie, Henrietta.
Schütze, Harrie Leslie Hugo, 1882–1946, vol. IV
Schütze, Henrietta; see Leslie, H.
Schwab, Charles M., 1862–1939, vol. III
Schwab, John Christopher, 1865–1916, vol. II
Schwabe, Maj.-Gen. George S.; see Salis-Schwabe.
Schwabe, Randolph, 1885–1948, vol. IV
Schwabe, Sir Walter George Salis, 1873–1931, vol. III
Schwartz, George Leopold, 1891–1983, vol. VIII
Schwarz, Ernest H. L., 1873–1928, vol. II
Schwarz, Rudolf, 1905–1994, vol. IX
Schwarzenberg, Johannes Erkinger, 1903–1978, vol. VII
Schwarzenberger, Georg, 1908–1991, vol. IX
Schweinitz, E. A. de, died 1904, vol. I
Schweitzer, Albert, 1875–1965, vol. VI
Schweitzer, Pierre-Paul, 1919–1994, vol. IX
Schwerdt, Captain Charles Max Richard, 1889–1968, vol. VI
Schwinger, Julian Seymour, 1918–1994, vol. IX
Sciama, Dennis William, 1926–1999, vol. X
Scicluna, Sir Hannibal Publius, 1880–1981, vol. VIII

Sciortino, Anthony, 1883–1947, vol. IV
Sclater, Charlotte Seymour, 1858–1942, vol. IV
Sclater, Edith Harriet, (Lady Sclater), died 1927, vol. II
Sclater, Gen. Sir Henry Crichton, 1855–1923, vol. II
Sclater, Very Rev. John Robert Paterson, 1876–1949, vol. IV
Sclater, Philip Lutley, 1829–1913, vol. I
Sclater, William Lutley, 1863–1944, vol. IV
Sclater-Booth, Hon. Charles Lutley, 1861–1931, vol. III
Sclater-Booth, Col Hon. Walter Dashwood, 1869–1953, vol. V
Scobell, Ven. Edward Chessall, 1850–1917, vol. II
Scobell, Maj.-Gen. Sir Henry Jenner, 1859–1912, vol. I
Scobell, Maj.-Gen. Sir John; see Scobell, Maj.-Gen. Sir S. J. P.
Scobell, Maj.-Gen. Sir (Sanford) John (Palairet), 1879–1955, vol. V
Scobie, Col Mackay John Graham, 1852–1930, vol. III
Scobie, Lt-Gen. Sir Ronald MacKenzie, 1893–1969, vol. VI
Scoble, Rt Hon. Sir Andrew Richard, 1831–1916, vol. II
Scoby-Smith, George, 1848–1929, vol. III
Scoggins, Air Vice-Marshal Roy, 1908–1970, vol. VI
Scogings, Very Rev. Frank, died 1976, vol. VII
Scollard, Clinton, 1860–1932, vol. III
Scollard, Rt Rev. David Joseph, 1862–1934, vol. III
Scoones, Gen. Sir Geoffry Allen Percival, 1893–1975, vol. VII
Scoones, Maj.-Gen. Sir Reginald Laurence, 1900–1991, vol. IX
Scopes, Sir Frederick, 1892–1978, vol. VII
Scopes, Sir Leonard Arthur, 1912–1997, vol. X
Scorgie, Mervyn Nelson, 1915–1986, vol. VIII
Scorgie, Sir Norman Gibb, 1884–1956, vol. V
Scorgie, Norman James, 1908–1958, vol. VI
Scorrer, Aileen Mona, 1905–1984, vol. VIII
Scot-Skirving, Archibald Adam, 1868–1930, vol. III
Scothern, Col Albert Edward, 1882–1970, vol. VI
Scotland, Sir Colley Harman, 1818–1903, vol. I
Scotland, James, 1917–1983, vol. VIII
Scotland, Rear-Adm. John Earl, 1911–1978, vol. VII
Scotson, Frederick Hector, 1900–1955, vol. V
Scott, Adrian Gilbert, 1882–1963, vol. VI
Scott, Agnes Catharine, 1875–1955, vol. V
Scott, Vice-Adm. Albert Charles, 1872–1969, vol. VI
Scott, Alexander, 1853–1947, vol. IV
Scott, Alexander MacCallum, 1874–1928, vol. II
Scott, Alexander R.; see Ritchie-Scott.
Scott, Alexander Whiteford, 1904–1993, vol. IX
Scott, Alfred Henry, 1868–1939, vol. III
Scott, Sir Andrew, 1857–1939, vol. III
Scott, Lt-Col Angel; see Scott, Lt-Col W. A.
Scott, Sir Angus Newton, 1876–1958, vol. V
Scott, Maj.-Gen. Anthony Gerald O'Carroll, 1899–1980, vol. VII
Scott, Very Rev. Archibald, 1837–1909, vol. I
Scott, Archibald Gifford, 1889–1980, vol. VII

Scott, Lt-Col Archibald Malcolm H.; *see* Henderson-Scott.

Scott, Sir (Arleigh) Winston, 1900–1976, vol. VII

Scott, Arthur, 1881–1953, vol. V

Scott, Maj.-Gen. Sir Arthur Binny, 1862–1944, vol. IV

Scott, Sir (Arthur) Guillum, 1842–1909, vol. I

Scott, Arthur William, 1846–1927, vol. II

Scott, Ven. Avison Terry, 1848–1925, vol. II

Scott, Sir Basil, 1859–1926, vol. II

Scott, Sir Benjamin, 1841–1927, vol. II

Scott, Benjamin Charles George, 1846–1929, vol. III

Scott, Sir Bernard Francis William, 1914–1987, vol. VIII

Scott, Col Bertal Hopton, 1863–1926, vol. II

Scott, Col Sir Buchanan, 1850–1937, vol. III

Scott, Catharine Amy D.; *see* Dawson Scott.

Scott, Charles, 1851–1934, vol. III

Scott, Rev. Charles Anderson, 1859–1941, vol. IV

Scott, Charles Clare, 1850–1925, vol. II

Scott, Rev. Canon Charles Harold, 1871–1940, vol. III (A), vol. IV

Scott, Maj.-Gen. Sir Charles Henry, 1848–1919, vol. II

Scott, Sir (Charles) Hilary, 1906–1991, vol. IX

Scott, Col Charles Inglis, 1866–1941, vol. IV

Scott, Charles Norman Lindsay Tollemache, 1852–1938, vol. III

Scott, Charles Paley, 1881–1950, vol. IV

Scott, Rt Rev. Charles Perry, 1847–1927, vol. II

Scott, Charles Prestwich, 1846–1932, vol. III

Scott, Charles Russell, 1898–1979, vol. VII

Scott, Rt Hon. Sir Charles Stewart, 1838–1924, vol. II

Scott, Charles Thomas, 1868–1953, vol. V

Scott, Lord Charles Thomas Montagu-Douglas-, 1839–1911, vol. I

Scott, Maj.-Gen. Charles Walker, 1875–1929, vol. III

Scott, Christopher Fairfax, 1894–1958, vol. V

Scott, Ven. Claud Syms, 1901–1983, vol. VIII

Scott, Clement William, 1841–1904, vol. I

Scott, Cyril Meir, 1879–1970, vol. VI

Scott, David, 1916–1996, vol. X

Scott, Ven. David, 1924–1996, vol. X

Scott, David Aylmer, 1892–1971, vol. VII

Scott, Sir David John Montagu Douglas, 1887–1986, vol. VIII

Scott, Hon. David Lynch, 1845–1924, vol. II

Scott, David Robert, *died* 1943, vol. IV

Scott, David Russell, *died* 1954, vol. V

Scott, Denis Herbert, 1899–1958, vol. V

Scott, Sir Donald; *see* Scott, Sir R. D.

Scott, Donald; *see* Scott, W. D.

Scott, Douglas, 1913–1990, vol. VIII

Scott, Maj.-Gen. Douglas Alexander, 1848–1924, vol. II

Scott, Sir Douglas Edward, 7th Bt (*cr* April 1806), 1863–1951, vol. V

Scott, Col. Sir Douglas Winchester, 2nd Bt, 1907–1984, vol. VIII

Scott, Dukinfield Henry, 1854–1934, vol. III

Scott, Duncan Campbell, 1862–1947, vol. IV

Scott, Rev. Edward Anderson Seymour, 1865–1941, vol. IV

Scott, Sir Edward Arthur Dolman, 8th Bt (*cr* April 1806), 1905–1980, vol. VII (AII)

Scott, Edward B.; *see* Baliol Scott.

Scott, Sir Edward Dolman, 6th Bt (*cr* April 1806), 1826–1905, vol. I

Scott, Edward Hey L.; *see* Laughton-Scott.

Scott, Edward John Long, 1840–1918, vol. II

Scott, Edward Taylor, 1883–1932, vol. III

Scott, Elisabeth Whitworth, 1898–1972, vol. VII

Scott, Sir Eric, 1891–1982, vol. VIII

Scott, Sir Ernest, 1868–1939, vol. III

Scott, Ernest Findlay, 1868–1954, vol. V

Scott, Ernest Newey, *died* 1952, vol. V

Scott, Hon. Sir Ernest Stowell, 1872–1953, vol. V

Scott, Ethleen Mary, 1896–1985, vol. VIII

Scott, Eustace Lindsay, 1885–1956, vol. V

Scott, Major Finlay Forbes, *died* 1949, vol. IV

Scott, Francis Clayton, 1881–1979, vol. VII

Scott, Maj.-Gen. Sir Francis Cunningham, 1834–1902, vol. I

Scott, Sir Francis David Sibbald, 4th Bt (*cr* Dec. 1806), 1851–1906, vol. I

Scott, Lt-Col Lord Francis George Montagu-Douglas-, 1879–1952, vol. V

Scott, Sir Francis Montagu Sibbald, 5th Bt (*cr* Dec. 1806), 1885–1945, vol. IV

Scott, Francis Reginald Fairfax, 1897–1969, vol. VI

Scott, Frank, (Francis Reginald), 1899–1985, vol. VIII

Scott, Col Frederick Beaufort, 1839–1903, vol. I

Scott, Ven. Frederick George, 1861–1944, vol. IV

Scott, Gavin, 1876–1933, vol. III

Scott, Lt-Col George, 1859–1955, vol. V

Scott, Sir George; *see* Scott, Sir J. G.

Scott, George Alexander, 1862–1933, vol. III

Scott, George Barclay, 1928–1990, vol. VIII

Scott, George Batley, 1844–1932, vol. III

Scott, Sir George Edward, 1903–1989, vol. VIII

Scott, George Edwin, 1925–1988, vol. VIII

Scott, George Ian, 1907–1989, vol. VIII

Scott, Lt-Col George John, 1858–1925, vol. II

Scott, George Walter, 1896–1963, vol. VI

Scott, Lord George William Montagu-Douglas-, 1866–1947, vol. IV

Scott, Col Gerald Bassett, 1875–1964, vol. VI

Scott, Geraldine Edith, (Lady Scott); *see* Mitton, G. E.

Scott, G(ilbert) Shaw, 1884–1969, vol. VI

Scott, Sir Giles Gilbert, 1880–1960, vol. V

Scott, Sir Guillum; *see* Scott, Sir A. G.

Scott, Rev. G(uthrie) Michael, 1907–1983, vol. VIII

Scott, Guy Harden Guillum, 1874–1960, vol. V

Scott, Hardiman; *see* Scott, P. H.

Scott, Sir Harold; *see* Scott, Sir Henry H.

Scott, Sir Harold Richard, 1887–1969, vol. VI

Scott, Major Harvey, 1868–1912, vol. I

Scott, Henry Cooper, 1915–1977, vol. VII

Scott, Col Lord Henry Francis Montagu-Douglas-, 1868–1945, vol. IV

Scott, Henry George, 1875–1935, vol. III

Scott, Sir (Henry) Harold, 1874–1956, vol. V

Scott, Brig. Sir Henry Lawrence, 1882–1971, vol. VII

Scott, Sir (Henry) Maurice, 1910–1976, vol. VII
Scott, Sir Henry Milne, 1876–1956, vol. V
Scott, Hon. Henry Robert H.; *see* Hepburne-Scott.
Scott, Brig. Henry St George Stewart, 1880–1940, vol. III
Scott, Lord Herbert Andrew Montagu-Douglas-, 1872–1944, vol. IV
Scott, Sir Herbert Septimus, 1873–1952, vol. V
Scott, Sir Hilary; *see* Scott, Sir C. H.
Scott, Hugh, 1885–1960, vol. V
Scott, Hugh Stowell; *see* Merriman, Henry Seton.
Scott, Jack Hardiman; *see* Scott, P. H.
Scott, James, 1850–1920, vol. II
Scott, Sir James, 1838–1925, vol. II
Scott, James, *died* 1929, vol. III
Scott, James, 1876–1939, vol. III
Scott, James Alexander, 1931–1997, vol. X
Scott, Maj.-Gen. James Bruce, 1892–1974, vol. VII
Scott, James Cospatrick Hepburne-, 1882–1942, vol. IV
Scott, Sir (James) George, 1851–1935, vol. III
Scott, James Henderson, 1913–1970, vol. VI
Scott, J(ames) M(aurice), 1906–1986, vol. VIII
Scott, Sir James Walter, 2nd Bt (*cr* 1962), 1924–1993, vol. IX
Scott, Sir James William, 1st Bt (*cr* 1909), 1844–1913, vol. I
Scott, Maj.-Gen. James Woodward, 1838–1914, vol. I
Scott, Col Sir Jervoise Bolitho, 1st Bt (*cr* 1962), 1892–1965, vol. VI
Scott, Sir John, 1814–1898, vol. I
Scott, John, 1830–1903, vol. I
Scott, Hon. Sir John, 1841–1904, vol. I
Scott, Rev. John, 1836–1906, vol. I
Scott, John, *died* 1919, vol. II
Scott, Sir John, 2nd Bt (*cr* 1907), 1854–1922, vol. II
Scott, Sir John, 1878–1946, vol. IV
Scott, Brig. John, 1887–1971, vol. VII
Scott, John Alexander, 1900–1965, vol. VI
Scott, Sir John Arthur G.; *see* Guillum Scott.
Scott, John Dick, 1917–1980, vol. VII
Scott, John Gordon Cameron, 1888–1946, vol. IV
Scott, John Halliday, *died* 1914, vol. I
Scott, Sir John Harley, *died* 1931, vol. III
Scott, John Healey, 1843–1925, vol. II
Scott, John Russell, 1879–1949, vol. IV
Scott, Maj.-Gen. John Walter Lennox, 1883–1960, vol. V
Scott, John Waugh, 1878–1974, vol. VII
Scott, Comdr John Wilfred, 1881–1926, vol. II
Scott, John William R.; *see* Robertson Scott.
Scott, Rev. Canon Joseph John, *died* 1931, vol. III
Scott, Kathleen, (Lady Scott); *see* Kennet, Lady.
Scott, Kenneth, *died* 1918, vol. II
Scott, Laurence Prestwich, 1909–1983, vol. VIII
Scott, Rt Hon. Sir Leslie Frederic, 1869–1950, vol. IV
Scott, Sir Lindsay; *see* Scott, Sir W. L.
Scott, Lt-Col Lothian Kerr, 1841–1919, vol. II
Scott, Hon. Louis Guy, 1850–1900, vol. I
Scott, Mackay Hugh Baillie, 1865–1945, vol. IV
Scott, Rear-Adm. Malcolm Maxwell-, 1883–1943, vol. IV

Scott, Col Sir Malcolm S.; *see* Stoddart-Scott.
Scott, Margaret, 1841–1917, vol. II
Scott, M(argaret) Audrey, 1904–1990, vol. VIII
Scott, Sir Maurice; *see* Scott, Sir H. M.
Scott, Hon. Mrs Maxwell, (Mary Monica), 1852–1920, vol. II
Scott, Rev. Melville, *died* 1929, vol. III
Scott, Ven. Melville Horne, 1827–1898, vol. I
Scott, Sir Michael Fergus M.; *see* Maxwell Scott.
Scott, Maj.-Gen. Michael Frederick, 1911–1995, vol. IX
Scott, Most Rev. Moses Nathanael Christopher Omobiala, 1911–1988, vol. VIII
Scott, Napier B.; *see* Baliol Scott.
Scott, Noel, 1890–1956, vol. V
Scott, Norman Carson, 1899–1975, vol. VII
Scott, Lt-Col Norman Emile Henry, 1875–1958, vol. V
Scott, Sir Oswald Arthur, 1893–1960, vol. V
Scott, Owen Stanley, 1852–1922, vol. II
Scott, Paul Mark, 1920–1978, vol. VII
Scott, Rev. Percy, 1910–1991, vol. IX
Scott, Adm. Sir Percy Moreton, 1st Bt (*cr* 1913), 1853–1924, vol. II
Scott, Rev. Percy Richard, 1850–1906, vol. I
Scott, Peter, *died* 1972, vol. VII
Scott, Peter Duncan, 1914–1977, vol. VII
Scott, (Peter) Hardiman, 1920–1999, vol. X
Scott, Peter Heathcote Guillum, 1913–1961, vol. VI
Scott, Sir Peter Markham, 1909–1989, vol. VIII
Scott, Brig.-Gen. Philip Clement J., 1871–1932, vol. III
Scott, Ralph Roylance, 1893–1978, vol. VII
Scott, Brig. Raymond S., *died* 1972, vol. VII
Scott, Richard, 1914–1983, vol. VIII
Scott, Rear-Adm. Richard James Rodney, 1887–1967, vol. VI
Scott, Hon. Sir Richard William, 1825–1913, vol. I
Scott, Sir Robert, 1903–1968, vol. VI
Scott, Robert, 1913–1996, vol. X
Scott, Maj.-Gen. Robert, 1929–1991, vol. IX
Scott, Sir Robert Claude, 7th Bt (*cr* 1821), 1886–1961, vol. VI
Scott, Sir (Robert) Donald, 1901–1974, vol. VII
Scott, Captain Robert Falcon, 1868–1912, vol. I
Scott, Very Rev. Robert Forrester Victor, 1897–1975, vol. VII
Scott, Sir Robert Forsyth, 1849–1933, vol. III
Scott, Robert George, 1857–1918, vol. II
Scott, Sir Robert Heatlie, 1905–1982, vol. VIII
Scott, Robert Henry, 1833–1916, vol. II
Scott, Robert Julian, 1861–1930, vol. III
Scott, Maj.-Gen. Robert Kellock, 1871–1942, vol. IV
Scott, Gen. Robert Nicholl D.; *see* Dawson-Scott.
Scott, Robert Pickett, 1856–1931, vol. III
Scott, Sir (Robert) Russell, 1877–1960, vol. V
Scott, Sir Robert Townley, 1841–1922, vol. II
Scott, Robin; *see* Scutt, R. H.
Scott, Ronald, 1927–1996, vol. X
Scott, Sir Ronald B.; *see* Bodley Scott.
Scott, Group Captain Roy Charles Edwin, 1918–1982, vol. VIII
Scott, Sir Russell; *see* Scott, Sir Robert R.
Scott, Rev. Samuel Cooper, 1838–1923, vol. II

Scott, Sir Samuel Edward, 6th Bt (*cr* 1821), 1873–1943, vol. IV
Scott, Rev. Samuel Gilbert, 1847–1916, vol. II
Scott, Sir Samuel Haslam, 2nd Bt (*cr* 1909), 1875–1960, vol. V
Scott, Sebastian Gilbert, 1879–1941, vol. IV
Scott, Sheila Christine, 1927–1988, vol. VIII
Scott, Rev. Sidney; *see* Scott, Rev. W. S.
Scott, Sydney Richard, *died* 1966, vol. VI
Scott, Sir Terence Charles Stuart M.; *see* Morrison-Scott.
Scott, Rev. Thomas, 1831–1914, vol. I
Scott, Maj.-Gen. Thomas, 1897–1968, vol. VI
Scott, Rt Rev. Thomas Arnold, 1879–1956, vol. V
Scott, Thomas Bodley, *died* 1924, vol. II
Scott, Lt-Gen. Sir Thomas Edwin, 1867–1937, vol. III
Scott, Rev. Thomas Errington, *died* 1930, vol. III
Scott, Thomas Gilbert, 1874–1933, vol. III
Scott, Maj.-Gen. Thomas Patrick David, 1905–1976, vol. VII
Scott, Tom, 1854–1927, vol. II
Scott, Col Wallace Arthur, *died* 1949, vol. IV (A), vol. V
Scott, Sir Walter, 1st Bt (*cr* 1907), 1826–1910, vol. I
Scott, Hon. Walter, 1867–1938, vol. III
Scott, Sir Walter, 3rd Bt (*cr* 1907), 1895–1967, vol. VI
Scott, Sir Walter, 1903–1981, vol. VIII
Scott, Sir Walter, 4th Bt (*cr* 1907), 1918–1992, vol. IX
Scott, Rev. Walter Henry, 1842–1931, vol. III
Scott, Maj.-Gen. Sir Walter Joseph Constable M.; *see* Maxwell-Scott.
Scott, Sir Walter Lawrence, 1880–1951, vol. V
Scott, Walter Montagu, 1867–1920, vol. II
Scott, Walter Samuel, 1870–1951, vol. V
Scott, Rev. (Walter) Sidney, 1900–1980, vol. VII
Scott, Warwick; *see* Trevor, E.
Scott, Sir (Warwick) Lindsay, 1892–1952, vol. V
Scott, Sir William, 1898–1965, vol. VI
Scott, William A., 1871–1918, vol. II
Scott, Lt-Col (William) Angel, 1857–1932, vol. III
Scott, Maj.-Gen. Sir William Arthur, 1899–1976, vol. VII
Scott, Col William Augustus, 1856–1930, vol. III
Scott, William Berryman, 1858–1947, vol. IV
Scott, William Clifford Munro, 1903–1997, vol. X
Scott, William Coxon, 1895–1968, vol. VI
Scott, Sir William Dalgliesh, 1890–1966, vol. VI
Scott, Col Sir William Dishington, 1878–1952, vol. V
Scott, (William) Donald, 1903–1996, vol. X
Scott, William Douglas R.; *see* Robson-Scott.
Scott, Ven. William Edward, *died* 1918, vol. II
Scott, Rev. William G.; *see* Gardiner-Scott.
Scott, William George, 1913–1989, vol. VIII
Scott, Rev. William Major, 1879–1932, vol. III
Scott, Sir William Monteath, 7th Bt (*cr* 1671), 1829–1902, vol. I
Scott, Rev. William Morris FitzGerald, 1912–1959, vol. V
Scott, William Robert, 1868–1940, vol. III

Scott, Maj.-Gen. William Walter Hopton, 1843–1906, vol. I
Scott, Lt-Col Lord William Walter Montagu-Douglas-, 1896–1958, vol. V
Scott, Winifred Mary, (Pamela Wynne), *died* 1959, vol. V
Scott, Sir Winston; *see* Scott, Sir A. W.
Scott-Barrett, Rev. Hugh, 1887–1958, vol. V
Scott-Batey, Rowland William John, 1913–1980, vol. VII
Scott Blair, George William, 1902–1987, vol. VIII
Scott-Brown, Walter Graham, 1897–1987, vol. VIII
Scott-Duff, Bt Lt-Col Arthur Abercromby, 1874–1951, vol. V
Scott Elliot Maj.-Gen. James, 1902–1996, vol. X
Scott-Elliot, Walter Travers, 1895–1977, vol. VII
Scott Fox, Sir David; *see* Scott Fox, Sir R. D. J.
Scott Fox, Sir (Robert) David (John), 1910–1985, vol. VIII
Scott-Gatty, Sir Alfred Scott, 1847–1918, vol. II
Scott Hall, Stewart, 1905–1961, vol. VI
Scott-Hill, Engr Rear-Adm. Walter, 1873–1963, vol. VI
Scott-Hopkins, Maj. Sir James Sidney Rawdon, 1921–1995, vol. IX
Scott-James, Rolfe Arnold, 1878–1959, vol. V
Scott-Kerr, Brig.-Gen. Robert, 1859–1942, vol. IV
Scott Makdougall, Hugh James Elibank, 1861–1934, vol. III
Scott-Malden, David; *see* Scott-Malden, F. D. S.
Scott-Malden, Air Vice-Marshal (Francis) David (Stephen), 1919–2000, vol. X
Scott-Miller, Comdr Ronald, 1904–1992, vol. IX
Scott-Moncrieff, Adm. Sir Alan Kenneth, *died* 1980, vol. VII
Scott Moncrieff, Charles Kenneth, 1889–1930, vol. III
Scott-Moncrieff, Sir Colin Campbell, 1836–1916, vol. II
Scott-Moncrieff, Maj.-Gen. Sir George Kenneth, 1855–1924, vol. II
Scott-Moncrieff, Joanna Constance, 1920–1978, vol. VII
Scott-Moncrieff, William, 1922–1997, vol. X
Scott-Moncrieff, William George, 1846–1927, vol. II
Scott O'Connor, Thomas Arthur Leslie, 1878–1944, vol. IV
Scott-Owen, Col Arthur Lewis, 1885–1944, vol. IV
Scott-Paine, Hubert, 1891–1954, vol. V
Scott-Smith, Sir Henry, 1865–1950, vol. IV
Scott-Taggart, Wing Comdr John, 1897–1979, vol. VII
Scott Thomson, Gladys, *died* 1966, vol. VI
Scotter, Sir Charles, 1st Bt, 1835–1910, vol. I
Scotter, Sir Frederick Charles, 2nd Bt, 1868–1911, vol. I
Scotter, Gen. Sir William Norman Roy, 1922–1981, vol. VIII
Scotti, Antonio, 1866–1936, vol. III
Scougal, Andrew E., 1846–1916, vol. II
Scourfield, Sir Owen Henry Philipps, 2nd Bt, 1847–1921, vol. II
Scovell, Sir Augustus Charles, 1840–1924, vol. II
Scovell, Lt-Col George Julian Selwyn, *died* 1948, vol. IV

Scovell, Rowley Fielding, 1902–1972, vol. VII
Scragg, Air Vice-Marshal Sir Colin, 1908–1989, vol. VIII
Scrase-Dickins, Col Spencer William; see Dickins.
Scrase-Dickins, Maj.-Gen. William Drummond, 1832–1914, vol. I
Scratchley, Herbert Arthur, 1855–1920, vol. II
Scratchley, Lt-Col Victor Henry Sylvester, 1870–1936, vol. III
Scriabin, Alexander, 1872–1915, vol. I
Scribner, Charles, 1890–1952, vol. V
Scrimgeour, H(ugh) Carron, 1883–1958, vol. V
Scrimgeour, James, 1903–1987, vol. VIII
Scrimgeour, John Stuart, 1887–1950, vol. IV
Scrimger, Lt-Col Francis Alexander Carron, 1880–1937, vol. III
Scriven, Ven. Augustine, died 1916, vol. II
Scrivener, Sir Patrick Stratford, 1897–1966, vol. VI
Scrivenor, Sir Thomas Vaisey, 1908–1998, vol. X
Scroggie, Rev. William Graham, 1877–1958, vol. V
Scroggie, Col William Reith John, 1876–1953, vol. V
Scroope, Arthur Edgar, died 1954, vol. V
Scrope, Henry Aloysius, 1862–1950, vol. IV
Scrutton, Hugh; see Scrutton, T. H.
Scrutton, James Herbert, 1858–1938, vol. III
Scrutton, Sir Thomas Edward, 1856–1934, vol. III
Scrutton, (Thomas) Hugh, 1917–1991, vol. IX
Scrymgeour, Edwin, 1866–1947, vol. IV
Scrymgeour, Norval, 1870–1952, vol. V
Scrymsoure-Steuart-Fothringham, Walter Thomas James, 1862–1936, vol. III
Scudamore, Brig.-Gen. Charles Philip, 1861–1929, vol. III
Scudder, Horace Elisha, 1838–1902, vol. I
Scullard, Rev. Herbert Hayes, 1862–1926, vol. II
Scullard, Howard Hayes, 1903–1983, vol. VIII
Scullin, Rt Hon. James Henry, 1876–1953, vol. V
Scully, Harry, died 1935, vol. III
Scully, James Aloysius, 1856–1929, vol. III
Scully, Major Vincent Joseph, 1876–1941, vol. IV
Scully, Lt-Col Vincent Marcus Barron, 1881–1941, vol. IV
Scully, Vincent William Thomas, 1900–1980, vol. VII
Scupham, John, 1904–1990, vol. VIII
Scupham, Brig. Sir William Eric Halstead, 1893–1958, vol. V
Scurfield, Harold, 1863–1941, vol. IV
Scurr, John, 1876–1932, vol. III
Scuse, Dennis George, 1921–1998, vol. X
Scutt, Robin Hugh, (Robin Scott), 1920–2000, vol. X
Seaborg, Glenn Theodore, 1912–1999, vol. X
Seaborn, Most Rev. Robert Lowder, 1911–1993, vol. IX
Sea-Lion; see Bennett, Captain G. M.
Seaborne Davies, David Richard; see Davies, D. R. S.
Seabrook, John, 1896–1985, vol. VIII
Seabrook, William, 1886–1945, vol. IV
Seabrooke, Elliott, died 1950, vol. IV
Seabrooke, Sir James Herbert, 1852–1933, vol. III
Seaby, Allen W., 1867–1953, vol. V
Seaby, Wilfred Arthur, 1910–1991, vol. IX

Seafield, 11th Earl of, 1876–1915, vol. I
Seafield, Countess of (12th in line), 1906–1969, vol. VI
Seafield, Countess of; (Caroline), died 1911, vol. I
Seaford, Sir Frederick Jacob, 1886–1968, vol. VI
Seaforth, 1st Baron, 1847–1923, vol. II
Seaforth, Lady; (Mary Margaret), died 1933, vol. III
Seager, Basil William, 1898–1977, vol. VII
Seager, Most Rev. Charles Allen, 1872–1948, vol. IV
Seager, Ven. Edward Leslie, 1904–1983, vol. VIII
Seager, Captain John Elliot, 1891–1955, vol. V
Seager, Philip Samuel, 1845–1924, vol. II
Seager, Samuel Hurst, 1855–1933, vol. III
Seager, Sir William Henry, 1862–1941, vol. IV
Seago, Edward Brian, 1910–1974, vol. VII
Seagram, Brig.-Gen. Tom Ogle, 1872–1958, vol. V
Seal, Sir Brajendranath, 1864–1938, vol. III
Seal, Sir Eric Arthur, 1898–1972, vol. VII
Seale, A. Barney, died 1957, vol. V
Seale, Douglas Robert, 1913–1999, vol. X
Seale, Rev. E. G., 1870–1936, vol. III
Seale, Sir John Carteret Hyde, 4th Bt, 1881–1964, vol. VI
Seale, Sir John Henry, 3rd Bt, 1843–1914, vol. I
Seales, Peter Clinton, 1929–1998, vol. X
Sealy, Sir John, 1807–1899, vol. I
Sealy, Patrick Persse, 1853–1938, vol. III
Seaman, Clarence Milton Edwards, 1908–1974, vol. VII
Seaman, Dick; see Seaman, R. J.
Seaman, Col Edwin Charles, 1867–1919, vol. II
Seaman, Edwin de Grey, 1908–1983, vol. VIII
Seaman, Sir Owen, 1st Bt, 1861–1936, vol. III
Seaman, Reginald Jasper, (Dick), 1923–1993, vol. IX
Seaman, Paymaster-Captain Tom, died 1943, vol. IV
Seamer, Rev. Arthur John, died 1963, vol. VI
Searcy, Philip Roy, 1914–1983, vol. VIII
Searight, Major Hugh fforde, 1875–1942, vol. IV
Searle, Alfred Broadhead, 1877–1967, vol. VI
Searle, Maj.-Gen. Arthur Thaddeus, 1830–1925, vol. II
Searle, Rev. Charles Edward, 1828–1902, vol. I
Searle, Col Frank, died 1948, vol. IV
Searle, George Frederick Charles, 1864–1954, vol. V
Searle, Herbert Victor, 1892–1968, vol. VI
Searle, Humphrey, 1915–1982, vol. VIII
Searle, Rear-Adm. Malcolm Walter St Leger, 1900–1994, vol. IX
Searle, Sir Malcolm William, died 1926, vol. II
Searle, Peter, 1941–1991, vol. IX
Searles-Wood, Herbert Duncan, 1853–1936, vol. III
Sears, Rear-Adm. Harold Baker, 1880–1959, vol. V
Sears, John Edward, 1857–1941, vol. IV
Sears, John Edward, 1883–1954, vol. V
Sears, William, died 1929, vol. III
Seath, Maj.-Gen. Gordon Hamilton, died 1952, vol. V
Seaton, 3rd Baron, 1854–1933, vol. III
Seaton, 4th Baron, 1863–1955, vol. V
Seaton, Albert Edward, 1848–1930, vol. III
Seaton, Colin Robert, 1928–1997, vol. X

Seaton, Rev. Douglas, 1839–1923, vol. II
Seaton, Edward Cox, 1847–1915, vol. I
Seaton, J. S., *died* 1929, vol. III
Seaton, Rt Rev. James Buchanan, 1868–1938, vol. III
Seaton, Reginald Ethelbert, 1899–1978, vol. VII
Seaver, Very Rev. Charles, 1820–1907, vol. I
Seaver, Very Rev. George, 1890–1976, vol. VII
Seaverns, Joel Herbert, 1860–1923, vol. II
Sebag-Montefiore, Edmund; *see* Montefiore.
Sebag-Montefiore, Sir Joseph; *see* Montefiore.
Sebastian, Rear-Adm. Brian Leonard Geoffrey, 1891–1983, vol. VIII
Sebastian, Erroll Graham, 1892–1978, vol. VII
Sebright, Sir Edgar Reginald Saunders, 11th Bt, 1854–1917, vol. II
Sebright, Sir Egbert Cecil Saunders, 10th Bt, 1871–1897, vol. I
Sebright, Lt-Col Sir Giles Edward, 13th Bt, 1896–1954, vol. V
Sebright, Sir Guy Thomas Saunders, 12th Bt, 1856–1933, vol. III
Sebright, Sir Hugo Giles Edmund, 14th Bt, 1931–1985, vol. VIII
Seccombe, Brig.-Gen. Archibald Kennedy, 1868–1931, vol. III
Seccombe, Thomas, 1866–1923, vol. II
Seccombe, Sir Thomas Lawrence, 1812–1902, vol. I
Secker, Martin, 1882–1978, vol. VII
Seckham, Lt-Col Bassett Thorne, 1863–1925, vol. II
Seckham, Lt-Col Douglas Thorne, 1873–1937, vol. III
Secombe, Maj.-Gen. Victor Clarence, 1897–1962, vol. VI
Secretan, Hubert Arthur, 1891–1969, vol. VI
Secretan, Walter Bernard, 1875–1966, vol. VI
Seddon, Charles Norman, 1870–1950, vol. IV
Seddon, Sir Harold, 1881–1958, vol. V
Seddon, Harry Sterratt, 1881–1944, vol. IV
Seddon, Sir Herbert John, 1903–1977, vol. VII
Seddon, James Andrew, 1868–1939, vol. III
Seddon, John, 1915–1991, vol. IX
Seddon, John Pollard, 1827–1906, vol. I
Seddon, Rt Hon. Richard John, 1845–1906, vol. I
Seddon-Brown, Lt-Col Sir Norman Seddon, 1880–1971, vol. VII
Sedgefield, W. J., 1866–1945, vol. IV
Sedgewick, Hon. George Herbert, 1878–1939, vol. III
Sedgwick, Adam, 1854–1913, vol. I
Sedgwick, Anne Douglas, 1873–1935, vol. III
Sedgwick, Rear-Adm. Cyril Gordon, 1885–1948, vol. IV
Sedgwick, Ellery, 1872–1960, vol. V
Sedgwick, Lt-Col Francis Roger, 1876–1955, vol. V
Sedgwick, Rev. Gordon, 1840–1921, vol. II
Sedgwick, Henry Dwight, 1861–1957, vol. V
Sedgwick, Patrick Cardinall Mason, 1911–1985, vol. VIII
Sedgwick, Richard Romney, 1894–1972, vol. VII
Sedgwick, Rev. S. N., 1872–1941, vol. IV
Sedgwick, William Thompson, 1855–1921, vol. II
Sedgwick, Rt Rev. William Walmsley, 1858–1948, vol. IV
See, Hon. Sir John, 1845–1907, vol. I

Sée, Peter Henri, 1910–1963, vol. VI
Seear, Baroness (Life Peer); Beatrice Nancy Seear, 1913–1997, vol. X
Seebohm, Baron (Life Peer); Frederic Seebohm, 1909–1990, vol. VIII
Seebohm, Frederic, 1833–1912, vol. I
Seebohm, Hugh Exton, 1867–1946, vol. IV
Seeds, Sir William, 1882–1973, vol. VII
Seefried, Irmgard Maria Theresia, 1919–1988, vol. VIII
Seel, Major Edward M.; *see* Molyneux-Seel.
Seel, Sir George Frederick, 1895–1976, vol. VII
Seeley, Edward Alexander, 1913–1979, vol. VII
Seeley, Ven. George Henry, *died* 1935, vol. III
Seeley, Harry Govier, 1839–1909, vol. I
Seely, Sir Charles, 1st Bt, 1833–1915, vol. I
Seely, Sir Charles Hilton, 2nd Bt, 1859–1926, vol. II
Seely, Sir Victor Basil John, 4th Bt, 1900–1980, vol. VII
Seeney, Noel Conway, 1926–1996, vol. X
Seers, Dudley, 1920–1983, vol. VIII
Seferiades, George, 1900–1971, vol. VII
Seferis, George; *see* Seferiades, G.
Sefton, 4th Earl of, 1835–1897, vol. I
Sefton, 5th Earl of, 1867–1901, vol. I
Sefton, 6th Earl of, 1871–1930, vol. III
Sefton, 7th Earl of, 1898–1972, vol. VII
Sefton, Anne Harriet, (Mrs Walter Sefton); *see* Fish, A. H.
Sefton-Cohen, Arthur, 1879–1968, vol. VI (AII)
Segal, Baron (Life Peer); Samuel Segal, 1902–1985, vol. VIII
Segar, George Xavier, 1838–1901, vol. I
Segar, Hugh William, 1868–1954, vol. V
Segonzac, André D. de; *see* Dunoyer de Segonzac.
Segovia Torres, Andrés, 1893–1987, vol. VIII
Segrave, Edmond, 1904–1971, vol. VII
Segrave, Brig.-Gen. Eric; *see* Segrave, Brig.-Gen. W. H. E.
Segrave, Major Sir Henry O'Neal Dehane, 1896–1930, vol. III
Segrave, Vice-Adm. John Roderick, 1871–1938, vol. III
Segrave, Captain Sir Thomas George, 1865–1941, vol. IV
Segrave, Brig.-Gen. (William Henry) Eric, 1875–1964, vol. VI
Segrè, Emilio, 1905–1989, vol. VIII
Séguel, George Gregory M., *died* 1954, vol. V
Segur, Marquis de; Pierre Marie Maurice Henri, 1853–1916, vol. II
Seifert, Jaroslav, 1901–1986, vol. VIII
Seigne, John Thomas, 1844–1922, vol. II
Seignobos, Charles, 1854–1942, vol. IV
Seillière, Baron Ernest, 1866–1955, vol. V
Seitz, John Arnold, 1883–1963, vol. VI
Sekers, Miki; *see* Sekers, Sir N. T.
Sekers, Sir Nicholas Thomas, (Miki Sekers), 1910–1972, vol. VII
Sekon, George Augustus, 1867–1948, vol. IV
Selbie, Rev. John A., 1856–1931, vol. III
Selbie, Robert Hope, 1868–1930, vol. III
Selbie, Rev. William Boothby, 1862–1944, vol. IV
Selborne, 2nd Earl of, 1859–1942, vol. IV
Selborne, 3rd Earl of, 1887–1971, vol. VII

Selby, 1st Viscount, 1835–1909, vol. I
Selby, 2nd Viscount, 1867–1923, vol. II
Selby, 3rd Viscount, 1911–1959, vol. V
Selby, 4th Viscount, 1942–1997, vol. X
Selby, Arthur Laidlaw, 1861–1942, vol. IV
Selby, Maj.-Gen. Arthur Roland, 1893–1966, vol. VI (AII)
Selby, Lt-Col Charles Westrope, 1883–1929, vol. III
Selby, Francis Guy, 1852–1927, vol. II
Selby, Francis James, 1867–1942, vol. IV
Selby, Harry, 1913–1984, vol. VIII
Selby, Sir Kenneth, 1914–1992, vol. IX
Selby, Percival Marchant, 1886–1955, vol. V
Selby, Ralph Walford, 1915–1997, vol. X
Selby, Rev. Thomas Gunn, 1846–1910, vol. I
Selby, Sir Walford Harmood Montague, 1881–1965, vol. VI
Selby, Lt-Col William, 1869–1916, vol. II
Selby, Rear-Adm. William Halford, 1902–1994, vol. IX
Selby, Rev. William John, 1858–1935, vol. III
Selby-Bigge, Sir Amherst; see Selby-Bigge, Sir L. A.
Selby-Bigge, Sir John Amherst, 2nd Bt, 1892–1973, vol. VII
Selby-Bigge, Sir (Lewis) Amherst, 1st Bt, 1860–1951, vol. V
Selby-Lowndes, Brig. Montacute William Worrall, 1896–1972, vol. VII
Selby-Lowndes, Col William; see Lowndes.
Selby Wright, Very Rev. Ronald William Vernon; see Wright.
Seldon Truss, Leslie, 1892–1990, vol. VIII
Self, Sir (Albert) Henry, 1890–1975, vol. VII
Self, Sir Henry; see Self, Sir A. H.
Self, Hugh Michael, 1921–1998, vol. X
Self, Peter John Otter, 1919–1999, vol. X
Self, Sir Robert Carr, 1840–1926, vol. II
Selfe, Sir William Lucius, 1845–1924, vol. II
Selfridge, Harry Gordon, 1858–1947, vol. IV
Seligman, Sir Charles David, 1869–1954, vol. V
Seligman, Charles Gabriel, 1873–1940, vol. III
Seligman, Edwin Robert Anderson, 1861–1939, vol. III
Seligman, Henry, 1909–1993, vol. IX
Seligman, Brig.-Gen. Herbert Spencer, 1872–1951, vol. V
Selincourt, Agnes de, 1872–1917, vol. II
Sélincourt, Anne de; see Sedgwick, Anne Douglas.
Selincourt, Ernest de, 1870–1943, vol. IV
Selincourt, Hugh de, 1878–1951, vol. V
Selkirk, 10th Earl of, 1906–1994, vol. IX
Selkirk, Countess of; (Cecely Louisa), died 1920, vol. II
Sell, Rev. Edward, 1839–1932, vol. III
Sell, William James, died 1915, vol. I
Sellar, Harry Harpham, 1893–1966, vol. VI
Sellar, Robert Watson, 1894–1965, vol. VI
Sellar, Lt-Col Thomas Byrne, 1865–1924, vol. II
Selleck, Sir Francis Palmer, 1895–1976, vol. VII
Sellers, Rt Hon. Sir Frederic Aked, 1893–1979, vol. VII
Sellers, Norman William Malin, 1919–1993, vol. IX
Sellers, Peter Richard Henry, 1925–1980, vol. VII
Sellers, Rev. Robert Victor, 1894–1973, vol. VII
Selley, Sir Harry Ralph, 1871–1960, vol. V

Sellheim, Maj.-Gen. Victor Conradsdorf Morisset, 1866–1928, vol. II
Sellon, Hugh Gilbert René, 1901–1974, vol. VII
Sellors, Sir Thomas Holmes, 1902–1987, vol. VIII
Sells, Arthur Lytton L.; see Lytton Sells.
Sells, Sir David Perronet, 1918–1993, vol. IX
Sells, Vice-Adm. William Fortescue, 1881–1966, vol. VI
Selly, Susan, (Mrs Clifford Selly); see Strange, S.
Selous, Frederick Courteney, 1851–1917, vol. II
Selous, Gerald Holgate, 1887–1978, vol. VII
Selsdon, 1st Baron, 1877–1938, vol. III
Selsdon, 2nd Baron, 1913–1963, vol. VI
Seltman, Charles Theodore, 1886–1957, vol. V
Selvon, Samuel Dickson, 1923–1994, vol. IX
Selway, Air Marshal Sir Anthony Dunkerton, 1909–1984, vol. VIII
Selway, Cornelius James, 1875–1948, vol. IV
Selwyn, Rev. Edward Carus, 1853–1918, vol. II
Selwyn, Very Rev. Edward Gordon, 1885–1959, vol. V
Selwyn, Rt Rev. George Theodore, 1887–1957, vol. V
Selwyn, Rt Rev. John Richardson, 1844–1898, vol. I
Selwyn, John Sidney Augustus, 1908–2000, vol. X
Selwyn, Rev. William, 1840–1914, vol. I
Selwyn, Rt Rev. William Marshall, 1880–1951, vol. V
Selwyn-Clarke, Sir Selwyn, 1893–1976, vol. VII
Selwyn-Lloyd, Baron (Life Peer); John Selwyn Brooke Selwyn-Lloyd, 1904–1978, vol. VII
Selznick, David Oliver, 1902–1965, vol. VI
Semenov, Nikolai Nikolaevich, 1896–1986, vol. VIII
Semmence, Adrian Murdoch, 1926–1999, vol. X
Semon, Sir Felix, 1849–1921, vol. II
Semon, Henry, 1881–1971, vol. VII
Semper, Dudley Henry, 1905–1982, vol. VIII
Sempill, 17th Lord, 1836–1905, vol. I
Sempill, 18th Lord, 1863–1934, vol. III
Sempill, 19th Lord, 1893–1965, vol. VI
Sempill, Lady, 20th in line, 1920–1995, vol. IX
Sempill, Major Hon. Douglas F.; see Forbes-Sempill.
Semple, Lt-Col Sir David, 1856–1937, vol. III
Semple, David; see Semple, W. D. C.
Semple, Dugald, 1884–1964, vol. VI
Semple, John Edward, 1903–1969, vol. VI
Semple, John Greenlees, 1904–1985, vol. VIII
Semple, Patrick, 1875–1954, vol. V
Semple, Hon. Robert, 1873–1955, vol. V
Semple, (William) David (Crowe), 1933–1994, vol. IX
Semple, William Hugh, 1900–1981, vol. VIII
Sen, Shri Binay Ranjan, 1898–1993, vol. IX
Sen, Jitendranath, 1875–1945, vol. IV
Sen, K. Chandra, 1888–1981, vol. VIII
Sen, Nirmul Chunder, 1869–1936, vol. III
Sen, Susil C., died 1946, vol. IV
Sen, Sir Usha Nath, 1880–1959, vol. V
Senanayake, Rt Hon. Don Stephen, 1884–1952, vol. V
Senanayake, Hon. Dudley Shelton, 1911–1973, vol. VII

Sencourt, Robert, (Robert Esmonde Gordon George), 1890–1969, vol. VI
Sendall, Bernard Charles, 1913–1996, vol. X
Sendall, Sir Walter Joseph, 1832–1904, vol. I
Sender, Ramón José, 1902–1982, vol. VIII
Senier, Alfred, 1853–1918, vol. II
Senier, Sir Frederic William, 1869–1951, vol. V
Senior, Albert, 1867–1929, vol. III
Senior, Bernard, 1865–1934, vol. III
Senior, Derek, 1912–1988, vol. VIII
Senior, Sir Edward Walters, 1902–1995, vol. IX
Senior, Col Henry William Richard, 1866–1935, vol. III
Senior, Mark, 1863–1927, vol. II
Senior, Ronald Henry, 1904–1988, vol. VIII
Senior, William, died 1920, vol. II
Senior, William Goodwin, 1894–1969, vol. VI
Senior, William Hirst, 1904–1984, vol. VIII
Senior, Hon. William Sidney, 1888–1938, vol. III
Senn, Charles Herman, died 1934, vol. III
Senna, Ayrton, 1960–1994, vol. IX
Sennett, Sir Richard, 1862–1947, vol. IV
Senter, George, 1874–1942, vol. IV
Senter, Sir John Watt, 1905–1966, vol. VI
Sepeku, Rt Rev. John, died 1983, vol. VIII
Sephton, Ven. Arthur, 1894–1982, vol. VIII
Sequeira, James Harry, died 1948, vol. IV
Serao, Matilde, 1856–1927, vol. II
Serby, John Edward, 1902–1999, vol. X
Serena, Arthur, died 1922, vol. II
Serena, Clara, died 1972, vol. VII
Sergeant, Adeline, 1851–1904, vol. I
Sergeant, Emily Frances Adeline; see Sergeant, Adeline.
Sergeant, Maj.-Gen. Frederick Cavendish H.; see Hilton-Sergeant.
Sergeant, (Herbert) Howard, 1914–1987, vol. VIII
Sergeant, Howard; see Sergeant, Herbert H.
Sergeant, Lewis, 1841–1902, vol. I
Sergent, René Edmond, 1904–1984, vol. VIII
Sergison, Captain Charles Warden, 1867–1911, vol. I
Sergison-Brooke, Lt-Gen. Sir Bertram Norman; see Brooke.
Series, George William, 1920–1995, vol. IX
Serjeant, Sir David Maurice, died 1929, vol. III
Serjeant, Robert Bertram, 1915–1993, vol. IX
Serjeant, Col Sir William Charles Eldon, 1857–1930, vol. III
Serkin, Rudolf, 1903–1991, vol. IX
Serle, Rev. Samuel Edward Bayard, 1866–1939, vol. III
Serocold, Brig.-Gen. Eric P.; see Pearce-Serocold.
Serocold, Oswald P.; see Pearce-Serocold.
Serpell, Henry Oberlin, 1853–1943, vol. IV
Serra Largo, Count de; Peter Alexander Cameron Mackenzie, 1856–1931, vol. III
Servaes, Vice-Adm. Reginald Maxwell, 1893–1978, vol. VII
Service, Hon. James, 1823–1899, vol. I
Service, Robert William, 1874–1958, vol. V
Seshadri, Tiruvenkata Rajendra, 1900–1975, vol. VII
Sessford, Rt Rev. George Minshull, 1928–1996, vol. X

Setalvad, Sir Chimanlal Harilal, died 1947, vol. IV
Setchell, Herbert Leonard, 1892–1976, vol. VII
Seth, Andrew, 1856–1931, vol. III
Seth, Arathoon, 1852–1918, vol. II
Seth, George, 1905–1990, vol. VIII
Seth, James, 1860–1924, vol. II
Seth-Smith, David, 1875–1963, vol. VI
Seth-Smith, Brig. Hugh Garden, 1885–1958, vol. V
Seth-Smith, W. H., 1852–1928, vol. II
Sethna, Hon. Sir Phiroze, 1866–1938, vol. III
Seton, Sir Alexander Hay, 10th Bt (cr 1663), 1904–1963, vol. VI
Seton, Alice Ida, (Lady Seton), died 1995, vol. IX
Seton, Anya, (Anya Seton Chase), died 1990, vol. VIII
Seton, Sir Bruce; see Seton, Sir C. B.
Seton, Col Sir Bruce Gordon, 9th Bt (cr 1663), 1868–1932, vol. III
Seton, Sir Bruce Lovat, 11th Bt (cr 1663), 1909–1969, vol. VI
Seton, Sir Bruce Maxwell, 8th Bt (cr 1663), 1836–1915, vol. I
Seton, (Christopher) Bruce, 12th Bt, 1909–1988, vol. VIII
Seton, Sir Claud Ramsay Wilmot, 1888–1982, vol. VIII
Seton, Ernest Thompson, 1860–1946, vol. IV
Seton, George, 1822–1908, vol. I
Seton, Grace Gallatin Thompson, died 1959, vol. V
Seton, Sir James Christall, 12th Bt (cr 1683), 1913–1998, vol. X
Seton, Captain Sir John Hastings, 10th Bt (cr 1683), 1888–1956, vol. V
Seton, Sir Malcolm Cotter Cariston, 1872–1940, vol. III
Seton, Miles Charles Cariston, 1874–1919, vol. II
Seton, Robert George, 1860–1939, vol. III
Seton, Sir Robert James, 11th Bt (cr 1683), 1926–1993, vol. IX
Seton, Robert S., died 1942, vol. IV
Seton, Walter Warren, 1882–1927, vol. II
Seton, Sir William Samuel, 9th Bt (cr 1683), 1837–1914, vol. I
Seton-Karr, Sir Henry, 1853–1914, vol. I
Seton-Karr, Heywood Walter, 1859–1938, vol. III
Seton Pringle, John; see Pringle, J. S. M.
Seton-Steuart, Sir Alan Henry; see Steuart.
Seton-Steuart, Sir Douglas Archibald; see Steuart.
Seton-Thompson; see Seton, E. T.
Seton-Watson, (George) Hugh (Nicholas), 1916–1984, vol. VIII
Seton-Watson, Hugh; see Seton-Watson, G. H. N.
Seton-Watson, Robert William, 1879–1951, vol. V
Settle, Alison, died 1980, vol. VII
Settle, Charles Arthur, 1905–1979, vol. VII
Settle, Lt-Gen. Sir Henry Hamilton, 1847–1923, vol. II
Settrington, Lord; Charles Henry Gordon-Lennox, 1899–1919, vol. II
Seuffert, Stanislaus, 1899–1986, vol. VIII
Ševčík, Otakar, 1852–1934, vol. III
Séverine, Madame, 1855–1929, vol. III
Severn, Arthur, died 1931, vol. III
Severn, Sir Claud, 1869–1933, vol. III
Severn, Walter, 1830–1904, vol. I

Seversky, Major Alexander P. de, 1894–1974, vol. VII

Sevestre, Robert, 1868–1949, vol. IV

Sewall, May Wright, *died* 1920, vol. II

Seward, Sir Albert Charles, 1863–1941, vol. IV

Seward, Sir Conrad; *see* Seward, Sir S. C.

Seward, Edwin, 1853–1924, vol. II

Seward, Sir Eric John, 1899–1981, vol. VIII

Seward, Sir (Samuel) Conrad, 1908–1976, vol. VII

Seward, Air Vice-Marshal Walter John, 1898–1972, vol. VII

Sewell, Sir Allan; *see* Sewell, Sir J. A.

Sewell, Rev. Archibald Hankey, 1874–1943, vol. IV

Sewell, Arnold Edward, 1886–1969, vol. VI

Sewell, Brig. Edgar Patrick, 1905–1957, vol. V

Sewell, Elizabeth Missing, 1815–1906, vol. I

Sewell, Col Evelyn Pierce, *died* 1960, vol. V

Sewell, Rev. Henry, 1847–1943, vol. IV

Sewell, Brig.-Gen. Horace Somerville, 1881–1953, vol. V

Sewell, Rev. James Edwards, 1810–1903, vol. I

Sewell, Sir (John) Allan, 1915–1988, vol. IX (AI)

Sewell, John Thomas Beadsworth, 1858–1930, vol. III

Sewell, Brig.-Gen. Jonathan William Shirley, 1872–1941, vol. IV

Sewell, Lt-Col Robert Beresford Seymour, 1880–1964, vol. VI

Sewell, Sir Sidney Valentine, 1880–1949, vol. IV

Sewell, Col Thomas Davies, 1832–1916, vol. II

Sexton, Maj.-Gen. (Francis) Michael, 1923–1995, vol. IX

Sexton, Frederic Henry, 1879–1955, vol. V

Sexton, Most Rev. Harold Eustace, 1888–1972, vol. VII

Sexton, Sir James, 1856–1938, vol. III

Sexton, Maj.-Gen. Michael; *see* Sexton, Maj.-Gen. F. M.

Sexton, Col Michael John, 1860–1922, vol. II

Sexton, Sir Robert, 1814–1901, vol. I

Sexton, T. M., *died* 1946, vol. IV (A), vol. V

Sexton, Thomas, 1848–1932, vol. III

Sexton, Walter, 1877–1941, vol. IV

Seyler, Athene, 1889–1990, vol. VIII

Seyler, Clarence Arthur, 1866–1959, vol. V

Seymour, Ven. Albert Eden, 1841–1908, vol. I

Seymour, Sir Albert Victor Francis, 2nd Bt (*cr* 1869), 1879–1949, vol. IV

Seymour, Alfred Wallace, 1881–1960, vol. V

Seymour, Very Rev. Algernon Giles, 1886–1933, vol. III

Seymour, Brig.-Gen. Archibald George, 1875–1933, vol. III

Seymour, Captain Arthur George, 1884–1935, vol. III

Seymour, Beatrice Kean, *died* 1955, vol. V

Seymour, Charles, 1885–1963, vol. VI

Seymour, Charles Derick, 1863–1935, vol. III

Seymour, Lt-Col Charles Hugh Napier, 1874–1933, vol. III

Seymour, Vice-Adm. Claude, 1876–1941, vol. IV

Seymour, Derek Robert Gurth, 1917–1986, vol. VIII

Seymour, Edgar William, 1868–1926, vol. II

Seymour, Major Sir Edward, 1877–1948, vol. IV

Seymour, Lord Edward Beauchamp, 1879–1917, vol. II

Seymour, Admiral of the Fleet Rt Hon. Sir Edward Hobart, 1840–1929, vol. III

Seymour, Lord Ernest James, 1850–1930, vol. III

Seymour, Sir George S.; *see* Seymour Seymour.

Seymour, Brig.-Gen. Lord Henry Charles, 1878–1939, vol. III

Seymour, Henry J., 1876–1954, vol. V

Seymour, Horace Alfred Damer, 1843–1902, vol. I

Seymour, Sir Horace James, 1885–1978, vol. VII

Seymour, Lady Katharine, 1900–1985, vol. VIII

Seymour, Leslie George, 1900–1976, vol. VII

Seymour, Sir Michael Culme-, 3rd Bt (*cr* 1809), 1836–1920, vol. II

Seymour, Vice-Adm. Sir Michael Culme-, 4th Bt (*cr* 1809), 1867–1925, vol. II

Seymour, Comdr Sir Michael Culme-, 5th Bt, 1909–1999, vol. X

Seymour, Michael Richard, 1880–1936, vol. III

Seymour, Comdr Ralph Frederick, 1886–1922, vol. II

Seymour, Lt-Col Sir Reginald Henry, 1878–1938, vol. III

Seymour, Richard, 1903–1982, vol. VIII

Seymour, Richard Sturgis, 1875–1959, vol. V

Seymour, Air Cdre Roland George, 1905–1983, vol. VIII

Seymour, Rosalind Herschel; *see* Wade, R. H.

Seymour, Rev. Lord Victor Alexander, 1859–1935, vol. III

Seymour, Gen. Lord William Frederick Ernest, 1838–1915, vol. I

Seymour, Gen. Sir William Henry, 1829–1921, vol. II

Seymour, William Kean, 1887–1975, vol. VII

Seymour-Lloyd, Sir John Hall, 1873–1939, vol. III

Seymour Seymour, Sir George, 1880–1962, vol. VI

Seys, Roland Alex. W.; *see* Wood-Seys.

Seznec, Jean Joseph, 1905–1983, vol. VIII

Sforza, Count Carlo, 1873–1952, vol. V

Sgambati, Giovanni, 1843–1914, vol. I

Shackle, Major Ernest William, 1862–1938, vol. III

Shackle, George Lennox Sharman, 1903–1992, vol. IX

Shackle, Robert Jones, 1895–1950, vol. IV

Shackleton, Baron (Life Peer); Edward Arthur Alexander Shackleton, 1911–1994, vol. IX

Shackleton, Sir David James, 1863–1938, vol. III

Shackleton, Edith; *see* Heald, E. S.

Shackleton, Major Sir Ernest Henry, 1874–1922, vol. II

Shackleton, Sir Harry Bertram, 1878–1958, vol. V

Shackleton, Robert, 1919–1986, vol. VIII

Shackleton, William, 1872–1933, vol. III

Shacklock, Constance, 1913–1999, vol. X

Shackman, Ralph, 1910–1981, vol. VIII

Shadbolt, Ernest Ifill, 1851–1936, vol. III

Shadi Lal, Rt Hon. Sir, 1874–1945, vol. IV

Shadwell, Arthur, 1854–1936, vol. III

Shadwell, Charles Lancelot, 1840–1919, vol. II

Shadwell, Lionel Lancelot, 1845–1925, vol. II

Shadwell, William L.; *see* Lucas-Shadwell.

Shafi, Sir Muhammad, 1869–1932, vol. III

Shafter, William Rufus, 1835–1906, vol. I

Shaftesbury, 9th Earl of, 1869–1961, vol. VI
Shaftesley, John Maurice, 1901–1981, vol. VIII
Shafto, Captain Arthur Duncombe, 1880–1914, vol. I
Shah, Hon. Sir Lallubhai Asharam, 1873–1926, vol. II
Shah, Khan Bahadur Sir Sayyid Mehdi, *died* 1927, vol. II, vol. III
Shahan, Rt Rev. Thomas Joseph, 1857–1932, vol. III
Shahpura, Raja Sir Nahar Singh Dhiraj, 1855–1932, vol. III
Shahub-ud-Din, Khan Bahadur Sir Chaudhri, *died* 1949, vol. IV (A), vol. V
Shaikh, Lt-Col Abdul Hamid, 1890–1963, vol. VI
Shairp, Lt-Col Alexander, 1873–1944, vol. IV
Shakerley, Sir Charles Watkin, 2nd Bt, 1833–1898, vol. I
Shakerley, Major Sir Cyril Holland, 5th Bt, 1897–1970, vol. VI
Shakerley, Major Geoffrey Charles, 1869–1915, vol. I
Shakerley, Sir Geoffrey Peter, 1906–1982, vol. VIII
Shakerley, Sir George Herbert, 4th Bt, 1863–1945, vol. IV
Shakerley, Sir Walter Geoffrey, 3rd Bt, 1859–1943, vol. IV
Shakespear, Alexander Blake, 1873–1949, vol. IV
Shakespear, Brig. Arthur Talbot, 1884–1964, vol. VI
Shakespear, Dame Ethel Mary Reader, 1871–1946, vol. IV
Shakespear, Maj.-Gen. George Robert James, 1842–1926, vol. II
Shakespear, Lt-Col John, 1861–1942, vol. IV
Shakespear, Col Leslie Waterfield, 1860–1933, vol. III
Shakespeare, Rt Hon. Sir Geoffrey Hithersay, 1st Bt, 1893–1980, vol. VII
Shakespeare, Rev. John Howard, 1857–1928, vol. II
Shakespeare, William, 1849–1931, vol. III
Shakespeare, Sir William Geoffrey, 2nd Bt, 1927–1996, vol. X
Shams-ul-Huda, Nawab Sir Syded, 1864–1922, vol. II
Shamsher Singh, Sir Sardar, Sardar Bahadur, 1860–1920, vol. II, vol. III
Shanahan, Col Daniel Davis, 1863–1954, vol. V
Shanahan, Foss, 1910–1964, vol. VI
Shand, 1st Baron, 1828–1904, vol. I
Shand, Alexander Faulkner, 1858–1936, vol. III
Shand, Alexander Innes, 1832–1907, vol. I
Shand, Sir Charles Lister, 1846–1925, vol. II
Shand, Sir James, 1908–2000, vol. X
Shand, Surg. Rear-Adm. Jonathan, 1865–1961, vol. VI
Shand, Philip Morton, 1888–1960, vol. V
Shand, Samuel James, 1882–1957, vol. V
Shand, Rev. Thomas Rodie, 1827–1914, vol. I
Shandon, 1st Baron, 1857–1930, vol. III
Shanker Shamsher Jang Bahadur Rana, Gen., 1909–1976, vol. VII
Shankland, Sir Thomas Murray, 1905–1986, vol. VIII
Shanks, Edward, 1892–1953, vol. V

Shanks, Ernest Pattison, 1911–1994, vol. IX
Shanks, Michael James, 1927–1984, vol. VIII
Shanks, S(eymour) Cochrane, 1893–1980, vol. VII
Shanks, W(illiam) Somerville, 1864–1951, vol. V
Shann, Edward Owen Giblin, 1884–1935, vol. III
Shann, Sir Keith Charles Owen, 1917–1988, vol. VIII
Shann, Sir Thomas Thornhill, 1846–1923, vol. II
Shannan, A. M'F., *died* 1915, vol. I
Shannon, 6th Earl of, 1860–1906, vol. I
Shannon, 7th Earl of, 1897–1917, vol. I
Shannon, 8th Earl of, 1900–1963, vol. VI
Shannon, Alastair, 1894–1982, vol. VIII
Shannon, Charles, 1863–1937, vol. III
Shannon, Godfrey Eccleston Boyd, 1907–1989, vol. VIII
Shannon, Howard Huntley, 1892–1976, vol. VII
Shannon, Sir James Jebusa, 1862–1923, vol. II
Shannon, Brig.-Gen. Lewis William, 1859–1936, vol. III
Shansfield, William Newton, *died* 1925, vol. II
Shapcott, Brig. Sir Henry, 1888–1967, vol. VI
Shapcott, John Dufour, 1857–1923, vol. II
Shapcott, Louis Edward, 1877–1950, vol. IV
Shapland, Cyril Dee, 1899–1980, vol. VII
Shapland, Maj.-Gen. John Dee, 1897–1971, vol. VII
Shapland, Rev. Richard Henry Bowden, 1877–1937, vol. III
Shapland, Sir William Arthur, 1912–1997, vol. X
Shapley, Harlow, 1885–1972, vol. VII
Shapley, Rt Rev. Ronald Norman, 1890–1964, vol. VI
Shapurji, Sir Burjorji Broacha, *died* 1920, vol. II
Share, Sir Hamnet Holditch, 1864–1937, vol. III
Sharfuddin, Syed, *born* 1856, vol. II
Sharkey, Sir Seymour John, 1847–1929, vol. III
Sharma, Shanker Dayal, 1918–1999, vol. X
Sharma, Vishnu Datt, 1921–1992, vol. IX
Sharman, Col Charles Henry Ludovic, 1881–1970, vol. VI
Sharman, Charlotte, 1832–1929, vol. III
Sharman, Thomas Charles, 1912–1990, vol. VIII
Sharman-Crawford, Col Rt Hon. Robert Gordon, 1853–1934, vol. III
Sharp, Baroness (Life Peer); Evelyn Adelaide Sharp, 1903–1985, vol. VIII
Sharp of Grimsdyke, Baron (Life Peer); Eric Sharp, 1916–1994, vol. IX
Sharp, Col Alexander Dunstan, 1870–1955, vol. V
Sharp, Air Vice-Marshal Alfred Charles Henry, 1904–1956, vol. V
Sharp, Alphonse, 1872–1942, vol. IV
Sharp, Sir Angus; *see* Sharp, Sir W. H. A.
Sharp, Rev. Arnold Mortimer, 1864–1938, vol. III
Sharp, Ven. Arthur Frederick, 1866–1960, vol. V
Sharp, Cecil James, 1859–1924, vol. II
Sharp, Christopher; *see* Sharp, J. C.
Sharp, Clifford Dyce, 1883–1935, vol. III
Sharp, David, 1840–1922, vol. II
Sharp, Dorothea, *died* 1955, vol. V
Sharp, Sir Edward, 1st Bt (*cr* 1922), 1854–1931, vol. III
Sharp, Sir Edward Herbert, 3rd Bt, 1927–1985, vol. VIII
Sharp, Elizabeth Amelia, 1856–1932, vol. III

Sharp, Ernest Hamilton, *died* 1922, vol. II
Sharp, Evelyn, 1869–1955, vol. V
Sharp, Francis Everard, 1890–1972, vol. VII
Sharp, Lt-Col Frederick Leonard, 1867–1916, vol. II
Sharp, Geoffrey Newton, 1914–1974, vol. VII
Sharp, Sir George, 1919–2000, vol. X
Sharp, Most Rev. Gerald, 1865–1933, vol. III
Sharp, Gilbert Granville-, 1894–1968, vol. VI
Sharp, Lt-Col Granville Maynard, 1906–1997, vol. X
Sharp, Harold Gregory, 1886–1972, vol. VII
Sharp, Sir Henry, 1869–1954, vol. V
Sharp, Henry Sutcliffe, 1910–1984, vol. VIII
Sharp, Sir Herbert Edward, 2nd Bt (*cr* 1922), 1879–1936, vol. III
Sharp, (James) Christopher, 1939–1997, vol. X
Sharp, Janet A.; *see* Achurch, J.
Sharp, Rev. John, 1837–1917, vol. II
Sharp, Rev. John Alfred, 1856–1932, vol. III
Sharp, Gen. Sir John Aubrey Taylor, 1917–1977, vol. VII
Sharp, Rev. Canon John Herbert, 1887–1950, vol. IV
Sharp, J(ohn) M(ichael) Cartwright, 1918–2000, vol. X
Sharp, Major John Reuben Philip, 1842–1922, vol. II
Sharp, Lauriston William, 1897–1959, vol. V
Sharp, Brig. Mainwaring Cato Ensor, 1897–1990, vol. VIII
Sharp, Margery, 1905–1991, vol. IX
Sharp, Michael Cartwright; *see* Sharp, J. M. C.
Sharp, Sir Milton, 2nd Bt (*cr* 1920), 1880–1941, vol. IV
Sharp, Sir Milton Reginald, 3rd Bt (*cr* 1920), 1909–1996, vol. X
Sharp, Sir Milton Sheridan, 1st Bt (*cr* 1920), 1856–1924, vol. II
Sharp, Noel Farquharson, 1905–1978, vol. VII
Sharp, Sir Percival, 1867–1953, vol. V
Sharp, Rear-Adm. Philip Graham, 1913–1988, vol. VIII
Sharp, Ven. Richard Lloyd, 1916–1982, vol. VIII
Sharp, Robert Farquharson, 1864–1945, vol. IV
Sharp, Thomas, 1901–1978, vol. VII
Sharp, Thomas Herbert, 1840–1918, vol. II
Sharp, W. H. Cartwright, 1883–1950, vol. IV
Sharp, William, 1856–1905, vol. I
Sharp, Mrs William; *see* Sharp, Elizabeth Amelia.
Sharp, Sir (William Harold) Angus, 1915–1993, vol. IX
Sharp, Rev. Canon William Hey, 1845–1928, vol. II
Sharpe, Sir Alfred, 1853–1935, vol. III
Sharpe, Charles W., *died* 1955, vol. V
Sharpe, Ven. Ernest Newton, *died* 1949, vol. IV
Sharpe, Sir Frank Victor, 1903–1988, vol. VIII
Sharpe, Rev. Harold Stephen, 1886–1960, vol. V
Sharpe, Rev. Henry Edmund, 1859–1939, vol. III
Sharpe, Hon. Sir John Henry, 1921–1999, vol. X
Sharpe, Joseph, 1859–1930, vol. III
Sharpe, Sir Montagu, 1856–1942, vol. IV
Sharpe, Peter Samuel, 1944–2000, vol. X
Sharpe, Phoebe Elizabeth, 1888–1941, vol. IV
Sharpe, Reginald Robinson, 1848–1925, vol. II

Sharpe, Sir Reginald Taaffe, 1898–1994, vol. IX
Sharpe, Richard Bowdler, 1847–1909, vol. I
Sharpe, Major Robert William, 1886–1943, vol. IV
Sharpe, Rev. Thomas Wetherherd, 1829–1905, vol. I
Sharpe, Major Wilfred Stanley, 1860–1917, vol. II
Sharpe, William, 1923–1999, vol. X
Sharpe, William Edward Thompson, 1834–1909, vol. I
Sharpe, William James, 1908–1994, vol. IX
Sharpe, Sir William Rutton Searle, 1881–1968, vol. VI
Sharpey-Schafer, Sir Edward Albert, 1850–1935, vol. III
Sharpey-Schafer, Edward Peter, 1908–1963, vol. VI
Sharpin, Ven. Frederick Lloyd, *died* 1921, vol. II
Sharples, Charles Norman, 1906–1954, vol. V
Sharples, Sir Richard Christopher, 1916–1973, vol. VII
Sharples, William Johnson, 1865–1948, vol. IV
Sharpley, Forbes Wilmot, 1897–1965, vol. VI
Sharrock, Rev. John Alfred, 1853–1932, vol. III
Sharrock, Roger Ian, 1919–1990, vol. VIII
Sharrock, Rev. Canon William R., *died* 1940, vol. III
Sharwood-Smith, Sir Bryan Evers, 1899–1983, vol. VIII
Sharwood-Smith, Edward, 1865–1954, vol. V
Shastri, Shri Lal Bahadur, 1904–1966, vol. VI
Shastri, Prabhu Dutt, *born* 1885, vol. IV
Shatford, Rev. Canon Allan P., 1873–1935, vol. III
Shattock, Clement Edward, 1887–1969, vol. VI
Shattock, Rear-Adm. Ernest Henry, 1904–1985, vol. VIII
Shattock, John Swithun Harvey, 1907–1993, vol. IX
Shattock, Samuel George, 1852–1924, vol. II
Shatwell, Kenneth Owen, 1909–1988, vol. VIII
Shaughnessy, 1st Baron, 1853–1923, vol. II
Shaughnessy, 2nd Baron, 1883–1938, vol. III
Shaw, Alan Frederick, 1910–1984, vol. VIII
Shaw, Albert, 1857–1947, vol. IV
Shaw, Alexander Malcolm, 1885–1974, vol. VII
Shaw, Sir Alexander William, 1847–1923, vol. II
Shaw, (Agnes) Maude; *see* Royden, A. M.
Shaw, Anne Gillespie, (Mrs J. H. Pirie), 1904–1982, vol. VIII
Shaw, Ven. Archibald, 1879–1956, vol. V
Shaw, Sir (Archibald) Douglas MacInnes, 1895–1957, vol. V
Shaw, Sir Archibald M'Innes, 1862–1931, vol. III
Shaw, Arnold John, 1909–1984, vol. VIII
Shaw, Rev. Arthur; *see* Shaw, Rev. B. A.
Shaw, Arthur, 1880–1939, vol. III
Shaw, Arthur Frederick Bernard, *died* 1947, vol. IV
Shaw, Arthur W.; *see* Winter-Shaw.
Shaw, Benjamin, 1906–1986, vol. VIII
Shaw, Bernard; *see* Shaw, G. B.
Shaw, Rev. (Bernard) Arthur, 1914–1988, vol. VIII
Shaw, Sir Bernard Vidal, 1891–1984, vol. VIII
Shaw, Byam; *see* Shaw, J. B. L.
Shaw, Sir Charles; *see* Shaw, Sir T. F. C. E.
Shaw, Very Rev. Charles Allan, 1927–1989, vol. VIII
Shaw, Charles James Dalrymple; *see* Baron Kilbrandon.

Shaw, Rev. Sir Charles John Monson, 8th Bt (*cr* 1665), 1860–1922, vol. II
Shaw, Charles Thomas K.; *see* Knox-Shaw.
Shaw, Clarice McNab, *died* 1946, vol. IV
Shaw, Captain (E) Cyril Arthur, 1894–1946, vol. IV
Shaw, Maj.-Gen. David G. Levinge, 1860–1930, vol. III
Shaw, Sir Douglas MacInnes; *see* Shaw, Sir A. D. M.
Shaw, Sir Doyle Money, 1830–1918, vol. II
Shaw, Rt Rev. Edward Domett, 1860–1937, vol. III
Shaw, Edward Wingfield, 1895–1916, vol. II
Shaw, Sir Evelyn Campbell, 1882–1974, vol. VII
Shaw, Sir Eyre Massey, 1830–1908, vol. I
Shaw, Col Francis Stewart Kennedy, 1871–1964, vol. VI
Shaw, Frank Howard, 1913–1990, vol. VIII
Shaw, Lt-Gen. Rt Hon. Sir Frederick Charles, 1861–1942, vol. IV
Shaw, Frederick John Freshwater, 1885–1936, vol. III
Shaw, Sir Frederick William, 5th Bt (*cr* 1821), 1858–1927, vol. II
Shaw, Geoffrey Mackintosh, 1927–1978, vol. VII
Shaw, Geoffrey Reginald Devereux, 1896–1960, vol. V
Shaw, Geoffrey Turton, 1879–1943, vol. IV
Shaw, George Anthony Theodore, 1917–1990, vol. VIII
Shaw, (George) Bernard, 1856–1950, vol. IV
Shaw, George Ernest, 1877–1958, vol. V
Shaw, George Ferdinand, 1821–1899, vol. I
Shaw, George Thomas, 1863–1938, vol. III
Shaw, Sir George Watson, 1858–1931, vol. III
Shaw, Rev. George William Hudson, *died* 1944, vol. IV
Shaw, Air Cdre Gerald Stanley, 1898–1976, vol. VII
Shaw, Sir Giles; *see* Shaw, Sir J. G. D.
Shaw, Harold Batty, 1867–1936, vol. III
Shaw, Harold K.; *see* Knox-Shaw.
Shaw, Harry Balmforth, 1899–1976, vol. VII
Shaw, Sir Havergal D.; *see* Downes-Shaw.
Shaw, Helen Brown, *died* 1964, vol. VI
Shaw, Henry Selby H.; *see* Hele-Shaw.
Shaw, Herman, 1891–1950, vol. IV
Shaw, Irwin, 1913–1984, vol. VIII
Shaw, Sir James Dods, *died* 1916, vol. II
Shaw, James John Sutherland, 1912–1994, vol. IX
Shaw, James Johnston, 1845–1910, vol. I
Shaw, John Byam Lister, 1872–1919, vol. II
Shaw, John Cecil Middleton, 1901–1961, vol. VI
Shaw, Sir John Charles Kenward, 7th Bt (*cr* 1665), 1829–1909, vol. I
Shaw, John Dennis Bolton, 1920–1989, vol. VIII
Shaw, Sir (John) Giles (Dunkerley), 1931–2000, vol. X
Shaw, Sir John Houldsworth, 1874–1962, vol. VI
Shaw, John James B.; *see* Byam Shaw.
Shaw, Sir John James Kenward B.; *see* Best-Shaw.
Shaw, Rev. John Mackintosh, 1879–1972, vol. VII
Shaw, Sir John Valentine Wistar, 1894–1982, vol. VIII
Shaw, John Woollands, 1875–1937, vol. III
Shaw, Joseph, 1856–1933, vol. III

Shaw, Kathleen Trousdell, 1870–1958, vol. V
Shaw, Lauriston Elgie, 1859–1923, vol. II
Shaw, Hon. Leslie Mortier, 1848–1932, vol. III
Shaw, Martin Fallas, 1875–1958, vol. V
Shaw, Mary, (Mrs Robert Shaw); *see* Ure, M.
Shaw, Maurice Elgie, 1894–1977, vol. VII
Shaw, Sir Napier; *see* Shaw, Sir W. N.
Shaw, Sir Patrick, 1913–1975, vol. VII
Shaw, Major Peter Stapleton-, 1888–1953, vol. V
Shaw, Philip Egerton, 1866–1949, vol. IV
Shaw, Reeves, 1886–1952, vol. V
Shaw, Richard James Herbert, 1885–1946, vol. IV
Shaw, Richard John Gildroy, 1936–1995, vol. IX
Shaw, Richard Norman, 1831–1912, vol. I
Shaw, Robert, 1927–1978, vol. VII
Shaw, Sir Robert de Vere, 6th Bt (*cr* 1821), 1890–1969, vol. VI
Shaw, Robert Macdonald, 1912–2000, vol. X
Shaw, Rt Hon. Sir Sebag, 1906–1982, vol. VIII
Shaw, Sinclair, *died* 1985, vol. VIII
Shaw, Sydney Herbert, 1903–1991, vol. IX
Shaw, Sir (Theodore Frederick) Charles (Edward), 1st Bt (*cr* 1908), 1859–1942, vol. IV
Shaw, Surg. Rear-Adm. Thomas Brown, 1879–1961, vol. VI
Shaw, Thomas Claye, 1841–1927, vol. II
Shaw, Thomas Edward, 1888–1935, vol. III
Shaw, Thomas K.; *see* Knox-Shaw.
Shaw, Thomas Richard, 1912–1989, vol. VIII
Shaw, Rt Hon. Tom, 1872–1938, vol. III
Shaw, Trevor Ian, 1928–1972, vol. VII
Shaw, Sir Walter Sidney, 1863–1937, vol. III
Shaw, Captain Walter William, 1868–1927, vol. II
Shaw, Wilfred, 1897–1953, vol. V
Shaw, William Arthur, 1865–1943, vol. IV
Shaw, William Barbour, 1868–1930, vol. III
Shaw, William Boyd Kennedy, 1901–1979, vol. VII
Shaw, Sir William Fletcher, 1878–1961, vol. VI
Shaw, Rev. William Francis, *died* 1904, vol. I
Shaw, Rev. William Frederick, 1843–1931, vol. III
Shaw, Sir (William) Napier, 1854–1945, vol. IV
Shaw, William R.; *see* Rawson-Shaw.
Shaw, William Thomas, 1879–1965, vol. VI
Shaw-Hamilton, Very Rev. Robert James, 1840–1908, vol. I
Shaw-Mackenzie, John Alexander, 1857–1933, vol. III
Shaw-Stewart, Col Basil Heron, 1877–1939, vol. III
Shaw-Stewart, Sir Euan Guy, 10th Bt, 1928–1980, vol. VII
Shaw-Stewart, Lt-Col Sir Guy; *see* Shaw-Stewart, Lt-Col Sir W. G.
Shaw-Stewart, Sir Hugh; *see* Shaw-Stewart, Sir M. H.
Shaw-Stewart, Sir (Michael) Hugh, 8th Bt, 1854–1942, vol. IV
Shaw-Stewart, Sir Michael Robert, 7th Bt, 1826–1903, vol. I
Shaw-Stewart, Lt-Col (Walter) Guy, 9th Bt, 1892–1976, vol. VII
Shaw-Stewart, Walter Richard, 1861–1934, vol. III
Shaw-Zambra, William Warren, 1898–1971, vol. VII
Shawcross, Christopher Nyholm, 1905–1973, vol. VII

Shawe, Lt-Col Charles, 1878–1951, vol. V
Shawe, Henry Benjamin, 1864–1943, vol. IV
Shawe-Taylor, Desmond Christopher, 1907–1995, vol. IX
Shawyer, Arthur Frederic, 1876–1954, vol. V
Shawyer, Robert Cort, 1913–1989, vol. VIII
Shaylor, Joseph, 1844–1923, vol. II
Shea, Lt-Col Alexander Gallwey, 1880–1935, vol. III
Shea, Hon. Sir Edward Dalton, 1820–1913, vol. I
Shea, Gen. Sir John Stuart Mackenzie, 1869–1966, vol. VI
Shea, Patrick, 1908–1986, vol. VIII
Shead, Sir Samuel George, 1871–1948, vol. IV
Sheals, John Gordon, 1923–1989, vol. VIII
Shearburn, Rt Rev. Victor George, 1900–1975, vol. VII
Sheard, Thomas Frederick Mason, 1866–1921, vol. II
Shearer, Sir Bruce, 1888–1971, vol. VII
Shearer, Cresswell, 1874–1941, vol. IV
Shearer, E., died 1945, vol. IV
Shearer, Brig. Eric James, 1892–1980, vol. VII
Shearer, Rt Hon. Ian Hamilton; see Avonside, Rt Hon. Lord.
Shearer, Sir James Greig, 1893–1966, vol. VI
Shearer, Sir John, 1843–1908, vol. I
Shearer, John Burt, 1904–1962, vol. VI
Shearer, Col Johnston, 1852–1917, vol. II
Shearer, Lt-Col Magnus, 1890–1961, vol. VI
Shearer, Thomas Hamilton, 1923–1995, vol. IX
Shearer, Rev. W(illiam) Russell, 1898–1987, vol. VIII
Shearing, Joseph; see Long, M. G.
Shearman, Arthur T., 1866–1937, vol. III
Shearman, Brig. Charles Edward Gowran, 1889–1968, vol. VI
Shearman, Sir Harold Charles, 1896–1984, vol. VIII
Shearman, Rt Hon. Sir Montague, 1857–1930, vol. III
Shearme, Edward, died 1920, vol. II
Shearme, Paymaster-Captain Edward Haweis, 1876–1925, vol. II
Shearme, Rev. John, 1842–1925, vol. II
Shears, Frederick Sidney, 1892–1932, vol. III
Shears, Maj.-Gen. Philip James, 1887–1972, vol. VII
Sheat, Sir Oliver; see Sheat, Sir W. J. O.
Sheat, Sir (William James) Oliver, 1864–1944, vol. IV
Shebbeare, Rev. Charles John, 1865–1945, vol. IV
Shebbeare, Edward Oswald, 1884–1964, vol. VI
Shedden, Sir Frederick Geoffrey, 1893–1971, vol. VII
Shedden, Sir George, 1856–1937, vol. III
Shedden, Sir Lewis, 1870–1941, vol. IV
Shedden, Rt Rev. Roscow George, 1882–1956, vol. V
Shedlock, John South, 1843–1919, vol. II
Shee, Sir George Richard Francis, 1869–1939, vol. III
Shee, Henry Gordon, 1847–1909, vol. I
Shee, Lt-Col Sir Martin A.; see Archer-Shee.
Sheean, (James) Vincent, 1899–1975, vol. VII
Sheean, Vincent; see Sheean, J. V.

Sheehan, Harold Leeming, 1900–1988, vol. VIII
Sheehan, Sir Henry John, 1883–1941, vol. IV
Sheehan, Most Rev. Michael, 1870–1945, vol. IV
Sheehan, Rev. Patrick Augustine, 1852–1913, vol. I
Sheehan, Most Rev. Richard Alphonsus, 1845–1915, vol. I
Sheehy, Sir Christopher, 1894–1960, vol. V
Sheehy, Sir John Francis, 1889–1949, vol. IV
Sheehy, Sir Joseph Aloysius, 1900–1971, vol. VII
Sheen, Alfred William, 1869–1945, vol. IV
Sheen, Engr-Rear-Adm. Charles C., 1871–1952, vol. V
Sheen, Most Rev. Fulton John, 1895–1979, vol. VII
Sheen, Air Vice-Marshal Walter Charles, 1907–1969, vol. VI (AII)
Sheepshanks, Rt Rev. John, 1834–1912, vol. I
Sheepshanks, Sir Thomas Herbert, 1895–1964, vol. VI
Sheepshanks, William, 1851–1928, vol. II
Sheerin, John Declan, 1932–1999, vol. X
Sheffield, 3rd Earl of, 1832–1909, vol. I
Sheffield, 4th Baron, and Stanley of Alderley, 4th Baron, 1839–1925, vol. II
Sheffield, 6th Baron, and Stanley of Alderley, 6th Baron, 1907–1971, vol. VII
Sheffield, 7th Baron, and Stanley of Alderley, 7th Baron, 1915–1971, vol. VII
Sheffield, Sir Berkeley Digby George, 6th Bt, 1876–1946, vol. IV
Sheffield, Edmund Charles Reginald, 1908–1977, vol. VII
Sheffield, Maj.-Gen. John, 1910–1987, vol. VIII
Sheffield, Sir Robert Arthur, 7th Bt, 1905–1977, vol. VII
Sheffield, Robert Stoney O.; see Oliphant-Sheffield.
Shehyn, Hon. Joseph, 1829–1918, vol. II
Sheil, Charles Leo, 1897–1968, vol. VI
Sheil, James, 1829–1908, vol. I
Sheil, John Devonshire, 1855–1935, vol. III
Sheild, Arthur Marmaduke, 1858–1922, vol. II
Sheilds, Francis Ernest W.; see Wentworth-Sheilds.
Sheilds, Rt Rev. Wentworth Francis W.; see Wentworth-Sheilds.
Sheils, George Kinglsey, 1894–1953, vol. V
Shekleton, Brig.-Gen. Hugh Pentland, 1860–1938, vol. III
Shelbourne, Sir Philip, 1924–1993, vol. IX
Sheldon, Charles Monroe, 1857–1946, vol. IV
Sheldon, Christine Mary, 1889–1970, vol. VI
Sheldon, John Prince, died 1913, vol. I
Sheldon, Sir Mark, 1871–1956, vol. V
Sheldon, Norman Lindsay, 1876–1946, vol. IV
Sheldon, Sir Wilfrid Percy Henry, 1901–1983, vol. VIII
Shelford, Frederic, 1871–1943, vol. IV
Shelford, Rev. Leonard Edmund, 1836–1914, vol. I
Shell, Rita, died 1950, vol. IV
Shelley, Col Bertram Arthur Graham, 1869–1947, vol. IV
Shelley, Sir Charles, 5th Bt (cr 1806), 1838–1902, vol. I
Shelley, Charles William Evans, 1912–1993, vol. IX
Shelley, Herbert John, 1895–1975, vol. VII
Shelley, Sir James, 1884–1961, vol. VI

Shelley, Sir John, 9th Bt (*cr* 1611), 1848–1931, vol. III
Shelley, Sir John Frederick, 10th Bt (*cr* 1611), 1884–1976, vol. VII
Shelley, Kew Edwin, 1894–1964, vol. VI
Shelley, Malcolm Bond, 1879–1968, vol. VI
Shelley, Sir Percy Bysshe, 7th Bt (*cr* 1806), 1872–1953, vol. V
Shelley, Sir Sidney Patrick, 8th Bt (*cr* 1806), 1880–1965, vol. VI
Shelley, Ursula, 1906–1993, vol. IX
Shelley-Rolls, Captain Sir John Courtown Edward, 6th Bt (*cr* 1806), 1871–1951, vol. V
Shellshear, Joseph Lexden, 1885–1958, vol. V
Shelmerdine, Lt-Col Sir Francis Claude, 1881–1945, vol. IV
Shennan, Sir Alfred Ernest, 1887–1959, vol. V
Shennan, Hay, 1859–1937, vol. III
Shennan, Theodore, *died* 1948, vol. IV
Shenstone, Allen Goodrich, 1893–1980, vol. VII
Shenstone, William Ashwell, 1850–1908, vol. I
Shentall, Sir Ernest, 1861–1936, vol. III
Shenton, Clive, 1946–1994, vol. IX
Shenton, Edward Warren Hine, 1872–1955, vol. V
Shenton, Hon. Sir George, 1842–1909, vol. I
Shenton, Sir William Edward Leonard, 1885–1967, vol. VI
Shepard, Ernest Howard, 1879–1976, vol. VII
Shepard, Helen Gould, 1868–1938, vol. III (A), vol. IV
Shepardson, Whitney Hart, 1890–1966, vol. VI
Shephard, Cecil Yaxley, 1900–1959, vol. V
Shephard, Lt-Col Charles Sinclair, 1848–1930, vol. III
Shephard, Firth, 1891–1949, vol. IV
Shephard, George Clifford, 1915–1994, vol. IX
Shephard, Air Cdre Harold Montague, 1918–2000, vol. X
Shephard, Sir Horatio Hale, *died* 1921, vol. II
Shephard, Rev. John, 1837–1926, vol. II
Shephard, Sidney, 1894–1953, vol. V
Shepheard, Major-Gen. Joseph Kenneth, 1908–1997, vol. X
Shepheard, Rex Beaumont, 1902–1980, vol. VII
Shepheard, Sir Victor George, 1893–1989, vol. VIII
Shepherd, 1st Baron, 1881–1954, vol. V
Shepherd, Rev. Ambrose, 1854–1915, vol. I
Shepherd, Arthur, 1884–1951, vol. V
Shepherd, Arthur Edmond, 1867–1942, vol. IV
Shepherd, Ven. Arthur Pearce, 1885–1968, vol. VI
Shepherd, Col Charles Herbert, 1846–1920, vol. II
Shepherd, Rear-Adm. Charles William Haimes, 1917–1998, vol. X
Shepherd, Lt-Col Claude Innes, 1884–1960, vol. V
Shepherd, Sir (Edward Henry) Gerald, 1886–1967, vol. VI
Shepherd, E(dwin) Colston, 1891–1976, vol. VII
Shepherd, Eric Andres, *died* 1937, vol. III
Shepherd, Eric William, 1913–1992, vol. IX
Shepherd, F. H. S., *died* 1948, vol. IV
Shepherd, Francis John, 1851–1929, vol. III
Shepherd, Sir Francis Michie, 1893–1962, vol. VI
Shepherd, Geoffrey Thomas, 1922–1993, vol. IX
Shepherd, George Anthony, 1931–1996, vol. X
Shepherd, Sir Gerald; *see* Shepherd, Sir E. H. G.

Shepherd, Gilbert David, 1880–1958, vol. V
Shepherd, Brig. Gilbert John Victor, 1887–1969, vol. VI
Shepherd, Harold Richard Bowman A.; *see* Adie-Shepherd.
Shepherd, Sir (Harry) Percy, *died* 1946, vol. IV
Shepherd, Henry Bryan, 1917–1974, vol. VII
Shepherd, Very Rev. Henry Young, *died* 1947, vol. IV
Shepherd, James Affleck, 1867–1946, vol. IV
Shepherd, Joseph Wilfrid, 1885–1975, vol. VII
Shepherd, Dame Margaret Alice, 1910–1990, vol. VIII
Shepherd, Air Vice-Marshal Melvin Clifford Seymour, 1922–1989, vol. VIII
Shepherd, Sir Percy; *see* Shepherd, Sir H. P.
Shepherd, Sir Peter Malcolm, 1916–1996, vol. X
Shepherd, Very Rev. Robert Henry Wishart, 1888–1971, vol. VII
Shepherd, Sir Walker; *see* Shpherd, Sir William W. F.
Shepherd, William Kidd Ogilvy, 1888–1941, vol. IV
Shepherd, William Morgan, 1905–1987, vol. VIII
Shepherd, Rev. William Mutrie, 1832–1910, vol. I
Shepherd, Sir (William) Walker (Frederick), 1895–1959, vol. V
Shepherd-Barron, Wilfrid Philip, 1888–1979, vol. VII
Shepherd-Cross, Herbert, 1847–1916, vol. II
Shepherd-Folker, Horace, 1859–1938, vol. III
Sheppard, Alfred Tresidder, 1871–1947, vol. IV
Sheppard, Adm. Sir Dawson; *see* Sheppard, Adm. Sir T. D. L.
Sheppard, Rev. Canon Edgar, 1845–1921, vol. II
Sheppard, Col George Sidney, 1867–1936, vol. III
Sheppard, Brig.-Gen. Herbert Cecil, *died* 1953, vol. V
Sheppard, Very Rev. Hugh Richard Lawrie, 1880–1937, vol. III
Sheppard, Sir John Tresidder, 1881–1968, vol. VI
Sheppard, Leslie Alfred, 1890–1985, vol. VIII
Sheppard, Tan Sri Dato Mervyn Cecil ffranck, 1905–1994, vol. IX
Sheppard, Oliver, *died* 1941, vol. IV
Sheppard, Percival Albert, (Peter), 1907–1977, vol. VII
Sheppard, Peter; *see* Sheppard, Percival A.
Sheppard, Philip Macdonald, 1921–1976, vol. VII
Sheppard, Sir Richard Herbert, 1910–1982, vol. VIII
Sheppard, Major Samuel Gurney, 1865–1915, vol. I
Sheppard, Samuel Townsend, 1880–1951, vol. V
Sheppard, Maj.-Gen. Seymour Hulbert, 1869–1957, vol. V
Sheppard, Thomas, 1876–1945, vol. IV
Sheppard, Adm. Sir (Thomas) Dawson Lees, 1866–1953, vol. V
Sheppard, Vivian Lee Osborne, 1877–1963, vol. VI
Sheppard, Sir William Didsbury, 1865–1933, vol. III
Sheppard, William Vincent, 1909–1985, vol. VIII
Sheppard Fidler, Alwyn Gwilym, 1909–1990, vol. VIII
Shepperson, Claude Allin, 1867–1921, vol. II

Shepperson, Sir Ernest Whittome, 1st Bt, 1874–1949, vol. IV
Shepstone, Arthur Jesse, 1852–1912, vol. I
Shepstone, John Wesley, 1827–1916, vol. II
Shepstone, Theophilus, 1843–1907, vol. I
Shera, Arthur Geoffrey, 1889–1971, vol. VII
Shera, Frank Henry, 1882–1956, vol. V
Sherard, 10th Baron, 1849–1902, vol. I
Sherard, 11th Baron, 1851–1924, vol. II
Sherard, 12th Baron, 1858–1931, vol. III
Sherard, Col Ralph Woodchurch, 1860–1922, vol. II
Sherard, Robert Harborough, 1861–1943, vol. IV
Sheraton, Rev. James Paterson, 1841–1906, vol. I
Sherborne, 4th Baron, 1831–1919, vol. II
Sherborne, 5th Baron, 1840–1920, vol. II
Sherborne, 6th Baron, 1873–1949, vol. IV
Sherborne, 7th Baron, 1911–1982, vol. VIII
Sherborne, 8th Baron, 1898–1985, vol. VIII
Sherbrooke, Captain Henry Graham, 1877–1940, vol. III
Sherbrooke, Rev. Henry Nevile, 1846–1916, vol. II
Sherbrooke, Col Nevile Hugh Cairns, 1880–1944, vol. IV
Sherbrooke, Rear-Adm. Robert St Vincent, 1901–1972, vol. VII
Sherbrooke-Walker, Col Ronald Draycott, 1897–1984, vol. VIII
Sherburn, Sir John, 1851–1926, vol. II
Shercliff, John Arthur, 1927–1983, vol. VIII
Sherek, Maj. (Jules) Henry, 1900–1967, vol. VI
Sherer, Brig.-Gen. James Donnelly, 1870–1959, vol. V
Sherer, John Walter, 1823–1911, vol. I
Sherfield, 1st Baron, 1904–1996, vol. X
Sheridan, Algernon Thomas Brinsley, 1845–1931, vol. III
Sheridan, Cecil Majella, 1911–2000, vol. X
Sheridan, Charles Cahill, *died* 1941, vol. IV
Sheridan, Clare Consuelo, 1885–1970, vol. VI
Sheridan, Sir Dermot Joseph, 1914–1978, vol. VII
Sheridan, Edward, *died* 1949, vol. IV
Sheridan, Rear-Adm. Henry A., 1884–1959, vol. V
Sheridan, Sir Joseph, 1882–1964, vol. VI
Sheridan, Sir Philip Cahill, 1871–1949, vol. IV
Sheriff, Rev. Thomas Holmes, *died* 1923, vol. II
Sheringham, George, 1884–1937, vol. III
Sheringham, Rev. Harry Alsager, 1852–1907, vol. I
Sheringham, Hugh Tempest, 1876–1930, vol. III
Sheringham, Ven. John William, *died* 1904, vol. I
Sherlock, Alexander, 1922–1999, vol. X
Sherlock, Sir Alfred Parker, 1876–1946, vol. IV
Sherlock, Col David John Christopher Eustace, 1879–1938, vol. III
Sherlock, David Thomas Joseph, 1881–1964, vol. VI
Sherlock, Frederick, 1853–1914, vol. I
Sherlock, Sir Philip Manderson, 1902–2000, vol. X
Sherlock, Ven. William, *died* 1919, vol. II
Sherman, Gina, (Mrs Alec Sherman); *see* Bachauer, G.
Sherman, John, 1823–1900, vol. I
Sherman, Most Rev. Louis Ralph, 1886–1953, vol. V
Sherrard, Col James William, *died* 1926, vol. II

Sherren, James, *died* 1945, vol. IV
Sherriff, Lt-Gen. John Pringle, 1831–1911, vol. I
Sherriff, Robert Cedric, 1896–1975, vol. VII
Sherrill, Brig.-Gen. Charles H., 1867–1936, vol. III
Sherrill, Rt Rev. Henry Knox, 1890–1980, vol. VII
Sherrington, Sir Charles Scott, 1857–1952, vol. V
Sherry, Mrs Vincent; *see* Robinson, Kathleen M.
Shersby, Sir (Julian) Michael, 1933–1997, vol. X
Shersby, Sir Michael; *see* Shersby, Sir J. M.
Sherston, Brig. John Reginald Vivian, 1888–1975, vol. VII
Sherston, Col William Maxwell, 1859–1925, vol. II
Sherston-Baker, Lt-Col Sir Dodington George Richard, 5th Bt, 1877–1944, vol. IV
Sherston-Baker, Sir Humphrey Dodington Benedict, 6th Bt, 1907–1990, vol. VIII
Sherwell, Arthur, 1863–1942, vol. IV
Sherwen, Ven. William, *died* 1915, vol. I
Sherwill, Sir Ambrose James, 1890–1968, vol. VI
Sherwin, Amy, *died* 1935, vol. III
Sherwin, Charles Edgar, 1909–1981, vol. VIII
Sherwin, Frederick George James, 1909–1984, vol. VIII
Sherwin-White, Adrian Nicholas, 1911–1993, vol. IX
Sherwood, 1st Baron, 1898–1970, vol. VI
Sherwood, Col Sir Arthur Percy, 1854–1940, vol. III
Sherwood, Rev. Edward Charles, *died* 1947, vol. IV
Sherwood, Frederic William, 1864–1931, vol. III
Sherwood, George Henry, 1877–1935, vol. III
Sherwood, Harry Leslie, 1863–1946, vol. IV
Sherwood, Leslie Robert, 1889–1974, vol. VII
Sherwood, Robert Emmet, 1896–1955, vol. V
Sherwood, Will, 1871–1955, vol. V
Sherwood, William Albert, 1855–1919, vol. II
Sherwood, Rev. William Edward, 1851–1927, vol. II
Sherwood-Kelly, Lt-Col John; *see* Kelly.
Sheshadri Iyar, K., Sir, *died* 1901, vol. I
Shevill, Rt Rev. Ian Wotton Allnutt, 1917–1988, vol. VIII
Shewan, Henry Alexander, 1906–1990, vol. VIII
Shewell, Brig. Eden Francis, 1877–1964, vol. VI
Shewell-Cooper, Wilfred Edward, 1900–1982, vol. VIII
Shiel, Rt Rev. Joseph, 1873–1931, vol. III
Shiel, Matthew Phipps, 1865–1947, vol. IV
Shield, George William, 1876–1935, vol. III
Shield, Hugh, 1831–1903, vol. I
Shields, Sir Douglas Andrew, 1878–1952, vol. V
Shields, Frederick James, 1833–1911, vol. I
Shields, Harry G., 1859–1935, vol. III
Shields, John Sinclair, 1903–1997, vol. X
Shields, John Veysie Montgomery, 1914–1966, vol. VI
Shields, Maj.-Gen. Ronald Frederick, 1912–1991, vol. IX
Shields, Ronald McGregor Pollock, 1921–1987, vol. VIII
Shields, Hon. Tasman, 1872–1950, vol. IV
Shiell, James Wyllie, 1912–1997, vol. X
Shiels, Sir Drummond; *see* Shiels, Sir T. D.
Shiels, Sir (Thomas) Drummond, 1881–1953, vol. V
Shiffner, Rev. Sir George Croxton, 4th Bt, 1819–1906, vol. I

Shiffner, Major Sir Henry Burrows, 7th Bt, 1902–1941, vol. IV
Shiffner, Sir John, 5th Bt, 1857–1914, vol. I
Shiffner, Sir John Bridger, 6th Bt, 1899–1918, vol. II
Shigemitsu, Mamoru, 1887–1957, vol. V
Shillaker, James Frederick, 1870–1943, vol. IV
Shillidy, George Alexander, 1886–1968, vol. VI
Shillidy, John Armstrong, 1882–1952, vol. V
Shillingford, John Parsons, 1914–1999, vol. X
Shillington, Courtenay Alexander Rives, 1902–1983, vol. VIII
Shillington, Major Rt Hon. David Graham, 1872–1944, vol. IV
Shillito, Charles Henry, 1922–1998, vol. X
Shillito, Rev. Edward, 1872–1948, vol. IV
Shillito, Edward Alan, 1910–1991, vol. IX
Shimeld, Kenneth Reeve, 1921–1984, vol. VIII
Shindler, George John, 1922–1994, vol. IX
Shine, Eustace Beverley, 1873–1952, vol. V
Shine, Col James Mathew Forrest, 1861–1931, vol. III
Shine, Most Rev. Thomas, 1872–1955, vol. V
Shiner, Lt-Col Sir Herbert, 1890–1962, vol. VI
Shiner, Ronald Alfred, 1903–1966, vol. VI
Shingleton, Frederick, 1846–1938, vol. III
Shinkwin, Col Ion Richard Staveley, 1875–1961, vol. VI
Shinn, Frederick George, 1867–1950, vol. IV
Shinnie, Andrew James, 1886–1963, vol. VI
Shinwell, Baron (Life Peer); Emanuel Shinwell, 1884–1986, vol. VIII
Shipley, Sir Arthur Everett, 1861–1927, vol. II
Shipley, Brig.-Gen. Charles Orby, 1867–1934, vol. III
Shipley, Col Charles Tyrell, 1863–1933, vol. III
Shipley, Hammond Smith, 1858–1930, vol. III
Shipley, Orby, 1832–1916, vol. II
Shipley, Lt-Col Reginald Burge, *died* 1924, vol. II
Shipley, Sir William Alexander, 1857–1922, vol. II
Shipman, Louis Evan, 1869–1933, vol. III
Shippard, Sir Sidney Godolphin Alexander, 1837–1902, vol. I
Shipstone, Sir Thomas, 1851–1940, vol. III
Shipton, Eric Earle, 1907–1977, vol. VII
Shipway, Sir Francis Edward, 1875–1968, vol. VI
Shipwright, Sqdn Leader Denis E. B. K., 1898–1984, vol. VIII
Shipwright, Lottie Adelina de Lara; *see* de Lara, Adelina.
Shircore, John Owen, 1882–1953, vol. V
Shirer, William Lawrence, 1904–1993, vol. IX
Shires, Sir Frank, 1899–1981, vol. VIII
Shirlaw, John Fenton, 1896–1975, vol. VII
Shirlaw, Matthew, 1873–1961, vol. VI
Shirley; *see* Skelton, Sir John.
Shirley, David Andrew, 1926–1999, vol. X
Shirley, Evelyn Philip Sewallis, 1900–1978, vol. VII
Shirley, Rev. (Frederick) John, 1890–1967, vol. VI
Shirley, Herbert John, 1868–1943, vol. IV
Shirley, Rev. John; *see* Shirley, Rev. F. J.
Shirley, Philip Hammond, 1912–1998, vol. X
Shirley, Hon. Ralph, 1865–1946, vol. IV
Shirley, Sewallis Evelyn, 1844–1904, vol. I

Shirley, Air Vice-Marshal Sir Thomas Ulric Curzon, 1908–1982, vol. VIII
Shirley, William, 1866–1930, vol. III
Shirley-Fox, John Shirley, *died* 1939, vol. III
Shirley-Smith, Sir Hubert, 1901–1981, vol. VIII
Shirras, George Findlay, 1885–1955, vol. V
Shirres, Major John Chivas, 1854–1899, vol. I
Shirtcliffe, Sir George, 1862–1941, vol. IV
Shoaib, Mohammad, 1905–1976, vol. VII
Shockley, Dr William Bradford, 1910–1989, vol. VIII
Shoenberg, Sir Isaac, 1880–1963, vol. VI
Shoesmith, Kenneth Denton, 1890–1939, vol. III
Sholl, Hon. Sir Reginald Richard, 1902–1988, vol. IX (AI)
Sholl, Richard Adolphus, 1846–1919, vol. II
Sholokhov, Mikhail Aleksandrovich, 1905–1984, vol. VIII
Shone, Sir Robert Minshull, 1906–1992, vol. IX
Shone, Rt Rev. Samuel, 1820–1897, vol. I
Shone, Sir Terence Allen, 1894–1965, vol. VI
Shone, Lt-Gen. Sir William Terence, 1850–1938, vol. III
Shonfield, Sir Andrew Akiba, 1917–1981, vol. VIII
Shoobert, Sir Harold; *see* Shoobert, Sir W. H.
Shoobert, Sir (Wilfred) Harold, 1896–1969, vol. VI
Shoobridge, Hon. Sir Rupert Oakley, 1883–1962, vol. VI
Shoolbred, Frederick Thomas, 1841–1922, vol. II
Shoolbred, Lt-Col Rupert, 1869–1946, vol. IV
Shoosmith, Maj.-Gen. Stephen Newton, 1900–1956, vol. V
Shoosmith, Thurston Laidlaw, 1865–1933, vol. III
Shoppee, Charles William, 1904–1994, vol IX
Shore, Bernard Alexander Royle, 1896–1985, vol. VIII
Shore, Lewis Erle, 1863–1944, vol. IV
Shore, Brig.-Gen. Offley Bohun Stovin Fairless, 1863–1922, vol. II
Shore, Robert S., *died* 1931, vol. III
Shore, Rev. Thomas Teignmouth, 1841–1911, vol. I
Shore, Thomas William, 1861–1947, vol. IV
Shore, W. Teignmouth, *died* 1932, vol. III
Shores, John Wallis, 1851–1935, vol. III
Shorrock, James Godby, 1910–1987, vol. VIII
Shorrock, William Gordon, 1879–1944, vol. IV
Short, Adrian Hugh H.; *see* Hassard-Short.
Short, Alfred, 1882–1938, vol. III
Short, Brig.-Gen. Anthony Holbeche, 1862–1940, vol. III
Short, Rt Rev. Hedley Vicars Roycraft, 1914–1996, vol. X
Short, Rev. John, 1896–1989, vol. IX (AI)
Shortt, Maj.-Gen. Arthur Charles, 1899–1984, vol. VIII
Short, Arthur Rendle, *died* 1953, vol. V
Short, Ernest Henry, 1875–1959, vol. V
Short, Lt-Col Ernest William George, 1877–1953, vol. V
Short, Sir Frank, 1857–1945, vol. IV
Short, Rev. Frank, 1895–1975, vol. VII
Short, Rev. Canon Frederick Winning H.; *see* Hassard-Short.
Short, Rev. Harry Lismer, 1906–1975, vol. VII
Short, Herbert Arthur, 1895–1967, vol. VI

Short, John, 1894–1967, vol. VI
Short, John Tregerthen, 1858–1933, vol. III
Short, Richard, 1841–1916, vol. II
Short, Thomas Sydney, *died* 1924, vol. II
Short, Vivian Augustus, 1883–1950, vol. IV
Short, Wilfrid Maurice, 1870–1947, vol. IV
Short, William, 1866–1929, vol. III
Short, Lt-Col William Ambrose, *died* 1917, vol. II
Shortall, Sir Patrick, 1872–1925, vol. II
Shorter, Clement King, 1857–1926, vol. II
Shorter, Dora, 1866–1918, vol. II
Shorthouse, Joseph Henry, 1834–1903, vol. I
Shortland, Adm. Edward George, 1855–1929,
   vol. III
Shortland, Captain Henry Vincent, *died* 1913, vol. I
Shorto, William Alfred Thomas, 1876–1951, vol. V
Shortt, Adam, 1859–1931, vol. III
Shortt, Rt Hon. Edward, 1862–1935, vol. III
Shortt, Col Henry Edward, 1887–1987, vol. VIII
Shortt, John, *died* 1932, vol. III
Shostakovich, Dmitry Dmitrievich, 1906–1975,
   vol. VII
Shott, Henry Hammond, 1877–1914, vol. I
Shotton, Edward, 1910–1998, vol. X
Shotton, Frederick William, 1906–1990, vol. VIII
Shotwell, James Thomson, 1874–1965, vol. VI
Shoubridge, Harry Oliver Baron, 1872–1934, vol. III
Shoubridge, Maj.-Gen. Herbert; *see* Shoubridge,
   Maj.-Gen. T. H.
Shoubridge, Maj.-Gen. (Thomas) Herbert,
   1871–1923, vol. II
Shove, Gerald Frank, 1887–1947, vol. IV
Shove, Captain Herbert William, 1886–1943,
   vol. IV
Shove, Ralph Samuel, 1889–1966, vol. VI
Shovelton, Sydney Taverner, 1881–1967, vol. VI
Showa, Emperor; *see* Hirohito, Emperor of Japan.
Showering, Sir Keith Stanley, 1930–1982, vol. VIII
Showers, Lt-Col Herbert Lionel, 1861–1916, vol. II
Shrapnell-Smith, Edward Shrapnell, 1875–1952,
   vol. V
Shreeve, George Harry, 1888–1960, vol. V
Shrewsbury and Waterford, 20th Earl of,
   1860–1921, vol. II
Shrewsbury and Waterford, 21st Earl of, 1914–1980,
   vol. VII
Shrewsbury, J. F. D., 1898–1971, vol. VII
Shrimsley, Anthony, 1934–1984, vol. VIII
Shrubsall, Frank Charles, *died* 1935, vol. III
Shrubsole, Rear-Adm. Percy Joseph, 1875–1958,
   vol. V
Shuard, Amy, (Mrs Peter Asher), 1924–1975,
   vol. VII
Shuckburgh, Sir (Charles Arthur) Evelyn,
   1909–1994, vol. IX
Shuckburgh, Sir Charles Gerald Stewkley, 12th Bt,
   1911–1988, vol. VIII
Shuckburgh, Sir Evelyn; *see* Shuckburgh, Sir
   C. A. E.
Shuckburgh, Evelyn Shirley, 1843–1906, vol. I
Shuckburgh, Sir Gerald Francis Stewkley, 11th Bt,
   1882–1939, vol. III
Shuckburgh, Sir John Evelyn, 1877–1953, vol. V
Shuckburgh, Robert Shirley, 1882–1954, vol. V

Shuckburgh, Sir Stewkley Frederick Draycott, 10th
   Bt, 1880–1917, vol. II
Shufeldt, Major Robert Wilson, 1850–1934, vol. III
Shufflebotham, Frank, *died* 1932, vol. III
Shuffrey, Paul, 1889–1955, vol. V
Shuffrey, Rev. William Arthur, 1851–1932, vol. III
Shuldham-Legh, Col Harry Shuldham, 1854–1915,
   vol. I
Shurmer, Percy Lionel Edward, *died* 1959, vol. V
Shute, Gen. Sir Cameron Deane, 1866–1936,
   vol. III
Shute, Gen. Sir Charles Cameron, 1816–1904, vol. I
Shute, Charles Cameron Donald, 1917–1999, vol. X
Shute, Lt-Col Cyril Aveling, 1886–1950, vol. IV
Shute, Geoffrey Gay, 1892–1951, vol. V
Shute, Col Henry Gwynn Deane, 1860–1909, vol. I
Shute, Col Sir John Joseph, *died* 1948, vol. IV
Shute, John Lawson, *born* 1901, vol. IX (AI)
Shute, Nevil; *see* Norway, N. S.
Shuter, Comdr Joseph Armand, 1876–1915, vol. I
Shuter, Brig.-Gen. Reginald Gauntlett, 1875–1957,
   vol. V
Shutt, Frank Thomas, 1859–1940, vol. III
Shuttleworth, 1st Baron, 1844–1939, vol. III
Shuttleworth, 2nd Baron, 1913–1940, vol. III
Shuttleworth, 3rd Baron, 1917–1942, vol. IV
Shuttleworth, 4th Baron, 1917–1975, vol. VII
Shuttleworth, Alfred, 1843–1925, vol. II
Shuttleworth, Brig. Betham Wilkins, 1880–1937,
   vol. III
Shuttleworth, Maj.-Gen. Sir Digby Inglis,
   1876–1948, vol. IV
Shuttleworth, Edward Cheke Smalley, 1866–1943,
   vol. IV
Shuttleworth, Edward James K.; *see*
   Kay-Shuttleworth.
Shuttleworth, Col Frank, 1845–1913, vol. I
Shuttleworth, George Edward, 1842–1928, vol. II
Shuttleworth, Rev. Henry Cary, 1850–1900, vol. I
Shuttleworth, Hon. Lawrence Ughtred K.; *see*
   Kay-Shuttleworth.
Shvernik, Nikolai Mikhailovich, 1888–1970, vol. VI
Siam, HM King of, Rama VI, 1881–1925, vol. II
Sibbald, Sir John, 1833–1905, vol. I
Sibbald, Maj.-Gen. Peter Frank Aubrey, 1928–1994,
   vol. IX
Sibbald, Rev. Samuel James Ramsay, 1869–1950,
   vol. IV
Sibbett, Cecil James, *died* 1967, vol. VI
Sibelius, Jean Julius Christian, 1865–1957, vol. V
Sibley, Walter Knowsley, 1862–1944, vol. IV
Sibly, Sir Franklin; *see* Sibly, Sir T. F.
Sibly, Sir (Thomas) Franklin, 1883–1948, vol. IV
Sibly, William Arthur, 1883–1959, vol. V
Siborne, Maj.-Gen. Herbert Taylor, 1826–1902,
   vol. I
Sibree, Rev. James, 1836–1929, vol. III
Sibthorpe, Surg.-Gen. Charles, 1847–1906, vol. I
Sich, Sir Rupert Leigh, 1908–1995, vol. IX
Sichel, Alan William Stuart, 1886–1966, vol. VI
Sichel, Edith, 1862–1914, vol. I
Sichel, Walter, 1855–1933, vol. III
Sickert, Walter Richard, 1860–1942, vol. IV
Sicot, Marcel Jean, 1898–1981, vol. VIII
Sidaner, Henri Le, 1862–1939, vol. III

Siddall, Joseph Bower, 1840–1925, vol. II
Siddeley, John Tennant Davenport, (3rd Baron Kenilworth), 1924–1981, vol. VIII
Siddiqui, Salimuzzaman, 1897–1994, vol. IX
Siddons, (Arthur) Harold (Makins), 1911–2000, vol. X
Siddons, Harold; *see* Siddons, A. H. M.
Sidebotham, Herbert, 1872–1940, vol. III
Sidebotham, John Biddulph, 1891–1988, vol. VIII
Sidebotham, Joseph Watson, 1857–1925, vol. II
Sidebottam, Tom Harrop, *died* 1908, vol. I
Sidebottom, William, *died* 1933, vol. III
Sidey, John MacNaughton, 1914–1990, vol. VIII
Sidey, Sir Thomas Kay, 1863–1933, vol. III
Sidgreaves, Sir Arthur Frederick, 1882–1948, vol. IV
Sidgreaves, Rev. Walter, 1837–1919, vol. II
Sidgwick, Alfred, 1850–1943, vol. IV
Sidgwick, Arthur, 1840–1920, vol. II
Sidgwick, Cecily, *died* 1934, vol. III
Sidgwick, Eleanor Mildred, 1845–1936, vol. III
Sidgwick, Ethel, 1877–1970, vol. VI
Sidgwick, Henry, 1838–1900, vol. I
Sidgwick, Mrs Henry; *see* Sidgwick, Eleanor Mildred.
Sidgwick, Rear-Adm. John Benson, 1891–1983, vol. VIII
Sidgwick, Nevil Vincent, 1873–1952, vol. V
Sidmouth, 3rd Viscount, 1824–1913, vol. I
Sidmouth, 4th Viscount, 1854–1915, vol. I
Sidmouth, 5th Viscount, 1882–1953, vol. V
Sidmouth, 6th Viscount, 1887–1976, vol. VII
Sidney, Herbert, *died* 1923, vol. II
Sidney, Thomas Stafford, 1863–1917, vol. II
Sidney-Humphries, Sydney, 1862–1941, vol. IV
Sidney-Wilmot, Air Vice-Marshal Aubrey, 1915–1989, vol. VIII
Sidwell, Rt Rev. Henry Bindley, 1857–1936, vol. III
Sidwell, Martindale, 1916–1998, vol. X
Sie, Sir Banja T.; *see* Tejan-Sie.
Sieff, Baron (Life Peer); Israel Moses Sieff, 1889–1972, vol. VII
Sieff, Joseph Edward, 1905–1982, vol. VIII
Sieff, Hon. Michael David, 1911–1987, vol. VIII
Siegbahn, (Karl) Manne (Georg), 1886–1978, vol. VII
Siegbahn, Manne; *see* Siegbahn, K. M. G.
Siegfried, André, 1875–1959, vol. V
Sieghart, Paul Henry Laurence Alexander, 1927–1988, vol. VIII
Siemens, Alexander, 1847–1928, vol. II
Sienkiewicz, Henryk, 1846–1916, vol. II
Siepmann, Charles Arthur, 1899–1985, vol. VIII
Siepmann, Harry Arthur, 1889–1963, vol. VI
Sieve, James Ezekiel Balfour, 1922–1983, vol. IX (AI)
Sieveking, Albert Forbes, 1857–1951, vol. V
Sieveking, Sir Edward Henry, 1816–1904, vol. I
Sieveking, Captain Lancelot de Giberne, 1896–1972, vol. VII
Sievier, Robert Standish, 1860–1939, vol. III
Sievwright, Andrew George Hume, 1885–1956, vol. V
Sievwright, J. D., 1863–1947, vol. IV
Sifton, Rt Hon. Arthur Lewis, 1858–1921, vol. II

Sifton, Hon. Sir Clifford, 1861–1929, vol. III
Sifton, Sir James David, 1878–1952, vol. V
Sifton, John William, 1925–1969, vol. VI
Sifton, Victor, 1897–1961, vol. VI
Sigerson, Dora; *see* Shorter, D.
Sigerson, George, *died* 1925, vol. II
Siggers, Ven. William C.; *see* Curzon-Siggers.
Signoret, Simone, (Simone Henriette Charlotte Montand), 1921–1985, vol. VIII
Sigrist, Frederick, 1884–1956, vol. V
Sigsbee, Rear-Adm. Charles Dwight, 1845–1923, vol. II
Sigurdsson, Asgeir Thorsteinn, 1864–1935, vol. III
Sikes, Alfred Walter, 1869–1948, vol. IV
Sikes, Edward Ernest, 1867–1940, vol. III
Sikes, Francis Henry, 1862–1943, vol. IV
Sikes, Howard Lecky, 1881–1943, vol. IV
Sikkim, Maharaja Kumar Sidkeong Tulku of, 1879–1914, vol. I
Sikkim, Maharaja Sidkeong Tulku of, *died* 1914, vol. I
Sikkim, Maharaja of, 1893–1963, vol. VI
Sikorski, Gen. Wladyslaw Eugeniusz, 1881–1943, vol. IV
Sikorsky, Igor Ivan, 1889–1972, vol. VII
Sikri, Mittra; *see* Sikri, S. M.
Sikri, Sarv Mittra, 1908–1992, vol. IX
Silberrad, Oswald John, 1878–1960, vol. V
Silberrad, Una L., 1872–1955, vol. V
Silburn, Col Percy Arthur Baxter, 1876–1929, vol. III
Silcock, Arnold, 1889–1953, vol. V
Silcock, Arthur Quarry, 1855–1904, vol. I
Silcock, Henry Thomas, 1882–1969, vol. VI
Silcock, Thomas Ball, 1854–1924, vol. II
Silcox, Albert Henry, 1895–1971, vol. VII
Silk, Paymaster Rear-Adm. Ernest Edwin, 1862–1940, vol. III
Silk, John Frederick William, 1858–1943, vol. IV
Silkin, 1st Baron, 1889–1972, vol. VII
Silkin of Dulwich, Baron (Life Peer); Samuel Charles Silkin, 1918–1988, vol. VIII
Silkin, Rt Hon. John Ernest, 1923–1987, vol. VIII
Silkin, Jon, 1930–1997, vol. X
Sillem, Maj.-Gen. Sir Arnold Frederick, 1865–1949, vol. IV
Sillery, Anthony, 1903–1976, vol. VII
Sillince, William Augustus, 1906–1974, vol. VII
Sillitoe, Leslie Richard, 1915–1996, vol. X
Sillitoe, Sir Percy Joseph, 1888–1962, vol. VI
Sills, George, 1832–1905, vol. I
Silone, Ignazio, 1900–1978, vol. VII
Siloti, Alexander, 1863–1945, vol. IV
Silsoe, 1st Baron, 1894–1976, vol. VII
Silver, Albert Harlow, 1875–1954, vol. V
Silver, Alfred Jethro, 1870–1935, vol. III
Silver, Gertrude; *see* Kingston, G.
Silver, Lt-Col John Payzant, 1868–1957, vol. V
Silver, Vice-Adm. Mortimer L'E., 1869–1946, vol. IV
Silver, Robert Simpson, 1913–1997, vol. X
Silverleaf, Alexander, 1920–1997, vol. X
Silverman, Herbert Albert, 1896–1980, vol. VII (AII)
Silverman, Julius, 1905–1996, vol. X

Silverman, (Samuel) Sydney, 1895–1968, vol. VI
Silverman, Sydney; *see* Silverman, S. S.
Silverstone, Arnold; *see* Baron Ashdown.
Silverwood-Cope, Maclachlan Alan Carl, 1915–1993, vol. IX
Silvester, Air Cdre James, 1898–1956, vol. V
Silvester, Norman Langton, 1894–1969, vol. VI (AII)
Silvester, Victor Marlborough, 1900–1978, vol. VII
Silvestri, Constantin, 1913–1969, vol. VI
Silyn Roberts, Air Vice-Marshal Glynn, 1906–1983, vol. VIII
Sim, Alastair, 1900–1976, vol. VII
Sim, Sir Alexander; *see* Sim, Sir G. A. S.
Sim, David, 1899–1987, vol. VIII
Sim, Sir (George) Alexander (Strachan), 1905–1980, vol. VII
Sim, Brig. George Edward Herman, 1886–1952, vol. V
Sim, George Gall, 1878–1930, vol. III
Sim, Col George Hamilton, 1852–1929, vol. III
Sim, Henry Alexander, 1856–1928, vol. II
Sim, James Duncan Stuart, 1849–1912, vol. I
Sim, John Mackay, 1917–1993, vol. IX
Sim, Sir Wilfrid Joseph, 1890–1974, vol. VII
Simcock, Rev. Canon James Alexander, 1897–1984, vol. VIII
Sime, John, 1842–1911, vol. I
Sime, William Arnold, 1909–1983, vol. VIII
Simenon, Georges, 1903–1989, vol. VIII
Simeon, Vice-Adm. Sir Charles Edward Barrington, 1889–1955, vol. V
Simeon, Sir Edmund Charles, 5th Bt, 1855–1915, vol. I
Simeon, Sir John Edmund Barrington, 7th Bt, 1911–1999, vol. X
Simeon, John Power Barrington, 1929–2000, vol. X
Simeon, Sir John Stephen Barrington, 4th Bt, 1850–1909, vol. I
Simeon, Sir John Walter Barrington, 6th Bt, 1886–1957, vol. V
Simeon, Stephen Louis, 1857–1937, vol. III
Simes, Charles Erskine Woollard, 1893–1978, vol. VII
Simey, Baron (Life Peer); Thomas Spensley Simey, 1906–1969, vol. VI
Simkin, Rt Rev. William John, 1883–1967, vol. VI
Simm, Matthew Turnbull, 1869–1928, vol. II
Simmonds, Arthur, 1892–1968, vol. VI
Simmonds, B(ernard) Sangster, 1886–1953, vol. V
Simmonds, Frederick, 1845–1921, vol. II
Simmonds, Herbert John, 1867–1950, vol. IV
Simmonds, Hugh Henry Dawes, 1886–1952, vol. V
Simmonds, Kenneth Royston, 1927–1995, vol. IX
Simmonds, Kenneth Willison, 1912–1991, vol. IX
Simmonds, Sir Oliver Edwin, 1897–1985, vol. VIII
Simmonds, Sidney, 1899–1977, vol. VII
Simmonds, William George, 1876–1968, vol. VI
Simmonds, William Henry, 1860–1934, vol. III
Simmons, Mrs Amy, *died* 1964, vol. VI
Simmons, Sir Anker; *see* Simmons, Sir W. A.
Simmons, Arthur Thomas, 1865–1921, vol. II
Simmons, Charles James, 1893–1975, vol. VII
Simmons, Ernest Bernard, 1913–1988, vol. VIII
Simmons, Ernest J., 1903–1972, vol. VII

Simmons, Maj.-Gen. Frank Keith, 1888–1952, vol. V
Simmons, Rev. Frederic Pearson Copland, 1902–1978, vol. VII
Simmons, Sir Frederick James, 1867–1955, vol. V
Simmons, Col George Francis Henry Le B.; *see* Le Breton-Simmons.
Simmons, Engr-Captain George Thomas, 1853–1933, vol. III
Simmons, George Thomas Wagstaffe, *died* 1954, vol. V
Simmons, Sir Ira Marcus, 1917–1974, vol. VII (AII)
Simmons, Jack, 1915–2000, vol. X
Simmons, Sir John Lintorn Arabin, 1821–1903, vol. I
Simmons, Major Sir Percy Coleman, 1875–1939, vol. III
Simmons, Robert J., 1894–1985, vol. VIII
Simmons, Sir (William) Anker, 1857–1927, vol. II
Simmons, William Foster, 1888–1985, vol. VIII
Simms, Ven. Arthur Hennell, 1853–1921, vol. II
Simms, Captain Charles Edward, 1900–1963, vol. VI
Simms, Most Rev. George Otto, 1910–1991, vol. IX
Simms, Very Rev. John Morrow, 1854–1934, vol. III
Simms, Ven. William, 1845–1932, vol. III
Simner, Col Sir Percy Reginald Owen Abel, 1878–1963, vol. VI
Simnett, William Edward, 1880–1958, vol. V
Simogun, Sir Petar, 1900–1987, vol. VIII
Simon, 1st Viscount, 1873–1954, vol. V
Simon, 2nd Viscount, 1902–1993, vol. IX
Simon, Viscountess; (Kathleen), 1871–1955, vol. V
Simon of Wythenshawe, 1st Baron, 1879–1960, vol. V
Simon of Wythenshawe, Lady; (Shena Dorothy), 1883–1972, vol. VII
Simon, André Louis, 1877–1970, vol. VI
Simon, Rev. D. W., 1830–1909, vol. I
Simon, (Ernest Julius) Walter, 1893–1981, vol. VIII
Simon, Sir Francis Eugene, 1893–1956, vol. V
Simon, George Percival, 1893–1963, vol. VI
Simon, Rt Rev. Glyn; *see* Simon, Rt Rev. W. G. H.
Simon, Sir John, 1818–1897, vol. I
Simon, Sir John, 1816–1904, vol. I
Simon, Rev. John Smith, 1843–1933, vol. III
Simon, Sir Leon, 1881–1965, vol. VI
Simon, Col Maximilian St Leger, 1876–1951, vol. V
Simon, Oliver, 1895–1956, vol. V
Simon, Sir Robert Michael, 1850–1914, vol. I
Simon, Ulrich Ernst, 1913–1997, vol. X
Simon, Walter; *see* Simon, E. J. W.
Simon, Walter, *died* 1967, vol. VI
Simon, Hon. William Edward, 1927–2000, vol. X
Simon, Rt Rev. (William) Glyn (Hughes), 1903–1972, vol. VI
Simond, Charles François, *died* 1957, vol. V
Simonds, 1st Viscount, 1881–1971, vol. VII
Simonds, Frank H., 1878–1936, vol. III
Simonds, Frederick Adolphus, 1881–1953, vol. V
Simonds, Lt-Gen. Guy Granville, 1903–1974, vol. VII
Simonds, John Hayes, 1879–1946, vol. IV

Simonds, Most Rev. Justin Daniel, 1890–1967, vol. VI

Simonds, William Barrow, 1820–1911, vol. I

Simons, Adm. Ernest Alfred, 1856–1928, vol. II

Simons, Very Rev. William Charles, *died* 1921, vol. II

Simonsen, Sir John Lionel, 1884–1957, vol. V

Simonson, Lee, 1888–1967, vol. VI

Simopoulos, Charalambos John, 1874–1942, vol. IV

Simpkin, Sir Oswald Richard Arthur, 1879–1936, vol. III

Simpkinson, Henry Walrond, 1853–1934, vol. III

Simpson, Lt-Col Adrian Francis Hugh Sibbald, 1880–1960, vol. V

Simpson, Alan, 1912–1998, vol. X

Simpson, Rev. Alan Haldane, 1875–1941, vol. IV

Simpson, Rev. Albert Edward, 1868–1947, vol. IV

Simpson, Sir Alexander Russell, 1835–1916, vol. II

Simpson, Alfred Allen, 1875–1939, vol. III

Simpson, Alfred Muller, 1843–1918, vol. II

Simpson, Archibald Henry, 1843–1918, vol. II

Simpson, Athol John Dundas, 1932–1999, vol. X

Simpson, Sir Basil Robert James, 2nd Bt (*cr* 1935), 1898–1968, vol. VI

Simpson, Sir Benjamin, 1831–1923, vol. II

Simpson, Bertie Soutar, 1896–1972, vol. VII

Simpson, Rt Rev. Bertram Fitzgerald, 1883–1971, vol. VII

Simpson, Bertram Lenox; *see* Weale, Putnam.

Simpson, (Cedric) Keith, 1907–1985, vol. VIII

Simpson, Col Charles Napier, 1856–1933, vol. III

Simpson, Maj.-Gen. Charles Rudyerd, 1856–1948, vol. IV

Simpson, Charles Valentine George, 1900–1987, vol. VIII

Simpson, Charles Walter, 1885–1971, vol. VII

Simpson, Sir Clement Bell, 1866–1933, vol. III

Simpson, Rear-Adm. Cortland Herbert, 1856–1943, vol. IV

Simpson, Very Rev. Cuthbert Aikman, 1892–1969, vol. VI

Simpson, Sir Cyril; *see* Simpson, Sir J. C. F.

Simpson, Rev. David Capell, 1883–1955, vol. V

Simpson, Edward Sydney, 1875–1939, vol. III

Simpson, Ernest Smith, 1921–1989, vol. VIII

Simpson, Esther Eleanor, 1919–1999, vol. X

Simpson, Miss Evelyn Blantyre, 1856–1920, vol. II

Simpson, Dame Florence Edith Victoria, 1874–1956, vol. V

Simpson, Gen. Sir Frank Ernest Wallace, 1899–1986, vol. VIII

Simpson, Col Sir Frank Robert, 1st Bt (*cr* 1935), 1864–1949, vol. IV

Simpson, Fred Brown, 1886–1939, vol. III

Simpson, Rev. Frederick Arthur, 1883–1974, vol. VII

Simpson, Frederick Moore, *died* 1928, vol. II

Simpson, Maj.-Gen. George, 1845–1908, vol. I

Simpson, Sir George Bowen, 1838–1915, vol. I

Simpson, Sir George Clarke, 1878–1965, vol. VI

Simpson, Col George Selden, 1878–1971, vol. VII

Simpson, Rear-Adm. George Walter Gillow, 1901–1972, vol. VII

Simpson, Gerald Gordon, 1918–1979, vol. VII

Simpson, Maj.-Gen. Hamilton Wilkie, 1895–1986, vol. VIII

Simpson, Harold, 1876–1974, vol. VII

Simpson, Harry Butler, 1861–1940, vol. III

Simpson, Helen de Guerry, 1897–1940, vol. III

Simpson, Col Henry Charles, 1879–1943, vol. IV

Simpson, Col Henry Cuthbert Connell Dunlop, 1854–1942, vol. IV

Simpson, Henry Fife Morland, 1859–1920, vol. II

Simpson, Henry George, 1917–1988, vol. VIII

Simpson, Sir Henry Lunnon, 1842–1900, vol. I

Simpson, Captain Henry Valentine, 1864–1937, vol. III

Simpson, Herbert Clayton, 1872–1947, vol. IV

Simpson, Sir James, 1858–1934, vol. III

Simpson, James, 1874–1939, vol. III

Simpson, Sir James Dyer, 1888–1979, vol. VII

Simpson, Sir James Fletcher, 1874–1967, vol. VI

Simpson, Very Rev. James Gilliland, 1865–1948, vol. IV

Simpson, Rev. James Harvey, 1825–1915, vol. I

Simpson, James Herbert, 1883–1959, vol. V

Simpson, Sir James Hope, 1864–1924, vol. II

Simpson, Sir James Joseph Trevor, 1908–1994, vol. IX

Simpson, Sir James Walter Mackay, 3rd Bt (*cr* 1866), 1882–1924, vol. II

Simpson, James Young, 1873–1934, vol. III

Simpson, John Alexander, 1892–1977, vol. VII

Simpson, Rt Rev. John Basil, *died* 1942, vol. IV

Simpson, Sir (John) Cyril (Finucane), 3rd Bt, 1899–1981, vol. VIII

Simpson, Rev. John Edmund, 1905–1970, vol. VI

Simpson, John Ferguson, 1902–1995, vol. IX

Simpson, Air Cdre John Herbert Thomas, 1907–1967, vol. VI

Simpson, Sir John Hope, 1868–1961, vol. VI

Simpson, John Liddle, 1912–1996, vol. X

Simpson, Sir John Roughton, 1899–1976, vol. VII

Simpson, Sir John William, 1858–1933, vol. III

Simpson, Joseph, 1879–1939, vol. III

Simpson, Sir Joseph, 1909–1968, vol. VI

Simpson, Keith; *see* Simpson, C. K.

Simpson, Kenneth John, 1914–1998, vol. X

Simpson, Lightly Stapleton, *died* 1942, vol. IV

Simpson, Mary Goudie, *died* 1934, vol. III

Simpson, Sir Maurice George, 1866–1954, vol. V

Simpson, Maxwell, 1815–1902, vol. I

Simpson, Melville William H.; *see* Hilton-Simpson.

Simpson, Maj.-Gen. Noel William, 1907–1972, vol. VII

Simpson, Oliver, 1924–2000, vol. X

Simpson, Rev. Patrick Carnegie, 1865–1947, vol. IV

Simpson, Percy, 1865–1962, vol. VI

Simpson, Rev. Percy John, 1864–1944, vol. IV

Simpson, Peter Miller, 1921–1988, vol. VIII

Simpson, Pierce Adolphus, 1837–1900, vol. I

Simpson, Rayene Stewart, 1926–1978, vol. VII

Simpson, Ven. Rennie, 1920–1997, vol. X

Simpson, Richard Jefferson, 1874–1936, vol. III

Simpson, Rev. Robert, 1900–1977, vol. VII

Simpson, Rt Hon. Robert, 1923–1997, vol. X

Simpson, Robert Gordon, 1887–1958, vol. V

Simpson, Col Robert John Shaw, 1858–1931, vol. III

Simpson, Col Robert Mills, 1865–1945, vol. IV (A)
Simpson, Sir Robert Russell, 1840–1923, vol. II
Simpson, Robert Wilfred Levick, 1921–1997, vol. X
Simpson, Samuel, 1876–1952, vol. V
Simpson, S(amuel) Leonard, 1900–1983, vol. VIII
Simpson, Scott, 1915–1981, vol. VIII
Simpson, Air Vice-Marshal Sturley Philip, 1896–1966, vol. VI
Simpson, Thomas, 1877–1964, vol. VI
Simpson, Thomas Blantyre, 1892–1954, vol. V
Simpson, Rear-Adm. (E) Thomas Harold, 1896–1952, vol. V
Simpson, Col Thomas Thomson, 1836–1916, vol. II
Simpson, Thomas Young, 1875–1963, vol. VI
Simpson, Trevor Claude, 1877–1929, vol. III
Simpson, Rev. W. J. Sparrow, 1859–1952, vol. V
Simpson, Sir Walter Grindlay, 2nd Bt (cr 1866), 1843–1898, vol. I
Simpson, Wilfred L., 1862–1937, vol. III
Simpson, William, 1823–1899, vol. I
Simpson, William Douglas, 1896–1968, vol. VI
Simpson, Col William George, 1876–1961, vol. VI
Simpson, Sir William John Ritchie, 1855–1931, vol. III
Simpson, William Marshall, 1868–1951, vol. V
Simpson, William Wynn, 1907–1987, vol. VIII
Simpson-Baikie, Brig.-Gen. Sir Hugh Archie Dundas; see Baikie.
Simpson-Hinchliffe, William Algernon, 1880–1963, vol. VI
Simpson-Orlebar, Sir Michael Keith Orlebar, 1932–2000, vol. X
Sims, Sir Alfred John, 1907–1977, vol. VII
Sims, Sir Arthur, 1877–1969, vol. VI
Sims, Arthur Mitford, 1889–1977, vol. VII
Sims, Charles, 1873–1928, vol. II
Sims, Ernest William Proctor-, 1868–1943, vol. IV
Sims, Francis John, 1856–1950, vol. IV
Sims, George Robert, 1847–1922, vol. II
Sims, Brig.-Gen. Reginald Frank Manley, 1878–1951, vol. V
Sims, Sir Thomas, 1858–1936, vol. III
Sims, Adm. William Sowden, 1858–1936, vol. III
Simson, Captain Sir Donald Petrie, 1878–1961, vol. VI
Simson, Harold F.; see Fraser-Simson.
Simson, Sir Henry John Forbes, 1872–1932, vol. III
Simson, Richard Arbuthnot, 1871–1958, vol. V
Simson, Col William Amor, 1872–1925, vol. II
Sinatra, Francis Albert, (Frank), 1915–1998, vol. X
Sinatra, Frank; see Sinatra, Francis A.
Sinbad; see Dingle, Aylward Edward.
Sinclair, 15th Lord, 1831–1922, vol. II
Sinclair, 16th Lord, 1875–1957, vol. V
Sinclair of Cleeve, 1st Baron, 1893–1979, vol. VII
Sinclair of Cleeve, 2nd Baron, 1919–1985, vol. VIII
Sinclair, Alexander Garden, 1859–1930, vol. III
Sinclair, Lt-Col Alfred Law, 1853–1911, vol. I
Sinclair, Allan Fergus Wilson, 1900–1980, vol. VII (AII)
Sinclair, Archibald, 1866–1922, vol. II
Sinclair, Arthur Henry Havens, 1868–1962, vol. VI
Sinclair, Rev. Hon. Charles Augustus, 1865–1944, vol. IV

Sinclair, Hon. Sir Colin Archibald, 1876–1956, vol. V
Sinclair, Surg.-Gen. David, 1847–1919, vol. II
Sinclair, Dep. Surg.-Gen. Edward Malcolm, 1832–1916, vol. II
Sinclair, Adm. Sir Edwyn Sinclair A.; see Alexander-Sinclair.
Sinclair, Ernest Keith, 1914–1995, vol. IX
Sinclair, Rear-Adm. Erroll Norman, 1909–1993, vol. IX
Sinclair, George Robertson, 1863–1917, vol. II
Sinclair, Hugh; see Herman, E.
Sinclair, Adm. Sir Hugh Francis Paget, 1873–1939, vol. III
Sinclair, Hugh Macdonald, 1910–1990, vol. VIII
Sinclair, Col Hugh Montgomerie, 1855–1924, vol. II
Sinclair, James, 1832–1910, vol. I
Sinclair, John, 1860–1938, vol. III
Sinclair, John, 1898–1979, vol. VII (AII)
Sinclair, John Alexander, 1885–1961, vol. VI
Sinclair, Maj.-Gen. Sir John Alexander, 1897–1977, vol. VII
Sinclair, John Alexis Clifford Cerda A.; see Alexander-Sinclair.
Sinclair, Sir John George Tollemache, 3rd Bt (cr 1786), 1825–1899, vol. I
Sinclair, John Houston, 1871–1961, vol. VI
Sinclair, Rt Hon. John Maynard, 1896–1953, vol. V
Sinclair, Sir John Robert, 1850–1940, vol. III
Sinclair, Sir John Rollo Norman Blair, 9th Bt (cr 1704), 1928–1990, vol. VIII
Sinclair, Sir John Rose George, 7th Bt (cr 1704), 1864–1926, vol. II
Sinclair, Ven. John Stewart, 1853–1919, vol. II
Sinclair, Sir Keith, 1922–1993, vol. IX
Sinclair, Captain Sir Kenneth Duncan Lecky, 1889–1973, vol. VII
Sinclair, Sir Leonard, 1895–1984, vol. VIII
Sinclair, Louis, 1861–1928, vol. II
Sinclair, Lt-Col Malcolm Cecil, 1899–1955, vol. V
Sinclair, May, 1870–1946, vol. IV
Sinclair, Meurice, 1878–1966, vol. VI
Sinclair, Sir Robert Charles, 9th Bt (cr 1636), 1820–1899, vol. I
Sinclair, Major Sir Ronald Norman John Charles Udny, 8th Bt (cr 1704, shown as 1631), 1899–1952, vol. V
Sinclair, Sir Ronald Ormiston, 1903–1996, vol. X
Sinclair, Rev. Canon Ronald Sutherland Brook, 1894–1953, vol. V
Sinclair, Shapton Donald, 1923–1974, vol. VII
Sinclair, Rt Hon. Thomas, 1838–1914, vol. I
Sinclair, Col Thomas, died 1940, vol. III
Sinclair, T(homas) Alan, 1899–1961, vol. VI
Sinclair, Col Thomas Charles, 1879–1948, vol. IV
Sinclair, Upton, 1878–1968, vol. VI
Sinclair, Lt-Col Sir Walrond Arthur Frank, 1880–1952, vol. V
Sinclair, Sir William, 1895–1976, vol. VII
Sinclair, William Angus, 1905–1954, vol. V
Sinclair, Sir William Japp, 1846–1912, vol. I
Sinclair, Ven. William Macdonald, 1850–1917, vol. II

Sinclair-Burgess, Maj.-Gen. Sir William Livingstone Hatchwell, 1880–1964, vol. VI

Sinclair Lockhart, Sir Graeme Alexander, 10th Bt (cr 1636); see Lockhart.

Sinclair-Lockhart, Sir Graeme Duncan Power, 12th Bt (cr 1636), 1897–1959, vol. V

Sinclair-Lockhart, Sir John Beresford, 13th Bt (cr 1636), 1904–1970, vol. VI

Sinclair-Lockhart, Sir Muir Edward, 14th Bt, 1906–1985, vol. VIII

Sinclair-Lockhart, Sir Robert Duncan, 11th Bt (cr 1636), 1856–1919, vol. II

Sinclair-Maclagan, Maj.-Gen. Ewen George, 1868–1948, vol. IV

Sinderson, Sir Harry Chapman, Pasha, 1891–1974, vol. VII

Sinding, Stephan, 1846–1922, vol. II

Sing, John Millington, 1863–1947, vol. IV

Sing, Roger Percy, 1865–1940, vol. III

Sing, Rt Rev. Tsae-Seng, 1861–1940, vol. III (A), vol. IV

Singer, Alfred Ernest, 1927–1999, vol. X

Singer, Charles, 1876–1960, vol. V

Singer, Brig.-Gen. Charles William, 1870–1936, vol. III

Singer, Dorothea Waley, 1882–1964, vol. VI

Singer, Isaac Bashevis, 1904–1991, vol. IX

Singer, Adm. Sir Morgan, 1864–1938, vol. III

Singer, Sir Mortimer, 1863–1929, vol. III

Singer, Rev. Canon Samuel Stanfield, 1920–1989, vol. VIII

Singer, Rev. Simeon, 1848–1906, vol. I

Singer, Washington Merritt Grant, 1866–1934, vol. III

Singers-Davies, Rev. R. W. F., died 1936, vol. III

Singh, Sardar Bahadur Sir D.; see Datar Singh.

Singh, Dinesh, 1925–1995, vol. IX

Singh, Prince Frederick D.; see Duleep Singh.

Singh, Sir Ganesh Dutta, 1868–1943, vol. IV

Singh, Giani Zail, 1916–1994, vol. IX

Singh, Kanwar Jasbir, 1889–1942, vol. IV

Singh, Raja Sir Maharaj, 1878–1959, vol. V

Singh, Nagendra, 1914–1988, vol. VIII

Singh, Raja Sir Padam, 1873–1947, vol. IV

Singh, Sardar Swaran, 1907–1994, vol. IX

Singh, Prince Victor Albert Jay D.; see Duleep Singh.

Singh Bahadur, Maharawal Shri Sir Lakshman, 1908–1989, vol. VIII

Singh Roy, Sir Bijoy Prosad, 1894–1961, vol. VI

Singhania, Sir Padampat, 1905–1979, vol. IX (AI)

Singhateh, Alhaji Sir Farimang Mohamadu, 1912–1977, vol. VII (AII)

Singhji Bahadur, Karni; see Bikaner, Maharaja of.

Singleton, Sir Edward Henry Sibbald, (Tim), 1921–1992, vol. IX

Singleton, Esther, died 1930, vol. III

Singleton, Col Henry Townsend Corbet, 1874–1934, vol. III

Singleton, Rt Rev. Hugh, 1851–1934, vol. III

Singleton, Rt Hon. Sir John Edward, 1885–1957, vol. V

Singleton, Rev. John J., 1838–1917, vol. II

Singleton, Tim; see Singleton, Sir E. H. S.

Singleton, Rear-Adm. Uvedale Corbet, 1838–1910, vol. I

Singleton, William Adam, 1916–1960, vol. V

Sington, Gerald Henry Adolphus, 1876–1946, vol. IV

Sinha, 1st Baron, 1864–1928, vol. II

Sinha, 2nd Baron, 1887–1967, vol. VI

Sinha, 3rd Baron, 1920–1989, vol. IX (AI)

Sinha, 4th Baron, 1953–1992, vol. X (AI)

Sinha, 5th Baron, 1930–1999, vol. X

Sinha, Narendra Prasanna, born 1858, vol. III

Sinha, Rajandhari, 1893–1976, vol. VII

Sinha, Sir Rajivaranjan Prashad, 1893–1948, vol. IV (A), vol. V

Sinker, Sir (Algernon) Paul, 1905–1977, vol. VII

Sinker, Rev. Canon Arthur, died 1940, vol. III

Sinker, Rev. Edmund, 1872–1941, vol. IV

Sinker, Rt Rev. George, 1900–1986, vol. VIII

Sinker, Very Rev. John, 1874–1936, vol. III

Sinker, Rev. Canon Michael Roy, 1908–1994, vol. IX

Sinker, Sir Paul; see Sinker, Sir A. P.

Sinker, Rev. Robert, 1838–1913, vol. I

Sinker, Rev. Canon Roy; see Sinker, Rev. Canon M. R.

Sinkinson, George, 1874–1939, vol. III

Sinnamon, Sir Hercules Vincent, 1899–1994, vol. IX

Sinnatt, Frank Sturdy, 1880–1943, vol. IV

Sinnatt, Oliver Sturdy, 1882–1965, vol. VI

Sinnett, Alfred Percy, 1840–1921, vol. II

Sinnott, Most Rev. Alfred A., 1877–1954, vol. V

Sinnott, Col Edward Stockley, 1868–1969, vol. VI

Sinnott, Ernest, 1909–1989, vol. VIII

Sinnott, John Joseph, 1882–1943, vol. IV

Sinton, Lt-Col John Alexander, 1884–1956, vol. V

Siqueland, Col Tryggve Albert, 1888–1937, vol. III

Sircar, Sir Nilratan, 1861–1943, vol. IV

Sircar, Sir Nripendra Nath, died 1945, vol. IV

Sire, Henry Alphonse, 1864–1947, vol. IV

Siriwardena, N. D. A. Silva-Wijayasinghe; see Wijayasinghe Siriwardena.

Sirmur (Nahan), Raja of, 1867–1911, vol. I

Sirmur, Maharaja of, 1888–1933, vol. III

Sirohi, HH Maharajadhiraj, 1888–1946, vol. IV

Sisam, Kenneth, 1887–1971, vol. VII

Sisley, Charles Percival, 1867–1934, vol. III

Sisnett, Sir Herbert Kortright McDonnell, 1862–1937, vol. III

Sisson, Charles Jasper, 1885–1966, vol. VI

Sisson, Sir (Eric) Roy, 1914–1993, vol. IX

Sisson, Marshall Arnott, 1897–1978, vol. VII

Sisson, Sir Roy; see Sisson, Sir E. R.

Sissons, Charles Bruce, 1879–1965, vol. VI

Sissons, Ven. Gilbert Holme, 1870–1940, vol. III

Sita Ram, Rai Bahadur Sir, 1885–1972, vol. VII

Sitwell, Dame Edith Louisa, 1887–1964, vol. VI

Sitwell, Rev. (Francis) Gerard, 1906–1993, vol. IX

Sitwell, Sir (Francis) Osbert, (Sacheverell), 5th Bt, 1892–1969, vol. VI

Sitwell, Sir George Reresby, 4th Bt, 1860–1943, vol. IV

Sitwell, Rev. Gerard; see Sitwell, Rev. F. G.

Sitwell, Maj.-Gen. Hervey Degge Wilmot, 1896–1973, vol. VII

Sitwell, Sir Osbert; *see* Sitwell, Sir F. O. S.
Sitwell, Sir Sacheverell, 6th Bt, 1897–1988, vol. VIII
Sitwell, Sir Sidney Ashley Hurt, 1871–1956, vol. V
Sitwell, Brig.-Gen. William Henry, 1860–1932, vol. III
Sivagnanam Pillai, Diwan Bahadur Sir Tinnevelly Nelliappa Pillai, *died* 1936, vol. III
Sivell, Robert, 1888–1958, vol. V
Sivewright, Hon. Sir James, 1848–1916, vol. II
Sivewright, Col Robert Charles Townsend, 1923–1994, vol. IX
Sixsmith, Maj.-Gen. Eric Keir Gilborne, 1904–1986, vol. VIII
Sixsmith, Guy; *see* Sixsmith, P. G. D.
Sixsmith, (Philip) Guy (Dudley), 1902–1984, vol. VIII
Skae, Victor Delvine Burnham, 1914–1979, vol. VII
Skaife, Brig. Sir Eric Ommanney, 1884–1956, vol. V
Skan, Peter Henry O.; *see* Ogle-Skan.
Skaug, Arne, 1906–1974, vol. VII
Skeaping, John Rattenbury, 1901–1980, vol. VII
Skeat, Rev. Walter William, 1835–1912, vol. I
Skeats, Ernest Willington, 1875–1953, vol. V
Skeen, Gen. Sir Andrew, 1873–1935, vol. III
Skeen, Brig. Andrew, 1906–1984, vol. VIII
Skeffington, Arthur Massey, 1909–1971, vol. VII
Skeffington, Hon. Oriel John Clotworthy Whyte Melville Foster-, 1871–1905, vol. I
Skeffington-Lodge, Thomas Cecil, 1905–1994, vol. IX
Skeffington Smyth, Lt-Col Geoffrey Henry Julian; *see* FitzPatrick, Lt-Col G. H. J.
Skeggs, Rev. Thomas Charles, *died* 1927, vol. II
Skelhorn, Sir Norman John, 1909–1988, vol. VIII
Skellerup, Sir Valdemar Reid, 1907–1982, vol. VIII
Skelmersdale, 5th Baron, 1876–1969, vol. VI
Skelmersdale, 6th Baron, 1896–1973, vol. VI
Skelton, Archibald Noel, 1880–1935, vol. III
Skelton, Rev. Charles Arthur, *died* 1913, vol. I
Skelton, Sir Charles Thomas, 1833–1913, vol. I
Skelton, Maj.-Gen. Dudley Sheridan, 1878–1962, vol. VI
Skelton, Rt Rev. Henry Aylmer, 1884–1959, vol. V
Skelton, Sir John, 1831–1897, vol. I
Skelton, Oscar Douglas, 1878–1941, vol. IV
Skelton, Rear-Adm. Peter, 1901–1994, vol. IX
Skelton, Engr Vice-Adm. Sir Reginald William, 1872–1956, vol. V
Skelton, Robert Lumley, 1896–1973, vol. VII
Skelton, Robin, 1925–1997, vol. X
Skelton, Rev. Canon Thomas, 1834–1915, vol. I
Skemp, Arthur Rowland, 1882–1918, vol. II
Skemp, Frank Whittingham, 1880–1971, vol. VII
Skemp, Joseph Bright, 1910–1992, vol. IX
Skemp, Terence Rowland Frazer, 1915–1996, vol. X
Skene, Macgregor, 1889–1973, vol. VII
Skene, Hon. Thomas, *died* 1910, vol. I
Skene, William Baillie, 1838–1911, vol. I
Skerrett, Hon. Sir Charles Perrin, 1863–1929, vol. III
Skerrington, Hon. Lord; William Campbell, 1855–1927, vol. II
Sketch, Ralph Yeo, 1877–1952, vol. V

Sketchley, Major Ernest Frederick Powys, 1881–1916, vol. II
Skevington, Sir Joseph Oliver, 1873–1952, vol. V
Skewes-Cox, Sir Thomas, 1849–1913, vol. I
Skey, Rev. Oswald William Laurie, 1878–1954, vol. V
Skidmore, Charles, 1839–1908, vol. I
Skiffington, Sir Donald Maclean, 1880–1963, vol. VI
Skikne, Larushka Mischa; *see* Harvey, Laurence.
Skilbeck, Dunstan, 1904–1989, vol. VIII
Skilbeck, William Wray, 1864–1919, vol. II
Skillicorn, Alice Havergal, 1894–1979, vol. VII
Skillicorn, William James Kinlay, 1883–1955, vol. V
Skillington, William Patrick Denny, 1913–1998, vol. X
Skimming, Ian Edward Bowring, 1920–1973, vol. VII
Skinnard, Frederick William, 1902–1984, vol. VIII
Skinner, Rev. Albert James, 1869–1949, vol. IV
Skinner, Allan Maclean, 1846–1901, vol. I
Skinner, Andrew Forrester, 1902–1995, vol. IX
Skinner, Arthur Banks, 1861–1911, vol. I
Skinner, Maj.-Gen. Bruce Morland, 1858–1932, vol. III
Skinner, Burrhus Frederic, 1904–1990, vol. VIII
Skinner, C(harles) William, 1895–1971, vol. VII
Skinner, Clarence Farringdon, 1900–1962, vol. VI
Skinner, Colin Marshall, 1882–1968, vol. VI
Skinner, Cornelia Otis, (Mrs A. S. Blodget), 1901–1979, vol. VII
Skinner, Maj.-Gen. Sir Cyriac; *see* Skinner, Maj.-Gen. Sir P. C. B.
Skinner, Col Edmund Grey, 1850–1917, vol. II
Skinner, Ernest Harry Dudley, 1892–1985, vol. VIII
Skinner, Maj.-Gen. Frank Hollamby Jerry, 1897–1979, vol. VII
Skinner, Col Frederick St Duthus, 1859–1938, vol. III
Skinner, Col George John, 1841–1930, vol. III
Skinner, Sir Gordon; *see* Skinner, Sir T. G.
Skinner, Lt-Col Harry Crawley R.; *see* Ross Skinner.
Skinner, Sir Harry Ross, 1867–1943, vol. IV
Skinner, Hon. Sir Henry Albert, 1926–1986, vol. VIII
Skinner, Herbert Wakefield Banks, 1900–1960, vol. V
Skinner, Sir Hewitt; *see* Skinner, Sir T. H.
Skinner, Horace Wilfrid, 1884–1955, vol. V
Skinner, Rev. James Henry, *died* 1913, vol. I
Skinner, Col James Tierney, 1845–1902, vol. I
Skinner, Rev. John, 1851–1925, vol. II
Skinner, John William, 1890–1955, vol. V
Skinner, Martyn, 1906–1993, vol. IX
Skinner, Maj.-Gen. Michael Timothy, 1931–1992, vol. IX
Skinner, Most Rev. Patrick James, *born* 1904, vol. VIII
Skinner, Maj.-Gen. Sir (Percy) Cyriac Burrell, 1871–1955, vol. V
Skinner, Robert, 1877–1955, vol. V
Skinner, Robert Peet, 1866–1960, vol. V
Skinner, Robert Taylor, 1867–1946, vol. IV

Skinner, Sidney, 1863–1944, vol. IV
Skinner, Sir Sydney Martyn, 1864–1941, vol. IV
Skinner, Sir Thomas, 1st Bt, 1840–1926, vol. II
Skinner, Sir Thomas Edward, 1909–1991, vol. IX
Skinner, Sir (Thomas) Gordon, 3rd Bt, 1899–1972, vol. VII
Skinner, Sir (Thomas) Hewitt, 2nd Bt, 1875–1968, vol. VI
Skinner, Thomas Monier, 1913–1995, vol. X (AI)
Skinner, Waldo W., 1878–1943, vol. IV
Skinner, Walter Robert, 1851–1924, vol. II
Skinner, Rev. William, 1859–1942, vol. IV
Skinner, William Goudie, died 1935, vol. III
Skipton, Rev. Horace Pitt Kennedy, 1861–1943, vol. IV
Skipwith, Col Frederick George, 1870–1964, vol. VI
Skipwith, Sir Grey Humberston d'Estoteville, 11th Bt, 1884–1950, vol. IV
Skipwith, Vice-Adm. Harry Louis d'Estoteville, 1868–1955, vol. V
Skipworth, Frank Markham, 1854–1929, vol. III
Skira, Albert, 1904–1973, vol. VII
Skirmunt, Constantine, 1866–1939, vol. III
Skirrow, Major Arthur George Walker, 1862–1941, vol. IV
Skirving, Archibald Adam S.; see Scot-Skirving.
Sklodowska, Marie; see Curie, Madame.
Skone James, Edmund Purcell, 1927–1992, vol. IX
Skottowe, Britiffe Constable, 1857–1925, vol. II
Skouras, Spyros Panayiotis, 1893–1971, vol. VII
Skrimshire of Quarter, Baroness (Life Peer); Margaret Betty Harvie Anderson, 1915–1979, vol. VII
Skrine, Sir Clarmont Percival, 1888–1974, vol. VII
Skrine, Francis Henry, 1847–1933, vol. III
Skrine, Henry Mills, 1844–1915, vol. I
Skrine, Rev. John Huntley, 1848–1923, vol. II
Skues, George Edward Mackenzie, 1858–1949, vol. IV
Skutsch, Otto, 1906–1990, vol. VIII
Skynner, (Augustus Charles) Robin, 1922–2000, vol. X
Skynner, Robin; see Skynner, A. C. R.
Skyrm, Llewellyn Sidgwick M., died 1964, vol. VI
Skyrme, Stanley James Beresford, 1912–1985, vol. VIII
Slack, Captain Charles, died 1925, vol. II
Slack, Geoffrey Layton, 1912–1991, vol. IX
Slack, Sir John B.; see Bamford-Slack.
Slack, Rev. Kenneth, 1917–1987, vol. VIII
Slack, Samuel Benjamin, 1859–1955, vol. V
Slacke, Francis Alexander, 1853–1940, vol. III
Slacke, Sir Owen Randal, 1837–1910, vol. I
Sladden, Sir Julius, 1847–1928, vol. II
Slade, Sir Alfred Fothringham, 5th Bt, 1898–1960, vol. V
Slade, Col Cecil Townley M.; see Mitford-Slade.
Slade, Cecil William Paulet, 1863–1943, vol. IV
Slade, Sir Cuthbert, 4th Bt, 1863–1908, vol. I
Slade, Adm. Sir Edmond John Warre, 1859–1928, vol. II
Slade, Lt-Gen. Frederick George, 1851–1910, vol. I
Slade, George Penkivil, 1899–1942, vol. IV
Slade, Sir Gerald Osborne, 1891–1962, vol. VI
Slade, Gordon; see Slade, R. G.

Slade, Sir James Benjamin, 1861–1950, vol. IV
Slade, Maj.-Gen. Sir John Ramsay, 1843–1913, vol. I
Slade, Leslie William, 1915–1995, vol. X (AI)
Slade, Mead, 1894–1954, vol. V
Slade, Sir Michael Nial, 6th Bt, 1900–1962, vol. VI
Slade, Richard Gordon, 1912–1981, vol. VIII
Slade, Roland Edgar, 1886–1968, vol. VI
Slade, William Ball, 1843–1938, vol. III
Slade, Wyndham, 1826–1910, vol. I
Slade, Wyndham Neave, 1867–1941, vol. IV
Sladen, Arthur French, 1866–1944, vol. IV
Sladen, Brig.-Gen. David Ramsay, 1869–1923, vol. II
Sladen, Douglas Brooke Wheelton, 1856–1947, vol. IV
Sladen, Francis Farquhar, 1875–1970, vol. VI
Sladen, Major Gerald Carew, 1881–1930, vol. III
Sladen, Hugh Alfred Lambart, 1878–1962, vol. VI
Sladen, Col Joseph, 1840–1930, vol. III
Sladen, Joseph Maurice, 1896–1956, vol. V
Sladen, Lt-Comdr Sir Sampson, 1868–1940, vol. III
Slaney, Col Francis Gerald K.; see Kenyon-Slaney.
Slaney, George Wilson, 1884–1978, vol. VII
Slaney, Major Philip Percy K.; see Kenyon-Slaney.
Slaney, Major Robert Orlando Rodolph K.; see Kenyon-Slaney.
Slaney, Sybil Anges, K.; see Kenyon-Slaney.
Slaney, Maj.-Gen. Walter Rupert K.; see Kenyon-Slaney.
Slaney, Rt Hon. William Slaney K.; see Kenyon-Slaney.
Slatcher, William Kenneth, 1926–1997, vol. X
Slater, Baron (Life Peer); Joseph Slater, 1904–1977, vol. VII
Slater, Sir (Alexander) Ransford, 1874–1940, vol. III
Slater, Arthur Edward, 1895–1982, vol. VIII
Slater, Charles, 1856–1940, vol. III
Slater, David A., 1866–1938, vol. III
Slater, Eliot Trevor Oakeshott, 1904–1983, vol. VIII
Slater, Ernest, died 1942, vol. IV
Slater, George, died 1941, vol. IV
Slater, George, 1874–1956, vol. V
Slater, Gilbert, 1864–1938, vol. III
Slater, Gordon Archbold, 1896–1979, vol. VII
Slater, Gordon Charles Henry, 1903–1997, vol. X
Slater, Gordon James Augustus, 1922–1995, vol. IX
Slater, Mrs Harriet, died 1976, vol. VII
Slater, John, 1847–1924, vol. II
Slater, John, 1889–1935, vol. III
Slater, Col John William, 1867–1936, vol. III
Slater, Leonard, 1908–1999, vol. X
Slater, Col Owen, 1890–1976, vol. VII
Slater, Sir Ransford; see Slater, Sir A. R.
Slater, Adm. Sir Robin Leonard Francis D.; see Durnford-Slater.
Slater, Samuel Henry, 1880–1967, vol. VI
Slater, Hon. William, 1890–1960, vol. V
Slater, Rev. William Fletcher, 1831–1924, vol. II
Slater, William Henry, 1896–1962, vol. VI
Slater, Sir William Kershaw, 1893–1970, vol. VI
Slatin Pacha, Baron Rudolf Carl, 1857–1932, vol. III
Slator, Instr Captain Thomas, 1872–1961, vol. VI

752

Slatter, Air Marshal Sir Leonard Horatio, 1894–1961, vol. VI
Slattery, Rt Rev. Charles Lewis, 1867–1930, vol. III
Slattery, John, 1886–1958, vol. V
Slattery, Rear-Adm. Sir Matthew Sausse, 1902–1990, vol. VIII
Slaughter, James Cameron, 1902–1982, vol. VIII
Slaughter, Lt-Col Reginald Joseph, 1874–1968, vol. VI
Slaughter, Sir William Capel, 1857–1917, vol. II
Slayter, Col Edward Wheeler, 1869–1946, vol. IV
Slayter, Adm. William Firth, 1867–1936, vol. III
Slayter, Adm. Sir William Rudolph, 1896–1971, vol. VII
Sleator, James Sinton, died 1950, vol. IV
Slee, Frederick Abraham, 1882–1963, vol. VI
Slee, Comdr John Ambrose, 1878–1944, vol. IV
Slee, Col Percy Henry, 1861–1929, vol. III
Sleeman, Cyril Montagu, 1883–1971, vol. VII
Sleeman, Col Sir James Lewis, 1880–1963, vol. VI
Sleeman, John Herbert, 1880–1963, vol. VI
Sleep, Arthur, 1894–1959, vol. V
Sleigh, Charles William, 1863–1949, vol. IV
Sleigh, Sir Hamilton Morton Howard, 1896–1979, vol. VII
Sleigh, Sir William Lowrie, 1865–1945, vol. IV
Sleight, Major Sir Ernest, 2nd Bt, 1873–1946, vol. IV
Sleight, Sir George Frederick, 1st Bt, 1853–1921, vol. II
Sleight, Sir John Frederick, 3rd Bt, 1909–1990, vol. VIII
Slemon, Air Marshal (Charles) Roy, 1904–1992, vol. IX
Slemon, Air Marshal Roy; see Slemon, Air Marshal C. R.
Slesinger, Edward Gustave, 1888–1975, vol. VII
Slesser, Rt Hon. Sir Henry Herman, 1883–1979, vol. VII
Slessor, Alexander Johnston, 1912–1954, vol. V
Slessor, Marshal of the Royal Air Force Sir John Cotesworth, 1897–1979, vol. VII
Slevin, Brian Francis Patrick, 1926–1995, vol. X (AI)
Sligo, 4th Marquess of, 1824–1903, vol. I
Sligo, 5th Marquess of, 1831–1913, vol. I
Sligo, 6th Marquess of, 1856–1935, vol. III
Sligo, 7th Marquess of, 1898–1941, vol. IV
Sligo, 8th Marquess of, 1867–1951, vol. V
Sligo, 9th Marquess of, 1873–1952, vol. V
Sligo, 10th Marquess of, 1908–1991, vol. IX
Slim, 1st Viscount, 1891–1970, vol. VI
Slimmings, Sir William Kenneth MacLeod, 1912–1995, vol. IX
Slinger, William, 1917–1998, vol. X
Slingo, Sir William, 1855–1935, vol. III
Sliwinski, Stanislaw, 1893–1940, vol. III (A), vol. IV
Sloan, Alexander, died 1945, vol. IV
Sloan, Alfred Pritchard, Jun., 1875–1966, vol. VI
Sloan, Hon. Gordon McGregor, 1898–1959, vol. V
Sloan, Maj.-Gen. John Macfarlane, 1872–1941, vol. IV
Sloan, John MacGavin, died 1926, vol. II
Sloan, Lawrence Gunn, 1859–1939, vol. III

Sloan, Norman Alexander, 1914–1999, vol. X
Sloan, Robert Patrick, 1874–1947, vol. IV
Sloan, Sir Tennant, 1884–1972, vol. VII
Sloane, Maj.-Gen. John Bramley Malet, 1912–1990, vol. VIII
Sloane, Mary Annie, died 1961, vol. VI
Sloane, William Milligan, 1850–1928, vol. II
Sloane-Stanley, Ronald Francis Assheton, 1867–1948, vol. IV
Slocock, Francis Samuel Alfred, died 1945, vol. IV
Slocombe, George Edward, 1894–1963, vol. VI
Slocum, Captain Frank Alexander, 1897–1982, vol. VIII
Slocum, William Frederick, 1851–1934, vol. III
Sloggett, Col Arthur John Henry, 1882–1950, vol. IV
Sloggett, Lt-Gen. Sir Arthur Thomas, 1857–1929, vol. III
Sloley, Sir Herbert Cecil, 1855–1937, vol. III
Sloman, Rev. Arthur, 1851–1919, vol. II
Sloman, Very Rev. Ernest, died 1918, vol. II
Sloman, Harold Newnham Penrose, 1885–1965, vol. VI
Sloman, Brig.-Gen. Henry Stanhope, 1861–1945, vol. IV
Slot, Gerald Maurice Joseph, died 1972, vol. VII
Slotki, Israel Wolf, 1884–1973, vol. VII
Sly, Sir Frank George, 1866–1928, vol. II
Sly, Henry Edward, 1876–1932, vol. III
Sly, Richard Meares, 1849–1929, vol. III
Slyne, Denis, 1859–1928, vol. II
Slyth, Arthur Roy, 1910–1989, vol. VIII
Smail, James Cameron, 1880–1970, vol. VI
Smail, William Mitchell, 1885–1971, vol. VII
Smailes, Arthur Eltringham, 1911–1984, vol. VIII
Smailes, George Mason, 1916–1988, vol. X (AI)
Smaldon, Catherine Agnes, 1903–1980, vol. VII
Smale, John Arthur, 1895–1993, vol. IX
Smale, Morton Alfred, 1847–1916, vol. II
Small, Sir Alexander Sym, 1887–1944, vol. IV
Small, Sir (Andrew) Bruce, 1895–1980, vol. VII (AII)
Small, Sir Bruce; see Small, Sir A. B.
Small, Sir Frank Augustus, 1903–1973, vol. VII
Small, James, 1889–1955, vol. V
Small, James, died 1968, vol. VI
Small, Very Rev. Leonard; see Small, Very Rev. R. L.
Small, Very Rev. (Robert) Leonard, 1905–1994, vol. IX
Small, William, 1843–1929, vol. III
Small, Col William George, died 1931, vol. III
Small, William Watson, 1909–1978, vol. VII
Smallbones, Robert Townsend, 1884–1976, vol. VII
Smalley, Beryl, 1905–1984, vol. VIII
Smalley, George Washburn, 1833–1916, vol. II
Smalley, Sir Herbert, 1851–1945, vol. IV
Smalley-Baker, Charles Ernest, 1891–1972, vol. VII
Smallfield, F., died 1915, vol. I
Smallman, Lt-Col Arthur Briton, 1873–1950, vol. IV
Smallman, Sir George; see Smallman, Sir H. G.
Smallman, Sir (Henry) George, 1854–1923, vol. II
Smallpiece, Sir Basil, 1906–1992, vol. IX
Smallwood, Arthur William, 1873–1938, vol. III

Smallwood, Air Chief Marshal Sir Denis Graham, 1918–1997, vol. X
Smallwood, Edward, 1861–1939, vol. III
Smallwood, Lt-Col Frank Graham, 1867–1919, vol. II
Smallwood, Geoffrey Arthur John, 1900–1973, vol. VII
Smallwood, Maj.-Gen. Gerald Russell, 1889–1977, vol. VII
Smallwood, Henry Armstrong, 1869–1942, vol. IV
Smallwood, Norah Evelyn, 1909–1984, vol. VIII
Smallwood, Oliver Daniel, 1889–1962, vol. VI
Smallwood, Richard Coningsby, 1879–1933, vol. III
Smart, Archibald Guelph Holdsworth, 1882–1964, vol. VI
Smart, Borlase, 1881–1947, vol. IV
Smart, Brig.-Gen. Charles Allan, 1868–1937, vol. III
Smart, Douglas Ian, *died* 1970, vol. VI (AII)
Smart, E. Hodgson, *died* 1942, vol. IV
Smart, Lt-Gen. Edward Kenneth, 1891–1961, vol. VI
Smart, Sir Eric Fleming, 1911–1973, vol. VII
Smart, Sir Harold Nevil, 1883–1950, vol. IV
Smart, Henry C., 1878–1951, vol. V
Smart, Henry Walter, 1908–1990, vol. VIII
Smart, Jack; *see* Smart, R. J.
Smart, John, 1838–1899, vol. I
Smart, Joseph McCaig, 1882–1953, vol. V
Smart, Leslie Masson, 1889–1972, vol. VII
Smart, Comdr Sir Morton, 1878–1956, vol. V
Smart, (Raymond) Jack, 1917–1998, vol. X
Smart, Maj.-Gen. Robert Arthur, 1914–1986, vol. VIII
Smart, V. Irving, 1874–1940, vol. III
Smart, Sir Walter Alexander, 1883–1962, vol. VI
Smart, Wilfred Wilmot, 1876–1961, vol. VI
Smart, William, 1853–1915, vol. I
Smart, William Marshall, 1889–1975, vol. VII
Smart, William Wilkinson, *died* 1943, vol. IV
Smartt, Rt Hon. Sir Thomas William, 1858–1929, vol. III
Smartt, Rev. William Hanbury, 1854–1933, vol. III
Smeall, James Leathley, 1907–1998, vol. X
Smeaton, Lt-Col (Charles) Oswald, 1862–1923, vol. II
Smeaton, Donald Mackenzie, 1848–1910, vol. I
Smeaton, Oliphant; *see* Smeaton, W. H. O.
Smeaton, Lt-Col Oswald; *see* Smeaton, Lt-Col C. O.
Smeaton, William Henry Oliphant, *died* 1914, vol. I
Smeddles, Thomas Henry, 1904–1987, vol. VIII
Smedley, Constance, *died* 1941, vol. IV
Smeed, Reuben Jacob, 1909–1976, vol. VII
Smeeton, Vice-Adm. Sir Richard Michael, 1912–1992, vol. IX
Smeeton, Captain Samuel Page, 1842–1916, vol. II
Smele, William Smauel George, 1912–1976, vol. VII
Smellie, Alexander, 1857–1923, vol. II
Smellie, Elizabeth Lawrie, 1884–1968, vol. VI
Smellie, James Maclure, 1893–1961, vol. VI
Smellie, Kingsley Bryce Speakman, 1897–1987, vol. VIII
Smellie, R(obert) Martin S(tuart), 1927–1988, vol. VIII

Smeterlin, Jan, 1892–1967, vol. VI
Smethurst, Albert H., 1868–1935, vol. III
Smethurst, Rev. Canon Arthur Frederick, 1904–1957, vol. V
Smethurst, Sir Thomas, 1860–1935, vol. III
Smiddy, Timothy A., 1875–1962, vol. VI
Smijth, Sir William Bowyer-, 12th Bt (*cr* 1661), 1840–1916, vol. II
Smijth-Windham, Brig. William Russell, 1907–1994, vol. IX
Smiles, Samuel, 1812–1904, vol. I
Smiles, Samuel, 1877–1953, vol. V
Smiles, Lt-Col Sir Walter Dorling, *died* 1953, vol. V
Smiles, William, 1824–1915, vol. I
Smiley, Sir Hugh Houston, 1st Bt, 1841–1909, vol. I
Smiley, Sir Hugh Houston, 3rd Bt, 1905–1990, vol. VIII
Smiley, Sir John, 2nd Bt, 1876–1930, vol. III
Smiley, Norman Bryce, 1909–1968, vol. VI
Smiley, Peter Kerr K.; *see* Kerr-Smiley.
Smillie, Robert, 1857–1940, vol. III
Smirk, Sir (Frederick) Horace, 1902–1991, vol. IX
Smirk, Sir Horace; *see* Smirk, Sir F. H.
Smit, Hon. Jacob Hendrik, 1881–1959, vol. V
Smit, Jacobus Stephanus, 1878–1960, vol. V
Smith, Baron (Life Peer); Rodney Smith, 1914–1998, vol. X
Smith, A. Reginald, *died* 1934, vol. III
Smith, Abel, 1829–1898, vol. I
Smith, Abel Henry, 1862–1930, vol. III
Smith, Hon. Sir Abercrombie; *see* Smith, Hon. Sir C. A.
Smith, Adam, 1854–1920, vol. II
Smith, Alan Guy E.; *see* Elliot-Smith.
Smith, Alan Oliver, 1929–1998, vol. X
Smith, Sir Alan R.; *see* Rae Smith.
Smith, Alastair Macleod M.; *see* Macleod Smith.
Smith, Albert, 1867–1942, vol. IV
Smith, Sir Albert, 1862–1944, vol. IV
Smith, Brig. Albert, 1896–1959, vol. V
Smith, Albert Hugh, 1903–1967, vol. VI
Smith, Albert William, 1863–1940, vol. III
Smith, Lt-Col Alexander Hugh Dickson, 1890–1960, vol. V
Smith, Sir Alexander Rowland, 1888–1988, vol. VIII
Smith, Alfred, *died* 1931, vol. III
Smith, Alfred Emanuel, 1873–1944, vol. IV
Smith, Alfred John, 1865–1925, vol. II, vol. III
Smith, Hon. Alfred Lee, *born* 1838, vol. II
Smith, Sir Alfred M.; *see* Mays-Smith.
Smith, Maj.-Gen. Alfred Travers Fairtlough, 1890–1965, vol. VI
Smith, Sir Alfred van W. L.; *see* Lucie-Smith.
Smith, Rt Rev. Alfred William, 1875–1958, vol. V
Smith, Lt-Col Algernon Fox Eric, 1857–1942, vol. IV
Smith, Alic Halford, 1883–1958, vol. V
Smith, Alick Drummond Buchanan-; *see* Baron Balerno.
Smith, Rt Hon. Alick Laidlaw B.; *see* Buchanan-Smith.
Smith, Sir Allan Chalmers, 1893–1980, vol. VII
Smith, Allan Frith, 1857–1935, vol. III
Smith, Sir Allan Gordon G.; *see* Gordon-Smith.

Smith, Sir Allan Macgregor, *died* 1941, vol. IV
Smith, Allan Ramsay, 1875–1926, vol. II
Smith, Andrew, 1849–1914, vol. I
Smith, Sir Andrew, 1880–1967, vol. VI
Smith, Andrew Thomas, 1884–1943, vol. IV
Smith, Comdr Andrew W.; *see* Wilmot-Smith.
Smith, Dame Anne Beadsmore, 1869–1960, vol. V
Smith, Annie Shepherd; *see* Smith, Mrs Burnett.
Smith, Dame Annis; *see* Gillie, Dame A. C.
Smith, Sir Anthony Paul G.; *see* Grafftey-Smith.
Smith, Anthony Robert, 1926–1988, vol. VIII
Smith, Rt Hon. Sir Archibald Levin, 1836–1901, vol. I
Smith, Arnold Cantwell, 1915–1994, vol. IX
Smith, (Arnold) John Hugh, 1881–1964, vol. VI
Smith, Arnold P.; *see* Pye-Smith.
Smith, Arthur C.; *see* Corbett-Smith.
Smith, Arthur Croxton, 1865–1952, vol. V
Smith, Rev. Arthur Edward, 1871–1952, vol. V
Smith, Lt-Gen. Sir Arthur Francis, 1890–1977, vol. VII
Smith, Vice-Adm. Arthur Gordon, 1873–1953, vol. V
Smith, Arthur H.; *see* Hopewell-Smith.
Smith, Arthur Hamilton, 1860–1941, vol. IV
Smith, Rev. Arthur Henderson, 1845–1932, vol. III
Smith, Sir Arthur Henry, 1905–1989, vol. VIII
Smith, Arthur Kirke, 1878–1937, vol. III
Smith, Arthur Lionel, 1850–1924, vol. II
Smith, Arthur Lionel Forster, 1880–1972, vol. VII
Smith, Arthur Llewellyn, 1903–1978, vol. VII
Smith, Lt-Col Arthur M.; *see* Murray-Smith.
Smith, Arthur Norman E.; *see* Exton-Smith.
Smith, Arthur William, 1880–1961, vol. VI
Smith, Sir Aubrey; *see* Smith, Sir Charles A.
Smith, Adm. Sir Aubrey Clare Hugh, 1872–1957, vol. V
Smith, Ven. Augustus Elder, *died* 1916, vol. II
Smith, Austin Geoffrey, 1918–1984, vol. VIII
Smith, Rev. Canon Basil Alec, 1908–1969, vol. VI
Smith, (Basil) Gerald P.; *see* Parsons-Smith.
Smith, Basil Gerrard, 1911–1993, vol. IX
Smith, Basil Guy Oswald, 1861–1928, vol. II
Smith, Basil Thomas P.; *see* Parsons-Smith.
Smith, Gen. Bedell; *see* Smith, Gen. W. B.
Smith, Rt Hon. Sir Ben, 1879–1964, vol. VI
Smith, Benjamin Eli, 1857–1913, vol. I
Smith, Ven. Benjamin Frederick, *died* 1900, vol. I
Smith, Bernard, 1881–1936, vol. III
Smith, Bernard Joseph G.; *see* Gilliat-Smith.
Smith, Sir Berry C.; *see* Cusack-Smith.
Smith, Col Bertram Abel, 1879–1947, vol. IV
Smith, Captain Bertram Hornsby, 1874–1945, vol. IV
Smith, Lt-Col Bertram M.; *see* Metcalfe-Smith.
Smith, Sir Bracewell, 1st Bt (*cr* 1947), 1884–1966, vol. VI
Smith, Brian A.; *see* Abel-Smith.
Smith, Ven. (Brian) John, 1933–2000, vol. X
Smith, Brian Percival, 1919–2000, vol. X
Smith, Major Brooke H.; *see* Heckstall-Smith.
Smith, Hon. Bruce, 1851–1937, vol. III
Smith, Sir Bryan Evers S.; *see* Sharwood-Smith.
Smith, Mrs Burnett, 1860–1943, vol. IV

Smith, Campbell Sherston (Campbell Williams), 1906–1992, vol. IX
Smith, Sir Carl Victor, 1897–1979, vol. VII
Smith, Carlton A., 1853–1946, vol. IV
Smith, Cecil Archibald, *died* 1948, vol. IV
Smith, Rt Hon. Sir Cecil Clementi, 1840–1916, vol. II
Smith, Sir Cecil F.; *see* Furness-Smith.
Smith, Sir Cecil Harcourt-, 1859–1944, vol. IV
Smith, Maj.-Gen. Sir Cecil Miller, 1896–1988, vol. VIII
Smith, Mrs Cecil W.; *see* Woodham-Smith.
Smith, Charles, 1844–1916, vol. II
Smith, Hon. Sir (Charles) Abercrombie, 1834–1919, vol. II
Smith, Lt-Col Charles Aitchison, 1871–1940, vol. III
Smith, Captain Charles Appleton, 1864–1928, vol. II
Smith, Sir (Charles) Aubrey, 1863–1948, vol. IV
Smith, Col Sir Charles Bean Euan-, 1842–1910, vol. I
Smith, Charles Bennett, 1870–1939, vol. III (A), vol. IV
Smith, Sir Charles Cunliffe, 3rd Bt (*cr* 1804), 1827–1905, vol. I
Smith, (Charles Edward) Gordon, 1924–1991, vol. IX
Smith, Air Cdre Sir Charles Edward K.; *see* Kingsford-Smith.
Smith, Charles Emory, 1842–1908, vol. I
Smith, Captain Charles Futcher, 1876–1925, vol. II
Smith, Air Cdre Charles Gainer, 1880–1948, vol. IV
Smith, Sir Charles Garden A.; *see* Assheton-Smith.
Smith, Hon. Sir Charles George, *died* 1941, vol. IV
Smith, Charles George Percy; *see* Baron Delacourt-Smith.
Smith, Charles H.; *see* Herbert-Smith.
Smith, Charles Harvard G.; *see* Gibbs-Smith.
Smith, Charles Henry C.; *see* Chichester Smith.
Smith, Sir (Charles) Herbert, 1871–1941, vol. IV
Smith, Maj.-Gen. Sir Charles Holled, 1846–1925, vol. II
Smith, C(harles) Holt, 1903–1984, vol. VIII
Smith, Charles Howard, 1888–1942, vol. IV
Smith, Rev. Charles John, *died* 1940, vol. III
Smith, Charles Johnston, 1880–1943, vol. IV
Smith, Charles Michie, 1854–1922, vol. II
Smith, Charles Nugent C.; *see* Close-Smith.
Smith, Very Rev. Charles Pressley, 1862–1935, vol. III
Smith, Sir (Charles) Robert, 1887–1959, vol. V
Smith, Rev. Charles Ryder, 1873–1956, vol. V
Smith, Charles Stewart, 1859–1934, vol. III
Smith, Charles Stuart, 1936–1991, vol. IX
Smith, Captain Charles Valentine, 1854–1932, vol. III
Smith, Mgr Charles William, 1873–1954, vol. V
Smith, Charlotte F.; *see* Fell-Smith.
Smith, Charlotte Susanna Wenban; *see* Rycroft, C. S.
Smith, Chilton Lind A.; *see* Addison-Smith.
Smith, (Christopher) Colin, 1927–1997, vol. X
Smith, Christopher Patrick Crawford, 1902–1984, vol. VIII

Smith, Cicely Fox, *died* 1954, vol. V
Smith, Sir Clarence, 1849–1941, vol. IV
Smith, Claude C.; *see* Croxton-Smith.
Smith, Rev. Clement, 1845–1921, vol. II
Smith, Lt-Gen. Clement John, 1831–1910, vol. I
Smith, Brig.-Gen. Clement Leslie, *died* 1927, vol. II
Smith, Sir Clifford Edward H.; *see* Heathcote-Smith.
Smith, Clifford P., 1869–1945, vol. IV
Smith, Colin, 1881–1940, vol. III
Smith, Colin; *see* Smith, Christopher C.
Smith, Sir Colville; *see* Smith, Sir P. C.
Smith, Surg.-Gen. Sir Colvin C.; *see* Colvin-Smith.
Smith, Constance Isabella Stuart, *died* 1930, vol. III
Smith, Cyril James, 1909–1974, vol. VII
Smith, Cyril Robert, 1907–1993, vol. IX
Smith, Dan; *see* Smith, T. D.
Smith, Rev. David, 1866–1932, vol. III
Smith, David B.; *see* Baird-Smith.
Smith, David Bonner-, 1890–1950, vol. IV
Smith, Hon. David John, 1907–1976, vol. VII
Smith, Very Rev. David MacIntyre Bell Armour, 1923–1997, vol. X
Smith, David MacLeish, 1900–1986, vol. VIII
Smith, David Murray, *died* 1952, vol. V
Smith, David Nichol, 1875–1962, vol. VI
Smith, David S.; *see* Seth-Smith.
Smith, Hon. Sir David Stanley, 1888–1982, vol. VIII
Smith, Sir David Wadsworth, 1883–1948, vol. IV
Smith, Dempster, *died* 1953, vol. V
Smith, Maj.-Gen. Desmond; *see* Smith, Maj.-Gen. J. D. B.
Smith, Desmond A.; *see* Abel Smith.
Smith, Dodie, 1896–1990, vol. VIII
Smith, Donald Charles, 1910–1995, vol. X (AI)
Smith, Donald MacKeen, 1923–1998, vol. X
Smith, Dorothy; *see* Smith, Dodie.
Smith, Douglas Alexander, 1915–1988, vol. VIII
Smith, Lt-Col Douglas Kirke, 1883–1923, vol. II
Smith, Sir Drummond Cospatric Hamilton-S., 5th Bt (*cr* 1804); *see* Spencer-Smith.
Smith, Sir Drummond Cuncliffe, 4th Bt (*cr* 1804), 1861–1947, vol. IV
Smith, Sir Dudley S.; *see* Stewart-Smith.
Smith, Maj.-Gen. E. Davidson-, *died* 1916, vol. II
Smith, E. W.; *see* Whitney-Smith.
Smith, Ean Kendal S.; *see* Stewart-Smith.
Smith, Edgar Albert, 1847–1916, vol. II
Smith, Edgar Charles B.; *see* Bate-Smith.
Smith, Edgar Dennis, 1911–1986, vol. VIII
Smith, Maj.-Gen. Sir Edmund H.; *see* Hakewill Smith.
Smith, Adm. Edmund Hyde, 1865–1939, vol. III
Smith, Edmund Robinson, 1856–1942, vol. IV
Smith, Sir Edmund Wyldbore-, 1877–1938, vol. III
Smith, Edward, 1839–1919, vol. II
Smith, Sir Edward, 1857–1926, vol. II
Smith, Edward B.; *see* Barclay-Smith.
Smith, Col Edward Castleman C.; *see* Castleman-Smith.
Smith, Edward John Gregg, 1930–1989, vol. VIII
Smith, Edward Orford, 1841–1915, vol. I
Smith, Lt-Col Edward Osborne, 1864–1930, vol. III
Smith, Major Edward Pelham, 1868–1937, vol. III

Smith, Major Edward Pendarves D.; *see* Dorrien-Smith.
Smith, Edward Percy, 1891–1968, vol. VI
Smith, Edward Rawdon R.; *see* Rawdon Smith.
Smith, Edward S.; *see* Sharwood-Smith.
Smith, Edward Shrapnell S.; *see* Shrapnell-Smith.
Smith, Edwin, 1870–1937, vol. III
Smith, Col Edwin Charles M.; *see* Montgomery-Smith.
Smith, Hon. Sir Edwin Thomas, 1830–1919, vol. II
Smith, Rev. Edwin W., 1876–1957, vol. V
Smith, Eileen S.; *see* Stamers-Smith.
Smith, Lady Eleanor, *died* 1945, vol. IV
Smith, Ellis, 1896–1969, vol. VI
Smith, Dame Enid Mary Russell R.; *see* Russell-Smith.
Smith, Captain Eric; *see* Smith, Captain Evan C. E.
Smith, Sir Eric; *see* Smith, Sir J. E.
Smith, Sir Eric Conran C.; *see* Conran-Smith.
Smith, Eric Martin, 1908–1951, vol. V
Smith, Eric Percival, 1890–1938, vol. III
Smith, Erik John, 1914–1972, vol. VII
Smith, Ernest, 1869–1945, vol. IV
Smith, Hon. Ernest D'Israeli, 1853–1948, vol. IV
Smith, Ernest Gardiner, *died* 1956, vol. V
Smith, Ernest Lester, 1904–1992, vol. IX
Smith, Ernest T.; *see* Thornton-Smith.
Smith, Brig. Ernest Thomas Cobley, 1895–1977, vol. VII
Smith, Sir Ernest Woodhouse, 1884–1960, vol. V
Smith, Eustace, *died* 1914, vol. I
Smith, Col Sir Eustace; *see* Smith, Col Sir T. E.
Smith, Eustace Abel, 1862–1938, vol. III
Smith, Captain Evan Cadogan Eric, 1894–1950, vol. IV
Smith, Everard Reginald Martin, 1875–1938, vol. III
Smith, Sir Ewart; *see* Smith, Sir. F. E.
Smith, Florence Margaret; *see* Smith, Stevie.
Smith, Sir Francis Edward James, 1863–1950, vol. IV
Smith, Francis Edward Viney, 1902–1979, vol. VII
Smith, Sir Francis H.; *see* Harrison-Smith.
Smith, Francis Hopkinson, 1838–1915, vol. I
Smith, Francis Jagoe, 1873–1969, vol. VI
Smith, (Francis) Raymond (Stanley), 1890–1981, vol. VIII
Smith, Francis St George M.; *see* Manners-Smith.
Smith, Sir Francis Villeneuve-, 1819–1909, vol. I
Smith, Sir Francis Whitmore, 1844–1931, vol. III
Smith, Francis William Head, 1886–1964, vol. VI
Smith, Hon. Sir Frank, *died* 1901, vol. I
Smith, Frank, 1854–1940, vol. III
Smith, Frank, 1882–1951, vol. V
Smith, Frank Braybrook, 1864–1950, vol. IV
Smith, Sir Frank Edward, 1879–1970, vol. VI
Smith, Sir Frank Edwin N.; *see* Newson-Smith.
Smith, Sir (Frank) Ewart, 1897–1995, vol. IX
Smith, Frank Guthrie, 1873–1932, vol. III
Smith, Frank Moffat, 1872–1940, vol. III
Smith, Fred, 1880–1940, vol. III
Smith, Fred John, 1857–1919, vol. II
Smith, Frederic G.; *see* Gordon-Smith.
Smith, Frederic Marlett B.; *see* Bell-Smith.
Smith, Maj.-Gen. Sir Frederick, 1857–1929, vol. III

Smith, Col Frederick, 1858–1933, vol. III
Smith, Sir Frederick, 1859–1945, vol. IV
Smith, Frederick A., 1887–1943, vol. IV
Smith, Frederick Bonham, *born* 1837, vol. II
Smith, Rev. Frederick J. J.; *see* Jervis-Smith.
Smith, Col Frederick John, 1866–1915, vol. I
Smith, Lt Col Frederick Lawrence C.; *see*
    Coldwell-Smith.
Smith, Frederick Llewellyn, 1909–1988, vol. VIII
Smith, Sir Frederick William, 1861–1926, vol. II
Smith, Frederick William, 1896–1981, vol. VIII
Smith, Garden Grant, 1860–1913, vol. I
Smith, Col Sir Gengoult; *see* Smith, Sir H. G.
Smith, Geoffrey, 1878–1910, vol. I
Smith, Geoffrey Ellrington Fane, 1903–1987,
    vol. VIII
Smith, Geoffrey R. H., 1901–1964, vol. VI
Smith, Geoffrey Samuel A.; *see* Abel-Smith.
Smith, Vice-Adm. Sir Geoffrey T.; *see*
    Thistleton-Smith.
Smith, Ven. Geoffry Bertram, 1889–1957, vol. V
Smith, George, 1833–1919, vol. II
Smith, George, 1870–1934, vol. III
Smith, Sir George, 1858–1938, vol. III
Smith, George, 1867–1957, vol. V
Smith, George, 1914–1994, vol. IX
Smith, George, 1919–1994, vol. IX
Smith, George A.; *see* Armitage-Smith.
Smith, Very Rev. Sir George Adam, 1856–1942,
    vol. IV
Smith, George Barnett, 1841–1909, vol. I
Smith, Brig.-Gen. George Barton, 1860–1921,
    vol. II
Smith, Sir George Basil H.; *see* Haddon-Smith.
Smith, Sir George Bracewell, 2nd Bt (*cr* 1947),
    1912–1976, vol. VII
Smith, George Charles Moore, 1858–1940, vol. III
Smith, George Douglas, 1865–1949, vol. IV
Smith, Brig.-Gen. George Edward, 1868–1944,
    vol. IV
Smith, Sir George Fenwick, 1914–1978, vol. VII
Smith, George Frederick Herbert, 1872–1953,
    vol. V
Smith, Rev. George Furness, 1849–1929, vol. III
Smith, George G.; *see* Gregory Smith.
Smith, George Geoffrey, 1885–1951, vol. V
Smith, Sir George Henry F.; *see* Fisher-Smith.
Smith, Rev. George Herbert, 1851–1923, vol. II
Smith, George Hill, 1833–1926, vol. II
Smith, Rt Rev. George John, 1840–1918, vol. II
Smith, Sir George John, 1845–1921, vol. II
Smith, Col George John, 1862–1946, vol. IV
Smith, George Lind A.; *see* Addison-Smith.
Smith, Rev. George Maberly, 1831–1917, vol. II
Smith, Lt-Col George Maciver Campbell,
    1869–1946, vol. IV
Smith, Col George Moultrie B.; *see* Bullen-Smith.
Smith, George Munro, 1856–1917, vol. II
Smith, George Murray, 1859–1919, vol. II
Smith, Sir George R.; *see* Reeves-Smith.
Smith, George S.; *see* Scoby-Smith.
Smith, George Stuart G.; *see* Graham-Smith.
Smith, George Tulloch B.; *see* Bisset-Smith.
Smith, George W. Duff A.; *see* Assheton-Smith.
Smith, George William Q.; *see* Quick-Smith.

Smith, Major George Wilson, 1880–1940, vol. IV
Smith, Gerald Dudley, 1866–1936, vol. III
Smith, Gerald P.; *see* Parsons-Smith.
Smith, Lt-Col Sir Gerard, 1839–1920, vol. II
Smith, Gerard Gustave L.; *see* Lind-Smith.
Smith, Gerard Thomas C.; *see* Corley Smith.
Smith, Brig.-Gen. Gilbert Boys, 1859–1937, vol. III
Smith, Rev. Gilbert Edward, *died* 1912, vol. I
Smith, Air Vice-Marshal Gilbert H.; *see*
    Harcourt-Smith.
Smith, Col Sir Gilbertson, 1867–1958, vol. V
Smith, Ven. Godfrey Scott, 1878–1944, vol. IV
Smith, Goldwin, 1823–1910, vol. I
Smith, Sir Gordon; *see* Smith, Sir W. G.
Smith, Gordon; *see* Smith, C. E. G.
Smith, Sir Grafton Elliot, 1871–1937, vol. III
Smith, Graham Burrell, 1880–1975, vol. VII
Smith, Granville, 1859–1925, vol. II
Smith, Col Granville Roland Francis, 1860–1917,
    vol. II
Smith, Rev. Granville V. V., 1838–1929, vol. III
Smith, Guy B.; *see* Bassett Smith, N. G.
Smith, Sir Guy B.; *see* Bracewell-Smith.
Smith, Guy Basil G.; *see* Gilliat-Smith.
Smith, Guy Bellingham, 1865–1945, vol. IV
Smith, Rt Rev. Guy Vernon, 1880–1957, vol. V
Smith, Rev. Gwilym, 1881–1939, vol. III
Smith, H. Herbert, 1851–1913, vol. I
Smith, Sir Hamilton Pym F.; *see* Freer Smith.
Smith, Sir Harold, 1876–1924, vol. II
Smith, Col Sir Harold Charles T.; *see*
    Templar-Smith.
Smith, Harold Clifford, 1876–1960, vol. V
Smith, Col Sir (Harold) Gengoult, 1890–1983,
    vol. VIII
Smith, Harold Hamel, 1867–1944, vol. IV
Smith, Harold Octavius, 1882–1952, vol. V
Smith, Harold Ross, 1906–1956, vol. V
Smith, Harry, 1870–1940, vol. III
Smith, Rev. Harry, 1865–1942, vol. IV
Smith, Sir Harry, 1874–1949, vol. IV
Smith, Lt-Col Harry Cyril, 1888–1983, vol. VIII
Smith, Ven. (Harry Kingsley) Percival, 1898–1965,
    vol. VI
Smith, Maj.-Gen. Sir Harry Reginald Walter
    Marriott, 1875–1955, vol. V
Smith, Harry Worcester, 1865–1945, vol. IV
Smith, Harvey Hall, 1880–1958, vol. V
Smith, Rev. Haskett, 1847–1906, vol. I
Smith, Rt Hon. Hastings Bertrand L.; *see*
    Lees-Smith.
Smith, Helen Gregory, *died* 1956, vol. V
Smith, Hely, 1862–1941, vol. IV
Smith, Sir Henry, *died* 1919, vol. II
Smith, Lt-Col Sir Henry, 1835–1921, vol. II
Smith, Rev. Henry, 1857–1939, vol. III
Smith, Lt-Col Henry, 1862–1948, vol. IV
Smith, Col Sir Henry A.; *see* Abel Smith.
Smith, Henry B.; *see* Batty-Smith.
Smith, Sir Henry Babington, 1863–1923, vol. II
Smith, Henry Bompas, 1867–1953, vol. V
Smith, Maj.-Gen. Henry C.; *see* Coape-Smith.
Smith, Engr Rear-Adm. Henry Frank, 1875–1939,
    vol. III
Smith, Rev. Henry Gibson, *died* 1931, vol. III

Smith, Brig. Henry Gilbertson, 1896–1977, vol. VII
Smith, Lt-Col Henry Lockhart, 1859–1935, vol. III
Smith, Sir Henry Martin, 1907–1979, vol. VII
Smith, Sir Henry Moncrieff, 1873–1951, vol. V
Smith, H(enry) Norman, 1890–1962, vol. VI
Smith, Col Henry Robert, 1843–1917, vol. II
Smith, Henry Roy William, 1891–1971, vol. VII
Smith, Sir Henry S.; see Scott-Smith.
Smith, Sir Henry Sutcliffe, 1864–1938, vol. III
Smith, Sir Henry Thompson, 1905–1986, vol. VIII
Smith, Henry W.; see Whitby-Smith.
Smith, Sir Henry W.; see White-Smith.
Smith, Sir Henry W.; see Wilson Smith.
Smith, Henry Wood, 1865–1906, vol. I
Smith, Sir Herbert; see Smith, Sir C. H.
Smith, Sir Herbert, 1st Bt (cr 1920), 1872–1943,
  vol. IV
Smith, Herbert, 1881–1953, vol. V
Smith, Sir Herbert, 2nd Bt (cr 1920), 1903–1961,
  vol. VI
Smith, Herbert Alexander, 1896–1976, vol. VII
Smith, Herbert Arthur, 1885–1961, vol. VI
Smith, Col Herbert Austen, 1866–1949, vol. IV
Smith, Herbert Cecil, 1893–1981, vol. VIII
Smith, Col Herbert Francis, 1859–1948, vol. IV
Smith, Lt-Col Herbert Frederick Edgar, 1888–1940,
  vol. III
Smith, Herbert Greenhough, died 1935, vol. III
Smith, Maj.-Gen. Sir Herbert Guthrie, 1864–1930,
  vol. III
Smith, Rev. Herbert Maynard, 1869–1949, vol. IV
Smith, Herbert S.; see Somerville Smith.
Smith, Major Herbert Stoney-, 1868–1915, vol. I
Smith, Herbert Williams, 1919–1987, vol. VIII
Smith, Horace, 1836–1922, vol. II
Smith, Howard; see Smith, P. H.
Smith, Sir Howard Frank Trayton, 1919–1996,
  vol. X
Smith, Col Howard William, 1858–1905, vol. I
Smith, Brig. Hubert Clementi, 1878–1958, vol. V
Smith, Sir Hubert Llewellyn, 1864–1945, vol. IV
Smith, Sir Hubert S.; see Shirley-Smith.
Smith, Hon. Hugh Adeane Vivian, 1910–1978,
  vol. VII
Smith, Hugh Alexander McC.; see McClure-Smith.
Smith, Lt-Col Sir Hugh Bateman P.; see
  Protheroe-Smith.
Smith, Hugh Bellingham, 1866–1922, vol. II
Smith, Hugh Colin, 1836–1910, vol. I
Smith, Hugh Crawford, died 1907, vol. I
Smith, Captain Hugh D.; see Dalrymple-Smith.
Smith, Brig. Hugh Garden S.; see Seth-Smith.
Smith, Hugh William H.; see Heckstall-Smith.
Smith, Vice-Adm. Humphrey Hugh, 1875–1940,
  vol. III
Smith, Ida Phyllis B.; see Barclay-Smith.
Smith, Rev. Irton, 1855–1933, vol. III
Smith, Rev. Isaac A., died 1940, vol. III
Smith, Rev. Isaac Gregory, 1826–1920, vol. II
Smith, J. Allister, 1866–1960, vol. V
Smith, J. T., died 1937, vol. III
Smith, Sir James, 1847–1932, vol. III
Smith, Most Rev. James A., 1841–1928, vol. II
Smith, James Aikman, 1914–1996, vol. X
Smith, James Alexander George, died 1942, vol. IV

Smith, Hon. Sir James Alfred, 1913–1993, vol. IX
Smith, Very Rev. James Allan, 1841–1918, vol. II
Smith, James Archibald Bruce, 1929–1996, vol. X
Smith, Col James Aubrey, 1877–1955, vol. V
Smith, Sir James Brown, 1845–1913, vol. I
Smith, Sir James Cowlishaw, 1873–1946, vol. IV
Smith, James Cruickshank, 1867–1946, vol. IV
Smith, James David Maxwell, 1895–1969, vol. VI
Smith, Maj.-Gen. (James) Desmond (Blaise),
  1911–1991, vol. IX
Smith, James Dury H.; see Hindley-Smith.
Smith, Sir James Edward M.; see Masterton-Smith.
Smith, Sir (James) Eric, 1909–1990, vol. VIII
Smith, James Hamblin, 1827–1901, vol. I
Smith, Hon. Sir (James) Joynton, 1855–1943,
  vol. IV
Smith, Surg.-Rear-Adm. James Lawrence,
  1862–1945, vol. IV
Smith, James Lorrain, died 1931, vol. III
Smith, James Maclaren G.; see Gray-Smith.
Smith, Rt Hon. James Parker, 1854–1929, vol. III
Smith, Lt-Col Sir James Robert Dunlop,
  1858–1921, vol. II
Smith, James Stewart, 1900–1987, vol. VIII
Smith, James Walter, 1868–1931, vol. III
Smith, Janet Buchanan A.; see Adam Smith.
Smith, Maj.-Gen. Jeremy Michael S.; see
  Spencer-Smith.
Smith, Rev. John, 1844–1905, vol. I
Smith, John, 1825–1910, vol. I
Smith, John, 1837–1922, vol. II
Smith, Very Rev. John, 1854–1927, vol. II
Smith, John, 1883–1964, vol. VI
Smith, Ven. John; see Smith, B. J.
Smith, Rt Hon. John, 1938–1994, vol. IX
Smith, John Alexander, 1863–1939, vol. III
Smith, Sir John Alfred L.; see Lucie-Smith.
Smith, Maj.-Gen. John Blackburne, 1865–1928,
  vol. II
Smith, Rear-Adm. John Edward D.; see Dyer-Smith.
Smith, John F.; see Forest Smith.
Smith, John George, 1881–1968, vol. VI
Smith, Sir John George Lawley V.; see
  Vassar-Smith.
Smith, John Gerald, 1907–1979, vol. VII
Smith, Lt-Col John Grant, died 1942, vol. IV
Smith, J(ohn) G(uthrie) Spence, 1880–1951, vol. V
Smith, John Henry E.; see Etherington-Smith.
Smith, John Hugh; see Smith, A. J. H.
Smith, John Hughes W.; see Wardle-Smith.
Smith, Sir John James, 1875–1957, vol. V
Smith, John Keats C.; see Catterson-Smith.
Smith, Sir John Kenneth N.; see Newson-Smith.
Smith, Lt-Col John Manners, 1864–1920, vol. II
Smith, John Mitchell Aitken, 1902–1974, vol. VII
Smith, John Obed, 1864–1937, vol. III
Smith, Rev. John Reader, died 1923, vol. II
Smith, John Roger B.; see Bickford Smith.
Smith, Rev. John Sandwith B.; see Boys Smith.
Smith, Sir John Smalman, 1847–1913, vol. I
Smith, Rt Rev. John Taylor, 1860–1938, vol. III
Smith, John William, 1864–1926, vol. II
Smith, Sir John Wilson, 1920–1995, vol. IX
Smith, Sir Jonah W.; see Walker-Smith.
Smith, Joseph, 1855–1939, vol. III

Smith, Maj.-Gen. Joseph Barnard, 1839–1925, vol. II

Smith, Sir Joseph Benjamin George, 1878–1950, vol. IV

Smith, Rt Rev. Joseph Oswald, 1854–1924, vol. II

Smith, Hon. Sir Joynton; see Smith, Hon. Sir James J.

Smith, K. W. A., 1899–1951, vol. V

Smith, Sir Keith Macpherson, 1890–1955, vol. V

Smith, Col Kenneth, 1885–1971, vol. VII

Smith, Kenneth Brooke Farley, 1913–1943, vol. IV

Smith, Brig.-Gen. Kenneth John K.; see Kincaid-Smith.

Smith, Kenneth Manley, 1892–1981, vol. VIII

Smith, Kenneth Shirley, 1900–1987, vol. VIII

Smith, Lancelot Grey Hugh, 1870–1941, vol. IV

Smith, Launcelot Eustace, 1868–1948, vol. IV

Smith, Sir Laurence Barton G.; see Graffley-Smith.

Smith, Lawrence Delpré, 1905–1996, vol. X

Smith, Sir Leonard Herbert, 1907–1989, vol. VIII

Smith, Col Leonard Kirke, 1877–1941, vol. IV

Smith, Lewis, 1869–1944, vol. IV

Smith, Captain Sir Lindsey, 1870–1960, vol. V

Smith, Brig.-Gen. Lionel A.; see Abel-Smith.

Smith, Col Lionel Fergus, 1869–1945, vol. IV

Smith, Lionel Graham Horton H.; see Horton-Smith.

Smith, Logan Pearsall, 1865–1949, vol. IV

Smith, Louis L.; see Laybourne-Smith.

Smith, Sir Louis W., died 1939, vol. III

Smith, Rt Rev. Lucius, 1860–1934, vol. III

Smith, Sir Lumley, 1834–1918, vol. II

Smith, Lyman Cornelius, died 1910, vol. I

Smith, Sir Malcolm, died 1935, vol. III

Smith, Lt-Col Malcolm K.; see Kincaid-Smith.

Smith, Marcella, died 1963, vol. VI

Smith, Maria Constance, died 1930, vol. III

Smith, Mark Barnet, 1917–1994, vol. IX

Smith, Marshall King, 1867–1946, vol. IV

Smith, Rt Rev. Martin Linton, 1869–1950, vol. IV

Smith, Martin Ridley, 1833–1908, vol. I

Smith, Mary Isobel Barr, died 1941, vol. IV

Smith, Mary Sybil, died 1952, vol. V

Smith, Sir Matthew Arnold Bracy, 1879–1959, vol. V

Smith, May, 1879–1968, vol. VI

Smith, Maynard, 1875–1928, vol. II

Smith, Maj.-Gen. Merton B.; see Beckwith-Smith.

Smith, Michael, 1932–2000, vol. X

Smith, Michael Garfield, 1921–1993, vol. IX

Smith, Michael James B.; see Babington Smith.

Smith, Michael Seymour S.; see Spencer-Smith.

Smith, Michael Wharton, 1927–1989, vol. VIII

Smith, Hon. Miles Staniforth Cater, 1869–1934, vol. III

Smith, Montague Bentley Talbot P.; see Paske-Smith.

Smith, Morton William, 1851–1925, vol. II

Smith, Naomi Gwladys R.; see Royde Smith.

Smith, Sir Nathaniel B.; see Bowden-Smith.

Smith, Nevil Digby B.; see Bosworth-Smith.

Smith, (Newlands) Guy B.; see Bassett Smith.

Smith, Noel James Gillies, born 1899, vol. VI

Smith, Norman, 1877–1963, vol. VI

Smith, Norman Kemp, 1872–1958, vol. V

Smith, Norman Lockhart, 1887–1968, vol. VI

Smith, Sir Norman Percival Arthur, 1892–1964, vol. VI

Smith, Captain Norman Wesley, 1900–1977, vol. VII

Smith, Nowell Charles, 1871–1961, vol. VI

Smith, Lt-Gen. Octavius Ludlow, 1828–1927, vol. II

Smith, Olivia Mary, (Mrs R. D. Smith); see Manning, O. M.

Smith, Lt-Col Osbert Walter Dudley, 1898–1973, vol. VII

Smith, Sir Osborne Arkell, 1876–1952, vol. V

Smith, Very Rev. Oswin Harvard G.; see Gibbs-Smith.

Smith, Owen Hugh, died 1958, vol. V

Smith, Owen Maurice, 1888–1957, vol. V

Smith, Patrick, 1858–1930, vol. III

Smith, Patrick Wykeham M.; see Montague-Smith.

Smith, Ven. Percival; see Smith, Ven. H. K. P.

Smith, Major Percy George D.; see Darvil-Smith.

Smith, Percy John Delf, died 1948, vol. IV

Smith, Surg.-Rear-Adm. Sir Percy W. B.; see Bassett-Smith.

Smith, Peter Caldwell, 1858–1923, vol. II

Smith, Philip, 1853–1922, vol. II

Smith, Philip, 1913–1999, vol. X

Smith, Sir (Philip) Colville, died 1937, vol. III

Smith, Philip George, 1911–1998, vol. X

Smith, Philip H. Law, 1866–1920, vol. II

Smith, Philip Henry P.; see Pye-Smith.

Smith, (Philip) Howard, 1845–1919, vol. II

Smith, Rear-Adm. P(hilip) Sydney, 1899–1973, vol. VII

Smith, Rev. Philip Vernon, 1845–1929, vol. III

Smith, Brig. Philip William Lilian B.; see Broke-Smith.

Smith, Phyllis B.; see Barclay-Smith.

Smith, Priestley, died 1933, vol. III

Smith, Sir Prince, 1st Bt (cr 1911), 1840–1922, vol. II

Smith, Sir Prince P., 2nd Bt (cr 1911); see Prince-Smith.

Smith, Ralph Emeric Kasope T; see Taylor-Smith.

Smith, Ralph G.; see Gordon-Smith.

Smith, Ralph Henry H.; see Hammersley-Smith.

Smith, Ralph Henry T.; see Tottenham-Smith.

Smith, Ravenscroft Elsey, 1859–1930, vol. III

Smith, Raymond; see Smith, F. R. S.

Smith, Reginald, vol. II

Smith, Rev. Reginald, 1844–1936, vol. III

Smith, Reginald Allender, died 1940, vol. III

Smith, Reginald Arthur, 1904–1985, vol. VIII

Smith, Reginald Eccles, 1887–1963, vol. VIII

Smith, Reginald Henry Macaulay A.; see Abel Smith.

Smith, Col Rt Hon. Sir Reginald Hugh D.; see Dorman-Smith.

Smith, Reginald John, 1857–1916, vol. II

Smith, Reginald John, 1895–1981, vol. VIII

Smith, Reginald Montagu B.; see Bosworth-Smith.

Smith, Reginald Norman M.; see Marsh Smith.

Smith, Sir Reginald V.; see Verdon-Smith.

Smith, Rennie, 1888–1962, vol. VI

Smith, Richard; see Smith, W. R.

Smith, Richard Edwin, 1910–1978, vol. VII

Smith, Richard G.; *see* Gordon-Smith.
Smith, Richard Henry S.; *see* Sandford Smith.
Smith, Richard Horton H.; *see* Horton-Smith.
Smith, Richard M.; *see* Mudie-Smith.
Smith, Sir Richard Rathborne V.; *see* Vassar-Smith.
Smith, Sir Richard Robert L.; *see* Law-Smith.
Smith, Maj.-Gen. Richard Talbot S.; *see* Snowden-Smith.
Smith, Sir Richard Vassar V.; *see* Vassar-Smith.
Smith, Sir Robert; *see* Smith, Sir C. R.
Smith, Robert Addison, 1846–1925, vol. II
Smith, Robert Allan, 1909–1980, vol. VII
Smith, Robert Cooper, 1859–1917, vol. II
Smith, Robert John, 1866–1942, vol. IV
Smith, Robert Macaulay, 1859–1927, vol. II
Smith, Sir Robert Murdoch, 1835–1900, vol. I
Smith, Robert Murray, 1831–1921, vol. II
Smith, Robert Paterson, 1903–1971, vol. VII
Smith, Robert Percy, *died* 1941, vol. IV
Smith, Robert Shingleton, 1845–1922, vol. II
Smith, Sir Robert Workman, 1st Bt (*cr* 1945), 1880–1957, vol. V
Smith, Rt Rev. Rocksborough Remington, 1872–1955, vol. V
Smith, Sir Roderick Philip, 1926–1981, vol. VIII
Smith, Gipsy Rodney, 1860–1947, vol. IV
Smith, Roger Thomas, 1863–1940, vol. III
Smith, Ron, 1915–1999, vol. X
Smith, Rev. Ronald Gregor, 1913–1968, vol. VI
Smith, Ronald Parkinson; *see* Parkinson, N.
Smith, Sir Ross G.; *see* Grey-Smith.
Smith, Sir Ross Macpherson, 1892–1922, vol. II
Smith, Sir Rudolph Hampden; *see* Smith, Sir T. R. H.
Smith, Col Rupert Alexander A.; *see* Alec-Smith.
Smith, Rupert Rawden R.; *see* Rawden-Smith.
Smith, Rutherfoord John P.; *see* Pye-Smith.
Smith, S. Catterson, 1849–1912, vol. I
Smith, Rt Hon. Samuel, 1836–1906, vol. I
Smith, Samuel, 1855–1921, vol. II
Smith, Samuel Harold, 1888–1971, vol. VII
Smith, Samuel Walter Johnson, 1871–1948, vol. IV
Smith, Sarah; *see* Stretton, Hesba.
Smith, Sheila K.; *see* Kaye-Smith.
Smith, Sidney, 1889–1979, vol. VII
Smith, Lt-Col Sidney Browning, *died* 1930, vol. III
Smith, Sidney Earle, 1897–1959, vol. V
Smith, Simon Harcourt N.; *see* Nowell-Smith.
Smith, Solomon Charles Kaines, *died* 1958, vol. V
Smith, Spence; *see* Smith, John G. S.
Smith, Stanley Alexander de; *see* de Smith.
Smith, Major Stanley Alwyn, 1882–1931, vol. III
Smith, Stanley G.; *see* Graham Smith.
Smith, Stanley Livingston, 1889–1958, vol. V
Smith, Stanley Parker, 1884–1953, vol. V
Smith, Stanley Wyatt-, 1887–1958, vol. V
Smith, Stephen Henry, 1865–1943, vol. IV
Smith, Col Steuart B.; *see* Bogle-Smith.
Smith, Stevie, (Florence Margaret Smith), 1902–1971, vol. VII
Smith, Stuart Hayne G.; *see* Granville-Smith.
Smith, Captain Sutton, *died* 1938, vol. III
Smith, Sir Swire, 1842–1918, vol. II
Smith, Maj.-Gen. Sir Sydenham Campbell Urquhart, 1859–1940, vol. III

Smith, Hon. Sydney, 1856–1934, vol. III
Smith, Sydney, 1900–1981, vol. VIII
Smith, Sir Sydney Alfred, *died* 1969, vol. VI
Smith, Sir Sydney Armitage A.; *see* Armitage-Smith.
Smith, Sydney David, 1873–1936, vol. III
Smith, Col Sydney Ernest, 1881–1943, vol. IV
Smith, Rev. Sydney Fenn, 1843–1921, vol. II
Smith, Sydney Herbert, 1885–1984, vol. VIII
Smith, Sydney M.; *see* Macdonald-Smith.
Smith, Sydney Ure, 1887–1949, vol. IV
Smith, Sydney William, 1878–1963, vol. VI
Smith, T. Gilbert, *died* 1904, vol. I
Smith, Theobald, 1859–1934, vol. III
Smith, Theodore Clarke, 1870–1960, vol. V (A), vol. VI (AI)
Smith, Thomas, 1817–1906, vol. I
Smith, Sir Thomas, 1st Bt (*cr* 1897), 1833–1909, vol. I
Smith, Sir Thomas, 1875–1963, vol. VI
Smith, Thomas, 1883–1969, vol. VI
Smith, Thomas Algernon D.; *see* Dorrien-Smith.
Smith, Sir Thomas Brown, 1915–1988, vol. VIII
Smith, Major Thomas Close, 1878–1946, vol. IV
Smith, Sir Thomas Cospatric Hamilton-S., 6th Bt (*cr* 1804); *see* Spencer-Smith.
Smith, Sir Thomas D. S.; *see* Straker-Smith.
Smith, T(homas) Dan, 1915–1993, vol. IX
Smith, Col Sir (Thomas) Eustace, 1900–1971, vol. VII
Smith, Rev. Canon Thomas G.; *see* Grigg-Smith.
Smith, Major Sir Thomas Gabriel Lumley L.; *see* Lumley-Smith.
Smith, Rt Rev. Thomas Geoffrey Stuart, 1901–1981, vol. VIII
Smith, Thomas I.; *see* Irvine Smith.
Smith, Sir Thomas James, *died* 1939, vol. III
Smith, Thomas James, 1905–1970, vol. VI
Smith, Thomas Roger, 1830–1903, vol. I
Smith, Sir (Thomas) Rudolph Hampden, 2nd Bt (*cr* 1897), 1869–1958, vol. V
Smith, Sir Thomas Turner, 3rd Bt (*cr* 1897), 1903–1961, vol. VI
Smith, (Thomas) Wareham, 1874–1938, vol. III
Smith, Thomas William, 1878–1946, vol. IV
Smith, Tom, 1886–1953, vol. IV
Smith, Sir Tom Elder B.; *see* Barr Smith.
Smith, Mrs Toulmin; *see* Meade, L. T.
Smith, Trafford, 1912–1975, vol. VII
Smith, Vernon Russell, 1849–1921, vol. II
Smith, Victor, 1879–1931, vol. III
Smith, Adm. Sir Victor Alfred Trumper, 1913–1998, vol. X
Smith, Vincent Arthur, 1848–1920, vol. II
Smith, Vivian Francis C.; *see* Crowther-Smith.
Smith, W. Harding, *died* 1922, vol. II
Smith, W. H. S.; *see* Seth-Smith.
Smith, W. P. Haskett-, *died* 1946, vol. IV
Smith, Sir Walter B.; *see* Buchanan-Smith.
Smith, Gen. (Walter) Bedell, 1895–1961, vol. VI
Smith, Walter Campbell, 1887–1988, vol. VIII
Smith, Rev. Walter Chalmers, 1824–1908, vol. I
Smith, Walter George, 1844–1932, vol. III
Smith, Rev. Walter Percy, 1848–1922, vol. II
Smith, Rev. Walter R., 1845–1921, vol. II

Smith, (Walter) Richard, 1926–1997, vol. X
Smith, Walter Riddell, 1914–1984, vol. VIII
Smith, Walter Robert, 1872–1942, vol. IV
Smith, Walter Robert George, 1887–1966, vol. VI
Smith, Walter William Marriott, 1846–1944, vol. IV
Smith, Wareham; see Smith, T. W.
Smith, Watson, 1845–1920, vol. II
Smith, Wilfred, 1903–1955, vol. V
Smith, Maj.-Gen. Wilfrid Edward Bownas, 1867–1942, vol. IV
Smith, Sir William, 1843–1916, vol. II
Smith, Maj.-Gen. William, 1835–1922, vol. II
Smith, William, 1859–1932, vol. III
Smith, Sir William Alexander, 1854–1914, vol. I
Smith, Col William Apsley, 1856–1927, vol. II
Smith, Vice-Adm. William B.; see Bowden Smith.
Smith, William Benjamin, 1850–1934, vol. III (A), vol. IV
Smith, William Binns, 1837–1911, vol. I
Smith, William Brownhill, died 1948, vol. IV
Smith, Sir William C.; see Cusack-Smith.
Smith, William Charles, 1849–1915, vol. I
Smith, William Charles Clifford, 1855–1931, vol. III
Smith, Maj.-Gen. Sir William Douglas, 1865–1939, vol. III
Smith, Maj.-Gen. William Dunlop, 1865–1940, vol. III
Smith, Sir William Edward, 1850–1930, vol. III
Smith, Hon. William Forgan, 1887–1953, vol. V
Smith, William Frederick Bottrill, 1903–1995, vol. X (AI)
Smith, Sir William Frederick Haynes, 1839–1928, vol. II
Smith, William French, 1917–1990, vol. VIII
Smith, Sir William George Verdon, 1876–1957, vol. V
Smith, Sir (William) Gordon, 2nd Bt, 1916–1983, vol. VIII
Smith, William Henry, 1894–1968, vol. VI
Smith, William Herbert G.; see Guthrie-Smith.
Smith, Rev. William Hodson, 1856–1943, vol. IV
Smith, Brig.-Gen. William Hugh Usher, 1869–1940, vol. III
Smith, Captain William Humphrey, 1879–1942, vol. IV
Smith, Rev. William Isaac Carr, died 1930, vol. III
Smith, Sir William James, 1853–1912, vol. I
Smith, Sir William Joseph P.; see Pearman-Smith.
Smith, William Owen Lester, 1888–1976, vol. VII
Smith, Sir William P.; see Prince-Smith.
Smith, Sir William Proctor, 1891–1963, vol. VI
Smith, Sir William R., died 1932, vol. III
Smith, William Ramsay, 1859–1937, vol. III
Smith, Sir William Reardon, 1st Bt (cr 1920), 1856–1935, vol. III
Smith, Sir William Reardon Reardon-, 3rd Bt (cr 1920), 1911–1995, vol. IX
Smith, Sir (William) Reginald V.; see Verdon-Smith.
Smith, Maj.-Gen. William Revell R.; see Revell-Smith.
Smith, Sir (William Robert) Dermot (Joshua) C.; see Cusack-Smith.
Smith, Sir William Rose, 1852–1934, vol. III

Smith, Most Rev. William Saumarez, 1836–1909, vol. I
Smith, William Sydney, 1866–1945, vol. IV
Smith, Sir William Sydney Winwood, 4th Bt (cr 1809), 1879–1953, vol. V
Smith, William W.; see Wenban-Smith.
Smith, Sir William Wright, 1875–1956, vol. V
Smith, Willie; see Smith, H. W.
Smith, Sir Willie Reardon-, 2nd Bt (cr 1920), 1887–1950, vol. IV
Smith, Wilson, 1897–1965, vol. VI
Smith, Winifred L. B.; see Boys-Smith.
Smith-Bingham, Brig.-Gen. Oswald Buckley Bingham; see Bingham.
Smith-Bosanquet, Major George Richard Bosanquet, 1866–1939, vol. III
Smith-Carington, Herbert Hanbury; see Carington.
Smith-Carington, Neville Woodford, 1878–1933, vol. III
Smith-Dodsworth, Sir Claude Matthew, 7th Bt, 1888–1940, vol. III
Smith-Dorrien, Olive Crofton, (Lady Smith-Dorrien), died 1951, vol. V
Smith-Dorrien, Gen. Sir Horace Lockwood, 1858–1930, vol. III
Smith-Dorrien, Rev. Walter Montgomery, died 1924, vol. II
Smith-Gordon, Sir Lionel Eldred, 2nd Bt, 1833–1905, vol. I
Smith-Gordon, Sir Lionel Eldred Pottinger, 3rd Bt, 1857–1933, vol. III
Smith-Gordon, Sir Lionel Eldred Pottinger, 4th Bt, 1889–1976, vol. VII
Smith-Marriott, Rev. Sir Hugh Randolph Cavendish, 9th Bt, 1868–1944, vol. IV
Smith-Marriott, Sir John Richard Wyldbore, 7th Bt, 1875–1942, vol. IV
Smith-Marriott, Sir Ralph George Cavendish, 10th Bt, 1900–1987, vol. VIII
Smith-Marriott, Sir William, 8th Bt, 1865–1943, vol. IV
Smith-Marriott, Sir William Henry, 5th Bt, 1835–1924, vol. II
Smith-Marriott, Sir William John, 6th Bt, 1870–1941, vol. IV
Smith-Neill, Col James William, 1865–1935, vol. III
Smith-Pearse, Thomas Lawrence, 1893–1972, vol. VII
Smith-Pearse, Rev. Thomas Northmore Hart, 1854–1943, vol. IV
Smith-Rewse, Rev. Gilbert Flesher, died 1935, vol. III
Smith-Rewse, Col Henry Whistler, 1850–1930, vol. III
Smith-Rose, Reginald Leslie, 1894–1980, vol. VII
Smith-Ryland, Sir Charles Mortimer Tollemache, 1927–1989, vol. VIII
Smithard, Major Richard Glass, 1891–1939, vol. III
Smithe, Ida Elizabeth, died 1951, vol. V
Smithe, Major Percy Bourdillon, 1860–1912, vol. I
Smithells, Arthur, 1860–1939, vol. III
Smitherman, Frank, 1913–1993, vol. IX
Smithers, Sir Alfred Waldron, 1850–1924, vol. II
Smithers, Sir Arthur Tennyson, 1894–1972, vol. VII
Smithers, Sir David Waldron, 1908–1995, vol. IX

Smithers, Donald William, 1905–1986, vol. VIII
Smithers, Geoffrey Victor, 1909–2000, vol. X
Smithers, Brig. Leonard Sueton Hirsch, 1879–1954, vol. V
Smithers, Hon. Sir Reginald Allfree, 1903–1994, vol. IX
Smithers, Sir Waldron, 1880–1954, vol. V
Smithson, Col Walter Charles, 1860–1938, vol. III
Smithwick, Rear-Adm. Algernon Robert, 1887–1948, vol. IV
Smithwick, John Francis, 1844–1913, vol. I
Smolka, H. P.; *see* Smollett, H. P.
Smollett, Maj.-Gen. Alexander Patrick Drummond T.; *see* Telfer-Smollett.
Smollett, Harry Peter, 1912–1980, vol. VII
Smollett, Captain James Drummond T.; *see* Telfer-Smollett.
Smoot, Reed, 1862–1941, vol. IV
Smout, Sir Arthur John Griffiths, 1888–1961, vol. VI
Smout, Charles Frederick Victor, 1895–1978, vol. VII
Smout, David Arthur Lister, 1923–1987, vol. VIII
Smuts, Field Marshal Rt Hon. Jan Christian, 1870–1950, vol. IV
Smuts, Johannes, 1865–1937, vol. III
Smylie, Air Cdre Gilbert Formby, 1895–1965, vol. VI
Smyly, Col Dennis Douglas Pilkington, 1913–1979, vol. VII
Smyly, J. Gilbart, 1867–1948, vol. IV
Smyly, Sir Philip Crampton, 1838–1904, vol. I
Smyly, Sir Philip Crampton, 1896–1953, vol. V
Smyly, William Cecil, 1840–1921, vol. II
Smyly, Sir William Josiah, 1850–1941, vol. IV
Smyth, Sir Alfred John Bowyer-, 13th Bt (*cr* 1661), 1850–1927, vol. II
Smyth, Austin Edward Arthur Watt, 1877–1949, vol. IV
Smyth, Col Charles Coghlan, 1842–1920, vol. II
Smyth, Charles Edward O.; *see* Owen-Smyth.
Smyth, Rev. Canon Charles Hugh Egerton, 1903–1987, vol. VIII
Smyth, David Henry, 1908–1979, vol. VII
Smyth, Dame Ethel Mary, 1858–1944, vol. IV
Smyth, Col Etwall Walter, 1843–1929, vol. III
Smyth, Lt-Col Geoffrey Henry Julian Skeffington; *see* FitzPatrick, Lt-Col G. H. J.
Smyth, George Watson, 1838–1910, vol. I
Smyth, Captain Gerald Brice Ferguson, 1885–1920, vol. II
Smyth, Hon. Gilbert Neville, 1864–1940, vol. III
Smyth, Rear-Adm. Harry Hesketh, 1872–1926, vol. II
Smyth, Lt-Col Henry, 1866–1943, vol. IV
Smyth, Gen. Sir Henry Augustus, 1825–1906, vol. I
Smyth, (Herbert) Warington, *died* 1943, vol. IV
Smyth, Major Humphrey Etwall, 1884–1927, vol. II
Smyth, James Richard, 1895–1953, vol. V
Smyth, John, 1864–1927, vol. II
Smyth, Brig.-Gen. John Ambard B.; *see* Bell-Smyth.
Smyth, John Andrew, 1893–1971, vol. VII
Smyth, Brig. Rt Hon. Sir John George, 1st Bt, 1893–1983, vol. VIII

Smyth, Lt-Col John Henry Graham Holroyd, 1846–1904, vol. I
Smyth, Sir John Henry Greville, 1st Bt, 1836–1901, vol. I
Smyth, Ven. John Paterson, *died* 1932, vol. III
Smyth, John William, 1880–1968, vol. VI
Smyth, Margaret Jane, 1897–1991, vol. IX
Smyth, Michael Joseph, *died* 1964, vol. VI
Smyth, Montague; *see* Smyth, W. M.
Smyth, Vice-Adm. Morris Henry, 1853–1940, vol. III
Smyth, Maj.-Gen. Sir Nevill Maskelyne, 1868–1941, vol. IV
Smyth, Col Owen Stuart, 1853–1923, vol. II
Smyth, Captain Sir Philip Weyland Bowyer-, 14th Bt, 1894–1978, vol. VII
Smyth, Reginald, 1917–1998, vol. X
Smyth, Sir Robert Middleton Watson, 1872–1939, vol. III
Smyth, Brig.-Gen. Robert Napier, 1868–1947, vol. IV
Smyth, Lt-Col Robert Riversdale, 1875–1946, vol. IV
Smyth, Sir Samuel Andrew, 1877–1953, vol. V
Smyth, Rev. Thomas Alexander, *died* 1936, vol. III
Smyth, Thomas Francis, 1875–1937, vol. III
Smyth, (Walter) Montague, 1863–1965, vol. VI
Smyth, Warington; *see* Smyth, H. W.
Smyth, Rev. William A. B.; *see* Blood-Smyth.
Smyth, William Bates, 1874–1946, vol. IV
Smyth, Rt Rev. William Edmund, 1858–1950, vol. IV
Smyth, Col William Ross, 1857–1932, vol. III
Smyth-Osbourne, Brig.-Gen. George Nowell Thomas, 1877–1942, vol. IV
Smyth-Osbourne, Air Cdre Sir Henry Percy, 1879–1969, vol. VI
Smyth-Pigott, Gp Captain (Joseph) Ruscombe (Wadham), 1889–1971, vol. VII
Smyth-Pigott, Gp Captain Ruscombe; *see* Smyth-Pigott, Gp Captain J. R. W.
Smythe, Albert Charles B.; *see* Butler-Smythe.
Smythe, Charles John, 1852–1918, vol. II
Smythe, Col David Murray, 1850–1928, vol. II
Smythe, Sir Edward Walter Joseph Patrick Herbert, 9th Bt, 1869–1942, vol. IV
Smythe, Rev. Canon Francis Henry Dumville, 1873–1966, vol. VI
Smythe, Francis Sydney, 1900–1949, vol. IV
Smythe, Henry James Drew-, 1916–1983, vol. VIII
Smythe, Sir (John) Walter, 8th Bt, 1827–1919, vol. II
Smythe, Lionel Percy, 1840–1918, vol. II
Smythe, Patricia Rosemary K.; *see* Koechlin-Smythe.
Smythe, Very Rev. Patrick Murray, 1860–1935, vol. III
Smythe, Captain Quentin George Murray, 1916–1997, vol. X
Smythe, Reginald; *see* Smyth, R.
Smythe, Sir Reginald Harry, 1905–1981, vol. VIII
Smythe, Lt-Col Rupert Cæsar, 1879–1943, vol. IV
Smythe, Sir Walter; *see* Smythe, Sir J. W.
Smythies, Evelyn Arthur, 1885–1975, vol. VII

Snadden, Sir William McNair, 1st Bt, 1896–1959, vol. V
Snagge, Vice-Adm. Arthur Lionel, 1878–1955, vol. V
Snagge, Sir Harold Edward, 1872–1949, vol. IV
Snagge, John Derrick Mordaunt, 1904–1996, vol. X
Snagge, Sir Mordaunt; *see* Snagge, Sir T. M.
Snagge, Dame Nancy Marion, 1906–1999, vol. X
Snagge, Sir (Thomas) Mordaunt, 1868–1955, vol. V
Snagge, Sir Thomas William, 1837–1914, vol. I
Snaith, John Collis, 1876–1936, vol. III
Snaith, Gp Captain Leonard Somerville, 1902–1985, vol. VIII
Snaith, Rev. Norman Henry, 1898–1982, vol. VIII
Snaith, Stanley, 1903–1976, vol. VII
Snape, Henry Lloyd, 1861–1933, vol. III
Snape, Thomas Peter, 1925–1997, vol. X
Snark, The; *see* Wood, Starr.
Snead-Cox, John, 1855–1939, vol. III
Snedden, Rt Hon. Sir Billy Mackie, 1926–1987, vol. VIII
Snedden, Sir Richard, 1900–1970, vol. VI
Sneddon, Ian Naismith, 1919–2000, vol. X
Snedden, Rev. James, 1871–1945, vol. IV
Sneddon, Robert, 1920–1997, vol. X
Snell, 1st Baron, 1865–1944, vol. IV
Snell, Alfred Walter S.; *see* Saxon-Snell.
Snell, Ven. Basil Clark, 1907–1986, vol. VIII
Snell, Rev. Bernard J., 1856–1934, vol. III
Snell, Frederick Rowlandson, 1903–1991, vol. IX
Snell, Rt Rev. Geoffrey Stuart, 1920–1988, vol. VIII
Snell, George Davis, 1903–1996, vol. X
Snell, Harvie Kennard, 1898–1969, vol. VI
Snell, Captain Ivan Edward, 1884–1958, vol. V
Snell, J. Herbert, 1861–1935, vol. III
Snell, Sir John Francis Cleverton, 1869–1938, vol. III
Snell, Simeon, *died* 1909, vol. I
Snell, William Edward, 1902–1990, vol. VIII
Snell, William Thomas, *died* 1951, vol. V
Snellgrove, Anthony; *see* Snellgrove, J. A.
Snellgrove, (John) Anthony, 1922–1999, vol. X
Snelling, Maj.-Gen. Arthur Hugh Jay, 1897–1965, vol. VI
Snelling, Sir Arthur Wendell, 1914–1996, vol. X
Snelson, Sir Edward Alec Abbot, 1904–1992, vol. IX
Snelus, Alan Roe, 1911–1990, vol. VIII
Snelus, George James, 1837–1906, vol. I
Sneyd, Ralph, 1863–1949, vol. IV
Sneyd, Vice-Adm. Ralph Stuart W.; *see* Wykes-Sneyd.
Sneyd, Maj.-Gen. Thomas William, 1837–1918, vol. II
Sneyd-Kynnersley, Charles Walter; *see* Kynnersley, C. W. S.
Snodgrass, William Robertson, 1890–1955, vol. V
Snow, Baron (Life Peer); Charles Percy Snow, 1905–1980, vol. VII
Snow, Lady; *see* Johnson, Pamela Hansford.
Snow, Rt Rev. George D'Oyly, 1903–1977, vol. VII
Snow, Edgar Parks, 1905–1972, vol. VII
Snow, Ernest Charles, 1886–1959, vol. V
Snow, Sir Frederick Sidney, 1899–1976, vol. VII

Snow, (George) Robert Sabine, 1897–1969, vol. VI
Snow, Sir Gordon Keith, 1898–1954, vol. V
Snow, Sir Harold Ernest, 1897–1971, vol. VII
Snow, Henry Martin, 1859–1931, vol. III
Snow, Herbert, 1847–1930, vol. III
Snow, Lt-Col Humphry Waugh, 1879–1969, vol. VI
Snow, Julian Ward; *see* Baron Burntwood.
Snow, Philip Chicheley Hyde, 1853–1931, vol. III
Snow, Robert Sabine; *see* Snow, G. R. S.
Snow, Sir Sydney, 1887–1958, vol. V
Snow, Lt-Gen. Sir Thomas D'Oyly, 1858–1940, vol. III
Snow, Thomas Maitland, 1890–1997, vol. X
Snowden, 1st Viscount, 1864–1937, vol. III
Snowden, Viscountess; (Ethel), 1881–1951, vol. V
Snowden, Sir Arthur, 1829–1918, vol. II
Snowden, Arthur de Winton, 1872–1950, vol. IV
Snowden, Rev. Arthur Hillersdon, 1856–1940, vol. III
Snowden, Lt-Col Sir Eccles; *see* Snowden, Lt-Col Sir R. E.
Snowden, James; *see* Snowden, Keighley.
Snowden, Rev. John Hampden, 1828–1907, vol. I
Snowden, Rt Rev. John Samuel Philip, *died* 1996, vol. X
Snowden, Joseph Stanley, 1901–1980, vol. VII
Snowden, Keighley, 1860–1947, vol. IV
Snowden, Lt-Col Sir (Robert) Eccles, 1880–1934, vol. III
Snowden, Tom, 1875–1949, vol. IV
Snowden-Smith, Maj.-Gen. Richard Talbot, 1887–1951, vol. V
Snoy, Baron Robert, 1879–1946, vol. IV
Snoy et d'Oppuers, Comte Jean-Charles, 1907–1991, vol. IX
Snyder, John Wesley, 1895–1985, vol. VIII
Soady, Brig.-Gen. George Joseph FitzMaurice, 1863–1940, vol. III
Soame, Sir Charles Buckworth-Herne-, 9th Bt, 1830–1906, vol. I
Soame, Sir Charles Buckworth-Herne-, 10th Bt, 1864–1931 (this entry was not transferred to Who Was Who).
Soame, Sir Charles Burnett Buckworth-Herne-, 11th Bt, 1894–1977, vol. VII (inserted in error in vol. III)
Soames, Baron (Life Peer); Arthur Christopher John Soames, 1920–1987, vol. VIII
Soames, Major Alfred, 1862–1915, vol. I
Soames, Arthur Gilstrap, 1854–1934, vol. III
Soames, Arthur Wellesley, 1852–1934, vol. III
Soames, Geoffrey Ewart, 1881–1952, vol. V
Soane, Leslie James, 1926–1999, vol. X
Soar, Joseph, 1878–1971, vol. VII
Soar, Leonard Charles, 1899–1969, vol. VI
Soares, Sir Ernest Joseph, 1864–1926, vol. II
Sobell, Sir Michael 1892–1993, vol. IX
Sobha Singh, Hon. Sardar Bahadur Sir Sardar, 1890–1978, vol. VII
Sobry, Henri, 1861–1937, vol. III
Soddy, Frederick, 1877–1956, vol. V
Soddy, Kenneth, 1911–1986, vol. VIII
Soden, Freiherr Hermann von, 1852–1914, vol. I
Soden, Thomas Spooner, 1837–1920, vol. II

Söderblom, Nathan Lars Olof Jonathan, 1866–1931, vol. III
Soertsz, Sir Francis Joseph, 1886–1951, vol. V
Soheily, Ali, 1896–1958, vol. V
Sokhey, Maj.-Gen. Sir Sahib Singh, 1887–1971, vol. VII
Solberg, Thorvald, 1852–1949, vol. IV (A), vol. V
Soldene, Emily, *died* 1912, vol. I
Sole, Brig. Denis Mavesyn Anslow, 1883–1962, vol. VI
Solé-Romeo, Luis Alberto, 1934–1993, vol. IX
Sollas, William Johnson, 1849–1936, vol. III
Sollberger, Edmond, 1920–1989, vol. VIII
Solley, Leslie Judah, 1905–1968, vol. VI
Solloway, Rev. John, 1860–1946, vol. IV (A)
Solly, S. Edwin, 1845–1906, vol. I
Solly-Flood, Maj.-Gen. Arthur, 1871–1940, vol. III
Solly-Flood, Maj.-Gen. Sir Frederick Richard, 1829–1909, vol. I
Solly-Flood, Brig.-Gen. Richard Elles, 1877–1954, vol. V
Sologub, Feodor, 1864–1927, vol. II
Solomon, 1902–1988, vol. VIII
Solomon, Hon. Albert Edgar, 1876–1914, vol. I
Solomon, Sir (Aubrey) Kenneth, 1884–1954, vol. V
Solomon, Sir David Arnold, 1907–1997, vol. X
Solomon, Hon. Sir Edward Philip, *died* 1914, vol. I
Solomon, Edwin, 1914–1985, vol. VIII
Solomon, Frank Oakley, 1867–1941, vol. IV
Solomon, Jonathan Hilali Moïse, 1939–2000, vol. X
Solomon, Sir Kenneth; *see* Solomon, Sir A. K.
Solomon, Sir Richard, 1850–1913, vol. I
Solomon, Saul, 1875–1960, vol. V
Solomon, Solomon Joseph, 1860–1927, vol. II
Solomon, Captain William Ewart Gladstone, 1880–1965, vol. VI
Solomon, Rt Hon. Sir William Henry, 1852–1930, vol. III
Solomons, Hon. Sir Adrian; *see* Solomons, Hon. Sir L. A.
Solomons, Bethel, *died* 1965, vol. VI
Solomons, David, 1912–1995, vol. IX
Solomons, Estella Frances, *died* 1968, vol. VI
Solomons, Henry, 1902–1965, vol. VI
Solomons, Hon. Sir (Louis) Adrian, 1922–1991, vol. IX
Soloveytchik, George Michael de, 1902–1982, vol. VIII
Soltau, Col Alfred Bertram, 1876–1930, vol. III
Soltau, Roger Henry, 1887–1953, vol. V
Soltau-Symons, Lt-Col George Algernon James, 1867–1947, vol. IV
Soltau-Symons, George William Culme, 1831–1916, vol. II
Solti, Sir Georg, 1912–1997, vol. X
Soltykoff, HSH Prince Dimitri, *died* 1903, vol. I
Solvay, Ernest, 1839–1922, vol. II
Sombart, Werner, 1863–1941, vol. IV
Somerfield, Stafford William, 1911–1995, vol. IX
Somerhough, Hon. Anthony George, 1906–1960, vol. V
Somerleyton, 1st Baron, 1857–1935, vol. III
Somerleyton, 2nd Baron, 1889–1959, vol. V
Somerleyton, Lady; (Phyllis), *died* 1948, vol. IV
Somers, 5th Baron, 1815–1899, vol. I

Somers, 6th Baron, 1887–1944, vol. IV
Somers, 7th Baron, 1864–1953, vol. V
Somers, 8th Baron, 1907–1995, vol. IX
Somers, Lady; (Finola), 1896–1981, vol. VIII
Somers, Thomas Peter Miller, 1877–1965, vol. VI
Somers-Cocks, Rev. Henry Lawrence, 1862–1940, vol. III
Somers-Cocks, John; *see* Somers, 8th Baron.
Somers Cocks, John Sebastian, 1907–1964, vol. VI
Somerscales, Thomas Lawrence, 1913–1996, vol. X
Somerset, 15th Duke of, 1846–1923, vol. II
Somerset, 16th Duke of, 1860–1931, vol. III
Somerset, 17th Duke of, 1882–1954, vol. V
Somerset, 18th Duke of, 1910–1984, vol. VIII
Somerset, Col Sir Alfred Plantagenet Frederick Charles, 1829–1915, vol. I
Somerset, Brig.-Gen. Charles Wyndham, 1862–1938, vol. III
Somerset, Lady Henry, (Isabella Caroline), 1851–1921, vol. II
Somerset, Sir Henry Beaufort, 1906–1995, vol. X (AI)
Somerset, Henry Charles Somers Augustus, 1874–1945, vol. IV
Somerset, Rt Hon. Lord Henry Richard Charles, 1849–1932, vol. III
Somerset, Henry Robert Somers Fitzroy de Vere, 1898–1965, vol. VI
Somerset, John Henry William, 1848–1928, vol. II, vol. III
Somerset, Brig. Hon. Nigel FitzRoy, 1893–1990, vol. VIII
Somerset, Richard Gay, 1848–1928, vol. II, vol. III
Somerset, Raglan Horatio Edwyn Henry, 1885–1956, vol. V
Somerset, Sir Thomas, 1870–1947, vol. IV
Somerset Fry, Peter George Robin Plantagenet, 1931–1996, vol. X
Somerset-Thomas, William Edwin, 1867–1946, vol. IV
Somervell of Harrow, Baron (Life Peer); Donald Bradley Somervell, 1889–1960, vol. V
Somervell, Sir Arnold Colin, 1883–1957, vol. V
Somervell, Sir Arthur, 1863–1937, vol. III
Somervell, David Churchill, 1885–1965, vol. VI
Somervell, James, 1845–1924, vol. II
Somervell, Rupert Churchill Gelderd, 1892–1969, vol. VI
Somervell, Theodore Howard, 1890–1975, vol. VII
Somervell, William Henry, 1860–1934, vol. III
Somerville, Sir Annesley Ashworth, 1858–1942, vol. IV
Somerville, Arthur Fownes, 1850–1942, vol. IV
Somerville, Vice-Adm. Boyle; *see* Somerville, Vice-Adm. H. B. T.
Somerville, Daniel Gerald, 1879–1938, vol. III
Somerville, David Hughes, 1840–1918, vol. II
Somerville, Edith Anna Œnone, 1858–1949, vol. IV
Somerville, Col George Cattell, 1878–1959, vol. V
Somerville, Vice-Adm. (Henry) Boyle (Townshend), 1863–1936, vol. III
Somerville, Howard, 1873–1952, vol. V
Somerville, Vice-Adm. Hugh Gaultier-Coghill, 1873–1950, vol. IV

Somerville, Lt-Col James Aubrey Henry Bellingham, 1884–1950, vol. IV
Somerville, Admiral of the Fleet Sir James Fownes, 1882–1949, vol. IV
Somerville, Col John Arthur Coghill, 1872–1955, vol. V
Somerville, Sir John Livingston, 1885–1964, vol. VI
Somerville, (Katherine) Lilian, 1905–1985, vol. VIII
Somerville, Lilian; see Somerville, K. L.
Somerville, Mary, 1897–1963, vol. VI
Somerville, Comdr Philip, 1906–1942, vol. IV
Somerville, Rev. Richard Neville, 1864–1932, vol. III
Somerville, Sir Robert, 1906–1992, vol. IX
Somerville, Maj.-Gen. Ronald Macaulay, 1919–1991, vol. IX
Somerville, Col Thomas Cameron FitzGerald, 1860–1942, vol. IV
Somerville, Walter Harold, 1881–1959, vol. V
Somerville, Sir William, 1860–1932, vol. III
Somerville, Lt-Col William Arthur Tennison Bellingham, 1882–1951, vol. V
Somerville, William Dennistoun, 1842–1917, vol. II
Somerville Smith, Herbert, 1890–1967, vol. VI
Somes, Michael George, 1917–1994, vol. IX
Somjee, Mahomedbhoy Alladinbhoy, 1889–1942, vol. IV
Sommer, André D.; see Dupont-Sommer.
Sommerlad, Hon. Ernest Christian, 1886–1952, vol. V
Sommerville, David, died 1937, vol. III
Sommerville, Duncan M'Laren Young, 1879–1934, vol. III
Sommerville, Vice-Adm. Frederick Avenel, 1883–1962, vol. VI
Sommerville, Norman, 1878–1941, vol. IV
Sonbarsa, Maharaja of, 1846–1907, vol. I
Sondes, 2nd Earl, 1861–1907, vol. I
Sondes, 3rd Earl, 1866–1941, vol. IV
Sondes, 4th Earl, 1914–1970, vol. VI
Sondes, 5th Earl, 1940–1996, vol. X
Sondheimer, Franz, 1926–1981, vol. VIII
Song Ong Siang, Sir, died 1941, vol. IV
Sonnenschein, Edward Adolf, 1851–1929, vol. III
Sonneborn, Tracy Morton, 1905–1981, vol. VIII
Sonnino, Baron Sidney, 1847–1922, vol. II
Sontag, Raymond James, 1897–1972, vol. VII
Soothill, Alfred, 1863–1926, vol. II
Soothill, Ronald Gray, 1898–1980, vol. VII
Soothill, Rev. William Edward, 1861–1935, vol. III
Soper, Baron, (Life Peer); Rev. Donald Oliver Soper, 1903–1998, vol. X
Soper, Frederick George, 1898–1982, vol. VIII
Soper, George, 1870–1942, vol. IV
Soper, Harry Tapley Tapley-, 1875–1951, vol. V
Soper, J. Dewey, 1893–1982, vol. VIII
Sopoushek, Mrs Jan; see Greig, Maysie.
Sopwith, Sir Charles Ronald, 1905–1996, vol. X
Sopwith, Douglas George, 1906–1970, vol. VI
Sopwith, Ven. Thomas Karl, 1873–1945, vol. IV
Sopwith, Sir Thomas Octave Murdoch, 1888–1989, vol. VIII
Sorabji, Cornelia, died 1954, vol. V
Sorby, Rev. Albert Ernest, 1859–1934, vol. III
Sorby, Henry Clifton, 1826–1908, vol. I

Soref, Harold Benjamin, 1916–1993, vol. IX
Sorel, Albert, 1842–1906, vol. I
Sorel Cameron, Brig. John, 1907–1986, vol. VIII
Sorell-Cameron, George Cecil Minett; see Cameron.
Sorensen, Baron (Life Peer); Reginald William Sorensen, 1891–1971, vol. VII
Sorine, Savely, 1886–1953, vol. V
Sorley, Herbert Tower, 1892–1968, vol. VI
Sorley, Air Marshal Sir Ralph Squire, 1898–1974, vol. VII
Sorley, William Ritchie, 1855–1935, vol. III
Sorn, Hon. Lord; James Gordon McIntyre, 1896–1983, vol. VIII
Sorokin, Pitirim Alexandrovitch, 1889–1968, vol. VI
Sorrell, Alan, 1904–1974, vol. VII
Sorrell, Alec Albert, 1925–1996, vol. X
Sorsbie, Sir Malin, 1906–1988, vol. VIII
Sorsbie, Brig.-Gen. Robert Fox, 1866–1948, vol. IV
Sorsby, Arnold, 1900–1980, vol. VII
Sorsby, Maurice, 1898–1949, vol. IV
Soskice, Frank; see Baron Stow Hill.
Soteriades, Antis Georghios, 1924–1988, vol. VIII
Sotheby, Sir Edward Southwell, 1813–1902, vol. I
Sotheby, Lt-Col Herbert George, 1871–1954, vol. V
Sothern, Edward H., 1859–1933, vol. III
Sotheron-Estcourt, Rev. Edmund Walter, 1850–1938, vol. III
Sotheron-Estcourt, Captain Thomas Edmund, 1881–1958, vol. V
Sothers, Donald Bevan, 1889–1979, vol. VII
Souchon, Sir (Hippolyte) Louis (Wiehe du Coudray), 1865–1957, vol. V
Souchon, Sir Louis; see Souchon, Sir H. L. W. du C.
Soukop, Wilhelm Josef, 1907–1995, vol. IX
Soulbury, 1st Viscount, 1887–1971, vol. VII
Soulby, Rev. Charles Frederick Hodgkinson, 1881–1952, vol. V
Soule, Malcolm H., 1896–1951, vol. V
Soulsby, Sir Llewellyn T. G., 1885–1966, vol. VI
Soulsby, Sir William Jameson, 1851–1937, vol. III
Soundy, Hon. Sir John, 1878–1960, vol. V (A), vol. VI (AI)
Soundy, Sir John Thomas, 1851–1935, vol. III
Sousa, John Philip, 1854–1932, vol. III
Soustelle, Jacques Emile, 1912–1990, vol. VIII
Soutar, Andrew, 1879–1941, vol. IV
Soutar, Brig. John James Macfarlane, 1889–1956, vol. V
Soutar, William, 1898–1943, vol. IV
Souter, Alexander, 1873–1949, vol. IV
Souter, Sir Charles Alexander, 1877–1958, vol. V
Souter, Sir Edward Matheson, 1891–1959, vol. V
Souter, Col Hugh Maurice Wellesley, 1873–1941, vol. IV
Souter, Sir William Alfred, 1879–1968, vol. VI
Souter, William Lochiel Berkeley, 1865–1945, vol. IV
South, Richard, died 1932, vol. III
Southall, Joseph Edward, 1861–1944, vol. IV
Southall, Reginald Bradbury, 1900–1965, vol. VI
Southall, Thomas Frederick, 1898–1965, vol. VI
Southam, Alexander William, 1898–1981, vol. VIII
Southam, Rev. Eric George, 1884–1952, vol. V
Southam, Frederick Armitage, died 1927, vol. II

Southam, Harry Stevenson, *died* 1954, vol. V

Southampton, 4th Baron, 1867–1958, vol. V

Southampton, 5th Baron (disclaimed for life); *see* FitzRoy, Charles.

Southborough, 1st Baron, 1860–1947, vol. IV

Southborough, 2nd Baron, 1889–1960, vol. V

Southborough, 3rd Baron, 1897–1982, vol. VIII

Southborough, 4th Baron, 1922–1992, vol. IX

Southby, Sir (Archibald) Richard (Charles), 2nd Bt, 1910–1988, vol. VIII

Southby, Comdr Sir Archibald Richard James, 1st Bt, 1886–1969, vol. VI

Southby, Sir Richard; *see* Southby, Sir A. R. C.

Southcott, Rev. Canon Ernest William, 1915–1976, vol. VII

Southee, Ethelbert Ambrook, 1890–1968, vol. VI

Southern, Sir James Wilson, 1840–1909, vol. I

Southern, Ralph Lang, 1893–1968, vol. VI (AII)

Southern, Richard, 1903–1989, vol. VIII

Southern, Sir Robert, 1907–1999, vol. X

Southerton, Sydney James, 1874–1935, vol. III

Southesk, 9th Earl of, 1827–1905, vol. I

Southesk, 10th Earl of, 1854–1941, vol. IV

Southesk, 11th Earl of, 1893–1992, vol. IX

Southey, Hon. Charles William, 1832–1924, vol. II

Southey, Air Cdre Harold Frederic George, 1906–1979, vol. VII

Southey, Reginald, 1835–1899, vol. I

Southey, Sir Richard, 1808–1901, vol. I

Southey, Col Richard George, 1844–1909, vol. I

Southey, Sir Robert John, 1922–1998, vol. X

Southey, Maj.-Gen. William Melvill, 1866–1939, vol. III

Southgate, Bernard Alfred, 1904–1975, vol. VII

Southgate, Very Rev. John Eliot, 1926–1999, vol. X

Southgate, Margaret Cecil Irene, 1918–1970, vol. VI

Southorn, Sir Thomas; *see* Southorn, Sir W. T.

Southorn, Sir (Wilfrid) Thomas, 1879–1957, vol. V

Southouse-Cheyney, Major Reginald Evelyn Peter; *see* Cheyney, Peter.

Southward, Sir Ralph, 1908–1997, vol. X

Southward, Rev. Walter Thomas, 1851–1919, vol. II

Southwark, 1st Baron, 1843–1929, vol. III

Southwell, 5th Viscount, 1872–1944, vol. IV

Southwell, 6th Viscount, 1898–1960, vol. V

Southwell, Sir (Charles Archibald) Philip, 1894–1981, vol. VIII

Southwell, Rt Rev. Henry Kemble, *died* 1937, vol. III

Southwell, Rev. Herbert Burrows, *died* 1922, vol. II

Southwell, Sir Philip; *see* Southwell, Sir C. A. P.

Southwell, Sir Richard Vynne, 1888–1970, vol. VI

Southwood, 1st Viscount, 1873–1946, vol. IV

Southwood, Albert Ray, *died* 1973, vol. VII

Southwood, Captain Horace Gerald, 1912–1997, vol. X

Southworth, Sir Frederick, 1910–1999, vol. X

Souttar, Sir Henry, 1875–1964, vol. VI

Souttar, Robinson, 1848–1912, vol. I

Soutter, Francis William, 1844–1932, vol. III

Sovereign, Rt Rev. Arthur Henry, 1881–1966, vol. VI (AII)

Soward, Sir Alfred Walter, 1856–1949, vol. IV

Sowby, Rev. Cedric Walter, 1902–1975, vol. VII

Sowden, John Percival, 1917–1997, vol. X

Sowden, Sir William John, 1858–1943, vol. IV

Sowerby, (Amy) Millicent, 1878–1967, vol. VI (AII)

Sowerby, Arthur de Carle, 1885–1954, vol. V

Sowerby, Lt-Col Harry John, 1867–1935, vol. III

Sowerby, Katherine Githa, (Mrs John Kendall), *died* 1970, vol. VI

Sowerby, Millicent; *see* Sowerby, A. M.

Sowler, Col Harry, *died* 1962, vol. VI

Sowman, Air Cdre John Edward Rudkin, 1902–1979, vol. VII

Sowrey, Gp Captain Frederick, 1893–1968, vol. VI

Sowrey, Air Cdre William, 1894–1968, vol. VI

Sowter, Ven. Francis Briggs, *died* 1928, vol. II

Sowton, Charles, 1865–1932, vol. III

Soysa, Sir Warusahennedige Abraham Bastian, *died* 1981, vol. IX (AI)

Spaak, Fernand Paul Jules, 1923–1981, vol. VIII

Spaak, Paul-Henri, 1899–1972, vol. VII

Spaatz, Gen. Carl Andrew, 1891–1974, vol. VII

Spackman, Air Vice-Marshal Charles Basil Slater, 1895–1971, vol. VII

Spackman, Cyril Saunders, 1887–1963, vol. VI

Spaght, Monroe Edward, 1909–1993, vol. IX

Spahlinger, Henry, 1882–1965, vol. VI

Spaight, James Molony, 1877–1968, vol. VI

Spain, Lt-Col George Redesdale Booker, 1877–1961, vol. VI

Spain, John Edward D.; *see* Dixon-Spain.

Spain-Dunk, Susan, 1880–1962, vol. VI

Spalding, Franklin Spencer, 1865–1914, vol. I

Spalding, Henry Norman, 1877–1953, vol. V

Spalding, Kenneth Jay, 1879–1962, vol. VI

Spalding, Col Warner, 1844–1920, vol. II

Spalding, William F., 1879–1963, vol. VI

Spann, Keith, 1922–1990, vol. IX (AI)

Spanswick, Albert; *see* Spanswick, E. A. G.

Spanswick, (Ernest) Albert (George), 1919–1983, vol. VIII

Spanton, Rev. Ernest Frederick, 1871–1936, vol. III

Sparey, John Raymond, 1924–1997, vol. X

Spargo, John, 1876–1966, vol. VI

Sparke, George Archibald, 1871–1970, vol. VI

Sparkes, Henry, 1871–1950, vol. IV

Sparkes, Sir James; *see* Sparkes, Sir W. B. J. G.

Sparkes, Rear-Adm. Robert C.; *see* Copland-Sparkes.

Sparkes, Stanley Robert, 1910–1976, vol. VII

Sparkes, Sir (Walter Beresford) James (Gordon), 1889–1974, vol. VII

Sparkes, Col William Spottiswoode, 1862–1906, vol. I

Sparkman, John Jackson, 1899–1985, vol. VIII

Sparks, Sir Ashley, 1877–1964, vol. VI

Sparks, Beatrice M., *died* 1953, vol. V

Sparks, Charles Pratt, 1866–1940, vol. III

Sparks, Sir Frederick James, 1881–1953, vol. V

Sparks, Rev. Hedley Frederick Davis, 1908–1996, vol. X

Sparks, Col Hubert Conrad, 1874–1933, vol. III

Sparks, Joseph Alfred, 1901–1981, vol. VIII

Sparks, Nathaniel, 1880–1957, vol. V

Sparrow, Rev. David Alan, 1936–1981, vol. VIII

Sparrow, John Hanbury Angus, 1906–1992, vol. IX

Sparrow, Col Richard, 1871–1953, vol. V

Sparrow, Walter Shaw, *died* 1940, vol. III
Sparshott, Margaret Elwin, 1870–1940, vol. III
Spater, Ernest George, 1886–1975, vol. VII
Spath, Leonard Frank, 1882–1957, vol. V
Spaul, Eric Arthur, 1895–1978, vol. VII
Speaight, Frederick William, 1869–1942, vol. IV
Speaight, Richard Langford, 1906–1976, vol. VII
Speaight, Richard Neville, 1875–1938, vol. III
Speaight, Robert William, 1904–1976, vol. VII
Speakman, Sir Harry, 1865–1946, vol. IV
Speakman, John Bamber, 1897–1969, vol. VI
Speakman, Lionel, *died* 1948, vol. IV
Spear, (Augustus John) Ruskin, 1911–1990,
    vol. VIII
Spear, Lt-Col Christopher Ronald, 1897–1942,
    vol. IV
Spear, Harold Cumming, 1909–1997, vol. X
Spear, Sir John Ward, 1848–1921, vol. II
Spear, Ruskin; *see* Spear, A. J. R.
Speares, Denis James, 1922–1970, vol. VI
Spearman, Sir Alexander Bowyer, 4th Bt,
    1917–1977, vol. VII
Spearman, Sir Alexander Cadwallader Mainwaring,
    1901–1982, vol. VIII
Spearman, Sir Alexander Young, 3rd Bt,
    1881–1959, vol. V
Spearman, Charles E., 1863–1945, vol. IV
Spearman, Clement, 1919–1997, vol. X
Spearman, Edmund Robert, 1837–1918, vol. II
Spearman, Sir Joseph Layton Elmes, 2nd Bt,
    1857–1922, vol. II
Spears, Maj.-Gen. Sir Edward Louis, 1st Bt,
    1886–1974, vol. VII
Spears, Mary, (Lady Spears); *see* Borden, Mary.
Speck, Rev. Jocelyn Henry, *died* 1922, vol. II
Spector, Walter Graham, 1924–1982, vol. VIII
Spedding, Major Charles Rodney, 1871–1915, vol. I
Spedding, Brig.-Gen. Edward Wilfrid, 1867–1939,
    vol. III
Speechly, Rt Rev. John Martindale, 1836–1898,
    vol. I
Speed, Sir Edwin Arney, 1869–1941, vol. IV
Speed, Sir Eric Bourne Bentinck, 1895–1971,
    vol. VII
Speed, Harold, 1872–1957, vol. V
Speed, James A.; *see* Andrews-Speed.
Speed, Lancelot, 1860–1931, vol. III
Speed, Marjorie Jane, 1903–1982, vol. VIII
Speed, Sir Robert William Arney, 1905–1999,
    vol. X
Speelman, Sir Cornelis Jacob, 7th Bt, 1881–1949,
    vol. IV
Speelman, Sir Cornelis Jacob Abraham, 5th Bt,
    1823–1898, did not have an entry in Who's
    Who.
Speelman, Sir Helenus, 6th Bt, 1852–1907, did not
    have an entry in Who's Who.
Speer, Rear-Adm. F. Shirley Litchfield-,
    1874–1922, vol. II
Speer, Robert Elliott, 1867–1947, vol. IV
Speidel, Gen. Hans, 1897–1984, vol. VIII
Speight, Harold Edwin Balme, 1887–1975, vol. VII
Speight, Johnny, 1920–1998, vol. X
Speight, Thomas Wilkinson, 1830–1915, vol. I
Speir, Col Guy Thomas, 1875–1951, vol. V

Speir, Wing Comdr Robert Cecil Talbot,
    1904–1980, vol. VII
Speir, Robert Thomas Napier, 1841–1922, vol. II
Speir, Sir Rupert Malise, 1910–1998, vol. X
Speirs, Alexander Archibald Hagart-, 1869–1958,
    vol. V
Speirs, William James McLaren, 1924–1998, vol. X
Spellman, Cardinal Francis J., 1889–1967, vol. VI
Spenale, Georges, 1913–1983, vol. VIII
Spence, Sir Alexander, 1866–1939, vol. III (A),
    vol. IV
Spence, Col Alexander Hierom Ogilvy, 1869–1936,
    vol. III
Spence, Allan William, 1900–1990, vol. VIII
Spence, Col Sir Basil Hamilton Hebden N.; *see*
    Neven-Spence.
Spence, Sir Basil Urwin, 1907–1976, vol. VII
Spence, Catherine Helen, 1825–1910, vol. I
Spence, Edward Fordham, 1860–1932, vol. III
Spence, Sir George Hemming, 1888–1962, vol. VI
Spence, Col Gilbert Ormerod, 1879–1925, vol. II
Spence, Henry Reginald, 1897–1981, vol. VIII
Spence, Sir James Calvert, 1892–1954, vol. V
Spence, James Knox, 1844–1919, vol. II
Spence, (James) Lewis (Thomas Chalmers),
    1874–1955, vol. V
Spence, Ven. John, *died* 1914, vol. I
Spence, John, 1878–1949, vol. IV
Spence, John Bowring, 1861–1918, vol. II
Spence, John Deane, 1920–1986, vol. VIII
Spence, Lewis; *see* Spence, J. L. T. C.
Spence, Sir Reginald, 1880–1961, vol. VI
Spence, Robert, 1870–1964, vol. VI
Spence, Robert, 1879–1966, vol. VI
Spence, Robert, 1905–1976, vol. VII
Spence, Most Rev. Robert William, 1860–1934,
    vol. III
Spence, Thomas William Leisk, 1845–1923, vol. II
Spence, William Robert Locke, 1875–1954, vol. V
Spence-Colby, Col Cecil John Herbert, 1873–1954,
    vol. V
Spence-Jones, Very Rev. Henry Donald Maurice,
    1836–1917, vol. II
Spencelayh, Charles, 1865–1958, vol. V
Spencer, 5th Earl, 1835–1910, vol. I
Spencer, 6th Earl, 1857–1922, vol. II
Spencer, 7th Earl, 1892–1975, vol. VII
Spencer, 8th Earl, 1924–1992, vol. IX
Spencer, Countess; (Cynthia Ellinor Beatrix),
    1897–1972, vol. VII
Spencer, Alan Douglas, 1920–2000, vol. X
Spencer, Rev. Arthur John, 1850–1922, vol. II
Spencer, Lt-Col Aubrey Vere, 1886–1973, vol. VII
Spencer, Augustus, 1860–1924, vol. II
Spencer, Sir Baldwin; *see* Spencer, Sir W. B.
Spencer, Brian, 1922–1985, vol. VIII
Spencer, Sir Charles Gordon Spencer, 1869–1934,
    vol. III
Spencer, Col Charles Louis, 1870–1948, vol. IV
Spencer, Cyril, 1924–1999, vol. X
Spencer, Dorothy, *died* 1969, vol. VI
Spencer, Sir Ernest, 1848–1937, vol. III
Spencer, Brig. Francis Elmhirst, 1881–1972,
    vol. VII
Spencer, Frederic, 1861–1942, vol. IV

Spencer, Air Vice-Marshal Geoffrey Roger Cole, 1901–1969, vol. VI
Spencer, Ven. George, *died* 1926, vol. II, vol. III
Spencer, George Alfred, 1872–1957, vol. V
Spencer, Gilbert, 1893–1979, vol. VII
Spencer, Sir Harris, 1863–1934, vol. III
Spencer, Sir Henry Francis, 1892–1964, vol. VI
Spencer, Herbert, 1820–1903, vol. I
Spencer, Herbert, 1915–1993, vol. IX
Spencer, Major Herbert Eames, 1871–1945, vol. IV
Spencer, Herbert Ritchie, 1860–1941, vol. IV
Spencer, Hugh, 1867–1926, vol. II
Spencer, Air Vice-Marshal Ian James, 1916–1994, vol. IX
Spencer, James Frederick, 1881–1950, vol. IV
Spencer, Brig.-Gen. John Almeric Walter, 1881–1952, vol. V
Spencer, Col John H.; *see* Heatly-Spencer.
Spencer, Sir Kelvin Tallent, 1898–1993, vol. IX
Spencer, Leonard James, 1870–1959, vol. V
Spencer, Surg.-Gen. Sir Lionel Dixon, 1842–1915, vol. I
Spencer, Col Maurice, 1863–1940, vol. III
Spencer, Noël, 1900–1986, vol. VIII
Spencer, Oscar Alan, 1913–1993, vol. IX
Spencer, Percival, 1864–1913, vol. I
Spencer, Rev. Percival L., 1845–1932, vol. III
Spencer, Captain Richard Austin, 1892–1956, vol. V
Spencer, Lt-Col Rowland Pickering, 1892–1965, vol. VI
Spencer, Sir Stanley, 1891–1959, vol. V
Spencer, Terence John Bew, 1915–1978, vol. VII
Spencer, Sir Thomas George, 1888–1976, vol. VII
Spencer, Sir (Walter) Baldwin, 1860–1929, vol. III
Spencer, Walter George, *died* 1940, vol. III
Spencer, William Kingdon, *died* 1955, vol. V
Spencer Chapman, Lt-Col Frederick, 1907–1971, vol. VII
Spencer-Churchill, Baroness (Life Peer); Clementine Ogilvy Spencer-Churchill, 1885–1977, vol. VII
Spencer-Churchill, Lord Edward; *see* Churchill.
Spencer-Churchill, Captain Edward George; *see* Churchill.
Spencer-Churchill, John George; *see* Churchill.
Spencer-Nairn, Sir Douglas Leslie; *see* Nairn.
Spencer-Nairn, Major Sir Robert, 1st Bt, 1880–1960, vol. V
Spencer-Phillips, Major John Charles, *died* 1937, vol. III
Spencer-Smith, Sir Drummond Cospatric Hamilton-, 5th Bt, 1876–1955, vol. V
Spencer-Smith, Maj.-Gen. Jeremy Michael, 1917–1985, vol. VIII
Spencer-Smith, Michael Seymour, 1881–1928, vol. II
Spencer-Smith, Sir Thomas Cospatric Hamilton-, 6th Bt, 1917–1959, vol. V
Spencer Wills, Sir John; *see* Wills.
Spender, A. F., *died* 1947, vol. IV
Spender, Arthur Edmund, 1871–1923, vol. II
Spender, E. Harold, 1864–1926, vol. II
Spender, Hugh Frederick, 1873–1930, vol. III
Spender, John Alfred, 1862–1942, vol. IV

Spender, Hon. Sir Percy Claude, 1897–1985, vol. VIII
Spender, Sir Stephen Harold, 1909–1995, vol. IX
Spender, Lt-Col Sir Wilfrid Bliss, 1876–1960, vol. V
Spender-Clay, Lt-Col Rt Hon. Herbert Henry, 1875–1937, vol. III
Spengler, Oswald, 1880–1936, vol. III
Spenlove-Spenlove, Frank, 1868–1933, vol. III
Spens, 1st Baron, 1885–1973, vol. VII
Spens, 2nd Baron, 1914–1984, vol. VIII
Spens, Ven. Andrew N. W., 1844–1932, vol. III
Spens, Col Hugh Baird, 1885–1958, vol. V
Spens, Maj.-Gen. James, 1853–1934, vol. III
Spens, Janet, 1876–1963, vol. VI
Spens, J(ohn) Ivan, 1890–1964, vol. VI
Spens, Nathaniel, 1850–1933, vol. III
Spens, Sir Will, 1882–1962, vol. VI
Spenser, Harry Joseph, 1866–1937, vol. III
Spenser-Wilkinson, Sir Thomas Crowe, 1899–1982, vol. VIII
Spensley, Philip Calvert, 1920–1994, vol. IX
Sperling, Sir Rowland Arthur Charles, 1874–1965, vol. VI
Sperrin-Johnson, John Charles, 1885–1948, vol. IV
Sperring, Digby, 1897–1969, vol. VI
Sperry, Roger Wolcott, 1913–1994, vol. IX
Sperry, Willard Learoyd, 1882–1954, vol. V
Speyer, Sir Edgar, 1st Bt, 1862–1932, vol. III
Spicer, Rt Hon. Sir Albert, 1st Bt, 1847–1934, vol. III
Spicer, Sir (Albert) Dykes, 2nd Bt, 1880–1966, vol. VI
Spicer, Sir Dykes; *see* Spicer, Sir A. D.
Spicer, Sir Evan, 1849–1937, vol. III
Spicer, Gerald Sydney, 1874–1942, vol. IV
Spicer, Henry Gage, 1875–1944, vol. IV
Spicer, Holmes W. T., 1860–1935, vol. III
Spicer, Sir Howard, 1872–1926, vol. II
Spicer, James Leonard, 1873–1949, vol. IV
Spicer, Hon. Sir John Armstrong, 1899–1978, vol. VII
Spicer, John Edmund Philip, 1850–1928, vol. II
Spicer, Rev. Canon John Maurice, *died* 1920, vol. II
Spicer, Lancelot Dykes, 1893–1979, vol. VII
Spicer, Sir Peter James, 4th Bt, 1921–1993, vol. IX
Spicer, Robert Henry Scanes, *died* 1925, vol. II
Spicer, Roy Godfrey Bullen, 1889–1946, vol. IV
Spicer, Captain Sir Stewart Dykes, 3rd Bt, 1888–1968, vol. VI
Spicer, W. T. H.; *see* Spicer, Holmes W. T.
Spicer-Jay, Edith Katharine; *see* Prescott, E. Livingston.
Spickernell, Sir Frank Todd, 1885–1956, vol. V
Spidle, Rev. Simeon, 1867–1954, vol. V
Spielman, Sir Meyer A., 1856–1936, vol. III
Spielmann, Sir Isidore, 1854–1925, vol. II
Spielmann, Mabel Henrietta, 1862–1938, vol. III
Spielmann, Marion Harry Alexander, 1858–1948, vol. IV
Spielmann, Percy Edwin, 1881–1964, vol. VI
Spiers, Frederick William, 1907–1993, vol. IX
Spiers, Harry Ratcliff, 1883–1956, vol. V
Spiers, Richard Phené, 1838–1916, vol. II
Spiers, Victor Julian Taylor, *died* 1937, vol. III

Spiller, John Wyatt, 1878–1949, vol. IV
Spilsbury, Alfred John, 1874–1940, vol. III
Spilsbury, Sir Bernard Henry, 1877–1947, vol. IV
Spinelli, Altiero, 1907–1986, vol. VIII
Spingarn, J. E., 1875–1939, vol. III (A), vol. IV
Spink, John Stephenson, 1909–1985, vol. VIII
Spinks, Alfred, 1917–1982, vol. VIII
Spinks, Maj.-Gen. Sir Charlton Watson, 1877–1959, vol. V
Spinks, Frederick Lowten, 1816–1899, vol. I
Spinks, Rev. George Stephens, 1903–1978, vol. VII
Spinks, Major John Thomas, 1889–1969, vol. VI
Spinner, Alice; see Fraser, Mrs Augusta Zelia.
Spinney, George Franklin, 1852–1926, vol. II
Spinney, George Wilbur, 1889–1948, vol. IV
Spire, Frederick, 1863–1951, vol. V
Spiro, Sidney, 1914–1991, vol. IX
Spitta, Edmund Johnson, 1853–1921, vol. II
Spitta, Harold Robert Dacre, 1877–1954, vol. V
Spittel, Richard Lionel, 1881–1969, vol. VI
Spitteler, Carl Friedrich Georg, 1845–1924, vol. II
Spitzer, Lyman, 1914–1997, vol. X
Spock, Benjamin McLane, 1903–1998, vol. X
Spoer, Mrs H. H.; see Goodrich-Freer, A. M.
Spofford, Charles Merville, 1902–1991, vol. IX
Spofforth, Markham, 1825–1907, vol. I
Spokes, Arthur Hewett, 1854–1922, vol. II
Spokes, Sir Peter, 1830–1910, vol. I
Spong, Major Charles Stuart, 1859–1925, vol. II
Spooner, Brig. Gen. Arthur Hardwicke, 1879–1945, vol. IV
Spooner, Charles Edwin, 1853–1909, vol. I
Spooner, Edgar Clynton Ross, 1908–1976, vol. VII
Spooner, Very Rev. Edward, died 1899, vol. I
Spooner, Edward Tenney Casswell, 1904–1995, vol. IX
Spooner, Edwin George, 1898–1977, vol. VII
Spooner, Rear-Adm. Ernest John, 1887–1942, vol. IV
Spooner, Ven. George Hardwicke, died 1933, vol. III
Spooner, Henry John, 1856–1940, vol. III
Spooner, Rev. Henry Maxwell, died 1929, vol. III
Spooner, Rev. William Archibald, 1844–1930, vol. III
Spooner, Rt Hon. Sir William Henry, 1897–1966, vol. VI
Spoor, Rt Hon. Benjamin Charles, 1878–1928, vol. II
Sporborg, Henry Nathan, 1905–1985, vol. VIII
Spottiswoode, John Roderick Charles Herbert, 1882–1946, vol. VI
Spottiswoode, Col Robert Collinson D'Esterre, 1841–1936, vol. III
Spottiswoode, William Hugh, 1864–1915, vol. I
Spowers, Col Allan, 1892–1968, vol. VI
Spragg, Cyril Douglas, 1894–1986, vol. VIII
Spragge, Lt-Col Basil Edward, 1852–1926, vol. II
Spragge, Brig.-Gen. Charles Henry, 1842–1920, vol. II
Spraggett, Col Richard William, died 1976, vol. VII
Sprague, Oliver Mitchell Wentworth, 1873–1953, vol. V
Sprague, Thomas Bond, 1830–1920, vol. II
Sprankling, Rt Rev. Mgr James, 1860–1935, vol. III

Spratt, Most Rev. Michael J., 1854–1938, vol. III
Sprawson, Maj.-Gen. Sir Cuthbert Allan, 1877–1956, vol. V
Sprawson, Evelyn Charles, 1881–1955, vol. V
Spreckels, Claus, 1828–1908, vol. I
Spreckels, John Diedrich, 1853–1926, vol. II
Spreckley, Air Marshal Sir Herbert Dorman, 1904–1963, vol. VI
Spreckley, Herbert William, 1857–1950, vol. IV
Spreckley, Sir (John) Nicholas (Teague), 1934–1994, vol. IX
Spreckley, Sir Nicholas; see Spreckley Sir J. N. T.
Sprengel, Hermann Johann Philipp, 1834–1906, vol. I
Spreull, James Spreull Andrew, 1908–1998, vol. X
Sprigg, Alfred Gordon, 1861–1921, vol. II
Sprigg, Rt Hon. Sir John Gordon, 1830–1913, vol. I
Sprigg, Stanhope William, died 1932, vol. III
Sprigge, Cecil Jackson Squire, 1896–1959, vol. V
Sprigge, Elizabeth Miriam Squire, 1900–1974, vol. VII
Sprigge, Sir Squire, 1860–1937, vol. III
Spriggs, Sir Edmund Ivens, died 1949, vol. IV
Spriggs, Sir Frank Spencer, 1895–1969, vol. VI
Spriggs, Leslie, 1910–1990, vol. IX (AI)
Spring, Sir Francis Joseph Edward, 1849–1933, vol. III
Spring, Frank Stuart, 1907–1997, vol. X
Spring, Brig.-Gen. Frederick Gordon, 1878–1963, vol. VI
Spring, Howard, 1889–1965, vol. VI
Spring-Rice, Rt Hon. Sir Cecil Arthur, 1859–1918, vol. II
Spring-Rice, Dominick, 1889–1940, vol. III
Spring-Rice, Stephen Edward, 1856–1902, vol. I
Springall, Harold Douglas, 1910–1982, vol. VIII
Springer, Axel Caesar, 1912–1985, vol. VIII
Springer, Sir Hugh Worrell, 1913–1994, vol. IX
Springer, Tobias, 1907–2000, vol. X
Springett, Jack Allan, 1916–1996, vol. X
Springett, Rev. William Douglas, 1850–1928, vol. II
Springfield, George, 1861–1939, vol. III
Springfield, Lincoln, died 1950, vol. IV
Springhall, Brig. Robert John, 1900–1965, vol. VI
Springman, Dame Ann Marcella, 1933–1987, vol. VIII
Sprot, Col Sir Alexander, 1st Bt, 1853–1929, vol. III
Sprot, Lt-Gen. John, 1830–1907, vol. I
Sprot, Major Mark, 1881–1946, vol. IV
Sprott, Sir Frederick Lawrence, 1863–1943, vol. IV
Sprott, Rt Rev. John Chappell, 1903–1982, vol. VIII
Sprott, Rt Rev. Thomas Henry, died 1942, vol. IV
Sprott, Walter John Herbert, 1897–1971, vol. VII
Sproul, Robert Gordon, 1891–1975, vol. VII
Sproule, Brig. James Chambers, 1887–1955, vol. V
Sproule, Percy Julian, 1873–1954, vol. V
Sproule, Hon. Robert, died 1948, vol. IV
Sproule, Thomas Simpson, 1843–1917, vol. II
Sproull, Maj.-Gen. Alexander Wallace, 1892–1961, vol. VI
Sprules, Dorothy Winifred, 1883–1972, vol. VII
Spry, Brig. Sir Charles Chambers Fowell, 1910–1994, vol. IX

Spry, Charles Gordon, 1872–1940, vol. III
Spry, Constance, *died* 1960, vol. V
Spry, Maj.-Gen. Daniel Charles, 1913–1989, vol. VIII
Spry, Graham, 1900–1983, vol. VIII
Spry, Sir John Farley, 1910–1999, vol. X
Spry, Lt-Col Leighton Hume-, 1871–1934, vol. III
Spurgeon, Sir Arthur, 1861–1938, vol. III
Spurgeon, Caroline F. E., 1869–1942, vol. IV
Spurgeon, Christopher Edward, 1879–1951, vol. V
Spurgeon, Rev. John, 1810–1902, vol. I
Spurgeon, Rev. Thomas, 1856–1917, vol. II
Spurgin, Sir John Blick, 1821–1903, vol. I
Spurling, Antony Cuthbert, 1906–1984, vol. VIII
Spurling, Hon. Sir (Arthur) Dudley, 1913–1986, vol. VIII
Spurling, Hon. Sir Dudley; *see* Spurling, Hon. Sir A. D.
Spurling, Rev. Frederick William, 1844–1914, vol. I
Spurling, Maj.-Gen. John Michael Kane, 1906–1980, vol. VII
Spurling, Sir Stanley, 1879–1961, vol. VI
Spurr, Frederic Chambers, 1862–1942, vol. IV
Spurrell, Walter Roworth, 1897–1966, vol. VI
Spurrier, Alfred Henry, 1862–1935, vol. III
Spurrier, Sir Henry, 1898–1964, vol. VI
Spurrier, Rev. Horatio, 1832–1913, vol. I
Spurrier, John Marston, 1886–1973, vol. VII
Spurrier, Mabel Annie, *died* 1979, vol. VII
Spurrier, Steven, *died* 1961, vol. VI
Spyers, Roper, 1868–1961, vol. I
Squair, John, 1850–1928, vol. II
Squibb, George Drewry, 1906–1994, vol. IX
Squire, Alice, *died* 1936, vol. III
Squire, Sir Giles Frederick, 1894–1959, vol. V
Squire, Herbert Brian, 1909–1961, vol. VI
Squire, Sir John Collings, 1884–1958, vol. V
Squire, John Edward, 1855–1917, vol. II
Squire, Rev. John Henry, *died* 1955, vol. V
Squire, John Rupert, 1915–1966, vol. VI
Squire, Sir Peter Wyatt, 1847–1919, vol. II
Squire, Ronald, 1886–1958, vol. V
Squire, Rose Elizabeth, 1861–1938, vol. III
Squire, Warwick Nevison, 1921–1992, vol. IX
Squire, William Barclay, 1855–1927, vol. II
Squire, William Henry, 1871–1963, vol. VI
Squires, Lt-Gen. Ernest Ker, 1882–1940, vol. III
Squires, Herbert Chavasse, 1880–1964, vol. VI
Squires, James Duane, 1904–1981, vol. VIII
Squires, Rt Hon. Sir Richard Anderson, 1880–1940, vol. III
Squirrell, Leonard Russell, 1893–1979, vol. VII
Sraffa, Piero, 1898–1983, vol. VIII
Srámek, Mgr Jan, 1870–1956, vol. V
Srawley, Rev. James Herbert, 1868–1954, vol. V
Srivastava, Sir Bisheshwar Nath, 1881–1938, vol. III
Srivastava, Sir Jwala Prasad, 1889–1954, vol. V
Staal, Baron de, 1822–1907, vol. I
Stabb, Sir Newton John, 1868–1931, vol. III
Stable, Daniel Wintringham, 1856–1929, vol. III
Stable, Maj.-Gen. Hugh Huntington, 1896–1985, vol. VIII
Stable, J. Joseph, 1883–1953, vol. V
Stable, Rt Hon. Sir Wintringham Norton, 1888–1977, vol. VII

Stableforth, Arthur Wallace, 1902–1978, vol. VII
Stabler, Arthur Fletcher, 1919–1997, vol. X
Stabler, Harold, 1872–1945, vol. IV
Stabler, Phœbe, *died* 1955, vol. V
Stables, William G.; *see* Gordon-Stables.
Stacey, Sir Ernest, 1896–1973, vol. VII
Stacey, Major Gerald Arthur, 1881–1916, vol. II
Stacey, Air Chief Marshal Sir John; *see* Stacey, Air Chief Marshal Sir W. J.
Stacey, Maurice, 1907–1994, vol. IX
Stacey, Reginald Stephen, 1905–1974, vol. VII
Stacey, Air Chief Marshal Sir (William) John, 1924–1981, vol. VIII
Stack, Austin, 1880–1929, vol. III
Stack, Rt Rev. Charles Maurice, 1825–1914, vol. I
Stack, Lt-Col Charles Spottiswoode, 1868–1943, vol. IV
Stack, Maj.-Gen. Sir Lee Oliver Fitzmaurice, 1868–1924, vol. II
Stack, Air Chief Marshal Sir Neville; *see* Stack, Air Chief Marshal Sir T. N.
Stack, Air Chief Marshal Sir (Thomas) Neville, 1919–1994, vol. IX
Stackhouse, J. Foster, *died* 1915, vol. I
Stacpole, Col John, 1849–1916, vol. II
Stacpoole, Florence, *died* 1942, vol. IV
Stacpoole, Frederic, 1813–1907, vol. I
Stacpoole, Lt-Col George William Robert, 1872–1939, vol. III
Stackpoole, Henry de Vere Stacpoole, 1863–1951, vol. V
Stacton, David Derek, 1925–1968, vol. VI
Stacy, Lt-Col Bertie Vandeleur, 1886–1971, vol. VII
Stacy, Reginald Joseph William, 1904–1981, vol. VIII
Stacy, Colman, David; *see* Colman.
Staddon, John Henry, *died* 1944, vol. IV
Stadler, Sir Sydney Martin, 1893–1976, vol. VII
Stafford, 11th Baron, 1833–1913, vol. I
Stafford, 12th Baron, 1859–1932, vol. III
Stafford, 13th Baron, 1864–1941, vol. IV
Stafford, 14th Baron, 1926–1986, vol. VIII
Stafford, Maj.-Gen. Boyle Torriano, 1828–1913, vol. I
Stafford, Hon. Sir Edward William, 1820–1901, vol. I
Stafford, Frank Edmund, 1895–1994, vol. IX
Stafford, Jack, 1909–1982, vol. VIII
Stafford, James William, 1884–1945, vol. IV
Stafford, Rev. John T. Wardle, 1861–1944, vol. IV
Stafford, Rt Hon. Sir Thomas, 1st Bt, 1857–1935, vol. III
Stafford, Brig.-Gen. William Francis Howard, 1854–1942, vol. IV
Stafford-Clark, David, 1916–1999, vol. X
Stafford-King-Harman, Sir Cecil William Francis, 2nd Bt, 1895–1987, vol. VIII
Stagg, Cecil, *died* 1955, vol. V
Stagg, James Martin, 1900–1975, vol. VII
Stagg, Air Cdre Walter Allan, 1903–1984, vol. VIII
Stagni, Most Rev. Pellegrino Francesco, 1859–1918, vol. II
Stahl, Ernest Ludwig, 1902–1992, vol. IX
Staig, Sir Bertie Munro, 1892–1952, vol. V

Staine, Sir Albert Llewellyn, 1928–1987, vol. VIII
Stainer, George Henry, *died* 1901, vol. I
Stainer, Sir John, 1840–1901, vol. I
Staines, Donald Victor, 1897–1960, vol. V
Staines, Herbert J., *died* 1958, vol. V
Staines, Michael, 1885–1955, vol. V
Stainforth, Graham Henry, 1906–1987, vol. VIII
Stainforth, Lt-Col Herbert Graham, 1865–1916, vol. II
Stainton, Sir Anthony Nathaniel, 1913–1988, vol. VIII
Stainton, Sir John Armitage, 1888–1957, vol. V
Stair, 10th Earl of, 1819–1903, vol. I
Stair, 11th Earl of, 1848–1914, vol. I
Stair, 12th Earl of, 1879–1961, vol. VI
Stair, 13th Earl of, 1906–1996, vol. IX
Stair, Alfred, 1845–1914, vol. I
Stairs, Gilbert S., 1882–1947, vol. IV
Stairs, Major Henry Bertram, 1871–1940, vol. III (A), vol. IV
Stalbridge, 1st Baron, 1837–1912, vol. I
Stalbridge, 2nd Baron, 1880–1949, vol. IV
Staley, Rt Rev. Thomas N., 1823–1898, vol. I
Staley, Rev. Vernon, 1852–1933, vol. III
Stalin, Generalissimo Joseph Vissarionovich, 1879–1953, vol. V
Stalker, Alexander Logie, 1920–1987, vol. VIII
Stalker, Alexander Mitchell, 1853–1932, vol. III
Stalker, Rev. James, 1848–1927, vol. II
Stallard, Col Hon. Charles Frampton, 1871–1971, vol. VII
Stallard, George, 1856–1912, vol. I
Stallard, Hyla Bristow, 1901–1973, vol. VII
Stallard, John Prince, 1857–1952, vol. V
Stallard, Sir Peter Hyla Gawne, 1915–1995, vol. IX
Stallard, Lt-Col Sidney, 1870–1949, vol. IV
Stallard, Brig.-Gen. Stacy Frampton, 1873–1961, vol. VI
Stallibrass, Geoffrey Ward, 1911–1994, vol. IX
Stallwood, Frank, 1910–1978, vol. VII
Stallworthy, Sir John Arthur, 1906–1993, vol. IX
Stallybrass, William Swan, 1855–1931, vol. III
Stallybrass, William Teulon Swan, 1883–1948, vol. IV
Stamer, Arthur Cowie, 1869–1944, vol. IV
Stamer, Sir Lovelace, 4th Bt, 1859–1941, vol. IV
Stamer, Rt Rev. Sir Lovelace Tomlinson, 3rd Bt, 1829–1908, vol. I
Stamer, Maj.-Gen. William Donovan, *died* 1963, vol. VI
Stamers-Smith, Eileen, 1929–1998, vol. X
Stamford, 9th Earl of, 1850–1910, vol. I
Stamford, 10th Earl of, 1896–1976, vol. VII
Stamford, Thomas William, 1882–1949, vol. IV
Stamfordham, 1st Baron, 1849–1931, vol. III
Stamler, Samuel Aaron, 1925–1994, vol. IX
Stamm, Air Vice-Marshal William Percivale, 1909–1986, vol. VIII
Stammers, Arthur Dighton, 1889–1971, vol. VII
Stammers, Francis Alan Roland, 1898–1982, vol. VIII
Stamp, 1st Baron, 1880–1941, vol. IV
Stamp, 2nd Baron, 1904–1941 (died with 1st Baron and did not have an entry in Who's Who).
Stamp, 3rd Baron, 1907–1987, vol. VIII

Stamp, Alfred Edward, 1870–1938, vol. III
Stamp, Hon. (Arthur) Maxwell, 1915–1984, vol. VIII
Stamp, Rt Hon. Sir Blanshard; *see* Stamp, Rt Hon. Sir E. B.
Stamp, Sir Dudley; *see* Stamp, Sir L. D.
Stamp, Edward, 1928–1986, vol. VIII
Stamp, Rt Hon. Sir (Edward) Blanshard, 1905–1984, vol. VIII
Stamp, Ernest, 1869–1942, vol. IV
Stamp, Sir (Laurence) Dudley, 1898–1966, vol. VI
Stamp, Hon. Maxwell; *see* Stamp, Hon. A. M.
Stampa, George Loraine, 1875–1951, vol. V
Stampe, Sir William Leonard, 1882–1951, vol. V
Stamper, James William, 1873–1947, vol. IV
Stamper, Thomas Henry Gilborn, 1884–1980, vol. VII
Stanbridge, Air Vice-Marshal Reginald Horace, 1897–1986, vol. VIII
Stanbury, Sydney William, 1919–1996, vol. X
Stancomb, William, 1850–1941, vol. IV
Stancliffe, Very Rev. Michael Staffurth, 1916–1987, vol. VIII
Stancomb-Wills, Dame Janet Stancomb Graham, *died* 1932, vol. III
Standage, Lt-Col Robert Fraser, 1868–1927, vol. II
Standen, Rev. Canon Aubrey Owen, 1898–1961, vol. VI
Standen, Sir Bertram Prior, 1867–1947, vol. IV
Standen, Edward James, 1836–1921, vol. II
Standen, Rev. James Edward, 1865–1933, vol. III
Standford, Col William, *died* 1926, vol. II
Standing, Rev. George, 1875–1966, vol. VI
Standing, Comdr Sir Guy, 1873–1937, vol. III
Standing, Michael Frederick Cecil, 1910–1984, vol. VIII
Standing, Percy Cross, *died* 1931, vol. III
Standish, Henry Noailles Widdrington, 1847–1920, vol. II
Standish, Col Ivon Tatham, 1883–1967, vol. VI
Standish, Major William Pery, 1860–1922, vol. II
Standish-White, Robert, 1888–1961, vol. VI
Stanes, Sir Robert, 1841–1936, vol. III
Stanfield, Richard, 1863–1950, vol. IV (A), vol. V
Stanford, Bedell; *see* Stanford, W. B.
Stanford, Gp-Captain C. E. C.; *see* Cortis-Stanford.
Stanford, Sir Charles T.; *see* Thomas-Stanford.
Stanford, Sir Charles Villiers, 1852–1924, vol. II
Stanford, Ernest, 1894–1966, vol. VI
Stanford, Rt Rev. Frederic, 1883–1964, vol. VI
Stanford, John Keith, 1892–1971, vol. VII
Stanford, Ven. Leonard John, 1896–1967, vol. VI
Stanford, Adm. Sir Peter Maxwell, 1929–1991, vol. IX
Stanford, Col Hon. Sir Walter Ernest Mortimer, 1850–1933, vol. III
Stanford, (William) Bedell, 1910–1984, vol. VIII
Stanford-Tuck, Wing Comdr Robert Roland, 1916–1987, vol. VIII
Stanger, Henry Yorke, 1849–1929, vol. III
Stanham, Maj.-Gen. Sir Reginald George, 1893–1957, vol. V
Stanhope, 6th Earl, 1838–1905, vol. I
Stanhope, 7th Earl, 1880–1967, vol. VI

Stanhope, Ven. Hon. Berkeley Lionel Scudamore, 1824–1919, vol. II
Stanhope, Hon. Charles Hay Scudamore, 1864–1937, vol. III
Stanhope, Hon. Evelyn Theodore Scudamore, 1862–1925, vol. II
Stanhope, Hon. Henry Augustus, 1845–1933, vol. III
Stanhope, James Banks, 1821–1904, vol. I
Stanhope, Hon. Richard Philip, 1885–1916, vol. II
Stanhope, Col Sir Walter Thomas William Spencer, 1827–1911, vol. I
Stanier, Brig. Sir Alexander Beville Gibbons, 2nd Bt, 1899–1995, vol. IX
Stanier, Sir Beville, 1st Bt, 1867–1921, vol. II
Stanier, Robert Spenser, 1907–1980, vol. VII
Stanier, Roger Yate, 1916–1982, vol. VIII
Stanier, Sir William Arthur, 1876–1965, vol. VI
Staniforth, John Arthur Reginald, 1912–1996, vol. X
Staniforth, Joseph Morewood, 1863–1921, vol. II
Stanistreet, Maj.-Gen. Sir George Bradshaw, 1866–1941, vol. IV
Stanistreet, Rt Rev. Henry Arthur, 1901–1981, vol. VIII
Stanley of Alderley, 3rd Baron, 1827–1903, vol. I
Stanley of Alderley, 4th Baron; see Sheffield.
Stanley of Alderley, 5th Baron, and Sheffield, 5th Baron, 1875–1931, vol. III
Stanley, Lord; Edward Montagu Cavendish Stanley, 1894–1938, vol. III
Stanley, Albert, 1863–1915, vol. I
Stanley, Rt Rev. Mgr the Hon. Algernon Charles, 1843–1928, vol. II
Stanley, Col Hon. Algernon Francis, 1874–1962, vol. VI
Stanley, Hon. Sir Arthur, 1869–1947, vol. IV
Stanley, Arthur; see Megaw, Arthur Stanley.
Stanley, Brian Taylor, 1907–1983, vol. VIII
Stanley, Carleton Wellesley, 1886–1971, vol. VII
Stanley, Charles Orr, 1899–1989, vol. VIII
Stanley, Charles Sidney Bowen W.; see Wentworth-Stanley.
Stanley, Captain Sir Charles Wentworth, 1860–1939, vol. III
Stanley, Dorothy, (Lady Stanley), died 1926, vol. II
Stanley, Edward Arthur Vesey, 1879–1941, vol. IV
Stanley, Edward James, 1826–1907, vol. I
Stanley, Brig.-Gen. Hon. Ferdinand Charles, 1871–1935, vol. III
Stanley, Lt-Col Hon. Frederick William, 1878–1942, vol. IV
Stanley, Col Geoffrey, 1855–1943, vol. IV
Stanley, Lt-Col Rt Hon. Sir George Frederick, 1872–1938, vol. III
Stanley, George J., 1852–1931, vol. III
Stanley, Harry Merridew, 1865–1945, vol. IV
Stanley, Sir Henry Morton, 1841–1904, vol. I
Stanley, Henry Sydney Herbert Cloete, 1920–1995, vol. IX
Stanley, Sir Herbert James, 1872–1955, vol. V
Stanley, Herbert Muggleton, 1903–1987, vol. VIII
Stanley, Rev. Howard Spencer, 1901–1975, vol. VII
Stanley, Sir John, 1846–1931, vol. III
Stanley, Lt-Col Joseph Henry, 1864–1937, vol. III

Stanley, Hon. Maude Alethea, 1833–1915, vol. I
Stanley, Michael Charles, 1921–1990, vol. VIII
Stanley, Rt Hon. Oliver Frederick George, 1896–1950, vol. IV
Stanley, Lt-Col Hon. Oliver Hugh, 1879–1952, vol. V
Stanley, Hon. Pamela Margaret, (Hon. Lady Cunynghame), 1909–1991, vol. IX
Stanley, Hon. Richard Oliver, 1920–1983, vol. VIII
Stanley, Sir Robert Christopher Stafford, 1899–1981, vol. VIII
Stanley, Robert Crooks, 1876–1951, vol. V
Stanley, Ronald Francis Assheton S.; see Sloane-Stanley.
Stanley, Adm. Hon. Sir Victor Albert, 1867–1934, vol. III
Stanley, Wendell Meredith, 1904–1971, vol. VII
Stanley, Captain William Blakeney, 1878–1935, vol. III
Stanley-Clarke, Brig. Arthur Christopher Lancelot, 1886–1983, vol. VIII
Stanley Price, Peter, 1911–1998, vol. X
Stanley-Wrench, Mollie Louise, died 1966, vol. VI
Stanmore, 1st Baron, 1829–1912, vol. I
Stanmore, 2nd Baron, 1871–1957, vol. V
Stannard, Mrs Arthur; see Stannard, H. E. V.
Stannard, H. Sylvester, 1870–1951, vol. V
Stannard, Henrietta Eliza Vaughan, 1856–1911, vol. I
Stannard, Henry, died 1920, vol. II
Stannard, John Anthony, 1931–1992, vol. IX
Stannard, Captain Richard Been, 1902–1977, vol. VII
Stannard, Rt Rev. Robert William, 1895–1986, vol. VIII
Stanner, William Edward Hanley, 1905–1981, vol. VIII
Stannus, Hugh Stannus, 1877–1957, vol. V
Stansbury, Captain Hubert, 1873–1949, vol. IV
Stansfeld, Maj.-Gen. Henry Hamer, 1839–1914, vol. I
Stansfeld, Rt Hon. Sir James, 1820–1898, vol. I
Stansfeld, Col James Rawdon, 1866–1936, vol. III
Stansfeld, Captain John, 1840–1928, vol. II
Stansfeld, Captain John Raymond Evelyn, 1880–1915, vol. I
Stansfeld, Captain Logan Sutherland, 1859–1936, vol. III
Stansfeld, Margaret, died 1951, vol. V
Stansfeld, Brig.-Gen. Thomas Wolryche, 1877–1935, vol. III
Stansfield, Alfred, died 1944, vol. IV
Stansfield, Sir Charles Henry Renn, 1856–1926, vol. II
Stansfield, Herbert, 1872–1960, vol. V
Stansfield, James Warden, 1906–1991, vol. IX
Stansfield, Knowles; see Stansfield, T. E. K.
Stansfield, (Thomas Edward) Knowles, 1862–1939, vol. III
Stansfield, Lt-Gen. Thomas Wolrich, 1829–1910, vol. I
Stansfield, Sir Walter, 1917–1984, vol. VIII
Stansfield, William, 1877–1946, vol. IV
Stansgate, 1st Viscount, 1877–1960, vol. V
Stantiall, William, 1865–1947, vol. IV

Stanton, Sir (Ambrose) Thomas, 1875–1938, vol. III

Stanton, Maj.-Gen. Anthony Francis, 1915–1988, vol. VIII

Stanton, Rev. Arthur Henry, 1839–1913, vol. I

Stanton, Blair Rowlands H.; see Hughes-Stanton.

Stanton, Charles Butt, 1873–1946, vol. IV

Stanton, Sir Edward, 1827–1907, vol. I

Stanton, Col Edward Alexander, 1867–1947, vol. IV

Stanton, Brig.-Gen. Frederick William Starkey, 1863–1930, vol. III

Stanton, Rt Rev. George Henry, 1835–1905, vol. I

Stanton, Major Harold James Clifford, 1859–1927, vol. II

Stanton, Maj.-Gen. Sir Henry Ernest, 1861–1943, vol. IV

Stanton, Sir Herbert H.; see Hughes-Stanton.

Stanton, Rev. Herbert Udny Weitbrecht, 1851–1937, vol. III

Stanton, Lt-Col John Percy, 1899–1974, vol. VII

Stanton, Lt-Col John Richard Guy, 1919–1990, vol. VIII

Stanton, Joseph, 1859–1935, vol. III

Stanton, Sir Joseph, 1884–1963, vol. VI

Stanton, Lionel William, 1843–1925, vol. II

Stanton, Sir Thomas, 1865–1931, vol. III

Stanton, Sir Thomas; see Stanton, Sir A. T.

Stanton, Rev. Vincent Henry, 1846–1924, vol. II

Stanton, Walter Kendall, 1891–1978, vol. VII

Stanton, Rev. William Henry, 1824–1910, vol. I

Stanton-Jones, Richard, 1926–1991, vol. IX

Stanton-Jones, Rt Rev. William, 1866–1951, vol. V

Stanuell, Lt-Col Herbert Stewart M'Cance, 1857–1930, vol. III

Stanway, Rt Rev. Alfred, 1908–1989, vol. VIII

Stanyforth, Lt-Col Edwin Wilfrid, 1861–1939, vol. III

Stanyforth, Lt-Col Ronald Thomas, 1892–1964, vol. VI

Stanyon, Sir Henry John, 1857–1934, vol. III

Stapf, Otto, 1857–1933, vol. III

Stapledon, Sir George; see Stapledon, Sir R. G.

Stapledon, Sir (Reginald) George, 1882–1960, vol. V

Stapledon, Sir Robert de Stapledon, 1909–1975, vol. VII

Stapledon, William Olaf, 1886–1950, vol. IV

Staples, Sir Gerald James Arland, 16th Bt, 1909–1999, vol. X

Staples, Irene E. Toye W.; see Warner-Staples.

Staples, Sir John Molesworth, 11th Bt, 1847–1933, vol. III

Staples, Sir John Richard, 14th Bt, 1906–1989, vol. VIII

Staples, Sir Nathaniel Alexander, 10th (shown as 8th) Bt, 1817–1899, vol. I

Staples, Sir Robert George Alexander, 13th Bt, 1894–1970, vol. VI

Staples, Sir Robert Ponsonby, 12th Bt, 1853–1943, vol. IV

Staples, Sir Thomas, 15th Bt, 1905–1997, vol. X

Stapleton, Sir Alfred; see Stapleton, Sir H. A.

Stapleton, Sir Francis George, 8th Bt, 1831–1899, vol. I

Stapleton, Brig. Francis Harry, 1876–1956, vol. V

Stapleton, Air Vice-Marshal Frederick Snowden, 1912–1974, vol. VII

Stapleton, Sir (Henry) Alfred, 10th Bt, 1913–1995, vol. IX

Stapleton, Henry Ernest, 1878–1962, vol. VI

Stapleton, Major Sir Miles Talbot, 9th Bt, 1893–1977, vol. VII

Stapleton-Bretherton, Frederick, 1841–1919, vol. II

Stapleton-Cotton, Adm. Richard Greville Arthur Wellington, 1873–1953, vol. V

Stapleton-Cotton, Col Hon. Richard Southwell George, 1849–1925, vol. II

Stapleton-Shaw, Major Peter; see Shaw.

Stapley, Sir Richard, 1842–1920, vol. II

Stapylton, Col Bryan Henry C.; see Chetwynd-Stapylton.

Stapylton, Granville Brian C.; see Chetwynd-Stapylton.

Stapylton, Lt-Gen. Granville George C.; see Chetwynd-Stapylton.

Stapylton, Rev. William C.; see Chetwynd-Stapylton.

Starey, Captain Stephen Helps, 1896–1972, vol. VII

Stark, Dame Freya Madeline, 1893–1993, vol. IX

Stark, Adm. Harold Raynsford, 1880–1972, vol. VII

Stark, Rev. James, 1838–1922, vol. II

Stark, John, 1865–1940, vol. III

Starke, Sir Hayden Erskine, 1871–1958, vol. V

Starke, Hon. Sir John Erskine, 1913–1994, vol. X (AI)

Starke, Leslie Gordon Knowles, 1898–1984, vol. VIII

Starkey, James Sullivan; see O'Sullivan, Seumas.

Starkey, Sir John Ralph, 1st Bt, 1859–1940, vol. III

Starkey, Lewis Randle, 1836–1910, vol. I

Starkey, Thomas Albert, 1872–1939, vol. III (A), vol. IV

Starkey, William Joseph Starkey B.; see Barber-Starkey.

Starkey, Lt-Col Sir William Randle, 2nd Bt, 1899–1977, vol. VII

Starkie, Enid Mary, died 1970, vol. VI

Starkie, Rev. Preb. Le Gendre George H.; see Horton-Starkie.

Starkie, Le Gendre Nicholas, 1828–1899, vol. I

Starkie, Robert Fitzwilliam, 1855–1934, vol. III

Starkie, Walter Fitzwilliam, 1894–1976, vol. VII

Starkie, Rt Hon. William Joseph Myles, 1860–1920, vol. II

Starley, Hubert Granville, 1909–1984, vol. VIII

Starling, Ernest Henry, 1866–1927, vol. II

Starling, Frederick Charles, 1886–1962, vol. VI

Starling, Hubert John, 1874–1950, vol. IV

Starling, John Henry, 1883–1966, vol. VI

Starling, Brig. John Sieveking, 1898–1986, vol. VIII

Starmer, Sir Charles Walter, 1870–1933, vol. III

Starr, Clarence L., 1868–1928, vol. II

Starr, Frederic Newton Gisborne, 1867–1934, vol. III

Starr, Sir Kenneth William, 1908–1976, vol. VII

Starr, Col William Henderson, 1861–1947, vol. IV

Starte, Oliver Harold Baptist, 1882–1969, vol. VI

Startin, Adm. Sir James, 1855–1948, vol. IV

Statham, Hon. Sir Charles Ernest, 1875–1946, vol. IV
Statham, Rev. George Herbert, 1842–1922, vol. II
Statham, Heathcote Dicken, 1889–1973, vol. VII
Statham, Henry Heathcote, 1839–1924, vol. II
Statham, Ira Cyril Frank, 1886–1967, vol. VI
Statham, Col John Charles Barron, 1872–1933, vol. III
Statham, Sir Randulph Meverel, 1890–1944, vol. IV
Statham, Reginald Samuel Sherard, 1884–1959, vol. V
Staton, Air Vice-Marshal William Ernest, 1898–1983, vol. VIII
Staudinger, Hermann, 1881–1965, vol. VI
Staughton, Captain Samuel Thomas, 1876–1903, vol. I
Staunton, Hugh Geoffrey, 1871–1951, vol. V
Staunton, Most Rev. James, 1889–1963, vol. VI
Staunton, Lt-Col Reginald Kirkpatrick Lynch, 1880–1918, vol. II
Staveley, Adm. Cecil Minet, 1874–1934, vol. III
Staveley, Martin Samuel, 1921–1998, vol. X
Staveley, Brig. Robert, 1892–1968, vol. VI
Staveley, Brig.-Gen. William Cathcart, 1865–1939, vol. III
Staveley, Adm. of the Fleet Sir William Doveton Minet, 1928–1997, vol. X
Staveley-Hill, Henry Staveley, 1865–1946, vol. IV
Stavert, Sir William Ewen, 1861–1937, vol. III
Stavert, Rev. William James, 1858–1932, vol. III
Stavridi, Sir John, 1867–1948, vol. IV
Stawell, Sir Richard Rawdon, 1864–1935, vol. III
Stawell, Mrs Rodolph, died 1949, vol. IV
Stawell, Maj.-Gen. William Arthur Macdonald, 1895–1987, vol. VIII
Stayner, Brig. Gerrard Francis Hood, 1900–1980, vol. VII
Staynes, Percy Angelo, died 1953, vol. V
Steacie, Edgar William Richard, 1900–1962, vol. VI
Steacy, Rev. Richard Henry, 1869–1950, vol. IV
Stead, Alfred, 1877–1933, vol. III
Stead, Lt-Col Alfred James, 1845–1909, vol. I
Stead, Sir Charles, 1877–1961, vol. VI
Stead, Christina Ellen, 1902–1983, vol. VIII
Stead, Francis Bernard, 1873–1954, vol. V
Stead, Francis Herbert, 1857–1928, vol. II
Stead, Gilbert, 1888–1979, vol. VII
Stead, James Lister, 1864–1915, vol. I
Stead, John Edward, 1851–1923, vol. II
Stead, Kingsley Willans, 1883–1950, vol. IV
Stead, William Thomas, 1849–1912, vol. I
Steadman, Frank St J., 1880–1943, vol. IV
Steadman, W. C., 1851–1911, vol. I
Steane, Bruce Harry Dennis, 1866–1939, vol. III
Steavenson, Arthur Paget, 1872–1934, vol. III
Steavenson, Hon. Brig.-Gen. Charles John, 1867–1933, vol. III
Steavenson, David Fenwick, 1844–1920, vol. II
Steavenson, William Herbert, 1894–1975, vol. VII
Stebbing, Edward Percy, 1870–1960, vol. V
Stebbing, (Lizzie) Susan, 1885–1943, vol. IV
Stebbing, Susan; see Stebbing, L. S.
Stebbing, Rev. Thomas Roscoe Rede, 1835–1926, vol. II
Stebbing, William, died 1926, vol. II

Stebbings, Sir John Chalmer, 1924–1988, vol. VIII
Stedeford, Sir Ivan Arthur Rice, 1897–1975, vol. VII
Stedman, Baroness (Life Peer); Phyllis Steadman, 1916–1996, vol. X
Stedman, Edgar, 1890–1975, vol. VII
Stedman, Edmund Clarence, 1833–1908, vol. I
Stedman, Gen. Sir Edward, 1842–1914, vol. I
Stedman, Air Vice-Marshal Ernest W., 1888–1957, vol. V
Stedman, Sir George Foster, 1895–1985, vol. VIII
Stedman, Sir Leonard Foster, 1871–1948, vol. IV
Stedman, Ralph Elliott, died 1964, vol. VI
Steed, Henry Wickham, 1871–1956, vol. V
Steedman, Air Chief Marshal Sir Alasdair; see Steedman, Air Chief Marshal Sir Alexander M. S.
Steedman, Air Chief Marshal Sir Alexander McKay Sinclair, (Sir Alasdair), 1922–1992, vol. IX
Steedman, Maj.-Gen. John Francis Dawes, 1897–1983, vol. VIII
Steeds-Bird, Elliott Beverley, 1881–1945, vol. IV
Steegman, John E. H., 1899–1966, vol. VI
Steegmuller, Francis, 1906–1994, vol. IX
Steel, Allan Gibson, 1858–1914, vol. I
Steel, Anthony Bedford, 1900–1973, vol. VII
Steel, Byron; see Steegmuller, Francis.
Steel, Charles, 1847–1925, vol. II
Steel, Brig. Charles Deane, 1901–1993, vol. IX
Steel, Sir Christopher Eden, 1903–1973, vol. VII
Steel, Edward, 1906–1976, vol. VII
Steel, Major Edward Anthony, 1880–1919, vol. II
Steel, Major Sir (Fiennes) William Strang, 2nd Bt, 1912–1992, vol. IX
Steel, Flora Annie, 1847–1929, vol. III
Steel, Gerald, 1895–1957, vol. V
Steel, Gerald Arthur, died 1963, vol. VI
Steel, Sir James, 1st Bt (cr 1903), 1830–1904, vol. I
Steel, Sir James, 1909–1994, vol. IX
Steel, Air Chief Marshal Sir John Miles, 1877–1965, vol. VI
Steel, Sir (Joseph) Lincoln (Spedding), 1900–1985, vol. VIII
Steel, Sir Lincoln; see Steel, Sir J. L. S.
Steel, Lt-Col Matthew Reginald, 1896–1941, vol. IV
Steel, Col Richard Alexander, 1873–1928, vol. II
Steel, Robert, 1839–1903, vol. I
Steel, Robert Walter, 1915–1997, vol. X
Steel, Major Sir Samuel Strang, 1st Bt (cr 1938), 1882–1961, vol. VI
Steel, William Strang, 1832–1911, vol. I
Steel, Maj. Sir William Strang; see Steel, Major Sir F. W. S.
Steel-Maitland, Rt Hon. Sir Arthur Herbert Drummond Ramsay, 1st Bt, 1876–1935, vol. III
Steel-Maitland, Sir (Arthur) James (Drummond Ramsay-), 2nd Bt, 1902–1960, vol. V
Steel-Maitland, Sir James; see Steel-Maitland, Sir A. J. D. R.
Steel-Maitland, Sir Keith Richard Felix Ramsay-, 3rd Bt, 1912–1965, vol. VI
Steele, Bertram Dillon, 1870–1934, vol. III
Steele, Col Charles Edward Beevor, 1876–1940, vol. III

Steele, Air Marshal Sir Charles Ronald, 1897–1973, vol. VII
Steele, Maj.-Gen. Sir Clive Selwyn, 1892–1955, vol. V
Steele, Fanny; see Steele, Francesca Maria.
Steele, Francesca Maria, died 1931, vol. III
Steele, Frank Fenwick, 1923–1997, vol. X
Steele, (Francis) Howard, 1929–1983, vol. VIII
Steele, Lt-Col Frederick William, 1858–1909, vol. I
Steele, Comdr Gordon Charles, 1892–1981, vol. VIII
Steele, Lt-Col Harwood Robert Elmes, 1897–1978, vol. VII
Steele, Sir Henry, 1879–1963, vol. VI
Steele, Howard; see Steele, F. H.
Steele, Gen. Sir James Stuart, 1894–1975, vol. VII
Steele, John, 1837–1922, vol. II
Steele, John Scott, 1870–1947, vol. IV
Steele, Maj.-Gen. Julian McCarty, 1870–1926, vol. II
Steele, Sir Kenneth Charles, 1913–1986, vol. VIII
Steele, Norman James, 1918–1977, vol. VII
Steele, Robert, 1860–1944, vol. IV
Steele, Col St George Loftus, 1859–1936, vol. III
Steele, Maj.-Gen. Sir Samuel Benfield, 1849–1919, vol. II
Steele, Thomas, 1905–1979, vol. VII
Steele, Col William Lawrence, 1878–1958, vol. V
Steele-Perkins, Surg. Vice-Adm. Sir Derek Duncombe, 1908–1994, vol. IX
Steell, David G., 1856–1930, vol. III
Steell, Graham, 1851–1942, vol. IV
Steen, Marguerite, 1894–1975, vol. VII
Steen, Robert Elsworth, 1902–1981, vol. VIII
Steen, Robert Hunter, 1870–1926, vol. II
Steen, Stephen Nicholas, 1907–1988, vol. VIII
Steenbock, Harry, 1886–1967, vol. VI
Steenkamp, Major William, 1868–1935, vol. III
Steer, Edward Pemberton, 1881–1938, vol. III
Steer, Francis William, 1912–1978, vol. VII
Steer, George Lowther, 1909–1944, vol. IV
Steer, Henry Reynolds, 1858–1928, vol. II
Steer, P. Wilson, 1860–1942, vol. IV
Steer, Rt Rev. Stanley Charles, 1900–1998, vol. X
Steer, Captain T. Bruce, died 1904, vol. I
Steer, William Bridgland, 1867–1939, vol. III (A), vol. IV
Steer, William Reed Hornby, 1899–1993, vol. IX
Steere, Sir Ernest Augustus L.; see Lee Steere.
Steere, Henry Charles Lee, 1859–1933, vol. III
Steere, Hon. Sir James George Lee, 1830–1903, vol. I
Steers, James Alfred, 1899–1987, vol. VIII
Steevens, Maj.-Gen. Sir John, 1855–1925, vol. II
Stefansson, Vilhjalmur, 1879–1962, vol. VI
Steggall, Charles, 1826–1905, vol. I
Steggall, John Edward Aloysius, 1855–1935, vol. III
Steggall, Reginald, 1867–1938, vol. III
Steil, John Wellesley, 1899–1983, vol. VIII
Stein, Adolphe, 1878–1938, vol. III
Stein, Sir Aurel, 1862–1943, vol. IV
Stein, Gertrude, 1874–1946, vol. IV
Stein, John, 1922–1985, vol. VIII
Stein, John Alan, 1888–1982, vol. VIII
Stein, Leonard Jacques, 1887–1973, vol. VII

Stein, William Howard, 1911–1980, vol. VII
Steinaecker, Lt-Col Francis Christian Ludwig, Baron von, born 1854, vol. II
Steinberg, Jack, 1913–1991, vol. IX
Steinbeck, John Ernst, 1902–1968, vol. VI
Steinberg, Sigfrid Henry, 1899–1969, vol. VI
Steinberg, William, 1899–1978, vol. VII
Steiner, Rear-Adm. Ottokar Harold Mojmir St John, 1916–1998, vol. X
Steinhardt, Laurence A., 1892–1950, vol. IV
Steinitz, (Charles) Paul (Joseph), 1909–1988, vol. VIII
Steinitz, Paul; see Steinitz, C. P. J.
Steinlen, Theophile Alexander, 1859–1923, vol. II
Stemp, Major Charles Hubert, 1871–1948, vol. IV
Stenbock, Count Otto, 1838–1915, vol. I
Stengel, Erwin, 1902–1973, vol. VII
Stenhouse, John Godwyn, 1908–1997, vol. X
Stenhouse, Sir Nicol, 1911–1998, vol. X
Stenhouse, Maj.-Gen. William, 1840–1914, vol. I
Stening, Sir George Grafton Lees, 1904–1996, vol. X
Stennett, Col Harry March, 1877–1941, vol. IV
Stenning, Sir Alexander Rose, 1864–1928, vol. II
Stenning, Ven. Ernest Henry, 1885–1964, vol. VI
Stenning, Rev. George Covey, 1840–1915, vol. I
Stenning, John Frederick, died 1959, vol. V
Stent, Percy John Hodsoll, 1888–1962, vol. VI
Stentiford, Charles Douglas, died 1920, vol. II
Stenton, Doris Mary, (Lady Stenton), 1894–1971, vol. VII
Stenton, Sir Frank Merry, 1880–1967, vol. VI
Step, Edward, 1855–1931, vol. III
Stephen, Sir Alastair Edward, 1901–1982, vol. VIII
Stephen, Captain Albert Alexander Leslie, 1879–1914, vol. I
Stephen, Sir Alexander Condie, 1850–1908, vol. I
Stephen, Sir Alexander Murray, 1892–1974, vol. VII
Stephen, Sir Andrew, 1906–1980, vol. VII
Stephen, Campbell, 1884–1947, vol. IV
Stephen, Col Charles Merton, 1874–1955, vol. V
Stephen, Sir Colin Campbell, 1872–1937, vol. III
Stephen, Edward Milner, 1870–1939, vol. III
Stephen, Col Fitzroy, 1835–1906, vol. I
Stephen, George, 1886–1972, vol. VII
Stephen, George Arthur, 1880–1934, vol. III
Stephen, Lt-Col Guy Neville, 1858–1932, vol. III
Stephen, Sir Harry Lushington, 3rd Bt, 1860–1945, vol. IV
Stephen, Sir Henry; see Stephen, Sir M. H.
Stephen, Sir Herbert, 2nd Bt, 1857–1932, vol. III
Stephen, Sir James Alexander, 4th Bt, 1908–1987, vol. VIII
Stephen, Katharine, 1856–1924, vol. II
Stephen, Sir Leslie, 1832–1904, vol. I
Stephen, Sir (Matthew) Henry, 1828–1920, vol. II
Stephen, Norman Kenneth, 1865–1948, vol. IV
Stephen, Rt Rev. Reginald, 1860–1956, vol. V
Stephen, Maj.-Gen. Robert Alexander, 1907–1983, vol. VIII
Stephen, Brig.-Gen. Robert Campbell, 1867–1947, vol. IV
Stephens, Maj.-Gen. Adolphus Haggerston, 1835–1916, vol. II

Stephens, Sir Alfred, 1871–1938, vol. III
Stephens, Alfred George Gower, *died* 1933, vol. III
Stephens, Air Comdt Dame Anne, 1912–2000, vol. X
Stephens, Arthur Veryan, 1908–1992, vol. IX
Stephens, Berkeley John Byng, 1871–1950, vol. IV
Stephens, Cedric John, 1921–1994, vol. IX
Stephens, Sir David, 1910–1990, vol. VIII
Stephens, Sir Edgar; *see* Stephens, Sir L. E.
Stephens, Brig. Frederick, 1906–1967, vol. VI
Stephens, Frederick James, 1903–1978, vol. VII
Stephens, George Arbour, 1870–1945, vol. IV
Stephens, George Henry, 1855–1927, vol. II
Stephens, Rear-Adm. George Leslie, 1889–1979, vol. VII
Stephens, George Washington, 1866–1942, vol. IV
Stephens, Henry Morse, 1857–1919, vol. II
Stephens, Herbert John, 1875–1957, vol. V
Stephens, Surg. Rear-Adm. Horace Elliott Rose, 1883–1959, vol. V
Stephens, Ian Melville, 1903–1984, vol. VIII
Stephens, James, *died* 1950, vol. IV
Stephens, James Brunton, 1835–1902, vol. I
Stephens, James Henry, 1862–1937, vol. III
Stephens, John Edward Robert, 1869–1941, vol. IV
Stephens, Rev. John Otter, 1832–1925, vol. II
Stephens, John William Watson, 1865–1946, vol. IV
Stephens, Maj.-Gen. Keith Fielding, 1910–1995, vol. IX
Stephens, Sir (Leon) Edgar, 1901–1977, vol. VII
Stephens, Engr Rear-Adm. Lindsay James, 1868–1958, vol. V
Stephens, Lockhart, 1858–1940, vol. III
Stephens, Rear-Adm. (S) Montague, *died* 1950, vol. IV
Stephens, Pembroke Scott, *died* 1914, vol. I
Stephens, Peter Scott, 1910–1981, vol. VIII
Stephens, Gen. Sir Reginald Byng, 1869–1955, vol. V
Stephens, Captain Richard Markham Tyringham, 1875–1967, vol. VI
Stephens, Maj. Robert, 1909–1994, vol. IX
Stephens, Sir Robert Graham, 1931–1995, vol. IX
Stephens, Lt-Col Rupert, 1884–1970, vol. VI
Stephens, Sir William, 1848–1929, vol. III
Stephens, William Francis, 1869–1963, vol. VI
Stephens, Sir William R.; *see* Reynolds-Stephens.
Stephens, Very Rev. William Richard Wood, 1839–1902, vol. I
Stephens Spinks, Rev. George; *see* Spinks.
Stephenson, Sir (Albert) Edward, 1864–1928, vol. II
Stephenson, Sir Albert Frederick, 1854–1934, vol. III
Stephenson, Lt-Col Arthur, *died* 1950, vol. IV
Stephenson, Sir Arthur George, 1890–1967, vol. VI
Stephenson, Sir Augustus Frederick William Keppel, 1827–1904, vol. I
Stephenson, Basil Ernest, 1901–1977, vol. VII
Stephenson, Donald, 1909–1993, vol. IX
Stephenson, Ven. Edgar, 1894–1984, vol. VIII
Stephenson, Sir Edward; *see* Stephenson, Sir A. E.
Stephenson, Edward F., 1868–1948, vol. IV
Stephenson, Col Eric Lechmere, 1892–1978, vol. VII
Stephenson, Eric Seymour, 1879–1915, vol. I

Stephenson, Lt-Col Sir Francis; *see* Stephenson, Lt-Col Sir H. F. B.
Stephenson, Francis Lawrance, 1845–1920, vol. II
Stephenson, Rev. Frank, *died* 1936, vol. III
Stephenson, Gen. Sir Frederick Charles Arthur, 1821–1911, vol. I
Stephenson, George Robert, 1819–1905, vol. I
Stephenson, Vice-Adm. Sir Gilbert Owen, 1878–1972, vol. VII
Stephenson, Gordon, 1908–1997, vol. X
Stephenson, Sir Guy, 1865–1930, vol. III
Stephenson, Sir Henry, 1826–1904, vol. I
Stephenson, Lt-Col Sir (Henry) Francis (Blake), 2nd Bt, 1895–1982, vol. VIII
Stephenson, Adm. Sir Henry Frederick, 1842–1919, vol. II
Stephenson, Lt-Col Sir Henry Kenyon, 1st Bt, 1865–1947, vol. IV
Stephenson, Henry Shepherd, 1905–1993, vol. IX
Stephenson, Rev. Henry Spencer, 1871–1957, vol. V
Stephenson, Sir Hugh Lansdown, 1871–1941, vol. IV
Stephenson, Sir Hugh Southern, 1906–1972, vol. VII
Stephenson, Ian; *see* Stephenson, J. I. L.
Stephenson, Rev. Jacob, 1844–1927, vol. II
Stephenson, (James) Ian (Love), 1934–2000, vol. X
Stephenson, Lt-Col John, 1871–1933, vol. III
Stephenson, Sir John Everard, 1893–1948, vol. IV
Stephenson, Rt Hon. Sir John Frederick Eustace, 1910–1998, vol. X
Stephenson, Air Vice-Marshal John Noel Tracy, 1907–1985, vol. VIII
Stephenson, Sir John Walker, *died* 1960, vol. V
Stephenson, Joseph, 1882–1965, vol. VI
Stephenson, Katharine J., 1874–1953, vol. V
Stephenson, Marjory, 1885–1948, vol. IV
Stephenson, Rt Rev. Percival William, 1888–1962, vol. VI
Stephenson, Sir Percy, 1909–1979, vol. VII
Stephenson, Philip Robert, 1914–1994, vol. IX
Stephenson, Lt-Col Robert, 1876–1959, vol. V
Stephenson, Sydney, 1862–1923, vol. II
Stephenson, Rev. T. Bowman, 1839–1912, vol. I
Stephenson, Maj.-Gen. Theodore Edward, 1856–1928, vol. II
Stephenson, Thomas, 1864–1938, vol. III
Stephenson, Thomas, 1889–1974, vol. VII
Stephenson, Thomas Alan, *died* 1961, vol. VI
Stephenson, Rev. Thomas Wilkinson, *died* 1936, vol. III
Stephenson, William, 1837–1919, vol. II
Stephenson, Sir William Haswell, 1836–1918, vol. II
Stephenson, Sir William Henry, 1811–1898, vol. I
Stephenson, William Lawrence, 1880–1963, vol. VI
Stephenson, Sir William Samuel, 1896–1989, vol. VIII
Stephenson, Willie, *died* 1938, vol. III (A), vol. IV
Stepney, Sir Emile Algernon Arthur Keppel C.; *see* Cowell-Stepney.
Steptoe, Harry Nathaniel, 1892–1949, vol. IV
Steptoe, Patrick Christopher, 1913–1988, vol. VIII
Sterling, Antoinette, 1843–1904, vol. I
Sterling, Herbert Harry, 1886–1959, vol. V

Sterling, Maj.-Gen. John Barton, 1840–1926, vol. II
Sterling, Sir Louis Saul, *died* 1958, vol. V
Sterling, Thomas Smith, 1883–1970, vol. VI
Stern, Lt-Col Sir Albert, 1878–1966, vol. VI
Stern, Sir Edward David, 1st Bt, 1854–1933, vol. III
Stern, Sir Frederick Claude, 1884–1967, vol. VI
Stern, Gladys Bertha, 1890–1973, vol. VII
Stern, Rev. Joseph Frederick, 1865–1934, vol. III
Stern, Joseph Peter Maria, 1920–1991, vol. IX
Stern, Philip, *died* 1933, vol. III
Stern-Salomons, Sir David Lionel Goldsmid-; *see* Salomons.
Sternberg, Hon. Joseph, 1855–1928, vol. II
Sternberg, Rudy; *see* Baron Plurenden.
Sterndale, 1st Baron, 1848–1923, vol. II
Sterndale, Robert Armitage, 1839–1902, vol. I
Sterndale-Bennett, T. C., *died* 1944, vol. IV
Sterne, Maurice, 1877–1957, vol. V
Sterrett, John Robert Sitlington, 1851–1914, vol. I
Sterry, Joseph A.; *see* Ashby-Sterry.
Sterry, Sir Wasey, 1866–1955, vol. V
Stettinius, Edward R., (Jr) 1900–1949, vol. IV
Steuart, Sir Alan Henry Seton-, 4th Bt, 1856–1913, vol. I
Steuart, Sir Douglas Archibald Seton-, 5th Bt, 1857–1930, vol. III
Steuart, Ethel Mary, *died* 1960, vol. V
Steuart, John Alexander, *died* 1932, vol. III
Steuart, Rev. Robert H. J., 1874–1948, vol. IV
Steuart-Fothringham, Walter Thomas James S.; *see* Scrymsoure-Steuart-Fothringham.
Steuart-Menzies, William George, 1858–1941, vol. IV
Steven, Temp. Captain Fraser; *see* Steven, Temp. Captain J. F.
Steven, Guy Savile, 1906–1980, vol. VII
Steven, Henry Marshall, 1893–1969, vol. VI
Steven, Temp. Captain (John) Fraser, *died* 1920, vol. II
Stevens, Air Marshal Sir Alick Charles, 1898–1987, vol. VIII
Stevens, Col Arthur Borlase, 1881–1965, vol. VI
Stevens, Col Arthur Cornish Jeremie, 1875–1962, vol. VI
Stevens, (Arthur) Edwin, 1905–1995, vol. IX
Stevens, Bertram, *died* 1922, vol. II
Stevens, Hon. Sir Bertram Sydney Barnsdale, 1889–1973, vol. VII
Stevens, Air Vice-Marshal Cecil Alfred, 1898–1958, vol. V
Stevens, Lt-Col Cecil Robert, 1867–1919, vol. II
Stevens, Engr-Rear-Adm. Charles, 1869–1933, vol. III
Stevens, Sir Charles Cecil, 1840–1909, vol. I
Stevens, Col Charles Frederick, 1866–1944, vol. IV
Stevens, Charles John, 1857–1917, vol. II
Stevens, Clement Henry, 1870–1959, vol. V
Stevens, E. S.; *see* Drower, Ethel May Stefana, (Lady Drower).
Stevens, Edwin; *see* Stevens, A. E.
Stevens, Ernest Hamilton, 1864–1945, vol. IV
Stevens, Hon. Ernest James, 1845–1922, vol. II
Stevens, Frank, 1850–1935, vol. III
Stevens, Lt-Col Sir Frank, 1877–1939, vol. III

Stevens, Frank Leonard, 1898–1991, vol. IX
Stevens, Frederick, 1840–1917, vol. II
Stevens, Frederick Guy, 1878–1944, vol. IV
Stevens, Frederick William, 1847–1900, vol. I
Stevens, Geoffrey Paul, 1902–1981, vol. VIII
Stevens, Brig.-Gen. George Archibald, 1875–1951, vol. V
Stevens, George Bridges, 1882–1937, vol. III
Stevens, George Cooper, 1905–1975, vol. VII
Stevens, Col Harold Raphael Gaetano, 1883–1961, vol. VI
Stevens, Sir Harold Samuel Eaton, 1892–1969, vol. VI
Stevens, Henry, 1885–1963, vol. VI
Stevens, Rev. Henry Bingham, 1835–1924, vol. II
Stevens, Hon. Henry Herbert, 1878–1973, vol. VII
Stevens, Herbert Lawrence, 1892–1978, vol. VII
Stevens, Maj.-Gen. Sir Jack Edwin Stawell, 1896–1969, vol. VI
Stevens, James Algernon, 1873–1934, vol. III
Stevens, Vice-Adm. Sir John Felgate, 1900–1989, vol. VIII
Stevens, Sir John Foster, 1845–1925, vol. II
Stevens, Engr Captain John Greet, 1857–1943, vol. IV
Stevens, Sir John Melior, 1913–1973, vol. VII
Stevens, Sir Joseph W.; *see* Weston-Stevens.
Stevens, Marshall, 1852–1936, vol. III
Stevens, Martin, 1929–1986, vol. VIII
Stevens, Lt-Col Nathaniel Melhuish Comins, 1868–1954, vol. V
Stevens, Norman Anthony, 1937–1988, vol. VIII
Stevens, Rt Rev. Percy, 1882–1966, vol. VI
Stevens, Philip Theodore, 1906–1992, vol. IX
Stevens, Richard William, 1924–1997, vol. X
Stevens, Sir Roger Bentham, 1906–1980, vol. VII
Stevens, Siaka Probyn, 1905–1988, vol. VIII
Stevens, Rt Rev. Thomas, 1841–1920, vol. II
Stevens, Thomas George, 1869–1953, vol. V
Stevens, Lt-Col Thomas Harry Goldsworthy, 1883–1970, vol. VI
Stevens, Thomas Stevens, 1900–2000, vol. X
Stevens, Thomas Terry Hoar; *see* Terry-Thomas.
Stevens, Thomas Wilson, 1901–1990, vol. VIII
Stevens, Walter Charles, 1904–1954, vol. V
Stevens, Rt Rev. William Bertrand, 1884–1947, vol. IV
Stevens, William C.; *see* Cleveland-Stevens.
Stevens, William Charles, 1900–1973, vol. VII
Stevens, William George, 1883–1971, vol. VII
Stevens, Maj.-Gen. William George, 1893–1974, vol. VII
Stevens, William Mitchell, 1868–1944, vol. IV
Stevens, William Oswald, 1891–1972, vol. VII
Stevenson, 1st Baron, 1873–1926, vol. II
Stevenson, Hon. Lord; James Stevenson, *died* 1963, vol. VI
Stevenson, Adlai Ewing, 1900–1965, vol. VI
Stevenson, Alan; *see* Stevenson, D. A.
Stevenson, Alan Carruth, 1909–1995, vol. IX
Stevenson, Alan Leslie, 1901–1985, vol. VIII
Stevenson, Sir Alexander, 1860–1936, vol. III
Stevenson, Maj.-Gen. Alexander Gavin, 1871–1939, vol. III
Stevenson, Alexander James, 1901–1970, vol. VI

Stevenson, Alexander Wight, 1886–1954, vol. V
Stevenson, Allan, 1878–1948, vol. IV
Stevenson, Rt Hon. Sir (Aubrey) Melford (Steed), 1902–1987, vol. VIII
Stevenson, D. E., 1892–1973, vol. VII
Stevenson, Sir Daniel Macaulay, 1st Bt, 1851–1944, vol. IV
Stevenson, Sir David; see Stevenson, Sir H. D.
Stevenson, D(avid) Alan, 1891–1971, vol. VII
Stevenson, David Watson, 1842–1904, vol. I
Stevenson, Air Vice-Marshal Donald Fasken, 1895–1964, vol. VI
Stevenson, Sir Edmond Sinclair, 1850–1927, vol. II
Stevenson, Lt-Col Sir Edward Daymonde, 1895–1958, vol. V
Stevenson, Brig.-Gen. Edward Hall, 1872–1964, vol. VI
Stevenson, Edward Irenæus Prime-, 1868–1942, vol. IV
Stevenson, Edward Snead Boyd, 1849–1917, vol. II
Stevenson, Flora Clift, died 1905, vol. I
Stevenson, Frances; see Lloyd George of Dwyfor, Countess.
Stevenson, Col Francis, 1851–1922, vol. II
Stevenson, Francis Seymour, 1862–1938, vol. III
Stevenson, Sir George Augustus, 1856–1931, vol. III
Stevenson, George Hope, 1880–1952, vol. V
Stevenson, Col George Ingram, 1882–1958, vol. V
Stevenson, Surg.-Gen. Henry Wickham, 1857–1944, vol. IV
Stevenson, Dame Hilda Mabel, 1895–1987, vol. VIII
Stevenson, Sir Hubert Craddock, 1888–1971, vol. VII
Stevenson, Vice-Adm. Sir (Hugh) David, 1918–1998, vol. X
Stevenson, Rev. J. Ross, 1866–1939, vol. III
Stevenson, Col James, 1838–1926, vol. II
Stevenson, James; see Stevenson, Hon. Lord.
Stevenson, James Alexander, 1881–1937, vol. III
Stevenson, James Arthur Radford, died 1974, vol. VII
Stevenson, James Cochran, 1825–1905, vol. I
Stevenson, James Verdier, 1858–1933, vol. III
Stevenson, Lt-Col John, 1895–1952, vol. V
Stevenson, Rear-Adm. John Bryan, 1876–1957, vol. V
Stevenson, John Horne, 1855–1939, vol. III
Stevenson, John Lynn, 1927–1971, vol. VII
Stevenson, Rev. John Sinclair, 1868–1930, vol. III
Stevenson, Air Vice-Marshal Leigh Forbes, 1895–1989, vol. VIII
Stevenson, Sir Malcolm, 1878–1927, vol. II
Stevenson, Margaret; see Stevenson, Mrs Sinclair.
Stevenson, Sir Matthew, 1910–1981, vol. VIII
Stevenson, Rt Hon. Sir Melford; see Stevenson, Rt Hon. Sir A. M. S.
Stevenson, Rev. Canon Morley, 1851–1930, vol. III
Stevenson, Gen. Nathaniel, 1840–1911, vol. I
Stevenson, R. Macaulay, died 1952, vol. V
Stevenson, Sir Ralph Clarmont Skrine, 1895–1977, vol. VII
Stevenson, Ralph Cornwallis, 1894–1967, vol. VI
Stevenson, Col Robert, 1845–1930, vol. III
Stevenson, Robert, 1905–1986, vol. VIII
Stevenson, Robert Alan Mowbray, 1847–1900, vol. I

Stevenson, Robert Barron Kerr, 1913–1992, vol. IX
Stevenson, Robert Scott, 1889–1967, vol. VI
Stevenson, Sir Roy Hunter, 1892–1963, vol. VI
Stevenson, Mrs Sinclair, (Margaret), 1875–1957, vol. V
Stevenson, Sir Thomas, 1838–1908, vol. I
Stevenson, Thomas Henry Craig, 1870–1932, vol. III
Stevenson, Maj.-Gen. Thomas Rennie, 1841–1923, vol. II
Stevenson, Walter Clegg, 1877–1931, vol. III
Stevenson, Sir William Alfred, died 1983, vol. VIII
Stevenson, William Barron, 1869–1954, vol. V
Stevenson, Lt-Col William David Henderson, died 1945, vol. IV
Stevenson, Maj.-Gen. William Flack, 1844–1922, vol. II
Stevenson, William Grant, 1849–1919, vol. II
Stevenson, Rt Rev. William Henry Webster, 1878–1945, vol. IV
Stevenson-Hamilton, Lt-Col James, 1867–1957, vol. V
Stevenson-Moore, Sir Charles James, 1866–1947, vol. IV
Steward, Rev. Edward, 1851–1930, vol. III
Steward, Maj.-Gen. Edward Harding, 1835–1918, vol. II
Steward, Maj.-Gen. Edward Merivale, 1881–1947, vol. IV
Steward, Francis James, died 1940, vol. III
Steward, Frederick Campion, 1904–1993, vol. IX
Steward, Lt-Col Sir George, 1866–1920, vol. II
Steward, George Coton, 1896–1989, vol. VIII
Steward, George Frederick, 1884–1952, vol. V
Steward, Col Godfrey Robert Viveash, 1881–1969, vol. VI
Steward, Sir Harold Macdonald, 1904–1977, vol. VII
Steward, Sir Henry Allan Holden, 1865–1954, vol. V
Steward, Rt Rev. John Manwaring, 1874–1937, vol. III
Steward, Nigel Oliver Willoughby, 1899–1991, vol. IX
Steward, Maj.-Gen. Reginald Herbert Ryrie, 1898–1975, vol. II
Steward, Stanley Feargus, 1904–1999, vol. X
Steward, Sir William Arthur, 1901–1987, vol. VIII
Stewardson Edward Alfred, 1904–1973, vol. VII
Stewart, Hon. Lord; Ewan George Francis Stewart, 1923–1987, vol. VIII
Stewart of Alvechurch, Baroness (Life Peer); Mary Elizabeth Henderson Stewart, 1903–1984, vol. VIII
Stewart of Fulham, Baron (Life Peer); Robert Michael Maitland Stewart, 1906–1990, vol. VIII
Stewart, Lt-Col Albert Fortescue, 1868–1925, vol. II
Stewart, Very Rev. Alexander, 1847–1915, vol. I
Stewart, Rev. Alexander, died 1916, vol. II
Stewart, Sir Alexander, 2nd Bt (cr 1920, of Balgownie), 1886–1934, vol. III
Stewart, Sir Alexander Anderson, 1877–1956, vol. V
Stewart, Alexander Bernard, 1908–1974, vol. VII
Stewart, Alexander Boyd, 1904–1981, vol. VIII

Stewart, Alexander Carmichael, 1865–1944, vol. IV
Stewart, Maj.-Gen. Alexander Charles Hector, 1838–1917, vol. II
Stewart, Lt-Col Alexander Dron, 1883–1969, vol. VI
Stewart, Brig.-Gen. Alexander Edward, 1867–1940, vol. III
Stewart, Alexander G.; see Graham-Stewart.
Stewart, Alexander MacKay, 1878–1952, vol. V
Stewart, Alfred Walter, died 1947, vol. IV
Stewart, Major Algernon Bingham Anstruther, 1869–1916, vol. II
Stewart, Allan, 1865–1951, vol. V
Stewart, Andrew, 1895–1972, vol. VII
Stewart, Andrew, 1904–1990, vol. VIII
Stewart, Andrew, 1907–1991, vol. IX
Stewart, Andrew Charles, 1907–1979, vol. VII
Stewart, Andrew Graham, 1901–1964, vol. VI
Stewart, Lt-Col Archibald Campbell, 1872–1936, vol. III
Stewart, Comdr Archibald Thomas, 1876–1968, vol. VI
Stewart, Arthur, 1877–1941, vol. IV
Stewart, Captain Arthur Courtenay, 1871–1958, vol. V
Stewart, Col Basil Heron S.; see Shaw-Stewart.
Stewart, Sir Bruce Fraser, 2nd Bt (cr 1920, of Fingask), 1904–1979, vol. VII (AII)
Stewart, Col Bryce, 1857–1936, vol. III
Stewart, Campbell; see Stewart, W. A. C.
Stewart, Charles, 1840–1907, vol. I
Stewart, Charles, 1840–1916, vol. II
Stewart, Hon. Charles, 1868–1946, vol. IV
Stewart, Charles Cosmo Bruce, 1912–1988, vol. VIII
Stewart, Col Charles Edward, 1836–1904, vol. I
Stewart, Lt-Col Charles Edward, 1868–1916, vol. II
Stewart, Rev. Charles Henry Hylton, died 1922, vol. II
Stewart, Charles Hunter, 1854–1924, vol. II
Stewart, Charles Hylton, 1884–1932, vol. III
Stewart, Sir Charles John, 1851–1932, vol. III
Stewart, Charles John, died 1954, vol. V
Stewart, Charlotte, 1863–1918, vol. II
Stewart, Air Vice-Marshal Colin Murray, 1910–1990, vol. VIII
Stewart, Brig.-Gen. Cosmo Gordon, 1869–1948, vol. IV
Stewart, Daniel, 1836–1912, vol. I
Stewart, Sir David, 1835–1919, vol. II
Stewart, Sir David Brodribb, 2nd Bt (cr 1960), 1913–1992, vol. IX
Stewart, Col David Brown Douglas, 1862–1935, vol. III
Stewart, David Macfarlane, 1878–1950, vol. IV
Stewart, David Mitchell, 1853–1924, vol. II
Stewart, Desmond Stirling, 1924–1981, vol. VIII
Stewart, Donald, 1894–1976, vol. VII
Stewart, Rt Hon. Donald James, 1920–1992, vol. IX
Stewart, Sir Donald Martin, 1st Bt (cr 1881), 1824–1900, vol. I
Stewart, Sir Donald William, 1860–1905, vol. I
Stewart, Lt-Col Douglas, 1875–1943, vol. IV
Stewart, Sir Douglas Law, 3rd Bt (cr 1881), 1878–1951, vol. V

Stewart, Douglas Roy, 1886–1939, vol. III
Stewart, Col Dudley Strathearn, 1859–1933, vol. III
Stewart of Appin, Sir Dugald Leslie Lorn, 1921–1984, vol. VIII
Stewart, Duncan George, 1904–1949, vol. IV
Stewart, Duncan Montgomery, 1930–1996, vol. X
Stewart, Edith Anne; see Robertson, E. A.
Stewart, Lt-Col Sir Edward, 1857–1948, vol. IV
Stewart, Sir Edward Orde MacTaggart-, 2nd Bt (cr 1892), 1883–1948, vol. IV
Stewart, Ellen Frances, died 1945, vol. IV
Stewart of Coll, Brig.-Gen. Ernest Moncrieff Paul, 1864–1942, vol. IV
Stewart, Sir Euan Guy S., see Shaw-Stewart.
Stewart, Ewen, 1926–2000, vol. X
Stewart, Sir Findlater; see Stewart, Sir S. F.
Stewart, Frances Henrietta, (Lady Stewart), 1883–1962, vol. VI
Stewart, Sir Francis Hugh, 1869–1921, vol. II
Stewart, Francis William, 1885–1963, vol. VI
Stewart, Francis William Sutton C.; see Cumbrae-Stewart.
Stewart, Frank Ogilvie, 1893–1964, vol. VI
Stewart, Rev. Frank White, 1867–1933, vol. III
Stewart, Col Sir Frederick Charles, died 1950, vol. IV
Stewart, Sir Frederick Harold, 1884–1961, vol. VI
Stewart, Maj.-Gen. George, 1839–1927, vol. II
Stewart, Rt Rev. George Craig, 1879–1940, vol. III
Stewart, Rt Hon. George Francis, 1851–1928, vol. II
Stewart, George Innes, 1896–1968, vol. VI
Stewart, Lt-Col Sir George Powell, 5th Bt (cr 1803), 1861–1945, vol. IV
Stewart, Sir Gershom, 1857–1929, vol. III
Stewart, Gordon William, 1906–1988, vol. VIII
Stewart, Haldane Campbell, 1868–1942, vol. IV
Stewart, Sir Halley, 1838–1937, vol. III
Stewart, Sir Harry Jocelyn Urquhart, 11th Bt (cr 1623), 1871–1945, vol. IV
Stewart, Sir Hector Hamilton, 1901–1980, vol. VII (AII)
Stewart, Henrietta; see Shell, Rita.
Stewart, Henry Cockburn, 1844–1899, vol. I
Stewart, Ven. Henry John, 1873–1960, vol. V
Stewart, Lt-Col Henry King, 1861–1907, vol. I
Stewart, Sir Herbert Ray, 1890–1989, vol. VIII
Stewart, Maj.-Gen. Herbert William Vansittart, 1886–1975, vol. VII
Stewart, Howard Hilton, 1900–1961, vol. VI
Stewart, Lt-Col Hugh, 1872–1931, vol. III
Stewart, Hugh, 1884–1934, vol. III
Stewart, Sir Hugh Charlie Godfray, 6th Bt (cr 1803), 1897–1994, vol. IX
Stewart, Rev. Hugh Fraser, 1863–1948, vol. IV
Stewart, Brig.-Gen. Sir Hugh Houghton, 4th Bt (cr 1803), 1858–1942, vol. IV
Stewart, Sir Hugh S.; see Shaw-Stewart.
Stewart, Brig.-Gen. Ian, 1874–1941, vol. IV
Stewart, Ian Struthers, 1876–1930, vol. III
Stewart, Sir Iain Maxwell, 1916–1985, vol. VIII
Stewart, James, 1846–1906, vol. I
Stewart, James, 1863–1931, vol. III
Stewart, James, 1867–1943, vol. IV
Stewart, Maj.-Gen. James Calder, 1840–1930, vol. III

Stewart, Brig.-Gen. James Campbell, 1884–1947, vol. IV

Stewart, Hon. James Charles, 1850–1931, vol. III

Stewart, Brig. James Crossley, 1891–1972, vol. VII

Stewart, Hon. James D., 1874–1933, vol. III

Stewart, James Douglas, 1869–1955, vol. V

Stewart, James Gill, 1907–1991, vol. IX

Stewart, Sir James H.; see Henderson-Stewart.

Stewart, James King, 1863–1938, vol. III

Stewart, James Lablache; see Granger, Stewart.

Stewart, James Maitland, 1908–1997, vol. X

Stewart, Maj.-Gen. Sir James Marshall, 1861–1943, vol. IV

Stewart, Sir James Purves-, 1869–1949, vol. IV

Stewart, Very Rev. James Stuart, 1896–1990, vol. VIII

Stewart, Sir James Watson, 1st Bt (cr 1920, of Balgownie), 1852–1922, vol. II

Stewart, Sir James Watson, 3rd Bt (cr 1920, of Balgownie), 1889–1955, vol. V

Stewart, Sir James Watson, 4th Bt (cr 1920, of Balgownie), 1922–1988, vol. VIII

Stewart, Sir Jocelyn Harry, 12th Bt, 1903–1982, vol. VIII

Stewart, Col John, 1833–1914, vol. I

Stewart, Lt-Col John, 1869–1931, vol. III

Stewart, Col John, 1848–1933, vol. III

Stewart, Sir John, 1867–1947, vol. IV

Stewart, Sir John, 1887–1958, vol. V

Stewart, John Alexander, 1846–1933, vol. III

Stewart, John Alexander, 1882–1948, vol. IV

Stewart, John Alexander, 1915–1974, vol. VII

Stewart of Ardvorlich, John Alexander MacLaren, 1904–1985, vol. VIII

Stewart, John Anthony Benedict, 1927–1995, vol. IX

Stewart, Captain John Christie, 1888–1978, vol. VII

Stewart, John Graham, died 1917, vol. II

Stewart, Sir John Henderson, 1st Bt (cr 1920 of Fingask), 1877–1924, vol. II

Stewart, Maj.-Gen. Sir (John Henry) Keith, 1872–1955, vol. V

Stewart, John Innes Mackintosh, 1906–1994, vol. IX

Stewart, Sir (John) Keith (Watson), 5th Bt, 1929–1990, vol. VIII

Stewart, John McKellar, 1878–1953, vol. V

Stewart, Sir John Marcus, 3rd Bt (cr 1803), 1830–1905, vol. I

Stewart, John Philip, 1900–1984, vol. VIII

Stewart, Brig.-Gen. John Smith, 1877–1970, vol. VI

Stewart, Maj.-Gen. John William, 1862–1938, vol. III

Stewart, Rev. Joseph Atkinson, died 1913, vol. I

Stewart, Joseph Francis, 1889–1964, vol. VI

Stewart, Maj.-Gen. Sir Keith; see Stewart, Maj.-Gen. Sir J. H. K.

Stewart, Sir Keith; see Stewart, Sir J. K. W.

Stewart, Maj.-Gen. Sir Keith Lindsay, 1896–1972, vol. VII

Stewart, Kenneth Albert, 1925–1996, vol. X

Stewart, Sir Kenneth Dugald, 1st Bt (cr 1960), 1882–1972, vol. VII

Stewart, Louisa Mary, 1861–1943, vol. IV

Stewart, Sir Malcolm; see Stewart, Sir P. M.

Stewart, Sir Mark John MacTaggart, 1st Bt (cr 1892), 1834–1923, vol. II

Stewart, Very Rev. Matthew, 1881–1952, vol. V

Stewart, Matthew John, 1885–1956, vol. V

Stewart, Sir Michael Hugh S.; see Shaw-Stewart.

Stewart, Sir Michael Norman Francis, 1911–1994, vol. IX

Stewart, Sir Michael Robert S.; see Shaw-Stewart.

Stewart, Major Noel St Vincent Ramsay, 1870–1940, vol. III

Stewart, Sir Norman Robert, 2nd Bt (cr 1881), 1851–1926, vol. II

Stewart, Major Oliver, 1895–1976, vol. VII

Stewart, Col Patrick Alexander Vansittart, 1875–1960, vol. V

Stewart, Rev. Percy, 1856–1934, vol. III

Stewart, Sir (Percy) Malcolm, 1st Bt (cr 1937), 1872–1951, vol. V

Stewart, Potter, 1915–1985, vol. VIII

Stewart, Rev. Ravenscroft, 1845–1921, vol. II

Stewart, Richard, 1920–1991, vol. IX

Stewart, Sir Richard Campbell, 1836–1904, vol. I

Stewart, Sir Robert, 1858–1937, vol. III

Stewart, Robert Bruce, 1863–1948, vol. IV

Stewart, Maj.-Gen. Robert Crosse, 1825–1913, vol. I

Stewart of Physgill, Adm. Robert Hathorn J.; see Johnston-Stewart of Physgill.

Stewart, Col Sir Robert King, 1854–1930, vol. III

Stewart, Gen. Sir Robert Macgregor, 1842–1919, vol. II

Stewart, Sir Robert Sproul, 1874–1969, vol. VI

Stewart, Robert Strother-, 1878–1954, vol. V

Stewart, Sir Ronald Compton, 2nd Bt (cr 1937), 1903–1999, vol. X

Stewart, Lt-Col Rupert, 1864–1930, vol. III

Stewart, Sir (Samuel) Findlater, 1879–1960, vol. V

Stewart, Stanley Toft, 1910–1992, vol. IX

Stewart, Stephen Malcolm, 1914–1995, vol. IX

Stewart, Sir Thomas Alexander, 1888–1964, vol. VI

Stewart, Brig. Thomas G.; see Grainger-Stewart.

Stewart, Thomas Grainger, died 1957, vol. V

Stewart, Valentine Peter Beardmore, 1882–1933, vol. III

Stewart, Lt-Col Sir Walter Guy S.; see Shaw-Stewart.

Stewart, Walter Richard S.; see Shaw-Stewart.

Stewart, Walter W., 1885–1958, vol. V

Stewart, Rt Rev. Weston Henry, 1887–1969, vol. VI

Stewart, Major William, 1859–1918, vol. II

Stewart, William, 1835–1919, vol. II

Stewart, William, 1856–1947, vol. IV (A), vol. V

Stewart, William, 1879–1964, vol. VI

Stewart, William, 1916–1975, vol. VII

Stewart, (William Alexander) Campbell, 1915–1997, vol. X

Stewart, Rt Rev. William Allen, 1943–1998, vol. X

Stewart, Lt-Col William Burton, 1872–1936, vol. III

Stewart, Hon. William Downie, 1878–1949, vol. IV

Stewart, William James, 1889–1969, vol. VI

Stewart, William John, 1849–1908, vol. I

Stewart, William John, died 1946, vol. IV

Stewart, William Joseph, died 1960, vol. V

Stewart, Air Vice-Marshal William Kilpatrick, 1913–1967, vol. VI

Stewart, William McCausland, 1900–1989, vol. VIII
Stewart, Lt-Col William Murray, 1875–1948, vol. IV
Stewart, Brig.-Gen. William Robert, 1862–1932, vol. III
Stewart, Maj.-Gen. William Ross, 1889–1966, vol. VI
Stewart, Hon. William Snodgrass, 1855–1938, vol. III (A), vol. IV
Stewart-Bam of Ards, Lt-Col Sir Pieter Canzius van Blommestein, 1869–1928, vol. II
Stewart-Brown, Ronald, 1872–1940, vol. III
Stewart-Brown, Ronald David, 1911–1963, vol. VI
Stewart-Clark, Sir John, 1st Bt, 1864–1924, vol. II
Stewart-Clark, Sir Stewart, 2nd Bt, 1904–1971, vol. VII
Stewart-Dick-Cunyngham, Sir William; see Cunyngham.
Stewart-Liberty, Captain Ivor; see Liberty.
Stewart-Richardson, Sir Edward Austin, 15th Bt; see Richardson.
Stewart-Richardson, Major Sir Ian Rorie Hay, 16th Bt, 1904–1969, vol. VI
Stewart-Richardson, Lt-Col Neil Graham; see Richardson.
Stewart-Richardson, Violet Roberta, 1882–1967, vol. VI
Stewart-Roberts, Walter Stewart, 1889–1975, vol. VII
Stewart-Smith, Sir Dudley, 1857–1919, vol. II
Stewart-Smith, Ean Kendal, 1907–1964, vol. VI
Stewart-Wallace, Sir John Stewart, died 1963, vol. VI
Stewart-Wilson, Sir Charles, 1864–1950, vol. IV
Stewartson, Keith, 1925–1983, vol. VIII
Steyn, Lucas Cornelius, 1903–1976, vol. VII
Steyn, Martinus Theunis, 1857–1916, vol. II
Sthamer, Friedrich, 1856–1931, vol. III
Stibbe, Edward Philip, 1884–1943, vol. IV
Stibbe, Philip Godfrey, 1921–1997, vol. X
Stiebel, Sir Arthur, 1875–1949, vol. IV
Stiebel, Herbert Cecil, 1876–1941, vol. IV
Stiebel, Victor Frank, 1907–1976, vol. VII
Stiff, Rt Rev. Hugh Vernon, 1916–1995, vol. X (AI)
Stiffe, Captain Arthur William, 1831–1912, vol. I
Stigand, Major Chauncey Hugh, died 1919, vol. II
Stigand, William, 1825–1915, vol. I
Stigler, George Joseph, 1911–1991, vol. IX
Stikeman, William Rucker, 1854–1927, vol. II
Stikker, Dirk Uipko, 1897–1979, vol. VII
Stileman, Rt Rev. Charles Harvey, 1863–1925, vol. II
Stileman, Rear-Adm. Sir Harry Hampson, 1860–1938, vol. III
Stileman, Maj.-Gen. William Croughton, died 1915, vol. I
Stiles, Charles Wardell, 1867–1941, vol. IV
Stiles, Lt-Col Sir Harold Jalland, 1863–1946, vol. IV
Stiles, Walter, 1886–1966, vol. VI
Stiles, Walter Stanley, 1901–1985, vol. VIII
Stilgoe, Henry Edward, died 1943, vol. IV
Still, Alexander William, 1860–1931, vol. III

Still, Dame Alicia Frances Jane Lloyd, died 1944, vol. IV
Still, Andrew, 1866–1939, vol. III
Still, Charles, 1849–1930, vol. III
Still, Sir George Frederic, 1868–1941, vol. IV
Still, Rev. John, died 1914, vol. I
Still, William Chester, 1878–1928, vol. II
Stillman, William James, 1828–1901, vol. I
Stilwell, Gen. Joseph Warren, 1883–1946, vol. IV
Stimson, Henry Lewis, 1867–1950, vol. IV
Stinson, Sir Charles Alexander, 1919–1989, vol. VIII
Stinton, T., 1886–1957, vol. V
Stirling, Mrs A. M. W., died 1965, vol. VI
Stirling, Brig. Alexander Dickson, 1886–1961, vol. VI
Stirling, Alfred T., 1902–1981, vol. VIII
Stirling, Adm. Anselan John Buchanan, 1875–1936, vol. III
Stirling, Brig.-Gen. Archibald, 1867–1931, vol. III
Stirling, Sir (Archibald) David, 1915–1990, vol. VIII
Stirling, Archibald William, died 1923, vol. II
Stirling, Carl Ludwig, 1890–1973, vol. VII
Stirling, Sir Charles Elphinstone Fleming, 8th Bt (cr 1666), 1831–1910, vol. I
Stirling, Sir Charles Norman, 1901–1986, vol. VIII
Stirling, Sir David; see Stirling, Sir A. D.
Stirling, Duncan Alexander, 1899–1990, vol. VIII
Stirling, Edward, 1891–1948, vol. IV
Stirling, Sir Edward Charles, 1848–1919, vol. II
Stirling, Col Sir George; see Stirling, Col Sir W. G.
Stirling, George Claudius Beresford, 1861–1929, vol. III
Stirling, Col Sir George Murray Home, 9th Bt (cr 1666), 1869–1949, vol. IV
Stirling, Gilbert, 1843–1915, vol. I
Stirling, Hon. Grote, 1875–1953, vol. V
Stirling, Hamish, 1938–1998, vol. X
Stirling, Rt Hon. Sir James, 1836–1916, vol. II
Stirling, Sir James; see Stirling, Sir R. J. L.
Stirling, Brig. James Erskine, 1898–1968, vol. VI
Stirling, Sir James Frazer, 1926–1992, vol. IX
Stirling, James Heron, 1867–1928, vol. II
Stirling, James Hutchison, 1820–1909, vol. I
Stirling, Hon. Brig.-Gen. James Wilfred, 1855–1926, vol. II
Stirling, Sir John, 1893–1975, vol. VII
Stirling, John Ashwell, 1891–1965, vol. VI
Stirling, John Bertram, 1888–1988, vol. VIII
Stirling, Hon. Sir (John) Lancelot, 1849–1932, vol. III
Stirling, John W., 1859–1923, vol. II
Stirling, Hon. Sir Lancelot; see Stirling, Hon. Sir J. L.
Stirling, Sir (Robert) James (Lindsay), 1907–1974, vol. VII
Stirling, Viola Henrietta Christian, 1907–1989, vol. VIII
Stirling, Rt Rev. Waite Hockin, 1829–1923, vol. II
Stirling, Brig. Walter Andrew, 1883–1972, vol. VII
Stirling, Lt-Col Walter Francis, 1880–1958, vol. V
Stirling, Col Sir (Walter) George, 3rd Bt (cr 1800), 1839–1934, vol. III
Stirling, Gen. Sir William, 1835–1906, vol. I

Stirling, William, 1851–1932, vol. III
Stirling, Brig.-Gen. William, 1878–1949, vol. IV
Stirling, Gen. Sir William Gurdon, 1907–1973, vol. VII
Stirling-Hamilton, Sir Bruce, 13th Bt, 1940–1989, vol. VIII
Stirling-Hamilton, Captain Sir Robert William, see Hamilton.
Stirling-Hamilton, Sir William; see Hamilton.
Stirling Home Drummond, Lt-Col Henry Edward, 1846–1911, vol. I
Stirling-Maxwell, Sir John M.; see Maxwell.
Stirton, Rev. John, 1871–1944, vol. IV
Stitt, Rear-Adm. Edward Rhodes, 1867–1948, vol. IV
Stoate, Richard Charles, 1952–1996, vol. X
Stobart, Col George Herbert, 1873–1943, vol. IV
Stobart, Lt-Col Hugh Morton, 1883–1952, vol. V
Stobart, Mrs St Clair, (Mrs Stobart Greenhalgh), died 1954, vol. V
Stobart, Patrick Desmond, 1920–1991, vol. IX
Stobie, Harry, 1882–1948, vol. IV
Stobie, William, 1886–1957, vol. V
Stoby, Sir Kenneth Sievewright, 1903–1985, vol. VIII
Stock, Allen Lievesley, 1906–1982, vol. VIII
Stock, Arthur Boy, died 1915, vol. I
Stock, Eugene, 1836–1928, vol. II
Stock, Francis Edgar, 1914–1997, vol. X
Stock, Henry John, 1853–1930, vol. III
Stock, James Henry, 1855–1907, vol. I
Stock, Keith Lievesley, 1911–1988, vol. VIII
Stock, Col Philip Graham, 1876–1975, vol. VII
Stock, Ralph, died 1962, vol. VI
Stockdale, Sir Edmund Villiers Minshull, 1st Bt, 1903–1989, vol. VIII
Stockdale, Frank Alleyne, 1910–1989, vol. VIII
Stockdale, Sir Frank Arthur, 1883–1949, vol. IV
Stockdale, Group Captain George William, 1932–1990, vol. VIII
Stockdale, Brig.-Gen. Herbert Edward, 1867–1953, vol. V
Stockdale, Herbert Fitton, 1868–1951, vol. V
Stockdale, Maj.-Gen. Reginald Booth, 1908–1979, vol. VII
Stockenström, Sir Anders Johan Booysen, 4th Bt, 1908–1957, vol. V
Stockenström, Sir Andries, 3rd Bt, 1868–1922, vol. II
Stockenström, Hon. Sir Gysbert Henry, 2nd Bt, 1841–1912, vol. I
Stocker, Edgar Percy, 1888–1959, vol. V
Stocker, Ven. Harry, died 1922, vol. II
Stocker, Rt Hon. Sir John Dexter, 1918–1996, vol. X
Stocker, Richard Dimsdale, 1877–1935, vol. III
Stockil, Sir Raymond Osborne, 1907–1984, vol. VIII
Stockings, Major Arthur Perry, 1880–1943, vol. IV
Stockley, Brig.-Gen. Arthur Uniacke, 1869–1939, vol. III
Stockley, Lt-Col Charles Hugh, 1882–1955, vol. V
Stockley, Col Charles More, 1845–1923, vol. II
Stockley, Cynthia, died 1936, vol. III
Stockley, David Dudgeon, 1900–1980, vol. VII

Stockley, Brig.-Gen. Ernest Norman, 1872–1946, vol. IV
Stockley, Gerald Ernest, 1900–1981, vol. VIII
Stockley, Major Sir Harry Hudson Fraser, 1878–1951, vol. V
Stockley, Brig.-Gen. Hugh Roderick, 1868–1935, vol. III
Stockley, Rev. Joseph John Gabbett, 1862–1949, vol. IV
Stockley, William F. P., 1859–1943, vol. IV
Stockman, Henry Watson, 1894–1982, vol. VIII
Stockman, Ralph, 1861–1946, vol. IV
Stockman, Sir Stewart, 1869–1926, vol. II
Stocks, Baroness (Life Peer); Mary Danvers Stocks, 1891–1975, vol. VII
Stocks, Alfred James, 1926–1988, vol. VIII
Stocks, Sir (Andrew) Denys, 1884–1961, vol. VI
Stocks, Arthur Hudson, 1889–1940, vol. III
Stocks, Charles Lancelot, 1878–1975, vol. VII
Stocks, Sir Denys; see Stocks, Sir A. D.
Stocks, Francis W., 1873–1929, vol. III
Stocks, Harold Carpenter Lumb, 1884–1956, vol. V
Stocks, Rev. John Edward, 1843–1926, vol. II
Stocks, John Leofric, 1882–1937, vol. III
Stocks, Percy, 1889–1974, vol. VII
Stockton, 1st Earl of, 1894–1986, vol. VIII
Stockton, Rear-Adm. Charles Herbert, 1845–1924, vol. II
Stockton, Sir Edwin Forsyth, 1873–1939, vol. III
Stockton, Francis Richard, 1834–1902, vol. I
Stockwell, Brig.-Gen. Clifton Inglis, 1879–1953, vol. V
Stockwell, Air Cdre Edmund Arthur, 1911–2000, vol. X
Stockwell, Hon. Maj.-Gen. George Clifton Inglis, 1863–1936, vol. III
Stockwell, Captain Henry, 1875–1962, vol. VI
Stockwell, Gen. Sir Hugh Charles, 1903–1986, vol. VIII
Stockwell, Col Ralph Frederick, 1885–1962, vol. VI
Stockwood, Rt Rev. (Arthur) Mervyn, 1913–1995, vol. IX
Stockwood, Ven. Charles Vincent, 1885–1958, vol. V
Stockwood, Rt Rev. Mervyn; see Stockwood, Rt Rev. A. M.
Stodart, Sqdn Ldr David Edmund, 1882–1938, vol. III
Stodart, James Carlyle, 1880–1956, vol. V
Stodart, Col Thomas, 1868–1934, vol. III
Stoddard, Charles Warren, 1843–1909, vol. I
Stoddard, Francis Hovey, 1847–1936, vol. III
Stoddard, Lothrop, 1883–1950, vol. IV (A)
Stoddart, Alexander Frederick Richard, 1904–1973, vol. VII
Stoddart, Andrew Ernest, 1863–1915, vol. I
Stoddart, Anna M., 1840–1911, vol. I
Stoddart, Adm. Archibald Peile, 1860–1939, vol. III
Stoddart, Sir Charles John, 1839–1913, vol. I
Stoddart, Jane T., died 1944, vol. IV
Stoddart, William Henry Butter, died 1950, vol. IV
Stoddart-Scott, Col Sir Malcolm, 1901–1973, vol. VII
Stoessel, Walter John, Jr, 1920–1986, vol. VIII
Stogdon, Rev. Edgar, 1870–1951, vol. V

Stogdon, Norman Francis, 1909–1996, vol. X
Stoker, Abraham; see Stoker, Bram.
Stoker, Bram, 1847–1912, vol. I
Stoker, Col Claude Bayfield, 1875–1948, vol. IV
Stoker, George, 1855–1920, vol. II, vol. III
Stoker, George Herbert, 1874–1935, vol. III
Stoker, Graves, 1864–1938, vol. III
Stoker, Captain Hew Gordon Dacre, 1885–1966, vol. VI
Stoker, Robert Burdon, 1859–1919, vol. II
Stoker, Thomas, 1849–1925, vol. II
Stoker, Sir Thornley; see Stoker, Sir W. T.
Stoker, William Henry, died 1944, vol. IV
Stoker, Sir (William) Thornley, 1st Bt, 1845–1912, vol. I
Stokes, A. G. Folliott, died 1939, vol. III
Stokes, Adrian, 1887–1927, vol. II
Stokes, Adrian, 1854–1935, vol. III
Stokes, Adrian Durham, 1902–1972, vol. VII
Stokes, Brig.-Gen. Alfred, 1860–1931, vol. III
Stokes, Rev. Anson Phelps, 1874–1958, vol. V
Stokes, Sir Arthur Romney, 2nd Bt, 1858–1916, vol. II
Stokes, Rev. Augustus Sidney, died 1922, vol. II
Stokes, Edith, died 1936, vol. III
Stokes, Eric Thomas, 1924–1981, vol. VIII
Stokes, Maj.-Gen. Sir Folliott Stuart Furneaux, 1849–1911, vol. I
Stokes, Sir (Frederick) Wilfrid Scott, 1860–1927, vol. II
Stokes, Sir Gabriel, 1849–1920, vol. II
Stokes, Sir George Gabriel, 1st Bt, 1819–1903, vol. I
Stokes, George Joseph, 1859–1935, vol. III
Stokes, Rev. George Thomas, 1843–1898, vol. I
Stokes, George Vernon, 1873–1954, vol. V
Stokes, Rear-Adm. Graham Henry, 1902–1969, vol. VI
Stokes, Haldane Day, 1885–1915, vol. I
Stokes, Sir Harold Frederick, 1899–1977, vol. VII
Stokes, Col Harold William Puzey, 1878–1949, vol. IV
Stokes, Sir Henry Edward, 1841–1926, vol. II
Stokes, Rev. Henry Paine, 1849–1931, vol. III
Stokes, Sir Hopetoun Gabriel, 1873–1951, vol. V
Stokes, Hugh, 1875–1932, vol. III
Stokes, Sir John, 1825–1902, vol. I
Stokes, Leonard Aloysius Scott, 1858–1925, vol. II
Stokes, Brig. Ralph Shelton Griffin, 1882–1979, vol. VII
Stokes, Rt Hon. Richard Rapier, 1897–1957, vol. V
Stokes, Sir Robert Baret, 1833–1899, vol. I
Stokes, Rear-Adm. Robert Henry Simpson, 1855–1914, vol. I
Stokes, Whitley, 1830–1909, vol. I
Stokes, Sir Wilfrid; see Stokes, Sir F. W. S.
Stokes, Sir William, 1839–1900, vol. I
Stokes, William Henry, 1894–1977, vol. VII
Stokowski, Leopold Boleslawowicz Stanislaw Antoni, 1882–1977, vol. VII
Stoll, Sir Oswald, 1866–1942, vol. IV
Stollery, Col John, 1852–1940, vol. III
Stone, Baron (Life Peer); Joseph Ellis Stone, 1903–1986, vol. VIII
Stone, Sir Alexander, 1907–1998, vol. X

Stone, Ven. Arthure Edward, 1852–1927, vol. II
Stone, Sir Benjamin; see Stone, Sir J. B.
Stone, Bertram Gilchrist, 1903–1978, vol. VII
Stone, Sir Charles, 1850–1931, vol. III
Stone, Christopher Reynolds, 1882–1965, vol. VI
Stone, Rev. Darwell, 1859–1941, vol. IV
Stone, Hon. Sir Edward Albert, 1844–1920, vol. II
Stone, Edward James, 1831–1897, vol. I
Stone, Brig.-Gen. Francis Gleadowe, 1857–1929, vol. III
Stone, George Frederick, 1855–1928, vol. II
Stone, Sir Gilbert, 1886–1967, vol. VI
Stone, Gilbert Seymour, 1915–1992, vol. IX
Stone, Harlan F., 1872–1946, vol. IV
Stone, Rev. Henry Cecil Brough, died 1936, vol. III
Stone, Henry Walter James, 1877–1954, vol. V
Stone, Air Vice-Marshal James Ambrose, 1885–1966, vol. VI
Stone, Sir (John) Benjamin, 1838–1914, vol. I
Stone, Sir (John) Leonard, 1896–1978, vol. VII
Stone, Sir (John) Richard (Nicholas), 1913–1991, vol. IX
Stone, John William, 1852–1936, vol. III
Stone, Sir Joseph Henry, 1858–1941, vol. IV
Stone, Julius, 1907–1985, vol. VIII
Stone, Lawrence, 1919–1999, vol. X
Stone, Sir Leonard; see Stone, Sir J. L.
Stone, Col Lionel George Tempest, 1874–1946, vol. IV
Stone, Marcus, 1840–1921, vol. II
Stone, Brig.-Gen. Percy Vere Powys, 1883–1959, vol. V
Stone, Reynolds, 1909–1979, vol. VII
Stone, Sir Richard; see Stone, Sir J. R. N.
Stone, Richard Evelyn, 1914–1980, vol. VII
Stone, Riversdale Garland, 1903–1985, vol. VIII
Stone, Lt-Gen. Robert Graham William Hawkins, 1890–1974, vol. VII
Stone, Rev. Samuel John, 1839–1900, vol. I
Stone, Thomas Archibald, 1900–1965, vol. VI
Stone, Rev. W. H., 1860–1920, vol. II
Stone, William, 1857–1958, vol. V
Stone, William George Rush, 1855–1939, vol. III
Stone, Very Rev. William Henry, died 1912, vol. I
Stone-Wigg, Rt Rev. Montagu John, 1861–1918, vol. II
Stoneham, Sir Ralph Thompson, 1888–1965, vol. VI
Stoneham, Robert Thompson Douglas, 1883–1962, vol. VI
Stonehaven, 1st Viscount, 1874–1941, vol. IV
Stonehewer Bird, Sir (Francis) Hugh (William), 1891–1973, vol. VI
Stonehewer Bird, Sir Hugh; see Stonehewer Bird, Sir F. H. W.
Stonehouse, Sir Edmund, 1854–1938, vol. III
Stonehouse, John Thomson, 1925–1988, vol. VIII
Stoneley, Robert, 1894–1976, vol. VII
Stoneman, Walter E., 1876–1958, vol. V
Stoner, Edmund Clifton, 1899–1968, vol. VI
Stones, Edward Lionel Gregory, 1914–1987, vol. VIII
Stones, Sir Frederick, 1886–1947, vol. IV
Stones, Hubert Horace, 1892–1965, vol. VI
Stones, James, died 1935, vol. III
Stones, William, 1904–1969, vol. VI

Stonestreet, George William, 1863–1940, vol. III
Stonex, Rev. Francis Tilney, 1857–1920, vol. II
Stoney, Bindon Blood, 1828–1909, vol. I
Stoney, Edith Anne, 1869–1938, vol. III
Stoney, Edward Waller, *died* 1931, vol. III
Stoney, Florence Ada, 1870–1932, vol. III
Stoney, George Gerald, 1863–1942, vol. IV
Stoney, George Johnstone, 1826–1911, vol. I
Stoney, Richard Atkinson, 1877–1966, vol. VI
Stoney-Smith, Major Herbert; *see* Smith.
Stonham, Baron (Life Peer); Victor John Collins, 1903–1971, vol. VII
Stonham, Charles, 1858–1916, vol. II
Stonham, Edwin Earle, 1867–1934, vol. III
Stonhouse, Sir Arthur Allan, 17th Bt, and 13th Bt, 1885–1967, vol. VI
Stonhouse, Sir Ernest Hay, 16th Bt, and 12th Bt, 1855–1937, vol. III
Stonhouse, Sir Philip Allan, 18th Bt, and 14th Bt, 1916–1993, vol. X (AI)
Stonhouse-Gostling, Maj.-Gen. Philip Le Marchant Stonhouse, 1899–1990, vol. VIII
Stonier, George Walter, 1903–1985, vol. VIII
Stonor, Most Rev. Mgr Hon. Edmund, 1831–1912, vol. I
Stonor, Hon. Edward Alexander, 1867–1940, vol. III
Stonor, Hon. Sir Harry, 1859–1939, vol. III
Stonor, Henry James, 1820–1908, vol. I
Stonor, Oswald Francis Gerard, 1872–1940, vol. III
Stoodley, Edwin Edward, 1844–1922, vol. II
Stoodley, Peter Ernest William, 1925–1995, vol. IX
Stooke, Sir George Beresford-, 1897–1983, vol. VIII
Stopes, Charlotte Carmichael, *died* 1929, vol. III
Stopes, Marie Charlotte Carmichael, *died* 1958, vol. V
Stopford of Fallowfield, Baron (Life Peer); John Sebastian Bach Stopford, 1888–1961, vol. VI
Stopford, Vice-Adm. Hon. Arthur, 1879–1955, vol. V
Stopford, Edward Kennedy, 1911–1983, vol. VIII
Stopford, Francis Powys, 1861–1935, vol. III
Stopford, Rear-Adm. Frederick Victor, 1900–1982, vol. VIII
Stopford, Lt-Gen. Hon. Sir Frederick William, 1854–1929, vol. III
Stopford, Captain Hon. Guy, 1884–1954, vol. V
Stopford, Hon. Horatia Charlotte Frances, 1835–1920, vol. II
Stopford, Rev. John Bird, 1859–1934, vol. III
Stopford, Maj.-Gen. Sir Lionel Arthur Montagu, 1860–1942, vol. IV
Stopford, Louise, *died* 1935, vol. III
Stopford, Gen. Sir Montagu George North, 1892–1971, vol. VII
Stopford, Robert Jemmett, 1895–1978, vol. VII
Stopford, Vice-Adm. Robert Wilbraham, 1844–1911, vol. I
Stopford, Rt Rev. and Rt Hon. Robert Wright, 1901–1976, vol. VII
Stopford Sackville, Col Nigel Victor, 1901–1972, vol. VII
Stopford-Taylor, Richard, 1884–1964, vol. VI
Stopp, Eric John Carl, 1894–1967, vol. VI

Stoppani, Rt Rev. Antonio, 1873–1940, vol. III (A), vol. IV
Stops, Col George, 1876–1940, vol. III
Stops, Gervase Frank Ashworth J.; *see* Jackson-Stops.
Storar, Leonore Elizabeth Therese, 1920–1997, vol. X
Storer, Bellamy, 1847–1922, vol. II
Storey, Charles Ambrose, 1888–1967, vol. VI
Storey, Major Charles Ernest, 1877–1943, vol. IV
Storey, Christopher, 1908–1994, vol. IX
Storey, Hon. Sir David, 1856–1924, vol. II
Storey, George Adolphus, 1834–1919, vol. II
Storey, Gladys; *see* Storey, M. G.
Storey, Harold Haydon, 1894–1969, vol. VI
Storey, Sir John Stanley, 1896–1955, vol. V
Storey, (Mary) Gladys, 1887–1978, vol. VII
Storey, Robert Holme, *died* 1956, vol. V
Storey, Samuel, 1840–1925, vol. II
Storey, Samuel; *see* Baron Buckton.
Storey, Sir Thomas, 1825–1898, vol. I
Storey, Sir Thomas James, 1851–1933, vol. III
Stork, Herbert Cecil, 1890–1983, vol. VIII
Stork, Joseph Whiteley, 1902–1990, vol. VIII
Storke, Arthur Ditchfield, 1894–1949, vol. IV
Storkey, Percy Valentine, 1893–1969, vol. VI
Storm, Lesley, *died* 1975, vol. VII
Stormonth-Darling, Hon. Lord; Moir Tod Stormonth-Darling, 1844–1912, vol. I
Stormonth Darling, Sir James Carlisle, (Sir Jamie), 1918–2000, vol. X
Stormonth Darling, Sir Jamie; *see* Stormonth Darling, Sir James C.
Stormonth-Darling, Major John Collier, 1878–1916, vol. II
Stormonth-Darling, Moir Tod; *see* Stormonth-Darling, Hon. Lord.
Storr, Francis, 1839–1919, vol. II
Storr, Lt-Col Lancelot, 1874–1944, vol. IV
Storr, Norman, 1907–1984, vol. VIII
Storr, Rev. Canon Vernon Faithfull, 1869–1940, vol. III
Storrar, Sir John, 1891–1984, vol. VIII
Storrar, Air Vice-Marshal Ronald Charles, 1904–1985, vol. VIII
Storrar, Air Vice-Marshal Sydney Ernest, 1895–1969, vol. VI
Storrs, Rt Rev. Christopher E., 1889–1977, vol. VII
Storrs, Very Rev. John, *died* 1928, vol. II
Storrs, Rear-Adm. Robert Francis, 1906–1968, vol. VI
Storrs, Sir Ronald, 1881–1955, vol. V
Storrs, William Hargrave, 1880–1964, vol. VI
Story, A. B. Herbert, *died* 1910, vol. I
Story, Alfred Thomas, 1842–1934, vol. III
Story, Arthur John, 1864–1938, vol. III
Story, Douglas, 1872–1921, vol. II
Story, Janet Leith, 1828–1926, vol. II
Story, John Benjamin, *died* 1926, vol. II
Story, Lt-Gen. Philip, 1840–1916, vol. II
Story, Very Rev. Robert Herbert, 1835–1907, vol. I
Story, Col William Frederick, *died* 1939, vol. III
Story, Adm. William Oswald, 1859–1938, vol. III
Story Maskelyne, Mervyn Herbert Nevil; *see* Maskelyne.

Stotesbury, Herbert Wentworth, 1916–1988, vol. VIII
Stothert, Sir Percy Kendall, 1863–1929, vol. III
Stott, Rt Hon. Lord; George Gordon Stott, 1909–1999, vol. X
Stott, Sir Arnold Walmsley, *died* 1958, vol. V
Stott, Edward, 1859–1918, vol. II
Stott, Sir George Edward, 2nd Bt, 1887–1957, vol. V
Stott, Rt Hon. George Gordon; *see* Stott, Rt Hon. Lord.
Stott, Maj.-Gen. Hugh, 1884–1966, vol. VI
Stott, May, (Lady Stott; May B. Lee), *died* 1977, vol. VII
Stott, Peter Frank, 1927–1993, vol. IX
Stott, Sir Philip Sidney, 1st Bt, 1858–1937, vol. III
Stott, Sir Philip Sidney, 3rd Bt, 1914–1979, vol. VII
Stott, Roger, 1943–1999, vol. X
Stott, Lt-Col William Henry, 1863–1930, vol. III
Stoughton, Rev. John, 1807–1897, vol. I
Stoughton, Raymond Henry, 1903–1979, vol. VII
Stourton, Col Hon. Edward Plantagenet Joseph Corbally, 1880–1966, vol. VI
Stourton, Sir Ivo Herbert Evelyn Joseph, 1901–1985, vol. VIII
Stourton, Hon. John Joseph, 1899–1992, vol. IX
Stourton, Rt Rev. Mgr Joseph, 1845–1921, vol. II
Stout, Alan Ker, 1900–1983, vol. VIII
Stout, Sir Duncan; *see* Stout, Sir T. D. M.
Stout, George Frederick, 1860–1944, vol. IV
Stout, Percy Wyfold, 1875–1937, vol. III
Stout, Rt Hon. Sir Robert, 1844–1930, vol. III
Stout, Sir (Thomas) Duncan (Macgregor), 1885–1979, vol. VII
Stow, Sir Alexander Montague, 1873–1936, vol. III
Stow, Sir Edmond Cecil P.; *see* Philipson-Stow.
Stow, Sir Elliot Philipson Philipson-, 2nd Bt, 1876–1954, vol. V
Stow, Sir Frederic Lawrence Philipson-, 3rd Bt, 1905–1976, vol. VII
Stow, Sir Frederic Samuel Philipson-, 1st Bt, 1849–1908, vol. I
Stow, Sir John Montague, 1911–1997, vol. X
Stow, Robert Frederic Philipson-, 1878–1949, vol. IV
Stow, Vincent Aubrey Stewart, 1883–1968, vol. VI
Stow Hill, Baron (Life Peer); Frank Soskice, 1902–1979, vol. VII
Stowe, Leonard, 1837–1920, vol. II
Stowell, Lt-Col Arthur Terence, 1873–1945, vol. IV
Stowell, Gordon William, 1898–1972, vol. VII
Stowell, Rev. Thomas Alfred, 1831–1916, vol. II
Stowell, Thomas Edmund Alexander, *died* 1970, vol. VI
Stowers, Arthur, 1897–1977, vol. VII
Stoy, Philip Joseph, 1906–2000, vol. X
Strabolgi, 9th Baron, 1853–1934, vol. III
Strabolgi, 10th Baron, 1886–1953, vol. V
Stracey, Sir Edward Paulet, 7th Bt, 1871–1949, vol. IV
Stracey, Maj.-Gen. Henry, 1839–1930, vol. III
Stracey, Sir Michael George Motley, 8th Bt, 1911–1971, vol. VII
Stracey-Clitherow, Lt-Col John Bourchier, 1853–1931, vol. III

Strachan, Hon. Lord; James Frederick Strachan, 1894–1978, vol. VII
Strachan, Sir Andrew Henry, 1895–1976, vol. VII
Strachan, Douglas, 1875–1950, vol. IV
Strachan, Gilbert Innes, 1888–1963, vol. VI
Strachan, Graham Robert, 1931–1994, vol. IX
Strachan, Lt-Col Harcus; *see* Strachan, Lt-Col Henry.
Strachan, Lt-Col Henry, 1884–1982, vol. VIII
Strachan, James, 1841–1917, vol. II
Strachan, James Frederick; *see* Strachan, Hon. Lord.
Strachan, John, 1838–1918, vol. II
Strachan, John, 1877–1934, vol. III
Strachan, Michael Francis, 1919 2000, vol. X
Strachan, Rev. Robert Harvey, 1873–1958, vol. V
Strachan, Robert Martin, 1913–1981, vol. VIII
Strachan, William Henry Williams, *died* 1921, vol. II
Strachan-Davidson, James Leigh, 1843–1916, vol. II
Strachey, Hon. Sir Arthur, 1858–1901, vol. I
Strachey, Sir Charles, 1862–1942, vol. IV
Strachey, Christopher, 1916–1975, vol. VII
Strachey, Sir Edward, 3rd Bt, 1812–1901, vol. I
Strachey, Rt Hon. (Evelyn) John (St Loe), 1901–1963, vol. VI
Strachey, (Giles) Lytton, 1880–1932, vol. III
Strachey, Jane Maria, (Lady Strachey), *died* 1928, vol. II
Strachey, Joan Pernel, 1876–1951, vol. V
Strachey, Sir John, 1823–1907, vol. I
Strachey, Rt Hon. John; *see* Strachey, Rt Hon. E. J. St L.
Strachey, John St Loe, 1860–1927, vol. II
Strachey, Lytton; *see* Strachey, G. L.
Strachey, Oliver, 1874–1960, vol. V
Strachey, Mrs Oliver; *see* Strachey, Ray.
Strachey, Philippa, 1872–1968, vol. VI
Strachey, Ray, 1887–1940, vol. III
Strachey, Lt-Gen. Sir Richard, 1817–1908, vol. I
Strachey, Col Richard John, 1861–1935, vol. III
Strachie, 1st Baron, 1858–1936, vol. III
Strachie, 2nd Baron, 1882–1973, vol. VII
Stradbroke, 3rd Earl of, 1862–1947, vol. IV
Stradbroke, 4th Earl of, 1903–1983, vol. VIII
Stradbroke, 5th Earl of, 1907–1983, vol. VIII
Stradling, Rt Rev. Leslie Edward, 1908–1998, vol. X
Stradling, Sir Reginald Edward, *died* 1952, vol. V
Stradling Thomas, Sir John, 1925–1991, vol. IX
Strafford, 3rd Earl of, 1830–1898, vol. I
Strafford, 4th Earl of, 1831–1899, vol. I
Strafford, 5th Earl of, 1835–1918, vol. II
Strafford, 6th Earl of, 1862–1951, vol. V
Strafford, 7th Earl of, 1904–1984, vol. VIII
Strafford, Countess of; (Alice), 1830–1928, vol. II
Strafford, Air Marshal Stephen Charles, 1898–1966, vol. VI
Straghan, Col Abel, 1836–1914, vol. I
Strahan, Sir Aubrey, 1852–1928, vol. II
Strahan, Lt-Gen. Charles, 1843–1930, vol. III
Strahan, Frank, 1886–1976, vol. VII
Strahan, Lt-Col Geoffrey Carteret, 1886–1973, vol. VII
Strahan, Rev. James, 1863–1926, vol. II
Strahan, James Andrew, 1858–1930, vol. III

Straight, Sir Douglas, 1844–1914, vol. I
Straight, Major Douglas Marshall, 1869–1949,
vol. IV
Straight, Whitney Willard, 1912–1979, vol. VII
Strain, Euphans H., died 1934, vol. III
Strain, Lt-Col Laurence Hugh, 1876–1952, vol. V
Straker, Herbert, 1856–1929, vol. III
Straker, John Coppin, 1847–1937, vol. III
Straker, Sir Michael Ian Bowstead, 1928–1998,
vol. X
Straker, William, 1855–1941, vol. IV
Straker-Smith, Sir Thomas Dalrymple, 1890–1970,
vol. VI
Strakosch, Sir Henry, 1871–1943, vol. IV
Stralia, Elsa, died 1945, vol. IV
Stranders, Michael O'Connell, 1911–1973, vol. VII
Strang, 1st Baron, 1893–1978, vol. VII
Strang, Lady; (Barbara Mary Hope), 1925–1982,
vol. VIII
Strang, Alexander Ronald, 1848–1926, vol. II
Strang, Barbara Mary Hope; see Strang, Lady.
Strang, Ian, 1886–1952, vol. V
Strang, John Martin, 1888–1970, vol. VI
Strang, William, 1859–1921, vol. II
Strang, William John, 1921–1999, vol. X
Strang Steel, Maj. Sir (Fiennes) William; see Steel,
Major Sir F. W. S.
Strang-Watkins, Watkin, 1869–1921, vol. II
Strange, 15th Baron, 1900–1982, vol. VIII
Strange of Knokin, Baroness; see St Davids,
Viscountess.
Strange, Rev. Cresswell, 1842–1905, vol. I
Strange, Lt-Col Edward Fairbrother, 1862–1929,
vol. III
Strange, Lt-Col Louis Arbon, 1891–1966, vol. VI
Strange, Brig.-Gen. Robert George, 1861–1949,
vol. IV
Strange, Susan, (Mrs Clifford Selly), 1923–1998,
vol. X
Strange, Maj.-Gen. Thomas Bland, 1831–1925,
vol. II
Stranger, Innes Harold, 1879–1936, vol. III
Stranger-Jones, Leonard Ivan, 1913–1983, vol. VIII
Strangman, James Gonville, 1902–1977, vol. VII
Strangman, Sir Thomas Joseph, 1873–1971,
vol. VII
Strangways, Arthur Henry Fox, 1859–1948, vol. IV
Strangways, Mary, died 1945, vol. IV
Strangways, Maurice Walter F.; see
Fox-Strangways.
Stranks, Ven. Charles James, 1901–1981, vol. VIII
Stranks, Donald Richard, 1929–1986, vol. VIII
Stransham, Sir Anthony Blaxland, 1805–1900,
vol. I
Strasser, Sir Paul, born 1911, vol. VIII
Strategicus; see O'Neill, H. C.
Stratford, Brig.-Gen. Cecil Vernon W.; see
Wingfield-Stratford.
Stratford, Esmé Cecil W.; see Wingfield-Stratford.
Stratford, Rt Hon. James, 1869–1952, vol. V
Strath, Sir William, 1906–1975, vol. VII
Strathalmond, 1st Baron, 1888–1970, vol. VI
Strathalmond, 2nd Baron, 1916–1976, vol. VII
Strathcarron, 1st Baron, 1880–1937, vol. III
Strathclyde, 1st Baron (cr 1914), 1853–1928, vol. II

Strathclyde, 1st Baron (cr 1955), 1891–1985,
vol. VIII
Strathcona and Mount Royal, 1st Baron, 1820–1914,
vol. I
Strathcona and Mount Royal, Baroness (2nd in line),
1854–1926, vol. II
Strathcona and Mount Royal, 3rd Baron, 1891–1959,
vol. V
Strathearn, Sir John Calderwood, 1878–1950,
vol. IV
Stratheden, 3rd Baron, and Campbell, 3rd Baron,
1829–1918, vol. II
Stratheden, 4th Baron, and Campbell, 4th Baron,
1899–1981, vol. VIII
Stratheden, 5th Baron, and Campbell, 5th Baron,
1901–1987, vol. VIII
Stratheden and Campbell, Lady; (Jean Helen), died
1956, vol. V
Strathie, Sir (David) Norman, 1886–1959, vol. V
Strathie, Sir Norman; see Strathie, Sir D. N.
Strathmore and Kinghorne, 13th Earl of, 1824–1904,
vol. I
Strathmore and Kinghorne, 14th Earl of, 1855–1944,
vol. IV
Strathmore and Kinghorne, 15th Earl of, 1884–1949,
vol. IV
Strathmore and Kinghorne, 16th Earl of, 1918–1972,
vol. VII
Strathmore and Kinghorne, 17th Earl of, 1928–1987,
vol. VIII
Strathon, Eric Colwill, 1908–1988, vol. VIII
Strathspey, 4th Baron, 1879–1948, vol. IV
Strathspey, 5th Baron, 1912–1992, vol. IX
Straton, Rt Rev. Norman Dumenil John,
1840–1918, vol. II
Stratten, Thomas Price, 1904–1980, vol. VII
Strattmann, HSH Edmund B.; see
Batthyany-Strattmann.
Stratton, Andrew, 1918–1994, vol. IX
Stratton, Arthur, died 1955, vol. V
Stratton, Ven. Basil, 1906–2000, vol. X
Stratton, Sir (Francis) John, 1906–1976, vol. VII
Stratton, Frederick John Marrian, 1881–1960,
vol. V
Stratton, Hon. J. R., 1858–1916, vol. II
Stratton, Sir John; see Stratton, Sir F. J.
Stratton, Rev. Joseph, 1839–1917, vol. II
Stratton, Julius Adams, 1901–1994, vol. IX
Stratton, Sir Richard James, 1924–1988, vol. VIII
Stratton, Mrs Roy Olin; see Dickens, Monica Enid.
Stratton, Lt-Col Wallace Christopher Ramsay,
1862–1942, vol. IV
Stratton, Lt-Gen. Sir William Henry, 1903–1989,
vol. VIII
Stratton-Porter, Gene; see Porter.
Straub, Marianne, 1909–1994, vol. IX
Strauchon, John, 1848–1934, vol. III
Straus, Bertram Stuart, 1867–1933, vol. III
Straus, Nathan, 1848–1931, vol. III
Straus, Oscar, 1870–1954, vol. V
Straus, Oscar S., 1850–1926, vol. II
Straus, Ralph, 1882–1950, vol. IV
Strauss, Baron (Life Peer); George Russell Strauss,
1901–1993, vol. IX

Strauss, Lady; Patricia Frances Strauss, 1909–1987, vol. VIII
Strauss, Arthur, 1847–1920, vol. II
Strauss, Edward Anthony, 1862–1939, vol. III
Strauss, Eric Benjamin, 1894–1961, vol. VI
Strauss, Franz Josef, 1915–1988, vol. VIII
Strauss, Hon. Jacobus Gideon Nel, 1900–1990, vol. IX (AI)
Strauss, Adm. Joseph, 1861–1948, vol. IV
Strauss, Lewis L., 1896–1974, vol. VII
Strauss, Richard, 1864–1949, vol. IV
Stravinsky, Igor, 1882–1971, vol. VII
Streat, Sir (Edward) Raymond, 1897–1979, vol. VII
Streat, Sir Raymond; see Streat, Sir E. R.
Streatfeild, Frank Newton, 1843–1916, vol. II
Streatfeild, Sir Geoffrey Hugh Benbow, 1897–1979, vol. VII
Streatfeild, Mrs Granville, (Lucy Anne Evelyn Streatfeild), died 1950, vol. IV
Streatfeild, Col Sir Henry, 1857–1938, vol. III
Streatfeild, Rev. Henry Bertram, 1852–1922, vol. II
Streatfeild, Henry Cuthbert, 1866–1950, vol. IV
Streatfeild, Lucy Anne Evelyn; see Streatfeild, Mrs Granville.
Streatfeild, (Mary) Noel, 1895–1986, vol. VIII
Streatfeild, Noel; see Streatfeild, M. N.
Streatfeild, Richard Alexander, 1866–1919, vol. II
Streatfeild, Brig. Richard John, 1903–1952, vol. V
Streatfeild, Rt Rev. William Champion, 1865–1929, vol. III
Streatfield, Captain Eric, died 1902, vol. I
Stredder, James Cecil, 1912–1991, vol. IX
Street, Lt-Col Alfred William Frederick, 1852–1911, vol. I
Street, Arthur George, 1892–1966, vol. VI
Street, Sir Arthur William, 1892–1951, vol. V
Street, Lt-Col Ashton, 1864–1946, vol. IV
Street, Captain Edmund Rochfort, died 1916, vol. II
Street, Fanny, 1877–1962, vol. VI
Street, Brig. Hon. Geoffrey Austin, 1894–1940, vol. III
Street, George Slythe, 1867–1936, vol. III
Street, Col Harold Edward, died 1917, vol. II
Street, John Hugh, 1914–1977, vol. VII
Street, Harry, 1919–1984, vol. VIII
Street, Hon. Sir Kenneth Whistler, 1890–1972, vol. VII
Street, Hon. Sir Philip Whistler, 1863–1938, vol. III
Street, Reginald Owen, 1890–1967, vol. VI
Street, Robert William, 1860–1954, vol. V
Street, Maj.-Gen. Vivian Wakefield, 1912–1970, vol. VI
Street, William P. R., 1841–1906, vol. I
Streeten, Frank; see Streeten, R. H.
Streeten, Reginald Hawkins, (Frank), 1928–1997, vol. X
Streeter, Rev. Burnett Hillman, 1874–1937, vol. III
Streeter, John Stuart, 1920–1996, vol. X
Streeter, Wilfrid A., 1877–1962, vol. VI
Streeton, Sir Arthur, 1867–1943, vol. IV
Streicher, Most Rev. Henry, 1863–1944, vol. IV
Streit, Clarence Kirshman, 1896–1986, vol. VIII
Strelcyn, Stefan, 1918–1981, vol. VIII
Stresemann, Gustav, 1878–1929, vol. III
Stretch, Rt Rev. John Francis, 1885–1919, vol. II

Strettell, Maj.-Gen. Sir C. B. Dashwood, 1881–1958, vol. V
Stretten, Charles James Derrickson, 1830–1919, vol. II
Stretton, Lt-Col Arthur John, 1863–1947, vol. IV
Stretton, Hesba, 1832–1911, vol. I
Stretton, Leonard Edward Bishop, 1893–1967, vol. VI
Strevens, Peter Derek, 1922–1989, vol. VIII
Stribling, Thomas Sigismund, 1881–1965, vol. VI
Strick, Col John, 1838–1903, vol. I
Strick, Maj.-Gen. John Arkwright, 1870–1934, vol. III
Strickland, 1st Baron, 1861–1940, vol. III
Strickland, Algernon Henry Peter, 1863–1928, vol. II
Strickland, Algernon Walter, 1891–1938, vol. III
Strickland, Rear-Adm. Sir Arthur Foster, 1882–1955, vol. V
Strickland, Barbara, (Lady Strickland), 1884–1977, vol. VII
Strickland, Sir Charles William, 8th Bt, 1819–1909, vol. I
Strickland, Claude Francis, 1881–1962, vol. VI
Strickland, Gen. Sir (Edward) Peter, 1869–1951, vol. V
Strickland, Maj.-Gen. Eugene Vincent Michael, 1913–1982, vol. VIII
Strickland, Frederic, 1867–1934, vol. III
Strickland, Henry H.; see Hornyold-Strickland.
Strickland, Hon. Mabel Edeline, 1899–1988, vol. VIII
Strickland, Hon. Mary Constance Elizabeth Christina H.; see Hornyold-Strickland.
Strickland, Captain Paul Sebring, 1885–1964, vol. VI
Strickland, Gen. Sir Peter; see Strickland, Gen. Sir E. P.
Strickland, Walter G., 1850–1928, vol. II
Strickland, Sir Walter William, 9th Bt, 1851–1938, vol. III
Strickland, Captain William Frederick, 1880–1954, vol. V
Strickland-Constable, Sir Henry Marmaduke, 10th Bt, 1900–1975, vol. VII
Strickland-Constable, Sir Robert Frederick, 11th Bt, 1903–1994, vol. IX
Striedinger, Col Oscar, 1875–1938, vol. III
Strijdom, Hon. Johannes Gerhardus, 1893–1958, vol. V
Strindberg, Auguste, 1849–1912, vol. I
Stringer, Donald Arthur, 1922–2000, vol. X
Stringer, Most Rev. Isaac O., 1866–1934, vol. III
Stringer, John Daniel, 1914–1971, vol. VII
Stringer, Sir (Thomas) Walter, 1855–1944, vol. IV
Stringer, Sir Walter; see Stringer, Sir T. W.
Stritch, His Eminence Cardinal Samuel Alphonsus, 1887–1958, vol. V
Strobl, Kisfalud Sigismund de, 1884–1975, vol. VII
Strode, Edward David C.; see Chetham-Strode.
Strode, Warren C.; see Chetham-Strode.
Strode-Jackson, Col Arnold Nugent Strode, 1891–1972, vol. VII
Strohmenger, Sir Ernest John, 1873–1967, vol. VI
Stromeyer, Charles E., 1856–1935, vol. III

Stronach, Ancell, 1901–1981, vol. VIII
Stronach, Catherine Geddes, *died* 1962, vol. VI
Stronach, John Clark, 1887–1967, vol. VI
Strong, Lt-Col Addington Dawsonne, 1875–1930, vol. III
Strong, Sir Archibald Thomas, 1876–1930, vol. III
Strong, Austin, 1881–1952, vol. V
Strong, Rev. Charles, 1844–1942, vol. IV
Strong, Sir Charles Love, 1908–1988, vol. VIII
Strong, Maj.-Gen. Dawsonne Melancthon, 1841–1903, vol. I
Strong, Rev. Canon Edward Herbert, *died* 1960, vol. V (A), vol. VI (AI)
Strong, Emilia Francis; *see* Dilke, E. F.
Strong, Eugénie, 1860–1943, vol. V
Strong, Lt-Col Henry Stuart, 1873–1949, vol. IV
Strong, Herbert A., *died* 1918, vol. II
Strong, Hugh W., 1861–1920, vol. II
Strong, John, 1868–1945, vol. IV
Strong, John Alexander, 1844–1917, vol. II
Strong, Maj.-Gen. Sir Kenneth William Dobson, 1900–1982, vol. VIII
Strong, Leonard Alfred George, 1896–1958, vol. V
Strong, Most Rev. Philip Nigel Warrington, 1899–1983, vol. VIII
Strong, Richard Pearson, 1872–1948, vol. IV
Strong, Rt Hon. Sir Samuel Henry, 1825–1909, vol. I
Strong, Sandford Arthur, 1863–1904, vol. I
Strong, Rt Rev. Thomas Banks, 1861–1944, vol. IV
Strong, Rt Hon. Sir (Thomas) Vezey, 1857–1920, vol. II
Strong, Rt Hon. Sir Vezey; *see* Strong, Rt Hon. Sir T. V.
Strong, Brig.-Gen. William, 1870–1956, vol. V
Stronge, Sir Charles Edmond Sinclair, 7th Bt, 1862–1939, vol. III
Stronge, Captain Rt Hon. Sir (Charles) Norman (Lockhart), 8th Bt, 1894–1981, vol. VIII
Stronge, Sir Francis William, 1856–1924, vol. II
Stronge, Sir Herbert Cecil, 1875–1963, vol. VI
Stronge, Brig. Humphrey Cecil Travell, 1891–1977, vol. VII
Stronge, Rt Hon. Sir James Henry, 5th Bt, 1849–1928, vol. II
Stronge, Sir John Calvert, 4th Bt, 1813–1899, vol. I
Stronge, Captain Rt Hon. Sir Norman; *see* Stronge, Captain Rt Hon. Sir C. N. L.
Stronge, Sir Walter Lockhart, 6th Bt, 1860–1933, vol. III
Stross, Sir Barnett, 1899–1967, vol. VI
Strother-Stewart, Robert; *see* Stewart.
Stroud, Dorothy Nancy, 1910–1997, vol. X
Stroud, Lt-Gen. Edward James, 1867–1935, vol. III
Stroud, Frederick, 1835–1912, vol. I
Stroud, Henry, 1861–1940, vol. III
Stroud, William, 1860–1938, vol. III
Stroyan, John, 1856–1941, vol. IV
Struben, William Charles Marinus, 1856–1928, vol. II, vol. III
Strudwick, Ethel, 1880–1954, vol. V
Strudwick, J. M., 1849–1937, vol. III
Strudwick, John Philip, 1914–1994, vol. IX
Strugnell, Surg. Rear-Adm. Lionel Frederick, 1892–1962, vol. VI

Struther, Jan, (Mrs A. K. Placzek), 1901–1953, vol. V
Struthers, Sir John, 1823–1899, vol. I
Struthers, Sir John, 1857–1925, vol. II
Strutt, Alfred William, 1856–1924, vol. II
Strutt, Vice-Adm. Hon. Arthur Charles, 1878–1973, vol. VII
Strutt, Sir Austin; *see* Strutt, Sir H. A.
Strutt, Hon. Charles Hedley, 1849–1926, vol. II
Strutt, Hon. Charles Richard, 1910–1981, vol. VIII
Strutt, Hon. Edward Gerald, 1854–1930, vol. III
Strutt, Lt-Col Edward Lisle, 1874–1948, vol. IV
Strutt, Geoffrey St John, 1888–1971, vol. VII
Strutt, George Herbert, 1854–1928, vol. II
Strutt, Sir (Henry) Austin, 1903–1979, vol. VII
Strutt, Maj.-Gen. John Rootsey, 1831–1909, vol. I
Strutt, Hon. Richard, 1848–1927, vol. II
Strutt, Rt Rev. Rupert Gordon, 1912–1985, vol. VIII
Strutt, William, *died* 1915, vol. I
Struve, Otto, 1897–1963, vol. VI
Stryker, M. Woolsey, 1851–1929, vol. III
Strzygowski, Josef, 1862–1941, vol. IV
Stuart, Viscount; David Andrew Noel Stuart, 1921–1942, vol. IV
Stuart, Viscount; Robert John Ochiltree Stuart, 1923–1944, vol. IV
Stuart of Findhorn, 1st Viscount, 1897–1971, vol. VII
Stuart of Findhorn, 2nd Viscount, 1924–1999, vol. X
Stuart of Wortley, 1st Baron, 1851–1926, vol. II
Stuart, Alan, 1894–1983, vol. VIII
Stuart, Sir Alexander M.; *see* Moody-Stuart.
Stuart, Alexander Mackenzie, 1877–1935, vol. III
Stuart, Alexander Moody, *died* 1915, vol. I
Stuart, Andrew Edmund Castlestuart, *died* 1936, vol. III
Stuart, Maj.-Gen. Sir Andrew Mitchell, 1861–1936, vol. III
Stuart, Arthur Constable M.; *see* Maxwell Stuart.
Stuart, Col Burleigh Francis Brownlow, 1868–1952, vol. V
Stuart, Sir Campbell, 1885–1972, vol. VII
Stuart, Charles Allan, 1864–1926, vol. II
Stuart, Rear-Adm. Charles Gage, 1887–1970, vol. VI
Stuart, Sir Charles James, 2nd Bt (*cr* 1840), 1824–1901, vol. I
Stuart, Lt-Col Charles Kennedy-Craufurd-, *died* 1942, vol. IV
Stuart, Charles Maddock, 1857–1932, vol. III
Stuart, Charles Rowell, 1928–1993, vol. IX
Stuart, Charles Russell, 1895–1975, vol. VII
Stuart, Lord Colum Edmund C.; *see* Crichton-Stuart.
Stuart, Rt Rev. Cyril Edgar, 1892–1982, vol. VIII
Stuart, Brig.-Gen. Donald MacKenzie, 1864–1946, vol. IV
Stuart, Dorothy Margaret, *died* 1963, vol. VI
Stuart, Maj.-Gen. Douglas, 1894–1955, vol. V
Stuart, Dudley, 1861–1939, vol. III
Stuart, Rev. Edward Alexander, 1853–1917, vol. II
Stuart, Sir Edward Andrew, 3rd Bt (*cr* 1840), 1832–1903, vol. I

Stuart, Rt Rev. Edward Craig, 1827–1911, vol. I
Stuart, Francis, 1902–2000, vol. X
Stuart, George Eustace B.; see Burnett-Stuart.
Stuart, George Moody, 1851–1940, vol. III
Stuart, Gerald Fitzgerald, 1897–1938, vol. III
Stuart, Major Godfrey Richard Conyngham, 1866–1955, vol. V
Stuart, Sir Harold Arthur, 1860–1923, vol. II
Stuart, Very Rev. Henry Venn, 1864–1933, vol. III
Stuart, Herbert Constable M.; see Maxwell-Stuart.
Stuart, Hilda Violet, died 1975, vol. VII
Stuart, Sir Houlton John, 8th Bt (cr 1660), 1863–1959, vol. V
Stuart, Ian Malcolm Bowen, 1902–1969, vol. VI
Stuart, Rev. James, 1841–1911, vol. I
Stuart, Rt Hon. James, 1843–1913, vol. I
Stuart, Rev. Sir James, 4th Bt (cr 1840), 1837–1915, vol. I
Stuart, John, 1836–1926, vol. II
Stuart, John, 1847–1931, vol. III
Stuart, Col John Alexander Man, 1841–1908, vol. I
Stuart, John Matthew Blackwood, 1882–1942, vol. IV
Stuart, Col John Patrick V.; see Villiers-Stuart.
Stuart, Gen. Sir John Theodosius B.; see Burnett-Stuart.
Stuart, John Windsor, 1846–1905, vol. I
Stuart, Lt-Gen. Kenneth, 1891–1945, vol. IV
Stuart, Leslie, 1866–1928, vol. II
Stuart, Rear-Adm. Leslie Creery, 1851–1908, vol. I
Stuart, Brig. Lionel Arthur, 1892–1959, vol. V
Stuart, Sir Louis, 1870–1949, vol. IV
Stuart, Malcolm Moncrieff, 1903–1991, vol. IX
Stuart, Captain Murray, 1882–1967, vol. VI
Stuart, Lord Ninian Edward C.; see Crichton-Stuart.
Stuart, Norman; see Teeling, Mrs Bartle.
Stuart, Maj.-Gen. Sir Robert Charles Ochiltree, 1861–1948, vol. IV
Stuart, Captain Hon. Robert Sheffield, 1886–1914, vol. I
Stuart, Captain Ronald Niel, 1886–1954, vol. V
Stuart, Ruth M'Enery, died 1917, vol. II
Stuart, Sir Simeon Henry Lechmere, 7th Bt (cr 1660), 1864–1939, vol. III
Stuart, Rt Rev. Simon; see Stuart, Rt Rev. C. E.
Stuart, Sir Thomas Anderson, 1856–1920, vol. II
Stuart, William C. S.; see Crawfurd-Stirling-Stuart.
Stuart, Maj.-Gen. William James, 1831–1914, vol. I
Stuart, Brig.-Gen. William V.; see Villiers-Stuart.
Stuart Black, (Ian) Hervey; see Black.
Stuart-Clark, Arthur Campbell, 1906–1973, vol. VII
Stuart-Cole, James, 1916–1992, vol. IX
Stuart-Forbes of Pitsligo, Sir Hugh; see Forbes of Pitsligo.
Stuart-Forbes-Trefusis, Hon. Henry Walter H.; see Trefusis.
Stuart-Forbes-Trefusis, Major Hon. John Frederick Hepburn; see Trefusis.
Stuart-Harris, Sir Charles Herbert, 1909–1996, vol. X
Stuart-Jones, Sir Henry, 1867–1939, vol. III
Stuart-Knill, Sir Ian, 3rd Bt, 1886–1973, vol. VII
Stuart-Low, William, 1857–1935, vol. III
Stuart-Menteth, Sir James; see Menteth.

Stuart-Menteth, Lt-Col Sir James Frederick; see Menteth.
Stuart-Menteth, Sir William Frederick; see Menteth.
Stuart Smith, Rt Rev. Thomas Geoffrey; see Smith.
Stuart Taylor, Sir Richard Laurence, 3rd Bt, 1925–1978, vol. VII
Stuart-Williams, Sir Charles; see Stuart-Williams, Sir S. C.
Stuart-Williams, Sir (Sydney) Charles, 1876–1960, vol. V
Stuart-Wortley, Lt-Gen. Hon. Sir (Alan) Richard Montagu-, 1868–1949, vol. IV
Stuart-Wortley, Hon. Clare Euphemia, 1889–1945, vol. IV
Stuart-Wortley, Maj.-Gen. Hon. Edward James Montagu-, 1857–1934, vol. III
Stuart-Wortley, Lt-Gen. Hon. Sir Richard; see Stuart-Wortley, Lt-Gen. Hon. Sir A. R. M.
Stuart-Wortley, Violet, (Hon. Mrs Edward Stuart Wortley), died 1953, vol. V
Stubber, Lt-Col John Henry H.; see Hamilton Stubber.
Stubblefield, Sir (Cyril) James, 1901–1999, vol. X
Stubblefield, Sir James; see Stubblefield, Sir. C. J.
Stubbs, Albert Ernest, 1877–1962, vol. VI
Stubbs, Rev. Arthur James, 1861–1945, vol. IV
Stubbs, Rt Rev. Charles William, 1845–1912, vol. I
Stubbs, Sir Edward; see Stubbs, Sir R. E.
Stubbs, George, 1864–1940, vol. III
Stubbs, Brig.-Gen. Guy Clifford, 1883–1939, vol. III
Stubbs, Sir James Wilfred, 1910–2000, vol. X
Stubbs, Lawrence Morley, 1874–1958, vol. V
Stubbs, Sir (Reginald) Edward, 1876–1947, vol. IV
Stubbs, Roy, 1897–1951, vol. V
Stubbs, Stanley, 1906–1976, vol. VII
Stubbs, Sydney, 1861–1953, vol. V
Stubbs, Rt Rev. William, 1825–1901, vol. I
Stubbs, William, 1911–1967, vol. VI
Stubbs, William Frederick, 1902–1987, vol. VIII
Stuchbery, Arthur Leslie, 1903–1986, vol. VIII
Stuck, Ven. Hudson, 1863–1920, vol. II
Stuckey, Reginald Robert, 1881–1948, vol. IV
Stucley, Maj. Sir Dennis Frederic Bankes, 5th Bt, 1907–1983, vol. VIII
Stucley, Sir Edward Arthur George, 3rd Bt, 1852–1927, vol. II
Stucley, Sir George Stucley, 1st Bt, 1812–1900, vol. I
Stucley, Sir Hugh Nicholas Granville, 4th Bt, 1873–1956, vol. V
Stucley, John Humphrey Albert, 1916–1988, vol. VIII
Stucley, Sir Lewis; see Stucley, Sir W. L.
Stucley, Sir (William) Lewis, 2nd Bt, 1836–1911, vol. I
Studd, C. T., died 1931, vol. III
Studd, Sir Eric, 2nd Bt, 1887–1975, vol. VII
Studd, Brig.-Gen. Herbert William, 1870–1947, vol. IV
Studd, Sir (John Edward) Kynaston, 1st Bt, 1858–1944, vol. IV
Studd, Sir Kynaston; see Studd, Sir J. E. K.
Studd, Sir Kynaston; see Studd, Sir R. K.
Studd, Brig. Malden Augustus, 1887–1973, vol. VII

Studd, Sir (Robert) Kynaston, 3rd Bt, 1926–1977, vol. VII
Studdert, Ven. Augustine John de Clare, 1901–1972, vol. VII
Studdert, Maj.-Gen. Robert Hallam, 1890–1968, vol. VI
Studdy, Sir Henry, 1894–1975, vol. VII
Studer, Paul, 1879–1927, vol. II
Studholme, Sir Henry Gray, 1899–1987, vol. VIII
Studholme, Lt-Col John, 1863–1934, vol. III
Studholme, Sir Paul Henry William, 2nd Bt, 1930–1990, vol. VIII
Studholme, Sir Richard Home, 1901–1963, vol. VI
Stungo, Adrian Paul, 1940–1998, vol. X
Stupart, Sir Frederic; see Stupart, Sir R. F.
Stupart, Sir (Robert) Frederic, 1857–1940, vol. III
Sturdee, Col Alfred Hobart, 1863–1939, vol. III
Sturdee, Admiral of the Fleet Sir Doveton; see Sturdee, Admiral of the Fleet Sir F. C. D.
Sturdee, Admiral of the Fleet Sir (Frederick Charles) Doveton, 1st Bt, 1859–1925, vol. II
Sturdee, Rear-Adm. Sir Lionel Arthur Doveton, 2nd Bt, 1884–1970, vol. VI
Sturdee, Rev. Robert James, 1879–1932, vol. III
Sturdee, Lt-Gen. Sir Vernon Ashton Hobart, 1890–1966, vol. VI
Sturdy, William Arthur, 1877–1958, vol. V
Sturge, Arthur Colwyn, 1912–1986, vol. VIII
Sturge, Arthur Lloyd, 1868–1942, vol. IV
Sturge, Harold Francis Ralph, 1902–1993, vol. IX
Sturge, Raymond Wilson, 1904–1984, vol. VIII
Sturge, William Allen, 1850–1919, vol. II
Sturges, Hugh Murray, 1863–1952, vol. V
Sturges, Lt-Gen. Sir Robert Grice, 1891–1970, vol. VI
Sturgess, Paymaster Rear-Adm. Richard Ernest Stanley, died 1933, vol. III
Sturgis, Julian Russell, 1848–1904, vol. I
Sturgis, Sir Mark Beresford Russell G.; see Grant-Sturgis.
Sturley, Major Albert Avern, 1887–1922, vol. II
Sturrock, Alick Riddell, 1885–1953, vol. V
Sturrock, Hon. Claud; see Sturrock, Hon. F. C.
Sturrock, Hon. (Frederick) Claud, 1882–1958, vol. V
Sturrock, Brig. George Colleymore, died 1935, vol. III
Sturrock, John, 1845–1926, vol. II
Sturrock, Sir John Christian Ramsay, 1875–1937, vol. III
Sturrock, John Leng, 1878–1943, vol. IV
Sturrock, William Duncan, 1880–1942, vol. IV
Sturt, Maj.-Gen. Charles Sheppey, 1838–1910, vol. I
Sturt, George, 1863–1927, vol. II
Sturt, Hon. Gerard Philip Montagu Napier, 1893–1918, vol. II
Sturt, Lt-Col Robert Ramsay Napier, 1852–1907, vol. I
Stutchbury, George Frederick, 1844–1934, vol. III
Stutfield, Hugh E. M., 1858–1929, vol. III
Stuttaford, Hon. Richard, 1870–1945, vol. IV
Stuttaford, Sir William Royden, 1928–1999, vol. X
Style, Sir Frederick Montague, 10th Bt, 1857–1930, vol. III

Style, Rev. George, died 1922, vol. II
Style, Lt-Comdr Sir Godfrey William, 1915–2000, vol. X
Style, Sir William Frederick, 11th Bt, 1887–1943, vol. IV
Style, Sir William Henry Marsham, 9th Bt, 1826–1904, vol. I
Style, Sir William Montague, 12th Bt, 1916–1981, vol. VIII
Styles, Frederick William, 1914–1998, vol. X
Styles, (Herbert) Walter, 1889–1965, vol. VI
Styles, Walter; see Styles, H. W.
Styles, William McNeil, 1941–1996, vol. X
Suárez, Eduardo, 1895–1976, vol. VII
Suart, Evelyn, (Lady Harcourt), died 1950, vol. IV
Suart, Brig.-Gen. William Hodgson, 1850–1923, vol. II
Subramanian, Chidambaram, 1910–2000, vol. X
Suckling, Rev. Charles William B.; see Baron-Suckling.
Suckling, Rev. Robert Alfred J., died 1917, vol. II
Sucksdorff, Mrs Åke; see Jonzen, Karin.
Sucksmith, Willie, 1896–1981, vol. VIII
Sucre-Trias, Juan Manuel, 1940–1983, vol. VIII
Sudborough, John Joseph, 1869–1963, vol. VI
Sudbury, Col Frederick Arthur, 1904–1983, vol. VIII
Suddards, Gaunt; see Suddards, H. G.
Suddards, (Henry) Gaunt, 1910–1992, vol. IX
Suddards, Roger Whitley, 1930–1995, vol. IX
Sudeley, 4th Baron, 1840–1922, vol. II
Sudeley, 5th Baron, 1870–1932, vol. III
Sudeley, 6th Baron, 1911–1941, vol. IV
Sudermann, Hermann, 1857–1928, vol. II
Sudmerson, Frederick William, died 1953, vol. V
Suenens, His Eminence Cardinal Leo Joseph, 1904–1996, vol. X
Sueter, Rear-Adm. Sir Murray Fraser, 1872–1960, vol. V
Suffian, Tun Mohamed, 1917–2000, vol. X
Suffield, 5th Baron, 1830–1914, vol. I
Suffield, 6th Baron, 1855–1924, vol. II
Suffield, 7th Baron, 1897–1943, vol. IV
Suffield, 8th Baron, 1907–1945, vol. IV
Suffield, 9th Baron, 1861–1946, vol. IV
Suffield, 10th Baron, 1865–1951, vol. V
Suffield, Sir (Henry John) Lester, 1911–1999, vol. X
Suffield, Sir Lester; see Suffield, Sir H. J. L.
Suffolk, 18th Earl of, and Berkshire, 11th Earl of, 1833–1898, vol. I
Suffolk, 19th Earl of, and Berkshire, 12th Earl of, 1877–1917, vol. II
Suffolk, 20th Earl of, and Berkshire, 13th Earl of, 1906–1941, vol. IV
Sugden, Alan Victor, 1877–1956, vol. V
Sugden, Sir Bernard, 1877–1954, vol. V
Sugden, General Sir Cecil Stanway, 1903–1963, vol. VI
Sugden, Charles, 1850–1921, vol. II
Sugden, Maj.-Gen. Francis George, 1938–1997, vol. X
Sugden, Frank, 1852–1927, vol. II
Sugden, Maj.-Gen. Sir Henry Haskins Clapham, 1904–1977, vol. VII

Sugden, Kaye Aspinall Ramsden, 1880–1966, vol. VI
Sugden, Sir Morris; *see* Sugden, Sir T. M.
Sugden, Brig.-Gen. Richard Edgar, 1871–1951, vol. V
Sugden, Gp Captain Ronald Scott, 1896–1971, vol. VII
Sugden, Samuel, 1892–1950, vol. IV
Sugden, Sir (Theodore) Morris, 1919–1984, vol. VIII
Sugden, Sir Wilfrid Hart, *died* 1960, vol. V
Sugerman, Sir Bernard, 1904–1976, vol. VII
Suggia, Guilhermina, 1888–1950, vol. IV
Suhrawardy, Sir Abdulla Al-Mamun, *died* 1935, vol. III
Suhrawardy, Lt-Col Sir Hassan, 1884–1946, vol. IV
Suhrawardy, Huseyn Shaheed, 1893–1963, vol. VI
Suhrawardy, Sir Zahhadur Rahim Zahid, 1870–1949, vol. IV
Sukhdeo Prasad Kak, Rao Bahadur Pandit Sir, 1862–1935, vol. III
Sukuna, Sir Joseva Lalabalavu Vanaaliali, *died* 1958, vol. V
Sulaiman, Sir Shah Muhammad, 1886–1941, vol. IV
Sulivan, Col Ernest Frederic, 1860–1928, vol. II
Sulivan, Vice-Adm. Norton Allen, 1879–1964, vol. VI
Sullivan, Albert Patrick Loisol, 1898–1981, vol. VIII
Sullivan, Alexander Martin, 1871–1959, vol. V
Sullivan, Rev. Arnold Moon, 1878–1943, vol. IV
Sullivan, Sir Arthur Seymour, 1842–1900, vol. I
Sullivan, Basil Martin, 1882–1946, vol. IV
Sullivan, Bernard Ponsonby, 1891–1958, vol. V
Sullivan, Hon. Daniel Giles, 1882–1947, vol. IV
Sullivan, Sir Desmond John, 1920–1996, vol. X
Sullivan, Donal, 1838–1907, vol. I
Sullivan, Edmund J., 1869–1933, vol. III
Sullivan, Rt Rev. Edward, *died* 1899, vol. I
Sullivan, Sir Edward, 2nd Bt (*cr* 1881), 1852–1928, vol. II
Sullivan, Brig.-Gen. Edward Langford, 1865–1949, vol. IV
Sullivan, Sir Edward Robert, 5th Bt (*cr* 1804), 1826–1899, vol. I
Sullivan, Francis Loftus, 1903–1956, vol. V
Sullivan, Sir Francis William, 6th Bt (*cr* 1804), 1834–1906, vol. I
Sullivan, Rev. Sir Frederick, 7th Bt (*cr* 1804), 1865–1954, vol. V
Sullivan, Henry Edward, 1830–1905, vol. I
Sullivan, James Frank, *died* 1936, vol. III
Sullivan, John William Navin, 1886–1937, vol. III
Sullivan, Joseph, 1866–1935, vol. III
Sullivan, Very Rev. Martin Gloster, 1910–1980, vol. VII
Sullivan, Sir Richard Benjamin Magniac, 8th Bt (*cr* 1804), 1906–1977, vol. VII
Sullivan, Timothy, 1874–1949, vol. IV
Sullivan, Timothy Daniel, 1827–1914, vol. I
Sullivan, Tod, 1934–1997, vol. X
Sullivan, Sir Wilfred; *see* Sullivan, Hon. Sir William W.
Sullivan, Sir William, 3rd Bt (*cr* 1881), 1860–1937, vol. III

Sullivan, Sir William, 1891–1967, vol. VI
Sullivan, William Charles, *died* 1926, vol. II
Sullivan, Sir William John, 1895–1971, vol. VII
Sullivan, Sir (William) Wilfred, 1843–1923, vol. II
Sully, James, 1842–1923, vol. II
Sully, Air Vice-Marshal John Alfred, 1892–1968, vol. VI (AII)
Sully, Leonard Thomas George, 1909–1994, vol. IX
Sulman, Sir John, 1849–1934, vol. III
Sultan, Syed Abdus, 1917–1991, vol. IX
Sulte, Benjamin, 1841–1923, vol. II
Sulzbach, Herbert, 1894–1985, vol. VIII
Sulzberger, Arthur Hays, 1891–1968, vol. VI
Sulzberger, Mayer, 1843–1923, vol. II
Sumichrast, Frederick C. de, 1845–1933, vol. III
Summerbell, Thomas, 1861–1910, vol. I
Summerfield, Sir John Crampton, 1920–1997, vol. X
Summerford, Engr Rear-Adm. Horace George, 1872–1963, vol. VI
Summerhayes, Sir Christopher Henry, 1896–1988, vol. VIII
Summerhayes, Lt-Col John Orlando, 1869–1942, vol. IV
Summerhays, Reginald Sherriff, 1881–1976, vol. VII
Summers, Rev. Alphonsus Joseph-Mary Augustus Montague, 1880–1948, vol. IV
Summers, Sir Felix Roland Brattan, 2nd Bt, 1918–1993, vol. X (AI)
Summers, Sir Geoffrey, 1st Bt, 1891–1972, vol. VII
Summers, Bt-Lt-Col Sir Gerald Henry, 1885–1925, vol. II
Summers, Sir (Gerard) Spencer, 1902–1976, vol. VII
Summers, James Woolley, 1849–1913, vol. I
Summers, Captain Joseph J., *died* 1954, vol. V
Summers, Sir Richard Felix, 1902–1977, vol. VII
Summers, Sir Spencer; *see* Summers, Sir G. S.
Summers, Thomas, *died* 1944, vol. IV
Summers, Walter Coventry, 1869–1937, vol. III
Summersby, Charles Harold, 1882–1961, vol. VI
Summerscale, Sir John Percival, 1901–1980, vol. VII
Summerskill, Baroness (Life Peer); Edith Summerskill, 1901–1980, vol. VII
Summerson, Sir John Newenham, 1904–1992, vol. IX
Summerson, Thomas Hawksley, 1903–1986, vol. VIII
Summerville, Sir Alan; *see* Summerville, Sir W. A. T.
Summerville, Sir (William) Alan (Thompson), 1904–1980, vol. VII
Sumner, 1st Viscount, 1859–1934, vol. III
Sumner, Benedict Humphrey, 1893–1951, vol. V
Sumner, Captain Berkeley H.; *see* Holme-Sumner.
Sumner, Donald; *see* Sumner, W. D. M.
Sumner, Rt Rev. George Henry, 1824–1909, vol. I
Sumner, James Batcheller, 1887–1955, vol. V
Sumner, Sir John, 1856–1934, vol. III
Sumner, John Richard Hugh, 1886–1971, vol. VII
Sumner, (William) Donald (Massey), 1913–1990, vol. VIII
Sumsion, Herbert Whitton, 1899–1995, vol. IX
Sundar Singh Majithia, Sirdar Sir, 1872–1941, vol. IV
Sundarlal, Hon. Pandit, 1857–1918, vol. II

Sunday, Rev. William Ashley, 1863–1935, vol. III
Sunderland, Earl of; John David Ivor
Spencer-Churchill, 1952–1955, vol. V
Sunderland, (George Frederick) Irvon, 1905–1984,
vol. VIII
Sunderland, Irvon; see Sunderland, G. F. I.
Sunderland, J. E., 1885–1956, vol. V
Sunderland, Col Marsden Samuel James,
1841–1929, vol. III
Sunderland, Septimus Philip, died 1950, vol. IV
Sunderland, Sir Sydney, 1910–1993, vol. IX
Sunley, Bernard, 1910–1964, vol. VI
Sunlight, Joseph, 1889–1978, vol. VII
Supervia, Conchita, 1899–1936, vol. III
Supomo, Raden, 1903–1958, vol. V
Supple, Col James Francis, 1843–1922, vol. II
Surfaceman; see Anderson, Alexander.
Surplice, Reginald Alwyn, 1906–1977, vol. VII
Surridge, Brewster Joseph, 1894–1982, vol. VIII
Surridge, Sir (Ernest) Rex (Edward), 1899–1990,
vol. VIII
Surridge, Sir Rex; see Surridge, Sir E. R. E.
Surtees, Col Charles Freville, 1823–1906, vol. I
Surtees, Brig.-Gen. Sir Conyers, 1858–1933, vol. III
Surtees, Maj.-Gen. George, 1895–1976, vol. VII
Surtees, Major (Henry) Siward (Balliol),
1873–1955, vol. V
Surtees, Major Siward; see Surtees, Major H. S. B.
Surtees, Rt Rev. William F., 1871–1956, vol. V
Surveyer, Hon. Edouard-Fabre, 1875–1957, vol. V
Susman, Maurice Philip, 1898–1988, vol. VIII
Susskind, (Jan) Walter, 1913–1980, vol. VII
Susskind, Walter; see Susskind, J. W.
Sutch, Ven. Ronald Huntley, 1890–1975, vol. VII
Sutcliff, Rosemary, 1920–1992, vol. IX
Sutcliffe, Edward Davis, 1917–1995, vol. IX
Sutcliffe, Frank Edmund, 1918–1983, vol. VIII
Sutcliffe, Geoffrey Scott, 1912–1999, vol. X
Sutcliffe, Halliwell, 1870–1932, vol. III
Sutcliffe, Sir Harold, 1897–1958, vol. V
Sutcliffe, Joseph Richard, 1897–1985, vol. VIII
Sutcliffe, Kenneth Edward, 1911–1991, vol. IX
Sutcliffe, Reginald Cockcroft, 1904–1991, vol. IX
Sutcliffe, Bt Col Richard Douglas, died 1941,
vol. IV
Sutcliffe, Tom, 1865–1931, vol. III
Sutcliffe, Air Cdre Walter Philip, 1910–1990,
vol. VIII
Sutcliffe, Very Rev. William Ormond, 1856–1944,
vol. IV
Suter, George Edward, 1869–1939, vol. III
Suter, Captain Roy Neville, 1884–1958, vol. V
Suther, Gen. Cuthbert Collingwood, 1839–1927,
vol. II
Suther, Brig. Percival, 1873–1945, vol. IV
Sutherland, 4th Duke of, 1851–1913, vol. I
Sutherland, 5th Duke of, 1888–1963, vol. VI
Sutherland, 6th Duke of, 1915–2000, vol. X
Sutherland, Duchess of; (Millicent Fanny),
1867–1955, vol. V
Sutherland, Alexander Malcolm G.; see Græme-
Sutherland.
Sutherland, Algernon Robert, 1854–1933, vol. III
Sutherland, Angus, 1848–1922, vol. II

Sutherland, Anthony Frederic Arthur, 1916–1996,
vol. X
Sutherland, Sir Arthur Munro, 1st Bt, 1867–1953,
vol. V
Sutherland, Sir (Benjamin) Ivan, 2nd Bt,
1901–1980, vol. VII
Sutherland, (Carol) Humphrey (Vivian), 1908–1986,
vol. VIII
Sutherland, Charles Leslie, 1839–1911, vol. I
Sutherland, D. M., died 1951, vol. V
Sutherland, David M., 1883–1973, vol. VII
Sutherland, Lt-Col David Waters, 1871–1939,
vol. III
Sutherland, Lt-Col Hon. Donald Matheson,
1879–1949, vol. IV
Sutherland, Earl Wilbur, Jr, 1915–1974, vol. VII
Sutherland, Edward Davenport, 1853–1923, vol. II
Sutherland, Sir (Frederick) Neil, 1900–1986,
vol. VIII
Sutherland, George Alexander, died 1939, vol. III
Sutherland, George Arthur, 1891–1970, vol. VI
Sutherland, Sir George Henry, 1866–1937, vol. III
Sutherland, Sir Gordon Brims Black McIvor,
1907–1980, vol. VII
Sutherland, Graham Vivian, 1903–1980, vol. VII
Sutherland, Halliday Gibson, 1882–1960, vol. V
Sutherland, Lt-Col Henry Homes, 1871–1940,
vol. III
Sutherland, Humphrey; see Sutherland, C. H. V.
Sutherland, Sir Iain Johnstone Macbeth, 1925–1986,
vol. VIII
Sutherland, Sir Ivan; see Sutherland, Sir B. I.
Sutherland, Hon. James, 1849–1905, vol. I
Sutherland, Sir James Runcieman, 1900–1996,
vol. X
Sutherland, Joan, died 1947, vol. IV
Sutherland, Sir John Donald, 1865–1952, vol. V
Sutherland, John Ebenezer, 1854–1918, vol. II
Sutherland, Lewis Robertson, 1863–1933, vol. III
Sutherland, Dame Lucy Stuart, 1903–1980, vol. VII
Sutherland, Mary Elizabeth, died 1972, vol. VII
Sutherland, Monica La Fontaine, 1897–1982,
vol. VIII
Sutherland, Sir Neil; see Sutherland, Sir F. N.
Sutherland, (Norman) Stuart, 1927–1998, vol. X
Sutherland, Rt Hon. Robert Franklin, 1859–1922,
vol. II
Sutherland, Scott, 1910–1984, vol. VIII
Sutherland, Stuart; see Sutherland, N. S.
Sutherland, Sir Thomas, 1834–1922, vol. II
Sutherland, Hon. William, 1857–1935, vol. III
Sutherland, William, died 1945, vol. IV
Sutherland, Rt Hon. Sir William, 1880–1949,
vol. IV
Sutherland, Hon. William Charles, 1865–1940,
vol. III
Sutherland-Dunbar, Sir George Cospatrick D.; see
Duff-Sutherland-Dunbar.
Sutherland-Dunbar, Sir George D.; see
Duff-Sutherland-Dunbar.
Sutherland-Gower, Rt Hon. Lord Ronald; see
Gower.
Sutherland-Harris, Lt-Col Alexander Sutherland,
1865–1934, vol. III

Sutherland-Harris, Sir Jack Alexander, 1908–1986, vol. VIII
Sutherland-Leveson Gower, Major Lord Alastair St Clair; *see* Leveson Gower.
Suthers, Rev. Canon George, 1908–1965, vol. VI
Sutro, Alfred, 1863–1933, vol. III
Suttie, Sir George Grant-, 7th Bt, 1870–1947, vol. IV
Suttie, Sir (George) Philip Grant-, 8th Bt, 1938–1997, vol. X
Suttie, Col Hubert Francis Grant-, 1884–1973, vol. VII
Suttie, Sir Philip; *see* Suttie, Sir G. P. G.
Suttill, Margaret Joan, (Mrs G. A. Pink), 1912–1996, vol. X
Suttner, Baroness Bertha Felicie Sophie von, 1843–1914, vol. I
Sutton, Sir Abraham, 1849–1921, vol. II
Sutton, Maj.-Gen. Alexander Arthur, 1861–1941, vol. IV
Sutton, Col Alfred, *died* 1922, vol. II
Sutton, Rev. Alfred, 1851–1938, vol. III
Sutton, Sir Arthur, 7th Bt (*cr* 1772), 1857–1948, vol. IV
Sutton, Rev. Arthur Frederick, *died* 1925, vol. II
Sutton, Arthur Warwick, 1854–1925, vol. II
Sutton, Air Marshal Sir Bertine Entwisle, 1886–1946, vol. IV
Sutton, Engr Rear-Adm. Charles Edwin, 1880–1968, vol. VI
Sutton, Charles William, 1848–1920, vol. II
Sutton, Denys Miller, 1917–1991, vol. IX
Sutton, Surg.-Rear-Adm. Edward, 1870–1940, vol. III
Sutton, Maj.-Gen. Evelyn Alexander, 1891–1964, vol. VI
Sutton, Maj.-Gen. F. A., 1884–1944, vol. IV
Sutton, Francis Henry Astley M.; *see* Manners-Sutton.
Sutton, Sir George, 1st Bt (*cr* 1922), 1856–1934, vol. III
Sutton, Sir George Augustus, 1st Bt, 1869–1947, vol. IV
Sutton, George Lowe, 1872–1964, vol. VI
Sutton, Hon. Sir George Morris, 1834–1913, vol. I
Sutton, Brig. George William, 1893–1971, vol. VII
Sutton, Sir Graham; *see* Sutton, Sir O. G.
Sutton, Sir Henry, 1845–1920, vol. II
Sutton, Rev. Henry, 1833–1921, vol. II
Sutton, Henry Cecil, 1868–1936, vol. III
Sutton, Maj.-Gen. Hugh Clement, 1867–1928, vol. II
Sutton, Janet Vida, (Mrs John Sutton); *see* Watson, J. V.
Sutton, John, 1919–1992, vol. IX
Sutton, John Edward, 1862–1945, vol. IV
Sutton, Sir John Smale, *died* 1942, vol. IV
Sutton, Leonard Goodhart, 1863–1932, vol. III
Sutton, Leslie Ernest, 1906–1992, vol. IX
Sutton, Martin Hubert Foquett, 1875–1930, vol. III
Sutton, Martin John, 1850–1913, vol. I
Sutton, Sir (Oliver) Graham, 1903–1977, vol. VII
Sutton, Peter John, 1917–1982, vol. VIII
Sutton, Ralph, 1881–1960, vol. V

Sutton, Sir Richard Vincent, 6th Bt (*cr* 1772), 1891–1918, vol. II
Sutton, Ven. Robert, 1832–1910, vol. I
Sutton, Sir Robert Lexington, 8th Bt, 1897–1981, vol. VIII
Sutton, Robert William, 1905–1997, vol. X
Sutton, Sir Stafford William Powell F.; *see* Foster-Sutton.
Sutton, Stanley Cecil, 1907–1977, vol. VII
Sutton, Thomas Francis, 1923–1994, vol. IX
Sutton, William Godfrey, 1894–1985, vol. VIII
Sutton, Brig. William Moxhay, 1885–1949, vol. IV
Sutton Curtis, John, 1913–1988, vol. VIII
Sutton Nelthorpe, Col Oliver, 1888–1963, vol. VI
Sutton-Nelthorpe, Robert Nassau, 1850–1937, vol. III
Sutton-Pratt, Brig. Reginald, 1898–1962, vol. VI
Suttor, Hon. Sir Francis Bathurst, 1839–1915, vol. I
Suvorin, Alexis, 1834–1912, vol. I
Suyematsu, Viscount Kencho, 1855–1920, vol. II
Svenningsen, Nils Thomas, 1894–1985, vol. VIII
Swabey, Christopher, 1906–1972, vol. VII
Swabey, Vice-Adm. Sir George Thomas Carlisle Parker, 1881–1952, vol. V
Swabey, Brig.-Gen. Wilfred Spedding, 1871–1939, vol. III
Swaby, Ven. J. A. R., *died* 1944, vol. IV
Swaby, Rt Rev. John Cyril Emerson, 1905–1975, vol. VII
Swaby, Rt Rev. William Proctor, 1844–1916, vol. II
Swaffer, Hannen, 1879–1962, vol. VI
Swain, Rt Rev. Edgar Priestley, 1881–1949, vol. IV
Swain, Rev. Edmund Gill, 1861–1938, vol. III
Swain, Air Cdre (Francis) Ronald Downs, 1903–1989, vol. VIII
Swain, Freda Mary, 1903–1985, vol. VIII
Swain, Very Rev. George Lill, 1870–1955, vol. V
Swain, Hon. Col George Llewellyn Douglas, 1858–1924, vol. II
Swain, James, *died* 1951, vol. V
Swain, Joseph, 1857–1927, vol. II
Swain, Percival Francis, 1888–1924, vol. II
Swain, Air Cdre Ronald; *see* Swain, Air Cdre F. R. D.
Swain, Thomas Henry, 1911–1979, vol. VII
Swain, Walter, 1876–1945, vol. IV
Swaine, Col Charles Edward, 1844–1928, vol. II
Swaine, Edward Thomas William, 1907–2000, vol. X
Swaine, Maj.-Gen. Sir Leopold Victor, 1840–1931, vol. III
Swainson, Maj.-Gen. Frederick Joseph, 1911–1965, vol. VI
Swainson, Willan, *died* 1970, vol. VI
Swaish, Sir John, 1852–1931, vol. III
Swales, A. B., *died* 1952, vol. V
Swales, John Douglas, 1935–2000, vol. X
Swales, John Kirby, 1879–1956, vol. V
Swallow, John Crossley, 1923–1994, vol. IX
Swallow, Rev. Richard Dawson, 1847–1930, vol. III
Swallow, Sir William, 1905–1997, vol. X
Swamikannu Pillai, Louis Dominic, 1865–1925, vol. II
Swan, Sir Alexander Brown, 1869–1941, vol. IV
Swan, Alice Macallan, *died* 1939, vol. III

Swan, Annie Shepherd; *see* Smith, Mrs Burnett.
Swan, Col Charles Arthur, 1854–1941, vol. IV
Swan, Sir Charles Sheriton, 1870–1944, vol. IV
Swan, Maj.-Gen. Dennis Charles Tarrant, 1900–1992, vol. IX
Swan, Captain Donald C.; *see* Cameron-Swan.
Swan, Rear-Adm. (S) Edgar Bocquet, 1874–1951, vol. V
Swan, Ernest William, 1883–1948, vol. IV
Swan, Harold Couch, 1890–1972, vol. VII
Swan, Henry Frederick, 1842–1908, vol. I
Swan, John Arthur Laing, 1877–1938, vol. III
Swan, John Edmund, 1877–1956, vol. V
Swan, John Macallan, 1847–1910, vol. I
Swan, Sir Joseph Wilson, 1828–1914, vol. I
Swan, Lt-Comdr Sir Kenneth Raydon, 1877–1973, vol. VII
Swan, Lionel Maynard, 1885–1969, vol. VI
Swan, Robert A., 1849–1937, vol. III
Swan, Robert Clayton, *died* 1929, vol. III
Swan, Russell Henry Jocelyn, 1876–1943, vol. IV
Swan, Sheriton Clements, 1909–1986, vol. VIII
Swan, Thomas, 1899–1981, vol. VIII
Swan, Lt-Col Sir William Bertram, 1914–1990, vol. VIII
Swan, Maj.-Gen. William Travers, 1861–1949, vol. IV
Swanborough, Baroness (Life Peer); *see* Reading, Marchioness of.
Swann, Baron (Life Peer); Michael Meredith Swann, 1920–1990, vol. VIII
Swann, Rev. Canon Alfred, *died* 1961, vol. VI
Swann, Sir Anthony Charles Christopher, 3rd Bt, 1913–1991, vol. IX
Swann, Rev. Cecil Gordon Aldersey, 1888–1969, vol. VI
Swann, Sir (Charles) Duncan, 2nd Bt, 1879–1962, vol. VI
Swann, Rt Hon. Sir Charles Ernest, 1st Bt, 1844–1929, vol. III
Swann, Donald Ibrahim, 1923–1994, vol. IX
Swann, Sir Duncan; *see* Swann, Sir C. D.
Swann, Rev. Ernest Henry, 1869–1948, vol. IV
Swann, (Frederick) Ralph (Holland), 1904–1992, vol. IX
Swann, Frederick Samuel Philip, *died* 1921, vol. II
Swann, Harry Kirke, 1871–1926, vol. II, vol. III
Swann, Maj.-Gen. John Christopher, 1856–1939, vol. III
Swann, Louis Herbert H.; *see* Hartland-Swann.
Swann, Air Vice-Marshal Sir Oliver, 1878–1948, vol. IV
Swann, Peter Geoffrey, 1921–1988, vol. VIII
Swann, Ralph; *see* Swann, F. R. H.
Swann, Robert Swinney, 1915–1986, vol. VIII
Swann, Rev. Sidney, 1862–1942, vol. IV
Swann, Rev. Canon Sidney Ernest, 1890–1976, vol. VII
Swann, William Francis Gray, 1884–1962, vol. VI
Swann-Mason, Rev. Richard Swann, *died* 1942, vol. IV
Swansea, 2nd Baron, 1848–1922, vol. II
Swansea, 3rd Baron, 1875–1934, vol. III
Swanson, Gloria May Josephine Swanson, 1899–1983, vol. VIII

Swanson, John Leslie, 1892–1974, vol. VII
Swanson, Sir John Warren, 1865–1924, vol. II
Swanston, Lt-Col Charles Oliver, 1865–1914, vol. I
Swanston, Comdr David, 1919–1987, vol. VIII
Swanston, John Francis Alexander, 1877–1958, vol. V
Swanton, Ernest William, 1907–2000, vol. X
Swanwick, Anna, 1813–1899, vol. I
Swanwick, Betty, 1915–1989, vol. VIII
Swanwick, Harold, *died* 1929, vol. III
Swanwick, Helena Maria, 1864–1939, vol. III
Swanzy, Very Rev. Henry Biddall, 1873–1932, vol. III
Swanzy, Sir Henry Rosborough, 1843–1913, vol. I
Swanzy, Rev. Thomas Erskine, 1869–1950, vol. IV
Swarbrick, John, 1879–1964, vol. VI
Swarbrick, Thomas, 1900–1965, vol. VI
Swart, Hon. Charles Robberts, 1894–1982, vol. VIII
Swash, Stanley Victor, 1896–1996, vol. X
Swayne, Col Charles Henry, 1848–1925, vol. II
Swayne, Charles Richard, 1843–1921, vol. II
Swayne, Brig.-Gen. Sir Eric John Eagles, 1863–1929, vol. III
Swayne, Col Harald George Carlos, 1860–1940, vol. III
Swayne, Maj.-Gen. James Dowell, 1827–1916, vol. II
Swayne, Lt-Gen. Sir John George des Réaux, 1890–1964, vol. VI
Swayne, Sir Ronald Oliver Carless, 1918–1991, vol. IX
Swayne, Walter Carless, 1862–1925, vol. II
Swayne, Rt Rev. William Shuckburgh, 1862–1941, vol. IV
Swaythling, 1st Baron, 1832–1911, vol. I
Swaythling, 2nd Baron, 1869–1927, vol. II
Swaythling, 3rd Baron, 1898–1990, vol. VIII
Swaythling, 4th Baron, 1928–1998, vol. X
Swaythling, Dowager Lady; Jean Marcia Montagu, 1908–1993, vol. IX
Sweaney, William Douglas, 1912–1996, vol. X
Sweatman, Most Rev. Arthur, 1834–1909, vol. I
Sweeney, Hon. Francis J., 1862–1921, vol. II, vol. III
Sweeney, Very Rev. Canon Garrett Daniel, 1912–1979, vol. VII
Sweeney, James Augustine, 1883–1945, vol. IV
Sweeney, Maj.-Gen. Joseph A., 1897–1980, vol. VII (AII)
Sweeny, Most Rev. James Fielding, 1857–1940, vol. III
Sweeny, Lt-Col Roger Lewis Campbell, 1878–1926, vol. II
Sweet, Lt-Col Edward Herbert, 1871–1966, vol. VI
Sweet, Henry, 1845–1912, vol. I
Sweet, Ven. John Hales Sweet, 1849–1929, vol. III
Sweet-Escott, Sir Bickham; *see* Sweet-Escott, Sir E. B.
Sweet-Escott, Sir (Ernest) Bickham, 1857–1941, vol. IV
Sweeting, Richard Deane, 1856–1913, vol. I
Sweeting, William Hart, 1909–1994, vol. IX
Sweetman, Sir Henry, 1858–1944, vol. IV
Sweetman, Seamus George, 1914–1985, vol. VIII
Sweett, Cyril, 1903–1991, vol. IX

Sweny, Captain William Halpin Paterson, 1871–1951, vol. V

Swete, Henry Barclay, 1835–1917, vol. II

Swetenham, Clement William, 1852–1927, vol. II

Swettenham, Sir Alexander, 1846–1933, vol. III

Swettenham, Sir Frank Athelstane, 1850–1946, vol. IV

Swettenham, Lt-Col George Kilner, 1866–1933, vol. III

Swettenham, Lt-Col William Alexander Whybault, 1870–1947, vol. IV

Swift, Brig.-Gen. Albert Edward, 1870–1948, vol. IV

Swift, Sir Brian Herbert, 1893–1969, vol. VI

Swift, Herbert Walker, 1894–1960, vol. V

Swift, Michael Charles, 1921–1999, vol. X

Swift, Reginald Stanley, 1914–1993, vol. IX

Swift, Sir Rigby Philip Watson, 1874–1937, vol. III

Swifte, Sir Ernest Godwin, 1839–1927, vol. II

Swinburn, Maj.-Gen. Henry Robinson, 1897–1981, vol. VIII

Swinburne, A. J., 1846–1915, vol. I

Swinburne, Algernon Charles, 1837–1909, vol. I

Swinburne, Hon. George, 1861–1928, vol. II

Swinburne, Sir Hubert, 8th Bt, 1867–1934, vol. III

Swinburne, Hon. Ivan Archie, 1908–1994, vol. IX

Swinburne, Sir James, 9th Bt, 1858–1958, vol. V

Swinburne, Sir John, 7th Bt, 1831–1914, vol. I

Swinburne, Nora; *see* Swinburne Johnson, Elinore.

Swinburne, Sir Spearman Charles, 10th Bt, 1893–1967, vol. VI

Swinburne, Lt-Col Thomas Robert, 1853–1921, vol. II

Swinburne-Hanham, John Castleman, 1860–1935, vol. III

Swinburne Johnson, Elinore, (Nora Swinburne), 1902–2000, vol. X

Swinburne-Ward, Col Henry Charles, 1879–1966, vol. VI

Swindell, Rev. Frank Guthrie, 1874–1975, vol. VII

Swindell, Rev. Canon Frederic Smith, *died* 1941, vol. IV

Swindells, Rev. Bernard Guy, 1887–1977, vol. VII

Swindlehurst, Joseph Eric, 1890–1972, vol. VII

Swindlehurst, Rt Rev. Owen Francis, 1928–1995, vol. IX

Swindley, Maj.-Gen. John Edward, 1831–1919, vol. II

Swiney, Brig.-Gen. Alexander John Henry, 1866–1933, vol. III

Swiney, Maj.-Gen. Sir (George Alexander) Neville, 1897–1970, vol. VI

Swiney, Maj.-Gen. John, 1832–1918, vol. II

Swiney, Maj.-Gen. Sir Neville; *see* Swiney, Maj.-Gen. Sir G. A. N.

Swinfen, 1st Baron, 1851–1919, vol. II

Swinfen, 2nd Baron, 1904–1977, vol. VII

Swing, Raymond, 1887–1968, vol. VI

Swingler, Bryan Edwin, 1924–1996, vol. X

Swingler, Rt Hon. Stephen Thomas, 1915–1969, vol. VI

Swinhoe, Lt-Gen. Frederick William, 1821–1907, vol. I

Swinley, Captain Casper Silas Balfour, 1898–1983, vol. VIII

Swinley, Maj.-Gen. George, 1842–1924, vol. II

Swinnerton, Frank Arthur, 1884–1982, vol. VIII

Swinnerton, Henry Hurd, 1875–1966, vol. VI

Swinnerton-Pilkington, Sir Thomas Edward Milborne-; *see* Pilkington.

Swinny, Shapland Hugh, 1857–1923, vol. II

Swinstead, Felix Gerald, 1880–1959, vol. V

Swinstead, Frank Hillyard, 1862–1937, vol. III

Swinstead, George Hillyard, 1860–1926, vol. II

Swinstead, Rev. John Howard, 1864–1924, vol. II

Swinton, 1st Earl of, 1884–1972, vol. VII

Swinton, Alan Archibald Campbell, 1863–1930, vol. III

Swinton, Brig. Alan Henry Campbell, 1896–1972, vol. VII

Swinton, Col Charles William, 1872–1935, vol. III

Swinton, Maj.-Gen. Sir Ernest Dunlop, 1868–1951, vol. V

Swinton, Lt-Col Francis Edward, 1866–1927, vol. II

Swinton, Captain George Herbert Tayler, 1852–1923, vol. II

Swinton, Captain George Sitwell Campbell, 1859–1937, vol. III

Swinton, John Edulf Blagrave, 1864–1941, vol. IV

Swinton, John Liulf Campbell, 1858–1920, vol. II

Swiny, Brig.-Gen. William Frederick, 1873–1950, vol. IV

Swire, John, 1861–1933, vol. III

Swire, John Kidston, 1893–1983, vol. VIII

Swire, Rev. S., 1866–1936, vol. III

Swire, William, 1862–1942, vol. IV

Swiss, Sir Rodney Geoffrey, 1904–1996, vol. X

Swithinbank, Bernard Winthrop, 1884–1958, vol. V

Swithinbank, Harold William, 1858–1928, vol. II

Swords, William Francis, 1873–1964, vol. VI

Swyer, Gerald Isaac Macdonald, 1917–1995, vol. IX

Swynnerton, Annie Louisa, *died* 1933, vol. III

Swynnerton, Charles Francis Massy, 1877–1938, vol. III

Swynnerton, Maj.-Gen. Charles Roger Alan, 1901–1973, vol. VII

Swynnerton, Sir Roger John Massy, 1911–2000, vol. X

Sycamore, Thomas Andrew Harding, 1907–1986, vol. VIII

Sydenham of Combe, 1st Baron, 1848–1933, vol. III

Sydenham, Engr-Rear-Adm. Ernest Dickerson, 1875–1952, vol. V

Sydenham, Engr Rear-Adm. Frederick William, 1871–1946, vol. IV

Sydnor, Charles Sackett, 1898–1954, vol. V

Syed, Sir Ali Imam, 1869–1932, vol. III

Syed Sirdar Ali Khan, Nawab, 1879–1942, vol. IV

Syer, William George, 1913–1988, vol. VIII

Syers, Sir Cecil George Lewis, 1903–1981, vol. VIII

Syers, Rev. Henry S., 1838–1915, vol. I

Syfret, Adm. Sir (Edward) Neville, 1889–1972, vol. VII

Syfret, Adm. Sir Neville; *see* Syfret, Adm. Sir E. N.

Sykes, Sir Alan John, 1st Bt (*cr* 1917), 1868–1950, vol. IV

Sykes, Vice-Adm. Alfred Charles, 1868–1933, vol. III

Sykes, Sir Arthur, 7th Bt (*cr* 1781), 1871–1934, vol. III
Sykes, Arthur Alkin, *died* 1939, vol. III
Sykes, Brig. Arthur Clifton, 1891–1967, vol. VI
Sykes, (Arthur) Frank (Seton), 1903–1980, vol. VII
Sykes, Lt-Col Arthur Patrick, 1906–1994, vol. IX
Sykes, Sir (Benjamin) Hugh, 2nd Bt (*cr* 1921), 1893–1974, vol. VII
Sykes, Bonar Hugh Charles, 1922–1998, vol. X
Sykes, Sir Charles, 1st Bt (*cr* 1921), 1867–1950, vol. IV
Sykes, Sir Charles, 1905–1982, vol. VIII
Sykes, Christopher, 1831–1898, vol. I
Sykes, Christopher Hugh, 1907–1986, vol. VIII
Sykes, Brig.-Gen. Clement Arthur, 1871–1938, vol. III
Sykes, Rev. Edward, 1862–1937, vol. III
Sykes, Ella Constance, *died* 1939, vol. III
Sykes, Ernest, 1870–1958, vol. V
Sykes, Sir Francis Godfrey, 9th Bt, 1907–1990, vol. VIII
Sykes, Frank; *see* Sykes, A. F. S.
Sykes, Rev. Canon Frank Morris, 1879–1939, vol. III
Sykes, Sir Frederic Henry, 5th Bt (*cr* 1781), 1826–1899, vol. I
Sykes, Rev. Sir Frederic John, 8th Bt (*cr* 1781), 1876–1956, vol. V
Sykes, Maj.-Gen. Rt Hon. Sir Frederick Hugh, 1877–1954, vol. V
Sykes, Sir Henry, 6th Bt (*cr* 1781), 1828–1916, vol. II
Sykes, Sir Hugh; *see* Sykes, Sir B. H.
Sykes, James, 1857–1929, vol. III
Sykes, John Bradbury, 1929–1993, vol. IX
Sykes, Sir John Charles Gabriel, 1869–1952, vol. V
Sykes, John Frederick Joseph, *died* 1913, vol. I
Sykes, Joseph, 1899–1967, vol. VI
Sykes, Keble Watson, 1921–1997, vol. X
Sykes, Lt-Col Sir Mark, 6th Bt (*cr* 1783), 1879–1919, vol. II
Sykes, Sir (Mark Tatton) Richard T., 7th Bt (*cr* 1783); *see* Tatton-Sykes.
Sykes, Very Rev. Norman, 1897–1961, vol. VI
Sykes, Brig.-Gen. Sir Percy Molesworth, 1867–1945, vol. IV
Sykes, Comdr Percy Stanley, 1878–1966, vol. VI
Sykes, Lt-Col Peter Thomas Wellesley, 1903–1975, vol. VII
Sykes, Reginald James, 1869–1940, vol. III
Sykes, Sir Richard Adam, 1920–1979, vol. VII
Sykes, Rev. Simon Joseph, 1867–1941, vol. IV
Sykes, Sir Tatton, 5th Bt (*cr* 1783), 1826–1913, vol. I
Sykes, Air Vice-Marshal William, 1920–1991, vol. IX
Sykes, Lt-Col William Ainley, 1857–1940, vol. III
Sykes, Sir William Edmund, 1884–1961, vol. VI
Sykes, William Stanley, 1894–1961, vol. VI
Sylva, Carmen, 1843–1916, vol. II
Sylvaine, Vernon, 1897–1957, vol. V
Sylvester, Albert James, 1889–1989, vol. VIII
Sylvester, Sir (Arthur) Edgar, 1891–1969, vol. VI
Sylvester, Sir Edgar; *see* Sylvester, Sir A. E.
Sylvester, George Harold, 1907–1994, vol. IX

Sylvester, George Oscar, 1898–1961, vol. VI
Sylvester, Asst Surgeon Henry Thomas, 1831–1920, vol. II
Sylvester, James Joseph, 1814–1897, vol. I
Sylvester, Rev. Samuel Augustus Kirwan, 1852–1928, vol. II
Sylvester-Bradley, Peter Colley, 1913–1978, vol. VII
Sym, John David, 1855–1931, vol. III
Sym, Maj.-Gen. Sir John Munro, 1839–1919, vol. II
Sym, William George, 1864–1938, vol. III
Syme, Sir Colin York, 1903–1986, vol. VIII
Syme, David, 1827–1908, vol. I
Syme, Sir Geoffrey, 1873–1942, vol. IV
Syme, Sir George Adlington, 1859–1929, vol. III
Syme, James, 1930–1999, vol. X
Syme, Sir Ronald, 1903–1989, vol. VIII
Symes, Sir Edward Spence, 1852–1901, vol. I
Symes, Lt-Col Sir (George) Stewart, 1882–1962, vol. VI
Symes, Maj.-Gen. George William, 1896–1980, vol. VII
Symes, Lt-Col Gustavus Phelps, 1857–1938, vol. III
Symes, Rev. John Elliotson, 1847–1921, vol. II
Symes, John Odery, 1867–1951, vol. V
Symes, Sir Robert Henry, 1837–1908, vol. I
Symes, Rev. Ronald, 1870–1935, vol. III
Symes, Lt-Col Sir Stewart; *see* Symes, Lt-Col Sir G. S.
Symes-Thompson, Edmund, 1837–1906, vol. I
Symes-Thompson, Henry Edmund, *died* 1952, vol. V
Symington, David, 1904–1984, vol. VIII
Symington, Herbert James, 1881–1965, vol. VI
Symington, John Alexander, 1887–1961, vol. VI
Symington, Johnson, 1851–1924, vol. II
Symington, Stuart; *see* Symington, W. S.
Symington, (William) Stuart, 1901–1988, vol. VIII
Symmers, W. St Clair, 1863–1937, vol. III
Symmers, William St Clair, 1917–2000, vol. X
Symmons, Israel Alexander, 1862–1923, vol. II
Symon, Sir Alexander Colin Burlington, 1902–1974, vol. VII
Symon, Rev. Dudley James, 1887–1961, vol. VI
Symon, Col Frank, 1879–1956, vol. V
Symon, Harold, 1896–1971, vol. VII
Symon, Jocelyn, (Mrs David Symon); *see* Moore, Miss J. A. M.
Symon, Hon. Sir Josiah Henry, 1846–1934, vol. III
Symon, Lt-Col Walter Conover, 1874–1949, vol. IV
Symonds, Sir Alfred Percival, *died* 1929, vol. III
Symonds, (Arthur) Leslie, 1910–1960, vol. V
Symonds, Sir Aubrey Vere, 1874–1931, vol. III
Symonds, Sir Charles Putnam, 1890–1978, vol. VII
Symonds, Sir Charters James, 1852–1932, vol. III
Symonds, Captain Frederick Cleave Loder-, 1846–1923, vol. II
Symonds, Vice-Adm. Frederick Parland Loder-, 1876–1952, vol. V
Symonds, Rev. Henry Herbert, 1885–1958, vol. V
Symonds, Joseph Bede, 1900–1985, vol. VIII
Symonds, Leslie; *see* Symonds, A. L.
Symonds, Robert Wemyss, 1889–1958, vol. V
Symonds, Ronald Charters, 1916–1997, vol. X
Symonds, Rev. William, 1832–1919, vol. II
Symonds-Tayler, Adm. Sir Richard Victor, 1897–1971, vol. VII

Symonette, Hon. Sir Roland Theodore, 1898–1980, vol. VII
Symons, Brig.-Gen. Adolphe, 1872–1954, vol. V
Symons, Albert James Alroy, 1900–1941, vol. IV
Symons, Arthur, 1865–1945, vol. IV
Symons, Col Charles Bertie Owen, 1874–1948, vol. IV
Symons, Rev. Charles Douglas, 1885–1949, vol. IV
Symons, Ernest Vize, 1913–1990, vol. VIII
Symons, Lt-Col Frank Albert, 1869–1917, vol. II
Symons, Lt-Col George Algernon James S.; see Soltau-Symons.
Symons, George James, 1838–1900, vol. I
Symons, George William Culme S.; see Soltau-Symons.
Symons, Maj.-Gen. Sir Henry; see Symons, Maj.-Gen. Sir T. H.
Symons, Hubert Wallace, 1890–1973, vol. VII
Symons, Julian Gustave, 1912–1994, vol. IX
Symons, Noel Victor Housman, 1894–1986, vol. VIII
Symons, Patrick Stewart, 1925–1993, vol. IX
Symons, Sir Robert F.; see Fox-Symons.
Symons, Ronald Stuart, 1904–1977, vol. VII
Symons, Maj.-Gen. Sir (Thomas) Henry, 1872–1948, vol. IV
Symons, Captain Thomas Raymond, 1866–1922, vol. II
Symons-Jeune, John Frederic; see Jeune.
Sympson, Edward Mansel, 1860–1922, vol. II
Synge, Sir Francis Robert Millington, 6th Bt, 1851–1924, vol. II
Synge, John Lighton, 1897–1995, vol. IX
Synge, John Millington, 1871–1909, vol. I

Synge, Major Mark, 1871–1921, vol. II
Synge, Richard Laurence Millington, 1914–1994, vol. IX
Synge, Sir Robert Follett, 1853–1920, vol. II
Synge, Sir Robert Millington, 7th Bt, 1877–1942, vol. IV
Synge, Victor Millington, 1893–1976, vol. VII
Synge-Hutchinson, Sir Edward; see Hutchinson, Sir E. S.
Synnot, Maj.-Gen. Arthur FitzRoy H.; see Hart-Synnot.
Synnot, Brig.-Gen. Arthur Henry Seton H.; see Hart-Synnot.
Synnot, Ronald Victor Okes H.; see Hart-Synnot.
Synnott, Nicholas Joseph, 1856–1920, vol. II
Synnott, Pierce Nicholas Netterville, 1904–1982, vol. VIII
Synnott, Bt Lt-Col Wilfrid Thomas, 1877–1941, vol. IV
Syrett, Herbert Sutton, died 1959, vol. V
Syrett, Netta, died 1943, vol. IV
Sysonby, 1st Baron, 1867–1935, vol. III
Sysonby, 2nd Baron, 1903–1956, vol. V
Sythes, Percy Arthur, 1915–1999, vol. X
Szarvasy, Frederick Alexander, died 1948, vol. IV
Szczepanski, Maj.-Gen. Henry Charles Antony, 1841–1923, vol. II
Szemerényi, Oswald John Louis, 1913–1996, vol. X
Szent-Györgyi, Albert, 1893–1986, vol. VIII
Szeryng, Henryk, 1918–1988, vol. VIII
Szigeti, Joseph, 1892–1973, vol. VII
Szlumper, Alfred Weeks, 1858–1934, vol. III
Szlumper, Gilbert Savil, 1884–1969, vol. VI
Szlumper, Sir James Weeks, 1834–1926, vol. II

T

Taaffe, George Joseph, 1866–1923, vol. II
Tabor, James, 1869–1938, vol. III
Tabor, Margaret Emma, died 1954, vol. V
Tabor, Richard John, died 1958, vol. V
Tabouis, Geneviève, 1892–1985, vol. VIII
Tabrar, Joseph, 1857–1931, vol. III
Tabuteau, Maj.-Gen. George Grant, 1881–1940, vol. III
Tachie-Menson, Sir Charles William, 1889–1962, vol. VI
Tacon, Sir Thomas Henry, 1838–1922, vol. II
Tadema, Miss Anna A.; see Alma-Tadema.
Tadema, Laura Theresa A.; see Alma-Tadema.
Tadema, Miss Laurence A.; see Alma-Tadema.
Tadema, Sir Lawrence A.; see Alma-Tadema.
Tafawa Balewa, Alhaji Rt Hon. Sir Abubakar, 1912–1966, vol. VI
Taflia, 4th Marquis of, 1837–1921, vol. II
Taft, Charles Phelps, 1897–1983, vol. VIII
Taft, Lorado, 1860–1936, vol. III
Taft, Robert Alphonso, 1889–1953, vol. V
Taft, William Howard, 1857–1930, vol. III
Tagart, Edward Samuel Bourn, 1877–1956, vol. V
Tagart, Maj.-Gen. Sir Harold Arthur Lewis, 1870–1930, vol. III

Tagg, Sir Arundel; see Arundel, Sir A. T.
Taggart, Sir James, 1849–1929, vol. III
Taggart, Wing Comdr John S.; see Scott-Taggart.
Tagore, Abanindra Nath, 1871–1951, vol. V
Tagone, Maharaja Bahadur Sir Joteendro Mohun, 1831–1908, vol. I
Tagone, Hon. Majharaja Bahadur Sir Prodyot Coomar, 1873–1942, vol. IV
Tagore, Sir Rabindranath, 1861–1941, vol. IV
Tagore, Raja Sir Sourindro Mohun, 1840–1914, vol. I
Tahourdin, Peter Anthony Ivan, 1920–1983, vol. VIII
Taillon, Hon. Sir Louis Olivier, 1840–1923, vol. II
Tailyour, Gen. Sir Norman Hastings, 1914–1979, vol. VII
Tailyour, Col Thomas Francis Bruce R.; see Renny-Tailyour.
Tainsh, Lt-Col Joseph Ramsay, 1874–1954, vol. V
Tait, Andrew Wilson, 1876–1930, vol. III
Tait, Rev. Arthur James, 1872–1944, vol. IV
Tait, Adm. Sir Campbell; see Tait, Adm. Sir W. E. C.
Tait, Ven. Donald, 1862–1932, vol. III
Tait, Sir Frank Samuel, 1883–1965, vol. VI

Tait, George Hope, 1861–1943, vol. IV
Tait, Hugh Nimmo, 1888–1960, vol. V
Tait, James, 1863–1944, vol. IV
Tait, Sir James Blair, 1890–1985, vol. VIII
Tait, Sir James Sharp, 1912–1998, vol. X
Tait, John, 1878–1944, vol. IV
Tait, Sir John, *died* 1972, vol. VII
Tait, Lt-Col John Spottiswood, 1875–1951, vol. V
Tait, Lawson, 1845–1899, vol. I
Tait, Sir Melbourne McTaggart, 1842–1917, vol. II
Tait, Sir Peter, 1915–1996, vol. X
Tait, Peter Guthrie, 1831–1901, vol. I
Tait, Sir Thomas, 1864–1940, vol. III (A), vol. IV
Tait, Thomas Smith, 1882–1954, vol. V
Tait, Air Vice-Marshal Sir Victor Hubert,
    1892–1988, vol. VIII
Tait, Adm. Sir (William Eric) Campbell,
    1886–1946, vol. IV
Taite, Charles Davis, 1872–1948, vol. IV
Taitt, Rt Rev. Francis Marion, 1862–1943, vol. IV
Takamine, Jokichi, 1854–1923, vol. II
Talbot de Malahide, 5th Baron, 1846–1921, vol. II
Talbot de Malahide, 6th Baron, 1874–1948, vol. IV
Talbot de Malahide, 7th Baron, 1912–1973, vol. VII
Talbot of Malahide, 8th Baron, 1897–1975, vol. VII
Talbot of Malahide, 9th Baron, 1899–1987, vol. VIII
Talbot, Lt-Col Sir Adelbert Cecil, 1845–1920,
    vol. II
Talbot, Very Rev. Albert Edward, 1877–1936,
    vol. III
Talbot, Vice-Adm. Sir (Arthur Allison) FitzRoy,
    1909–1998, vol. X
Talbot, Vice-Adm. Arthur George, 1892–1960,
    vol. V
Talbot, Rev. Arthur Henry, 1855–1927, vol. II
Talbot, Benjamin, 1864–1947, vol. IV
Talbot, Bertram, 1865–1936, vol. III
Talbot, Bridget Elizabeth, *died* 1971, vol. VII
Talbot, Vice-Adm. Sir Cecil Ponsonby, 1884–1970,
    vol. VI
Talbot, Charles Henry, 1842–1916, vol. II
Talbot, Maj.-Gen. Dennis Edmund Blaquière,
    1908–1994, vol. IX
Talbot, Rev. Edward Keble, 1877–1949, vol. IV
Talbot, Rt Rev. Edward Stuart, 1844–1934, vol. III
Talbot, Emily Charlotte, *died* 1918, vol. II
Talbot, Rt Rev. Ethebert, 1848–1928, vol. II
Talbot, Vice-Adm. Sir FitzRoy, *see* Talbot,
    Vice-Adm. Sir A. A. F.
Talbot, Frank Heyworth, 1895–1990, vol. VIII
Talbot, George, 1823–1914, vol. I
Talbot, Lt-Col George James Francis, 1857–1941,
    vol. IV
Talbot, Rt Hon. Sir George John, 1861–1938,
    vol. III
Talbot, Sir Gerald Francis, 1881–1945, vol. IV
Talbot, Godfrey Walker, 1908–2000, vol. X
Talbot, Gustavus Arthur, 1848–1920, vol. II
Talbot, Howard, 1865–1928, vol. II
Talbot, John Ellis, 1906–1967, vol. VI
Talbot, Rt Hon. John Gilbert, 1835–1910, vol. I
Talbot, Matilda Theresa, 1871–1958, vol. V
Talbot, Very Rev. Maurice John, 1912–1999, vol. X
Talbot, Dame Meriel Lucy, 1866–1956, vol. V
Talbot, Michael Chetwynd-; *see* Talbot, R. M. A. C.

Talbot, Col Hon. Milo George, 1854–1931, vol. III
Talbot, Rt Rev. Neville Stuart, *died* 1943, vol. IV
Talbot, Lt-Gen. Sir Norman Graham Guy,
    1914–1979, vol. VII
Talbot, Hon. Sir Patrick Wellington, 1817–1898,
    vol. I
Talbot, Percy Amaury, 1877–1945, vol. IV
Talbot, Maj.-Gen. Hon. Sir Reginald Arthur James,
    1841–1929, vol. III
Talbot, Comdr Reginald George Chetwynd,
    1881–1939, vol. III
Talbot, Hon. Reginald Gilbert Murray, 1849–1930,
    vol. III
Talbot, Very Rev. Reginald Thomas, 1862–1935,
    vol. III
Talbot, Richard Michael Arthur Chetwynd-,
    1911–1993, vol. IX
Talbot, Sir Samuel Thomas, *died* 1931, vol. III
Talbot, Thomas, *died* 1929, vol. III
Talbot, Thomas George, 1904–1992, vol. IX
Talbot, Walter Stanley, 1869–1935, vol. III
Talbot, Sir William Henry, 1831–1919, vol. II
Talbot, Sir William J., 1872–1947, vol. IV
Talbot, William John, 1859–1923, vol. II
Talbot Rice, David; *see* Rice.
Talfan Davies, Sir Alun; *see* Davies.
Tallack, Sir Hugh M.; *see* Mackay-Tallack.
Tallberg, Axel, 1860–1928, vol. II
Tallents, George William, 1856–1924, vol. II
Tallents, Philip Cubitt, 1886–1962, vol. VI
Tallents, Sir Stephen George, 1884–1958, vol. V
Tallerman, Kenneth Harry, 1894–1981, vol. VIII
Tallis, Sir George, 1869–1948, vol. IV
Tallis, Gillian Helen; *see* Mackay, G. H.
Talmage, Algernon, *died* 1939, vol. III
Tamagno, Francisco, 1851–1905, vol. I
Tame, William Charles, 1909–1995, vol. IX
Tamm, Igor Evgenievich, 1895–1971, vol. VII
Tamplin, Herbert Travers, 1853–1925, vol. II
Tan, Dato Sir Cheng-lock, 1883–1960, vol. V
Tancock, Lt-Col Alexander Charles, *died* 1966,
    vol. VI
Tancock, Rev. Charles Coverdale, 1851–1922,
    vol. II
Tancock, Col Osborne Kendall, 1866–1946, vol. IV
Tancock, Rev. Osborne William, 1839–1930,
    vol. III
Tancred, Vice-Adm. James Charles, 1864–1943,
    vol. IV
Tancred, Maj.-Gen. Thomas Angus, 1867–1944,
    vol. IV
Tancred, Sir Thomas Selby, 8th Bt, 1840–1910,
    vol. I
Tancred, Major Sir Thomas Selby L.; *see*
    Lawson-Tancred.
Tandy, Sir Arthur Harry, 1903–1964, vol. VI
Tandy, Brig. Sir Edward Aldborough, 1871–1950,
    vol. IV
Tandy, Brig.-Gen. Ernest Napper, 1879–1953,
    vol. V
Tandy, Jessica Alice, 1909–1994, vol. IX
Tandy, Col Maurice O'Connor, 1873–1942, vol. IV
Tang, Sir Shiu-kin, 1901–1986, vol. VIII
Tangley, Baron (Life Peer); Edwin Savory Herbert,
    1899–1973, vol. VII

Tangney, Dame Dorothy Margaret, 1911–1985, vol. VIII
Tangye, Captain Sir Basil Richard Gilzean, 2nd Bt, 1895–1969, vol. VI
Tangye, Claude Edward, 1877–1952, vol. V
Tangye, Sir (Harold) Lincoln, 1st Bt, 1866–1935, vol. III
Tangye, Sir Lincoln; *see* Tangye, Sir H. L.
Tangye, Sir Richard, 1833–1906, vol. I
Tangye, Lt-Col Richard Trevithick Gilbertstone, 1875–1944, vol. IV
Tankerville, 6th Earl of, 1810–1899, vol. I
Tankerville, 7th Earl of, 1852–1931, vol. III
Tankerville, 8th Earl of, 1897–1971, vol. VII
Tankerville, 9th Earl of, 1921–1980, vol. VII
Tann, Florence Mary, 1892–1981, vol. VIII
Tanner, Archibald Gerard, 1895–1937, vol. III
Tanner, Bernice Alture, 1917–1991, vol. IX
Tanner, Charles Elliott, 1857–1946, vol. IV
Tanner, Sir Edgar Stephen, 1914–1979, vol. VII
Tanner, Maj.-Gen. Edward, 1839–1916, vol. II
Tanner, Dame Emmeline Mary, 1876–1955, vol. V
Tanner, Lt-Col Frederick Courtney, 1879–1965, vol. VI
Tanner, Frederick John Shirley; *see* Tanner, Jack.
Tanner, Col Sir Gilbert, 1877–1953, vol. V
Tanner, Sir Henry, 1849–1935, vol. III
Tanner, Henry, 1876–1947, vol. IV
Tanner, Henry William Lloyd, 1851–1915, vol. I
Tanner, Herbert George, 1882–1974, vol. VII
Tanner, Jack, (Frederick John Shirley Tanner), 1889–1965, vol. VI
Tanner, Brig.-Gen. John Arthur, 1858–1917, vol. II
Tanner, John Arthur Charles, 1854–1928, vol. II
Tanner, John Edward, 1834–1906, vol. I
Tanner, Joseph Robson, 1860–1931, vol. III
Tanner, Lawrence Edward, 1890–1979, vol. VII
Tanner, Norman Cecil, 1906–1982, vol. VIII
Tanner, Lt-Gen. Sir Oriel Viveash, 1832–1911, vol. I
Tanner, Paul Antony, (Tony), 1935–1998, vol. X
Tanner, Lt-Col Richard Morrison, 1871–1936, vol. III
Tanner, Tony; *see* Tanner, P. A.
Tanner, William Edward, 1889–1951, vol. V
Tanner, Maj.-Gen. William Ernest Collins, 1875–1943, vol. IV
Tanqueray, Rev. Truman, 1888–1960, vol. V
Tanquerey, F. J., *died* 1942, vol. IV
Tansley, Sir Arthur George, 1871–1955, vol. V
Tansley, Sir Eric Crawford, 1901–1992, vol. IX
Tapley, Harold Livingstone, 1875–1932, vol. III
Tapley, Maj.-Gen. James John Bonifant, 1877–1958, vol. V
Tapley-Soper, Harry Tapley; *see* Soper.
Taplin, Walter, 1910–1986, vol. VIII
Tapp, Maj.-Gen. Sir Nigel Prior Hanson, 1904–1991, vol. IX
Tapp, Norman Charles, 1925–1977, vol. VII
Tapp, Percy John Rutty, 1886–1964, vol. VI
Tapper, Sir Walter John, 1861–1935, vol. III
Tapper-Jones, Sydney, 1904–1991, vol. IX
Tapps-Gervis-Meyrick, Sir George Augustus Eliott; *see* Meyrick.

Tapps-Gervis-Meyrick, Major Sir George Llewelyn; *see* Meyrick.
Tarbat, Sir John Allan, 1891–1977, vol. VII
Tarbet, Lt-Col Alexander Francis, 1860–1939, vol. III
Tarbet, Captain William Godfrey, 1878–1911, vol. I
Tarbolton, Harold Ogle, *died* 1947, vol. IV
Tardieu, André Pierre Gabriel Amedée, 1876–1945, vol. IV
Tardrew, Rev. Canon Thomas Hedley, 1889–1966, vol. VI
Targett, James Henry, *died* 1913, vol. I
Targett, Sir Robert William, 1891–1965, vol. VI
Tarkington, Booth, 1869–1946, vol. IV
Tarleton, Captain Alfred Henry, 1862–1921, vol. II
Tarleton, Francis Alexander, 1841–1920, vol. II
Tarn, Sir William Woodthorpe, 1869–1957, vol. V
Tarrant, Dorothy, 1885–1973, vol. VII
Tarrant, Surg.-Gen. Thomas, 1830–1909, vol. I
Tarrant, William Charles, 1881–1941, vol. IV
Tarrant, Rev. William George, 1853–1928, vol. II
Tarring, Sir Charles James, 1845–1923, vol. II
Tarry, Frederick Thomas, 1896–1976, vol. VII
Tarte, Hon. Joseph Israel, 1848–1907, vol. I
Tarver, Maj.-Gen. Alexander Leigh, 1871–1941, vol. IV
Tarver, Maj.-Gen. Charles Herbert, 1908–1982, vol. VIII
Tarver, J. C., *died* 1926, vol. II
Tarver, Maj.-Gen. William Knapp, 1872–1952, vol. V
Tasadduk Rasul Khan, Raja Sir, *died* 1928, vol. II
Taschereau, His Eminence Cardinal Elzéar Alexander, 1820–1898, vol. I
Taschereau, Rt Hon. Sir Henri Elzéar, 1836–1911, vol. I
Taschereau, Sir Henri Thomas, 1841–1909, vol. I
Taschereau, Hon. Louis Alexandre, 1867–1952, vol. V
Taschereau, Rt Hon. Robert, 1896–1970, vol. VI
Tasker, Antony Greaves, 1916–1990, vol. VIII
Tasker, Rev. Canon Derek Morris Phipps, 1916–1978, vol. VII
Tasker, Rev. John Greenwood, 1853–1936, vol. III
Tasker, Rev. Randolph Vincent Greenwood, 1895–1976, vol. VII
Tasker, Major Sir Robert Inigo, 1868–1959, vol. V
Tasker, Sir Theodore James, 1884–1981, vol. VIII
Tasma; *see* Couvreur, Jessie.
Tassell, Alick James, 1865–1932, vol. III
Tata, Sir Dorabji Jamsetji, 1859–1932, vol. III
Tata, Jamsetjee Nasarwanji, 1839–1904, vol. I
Tata, Sir Ratanji Jamsetji, 1871–1918, vol. II
Tatchell, Sydney Joseph, 1887–1965, vol. VI
Tate, Col Alan Edmondson, 1859–1934, vol. III
Tate, Adm. Alban Giffard, 1853–1930, vol. III
Tate, Lt-Col Arthur Wignall, 1888–1939, vol. III
Tate, Charles James Gerrard, 1880–1951, vol. V
Tate, D'Arcy, 1866–1935, vol. III
Tate, Ellalice; *see* Hibbert, Eleanor.
Tate, Francis Herbert, 1913–1998, vol. X
Tate, Sir Ernest William, 3rd Bt, 1867–1939, vol. III
Tate, Frank, 1863–1939, vol. III
Tate, George Vernon, 1890–1955, vol. V

Tate, Col Gerard William, 1866–1937, vol. III
Tate, Maj.-Gen. Godfrey, 1873–1944, vol. IV
Tate, Harry, *died* 1940, vol. III
Tate, Sir Henry, 1st Bt, 1819–1899, vol. I
Tate, Lt-Col Sir Henry, 4th Bt, 1902–1994, vol. IX
Tate, James William, 1875–1922, vol. II
Tate, Jonathan, 1899–1958, vol. V
Tate, Mavis Constance, *died* 1947, vol. IV
Tate, Phyllis Margaret Duncan, (Mrs Alan Frank), 1911–1987, vol. VIII
Tate, Col Robert Ward, 1864–1938, vol. III
Tate, Major Sir Robert William, 1872–1952, vol. V
Tate, Thomas Bailey, 1882–1957, vol. V
Tate, Walter William Hunt, 1865–1916, vol. II
Tate, Sir William Henry, 2nd Bt, 1842–1921, vol. II
Tatham, Brig.-Gen. Arthur Glanville, 1856–1933, vol. III
Tatham, Rev. Edward Henry Ralph, 1857–1938, vol. III
Tatham, Lt-Col Hon. Frederic Spence, 1865–1934, vol. III
Tati, Jacques, (Jacques Tatischeff), 1908–1982, vol. VIII
Tatischeff, Jacques; *see* Tati, J.
Tatlock, Robert Rattray, 1889–1954, vol. V
Tatlow, Frank, 1861–1934, vol. III
Tatlow, Joseph, 1851–1929, vol. III
Tatlow, Hon. Robert Garnett, 185–1910, vol. I
Tatlow, Rev. Canon Tissington, 1876–1957, vol. V
Tattersall, Creassey Edward Cecil, 1877–1957, vol. V
Tattersall, Lt-Col Edmund Harry, 1897–1968, vol. VI
Tattersall, John Lincoln, 1865–1942, vol. IV
Tattersall, Rev. Thomas Newell, 1879–1943, vol. IV
Tattersall, William, *died* 1914, vol. I
Tattersall, William Boothman, 1873–1943, vol. IV
Tatton Brown, William Eden, 1910–1997, vol. X
Tatton-Sykes, Sir (Mark Tatton) Richard, 7th Bt, 1905–1978, vol. VII
Tatum, E(dward) L(awrie), 1909–1975, vol. VII
Tauber, Richard, 1892–1948, vol. IV
Taubman, Frank Mowbray, 1868–1946, vol. IV
Taukalo, Sir (David) Dawea, 1920–1995, vol. IX
Taukalo, Sir Dawea; *see* Taukalo, Sir David D.
Taunton, Agnes, 1877–1941, vol. IV
Taunton, Doidge Estcourt, 1902–1991, vol. IX
Taunton, Sir Ivon Hope, 1890–1957, vol. V
Taussig, Francis William, 1859–1940, vol. III (A), vol. IV
Taveggia, Rt Rev. Santino, 1855–1928, vol. II, vol. III
Taverner, Hon. Sir John William, 1852–1923, vol. II
Taverner, William Burgoyne, 1879–1958, vol. V
Taw Sein Ko, 1864–1930, vol. III
Tawney, Charles Henry, 1837–1922, vol. II
Tawney, Richard Henry, 1880–1962, vol. VI
Tawse, Col Harry Storey, 1889–1959, vol. V
Tay, Waren, *died* 1927, vol. II
Tayler, Alan Breach, 1931–1995, vol. IX
Tayler, Albert Chevallier, 1862–1925, vol. II
Tayler, Lt-Col Francis Lionel, 1883–1933, vol. III
Tayler, Maj.-Gen. John Charles, 1834–1913, vol. I

Tayler, Adm. Sir Richard Victor S.; *see* Symonds-Tayler.
Tayler, Roger John, 1929–1997, vol. X
Taylor, Baron (Life Peer); Stephen James Lake Taylor, 1910–1988, vol. VIII
Taylor of Gosforth, Baron (Life Peer); Peter Murray Taylor, 1930–1997, vol. X
Taylor of Hadfield, Baron (Life Peer); Francis Taylor, 1905–1995, vol. IX
Taylor of Mansfield, Baron (Life Peer); Harry Bernard Taylor, 1895–1991, vol. IX
Taylor, Lady; (May Doris) Charity Taylor, 1914–1998, vol. X
Taylor, Alan Carey, 1905–1975, vol. VII
Taylor, Alan John Percivale, 1906–1990, vol. VIII
Taylor, Rt Hon. Sir Alan Russell, 1901–1969, vol. VI (AII)
Taylor, Albert Booth, 1896–1971, vol. VII
Taylor, Alec C.; *see* Clifton-Taylor.
Taylor, Sir Alexander, 1826–1912, vol. I
Taylor, Alexander, 1872–1917, vol. II
Taylor, Alexander Burt, 1904–1972, vol. VII
Taylor, Sir Alexander Thomson, 1873–1953, vol. V
Taylor, Alfred Edward, 1869–1945, vol. IV
Taylor, Rear-Adm. Alfred Hugh, 1886–1972, vol. VII
Taylor, (Alfred) Maurice, 1903–1979, vol. VII
Taylor, Sir Allen, 1864–1940, vol. III
Taylor, Sir Alvin B.; *see* Burton-Taylor.
Taylor, Sir Andrew Thomas, 1850–1937, vol. III
Taylor, Brig.-Gen. Arthur Henry Mendle, 1870–1934, vol. III
Taylor, Lt-Col Arthur James, 1876–1949, vol. IV (A), vol. V
Taylor, Arthur John, 1919–1992, vol. IX
Taylor, Arthur John Ernest, 1913–1979, vol. VII
Taylor, Captain Arthur Lombe, 1882–1968, vol. VI
Taylor, Captain Arthur Trevelyan, 1864–1956, vol. V
Taylor, Arthur William Charles, 1913–1992, vol. IX
Taylor, Lt-Col Arthur William Neufville, 1863–1930, vol. III
Taylor, Arthur Wood, 1909–1987, vol. VIII
Taylor, Austin, *died* 1955, vol. V
Taylor, Col Bertie Harry Waters, *died* 1946, vol. IV
Taylor, Rear-Adm. Bertram Wilfrid, 1906–1970, vol. VI
Taylor, Maj.-Gen. Sir Brian; *see* Taylor, Maj.-Gen. Sir G. B. O.
Taylor, Brian Hyde, 1931–2000, vol. X
Taylor, Charity; *see* Taylor, Lady.
Taylor, Rev. Charles, 1840–1908, vol. I
Taylor, Charles Allison, 1885–1965, vol. VI
Taylor, Charles Bell, 1829–1909, vol. I
Taylor, Charles Edward, 1853–1924, vol. II
Taylor, Lt-Col Charles Newton, 1866–1949, vol. IV
Taylor, Rev. Charles Reeve, 1845–1931, vol. III
Taylor, Sir Charles Stuart, 1910–1989, vol. VIII
Taylor, Charles William, 1878–1960, vol. V
Taylor, Very Rev. Charles William Gray, 1879–1950, vol. IV
Taylor, Christopher Albert, 1915–1981, vol. VIII
Taylor, Claude, 1877–1957, vol. V
Taylor, Rev. Decimus A. G., 1871–1933, vol. III
Taylor, Derek, 1930–2000, vol. X

Taylor, Desmond Christopher S.; *see* Shawe-Taylor.
Taylor, Desmond Maxwell, 1928–1978, vol. VII
Taylor, Dorothy Daisy C.; *see* Cottington-Taylor.
Taylor, Dorothy Mary, 1902–1983, vol. VIII
Taylor, Douglas, 1915–1971, vol. VII
Taylor, Col Edward, 1860–1931, vol. III
Taylor, Ven. Edward, 1921–1982, vol. VIII
Taylor, Lt-Col Edward Harrison Clough, 1849–1921, vol. II
Taylor, Edward Henry, *died* 1922, vol. II
Taylor, Edward Plunket, 1901–1989, vol. VIII
Taylor, Edward R., 1838–1911, vol. I
Taylor, (Edward) Wilfred, 1891–1980, vol. VII
Taylor, Edwin, 1881–1972, vol. VII
Taylor, Edwin, 1905–1973, vol. VII
Taylor, Elizabeth, (Mrs J. W. K. Taylor), 1912–1975, vol. VII
Taylor, Eric Scollick, 1918–1995, vol. IX
Taylor, Sir Eric Stuart, 2nd Bt (*cr* 1917), 1889–1977, vol. VII
Taylor, Eric W., 1909–1999, vol. X
Taylor, Vice-Adm. Sir Ernest Augustus, 1876–1971, vol. VII
Taylor, Ernest Edward, 1897–1974, vol. VII
Taylor, Col Ernest Fitzwilliam, 1867–1944, vol. IV
Taylor, Ernest Richard, 1910–1993, vol. IX
Taylor, Lt-Col Eustace Trevor Neave, 1894–1971, vol. VII
Taylor, Eva Germaine Rimington, *died* 1966, vol. VI
Taylor, Fanny Isabel, *died* 1947, vol. IV
Taylor, Lt-Col Hon. Fawcett Gowler, 1878–1940, vol. III (A), vol. IV
Taylor, Francis, 1845–1915, vol. I
Taylor, Sir Francis Edward W.; *see* Worsley-Taylor.
Taylor, Francis Henry, 1903–1957, vol. V
Taylor, Rt Rev. Francis John, 1912–1971, vol. VII
Taylor, Francis Maurice Gustavus D. P.; *see* Du-Plat-Taylor.
Taylor, Col Francis Pitt Stewart, 1869–1924, vol. II
Taylor, Frank, 1915–1999, vol. X
Taylor, Frank, 1910–2000, vol. X
Taylor, Frank Alwyn, 1890–1960, vol. V
Taylor, Frank Herbert Graham, 1890–1971, vol. VII
Taylor, F(rank) Sherwood, 1897–1956, vol. V
Taylor, Franklin, 1843–1919, vol. II
Taylor, Fred, 1875–1963, vol. VI
Taylor, Ven. Frederic Norman, 1871–1960, vol. V
Taylor, Frederic Richard, 1876–1929, vol. III
Taylor, Sir Frederick, 1st Bt (*cr* 1917), 1847–1920, vol. II
Taylor, Rt Rev. Frederick Adrian, 1892–1961, vol. VI
Taylor, Sir Frederick W.; *see* Williams-Taylor.
Taylor, Frederick William, 1909–1989, vol. VIII
Taylor, Sir Geoffrey Ingram, 1886–1975, vol. VII
Taylor, Hon. George, 1840–1919, vol. II
Taylor, Sir George, 1904–1993, vol. IX
Taylor, Maj.-Gen. Sir (George) Brian (Ogilvie), *died* 1973, vol. VII
Taylor, George Francis, 1903–1979, vol. VII
Taylor, Sir George L.; *see* Langley-Taylor.
Taylor, George Paul, 1860–1917, vol. II
Taylor, George Reginald Thomas, 1876–1965, vol. VI

Taylor, George Simon Arthur W.; *see* Watson-Taylor.
Taylor, George William, 1864–1929, vol. III
Taylor, Rear-Adm. George William, 1883–1964, vol. VI
Taylor, Brig.-Gen. Gerald Kyffin-, 1863–1949, vol. IV
Taylor, Gerard William, 1920–1995, vol. IX
Taylor, Dame Gladys, 1890–1950, vol. IV
Taylor, Sir Gordon G.; *see* Gordon-Taylor.
Taylor, Gordon Rattray, 1911–1981, vol. VIII
Taylor, Greville Laughton, 1902–1993, vol. IX
Taylor, Griffith; *see* Taylor, T. G.
Taylor, Col H. Brooke, 1855–1923, vol. II
Taylor, H. Stanley, 1871–1959, vol. V
Taylor, Major Harold Blake, 1862–1936, vol. III
Taylor, Harold George K.; *see* Kirwan-Taylor.
Taylor, Harold Joseph, 1904–1993, vol. IX
Taylor, Harold McCarter, 1907–1995, vol. IX
Taylor, Rev. Harold Milman Strickland, 1890–1966, vol. VI
Taylor, Harold Victor, *died* 1965, vol. VI
Taylor, Harry Ashworth, *died* 1907, vol. I
Taylor, Harry Mead, 1872–1928, vol. II
Taylor, Harry Willoughby O.; *see* Oddin-Taylor.
Taylor, Col Haydon D'Aubrey Potenger, 1860–1939, vol. III
Taylor, Henry Archibald, *died* 1980, vol. VII
Taylor, Henry G.; *see* Gawan Taylor.
Taylor, Rev. Henry James, *died* 1945, vol. IV
Taylor, Henry Martyn, 1842–1927, vol. II
Taylor, Sir Henry Milton, 1903–1994, vol. IX
Taylor, Henry Osborn, 1856–1941, vol. IV
Taylor, Sir Henry Wilson W.; *see* Worsley-Taylor.
Taylor, Herbert, 1885–1970, vol. VI (AII)
Taylor, Captain Herbert Bardsley, 1884–1947, vol. IV
Taylor, Col Herbert James Cox-, 1872–1936, vol. III
Taylor, Sir Herbert John, 1865–1943, vol. IV
Taylor, Hobart Chatfield C.; *see* Chatfield-Taylor.
Taylor, Horace, 1881–1934, vol. III
Taylor, Lt-Col Hugh Neufville, 1859–1931, vol. III
Taylor, Sir Hugh Stott, 1890–1974, vol. VII
Taylor, Rev. Isaac, 1829–1901, vol. I
Taylor, Col Jack H.; *see* Hulme Taylor.
Taylor, Rev. Jackson, *died* 1929, vol. III
Taylor, James, 1871–1944, vol. IV
Taylor, James, 1859–1946, vol. IV
Taylor, Sir James, 1902–1994, vol. IX
Taylor, James Benjamin, 1860–1944, vol. IV
Taylor, Sir James Braid, 1891–1943, vol. IV
Taylor, Air Vice-Marshal James Clarke, 1910–1978, vol. VII
Taylor, James Haward, 1909–1968, vol. VI
Taylor, James Henry, 1861–1926, vol. II
Taylor, James Monroe, 1848–1916, vol. II
Taylor, Lt-Col Sir James W.; *see* Worsley-Taylor.
Taylor, Joe, 1906–1989, vol. VIII
Taylor, Sir John, 1833–1912, vol. I
Taylor, John, 1834–1922, vol. II
Taylor, John, 1857–1936, vol. III
Taylor, John, 1861–1945, vol. IV
Taylor, Maj.-Gen. Sir John, 1884–1959, vol. V
Taylor, John, 1902–1962, vol. VI

Taylor, Sir John, 1876–1971, vol. VII
Taylor, Brig. John Alexander Chisholm, 1891–1981, vol. VIII
Taylor, John Barrington, 1914–1993, vol. IX
Taylor, Rev. John Edward, 1899–1966, vol. VI
Taylor, Captain Sir John Godfrey W.; see Worsley-Taylor.
Taylor, John Gray, 1890–1944, vol. IV
Taylor, John Hugh, 1916–1985, vol. VIII
Taylor, John Idowu Conrad, 1917–1973, vol. VII
Taylor, Sir John James, 1859–1945, vol. IV
Taylor, Col John Lowther Du Plat, 1829–1904, vol. I
Taylor, John Norman, died 1945, vol. IV
Taylor, John Ralph Carlisle, 1902–1991, vol. IX
Taylor, Rt Rev. John Ralph Strickland, 1883–1961, vol. VI
Taylor, John T., 1840–1908, vol. I
Taylor, Sir John W.; see Wilson-Taylor.
Taylor, John William, 1851–1910, vol. I
Taylor, Sir John William, 1895–1974, vol. VII
Taylor, Mrs John William Kendell; see Taylor, Elizabeth.
Taylor, John William Ransom, 1922–1999, vol. X
Taylor, Joseph Charlton, 1913–1971, vol. VII
Taylor, Sir Joshua R.; see Ross-Taylor.
Taylor, Julian, 1889–1961, vol. VI
Taylor, Keith Henry, 1938–2000, vol. X
Taylor, Kenneth, 1923–1990, vol. VIII
Taylor, Kenneth John, 1929–1995, vol. IX
Taylor, Kenneth Roy E.; see Eldin-Taylor.
Taylor, Most Rev. Leo Hale, 1889–1965, vol. VI
Taylor, Leon Eric Manners, 1917–1995, vol. IX
Taylor, Leonard Campbell, 1874–1969, vol. VI
Taylor, Leonard Whitworth, 1880–1979, vol. VII
Taylor, Sir Lionel Goodenough, 1871–1963, vol. VI
Taylor, Lionel Robert Stewart, 1915–1972, vol. VII
Taylor, Luke, 1876–1916, vol. II
Taylor, Rev. Malcolm Campbell, died 1922, vol. II
Taylor, Gen. Sir Malcolm Cartwright C.; see Cartwright-Taylor.
Taylor, Air Vice-Marshal Malcolm Lincoln, 1893–1970, vol. VI
Taylor, Hon. Mrs Margaret Sophia, 1877–1962, vol. VI
Taylor, Margerie Venables, 1881–1963, vol. VI
Taylor, Mark Ronald, died 1942, vol. IV
Taylor, Martin, 1885–1981, vol. VIII
Taylor, Maurice; see Taylor, A. M.
Taylor, Gen. Sir Maurice Grove, 1881–1960, vol. V
Taylor, Gen. Maxwell Davenport, 1901–1987, vol. VIII
Taylor, Sir Michael Goodiff, 1929–1991, vol. IX
Taylor, Myron C., 1874–1959, vol. V
Taylor, Nicholas George Frederick, born 1917, vol. X (AI)
Taylor, Captain Sir Patrick Gordon, died 1966, vol. VI
Taylor, Peter, 1924–1999, vol. X
Taylor, Peter Athol, 1926–1976, vol. VII
Taylor, Peter John, 1929–1987, vol. VIII
Taylor, Col Philip Beauchamp, died 1939, vol. III
Taylor, Rear-Adm. Philip Cardwell, 1902–1965, vol. VI
Taylor, Rachel Annand, 1876–1960, vol. V

Taylor, Raymond Charles, 1926–1977, vol. VII
Taylor, Brig.-Gen. Reginald O'Bryen, 1872–1949, vol. IV
Taylor, Sir Reginald William, 1895–1971, vol. VII
Taylor, Brig.-Gen. Reynell Hamilton Baylay, 1858–1942, vol. IV
Taylor, Rev. Richard, died 1922, vol. II
Taylor, Sir Richard Chambré Hayes, 1819–1904, vol. I
Taylor, Sir Richard Laurence S.; see Stuart Taylor.
Taylor, Richard S.; see Stopford-Taylor.
Taylor, Richard Sanderson, died 1932, vol. III
Taylor, Sir Richard Stephens, 1842–1928, vol. II
Taylor, Richard Whately C.; see Cooke-Taylor.
Taylor, Sir Robert, 1855–1921, vol. II
Taylor, Robert, died 1969, vol. VI
Taylor, Robert Arthur, 1886–1934, vol. III
Taylor, Robert Bruce, 1869–1954, vol. V
Taylor, Robert George, 1932–1981, vol. VIII
Taylor, Rt Hon. Robert John, 1881–1954, vol. V
Taylor, Col Robert Lewis, 1822–1906, vol. I
Taylor, Sir Robert Mackinlay, 1912–1985, vol. VIII
Taylor, Robert Martin, 1914–1992, vol. IX
Taylor, Very Rev. Robert Oswald Patrick, 1873–1944, vol. IV
Taylor, (Robert) Ronald, 1916–1999, vol. X
Taylor, Robert Richardson, 1919–1993, vol. IX
Taylor, Most Rev. Robert Selby, 1909–1995, vol. IX
Taylor, Robert Walter, 1883–1972, vol. VII
Taylor, Ronald; see Taylor, Robert R.
Taylor, Rupert Sutton, 1905–1986, vol. VIII
Taylor, Lt-Col St John Louis Hyde du Plat-, 1865–1936, vol. III
Taylor, Samuel C.; see Coleridge-Taylor.
Taylor, Rt Rev. Samuel Mumford, 1859–1929, vol. III
Taylor, Selwyn Francis, 1913–2000, vol. X
Taylor, Seymour, 1851–1931, vol. III
Taylor, Sidney Berald, 1900–1960, vol. V
Taylor, Stanley Grisewood, 1893–1980, vol. VII
Taylor, Stanley Shelbourne, 1875–1965, vol. VI
Taylor, Theodore Cooke, 1850–1952, vol. V
Taylor, Thomas, 1851–1916, vol. II
Taylor, Thomas, 1849–1938, vol. III
Taylor, Rev. Thomas, 1858–1938, vol. III
Taylor, Sir Thomas, 1876–1941, vol. IV
Taylor, (Thomas) Griffith, 1880–1963, vol. VI
Taylor, Sir Thomas Marris, 1871–1941, vol. IV
Taylor, Sir Thomas Murray, 1897–1962, vol. VI
Taylor, Rt Rev. Mgr Thomas N., died 1963, vol. VI
Taylor, Sir Thomas Wardlaw, 1833–1917, vol. II
Taylor, Sir Thomas Weston Johns, 1895–1953, vol. V
Taylor, Thomas Whiting, 1907–1981, vol. VIII
Taylor, Tom Lancelot, 1878–1960, vol. V
Taylor, Rev. Vincent, 1887–1968, vol. VI
Taylor, Walter R.; see Ross Taylor.
Taylor, Maj.-Gen. Walter Reynell, 1928–1996, vol. X
Taylor, Rev. Walter Ross, 1838–1907, vol. I
Taylor, Gen. Sir Walter William P.; see Pitt-Taylor.
Taylor, Wilfred; see Taylor, E. W.
Taylor, Surg.-Gen. Sir William, 1843–1917, vol. II
Taylor, Col Sir William, 1871–1933, vol. III

Taylor, William, 1865–1937, vol. III
Taylor, William, 1892–1977, vol. VII
Taylor, William Benjamin, 1875–1932, vol. III
Taylor, William Ernest, 1900–1965, vol. VI
Taylor, Ven. William Francis, *died* 1906, vol. I
Taylor, Lt-Col William Herbert, 1885–1959, vol. V
Taylor, Lt Comdr William Horace, 1908–1999, vol. X
Taylor, Sir William Johnson, 1st Bt (*cr* 1963), 1902–1972, vol. VII
Taylor, Sir William Ling, 1882–1969, vol. VI
Taylor, William Leonard, 1916–1991, vol. IX
Taylor, William T., 1843–1933, vol. III
Taylor, Sir William Thomas, 1848–1931, vol. III
Taylor-Smith, Ralph Emeric Kasope, 1924–1987, vol. IX (AI)
Tayside, Baron (Life Peer); David Lauchlan Urquhart, 1912–1975, vol. VII
Tchigorin, T., 1850–1908, vol. I
Teacher, Anthony Donald Macdonald, 1905–1969, vol. VI
Teacher, John Hammond, 1869–1930, vol. III
Teago, Frederick Jerrold, 1886–1964, vol. VI
Teague, Col John, 1896–1983, vol. VII
Teague, Rev. John Jessop, 1856–1929, vol. III
Teakle, Laurence John Hartley, 1901–1979, vol. VII
Teale, Sir Edmund Oswald, 1874–1971, vol. VII
Teale, Sir Francis Hugo, *died* 1959, vol. V
Teale, Rear-Adm. Godfrey Benjamin, 1908–1978, vol. VII
Teale, Major Joseph William, 1876–1926, vol. II
Teale, Thomas Pridgin, 1831–1923, vol. II
Teall, Major George Harris, 1880–1939, vol. III
Teall, Sir Jethro Justinian Harris, 1849–1924, vol. II
Teare, Douglas; *see* Teare, H. D.
Teare, (Hugo) Douglas, 1917–1991, vol. IX
Teare, Robert Donald, 1911–1979, vol. VII
Tearle, Sir Godfrey Seymour, 1884–1953, vol. V
Tearsdale, Sir John Smith, 1881–1962, vol. VI
Tebb, William, 1830–1918, vol. II
Tebbitt, Sir Alfred St Valery, *died* 1941, vol. IV
Tebble, Norman, 1924–1998, vol. X
Tebbs, Herbert Louis, 1868–1940, vol. III
Tebbutt, Edward G. F., *died* 1934, vol. III
Tebbutt, Dame Grace, 1893–1983, vol. VIII
Tebbutt, Rev. Henry Jemson, *died* 1915, vol. I
Teck, HH the Duke of; Francis Paul Louis Alexander, 1837–1900, vol. I
Teck, HSH Prince Francis Joseph Leopold Frederick of, 1870–1910, vol. I
Tedder, 1st Baron, 1890–1967, vol. VI
Tedder, 2nd Baron, 1926–1994, vol. IX
Tedder, Sir Arthur John, 1851–1931, vol. III
Tedder, Henry Richard, 1850–1924, vol. II
Tee, Lt-Col James Henry Stanley, 1876–1951, vol. V
Teed, Frank Litherland, 1858–1937, vol. III
Teeling, Bartholomew, 1848–1921, vol. II
Teeling, Mrs Bartle, *died* 1906, vol. I
Teeling, Charles Hamilton, *died* 1921, vol. II
Teeling, Luke Alexander, 1856–1943, vol. IV
Teeling, Sir (Luke) William (Burke), 1903–1975, vol. VII
Teeling, Sir William; *see* Teeling, Sir L. W. B.
Teelock, Sir Leckraz, 1909–1982, vol. VIII

Teesdale, Edmund Brinsley, 1915–1997, vol. X
Teesdale, Rev. Frederic Dobree, 1845–1935, vol. III
Teetzel, James Vernal, 1853–1926, vol. II
Teevan, Thomas Leslie, 1927–1954, vol. V
Tegart, Sir Charles Augustus, 1881–1946, vol. IV
Tegetmeier, William Bernhard, 1816–1912, vol. I
Te Heuheu, Sir Hepi Hoani, 1919–1997, vol. X
Tehri, HH Raja Sir Keerti Shah, 1874–1913, vol. I
Tehri-Garhwal, Maharaja of, 1898–1950, vol. IV (A), vol. V
Tei Abal, Sir, 1932–1995, vol. IX
Teichman, Sir Eric, 1884–1944, vol. IV
Teichman, Major Oskar, 1880–1959, vol. V
Teichman-Derville, Major Max, 1876–1963, vol. VI
Teignmouth, 3rd Baron, 1840–1915, vol. I
Teignmouth, 4th Baron, 1844–1916, vol. II
Teignmouth, 5th Baron, 1847–1926, vol. II
Teignmouth, 6th Baron, 1881–1964, vol. VI
Teignmouth, 7th Baron, 1920–1981, vol. VIII
Teixeira de Mattos, Alexander Louis, 1865–1921, vol. II
Tejam-Sie, Sir Banja, 1917–2000, vol. X
Tek Chand, Sir, 1883–1962, vol. VI
Telfer, Rev. Andrew Cecil, 1893–1978, vol. VII
Telfer, Rev. Canon William, 1886–1968, vol. VI
Telfer-Smollett, Maj.-Gen. Alexander Patrick Drummond, 1884–1954, vol. V
Telfer-Smollett, Captain James Drummond, 1824–1909, vol. I
Telford, Evelyn Davison, 1876–1961, vol. VI
Telford, Rev. John, 1851–1936, vol. III
Telford Beasley, John, 1929–1998, vol. X
Tellier, Hon. Sir Joseph Mathias, 1861–1952, vol. V
Tellier, Louis, 1844–1935, vol. III
Telling, Harry George, 1880–1961, vol. VI
Temin, Howard Martin, 1934–1994, vol. IX
Tempany, Sir Harold Augustin, 1881–1955, vol. V
Tempel, Frederik Jan, 1900–1974, vol. VII
Temperley, Rev. Canon Arthur, 1850–1927, vol. II
Temperley, Maj.-Gen. Arthur Cecil, 1877–1940, vol. III
Temperley, Major Harold William Vazeille, 1879–1939, vol. III
Tempest, Major Adolphus V.; *see* Vane-Tempest.
Tempest, Lord Henry John V.; *see* Vane-Tempest.
Tempest, Lord Henry V.; *see* Vane-Tempest.
Tempest, Margaret Mary, (Lady Mears), *died* 1982, vol. VIII
Tempest, Dame Mary Susan, 1866–1942, vol. IV
Tempest, Norton Robert, 1904–1985, vol. VIII
Tempest, Sir Percy Crosland, 1861–1924, vol. II
Tempest, Sir Robert Tempest, 3rd Bt, 1836–1901, vol. I
Tempest, Brig.-Gen. Roger Stephen, 1876–1948, vol. IV
Tempest, Sir Tristram Tempest, 4th Bt, 1865–1909, vol. I
Tempest-Hicks, Brig.-Gen. Henry, 1852–1922, vol. II
Templar-Smith, Col Sir Harold Charles, 1890–1970, vol. VI
Temple of Stowe, 5th Earl, 1871–1940, vol. III
Temple of Stowe, 6th Earl, 1909–1966, vol. VI
Temple of Stowe, 7th Earl, 1910–1988, vol. VIII
Temple, Sir Alfred George, 1848–1928, vol. II

Temple, Maj.-Gen. Bertram, 1896–1973, vol. VII
Temple, Charles Lindsay, 1871–1929, vol. III
Temple, Edwin, *died* 1932, vol. III
Temple, Sir (Ernest) Sanderson, 1921–1999, vol. X
Temple, Frances Gertrude Acland, (Mrs William Temple), 1890–1984, vol. VIII
Temple, Col Frank Valiant, 1879–1937, vol. III
Temple, Most Rev. and Rt Hon. Frederick, 1821–1902, vol. I
Temple, Frederick Charles, 1879–1957, vol. V
Temple, Rt Rev. Frederick Stephen, 1916–2000, vol. X
Temple, George Frederick James, 1901–1992, vol. IX
Temple, Comdr Grenville Mathias, 1897–1965, vol. VI
Temple, Rev. Henry, *died* 1906, vol. I
Temple, Lt-Col Henry Martindale, 1853–1905, vol. I
Temple, Hope, 1859–1938, vol. III
Temple, John, 1839–1922, vol. II
Temple, Sir John Meredith, 1910–1994, vol. IX
Temple, Sir Rawden John Afamado, 1908–2000, vol. X
Temple, Lt-Gen. Reginald Cecil, 1877–1959, vol. V
Temple, Rt Hon. Sir Richard, 1st Bt, 1826–1902, vol. I
Temple, Lt-Col Sir Richard Carnac, 2nd Bt, 1850–1931, vol. III
Temple, Col Sir Richard Durand, 3rd Bt, 1880–1962, vol. VI
Temple, Sir Sanderson; *see* Temple, Sir E. S.
Temple, Lt-Col William, 1833–1919, vol. II
Temple, Most Rev. and Rt Hon. William, 1881–1944, vol. IV
Temple-Gore-Langton, Hon. Chandos Graham, 1873–1921, vol. II
Temple-Gore-Langton, Comdr Hon. Evelyn Arthur Grenville, 1884–1972, vol. VII
Temple-Morris, Sir Owen, 1896–1985, vol. VIII
Templeman, Geoffrey, 1914–1988, vol. VIII
Templeman, Philip George, 1910–1972, vol. VII
Templeman, Hon. William, 1844–1914, vol. I
Templemore, 2nd Baron, 1821–1906, vol. I
Templemore, 3rd Baron, 1854–1924, vol. II
Templemore, 4th Baron, 1880–1953, vol. V
Templer, Brig.-Gen. Cyril Frank, 1869–1947, vol. IV
Templer, Frederic Gordon, 1849–1918, vol. II
Templer, Field Marshal Sir Gerald Walter Robert, 1898–1979, vol. VII
Templer, Col J. L. B., 1846–1924, vol. II
Templer, Lt-Col Walter Francis, 1865–1942, vol. IV
Templeton, Archibald Angus, 1893–1969, vol. VI
Templeton, Charles Perry, 1884–1929, vol. III
Templeton, James Stanley, 1906–1977, vol. VII
Templeton, Col John Montgomery, 1840–1908, vol. I
Templeton, William Paterson, 1876–1938, vol. III
Templetown, 4th Viscount, 1853–1939, vol. III
Templetown, 5th Viscount, 1894–1981, vol. VIII
Templewood, 1st Viscount, 1880–1959, vol. V
Tenby, 1st Viscount, 1894–1967, vol. VI
Tenby, 2nd Viscount, 1922–1983, vol. VIII
Tengbom, Ivar Justus, 1878–1968, vol. VI

Tenison, Marika H.; *see* Hanbury Tenison.
Tenison, Lt-Col William Percival Cosnahan, 1884–1983, vol. VIII
Tennant, Sir Charles, 1st Bt, 1823–1906, vol. I
Tennant, Charles Coombe, 1852–1928, vol. II
Tennant, Hon. Sir David, 1829–1905, vol. I
Tennant, Francis John, 1861–1942, vol. IV
Tennant, Rev. Frederick Robert, 1866–1957, vol. V
Tennant, Rt Hon. Harold John, 1865–1935, vol. III
Tennant, Hercules, 1850–1925, vol. II
Tennant, Lt-Gen. James Francis, 1829–1915, vol. I
Tennant, Lt-Col John Edward, 1890–1941, vol. IV
Tennant, Major John Trenchard, 1841–1904, vol. I
Tennant, Sir Mark Dalcour, 1911–1990, vol. VIII
Tennant, May, 1869–1946, vol. IV
Tennant, Sir Peter Frank Dalrymple, 1910–1996, vol. X
Tennant, Robert Hugh, 1860–1936, vol. III
Tennant, Adm. Sir William George, 1890–1963, vol. VI
Tennant, Sir William Robert, 1892–1969, vol. VI
Tennant, Thomas, 1900–1962, vol. VI
Tenney, John, 1856–1944, vol. IV
Tenniel, Sir John, 1820–1914, vol. I
Tennstedt, Klaus, 1926–1998, vol. X
Tennyson, 2nd Baron, 1852–1928, vol. II
Tennyson, 3rd Baron, 1889–1951, vol. V
Tennyson, 4th Baron, 1919–1991, vol. IX
Tennyson, Sir Charles Bruce Locker, 1879–1977, vol. VII
Tennyson, Frederick, 1807–1898, vol. I
Tennyson-d'Eyncourt, Edmund Charles, 1855–1924, vol. II
Tennyson d'Eyncourt, Adm. Edwin Clayton; *see* d'Eyncourt.
Tennyson d'Eyncourt, Sir (Eustace) Gervais, 2nd Bt, 1902–1971, vol. VII
Tennyson-d'Eyncourt, Sir Eustace Henry William, 1st Bt, 1868–1951, vol. V
Tennyson-d'Eyncourt, Sir Gervais; *see* Tennyson d'Eyncourt, Sir E. G.
Tennyson d'Eyncourt, Sir Giles Gervais, 4th Bt, 1935–1989, vol. VIII
Tennyson-d'Eyncourt, Sir Jeremy; *see* Tennyson-d'Eyncourt, Sir J. J. E.
Tennyson-d'Eyncourt, Sir (John) Jeremy (Eustace), 3rd Bt, 1927–1988, vol. VIII
Tenterden, 4th Baron, 1865–1939, vol. III
Tenzing Norgay, 1914–1986, vol. VIII
Teō, Sir (Fiatau) Penitala, 1911–1998, vol. X
Teō, Sir Penitala; *see* Teō, Sir F. P.
Teresa, Mother, (Agnes Gonxha Bojaxhiu), 1910–1997, vol. X
Ternan, Brig.-Gen. Trevor Patrick Breffney, 1860–1949, vol. IV
Terrell, Arthur Koberwein à Beckett, 1881–1956, vol. V
Terrell, Sir Courtney, 1881–1938, vol. III
Terrell, Edward, 1902–1979, vol. VII
Terrell, George, 1862–1952, vol. V
Terrell, Henry, 1856–1944, vol. IV
Terrell, Captain Sir Reginald; *see* Terrell, Captain Sir T. A. R.
Terrell, Thomas, *died* 1928, vol. II

Terrell, Captain Sir (Thomas Antonio) Reginald, 1889–1979, vol. VII
Terrey, Henry, died 1954, vol. V
Terrington, 1st Baron, 1852–1921, vol. II
Terrington, 2nd Baron, 1877–1940, vol. III
Terrington, 3rd Baron, 1887–1961, vol. VI
Terrington, 4th Baron, 1915–1998, vol. X
Terriss, William, 1852–1897, vol. I
Terrot, Brig. Charles Russell, died 1944, vol. IV
Terry, Sir Andrew Henry Bouhier I.; see Imbert-Terry.
Terry, Charles Sanford, 1864–1936, vol. III
Terry, Lt-Col Claude Henry Maxwell I.; see Imbert-Terry.
Terry, Major Sir Edward Henry Bouhier I.; see Imbert-Terry.
Terry, Edward O'Connor, 1844–1912, vol. I
Terry, Dame Ellen (Alice), 1847–1928, vol. II
Terry, Sir Francis William, 1877–1960, vol. V
Terry, Fred, 1863–1933, vol. III
Terry, Captain Frederic Bouhier Imbert-, 1887–1963, vol. VI
Terry, Sir George Walter Roberts, 1921–1995, vol. IX
Terry, Rev. Canon George Frederick, 1864–1919, vol. II
Terry, George Percy Warner, 1867–1949, vol. IV
Terry, Harold; see Terry, J. E. H.
Terry, Lt-Col Sir Henry Bouhier I.; see Imbert-Terry.
Terry, Sir Henry Machu I.; see Imbert-Terry.
Terry, Captain Herbert Durell, 1847–1911, vol. I
Terry, Sir John Elliott, 1913–1995, vol. IX
Terry, Sir Joseph, 1827–1898, vol. I
Terry, (Joseph Edward) Harold, 1885–1939, vol. III
Terry, Joseph Pitches, 1880–1955, vol. V
Terry, Julia; see Neilson, J.
Terry, Marion, died 1930, vol. III
Terry, Michael, 1899–1981, vol. VIII
Terry, Phyllis N.; see Neilson-Terry.
Terry, Sir Richard Runciman, 1865–1938, vol. III
Terry, Major Robert Joseph Atkinson, 1869–1915, vol. I
Terry, Stephen Harding, 1853–1924, vol. II
Terry, Walter, 1924–1991, vol. IX
Terry-Thomas, (Thomas Terry Hoar Stevens), 1911–1990, vol. VIII
Tertis, Lionel, 1876–1975, vol. VII
Teschemacher, Edward, 1876–1940, vol. III (A), vol. IV
Tesla, Nikola, 1857–1943, vol. IV
Tessier, Hon. Auguste, 1853–1938, vol. III
Tessier, Hon. Jules, 1852–1934, vol. III
Tester, Air Cdre John Andrews, 1907–1972, vol. VII
Tester, Leslie, 1891–1975, vol. VII
Teternikov, Feodor Kuzmich; see Sologub, Feodor.
Tetley, Sir Herbert, 1908–1999, vol. X
Tetley, Rev. James George, 1843–1924, vol. II
Tetley, Brig. James Noel, 1898–1971, vol. VII
Tetley, Kenneth James, 1921–1993, vol. IX
Tetrazzini, Luisa, 1871–1940, vol. III
Teunon, Sir William, 1863–1926, vol. II
Teusner, Hon. Berthold Herbert, 1907–1996, vol. X (AI)

Teversham, Brig. Mark Symonds, 1895–1973, vol. VII
Teversham, Col Richard Kinlock, 1856–1929, vol. III
Teviot, 1st Baron, 1874–1968, vol. VI
Tew, Lt-Col Harold Stuart, 1869–1945, vol. IV
Tew, Sir Mervyn Lawrence, 1876–1963, vol. VI
Tew, Percy, 1840–1921, vol. II
Tew, Thomas Percy, 1876–1953, vol. V
te Water, Charles Theodore, 1887–1964, vol. VI
Tewsley, Cyril Hocken, 1878–1950, vol. IV
Tewson, Sir (Harold) Vincent, 1898–1981, vol. VIII
Tewson, Sir Vincent; see Tewson, Sir H. V.
Tey, Josephine; see Daviot, Gordon.
Teyen, Charles St Leger, 1877–1947, vol. IV
Teynham, 18th Baron, 1867–1936, vol. III
Teynham, 19th Baron, 1896–1972, vol. VII
Teyte, Dame Maggie, (Dame Margaret Cottingham), 1888–1976, vol. VII
Thacker, Charles, 1897–1982, vol. VIII
Thacker, Maj.-Gen. Herbert Cyril, 1870–1953, vol. V
Thacker, Maj.-Gen. Percival Edward, 1873–1945, vol. IV
Thacker, Ransley Samuel, 1891–1965, vol. VI
Thacker, Thomas William, 1911–1984, vol. VIII
Thackeray, Col Charles Bouverie, 1875–1938, vol. III
Thackeray, Col Edward Francis, 1870–1956, vol. V
Thackeray, Col Sir Edward Talbot, 1836–1927, vol. II
Thackeray, Rev. Francis St John, 1832–1919, vol. II
Thackeray, Brig.-Gen. Frank Staniford, 1880–1960, vol. V
Thackeray, Lance, died 1916, vol. II
Thackersey, Sir Vithaldas Damodher, 1873–1922, vol. II
Thackstone, Howard Harrison, 1905–1969, vol. VI
Thackwell, Major Charles Joseph, 1870–1933, vol. III
Thackwell, Col Colquhoun Grant Roche, 1857–1931, vol. III
Thackwell, Gen. Joseph Edwin, 1813–1900, vol. I
Thackwell, Maj.-Gen. William de Wilton Roche, 1834–1910, vol. I
Thaddeus, Henry Jones, 1860–1929, vol. III
Thaine, Robert Niemann, 1875–1943, vol. IV
Thakorram Kapilram, Diwan Bahadur, born 1868, vol. V
Thakurdas, Sir Purshotamdas, 1879–1961, vol. VI
Thalben-Ball, Sir George Thomas, 1896–1987, vol. VIII
Thalmann, Ernesto, 1914–1993, vol. IX
Thane, Sir George Dancer, 1850–1930, vol. III
Thankerton, Baron (Life Peer); William Watson, 1873–1948, vol. IV
Thant, U Maung, 1909–1974, vol. VII
Thapa, Hon. Captain Lalbahadur, 1907–1968, vol. VI
Thapar, Prem Nath, 1903–1982, vol. VIII
Tharp, Arthur Keane, 1848–1928, vol. II
Tharp, Philip Anthony, 1890–1958, vol. V
That; see Tate, James William.
Thatcher, J. Wells, 1856–1946, vol. IV
Thatcher, Sir Reginald Sparshatt, 1888–1957, vol. V

Thatcher, William Sutherland, 1888–1966, vol. VI
Thavenot, Alexander Frank Noel, 1883–1947, vol. IV
Thayer, William Sydney, *died* 1932, vol. III
Thayre, Albert Jesse, 1917–1988, vol. VIII
Theak, Air Vice-Marshal William Edward, 1898–1955, vol. V
Theaker, Harry G., 1873–1954, vol. V
Theiler, Sir Arnold, 1867–1936, vol. III
Theiler, Max, 1899–1972, vol. VII
Theis, Otto Frederick, 1881–1966, vol. VI
Thelwall, John Walter Francis, 1884–1934, vol. III
Thelwell, Sir Arthur Frederick, 1889–1966, vol. VI
Theobald, Rev. Charles, 1831–1930, vol. III
Theobald, Frederic Vincent, 1868–1930, vol. III
Theobold, Sir Henry Studdy, 1847–1934, vol. III
Theodore, Hon. Edward Granville, 1884–1950, vol. IV
Theorell, (Axel) Hugo (Teodor), 1903–1982, vol. VIII
Theorell, Hugo; *see* Theorell, A. H. T.
Theotonio Pereira, Pedro, 1902–1972, vol. VII
Theron, Maj.-Gen. François Henri, 1891–1967, vol. VI
Thesiger, Arthur Lionel Bruce, 1872–1968, vol. VI
Thesiger, Adm. Sir Bertram Sackville, 1875–1966, vol. VI
Thesiger, Lt-Gen. Hon. Charles Wemyss, 1831–1903, vol. I
Thesiger, Hon. Sir Edward Peirson, 1842–1928, vol. II
Thesiger, Ernest, 1879–1961, vol. VI
Thesiger, Brig.-Gen. George Handcock, 1868–1915, vol. I
Thesiger, Sir Gerald Alfred, 1902–1981, vol. VIII
Thesiger, Captain Hon. Wilfred Gilbert, 1871–1920, vol. II
Theunis, Georges, 1873–1966, vol. VI
Theunissen, Most Rev. John Baptist Hubert, 1905–1979, vol. VII (AII)
Theuriet, Claude André, *died* 1907, vol. I
Thew, Sir Edgar William, 1879–1942, vol. IV
Thibaudeau, Hon. Alfred Arthur, 1860–1926, vol. II
Thibault, Jacques Anatole François; *see* France, A.
Thibaut, George Frederick William, 1848–1914, vol. I
Thicknesse, Very Rev. Cuthbert Carroll, 1887–1971, vol. VII
Thicknesse, Rt Rev. Francis Henry, 1829–1921, vol. II
Thicknesse, Ven. Francis Norman, 1858–1946, vol. IV
Thiess, Sir Leslie Charles, 1909–1993, vol. IX
Thiman, Eric Harding, 1900–1975, vol. VII
Thimann, Kenneth Vivian, 1904–1997, vol. X
Thin, Robert, 1861–1941, vol. IV
Thirkell, Angela Margaret, (Mrs G. L. Thirkell), 1890–1961, vol. VI
Thirkell, Lancelot George, 1921–1989, vol. VIII
Thirkettle, Ellis; *see* Thirkettle, W. E.
Thirkettle, (William) Ellis, 1904–2000, vol. X
Thirkhill, Sir Henry, 1886–1971, vol. VII
Thirlmere, Rowland, 1861–1932, vol. III
Thirlwall, Air Vice-Marshal George Edwin, 1924–2000, vol. X

Thirtle, James William, 1854–1934, vol. III
Thiselton-Dyer, Sir William Turner, 1843–1928, vol. II
Thistleton-Smith, Vice-Adm. Sir Geoffrey, 1905–1986, vol. VIII
Thoday, David, 1883–1964, vol. VI
Thode, Henry George, 1910–1997, vol. IX
Thody, Philip Malcolm Waller, 1928–1999, vol. X
Thom, Alexander, 1894–1985, vol. VIII
Thom, Donaldson Rose, *died* 1920, vol. II
Thom, Col George St Clair, *died* 1935, vol. III
Thom, Herbert James, 1895–1972, vol. VII
Thom, James Robert, 1910–1981, vol. VIII
Thom, Lt-Col Sir John Gibb, 1891–1941, vol. IV
Thom, Sir William, *died* 1939, vol. III
Thomas, Baron (Life Peer); William Miles Webster Thomas, 1897–1980, vol. VII
Thomas, Abel, 1848–1912, vol. I
Thomas, Sir (Abraham) Garrod, 1853–1931, vol. III
Thomas, Alan Ernest Wentworth, 1896–1969, vol. VI
Thomas, Rt Rev. Albert Reuben Edward, 1908–1983, vol. VIII
Thomas, Rev. Alexander, *died* 1918, vol. II
Thomas, Rev. Canon Alfred, *died* 1957, vol. V
Thomas, Sir (Alfred) Brumwell, 1868–1948, vol. IV
Thomas, Alfred Patten, 1860–1931, vol. III
Thomas, Sir Algernon Phillips Withiel, 1857–1937, vol. III
Thomas, Alston Havard Rees, 1925–1999, vol. X
Thomas, Ambler Reginald, 1913–1996, vol. X
Thomas, Annie, 1838–1918, vol. II
Thomas, Brig. Arthur Frank Friend, 1897–1987, vol. VIII
Thomas, Col Arthur Havilland, 1860–1919, vol. II
Thomas, Arthur Hermann, 1877–1971, vol. VII
Thomas, Rt Rev. Arthur Nutter, 1869–1954, vol. V
Thomas, (Aubrey) Ralph, 1879–1957, vol. V
Thomas, Augustus, 1857–1934, vol. III
Thomas, Sir Ben Bowen, 1899–1977, vol. VII
Thomas, Bert, *died* 1966, vol. VI
Thomas, Bertie P.; *see* Pardoe-Thomas.
Thomas, Bertram Sidney, 1892–1950, vol. IV
Thomas, Brandon, 1849–1914, vol. IV
Thomas, Brian Dick Lauder, 1912–1989, vol. VIII
Thomas, Brinley, 1906–1994, vol. IX
Thomas, Sir Brumwell; *see* Thomas, Sir A. B.
Thomas, Carmichael, 1856–1942, vol. IV
Thomas, Cecil, 1885–1976, vol. VII
Thomas, Cecil James, 1902–1973, vol. VII
Thomas, Maj.-Gen. Charles Frederick, *died* 1922, vol. II
Thomas, Sir (Charles) Inigo, 1846–1929, vol. III
Thomas, Lt-Col Sir Charles John Howell, 1874–1943, vol. IV
Thomas, Captain Charles William, 1854–1935, vol. III
Thomas, Claudius Cornelius, 1928–1987, vol. VIII
Thomas, Sir Clement P.; *see* Price Thomas.
Thomas, Daniel, 1880–1938, vol. III
Thomas, Sir Daniel Lleufer, 1863–1940, vol. III
Thomas, David Emlyn, 1892–1954, vol. V
Thomas, Rev. David John, 1862–1936, vol. III
Thomas, David Monro, 1915–1996, vol. X
Thomas, Ven. David Richard, *died* 1916, vol. II

Thomas, David Rowland, *died* 1955, vol. V
Thomas, Rev. David Walter, *died* 1905, vol. I
Thomas, Ven. David William, *died* 1951, vol. V
Thomas, David Winton, 1901–1970, vol. VI
Thomas, Rev. Canon Dennis Daven-, 1913–1973, vol. VII
Thomas, Dewi Alun, 1917–1996, vol. X
Thomas, Dewi-Prys, 1916–1985, vol. VIII
Thomas, Dylan Marlais, 1914–1953, vol. V
Thomas, Ebenezer Rhys, 1885–1979, vol. VII
Thomas, Edgar, 1900–1979, vol. VII
Thomas, Edgar William, 1879–1963, vol. VI
Thomas, Edward; *see* Thomas, P. E.
Thomas, Brig.-Gen. Edward Algernon D'Arcy, 1858–1937, vol. III
Thomas, Edward Francis, 1880–1954, vol. V
Thomas, Elbert Duncan, 1883–1953, vol. V
Thomas, Sir Eric; *see* Thomas, Sir W. E.
Thomas, Ethel Nancy Miles, *died* 1944, vol. IV
Thomas, Sir Eustace; *see* Thomas, Sir W. E. R.
Thomas, Evan Kyffin, 1866–1935, vol. III
Thomas, Evan Lewis, *died* 1935, vol. III
Thomas, Rev. Evan Lorimer, 1872–1953, vol. V
Thomas, Wing Comdr Forest Frederick Edward Y.; *see* Yeo-Thomas.
Thomas, Rt Rev. Francis Gerard, 1930–1988, vol. VIII
Thomas, Col Francis Herbert Sullivan, 1862–1944, vol. IV
Thomas, Gen. Sir Francis William, 1832–1925, vol. II
Thomas, Frank; *see* Thomas, J. F. P.
Thomas, Lt-Col Frank S. W.; *see* Williams-Thomas.
Thomas, Frederic George, 1872–1937, vol. III
Thomas, Frederic William W.; *see* Watkyn-Thomas.
Thomas, Frederick Maginley, 1908–1984, vol. VIII
Thomas, Frederick William, 1867–1956, vol. V
Thomas, Sir Frederick William, 1906–1999, vol. X
Thomas, Sir Garrod; *see* Thomas, Sir A. G.
Thomas, Air Vice-Marshal Geoffrey Percy Sansom, 1915–1992, vol. IX
Thomas, Sir George Alan, 7th Bt (*cr* 1766), 1881–1972, vol. VII
Thomas, George Arthur, 1877–1950, vol. IV
Thomas, Maj.-Gen. George Arthur, 1906–1992, vol. IX
Thomas, George H.; *see* Holt-Thomas.
Thomas, Sir George Hector, 1884–1965, vol. VI
Thomas, George Ross, 1876–1955, vol. V
Thomas, Sir George Sidney Meade, 6th Bt (*cr* 1766), 1847–1918, vol. II
Thomas, Gerwyn Pascal, 1895–1956, vol. V
Thomas, Gilbert Oliver, 1891–1978, vol. VII
Thomas, Rt Hon. Sir Godfrey John Vignoles, 10th Bt (*cr* 1694), 1889–1968, vol. VI
Thomas, Brig.-Gen. Sir Godfrey Vignoles, 9th Bt (*cr* 1694), 1856–1919, vol. II
Thomas, Sir Griffith, 1847–1923, vol. II
Thomas, Grosvenor, 1856–1923, vol. II
Thomas, Gwilym Ewart A.; *see* Aeron-Thomas.
Thomas, Gen. Sir (Gwilym) Ivor, 1893–1972, vol. VII
Thomas, Gwyn, 1913–1981, vol. VIII
Thomas, Brig.-Gen. Gwyn G.; *see* Gwyn-Thomas.
Thomas, Harold, 1847–1917, vol. II

Thomas, Rt Rev. Harry, 1897–1955, vol. V
Thomas, Sir Henry, 1878–1952, vol. V
Thomas, Henry Arnold, 1848–1924, vol. II
Thomas, Henry Hugh, 1904–1967, vol. VI
Thomas, Brig.-Gen. Henry Melville, 1870–1940, vol. III
Thomas, Herbert Henry, 1876–1935, vol. III
Thomas, Herbert J., 1892–1947, vol. IV
Thomas, Herbert James, 1882–1960, vol. V
Thomas, Herbert P.; *see* Preston-Thomas.
Thomas, Herbert Percival, 1879–1972, vol. VII
Thomas, Horatio Oritsejolomi, 1917–1979, vol. VII
Thomas, Howard, 1909–1986, vol. VIII
Thomas, Lt-Col Hubert St George, 1862–1936, vol. III
Thomas, Adm. Sir Hugh E.; *see* Evan-Thomas.
Thomas, Hugh Hamshaw, 1885–1962, vol. VI
Thomas, Major Sir Hugh James Protheroe, 1879–1924, vol. II
Thomas, Hugh Lloyd, 1888–1938, vol. III
Thomas, Hugh Whitelegge, *died* 1960, vol. V
Thomas, Sir Illtyd, 1864–1943, vol. IV
Thomas, Sir Inigo; *see* Thomas, Sir C. I.
Thomas, Iorwerth Rhys, 1895–1966, vol. VI
Thomas, Gen. Sir Ivor; *see* Thomas, Gen. Sir G. I.
Thomas, Ivor B.; *see* Bulmer-Thomas.
Thomas, Sir Ivor Broadbent, 1890–1955, vol. V
Thomas, Ivor Cradock, 1861–1942, vol. IV
Thomas, Ivor Owen, 1898–1982, vol. VIII
Thomas, J. Havard, 1854–1921, vol. II
Thomas, Rt Hon. James Henry, 1874–1949, vol. IV
Thomas, James Jonathan, 1850–1919, vol. II
Thomas, Sir (James William) Tudor, 1893–1976, vol. VII
Thomas, Jeffrey, 1933–1989, vol. VIII
Thomas, Sir John, 1834–1920, vol. II
Thomas, John Aeron, 1850–1935, vol. III
Thomas, (John) Frank (Phillips), 1920–2000, vol. X
Thomas, John Herbert, 1895–1960, vol. V
Thomas, Rt Rev. John James Absalom, 1908–1995, vol. IX
Thomas, Sir John L.; *see* Lynn-Thomas.
Thomas, Gen. Sir (John) Noel, 1915–1983, vol. VIII
Thomas, John Owen, 1862–1928, vol. II
Thomas, John Richard, 1897–1968, vol. VI
Thomas, Rev. John Roland Lloyd, 1908–1984, vol. VIII
Thomas, Sir John S.; *see* Stradling Thomas.
Thomas, Lt-Gen. Sir John Wellesley, 1822–1908, vol. I
Thomas, Joseph Anthony Charles, 1923–1981, vol. VIII
Thomas, Rev. Joseph Llewelyn, *died* 1940, vol. III
Thomas, Joseph Silvers Williams-, 1848–1933, vol. III
Thomas, Hon. Josiah, 1863–1933, vol. III
Thomas, Ven. Lawrence, 1889–1960, vol. V
Thomas, Maj.-Gen. Lechmere Cay, 1897–1981, vol. VIII
Thomas, Leonard Charles, 1879–1964, vol. VI
Thomas, Sir Leslie Montagu, 1906–1971, vol. VII
Thomas, (Lewis John) Wynford V.; *see* Vaughan-Thomas.
Thomas, Col Lionel B.; *see* Beaumont-Thomas.
Thomas, Llewelyn E.; *see* Evan-Thomas.

807

Thomas, Lowell Jackson, 1892–1981, vol. VIII
Thomas, Sir Lynn U.; *see* Ungoed-Thomas, Sir A. L.
Thomas, Margaret, *died* 1929, vol. III
Thomas, Meirion, 1894–1977, vol. VII
Thomas, Melbourne, 1906–1989, vol. VIII
Thomas, Air Vice Marshal Meredith, 1892–1984, vol. VIII
Thomas, Captain Mervyn Somerset, 1900–1947, vol. IV
Thomas, Rt Rev. Nathaniel Seymour, 1867–1937, vol. III
Thomas, Gen. Sir Noel; *see* Thomas, Gen. Sir J. N.
Thomas, Oldfield, 1858–1929, vol. III
Thomas, Sir Patrick Muirhead, 1914–1990, vol. VIII
Thomas, Percy, *died* 1922, vol. II
Thomas, Sir Percy Edward, 1883–1969, vol. VI
Thomas, Percy Goronwy, 1875–1954, vol. V
Thomas, Major Peter David, 1873–1952, vol. V
Thomas, (Philip) Edward, 1878–1917, vol. II
Thomas, Philip Henry, 1854–1920, vol. II
Thomas, Philip Martin, 1924–1968, vol. VI
Thomas, Ralph; *see* Thomas, A. R.
Thomas, Rees Griffith, 1870–1934, vol. III
Thomas, Lt-Col Sir Reginald Aneurin, 1879–1975, vol. VII
Thomas, Lt-Col Reginald Silvers W.; *see* Williams-Thomas.
Thomas, Rt Rev. Richard, 1881–1958, vol. V
Thomas, Richard, 1890–1977, vol. VII
Thomas, Adm. Sir Richard; *see* Thomas, Adm. Sir W. R. S.
Thomas, Rev. Richard Albert, 1873–1943, vol. IV
Thomas, Richard Macaulay, 1857–1937, vol. III
Thomas, Ven. Richard Rice, *died* 1942, vol. IV
Thomas, Robert Anthony C.; *see* Clinton-Thomas.
Thomas, Robert Clifford Lloyd, 1893–1969, vol. VI
Thomas, Brig. Robert Henry, 1877–1946, vol. IV
Thomas, Sir Robert John, 1st Bt (*cr* 1918), 1873–1951, vol. V
Thomas, Sir Robert Kyffin, 1851–1910, vol. I
Thomas, Sir Roger, 1886–1960, vol. V
Thomas, Roger Gareth, 1925–1994, vol. IX
Thomas, Ronald Hamilton Eliot, 1896–1977, vol. VII
Thomas, Rev. Ronald Stuart, 1913–2000, vol. X
Thomas, Ruth Rees-, (Mrs William Rees-Thomas); *see* Darwin, R.
Thomas, Ryland Lowell Degwel, 1914–1982, vol. VIII
Thomas, Salusbury Vaughan, 1856–1943, vol. IV
Thomas, Sir Samuel Joyce, *died* 1952, vol. V
Thomas, Sir Shenton; *see* Thomas, Sir T. S. W.
Thomas, Stephen Peter John Quao, 1904–1975, vol. VII
Thomas, Rev. Sutcliffe, *died* 1930, vol. III
Thomas, Terry; *see* Terry-Thomas.
Thomas, Terry, 1888–1978, vol. VII
Thomas, Theodore, 1835–1905, vol. I
Thomas, Sir Theodore Eastaway, 1882–1951, vol. V
Thomas, Theodore Lynam, 1900–1976, vol. VII
Thomas, Thomas; *see* Lewis, Richard.
Thomas, Thomas Henry, 1839–1915, vol. I
Thomas, Sir Thomas Powell, *died* 1932, vol. III

Thomas, Sir (Thomas) Shenton (Whitelegge), 1879–1962, vol. VI
Thomas, Trevor, 1907–1993, vol. IX
Thomas, Trevor Cawdor, 1914–1985, vol. VIII
Thomas, Sir Tudor; *see* Thomas, Sir J. W. T.
Thomas, Maj.-Gen. Vivian Davenport, 1897–1984, vol. VIII
Thomas, Sir (Walter) Eric, 1889–1963, vol. VI
Thomas, Rt Rev. Wilfrid William Henry, *died* 1953, vol. V
Thomas, William, 1891–1958, vol. V
Thomas, William, 1890–1974, vol. VII
Thomas, Sir William Beach, 1868–1957, vol. V
Thomas, Sir William Bruce, 1878–1952, vol. V
Thomas, Rev. William Ceidrych, 1850–1937, vol. III
Thomas, William Edwin S.; *see* Somerset-Thomas.
Thomas, Sir (William) Eustace) (Rhyddlad), 2nd Bt (*cr* 1918), 1909–1957, vol. V
Thomas, Sir William Henry, 1859–1947, vol. IV
Thomas, Rev. William Henry Griffith, 1861–1924, vol. II
Thomas, William Herbert Evans, 1886–1979, vol. VII
Thomas, Sir William James, 1st Bt (*cr* 1919), 1867–1945, vol. IV
Thomas, William Luson, 1830–1900, vol. I
Thomas, William Moy, 1828–1910, vol. I
Thomas, William Norman, 1885–1960, vol. V
Thomas, William R.; *see* Rees-Thomas.
Thomas, Adm. Sir (William) Richard Scott, 1932–1998, vol. X
Thomas, William Stanley Russell, 1896–1957, vol. V
Thomas, William Thelwall, 1865–1927, vol. II
Thomas, Wynford V.; *see* Vaughan-Thomas, L. J. W.
Thomas-Stanford, Sir Charles, 1st Bt, 1858–1932, vol. III
Thomason, Maj.-Gen. Charles Simson, 1833–1911, vol. I
Thomasson, Lt-Col Franklin, *died* 1941, vol. IV
Thomasson, John Pennington, *died* 1904, vol. I
Thomlinson, Lt-Col Sir William, 1854–1943, vol. IV
Thompson, Col Albert George, *died* 1940, vol. III
Thompson, Alexander Hamilton, 1873–1952, vol. V
Thompson, Alexander M., 1861–1948, vol. IV
Thompson, Alfred Corderoy, *died* 1928, vol. II
Thompson, Captain Sir Algar de Clifford Charles M.; *see* Meysey-Thompson.
Thompson, Lt-Gen. Arnold Bunbury, 1822–1917, vol. II
Thompson, Rev. Arthur Charles, 1868–1933, vol. III
Thompson, Arthur Hugh, *died* 1937, vol. III
Thompson, Ven. Arthur Huxley, 1872–1951, vol. V
Thompson, Rev. Arthur Wellington, *died* 1937, vol. III
Thompson, Aubrey Denzil F.; *see* Forsyth-Thompson.
Thompson, Rev. Austin Henry, 1870–1941, vol. IV
Thompson, Brenda, (Mrs Gordon Thompson), 1935–1989, vol. VIII
Thompson, Lt-Col Cecil Henry Farrer, 1882–1975, vol. VII

Thompson, Charles, 1930–1991, vol. IX
Thompson, Charles Henry, 1865–1948, vol. IV
Thompson, Charles John S., *died* 1943, vol. IV
Thompson, Charles Paxton, 1911–1985, vol. VIII
Thompson, Comdr Charles Ralfe, 1894–1966, vol. VI
Thompson, Maj.-Gen. Charles William, 1859–1940, vol. III
Thompson, Captain Hon. Claude Henry M.; *see* Meysey-Thompson.
Thompson, Claude Metford, 1855–1933, vol. III
Thompson, Lt-Col Cyril Powney, 1864–1924, vol. II
Thompson, Daniel Varney, 1902–1980, vol. VII
Thompson, Sir D'Arcy Wentworth, 1860–1948, vol. IV
Thompson, David Richard, 1916–1995, vol. IX
Thompson, Dorothy, 1894–1961, vol. VI
Thompson, Rev. Douglas Weddell, 1903–1981, vol. VIII
Thompson, Mrs E. Roffe; *see* Lejeune, C. A.
Thompson, Lt-Col Edgar Hynes, 1910–1976, vol. VII
Thompson, Edith Marie, *died* 1961, vol. VI
Thompson, Edmund S.; *see* Symes-Thompson.
Thompson, Edward, 1881–1954, vol. V
Thompson, Edward Arthur, 1914–1994, vol. IX
Thompson, Edward Charles, 1851–1933, vol. III
Thompson, Edward Herbert, 1860–1935, vol. III
Thompson, Sir Edward Hugh Dudley, 1907–1994, vol. IX
Thompson, Edward John, 1886–1946, vol. IV
Thompson, Sir Edward Maunde, 1840–1929, vol. III
Thompson, Edward Palmer, 1924–1993, vol. IX
Thompson, Edward Raymond, 1872–1928, vol. II
Thompson, Edward Vincent, 1880–1976, vol. VII
Thompson, Sir Edward Walter, 1902–1989, vol. VIII
Thompson, Edwin, 1881–1967, vol. VI
Thompson, Edwin Reginald R.; *see* Roe-Thompson.
Thompson, Eric, 1905–1969, vol. VI
Thompson, Sir Eric; *see* Thompson, Sir J. E. S.
Thompson, Sir Ernest, 1865–1941, vol. IV
Thompson, Ernest; *see* Thompson, R. E.
Thompson, Ernest Claude M.; *see* Meysey-Thompson.
Thompson, E(rnest) Heber, 1891–1971, vol. VII
Thompson, Estelle Merle O'Brien; *see* Oberon, Merle.
Thompson, Francis, 1859–1907, vol. I
Thompson, Francis L.; *see* Longstreth-Thompson.
Thompson, Frank Charles, 1890–1977, vol. VII
Thompson, Fred, 1884–1949, vol. IV
Thompson, Fred, 1883–1951, vol. V
Thompson, Frederick Charles, *died* 1919, vol. II
Thompson, Brig.-Gen. Frederick Hacket-, 1858–1944, vol. IV
Thompson, Air Cdre Frederick William, 1914–1994, vol. IX
Thompson, Sir Geoffrey Harington, 1898–1967, vol. VI
Thompson, Lt-Gen. Sir Geoffrey Stuart, 1905–1983, vol. VIII
Thompson, Rev. George, *died* 1941, vol. IV
Thompson, George Henry Main, 1882–1957, vol. V

Thompson, Rev. Gerald Alexander, 1868–1939, vol. III
Thompson, Gerald Francis Michael Perronet, 1910–1994, vol. IX
Thompson, Gertrude C.; *see* Caton-Thompson.
Thompson, Gibson, *died* 1917, vol. II
Thompson, Gustav Weber, 1878–1944, vol. IV
Thompson, Captain Harold, 1881–1917, vol. II
Thompson, Sir Harold Warris, 1908–1983, vol. VIII
Thompson, Maj.-Gen. Sir Harry Neville, 1861–1925, vol. II
Thompson, Harry Sydney, 1878–1966, vol. VI
Thompson, Sir Henry, 1st Bt (*cr* 1899), 1820–1904, vol. I
Thompson, Rev. Henry, *died* 1916, vol. II
Thompson, Henry Edmund S.; *see* Symes-Thompson.
Thompson, Sir (Henry Francis) Herbert, 2nd Bt (*cr* 1899), 1859–1944, vol. IV
Thompson, Rt Rev. Henry Gregory, 1871–1942, vol. IV
Thompson, Henry Nilus, *died* 1938, vol. III
Thompson, Rev. (Henry) Percy, 1858–1935, vol. III
Thompson, Henry Yates, 1838–1928, vol. II
Thompson, Herbert, 1856–1945, vol. IV
Thompson, Herbert, 1870–1949, vol. IV
Thompson, Sir Herbert; *see* Thompson, Sir Henry F. H.
Thompson, Sir Herbert; *see* Thompson, Sir J. H.
Thompson, Herbert Marshall, *died* 1945, vol. IV
Thompson, Col Horace Cuthbert Rees, 1893–1975, vol. VII
Thompson, Hubert Charles M.; *see* Meysey-Thompson.
Thompson, Vice-Adm. Sir Hugh Leslie Owen, 1931–1996, vol. X
Thompson, Sir Ivan, 1894–1970, vol. VI
Thompson, J. Ashburton, 1846–1915, vol. I
Thompson, Sir James, 1835–1906, vol. I
Thompson, James Coulthred, *died* 1935, vol. III
Thompson, Rt Rev. James Denton, 1856–1924, vol. II
Thompson, Rev. James Matthew, 1878–1956, vol. V
Thompson, Maj.-Gen. John, 1830–1915, vol. I
Thompson, Sir John, 1907–1995, vol. IX
Thompson, John Baird, 1868–1948, vol. IV
Thompson, John Crighton, 1902–1982, vol. VIII
Thompson, Sir (John) Eric (Sidney), 1898–1975, vol. VII
Thompson, John Fairfield, 1881–1968, vol. VI
Thompson, (John) Kenneth, 1913–1985, vol. VIII
Thompson, John McLean, 1887–1977, vol. VII
Thompson, Air Cdre John Marlow, 1914–1994, vol. IX
Thompson, John Ockelford, 1872–1940, vol. III
Thompson, Sir John Perronet, 1873–1935, vol. III
Thompson, John William Howard, *died* 1959, vol. V
Thompson, Rear-Adm. John Yelverton, 1909–1998, vol. X
Thompson, Sir (Joseph) Herbert, 1898–1984, vol. VIII
Thompson, Kenneth; *see* Thompson, J. K.
Thompson, Rt Rev. Kenneth George, 1909–1975, vol. VII

Thompson, Sir Kenneth Pugh, 1st Bt, 1909–1984, vol. VIII
Thompson, Sir Lionel; see Thompson, Sir Louis L. H.
Thompson, Llewellyn E., 1904–1972, vol. VII
Thompson, Maj. Lloyd H.; see Hall-Thompson.
Thompson, Sir Lionel; see Thompson, Sir T. L. T.
Thompson, Sir (Louis) Lionel (Harry), 1893–1983, vol. VIII
Thompson, Sir Luke, 1867–1941, vol. IV
Thompson, Sir Matthew William, 3rd Bt (cr 1890), 1872–1956, vol. V
Thompson, Maurice, died 1901, vol. I
Thompson, Merrick Arnold Bardsley D.; see Denton-Thompson.
Thompson, Oliver Frederic, 1905–1993, vol. IX
Thompson, Owen, 1868–1958, vol. V
Thompson, Rev. Sir Peile, 2nd Bt (cr 1890), 1844–1918, vol. II
Thompson, Sir Peile, 5th Bt, 1911–1985, vol. VIII
Thompson, Sir Peile Beaumont, 4th Bt (cr 1890), 1874–1972, vol. VII
Thompson, Adm. Percival Henry H.; see Hall-Thompson.
Thompson, Sir Percy, 1872–1946, vol. IV
Thompson, Rev. Percy; see Thompson, Rev. H. P.
Thompson, Peter, 1871–1921, vol. II
Thompson, Piers Gilchrist, 1893–1969, vol. VI
Thompson, Sir Ralph Patrick, 1916–1991, vol. IX
Thompson, Rev. Ralph Wardlaw, died 1916, vol. II
Thompson, Rt Hon. Sir Ralph Wood, 1830–1902, vol. I
Thompson, Reginald Aubrey, 1905–1998, vol. X
Thompson, Reginald Campbell, 1876–1941, vol. IV
Thompson, Reginald Edward, 1834–1912, vol. I
Thompson, Reginald Harry, 1925–1992, vol. IX
Thompson, (Reginald) Stanley, 1899-1994, vol. IX
Thompson, Rev. Reginald William, died 1953, vol. V
Thompson, Col Richard, 1852–1932, vol. III
Thompson, Col Richard Frederick M.; see Meysey-Thompson.
Thompson, Sir Richard Hilton Marler, 1st Bt (cr 1963), 1912–1999, vol. X
Thompson, Lt-Col Richard James Campbell, 1880–1946, vol. IV
Thompson, Maj.-Gen. Richard Lovell Brereton, 1874–1957, vol. V
Thompson, Rt Hon. Robert, 1839–1918, vol. II
Thompson, Robert Cyril, 1907–1967, vol. VI
Thompson, Sir Robert Grainger Ker, 1916–1992, vol. IX
Thompson, Robert Henry Stewart, 1912–1998, vol. X
Thompson, Sir Robert James, 1845–1926, vol. II
Thompson, Robert John, 1867–1951, vol. V
Thompson, Maj. Robert Lloyd H.; see Hall-Thompson.
Thompson, Sir Robert Norman, 1878–1951, vol. V
Thompson, Lt-Col Roland-Wycliffe, 1864–1940, vol. III
Thompson, (Russell) Ernest, 1936–1998, vol. X
Thompson, Lt-Col Rt Hon. S. H. H.; see Hall-Thompson.
Thompson, Samuel Nock, 1851–1938, vol. III

Thompson, Silvanus Phillips, 1851–1916, vol. II
Thompson, Stanley; see Thompson, R. S.
Thompson, Major Stephen John, 1875–1955, vol. V
Thompson, Sylvia, (Mrs Peter Luling), 1902–1968, vol. VI
Thompson, Theodore, 1878–1935, vol. III
Thompson, Hon. Thomas, vol. II
Thompson, Sir (Thomas) Lionel (Tennyson), 5th Bt (cr 1806), 1921–1999, vol. X
Thompson, Sir Thomas Raikes, 3rd Bt (cr 1806), 1852–1904, vol. I
Thompson, Lt-Col Sir Thomas Raikes Lovett, 4th Bt (cr 1806), 1881–1964, vol. VI
Thompson, Maj.-Gen. Sir Treffry Owen, 1888–1979, vol. VII
Thompson, Vernon Cecil, 1905–1995, vol. IX
Thompson, Viginti Tertius, 1862–1946, vol. IV
Thompson, Sir Walter, 1875–1951, vol. V
Thompson, Walter Scott, 1885–1966, vol. VI
Thompson, Rev. William, died 1909, vol. I
Thompson, Brig.-Gen. William Arthur Murray, 1866–1938, vol. III
Thompson, William David James C.; see Cargill Thompson.
Thompson, William George, 1863–1953, vol. V
Thompson, Brig.-Gen. William George Hemsley, 1871–1944, vol. IV
Thompson, William Harding, 1887–1946, vol. IV
Thompson, Sir William Henry, died 1918, vol. II
Thompson, William Hugh, 1885–1966, vol. VI
Thompson, Rt Rev. William Jameson, 1885–1975, vol. VII
Thompson, Sir William John, 1861–1929, vol. III
Thompson, William John, 1871–1959, vol. V
Thompson, William John, died 1971, vol. VII
Thompson, William Marcus, 1857–1907, vol. I
Thompson, Lt-Col William Maxwell, 1869–1934, vol. III
Thompson, Col William Oliver, 1844–1917, vol. II
Thompson, William Robin, 1887–1972, vol. VII
Thompson, William Whitaker, 1857–1920, vol. II
Thompson-McCausland, Lucius Perronet, 1904–1984, vol. VIII
Thompstone, Sir Eric Westbury, 1897–1974, vol. VII
Thompstone, Sydney Wilson, 1863–1935, vol. III
Thoms, Lt-Col Nathaniel William Benjamin Butler, 1880–1957, vol. V
Thomson, 1st Baron, 1875–1930, vol. III
Thomson, Hon. Lord; Alexander Thomson, 1914–1979, vol. VII
Thomson, Rt Hon. Lord; George Reid Thomson, 1893–1962, vol. VI
Thomson of Fleet, 1st Baron, 1894–1976, vol. VII
Thomson, Ada; see Merchant, Vivien.
Thomson, Sir Adam, 1926–2000, vol. X
Thomson, A(dam) Bruce, 1885–1976, vol. VII
Thomson, Addison Yalden, 1863–1931, vol. III
Thomson, Brig. Alan Fortescue, 1880–1957, vol. V
Thomson, Engr Captain Alan Leslie, 1890–1970, vol. VI
Thomson, Alexander; see Thomson, Hon. Lord.
Thomson, Lt-Col Alexander Guthrie, 1873–1953, vol. V
Thomson, Col Alexander M.; see Milne-Thomson.

Thomson, Hon. Alexander Macdonald, 1863–1924, vol. II

Thomson, Alexander Stuart Duff, 1854–1927, vol. II

Thomson, Alfred Reginald, *died* 1979, vol. VII

Thomson, Rev. Andrew, 1814–1901, vol. I

Thomson, Brig.-Gen. Andrew Graham, 1858–1926, vol. II

Thomson, Captain Anthony Standidge, 1851–1925, vol. II

Thomson, Arthur, 1858–1935, vol. III

Thomson, Sir Arthur; *see* Thomson, Sir J. A.

Thomson, Sir (Arthur) Landsborough, 1890–1977, vol. VII

Thomson, Sir Arthur Peregrine, 1890–1977, vol. VII

Thomson, Sir Basil Home, 1861–1939, vol. III

Thomson, Benjamin, *died* 1934, vol. III

Thomson, Bryden, 1928–1991, vol. IX

Thomson, César, 1856–1931, vol. III

Thomson, Air Chief Marshal Sir (Charles) John, 1941–1994, vol. IX

Thomson, Rev. Canon Clement R., 1870–1953, vol. V

Thomson, Sir Daniel, 1912–1976, vol. VII

Thomson, David, 1912–1970, vol. VI

Thomson, David Alexander, 1872–1922, vol. II

Thomson, David Couper, 1861–1954, vol. V

Thomson, David Croal, 1855–1930, vol. III

Thomson, Lt-Col David George, 1856–1923, vol. II

Thomson, David Kinnear, 1910–1992, vol. IX

Thomson, David Landsborough, 1901–1964, vol. VI

Thomson, Donald F., 1901–1970, vol. VI (AII)

Thomson, Sir Douglas; *see* Thomson, Sir J. D. W.

Thomson, Hon. Dugald, 1848–1922, vol. II

Thomson, Edward William, 1849–1924, vol. II

Thomson, Elihu, 1853–1937, vol. III

Thomson, Eric Hugh, 1909–1973, vol. VII

Thomson, Sir Evan Rees Whitaker, 1919–1993, vol. IX

Thomson, Vice-Adm. Evelyn Claude Ogilvie, 1884–1941, vol. IV

Thomson, Ewen Cameron, 1915–1988, vol. VIII

Thomson, Rt Rev. Francis, 1917–1987, vol. VIII

Thomson, Francis Paul, 1914–1998, vol. X

Thomson, Sir (Francis) Vernon, 1st Bt (*cr* 1938), 1881–1953, vol. V

Thomson, Frank David, 1877–1934, vol. III

Thomson, Sir Frederick Charles, 1st Bt (*cr* 1929), 1875–1935, vol. III

Thomson, Sir Frederick Whitley W.; *see* Whitley-Thomson.

Thomson, Surg.-Col Sir George, 1843–1903, vol. I

Thomson, George, *died* 1939, vol. III

Thomson, Major George, 1889–1970, vol. VI

Thomson, George Derwent, 1903–1987, vol. VIII

Thomson, George Ewart, 1897–1981, vol. VIII

Thomson, Rev. George Ian Falconer, 1912–1987, vol. VIII

Thomson, George Malcolm, 1848–1933, vol. III

Thomson, George Malcolm, 1899–1996, vol. X

Thomson, Sir George Paget, 1892–1975, vol. VII

Thomson, Rear-Adm. Sir George Pirie, 1887–1965, vol. VI

Thomson, Rt Hon. George Reid; *see* Thomson, Rt Hon. Lord.

Thomson, Lt-Col George Ritchie, *died* 1946, vol. IV

Thomson, Rev. George Thomas, 1887–1958, vol. V

Thomson, George Walker, 1883–1949, vol. IV

Thomson, George William, 1845–1928, vol. II

Thomson, Gladys S.; *see* Scott Thomson.

Thomson, Sir Godfrey Hilton, 1881–1955, vol. V

Thomson, Sir Graeme, 1875–1933, vol. III

Thomson, Harry Redmond, 1860–1917, vol. II

Thomson, Harry Torrance, 1868–1944, vol. IV

Thomson, Henry, 1840–1916, vol. II

Thomson, Maj.-Gen. Henry, 1851–1932, vol. III

Thomson, Henry Alexis, 1863–1924, vol. II

Thomson, Henry John, *died* 1966, vol. VI

Thomson, Henry Wagstaffe, 1874–1941, vol. IV

Thomson, Herbert Campbell, 1870–1940, vol. III

Thomson, Hugh, 1860–1920, vol. II

Thomson, Col Sir Hugh Davie W.; *see* White-Thomson.

Thomson, Maj.-Gen. Hugh Gordon, 1830–1910, vol. I

Thomson, Very Rev. Ian Hugh W.; *see* White-Thomson.

Thomson, Ian Mackenzie, 1926–2000, vol. X

Thomson, Sir Ivo Wilfrid Home, 2nd Bt (*cr* 1925), 1902–1991, vol. IX

Thomson, Sir James, 1848–1929, vol. III

Thomson, Maj.-Gen. James, 1862–1953, vol. V

Thomson, James, 1895–1959, vol. V

Thomson, James Alexander Kerr, 1879–1959, vol. V

Thomson, Tun Sir James Beveridge, 1902–1983, vol. VIII

Thomson, Sir (James) Douglas (Wishart), 2nd Bt (*cr* 1929), 1905–1972, vol. VII

Thomson, James Frederick Gordon; *see* Hon. Lord Migdale.

Thomson, James Leonard, 1905–1997, vol. X

Thomson, James Moffat, *died* 1953, vol. V

Thomson, Maj.-Gen. James Noel, 1888–1978, vol. VII

Thomson, James Oliver, 1889–1971, vol. VII

Thomson, James Park, 1854–1941, vol. IV

Thomson, Very Rev. James Sutherland, 1892–1972, vol. VII

Thomson, Lt-Col Sir James Wishart, 1871–1929, vol. III

Thomson, Captain Jocelyn Home, 1859–1908, vol. I

Thomson, Air Chief Marshal Sir John; *see* Thomson, Air Chief Marshal Sir C. J.

Thomson, John, 1856–1926, vol. II

Thomson, John, 1903–1974, vol. VII

Thomson, Sir John, 1908–1998, vol. X

Thomson, John A.; *see* Anstruther-Thomson.

Thomson, Sir (John) Arthur, 1861–1933, vol. III

Thomson, John Ebenezer Honeyman, 1841–1923, vol. II

Thomson, Lt-Col John Ferguson, 1880–1937, vol. III

Thomson, John Gordon, *died* 1937, vol. III

Thomson, Sir John Mackay, 1887–1974, vol. VII

Thomson, John Millar, 1849–1933, vol. III

Thomson, J(ohn) Murray, 1885–1974, vol. VII

Thomson, John Stuart, 1888–1973, vol. VII

Thomson, Sir Joseph John, 1856–1940, vol. III

Thomson, Sir Landsborough; *see* Thomson, Sir A. L.

Thomson, Rt Rev. Leonard Jauncey W.; *see* White-Thomson.
Thomson, Leslie, *died* 1929, vol. III
Thomson, Louis Melville M.; *see* Milne-Thomson.
Thomson, Mark Alméras, 1903–1962, vol. VI
Thomson, (Matthew) Sydney, 1894–1969, vol. VI
Thomson, Sir Mitchell M.; *see* Mitchell-Thomson.
Thomson, Gen. Sir Mowbray, 1832–1917, vol. II
Thomson, Brig.-Gen. Noel Arbuthnot, 1872–1959, vol. V
Thomson, Very Rev. P. D., 1872–1955, vol. V
Thomson, Peter, 1914–1991, vol. IX
Thomson, Robert Norman, 1935–1994, vol. IX
Thomson, Col Sir Robert Thomas W.; *see* White-Thomson.
Thomson, Col Roger Gordon, 1878–1976, vol. VII
Thomson, Air Vice-Marshal Ronald Bain, 1912–1984, vol. VIII
Thomson, Sir Ronald Jordan, 1895–1978, vol. VII
Thomson, Roy Harry Goodisson, 1891–1974, vol. VII
Thomson, Sir St Clair, 1859–1943, vol. IV
Thomson, Col Samuel John, 1853–1936, vol. III
Thomson, Sydney; *see* Thomson, M. S.
Thomson, Theodore, 1857–1916, vol. II
Thomson, Rev. T(homas) B(entley) Stewart, 1889–1973, vol. VII
Thomson, Thomas Davidson, 1911–1989, vol. VIII
Thomson, Trevelyan, 1875–1928, vol. II
Thomson, Sir Vernon; *see* Thomson, Sir F. V.
Thomson, Walter Henry, 1856–1917, vol. II
Thomson, Sir Wilfrid Forbes Home, 1st Bt (*cr* 1925), 1858–1939, vol. III
Thomson, Sir William, 1843–1910, vol. I
Thomson, Sir William, 1856–1947, vol. IV
Thomson, Sir William, 1916–1971, vol. VII
Thomson, Sir William Brown, 1863–1937, vol. III
Thomson, William Archibald Robson, 1906–1983, vol. VIII
Thomson, Col William David, 1858–1941, vol. IV
Thomson, Sir William Gardner, 1874–1938, vol. III
Thomson, Sir William Johnston, 1881–1949, vol. IV
Thomson, Lt-Gen. Sir William Montgomerie, 1877–1963, vol. VI
Thomson, Sir William R.; *see* Rowan-Thomson.
Thomson, Sir William Willis Dalziel, *died* 1950, vol. IV
Thomson-Walker, Sir John William, *died* 1937, vol. III
Thorburn, Archibald, 1860–1935, vol. III
Thorburn, Col Harold Hay, 1882–1937, vol. III
Thorburn, J. Hay, 1848–1931, vol. III
Thorburn, James Jamieson, 1864–1929, vol. III
Thorburn, Sir Michael Grieve, 1851–1934, vol. III
Thorburn, Hon. Sir Robert, 1836–1906, vol. I
Thorburn, Septimus Smet, 1844–1924, vol. II
Thorburn, Thomas, *died* 1927, vol. II
Thorburn, Rev. Thomas James, 1858–1923, vol. II
Thorburn, Sir Walter, 1842–1908, vol. I
Thorburn, Sir William, *died* 1923, vol. II
Thorburn, Lt-Col William, 1881–1959, vol. V
Thorby, Hon. Harold Victor Campbell, 1888–1973, vol. VII
Thorley, George Earlam, 1830–1904, vol. I
Thorley, Sir Gerald Bowers, 1913–1988, vol. VIII

Thorley, Wilfrid, 1878–1963, vol. VI
Thorman, Rt Rev. Joseph, 1871–1936, vol. III
Thorn, Sir Jules, 1899–1980, vol. VII
Thorn-Drury, George; *see* Drury.
Thorndike, Dame (Agnes) Sybil, 1882–1976, vol. VII
Thorndike, (Arthur) Russell, 1885–1972, vol. VII
Thorndike, Russell; *see* Thorndike, A. R.
Thorndike, Dame Sibyl; *see* Thorndike, Dame A. S.
Thorne, Alfred Charles, 1870–1952, vol. IV
Thorne, Gen. Sir Andrew; *see* Thorne, Gen. Sir A. F. A. N.
Thorne, Atwood, 1867–1932, vol. III
Thorne, Gen. Sir (Augustus Francis) Andrew (Nicol), 1885–1970, vol. VI
Thorne, Charles, *died* 1933, vol. III
Thorne, Christopher Guy, 1934–1992, vol. IX
Thorne, Maj.-Gen. Sir David Calthrop, 1933–2000, vol. X
Thorne, Edward Henry, 1834–1916, vol. II
Thorne, Rt Rev. Frank Oswald, 1892–1981, vol. VIII
Thorne, George Rennie, 1853–1934, vol. III
Thorne, Gordon, 1912–1965, vol. VI
Thorne, Guy; *see* Gull, Cyril Arthur Edward Ranger.
Thorne, Sir John Anderson, 1888–1964, vol. VI
Thorne, Sir Richard Thorne, 1841–1899, vol. I
Thorne, Air Vice-Marshal Walter, 1890–1960, vol. V
Thorne, Rt Hon. Will; *see* Thorne, Rt Hon. W. J.
Thorne, Sir William, 1839–1917, vol. II
Thorne, Sir William Calthrop, 1864–1935, vol. III
Thorne, William Hobart Houghton, 1875–1931, vol. III
Thorne, William Huxtable, 1882–1951, vol. V
Thorne, Rt Hon. William James, (Will), 1857–1946, vol. IV
Thorne-Waite, Robert, 1842–1935, vol. III
Thorneloe, Most Rev. George, 1848–1935, vol. III
Thornely, Sir Arnold, 1870–1953, vol. V
Thornely, P. Wilfrid, 1879–1926, vol. II
Thornely, Thomas, 1855–1949, vol. IV
Thorneycroft, Baron (Life Peer); (George Edward) Peter Thorneycroft, 1909–1994, vol. IX
Thorneycroft, Maj.-Gen. Alexander Whitelaw, 1859–1931, vol. III
Thorneycroft, Major George Edward Mervyn, 1883–1943, vol. IV
Thorneycroft, Harry, 1892–1956, vol. V
Thorneycroft, Thomas Hamo, *died* 1970, vol. VI
Thorneycroft, Wallace, 1864–1954, vol. V
Thornhill, Sir Anthony John Compton-, 2nd Bt, 1868–1949, vol. IV
Thornhill, Arthur Horace, 1895–1970, vol. VI
Thornhill, Arthur John, 1850–1930, vol. III
Thornhill, Col Cudbert John Massy, 1883–1952, vol. V
Thornhill, Lt-Col Edmund Basil, 1898–1998, vol. X
Thornhill, George, *died* 1908, vol. I
Thornhill, Col George B.; *see* Badham-Thornhill.
Thornhill, Lt-Col Sir Henry Beaufoy, 1854–1942, vol. IV
Thornhill, Noel, 1881–1955, vol. V
Thornhill, Dame Rachel; *see* Crowdy, Dame R. E.

Thornhill, Sir Thomas, 1st Bt, 1837–1900, vol. I
Thornhill, Thomas Bryan C.; see Clarke-Thornhill.
Thornley, Sir Colin Hardwick, 1907–1983, vol. VIII
Thornley, Sir Hubert Gordon, 1884–1962, vol. VI
Thornley, Reginald Ernest, 1872–1942, vol. IV
Thornley, Major Samuel Kerr, 1871–1947, vol. IV
Thornton, Alfred Henry Robinson, 1863–1939, vol. III
Thornton, Lt-Col Arthur Parry, 1848–1909, vol. I
Thornton, Rev. Augustus Vansittart, 1851–1913, vol. I
Thornton, Lt-Col Charles Edward, 1867–1946, vol. IV
Thornton, Charles Inglis, 1850–1929, vol. III
Thornton, (Clara) Grace, 1913–1987, vol. VIII
Thornton, Ven Claude Cyprian, died 1939, vol. III
Thornton, Edna, died 1964, vol. VI
Thornton, Rt Hon. Sir Edward, 1817–1906, vol. I
Thornton, Brig. Sir Edward Newbury, 1878–1946, vol. IV
Thornton, Ernest, 1905–1992, vol. IX
Thornton, Sir Ernest Hugh, 1884–1951, vol. V
Thornton, Rev. Frederick Ferdinand Martin S., died 1938, vol. III
Thornton, George Edwin, 1899–1983, vol. VIII
Thornton, George Lestock, 1872–1951, vol. V
Thornton, Rev. George Ruthven, 1882–1964, vol. VI
Thornton, Sir Gerard; see Thornton, Sir H. G.
Thornton, Grace; see Thornton, C. G.
Thornton, Sir (Henry) Gerard, 1892–1977, vol. VII
Thornton, Air Vice-Marshal Henry Norman, 1896–1971, vol. VII
Thornton, Sir Henry Worth, 1871–1933, vol. III
Thornton, Rev. Herbert Parry, died 1923, vol. II
Thornton, Hugh Aylmer, 1872–1962, vol. VI
Thornton, Sir Hugh Cholmondeley, 1881–1962, vol. VI
Thornton, Jack Edward Clive, 1915–1996, vol. X
Thornton, James Cholmondeley, 1906–1969, vol. VI
Thornton, Sir James Howard, 1834–1919, vol. II
Thornton, Lt-Gen. Sir Leonard Whitmore, 1916–1999, vol. X
Thornton, Col Leslie Heber, 1873–1937, vol. III
Thornton, Rev. Lionel Spencer, 1884–1960, vol. V
Thornton, Maxwell Ruthven, 1878–1950, vol. IV
Thornton, Michael James, 1919–1989, vol. VIII
Thornton, Percy Melville, 1841–1918, vol. II
Thornton, R. M., 1841–1913, vol. I
Thornton, Major Robert Lawrence, 1865–1947, vol. IV
Thornton, Hon. Robert Stirton, 1863–1936, vol. III
Thornton, Major Roland Hobhouse, 1892–1967, vol. VI
Thornton, Sir Ronald George, 1901–1981, vol. VIII
Thornton, Russel William, 1881–1966, vol. VI
Thornton, Rt Rev. Samuel, 1835–1917, vol. II
Thornton, Rev. Stephen Augustine Lawrence, 1871–1936, vol. III
Thornton, Swinford Leslie, 1853–1939, vol. III
Thornton, Sir Thomas, 1829–1903, vol. I
Thornton, Col Thomas Anson, 1887–1978, vol. VII
Thornton, Thomas Henry, 1832–1913, vol. I
Thornton, William Mundell, 1870–1944, vol. IV

Thornton-Berry, Trevor, 1895–1967, vol. VI
Thornton Cook, Elsie; see Cook.
Thornton-Duesbury, Rt Rev. Charles Leonard, 1867–1928, vol. II
Thornton-Duesbery, Rev. Canon Julian Percy, 1902–1985, vol. VIII
Thornton-Kemsley, Col Sir Colin Norman, 1903–1977, vol. VII
Thornton-Smith, Ernest T., 1881–1971, vol. VII
Thornycroft, Lt-Col Charles Mytton, 1879–1948, vol. IV
Thornycroft, Sir Hamo; see Thornycroft, Sir W. H.
Thornycroft, Sir John Edward, 1872–1960, vol. V
Thornycroft, Sir John Isaac, 1843–1928, vol. II
Thornycroft, John Ward, 1899–1989, vol. VIII
Thornycroft, Oliver, 1885–1956, vol. V
Thornycroft, Sir (William) Hamo, 1850–1925, vol. II
Thoroddsen, Thorvald, 1855–1921, vol. II
Thorogood, Horace Walter, died 1962, vol. VI
Thorogood, Stanley, 1873–1953, vol. V
Thorold, Algar Labouchere, 1866–1936, vol. III
Thorold, Captain Sir Anthony Henry, 15th Bt, 1903–1999, vol. X
Thorold, Rev. Ernest Hayford, 1879–1940, vol. III
Thorold, Sir Guy Frederick, 1898–1970, vol. VI
Thorold, Col Hayford Douglas, 1859–1934, vol. III
Thorold, Air Vice-Marshal Henry Karslake, 1896–1966, vol. VI
Thorold, Sir James Ernest, 14th Bt, 1877–1965, vol. VI
Thorold, Sir John George, 13th Bt, 1870–1951, vol. V
Thorold, Sir John Henry, 12th Bt, 1842–1922, vol. II
Thorold, Montague George, 1844–1920, vol. II
Thorold, William James, 1871–1942, vol. IV (A), vol. V
Thorold, Lt-Col Charles Julian, 1875–1939, vol. III
Thorp, Lt-Col Arthur Hugh, 1869–1955, vol. V
Thorp, Austin, 1873–1918, vol. II
Thorp, Adm. Charles Frederick, 1869–1954, vol. V
Thorp, Col Herbert Walter Beck, 1879–1934, vol. III
Thorp, J. Walter H., 1851–1912, vol. I
Thorp, Sir John Kingsmill Robert, 1912–1961, vol. VI
Thorp, Joseph Peter, 1873–1962, vol. VI
Thorp, Linton Theodore, 1884–1950, vol. IV
Thorp, Brig. Robert Allen Fenwick, 1900–1966, vol. VI
Thorp, William Henry, 1852–1944, vol. IV
Thorpe, A(rthur) Winton, 1865–1952, vol. V
Thorpe, Bernard, 1895–1987, vol. VIII
Thorpe, Sir Edward; see Thorpe, Sir T. E.
Thorpe, Brig.-Gen. Edward Ivan de Sausmarez, 1871–1942, vol. IV
Thorpe, Frank Gordon, 1885–1967, vol. VI
Thorpe, Col Sir Fred Garner, 1893–1970, vol. VI
Thorpe, Maj.-Gen. Gervase, 1877–1962, vol. VI
Thorpe, Harry, 1913–1977, vol. VII
Thorpe, James, 1876–1949, vol. IV
Thorpe, Sir Jocelyn Field, 1872–1940, vol. III
Thorpe, John Henry, 1887–1944, vol. IV
Thorpe, Ven. John Henry, died 1932, vol. III

Thorpe, Lewis Guy Melville, 1913–1977, vol. VII
Thorpe, Col Sir Ronald Laurence G.; see
   Gardner-Thorpe.
Thorpe, Sir (Thomas) Edward, 1845–1925, vol. II
Thorpe, Surg. Rear-Adm. Vidal Gunson,
   1864–1948, vol. IV
Thorpe, William Geoffrey, 1909–1975, vol. VII
Thorpe, William Homan, 1902–1986, vol. VIII
Thorson, Hon. Joseph T., 1889–1978, vol. VII
Thorvaldson, Gunnar S., 1901–1969, vol. VI
Thorvardsson, Stefan, 1900–1951, vol. V
Thoseby, William Martin, 1901–1959, vol. V
Thouless, Robert Henry, 1894–1984, vol. VIII
Thoyts, Robert Francis Newman, 1913–1991,
   vol. IX
Threipland, Col William M.; see
   Murray-Threipland.
Threlfall, Sir Richard, 1861–1932, vol. III
Threlfall, Richard Ian, 1920–1997, vol. X
Threlfall, Thomas, 1842–1907, vol. I
Threlford, Sir William Lacon, 1883–1958, vol. V
Thresh, John Clough, 1850–1932, vol. III
Thresher, Lt-Col James Henville, 1870–1943,
   vol. IV
Thrift, Sir John Edward, 1845–1926, vol. II
Thrift, William Edward, 1870–1942, vol. IV
Thring, 1st Baron, 1818–1907, vol. I
Thring, Sir Arthur Theodore, 1860–1932, vol. III
Thring, Captain Ernest Walsham Charles,
   1875–1970, vol. VI
Thring, George Herbert, 1859–1941, vol. IV
Thring, Captain Walter Hugh Charles Samuel,
   1873–1949, vol. IV
Throckmorton, Sir Anthony John Benedict, 12th Bt,
   1916–1994, vol. IX
Throckmorton, Geoffrey William Berkeley,
   1883–1976, vol. VII
Throckmorton, Sir Nicholas William George, 9th
   Bt, 1838–1919, vol. II
Throckmorton, Sir Richard Charles Acton, 10th Bt,
   1839–1927, vol. II
Throckmorton, Sir Robert George Maxwell, 11th Bt,
   1908–1989, vol. VIII
Throssell, Arthur Graham, 1881–1942, vol. IV
Throssell, Hon. George, 1840–1910, vol. I
Throssell, Hugo Vivian Hope, 1884–1933, vol. III
Thrower, Frank James, 1932–1987, vol. VIII
Thrower, Percy John, 1913–1988, vol. VIII
Thubron, John Brown Sydney, 1879–1949, vol. IV
Thuillier, Sir Henry Edward Landor, 1813–1906,
   vol. I
Thuillier, Maj.-Gen. Sir Henry Fleetwood,
   1868–1953, vol. V
Thuillier, Sir Henry Ravenshaw, 1838–1922, vol. II
Thuillier, Lt-Col Henry Shakespear, 1895–1982,
   vol. VIII
Thuillier, Maj.-Gen. Lesle de Malapert, (Pete),
   1905–1999, vol. X
Thuillier, Maj.-Gen. Pete; see Thuillier, Maj.-Gen.
   L. de M.
Thuillier, Brig.-Gen. Willoughby, 1860–1941,
   vol. IV
Thulrai, Taluqdar of, 1865–1920, vol. II, vol. III
Thumboo Chetty, Amatyasiromani Sir Bernard T.,
   1877–1952, vol. V (A), vol. VI (AI)

Thunder, Lt-Col Stuart Harman Joseph, 1879–1948,
   vol. IV
Thurber, James Grover, 1894–1961, vol. VI
Thurburn, Edward Alexander, 1841–1915, vol. I
Thurburn, Gwynneth Loveday, 1899–1993, vol. IX
Thurburn, Col James White, 1848–1930, vol. III
Thurburn, Brig. Roy Gilbert, 1901–1990, vol. VIII
Thureau-Dangin, François, 1872–1944, vol. IV
Thureau-Dangin, Paul Marie Pierre, 1837–1913,
   vol. I
Thurles, Viscount; James Anthony Butler,
   1916–1940, vol. III
Thurlow, 5th Baron, 1838–1916, vol. II
Thurlow, 6th Baron, 1869–1952, vol. V
Thurlow, 7th Baron, 1910–1971, vol. VII
Thurlow, Very Rev. Alfred Gilbert Goddard,
   1911–1991, vol. IX
Thurlow, Very Rev. Gilbert; see Thurlow, Very
   Rev. A. G. G.
Thurnam, Walter Digby, 1854–1934, vol. III
Thurnheer, Walter, 1884–1945, vol. IV
Thursby, Adm. Sir Cecil Fiennes, 1861–1936,
   vol. III
Thursby, Sir George James, 3rd Bt, 1869–1941,
   vol. IV
Thursby, Sir John Hardy, 1st Bt, 1826–1901, vol. I
Thursby, Sir John Ormerod Scarlett, 2nd Bt,
   1861–1920, vol. II
Thursby-Pelham, James, 1869–1947, vol. IV
Thursfield, (Edward) Philip, 1876–1962, vol. VI
Thursfield, Rear-Adm. Henry George, 1882–1963,
   vol. VI
Thursfield, Hugh, died 1944, vol. IV
Thursfield, Sir James Richard, 1840–1923, vol. II
Thursfield, Philip; see Thursfield, E. P.
Thursfield, Captain (S) Raymond Spencer,
   1882–1953, vol. V
Thurso, 1st Viscount, 1890–1970, vol. VI
Thurso, 2nd Viscount, 1922–1995, vol. IX
Thurstan, Edward William Paget, 1880–1947,
   vol. IV
Thurstan, Violetta, died 1978, vol. VII
Thurston, Albert Peter, 1881–1964, vol. VI
Thurston, E. Temple, 1879–1933, vol. III
Thurston, Edgar, 1855–1935, vol. III
Thurston, Frederick John, 1901–1953, vol. V
Thurston, Gavin Leonard Bourdas, 1911–1980,
   vol. VII
Thurston, Sir George; see Thurston, Sir T. G. O.
Thurston, Rev. Herbert, 1856–1939, vol. III
Thurston, Col Hugh Champneys, 1862–1919, vol. II
Thurston, Col Hugh Stanley, 1869–1945, vol. IV
Thurston, Katherine Cecil, 1875–1911, vol. I
Thurston, Sir (T.) George (O.), died 1950, vol. IV
Thurtle, Ernest, 1884–1954, vol. V
Thwaite, Hartley, 1903–1978, vol. VII
Thwaites, Brian St George, 1912–1989, vol. VIII
Thwaites, Lt-Col Norman Graham, 1872–1956,
   vol. V
Thwaites, Brig. Peter Trevenen, 1926–1991, vol. IX
Thwaites, Gen. Sir William, 1868–1947, vol. IV
Thwing, Charles Franklin, 1853–1937, vol. III
Thyateira, Archbishop of; see Athenagoras,
   Archbishop.
Thyne, William, 1901–1978, vol. VII

Thynne, Lord Alexander George, 1873–1918, vol. II
Thynne, Major Algernon Carteret, 1868–1917, vol. II
Thynne, Col Hon. Andrew Joseph, 1847–1927, vol. II
Thynne, Rev. Arthur Barugh, 1840–1917, vol. II
Thynne, Rev. Arthur Christopher, 1832–1908, vol. II
Thynne, Captain Denis Granville, 1875–1955, vol. V
Thynne, Francis John, 1830–1910, vol. I
Thynne, Sir Henry, 1839–1915, vol. I
Thynne, Rt Hon. Lord Henry Frederick, 1832–1904, vol. I
Thynne, Maj.-Gen. Sir Reginald Thomas, 1843–1926, vol. II
Thynne, Col Ulric Oliver, 1871–1957, vol. V
Tiarks, Frank Cyril, 1874–1952, vol. V
Tiarks, Rt Rev. Geoffrey Lewis, 1909–1987, vol. VIII
Tiarks, Henry Frederic, 1900–1995, vol. IX
Tiarks, Rt Rev. John Gerhard, 1903–1974, vol. VII
Tibbits, Vice-Adm. Charles, 1872–1947, vol. IV
Tibbits, Charles John, 1861–1935, vol. III
Tibbits, Sir Cliff; see Tibbits, Sir J. C.
Tibbits, Sir (Jabez) Cliff, 1884–1974, vol. VII
Tibble, John William, 1901–1972, vol. VII
Tibbles, Sydney Granville, 1884–1960, vol. V
Tibbles, William, 1859–1928, vol. II
Tichborne, Sir Anthony Joseph Henry Doughty Doughty-, 14th Bt, 1914–1968, vol. VI
Tichborne, Charles Robert, died 1905, vol. I
Tichborne, Rt Rev. Ford, died 1940, vol. III
Tichborne, Sir Henry Alfred Joseph Doughty-, 12th Bt, 1866–1910, vol. I
Tichborne, Sir Joseph Henry Bernard Doughty-, 13th Bt, 1890–1930, vol. III
Tickell, Lt-Col Edward James, 1861–1942, vol. IV
Tickell, Maj.-Gen. Sir Eustace Francis, 1893–1972, vol. VII
Tickell, Rear-Adm. Frederick, 1857–1919, vol. II
Tickell, Richard Hugh, died 1948, vol. IV
Tickle, Ernest William, 1882–1947, vol. IV
Tickle, Rt Rev. Gerard William, 1909–1994, vol. IX
Tickler, Thomas George, 1852–1938, vol. III
Tidbury-Beer, Sir Frederick Tidbury, 1892–1959, vol. V
Tiddeman, Lizzie Ellen, died 1937, vol. III
Tidswell, Brig.-Gen. Edward Cecil, 1862–1937, vol. III
Tidy, Sir Henry Letheby, 1877–1960, vol. V
Tiegs, Oscar Werner, 1897–1956, vol. V
Tierney, Dom Alphonsus; see Tierney, Dom F. A.
Tierney, Dom Francis Alphonsus, 1910–1992, vol. IX
Tierney, Michael, 1894–1975, vol. VII
Tiffany, Stanley, 1908–1971, vol. VII
Tiffin, Arthur Ernest, 1896–1955, vol. V
Tigar, Edward, 1851–1937, vol. III
Tighe, Maj.-Gen. Anthony; see Tighe, Maj.-Gen. P. A. M.
Tighe, Edward Kenrick Banbury, 1862–1917, vol. II
Tighe, Henry, (Harry), 1877–1946, vol. IV
Tighe, Lt-Gen. Sir Michael Joseph, 1864–1925, vol. II

Tighe, Maj.-Gen. Patrick Anthony Macartan, 1923–1989, vol. VIII
Tighe, Thomas, 1829–1914, vol. I
Tighe, Major Vincent John, 1865–1919, vol. II
Tighe, Rear-Adm. Wilfred Geoffrey Stuart, 1905–1975, vol. VII
Tilbe, Douglas Sidney, 1931–1984, vol. VIII
Tilberis, Elizabeth Jane, 1947–1999, vol. X
Tilby, A. Wyatt, 1880–1948, vol. IV
Tilden, Philip Armstrong, 1887–1956, vol. V
Tilden, Sir William Augustus, 1842–1926, vol. II
Tilden, William Tatem, 1893–1953, vol. V
Tilea, Viorel Virgil, 1896–1972, vol. VII
Tiley, Arthur, 1910–1994, vol. IX
Tillard, Col Arthur Basil, 1870–1938, vol. III
Tillard, Rear-Adm. Sir Aubrey Thomas, 1881–1952, vol. V
Tillard, Maj.-Gen. John Arthur, 1837–1928, vol. II
Tillard, Maj.-Gen. Philip Blencowe, 1923–1994, vol. IX
Tillard, Adm. Philip Francis, 1852–1933, vol. III
Tillett, Benjamin, 1860–1943, vol. IV
Tillett, Emmie Muriel, 1896–1982, vol. VIII
Tillett, John Varnell, 1868–1931, vol. III
Tillett, Louis John, 1865–1929, vol. III
Tilley, Arthur Augustus, 1851–1942, vol. IV
Tilley, Cecil Edgar, 1894–1973, vol. VII
Tilley, Sir George, 1866–1948, vol. IV
Tilley, George Reginald Louis, 1904–1963, vol. VI
Tilley, Herbert, died 1941, vol. IV
Tilley, Sir John, 1813–1898, vol. I
Tilley, Rt Hon. Sir John Anthony Cecil, 1869–1952, vol. V
Tilley, Leonard Percy De Wolfe, 1870–1947, vol. IV
Tilley, Vesta, (Lady de Frece; Matilda Alice), 1864–1952, vol. V
Tillich, Paul, 1886–1965, vol. VI
Tillie, Lt-Col William Kingsley, died 1939, vol. III
Tilling, Richard Stephen, 1851–1929, vol. III
Tillinghast, Charles Carpenter, Jr, 1911–1998, vol. X
Tillotson, Geoffrey, 1905–1969, vol. VI
Tilly, Maj.-Gen. Justice Crosland, 1888–1941, vol. IV
Tillyard, Eustace Mandeville Wetenhall, 1889–1962, vol. VI
Tillyard, Sir Frank, 1865–1961, vol. VI
Tillyard, Henry Julius Wetenhall, 1881–1968, vol. VI
Tillyard, Robin John, 1881–1937, vol. III
Tilman, Harold William, 1898–1977/8, vol. VII
Tilmouth, Michael, 1930–1987, vol. VIII
Tilney, Frederick Colin, 1870–1951, vol. V
Tilney, Dame Guinevere, 1916–1997, vol. X
Tilney, John Deane, 1841–1909, vol. I
Tilney, Sir John Dudley Robert Tarleton, 1907–1994, vol. IX
Tilney, Lt-Col Norman Eccles, 1872–1950, vol. IV
Tilney, Brig. Robert Adolphus George, 1903–1981, vol. VIII
Tilsley, Frank, 1904–1957, vol. V
Tilston, Col Frederick Albert, 1906–1992, vol. IX
Tiltman, H(ugh) Hessell, 1897–1976, vol. VII
Tiltman, Brig. John Hessell, 1894–1982, vol. VIII
Timbury, Gerald Charles, 1929–1985, vol. VIII

Timins, Rev. Francis Charles, 1866–1941, vol. IV
Timmins, Samuel, *died* 1903, vol. I
Timmis, Col Reginald Symonds, 1884–1968, vol. VI
Timmis, Shirley Sutton, 1875–1957, vol. V
Timms, Cecil, 1911–1998, vol. X
Timms, Ven. George Boorne, 1910–1997, vol. X
Timoshenko, Marshal Semyon Konstantinovich, 1895–1970, vol. VI
Timoshenko, Stephen, 1878–1972, vol. VII
Timpson, Sir John, 1863–1937, vol. III
Tims, Henry William Marett, 1863–1954, vol. V
Tims, Ven. John William, 1857–1945, vol. IV
Tinayre, Marcelle; *see* Tinayre, M. S. M.
Tinayre, (Marguerite Suzanne) Marcelle, *died* 1948, vol. IV
Tinbergen, Jan, 1903–1994, vol. IX
Tinbergen, Nikolaas, 1907–1988, vol. VIII
Tindal, Rev. William Strang, 1899–1965, vol. VI
Tindal-Carill-Worsley, Air Cdre Geoffrey Nicolas Ernest, 1908–1996, vol. X
Tindal-Carill-Worsley, Philip Ernest, 1881–1946, vol. IV
Tindale, Lawrence Victor Dolman, 1921–1996, vol. X
Tindall, Albert Alfred, 1840–1931, vol. III
Tindall, Benjamin Arthur, *died* 1963, vol. VI
Tindall, Christian, 1878–1951, vol. V
Tindall, Rev. Canon Frederick Cryer, 1900–1995, vol. IX
Tindall, Rt Rev. Gordon Leslie, *died* 1969, vol. VI
Tindall, Rev. Peter Francis, *died* 1931, vol. III
Tindall, William Edwin, 1863–1938, vol. III
Tindaro, Count del; *see* Rampolla, Cardinal Mariano.
Tingley, Katherine, 1852–1929, vol. III
Tinker, Brian, 1892–1977, vol. VII
Tinker, Chauncey Brewster, 1876–1963, vol. VI
Tinker, Hugh Russell, 1921–2000, vol. X
Tinker, John Joseph, 1875–1957, vol. V
Tinkler, Charles Kenneth, 1881–1951, vol. V
Tinley, Col Gervase Francis Newport, 1857–1918, vol. II
Tinling, Rev. Edward Douglas, *died* 1898, vol. I
Tinn, James, 1922–1999, vol. X
Tinne, John Abraham, 1877–1933, vol. III
Tinsley, Charles Henry, 1914–1995, vol. IX
Tinsley, Rt Rev. (Ernest) John, 1919–1992, vol. IX
Tinsley, Rt Rev. John; *see* Tinsley, Rt Rev. E. J.
Tinsley, Captain Richard Bolton, 1875–1944, vol. IV
Tinton, Major Ben Thomas, 1897–1966, vol. VI
Tinworth, George, 1843–1913, vol. I
Tipperah, Hill, Raja of, 1857–1909, vol. I
Tippet, Captain Arthur Grendon, 1885–1943, vol. IV
Tippett, Sir Michael Kemp, 1905–1998, vol. X
Tippetts, Sydney Atterbury, 1878–1946, vol. IV
Tipping, Col Robert Francis G.; *see* Gartside-Tipping.
Tippinge, Captain Leicester Francis Gartside, 1855–1938, vol. III
Tirard, Sir Nestor Isidore Charles, 1853–1928, vol. II
Tirebuck, William Edwards, *died* 1900, vol. I

Tireman, Henry Stainton, 1871–1951, vol. V
Tirikatene, Sir Eruera Tihema, 1895–1967, vol. VI
Tisdale, Lt-Col Hon. David, 1835–1913, vol. I
Tisdall, Col Arthur Lance, 1860–1927, vol. II
Tisdall, Rev. William St Clair, 1859–1928, vol. II
Tiselius, Arne Wilhelm Kaurin, 1902–1971, vol. VII
Tisserant, His Eminence Cardinal Eugène, 1884–1972, vol. VII
Titchell, John, 1926–1998, vol. X
Titchener, (John) Lanham Bradbury, 1912–1998, vol. X
Titchener, Lanham; *see* Titchener, J. L. B.
Titchener-Barrett, Sir Dennis Charles, *died* 1996, vol. X
Titchmarsh, Edward Charles, 1899–1963, vol. VI
Titford, Rear-Adm. Donald George, 1925–2000, vol. X
Titheradge, Madge, *died* 1961, vol. VI
Titheridge, Lieut Benjamin, *died* 1918, vol. II
Titman, Sir George Alfred, 1889–1980, vol. VII
Titmas, Air Cdre John Francis, 1898–1973, vol. VII
Titmuss, Richard Morris, 1907–1973, vol. VII
Tito, President (Josip Broz), 1892–1980, vol. VII
Tito, Pittore Ettore, 1860–1941, vol. IV
Titta, Commendatore Ruffo, 1877–1953, vol. V
Titterington, Meredith Farrar, 1886–1949, vol. IV
Titterton, Major David Maitland M.; *see* Maitland-Titterton.
Titterton, Sir Ernest William, 1916–1990, vol. VIII
Titterton, Frank, 1882–1956, vol. V
Tittle, Walter Ernest, 1883–1966, vol. VI
Tittoni, Tommaso, 1855–1931, vol. III
Titulesco, Nicolas, 1883–1941, vol. IV
Titus, Rev. Murray Thurston, 1885–1964, vol. VI
Titzell, Anne; *see* Parrish, A.
Tivey, Maj.-Gen. Edwin, 1866–1947, vol. IV
Tivey, Sir John Proctor, 1882–1968, vol. VI
Tivy, Henry Lawrence, 1848–1929, vol. III
Tiwana, Al-Haj Lt-Col Nawab Sir Malik Khizar Hayat Khan, 1900–1975, vol. VII
Tizard, Sir Henry Thomas, 1885–1959, vol. V
Tizard, Jack, 1919–1979, vol. VII
Tizard, Sir (John) Peter (Mills), 1916–1993, vol. IX
Tizard, Sir Peter; *see* Tizard, Sir J. P. M.
Tizard, Captain Thomas Henry, 1839–1923, vol. II
Tobias, Rt Rev. George Wolfe Robert, 1882–1974, vol. VII
Tobias, Stephen Albert, 1920–1986, vol. VIII
Tobin, Sir Alfred Aspinall, 1855–1939, vol. III
Tobin, Maurice J., 1901–1953, vol. V
Tobler, Adolf, 1835–1910, vol. I
Toby, MP; *see* Lucy, Sir Henry.
Tocher, Rev. Forbes Scott, 1885–1973, vol. VII
Tocher, James Fowler, 1864–1945, vol. IV
Tocker, Albert Hamilton, 1884–1964, vol. VI
Tod, Sir Alan Cecil, 1887–1970, vol. VI
Tod, Hunter F., *died* 1923, vol. II
Tod, James Niebuhr, 1876–1947, vol. IV
Tod, Air Marshal Sir John Hunter H.; *see* Hunter-Tod.
Tod, Col John Kelso, *died* 1946, vol. IV
Tod, Marcus Niebuhr, 1878–1974, vol. VII
Tod, Murray Macpherson, 1909–1974, vol. VII
Todd, Baron (Life Peer) of Trumpington; Alexander Robertus Todd, 1907–1997, vol. X

Todd, Adam Brown, 1822–1915, vol. I
Todd, Alan Livesey Stuart, 1900–1976, vol. VII
Todd, Lt-Col Alfred John Kennett, 1890–1970, vol. VI
Todd, (Alfred) Norman, 1904–1990, vol. VIII
Todd, Ann, 1909–1993, vol. IX
Todd, Col Arthur George, died 1954, vol. V
Todd, Arthur Henry Ashworth, 1884–1938, vol. III
Todd, Arthur James Stewart, 1895–1978, vol. VII
Todd, Arthur Ralph Middleton, died 1966, vol. VI
Todd, Sir Bryan James, 1902–1987, vol. VIII
Todd, Sir Charles, 1826–1910, vol. I
Todd, Charles, 1869–1957, vol. V
Todd, Col Charles Campbell, 1870–1956, vol. V
Todd, Sir Desmond Henry, 1897–1970, vol. VI
Todd, Frederick, died 1940, vol. III (A), vol. IV
Todd, Frederick Augustus, 1880–1944, vol. IV
Todd, Sir Geoffrey Sydney, 1900–1986, vol. VIII
Todd, George, 1844–1912, vol. I
Todd, George E.; see Eyre-Todd.
Todd, George William, 1886–1950, vol. IV
Todd, Guy Mansfield, 1883–1958, vol. V
Todd, Sir Herbert John, 1893–1985, vol. VIII
Todd, Howard, 1855–1925, vol. II
Todd, James Eadie, died 1949, vol. IV
Todd, James Maclean, 1907–1988, vol. VIII
Todd, John Aiton, 1875–1954, vol. V
Todd, John Arthur, 1908–1994, vol. IX
Todd, John L., 1876–1949, vol. IV
Todd, (John) Spencer Brydges, 1840–1921, vol. II
Todd, John William, 1882–1957, vol. V
Todd, Sir Joseph White, 1st Bt, 1846–1926, vol. II
Todd, Margaret; see Travers, Graham.
Todd, Norman; see Todd, A. N.
Todd, Ronald Ruskin, 1902–1980, vol. VII
Todd, Spencer Brydges; see Todd, J. S. B.
Todd, Thomas Robert Rushton, 1895–1975, vol. VII
Todd, W. J. Walker, 1884–1944, vol. VI
Todd, Sir William Alexander Forster, died 1946, vol. IV
Todd, Hon. William Frederic, 1854–1935, vol. III
Todd, Captain Sir William Henry W.; see Wilson-Todd.
Todd, Captain Sir William Pierrepoint W.; see Wilson-Todd.
Todd-Jones, Sir Basil; see Todd-Jones, Sir G. B.
Todd-Jones, Sir (George) Basil, 1898–1980, vol. VII
Todhunter, Sir Charles George, 1869–1949, vol. IV
Todhunter, Brig. Edward Joseph, 1900–1976, vol. VII
Todhunter, Col Herbert William, 1875–1936, vol. III
Todhunter, John, 1839–1916, vol. II
Toft, Albert, 1862–1949, vol. IV
Toft, Alfonso, died 1964, vol. VI
Togo, Adm. Marquis Heihachiro, 1847–1934, vol. III
Tohill, Rt Rev. John, 1855–1914, vol. I
Toker, Maj.-Gen. Sir Alliston Champion, 1843–1936, vol. III
Tolansky, Samuel, 1907–1973, vol. VII
Tole, Hon. Joseph Augustus, died 1920, vol. II
Toler, Hector Robert Graham, 1847–1899, vol. I
Toler, Otway Scarlett Graham, 1886–1941, vol. IV
Tolerton, Sir Robert Hill, 1887–1956, vol. V

Tolkien, John Ronald Reuel, 1892–1973, vol. VII
Tollemache, 2nd Baron, 1832–1904, vol. I
Tollemache, 3rd Baron, 1883–1955, vol. V
Tollemache, 4th Baron, 1910–1975, vol. VII
Tollemache, Arthur Frederick Churchill, 1860–1923, vol. II
Tollemache, Sir (Cecil) Lyonel (Newcomen), 5th Bt, 1886–1969, vol. VI
Tollemache, David, died 1918, vol. II
Tollemache, Lt-Col Hon. Denis Plantagenet, 1884–1942, vol. IV
Tollemache, Hon. Douglas Alfred, 1862–1944, vol. IV
Tollemache, Maj.-Gen. Edward Devereux Hamilton, 1885–1947, vol. IV
Tollemache, Henry James, 1846–1939, vol. III
Tollemache, Maj.-Gen. Sir Humphry Thomas, 6th Bt, 1897–1990, vol. VIII
Tollemache, Hon. Lionel Arthur, 1838–1919, vol. II
Tollemache, Sir Lyonel; see Tollemache, Sir C. L. N.
Tollemache, Sir Lyonel Felix Carteret Eugene, 4th Bt, 1854–1952, vol. V
Tollemache, Lyonulph De Oreliana, 1892–1966, vol. VI
Tollemache, Hon. Mortimer Granville, 1872–1950, vol. IV
Tollemache, Hon. Stratford, 1864–1937, vol. III
Toller, Arthur Thomas, 1857–1899, vol. I
Toller, Ernst, 1893–1939, vol. III
Toller, Brig. Hamlet Bush, 1871–1950, vol. IV
Toller, William Stark, 1884–1968, vol. VI
Tollerfield, Albert Edward, 1906–1984, vol. VIII
Tolley, Major Cyril James Hastings, 1895–1978, vol. VII
Tolley, Leslie John, 1913–1995, vol. IX
Tolley, Louis, died 1959, vol. V
Tollinton, Henry Phillips, 1870–1937, vol. III
Tollinton, Rev. Richard Bartram, 1866–1932, vol. III
Tollinton, Richard Bartram Boyd, 1903–1978, vol. VII
Tollit, Percy Kitto, 1863–1942, vol. IV
Tollner, Col Barrett Lennard, 1839–1918, vol. II
Tolmie, Hon. James, 1862–1939, vol. III (A), vol. IV
Tolmie, Hon. Simon Fraser, 1867–1937, vol. III
Tolstoy, Alexandra, 1884–1979, vol. VII
Tolstoy, Dimitry, (Dimitry Tolstoy-Miloslavsky), 1912–1997, vol. X
Tolstoy, Count Leo, 1828–1910, vol. I
Tom, Henry, 1881–1937, vol. III
Tomasson, Captain Sir William Hugh, 1858–1922, vol. II
Tomb, John Walker, 1882–1948, vol. IV
Tomblings, Douglas Griffith, 1889–1970, vol. VI
Tombs, Robert Charles, 1842–1923, vol. II
Tomes, Sir Charles Sissmore, 1846–1928, vol. II
Tomes, Brig. Clement Thurstan, 1882–1972, vol. VII
Tomkins, Sir Alfred George, 1895–1975, vol. VII (AII)
Tomkins, Ernest William, 1872–1925, vol. II
Tomkins, Lt-Col Harry Leith, 1870–1926, vol. II
Tomkins, Herbert Gerard, 1869–1934, vol. III

Tomkins, Sir Lionel Linton, 1871–1936, vol. III
Tomkins, Rt Rev. Oliver Stratford, 1908–1992, vol. IX
Tomkins, Stanley Charles, *died* 1946, vol. IV
Tomkins, William Douglas, 1882–1959, vol. V
Tomkins, Gen. William Percival, 1841–1922, vol. II
Tomkinson, Charles, 1893–1976, vol. VII
Tomkinson, Sir Geoffrey Stewart, 1881–1963, vol. VI
Tomkinson, Brig. Henry Archdale, 1881–1937, vol. III
Tomkinson, John Stanley, 1916–1992, vol. IX
Tomkinson, Joseph Goodwin-, *died* 1940, vol. III
Tomkinson, Michael, 1841–1921, vol. II
Tomkinson, Vice-Adm. Wilfred, 1877–1971, vol. VII
Tomley, John Edward, 1874–1951, vol. V
Tomlin of Ash, Baron (Life Peer); Thomas James Chesshyre Tomlin, 1867–1935, vol. III
Tomlin, Eric Walter Frederick, 1913–1988, vol. VIII
Tomlin, Vice-Adm. George Napier, 1875–1947, vol. IV
Tomlin, Rev. James William Sackett, 1871–1959, vol. V
Tomlin, Lt-Col Julian Latham, 1886–1960, vol. V
Tomlinson, Rev. Cyril Edric, 1886–1968, vol. VI
Tomlinson, David Cecil MacAlister, 1917–2000, vol. X
Tomlinson, Sir (Frank) Stanley, 1912–1994, vol. IX
Tomlinson, Rt Hon. George, 1890–1952, vol. V
Tomlinson, Rt Rev. Mgr George Arthur, 1906–1985, vol. VIII
Tomlinson, Sir George John Frederick, 1876–1963, vol. VI
Tomlinson, H. M., 1873–1958, vol. V
Tomlinson, Harry, 1846–1938, vol. III
Tomlinson, Herbert, 1845–1931, vol. III
Tomlinson, Maj.-Gen. Michael John, 1929–1997, vol. X
Tomlinson, Maj.-Gen. Sir Percy Stanley, 1884–1951, vol. V
Tomlinson, Reginald Robert, 1885–1978, vol. VII
Tomlinson, Robert Parkinson, *died* 1943, vol. IV
Tomlinson, Ruth, *died* 1972, vol. VII
Tomlinson, Sir Stanley; *see* Tomlinson, Sir F. S.
Tomlinson, Sir Thomas, 1877–1957, vol. V
Tomlinson, Sir Thomas Symonds, 1877–1965, vol. VI
Tomlinson, Sir William Edward Murray, 1st Bt, 1838–1912, vol. I
Tomney, Frank, 1908–1984, vol. VIII
Tomonaga, Sin-itiro, 1906–1979, vol. VII
Tomory, Maj.-Gen. Kenneth Alexander Macdonald, 1891–1968, vol. VI
Tompkins, Engr Captain Albert Edward, 1863–1927, vol. II
Tompkins, Frederick Clifford, 1910–1995, vol. IX
Tompkins, (Granville) Richard (Francis), 1918–1992, vol. IX
Tompkins, Richard; *see* Tompkins, G. R. F.
Tompson, Col Hew Wakeman, 1870–1933, vol. III
Tompson, Rev. Reginald, 1845–1907, vol. I
Tompson, Maj.-Gen. Reginald Henry Dalrymple, 1879–1937, vol. III

Tompson, Maj.-Gen. William Dalrymple, 1833–1916, vol. II
Toms, Carl, 1927–1999, vol. X
Toms, Frederick, *died* 1900, vol. I
Tomson, Rev. John, *died* 1926, vol. II
Toner, Rt Rev. John, 1857–1949, vol. IV
Tong, Sir Walter Wharton, 1890–1978, vol. VII
Tonga, HM the Queen of; Queen Salote Tupou, 1900–1965, vol. VI
Tonge, (Cecil) Howard, 1915–1992, vol. IX
Tonge, Rev. David Theophilus, 1930–1995, vol. IX
Tonge, Francis Henry, 1855–1936, vol. III
Tonge, George Edward, 1876–1956, vol. V
Tonge, George Edward, 1910–1979, vol. VII
Tonge, Howard; *see* Tonge, C. H.
Tonge, Col William Corrie, 1862–1943, vol. IV
Tonk, HH Amin-ud-Daula Wazir-ul Mulk Nawab Sir Hafiz Muhammad Ibrahim Ali Khan Bahadur, Saulat Jung, 1848–1930, vol. III
Tonk, HH Said-ud-Daulah Wazir-ul-Mulk Nawab Hafiz Sir Mohammed Saadat Ali Khan Bahadur Sowlat-i-Jung, 1879–1947, vol. IV
Tonkin, David Oliver, 1929–2000, vol. X
Tonkinson, Harry, 1880–1937, vol. III
Tonks, Rt Rev. Basil, *born* 1930, vol. VIII
Tonks, Ven. Charles Frederick, 1881–1957, vol. V
Tonks, Henry, 1862–1937, vol. III
Tonks, Rt Rev. Horace Norman Vincent, 1891–1959, vol. V
Tonnochy, Alec Bain, *died* 1963, vol. VI
Tonypandy, 1st Viscount, 1909–1997, vol. X
Toogood, Col Cyril George, 1894–1962, vol. VI
Tooker, Hyde Charnock W.; *see* Whalley-Tooker.
Tookey, Geoffrey William, 1902–1976, vol. VII
Toole, John Lawrence, 1830–1906, vol. I
Toole, Joseph, 1887–1945, vol. IV
Tooley, Sarah A., *died* 1946, vol. IV
Toomer, Air Vice-Marshal Sydney Edward, 1895–1954, vol. V
Toone, Sir Frederick Charles, 1868–1930, vol. III
Toone, Rev. John, 1844–1934, vol. III
Toop, Engr-Rear-Adm. William, *died* 1950, vol. IV
Toosey, Sir Philip John Denton, 1904–1975, vol. VII
Tooth, Sir (Archibald) Leonard (Lucas) L.; *see* Lucas-Tooth.
Tooth, Hon. Sir Douglas; *see* Tooth, Hon. Sir S. D.
Tooth, Sir Edwin Marsden, 1886–1957, vol. V
Tooth, Geoffrey Cuthbert, 1908–1998, vol. X
Tooth, Howard Henry, 1856–1925, vol. II
Tooth, Sir Hugh Vere Huntly Duff M. L.; *see* Munro-Lucas-Tooth.
Tooth, Sir Robert Lucas L.; *see* Lucas-Tooth.
Tooth, Hon. Sir (Seymour) Douglas, 1904–1982, vol. VIII (A)
Toothill, Sir John Norman, 1908–1986, vol. VIII
Tootill, Robert, 1850–1934, vol. III
Toovey, Maj.-Gen. Cecil Wotton, 1891–1954, vol. V
Toovey, Rev. Henry, 1843–1922, vol. II
Tope, Maj.-Gen. Wilfrid Shakespeare, 1892–1962, vol. VI
Topham, Alfred Frank, 1874–1952, vol. V
Topham, Frank W. W., 1838–1924, vol. II
Topham, Rev. John, 1863–1955, vol. V
Topham, Lt-Col Thomas H.; *see* Harrison-Topham.

Topley, William Whiteman Carlton, 1886–1944, vol. IV
Toplis, James, 1876–1961, vol. VI
Topolski, Feliks, 1907–1989, vol. VIII
Topp, Charles Alfred, 1847–1932, vol. III
Topp, Brig.-Gen. Charles Beresford, 1893–1976, vol. VII
Topp, Wilfred Bethridge, 1891–1978, vol. VII
Toppin, Aubrey John, 1881–1969, vol. VI
Topping, Andrew, 1890–1955, vol. V
Topping, Sir (Hugh) Robert, 1877–1952, vol. V
Topping, James, 1904–1994, vol. IX
Topping, Sir Robert; see Topping, Sir H. R.
Topping, Col Thomas Edward, 1871–1926, vol. II
Topping, Rt Hon. Walter William Buchanan, 1908–1978, vol. VII
Torlesse, Rear-Adm. Arthur David, 1902–1995, vol. IX
Tornaritis, Criton George, 1902–1997, vol. X
Torney, Thomas William, 1915–1998, vol. X
Torphichen, 12th Lord, 1846–1915, vol. I
Torphichen, 13th Lord, 1886–1973, vol. VII
Torphichen, 14th Lord, 1917–1975, vol. VII
Torphichen, Master of; Hon. James Archibald Douglas Sandilands, 1884–1909, vol. I
Torr, Cecil, 1857–1928, vol. II
Torr, James Fenning, died 1915, vol. I
Torr, Rev. William Edward, 1851–1924, vol. II
Torr, Brig. (William) Wyndham (Torre), 1890–1963, vol. VI
Torr, Brig. Wyndham; see Torr, Brig. W. W. T.
Torrance, Sir A. M., died 1909, vol. I
Torre-Diaz, Count de; Brodie Manuel de Zulueta, 1842–1918, vol. II
Torrens, James Aubrey, 1881–1954, vol. V
Torres Bodet, Jaime, 1902–1974, vol. VII
Torrey, Charles Cutler, 1863–1956, vol. V
Torrey, Reuben Archer, 1856–1928, vol. II
Torriano, Col Charles Edward, 1833–1908, vol. I
Torrie, Lt-Col Claud Jameson, 1879–1936, vol. III
Torrington, 9th Viscount, 1886–1944, vol. IV
Torrington, 10th Viscount, 1876–1961, vol. VI
Tortelier, Paul, 1914–1990, vol. VIII
Tortise, Col Herbert James, died 1954, vol. V
Tory, Henry Marshall, 1864–1947, vol. IV
Tory, Hon. James Cranswick, died 1944, vol. IV
Toscanini, Arturo, 1867–1957, vol. V
Toseland, Charles Stephen, 1894–1971, vol. VII
Tostevin, Engr-Captain Harold Bertram, 1884–1956, vol. V
Tosti, Sir (Francesco) Paolo, 1847–1916, vol. II
Tosti, Sir Paolo; see Tosti, Sir F. P.
Tothill, Adm. Sir Hugh Henry Darby, 1865–1927, vol. II
Tothill, John Douglas, 1888–1969, vol. VI
Totman, Grenfell William, 1911–1986, vol. VIII
Tottenham, Sir Alexander Robert Loftus, 1873–1946, vol. IV
Tottenham, Major Charles Bosvile, 1869–1911, vol. I
Tottenham, Col Charles George, 1835–1918, vol. II
Tottenham, Charles Gore Loftus, 1861–1929, vol. III
Tottenham, Rear-Adm. Edward Loftus, 1896–1974, vol. VII

Tottenham, Adm. Sir Francis Loftus, 1880–1967, vol. VI
Tottenham, Very Rev. George, 1825–1911, vol. I
Tottenham, Sir (George) Richard (Frederick), 1890–1977, vol. VII
Tottenham, Adm. Henry Loftus, 1860–1950, vol. IV
Tottenham, Percy Marmaduke, 1873–1975, vol. VII
Tottenham, Sir Richard; see Tottenham, Sir G. R. F.
Tottenham, Richard E., died 1971, vol. VII
Tottenham-Smith, Ralph Henry, 1893–1971, vol. VII
Totterdell, Sir Joseph, 1885–1959, vol. V
Touch, Arthur Gerald, 1911–1994, vol. IX
Touch, Gerald; see Touch, A. G.
Touche, Sir George Alexander, 1st Bt (cr 1920), 1861–1935, vol. III
Touche, Rt Hon. Sir Gordon Cosmo, 1st Bt (cr 1962), 1895–1972, vol. VII
Touche, Sir Norman George, 2nd Bt (cr 1920), 1888–1977, vol. VII
Toulmin, Sir George, 1857–1923, vol. II
Toulmin Smith, Elizabeth Thomasina; see Meade, L. T.
Tours, Berthold George, 1871–1944, vol. IV
Tours, Frank E., 1877–1963, vol. VI
Tours, Kenneth Cecil, 1908–1987, vol. VIII
Tout, Sir Frederick Henry, died 1950, vol. IV
Tout, Herbert, 1904–1997, vol. X
Tout, Thomas Frederick, 1855–1929, vol. III
Tout, W. J., 1870–1946, vol. IV
Tovell, Laurence, 1919–1998, vol. X
Tovell, Brig. Raymond Walter, 1890–1966, vol. VI
Tovey, 1st Baron, 1885–1971, vol. VII
Tovey, Sir Donald Francis, 1875–1940, vol. III
Tovey, Lt-Col George Strangways, 1875–1943, vol. IV
Towell, Brig. Rowland Henry, 1891–1973, vol. VII
Tower, Bernard Henry, died 1933, vol. III
Tower, Charlemagne, 1848–1923, vol. II
Tower, Christopher Joan Hume, 1841–1924, vol. II
Tower, Adm. Cyril Everard, 1861–1929, vol. III
Tower, Comdr Francis FitzPatrick, 1859–1944, vol. IV
Tower, Vice-Adm. Sir Francis Thomas Butler, 1885–1964, vol. VI
Tower, Rev. Henry, 1862–1948, vol. IV
Tower, Rev. Henry Bernard, 1882–1964, vol. VI
Tower, Sir Reginald Thomas, 1860–1939, vol. III
Towers, Graham Ford, 1897–1975, vol. VII
Towers, Samuel, 1863–1943, vol. IV
Towers-Clark, James, 1852–1926, vol. II
Towle, Arthur Edward, 1878–1948, vol. IV
Towle, Lt-Col Sir Francis William, 1876–1951, vol. V
Towle, Margery; see Lawrence, M.
Towle, Sir William, 1849–1929, vol. III
Towler, Eric William, 1900–1987, vol. VIII
Town, Sir (Hugh) Stuart, 1893–1972, vol. VII
Town, Sir Stuart; see Town, Sir H. S.
Townend, Arnold Ernest, 1880–1970, vol. VI (AII)
Townend, Donald Thomas Alfred, 1897–1984, vol. VIII
Townend, Harry, 1872–1949, vol. IV
Townend, Sir Harry Douglas, 1891–1976, vol. VII

Townend, Herbert Patrick Victor, 1887–1950, vol. IV

Towner, Major Edgar Thomas, 1890–1972, vol. VII

Townesend, Air Cdre Ernest John Dennis, 1896–1975, vol. VII

Townesend, Stephen, *died* 1914, vol. I

Townley, Athol Gordon, 1907–1963, vol. VI

Townley, Rev. Charles Francis, 1856–1930, vol. III

Townley, Rev. Charles Gale, 1848–1942, vol. IV

Townley, Frank, 1924–1982, vol. VIII

Townley, Rt Rev. George Frederick, 1891–1977, vol. VII

Townley, Sir John Barton, 1914–1990, vol. VIII

Townley, Maximilian Gowran, 1864–1942, vol. IV

Townley, Reginald Colin, 1904–1982, vol. VIII

Townley, Sir Walter Beaupre, 1863–1945, vol. IV

Townroe, Bernard Stephen, 1885–1962, vol. VI

Townroe, Rev. James Weston, *died* 1934, vol. III

Townsend, Alexander Cockburn, 1905–1964, vol. VI

Townsend, Crewe Armand Hamilton, *died* 1954, vol. V

Townsend, Adm. Cyril Samuel, 1875–1949, vol. IV

Townsend, Surg.-Gen. Sir Edmond, 1845–1917, vol. II

Townsend, Major Edward Neville, 1871–1938, vol. III

Townsend, Brig. Edward Philip, 1909–1978, vol. VII

Townsend, Frederick Henry, 1868–1920, vol. II

Townsend, Rev. Henry, *died* 1955, vol. V

Townsend, Sir John Sealy Edward, 1868–1957, vol. V

Townsend, Sir Lance; *see* Townsend, Sir S. L.

Townsend, Rear-Adm. Sir Leslie William, 1924–1999, vol. X

Townsend, Rear-Adm. Michael Southcote, 1908–1984, vol. VIII

Townsend, Gp Captain Peter Wooldridge, 1914–1995, vol. IX

Townsend, Sir Reginald, 1882–1938, vol. III

Townsend, Stephen Chapman, 1826–1901, vol. I

Townsend, Sir (Sydney) Lance, 1912–1983, vol. VIII

Townsend, Thomas Sutton, 1847–1918, vol. II

Townsend, Air Vice-Marshal William Edwin, *born* 1916, vol. VIII

Townsend, Rev. William John, 1835–1915, vol. I

Townsend-Farquhar, Sir Robert; *see* Farquhar.

Townshend, 5th Marquess, 1831–1899, vol. I

Townshend, 6th Marquess, 1866–1921, vol. II

Townshend, Sir Charles James, 1844–1924, vol. II

Townshend, Maj.-Gen. Sir Charles Vere Ferrers, 1861–1924, vol. II

Townshend, Col Frederick Trench, 1838–1924, vol. II

Townshend, Captain Harry Leigh, 1842–1924, vol. II

Townshend, Hugh, 1890–1974, vol. VII

Townshend, James, *died* 1949, vol. IV

Townshend, Hon. Robert M.; *see* Marsham-Townshend.

Townshend, Samuel Nugent, 1844–1910, vol. I

Townshend, William Tower, 1855–1943, vol. IV

Townsing, Sir Kenneth Joseph, 1914–1997, vol. X

Towse, Captain Sir Beachcroft; *see* Towse, Captain Sir E. B. B.

Towse, Captain Sir (Ernest) Beachcroft Beckwith, 1864–1948, vol. IV

Towse, Sir (John) Wrench, 1848–1929, vol. III

Towse, Sir Wrench; *see* Towse, Sir J. W.

Towsey, Brig.-Gen. Francis William, *died* 1948, vol. IV

Toy, Carter; *see* Toy, F. C.

Toy, Crawford Howell, 1836–1919, vol. II

Toy, Francis Carter, 1892–1988, vol. VIII

Toy, Sir Henry, 1862–1939, vol. III

Toye, Brig. Alfred Maurice, 1897–1955, vol. V

Toye, Dudley Bulmer, 1888–1968, vol. VI

Toye, Major Edward Geoffrey, 1889–1942, vol. IV

Toye, Francis; *see* Toye, J. F.

Toye, Herbert Graham Donovan, 1911–1969, vol. VI

Toye, (John) Francis, 1883–1964, vol. VI

Toynbee, Arnold Joseph, 1889–1975, vol. VII

Toynbee, Brig. Guy Elliston, 1884–1947, vol. IV

Toynbee, Jocelyn Mary Catherine, 1897–1985, vol. VIII

Toynbee, Paget, 1855–1932, vol. III

Toynbee, Philip; *see* Toynbee, T. P.

Toynbee, (Theodore) Philip, 1916–1981, vol. VIII

Toyne, Rev. Frederick Elijah, *died* 1927, vol. II

Toyne, Stanley Mease, *died* 1962, vol. VI

Tozer, Basil, 1896–1949, vol. IV

Tozer, Beatrice Cordelia Auchmuty, (Mrs Basil Tozer); *see* Langley, B.

Tozer, Rev. Henry Fanshawe, 1829–1916, vol. II

Tozer, Hon. Sir Horace, 1844–1916, vol. II

Tozer, Major Sir James Clifford, 1889–1970, vol. VI

Tozer, Col William, 1894–1971, vol. VII

Tozer, Rt Rev. William George, *died* 1899, vol. I

Tracey, Herbert Trevor, 1884–1955, vol. V

Tracey, Sir Richard Edward, 1837–1907, vol. I

Tracy, Major Hon. Algernon Henry Charles H.; *see* Hanbury-Tracy.

Tracy, Frederick, 1862–1951, vol. V

Tracy, Hon. Frederick Stephen Archibald H.; *see* Hanbury-Tracy.

Tracy, Louis, 1863–1928, vol. II

Tracy, Spencer, 1900–1967, vol. VI

Tracy, Walter Valentine, 1914–1995, vol. IX

Tracy-Inglis, Col Russell; *see* Inglis.

Trafalgar, Viscount; Herbert Horatio Nelson, 1854–1905, vol. I

Trafford, Baron (Life Peer); Joseph Anthony Porteous Trafford, 1932–1989, vol. VIII

Trafford, Edward Southwell, 1838–1912, vol. I

Trafford, F. G.; *see* Riddell, C. E. L.

Trafford, Marcus Antonius Johnston de L.; *see* de Lavis-Trafford.

Trafford, Rt Rev. Ralph Sigebert, 1886–1976, vol. VII

Tragett, Margaret Rivers; *see* Larminie, M. R.

Trahan, Hon. Arthur, 1877–1950, vol. IV (A), vol. V

Traherne, Sir Cennydd George, 1910–1995, vol. IX

Trail, James William Helenus, 1851–1919, vol. II

Trail, Richard Robertson, 1894–1971, vol. VII

Traill, Anthony, 1838–1914, vol. I

Traill, Major Cecil James, 1888–1968, vol. VI
Traill, Maj.-Gen. George Balfour, 1833–1913, vol. I
Traill, Henry Duff, 1842–1900, vol. I
Traill, Lt-Col John Charles Merriman, 1881–1942, vol. IV
Traill, Peter; see Morton, Guy Mainwaring.
Traill, Major Thomas Balfour, 1881–1920, vol. II
Traill, Air Vice-Marshal Thomas Cathcart, 1899–1973, vol. VII
Traill, Lt-Col William Henry, 1871–1951, vol. V
Traill, Lt-Col William Stewart, 1868–1959, vol. V
Train, Arthur, 1875–1945, vol. IV
Train, George Francis, 1829–1904, vol. I
Train, Sir John, 1873–1942, vol. IV
Train, Rev. John Gilkison, 1847–1920, vol. II
Train, Sir (John) Landale, 1888–1969, vol. VI
Train, Sir Landale; see Train, Sir J. L.
Trainor, James P., 1914–1989, vol. VIII
Tranmire, Baron (Life Peer); Robert Hugh Turton, 1903–1994, vol. IX
Transjordan, King of; HH Abdullah Ibn Hussein, died 1951, vol. V
Trant, John Philip, 1889–1953, vol. V
Tranter, Clement John, 1909–1991, vol. IX
Tranter, Nigel Godwin, 1909–2000, vol. X
Trapani, Lt-Col Alfred, 1859–1928, vol. II, vol. III
Trapnell, Alan Stewart, 1913–1986, vol. VIII
Trapnell, John Arthur, 1913–1997, vol. X
Trapnell, John Graham, died 1949, vol. IV
Trapp, Rt Rev. Eric Joseph, 1910–1993, vol. IX
Trappes-Lomax, Michael Roger, 1900–1972, vol. VII
Trappes-Lomax, Brig. Thomas Byrnand, 1895–1962, vol. VI
Traquair, Harry Moss, 1875–1954, vol. V
Traquair, Ramsay, 1874–1952, vol. V
Traquair, Ramsay Heatley, 1840–1912, vol. I
Trask, Katrina, died 1922, vol. II
Tratman, David William, died 1953, vol. V
Tratman, Edgar Kingsley, 1899–1978, vol. VII
Travancore, Maharajah of, 1857–1924, vol. II
Travancore, Rajpramukh of, 1912–1991, vol. IX
Travers, Basil Holmes, 1919–1998, vol. X
Travers, Ben, 1886–1980, vol. VII
Travers, Rt Rev. Mgr Brendan, 1931–1992, vol. IX
Travers, Captain Francis Eaton, died 1953, vol. V
Travers, Lt-Col George Alfred, 1867–1950, vol. IV
Travers, Graham, 1859–1918, vol. II
Travers, Sir Guy Francis Travers Clarke-, 3rd Bt (cr 1804), 1842–1905, vol. I
Travers, Col Henry Cecil, died 1958, vol. V
Travers, Brig.-Gen. Jonas Hamilton du Boulay, 1861–1933, vol. III
Travers, Brig.-Gen. Joseph Oates, 1867–1936, vol. III
Travers, Sir Lancelot, see Travers, Sir W. L.
Travers, Morris William, 1872–1961, vol. VI
Travers, Lt-Gen. Sir Paul Anthony, 1927–1983, vol. VIII
Travers, Sir Thomas à Beckett, 1902–1999, vol. X
Travers, Sir (Walter) Lancelot, 1880–1937, vol. III
Travis, Comdr Sir Edward Wilfrid Harry, 1888–1956, vol. V
Travis, Harry, 1858–1927, vol. II
Travis, Rev. James, 1840–1919, vol. II

Travis, Rev. William Travis, died 1924, vol. II
Travis-Clegg, Sir James Travis, 1874–1942, vol. IV
Trayner, Hon. Lord; John Trayner, 1834–1929, vol. III
Trayner, John; see Hon. Lord Trayner.
Treacher, Rev. Preb. Hubert Harold, 1891–1964, vol. VI
Treacher, Sir William Hood, 1849–1919, vol. II
Treacy, Rt Rev. Eric, 1907–1978, vol. VII
Treadgold, Group Captain Henry A., 1883–1941, vol. IV
Treadwell, Brig. John William Ferguson, 1901–1968, vol. VI
Treanor, Ven. James, died 1926, vol. II
Trease, Geoffrey; see Trease, R. G.
Trease, George Edward, 1902–1986, vol. VIII
Trease, (Robert) Geoffrey, 1909–1998, vol. X
Treasure, Col Kenneth David, 1913–1983, vol. VIII
Treasure, William Houston, died 1916, vol. II
Treatt, Hon. Sir Vernon Haddon, 1897–1984, vol. VIII
Treble, Rev. Edmund John, died 1924, vol. II
Treble, Col George Walker, 1865–1929, vol. III
Tredcroft, Lt-Col Charles Lennox, 1832–1917, vol. II
Tredegar, 1st Viscount (cr 1905), 1830–1913, vol. I
Tredegar, 1st Viscount (cr 1926), 1867–1934, vol. III
Tredegar, 2nd Viscount (cr 1926), 1893–1949, vol. IV
Tredegar, 5th Baron, 1873–1954, vol. V
Tredegar, 6th Baron, 1908–1962, vol. VI
Tredennick, (George) Hugh (Percival Phair), 1899–1981, vol. VIII
Tredennick, Rev. George Nesbitt Haydon, 1860–1942, vol. IV
Tredennick, Hugh; see Tredennick, G. H. P. P.
Tredennick, Rev. John Nesbitt Ernest, 1892–1976, vol. VII
Tredgold, Alfred Frank, 1870–1952, vol. V
Tredgold, Sir Clarkson Henry, 1865–1938, vol. III
Tredgold, Joan Alison, 1903–1989, vol. VIII
Tredgold, Rt Hon. Sir Robert Clarkson, 1899–1977, vol. VII
Tredgold, Roger Francis, 1911–1975, vol. VII
Tree, Charles, died 1940, vol. III
Tree, Sir Herbert Beerbohm, 1853–1917, vol. II
Tree, Maud, (Lady Tree), 1864–1937, vol. III
Tree, Ronald, 1897–1976, vol. VII
Tree, Ven. Ronald James, 1914–1970, vol. VI
Treeby, Lt-Col Henry Paul, 1858–1935, vol. III
Treffry, Charles Ebenezer, 1842–1924, vol. II
Treffry, Col Edward, 1869–1942, vol. IV
Treffry, Mary Beatrice, 1865–1942, vol. IV
Trefgarne, 1st Baron, 1894–1960, vol. V
Trefle, Hon. John Louis, died 1915, vol. I
Trefusis, Hon. Henry Walter Hepburn-Stuart-Forbes-, 1864–1948, vol. IV
Trefusis, Major Hon. John Frederick Hepburn-Stuart-Forbes-, 1878–1915, vol. I
Trefusis, Col Hon. John Schomberg, 1852–1932, vol. III
Trefusis, Lady Mary, 1869–1927, vol. II
Trefusis, Rt Rev. Robert Edward, 1843–1930, vol. III

Tregarthen, John Coulson, 1854–1933, vol. III
Tregear, Edward, 1846–1931, vol. III
Tregear, Maj.-Gen. Sir Vincent William, 1842–1925, vol. II
Tregoning, Wynn Harold, 1876–1930, vol. III
Treharne, Kenneth John, 1939–1989, vol. VIII
Treharne, Reginald Francis, 1901–1967, vol. VI
Trehearne, Alfred Frederick Aldridge, 1874–1962, vol. VI
Trehearne, Frank William, 1881–1956, vol. V
Treherne, Rev. Charles Albert, 1856–1919, vol. II
Treherne, Maj.-Gen. Sir Francis Harper, 1858–1955, vol. V
Treherne, John Edwin, 1929–1989, vol. VIII
Trelawny, Horace Dormer, 1824–1906, vol. I
Trelawny, Maj.-Gen. John I.; see Iago-Trelawny.
Trelawny, Sir John William Robin Maurice Salusbury-, 12th Bt, 1908–1956, vol. V
Trelawny, Sir John William Salusbury-, 11th Bt, 1869–1944, vol. IV
Trelawny, Sir William Lewis Salusbury-, 10th Bt, 1844–1917, vol. II
Trelawny-Ross, Rev. John Trelawny, 1852–1935, vol. III
Treloar, Sir William Purdie, 1st Bt, 1843–1923, vol. II
Trematon, Viscount; Rupert Alexander George Augustus Cambridge, 1907–1928, vol. II
Tremayne, Lt-Col Arthur, 1827–1905, vol. I
Tremayne, Arthur, 1879–1954, vol. V
Tremayne, Harold, died 1908, vol. I
Tremayne, John, 1825–1901, vol. I
Tremayne, Air Marshal Sir John Tremayne, 1891–1979, vol. VII
Tremblay, Maj.-Gen. Thomas Louis, 1886–1951, vol. V
Tremellen, Norman Cleverton, 1895–1979, vol. VII
Tremlett, Rt Rev. Anthony Paul, 1914–1992, vol. IX
Tremlett, Charles Hugh, 1876–1939, vol. III
Tremlett, Col Colin Percy, 1880–1972, vol. VII
Tremlett, Maj.-Gen. Erroll Arthur Edwin, 1893–1982, vol. VIII
Trenam, Edwin, 1843–1909, vol. I
Trench, Anthony C.; see Chenevix-Trench.
Trench, Col Arthur Henry C.; see Chenevix-Trench.
Trench, Charles Godfrey C.; see Chenevix-Trench.
Trench, Hon. Cosby Godolphin, 1844–1925, vol. II
Trench, Sir David Clive Crosbie, 1915–1988, vol. VIII
Trench, Ernest Frederic Crosbie, 1869–1960, vol. V
Trench, Col Frederic John Arthur, 1857–1942, vol. IV
Trench, Hon. Frederic Sydney, 1894–1916, vol. II
Trench, Lt-Col Frederick Amelius Le P.; see Le Poer Trench.
Trench, Hon. Frederick Le P.; see Le Poer Trench.
Trench, Lt-Col George Frederick C.; see Chenevix-Trench.
Trench, Herbert, 1865–1923, vol. II
Trench, Col Lawrence C.; see Chenevix-Trench.
Trench, Brig. Ralph C.; see Chenevix-Trench.
Trench, Lt-Col Sir Richard Henry C.; see Chenevix-Trench.
Trench, Wilbraham Fitz-John, 1873–1939, vol. III

Trench, Hon. William Cosby, 1869–1944, vol. IV
Trench, William Launcelot Crosbie, died 1949, vol. IV
Trench, Col Hon. William Le-P.; see Le-Poer-Trench.
Trench, Rev. William Robert, 1838–1913, vol. I
Trenchard, 1st Viscount, 1873–1956, vol. V
Trenchard, 2nd Viscount, 1923–1987, vol. VIII
Trend, Baron (Life Peer); Burke St John Trend, 1914–1987, vol. VIII
Trend, John Brande, 1887–1958, vol. V
Trendall, Arthur Dale, 1909–1995, vol. IX
Trendell, Sir Arthur James Richens, 1836–1909, vol. I
Trendell, Herbert Arthur Previté, 1864–1929, vol. III
Trenholme, Norman William, 1837–1919, vol. II
Trent, 1st Baron, 1850–1931, vol. III
Trent, 2nd Baron, 1889–1956, vol. V
Trent, Col George Alexander, 1870–1930, vol. III
Trent, Group Captain Leonard Henry, 1915–1986, vol. VIII
Trent, Newbury Abbot, 1885–1953, vol. V
Trentham, Everard Noel Rye, 1888–1963, vol. VI
Trentham, George Percy, died 1940, vol. III
Treowen, 1st Baron, 1851–1933, vol. III
Tresidder, Lt-Col Alfred Geddes, 1881–1970, vol. VI
Tresidder, Gerald Charles, 1912–1996, vol. X
Tresidder, Captain Tolmie John, 1850–1931, vol. III
Treston, Hubert Joseph, 1888–1959, vol. V
Treston, Col Maurice Lawrence, 1891–1970, vol. VI
Trestrail, Major Alfred Ernest Yates, 1876–1935, vol. III
Trethowan, Hon. Sir Arthur King, 1863–1937, vol. III
Trethowan, Sir Ian; see Trethowan, Sir J. I. R.
Trethowan, Sir (James) Ian (Raley), 1922–1990, vol. VIII
Trethowan, Sir William Henry, 1917–1995, vol. IX
Treuhaft, Mrs Jessica; see Mitford, J. L.
Trevail, Silvanus, 1851–1903, vol. I
Trevan, John William, 1887–1956, vol. V
Trevaskis, Sir (Gerald) Kennedy (Nicholas), 1915–1990, vol. VIII
Trevaskis, Rev. Hugh Kennedy, 1882–1962, vol. VI
Trevaskis, Sir Kennedy; see Trevaskis, Sir G. K. N.
Trevelyan, Baron (Life Peer); Humphrey Trevelyan, 1905–1985, vol. VIII
Trevelyan, Rt Hon. Sir Charles Philips, 3rd Bt (cr 1874), 1870–1958, vol. V
Trevelyan, Edmond Fauriel, died 1911, vol. I
Trevelyan, Sir Ernest John, 1850–1924, vol. II
Trevelyan, Sir George Lowthian, 4th Bt (cr 1874), 1906–1996, vol. X
Trevelyan, George Macaulay, 1876–1962, vol. VI
Trevelyan, Rt Hon. Sir George Otto, 2nd Bt (cr 1874), 1838–1928, vol. II
Trevelyan, Hilda, died 1959, vol. V
Trevelyan, Janet Penrose, 1879–1956, vol. V
Trevelyan, Julian Otto, 1910–1988, vol. VIII
Trevelyan, Mary, 1897–1983, vol. VIII
Trevelyan, Sir Norman Irving, 10th Bt (cr 1662), 1915–1996, vol. X
Trevelyan, Robert Calverley, 1872–1951, vol. V

Trevelyan, Sir Walter John, 8th Bt (*cr* 1662), 1866–1931, vol. III
Trevelyan, Rev. William Bouverie, 1853–1929, vol. III
Trevelyan, Sir Willoughby John, 9th Bt (*cr* 1662), 1902–1976, vol. VII
Treves, Sir Frederick, 1st Bt, 1853–1923, vol. II
Trevethin, 1st Baron, 1843–1936, vol. III
Trevethin, 2nd Baron, 1879–1959, vol. V
Trevethin, 3rd Baron, **and Oaksey** 1st Baron, 1880–1971, vol. VII
Trevithick, Arthur Reginald, 1858–1939, vol. III
Trevor, 2nd Baron, 1852–1923, vol. II
Trevor, 3rd Baron, 1863–1950, vol. IV
Trevor, 4th Baron, 1928–1997, vol. X
Trevor, Lady; (Rosamond Catherine), 1857–1942, vol. IV
Trevor, Sir Arthur Charles, 1841–1920, vol. II
Trevor, Arthur Hill, 1858–1924, vol. II
Trevor, Lt-Col Arthur Prescott, 1872–1930, vol. III
Trevor, Sir Cecil; *see* Trevor, Sir Charles C.
Trevor, Sir Cecil Russell, 1899–1971, vol. VII
Trevor, Sir (Charles) Cecil, 1830–1921, vol. II
Trevor, Sir (Charles) Gerald, 1882–1959, vol. V
Trevor, David, 1906–1988, vol. VIII
Trevor, Elleston, 1920–1995, vol. IX
Trevor, Surg.-Gen. Sir Francis Woollaston, 1851–1922, vol. II
Trevor, Frederick George Brunton, 1838–1924, vol. II
Trevor, Hon. George Edwyn Hill-, 1859–1922, vol. II
Trevor, Col George Herbert, 1840–1927, vol. II
Trevor, Sir Gerald; *see* Trevor, Sir C. G.
Trevor, Brig.-Gen. Herbert Edward, 1871–1939, vol. III
Trevor, Meriol, 1919–2000, vol. X
Trevor, Col Philip Christian William, 1863–1932, vol. III
Trevor, Rev. Thomas Warren, 1839–1924, vol. II
Trevor, Col William Herbert, 1872–1936, vol. III
Trevor, Maj.-Gen. William Spottiswoode, 1831–1907, vol. I
Trevor-Battye, Aubyn Bernard Rochfort, *died* 1922, vol. II
Trevor Jones, Alan; *see* Jones.
Trew, Brig.-Gen. Edward Fynmore, 1879–1935, vol. III
Trewavas, Joseph, 1835–1905, vol. I
Trewby, Vice-Adm. George, 1874–1953, vol. V
Trewin, John Courtenay, 1908–1990, vol. VIII
Trias, Juan Mannel S.; *see* Sucre-Trias.
Tribe, Sir Frank Newton, 1893–1958, vol. V
Trickett, Sir Henry Whittaker, 1857–1913, vol. I
Trickett, (Mabel) Rachel, 1923–1999, vol. X
Trickett, Rachel; *see* Trickett, M. B.
Trickett, William, 1840–1928, vol. II, vol. III
Trickett, Hon. William Joseph, 1844–1916, vol. II
Triger, David Ronald, 1941–1993, vol. IX
Triggs, H. Inigo, 1876–1923, vol. II
Triggs, William Henry, 1855–1934, vol. III
Trilling, Lionel, 1905–1975, vol. VII
Trillo, Rt Rev. (Albert) John, 1915–1992, vol. IX
Trillo, Rt Rev. John; *see* Trillo, Rt Rev. A. J.
Trimble, Brig. Arthur Philip, 1909–1984, vol. VIII

Trimble, Charles Joseph, 1856–1944, vol. IV
Trimble, S. Delmege, 1857–1947, vol. IV
Trimble, William Copeland, 1851–1941, vol. IV
Trimen, Roland, 1840–1916, vol. II
Trimingham, Sir Eldon Harvey, 1889–1959, vol. V
Trimlestown, 18th Baron, 1862–1937, vol. III
Trimlestown, 19th Baron, 1899–1990, vol. VIII
Trimlestown, 20th Baron, 1928–1997, vol. X
Trimmer, Sir George William Arthur, 1882–1972, vol. VII
Trimnell, Col William Duncan Conabeare, 1874–1953, vol. V
Trinder, Sir (Arnold) Charles, 1906–1989, vol. VIII
Trinder, Sir Charles; *see* Trinder, Sir A. C.
Trinder, Air Vice-Marshal Frank Noel, 1895–1991, vol. IX
Trinder, Thomas Edward, 1909–1989, vol. VIII
Trine, Ralph Waldo, 1866–1958, vol. V
Trinkler, Emil, 1896–1931, vol. III
Tripp, Sir Alker; *see* Tripp, Sir H. A.
Tripp, Bernard Edward Howard, 1868–1940, vol. III (A), vol. IV
Tripp, George Henry, 1860–1922, vol. II
Tripp, Sir (Herbert) Alker, 1883–1954, vol. V
Tripp, Lt-Gen. William Henry Lainson, 1881–1959, vol. V
Trippe, Juan Terry, 1899–1981, vol. VIII
Trippel, Sir Francis, 1866–1930, vol. III
Tripura, Maharaja of, 1908–1947, vol. IV
Triscott, Col Charles Prideaux, 1857–1926, vol. II
Tristram, Ernest William, 1882–1952, vol. V
Tristram, Rev. Henry, 1881–1955, vol. V
Tristram, Rev. Henry Baker, 1822–1906, vol. I
Tristram, Henry Barrington, 1861–1946, vol. IV
Tristram, Rev. John William, *died* 1926, vol. II
Tristram, Katharine Alice Salvin, 1858–1948, vol. IV
Tristram, Thomas H., 1825–1912, vol. I
Tristram, William John, 1896–1992, vol. IX
Tritton, Sir Alfred Ernest, 2nd Bt, 1873–1939, vol. III
Tritton, Arthur Henry, 1855–1936, vol. III
Tritton, Arthur Stanley, 1881–1973, vol. VII
Tritton, Sir (Charles) Ernest, 1st Bt, 1845–1918, vol. II
Tritton, Sir Ernest; *see* Tritton, Sir C. E.
Tritton, Major Sir Geoffrey Ernest, 3rd Bt, 1900–1976, vol. VII
Tritton, Herbert Leslie Melville, 1870–1940, vol. III
Tritton, Joseph Herbert, 1844–1923, vol. II
Tritton, Julian Seymour, 1889–1979, vol. VII
Tritton, Sir Seymour Biscoe, 1860–1937, vol. III
Tritton, Sir William Ashbee, 1876–1946, vol. IV
Trivedi, Sir Chandulal Madhavlal, 1893–1980, vol. VII (AII)
Trofimov, M. V., *died* 1948, vol. IV
Trollip, Arthur Stanley, 1888–1963, vol. VI
Trollope, Sir Anthony Owen Clavering, 16th Bt, 1917–1987, vol. VIII
Trollope, Lt-Col Sir Arthur Grant, 13th Bt, 1866–1937, vol. III
Trollope, Fabian George, 1872–1960, vol. V
Trollope, Sir Frederic Farrand, 14th Bt, 1875–1957, vol. V

Trollope, Sir Gordon Clavering, 15th Bt, 1885–1958, vol. V

Trollope, Sir Henry Cracroft, 12th Bt, 1860–1935, vol. III

Trollope, Brig. Hugh Charles Napier, 1895–1953, vol. V

Trollope, Rt Rev. Mark Napier, 1862–1930, vol. III

Trollope, Hon. Robert Cranmer, 1852–1908, vol. I

Trollope, Sir Thomas Ernest, 11th Bt, 1858–1927, vol. II

Trollope, Sir William Henry, 10th Bt, 1858–1921, vol. II

Troop, Rev. G. Osborne, 1854–1932, vol. III

Trotman, Arthur Edwin, 1906–1961, vol. VI

Trotman, Gen. Sir Charles Newsham, 1864–1929, vol. III

Trotman, Rev. Edward Fiennes, 1828–1910, vol. I

Trotman-Dickenson, Rev. Lenthall Greville, 1864–1931, vol. III

Trotsky, Lev Davidovich, 1879–1940, vol. III

Trott, Alan Charles, 1895–1959, vol. V

Trott, Charles Edmund, 1911–1984, vol. VIII

Trott, George Henry, 1889–1972, vol. VII

Trott, Hon. Sir Howard; see Trott, Hon. Sir W. J. H.

Trott, Hon. Sir (William James) Howard, 1883–1971, vol. VII

Trotter, Alexander Cooper, 1902–1975, vol. VII

Trotter, Alexander Pelham, 1857–1947, vol. IV

Trotter, Col Charles William, 1865–1931, vol. III

Trotter, Edith, died 1962, vol. VI

Trotter, Rev. Canon Edward Bush, 1842–1920, vol. II

Trotter, Major Edward Henry, 1872–1916, vol. II

Trotter, Col Gerald Frederic, 1871–1945, vol. IV

Trotter, Maj-Gen. Sir Henry, 1844–1905, vol. I

Trotter, Lt-Col Sir Henry, 1841–1919, vol. II

Trotter, Henry Alexander, 1869–1949, vol. IV

Trotter, Rev. Henry Eden, 1844–1922, vol. II

Trotter, Hugh, 1890–1965, vol. VI

Trotter, Maj.-Gen. Sir James Keith, 1849–1940, vol. III

Trotter, Rev. John Crawford, 1848–1942, vol. IV

Trotter, Rev. John George, 1848–1917, vol. II

Trotter, Lt-Col John Moubray, 1842–1924, vol. II

Trotter, Rev. Mowbray, 1848–1913, vol. I

Trotter, Col Sir Philip, 1844–1918, vol. II

Trotter, Reginald George, 1888–1951, vol. V

Trotter, Captain Richard Durant, 1887–1968, vol. VI

Trotter, Richard Stanley, 1903–1974, vol. VII

Trotter, Thomas, 1868–1944, vol. IV

Trotter, Thomas Henry Yorke, 1854–1934, vol. III

Trotter, Sir Victor Murray Coutts, 1874–1929, vol. III

Trotter, Wilfred, died 1939, vol. III

Trotter, William, 1839–1908, vol. I

Trotter, William Finlayson, 1871–1945, vol. IV

Troubetskoi, Prince, died 1915, vol. I

Troubetskoy, Princess Pierre; see Rives, Amélie.

Troubridge, Adm. Sir Ernest Charles Thomas, 1862–1926, vol. II

Troubridge, Laura, (Lady Troubridge), died 1946, vol. IV

Troubridge, Sir Peter, 6th Bt, 1927–1988, vol. VIII

Troubridge, Lt-Col Sir St Vincent; see Troubridge, Lt-Col T. St V. W.

Troubridge, Sir Thomas Herbert Cochrane, 4th Bt, 1860–1938, vol. III

Troubridge, Vice-Adm. Sir Thomas Hope, 1895–1949, vol. IV

Troubridge, Lt-Col Sir (Thomas) St Vincent (Wallace), 5th Bt, 1895–1963, vol. VI

Troughton, Rev. Arthur Perceval, 1858–1937, vol. III

Troughton, Sir Charles Hugh Willis, 1916–1991, vol. IX

Troughton, Henry Lionel, 1914–1994, vol. IX

Troughton, John Frederick George, 1902–1975, vol. VII

Trouncer, Cecil, 1898–1953, vol. V

Trouncer, Harold Moltke, 1871–1948, vol. IV

Troup, Lt-Col Alan Gordon, 1879–1931, vol. III

Troup, Sir (Charles) Edward, 1857–1941, vol. IV

Troup, Sir Edward; see Troup, Sir C. E.

Troup, Francis William, 1859–1941, vol. IV

Troup, Sir George Alexander, 1863–1941, vol. IV

Troup, James, 1840–1925, vol. II

Troup, Vice-Adm. Sir James Andrew Gardiner, 1883–1975, vol. VII

Troup, Robert Scott, 1874–1939, vol. III

Trousdale, Major Robert Cecil, 1876–1934, vol. III

Trout, Sir (Herbert) Leon, 1906–1978, vol. VII

Trout, Sir Leon; see Trout, Sir H. L.

Troutbeck, John, 1860–1912, vol. I

Troutbeck, Sir John Monro, 1894–1971, vol. VII

Trouton, Frederick Thomas, 1863–1922, vol. II

Trow, Albert Howard, died 1939, vol. III

Trowbridge, John Townsend, 1827–1916, vol. II

Trower, Col Courtney Vor, 1856–1947, vol. IV

Trower, Rt Rev. Gerard, 1860–1928, vol. II

Trower, John Henry Peter, 1913–1968, vol. VI

Trower, Sir Walter, 1853–1924, vol. II

Trower, Sir William Gosselin, 1889–1963, vol. VI

Troy, Hon. Michael Francis, 1877–1953, vol. V

Troyte, Sir Gilbert John A.; see Acland-Troyte.

Troyte-Bullock, Lt-Col Edward George, 1862–1942, vol. IV

Trubshaw, Dame Gwendoline Joyce, died 1954, vol. V

Trubshaw, Wilfred, 1870–1944, vol. IV

Trudeau, Edward Livingston, 1848–1915, vol. I

Trudeau, Rt Hon. Pierre Elliott, 1919–2000, vol. X

Truell, Maj.-Gen. Robert Holt, 1837–1900, vol. I

Trueman, Sir Arthur Elijah, 1894–1956, vol. V

Trueman, Edwin Royden, 1922–2000, vol. X

Trueman, George Johnstone, 1872–1949, vol. IV

Trueta, Joseph, 1897–1977, vol. VII

Truffaut, François, 1932–1984, vol. VIII

Truman, Charles Edwin, died 1938, vol. III

Truman, Lt-Col Egerton Danford, died 1938, vol. III

Truman, Harry S., 1884–1972, vol. VII

Truman, Maj.-Gen. William Robinson, died 1905, vol. I

Trumble, Thomas, 1872–1954, vol. V

Trump, John, 1858–1941, vol. IV

Trumpler, Stephen Alfred Herman, 1879–1963, vol. VI

Truninger, Lionel, 1870–1961, vol. VI

Truro, 3rd Baron, 1856–1899, vol. I
Truscott, Sir Denis Henry, 1908–1989, vol. VIII
Truscott, Sir Eric Homewood Stanham, 2nd Bt, 1898–1973, vol. VII
Truscott, Sir George Wyatt, 1st Bt, 1857–1941, vol. IV
Truscott, Samuel John, 1870–1950, vol. IV
Truss, Leslie S.; see Seldon Truss.
Trust, Helen, died 1953, vol. V
Trustam, Sir Charles Frederick, 1900–1964, vol. VI
Trusted, Sir Harry Herbert, 1888–1985, vol. VIII
Trutch, Sir Joseph William, 1826–1904, vol. I
Truter, Sir Theodore Gustaff, 1873–1949, vol. IV
Trye, Captain John Henry, 1875–1959, vol. V
Tryhorn, Frederick Gerald, 1893–1972, vol. VII
Tryon, 1st Baron, 1871–1940, vol. III
Tryon, 2nd Baron, 1906–1976, vol. VII
Trypanis, Constantine Athanasius, 1909–1993, vol. IX
Trythall, Rear-Adm. John Douglas, 1914–1991, vol. IX
Tschiffeley, Aimé Felix, 1895–1954, vol. V
Tschudi, Hugo von, 1851–1911, vol. I
Tsen, Rt Rev. P(hilip) Lindel, died 1954, vol. V
Tsibu Darku, Nana Sir, 1902–1982, vol. VIII
Tubb, Carrie, (Mrs A. J. E. Oliveira), 1876–1976, vol. VII
Tubb, Captain Frederick Harold, died 1917, vol. II
Tubbs, Francis Ralph, 1907–1980, vol. VII
Tubbs, Rt Rev. Norman H., 1879–1965, vol. VI
Tubbs, Oswald Sydney, 1908–1993, vol. IX
Tubbs, Percy Burnell, 1868–1933, vol. III
Tubbs, Ralph, 1912–1996, vol. X
Tubbs, Sir Stanley William, 1st Bt, 1871–1941, vol. IV
Tubby, Alfred Herbert, 1862–1930, vol. III
Tuck, Sir Adolph, 1st Bt, 1854–1926, vol. II
Tuck, Col Charles Harold Amys, 1880–1951, vol. V
Tuck, Maj.-Gen. George Newsam, 1901–1981, vol. VIII
Tuck, Col Gerald Louis Johnson, 1889–1966, vol. VI
Tuck, Gustave, 1857–1942, vol. IV
Tuck, Sir Raphael Herman, 1910–1982, vol. VIII
Tuck, Major Sir Reginald; see Tuck, Major Sir W. R.
Tuck, Wing Comdr Robert Roland S.; see Stanford-Tuck.
Tuck, William Henry, 1840–1922, vol. II
Tuck, Major Sir (William) Reginald, 2nd Bt, 1883–1954, vol. V
Tucker, Baron (Life Peer); Frederick James Tucker, 1888–1975, vol. VII
Tucker, Alexander Lauzun Pendock, 1861–1941, vol. IV
Tucker, Alfred Brook, 1861–1945, vol. IV
Tucker, Rt Rev. Alfred Robert, 1849–1914, vol. I
Tucker, Archibald Norman, 1904–1980, vol. VII
Tucker, Arthur, 1864–1929, vol. III
Tucker, Col Aubrey Hervey, 1833–1907, vol. I
Tucker, Rt Rev. Beverley Dandridge, 1846–1930, vol. III
Tucker, Lt-Gen. Sir Charles, 1838–1935, vol. III
Tucker, Rt Rev. Cyril James, 1911–1992, vol. IX
Tucker, David Gordon, 1914–1990, vol. VIII

Tucker, Sir Edward George, 1896–1961, vol. VI
Tucker, Edward William, 1908–1995, vol. IX
Tucker, Francis Ellis, 1844–1921, vol. II
Tucker, Frederick St George de Lautour B.; see Booth Tucker.
Tucker, Rev. George, 1835–1908, vol. I
Tucker, Gordon; see Tucker, D. G.
Tucker, Harold Herbert, 1925–1996, vol. X
Tucker, Hon. Sir Henry James, 1903–1986, vol. VIII
Tucker, Howard Archibald, 1889–1963, vol. VI
Tucker, Sir James Millard, 1892–1963, vol. VI
Tucker, Rev. John Savile, 1866–1954, vol. V
Tucker, Keith Ravenscroft, 1890–1963, vol. VI
Tucker, Maj.-Gen. Louis Henry Emile, 1843–1925, vol. II
Tucker, Sir Norman Sanger, 1895–1965, vol. VI
Tucker, Norman Walter Gwynn, 1910–1978, vol. VII
Tucker, Robert St John P.; see Pitts-Tucker.
Tucker, Captain S. N., 1876–1902, vol. I
Tucker, Thomas George, 1859–1946, vol. IV
Tucker, William, died 1909, vol. I
Tucker, William Eldon, 1903–1991, vol. IX
Tucker, Very Rev. William Frederic, 1856–1934, vol. III
Tucker, Maj.-Gen. William Guise, 1850–1906, vol. I
Tucker, William Kidger, 1857–1944, vol. IV
Tucker, Lt-Col William Kington, 1877–1956, vol. V
Tuckey, Rev. Canon James Grove White, 1864–1947, vol. IV
Tuckwell, Sir Edward George, 1910–1988, vol. VIII
Tuckwell, Gertrude Mary, 1861–1951, vol. V
Tuckwell, Rev. W., 1829–1919, vol. II
Tudball, Peter Colum, 1933–2000, vol. X
Tudball, Sir William, 1866–1939, vol. III
Tudhope, David Hamilton, 1921–1996, vol. X
Tudhope, George Ranken, 1893–1955, vol. V
Tudor, Sir Daniel Thomas, 1866–1928, vol. II
Tudor, Hon. Frank Gwynne, 1866–1922, vol. II
Tudor, Adm. Sir Frederick Charles Tudor, 1863–1946, vol. IV
Tudor, Maj.-Gen. Sir H. Hugh, 1871–1965, vol. VI
Tudor, Sir James Cameron, 1919–1995, vol. IX
Tudor-Craig, Major Sir Algernon Tudor, 1873–1943, vol. IV
Tudor Davies, William; see Davies.
Tudor-Evans, Rev. George Simon, 1867–1935, vol. III
Tudor Price, Hon. Sir David William, 1931–1986, vol. VIII
Tudsbery, Sir Francis Cannon Tudsbery, 1888–1968, vol. VI
Tudsbery, Col Henry Tudsbery, 1886–1946, vol. IV
Tudsbery, J. H. T., 1859–1939, vol. III
Tudsbery, Marmaduke Tudsbery, 1892–1983, vol. VIII
Tudway, Brig.-Gen. Robert John, 1859–1944, vol. IV
Tuer, Andrew White, 1838–1900, vol. I
Tuff, Charles, 1855–1929, vol. III
Tuff, Sir Charles, 1881–1961, vol. VI
Tuffier, Sir Theodore Martin, 1857–1929, vol. III

Tuffill, Comdr (S) Harold Birch, 1870–1950, vol. IV
Tufnell, Col Arthur Wyndham, *died* 1920, vol. II
Tufnell, Lt-Col Edward, 1848–1909, vol. I
Tufnell, Brig.-Gen. Lionel Charles Gostling, 1865–1941, vol. IV
Tufnell, Adm. Lionel Grant, 1857–1930, vol. III
Tufnell, Lt-Comdr Richard Lionel, 1896–1956, vol. V
Tufnell, Col William Nevill, 1838–1922, vol. II
Tufnell-Barrett, Hugh, 1900–1981, vol. VIII
Tufton, Hon. Charles Henry, 1879–1923, vol. II
Tufts, J. F., *died* 1921, vol. II
Tufts, James Hayden, 1862–1942, vol. IV
Tugendhat, Georg, 1898–1973, vol. VII
Tugwell, Rt Rev. Herbert, *died* 1936, vol. III
Tugwell, Ven. Lewen Greenwood, *died* 1937, vol. III
Tu'ipelehake, HRH Prince Fatafehi, 1922–1999, vol. X
Tuite, Sir Brian Hugh Morgan, 12th Bt, 1897–1970, vol. VI
Tuite, Sir Denis George Harmsworth, 13th Bt, 1904–1981, vol. VIII
Tuite, James, 1849–1916, vol. II
Tuite, Sir Mark Anthony Henry, 10th Bt, 1808–1898, vol. I
Tuite, Sir Morgan Harry Paulet, 11th Bt, 1861–1946, vol. IV
Tuke, Anthony William, 1897–1975, vol. VII
Tuke, Lt-Col George Francis Stratford, 1876–1948, vol. IV
Tuke, Captain Godfrey, 1871–1944, vol. IV
Tuke, Henry Scott, 1858–1929, vol. III
Tuke, Sir John Batty, 1835–1913, vol. I
Tuke, Col John Melville, 1885–1958, vol. V
Tuke, Dame Margaret Janson, 1862–1947, vol. IV
Tuke, Comdr Seymour Charles, 1903–1994, vol. IX
Tuke, William Favill, 1863–1940, vol. III
Tuker, Lt-Gen. Sir Francis Ivan Simms, 1894–1967, vol. VI
Tull, Thomas Stuart, 1914–1982, vol. VIII
Tullis, Ramsey, 1916–1991, vol. IX
Tulloch, Maj.-Gen. Sir Alexander Bruce, 1838–1920, vol. II
Tulloch, Angus Alexander Gegorie, 1867–1932, vol. III
Tulloch, Maj.-Gen. Derek; *see* Tulloch, Maj.-Gen. Donald D. C.
Tulloch, Maj.-Gen. (Donald) Derek (Cuthbertson), 1903–1974, vol. VII
Tulloch, Major Hector, 1835–1922, vol. II
Tulloch, Brig.-Gen. James Bruce Gregorie, *died* 1946, vol. IV
Tulloch, Brig.-Gen. John Arthur Stamford, 1865–1946, vol. IV
Tulloch, Maj.-Gen. John Walter Graham, 1861–1934, vol. III
Tulloch, Rev. W. W., 1846–1920, vol. II
Tulloch, William John, 1887–1966, vol. VI
Tulloh, Maj.-Gen. John Stewart, 1827–1901, vol. I
Tully, Jasper, 1858–1938, vol. III
Tully, Kivas, 1820–1905, vol. I
Tully, Sydney Strickland, *died* 1911, vol. I
Tun, Hon. Sir Paw, *died* 1953, vol. V

Tunbridge, Sir Ronald Ernest, 1906–1984, vol. VIII
Tunbridge, Brig.-Gen. Walter Howard, 1856–1943, vol. IV
Tunc, André Robert, 1917–1999, vol. X
Tunnard, John Samuel, 1900–1971, vol. VII
Tunnecliffe, Hon. Thomas, 1869–1948, vol. IV
Tunnicliffe, Charles Frederick, 1901–1979, vol. VII
Tunnicliffe, Francis Whittaker, *died* 1928, vol. II
Tunstall, Brian; *see* Tunstall, W. C. B.
Tunstall, (William Cuthbert) Brian, 1900–1970, vol. VI
Tuohy, Frank; *see* Tuohy, J. F.
Tuohy, James M., 1859–1923, vol. II
Tuohy, John Francis, (Frank), 1925–1999, vol. X
Tuohy, Patrick Joseph, 1894–1930, vol. III
Tuominen, Leo Olavi, 1911–1981, vol. VIII
Tuplin, William Alfred, *died* 1975, vol. VII
Tupolev, Andrei Nikolaevich, 1888–1972, vol. VII
Tupou, Queen Salote; *see* Tonga, HM the Queen of.
Tupp, Alfred Cotterell, 1840–1914, vol. I
Tupper, Rt Hon. Sir Charles, 1st Bt, 1821–1915, vol. I
Tupper, Sir Charles, 3rd Bt, 1880–1962, vol. VI
Tupper, Hon. Sir Charles Hibbert, 1855–1927, vol. II
Tupper, Sir (Charles) Lewis, 1848–1910, vol. I
Tupper, Sir Charles Stewart, 2nd Bt, 1884–1960, vol. V
Tupper, Sir Daniel Alfred Anley, 1849–1922, vol. II
Tupper, Gen. Gaspard le Marchant, 1826–1906, vol. I
Tupper, J. Stewart, 1851–1915, vol. I
Tupper, Sir James Macdonald, 4th Bt, 1887–1967, vol. VI
Tupper, Sir Lewis; *see* Tupper, Sir C. L.
Tupper, Adm. Sir Reginald Godfrey Otway, 1859–1945, vol. IV
Tupper, William Johnston, 1862–1947, vol. IV
Tupper-Carey, Rev. Albert Darell, 1866–1943, vol. IV
Turbayne, Albert Angus, 1866–1940, vol. III
Turbervill, Edith P.; *see* Picton-Turbervill.
Turberville, Arthur Stanley, 1888–1945, vol. IV
Turberville, Geoffrey, 1899–1993, vol. X (AI)
Turck, Hermann, 1856–1933, vol. III
Turgeon, Hon. Adelard, 1863–1930, vol. III
Turgeon, Hon. William Ferdinand Alphonse, 1877–1969, vol. VI
Turing, Alan Mathison, 1912–1954, vol. V
Turing, Harvey Doria, 1877–1950, vol. IV
Turing, Henry, 1843–1922, vol. II
Turing, Sir James Walter, 9th Bt, 1862–1928, vol. II
Turing, Sir John Leslie, 11th Bt, 1895–1987, vol. VIII
Turing, Sir Robert Andrew Henry, 10th Bt, 1895–1970, vol. VI
Turing, Sir Robert Fraser, 8th Bt, 1827–1913, vol. I
Turle, Rear-Adm. Charles Edward, 1883–1966, vol. VI
Turle, Henry Bernard, 1885–1974, vol. VII
Turley, Henry, *died* 1929, vol. III
Turnbull, Col Alan William, 1893–1964, vol. VI
Turnbull, Sir Alexander Cuthbert, 1925–1990, vol. VIII

826

Turnbull, Sir Alfred Clarke, *died* 1962, vol. VI
Turnbull, Col Bruce, 1880–1952, vol. V
Turnbull, Dora Amy; *see* Turnbull, Mrs George.
Turnbull, Brig. Douglas John Tulloch, 1901–1973, vol. VII
Turnbull, Major Dudley Ralph, 1891–1917, vol. II
Turnbull, Edwin Laurence, 1888–1968, vol. VI
Turnbull, Sir Francis Fearon, (Sir Frank Turnbull), 1905–1988, vol. VIII
Turnbull, Mrs George, (Dora Amy), *died* 1961, vol. VI
Turnbull, George Henry, 1889–1961, vol. VI
Turnbull, Sir George Henry, 1926–1992, vol. IX
Turnbull, Gilbert Learmonth, 1895–1981, vol. VIII
Turnbull, Herbert Westren, 1885–1961, vol. VI
Turnbull, Hubert Maitland, 1875–1955, vol. V
Turnbull, Lt-Col Sir Hugh Stephenson, 1882–1973, vol. VII
Turnbull, Cdre James, 1874–1964, vol. VI
Turnbull, Jane Holland, *died* 1958, vol. V
Turnbull, Col John, 1864–1937, vol. III
Turnbull, Ven. John William, 1905–1979, vol. VII
Turnbull, Sir March; *see* Turnbull, Sir R. M. K.
Turnbull, Maj.-Gen. Peter Stephenson, 1836–1921, vol. II
Turnbull, Reginald March Graham, 1907–1995, vol. IX
Turnbull, Sir (Reginald) March Kesterson, 1878–1943, vol. IV
Turnbull, Sir Richard Gordon, 1909–1998, vol. X
Turnbull, Robert, 1823–1901, vol. I
Turnbull, Sir Robert, 1852–1926, vol. II
Turnbull, Sir Roland Evelyn, 1905–1960, vol. V
Turnbull, Lt-Col Thomas, *died* 1929, vol. III
Turnbull, Sir Winton George, 1899–1980, vol. VII
Turner, Sir Adolphus Hilgrove, *died* 1911, vol. I
Turner, Sir Alan George, 1906–1978, vol. VII (AII)
Turner, Sir Alexander Kingcome, 1901–1993, vol. IX
Turner, Alfred, 1874–1922, vol. II
Turner, Alfred, 1874–1940, vol. III
Turner, Sir Alfred Charles; *see* Turner, Sir V. A. C.
Turner, Maj.-Gen. Sir Alfred Edward, 1842–1918, vol. II
Turner, Rt Rev. Arthur Beresford, 1862–1910, vol. I
Turner, Adm. Sir (Arthur) Francis, 1912–1991, vol. IX
Turner, Arthur James, 1889–1971, vol. VII
Turner, Brig.-Gen. Arthur Jervois, 1878–1952, vol. V
Turner, Arthur Logan, 1865–1939, vol. III
Turner, Engr Rear-Adm. Arthur William, 1859–1928, vol. II
Turner, Col Augustus Henry, 1842–1925, vol. II
Turner, Beatrice Ethel, 1891–1964, vol. VI
Turner, Sir Ben, 1863–1942, vol. IV
Turner, Captain Bingham Alexander, 1877–1914, vol. I
Turner, Comdr Bradwell Talbot, 1907–1990, vol. VIII
Turner, Air Vice-Marshal Cameron Archer, 1915–1999, vol. X
Turner, Maj.-Gen. Cecil Douglas Lovett, 1898–1976, vol. VII

Turner, Sir Cedric Oban, 1907–1982, vol. VIII
Turner, Sir Charles Arthur, 1833–1907, vol. I
Turner, Major Charles Cyril, 1870–1952, vol. V
Turner, Col Charles Edward, 1876–1961, vol. VI
Turner, Brig. Charles Edward Francis, 1899–1990, vol. VIII
Turner, Charles George, 1838–1913, vol. I
Turner, Rt Rev. Charles Henry, 1842–1923, vol. II
Turner, Sir Charles William Aldis, 1879–1938, vol. III
Turner, Vice-Adm. Charles Wolfran R.; *see* Round-Turner.
Turner, Major Clarence Roy, 1891–1957, vol. V
Turner, Air Cdre Clifford John, 1918–1992, vol. IX
Turner, Cuthbert Hamilton, 1860–1930, vol. III
Turner, Dawson, 1857–1928, vol. II
Turner, Douglas William, 1894–1977, vol. VII
Turner, Dudley Charles, 1885–1958, vol. V
Turner, E. A., (Lady Turner); *see* Robertson, E. Arnot.
Turner, E. L., *died* 1940, vol. III
Turner, Edmund Robert, 1826–1899, vol. I
Turner, Edward Beadon, 1854–1931, vol. III
Turner, Edward Raymond, 1881–1929, vol. III
Turner, Elston G.; *see* Grey-Turner.
Turner, Eric, 1918–1980, vol. VII
Turner, Sir Eric Gardner, 1911–1983, vol. VIII
Turner, Ernest George, 1874–1932, vol. III
Turner, Ernest James, 1877–1966, vol. VI
Turner, Maj.-Gen. Ernest Vere, *died* 1949, vol. IV
Turner, Ethel, (Mrs H. R. Curlewis), 1872–1958, vol. V
Turner, Eustace Ebenezer, 1893–1966, vol. VI
Turner, Dame Eva, 1892–1990, vol. VIII
Turner, Brig. Dame Evelyn Marguerite (Brig. Dame Margot), 1910–1933, vol. IX
Turner, Adm. Sir Francis; *see* Turner, Adm. Sir A. F.
Turner, Lt-Col Francis Charles, 1866–1942, vol. IV
Turner, Francis McDougall Charlewood, 1897–1982, vol. VIII
Turner, Frank Douglas, 1871–1957, vol. V
Turner, Franklyn Lewis, 1866–1933, vol. III
Turner, Fred, 1852–1939, vol. III
Turner, Frederick Bancroft, *died* 1966, vol. VI
Turner, Frederick Charles, 1872–1950, vol. IV
Turner, Vice-Adm. Sir Frederick Richard Gordon, 1889–1976, vol. VII
Turner, Sir George, *died* 1915, vol. I
Turner, Rt Hon. Sir George, 1851–1916, vol. II
Turner, George Charlewood, 1891–1967, vol. VI
Turner, Col George Frederick Brown, 1876–1941, vol. IV
Turner, George Grey, 1877–1951, vol. IV
Turner, George Henry, 1837–1903, vol. I
Turner, George James, *died* 1946, vol. IV
Turner, Sir George Robertson, 1855–1941, vol. IV
Turner, Sir George Wilfred, 1896–1974, vol. VII
Turner, Rt Rev. Gilbert Price Lloyd, 1888–1968, vol. VI
Turner, Maj.-Gen. Guy Roderick, 1889–1963, vol. VI
Turner, Harold Goodhew, 1906–1981, vol. VIII
Turner, Harold H.; *see* Horsfall Turner.
Turner, Captain Harry Gordon, *born* 1862, vol. III

Turner, Sir Harvey, 1889–1983, vol. VIII
Turner, Hawes Harison, 1851–1939, vol. III
Turner, Henry Blois Hawkins, 1839–1909, vol. I
Turner, Sir Henry Ernest, *died* 1961, vol. VI
Turner, Rev. Henry Ernest William, (Hugh), 1907–1995, vol. IX
Turner, H(enry) F(rederic) Lawrence, 1908–1977, vol. VII
Turner, Col Henry Fyers, 1840–1909, vol. I
Turner, Sir Henry Samuel Edwin, 1887–1978, vol. VII
Turner, Herbert Arthur, 1912–1972, vol. VII
Turner, Herbert Arthur Frederick, 1919–1998, vol. X
Turner, Herbert Hall, 1861–1930, vol. III
Turner, Rt Rev. Herbert Victor, 1888–1968, vol. VI
Turner, Rev. Herbert William, 1846–1922, vol. II
Turner, Rev. Hugh; *see* Turner, Rev. H. E. W.
Turner, Maj.-Gen. James Gibbon, 1859–1950, vol. IV
Turner, James Grant Smith, 1897–1985, vol. VIII
Turner, James Neil Frederick, 1932–1984, vol. VIII
Turner, Sir John, 1858–1931, vol. III
Turner, John Andrew, 1858–1922, vol. II
Turner, Ven. John Carpenter, 1867–1952, vol. V
Turner, Col John Eamer, 1880–1955, vol. V
Turner, Col Sir John Fisher, 1881–1958, vol. V
Turner, John Hastings, 1892–1956, vol. V
Turner, John Herbert, 1833–1923, vol. II
Turner, John Sidney, 1843–1920, vol. II
Turner, John William Aldren, 1911–1980, vol. VII
Turner, Sir Joseph, 1868–1939, vol. III
Turner, Joseph Harling, 1859–1942, vol. IV
Turner, Rear-Adm. Laurence, 1882–1963, vol. VI
Turner, Laurence Beddome, 1886–1963, vol. VI
Turner, Sir Llewelyn, 1823–1903, vol. I
Turner, Lloyd Charles, 1938–1996, vol. X
Turner, Brig. Dame Margot; *see* Turner, Brig. Dame E. M.
Turner, Sir Mark; *see* Turner, Sir R. M. C.
Turner, Brig.-Gen. Martin Newman, 1865–1944, vol. IV
Turner, Maxwell Joseph Hall, 1907–1960, vol. V
Turner, Sir Michael William, 1905–1980, vol. VII
Turner, Sir Montagu Cornish, 1853–1934, vol. III
Turner, Paul, 1933–1994, vol. IX
Turner, Brig.-Gen. Percy Alexander, 1868–1940, vol. III
Turner, Percy Frederick, 1878–1926, vol. II
Turner, Philip, 1873–1955, vol. V
Turner, Philip, 1913–1995, vol. IX
Turner, Surg. Rear-Adm. (D) Philip Stanley, 1905–1997, vol. X
Turner, Lt-Col Ralph Beresford, 1879–1972, vol. VII
Turner, Sir Ralph Lilley, 1888–1983, vol. VIII
Turner, Raymond C.; *see* Clifford-Turner.
Turner, Lt-Col Reginald, 1870–1953, vol. V
Turner, Col Reginald George, 1870–1953, vol. V
Turner, Richard, 1909–1994, vol. IX
Turner, Lt-Gen. Sir Richard Ernest William, 1871–1961, vol. VI
Turner, Richard Wainwright Duke, 1909–1992, vol. IX
Turner, Richard Whitbourn, 1867–1932, vol. III

Turner, Robert Noel, 1912–1987, vol. VIII
Turner, Vice-Adm. Sir Robert Ross, 1885–1977, vol. VII
Turner, Sir (Ronald) Mark (Cunliffe), 1906–1980, vol. VII
Turner, Sir Samuel, 1840–1924, vol. II
Turner, Sir Samuel, 1878–1955, vol. V
Turner, Maj.-Gen. Samuel Compton, *died* 1900, vol. I
Turner, Sir Sidney, 1882–1966, vol. VI
Turner, Sir Skinner, 1868–1935, vol. III
Turner, Sydney George, 1880–1967, vol. VI
Turner, Theodora, 1907–1999, vol. X
Turner, Theodore Francis, 1900–1986, vol. VIII
Turner, Thomas, 1861–1951, vol. V
Turner, Sir Victor Alfred Charles, 1892–1974, vol. VII
Turner, Lt-Col Victor Buller, 1900–1972, vol. VII
Turner, Sir Walford Hollier, 1881–1962, vol. VI
Turner, Walter James Redfern, 1889–1946, vol. IV
Turner, Rt Rev. William, 1844–1914, vol. I
Turner, Sir William, 1832–1916, vol. II
Turner, William, 1856–1936, vol. III
Turner, Rt Hon. Sir William, 1872–1937, vol. III
Turner, Lt-Col William, 1859–1940, vol. III
Turner, William, *died* 1944, vol. IV
Turner, William Aldren, 1864–1945, vol. IV
Turner, William Ernest Stephen, 1881–1963, vol. VI
Turner, Lt-Gen. Sir William Francis Robert, 1907–1989, vol. VIII
Turner, Sir William Henry, 1868–1923, vol. II
Turner, William Hovell, 1891–1979, vol. VII
Turner, William Percy Whitford, 1884–1962, vol. VI
Turner Cain, Maj.-Gen. George Robert, 1912–1996, vol. X
Turner-Samuels, Moss, *died* 1957, vol. V
Turney, Sir John, 1839–1927, vol. II
Turnor, Algernon, 1845–1921, vol. II
Turnor, Christopher Hatton, 1873–1940, vol. III
Turnor, Edmund, 1838–1903, vol. I, vol. III
Turnór, Lady Mary Katherine, *died* 1930, vol. III
Turnour, Rear-Adm. Edward Winterton, 1821–1901, vol. I
Turnour-Fetherstonhaugh, Hon. Keith; *see* Fetherstonhaugh.
Turpin, Edmund Hart, 1885–1907, vol. I
Turpin, George Sherbrooke, *died* 1948, vol. IV
Turpin, Maj.-Gen. Patrick George, 1911–1996, vol. X
Turpin, Sir William Gibbs, 1854–1940, vol. III
Turpin, Ven. William Homan, *died* 1920, vol. II
Turquan, Joseph, *died* 1928, vol. II
Turquet, André, *died* 1940, vol. III
Turquet, Gladys, *died* 1977, vol. VII
Turrell, Charles, 1846–1932, vol. III
Turrell, Harry Joseph, 1863–1936, vol. III
Turrell, Walter John, 1865–1943, vol. IV
Turrill, William Bertram, 1890–1961, vol. VI
Turton, family name of Baron Tranmire.
Turton, Sir Edmund Russborough, 1st Bt, 1857–1929, vol. III
Turton, Col Ralph Douglas, 1862–1936, vol. III
Turton, Lt-Col William Harry, 1856–1938, vol. III

Turton-Hart, Sir Francis Edmund, 1908–1993, vol. IX

Turvey, Isaiah, 1845–1934, vol. III

Turville-Petre, Edward Oswald Gabriel, 1908–1978, vol. VII

Turville-Petre, Lt-Col Oswald Henry Philip, 1862–1941, vol. IV

Tushingham, Sidney, died 1968, vol. VI

Tuson, Alan Arthur Lancelot, 1890–1968, vol. VI

Tuson, Brig.-Gen. Harry Denison, 1866–1958, vol. V

Tuson, Sir Henry Brasnell, 1836–1916, vol. II

Tussaud, John Theodore, 1858–1943, vol. IV

Tustin, Arnold, 1899–1994, vol. IX

Tute, Sir Richard Clifford, 1874–1950, vol. IV

Tute, Warren Stanley, 1914–1989, vol. VIII

Tutin, Thomas Gaskell, 1908–1987, vol. VIII

Tutt, James William, 1858–1911, vol. I

Tuttiett, Mary Gleed; see Gray, Maxwell.

Tuttle, Rt Rev. Daniel Sylvester, 1837–1923, vol. II

Tuttle, Sir Geoffrey William, 1906–1989, vol. VIII

Tuttle, Wilbur C., 1883–1969, vol. VI

Tutton, Alfred Edwin Howard, 1864–1938, vol. III

Tuxford, Brig.-Gen. George Stuart, 1870–1943, vol. IV

Tuzo, Gen. Sir Harry Craufurd, 1917–1998, vol. X

Twain, Mark, 1835–1910, vol. I

Tweddle, Sir William, 1914–1982, vol. VIII

Tweed, Rev. Henry Earle, 1827–1910, vol. I

Tweed, John, 1869–1933, vol. III

Tweed, Lt-Col Thomas Frederic, 1890–1940, vol. III

Tweedale, Rev. Charles L., died 1944, vol. IV

Tweedale, Violet, died 1936, vol. III

Tweeddale, 10th Marquess of, 1826–1911, vol. I

Tweeddale, 11th Marquess of, 1884–1967, vol. VI

Tweeddale, 12th Marquis of, 1921–1979, vol. VII

Tweeddale, Marchioness of; (Julia), died 1937, vol. III

Tweedie, Mrs Alec, died 1940, vol. III

Tweedie, Lt-Col David Keltie, 1878–1941, vol. IV

Tweedie, Adm. Sir Hugh Justin, 1877–1951, vol. V

Tweedie, Jill Sheila, 1936–1993, vol. IX

Tweedie, Col John Lannoy, 1842–1920, vol. II

Tweedie, Brig. John William, 1907–1991, vol. IX

Tweedie, Hon. Lemuel John, 1849–1917, vol. II

Tweedie, Mary, 1875–1961, vol. VI

Tweedie, Maj.-Gen. Michael, 1836–1917, vol. II

Tweedie, Maj.-Gen. William, 1836–1914, vol. I

Tweedie, Col William John Bell, 1869–1929, vol. III

Tweedmouth, 2nd Baron, 1849–1909, vol. I

Tweedmouth, 3rd Baron, 1874–1935, vol. III

Tweedsmuir, 1st Baron, 1875–1940, vol. III

Tweedsmuir, 2nd Baron, 1911–1996, vol. X

Tweedsmuir, Lady; (Susan Charlotte), 1882–1977, vol. VII

Tweedsmuir of Belhelvie, Baroness (Life Peer); Priscilla Jean Fortescue Buchan, 1915–1978, vol. VII

Tweedy, Ernest Hastings, 1862–1945, vol. IV

Tweedy, George Alfred, died 1934, vol. III

Tweedy, Sir John, 1849–1924, vol. II

Twells, Rt Rev. Edward, 1828–1898, vol. I

Twemlow, Col Francis Randle, 1852–1927, vol. II

Twemlow, George Fletcher Fletcher-, 1857–1935, vol. III

Twentyman, Col Augustus Charles, 1836–1913, vol. I

Twentyman-Jones, Hon. Percy Sydney, 1876–1954, vol. V

Twidale, Lt-Col Cecil; see Twidale, Lt-Col W. C. E.

Twidale, Lt-Col (William) Cecil Erasmus, 1877–1949, vol. IV

Twigg, Surg. Rear-Adm. Francis John Despard, 1888–1962, vol. VI

Twigg, Sir John, 1856–1935, vol. III

Twigg, John James, 1825–1920, vol. II

Twigg, Brig.-Gen. Robert Henry, 1860–1956, vol. V

Twinberrow, James Frederick, 1866–1931, vol. III

Twining, Baron (Life Peer); Edward Francis Twining, 1899–1967, vol. VI

Twining, Louisa, 1820–1911, vol. I

Twining, Gen. Nathan Farragut, 1897–1982, vol. VIII

Twining, Maj.-Gen. Sir Philip Geoffrey, 1862–1920, vol. II

Twining, Richard Haynes, 1889–1979, vol. VII

Twinn, Frank Charles George, 1885–1972, vol. VII

Twisaday, Major C. E. J., 1850–1925, vol. II

Twisden, Rev. Sir John Francis, 11th Bt, 1825–1914, vol. I

Twisden, Sir John Ramskill, 12th Bt, 1856–1937, vol. III

Twisleton-Wykeham-Fiennes, Gerard Francis Gisborne, 1906–1985, vol. VIII

Twisleton-Wykeham-Fiennes, Sir John Saye Wingfield, 1911–1996, vol. X

Twisleton-Wykeham-Fiennes, Lt-Col Sir Ranulph; see Fiennes.

Twiss, Brig.-Gen. Francis Arthur, 1871–1952, vol. V

Twiss, Adm. Sir Frank Roddam, 1910–1994, vol. IX

Twiss, Lt-Col George Edward, 1856–1921, vol. II

Twiss, Vice-Adm. Guy Ouchterlony, 1834–1918, vol. II

Twiss, Brig.-Gen. John Henry, 1867–1941, vol. IV

Twiss, Maj.-Gen. Sir William Louis Oberkirch, 1879–1962, vol. VI

Twist, Henry, 1870–1934, vol. III

Twist, Henry Aloysius, 1914–1997, vol. X

Twitchell, Rt Rev. Thomas Clayton, 1864–1947, vol. IV

Twitchett, Ven. Cyril Frederick, 1890–1950, vol. IV

Twohig, Brig. Joseph Patrick O.; see O'Brien Twohig.

Twohig, Col Michael Joseph O.; see O'Brien-Twohig.

Twomey, Sir Daniel Harold Ryan, 1864–1935, vol. III

Twopeny, Richard Ernest Nowell, 1857–1915, vol. I

Twort, Frederick William, 1877–1950, vol. IV

Twyford, Sir Harry Edward Augustus, 1870–1967, vol. VI

Twyford, Thomas William, 1849–1921, vol. II

Twyman, Frank, died 1959, vol. V

Twynam, Sir Henry Joseph, 1887–1966, vol. VI

Twynam, Major Humphrey Martin, 1858–1913, vol. I

Twynam, Col Philip Alexander Anstruther, 1832–1920, vol. II

Twynam, Sir William Crofton, *died* 1922, vol. II
Twysden, Sir Anthony Roger Duncan, 11th Bt, 1918–1946, vol. IV
Twysden, Sir Louis John Francis, 9th Bt, 1831–1911, vol. I
Twysden, Sir Roger Thomas, 10th Bt, 1894–1934, vol. III
Twysden, Sir William Adam Duncan, 12th Bt, 1897–1970, vol. VI
Tyabji, Badruddin, 1844–1906, vol. I
Tydeman, Col Frank William Edward, 1901–1995, vol. X (AI)
Tye, James, 1921–1996, vol. X
Tye, Walter, 1912–1998, vol. X
Tyerman, Donald, 1908–1981, vol. VIII
Tylden, Brig.-Gen. William, *died* 1942, vol. IV
Tylden-Pattenson, Major Arthur Henry, 1856–1938, vol. III
Tylden-Pattenson, Lt-Col Edwin Cooke; *see* Pattenson.
Tylecote, Edward Ferdinando Sutton, 1849–1938, vol. III
Tylecote, Frank Edward, *died* 1965, vol. VI
Tylecote, Dame Mabel, 1896–1987, vol. VIII
Tyler, Sir Alfred, 1869–1936, vol. III
Tyler, Brig. Arthur Catchmay, 1913–1998, vol. X
Tyler, Brig.-Gen. Arthur Malcolm, 1866–1950, vol. IV
Tyler, Cyril, 1911–1996, vol. X
Tyler, Sir Frederick Charles, 2nd Bt, 1865–1907, vol. I
Tyler, Froom; *see* Tyler, G. C. F.
Tyler, (George Charles) Froom, 1904–1983, vol. VIII
Tyler, Sir George Robert, 1st Bt, 1835–1897, vol. I
Tyler, Rev. Henry Francis Macdonald, 1846–1929, vol. III
Tyler, Sir Henry Hewey Francis M.; *see* Macdonald-Tyler.
Tyler, Sir Henry Whatley, 1827–1908, vol. I
Tyler, Brig.-Gen. James Arbuthnot, 1867–1945, vol. IV
Tyler, Sir John William, 1939–1913, vol. I
Tyler, Maj.-Gen. Sir Leslie Norman, 1904–1992, vol. IX
Tyler, Maj.-Gen. Trevor Bruce, 1841–1923, vol. II
Tylor, Alfred, 1888–1958, vol. V
Tylor, Sir Edward Burnett, 1832–1917, vol. II
Tylor, Sir Theodore Henry, 1900–1968, vol. VI
Tymms, Sir Frederick, 1889–1987, vol. VIII
Tymms, Ralph Vincent, 1913–1987, vol. VIII
Tymms, Rev. T. Vincent, 1842–1921, vol. II
Tynan, Katharine, 1861–1931, vol. III
Tynan, Kenneth Peacock, 1927–1980, vol. VII
Tyndale, Geoffrey Clifford, 1887–1966, vol. VI
Tyndale, Henry Edmund Guise, 1887–1948, vol. IV
Tyndale, Walter, 1855–1943, vol. IV
Tyndale, Lt-Col Wentworth Francis, 1874–1964, vol. VI
Tyndale-Biscoe, Rear-Adm. Alec Julian, 1906–1997, vol. X
Tyndale-Biscoe, Rev. Cecil Earle, 1863–1949, vol. IV
Tyndale-Biscoe, Brig.-Gen. Julian Dallas Tyndale, 1867–1960, vol. V

Tyndall, Sir Arthur, 1891–1979, vol. VII
Tyndall, Arthur Mannering, 1881–1961, vol. VI
Tyndall, Rt Rev. Charles John, 1900–1971, vol. VII
Tyndall, Lt-Col Henry Stuart, 1875–1942, vol. IV
Tyndall, Maj.-Gen. William Ernest, 1891–1975, vol. VII
Tyndall, Lt-Col William Ernest Marriott, 1875–1916, vol. II
Tyner, Rt Rev. Richard, *died* 1958, vol. V
Tynte, Fortescue Joseph Pratt-, 1841–1907, vol. I
Tyrer, Anderson; *see* Tyrer, F. A.
Tyrer, (Frank) Anderson, *died* 1962, vol. VI
Tyrer, William Henry, 1876–1947, vol. IV
Tyrrell, 1st Baron, 1866–1947, vol. IV
Tyrrell, Col Charles Robert, 1859–1934, vol. III
Tyrrell, Sir Francis Graeme, *died* 1964, vol. VI
Tyrrell, Rev. George, 1861–1909, vol. I
Tyrrell, George Walter, 1883–1961, vol. VI
Tyrrell, Lt-Col Gerald Ernest, 1871–1917, vol. II
Tyrrell, Gerald Fraser, 1907–1993, vol. IX
Tyrrell, Lt-Col Jasper Robert Joly, *died* 1951, vol. V
Tyrrell, Col John Frederick, 1872–1944, vol. IV
Tyrrell, Sir Murray Louis, 1913–1994, vol. IX
Tyrrell, Robert Yelverton, 1844–1914, vol. I
Tyrrell, Thomas, 1857–1929, vol. III
Tyrrell, Air Vice-Marshal Sir William, 1885–1968, vol. VI
Tyrrell, Brig. William Grant, 1882–1961, vol. VI
Tyrrell-Green, Rev. Edmund; *see* Green.
Tyrwhitt, Hon. Clement, 1857–1938, vol. III
Tyrwhitt, Captain Hon. Hugh, 1856–1907, vol. I
Tyrwhitt, Rev. Hon. Leonard Francis, 1863–1921, vol. II
Tyrwhitt, Brig. Dame Mary Joan Caroline, 1903–1997, vol. X
Tyrwhitt, Adm. of the Fleet Sir Reginald Yorke, 1st Bt, 1870–1951, vol. V
Tyrwhitt, Adm. Sir St John Reginald Joseph, 2nd Bt, 1905–1961, vol. VI
Tyrwhitt, Walter Spencer-Stanhope, 1859–1932, vol. III
Tyrwhitt-Drake, Sir Garrard; *see* Drake.
Tyrwhitt-Drake, Hon. Montague W.; *see* Drake.
Tyser, Sir Charles Robert, 1848–1926, vol. II
Tyser, Granville, 1884–1970, vol. VI
Tyson, Alan Walker, 1926–2000, vol. X
Tyson, Dorothy Estelle Esmé W.; *see* Wynne-Tyson.
Tyson, Geoffrey William, 1898–1971, vol. VII
Tyson, George Alfred, 1888–1972, vol. VII
Tyson, Sir John Dawson, 1893–1976, vol. VII
Tyson, Moses, 1897–1969, vol. VI
Tyson, William Joseph, 1851–1927, vol. II
Tyssen, Air Vice-Marshal John Hugh Samuel, 1889–1953, vol. V
Tytler, Adam Gillies, 1845–1929, vol. III
Tytler, Christian Helen F.; *see* Fraser-Tytler.
Tytler, Rt Rev. Donald Alexander, 1925–1992, vol. IX
Tytler, Edward Grant F.; *see* Fraser-Tytler.
Tytler, Maj.-Gen. Sir Harry Christopher, 1867–1939, vol. III
Tytler, Sir James Macleod Bannatyne F.; *see* Fraser-Tytler.
Tytler, Bt Col Neil F.; *see* Fraser-Tytler.

Tytler, Maj.-Gen. Robert Francis Christopher
Alexander, *died* 1916, vol. II
Tytler, Sarah; *see* Keddie, Henrietta.
Tytler, William Howard, 1885–1957, vol. V

Tytler, Lt-Col Sir William Kerr F.; *see*
Fraser-Tytler.
Tyzack, Group Captain John Edward Valentine,
1904–1979, vol. VII

U

Uatioa, Dame Mere, 1924–1979, vol. X (AI)
Ubbelohde, (Alfred Rene John) Paul, 1907–1988,
vol. VIII
Ubbelohde, Paul; *see* Ubbelohde, A. R. J. P.
Ubee, Air Vice-Marshal Sydney Richard,
1903–1998, vol. X
Udaipur, HH Maharajahdhiraja Maharana of,
1849–1930, vol. III
Udaipur, HH Maharana of, 1884–1955, vol. V
Udal, (Nicholas) Robin, 1883–1964, vol. VI
Udal, Robin; *see* Udal, N. R.
ud-Din, Rt Rev. Khair-, 1921–1997, vol. X
Udoma, Hon. Sir Udo; *see* Udoma, Hon. Sir E. U.
Udoma, Hon. Sir (Egbert) Udo, 1917–1998, vol. X
Udny, John Henry Fullarton, 1853–1934, vol. III
Udny, Sir Richard, 1847–1923, vol. II
Uglow, Euan Ernest Richard, 1932–2000, vol. X
Uhr, Sir Clive Wentworth, *died* 1974, vol. VII
Uhthoff, John Caldwell, 1856–1927, vol. II
Ulanova, Galina Sergeyevna, 1910–1998, vol. X
Ullah, Rev. Ihsan, 1857–1929, vol. III
Ullman, Maj.-Gen. Peter Alfred, 1897–1972,
vol. VII
Ullmann, Stephen, 1914–1976, vol. VII
Ullmann, Walter, 1910–1983, vol. VIII
Ullswater, 1st Viscount, 1855–1949, vol. IV
Ulrich, Ruy E.; *see* Ennes Ulrich.
Umfreville, Col Percy, 1868–1922, vol. II
Umfreville, Lt-Col Ralph Brunton, *died* 1937,
vol. III
Umfreville, William Henry, 1893–1984, vol. VIII
Umney, John Charles, 1868–1919, vol. II
Umpherston, Francis Albert, 1869–1940, vol. III
Unbegaun, Boris Ottokar, 1898–1973, vol. VII
Underdown, Emanuel Maguire, *died* 1913, vol. I
Underdown, Thomas H. J., 1872–1953, vol. V
Underhill, Baron (Life Peer); Henry Reginall
Underhill, 1914–1993, vol. IX
Underhill, Sir Arthur, 1850–1939, vol. III
Underhill, Charles Edward, 1845–1908, vol. I
Underhill, Adm. Edwin Veale, 1868–1928, vol. II
Underhill, Evelyn, 1875–1941, vol. IV
Underhill, Rt Rev. Francis, 1878–1943, vol. IV
Underhill, Michael Thomas Ben, 1918–1987,
vol. VIII
Underhill, Rev. Percy Cyril, 1883–1963, vol. VI
Underwood, Rev. Alfred Clair, 1885–1948, vol. IV
Underwood, Arthur Swayne, *died* 1916, vol. II
Underwood, Edgar Ashworth, 1899–1980, vol. VII
Underwood, Eric Gordon, *died* 1952, vol. V
Underwood, Eric John, 1905–1980, vol. VII
Underwood, John Ernest Alfred, 1886–1960, vol. V
Underwood, Brig. John Percy Delabene, 1882–1958,
vol. V

Underwood, Leon, 1890–1975, vol. VII
Underwood, Michael; *see* Evelyn, J. M.
Undset, Sigrid, 1882–1949, vol. IV
Unett, Captain John Alfred, 1868–1932, vol. III
Unger, Gladys Buchanan, *died* 1940, vol. III,
vol. IV
Unger, Josef, 1912–1967, vol. VI
Ungoed-Thomas, Sir (Anwyn) Lynn, 1904–1972,
vol. VII
Ungoed-Thomas, Sir Lynn; *see* Ungoed-Thomas, Sir
A. L.
Uniacke, Lt-Gen. Sir Herbert Crofton Campbell,
1866–1934, vol. III
Uniacke-Penrose-Fitzgerald, Sir Robert; *see*
Fitzgerald.
Unmack, Randall Carter, 1899–1978, vol. VII
Unstead, Robert John, 1915–1988, vol. VIII
Untermeyer, Louis, 1885–1977, vol. VII
Unwin, Edward, 1840–1933, vol. III
Unwin, Captain Edward, 1864–1950, vol. IV
Unwin, Francis Sydney, 1885–1925, vol. II
Unwin, Col Garton Bouverie, 1859–1928, vol. II
Unwin, Rear-Adm. John Harold, 1906–1970,
vol. VI
Unwin, Joseph Daniel, 1895–1936, vol. III
Unwin, Sir Keith, 1909–1990, vol. VIII
Unwin, Nora Spicer, 1907–1982, vol. VIII
Unwin, Sir Raymond, 1863–1940, vol. III
Unwin, Rayner Stephens, 1925–2000, vol. X
Unwin, Sir Stanley, 1884–1968, vol. VI
Unwin, Thomas Fisher, 1848–1935, vol. III
Unwin, William Cawthorne, 1838–1933, vol. III
Upcher, Rev. Abbot Roland, 1849–1929, vol. III
Upcher, Rev. Arthur Charles Wodehouse,
1846–1938, vol. III
Upcher, Sir Henry Edward Sparke, 1870–1954,
vol. V
Upcher, Henry Morris, 1839–1921, vol. II
Upcher, Ven. James Hay, *died* 1931, vol. III
Upcher, Maj.-Gen. Russell, 1844–1936, vol. III
Upcott, Ven. Arthur William, 1857–1922, vol. II
Upcott, Sir Frederick Robert, 1847–1918, vol.II
Upcott, Sir Gilbert Charles, 1880–1967, vol. VI
Updike, Daniel Berkeley, 1860–1941, vol. IV
Upham, Captain Charles Hazlitt, 1908–1994,
vol. IX
Upington, Sir Thomas, 1844–1898, vol. I
Upjohn, Baron (Life Peer); Gerald Ritchie Upjohn,
1903–1971, vol. VII
Upjohn, Howard Emlyn, 1925–1980, vol. VII
Upjohn, Sir William George Dismore, 1888–1980,
vol. VII
Upjohn, William Henry, 1853–1941, vol. IV
Upperton, Maj.-Gen. John, 1838–1924, vol. II

Upson, Rt Rev. Dom Wilfrid, 1880–1963, vol. VI
Upton, Charles B., 1831–1920, vol. II
Upton, Captain Edward James Gott, *died* 1943, vol. IV
Upton, Hon. Eric Edward Montagu John, 1885–1915, vol. I
Upton, Sir Everard; *see* Upton, Sir T. E. T.
Upton, Florence, *died* 1922, vol. II
Upton, James Bryan, 1900–1976, vol. VII
Upton, John Herbert, 1865–1930, vol. III
Upton, Leslie William Stokes, 1900–1979, vol. VII
Upton, Sir (Thomas) Everard (Tichborne), 1871–1937, vol. III
Upton, Rev. William Clement, *died* 1922, vol. II
Upward, Allen, 1863–1926, vol. II
Upward, Herbert, *died* 1944, vol. IV
Urban, Wilbur Marshall, 1873–1952, vol. V
Ure, Alexander; *see* Baron Strathclyde.
Ure, Mary Eileen (Mrs Robert Shaw), 1933–1975, vol. VII
Ure, Percy Neville, 1879–1950, vol. IV
Ure, Peter, 1919–1969, vol. VI
Uren, Reginald Harold, 1906–1988, vol. VIII
Urey, Harold Clayton, 1893–1981, vol. VIII
Urgüplü, Ali Suad Hayri, 1903–1981, vol. VIII
Uriburu, José Evaristo, *died* 1956, vol. V
Urich, John, 1849–1939, vol. III (A), vol. IV
Urling Clark, Sir Henry Laurence, 1883–1975, vol. VII
Urmson, George Harold, 1851–1907, vol. I
Urmson, Rev. Thomas, *died* 1926, vol. II
Urmston, Col Edward Brabazon, 1858–1920, vol. II
Urquhart, Alexander, 1867–1942, vol. IV
Urquhart, Sir Andrew, 1918–1988, vol. VIII
Urquhart, David Lanchlan; *see* Baron Tayside.
Urquhart, Donald John, 1909–1994, vol. IX
Urquhart, Lt-Col Francis Edward Romulus P.; *see* Pollard-Urquhart.
Urquhart, Francis Fortescue, 1868–1934, vol. III
Urquhart, Frederic Charles, 1858–1936, vol. III
Urquhart, George A., 1888–1951, vol. V
Urquhart, Sir James, 1864–1930, vol. III
Urquhart, John Leslie, 1874–1933, vol. III
Urquhart, Col Robert, 1845–1922, vol. II
Urquhart, Maj.-Gen. Robert Elliott, 1901–1988, vol. VIII
Urquhart, Sir Robert William, 1896–1983, vol. VIII
Urquhart, Maj.-Gen. Ronald Walton, 1906–1968, vol. VI
Urquhart, Rev. William Spence, 1877–1964, vol. VI
Urton, Sir William Holmes Lister, 1908–1982, vol. VIII
Urwick, Edward Johns, 1867–1945, vol. IV
Urwick, Col Frank Davidson, 1874–1936, vol. III
Urwick, Sir Henry, 1859–1931, vol. III
Urwick, Lyndall Fownes, 1891–1983, vol. VIII
Urwick, Sir Thomas Hunter, 1865–1939, vol. III
Urwin, Charles Henry, (Harry), 1915–1996, vol. X
Urwin, Harry; *see* Urwin, C. H.
Urwin, Rt Hon. Thomas William, 1912–1985, vol. VIII

Usborne, Vice-Adm. Cecil Vivian, 1880–1951, vol. V
Usborne, Henry Charles, 1909–1996, vol. X
Usborne, Thomas, 1840–1915, vol. I
Usher, Col Charles Milne, 1891–1981, vol. VIII
Usher, Sir George Clemens, 1889–1963, vol. VI
Usher, Herbert Brough, 1892–1969, vol. VI
Usher, James Ward, *died* 1921, vol. II
Usher, Sir John, 1st Bt, 1828–1904, vol. I
Usher, Sir John; *see* Usher, Sir W. J. T.
Usher, Col Sir John Turnbull, 3rd Bt, 1891–1951, vol. V
Usher, Sir Peter Lionel, 5th Bt, 1931–1990, vol. VIII
Usher, Rev. Philip Charles Alexander, 1899–1941, vol. IV
Usher, Sir Robert, 2nd Bt, 1860–1933, vol. III
Usher, Sir Robert Edward, 6th Bt, 1934–1994, vol. IX
Usher, Sir (Robert) Stuart, 4th Bt, 1898–1962, vol. VI
Usher, Sir Stuart; *see* Usher, Sir R. S.
Usher, Brig. Thomas Clive, 1907–1982, vol. VIII
Usher, Sir (William) John Tevenar, 7th Bt, 1940–1998, vol. X
Usher-Wilson, Rt Rev. Lucian Charles, 1903–1984, vol. VIII
Usherwood, John F., *died* 1964, vol. VI
Usherwood, Kenneth Ascough, 1904–1988, vol. VIII
Usherwood, Ven. Thomas Edward, 1841–1939, vol. III
Usman, Sir Mahomed, 1884–1960, vol. V
Ussher, Col Allan Vesey, 1860–1941, vol. IV
Ussher, Captain Edward, *died* 1902, vol. I
Ussishkin, Menahem, *died* 1941, vol. IV
Uthwatt, Baron (Life Peer); Augustus Andrewes Uthwatt, 1879–1949, vol. IV
Uthwatt, Ven. William Andrewes, *died* 1952, vol. V
Utiger, Ronald Ernest, 1926–1995, vol. IX
Utley, Clifton Maxwell, 1904–1978, vol. VII
Utley, Peter; *see* Utley, T. E.
Utley, Thomas Edwin, (Peter), 1921–1988, vol. VIII
Utrillo, Maurice, (Maurice Valadon), 1883–1955, vol. V
Utterson, Maj.-Gen. Archibald Hammond, 1836–1912, vol. I
Utterson-Kelso, Maj.-Gen. John Edward, 1893–1972, vol. VII
Utterton, Ven. Frank Ernest, *died* 1908, vol. I
Utting, Sir John, *died* 1927, vol. II
Uttley, Albert Maurel, 1906–1985, vol. VIII
Uttley, Alison, 1884–1976, vol. VII
Uttley, George Harry, 1879–1960, vol. V
Uvarov, Sir Boris Petrovitch, 1889–1970, vol. VI
Uvedale of North End, 1st Baron, 1885–1974, vol. VII
Unwins, Cyril Frank, 1896–1972, vol. VII
Uzanne, Octave, 1852–1931, vol. III
Uzès, Duchesse d', 1848–1933, vol. III
Uzielli, Herbert Rex, 1890–1961, vol. VI
Uzielli, Col Theodore John, 1882–1934, vol. III

V

Vacaresco, Helen, *died* 1947, vol. IV
Vachell, Benjamin Garnet L.; *see* Lampard-Vachell.
Vachell, Charles Francis, 1854–1935, vol. III
Vachell, Horace Annesley, 1861–1955, vol. V
Vachon, Most Rev. Mgr Alexandre, 1885–1953, vol. V
Vade-Walpole, Henry Spencer, 1837–1913, vol. I
Vade-Walpole, Thomas Henry Bourke, 1879–1915, vol. I
Vaes, Baron Robert, 1919–2000, vol. X
Vaghjee, Sir Harilal Ranchhordas, 1912–1979, vol. VII
Vaillancourt, Hon. Cyrille, 1892–1969, vol. VII (AI)
Vailland, Roger, 1907–1965, vol. VI
Vaisey, Dame Dorothy May, *died* 1969, vol. VI
Vaisey, Sir Harry Bevir, 1877–1965, vol. VI
Vaithianathan, Sir Kanthiah, 1896–1965, vol. VI
Vaizey, Baron (Life Peer); John Ernest Vaizey, 1929–1984, vol. VIII
Vaizey, Mrs G. de Horne, *died* 1927, vol. II
Vakil, Sardar Khan Bahadur Sir Rustom Jehangir, 1879–1933, vol. III
Valadier, Sir Auguste Charles, 1873–1931, vol. III
Valadon, Maurice; *see* Utrillo, M.
Valantine, Louis Francis, 1907–1977, vol. VII
Valdar, Colin Gordon, 1918–1996, vol. X
Valdés, Armando P.; *see* Palacio Valdés.
Vale, Brig. Croxton Sillery, 1896–1975, vol. VII
Vale, Edmund; *see* Vale, H. E. T.
Vale, (Henry) Edmund (Theodoric), 1888–1969, vol. VI
Vale, Captain Seymour Douglas, 1865–1931, vol. III
Valentia, 11th Viscount, 1843–1927, vol. II
Valentia, 12th Viscount, 1883–1949, vol. IV
Valentia, 13th Viscount, 1875–1951, vol. V
Valentia, 14th Viscount, 1888–1983, vol. VIII
Valentine; *see* Pechey, Archibald T.
Valentine, Sir Alec, (Alexander Balmain Bruce Valentine), 1899–1977, vol. VII
Valentine, Alfred Buyers, 1894–1970, vol. VI
Valentine, Charles Wilfrid, 1879–1964, vol. VI
Valentine, David Henriques, 1912–1987, vol. VIII
Valentine, George Donald, 1877–1946, vol. IV
Valentine, Wing-Comdr George Engebret, 1909–1941, vol. IV
Valentine, William Alexander, 1869–1959, vol. V
Valéry, Paul, 1871–1945, vol. IV
Valintine, Thomas Harcourt Ambrose, 1865–1945, vol. IV
Vallance, Lt-Col Aylmer, (George Alexander Gerald Vallance), 1892–1955, vol. V
Vallance, David James, 1849–1915, vol. I
Vallance, George Alexander Gerald; *see* Vallance, Lt-Col Aylmer.
Vallance, William Fleming, 1827–1904, vol. I
Vallery-Radot Pasteur, Louis, 1886–1970, vol. VI
Valluy, Général d'Armée Jean Étienne, 1899–1970, vol. VI
Valon, Maj.-Gen. Albert Robert, 1885–1971, vol. VII

Valpy, Rev. Arthur Sutton, *died* 1909, vol. I
Valtorta, Rt Rev. Mgr Henry Paschal, 1883–1951, vol. V
Vambery, Arminius, 1832–1913, vol. I
van Allen, Rev. William Harman, 1870–1931, vol. III
van Anrooy, A., 1870–1949, vol. IV
Van Beinum, Eduard, 1900–1959, vol. V
van Bellinghen, Jean-Paul, 1925–1993, vol. IX
Van Beneden, Edward, *died* 1910, vol. I, vol. III
van Boeschoten, Sir Johannes Gerard, 1862–1937, vol. III
van Broekhuizen, Herman Dirk, 1872–1953, vol. V
Vanbrugh, Dame Irene, 1872–1949, vol. IV
Vanbrugh, Violet, 1867–1942, vol. IV
Van Buren, Rt Rev. James Heartt, 1850–1917, vol. II
Vance, Very Rev. George Oakley, 1828–1910, vol. I
Vance, Rt Rev. John Gabriel, 1885–1968, vol. VI
Van Cuylenburg, Sir Hector, 1847–1915, vol. I
Vandal, Louis Jules Albert, 1853–1910, vol. I
Vandam, Albert Dresden, 1843–1903, vol. I
Vandeleur, Lt-Col Cecil Foster Seymour, 1869–1901, vol. I
Vandeleur, Captain Hector Stewart, 1836–1909, vol. I
Vandeleur, Brig. Henry Martley, 1875–1951, vol. V
Vandeleur, Maj.-Gen. John Ormsby, 1832–1908, vol. I
Vandeleur, Brig.-Gen. Robert Seymour, 1869–1956, vol. V
Vanden-Bempde-Johnstone, Hon. Sir Alan; *see* Johnstone.
Vandenberg, Arthur Hendrick, 1884–1951, vol. V
Van Den Berg, Frederick, 1893–1957, vol. V
Van den Bergh, Donald Stanley, 1888–1949, vol. IV
Van den Bergh, Henry, 1851–1937, vol. III
Van Den Bergh, James Philip, 1905–1988, vol. VIII
Van den Bogaerde, Sir Derek Niven, (Sir Dirk Bogarde), 1921–1999, vol. X
van den Heever, C. M., 1902–1957, vol. V
Vanden Heuvel, Frederick, 1885–1963, vol. VI
Vandepeer, Sir Donald Edward, 1890–1968, vol. VI
van der Bijl, Hendrik Johannes, 1887–1948, vol. IV
Vanderbilt, Alfred Gwynne, 1877–1915, vol. I
Vanderbilt, Brig.-Gen. Cornelius, 1873–1942, vol. IV
Vanderbilt, Cornelius, 1898–1974, vol. VII
Vanderbilt, Frederick William, 1856–1938, vol. III
Vanderbilt, George Washington, 1862–1914, vol. I
Vanderbilt, William Kissam, 1849–1920, vol. II
Van der Byl, Brig. John, 1878–1953, vol. V
van der Byl, Major Hon. Pieter Voltelyn Graham, 1889–1975, vol. VII
Vanderbyl, Captain P. B., 1867–1930, vol. III
Van Der Hoeve, Jan, 1878–1952, vol. V
Van der Kiste, Lt-Col Freegift William, 1875–1948, vol. IV
Van Der Kiste, Wing Comdr Robert Edgar Guy, 1912–1999, vol. X
Vanderlip, Frank Arthur, 1864–1937, vol. III

Vanderlyn, Nathan, 1872–1946, vol. IV
van der Meulen, Daniel, 1894–1989, vol. VIII
Van der Meulen, Sir Frederick Alan, 1875–1935,
vol. III
Vander-Meulen, Adm. Frederick Samuel,
1839–1913, vol. I
Vanderpant, Sir Harry Sheil Elster, 1866–1955,
vol. V
Van der Poorten-Schwartz, Joost Marius Willem; see
Maartens, Maarten.
van der Post, Jan Laurens, 1928–1984, vol. VIII
Van der Post, Sir Laurens Jan, 1906–1996, vol. X
Van der Riet, Frederick John Werndly, died 1929,
vol. III
Van der Smissen, William Henry, 1844–1929,
vol. III
Van der Veer, John Conrad, 1869–1928, vol. II
Vandervelde, Emile, died 1938, vol. III
Vandervell, Harry, 1870–1956, vol. V
Van der Vlugt, W., 1853–1928, vol. II
Van der Waals, Johannes Diedevik, 1837–1923,
vol. II
Vanderzee, Maj.-Gen. Francis Henry, 1841–1909,
vol. I
Van Deventer, Hon. Lt-Gen. Sir Louis Jacob, died
1922, vol. II
Van de Weyer, Victor William Bates, 1839–1915,
vol. I
Van de Weyer, Major William John Bates,
1870–1946, vol. IV
Van Dine, S. S.; see Wright, Willard Huntington.
Van Druten, John William, 1901–1957, vol. V
Vandry, Rt Rev. Mgr Ferdinand, 1887–1967,
vol. VI (AII)
Van Dyck, Ernest Marie Hubert, 1861–1923, vol. II
Van Dyke, Rev. Henry, 1852–1933, vol. III
Vane, Major Sir Francis Patrick Fletcher, 5th Bt,
1861–1934, vol. III
Vane, Frederick William, 1852–1935, vol. III
Vane, Harry Tempest, died 1943, vol. IV
Vane, Captain Hon. Henry Cecil, 1882–1917, vol. II
Vane, Sir Henry Ralph Fletcher, 4th Bt, 1830–1908,
vol. I
Vane, Hon. Ralph Frederick, 1891–1928, vol. II
Vane, Hon. William Lyonel, 1859–1920, vol. II
Vane-Tempest, Major Adolphus; see Vane-Tempest,
Major F. A.
Vane-Tempest, Major (Francis) Adolphus,
1863–1932, vol. III
Vane-Tempest, Lord Henry; see Vane-Tempest,
Lord Herbert L. H.
Vane-Tempest, Lord Henry John, 1854–1905, vol. I
Vane-Tempest, Lord (Herbert Lionel) Henry,
1862–1921, vol. II
van Eyck, Aldo Ernest, 1918–1999, vol. X
Vangeke, Most Rev. Sir Louis, 1904–1982,
vol. VIII
van Geyzel, Lt-Col John Lawrence, 1857–1932,
vol. III
Van Heerden, Hon. H. C., 1862–1933, vol. III
van Heyningen, William Edward, 1911–1989,
vol. VIII
Van Horne, William Cornelius, 1843–1915, vol. I
Van Hulsteyn, Sir Willem, 1865–1939, vol. III

Vanier, Gen. Rt Hon. Georges Philias, 1888–1967,
vol. VI
Van Koughnet, Captain Edmund Barker,
1849–1905, vol. I
Van Lare, William Bedford, 1904–1969, vol. VI
van Lennep, Jonkheer Emile, 1915–1996, vol. X
van Loon, Hendrik Willem, died 1944, vol. IV
van Meerbeke, René Louis Joseph Marie,
1895–1983, vol. VIII
Van Miltenburg, Most Rev. Mgr Alcuin,
1909–1966, vol. VI
Vanneck, Hon. Andrew Nicolas Armstrong,
1890–1965, vol. VI
Vanneck, Air Cdre Hon. Sir Peter Beckford Rutgers,
1922–1999, vol. X
Van Neck, Captain Stephen Hugh, 1889–1963,
vol. VI
Vanneck, Hon. William Arcedeckne, 1845–1912,
vol. I
Van Notten-Pole, Sir Cecil Pery; see Pole.
Vanoc; see White, Arnold.
Van Oss, (Adam) Oliver, 1909–1992, vol. IX
Van Oss, Oliver; see Van Oss, A. O.
van Praag, Louis, 1926–1993, vol. IX
Van Praagh, Dame Peggy, 1910–1990, vol. VIII
van Raalte, Charles, 1857–1907, vol. I
Van Reeth, Rt Rev. Joseph, 1843–1923, vol. II
Van Rhyn, Albertus Johannes Roux, 1890–1971,
vol. VII
Van Roey, His Eminence Cardinal Joseph Ernest,
1874–1961, vol. VI
Van Roijen, Jan Herman; see Roijen.
Van Ryneveld, Gen. Sir Pierre Helperus Andrias,
1891–1972, vol. VII
Vans Agnew, Lt-Col John, 1859–1943, vol. IV
Van Scoy, Thomas, 1848–1901, vol. I
Vansittart, 1st Baron, 1881–1957, vol. V
Vansittart, Arthur George, 1854–1911, vol. I
Vansittart, Col Eden, 1856–1936, vol. III
Vansittart, Adm. Edward Westby, 1818–1904, vol. I
Vansittart, Guy Nicholas, 1893–1989, vol. VIII
Vansittart, Ronald Arnold, 1851–1938, vol. III
Vansittart, Spencer Charles Patrick, 1860–1928,
vol. II
Vansittart-Neale, Sir Henry James; see Neale.
Van Someren, William Taylor, 1855–1944, vol. IV
Van Someren, Major William Weymouth,
1876–1939, vol. III
Vanston, Sir George Thomas Barrett, 1853–1923,
vol. II
van Straubenzee, Maj.-Gen. Sir Casimir Cartwright,
1867–1956, vol. V
van Straubenzee, Brig.-Gen. Casimir Henry Claude,
1864–1943, vol. IV
van Straubenzee, Maj.-Gen. Turner, 1838–1920,
vol. II
van Straubenzee, Sir William Radcliffe, 1924–1999,
vol. X
Van Swinderen, Jonkheer Rene de Marees-,
1860–1955, vol. V
Van Vechten, Carl, 1880–1964, vol. VI
van Verduynen, (Edgar) Michiels, 1885–1952,
vol. V
van Verduynen, Michiels; see van Verduynen, E. M.
Van Vleck, John Hasbrouch, 1899–1980, vol. VII

Van Wyck, Robert Anderson, 1849–1918, vol. II
van Zeeland, Paul, Vicomte, 1893–1973, vol. VII
Van Zyl, Rt Hon. Gideon Brand, 1873–1956, vol. V
Vapereau, Louis Gustave, 1819–1906, vol. I
Varah, (Doris) Susan, 1916–1993, vol. IX
Varah, Susan; see Varah, D. S.
Varcoe, Frederick Percy, 1889–1965, vol. VI
Vardon, Harry, 1870–1937, vol. III
Vardy, Rev. Albert Richard, 1841–1900, vol. I
Varey, John Earl, 1922–1999, vol. X
Varin, René Louis, 1896–1976, vol. VII
Varjivandas, Sir Jugmohandas; see Jugmohandas
  Varjivandas.
Varley, Frank Bradley, died 1929, vol. III
Varley, George Copley, 1910–1983, vol. VIII
Varley-Haigh, Ernest; see Haigh.
Varrier-Jones, Sir Pendrill Charles, 1883–1941,
  vol. IV
Varvill, Michael Hugh, 1909–1988, vol. VIII
Vasey, Sir Ernest Albert, 1901–1984, vol. VIII
Vasey, Maj.-Gen. George Alan, 1895–1945, vol. IV
Vaskess, Henry Harrison, 1891–1969, vol. VI
Vassal, Gabrielle M., died 1959, vol. V
Vassall-Phillips, Father Oliver Rodie, died 1932,
  vol. III
Vassar-Smith, Sir John George Lawley, 2nd Bt,
  1868–1942, vol. IV
Vassar-Smith, Maj. Sir Richard Rathborne, 3rd Bt,
  1909–1995, vol. IX
Vassar-Smith, Sir Richard Vassar, 1st Bt,
  1843–1922, vol. II
Vasse, Air Cdre Gordon Herbert, 1899–1965,
  vol. VI
Vatcher, Rev. James Raynold Morley, 1861–1931,
  vol. III
Vaucher, Paul, 1887–1966, vol. VI
Vaudin, William Marshall, 1866–1919, vol. II
Vaudrey, Sir William Henry, 1855–1926, vol. II
Vaudrey-Barker-Mill, William Claude Frederick,
  1874–1916, vol. II
Vaughan, Rev. Bernard, 1847–1922, vol. II
Vaughan, Major Charles Davies, 1868–1915, vol. I
Vaughan, Charles Edwyn, 1854–1922, vol. II
Vaughan, Brig. (Charles) Hilary (Vaughan),
  1905–1976, vol. VII
Vaughan, Col Charles Jerome, 1873–1948, vol. IV
Vaughan, Very Rev. Charles John, 1816–1897,
  vol. I
Vaughan, Hon. Crawford, 1874–1947, vol. IV
Vaughan, David, 1873–1938, vol. III
Vaughan, Rev. David James, 1825–1905, vol. I
Vaughan, David Thomas G.; see Gwynne-Vaughan.
Vaughan, David Wyamar, 1906–1982, vol. VIII
Vaughan, Sir Edgar; see Vaughan, Sir G. E.
Vaughan, Brig.-Gen. Edward, 1866–1956, vol. V
Vaughan, Brig.-Gen. Edward James Forrester,
  1875–1957, vol. V
Vaughan, Brig. Edward William Drummond,
  1894–1953, vol. V
Vaughan, Ernest James, 1901–1987, vol. VIII
Vaughan, Major Eugene Napoleon Ernest Mallet,
  1878–1934, vol. III
Vaughan, Francis Baynham, 1844–1919, vol. II
Vaughan, Rt Rev. Francis John, 1877–1935, vol. III
Vaughan, Frankie, 1928–1999, vol. X

Vaughan, Captain George Augustus, 1833–1914,
  vol. I
Vaughan, Sir (George) Edgar, 1907–1994, vol. IX
Vaughan, Dame Helen Charlotte Isabella G.; see
  Gwynne-Vaughan.
Vaughan, Rev. Henry, 1848–1920, vol. II
Vaughan, Henry William Campbell, 1919–1991,
  vol. IX
Vaughan, His Eminence Cardinal Herbert,
  1932–1903, vol. I
Vaughan, Very Rev. Herbert, 1874–1936, vol. III
Vaughan, Herbert Millingchamp, 1870–1948,
  vol. IV
Vaughan, Col Herbert Radclyffe, 1864–1947,
  vol. IV
Vaughan, Brig. Hilary; see Vaughan, Brig. C. H. V.
Vaughan, Hilda, (Mrs Charles Morgan), 1892–1985,
  vol. VIII
Vaughan, Maj.-Gen. Hugh Thomas J.; see
  Jones-Vaughan.
Vaughan, Sir James, 1814–1906, vol. I
Vaughan, Dame Janet Maria, 1899–1993, vol. IX
Vaughan, Rev. Canon John, 1841–1918, vol. II
Vaughan, Rev. Canon John, 1855–1922, vol. II
Vaughan, Maj.-Gen. John, 1871–1956, vol. V
Vaughan, Sir (John Charles) Tudor (St Andrew-),
  1870–1929, vol. III
Vaughan, John Edwards, 1863–929, vol. III
Vaughan, John Godfrey, 1916–1984, vol. VIII
Vaughan, John Henry, 1892–1965, vol. VI
Vaughan, John Howard, 1879–1955, vol. V
Vaughan, (John) Keith, 1912–1977, vol. VII
Vaughan, Sir John Luther, 1820–1911, vol. I
Vaughan, Rt Rev. John Stephen, 1853–1925, vol. II
Vaughan, Keith; see Vaughan, J. K.
Vaughan, Lt-Col Joseph Charles Stoelke,
  1862–1932, vol. III
Vaughan, Lt-Gen. Sir Louis Ridley, 1875–1942,
  vol. IV
Vaughan, Margaret; see Vaughan, Mrs William
  Wyamar.
Vaughan, Reginald Charles, 1874–1935, vol. III
Vaughan, Reginald Charles, 1896–1960, vol. V
Vaughan, Sir Robert, 1866–1941, vol. IV
Vaughan, Robert Charles, 1883–1966, vol. VI
Vaughan, Maj.-Gen. Robert Edward, 1866–1946,
  vol. IV
Vaughan, Sir Tudor; see Vaughan, Sir J. C. T. St A.
Vaughan, Victor C., 1851–1929, vol. III
Vaughan, Rt Rev. William, 1814–1902, vol. I
Vaughan, William Hubert, 1894–1959, vol. V
Vaughan, William Randal, 1912–1998, vol. X
Vaughan, William Wyamar, 1865–1938, vol. III
Vaughan, Mrs William Wyamar, (Margaret
  Vaughan), 1869–1925, vol. II
Vaughan-Hughes, Brig. Gerald Birdwood,
  1896–1983, vol. VIII
Vaughan-Lee, Col Arthur Vaughan Hanning,
  1862–1933, vol. III
Vaughan-Lee, Charles Guy, 1913–1984, vol. VIII
Vaughan-Lee, Adm. Sir Charles Lionel, 1867–1928,
  vol. II
Vaughan-Morgan, family name of Baron Reigate.
Vaughan-Morgan, Sir Kenyon Pascoe, 1873–1933,
  vol. III

Vaughan-Russell, John Francis Robert, 1895–1958, vol. V
Vaughan-Sawyer, Ethel, 1868–1949, vol. IV
Vaughan-Thomas, (Lewis John) Wynford, 1908–1987, vol. VIII
Vaughan-Thomas, Wynford; see Vaughan-Thomas, L. J. W.
Vaughan Wilkes, Rev. John Comyn, 1902–1986, vol. VIII
Vaughan-Williams, Major Francis, 1856–1920, vol. II
Vaughan Williams, Ralph, 1872–1958, vol. V
Vautelet, Renée G., (Mme H. E. Vautelet), 1897–1980, vol. VII (AII)
Vaux of Harrowden, 7th Baron, 1860–1935, vol. III
Vaux of Harrowden, Baroness (8th in line), 1887–1958, vol. V
Vaux of Harrowden, 9th Baron, 1914–1977, vol. VII
Vaux, Lt-Col Ernest, 1865–1925, vol. II
Vaux, Lt-Col Henry George, 1883–1957, vol. V
Vaux, Sir Richard Augustus, 1869–1946, vol. IV
Vavasour, Comdr Sir Geoffrey William, 5th Bt, 1914–1997, vol. X
Vavasour, Sir Henry Mervin, 3rd Bt (cr 1801), 1814–1912, vol. I
Vavasour, Captain Sir Leonard Pius, 4th Bt (cr 1828), 1881–1961, vol. VI
Vavasour, Sir William Edward, 3rd Bt (cr 1828), 1846–1915, vol. I
Vavasseur, Josiah, 1834–1908, vol. I
Vawdrey, Col George, 1872–1961, vol. VI
Vawdrey, Rev. John Cossham, died 1931, vol. III
Veale, Sir Douglas, 1891–1973, vol. VII
Veale, Sir Geoffrey, 1906–1971, vol. VII
Veall, Harry Truman, 1901–1983, vol. VIII
Veasey, Brig. Harley Gerald, 1896–1982, vol. VIII
Veblen, Oswald, 1880–1960, vol. V
Vecqueray, Rev. Gerard Cokayne, 1851–1933, vol. III
Vedder, Elihu, 1836–1923, vol. II
Vedrenne, John E., 1867–1930, vol. III
Veidt, Conrad, 1893–1943, vol. IV
Veira, Sir Philip Henry, 1921–1991, vol. IX
Veitch, Allan, 1900–1971, vol. VII
Veitch, George Stead, 1885–1943, vol. IV
Veitch, Sir Harry James, 1840–1924, vol. II
Veitch, Marian, (Mrs Donald Barnie), 1913–1973, vol. VII
Veitch, William, 1885–1968, vol. VI
Veitch, Maj.-Gen. William Lionel Douglas, 1901–1969, vol. VI
Velázquez, Carlos María, 1918–1970, vol. VI
Veley, Lilian Jane, 1861–1936, vol. III
Veley, Victor Herbert, 1856–1933, vol. III
Vella, Hon. Tom, born 1849, vol. II
Vella, Col Victor George, 1901–1963, vol. VI
Vellacott, Paul Cairn, 1891–1954, vol. V
Venables, Major Charles John, 1865–1915, vol. I
Venables, Rev. Canon E(dward) Malcolm, 1884–1957, vol. VII
Venables, Rev. George, 1821–1908, vol. I
Venables, Harry Archbutt, 1858–1944, vol. IV
Venables, Oswald Eric, 1891–1960, vol. V
Venables, Sir Peter Percy Frederick Ronald, 1904–1979, vol. VII

Venables-Llewelyn, Sir Charles Leyshon Dillwyn-, 2nd Bt, 1870–1951, vol. V
Venables-Llewelyn, Brig. Sir (Charles) Michael Dillwyn-, 3rd Bt, 1900–1976, vol. VII
Venables-Llewelyn, Brig. Sir Michael Dillwyn-; see Venables-Llewelyn, Brig. Sir C. M. D.
Venables-Vernon, Sir William Henry; see Vernon.
Venis, Arthur, 1857–1918, vol. II
Venizelos, Eleutherios, 1864–1936, vol. III
Venkata Reddi Naidu, Sir Kurma, 1875–1942, vol. IV
Venkatagiri, Rajah of, 1857–1916, vol. II
Venkatagiri, Maharajah of, died 1937, vol. III
Venkatanarayana Nayudu, Diwan Bahadur J., 1875–1958, vol. V
Venkataratnam Nayudu, Sir R., 1862–1939, vol. III
Venkatasweta Chalapati Runga-Rao Bahadur, Maharajah Sir Ravu, Maharajah of Bobbili, 1862–1920, vol. II
Venmore, Arthur, 1883–1961, vol. VI
Venn, Albert John, 1840–1919, vol. II
Venn, Edward James Alfred, 1919–1989, vol. VIII
Venn, Air Cdre George Oswald, 1892–1984, vol. VIII
Venn, George William Cavendish, died 1933, vol. III
Venn, Rev. Henry, 1838–1923, vol. II
Venn, John, 1834–1923, vol. II
Venn, John Archibald, 1883–1958, vol. V
Venner, Sir Edwin John, 1871–1955, vol. V
Venner, John Franklyn, 1902–1955, vol. V
Venning, Alfred Reid, 1846–1927, vol. II
Venning, Sir Edgcombe, 1837–1920, vol. II
Venning, Brig. Francis Esmond Wingate, 1882–1970, vol. VI
Venning, Lieut Gordon Ralph, died 1902, vol. I
Venning, Gen. Sir Walter King, 1882–1964, vol. VI
Veno, Sir William Henry, 1866–1933, vol. III
Venour, Major Wilfred John, 1870–1914, vol. I
Venter, Gen. Christoffel Johannes, 1892–1977, vol. VII
Ventris, Maj.-Gen. Francis, 1857–1929, vol. III
Ventry, 4th Baron, 1828–1914, vol. I
Ventry, 5th Baron, 1861–1923, vol. II
Ventry, 6th Baron, 1864–1936, vol. III
Ventry, 7th Baron, 1898–1987, vol. VIII
Verco, Sir Joseph Cooke, 1851–1933, vol. III
Vercors, (Jean Marcel Bruller), 1902–1991, vol. IX
Verdi, Guiseppe, 1813–1901, vol. I
Verdin, Sir Joseph, 1st Bt, 1838–1920, vol. II
Verdin, Lt-Col Sir Richard Bertram, 1912–1978, vol. VII
Verdin, William Henry, 1848–1929, vol. III
Verdon, Rt Rev. Michael, 1838–1918, vol. II
Verdon-Roe, Sir Alliott; see Roe.
Verdon-Smith, Sir Reginald; see Verdon-Smith, Sir W. R.
Verdon-Smith, Sir (William) Reginald, 1912–1992, vol. IX
Vere, James Charles H.; see Hope-Vere.
Vere, Very Rev. Langton George, 1844–1924, vol. II
Vere Hodge, John Douglass; see Hodge.
Vere-Laurie, Lt-Col George Halliburton Foster Peel, 1906–1981, vol. VIII

Vereker, Sir (George) Gordon (Medlicott), 1889–1976, vol. VII
Vereker, Sir Gordon; *see* Vereker, Sir G. G. M.
Vereker, Hon. Henry Prendergast, 1824–1904, vol. I
Veresmith, Daniel Albert, 1861–1932, vol. III
Veresmith, Emile, vol. III
Verestchagin, Vassili, 1842–1904, vol. I
Verey, David Cecil Wynter, 1913–1984, vol. VIII
Verey, Lt-Col Henry Edward, 1877–1968, vol. VI
Verey, Sir Henry William, 1836–1920, vol. II
Verey, Rev. Lewis, 1874–1961, vol. VI
Verey, Michael John, 1912–2000, vol. X
Verhaeren, Emil, 1855–1916, vol. II
Verity, Gp Captain Conrad Edward Howe, 1901–1984, vol. VIII
Verity, Sir Edgar William, 1891–1975, vol. VII
Verity, Francis Thomas, *died* 1937, vol. III
Verity, George, 1867–1936, vol. III
Verity, Rev. Heron Beresford, *died* 1940, vol. III (A), vol. IV
Verity, Sir John, 1892–1970, vol. VI
Verne, Adela, 1886–1952, vol. V
Verne, Jules, 1828–1905, vol. I
Verner, Sir Edward Derrick Wingfield, 6th Bt, 1907–1975, vol. VII
Verner, Sir Edward Wingfield, 4th Bt, 1830–1899, vol. I
Verner, Captain Sir Edward Wingfield, 5th Bt, 1865–1936, vol. III
Verner, Maj.-Gen. Thomas Edward, 1845–1931, vol. III
Verner, Col William Willoughby Cole, 1852–1922, vol. II
Verneuil, Louis, 1893–1952, vol. V
Verney, Sir Edmund Hope, 3rd Bt (*cr* 1818), 1838–1910, vol. I
Verney, Ernest Basil, 1894–1967, vol. VI
Verney, Frank Arthur, 1874–1952, vol. V
Verney, Frederick William, 1846–1913, vol. I
Verney, Maj.-Gen. Gerald Lloyd, 1900–1957, vol. V
Verney, Sir Harry Calvert Williams, 4th Bt (*cr* 1818), 1881–1974, vol. VII
Verney, Sir Harry Lloyd, 1872–1950, vol. IV
Verney, Sir John, 2nd Bt (*cr* 1946), 1913–1993, vol. IX
Verney, Margaret Maria, (Lady Verney), 1844–1930, vol. III
Verney, Lt-Col Sir Ralph, 1st Bt (*cr* 1946), 1879–1959, vol. V
Verney, Air Cdre Reynell Henry, 1886–1974, vol. VII
Vernham, John Edward, 1854–1921, vol. II
Vernier-Palliez, Bernard Maurice Alexandre, 1918–1999, vol. X
Vernon, 7th Baron, 1854–1898, vol. I
Vernon, 8th Baron, 1888–1915, vol. I
Vernon, 9th Baron, 1889–1963, vol. VI
Vernon, 10th Baron, 1923–2000, vol. X
Vernon, Ambrose White, 1870–1951, vol. V
Vernon, Sir (Bowater) George (Hamilton), 2nd Bt (*cr* 1885), 1865–1940, vol. III
Vernon, Rev. Canon C. W., 1871–1934, vol. III
Vernon, Major Frank, 1875–1940, vol. III

Vernon, Air Cdre Frederick Edward, 1899–1963, vol. VI
Vernon, Sir George; *see* Vernon, Sir B. G. H.
Vernon, Rt Rev. Gerald Richard, 1899–1963, vol. VI
Vernon, Hon. Greville Richard, 1835–1909, vol. I
Vernon, Harold Anselm Bellamy, 1874–1945, vol. IV
Vernon, Sir Harry Foley, 1st Bt (*cr* 1885), 1834–1920, vol. II
Vernon, Brig.-Gen. Henry Albemarle, 1879–1943, vol. IV
Vernon, Sir Herbert, *see* Vernon, Sir J. H.
Vernon, Horace Middleton, 1870–1951, vol. V
Vernon, Captain Hubert Edward, 1867–1902, vol. I
Vernon, Rev. James Edmund, 1837–1928, vol. II
Vernon, James William, 1915–1999, vol. X
Vernon, Sir (John) Herbert, 2nd Bt (*cr* 1914), 1858–1933, vol. III
Vernon, Magdalen Dorothea, 1901–1991, vol. IX
Vernon, Sir Norman; *see* Vernon, Sir W. N.
Vernon, Philip Ewart, 1905–1987, vol. VIII
Vernon, Roland Venables, *died* 1942, vol. IV
Vernon, Rupert Robert, 1872–1940, vol. III
Vernon, Sir Sydney, 1876–1966, vol. VI
Vernon, Sir Wilfred Douglas, 1897–1973, vol. VII
Vernon, Major Wilfrid Foulston, 1882–1975, vol. VII
Vernon, Sir William, 1st Bt (*cr* 1914), 1835–1919, vol. II
Vernon, Sir William Henry Venables-, 1852–1934, vol. III
Vernon, Sir (William) Norman, 3rd Bt (*cr* 1914), 1890–1967, vol. VI
Vernon Harcourt, Augustus George, 1834–1919, vol. II
Vernon-Harcourt, Leveson Francis, 1839–1907, vol. I
Vernon-Harcourt, Rt Hon. Sir William George Granville Venables; *see* Harcourt.
Vernon-Hunt, Ralph Holmes, 1923–1987, vol. VIII
Vernon-Jones, Vernon Stanley, 1875–1955, vol. V
Vernon-Wentworth, Captain Bruce Canning, 1862–1951, vol. V
Vernon-Wentworth, Captain Frederick Charles Ulick, 1866–1947, vol. IV
Veronese, Senator Giuseppe, *born* 1854, vol. II
Veronese, Vittorino, 1910–1986, vol. VIII
Verpilleux, Antoine Emile, 1888–1964, vol. VI
Verrall, Arthur Woollgar, 1851–1912, vol. I
Verrall, George Henry, 1848–1911, vol. I
Verrall, Sir Jenner; *see* Verrall, Sir T. J.
Verrall, Paul Jenner, 1883–1951, vol. V
Verrall, Sir (Thomas) Jenner, 1852–1929, vol. III
Verrett, Lt-Col Hector Bacon, 1874–1926, vol. II
Verrieres, Albert Claude, 1871–1940, vol. III
Verrill, Alpheus Hyatt, 1871–1954, vol. V
Verry, Frederick William, 1899–1981, vol. VIII
Verschoyle, Arthur Robert, 1859–1937, vol. III
Verschoyle, Beresford St George, *died* 1962, vol. VI
Verschoyle, Derek Hugo, 1911–1973, vol. VII
Verschoyle, James Kynaston Edwards, 1858–1907, vol. I
Verschoyle-Campbell, Maj.-Gen. William Henry McNeile, 1884–1964, vol. VI

Versey, Henry Cherry, 1894–1990, vol. VIII
Verstone, Philip Eason, 1882–1973, vol. VII
Verteillac, Herminie de; see Rohan, Duchess de.
Vertue, Rt Rev. John, 1826–1900, vol. I
Verulam, 3rd Earl of, 1852–1924, vol. II
Verulam, 4th Earl of, 1880–1949, vol. IV
Verulam, 5th Earl of, 1910–1960, vol. V
Verulam, 6th Earl of, 1912–1973, vol. VII
Verykios, Panaghiotis Andrew, 1910–1990, vol. VIII
Verwoerd, Hendrik Frensch, 1901–1966, vol. VI
Vesey, Captain Charles Nicholas C.; see Colthurst-Vesey.
Vesey, Ven. Francis Gerald, 1832–1915, vol. I
Vesey, Sir Henry; see Vesey, Sir N. H. P.
Vesey, Gen. Sir Ivo Lucius Beresford, 1876–1975, vol. VII
Vesey, Sir (Nathaniel) Henry Peniston, 1901–1998, vol. X
Vesey, Lt-Col Hon. Sir Osbert Eustace, 1884–1957, vol. V
Vesey, Sidney Philip Charles, 1873–1932, vol. III
Vesey, Col Hon. Thomas Eustace, 1885–1946, vol. IV
Vesey-Fitzgerald, Brian Percy Seymour, 1900–1981, vol. VIII
Vesey-Fitzgerald, James Foster-; see Fitzgerald.
Vesey-FitzGerald, John Foster, died 1932, vol. III
Vesey-FitzGerald, John Vesey, 1848–1929, vol. III
Vesey-Fitzgerald, Seymour Gonne, 1884–1954, vol. V
Vesnin, Victor, 1882–1950, vol. IV (A)
Vestal, Stanley; see Campbell, W. S.
Vestey, 1st Baron, 1859–1940, vol. III
Vestey, 2nd Baron, 1882–1954, vol. V
Vestey, Sir Edmund Hoyle, 1st Bt, 1866–1953, vol. V
Vestey, Ronald Arthur, 1898–1987, vol. VIII
Vetch, Col Robert Hamilton, 1841–1916, vol. II
Vetch, Maj.-Gen. William Francis, 1845–1910, vol. I
Vevers, Geoffrey Marr, 1890–1970, vol. VI
Veysey, Geoffrey Charles, 1895–1984, vol. VIII
Vezin, Hermann, 1829–1910, vol. I
Vial, Rev. Frank Gifford, 1872–1948, vol. IV
Vialls, Lt-Col Harry George, 1859–1918, vol. II
Vian, Admiral of the Fleet Sir Philip, 1894–1968, vol. VI
Viant, Samuel Philip, 1882–1964, vol. VI
Viardot, Michelle Pauline, 1821–1910, vol. I
Viaud, Louis Marie Julien; see Loti, Pierre.
Vibart, Col Henry Meredith, 1839–1917, vol. II
Vibart, Captain John Fleming, 1877–1948, vol. IV (A), vol. V
Vibart, Bt Lt-Col Noel Meredith, 1893–1935, vol. III
Vibert, Captain Frederick William, 1859–1935, vol. III
Vibert, McInroy Este, 1894–1986, vol. VIII
Vicars, Sir Arthur Edward, 1864–1921, vol. II
Vicars, Edward Robert Eckersall, 1869–1949, vol. IV
Vicars, Sir John, 1857–1936, vol. III
Vicars, Sir William, 1859–1940, vol. III
Vicars-Harris, Noël Hedley, 1901–1991, vol. IX

Vicary, Col Alexander Craven, 1888–1975, vol. VII
Viccars, John Ellis, 1882–1940, vol. III
Vick, Sir Arthur; see Vick, Sir F. A.
Vick, Sir (Francis) Arthur, 1911–1998, vol. X
Vick, Sir Godfrey Russell, 1892–1958, vol. V
Vick, Reginald Martin, died 1971, vol. VII
Vick, Richard William, 1917–1997, vol. X
Vickers, Baroness (Life Peer); Joan Helen Vickers, 1907–1994, vol. IX
Vickers, Albert, 1838–1919, vol. II
Vickers, Allan Robert Stanley, 1901–1967, vol. VI
Vickers, Sir (Charles) Geoffrey, 1894–1982, vol. VIII
Vickers, Douglas, 1861–1937, vol. III
Vickers, Sir Geoffrey; see Vickers, Sir C. G.
Vickers, Harold James, 1895–1970, vol. VI
Vickers, Kenneth Hotham, 1881–1957, vol. V
Vickers, Thomas Douglas, 1916–1999, vol. X
Vickers, Col Thomas Edward, 1833–1915, vol. I
Vickers, Vincent Cartwright, 1879–1939, vol. III
Vickers, William John, 1898–1979, vol. VII
Vickers, Lt-Gen. Wilmot Gordon Hilton, 1890–1987, vol. VIII
Vickery, Col Charles Edwin, 1881–1951, vol. V
Vickery, Sir Philip Crawford, 1890–1987, vol. VIII
Vicky; see Weisz, Victor.
Victor, Rt Rev. Dennis, 1882–1949, vol. IV
Vidal, Col Francis Peter, 1879–1952, vol. V
Vidal, Rt Rev. Julian, 1846–1922, vol. II
Vidler, Rev. Alexander Roper, 1899–1991, vol. IX
Vidor, King Wallis, 1896–1982, vol. VIII
Vieler, Geoffrey Herbert, 1910–1997, vol. X
Viener, Rev. Harry Dan Leigh, 1868–1947, vol. IV
Vigne, Lt-Col Robert Austen, 1862–1940, vol. III
Vignoles, Charles Malcolm, 1901–1961, vol. VI
Vigors, Edward Cliffe, died 1945, vol. IV
Vigors, Captain Philip Urban, 1875–1917, vol. II
Vigors, Major Philip Urban Walter, 1863–1935, vol. III
Viljoen, Hon. Sir Antonie Gysbert, 1858–1918, vol. II
Viljoen, W. J., 1869–1929, vol. III
Villa-Urrutia, Marquis de, 1850–1933, vol. III
Villalobar, Marquis of, 1866–1926, vol. II
Villar, Captain George, 1887–1970, vol. VI
Villard, Oswald Garrison, 1872–1949, vol. IV
Villars, Henry G.; see Gauthier-Villars.
Villars, Paul, 1849–1935, vol. III
Villasante, Julian Martinez-Villasante y Navarro, 1876–1945, vol. IV
Villeneuve, Son Eminence le Cardinal J. M. Rodrigue, 1883–1947, vol. IV
Villeneuve-Smith, Sir Francis; see Smith.
Villiers, Viscount; George Henry Child Villiers, 1948–1998, vol. X
Villiers, Alan John, 1903–1982, vol. VIII
Villiers, Hon. Arthur George Child, 1883–1969, vol. VI
Villiers, Lt-Col Charles Hyde, died 1947, vol. IV
Villiers, Sir Charles Hyde, 1912–1992, vol. IX
Villiers, Rt Hon. Charles Pelham, 1802–1898, vol. I
Villiers, Lt-Col Charles Walter, 1873–1938, vol. III
Villiers, Sir Edward; see Villiers, Sir F. E. E.
Villiers, Rear-Adm. Edward Cecil, 1866–1939, vol. III

Villiers, Col Ernest, 1838–1921, vol. II
Villiers, Ernest Amherst, 1863–1923, vol. II
Villiers, Lt-Col Evelyn Fountaine, 1875–1955, vol. V
Villiers, Sir (Francis) Edward Earle, 1889–1967, vol. VI
Villiers, Rt Hon. Sir Francis Hyde, 1852–1925, vol. II
Villiers, Francis John, 1851–1925, vol. II
Villiers, Frederic, 1852–1922, vol. II
Villiers, Gerald Hyde, 188?–1953, vol. V
Villiers, Rev. Henry Montagu, 1837–1908, vol. I
Villiers, Vice-Adm. Sir (John) Michael, 1907–1990, vol. VIII
Villiers, Maria Theresa; see Earle, Mrs C. W.
Villiers, Vice-Adm. Sir Michael; see Villiers, Vice-Adm. Sir J. M.
Villiers, Richard J., 1850–1913, vol. I
Villiers, Brig. Richard Montagu, 1905–1973, vol. VII
Villiers, Sir Thomas Lister, 1869–1959, vol. V
Villiers-Stuart, Col John Patrick, 1879–1958, vol. V
Villiers-Stuart, Brig.-Gen. William, 1872–1961, vol. VI
Vinall, Joseph William Topham, 1873–1953, vol. V
Vinaver, Eugène, 1899–1979, vol. VII
Vince, Charles Anthony, 1855–1929, vol. III
Vincent, Sir Alfred, 1891–1967, vol. VI
Vincent, Sir Anthony Francis, 14th Bt (cr 1620), 1894–1936, vol. III
Vincent, Col Arthur Craigie Fitz-Hardinge, 1857–1929, vol. III
Vincent, Arthur Rose, 1876–1956, vol. V
Vincent, Brig.-Gen. Sir Berkeley, 1871–1963, vol. VI
Vincent, Rt Rev. Boyd, 1845–1935, vol. III
Vincent, Sir (Charles Edward) Howard, 1849–1908, vol. I
Vincent, Air Vice-Marshal Claude McClean, 1896–1967, vol. VI
Vincent, Maj.-Gen. Douglas, 1916–1995, vol. X (AI)
Vincent, Eric Reginald Pearce, 1894–1978, vol. VII
Vincent, Ethel Gwendoline (Lady Vincent), 1861–1952, vol. V
Vincent, Sir Francis Erskine, 13th Bt (cr 1620), 1869–1935, vol. III
Vincent, Frank Arthur Money, 1875–1950, vol. IV
Vincent, Sir Frederick d'Abernon, 15th Bt (cr 1620), 1852–1936, vol. III
Vincent, George Edgar, 1864–1941, vol. IV
Vincent, Sir Graham; see Vincent, Sir H. G.
Vincent, Sir (Harold) Graham, 1891–1981, vol. VIII
Vincent, Sir Harry, 1874–1952, vol. V
Vincent, Brig.-Gen. Henry Osman, 1863–1945, vol. IV
Vincent, Sir Howard; see Vincent, Sir C. E. H.
Vincent, Sir Hugh Corbet, died 1931, vol. III
Vincent, Ivor Francis Sutherland, 1916–1994, vol. IX
Vincent, James Edmund, 1857–1909, vol. I
Vincent, Rt Rev. John Dacre, 1894–1960, vol. V
Vincent, John Lewis, 1845–1915, vol. I
Vincent, Very Rev. John Ranulph, died 1914, vol. I
Vincent, Lady Kitty; see Ritson, Lady K.

Vincent, Sir Lacey Eric, 2nd Bt (cr 1936), 1902–1963, vol. VI
Vincent, Marvin Richardson, 1834–1922, vol. II
Vincent, Sir Percy, 1st Bt (cr 1936), 1868–1943, vol. IV
Vincent, Ralph, 1870–1922, vol. II
Vincent, Robert William Edward Hampe, 1841–1914, vol. I
Vincent, Rev. Samuel, 1839–1910, vol. I
Vincent, Air Vice-Marshal Stanley Flamank, 1897–1976, vol. VII
Vincent, Swale, 1868–1933, vol. III
Vincent, Sir William, 12th Bt (cr 1620), 1834–1914, vol. I
Vincent, Sir William Henry Hoare, 1866–1941, vol. IV
Vincent, William James Nathaniel, 1867–1953, vol. V
Vincent, Sir William Wilkins, 1843–1916, vol. II
Vincent-Gompertz, Frank Priestly, died 1968, vol. VI
Vincent-Jackson, Rev. William, died 1919, vol. II
Vincent-Jones, Captain Desmond, 1912–1992, vol. IX
Vincze, Paul, 1907–1994, vol. IX
Vinden, Brig. Frederick Hubert, 1898–1977, vol. VII
Vine, Rev. Aubrey Russell, 1900–1973, vol. VII
Vine, Francis Seymour, 1904–1961, vol. VI
Vine, Sir John Richard Somers, 1847–1929, vol. III
Vine, Laurence Arthur, 1885–1954, vol. V
Vine, Rev. Marshall George, 1850–1918, vol. II
Viney, Lt-Col Horace George, 1885–1972, vol. VII
Vine, Norman Douglas, 1890–1966, vol. VI
Vine, Philip Mesban, 1919–1992, vol. IX
Vines, Col Clement Erskine, 1878–1964, vol. VI
Vines, Howard William Copland, 1893–1982, vol. VIII
Vines, Sydney Howard, 1849–1934, vol. III
Vines, Rev. Thomas Hotchkin, died 1928, vol. II
Viney, Col Oscar Vaughan, 1886–1976, vol. VII
Vining, Most Rev. Leslie Gordon, 1885–1955, vol. V
Vinogradoff, Sir Paul Gavrilovitch, 1854–1925, vol. II
Vinson, Frederick Moore, 1890–1953, vol. V
Vintcent, Sir Joseph, 1861–1914, vol. I
Vinter, Geoffrey Odell, 1900–1981, vol. VIII
Vintras, George Charles Louis Bartlett, 1864–1934, vol. III
Viollet, Paul, 1840–1914, vol. I
Vipan, Alfred, 1884–1947, vol. IV
Vipan, Major Charles, 1849–1921, vol. II
Vipan, Captain John Alexander Maylin, 1849–1939, vol. III
Virchow, Rudolf, 1821–1902, vol. I
Virgo, Charles G., 1843–1907, vol. I
Virgo, John James, 1865–1956, vol. V
Virtanen, Artturi Ilmari, 1895–1973, vol. VII
Virtue, Hon. Sir John Evenden, 1905–1986, vol. VIII
Vischer, Sir Hanns, 1876–1945, vol. IV
Visconti, Luchino, 1906–1976, vol. VII
Visetti, Albert, 1846–1928, vol. II
Visger, Mrs Owen; see Owen, Jean A.
Vissanji, Sir Mathuradas, 1881–1949, vol. IV

Visser't Hooft, Willem Adolf, 1900–1985, vol. VIII
Visvesvaraya, Sir Mokshagundam, 1861–1962, vol. VI
Viswa Nath, Rao Bahadur Bhagavatula, 1889–1964, vol. VI
Vivenot, Baroness de, 1907–1992, vol. IX
Vivian, 4th Baron, 1878–1940, vol. III
Vivian, 5th Baron, 1906–1991, vol. IX
Vivian, Adm. Algernon W. H.; see Walker-Heneage-Vivian.
Vivian, Captain Anthony Hamilton, 1880–1937, vol. III
Vivian, Arthur Henry Seymour, 1899–1985, vol. VIII
Vivian, Sir Arthur Pendarves, 1834–1926, vol. II
Vivian, Hon. Claud Hamilton, 1849–1902, vol. I
Vivian, Captain Gerald William, 1869–1921, vol. II
Vivian, Graham Linsell, 1887–1978, vol. VII
Vivian, Henry, 1868–1930, vol. III
Vivian, Herbert, 1865–1940, vol. III
Vivian, Vice-Adm. John Guy Protheroe, 1887–1963, vol. VI
Vivian, Preston G.; see Graham-Vivian, R. P.
Vivian, Lt-Col Ralph, 1845–1924, vol. II
Vivian, Sir Sylvanus Percival, 1880–1958, vol. V
Vivian, Lt-Col Valentine, 1880–1948, vol. IV
Vivian, Lt-Col Valentine Patrick Terrel, 1886–1969, vol. VI
Vivian, William Graham, 1827–1912, vol. I
Vizard, Brig.-Gen. Robert Davenport, 1861–1941, vol. IV
Vizetelly, Ernest Alfred, 1853–1922, vol. II
Vizetelly, Francis Horace, (Frank), 1864–1938, vol. III
Vizianagram, Rajkumar of, 1905–1965, vol. VI
Vlasto, Michael, 1888–1979, vol. VII
Vlieland, Alice Edith, died 1944, vol. IV
Vodden, Rt Rev. Henry Townsend, 1887–1960, vol. V
Voelcker, Arthur Francis, 1861–1946, vol. IV
Voelcker, Francis William, 1896–1954, vol. V
Voelcker, John Augustus, 1854–1937, vol. III
Vogel, Harry Benjamin, 1868–1947, vol. IV
Vogel, Hon. Sir Julius, 1835–1899, vol. I
Vogt, Alfred, 1879–1943, vol. IV
Vogt, Paul Benjamin, 1863–1947, vol. IV
Vogüé, Marquis Charles Jean Melchior de, 1829–1916, vol. II
Voigt, F. A., 1892–1957, vol. V
Vokes, Maj.-Gen. Christopher, 1904–1985, vol. VIII
Volkers, Robert Charles Francis, died 1929, vol. III
von Anrep, Boris, 1883–1969, vol. VI
Von Arnheim, Edward Henry Silberstein; see Arnheim.
von Berg, Clement, 1853–1936, vol. III
von Bibra, Major Sir Eric Ernest, 1895–1958, vol. V
von Braun, Wernher, 1912–1977, vol. VII
von Bülow, Prince Bernhard Henry Martin Charles, 1849–1929, vol. III
von Clemm, Michael, 1935–1997, vol. X
Von der Heyde, Brig. John Leslie, 1896–1974, vol. VII
von Donop, Lt-Col Pelham George, 1851–1921, vol. II

von Donop, Maj.-Gen. Sir Stanley Brenton, 1860–1941, vol. IV
von Euler, Ulf Svante, 1905–1983, vol. VIII
von Franckenstein, Baroness Joseph; see Boyle, Kay.
von Frisch, Karl Ritter, 1886–1982, vol. VIII
von Hagen, Victor Wolfgang, born 1908, vol. VIII
von Halle, Ernst, 1868–1909, vol. I
von Karajan, Herbert, 1908–1989, vol. VIII
Vonier, Rt Rev. Dom Anscar, 1875–1938, vol. III
von Karman, Theodore, 1881–1963, vol. VI
von Laue, Max Theodor Felix, 1879–1960, vol. V
von Neumann, John, 1903–1957, vol. V
von Neurath, Freiherr Constantin, 1873–1956, vol. V
Vonnoh, Bessie Potter, 1872–1955, vol. V
Vonnoh, Robert, 1858–1933, vol. III
von Nordenwall, Oswald Hans Carl Maria; see von Stroheim, Erich.
von Purucker, (Hobart Lorenz) Gottfried; see Purucker.
von Ribbentrop, Joachim; see Ribbentrop.
von Sauer, Emil, 1862–1942, vol. IV
von Schröder, Baron William Henry, 1841–1912, vol. I
von Seeckt, Gen., 1866–1936, vol. III
von Stroheim, Erich, (Oswald Hans Carl Maria von Nordenwall), 1885–1957, vol. V
Vonwiller, Oscar Ulrich, 1882–1972, vol. VII
Vora, Sir Manmohandas Ramji, 1857–1934, vol. III (A), vol. V
Vorley, Lt-Col John Stuart, 1898–1953, vol. V
Voronoff, Serge, 1866–1951, vol. V
Voroshilov, Kliment Efremovich, 1881–1969, vol. VI
Vorster, Hon. Balthazar Johannes, 1915–1983, vol. VIII
Vos, Philip, 1891–1948, vol. IV
Vosper, Dennis Forwood; see Baron Runcorn.
Vosper, Sydney Curnow, 1866–1942, vol. IV
Vouel, Raymond, 1923–1987, vol. VIII
Voules, Arthur Blennerhassett, 1870–1954, vol. V
Voules, Sir Francis Minchin, 1867–1947, vol. IV
Voules, Sir Gordon Blennerhassett, 1839–1924, vol. II
Voules, Horace St George, 1844–1909, vol. I
Vousden, William John, 1845–1902, vol. I
Vowden, Desmond Harvey Weight, 1921–1990, vol. VIII
Voynich, Wilfrid Michael, 1865–1930, vol. III
Voysey, Rev. Charles, 1828–1912, vol. I
Voysey, Charles C.; see Cowles-Voysey.
Voysey, Charles Francis Annesley, 1857–1941, vol. IV
Voysey, Reginald George, 1916–1993, vol. IX
Voysey, Violet Mary Annesley, 1880–1943, vol. IV
Vroom, Ven. Fenwick Williams, 1856–1944, vol. IV
Vulliamy, Colwyn Edward, 1886–1971, vol. VII
Vulliamy, Maj.-Gen. Colwyn Henry Hughes, 1894–1972, vol. VII
Vulliamy, Edward, 1876–1962, vol. VI
Vulliamy, Grace, 1878–1957, vol. V
Vyle, Sir Gilbert Christopher, 1870–1933, vol. III
Vyner, Clare George, 1894–1989, vol. VIII

Vyner, Robert Charles de Grey, 1842–1915, vol. I
Vynne, Nora, *died* 1914, vol. I
Vyse, Charles, 1882–1971, vol. VII
Vyse, Lt-Gen. Sir Edward D. H.; *see* Howard-Vyse.
Vyse, Lt-Gen. Edward H.; *see* Howard-Vyse.
Vyse, Howard Henry H.; *see* Howard-Vyse.
Vyse, Maj.-Gen. Sir Richard Granville Hylton H.; *see* Howard-Vyse.
Vyshinsky, Andrei Yanuarievich, 1883–1954, vol. V
Vyvyan, Col Sir Courtenay Bourchier, 10th Bt, 1858–1941, vol. IV
Vyvyan, Captain Sir George Rawlinson, 1838–1914, vol. I
Vyvyan, Jennifer Brigit, 1925–1974, vol. VII

Vyvyan, Sir John Stanley, 12th Bt, 1916–1995, vol. IX
Vyvyan, Maj.-Gen. Ralph Ernest, 1891–1971, vol. VII
Vyvyan, Sir Richard Philip, 11th Bt, 1891–1978, vol. VII
Vyvyan, Major Richard Walter Comyn, 1859–1931, vol. III
Vyvyan, Air Vice-Marshal Sir Vyell, 1875–1935, vol. III
Vyvyan, Rev. Sir Vyell Donnithorne, 9th Bt, 1826–1917, vol. II
Vyvyan, Rt Rev. Wilmot Lushington, 1861–1937, vol. III

W

Waal, Hon. Sir Frederic de; *see* Waal, Hon. Sir N. F. de.
Waal, Hon. Sir (Nicholas) Frederic de, 1853–1932, vol. III
Wace, Alan John Bayard, 1879–1957, vol. V
Wace, Sir Blyth; *see* Wace, Sir F. B.
Wace, Brig.-Gen. Edward Gurth, 1876–1962, vol. VI
Wace, Col Ernest Charles, 1850–1927, vol. II
Wace, Ernest William Cornish, 1894–1977, vol. VII
Wace, Sir (Ferdinand) Blyth, 1891–1964, vol. VI
Wace, Very Rev. Henry, 1836–1924, vol. II
Wace, Herbert, *died* 1906, vol. I
Wace, Maj.-Gen. Richard, 1842–1920, vol. II
Wacha, Sir Dinsha Edulji, 1844–1936, vol. III
Wacher, David Mure, 1909–1989, vol. VIII
Wackett, Air Vice-Marshal Ellis Charles, 1901–1984, vol. VIII
Wackett, Sir Lawrence James, 1896–1982, vol. VIII
Waddams, Rev. Canon Herbert Montague, 1911–1972, vol. VII
Waddell, Sir Alexander Nicol Anton, 1913–1999, vol. X
Waddell, Hon. Sir (Charles) Graham, 1877–1960, vol. V (A)
Waddell, Gilbert, 1894–1967, vol. VI
Waddell, Hon. Sir Graham; *see* Waddell, Hon. Sir C. G.
Waddell, Helen, 1889–1965, vol. VI
Waddell, John J.; *see* Jeffrey-Waddell.
Waddell, Alexander Peddie-, 1832–1917, vol. II
Waddell, John, *died* 1923, vol. II
Waddell, John J.; *see* Jeffrey-Waddell.
Waddell, Lt-Col Laurence Austine, 1854–1938, vol. III
Waddell, Hon. Thomas, 1854–1940, vol. III
Waddell, William Gillan, 1884–1945, vol. IV
Waddilove, Douglas Edwin, 1918–1976, vol. VII
Waddilove, Sir Joshua Kelley, *died* 1920, vol. II
Waddilove, Lewis Edgar, 1914–2000, vol. X
Waddington, Charles Willoughby, 1865–1946, vol. IV
Waddington, Conrad Hal, 1905–1975, vol. VII
Waddington, Sir (Eubule) John, 1890–1957, vol. V
Waddington, Gerald Eugene, 1909–1996, vol. X

Waddington, John, 1855–1935, vol. III
Waddington, Sir John; *see* Waddington, Sir E. J.
Waddington, Very Rev. John Albert Henry, 1910–1994, vol. IX
Waddington, Mary King, *died* 1923, vol. II
Waddington, Sir Robert, 1868–1941, vol. IV
Waddington, Samuel, 1844–1923, vol. II
Waddington, Maj.-Gen. Thomas, 1827–1921, vol. II
Waddington, Brig. Thomas Thelwall, 1888–1958, vol. V
Waddy, Bentley Herbert, 1893–1956, vol. V
Waddy, Dorothy Knight, 1909–1970, vol. VI
Waddy, Henry Turner, 1863–1926, vol. II
Waddy, Rev. Percival Stacy, 1875–1937, vol. III
Waddy, Samuel Danks, 1830–1902, vol. I
Wade, Baron (Life Peer); Donald William Wade, 1904–1988, vol. VIII
Wade, Sir Armigel de Vins, 1880–1966, vol. VI
Wade, Arthur Shepherd, *died* 1941, vol. IV
Wade, Maj.-Gen. Ashton; *see* Wade, Maj.-Gen. D. A. L.
Wade, Hon. Sir Charles Gregory, 1863–1922, vol. II
Wade, Maj.-Gen. (Douglas) Ashton (Lofft), 1898–1996, vol. X
Wade, Emlyn Capel Stewart, 1895–1978, vol. VII
Wade, Brig. Ernest Wentworth, 1889–1970, vol. VI
Wade, Hon. Frederick Coate, 1860–1924, vol. II
Wade, Surg.-Maj.-Gen. Frederick William, *died* 1906, vol. I
Wade, Col Sir George Albert, 1891–1986, vol. VIII
Wade, George Edward, 1853–1933, vol. III
Wade, Major George Frederick Dennis, 1899–1968, vol. VI
Wade, Rev. George Woosung, 1858–1941, vol. IV
Wade, Sir Henry, 1877–1955, vol. V
Wade, Col Henry Oswald, 1869–1941, vol. IV
Wade, John Charles, 1908–1984, vol. VIII
Wade, John Roland, 1890–1984, vol. VIII
Wade, Philip Harold, 1860–1930, vol. III
Wade, Sir Robert Blakeway, 1874–1954, vol. V
Wade, Maj.-Gen. Ronald Eustace, 1905–1995, vol. X
Wade, Rosalind Herschel, (Mrs R. H. Seymour), 1909–1989, vol. VIII

Wade, Rt Rev. (Sydney) Walter, 1909–1976, vol. VII
Wade, Sqdn Ldr Trevor Sidney, 1920–1951, vol. V
Wade, Rt Rev. Walter; see Wade, Rt Rev. S. W.
Wade, Sir William, 1849–1935, vol. III
Wade, Sir Willoughby Francis, 1827–1906, vol. I
Wade-Evans, Rev. Arthur Wade, 1875–1964, vol. VI
Wade-Gery, Henry Theodore, 1888–1972, vol. VII
Wadel, William, 1868–1946, vol. IV
Wadely, Frederick William, 1882–1970, vol. VI
Wadeson, Maj.-Gen. Frederick William George, 1860–1920, vol. II
Wadham, Arthur, 1852–1923, vol. II
Wadham, Sir Samuel MacMahon, 1891–1972, vol. VII
Wadia, Sir Bomanji Jamsetji, 1881–1947, vol. IV
Wadia, Sir Cusrow, 1869–1950, vol. IV
Wadia, D. N., 1883–1969, vol. VI
Wadia, Sir Hormasji Ardeshir, died 1928, vol. II
Wadia, Sir Ness Nowrosjee, 1873–1952, vol. V
Wadley, Sir Douglas, 1904–1984, vol. VIII
Wadley, Lt-Col Edward John, 1880–1950, vol. IV
Wadley, Walter Joseph Durham, 1903–1982, vol. VIII
Wadsley, Olive, died 1959, vol. V
Wadson, Hon. Sir Thomas John, 1844–1921, vol. II
Wadsworth, Alfred Powell, 1891–1956, vol. V
Wadsworth, Edward Alexander, 1889–1949, vol. IV
Wadsworth, George, 1902–1979, vol. VII (AII)
Wadsworth, John, 1850–1921, vol. II
Wadsworth, Sir Sidney, 1888–1976, vol. VII
Wadsworth, Vivian Michael, 1921–1992, vol. IX
Waechter, Sir d'Arcy; see Waechter, Sir H. L. d'A.
Waechter, Sir Harry, 1st Bt, 1871–1929, vol. III
Waechter, Sir (Harry Leonard) d'Arcy, 2nd Bt, 1912–1987, vol. VIII
Waechter, Sir Max Leonard, 1837–1924, vol. II
Wager, Harold, 1862–1929, vol. III
Wager, Lawrence Rickard, 1904–1965, vol. VI
Wagg, Alfred Ralph, 1877–1969, vol. VI
Waggett, Ernest Blechynden, 1866–1939, vol. III
Waggett, Rev. Philip Napier, 1862–1939, vol. III
Waghorn, Brig.-Gen. Sir William Danvers, died 1936, vol. III
Wagner, Sir Anthony Richard, 1908–1995, vol. IX
Wagner, Franz William, 1905–1985, vol. VIII
Wagner, Wieland Adolf Gottfried, 1917–1966, vol. VI
Wagner, Very Rev. William Wolfe, died 1937, vol. III
Wagstaff, Charles John Leonard, 1875–1981, vol. VIII
Wagstaff, Maj.-Gen. Cyril Mosley, 1878–1934, vol. III
Wagstaff, Col Henry Wynter, 1890–1992, vol. IX
Wagstaff, John Edward Pretty, 1890–1963, vol. VI
Wagstaff, Lt-Col Lewis Cecil, 1882–1951, vol. V
Wagstaff, William George, 1837–1918, vol. II
Wahab, Col Robert Alexander; see Wauhope, Col R. A.
Wahba, Sheikh Hafiz, 1889–1967, vol. VI
Wahlstatt, Blucher von, 3rd Prince, 1836–1916, vol. II
Wahlström, Gen. Jarl Holger, 1918–1999, vol. X

Waight, Leonard, 1895–1970, vol. VI
Waights, Rev. Kenneth Laws, 1909–1984, vol. VIII
Wain, John Barrington, 1925–1994, vol. IX
Wain, Louis; see Wain, R. L.
Wain, Louis William, 1860–1939, vol. III
Wain, (Ralph) Louis, 1911–2000, vol. X
Wainewright, Brig.-Gen. Arthur Reginald, 1874–1970, vol. VI
Wainright, Maj.-Gen. Charles Brian, 1893–1968, vol. VI
Wainwright, Desmond; see Wainwright, E. D.
Wainwright, (Edward) Desmond, 1902–1976, vol. VII
Wainwright, Edwin, 1908–1998, vol. X
Wainwright, Elsie, died 1964, vol. VI
Wainwright, Rev. Frederick, died 1921, vol. II
Wainwright, Sir Gilbert Cochrane, 1871–1954, vol. V
Wainwright, Sir James Gadesden, 1837–1929, vol. III
Wainwright, Robert Everard, 1913–1990, vol. VIII
Wainwright, Rear-Adm. Rupert Charles Purchas, 1913–1991, vol. IX
Wainwright, William J., 1855–1931, vol. III
Waistell, Adm. Sir Arthur Kipling, 1873–1953, vol. V
Wait, Air Vice-Marshal George Enoch, 1895–1972, vol. VII
Wait, Col Hugh Godfrey Killigrew, 1871–1948, vol. IV
Wait, Walter Ernest, 1878–1961, vol. VI
Waite, Arthur Edward, 1857–1942, vol. IV
Waite, Clifford, 1896–1974, vol. VII
Waite, Col Hon. Fred, 1885–1952, vol. V
Waite, Herbert William, 1887–1967, vol. VI
Waite, Rev. Joseph, 1824–1908, vol. I
Waite, Air Cdre Reginald Newnham, 1901–1975, vol. VII
Waite, Robert T.; see Thorne-Waite.
Waithman, Robert William, 1828–1914, vol. I
Waithman, William Sharp, 1853–1922, vol. II
Wake, Major Charles St Aubyn, 1861–1938, vol. III
Wake, Adm. Sir Drury St Aubyn, 1863–1935, vol. III
Wake, Lt-Col Edward St Aubyn, 1862–1944, vol. IV
Wake, Sir Herewald, 12th Bt, 1852–1916, vol. II
Wake, Herewald Crawfurd, 1828–1901, vol. I
Wake, Maj.-Gen. Sir Hereward, 13th Bt, 1876–1963, vol. VI
Wake, Hereward Baldwin Lawrence, 1900–1983, vol. VIII
Wake, Major Hugh St Aubyn, 1870–1914, vol. I
Wake, Joan, 1884–1974, vol. VII
Wake, Vice-Adm. Sir St Aubyn Baldwin, 1882–1951, vol. V
Wake, William St Aubyn, 1871–1900, vol. I
Wake-Walker, Adm. Sir William Frederic, 1888–1945, vol. IV
Wakefield, 1st Viscount, 1859–1941, vol. IV
Wakefield of Kendal, 1st Baron, 1898–1983, vol. VIII
Wakefield, Arthur John, 1900–1973, vol. VII
Wakefield, Sir Edward Birkbeck, 1st Bt, 1903–1969, vol. VI

Wakefield, George Edward Campbell, 1873–1944, vol. IV
Wakefield, Rev. Gordon Stevens, 1921–2000, vol. X
Wakefield, Rt Rev. Henry Russell, 1854–1933, vol. III
Wakefield, Hubert George; see Wakefield, Hugh.
Wakefield, Maj.-Gen. Hubert Stephen, 1883–1962, vol. VI
Wakefield, Hugh, (Hubert George), 1915–1984, vol. VIII
Wakefield, Roger Cuthbert, 1906–1986, vol. VIII
Wakefield, Lt-Col Thomas Montague, 1878–1936, vol. III
Wakefield-Harrey, Cyril Ogden, 1894–1971, vol. VII
Wakeford, Edward Felix, 1914–1973, vol. VII
Wakeford, John Chrysostom Barnabas, 1898–1989, vol. VIII
Wakeford, Major Richard, 1921–1972, vol. VII
Wakeham, Rev. Charles Thomas, 1852–1931, vol. III
Wakehurst, 1st Baron, 1861–1936, vol. III
Wakehurst, 2nd Baron, 1895–1970, vol. VI
Wakehurst, Dowager Lady; Dame Margaret Wakehurst, 1899–1994, vol. IX
Wakelam, Lt-Col Henry Blythe Thornhill, 1893–1963, vol. VI
Wakeley, Sir Cecil Pembrey Grey, 1st Bt, 1892–1979, vol. VII
Wakely, Maj.-Gen. Arthur Victor Trocke, 1886–1959, vol. V
Wakely, Sir Clifford Holland, 1891–1976, vol. VII
Wakely, John, 1861–1942, vol. IV
Wakely, Sir Leonard Day, 1880–1961, vol. VI
Wakely, Leonard John Dean, 1909–1995, vol. IX
Wakeman, Sir David; see Wakeman, Sir O. D.
Wakeman, Henry Offley, 1852–1899, vol. I
Wakeman, Sir Offley, 3rd Bt, 1850–1929, vol. III
Wakeman, Captain Sir Offley, 4th Bt, 1887–1975, vol. VII
Wakeman, Sir (Offley) David, 5th Bt, 1922–1991, vol. IX
Wakerley, Rev. John E., 1858–1923, vol. II
Wakley, Thomas, 1851–1909, vol. I
Wakley, Thomas Henry, 1821–1907, vol. I
Waksman, Selman Abraham, 1888–1973, vol. VII
Walbrook, Anton, 1900–1967, vol. VI
Walbrook, Henry Mackinnon, died 1941, vol. IV
Walby, Herbert Charles, 1897–1966, vol. VI
Walch, Sir Geoffrey Archer, 1898–1971, vol. VII
Walcot, Lt-Col Basil, 1880–1918, vol. II
Walcot, William, 1874–1943, vol. IV
Walcott, Charles Doolittle, 1850–1927, vol. II
Walcott, Captain Colpoys Cleland, 1878–1961, vol. VI
Walcott, Col Edmund Scopoli, 1842–1923, vol. II
Walcott, Sir Henry Barclay, 1866–1931, vol. III
Wald, George, 1906–1997, vol. X
Walde, Ernest Herman Stewart, 1874–1958, vol. V
Waldeck-Rousseau, Pierre Marie, 1846–1904, vol. I
Waldegrave, 9th Earl, 1851–1930, vol. III
Waldegrave, 10th Earl, 1882–1933, vol. III
Waldegrave, 11th Earl, 1854–1936, vol. III
Waldegrave, 12th Earl, 1905–1995, vol. IX
Waldegrave, Countess; (Mary), 1850–1933, vol. III
Waldegrave-Leslie, Hon. George; see Leslie.

Walden, Alfred Edward, 1893–1968, vol. VI
Walden, Sir Robert Woolley, died 1929, vol. III
Walden, Stanley Arthur, 1905–1980, vol. VII
Walden, Trevor Alfred, 1916–1979, vol. VII
Walder, (Alan) David, 1928–1978, vol. VII
Walder, David; see Walder, A. D.
Walder, Hon. Sir Samuel Robert, 1879–1946, vol. IV
Waldersee, Field-Marshal Count Von, 1832–1904, vol. I
Waldie-Griffith, Sir Richard John; see Griffith.
Waldman, Milton, 1895–1976, vol. VII
Waldman, Ronald Hartley, 1914–1978, vol. VII
Waldman, Stanley John, 1923–1989, vol. VIII
Waldo, Frederick Joseph, 1852–1933, vol. III
Waldock, Sir (Claud) Humphrey (Meredith), 1904–1981, vol. VIII
Waldock, Sir Humphrey; see Waldock, Sir C. H. M.
Waldram, Percy John, 1869–1949, vol. IV
Waldron, Rev. Arthur John, 1868–1925, vol. II
Waldron, Brig.-Gen. Francis, 1853–1932, vol. III
Waldron, Brig. John Graham Claverhouse, 1909–1993, vol. IX
Waldron, Rt Hon. Laurence Ambrose, 1858–1923, vol. II
Waldron, Sir John Lovegrove, 1909–1975, vol. VII
Waldron, Col Sir William James, 1876–1957, vol. V
Waldstein, Sir Charles; see Walston, Sir Charles.
Waldstein, Louis, 1853–1915, vol. I
Waldteufel, Emile, 1837–1915, vol. I
Waleran, 1st Baron, 1849–1925, vol. II
Waleran, 2nd Baron, 1905–1966, vol. VI
Wales, Sir (Alexander) George, 1885–1962, vol. VI
Wales, Rev. Arthur Philip, 1896–1964, vol. VI
Wales, Geoffrey, 1912–1990, vol. VIII
Wales, Sir George; see Wales, Sir A. G.
Wales, Horace Geoffrey Quaritch, 1900–1981, vol. VIII
Wales, Hubert, 1870–1943, vol. IV
Wales, Quaritch; see Wales, H. G. Q.
Waley, (Andrew) Felix, 1926–1995, vol. IX
Waley, Sir David; see Waley, Sir S. D.
Waley, Alfred Joseph, 1861–1953, vol. V
Waley, Arthur David, 1889–1966, vol. VI
Waley, Felix; see Waley, A. F.
Waley, Sir Frederick George, 1860–1933, vol. III
Waley, Sir (Sigismund) David, 1887–1962, vol. VI
Waley-Cohen, Sir Bernard Nathaniel, 1st Bt, 1914–1991, vol. IX
Walford, Maj.-Gen. Alfred Ernest, 1896–1990, vol. VIII
Walford, Col J. A., died 1903, vol. I
Walford, Lucy Bethia, 1845–1915, vol. I
Walkden, 1st Baron, 1873–1951, vol. V
Walkden, Evelyn, 1893–1970, vol. VI
Walkem, Joseph B., 1842–1938, vol. III
Walker, Hon. Lord; James Walker, 1890–1972, vol. VII
Walker, Sir Alan, died 1978, vol. VII
Walker, Sir Alan Grierson, 1907–1994, vol. IX
Walker, Major Alan Richard H.; see Hill-Walker.
Walker, Maj.-Gen. Albert Lancelot, 1839–1918, vol. II
Walker, Maj.-Gen. Alexander, 1838–1905, vol. I

Walker, Alexander, 1866–1945, vol. IV
Walker, Sir Alexander, 1869–1950, vol. IV
Walker, Sir Alexander Arthur, 2nd Bt (cr 1906), 1857–1932, vol. III
Walker, Alexander Neilson Strachan, 1921–1980, vol. VII
Walker, Andrew Barclay, 1865–1930, vol. III
Walker, Archibald, 1858–1945, vol. IV
Walker, Archibald Stodart, 1869–1934, vol. III
Walker, Sir Arnold Learoyd, died 1968, vol. VI
Walker, Rev. Arthur, died 1918, vol. II
Walker, Arthur George, 1861–1939, vol. III
Walker, Rear-Adm. Arthur Horace, 1881–1947, vol. IV
Walker, Air Chief Marshal Sir Augustus; see Walker, Air Chief Marshal Sir G. A.
Walker, Augustus Merrifield, 1880–1965, vol. VI
Walker, Sir Baldwin Wake, 2nd Bt (cr 1856), 1846–1905, vol. I
Walker, Bernard F.; see Fleetwood-Walker.
Walker, Bertram James, 1880–1947, vol. IV
Walker, Bobby; see Walker, W. B. S.
Walker, Sir (Byron) Edmund, 1848–1924, vol. II
Walker, Major Sir Cecil Edward, 3rd Bt cr 1906), 1882–1964, vol. VI
Walker, Sir Charles, 1871–1940, vol. III
Walker, Charles Alfred le Maistre, 1873–1961, vol. VI
Walker, Charles Clement, 1877–1968, vol. VI
Walker, Charles Edward, died 1953, vol. V
Walker, Rear-Adm. Charles Francis, 1836–1925, vol. II
Walker, Vice-Adm. Sir (Charles) Peter (Graham), 1911–1989, vol. VIII
Walker, Col Charles William Garne, 1882–1974, vol. VII
Walker, Lt-Col Claude Edward Forestier-, died 1932, vol. III
Walker, Sir Clive Radzivill Forestier-, 5th Bt, 1922–1983, vol. VIII
Walker, Sir Colin John Shedlock, 1934–1999, vol. X
Walker, Cyril Herbert, 1888–1970, vol. VI
Walker, Cyril Hutchinson, 1861–1955, vol. V
Walker, Daniel Pickering, 1914–1985, vol. VIII
Walker, David Esdaile, 1907–1968, vol. VI
Walker, Maj. David Harry, 1911–1992, vol. IX
Walker, Rev. Dawson D.; see Dawson-Walker.
Walker, Douglas Learoyd, 1894–1962, vol. VI
Walker, Dame Eadith Campbell, 1874–1937, vol. III
Walker, Sir Edmund; see Walker, Sir B. E.
Walker, Edmund W., 1832–1919, vol. II
Walker, Sir Edward Daniel, 1840–1919, vol. II
Walker, Rev. Edward Mewburn, 1857–1941, vol. IV
Walker, Sir Edward Noel-, 1842–1908, vol. I
Walker, Sir E(dward) Ronald, 1907–1988, vol. VIII
Walker, Sir Emery, 1851–1933, vol. III
Walker, Eric Anderson, 1886–1976, vol. VII
Walker, Ernest, 1870–1949, vol. IV
Walker, Maj.-Gen. Sir Ernest Alexander, 1880–1944, vol. IV
Walker, Ernest Octavius, 1850–1919, vol. II
Walker, Ernest William A.; see Ainley-Walker.

Walker, Dame Ethel, 1861–1951, vol. V
Walker, Sir Francis Elliot, 3rd Bt (cr 1856), 1851–1928, vol. II
Walker, Francis John, died 1940, vol. III
Walker, Rev. Francis Joseph, 1876–1933, vol. III
Walker, Francis S., 1848–1916, vol. II
Walker, Lt-Col Francis Spring, 1876–1941, vol. IV
Walker, Sir Francis William, 1887–1968, vol. VI
Walker, Frank Stockdale, 1895–1989, vol. VIII
Walker, Captain Frederic John, 1896–1944, vol. IV
Walker, Lt-Col Frederic William, 1870–1954, vol. V
Walker, Frederick James, 1835–1913, vol. I
Walker, Frederick William, 1830–1910, vol. I
Walker, Gen. Sir Frederick William Edward Forestier Forestier-, 1844–1910, vol. I
Walker, Sir G. Bernard L.; see Lomas-Walker.
Walker, Garrett William, 1856–1932, vol. III
Walker, Geoffrey Basil W.; see Woodd Walker.
Walker, Maj.-Gen. George, 1869–1936, vol. III
Walker, George Abram, 1879–1959, vol. V
Walker, Air Chief Marshal Sir (George) Augustus, 1912–1986, vol. VIII
Walker, Sir George Casson, 1854–1925, vol. II
Walker, George Edward Orr, 1909–1973, vol. VII
Walker, Sir George Ferdinand Forestier-, 3rd Bt (cr 1835), 1855–1933, vol. III
Walker, Major Sir George Ferdinand Forestier-, 4th Bt (cr 1835), 1899–1976, vol. VII
Walker, Major George Goold, died 1955, vol. V
Walker, Sir George Gustavus, 1831–1897, vol. I
Walker, Col George Gustavus, 1897–1972, vol. VII
Walker, George Henry, 1874–1954, vol. V
Walker, George Herbert Dacres, 1845–1929, vol. III
Walker, Col George Kemp, 1872–1942, vol. IV
Walker, Maj.-Gen. Sir George Townshend Forestier-, 1866–1939, vol. III
Walker, George Walker, 1874–1921, vol. II
Walker, Gen. George Warren, 1823–1920, vol. II
Walker, Rev. Gilbert George, 1858–1933, vol. III
Walker, Gilbert James, 1907–1982, vol. VIII
Walker, Sir Gilbert Thomas, 1868–1958, vol. V
Walker, Lt-Gen. Sir Harold Bridgwood, 1862–1934, vol. III
Walker, Adm. Sir Harold Thomas Coulthard, 1891–1975, vol. VII
Walker, Sir Henry, 1873–1954, vol. V
Walker, Henry; see Walker, R. St J.
Walker, Brig.-Gen. Henry Alexander, 1874–1953, vol. V
Walker, Henry Claude, 1851–1939, vol. III
Walker, Henry de Rosenbach, 1867–1923, vol. II
Walker, Sir Herbert Ashcombe, 1868–1949, vol. IV
Walker, Lt-Col Herbert Sutherland, 1864–1932, vol. III
Walker, Hirst, 1868–1957, vol. V
Walker, Sir (Horace) Alan; see Walker, Sir Alan.
Walker, Sir Hubert Edmund, 1891–1969, vol. VI
Walker, Hugh, 1855–1939, vol. III
Walker, Sir Hugh Selby N.; see Norman-Walker.
Walker, Ian Royaards, 1927–1985, vol. VIII
Walker, J. Wallace, died 1932, vol. III
Walker, Sir James, 1864–1933, vol. III
Walker, Sir James, 1863–1935, vol. III
Walker, Lt-Col James, died 1940, vol. III

Walker, James, *died* 1945, vol. IV
Walker, James; *see* Walker, Hon. Lord.
Walker, James, 1916–1995, vol. IX
Walker, James Arthur H.; *see* Higgs-Walker.
Walker, James Atkinson, 1878–1954, vol. V
Walker, James Douglas, 1841–1920, vol. II
Walker, Maj.-Gen. James Grant Duff, 1842–1921, vol. II
Walker, Captain Sir James Heron, 3rd Bt (*cr* 1868), 1865–1900, vol. I
Walker, Sir James Lewis, 1845–1927, vol. II
Walker, Sir James Robert, 2nd Bt, 1829–1898, vol. I
Walker, Hon. James Thomas, 1841–1923, vol. II
Walker, Major James Thomas, *died* 1930, vol. III
Walker, Brig.-Gen. James Workman, 1873–1945, vol. IV
Walker, Jane Harriett, 1859–1938, vol. III
Walker, Rev. John, 1837–1910, vol. I
Walker, John, 1900–1964, vol. VI
Walker, John; *see* Thirlmere, Rowland.
Walker, Sir John, 1906–1984, vol. VIII
Walker, John, 1906–1995, vol. IX
Walker, John Bayldon, 1854–1927, vol. II
Walker, John Brisben, 1847–1931, vol. III
Walker, John Crampton, 1890–1942, vol. IV
Walker, John Henry, 1915–1974, vol. VII
Walker, Col John Norman N.; *see* Norman-Walker.
Walker, John Reid, 1855–1934, vol. III
Walker, John Riddell Bromhead, 1913–1984, vol. VIII
Walker, Sir John William T.; *see* Thomson-Walker.
Walker, Kenneth, 1874–1947, vol. IV
Walker, Kenneth Macfarlane, *died* 1966, vol. VI
Walker, Kenneth Richard, 1931–1989, vol. VIII
Walker, Sir Leolin F.; *see* Forestier-Walker, Sir C. L.
Walker, Leonard, *died* 1964, vol. VI
Walker, Malcolm Thomas, 1915–1980, vol. VII
Walker, Sir Mark, 1827–1902, vol. I
Walker, Miles, *died* 1941, vol. IV
Walker, Sir Norman, 1862–1942, vol. IV
Walker, Norman, 1907–1963, vol. VI
Walker, Norman Macdonald Lockhart, 1889–1975, vol. VII
Walker, Norman Marshall, 1882–1956, vol. V
Walker, Oliver Ormerod, 1833–1914, vol. I
Walker, Patrick Chrestien G.; *see* Baron Gordon-Walker.
Walker, Paul Francis, 1932–1999, vol. X
Walker, Vice-Adm. Sir Peter; *see* Walker, Vice-Adm. Sir C. P. G.
Walker, Sir Peter Carlaw, 2nd Bt (*cr* 1886), 1854–1915, vol. I
Walker, Philip Gordon, 1912–1994, vol. X (AI)
Walker, Raymond St John, (Henry), 1917–1980, vol. VII
Walker, Paymr Captain Reginald Phelps, 1871–1958, vol. V
Walker, Major Reginald Selby, 1871–1918, vol. II
Walker, Richard Cornelius Critchett, 1841–1903, vol. I
Walker, Richard Johnson, 1868–1934, vol. III
Walker, (Richard) Sebastian (Maynard), 1942–1991, vol. IX

Walker, Robert, *died* 1910, vol. I
Walker, Robert, 1842–1920, vol. II
Walker, Sir Robert Bryce, 1873–1956, vol V
Walker, Ven. Robert Henry, 1857–1939, vol. III
Walker, Major Sir Robert James Milo, 4th Bt (*cr* 1868), 1890–1930, vol. III
Walker, Robert John, 1870–1936, vol. III
Walker, Robert Milnes, 1903–1985, vol. VIII
Walker, Lt-Col Robert Sandilands Frowd, 1850–1917, vol. II
Walker, Robert Scott, 1913–1995, vol. IX
Walker, Bt-Col Roland Stuart Forestier-, 1871–1938, vol. III
Walker, Sir Ronald; *see* Walker, Sir E. R.
Walker, Col Ronald Draycott S.; *see* Sherbrooke-Walker.
Walker, Sir Ronald Fitz-John, 1880–1971, vol. VII
Walker, Ronald Leslie, 1896–1984, vol. VIII
Walker, Rt Hon. Sir Samuel, 1st Bt (*cr* 1906), 1832–1911, vol. I
Walker, Samuel, 1875–1945, vol. IV
Walker, Samuel Richard, 1892–1989, vol. VIII
Walker, Sebastian; *see* Walker, R. S. M.
Walker, Air Cdre Sidney George, 1911–1975, vol. VII
Walker, Stanley Kenneth, 1916–1993, vol. IX
Walker, Dame Susan Armour, 1906–1993, vol. IX
Walker, Rev. Thomas, *died* 1929, vol. III
Walker, Hon. Thomas, 1858–1932, vol. III
Walker, Rev. Thomas Alfred, 1862–1935, vol. III
Walker, Very Rev. Thomas Gordon, *died* 1916, vol. II
Walker, Sir Thomas Gordon, 1849–1917, vol. II
Walker, Lt-Col Thomas Henry, 1877–1955, vol. V
Walker, Thomas Hollis, 1860–1945, vol. IV
Walker, Thomas Kennedy, 1893–1970, vol. VI
Walker, Thomas Leonard, 1867–1942, vol. IV
Walker, Adm. Thomas Philip, *died* 1932, vol. III
Walker, Timothy Ashley Peter, 1942–1988, vol. VIII
Walker, Walter Basil Scarlett (Bobby), 1915–1996, vol. X
Walker, Very Rev. William, *died* 1911, vol. I
Walker, Sir William, 1863–1930, vol. III
Walker, Sir William, *died* 1961, vol. VI
Walker, William, 1920–1984, vol. VIII
Walker, William Anderson Macpherson, 1891–1962, vol. VI
Walker, Hon. William Campbell, 1837–1904, vol. I
Walker, Col William Eric, 1885–1949, vol. IV
Walker, William Eyre, 1847–1930, vol. III
Walker, Adm. Sir William Frederic W.; *see* Wake-Walker.
Walker, Maj.-Gen. William George, 1863–1936, vol. III
Walker, Sir William Giles Newsom, 1905–1989, vol. VIII
Walker, William Gregory, 1848–1910, vol. I
Walker, William Henry, 1864–1933, vol. III
Walker, William James Dickson, 1854–1926, vol. II
Walker, William James Stirling, 1897–1958, vol. V
Walker, Rev. William Lowe, 1845–1930, vol. III
Walker, William Sylvester, 1846–1926, vol. II
Walker-Heneage-Vivian, Adm. Algernon, 1871–1952, vol. V

Walker Lee, Rev. William; see Lee.
Walker-Okeover, Col Sir Ian Peter Andrew Monro, 3rd Bt, 1902–1982, vol. VIII
Walker-Smith, family name of Baron Broxbourne.
Walker-Smith, Sir Jonah, 1874–1964, vol. VI
Walkey, Rear-Adm. Howarth Seymour, 1900–1970, vol. VI
Walkey, Rev. James Rowland, 1880–1960, vol. V
Walkey, Maj.-Gen. John Christopher, 1903–1989, vol. VIII
Walkinton, John James Gordon, 1895–1968, vol. VI
Walkley, Arthur Bingham, 1855–1926, vol. II
Walkley, Sir William Gaston, 1896–1976, vol. VII
Walkling, Maj.-Gen. Alec Ernest, 1918–1988, vol. VIII
Wall, Baron (Life Peer); John Edward Wall, 1913–1980, vol. VII
Wall, Arnold, died 1966, vol. VI
Wall, Arthur Joseph, died 1927, vol. II
Wall, Rt Rev. Bernard Patrick, 1894–1976, vol. VII
Wall, (Charles) Patrick, 1933–1990, vol. VIII
Wall, Col Edward Watkin, 1866–1954, vol. V
Wall, Rt Rev. Francis Joseph, 1866–1947, vol. IV
Wall, Col Frank, 1868–1950, vol. IV
Wall, Sir Frederick Joseph, 1858–1944, vol. IV
Wall, Sir (George) Rolande (Percival), 1898–1972, vol. VII
Wall, Hon. Sir Gerard Aloysius, 1920–1992, vol. IX
Wall, Engr Rear-Adm. Henry, 1867–1950, vol. IV
Wall, John William, 1910–1989, vol. VIII
Wall, Patrick; see Wall, C. P.
Wall, Maj. Sir Patrick Henry Bligh, 1916–1998, vol. X
Wall, Reginald Cecil Bligh, 1869–1947, vol. IV
Wall, Sir Rolande; see Wall, Sir G. R. P.
Wall, Ronald George Robert, 1910–1991, vol. IX
Wallace of Campsie, Baron (Life Peer); George Wallace, 1915–1997, vol. X
Wallace, Abraham, died 1930, vol. III
Wallace, Maj.-Gen. Sir Alexander, 1858–1922, vol. II
Wallace, Alexander Falconer, 1836–1925, vol. II
Wallace, Very Rev. Alexander Ross, 1891–1982, vol. VIII
Wallace, Alfred Russel, 1823–1913, vol. I
Wallace, Sir Arthur Robert, 1837–1912, vol. I
Wallace, Rev. Charles Hill, 1833–1912, vol. I
Wallace, Maj.-Gen. Charles John, 1890–1943, vol. IV
Wallace, Charles Redwood Vachel, 1877–1944, vol. IV
Wallace, Rev. Charles Stebbing, died 1914, vol. I
Wallace, Charles William, 1865–1932, vol. III
Wallace, Col the Hon. Clarence, 1894–1982, vol. VIII
Wallace, Sir Cuthbert Sidney, 1st Bt (cr 1937), 1867–1944, vol. IV
Wallace, Sir David, 1862–1952, vol. V
Wallace, Captain Rt Hon. (David) Euan, 1892–1941, vol. IV
Wallace, Major David Johnston, 1886–1965, vol. VI
Wallace, David Mitchell, 1913–1992, vol. IX
Wallace, Denis Bowes J.; see Johnstone-Wallace.
Wallace, Sir Donald Mackenzie, 1841–1919, vol. II

Wallace, Doreen, (Mrs Dora Eileen A. Rash), 1897–1989, vol. VIII
Wallace, Edgar; see Wallace, R. H. E.
Wallace, Sir Edward Hamilton, 1873–1943, vol. IV
Wallace, Edward Wilson, 1880–1941, vol. IV
Wallace, Captain Rt Hon. Euan; see Wallace, Captain Rt Hon. D. E.
Wallace, Rev. Francis Huston, 1851–1930, vol. III
Wallace, George, 1854–1927, vol. II
Wallace, Col George Smith, 1878–1951, vol. V
Wallace, George Williamson, 1862–1952, vol. V
Wallace, Sir Gordon, 1900–1987, vol. VIII
Wallace, Harold Frank, 1881–1962, vol. VI
Wallace, Harry Wright, 1885–1973, vol. VII
Wallace, Henry Agard, 1888–1965, vol. VI
Wallace, Captain Henry Steuart Macnaghten H.; see Harrison-Wallace.
Wallace, Maj.-Gen. Hill, 1823–1899, vol. I
Wallace, Hugh Campbell, 1863–1931, vol. III
Wallace, Lt-Col Hugh Robert, 1861–1924, vol. II
Wallace, Irving, 1916–1990, vol. VIII
Wallace, Air Cdre James, 1918–1980, vol. VII
Wallace, James Sim, 1869–1951, vol. V
Wallace, Sir John, 1868–1949, vol. IV
Wallace, Air Vice-Marshal John Brown, 1907–1980, vol. VII
Wallace, John Henry, 1903–1960, vol. V
Wallace, John Madder, 1887–1975, vol. VII
Wallace, Sir John Stewart S.; see Stewart-Wallace.
Wallace, Col Sir Johnstone, 1861–1922, vol. II
Wallace, Sir Lawrence Aubrey, 1857–1942, vol. IV
Wallace, Gen. Lew, (Lewis), 1827–1905, vol. I
Wallace, Malcolm William, 1873–1960, vol. V
Wallace, Sir Martin Kelso, 1898–1978, vol. VII
Wallace, Sir Matthew Gemmill, 1st Bt (cr 1922), 1854–1940, vol. III
Wallace, Hon. Nathaniel Clarke, 1844–1901, vol. I
Wallace, Col Nesbit Willoughby, 1839–1931, vol. III
Wallace, O. C. S., 1856–1947, vol. IV
Wallace, Percy Maxwell, 1863–1943, vol. IV
Wallace, Philip Adrian H.; see Hope-Wallace.
Wallace, (Richard Horatio) Edgar, 1875–1932, vol. III
Wallace, Rear-Adm. Richard Roy, 1895–1963, vol. VI
Wallace, Robert, 1831–1899, vol. I
Wallace, Robert, 1878–1931, vol. III
Wallace, Sir Robert, 1850–1939, vol. III
Wallace, Robert, 1853–1939, vol. III
Wallace, Robert, 1911–1995, vol. IX
Wallace, Robert Charles, 1881–1955, vol. V
Wallace of that Ilk, Col Robert Francis Hurter, 1880–1970, vol. VI
Wallace, Col Rt Hon. Robert Hugh, 1860–1929, vol. III
Wallace, Robert John, 1846–1909, vol. I
Wallace, Robert Johnston, 1886–1967, vol. VI
Wallace, Sir Robert Strachan, 1882–1961, vol. VI
Wallace, Roger William, 1854–1926, vol. II
Wallace, Lt-Gen. Rowland Robert, 1830–1915, vol. I
Wallace, S. Williamson, 1855–1932, vol. III
Wallace, Samuel Thomas Dickson, 1892–1968, vol. VI

Wallace, Thomas, 1891–1965, vol. VI
Wallace, Thomas Brown, 1865–1951, vol. V
Wallace, Walter Ian James, 1905–1993, vol. IX
Wallace, Sir William, 1856–1916, vol. II
Wallace, William, 1843–1921, vol. II
Wallace, William, 1860–1922, vol. II
Wallace, William, 1860–1940, vol. III
Wallace, Sir William, 1881–1963, vol. VI
Wallace, William, 1891–1976, vol. VII
Wallace, William, 1911–1990, vol. VIII
Wallace, Col William Arthur James, 1842–1902,
    vol. I
Wallace, Lt-Col William Berkeley, died 1934,
    vol. III
Wallace, William Kelly, 1883–1969, vol. VI
Wallace, William Reeve, 1873–1966, vol. VI
Wallace, William Stewart, 1884–1970, vol. VI
Wallace-Copland, Harold, 1893–1973, vol. VII
Wallace-Hadrill, John Michael, 1916–1985, vol. VIII
Wallace Whitfield, Sir Cecil Vincent, 1930–1990,
    vol. VIII
Wallach, Lewis Charles, 1871–1964, vol. VI
Wallack, Maj.-Gen. Ernest Townshend, 1857–1932,
    vol. III
Wallas, Graham, 1858–1932, vol. III
Wallas, Katharine Talbot, 1864–1944, vol. IV
Waller, Alfred Rayney, 1867–1922, vol. II
Waller, Vice-Adm. Arthur Craig, 1872–1943,
    vol. IV
Waller, Augustus Désiré, 1856–1922, vol. II
Waller, Rev. Bolton Charles, 1890–1936, vol. III
Waller, Sir Charles, 6th Bt (cr 1780), 1835–1912,
    vol. I
Waller, Rev. Charles Cameron, 1869–1944, vol. IV
Waller, Very Rev. Charles Kempson, 1891–1951,
    vol. V
Waller, Sir David Grierson, 1872–1949, vol. IV
Waller, Sir Edmund, 6th Bt (cr 1815), 1871–1954,
    vol. V
Waller, Very Rev. Edward Hardress, 1859–1933,
    vol. III
Waller, Rt Rev. Edward Harry Mansfield,
    1871–1942, vol. IV
Waller, Sir Francis Ernest, 4th Bt (cr 1815),
    1880–1914, vol. I
Waller, Rt Hon. Sir George Stanley, 1911–1999,
    vol. X
Waller, Maj.-Gen. John Edmund, 1841–1934,
    vol. III
Waller, Captain John Hampden, 1839–1934, vol. III
Waller, Sir (John) Keith, 1914–1992, vol. IX
Waller, Sir John Stanier, 7th Bt (cr 1815),
    1917–1995, vol. IX
Waller, Vice-Adm. John William Ashley,
    1892–1975, vol. VII
Waller, Sir Keith; see Waller, Sir J. K.
Waller, Lewis, (William Waller Lewis), 1860–1915,
    vol. I
Waller, Mary Lemon, died 1931, vol. III
Waller, Sir Maurice Lyndham, 1875–1932, vol. III
Waller, Mervyn Napier, 1893–1972, vol. VII
Waller, Brig.-Gen. Richard Lancelot, 1875–1961,
    vol. VI
Waller, Sir Roland Edgar, 8th Bt (cr 1780),
    1892–1958, vol. V

Waller, Ross Douglas, 1899–1988, vol. VIII
Waller, Samuel Edmund, 1850–1903, vol. I
Waller, Col Stainier, 1844–1930, vol. III
Waller, Sir Wathen Arthur, 5th Bt (cr 1815),
    1881–1947, vol. IV
Waller, Sir William Edgar, 7th Bt (cr 1780),
    1863–1943, vol. IV
Wallers, Sir Evelyn Ashley, 1876–1934, vol. III
Wallerston, Brig.-Gen. Francis Edward, 1856–1926,
    vol. II
Wallhead, Richard Collingham, 1869–1934, vol. III
Walling, Robert Alfred John, 1869–1949, vol. IV
Wallinger, Lt-Col Ernest Arnold, 1875–1934,
    vol. III
Wallinger, Sir Geoffrey Arnold, 1903–1979,
    vol. VII
Wallinger, Sir John Arnold, 1872–1931, vol. III
Wallingford, Air Cdre Sidney, 1898–1978, vol. VII
Wallington, Sir Edward William, 1854–1933,
    vol. III
Wallington, Hon. Sir Hubert Joseph, died 1962,
    vol. VI
Wallington, Col Sir John Williams, 1822–1910,
    vol. I
Wallis, Captain Arthur Hammond, 1903–1989,
    vol. VIII
Wallis, Arthur Henry, 1847–1929, vol. III
Wallis, Sir Barnes Neville, 1887–1979, vol. VII
Wallis, Major Charles Braithwaite, died 1945,
    vol. IV
Wallis, Charles Edward, died 1927, vol. II
Wallis, Rev. Charles Steel, 1875–1959, vol. V
Wallis, Claude Edgar, 1886–1980, vol. VII
Wallis, Rt Rev. Frederic, 1853–1928, vol. II
Wallis, Sir Frederick Charles, 1859–1912, vol. I
Wallis, Frederick Samuel, 1857–1939, vol. III (A),
    vol. IV
Wallis, George Harry, died 1936, vol. III
Wallis, Harry Bernard, 1882–1956, vol. V
Wallis, Henry Aubrey Beaumont, died 1926, vol. II
Wallis, Henry Richard, 1866–1946, vol. IV
Wallis, Col Hugh Macdonell, 1893–1991, vol. IX
Wallis, Rt Hon. Sir John Edward Power,
    1861–1946, vol. IV
Wallis, Rev. Canon John Eyre Winstanley,
    1886–1957, vol. V
Wallis, Leonard George C.; see Coke Wallis.
Wallis, Mrs Ransome, 1858–1928, vol. II
Wallis, Victor Harry, 1922–1995, vol. X (AI)
Wallis, Sir Whitworth, 1855–1927, vol. II
Wallop, Hon. Frederick Henry Arthur, 1870–1953,
    vol. V
Walls, Daniel Frank, 1942–1999, vol. X
Walls, Hamish; see Walls, Henry J.
Walls, Henry James, 1907–1988, vol. VIII
Walls, Rev. John W., 1858–1924, vol. II
Walls, Tom, 1883–1949, vol. IV
Walls, William, 1860–1942, vol. IV
Wallscourt, 4th Baron, 1841–1918, vol. II
Wallscourt, 5th Baron, 1876–1920, vol. II
Walmesley White, Brig. Arthur, 1917–1985,
    vol. VIII
Walmsley, Allan, 1889–1963, vol. VI
Walmsley, (Arnold) Robert, 1912–2000, vol. X
Walmsley, Ben, 1871–1960, vol. V (A), vol. VI (AI)

Walmsley, Charles; see Walmsley, R. C.
Walmsley, Sir Hugh, 1871–1950, vol. IV
Walmsley, Air Marshal Sir Hugh Sydney Porter, 1898–1985, vol. VIII
Walmsley, Rt Rev. John, died 1922, vol. II
Walmsley, Air Cdre John Banks, 1896–1976, vol. VII
Walmsley, Kenneth Maurice, 1914–1977, vol. VII
Walmsley, Leo, 1892–1966, vol. VI
Walmsley, Robert; see Walmsley, A. R.
Walmsley, Robert, 1906–1998, vol. X
Walmsley, Robert Mullineux, died 1924, vol. II
Walmsley, (Ronald) Charles, 1909–1983, vol. VIII
Walmsley, Thomas, died 1951, vol. V
Waln, Nora, 1895–1964, vol. VI
Walpole, 9th Baron, 1913–1989, vol. VIII
Walpole, Sir Charles George, 1848–1926, vol. II
Walpole, George Frederick, 1892–1975, vol. VII
Walpole, Rt Rev. George Henry Somerset, 1854–1929, vol. III
Walpole, Henry Spencer V.; see Vade-Walpole.
Walpole, Sir Horatio George, 1843–1923, vol. II
Walpole, Sir Hugh Seymour, 1884–1941, vol. IV
Walpole, Kathleen Annette, 1899–1987, vol. VIII
Walpole, Ralph Charles, 1844–1928, vol. II
Walpole, Sir Spencer, 1839–1907, vol. I
Walpole, Rt Hon. Spencer Horatio, 1806–1898, vol. I
Walpole, Thomas Henry Bourke V.; see Vade-Walpole.
Walrond, Arthur Melville Hood, 1861–1946, vol. IV
Walrond, Col Henry, 1841–1917, vol. II
Walrond, Main Swete Osmond, 1870–1927, vol. II
Walrond, Hon. William Lionel Charles, 1876–1915, vol. I
Walser, Ven. David, 1923–1993, vol. IX
Walsh, Sir Alan, 1916–1998, vol. X
Walsh, Hon. Sir Albert Joseph, died 1958, vol. V
Walsh, Arthur Donald, 1916–1977, vol. VII
Walsh, Brian, 1935–2000, vol. X
Walsh, Sir Cecil, 1869–1946, vol. IV
Walsh, Sir Charles Arthur, 1869–1949, vol. IV
Walsh, Rt Hon. Sir Cyril Ambrose, 1909–1973, vol. VII
Walsh, Sir David Philip, 1902–1989, vol. VIII
Walsh, Surg. Rear-Adm. Dermot Francis, 1901–1992, vol. IX
Walsh, Ernest Herbert Cooper, 1865–1952, vol. V
Walsh, Ernst P.; see Pakenham-Walsh.
Walsh, Rt Rev. Francis, 1901–1974, vol. VII
Walsh, Maj.-Gen. Francis James, 1900–1987, vol. VIII
Walsh, Geoffrey, 1884–1946, vol. IV
Walsh, Lt-Gen. Geoffrey, 1909–1999, vol. X
Walsh, Maj.-Gen. George Peregrine, 1899–1972, vol. VII
Walsh, Air Vice-Marshal George Victor, 1893–1960, vol. V
Walsh, Hon. Gerald, 1864–1925, vol. II
Walsh, Rt Rev. Gordon John, 1880–1971, vol. VII
Walsh, Col Henry Alfred, 1853–1918, vol. II
Walsh, Henry Francis Chester, 1891–1977, vol. VII
Walsh, Rt Rev. Herbert Pakenham P.; see Pakenham-Walsh.

Walsh, Sir Hunt Henry Allen Johnson-, 5th Bt, 1864–1953, vol. V
Walsh, Very Rev. James Hornidge, died 1919, vol. II
Walsh, James J., 1865–1942, vol. IV
Walsh, James Joseph, 1880–1948, vol. IV
Walsh, James Mark, 1909–1997, vol. X
Walsh, James Morgan, 1897–1952, vol. V
Walsh, John, 1856–1925, vol. II
Walsh, John James, 1917–1992, vol. IX
Walsh, Most Rev. Joseph, 1888–1973, vol. VII
Walsh, Langton Prendergast, 1856–1927, vol. II
Walsh, Leslie, 1903–1986, vol. VIII
Walsh, Brig. Mainwaring Ravell, 1876–1940, vol. III
Walsh, Maurice, 1879–1964, vol. VI
Walsh, Hon. Nigel Christopher, 1867–1931, vol. III
Walsh, Hon. Patrick Joseph Stanislaus, 1872–1943, vol. IV
Walsh, Ven. Philip, 1843–1914, vol. II
Walsh, Richard; see Walsh, W. H.
Walsh, Brig.-Gen. Richard Knox, 1873–1960, vol. V
Walsh, Maj.-Gen. Ridley P. P.; see Pakenham-Walsh.
Walsh, Ven. Robert, died 1917, vol. II
Walsh, Col Robert Henry, 1884–1968, vol. VI
Walsh, Rt Hon. Stephen, 1859–1929, vol. III
Walsh, Lt-Col Theobald Alfred, 1882–1935, vol. III
Walsh, Valentine John Hussey-, 1862–1925, vol. II
Walsh, Walter, 1847–1912, vol. I
Walsh, Rev. Walter, 1857–1931, vol. III
Walsh, Rt Rev. William, 1836–1918, vol. II
Walsh, William, 1916–1996, vol. X
Walsh, Lt-Col William H.; see Hussey-Walsh.
Walsh, William Henry, 1913–1986, vol. VIII
Walsh, Most Rev. William J., 1841–1921, vol. II
Walsh, William Joseph, 1919–1978, vol. VII
Walsh, Hon. William Legh, 1857–1938, vol. III
Walsh, Rt Rev. William Pakenham, 1820–1902, vol. I
Walsh-Atkins, Leonard Brian, 1915–1997, vol. X
Walsham, Hugh, died 1924, vol. II
Walsham, Sir John, 2nd Bt, 1830–1905, vol. I
Walsham, Sir John Scarlett, 3rd Bt, 1869–1940, vol. III
Walsham, Rear-Adm. Sir John Scarlett Warren, 4th Bt, 1910–1992, vol. IX
Walsham, William Johnson, 1847–1903, vol. I
Walshe, Sir Francis Martin Rouse, died 1973, vol. VII
Walshe, Brig.-Gen. Frederick William Henry, died 1931, vol. III
Walshe, Lt-Col Henry Ernest, 1866–1947, vol. IV
Walshe, Lt-Col Sarsfield James Ambrose Hall, 1881–1959, vol. V
Walshe, Rt Rev. Mgr T. J., 1861–1938, vol. III
Walsingham, 6th Baron, 1843–1919, vol. II
Walsingham, 7th Baron, 1849–1929, vol. III
Walsingham, 8th Baron, 1884–1965, vol. VI
Walston, Baron (Life Peer); Henry David Leonard George Walston, 1912–1991, vol. IX
Walston, Sir Charles, 1856–1927, vol. II
Waltari, Mika, 1908–1979, vol. VII
Walter, Arthur, 1874–1921, vol. II

Walter, Arthur Fraser, 1846–1910, vol. I
Walter, Arthur James, *died* 1919, vol. II
Walter, Bruno, 1876–1962, vol. VI
Walter, Lt-Col Edmund, 1881–1951, vol. V
Walter, Sir Edward, 1823–1904, vol. I
Walter, Major Frederick Edward, 1848–1931, vol. III
Walter, Hon. Sir Harold Edward, 1920–1992, vol. X (AI)
Walter, Hubert, 1870–1933, vol. III
Walter, John, 1873–1968, vol. VI
Walter, Maj.-Gen. John McNeill, 1861–1951, vol. V
Walter, Rear-Adm. Keith McNeil C.; *see* Campbell-Walter.
Walter, Louis Heathcote, *died* 1922, vol. II
Walter, Madison Melville, 1897–1960, vol. V
Walter, Captain Philip Norman, 1898–1984, vol. VIII
Walter, Robert, *died* 1959, vol. V
Walter, William, 1852–1942, vol. IV
Walter, W(illiam) Grey, 1910–1977, vol. VII
Walters, Air Vice-Marshal Allan Leslie, 1905–1968, vol. VI
Walters, Arthur Melmoth, 1865–1941, vol. IV
Walters, Rev. Charles Ensor, 1872–1938, vol. III
Walters, Rev. David John, 1893–1979, vol. VII
Walters, Very Rev. Derrick; *see* Walters, Very Rev. R. D. C.
Walters, Francis Paul, 1888–1976, vol. VII
Walters, Frank Bridgman, 1851–1899, vol. I
Walters, Rev. Harold Crawford, *died* 1958, vol. V
Walters, Henry Beauchamp, 1867–1944, vol. IV
Walters, Hubert Algernon, 1898–1969, vol. VI
Walters, Lt-Col Hubert de Lancey, 1868–1936, vol. III
Walters, John Cuming, *died* 1933, vol. III
Walters, Rt Hon. Sir (John) Tudor, 1868–1933, vol. III
Walters, Peter Ernest, 1913–1999, vol. X
Walters, Peter Hugh Bennetts Ensor, 1912–1994, vol. IX
Walters, Very Rev. (Rhys) Derrick (Chamberlain), 1932–2000, vol. X
Walters, Rt Hon. Sir Tudor; *see* Walters, Rt Hon. Sir J. T.
Walters, W. C. Flamstead, *died* 1927, vol. II
Walters, Rev. W. D., 1839–1913, vol. I
Walters, Ven. William, *died* 1912, vol. I
Walters, Col William Barker, 1839–1929, vol. III
Walters, Sir William Howell, 1857–1934, vol. III
Walters, William Melmoth, 1835–1925, vol. II
Walthall, Brig.-Gen. Edward Charles Walthall Delves, 1874–1961, vol. VI
Walther, David Philippe, 1909–1973, vol. VII
Walthew, Richard Henry, 1872–1951, vol. V
Walton, Allan, 1891–1948, vol. IV
Walton, Anthony Michael, 1925–2000, vol. X
Walton, Cecil Simpson, 1905–1955, vol. V
Walton, Col Sir Cusack, 1878–1966, vol. VI
Walton, Lt-Col Edgar Brocas, 1880–1964, vol. VI
Walton, Hon. Sir Edgar Harris, 1856–1942, vol. IV
Walton, Edward Arthur, 1860–1922, vol. II
Walton, Ernest Thomas Sinton, 1903–1993, vol. IX
Walton, Frank, 1840–1928, vol. II
Walton, Frederick Parker, 1858–1948, vol. IV

Walton, Frederick Thomas Granville, 1840–1925, vol. II
Walton, Brig. Sir George Hands, *died* 1976, vol. VII
Walton, Sir George O'Donnell, 1871–1950, vol. IV
Walton, Col Granville, 1888–1974, vol. VII
Walton, Henry George, 1876–1962, vol. VI
Walton, Rev. Herbert Arthur, *died* 1955, vol. V
Walton, Herbert Francis Raine, 1869–1929, vol. III
Walton, James, 1867–1924, vol. II
Walton, Sir James, 1881–1955, vol. V
Walton, James Ratcliffe, 1898–1973, vol. VII
Walton, John, 1895–1971, vol. VII
Walton, Sir John Charles, 1885–1957, vol. V
Walton, Sir John Lawson, 1852–1908, vol. I
Walton, Sir John Robert, 1904–1998, vol. X
Walton, Sir Joseph, 1845–1910, vol. I
Walton, Sir Joseph, 1st Bt, 1849–1923, vol. II
Walton, Kenneth, 1923–1979, vol. VII
Walton, Leslie Bannister, 1895–1960, vol. V
Walton, Norman Burdett, 1884–1950, vol. IV
Walton, Sir Raymond Henry, 1915–1988, vol. VIII
Walton, Sir Richmond, 1888–1971, vol. VII
Walton, Sir Robert, 1843–1914, vol. I
Walton, Lt-Col Robert Henry, 1877–1959, vol. V (A)
Walton, Sydney, 1882–1964, vol. VI
Walton, Sir William, 1844–1929, vol. III
Walton, Brig.-Gen. William Crawford, 1864–1937, vol. III
Walton, William Stanley, 1901–1979, vol. VII
Walton, Sir William Turner, 1902–1983, vol. VIII
Waltz, Jacques; *see* Hansi.
Walwyn, Algernon Edward Vere, 1888–1970, vol. VI
Walwyn, Eileen Mary, (Lady Walwyn), *died* 1973, vol. VII
Walwyn, Fulke Thomas Tyndall, 1910–1991, vol. IX
Walwyn, Vice-Adm. Sir Humphrey Thomas, 1879–1957, vol. V
Walwyn, Rear-Adm. James Humphrey, 1913–1986, vol. VIII
Walzer, Richard Rudolf, 1900–1975, vol. VII
Wanamaker, John, 1838–1922, vol. II
Wanamaker, Rodman, *died* 1928, vol. II
Wanamaker, Sam, 1919–1993, vol. IX
Wand, Rt Rev. and Rt Hon. (John) William (Charles), 1885–1977, vol. VII
Wand, Solomon, 1899–1984, vol. VIII
Wand, Rt Rev. and Rt Hon. William; *see* Wand, Rt Rev. and Rt Hon. J. W. C.
Wandsworth, 1st Baron, 1845–1912, vol. I
Wang, Chunk-Yik, 1888–1930, vol. III
Wani, Most Rev. Silvanus, 1916–1998, vol. X
Wankaner, Maharana Raj Saheb of, 1879–1954, vol. V
Wanklyn, Lt-Comdr Malcolm David, 1911–1942, vol. IV
Wanless, Sir William James, 1865–1933, vol. III
Wanless-O'Gowan, Maj.-Gen. Robert, 1864–1947, vol. IV
Wanliss, Col David Sydney, 1864–1943, vol. IV
Wanliss, Captain Harold Boyd, 1891–1917, vol. II
Wannell, Lt-Col George Edward, 1882–1933, vol. III

Wannop, Rev. Thomas Nicholson, 1822–1910, vol. I

Wansbrough, George, 1904–1979, vol. VII

Wansbrough, Hon. Lt-Col Thomas Percival, 1875–1943, vol. IV

Wansbrough-Jones, Maj.-Gen. Llewelyn, 1900–1974, vol. VII

Wansbrough-Jones, Sir Owen Haddon, 1905–1982, vol. VIII

Wanstall, Rev. Walter, 1847–1918, vol. II

Wantage, 1st Baron, 1832–1901, vol. I

Wantage, Lady; (Harriet Sarah), 1837–1920, vol. II

Wapshare, Lt-Gen. Sir Richard, 1860–1932, vol. III

Warbey, William Noble, 1903–1980, vol. VII

Warburg, Frederic John, 1898–1981, vol. VIII

Warburg, Sir Oscar Emanuel, 1876–1937, vol. III

Warburg, Otto Heinrich, 1883–1970, vol. VI

Warburg, Sir Siegmund George, 1902–1982, vol. VIII

Warburton, A. Bannerman, 1852–1929, vol. III

Warburton, Eric John Newnham, 1904–1989, vol. VIII

Warburton, Geoffrey E.; *see* Egerton-Warburton.

Warburton, John E.; *see* Egerton-Warburton.

Warburton, John Paul, 1840–1919, vol. II

Warburton, Piers E.; *see* Egerton-Warburton.

Warburton, Col Sir Robert, *died* 1899, vol. I

Warburton, Lt-Col William Melvill, 1877–1952, vol. V

Warburton, Col William Pleace, 1843–1911, vol. I

Ward of North Tyneside, Baroness (Life Peer); Irene Mary Bewick Ward, 1895–1980, vol. VII

Ward of Witley, 1st Viscount, 1907–1988, vol. VIII

Ward, Sir Adolphus William, 1837–1924, vol. II

Ward, Col Sir (Albert) Lambert, 1st Bt (*cr* 1929), 1875–1956, vol. V

Ward, Gen. Sir (Alfred) Dudley, 1905–1991, vol. IX

Ward, Ven. Algernon, 1869–1947, vol. IV

Ward, Anthony Edward Walter, 1905–1968, vol. VI

Ward, Arnold Sandwith, 1876–1950, vol. IV

Ward, Lt-Col Arthur, 1866–1935, vol. III

Ward, Lt-Col Arthur Blackwood, 1870–1950, vol. IV

Ward, Arthur Claud, 1878–1914, vol. I

Ward, Rev. Canon Arthur Evelyn, 1877–1944, vol. IV

Ward, Ven. Arthur Frederick, 1912–1998, vol. X

Ward, Sir Arthur Hugh, 1906–1993, vol. IX

Ward, (Arthur) Neville, 1922–1989, vol. VIII

Ward, Arthur Samuel, *died* 1952, vol. V

Ward, Arthur William, 1858–1919, vol. II

Ward, Sir Ashley Skelton, 1877–1959, vol. V

Ward, Sir Aubrey Ernest, 1899–1987, vol. VIII

Ward, Barbara; *see* Jackson of Lodsworth, Baroness.

Ward, Basil Robert, 1902–1976, vol. VII

Ward, Rt Rev. Mgr Bernard, 1857–1920, vol. II

Ward, Lt-Gen. Hon. Bernard Matthew, 1831–1918, vol. II

Ward, Col Bernard Rowland, 1863–1933, vol. III

Ward, Bill; *see* Ward, I. W.

Ward, Rear-Adm. (S) Cecil Arthur, 1881–1954, vol. V

Ward, Charles James, *died* 1913, vol. I

Ward, Rev. Canon Charles Leslie, 1916–1994, vol. IX

Ward, Rev. Charles Triffit, *died* 1925, vol. II

Ward, Cyril, 1863–1935, vol. III

Ward, Captain Hon. Cyril Augustus, 1876–1930, vol. III

Ward, Sir Cyril Rupert Joseph, 2nd Bt (*cr* 1911), 1884–1940, vol. III

Ward, David, 1922–1983, vol. VIII

Ward, Sir Deighton Harcourt Lisle, 1909–1984, vol. VIII

Ward, Denzil Anthony Seaver, 1909–1989, vol. VIII

Ward, Dudley, 1885–1957, vol. V

Ward, Gen. Sir Dudley; *see* Ward, Gen. Sir A. D.

Ward, Ebenezer Thomas, 1879–1942, vol. IV

Ward, Edmund Fisher, 1912–1998, vol. X

Ward, Edward, *died* 1921, vol. II

Ward, Edward; *see* Bangor, 7th Viscount.

Ward, Lt-Col Edward Francis, 1870–1935, vol. III

Ward, Edward Rex, 1902–1984, vol. VIII

Ward, Captain Sir Edward Simons, 2nd Bt (*cr* 1914), 1882–1930, vol. III

Ward, Col Sir Edward Willis Duncan, 1st Bt (*cr* 1914), 1853–1928, vol. II

Ward, Edwin, 1880–1934, vol. III

Ward, Lt-Col Ellacott Leamon, 1873–1968, vol. VI

Ward, Air Cdre Ellacott Lyne Stephens, 1905–1991, vol. IX

Ward, Enoch, 1859–1922, vol. II

Ward, F. K.; *see* Kingdon-Ward.

Ward, Francis Alan Burnett, 1905–1990, vol. VIII

Ward, Maj.-Gen. Francis William, 1840–1919, vol. II

Ward, Rev. Frederick Hubert, 1858–1918, vol. II

Ward, Frederick John, 1922–1986, vol. VIII

Ward, Frederick Josiah, 1861–1941, vol. IV

Ward, Frederick Temple B.; *see* Barrington-Ward.

Ward, Rev. Frederick William Orde, 1843–1922, vol. II

Ward, Genevieve, Countess de Guerbel, 1837–1922, vol. II

Ward, George, 1878–1951, vol. V

Ward, George Edgar Septimus, 1888–1969, vol. VI

Ward, Ven. George Herbert, 1862–1946, vol. IV

Ward, Hon. Gerald Ernest Francis, 1877–1914, vol. I

Ward, Lt-Col Guy Bernard Campbell, 1875–1933, vol. III

Ward, Col Harry, 1876–1939, vol. III

Ward, Harry Marshall, 1854–1905, vol. I

Ward, Henrietta Mary Ada, *died* 1924, vol. II

Ward, Col Henry Charles S.; *see* Swinburne-Ward.

Ward, Col Henry Constantine Evelyn, 1837–1907, vol. I

Ward, Maj.-Gen. Henry Dudley Ossulston, 1872–1947, vol. IV

Ward, Herbert, *died* 1919, vol. II

Ward, Herbert, 1866–1938, vol. III

Ward, Mrs Humphry, (Mary Augusta Ward), 1851–1920, vol. II

Ward, Ida Caroline, 1880–1949, vol. IV

Ward, Ivor William, (Bill), 1916–1999, vol. X

Ward, James, 1851–1924, vol. II

Ward, James, 1843–1925, vol. II

Ward, Rt Rev. James, 1905–1973, vol. VII
Ward, Sir John, *died* 1908, vol. I
Ward, John, 1832–1912, vol. I
Ward, Lt-Col John, 1866–1934, vol. III
Ward, Col Sir John Chappell, 1877–1942, vol. IV
Ward, John Clive, 1924–2000, vol. X
Ward, John Frederick, 1883–1954, vol. V
Ward, John Grosvenor B.; *see* Barrington-Ward.
Ward, Sir John Guthrie, 1909–1991, vol. IX
Ward, Major Hon. Sir John Hubert, 1870–1938, vol. III
Ward, John Manning, 1919–1990, vol. VIII
Ward, Captain John Richard Le Hunte, 1870–1953, vol. V
Ward, Engr-Captain John Tom Hickman, *died* 1939, vol. III
Ward, Rev. John William, 1874–1938, vol. III
Ward, Joseph, *died* 1963, vol. VI
Ward, Rt Hon. Sir Joseph George, 1st Bt (*cr* 1911), 1856–1930, vol. III
Ward, Sir Joseph George Davidson, 3rd Bt (*cr* 1911), 1909–1970, vol. VI
Ward, Col Sir Lambert; *see* Ward, Col Sir A. L.
Ward, Sir Lancelot Edward B.; *see* Barrington-Ward.
Ward, Lt-Col Lancelot Edward Seth, 1875–1929, vol. III
Ward, Sir Leslie, 1851–1922, vol. II
Ward, Leslie Moffat; *see* Ward, P. L. M.
Ward, Lester F., 1841–1913, vol. I
Ward, Rev. Mark James B.; *see* Barrington-Ward.
Ward, Martyn Eric, 1927–1991, vol. IX
Ward, Mary Augusta; *see* Ward, Mrs Humphry.
Ward, Comdr Sir Melvill Willis, 3rd Bt (*cr* 1914), 1885–1973, vol. VII
Ward, Sir Michael B.; *see* Barrington-Ward.
Ward, Neville; *see* Ward, A. N.
Ward, Air Vice-Marshal Peter Alexander, 1930–1996, vol. X
Ward, Philip, 1845–1916, vol. II
Ward, (Philip) Leslie Moffat, 1888–1978, vol. VII
Ward, Adm. Philip N.; *see* Nelson-Ward.
Ward, Captain Hon. Reginald, 1874–1904, vol. I
Ward, Gen. Sir Richard Erskine, 1917–1989, vol. VIII
Ward, Richard Percyvale, 1894–1945, vol. IV
Ward, Hon. Robert Arthur, 1871–1942, vol. IV
Ward, Robert De Courcy, 1867–1931, vol. III
Ward, Robert M'Gowan B.; *see* Barrington-Ward.
Ward, Robert Percy, 1868–1936, vol. III
Ward, Ronald, 1909–1973, vol. VII
Ward, Ronald Ogier, 1886–1971, vol. VII
Ward, Sarah Adelaide, *died* 1969, vol. VI
Ward, Captain Hon. Somerset Richard Hamilton Augusta, 1833–1912, vol. I
Ward, Stacey George, 1906–1980, vol. VII
Ward, Sir Terence George, 1906–1991, vol. IX
Ward, Brig.-Gen. Thomas, 1861–1949, vol. IV
Ward, Thomas Humphry, 1845–1926, vol. II
Ward, Adm. Thomas Le Hunte, 1830–1907, vol. I
Ward, Sir Thomas Robert John, 1863–1944, vol. IV
Ward, Thomas William, 1918–2000, vol. X
Ward, Sir (Victor) Michael B.; *see* Barrington-Ward.
Ward, Col Walter, *died* 1948, vol. IV

Ward, Brig.-Gen. Walter Reginald, 1869–1952, vol. V
Ward, Wilfrid Arthur, 1892–1981, vol. VIII
Ward, Wilfrid Philip, 1856–1916, vol. II
Ward, Sir William, 1841–1927, vol. II
Ward, Rt Hon. William Dudley, 1877–1946, vol. IV
Ward, William Ernest Frank, 1900–1994, vol. IX
Ward, Sir William Erskine, 1838–1916, vol. II
Ward, Rev. William Hayes, 1835–1916, vol. II
Ward, William Kenneth, 1918–1995, vol. X (AI)
Ward-Harrison, Maj.-Gen. John Martin Donald, 1918–1985, vol. VIII
Ward-Jackson, Adrian Alexander, 1950–1991, vol. IX
Ward-Jackson, Major Charles Lionel Atkins, 1869–1930, vol. III
Ward-Perkins, John Bryan, 1912–1981, vol. VIII
Wardale, Edith Elizabeth, 1863–1943, vol. IV
Wardale, John Dobson, *died* 1958, vol. V
Warde, Beatrice Lamberton, 1900–1969, vol. VI
Warde, Lt-Col Charles Arthur Madan, 1839–1912, vol. I
Warde, Col Sir Charles Edward, 1st Bt, 1845–1937, vol. III
Warde, Rt Rev. Geoffrey Hodgson, 1889–1972, vol. VII
Warde, Lt-Col Henry Murray Ashley, 1850–1940, vol. III
Warde, John Robins, 1920–1999, vol. X
Warde, Engr Rear-Adm. Thomas Herbert, 1882–1960, vol. V
Warde-Aldam, Col William St Andrew, 1882–1958, vol. V
Wardell, Lt-Col Henry, *died* 1933, vol. III
Wardell, John Henry, 1878–1957, vol. V
Wardell-Yerburgh, Rev. Oswald Pryor, 1858–1913, vol. I
Warden, Archibald A., 1869–1943, vol. IV
Warden, Florence; *see* James, Florence.
Warden, Herbert Lawton, 1877–1946, vol. IV
Warden, William Luck, *died* 1942, vol. IV
Warder, John Arthur, 1909–1989, vol. VIII
Wardington, 1st Baron, 1869–1950, vol. IV
Wardlaw, Hon. Alan Lindsay, 1887–1938, vol. III
Wardlaw, Rear-Adm. Alexander Livingston Penrose M.; *see* Mark-Wardlaw.
Wardlaw, Claude Wilson, 1901–1985, vol. VIII
Wardlaw, Sir Henry, 18th Bt, 1822–1897, vol. I
Wardlaw, Sir Henry, 19th Bt, 1867–1954, vol. V
Wardlaw, Sir Henry, 20th Bt, 1894–1983, vol. VIII
Wardlaw, Rev. James Tait P.; *see* Plowden-Wardlaw.
Wardlaw, William, 1892–1958, vol. V
Wardlaw, Rear-Adm. William Penrose M.; *see* Mark-Wardlaw.
Wardlaw-Milne, Sir John Sydney, *died* 1967, vol. VI
Wardle, Air Cdre Alfred Randles, 1898–1989, vol. VIII
Wardle, Arthur, 1864–1949, vol. IV
Wardle, Captain Ernest Vivian Livesey, 1878–1931, vol. III
Wardle, George James, 1865–1947, vol. IV
Wardle, Sir Thomas, 1831–1909, vol. I
Wardle, Sir Thomas Edward Jewell, 1912–1997, vol. X

Wardle, Vice-Adm. Thomas Erskine, 1877–1944, vol. IV
Wardle, Ven. Walter Thomas, 1900–1982, vol. VIII
Wardle, Rev. William Lansdell, 1877–1946, vol. IV
Wardle-Smith, John Hughes, 1909–1968, vol. VI
Wardley, Donald Joule, 1893–1950, vol. IV
Wardrop, Maj.-Gen. Alexander, 1831–1908, vol. I
Wardrop, Gen. Sir Alexander, 1872–1961, vol. VI
Wardrop, Col Douglas, 1854–1937, vol. III
Wardrop, Col Frederick Meyer, 1847–1905, vol. I
Wardrop, Rev. James, died 1909, vol. I
Wardrop, Sir (John) Oliver, 1864–1948, vol. IV
Wardrop, Sir Oliver; see Wardrop, Sir J. O.
Wardrope, William Hugh, 1860–1947, vol. IV
Wards, Brig. George Thexton, 1897–1991, vol. IX
Ware, Maj.-Gen. Sir Fabian Arthur Goulstone, 1869–1949, vol. IV
Ware, Sir Frank, 1886–1968, vol. VI
Ware, Lt-Col Frank Cooke W.; see Webb-Ware.
Ware, Lt-Col George William Webb, died 1943, vol. IV
Ware, Sir Henry Gabriel, 1912–1989, vol. VIII
Ware, Martin, 1915–1998, vol. X
Ware, Rev. Martin Stewart, died 1934, vol. III
Wareham, Arthur George, 1908–1988, vol. VIII
Wareing, Alfred, 1876–1942, vol. IV
Wareing, Eustace Bernard Foley, 1890–1958, vol. V
Wareing, Philip Frank, 1914–1996, vol. X
Warfield, Benjamin Breckinridge, 1851–1921, vol. II
Wargrave, 1st Baron, 1862–1936, vol. III
Waring, 1st Baron, 1860–1940, vol. III
Waring, Sir (Alfred) Harold, 2nd Bt, 1902–1981, vol. VIII
Waring, Col Anthony Henry, 1871–1941, vol. IV
Waring, Sir (Arthur) Bertram, 1893–1974, vol. VII
Waring, Captain Arthur Cunliffe Bernard C.; see Critchley-Waring.
Waring, Sir Bertram; see Waring, Sir A. B.
Waring, Lady Clementine; see Waring, Lady S. E. C.
Waring, Sir Douglas Tremayne, 1904–1980, vol. VII
Waring, Francis John, 1843–1924, vol. II
Waring, Sir Harold; see Waring, Sir A. H.
Waring, Sir Henry John, 1817–1903, vol. I
Waring, (Henry) William (Allen), 1906–1962, vol. VI
Waring, Herbert, 1857–1932, vol. III
Waring, Sir Holburt Jacob, 1st Bt, 1866–1953, vol. V
Waring, Rev. Canon John, 1890–1967, vol. VI
Waring, Margaret Alicia, 1887–1968, vol. VI
Waring, Lady (Susan Elizabeth) Clementine, died 1964, vol. VI
Waring, Col Thomas, died 1898, vol. I
Waring, Walter, 1876–1930, vol. III
Waring, William; see Waring, H. W. A.
Warington, Robert, 1838–1907, vol. I
Wark, Hon. Lord; John Lean Wark, 1877–1943, vol. IV
Wark, Anna Elisa, 1867–1944, vol. IV
Wark, Lt-Col Blair Anderson, 1894–1941, vol. IV
Wark, Sir Ian William, 1899–1985, vol. VIII
Wark, John Lean; see Wark, Hon. Lord.

Warleigh, Captain Percival H., 1873–1933, vol. III
Warlow, Ven. Edmund John, 1863–1937, vol. III
Warlow-Davies, Eric John, 1910–1964, vol. VI
Warman, Ven. Francis Frederic Guy, 1904–1991, vol. IX
Warman, Rt Rev. (Frederic Sumpter) Guy, 1872–1953, vol. V
Warman, Rt Rev. Guy; see Warman, Rt Rev. F. S. G.
Warmington, Sir Cornelius Marshall, 1st Bt, 1842–1908, vol. I
Warmington, Eric Herbert, 1898–1987, vol. VIII
Warmington, Sir Malcolm; see Warmington, Sir Marshall D. M.
Warmington, Sir Marshall Denham, 2nd Bt, 1871–1935, vol. III
Warmington, Sir (Marshall Denham) Malcolm, 4th Bt, 1934–1996, vol. X
Warmington, Lt-Comdr Sir Marshall George Clitheroe, 3rd Bt, 1910–1995, vol. IX
Warne, Rt Rev. Francis Wesley, 1854–1932, vol. III
Warne, George Henry, 1881–1928, vol. II
Warne, Rear-Adm. Robert Spencer, 1903–1990, vol. VIII
Warne-Browne, Air Marshal Sir Thomas Arthur, 1898–1962, vol. VI
Warner, Hon. Sir Arthur George, 1899–1966, vol. VI
Warner, Brodrick Ashton, 1888–1942, vol. IV
Warner, Charles Dudley, 1829–1900, vol. I
Warner, Rev. Canon Charles Edward, 1868–1945, vol. IV
Warner, Sir Christopher Frederick Ashton, 1895–1957, vol. V
Warner, Sir Courtenay; see Warner, Sir T. C. T.
Warner, Col Sir Edward Courtenay Thomas, 2nd Bt, 1886–1955, vol. V
Warner, Edward Handley, 1850–1925, vol. II
Warner, Edwin Charles, 1900–1968, vol. VI
Warner, Francis, 1847–1926, vol. II
Warner, Sir Frank, 1862–1930, vol. III
Warner, Sir Frederick Archibald, 1918–1995, vol. IX
Warner, Frederick Sydney, 1903–1987, vol. VIII
Warner, Sir George Frederic, 1845–1936, vol. III
Warner, Sir George Redston, 1879–1978, vol. VII
Warner, Lt-Col Harry Granville L.; see Lee-Warner.
Warner, Jack, (Jack Waters), 1896–1981, vol. VIII
Warner, Rev. John, 1860–1933, vol. III
Warner, Sir Joseph Henry, 1836–1897, vol. I
Warner, Rt Rev. Kenneth Charles Harman, 1891–1983, vol. VIII
Warner, Leonard William, died 1959, vol. V
Warner, Sir Lionel Ashton Piers, 1875–1953, vol. V
Warner, Michael Henry Charles, 1927–1994, vol. IX
Warner, Oliver, 1903–1976, vol. VII
Warner, Sir Pelham Francis, 1873–1963, vol. VI
Warner, Philip Henry L.; see Lee Warner.
Warner, Rex, 1905–1986, vol. VIII
Warner, Rev. Richard Edward, 1836–1910, vol. I
Warner, Robert Stewart Aucher, 1859–1944, vol. IV
Warner, Robert Townsend, 1868–1938, vol. III

Warner, Rev. Canon Stephen Mortimer, 1873–1947, vol. IV
Warner, Sydney Jeannetta, 1890–1979, vol. VII
Warner, Sylvia Townsend, 1893–1978, vol. VII
Warner, Sir (Thomas) Courtenay Theydon, 1st Bt, 1857–1934, vol. III
Warner, Sir William L.; see Lee-Warner.
Warner, Brig.-Gen. William Ward, 1867–1950, vol. IV
Warner-Staples, Irene E. Toye, died 1954, vol. V
Warnock, Rt Hon. Edmond, 1887–1971, vol. VII
Warnock, Frederick Victor, 1893–1976, vol. VII
Warnock, Sir Geoffrey James, 1923–1995, vol. IX
Warnock, John, 1864–1942, vol. IV
Warnock, Rt Hon. (John) Edmond; see Warnock, Rt Hon. E.
Warnock, William Robertson Lyon, 1916–1971, vol. VII
Warr, Augustus Frederick, 1847–1908, vol. I
Warr, Very Rev. Charles Laing, 1892–1969, vol. VI
Warr, George Charles Winter, 1845–1901, vol. I
Warr, Sir George Godfrey, 1882–1943, vol. IV
Warr, George Michael, 1915–1989, vol. VIII
Warrack, Grace Harriet, 1855–1932, vol. III
Warrack, Guy Douglas Hamilton, 1900–1986, vol. VIII
Warrack, Sir James Howard, 1855–1926, vol. II
Warrand, Maj.-Gen. William Edmund, 1831–1910, vol. I
Warre, Rev. Edmond, 1837–1920, vol. II
Warre, Felix Walter, 1879–1953, vol. V
Warre, Rev. Francis, died 1917, vol. II
Warre, Captain George Francis, 1876–1957, vol. V
Warre, Lt-Col Henry Charles, 1866–1934, vol. III
Warre, Sir Henry James, 1819–1898, vol. I
Warren, Albert Henry, 1830–1911, vol. I
Warren, Alec Stephen, 1894–1982, vol. VIII
Warren, Sir Alfred Haman, 1856–1927, vol. II
Warren, Sir Alfred Henry, (Sir Freddie), 1915–1990, vol. VIII
Warren, Dame (Alice) Josephine (Mary Taylor); see Barnes, Dame A. J. M. T.
Warren, Rt Rev. Alwyn Keith, 1900–1988, vol. VIII
Warren, Arthur, 1860–1924, vol. II
Warren, Maj.-Gen. Sir Arthur Frederick, 1830–1913, vol. I
Warren, Arthur George, 1887–1967, vol. VI
Warren, Sir (Augustus George) Digby, 7th Bt, 1898–1958, vol. V
Warren, Sir Augustus Riversdale, 5th Bt, 1833–1914, vol. I
Warren, Sir Augustus Riversdale John Blennerhasset, 6th Bt, 1865–1914, did not have an entry in Who's Who.
Warren, Sir Brian; see Warren, Sir H. B. S.
Warren, Gen. Sir Charles, 1840–1927, vol. II
Warren, Charles, 1868–1954, vol. V
Warren, Clarence Henry, 1895–1966, vol. VI
Warren, Cuthbert L.; see Leicester-Warren.
Warren, Maj.-Gen. Dawson Stockley, 1830–1908, vol. I
Warren, Sir Digby; see Warren, Sir A. G. D.
Warren, Douglas Daintry, 1897–1972, vol. VII

Warren, Douglas Ernest, 1918–1993, vol. IX
Warren, Earl, 1891–1974, vol. VII
Warren, Hon. Sir Edward Emerton, 1897–1983, vol. VIII
Warren, Brig. Edward Galwey, 1893–1975, vol. VII
Warren, Edward Prioleau, 1856–1937, vol. III
Warren, Ernest, 1871–1946, vol. IV
Warren, Falkland George Edgeworth, 1834–1908, vol. I
Warren, Sir Freddie; see Warren, Sir A. H.
Warren, Rev. Frederick Edward, 1842–1930, vol. III
Warren, Frederick Lloyd, 1911–1999, vol. X
Warren, Frederick Samuel Edward Wright, 1878–1952, vol. V
Warren, Major George Ernest, 1871–1942, vol. IV
Warren, Rear-Adm. Guy Langton, 1888–1961, vol. VI
Warren, Sir (Harold) Brian (Seymour), 1914–1996, vol. X
Warren, Rev. Henry George, 1851–1942, vol. IV
Warren, Sir (Henry William) Hugh, 1891–1961, vol. VI
Warren, Sir Herbert; see Warren, Sir T. H.
Warren, Adm. Herbert Augustus, 1855–1926, vol. II
Warren, Howard Crosby, 1867–1934, vol. III
Warren, Sir Hugh; see Warren, Sir Henry W. H.
Warren, John, 1830–1919, vol. II
Warren, Vice-Adm. John Borlase, 1838–1919, vol. II
Warren, John Herbert, 1895–1960, vol. V
Warren, Lt-Col John Leighton Byrne L.; see Leicester-Warren.
Warren, Col John Raymond, 1888–1956, vol. V
Warren, Rev. John Shrapnel, died 1925, vol. II
Warren, Dame Josephine; see Barnes, Dame A. J. M. T.
Warren, Ven. Latham Coddington, died 1912, vol. I
Warren, Low, died 1941, vol. IV
Warren, Rev. Max Alexander Cunningham, 1904–1977, vol. VII
Warren, Sir Mortimer Langton, 1903–1972, vol. VII
Warren, Nigel Sebastian Sommerville, 1912–1967, vol. VI
Warren, Sir Norcot Hastings yeeles, 1864–1947, vol. IV
Warren, Sir Pelham Laird, 1845–1923, vol. II
Warren, Col Peter, 1866–1952, vol. V
Warren, Philip David, 1851–1928, vol. II
Warren, Phillip; see Warren, W. P.
Warren, Richard, 1876–1957, vol. V
Warren, Robert Penn, 1905–1989, vol. VIII
Warren, Rt Hon. Robert Richard, 1817–1897, vol. I
Warren, Thomas Alfred, 1882–1968, vol. VI
Warren, Sir (Thomas) Herbert, 1853–1930, vol. III
Warren, Col Sir Thomas Richard Pennefather, 8th Bt, 1885–1961, vol. VI
Warren, Sir Victor Dunn, 1903–1953, vol. V
Warren, Wilfrid, 1910–1991, vol. IX
Warren, William Fairfield, 1833–1929, vol. III
Warren, William Henry, 1852–1926, vol. II
Warren, William Phillip, 1924–1988, vol. VIII

Warren, Hon. William Robertson, 1879–1927, vol. II
Warren, Col William Robinson, 1882–1969, vol. VI
Warrender, Sir George, 6th Bt, 1825–1901, vol. I
Warrender, Vice-Adm. Sir George John Scott, 7th Bt, 1860–1917, vol. II
Warrender, Lt-Col Hugh Valdave, 1868–1926, vol. II
Warrender, Lady Maud, 1870–1945, vol. IV
Warriner, John, 1860–1938, vol. III
Warrington of Clyffe, 1st Baron, 1851–1937, vol. III
Warrington, Anthony, 1929–1990, vol. VIII
Warrington-Morris, Air Cdre Alfred Drummond, 1883–1962, vol. VI
Warry, George Deedes, 1831–1904, vol. I
Warry, William Taylor, 1836–1906, vol. I
Warsop, Rear-Adm. John Charles, 1927–1995, vol. IX
Warter, Sir Philip Allan, 1903–1971, vol. VII
Wartiovaara, Otso Uolevi, 1908–1992, vol. IX
Warton, Rear-Adm. John Fenwick, 1877–1950, vol. IV
Warwick, 5th Earl of, 1853–1924, vol. II
Warwick, 6th Earl of, 1882–1928, vol. II
Warwick, 7th Earl of, 1911–1984, vol. VIII
Warwick, 8th Earl of, 1934–1996, vol. X
Warwick, Countess of; (Frances), 1861–1938, vol. III
Warwick, Countess of; (Marjorie), 1887–1943, vol. IV
Warwick, Cyril Walter, 1899–1985, vol. VIII
Warwick, Rt Rev. Mgr J. V., 1857–1939, vol. III
Warwick, Captain John Abraham, 1871–1937, vol. III
Warwick, Sir Norman Richard Combe, 1892–1962, vol. VI
Warwick, Roger, 1912–1991, vol. IX
Warwick, Walter Curry, 1877–1963, vol. VI
Warwick, Captain William Eldon, 1912–1999, vol. X
Warwick, Rev. William Geoffrey, 1898–1955, vol. V
Warwick, William Turner, 1888–1949, vol. IV
Washbourn, John Wichenford, 1863–1902, vol. I
Washbourn, Rear-Adm. Richard Everley, 1910–1988, vol. VIII
Washbourn, William, 1862–1959, vol. V
Washington, Vice-Adm. Basil George, died 1940, vol. III
Washington, Booker T., died 1915, vol. I
Washington, Horace Lee, 1864–1938, vol. III
Washington, Rev. Marmaduke, 1846–1935, vol. III
Wason, Rear-Adm. Cathcart Romer, 1874–1941, vol. IV
Wason, Rt Hon. Eugene, 1846–1927, vol. II
Wason, John Cathcart, 1848–1921, vol. II
Wason, Lt-Gen. Sydney Rigby, 1887–1969, vol. VI
Wass, Charles Alfred Alan, 1911–1989, vol. VIII
Wass, Samuel Hall, 1907–1970, vol. VI
Wassermann, Jakob, 1873–1934, vol. III
Wasserstein, Abraham, 1921–1995, vol. IX
Wastie, Winston Victor, 1900–1996, vol. X
Watchorn, Col Edwin Thomas, 1856–1940, vol. III(A), vol. V
Waterer, Sir Bernard; see Waterer, Sir R. B.

Waterer, Sir (Robert) Bernard, 1891–1971, vol. VII
Waterfall, Sir Charles Francis, 1888–1954, vol. V
Waterfall, William Duncan, 1889–1970, vol. VI
Waterfield, Sir (Alexander) Percival, 1888–1965, vol. VI
Waterfield, Bt-Col Arthur Charles Mallison, 1866–1943, vol. IV
Waterfield, Sir Henry, 1837–1913, vol. I
Waterfield, Maj.-Gen. Henry Gordon, 1840–1901, vol. I
Waterfield, Lina, 1874–1964, vol. VI
Waterfield, Sir Percival; see Waterfield, Sir A. P.
Waterfield, Very Rev. Reginald, 1867–1967, vol. VI
Waterford, 6th Marquess of, 1875–1911, vol. I
Waterford, 7th Marquess of, 1901–1934, vol. III
Waterhouse, Alfred, 1830–1905, vol. I
Waterhouse, Captain Rt Hon. Charles, 1893–1975, vol. VII
Waterhouse, Charles Owen, 1843–1917, vol. II
Waterhouse, Douglas Frew, 1916–2000, vol. X
Waterhouse, Eben Gowrie, 1881–1977, vol. VII
Waterhouse, Edwin, 1841–1917, vol. II
Waterhouse, Sir Ellis Kirkham, 1905–1985, vol. VIII
Waterhouse, Rev. Eric Strickland, 1879–1964, vol. VI
Waterhouse, Maj.-Gen. George Guy, 1886–1975, vol. VII
Waterhouse, Gilbert, 1888–1977, vol. VII
Waterhouse, Sir Herbert Furnivall, 1864–1931, vol. III
Waterhouse, J. W., died 1917, vol. II
Waterhouse, Maj.-Gen. James, 1842–1922, vol. II
Waterhouse, Michael Theodore, 1888–1968, vol. VI
Waterhouse, Sir Nicholas Edwin, 1877–1964, vol. VI
Waterhouse, Osborn, 1881–1945, vol. IV
Waterhouse, Paul, 1861–1924, vol. II
Waterhouse, Lt-Col Sir Ronald, 1878–1942, vol. IV
Waterhouse, Rupert, 1873–1958, vol. V
Waterhouse, Thomas, 1878–1961, vol. VI
Waterhouse, Walter Lawry, 1887–1969, vol. VI
Waterloo, Stanley, 1846–1913, vol. I
Waterlow, David Sydney, 1857–1924, vol. II
Waterlow, Sir Edgar Lutwyche, 3rd Bt (cr 1873), 1870–1954, vol. VI
Waterlow, Sir Ernest Albert, 1850–1919, vol. II
Waterlow, Col Sir James; see Waterlow, Col Sir W. J.
Waterlow, Col James Francis, 1869–1942, vol. IV
Waterlow, Sir Philip Alexander, 4th Bt (cr 1873), 1897–1973, vol. VII
Waterlow, Sir Philip Hickson, 2nd Bt (cr 1873), 1847–1931, vol. III
Waterlow, Sir Sydney Hedley, 1st Bt (cr 1873), 1822–1906, vol. I
Waterlow, Sir Sydney Philip, 1878–1944, vol. IV
Waterlow, Sir Thomas Gordon, 3rd Bt, 1911–1982, vol. VIII
Waterlow, Sir William Alfred, 1st Bt (cr 1930), 1871–1931, vol. III
Waterlow, Col Sir (William) James, 2nd Bt (cr 1930), 1905–1969, vol. VI
Waterman, Sir Ewen McIntyre, 1901–1982, vol. VIII

Waterman, Rt Rev. Robert Harold, 1894–1984, vol. VIII
Watermeyer, Rt Hon. Ernest Frederick, 1880–1958, vol. V
Waterpark, 4th Baron, 1839–1912, vol. I
Waterpark, 5th Baron, 1883–1932, vol. III
Waterpark, 6th Baron, 1876–1948, vol. IV
Waters, Alfred Charles, 1848–1912, vol. I
Waters, Alwyn Brunow, 1906–1988, vol. VIII
Waters, Major Sir Arnold Horace Santo, 1886–1981, vol. VIII
Waters, Arthur George, 1888–1953, vol. V
Waters, Denise Jeanne Marie Lebreton, (Mrs Frank Waters); see Brown, D. J. M. L.
Waters, Edwin George Ross, 1890–1930, vol. III
Waters, Rev. Francis Edward, 1847–1929, vol. III
Waters, Frank George, 1911–1974, vol. VII
Waters, Frank Henry, 1908–1954, vol. V
Waters, Garth Rodney, 1944–1995, vol. IX
Waters, George, died 1905, vol. I
Waters, Sir George Alexander, 1880–1967, vol. VI
Waters, Sir Harry G., 1868–1946, vol. IV
Waters, Jack; see Warner, Jack.
Waters, James, died 1923, vol. II
Waters, John Dallas, 1889–1967, vol. VI
Waters, Montague, 1917–1999, vol. X
Waters, Lt-Col Robert, died 1927, vol. II
Waters, Rev. Thomas Brocas, died 1922, vol. II
Waters, Brig.-Gen. Wallscourt Hely-Hutchinson, 1855–1945, vol. IV
Waters, William Alexander, 1903–1985, vol. VIII
Waterson, Anthony Peter, 1923–1983, vol. VIII
Waterson, David, died 1942, vol. IV
Waterson, David, 1870–1954, vol. V
Waterson, Hon. Sidney Frank, 1896–1976, vol. VII
Waterston, David James, 1910–1985, vol. VIII
Wates, George Leslie, 1884–1958, vol. V
Wates, Sir Ronald Wallace, 1907–1986, vol. VIII
Wathen, Gerald Anstruther, 1878–1958, vol. V
Watherston, Lt-Col Alan Edward Garrard, 1867–1909, vol. I
Watherston, Charles Fell, 1875–1940, vol. III
Watherston, Sir David Charles, 1907–1977, vol. VII
Watkin, Rt Rev. Abbot Aelred; see Watkin, Rt Rev. Abbot C. A. P.
Watkin, Sir Alfred Mellor, 2nd Bt, 1846–1914, vol. I
Watkin, Rt Rev. Abbot (Christopher) Aelred Paul, 1918–1997, vol. X
Watkin, Sir Edward William, 1st Bt, 1819–1901, vol. I
Watkin, Ernest Lucas, 1876–1951, vol. V
Watkin, Col Henry Samuel Spiller, 1843–1905, vol. I
Watkin, Sir Herbert George, died 1966, vol. VI
Watkin, Morgan, 1878–1970, vol. VI
Watkin, Thomas Morgan Joseph, 1856–1915, vol. I
Watkin-Davies, Rev. Francis Parry, 1862–1939, vol. III
Watkin-Jones, Rev. Howard, 1888–1953, vol. V
Watkin Williams, Sir Peter, 1911–1996, vol. X
Watkin-Williams, Robert Thesiger, 1867–1953, vol. V
Watkins, Baron (Life Peer); Tudor Elwyn Watkins, 1903–1983, vol. VIII

Watkins, Arthur Ernest, 1898–1967, vol. VI
Watkins, Arthur Goronwy, 1903–1990, vol. VIII
Watkins, Brig. Bernard Springett, 1900–1977, vol. VII
Watkins, Col Charles Bell, 1859–1929, vol. III
Watkins, Ven. D. Glyn, 1844–1907, vol. I
Watkins, Frederick Charles, 1883–1954, vol. V
Watkins, Frederick Henry, 1859–1928, vol. II, vol. III
Watkins, Col Frederic Mostyn, 1873–1946, vol. IV
Watkins, Rear-Adm. Geoffrey Robert Sladen, 1885–1950, vol. IV
Watkins, Harold James, 1914–1983, vol. VIII
Watkins, Henry George, 1907–1932, vol. III
Watkins, Col Henry George, 1880–1935, vol. III
Watkins, Ven. Henry William, 1844–1922, vol. II
Watkins, Lt-Col Hubert Bromley, 1897–1984, vol. VIII
Watkins, Rt Rev. Ivor Stanley, 1896–1960, vol. V
Watkins, James William, 1890–1959, vol. V
Watkins, Rear-Adm. John Kingdom, 1913–1970, vol. VI
Watkins, Mary Gwendolen, 1905–1981, vol. VIII
Watkins, Sir Metford, 1900–1950, vol. IV
Watkins, Michael John, 1875–1945, vol. IV
Watkins, Ven. Oscar Daniel, 1848–1926, vol. II
Watkins, Lt-Col Oscar Ferris, 1877–1943, vol. IV
Watkins, Rev. Owen Spencer, 1873–1957, vol. V
Watkins, Sir Percy Emerson, 1871–1946, vol. IV
Watkins, Stanley Heath, died 1967, vol. VI
Watkins, Rev. Thomas Benjamin, 1856–1933, vol. III
Watkins, Vernon Phillips, 1906–1967, vol. VI
Watkins, Watkin S.; see Strang-Watkins.
Watkins, William Henry, 1877–1964, vol. VI
Watkins-Pitchford, Denys James, 1905–1990, vol. VIII
Watkins-Pitchford, Lt-Col Herbert, died 1951, vol. V
Watkins-Pitchford, John, 1912–1994, vol. IX
Watkinson, 1st Viscount, 1910–1995, vol. IX
Watkinson, Arnold Edwards, 1893–1953, vol. V
Watkinson, Sir (George) Laurence, 1896–1974, vol. VII
Watkinson, Sir Laurence; see Watkinson, Sir G. L.
Watkinson, William Henry, 1860–1932, vol. III
Watkinson, Rev. William L., 1838–1925, vol. II
Watkis, Gen. Sir Henry Bulckley Burlton, 1860–1931, vol. III
Watkiss, Ronald Frederick, 1920–1991, vol. IX
Watkyn-Thomas, Frederic William, died 1963, vol. VI
Watling, Col Francis Wyatt, 1869–1953, vol. V
Watlington, Sir Henry William, 1866–1942, vol. IV
Watmough, John Edwin, 1860–1939, vol. III
Watney, Col Charles Norman, 1868–1956, vol. V
Watney, Dendy, 1865–1955, vol. V
Watney, Col Sir Frank Dormay, 1870–1965, vol. VI
Watney, Sir John, 1834–1923, vol. II
Watney, Oliver Vernon, 1902–1966, vol. VI
Watney, Vernon James, 1860–1928, vol. II
Watson, Baron (Life Peer); William Watson, 1828–1899, vol. I
Watson, Aaron, 1850–1926, vol. II
Watson, Very Rev. Alan Cameron, 1900–1976, vol. VII

Watson, Alexandra Mary Chalmers, 1873–1936, vol. III
Watson, Alfred Edward Thomas, 1849–1922, vol. II
Watson, Sir Alfred Henry, 1874–1967, vol. VI
Watson, Sir Alfred William, 1870–1936, vol. III
Watson, Col Andrew Alexander, *died* 1931, vol. III
Watson, A(ndrew) Aiken, 1897–1969, vol. VI
Watson, Andrew Gordon, *died* 1949, vol. IV
Watson, Sir Angus; *see* Watson, Sir J. A.
Watson, Archibald, 1849–1940, vol. III(A), vol. IV
Watson, Sir Arthur, 1873–1954, vol. V
Watson, Arthur E., 1880–1969, vol. VI
Watson, Sir Arthur Egerton, 1882–1967, vol. VI
Watson, Arthur George, 1829–1916, vol. II
Watson, Ven. Arthur Herbert, 1864–1952, vol. V
Watson, Arthur Kenelm, 1867–1947, vol. IV
Watson, Sir Arthur Townley, 2nd Bt (*cr* 1866), 1830–1907, vol. I
Watson, Arthur William, 1874–1925, vol. II
Watson, Basil Bernard, *died* 1941, vol. IV
Watson, Benjamin Philip, 1880–1976, vol. VII
Watson, Vice-Adm. Bertram Chalmers, 1887–1976, vol. VII
Watson, Sir Bertrand, 1878–1948, vol. IV
Watson, Rear-Adm. Burges, 1846–1902, vol. I
Watson, Most Rev. Campbell West W.; *see* West-Watson.
Watson, Chalmers, 1870–1946, vol. IV
Watson, Sir Charles Cuningham, 1874–1934, vol. III
Watson, Brig.-Gen. Charles Frederic, 1877–1948, vol. IV
Watson, Maj.-Gen. Sir Charles G.; *see* Gordon-Watson.
Watson, Col Sir Charles Moore, 1844–1916, vol. II
Watson, Sir Charles Rushworth, 3rd Bt (*cr* 1866), 1865–1922, vol. II
Watson, Gen. Sir Daril G., 1888–1967, vol. VI
Watson, Maj.-Gen. Sir David, 1871–1922, vol. II
Watson, David, *died* 1940, vol. III
Watson, David Archibald Beverley, 1905–1971, vol. VII
Watson, Hon. David John, 1911–1959, vol. V
Watson, Sir David M.; *see* Milne-Watson.
Watson, David Meredith Seares, 1886–1973, vol. VII
Watson, Sir (David) Ronald M.; *see* Milne-Watson.
Watson, Dennis George, *died* 1977, vol. VII
Watson, Captain Sir Derrick William Inglefield Inglefield-, 4th Bt, 1901–1987, vol. VIII
Watson, Sir Duncan, 1873–1959, vol. V
Watson, Sir Duncan; *see* Watson, Sir N. D.
Watson, Vice-Adm. Sir Dymock; *see* Watson, Vice-Adm. Sir R. D.
Watson, Edith Margaret, *died* 1953, vol. V
Watson, Edmund Henry Lacon, 1865–1948, vol. IV
Watson, Rev. Edward William, 1859–1936, vol. III
Watson, Elliot Lovegood Grant, 1885–1970, vol. VI
Watson, Rear-Adm. Fischer Burges, 1884–1960, vol. V
Watson, Lt-Col Forrester Colvin, 1878–1951, vol. V
Watson, Foster, 1860–1929, vol. III
Watson, Sir Francis, 1864–1947, vol. IV
Watson, Sir Francis John Bagott, 1907–1992, vol. IX

Watson, Col Francis William, 1893–1966, vol. VI
Watson, Sir Frank Pears, 1878–1941, vol. IV
Watson, Rev. Frederick, 1844–1906, vol. I
Watson, Frederick, 1885–1935, vol. III
Watson, Frederick, 1880–1947, vol. IV
Watson, Rev. Frederick Vincent, 1869–1954, vol. V
Watson, Rear-Adm. Garth; *see* Watson, Rear-Adm. J. G.
Watson, Sir Geoffrey Lewin, 3rd Bt (*cr* 1918), 1879–1959, vol. V
Watson, George, 1845–1927, vol. II
Watson, George, 1872–1937, vol. III
Watson, Sir George; *see* Watson, Sir W. G.
Watson, George Lennox, 1851–1904, vol. I
Watson, George Spencer, 1869–1934, vol. III
Watson, Ven. George Wade, 1838–1915, vol. I
Watson, Sir George Willes, 1827–1897, vol. I
Watson, George William, 1877–1956, vol. V
Watson, Gilbert, *died* 1920, vol. II
Watson, Gilbert, 1864–1941, vol. IV
Watson, Gilbert, 1882–1987, vol. VIII
Watson, Maj.-Gen. Gilbert France, 1895–1976, vol. VII
Watson, G(ordon) G(raham) Gibbes, 1891–1971, vol. VII
Watson, Harold Argyle, 1884–1959, vol. V
Watson, Lt-Col Harold Farnell, 1876–1941, vol. IV
Watson, Harrison, 1864–1948, vol. IV
Watson, Harry, 1871–1936, vol. III
Watson, Maj.-Gen. Sir Harry Davis, 1866–1945, vol. IV
Watson, Henry Angus, 1863–1952, vol. V
Watson, Henry Brereton Marriott, 1863–1921, vol. II
Watson, Henry C.; *see* Cradock-Watson.
Watson, Sir Henry Edmund, 1815–1901, vol. I
Watson, Hon. Sir (Henry) Keith, 1900–1973, vol. VII
Watson, Rev. Henry Lacon, 1823–1903, vol. I
Watson, Brig. Henry Neville Grylls, 1885–1976, vol. VII
Watson, Rev. Henry William, 1827–1903, vol. I
Watson, Herbert Adolphus G.; *see* Grant Watson.
Watson, Rev. Herbert Armstrong, 1860–1937, vol. III
Watson, Herbert Edmeston, 1886–1980, vol. VII
Watson, Major Herbert Frazer, 1881–1937, vol. III
Watson, Herbert James, 1895–1988, vol. VIII
Watson, Homer, 1855–1936, vol. III
Watson, Captain Horace Cyril, 1876–1949, vol. IV
Watson, Hubert Digby, 1869–1947, vol. IV
Watson, Rev. Hubert Luing, 1892–1985, vol. VIII
Watson, Sir Hugh, 1897–1966, vol. VI
Watson, Adm. Sir Hugh Dudley Richards, 1872–1954, vol. V
Watson, Hugh Gordon, 1912–1989, vol. VIII
Watson, Sir Hugh Wesley Allen, 1875–1953, vol. V
Watson, Maj.-Gen. Hugh Wharton Myddleton, 1881–1938, vol. III
Watson, Sir James Anderson Scott, 1889–1966, vol. VI
Watson, Sir (James) Angus, 1874–1961, vol. VI
Watson, Lt-Col James Kiero, 1865–1942, vol. IV
Watson, James Murray, 1888–1955, vol. V
Watson, Very Rev. James P.; *see* Pitt-Watson.

Watson, James Wreford, 1915–1990, vol. VIII
Watson, Janet Vida, (Mrs John Sutton), 1923–1985, vol. VIII
Watson, Sir John, 1st Bt (*cr* 1895), 1819–1898, vol. I
Watson, Sir John, 2nd Bt (*cr* 1895), 1860–1903, vol. I
Watson, Rev. John, 1850–1907, vol. I
Watson, John, *died* 1908, vol. I
Watson, Sir John, 3rd Bt (*cr* 1895), 1898–1918, vol. II
Watson, Gen. Sir John, 1829–1919, vol. II
Watson, John, *died* 1928, vol. II
Watson, Rev. John, 1843–1930, vol. III
Watson, John, *died* 1936, vol. III
Watson, John, 1847–1939, vol. III
Watson, John Alfred, *died* 1931, vol. III
Watson, John Arthur Fergus, 1903–1978, vol. VII
Watson, Sir John Ballingall Forbes, 1879–1952, vol. V
Watson, Sir John Charles, 1883–1944, vol. IV
Watson, Hon. John Christian, 1867–1941, vol. IV
Watson, John Duncan, 1860–1946, vol. IV
Watson, Brig.-Gen. John Edward, 1859–1951, vol. V
Watson, Rear Adm. John Garth, 1914–1992, vol. IX
Watson, John Harry, 1875–1944, vol. IV
Watson, Sir John Mathewson, *died* 1942, vol. IV
Watson, John Parker, 1909–1989, vol. VIII
Watson, (John) Steven, 1916–1986, vol. VIII
Watson, Rev. John T., 1904–1992, vol. IX
Watson, Lt-Col John William, 1874–1962, vol. VI
Watson, Joseph Stanley, 1910–1991, vol. IX
Watson, Hon. Sir Keith; *see* Watson, Hon. Sir H. K.
Watson, Laurence H.; *see* Hill Watson, Hon. Lord
Watson, Engr Rear-Adm. Lewis Jones, 1871–1942, vol. IV
Watson, Sir Logie Pirie, 1864–1933, vol. III
Watson, Malcolm, 1853–1929, vol. III
Watson, Sir Malcolm, 1873–1955, vol. V
Watson, Air Cdre Michael, 1909–1991, vol. IX
Watson, Sir Michael M.; *see* Milne-Watson.
Watson, Sir (Noel) Duncan, 1915–1999, vol. X
Watson, Sir Norman James, 2nd Bt, 1897–1983, vol. VIII
Watson, Maj.-Gen. Norman Vyvyan, 1898–1974, vol. VII
Watson, P. F.; *see* Fletcher-Watson.
Watson, Sir Patrick Heron, 1832–1907, vol. I
Watson, Reginald Frank William, 1921–1989, vol. VIII
Watson, Reginald George, 1862–1926, vol. II
Watson, Reginald Gordon Harry, (Rex), 1928–2000, vol. X
Watson, Captain Reginald James Newall, 1877–1930, vol. III
Watson, Sir Renny; *see* Watson, Sir W. R.
Watson, Rex; *see* Watson, Reginald G. H.
Watson, Rt Rev. Richard Charles Challinor, 1923–1998, vol. X
Watson, Hon. Robert, 1853–1929, vol. III
Watson, Hon. Robert, 1868–1930, vol. III
Watson, Robert, 1882–1948, vol. IV
Watson, Robert, 1894–1977, vol. VII
Watson, Rev. Robert A., 1845–1921, vol. II

Watson, Vice-Adm. Sir (Robert) Dymock, 1904–1988, vol. VIII
Watson, Rt Hon. Robert Spence, 1837–1911, vol. I
Watson, Robert William S.; *see* Seton-Watson.
Watson, Roderick Anthony, 1920–1993, vol. IX
Watson, Sir Ronald M.; *see* Milne-Watson, Sir D. R.
Watson, Col Ronald Macgregor, 1887–1936, vol. III
Watson, Samuel, 1898–1967, vol. VI
Watson, Lt-Col Stancliffe Wallace, 1889–1947, vol. IV
Watson, Sir Stephen John, 1898–1976, vol. VII
Watson, Steven; *see* Watson, J. S.
Watson, Sydney, 1903–1991, vol. IX
Watson, Lt-Col Sydney Twells, 1879–1936, vol. III
Watson, Thomas, 1844–1914, vol. I
Watson, Sir Thomas Aubrey, 4th Bt (*cr* 1866), 1911–1941, vol. IV
Watson, Lt-Col Thomas Colclough, 1867–1917, vol. II
Watson, Sir Thomas Edward, 1st Bt (*cr* 1918), 1851–1921, vol. II
Watson, Thomas Frederick, 1906–1994, vol. IX
Watson, Thomas J., 1847–1912, vol. I, vol. III
Watson, Thomas William, 1889–1957, vol. V
Watson, Thomas Yirrell, 1906–1996, vol. X
Watson, Ven. W. C., 1867–1916, vol. II, vol. III
Watson, Sir Wager Joseph, 4th Bt (*cr* 1760), 1837–1904, vol. I
Watson, Rev. Wentworth, 1848–1925, vol. II
Watson, Sir Wilfrid Hood, 2nd Bt (*cr* 1918), 1875–1922, vol. II
Watson, William, 1843–1909, vol. I
Watson, Sir William, 1842–1918, vol. II
Watson, William, 1868–1919, vol. II
Watson, Sir William, 1858–1935, vol. III
Watson, Major William, 1885–1942, vol. IV
Watson, Sir William, 1902–1984, vol. VIII
Watson, William; *see* Baron Thankerton.
Watson, Maj.-Gen. William Arthur, 1860–1944, vol. IV
Watson, Sir (William) George, 1st Bt (*cr* 1912), 1861–1930, vol. III
Watson, William Henry Lowe, 1891–1932, vol. III
Watson, William John, 1865–1948, vol. IV
Watson, William Law, 1883–1958, vol. V
Watson, William Livingstone, 1835–1903, vol. I
Watson, William McLean, 1874–1962, vol. VI
Watson, William Peter, *died* 1932, vol. III
Watson, Sir (William) Renny, 1838–1900, vol. I
Watson, William Trevor, 1886–1943, vol. IV
Watson, Lt-Col William Walter Russell, 1875–1924, vol. II
Watson, Wreford; *see* Watson, J. W.
Watson-Jones, Sir Reginald, 1902–1972, vol. VII
Watson-Kennedy, Lt-Col Thomas Francis Archibald, 1856–1935, vol. III
Watson Stewart, Sir James; *see* Stewart.
Watson-Taylor, George Simon Arthur, 1850–1942, vol. IV
Watson-Watt, Air Chief Comdt Dame Katherine Jane Trefusis, 1899–1971, vol. VII
Watson-Watt, Sir Robert Alexander, 1892–1973, vol. VII
Watson-Williams, Eric, 1890–1964, vol. VI

Watson-Williams, Patrick, 1863–1938, vol. III
Watt, Sir Alan Stewart, 1901–1988, vol. VIII
Watt, Lt-Col Alexander Fitzgerald, 1871–1957, vol. V
Watt, Alexander Pollock, *died* 1914, vol. I
Watt, Alexander Strahan, *died* 1948, vol. IV
Watt, Alexander Stuart, 1892–1985, vol. VIII
Watt, Andrew, 1909–1996, vol. X
Watt, Very Rev. Archibald, 1901–1981, vol. VIII
Watt, David, 1932–1987, vol. VIII
Watt, Brig-Gen. Donald Munro, 1871–1942, vol. IV
Watt, Lt-Col Edward William, 1877–1955, vol. V
Watt, Commissary-Gen. FitzJames Edward, 1822–1902, vol. I
Watt, Francis, 1849–1927, vol. II
Watt, Francis Clifford, 1896–1971, vol. VII
Watt, Sir George, 1851–1930, vol. III
Watt, George, 1854–1940, vol. III
Watt, George Fiddes, 1873–1960, vol. V
Watt, George Percival Norman, 1890–1983, vol. VIII
Watt, Sir George Steven H.; *see* Harvie-Watt.
Watt, Harry Anderson, 1863–1929, vol. III
Watt, Henry J., 1879–1925, vol. II
Watt, Very Rev. Hugh, 1879–1968, vol. VI
Watt, Rt Hon. Hugh, 1912–1980, vol. VII
Watt, Ian Buchanan, 1916–1988, vol. VIII
Watt, James, 1867–1929, vol. III
Watt, Sir James, *died* 1935, vol. III
Watt, James, 1863–1945, vol. IV
Watt, James, 1870–1945, vol. IV
Watt, James Crabb, 1853–1917, vol. II
Watt, James Cromar, 1862–1940, vol. III(A), vol. IV
Watt, Rev. John, 1862–1930, vol. III
Watt, John Mitchell, 1892–1980, vol. VII
Watt, Dame Katherine Christie, 1886–1963, vol. VI
Watt, Air Chief Comdt Dame Katherine Jane Trefusis W.; *see* Watson-Watt.
Watt, Langmuir; *see* Watt, W. L.
Watt, Very Rev. Lauchlan MacLean, *died* 1957, vol. V
Watt, Rev. Lewis, 1885–1965, vol. VI
Watt, Michael Herbert, 1887–1967, vol. VI
Watt, Richard Lorimer, 1921–1991, vol. IX
Watt, Sir Robert Alexander W.; *see* Watson-Watt.
Watt, Robert Cameron, 1898–1983, vol. VIII
Watt, Sir Robert Dickie, 1881–1965, vol. VI
Watt, Samuel, 1876–1927, vol. II
Watt, Captain Samuel Alexander, 1876–1950, vol. IV
Watt, Theodore, 1884–1946, vol. IV
Watt, Hon. Sir Thomas, 1857–1947, vol. IV
Watt, Sir Thomas, 1882–1955, vol. V
Watt, (Walter) Langmuir, 1876–1953, vol. V
Watt, William, 1912–1985, vol. VIII
Watt, Rt Hon. William Alexander, 1871–1946, vol. IV
Watt, William Robert, 1888–1949, vol. IV
Watt, William Warnock, 1890–1963, vol. VI
Watterson, Hon. Henry, 1840–1921, vol. II
Watterston, David, 1845–1931, vol. III
Wattie, Sir James, 1902–1974, vol. VII
Wattie, James MacPherson, 1862–1943, vol. IV

Watton, Rt Rev. James Augustus, 1915–1995, vol. X (AI)
Watts, Arthur, *died* 1935, vol. III
Watts, Arthur Francis, 1916–1972, vol. VII
Watts, Arthur Frederick, 1897–1970, vol. VI(AII)
Watts, Rev. Arthur Herbert, 1886–1960, vol. V
Watts, Charles Albert, 1858–1946, vol. IV
Watts, Maj.-Gen. Charles Donald Raynsford, 1871–1943, vol. IV
Watts, Rt Rev. Christopher Charles, *died* 1958, vol. V
Watts, Sir (Fenwick) Shadforth, 1858–1926, vol. II
Watts, Sir Francis, 1859–1930, vol. III
Watts, George Frederick, 1817–1904, vol. I
Watts, Gordon Edward, 1902–1974, vol. VII
Watts, Henry Edward, 1832–1904, vol. I
Watts, Lt-Gen. Sir Herbert Edward, 1858–1934, vol. III
Watts, Rt Rev. Horace Godfrey, 1901–1959, vol. V
Watts, Sir Hugh Edmund, 1888–1958, vol. V
Watts, James, 1903–1961, vol. VI
Watts, James T., *died* 1930, vol. III
Watts, John Hylton, 1890–1972, vol. VII
Watts, Leonard, 1871–1951, vol. V
Watts, Maurice Emygdius, 1878–1933, vol. III
Watts, Col Sir Philip, 1846–1926, vol. II
Watts, Rev. Robert Rowley, *died* 1911, vol. I
Watts, Ronald George Henry, 1914–1993, vol. IX
Watts, Sir Roy, 1925–1993, vol. IX
Watts, Sir Shadforth; *see* Watts, Sir F. S.
Watts, Rev. Sidney Maurice, 1892–1979, vol. VII
Watts, Sir Thomas, 1868–1951, vol. V
Watts, Weldon Patrick Tyrone, 1897–1972, vol. VII
Watts, Col Sir William, 1858–1922, vol. II
Watts, William John, 1923–1983, vol. VIII
Watts, William Marshall, 1844–1919, vol. II
Watts, William Walter, 1862–1948, vol. IV
Watts, William Whitehead, 1860–1947, vol. IV
Watts-Ditchfield, Rt Rev. John Edwin, 1861–1923, vol. II
Watts-Dunton, Walter Theodore, 1832–1914, vol. I
Wauchope, Gen. Sir Arthur Grenfell, 1874–1947, vol. IV
Wauchope, Lt-Col David Alexander, 1871–1929, vol. III
Wauchope, Mrs, (Jean Mary Wauchope), *died* 1942, vol. IV
Wauchope, Sir John Douglas Don-, 9th Bt, 1859–1951, vol. V
Wauchope, Sir Patrick George Don-, 10th Bt, 1898–1989, vol. VIII
Waud, Christopher Denis George Pierre, 1928–1995, vol. IX
Waugh, Alec, 1898–1981, vol. VIII
Waugh, Sir (Alexander) Telford, 1865–1950, vol. IV
Waugh, Arthur, 1866–1943, vol. IV
Waugh, Sir Arthur Allen, 1891–1968, vol. VI
Waugh, Ven. Arthur Thornhill, 1842–1922, vol. II
Waugh, Rev. Benjamin, 1839–1908, vol. I
Waugh, Evelyn Arthur St John, 1903–1966, vol. VI
Waugh, George Ernest, *died* 1940, vol. III
Waugh, Sir Telford; *see* Waugh, Sir A. T.
Waugh, William James, 1856–1931, vol. III
Waugh, William Templeton, 1884–1932, vol. III

Wauhope, Col Robert Alexander, 1855–1921, vol. II
Wauters, Emile, 1846–1933, vol. III
Wauton, Edric Brenton, 1883–1957, vol. V
Wavell, 1st Earl, 1883–1950, vol. IV
Wavell, 2nd Earl, 1916–1953, vol. V
Wavell, Maj.-Gen. Archibald Graham, 1843–1935, vol. III
Waverley, 1st Viscount, 1882–1958, vol. V
Waverley, 2nd Viscount, 1911–1990, vol. VIII
Waverley, Viscountess; (Ava), 1896–1974, vol. VII
Wavertree, 1st Baron, 1856–1933, vol. III
Wavertree, Lady; (Sophie Florence Lothrop), (Mrs F. M. B. Fisher), *died* 1952, vol. V
Way, Andrew Greville Parry, 1909–1974, vol. VII
Way, Arthur S., 1847–1930, vol. III
Way, Lt-Col Benjamin Irby, 1869–1932, vol. III
Way, Lt-Col Bromley George Vere, 1873–1940, vol. III
Way, Rev. Charles Parry, 1870–1949, vol. IV
Way, Christine Stella, 1895–1975, vol. VII
Way, Col George Augustus, 1837–1899, vol. I
Way, Gerald Oscar, 1875–1938, vol. III
Way, Rev. John Hugh, 1834–1912, vol. I
Way, Rev. John Pearce, 1850–1937, vol. III
Way, Maj.-Gen. Nowell FitzUpton Sampson-, 1838–1926, vol. II
Way, Sir Richard George Kitchener, 1914–1998, vol. X
Way, Rt Hon. Sir Samuel James, 1st Bt, 1836–1916, vol. II
Way, Rt Rev. Wilfrid Lewis Mark, 1905–1982, vol. VIII
Way, Captain William, 1847–1927, vol. II
Wayland, Edward James, 1888–1966, vol. VI
Wayland, Lt-Col Edward Robert, 1871–1939, vol. III
Wayland, Lt-Col Sir William Abraham, 1869–1950, vol. IV
Wayman, Lt-Col Harry Reginald Bland, 1877–1931, vol. III
Wayman, Lt-Col Sir Myers, 1890–1959, vol. V
Wayman, Thomas, 1833–1901, vol. I
Waymouth, Adm. Arthur William, 1863–1936, vol. III
Waymouth, Charity, 1915–2000, vol. X
Waymouth, Paymaster-Captain Frederick Richard, 1862–1927, vol. II
Wayne, Sir Edward Johnson, 1902–1990, vol. VIII
Wayne, Naunton, 1901–1970, vol. VI
Wayne, Richard St John Ormerod, 1904–1959, vol. V
Waynforth, Harry Morton, 1867–1916, vol. II
Wayte, Lt-Col Adrian Barclay, 1882–1934, vol. III
Wazir Hasan, Hon. Sir Saiyid, 1874–1947, vol. IV(A), vol. V
Weakley, Ernest, 1861–1923, vol. II
Weale, Putnam, 1877–1930, vol. III
Weale, W. H. James, 1832–1917, vol. II
Wear, Col Algernon Edward Luke, 1866–1941, vol. IV
Weardale, 1st Baron, 1847–1923, vol. II
Weare, Sir Henry Edwin, 1825–1898, vol. I
Wearing, John Frederick, 1922–1974, vol. VII
Weatherall, Col Henry Burgess, *died* 1917, vol. II
Weatherall, John Henry, 1868–1950, vol. IV

Weatherburn, Charles Ernest, 1884–1974, vol. VII
Weatherby, Sir Francis, 1885–1969, vol. VI
Weatherhead, Arthur Evelyn, 1880–1956, vol. V
Weatherhead, Rev. Arthur Swinton, 1866–1937, vol. III
Weatherhead, Sir Arthur Trenham, 1905–1984, vol. VIII
Weatherhead, Rev. Herbert Thomas Candy, 1875–1930, vol. III
Weatherhead, Very Rev. James, 1863–1944, vol. IV
Weatherhead, Rev. Leslie Dixon, 1893–1976, vol. VII
Weatherhead, Rev. Robert Johnston, 1839–1912, vol. I
Weatherill, Charles, 1874–1944, vol. IV
Weatherill, Rev. Canon David, 1866–1933, vol. III
Weatherill, Henry, 1868–1943, vol. II
Weatherly, Frederic Edward, 1848–1929, vol. III
Weatherstone, Sir Duncan Mackay, 1898–1972, vol. VII
Weaver, Mrs Baillie, (Gertrude Weaver), *died* 1926, vol. II
Weaver, Gertrude; *see* Weaver, Mrs Baillie.
Weaver, Herbert Parsons, 1872–1945, vol. IV
Weaver, John Reginald Homer, 1882–1965, vol. VI
Weaver, Sir Lawrence, 1876–1930, vol. III
Weaver, Percy William, 1882–1943, vol. IV
Weaver, Warren, 1894–1978, vol. VII
Web-Gilbert, Charles, 1869–1925, vol. II
Webb, Rt Rev. Allan Becher, 1839–1907, vol. I
Webb, Sir (Ambrose) Henry, 1882–1964, vol. VI
Webb, Lt-Col Andrew Henry, 1873–1949, vol. IV
Webb, Anthony Michael Francis, 1914–1998, vol. X
Webb, Sir Arthur Lewis, 1860–1921, vol. II
Webb, Col Sir (Arthur) Lisle Ambrose, 1871–1945, vol. IV
Webb, Sir Aston, 1849–1930, vol. III
Webb, Augustus D., 1880–1953, vol. V
Webb, Beatrice; *see* Webb, Mrs Sidney.
Webb, C. Locock, 1822–1898, vol. I
Webb, Cecil Richard, 1887–1974, vol. VII
Webb, Sir Charles Morgan, 1872–1963, vol. VI
Webb, Clement Charles Julian, 1865–1954, vol. V
Webb, Clifford, 1895–1972, vol. VII
Webb, Hon. Sir Clifton; *see* Webb, Hon. Sir T. C.
Webb, Douglas Edward, 1909–1988, vol. VIII
Webb, Francis Gilbert, 1853–1941, vol. IV
Webb, Frederick William, 1837–1919, vol. II
Webb, Geoffrey Fairbank, 1898–1970, vol. VI
Webb, Lt-Col George Ambrose Congreve, 1869–1942, vol. IV
Webb, Brig. George Clifford, 1905–1945, vol. IV
Webb, Lt-Col Sir Henry, 1st Bt, 1866–1940, vol. III
Webb, Sir Henry; *see* Webb, Sir A. H.
Webb, Mrs Henry Bertram Law; *see* Webb, Mary.
Webb, James, 1918–1982, vol. VIII
Webb, Col James B., *see* Baldwin-Webb.
Webb, John, 1885–1954, vol. V
Webb, John Curtis, 1868–1949, vol. IV
Webb, John Victor Duncombe, 1930–1983, vol. VIII
Webb, Katharine, (Katharine Adams), 1862–1952, vol. V
Webb, Kaye, 1914–1996, vol. X

Webb, Col Sir Lisle; *see* Webb, Col Sir A. L. A.
Webb, Marion St John, *died* 1930, vol. III
Webb, Mary, 1881–1927, vol. II
Webb, Maurice, 1880–1946, vol. IV
Webb, Rt Hon. Maurice, 1904–1956, vol. V
Webb, Maurice Everett, 1880–1939, vol. III
Webb, Millicent Vere, 1878–1969, vol. VI
Webb, Sir Montagu de Pomeroy, 1869–1938, vol. III
Webb, Montague, 1847–1930, vol. III
Webb, Percy Henry, 1856–1937, vol. III
Webb, Philip George Lancelot, 1856–1937, vol. III
Webb, Adm. Sir Richard, 1870–1950, vol. IV
Webb, Lt-Gen. Sir Richard James Holden, 1919–1990, vol. IX (AI)
Webb, Robert Alexander, 1891–1978, vol. VII
Webb, Mrs Sidney, (Beatrice Webb), 1858–1943, vol. IV
Webb, Stella Dorothea, (Mrs A. B. Webb); *see* Gibbons, S. D.
Webb, Sir Sydney, 1816–1898, vol. I
Webb, Hon. Sir (Thomas) Clifton, 1889–1962, vol. VI
Webb, Thomas Ebenezer, 1827–1903, vol. I
Webb, Lt-Col Walter Edward, *died* 1934, vol. III
Webb, Col Walter George, 1838–1919, vol. II
Webb, Walter Prescott, 1888–1963, vol. VI
Webb, Lt-Col Wilfred Francis, 1897–1973, vol. VII
Webb, Wilfred Mark, 1868–1952, vol. V
Webb, William Flood, 1887–1972, vol. VII
Webb, William Harcourt, 1875–1968, vol. VI
Webb, William Seward, 1851–1926, vol. II
Webb, Rt Rev. William Walter, 1857–1934, vol. III
Webb-Bowen, Col Hildred Edward, 1882–1958, vol. V
Webb-Bowen, Air Vice-Marshal Sir Tom Ince, 1879–1956, vol. V
Webb-Johnson, 1st Baron, 1880–1958, vol. V
Webb-Johnson, Cecil, *died* 1930, vol. III
Webb-Johnson, Stanley, 1888–1965, vol. VI
Webb-Jones, James William, 1904–1965, vol. VI
Webb-Peploe, Rev. Hanmer William, 1837–1923, vol. I
Webb-Ware, Lt-Col Frank Cooke, 1866–1934, vol. III
Webbe, Alexander Josiah, 1855–1941, vol. IV
Webbe, Sir Harold, 1885–1965, vol. VI
Webber, Brig.-Gen. Adrian Beare I.; *see* Incledon-Webber.
Webber, Sir Arthur Frederick Clarence, 1873–1952, vol. V
Webber, Maj.-Gen. Charles Edmund, 1838–1904, vol. I
Webber, Fernley Douglas, 1918–1991, vol. IX
Webber, Lt-Col Godfrey Sturdy I.; *see* Incledon-Webber.
Webber, Harold Norris, 1881–1954, vol. V
Webber, Lt-Col Horace Armine William, 1880–1940, vol. III
Webber, Brig.-Gen. Norman William, 1881–1950, vol. IV
Webber, Robert Bryan, 1860–1934, vol. III
Webber, Sir Robert John, 1884–1962, vol. VI
Webber, William Downes, 1834–1924, vol. II

Webber, Sir William James Percival, 1901–1982, vol. VIII
Webber, William Southcombe L.; *see* Lloyd Webber.
Webber, Rt Rev. William Thomas Thornhill, 1837–1903, vol. I
Weber, (Derek) Edmund (Craig), 1921–1996, vol. X
Weber, Edmund; *see* Weber, D. E. C.
Weber, F. Parkes, 1863–1962, vol. VI
Weber, Sir Herman, 1823–1918, vol. II
Weber, Col William Hermann Frank, 1875–1936, vol. III
Weber-Brown, Lt-Col Arthur Miles, 1898–1965, vol. VI
Webley-Parry-Pryse, Sir Edward John; *see* Pryse.
Webster, Adam Blyth, 1882–1956, vol. V
Webster, Amy Marjorie, 1901–1967, vol. VI
Webster, Col Arthur George, 1837–1916, vol. II
Webster, Hon. Arthur Harold, 1874–1902, vol. I
Webster, Sir Augustus Frederick Walpole Edward, 8th Bt, 1864–1923, vol. II
Webster, Benjamin, 1864–1947, vol. IV
Webster, Brian Mackenzie, 1938–1985, vol. VIII
Webster, Sir Charles Kingsley, 1886–1961, vol. VI
Webster, Sir David Lumsden, 1903–1971, vol. VII
Webster, David William Ernest, 1923–1969, vol. VI
Webster, Rev. Canon Douglas, 1920–1986, vol. VIII
Webster, Edmund Forster, *died* 1913, vol. I
Webster, Sir Francis, 1850–1924, vol. II
Webster, Rev. Francis Scott, *died* 1920, vol. II
Webster, George Frederick, 1889–1959, vol. V
Webster, George Henry, 1887–1955, vol. V
Webster, Rev. George Russell B.; *see* Bullock-Webster.
Webster, Rt Rev. Hedley, 1880–1954, vol. V
Webster, Herbert Cayley, *died* 1917, vol. II
Webster, Herman Armour, 1878–1970, vol. VII (AI)
Webster, Sir Hugh Calthrop, 1869–1941, vol. IV
Webster, Hugh Colin, 1905–1979, vol. VII (AII)
Webster, James Alexander, 1877–1964, vol. VI
Webster, James Mathewson, *died* 1973, vol. VII
Webster, John, 1891–1947, vol. IV
Webster, Captain John Alexander, 1874–1924, vol. II
Webster, John Alexander R.; *see* Riddell-Webster.
Webster, John Clarence, 1863–1950, vol. IV
Webster, John Edward, 1870–1943, vol. IV
Webster, John Henry Douglas, 1882–1975, vol. VII
Webster, John Roger, 1926–1995, vol. IX
Webster, Sir Lonsdale; *see* Webster, Sir T. L.
Webster, Lorne C., 1871–1941, vol. IV
Webster, Margaret, 1905–1972, vol. VII
Webster, Dame May, 1865–1948, vol. IV
Webster, Very Rev. Reginald Godfrey Michael, 1860–1913, vol. I
Webster, Sir Richard James, 1913–1986, vol. VIII
Webster, Robert Grant, *died* 1925, vol. II
Webster, Sir Robert Joseph, 1891–1981, vol. VIII
Webster, Thomas Bertram Lonsdale, 1905–1974, vol. VII
Webster, Lt-Gen. Thomas Edward, 1830–1909, vol. I
Webster, Sir (Thomas) Lonsdale, 1868–1930, vol. III

Webster, Gen. Sir Thomas Sheridan R.; *see* Riddell-Webster.
Webster, Tom, 1886–1962, vol. VI
Webster, Walter Ernest, 1878–1959, vol. V
Webster, Col William, 1865–1934, vol. III
Webster, William, 1866–1953, vol. V
Webster, Major William Henry Albert, 1884–1968, vol. VI
Weck, Richard, 1913–1986, vol. VIII
Wedd, Major Aubrey Pattison Wallman, 1885–1945, vol. IV
Wedd, Nathaniel, *died* 1940, vol. III
Wedd, Brig. William Basil, 1890–1966, vol. VI
Weddell, (Alexander) Graham (McDonnell), 1908–1990, vol. VIII
Weddell, Graham; *see* Weddell, A. G. M.
Weddell, Col John Murray, 1884–1966, vol. VI
Wedderburn, Alexander, 1854–1931, vol. III
Wedderburn, Alexander Henry Melvill, 1892–1968, vol. VI
Wedderburn, Sir Ernest Maclagan, 1884–1958, vol. V
Wedderburn, Henry Scrymgeour, 1840–1914, vol. I
Wedderburn, Lt-Col Henry Scrymgeour, 1872–1924, vol. II
Wedderburn, Sir John Andrew O.; *see* Ogilvy-Wedderburn.
Wedderburn, Comdr Sir (John) Peter O.; *see* Ogilvy-Wedderburn.
Wedderburn, Joseph Henry Maclagan, 1882–1948, vol. IV
Wedderburn, Sir Maxwell MacLagan, 1883–1953, vol. V
Wedderburn, Sir William, 10th and 4th Bt, 1838–1918, vol. II
Wedderburn-Maxwell, Major James Andrew Colvile, 1849–1917, vol. II
Wedderspoon, Sir Thomas Adam, 1904–1987, vol. VIII
Wedega, Dame Alice, 1905–1987, vol. IX (AI)
Wedgwood, 1st Baron, 1872–1943, vol. IV
Wedgwood, 2nd Baron, 1898–1959, vol. V
Wedgwood, 3rd Baron, 1921–1970, vol. VI
Wedgwood, Hon. Camilla Hildegarde, 1901–1955, vol. V
Wedgwood, Major Cecil, *died* 1916, vol. II
Wedgwood, Dame (Cicely) Veronica, 1910–1997, vol. X
Wedgwood, Francis Hamilton, *died* 1930, vol. III
Wedgwood, Geoffrey Heath, 1900–1977, vol. VII (AII)
Wedgwood, Dame Ivy Evelyn, *died* 1975, vol. VII
Wedgwood, Sir John Hamilton, 2nd Bt, 1907–1989, vol. VIII
Wedgwood, Hon. Josiah, 1899–1968, vol. VI
Wedgwood, Julia, 1833–1913, vol. I
Wedgwood, Sir Ralph Lewis, 1st Bt, 1874–1956, vol. V
Wedgwood, Dame Veronica; *see* Wedgwood, Dame C. V.
Wedlake, John, 1892–1958, vol. V
Wedmore, Edmund Basil, 1876–1956, vol. V
Wedmore, Sir Frederick, 1844–1921, vol. II
Weech, William Nassau, 1878–1961, vol. VI
Weedon, Augustus Walford, *died* 1908, vol. I

Weedon, Air Marshal Sir Colin Winterbotham, 1901–1975, vol. VII
Weedon, Hon. Sir Henry, 1859–1921, vol. II
Weekes, Ven. Christian William Hampton, 1880–1948, vol. IV
Weekes, Rev. George Arthur, 1869–1953, vol. V
Weekes, Col Henry Wilson, 1870–1943, vol. IV
Weekes, Paymaster Rear-Adm. Victor Herbert Thomas, 1873–1937, vol. III
Weekes, Rev. William Haye, 1867–1945, vol. IV
Weekley, Charles Montague, 1900–1982, vol. VIII
Weekley, Ernest, *died* 1954, vol. V
Weeks, 1st Baron, 1890–1960, vol. V
Weeks, Alan Frederick, 1923–1996, vol. X
Weeks, Edward Augustus, 1898–1989, vol. VIII
Weeks, Engr Rear-Adm. Edward John, 1868–1954, vol. V
Weeks, Maj.-Gen. Ernest Geoffrey, 1896–1987, vol. VIII
Weeks, Sir Hugh Thomas, 1904–1992, vol. IX
Weevers, Theodoor, 1904–1992, vol. IX
Wegg-Prosser, Francis Richard, 1824–1911, vol. I
Weguelin, Mrs Arthur, *died* 1931, vol. III
Weguelin, John Reinhard, 1849–1927, vol. II
Wei Yuk, Sir Boshan, 1849–1921, vol. II
Weidlein, Edward Ray, 1887–1983, vol. VIII
Weigall, Albert Bythesea, 1840–1912, vol. I
Weigall, Lt-Col Sir Archibald; *see* Weigall, Lt-Col Sir W. E. G. A.
Weigall, Arthur Edward Pearse Brome, 1880–1934, vol. III
Weigall, Cecil Edward, 1870–1955, vol. V
Weigall, Henry, 1829–1925, vol. II
Weigall, Julian William Wellesley, 1868–1945, vol. IV
Weigall, Peter Raymond, 1922–1999, vol. X
Weigall, Lady Rose Sophia Mary, 1834–1921, vol. II
Weigall, Theyre à Beckett, 1860–1926, vol. II
Weigall, Lt-Col Sir (William Ernest George) Archibald, 1st Bt, 1874–1952, vol. V
Weigh, Brian, 1926–1997, vol. X
Weighill, Air Cdre Robert Harold George, 1920–2000, vol. X
Weight, Carel Victor Morlais, 1908–1997, vol. X
Weight, Rev. Thomas Joseph, 1845–1922, vol. II
Weightman, Sir Hugh, 1898–1949, vol. IV
Weightman, William Henry, 1887–1970, vol. VI
Weighton, Robert Lunan, 1851–1937, vol. III
Weill, David D.; *see* David-Weill.
Weinberger, Jaromir, 1896–1967, vol. VI
Weiner, Joseph Sidney, 1915–1982, vol. VIII
Weingartner, Felix, 1863–1942, vol. IV
Weinthal, Leo, 1865–1930, vol. III
Weipers, Sir William Lee, 1904–1990, vol. VIII
Weir, 1st Viscount, 1877–1959, vol. V
Weir, 2nd Viscount, 1905–1975, vol. VII
Weir, Very Rev. Andrew John, (Jack), 1919–2000, vol. X
Weir, Archibald A. E., 1859–1935, vol. III
Weir, Rev. Cecil James Mullo, 1897–1995, vol. IX
Weir, Sir Cecil McAlpine, 1890–1960, vol. V
Weir, Air Vice-Marshal Cecil Thomas, 1913–1965, vol. VI
Weir, Lt-Col Donald Lord, 1885–1921, vol. II

Weir, Gen. Sir George Alexander, 1876–1951, vol. V
Weir, George Moir, 1885–1949, vol. IV
Weir, Harrison William, 1824–1906, vol. I
Weir, Helen Stuart, *died* 1969, vol. VI
Weir, Very Rev. Jack; *see* Weir, Very Rev. A. J.
Weir, James Galloway, 1839–1911, vol. I
Weir, James George, 1887–1973, vol. VII
Weir, Lt-Col James Leslie Rose, 1883–1950, vol. IV
Weir, Sir John, 1879–1971, vol. VII
Weir, Sir John Charles, 1872–1936, vol. III
Weir, (Lauchlan) MacNeill, 1877–1939, vol. III
Weir, MacNeill; *see* Weir, L. MacN.
Weir, Neil Archibald Campbell, 1895–1967, vol. VI
Weir, Maj.-Gen. Sir Norman William McDonald, 1893–1961, vol. VI
Weir, Rt Rev. Mgr Peter John, 1831–1917, vol. II
Weir, Ralph Somerville, 1884–1962, vol. VI
Weir, Major Hon. Robert, 1882–1939, vol. III
Weir, Robert Fulton, 1838–1927, vol. II
Weir, Robert Hendry, 1912–1985, vol. VIII
Weir, Robert Stanley, 1856–1926, vol. II
Weir, Brig.-Gen. Stanley Price, 1866–1944, vol. IV
Weir, Maj.-Gen. Sir Stephen Cyril Ettrick, 1905–1969, vol. VI
Weir, Hon. William Alexander, 1858–1929, vol. III
Weir, Rev. Canon William Mortimer, 1868–1936, vol. III
Weirter, Louis, 1873–1932, vol. III
Weis-Fogh, Torkel, 1922–1975, vol. VII
Weisberg, Hyman, 1890–1976, vol. VII
Weismann, August, 1834–1914, vol. I
Weiss, Sir Eric, 1908–1990, vol. VIII
Weiss, Frederick Ernest, 1865–1953, vol. V
Weiss, Joseph J., 1907–1972, vol. VII
Weiss, Peter Ulrich, 1916–1982, vol. VIII
Weiss, Roberto, 1906–1969, vol. VI
Weisz, Victor, 1913–1966, vol. VI
Weitnauer, Albert, 1916–1984, vol. VIII
Weitzman, David, 1898–1987, vol. VIII
Weizmann, Chaim, 1874–1952, vol. V
Welbourne, Edward, 1894–1966, vol. VI
Welby, 1st Baron, 1832–1915, vol. I
Welby, Sir Alfred Cholmeley Earle, 1849–1937, vol. III
Welby, Charles Cornwallis Anderson P.; *see* Pelham Welby.
Welby, Sir Charles Glynne Earle, 5th Bt, 1865–1938, vol. III
Welby, Edward Montague Earle, 1836–1926, vol. II
Welby, Euphemia Violet, 1891–1987, vol. VIII
Welby, Sir George Earle, 1851–1936, vol. III
Welby, Hugh Robert Everard Earle, 1885–1970, vol. VI
Welby, John Earle, 1820–1905, vol. I
Welby, Sir Oliver Charles Earle, 6th Bt, 1902–1977, vol. VII
Welby, Rt Rev. Thomas Earle, 1811–1899, vol. I
Welby, Thomas Earle, 1881–1933, vol. III
Welby-Everard, Maj.-Gen. Sir Christopher Earle, 1909–1996, vol. X
Welby-Everard, Edward Everard Earle, 1870–1951, vol. V
Welch, Rev. Adam Cleghorn, 1864–1943, vol. IV

Welch, Anthony Edward, 1906–1993, vol. IX
Welch, Charles, 1848–1924, vol. II
Welch, Colin; *see* Welch, J. C. R.
Welch, Col Sir Cullum; *see* Welch, Col Sir G. J. C.
Welch, David, 1933–2000, vol. X
Welch, Sir David Nairne, 1820–1912, vol. I
Welch, Rev. Edward Ashurst, 1860–1932, vol. III
Welch, Air Vice-Marshal Edward Lawrence C.; *see* Colbeck-Welch.
Welch, Surg.-Rear-Adm. Sir George, 1858–1947, vol. IV
Welch, Col Sir (George James) Cullum, 1st Bt, 1895–1980, vol. VII
Welch, Col George Osbaldeston, 1861–1935, vol. III
Welch, Sir Gordon; *see* Welch, Sir H. G. G.
Welch, Sir (Henry George) Gordon, 1890–1960, vol. V
Welch, Henry John, 1872–1958, vol. V
Welch, James, 1865–1917, vol. II
Welch, (James) Colin (Ross), 1924–1997, vol. X
Welch, James William, 1900–1967, vol. VI
Welch, John Joseph, 1871–1950, vol. IV
Welch, Lucy Elizabeth K.; *see* Kemp-Welch.
Welch, Brig.-Gen. Malcolm Hammond Edward, 1872–1946, vol. IV
Welch, Margaret K.; *see* Kemp-Welch.
Welch, Brig.-Gen. Martin K.; *see* Kemp-Welch.
Welch, Rt Rev. Neville; *see* Welch, Rt Rev. W. N.
Welch, Robert Radford, 1929–2000, vol. X
Welch, William Henry, 1850–1934, vol. III
Welch, Rt Rev. (William) Neville, 1906–1999, vol. X
Welch, William Tom, 1910–1979, vol. VII
Welchman, Col Edmund Walter St George, 1857–1933, vol. III
Welchman, Edward Theodore, 1881–1914, vol. I
Welchman, Ven. William, 1866–1954, vol. V
Weld, Brig. Charles Joseph, 1893–1962, vol. VI
Weld, Francis Joseph, 1873–1958, vol. V
Weld, Rt Rev. George, 1883–1959, vol. V
Weld, Harry Porter, 1877–1970, vol. VI(AII)
Weld, Herbert, *died* 1935, vol. III
Weld, Col Sir Joseph William, 1909–1992, vol. IX
Weld, Reginald Joseph, 1842–1923, vol. II
Weld, Rev. Walter Joseph, 1881–1969, vol. VI
Weld-Blundell, Charles Joseph, 1845–1927, vol. II
Weld-Forester, Hon. Charles Cecil Orlando; *see* Forester.
Weld-Forester, Major Hon. Edric Alfred Cecil; *see* Forester.
Weld-Forester, Lt-Comdr Wolstan Beaumont Charles, 1899–1961, vol. VI
Weldon, Col Sir Anthony Arthur, 6th Bt, 1863–1917, vol. II
Weldon, Sir Anthony Crosdill, 5th Bt, 1827–1900, vol. I
Weldon, Sir Anthony Edward Wolseley, 7th Bt, 1902–1971, vol. VII
Weldon, Lt-Col Ernest Steuart, 1877–1946, vol. IV
Weldon, Major Francis Harry, 1869–1920, vol. II
Weldon, George, 1908–1963, vol. VI
Weldon, Surg.-Rear-Adm. Gerald; *see* Weldon, Surg.-Rear-Adm. S. G.
Weldon, Brig. Hamilton Edward Crosdill, 1910–1985, vol. VIII

Weldon, Surg.-Rear-Adm. (Samuel) Gerald, 1900–1958, vol. V
Weldon, Col Thomas, 1834–1905, vol. I
Weldon, Sir Thomas Brian, 8th Bt, 1905–1979, vol. VII
Weldon, Thomas Dewar, 1896–1958, vol. V
Weldon, Walter Frank Raphael, 1860–1906, vol. I
Weldon, Sir William Henry, 1837–1919, vol. II
Welensky, Rt Hon. Sir Roland, (Sir Roy), 1907–1991, vol. IX
Welensky, Rt Hon. Sir Roy; see Welensky, Rt Hon. Sir Roland.
Welford, Richard, 1836–1919, vol. II
Welford, Walter Thompson, 1916–1990, vol. VIII
Welham, David Richard, 1930–1989, vol. VIII
Welland, Rt Rev. Thomas James, 1830–1907, vol. I
Wellborne, Lt-Col Cyril de Montfort, 1884–1965, vol. VI
Wellcome, Sir Henry, 1853–1936, vol. III
Welldon, Rt Rev. James Edward Cowell, 1854–1937, vol. III
Weller, Major Bernard George, 1881–1941, vol. IV
Weller, Bernard Williams, 1870–1943, vol. IV
Weller, Rt Rev. John Reginald, 1880–1969, vol. VI
Weller, Rt Rev. Reginald Heber, 1857–1935, vol. III
Weller-Poley, Thomas, 1850–1924, vol. II
Welles, (George) Orson, 1915–1985, vol. VIII
Welles, Orson; see Welles, G. O.
Welles, Sumner, 1892–1961, vol. VI
Wellesley, Col Hon. Frederick Arthur, 1844–1931, vol. III
Wellesley, Julian Valerian, 1933–1996, vol. X
Wellesley, Lord George, 1889–1967, vol. VI
Wellesley, Sir George Greville, 1814–1901, vol. I
Wellesley, Lord Richard, 1879–1914, vol. I
Wellesley, Brig.-Gen. Richard Ashmore Colley, 1868–1939, vol. III
Wellesley, Sir Victor Alexander Augustus Henry, 1876–1954, vol. V
Wellesz, Egon Joseph, 1885–1974, vol. VII
Wellings, Milton, 1850–1929, vol. III
Wellington, 3rd Duke of, 1846–1900, vol. I
Wellington, 4th Duke of, 1849–1934, vol. III
Wellington, 5th Duke of, 1876–1941, vol. IV
Wellington, 6th Duke of, 1912–1943, vol. IV
Wellington, 7th Duke of, 1885–1972, vol. VII
Wellington, Arthur Robartes, 1877–1961, vol. VI
Wellington, Gilbert Trevor, 1882–1963, vol. VI
Wellington, Hubert Lindsay, 1879–1967, vol. VI
Wellington, Rt Rev. John, 1889–1976, vol. VII
Wellington, Sir Lindsay; see Wellington, Sir R. E. L.
Wellington, Sir (Reginald Everard) Lindsay, 1901–1985, vol. VIII
Wellish, Edward Montague, 1882–1948, vol. IV
Wellock, Wilfred, 1879–1972, vol. VII
Wells, Arthur Collings, 1857–1922, vol. II
Wells, Arthur Quinton, 1896–1956, vol. V
Wells, Sir Arthur Spencer, 2nd Bt (cr 1883), 1866–1906, vol. I
Wells, Carveth; see Wells, G. C.
Wells, Charles, died 1917, vol. II
Wells, Charles, 1859–1932, vol. III
Wells, Charles Alexander, 1898–1989, vol. VIII
Wells, Sir Charles Maltby, 2nd Bt, 1908–1996, vol. X

Wells, Cyril Mowbray, 1871–1963, vol. VI
Wells, Rear-Adm. David Charles, 1911–1983, vol. VIII
Wells, Denys George, 1881–1973, vol. VII
Wells, Eugene, died 1925, vol. II
Wells, Frederick Arthur, 1901–1971, vol. VII
Wells, Sir Frederick Michael, 1st Bt (cr 1948), 1884–1966, vol. VI
Wells, Rt Rev. George Anderson, 1877–1964, vol. VI
Wells, George Philip, 1901–1985, vol. VIII
Wells, Vice-Adm. Sir Gerard Aylmer, died 1943, vol. IV
Wells, (Grant) Carveth, died 1957, vol. V
Wells, Air Cdre Hardy Vesey, 1877–1956, vol. V
Wells, Lt-Gen. Sir Henry, 1898–1973, vol. VII
Wells, Henry Bensley, 1891–1967, vol. VI
Wells, Henry Tanworth, 1828–1903, vol. I
Wells, Sir Henry Weston, 1911–1971, vol. VII
Wells, Herbert George, 1866–1946, vol. IV
Wells, Lt-Col Herbert James, 1897–1993, vol. IX
Wells, Rev. Herbert Methuen, 1862–1931, vol. III
Wells, Rev. James, 1838–1924, vol. II
Wells, Sister Janet; see King J.
Wells, Brig.-Gen. John Bayford, 1881–1952, vol. V
Wells, John Chancellor, 1936–1998, vol. X
Wells, John Sanderson S.; see Sanderson-Wells.
Wells, Captain John Stanhope Collings, 1880–1918, vol. II
Wells, Major John Stuart Kerr, 1873–1937, vol. III(A), vol. IV
Wells, Joseph, 1855–1929, vol. III
Wells, Rt Rev. Lemuel H., 1841–1936, vol. III
Wells, Captain Sir Lionel de Lautour, 1859–1929, vol. III
Wells, Adm. Sir Lionel Victor, 1884–1965, vol. VI
Wells, Madeline, died 1959, vol. V
Wells, Percy Lawrence, 1891–1964, vol. VI
Wells, Reginald F., 1877–1951, vol. V
Wells, Sir Richard; see Wells, Sir S. R.
Wells, Robert Douglas, 1875–1963, vol. VI
Wells, Sidney Herbert, 1865–1923, vol. II
Wells, Stanley Walter, 1887–1975, vol. VII
Wells, Sir Sydney R.; see Russell-Wells.
Wells, Sir (Sydney) Richard, 1st Bt (cr 1944), 1879–1956, vol. V
Wells, Thomas Bucklin, 1875–1944, vol. IV
Wells, Thomas Grantham, 1901–1943, vol. IV
Wells, Thomas Henry S.; see Sanderson-Wells.
Wells, Sir William Henry, 1871–1933, vol. III
Wells, William Page Atkinson, 1872–1923, vol. II
Wells, William Thomas, 1908–1990, vol. VIII
Wells-Cole, Lt-Col Henry, 1864–1914, vol. I
Wells-Durrant, Frederick Chester, 1864–1934, vol. III
Wells-Pestell, Baron (Life Peer); Reginald Alfred Wells-Pestell, 1910–1991, vol. IX
Wellstood, Frederick Christian, 1884–1942, vol. IV
Wellwood, William, 1893–1971, vol. VII
Welman, Captain Arthur Eric Pole, 1893–1966, vol. VI
Welman, Douglas Pole, 1902–1996, vol. X
Welman, Maj.-Gen. William Henry Dowling Reeves, 1828–1906, vol. I
Welpton, William P., 1872–1939, vol. III

Welsford, Sir Robert Mills, 1861–1933, vol. III
Welsh, Hon. Sir Allan Ross, 1875–1957, vol. V
Welsh, Brig. David, 1908–1987, vol. VIII
Welsh, David Arthur, died 1948, vol. IV
Welsh, Elizabeth, died 1921, vol. II
Welsh, Harry Lambert, 1910–1984, vol. VIII
Welsh, James, 1881–1969, vol. VI
Welsh, James C., 1880–1954, vol. V
Welsh, John, 1887–1950, vol. IV
Welsh, John Aitken, 1871–1940, vol. III
Welsh, Rt Rev. John Francis, died 1916, vol. II
Welsh, Dame Mary; see Welsh, Dame R. M. E.
Welsh, Rev. Robert E., 1857–1935, vol. III
Welsh, Dame (Ruth) Mary (Eldridge), 1896–1986, vol. VIII
Welsh, Rev. Thomas, died 1920, vol. II, vol. III
Welsh, Air Marshal Sir William Lawrie, died 1962, vol. VI
Welsh, Brig. William Miles Moss O'Donnell, 1888–1965, vol. VI
Welsted, Col Reginald Hugh P.; see Penrose-Welsted.
Welton, James, 1854–1942, vol. IV
Welwood, John Allan Maconochie, died 1934, vol. III
Wemyss, 10th Earl of, and March, 6th Earl of, 1818–1914, vol. I
Wemyss, 11th Earl of, and March, 7th Earl of, 1857–1937, vol. III
Wemyss, Gen. Sir Colville; see Wemyss, Gen. Sir H. C. B.
Wemyss, Sir Francis C.; see Colchester-Wemyss.
Wemyss, Gen. Sir (Henry) Colville (Barclay), 1891–1959, vol. V
Wemyss, Maj.-Gen. Henry Manley, 1831–1915, vol. I
Wemyss, Maynard Willoughby C.; see Colchester Wemyss.
Wemyss, Randolph Gordon Erskine, died 1908, vol. I
Wenban-Smith, Charlotte Susanna; see Rycroft, C. S.
Wenban-Smith, William, 1908–2000, vol. X
Wendell, Barrett, 1855–1921, vol. II
Wenden, Henry Charles Edward, died 1919, vol. II
Wendover, Viscount; Albert Edward Samuel Charles Robert Wynn-Carrington, 1895–1915, vol. I
Wendt, Henry Lorenz, 1858–1911, vol. I
Wenger, Adolph Henry Charles, 1877–1954, vol. V
Wenger, Marjorie Lawson, 1910–1981, vol. VIII
Wenham, Brian George, 1937–1997, vol. X
Wenham, Edward Gordon, 1884–1956, vol. V
Wenham, Sir John Henry, 1891–1970, vol. VI
Wenley, Robert Mark, 1861–1929, vol. III
Wenlock, 3rd Baron, 1849–1912, vol. I
Wenlock, 4th Baron, 1856–1918, vol. II
Wenlock, 5th Baron, 1857–1931, vol. III
Wenlock, 6th Baron, 1860–1932, vol. III
Wenlock, Lady; (Annie Allen), died 1944, vol. IV
Wensinck, Arent Jan, 1882–1939, vol. III(A), vol. IV
Went, Rev. James, 1845–1936, vol. III
Wentworth, Baroness (14th in line), 1871–1917, vol. II

Wentworth, Baroness (15th in line), 1837–1917, vol. II
Wentworth, Baroness (16th in line), 1873–1957, vol. V
Wentworth, Captain Bruce Canning V.; see Vernon-Wentworth.
Wentworth, Captain Frederick Charles Ulick V.; see Vernon-Wentworth.
Wentworth, Patricia; see Turnbull, Mrs George.
Wentworth-Fitzwilliam, George Charles; see Fitzwilliam.
Wentworth-Fitzwilliam, Captain Hon. Sir (William) Charles; see Fitzwilliam.
Wentworth-Fitzwilliam, Hon. William Henry; see Fitzwilliam.
Wentworth-Sheilds, Francis Ernest, 1869–1959, vol. V
Wentworth-Sheilds, Rt Rev. Wentworth Francis, 1867–1944, vol. IV
Wentworth-Stanley, Charles Sidney Bowen, 1892–1960, vol. V
Wenyon, Charles Morley, died 1948, vol. IV
Wenyon, Herbert John, 1888–1944, vol. IV
Were, Cecil Allan Walter, 1889–1977, vol. VII
Were, Rt Rev. Edward Ash, 1846–1915, vol. I
Were, Major Harry Harris, 1865–1925, vol. II
Werfel, Franz, 1890–1945, vol. IV
Werner, Alfred, 1866–1919, vol. II
Werner, Alice, 1859–1935, vol. III
Werner, E. A., died 1951, vol. V
Werner, Edward Theodore Chalmers, 1864–1954, vol. V
Werner, Louis, died 1936, vol. III
Wernham, Archibald Garden, 1916–1989, vol. VIII
Wernham, Richard Bruce, 1906–1999, vol. X
Wernher, Sir Derrick Julius, 2nd Bt, 1889–1948, vol. IV
Wernher, Hon. Maj.-Gen. Sir Harold Augustus, 3rd Bt, 1893–1973, vol. VII
Wernher, Sir Julius Charles, 1st Bt, 1850–1912, vol. I
Wertenbaker, Thomas Jefferson, 1879–1966, vol. VI
Werth, Albertus Johannes, 1888–1948, vol. IV
Werth, Alexander, 1901–1969, vol. VI
Wertheimer, Julius, died 1924, vol. II
Wesbrook, F. F., 1868–1918, vol. II
Wessel, Robert Leslie, 1912–1995, vol. IX
Wesselitsky, Gabriel de, 1841–1930, vol. III
Wessels, Hon. Sir Cornelius Hermanus, 1851–1924, vol. II
Wessels, Rt Hon. Sir Johannes Wilhelmus, 1862–1936, vol. III
West, Brig. Alexander Henry Delap, 1877–1959, vol. V
West, Alfred Slater, 1846–1932, vol. III
West, Rt Hon. Sir Algernon, 1832–1921, vol. II
West, Andrew F., 1853–1943, vol. IV
West, Anthony Panther, 1914–1987, vol. VIII
West, Rev. Arthur George Bainbridge, 1864–1952, vol. V
West, Cecil McLaren, 1893–1951, vol. V
West, Charles Ernest, died 1951, vol. V
West, Charles Henry, 1859–1923, vol. II
West, Christopher, 1915–1967, vol. VI
West, Christopher Robin, 1944–1994, vol. IX

West, Maj.-Gen. Clement Arthur, 1892–1972, vol. VII
West, Daniel Granville; *see* Baron Granville-West.
West, David, *died* 1936, vol. III
West, Rev. Edward Courtenay, 1872–1938, vol. III
West, Air Cdre Ferdinand Maurice Felix, 1896–1988, vol. VIII
West, Fielding Reginald, 1892–1935, vol. III
West, Rt Rev. Francis Horner, 1909–1999, vol. X
West, Sir Frederick John, 1897–1971, vol. VII
West, Sir Frederick Joseph, 1872–1959, vol. V
West, Rt Rev. George Algernon, 1893–1930, vol. VII
West, Major George F. M. C.; *see* Cornwallis-West.
West, George Stephen, 1876–1919, vol. II
West, Gladys; *see* Young, G.
West, Sir Glynn Hamilton, 1877–1945, vol. IV
West, Sir Harold Ernest Georges, 1895–1968, vol. VI
West, Sir James Grey, 1885–1951, vol. V
West, John Henry Rickard, 1846–1920, vol. II
West, Col John Milns, 1897–1973, vol. VII
West, Maj.-Gen. John Weir, 1875–1949, vol. IV
West, Joseph Walter, *died* 1933, vol. III
West, Sir Leonard Henry, 1864–1950, vol. IV
West, Leonard R., 1859–1910, vol. I
West, Mary, (Mrs James West); *see* McCarthy, M.
West, Gen. Sir Michael Montgomerie Alston Roberts, 1905–1978, vol. VII
West, Morris Langlo, 1916–1999, vol. X
West, Ralph Winton, 1895–1968, vol. VI
West, Sir Raymond, 1832–1911, vol. I
West, Dame Rebecca, 1892–1983, vol. VIII
West, Samuel, 1848–1920, vol. II
West, Stewart Ellis Lawrence, 1890–1968, vol. VI
West, Hon. V. M. S.; *see* Sackville-West.
West, Sir Walter Wooll, 1861–1952, vol. V
West, William Cornwallis Cornwallis-, 1835–1917, vol. II
West, William Dixon, 1901–1994, vol. IX
West, William Frederick, 1882–1954, vol. V
West-Watson, Most Rev. Campbell West, 1877–1953, vol. V
Westall, Bernard Clement, 1893–1970, vol. VI
Westall, Gen. Sir John Chaddesley, 1901–1986, vol. VIII
Westall, Robert Atkinson, 1929–1993, vol. IX
Westall, Rupert Vyvyan Hawksley, 1899–1992, vol. IX
Westall, Rt Rev. Wilfrid Arthur Edmund, 1900–1982, vol. VIII
Westall, William Bury, 1834–1903, vol. I
Westaway, Katharine Mary, 1893–1973, vol. VII
Westbrook, Bernard Anson, 1884–1969, vol. VI
Westbrook, Trevor Cresswell Lawrence, 1901–1978, vol. VII
Westbury, 3rd Baron, 1852–1930, vol. III
Westbury, 4th Baron, 1914–1961, vol. VI
Westbury, Lt-Col Frederic Newell, 1877–1946, vol. IV
Westbury, Marjorie; *see* Westbury, R. M.
Westbury, (Rose) Marjorie, 1905–1989, vol. VIII
Westcar, Lt-Col Sir William Villiers Leonard P.; *see* Prescott-Westcar.
Westcott, Rt Rev. Brooke Foss, 1825–1901, vol. I

Westcott, Rt Rev. Foss, 1863–1949, vol. IV
Westcott, Ven. Frederick Brooke, 1857–1918, vol. II
Westcott, George Foss, 1893–1987, vol. VIII
Westcott, Rt Rev. George Herbert, *died* 1916, vol. II
Westcott, J. B., *died* 1907, vol. I
Westcott, Col Sinclair, 1859–1923, vol. II
Westcott, William Wynn, 1848–1925, vol. II
Westell, William Percival, 1874–1943, vol. IV
Wester Wemyss, 1st Baron, 1864–1933, vol. III
Westerman, Percy F., 1876–1959, vol. V
Westermann, Diedrich H., 1875–1956, vol. V
Westermarck, Edward Alexander, 1862–1939, vol. III
Western, Lt-Col Bertram Charles Maximilian, 1886–1942, vol. IV
Western, Col Charles Maximilian, *died* 1915, vol. I
Western, Rt Rev. Frederick James, 1880–1951, vol. V
Western, George Trench, 1877–1948, vol. IV
Western, Lt-Col James Halifax, 1842–1917, vol. II
Western, John Henry, 1906–1981, vol. VIII
Western, Col John Sutton Edward, *died* 1931, vol. III
Western, Sir Thomas Charles Callis, 3rd Bt, 1850–1917, vol. II
Western, Maj.-Gen. Sir William George Balfour, 1861–1936, vol. III
Westhoven, Joseph Charles, 1876–1957, vol. V
Westinghouse, George, 1846–1914, vol. I
Westlake, Alan Robert Cecil, 1894–1978, vol. VII
Westlake, Col Almond Paul, 1858–1927, vol. II
Westlake, Sir Charles Redvers, 1900–1972, vol. VII
Westlake, Henry Dickinson, 1906–1992, vol. IX
Westlake, Rev. Herbert Francis, 1879–1925, vol. II
Westlake, John, 1828–1913, vol. I
Westlake, Nathaniel Hubert John, 1833–1921, vol. II
Westland, Sir James, 1842–1903, vol. I
Westley, Lt-Col Joseph Harold Stops, 1882–1959, vol. V
Westmacott, Brig.-Gen. Claude Berners, 1865–1948, vol. IV
Westmacott, Frederic Hibbert, 1867–1935, vol. III
Westmacott, Percy Graham Buchanan, 1830–1917, vol. II
Westmacott, Maj.-Gen. Sir Richard, 1841–1925, vol. II
Westmacott, Rev. Walter, 1853–1939, vol. III
Westmeath, 11th Earl of, 1870–1933, vol. III
Westmeath, 12th Earl of, 1880–1971, vol. VII
Westminster, 1st Duke of, 1825–1899, vol. I
Westminster, 2nd Duke of, 1879–1953, vol. V
Westminster, 3rd Duke of, 1894–1963, vol. VI
Westminster, 4th Duke of, 1907–1967, vol. VI
Westminster, 5th Duke of, 1910–1979, vol. VII
Westminster, Viola Dowager Duchess of; Viola Maud Grosvenor, 1912–1987, vol. VIII
Westmorland, 13th Earl of, 1859–1922, vol. II
Westmorland, 14th Earl of, 1893–1948, vol. IV
Westmorland, 15th Earl of, 1924–1993, vol. IX
Westmorland, Brig.-Gen. Charles Henry, 1856–1916, vol. II
Westmorland, Lt-Col Percy Thuillier, 1863–1929, vol. III
Westoby, Jack Cecil, 1912–1988, vol. VIII

Westoll, James, 1918–1999, vol. X
Westoll, Thomas Stanley, 1912–1995, vol. IX
Weston, Dame Agnes Elizabeth, 1840–1918, vol. II
Weston, Rev. Arthur Ernest, 1890–1971, vol. VII
Weston, Captain Arthur Fullam, 1879–1962, vol. VI
Weston, Sir Arthur Reginald Astley, 1892–1969, vol. VI
Weston, Lt-Gen. Sir Aylmer H.; see Hunter-Weston.
Weston, Bertram John, 1907–1997, vol. X
Weston, Rear-Adm. Charles Arthur Winfield, 1922–1998, vol. X
Weston, Col Claude Horace, 1879–1946, vol. IV
Weston, Sir Eric, 1892–1976, vol. VII
Weston, Lt-Gen. Eric Culpeper, 1888–1950, vol. IV
Weston, Lt-Col Ernest Arthur, 1880–1940, vol. III
Weston, Rt Rev. Frank, 1871–1924, vol. II
Weston, Garfield; see Weston, W. G.
Weston, Geoffrey Harold, 1920–1999, vol. X
Weston, George, 1878–1956, vol. V
Weston, Maj.-Gen. Gerald Patrick Linton, 1910–1977, vol. VII
Weston, Lt-Col Gould H.; see Hunter-Weston.
Weston, Jessie Laidlay, died 1928, vol. II
Weston, John Carruthers, 1917–1999, vol. X
Weston, Air Vice-Marshal Sir John Gerard Willsley, 1908–1979, vol. VII
Weston, Hon. Brig. John Leslie, 1882–1963, vol. VI
Weston, Sir John Wakefield, 1st Bt, 1852–1926, vol. II
Weston, Kenneth Southwold, 1899–1971, vol. VII
Weston, Laurence, 1909–1972, vol. VII
Weston, Lt-Col Reginald Salter, 1867–1944, vol. IV
Weston, Ronald, 1929–1990, vol. VIII
Weston, Brig.-Gen. Spencer Vaughan Percy, 1883–1973, vol. VII
Weston, Rev. Walter, 1861–1940, vol. III
Weston, (Willard) Garfield, 1898–1978, vol. VII
Weston, William Guy, 1907–1980, vol. VII
Weston, Rear-Adm. William Kenneth, 1904–1992, vol. IX
Weston-Stevens, Sir Joseph, 1861–1917, vol. II
Westphal, Bishop Augustus, 1864–1939, vol. III (A), vol. IV
Westrop, Brig. Sidney Albert, 1895–1979, vol. VII
Westropp, Col George O'C.; see O'Callaghan-Westropp.
Westropp, Col George Ralph Collier, 1859–1934, vol. III
Westropp, Col John M.; see Massy-Westropp.
Westropp, Maj.-Gen. Roberts Michael, 1824–1910, vol. I
Westropp, Maj.-Gen. Victor John Eric, 1897–1974, vol. VII
Westrup, Sir Jack Allan, 1904–1975, vol. VII
Westwood, 1st Baron, 1880–1953, vol. V
Westwood, 2nd Baron, 1907–1991, vol. IX
Westwood, Earle Cathers, 1909–1980, vol. VII (AII)
Westwood, John David, 1881–1964, vol. VI
Westwood, Rt Hon. Joseph, 1884–1948, vol. IV
Westwood, Rt Rev. William John, 1925–1999, vol. X
Wetherall, Lt-Gen. Sir Edward; see Wetherall, Lt-Gen. Sir H. E. de R.
Wetherall, Lt-Gen. Sir (Harry) Edward de Robillard, 1889–1979, vol. VII

Wetherall, Rev. Canon Theodore Sumner, 1910–1990, vol. VIII
Wetherall, Col William Alexander, 1847–1935, vol. III
Wetherbee, George, 1851–1920, vol. II
Wethered, Ernest Handel Cossham, 1878–1975, vol. VII
Wethered, Lt-Col Francis Owen, 1864–1922, vol. II
Wethered, Frank Joseph, 1860–1928, vol. II
Wethered, Brig. Herbert Lawrence, 1877–1953, vol. V
Wethered, Col Joseph Robert, 1873–1942, vol. IV
Wethered, Joyce, (Lady Heathcoat Amory), 1901–1997, vol. X
Wethered, Thomas Owen, 1832–1921, vol. II
Wethered, Vernon, 1865–1952, vol. V
Wetherell, Alan Marmaduke, 1932–1998, vol. X
Wetherell, Col Robert May, 1874–1960, vol. V
Wetherill, Henry Buswell, 1876–1959, vol. V
Wethey, Captain Edwin Howard, 1887–1963, vol. VI
Wetmore, Hon. Edward Ludlow, 1841–1922, vol. II
Wetton, Henry Davan, 1862–1928, vol. II
Weyer, Deryk Vander, 1925–1990, vol. VIII
Weygand, Général Maxime, 1867–1965, vol. VI
Weyler y Nicolau, Valeriano, 1838–1930, vol. III
Weyman, Stanley John, 1855–1928, vol. II
Weymouth, Viscount; John Alexander Thynne, 1895–1916, vol. II
Whaite, Col Thomas du Bédat, 1862–1943, vol. IV
Whale, George, 1849–1925, vol. II
Whale, George Harold Lawson, 1876–1943, vol. IV
Whale, Rev. John Seldon, 1896–1997, vol. X
Whale, Philip Barrett, 1898–1950, vol. IV
Whale, Winifred Stephens, died 1944, vol. IV
Whalley, Frank Douglas, 1877–1932, vol. III
Whalley, Philip Guy Rothay, 1901–1950, vol. IV
Whalley, Major Richard Cyril Rae, 1896–1944, vol. IV
Whalley-Tooker, Hyde Charnock, 1900–1992, vol. IX
Wharhirst, Sir Robert William, 1885–1949, vol. IV
Wharncliffe, 1st Earl of, 1827–1899, vol. I
Wharncliffe, 2nd Earl of, 1856–1926, vol. II
Wharncliffe, 3rd Earl of, 1892–1953, vol. V
Wharncliffe, 4th Earl of, 1935–1987, vol. VIII
Wharry, Harry Mortimer, 1891–1933, vol. III
Wharton, 8th Baron, 1876–1934, vol. III
Wharton, 9th Baron, 1908–1969, vol. VI
Wharton, Baroness (10th in line), 1906–1974, vol. VII
Wharton, Baroness (11th in line), 1934–2000, vol. X
Wharton, Anthony, 1877–1943, vol. IV
Wharton, Sir Anthony; see Wharton, Sir G. A.
Wharton, Rev. Edgar, died 1936, vol. III
Wharton, Edith, 1862–1937, vol. III
Wharton, Sir (George) Anthony, 1917–1980, vol. VII
Wharton, Rt Hon. John Lloyd, 1837–1912, vol. I
Wharton, William Henry Anthony, 1859–1938, vol. III
Wharton-Duff, John Wharton; see Duff.
Whately, Ven. Herbert Edward, 1876–1947, vol. IV
Whately, William, died 1937, vol. III

Whateley, Dame Leslie Violet Lucy Evelyn Mary, 1899–1987, vol. VIII
Whates, Harry Richard, *died* 1923, vol. II
Whatham, Rev. William Laurence T., 1866–1938, vol. III
Whatley, Norman, 1884–1965, vol. VI
Whatley, William Henry Potts, 1922–1997, vol. X
Whatman, George Dunbar, 1846–1923, vol. II
Whatman, Col William Douglas, 1860–1929, vol. III
Whatmough, Joshua, 1897–1964, vol. VI
Whayman, Engr Rear-Adm. William Matthias, 1871–1955, vol. V
Wheare, Sir Kenneth Clinton, 1907–1979, vol. VII
Wheatcroft, Edward Lewis Elam, 1896–1982, vol. VIII
Wheatcroft, Rev. Frank Elam, *died* 1930, vol. III
Wheatcroft, George Shorrock Ashcombe, 1905–1987, vol. VIII
Wheatcroft, Harry, 1898–1977, vol. VII
Wheatley, Baron (Life Peer); John Wheatley, 1908–1988, vol. VIII
Wheatley, Sir Andrew; *see* Wheatley, Sir G. A.
Wheatley, Major Cyril Moreton, 1870–1942, vol. IV
Wheatley, Dennis Yates, 1897–1977, vol. VII
Wheatley, Edith Grace, *died* 1970, vol. VI
Wheatley, Frederick William, 1871–1955, vol. V
Wheatley, Sir (George) Andrew, 1908–1991, vol. IX
Wheatley, Henry Benjamin, *died* 1917, vol. II
Wheatley, Col Henry Spencer, 1851–1932, vol. III
Wheatley, Rt Hon. John, 1869–1930, vol. III
Wheatley, John, 1892–1955, vol. V
Wheatley, Joseph Larke, 1846–1932, vol. III
Wheatley, Brig.-Gen. Leonard Lane, 1876–1954, vol. V
Wheatley, Major Sir Mervyn James, 1880–1974, vol. VII
Wheatley, Maj.-Gen. Mervyn Savile, 1900–1979, vol. VII
Wheatley, Col Moreton John, 1837–1916, vol. II
Wheatley, Maj.-Gen. (Percival) Ross, 1909–1988, vol. VIII
Wheatley, Brig.-Gen. Philip, 1871–1935, vol. III
Wheatley, Robert Albert, 1873–1954, vol. V
Wheatley, Maj.-Gen. Ross; *see* Wheatley, Maj.-Gen. P. R.
Wheatley, Major William Prescott Ross, 1878–1925, vol. II
Wheatley, Sir Zachariah, 1865–1950, vol. IV
Wheeldon, Edward Christian, 1907–1980, vol. VII
Wheeldon, Rt Rev. Philip William, 1913–1992, vol. IX
Wheeldon, William Edwin, 1898–1960, vol. V
Wheeler, Rev. Alfred, *died* 1949, vol. IV
Wheeler, Sir Arthur, 1st Bt, 1860–1943, vol. IV
Wheeler, Sir Arthur F. P., 2nd Bt, 1900–1964, vol. VI
Wheeler, Arthur H., *died* 1935, vol. III
Wheeler, Rear-Adm. Aubrey John, 1894–1970, vol. VI
Wheeler, Burton Kendall, 1882–1975, vol. VII
Wheeler, Sir Charles Reginald, 1904–1975, vol. VII
Wheeler, Sir Charles Thomas, 1892–1974, vol. VII
Wheeler, Denis Edward, 1910–1977, vol. VII

Wheeler, Brig. Sir (Edward) Oliver, 1890–1962, vol. VI
Wheeler, Edwin Paul, 1897–1944, vol. IV
Wheeler, Lt-Comdr Sir (Ernest) Richard, 1917–1990, vol. VIII
Wheeler, Sir Frederick Henry, 1914–1994, vol. X (AI)
Wheeler, Geoffrey, 1909–1987, vol. VIII
Wheeler, Lt-Col Geoffrey Edleston, 1897–1990, vol. VIII
Wheeler, Rt Rev. Gordon; *see* Wheeler W. G.
Wheeler, Sir Henry, 1870–1950, vol. IV
Wheeler, Major Henry Littelton, 1868–1924, vol. II
Wheeler, Rev. Hugh Trevor, 1874–1949, vol. IV
Wheeler, Gen. Joseph, 1836–1906, vol. I
Wheeler, Hon. Sir Kenneth Henry, 1912–1996, vol. X
Wheeler, Michael Mortimer, 1915–1992, vol. IX
Wheeler, Sir Mortimer; *see* Wheeler, Sir R. E. M.
Wheeler, Maj.-Gen. Norman; *see* Wheeler, Maj.-Gen. T. N. S.
Wheeler, Dame Olive Annie, *died* 1963, vol. VI
Wheeler, Brig. Sir Oliver; *see* Wheeler, Brig. Sir E. O.
Wheeler, Brig. Ralph Pung, 1898–1977, vol. VII
Wheeler, Lt-Comdr Sir Richard; *see* Wheeler, Lt-Comdr Sir E. R.
Wheeler, Maj.-Gen. Richard Henry Littleton, 1906–1994, vol. IX
Wheeler, Richard Vernon, 1883–1939, vol. III
Wheeler, Sir (Robert Eric) Mortimer, 1890–1976, vol. VII
Wheeler, Rev. Thomas Littleton, 1834–1910, vol. I
Wheeler, Maj.-Gen. (Thomas) Norman (Samuel), 1915–1990, vol. VIII
Wheeler, Thomas Sherlock, 1899–1962, vol. VI
Wheeler, Thomas Whittenbury, *died* 1923, vol. II
Wheeler, William, *died* 1926, vol. II
Wheeler, Rt Rev. (William) Gordon, 1910–1998, vol. X
Wheeler, William Henry, 1907–2000, vol. X
Wheeler, Sir William Ireland de Courcy, 1879–1943, vol. IV
Wheeler-Bennett, John Wheeler, *died* 1926, vol. II
Wheeler-Bennett, Sir John Wheeler, 1902–1975, vol. VII
Wheeler-Cuffe, Sir Charles Frederick Denny; *see* Cuffe.
Wheeler-Cuffe, Sir Otway Fortescue Luke; *see* Cuffe.
Wheelock, Frank E., 1877–1941, vol. IV
Wheelwright, Charles Apthorpe, 1873–1954, vol. V
Wheelwright, Rowland, 1870–1955, vol. V
Wheen, Rear-Adm. Charles Kerr Thorneycroft, 1912–1989, vol. VIII
Whelan, Air Cdre James Roger, 1914–1985, vol. VIII
Whelan, Leo, 1892–1956, vol. V
Whelan, Robert Ford, 1922–1984, vol. VIII
Wheldon, Sir Huw Pyrs, 1916–1986, vol. VIII
Wheldon, Robert William, 1893–1954, vol. V
Wheldon, Sir Wynn Powell, 1879–1961, vol. VI
Wheler, Sir Edward, 12th Bt (*cr* 1660), 1857–1903, vol. I

867

Wheler, Sir Granville Charles Hastings, 1st Bt (*cr* 1925), 1872–1927, vol. II
Wheler, Sir Trevor, 11th Bt (*cr* 1660), 1828–1900, vol. I
Wheler, Captain Sir Trevor Wood, 13th Bt, 1889–1986, vol. VIII
Whelpton, Rev. Henry Urling, 1860–1935, vol. III
Wherry, George Edward, 1852–1928, vol. II
Whetham, Rear-Adm. Edye Kington B.; *see* Boddam-Whetham.
Whetham, Major Sydney A. B.; *see* Boddam-Whetham.
Whettnall, Baron Edward Charles Stephen, 1840–1903, vol. I
Whetton, John Thomas, 1894–1979, vol. VII
Whewell, Charles Smalley, 1912–1995, vol. IX
Whewell, Herbert, 1863–1951, vol. V
Whibley, Charles, 1859–1930, vol. III
Whibley, Leonard, 1863–1941, vol. IV
Whichcote, Sir George, 9th Bt, 1870–1946, vol. IV
Whichcote, Sir Hugh Christopher, 10th Bt, 1874–1949, vol. IV
Whidden, Howard Primrose, 1871–1952, vol. V
Whiddington, Richard, 1885–1970, vol. VI
Whigham, Gen. Sir Robert Dundas, 1865–1950, vol. IV
Whigham, Walter Kennedy, 1878–1948, vol. IV
Whillis, James, 1900–1955, vol. V
Whinney, Sir Arthur, 1865–1927, vol. II
Whinney, Margaret Dickens, 1897–1975, vol. VII
Whipham, Thomas Rowland Charles, 1871–1945, vol. IV
Whipham, Thomas Tillyer, *died* 1917, vol. II
Whipple, Dorothy, *died* 1966, vol. VI
Whipple, Francis John Welsh, 1876–1943, vol. IV
Whipple, George Hoyt, 1878–1976, vol. VII
Whipple, Rt Rev. Henry Benjamin, 1823–1901, vol. I
Whipple, Robert Stewart, 1871–1953, vol. V
Whishaw, Sir Ralph, 1895–1976, vol. VII
Whiskard, Sir Geoffrey Granville, 1886–1957, vol. V
Whistler, Sir (Alan Charles) Laurence, 1912–2000, vol. X
Whistler, Maj.-Gen. Alwyne Michael Webster, 1909–1993, vol. IX
Whistler, Rev. Charles Watts, 1856–1913, vol. I
Whistler, Group Captain Harold Alfred, 1896–1940, vol. III
Whistler, James Abbott McNeill, 1834–1903, vol. I
Whistler, Gen. Sir Lashmer Gordon, 1898–1963, vol. VI
Whistler, Sir Laurence; *see* Whistler, Sir A. C. L.
Whistler, Maj.-Gen. Michael; *see* Whistler, Maj.-Gen. A. M. W.
Whiston, Peter Rice, 1912–1999, vol. X
Whitaker, Col Sir Albert Edward, 1st Bt, 1860–1945, vol. IV
Whitaker, Sir Arthur; *see* Whitaker, Sir F. A.
Whitaker, Charles Kenneth, 1919–1981, vol. VIII
Whitaker, Sir Cuthbert Wilfrid, 1873–1950, vol. IV
Whitaker, Edgar, *died* 1903, vol. I
Whitaker, (Edgar) Haddon, 1908–1982, vol. VIII
Whitaker, Enid Rosamond, (Mrs G. C. F. Whitaker); *see* Love, E. R.

Whitaker, Ernest Gillett, 1903–1975, vol. VII
Whitaker, Frank, *died* 1962, vol. VI
Whitaker, Frank Howard, 1909–1987, vol. VIII
Whitaker, Sir (Frederick) Arthur, 1893–1968, vol. VI
Whitaker, Major George Cecil, 1880–1959, vol. V
Whitaker, George Herbert, 1862–1933, vol. III
Whitaker, Haddon; *see* Whitaker, E. H.
Whitaker, James, 1863–1946, vol. IV
Whitaker, Sir James Herbert Ingham, 3rd Bt, 1925–1999, vol. X
Whitaker, Sir James Smith, 1866–1936, vol. III
Whitaker, Maj.-Gen. Sir John Albert Charles, 2nd Bt, 1897–1957, vol. V
Whitaker, William, 1836–1925, vol. II
Whitaker, William Ingham, 1866–1936, vol. III
Whitamore, Charles Eric, 1890–1965, vol. VI
Whitbread, Francis Pelham, 1867–1941, vol. IV
Whitbread, Col Sir Howard, 1836–1908, vol. I
Whitbread, Samuel, 1830–1915, vol. I
Whitbread, Samuel Howard, 1858–1944, vol. IV
Whitbread, Major Simon, 1904–1985, vol. VIII
Whitbread, William Henry, 1900–1994, vol. IX
Whitburgh, 1st Baron, 1874–1967, vol. VI
Whitby, Anthony Charles, 1929–1975, vol. VII
Whitby, Beatrice Janie, *died* 1931, vol. III
Whitby, Sir Bernard James, 1892–1973, vol. VII
Whitby, G. Stafford, 1887–1972, vol. VII
Whitby, Harry, 1910–1984, vol. VIII
Whitby, Sir Lionel Ernest Howard, 1895–1956, vol. V
Whitby, Lionel Gordon, 1926–2000, vol. X
Whitby, Rev. Thomas, 1835–1918, vol. II
Whitby-Smith, Henry, 1858–1934, vol. III
Whitchurch, Major Harry Frederick, 1866–1907, vol. I
Whitcombe, Maj.-Gen. Philip Sidney, 1893–1989, vol. VIII
Whitcombe, Rt Rev. Robert Henry, 1862–1922, vol. II
White, Baroness (Life Peer); Eirene Lloyd White, 1909–1999, vol. X
White of Hull, Baron (Life Peer); Vincent Gordon Lindsay White, 1923–1995, vol. IX
White, Adam Seaton, *died* 1950, vol. IV
White, Adrian Nicholas S.; *see* Sherwin-White.
White, Alan Richard, 1922–1992, vol. IX
White, Hon. Albert Scott, 1855–1931, vol. III
White, Alexander Hay, 1898–1975, vol. VII
White, Sir (Alfred Edward) Rowden, 1876–1963, vol. VI
White, Alfred George Hastings, 1859–1945, vol. IV
White, Hon. Sir Alfred John, 1902–1987, vol. VIII
White, Amber B.; *see* Blanco White.
White, Andrew Dickson, 1832–1918, vol. II
White, Anne Margaret Wilson, 1916–1976, vol. VII
White, Antonia, 1899–1980, vol. VII
White, Sir Archibald Woollaston, 4th Bt (*cr* 1802), 1877–1945, vol. IV
White, Col Archie Cecil Thomas, 1891–1971, vol. VII
White, Arnold, 1848–1925, vol. II
White, Sir Arnold; *see* White, Sir C. A.
White, Ven. Arthur, 1880–1961, vol. VI
White, Lt-Col Arthur Denham, 1879–1950, vol. IV

White, Arthur John Stanley, 1896–1991, vol. IX
White, Arthur Silva, 1859–1932, vol. III
White, Maj.-Gen. Arthur Thomas, 1860–1947, vol. IV
White, Brig. Arthur W.; *see* Walmesley White.
White, Aubrey, *died* 1915, vol. II
White, Sir Bernard Kerr, 1888–1964, vol. VI
White, Sir Bruce Gordon, 1885–1983, vol. VIII
White, Gen. Sir Brudenell; *see* White, Gen. Sir C. B. B.
White, Maj.-Gen. Cecil Meadows Frith, 1897–1985, vol. VIII
White, Cedric Masey, 1898–1993, vol. IX
White, Sir (Charles) Arnold, 1858–1931, vol. III
White, Charles Francis, 1890–1966, vol. VI
White, Charles Frederick, 1863–1923, vol. II
White, Charles Frederick, 1891–1956, vol. V
White, Major Hon. Charles James, 1860–1930, vol. III
White, Major Charles James B.; *see* Brooman-White.
White, Charles Percival, *died* 1928, vol. II
White, Charles Powell, 1867–1930, vol. III
White, Claude G.; *see* Graham-White.
White, Clifford, 1881–1957, vol. V
White, Gen. Sir (Cyril) Brudenell (Bingham), 1876–1940, vol. III
White, Cyril Grove C.; *see* Costley-White.
White, Cyril Montgomery, 1897–1980, vol. VII
White, Lt-Col David Archibald P.; *see* Price-White.
White, Sir Dennis Charles, 1910–1983, vol. VIII
White, Sir Dick Goldsmith, 1906–1993, vol. IX
White, Dudley, 1873–1930, vol. III
White, Sir Edward, 1847–1914, vol. I
White, Edward, *died* 1952, vol. V
White, Brig.-Gen. Edward Dalrymple, 1865–1929, vol. III
White, Edwin George, 1911–1988, vol. VIII
White, (Elizabeth) Evelyne (McIntosh), *died* 1972, vol. VII
White, Elwyn Brooks, 1899–1985, vol. VIII
White, Sir Eric Henry W.; *see* Wyndham White.
White, Very Rev. Eric M.; *see* Milner-White.
White, Sir (Eric) Richard Meadows, 2nd Bt (*cr* 1937), 1910–1972, vol. VII
White, Brig. Eric Stuart, 1888–1979, vol. VII
White, Erica, 1904–1991, vol. IX
White, Sir Ernest, 1867–1949, vol. IV
White, Sir Ernest Keith, 1892–1983, vol. VIII
White, Lt-Col Ernest William, 1851–1935, vol. III
White, Errol Ivor, 1901–1985, vol. VIII
White, Ethelbert, 1891–1972, vol. VII
White, Evelyne; *see* White, Elizabeth E. M.
White, Col Frank Augustin Kinder, 1873–1948, vol. IV
White, Frank Faulder, 1861–1939, vol. III
White, Lt-Col Frederick, 1847–1918, vol. II
White, Col Frederick, 1861–1924, vol. II
White, Major Frederick Alexander, 1872–1919, vol. II
White, Frederick Meadows, 1829–1898, vol. I
White, Major Frederick Norman, 1877–1964, vol. VI
White, Sir Frederick William George, 1905–1994, vol. IX

White, Gabriel Ernest Edward Francis, 1902–1988, vol. VIII
White, Geoffrey Charles, 1912–1961, vol. VI
White, Geoffrey Henllan, 1873–1969, vol. VI
White, Maj.-Gen. Geoffrey Herbert Anthony, 1870–1959, vol. V
White, Sir George, 1840–1912, vol. I
White, Sir George, 1st Bt (*cr* 1904), 1854–1916, vol. II
White, Brig.-Gen. George Francis, *died* 1938, vol. III
White, Brig. George Frederick Charles, 1882–1953, vol. V
White, George Gilbert, 1857–1916, vol. II
White, Air Vice-Marshal George Holford, 1904–1965, vol. VI
White, George Rivers Blanco, 1883–1966, vol. VI
White, Sir (George) Stanley, 2nd Bt (*cr* 1904), 1882–1964, vol. VI
White, Sir George Stanley Midelton, 3rd Bt, 1913–1983, vol. VIII
White, Field-Marshal Sir George Stuart, 1835–1912, vol. I
White, Col Hon. Gerald Verner, 1879–1948, vol. IV
White, Rt Rev. Gilbert, 1859–1933, vol. III
White, Gleeson, 1851–1898, vol. I
White, Lt-Col Sir Godfrey Dalrymple D.; *see* Dalrymple-White.
White, Ven. Graham, *born* 1884, vol. IV
White, Rt Hon. Graham; *see* White, Rt Hon. H. G.
White, Very Rev. Harold C.; *see* Costley-White.
White, Lt-Col Harold Fletcher, 1883–1971, vol. VII
White, Sir Harold Leslie, 1905–1992, vol. IX
White, Rt Rev. Harry Vere, 1853–1941, vol. IV
White, Sir Headley Dymoke, 3rd Bt (*cr* 1922), 1914–1971, vol. VII
White, Henrietta Margaret, *died* 1936, vol. III
White, Henry, 1850–1927, vol. II
White, Henry, 1890–1964, vol. VI
White, Sir Henry Arthur, 1849–1922, vol. II
White, Henry Bantry, *died* 1929, vol. III
White, Surg. Rear-Adm. Sir Henry Ellis Yeo, 1888–1976, vol. VII
White, Hon. Henry Frederic, 1859–1903, vol. I
White, Maj.-Gen. Henry George, 1835–1906, vol. I
White, Rt Hon. (Henry) Graham, *died* 1965, vol. VI
White, Lt-Col Henry Herbert Ronald, 1879–1939, vol. III
White, Henry James, 1898–1961, vol. VI
White, Very Rev. Henry Julian, 1859–1934, vol. III
White, Sir Henry M.; *see* Milner-White.
White, Herbert Arthur, 1876–1958, vol. V
White, Sir Herbert Edward, 1855–1947, vol. IV
White, Herbert Martyn Oliver, 1885–1963, vol. VI
White, Maj.-Gen. Herbert Southey Neville, 1862–1938, vol. III
White, Sir Herbert Thirkell, 1855–1931, vol. III
White, Horace, 1834–1916, vol. II
White, Horace Powell W.; *see* Winsbury-White.
White, Hugh Fortescue Moresby, 1891–1979, vol. VII
White, Air Vice-Marshal Hugh Granville, 1898–1983, vol. VIII
White, James, 1878–1927, vol. II
White, James, 1863–1928, vol. II

White, James, 1908–1988, vol. VIII
White, James, 1937–1994, vol. IX
White, James Charles Napoleon, *died* 1923, vol. II
White, James Cobb, 1855–1927, vol. II
White, J(ames) Dundas, 1866–1951, vol. V
White, Col James G.; *see* Grove-White.
White, James Martin, 1857–1928, vol. II
White, James William, 1850–1916, vol. II
White, Jessie, 1865–1958, vol. V
White, John, 1839–1912, vol. I
White, Hon. John, 1852–1922, vol. II
White, John, 1851–1933, vol. III(A), vol. IV
White, Instr Captain John, 1870–1934, vol. III
White, Rt Rev. John, 1867–1951, vol. V
White, John Alan, 1905–1991, vol. IX
White, John B.; *see* Bazley-White.
White, Lt-Col John Baker, 1902–1988, vol. VIII
White, John Bell, 1857–1934, vol. III
White, Maj.-Gen. John Burton, 1874–1945, vol. IV
White, John Claude, *died* 1918, vol. II
White, Lt-Col John Henry, 1868–1942, vol. IV
White, Maj.-Gen. John Hubbard, 1834–1910, vol. I
White, John W., *died* 1919, vol. II
White, John Williams, 1849–1917, vol. II
White, Joseph Henry Lachlan, 1859–1940, vol. III
White, Lt-Col Joshua Chaytor, 1864–1924, vol. II
White, Kenneth James Macarthur, 1894–1969,
   vol. VI
White, Leslie Gordon, 1889–1979, vol. VII
White, Sir Luke, 1845–1920, vol. II
White, Margaret B.; *see* Bourke-White.
White, Maude Valérie, 1855–1937, vol. III
White, Lt-Gen. Sir Maurice Fitzgibbon G.; *see*
   Grove-White.
White, Michael James Denham, 1910–1983,
   vol. VIII
White, Air Vice-Marshal Michael William Langtry,
   1915–1984, vol. VIII
White, Montagu, *died* 1916, vol. II
White, Maj.-Gen. Napier; *see* White, Maj.-Gen.
   P. N.
White, Rev. Newport John Davis, 1860–1936,
   vol. III
White, Norman Lewis, *died* 1978, vol. VII
White, Lt-Col Oliver Woodhouse, 1884–1940,
   vol. III
White, Oswald, 1884–1970, vol. VI
White, P. Bruce, *died* 1949, vol. IV
White, Patrick Victor Martindale, 1912–1990,
   vol. VIII
White, Paul Dudley, 1886–1973, vol. VII
White, Maj.-Gen. (Percival) Napier, 1901–1982,
   vol. VIII
White, Percy, 1852–1938, vol. III
White, Maj.-Gen. Percy C.; *see* Carr-White.
White, Philip Jacob, *died* 1929, vol. III
White, Raymond Walter Ralph, 1923–1998, vol. X
White, Col Reginald Strelley Moresby, 1893–1947,
   vol. IV
White, Sir Richard, *died* 1925, vol. II
White, Sir Richard; *see* White, Sir E. R. M.
White, Richard Charles B.; *see* Brooman-White.
White, Adm. Richard Dunning, 1813–1899, vol. I
White, Richard Hamilton Hayden, 1939–1998,
   vol. X

White, Col Richard Stephen Murray, 1876–1942,
   vol. IV
White, Captain Richard Taylor, 1908–1995, vol. IX
White, Vice-Adm. Richard William, 1849–1924,
   vol. II
White, Sir Robert, 1827–1902, vol. I
White, Brig.-Gen. Hon. Robert, 1861–1936, vol. III
White, Robert, 1872–1959, vol. V
White, Sir Robert Eaton, 1st Bt (*cr* 1937),
   1864–1940, vol. III
White, Robert George, 1885–1976, vol. VII
White, Robert George, 1917–1982, vol. VIII
White, Lt-Col Robert L; *see* Lynch-White.
White, Robert Prosser, 1855–1934, vol. III
White, Robert S.; *see* Standish-White.
White, Roger Lowrey, 1928–2000, vol. X
White, Sir Rowden; *see* White, Sir A. E. R.
White, Sir Rudolph Dymoke, 2nd Bt (*cr* 1922),
   1888–1968, vol. VI
White, Rt Rev. Russell Berridge, 1896–1978,
   vol. VII
White, Captain Samuel Albert, 1870–1954, vol. V
White, Lt-Col Samuel Robert Llewellyn,
   1863–1925, vol. II
White, Sinclair, 1858–1920, vol. II
White, Stanford, 1853–1906, vol. I
White, Sir Stanley; *see* White, Sir G. S.
White, Stuart Arthur Frank, *died* 1951, vol. V
White, Sir Sydney Arthur, 1884–1958, vol. V
White, T. Charters, 1828–1916, vol. II
White, Terence de Vere, 1912–1994, vol. IX
White, Terence Hanbury, 1906–1964, vol. VI
White, Sir Thomas, *died* 1938, vol. III
White, Rt Hon. Sir Thomas; *see* White, Rt Hon. Sir
   W. T.
White, Sir Thomas Astley Woollaston, 5th Bt (*cr*
   1802), 1904–1996, vol. X
White, Thomas Cyril, 1911–1981, vol. VIII
White, Group Captain Hon. Sir Thomas Walter,
   1888–1957, vol. V
White, Sir Thomas Woollaston, 3rd Bt (*cr* 1802),
   1828–1907, vol. I
White, Wilbert Webster, 1863–1944, vol. IV
White, Brig.-Gen. Wilfred Arthur, 1870–1935,
   vol. III
White, Wilfrid H.; *see* Hyde White.
White, William, *died* 1912, vol. I
White, Rt Rev. William Charles, 1865–1943,
   vol. IV
White, Rt Rev. William Charles, 1873–1960, vol. V
White, Sir William H.; *see* Hale-White.
White, William Hale, 1831–1913, vol. I
White, William Harry, 1851–1914, vol. I
White, Sir William Henry, 1845–1913, vol. I
White, Col William Lambert, 1849–1929, vol. III
White, Brig.-Gen. William Lewis, 1856–1931,
   vol. III
White, William Lindsay, 1900–1973, vol. VII
White, Brig. William Nicholas, 1879–1951, vol. V
White, William Rogerson, 1850–1913, vol. I
White, Rt Hon. Sir (William) Thomas, 1866–1955,
   vol. V
White, Col William Westropp, 1862–1927, vol. II
White, Rev. Wilson Woodhouse, 1864–1941,
   vol. IV

White, Sir Woolmer Rudolph Donati, 1st Bt (*cr* 1922), 1858–1931, vol. III
White-Jervis, Sir Henry Felix Jervis; *see* Jervis.
White-Jervis, Col Sir John Henry Jervis; *see* Jervis.
White-Smith, Sir Henry, 1878–1943, vol. IV
White-Thomson, Col Sir Hugh Davie, 1866–1922, vol. II
White-Thomson, Very Rev. Ian Hugh, 1904–1997, vol. X
White-Thomson, Rt Rev. Leonard Jauncey, 1863–1933, vol. III
White-Thomson, Col Sir Robert Thomas, 1831–1918, vol. II
White-Winton, Meryon, *died* 1921, vol. II
Whiteaves, Joseph Frederick, 1835–1909, vol. I
Whitechurch, Rev. Victor Lorenzo, 1868–1933, vol. III
Whitefoord, Rev. Canon Benjamin, 1848–1911, vol. I
Whitefoord, Maj.-Gen. Philip Geoffrey, 1894–1975, vol. VII
Whitehead, Alfred North, 1861–1947, vol. IV
Whitehead, Arnold Sydney, 1895–1966, vol. VI
Whitehead, Arthur Longley, *died* 1930, vol. III
Whitehead, Sir Charles, 1834–1912, vol. I
Whitehead, Rt Rev. Cortlandt, 1842–1922, vol. II
Whitehead, Sir Edgar Cuthbert Fremantle, 1905–1971, vol. VII
Whitehead, Comdr Edward, 1908–1978, vol. VII
Whitehead, Frank Henry, 1918–1988, vol. VIII
Whitehead, Vice-Adm. Frederic Aubrey, 1874–1958, vol. V
Whitehead, Frederick, *died* 1938, vol. III
Whitehead, Sir George Hugh, 2nd Bt, 1861–1931, vol. III
Whitehead, George Sydney, 1915–1998, vol. X
Whitehead, Maj.-Gen. Sir Hayward Reader, 1855–1925, vol. II
Whitehead, Henry, 1842–1921, vol. II
Whitehead, Sir Henry, 1859–1928, vol. II
Whitehead, Rt Rev. Henry, 1853–1947, vol. IV
Whitehead, Sir James, 1st Bt, 1834–1917, vol. II
Whitehead, James, *died* 1936, vol. III
Whitehead, Brig. James, 1880–1955, vol. V
Whitehead, Sir James Beethom, 1858–1928, vol. II
Whitehead, Col James Buckley, 1898–1983, vol. VIII
Whitehead, John Henry Constantine, 1904–1960, vol. V
Whitehead, Col John Herbert, 1869–1928, vol. II
Whitehead, Major Sir Philip Henry Rathbone, 4th Bt, 1897–1953, vol. V
Whitehead, Maj.-Gen. Robert Children, 1833–1905, vol. I
Whitehead, Sir Rowland Edward, 3rd Bt, 1863–1942, vol. IV
Whitehead, Rev. Silvester, 1841–1917, vol. II
Whitehead, Spencer, 1845–1922, vol. II
Whitehead, Thomas Alec, 1886–1959, vol. V
Whitehead, Thomas Henderson, 1851–1933, vol. III
Whitehead, Lt-Col Wilfred James, 1873–1934, vol. III
Whitehead, Lt-Col Wilfrid Arthur, 1898–1981, vol. VIII
Whitehill, Clarence Eugene, 1871–1932, vol. III

Whitehorn, Joseph Hammond, 1861–1935, vol. III
Whitehorn, Rev. Roy Drummond, 1891–1976, vol. VII
Whitehorne, James Charles, *died* 1905, vol. I
Whitehouse, Arthur Wildman, 1865–1944, vol. IV
Whitehouse, Cyril John Arthur, 1913–1982, vol. VIII
Whitehouse, Sir George, 1857–1938, vol. III
Whitehouse, Sir Harold Beckwith, 1882–1943, vol. IV
Whitehouse, John Howard, 1873–1955, vol. V
Whitehouse, Sir Julian Osborn, 1876–1942, vol. IV
Whitehouse, Rev. Owen Charles, 1849–1916, vol. II
Whitehouse, Wallace Edward, 1882–1963, vol. VI
Whitehouse, William Edward, 1859–1935, vol. III
Whitehouse, Major William Henry, 1873–1963, vol. VI
Whiteing, Richard, 1840–1928, vol. II
Whitelaw, 1st Viscount, 1918–1999, vol. X
Whitelaw, Alexander, 1862–1938, vol. III
Whitelaw, Anne Watt, 1875–1966, vol. VI
Whitelaw, David, 1876–1971, vol. VII
Whitelaw, Græme Alexander Lockhart, 1863–1928, vol. II
Whitelaw, Maj.-Gen. John Stewart, 1894–1964, vol. VI
Whitelaw, Robert Pender, 1865–1934, vol. III
Whitelaw, Thomas, 1840–1917, vol. II
Whitelaw, William, 1868–1946, vol. IV
Whitelegge, Sir (B.) Arthur, 1852–1933, vol. III
Whiteley, Cecil, 1875–1942, vol. IV
Whiteley, Frank, 1856–1933, vol. III
Whiteley, Maj.-Gen. Gerald Abson, 1915–1997, vol. X
Whiteley, Sir Gerald Charles, 1891–1958, vol. V
Whiteley, Sir Herbert Huntington-, 1st Bt, 1857–1936, vol. III
Whiteley, Captain Sir (Herbert) Maurice H.; *see* Huntington-Whiteley.
Whiteley, Gen. Sir John Francis Martin, 1896–1970, vol. VI
Whiteley, Brig. John Percival, *died* 1943, vol. VI
Whiteley, Martha Annie, 1866–1956, vol. V
Whiteley, Wilfrid, 1882–1970, vol. VI
Whiteley, Rt Hon. William, 1882–1955, vol. V
Whitelock, Dorothy, 1901–1982, vol. VIII
Whitelocke, R. Henry Anglin, 1861–1927, vol. II
Whiteman, Anne; *see* Whiteman, E. A. O.
Whiteman, (Elizabeth) Anne (Osborn), 1918–2000, vol. X
Whiteman, George W., 1903–1974, vol. VII
Whiteman, William Meredith, 1905–1989, vol. VIII
Whiteside, Borras Noel Hamilton, 1903–1948, vol. IV
Whiteside, Sir Cuthbert William, 1880–1969, vol. VI(AII)
Whiteside, Surg. Rear-Adm. Henry Cadman, *died* 1949, vol. IV
Whiteside, Most Rev. Thomas, 1857–1921, vol. II
Whiteway, Ronald Harry Clift, 1885–1951, vol. V
Whiteway, Rt Hon. Sir William Vallance, 1828–1908, vol. I
Whitfeld, Hubert Edwin, 1875–1939, vol. III
Whitfield, Arthur, *died* 1947, vol. IV

Whitfield, Sir Cecil Vincent W.; *see* Wallace Whitfield.
Whitfield, George, 1891–1983, vol. VIII
Whitfield, Rev. George Joshua Newbold, 1909–2000, vol. X
Whitfield, John Humphreys, 1906–1995, vol. IX
Whitfield, Maj.-Gen. John Yeldham, 1899–1971, vol. VII
Whitfield-Jackson, John; *see* Jackson, J. W.
Whitford, Air Vice-Marshal Sir John, 1893–1966, vol. VI
Whitham, Rev. Arthur Richard, 1863–1930, vol. III
Whitham, Gilbert Shaw, 1889–1970, vol. VI
Whitham, Lt-Gen. John Lawrence, 1881–1952, vol. V
Whitham, Air Cdre Robert Parker Musgrave, 1895–1943, vol. IV
Whiting, Arthur John, *died* 1941, vol. IV
Whiting, Rev. Charles Edwin, 1871–1953, vol. V
Whiting, Frederic, *died* 1962, vol. VI
Whiting, John Robert, 1917–1963, vol. VI
Whiting, Maurice Henry, 1885–1984, vol. VIII
Whiting, William Henry, 1854–1927, vol. II
Whiting, William Robert Gerald, 1884–1947, vol. IV
Whiting, Winifred Ada, 1898–1979, vol. VII
Whitington, Ven. Frederick Taylor, 1853–1938, vol. III
Whitla, Sir William, 1851–1933, vol. III
Whitley, Brig.-Gen. Sir Edward Nathan, 1873–1966, vol. VI
Whitley, Very Rev. Henry Charles, 1906–1976, vol. VII
Whitley, Rt Rev. Jabez Cornelius, 1837–1904, vol. I
Whitley, Rt Hon. John Henry, 1866–1935, vol. III
Whitley, Air Marshal Sir John René, 1905–1997, vol. X
Whitley, John Robinson, 1843–1922, vol. II
Whitley, Kate Mary, *died* 1920, vol. II
Whitley, Sir Michael Henry, 1872–1959, vol. V
Whitley, Sir Norman Henry Pownall, 1883–1957, vol. V
Whitley, William Thomas, 1858–1942, vol. IV
Whitley, William Thomas, 1861–1947, vol. IV
Whitley-Jones, Ernest, 1890–1965, vol. VI
Whitley-Thomson, Sir Frederick Whitley, 1851–1925, vol. II
Whitlock, Brand, 1869–1934, vol. III
Whitlock, Col George Frederic Ashford, 1868–1936, vol. III
Whitman, Alfred Charles, 1860–1910, vol. I
Whitman, Sidney, *died* 1925, vol. II
Whitmarsh, Gerald Edward Leaman, 1908–1980, vol. VII (AII)
Whitmarsh, Rev. Robert Thomas, *died* 1921, vol. II
Whitmee, Harold James Conder, 1901–1954, vol. V
Whitmore, Charles Algernon, 1851–1908, vol. I
Whitmore, Francis, 1903–1975, vol. VII
Whitmore, Col Sir Francis Henry Douglas Charlton, 1st Bt, 1872–1962, vol. VI
Whitmore, Hon. Col Sir George Stoddart, 1830–1903, vol. I
Whitnall, S. E., 1876–1950, vol. IV
Whitney, Sir Benjamin, 1833–1916, vol. II
Whitney, Caspar, 1864–1929, vol. III

Whitney, Sir Cecil Arthur, 1862–1956, vol. V
Whitney, George, 1885–1963, vol. VI
Whitney, Harry Payne, 1872–1930, vol. III
Whitney, Henry Ernest William F.; *see* Fetherstonhaugh-Whitney.
Whitney, Hon. Sir James Pliny, 1843–1914, vol. I
Whitney, James Pounder, 1857–1939, vol. III
Whitney, John Hay, 1904–1982, vol. VIII
Whitney, William Collins, 1841–1904, vol. I
Whitney, William Dwight, 1899–1973, vol. VII
Whitney-Smith, E., 1880–1952, vol. V
Whitsey, Rt Rev. Hubert Victor, 1916–1987, vol. VIII
Whitsey, Rt Rev. Victor; *see* Whitsey, Rt Rev. H. V.
Whitson, Sir Thomas Barnby, 1869–1948, vol. IV
Whittaker, Arnold, 1900–1984, vol. VIII
Whittaker, Sir Edmund Taylor, 1873–1956, vol. V
Whittaker, John Macnaghten, 1905–1984, vol. VIII
Whittaker, Sir (Joseph) Meredith, 1914–1984, vol. VIII
Whittaker, Sir Meredith; *see* Whittaker, Sir J. M.
Whittaker, Sir Meredith Thompson, 1841–1931, vol. III
Whittaker, Maj.-Gen. Robert Frederick Edward, 1894–1967, vol. VI
Whittaker, Thomas, 1856–1935, vol. III
Whittaker, Rt Hon. Sir Thomas Palmer, 1850–1919, vol. II
Whittaker, William Gillies, 1876–1944, vol. IV
Whittaker, William Joseph, 1868–1931, vol. III
Whittall, Sir (James) William, 1838–1910, vol. I
Whittall, Lionel Harry, 1907–1977, vol. VII
Whittall, Lt-Col Percival Frederick, 1877–1943, vol. IV
Whittall, Sir William; *see* Whittall, Sir J. W.
Whittard, Walter Frederick, 1902–1966, vol. VI
Whittemore, Ernest William, 1916–1995, vol. IX
Whitten, Wilfred, *died* 1942, vol. IV
Whitten-Brown, Sir Arthur, 1886–1948, vol. IV
Whitteridge, David, 1912–1994, vol. IX
Whitteridge, Sir Gordon Coligny, 1908–1995, vol. IX
Whittet, Thomas Douglas, 1915–1987, vol. VIII
Whittick, Henry John, 1870–1937, vol. III
Whitting, Brig. Everard Le Grice, 1881–1953, vol. V
Whittingham, Col Charles Herbert, 1873–1932, vol. III
Whittingham, Rev. George Gustavus Napier, 1866–1941, vol. IV
Whittingham, Air Marshal Sir Harold Edward, 1887–1983, vol. VIII
Whittingham, Rt Rev. Walter Godfrey, *died* 1941, vol. IV
Whittingham, Engr-Rear-Adm. William, 1862–1940, vol. III
Whittingstall, Francis Herbert F.; *see* Fearnley-Whittingstall.
Whittingstall, William Arthur F.; *see* Fearnley-Whittingstall.
Whittington, Brig.-Gen. Cecil Henry, 1878–1934, vol. III
Whittington, Charles Richard, 1908–1992, vol. IX
Whittington, Col George John Charles, 1836–1916, vol. II

Whittington, Joseph Basil, 1921–1995, vol. IX
Whittington, Rev. Richard, 1825–1900, vol. I
Whittington, Sir Richard, 1905–1975, vol. VII
Whittington-Ince, Captain Edward Watkins, 1886–1976, vol. VII
Whittle, Alfred Thomas, 1836–1913, vol. I
Whittle, Claude Howard, 1896–1986, vol. VIII
Whittle, Air Cdre Sir Frank, 1907–1996, vol. X
Whittle, Ven. John Tyler, 1889–1969, vol. VI
Whittome, Sir Maurice Gordon, 1902–1974, vol. VII
Whitton, Charlotte Elizabeth, 1896–1975, vol. VII
Whitton, Cuthbert Henry, 1905–1995, vol. IX
Whitton, Lt-Col Frederick Ernest, 1872–1940, vol. III
Whitton, James Reid, died 1919, vol. II
Whittuck, Gerald Saumarez, 1912–1997, vol. X
Whitworth, Gp Captain Frank, 1910–1995, vol. IX
Whitworth, Hugh Hope Aston, 1914–1996, vol. X
Whitty, Maj.-Gen. Henry Martin, 1896–1961, vol. VI
Whitty, Sir John Tarlton, 1876–1948, vol. IV
Whitty, Dame May; see Webster, Dame May.
Whitty, Brig. Noel Irwine, 1885–1964, vol. VI
Whitty, Sir Reginald Ramson, 1891–1960, vol. V
Whitwell, Edward Robson, 1843–1922, vol. II
Whitwell, Joseph Fry, 1869–1932, vol. III
Whitwell, William Fry, 1867–1942, vol. IV
Whitwill, Col Mark, 1889–1967, vol. VI
Whitworth, Arthur, 1875–1972, vol. VII
Whitworth, Charles Stanley, 1880–1963, vol. VI
Whitworth, Clifford, 1906–1983, vol. VIII
Whitworth, Cyril, 1904–1968, vol. VI
Whitworth, Brig. Dysart Edward, 1890–1974, vol. VII
Whitworth, Eric Edward Allen, died 1971, vol. VII
Whitworth, Geoffrey Arundel, 1883–1951, vol. V
Whitworth, Harry, 1870–1930, vol. III
Whitworth, Air Cdre John Nicholas Haworth, 1912–1974, vol. VII
Whitworth, Thomas, 1917–1979, vol. VII
Whitworth, Rev. William Allen, 1840–1905, vol. I
Whitworth, William Hervey Allen, died 1960, vol. V
Whitworth, Adm. Sir William Jock, 1884–1973, vol. VII
Whitworth Jones, Air Chief Marshal Sir John; see Jones.
Whorlow, Rev. Alfred, 1852–1937, vol. III
Whyatt, Sir John, 1905–1978, vol. VII
Whyham, William Henry, born 1848, vol. II
Whymper, Charles, 1853–1941, vol. IV
Whymper, Edward, 1840–1911, vol. I
Whymper, Josiah Wood, 1813–1903, vol. I
Whyte, Rev. Alexander, 1836–1921, vol. II
Whyte, Sir (Alexander) Frederick, 1883–1970, vol. VI
Whyte, Angus H.; see Hedley-Whyte.
Whyte, Frederic, 1867–1941, vol. IV
Whyte, Sir Frederick; see Whyte, Sir A. F.
Whyte, Gabriel Thomas, 1925–1986, vol. VIII
Whyte, Sir Hamilton; see Whyte, Sir. W. E. H.
Whyte, Ian, 1901–1960, vol. V
Whyte, J. Mackie, 1858–1930, vol. III
Whyte, James Wilkinson, 1852–1923, vol. II

Whyte, Jardine Bell, 1880–1954, vol. V
Whyte, Major John Nicholas, 1864–1906, vol. I
Whyte, Lewis Gilmour, 1906–1986, vol. VIII
Whyte, Ven. Richard Athenry, died 1917, vol. II
Whyte, Air Comdt Dame Roberta Mary, 1897–1979, vol. VII
Whyte, Sir William, 1843–1914, vol. I
Whyte, Sir William, died 1945, vol. IV
Whyte, Sir William Edward, died 1950, vol. IV
Whyte, Sir (William Erskine) Hamilton, 1927–1990, vol. VIII
Whyte, William Hamilton, 1885–1973, vol. VII
Whyte, Sir William Marcus Charles Beresford, 1863–1932, vol. III
Whytehead, Rev. Henry Robert, 1849–1937, vol. III
Whytehead, Rev. Canon Ralph Layard, 1883–1956, vol. V
Whytlaw-Gray, Robert Whytlaw, 1877–1958, vol. V
Wibberley, Charles, 1851–1929, vol. III
Wibberley, Gerald Percy, 1915–1993, vol. IX
Wibberley, T., 1880–1930, vol. III
Wickberg, Gen. Erik E., 1904–1996, vol. X
Wickenden, Keith David, 1932–1983, vol. VIII
Wickens, Charles Henry, 1872–1939, vol. III
Wickham, Rev. Archdale Palmer, 1855–1935, vol. III
Wickham, Lt-Col Sir Charles George, 1879–1971, vol. VII
Wickham, Very Rev. Edward Charles, 1834–1910, vol. I
Wickham, Rt Rev. Edward Ralph, 1911–1994, vol. IX
Wickham, Lt-Col Edward Thomas Ruscombe, 1890–1957, vol. V
Wickham, Rev. Gordon Bolles, 1850–1920, vol. II
Wickham, Sir Henry, 1846–1928, vol. II
Wickham, Lt-Col Henry, 1855–1933, vol. III
Wickham, Col Henry Francis, 1874–1931, vol. III
Wickham, Brig. John Charles, 1886–1970, vol. VI
Wickham, Major Thomas Edmund Palmer, 1879–1917, vol. II
Wickham, Captain Thomas Strange, 1878–1914, vol. I
Wickham, William, 1831–1897, vol. I
Wickham, Col William James Richard, 1860–1932, vol. III
Wickham, William Reginald Lamplugh, 1908–1956, vol. V
Wickham-Boynton, Captain Thomas Lamplugh, 1869–1942, vol. IV
Wickins, Bt-Col George Cradock, 1884–1973, vol. VII
Wickins, Ven. William John, died 1933, vol. III
Wicklow, 7th Earl of, 1877–1946, vol. IV
Wicklow, 8th Earl of, 1902–1978, vol. VII
Wickreme, Alfred Silva K.; see Kohoban-Wickreme.
Wickremasinghe, N. Don Martino de Zilva, 1865–1937, vol. III
Wickremesinghe, Cyril Leonard, 1890–1945, vol. IV
Wickremesinghe, Walter Gerald, 1897–1986, vol. X (AI)
Wicks, David Vaughan, 1918–1996, vol. X
Wicks, Frederick, 1840–1910, vol. I
Wicks, Sir James, 1909–1989, vol. VIII
Wicks, Sir James Albert, 1910–1996, vol. X

Wicks, Margaret Campbell Walker, 1893–1970, vol. VI
Wicks, Pembroke, 1882–1957, vol. V
Wicks, Rt Rev. Ralph Edwin, 1921–1997, vol. X
Wicksteed, Joseph Hartley, 1842–1919, vol. II
Wicksteed, Rev. Philip Henry, 1844–1927, vol. II
Wicksteed, Thomas Frederic, 1848–1901, vol. I
Widdecombe, James Murray, 1910–1999, vol. X
Widdess, Rev. Canon Arthur Geoffrey, 1920–1982, vol. VIII
Widdicombe, Lt-Col George Templer, 1867–1952, vol. V
Widdicombe, Rev. John, 1839–1927, vol. II
Widdows, Archibald Edwards, 1878–1942, vol. IV
Widdowson, Elsie May, 1906–2000, vol. X
Widdowson, Thomas William, 1877–1956, vol. V
Widdrington, Brig.-Gen. Bertram FitzHerbert, 1873–1942, vol. IV
Widdrington, Major Shallcross Fitzherbert, 1826–1917, vol. II
Widener, Joseph E., *died* 1943, vol. IV
Widener, Peter A. Brown, 1834–1915, vol. I
Widgery, Baron (Life Peer); John Passmore Widgery, 1911–1981, vol. VIII
Widgery, Alban Gregory, 1887–1968, vol. VI
Widor, Charles-Marie, 1847–1937, vol. III
Wieland, Heinrich Otto, 1877–1957, vol. V
Wieler, Brig. Leslie Frederic Ethelbert, 1899–1965, vol. VI
Wien, Hon. Sir Phillip Solly, 1913–1981, vol. VIII
Wiener, Leo, 1862–1939, vol. III(A), vol. IV
Wiener, Norbert, 1894–1964, vol. VI
Wiesner, Jerome Bert, 1915–1994, vol. IX
Wiesner, Karel František, 1919–1986, vol. VIII
Wigan, Sir Alan Lewis, 5th Bt, 1913–1996, vol. X
Wigan, Alfred Edmund, 1855–1940, vol. III
Wigan, Charles, 1860–1937, vol. III
Wigan, Sir Frederick, 1st Bt, 1827–1907, vol. I
Wigan, Sir Frederick Adair, 4th Bt, 1911–1979, vol. VII
Wigan, Sir Frederick William, 2nd Bt, 1859–1907, did not have an entry in Who's Who.
Wigan, Brig.-Gen. John Tyson, 1877–1952, vol. V
Wigan, Sir Roderick Grey, 3rd Bt, 1886–1954, vol. V
Wigg, Baron (Life Peer); George Edward Cecil Wigg, 1900–1983, vol. VIII
Wigg, Rt Rev. Montagu John S.; *see* Stone-Wigg.
Wiggin, Alfred Harold, 1864–1933, vol. III
Wiggin, Arthur Francis Holme, 1892–1935, vol. III
Wiggin, Sir Charles Douglas, 1922–1977, vol. VII
Wiggin, Sir Charles Richard Henry, 3rd Bt, 1885–1972, vol. VII
Wiggin, Brig.-Gen. Edgar Askin, 1867–1939, vol. III
Wiggin, Sir Henry Samuel, 1st Bt, 1824–1905, vol. I
Wiggin, Sir Henry Arthur, 2nd Bt, 1852–1917, vol. II
Wiggin, Sir John Henry, 4th Bt, 1921–1991, vol. IX
Wiggin, Kate Douglas, 1856–1923, vol. II
Wiggin, Lt-Col Walter William, 1856–1936, vol. III
Wiggin, Lt-Col Sir William Henry, 1888–1951, vol. V
Wiggins, Rev. Clare Aveling, *died* 1965, vol. VI

Wiggins, Captain Joseph, 1832–1905, vol. I
Wiggins, William Denison Clare, 1905–1971, vol. VII
Wiggins, William Martin, 1870–1950, vol. IV
Wigglesworth, Air Cdre Cecil George, 1893–1961, vol. VI
Wigglesworth, Air Marshal Sir (Horace Ernest) Philip, 1896–1975, vol. VII
Wigglesworth, Air Marshal Sir Philip; *see* Wigglesworth, Air Marshal Sir H. E. P.
Wigglesworth, Sir Vincent Brian, 1899–1994, vol. IX
Wigglesworth, Walter Somerville, 1906–1972, vol. VII
Wigham, Eric Leonard, 1904–1990, vol. VIII
Wigham, Joseph Theodore, 1874–1951, vol. V
Wigham Richardson, Sir George; *see* Richardson.
Wight, Sir Gerald Robert, 1898–1962, vol. VI
Wight, James Alfred, 1916–1995, vol. IX
Wight, Martin; *see* Wight, R. J. M.
Wight, (Robert James) Martin, 1913–1972, vol. VII
Wight-Boycott, Lt-Col T. A., 1872–1916, vol. II
Wightman, Sir Owen William, 1869–1948, vol. IV
Wightman, Ralph, 1901–1971, vol. VII
Wightwick, Humphrey Wolseley, 1889–1962, vol. VI
Wigley, Frederick George, 1855–1918, vol. II
Wigley, Sir George, 1837–1925, vol. II
Wigley, Sir Henry Rodolph, 1913–1980, vol. VII (AII)
Wigley, Rev. Henry Townsend, 1893–1970, vol. VI
Wigley, John Edwin Mackonochie, 1892–1962, vol. VI
Wigley, Sir Wilfrid Murray, 1876–1959, vol. V
Wigmore, John Henry, 1863–1943, vol. IV
Wignall, Frederick William, *died* 1939, vol. III
Wignall, James, 1865–1925, vol. II
Wignall, Joshua Jennings, 1859–1941, vol. IV
Wigner, Eugene Paul, 1902–1995, vol. IX
Wigram, 1st Baron, 1873–1960, vol. V
Wigram, Alfred Money, 1856–1899, vol. I
Wigram, Sir Charles Hampden, 1826–1903, vol. I
Wigram, Rev. Canon Sir Clifford Woolmore, 7th Bt, 1911–2000, vol. X
Wigram, Derek Roland, 1908–1996, vol. X
Wigram, Sir Edgar Thomas Ainger, 6th Bt, 1864–1935, vol. III
Wigram, Vice-Adm. Ernest, 1877–1944, vol. IV
Wigram, Maj.-Gen. Godfrey James, 1836–1908, vol. I
Wigram, Sir Henry Francis, 1857–1934, vol. III
Wigram, Gen. Sir Kenneth, 1875–1949, vol. IV
Wigram, Loftus Edward, 1877–1963, vol. VI
Wigram, Ralph Follet, 1890–1936, vol. III
Wigram, Rev. William Ainger, 1872–1953, vol. V
Wigram, Rev. Woolmore, 1831–1907, vol. I
Wijayasinghe Siriwardena, N. D. A. Silva-, 1888–1949, vol. IV(A)
Wijeyekoon, Sir Gerard, 1878–1952, vol. V
Wijeyeratne, Sir Edwin Aloysius Perera, 1890–1968, vol. VI
Wijeyewardene, Hon. Sir Arthur; *see* Wijeyewardene, Hon. Sir E. A. L.
Wijeyewardene, Hon. Sir (Edwin) Arthur (Lewis), 1887–1964, vol. VI

Wijhe, J. W. van, 1856–1935, vol. III
Wikeley, Thomas, 1902–1984, vol. VIII
Wilberforce, Ven. Albert Basil Orme, 1841–1916, vol. II
Wilberforce, Edward, 1834–1914, vol. I
Wilberforce, Rt Rev. Ernest Roland, 1840–1907, vol. I
Wilberforce, Col Harold Hartley, 1881–1943, vol. IV
Wilberforce, Brig.-Gen. Sir Herbert William, 1866–1952, vol. V
Wilberforce, Sir Herbert William Wrangham, 1864–1941, vol. IV
Wilberforce, Lionel Robert, 1861–1944, vol. IV
Wilberforce, Robert Francis, 1887–1990, vol. VIII
Wilberforce, Samuel, 1874–1954, vol. V
Wilberforce-Bell, Lt-Col Sir Harold, 1885–1956, vol. V
Wilbraham, Lt-Col Bernard Hugh, died 1942, vol. IV
Wilbraham, Edward; see Lathom, 3rd Earl of.
Wilbraham, Sir George Barrington Baker-, 5th Bt, 1845–1912, vol. I
Wilbraham, Hugh Edward, 1857–1930, vol. III
Wilbraham, Sir Philip Wilbraham Baker, 6th Bt, 1875–1957, vol. V
Wilbraham, Sir Randle John Baker, 7th Bt, 1906–1980, vol. VII
Wilbraham, Sir Richard, 1811–1900, vol. I
Wilby, Col (Arthur William) Roger, 1875–1942, vol. IV
Wilby, John Ronald William, 1906–1989, vol. VIII
Wilby, Col Roger; see Wilby, Col A. W. R.
Wilcher, Lewis Charles, 1908–1983, vol. VIII
Wilcock, Alfred William, died 1953, vol. V
Wilcock, Gp Captain Clifford Arthur Bowman, died 1962, vol. VI
Wilcock, John Stewart, 1905–1951, vol. V
Wilcocks, Hon. Carl Theodorus Muller, 1861–1936, vol. III
Wilcocks, C(harles), 1896–1977, vol. VII
Wilcockson, Rear-Adm. Kenneth Dilworth East, 1927–1986, vol. VIII
Wilcox, Rev. Arthur John, 1889–1960, vol. V
Wilcox, Bernard Herbert, 1917–1980, vol. VII
Wilcox, Claude Henry Marwood, 1908–1981, vol. VIII
Wilcox, Desmond John, 1931–2000, vol. X
Wilcox, Ella Wheeler, 1855–1919, vol. II
Wilcox, Dame (Florence) Marjorie; see Neagle, Dame Anna.
Wilcox, Herbert Sydney, 1892–1977, vol. VII
Wilcox, Sir Malcolm George, 1921–1986, vol. VIII
Wilcox, Dame Marjorie; see Neagle, Dame Anna.
Wild, Albert, 1899–1971, vol. VII
Wild, Maj.-Gen. Edward John, died 1914, vol. I
Wild, Rt Rev. Eric, 1914–1991, vol. IX
Wild, Sir Ernest Edward, 1869–1934, vol. III
Wild, F. Percy, died 1950, vol. IV
Wild, Frank, 1874–1939, vol. III
Wild, Captain Geoffrey Alan, 1904–1985, vol. VIII
Wild, Maj. Hon. Gerald Percy, 1908–1996, vol. X
Wild, Rt Rev. Herbert Louis, 1865–1940, vol. III
Wild, Rt Hon. Sir (Herbert) Richard (Churton), 1912–1978, vol. VII

Wild, Ira, 1895–1974, vol. VII
Wild, Jack, 1927–1988, vol. VIII
Wild, James Anstey, 1853–1922, vol. II
Wild, Very Rev. John Herbert Severn, 1904–1992, vol. IX
Wild, Rev. Marshall, 1834–1916, vol. II
Wild, Ralph Bagnall B.; see Bagnall-Wild.
Wild, Brig.-Gen. Ralph Kirkby B.; see Bagnall-Wild.
Wild, Rt Hon. Sir Richard; see Wild, Rt Hon. Sir H. R. C.
Wild, Robert Briggs, 1862–1941, vol. IV
Wild, Lt-Col Wilfrid Hubert, 1874–1953, vol. V
Wilde, Derek Edward, 1912–1993, vol. IX
Wilde, Henry, 1833–1919, vol. II
Wilde, Johannes, 1891–1970, vol. VI
Wilde, Percy, 1857–1929, vol. III
Wilden-Hart, Bernard John, 1881–1932, vol. III
Wildenburg, Count Paul von H.; see Hatzfeldt-Wildenburg.
Wilder, Thornton Niven, 1897–1975, vol. VII
Wildey, Alexander Gascoigne, 1860–1934, vol. III
Wilding, Anthony Frederick, 1883–1915, vol. I
Wilding, Brig.-Gen. Charles Arthur, 1868–1953, vol. V
Wilding, Edward, 1875–1939, vol. III
Wilding, Longworth Allen, 1902–1963, vol. VI
Wilding, Michael, 1912–1979, vol. VII
Wilding, Captain Michael Henry, 1875–1933, vol. III
Wildish, Engr Rear-Adm. Sir Henry William, 1884–1973, vol. VII
Wildman-Lushington, Maj.-Gen. Godfrey Edward, 1897–1970, vol. VI
Wildy, (Norman) Peter (Leete), 1920–1987, vol. VIII
Wildy, Peter; see Wildy, N. P. L.
Wile, Frederic William, 1873–1941, vol. IV
Wileman, Alfred Ernest, 1860–1929, vol. III
Wilenski, Reginald Howard, 1887–1975, vol. VII
Wiles, Sir Donald Alonzo, 1912–1999, vol. X
Wiles, Sir Gilbert, 1880–1961, vol. VI
Wiles, Sir Harold Herbert, 1892–1965, vol. VI
Wiles, Peter John de la Fosse, 1919–1997, vol. X
Wiles, Philip, 1899–1967, vol. VI
Wiles, Reid, 1919–1975, vol. VII
Wiles, Rt Hon. Thomas, died 1951, vol. V
Wiley, Very Rev. C. Ormsby, 1839–1915, vol. I
Wiley, Charles Joseph, 1873–1939, vol. III
Wiley, Louis, 1869–1935, vol. III
Wilford, Rev. Canon John Russell, 1877–1954, vol. V
Wilford, Sir Thomas Mason, died 1939, vol. III
Wilgar, Lt-Col William Percy, 1877–1940, vol. III(A), vol. IV
Wilgress, Rev. George Frederick, 1868–1953, vol. V
Wilgress, L. Dana, 1892–1969, vol. VI
Wilhelm, C.; see Pitcher, W. J. C.
Wilhelm, Most Rev. Joseph Lawrence, 1909–1995, vol. X (AI)
Wilkes, Rev. John Comyn V.; see Vaughan Wilkes.
Wilkes, Lyall, 1914–1991, vol. IX
Wilkes, Richard Leslie Vaughan, 1904–1970, vol. VI
Wilkie, Alexander, 1850–1928, vol. II

Wilkie, Alexander Mair, 1917–1966, vol. VI
Wilkie, Rev. Arthur West, 1875–1958, vol. V
Wilkie, Daniel R., 1846–1914, vol. I
Wilkie, Sir David Percival Dalbreck, 1882–1938, vol. III
Wilkie, Douglas Robert, 1922–1998, vol. X
Wilkie, Hugh Graham, 1893–1969, vol. VI
Wilkie, James, 1890–1957, vol. V
Wilkie, James, 1896–1987, vol. VIII
Wilkie-Dalyell, Major Sir James Bruce; see Dalyell.
Wilkin, Sir Albert Scholick, 1883–1943, vol. IV
Wilkin, (Frederick) John, 1916–1997, vol. X
Wilkin, Vice-Adm. Henry Douglas, 1862–1931, vol. III
Wilkin, John; see Wilkin, F. J.
Wilkin, Sir Walter Henry, 1842–1922, vol. II
Wilkins, Augustus Samuel, 1843–1905, vol. I
Wilkins, Charles Timothy, 1905–1979, vol. VII
Wilkins, Major Cyril Francis, died 1935, vol. III
Wilkins, Frederick Charles, 1901–1987, vol. VIII
Wilkins, Rev. George, died 1920, vol. II
Wilkins, Sir (George) Hubert, 1888–1958, vol. V
Wilkins, Sir Henry John Arthur, died 1936, vol. III
Wilkins, Rev. Henry Russell, 1859–1924, vol. II
Wilkins, Sir Hubert; see Wilkins, Sir G. H.
Wilkins, Col James Sutherland, 1851–1916, vol. II
Wilkins, Mary E., died 1930, vol. III
Wilkins, Lt-Gen. Sir Michael Compton Lockwood, 1933–1994, vol. IX
Wilkins, Roland Field, 1872–1950, vol. IV
Wilkins, William Albert, 1899–1987, vol. VIII
Wilkins, William Henry, 1860–1905, vol. I
Wilkins, William Vaughan, 1890–1959, vol. V
Wilkinson, Andrew Wood, 1914–1995, vol. IX
Wilkinson, Col Arthur Clement, 1870–1950, vol. IV
Wilkinson, Rev. Arthur Henry, 1885–1973, vol. VII
Wilkinson, Rev. Arthur Rupert B.; see Browne-Wilkinson.
Wilkinson, Engr Rear-Adm. Brian John Hamilton, died 1963, vol. VI
Wilkinson, Rt Rev. (Charles Robert) Heber, 1900–1979, vol. VII
Wilkinson, Ven. Charles Thomas, 1823–1910, vol. I
Wilkinson, Col Charles William, 1868–1954, vol. V
Wilkinson, Clennell Anstruther, 1883–1936, vol. III
Wilkinson, Clennell Frank Massy D.; see Drew-Wilkinson.
Wilkinson, Cyril Hackett, 1888–1960, vol. V
Wilkinson, Cyril Theodore Anstruther, 1884–1970, vol. VI
Wilkinson, Sir David; see Wilkinson, Sir L. D.
Wilkinson, Edgar Riley, 1898–1977, vol. VII
Wilkinson, Edward Sheldon, 1883–1950, vol. IV
Wilkinson, Rt Hon. Ellen Cicely, 1891–1947, vol. IV
Wilkinson, Fanny Rollo, died 1951, vol. V
Wilkinson, Most Rev. Francis Oliver G.; see Green-Wilkinson.
Wilkinson, Frank, 1900–1970, vol. VI
Wilkinson, Frank Clare, 1889–1979, vol. VII
Wilkinson, Frederick 1891–1978, vol. VII
Wilkinson, Frederick Edgar, 1871–1950, vol. IV
Wilkinson, Lt-Gen. Frederick G.; see Green-Wilkinson.
Wilkinson, Sir Geoffrey, 1921–1996, vol. X

Wilkinson, George, 1867–1956, vol. V
Wilkinson, Col George Alexander Eason, 1860–1941, vol. IV
Wilkinson, Maj.-Gen. George Allix, 1828–1919, vol. II
Wilkinson, Sir George Henry, 1st Bt, 1885–1967, vol. VI
Wilkinson, Rt Rev. George Howard, 1833–1907, vol. I
Wilkinson, Sir Harold, 1903–1986, vol. VIII
Wilkinson, Rt Rev. Heber; see Wilkinson, Rt Rev. C. R. H.
Wilkinson, Hector Russell, 1888–1972, vol. VII
Wilkinson, Lt-Col Henry Benfield Des Vœux, 1870–1943, vol. IV
Wilkinson, Lt-Gen. Sir Henry Clement, 1837–1908, vol. I
Wilkinson, (Henry) Spenser, 1853–1937, vol. III
Wilkinson, Hiram Parkes, 1866–1935, vol. III
Wilkinson, Sir Hiram Shaw, 1840–1926, vol. II
Wilkinson, Ven. Hubert Seed, 1897–1984, vol. VIII
Wilkinson, Hon. James, 1854–1915, vol. I
Wilkinson, James Hardy, 1919–1986, vol. VIII
Wilkinson, Rev. John, 1856–1935, vol. III
Wilkinson, John Frederick, 1897–1998, vol. X
Wilkinson, Brig. John Shann, 1884–1977, vol. VII
Wilkinson, Sir Joseph Loftus, 1845–1903, vol. I
Wilkinson, Vice-Adm. Julian Charles Allix, 1859–1917, vol. II
Wilkinson, Kenneth Douglas, 1886–1951, vol. V
Wilkinson, Kenneth Grahame, 1917–1990, vol. VIII
Wilkinson, Lancelot Craven, died 1923, vol. II
Wilkinson, (Lancelot) Patrick, 1907–1985, vol. VIII
Wilkinson, Sir (Leonard) David, 2nd Bt, 1920–1972, vol. VII
Wilkinson, Leslie, 1882–1973, vol. VII
Wilkinson, Brig.-Gen. Lewis Frederic G.; see Green-Wilkinson.
Wilkinson, Louis Umfreville, 1881–1966, vol. VI
Wilkinson, Dame Louisa Jane, 1889–1968, vol. VI
Wilkinson, Sir Martin; see Wilkinson, Sir R. F. M.
Wilkinson, Brig. Maurice Lean, 1873–1946, vol. IV
Wilkinson, Rev. Michael Marlow Umfreville, 1831–1916, vol. II
Wilkinson, Brig.-Gen. Montagu Grant, 1857–1943, vol. IV
Wilkinson, Major Sir Nevile Rodwell, 1869–1940, vol. III
Wilkinson, Norman, 1882–1934, vol. III
Wilkinson, Norman, 1878–1971, vol. VII
Wilkinson, Maj.-Gen. Osborn, 1822–1906, vol. I
Wilkinson, Patrick; see Wilkinson, L. P.
Wilkinson, Maj.-Gen. Sir Percival Spearman, 1865–1953, vol. V
Wilkinson, Peter, 1918–1981, vol. VIII
Wilkinson, Sir Peter Allix, 1914–2000, vol. X
Wilkinson, Rev. Canon Raymond Stewart, 1919–1995, vol. IX
Wilkinson, Reginald Warren Hale, 1882–1973, vol. VII
Wilkinson, Richard Edward, 1901–1972, vol. VII
Wilkinson, Richard James, 1867–1941, vol. IV
Wilkinson, Sir (Robert Francis) Martin, 1911–1900, vol. VIII
Wilkinson, Sir Robert Pelham, 1883–1962, vol. VI

Wilkinson, Sir Russell Facey, 1888–1968, vol. VI
Wilkinson, Spenser; *see* Wilkinson, H. S.
Wilkinson, Stephen, 1876–1962, vol. VI
Wilkinson, Sydney Frank, 1894–1988, vol. VIII
Wilkinson, Sir Thomas Crowe S.; *see*
  Spenser-Wilkinson.
Wilkinson, Rt Rev. Thomas Edward, *died* 1914,
  vol. I
Wilkinson, Major Thomas Henry Des Vœux,
  1858–1928, vol. II
Wilkinson, Rt Rev. Thomas W., 1825–1909, vol. I
Wilkinson, Walter Sutherland, 1875–1943, vol. IV
Wilkinson, William, 1882–1944, vol. IV
Wilkinson, William Dale, 1893–1973, vol. VII
Wilkinson, Rev. Canon William Evans, 1891–1967,
  vol. VI
Wilkinson, Sir William Henry, 1858–1930, vol. III
Wilkinson, Sir William Henry Nairn, 1932–1996,
  vol. X
Wilkinson-Guillemard, Hugh; *see*
  Wilkinson-Guillemard, W. H. J.
Wilkinson-Guillemard, (Walter) Hugh (John),
  1874–1939, vol. III
Wilks, Dick Lloyd, 1923–1985, vol. VIII
Wilks, Jim; *see* Wilks, Stanley David.
Wilks, Stanley David, (Jim), 1920–1997, vol. X
Wilks, Rev. William, 1843–1923, vol. II
Will, John Shiress, 1840–1910, vol. I
Will, Robert Ross, 1883–1968, vol. VI
Willan, Col Frank, 1846–1931, vol. III
Willan, Group Captain Frank Andrew, 1915–1981,
  vol. VIII
Willan, Brig.-Gen. Frank Godfrey, 1878–1957,
  vol. V
Willan, Sir Harold Curwen, 1896–1971, vol. VII
Willan, Healey, 1880–1968, vol. VI
Willan, Col Henry Percy Douglas, 1848–1912,
  vol. I
Willan, Col Robert Hugh, 1882–1960, vol. V
Willan, Robert Joseph, 1878–1955, vol. V
Willan, Thomas Stuart, 1910–1994, vol. IX
Willans, Sir Frederic Jeune, *died* 1949, vol. IV
Willans, Maj.-Gen. Harry, 1892–1943, vol. IV
Willans, Lt-Col Thomas James, 1872–1922, vol. II
Willans, William Henry, 1833–1904, vol. I
Willar, Paul; *see* Villars, Paul.
Willard, E. S. *died* 1915, vol. I
Willard, Frances Elizabeth, 1839–1898, vol. I
Willasey-Wilsey, Maj.-Gen. Anthony Patrick,
  1920–1985, vol. VIII
Willatt, Sir Hugh, 1909–1996, vol. X
Willcock, Rev. John, 1853–1931, vol. III
Willcock, Hon. John Collings, 1879–1956, vol. V
Willcock, Major Ralph, 1887–1969, vol. VI
Willcocks, G. Waller, *died* 1918, vol. II
Willcocks, Gen. Sir James, 1857–1926, vol. II
Willcocks, Sir William, 1852–1932, vol. III
Willcox, Arthur, 1909–1963, vol. VI
Willcox, Lt-Gen. Sir Henry Beresford Dennitts,
  1889–1968, vol. VI
Willcox, Captain Howard James Lionel Walter Kox,
  died 1936, vol. III
Willcox, Lt-Col Walter Temple, 1869–1943, vol. IV
Willcox, Sir William Henry, 1870–1941, vol. IV
Willert, Sir Arthur, 1882–1973, vol. VII

Willert, Paul Ferdinand, 1844–1912, vol. I
Willes, Lt-Col Charles Edward, 1870–1952, vol. V
Willes, Adm. Sir George Lambart A.; *see*
  Atkinson-Willes.
Willes, Sir George Ommanney, 1823–1901, vol. I
Willes, Richard Augustus, 1881–1966, vol. VI
Willes, William, 1855–1924, vol. II
Willets, Lt-Col Charles Richard Edward,
  1880–1931, vol. III
Willett, Alfred, 1837–1913, vol. I
Willett, Archibald Anthony, 1924–1992, vol. IX
Willett, Captain Basil Rupert, 1896–1966, vol. VI
Willett, Frederick John, 1922–1993, vol. IX
Willett, Guy William, 1913–1990, vol. VIII
Willett, John Eddowes, 1853–1937, vol. III
Willett, Comdr William Basil, 1919–1976, vol. VII
Willetts, Bernard Frederick, 1927–1993, vol. IX
Willetts, Bill; *see* Willetts, B. F.
Willey, Arthur, 1867–1942, vol. IV
Willey, Basil, 1897–1978, vol. VII
Willey, Rt Hon. Frederick Thomas, 1910–1987,
  vol. VIII
Willey, Octavius George, 1886–1952, vol. V
William-Powlett, Vice-Adm. Sir Peveril Barton
  Reibey Wallop, 1898–1985, vol. VIII
Williams, 1st Baron, 1892–1966, vol. VI
Williams of Barnburgh, Baron (Life Peer); Thomas
  Williams, 1888–1967, vol. VI
Williams, A. Franklyn, 1907–1979, vol. VII
Williams, Rt Rev. Aidan; *see* Williams, Rt Rev.
  Augustine A.
Williams, Alan Frederick, 1945–1992, vol. IX
Williams, Sir Alan Meredith, 1909–1972, vol. VII
Williams, Captain Albert, 1864–1926, vol. II
Williams, (Albert) Clifford, *born* 1905, vol. VIII
Williams, Maj.-Gen. Sir Albert Henry Wilmot,
  1832–1919, vol. II
Williams, Ven. Aldred; *see* Williams, Ven. E. D. A.
Williams, Alexander, *died* 1930, vol. III
Williams, Sir Alexander Thomas, 1903–1984,
  vol. VIII
Williams, Alfred Cecil, 1899–1976, vol. VII
Williams, Col Alfred Ernest, 1871–1941, vol. IV
Williams, Alfred Martyn, 1897–1985, vol. VIII
Williams, Alice Helena Alexandra, 1863–1957,
  vol. V
Williams, Rt Rev. Alwyn Terrell Petre, 1888–1968,
  vol. VI
Williams, Alyn, *died* 1941, vol. IV
Williams, Aneurin, 1859–1924, vol. II
Williams, Anna, *died* 1924, vol. II
Williams, Sir Anthony James, 1923–1990, vol. VIII
Williams, Rt Rev. Anthony Lewis Elliott,
  1892–1975, vol. VII
Williams, Arnold, 1890–1958, vol. V
Williams, Rt Rev. Arthur Acheson, *died* 1914, vol. I
Williams, Brig.-Gen. Arthur Blount Cuthbert,
  1860–1918, vol. II
Williams, Lt-Col Arthur Cecil, 1871–1940, vol. III
Williams, Ven. Arthur Charles, 1899–1974, vol. VII
Williams, Arthur de Coetlogon, 1890–1973, vol. VII
Williams, A(rthur) Emlyn, 1910–1976, vol. VII
Williams, (Arthur Frederic) Basil, 1867–1950,
  vol. IV

Williams, Col Arthur Frederick Carlisle, 1876–1934, vol. III
Williams, Arthur James, 1880–1962, vol. VI
Williams, Arthur John, 1835–1911, vol. I
Williams, Brig.-Gen. Sir Arthur John A.; *see* Allen-Williams.
Williams, Sir (Arthur) Leonard, 1904–1972, vol. VII
Williams, Rt Rev. Arthur Llewellyn, 1856–1919, vol. II
Williams, Rev. Arthur Lukyn, 1853–1943, vol. IV
Williams, Maj.-Gen. Arthur Nicholl, 1894–1982, vol. VIII
Williams, Sir (Arthur) Osmond, 1st Bt (*cr* 1909), 1849–1927, vol. II
Williams, Arthur Vivian, 1909–1993, vol. IX
Williams, Captain Ashley Paget Wilmot, 1867–1913, vol. I
Williams, Maj.-Gen. Aubrey Ellis, 1888–1977, vol. VII
Williams, Rt Rev. (Augustine) Aidan, 1904–1965, vol. VI
Williams, Brig. Augustus John, 1876–1945, vol. IV
Williams, B. Francis, 1845–1914, vol. I
Williams, Barbara M.; *see* Moray Williams.
Williams, Basil; *see* Williams, A. F. B.
Williams, Basil Hugh G.; *see* Garnons Williams.
Williams, Sir Benjamin Allen, *died* 1968, vol. VI
Williams, Benjamin H.; *see* Haydn Williams.
Williams, Captain Berkeley Cole Wilmot, 1865–1938, vol. III
Williams, Bernard Warren, 1895–1970, vol. VI
Williams, Sir Brandan Meredith R.; *see* Rhys Williams.
Williams, Lt-Col Brian Robertson, 1909–1980, vol. VII
Williams, Sir Burton Robert, 6th Bt (*cr* 1866), 1889–1917, vol. II
Williams, C. F. Abdy, 1855–1923, vol. II
Williams, Campbell Sherston; *see* Smith, Campbell Sherston.
Williams, Carrington Bonsor, 1889–1981, vol. VIII
Williams, Catrin Mary, 1922–1998, vol. X
Williams, Cecil Beaumont, 1925–1998, vol. X
Williams, Brig. Cecil James, 1898–1948, vol. IV
Williams, Charles, 1834–1900, vol. I
Williams, Charles, 1838–1904, vol. I
Williams, Rt Hon. Charles, 1886–1955, vol. V
Williams, Lt-Col Charles Augustus M; *see* Muspratt-Williams.
Williams, Rt Rev. Charles David, 1860–1923, vol. II
Williams, Major Charles Edward, 1873–1955, vol. V
Williams, Charles Frederick Victor, 1898–1984, vol. VIII
Williams, Charles Garrett, 1901–1976, vol. VII
Williams, Charles Hanson Greville, 1829–1910, vol. I
Williams, Charles Harold, 1895–1981, vol. VIII
Williams, Sir Charles Henry Trelease, (Sir Harry), 1898–1982, vol. VIII
Williams, Charles Riby, 1857–1924, vol. II
Williams, Sir Charles S.; *see* Stuart-Williams.
Williams, Captain Charles Shrine, 1895–1973, vol. VII
Williams, Charles Theodore, 1838–1912, vol. I

Williams, Charles Walter Stansby, 1886–1945, vol. IV
Williams, Charles Wodehouse, 1899–1957, vol. V
Williams, Chisholm, 1866–1928, vol. II
Williams, Christmas Price, *died* 1965, vol. VI
Williams, Christopher A.; *see* Addams Williams.
Williams, Hon. Christopher Alexander S.; *see* Sapara-Williams.
Williams, Christopher David, 1873–1934, vol. III
Williams, Cicely Delphine, 1893–1992, vol. IX
Williams, Clarence Faithfull M.; *see* Monier-Williams.
Williams, Clifford; *see* Williams, A. C.
Williams, Conrad Veale, 1903–1969, vol. VI
Williams, Major Craufurd Victor M.; *see* Monier-Williams.
Williams, Cyril Herbert, 1908–1983, vol. VIII
Williams, Cyril Robert, 1895–1991, vol. IX
Williams, Daniel, 1876–1944, vol. IV
Williams, Sir (Daniel) Thomas, *died* 1973, vol. VII
Williams, David, 1877–1927, vol. II
Williams, Ven. David, 1841–1929, vol. III
Williams, Most Rev. David, 1859–1931, vol. III
Williams, Ven. David, 1862–1936, vol. III
Williams, David, 1865–1941, vol. IV
Williams, David, 1900–1978, vol. VII
Williams, David, 1898–1984, vol. VIII
Williams, Rear-Adm. David Apthorp, 1911–1995, vol. IX
Williams, David Barry, 1931–1995, vol. IX
Williams, David Carlton, 1912–1994, vol. IX
Williams, David Davey, 1874–1954, vol. V(A)
Williams, Ven. David Edward, 1847–1920, vol. II
Williams, David Gwynne, 1886–1975, vol. VII
Williams, David Iorwerth, 1913–1994, vol. IX
Williams, David James, 1897–1972, vol. VII
Williams, David L.; *see* Llewelyn-Williams.
Williams, David Parry, 1842–1909, vol. I
Williams, Sir David Philip, 3rd Bt (*cr* 1915), 1909–1970, vol. VI
Williams, Lt-Gen. David Walter, 1839–1909, vol. I
Williams, Sir Dawson, 1854–1928, vol. II
Williams, Denis John, 1908–1990, vol. VIII
Williams, Donald; *see* Williams, W. D.
Williams, Dorian Joseph George, 1914–1985, vol. VIII
Williams, Dorothy Sylvia L.; *see* Lloyd-Williams.
Williams, Captain Douglas, 1892–1975, vol. VII
Williams, D(ouglas) Graeme, 1909–1970, vol. VI
Williams, Hon. Sir Dudley, 1889–1963, vol. VI
Williams, E. C., 1892–1973, vol. VII
Williams, E. G. Harcourt, 1880–1957, vol. V
Williams, Edith, *died* 1919, vol. II
Willaims, Sir Edgar Trevor, 1912–1995, vol. IX
Williams, Rev. Edward Adams, 1826–1913, vol. I
Williams, Maj.-Gen. Edward Alexander Wilmot, 1910–1994, vol. IX
Williams, Edward Cecil, 1867–1939, vol. III
Williams, Maj.-Gen. Edward Charles Ingouville, 1861–1916, vol. II
Williams, Sir Edward Charles Sparshott, 1831–1907, vol. I
Williams, Major Edward Ernest, 1875–1915, vol. I
Williams, Edward Francis; *see* Baron Francis-Williams.

Williams, Brig.-Gen. Edward George, 1867–1941, vol. IV

Williams, Rt Hon. Sir Edward John, 1890–1963, vol. VI

Williams, Sir Edward Leader, 1828–1910, vol. I

Williams, Brig. Edward Stephen Bruce, 1892–1977, vol. VII

Williams, Hon. Sir Edward Stratten, 1921–1999, vol. X

Williams, Edward Taylor, 1911–1997, vol. X

Williams, Edward Wilmot, 1826–1913, vol. I

Williams, Rev. Eleazar, died 1905, vol. I

Williams, Lt-Col Eliot C.; see Crawshay-Williams.

Williams, Rt Hon. Sir Ellis H.; see Hume Williams.

Williams, Emlyn; see Williams, G. E.

Williams, Eric, 1911–1983, vol. VIII

Williams, Eric Charles, 1915–1980, vol. VII

Williams, Rt Hon. Eric Eustace, 1911–1981, vol. VIII

Williams, Eric W.; see Watson-Williams.

Williams, Ernest Edwin, 1866–1935, vol. III

Williams, Sir Ernest H.; see Hodder-Williams, Sir J. E.

Williams, Sir Ernest Hillas, 1899–1965, vol. VI

Williams, (Ernest) Rohan, 1906–1963, vol. VI

Williams, Ethel Mary Nucella, 1863–1948, vol. IV

Williams, Sir Evan, 1st Bt (cr 1935), 1871–1959, vol. V

Williams, Ven. (Evan Daniel) Aldred, 1879–1951, vol. V

Williams, Evan James, 1903–1945, vol. IV

Williams, Sir (Evan) Owen, 1890–1969, vol. VI

Williams, Bt-Col Evelyn Hugh Watkin, 1884–1934, vol. III

Williams, F. Harald; see Ward, Rev. Frederick, W. O.

Williams, Sir Francis John Watkin, 8th Bt (cr 1798), 1905–1995, vol. IX

Williams, Major Francis V.; see Vaughan-Williams.

Williams, Francis Wigley Greswolde G.; see Greswolde-Williams.

Williams, Surg. Rear-Adm. (D) Frank Reginald Parry, 1897–1965, vol. VI

Williams, Franklyn; see Williams, A. F.

Williams, Sir Frederic Calland, 1911–1977, vol. VII

Williams, Rev. Frederick Billingsley Ambrose, 1870–1932, vol. III

Williams, Brig. and Chief Paymaster Frederick Christian, 1891–1970, vol. VI

Williams, Rev. Frederick Farewell Sanigear, 1870–1956, vol. V

Williams, Sir Frederick Law, 7th Bt (cr 1866), 1862–1921, vol. II

Williams, Frederick Sims, 1855–1941, vol. IV

Williams, Sir Frederick William, 5th Bt (cr 1866), 1888–1913, vol. I

Williams, Brig.-Gen. G. Coventry, 1860–1947, vol. IV

Williams, Very Rev. Garfield Hodder, 1881–1960, vol. V

Williams, Geoffrey Milson John, 1923–1988, vol. VIII

Williams, Geoffrey Sydney, 1871–1952, vol. V

Williams, Sir George, 1821–1905, vol. I

Williams, George, 1879–1951, vol. V

Williams, Sir George Clark, 1st Bt (cr 1955), 1878–1958, vol. V

Williams, Comdr George Davies, 1879–1947, vol. IV

Williams, (George) Emlyn, 1905–1987, vol. VIII

Williams, Rev. George H., 1859–1926, vol. II

Williams, George L; see Lowsley-Williams.

Williams, Brig.-Gen. George Mostyn, 1868–1943, vol. IV

Williams, George W.; see Wynn-Williams.

Williams, Gerald Wellington, 1903–1989, vol. VIII

Williams, Rt Rev. Gershom Mott, 1857–1923, vol. II

Williams, Gertrude, (Lady Williams), 1897–1983, vol. VIII

Williams, Gilbert Milner, 1898–1979, vol. VII

Williams, Glanville Llewelyn, 1911–1997, vol. X

Williams, Rev. Glen Garfield, 1923–1994, vol. IX

Williams, Maj.-Gen. Sir Godfrey, 1859–1940, vol. III

Williams, Godfrey Herbert, 1875–1956, vol. V

Williams, Sir Griffith Goodland, 1890–1974, vol. VII

Williams, Gen. Sir Guy Charles, 1881–1959, vol. V

Williams, Gwilym, 1839–1906, vol. I

Williams, Sir Gwilym Ffrangcon, 1902–1969, vol. VI

Williams, Rt Rev. Gwilym Owen, 1913–1990, vol. VIII

Williams, Sir Gwilym Tecwyn, 1913–1989, vol. VIII

Williams, Gwyn, 1904–1955, vol. V

Williams, Gwynne Evan Owen, died 1958, vol. V

Williams, Harcourt; see Williams, E. G. H.

Williams, Harley; see Williams, J. H. H.

Williams, Lt-Gen. Sir Harold, 1897–1971, vol. VII

Williams, Harold Beck, 1889–1969, vol. VI

Williams, Very Rev. Harold Claude Noel, 1914–1990, vol. VIII

Williams, Air Vice-Marshal Harold Guy L.; see Leonard-Williams.

Williams, Harold H.; see Heathcote-Williams.

Williams, Sir Harold Herbert, 1880–1964, vol. VI

Williams, Harri Llwyd H.; see Hudson-Williams.

Williams, Sir Harry; see Williams, Sir C. H. T.

Williams, Hon. Sir Hartley, 1843–1929, vol. III

Williams, Henry, 1850–1933, vol. III

Williams, Col Henry David, 1854–1924, vol. II

Williams, Lt-Gen. Sir Henry Francis, 1825–1907, vol. I

Williams, Rt Rev. Henry Herbert, 1872–1961, vol. VI

Williams, Rev. (Henry) Howard, 1918–1991, vol. IX

Williams, Lt-Col Henry John, 1870–1935, vol. III

Williams, Sir Henry Morton Leech, 1913–1989, vol. VIII

Williams, Henry Owen, 1855–1943, vol. IV

Williams, Herbert, 1862–1916, vol. II

Williams, Sir Herbert Geraint, 1st Bt (cr 1953), 1884–1954, vol. V

Williams, Rt Rev. Herbert William, died 1937, vol. III

Williams, Howard, 1837–1931, vol. III

Williams, Rev. Howard; see Williams, Rev. Henry H.

Williams, Sir Howell Jones, *died* 1939, vol. III
Williams, Hubert Llewelyn, 1890–1964, vol. VI
Williams, Rev. Hugh, 1843–1911, vol. I
Williams, Hugh Anthony Glanmore, 1904–1969, vol. VI
Williams, Maj.-Gen. Sir Hugh Bruce Bruce-, 1865–1942, vol. IV
Williams, Rev. Hugh Cernyw, 1843–1937, vol. III
Williams, Sir Hugh Grenville, 6th Bt (*cr* 1798), 1889–1961, vol. VI
Williams, Hugh L.; *see* Lloyd-Williams.
Williams, Hugh Noel, 1870–1925, vol. II
Williams, Adm. Hugh Pigot, 1858–1934, vol. III
Williams, Sir (I.) Thomas, 1853–1941, vol. IV
Williams, Ian Malcolm Gordon, 1914–1997, vol. X
Williams, Sir Ifor, 1881–1965, vol. VI
Williams, Iolo Aneurin, 1890–1962, vol. VI
Williams, Isaac John, 1875–1939, vol. III
Williams, Ivor Maredydd B.; *see* Bankes-Williams.
Williams, J. H., 1855–1942, vol. IV
Williams, J. Lloyd, *died* 1945, vol. IV
Williams, Jack F.; *see* Fox-Williams.
Williams, James, 1851–1911, vol. I
Williams, James Alexander, 1856–1937, vol. II
Williams, Ven. James Evan, *died* 1953, vol. V
Williams, Captain James Evan L.; *see* Lloyd-Williams.
Williams, James Howard, 1897–1958, vol. V
Williams, James Leslie, 1870–1949, vol. IV
Williams, Hon. James Rowland, 1860–1916, vol. II
Williams, James Vaughan, 1912–1994, vol. IX
Williams, John, 1861–1922, vol. II
Williams, Sir John, 1st Bt, 1840–1926, vol. II
Williams, Lt-Col John, 1874–1942, vol. IV
Williams, John, *died* 1951, vol. V
Williams, John Basil, 1906–1953, vol. V
Williams, John Carvell, 1821–1907, vol. I
Williams, John Charles, 1861–1939, vol. III
Williams, Sir John Coldbrook H.; *see* Hanbury-Williams.
Williams, John David, 1853–1923, vol. II
Williams, John Ellis Caerwyn, 1912–1999, vol. X
Williams, John Elwyn, 1921–1990, vol. VIII
Williams, Sir John Fischer, 1870–1947, vol. IV
Williams, Sir John Francis, 1901–1982, vol. VIII
Williams, Very Rev. John Frederick, 1907–1983, vol. VIII
Williams, Maj.-Gen. Sir John H.; *see* Hanbury-Williams.
Williams, John H.; *see* Haynes-Williams.
Williams, (John Hargreaves) Harley, *died* 1974, vol. VII
Williams, John Haulfryn, 1908–1980, vol. VII
Williams, John Henry, 1870–1936, vol. III
Williams, Sir (John) Leslie, 1913–1993, vol. IX
Williams, Sir John Lias Cecil C.; *see* Cecil-Williams.
Williams, Sir (John Lloyd Vaughan) Seymour, 1868–1945, vol. IV
Williams, John Meredith, 1926–1996, vol. X
Williams, Rev. John Owen, 1853–1932, vol. III
Williams, Captain Sir John Protheroe, *born* 1896, vol. VIII
Williams, Sir John Robert, 1922–2000, vol. X
Williams, Sir John Rolleston L.; *see* Lort-Williams.

Williams, John Trevor, 1921–1987, vol. VIII
Williams, Maj.-Gen. John William C.; *see* Channing Williams.
Williams, Sir John William Collman, 1823–1911, vol. I
Williams, John Williams, 1885–1957, vol. V
Williams, Joseph Grout, 1848–1923, vol. II
Williams, Rt Hon. Joseph Powell, 1840–1904, vol. I
Williams, Rt Rev. Joseph Watkin, 1857–1934, vol. III
Williams, Rt Hon. Sir Joshua Strange, 1837–1915, vol. I
Williams, Katharine Georgina L.; *see* Lloyd-Williams.
Williams, Kenneth; *see* Williams, O. K.
Williams, Kenneth Charles, 1926–1988, vol. VIII
Williams, Lt-Col Kenneth Greville, 1892–1972, vol. VII
Williams, L. Gwendolen, *died* 1955, vol. V
Williams, Laurence Frederic Rushbrook, 1890–1978, vol. VII
Williams, Maj.-Gen. Lawrence Henry, 1834–1916, vol. II
Williams, Rt Rev. Lennox Waldron, 1859–1958, vol. V
Williams, Sir Leonard; *see* Williams, Sir A. L.
Williams, Leonard John, 1894–1975, vol. VII
Williams, Leonard Llewelyn Bulkeley, 1861–1939, vol. III
Williams, Sir Leslie; *see* Williams, Sir J. L.
Williams, Ven. Leslie Arthur, 1909–1996, vol. X
Williams, Col Leslie Gwatkin, 1878–1926, vol. II
Williams, Maj.-Gen. Sir Leslie Hamlyn, 1892–1965, vol. VI
Williams, Leslie Harry, 1909–1978, vol. VII
Williams, Leslie Henry, 1903–1991, vol. IX
Williams, Leslie Herbert Whitby, 1893–1972, vol. VII
Williams, Leslie Thomas Douglas, 1905–1976, vol. VII
Williams, Lily, 1874–1940, vol. III
Williams, Llywelyn, 1911–1965, vol. VI
Williams, Margaret Lindsay, *died* 1960, vol. V
Williams, Mary, 1882–1977, vol. VII
Williams, Mary Atkinson, *died* 1949, vol. IV
Williams, Mary Bridget, 1933–1989, vol. VIII
Williams, Michael Edward John, 1933–1997, vol. X
Williams, Sir Michael Sanigear, 1911–1984, vol. VIII
Williams, Monier Faithful M.; *see* Monier-Williams.
Williams, Sir Monier M.; *see* Monier-Williams.
Williams, Montagu Sneade Faithful M.; *see* Monier-Williams.
Williams, Morgan Stuart, 1846–1909, vol. I
Williams, Captain Nevill Glennie G.; *see* Garnons Williams.
Williams, Neville John, 1924–1977, vol. VII
Williams, Rev. Norman Powell, 1883–1943, vol. IV
Williams, Brig.-Gen. Oliver de Lancey, 1875–1959, vol. V
Williams, Orlando Cyprian, (Orlo), 1883–1967, vol. VI
Williams, Sir Osmond; *see* Williams, Sir A. O.
Williams, Sir Owen; *see* Williams, Sir E. O.
Williams, Owen Gwyn Revell, 1886–1954, vol. V

Williams, Owen Herbert, 1884–1962, vol. VI
Williams, Owen John, 1850–1908, vol. I
Williams, (Owen) Kenneth, 1928–1984, vol. VIII
Williams, Owen Lenn, 1914–1998, vol. X
Williams, Lt-Gen. Owen Lewis Cope, 1836–1904, vol. I
Williams, Owen Thomas, 1877–1913, vol. I
Williams, Patrick W.; see Watson-Williams.
Williams, Penry, 1866–1945, vol. IV
Williams, Peter H.; see Havard-Williams.
Williams, Peter Lancelot, 1914–1995, vol. IX
Williams, Sir Peter W.; see Watkin Williams.
Williams, Rev. Philip, died 1933, vol. III
Williams, Sir Philip Francis Cunningham, 2nd Bt (cr 1915), 1884–1958, vol. V
Williams, Philip Maynard, 1920–1984, vol. VIII
Williams, Sir Ralph Champneys, 1848–1927, vol. II
Williams, Ralph Paul, 1874–1939, vol. III
Williams, Ralph V.; see Vaughan Williams.
Williams, Ralph Wilfred H.; see Hodder-Williams.
Williams, Brig.-Gen. Raymond Burlton, 1855–1929, vol. III
Williams, Raymond Henry, 1921–1988, vol. VIII
Williams, Sir Reginald Lawrence William, 7th Bt (cr 1798), 1900–1971, vol. VII
Williams, Lt-Col Sir Rhys Rhys-, 1st Bt (cr 1918), 1865–1955, vol. V
Williams, Air Marshal Sir Richard, 1890–1980, vol. VII
Williams, Richard Aelwyn Ellis, 1901–1981, vol. VIII
Williams, Richard James, 1876–1964, vol. VI
Williams, Sir Richard John, 1853–1941, vol. IV
Williams, Richard Tecwyn, 1909–1979, vol. VII
Williams, Robert, 1881–1936, vol. III
Williams, Sir Robert, 1st Bt (cr 1928), 1860–1938, vol. III
Williams, Ven. Robert, 1863–1938, vol. III
Williams, Col Sir Robert, 1st Bt (cr 1915), 1848–1943, vol. IV
Williams, Robert Allan, died 1951, vol. V
Williams, Rev. Robert C.; see Camber-Williams.
Williams, Lt-Col Robert Carlisle, 1880–1964, vol. VI
Williams, Robert Emmanuel, 1900–1988, vol. VIII
Williams, Maj.-Gen. Robert Ernest, 1855–1943, vol. IV
Williams, Sir Robert Ernest, 9th Bt (cr 1866), 1924–1976, vol. VII
Williams, Robert James P.; see Probyn-Williams.
Williams, Robert Percy H.; see Hodder-Williams.
Williams, Robert Stenhouse, 1871–1932, vol. III
Williams, Robert Thesiger W.; see Watkin-Williams.
Williams, Rohan; see Williams, E. R.
Williams, Roland Edmund Lomax Vaughan, 1866–1949, vol. IV
Williams, Rt Hon. Sir Roland Lomax Bowdler Vaughan, 1838–1916, vol. II
Williams, Sir Rolf Dudley D.; see Dudley-Williams.
Williams, Romer, 1850–1942, vol. IV
Williams, Rt Rev. Ronald Ralph, 1906–1979, vol. VII
Williams, Major Ronald Samuel Ainslie, 1890–1971, vol. VII
Williams, Ronald Watkins, 1907–1958, vol. V

Williams, Sir Roy Ellis H.; see Hume-Williams.
Williams, Captain Rupert Stanley G.; see Gwatkin-Williams.
Williams, Ven. Samuel, 1822–1907, vol. I
Williams, Rev. Samuel Blackwell G.; see Guest Williams.
Williams, Samuel Charles Evans, 1842–1926, vol. II
Williams, Sir Seymour; see Williams, Sir J. L. V. S.
Williams, Stanley, 1911–1990, vol. VIII
Williams, Lt-Col. Stanley Price, 1885–1977, vol. VII
Williams, Stuart Graeme, 1914–1986, vol. VIII
Williams, Brig.-Gen. Sydney Frederick, 1866–1942, vol. IV
Williams, Tennessee, (Thomas Lanier Williams) 1911–1983, vol. VIII
Williams, Terrick, 1860–1936, vol. III
Williams, Theodore Rowland, 1889–1964, vol. VI
Williams, Rev. Thomas, died 1915, vol. I
Williams, Sir Thomas, 1893–1967, vol. VI
Williams, Sir Thomas; see Williams, Sir D. T.
Williams, Sir Thomas; see Williams, Sir I. T.
Williams, Sir Thomas; see Williams, Sir W. T.
Williams, Very Rev. Thomas Alfred, 1870–1941, vol. IV
Williams, Rev. Thomas Charles, died 1927, vol. II
Williams, Thomas Christopher, 1913–1972, vol. VII
Williams, Thomas; see Hudson-Williams.
Williams, Sir Thomas Herbert P.; see Parry-Williams.
Williams, Thomas Jeremiah, 1872–1919, vol. II
Williams, Ven. Thomas John, 1889–1956, vol. V
Williams, Thomas Lanier; see Williams, Tennessee.
Williams, Most Rev. Thomas Leighton, 1877–1946, vol. IV
Williams, Sir Thomas Marchant, 1845–1914, vol. I
Williams, Air Marshal Sir Thomas Melling, 1899–1956, vol. V
Williams, Rev. Thomas Rhondda, 1860–1945, vol. IV
Williams, Maj.-Gen. Thomas Rhys, 1884–1950, vol. IV
Williams, Lt-Col Thomas Samuel Beauchamp, 1877–1927, vol. II
Williams, Thurston Monier, 1924–1985, vol. VIII
Williams, Trevor Illtyd, 1921–1996, vol. X
Williams, Valentine, 1883–1946, vol. IV
Williams, Vaughan; see Williams, J. V.
Williams, Victor Erle N.; see Nash-Williams.
Williams, W. H.; see Howard-Williams.
Williams, W. Llewelyn, 1867–1922, vol. II
Williams, W. Phillpotts, 1860–1916, vol. II
Williams, Walter Gordon Mason, 1923–2000, vol. X
Williams, Engr-Comdr Walter Kent, died 1914, vol. I
Williams, Maj.-Gen. Walter David Abbott, 1897–1973, vol. VII
Williams, Walter Nalder, 1880–1966, vol. VI
Williams, Rt Rev. Watkin Herbert, 1845–1944, vol. IV
Williams, Rev. Watkin Wynn, 1859–1944, vol. IV
Williams, Maj.-Gen. Weir De Lancey, 1872–1961, vol. VI
Williams, Very Rev. William, died 1930, vol. III

Williams, Engr-Captain William Arthur, 1882–1953, vol. V

Williams, William Daniel, 1888–1970, vol. VI

Williams, Surg.-Gen. Sir William Daniel Campbell, 1856–1919, vol. II

Williams, (William) Donald, 1919–1990, vol. VIII

Williams, Sir William Emrys, 1896–1977, vol. VII

Williams, Sir William Frederick, 4th Bt (cr 1866), 1886–1905, vol. I

Williams, Sir William Grenville, 4th Bt (cr 1798), 1844–1904, vol. I

Williams, William Henry, 1852–1941, vol. IV

Williams, Col William Hugh, 1857–1938, vol. III

Williams, Sir William John, 1828–1903, vol. I

Williams, William John, 1878–1952, vol. V

Williams, Lt-Col Sir William Jones, 1904–1976, vol. VII

Williams, Sir William Law, 8th Bt (cr 1866), 1907–1960, vol. V

Williams, Rt Rev. William Leonard, 1829–1916, vol. II

Williams, Hon. William Micah, died 1924, vol. II

Williams, William Owen, 1860–1911, vol. I

Williams, William Penry, 1892–1981, vol. VIII

Williams, Col William Picton B.; see Bradley-Williams.

Williams, Sir William Richard, 1879–1961, vol. VI

Williams, William Richard, 1895–1963, vol. VI

Williams, Sir William Robert, 3rd Bt (cr 1866), 1860–1903, vol. I

Williams, William St John F.; see Francis-Williams.

Williams, Sir (William) Thomas, 1915–1986, vol. VIII

Williams, William Thomas, 1913–1995, vol. IX

Williams, Sir William Willoughby, 5th Bt (cr 1798), 1888–1932, vol. III

Williams, Yvonne Lovat, 1920–1994, vol. IX

Williams-Bulkeley, Sir Richard Harry David, 13th Bt, 1911–1992, vol. IX

Williams-Bulkeley, Sir Richard Henry; see Bulkeley.

Williams-Drummond, Sir James Hamlyn Williams; see Drummond.

Williams-Drummond, Sir William Hugh Dudley; see Drummond.

Williams-Ellis, Amabel, (Lady Williams-Ellis); see Williams-Ellis, M. A. N.

Williams-Ellis, Sir (Bertram) Clough, 1883–1978, vol. VII

Williams-Ellis, Sir Clough; see Williams-Ellis, Sir B. C.

Williams-Ellis, Mary Annabel Nassau, (Amabel), (Lady Williams-Ellis), 1894–1984, vol. VIII

Williams-Freeman, Comdr Frederick Arthur Peere, 1889–1939, vol. III

Williams-Taylor, Sir Frederick, 1863–1945, vol. IV

Williams-Thomas, Lt-Col Frank S., 1879–1942, vol. IV

Williams-Thomas, Joseph Silvers; see Thomas.

Williams-Thomas, Lt-Col Reginald Silvers, 1914–1990, vol. VIII

Williams Wynn, Frederick R., 1865–1940, vol. III

Williams-Wynn, Col Sir Herbert Lloyd Watkin, 7th Bt, 1860–1944, vol. IV

Williams-Wynn, Col Sir (Owen) Watkin, 10th Bt, 1904–1988, vol. VIII

Williams-Wynn, Col Sir Robert William Herbert Watkin, 9th Bt, 1862–1951, vol. V

Williams-Wynn, Col Sir Watkin; see Williams-Wynn, Col Sir O. W.

Williams-Wynn, Sir Watkin, 8th Bt, 1891–1949, vol. IV

Williams-Wynne, Col John Francis, 1908–1998, vol. X

Williamson, Baron (Life Peer); Thomas Williamson 1897–1983, vol. VIII

Williamson, Captain Adolphus Huddleston, 1869–1918, vol. II

Williamson, Alec, 1886–1975, vol. VII

Williamson, Sir Alexander, 1879–1971, vol. VII

Williamson, Alexander William, 1824–1904, vol. I

Williamson, Air Comdt Dame Alice Mary, 1903–1983, vol. VIII

Williamson, Alice Muriel, 1869–1933, vol. III

Williamson, Andrew, died 1937, vol. III

Williamson, Rt Rev. Andrew Wallace, 1856–1926, vol. II

Williamson, Benjamin, 1827–1916, vol. II

Williamson, Bruce, 1893–1984, vol. VIII

Williamson, Mrs Catherine Ellis, 1896–1977, vol. VII

Williamson, Rev. Charles David Robertson, 1853–1943, vol. IV

Williamson, Sir Charles Hedworth, 10th Bt, 1903–1946, vol. IV

Williamson, Charles Norris, 1859–1920, vol. II

Williamson, Mrs Charles Norris; see Williamson, Alice Muriel.

Williamson, Colin Martin, 1887–1976, vol. VII

Williamson, David, 1868–1955, vol. V

Williamson, David, 1916–1980, vol. VII

Williamson, David Robertson, 1830–1913, vol. I

Williamson, David Theodore Nelson, (Theo), 1923–1992, vol. IX

Williamson, Rt Rev. Edward William, 1892–1953, vol. V

Williamson, Francis John, 1833–1920, vol. II

Williamson, Frank Edger, 1917–1998, vol. X

Williamson, Brig.-Gen. Sir Frederic Herbert, 1876–1939, vol. III

Williamson, Frederick, 1891–1935, vol. III

Williamson, Sir George Alexander, 1898–1975, vol. VII

Williamson, George Charles, 1858–1942, vol. IV

Williamson, George Watkins, 1875–1957, vol. V

Williamson, Harold, 1872–1935, vol. III

Williamson, Sir Hedworth, 8th Bt, 1827–1900, vol. I

Williamson, Sir Hedworth, 9th Bt, 1867–1942, vol. IV

Williamson, Henry, 1895–1977, vol. VII

Williamson, Rev. Henry Drummond, 1854–1926, vol. II

Williamson, Rev. Henry Trevor, died 1940, vol. III

Williamson, Herbert, 1872–1924, vol. II

Williamson, Sir Horace, 1880–1965, vol. VI

Williamson, Gp Captain Hugh Alexander, 1885–1979, vol. VII

Williamson, Hugh R.; see Ross Williamson.

Williamson, Sir James, 1839–1932, vol. III

Williamson, Sir James, 1877–1959, vol. V

Williamson, James Alexander, 1886–1964, vol. VI

Williamson, John, 1915–1982, vol. VIII
Williamson, Col John Francis, 1851–1930, vol. III
Williamson, John Thoburn, 1907–1958, vol. V
Williamson, Kenneth Bertram, 1875–1959, vol. V
Williamson, Lawrence Collingwood, 1886–1955, vol. V
Williamson, Ven. Montague Blamire, 1863–1939, vol. III
Williamson, Sir Nicholas Frederick Hedworth, 11th Bt, 1937–2000, vol. X
Williamson, Oliver Key, died 1941, vol. IV
Williamson, Air Vice-Marshal Peter Greville Kaye, 1923–1982, vol. VIII
Williamson, Reginald Pole R.; see Ross Williamson.
Williamson, Richard Harcourt, 1879–1941, vol. IV
Williamson, Richard Thomas, 1862–1937, vol. III
Williamson, Col Robert Frederic, 1843–1938, vol. III
Williamson, Robert Wood, 1856–1932, vol. III
Williamson, Samuel, died 1950, vol. IV
Williamson, Stephen, 1827–1903, vol. I
Williamson, Theo; see Williamson, D. T. N.
Williamson, Thomas Bateson, 1915–1985, vol. VIII
Williamson, Thomas Broadwood, 1911–1963, vol. VI
Williamson, Victor Alexander, 1838–1924, vol. II
Williamson, Sir Walter James Franklin, 1867–1954, vol. V
Williamson, Rev. William, 1851–1936, vol. III
Williamson-Noble, Frederick Arnold, 1889–1969, vol. VI
Willingdon, 1st Marquis of, 1866–1941, vol. IV
Willingdon, 2nd Marquess of, 1899–1979, vol. VII
Willingdon, Marchioness of; (Marie Adelaide), 1875–1960, vol. V
Willink, Rt Hon. Sir Henry Urmston, 1st Bt, 1894–1973, vol. VII
Willink, Very Rev. John Wakefield, 1858–1927, vol. II
Willis, Baron (Life Peer); Edward Henry Willis, 1914–1992, vol. IX
Willis, Sir Addington; see Willis, Sir W. A.
Willis, Hon. Albert Charles, 1876–1954, vol. V
Willis, Rt Rev. Alfred, 1836–1920, vol. II
Willis, Admiral of the Fleet Sir Algernon Usborne, 1889–1976, vol. VII
Willis, Anthony Armstrong, 1897–1976, vol. VII
Willis, Arthur d'Anyers, 1879–1953, vol. V
Willis, Charles Armine, 1881–1975, vol. VII
Willis, Col Charles Fancourt, 1854–1918, vol. II
Willis, Lt-Col Charles Hope, 1859–1940, vol. III
Willis, Charles Reginald, 1906–1995, vol. X (AI)
Willis, Maj.-Gen. Edward Henry, 1870–1961, vol. VI
Willis, Sir Edward William, 1849–1941, vol. IV
Willis, Hon. Sir Eric Archibald, 1922–1999, vol. X
Willis, Ernest William, 1874–1939, vol. III
Willis, Rt Hon. Eustace George, 1903–1987, vol. VIII
Willis, Frank, 1865–1932, vol. III
Willis, Sir Frank; see Willis, Sir Z. F.
Willis, Captain Frank Reginald, 1881–1964, vol. VI
Willis, Frank William, 1947–1999, vol. X
Willis, Rev. Frederic Earle d'Anyers, 1869–1940, vol. III

Willis, Rev. Frederic William, 1842–1930, vol. III
Willis, Sir Frederick James, 1863–1946, vol. IV
Willis, Rt Rev. Frederick Roberts, 1900–1976, vol. VII
Willis, Gaspard; see Willis, R. W. G.
Willis, Sir George Henry Smith, 1823–1900, vol. I
Willis, Col Sir George Henry, 1875–1940, vol. III
Willis, Paymaster Captain George Hughlings Armstrong, 1863–1934, vol. III
Willis, Harold Infield, 1902–1986, vol. VIII
Willis, Hector Ford, 1909–1989, vol. VIII
Willis, Hon. Henry, 1860–1950, vol. IV
Willis, John Brooke, 1906–1996, vol. X
Willis, John Christopher, 1868–1958, vol. V
Willis, Maj.-Gen. John Christopher Temple, 1900–1969, vol. VI
Willis, John Henry, 1887–1989, vol. VIII
Willis, Rt Rev. John Jamieson, 1872–1954, vol. V
Willis, Sir John Ramsay, 1908–1988, vol. VIII
Willis, John Robert, 1896–1982, vol. VIII
Willis, John Trueman, 1918–1998, vol. X
Willis, Joseph George, 1861–1924, vol. II
Willis, Rear-Adm. Kenneth Henry George, died 1998, vol. X
Willis, Olive Christine, (Lady Willis), 1895–1987, vol. VIII
Willis, Col Richard ffolliott, 1875–1960, vol. V
Willis, Major Richard Raymond, 1876–1966, vol. VI
Willis, (Robert William) Gaspard, 1905–1997, vol. X
Willis, Roger Blenkiron, 1906–1996, vol. X
Willis, Rupert Allan, 1898–1980, vol. VII
Willis, Samuel William Ward, 1870–1948, vol. IV
Willis, Ted; see Willis, Baron.
Willis, Sir (Walter) Addington, 1862–1953, vol. V
Willis, Sir William, 1821–1906, vol. I
Willis, Comdr William John Adlam, 1894–1982, vol. VIII
Willis, Ven. William Newcombe de Laval, 1846–1916, vol. II
Willis, William Outhwaite, 1870–1940, vol. III
Willis, Sir (Zwinglius) Frank, 1890–1974, vol. VII
Willis-Bund, John William, 1843–1928, vol. II
Willis-O'Connor, Col Henry; see O'Connor.
Willison, Brig. Arthur Cecil, 1896–1966, vol. VI
Willison, Herbert, died 1943, vol. IV
Willison, Sir John Stephen, 1856–1927, vol. II
Willkie, Wendell Lewis, 1892–1944, vol. IV
Willmer, Rt Hon. Sir Gordon; see Willmer, Rt Hon. Sir H. G.
Willmer, Rt Hon. Sir (Henry) Gordon, 1899–1983, vol. VIII
Willmore, Henry Horace Albert, 1871–1919, vol. II
Willmot, Joseph William, 1849–1929, vol. III
Willmot, Roger Boulton, 1892–1964, vol. VI
Willmott, Harry, 1851–1931, vol. III
Willmott, Sir Maurice Gordon, 1894–1977, vol. VII
Willmott, Peter, 1923–2000, vol. X
Willock, Brig.-Gen. Frederick George, died 1955, vol. V
Willock, Air Vice-Marshal Robert Peel, 1893–1973, vol. VII
Willock-Pollen, Henry Court, 1860–1934, vol. III

Willott, Lt-Col Roland Lancaster, 1912–1984, vol. VIII
Willoughby de Broke, 18th Baron, 1844–1902, vol. I
Willoughby de Broke, 19th Baron, 1869–1923, vol. II
Willoughby de Broke, 20th Baron, 1896–1986, vol. VIII
Willoughby de Eresby, Lord; Timothy Gilbert Heathcote-Drummond-Willoughby, 1936–1963, vol. VI
Willoughby, Brig.-Gen. Hon. Charles Strathavon Heathcote-Drummond-, 1870–1949, vol. IV
Willoughby, Lt-Col Hon. Claud Heathcote-Drummond, 1872–1950, vol. IV
Willoughby, Col Hon. Claude Henry Comaraich, 1862–1932, vol. III
Willoughby, Ven. David Albert, 1931–1998, vol. X
Willoughby, Col Douglas Vere, 1882–1949, vol. IV
Willoughby, Rear-Adm. Guy, 1902–1987, vol. VIII
Willoughby, Maj.-Gen. James Fortnom, 1844–1922, vol. II
Willoughby, Major Sir John Christopher, 5th Bt, 1859–1918, vol. II
Willoughby, Maj.-Gen. Sir John Edward Francis, 1913–1991, vol. IX
Willoughby, Leonard Ashley, 1885–1977, vol. VII
Willoughby, Brig.-Gen. Michael Edward, 1864–1939, vol. III
Willoughby, Lt-Gen. Michael Weekes, 1833–1925, vol. II
Willoughby, Percival Robert Augustus, 1868–1913, vol. I
Willoughby, Wellington Bartley, 1859–1932, vol. III
Willoughby-Osborne, Col Arthur de Vere, 1869–1933, vol. III
Willox, Sir John Archibald, 1842–1905, vol. I
Wills, Rt Hon. Sir Alfred, 1828–1912, vol. I
Wills, Captain Arnold Stancomb, 1877–1961, vol. VI
Wills, Arthur Walters, 1868–1948, vol. IV
Wills, Lt-Col Caleb Shera, 1834–1906, vol. I
Wills, Cecil Upton, died 1954, vol. V
Wills, Charles James, 1842–1912, vol. I
Wills, Vice-Adm. Charles Samuel, died 1931, vol. III
Wills, Colin Spencer, 1937–1997, vol. X
Wills, Sir David; see Wills, Sir H. D. H.
Wills, Edith Agnes, 1892–1970, vol. VI
Wills, Lt-Col Sir Edward; see Wills, Lt-Col Sir Ernest E. de W.
Wills, Sir Edward Chaning, 2nd Bt (cr 1904), 1861–1921, vol. II
Wills, Sir Edward Payson, 1st Bt (cr 1904), 1834–1910, vol. I
Wills, Lt-Col Sir (Ernest) Edward (de Winton), 4th Bt, 1903–1983, vol. VIII
Wills, Sir Ernest Salter, 3rd Bt, (cr 1904), 1869–1958, vol. V
Wills, Sir Frank William, 1852–1932, vol. III
Wills, Sir Frederick, 1st Bt (cr 1897), 1838–1909, vol. I
Wills, Rev. Freeman, died 1913, vol. I
Wills, Sir George Alfred, 1st Bt (cr 1923), 1854–1928, vol. II

Wills, Sir (George) Peter (Vernon), 3rd Bt (cr 1923), 1922–1945, vol. IV
Wills, Sir George Vernon Proctor, 2nd Bt (cr 1923), 1887–1931, vol. III
Wills, Sir Gerald, 1905–1969, vol. VI
Wills, Helen; see Roark, H. W.
Wills, Henry Herbert, 1856–1922, vol. II
Wills, Herbert W., died 1937, vol. III
Wills, Sir (Hugh) David (Hamilton), 1917–1999, vol. X
Wills, Dame Janet Stancomb Graham S.; see Stancomb-Wills.
Wills, John Joseph, 1877–1971, vol. VII
Wills, Sir John Spencer, 1904–1991, vol. IX
Wills, Sir John Vernon, 4th Bt (cr 1923), 1928–1998, vol. X
Wills, Joseph Lyttleton, born 1899, vol. VIII
Wills, Brig. Sir Kenneth Agnew, 1896–1977, vol. VII
Wills, Leonard Johnston, 1844–1979, vol. VII
Wills, Rev. Percival Banks, died 1936, vol. III
Wills, Sir Peter; see Wills, Sir G. P. V.
Wills, Philip Aubrey, 1907–1978, vol. VII
Wills, Richard Lloyd Joseph, 1914–1969, vol. VI
Wills, Dame Violet Edith, died 1964, vol. VI
Wills, Walter Kenneth, 1872–1968, vol. VI
Wills, Wilfrid Dewhurst, 1898–1954, vol. V
Wills, Major William Arthur, 1863–1937, vol. III
Willshire, Sir Arthur Reginald Thomas Maxwell-, 2nd Bt, 1850–1919, vol. II
Willshire, Sir Gerard Arthur Maxwell-, 3rd Bt, 1892–1947, vol. IV
Willson, Rev. Archdall Beaumont Wynne, died 1958, vol. V
Willson, Beckles, 1869–1942, vol. IV
Willson, Douglas James, 1906–1993, vol. IX
Willson, Leslie, died 1924, vol. II
Willson, Maj.-Gen. Sir Mildmay Willson, 1847–1912, vol. I
Willson, Rt Rev. St J. Basil Wynne, 1868–1946, vol. IV
Willson, Rev. Thomas B., 1851–1932, vol. III
Willson, Thomas Olaf, 1880–1973, vol. VII
Willson, Sir Walter Stuart James, 1876–1952, vol. V
Willson, William Thomas C.; see Curtis-Willson.
Willway, Brig. Alfred Cedric Cowan, 1898–1980, vol. VII
Willway, Brig. Cedric; see Willway, Brig. A. C. C.
Willy; see Gauthier-Villars, Henry.
Willyams, Arthur Champion Phillips, 1837–1917, vol. II
Willyams, Edward Brydges, 1836–1916, vol. II
Willyams, Bt Col Edward Neynoe, 1891–1964, vol. VI
Wilmer, Brig. Eric Randal Gordon, 1882–1958, vol. V
Wilmer, Rev. John Kidd, died 1928, vol. II, vol. III
Wilmers, John Geoffrey, 1920–1984, vol. VIII
Wilmington, Joseph Robert, 1932–1999, vol. X
Wilmot of Selmeston, 1st Baron, 1895–1964, vol. VI
Wilmot, Hon. Alexander, 1836–1923, vol. II
Wilmot, Col Arthur E.; see Eardley-Wilmot.
Wilmot, Captain Sir Arthur Ralph, 7th Bt (cr 1759), 1909–1942, vol. IV

Wilmot, Air Vice-Marshal Aubrey S.; *see* Sidney-Wilmot.

Wilmot, Chester, (Reginald William Winchester Wilmot), 1911–1954, vol. V

Wilmot, Sir Henry, 5th Bt (*cr* 1759), 1831–1901, vol. I

Wilmot, Captain Cecil F. E.; *see* Eardley-Wilmot.

Wilmot, Rev. Ernest Augustus E.; *see* Eardley-Wilmot.

Wilmot, Harold, 1895–1966, vol. VI

Wilmot, Hugh Eden E.; *see* Eardley-Wilmot.

Wilmot, Sir John Assheton E.; *see* Eardley-Wilmot.

Wilmot, Sir John E., *see* Eardley Wilmot

Wilmot, May E.; *see* Eardley-Wilmot.

Wilmot, Sir Ralph Henry Sacheverel, 6th Bt (*cr* 1759), 1875–1918, vol. II

Wilmot, Reginald William Winchester; *see* Wilmot, C.

Wilmot, Maj.-Gen. Revell E.; *see* Eardley-Wilmot.

Wilmot, Sir Robert Arthur, 8th Bt, 1939–1974, (*cr* 1759), vol. VII

Wilmot, Sir Robert Rodney, 6th Bt (*cr* 1772), 1853–1931, vol. III

Wilmot, Sir Sainthill E.; *see* Eardley-Wilmot.

Wilmot, Rear-Adm. Sir Sydney Marow E.; *see* Eardley-Wilmot.

Wilmot-Smith, Comdr Andrew, *died* 1937, vol. III

Wilmott, Alfred James, 1888–1950, vol. IV

Wilmshurst, Thomas Percival, *died* 1950, vol. IV

Wilsden, Rev. Joseph Samuel, 1835–1914, vol. I

Wilsey, Maj.Gen. Anthony Patrick W.; *see* Willasey-Wilsey.

Wilsey, Maj.-Gen. John Harold Owen, 1904–1961, vol. VI

Wilshaw, Sir Edward, 1879–1968, vol. VI

Wilshere, Alfred Henry, 1854–1927, vol. II, vol. III

Wilshire, Frederick Allen, 1868–1944, vol. IV

Wilsmore, Norman T. M., 1868–1940, vol. III

Wilson, 1st Baron, 1881–1964, vol. VI

Wilson of High Wray, Baron (Life Peer); Paul Norman Wilson, 1908–1980, vol. VII

Wilson of Langside, Baron (Life Peer); Henry Stephen Wilson, 1916–1997, vol. X

Wilson of Radcliffe, Baron (Life Peer); Alfred Wilson, 1909–1983, vol. VIII

Wilson of Rievaulx, Baron (Life Peer); James Harold Wilson, 1916–1995, vol. IX

Wilson, Adam, 1882–1951, vol. V

Wilson, Alan, 1896–1959, vol. V

Wilson, Rear-Adm. Alan Christopher Wyndham, 1919–1985, vol. VIII

Wilson, Sir Alan Herries, 1906–1995, vol. IX

Wilson, Lt-Col Alban; *see* Wilson, Lt-Col J. A.

Wilson, Albert Edward, *died* 1960, vol. V

Wilson, Sir Alexander, 1st Bt (*cr* 1897), 1837–1907, vol. I

Wilson, Sir Alexander, 1843–1907, vol. I

Wilson, Maj.-Gen. Sir Alexander, 1858–1937, vol. III

Wilson, Alexander, 1917–1978, vol. VII

Wilson, Captain Alexander Guy Berners, 1890–1942, vol. IV

Wilson, Alexander Johnstone, 1841–1921, vol. II

Wilson, Alfred Harold, 1895–1984, vol. VIII

Wilson, Allan Charles, 1934–1991, vol. IX

Wilson, Alpheus Waters, 1834–1916, vol. II

Wilson, Rev. Ambrose John, 1853–1929, vol. III

Wilson, Andrew, 1852–1912, vol. I

Wilson, Andrew, 1909–1974, vol. VII

Wilson, Rev. Canon Andrew, 1920–1985, vol. VIII

Wilson, Sir Angus Frank Johnstone, 1913–1991, vol. IX

Wilson, Sir (Archibald) Duncan, 1911–1983, vol. VIII

Wilson, Archibald Wayet, *died* 1950, vol. IV (A), vol. V

Wilson, Lt-Col Sir Arnold Talbot, 1884–1940, vol. III

Wilson, Arthur, 1836–1909, vol. I

Wilson, Rt Hon. Sir Arthur, 1837–1915, vol. I

Wilson, Maj.-Gen. Arthur Gillespie, 1900–1982, vol. IX (AI)

Wilson, Col Arthur Harry H.; *see* Hutton-Wilson.

Wilson, Arthur James Cochran, 1914–1995, vol. IX

Wilson, Adm. Sir Arthur Knyvet, 3rd Bt (*cr* 1857), 1842–1921, vol. II

Wilson, Arthur Stanley, 1868–1938, vol. III

Wilson, Sir Arton, 1893–1977, vol. VII

Wilson, Sir Austin George, 1906–1987, vol. VIII

Wilson, Rev. Barton Worsley, *died* 1920, vol. II

Wilson, Rev. Bernard Robert, 1857–1909, vol. I

Wilson, Sir Bertram, 1893–1974, vol. VII

Wilson, Bertram Martin, 1896–1935, vol. III

Wilson, Beryl Charlotte Mary, *died* 1951, vol. V

Wilson, Maj.-Gen. Bevil Thomson, 1885–1975, vol. VII

Wilson, Brian Harvey, 1915–2000, vol. X

Wilson, Col Campbell Aubrey Kenneth I.; *see* Innes-Wilson.

Wilson, Rt Rev. Cecil, 1860–1941, vol. IV

Wilson, Cecil Claude, 1885–1968, vol. VI

Wilson, Cecil Henry, 1862–1945, vol. IV

Wilson, Rt Rev. Cecil Wilfred, 1875–1937, vol. III

Wilson, Major Cecil William, 1870–1937, vol. III

Wilson, Charles Ashley C.; *see* Carus-Wilson.

Wilson, Mrs Charles Ashley C.; *see* Carus-Wilson.

Wilson, Captain Charles Benjamin, 1885–1957, vol. V

Wilson, Charles Edward, 1848–1938, vol. III (A), vol. IV

Wilson, Rev. Charles Edward, 1871–1956, vol. V

Wilson, Charles Edward, 1886–1972, vol. VII

Wilson, Charles Erwin, 1890–1961, vol. VI

Wilson, Sir Charles Henry, 1859–1930, vol. III

Wilson, Charles Henry, 1858–1937, vol. III

Wilson, Charles Henry, 1914–1991, vol. IX

Wilson, Col Charles Henry Luttrell Fahie, 1858–1935, vol. III

Wilson, Charles Paul, 1900–1970, vol. VI

Wilson, Sir Charles Rivers, 1831–1916, vol. II

Wilson, Sir Charles S.; *see* Stewart-Wilson.

Wilson, Brig.-Gen. Charles Stuart, 1867–1933, vol. III

Wilson, Charles Thomson Rees, 1869–1959, vol. V

Wilson, Rev. Charles William Goodall, 1860–1948, vol. IV

Wilson, Christopher James, 1879–1956, vol. V

Wilson, Christopher Maynard, 1928–1997, vol. X

Wilson, Col Christopher Wyndham, 1844–1918, vol. II

Wilson, Claude, 1860–1937, vol. III
Wilson, Clifford, 1906–1997, vol. X
Wilson, Clive Henry Adolphus, 1876–1921, vol. II
Wilson, Clyde Tabor, 1889–1971, vol. II
Wilson, Sir Courthope; *see* Wilson, Sir William C. T.
Wilson, Col Cyril Edward, 1873–1938, vol. III
Wilson, D. Forrester, *died* 1950, vol. IV
Wilson, Rev. Daniel Frederic, 1830–1918, vol. II
Wilson, Hon. Daniel Martin, 1862–1932, vol. III
Wilson, Sir David, 1838–1924, vol. II
Wilson, Sir David, 1st Bt (*cr* 1920), 1855–1930, vol. III
Wilson, David Alec, 1864–1933, vol. III
Wilson, Very Rev. David Frederick Ruddell, 1871–1957, vol. V
Wilson, David Mackay, 1863–1929, vol. III
Wilson, Douglas George, 1924–1991, vol. IX
Wilson, Rt Rev. Douglas John, 1903–1980, vol. VII
Wilson, Sir Duncan; *see* Wilson, Sir A. D.
Wilson, Sir Duncan Randolph, 1875–1945, vol. IV
Wilson, Major Duncan William, 1881–1935, vol. III
Wilson, Lt-Col Edmond Munkhouse, 1855–1921, vol. II
Wilson, Edmund, 1895–1972, vol. VII
Wilson, Edmund Beecher, 1856–1939, vol. III
Wilson, Col Edward Hales, 1845–1917, vol. II
Wilson, Edward Meryon, 1906–1977, vol. VII
Wilson, Brig. Edward William Gravatt, 1888–1971, vol. VII
Wilson, Edwin John B.; *see* Boyd-Wilson.
Wilson, Eleanora Mary C.; *see* Carus-Wilson.
Wilson, Ellis; *see* Wilson, H. E. C.
Wilson, Maj.-Gen. Erastus William, 1860–1922, vol. II
Wilson, Brig. Sir Eric Edward Boketon H.; *see* Holt-Wilson.
Wilson, Ernest, *died* 1932, vol. III
Wilson, Ernest Henry, 1876–1930, vol. III
Wilson, Florence Roma Muir; *see* Wilson, Romer.
Wilson, Forsyth James, 1880–1944, vol. IV
Wilson, Maj.-Gen. Francis Adrian, 1874–1954, vol. V
Wilson, Maj.-Gen. Francis Edward Edwards, 1839–1905, vol. I
Wilson, Hon. Frank, 1859–1918, vol. II
Wilson, Captain Sir Frank O'Brien, 1883–1962, vol. VI
Wilson, Frank Percy, 1889–1963, vol. VI
Wilson, Col Frank Walter, 1869–1953, vol. V
Wilson, Lt-Col Frederick Alfred, 1863–1932, vol. III
Wilson, Frederick James, 1858–1926, vol. II
Wilson, Maj.-Gen. Frederick Maurice, 1868–1956, vol. V
Wilson, Sir Frederick William, 1844–1924, vol. II
Wilson, Sir Garnet Douglas, 1885–1975, vol. VII
Wilson, Geoffrey; *see* Wilson, H. G. B.
Wilson, Maj.-Gen. Geoffrey Boyd, 1927–1984, vol. VIII
Wilson, Captain George, 1849–1932, vol. III
Wilson, Lt-Col George, 1869–1935, vol. III
Wilson, George, 1862–1943, vol. IV
Wilson, Sir George, 1900–1979, vol. VII
Wilson, George Ambler, 1906–1977, vol. VII

Wilson, George Bailey, 1863–1952, vol. V
Wilson, George Frederick, 1886–1970, vol. VI
Wilson, George Hamilton Bracher, 1895–1963, vol. VI
Wilson, Sir George Henry, 1869–1939, vol. III
Wilson, Rev. Canon George Herbert, 1870–1952, vol. V
Wilson, George Heron, 1868–1959, vol. V
Wilson, George Maryon Maryon-, 1861–1941, vol. IV
Wilson, Rev. Canon Sir George Percy Maryon M.; *see* Maryon-Wilson.
Wilson, Lt-Col George Robert Stewart, 1896–1958, vol. V
Wilson, (Gerald) Roy, 1930–1997, vol. X
Wilson, Gerald Sidney, 1880–1960, vol. V
Wilson, Gilbert, 1908–1994, vol. IX
Wilson, Godfrey Harold Alfred, 1871–1958, vol. V
Wilson, Maj.-Gen. Sir Gordon, 1887–1971, vol. VII
Wilson, Lt-Col Gordon Chesney, 1865–1914, vol. I
Wilson, Gordon Wallace, 1926–2000, vol. X
Wilson, Grace Margaret, (Mrs Bruce Campbell), *died* 1957, vol. V
Wilson, Graeme McDonald, 1919–1992, vol. IX
Wilson, Graham Malcolm, 1917–1977, vol. VII
Wilson, Sir Graham Selby, 1895–1987, vol. VIII
Wilson, Gregg, 1865–1951, vol. V
Wilson, Rear-Adm. Guy Austen Moore, 1906–1986, vol. VIII
Wilson, Rt Hon. Sir Guy Douglas Arthur Fleetwood, 1850–1940, vol. III
Wilson, Col Hon. Guy Greville, 1877–1943, vol. IV
Wilson, Rev. Canon Harold, 1919–1975, vol. VII
Wilson, Harold Albert, 1874–1964, vol. VI
Wilson, Air Vice-Marshal Harold Arthur Cooper B.; *see* Bird-Wilson.
Wilson, Harold Fitzhardinge Wilson, 1913–1984, vol. VIII
Wilson, Col Harold René, 1890–1941, vol. IV
Wilson, Harold William, *died* 1959, vol. V
Wilson, Harry, 1852–1928, vol. II
Wilson, (Harry) Ellis (Charter), 1899–1987, vol. VIII
Wilson, Rear-Adm. (S) Harry George, 1874–1947, vol. IV
Wilson, Harry Lawrence L.; *see* Lawrence-Wilson.
Wilson, Harry Leon, 1867–1939, vol. III
Wilson, Helen Russell, *died* 1924, vol. II
Wilson, Rt Rev. Henry Albert, 1876–1961, vol. VI
Wilson, Rev. Henry Austin, 1854–1927, vol. II
Wilson, Sir Henry Francis, (Harry), 1859–1937, vol. III
Wilson, Lt-Gen. Sir Henry Fuller Maitland, 1859–1941, vol. IV
Wilson, Field-Marshal Sir Henry Hughes, 1st Bt (*cr* 1919), 1864–1922, vol. II
Wilson, (Henry) James, 1916–1990, vol. VIII
Wilson, Col Henry James, 1904–1985, vol. VIII
Wilson, Henry Joseph, 1833–1914, vol. I
Wilson, Henry Leonard, 1897–1968, vol. VI
Wilson, Henry Moir, 1910–1992, vol. IX
Wilson, Henry Wilcox, 1895–1974, vol. VII
Wilson, Herbert, 1862–1927, vol. II, vol. III
Wilson, Captain Herbert Haydon, 1875–1917, vol. II
Wilson, Sir Herbert W. L.; *see* Lush-Wilson.

Wilson, Herbert Wrigley, 1866–1940, vol. III
Wilson, Sir Horace John, 1882–1972, vol. VII
Wilson, Sir Hubert Guy Maryon M.; *see*
Maryon-Wilson.
Wilson, Hubert Wilberforce, 1867–1949, vol. IV
Wilson, Sir Hugh; *see* Wilson, Sir L. H.
Wilson, (Hugh) Geoffrey (Birch), 1903–1975,
vol. VII
Wilson, Hon. Sir Ian; *see* Wilson, Hon. Sir T. I. F.
Wilson, Rev. Canon Ian George MacQueen,
1920–1988, vol. VIII
Wilson, Sir Isaac Henry, *died* 1944, vol. IV
Wilson, Isabel Grace Hood, 1895–1982, vol. VIII
Wilson, Sir Jacob, 1836–1905, vol. I
Wilson, James; *see* Wilson, H. J.
Wilson, Rev. James, 1856–1923, vol. II
Wilson, James, 1847–1924, vol. II
Wilson, Sir James, 1853–1926, vol. II
Wilson, James, 1861–1941, vol. IV
Wilson, James, 1879–1943, vol. IV
Wilson, James, 1899–1978, vol. VII (AII)
Wilson, Lt-Col (James) Alban, 1865–1928, vol. II
Wilson, Rev. James Allen, 1827–1917, vol. II
Wilson, Sir James Arthur, 1877–1950, vol. IV
Wilson, Maj.-Gen. James Barnett, 1862–1936,
vol. III
Wilson, Sir James Glenny, 1849–1929, vol. III
Wilson, Ven. James Maurice, 1836–1931, vol. III
Wilson, Sir James Robertson, 2nd Bt (*cr* 1906),
1883–1964, vol. VI
Wilson, Sir (James) Steuart, 1889–1966, vol. VI
Wilson, Air Vice-Marshal James Stewart,
1909–1994, vol. IX
Wilson, James Thomas, 1861–1945, vol. IV
Wilson, James Thomas Pither, 1884–1976, vol. VII
Wilson, Sir Jeremiah, *died* 1930, vol. III
Wilson, John, 1837–1915, vol. I
Wilson, Sir John, 1st Bt (*cr* 1906), 1844–1918,
vol. II
Wilson, John, 1837–1928, vol. II
Wilson, John, 1860–1938, vol. III
Wilson, Rev. John, 1854–1939, vol. III
Wilson, John; *see* Ashmore, Hon. Lord.
Wilson, John Anthony Burgess; *see* Burgess, A.
Wilson, Sir John Carnegie Dove-, 1865–1935,
vol. III
Wilson, John Dove, 1833–1908, vol. I
Wilson, John Dover, 1881–1969, vol. VI
Wilson, Sir John Foster, 1919–1999, vol. X
Wilson, Sir John Gardiner, 1913–1994, vol. IX
Wilson, Col John George Yule, 1853–1935, vol. III
Wilson, Col John Gerald, 1841–1902, vol. I
Wilson, John Gideon, 1876–1963, vol. VI
Wilson, John Graham, 1911–1994, vol. X (AI)
Wilson, John Gray, 1915–1968, vol. VI
Wilson, J(ohn) Greenwood, 1897–1990, vol. VIII
Wilson, John Henry, 1862–1932, vol. III
Wilson, Rev. John Kenneth, 1890–1949, vol. IV
Wilson, Rt Rev. John Leonard, 1897–1970, vol. VI
Wilson, Sir John Martindale, 1915–1993, vol. IX
Wilson, Sir John Menzies, 3rd Bt (*cr* 1906),
1885–1968, vol. VI
Wilson, Sir John Mitchell Harvey, 2nd Bt (*cr* 1920),
1898–1975, vol. VII
Wilson, Very Rev. John Skinner, 1849–1926, vol. II

Wilson, Col John Skinner, 1888–1969, vol. VI
Wilson, John Spark, 1922–1993, vol. IX
Wilson, John Stuart Gladstone, 1916–1996, vol. X
Wilson, John Thomson, 1855–1930, vol. III
Wilson, (John) Tuzo, 1908–1993, vol. IX
Wilson, Rt Hon. John William, 1858–1932, vol. III
Wilson, Joseph Havelock, 1859–1929, vol. III
Wilson, Rev. Joseph Kershaw, 1854–1930, vol. III
Wilson, Joseph Maitland, 1868–1940, vol. III
Wilson, Hon. Joseph Marcellin, 1859–1940, vol. III
(A), vol. IV
Wilson, Joseph Vivian, 1894–1977, vol. VII
Wilson, Joseph William, 1851–1930, vol. III
Wilson, Sir Keith Cameron, 1900–1987, vol. VIII
Wilson, Kenneth Henry, 1885–1969, vol. VI
Wilson, Brig.-Gen. Lachlan Chisholm, 1871–1947,
vol. IV
Wilson, Col Lancelot Machell, 1873–1950, vol. IV
Wilson, Sir Leonard, 1888–1980, vol. VII
Wilson, Sir (Leslie) Hugh, 1913–1985, vol. VIII
Wilson, Col Rt Hon. Sir Leslie Orme, 1876–1955,
vol. V
Wilson, Rev. Canon L(eslie) Rule, 1909–1991,
vol. IX
Wilson, Rt Rev. Lucian Charles U.; *see*
Usher-Wilson.
Wilson, Sir Mark, 1896–1956, vol. V
Wilson, Sir Martin; *see* Wilson, Sir Mathew M.
Wilson, Sir Mathew Amcotts, 3rd Bt (*cr* 1874),
1853–1914, vol. I
Wilson, Sir (Mathew) Martin, 5th Bt (*cr* 1874),
1906–1991, vol. IX
Wilson, Lt-Col Sir Mathew Richard Henry, 4th Bt
(*cr* 1874), 1875–1958, vol. V
Wilson, Sir Mathew Wharton, 2nd Bt (*cr* 1874),
1827–1909, vol. I
Wilson, Matthew, 1854–1920, vol. II
Wilson, Maurice, 1862–1936, vol. III
Wilson, Sir Maurice B.; *see* Bromley-Wilson.
Wilson, Sir Michael Thomond, 1911–1983, vol. VIII
Wilson, Mona, 1872–1954, vol. V
Wilson, Morris W., 1883–1946, vol. IV
Wilson, Lt-Col Sir Murrough John, 1875–1946,
vol. IV
Wilson, Lt-Col Nathaniel, *died* 1944, vol. IV
Wilson, Captain Neville Frederick Jarvis,
1865–1947, vol. IV
Wilson, Maj.-Gen. Nigel Maitland, 1884–1950,
vol. IV
Wilson, Norman George, 1911–1992, vol. IX
Wilson, Maj.-Gen. Norman Methven, 1881–1961,
vol. VI
Wilson, Oscar, 1867–1930, vol. III
Wilson, P. Macgregor, *died* 1928, vol. II, vol. III
Wilson, Lt-Col Patrick Hogarth, 1874–1939, vol. III
Wilson, Percy, 1904–1986, vol. VIII
Wilson, Rev. Canon Sir Percy M.; *see*
Maryon-Wilson.
Wilson, Lt-Col Percy Norton Whitestone,
1886–1933, vol. III
Wilson, Peter Cecil, 1913–1984, vol. VIII
Wilson, Peter Humphrey St John, 1908–1987,
vol. VIII
Wilson, Philip Duncan, 1886–1969, vol. VI
Wilson, Philip Whitwell, 1875–1956, vol. V

Wilson, Rt Rev. Piers Holt, *died* 1956, vol. V
Wilson, Ralph Darrell, 1892–1967, vol. VI
Wilson, Raymond, 1925–1995, vol. IX
Wilson, Reginald Appleby, 1878–1955, vol. V
Wilson, Rev. Reginald Francis, 1873–1937, vol. III
Wilson, Reginald Henry Rimington Rimington-, 1852–1927, vol. II
Wilson, Sir Reginald Holmes, 1905–1999, vol. X
Wilson, Reginald Page, *died* 1950, vol. IV
Wilson, Hon. Sir (Reginald) Victor, 1877–1957, vol. V
Wilson, Col Richard Henry, 1886–1969, vol. VI
Wilson, Lt-Col Richard Henry Francis Wharton, 1855–1936, vol. III
Wilson, Richard Henry George, 1874–1944, vol. IV
Wilson, Rev. Richard Mercer, 1887–1976, vol. VII
Wilson, Richard Middlewood, 1908–1995, vol. X (AI)
Wilson, Robert, 1871–1920, vol. II
Wilson, Sir Robert, 1865–1943, vol. IV
Wilson, Captain Robert Amcotts, 1882–1960, vol. V
Wilson, Robert Andrew, 1905–1984, vol. VIII
Wilson, Hon. Sir Robert Christian, 1896–1973, vol. VII
Wilson, Lt-Col Robert Edward, 1884–1936, vol. III
Wilson, Robert Graham, 1917–1982, vol. VIII
Wilson, Rev. Robert James, *died* 1897, vol. I
Wilson, Robert John, 1865–1946, vol. IV
Wilson, Very Rev. Robert John, 1893–1981, vol. VIII
Wilson, Robert McNair, 1882–1963, vol. VI
Wilson, Sir Robert Michael Conal; *see* McNair-Wilson.
Wilson, Sir (Roderick) Roy, 1876–1942, vol. IV
Wilson, Gen. Sir Roger Cochrane, 1882–1966, vol. VI
Wilson, Roger Cowan, 1906–1991, vol. IX
Wilson, Lt-Col Roger Parker, 1870–1943, vol. IV
Wilson, Sir Roland, 1904–1996, vol. X
Wilson, Sir Roland Knyvet, 2nd Bt (*cr* 1857), 1840–1919, vol. II
Wilson, Romer, 1891–1930, vol. III
Wilson, Sir Roy; *see* Wilson, Sir Roderick R.
Wilson, Roy; *see* Wilson, G. R.
Wilson, Sheriff Roy Alexander, 1927–1985, vol. VIII
Wilson, Sir Roy Mickel, 1903–1982, vol. VIII
Wilson, Rule; *see* Wilson, L. R.
Wilson, Sir Samuel, 1861–1937, vol. III
Wilson, Samuel Alexander Kinnier, 1874–1937, vol. III
Wilson, Brig.-Gen. Sir Samuel Herbert, 1873–1950, vol. IV
Wilson, Lady Sarah Isabella Augusta, 1865–1929, vol. III
Wilson, Sir Spencer Maryon Maryon, 10th Bt (*cr* 1661), 1829–1897, vol. I
Wilson, Sir Spencer Pocklington Maryon Maryon-, 11th Bt (*cr* 1661), 1859–1944, vol. IV
Wilson, Stanley Livingstone, 1905–1990, vol. IX (AI)
Wilson, Stanley Reginald, 1890–1973, vol. VII
Wilson, Stephen Shipley, 1904–1989, vol. VIII
Wilson, Sir Steuart; *see* Wilson, Sir J. S.
Wilson, Sydney Ernest, *died* 1973, vol. VII

Wilson, T. Henry, *died* 1941, vol. IV
Wilson, Theodora Wilson, *died* 1941, vol. IV
Wilson, Theodore Stacey, 1861–1949, vol. IV
Wilson, Col Thomas, 1831–1915, vol. I
Wilson, Sir Thomas, 1863–1930, vol. III
Wilson, Thomas, 1905–1988, vol. VIII
Wilson, Maj.-Gen. Thomas Arthur Atkinson, 1882–1958, vol. V
Wilson, Ven. Thomas Bowstead, 1882–1961, vol. VI
Wilson, Thomas Corby, *died* 1934, vol. III
Wilson, Captain Sir Thomas Douglas, 4th Bt, 1917–1984, vol. VIII
Wilson, Rev. Thomas Erskine, 1874–1951, vol. V
Wilson, Sir Thomas Fleming, 1862–1929, vol. III
Wilson, Sir Thomas George, 1876–1958, vol. V
Wilson, Sir (Thomas) George; *see* Wilson, Sir G.
Wilson, Thomas Marcus, 1913–1996, vol. X
Wilson, Maj.-Gen. Thomas Needham Furnival, 1896–1961, vol. VI
Wilson, (Thomas) Woodrow, 1856–1924, vol. II
Wilson, Hon. Sir (Tom) Ian (Findley), 1904–1971, vol. VI
Wilson, Tuzo; *see* Wilson, J. T.
Wilson, Hon. Sir Victor; *see* Wilson, Hon. Sir R. V.
Wilson, Gp Captain Walter Carandini, 1885–1968, vol. VI
Wilson, Walter Gordon, 1874–1957, vol. V
Wilson, Hon. Walter Horatio, 1839–1902, vol. I
Wilson, Sir Wemyss G.; *see* Grant-Wilson.
Wilson, William, 1884–1944, vol. IV
Wilson, William, 1875–1965, vol. VI
Wilson, William, 1920–1972, vol. VII
Wilson, William Adam, 1928–1994, vol. IX
Wilson, Engr-Captain William Anderson, 1868–1957, vol. V
Wilson, William Combe, 1897–1974, vol. VII
Wilson, Sir (William) Courthope (Townshend), 1865–1944, vol. IV
Wilson, Surg.-Gen. Sir William Deane, 1843–1921, vol. II
Wilson, William Edward, 1851–1908, vol. I
Wilson, Sir William G.; *see* Grey-Wilson.
Wilson, Rt Rev. William Gilbert, 1918–1999, vol. X
Wilson, Very Rev. William Hay, *died* 1925, vol. II
Wilson, Maj. William Herbert, 1866–1928, vol. II
Wilson, William James, 1879–1954, vol. V
Wilson, William Joseph Robinson, 1909–1982, vol. VIII
Wilson, William Lawrence, 1912–1993, vol. IX
Wilson, William Lyne, 1843–1900, vol. I
Wilson, Gp Captain William Proctor, 1902–1980, vol. VII
Wilson, William Robert, 1844–1928, vol. II
Wilson, Sir William Tweedley, 1882–1942, vol. IV
Wilson, William Tyson, 1855–1921, vol. II
Wilson, William Wright, 1843–1919, vol. II
Wilson, Woodrow; *see* Wilson, T. W.
Wilson-Farquharson, Lt-Col David Lorraine; *see* Farquharson.
Wilson-Fox, Hon. Mrs Eleanor Birch, *died* 1963, vol. VI
Wilson-Fox, Henry; *see* Fox.
Wilson-Haffenden, Maj.-Gen. Donald James, 1900–1986, vol. VIII

Wilson-Johnston, Joseph; *see* Johnston.
Wilson-Johnston, Maj.-Gen. Walter Edward; *see* Johnston.
Wilson Smith, Sir Henry, 1904–1978, vol. VII
Wilson Taylor, Sir John, *died* 1943, vol. IV
Wilson-Todd, Captain Sir William Henry, 1st Bt, 1828–1910, vol. I
Wilson-Todd, Captain Sir William Pierrepoint, 2nd Bt, 1857–1925, vol. II
Wilsone, Arthur Henry, 1860–1939, vol. III
Wilthew, Gerard Herbert Guy, 1876–1913, vol. I, vol. III
Wilton, 4th Earl of, 1839–1898, vol. I
Wilton, 5th Earl of, 1863–1915, vol. I
Wilton, 6th Earl of, 1896–1927, vol. II
Wilton, 7th Earl of, 1921–1999, vol. X
Wilton, Sir Ernest Colville Collins, 1870–1952, vol. V
Wilton, George Wilton, 1862–1964, vol. VI
Wilton, Herbert George, 1882–1959, vol. V
Wilton, Captain Sir James M., *died* 1946, vol. IV
Wilton, Gen. Sir John Gordon Noel, 1910–1981, vol. VIII
Wilton, John Raymond, 1884–1944, vol. IV
Wilton, Sir Thomas, 1861–1929, vol. III
Wiltshire, Aubrey Roy Liddon, 1891–1969, vol. VI
Wiltshire, Sir Frank H. C., 1881–1949, vol. IV
Wiltshire, Sir Frederick Munro, 1911–1994, vol. IX
Wiltshire, Harold Waterlow, 1879–1937, vol. III
Wiltshire, Samuel Paul, 1891–1967, vol. VI
Wimberley, Col Charles Neil Campbell, 1867–1949, vol. IV
Wimberley, Maj.-Gen. Douglas Neil, 1896–1983, vol. VIII
Wimble, Ernest Walter, 1887–1979, vol. VII
Wimble, Sir John Bowring, 1868–1927, vol. II
Wimborne, 1st Baron, 1835–1914, vol. I
Wimborne, 1st Viscount, 1873–1939, vol. III
Wimborne, 2nd Viscount, 1903–1967, vol. VI
Wimborne, 3rd Viscount, 1939–1993, vol. IX
Wimbush, Rt Rev. Richard Knyvet, 1909–1994, vol. IX
Wimperis, Arthur Harold, 1874–1953, vol. V
Wimperis, Harry Egerton, 1876–1960, vol. V
Wimshurst, James, 1832–1903, vol. I
Winans, Walter, *died* 1920, vol. II
Winant, Hon. John Gilbert, 1889–1947, vol. IV
Winby, Lt-Col Lewis Phillips, 1874–1956, vol. V
Winchell, Walter, 1897–1972, vol. VII
Winchester, 15th Marquess of, 1858–1899, vol. I
Winchester, 16th Marquess of, 1862–1962, vol. VI
Winchester, 17th Marquess of, 1905–1968, vol. VI
Winchester, Clarence Arthur C.; 1895–1981, vol. VIII
Winchester, Ian Sinclair, 1931–1994, vol. IX
Winchester, Tarleton, 1895–1967, vol. VI
Winchilsea, 12th Earl of, and Nottingham, 7th Earl of, 1851–1898, vol. I
Winchilsea, 13th Earl of, and Nottingham, 8th Earl of, 1852–1927, vol. II
Winchilsea, 14th Earl of, and Nottingham, 9th Earl of, 1885–1939, vol. III
Winchilsea, 15th Earl of, and Nottingham, 10th Earl of, 1911–1950, vol. IV

Winchilsea, 16th Earl, and Nottingham, 11th Earl, 1936–1999, vol. X
Winckles, Kenneth, 1918–1999, vol. X
Winckley, Rev. Canon Sidney Thorold, 1858–1937, vol. III
Winckworth, Chauncey P. Tietjens, 1896–1954, vol. V
Wincott, Harold Edward, 1906–1969, vol. VI
Wind, Edgar, 1900–1971, vol. VII
Windaus, Adolf Otto Reinhold, 1876–1959, vol. V
Winder, Sir Arthur Benedict, 1875–1953, vol. V
Winder, Col John Lyon C.; *see* Corbett-Winder.
Winder, Lt-Col Maurice Guy, *died* 1932, vol. III
Winder, Captain Robert Cecil, *died* 1920, vol. II
Winder, Very Rev. Thomas Edward, *died* 1926, vol. II
Winder, Major William John C.; *see* Corbett-Winder.
Windeyer, Sir Brian Wellingham, 1904–1994, vol. IX
Windeyer, John Cadell, 1875–1951, vol. V
Windeyer, Rt Hon. Sir Victor; *see* Windeyer, Rt Hon. Sir W. J. V.
Windeyer, Sir William Charles, 1834–1897, vol. I
Windeyer, Rt Hon. Sir (William John) Victor, 1900–1987, vol. VIII
Windham, Vice-Adm. Charles, 1851–1916, vol. II
Windham, Lt-Col Charles Joseph, 1867–1941, vol. IV
Windham, Sir Ralph, 1905–1980, vol. VII
Windham, Comdr Sir Walter George, 1868–1942, vol. IV
Windham, Sir William, 1864–1961, vol. VI
Windham, William Evan, 1904–1977, vol. VII
Windham, Brig. William Russell S.; *see* Smijth-Windham.
Windle, Sir Bertram Coghill Alan, 1858–1929, vol. VII
Windlesham, 1st Baron, 1877–1953, vol. V
Windlesham, 2nd Baron, 1903–1962, vol. VI
Windlesham, Lady; *see* Glynn, P. L.
Windley, Sir Edward Henry, 1909–1972, vol. VII
Windsor, Viscount; Other Robert Windsor-Clive, 1884–1908, vol. I
Windsor, Bt-Col Arthur Herbert, 1880–1972, vol. VII
Windsor, Lt-Col Frank Needham, 1868–1951, vol. V
Windsor, Robert, 1916–1980, vol. VII
Windsor, Walter, *died* 1945, vol. IV
Windsor-Aubrey, Henry Miles, 1901–1986, vol. VIII
Windsor-Clive, Lt-Col George, 1878–1968, vol. VI
Windsor-Clive, Lt-Col Hon. George Herbert Windsor, 1835–1918, vol. II
Windsor Lewis, Brig. James Charles, 1907–1964, vol. VI
Winegarten, Asher, 1922–1979, vol. VII
Winfield, Rev. Benjamin, *died* 1933, vol. III
Winfield, Sir Percy Henry, 1878–1953, vol. V
Winfield, Peter Stevens, 1927–1999, vol. X
Winfrey, Sir Richard, 1858–1944, vol. IV
Wing, Brig.-Gen. Frederick Drummond Vincent, 1860–1915, vol. I
Wing, Thomas Edward, 1853–1935, vol. III

Wingate, Col Alfred Woodrow Stanley, 1861–1938, vol. III
Wingate, Sir Andrew, 1846–1937, vol. III
Wingate, Col Basil Fenton, *died* 1940, vol. III
Wingate, Gen. Sir (Francis) Reginald, 1st Bt, 1861–1953, vol. V
Wingate, Col George, 1852–1936, vol. III
Wingate, Henry Smith, 1905–1982, vol. VIII
Wingate, Sir (James) Lawton, 1846–1924, vol. II
Wingate, Sir Lawton; *see* Wingate, Sir J. L.
Wingate, Captain Malcolm Roy, 1893–1918, vol. II
Wingate, Maj.-Gen. Orde Charles, 1903–1944, vol. IV
Wingate, Gen. Sir Reginald; *see* Wingate, Gen. Sir F. G.
Wingate, Sir Ronald Evelyn Leslie, 2nd Bt, 1889–1978, vol. VII
Wingate, William Granville, 1911–1990, vol. VIII
Wingate-Saul, Bazil Sylvester, 1906–1975, vol. VII
Wingate-Saul, Sir Ernest Wingate, 1873–1944, vol. IV
Winge, Ojvind, 1886–1964, vol. VI
Wingfield, Sir Anthony H., 1857–1952, vol. V
Wingfield, Sir Charles John FitzRoy Rhys, 1877–1960, vol. V
Wingfield, Sir Edward, 1834–1910, vol. I
Wingfield, Lt-Col John Maurice, 1863–1931, vol. III
Wingfield, Ven. John William, 1915–1983, vol. VIII
Wingfield, Maj.-Gen. Hon. Maurice Anthony, 1883–1956, vol. V
Wingfield, Maurice Edward, 1869–1937, vol. III
Wingfield, Mervyn Edward George Rhys, 1872–1952, vol. V
Wingfield, Major Walter Clopton, 1833–1912, vol. I
Wingfield, Rev. Lt-Col William Edward, 1867–1927, vol. II
Wingfield Digby, George F.; *see* Digby.
Wingfield Digby, Simon; *see* Digby.
Wingfield Digby, Ven. Stephen Basil, 1910–1996, vol. X
Wingfield-Stratford, Brig.-Gen. Cecil Vernon, 1853–1939, vol. III
Wingfield-Stratford, Esmé Cecil, 1882–1971, vol. VII
Wingrave, Vitruvius Harold Wyatt, 1858–1938, vol. III
Winks, William Edward, 1842–1926, vol. II
Winlaw, Ashley William Edgell, 1914–1988, vol. VIII
Winlock, Herbert Eustis, 1884–1950, vol. IV
Winmill, Thomas Field, 1888–1953, vol. V
Winn, Rt Hon. Sir (Charles) Rodger (Noel), 1903–1972, vol. VII
Winn, Air Vice-Marshal Charles Vivian, 1918–1988, vol. VIII
Winn, Godfrey Herbert, 1908–1971, vol. VII
Winn, Rt Hon. Sir Rodger; *see* Winn, Rt Hon. Sir C. R. N.
Winn, Lt-Comdr Sydney Thornhill, 1888–1924, vol. II
Winneke, Hon. Sir Henry Arthur, 1908–1985, vol. VIII
Winner, Dame Albertine Louise, 1907–1988, vol. VIII
Winner, Harold Ivor, 1918–1992, vol. IX

Winnicott, Sir Frederick; *see* Winnicott, Sir J. F.
Winnicott, Sir (John) Frederick, 1855–1948, vol. IV
Winnifrith, Sir (Alfred) John (Digby), 1908–1993, vol. IX
Winnifrith, Sir John; *see* Winnifrith, Sir A. J. D.
Winning, Theodore Norman, 1884–1946, vol. IV
Winnington, Sir Francis Salwey, 5th Bt, 1849–1931, vol. III
Winnington, Lt-Col John Francis Sartorius, 1876–1918, vol. II
Winnington Ingram, Rt Rev. and Rt Hon. Arthur Foley; *see* Ingram.
Winnington-Ingram, Ven. Arthur John, 1888–1965, vol. VI
Winnington-Ingram, Rev. Edward Henry; *see* Ingram.
Winnington-Ingram, Reginald Pepys, 1904–1993, vol. IX
Winsbury-White, Horace Powell, *died* 1962, vol. VI
Winser, Col Charles Rupert Peter, 1880–1961, vol. VI
Winser, (Cyril) Legh, 1884–1983, vol. VIII
Winser, Legh; *see* Winser, C. L.
Winsloe, Adm. Sir Alfred Leigh, 1852–1931, vol. III
Winsloe, Col Alfred Raynaud, 1868–1932, vol. III
Winsloe, Lt-Col Herbert Edward, 1873–1921, vol. II
Winsloe, Col Richard William Charles, 1835–1917, vol. II
Winslow, Rev. Forbes Edward, 1842–1913, vol. I
Winslow, L. Forbes, 1844–1913, vol. I
Winslow, Rev. William Copley, 1840–1925, vol. II
Winstanley, Baron (Life Peer); Michael Platt Winstanley, 1918–1993, vol. IX
Winstanley, Denys Arthur, 1877–1947, vol. IV
Winstedt, Sir Richard Olaf, 1878–1966, vol. VI
Winster, 1st Baron, 1885–1961, vol. VI
Winston, Charles Edward, 1898–1989, vol. VIII
Winstone, (Frank) Reece, 1909–1991, vol. IX
Winstone, Reece; *see* Winstone, F. R.
Wint, Arthur Stanley, 1920–1992, vol. IX
Wint, Hon. Dunbar Theophilus, 1879–1938, vol. III
Winter, Rt Rev. Allen Ernest, 1903–1997, vol. X
Winter, Carl, 1906–1966, vol. VI
Winter, Charles Milne, 1933–1996, vol. X
Winter, Col Clifford Boardman, 1869–1930, vol. III
Winter, Rt Rev. Colin O'Brien, 1928–1981, vol. VIII
Winter, Rev. Edward George Adlington, 1853–1933, vol. III
Winter, Edwin, 1840–1915, vol. I
Winter, Lt-Col Ernest Arthur, 1874–1925, vol. II
Winter, Hon. Sir Francis Pratt, 1848–1919, vol. II
Winter, Rev. Canon George Percival Thomas Horden, 1885–1953, vol. V
Winter, Hon. Henry Daniel, 1851–1927, vol. II
Winter, James Alexander, 1886–1971, vol. VII
Winter, Sir James Spearman, 1845–1911, vol. I
Winter, John Strange; *see* Stannard, H. E. V.
Winter, Keith, 1906–1983, vol. VIII
Winter, Hon. Sir Marmaduke George, 1857–1936, vol. III
Winter, Brig.-Gen. Sir Ormonde de l'Epée, 1875–1962, vol. VI
Winter, Reginald Keble, 1883–1955, vol. V
Winter, Robert Pearson, 1897–1973, vol. VII

Winter, Col Samuel Henry, 1854–1938, vol. III
Winter, Thomas, 1866–1912, vol. I
Winter, W. Tatton, *died* 1928, vol. II
Winter, William, 1836–1917, vol. II
Winter-Shaw, Arthur, *died* 1948, vol. IV
Winterbotham, Gp Capt. Frederick William, 1897–1990, vol. VIII
Winterbotham, Sir Geoffrey Leonard, *died* 1966, vol. VI
Winterbotham, Brig. Harold St John Lloyd, 1878–1946, vol. IV
Winterbotham, Sir Henry Martin, 1847–1932, vol. III
Winterbotham, Rev. Rayner, *died* 1924, vol. II
Winterbotham, Sir William Howard, 1843–1926, vol. II
Winterbottom, Baron (Life Peer); Ian Winterbottom, 1913–1992, vol. IX
Winterbottom, Lt-Col Archibald Dickson, 1885–1942, vol. IV
Winterbottom, Richard Emanuel, 1899–1968, vol. VI
Winters, Ellen Dorothea Margaret, 1894–1956, vol. V
Winterstoke, 1st Baron, 1830–1911, vol. I
Winterton, 5th Earl, 1837–1907, vol. I
Winterton, 6th Earl, 1883–1962, vol. VI
Winterton, 7th Earl, 1915–1991, vol. IX
Winterton, George Ernest, 1873–1942, vol. IV
Winterton, Maj.-Gen. Sir John; *see* Winterton, Maj.-Gen. Sir T. J. W.
Winterton, Ralph; *see* Winterton, W. R.
Winterton, Maj.-Gen. Sir (Thomas) John (Willoughby), 1898–1987, vol. VIII
Winterton, (William) Ralph, 1905–1988, vol. VIII
Wintle, Col Charles Edmund Hunter, *died* 1969, vol. VI
Wintle, Col Frank Graham, 1852–1907, vol. I
Winton, Frank Robert, 1894–1985, vol. VIII
Winton, Meryon W.; *see* White-Winton.
Wintour, Charles Vere, 1917–1999, vol. X
Wintour, Maj.-Gen. Fitzgerald, 1860–1949, vol. IV
Wintour, Ulick Fitzgerald, 1877–1947, vol. IV
Wintringham, Col John Workman, 1894–1980, vol. VII
Wintringham, Margaret, *died* 1955, vol. V
Wintringham, Thomas, 1867–1921, vol. II
Wintringham, Thomas Henry, 1898–1949, vol. IV
Wintz, Adm. Lewis Edmund, 1849–1933, vol. III
Wintz, Dame Sophia Gertrude, *died* 1929, vol. III
Winwood, Lt-Col William Quintyne, 1873–1954, vol. V
Wippell, Adm. Sir Henry Daniel P.; *see* Pridham-Wippell.
Wippell, Rev. Canon John Cecil, 1883–1978, vol. VII
Wirgman, Ven. Augustus Theodore, 1846–1917, vol. II
Wirgman, Theodore Blake, 1848–1925, vol. II
Wirkkala, Tapio, 1915–1985, vol. VIII
Wisdom, Arthur John Terence Dibben, 1904–1993, vol. IX
Wisdom, Brig.-Gen. Evan Alexander, 1869–1945, vol. IV
Wisdom, George Evan Cameron, 1899–1958, vol. V

Wisdom, John; *see* Wisdom A. J. T. D.
Wise, 1st Baron, 1887–1968, vol. VI
Wise, Alfred Gascoyne, 1854–1923, vol. II
Wise, Lt-Col Alfred Roy, 1901–1974, vol. VII
Wise, Audrey, 1935–2000, vol. X
Wise, Hon. Bernhard Ringrose, 1858–1916, vol. II
Wise, Rear-Adm. Cyril Hubert Surtees, 1913–1982, vol. VIII
Wise, Edward Frank, 1885–1933, vol. III
Wise, Ernie; *see* Wiseman, Ernest.
Wise, Francis Hubert, 1869–1917, vol. II
Wise, Sir Fredric, 1871–1928, vol. II
Wise, Hon. George Henry, 1853–1950, vol. IV
Wise, Lt-Col Henry Edward Disbrowe Disbrowe-, 1868–1948, vol. IV
Wise, Rear-Adm. John; *see* Wise, Rear-Adm. C. H. S.
Wise, Sir John Humphrey, 1890–1984, vol. VIII
Wise, Sir Lloyd; *see* Wise, Sir W. L.
Wise, Gp Captain Percival Kinnear, 1885–1968, vol. VI
Wise, Very Rev. Randolph George, 1925–1999, vol. X
Wise, Rabbi Stephen S., 1874–1949, vol. IV
Wise, Thomas James, 1859–1937, vol. III
Wise, Sir (William) Lloyd, 1845–1910, vol. I
Wiseham, Sir Joseph Angus Lucien, 1906–1972, vol. VII
Wiseman, Arthur Maurice, 1893–1948, vol. IV
Wiseman, Christopher Luke, 1893–1987, vol. VIII
Wiseman, Gen. Clarence Dexter, 1907–1985, vol. VIII
Wiseman, Ernest, (Ernie Wise), 1925–1999, vol. X
Wiseman, Rev. Frederick Luke, 1858–1944, vol. IV
Wiseman, Very Rev. James, *died* 1925, vol. II
Wiseman, Air Cdre Percy John, 1888–1948, vol. IV
Wiseman, Robert Arthur, 1886–1955, vol. V
Wiseman, Stephen, 1907–1971, vol. VII
Wiseman, Sir William George Eden, 10th Bt, 1885–1962, vol. VI
Wiseman-Clarke, Lt-Gen. Somerset Molyneux, 1830–1905, vol. I
Wishart, D. J. Gibb, 1859–1934, vol. III
Wishart, George Macfeat, 1895–1958, vol. V
Wishart, John, 1898–1956, vol. V
Wishart, John, 1879–1970, vol. VI
Wishart, Rear-Adm. John Webster, 1892–1968, vol. VI
Wishart, Captain Robert, 1875–1938, vol. III (A), vol. IV
Wishart, Col Sir Sidney, 1854–1935, vol. III
Wiskemann, Elizabeth Meta, 1901–1971, vol. VII
Wissman, Major Herman von, 1853–1905, vol. I
Wister, Owen, 1860–1938, vol. III
Witham, Col James Kirkconnell Maxwell, 1848–1937, vol. III
Witham, Philip, 1842–1921, vol. II
Witherby, Harry Forbes, 1873–1943, vol. IV
Witherington, Giles Somerville Gwynne, 1919–1996, vol. X
Withers, Alfred, *died* 1932, vol. III
Withers, Col Charles M'Gregor, 1876–1958, vol. V
Withers, Captain Edgar Clements, 1883–1951, vol. V
Withers, Harry Livingston, 1864–1902, vol. I

Withers, Hartley, 1867–1950, vol. IV
Withers, Lt-Col Henry Hastings Cavendish, 1904–1948, vol. IV
Withers, Isobelle; *see* Dods-Withers.
Withers, Sir John James, 1863–1939, vol. III
Withers, John Keppel Ingold D.; *see* Douglas-Withers.
Withers, Percy, 1867–1945, vol. IV
Withers, Rupert Alfred, 1913–1995, vol. IX
Withers, Lt-Col Samuel Henry, *died* 1942, vol. IV
Withy, George, 1924–1998, vol. X
Withycombe, Brig.-Gen. William Maunder, 1869–1951, vol. V
Witney, John Humphrey, 1879–1964, vol. VI
Witney, Kenneth Percy, 1916–1999, vol. X
Witt, Rt Rev. Howell Arthur John, 1920–1998, vol. X
Witt, Sir John Clermont, 1907–1982, vol. VIII
Witt, Maj.-Gen. John Evered, 1897–1989, vol. VIII
Witt, John George, *died* 1906, vol. I
Witt, Sir Robert Clermont, *died* 1952, vol. V
Witt, Tansley, 1839–1915, vol. I
Witte, Count Sergius, 1849–1915, vol. I
Witte, William, 1907–1992, vol. IX
Wittenham, 1st Baron, 1852–1931, vol. III
Wittenoom, Hon. Sir Edward Horne, 1854–1936, vol. III
Wittet, John, 1868–1952, vol. V
Wittewronge, Sir Charles L.; *see* Lawes-Wittewronge.
Wittewronge, Sir John Bennet L.; *see* Lawes-Wittewronge.
Wittewronge, Sir John Claud Bennet Lawes; *see* Lawes, Sir J. C. B.
Wittig, Georg, 1897–1987, vol. VIII
Wittgenstein, Ludwig, 1889–1951, vol. V
Wittkower, Rudolf, 1901–1971, vol. VII
Witton-Davies, Ven. Carlyle, 1913–1993, vol. IX
Wittrick, William Henry, 1922–1986, vol. VIII
Witts, Rev. Francis Edward Broome, 1840–1913, vol. I
Witts, Brig. Frank Hole, 1887–1941, vol. IV
Witts, Maj.-Gen. Frederick Vavasour Broome, 1889–1969, vol. VI
Witts, Leslie John, 1898–1982, vol. VIII
Woakes, Claud Edward, 1868–1936, vol. III
Wodehouse, Hon. Armine, 1860–1901, vol. I
Wodehouse, Rev. Armine, 1860–1938, vol. III
Wodehouse, Edmond Henry, 1837–1923, vol. II
Wodehouse, Rt Hon. Edmond Robert, 1835–1914, vol. I
Wodehouse, Major Sir (Edwin) Frederick, 1851–1934, vol. III
Wodehouse, Major Ernest Charles Forbes, 1871–1915, vol. I
Wodehouse, Lt-Col Frederic William, 1867–1961, vol. VI
Wodehouse, Major Sir Frederick; *see* Wodehouse, Major Sir E. F.
Wodehouse, Helen Marion, 1880–1964, vol. VI
Wodehouse, Henry Ernest, 1845–1929, vol. III
Wodehouse, Gen. Sir Josceline Heneage, 1852–1930, vol. III
Wodehouse, Vice-Adm. Norman Atherton, 1887–1941, vol. IV

Wodehouse, Sir Pelham Grenville, 1881–1975, vol. VII
Wodehouse, Rev. Philip John, 1836–1917, vol. II
Wodehouse, Philip Peveril John, 1877–1951, vol. V
Wodeman, Guy Stanley, 1886–1970, vol. VI
Woden, George; *see* Slaney, G. W.
Woelmont, Henry, Baron de, 1881–1931, vol. III
Wofinden, Robert Cavill, 1914–1975, vol. VII
Woinarski, Casimir Julius Z.; *see* Zichy-Woinarski.
Wolf, Abraham, 1876–1948, vol. IV
Wolf, Lucien, 1857–1930, vol. III
Wolf-Ferrari, Ermanno, 1876–1948, vol. IV
Wolfe, Very Rev. Charles William, 1914–1980, vol. VII (AII)
Wolfe, Rev. Clarence Albert Edward, 1892–1967, vol. VI
Wolfe, Frederick John, *died* 1962, vol. VI
Wolfe, George, 1859–1941, vol. IV
Wolfe, Herbert Robert Inglewood, 1907–1970, vol. VI
Wolfe, Humbert, 1886–1940, vol. III
Wolfe, James Nathan, 1927–1988, vol. VIII
Wolfe, Nathan; *see* Wolfe, J. N.
Wolfe-Barry, Sir John Wolfe; *see* Barry.
Wolfe-Murray, Lt-Col Arthur Alexander, 1866–1918, vol. II
Wolfenden, Baron (Life Peer); John Frederick Wolfenden, 1906–1985, vol. VIII
Wolff, Hon. Sir Albert Asher, 1899–1977, vol. VII
Wolff, Lt-Co. Arnold Johnston, 1873–1941, vol. IV
Wolff, Edna; *see* Best, E.
Wolff, Ernest Charteris Holford, 1875–1946, vol. IV
Wolff, Eugene, 1896–1954, vol. V
Wolff, Frederick Ferdinand, 1910–1988, vol. VIII
Wolff, Gustav William, 1834–1913, vol. I
Wolff, Henry D.; *see* Drummond-Wolff.
Wolff, Rt Hon. Sir Henry Drummond Charles, 1830–1908, vol. I
Wolff, Henry William, 1840–1931, vol. III
Wolff, Johannes, *born* 1862, vol. IV
Wolff, John Arnold Harrop, 1912–1984, vol. VIII
Wolff, Michael, 1930–1976, vol. VII
Wolfflin, Heinrich, 1864–1945, vol. IV
Wolffsohn, Sir Arthur Norman, 1888–1967, vol. VI
Wolfit, Sir Donald, 1902–1968, vol. VI
Wolfson, Sir Isaac, 1st Bt, 1897–1991, vol. IX
Wolkind, Jack, 1920–1997, vol. X
Wollaston, Alexander Frederick Richmond, 1875–1930, vol. III
Wollaston, Sir Arthur Naylor, 1842–1922, vol. II
Wollaston, Sir Gerald Woods, 1874–1957, vol. V
Wollaston, Sir Harry Newton Phillips, 1846–1921, vol. II
Wollaston, Henry Woods, 1916–1989, vol. VIII
Wollaston, Vice-Adm. Herbert Arthur Buchanan-, 1878–1975, vol. VII
Wollen, Sir (Ernest) Russell (Storey), 1902–1986, vol. VIII
Wollen, Sir Russell; *see* Wollen, Sir E. R. S.
Wollen, William Barnes, 1857–1936, vol. III
Wolley, Sir Clive P.; *see* Phillipps-Wolley.
Wolley, Rev. Henry Francklyn, 1839–1915, vol. I
Wolley-Dod, Brig.-Gen. Owen Cadogan, 1863–1942, vol. IV
Wolmark, Alfred Aaran, 1877–1961, vol. VI

Wolmer, Viscount; William Matthew Palmer, 1912–1942, vol. IV
Wolpe, Berthold Ludwig, 1905–1989, vol. VIII
Wolrige-Gordon, Henry, 1831–1906, vol. I
Wolrige-Gordon, Col John Gordon, 1859–1925, vol. II
Wolrige Gordon, Captain Robert, *died* 1939, vol. III
Wolseley, 1st Viscount, 1833–1913, vol. I
Wolseley, Viscountess (2nd in line), 1872–1936, vol. III
Wolseley, Sir Capel Charles, 9th Bt (*cr* 1744), 1870–1923, vol. II
Wolseley, Sir Charles Michael, 9th Bt (*cr* 1628), 1846–1931, vol. III
Wolseley, Sir Edric Charles Joseph, 10th Bt (*cr* 1628), 1886–1954, vol. V
Wolseley, Sir Garnet, 12th Bt (*cr* 1745), 1915–1991, vol. IX
Wolseley, Garnet Ruskin, 1884–1967, vol. VI
Wolseley, Gen. Sir George Benjamin, 1839–1921, vol. II
Wolseley, Sir Reginald Beatty, 10th Bt (*cr* 1744), 1872–1933, vol. III
Wolseley, Rev. Sir William Augustus, 11th Bt (*cr* 1744), 1865–1950, vol. IV
Wolseley-Lewis, Mary, 1865–1955, vol. V
Wolstencroft, Frank, 1882–1952, vol. V
Wolstenholme, William, 1865–1931, vol. III
Wolters, Very Rev. Conrad Clifton, 1909–1991, vol. IX
Wolverhampton, 1st Viscount, 1830–1911, vol. I
Wolverhampton, 2nd Viscount, 1870–1943, vol. IV
Wolverson, William Alfred, 1905–1974, vol. VII
Wolverton, 4th Baron, 1861–1932, vol. III
Wolverton, 5th Baron, 1904–1986, vol. VIII
Wolverton, 6th Baron, 1913–1988, vol. VIII
Wolvin, Roy Mitchell, 1880–1945, vol. IV
Wombwell, Lt-Gen. Arthur, 1821–1914, vol. I
Wombwell, Sir (Frederick) Philip (Alfred William), 6th Bt, 1910–1977, vol. VII
Wombwell, Sir George Orby, 4th Bt, 1832–1913, vol. I
Wombwell, Captain Sir Henry Herbert, 5th Bt, 1840–1926, vol. II
Wombwell, Sir Philip; *see* Wombwell, Sir F. P. A. W.
Womersley, J(ohn) Lewis, 1910–1990, vol. VIII
Womersley, Rt Hon. Sir Walter James, 1st Bt, 1878–1961, vol. VI
Wonham, Rear-Adm. (S) Charles Scrivener, 1870–1946, vol. IV
Wonnacott, Ven. Thomas Oswald, 1869–1957, vol. V
Wontner, Arthur, 1875–1960, vol. V
Wontner, Sir Hugh Walter Kingwell, 1908–1992, vol. IX
Wood, Sir Alexander, 1849–1924, vol. II
Wood, Rt Rev. Alexander, *died* 1937, vol. III
Wood, Alexander, 1879–1950, vol. IV
Wood, Major Alexander Vaughan Leipsic, 1867–1933, vol. III
Wood, Alfred, 1836–1906, vol. I
Wood, Sir Alfred, 1878–1960, vol. V
Wood, Alfred Arden, 1926–1995, vol. IX
Wood, Alfred Cecil, 1896–1968, vol. VI

Wood, Ven. Alfred Maitland, 1840–1918, vol. II
Wood, Allan Fergusson, 1876–1966, vol. VI
Wood, Rev. Andrew, 1833–1917, vol. II
Wood, Rear-Adm. Arthur Edmund, 1875–1961, vol. VI
Wood, Arthur Henry, 1870–1964, vol. VI
Wood, Sir (Arthur) Michael, 1919–1987, vol. VIII
Wood, Sir Arthur Nicholas Lindsay, 2nd Bt (*cr* 1897), 1875–1939, vol. III
Wood, Captain Sir Basil Samuel Hill H.; *see* Hill-Wood.
Wood, Brooks Crompton, *died* 1946, vol. IV
Wood, Butler, 1854–1934, vol. III
Wood, Catherine Jane, *died* 1930, vol. III
Wood, Col Cecil Ernest, *died* 1932, vol. III
Wood, Cecil Godfrey, 1851–1906, vol. I
Wood, Rt Rev. Cecil John, 1874–1957, vol. V
Wood, Rev. Canon Cecil Thomas, 1903–1980, vol. VII
Wood, Sir (Charles) Edgar, 1877–1941, vol. IV
Wood, Charles Frederick, 1867–1937, vol. III
Wood, Charles Malcolm, 1846–1915, vol. I
Wood, Col Charles Michell Aloysius, 1873–1936, vol. III
Wood, Lt-Col Charles Peevor Boileau, *died* 1932, vol. III
Wood, Rt Rev. Claud Thomas Thellusson, 1885–1961, vol. VI
Wood, Lt-Col Cyril, 1852–1904, vol. I
Wood, Lt-Col David Edward, 1853–1927, vol. II
Wood, Sir David John Hatherley P., 7th Bt (*cr* 1837); *see* Page Wood.
Wood, Derek Rawlins, 1921–1997, vol. X
Wood, Sir Edgar; *see* Wood, Sir C. E.
Wood, Rev. Edmund Gough De Salis, 1842–1932, vol. III
Wood, Edmund Walter Hanbury, 1898–1947, vol. IV
Wood, Sir Edward, 1839–1917, vol. II
Wood, Maj.-Gen. Edward Alexander, 1841–1898, vol. I
Wood, Brig.-Gen. Edward Allan, 1872–1930, vol. III
Wood, Sir (Edward) Graham, 1854–1930, vol. III
Wood, Edward James, 1902–1993, vol. IX
Wood, Edward Stephen, 1890–1948, vol. IV
Wood, Maj.-Gen. Sir Elliott, 1844–1931, vol. III
Wood, Eric Rawlinson, 1893–1977, vol. VII
Wood, Lt-Gen. Sir Ernest, 1894–1971, vol. VII
Wood, Ernest Clement, 1890–1970, vol. VI
Wood, Brig.-Gen. Ernest Joseph MacFarlane, 1867–1939, vol. III
Wood, Ethel Mary, *died* 1970, vol. VI
Wood, Field-Marshal Sir Evelyn; *see* Wood, Field-Marshal Sir H. E.
Wood, Hon. Col Evelyn Fitzgerald Michell, 1869–1943, vol. IV
Wood, Francis Derwent, 1871–1926, vol. II
Wood, Sir Frank, 1913–1974, vol. VII
Wood, Franklin Garrett, *died* 1978, vol. VII
Wood, Frederick Benjamin, 1849–1928, vol. II
Wood, Frederick Lloyd Whitfeld, 1903–1989, vol. VIII
Wood, George Arnold, 1865–1928, vol. II

Wood, Sir George Ernest Francis, 1900–1978, vol. VII (AII)
Wood, Maj.-Gen. George Neville, 1898–1982, vol. VIII
Wood, Gervase E., 1877–1954, vol. V
Wood, Sir Graham; see Wood, Sir E. G.
Wood, Harrie Dalrymple, 1869–1937, vol. III
Wood, Col Hastings St Leger, 1856–1933, vol. III
Wood, Haydn, 1882–1959, vol. V
Wood, Col Henry, 1835–1919, vol. II
Wood, Col Henry, 1872–1940, vol. III
Wood, Henry Ernest, 1868–1946, vol. IV
Wood, Field-Marshal Sir (Henry) Evelyn, 1838–1919, vol. II
Wood, Sir Henry Hastings Affleck, 1826–1904, vol. I
Wood, Sir Henry Joseph, 1869–1944, vol. IV
Wood, Sir Henry Peart, 1908–1994, vol. IX
Wood, Rev. Henry Thellusson, died 1928, vol. II
Wood, Sir Henry Trueman, 1845–1929, vol. III
Wood, Herbert, 1893–1950, vol. IV
Wood, Herbert Duncan S.; see Searles-Wood.
Wood, Herbert George, 1879–1963, vol. VI
Wood, Hubert Lyon-Campbell, 1903–1982, vol. VIII
Wood, Hugh McKinnon, 1884–1955, vol. V
Wood, Rev. Hugh Singleton, 1859–1941, vol. IV
Wood, I. Hickory, died 1913, vol. I
Wood, Sir Ian Jeffreys, 1903–1986, vol. VIII
Wood, Captain Sir Ian Lindsay, 3rd Bt (cr 1897), 1909–1946, vol. IV
Wood, J. S. 1853–1920, vol. II
Wood, James, died 1936, vol. III
Wood, Lt-Col Sir James L.; see Leigh-Wood.
Wood, Sir James Lockwood, died 1941, vol. IV
Wood, James Maxwell, (Max Wood), 1914–1982, vol. VIII
Wood, Rev. John, 1833–1929, vol. III
Wood, Sir John, 1st Bt (cr 1918), 1857–1951, vol. V
Wood, John, 1880–1952, vol. V
Wood, Sir John Arthur Haigh, 2nd Bt (cr 1918), 1888–1974, vol. VII
Wood, Sir John Barry, 1870–1933, vol. III
Wood, Lt-Col John Bruce, 1886–1927, vol. II
Wood, Hon. John Dennistoun, 1829–1914, vol. I
Wood, John Gathorne, 1839–1929, vol. III
Wood, Captain John Lockhart, 1871–1915, vol. I
Wood, Lt-Col John Nicholas Price, 1877–1962, vol. VI
Wood, Major Sir John Page, 5th Bt (cr 1837), 1860–1912, vol. I
Wood, John Philip, died 1906, vol. I
Wood, Sir John Stuart Page, 6th Bt (cr 1837), 1898–1955, vol. V
Wood, John Vincent, 1905–1952, vol. V
Wood, Lt-Col John William Massey, 1855–1916, vol. II
Wood, Rev. Joseph, 1842–1921, vol. II
Wood, Josiah, 1843–1927, vol. II
Wood, Kenneth Maynard, 1916–1997, vol. X
Wood, Sir Kenneth Millns, 1909–1986, vol. VIII
Wood, Kenneth Spencer, 1897–1963, vol. VI
Wood, Rt Hon. Sir Kingsley, 1881–1943, vol. IV
Wood, Lawson, 1878–1957, vol. V

Wood, Leslie Stuart, 1873–1948, vol. IV
Wood, Sir Lindsay, 1st Bt (cr 1897), 1834–1920, vol. II
Wood, Rev. Llewellyn, died 1929, vol. III
Wood, Mary Hay, died 1934, vol. III
Wood, Sir Matthew, 4th Bt (cr 1837), 1857–1908, vol. I
Wood, Max; see Wood, J. M.
Wood, Metcalfe, died 1944, vol. IV
Wood, Sir Michael; see Wood, Sir A. M.
Wood, Major Sir Murdoch McKenzie, 1881–1949, vol. IV
Wood, Oswald Edward, 1899–1974, vol. VII
Wood, Lt-Col Oswald Gillespie, 1851–1902, vol. I
Wood, Paul Hamilton, 1907–1962, vol. VI
Wood, Percival Arthur Gilbert, 1866–1945, vol. IV
Wood, Philip Francis, 1858–1939, vol. III
Wood, Brig.-Gen. Philip Richard, 1868–1845, vol. IV
Wood, Ralph, 1921–1986, vol. VIII
Wood, Sir Richard, 1806–1900, vol. I
Wood, Gen. Robert E., 1879–1969, vol. VI
Wood, Robert Eric, 1909–1995, vol. IX
Wood, Robert Henry, 1860–1930, vol. III
Wood, Sir Robert Stanford, 1886–1963, vol. VI
Wood, Robert Williams, 1868–1955, vol. V
Wood, Roger L.; see Leigh-Wood.
Wood, R(onald) McKinnon, 1892–1967, vol. VI
Wood, Maj.-Gen. Sam; see Wood, Maj.-Gen. G. N.
Wood, Sam, 1911–1992, vol. IX
Wood, Major Sir Samuel Hill H.; see Hill-Wood.
Wood, Starr, 1870–1944, vol. IV
Wood, Stuart Zachary Taylor, 1889–1966, vol. VI
Wood, Sydney Herbert, 1884–1958, vol. V
Wood, Rev. Theodore, 1862–1923, vol. II
Wood, Col Thomas, 1853–1933, vol. III
Wood, Thomas, 1892–1950, vol. IV
Wood, Rev. Thomas, 1919–1987, vol. VIII
Wood, Thomas Alfred, 1867–1944, vol. IV
Wood, Thomas Andrew Urquhart, 1914–1975, vol. VII
Wood, Thomas Barlow, 1869–1929, vol. III
Wood, Brig.-Gen. Thomas Birchall, 1865–1944, vol. IV
Wood, Rt Hon. Thomas McKinnon, 1855–1927, vol. II
Wood, Thomas Outterson, died 1930, vol. III
Wood, W. H., 1888–1954, vol. V
Wood, Walter, 1866–1961, vol. Vi
Wood, Walter, 1914–1997, vol. X
Wood, Walter Gunnell, 1861–1942, vol. IV
Wood, Sir Wilfred William Hill H.; see Hill-Wood.
Wood, Wilfrid Burton, 1883–1943, vol. IV
Wood, Rev. William, 1829–1919, vol. II
Wood, William Alfred Rae, 1878–1970, vol. VI
Wood, William Charles Henry, died 1947, vol. IV (A)
Wood, William Francis John, 1876–1934, vol. III
Wood, William Henry Heton A.; see Arden Wood.
Wood, William K.; see King-Wood.
Wood, William L.; 1879–1958, vol. V
Wood, William Thomas, 1877–1958, vol. V
Wood, Sir William Valentine, 1883–1959, vol. V
Wood, William Walter, 1896–1982, vol. VIII
Wood, William Wightman, 1846–1914, vol. I

Wood, Sir William Wilkinson, 1879–1963, vol. VI
Wood, Lt-Col Wyndham Madden Pierpoint, *died* 1950, vol. IV
Wood, Zachary Taylor, 1860–1915, vol. I
Wood-Martin, William Gregory, 1847–1917, vol. II
Wood-Samuel, Rev. Richard, *died* 1939, vol. III
Wood-Seys, Roland Alex., 1854–1919, vol. II
Woodall, Sir Corbet, 1841–1916, vol. II
Woodall, Col Frederic, 1866–1956, vol. V
Woodall, Lt-Col Harold Whiteman, 1872–1951, vol. V
Woodall, Lt-Gen. Sir John Dane, 1897–1985, vol. VIII
Woodall, Mary, 1901–1988, vol. VIII
Woodall, William, 1832–1901, vol. I
Woodard, Rev. Canon Alfred Lambert, 1880–1971, vol. VII
Woodard, Rev. Lambert, 1848–1924, vol. II
Woodberry, George Edward, 1855–1930, vol. III
Woodbine Parish, Sir David Elmer, 1911–1998, vol. X
Woodbridge, 1st Baron, 1867–1949, vol. IV
Woodburn, Rt Hon. Arthur, 1890–1978, vol. VII
Woodburn, Rev. George, 1867–1947, vol. IV
Woodburn, Hon. Sir John, 1843–1902, vol. I
Woodburn, Lt-Col Thomas Stanley, 1881–1965, vol. VI
Woodcock, Eric Charles, 1904–1978, vol. VII
Woodcock, Rt Hon. George, 1904–1979, vol. VII
Woodcock, George, 1912–1995, vol. IX
Woodcock, Co. Herbert Charles, 1871–1950, vol. IV
Woodcock, Hubert Bayley Drysdale, 1867–1957, vol. V
Woodcock, John, 1920–1981, vol. VIII
Woodcock, T. A., 1897–1965, vol. VI
Woodcock, Brig.-Gen. Wilfrid James, 1878–1960, vol. V
Woodd, Ven. Henry Alexander, 1865–1954, vol. V
Woodd Walker, Geoffrey Basil, 1900–1991, vol. IX
Woodeson, Sir James Brewis, 1917–1980, vol. VII
Woodfall, Robert, 1855–1920, vol. II
Woodfield, Sir Philip John, 1923–2000, vol. X
Woodfield, Ven. Samuel Percy, 1889–1983, vol. VIII
Woodford, Charles Morris, 1852–1927, vol. II
Woodford, Colin Godwin Patrick, 1934–1993, vol. IX
Woodford, Brig. Edward Cecil James, 1901–1988, vol. VIII
Woodford, James, 1893–1976, vol. VII
Woodford, Stewart Lyndon, 1835–1913, vol. I
Woodford, Thomas Gordon Charles, 1911–1962, vol. VI
Woodforde, Very Rev. Christopher, 1907–1962, vol. VI
Woodgate, Sir Alfred, 1860–1943, vol. IV
Woodgate, Maj.-Gen. Edward Robert Prevost, 1845–1900, vol. I
Woodgate, (Hubert) Leslie, 1902–1961, vol. VI
Woodgate, Leslie; see Woodgate, H. L.
Woodgate, Walter Bradford, 1840–1920, vol. II
Woodger, Joseph Henry, 1894–1981, vol. VIII
Woodhall, Lt-Comdr Eric Langton, 1899–1940, vol. III
Woodham, Ronald Ernest, 1912–1998, vol. X

Woodham-Smith, Cecil (Blanche), 1896–1977, vol. VII
Woodhams, Ven. Brian Watson, 1911–1992, vol. IX
Woodhams, Herbert Martin, 1890–1965, vol. VI
Woodhead, Arthur Longden, 1862–1957, vol. V
Woodhead, Ernest, 1857–1944, vol. IV
Woodhead, Sir German Simms, 1855–1921, vol. II
Woodhead, Henry George Wandesford, 1883–1959, vol. V
Woodhead, Jane; see Woodhead, S. J.
Woodhead, Sir John Ackroyd, 1881–1973, vol. VII
Woodhead, (Susan) Jane, 1954–1993, vol. IX
Woodhouse, Albert Cyril, 1887–1940, vol. IV
Woodhouse, Arthur William Webster, 1867–1961, vol. VI
Woodhouse, Adm. Sir Charles Henry Lawrence, 1893–1978, vol. VII
Woodhouse, Rev. Frederick Charles, 1827–1905, vol. I
Woodhouse, Brig. Harold Lister, 1887–1960, vol. V
Woodhouse, Rear-Adm. Hector Roy Mackenzie, 1889–1971, vol. VII
Woodhouse, Henry, 1913–1990, vol. VIII
Woodhouse, Rev. Henry George, 1852–1930, vol. III
Woodhouse, Herbert, 1859–1957, vol. V
Woodhouse, Rt Rev. John Walker, 1884–1955, vol. V
Woodhouse, Sir Percy, 1856–1931, vol. III
Woodhouse, Maj.-Gen. Sir Percy; see Woodhouse, Maj.-Gen. Sir T. P.
Woodhouse, Ven. Samuel Mostyn Forbes, 1912–1995, vol. IX
Woodhouse, Sir Stewart, 1846–1921, vol. II
Woodhouse, Thomas, 1862–1933, vol. III
Woodhouse, Maj.-Gen. Sir (Tom) Percy, 1857–1931, vol. III
Woodhouse, Vernon Kerslake, *died* 1936, vol. III
Woodhouse, William Bradley, 1873–1940, vol. III
Woodhouse, William John, 1866–1937, vol. III
Woodhull, Zula Maud, *died* 1940, vol. III
Woodifield, Rear-Adm. Anthony, 1912–1986, vol. VIII
Woodifield, Col Anthony Hudson, 1867–1946, vol. IV
Wooding, Rt Hon. Sir Hugh Olliviere Beresford, 1904–1974, vol. VII
Wooding, John Conrad, 1901–1954, vol. V
Woodland, Col Arthur Law, 1849–1921, vol. II
Woodland, Austin William, 1914–1990, vol. VIII
Woodland, William Norton Ferrier, 1879–1952, vol. V
Woodley, Sir (Frederick George) Richard, *died* 1971, vol. VII
Woodley, Sir Richard; see Woodley, Sir F. G. R.
Woodlock, Rev. Francis, 1871–1940, vol. III
Woodlock, Jack Terence, 1919–1998, vol. X
Woodman, Sir George Joseph, 1847–1915, vol. I
Woodman, John, 1888–1971, vol. VII
Woodnutt, Harold Frederick Martin; see Woodnutt, Mark.
Woodnutt, Mark, (Harold Frederick Martin Woodnutt), 1918–1974, vol. VII
Woodroffe, Brig.-Gen. Charles Richard, 1878–1965, vol. VI

Woodroffe, Hon. James T., 1838–1908, vol. I
Woodroffe, Sir John George, 1865–1936, vol. III
Woodroffe, Paul Vincent, 1875–1954, vol. V
Woodrooffe, Very Rev. Henry Reade, 1834–1913, vol. I
Woodrow, Maj.-Gen. (Albert) John, 1919–1988, vol. VIII
Woodrow, David, 1920–1999, vol. X
Woodrow, Gayford William, 1922–1999, vol. X
Woodrow, Maj.-Gen. John; see Woodrow, Maj.-Gen. A. J.
Woodruff, Alan Waller, 1916–1992, vol. IX
Woodruff, Douglas; see Woodruff, J. D.
Woodruff, Harold Addison, died 1966, vol. VI
Woodruff, (John) Douglas, 1897–1978, vol. VII
Woodruff, Keith Montague Cumberland, 1891–1978, vol. VII
Woodruff, Philip; see Mason, Philip.
Woodruff, Timothy Lester, 1858–1913, vol. I
Woods, Albert, died 1944, vol. IV
Woods, Lt-Col Albert Edward, 1862–1938, vol. III
Woods, Sir Albert William, 1816–1904, vol. I
Woods, Rev. Vice-Adm. Alexander Riall Wadham, 1880–1954, vol. V
Woods, Alice, 1849–1941, vol. IV
Woods, Maj.-Gen. Charles William, 1917–1996, vol. X
Woods, Donald Devereux, 1912–1964, vol. VI
Woods, Maj.-Gen. Edward Ambrose, 1891–1957, vol. V
Woods, Rt Rev. Edward Sydney, 1877–1953, vol. V
Woods, Most Rev. Frank, 1907–1992, vol. IX
Woods, Rt Rev. Frank Theodore, 1874–1932, vol. III
Woods, George David, 1901–1982, vol. VIII
Woods, Rev. George Frederick, 1907–1966, vol. VI
Woods, Rev. George Saville, 1886–1951, vol. V
Woods, Col Harold, 1879–1952, vol. V
Woods, Henry, 1846–1921, vol. II
Woods, Henry, 1868–1952, vol. V
Woods, Henry Charles, 1841–1931, vol. III
Woods, Henry Charles, 1881–1939, vol. III
Woods, Adm. Sir Henry Felix, 1843–1929, vol. III
Woods, Rev. Henry George, 1842–1915, vol. I
Woods, Hon. Henry John Bacon, 1842–1916, vol. II
Woods, Brig.-Gen. Hugh Kennedy, 1877–1964, vol. VI
Woods, Irene Charlotte, 1891–1976, vol. VII
Woods, Sir James Edward, 1850–1944, vol. IV
Woods, Hon. Lt-Col James Hossack, 1867–1941, vol. IV
Woods, Sir James William, died 1941, vol. IV
Woods, Sir John Harold Edmund, 1895–1962, vol. VI
Woods, Joseph Ainsworth, 1870–1947, vol. IV
Woods, Joseph Andrews, died 1925, vol. II
Woods, Margaret Louisa, 1856–1945, vol. IV
Woods, Matthew Snooke Grosvenor, 1838–1925, vol. II
Woods, Maurice Henry, 1882–1929, vol. III
Woods, Oliver Frederick John Bradley, 1911–1972, vol. VII
Woods, Percy, 1842–1922, vol. II
Woods, Col Philip James, 1880–1961, vol. Vi
Woods, Sir Raymond Wybrow, 1882–1943, vol. IV

Woods, Reginald Salisbury, (Rex Woods), 1891–1986, vol. VIII
Woods, Rex; see Woods, Reginald S.
Woods, Richard Lennox, 1838–1918, vol. II
Woods, Sir Robert Henry, 1865–1938, vol. III
Woods, Sir Robert Stanton, 1877–1954, vol. V
Woods, Rt Rev. Robert Wilmer, 1914–1997, vol. X
Woods, Samuel, 1846–1915, vol. I
Woods, Samuel Moses James, 1867–1931, vol. III
Woods, Maj.-Gen. Thomas Frederic Mackie, 1904–1982, vol. VIII
Woods, Walter Sainsbury, 1884–1960, vol. V(A)
Woods, Adm. Sir Wilfrid John Wentworth, 1906–1975, vol. VII
Woods, Sir Wilfrid Wentworth, 1876–1947, vol. IV
Woods, William, 1855–1932, vol. III
Woods, William Forster, 1865–1942, vol. IV
Woods, Col William Talbot, 1891–1975, vol. VII
Woods, William Wilson, 1884–1972, vol. VII
Woods Ballard, Lt-Col Basil, 1900–1980, vol. VII
Woodthorpe, John Frederick, 1897–1966, vol. VI
Woodthorpe, Ven. Robert Augustus, 1861–1931, vol. III
Woodthorpe, Col Robert Gosset, 1844–1898, vol. I
Woodville, Richard Caton, 1856–1927, vol. II
Woodward, Sir (Alfred) Chad (Turner), 1880–1957, vol. V
Woodward, Arthur Maurice, 1883–1973, vol. VII
Woodward, Sir Arthur Smith, 1864–1944, vol. IV
Woodward, Sir Chad; see Woodward, Sir A. C. T.
Woodward, Rt Rev. Clifford Salisbury, 1878–1959, vol. V
Woodward, Comer Vann, 1908–1999, vol. X
Woodward, Denys Cuthbert, 1902–1972, vol. VII
Woodward, Edward Gilbert, 1900–1950, vol. IV
Woodward, Lt-Col Edward Hamilton Everard, 1888–1976, vol. VII
Woodward, Maj.-Gen. Sir Edward Mabbott, 1861–1943, vol. IV
Woodward, Lt-Gen. Sir Eric Winslow, 1899–1967, vol. VI
Woodward, Sir (Ernest) Llewellyn, 1890–1971, vol. VII
Woodward, (Foster) Neville, 1905–1985, vol. VIII
Woodward, Col Francis Willoughby, 1872–1926, vol. II
Woodward, Geoffrey Frederick, 1924–1997, vol. X
Woodward, Geoffrey Royston, 1921–1991, vol. IX
Woodward, George Ernest, 1865–1939, vol. III
Woodward, Henry, 1832–1921, vol. II
Woodward, Rear-Adm. Sir Henry William, 1879–1959, vol. V
Woodward, Rev. Herbert Willoughby, 1854–1932, vol. III
Woodward, Horace Bolingbroke, 1848–1914, vol. I
Woodward, Joan; see Woodward, W. J.
Woodward, Joan, (Mrs L. T. Blakeman), 1916–1971, vol. VII
Woodward, Col John Henry, 1849–1918, vol. II
Woodward, Sir Lionel Mabbott, 1864–1925, vol. II
Woodward, Sir Llewellyn; see Woodward, Sir E. L.
Woodward, Marcus, died 1940, vol. III
Woodward, Rev. Max Wakerley, 1908–1996, vol. IX
Woodward, Neville; see Woodward, F. N.

Woodward, Oliver Holmes, 1885–1966, vol. VI
Woodward, Adm. Robert, 1838–1907, vol. I
Woodward, Robert Burns, 1917–1979, vol. VII
Woodward, Robert Simpson, 1849–1924, vol. II
Woodward, William Harrison, 1855–1941, vol. IV
Woodward, (Winifred) Joan, 1907–1981, vol. VIII
Woodward-Nutt, Arthur Edgar, 1902–1980, vol. VII
Woodwark, Sir (Arthur) Stanley, *died* 1945, vol. IV
Woodwark, Col (George) Graham, 1874–1938, vol. III
Woodwark, Col Graham; *see* Woodwark, Col George G.
Woodwark, Sir Stanley; *see* Woodwark, Sir A. S.
Woodwright, Surg. Rear-Adm. Charles Sharman, 1870–1949, vol. IV
Woodyatt, Maj.-Gen. Nigel Gresley, 1861–1936, vol. III
Woof, Robert Edward, 1911–1997, vol. X
Woof, Rowsby, 1883–1943, vol. IV
Wookey, Eric Edgar, 1892–1985, vol. VIII
Woolacott, John Evans, 1862–1936, vol. III
Woolavington, 1st Baron, 1849–1935, vol. III
Woolcock, William James Uglow, 1878–1947, vol. IV
Wooldridge, George Henry, *died* 1957, vol. V
Wooldridge, Harry Ellis, 1845–1917, vol. II
Wooldridge, Henry, 1908–1975, vol. VII
Wooldridge, Sidney William, 1900–1963, vol. VI
Wooldridge, Walter Reginald, 1900–1966, vol. VI
Woolf, Albert Edward Mortimer, 1884–1957, vol. V
Woolf, Rev. Bertram Lee, *died* 1956, vol. V
Woolf, Charles H.; *see* Hyatt-Woolf.
Woolf, Sir John, 1913–1999, vol. X
Woolf, Leonard Sidney, 1880–1969, vol. VI
Woolf, Virginia, 1882–1941, vol. IV
Woolfe, Brig. Richard Dean Townsend, 1888–1966, vol. VI
Woolford, Sir Eustace Gordon, 1876–1966, vol. VI
Woolford, Harry Russell Halkerston, 1905–1999, vol. X
Woolfryes, Surg.-Gen. Sir John Andrews, 1823–1912, vol. I
Woolfson, Mark, 1911–2000, vol. X
Woolgar, Alfred John, 1879–1968, vol. VI
Woolhouse, Harold William, 1932–1996, vol. X
Wooll, Edward, 1878–1970, vol. VI
Woollam, Rev. Canon J., 1827–1909, vol. I
Woollard, Herbert Henry, 1889–1939, vol. III
Woollaston, Sir (Mountford) Tosswill, 1910–1998, vol. X
Woollaston, Sir Tosswill; *see* Woollaston, Sir M. T.
Woollcombe, Captain Charles George Ley, 1884–1962, vol. VI
Woollcombe, Lt-Gen. Sir Charles Louis, 1857–1934, vol. III
Woollcombe, Rt Rev. Henry St John Stirling, 1869–1941, vol. IV
Woollcombe, Dame Jocelyn May, 1898–1986, vol. VIII
Woollcombe, Adm. Louis Charles Stirling, 1872–1951, vol. V
Woollcombe, Major Malcolm Louis, 1891–1968, vol. VI
Woollcombe, Adm. Maurice, 1868–1930, vol. III
Woollcott, Alexander, 1887–1943, vol. IV

Woollen, James, 1854–1921, vol. II
Wooller, Arthur, 1912–1989, vol. VIII
Woolley, Baron (Life Peer); Harold Woolley, 1905–1986, vol. VIII
Woolley, Rev. (Alfred) Russell, 1899–1986, vol. VIII
Woolley, Charles, 1846–1922, vol. II
Woolley, Lt-Col Sir Charles Augustus, 1859–1936, vol. III
Woolley, Sir Charles Campbell, 1893–1981, vol. VIII
Woolley, Paymaster Rear-Adm. Charles Edward Allen, 1863–1940, vol. III
Woolley, Sir (Charles) Leonard, 1880–1960, vol. V
Woolley, Frank Edward, 1887–1978, vol. VII
Woolley, Rev. Geoffrey Harold, 1892–1968, vol. VI
Woolley, Howard Mark, 1879–1971, vol. VII
Woolley, Sir Leonard; *see* Woolley, Sir C. L.
Woolley, Rev. Reginald Maxwell, 1877–1931, vol. III
Woolley, Richard, 1916–1986, vol. VIII
Woolley, Sir Richard van der Riet, 1906–1986, vol. VIII
Woolley, Rev. Russell; *see* Woolley, Rev. A. R.
Woolley, Samuel Walter, 1865–1927, vol. II
Woolley, William Edward, 1901–1989, vol. VIII
Woolley-Hart, Arthur, 1859–1941, vol. IV
Woolmer, Rt Rev. Laurence Henry, 1906–1977, vol. VII
Woolmer, Ronald Francis, 1908–1962, vol. VI
Woolner, Alfred Cooper, *died* 1936, vol. III
Woolner, Maj.-Gen. Christopher Geoffrey, 1893–1984, vol. VIII
Woolnough, Rev. Canon Howard Frank, 1886–1973, vol. VII
Woolnough, Walter George, 1876–1958, vol. V
Woolrych, H. R., 1858–1917, vol. II
Wools-Sampson, Col Sir Aubrey, *died* 1924, vol. II
Woolston, Thomas Henry, 1855–1927, vol. II
Woolton, 1st Earl of, 1883–1964, vol. VI
Woolton, 2nd Earl of, 1922–1969, vol. VI
Woolveridge, Air Cdre Harry Leonard, 1887–1960, vol. V
Woon, Gen. Sir John Blaxall, 1856–1938, vol. III
Woosnam, Ven. Charles Maxwell, 1856–1930, vol. III
Woosnam, R. B., *died* 1915, vol. I
Wootten, Aubrey Francis Wootten, 1866–1923, vol. II
Wootten, Maj.-Gen. Sir George Frederick, 1893–1970, vol. VI
Wootten, Maj.-Gen. Richard Montague, 1889–1979, vol. VII
Wootton of Abinger, Baroness (Life Peer); Barbara Frances, 1897–1988, vol. VIII
Wootton, Gordon Henry, 1927–1991, vol. IX
Wootton, Harold Samuel, 1891–1989, vol. VIII
Wootton, Hubert Arthur, 1884–1947, vol. IV
Wootton-Davies, James Henry, 1884–1964, vol. VI
Worboys, Sir Arthur Thomas, *died* 1966, vol. VI
Worboys, Sir Walter John, 1900–1969, vol. VI
Worden, Alastair Norman, 1916–1987, vol. VIII
Wordie, Sir James Mann, 1889–1962, vol. VI
Wordie, Sir John Stewart, 1924–1997, vol. X
Wordingham, Charles Henry, 1866–1925, vol. II

Wordsworth, Rev. Christopher, 1848–1938, vol. III
Wordsworth, Dame Elizabeth, 1840–1932, vol. III
Wordsworth, Rt Rev. John, 1843–1911, vol. I
Wordsworth, Maj.-Gen. Robert Harley, 1894–1984, vol. VIII
Wordsworth, William, 1835–1917, vol. II
Wordsworth, William Christopher, 1878–1950, vol. IV
Wordsworth, Captain Sir William Henry Laycock, 1880–1960, vol. V
Worgan, Lt-Gen. John, 1821–1909, vol. I
Worgan, Brig.-Gen. Rivers Berney, died 1936, vol. III
Worgan, Col Sydney Drummond, 1872–1950, vol. IV
Workman, Charles Rufus Marshall, died 1942, vol. IV
Workman, Fanny Bullock, 1859–1925, vol. II
Workman, Harold, 1897–1975, vol. VII
Workman, Rev. Herbert Brook, 1862–1951, vol. V
Workman, Mark, 1864–1936, vol. III
Workman, Robert Little, 1914–1994, vol. IX
Workman, Walter Percy, 1863–1918, vol. II
Workman, William Arthur, 1877–1956, vol. V
Workman, William Hunter, 1847–1937, vol. III
Workman, William Thomas, died 1971, vol. VII
Workman-Macnaghten, Rt Hon. Sir Francis Edmund; see Macnaghten.
Worley, Sir Arthur, 1st Bt, 1871–1937, vol. III
Worley, Frederick Palliser, 1880–1960, vol. V(A)
Worley, Sir Newnham Arthur, 1892–1976, vol. VII
Worlledge, Rev. Arthur John, 1848–1919, vol. II
Worlledge, Sir John Leonard, 1895–1968, vol. VI
Worlock, Most Rev. Derek John Harford, 1920–1996, vol. X
Wormald, Maj.-Gen. Derrick Bruce, 1916–1994, vol. IX
Wormald, Dame Ethel May, 1901–1993, vol. IX
Wormald, Francis, 1904–1972, vol. IX
Wormald, Sir John, 1859–1933, vol. III
Wormall, Arthur, 1900–1964, vol. VI
Wormell, Donald Ernest Wilson, 1908–1990, vol. VIII
Wormell, Richard, 1838–1914, vol. I
Worms, 2nd Baron de, 1829–1912, vol. I
Worms, 3rd Baron de, 1869–1938, vol. III
Worms, Percy George de, 1873–1941, vol. IV
Wörner, Manfred, 1934–1994, vol. IX
Wornum, George Grey, 1888–1957, vol. V
Wornum, Ralph Selden, 1847–1910, vol. I
Worrall, Alfred Stanley, 1912–1991, vol. IX
Worrall, Arthur Hardey, 1868–1960, vol. V
Worrall, Air Vice-Marshal John, 1911–1988, vol. VIII
Worrell, Most Rev. Clarendon Lamb, 1853–1934, vol. III
Worrell, Sir Frank Mortimer Maglinne, 1924–1967, vol. VI
Worrell, John Austin, 1852–1927, vol. II
Worsfold, Sir Thomas Cato, 1st Bt, died 1936, vol. III
Worsfold, William Basil, 1858–1939, vol. III
Worsley, Lord; Charles Sackville Pelham, 1887–1914, vol. I

Worsley, Lady; (Alexandra Mary Freesia), 1890–1963, vol. VI
Worsley, Rev. Edward, 1844–1923, vol. II
Worsley, Comdr Frank Arthur, 1872–1943, vol. IV
Worsley, Air Cdre Geoffrey Nicolas Ernest T-C.; see Tindal-Carill-Worsley.
Worsley, Very Rev. Godfrey Stuart Harling, 1906–1990, vol. VIII
Worsley, Very Rev. Gordon; see Worsley, Very Rev. Godfrey S. H.
Worsley, Col Henry Robert Brown, 1833–1902, vol. I
Worsley, Lt-Gen. Sir John Francis, 1912–1987, vol. VIII
Worsley, Philip Ernest T. C.; see Tindal-Carill-Worsley.
Worsley, Ralph Marcus Meaburn, 1887–1939, vol. III
Worsley, Rev. Richard, 1889–1972, vol. VII
Worsley, Lt-Col Richard Stanley, 1879–1917, vol. II
Worsley, Major Ronald Henry Warton, 1886–1932, vol. III
Worsley, Col Sidney John, 1895–1974, vol. VII
Worsley, Col Sir William Arthington, 4th Bt, 1890–1973, vol. VII
Worsley, Sir William Cayley, 2nd Bt, 1828–1897, vol. I
Worsley, Sir William Henry Arthington, 3rd Bt, 1861–1936, vol. III
Worsley-Gough, Lt-Col Henry Worsley; see Gough.
Worsley-Taylor, Sir Francis Edward, 4th Bt, 1874–1958, vol. V
Worsley-Taylor, Sir Henry Wilson, 1st Bt, 1847–1924, vol. II
Worsley-Taylor, Lt-Col Sir James, 2nd Bt, 1872–1933, vol. III
Worsley-Taylor, Captain Sir John Godfrey, 3rd Bt, 1915–1952, vol. V
Worsnop, Bernard Lister, 1892–1980, vol. VII
Worster-Drought, Charles, died 1971, vol. VII
Worswick, Thomas, died 1932, vol. III
Wort, Sir Alfred William Ewart, 1883–1976, vol. VII
Worth, Arthur Hovenden, 1877–1955, vol. V
Worth, Claud, died 1936, vol. III
Worth, George Arthur, 1907–1995, vol. IX
Wortham, Maj.-Gen. Geoffrey Christopher Hale, 1913–1967, vol. VI
Wortham, Col Harold Charles Webster Hale, 1878–1939, vol. III
Wortham, Hugh Evelyn, 1884–1959, vol. V
Wortham, Brig. Philip William Temple Hale, 1874–1955, vol. V
Worthington, Albert Octavius, 1844–1918, vol. II
Worthington, Arthur Furley, 1874–1964, vol. VI
Worthington, Arthur Mason, 1852–1916, vol. II
Worthington, Charles Edward, 1897–1970, vol. VI
Worthington, Col Edward Bruen, 1860–1945, vol. IV
Worthington, Col Sir Edward Scott, 1876–1953, vol. V
Worthington, Frank, 1874–1964, vol. VI
Worthington, Maj.-Gen. Frederic Frank, 1889–1967, vol. VI

Worthington, Air Vice-Marshal Sir Geoffrey, 1903–1992, vol. IX
Worthington, Henry Hugo, 1857–1924, vol. II
Worthington, Sir Hubert, 1886–1963, vol. VI
Worthington, John Morton, 1883–1956, vol. V
Worthington, Sir John Vigers, 1872–1951, vol. V
Worthington, Sir Percy Scott, 1864–1939, vol. III
Worthington, Rear-Adm. Roger Ernest, 1889–1967, vol. VI
Worthington, Thomas, 1850–1933, vol. III
Worthington, William Barton, 1854–1939, vol. III
Worthington-Evans, Rt Hon. Sir Laming, 1st Bt, 1868–1931, vol. III
Worthington-Evans, Sir Shirley; see Worthington-Evans, Sir W. S. W.
Worthington-Evans, Sir (William) Shirley (Worthington), 2nd Bt, 1904–1971, vol. VII
Wortley, Ben Atkinson, 1907–1989, vol. VIII
Wortley, Hon. Clare Euphemia S.; see Stuart-Wortley.
Wortley, Maj.-Gen. Hon. Edward James Montagu S.; see Stuart-Wortley.
Wortley, Rev. Edward Jocelyn, died 1928, vol. II
Wortley, Edward Jocelyn, 1884–1942, vol. IV
Wortley, Hon. Mrs Edward S.; see Stuart Wortley, Violet.
Wortley, Harry Almond Saville, 1885–1947, vol. IV
Wortley, Lt-Gen. Hon. Sir Richard Montagu S.; see Stuart-Wortley.
Worton, Albert Samuel, 1874–1940, vol. III
Wotherspoon, (George) Ralph (Howard), 1897–1979, vol. VII
Wotherspoon, Ralph; see Wotherspoon, G. R. H.
Wotherspoon, Robert Andrew, 1912–1975, vol. VII
Wragg, Sir Herbert, died 1956, vol. V
Wragg, Hon. Sir Walter Thomas, 1842–1913, vol. I
Wragge, Clement Lindley, 1852–1922, vol. II
Wragge, Robert Horton Vernon, 1854–1933, vol. III
Wraight, Ernest Alfred, 1879–1946, vol. IV
Wraight, Sir John Richard, 1916–1997, vol. X
Wraith, Col Ernest Arnold, 1876–1937, vol. III
Wrangel, Count Herman, 1857–1934, vol. III
Wrangham, Cuthbert Edward, 1907–1982, vol. VIII
Wrangham, Dennis; see Wrangham, C. E.
Wrangham, Rev. Francis, died 1941, vol. IV
Wrangham, Sir Geoffrey Walter, 1900–1986, vol. VIII
Wratislaw, Albert Charles, 1862–1938, vol. III
Wratislaw, Adm. Henry Rushworth, 1832–1913, vol. I
Wraxall, 1st Baron, 1873–1931, vol. III
Wraxall, Sir Charles Frederick Lascelles, 7th Bt, 1896–1951, vol. V
Wraxall, Sir Morville William, 6th Bt, 1862–1902, did not have an entry in Who's Who.
Wraxall, Sir Morville William Lascelles, 8th Bt, 1922–1978, vol. VII
Wraxall, Sir Morville William Nathaniel, 5th Bt, 1834–1898, vol. I
Wray, Brig.-Gen. Cecil; see Wray, Brig.-Gen. J. C.
Wray, Vice-Adm. Fawcet, 1873–1932, vol. III
Wray, Rev. Frederick William, 1864–1943, vol. IV
Wray, Brig.-Gen. (John) Cecil, 1864–1947, vol. IV
Wray, Captain Kenneth Mackenzie, 1855–1927, vol. II

Wray, Sir Kenneth Owen R.; see Roberts-Wray.
Wray, Leonard, died 1942, vol. IV
Wray, Martin Osterfield, 1912–1991, vol. IX
Wray, Captain Thomas Henry Roberts-, died 1943, vol. IV
Wray, W. Fitzwater, died 1938, vol. III
Wreford, Sir Ernest Henry, 1866–1938, vol. III
Wreford, George, 1843–1919, vol. II
Wreford, James; see Watson, J. W.
Wreford-Brown, Captain Claude Wreford, 1876–1915, vol. I
Wren, Maj.-Gen. John, 1896–1958, vol. V
Wren, Percival Christopher, 1885–1941, vol. IV
Wren, Walter, died 1898, vol. I
Wrenbury, 1st Baron, 1845–1935, vol. III
Wrenbury, 2nd Baron, 1890–1940, vol. III
Wrench, Sir Charles Arthur, 1875–1948, vol. IV
Wrench, Edward Mason, 1833–1912, vol. I
Wrench, Sir Evelyn; see Wrench, Sir J. E. L.
Wrench, Rt Hon. Frederick Stringer, 1849–1926, vol. II
Wrench, Hylda Henrietta, (Lady Wrench), died 1955, vol. V
Wrench, Sir (John) Evelyn (Leslie), 1882–1966, vol. VI
Wrench, John Mervyn Dallas, 1883–1961, vol. VI
Wrench, Mollie Louise S.; see Stanley-Wrench.
Wrenfordsley, Sir Henry Thomas, died 1908, vol. I
Wrenn, Charles Leslie, 1895–1969, vol. VI
Wrey, Rev. Sir Albany Bourchier Sherard, 13th Bt, 1861–1948, vol. IV
Wrey, Sir Bourchier; see Sir C. R. B.
Wrey, Sir Bourchier; see Wrey, Sir R. B. S.
Wrey, Sir (Castel Richard) Bourchier, 14th Bt, 1903–1991, vol. IX
Wrey, Sir Henry Bourchier Toke, 10th Bt, 1829–1900, vol. I
Wrey, Sir Philip Bourchier Sherard, 12th Bt, 1858–1936, vol. III
Wrey, Sir (Robert) Bourchier (Sherard), 11th Bt, 1855–1917, vol. II
Wrey, Captain William Bourchier Sherard, 1865–1926, vol. II
Wright, Baron (Life Peer); Robert Alderson Wright, 1869–1964, vol. VI
Wright of Ashton under Lyne, Baron (Life Peer); Lewis Tatham Wright, 1903–1974, vol. VII
Wright, Adam Henry, 1846–1930, vol. III
Wright, Alastair William, 1913–1985, vol. VIII
Wright, Albert Allen, 1846–1905, vol. I
Wright, Albert Ernest, 1902–1960, vol. V
Wright, Comdr Alexander Galloway, 1874–1943, vol. IV
Wright, Sir Alexander Kemp, 1859–1933, vol. III
Wright, Hon. Alison Elizabeth, 1945–2000, vol. X
Wright, Sir Almroth Edward, 1861–1947, vol. IV
Wright, Sir Andrew Barkworth, 1895–1971, vol. VII
Wright, Brig.-Gen. Archibald John Arnott, 1851–1943, vol. IV
Wright, Arnold, died 1941, vol. IV
Wright, Rev. Arthur, 1831–1920, vol. II
Wright, Rev. Arthur, 1843–1924, vol. II
Wright, Arthur Alban, 1887–1967, vol. VI
Wright, Sir Arthur Cory C.; see Cory-Wright.

Wright, A(rthur) Dickson, *died* 1976, vol. VII
Wright, Arthur Francis Stevenson, 1918–1997, vol. X
Wright, Arthur Robinson, 1862–1932, vol. III
Wright, Lt-Col Bache Allen, 1874–1932, vol. III
Wright, Basil Charles, 1907–1987, vol. VIII
Wright, Bernard Arker, 1893–1973, vol. VII
Wright, Sir Bernard Swanwick, 1876–1961, vol. VI
Wright, Billy; *see* Wright, W. A.
Wright, Cecily Gertrude, *died* 1942, vol. IV
Wright, Col Sir Charles; *see* Wright, Col Sir W. C.
Wright, Charles Edward, *died* 1945, vol. IV
Wright, Charles Henry, 1864–1941, vol. IV
Wright, Charles Henry Conrad, 1869–1957, vol. V
Wright, Rev. Charles Henry Hamilton, 1836–1909, vol. I
Wright, Charles Ichabod, 1828–1905, vol. I
Wright, Sir Charles Seymour, 1887–1975, vol. VII
Wright, Sir Charles Theodore Hagberg, 1862–1940, vol. III
Wright, Sir Cory Francis C.; *see* Cory-Wright.
Wright, Dickson; *see* Wright, A. D.
Wright, Donald Arthur, 1911–1988, vol. VIII
Wright, Sir Douglas; *see* Wright, Sir R. D.
Wright, Dudley, 1868–1949, vol. IV
Wright, Dudley d'Auvergne, 1867–1948, vol. IV
Wright, (Edmund) Kenneth, 1909–1991, vol. IX
Wright, Edward Fitwalter, 1902–1957, vol. V
Wright, Edward Fortescue, 1858–1904, vol. I
Wright, Edward Perceval, 1834–1910, vol. I
Wright, Rev. Edwin Henry, 1843–1937, vol. III
Wright, Eric Blackwood, 1860–1940, vol. III
Wright, Ernest, 1882–1974, vol. VII
Wright, Fowler; *see* Wright, S. F.
Wright, Frank, 1853–1922, vol. II
Wright, Frank Arnold, 1874–1961, vol. VI
Wright, Frank Joseph Henry, 1901–1970, vol. VI
Wright, Frank Lloyd, 1869–1959, vol. V
Wright, Frank Trueman W.; *see* Wynyard-Wright.
Wright, Frederick Adam, 1869–1946, vol. IV
Wright, Lt-Col Frederick William, 1850–1927, vol. II
Wright, Frederick Matthew, 1916–1990, vol. VIII
Wright, Sir Geoffrey C.; *see* Cory-Wright.
Wright, George, *died* 1913, vol. I
Wright, Sir George, *died* 1927, vol. II
Wright, Col George, 1860–1942, vol. IV
Wright, George Arthur, *died* 1920, vol. II
Wright, George Maurice, *died* 1956, vol. V
Wright, George Payling, 1898–1964, vol. VI
Wright, Rt Rev. George William, 1873–1956, vol. V
Wright, Lt-Col Guy Jefferys H.; *see* Hornsby-Wright.
Wright, H. C. Seppings, *died* 1937, vol. III
Wright, Harold, 1858–1908, vol. I
Wright, Harold Bell, 1872–1944, vol. IV
Wright, Harold Edward, 1868–1946, vol. IV
Wright, Rev. Harold Hall, 1859–1926, vol. II
Wright, Lt-Col Harry, 1856–1942, vol. IV
Wright, Major Hedley, 1859–1903, vol. I
Wright, Hedley Duncan, 1891–1942, vol. IV
Wright, Maj.-Gen. Henry Brooke Hagstromer, 1864–1948, vol. IV
Wright, Rev. Henry Dixon D.; *see* Dixon-Wright.

Wright, Sir Henry Edward, 1893–1966, vol. VI
Wright, Henry FitzHerbert, 1870–1947, vol. IV
Wright, Henry Robert, 1877–1951, vol. V
Wright, Henry Smith, 1839–1910, vol. I
Wright, Sir Herbert, 1874–1940, vol. III
Wright, Lt-Col Herbert James, 1888–1974, vol. VII
Wright, Huntley, 1869–1941, vol. IV
Wright, Sir James, 1823–1899, vol. I
Wright, James, *died* 1947, vol. IV
Wright, James Brown, 1861–1926, vol. II
Wright, Adm. Jerauld, 1898–1995, vol. IX
Wright, John, 1857–1933, vol. III
Wright, Air Cdre John Allan Cecil C.; *see* Cecil-Wright.
Wright, Most Rev. John Charles, 1861–1933, vol. III
Wright, John George, 1897–1971, vol. VII
Wright, John Graham, 1873–1949, vol. IV
Wright, John Henry, 1910–1984, vol. VIII
Wright, John Keith, 1928–1994, vol. IX
Wright, John Moncrieff, 1884–1971, vol. VII
Wright, John Nicholson, 1896–1982, vol. VIII
Wright, Col Sir John Roper, 1st Bt, 1843–1926, vol. II
Wright, Sir Johnstone, 1883–1953, vol. V
Wright, Joseph, 1855–1930, vol. III
Wright, Joshua Butler, 1877–1939, vol. III
Wright, Judith, (Mrs J. P. McKinney), 1915–2000, vol. X
Wright, Kenneth; *see* Wright, E. K.
Wright, Kenneth Anthony, 1899–1975, vol. VII
Wright, Sir Leonard Morton, 1906–1967, vol. VI
Wright, Rev. Leslie, 1899–1972, vol. VII
Wright, Louis Booker, 1899–1984, vol. VIII
Wright, Louise, *died* 1944, vol. IV
Wright, Mabel Osgood, 1859–1934, vol. III
Wright, Mark Robinson, 1854–1944, vol. IV
Wright, Sir Michael Robert, 1901–1976, vol. VII
Wright, Rear-Adm. Noel, 1890–1975, vol. VII
Wright, Sir Norman Charles, 1900–1970, vol. VI
Wright, Orville, 1871–1948, vol. IV
Wright, Percy Malcolm, 1906–1959, vol. V
Wright, Peter Harold, 1916–1990, vol. VIII
Wright, Philip Arundell, 1889–1970, vol. VI
Wright, R. Ramsay, 1852–1933, vol. III
Wright, Hon. Sir Reginald Charles, 1905–1990, vol. VIII
Wright, Sir Robert Brash, 1915–1981, vol. VIII
Wright, Lt-Col Robert Ernest, 1884–1977, vol. VII
Wright, Sir Robert Patrick, 1857–1938, vol. III
Wright, Sir Robert Samuel, 1839–1904, vol. I
Wright, Col Robert Wallace, 1863–1928, vol. II
Wright, Very Rev. Ronald William Vernon Selby, 1908–1995, vol. IX
Wright, Sir Rowland Sydney, 1915–1991, vol. IX
Wright, Sir (Roy) Douglas, 1907–1990, vol. VIII
Wright, Roy William, 1914–1994, vol. IX
Wright, Adm. Sir Royston Hollis, 1908–1977, vol. VII
Wright, Samson, *died* 1956, vol. V
Wright, Samuel, 1895–1975, vol. VII
Wright, Samuel John, 1899–1975, vol. VII
Wright, Sewall, 1889–1988, vol. VIII
Wright, Lt-Col Stephen, 1863–1936, vol. III
Wright, (Sydney) Fowler, 1874–1965, vol. VI

Wright, Sir Thomas, 1838–1905, vol. I
Wright, Gen. Sir Thomas, 1825–1910, vol. I
Wright, Thomas, 1859–1936, vol. III
Wright, Thomas Erskine, 1902–1986, vol. VIII
Wright, Thomas G., 1878–1929, vol. III
Wright, Thomas Rowland Drake, 1853–1926, vol. II
Wright, Uriah John, 1840–1914, vol. I
Wright, Verna, 1928–1998, vol. X
Wright, Vincent, 1937–1999, vol. X
Wright, Brig.-Gen. Wallace Duffield, died 1953, vol. V
Wright, Walter Page, 1864–1940, vol. III
Wright, Wilfrid Thomas Mermoud, 1882–1946, vol. IV
Wright, Willard Huntington, 1888–1939, vol. III
Wright, William, 1862–1931, vol. III
Wright, William, 1874–1937, vol. III
Wright, William, 1918–1985, vol. VIII
Wright, William Alan, born 1895, vol. VIII
Wright, William Aldis, 1831–1914, vol. I
Wright, William Ambrose (Billy), 1924–1994, vol. IX
Wright, Col William Burgess, died 1930, vol. III
Wright, Col Sir (William) Charles, 2nd Bt, 1876–1950, vol. IV
Wright, William David, 1906–1997, vol. X
Wright, Major William Gordon, 1883–1930, vol. III
Wright, William Hammond, 1871–1959, vol. V(A)
Wright, Rev. William Herbert Thomas, died 1929, vol. III
Wright, Rev. Canon William Joseph, 1881–1954, vol. V
Wright, Most Rev. William Lockridge, 1904–1990, vol. VIII
Wright, Sir William Owen, 1882–1951, vol. V
Wright, Gen. Sir William Purvis, 1846–1910, vol. I
Wright, Sir William Shaw, 1843–1914, vol. I
Wright, Lt-Col Rev. William Thomas, died 1938, vol. III
Wright-Henderson, Rev. Patrick Arkley, 1841–1922, vol. II
Wrighton, Edward, 1880–1937, vol. III
Wrightson, Captain Charles Archibald Wise, 1874–1953, vol. V
Wrightson, Edmund Harry Paul Garmondsway, 1919–1972, vol. VII
Wrightson, Sir Guy; see Wrightson, Sir T. G.
Wrightson, John, 1840–1916, vol. II
Wrightson, Sir John Garmondsway, 3rd Bt, 1911–1983, vol. VIII
Wrightson, Oliver, 1920–1987, vol. VIII
Wrightson, Sir Thomas, 1st Bt, 1839–1921, vol. II
Wrightson, Sir Thomas Garmondsway, (Sir Guy), 2nd Bt, 1871–1950, vol. IV
Wrightson, Walsh, 1852–1935, vol. III
Wrigley, Arthur Joseph, 1902–1983, vol. VIII
Wrigley, Hon. Brig.-Gen. Clement Carr, 1870–1934, vol. III
Wrigley, Fred, 1909–1982, vol. VIII
Wrigley, Air Vice-Marshal Henry Bertram, 1909–1999, vol. X
Wrigley, Sir John Crompton, 1888–1977, vol. VII
Wrigley, Rev. Joseph Henry, died 1938, vol. III
Wrigley, Leslie James, died 1933, vol. III

Wrigley, Michael Harold, 1924–1995, vol. IX
Wrinch, Dorothy, died 1976, vol. VII
Wrisberg, Lt-Gen. Sir (Frederick) George, 1895–1982, vol. VIII
Wrisberg, Lt-Gen. Sir George; see Wrisberg, Lt-Gen. Sir F. G.
Wrixon, Hon. Sir Henry John, 1839–1913, vol. I
Wrixon-Becher, Sir Eustace William Windham; see Becher.
Wrixon-Becher, Lt-Col Henry; see Becher.
Wrixon-Becher, Sir John; see Becher.
Wrixon-Becher, Maj. Sir William Fane; see Becher.
Wroblewski, Wladyslaw, 1875–1952, vol. V
Wrong, Edward Murray, 1889–1928, vol. II
Wrong, George Mackinnon, 1860–1948, vol. IV
Wrong, Humphrey Hume, 1894–1954, vol. V
Wroth, (Charles) Peter, 1929–1991, vol. IX
Wroth, Peter; see Wroth, C. P.
Wrottesley, 3rd Baron, 1824–1910, vol. I
Wrottesley, 4th Baron, 1873–1962, vol. VI
Wrottesley, 5th Baron, 1918–1977, vol. VII
Wrottesley, Captain Francis Robert, 1877–1954, vol. V
Wrottesley, Rt Hon. Sir Frederic John, 1880–1948, vol. IV
Wroughton, Brig.-Gen. John Bartholomew, 1874–1940, vol. III
Wroughton, Philip, 1846–1910, vol. I
Wroughton, Major Philip Musgrave Neeld, 1887–1917, vol. II
Wroughton, William Musgrave, 1850–1928, vol. II
Wunderly, Sir Harry Wyatt, 1892–1971, vol. VII
Wurth, Wallace Charles, 1896–1960, vol. V(A)
Wurtzburg, Charles Edward, 1891–1952, vol. V
Wuttke, Hans A., 1923–2000, vol. X
Wyard, Stanley, 1887–1946, vol. III
Wyatt of Weeford, Baron (Life Peer); Woodrow Lyle Wyatt, 1918–1997, vol. X
Wyatt, Brig. Arthur Geoffrey, 1900–1960, vol. V
Wyatt, Vice-Adm. Sir (Arthur) Guy (Norris), 1893–1981, vol. VIII
Wyatt, Col Ernest Robert Caldwell, 1880–1957, vol. V
Wyatt, Major Francis Ogilvy, 1871–1919, vol. II
Wyatt, Vice-Adm. Sir Guy; see Wyatt, Vice-Adm. Sir A. G. N.
Wyatt, Harold Frazer, died 1925, vol. II
Wyatt, Horace Matthew, 1876–1954, vol. V
Wyatt, James Montagu, 1883–1953, vol. V
Wyatt, Rev. Joseph Light, 1841–1936, vol. III
Wyatt, Brig.-Gen. Louis John, 1874–1955, vol. V
Wyatt, Sir Myles Dermot Norris, 1903–1968, vol. VI
Wyatt, Rev. Paul Williams, 1856–1935, vol. III
Wyatt, Sir Stanley, 1877–1968, vol. VI
Wyatt, Thomas Henry, 1841–1920, vol. II
Wyatt, Travers Carey, 1887–1954, vol. V
Wyatt, Sir William Henry, 1823–1898, vol. I
Wyatt-Paine, Wyatt, died 1935, vol. III
Wyatt-Smith, Stanley; see Smith.
Wyburn, George McCreath, 1903–1985, vol. VIII
Wyche, Rev. Cyrill John, 1867–1945, vol. IV
Wycherley, Sir Bruce; see Wycherley, Sir R. B.
Wycherley, Sir (Robert) Bruce, 1894–1965, vol. VI
Wyeth, Paul James Logan, 1920–1982, vol. VIII

Wyeth, Rex, 1914–1978, vol. VII
Wyfold, 1st Baron, 1851–1937, vol. III
Wyfold, 2nd Baron, 1880–1942, vol. IV
Wyfold, 3rd Baron, 1915–1999, vol. X
Wyke, Rt Hon. Sir Charles Lennox, 1815–1897, vol. I
Wykeham, Air Marshal Sir Peter Guy, 1915–1995, vol. IX
Wykeham-Martin, Cornwallis Philip; *see* Martin.
Wykeham-Musgrave, Herbert Wenman, 1871–1931, vol. III
Wykes, James Cochrane, 1913–1992, vol. IX
Wykes, John Arthur, 1891–1970, vol. VI
Wykes-Finch, Rev. William Robert, 1855–1922, vol. II
Wykes-Sneyd, Vice-Adm. Ralph Stuart, 1882–1951, vol. V
Wyld, Rev. Edwin George, *died* 1919, vol. II
Wyld, Henry Cecil Kennedy, 1870–1945, vol. IV
Wyldbore-Smith, Sir Edmund; *see* Smith.
Wylde, Rt Rev. Arnold Lomas, 1880–1958, vol. V
Wylde, Col Charles Fenwick, 1867–1946, vol. IV
Wylde, Gen. Edward Andrée, 1858–1925, vol. II
Wylde, Everard William, *died* 1911, vol. I
Wylde, Rev. John, 1841–1941, vol. IV
Wylde, John Truro, 1849–1927, vol. II
Wylde, Rev. Robert, *died* 1927, vol. II
Wylde, William Henry, 1819–1909, vol. I
Wyler, William, 1902–1981, vol. VIII
Wyles, Lilian Mary Elizabeth, 1895–1975, vol. VII
Wyley, Col Sir William Fitzthomas, 1852–1940, vol. III
Wylie, Alexander, *died* 1921, vol. II
Wylie, Andrew, *died* 1935, vol. III
Wylie, Sir Campbell, 1905–1992, vol. IX
Wylie, Major Charles Hotham Montagu Doughty-, 1868–1915, vol. I
Wylie, David Storer, 1876–1965, vol. VI
Wylie, Derek; *see* Wylie, W. D.
Wylie, Sir Francis James, 1865–1952, vol. V
Wylie, Sir Francis Verner, 1891–1970, vol. VI
Wylie, Maj.-Gen. Henry, 1844–1918, vol. II
Wylie, Miss I. A. R., *died* 1959, vol. V
Wylie, James, 1875–1941, vol. IV
Wylie, James Hamilton, 1844–1914, vol. I
Wylie, Rt Hon. James Owens, 1845–1935, vol. III
Wylie, Brig.-Gen. James Scott, 1862–1937, vol. III
Wylie, John, *died* 1936, vol. III
Wylie, Major John Price, 1888–1939, vol. III
Wylie, Lt-Col Macleod, 1881–1952, vol. V
Wylie, (William) Derek, 1918–1998, vol. X
Wylie, Hon. William Evelyn, 1881–1964, vol. VI
Wyllarde, Dolf, *died* 1950, vol. IV
Wyllie, Lt-Col Alexander Keith, 1853–1928, vol. II
Wyllie, Charles William, 1853–1923, vol. II
Wyllie, Lt-Col Harold, 1880–1973, vol. VII
Wyllie, John, *died* 1916, vol. II
Wyllie, Robert Lyon, 1897–1995, vol. IX
Wyllie, William Gifford, *died* 1969, vol. VI
Wyllie, Lt-Col Sir William Hutt Curzon, 1848–1909, vol. I
Wyllie, William Lionel, 1851–1931, vol. III
Wylly, Col Guy George Egerton, 1880–1962, vol. VI
Wylly, Col Harold Carmichael, 1858–1932, vol. III

Wylson, Oswald Cane, 1858–1925, vol. II
Wyman, John Bernard, 1916–1994, vol. IX
Wymark, Patrick Carl, (A. K. A. Cheeseman), 1926–1970, vol. VI
Wymer, Francis John, 1898–1976, vol. VII
Wyne-Harris, Sir Percy, 1903–1979, vol. VII
Wynch, Lionel Maling, 1864–1955, vol. V
Wyncoll, Col Charles Edward, 1857–1943, vol. IV
Wyndham, Sir Charles, 1837–1919, vol. II
Wyndham, Lt-Col Charles John, 1844–1930, vol. III
Wyndham, Rt Hon. George, 1863–1913, vol. I
Wyndham, Sir (George) Hugh, 1836–1916, vol. II
Wyndham, Col Guy Percy, 1865–1941, vol. IV
Wyndham, Major Guy Richard Charles, 1896–1948, vol. IV
Wyndham, Sir Harold Stanley, 1903–1988, vol. VIII
Wyndham, Henry Saxe, 1867–1940, vol. III
Wyndham, Horace Cowley, 1873–1970, vol. VI
Wyndham, Sir Hugh; *see* Wyndham, Sir G. H.
Wyndham, Mary, (Lady Wyndham); *see* Moore, Mary.
Wyndham, Sir Percy, 1864–1943, vol. IV
Wyndham, Percy, 1867–1947, vol. IV
Wyndham, Hon. Percy Scawen, 1835–1911, vol. I
Wyndham, Lady Sibell Mary; *see* Grosvenor, Countess.
Wyndham, Col Walter George Crole, 1857–1948, vol. IV
Wyndham, Captain William, 1842–1930, vol. III
Wyndham, Hon. William Reginald, 1876–1914, vol. I
Wyndham-Quin, Captain Hon. Valentine Maurice, 1890–1983, vol. VIII
Wyndham White, Sir Eric, 1913–1980, vol. VII
Wynford, 3rd Baron, 1826–1899, vol. I
Wynford, 4th Baron, 1829–1903, vol. I
Wynford, 5th Baron, 1834–1904, vol. I
Wynford, 6th Baron, 1871–1940, vol. III
Wynford, 7th Baron, 1874–1943, vol. IV
Wynn, Hon. Charles Henry, 1847–1911, vol. I
Wynn, Hon. Frederick George, 1853–1932, vol. III
Wynn, Frederick R. W.; *see* Williams Wynn.
Wynn, Rt Rev. Harold Edward, 1889–1956, vol. V
Wynn, Col Sir Herbert Lloyd Watkin W.; *see* Williams-Wynn.
Wynn, Col Sir (Owen) Watkin W.; *see* Williams-Wynn.
Wynn, Col Sir Robert William Herbert Watkin W.; *see* Williams-Wynn.
Wynn, Hon. Rowland Tempest Beresford, 1898–1977, vol. VII
Wynn, Rev. Walter, 1865–1951, vol. V
Wynn, Sir Watkin W.; *see* Williams-Wynn.
Wynn, William Henry, 1878–1956, vol. V
Wynn Parry, Hon. Sir Henry, 1899–1964, vol. VI
Wynn-Williams, George, 1911–1993, vol. IX
Wynn-Wynne, Major Reginald, 1857–1913, vol. I
Wynne, Hon. Agar, 1850–1934, vol. III
Wynne, Anthony; *see* Wilson, Robert McNair.
Wynne, Rev. Arthur Edwin, 1864–1964, vol. VI
Wynne, Gen. Sir Arthur Singleton, 1846–1936, vol. III
Wynne, Charles Gorrie, 1911–1999, vol. X
Wynne, Esmé; *see* Wynne-Tyson, D. E. E.
Wynne, Major Francis George, 1885–1918, vol. II

Wynne, Frederick Horton, 1877–1943, vol. IV
Wynne, Ven. G. R., 1838–1912, vol. I
Wynne, George, 1839–1912, vol. I
Wynne, Rt Hon. Sir Henry Arthur, 1867–1943, vol. IV
Wynne, Lt-Col Henry Ernest Singleton, 1877–1962, vol. VI
Wynne, Col John Francis W.; *see* Williams-Wynne.
Wynne, May; *see* Knowles, Mabel Winifred.
Wynne, Pamela; *see* Scott, Winifred Mary.
Wynne, Major Reginald W.; *see* Wynn-Wynne.
Wynne, Sir Trevredyn Rashleigh, 1853–1942, vol. IV
Wynne, William Palmer, 1861–1950, vol. IV
Wynne, William Robert Maurice, 1840–1909, vol. I
Wynne-Edwards, Rev. John Rosindale, 1864–1943, vol. IV
Wynne-Edwards, Sir Robert Meredydd, 1897–1974, vol. VII
Wynne-Edwards, Vero Copner, 1906–1997, vol. X
Wynne-Eyton, Alan John F.; *see* Fairbairn-Wynne-Eyton.
Wynne-Eyton, Mrs Frances; *see* Wynne-Eyton, Mrs S. F.
Wynne-Eyton, Mrs Selena Frances, 1898–1982, vol. VIII
Wynne Finche, Col John Charles, 1891–1982, vol. VIII
Wynne Finch, Col Sir William Heneage, 1893–1961, vol. VI
Wynne-Jones, Baron (Life Peer); William Francis Kenrick Wynne-Jones, 1903–1982, vol. VIII
Wynne-Jones, Major Charles Llewelyn, 1890–1974, vol. VII

Wynne-Jones, Very Rev. Llewelyn, *died* 1936, vol. III
Wynne-Jones, Tom Neville, 1893–1979, vol. VII
Wynne Mason, Walter, 1910–1992, vol. IX
Wynne-Tyson, Dorothy Estelle Esmé, 1898–1972, vol. VII
Wynter, Bryan Herbert, 1915–1975, vol. VII
Wynter, Brig.-Gen. Francis Arthur, 1870–1942, vol. IV
Wynter, Maj.-Gen. Henry Douglas, 1886–1945, vol. IV
Wynter, Brig. Henry Walter, 1882–1959, vol. V
Wynter, Sir Luther Reginald, 1899–1984, vol. VIII
Wynter, Walter Essex, 1860–1945, vol. IV
Wynter-Morgan, Air Cdre Wilfred, 1894–1968, vol. VI
Wynyard, Diana, 1906–1964, vol. VI
Wynyard, Major Edward George, 1861–1936, vol. III
Wynyard, Col Rowley, 1855–1931, vol. III
Wynyard-Wright, Frank Trueman, 1884–1979, vol. VII
Wyon, Sir Albert William, 1869–1937, vol. III
Wyon, Allan, 1843–1907, vol. I
Wyon, Rev. Allan Gairdner, 1882–1962, vol. VI
Wyrall, Everard; *see* Wyrall, R. E.
Wyrall, Reginald Everard, 1878–1933, vol. III
Wyse, Andrew Nicholas B.; *see* Bonaparte-Wyse.
Wyse, Henry Taylor, 1870–1951, vol. IV
Wyse, Marjorie Anne E.; *see* Erskine-Wyse.
Wyss, Sophie Adele, 1897–1983, vol. VIII
Wythes, Ernest James, 1868–1949, vol. IV
Wyvill, Marmaduke D'Arcy, 1849–1918, vol. II

Y

Yahuda, Abraham Shalom Ezekiel, 1877–1951, vol. V
Yahya Khan, Gen. Agha Muhammad, 1917–1980, vol. VII
Yain, Sir Lee Ah, 1874–1932, vol. III
Yakub, Moulvi Sir Mohammad, 1879–1942, vol. IV
Yaldwin, Lt-Col Alfred George, 1847–1905, vol. I
Yale, Col James Corbet, 1859–1936, vol. III
Yamagata, Aritomo, Field-Marshal Prince, 1838–1922, vol. II
Yamin Khan, Sir Mohammed, *died* 1966, vol. VI
Yang Shangkun, 1907–1998, vol. X
Yapp, Sir Arthur Keysall, 1869–1936, vol. III
Yapp, Sir Frederick Charles, 1880–1958, vol. V
Yapp, Richard Henry, *died* 1929, vol. III
Yarborough, 4th Earl of, 1859–1936, vol. III
Yarborough, 5th Earl of, 1888–1948, vol. IV
Yarborough, 6th Earl of, 1893–1966, vol. VI
Yarborough, 7th Earl, 1920–1991, vol. IX
Yarborough, Countess of; (Marcia Amelia Mary); *see* Fauconberg and Conyers, Baroness.
Yarborough, George Eustace C.; *see* Cooke-Yarborough.
Yarborough, Rev. John James Cooke-, 1855–1941, vol. IV

Yarde, Air Vice-Marshal Brian Courtenay, 1905–1986, vol. VIII
Yarde-Buller, Brig.-Gen. Hon. Sir Henry, 1862–1928, vol. II
Yarde-Buller, Hon. Walter, 1859–1935, vol. III
Yardley, Captain John Henry Reginald, 1881–1938, vol. III
Yardley, Col John Watkins, 1858–1920, vol. II
Yardley, Samuel, 1839–1902, vol. I
Yarr, Maj.-Gen. Sir Thomas, 1862–1937, vol. III
Yarrow, Sir Alfred Fernandez, 1st Bt, 1842–1932, vol. III
Yarrow, Eleanor Cecilia, (Lady Yarrow), *died* 1953, vol. V
Yarrow, Sir Harold Edgar, 2nd Bt, 1884–1962, vol. VI
Yarwood, Dame Elizabeth Ann, 1900–1989, vol. VIII
Yarworth-Jones, Sir William, 1870–1953, vol. V
Yashiro, Yukio, 1890–1975, vol. VII
Yate, Lt-Col Arthur Campbell, 1853–1929, vol. III
Yate, Col Sir Charles Edward, 1st Bt, 1849–1940, vol. III
Yate, Rev. George Edward, *died* 1908, vol. I
Yate-Lee, Lawford, 1838–1901, vol. I

Yates, Col Clarence Montague, 1881–1952, vol. V
Yates, Lt-Gen. Sir David P.; *see* Peel Yates.
Yates, Lt-Col Donald, 1893–1960, vol. V (A), vol. VI (AI)
Yates, Dornford; *see* Mercer, Major Cecil William.
Yates, Dame Frances Amelia, 1899–1981, vol. VIII
Yates, Frank, 1902–1994, vol. IX
Yates, Lt-Col Hubert Peel, 1874–1938, vol. III
Yates, Bt-Col James Ainsworth, 1883–1929, vol. III
Yates, John Ernest, 1887–1969, vol. VI
Yates, Joseph Maghull, 1844–1916, vol. II
Yates, Rev. Thomas, 1873–1936, vol. III
Yates, Sir Thomas, 1896–1978, vol. VII
Yates, Victor Francis, 1900–1969, vol. VI
Yates, Walter Baldwyn, *died* 1947, vol. IV
Yates, Rev. Canon William R., 1870–1951, vol. V
Yates-Bell, Geoffrey; *see* Yates-Bell, J. G.
Yates-Bell, John Geoffrey, 1902–1991, vol. IX
Yatman, Col Arthur Hamilton, 1874–1947, vol. IV
Yatman, Brig.-Gen. Clement, 1871–1940, vol. III
Yeabsley, Sir Richard Ernest, 1898–1983, vol. VIII
Yeaman, Sir Ian David, 1889–1977, vol. VII
Yeames, William Frederick, 1835–1918, vol. II
Yearsley, Macleod; *see* Yearsley, P. M.
Yearsley, (Percival) Macleod, *died* 1951, vol. V
Yeates, Keith; *see* Yeates, W. K.
Yeates, W(illiam) Keith, 1920–1992, vol. IX
Yeatman-Biggs, Rt Rev. Huyshe Wolcott, 1845–1922, vol. II
Yeats, Gerald Aylmer L.; *see* Levett-Yeats.
Yeats, Jack Butler, *died* 1957, vol. V
Yeats, John Butler, 1839–1922, vol. II
Yeats, William Butler, 1865–1939, vol. III
Yeats-Brown, Francis, 1886–1944, vol. IV
Yeats-Brown, Montagu, 1834–1921, vol. II
Yeatts, Maurice William Walter Murray, 1894–1950, vol. IV
Yeaxlee, Basil Alfred, 1883–1967, vol. VI
Yeend, Sir Geoffrey John, 1927–1994, vol. IX
Yeilding, Col William Richard, 1856–1934, vol. III
Yeld, Edward, 1839–1921, vol. II
Yellowlees, Henry, 1888–1971, vol. VII
Yelverton, Adm. Bentinck John Davies, *died* 1959, vol. V
Yelverton, Hon. Roger Dawson, *died* 1912, vol. I
Yelverton, William Henry Morgan, 1840–1909, vol. I
Yemm, Edmund William, 1909–1993, vol. IX
Yen, W. W., 1877–1950, vol. IV(A), vol. V
Yencken, Arthur F., 1894–1944, vol. IV
Yendell, Rear-Adm. William John, 1903–1988, vol. VIII
Yeo, Sir Alfred William, 1863–1928, vol. II
Yeo, Gerald Francis, 1845–1909, vol. I
Yeo, Rt Rev. Mgr Henry D., 1872–1952, vol. V
Yeo, J. Burney, *died* 1914, vol. I
Yeo, Sir William, 1896–1972, vol. VII
Yeo-Thomas, Wing Comdr Forest Frederick Edward, 1901–1964, vol. VI
Yeoman, Rev. Alexander Ross, 1874–1956, vol. V
Yeoman, Ven. Henry Walker, *died* 1897, vol. I
Yeoman, Philip Metcalfe, 1923–1997, vol. X
Yerburgh, Rev. Oswald Pryor W.; *see* Wardell-Yerburgh.
Yerburgh, Richard Eustre, 1847–1939, vol. III

Yerburgh, Robert Armstrong, 1853–1916, vol. II
Yerbury, Francis Rowland, 1885–1970, vol. VI
Yerbury, Air Vice-Marshal Richard Olyffe, 1914–1971, vol. VII
Yerby, Frank Garvin, 1916–1991, vol. IX
Yerkes, Charles Tyson, 1837–1905, vol. I
Yerkes, Robert Mearns, 1876–1956, vol. V
Yetts, W. Perceval, 1878–1957, vol. V
Yew, Loke, *died* 1917, vol. II
Yexley, Lionel, 1861–1933, vol. III
Yglesias, V. P., *died* 1911, vol. I
Yin, Leslie Charles Bowyer; *see* Charteris, L.
Yoffey, Joseph Mendel, 1902–1994, vol. IX
Yolland, John Horatio, 1863–1944, vol. IV
Yonge, Sir (Charles) Maurice, 1899–1986, vol. VIII
Yonge, Charlotte Mary, 1823–1901, vol. I
Yonge, Dame Felicity; *see* Yonge, Dame I. F. A.
Yonge, Dame (Ida) Felicity (Ann), 1921–1995, vol. IX
Yonge, Sir Maurice; *see* Yonge, Sir C. M.
Yonge, Lt-Col Philip Caynton, 1877–1928, vol. II
Yool, Air Vice-Marshal William Munro, 1894–1978, vol. VII
York, Christopher, 1909–1999, vol. X
York, Ven. George William, *died* 1944, vol. IV
York, Thomas John Pinches, 1898–1970, vol. VI
Yorke, Hon. Alexander Grantham, 1847–1911, vol. I
Yorke, Hon. Alfred Ernest Frederick, 1871–1928, vol. II
Yorke, Lt-Col Sir Arthur; *see* Yorke, Lt-Col Sir H. A.
Yorke, Curtis, *died* 1930, vol. III
Yorke, Dorothy, 1879–1946, vol. IV
Yorke, Francis Reginald Stevens, 1906–1962, vol. VI
Yorke, Lt-Col Sir (H.) Arthur, 1848–1930, vol. III
Yorke, Sir Henry Francis Redhead, 1842–1914, vol. I
Yorke, Henry Vincent; *see* Green, H.
Yorke, John Reginald, 1836–1912, vol. I
Yorke, Brig. Philip Gerard, 1882–1968, vol. VI
Yorke, Brig.-Gen. Ralph Maximilian, 1874–1951, vol. V
Yorke, Richard Michael, 1930–1991, vol. IX
Yorke, Robert Langdon, 1887–1954, vol. V
Yorke, Simon, 1903–1966, vol. VI
Yorke, Vincent Wodehouse, 1869–1957, vol. V
Yorke, Warrington, 1883–1943, vol. IV
Yorston, Sir Keith; *see* Yorston, Sir R. K.
Yorston, Sir (Robert) Keith, 1902–1983, vol. VIII
Yorstoun, Brig.-Gen. Archibald Mordern C.; *see* Carthew-Yorstoun.
Yoshida, Shigeru, 1878–1967, vol. VI
Yost, Charles Woodruff, 1907–1981, vol. VIII
Youard, Very Rev. Wilfrid Wadham, 1869–1964, vol. VI
Youde, Sir Edward, 1924–1986, vol. VIII
Youell, Rev. Canon George, 1910–1995, vol. IX
Youens, Rev. Canon Fearnley Algernon Cyril, 1886–1967, vol. VI
Youens, Ven. John Ross, 1914–1993, vol. IX
Youens, Rt Rev. Laurence W., *died* 1939, vol. III
Youens, Sir Peter William, 1916–2000, vol. X
Youl, Sir James Arndell, 1809–1904, vol. I

Young, Rt Hon. Lord; George Young, 1819–1907, vol. I
Young, Sir Alastair Spencer Templeton, 2nd Bt (cr 1945), 1918–1963, vol. VI
Young, Sir Alban; see Young, Sir C. A.
Young, Hon. Sir Alexander; see Young, Hon. Sir J. A.
Young, Maj.-Gen. Alexander, 1915–1983, vol. VIII
Young, Alexander; see Young, B. A.
Young, (Alexander Bell) Filson, 1876–1938, vol. III
Young, Alfred, died 1900, vol. I
Young, Rev. Alfred, 1873–1940, vol. III
Young, Alfred Harry, died 1912, vol. I
Young, Sir Alfred Karney, 1865–1942, vol. IV
Young, Rev. Allan, 1925–1979, vol. VII
Young, Sir Allen William, 1827–1915, vol. I
Young, Allyn Abbott, 1876–1929, vol. III
Young, Andrew, 1873–1937, vol. III
Young, Andrew, 1858–1943, vol. IV
Young, Rev. Canon Andrew John, 1885–1971, vol. VII
Young, Col Archibald, 1865–1931, vol. III
Young, Archibald, 1873–1939, vol. III
Young, Archibald Hope, 1863–1935, vol. III
Young, Lt-Col Arthur Davidson, 1862–1937, vol. III
Young, Col Sir Arthur Edwin, 1907–1979, vol. VII
Young, Captain Sir Arthur Henderson, 1854–1938, vol. III
Young, Arthur Primrose, 1885–1977, vol. VII
Young, Sir Arthur Stewart Leslie, 1st Bt (cr 1945), 1889–1950, vol. IV
Young, Rev. Augustus Blayney Russell, 1845–1941, vol. IV
Young, (Basil) Alexander, 1920–2000, vol. X
Young, Maj.-Gen. Bernard Keith, 1892–1969, vol. VI
Young, Air Vice-Marshal Brian Pashley, 1918–1992, vol. IX
Young, Carmichael Aretas, 1913–1986, vol. VIII
Young, Rev. Canon (Cecil) Edwyn, 1913–1988, vol. VIII
Young, Sir (Charles) Alban, 9th Bt (cr 1769), 1865–1944, vol. IV
Young, Col Charles Augustus, 1863–1944, vol. IV
Young, Rev. Canon Charles Edgar, 1897–1977, vol. VII
Young, Charles Edward Baring, 1850–1928, vol. II
Young, Maj.-Gen. Charles Frederic Gordon, 1859–1956, vol. V
Young, (Charles) Kenneth, 1916–1985, vol. VIII
Young, Christopher Alwyne Jack, 1912–1978, vol. VII
Young, Clyde, 1871–1948, vol. IV
Young, Sir Cyril Roe Muston, 4th Bt (cr 1821), 1881–1955, vol. V
Young, Rev. Daniel Eliott, 1851–1935, vol. III
Young, Daniel Henderson Lusk, 1861–1921, vol. II
Young, Lt-Col David Douglas, 1857–1940, vol. III
Young, Lt-Gen. Sir David Tod, 1926–2000, vol. X
Young, Rev. Dinsdale Thomas, 1861–1938, vol. III
Young, Douglas, 1882–1967, vol. VI
Young, Sir Douglas; see Young, Sir J. D.
Young, Sir Douglas; see Young, Sir W. D.
Young, Edith Isabella, 1904–1988, vol. VIII

Young, Rev. Canon Edwyn; see Young, Rev. Canon C. E.
Young, Rev. Egerton Ryerson, 1840–1909, vol. I
Young, Emily Hilda, 1880–1949, vol. IV
Young, Sir Eric; see Young, Sir T. E. B.
Young, Eric Edgar, 1912–1986, vol. VIII
Young, Eric William, 1896–1987, vol. VIII
Young, Ernest, 1869–1952, vol. V
Young, Brig.-Gen. Ernest Douglas, 1872–1957, vol. V
Young, Ernest Herbert, 1878–1921, vol. II, vol. III
Young, Evelyn Lucy, 1879–1960, vol. V
Young, F. E. Mills, died 1945, vol. IV
Young, Filson, see Young, A. B. F.
Young, Francis Brett, 1884–1954, vol. V
Young, Rev. Francis Samuel, 1871–1934, vol. III
Young, Francis Watson, 1851–1941, vol. IV
Young, Sir Frank George, 1908–1988, vol. VIII
Young, Lt-Col Sir Frank Popham, 1863–1940, vol. III
Young, Captain Sir Frederic William, 1859–1927, vol. II
Young, Sir Frederick, 1817–1913, vol. I
Young, Frederick, 1890–1948, vol. IV
Young, Col Frederick de Bude, 1865–1920, vol. II
Young, Frederick George Charles, 1877–1955, vol. V
Young, Frederick Hugh, 1892–1969, vol. VI
Young, Frederick Trestrail Clive, 1887–1982, vol. VIII
Young, Sir Frederick William, 1876–1948, vol. IV
Young, Frieda Margaret, 1913–1998, vol. X
Young, Geoffrey Winthrop, 1876–1958, vol. V
Young, Sir George, 3rd Bt (cr 1813), 1837–1930, vol. III
Young, Sir George, 4th Bt (cr 1813), 1872–1952, vol. V
Young, George; see Young, Rt Hon. Lord.
Young, Rt Hon. George Charles Gillespie, 1876–1939, vol. III
Young, Very Rev. George Edward, died 1937, vol. III
Young, Brig.-Gen. George Frederick, 1846–1919, vol. II
Young, George Kennedy, 1911–1990, vol. VIII
Young, George Malcolm, 1882–1959, vol. V
Young, Sir George Peregrine, 5th Bt (cr 1813), 1908–1960, vol. V
Young, Mrs George Washington; see Nordica, Lillian.
Young, Gerard Mackworth-, 1884–1965, vol. VI
Young, Gladys, 1887–1975, vol. VII
Young, Air Vice-Marshal Gordon, 1919–1993, vol. IX
Young, Maj.-Gen. Gordon Drummond, 1896–1964, vol. VI
Young, Grace Chisholm, 1868–1944, vol. IV
Young, Most Rev. Sir Guilford Clyde, 1916–1988, vol. VIII
Young, Lt-Col Harry Norman, 1874–1944, vol. IV
Young, Brig.-Gen. Henry Alfred, 1867–1941, vol. IV
Young, Henry Alfred, died 1942, vol. IV
Young, Brig. Henry Ayerst, 1895–1952, vol. V
Young, Hon. Henry Esson, 1867–1939, vol. III

Young, Brig.-Gen. Henry George, 1870–1956, vol. V

Young, Hilda Beatrice, (Sister Pauline), *died* 1967, vol. VI

Young, Major Sir Hubert Winthrop, 1885–1950, vol. IV

Young, Maj.-Gen. Hugh A., 1898–1982, vol. VIII

Young, Hugh Hampton, 1870–1945, vol. IV

Young, Hugo Joseph, 1847–1929, vol. III

Young, James, 1883–1963, vol. VI

Young, James, 1887–1975, vol. VII

Young, Hon. Sir (James) Alexander, 1875–1956, vol. V

Young, James Barclay Murdoch, 1897–1957, vol. V

Young, James Carleton, 1856–1918, vol. II

Young, Maj.-Gen. James Charles, 1858–1926, vol. II

Young, Gen. James Nowell, 1824–1917, vol. II

Young, Sir James Reid, 1888–1971, vol. VII

Young, Maj.-Gen. James Vernon, 1891–1961, vol. VI

Young, John, 1835–1902, vol. I

Young, Rt Hon. John, 1826–1915, vol. I

Young, John, 1845–1925, vol. II

Young, Rev. John, 1844–1930, vol. III

Young, Major John Darling, 1910–1988, vol. VIII

Young, Sir (John) Douglas, 1883–1973, vol. VII

Young, Col Sir John Smith, 1843–1932, vol. III

Young, John Stirling, 1894–1971, vol. VII

Young, Sir John William Roe, 5th Bt, 1913–1981, vol. VIII

Young, John Zachary, 1907–1997, vol. X

Young, Brig.-Gen. Sir Julian Mayne, 1872–1961, vol. VI

Young, Brig.-Gen. Julius Ralph, 1864–1961, vol. VI

Young, Karl, 1879–1943, vol. IV

Young, Brig. Keith de Lorentz, 1889–1962, vol. VI

Young, Keith Downes, 1848–1929, vol. III

Young, Kenneth; *see* Young, C. K.

Young, Leslie, 1911–1992, vol. IX

Young, M'Gregor, 1864–1942, vol. IV

Young, Mark, 1929–1991, vol. IX

Young, Sir Mark Aitchison, 1886–1974, vol. VII

Young, Mary Lavinia Bessie, 1911–1986, vol. VIII

Young, Morris Yudlevitz, *died* 1950, vol. IV

Young, Major Norman Edward, 1862–1902, vol. I

Young, Norman Egerton, 1892–1964, vol. VI

Young, Sir Norman Smith, 1911–1999, vol. X

Young, Norwood, 1860–1943, vol. IV

Young, Comdr Oliver, 1855–1908, vol. I

Young, Owen D., 1874–1962, vol. VI

Young, Patrick Charles, 1880–1951, vol. V

Young, Brig. Peter, 1915–1988, vol. VIII

Young, Ven. Peter Claude, 1916–1987, vol. VIII

Young, Maj.-Gen. Peter George Francis, 1912–1976, vol. VII

Young, Pierre Henry John, 1926–1985, vol. VIII

Young, Reginald Stanley, (Robert), 1891–1985, vol. VIII

Young, Rt Rev. Richard, 1843–1905, vol. I

Young, Robert; *see* Young, Reginald S.

Young, Rt Hon. Robert, 1822–1917, vol. II

Young, Robert, 1860–1932, vol. III

Young, Maj.-Gen. Robert, 1877–1953, vol. V

Young, Sir Robert, 1872–1957, vol. V

Young, Sir Robert Arthur, 1871–1959, vol. V

Young, Sir Robert Christopher M.; *see* Mackworth-Young

Young, Robert Fitzgibbon, *died* 1960, vol. V

Young, Robert Henry, 1903–1997, vol. X

Young, Robert Magill, 1851–1925, vol. II

Young, Ruth, 1884–1983, vol. VIII

Young, Samuel, 1822–1918, vol. II

Young, Stephen, 1894–1972, vol. VII

Young, Stuart, 1934–1986, vol. VIII

Young, Sydney, 1857–1937, vol. III

Young, Thomas, 1896–1977, vol. VII

Young, Maj.-Gen. Thomas, 1893–1979, vol. VII

Young, Sir (Thomas) Eric (Boswell), 1891–1973, vol. VII

Young, Thomas Moffat, 1873–1946, vol. IV

Young, Lt-Col Walter Herbert, *died* 1940, vol. III

Young, Sir Walter James, 1872–1940, vol. III

Young, Rev. William, 1840–1915, vol. I

Young, William, 1863–1942, vol. IV

Young, Sir William, 1875–1957, vol. V

Young, William, 1885–1965, vol. VI(AII)

Young, Sir William, 1905–1980, vol. VII

Young, William Arthur, 1867–1955, vol. V

Young, William Arthur, 1890–1955, vol. V

Young, Sir (William) Douglas, 1859–1943, vol. IV

Young, William Henry, 1863–1942, vol. IV

Young, William John, 1878–1942, vol. IV

Young, Sir William Lawrence, 8th Bt (*cr* 1769), 1864–1921, vol. II

Young, Sir William Mackworth, 1840–1924, vol. II

Young, Sir William Muston Need, 3rd Bt (*cr* 1821), 1847–1934, vol. III(A), vol. IV

Young, Rt Hon. William Robert, 1856–1933, vol. III

Young-Herries, Sir Michael Alexander Robert; *see* Herries.

Young-Jamieson, Vice-Adm. Douglas, 1893–1955, vol. V

Younger of Leckie, 1st Viscount, 1851–1929, vol. III

Younger of Leckie, 2nd Viscount, 1880–1946, vol. IV

Younger of Leckie, 3rd Viscount, 1906–1997, vol. X

Younger, Brig. Arthur Allan Shakespear, 1881–1960, vol. V

Younger, Charles Frank Johnston, 1908–1995, vol. IX

Younger, Harry George, 1866–1951, vol. V

Younger, Sir James Paton, 1891–1974, vol. VII

Younger, Maj.-Gen. John Edward Talbot, 1888–1974, vol. VII

Younger, Rt Hon. Sir Kenneth Gilmour, 1908–1976, vol. VII

Younger, Maj.-Gen. Ralph, 1904–1985, vol. VIII

Younger, Robert; *see* Baron Blanesborough.

Younger, Robert Tannahill, 1860–1906, vol. I

Younger, Sir William, 1st Bt, 1862–1937, vol. III

Younger, Rev. William, 1869–1956, vol. V

Younger, Sir William McEwan, 1st Bt (*cr* 1964), 1905–1992, vol. IX

Younger, Sir William Robert, 2nd Bt, 1888–1973, vol. VII

Younghusband, Arthur Delaval, 1854–1931, vol. III
Younghusband, Charles Wright, 1821–1899, vol. I
Younghusband, Dame Eileen Louise, 1902–1981, vol. VIII
Younghusband, Sir Francis Edward, 1863–1942, vol. IV
Younghusband, Maj.-Gen. Sir George John, 1859–1944, vol. IV
Younghusband, Maj.-Gen. John William, 1823–1907, vol. I
Younghusband, Maj.-Gen. Leslie Napier, *died* 1939, vol. III
Younghusband, Gen. Robert Romer, 1819–1905, vol. I
Younghusband, Romer Edward, 1858–1933, vol. III
Youngman, Annie Mary, *died* 1919, vol. II
Youngman, William, 1880–1963, vol. VI
Yousuf, Lt-Gen. Mohammed, 1908–1981, vol. VIII
Yoxall, Harry Waldo, 1896–1984, vol. VIII

Yoxall, Sir James Henry, 1857–1925, vol. II
Ypres, 1st Earl of, 1852–1925, vol. II
Ypres, 2nd Earl of, 1881–1958, vol. V
Ypres, 3rd Earl of, 1921–1988, vol. VIII
Ysaye, Eugene, 1858–1931, vol. III
Ystwyth, 1st Baron, 1840–1935, vol. III
Yudkin, John, 1910–1995, vol. IX
Yuill, Lt-Col Harry Hogg, 1886–1935, vol. III
Yukawa, Hideki, 1907–1981, vol. VIII
Yule, Annie Henrietta, (Lady Yule), *died* 1950, vol. IV
Yule, Sir David, 1st Bt, 1858–1928, vol. II
Yule, George Udny, 1871–1951, vol. V
Yule, Col James Herbert, 1847–1920, vol. II
Yusuf, Sir Mohamad, *died* 1965, vol. VI(AII)
Yusuf, Nawab Sir Muhammad, *born* 1895, vol. VI
Yutang, Lin; *see* Lin Yutang.
Yves-Guyot, 1843–1928, vol. II

Z

Zacharewitsch, Michael, 1878–1953, vol. V
Zaehner, Robert Charles, 1913–1974, vol. VII
Zafar Ali, Sir, Khan Bahadur, Mirza, 1870–1942, vol. IV
Zafrulla Khan, Hon. Chaudhri Sir Muhammad, 1893–1985, vol. VIII
Zaharoff, Sir Basil, 1850–1936, vol. III
Zaidi, Bashir Husain Syed, 1898–1992, vol. IX
Zaimis, Eleanor, 1915–1982, vol. VIII
Zambra, William Warren S.; *see* Shaw-Zambra.
Zammit, Salvatore Cachia, *died* 1918, vol. II
Zammit, Sir Temistocle, 1864–1935, vol. III
Zamora y Torres, Don Niceto Alcalá, 1877–1949, vol. IV
Zanardelli, Guiseppe, 1829–1903, vol. I
Zangwill, Edith Ayrton, *died* 1945, vol. IV
Zangwill, Israel, 1864–1926, vol. II
Zangwill, Louis, 1869–1938, vol. III
Zangwill, Oliver Louis, 1913–1987, vol. VIII
Zanuck, Darryl Francis, 1902–1979, vol. VII
Zanzibar, Sultan of, *died* 1902, vol. I
Zanzibar, Sultan of, 1879–1960, vol. V
Zaphiro, Photius Philip Constantine, 1877–1933, vol. III
Zaroubin, Georgi Nikolaevitch, 1900–1968, vol. VI
Zavertal, Hon. Captain Ladislao Joseph Philip Paul, 1849–1942, vol. IV
Zeal, Hon. Sir William Austin, 1830–1912, vol. I
Zealley, Sir Alec Thomas Sharland, 1893–1970, vol. VI
Zeidler, Sir David Ronald, 1918–1998, vol. X
Zeiller, Charles René, 1847–1915, vol. I
Zelie, Rev. John Sheridan, 1866–1942, vol. IV
Zepler, Eric Ernest, 1898–1980, vol. VII
Zeppelin, Count Ferdinand von, 1838–1917, vol. II
Zernike, Frits, 1888–1966, vol. VI
Zetland, 1st Marquess of, 1844–1929, vol. III
Zetland, 2nd Marquess of, 1876–1961, vol. VI
Zetland, 3rd Marquess of, 1908–1989, vol. VIII

Zetterling, Mai Elizabeth, 1925–1994, vol. IX
Zeuner, Frederick Everard, 1905–1963, vol. VI
Zhukov, Marshal Georgi Konstantinovich, 1896–1974, vol. VII
Ziaur Rahman, General, 1935–1981, vol. VIII
Zichy-Woinarski, Casimir Julius, 1863–1935, vol. III
Ziegler, Henri Alexandre Léonard, 1906–1998, vol. X
Ziegler, Karl, 1898–1973, vol. VII
Zielinski, Thaddeus, 1859–1944, vol. IV
Zigomala, Hilda, 1869–1946, vol. IV
Zilliacus, Konni, 1894–1967, vol. VI
Ziman, Herbert David, 1902–1983, vol. VIII
Zimbalist, Efrem, 1890–1985, vol. VIII
Zimmer, George Frederick, 1854–1935, vol. III
Zimmermann, Agnes Marie, 1845–1925, vol. II
Zimmern, Sir Alfred, 1879–1957, vol. V
Zimmern, Alice, 1855–1939, vol. III
Zimmern, Archibald, 1917–1985, vol. VIII
Zimmern, Helen, 1846–1934, vol. III
Zinkeisen, Anna Katrina, *died* 1976, vol. VII
Zinn, Maj. William Victor, 1903–1989, vol. VIII
Zinnemann, Fred, 1907–1997, vol. X
Ziwer, Ahmad Pasha, 1864–1945, vol. IV
Zohrab, Gen. Sir Edward Henry, 1850–1909, vol. I
Zola, Emile Edouard Charles Antoine, 1840–1902, vol. I
Zoppi, Count Vittorio, 1898–1967, vol. VI
Zorn, Anders Leonard, 1860–1920, vol. II
Zouche, 15th Baron, 1851–1914, vol. I
Zouche, Baroness (16th in line), 1860–1917, vol. II
Zouche, Baroness (17th in line), 1875–1965, vol. VI
Zsögöd, Géza B. G.; *see* Grosschmid-Zsögöd, G. B.
Zuckerman, Baron (Life Peer); Solly Zuckerman, 1904–1993, vol. IX
Zukor, Adolph, 1873–1976, vol. VII
Zulfikar Ali Khan, Sir, 1875–1933, vol. III
Zuloaga, Ignacio, 1870–1945, vol. IV

Notes

Notes

Notes

Notes

Notes

Notes

Notes

Notes

Notes

Notes

Notes

Notes

Notes

Notes